Dictionary of
Missouri Biography

Dictionary

7 October 1999

To Faye Carter
with warm regards
Lawrence O. Christensen

Kenneth H. Winn

To Faye Carter,
With whom I shared the Lincoln
experience, With warmest
regards, Gary R. Kremer

# of Missouri Biography

Edited by Lawrence O. Christensen,
William E. Foley, Gary R. Kremer,
and Kenneth H. Winn

University of Missouri Press
COLUMBIA AND LONDON

Publication of this book has been supported by generous contributions from
Central Missouri State University and the Clifford Willard Gaylord Foundation.

Copyright © 1999 by
The Curators of the University of Missouri
University of Missouri Press, Columbia, Missouri 65201
Printed and bound in the United States of America
All rights reserved
5   4   3   2   1   03   02   01   00   99

Library of Congress Cataloging-in-Publication Data

Dictionary of Missouri biography / edited by Lawrence O. Christensen
   . . . et al.].
      p.   cm.
   Includes bibliographical references.
   ISBN 0-8262-1222-0 (alk. paper)
   1. Missouri Biography.   I. Christensen, Lawrence O.
CT244.D53   1999
920.0778—dc21
[B]   99-15518
                                                        CIP

⊗™ This paper meets the requirements of the
American National Standard for Permanence of Paper
for Printed Library Materials, Z39.48, 1984.

Jacket designer: Kristie Lee
Text designer: Mindy Shouse
Typesetter: Bookcomp,Inc.
Printer and binder: Sheridan Books, Inc.
Typefaces: Times Roman, Caslon Open Face

Preface

The women and men featured in this volume either were born in Missouri or through their lives and careers touched the state in a significant way. They came from all walks of life and achieved distinction or notoriety in diverse arenas. Some are instantly recognizable and familiar to all, while others will be known to only a few. They mirror Missouri's cultural diversity and its regional variations, and their collective stories support the proposition that the history of Missouri is, in large measure, a microcosm of the larger American experience.

Situated at the confluence of North America's great central river system, the place we now call Missouri has for centuries occupied a significant niche in regional, national, and international developments. Long before Missouri became a part of the United States, Indian peoples and subsequently rival European powers competed to control this strategic locality in the continental heartland. Throughout history, Missouri's abundant resources and its scenic beauty have attracted diverse peoples from many different places. By the time of the Louisiana Purchase in 1803, the region already boasted a cultural heritage containing Native American, French, Spanish, African, Anglo, and scattered other strains. Not all early Missourians were equal partners in the emerging order. The Indians were systematically pushed beyond the territory's western border, and the vast majority of African Americans were enslaved and treated as chattel.

Missouri's application for statehood in 1818 precipitated a major national debate over slavery extension that signaled a troubled future for both the state and the nation. The democratic impulses of the Jacksonian movement that took root in Missouri following statehood failed to ameliorate the plight of its slaves or to make a place for the Mormons who were driven from the state. As the gateway to the West, Missouri played a vital role in the settlement and development of the western half of the North American continent. Not only did it serve as the point of departure for vast numbers of westering Americans, but it also became a depot and warehouse for much of the region's produce.

During the troubled years of the Civil War and Reconstruction, Missouri was a border state reflecting to an unusual degree the national divisions and traumas. Beginning with the bloody contest in neighboring Kansas in the 1850s and continuing as the nation was plunged into an extended and bitter conflict, Missourians remained deeply divided as they struggled to chart their state's course. Influential residents who traced their origins to the Old South clashed with the state's expanding Yankee and Germanic populace over questions of slavery and the Union. Even after the guns had been silenced, the debate continued as African Americans, disfranchised former Confederates, new immigrants, and women fought to attain equal standing. The ascendancy of railroad transportation brought dramatic changes that compelled Missourians to confront the consequences of industrialization and modernization. Amid an economic transformation that made Missouri a national leader in manufacturing, many of its citizens remained devoted to the ideals and values associated with rural and small-town living. America's urban-rural dichotomy was, and is, deeply imbedded in the Missouri experience.

From the farmer and labor protests of the late nineteenth century to the debates a century later over welfare reform, social issues, and the consequences of a global economy, Missouri has, to a remarkable degree, mirrored national developments. Because twentieth-century Missouri typified, in so many ways, the national experience, the state and its people have come to be viewed as credible barometers for national trends and opinions. The story of Missouri is the story of its people, and the biographical sketches contained in this work testify eloquently to their achievements and in many instances to their greatness. Not only do these Missourians exemplify the excitement and richness of their state's past, but they also foreshadow the promise of its future.

The *Dictionary of Missouri Biography* is intended to serve as an authoritative reference to which scholars, researchers, and general readers can turn for accessible, reliable information about noteworthy Missourians. With the singular exception of *Show Me Missouri Women,* a valuable two-volume set featuring the biographies of Missouri women, edited by Mary K. Dains and Sue Sadler for the Missouri State American Association of University Women and published in 1989 and 1993, Floyd Shoemaker's long-out-of-print 1943 edition of *Missouri and Missourians* is still the most reliable comprehensive reference for Missouri biography. The obvious need for a modern Missouri biographical dictionary prompted Beverly Jarrett, the director of the University of Missouri Press, and Clair Willcox, the acquisitions editor, to propose publication of such a volume.

In 1991, following a series of exploratory discussions about the project's feasibility, the four editors whose names appear on the title page consented to oversee the preparation of the *Dictionary of Missouri Biography,* which would be based on the best current scholarship. To expedite work on what promised to be a monumental undertaking, the editors decided to divide their assignments by chronological period, with William E. Foley assuming responsibility for the prestatehood era, Kenneth H. Winn for the years 1821 to 1875, Gary R. Kremer for the period 1876 to 1925, and Lawrence O. Christensen for the post-1926 era.

The *Dictionary of Missouri Biography* contains the biographies of 724 Missourians who made distinctive contributions to the course of state and national history. Living persons have been excluded, along with anyone deceased after January 1, 1994. In making their selections, the editors attempted to choose men and women who were representative of the state's cultural, racial, and ethnic diversity. They likewise sought to include Missourians who distinguished themselves in wide-ranging fields of endeavor, including government and politics, business and industry, agriculture, the arts, entertainment, sports, education, military service, diplomacy, social reform, civic improvements, science, and religion. The editors also tried to ensure that persons from all time periods and from all regions of the state were represented. The only automatic selections were Missouri's governors and its U.S. senators. The editors solicited nominations from professional colleagues and outside reviewers. While every effort has been made to include those Missourians most deserving of attention, there are numerous influential figures who, for one reason or another, have been omitted. Readers and reviewers will inevitably take exception with some of the editors' choices. They will lament the absence of particular individuals, many of whom undoubtedly will be candidates for inclusion in future editions.

The biographies vary in length in accordance with the relative importance of the subject. Each entry includes a sketch of the subject's life, organized chronologically, with specific dates and facts. The authors and the editors have made every effort to provide essential information, but in some cases vital facts, such as dates of birth and death, could not be located. Authors have also been asked to place persons within the context of their times, assess their significance, and provide some impression of their personality. A brief bibliography has been appended to each entry.

The usefulness and value of this volume must depend on the quality of its entries. Fortunately, in assembling this work, the editors were able to recruit talented researchers and gifted writers. Readers will recognize the names of many distinguished scholars among the contributors, and the editors gratefully acknowledge each of the authors for their important contributions. Inevitably with so many contributors, the individual entries differ in style and approach, but the editors believe that the benefits of utilizing the expertise of individuals with special knowledge easily outweigh any possible disadvantages resulting from a lack of uniformity.

A project of this magnitude would be impossible without the encouragement and support of many people and organizations. Although most of them also served as contributors, several individuals merit special recognition for the additional advice and counsel they provided. The editors are particularly grateful to Mary K. Dains for her assistance with the compilation of the subject list. Arvarh Strickland, Richard McKenzie, Duane Meyer, Sally Miller, and James W. Goodrich also reviewed the list and offered helpful suggestions. Grants from the State Historical Society of Missouri's Richard S. Brownlee Fund in 1992, 1993, and 1996 helped defray many ongoing project expenses. In particular, the Brownlee Fund supported the employment of Laura Robinson Jolley as a part-time project coordinator and Dennis Boman as a researcher. Jolley's diligent efforts, watchful eye, and unwavering commitment helped bring order out of chaos in the often unwieldy process. Janelle L. Lambert, Rochelle Horn, and Cynthia Heimberger of the University of Missouri–Rolla assisted Jolley with the task of keyboarding and preparing a machine-readable copy of the manuscript. Dennis Boman served ably as a researcher. Annette Wenda deftly managed the daunting assignment of copyediting a lengthy manuscript that was the work of so many different hands. Jane Lago also provided welcome assistance at several critical moments in the production process. Finally, the guiding hand and constant but gentle prodding of Clair Willcox helped keep the project on track and bring it to final closure. The eventual completion of this lengthy process owes much to his methodical and good-humored oversight.

Subventions provided by Central Missouri State University, through the offices of President Ed Elliott, and by the Clifford Willard Gaylord Foundation, with the assistance of Francis M. Barnes III, helped underwrite some production costs for this sizable volume.

LAWRENCE O. CHRISTENSEN
WILLIAM E. FOLEY
GARY R. KREMER
KENNETH H. WINN

Contributors

Aamodt, David C.
Adair, Bianca
Adams, Henry
Albertini, Virgil
Anders, R. Leslie
Anderson, Paul G.
Anderson, R. D.
Archer, Stephen M.
Armitage, Shelley S.
Ashman, Patricia
Bagg, Sharon
Bailey, Elizabeth J.
Beggs, Margaret
Behan, Hugh F.
Beveridge, Mary I.
Billington, David P.
Bloom, Jo Tice
Blunt, Roy D.
Boman, Dennis K.
Boxerman, Burton A.
Boyd, Kent C.
Boyd, Mary Ellen
Boyd, Robert C.
Boyle, Michael P.
Bradbury, John F., Jr.
Bradley, Jennifer
Bradley, Lenore K.
Brandon-Falcone, Janice
Brennan, Michael
Brown, Bernard M.
Buckingham, Peter H.
Burnett, Robyn
Camenzind, Krista
Campbell, Janet Bruce
Capeci, Dominic J., Jr.
Carneal, Thomas W.
Carter, Quentin R.
Carver, Laurence R., II
Cash, Jon David
Cassity, Michael
Cates, Misty
Chalfant, Rhonda
Christensen, Lawrence O.
Christensen, Maxine J.
Claycomb, William B.
Coalier, Paula
Cochran, David
Cogell, Donna K.
Cohen, Herbert R.
Collings, Carolyn K.
Cooke, Thomas D.

Corbett, Katharine T.
Cotner, Richard
Cramer, Deborah L.
Curran, Pat
Curtis, Susan
Dains, Mary K.
Dalton-Cooper, Fran
Danisi, Thomas
Davis, Cyprian
Denny, James M.
DeWitt, Petra
Dicks, Samuel E.
Dillon, Merton L.
Dorsett, Lyle W.
Dougan, Michael B.
Dyer, Robert L.
Eby, Clare Virginia
Ehrlich, George
Ehrlich, Walter
Ekberg, Carl J.
Elley, Christyn L.
Engle, Stephen D.
Faherty, William B.
Farnsworth, Robert M.
Farrar, Ronald T.
Faust, Robert
Feezor, Joan
Ferrell, Robert H.
Finkelston, Theodore
Fischer, Lisa
Fisher, James T.
Fivel, Sharon
Flader, Susan
Flanders, Robert
Foley, William E.
Fry, Dawn
Gentzler, Lynn Wolf
Gerteis, Louis S.
Giffen, Jerena E.
Giffen, Lawrence E., Sr.
Giglio, Frances T.
Giglio, James N.
Gilbert, Judith A.
Goldman, Helen
Goodrich, James W.
Greene, Debra F.
Hamby, Alonzo L.
Hatfield, Joseph T.
Havig, Alan R.
Havird, Lawrence
Hays, Christopher K.

Hays, John
Heidenreich, Donald E., Jr.
Heimberger, Cynthia
Heming, Carol
Herr, Pamela
Hervey, Martha
Hier, Marshall D.
Hively, Kay
Holland, Antonio F.
Holsinger, J. Calvin
Holt, Earl K., III
Holtz, William
Hoover, John Neal
Horsman, Reginald
Houser, Steven
Hubbard, Dolan
Huber, Patrick J.
Hudson, Mark S.
Huggins, Marvin A.
Hulston, John K.
Hurt, R. Douglas
Iarocci, Louisa
Johnson, Betsy
Johnson, Vicki
Johnson, Yvonne
Jones, Charles T., Jr.
Kamphoefner, Walter D.
Kane, Marie Louise
Kasper, Shirl
Kaufman, Kenneth C.
Ketner, Joseph D.
Kilgo, Dolores A.
Killoren, John J.
Kinder, Rose Marie
Kinsey, Joni L.
Kirkendall, Richard S.
Knutson, Kaia A.
Koerting, Gayla
Kohl, Martha
Kremer, Gary R.
Kremer, Lisa A.
Laas, Virginia J.
Lance, Donald M.
Larsen, Lawrence H.
Launius, Roger D.
Lecompte, Janet S.
Leighton, Denys P.
Lemons, Shelly L.
Leslie, Edward E.
Lipsitz, George
Long, Michael

Long, Suzanna Maupin
Lovelace, Eldridge
Luebbering, Kenneth
Machon, Charles
Maidment, Stephen
March, David D.
Marcrum-Phelps, Catherine L.
Marra, Dorothy B.
Marszalek, John F.
Matson, Madeline
Mattingly, Arthur H.
Mauer, Cathlin Maloney
Maurer, Julie
McCall, Edith
McCandless, Perry
McClure, Arthur F.
McKinney, Edgar D.
McLaurin, Melton A.
McMillen, Margot Ford
McNamee, M. B.
Meagher, Michael E.
Melton, John E.
Meyer, Duane G.
Miller, John E.
Miller, Sally M.
Mink, Charles R.
Mitchell, Franklin D.
Molitor, Donald F.
Mooney, Catherine M.
Morasch, Mark
Morris, Ann
Morrison, Geoffrey Fahy
Morrissey, Thomas E.
Morrow, Lynn
Moulton, Gary E.
Nelson, Erika K.
Nichols, Ann
Norall, Frank
Northcott, Dennis
O'Brien, Michael J.
O'Brien, William Patrick
O'Connor, Candace
Ogilvie, Leon P.
Ohman, Marian M.
Olpin, Larry

Olson, James C.
O'Neal, Stephanie L.
Oster, Donald B.
Page, James W., III
Parke, Catherine N.
Parrish, William E.
Phelps, Marshall Ted
Phillips, Christopher
Piott, Steven L.
Pond, Gary W.
Potts, Donna L.
Potts, Louis W.
Prawl, Toni M.
Priddy, Bob
Prinsloo, Oleta
Quirk, Tom
Rafferty, Edward C.
Rawley, James A.
Renfrow, Louis A.
Rice, C. David
Richardson, Vivian
Ridley, Jack B.
Ridley, Katharine L.
Roberts, Gary L.
Rottman, Betty Cook
Rowan, Steven
Rowe, Mary Ellen
Rubin, Beth
Sandweiss, Eric
Saum, Lewis O.
Sayad, Elizabeth Gentry
Schirmer, Sherry Lamb
Schneider, Nicholas
Schnell, J. Christopher
Schroeder, Adolf E.
Schroeder, Rebecca B.
Schroeder, Walter A.
Seematter, Mary E.
Selvidge, Marla J.
Setran, David P.
Sherwood, Dolly
Simon, John Y.
Smith, Harold F.
Smith, Jeffrey E.
Snodgrass, Michael R.

Sonntag, Mark
Stadler, Frances H.
Stebbins, Chad
Steiner, Roger W.
Stepenoff, Bonnie
Steward, Deborah
Steward, Dick
Stilwell, Kristine
Stone, Ilene
Strickland, Arvarh E.
Swanson, Keith D.
Thomas, Kenn
Thorne, Tanis C.
Towne, Ruth Warner
Trefousse, Hans L.
Tucker, Phillip Thomas
Turner, Wilma Leonard
Twomey, Alfred E.
Vogt, Mary
Volpe, Vernon L.
Vonalt, Larry
Vostral, Sharra
Wade, Clyde G.
Waide, John
Walker, Stephen P.
Ware, Leland
Weekley, Rachel Franklin
Weil, Lisa Heffernan
Westcott, Timothy C.
White, Bob
White, Paul A.
Whites, LeeAnn
Whiteside, James
Wiley, Robert S.
Williams, J. Wayman
Wilson, Jerry E.
Wilson, Thomas D.
Winfield, Betty Houchin
Winn, Kenneth H.
Winter, William C.
Wixson, Douglas
Wolfman, Sharren G.
Worley, William S.
Wyman, Linda

Missouri's Counties.

Dictionary of
Missouri Biography

ACE, GOODMAN (1899–1982)

Goodman Ace, a humorist, was born Goodman Aiskowitz in Kansas City, Missouri, on January 15, 1899. The son of Latvian Jewish parents who emigrated in 1896 and married in the United States, Goodman anglicized his name in the early 1920s. He became the chief financial support of his mother and two sisters after his father's death in 1918, and, exempt from military service, he studied journalism at the Kansas City Polytechnic Institute while working at a succession of jobs. Already an aspiring author, Ace wrote a column titled "The Dyspeptic" for the school paper.

In 1919 he left the employ of the Wormser Hat Store after persuading the editor of the *Kansas City Post* to hire him as the paper's drama and movie critic. This young author of the *Post*'s reviews and "The Movie Man" column already displayed a brash, jaunty writing style. He fearlessly critiqued the film and stage productions that passed through Kansas City, and penned puckish responses to letters from youthful Missouri and Kansas movie fans. Many readers asked for advice about breaking into the movies. Ace invariably discouraged them. "Flapper" of Kansas City inquired in 1922 about "the ways and means of becoming a movie star." Ace wrote: "I'll admit the way is mean. You'd better try flapping in another field." An aspiring "authoress" of film scenarios announced that she would be writing for the movies "p.d.q." Ace agreed: "I think it is pretty darned questionable too."

In 1922 Ace married Jane Sherwood (born Epstein), whom he had met while a student at Central High School. His partner in a fifty-two-year marriage, Jane in 1929 became his partner in comedy radio broadcasting. At the conclusion of his movie and theater talk show on KMBC one evening, Ace and Jane, who was visiting the studio, improvised a humorous dialogue on playing bridge when the station engineer failed to pick up the scheduled CBS program. Impressing listeners, including a local advertising man, the Aces' ad-libbing led to a sponsored, regularly scheduled program named *Easy Aces,* which moved from KMBC to the CBS Network and broadcast from Chicago beginning in October 1931. Unsure of their future in the new medium, Goodman continued to write for what was now the *Journal-Post* in Kansas City.

The Aces' experience during the Great Depression ran counter to that of most Americans. Their second network contract with sponsor Lavoris mouthwash paid $1650 per week during the 1932–1933 radio season, for example. In 1933 the Aces took their program to New York City where producer Frank Hummert added it to his stable of serials, most of which were daytime soap operas. Appropriately, John Dunning has categorized *Easy Aces* as a "comedy serial." During the greater part of its long run on the NBC Blue Network, from 1933 to 1942, *Easy Aces* was broadcast for fifteen minutes, three evenings a week, presenting listeners with to-be-continued narratives about the humorously complicated dilemmas that filled the lives of "Mr. Ace" (listeners never knew his first name) and **Jane Ace.** Goodman was the show's only writer, and he readily admitted that his program's story lines were secondary to the delineation of strong characters. "The malaprops were Jane's," he recalled in 1977, "and she was the star of the show." Ace's forte as a humorist was exploring the comic possibilities of language, which made radio, whose writers necessarily shaped program content for a listening-only audience, the medium that he found most satisfying. As Jane's verbal faux pas became legendary, Ace's scripts influenced American English. Listeners found unexpected truth imbedded in such "janeaceisms" as "up at the crank of dawn," "familiarity breeds attempt," and "time wounds all heels." The point of the malaprop was more pertinent than that of the original cliché. The Aces and their supporting cast continued to broadcast, while seated around a card table with a concealed microphone to allay on-air nervousness, through transitions back to CBS in 1942 and to a thirty-minute format in 1943. A disagreement between Ace, who ferociously defended his creative freedom, and sponsor Anacin led to the program's cancellation after the broadcast of January 10, 1945. A mildly successful revival, *mr. ace and jane,* appeared on CBS Radio from February 1948 to May 1949.

Goodman Ace's writing career flourished after the demise of his own radio program, and for a time he became broadcasting's most successful comedy writer. For CBS Radio he wrote for the Danny Kaye show in 1945–1946, served as "supervisor of comedy" in 1946–1947, and as a script "doctor" to programs whose ratings needed improvement, and in 1947 he ran a School for Comedy Writers whose students included Neil Simon and Paddy Chayefsky. In 1947 Ace also created the historical drama series *You Are There* for CBS. Featuring Walter Cronkite, the show later had a successful run on CBS Television. In 1950 Ace began work at NBC as head writer for *The Big Show,* which starred Tullulah Bankhead and featured prominent guest stars and a lavish budget, all devoted to staving off television's assault on radio's listening audience and advertising revenues. The effort failed; *The Big Show* became a memory in April 1952.

Although Ace preferred radio to television, he spent the years 1952 to 1967 writing for the latter, at salaries few writers would reject to preserve principle. He transformed Milton Berle's program between 1952 and 1955 to restore the ratings that "Mr. Television" had enjoyed in the late 1940s. Ace also wrote for Sid Caesar's program in 1963–1964, and for Perry Como's popular variety show from 1955 to 1967. While working as head writer for the relaxed, unflappable Como, Ace earned $10,000 per week. Ace never hid his dislike of television, even as he profited from it. As he remarked to Groucho Marx: "TV [is] a clever contraction derived from the words Terrible Vaudeville." "We call it a medium," he often said, "because nothing's well done."

After he left television, Ace continued to reside in New York City, endured the death of Jane in 1974, and returned to print journalism. He wrote a regular column for the *Saturday Review* titled "Top of My Head," the subject matter evolving from radio-television criticism to commentary on all of show business and public affairs as well. In the mid-1970s Ace appeared several times per month on National Public Radio's *All Things Considered.* He published several collections of his work, including *Ladies and Gentlemen, Easy Aces* (consisting of radio scripts), and *The Better of Goodman Ace* (a compilation of magazine pieces). In his conversation as well as in his writing, interviewer Mark Singer found in 1977, "Ace's primary instinct is to be funny, and he almost always is."

Although for years he lived far from Missouri, Goodman Ace was living evidence of the state's rich heritage of humor, which includes the works of **Mark Twain, Homer Croy, Eugene Field,** and Paul Henning, among others. The fact that much of Ace's comedy resides in scripts that are all but inaccessible to readers hinders recognition of his achievement. Goodman Ace died in New York City on March 25, 1982. He was buried in Kansas City, beside Jane.

ALAN R. HAVIG

Ace, Goodman. *The Better of Goodman Ace.* Garden City, N.Y.: Doubleday, 1971.

————. *Ladies and Gentlemen, Easy Aces.* Garden City, N.Y.: Doubleday, 1971.
Dunning, John. "The Easy Aces." In *Tune in Yesterday: The Ultimate Encyclopedia of Old-Time Radio, 1925–1976,* 175–77. Englewood Cliffs, N.J.: Prentice Hall, 1976.
Marx, Groucho. *The Groucho Letters: Letters to and from Groucho Marx.* 1967. Reprint, New York: Manor Books, 1974.
New York Times, March 27, 1982.
Singer, Mark. "Profiles—Goody." *New Yorker* 53 (April 4, 1977): 41–80.

ACE, JANE (1900?–1974)

Jane Ace, a radio actress who was born Jane Epstein and known professionally as Jane Sherwood, was born in Kansas City, Missouri. The secondary sources yield no reliable birth dates. Said to have been seventy-four at the time of her death in 1974, she was probably born in 1900 or 1901. The date of her marriage to **Goodman Ace,** a *Kansas City Post* journalist, is equally uncertain. Although many sources contend it was 1928, the most reliable, Mark Singer's article in the *New Yorker,* says 1922. Ace's marriage alienated her father, Jacob Epstein, who wanted a son-in-law to join him in the retail clothing business. The Aces' marriage lasted for fifty-two years.

An attractive, blue-eyed blond, Ace gained national fame through her nasal voice, not her appearance, as radio's Mrs. Malaprop. Teamed with her husband on the comedy program *Easy Aces,* first broadcast in 1929 on KMBC in Kansas City and then on networks from Chicago and New York City beginning in 1931, Jane confused similar-sounding words for comic effect as she read Goodman's scripts.

Although cast in the "Dumb Dora" stereotype that had evolved through decades of vaudeville experience, Ace, like Gracie Allen, possessed a talent for interpreting and delivering comic dialogue. Unlike Allen and her husband, George Burns, who started in vaudeville and the movies before coming to radio, Jane and Goodman Ace were the first male-female team on radio to derive comedy from language mix-ups, and they restricted their language play to radio, the entertainment medium that relied solely on sound to produce humor. "Janeaceisms," as Goodman called them, included: "You're making a mountain out of a moleskin"; "That remark has all the earmuffs of a dirty dig"; "I understand, in a sort of roustabout way"; "Say it in words of one cylinder"; "I need the money for purposes too humorous to mention": "We're insufferable friends"; "It's our clowning achievement"; "He's a ragged individualist"; "Be it ever so hovel, there's no place like home"; "On the Lower East Side you find those

Old Testament houses"; "They're living in squander"; "We're all cremated equal"; "The food in that restaurant was abdominal"; "Congress is still in season"; "You monotonize the conversation"; and "New Year's resolutions go in one year and out the other."

Jane Ace's seventeen-year career as a comedienne on *Easy Aces* abruptly ended in January 1945 when a disagreement with the sponsor led to the show's cancellation. She came out of retirement twice: in 1948–1949 for a revival of the Aces' old program, called *mr. ace and jane,* and in 1952 for *Jane Ace, Disk Jockey,* which mixed record playing and light patter. Both efforts to revive Ace's on-air distortions of reality were mere echoes of the original *Easy Aces.* She never attempted a career in television acting.

Residing with her husband at the Ritz Towers Hotel in New York City, Ace made annual visits to family in Kansas City. She died in New York on November 11, 1974, and was buried in Kansas City.

ALAN R. HAVIG

Ace, Goodman. *Ladies and Gentlemen, Easy Aces.* Garden City, N.Y.: Doubleday, 1970.

Ace, Goodman, and Jane Goodman. Clipping File. Billy Rose Theatre Collection, New York Public Library at Lincoln Center.

Kansas City Times, November 12, 1974.

New York Times, November 12, 1974.

Singer, Mark. "Profiles—Goody." *New Yorker* 53 (April 4, 1977): 41–80.

AKINS, ZOË BYRD (1886–1958)

Zoë Byrd Akins was born on October 30, 1886, in Humansville, Missouri, the second of three children of Thomas Jasper and Sarah Elizabeth Green Akins, who was for many years chair of the Missouri Republican Party. Through her mother, Akins claimed kinship to a number of prominent Americans, including George Washington and **Duff Green.**

When her family moved to St. Louis just before the turn of the century, Akins was sent to be educated first at Monticello Seminary in Godfrey, Illinois, and later to Hosmer Hall, a preparatory school in St. Louis. While a student at Monticello Seminary, Akins wrote her first play, a parody of a Greek tragedy. While attending Hosmer Hall, she attended Saturday matinees every weekend. By the time she graduated from Hosmer Hall in 1903, she knew that she wanted a career in the theater, and she considered both acting and writing. In 1905 she acted walk-ons for several weeks with the Odeon Stock Company in St. Louis. Although for a few years she continued to act, she knew that her main talent lay in writing lines rather than in performing them.

By 1910 Akins had turned her attention seriously to dramatic writing, the work for which she became best known professionally. Early plays include *Iseult, the Fair* (which Akins dated from 1905), *The Learned Lady: A Comedy in Three Acts* (copyrighted 1910), *Such a Charming Young Man* (first produced in 1915), and *A Portrait of Tiero* (an adaptation of a 1915 story). Her first published play, *Papa: An Amorality in Three Acts* (1913), was chosen for the important *Modern Drama Series* published by Mitchell Kennerley and edited by Edwin Björkman. It was subsequently produced in Los Angeles in 1916, and then on Broadway with limited success two years later. Akins's first New York City production was her verse play *The Magical City,* produced by the Washington Square Players in 1915.

Meanwhile, Akins was also writing theater and music reviews for several St. Louis newspapers and weekly magazines. A first collection of her own poems, *Interpretations* (1912), was published in England and the United States. These poems, like those collected twenty-five years later in *The Hills Grow Smaller,* exhibit Akins's distinctive interest in lyric poetry and the dramatic monologue written chiefly for historical and fictional women characters.

William Marion Reedy, editor of *Reedy's Mirror,* the important St. Louis weekly that was distributed in the United States and abroad, asked Akins to write a series of critical essays on the new poetry. From February 19 to August 13, 1915, she wrote twenty-three weekly essays, titled *In the Shadow of Parnassus: A Critical Anthology of Contemporary American Poetry.* The series featured work by more than sixty poets whose poetry was beginning to appear in the years just before World War I, including Robert Frost, Amy Lowell, Edgar Lee Masters, Edna St. Vincent Millay, Ezra Pound, Edwin Arlington Robinson, Carl Sandburg, and **Sara Teasdale.** Akins focused her attention on the new young poets of her generation. Many of them came from the Midwest, a region that was developing a self-conscious sense of its literary identity in competition with the East and West Coasts. Akins and her contemporaries aimed to revitalize the stale conventions of Victorian poetry by returning American poetics to their revolutionary roots in Walt Whitman and Emily Dickinson and making connections with other experimental verse forms worldwide.

Akins continued to live and work in Jennings, near St. Louis, and to visit New York City during the winter theater seasons. In 1919 she moved to Manhattan following the publication of her first novel, *Cake upon the Waters,* and the success of her first Broadway hit, *Déclassée,* a melodrama cast auspiciously with Ethel Barrymore in the starring role of Lady Helen Haden. *Déclassée* introduced one of Akins's classic female protagonists, a flamboyant and glamorous, yet delicately sentimental, character caught in a tug-of-war between high romance and high principle.

In the sixteen years following her first big success Akins had sixteen plays on Broadway, including *Footloose,* an adaptation of a melodrama (1920); *Daddy's Gone A-Hunting* and *The Varying Shore,* original dramas (1921); *The Texas Nightingale,* an original comedy (1922); *A Royal Fandango,* an original comedy (1923); *The Moonflower,* a drama adaptation (1924); *First Love,* an adaptation (1926); *Thou Desperate Pilot,* an original drama, and *The Crown Prince,* an adaptation (1927); *The Furies,* an original drama (1928); and *The Love Duel* and *Careers,* both adaptations (1929).

In 1930 William Harris Jr. produced Akins's original farce *The Greeks Had a Word for It,* which was about a trio of depression-era gold diggers; it ran for more than two hundred performances and remains her best-known play. The actresses and actors cast in her plays—Emily Stevens, Marjorie Rambeau, Frank Conroy, Cyril Knightley, Laurette Taylor, Elsie Ferguson, and Fay Bainter, among them—indicate the measure of Akins's box-office appeal.

Akins's interest in varieties of dramatic writing led her to lucrative associations with Hollywood film companies. By the mid-1920s film companies were buying screen rights to her plays, including *Déclassée* and *Daddy's Gone A-Hunting.* For *The Moonflower,* filmed as *Eve's Secret* in 1925, Akins was paid eight thousand dollars, then a substantial sum. And in 1930 Samuel Goldwyn paid her ten times that amount for *The Greeks Had a Word for It.* In 1929 Akins moved to California and became a valuable screenwriter as sound transformed the art of motion pictures. Between 1930 and 1938 Akins wrote or collaborated on thirteen screenplays, with another eight films credited to her stories or other material. Akins received screenplay credit for *Anybody's Woman, The Right to Love,* and *Sarah and Son* (1930); *Once a Lady, Working Girls,* and *Women Love Once* (1931); *Christopher Strong* (1933); *Outcast Lady* (1934); *Camille* and *Lady of Secrets* (1936); *The Toy Wife* and *Zaza* (1938); and *Desire Me* (1947). Movies based on her work include *Morning Glory* (1932), notable for Katharine Hepburn's Oscar-winning performance, *Girls about Town* (1931), and *The Greeks Had a Word for It* (1932). Greta Garbo, Ruth Chatterton, Kay Francis, Billie Burke, Herbert Marshall, Melvyn Douglas, Douglas Fairbanks Jr., Joel McCrea, and Frederic March starred in her films. And Akins worked with such able and innovative directors as Dorothy Arzner and George Cukor.

Throughout the Hollywood years, Akins continued writing for the stage. *The Old Maid,* her adaptation of Edith Wharton's novella, was a Broadway success starring Judith Anderson and Helen Menken. The play won Akins the 1935 Pulitzer Prize in drama. The following year *O Evening Star!* played on Broadway, and two years later an adaptation, *I Am Different,* toured without reaching New York City. The year 1941 saw the production of her adaptation of Claude-André Puget's story, *The Happy Days,* and the publication of a second novel, *Forever Young.* *Mrs. January and Mr. Ex-* (1944) was her last Broadway play. Yet, until her death, Akins continued writing. She wrote plays produced by Midwestern theater companies, collaborated with a composer on a musical version of her play *The Varying Shore,* worked on Hollywood film projects, wrote scripts for radio and television programs, and wrote substantial portions of a St. Louis novel, "The White Doe," and her memoirs, "Others Than Myself." She died on October 29, 1958.

Zoë Akins was a professional writer for more than fifty years. She lived at Green Fountains, her Pasadena home, and remained unmarried until her mid-forties, when in 1932 she married Hugo Rumbold, a British theatrical designer, artist, and lieutenant in the Grenadier Guards who died eight months later. Throughout her career, Akins wrote in all the major literary genres: drama, poetry, fiction, and nonfiction prose. A promising young writer in St. Louis, later productive in both New York City and Hollywood, she epitomizes the new professional woman writer of the first half of the twentieth century. The woman who works, Akins once observed, is the "new romantic heroine of our time." She might well have been describing herself.

JENNIFER BRADLEY AND CATHERINE N. PARKE

Akins, Zoë. *In the Shadow of Parnassus: Zoë Akins's Essays on American Poetry.* Ed. Catherine N. Parke. Selinsgrove, Pa.: Susquehanna University Press, 1994.

Bradley, Jennifer. "Zoë Akins and the Age of Excess: Broadway Melodrama in the 1920s." In *Modern American Drama: The Female Canon,* ed. June Schlueter, 86–96. Rutherford, N.J.: Fairleigh Dickinson University Press, 1990.

Cranmer, Catherine. "Little Visits with Literary Missourians: Zoë Akins." *Missouri Historical Review* 20 (October 1925–July 1926): 252–61.

Dictionary of Literary Biography. Vol. 26. S.v. "Akins, Zoë."

Mielech, Ronald Albert. "The Plays of Zoë Akins Rumbold." Ph.D diss., Ohio State University, 1974.

Yongue, Patricia Lee. "Zoë Akins." In *American Women Writers: A Reference Guide from Colonial Times to the Present,* ed. Langdon Lynne Faust, 13–14. New York: Frederick Ungar, 1988.

ALEXANDER, ARCHER (1828–1880?)

On April 14, 1876, the eleventh anniversary of Abraham Lincoln's assassination, a handsome bronze statue called Freedom's Memorial was unveiled in Washington, D.C. The piece presented two figures: Lincoln and a newly freed slave, just rising from his knees and grasping a broken chain. The statue, which still stands in Washington's Lincoln Park with a copy at Washington University in St. Louis, was erected with contributions from hundreds of former slaves who wanted to honor the president who had proclaimed their freedom in 1863. But it also commemorates a slave, Archer Alexander, who found refuge in St. Louis during the Civil War and later served as the model for the freedman in the statue. The moving force behind the statue was Rev. **William Greenleaf Eliot,** a prominent Unitarian minister in St. Louis who rescued Alexander, employed him, and became his friend. In 1885 Eliot published a moving biography, *The Story of Archer Alexander,* in which he wrote, "I never knew a man, white or black, more thoroughly Christian . . . in all conduct and demeanor."

As Eliot described it, Alexander was born in 1828 on the Virginia plantation of a Reverend Mr. Delaney. When Alexander was a young boy, his father was sold south to pay Delaney's debts. Soon Delaney died and Alexander was settled on a son, Tom Delaney, who moved to Missouri, taking his slave with him. Alexander's mother, left behind, died within months. Delaney spent several years in St. Louis, hiring Alexander out to local brickyards. But Delaney was a spendthrift and needed money; he sold Alexander, who had married a slave woman named Louisa, to a farmer, James Hollman, living on the border between St. Charles and Warren Counties. Alexander spent more than twenty years working faithfully for Hollman and served as a kind of overseer on the farm. Meanwhile, he and Louisa had become parents of a large family; some of the children, though, were "sent away" by Hollman, who did not like their unruly behavior.

On the eve of the Civil War, Alexander listened to the political talk that swirled around him. He decided, Eliot wrote, "that freedom was his rightful inheritance, under the law of Christ. . . . He had pretty well outgrown the spirit of bondage, and . . . was quite prepared to do his part in breaking his chains." In February 1863 he got his chance: he slipped a warning to Union troops that a bridge they planned to cross had been sabotaged by Southern sympathizers. Under suspicion, Alexander had to flee. Kidnapped by slave catchers, he managed to escape and make his way to St. Louis, where he looked for work in a downtown public market. Luckily, Eliot's wife was also there, hoping to hire

a servant. She brought Alexander, who was reticent about his background, to her home. Eliot guessed that Alexander was a fugitive slave and knew how he had to act. In a controversial 1849 sermon he had declared that he would never return a fugitive slave to his master. But how to prevent possible recapture? Eliot hurried to the local provost-marshal's office, where he received a permit to keep Alexander for thirty days. He then asked a judicial friend to write to Hollman, offering six hundred dollars if he would renounce any claim to his slave, whom Eliot intended to free. But Hollman sent back a verbal threat, according to Eliot. "He'd have the nigger yet, and take it out of his black hide."

Two days before the permit was to expire, Alexander was kidnapped by slave catchers, who had clearly been sent by Hollman. With the help of the provost-marshal, Eliot managed to find Alexander and keep him safe until the emancipation of the slaves. Alexander and his wife were reunited, but in 1866—against Eliot's advice—she decided it would be safe to return to Hollman's house for some things she had left behind. The possessions came back without her. Hollman sent word that Louisa had died, two days after her arrival, of a mysterious sickness.

In 1869 Eliot was working on behalf of the Western Sanitary Commission, a St. Louis–based relief organization that aided Civil War victims, to erect a statue honoring Lincoln. Sculptor Thomas Ball had a suitable model already made, but the commission wanted it to represent a real freedman, not an idealized figure. Eliot gave Ball a photo of his employee, Archer Alexander. A sparkling array of dignitaries attended the 1876 unveiling, including President Ulysses S. Grant, members of his cabinet, Supreme Court justices, senators, and foreign ministers. Frederic Douglass, himself a former slave, gave an address. Neither Eliot nor Alexander were present, but Eliot was at his friend's bedside when he died a few years later, around 1880. Archer Alexander's last words, Eliot wrote, "were a prayer of thanksgiving that he had died in freedom."

CANDACE O'CONNOR

Eliot, William G. *The Story of Archer Alexander: From Slavery to Freedom, March 30, 1863.* Boston: Cupples, Upham, 1885.

ALEXANDER, GROVER CLEVELAND (1887–1950)

Born on February 26, 1887, in Elba, Nebraska, Alexander graduated from St. Paul High School in St. Paul, Nebraska. He worked as a telephone lineman before becoming a professional baseball player at the age of twenty-two. In 1911 he reached the major leagues as a pitcher for the Philadelphia Phillies of the National League (NL).

Thus began a sensational career in which Alexander recorded twenty-eight wins, seven shutouts, and thirty-one complete games in his rookie season. He soon supplanted Christy Mathewson as the NL's leading pitcher. In 1915 he won thirty-one games with an earned run average of 1.22, the NL's third all-time lowest. He again won thirty games over the next two seasons, making him the only pitcher in the twentieth century besides Mathewson to record thirty victories over three consecutive seasons. In 1916 the right-handed Alexander pitched sixteen shutouts, a major league record. Remarkably he performed brilliantly in Baker Bowel in Philadelphia where the right-field fence was only 280 feet from home plate. Due to his efforts, Philadelphia won its first NL pennant in 1915, losing to the Boston Red Sox in the World Series in five games. Alexander recorded Philadelphia's only World Series victory that year.

World War I disrupted Alexander's professional career. Following his marriage to Aimee Marie Arrants on May 31, 1918, he departed for France as an artilleryman in the 342nd Battalion of the Eighty-ninth Division. Alexander returned an alcoholic and an epileptic. For the remainder of his career he suffered epileptic seizures on the bench, forcing teammates to restrain him and to pour brandy into his mouth. Never the pitcher he once was, Alexander nonetheless won 128 games for the NL's Chicago Cubs from 1919 through 1925, representing 25 percent of their victories.

In 1926 the National League's St. Louis Cardinals purchased the thirty-nine-year-old Alexander's contract. As it turned out, the Cardinals probably would not have won their first World Series without him. Not only did he win nine games during the regular season, he became a World Series hero with his two victories. Moreover, after pitching the sixth game of the series, he relieved Jesse Haines the next day in the dramatic seventh game. Despite a hangover, Alexander struck out Tony Lazzeri of the New York Yankees with the bases loaded in the seventh inning and then pitched the last two innings to preserve a three-to-two victory. Alexander came back to win twenty-one games for the Cardinals the following season and pitched effectively for them in their 1928 pennant-winning season. He closed out his major league career with the Phillies in 1930 but continued pitching for semipro teams until the age of fifty-one. He died on November 4, 1950, in St. Paul, Nebraska.

The six-foot-one, 185-pound Alexander will always be remembered for his grace and economy on the mound. Games rarely lasted more than an hour and a half when he pitched. He wasted no time between deliveries, and he threw mostly strikes.

Often he retired the opposing side on five or six pitches. Known as "Old Low and Away" because of his knee-high strikes, he relied on pinpoint control and an excellent screwball and curve. Alexander's career statistics include 373 wins and 208 losses, 5,189 innings pitched, 2,199 strikeouts, and an average of only 1.65 bases on balls per nine-inning games. He won fifty-five games and lost thirty-four in his four years with the Cardinals. Alexander was elected to the National Baseball Hall of Fame in 1938.

JAMES N. GIGLIO

Biographical Dictionary of American Sports: Baseball. S.v. "Alexander, Grover Cleveland."

Rains, Rob. *The St. Louis Cardinals: The 100th Anniversary History.* New York: St. Martin's, 1992.

Ritter, Lawrence S. *The Glory of Their Times: The Story of the Early Days of Baseball Told by the Men Who Played It.* New York: Vintage, 1985.

Seymour, Harold. *Baseball: The Golden Age.* New York: Oxford University Press, 1971.

ALLEN, FORREST C. "PHOG" (1885–1974)

Forrest C. "Phog" Allen, whose foghorn voice earned him his nickname, was a masterful, outspoken basketball coach, so dedicated to the sport that he won the honorary title "Mr. Basketball." He found a game in a gymnasium and almost single-handedly made it an international sport.

Forrest Claire Allen was born in Jamesport, Missouri, on November 15, 1885, to William T. and Mary E. Allen. Allen's grandfather George P. Allen moved the family from Virginia to Daviess County, Missouri, in 1866, where he was a county surveyor. William and Mary Allen had five other sons, and together the boys composed the "Allen Brothers Basket Ball Team."

While a student at Independence High School, Allen was interested in athletics and became a member of every athletic organization and played on every team. During a game in 1903 Allen first met James Naismith, inventor of the game of basketball, who was director of sports at the University of Kansas. Allen entered the university in 1904 and lettered in basketball in 1905, 1906, and 1907 and in baseball in 1906 and 1907. On June 25, 1907, he married Bessie E. Milton of Jackson County, Missouri. They had four children, two boys and two girls.

In 1905 Allen managed and played guard for the Kansas City Athletic Club (KCAC), which won two of three games against the Buffalo Germans, the world-champion team touring the country. His team proclaimed themselves the new national champions after beating the Buffalo team, who had earned their title by winning both the Pan American and the St. Louis World's Fair tournaments.

Allen's formal coaching career began at the University of Kansas in 1908 and spanned forty-six years. He also coached at Baker University in Baldwin, Kansas, in 1908 and 1909. Following his graduation from the University of Kansas in 1909, Allen left coaching for the next four years to study osteopathic medicine. He returned to college athletics in 1912 as coach of all sports at Warrensburg Normal (now Central Missouri State University), where his football, basketball, and baseball teams won numerous championships during his seven-year tenure. Allen resigned in 1919 when the school's board of regents rehired him with a raise in pay on the condition that he drop his osteopathic practice and devote his full attention to coaching.

In 1919 he returned to the University of Kansas to serve as director of athletics and football coach for one season, but chiefly as head basketball coach, a game he came to dominate thoroughly by the force of his ideas and his personality. He served as the university's basketball coach until thrust into mandatory retirement in 1956 when he became professor emeritus of physical education. He referred to the university's retirement policy as the age of "statutory senility."

Of all his accomplishments, Allen most cherished his successful effort to have basketball awarded Olympic status. During the 1920s and early 1930s Allen conducted a one-man crusade to convince Olympic officials to include basketball in the world games. His untiring work was finally rewarded when the American-invented game was added to the 1936 Olympics in Berlin.

Coaches around the world read Allen's books about basketball. In 1952 he served as a coach for the U.S. Olympic team, comprised in large part of the University of Kansas players who had won the NCAA championship that year, and won the gold medal at Helsinki, Finland. Allen was a founder and the first president of the National Basketball Coaches Association. Twice he was named Coach of the Year and once Basketball Man of the Year. He was elected to the Missouri Sports Hall of Fame, the Kansas Centennial Hall of Fame, and the Naismith Hall of Fame in Springfield, Massachusetts. The 17,500-seat arena at the University of Kansas was named in his honor in March 1955. Allen died on September 16, 1974.

ARTHUR F. MCCLURE AND VIVIAN RICHARDSON

Cockrell, Ewing. *History of Johnson County, Missouri.* Topeka, Kans.: Historical Publishing, 1918.
Kansas City Times, September 17, 1974.

ALLEN, THOMAS (1813–1882)

Thomas Allen was among the most prominent and powerful individuals who led St. Louis in its transition from commercial outpost to industrial metropolis. Best known for his political service and for his leadership in establishing the Pacific Railroad, Allen played an equally important role in the development of St. Louis land during the city's most rapid period of growth. Perhaps more significantly, Allen's career bridged the period when the city's fortunes rested in the hands of a small group of locally prominent citizens to the era of corporate control, in which personal power was based on connections to national finance and influence.

Allen was born in 1813 in Pittsfield, Massachusetts, a town to which he would return throughout his life. Early biographers emphasized the prominence and status of his father's family, which had resided in Massachusetts since the seventeenth century. At the same time, however, Allen is portrayed as a man who built his own fortunes. His father, having suffered a series of business reversals, was said to have given the young Allen twenty-five dollars, telling him, "Go and take care of yourself." In spite of his privileged origins, then, Allen would later claim, "I also started at the bottom of the ladder."

Allen left Pittsfield for Union College in New York, then studied for the bar in Albany. In 1832 he moved to New York City, where he found a livelihood not in the practice of law but in publishing. He edited *Family Magazine* and also compiled and published a digest of state laws. With the small stake he had acquired from these ventures, he moved again four years later, to Washington, D.C.

It was in Washington that a combination of professional ambition and political good fortune elevated Allen to national prominence. An early supporter of the new administration of Martin Van Buren, he became, after the panic of 1837, one of the president's most outspoken critics. His prominence in the political scene was obtained largely through his position as the editor of a new journal, the *Madisonian.* This job also allowed him to secure the printing contract for the House of Representatives from 1837 to 1839, and for the Senate in the three years that followed. With his professional standing and his rhetorical skills, he quickly endeared himself to Van Buren's Whig opponent in 1840, **William Henry Harrison.**

Allen remained close to the short-lived president, and was allegedly present at Harrison's deathbed. He supported Harrison's successor, John Tyler, but left Washington (and the *Madisonian*) a short time later, in 1842. This move proved the most important of his young career.

Why Allen came to St. Louis is unclear. He may have envisioned more room for his political ambitions outside the tightly drawn circles of Washington; he may simply have longed for the adventure of a life on the frontier. In any case, he arrived in the spring of the year, and within months had found personal happiness and, for the first time, lasting financial security. Both came in the person of Ann Russell, whom Allen married in July of the same year.

Allen's new father-in-law, William Russell, had come to the city just after the American takeover to serve as the new government's land surveyor. In the course of his work, he had acquired vast amounts of land in his own right, much of it surrounding his home on the southern edge of the city. In bequeathing this land to his son-in-law, Russell obligated Allen to provide Ann with an annual income from the property. Allen proceeded to develop the rolling prairie around the family estate into an even grid of streets, blocks, and house lots. Either selling these lots outright or renting them through long-term leases, Allen developed much of the area from the Carondelet Road (now South Broadway) west to Jefferson Avenue, between Soulard Market to the north and Benton Park to the south. Much of this land, which was soon closely built and heavily populated by working-class immigrant families, remained in his possession until his death. At the time, it represented the largest tract of property in St. Louis to be developed by a single person.

When not surveying and developing his lands, Allen devoted his early years in St. Louis to the craft of political pamphleteering, always in the interests of himself and his adopted city. In one work he excoriated American delinquency in affirming French and Spanish land grants in the former Louisiana Territory (his own claim to the Russell property rested on the security of several such grants). In another, Allen called on the federal government to spend more toward making navigable the country's inland waterways.

The accomplishment with which Allen will forever be most closely identified, however, was his successful advocacy of a different kind of federal improvement: a transcontinental railroad, headed west to California by way of St. Louis. In 1849, writing in anticipation of the great railroad convention held in the city that year, Allen made his claim for "a Western route to Asia," along "a CENTRAL HIGHWAY that shall be most useful and most acceptable to all parts of our country. With the support of **Thomas Hart Benton,** Allen—elected president of the new Pacific Railroad in 1850—traveled across the state, as well as east to New York and Washington, in pursuit of support for the venture. As a state senator, he engineered government loan guarantees and land grants that put the fledgling company on its feet. In addition to the originally planned route from St. Louis to Kansas City, he oversaw the opening of a southwestern route, which opened up the mining regions west of the Ozarks for widespread commercial exploitation.

In 1854 the railroad suffered the first of what would become a recurrent series of financial crises, and Allen was implicated in public rumors of board mismanagement. He offered his resignation on the eve of a St. Louis County bond issue designed to offer emergency relief to the company. The bonds were approved, but Allen had lost his key place in the railroad's development.

Allen returned to his land-development business, dabbled in banking, and ran, unsuccessfully, for Congress in 1862. In 1867 he reentered the railroad business, but his sights were now set closer to home than on the grandiose "Western route to Asia" that had first inspired him. In the Iron Mountain Railroad, Allen saw a route, nearly as old as the Pacific, that reached south into a trade territory not yet tapped by rival transportation centers such as Chicago. Within five years he had extended the road beyond its original terminus in the area of Iron Mountain all the way to Texarkana. His enterprise took on ever greater proportions as he absorbed first one and then another line into the Iron Mountain system, until by 1874 Allen conglomerated his holdings into the St. Louis, Iron Mountain, and Southern Railroad.

By the late 1870s Allen, extremely wealthy and secure in his financial ventures, had once again begun to consider a return to Washington. In 1878 he returned to his old craft, political pamphleteering, to publicize his positions. Most were unsurprising for a man of his station: he warned of "the spirit of discontent and revolution" brewing in America's cities, he advocated keeping the Chinese in Asia and returning American blacks to Africa, and he proposed to economically colonize Mexico and "make it our own."

Allen was elected as the Democratic representative to Missouri's Second District in 1880. The following year, as he began his term, he sold his railroad holdings to Jay Gould and erected the Southern Hotel in downtown St. Louis. If his capacity for spending and making money seemed undiminished, his health did not. By the time of the election, Allen had begun to feel the effects of what was later described as cancer of either the stomach or the bladder; his condition deteriorated sharply after he came to Washington.

Like his early patron, William Henry Harrison, Thomas Allen's term in the capital was cut short. He died on April 8, 1882, and his body was returned to his hometown of Pittsfield for burial. The persona he had encouraged in life—of a tireless and dedicated public servant—was eagerly taken up after his death; Allen's eulogizer reported that he had died murmuring: "I would like to live a few years longer. There are some things I would like to do for Missouri."

ERIC SANDWEISS

Allen, Thomas. "Pacific Railroad Commenced: Address of Thomas Allen, Esq., of St. Louis, to the Board of Directors of the Pacific Railroad Company." St. Louis: Republican, 1850.

Dacus, J. A., and James W. Buel. *A Tour of St. Louis, or the Inside Life of a Great City.* St. Louis: Western Publishing, 1878.

History of the Pacific Railroad, from Its Inception to Its Final Completion. St. Louis: Democrat Book and Job Printing House, 1865.

Memorial Addresses on the Life and Character of Thomas Allen. Washington, D.C.: U.S. Government Printing Office, 1884.

ANDERSON, GALUSHA (1832–1918)

Of the various eyewitness accounts of Civil War St. Louis, one written nearly a half century afterward gives perhaps the freshest and most vivid description of the city and its people during this tumultuous period. This account, *The Story of a Border City during the Civil War,* was written in 1908 by the Reverend Galusha Anderson, who was pastor of Second Baptist Church in St. Louis during the war.

Anderson was born March 7, 1832, on a farm near Clarendon, New York. From the time of his religious conversion and baptism at age twelve, the young Anderson set his heart on the ministry. After graduating from a private academy in 1851, he received his bachelor's degree in 1854 from the newly founded University of Rochester and his doctorate of divinity from the Rochester Theological Seminary in 1856. Upon graduation he accepted his first pastorate at the Baptist Church of Janesville, Wisconsin. Two years after his arrival in Wisconsin, word of the success of the dynamic and handsome young pastor became known throughout Baptist circles, and Anderson was asked to become pastor of the Second Baptist Church of St. Louis, then the largest and most influential Baptist church west of the Mississippi River.

Like fellow abolitionist St. Louis pastors **Truman Marcellus Post** of First Trinity Congregational Church and Henry A. Nelson of First Presbyterian Church, Galusha Anderson discovered that his St. Louis congregation included slaveholders, some of whom were wealthy and prominent. Despite their differing beliefs on slavery, pastor and congregation achieved an understanding prior to the war, whereby Anderson carefully avoided preaching on slavery and those favoring slavery in his congregation focused on their pastor's other qualities. On the eve of the Civil War, even the proslavery *Missouri Republican* acknowledged that abolitionist Anderson was "exceedingly popular as a preacher," and the newspaper encouraged attendance at his public lecture on the subject of bigotry.

Anderson's *Story of a Border City* is an entertaining, accurate, and, given that its author was an ardent Unionist and abolitionist, surprisingly balanced narrative and has become one of the most quoted sources on Civil War St. Louis. From his descriptions of the provocative actions of the pro-Confederate Minutemen to the chaos following **Nathaniel Lyon**'s capture of Camp Jackson, Anderson gives a fascinating picture of his fellow St. Louisans in the crucial first months of the war. Former Confederate general and Minutemen captain **Basil Wilson Duke** also wrote an excellent description of this period in St. Louis history, but Duke fled St. Louis after Camp Jackson for service in the Confederate army. Anderson, on the other hand, lived in St. Louis for the duration of the war and wrote of important events in St. Louis throughout the conflict. For example, Anderson sheds valuable light on the great Mississippi Valley Sanitary Fair of 1864 that raised record amounts of money for the Union cause. Equally valuable are Anderson's insightful and sympathetic descriptions of black St. Louisans, especially the charismatic, self-educated black pastor John Richard Anderson, who pastored the largest black church in St. Louis.

Galusha Anderson was not merely an observer but also a significant participant in many of the events that he described. After he dared to preach the first overtly pro-Union sermon in St. Louis in April 1861, Anderson was targeted by pro-Confederate bullies, who mistakenly attacked the better-known Samuel J. P. Anderson, pastor of Central Presbyterian Church, who, ironically, was very pro-Southern in philosophy. Throughout the war, Galusha Anderson took a leading role in promoting various Union causes, including the Sanitary Fair, and was regarded by many as being unseemly partisan on behalf of the Union. In 1864, after a series of bloody Union defeats, Anderson delivered a sermon in which he urged the Union to continue the war until slavery was ended, even if it took more than eighty years. His remarks were met with scorn from the once-laudatory *Missouri Republican,* which now lampooned him as "a Preacher on the War Path."

In 1866, shortly after the end of the Civil War, Anderson left St. Louis and taught for seven years at the Newton Theological Institution in Massachusetts and then spent the next six years occupying influential Baptist pastorates in Brooklyn and Chicago. In 1878 he was appointed president of the "old" University of Chicago and in 1887 of Denison University in Granville, Ohio. From 1890 until 1892 he taught at a Baptist theological school in Illinois. In 1892 Anderson was one of nine former college and seminary presidents specially selected for the initial faculty of the well-endowed "new" University of Chicago, where he would remain as a professor in the Divinity School until his retirement in 1904. From 1904 until his death on July 20, 1918, in Massachusetts, he devoted much of his retirement to writing numerous articles and books, including *The Story of a Border City.*

MARSHALL D. HIER

Anderson, Frederick. *Galusha Anderson: Preacher and Educator, 1832–1918.* Newton Center, Mass.: Elbridge R. Anderson, 1933.

Anderson, Galusha. *The Story of a Border City during the Civil War.* Boston: Little, Brown, 1908.

Dictionary of American Biography. Vol. 1. S.v. "Anderson, Galusha."

Missouri Republican, October 25, 1860–September 26, 1864.

ANDERSON, WILLIAM T. "BLOODY BILL" (1838?–1864)

The facts concerning the early life of Bloody Bill Anderson are as elusive as he was as a Confederate irregular. He was born in 1838 or 1839 in Jefferson County or Salt Springs Township in Randolph County, Missouri. His parents probably came from Kentucky, and he had three sisters and at least one brother. Bill and his brother James attended a local school in Huntsville, Missouri. **Richard S. Brownlee,** in his study of guerrilla warfare in Missouri, *Gray Ghosts of the Confederacy,* stated: "In the annals of the border war Bill Anderson is truly a mysterious figure, for little is known about the background of this terrible young man. . . ." Notwithstanding his obscure origins, we know that he became one of the most violent and fiendish characters on either side during the Civil War.

Anderson's father, a hatter, moved the family to Kansas in 1856 or 1857. The Kansas and Missouri border was, at that time, a tinderbox. The Andersons moved into this storm in which lines had been drawn between proslavery and antislavery factions. Civil disorder, murder, arson, and thievery had become a way of life on the border, long before the nation was swept into the Civil War. The family passed through the turbulent eastern counties of Kansas and squatted on a sparsely settled prairie near Council Grove. The Andersons, because of their Southern sympathies and their refusal to take up arms against the South, soon found themselves at odds with their neighbors. The ferocious passion on both sides seemed a fitting training ground for someone with Bloody Bill's personality.

The Andersons soon gained a reputation for shady dealings. In early 1862 a local judge accused the Andersons and their friends of horse stealing, and in a confrontation the elder Anderson was killed. The family then returned to the supposed safety of Missouri. But Bill and several friends returned to Council Grove seeking revenge against his father's killer. They gunned down the judge and his brother-in-law and set on fire a store owned by the judge. This was the beginning of Anderson's intense vendetta against all Free Staters and later Union soldiers.

Anderson's appearance is described as "most handsome." He stood just under six feet, was slender with long, thick, curly dark hair and piercing blue-gray eyes. He was an excellent horseman and exhibited no fear of battle or death. His viciousness and show of emotions soon earned him the name "Bloody Bill."

Gen. **Thomas Ewing Jr.** became commander of the District of the Border in June 1863 with headquarters in Kansas City, Missouri, which was located near the center of guerrilla activities. Ewing, aware that the guerrillas depended on friends and relatives for information, shelter, and supplies, stepped up the arrest and confinement of suspected guerrilla supporters, including women. The women prisoners were housed in a three-story brick building that collapsed on August 14, 1863, killing four women, including Josephine Anderson, Bill's sister. Another sister, Mary, was crippled. Anderson, like most guerrillas, became outraged when he learned of the death and injury of loved ones. From that time, Anderson was determined to kill every Union supporter he encountered. The die had been cast, and, according to Brownlee, Anderson became a "homicidal maniac."

The cry for vengeance was soon answered, as the guerrillas, led by **William Clarke Quantrill,** decided to enter Kansas and destroy the hotbed of abolitionists in Lawrence. Many now believe the death of the women was the impetus Quantrill needed to persuade his men to raid Lawrence. Anderson was reported to have stated: "Lawrence or hell, but with one proviso, that we kill every male thing." On August 21, 1863, Quantrill ordered his men to move into Lawrence. Bill Anderson's band was credited with more killing than any other company. When they left Lawrence four hours later, the guerrillas had killed 150 unarmed men. The irregulars then fled to Missouri and divided into small groups seeking safety and shelter from their friends and relatives.

The Union commander, General Ewing, issued General Order No. 11. This order banished twenty thousand inhabitants, all but those of proven Northern sympathies, from the four western border counties in an effort to curtail further guerrilla activities and to keep the revenge-seeking Kansans out of Missouri.

The guerrillas remained in hiding until late September when they began their yearly journey to winter quarters in Texas. As usual, they killed and plundered along the way, and their arrival in Sherman, Texas, was not welcomed by the citizens. The band robbed and murdered local residents and even shot at the church steeple. The guerrillas soon wore out their welcome in Texas and began their trek north to Missouri.

On June 11, 1864, Missourians realized the guerrillas had returned when it was discovered that twelve Union soldiers had been killed and mutilated—a common practice of the Anderson irregulars. Bloody Bill Anderson took center stage as the most feared and vicious bushwhacker in Missouri. Albert Castel, in his study of Quantrill, stated of Anderson: "Between July and October he made more raids, rode more miles, and killed more men than any other guerrilla chieftain, including Quantrill, ever did."

The people of central Missouri lived in fear as Anderson moved from county to county. He robbed and murdered in Carroll and Chariton Counties and even in his hometown of Huntsville. He entered Shelby County and burned the railroad bridge at Salt River. In Rocheport his men killed, scalped, and slit the throats of Union troops. Anderson and his men committed unspeakable atrocities on both the living and the dead. The name "Bloody Bill" was more than justified.

In September 1864, Gen. **Sterling Price** sent word to the guerrillas that he would enter southeast Missouri and asked them to harass the Union troops. Anderson, seeking news of Price's army, entered Centralia, Missouri, on September 27, 1864. After robbing the stores, he and his men became drunk. The noon train arrived, and Anderson ordered the Union soldiers on it to disrobe. He then directed his men to "muster out" the soldiers. The guerrillas opened fire at point-blank range. On returning to their camp, they learned that a mounted Union infantry unit from Paris was approaching. To Anderson's amazement, Maj. A. V. E. Johnson, the Union commander, ordered his men to dismount. Within a few minutes, Johnson's Thirty-ninth Missouri Infantry was massacred. Even the wounded were killed. Bodies were mutilated: heads were severed, ears and noses were sliced, and many were scalped.

Anderson finally found Price in Boonville, but Price refused to meet with Anderson until he and his men disposed of the scalps and other trophies. Price then ordered Anderson to destroy the North Missouri Railroad bridge.

On October 26, 1864, Bloody Bill fought his final battle. The Missouri State Militia found his camp near Albany. A little after noon Anderson encountered an ambush by the Missouri troops. With a Rebel cry, he charged the bluecoats. He broke their ranks but was shot twice in the back of the head. His body was placed in a wagon and taken to Richmond, where it was put on public display and the town photographer took Anderson's most famous photograph. It was reported the militia removed his head and placed it on a telegraph pole.

Anderson's death ended the spree of one of the most cruel and vicious men in Missouri history. Anderson was no doubt brave, but his mental imbalance and homicidal urges overshadowed his courage.

Charles R. Mink

Brownlee, Richard S. *Gray Ghosts of the Confederacy: Guerrilla Warfare in the West.* Baton Rouge: Louisiana State University Press, 1958.

Castel, Albert. *William Clarke Quantrill: His Life and Time.* New York: Frederick Fell, 1962.

Connelly, William Elsey. *Quantrill and the Border Wars.* New York: Pagent, 1956.

Goodman, Thomas M. *A Thrilling Record Founded on Facts and Observations Obtained during Ten Days' Experience with Col. Wm. T. Anderson.* Columbia, Mo.: State Historical Society, 1868.

Goodrich, Thomas. *Bloody Dawn: The Story of the Lawrence Massacre.* Kent, Ohio: Kent State University Press, 1991.

Hale, Donald, *The Life of William Anderson: Missouri Guerrilla.* Clinton, Mo.: Printery, 1975.

ANDREIS, FELIX DE (1778–1820)

Felix de Andreis, the pioneer professor of theology in the American West, came to America at the invitation of Bishop **Louis William DuBourg** of Louisiana Territory, in the summer of 1817. Born on May 1, 1778, in the Province of Piemonte in northern Italy, Andreis had joined the Vincentian Congregation and taught theology at the College of the Propaganda in Rome, which prepared priests for work in distant mission fields. In 1815 the newly consecrated DuBourg recruited Andreis and many others to work in his vast diocese. DuBourg had successfully enlisted the aid of Pope Pius VII in securing the release of Andreis from his work in Rome.

The missionary team that accompanied Andreis to the United States in 1817 included four Vincentian priests, one coadjutor brother, two priests, four seminarians, and three young men who intended to join the Vincentians in America. One of the priests was Joseph Rosati, a future bishop of St. Louis. A thoughtful man with a tenacious memory, but of frail physique, Andreis spoke Latin fluently, and knew Greek and Hebrew. He enjoyed poetry and wrote religious songs. He could read French and presumably could speak it well enough to begin work among the people of New Orleans. But ever enthusiastic and constantly changing DuBourg decided instead to send his recruits to St. Louis.

Many reasons may account for this change in plans. Perhaps the greatest was the presence in New Orleans of the popular and powerful pastor of the cathedral, the Spanish Capuchin, Fray Antonio de Sedella, who had received his appointment from the king of Spain before the Louisiana Purchase. Andreis necessarily altered his own plans. He accepted the hospitality of Bishop Benedict Joseph Flaget and the people of Bardstown, Kentucky, and established his seminary there for a year, teaching theology and studying English.

When Andreis arrived in St. Louis to be rector of the church in October 1817, the parish had not had a pastor for almost ten years. A priest from Cahokia, across the river, had occasionally come. The new pastor found the French residents unconcerned about the differences between Catholic and Protestant doctrines, while the Irish were ready to fight over every point of faith and Catholic practice. Further, the rough ways of a French-American river town proved trying for the quiet, scholarly, and feeble theology professor.

The always-moving DuBourg appointed Andreis his assistant for Upper Louisiana with the title "Vicar-General." Andreis also directed the Congregation of the Mission in America, the diocesan seminary, and the Vincentian novitiate. For a short time he was the spiritual director of Mother **Rose Philippine Duchesne** and the nuns of the Sacred Heart who came from France to teach girls.

In early December, DuBourg arrived at Baltimore with an additional twenty-nine recruits. Early in January 1818, DuBourg arrived in St. Louis. He planned to build a cathedral, open an academy, and establish a seminary in Perryville. While this latter project was under way, Andreis continued to teach the prospective priests in St. Louis. The first to be ordained, François Niel, directed DuBourg's academy when it opened in the fall of 1818.

Andreis chose Rosati to take charge of the seminary and the Vincentian missionary efforts in Perryville. Rosati found Maryland Catholics there a devout people. Their English and Irish ancestors had long known how to preserve their religious spirit in a pluralistic society, while the French had met few Protestants before the Louisiana Purchase.

Andreis hoped to work among the tribes of the West and planned to prepare religious instructions in the native tongues. He talked to Native American leaders visiting St. Louis about future missions. That opportunity never arose. His many cares overrode his already weak frame. He became ill and died October 15, 1820, at the age of forty-two.

WILLIAM B. FAHERTY

Rosati, Joseph. *Sketches of the Life of the Very Rev. Felix de Andreis.* St. Louis: B. Gerder, 1900.

Rothensteiner, John E. *History of the Archdiocese of St. Louis in Its Various Stages of Development from* A.D. *1637 to* A.D. *1928.* Vol. 1. St. Louis: Blackwell Wielandy, 1928.

ARMSTRONG, ORLAND KAY (1893–1987)

Orland Kay "O. K." Armstrong was a social crusader who used a combination of political skills, gained as a legislator and congressman, and writing skills to advance a number of issues. He championed the pre–World War II isolationist movement, advocated increased civil rights for American Indians, and helped organize the antipornography movement in the 1960s and 1970s. Armstrong served three terms in the Missouri House, one in Congress, established the journalism department at the University of Florida–Gainesville, created an international incident at the Japanese Allied Peace Conference by accusing the Soviets of maintaining slave-labor camps, and worked either as a writer for, or on the editorial staff of, *Reader's Digest* for more than three decades.

Armstrong was born October 2, 1893, in Willow Springs, Missouri, the third of nine children to the Reverend William Armstrong, a schoolteacher. Since the reverend was involved in founding new churches, the family moved often but always stayed in the southern Missouri Ozarks during O. K. Armstrong's years at home.

In 1907 the family relocated to Carterville, Missouri, where Armstrong graduated from high school in 1912 as class valedictorian. From there he entered Drury College, in Springfield, Missouri, to pursue the first of five college degrees he would earn by the time he was thirty-two. In 1916 he graduated summa cum laude from Drury with a bachelor's degree in education.

The next year Armstrong began his first professional position as an English teacher at Southwest Baptist College (now University) in Bolivar, Missouri, where he also coached basketball and managed the men's dorm. His maternal grandfather, the Reverend Daniel Preston, had been a moving force in the founding of the school.

War raged in Europe, and Armstrong left Southwest Baptist after his first year to enlist in the aviation division of the United States Signal Corps. Initially trained as a pilot, he later served as an instructor, rising from private to second lieutenant at what would later become Maxwell Air Force Base near Montgomery, Alabama. While in the army he received his first taste of professional journalism by serving as the editor of an aviation magazine, the *Propeller.*

Disappointed that he had not been sent to France as had two brothers, Armstrong volunteered to work as a civilian in France for the YMCA in 1919. He served with the Russian prisoners of war in eight camps, organizing recreational and cultural activities for the prisoners while they awaited return to the newly formed Soviet Union.

Armstrong's return to the United States in 1920 entailed a number of rapid changes. His parents had moved to Florida to establish churches, and Armstrong served for two years as the first state director of the Florida Baptist Young People's Union. While serving with this organization he met Louise McCool, who would become his first wife.

The restless Armstrong then moved to Cumberland University in Tennessee where he earned a law degree and a bachelor's degree in oratory, and then married Louise McCool in Jacksonville, Florida, in 1922. Although admitted to the Missouri bar, he never practiced law. Instead, he declared that he "wanted to make an honest living" and had decided to be a journalist. That decision necessitated a move to Columbia, Missouri, where he attended the University of Missouri, receiving both a bachelor's and a master's degree in journalism in 1925. While attending school he also worked as circulation manager of the *Columbia Missourian.* The publisher was **Walter Williams,** who was also the dean of the Journalism School.

Williams arranged for Armstrong to be offered immediate teaching positions at the College of William and Mary in Virginia and the University of Florida–Gainesville. Armstrong chose the University of Florida in part because it allowed him to be close to his parents. The university planned to establish a school of journalism, where Armstrong served as the only full-time faculty member as well as its first director.

During his three years at the university, Armstrong also outlined a high school journalism textbook, wrote the biography of University of Florida president A. A. Murphree, authored a Boy Scouts pamphlet giving career guidance for those interested in journalism, and began collecting material for a book about the lives of African American slaves. He left the university and moved from Florida after suffering financial reversals in land speculation.

A turning point came in Armstrong's life in 1927. He had traveled to Washington to see the activities surrounding the return of **Charles A. Lindbergh** from history's first New York–Paris solo flight. Armstrong met Frank Robertson, who had been one of Lindbergh's early flying instructors. Robertson then arranged an invitation for Armstrong to a private meeting with Lindbergh. That meeting started a long-term friendship between the two Missourians. Lindbergh granted Armstrong the only interview he gave on that trip. Armstrong was representing the Boy Scouts at the festivities, and the Lindbergh interview was published first in *Boy's Life* and then in newspapers around the United States.

Armstrong returned to Springfield, Missouri, and to Drury College where he took a part-time job handling the school's public relations. He also began a freelance writing career that would span six decades. Armstrong's first freelance article appeared in the *American Legion Magazine* in November 1929. The article featured the Legion's Hospital for Crippled Children in St. Petersburg, Florida, and so began an era of his life that would provide both an income and a wide-ranging forum for almost fifty years.

In 1930 Armstrong ran for the Missouri State Senate. Although he was not successful in that effort, he began his governmental career that same year when Gov. **Henry Stewart Caulfield** appointed him as executive secretary of the Century of Progress Committee, which was preparing the state's exhibit for the 1933 Chicago World's Fair.

Armstrong defied the Democratic landslide in 1932 and won his first race for the General Assembly. He was one of only ten Republicans elected to the 150-member Missouri House of Representatives. As one of the few lawyers in the House, Armstrong did manage to have an impact by acting as a bill drafter for leading Democratic lawmakers. He won an additional term in 1934 but lost in 1936.

While serving in the legislature Armstrong continued his career as a journalist. Some of his writing was very much a part of his governmental and political agenda. In 1934 he wrote a syndicated series of exposé articles about **Thomas J. Pendergast** and Kansas City political corruption and gambling. As a result of those articles, and a chance encounter at a national governors' meeting in Oklahoma City with Missouri governor **Lloyd Stark,** Armstrong became an undercover investigator in 1938. He was the first person called to appear before the Jackson County grand jury investigating Pendergast in 1939.

That year Armstrong's activities had both a national and an international focus. He was hired to handle public relations for Adm. Richard E. Byrd after the admiral's return from the Antarctic in 1939. And then as war clouds rolled across both Europe and Asia, Armstrong and Lindbergh became enmeshed in a national effort to keep the United States out of war. Armstrong was part of the earliest discussions that led to the formation of the America First Committee, and in 1940 he, Lindbergh, and others formed the No War Committee of which Armstrong was the director. After the attack on Pearl Harbor, though, Armstrong supported the war.

He began his association with *Reader's Digest* in 1942 when he submitted a freelance article on trade barriers between states. He became a staff writer in 1944. He contributed 125 articles in his own name and pen names before retiring in 1974. Perhaps his best-remembered articles are "Great Moments in American History" written between 1973 and 1975 as the cornerstone of *Reader's Digest*'s Bicentennial efforts. Armstrong used his position with the magazine to champion civil rights for American

Indians, to attack the national deficit, and to oppose pornography.

Armstrong was reelected to the Missouri House of Representatives in 1942. His last term in the Missouri legislature was far different from his first. Republicans controlled the House, and Armstrong was able to chair the budget subcommittee on the University of Missouri and to draft substantive legislation in his own name. That legislation reorganized significant areas in state government, including civil services, education, and corrections. He was credited with founding the State Department of Resources and Development, which eventually became the Department of Economic Development.

Armstrong left the Missouri House to run for lieutenant governor in 1944 but lost the Republican primary. His governmental activity then shifted to advisory roles. He served as a member of the Missouri Children's Code Commission from 1947 to 1949 and as chairman of a U.S. Senate Study Commission on the executive branch in 1947–1948.

In 1947 Armstrong's first wife, Louise, died of cancer. The couple had five children. In 1949 Armstrong married Marjorie Moore, a fellow writer who had once edited his work. He ran for Congress in 1950 and was elected to represent Missouri's Sixth District. As a freshman congressman, Armstrong introduced bills and resolutions to eliminate the Bureau of Indian Affairs, create public holidays commemorating **George Washington Carver** and Booker T. Washington, and proposed changes in the Civil Service Retirement Act. None of the laws he proposed were enacted. The Armstrongs returned to Missouri in 1965.

Congressman Armstrong did, however, make his presence felt, especially during a 1951 trip to Korea. He met in Taiwan with President Chiang Kai-shek. Armstrong became the liaison between Congress and President Chiang regarding a plan to bring nationalist Chinese forces into the Korean War to attack communist China. The plan had been drafted with Gen. Douglas MacArthur and Gen. Clair Chennault. The day Armstrong met with President Chiang, however, President **Harry S. Truman** fired MacArthur, bringing the plan to an end.

On that same trip Armstrong became convinced that the rumor President Truman would soon give the island of Taiwan to communist China was true. Hoping to force the government to take a position committed to defending Chiang Kai-shek's government in exile on the island, Armstrong called a news conference to refute the rumors. The State Department responded by denying that such a plan was under consideration.

In 1951 Armstrong helped create an international incident at the Japanese Allied Peace Conference in San Francisco. During heated discussions with the Soviet's chief delegate, Andrey Gromyko

(the eventual Soviet prime minister), Armstrong upbraided the Soviet leadership for maintaining slave-labor camps. Gromyko denied the charge, but Armstrong produced a map showing the existence of the camps.

The redrawing of Missouri's congressional districts in 1952 forced Armstrong to decide whether to run against his friend and senior in the Congress, **Dewey Jackson Short.** Armstrong chose not to run again. Soon after the election his longtime acquaintance John Foster Dulles appointed Armstrong director of public relations for the Department of State. But Armstrong never got the job, because the Internal Revenue Service notified Dulles that they were filing a request for criminal action against Armstrong.

The IRS case took twelve years to fully resolve. In 1955 Armstrong was convicted on three counts of tax evasion and paid all the required back taxes, but he countersued and eventually recovered all the money. His public-service career, however, ended with the IRS action.

Now Armstrong concentrated on his journalism career. In 1957 he began a twenty-year crusade against pornography, beginning with stories in *Reader's Digest.* In 1970 he founded the Springfield Citizens' Council for Decency based on articles he had written about a similar group in Coral Gables, Florida. He also wrote a series of stories on the plight of the American Indians and the need for reforming their federal assistance.

Armstrong ran unsuccessfully for the General Assembly in 1966 when his efforts to lead a boycott of the movie *Who's Afraid of Virginia Woolf?* became a major feature of the campaign. His final campaign took place in 1982 when he ran for the Missouri House against two much younger opponents. He was defeated in the Republican primary. O. K. and Marjorie Armstrong spent their final years together at a home they called the Highlands just north of Wilson's Creek National Battlefield. O. K. Armstrong died there on April 15, 1987, following a stroke.

ROY D. BLUNT

Kansas City Times, May 11, 1982.

Lindbergh, Charles A. *The Wartime Journals of Charles A. Lindbergh.* New York: Harcourt Brace Jovanovich, 1970.

Republican Monitor, April 14, 1966.

Sirianni, Anararcia. "O. K. Armstrong." Master's thesis, University of Florida–Gainesville, 1992.

Springfield News and Leader, April 20, 1975–April 16, 1987.

ARMSTRONG, PAUL (1869–1915)

Paul Armstrong, a journalist and playwright, was born in Kidder, Missouri, near St. Joseph, on April

25, 1869. He attended the public schools of Kidder and Bay City, Michigan, the town to which he moved while still a boy.

Pursuing his father's occupation, Armstrong worked for five years on Great Lakes steamboats, earning a master's license at the age of twenty-one. The short stories that he wrote during these years failed to find publishers, but Armstrong developed a writing style and built a fund of experience that later served him well as a playwright.

The same may be said of Armstrong's years as a journalist, from the early 1890s to 1904. Specializing in crime and sports reporting, he worked in Buffalo until 1896 for the *Express,* the *Courier,* and the *News;* in Chicago from 1896 to 1898 for the *Inter-Ocean* and the *Times-Herald;* and in New York from 1898 to 1904 for several papers, including William Randolph Hearst's *Journal.* While working for the *Express,* he solved a murder that had baffled Buffalo police. While residing in Chicago, he wrote anti–free silver propaganda for William McKinley's 1896 Republican presidential campaign. As a Hearst journalist, Armstrong was the first author of the syndicated boxing column "Right Cross."

Armstrong's success in the theater came only after grim persistence. While in New York he freelanced monologues for vaudeville comics and wrote one-act plays for vaudeville and full-length dramas for the Broadway stage. From his first success, *The Heir to the Hoorah* (1905), until his health declined in 1913, Armstrong was among the most popular and financially successful of American playwrights. He is best known for *Alias Jimmy Valentine* (1909), which he wrote in five days and from which he had earned a reported seventy-six thousand dollars in royalties by August 1913. About a reformed criminal, the play represented Armstrong's specialty: melodramas of the underworld featuring hard-bitten, slangy crime characters with hearts of gold.

Armstrong's greatest stage successes were melodramas that fit two patterns: adaptations of others' material (*Alias Jimmy Valentine* was based on an O'Henry character, while *Salomy Jane* [1907] was adapted from a Bret Harte story) and collaborations. His coauthors included Rex Beach, Newton Macmillan, and Wilson Mizner. A financially successful storyteller, Armstrong wrote nothing of permanent importance.

Armstrong married twice: in 1899 in London, England, to Rella Abell of Kansas City, Missouri; and in 1913 to Kittie Cassidy (stage name Catharine Calvert). He died of heart failure in New York City on August 30, 1915, at the age of forty-six.

ALAN R. HAVIG

Armstrong, Paul. Clipping File. Billy Rose Theatre Collection, New York Public Library at Lincoln Center.

Collins, Charles W. "Paul Armstrong—Apostle of 'The Punch.' " *Green Book* 11 (April 1914): 651–56.

Dictionary of American Biography. S.v. "Armstrong, Paul."

New York Times, August 31, 1915.

ASHLEY, GRACE. *See* Papin, Grace.

ASHLEY, WILLIAM HENRY (1778?–1838)

William Henry Ashley, a fur trader, entrepreneur, and political leader, was born about 1778, in Powhatan County, Virginia. While Ashley said little about his ancestry, it appears his father was a shopkeeper or craftsman, and his grandfather a Revolutionary War soldier. There are no records of Ashley's education, but his ability with the written language and skills of bookkeeping and surveying indicate some formal schooling.

Ashley moved to Missouri around 1802. In a September 1831 letter to a St. Louis newspaper, Ashley mentioned that he entered Missouri before it was ceded to the United States and that he had been involved in Missouri land claims for twenty years. When he first arrived, he may have resided briefly in Cape Girardeau, but his earliest-known activities are associated with Ste. Genevieve. There he became a justice of the peace, a captain in the local militia, and a participant in nearby lead mining.

As the War of 1812 approached, Ashley formed a volunteer company of rangers to protect the area from hostile British and Indian forces. A popular officer, he rose steadily in rank, and by the war's end he was a lieutenant colonel. On a hunting trip in the Missouri Ozarks during the war, Ashley encountered some strange soil, which he noted contained potassium nitrate. Further investigation led him to the enormous Ashley Cave, near what is now Houston in Texas County, which he identified as the source of these minerals. Ashley and a partner established a factory to turn the saltpeter into gunpowder, but by 1818 numerous explosions and the changing markets forced the closing of this factory.

Ashley moved in 1819 to St. Louis and became involved in real estate. He prospered, purchased a fine home, and joined nineteen other families in organizing Christ Episcopal Church, of which he was a lifetime member and briefly a vestryman. His growing prominence made possible his 1820 election as the first lieutenant governor of Missouri. He presided over the Missouri Senate that ratified the state's admission to the Union. That same year, 1821, he became a brigadier general in the Missouri militia.

Although he was a Missouri mining and real estate developer, a politician, and a director of the St. Louis branch of U.S. Bank, Ashley's real place in Missouri and American history is associated with the development of the fur trade, which strengthened the St. Louis economy and encouraged exploration and settlement of the West.

The American fur business had generally operated from trading posts to which persons brought furs and exchanged the pelts for supplies. Ashley and his partner, Andrew Henry, decided that the traditional system was expensive and unreliable. With financial backing from St. Louis merchants, Ashley is credited with introducing an innovative system known as the "annual rendezvous." In 1822, instead of relying on hired employees, Indian trappers, and trading posts, Ashley secured through newspaper advertisements hundreds of venturesome young men to live in the West and trap beaver. His initial recruits included such fur-trade luminaries as **Jedediah Smith,** Tom Fitzpatrick, **William Sublette, Jim Bridger,** Hugh Glass, and David Jackson. Ashley transported these free-agent trappers to the West, supplied their needs, and bought their pelts at large "fur rendezvous." The advantages of these rendezvous were that they could be moved closer to the trappers and were less expensive to operate. These quasi-independent "mountain men" developed more initiative through this innovation, and the industry flourished. In 1826 Ashley sold his Rocky Mountain Fur Company, but he continued to market supplies to its new partners.

With his modest fortune now made, Ashley turned back to Missouri politics. In 1831 he was elected to Congress as a Jacksonian Democrat to fill the seat of Congressman **Spencer Darwin Pettis** who had been killed in a duel. During his congressional terms from 1831 to 1837, Ashley was considered a maverick Jacksonian—generally voting with the Jacksonians but at times (such as the U.S. Bank recharter) siding with Jackson's opponents. Although he was never a major force in Congress, Ashley remained popular with Missouri voters because he successfully looked after the state's interests. In 1836 he declined to seek reelection to a fourth term in Congress in order to enter the race for governor. In that contest, Ashley continued to present himself as an independent Jacksonian, but regular Democrats, long frustrated by what they considered his apostasy, rallied behind **Lilburn W. Boggs,** who won handily. After his defeat, Ashley moved closer to the state's emerging Whig Party as he made plans to run for Congress again in 1838. However, his health was failing, and he died of pneumonia on March 26, 1838, well before the election. As he requested he was buried on top of an Indian mound where the Lamine River joins the Missouri. He had married three times (Mary Able in 1806, Eliza Christy in 1825, and Elizabeth Moss Wilcox in 1832) but had no children. At his funeral, prominent clergyman **William Greenleaf Eliot** eulogized Ashley as a good representative of "the first enterprising settlers of the West."

J. CALVIN HOLSINGER

Chittenden, Hiram Martian. *The American Fur Trade of the Far West.* Vol. 1. Stanford: Academic Reprints, 1954.

Clokey, Richard M. *William H. Ashley: Enterprise and Politics in the Trans-Mississippi West.* Norman: University of Oklahoma Press, 1980.

Dale, Harrison Clifford. *The Explorations of William H. Ashley and Jedediah Smith, 1822–1829.* Lincoln: University of Nebraska Press, 1991.

ATCHISON, DAVID RICE (1807–1886)

David Rice Atchison, a U.S. senator, was born in Frogtown, Kentucky, on August 11, 1807, the son of William and Catherine Allen Atchison. The young Atchison's father was a farmer who, realizing the importance of a good education for his son, enrolled him in the preparatory school of Transylvania University in nearby Lexington. He entered the university itself as a freshman at age fourteen. There he met five classmates who would later serve with him in the United States Senate: Solomon W. Downs of Louisiana, Jesse D. Bright of Indiana, Edward A. Hannegan of Indiana, Jefferson Davis of Mississippi, and George W. Jones of Iowa. Of this group he became particularly close friends with the last three. Following his graduation in 1825, Atchison studied law with several prominent local preceptors and was admitted to the bar two years later.

After practicing law for three years in Carlisle, Kentucky, Atchison moved to Liberty, Missouri, which then had only one attorney. Many years later, **Alexander W. Doniphan** recalled that Atchison at this time "was a very ripe scholar; of fine literary taste and very familiar with all the English classics." Among Atchison's earliest clients were the Mormons, who had recently been driven from their homes in Jackson County. Although unsuccessful in helping them regain their lost property, he assisted them in resettling in Clay County.

Elected to the General Assembly in 1834, Atchison initially acted with the anti-Democratic element, serving as its unsuccessful candidate for Speaker. By the end of the session, however, he had been converted to the Democratic faith, introducing several resolutions in support of the antibank policies of Andrew Jackson. He also sought unsuccessfully to secure redress for his Mormon clients. After losing his reelection bid in 1836 as Clay County fell into the Whig column, he returned to his law practice.

Atchison became active in the state militia, rising rapidly to the rank of major general. This placed him in an uncomfortable position when renewed difficulties between the Mormons and their neighbors led to full-scale warfare in western Missouri in the fall of 1838. He sought unsuccessfully to mediate between the two groups, but Gov. **Lilburn W. Boggs,** whose home was in Jackson County and who had been active in the anti-Mormon movement there, placed the blame on the Mormon leaders and initiated his "extermination policy" that resulted in the Mormons being driven from the state. That same fall Atchison secured election to a second term in the legislature where he performed his most notable service as chairman of the joint committee to investigate charges levied against Missouri troops in the Seminole War. He also called unsuccessfully for a new constitutional convention to reapportion the lower house of the General Assembly and make certain judicial changes.

When the General Assembly created the Twelfth Judicial Circuit out of the recently acquired Platte Purchase and Clinton County, Gov. **Thomas Reynolds** appointed Atchison as its first judge in February 1841. The new jurist thereupon moved to Platte City, where he would make his home until 1857. None of the counties then had courthouses, and Atchison frequently held court in an arbor, especially constructed for this purpose, when the weather allowed.

Governor Reynolds was favorably impressed by the new judge, and when U.S. Senator **Lewis F. Linn** died suddenly in October 1843, the governor appointed Atchison as his successor. At age thirty-six Atchison became the first senator from western Missouri as well as the youngest man ever to enter the Senate from Missouri. In the Senate, Atchison quickly took up a cause to which Linn had given strong support—the protection of immigrants, many of them Missourians, going to Oregon. He found himself at variance with his senior senatorial colleague, **Thomas Hart Benton,** over the annexation of Texas. Benton strongly opposed annexation for fear it would lead to war with Mexico. Atchison realized that his constituents favored it, however, as a first step on the road to Manifest Destiny. His strong actions in favor of expansion in both Oregon and Texas helped bring his election to a full term when the legislature voted in the fall of 1844.

When the new Congress convened a year later, Atchison was again in the forefront of the movement to acquire Oregon, which proved successful in June 1846 through a treaty with Great Britain dividing the area at the forty-ninth parallel. Atchison voted against the treaty, however, because of his belief that the United States should have held out for all of Oregon, up to fifty-four degrees forty minutes. As chair of the Senate Militia Committee, he strongly supported the Mexican War that had broken out the previous month while pushing for reliance on volunteers to bear the brunt of the conflict.

The Senate first elected Atchison president pro tempore in August 1846, less than three years after he had arrived. His Senate colleagues would bestow that honor on him sixteen times over the next eight years whenever they needed someone to preside in the absence of the vice president. His service in this post led to the assertion by some that Atchison became president for one day on March 4, 1849. That date fell on Sunday, and President-elect Zachary Taylor refused to take the oath until the following day. In an interview many years later, Atchison, who had been presiding over the Senate late into the night, laughingly remarked that he had slept through his entire term. In reality he made no claim to the position. During his last two years in the Senate, 1853 to 1855, he was next in line to the presidency after the death of Vice President William R. Ring.

Atchison had been reelected to a second term by the Missouri General Assembly in January 1849. In the controversies over slavery expansion following the Mexican War, he found himself increasingly allied with the southern ultras under the leadership of Senator John C. Calhoun of South Carolina. Atchison alone of the entire Missouri delegation signed the Southern Address of January 1849, which denounced the Free Soil movement and called upon the southern states to stand firmly for their rights. When the Missouri legislature took a similar stance in the form of the Jackson Resolutions, Atchison's senior colleague, Senator Benton, denounced the action and thereby created a split in the ranks of the Missouri Democracy. Atchison now took charge of the proslavery wing of the Missouri Democratic Party and the following year helped engineer the defeat of Benton, who had served in the Senate since 1821. The party would remain divided throughout the remainder of the 1850s.

Atchison now stood as the dean of Senate Democrats and in 1852 was reelected president pro tempore by his colleagues. He formed a close alliance with three other southern senators and close friends: James M. Mason of Virginia, chairman of the Foreign Relations Committee; Robert M. T. Hunter of Virginia, chairman of the Finance Committee; and Andrew P. Butler, chairman of the Judiciary Committee. These four men lived as messmates in the same boardinghouse, and through their key leadership positions they exercised considerable influence on patronage and legislation behind the scenes.

Although many believed that the Compromise of 1850 had settled the question of slavery extension once and for all through its application of the doctrine of popular sovereignty in the territories of Utah and New Mexico, the issue really had been laid to rest only temporarily. Forces seeking the organization of Nebraska Territory to the west of Missouri as a natural route for a transcontinental railroad to California quickly mobilized. The region was barred to slavery under the Missouri Compromise of 1820, which caused Atchison to question the feasibility of extinguishing Indian claims and opening it to settlement. Benton, however, chose the issue of the railroad's value to Missouri and the subsequent necessity of Nebraska's organization as his vehicle to seek to replace Atchison in the Senate when the latter's term expired in 1855. This spurred Atchison to soften his opposition while demanding equal access to lands in Nebraska for slaveholders.

When it became obvious that legislation to organize Nebraska would pass in the spring of 1854, Atchison and his messmates worked diligently to make certain that it provided for the repeal of the Missouri Compromise, thus allowing Missouri slaveholders to settle there on an equal basis. The result was the Kansas-Nebraska Act, which provided for two territories at the insistence of the Iowa delegation. Atchison returned home at the close of the session to organize the proslavery men along Missouri's western border for the task of ensuring that Kansas would become a slave state. Assisted by Benjamin F. Stringfellow and John H. Stringfellow, among others, he stumped western Missouri that fall and winter, establishing "blue lodges" for this purpose. The Missourians helped establish several proslavery towns on the western side of the Missouri River between Kansas City and the Nebraska line, including one that was named after the senator.

When a territorial election was held in November 1854 to choose a delegate to Congress, Atchison led a large group of Missourians across the border to vote and ensure the selection of the proslavery candidate. This would be the first of several elections held in the territory in which Atchison and his followers would participate. Atchison contended that the Kansas-Nebraska Act made no provision for residency requirements for voting, in spite of his efforts to secure some, and the Missourians' votes were needed to keep Free Soilers from seizing control of the territory.

As Free Soilers began moving into Kansas from the eastern states, battle lines were drawn, and the territory became the scene of a number of bloody encounters between the two groups over the next three years. One of the most controversial of these came on May 21, 1856, when Atchison led a group of followers into the Free State town of Lawrence where they destroyed the local hotel and the newspaper presses in a rampage of pillage. This led to retaliation three days later at Pottawatomie Creek in the southern

part of the territory when John Brown called from their homes five proslavery settlers, who had had nothing to do with the raid, and murdered them.

Atchison in the meantime also traveled extensively throughout the South attempting to recruit proslavery immigrants to the territory, with moderate success. On the home front he found himself locked in a three-way race for reelection before the Missouri legislature in January 1855. That body, unable to muster a majority for either Atchison or his two opponents, Thomas Hart Benton and Alexander W. Doniphan, adjourned without electing, thereby leaving the seat vacant for the next two years.

By the summer of 1857, Atchison had generally concluded that the proslavery effort in Kansas was a lost cause. When the Free Staters carried the election for a new territorial legislature the following October, Atchison retired from the scene. He took no part in the subsequent fiasco surrounding the Lecompton Constitution. Over the years, Atchison had acquired some fifteen hundred acres, part of it in conjunction with his brother Ben, in Clinton County. When the latter died in December 1856, Atchison moved to his farmstead near present-day Gower to assist Ben's widow in the management of the property. The 1860 census revealed that the senator-turned-farmer owned sixteen slaves ranging in age from three to forty-eight years. Atchison never married.

In the election of 1860, Atchison stumped the state in behalf of the presidential bid of his friend John C. Breckinridge, the candidate of the breakaway Democrats. When the Civil War broke out, he supported the pro-Confederate regime of Gov. **Claiborne Fox Jackson.** After Jackson was driven from Jefferson City by Gen. **Nathaniel Lyon** in June 1861, Atchison volunteered his services to the governor and was present at the Battle of Carthage on July 5 when the state forces defeated federal troops under Gen. **Franz Sigel.**

Shortly thereafter, Atchison and Jackson headed south through Arkansas on their way to Richmond to seek the support of the Confederate government for the Missouri State Guard, now headed by **Sterling Price.** Atchison's longtime friendship with Jefferson Davis played a significant role in ensuring the success of their mission, which gained the Confederate president's promise to pay Missouri troops in the field as soon as the money could be appropriated by the Confederate Congress. Returning to Missouri, the two men determined on a proclamation of secession, which Jackson issued from New Madrid on August 5. They rejoined Price's army in western Missouri as it moved against Lexington. Atchison was apparently present when the rump legislature met at Neosho on October 21 to formally vote secession. Thereafter his movements are not certain, but it is believed that he accompanied Governor Jackson on an extended trip through southeast Missouri, Tennessee, and Louisiana before rejoining Price in time to participate in the Battle of Pea Ridge, Arkansas, on March 6 and 7, 1862.

By the spring of 1864 he had settled in Grayson County, Texas, where he remained until 1867. He then returned to his Clinton County farm where he spent the remainder of his life in semiretirement, generally eschewing politics but making occasional appearances at local fairs and other special events. He died January 26, 1886.

A controversial figure throughout the 1850s, Atchison, nevertheless, sincerely believed in the causes he championed, particularly western expansion, whether Oregon, Texas, or Kansas. Ardently proslavery, he was concerned that the territories be opened to Northerners and Southerners alike. He was held in high esteem by his colleagues as attested by his service as Senate president pro tempore and numerous testimonials by friends and foes alike in that body.

WILLIAM E. PARRISH

Atchison, David Rice. Papers. Western Historical Manuscripts Collection, Columbia.

Parrish, William E. *David Rice Atchison of Missouri: Border Politician.* Columbia: University of Missouri Press, 1961.

ATHERTON, LEWIS E. (1905–1989)

One of Missouri's most distinguished scholars and teachers, Lewis E. Atherton was born in Bosworth, Missouri, on March 1, 1905. Atherton's early years were spent on the family farm. He attended high school in nearby Carrollton and then matriculated to the University of Oklahoma. In 1925 Atherton transferred to the University of Missouri, from which he graduated Phi Beta Kappa in 1927.

The following year Atherton gained a teaching position at New Mexico Military Institute. While teaching in New Mexico, he met and on June 5, 1929, married Mary Louise Webb. Later in the year the newlyweds left New Mexico so Atherton could teach at a community college in St. Joseph, Missouri. He taught in St. Joseph for two years and then accepted a teaching assignment at Wentworth Military Academy in Lexington, Missouri, a position that he held from 1931 to 1936.

During the summers of 1930 to 1935 Atherton attended graduate school at the University of Missouri, where he also worked as an instructor in the history department. His friend and mentor, **Elmer Ellis,** served as Atherton's Ph.D. adviser. Atherton completed the degree in 1937.

Two years later the history department's members, with some exhibiting trepidation toward hiring one of their own students, made Atherton an assistant professor. Those who questioned Atherton's appointment found their objections meaningless as the young Ph.D. rose through the ranks. In 1942 he was promoted to associate professor, and four years later he became a professor of history, a rank he held until his retirement in 1973.

Atherton's speedy ascension through the professorial ranks resulted from his excellent teaching skills, his unselfish work as an adviser, and his research and writing abilities. He compiled a lengthy and impressive publication list, which included four monographs and more than thirty articles. Atherton devoted most of his research and writing to the fields of the American South, the Midwest, and the West. His well-received *Pioneer Merchant in Mid-America,* published in 1939, was revised and expanded in 1971 and titled *The Frontier Merchant in Mid-America.* Atherton's 1949 monograph, *The Southern Country Store,* proved to be another critically acclaimed, groundbreaking study. Probably his most important book was published in 1954. Titled *Main Street on the Middle Border,* Atherton's study of small towns in the Midwest received rave reviews and became a classic. His last monograph, *The Cattle Kings,* published in 1961, also elicited laudatory reviews.

Through the years, Atherton received prestigious grants that allowed him to devote lengths of time entirely to research. He received a Guggenheim Fellowship in 1940. Ten years later the Newberry Library granted him a fellowship. In 1953 Atherton won a Rockefeller Foundation award, and the Social Science Research Foundation provided him with a research grant for 1958–1959.

Atherton also excelled in the classroom by presenting exciting and thought-provoking lectures. Despite lengthy reading assignments, his popular undergraduate courses attracted students from various academic disciplines. Atherton also proved to be an unselfish adviser to hundreds of undergraduate students besides those majoring in history. His outstanding teaching skills and his genuine concern for the students earned him the first annual Distinguished Faculty Award presented by the University's Alumni Association in 1960.

Atherton further distinguished himself through his work with graduate students. His graduate seminars promoted spirited discussions and oftentimes contentious debates. The professor greatly enjoyed the intellectual arguments prompted by his insightful questions. In addition to supervising countless M.A. candidates, Atherton served as the principal adviser of more than fifty graduate students who earned the Ph.D. degree.

During his academic years, Atherton served as a member of the executive committees of the Mississippi Valley Historical Association and the Agricultural History Society. The latter organization chose him as its president in 1952. Three important historical journals sought his talents for their editorial boards: *Agricultural History,* the *Journal of Southern History,* and the *Mississippi Valley Historical Review.*

Besides teaching and writing history, Atherton collected history for repositories. The University of Missouri established its Western Historical Manuscripts Collection in 1943 to complement the collecting activities of the State Historical Society of Missouri, located on the Columbia campus. Atherton served as its temporary director from 1951 to 1953, its director from 1957 to 1963, and continued to support its activities over the years.

Atherton became a member of the State Historical Society in 1934 and constantly promoted the state's past through his service to that specialized research library. The society's quarterly, the *Missouri Historical Review,* published six of his historical contributions. In 1966 he became a trustee of the society and served in that capacity until his death. A member of the society's executive (finance) committee from 1975 to 1985, Atherton was also elected in 1980 to a three-year term as president of the organization. For his longtime commitment to the society, he received its Distinguished Service Award in 1980.

Atherton earned a number of honors during his lifetime. Besides the Distinguished Faculty Award, the university also bestowed upon him the Thomas Jefferson Award in 1971 and the Distinguished Alumni Award in 1989. The Western History Association honored him with its Award of Merit in 1981 and then granted him an honorary membership in 1986. One honor that especially pleased Atherton occurred during the Missouri Conference on History in 1969, when friends, colleagues, and former students established a history-graduate-student research fund in his name. Seventeen years later, in April, the department of history and the State Historical Society honored him with Atherton Recognition Day in Columbia.

After retiring Atherton continued work on behalf of the State Historical Society. He also pursued his favorite avocations—Democratic politics, reading, classical music, bird-watching, gardening, and Missouri basketball. He and his wife also designed and built a new home that provided them hours of enjoyment. Louise Atherton died at home on September 2, 1987. Her husband continued to live there until, after a brief hospital stay, he died on March 25, 1989. The Athertons were preceded in death by a son, Richard Franklin, in 1935, and two adopted daughters, Mary Ann in 1965 and Barbara Lee in 1984.

JAMES W. GOODRICH

"Distinguished Scholar: Lewis E. Atherton." *Missouri Alumnus* 48 (April 1960): 2–3, 8.

Goodrich, James W. "Lewis E. Atherton (1905–1989)." *Missouri Historical Review* 83 (July 1989): 448–58.

Grant, Roger H. "Lewis Atherton." *Great Plains Journal* 18 (1979): 10–14.

March, David D. *The History of Missouri.* New York: Lewis Historical Publishing, 1967.

AULL, ARTHUR (1872–1948)

Arthur Aull, who edited the *Lamar (Mo.) Democrat* from 1900 until his death in 1948, was known coast-to-coast as one of the most colorful figures in country journalism. His sensationalistic, all-the-news-is-fit-to-print philosophy brought him subscribers in all forty-eight states plus Canada and England. He was also widely quoted by the metropolitan press and syndicated columnists O. O. McIntyre and Ted Cook.

Aull was sued for libel three times, assaulted with a club, threatened with other kinds of bodily harm, and cursed by many. But he persisted in printing every scandal and piece of gossip that he could turn up. He detested the syndicated material that other country papers used and insisted on filling his paper, an afternoon daily, with the stories he gathered every morning. He realized early on that newspapering was a business, above all else, and that sensationalism sold papers. Consequently, his entire career was spent looking for the shocking, the scurrilous, the comical, even the grim and grisly story that might encourage someone to pick up his *Democrat.*

Aull's stories were amusing, disturbing, even vulgar at times. Many told of misfortune and death. Some were preposterous. But they all contained a sensational element, something his readers could gossip about. Circulation figures support Aull's assertion that scandal sold newspapers. The *Democrat*'s circulation exceeded the population of Lamar for most of his editorship. A few irate readers canceled their subscriptions along the way, but they usually managed to borrow someone else's copy.

Arthur Fabian Aull was born November 18, 1872, in Daviess County, Kentucky. He moved to Barton County, Missouri, in 1884 and attended the rural school in Nashville. He later studied history, language, and literature at Fort Scott Normal School in Kansas, a small college across the state line. Aull taught school and dabbled in politics (he was elected surveyor of Barton County in 1896) until purchasing the *Lamar Democrat* for six thousand dollars shortly after the turn of the century.

The newly minted editor immediately decided to apply the formula of William Randolph Hearst's "yellow press" to his own paper, figuring that his rural readers also yearned for the unusual and sensational. Stories of grisly accidents, murders, rapes, juvenile crimes, suicides and attempted suicides, and scandalous divorces became Aull's trademark. But he embellished nearly all his sensational stories with a personal, homespun flavor, and that is what caught the attention of the syndicated columnists, metropolitan press, and popular magazines toward the latter part of his career.

The rise of **Harry S. Truman,** first as the Democratic nominee for vice president and later as the nation's thirty-third president, also helped make Aull a national curiosity. The national media frequently came to Lamar in search of a human-interest piece about Truman's birthplace and more than once came away with a story about Aull instead. *Life* devoted two pages to the country editor in 1945, and news of his death on May 7, 1948, was carried by newspapers ranging from the *New York Times* to the *San Francisco Examiner* and such magazines as *Time* and *Newsweek.*

Luanna Aull (1873–1968) assumed the role of publisher upon her husband's death, and their eldest daughter, Madeleine Aull Van Hafften, took over as editor. Van Hafften (1896–1977) struggled to carry on the Aull tradition until her brother-in-law, Stanley White, arrived in 1953 to become advertising manager. Her sister, Betty Aull White, handled much of the society news and helped in the office. The Aull family sold the *Democrat* in 1972 to Missouri Secretary of State James Kirkpatrick and his son, Don.

CHAD STEBBINS

Cauley, John R. "Aull Prints All the News." *Life* (February 26, 1945): 8, 10.
Chicago Daily News, December 23–24, 1972.
Eddy, Don. "Ripsnorting News." *American Magazine* (June 1949): 134–37.
Gilmer, Carol Lynn. "Missouri's One-Family Newspaper." *Harper's Magazine* (October 1954): 52–57.
St. Louis Post-Dispatch, June 30, 1946.
Stebbins, Chad. *All the News Is Fit to Print: A Country Editor in Missouri.* Columbia: University of Missouri Press, 1998.

AUSTIN, MOSES (1761–1821)

Moses Austin has been aptly called the lead king of Missouri. But the king had many pretenders to the throne during his reign in the colonial and territorial periods. This was an extremely turbulent era in Missouri history, and it required men of courage, self-reliance, and a spirit of adventure. Austin shared these traits with many of his challengers.

Nevertheless, for a considerable period of time, Austin fought off his assailants and retained his title as lead king. Eventually his rule ended in a rather inglorious denouement brought about by a combination of failures partly of his own doing and partly by forces beyond his control. In 1797, however, when he arrived in Spanish Missouri the future looked extremely promising. In fact, Austin seemed ideally suited for a long and successful tenure as the mineral sovereign of the lead-mining region.

Austin was in many respects the prototypical American entrepreneur. He was born October 4, 1761, in Durham, Connecticut, to a modestly well-to-do family of traditional Congregationalist values. It was an environment that inculcated the young Austin with the spirit of hard work and venture capitalism. Adversity also conditioned the youth's character. Orphaned at the age of fourteen, he never tired in his quest for financial stability, independence, and success. Like many budding entrepreneurs, Moses left New England for greater economic opportunities. He found a home first in Virginia where he began his lifelong career with minerals. During the 1790s, as he struggled to master the intricacies of the mining industry, Austin confronted formidable competition from the Missouri lead mines. As the stories and tales of the richness of the western mines continued to float across the Mississippi, the adopted Virginian became increasingly intrigued by the potential for wealth and power far beyond what the Commonwealth of Virginia could ever offer. His assessment of the richness of the Missouri mines was underscored by a 1796 pamphlet written by **Pierre-Charles Delassus de Luzières** of New Bourbon, a small settlement near Ste. Genevieve. Austin set out for the Spanish frontier to determine for himself what possibilities he could exploit. He was thirty-five when he made this momentous decision.

Austin arrived in Missouri in January 1797 and received an invitation to meet **Zenon Trudeau,** the Spanish governor of the territory. The meeting with Trudeau went well, and Austin soon left for his first inspection of the mining region. At Ste. Genevieve he was introduced to a leading French resident, **François Vallé II,** and an American businessman, **John Rice Jones.** From there he made his way to Breton Creek, in the heart of the lead district. Much to his surprise and pleasure, the richness of the area confirmed his greatest hopes. Returning to Ste. Genevieve, Austin penned a letter to the Governor General of Louisiana in New Orleans, the Baron de Carondelet. He requested a virtual empire on the raw edges of the frontier. He would need, the letter stated, sixteen leagues, or approximately 70,000 acres of land, to establish a self-sufficient community. This vast amount of land was required, he wrote, in order to harvest the wood essential in the smelting of the lead as well as to raise the livestock and the crops necessary to ensure the viability of the new settlement. The letter was couched in language that made the request appear to be in the best interests of both guest and patron. The extraction of vast amounts of lead, he reminded Carondelet, could, among other advantages, assist the mother country in the defense of her colonies.

The petition came at a most propitious time. Spanish diplomatic and military strategists in the last decade of the eighteenth century, believing that the British posed the most immediate geopolitical threat to their trans-Mississippi empire, had begun to welcome a select number of Americans to Missouri to serve as buffers to Anglo expansion. Austin, with his mining expertise and his ambitious designs, dovetailed into this new imperial strategy. Working with a speed uncommon for the Spanish bureaucracy, the authorities in Louisiana granted Austin's request but pared down the size of the land grant to one league, or approximately 4,250 acres. From these "humble" beginnings, the Yankee emigrant began the construction of his lead kingdom. One of the first displays of Austin's newfound power was the construction of Durham Hall, a frontier castle on the banks of Breton Creek near the present town of Potosi in Washington County. Historian **Floyd Calvin Shoemaker** called it "the most impressive private residence" in all the territory.

During these twilight years of Spanish rule in Missouri, Austin, his wife, Maria, and the Americans around the mines, now called Mine à Breton, prospered. The settlement also contained African slaves, mainly owned by Austin and a few farmers and miners. The French natives who had previously worked the land and mines, although far less systematically than the Americans, were not overjoyed with the usurpers. **Rufus Easton,** another Yankee transplant to Missouri, wrote to Austin, "The French are violently prejudiced against you. . . ." Nevertheless, Spanish authorities maintained a semblance of order in the mining district until the eve of its transfer to the United States. The Louisiana Purchase factionalized the mineral area and produced violence on a level not to be equaled until the Civil War.

In the meantime, Austin revolutionized the practice of lead mining, using many of the techniques he had previously employed in Virginia. He utilized better technologies for smelting the ore and gathering the residue from the ashes. His reverberatory furnace, built at a cost of eight thousand dollars, was so efficient that other miners found it more profitable to deal with him rather than to smelt their own lead. Furthermore, he vertically integrated his operation by means of a company store, a flour mill, a sawmill, and a blacksmith shop. He built a road from Mine à Breton to the high limestone bluffs overlooking the Mississippi River and constructed shot towers that provided operational outlets to markets in New

Orleans and other parts of the American West. In addition, he fortified his residence with cannons and arms. Ostensibly, these weapons were to ward off marauding Osage Indians; in reality they served to deter his principal rivals. Over the course of the next decade both he and his adversaries hired sizable armies to protect their properties and maintain their influence in the region.

After the transfer of Louisiana to the United States, Austin was able to use his economic influence to enhance his political power. He became, for example, chief justice of the Ste. Genevieve Court of Common Pleas and Quarter Sessions. No doubt he aspired to even higher state and national offices. But power bred enmity, and enmity spawned conflict. His principal protagonists during these early territorial years were Gen. **James Wilkinson,** appointed by President Jefferson as territorial governor, and **John Smith T,** the main challenger to Austin's mineral supremacy. These two foes wanted to control the lead-mining district and use its resources as a launching pad for filibustering activities in the Southwest. Moses Austin stood in the way of these plans. The governor first removed Austin from his official positions in the Ste. Genevieve district and gave them to Smith T. The latter was also named a colonel in the militia. Next, Wilkinson began removing Austin's supporters from political and military assignments in the region.

Austin confronted an even more serious challenge to his title as lead king on the economic front. Taking advantage of the confusion surrounding Spanish land titles, Austin's enemies, especially Smith T, began claiming more and more of his properties. This set off a war in the mining region that raged intermittently from the Louisiana Purchase until the War of 1812. Austin was abetted somewhat in this power struggle by the removal in 1807 of Governor Wilkinson from the territory and by the removal of all Smith T's official duties by **Frederick Bates,** who served as the acting governor after Wilkinson's departure. Although Austin welcomed these moves, they were not enough to restore him to the preeminence that he once enjoyed.

By the late territorial period Austin and his son, Stephen, were beginning to experience severe financial difficulties. The expenses of the mineral wars, along with additional competitors in the lead-mining field, were beginning to take their toll. Consequently, the Austins searched for alternative business ventures that might rectify their economic setbacks. Unfortunately for Austin, his choice of investments proved disastrous. First, he became heavily involved in land speculation around the Potosi region, hoping that this mineral town would become the first state capital. Second, he purchased a sizable number of New Madrid land certificates that he was forced in

1819 to sell at a loss. Third, he invested a good deal of his dwindling resources in the Bank of St. Louis. The panic of 1819 and the selection of St. Charles as the new state of Missouri's temporary capital destroyed these dreams and financially ruined the Austins. On April 8, 1821, in a letter to James Austin, he confessed that "I am ruined" in this country.

By the time of this admission of bankruptcy, Moses Austin had launched the project that would gain him immortality. He would leave Missouri for greener pastures in the Southwest. In December 1820 he arrived at San Antonio de Bexar, the capital of Texas, and discussed with Gov. Antonio Maria Martínez a colonization scheme. Specifically, he proposed leading three hundred American families to Texas. No doubt his past experiences with the Spanish in Missouri helped persuade the officials in Texas to honor his request.

Before the colonization plans could progress, Austin's health began to decline. Exhausted from the long rides to and from Texas and from his endless political and economic worries, the miner-speculator-turned-colonizer fell seriously ill. Fever began to ravage his body. Before he died, he made Stephen promise to carry on the Texas venture. The goodwill he had established with the Mexican government laid a foundation of trust that paved the way for Stephen to carry out his father's final wishes. With his plans somewhat secure, Moses Austin died on June 10, 1821, in St. Francois County, Missouri, and was buried in a family plot there. A decade later his remains were reinterred in the Presbyterian cemetery in Potosi. Shortly following Austin's death, his son, Stephen, established an American settlement on the Brazos River. Thus, from the dreams of Moses Austin sprang the reality of a permanent American presence in Texas.

DICK STEWARD

Austin, Moses. Papers. Vol. 1, pts. 1, 2. 1785–1812. Eugene Barker Library. University of Texas, Austin.

Foley, William E. *The Genesis of Missouri: From Wilderness Outpost to Statehood.* Columbia: University of Missouri Press, 1989.

Gardner, James A. "The Business Career of Moses Austin in Missouri, 1798–1821." *Missouri Historical Review* 50 (April 1956): 235–47.

———. *Lead King: Moses Austin.* St. Louis: Sunrise Publishing, 1980.

Gracy, David B., II. *Moses Austin: His Life.* San Antonio: Trinity University Press, 1987.

BAKER, JOSEPHINE (1906–1975)

Josephine Baker escaped a childhood marked by poverty and racism to become an international superstar and the personification of Jazz Age exoticism as lead dancer for the Folies-Bergères Revue in Paris in the 1920s. In a career that spanned five decades, Baker earned acclaim as a dancer, singer, stage and film actress, and political activist. Despite her success, though, she never forgot her humble origins, and devoted her life to fighting prejudice and helping the oppressed, playing an active role in the French resistance against Nazism during World War II, as well as in the American civil rights movement in the 1950s and 1960s.

Baker was born June 3, 1906, in St. Louis. Her mother, Carrie McDonald, a domestic worker and amateur dancer, had arrived in St. Louis two years earlier from South Carolina. Josephine's father, Eddie Carson, a musician who played in bands around the Chestnut valley, a red-light district near Union Station, deserted the family shortly after the birth of the couple's second child in 1907. Baker grew up in abject poverty. As a child, she was sent with her brother to Soulard Market to scavenge for food and to Union Station to steal coal from the freight cars. As she later commented, "I started to dance to keep warm" during the cold Missouri winters.

At the age of eleven, Baker observed in horror the July 1917 race riot in East St. Louis, a signal event in her developing consciousness. As thousands of blacks fled across Eads Bridge to St. Louis, she remembered, "We children stood huddled together in bewilderment. We were hiding behind the skirts of grown-ups, frightened to death." Afterward, St. Louis served as a negative reference point, a symbol of everything she sought to escape. "For me," she said, "St. Louis represents a city of fear and humiliation."

After a brief marriage at age thirteen, Baker joined a group of street performers called the Jones Family Band, which played in the area around the Booker T. Washington Theater, a black vaudeville house at Market and Twenty-third Streets. Mrs. Jones taught Baker to play trombone, and the band played ragtime, passing the hat for money. When a troupe called the Dixie Steppers played the Booker T. Washington, the Jones Family Band was brought in as an opening act. The band was invited to accompany the Steppers when they left St. Louis to tour the South. When the band dissolved shortly thereafter, Baker remained on the tour as a dresser for one of the stars, blues singer Clara Smith. Eventually she worked her way into the chorus line.

Following another brief marriage at age fifteen to Willie Baker, in 1921 Baker earned a spot in the Broadway show *Shuffle Along,* with music by Noble Sissle and Eubie Blake. Beginning in the chorus, Baker's improvisational dancing and comedic talents quickly propelled her to star status. When the successful *Shuffle Along* finally closed, she gained a part in Sissle and Blake's next show, *The Chocolate Dandies.* In 1925 she traveled to Paris to perform in *La Revue Negro,* a black song-and-dance revue.

An instant success in Paris, Baker quickly became the star of the Folies-Bergères Revue, where her nearly nude jazz dancing caused a sensation. Throughout France, her popularity was extraordinary, as people bought Josephine Baker perfumes, dolls, and costumes, and many women imitated her slicked-down, short haircut. She was constantly in the news, whether for her exotic menagerie, which included a pet leopard, or her many public love affairs. Throughout Europe, Baker associated with the rich and famous, including such prominent artists and intellectuals as Max Reinhardt, Georges Simenon, and Colette. Erich Maria Remarque commented that Baker "brought a blast of jungle air, elemental power, and beauty, into the tired stages of Western civilization."

Although she rose to fame as a dancer, Baker began singing publicly in the early 1930s. Her signature song was Vincent Scotto's "J'ai deux amours," which told of her two loves, her country and Paris. She also starred in such French films as *Zou-Zou* (1934) and *Princess Tam-Tam* (1935). In 1936 she sought to return to America and gain success in her home country, starring in the Ziegfeld's Follies. But the reaction of the mainstream press was not friendly. Much of the response reflected the American reluctance to let an African American performer succeed in anything other than stereotypical roles. As *Time*'s critic wrote:

> Josephine Baker is a St. Louis washer-woman's daughter who stepped out of a Negro burlesque show into a life of adulation and luxury in Paris during the booming 1920s. In sex appeal to jaded Europeans of the jazz-loving type, a Negro wench always has a head start. . . . But to Manhattan theater goers last week she was just a slightly buck-toothed young Negro woman whose figure

might be matched in any night-club show, and whose dancing and singing might be topped practically anywhere outside of Paris.

Returning to Paris, Baker married again, this time to the wealthy Jewish sugar-broker Jean Lion. Although the two filed for divorce only a year after their wedding, they were still officially married when the Germans invaded France in 1940, making Baker a member of two groups victimized by Nazi policies— Negroes and Jews. During the occupation, Baker refused to perform in Nazi-controlled areas, living in southern France and later northern Africa. An early partisan of Charles de Gaulle, Baker helped several people escape France and used her connections in Italy to gain information concerning Mussolini's Fascist government, which she passed to the Allies. While living in Africa, she developed a severe case of septicemia that nearly killed her and forced an extended convalescence. Upon her recovery, she toured north Africa and the Middle East, entertaining Allied troops and performing benefits for the resistance. In honor of her services, Baker was made a sublieutenant in the Women's Auxiliary of the French Air Force and earned a Medal of the Resistance. In awarding her the medal, de Gaulle stated he was "touched by the enthusiasm with which she had dedicated her talent to the cause of the resistance."

After the war Baker devoted herself to the cause of civil rights for African Americans. During her 1951 tour of the United States, she refused to perform before segregated audiences, a demand that broke color barriers in such cities as Miami and Las Vegas. She publicly associated herself with several controversial civil rights cases, including that of Willie McGee, a black Mississippi truck driver sentenced to death for raping a white woman. On August 28, 1963, Baker spoke at the March on Washington, wearing her World War II uniform, where she told the crowd, "You are on the eve of a complete victory. You can't go wrong. The world is behind you."

As further proof of her commitment to racial equality, Baker and her fourth husband, French orchestra leader Jo Bouillon, bought Les Milandes, a fifteenth-century estate in Dordogne, France, where they planned to create a multiracial and multicultural family. Eventually they adopted twelve children of various cultural, racial, and ethnic backgrounds in a family that Baker would dub her "Rainbow tribe."

Baker continued to perform throughout her life, and on April 8, 1975, opened in Paris a sold-out, musical retrospective of her career. It was to be her last show. On April 14, 1975, she died of a cerebral hemorrhage. Her state funeral was televised throughout France, where she would always be a hero.

DAVID COCHRAN

Haney, Lynn. *Naked at the Feast: A Biography of Josephine Baker.* New York: Dodd, Mead, 1981.
Rose, Phyllis. *Jazz Cleopatra: Josephine Baker in Her Time.* New York: Doubleday, 1989.

BAKER, SAMUEL AARON (1874–1933)

School administrator, state superintendent of schools, and thirty-sixth governor of Missouri, Sam A. Baker was born November 7, 1874, in Patterson, in Wayne County, Missouri. His father, Samuel Aaron Baker, died shortly before his son was born, and the reduced family fortune required Sam to contribute materially to his own education. He attended school in the village of Mill Springs, Missouri, and taught for a short time in various country schools. Determined to go to college, he earned the necessary funds by working as a railroad section hand and in the planing mill of a southeast Missouri lumber firm. After graduating in 1887 with a bachelor's degree in pedagogy from the state teachers college at Cape Girardeau (now Southeast Missouri State University), he later earned an A.B. degree at Missouri Wesleyan College.

Baker's career as a Missouri school administrator began with his appointment as superintendent of schools at Piedmont in 1897. His next assignment came as principal of high schools at Jefferson City in 1899 and at Joplin in 1910. After completing a three-year tenure as superintendent of schools at Richmond, he returned to Jefferson City in 1913 and resided there for the remainder of his life. As superintendent of schools in the Missouri capital city, Baker gave leadership for the issuance of $100,000 in school bonds that permitted the district to improve facilities, provide students with free textbooks, and expand the curriculum to include commercial studies, manual training, and a teachers' training course. These accomplishments led to his election in 1918 as state superintendent of schools on the Republican ticket.

During Baker's four-year term as Missouri's school chief, the state's public schools registered substantial achievements. Increased funds were earmarked for rural schools that had fallen behind the schools of the cities, vocational and rehabilitation education was boosted, and teaching efficiency was enhanced through new training facilities, programs, and a doubling of teachers' salaries. Despite this record, Baker was defeated in his reelection bid.

In 1923 Baker set his sights on the governorship. Without funds or organizational backing, he demonstrated sufficient statewide support to gain the endorsement of the outgoing Hyde administration. He won the gubernatorial election in 1924 by a scant

5,872-vote margin over his Democratic opponent, Arthur W. Nelson. As governor, Baker demonstrated his independence of the Republican organization by naming persons friendly and loyal to him to state offices. The resulting political rows over Baker's appointment policy made his term contentious.

Despite the general prosperity of the midtwenties, when Baker took office the state's operating costs exceeded anticipated revenues, thus forcing a strict economy upon his administration. Moreover, the economy-minded legislators denied his request for the establishment of a permanent school fund created through taxes on inheritances, amusements, and tobacco. His recommendations for the establishment of a teachers' retirement fund and a statewide school redistricting plan to eliminate costly and backward school districts were also rejected by the state legislature. The legislature approved the governor's call for a workers' compensation law but showed no interest in his request for an additional state prison for hardened criminals. When two powerful groups, the Automobile Club of Missouri and the State Highway Commission, were $40 million apart on the amount to be requested of voters on a bond issue for highway construction and road improvements, Baker secured a compromise for a $75 million bond issue that voters approved during his term.

Baker's service to education led Missouri Valley College to confer upon him the honorary degree of LL.D. in 1922. His professional associates elected him president of the Missouri State Teachers Association and vice president of the National Education Association. His secretaries and aides in the governor's office, many of them his students when he was superintendent of schools in Jefferson City, called him "Professor" rather than "Governor."

Baker was an elder of the Presbyterian Church of Jefferson City for many years. He and his wife, the former Nelle R. Tuckley, practiced tithing, contributing one-tenth of their income for religious and charitable purposes. The Bakers had one child, Mary Elizabeth. Baker's only vice was smoking cigars. When his associates advised him to take up golf, he remarked that it was "an old man's game" that he would take up when he could not do anything else.

Baker's health began to decline during the last year of his governorship. A few months after he left office in January 1929 he suffered two paralytic strokes that kept him confined to bed for most of the remaining years of his life. He was fifty-eight when he died in Jefferson City on September 16, 1933.

During Baker's service as state superintendent of schools, he assisted the development of teacher professionalism through the understanding and programs that he brought to his office. As governor, he demonstrated as well that a former school superintendent could administer state government while advocating measures to upgrade public education in Missouri. However, he failed to achieve his major goal—the creation of a permanent school fund—and thus enjoyed less success in educational improvement as governor than he did as the state's chief of Missouri's public schools.

FRANKLIN D. MITCHELL

The National Cyclopedia of American Biography. S.v. "Baker, Samuel Aaron."

Shoemaker, Floyd Calvin. *Missouri and Missourians: Land of Contrasts and People of Achievements.* Vol. 2. Chicago: Lewis Publishing, 1943.

St. Louis Post-Dispatch, September 16, 1933.

BALDWIN, JOSEPH (1827–1899)

Founder and first president of the oldest normal school in Missouri and educational reformer, Joseph Baldwin was born October 31, 1827, near New Castle, Pennsylvania. After attending Bethany College in Virginia, an academy founded by Alexander Campbell to prepare ministers for his new sect (later known as Disciples of Christ), Baldwin became a preacher. Because the fledgling denomination was unable to support resident pastors, its preachers needed another occupation. Baldwin became a teacher and married a woman who was an equally dedicated Campbellite and teacher, Ellen Sophronia Fluhart, who was even more reform-minded than her husband and helped him develop his ideas about teacher education. Baldwin moved frequently from various principalships of private and county academies and normal schools. His career brought him to Missouri, to Pennsylvania, and later to Indiana.

Normal schools established in the 1850s and 1860s in the East required six to eight weeks of study. Through lectures, demonstrations, and discussions, the principal drilled teachers in the correct, or "normal," way to present the different subjects of the common school. Although adept at such instruction, Baldwin became dissatisfied with it.

As Baldwin refined his ideas about teacher education, he rejected the normal-institute approach. Instead, he combined traditional liberal arts with new European ideas about pedagogy, and began to think of founding a school where he could put his ideas into practice. His wife suggested a state west of the Mississippi where normal schools had not yet been established. Already acquainted with educational leaders in St. Louis, Baldwin decided to visit Missouri in February 1867.

Baldwin had intended to return to western Missouri, but educators in St. Louis urged him to consider the northeastern part of the state, and a kinsman in Kirksville dangled before him the offer of a building constructed for an academy but not used since the

Civil War. Baldwin found eager support among the townspeople, and the building, with some repairs and additions, seemed suitable. He spent the summer recruiting faculty and students and was able to open the North Missouri Normal School and Commercial College on September 2, 1867.

Efforts were already under way to establish a state normal school, and in 1870 legislators enacted a law providing for two schools. With the aid of Adair County citizens Baldwin persuaded the state board to designate his school as the one to be located north of the Missouri River. On January 1, 1871, the institution at Kirksville became the First District Normal School of Missouri (later Truman State University) with Joseph Baldwin as its president.

Baldwin attempted within the limitations imposed by his resources to implement his theories of teacher education. Their education must be equal in every way, he argued, with the work offered at the best liberal arts institutions. Graduation required 120 credits, three-fourths of which were to be taken in the liberal arts. The required thirty hours of pedagogy study focused both on how to teach a specific subject and on theories about learning supplemented by practice in the demonstration school. Mathematics through integral calculus, the principal areas of science, languages (both ancient and modern), literature, history, and the fine arts formed the bulk of the future teacher's course work.

Baldwin's tenure brought successes such as the construction of a three-story brick building on a fifteen-acre campus located at the then southern edge of town. Enrollment produced as many or more students as the school could absorb, and the faculty was capable. Nevertheless, Baldwin grew dissatisfied with the inadequate state support of the school and resigned in 1881 to become president of Sam Houston State Normal School in Huntsville, Texas. In 1891 he accepted a chair of pedagogy at the University of Texas and discovered sentiment favored the eastern normal-school style of training. His resignation in 1897 ended his professional career, and he died January 13, 1899.

RUTH WARNER TOWNE

Baldwin, Joseph. Papers. Northeast Missouri State University, Kirksville.

Ryle, Walter H. *Centennial History of Northeast Missouri State Teachers College.* Kirksville, Mo.: Board of Regents, 1972.

Simmons, Lucy, and P. O. Selby. "The Northeast Missouri State Teachers College and Its Founder, Joseph Baldwin." *Missouri Historical Review* 22 (January 1928): 157–70.

Violette, E. M. *History of Adair County.* Reprint, Kirksville, Mo.: Journal Printing, 1977.

BALDWIN, ROGER NASH (1884–1981)

Roger Nash Baldwin is best known as the founder of the American Civil Liberties Union (ACLU), an organization dedicated to "the defense of the principles of the Bill of Rights." The eldest of seven children, Baldwin was born January 21, 1884, into a well-to-do Unitarian family in Wellesley, Massachusetts, an elite Boston suburb, where at age ten he joined his church's Lend-a-Hand Society. Among Boston Unitarians, he later explained, "it was an accepted assumption that you had to help the underdog." At age seventeen, he enrolled in Harvard University, where he continued to participate in helping-hand activities before graduating with both a bachelor's and a master's degree in four years. In 1906, after a year in Europe, Baldwin accepted a position in St. Louis to found the sociology department at Washington University and to serve as the director of a neighborhood settlement house.

For Baldwin, St. Louis was a liberating change from Boston, where the pressures of his prominent family confined him. He remembered later, "The caste system which I grew up with was entirely absent." Although St. Louis was more class-bound than he remembered, Baldwin himself was socially mobile and friendly with Progressive Era reformers of all types, from radical unionists to business people.

Juvenile delinquency was a major problem in the neighborhood where Baldwin lived as settlement-house director, so he became involved in shaping St. Louis's new juvenile court system. He served as the court's chief probation officer from 1907 to 1910. Active in professionalizing the role of the probation officer, Baldwin organized the first national association of probation officers, and with Bernard Flexner, a Louisville, Kentucky, lawyer, he published in 1912 *Juvenile Courts and Probation,* which remained the field's standard text for some time.

Baldwin excelled as a networker and creator of organizations. Soon after he arrived in St. Louis he organized the Social Service Conference for St. Louisans involved in social service and the St. Louis City Club (a men-only luncheon club that hosted speakers on political issues), and he helped form the Joint Committee for Social Service among Colored People (later the St. Louis Urban League). His contributions to St. Louis were highly valued: in 1915 the *St. Louis Post-Dispatch* named him one of the city's ten most influential citizens.

In 1910 Baldwin resigned from the juvenile court to accept a position as secretary of the Civic League, a "city beautiful" organization dominated by professionals and businessmen. Baldwin committed himself to expanding the league's membership and concentrating its efforts on "democratizing the city instead of just [creating] a city beautiful." Under Baldwin's direction the Civic League promoted reform for workhouses, housing, and the city charter as well as antipollution measures and good government. Yet, for most working-class St. Louisans, the league never shed its upper-class image, which, along with the resignation of many elites who objected to Baldwin's more democratic notions, stymied the league's effectiveness.

Baldwin did not let his position of Civic League secretary prevent him from associating with other more left-wing organizations, such as the Single Tax League (which proposed taxes on unimproved lands as a method of redistributing wealth) and the Industrial Workers of the World (for whom he worked to established a free municipal boardinghouse and soup kitchen in 1912). As Civic League secretary, Baldwin successfully lobbied for the inclusion of initiative and referendum provisions in the new city charter of 1914. The addition of those provisions won over enough of the charter's earlier opponents to secure its enactment.

Progressives celebrated the passage of the new charter as a democratic victory, but much of the support had come from racists eager to use the democratic reforms to institute residential segregation. In fact, a segregation ordinance taught Baldwin the bitter lesson that "where minority rights are concerned, you can't trust the majority." Baldwin later recalled that he became an "instant convert" to the concept of "judicial supremacy" in 1917 when the Supreme Court ruled against a similar ordinance passed in Louisville. Actually, the courts usually ruled against minority rights in the 1910s and 1920s, and Baldwin retained a healthy skepticism toward overreliance on legal remedies, working both within and without the court system to create a favorable social climate for civil liberties.

If Baldwin first experienced disillusionment with direct democracy in St. Louis, he also entered his first free-speech fight there. When a St. Louis theater owner yielded to Catholic protests and revoked his contract with birth-control advocate Margaret Sanger, who came to lecture in St. Louis in 1916, Baldwin organized a protest in support of Sanger on the theater's front steps.

In an interview in the 1970s Baldwin characterized himself upon his arrival in St. Louis as a "social worker and reformer with little understanding of the realities of universal thought and experience." Around 1910, however, he attended a lecture by anarchist-feminist Emma Goldman, an experience that he later called "a turning point in my intellectual life." Predisposed to dismiss Goldman's message, Baldwin became a convert to her "vision of the end of poverty and injustice by free association of those who worked. . . . In the years since . . . I have never departed far from . . . the goal of a society with a minimum of compulsion, a maximum of individual

freedom and of voluntary association, and the abolition of exploitation and poverty."

If Baldwin adopted a revolutionary ideology, in practice he remained a reformer. He continued working with the elite Civic League for several years after his encounter with Goldman, and throughout his career he remained a pragmatist, often willing to sacrifice principle for effectiveness. For example, in 1942 Baldwin dismissed a black ACLU lawyer because he believed the lawyer's race would make it difficult for him to persuade presumably prejudiced white jurors.

Baldwin left St. Louis in 1917 to become director of the American Union Against Militarism (AUAM), a New York–based organization that opposed World War I. With the violations of the civil liberties of radicals, unionists, and pacifists and the attack on free speech that accompanied America's entry into the war, the AUAM spawned a new organization, the National Civil Liberties Bureau (NCLB), of which Baldwin became the director. The NCLB became a clearinghouse for information for conscientious objectors and fought for Americans' rights to speak out against the war. Himself a conscientious objector, Baldwin was sentenced on Armistice Day and spent nearly a year in jail for refusing to report for his physical. Oral James, one of two young men Baldwin adopted in St. Louis, also resisted the war and served his sentence in a military prison camp at Fort Leavenworth, Kansas.

The postwar Palmer raids—in which federal marshals and local police ransacked the homes and offices of thousands of radicals—convinced Baldwin that the rights of those with unpopular opinions would always need protecting. After the war the Civil Liberties Bureau changed its name to the American Civil Liberties Union to reflect its expanded purpose. With Baldwin at its head, the ACLU initiated many landmark civil liberties cases: opposing ordinances prohibiting the freedom of assembly, challenging the Tennessee law that prohibited the teaching of evolution in schools, attacking the censorship of imported books, and defending Jehovah's Witnesses children who refused to salute the American flag. Under Baldwin's leadership, the ACLU also cooperated in such celebrated trials as those of Sacco and Vanzetti and the Scottsboro boys.

A consummate coalition builder, Baldwin joined several "popular front" organizations during the 1920s and 1930s, including the League Against Imperialism, the League Against War and Fascism, and the American Committee for Loyalist Spain. After the Hitler-Stalin pact, Baldwin became a virulent anticommunist and, embarrassed by his earlier associations, frequently denounced communism. In fact, the ACLU purged its board—but not its membership— of communists in 1940, becoming one of the first organizations to institute the sort of loyalty oath later identified with McCarthyism.

In 1947 Baldwin visited Japan at the invitation of Gen. Douglas MacArthur, who was in charge of the occupying forces, to advise the general on civil liberties issues. Baldwin turned his attention to international civil liberties full-time in 1949, when he resigned as director of the ACLU at age sixty-five. As chairman of the International League of the Rights of Man, one of the first nongovernmental organizations to be recognized by the United Nations, Baldwin committed himself to the fight against colonialism and to the extension of civil liberties worldwide.

Baldwin was married twice, first in 1919 to prominent feminist lawyer Madeleine Doty. They separated in 1925 when Doty took a position in Geneva as secretary for the Women's International League for Peace. Baldwin and Doty divorced in 1935 so Baldwin could marry independently wealthy labor activist Evelyn Preston, whose love affair with Baldwin ended her marriage to prominent liberal Steve Raushenbush. Baldwin and Preston raised Preston's two sons, Roger and Carl. Together they had one daughter, Helen. Years earlier in St. Louis, Baldwin adopted two wards of the court, Otto Stoltz and Oral James. Stoltz committed suicide in February 1930, and Helen also predeceased her father. Baldwin died of heart failure in Ridgewood, New Jersey, near his home in Oakland, on August 26, 1981, at the age of ninety-seven.

MARTHA KOHL

Baldwin, Roger. "Recollections of a Life in Civil Liberties—I." *Civil Liberties Review* 2:2 (spring 1975): 39–72.

———. "Recollections of a Life in Civil Liberties—II." *Civil Liberties Review* 2:4 (fall 1975): 10–40.

Lamson, Peggy. *Roger Baldwin: Founder of the American Civil Liberties Union.* Boston: Houghton Mifflin, 1976.

Walker, Samuel. *In Defense of American Liberties: A History of the ACLU.* New York: Oxford University Press, 1990.

BANNON, JOHN B. (1829–1913)

Father John B. Bannon deserves his recognition as a leading Confederate religious figure. No religious personality of the South contributed more to the cause of Confederate independence than Bannon: from 1861 to 1863 he served as the "Fighting Chaplain" of the First Missouri Confederate Brigade, he was the Confederacy's first diplomatic agent to the Vatican in an effort to win recognition from the pope, and he performed invaluable service as a daring Confederate secret agent in Ireland on a mission of considerable importance. Some have called him "the most notable chaplain in the Civil War," and he was widely known as "the Catholic priest who always went into battle." However, Bannon and his accomplishments were relegated to obscurity, and his important contributions are generally ignored by Civil War historians.

Bannon was born near Dublin, Ireland, on December 29, 1829. After receiving a good academic and religious education, the newly ordained priest was sent to Missouri. Leaving Ireland for the first time in his life, he reached St. Louis in 1853. He faithfully administered to the large Irish population of St. Louis with an enthusiasm that soon made him one of the city's best-liked priests. In November 1858 Bannon became pastor of St. John's Parish in western St. Louis where he became the driving force behind the construction of one of the city's most beautiful churches, St. John the Apostle and Evangelist.

Besides his many religious duties, Bannon also served with the Missouri Volunteer Militia of St. Louis during the antebellum period, administering to the many Irish Catholic soldiers in the ranks. As a militia chaplain, he was a brief participant in the Southeast Expedition of December 1860. Bannon, in a blue militia uniform, was captured at Camp Jackson by Unionists in May 1861. Of strong pro-Southern beliefs, Bannon left his St. Louis church and promising religious career in late 1861 to join the pro-Southern Missouri forces of Gen. **Sterling Price,** and he became chaplain of the First Missouri Confederate Brigade.

During the Battle of Pea Ridge, Arkansas, Bannon served with distinction on the battlefield. Instead of following orders and remaining in the rear with the other Rebel chaplains, he was on the front lines during the two-day battle, helping the wounded and dying and inspiring the faithful. When cannoneers were killed, he joined an artillery crew and assisted the Rebel gunners.

Upon the transfer of Gen. Earl Van Dorn's Southern army to the eastern side of the Mississippi, Bannon was involved in the Mississippi battles of Iuka and Corinth in 1862, followed by Grand Gulf, Port Gibson, Champion Hill, and the siege of Vicksburg in 1863. As throughout his remarkable career, Bannon's feats of bravery at Vicksburg became legendary.

After the surrender of Vicksburg in July 1863, Bannon journeyed east to the Confederate capital at Richmond, Virginia, where President Jefferson Davis presented him with a key mission: travel to Ireland and begin a career as a Confederate secret agent to convince Irish immigrants not to join the Union army when they reach America's shores. This mission was important because the war-weary Union was drawing upon thousands of Irish immigrants to replenish its battered armies in anticipation of the 1864 campaigns for Atlanta and Richmond.

Bannon proposed that President Jefferson Davis also send a special diplomatic mission to the Vatican. Fully realizing that the Confederacy had missed a diplomatic opportunity, Bannon developed a bold plan to solicit recognition for the Confederacy from the pope. If the pope bestowed recognition on the new Southern nation, he believed, a small European Catholic country might follow with recognition. This in turn might draw France, and then Britain, closer to recognition, which could affect the war's outcome. Bannon also saw the mission as a chance to recapture the moral high ground that the Confederacy had lost when Lincoln issued the Emancipation Proclamation.

Diplomat-agent Bannon accomplished a great deal during both his Vatican and Ireland missions, performing capable, if not brilliant, service under demanding circumstances. He effectively laid the Confederacy's case before Pope Pius IX, and felt encouraged about the prospects for recognition. Bannon's masterful propaganda campaign in Ireland during 1863 and 1864 also helped keep a large number of Irish out of the Union army. His accomplishments were the most impressive diplomatic successes of the Confederacy in Ireland. By any measure, his many contributions to the cause of Southern independence made him an outstanding Confederate religious figure.

Bannon joined the Jesuit Order in 1864, becoming one of the most famous and popular priests in his native Ireland. He died on his beloved Emerald Isle on July 14, 1913.

PHILLIP THOMAS TUCKER

Tucker, Phillip Thomas. *The Confederacy's Fighting Chaplain: Father John B. Bannon.* Tuscaloosa: University of Alabama Press, 1992.

BARTHOLOMEW, HARLAND (1889–1989)

Harland Bartholomew was born near Boston, Massachusetts, on September 4, 1889. He died in St. Louis at the age of one hundred on December 2, 1989. He studied civil engineering at Rutgers University but left before receiving a degree. Rutgers later awarded him two honorary degrees: civil engineer in 1921 and doctor of science in 1952.

Early in his career Bartholomew was employed by E. P. Goodrich, a New York civil engineer. Goodrich, associated with architect George P. Ford, was engaged to prepare a comprehensive city plan for Newark, New Jersey, in 1911. Bartholomew was assigned to this work and, as it was nearing completion, was engaged by Newark as its "city plan engineer," becoming the first full-time planner employed by an American city. Because of his work

in Newark, Bartholomew became well known in the infant city-planning movement.

In 1916 Bartholomew accepted a similar assignment in St. Louis and immediately began preparation of a city plan. A major street plan that guided an active program of widening and connecting important streets, a zoning ordinance that finally took effect in 1922 after two trips to the state supreme court, and a $83 million bond issue in 1923 that brought the civic center and the mall from downtown to Union Station were all extraordinary achievements that drew national attention. In 1918 Bartholomew was appointed professor of civil design at the University of Illinois, a nonresident position he held until 1956.

The compelling need to manage urban growth and Bartholomew's record of accomplishment in Newark and St. Louis compelled many cities to seek his advice. He quickly found the "in and out expert" practice unsatisfactory because his clients were not producing the comprehensive city plans that he deemed essential to real accomplishment. Consequently, he founded the firm of Harland Bartholomew and Associates in 1919. An association of civil engineers, architects, and landscape architects, the company's primary purpose was the preparation of comprehensive plans. The firm still exists, having completed six thousand major professional assignments, including six hundred comprehensive plans (one hundred in Missouri). The company provides planning, environmental, and landscape architectural work throughout the world, all coordinated from its office in St. Louis County, one of five in the country.

In 1928 the St. Louis Planning Commission proposed the Central Riverfront Plan, creating a great open space on the Mississippi River and a new expressway along Third Street. The Jefferson National Expansion Memorial (the Arch), the symbol of St. Louis, carried to completion the 1928 plans.

A 1934 Regional Plan for St. Louis brought establishment of the Bistate Development Agency and the gift of Babler State Park. The 1936 Urban Land Policy Report brought attention to the alarming deterioration of older sections of St. Louis. The summary outlined how to rebuild obsolete areas, rehabilitate blighted districts, and protect satisfactory residential neighborhoods. Ignored locally, the report was influential nationally, responsible in part for federal-housing and urban-renewal legislation. A direct result of the report was Missouri Law 353, passed in 1943, enabling tax credits for private redevelopment corporations, which, in turn, was responsible for the rebuilding of the downtown areas of St. Louis and Kansas City.

In 1940 President Roosevelt appointed Bartholomew a member of the Interregional Highway Committee. The report of this panel made in 1944 and approved by Congress in 1947 formed the basis for the U.S. system of interstate highways. Bartholomew was responsible for the section that dealt with highways in urban areas, probably his greatest influence on the American city.

President Eisenhower appointed Bartholomew chairman of the National Capital Park and Planning Commission in 1953. During his seven-year tenure, he established regional planning for Washington, D.C., and prepared the studies that brought about the city's metro system. After the Washington appointment ended, Bartholomew managed the Washington office of Harland Bartholomew and Associates for two years and then resigned his partnership in 1963, remaining a consultant until his death in 1989.

Bartholomew was a pioneer in the American planning movement. He systematized approaches to planning and brought acceptance of planning as a governmental responsibility. He helped to develop planning as a rational discipline that could be taught. He discovered basic land-use relationships and wrote two books about them. Bartholomew believed that planning without accomplishment was worthless. He devised mechanisms and procedures, capital-improvements programs, advanced zoning techniques, financial inducements, public-participation procedures, and urban-redevelopment corporations to carry out the comprehensive plans.

Bartholomew received the highest award of honorary membership from the American Society of Civil Engineers in 1962 and from the American Society of Landscape Architects in 1958. He received the Distinguished Service Award from the American Institute of Planners in 1955.

ELDRIDGE LOVELACE

Bartholomew, Harland. *Land Uses in American Cities.* Cambridge: Harvard University Press, 1955.

———. *Urban Land Policy for St. Louis.* Report prepared for the St. Louis City Plan Commission, 1936.

———. *Urban Land Uses.* Harvard City Planning Studies Series, vol. 4. Cambridge: Harvard University Press, 1932.

Lovelace, Eldridge. *Harland Bartholomew: His Contributions to American Urban Planning.* Urbana: University of Illinois Press, 1993.

BARTLE, H. ROE (1896–1974)

Twice elected mayor of Kansas City, Missouri, and known as "Chief" to tens of thousands of Boy Scouts across western Missouri, H. Roe Bartle cut a big swath through part of Missouri history. The original big-and-tall role model, Bartle stood more than six-foot-three and weighed at least three hundred pounds. His booming baritone voice brought him attention and respect as a public speaker and an advocate for character-building organizations such as the Boy Scouts of America.

Born in Richmond, Virginia, on June 25, 1896, of Scottish Presbyterian stock, Bartle grew up with southern upbringing and Scottish thrift and public service as his models. His father was an ordained clergyman in the southern branch of the Presbyterian Church and encouraged him to enter the ministry. Instead, the younger Bartle studied law at the University of Chattanooga and practiced corporate law in Kentucky for four years in the early 1920s.

Knowledge of businesses and their value led to sound investments during Bartle's legal career. He accumulated the basis of a significant investment income that subsidized his long years at lower pay in public service. While in Kentucky he became interested in the Boy Scouts, and he gradually moved out of legal practice and into a Scout executive position in the mid-1920s. By 1928 he had served as a Scout executive in Wyoming and St. Joseph, Missouri; that year he took the same position in Kansas City, Missouri. Among Bartle's accomplishments over the next twenty-five years in the executive position was the creation of the Tribe of Mic-O-Say Scouting honorary camping organization. He also attracted the largest group of Eagle Scouts per capita of any Scouting district in the country.

Besides his Scouting responsibilities, Bartle served simultaneously as president of Missouri Valley College, a Presbyterian institution in Marshall, from 1948 to 1952. During his presidency, he formed a curriculum for the training of young men and women to work in voluntary public-service positions with youth, such as the Boy Scouts, the Girl Scouts, and similar organizations. He was much in demand as a public speaker, often giving as many as seven hundred formal speeches in one year.

Former Scouts prevailed upon Bartle to run for mayor of Kansas City in 1955. Since the "Clean-up" campaign of 1940 that defeated most of the Pendergast organization, the nonpartisan Citizens Association had dominated the electoral process. Bartle refused to run on the Citizens ticket, preferring to campaign as an independent who had not promised anything to anyone. He officially declined the support of the remnant of the Pendergast Democrats as well.

When it came time for reelection in 1957, however, Bartle accepted unofficial support from the Democrats, which raised fears in Kansas City of a possible revival of "boss politics." The fears proved groundless; while Bartle did appoint some machine supporters to a few positions, the office of mayor in Kansas City is little more than that of a city council member elected at large. Needless to say, Bartle performed the ceremonial aspects of the mayoralty quite well.

During Bartle's two terms, Kansas City became a major-league city in two sports. The Philadelphia Athletics relocated there in 1955, and the Dallas Texans moved north early in the next decade. Indeed, the mayor's nickname of "Chief" was adopted by the new American Football League franchise. The Kansas City Chiefs adopted the Indian connotations of the name rather quickly, which led Missourians to forget the original source of the name.

Bartle was most proud of founding the American Humanics Foundation, which is still headquartered in Kansas City.

Bartle died in Kansas City on May 8, 1974. Kansas City's convention and exhibition center, Bartle Hall, is named in honor of the former mayor.

WILLIAM S. WORLEY

Fowler, Dick. *Leaders in Our Town*. Kansas City: Burd and Fletcher, 1952.

Green, George Fuller. "H. Roe Bartle." In *A Condensed History of the Kansas City Area*. Kansas City: Lowell Press, 1968.

Spence, Hartzell. "The Colossal Mayor of Kansas City." *Saturday Evening Post* (January 28, 1956): 17–18, 79–80.

BARTON, DAVID (1783–1837)

David Barton was born near Greenville, North Carolina, now in eastern Tennessee, on December 14, 1783. He was the fifth of twelve children born to Isaac and Keziah Barton. A frontier Baptist minister, Isaac Barton probably struggled to provide for his large family. David, however, apparently received a good education. According to traditional accounts, he attended Greenville College, studied law with a distinguished Tennessee judge and attorney, and was admitted to the Tennessee bar.

The best evidence indicates that the young lawyer moved to Missouri in 1809, and appears to have been well received in St. Louis. Barton made early connections with some of the leading lawyers and political figures of the Missouri Territory, and within a short time had established a successful law practice and launched his political career.

In March 1812 Barton joined a company of mounted rangers organized by **Nathan Boone.** He was appointed ensign but resigned his commission after three months. The following year, Gov. **William Clark** appointed Barton as the territory's attorney general. During his term Barton joined a company of volunteer Missouri rangers under the command of Gen. **Henry Dodge** that marched into the Boonslick country in September 1814 to deal with Indian unrest. Barton saw no combat, but his two stints in the rangers helped establish his popularity throughout the Missouri Territory.

In 1815 Governor Clark appointed Barton as the first circuit judge of the Northern District of Missouri, then comprising St. Charles and St. Louis Counties (Howard County was added to the district in 1816). In this office, Barton apparently gained new friends and clients, and he resigned the judgeship to attend to his growing law practice. In 1818 he returned to politics, winning a seat in the territorial House of Representatives, which chose him as its Speaker. Barton was well on his way to a promising political career.

As Missouri advanced toward statehood, Barton was elected as a member of the Constitutional Convention, whose delegates elected him as the presiding officer. Barton apparently played such a leading role in writing Missouri's first constitution that it has been called "the Barton Constitution." While scant records of the convention's proceedings make it difficult to trace his precise role, Barton clearly influenced the shape of the document, especially the judicial branch and its other conservative features.

Credited by some historians as having been the most popular man in Missouri by 1820, the Missouri General Assembly elected Barton as the state's first U.S. senator. Although chosen by a large majority, Barton did not receive the unanimous vote traditionally accorded him in Missouri political lore. Barton's statewide popularity and the impressive vote for senator stemmed from his ranger service, from his territorial political career, and from his nonaffiliation with either the St. Louis junto or the antijunto factions that were struggling for control of the state. In a much closer contest, the General Assembly elected **Thomas Hart Benton,** then connected with the St. Louis junto, as Missouri's second U.S. senator. Barton drew by lot the four-year term assigned to one of the new state's first U.S. senators.

Barton probably reached the peak of his political popularity and power in 1820. He won reelection to the Senate in 1824, in spite of opposition from Benton and others. Although he continued for several years to be an influential political leader, Barton increasingly represented a conservative minority that opposed the rising tide of Jacksonian Democracy led in Missouri by Benton.

Barton's appearance, habits, and general demeanor are not fully clear. Some historians have questioned the authentication of the portrait most often used in Missouri history books. In general, his contemporaries described Barton as small, thin, habitually careless, even untidy in dress, and physically unimpressive. Yet, friends called him a cultured gentleman, one whose oratorical eloquence and skill surprised first-time listeners. He could speak with ease, revealing a knowledge of his subject and making his points with decisive logic. He has also been described as a forceful and fighting speaker. With a hard-hitting sarcasm, often bitter and vindictive, Barton attacked his opponents and held his own in Missouri's rough, personal, and frontier-style politics. His rough and ready behavior extended to hard drinking. He may not have been as intemperate as his enemies sometimes charged, but his frequent bouts with the bottle spawned rumors, and the unfortunate habit became a highly detrimental factor in his final years.

In the national election of 1824, Barton campaigned, as did Benton, for Henry Clay, the clear presidential favorite in Missouri. But when the absence of a majority vote sent the presidential election to the House of Representatives as a contest between John Quincy Adams and Andrew Jackson, the two Missouri senators parted company and launched their roles as leaders of the two diverging political factions in Missouri. In time, the Barton faction would relate to the National Republican Party of Clay and Adams, while the Benton faction generally became the Democratic Party of Jackson.

In the election of a president, Barton advised **John Scott,** Missouri's representative, to vote for Adams. While recognizing the accountability of a representative to his constituents, Barton argued that, in this case, the representative's vote was cast under the authority of the Union and not the state. Thus, the representative should act in the interest of the nation and vote for the best man to be president—and Barton believed that man was Adams. Barton's reasoning had merit, but more Missourians agreed with Benton's passionate oratory that because the people of Missouri wanted Jackson, Scott had no choice but to honor their wishes and vote accordingly.

Only a short time earlier, Barton had opposed Benton's proposals for a constitutional amendment to abolish the electoral college and provide for a more direct election for the president and for a law to graduate downward the price of public land. In this negative stance, Barton stood opposed to the growing strength of the Jacksonian movement in Missouri with its popular advocacy of a greater political democracy and greater equality of economic opportunity.

As Barton emerged as the Missouri leader for the Adams-Clay position, he urged a more positive view of national government, strongly disapproving of those who charged the federal government with trying to destroy states' rights. In asserting the benefits of national power, he supported Clay's proposed American System of protective tariffs for American producers and national internal improvements as beneficial to all Americans.

As a political conservative, Barton feared the excesses of popular democracy, and he believed those excesses less likely to affect the national than the state governments. He always held the judicial branch of government in high esteem, and he saw the United States Supreme Court as the check upon abuse of power by the people, the executive, and the Congress. On the other hand, he favored a liberal interpretation of the Constitution to accomplish the programs and goals of Clay's American System.

Benton's reelection in 1826, despite Barton's opposition, revealed further the divergence of the two Missouri leaders and their respective factions. In 1828 a correspondent for the *New York Commercial Advertiser* wrote that Barton and Benton were uniformly opposed on every subject. The 1828 sweeping victories of Jackson nationally and in Missouri elevated the Jackson party, along with Benton, to a clear political dominance in the state. At the same time, that election marked a rapid decline in Barton's political fortunes.

Perhaps the final straw in Barton's political downfall was his vote against Benton's land-graduation bill in 1829—the only western senator to vote against it in that session. He voted against graduation even as he recognized that the great majority of Missourians favored it. He distrusted the direct mass democracy he saw stemming from Benton's proposal to abolish the electoral college, and he saw graduation as an example of politicians inflaming passions and hopes of the masses founded on unsound programs to gain votes and political power. He set forth a well-reasoned explanation for his stance: to lower the price of public land, he argued, would not help the poor who had no money, but would result in vast sales of the public lands to speculators. Rather, he proposed reducing the minimum price of public land from $1.25 to $1.00 per acre, and from those lands not sold after five years make direct grants to the poor who would settle on them. But Missourians would not listen to Barton's land proposal. Finally, in 1830, recognizing the then popular "right of instruction," Barton complied with instructions from the Missouri General Assembly and voted for a graduation bill. The bill, however, failed passage in the Congress.

The only major office at stake in the Missouri elections of 1830 was Barton's seat in the United States Senate. Given his representation of a Missouri minority, widespread reports of his intemperance, and the Jackson-Benton party's determination to bring him down, Barton accepted the advice of friends and did not seek reelection.

Barton did not, however, withdraw from the political arena. Making his home in St. Louis, he made an unsuccessful run for election to the United States House of Representatives in 1831. In 1834, however, he won election to the state senate, although he took little part in the Senate proceedings. His associates described him as melancholy and moody, and he resigned his post before the close of the session.

Barton moved to Boonville in December 1836. Although he engaged in law practice there, his physical and mental health made it difficult for him to attract new business or handle more than a few cases; in fact, he was unable to finish some cases. His increasingly strange and irrational, sometimes violent, behavior caused his friends to worry about his own safety as well as that of others. Just how much his excessive use of alcohol contributed to his deteriorating mental and physical health is not clear. His conditioned so worsened that in August 1837 the county court ordered the sheriff to summon a jury to investigate Barton's mental faculties. The jurors pronounced him insane and appointed his brother Isaac as his guardian. Barton died in Boonville on September 28, 1837.

Barton's unfortunate demise was a tragic end for the career of a Missourian who, with great ability, distinction, and integrity, had served his state in several important public posts. If he did not always represent a majority position on public issues, he based his actions on sound principles backed by equally sound and valid reasoning.

PERRY MCCANDLESS

Foley, William E. "The Political Philosophy of David Barton." *Missouri Historical Review* 58 (April 1964): 287–89.

McCandless, Perry. "Benton v Barton: The Formation of the Second-Party System in Missouri." *Missouri Historical Review* 79 (July 1985): 425–38.

Van Ravenswaay, Charles. "The Tragedy of David Barton." *Missouri Historical Society Bulletin* 7 (October 1950): 35–56.

BARTON, JOSHUA (1788–1823)

Like so many men of his kind and class, Joshua Barton was a southern gentlemen who hitched his proverbial star to territorial Missouri. And, like a few of the most unlucky, he saw it prematurely snuffed out. In many ways Barton epitomized the early ruling class in Missouri. He was, according to an early biographer, motivated in part by the spirit of chivalry and knight-errantry so characteristic of that generation of elites. Born into a well-to-do Tennessee family in 1788, he moved to St. Louis in 1809 to seek his fortune. Like many other early transplants, Barton relied upon family connections to solidify his standing. His father, the Reverend Isaac Barton, was a Scotsman with a fine reputation. The family had first moved to Maryland and then struck out for Tennessee. It was only logical that the trans-Mississippi West and the call of a new and promising frontier would beckon to these young adventurers. His older brother David had already established himself among the prominent families of St. Charles

and St. Louis as a brilliant orator, lawyer, and future statesman. Another brother, named after his father, also resided in St. Louis. It was generally agreed that all three young men had illustrious careers in store.

Upon his arrival in St. Louis, Barton put his formal education to use. First he read and studied law under the preceptorship of **Rufus Easton,** who would shortly serve as Missouri's second territorial representative to the national capital. This mentorship subsequently led to Barton's admission to the bar and a professional legal association with another prominent individual, **Edward Bates,** who would subsequently serve as Missouri's first attorney general. Bates later claimed that Barton possessed the best legal mind in the city. With the influence of his brother David, who had only recently become the state's first U.S. senator, Barton was appointed as Missouri's secretary of state on September 26, 1820. Less than a year later, at President James Monroe's behest, he resigned his position to become the U.S. district attorney in St. Louis.

Even the most cursory of biographical sketches reveal that frontier elites such as Barton did not personify the stereotypical traits of rugged individualism and social independence. Success was as much a consequence of breeding as it was of boldness and sagacity. Missouri society was characterized by marked economic differentiation, political hierarchy, and clearly recognized class distinctions. Struggles for power and prestige therefore were waged more within the upper echelons of the social structure rather than between classes. Barton fell victim to this intense factional discord.

Of the many methods of silencing an opponent, the code duello was most effective, sending Barton and many other young gentlemen to an early grave. Dueling was one visible manifestation of upper-class respectability. Among other social customs it had found its way to Missouri from the South. Unlike their counterparts in the Deep South, however, Missouri duels were less theatrical and more lethal.

Barton was no stranger to the field of honor. In 1816 he dueled Thomas Hempstead, the brother of **Edward Hempstead,** Missouri's first territorial representative. Barton's second in this affair was his law partner, Edward Bates. **Thomas Hart Benton** served as Hempstead's second. It was not unusual during this period to find prominent citizens engaged in political duels. Although the 1816 encounter ended without bloodshed, all the parties involved gained considerable notoriety. The following year, Barton twice ventured to the field of honor as **Charles Lucas**'s second in his duels with Benton. It was in the second of these affairs that Lucas received a mortal wound. This experience should have made Barton realize that duels in Missouri did not always end harmlessly.

In 1823 violent political partisanship again reared its head and once again claimed an aspiring youth as its victim. On June 25, 1823, there appeared in the *St. Louis Republican* an article signed anonymously by "Philo" outlining a series of charges, including corruption and nepotism, against Gen. William C. Rector, the surveyor-general of Illinois, Missouri, and Arkansas. **David Barton** had supplied the evidence, but it was Joshua who published the results. Rector's brother Thomas demanded from the *Republican* the identity of "Philo." Upon obtaining the information, he promptly challenged Joshua. On June 30, 1823, at six in the evening they met on a sandbar by that time dubbed, appropriately, Bloody Island. Barton fell on first fire and died within minutes. He was buried in St. Charles. The *Republican,* without even a hint of its own culpability, lamented Missouri's loss of "one of her ablest and worthiest citizens." Rector's victory, however, was Pyrrhic in that he was soon fired by President Monroe and subsequently died penniless. As for Thomas Rector, he was killed two years later in a St. Louis knife fight.

DICK STEWARD

"Joshua Barton, 1820–1821." Vertical File. Missouri State Archives, Jefferson City.

Letter. J. B. C. Lucas to Rufus King, November 20, 1823. John B. C. Lucas Collection. Missouri Historical Society, St. Louis.

Letter. William Rector to James Monroe, July 25, 1823. Vol. A, pp. 278–81, U.S. Surveyor General of Missouri, Outgoing Correspondence. Missouri State Archives, Jefferson City.

Stevens, Walter B. *Centennial History of Missouri.* Vol. 1. St. Louis: S. J. Clarke, 1921.

———. *Missouri: The Center State, 1821–1915.* Vol. 1. St. Louis: S. J. Clarke, 1915.

BARTON, RALPH (1891–1931)

Ralph Waldo Emerson Barton was born August 14, 1891, in Kansas City, Missouri, to Abraham and Catherine Barton, and was the youngest of four children. Not long before Barton's birth, his father gave up his career as an attorney to pursue with his wife the publication of various metaphysical journals. Catherine Barton was also a portrait painter and operated a successful art studio.

In 1908 Ralph Barton left Westport High School before graduating "to study art," having already published cartoons and illustrations in the *Kansas City Star* and the *Kansas City Post.* He left Kansas City in 1909 to attend school at the Art Institute of Chicago but disliked the confines of its teaching. "I don't like Chicago or Chicago people and worst of all the Art Institute. I could learn twice as much at work," he wrote to his mother. Barton received no formal art education; most of what he knew he learned from his mother, those who frequented her art studio, and his own self-study of the old masters.

Shortly after returning to Kansas City in 1909, Barton married his first wife, Marie Jennings, and they had a daughter, Natalie, in 1910. Barton supported them with income earned from the *Star* and the *Post.* He sold his first drawing to the humor magazine *Puck* in 1912 for three dollars and soon thereafter moved his family to New York City. His departure marked the beginning of his rise from obscurity to the wealth and notoriety he would experience in the 1920s. It also represented the start of his unceasing quest for the urbane and sophisticated, escaping what he considered the provincialism of the Midwest.

Barton's early days in New York were spent drawing for such magazines as *Puck* and *McCall's.* Unhappy with their new life, his wife soon left him and returned to Kansas City. Barton rented studio space in the Lincoln Arcade, a building with cheap rent that made it a haven for the city's bohemians. He shared the studio with another Missouri native, **Thomas Hart Benton,** and the two became good friends. In his autobiography, Benton later wrote that Ralph Barton was pretentious and that his drawing ability was limited only to a marketable style.

By 1913 Barton's distinctive style of caricature and social commentary was clearly emerging. The flat lines delineating his hollow doll-like figures were likely influenced by the stylized, elongated figures of art-nouveau illustrator Aubrey Beardsley. Barton himself claimed the influence of the flat planes and lines of ancient Egyptian art.

Barton's enthrallment with France and his affected European snobbery began in 1915 when *Puck* sent him to Paris to record images of the war. The midwestern expatriate became a Francophile, living in Paris periodically for the rest of his life. His friend Thomas Craven wrote of him, "he out fopped the French at their own game, dressed like something midway between a toreador and an aesthete. . . ."

The 1920s brought professional success to Barton, who at times earned as much as fifteen hundred dollars per drawing. In 1922 he was commissioned to execute an intermission curtain for a Russian revue called *Chauve Souris* written by Nikita Balieff. Decorated with 135 celebrity caricatures, the curtain brought Barton public acclaim. When the *New Yorker* was founded in 1925, Barton served as an advisory editor, stockholder, and occasional contributor of theatrical caricatures. Barton also illustrated one of the 1920s' most popular books, Anita Loos's *Gentlemen Prefer Blondes.* In 1927 France awarded Barton the Cross of the Legion of Honor.

Barton's professional achievements were not reflected in his personal life. By the end of the 1920s, his reputation for casual affairs contributed to three failed marriages: to model Anne Minnerly who later married poet e. e. cummings and with whom he had a daughter, Diana; to actress Carlotta Monterey who later married playwright Eugene O'Neill; and to French composer Germaine Tailleferre. In addition, his 1929 book *God's Country,* a satirical look at U.S. history in drawings, was not well received.

Undoubtedly these disappointments contributed to Barton's depression, ultimately leading to his suicide on May 20, 1931, at age thirty-nine in his New York penthouse apartment. Before shooting himself, he left a note titled "OBIT" emphasizing his self-diagnosed melancholia: "It has made it impossible for me to enjoy the simple pleasures of life. I have run from wife to wife, from house to house and from country to country in a ridiculous effort to escape from myself. . . ." Barton was eulogized in New York and Kansas City newspapers, but public interest in him quickly waned, returning him to obscurity. His ashes were returned to Kansas City for interment in Mount Moriah Cemetery, an ironic twist given his frequent reference to "climbing out of the Kansas City mud." Little interest was shown in his work until a 1968 exhibition at the Rhode Island School of Design.

Perhaps Barton would scoff at his inclusion in the *Dictionary of Missouri Biography* given his disdain of his hometown, a disdain well exemplified in a letter to his sister after hearing that the touring *Chauve Souris* got little attention in Kansas City: "In Kansas City, Balieff and all the music, dancing and acting in Russian aren't half as interesting as the oiling of Gillham Road."

MARY ELLEN BOYD

Barton, Ralph. *God's Country.* New York: Knopf, 1929.

———. *The Jazz Age as Seen through the Eyes of Ralph Barton, Miguel Covarrubias, and John Held, Jr.* Providence: Museum of Art, Rhode Island School of Design, 1968.

Kellner, Bruce. *The Last Dandy, Ralph Barton: American Artist, 1891–1931.* Foreword by John Updike. Columbia: University of Missouri Press, 1991.

Loos, Anita. *Gentlemen Prefer Blondes: The Illuminating Diary of a Professional Lady.* New York: Boni and Liveright, 1925.

Updike, John. "A Case of Melancholia." In *Just Looking: Essays on Art.* New York: Knopf, 1989.

BASIE, WILLIAM "COUNT" (1904–1984)

Born on August 21, 1904, in Red Bank, New Jersey, William Basie's earliest ambition was to leave his birthplace and earn enough money to allow his mother to give up her laundry work. Because education struck him as an unlikely route to his goal, he left school in junior high, having refused to learn anything but reading and arithmetic. Music, not geography, enthralled him. While he preferred the drums, his parents owned a piano, and his mother insisted on piano lessons. Too independent to learn sight reading, young Willie discovered that he could pick out on the keyboard almost any tune he had heard—a talent that enabled him to take over as piano player at a Red Bank movie house while he was still in knee pants and to play gigs with local musicians. Equally captivated by the traveling performers and carnival troupes who came to town, Basie yearned to take to the road with his music. Around 1923 he made his break, taking the train with a friend to Asbury Park where the two lived hand-to-mouth, picking up odd jobs and a few gigs before moving to Harlem the next year.

In Harlem Basie found a job touring with a burlesque show on the Columbia Circuit. After two seasons on tour, Basie obtained his first permanent club engagement in Harlem, where he learned to play the organ after-hours with Fats Waller. But Basie's inability to read music cost him jobs. He struggled to make a living until 1926 when he joined a band playing in the Gonzelle White Company and traveling for the Theatre Owners' Booking Association, the so-called TOBA circuit of black vaudeville houses. The tours took him to Kansas City occasionally. The vibrant nightlife there and the many talented musicians who circulated around Eighteenth and Vine Streets in the city's ghetto so impressed him that, when White dissolved her stranded company in Kansas City in 1929, Basie chose to remain in the Missouri River jazz center.

Basie took a job at the black-owned Eblon Theatre on Eighteenth Street, accompanying the silent films on the organ. After hours, he sat in at the clubs in the Eighteenth and Vine district. And there was no shortage of clubs. Under **Thomas J. Pendergast**'s machine rule, Kansas City sprouted scores of nightclubs, most of them located in the ghetto, where white gangsters and solid citizens alike partook of jazz and the illicit trades that accompanied it—all under the protection of a corrupt police force. When depression closed clubs elsewhere in the region, Boss Tom's lavish public spending provided Kansas Citians with sufficient incomes to continue their club hopping. Consequently, musicians flocked to the city, where African American club managers such as Piney Brown and Ellis Burton befriended them with food and money and allowed neophytes like Basie to jam with the house combos. Preferring to sit in at the Sunset Club or the Subway, the diffident young musician fled to the lesser dives when stellar pianists such as Mary Louise Williams or Pete Johnson showed up, thinking his skills were no match for theirs.

Yet, Basie began scheming to get a place in the **Bennie Moten** band—a bold ambition given that Moten himself was the pianist and Basie discounted his own talents at the keyboard. Moten's was the premier outfit among the so-called territory bands that toured the Southwest from a base in Kansas City. With top players, popular recordings, and a steady schedule of engagements to its credit, the Moten band represented the pinnacle of success for local musicians. Basie fell in with Eddie Durham, one of Moten's trombonists. Together, they worked up some new arrangements as Basie played and Durham wrote down Basie's keyboarding. Moten liked the new charts and took Basie on tour as his staff arranger, gradually letting the young man sit in at the piano on stage and then on recordings.

While the band extended its audience with play dates in Chicago and recordings for Victor, Durham and Basie plotted to enliven the band's sound. They convinced Moten to hire vocalist Jimmy Rushing and trumpeter Oran "Hot Lips" Page, whom Basie had met when he performed briefly with Walter Page's territory band, the Blue Devils. Basie and Durham worked up complicated arrangements using five-part harmonies and spotlighting the "hot" styling of the former Blue Devils.

In so doing, Basie incorporated the driving, improvisational sound characteristic of Kansas City jazz in the twenties and thirties. Kansas City style rested on the "riff," a simple musical phrase repeated and reinterpreted by successive instrument sections and used as background to solo improvisations. Most often, these phrases employed a twelve-bar blues progression that translated standard blues vocals into an orchestral form that drove with an increasing intensity toward a crescendo of emotion. Rhythm glued the riffs together into a coherent whole by maintaining an aggressive but constant tempo, a styling called "swing" that made dancing, clapping, or foot tapping irresistible.

At first the Moten veterans disliked the hot sound, but Moten approved, and the band's sound on records won over the rest of the outfit. A succession of engagements in eastern cities, including New York at the Savoy Ballroom, attracted attention from larger audiences who liked "Moten's Swing" style. "They couldn't understand it," Basie recalled, "but they knew they could pat their feet and dance to it." Still, big-time bookings were interspersed with lean times when the band slept on the bus or dined from the common stew pot in a Harlem bar. Periodic returns to Kansas City for engagements at Fairyland Park and battle-of-the-bands competitions made welcome respites.

Money was a growing concern for Basie. He learned that his parents had separated. More than ever, his mother needed the cash he sent whenever he could. On a return to Kansas City, he bought his first car and married his first wife, Vivian Wynn. Not long after, he had lost both—one to repossession and the other to divorce. And he had acquired a nickname. Legend says that a Kansas City radio announcer coined the name "Count," but Basie claimed that he gave himself the moniker for reasons he did not recall. Durham, however, remembered that it originated in Moten's frustrated hunts for his arranger. Basie was accustomed to laying down an arrangement on the piano, then leaving to drink and flirt while Durham wrote out the chart. He was missing so often that Bennie Moten was frequently heard asking where that "no 'count rascal" was.

By 1934 some of the band members were dissatisfied with Moten's leadership. That summer the orchestra accepted an engagement performing in the new Cherry Blossom, a Kansas City nightclub located in the former Eblon Theatre. Moten disliked the booking. With some other plan in mind for making the big time, Moten wanted to pull out of the Cherry Blossom, but many of the band members wanted to stay. Because the orchestra was a commonwealth band, granting members a vote in the band's policies and shares of the profits in lieu of salaries, the outfit voted Moten out and a reluctant Basie in as new bandleader. Now billed as Count Basie and His Cherry Blossom Orchestra, the outfit promptly lost all but two of its members while touring the territories, some of them drifting back to Moten's new organization. Threadbare and nearly starving, Basie made his way back to Kansas City to rejoin Moten.

The next year while on tour, the new organization learned that its leader Bennie Moten had bled to death during a tonsillectomy in Kansas City. Disheartened, the band split up, and Basie took a job at the Reno, a cabaret in downtown Kansas City. Shortly, the club's owner made Basie the band's leader, and the Count began hiring musicians who could play the kind of sound he wanted—the kind he had heard in his imagination for years. Most of the new members were Blue Devils or Moten veterans, including bassist Walter Page, tenor saxophonist Lester Young, and trumpeter Hot Lips Page. Club patrons liked the result. So did listeners to a local radio station, which began broadcasting Count Basie and His Barons of Rhythm from the Reno. Hard-pressed to come up with enough arrangements to fill air time with fresh material, the band improvised. Basie made up titles on the spur of the moment to give the announcer, then played whatever occurred to him. The band took up the line, "and we hit it with the rhythm section and went into the riffs, and the riffs just stuck." Several of Basie's signature tunes, including "One O'Clock Jump," originated in these improvised sessions on the air.

John Hammond also liked what he heard when he picked up a broadcast from the Reno on his shortwave radio. A passionate jazz fan and writer for *Down Beat* magazine, Hammond asked to come to Kansas City from New York to hear Basie's group play. Basie gave Hammond little thought, but the writer persisted. When they finally met, on Basie's piano bench at the Reno, they became close friends. Using his extensive connections in the music world, Hammond arranged for the top booking agent Willard Alexander to represent the group, and Alexander put together an extensive tour. Meanwhile, the band left the Reno's tiny bandstand and went into rehearsals, adding tenor saxophonist Hershel Evans and Buck Clayton, who replaced Page on trumpet. After a rousing farewell appearance at Paseo Dance Hall, Count Basie and His Orchestra left Kansas City for a big-city tour in 1936.

The tour began badly. Adding new musicians made the group's playing sluggish, and patrons of eastern supper clubs and ballrooms such as New York's Roseland were more accustomed to "sweet" music. They did not seem to know what to make of the Kansas City swing style. While the diffident Basie agonized, John Hammond followed the band offering support and encouragement. With Hammond's advice, Basie added guitarist Freddie Greene and female singer Billie Holiday, who joined Jimmy Rushing in providing blues vocals for the next two years. By the time the band played New York's Apollo, Basie's musicians had polished their sound, and audiences were ready to embrace it.

Basie's distinctive sound depended on inventive musicianship combined with intricate ensemble playing. In rehearsals at the Woodside Hotel, the reed section might play its own interpretation of a tune while the brass kept up a background riff of its own. As the reeds' motif faded, the brass brought its interpretation to the fore so that, characteristic of the Kansas City style, a single number interwove several interpretations by the various orchestra sections. Once having played the improvised arrangement, the musicians could repeat the same performance on stage without charts by relying on so-called head arrangements. No matter the tune or the tempo, however, the Count's musicians gave it a swing rhythm and an aggressive beat. Basie's own invention pitted tenor saxophonists Evans and Young in competitions resembling a battle of the bands, with each tenor trying to outdo the other in alternating solo interpretations. Basie tied the elements together by using his own spare piano phrases to introduce the riffs and drummer Jo Jones's impeccable rhythm to anchor the tempo.

A widening jazz audience came to love the resulting sound so well represented in the 1938 Basie hit "Jumpin' at the Woodside." Following a triumphal return engagement in Kansas City and a battle of the bands with Chick Web at the Savoy Ballroom in New York, the Basie band was booked into the Famous Door in New York in 1938. As part of the agreement, Hammond and Alexander arranged for the CBS Radio network to broadcast Basie's performances at the club to a nationwide audience, netting great publicity, more fans, and a better record contract with Columbia.

Basie particularly welcomed his orchestra's success because his own financial obligations had mounted. A serious injury to his mother left her in need of round-the-clock nursing care. And he had attracted the attention of a beautiful dancer named Catherine Morgan. Basie had first encountered Morgan when he was with the Moten band and she was appearing as one of the dancing Whitman Sisters, but she had ignored him because she was just sixteen and her company kept strict watch over its juvenile dancers. Later, when Morgan began catching Basie's act at the Famous Door, the orchestra leader tried, to no avail, to interest her in a date. Friends had warned the abstemious Morgan against dating jazzmen. Over the next three years, however, while the Basie orchestra headlined engagements, broke the color line at posh hotels, and smashed attendance records around the country, the two dated. But Morgan refused the Count's repeated proposals of marriage because she did not want to give up her own career as a singer and dancer. Finally, in 1943, Morgan relented, and she and Basie were married. A year later their daughter, Diane, was born, and Catherine established a home for the family in New York. Only Catherine's death in 1983 severed a marriage that remained a strong and loving relationship, in spite of the temptations and long absences that life on the road entailed.

Marriage and family helped sustain the Count during tough times. By 1950 swing music played by big bands had lost much of its popularity, while bebop and so-called modern jazz competed for the allegiances of remaining jazz fans. That year Basie dissolved his orchestra and replaced it with a small combo. In 1951, however, he defied pop-music trends and assembled a second big band incorporating some of his former players. He altered the new orchestra's sound slightly, de-emphasizing flashy solos that electrified ballroom patrons and featuring the tighter ensemble playing that suited jazz-concert venues. Yet, Basie retained the key elements of Kansas City style in its insistence on a swinging rhythm and its reproduction of a blues structure in orchestral form. Gifted new arrangers such as Neal Hefti and Quincy Jones created fresh charts adapting the style to modern tastes.

The Count Basie Orchestra attracted a new generation of fans in the United States, Europe, and Asia, as revenues from concert tickets and album sales attested. Command performances for presidents and crowned heads signaled the wide appreciation Basie had helped to win for a music form once condemned as barbaric and decadent. In 1981, Basie received an achievement award from the Kennedy Center for Performing Arts, and in 1982 the Black Music Association honored him with a tribute gala. At the time of his death in Hollywood, Florida, on April 26, 1984, Basie was keeping a full tour schedule.

Count Basie's legacy touched most areas of jazz. Among his contributions was his own style at the keyboard. In Kansas City he gave up rag and stride for an elegant, quiet simplicity of his own design. He never played an unnecessary note. When he brought his piano style to New York in 1936, other musicians were riveted by his understated artistry and strove to imitate his playing. The minimalist style of modern jazz artists such as Thelonious Monk bears witness to the impact of the Count's keyboard innovations. Also in the thirties, Basie took the lead in introducing Kansas City's jazz style to a national audience. The big-band sound and bebop both emerged from that introduction. Ironically, by organizing his second orchestra Basie helped to preserve the big-band sound from oblivion, thus making the Basie Orchestra a riff linking the disparate and seemingly antagonistic jazz forms of swing, bebop, and modern jazz and tying the three to the older blues song.

SHERRY LAMB SCHIRMER

Basie, Count, and Albert Murray. *Good Morning Blues: The Autobiography of Count Basie.* New York: Random House, 1985.

Dance, Stanley. *The World of Count Basie.* New York: Da Capo Press, 1980.

Horricks, Raymond. *Count Basie and His Orchestra: Its Music and Its Musicians.* Westport, Conn.: Negro Universities Press, 1957.

Pearson, Nathan W., Jr. *Goin' to Kansas City.* Urbana: University of Illinois Press, 1987.

Russell, Ross. *Jazz Style in Kansas City and the Southwest.* Berkeley and Los Angeles: University of California Press, 1971.

BASS, TOM (1859–1934)

Tom Bass was born a slave on the Hayden plantation in Boone County, Missouri, on January 5, 1859. He was the child of his owner, William H. Bass, and a slave girl, but he was raised by two other slaves on the plantation, Presley and Eliza Grey. It was on the Bass estate that Tom gained his first understanding of animals, first with cattle, then with horses. By popular consensus, Tom Bass was one of the most skillful and popular horsemen who ever lived. At the time of his death in 1934, his home in Mexico, Missouri, was overflowing with awards he had collected throughout his lifetime as a rider and trainer of fine show horses.

Bass's early life as a slave, his path to freedom, and his youth are somewhat of a mystery, but it appears that he began his career handling horses shortly following the end of the Civil War in Mexico, Missouri. There he eventually found employment training and selling horses for the Mexico Horse Sales Company. During these early years his expertise with horses became widely recognized throughout the state. Riders throughout the region discovered that it was wise to ask his advice before making an expensive purchase, and Bass rarely failed them. He had the apparent ability to judge what would and would not make a fine show horse. It was also during this period that he developed the Tom Bass horse bit, which prevented the abuse of horses during training. The "Bass bit," as it came to be called, is still considered standard equipment in many stables today.

By the late 1880s Bass's skill and knowledge came to the attention of a group of prosperous businessmen in Kansas City, Missouri, who asked him if he would take charge of their stables. Apparently, these boosters wanted to make Kansas City as important an equestrian center as their rival—St. Louis. Bass agreed, and he and his wife, Angel, relocated. In Kansas City, Bass built on his reputation and busied himself training horses and riders for the city's local elite. It has been suggested that Bass personally trained **Loula Long Combs,** at one time one of the nation's top female equestrians. He also won many prizes and widespread acclaim as a horse trainer and rider of outstanding ability.

Bass's national reputation was established when he represented Missouri at the Columbian Exposition in Chicago in 1893, where he drew widespread acclaim for his gentle gliding style. Afterward, the wealthy and powerful sought Bass for advice and instruction. Subsequently, Bass counted among his personal friends many famous individuals, including Buffalo Bill Cody, William Jennings Bryan, and Will Rogers.

Bass trained many great riders as well as horses, including Rex McDonald, one of the most famous and successful animals ever. In 1897 Bass was asked by the Vanderbilt family if he would participate in a show at Madison Square Garden in New York City. He consented and became the first African American to perform there.

After having spent so much time and energy in making Kansas City a focal point for equestrianism, Bass decided to return to Mexico, Missouri, where he spent the remainder of his career doing what he loved best, working with fine horses. However, it is difficult to say that he lived anywhere permanently, as he was constantly on the road traveling from one engagement to another. In so doing, he was instrumental in making Mexico the "Saddle Horse Capital of the World." During his lifetime, he came into contact with many notable personalities, including Presidents Calvin Coolidge, William McKinley, and William Howard Taft. Bass was also instrumental in developing what has become a national institution, the American Royal Horse Show, in Kansas City, for which he performed until 1928. The show has, over the years, become an important event in the equestrian world.

One of Bass's most famous mounts, Belle Beach, was a nationally recognized "high school" horse that amazed and amused audiences for years. One of his favorite routines was to ride Belle Beach into an arena accompanied by marital music, run the horse into a low bow, then a curtsy, have her lie down, and finally get the animal to dance a waltz or foxtrot.

Bass was an exceptional character in Missouri history. He began his life as a slave and ended it as a nationally recognized equestrian artist. It is remarkable that he did all of these things in a particularly unfriendly racial atmosphere that characterized the period from the Civil War to the Great Depression and that he was able to win the respect of both whites and blacks throughout the country. Bass died at his home in Mexico on November 4, 1934, at the age of seventy-five.

CHRISTOPHER K. HAYS

Downey, Bill. *Tom Bass: Black Horseman.* St. Louis: Saddle and Bridle, 1975.
Kansas City Star, November 20, 1934.
New York Times, June 25, 1961.

BATES, EDWARD (1793–1869)

Edward Bates, a political leader and attorney general of the United States, was born September 4, 1793, in Belmont, in Goochland County, Virginia, to Thomas Fleming and Caroline Matilda Woodson Bates, the youngest son in a family of twelve children. His father had served with valor in the Revolutionary War but had been read out of his Quaker congregation for doing so. The senior Bates suffered heavy financial losses as a result of his Revolutionary service and died when Edward was twelve, leaving the family in straitened circumstances. Edward went first to live with an older brother in Northumberland, Virginia, but two years later came under the fortunate tutelage of a cousin, Benjamin Bates of Hanover, Maryland, who later sent him to nearby Charlotte Hall Academy. An introspective individual, young Bates read exhaustively in philosophy, history, and natural science, which stood him in good stead for his later career.

Bates declined an appointment as a naval midshipman because of his mother's objection, but with the outbreak of the War of 1812 he volunteered for the Virginia militia in February 1813 and served until October, rising to the rank of sergeant. Following his discharge he decided to join his brother Frederick in frontier St. Louis. There he studied law under **Rufus Easton,** one of Missouri Territory's foremost lawyers, and was admitted to the bar in November 1816. With his brother's and Easton's connections, he quickly established his legal practice among St. Louis's wealthy business and landholding elements. Gov. **William Clark** appointed him attorney for the Northern District of Missouri in 1818. Simultaneously, Bates formed a legal partnership with **Joshua Barton,** which continued until Barton was killed in a duel in 1823. Bates also engaged extensively in land speculation and, for a time, managed a steam mill company.

Active in the movement for Missouri statehood, Bates was elected as a delegate to the first Constitutional Convention on a platform calling for free white–manhood suffrage, although with property qualification attached, and the unrestricted importation of slaves into Missouri. With little faith in mass democratic rule, Bates believed that "a natural aristocracy of talent and ambition directed the course of any society," a view that would sustain him throughout his political career.

Gov. **Alexander McNair** appointed Bates as Missouri's first attorney general in 1821. He served one term in the legislature, in 1822–1823, before accepting an appointment as U.S. district attorney. In the quarrel between **Thomas Hart Benton** and **David Barton,** Missouri's two senators, over the election of President John Quincy Adams, Bates sided with the Barton faction, which would ultimately lead him into a leadership position in Missouri's Whig Party as the old Jeffersonian republicans divided in the late 1820s. He had been elected to Congress in 1826 but was defeated for reelection because of the power of the new Jacksonian Democracy, which counted Benton as its Missouri leader. He moved to St. Charles County, to a farm on Dardenne Prairie, while continuing his extensive law practice. He served one term in the Missouri State Senate (from 1830 to 1833) and another in the Missouri House (from 1834 to 1835), but thereafter contented himself with a behind-the-scenes role within Missouri's Whig Party, which found itself a decided minority in the heady days of Jacksonian rule.

Bates emerged from political obscurity in 1847 when he served as president of the Chicago River and Harbor Improvement Convention, where he spoke eloquently on national unity and western expansionism, causing him to emerge as a national figure. Simultaneously, the division of the Benton Democracy in Missouri over the issue of free soil allowed the state's Whigs to wield a playmaker role in the turbulent politics that followed. Bates declined appointment as secretary of war at the hands of President Millard Fillmore in 1850 because of personal and family commitments, but increasingly his views were sought by Whig leaders at all levels. He opposed the repeal of the Missouri Compromise, although he declined to be openly associated with the Free Soil cause. As both of Missouri's political parties divided over the slavery issue in the 1850s, Bates clung tenaciously to his Clay Whig principles. He presided over the last national Whig convention in 1856, which endorsed the American or Know-Nothing ticket. Thereafter he drifted toward the fledgling Republican Party, opposing the admission of Kansas under the Lecompton Constitution. As he gained increasing national attention, Harvard College awarded him an honorary LL.D. degree in 1858.

With the approach of the 1860 election, **Frank Blair** and others in Missouri launched a Bates-for-president movement within Republican circles, contending that a free-soil Whig could carry the border states and help avert secession. The Republican nomination went instead to Abraham Lincoln. Although Bates gave only limited support to the ticket, the new president appointed him attorney general. In the turbulent days that followed Lincoln's inauguration, Bates counseled a conservative course with regard to the pro-Southern tendencies of the **Claiborne Fox Jackson** regime in Missouri, thus breaking with Frank and **Montgomery Blair** in this regard. When the Jackson group was driven from Jefferson City, Bates's brother-in-law, **Hamilton Rowan Gamble,** became provisional governor and through the attorney general had ready entrée to the president.

A basic conservative where legal affairs were concerned, Bates performed his duties as attorney general conscientiously, seeking to uphold civil law wherever possible in the face of the encroachments by military authority and carefully circumscribing the elements of proof in confiscation cases. In this regard, he found himself in frequent conflict with his fellow cabinet officers: Secy. of State William H. Seward and Secy. of War Edwin M. Stanton. In the matter of the blockade and belligerency, he sided with Lincoln in ambiguous policy regarding the confiscation of neutral as opposed to Confederate vessels. During the *Trent* affair, however, he diligently sought to avert war with England by urging that the question of legal rights be waived.

Increasingly, as the war progressed, Bates's influence waned. He split with Lincoln over the admission of West Virginia as a separate state in 1863, arguing unsuccessfully that this was nothing more than a form of secession. On the critical issue of slavery, Bates regarded military emancipation as unlawful and worked to keep the issue under executive control in the face of an increasingly zealous Congress. He supported Lincoln's 1862 program of compensated gradual emancipation and pushed Governor Gamble to get Missouri to act on it. When Lincoln proposed his Emancipation Proclamation, Bates approved, believing it would allow the president to gain the upper hand on his more vehement Radical critics. He agreed with the rest of the cabinet, however, on postponing its announcement until after significant Union military successes. Unlike many of his cabinet colleagues, he hoped that emancipation could be coupled with some kind of colonization scheme.

Following Lincoln's reelection Bates resigned as attorney general on November 24, 1864, disheartened by the electoral triumph of the Radicals in Missouri. He strongly opposed the Radical state constitution of 1865 and its stringent test oath of voters. He was also dismayed at the Radical's purging of state judicial personnel in their Ouster Ordinance. He published a series of articles denouncing the work of the state convention during the ratification campaign for the constitution. Shortly thereafter, Bates's health began to decline, and he died March 25, 1869.

WILLIAM E. PARRISH

Bates, Edward. Papers. Library of Congress, Washington, D.C.
———. Papers. Missouri Historical Society, St. Louis.
———. Papers. State Historical Society of Missouri, Columbia.
Beale, Howard K., ed. *The Diary of Edward Bates, 1859–1866.* Annual Report of the American Association for the Year 1930. Vol. 4. Washington: American Historical Association, 1933.
Cain, Marvin R. *Lincoln's Attorney General: Edward Bates of Missouri.* Columbia: University of Missouri Press, 1965.
Mering, John V. *The Whig Party in Missouri.* Columbia: University of Missouri Press, 1967.

BATES, FREDERICK (1777–1825)

Frederick Bates was the fourth of twelve children born to Thomas Fleming and Caroline Matilda Woodson Bates of Goochland County, Virginia. He was born during the American Revolution, on June 23, 1777.

Although little is known about his early education, in late 1794 or early 1795, at the age of seventeen, Bates entered the law office of William Miller, the clerk of the county court of Goochland County. While studying law there Bates became a deputy court clerk and a postmaster. In the fall of 1797 he received a federal appointment in the quartermaster department of the Army of the Northwest. He proceeded to Detroit by horseback to take up his duties. From there he conducted army business at Lexington, Michilimackinac, and Fort Wayne.

In 1800 young Bates left the army quartermaster office and entered private business as a merchant in Detroit. He continued in business until the summer of 1805, when a large fire in Detroit destroyed most of his possessions. During his excursion into private business Bates did not completely abandon the federal service. In October 1802 he became the deputy postmaster at Detroit. During a brief earlier period in his life Bates flirted with the Federalist Party, but he soon returned to his roots of Jeffersonian Republicanism. Indeed, his Virginia heritage, family friendships, and allegiance to President Thomas Jefferson soon opened additional professional doors to him.

When Michigan Territory was created in late 1804, Bates acquired an important territorial position, as receiver of federal monies at Detroit. He also became the local federal land commissioner. In March 1805 he received a Jefferson administration appointment as associate judge of Michigan Territory. However, all his appointments occurred before he left his private mercantile venture. Understandably, some in Detroit believed that his public and private interests were in conflict. Bates even drew local criticism because he dated young women from British Canada. Nevertheless, he gained invaluable governmental experience in Michigan that would prove useful in Missouri.

After the Louisiana Purchase, Congress created the District of Louisiana in March 1804. For the moment, administratively, that area was attached to Indiana Territory with **William Henry Harrison** in command. Harrison arrived in St. Louis in October 1804. In March 1805 Congress separated the territory of Louisiana from Indiana Territory, and President Jefferson appointed Gen. **James Wilkinson** territorial governor.

In 1806 Bates left Detroit and lived in Washington, D.C., for a time. While there he solidified his contacts with the Jefferson administration. Then, when the Burr-Wilkinson conspiracy broke into the open, Bates helped fill the administrative vacuum. Jefferson appointed **Meriwether Lewis** to replace Wilkinson as governor of the territory of Louisiana, and he appointed the still young but now experienced Frederick Bates as secretary of Louisiana Territory and the recorder of land titles. In taking those positions Bates replaced an associate of James Wilkinson and the brother-in-law of Aaron Burr.

On the surface Bates had little significant power, but in actuality he had a great deal, for in the absence of the territorial governor, the secretary of the territory served as acting governor. Bates, in effect, was the governor of the territory of Louisiana between April 1, 1807, when he arrived in future Missouri for the first time, until March 8, 1808, when Gov. Meriwether Lewis finally took over. As acting governor, Bates, with the assistance of **William Clark,** the U.S. Indian agent, organized the territorial militia and attended to Indian affairs. In addition, he kept the position of recorder of land titles.

Ironically, once Lewis did arrive in St. Louis, he and Bates clashed over patronage appointments and Indian policy. Bates thought Lewis's military habits made him difficult to work with. As secretary of the territory, Bates produced *A Compilation of the Laws of Louisiana Territory* in 1808, the first book to be published within the confines of what would become Missouri.

On October 11, 1809, Governor Lewis died. Again, Bates became acting governor. President James Madison, another fellow Virginian, wanted to make Bates the permanent governor, but Bates refused the position because it would have meant a reduction in pay. Instead, he kept his other positions while continuing to act as governor until the newly appointed governor, **Benjamin Howard,** arrived. Bates supervised the 1810 census in the territory, and he spent a great deal of his time participating in land-title board decisions regarding the validity of land claims. Conflicting French, Spanish, and American claims made that position very important. By 1812 three thousand decisions had been rendered.

When Congress created the Missouri Territory in June 1812, Bates retained his secretary and land title–recorder positions and for a third time served as acting governor. Two weeks later Congress declared war on Great Britain. In March 1813 acting governor Bates instructed volunteer militia companies to muster. Finally, on July 1, 1813, Bates stepped down from territorial command for the last time. Around this same time, **Edward Bates,** Frederick's younger brother, moved to St. Louis from Virginia and started the study of law. Edward would eventually become President Abraham Lincoln's attorney general.

In 1816 Frederick Bates traveled to Washington, D.C., and presented his land-claims report to Josiah Meigs, commissioner of the General Land Office. When statehood came in 1821, Bates relinquished his secretary's position, but continued to hold the land-title office until 1824.

In the process of dealing with land titles and claims, Bates invested in some land on his own. He developed his estate, Thornhill, in Bonhomme Township, in St. Louis County, near present Chesterfield. It was to that estate that Bates, at age forty-two, took his bride, Opie Ball of St. Louis County, after their marriage on March 4, 1819. The couple produced four children between 1820 and 1826: Emily Caroline, Lucius Lee, Woodville, and Frederick (who was born after the death of his father).

When Missouri became a state, merchants and professionals living in the St. Louis area, people with whom he had long associations, wanted Bates to be a candidate for the United States Senate. He chose not to run, but he and his associates did support William Clark's candidacy for the governorship. However, Clark lost to **Alexander McNair,** who had out-state support.

In the next statewide elections Bates did become a candidate for governor. Senator **David Barton,** who had affiliated with John Quincy Adams, backed him. Fur entrepreneur **William Henry Ashley,** the state's lieutenant governor, ran against Bates, but Sen. **Thomas Hart Benton** and Kentucky's Henry Clay supported him. Bates won the election.

Upon taking office in November 1824 Bates claimed to be an old Jeffersonian Republican who stood above party. Two issues hallmarked his administration. He vetoed a bill that would have discouraged dueling, because he thought the penalties were too harsh for those who violated the law. He also refused to officially welcome the American Revolution hero the Marquis de Lafayette when he came to St. Louis in April 1825. Bates claimed he had no appropriations to finance the welcome. In truth, Bates had an anti-French bias, although he was close to the highly influential **Chouteau** family of St. Louis.

On August 4, 1825, Bates experienced an attack of pleurisy and died unexpectedly at the age of forty-eight. As acting governor of the territories of Louisiana and Missouri, territorial secretary, federal recorder of land titles, and the state's second governor, Frederick Bates left a strong mark on Missouri.

DONALD B. OSTER

Biographical Dictionary of the Governors of the United States, 1789–1978. Vol. 2. S.v. "Bates, Frederick."

Foley, William E. *The Genesis of Missouri: From Wilderness Outpost to Statehood.* Columbia: University of Missouri Press, 1989.

Marshall, Thomas Maitland, ed. *The Life and Papers of Frederick Bates.* St. Louis: Missouri Historical Society, 1926.

BAXTER, ANNIE WHITE (1864–1944)

Almost thirty years before women received the right to vote through the Nineteenth Amendment, Annie White Baxter ran for the office of Jasper County clerk on the Democratic ticket in 1890 and won the election by more than four hundred votes. She became the first female county clerk in the United States and the first elected woman official in Missouri. Baxter assumed her duties as Jasper County clerk in January 1891 in the Carthage office, despite an election challenge by one of her opponents. Julius Fischer claimed Baxter's votes were not legal because of her sex, but a few months later the Greene County Circuit Court upheld her election. The judge ruled that Baxter had won the election and Fischer should pay her legal fees.

Baxter was born March 2, 1864, in Pittsburgh, Pennsylvania, the daughter of John B. and Jennie Black White. Her father, a cabinetmaker, moved the family to Ohio, and then to Carthage, Missouri, in 1876.

Baxter was one of six persons who graduated from Carthage High School in 1882. A short time later she started working for County Clerk George Balkeney. Additional work in the recorder's office, as well as the county collector's office, gave her a good understanding of county government. She later served as deputy clerk under county clerks John N. Wilson and Jesse Rhoads, retiring only briefly after marriage to Charles W. Baxter on January 19, 1888.

At the end of Rhoads's term of office, the Democratic County Convention in 1890 nominated Annie Baxter as their candidate for county clerk. The local newspaper debated whether Baxter could legally be elected because of her sex.

During Baxter's term the county made plans to construct a new courthouse, and voters approved the bonds and authorized the construction. She did create a controversy when she employed her husband as an assistant clerk and gave him a substantial raise in salary. Nevertheless, some regarded Baxter as the best county clerk in the state, and Gov. **David R. Francis** named her an honorary colonel on his staff. In 1894 Baxter was nominated for a second term, but she lost in a Republican landslide.

After her defeat the Baxters lived in St. Louis and then moved to Jefferson City where she worked for Cornelius Roach, who won election as secretary of state in 1908. As land registrar under Roach from 1908 to 1916, Baxter reorganized the staff and instituted efficient record-keeping techniques. In 1922 she became financial secretary for the Missouri Constitutional Commission—the only woman on the staff.

Baxter served as secretary to James T. Quarles, dean of the University of Missouri's School of Fine Arts in Columbia. She later returned to Jefferson City where she continued her interest in state government and Democratic politics. She last visited Jasper County in May 1936 when she was a delegate to the Democratic State Convention in Joplin. She died on June 28, 1944, in Jefferson City.

A Joplin street is named for Annie Baxter, and a stone is embedded near the Jasper County Courthouse, recalling her role in the construction of the building. Her achievements inspired other Missouri women in their struggles for suffrage and political and economic equality.

MARY K. DAINS

Carthage Evening Press, March 2, 1971.

Dains, Mary K., ed. *Show Me Missouri Women: Selected Biographies.* Vol. 1. Kirksville, Mo.: Thomas Jefferson University Press, 1989.

Priddy, Bob. "Across Our Wide Missouri, God Bless Annie Baxter!—Before Women Could Vote, She Won Elected Office." *Missouri Life* 10 (May–June 1982): 20–22.

Zophy, Angela Howard, ed. *Handbook of American Women's History.* Vol. 696 in Garland Reference Library of the Humanities. N.p., 1990.

BEARDSLEY, HENRY MAHAN (1858–1938)

During the Progressive Era in the early twentieth century, Henry M. Beardsley can justifiably be called Kansas City's best representative. For more than a quarter of a century Beardsley led that city's civic-minded structural reformers who believed that municipal governmental structure needed to be streamlined, more businesslike, and less politically partisan. Between 1905 and 1925 Beardsley led the effort to acquire modern government for Kansas City. After five attempts, his and others' efforts finally resulted in the passage of the 1925 municipal charter that initiated city-manager government for the city. However, unlike most structural Progressives, Beardsley also participated in the social-justice side of the movement, genuinely concerning himself with the needs of the less fortunate.

Henry Mahan Beardsley was born on October 20, 1858, on a farm near Mount Vernon, Ohio. In 1879 he earned a law degree, with Phi Beta Kappa honors, and in 1880 an advanced law degree, both from the University of Illinois. He became a member of the Illinois bar in 1882, and in 1883 he married Marietta Davis, from Monticello, Illinois. They had three children: Eleanor M., George D., and Henry S.

In 1886 the Beardsleys moved to Kansas City. He went to work for Jarvis and Conklin Mortgage Trust Company, but soon formed a law partnership with Alfred Gregory, an Illinois friend. Beardsley quickly established his law practice and began to express his civic-mindedness. He also put his religion, Christianity, into practice. In 1892 he became president of the Kansas City Young Men's Christian Association, a position he held until his death. In 1895 his law colleagues recognized his abilities by electing him president of the Kansas City Bar Association.

Always civic-minded, Beardsley ran for a seat in the city council's upper house in 1898 as a Republican. He won, and voters reelected him in 1902 for another four-year term. In 1900 he became the president of the upper house, which placed him on the board of public works. In 1900 he also became a member of the newly created Civic League, a local

arm of the National Municipal League that worked to bring better municipal government through charter reform. Beardsley worked to obtain the passage of proposed charter reform in 1905, but the proposal lost, although he did not stop trying to bring structural change.

In 1906 Beardsley successfully ran for the office of mayor of Kansas City. As mayor he attempted to run the city in a businesslike fashion, while providing aid to lower socioeconomic segments of the population. In addition, he nominated a board of freeholders who would, if elected, construct a charter proposal for the electorate's consideration. In the April 1908 municipal elections the voters approved the board of freeholders but did not elect Beardsley for a second term; the voters subsequently did approve the 1908 charter proposal.

Although Beardsley never held elective office again, he remained active. He provided free legal advice to individuals who could not otherwise afford the services of a lawyer. In 1915 he began a two-year term as the moderator of the Council of Congregational Churches of America. He also continued his efforts to bring modern governmental structure to Kansas City, joining the Model Charter and Good Government League, an organization that supported the city-manager form for municipal administrations.

In 1918 Beardsley became chairman of the Kansas City Chamber of Commerce Committee devoted to obtaining an amendment to the Missouri state constitution that would allow municipal governments to use any form of representative government they wished instead of only bicameral councils. That effort failed in 1918, but it passed in 1920. In 1918 Beardsley also became the president of the newly founded Citizens' League, a local organization dedicated to governmental reform. In 1920 he became the chairman of the Jackson County Republican Committee.

In 1921 Beardsley helped create the Citizens' Charter Commission, a coalition of civic groups supporting the city-manager concept. In 1922 he became a member of the Citizens' Water and Charter Committee, for which he chaired a subcommittee called the Committee of Seven, which was charged with studying municipal charter possibilities and supporting the city-manager form. In 1925 Kansas City voters approved a new city-manager municipal charter.

Described as "self-effacing" and not the crusading type, nevertheless, Beardsley did crusade. On April 19, 1938, at the age of seventy-nine, he experienced a heart attack at his home and died.

DONALD B. OSTER

Green, George Fuller. *A Condensed History of the*

Kansas City Area, Its Mayors and Some V.I.P.'s. Kansas City: Lowell Press, 1968.

Muraskin, Jack. "Municipal Reform in Two Missouri Cities." *Missouri Historical Society Bulletin* 25 (April 1969): 213–28.

Oster, Donald B. "Reformers, Factionalists and Kansas City's 1925 City Manager Charter." *Missouri Historical Review* 72 (April 1978): 296–327.

BEAUMONT, WILLIAM (1785–1853)

William Beaumont, who spent most of the last two decades of his life in St. Louis, achieved fame for his research on human digestion and was the first American physiologist to gain an international reputation. He was born in Lebanon, Connecticut, on November 21, 1785, the son of Samuel Beaumont, a farmer, and Lucretia Abel Beaumont. It is likely that he received his basic education in Lebanon at Nathan Tisdale's school, regarded as one of the best in New England.

In the winter of 1806–1807, Beaumont left home to settle in the frontier community of Champlain, near the Canadian border in northern New York. Beaumont had begun to read medical books, and in the spring of 1811 he moved across Lake Champlain to study medicine as an apprentice of Dr. Benjamin Chandler. This apprenticeship was the only formal medical education that Beaumont ever received. In June 1812 he was licensed to practice medicine and surgery.

The outbreak of the War of 1812 gave Beaumont the opportunity to further both his medical career and his ardent Jeffersonian principles. In September 1812 he recrossed Lake Champlain to Plattsburgh to volunteer as a surgeon's mate in the United States Army. He saw considerable action in the war, taking part in the attack of York (now Toronto), in upper Canada, in April 1813; coming under fire when the Americans attacked Fort George in the following month; and receiving favorable mention for his bravery during the British attack on Plattsburgh in September 1814.

At the end of the war, Beaumont resigned to open a private practice in Plattsburgh. Rejoining the army medical department in 1820, he was first stationed at Mackinac, where, in June 1822, the accident that enabled Beaumont to achieve permanent fame occurred. On June 6 he was called to treat a French Canadian voyageur, Alexis St. Martin, who had been shot in the stomach at short range. St. Martin's wound healed in such a manner as to leave a permanent fistula, allowing the stomach to be observed and food and other objects to be inserted through the cavity.

By the summer of 1825 Beaumont, with the encouragement of the army surgeon general, Joseph Lovell, began what was to become a long series of experiments on the process of human digestion.

Although there had been earlier recorded cases of human gastric fistulas, Beaumont was the first researcher to take full advantage of the situation and undertake systematic and extended experiments, which were often carried out under unfavorable conditions. He was transferred from Fort Mackinac to Fort Niagara in 1825, to Fort Howard at Green Bay in 1826, and to Fort Crawford at Prairie du Chien in 1828. His research was delayed for four years when St. Martin returned to Canada, but Beaumont was able to complete most of his experiments in 1832 and 1833 when he was granted a six-month furlough for research purposes.

Late in 1833 Beaumont published an extensive account of his experiments and conclusions in *Experiments and Observations on the Gastric Juice and the Physiology of Digestion.* He provided proof for those who had defended the idea that human digestion was a chemical process and that gastric juice was an acid that acted as a solvent both inside and outside the stomach.

In the summer of 1834 Beaumont was transferred to Jefferson Barracks, south of St. Louis, and in the following year moved into the city itself after he was given an appointment at the arsenal as a medical purchasing agent. With his family Beaumont made St. Louis his home for the rest of his life. In 1821 Beaumont had married Deborah Green Platt of Plattsburgh. At the time they moved to St. Louis, they had three children: Sarah, Lucretia, and Israel. In his early years in St. Louis, Beaumont, while continuing his military duties, quickly developed an extensive and lucrative private practice. He and his family also became intimate friends of Capt. Robert E. Lee and his family when Lee was in St. Louis to improve the harbor. Beaumont's army career came to an end largely as a result of the death in 1836 of Surgeon General Joseph Lovell and the succession to that post of Thomas Lawson, who resented the special privileges that had been granted to Beaumont by his predecessor and in 1839 ordered Beaumont to Florida. Now well established in St. Louis, Beaumont threatened resignation if the order were not rescinded. After acrimonious exchanges between the two thin-skinned men, Beaumont's resignation was accepted as of December 31, 1839.

While Beaumont achieved considerable success as a physician in St. Louis, his residence there was not always serene. From his earliest years, he forcefully defended what he considered to be his rights. He had a close-knit, apparently loving family circle, with a number of warm and intimate friends, but disagreements with others often flared into complete estrangement. Although he twice brought in partners to help him with his burgeoning practice, both partnerships ended in controversy.

Beaumont's first St. Louis partnership, with Dr. James Sykes, even began in controversy in 1839 when Sykes put an advertisement in the *Missouri Republican*, which some members of the Missouri Medical Society of St. Louis thought was against their rules. Although medical advertising was common in St. Louis in those years, the recently formed society was attempting to regulate it. Rather than smoothing over the matter, Beaumont chose to fight it, further dividing the already acrimonious society.

In the following year, Beaumont again figured prominently in local controversy when he became entangled in the notorious Darnes-Davis murder case. The political infighting that resulted in the public beating and death of newspaper owner Andrew Jackson Davis by William P. Darnes had its parallel in the increased acrimony among the members of the St. Louis medical profession created by the subsequent trial. Beaumont was called in to treat the dying Davis and performed a trephination, which involved drilling holes in the skull. At Darnes's trial for murder, the defense lawyers tried to show that Beaumont's operation, not the original beating, had killed Davis, and even suggested that a taste for experimentation acquired in his research on St. Martin had contributed to his decision on treatment. The tactic was given credibility by some of Beaumont's enemies among the St. Louis physicians who appeared for the defense, criticizing Beaumont. Darnes was found guilty of manslaughter and fined five hundred dollars, but Beaumont had endured a public attack on his professional skill.

That Beaumont had many professional defenders was soon made obvious, for in 1841 he became president of the Missouri Medical Society of St. Louis. He made no attempt to reconcile the warring elements in the St. Louis medical profession, devoted his inaugural address to an attack on the tactics of his enemies, and subsequently resigned from the society.

Beaumont's partnership with Sykes ended in the St. Louis courts, where they argued about the original terms of their agreement and the allocation of fees from their combined practice. Beaumont, who for many years had little money, was extremely cautious in financial matters. Another attempt at partnership—this time with Dr. George Johnson—ended in a similar argument over the allocation of fees.

In 1844 Beaumont was again in court, this time in a malpractice case that further divided the St. Louis medical community. One of Dr. Stephen Adreon's patients, Mary Dugan, was encouraged by some local physicians to sue him for malpractice. Beaumont, who had been called in as a consultant, was linked with Adreon in the suit. He claimed, probably with good reason, that he had been brought into the suit in this way to prevent his testifying for the defense. Beaumont escaped unscathed in the suit, but the experience increased his tendency to devote himself exclusively to his practice and his family.

Public controversy apparently did little to harm Beaumont's practice or his general reputation. As St. Louis grew, Beaumont prospered, and he was able to continue his earlier interest in land speculation. He invested in land on the outskirts of St. Louis, in Green Bay, in Prairie du Chien, and in southwestern Wisconsin.

Throughout the 1840s and into the early 1850s Beaumont had hopes that he would renew his experiments on Alexis St. Martin. At various times he almost succeeded in persuading St. Martin to come from Canada to join him in St. Louis. He was hindered, however, by his financial caution and his fear that St. Martin, who at times drank a great deal, would simply squander any money advanced to him for the trip. Beaumont never renewed his experiments after 1833, although St. Martin lived into the 1880s.

In March 1853 Beaumont, while returning from visiting a patient, slipped on the ice and hit his head. His condition deteriorated in the following weeks, and he died on April 25, 1853, and was buried in Bellefontaine Cemetery. Beaumont was a largely self-trained, extremely hard-working doctor with a strong sense of duty and a prickly exterior, perhaps accentuated by his increasing deafness in his later years. He achieved fame by taking full advantage of the single opportunity that was given him and by demonstrating an innate, practical grasp of the principles of dispassionate scientific research.

REGINALD HORSMAN

Beaumont, William. Collection. School of Medicine Library, Washington University, St. Louis.

———. Papers. Beaumont Medical Club, Medical Library, Yale University, New Haven, Conn.

———. Papers. Joseph Regenstein Library, University of Chicago.

Horsman, Reginald. *Frontier Doctor: William Beaumont, America's First Great Medical Scientist.* Columbia: University of Missouri Press, 1996.

Myer, Jesse S. *Life and Letters of Dr. William Beaumont.* St. Louis: C. V. Mosby, 1912.

Nelson, Rodney B. *Beaumont: America's First Physiologist.* Geneva, Ill.: Grant House Press, 1990.

Pitcock, Cynthia DeHaven. "The Career of William Beaumont, 1785–1853: Science and the Self-Made Man in America." Ph.D. diss., Memphis State University, 1985.

BECK, HELEN GOULD (SALLY RAND) (1904–1979)

Helen Gould Beck, who became a celebrity under the stage name Sally Rand, was born on January 2, 1904, in Hickory County, Missouri, in the village of

Elkton. Her father was a West Point graduate who retired from the army with the rank of colonel. Her mother was a schoolteacher who also acted as a correspondent for several small area papers. Helen Gould Beck's family moved from Hickory County to Jackson County, Missouri, when she was still in elementary school.

Beck showed an early interest in show business. At the age of thirteen she danced as a chorus girl in vaudeville performances at the Empress Theatre in Kansas City. **Goodman Ace,** drama critic for the *Kansas City Journal,* discovered her in a Kansas City nightclub and wrote approvingly of her stage potential. Gus Edwards, who at one time acted as an agent for such stars as Eddie Cantor and George E. Jessel, agreed with Ace's earlier evaluation. Edwards suggested to Beck that she study ballet, drama, and voice. She followed his advice, and before long relocated to Hollywood, where she found work in silent movies. On the way to Hollywood she served briefly as an acrobat in the Ringling Brothers Circus and even appeared for a short time in summer stock with Humphrey Bogart.

Cecil B. DeMille cast her in several silent movies in the 1920s. Believing she needed a new name, DeMille is reputed to have selected her surname from the cover of the *Rand McNally Atlas.* When he cast her as a slave girl to Mary Magdalene in *King of Kings* he identified her in the screen credits as Sally Rand, and thus she was known for the rest of her long professional life. Rand played roles in such silent movies as *Bolero, Dressmaker from Paris, Getting Gertie's Garter, Man Bait, The Fighting Eagle, The Night of Love,* and *A Girl in Every Port.*

When the Chicago World's Fair opened in 1933, Rand was appearing in a risqué revue at the Paramount Club, a speakeasy in the Windy City, having earlier given up movies as a career. The administration of the Chicago World's Fair had given permission for a "girl show" to operate on the midway, to be named "The Streets of Paris." When Rand's application for a place in the show was rejected, she and her agent devised a plan to win her a spot in the revue. On the first day of the fair, she rode around the grounds on a rented white horse impersonating Lady Godiva. After city police arrested her for indecent exposure four times that day, news of her antics were reported from coast to coast. Eager to capitalize on the publicity, the director of "The Streets of Paris" reversed his position and hired her to dance in his show, ultimately paying her the then exorbitant sum of five thousand dollars per week.

Rand was billed as the "inventor" of the fan dance. She employed two large fans of ostrich plumes—each seven feet long—to cover her body as she danced in pink and blue spotlights to the strains of such classics as "Clair de Lune." A small, athletic woman, she stood only five feet tall and weighed just 109 pounds. She moved rapidly across the stage in such a way, according to the *Los Angeles Times,* "as to reveal momentary but titillating glimpses of her petite and shapely figure." Rand also claimed credit for "inventing" the bubble dance, substituting huge rubber balloons for her ostrich feather fans. When reporters asked about her rapid dancing style she told them with characteristic wit to remember that "the Rand is quicker than the eye."

With all the notoriety she gained as a star at the Chicago World's Fair in 1933–1934, it was to be expected that Rand would be invited to perform at the next World's Fair in San Francisco in 1939. She performed both her fan dance and her bubble dance at the "Nude Ranch" sideshow. For the next forty years she fulfilled dancing contracts across the United States. In 1950 she estimated that approximately 17 million people had by that time paid admission to see her dance. Her last performances were in Albuquerque and Santa Fe in May 1979, only three months before her death in her adopted hometown of Glendora, California, at the age of seventy-five.

Rand had recognized that acting and singing were not her greatest gifts, so she abandoned them to specialize in dancing. Her creativity and originality set her apart from other performers. In addition, she had the good sense to hire competent press agents and business managers and follow their advice. Her witty comments endeared her to reporters who relayed her remarks to an amused American public. Last, and perhaps most important, Rand seemed truly to enjoy being in the limelight. When a reporter asked why she was still doing fan dances in her seventies she responded, "It's a lot better than doing needle point on the patio."

Rand lived in a Frank Lloyd Wright–designed mansion in Glendora, near Los Angeles, for more than fifty years. She was first married in 1942 to "Turk" Greenough, a rodeo cowboy. Her second and third husbands were Harry Finkelstein, a businessman, and Fred Lalla, a plaster contractor. All three marriages ended in divorce. Rand died on August 31, 1979, and was buried in Oakdale Cemetery in Glendora. She was survived by her adopted son, Sean, and two grandchildren.

Rand, with her love of puns, would have enjoyed the headline announcing her death in the *Chicago Tribune:* "Sally Rand Dies at 75: Leaves Many Fans Behind."

DUANE G. MEYER

Chicago Tribune, September 1, 1979.

Dains, Mary K., ed. *Show Me Missouri Women: Selected Biographies.* Kirksville, Mo.: Thomas Jefferson University Press, 1989.

Los Angeles Times, September 1, 1979.
New York Times, September 1, 1979.
Rand, Sally. "Bubbles Become Big Business." *Review of Reviews* 91 (April 1935): 40–41.
Washington Post, September 1, 1979.

BECKNELL, WILLIAM (1787–1856)

The early life of William Becknell, generally known by American historians as "the Father of the Santa Fe Trail," is obscure. He was born in the Rockfish Creek area of Amhearst County, Virginia (later Nelson County), to Micajah and Pheby Landrum Becknell sometime in 1787. He married Jane Trusler in 1807. He arrived in the Missouri country about 1810 and was at Gatty's Emplacement west of St. Charles by 1811. He worked for James and Jesse Morrison, brothers of Kaskaskia trader William Morrison. In 1813 he joined Capt. **Daniel Morgan Boone**'s United States Mounted Rangers, belonging to Col. William Russell's regiment. He was discharged from duty on June 20, 1815.

After his military service, Becknell engaged in a variety of commercial and trading pursuits. His wife evidently died, and he married Mary Cribbs of Pennsylvania by 1817. The Becknells made their home in Howard County, Missouri, where they had a son, William Alexander Becknell Jr. The elder Becknell purchased two town lots at Franklin, Missouri, in August 1817. He worked as a ferryman and managed the Boon's Lick Salt Works, a business in which he later became a partner. On January 8, 1820, Becknell bought 180 acres of land in Howard County and in the ensuing months took out substantial loans and dabbled in Missouri politics.

By 1821 Becknell, now signing himself as "William Becknell and Co." was seriously in debt. Possibly in an effort to extricate himself from his predicament, he decided to enter into trade with Mexico. He left Missouri in September, arriving in New Mexico on November 16. Instead of following earlier routes, Becknell left the Arkansas River somewhere near Dodge City, Kansas, and crossed the Cimmaron to the South Fork. From there he moved to the forks of the Canadian, and thence through the mountains to San Miguel, thus establishing one of the main routes of the trail. Becknell's was not the only trading expedition to set out for Santa Fe that year, but his was the first to arrive.

Becknell realized substantial profits from his first venture. The next year, in 1822, he placed an advertisement in the *Missouri Intelligencer,* hired twenty-one hands (including William Wolfskill, Henry Ferril, and Ewing Young), loaded three wagons instead of pack animals, and set off from Fort Osage, Missouri. Becknell's second return route differed somewhat from his first, shortening his travel time, according

to his report, by forty-eight days. This venture also proved profitable, and Becknell's investors were well served, including Fanny Marshall whose sixty-dollar investment returned nine hundred dollars. Becknell suggested in the *Missouri Intelligencer* in 1823 that a good road could be made between Missouri and Santa Fe.

In 1824 Becknell made at least one other venture into New Mexico. From there he traveled to Green River, Colorado, on a trapping expedition. In 1825 he helped survey the trail from Fort Osage, Missouri, to Santa Fe, New Mexico. By 1827 he had relocated to Arrow Rock, in Saline County, Missouri, where he served as justice of the peace. He was also elected to the Missouri House of Representatives in 1828 and 1830.

By 1830 his family included two daughters and two sons; he also owned five slaves. He participated in quelling Indian depredations in Missouri between 1829 and 1832 as a captain in the Missouri militia and served in the Black Hawk War. In 1835, after selling some of his property, Becknell and his family moved from Howard County to present-day Red River County, Texas, then part of Mexico. During the Texas Rebellion in 1836, he organized a military unit known as the Red River Blues, and also briefly served as a member of congress in the Republic of Texas.

Becknell returned to his farm where he continued to work with his sons and participate in militia activities. By 1840 he owned thirty-five hundred acres. Five years later he had added town lots in Clarksville and owned 215 head of cattle. By 1850 he was listed as holding three thousand dollars in real estate and a bridge spanning the Sulphur River. He remained active in local politics and continued to be successful in business and agriculture.

William Becknell died April 25, 1856, at the age of sixty-eight or sixty-nine and was buried at Becknell's Prairie. In 1957 the Texas legislature marked the grave site with a large granite stone.

WILLIAM PATRICK O'BRIEN

Barry, Louis. *The Beginning of the West: Annals of the Kansas Gateway to the American West, 1540–1854.* Topeka: Kansas State Historical Society, 1972.

Beachum, Larry. *William Becknell: Father of the Santa Fe Trail.* El Paso: Texas Western Press, 1982.

Gregg, Josiah. *The Commerce of the Prairies.* Ed. Milo Milton Quaife. Lincoln: University of Nebraska Press, 1967.

Weber, David J. *The Mexican Frontier, 1821–1846: The American Southwest under Mexico.* Albuquerque: University of New Mexico Press, 1982.

BECKWOURTH (BECKWITH), JAMES PIERSON (1798–1866)

James Pierson Beckwith, better known as Jim Beckwourth following the publication of his autobiography, was a notable African American fur trapper, mountain man, army scout, and pioneer settler. Beckwourth, the son of Jennings Beckwith and an unidentified African slave woman, was born in Virginia, probably Frederick County, on April 26, 1798. The elder Beckwith moved his family to the Louisiana Territory sometime prior to September 1809. The next year he purchased land in the isolated backwoods near Portage des Sioux, in the District of St. Charles, perhaps in an attempt to give his biracial progeny greater opportunities.

Although Beckwourth was born a slave, his father did not treat him as one. He sent the lad to St. Louis for schooling when he was about ten years old, and during the two years that he studied there, Jim learned to read and to write legibly. Young Beckwourth served a brief apprenticeship with blacksmiths George Casner and John Sutton, but he abruptly left their employ in 1819 following a dispute. In 1822 he worked at the mines at Fever River (later Galena), Illinois, before setting out for New Orleans on a steamboat, probably as a deckhand.

After contracting yellow fever in New Orleans, Beckwourth returned home to recuperate, but by then he had acquired the wanderlust that claimed so many pioneering Americans. In 1824 he signed on as a member of the overland trapping expedition that **William Henry Ashley** was organizing. Prior to Beckwourth's departure, his father appeared in a St. Louis court to execute a deed making his son's emancipation official. When Beckwourth set out for the fabled Rocky Mountains with Ashley's party, he did so as a free man. After a difficult winter journey during which expedition members endured privation and traveled through deep snowdrifts, they reached the vicinity of Greeley, Colorado, where Beckwourth first learned to trap in frozen streams. The Ashley expedition proceeded northwest to the Laramie Plains, crossed the North Platte River, and traversed the Continental Divide before reaching the Green River. After spending two months trapping in that region with a party headed by James Clyman, Beckwourth attended the 1825 trade fair and rendezvous on Henry's Fork. That event, along with his experiences in the mountains, convinced Beckwourth that trapping was the life for him.

He left St. Louis in 1824 as a hired hand and returned a year later as a confirmed mountain man. Following a brief visit with his family, Beckwourth enlisted as a free trapper with Ashley's new field partner, **Jedediah Strong Smith,** and set out once again for the West. After Ashley sold his interest in the Rocky Mountain trade to Smith, **William Sublette,** and David Jackson, Beckwourth worked for them as an independent trapper until 1829. In that year he decided to join the Crow people, and for the next seven years he called their villages home. During that time, he learned their language and customs, took several Indian wives, adopted a preference for Indian dress, won standing as a Crow leader, and traded with the American Fur Company. But ten years of trapping and trading in the mountains was enough for Beckwourth, who was ready to try something new. When he returned to St. Louis in 1836, he found himself a stranger in a much altered city and learned that his family had moved from the area.

Seeking new opportunities, he traveled to Florida to work for the United States Army as a civilian employee during the Second Seminole War. Beckwourth served as a muleteer, express rider, teamster, and assistant wagon master, and he was present at the Battle of Okeechobee on Christmas Day in 1837. He tired of life in the Everglades and returned to St. Louis, where Louis Vásquez and Andrew Sublette employed him to join their trading operations with Indians on the southern plains.

Beckwourth set out for the American Southwest via the Santa Fe Trail in the summer of 1838. During the next decade he traded with the Cheyennes; participated in a successful horse-stealing raid in California; joined with other families in establishing a settlement at Pueblo, Colorado; fought in the California Revolution of 1845; operated a hotel in Santa Fe; served as a guide, interpreter, and messenger for the U.S. military; and assisted the American forces in suppressing the Taos Revolt in 1847.

Following the discovery of gold in California, Beckwourth joined the Forty-Niners who flocked there seeking their fortunes, but he spent more time working as a trader and a guide than as a prospector. He guided overland travelers into California through the Beckwith Pass, which he had discovered in 1851, and occupied himself variously as a hotelman, merchant, and rancher. While in California, Beckwourth met Thomas D. Bonner, a colorful, itinerant justice of the peace and onetime New England journalist who agreed to record and publish his autobiography. That work, *The Life and Adventures of James P. Beckwourth: Mountaineer, Scout, and Pioneer, and Chief of the Crow Nation of Indians,* first published in 1856, brought fame and attention to Beckwourth. It was Bonner who changed the spelling of Jim's surname from Beckwith to Beckwourth.

Beckwourth, now renowned as a storyteller, left California in 1858 and headed back to Missouri where his presence attracted mention in Kansas City and St. Louis newspapers. His old friend Louis Vásquez hired him to be his firm's agent-trader in Denver. While serving as a storekeeper in the Colorado city, Beckwourth also acted as the local Indian agent. He occasionally worked as a guide for the military and was present at the infamous Sand Creek Massacre in 1864. Shortly thereafter, Beckwourth left Denver, serving briefly as a United States Army scout before returning to the Crow villages where he died probably in late October 1866.

In death, Beckwourth failed to achieve the recognition he rightly deserved, largely because of his race. Historians and others who wrote about the West branded him a "gaudy liar" and sought to discredit his accounts as mostly fabrication. While it is true that as a storyteller Beckwourth, like most of his contemporaries, embellished his tales with exaggeration, modern historical research has demonstrated that his recollections were for the most part factual and sustained by the evidence.

WILLIAM E. FOLEY

Bonner, T. D. *The Life and Adventures of James P. Beckwourth: Mountaineer, Scout, and Pioneer, and Chief of the Crow Nation of Indians.* New York: Harper and Brothers, 1856.

Oswald, Delmont R. "James P. Beckwourth." In *The Mountain Men and the Fur Trade of the Far West,* ed. LeRoy R. Hafen, 6:37–60. Glendale, Calif.: Arthur H. Clark, 1968.

Wilson, Elinor. *Jim Beckwourth: Black Mountain Man and War Chief of the Crows.* Norman: University of Oklahoma Press, 1972.

BEERY, NOAH, SR. (1884–1946)

Noah Beery Sr., a film actor, was born on a Clay County, Missouri, farm several miles northwest of Smithville on January 17, 1884. Although he was the son of Noah Webster Beery, the subject of this biography was known as Noah Beery Sr.; his son, who played James Garner's father in television's *Rockford Files,* is Noah Beery Jr. Beery Sr. left the farm when his father became a Kansas City policeman in the 1890s, and there he and two brothers matured in the neighborhood centered in Seventeenth Street and the Paseo. Among his boyhood jobs, Beery sold lemon drops from the aisles of Kansas City's Gillis Theater. An actor's advice to cultivate his deep, booming voice led to singing lessons, transforming a budding career in salesmanship into one in show business.

After singing for a summer at Electric Park amusement park, Beery went to New York, where he sang in vaudeville and musical-comedy choruses, and then began to act in melodrama under William A. Brady's direction. Noah and brother **Wallace Beery,** who also began an acting career on New York's popular stage, toured together in a road-company presentation of *Trail of the Lonesome Pine.* Beery married actress Marguerite Abbott, his wife of thirty-six years, in 1910. The couple's son, Noah Jr., became seriously ill in 1912, and to better his chances of retiring an eight-thousand-dollar medical bill, as well as to provide his son with a healthier climate, Beery moved his family to Hollywood. Appearing in his first two movies in 1916, the actor soon found steady employment in the film studios.

In a career of acting in more than one hundred silent and sound films, Noah Beery Sr. specialized in villainous characters, often of unredeemable evil. Although he once quipped that "villainy is its own reward," this kind man who took his work seriously was at times haunted by the sadism his roles required. He regretted, for example, having played a brutal reformatory guard who tortured children in *The Godless Girl* (sound, 1929). He played his "man-you-love-to-hate" roles in such well-known films as Jack London's *The Sea Wolf* (silent, 1920), in which he portrayed Captain "Wolf" Larsen; *The Mark of Zoro* (silent, 1920); Sinclair Lewis's *Main Street* (silent, 1923); and Mae West's *She Done Him Wrong* (sound, 1933). In the sound era, Noah became chiefly a character actor whose career fell under the shadow of that of his more renowned brother Wallace. In the 1940s he appeared in several Metro-Goldwyn-Mayer films starring Wallace.

No friction resulted from the disparities in the brothers' careers. On vacation from his role as Boss Tweed in the Broadway play *Up in Central Park,* Noah Beery Sr. died in his brother's arms following a heart attack suffered on Wallace's birthday, April 1, 1946, at the latter's Los Angeles home. He was sixty-two. The brothers were rehearsing their parts in a radio play to be broadcast later that evening. Wallace met the commitment.

ALAN R. HAVIG

Kansas City Star, April 1, 1946.

New York Times, April 2, 1946.

"Noah Beery, Sr." In *Eighty Silent Film Stars: Biographies and Filmographies of the Obscure to the Well-Known,* by George A. Katchmer, 34–48. Jefferson, N.C.: McFarland, 1991.

"Noah Beery, Sr." In *Hollywood Character Actors,* by James Robert Parish, 59–60. New Rochelle, N.Y.: Arlington House, 1978.

Smithville (Mo.) Democrat-Herald, April 5, 1946.

BEERY, WALLACE FITZGERALD (1885–1949)

Standard reference works list film actor Wallace Beery's birthplace as Kansas City, Missouri, and disagree on his birth date. In fact, this youngest of three sons of Noah Webster and Margaret Fitzgerald

Beery was born April 1, 1885, on a farm several miles northwest of Smithville in Clay County. In the mid-1890s, when father Beery became a Kansas City policeman, the family relocated. An indifferent student both at the Chase School and at his mother's piano, Beery ran away from home, soon returning to take a job as an engine wiper in the Santa Fe Railroad yards.

Beery left home a second time around 1900 to join a circus. He became the Ringling Brothers' head elephant trainer before joining brother **Noah Beery Sr.** in 1904 in the chorus of a Broadway musical. For several years Wallace sang in the productions of a musical-comedy company and performed in summer stock. His most important stage role was the lead in the 1907 *The Yankee Tourist.* In 1913 he left the stage to join the Essanay film studio in Chicago as a writer-director.

Beery's thirty-six-year film career, from 1913 to 1949, featured an actor who adapted a seemingly limited persona to a surprising variety of genres. He portrayed what his *New York Times* obituary described as "a lusty, hard-boiled, lumbering character" that screenwriters and Beery himself could toughen for villainous roles, sentimentalize for tearjerkers, and lighten for comedies. Sent by Essanay to Niles, California, in 1915 to manage the firm's new West Coast studio, Beery landed in Hollywood when the business venture failed. Already a veteran of short comedy films—a 225-pound, six-foot male, he had played a Swedish maid in a series of "Swedie" comedies for Essanay in 1914—Beery soon found a place in Mack Sennett's famed Keystone Comedies. One of his roles was the villain in *Teddy at the Throttle* in 1917, a parody of Victorian melodrama and harrowing rescue films that featured the dog Teddy. In 1916 the thirty-one-year-old actor married another of Sennett's slapstick comics, sixteen-year-old Gloria Swanson. That marriage ended in divorce in 1918. Beery's second marriage, to actress Rita Gilman in 1924, terminated in a 1939 divorce.

From the 1920s through the 1940s, while working for several studios, Beery played scores of villains. He was the evil Huron brave Magua in *The Last of the Mohicans* (silent, 1920), and the hard-bitten convict Butch in the prison drama *The Big House* (sound, 1930). But the warmer side of his character showed in Beery's 1931 Oscar-winning role in *The Champ,* and in a series of films costarring Keystone alumna Marie Dressler, including *Min and Bill* in 1930. As co–best actor in 1931, Beery played an aging, drunken boxer who wins one last fight for his young son, played by Jackie Cooper.

Wallace Beery had no illusions or pretensions as an actor: "I just put on dirty clothes and am myself," he once commented. He appeared in more than 250 films and was several times among the top-ten box-office attractions during the 1930s. A pilot, Beery was a lieutenant commander in the naval reserve at the time of his death. He died of heart failure in his Hollywood home on April 15, 1949.

ALAN R. HAVIG

Dictionary of American Biography. Supplement 4. S.v. "Beery, Wallace Fitzgerald."
Kansas City Star, April 16, 1949.
New York Times, April 17, 1949.
Osborne, Robert. *Fifty Golden Years of Oscar: The Official History of the Academy of Motion Picture Arts and Sciences.* LaHabra, Calif.: ESE California, 1979.
Variety, April 20, 1949.
"Wallace Beery." In *Eighty Silent Film Stars: Biographies and Filmographies of the Obscure to the Well-Known,* by George A. Katchmer, 49–67. Jefferson, N.C.: McFarland, 1991.

BEHRENS, ERNEST T. (1866–1947)

Ernest T. Behrens of Sedalia served as an early leader of the Socialist Party in Missouri. Born September 15, 1866, in Cole Camp, Missouri, he was educated in the public schools of Sedalia and learned the trade of cigar making at the age of fifteen. Sedalia was a focal point in the railroad strikes of 1885 and 1886, and those conflicts helped launch the youthful Behrens into the trade-union movement. As a follower of Henry George and a member of the Knights of Labor, he helped organize local workers for action. He later recalled that he "lectured nightly on trade unionism, economics, and social problems with special emphasis on working class political action."

Behrens affiliated with the People's Party and served as a congressional committee member of the Seventh District in 1893–1894. In 1900 when the Social Democratic Party was organized in Missouri, Behrens attended the state convention held in St. Louis and helped draft the platform endorsing the nomination of Eugene V. Debs. As president of the Missouri Federation of Labor and a member of the Local Quorum, Behrens may have played a role in the relocation of the Missouri party headquarters from St. Louis to Sedalia in June 1902.

In 1904 Behrens attended the Socialist Convention in Chicago as one of the Missouri delegates. During the same year state party leaders chose him to run as their gubernatorial candidate. While Behrens received endorsements from trade and industrial unionists in St. Louis, St. Joseph, and Kansas City, he polled only 11,031 votes, 4,429 of which were tallied in St. Louis. Undaunted, Behrens ran for superintendent of public instruction in 1906 on the Socialist ticket, but his attempt to win public office was again unsuccessful.

Continuing to play a major role in the party, Behrens attended the Socialist National Conventions held in Chicago in 1906, 1908, and 1910. He and L. G. Pope of St. Louis were members of the Socialist Party's national committee in 1908. Behrens also served on the committee in 1909 and 1910. As secretary and treasurer of the Sedalia Federation of Labor in 1910, he also participated in the Missouri State Federation of Labor Convention held in Jefferson City, joining four other members on the committee of resolutions.

At the May 1912 national convention, Behrens attended as a Missouri delegate and addressed the labor committee. He opposed dual unionism, and, consequently, the focus of his presentation centered on the socialist position with relations to trade unions. At one time he also served as editor of the *Railway Federationist,* the major railroad labor paper in the state. Behrens died in August 1947.

JOAN FEEZOR

Bureau of Labor Statistics. *Thirty-Second Annual Report.* Jefferson City: Hugh Stephens Printing, 1911.

Cassity, Michael. *Defending a Way of Life: An American Community in the Nineteenth Century.* Albany: State University of New York Press, 1989.

1910 Census of the United States. Pettis County, Missouri.

Official Manual of the State of Missouri, 1893–1894. Jefferson City: Secretary of State, 1894.

Official Manual of the State of Missouri, 1905–1906. Jefferson City: Secretary of State, 1906.

Official Manual of the State of Missouri, 1909–1910. Jefferson City: Secretary of State, 1910.

BELDEN, HENRY MARVIN (1865–1954)

Henry Marvin Belden, a pioneer in the study of Missouri balladry and song, was born October 3, 1865, in Wilton, Connecticut, the second of five sons of an old New England family of modest means. He graduated from Trinity College in Hartford, Connecticut, in 1888 and taught at a private training school for West Point candidates until a small inheritance from his grandmother enabled him to begin graduate work in English at Johns Hopkins University in 1889. In 1893 he spent a year at the University of Nebraska, where he met Louise Pound, who became a lifelong friend and ally in ballad-scholarship controversies. After spending the subsequent year at the University of Strasbourg to complete his thesis, Belden received his doctorate, and in 1895 he accepted a position at the University of Missouri in Columbia.

In 1903 Belden learned from his students that traditional English and Scottish ballads, thought by scholars of the time to have virtually disappeared in both England and North America, flourished in Missouri, and the collection and study of ballad and song texts became his major scholarly interest. He enlisted students in the effort to collect songs extant in their local communities, and in 1906 he organized the Missouri Folk-Lore Society to further the work. In August 1907 he published and circulated a brochure, "A Partial List of Song-Ballads and Other Popular Poetry Known in Missouri with Some Hints for the Collector." The list described seventy-six songs already collected, including about a dozen songs originating in the United States, such as "Jesse James" and "Charles Guiteau," as well as Civil War ballads and other songs relating to American history. Suggestions for prospective collectors urged that all popular songs learned by ear be preserved, "whether tragic, comic, or sentimental, religious, historic or didactic." Among the many scholars and collectors who followed him in the next four decades, Belden's approach was notable in its inclusiveness and in that he found American ballads and songs more interesting than survivals of the traditional body of balladry brought to America by early British settlers. Although, like others, he collected the ballads included in Francis James Child's *English and Scottish Popular Ballads,* published in five volumes in Boston from 1882 to 1898, and considered by many twentieth-century scholars the ballad canon, Belden thought the songs not included in Child's book were of greater interest in the study of popular and folk culture.

In 1908 Belden spent a semester at the British Museum to study broadside ballads, topical and other songs circulated widely on broadside sheets, which were not available in published collections. On his return to Missouri, he joined with Mary Alicia Owen of St. Joseph, Missouri, a pioneering collector of Native American and African American folklore, to promote further collection of the state's verbal lore. To broaden the scope of its work the Folk-Lore Society published "Suggestions for Collectors of Negro and Indian Folk-Lore in Missouri," outlining the types of superstitious beliefs and practices believed to exist, and a second edition of "A Partial List of Song-Ballads." With Belden as secretary and Owen as president, the society quickly gained a loyal statewide membership.

The success of the song-collecting effort in Missouri and Belden's enthusiastic reports of the results at meetings and in German and American journals brought him national attention, and he served as president of the American Folklore Society in 1910 and 1911. He spent 1916–1917 on leave at Harvard to work on notes for his song collection and made arrangements for an anticipated volume of Missouri folklore to be published by the American Folklore Society. World War I brought an end to plans for the publication and eventually to the Missouri Folk-Lore Society, which held its last meeting for many years in 1920. Owen, the longtime president and supporter of the society, whom Belden had counted on to provide the African American and Native American materials, suffered several years of poor health before her death in 1934 ended any hope for publication of a comprehensive collection of Missouri folklore.

Belden retired from teaching in 1936 with his own collection still unpublished, but in 1940 his colleagues in the English department arranged for the publication of *Ballads and Songs Collected by the Missouri Folk-Lore Society* as a volume of the University of Missouri Studies. By that time a number of state collections had been published, but *Ballads and Songs* was widely praised for its scholarly notes and careful editing and its studies of such local songs as those relating to the Meeks-family murders. It is still considered a model state collection.

Ballads and Songs is a testament to Belden's dedication to the task of preserving Missouri's heritage of song and the dedication of his students in carrying on the work in their own communities. Although he was influenced to some extent by the scholarly views of his time, Belden remained a pioneer in his study of broadside and Native American balladry, at first for clues to problems of ballad definition and origin, and later because he valued the knowledge gained by tracing the songs and the events that inspired them. Because of his broad interest in documenting all aspects of the oral culture in the state, many songs relating to Missouri history were preserved through his work.

After *Ballads and Songs* gained national praise, Belden was instrumental in helping with the publication of **Vance Randolph**'s monumental four-volume collection, *Ozark Folksongs,* published by the State Historical Society of Missouri from 1946 to 1950. Belden served, with Arthur P. Hudson, as coeditor of the two volumes of ballads and folksongs included in the seven-volume *Frank C. Brown Collection of North Carolina Folklore,* which was published in 1952 when he was eighty-seven, bringing to the tasks the same enthusiasm and energy he had devoted to the collection and documentation of Missouri's folksongs, considered his greatest scholarly achievement. He died May 17, 1954, in Columbia, Missouri, and is buried there.

REBECCA B. SCHROEDER

Belden, Henry M. "Autobiographical Notes." In *A Belden Lineage, 1066–1976,* by Allen Belden. Washington, D.C.: Belden, 1976.

———, ed. *Ballads and Songs Collected by the Missouri Folk-Lore Society.* Columbia: University of Missouri Studies, 1940.

Missouri Folk-Lore Society. "Ballads, Songs, Rimes, Riddles, etc. Collected between 1903 and 1917." Typescript deposited at Harvard University Library, by H. M. Belden, in 1917.

Pentlin, Susan, and Rebecca B. Schroeder. "H. M. Belden, the English Club and the Missouri Folk-Lore Society." *Missouri Folklore Society Journal* 8–9 (1986–1987): 1–42.

BELL, GERTRUDE (1911–1987)

Gertrude Bell was born in Liberty, Missouri, on January 28, 1911, and was a resident of that city for most of her life. Shortly before her death, she moved to California, Missouri, where she died on March 31, 1987. She received an A.B. degree in English in 1933 from William Jewell College in Liberty, and looked forward to a job teaching English, but the depression made teaching jobs scarce, so she took a job at Liberty City Hall as a municipal utility clerk. Writing at night and on weekends, she worked at the city hall until 1945, when, apparently at the urging of her parents, she quit her job to become a full-time writer.

Bell took full advantage of her time and became a prolific writer. She wrote many stories for such diverse publications as the confession magazines *Secrets* and *Modern Love* and Christian publications such as the *Christian Home* and the *Catholic Boy.* The seeming disparity between these two genres characterizes Bell as a writer. Her ability to write "respectable" stories and articles for Christian publications while at the same time writing for the more "lurid" confession magazines underlines her skill in fitting subject to audience. It was a versatility she felt good about. According to her sister, Betty Hood, Bell never "wrote a thing she was not proud of."

It is, however, a third type of writing for which Bell is and will be remembered. She published four juvenile works of fiction, set mostly in nineteenth-century Jackson and Clay Counties in Missouri before or at the time of the Civil War. The first of these, *A Posse of Two,* is set against the turmoil of the times just before the war in Clay County. Her next three Missouri Civil War novels were all published in Independence, Missouri. *Roundabout Road* (1972) deals with a hazardous trip across Missouri in the first year of the war. *First Crop* (1973) recounts the effects of Order Number 11 on western Missouri during the war, and finally *Where Runs the River* (1976) focuses on the war against the image of the possibility of flight from its destructive force on the Missouri River. A fifth book, written for a younger audience, is *A Ladder of Silvanus* (1974), about a squirrel who, lacking confidence, cannot stay in a tree until he gets a ladder of confidence.

Bell won a number of awards for her writing. Chief among these are the Missouri Writers Guild Award and the National League of American Pen Women for *A Posse of Two* in 1965, the Missouri Library Association Literary Award in 1975, and a nomination for the Mark Twain Award for *First Crop* in 1975. She was also active in meeting with various groups such as historical societies and children's literary groups throughout her adult life.

Bell's four historical novels demonstrate her awareness of history, which is informed both by an awareness of the general history of the times and by the oral tradition of her family whose roots extend five generations in Clay County. Yet, while each of the novels is firmly embedded in local history and tradition, the major accomplishment is in the story-telling itself. In keeping with her view that "stories are what make history real and alive to young people," Bell wrote fast-paced, well-told stories that are well suited for an adolescent audience.

LARRY OLPIN

Dains, Mary K., ed. *Show Me Missouri Women: Selected Biographies.* Kirksville, Mo.: Thomas Jefferson University Press, 1989.

Gertrude, Bell. Ophelia Gilbert Room: A Research Collection in Literature for Children and Young Adults. Ward Edwards Library. Central Missouri State University, Warrensburg.

North Kansas City Press Dispatch, April 13, 1977.

BELL, JAMES "COOL PAPA" (1903–1991)

Pitching immortal **Satchel Paige,** noted for his tall tales as much as his pitching, claimed that Cool Papa Bell could run so fast—in the outfield or on the base paths—that when he turned out the light at night, he was in bed before the room got dark. Then there was the time, said Paige, that Bell hit a line drive up the middle between the pitcher's legs, but was called out because the ball hit him as he slid into second.

Fast, indeed. James "Cool Papa" Bell ranked among the fastest men ever to play baseball, among the top base stealers in history, and among the great hitters. He stole 175 bases in the 1933 season, while with the Pittsburgh Crawfords in the Negro National League (NNL), and was once timed at running around the bases in twelve seconds. Bell played his entire career in the NNL, before Jackie Robinson became the first African American to integrate the other two modern major leagues.

Born James Bell on May 17, 1903, in Starkville, Mississippi, Bell moved to St. Louis in 1920 and started work for the Independent Packing Company;

when not working, he joined four of his brothers playing for the all-black Compton Hill Cubs. After the Cubs disbanded following the 1921 season, Bell joined the St. Louis Stars in the NNL for $90 a month; $450 per month was the most he ever received for playing professional baseball.

Bell started his career as a pitcher, which is where he acquired his nickname. Stars manager Bill Gatewood dubbed him "Cool Papa" for remaining so coolheaded in pitching to Oscar Charleston in a clutch situation. Bell was also an excellent hitter, so, as with Babe Ruth, he was converted to an outfielder in 1924 to hit in the lineup every day. He remained a center fielder for the rest of his career.

The Stars disbanded after the 1931 season, even though they won the NNL championships in 1930 and 1931, leaving Bell in search of a new employer in the African American major league. Bell joined the Kansas City Monarchs in 1932, then moved to the Pittsburgh Crawfords in 1933 with Josh Gibson, Satchel Paige, Oscar Charleston, Jimmie Crutchfield, and Judy Johnson as teammates. Like several African American players, Bell played several years in Latin America, avoiding the racial discrimination of the national pastime in the United States. He played in the Dominican Republic and Mexico through the 1941 season before returning to the NNL.

Bell may have had his finest year in 1946, at age forty-three, with the Homestead Grays, hitting .412. He followed it with a .407 mark the following year with the Kansas City Monarchs, as a player-manager. He managed the Kansas City Stars, a black minor-league team, through 1951, then became a scout for the St. Louis Browns for three years. Browns owner Bill Veeck even offered Bell a position as a player in 1952, which he turned down because of his age. While with the Monarchs, Bell played a role in the development of youngsters who became great players in their own right, including **Elston Howard,** Ernie Banks, and Jackie Robinson.

During the 1930s and 1940s, integrated barnstorming tours of major leaguers traveled after the end of the season. African American teams were usually headed by Satchel Paige, and white teams by such popular players as Bob Feller or **Jay Hanna "Dizzy" Dean.** Bell posted a .373 average in these all-star games over his career. In one of those games, he became the only player to ever steal home against pitcher Dizzy Dean.

Bell was among the first players from the black leagues to be inducted into the Baseball Hall of Fame in Cooperstown, New York. He was inducted in 1974, the same year as teammate Satchel Paige. James "Cool Papa" Bell died in St. Louis on March 3, 1991.

JEFFREY E. SMITH

Bruce, Janet. *The Kansas City Monarchs: Champions of Black Baseball.* Lawrence: University Press of Kansas, 1985.

Jet, March 5, 1990; March 25, 1991.

Levy, Scott Jarman. "Tricky Ball: 'Cool Papa' Bell and Life in the Negro Leagues." *Gateway Heritage* 9 (spring 1989): 26–35.

New York Times, March 9, 1991.

BELL, MORRIS FREDERICK (1849–1929)

"I saved enough money to buy a railroad ticket from Maryland to Missouri, where I landed with $2.50 in cash, a stranger in a strange land," recalled Morris Frederick Bell in 1903, describing his May 1869 entry into Missouri when he was not yet twenty years of age. Bell had been born in Hagerstown, Maryland, on August 18, 1849. His father, Frederick Bell, served as a county judge, but earned his living farming and milling. The son, who called himself M. Fred Bell, claimed that he started his career as apprentice to a builder in Martinsburg, West Virginia, earning twelve cents a day, plus board. He may have completed a course at Duff's College in Pittsburgh, Pennsylvania.

In Missouri Bell worked on the courthouse in Mexico, before settling in Fulton. He married Maria Dreps, daughter of a Fulton tailor in 1873, and they had two daughters. Bell's income never exceeded sixty dollars per month for the first eight years, but his habits of hard work, frugal living, and saving persisted. For more than sixty years Bell's talent and enthusiasm embraced the diverse fields of architecture, business, politics, and public service in his adopted state.

Once his reputation as a responsible builder became known, commissions flowed in, and in a society growing respectful of professionalism Bell the builder, without benefit of any formal training, became an "architect." By 1881 he was admitted to the American Institute of Architects.

Bell's career as a supervising architect (one who not only designs but also supervises construction on the site) spans the years 1883 to 1929. He was working on plans for William Woods College at the time of his death. An initial survey identified more than fifty examples of his work.

Bell produced many monuments for the state, most of them executed before 1900. He was frequently asked to remodel or enlarge existing buildings. He understood that boards and commissions operated with limited resources, and he cooperated, offering them choices and willingly revising his drawing-board plans.

The first-known significant work that Bell created dates from 1883 when he was appointed associate architect with H. W. Kirchner to enlarge Academic Hall on the University of Missouri campus (Kirchner's plan placed first in the competition, Bell's second). The university's board of curators praised Bell's managerial ability and complimented his accuracy when estimating building costs.

Most notable of his entire output, perhaps, is the Quadrangle at the University of Missouri (1892–1895), now listed in the National Register of Historic Places. Other state projects include a school for the deaf at Fulton (1893); mental hospitals at Nevada (1885) and Fulton (1889, 1903, and 1922); and correctional facilities at Boonville (1889), Chillicothe (1889), and Tipton (1916). He drew numerous plans for school buildings: Central Female College at Lexington (1884), Stephens College (an addition to Senior Hall, 1889), and the Orphans Home of the Christian Churches of Missouri (later William Woods College) in Fulton (1890); and public high schools at Centralia (1909) and Fulton (1917). Libraries and commercial structures, too, mark his work: a Lexington bank (1884), Herald Building in Columbia (1893), and the Fulton Opera House (1903). He designed and constructed untold numbers of houses.

The telephone fascinated Bell. In 1881 he wrote Alexander Graham Bell (no relation) and asked to purchase fifty telephones; the inventor referred him to the Kansas City company that controlled the territorial franchise. In 1882 he initiated telephone service in Fulton, the first installation in Missouri outside Kansas City and St. Louis; throughout numerous changes of ownership, Bell continued as general manager of the Fulton exchange for forty-seven years. While working in Nevada on the hospital he found the telephone service inferior, complained, and became general manager, a position he retained for several years.

Bell appreciated the value of marketing and sometimes undertook his own. He prepared and sold pamphlets describing his architecture, including "Pleasant Homes and How to Make Them" or "Typical American Homes." Advertisements in the *Missouri State Gazetteer and Business Directory* identified him as secretary of the Howard Fire Clay Manufacturing Company and listed stoneware, firebrick, drain tile, and so on, among its products; a partner in a real estate firm with William E. Jameson; state architect for Missouri; and an agent for the New York Life Insurance Company. He and a son-in-law jointly owned a mercantile establishment in Fulton. Other ventures included the Sun Printing Company that also published a newspaper, the *Fulton Sun;* real estate investment and development; loans; and farming.

Bell, a staunch Democrat, participated in politics at the local, state, and occasionally national level. In Fulton he served many terms as city councilman. In 1893 Gov. **William Joel Stone** appointed him paymaster general of the state militia, and Gov.

Lawrence "Lon" Vest Stephens appointed him adjutant general during the Spanish American War. Gov. **Alexander M. Dockery** included him on his personal staff and promoted him to brigadier general. Bell sat on the board of managers for the school for the deaf and the boys correctional school in Boonville. In 1908 he was assistant to the sergeant at arms at the Democratic National Convention in Denver.

As a young man Bell associated with older, experienced men from whom he claimed he learned habits of industry and honesty, and he in turn extended his helping hand to others. When W. Ed Jameson, a Fulton resident, was only nineteen, Bell proposed they enter the insurance business together. Jameson later said no boy ever felt more complimented than when Bell made the offer.

To encourage self-sufficiency Bell helped set up a carpenters' training shop at the state school for the deaf in 1876, and acted as foreman until 1883. In 1889 resident boys helped construct their new school buildings.

An active participant in civic affairs, Bell was president of the Fulton Commercial Club, a Rotarian, and prominent in the Masonic organization.

The twentieth century opened to an era of heightened professionalism. New laws and standards required formal education, and for the designation "architect," "teacher," or "doctor," certification became imperative. Architecture grew more complex; major projects called for national competitions with entries from reputed architects to be rigorously judged. Such expertise was beyond Bell's capability; he permitted his membership in the American Institute of Architects to lapse in 1897.

Bell typifies a popular nineteenth-century image—a versatile, independent, lively citizen who joyfully participated in civic affairs. Such high energy and ambition frequently are associated with men of strong egos and those driven to accumulate great wealth, but nowhere is this evident in Bell's life. He accepted meager salaries, submitted inordinately low bids on most projects, and practiced economy at every turn.

Bell provided structures that were reasonably fashionable so most people could take pride in the building's appearance and feel comfortable within its walls. And although large-scale commissions were not forthcoming, he continued building small-town banks, schools, libraries, and other useful buildings.

On August 2, 1929, Bell died at his home in Fulton and is buried in Hillcrest Cemetery. This stranger from Maryland had long ceased to be a stranger, and he intimately knew the land. People liked him, admired his spirit, and respected his work. Bell understood Missouri's needs and served her people well; he was the right man, in the right place, at the right time.

MARIAN M. OHMAN

Columbia Missouri Herald, April 1895.
Conard, Howard L., ed. *Encyclopedia of the History of Missouri.* New York: Southern History, 1901.
Fulton Daily Sun Gazette, August 2, 1929.
Ohman, Marian M. "Initial Study of Architect M. F. Bell." Master's thesis, University of Missouri, 1970.

BELLAMANN, HENRY (1882–1945)

Henry Bellamann is known mostly for his best-selling 1940 novel *Kings Row* and for the uproar it and its filmed version in 1942 caused among some of the citizens of his hometown of Fulton, Missouri. These citizens believed that Kings Row, the name of the town in Bellamann's novel, was Fulton and that Bellamann, in the words of the local newspaper, "intended to besmirch Fulton." The offended citizens thought that Bellamann's depiction of his midwestern town was retaliation for insults he had suffered while growing up in Fulton.

The insults concerned Bellamann's birth. Born on April 28, 1882, in Fulton to George Henrik and Caroline Krahenbuhl Bellamann, Henry's German ancestry immediately excluded him from the finer circles of Fulton society. In addition, speculation existed that George Bellamann was not Henry's biological father. Jay Miles Karr, in examining this speculation, finds no conclusive evidence but indicates how important the theme of parental alienation is in Bellamann's fiction.

Bellamann graduated from Fulton High School in 1899 and attended Westminster College for one year. From 1901 to 1903 he studied piano and organ with faculty at the University of Denver Conservatory of Music. In 1904 he began teaching music at female academies in the South. While teaching in Tuscaloosa, Alabama, he met Katherine McKee Jones, a voice teacher. On September 3, 1907, they married and then moved to Greenville, South Carolina, where they both taught in the music department of Chicora College.

From 1908 to 1913 Albert Berghouser, Bellamann's friend from Fulton, lived with the Bellamanns and also taught music at Chicora. During the summers all three traveled to Europe where Bellamann studied piano and organ with the French masters Isidor Philip and Charles Marie Widor. In 1924 the French government named Bellamann officer de l'instruction publique for his many years of promoting French music.

Bellamann had a distinguished musical career. In 1924, after serving as head of Chicora College's music department for seventeen years, Bellamann became the chairman of the Juilliard Musical Foundation's examining board and acting dean of the graduate school. In 1926 DePaul University awarded him an honorary doctorate in music. His articles about Charles Ives were among the earliest to recognize the importance of the American composer. In 1932 Bellamann served as dean of Curtis Institute of Music in Philadelphia.

When Chicora College moved to Columbia, South Carolina, in 1915, Bellamann's interest in the literary world grew. He began writing and publishing poems in some of the leading literary journals. During the 1920s he published three books of poems: *A Music Teacher's Notebook* (1920), *Cups of Illusion* (1923), and *The Upward Pass* (1927). From 1923 until 1932, Bellamann wrote a weekly literary column for the Columbia newspapers. In his column he championed, among others, the work of DuBose Heyward and the Pulitzer Prize–winning novelist Julia Peterkin.

In 1926 Bellamann published his first novel, *Petenera's Daughter,* a story of a woman who falls in love with a farmer who deserts her when she becomes pregnant. In his 1928 work *Crescendo,* Bellamann tells of an artist who is in love with both his wife, a noted concert pianist, and a young woman of society. *The Richest Woman in Town,* published in 1932, perhaps combines the themes of Bellamann's first two novels and points to some of the concerns of *Kings Row.* It is a story of love between a colorful gambler and a poor country widow. As the gambler's mistress, the woman lives comfortably, but when he dies she faces the jealousy of the town.

For his fourth novel, Bellamann radically shifted modes and, rather than writing a love story, wrote a mystery, *The Gray Man Walks,* in 1936. In 1940 came *Kings Row,* which brought him money and fame. Harry McBrayer Bayne contends that *Kings Row* is important as a prototype of novels such as Grace Metalious's *Peyton Place* and Truman Capote's *Other Voices, Other Rooms.* After *Kings Row,* Bellamann wrote two more novels: *Floods of Spring* in 1942 and *Victoria Grandolet* in 1943. Henry Bellamann died on June 16, 1945, of a heart attack in New York City, where he had lived since 1924.

Although he had two distinguished careers—one as a music teacher and one as a novelist—Henry Bellamann will be remembered for *Kings Row,* his long novel about life around the turn of the twentieth century in a small midwestern town.

LARRY VONALT

Bayne, Harry McBrayer. "A Critical Study of Henry Bellamann's Life and Work." Ph.D. diss., University of Mississippi, 1990.

Bellamann, Henry, and Katherine Bellamann. Collection. John Davis Williams Library, Division of Archives and Special Collections. University of Mississippi, Oxford.

Karr, Jay Miles. "Rediscovering the Author of *Kings Row.*" Fulton, Mo.: Westminster Library, 1979.

BENNETT, ROBERT RUSSELL (1894–1981)

Robert Russell Bennett was born on June 15, 1894, in Kansas City, Missouri, the only son of George Robert and Mary Bradford Bennett. Both parents were of Yankee stock going back to the early colonial era. His mother was a descendant of an early governor of Plymouth Colony, William Bradford. Both parents were musical: his father played the trumpet and violin in the Kansas City Philharmonic, and his mother was a piano teacher.

At the age of three, Bennett demonstrated an aptitude for music, surprising his mother by playing a Beethoven sonata he had heard. His parents were responsible for much of his musical education. At four years of age, Bennett contracted polio, and to aid in his recovery the family moved to a farm south of Kansas City. Bennett's father extended his son's musical education during this period by teaching him most of the band instruments.

The family moved back to Kansas City in 1909, where Bennett continued his musical education. He studied composition with the Danish American musician Carl Busch and played violin in the Kansas City Symphony and third base for a local ball team. In addition to these activities, and to help support himself and his musical studies, he played piano in movie houses, theater pits, and dance halls.

In 1916 Bennett went to New York where he found employment in a variety of musical activities, including a job as copyist for the music publisher G. Schirmer. When the United States entered World War I in 1917, Bennett joined the army. He was assigned to organize and conduct army bands and to score musical arrangements. After the war ended he returned to New York where he married Louise Merrill. In 1919 he was hired by the firm of T. B. Harms to orchestrate theatrical songs. Bennett continued to study privately and in 1927 received a Guggenheim Fellowship. Accompanied by his wife and daughter, Beatrice, he went to Paris to study with the famous Nadia Boulanger. While there he studied alongside a number of Americans, including Aaron Copland, Roy Harris, and Marc Blitzstein. Bennett spent the next three years in Paris, London, and Berlin. It was during this period he composed the *Abraham Lincoln Symphony* and the tone poem *Sight and Sound.*

In 1931 after Bennett returned to the United States he entered a symphonic contest sponsored by RCA-

Victor. He shared the prize of twenty-five thousand dollars with two other contestants. Encouraged by his success, Bennett committed himself to further composition as well as a career as a scorer and arranger. During his career, he established a reputation in both popular and serious music. He created an impressive number of compositions, including the operas *Maria Malibran* and *The Enchanted Kiss,* numerous works for orchestra, pieces for band, chamber music for various ensembles, concertos, and orchestrations and original music for more than thirty motion pictures and many major television programs.

Bennett's greatest fame came as Broadway's leading arranger of musical-comedy scores. Between 1926 and 1960 he scored some three hundred shows. He created arrangements for every important composer on Broadway, including George Gershwin, Cole Porter, Rudolph Frimil, Richard Rodgers, Fritz Loewe, and Jerome Kern. The shows included *Show Boat, Carousel, Oklahoma, South Pacific, My Fair Lady, The Sound of Music, Porgy and Bess,* and *Carmen Jones.* He had as many as twenty-two different shows appearing at the same time.

During the latter part of the 1930s, Bennett worked in Hollywood, where he scored or composed original music for numerous films, notably *The Hunchback of Notre Dame, Rebecca,* and the musical *Swingtime.* In 1955 Richard Rodgers undertook a commission from NBC Television to provide continuous musical background for twenty-six half-hour installments for a documentary on the United States Navy in World War II, called *Victory at Sea.* Rodgers asked Bennett to collaborate with him on the project. The series proved highly popular, and an RCA-Victor recording of the show, arranged and conducted by Bennett, became a best-selling record. His work on *Victory at Sea* earned Bennett the appointment as musical director for the NBC network. In 1975 he published a book on orchestration, *Instrumentally Speaking.*

A frequent visitor to Kansas City, Bennett's last visit was in 1977 to receive an honorary life membership in the University of Missouri–Kansas City Alumni Association. Bennett was a member of the American National Theater and Academy and the National Association of Authors, Composers, and Conductors. Despite the great acclaim he won in New York and Hollywood, he remained a Kansas Citian at heart. He died in New York on August 18, 1981.

ALFRED E. TWOMEY

Current Biography. New York: H. W. Wilson, 1962.

Holmes, John L. *Conductors on Record.* Westport, Conn.: Greenwood Press, 1982.

Vacha, John E. "The Sound of Musicals." *Opera News* 58 (July 1993): 22.

BENT, SILAS (1768–1827)

Born in Massachusetts on April 4, 1768, Silas Bent was educated in Rutland, Massachusetts. He moved with his parents and siblings to Marietta, Ohio, in 1788. Later, Bent moved to Virginia where he married Martha Kerr. Over the next several years, he studied law, opened a mercantile store, and was a postmaster. He later returned to Marietta where he worked as a surveyor and served as an associate judge of the court of common pleas in Washington County, Ohio.

Bent was appointed principal deputy surveyor for Upper Louisiana and moved his wife and children to St. Louis, where they arrived on September 17, 1806. Bent's tenure was difficult due to the haphazard and confusing system of Spanish land grants, and he found the work of his predecessor, **Antoine Soulard,** to be inaccurate and full of alterations. Bent, whose income depended on the number of surveys he performed, struggled financially when the Board of Land Commissioners, created by Congress to settle private land claims in the territory, refused to order new surveys.

Bent served as a judge following his appointment to the Court of Common Pleas for the District of St. Louis in 1807. He was also auditor of the public accounts for the District of St. Louis. Judge Bent signed the charter for the town of St. Louis in 1809.

On February 18, 1813, President Monroe appointed Bent as a judge of the Superior Court of the Missouri Territory and reappointed him on January 21, 1817. Bent held the post until the court was abolished when Missouri became a state.

During the Missouri Constitutional Convention of 1820, Bent administered the oath of office to the delegates. In 1820 the voters elected him to the Missouri State Senate, where his colleagues unanimously chose him to serve as president pro tempore.

Bent served as clerk of the St. Louis County court until his death on November 27, 1827. Several of his eleven children were notable. Charles and his younger brother William, fur traders on the Colorado–New Mexico frontier, located and built Bent's Fort in Colorado. Charles became the first civil governor of New Mexico, while Silas Bent Jr. chartered ocean currents as a naval officer.

ROGER W. STEINER

Bay, W. V. N. *Reminiscences of the Bench and Bar of Missouri.* St. Louis: F. H. Thomas, 1878.

Lavender, David. *Bent's Fort.* Garden City, N.Y.: Doubleday, 1954.

March, David D. *The History of Missouri.* New York: Lewis Historical Publishing, 1967.

Richardson, Lemont K. "Private Land Claims in Missouri." Parts 1 and 2. *Missouri Historical*

Review 50 (January 1956): 143–44; (April 1956): 277.

Scharf, J. Thomas. *History of St. Louis City and County: From Earliest Periods to the Present Day.* Vol. 2. Philadelphia: Everts, 1883.

BENTON, THOMAS HART (1782–1858)

First elected to the United States Senate from Missouri in 1820, Thomas Hart Benton soon emerged as the state's most prominent and powerful political leader and as a nationally recognized advocate of Jacksonian Democracy. His five successive terms in the Senate enabled Benton to play a leading part in nearly every major national political debate from the Missouri statehood controversy in 1820 to the crisis of disunion in the early 1850s.

Democratic Party leaders put Benton's name forward as a possible presidential candidate in each election year from 1836 through 1856, but he rejected unequivocally all suggestions that he run for the presidency, choosing instead to play out his political life in the United States Senate. His personal inclinations and personality better suited him to be an aggressive advocate of idealism rather than an administrator assigned to implement existing law.

Born on March 14, 1782, near Hillsborough, North Carolina, as the first son of Jesse and Ann Gooch Benton, young Thomas seemed destined to a life of the gentry. Unexpected events, however, altered his future.

Tuberculosis cut Jesse Benton's life short in the winter of 1791–1792. Jesse's speculative business ventures and land purchases left his widow and eight minor children heavily in debt with an estate consisting mostly of undeveloped western lands. The young widow (commonly called Nancy) struggled to raise her children in the style of her class, but she managed to send Thomas to the University of North Carolina.

At the university, Benton joined the prestigious Philanthropic Society, but allegations by his roommates that he stole small amounts of money led to his expulsion from the Philanthropic Society and in effect from the university. He may have taken the money when the allowance from his mother was late with the intention of making restitution before the small sums were missed. Regardless, Benton left the university in disgrace.

In 1801 Nancy Benton moved her large family to lands Jesse had acquired on the Tennessee frontier. With two thousand acres of land and several slaves, the Bentons were not common pioneering folks. As a young man Thomas helped improve the land, but he never liked farm life. He left the family farm to teach school, and began to study law on his own.

When Benton received a license to practice law in Tennessee in 1806, a political career was just over the horizon.

A large man, physically strong, aggressive, self-confident, combative in debate, totally without fear, and inherently capable, Benton fitted well into the world of frontier legal practice and politics. Speaking out in the interests of the common people, Benton won election to the Tennessee State Senate in 1809. He cut short his first venture into politics to volunteer for military service during the War of 1812. Advancing to the rank of colonel, Benton became a regimental commander and first aide to Gen. Andrew Jackson.

A disappointed Benton never saw combat. Further, his close connection with the influential Jackson was severed after Jackson acted as a second for William Carroll in a duel with Benton's brother Jesse. Mutual friends averted a possible duel between Benton and Jackson, but later Jackson and some friends engaged the Benton brothers in a street brawl in Nashville. After that fracas, the general left Colonel Benton in Tennessee on recruiting duty while he marched off to victory over the British and national glory at New Orleans.

When the war ended, Benton realized that if he stayed in Tennessee he would face the opposition of the state's most popular and powerful political figure. However, Benton also foresaw a large western migration creating great opportunities on a new frontier for a man of his interests and abilities. In 1815, at the age of thirty-three, he moved to St. Louis in the Missouri Territory.

Through a chance meeting, **Charles Gratiot,** a prominent business leader with ties to the powerful **Chouteau** family, became Benton's first close friend in St. Louis. With such connections, Benton quickly established himself as a leading member of the St. Louis bar. He drew clients and friends from a conservative St. Louis elite consisting of businessmen, fur traders, and speculators in disputed Spanish land claims.

In 1817 Benton challenged **Charles Lucas** to a duel. He considered certain comments Lucas had made an affront to his honor and perhaps also desired to prove his courage in his new community. When the two men faced off and fired, each received a minor injury. Rumors about the initial encounter prompted Benton to demand a second engagement. This time Lucas fell dead from Benton's fire. The tragic result had a sobering effect on a remorseful Benton who refused to ever discuss the matter.

In August 1818 Benton turned his energies to the editorship of the *St. Louis Enquirer,* which he used to launch his political career in Missouri. Through his editorials Benton spoke out, forcefully and in dramatic prose, about political issues—especially those relating to the interests of Missouri and Missourians. For his St. Louis friends, he called for the national government to confirm the old Spanish land grants and to provide more aid and protection for the western fur trade. But of more importance to his political future, he proposed a more liberal public land policy to help common people secure family farms, and he established himself as a foe of paper currency and nonspecie banks. He also launched his lifelong advocacy of western expansion as part of America's destiny.

A strong advocate of statehood, Benton became a leading and outspoken critic of congressional efforts to delay Missouri's admission into the Union or to impose restrictions on slavery in the new state. Benton argued that Missouri had the constitutional right to decide on the question of slavery within its own borders.

During the summer of 1820, Benton eyed a seat in the United States Senate. Recognizing that the state assembly would select Missouri's first two U.S. senators, Benton carefully watched the outcome of the state's first general election. The election results surprised Benton and the established territorial leadership with whom he was associated. **William Clark,** territorial governor and candidate for governor, was defeated, and votes from the common people put many new political faces in the General Assembly. Yet, Benton's statewide recognition as a spokesman for Missouri persuaded the assembly to elect him along with **David Barton** to represent the state in the United States Senate. From the 1820 elections Benton appears to have concluded that, henceforth, political power rested with the masses—not the upper-class elite.

During his first term, Senator Benton introduced two bills that became foundations for his future career. In 1823 he proposed a constitutional amendment to abolish the electoral-college system and substitute a more direct popular election of the president. As a spokesman for greater political democracy, Benton made electoral-college reform a key issue throughout his political career. His second bill, introduced in 1824, called for a downward graduation in the price of public land by twenty-five cents per acre each year that it remained unsold on the market. He proposed that any land not sold after five years be given without charge to poor families who would settle on it. Speaking and writing extensively about his land policy, Benton made graduation a symbol of economic opportunity, aligning himself squarely with the growing popular forces of Jacksonian Democracy.

Benton unsuccessfully supported Jackson over John Quincy Adams when the 1824 presidential election was sent to the House of Representatives. Jackson's sweeping presidential victory four years later thrust Benton into a position of power and leadership within the emerging Democratic Party, which became the dominant force in state and national politics for at least two decades.

During the 1830s Benton spoke for a rural, small-scale entrepreneurial economy with a politically broad democratic base. A fiery fighter for the common man, his stand for gold and silver currency won him the popular title of "Old Bullion." Benton used eloquent, if somewhat verbose, prose to launch a full-scale attack upon monopolies, corporations, special privileges, paper currency in general, and the "monster" Bank of the United States in particular, all of which helped formulate a radical agenda for Jacksonian Democracy.

As a leading Jacksonian spokesman for western interests, Benton also endeavored to unite the West and the South as a common agrarian front. Despite his strong commitment to states' rights, Benton remained a Unionist. He rejected John C. Calhoun's doctrine of nullification and his defense of a state's right to secede from the Union.

Benton projected an image, partially contrived, that presented him as a charismatic natural leader. That persona helped him win and hold a political following for many years. Contemporaries described him as one of the most striking figures of his time— a man who carried himself with great dignity and poise, and one who gave the appearance of being a great leader.

Benton viewed the Senate as a body of great power, responsibility, and dignity that set its members apart from the more common roles in public or private life. Although an aggressive advocate of policies and programs appealing to the masses, Benton never projected himself as, or played the role of, a common man. Always standing aloof from the crowd, Benton was by nature an aristocrat. He never altered his upper-class manners or lifestyle. His career demonstrates that one did not have to be born in a log cabin or become a hand-shaking sycophant to win mass political support in the antebellum American West.

The decade of the 1840s brought major changes to Benton's Missouri and to the nation as a whole. A more dynamic and highly organized commercial urban-based economy began to assume a primacy over the earlier and simpler agrarian, small-business economy. These new forces in American life made many policies of a radical Jacksonian Democracy, especially hard money and an unyielding opposition to banks and corporations, seem out of place.

During Benton's fourth term in 1838–1844, banking and currency questions overshadowed other political issues in Missouri. Then, just prior to the election of 1844, proposals to annex Texas opened an intense sectional controversy over the extension of slavery that marked the nation's history until the Civil War. Benton and his hard-money policy had long been supported by a powerful group of central-Missouri politicians. But these men were also Southerners, and he lost their support when he opposed the immediate annexation of Texas—an act that, he asserted, would bring on an unjustified war with Mexico.

Benton foresaw the danger of the Union being dissolved over the slavery controversy, and, as the decade proceeded, he concluded that Southern extremists posed the greatest danger to the nation. Turning his primary attention to the preservation of the Union, Benton became less a Missouri senator and more a national statesman, less a western man and more a nationalist. To some this new role seemed to cast him with the North, and his enemies charged him with being a traitor to Missouri and to the South. Benton won reelection in 1844, but with a smaller majority than in previous elections. In the heat of the political wars of the late forties, the University of Missouri bestowed upon Benton the honorary doctor of laws degree in recognition of his national stature.

When John C. Calhoun of South Carolina brought before the Senate a set of resolutions setting forth the constitutional right of slaveholders to carry their slaves into any U.S. territory, Benton leveled repeated and heated attacks upon Calhoun in statements on the Senate floor, in public speeches, and in the press. His former proslavery, pro-Southern supporters in central Missouri responded by moving to oust him from the Senate. In 1851 these men, joined with the Whigs, who disliked Benton's money and banking policies, to deny him a sixth term in the Senate.

Although sixty-eight years old, Benton had no intention of retiring from public life. In 1852 he ran for and won election to the United States House of Representatives from Missouri's First Congressional District, but he was defeated in his bid for reelection two years later. Undaunted, with his fighting instincts still intact, Benton announced his candidacy to replace **David Rice Atchison** whose term in the Senate was about to expire. When the General Assembly took up the election of a senator in 1855, old-line Benton supporters voted for him, but he ran third behind Atchison and **Alexander W. Doniphan.** Repeated balloting brought no major change in the results, and the deadlock kept the Senate seat unfilled until 1857.

Unwilling to leave the political arena, Benton accepted the nomination of the Benton wing of the Democratic Party for governor in 1856. At the age of seventy-four, Benton traveled an estimated twelve hundred miles during the summer heat by rail, buggy, and horseback and delivered at least twenty-five major speeches. Large crowds turned out to hear him—still a master orator of that period—as he tore with heavy invective into all who opposed him. But Benton's time had passed. **Trusten W.**

Polk, an uncompromising proslavery, pro-Southern Democrat, won the election.

Continuing to live in Washington, D.C., Benton devoted most of his time in his later years to writing. He wrote two massive volumes titled *Thirty Years' View: A History of the Workings of the American Government for Thirty Years, from 1820 to 1850.* Completed in 1856 these volumes show Benton's continued pride and faith in Jacksonian political and economic democracy. Old and quite ill, Benton retained an amazing energy and determination to complete his *Abridgment of the Debates in Congress from 1789 to 1856,* which he had started in 1856.

Although working furiously to finish this project, he took time to challenge the United States Supreme Court's decision in the *Dred Scott* case in a lengthy work titled *Historical and Legal Examination [of the] Dred Scott Case* in 1857. Returning to his work on the abridgment of the congressional debates, Benton completed volume 16, carrying the debates through 1850, and the following day, April 10, 1858, he died.

A special train carried Benton's body westward to St. Louis. There a massive throng paid homage to this Missourian who, in serving his state and nation as a U.S. senator for thirty years, had left an indelible mark as a leader of Jacksonian Democracy and as a Unionist upon their respective histories. He was buried in Bellefontaine Cemetery beside his beloved wife, Elizabeth Preston McDowell Benton, who had preceded him in death in 1854. The Bentons had six children, including **Jessie Benton Frémont,** wife of **John C. Frémont,** who made a mark in her own right.

PERRY MCCANDLESS

Benton, Thomas H. *Thirty Years' View: A History of the Workings of the American Government for Thirty Years, from 1820 to 1850.* 2 vols. New York: D. Appleton, 1854–1856.
Chambers, William N. *Old Bullion Benton: Senator from the New West.* Boston: Little, Brown, 1956.
Smith, Elbert B. *Magnificent Missourian: The Life of Thomas Hart Benton.* Philadelphia: J. B. Lippincott, 1958.

BENTON, THOMAS HART (1889–1975)

Thomas Hart Benton, an outstanding muralist, writer, and musician, was the leader of the regionalist movement in painting that dominated American art during the 1930s. Born in Neosho, Missouri, on April 15, 1889, the artist was the eldest child of Maecenas Eason and Elizabeth Wise Benton. Benton's family had long been prominent in Missouri politics: his great-uncle **Thomas Hart Benton,** for whom he was named, served in the United States Senate for thirty years and vigorously promoted western interests; his father was a highly successful lawyer who gained appointment as U.S. attorney for Missouri.

At an early age, Benton showed a precocious ability to draw, a talent that was supported by his mother but opposed by his father, who felt that a Benton should devote himself to politics or law. In 1896 the elder Benton was elected to the United States Congress, and the time the family spent in Washington encouraged his son's artistic interests. The first sight of the splendid interior of the newly opened Library of Congress convinced the boy that he wanted to become a mural painter. Moreover, under the influence of Clifford Berryman, the cartoonist of the *Washington Post,* Benton developed great skill in making caricatures.

In 1904 Maecenas Benton was defeated for reelection, and the family returned to Neosho. Although he later became a spokesman for the Midwest, at this point in his life Benton was not happy to return to Missouri. He found the adjustment difficult and was twice hauled into police court and fined for fighting with the local boys. In the summer of 1906, eager to get away from home, he worked with a surveying outfit in Joplin, Missouri, where lead and zinc had just been discovered. Due to a chance meeting in a barroom, he then found a better-paying job as the staff artist for the local newspaper, the *Joplin American.* There he drew humorous portraits of local citizens in the manner of Berryman for the lofty sum of fourteen dollars a week.

Armed with this proof of his ability, Benton tried to persuade his father to send him to art school. Instead, Maecenas Benton packed him off to military school in Upper Alton, Illinois. He stayed there little more than a term, and by the spring of 1907 had persuaded his father to allow him to study painting at the Art Institute of Chicago.

In Chicago Benton proved to be a pushy student, elbowing his way into the advanced classes and, on one occasion, pushing a rival who had taunted him down a coal chute. Nevertheless, his talent attracted the attention of the watercolor teacher, Frederic Oswald, and he became the star student in Oswald's classes.

As Benton's skill grew, so did his ambition, and in 1908 he persuaded his parents to send him to Paris. Arriving in June 1908 he began by taking classes at the Académie Julian and drawing from the model at Colarossi's. After a few months, however, he ceased to follow this traditional routine and began a program of independent study, which combined copying old-master drawings in the Louvre with making bold landscape studies outdoors. In the winter of 1909 he met the young California painter Stanton Macdonald-Wright. The two soon became close friends, and under Macdonald-Wright's influence Benton began experimenting with brilliant color and simplified form. During the summer of 1910 he worked in the south of France, at Saint-Augustin just outside of Tulle, where he painted landscapes inspired by the pointillism of Paul Signac. These were the best paintings he produced in France, but when he exhibited them after his return to Paris only three visitors came.

In March 1911 Benton's artistic studies were rudely interrupted when his mother arrived unexpectedly in Paris, discovered that her son was keeping a mistress, and decided to take him home. Benton returned to Neosho late in July 1911. His father was shocked by the modern work he had produced in Paris, and to appease his anger Benton produced some portraits in a realistic style. Over the last few years Maecenas had suffered financial reverses, and he made it clear to his son that he could no longer support him. Accordingly, after an abortive attempt to settle in Kansas City, Benton left for New York in June 1912, with train fare and $150 to get started. He had assured his parents that he would be able to support himself with portraiture, but this turned out to be untrue: he was unable to produce satisfactory commercial work, and his paintings in a modern style were impossible to sell. At one point he had to steal food to survive. Fortunately, one of his friends, **Ralph Barton,** who had grown up in Kansas City, became an extremely successful cartoonist and provided handouts. Another friend, Rex Ingram, who became a film director, gave him jobs designing movie sets.

During the teens Benton was most strongly influenced by the synchronism of his friend Macdonald-Wright—a kind of cubism with brilliant prismatic colors. This phase of development was interrupted by World War I. Benton used family influence to get a safe berth in the navy, and spent several months making descriptive drawings of the buildings, ships, and machinery at the Norfolk navy base. He would later view this period as a fundamental turning point in his career, the point at which he turned from abstraction to representational styles. After his release from the navy, Benton spent several years perfecting a new manner of planning his paintings, using clay models to work out the spatial and rhythmic organization of the design.

Throughout this period, Benton was generally viewed as a modernist. In 1914, due to his friendship with Macdonald-Wright, he showed his work in the forum Exhibition, the first group show of work by modernist American artists; and in the early 1920s he attracted the attention of the collector and scholar of modern painting Alfred Barnes.

By this time, however, Benton was beginning to move away from abstract concerns toward representation of American life. Around 1920 he began to make portrait studies of curious local characters on Martha's Vineyard. He also started an ambitious mural cycle, *The American Historical Epic,* which combined modern handling of form with Marxism to create a "people's history" of the United States. The real turning point in his career, however, came in 1924 when he went to Springfield, Missouri, to visit his dying father, whom he had not seen in many years. The experience reawakened early memories and prompted him to revisit the scenes of his childhood. In 1926 he made a sketching trip through the Ozarks, and two years later embarked on a much longer trip, during which he traversed the United States sketching steel mills, coal mines, logging camps, cotton fields, riverboats, oil fields, and cowboys. He returned to New York with a mountain of pictorial material that he would mine for the next decade.

Over the next six years Benton painted the four gigantic murals of American life that established his national fame. Whereas earlier American mural paintings had been executed in a nineteenth-century allegorical style, with pale colors influenced by the French artist Puvis de Chavannes, Benton's murals focused on the realities of the American working man, and were bold in form and forceful in color.

In 1929–1930 he produced *America Today* for the New School for Social Research, a center of liberal educational policy and ideas. The introductory scene, *Instruments of Power,* showed machines that had transformed human life. The other panels showed Americans at work, with scenes such as *Deep South, Midwest, Changing West, Steel, City Building,* and *Urban Activities.* For the first time an American artist had looked at America as a whole, penetrating regions of America such as the Far West and Deep South that had remained virtually unexplored by artists up to that time.

In 1932 he produced *The Arts of Life in America* for the library of the Whitney Museum of American Art. It portrayed the leisure activities of ordinary Americans, and included bootleggers, gangsters, radio performers, bums, cowboys, and black gospel singers. The painting was widely denounced for the vulgarity of its subject matter.

In 1933 he painted *A Social History of Indiana,* an irreverent view of Indiana life from pioneer times to the Great Depression, for the Indiana Pavilion at the Century of Progress Exposition in Chicago. One of the most controversial panels depicted a cross-burning Klavern of the Ku Klux Klan, which Benton argued was an intrinsic part of Indiana history. The completed painting was 14 feet high and more than 250 feet long, with hundreds of life-size figures. Benton designed the program in a mere four months, and executed the entire work in just sixty-two days.

Benton's murals brought him national fame but also enemies. Conservatives and local boosters disliked his frank treatment of the vulgar side of American life, as well as his depiction of such disagreeable historical episodes as the mistreatment of Native and African Americans. Communists and leftists, on the other hand, felt that Benton's art did not sufficiently promote the overthrow of the capitalist system and that his view of the American proletariat was too satirical. Fanning the flames was Benton's friend and former roommate, Thomas Craven, an immensely popular art critic. Craven combined lavish praise of Benton with savage personal attacks on other artists. Throughout the decade Benton engaged in battles with various members of the art world, including Alfred Stieglitz, Diego Rivera, and the abstract painter Stuart Davis. (Curiously, Davis, who at the time was a supporter of Stalin, did not attack Benton's realism. Instead he attacked his failure to follow communist doctrine.)

On December 24, 1934, Benton was featured on the cover of *Time,* a position usually reserved for statesmen, movie stars, and financiers, but never before awarded to a painter. In a single stroke he achieved a degree of fame never before attained by an American artist. The accompanying article proposed that Benton was the leader of a realist movement in American art that focused on American rather than foreign subject matter. The heroes of the article were three painters who had grown up in the Midwest: Benton from Missouri, Grant Wood from Iowa, and John Steuart Curry from Kansas.

Soon afterward, in April 1935, Benton decided to leave New York, where he had lived for more than twenty years, and return to his home state of Missouri. To mark the occasion he penned a vitriolic "Farewell to New York" in which he declared that "the big cities are dead," and went on to denounce, in turn, conservatives, communists, and homosexuals.

Settling in Kansas City in September 1935, Benton took up teaching at the Kansas City Art Institute. He also began work on a large mural for the state capitol in Jefferson City, which he completed early in 1937. Titled *A Social History of Missouri,* the mural contained a number of controversial vignettes: fur traders selling whiskey to the Indians, slaves being sold and lynched, Mormons being tarred and feathered, **Jessie James** robbing a bank, and Frankie gunning down Johnnie in a St. Louis saloon. One of the most controversial panels depicted the notorious Kansas City political boss **Thomas J. Pendergast** sitting in a saloon with two of the trustees of the newly opened Nelson-Atkins Museum of Art. The week after it was unveiled the mural drew fifty thousand spectators, but it was also heatedly attacked, and a bill was introduced in the state legislature to have it whitewashed.

Benton followed this mural with a flood of activity. He took sketching trips to flooded areas of southeast Missouri, to Hollywood, and to Detroit, which was racked with labor conflict. He staged shows of his paintings and drawings in New York and Chicago. In October 1937 he published a lively autobiography, which was praised by such figures as Bruce Catton and Clifton Fadiman for its literary flair. "Here is a rare thing," wrote Sinclair Lewis in *Newsweek,* "a painter who can write."

In the summer of 1938 Benton was nearly fired from the Art Institute, due to a gate campaign waged by a local moralist, Howard Huselton. Benton went on to paint two controversial nudes, *Susanna and the Elders* and *Persephone,* which gave these ancient stories an unexpected piquancy by placing them in a modern setting. When *Susanna* was shown at the St. Louis Museum it was widely denounced: one local pastor complained that "the nude is stark naked."

In 1939 Benton held a retrospective exhibition of his work at the Associated American Artists (AAA) in New York. It was a commercial and critical success. In 1941, however, he unwisely opened his next exhibition at the AAA with a press conference in which he denounced the effeminacy of the American art world and made unmistakable references to the homosexuality of specific staff members of the Nelson-Atkins Museum of Art. The interview caused social tremors in Kansas City, and on May 5, 1941, Benton was fired from his teaching position at the Kansas City Art Institute.

Benton remained active throughout the 1940s. In 1941 Decca issued a record in which he performed folk tunes on the harmonica. He had taken up the instrument in 1930, and had even devised a new system of musical notation for it, which is still used by professional music publishers. Following the bombing of Pearl Harbor, he produced a series of horrific propaganda paintings, *Year of Peril,* reproductions of which were distributed by the millions. In the mid-1940s he produced several of his best-known midwestern landscapes, such as *July Hay,* and also accepted commissions from advertisers and Hollywood producers.

After the war, however, the regionalist movement gradually declined, the victim of savage attacks by such advocates of modern and abstract art as the European-trained art historian H. W. Janson, who denounced Benton as a fascist and know-nothing in the May 1946 number of the *Magazine of Art.* Grant Wood died in 1942 and John Steuart Curry in 1946. In 1947 Benton broke ties with his New York art gallery, AAA. Ironically, this same period saw the rise to fame of Benton's renegade former pupil, the abstract expressionist Jackson Pollock.

During the remainder of his career, Benton concentrated mainly on landscapes such as *Trail Riders* (1964–1965), a view of Mount Assiniboine in the Canadian Rockies. He also continued to paint murals, including *Achelous and Hercules* (1947), *Trading at Westport Landing* (1956), *Jacques Cartier* (1957),

Father Hennepin at Niagara Falls (1961), *Independence and the Opening of the West* (1959–1962), *Turn of the Century Joplin* (1972), and *The Sources of Country Music* (1975). All dealt with mythological or historical subjects instead of contemporary life, and lacked the biting satire and social commentary of his early work. In addition, the works do not surround the spectator, but are essentially large-scale easel paintings.

At the close of his career, critical attitudes toward Benton softened somewhat, and he began to be regarded as a living American old master. He was featured in such national magazines as *Life, American Heritage,* and *Sports Illustrated,* and frequently appeared on radio and television. In 1969 Benton published *An American in Art,* an artistic and technical biography, and during the last years of his life he worked on a third unfinished autobiography, *The Intimate Story,* substantial parts of which exist in manuscript form.

Benton continued to paint until the end. About eight in the evening, on January 19, 1975, he died of a heart attack in his Kansas City studio, while looking over his mural of *The Sources of Country Music,* which he had completed the day before.

HENRY ADAMS

Adams, Henry. *Thomas Hart Benton: An American Original.* New York: Knopf, 1989.

———. *Thomas Hart Benton: Drawing from Life.* New York: Abbeville Press, 1990.

Baigell, Matthew. *Thomas Hart Benton.* New York: Abrams, 1974.

Benton, Thomas Hart. *An Artist in America.* 4th ed. Columbia: University of Missouri Press, 1983.

Pickering, Ruth. "Thomas Hart Benton on His Way Back to Missouri." *Arts and Decoration* 42 (February 1935): 15–20.

Priddy, Bob. *Only the Rivers Are Peaceful: Thomas Hart Benton's Missouri Mural.* Independence, Mo.: Independence Press, Herald Publishing House, 1989.

BEVERIDGE, THOMAS ROBINSON (1918–1978)

Thomas Robinson Beveridge was born June 30, 1918, in Sandwich, Illinois, the third child of Merritt Hoy and Isabelle Robinson Beveridge. He received a bachelor of science degree in geology from Monmouth College of Illinois in 1939 and a bachelor's degree in petroleum engineering from the Missouri School of Mines and Metallurgy in 1942. During World War II he served in the Army Air Corps as a navigator aboard a B-24, flying missions over Europe, and was wounded when his plane was shot down in July 1944. Upon discharge from the service in 1945, Beveridge enrolled in graduate school at the University of Iowa from which he earned a master's degree in geology in 1947 and a doctorate in 1949. In 1946 he married the former Nancy Mary Lytle.

Beveridge worked for the Missouri Geological Survey during the summers of 1947 and 1948, and the survey published his doctoral dissertation, "The Geology of the Weaubleau Creek Area, Missouri," as part of its Reports series in 1951. After completion of his doctorate Beveridge joined the permanent staff of the survey as a geologist in charge of mapping and manuscript editing. In 1955 Beveridge was appointed state geologist and an ex-officio member of the State Highway Commission.

While state geologist, Beveridge oversaw the publication by the survey of volumes about caves and subsurface geology; guidebooks to the northeastern, western, and Ozark regions of the state; and a revised state geologic map in 1961. The survey expanded its responsibilities during this period to include investigations of waste-disposal facilities, dam sites, landslides, and mine collapses. Beveridge successfully lobbied for legislative funding for a new building for the Missouri Division of Geology and Land Survey and oversaw much of its construction. He frequently contributed articles about geological features of the state to the *Missouri Conservationist.*

In 1964 Beveridge resigned as state geologist to accept a position as professor of geology and geological engineering at the University of Missouri–Rolla. He served as chair of the department from 1965 to 1971 and remained at the university until his death in Rolla from cancer on August 24, 1978.

In the early 1950s Beveridge began a card file of natural bridges in Missouri. During his tenure as state geologist he added categories such as shut-ins, caves, waterfalls, and rapids as he noted features of geologic interest in his travels throughout the state. This research became the basis for his book *Geologic Wonders and Curiosities of Missouri,* which the Geological Survey published shortly after his death. Intended as a layman's guide to the geological features of the state, it includes directions and descriptions of more than two hundred places of interest.

Although not a native Missourian, Beveridge developed a love of the state that he summarized in a 1972 article for *Interface,* a publication of the University of Missouri–Rolla: "Often a convert is the most devout member of his faith. As a northern Illinoisan from the farm, I find that I am now an Ozark fanatic. Flat land, cities, and people who won't take time for the rural social amenities worry me."

Missouri was a geologist's dream, Beveridge believed, because of the wealth and variety of its natural features. His affection for the state went beyond landforms, however. The language and culture of the people whom he encountered doing fieldwork, particularly those of the Ozarks, fascinated him. He delivered slide presentations on the geology and also the culture of the Ozark region to groups throughout the state. His observations and extensive reading on Ozark history and folklore were also recounted in a series of articles called "Hardscrabble Village" for the *Rolla Daily News,* collected and published posthumously as *Tom Beveridge's Ozarks.*

MARY I. BEVERIDGE

Beveridge, Thomas R. *Geologic Wonders and Curiosities of Missouri.* Missouri Department of Natural Resources, Division of Geology and Land Survey. Educational Series 4. Rolla, Mo.: The Survey, 1978.
———. *Geology of the Weaubleau Creek Area, Missouri.* Missouri Division of Geological Survey and Water Resources. 2d series, no. 32. Rolla, Mo.: The Survey, 1951.
———. "Look at the Ozarks." *Interface* 3 (January 1972): 3–9.
———. *Tom Beveridge's Ozarks.* Pacific Grove, Calif.: Boxwood Press, 1979.
———. "What Are the Ozarks?" *Missouri Conservationist* 23 (May 1962): 4–7.

BIDDLE, ANN MULLANPHY (1800?–1846)

From all reports, Ann Mullanphy Biddle was a puzzling mixture of personality traits: charitable and tightfisted, sociable and lonely, delightful to her distinguished guests but shrewish and litigious toward her help. Her life also contained its share of opposites. Although blessed by birth and marriage with immense wealth, she suffered the early loss of her husband, who was killed in a duel.

Born around 1800 before her family arrived in St. Louis, Ann was the daughter of **John Mullanphy,** an Irish-born emigrant who amassed a fortune from trade and real estate speculation. He and his wife, Elizabeth, had fifteen children of whom eight— seven girls and one boy—survived to adulthood. Like her sisters Ann was educated largely abroad, at Ursuline convents in France. In 1819 the family settled permanently in St. Louis where the girls married prominent citizens.

Ann Mullanphy married Maj. **Thomas Biddle** of Philadelphia, who became paymaster of the United States Army and a director of the St. Louis branch of the Bank of the United States. His brother, Nicholas Biddle, president of the bank, was a nationally known figure in banking circles.

The Biddles' home became the scene of lavish parties. In 1828 Margaret Hunter Hall spoke to Biddle about the problem of training servants to support this elegant social life. Biddle replied tartly, "I have to attend to the washing of my cook's face as if she were a child of five years old. And when I give a party I have to go to bed for a week afterwards because I am so exhausted from superintending the servants."

During the 1831 campaign for the United States Congress, candidate **Spencer Darwin Pettis** opposed the rechartering of the national bank; he attacked both the bank and Nicholas Biddle. Outraged, Major Biddle sent anonymous letters to the newspaper and finally gave Pettis a whip lashing. On August 26 the two men met on Bloody Island in a duel, at a distance of five feet. Both were mortally wounded; Biddle died three days later.

Ann Biddle may not have known of the duel until her husband was brought home to die. But a few months later Harriet Radford Clark, wife of Gen. **William Clark,** told her son, "Mrs. Biddle is Sole Aire & Adminestratrix & finds She can Live & Sustane hir loss." In fact, Biddle became an exceedingly shrewd administrator of the estate she inherited from her husband and from her father after his death in 1833.

Biddle also became known for her fondness of lawsuits. An 1839 letter from Nicholas Biddle to Col. **John O'Fallon** of St. Louis expresses Nicholas's shock at a letter he had received from a tradesman, John McEvoy, who said he had been hired by Ann Biddle to build a stone monument for her husband's grave. McEvoy had written to Nicholas Biddle that, "being aware of Mrs. Biddle's propensity for litigation, with all those with whom she had dealings, I suggested the propriety of making out a written contract or agreement. To this . . . she replied that 'her word was her bond,' and I unfortunately in this case . . . gave her credit for sincerity and believed her." McEvoy went on to say that after the monument was complete Biddle had changed her mind and decided she wanted marble instead. He sued for nonpayment, but, despite one judgment against her, she had succeeded in tying the case up in court. Nicholas Biddle told O'Fallon to pay McEvoy and prevent the suit from again going to trial.

On the other hand, Ann Biddle became widely known for her philanthropic work. She gave land for the Visitation Convent and for St. Patrick's Church and money to the Girls' Orphan Asylum. She also founded the Biddle Foundling Asylum and Lying-In Hospital. In her will, she gave money to many charities.

Childless and said to be lonely, Biddle was known for the brilliant parties held in her home at the southwest corner of Broadway and O'Fallon. "Her salon was the resort of all that was best and most brilliant in St. Louis," said one source, and, "owing to her facility in several languages, she was always expected to entertain the distinguished strangers who passed through St. Louis."

Biddle died in St. Louis on January 10, 1846, and was buried next to her husband in a plot at the corner of Tenth and Biddle Streets. Later their bodies were moved to Calvary Cemetery; today they rest inside a crumbling limestone mausoleum. The bas-relief faces of Ann and Thomas Biddle still face each other on opposite walls of the tomb.

CANDACE O'CONNOR

Letter. Harriet Radford Clark to M. L. Clark, November 6, 1831. Clark Family Papers. Missouri Historical Society, St. Louis.

Letter. Nicholas Biddle to Col. John O'Fallon, November 6, 1838. O'Fallon Collection. Missouri Historical Society, St. Louis.

Hall, Margaret Hunter. *The Aristocratic Journey.* New York: G. P. Putnam's Sons, 1931.

Hyde, William, and Howard L. Conard, eds. *Encyclopedia of the History of St. Louis.* New York: Southern History, 1899.

Picot, Louis G. *The Last Will and Testament of Mrs. Ann Biddle.* St. Louis, 1846.

BIDDLE, THOMAS (1790–1831)

Posterity normally defines the most outstanding moments of a person's public or private career by the major contributions throughout a lifetime. Unfortunately for Thomas Biddle, he will always be remembered for how he died rather than how he lived. His tragedy, along with that of his protagonist, **Spencer Darwin Pettis,** became a defining moment in the history of antebellum violence in Missouri.

Biddle was born in Philadelphia on November 21, 1790. His pedigree was rich in history. His father had served as a Revolutionary War officer and later vice president of the executive council of Pennsylvania at the time Benjamin Franklin was council president. Two brothers had served in the U.S. military with distinction. Another brother, Nicholas, had become president of the Bank of the United States. Thomas had served as a captain of artillery during the War of 1812 and was a war hero. At the bloody battle of Lundy's Lane he captured the only British artillery piece taken that day; it was later preserved in Washington, D.C. He also fought bravely during the siege of Fort Eric. At the end of the war he was promoted to major and assigned to St. Louis as paymaster of the army.

Shortly after his arrival in Missouri, Biddle married a daughter of John Mullanphy, reportedly the state's first millionaire. Economically and socially secure, the major was a highly regarded figure in the community. According to historian **Floyd Calvin**

Shoemaker, Biddle was not only handsome and gallant but also one of the most dashing figures in St. Louis. In many ways the city in the early 1830s appeared to have outgrown the paroxysms of institutionalized violence that characterized the previous quarter of a century. Dueling, a manifestation of the violence during the years of bitter personal and factional discord, had subsided by this time. Biddle was soon to assist in its bloody revival.

Political maturation had scarcely begun in 1831. It was a time when the Jacksonians in Missouri, led by **Thomas Hart Benton,** engaged in a number of land, banking, and currency debates that would define their philosophy. The growing pains of political-party development, however, turned extremely vexatious when personal and family attacks began to appear in two rival St. Louis newspapers. Biddle's resort to the code duello must therefore be placed within the context of this fierce partisanship.

Spencer Pettis, the third U.S. congressman from Missouri and a Benton protégé, was engaged in a bitter contest for reelection. During the campaign he repeatedly criticized the Bank of the United States and its president, Nicholas Biddle. For Thomas the attacks bordered on calumny and impugned the family's name and honor. Using the *St. Louis Beacon* as a forum for his outrage, he replied with a series of insults, calling Pettis on one occasion "a dish of skimmed milk." The congressman responded in kind, even going so far as to question the major's manhood. The skirmish was only a small but dramatic part of the bank war.

At this juncture Thomas Biddle, on July 9, 1831, took matters into his own hands. Upon hearing that Pettis was in his room at the City Hotel in St. Louis and suffering from a bilious attack, Biddle entered the room and repeatedly struck the congressman with a rawhide whip. Fortunately, other guests in the hotel heard the disturbance and broke up the beating. As soon as he recovered, Pettis had Biddle arrested. The cowhiding, the term used to describe attacks of this kind, was inexcusable. It also set in motion a chain of events that ended in the most sensational and senseless duel in Missouri history.

If Biddle believed that the cowhiding would dishonor Pettis and thus prejudice his chances for reelection, he was mistaken. The beating did not sit well with the citizenry and may have in fact gained Pettis some sympathy votes since he was reelected by a sizable majority. Pettis waited until he secured his political victory before issuing a challenge on August 21, carried by Capt. Martin Thomas. As the challenged party Biddle had the privilege of choosing the place, distance, and type of weapons. Only in his wildest nightmares could Pettis have imagined what would next transpire. Because of nearsightedness, Biddle chose pistols at five feet. This meant that each man would take one small step, turn, and fire—the pistols actually overlapping.

Perhaps Biddle was surprised when Pettis agreed to the terms, but the die had been cast. On the afternoon of Friday, August 26, 1831, as curious crowds lined the river's edge and crowded onto rooftops, two skiffs headed for an island sandbar and destiny. Once on the island, the formalities were quickly dispensed, and the seconds, Captain Thomas for Pettis and Maj. **Benjamin O'Fallon** for Biddle, were instructed to shoot down either man if he violated the terms of the duel and shot too quickly. The command was brief. "Are you ready?" inquired a second. "We are," came the reply. Then came the word: "One, two, three . . ." In a burst of sound and smoke it was over. Both men lay mortally wounded. Before being carried from the field both men forgave the other. Pettis died the following day, and Biddle expired on August 29. Biddle was buried with full military honors at Jefferson Barracks, and his funeral was one of the largest in the history of the city.

DICK STEWARD

St. Louis Beacon, September 8, 1831.
Stevens, Walter B. *Centennial History of Missouri.* Vol. 1. Chicago: S. J. Clarke, 1921.
———. *Missouri: The Center State, 1821–1915.* Vol. 1. Chicago: S. J. Clarke, 1915.

BIG SOLDIER (1773?–1844)

Big Soldier, a Little Osage war leader, was probably born in 1773 in a village near the Missouri River, in present Saline County. His Osage name is variously rendered Mo'n-Sho'n A-ki-Da Tonka (Great Protector of the Land), Marchar-thitah-toogah, Nika-ouassatanga, Manuaquida', and Mant sa. He distinguished himself for bravery and leadership at an early age. Among the government medals requested by Lt. Gov. **Zenon Trudeau** for Osage leaders in 1794 was a gorget for "Mauaquida', Le Soldat," of the Little Osage. Such recognition suggests Trudeau's acknowledgment of the young, rising war captain. Big Soldier's name itself reflects his status. The "akida tonkah" (great soldier or protector) was an important officer selected by the head chief to assist him in leading buffalo hunts and keeping peace.

Big Soldier played a prominent role in early diplomatic contacts between the Little Osage and American officials. He accompanied a delegation of Osage and Pawnee leaders to Washington, D.C., in 1805, returning to Osage lands with the Zebulon Pike expedition in 1806. Pike appointed him leader of the Osage in the party, despite considerable rivalry between Big Soldier and another Little Osage war leader, Sans Oreille.

In 1808 Big Soldier led a party to St. Louis to return horses stolen from American citizens, a good-will gesture to smooth the way for the establishment of a U.S. factory, or trading post, among his people. **George Champlin Sibley,** in charge of the government factory at Fort Osage, considered Chief Ne-zu-mone and war leaders Sans Oreille and Big Soldier to be the most influential men among the Little Osage during the years of the factory's operation, from 1808 to 1822.

The rivalry between Big Soldier and Sans Oreille apparently continued during those years, for the two seemed ever at odds, each seizing any opportunity to enhance his own status among the Osage or the Americans at the other's expense. In October 1809 a group of Osage attempted to prevent a private trader's boats from ascending the Missouri to trade with rival tribes. Sans Oreille convinced Sibley that Ne-zu-mone and Big Soldier were the ringleaders of the trouble, and presented himself as peacemaker. Some months passed before Big Soldier worked his way back into Sibley's favor. Sibley considered Big Soldier to be "certainly a man of good sense, but not decided and firm in his measures as many others." Still, Big Soldier was blunt enough to chide Sibley that "the Americans are afraid of (Pierre) Chouteau and dare not oppose his Measures."

Big Soldier figured prominently in treaty councils of the early 1800s, amply demonstrating why he was sometimes called "the Orator." He strongly supported cooperation with the U.S. government, and generally spoke in favor of treaty agreements, though he did not hesitate to chastise government officials for failing to uphold promises made in those treaties.

While among the Osage in January 1820, Steven H. Long's expedition encountered Big Soldier at the height of his power, leading successful raids against enemy tribes and as a major participant in the "jealousies and intrigues" then disrupting Osage affairs. The pressures created by American expansion and the intrusion of eastern refugee tribes into Osage lands undermined the prestige of the chiefs. Long reported that the Osage chiefs other than **Clermont** were "weak and unpopular," while "war captains" such as Big Soldier were jockeying for control of their villages.

In his quest for prestige Big Soldier welcomed the scheme of David Delaunay and other St. Louis promoters who planned to take a party of "wild Indians" on a European tour as a moneymaking venture. They persuaded six Osage, including Big Soldier, to make the trip. Arriving in France in July 1827, the Osage were instant celebrities, besieged by crowds and entertained by the Paris elite. By December, however, few people were still willing to pay to see the Indians. An old creditor had Delaunay imprisoned for debt. The Osage wandered through Belgium, Germany, Switzerland, and Italy, sometimes with and sometimes without their St. Louis chaperons, usually in great want and misery. They made their way back to France, where humanitarians, including the Marquis de Lafayette, raised the funds to return them home. Big Soldier and his companions finally reached their villages in June 1830. What impact the harrowing adventure had on Big Soldier's life and status is difficult to judge, but he treasured a medal presented to him by Lafayette and in later years proudly wore it on every public occasion.

French tourist Victor Tixier encountered Big Soldier in his travels among the Osage in 1840, and understood him to be a pompous but minor functionary pretending to much greater honor than his due. The old warrior enjoyed his accustomed prominence at a large intertribal council held at Tahlequah in 1843, however, and deeply impressed the painter John Mix Stanley, who befriended him and painted his portrait. Big Soldier died in the summer of 1844, his lifelong quest for rank and prestige finally ended.

MARY ELLEN ROWE

Foreman, Grant. "Our Indian Ambassadors to Europe." *Missouri Historical Society Collection* 5 (February 1928): 109–28.

Mathews, John Joseph. *The Osage: Children of the Middle Waters.* Norman: University of Oklahoma Press, 1961.

McDermott, John Francis, ed. *Tixler's Travels on the Osage Prairies.* Norman: University of Oklahoma Press, 1940.

Rollings, Willard H. *The Osage: An Ethnohistorical Study of Hegemony on the Prairie-Plains.* Columbia: University of Missouri Press, 1995.

Sibley, George C. Papers. Missouri Historical Society, St. Louis.

BILLON, FREDERIC L. (1801–1895)

Frederic L. Billon's amateur antiquarian pursuits in the mid-nineteenth century resulted in the production of highly successful works about St. Louis that are still useful for historians. Born in Philadelphia on April 23, 1801, the son of Charles F. Billon, a Swiss jeweler, silversmith, and watch dealer, he emigrated with his family to St. Louis in 1818 during financial hard times. As a teenager Frederic entered the family business and soon assumed sole management of its affairs.

Billon's long life in St. Louis spanned the end of the territorial period to the years immediately preceding the turn of the twentieth century. When he died in St. Louis on October 20, 1895, he was the city's longest resident. His position as a member of the pioneering generation placed him in a good position to document the history of the city he called home. One of his earliest writings, a diary of his 1818 journey from Philadelphia to St. Louis, titled *Reminiscences of Our Removal to St. Louis,* briefly describes the early settlements in Illinois and Missouri.

As a prosperous young shopkeeper selling fancy goods, Billon came to know the first citizens of the bustling little town of St. Louis. The optimistic, handsome young merchant made friends easily. In his youth he joined the dashing St. Louis Grays, an early militia guard composed of the city's most prominent male citizens.

In the late 1820s Billon became active in St. Louis government and civic affairs. He was an alderman and twice held the office of comptroller. As leaders in the growing city put their energies behind railroad promotion and enterprise, Billon became involved in the development of the Missouri Pacific Railroad, holding financial posts with the company in the key decade of the 1850s. Like so many other St. Louisans of his day, the West beckoned him, at least briefly. In 1834 he left his business activities to make an overland trip to Santa Fe and the Rockies. Clearly he was fascinated with St. Louis's potential for economic leadership within a vast inland empire.

A keen observer of St. Louis and its citizens for many generations, Billon was consumed with collecting and compiling data on the city's early history. He became St. Louis's unofficial archivist and historian. He used interviews with early inhabitants, research in territorial archives, scattered diaries, scrapbooks, journals, and other manuscript records to produce a detailed and useful chronology of early St. Louis. His two classic works were published late in life, *Annals of St. Louis in Its Early Days under the French and Spanish Dominations, 1764–1804* (1886) and *Annals of St. Louis in Its Territorial Days from 1804 to 1821* (1888).

Although Billon's historical works are only loosely organized by date and subject, nonfocused, and lacking in analysis, they remain valuable sources containing documentary details about the city's physical appearance and its early inhabitants. Today Billon's *Annals* can still be consulted profitably for information about early life in St. Louis and Missouri.

As a young pioneer looking for a home in the Far West, Billon grasped the potential of the city he saw in its infancy. He had the energetic drive and intellectual resources to produce extensive texts that became hallmarks in the historiography of St. Louis. His Swiss background, fluency in French, and likable manner won over the old French families. They shared with him the memories, traditions, and documents of the colonial era, which make up some of the most useful data in his *Annals.* By working with original documents, letters, and other archives, and massive amounts of printed historical materials, Billon earned the title of St. Louis's first true chronicler. As he put it in the preface to his *Annals,* he "presented the facts in all cases as I found them." He verified these facts to the extent of his untrained capabilities and thus produced a useful documentary history and profile of St. Louis's first century.

J OHN N EAL H OOVER

Billon, Frederic L. *Annals of St. Louis in Its Early Days under the French and Spanish Dominations, 1764–1804.* St. Louis, 1886.
———. *Annals of St. Louis in Its Territorial Days from 1804 to 1821.* St. Louis, 1888.
———. Papers. Missouri Historical Society, St. Louis.

BILLUPS, KENNETH BROWN, SR. (1918–1985)

Kenneth Brown Billups Sr. was born in St. Louis, Missouri, on April 14, 1918, the son of Louis and Ellen Brown Billups. He grew up in an elite African American neighborhood known as the Ville. He was one of two sons of a longtime minister of the Antioch Baptist Church, one of the most important social anchors of the Ville. In later years Billups served as minister of music and director of the chancel choir at the church.

Billups attended segregated schools in St. Louis, including Sumner High School, the oldest African American high school west of the Mississippi River. He attended Lincoln University in Jefferson City on a music scholarship and also played varsity basketball for three years. He graduated from Lincoln with a degree in biology in 1940. In 1947 Billups earned a master's of music degree from Northwestern University.

Billups began his teaching at the old Douglas High School in St. Louis, although most of his professional career as a music teacher was spent at Sumner High School. He founded the honors music program in the St. Louis public schools and became their supervisor of music. He served as adjunct professor of music at the University of Missouri–St. Louis during the late 1970s.

Billups received many awards for his accomplishments in the field of music, including the Urban League Award of Merit in 1979, the National Association of Negro Musicians' W. C. Handy Award in 1969 and Gold Record Award in 1976, and the Missouri Music Educators' Honors Award in 1977. Billups was elected president of the National Association of Negro Musicians in 1959.

Billups's greatest fame came as a choir director. His protégés include Cheryl Bibbs, Grace Bumbry, Felicia Weathers, and Robert McFerrin. In 1940

Billups, then in his early twenties, founded a choral group known as the Legend Singers. The group consisted of eighteen singers who were enrolled in the National Youth Act Music Project, a program of the Works Progress Administration, directed by Billups. Over the years, the Legend Singers performed with such groups as the St. Louis Symphony Orchestra, the Southern Illinois University Symphony, and the Indianapolis Symphony Orchestra. Billups and his Legend Singers performed at the Missouri Historical Society's ninetieth-anniversary dinner in 1956 and at the Kiel Opera House for a bicentennial program titled "200 Years of Black Music" in 1976. During his later years Billups also hosted a television show titled *God's Musical World.*

Billups was still actively directing the Legend Singers when he died. In fact, he died on October 10, 1985, during the group's rehearsal at the Phillis Wheatley branch of the YMCA in St. Louis. Billups was survived by his wife, Florence; a son, Kenneth B. Billups Jr.; and three daughters: Kathleen Buie, Karla Philips, and Karyl Boozer. Kenneth Billups Sr. is buried in Oak Grove Cemetery in University City, Missouri. Billups Avenue, formerly a section of Pendleton Avenue in the Ville, is named in his honor.

GARY R. KREMER

Smith, Joann Adams. *Selected Neighbors and Neighborhoods of North St. Louis and Selected Related Events.* St. Louis: Friends of Vaughn Cultural Center, 1988.

St. Louis Globe-Democrat, March 3, 1966.

St. Louis Post-Dispatch, August 23, 1959–October 12, 1985.

Wright, John A. *Discovering African-American St. Louis: A Guide to Historic Sites.* St. Louis: Missouri Historical Society Press, 1994.

BINGHAM, GEORGE CALEB (1811–1879)

During his lifetime George Caleb Bingham, one of America's greatest painters, was nationally known as "the Missouri Artist." While today this seems oddly parochial, easterners in Bingham's prime thought Missouri exotic. In the 1840s it was the farthest state west, hanging on America's periphery, the very border of civilization. That a talent such as Bingham's could come out of the untamed West fascinated cultivated people in the country's older regions. In no small measure Bingham's appeal to easterners was so strong because he could both titillate and reassure them. He gave them the western exotica they wanted—fur traders, flatboatmen, and primitive settlers—but in a manner sufficiently reassuring to calm the fears of nervous conservative audiences. Bingham's flatboatmen are, thus, "jolly" rather than the drunken, violent Mike Finks of legend, who "cock-a-doodle-doed" about being "half-horse and half-alligator." Bingham's masterpiece, *Fur Traders Descending the Missouri,* was once called *French Trapper and His Half-Breed Son,* but he subsequently changed the title so as not to offend prudish sensibilities about interracial relationships between whites and Indians. In *The County Election* frontier democracy mythically rises above the scalawags, drunks, and brawlers at the polling place. Despite the rawness of western society, his images inspired confidence that American progress marched forward on the frontier. Yet, while Bingham had a calculating eye for commercial success, he took his art seriously. He was tough, courageous, ambitious, vain, generous, and possessed of a paradoxical brilliance that let him embody conflicting desires that both limited him as an artist and laid the basis of his genius.

George Caleb Bingham, the second of Henry Vest and Mary Amend Bingham's seven children, was born in prosperous circumstances in Augusta County, Virginia, on March 20, 1811. The fortunate conditions of his birth, however, came to an abrupt end in 1818. Shortly after Henry Bingham generously pledged his substantial landholdings as security on a friend's debt, the friend died and the Binghams were suddenly without a home. The Bingham family's misfortune, however, coincided with a national land rush into central Missouri. Packing up his family, some seven slaves, and his father-in-law, Henry Bingham in 1819 moved to Franklin, Missouri, the heart of the rush area. The change seemed a good one as the Binghams' fortunes quickly improved: Henry opened a tobacco warehouse and bought new farmland, and his neighbors elected him justice of the peace and, later, circuit judge for Howard County. Then misfortune struck again when Henry Bingham died unexpectedly in December 1823, just before the spreading ripples of the panic of 1819 consumed most of the Bingham family property. In straitened circumstances once more, Mary Bingham opened a girls' school. When the flooding Missouri River drowned Franklin out of existence, she moved her family to a farm outside the village of Arrow Rock and reopened her school.

From selected elements of his early life comes the Bingham miracle story about how a poor fatherless lad, with no education, living in the most primitive of societies, somehow became a giant of American art. Yet, if the Binghams did not come from the top of Virginia society, they had been neither poor nor poorly educated; they were not frontier squatters, nor were their Missouri friends. They were, on the contrary, ambitious people aiming to improve on the reasonably successful life they had left behind.

Why Bingham became a painter is partly obscured from history. According to family tradition he was encouraged to draw from a young age. More concretely, new evidence has confirmed an old story about Bingham and the painter **Chester Harding,** a soon-to-be-famous Boston portraitist who had come west, brush in hand, in search of the aged **Daniel Boone**. Harding succeeded, and upon leaving Boone he went to Franklin where he stayed at Henry Bingham's inn. There he let nine-year-old George serve as his assistant while he put the finishing touches on the frontiersman's portrait. Harding's visit made a lasting impression on Bingham. Nonetheless, as Bingham approached manhood he tried on various vocational hats, ranging from minister to lawyer, before settling on art as his profession sometime after 1828. While he soon obtained portrait commissions, none survives prior to the 1834 portraits of Arrow Rock village grandee **John S. Sappington** and his wife, Jane.

Whatever the source of Bingham's ambition to be a painter, it burned with white-hot intensity. Early on he declared that "there is no honourable sacrifice which I would not make to attain eminence in the art to which I have devoted myself," and he meant it. Some of this intensity is easily seen in his 1834–1835 self-portrait, with its combative, even arrogant features.

It was fortunate that Bingham's devotion to art was intense, for he would be sorely tried in the years ahead, most of them spent on the move endlessly searching for portrait commissions. Having painted much of the village elite of central Missouri by 1835, he felt he was ready to tackle St. Louis. Unfortunately, he caught the town unprepared for his talent and left in failure after a brief stay. While en route to Liberty, Missouri, by steamboat in May 1835, he became extremely ill with what has been variously called smallpox or the measles. Although Bingham recovered, his hair did not, and proud and vain man that he was he wore a wig for the rest of his life.

By the winter of 1835–1836 Bingham was ready to try St. Louis again. Writing from that city to his fiancée, Sarah Elizabeth Hutchinson, in 1835, he said that he was "fully aware of [his] many deficiencies" as a painter. "Nearly three years have elapsed," he said, "and I have yet scarsely [*sic*] learned to paint the human face." Yet, while "I am frequently under the influence of melancholy when my prospects appear dark and gloomy before me, yet I have never entirely despaired, and the determination to do my utmost to rise in my profession has ever remained strong in my mind." Uncertain prospects or no, Hutchinson married Bingham shortly thereafter, and in 1837 they settled in Arrow Rock.

That is, Elizabeth settled in Arrow Rock. George took up his itinerant wandering almost immediately upon their marriage. It was painfully clear to him by this time, however, that if he were ever to improve as a painter he needed to learn more about his craft from others. In 1838 he went to Philadelphia. His six months' stay proved profitable, because of both his exposure to the Academy of Fine Arts and more specifically his first contact with so-called genre art: the painting of realistic scenes of everyday life. While Bingham would one day become America's most famous practitioner of genre art, he did not achieve that in 1838. Inspired, he attempted at least one genre piece, *Western Boatman Ashore* (which is now lost), and returned to Missouri and portraiture.

Whatever troubles Bingham had throughout his adult life, he also had the special advantage of his friendship with **James Sidney Rollins.** In 1834 Bingham was painting in a studio on Guitar Street in Columbia. Rollins, then a young attorney, worked in the same building, and the two quickly became friends. There was a real sense of presence about Rollins that would make him the leader of Missouri's Whig Party, a burning passion about education that would make him the father of the University of Missouri, and a business talent that would make him even wealthier. Rollins was rich, handsome, and politically influential, and, convinced of Bingham's genius, he gladly put all his assets at the artist's disposal. When there were no commissions to be had, Rollins rounded up his parents, friends, and colleagues—whomever he could—to sit for Bingham. Later he secured from several Democratic-dominated Missouri legislatures lucrative commissions for paintings for the capitol. Rollins was frequently called upon to serve as Bingham's financial backer and would later pay for the engraving of one of Bingham's most famous paintings, *Order No. 11*. However, Bingham's needs were not all financial, and Rollins's friendship sustained Bingham through a long series of personal troubles. While the artist had materially less to give, he returned Rollins's friendship with equal warmth. Symbolic of their friendship, both men would later name one of their children after the other. It was Rollins's careful preservation of the artist's letters that makes a credible biography of Bingham possible.

From Rollins Bingham derived an enthusiasm for Whig Party politics. Yet, even as the artist had a genuine passion for politics and his political beliefs sometimes colored his paintings, he was also very much interested in having politics serve his art, which was most vividly first demonstrated when he moved his family to Washington, D.C., following **William Henry Harrison**'s election as president in 1840. There he successfully obtained a studio in the Capitol basement, thinking he would be able to draw upon his party connections to gain fame and fortune as the painter of America's foremost politicians. The result was a personal and professional disaster. Most devastating was the death of his much beloved eight-year-old son, Newton, which sent Bingham into a long depression. His personal grief was matched by his professional disappointment at being unable to convince America's important politicians to sit for him. The one exception was John Quincy Adams, who sat for him in 1844, but the reality was that Bingham was sharing a studio with Adams's cousin John Cranch, and Bingham merely secured permission to paint Adams at the same time. (Adams found the portrait inadequate.) In 1844, his plans lying prostrate before him, Bingham threw in the towel and returned to Missouri.

While Bingham's failure in Washington may have been the nadir of his career, it proved a most fortunate fall. Prior to leaving the East, he revisited the Philadelphia Academy of Fine Arts and left inspired to try his hand at genre art once more. With his return to Missouri, Bingham's moment had arrived. For twelve years he could hardly misstep. His first surviving painting from the period, *Fur Traders Descending the Missouri,* with its hypnotic sensuousness, is commonly regarded as his masterpiece. While Bingham created some extraordinary pictures of life on the Missouri frontier, such as *Shooting for the Beef* (1850), and a history painting called *The Emigration of Daniel Boone* (1851), his best genre pictures are principally divided into those portraying life on the river, such as *The Jolly Flatboatmen* and *Raftsmen Playing Cards,* and his great series of political pictures, typified by *The County Election* (1851), *Stump Speaking* (1853), and *Verdict of the People* (1855). By the time Bingham was painting *Stump Speaking* he had long since lost any youthful doubts about his ability. Writing to Rollins about the painting's progress he was exuberant: "The fact is that I am getting quite conceited, whispering sometimes to myself, that in the familiar line which I have chosen, I am greatest among the disciples of the brush, which my native country has produced."

While the painting of *Fur Traders,* and many of the pictures that followed, made Bingham into a great painter, it was the American Art Union that made him famous and helped him, at last, to achieve a measure of financial security. Based in New York City, the goal of the Art Union was to promote an appreciation of American art and encourage American artists. The union, accordingly, purchased jury-selected paintings from those submitted by artists, exhibited and engraved them, made prints, and sent the prints to their mostly middle-class members around the country. As an additional benefit to their members the original paintings were distributed to their members by lottery. In 1845 Bingham sent *Fur Traders* and three other paintings to the Art Union. It was a clean sweep: all four were purchased. Before Bingham broke with the Art Union in 1852 over a critic's remarks in one of its publications, it had purchased more than twenty of his pictures. By the time of the break, Bingham's national reputation was ensured.

Unfortunately, Bingham's great triumph as a painter was marred by the heart-wrenching death of his wife, Elizabeth, in late 1848. Unhappy and longing for married companionship, with the ever ready help of James Rollins, Bingham met and married Eliza Thomas, the daughter of a University of Missouri professor, in 1849.

Fame notwithstanding, by the mid-1850s Bingham had once again become artistically restless. Believing that history painting was an artist's highest calling, he became determined to live abroad, thinking he could further his skills through direct contact with European art. With his economic support guaranteed by a commission from the Missouri state legislature to paint grand-scale portraits of George Washington and Thomas Jefferson, he departed in 1856 for Europe, eventually settling in Düsseldorf, which had a substantial artistic émigré community. There he put the final touches on *The Jolly Flatboatmen in Port* in 1857, generally considered the last of his great genre works. Upon fulfilling Bingham's commission, the appreciative Missouri legislature awarded him an additional commission to paint portraits of Henry Clay and Andrew Jackson. Following the death of Eliza's father, the Bingham family returned to Missouri. Although Bingham had left Europe with greater faith than ever in his new artistic direction, most art historians, disliking new melodramatic effects in his paintings, regard his most important work at an end by his return to the United States.

When Bingham returned to Missouri, however, he returned not principally to painting, but to politics. Through all his artistic success he had never lost his taste for political battle. In the 1844 election he was readily enlisted to paint Whig banners for the state party convention in Boonville. In 1846 he apparently won election to the Missouri legislature only to see his victory overturned by a Democratic house that seated his opponent. Two years later, however, he claimed vindication with a more decisive victory over the same opponent.

Like many of his countrymen, Bingham's enthusiasm for party competition turned to anger at the sweep of events during the 1850s. He now painted former Missouri senator **Thomas Hart Benton,** formerly the worst of political villains in Bingham's eyes, as a noble Roman statesman in modern dress for his fierce stand against the pro-Southern faction that had taken over Missouri's Democratic Party. Bingham, however, was no abolitionist. Although sometime before he left for Europe he disposed of his slaves, for much of his life he had been a slaveholder, and his friend Rollins was one of the largest slave owners in the state. Yet, while Bingham did dislike the institution of slavery, he despised those he felt guilty of disunionism. He viewed the border struggles between slavery-sympathizing Missourians and free-soil Kansans with sickened disgust, writing Rollins: "I have gone clean over to the black republicans."

During the secession winter of 1860–1861 Bingham took his large portrait of Jackson on a tour of the state in an attempt to shame Democrats with the image of the great chieftain who had forced John C. Calhoun and South Carolinians to back down during the nullification crisis. When war broke out Bingham was immediately elected captain of a Kansas City company of home guards. Shortly thereafter Constitutional Convention delegates named **Hamilton Rowan Gamble** to head the pro-Union government, and he, in turn, named Bingham state treasurer. Bingham served with distinction, although without pleasure, in this position until the war's end, and endured yet more pain when his son Horace was killed in the conflict.

During the course of the war, however, Bingham's pro-Union enthusiasm was dampened when federal military authorities commandeered a house he had inherited in Kansas City to house female relations of pro-Confederate guerrillas. When the house collapsed, killing a number of the women, the guerrillas retaliated with a cruel and unmerciful raid on Lawrence, Kansas. In the continuing escalation of border warfare on August 25, 1863, Union general **Thomas Ewing Jr.** ordered the forced exile of all Missourians, except a handful of demonstrably pro-Union families, from a four-county area along the Kansas border. Before the order was implemented Bingham tried to intercede with Ewing, but to no avail. A general looting and burning of Missouri houses followed.

By the war's end Bingham was a Democrat, and he spent much of his political and artistic energies denouncing the repressive measures being levied at those considered pro-Southern, or simply anti-Republican. In particular, he lavished a great deal of attention on a large theatrical painting of the forced evacuation of western Missouri titled *Order No. 11,* which he sent to Ohio to follow Ewing when he ran for governor there. Another well-known picture from the period titled *Major Dean in Jail* celebrated the incarceration of Baptist minister "and Union Army Major" Abner Dean, who was jailed because he felt he could not take the loyalty oath demanded of all ministers before they could preach.

When the Democrats came back into power Bingham's political fortunes rose once again. In 1875 Gov. **Charles Henry Hardin** appointed Bingham Missouri's adjutant general. His brief two-year term was eventful, with much of it spent in Washington attempting to settle Missouri's war claims against the federal government. He also actively suppressed vigilante violence in southern Missouri and, on behalf of the governor, investigated the bombing of **Jesse James**'s mother's home in 1876.

The end of George Caleb Bingham's government service coincided with a hard time in his life. His wife, Eliza, who had long suffered from mental difficulties, became delusional and after a brief stay died at the Missouri State Lunatic Asylum in Fulton. In 1878 Bingham married for a third time. His new wife was the lively Martha Livingston Lykins, a descendant of a signer of the Declaration of Independence, second cousin to Stonewall Jackson, and recent widow of a former mayor of Kansas City. During the Civil War federal authorities had considered her so pro-Confederate in her views that they exiled her to St. Louis.

Despite the happy respite offered by their marriage, life was, nevertheless, becoming increasingly hard for the painter. Weak in health, Bingham spent his honeymoon in Colorado in an attempt to shake a chronic cough. Rollins attempted to come to Bingham's financial aid again by securing for him an appointment as the University of Missouri's first professor of art, but Bingham made only a gesture at serving in the position. Immediately upon his return from a long visit with Rollins in Columbia, Bingham became ill with cholera and died in Kansas City on July 7, 1879. Rollins delivered the eulogy.

By the time of his death Bingham had mostly faded from national memory. His wife, known as Mattie, tried to keep his memory alive, but the artist's own collection of his paintings was sold and scattered at her death, the proceeds going to support the Confederate Soldier's Home in Higginsville. Of all the painters of his day Bingham best memorialized his time. Time has now remembered him. A full-scale revival of interest in his art began in 1933 when the Metropolitan Museum of Art in New York purchased *Fur Traders Descending the Missouri.* The following year the St. Louis Art Museum organized a major exhibition, which received national attention when it, too, traveled to the Metropolitan Museum. Painter **Thomas Hart Benton** helped as well through his vigorous championship of Bingham's work. In the last half of the twentieth century George Caleb Bingham emerged as one of America's most popular and securely established painters.

KENNETH H. WINN

Bloch, Maurice. *George Caleb Bingham: The Evolution of an Artist.* Berkeley and Los Angeles: University of California Press, 1967.

McDermott, John F. *George Caleb Bingham: River Portraitist.* Norman: University of Oklahoma Press, 1959.

Rash, Nancy. *The Painting and Politics of George*

Caleb Bingham. New Haven: Yale University Press, 1991.

Shapiro, Michael Edward. *George Caleb Bingham.* New York: Harry N. Abrams Publishers, in association with the National Museum of American Art, Smithsonian Institution, 1993.

Shapiro, Michael, et al. *George Caleb Bingham.* New York: St. Louis Art Museum, in association with Harry N. Abrams Publishers, 1990.

BIRCH, JAMES H. (1804–1878)

James H. Birch, who served on the Missouri Supreme Court from 1849 to 1851, is better remembered for his vitriolic prose as a journalist, his long-standing feud with Sen. **Thomas Hart Benton,** and his political inconsistencies than for his service on the bench. His supreme-court term proved relatively uneventful. Birch's abbreviated term expired before the justices had an opportunity to issue a ruling in the landmark *Dred Scott* case, then pending before the high court, and his most notable opinion clarified a law regarding the calculation of interest.

Born March 27, 1804, in Montgomery County, Virginia, Birch spent some time in Kentucky before arriving in St. Louis in 1826. Ironically in light of future events, he found work editing Benton's *St. Louis Enquirer.* In 1827 he moved to Fayette, Missouri, where he established a newspaper, the *Western Monitor,* to support the presidential ambitions of Andrew Jackson. Through his editorials, Birch soon became known for his outspokenness.

Birch protested the treatment of Native Americans taken prisoner in 1829 during the Big Neck Affair, a land dispute between settlers and members of the Iowa tribe in northeast Missouri that resulted in casualties on both sides. He acted as a defense lawyer for the Native Americans and used his newspaper to denounce Ignatius Owen, leader of the force that had fired upon the Indians. His charges led to Owen's arrest and trial.

In 1828 Birch was appointed chief clerk of the Missouri House of Representatives. In 1832 he was elected to the Missouri State Senate and named chairman of the joint committee to revise laws. His unsuccessful bid for a seat in the United States House of Representatives in 1835 further complicated efforts by Democrats to present a more unified front. He ran as a Jackson man without backing from the Democrats. Two years later Birch changed his newspaper's name to the *Missourian* and its political affiliation to Whig. In 1840 he endorsed the candidacy of **William Henry Harrison** for president.

Birch actively supported the Platte Purchase, which extended Missouri's northwestern boundary westward to the Missouri River. In 1843 he moved to Plattsburg following his appointment as register of lands. By then Birch had become an outspoken foe of Senator Benton. Their differences began during the debates in the 1840s over currency policies. Birch advocated a system based on paper currency while Benton adamantly supported the gold standard. The animosity between them grew after Birch's failed attempts to prevent Benton's reelection to the Senate in 1844. During the 1848 elections Birch, a staunch proslavery advocate, denounced Martin Van Buren and the Free Soilers.

Birch became a leading proponent of the Jackson Resolutions engineered by **Claiborne Fox Jackson** and anti-Benton Democrats to embarrass Senator Benton and to hamper his bid for reelection in 1850. After Birch returned to the Democratic fold as a supporter of the anti-Benton faction, Gov. **Austin A. King** appointed him to the Missouri Supreme Court in 1849. Politics loomed large during Birch's brief stint on the high court. He and his fellow justice **William Barclay Napton** saw the pending *Dred Scott* case as an opportunity to further discredit Benton. They intended to reverse earlier judicial precedent by ruling that Congress had no authority to legislate on slavery in the territories. But following an 1850 reorganization of the Missouri Supreme Court requiring the election of judges, Missouri voters turned Birch and Napton out of office before they had a chance to issue their opinion in the case.

During Benton's reelection campaign, Birch routinely thrashed the senator in print and in speeches, which provoked Benton, fighting for his political life, to ask publicly, "I wonder when the damned scoundrel whipped his wife last?" Benton also accused Birch of knocking out three of his wife's teeth during a quarrel over his black mistress, and called Birch "that cur dog—yes, that son of a cur—yes, a damned sheep-killing dog." Birch sued Benton for slander. The trial and appeals dragged on until 1858 when on technical grounds the Missouri Supreme Court reversed an 1853 lower-court verdict that awarded Birch five thousand dollars.

After Birch left the bench in 1851, he was again appointed register of lands in northwest Missouri, a position he held until 1861. He repeatedly ran without success for a congressional seat. As editor of Plattsburg's *Clinton County Register,* he ardently supported the Union, and as a member of the 1861 state convention, he opposed secession.

Birch died on January 10, 1878, a man who remained uncompromising in his views and maintained the respect of his friends and enemies alike for his strength of character.

JERRY E. WILSON

Bay, W. V. N. *Reminiscences of the Bench and Bar of Missouri.* St. Louis: F. H. Thomas, 1878.

Meyer, Duane G. *The Heritage of Missouri*. St. Louis: River City Publishers, 1982.

Shoemaker, Floyd Calvin. *Missouri and Missourians: Land of Contrasts and People of Achievements.* Chicago: Lewis Publishing, 1943.

Stewart, A. J. D., ed. *The History of the Bench and Bar of Missouri.* St. Louis: Legal Publishing, 1898.

BIRKBECK, MORRIS (1764–1825)

An early pioneer–farming expert and author, Morris Birkbeck exerted an enormous influence in publicizing the Illinois and Missouri Territories not only to his planned colony of English families, but also to waves of American and continental European settlers. Born in Sette, England, on January 23, 1764, Birkbeck was the son of Morris and Hannah Bradford Birkbeck, parents of some means and standing. As he grew into manhood in England, the younger Birkbeck prospered at farming and sheep raising and acquired substantial landholdings, but he became increasingly dissatisfied with the restrictive political and economic situation in the British Isles.

In 1817 Birkbeck emigrated to the United States with his large family and with his friend George Flower, also a successful landowner and farmer. In America the two men set about to create a colony for English settlers on the Illinois prairies. A former acquaintance in England, Edward Coles, who later became the second governor of Illinois, told Birkbeck of the vast expanses of open, untilled lands in the heart of America needing relatively little timber clearing. Birkbeck acquired tens of thousands of acres of virgin Illinois land, raised money, and wrote several books to lure English settlers to his American venture. Birkbeck's publications, most notably his *Notes on a Journey in America from the Coast of Virginia to the Territory of Illinois* (1817) and *Letters from Illinois* (1818), eloquently described the new regions he intended to open up to productive farming.

In his promotional books Birkbeck touted the relative cheapness of the western lands nearer the Mississippi Valley as opposed to the more expensive, "improved" areas of the central Ohio Valley, already damaged by improper clearing and poor drainage. In Birkbeck's time eastern speculators routinely offered dubious land to unwary purchasers. A strong feature of Birkbeck's writing was his detailed accounting of the capital outlays English farmers needed to become landholders in the New World. He also extolled the ease of travel and communication via heavily used water routes linking the remote mid-American territory with New Orleans and the eastern seaboard.

Birkbeck optimistically looked upon the Illinois prairies as offering a new chapter in American agricultural development. He was one of the first writers to pull settlers away from the tradition that the good agricultural land was limited to the wooded bottoms closest to the major rivers. With a farmer's careful perspective, he weighed the advantages and disadvantages of striking out boldly for the natural, almost parklike pastures and open prairies.

Birkbeck's works went through numerous editions, and created worldwide interest in settlement theories. Land promoters protested his assertions, and the controversy increased interest in the western territories. In fact, his books contributed to the stepped-up settlement in the Mississippi Valley in the 1820s. According to historian Solon Buck, Birkbeck called attention "not only to the English settlement itself but to Illinois and the West as a whole, and undoubtedly helped to promote emigration both from abroad and from the eastern states."

Well informed regarding agricultural practices, Birkbeck became the first president of the earliest agricultural society in Illinois, one of the oldest in the West. He helped win acceptance for a scientific approach to farming in Illinois and the American Midwest. He drew upon his own observations on the Illinois frontier to formulate his ideas about farming. No mere speculator's advertisements, his books documented successful early experiments in tilling the endless prairie lands of Illinois and Missouri. His ideas appealed not only to the sturdy, dedicated farmers and artisans he attracted from England, but to many others as well. Birkbeck also helped infuse Illinois with early settlers who shared his abhorrence for slavery and fought its introduction into the state. He allied himself with early Methodist and Baptist leaders in the region.

The English colony that Birkbeck established did not survive following his tragic death by drowning on June 4, 1825. But through his writings and his efforts to establish English settlements in the seemingly endless ocean of grasslands in the Illinois country, Birkbeck facilitated the subsequent growth of an agricultural empire in the central states.

JOHN NEAL HOOVER

Boewe, Charles. *Prairie Albion: An English Settlement in Pioneer Illinois.* Carbondale: Southern Illinois University Press, 1962.

Birkbeck, Morris. *Letters from Illinois.* Philadelphia: Carey, 1818.

———. *Notes on a Journey from the Coast of Virginia to the Territory of Illinois.* London: Ridgeway, 1818.

Buck, Solon. *Illinois in 1818.* Reprint, Urbana: University of Illinois Press, 1967.

Faux, William. *Memorable Days in America, . . . Including Accounts of Mr. Birkbeck's Settlement in the Illinois (1819–1820).* Vols. 9 and 12 of *Early*

Western Travels, 1748–1846, ed. R. G. Thwaites. Cleveland: Arthur H. Clark, 1905.

Sparks, Edwin Erle. *The English Settlement in the Illinois: Reprints of Three Rare Tracts on the Illinois Country.* Cedar Rapids, Iowa: Torch Press, 1907.

BISSELL, DANIEL (1768?–1833)

The builder and commandant of Fort Bellefontaine, Gen. Daniel Bissell served with distinction as military commander of Upper Louisiana in the key period after the French cession of the Louisiana Territory to the United States. Born in Windsor, Connecticut, around 1768, Bissell was the son of Ozias and Mabel Robarts Bissell. He came from a family of soldiers and military leaders. His father once proudly remarked that he and his sons alone had given 120 years of service to their country.

During the Revolutionary War, Bissell was a fifer and carried out numerous other tasks with distinction. One of his earliest exploits concerned the carrying of important military documents and dispatches alone between Philadelphia and Pittsburgh in hostile Indian territory. After the Revolution Bissell was destined to remain in the military as a professional army officer. He became a noted Indian fighter in the regular army as it attempted to secure the frontier. He was with Maj. Gen. Arthur St. Clair at the battle of November 4, 1791, widely known as St. Clair's Defeat in the central Ohio Valley and fought with great heroics.

Bissell rose steadily in the military ranks, from cadet in 1791 to lieutenant to captain, next to lieutenant colonel, and finally to colonel at the time he took command at Fort Bellefontaine in 1808, a military post that Gen. **James Wilkinson** had established three years earlier. Bissell had previously commanded Fort Massac, a port of entry on the Ohio River, where he also served as a customs officer between Spanish Louisiana and the United States. In 1804 he officiated at the formal ceremony of transfer of New Madrid to American rule, one of the few such observances in Upper Louisiana.

At the time Bissell established his military command at Fort Bellefontaine a few miles north of St. Louis, the installation was already in disrepair and probably indefensible. Bissell took steps to rebuild the cantonment to make it a useful and strategic base for frontier defense. While in command at Fort Bellefontaine between 1808 and 1813, Bissell assumed a key role in providing for the security of the territory during a time of increasing unrest and uncertainty.

Bissell advocated strong defensive measures along the young American republic's western border but managed to remain aloof from the political squabbles and factionalism that raged in the Louisiana Territory in the early years of American domination. Bissell was a friend of **Daniel Boone** and provided the Lewis and Clark Corps of Discovery with useful advice. He was able to work effectively with individuals of varied temperaments and strong personalities such as Wilkinson, **Frederick Bates, Auguste Chouteau,** and Ninian Edwards.

During the War of 1812 Bissell participated in the American victory at Lyon's Creek, in October 1814. After the war, while serving at posts on the lower Mississippi at Baton Rouge and New Orleans, he waged a prolonged and embittered struggle to preserve his rank of brigadier general and his commission during a time of general military retrenchment. The proud, old career soldier, with many honors to his credit, resisted efforts to dismiss him from military service. For ten years he utilized powerful intermediaries such as Sen. **Thomas Hart Benton** to seek an overturn of his forced retirement. During that time he improved his beloved farm, Franklinton, above St. Louis near the old fortress and military camp he had rehabilitated in earlier days. The personal strife of these years was alleviated by the wide respect he commanded in St. Louis, where he was considered one of the first men of the city. In 1825 Bissell was a leader in arranging for the Marquis de Lafayette's visit to St. Louis in the autumn of that year.

Bissell was undoubtedly an ambitious soldier in the early days of national expansion. His gifts for building defensive fortifications and maintaining military discipline enabled him to advance in rank. His successful oversight of western military operations contributed to the establishment of St. Louis as a major center of American military operations. At the time of his death on December 14, 1833, Bissell projected an image of a prosperous country squire along the Bellefontaine Road, the old military road he had improved. He amassed a farm of several thousand acres and exemplified the successful American settlers who came to early Missouri. His activities as a Missouri version of an aging Cincinnatus came to symbolize the growing peace and prosperity that nurtured the Mississippi Valley as the frontier moved ever westward.

JOHN NEAL HOOVER

Bissell, Daniel. Letters. St. Louis Mercantile Library, St. Louis.

———. Papers. Missouri Historical Society, St. Louis.

Brockhoff, Dorothy Adele. *The Bissell Saga.* St. Louis: St. Louis County Department of Parks and Recreation, 1962.

Gregg, Kate L. "The War of 1812 on the Missouri Frontier." Parts 1–3. *Missouri Historical Review* 33 (October 1938): 3–22; (January 1939): 184–202; (April 1939): 326–48.

Jessop, Edith Newbold. *General Daniel Bissell: His Ancestors and Descendants.* New York [Philadelphia: William F. Fell, printers], 1927.

Ryan, Harold W. "Daniel Bissell—'Late General.'" *Bulletin of the Missouri Historical Society* 15 (October 1958): 20–28.

BIXBY, WILLIAM KEENEY
(1857–1931)

One of the key St. Louis businessmen and philanthropists of his generation in St. Louis, William K. Bixby left a legacy in connoisseurship by gathering an important collection of art, rare books, and literary and historical manuscripts on a scale that has seldom been equaled in the United States. Born in Adrian, Michigan, on January 2, 1857, the son of Alonzo and Emma Louise Bixby, William was reared in a household that respected the great passions of his family: history and art.

As a young man this cultural appreciation was temporarily held in check as Bixby made his way in life. He began work as a newspaperman in his hometown. Next, he became a bank clerk in Detroit, without pay, in order, as he put it, to make his way in the world of business and finance, learning from the ground up numerous procedures and practices that he would find useful in his subsequent career. His formal schooling ended with a high school degree, and he went to work in Texas in various capacities, such as watchman, freight clerk, and baggage man for the International and Great Northern Railroad. He thus began to "make his own place" in the business world, barely out of his teens, as one newspaper put it, initially earning the humble sum of fifty dollars per month. From this time onward, Bixby's business career would be associated with railroading and rail parts manufacturing.

By the early 1880s, after working briefly for the Missouri Pacific Railroad, Bixby became the printing and stationary agent for the entire Jay Gould system. Next he was lumber agent for the Missouri Car and Foundry Company of St. Louis, later becoming the purchasing agent, treasurer, vice president, general manager, and ultimately president of what eventually evolved into the American Car and Foundry Company.

In the business of railroad-car building in Missouri, Bixby increased his company's stock through mergers and acquisitions. So successful were his financial decisions that he retired in 1905 from an active role in the railroad business. Yet, he continued to be involved in such companies as the Laclede Gas and Light Company and various St. Louis banking concerns, as well as the Wabash Railroad.

By midlife Bixby had thus acquired the means to embark upon a second career in collecting art, rare books, and artifacts. These endeavors occupied him for the rest of his days. Bixby channeled his wealth and collecting genius into the development of the budding educational and cultural institutions of St. Louis. He thus had a direct impact on their future; perhaps more far-reaching than any St. Louisan of his time.

Bixby had an extremely progressive, farsighted view toward philanthropy. He looked at St. Louis's cultural organizations in totality, making substantial material gifts and providing financial support for capital improvements, operating expenses, and designated funds. He helped weave the cultural fabric for arts and education in St. Louis.

In the later decades of his life, Bixby held the presidency of Washington University, succeeding **Robert Brookings.** He was also president of the City Art Museum of St. Louis and a trustee of the St. Louis Public Library. He endowed, either through gifts of rare books, art objects, or financial assistance, the School of Fine Arts and the libraries at Washington University, the Missouri Historical Society, the Mercantile Library, the St. Louis Academy of Science, and the St. Louis Artists' Guild. Bixby served on the board of directors of the Louisiana Purchase Exposition and the Commission on Fine Arts. Often, as in the case of the City Art Museum, the Missouri Historical Society, or the Washington University School of Fine Arts, his participation became instrumental in securing permanent structures to house collections and programs.

Bixby was known far beyond the bounds of Missouri as an international collector of manuscript Americana, and literary manuscripts of the world classics. Both Washington University and the Missouri Historical Society benefited from this prodigious collecting. He gave the society a large collection of Lincoln and Washington correspondence, and the largest collection of Thomas Jefferson letters amassed privately up to that time.

One of the most interesting features of Bixby's book- and manuscript-collecting genius was his privately funded publishing program for works he had acquired. Often he created highly useful first printings of original correspondence and disseminated it to libraries nationwide. In this way he produced and distributed the famous *Journal* of Maj. John André, Alexander Hamilton's *Itinerarium,* and the *Private Journal of Aaron Burr.* Bixby also published works of local Missouri interest such as *Grant in St. Louis,* by Walter Stevens, and *The Brown-Reynolds Duel: A Complete Documentary of the Last Bloodshed under the Code between St. Louisans.* He also published various poems of **Eugene Field** in elaborately illustrated editions.

Bixby's library became huge. Through a series of great sales at auction, Bixby helped place many important rarities in the hands of other collectors whose libraries formed the nuclei for several noted research libraries. He associated with Henry E. Huntington, founder of the Huntington Library in San Marino, California; A. S. W. Rosenback, the famed bookseller; and other bibliophiles of his time. Before dispersal Bixby's collections held a staggering array of American, British, and French literary manuscripts, literary first editions, and early printings of classic American works, including the double elephant folio of John James Audubon's *Birds of America.* He possessed other noted works as varied as the letters of Lord Byron or Samuel Taylor Coleridge to manuscripts by Davy Crockett, the war correspondence of **Ulysses S. Grant,** and a most extensive collection of letters by Nathaniel Hawthorne.

Virtually all the newly developing bibliographical organizations of a century past—from the Bibliographical Society of America, to the Grolier Club, to the Bibliophile Society (for which he published numerous works), to the Club of Odd Volumes in Boston—counted Bixby among their strongest friends and supporters. In St. Louis Bixby aided the Franklin Club, which exhibited collections based on his research; the Round Table, an organization of civic leaders; and the Burns Club. He also was a supporter of the American Red Cross.

St. Louisans long appreciated Bixby's role as a great cultural benefactor to their city. He was considered the guiding spirit for the city's art museums, libraries, and universities in the early years of this century. At his death on October 29, 1931, St. Louis poured out its respect to one of its first citizens. The City Art Museum closed at noon on the day of the funeral, and the west wing of the Jefferson Memorial closed for a day. There were 180 honorary pallbearers, including **August A. Busch,** W. H. Danforth, John H. Olin, **John Joseph Glennon,** Morton May, and Edward Mallinckrodt, a final testament of the civic leadership Bixby had inspired.

JOHN NEAL HOOVER

Bixby, William K. *List of Books Privately Printed by William K. Bixby.* St. Louis and Boston: Merrymount Press, 1919.

Defty, Sally Bixby. *The First Hundred Years.* St. Louis: Washington University School of Fine Arts, 1979.

Hoover, John Neal. "The Forgotten Legacy of William K. Bixby: Philanthropist, Book Collector, and Friend of Libraries." St. Louis Mercantile Library Association Annual Report, 1987.

Shaddy, Robert A. "Book Collecting in Missouri: Three Custodians of Culture." *Missouri Historical Review* 86:4 (July 1992): 363–85.

St. Louis Globe-Democrat. Clipping files and morgue. St. Louis Mercantile Library Special Collections, St. Louis.

BLAIR, EMILY NEWELL (1877–1951)

Writer, suffragist, national Democratic Party political leader, and feminist, Emily Newell Blair was born in Joplin, Missouri, on January 9, 1877, the eldest daughter of James Patton and Ann Cynthia Gray Newell. After graduating from Carthage High School in 1894, she attended the Woman's College of Baltimore (later Goucher College) and the University of Missouri. When her father died, she returned to her family's home in Carthage, Missouri, to help support and care for her brother and three sisters. For a time, she taught school in Sarcoxie, Missouri.

On Christmas Eve 1900 Newell married high school classmate Harry Wallace Blair. After he graduated from Columbian Law School (later George Washington University), they moved to Carthage where Harry practiced law and Emily devoted herself to homemaking, rearing their two children (Harriet and Newell), and participating in various social and civic activities. On September 16, 1909, the Blairs joined an innovative group of Carthage residents in establishing a cooperative kitchen. Renting a home and hiring a manager, they turned the first floor into a dining area and rented out the upstairs rooms. Until January 1, 1912, the cooperative provided three meals a day for participating families.

With her husband's encouragement, Blair began her writing career in 1909 when she sold her first article, "Letters of a Contented Wife," to *Cosmopolitan.* After quickly selling two more, she began writing on a regular basis. At the same time, her work on a countywide bond campaign for the almshouse sparked her interest in the world beyond her limited Carthage social circle. With the rejuvenation of the suffrage issue, Blair became active in the local campaign, moving to a state position in 1914 when she became publicity chair for the Missouri Equal Suffrage Association and the first editor of its monthly publication, the *Missouri Woman.*

After U.S. entry into World War I, Blair became vice chairman of the Missouri Woman's Committee of the Council of Defense. When her husband went abroad for the YMCA, she moved to Washington and accepted a position in the publicity department of the Women's Committee of the Council of Defense, working for Ida Tarbell and Anna Howard Shaw. In 1920 Blair published its history, *The Woman's Committee, U.S. Council of National Defense: An Interpretive Report.*

Although she had been a founder of the League of Women Voters, Blair turned her talents to working within the state Democratic Party structure. In 1921 she was elected Missouri's committeewoman on the Democratic National Committee, and in the following year she was chosen to be vice chairman in charge of organizing women voters, a position she held until 1928. Relying on experience gained in the suffrage campaign and defense work, Blair organized more than two thousand Democratic women's clubs, established regional training programs for women party workers, and created a national Democratic Women's Clubhouse in Washington, D.C.

Petite, poised, and quietly effective, Blair was every inch a lady; she was also a cool, polished, and practical politician. The author of one profile referred to "that gentle exterior and feminine beauty of hers which masks an analytical mind and a steel will." In her autobiography Blair remembered how she was described by Virginia's Democratic senator Carter Glass: "I was like the drink called Southern Comfort which goes down so smooth and easily but has an awful kick afterwards."

Early in her political career Blair had thought that with training and experience, women could become the "co-partners" of men by "boring from within" in party politics, gaining power on merit without regard to gender. Her tenure on the national committee changed her mind. Since gaining suffrage, women had lost political clout. Men had realized that since women did not vote as a bloc, male politicians could conveniently ignore them. Blair's solution was feminism. Because men did not accept female leadership, women's only alternative was to build their own power base within existing party structures. They must, Blair contended, organize and support strong women candidates for office who could lead the demand for equality.

While deeply involved in politics, Blair never neglected her writing career, publishing articles on the home as well as on political and feminist topics. From 1925 to 1933 she was an associate editor of *Good Housekeeping,* writing a monthly book column. In 1930 she published a book on home decorating, *The Creation of a Home,* and in 1931 a novel, *A Woman of Courage.*

In 1932 Blair worked hard for the Democratic Party as director of the Bureau of Women's Clubs. She was part of the network of prominent women who were active in securing positions for women in the New Deal. Appointed to the Consumers' Advisory Board of the National Industrial Recovery Act, she became its chairman in 1935. Her last public service came in 1942 when she was appointed chief of the women's interest section of the War Department's Bureau of Public Relations. In 1944 she suffered a stroke. Emily Newell Blair died in Alexandria, Virginia, on August 3, 1951.

VIRGINIA J. LAAS

Blair, Emily Newell. Papers. "Autobiography." Western Reserve Historical Society Manuscript Collection, Cleveland.

Evans, Ernestine. "Women in the Washington Scene." *Century Magazine* (August 1923): 507–17.

Hard, Ann. "Emily Newell Blair, 'Politician.' " *Woman Citizen* (April 1926): 15–16, 40, 42.

Laas, Virginia Jeans, ed. *Bridging Two Eras: The Autobiography of Emily Newell Blair, 1877–1951.* Columbia: University of Missouri Press, 1999.

"Profile of Emily Newell Blair." *Missouri Historical Review* 63 (October 1968): 135.

Ware, Susan. *Beyond Suffrage: Women in the New Deal.* Cambridge: Harvard University Press, 1981.

BLAIR, FRANCIS PRESTON, JR. (1821–1875)

Frank Blair, Union general, congressman, and senator, was born February 19, 1821, at Lexington, Kentucky, the third and youngest son of Francis Preston and Eliza Gist Blair. At the time his father was the circuit-court clerk of Franklin County, but the senior Blair would gain fame later as a newspaper editor, particularly after Andrew Jackson called him to Washington in 1830 to take charge of the *Washington Globe.* The father's political influence would be a dominant factor in the development of Frank's career, with the senior Blair eventually harboring strong presidential ambitions for his youngest son.

Frank Blair grew up in the shadow of the Jackson White House, and he would maintain a lifelong devotion to Old Hickory and the ideals of Jacksonian Democracy, as he understood them. Educated in private schools, he proved popular with his fellow students but was hardly dedicated to his studies. He attended both Yale University and the University of North Carolina, from both of which he was expelled, before graduating from Princeton University in 1842, his degree held back for a year because of a riotous party a few weeks before he was originally due to graduate. In the meantime he had gone to Transylvania University Law School in Lexington, from which he graduated in 1843. He spent that spring and summer in Washington writing editorials for his father at the *Globe* before going to St. Louis in the fall to begin the practice of law with his brother **Montgomery Blair.**

In the fall of 1845, having suffered some health problems, Frank Blair decided to join a "buffalo hunt" along the Santa Fe Trail. He spent the winter with his cousin George Bent in Bent's Fort in eastern Colorado. He was still there when the Mexican War broke out the following spring. Caught up in the excitement, he joined Gen. **Stephen Watts Kearny**'s expedition when it came through on the way to Santa Fe. Kearny appointed Blair attorney general at Santa Fe. Working with **Alexander W. Doniphan, Willard Preble Hall,** and **David Waldo,** Blair drew up an American Code of Law for the liberated region of New Mexico and tried several cases in the newly established circuit court there before returning to St. Louis in the summer of 1847. On September 8, 1847, he married Appoline Alexander of Woodford County, Kentucky, a distant cousin, and they established their permanent home in St. Louis where Frank resumed the practice of law. They had eight children.

To Frank Blair, however, his legal practice always took second place to his interest in politics. Although owning slaves himself, he became a strong supporter of the Free Soil movement and in the presidential election of 1848 briefly established a Free Soil newspaper, the *Barnburner,* to champion the cause of Martin Van Buren. A devotee of his father's close friend Sen. **Thomas Hart Benton,** in whose law office he had taken additional training, Blair took an active role in Benton's unsuccessful campaign to save his Senate seat in 1850 following his split with **Claiborne Fox Jackson** and **David Rice Atchison** over the question of slavery extension. He would continue to champion Benton's cause throughout numerous other election campaigns in the 1850s.

Blair joined his cousin **B. Gratz Brown** and several others in July 1852 to purchase the *St. Louis Morning Signal,* which they promptly renamed the *Missouri Democrat.* Blair and Brown used this organ to promote their successful candidacies for the Missouri legislature that fall as well as the election of Benton to the United States House of Representatives. Through the editorial pages of the *Democrat* as well as their newly gained legislative seats, the two men openly opposed the extension of slavery into new territories and denounced the Kansas-Nebraska Act of 1854, which opened the door for proslavery settlers to enter Kansas.

In the 1856 presidential election Blair supported **John Charles Frémont** while securing his own election to Congress as a Free Soiler. In his maiden speech in Congress Blair argued that slavery was doomed in the South and urged the adoption of a policy of gradual emancipation coupled with the deportation and colonization of the freed slaves in Central America. This remained a major theme as he moved to the forefront of the newly emerging Republican Party and became one of its chief spokesmen in the late 1850s. He assisted Abraham Lincoln in his 1858 unsuccessful Illinois senatorial contest with Stephen A. Douglas and thereby developed a strong friendship that would continue throughout the Civil War. Blair's own contest for reelection also appeared unsuccessful that fall as initial returns indicated that his opponent Richard Barret had won by 426 votes. Blair contested

the election, however, and was eventually seated by the House of Representatives in a narrow vote. Over the next two years he suffered a series of financial reverses brought on by his bad habit of co-signing notes for various relatives and friends.

Although initially supporting the candidacy of Missouri's favorite son **Edward Bates** for the Republican presidential nomination in 1860, Blair quickly endorsed Lincoln's candidacy when the Republican convention turned to the Illinoisan. He himself was running for reelection to Congress. He organized a support group known as the Wide Awakes, who marched with him from one rally to another, often battling with supporters of other candidates who sought to break up Republican rallies. Following his own reelection in August, Blair campaigned extensively for Lincoln throughout Missouri, Illinois, and Pennsylvania. In the aftermath of Lincoln's election, Frank's brother Montgomery was chosen postmaster general in the new cabinet, while his father became a close personal adviser to the new president. Frank himself visited Lincoln in Springfield to strengthen the already existing bond between the two.

With the election of **Claiborne Fox Jackson** as governor, Missouri found itself divided between a pro-Confederate state executive and a majority of citizens who wished to remain neutral in any impending contest between North and South. Blair, on the other hand, was staunchly committed to the preservation of the Union with Missouri an integral part of it. He reorganized his Wide Awakes into Home Guards, drilling them secretly to prepare for any untoward move by the governor. When Jackson refused to furnish volunteers for the Union army in the wake of Fort Sumter, Blair and a newfound ally, Capt. **Nathaniel Lyon,** offered the Home Guards, who were promptly accepted. Having organized a Committee of Public Safety, the two men developed a plan of defense for the federal arsenal in south St. Louis with its sixty thousand stand of arms.

When Governor Jackson mustered the state militia into a weeklong training operation in early May 1861, Blair and Lyon immediately suspected that the governor had designs on the arsenal. On May 10 they surrounded the St. Louis encampment known as Camp Jackson with their newly mustered Home Guards and demanded its surrender. Although the militia complied, bloodshed occurred in the aftermath, and St. Louis was plunged into panic. The state legislature, meeting at Jefferson City, quickly passed bills giving the governor broad military powers to defend the state. A temporary truce between state and federal forces lasted a month until Blair and Lyon forced a showdown with state officials at the Planters' House in St. Louis on June 11. The state government was now driven into exile as Lyon and Blair moved forces up the Missouri River to occupy the state capital and defeat Jackson's newly organized Missouri State Guard at Boonville.

When Congress convened the following month, Blair was defeated for Speaker of the House by Galusha Grow of Pennsylvania but was chosen chairman of the Committee on Military Defense where he did yeoman's work to help organize the war effort. At the instigation of the Blairs, Gen. **John C. Frémont** was appointed to command the Department of the West at St. Louis. Blair quickly became disillusioned with Frémont, however, because of his failure to support Lyon in the field and disputes over procurement contracts. His criticism of Frémont led to his arrest by the general, but in the end the Blairs prevailed as Frémont was removed from his command by Lincoln. This caused Frank to lose much of the German support, which had previously been his, because of the Germans' enthusiasm for Frémont's emancipation policy.

In the late summer of 1862, Blair raised seven regiments from throughout the Mississippi Valley for the Union cause and received an appointment as brigadier general. He fought with valor at Chickasaw Bayou near Vicksburg in December and actively participated throughout the entire Vicksburg campaign. Promoted to major general, he later commanded the Fifteenth and Seventeenth Corps, respectively, during the Chattanooga and Atlanta campaigns.

In the interim, between the two campaigns Blair returned to Congress at Lincoln's request to help defend his plan for Reconstruction against Radical assaults. In two fiery speeches on February 5 and 27, 1864, Blair attacked Secy. of the Treasury Salmon Chase for his policies in the Mississippi Valley and his presidential ambitions while deriding Missouri Radicals, who had falsely accused him of misappropriating funds while in the military. He then returned to his military command, leaving his enemies in Congress sufficiently infuriated that they unseated him in favor of Samuel Knox, who had been contesting his election.

Blair ably led the Seventeenth Corps with Gen. **William T. Sherman** in the fight for Atlanta and the March to the Sea and through the Carolinas. Declining a postwar military career, Blair returned to Missouri to take up his law practice and try to salvage his political career. Financially ruined by having devoted so much to the Union cause, he tried without success to retrieve his lost fortune through the leasing of a cotton plantation in Mississippi. Frank strongly opposed the Radical Constitution of 1865 and the proscriptive policies of that party, which now controlled Missouri. He challenged the test oath for voting in the courts, but ultimately lost the case on a tie vote in the United States Supreme Court.

Blair helped reorganize the Democratic Party in opposition and campaigned extensively throughout the state for its candidates in the elections of 1866 and 1868. Gaining widespread national recognition for his attacks on Radical Reconstruction, he was nominated by the national party for vice president in 1868. His highly controversial letter to **James Broadhead,** in which he advocated the overthrow of congressional Reconstruction by strong presidential authority, greatly handicapped the campaign, however, and helped lead to the Democratic defeat.

In the wake of the Liberal Republican split with the Radicals in Missouri in 1870, Blair advocated the "possum policy" of support for the Liberal Republican state ticket while running Democratic candidates in the legislative races. This proved successful, resulting in the election of his cousin B. Gratz Brown as governor. In the aftermath Blair was elected to the United States Senate to replace **Charles Daniel Drake,** who had resigned to accept a federal judgeship. In the Senate Blair strongly defended the course of the South in challenging Radical Reconstruction through such organizations as the Ku Klux Klan. He played a major role in arranging the 1872 Liberal Republican ticket of Horace Greeley and B. Gratz Brown.

In the aftermath of the election, Blair was stricken by a crippling stroke in November 1872, and sought recovery in a sanitarium at Clifton Springs, New York. In view of this, the Democrats in the state legislature rejected his bid for reelection to a full Senate term that winter. Gov. **Silas Woodson** appointed him state superintendent of insurance to help provide income, but the work of the office was largely left to deputies as Blair continued to pursue efforts to regain his health. He died at his home in St. Louis on July 9, 1875, following a fall. At his death there was a large outpouring of sympathy for the man who had dominated Missouri politics for the past twenty years. His friends raised funds for the erection of a statue that stands in Forest Park in St. Louis, and he is commemorated, together with Benton, as one of Missouri's two representatives in Statuary Hall in the national Capitol.

Highly controversial in his lifetime, Frank Blair was either strongly admired or hated by the public and political figures of his day. Convivial and generous to a fault, he could also excoriate his enemies in biting terms. An impassioned orator, he held strongly to opinions with which he had been imbued in his Jacksonian youth as his world changed dramatically around him.

Acclaimed by both Sherman and Grant as one of the best of the non–West Point–trained generals during the war, he lived and breathed politics, which became his consuming passion.

WILLIAM E. PARRISH

Blair Family. Papers. Library of Congress, Washington, D.C.

Blair Family. Papers. Missouri Historical Society, St. Louis.

Blair-Lee Family. Papers. Firestone Library, Princeton University, Princeton, N.J.

Laas, Virginia Jeans. *Wartime Washington: The Civil War Letters of Elizabeth Blair Lee.* Urbana: University of Illinois Press, 1991.

Parrish, William E. *Frank Blair: Lincoln's Conservative.* Columbia: University of Missouri Press, 1998.

Smith, William E. *The Francis Preston Blair Family in Politics.* 2 vols. New York: Macmillan, 1933.

BLAIR, JAMES THOMAS, JR. (1902–1962)

As the forty-fifth governor of Missouri, James T. Blair Jr. addressed a wide array of problems, including human rights, welfare, and education. Legislation passed during his term promised to improve the quality of life for Missourians of all races and ages, but emphasized providing equal opportunities for the disadvantaged.

Born March 15, 1902, in Maysville, Missouri, Blair attended public schools in Jefferson City and the Staunton Military Academy in Virginia. As a young child Blair played with the sons of Gov. **Herbert Hadley** and dreamed of living in the Governor's Mansion in Jefferson City. With the encouragement of his father, a Missouri Supreme Court justice, two-term representative in the Missouri General Assembly, and St. Louis attorney, Blair pursued his childhood dreams. He attended Southwest Missouri State Teachers College and the University of Missouri. He then earned his law degree from Tennessee's Cumberland University in 1924, and after passing the bar exam began practicing law in Jefferson City. On July 17, 1926, Blair married Emilie Chorn of Kansas City, Missouri. The Blairs raised two children, James Thomas III and Mary Margaret.

Blair's political career took off during the Republican landslide of 1925 when he achieved the sole Democratic victory in Jefferson City with his election to the office of city attorney. In 1928 the voters of Cole County elected Blair to the Missouri House of Representatives. In 1930 the Missouri State Bar Association elected Blair as its president. Reelected to a second term in the legislature, he won the position of majority floor leader in 1931, the youngest Missourian to do so. In 1932 he returned to his law practice in Jefferson City. Blair acted as chairman of the Cole County Democratic Committee for eight years, and served as a delegate to the Democratic National Convention in Philadelphia in 1936.

During World War II Blair served as an officer in the air force in the European theater. He received several medals for his efforts during the war, including the Air Medal for his participation in night flights from England to Africa, which the War Department hailed as "the longest massed, unescorted nonstop troop-carrier flight ever successfully performed . . . in spite of adverse weather conditions and communication conditions and in the face of enemy fighter activity." The air force promoted Blair from major to lieutenant colonel after he helped organize the placement of airborne troops into the Cherbourg peninsula in France to prepare for the arrival of seaborne troops. Blair also received the Bronze Star, the Legion of Merit, the Presidential Unit Citation, and eleven battle stars. He returned to Missouri after his discharge in 1945.

In 1947 Blair ran successfully for mayor of Jefferson City and became known as one of the most innovative mayors of his time. The next year he resigned following his election as lieutenant governor of Missouri, an office he held for eight years. In 1956 Blair won the governorship, defeating Republican Lon Hocker by a margin of 74,718 votes.

As governor Blair fought to end discrimination and segregation in Missouri. He proposed to establish a committee to work toward mutual respect and understanding among ethnic, racial, and religious groups. Governor Blair boldly proclaimed to the General Assembly, "Always and everywhere I will identify myself with any victim of oppression or discrimination, whoever or wherever he may be, and I will support him. . . ." In May 1957 the Missouri General Assembly created the Missouri Commission on Human Rights.

By April 1958 the United States faced a recession with unemployment topping 5 million. Blair believed that the federal government should support the state's public-assistance programs, which were consuming one-third of Missouri's tax revenue. When the federal government announced its intention to limit matching funds for the administrative costs of public-assistance programs, Blair appealed to U.S. Representative **Clarence A. Cannon** to overturn the decision. He also worked to improve what he considered to be an inefficient and inadequate welfare system in Missouri. Blair believed that liberal requirements for welfare recipients allowed too many people to obtain financial assistance, thus decreasing the stipends for those who needed them most. The welfare system also lacked an adequate health-care program for public-assistance recipients. Blair wanted to increase the number of public-health units and improve the Federal Disability Insurance Program by extending aid to all disabled persons, regardless of age.

Blair's experiences as a member and two-time president of the Jefferson City Board of Education helped shape his education policies. As governor he established a Council on Higher Education to deal with such issues as enrollment, finances, and curriculum in Missouri colleges. He supported legislation that established a number of junior colleges in Missouri, which lessened the strain on four-year colleges and reduced educational expenses for students. Blair supported the addition of a four-year school of medicine at the University of Missouri. He also established a commission to look after the educational needs of handicapped and retarded children.

A champion of the elderly citizens of Missouri, Blair set up an agency to investigate the needs of the aged and to make recommendations to the legislature. He wanted to transfer a number of senile people out of state mental institutions into homes for the aged or to family care. Blair supported the Nursing Home Licensing Law that tightened the regulations on safety in nursing homes and provided for inspections and tougher penalties for homes that did not comply.

In addition, Blair established the first effective system for controlling state governmental financing by creating the budget review and control office. He also placed the state's idle funds in interest-bearing accounts. He secured motor-vehicle speed limits, while increasing the ability of the State Highway Patrol to oversee Missouri's highways. Finally, his administration sponsored improvements in penal and mental-health programs.

After completing his term as governor, Blair continued to be involved in politics. He supported Missouri's U.S. senator **William Stuart Symington** in his bid for the presidential nomination at the 1960 Democratic National Convention. Blair himself was considered to be a vice presidential possibility had the presidential nominee been an easterner. When controversy arose over John F. Kennedy's Catholicism during the 1960 presidential campaign, Blair supported him, feeling that religion should not be a factor.

Two years after leaving office, Blair and his wife, Emilie, died of carbon-monoxide poisoning in their home in Jefferson City on July 12, 1962.

ERIKA K. NELSON

Blair, James T., Jr. Papers. 1902–1962. Western Historical Manuscripts Collection, Columbia.
March, David D. *The History of Missouri.* New York: Lewis Historical Publishing, 1967.
"Historical Notes and Comments." *Missouri Historical Review* 57 (October 1962): 98–100.
New York Times, July 13, 1962.
Official Manual of the State of Missouri, 1957–1958. Jefferson City: Secretary of State, 1958.

BLAIR, MONTGOMERY (1813–1883)

Montgomery Blair, a lawyer and postmaster general, was born May 10, 1813, in Franklin County, Kentucky, the eldest son of Francis Preston and Eliza Gist Blair. His father was active in local politics but moved into a position of national prominence following the presidential election of Andrew Jackson, when he became editor of the *Washington Globe.* As in the case of Montgomery's younger brother, **Frank Blair,** the father's political influence would play a major role in his elder son's career. The Blairs were a close-knit family, constantly consulting with one another in matters political and personal.

Educated in the local Kentucky schools, Montgomery Blair entered Transylvania University in 1830 to pursue a legal career. The following year, at his father's insistence, he reluctantly accepted an appointment from President Jackson to the United States Military Academy at West Point. He graduated with honors in 1836, having taken an extra year because of illness. Following a year's service in the Seminole War, he resigned his commission as a second lieutenant to resume his legal studies at Transylvania University.

Admitted to the bar in 1839, Blair settled in St. Louis as a protégé of **Thomas Hart Benton,** a longtime family friend. The Benton connection proved beneficial as Blair immersed himself in cases dealing with Spanish land claims and corporate law, securing the business of several railroad companies. He also engaged in extensive real estate speculation in the rapidly growing community and became active in local Democratic politics. Appointed U.S. district attorney in 1841, he served until early 1844 when he accepted a judgeship on the court of common pleas. He also served one term as mayor of St. Louis, from 1842 to 1843. He continued on the court until 1849 when he resigned to return to private practice with his brother Frank, who had moved to St. Louis in 1843.

The Blair brothers became actively involved in Martin Van Buren's campaign for the presidency on the Free Soil ticket in 1848, briefly establishing a Free Soil newspaper, the *Barnburner,* in St. Louis to champion the cause. They and their father remained committed to the Free Soil movement throughout the 1850s, though Montgomery left the active pursuit of politics to Frank while he concentrated on his legal practice.

At the strong urging of his father, Montgomery moved to Washington, D.C., in 1853 and took up residence at 1651 Pennsylvania Avenue, across from the White House, in a home that his father had given him. The Blair mansion quickly became a social center for official Washington. Montgomery also maintained a home near his parents in Silver Spring, Maryland, and became actively involved in political affairs there. He soon built a reputable law practice, practicing chiefly before the United States Supreme Court. President Pierce appointed him solicitor of the U.S. Court of Claims in 1855, but President Buchanan removed him two years later because of his adherence to the new Republican Party. In the interim he served as attorney for the slave **Dred Scott** in his appeal to the Supreme Court, which greatly increased Blair's stature with the antislavery forces.

Blair presided over the Maryland Republican convention in 1860 and served as a delegate to the national-party conclave in Chicago. As a result of the strong activity of the Blair family on behalf of the Lincoln ticket, Montgomery was appointed postmaster general in the new president's cabinet. He performed admirably in this post, instituting a number of important changes, including free delivery in the cities, money orders, and the sorting and distribution of mail on postal railroad cars. He championed a uniform system for the international exchange of mail and took the lead in calling a conference of fifteen nations at Paris in 1863 that ultimately resulted in the creation of the Universal Postal Union. Blair also organized an efficient military mail system in which each regiment had its own postmaster, and service personnel could send mail unstamped with the postage paid by the recipients.

Politically, Montgomery Blair constituted part of the conservative wing of the Lincoln cabinet, together with Atty. Gen. **Edward Bates** and Secy. of the Navy Gideon Welles. He was the lone cabinet supporter of Lincoln's plan to reinforce Fort Sumter in 1861 and remained one of the president's closest advisers throughout the war. The Blair family supported compensated emancipation with colonization, which led them into direct conflict with the emerging Radical wing of the Republican Party. This ultimately led Lincoln to reluctantly request Montgomery's resignation in the fall of 1864 as a part of his reelection program.

In the aftermath of the Civil War, Blair became a close adviser to President Andrew Johnson, urging him in vain to reorganize the cabinet. He supported the Lincoln-Johnson moderate plan of Reconstruction as the best hope for reconciling the South to the Union, decrying the disfranchisement of Southern whites and the enfranchisement of the freedmen. This again brought him and his family into conflict with the Radicals, and by 1868 they were back in the Democratic Party, where Montgomery remained until his death on July 27, 1883. He championed the cause of Samuel J. Tilden in the presidential contest of 1876, helping to establish a Washington-based paper, the *Union,* to uphold his claims and serving as his counsel before the electoral commission charged with making the final decision. Blair's only political race came in 1882 when he was an unsuccessful candidate for Congress.

An outstanding lawyer who researched and argued his cases well, Blair was a familiar figure before the United States Supreme Court. He strongly supported the political and military career of his brother Frank in Missouri and, together with their father, served him as a key adviser. Montgomery Blair married twice: in 1836 to Caroline Buckner of Virginia, who died in childbirth in 1844, leaving him with two children, the youngest of whom died shortly thereafter; and in 1846 to Mary Elizabeth Woodbury of New Hampshire, with whom he had five children.

WILLIAM E. PARRISH

Blair Family. Papers. Library of Congress, Washington, D.C.

Blair Family. Papers. Missouri Historical Society, St. Louis.

Blair-Lee Family. Papers. Firestone Library, Princeton University, Princeton, N.J.

Laas, Virginia Jeans, ed. *Wartime Washington: The Civil War Letters of Elizabeth Blair Lee.* Urbana: University of Illinois Press, 1991.

Smith, Elbert B. *Francis Preston Blair.* New York: Free Press, 1980.

Smith, William E. *The Francis Preston Blair Family in Politics.* 2 vols. New York: Macmillan, 1933.

BLAND, RICHARD PARKS (1835–1899)

Bland, a member of the United States House of Representatives from Missouri for twenty-four years, was so inextricably tied to the silver issue that he was known as "Silver Dick." He was born in Kentucky on August 19, 1835, to Stoughton and Margaret Parks Nall Bland. Orphaned at fourteen he worked as a farm laborer until he migrated to Missouri in 1854. Two years later he joined a band heading for California, but he discovered he was too late to gain riches in gold. He drifted into the Nevada Territory where the silver strikes had begun. By day he worked in the mines; at night he read law books. Even though he had only a common-school education, Bland aspired to become a lawyer.

In 1869 Bland returned to Missouri, began a law practice in Rolla, and engaged in local Democratic activities. In 1872 the congressional-district convention chose Bland as the Democratic candidate for representative from the Fifth District. He won the election, leading to a long career in Washington, D.C.

When Bland took office in December 1873, currency had become the paramount question for many citizens. The issue was anything but simple, nor were its implications understood even by the economists of the day, much less the politicians or their constituents. Economics itself had not yet become a science but was still associated with moral philosophy; hence the arguments tended to be waged in moral terms. To say that Bland lacked understanding of the issue or of the implications of the course he espoused is only to say he was one of a very large company. However, as time passed and the new social sciences began to appear in some leading universities, Bland failed to study their findings or change his preconceived ideas.

Bland claimed that by increasing the volume of money the federal government could ensure the prosperity of farmers and laborers. By 1873, as the silver strikes uncovered great lodes, coining all the silver brought to the mint would tremendously enlarge the number of dollars in circulation. Just prior to Bland's arrival, Congress had dropped the silver dollar from the list of coins because so little silver was coming to the mint. When the discovery of new lodes changed that situation, the silver producers began a campaign for the resumption of silver coinage. Depressed farmers, confused by the new style of commercial agriculture brought about by the development of a world market, joined the demand for unlimited coinage of silver at the old ratio. Urban laborers, on the other hand, viewed inflated currency in terms of prices rising faster than wages. Repeatedly, Bland offered bills calling for silver coinage that reflected farmers' desires but not laborers'. One such measure, the Bland-Allison Act, passed, although Congress amended it to limit the amount of silver coined.

The silver issue came to a climax in 1896. Silverites gained control of Democratic local and state organizations in states and territories of the South, Far West, and central Midwest to command a two-thirds majority in the national convention, giving them the ability to write the platform and choose the presidential candidate. In recognition of his long identification with silver, the Missouri State Democratic Convention instructed the state's delegates to support Bland.

Those who were masterminding silver strategy were less than enthusiastic about Bland. Obviously, they wanted a winner, and Bland did not look like one. He was colorless, plodding, and unimaginative. Beyond the sobriquet of "Silver Dick," he was little known outside the halls of Congress and his own state. He was not clearly associated with any other issue, but even his chances of attracting silver Republicans or members of the third party were dim. On the new issues facing the nation, Bland's views were negative and retrogressive.

The Missouri delegation fulfilled its obligation by nominating Bland and staying with him for five ballots. When the stampede for William Jennings Bryan began on the sixth ballot, Bland's candidacy ended. Since he had remained on his farm near Lebanon perhaps he was not greatly surprised or displeased. Although he had not entered the congressional race in 1896, he ran again in 1898, won and returned to Congress for the final time. He came home in 1899 to recover, he hoped, from a severe throat infection that had plagued him in the spring. Instead, he suffered a relapse, grew progressively worse, and died on July 15. By then the silver issue had ended, with returning prosperity, rising opportunities for more people to attain middle-class status, and increasing availability of new products that made life more comfortable.

Bland was not a leader in the broader sense. He failed to comprehend the profound alteration of American society that took place in the late nineteenth century; consequently he could not deal with its problems. He followed the thinking of his constituents.

RUTH WARNER TOWNE

Clevenger, Homer. "Agrarian Politics in Missouri, 1880–1895." Ph.D. diss., University of Missouri, 1940.

Haswell, Harold Atchison, Jr. "The Public Life of Congressman Richard Parks Bland." Ph.D. diss., University of Missouri, 1951.

Redfield, Maynard Gregg. "The Political Campaign of 1896 in Missouri." Master's thesis, University of Missouri, 1946.

Towne, Ruth Warner. *Senator William J. Stone and the Politics of Compromise.* Port Washington, N.Y.: Kennikat Press, 1979.

BLOW, HENRY TAYLOR (1817–1875)

Henry Taylor Blow, U.S. congressman and noted St. Louis businessman and civic leader during the Civil War period, is most often remembered as a benefactor in **Dred Scott**'s famous slave suit for freedom and as the father of **Susan Elizabeth Blow,** founder of the first kindergarten in America in 1873.

Born July 15, 1817, in Virginia, Blow was one of ten children born to Peter and Elizabeth Blow. When he was still a child, his family migrated west, arriving in St. Louis in 1830 along with their slaves, including one named Dred Scott. With no money for land, the family rented a large house at Seventh and Market Streets and opened a hotel. Money problems continued, and the slave Dred Scott was sold to a United States Army surgeon named John Emerson. Shortly after, Peter and Elizabeth Blow died, and the Blow children were left on their own.

Fortunately, one of the older Blow daughters married **Joseph Charless Jr.,** a member of a wealthy and well-established St. Louis family, and he soon began handling the Blow family affairs, enrolling Henry Blow in St. Louis College. After graduation, Blow studied law but abandoned that idea in favor of commercial pursuits, joining his brother-in-law's wholesale drug and paint firm as a clerk. Blow did well and in 1836 at age nineteen became a partner in the company, and the firm's name was changed to Charless, Blow, and Company. In 1840 Blow married Minerva Grimsley, daughter of **Thornton Grimsley,** a prominent manufacturer of saddles and member of the St. Louis Board of Aldermen. To this union six children were born, one of whom was Susan, born in 1843.

Blow continued to prosper in business, and when Charless and Blow dissolved their partnership in 1844, Blow kept the manufacturing portion and developed it into the Collier White Lead and Oil Company, one of the largest manufacturing firms in the city. Later it expanded to include a large lead-mining and smelting works in Newton County, Missouri.

In 1846 when Dred Scott filed for freedom, Blow, along with other members of the family, supported the slave, often providing attorneys and sometimes money. Blow testified on behalf of Scott on June 30, 1847, at his first state-court trial. Reports that Blow encouraged Scott to file his freedom suit are not supported, but the Blow family, including Henry, stood by the Scott family during the long eleven years of litigation and arranged for the family's eventual freedom after it was denied them by the United States Supreme Court in 1857.

Blow's political leanings were pro-Union and antislavery, and of all the Blow sons, he alone supported the Union cause during the Civil War. Active in the Free Soil movement, Blow later became a Republican and was a delegate to the 1860 Republican National Convention that nominated Abraham Lincoln.

In 1861 President Lincoln named Blow minister to Venezuela, but after a short time Blow resigned and returned to St. Louis. In 1862 he ran for the United States House of Representatives, and though his only other political office had been two terms in the Missouri State Senate, he was elected to Congress by a ten-to-one margin. He served two terms, from 1863 to 1867. As congressman he served on the committee on Reconstruction following the Civil War.

Blow declined to run for a third term, devoting time to other interests. Earlier he had been one of the five founders of the St. Louis Philharmonic Society. He also helped establish the Western Academy of Art and in 1866 organized the first public school in the French village of Carondelet, south of St. Louis. Blow and his family had fled to Carondelet in 1849 to escape the cholera in St. Louis. There on sixteen acres of wooded land he built a large Greek Revival mansion.

In 1869 Blow was appointed minister to Brazil, and in 1874, a year before his death, to the board of commissioners for the newly created District of Columbia, which had been upgraded by Congress from territorial status. Henry Blow died at Saratoga, New York, on September 11, 1875. In St. Louis an elementary school and a street bear his name.

KENNETH C. KAUFMAN

Bryan, John A. "The Blow Family and Their Slave Dred Scott." Parts 1 and 2. *Missouri Historical Society Bulletin* 4 (July 1948): 223–31; 5 (October 1948): 19–33.

Conard, Howard L., ed. *Encyclopedia of the History of Missouri.* New York: Southern History, 1901.

Lawson, John D. *American State Trials.* Vol. 14. St. Louis: Thomas Law Book Company, 1921.

Scharf, J. Thomas. *History of St. Louis City and County: From Earliest Periods to the Present Day.* Philadelphia: Everts, 1883.

BLOW, SUSAN ELIZABETH (1843–1916)

Susan Elizabeth Blow was born in St. Louis on June 7, 1843, during the turbulent years that preceded the Civil War. In those politically charged times, Blow came of age in a prominent and intellectual family. The eldest of six children, her family life directed her naturally toward education, and she eventually led the entire nation in establishing standards for schools in kindergarten education.

Blow's parents, Henry and Minerva Grimsley came from old-stock St. Louis families who emigrated from the South. Slave owners, they were also industrialists who earnestly desired to preserve the Union and end slavery. Henry's career in the lead industry enabled him to build a fortune. In 1849, when cholera claimed as many as seven thousand lives in St. Louis and a great fire destroyed most of the riverfront, including their home, Henry moved his wife and children to Carondelet, south of St. Louis.

Susan Blow's early education was typical and appropriate for a young lady of the time. Lessons began at home with her governesses, from whom she learned French. At age nine, she spent a year at William McCauley's School in New Orleans where she focused on grammar, arithmetic, reading, and French. She also tutored her younger siblings.

Blow's father recognized when she was young that she had an extraordinary intellect. "Sue must have the best advantage in education" he wrote home in 1857. On a business trip he discovered Miss Haines' School in New York City, and Susan Blow was enrolled in 1858. The school put into practice the latest educational trends from Western Europe. Blow attended until school was suspended in 1861 at the onset of the Civil War.

Back in St. Louis, with the encouragement of her father, Blow took her education further—reading voraciously from the family library. During the war her father was active as a Unionist and a Republican, and Blow no doubt absorbed his thinking and opinions.

Blow was introduced to a philosophical group called the St. Louis Society early in its history. This group of American and European intellectuals, which met to discuss Western European philosophy on Sunday afternoons, was officially formed in 1866 to back the publication of a translation of Hegel's *Larger Logic,* which had been rendered by one of its members. The group failed to achieve this goal but its meetings and the other publications of its members helped make St. Louis a national cultural center. Three men—**Henry Conrad Brokmeyer, William Torrey Harris,** and **Denton Jacques Snider**—are credited as founders. Snider, however, wrote of a fourth early member: Susan Blow.

Many community leaders participated in the society, wrestling with idealism, free thought, and interpretations of music, sculpture, literature, law, education, social organization, and all knowledge. Blow and Harris, who was St. Louis's superintendent of schools from 1867 to 1880, discussed education and the work of Frederick Froebel, a pioneer in early-childhood education.

After the Civil War, in 1869, President **Ulysses S. Grant** appointed **Henry Blow** minister to Brazil. Susan Blow accompanied her father as his secretary. Two years later, when the appointment ended, the family traveled to Europe and was given a grand tour by a Russian count, the beau and future husband of Susan's sister Nellie.

The tour was Susan Blow's opportunity to seek out Frederick Froebel and observe his series of classroom exercises for children ages three to six. In Froebel's plan, as children progressed, they were introduced to certain objects, called "Froebel's Gifts," to develop skills and intellectual powers. Gift one, for the youngest, was a set of six soft colored balls to teach color and, when rolled toward or away from the child, direction. Gift two—a solid sphere, cube, and cylinder—taught form and pointed out similarity and difference between objects. Gift three was a large cube cut into eight equal cubes, illustrating the idea of fractions. Using the gifts children were taught through play, first with their mothers and then in the kindergarten.

When they returned to Carondelet, the Blows found their community had been annexed to St. Louis and that a new school building was being planned. Blow met with Harris and persuaded him to explore the concept of kindergarten with his board. Harris appointed a committee. In their research, they learned that one public school system, in Newark, New Jersey, had a play school for young children and that those who attended benefited greatly. The committee recommended that the board proceed with a kindergarten program.

Blow returned to Miss Haines' School to meet with her old teacher and Maria Boelte, a German disciple of Froebel's who had come to New York to start a kindergarten. Throughout 1872 and part of 1873, Haines, Boelte, and Blow worked to develop a program for public schools that would influence education forever.

Kindergarten, according to Blow, should be a time of learning through play and creativity. "Through play the child becomes original and conscious of originality. He feels himself a creative first cause; rejoices in his sense of freedom; and is impelled to further exercise of creative activity. . . . Without this self-creative activity all human beings would tend to become tiresome repetitions of one dull pattern," she wrote in *Educational Issues* in 1909.

The Carondelet kindergarten room, in contrast to other classrooms of the time, was bright and colorful. Plants grew on the windowsills, and children sat on benches around low tables to play with blocks and string yarn through perforated pictures. Children learned about color, shapes, and fractions. There were lessons in hygiene, nutrition, and physical education. After this first year of exposure to structure and basic skills, children entered school ready to learn.

The kindergarten was successful. By 1879 the St. Louis school system had fifty-three kindergarten rooms, all designed by Blow. She found herself in demand as a teacher of teachers, a consultant and lecturer on the subjects called today early-childhood education, creativity, and self-esteem. One of two hundred women enrolled in an early class left an account: "I leaned forward to see one of the world's greatest educators. . . . She was small in stature with a slight, well-rounded face and graceful figure, a refined and keenly intellectual face, light brown hair and expressive blue eyes. She was altogether attractive and distinguished in appearance."

Harris left his post as superintendent in 1880. Although kindergartens were firmly established in the system, the loss of her old friend and colleague was certainly disheartening to Blow. Family obligations after the deaths of several siblings and both parents, plus the unbroken pace of her work, took their toll on her health. In 1887 she was diagnosed with Graves' disease. In 1891 her worsening illness prompted her to move to Cazenovia, New York, a beautiful and peaceful town far from the demands of St. Louis life, to recuperate.

Family members expected that she would not live, but Blow recovered and by 1895 took up her work again. She served as a board member on many national educational organizations and in 1898 began lecturing at Columbia University's Teachers College. Her six important books, *The Study of Dante, Symbolic Education, Mottoes and Commentaries of Froebel's Mother Play, Songs and Music of Froebel's*

Mother Play, Letters to a Mother, and *Educational Issues in the Classroom,* were published between 1890 and 1909.

Many of the ideas of Blow's time ring throughout her writings. Freedom, emancipation, self-expression, self-determination, and the opposite values of work and play are all discussed in her works. References to a wide variety of sources—from Sojourner Truth, to Martin Luther, to Oliver Cromwell, to the Koran—color her discussions, but mostly there is a focus on young children. "If we create in children a love for work, we shall not have a difficulty in making them persistently industrious," she wrote. "If we can make children love intellectual effort, we shall prolong habits of study beyond school years, and, if we can insure to children every day four hours of pleasurable activity without excitement, we lay a foundation for a strong, centered disposition."

As an old woman, Blow continued her career as a lecturer, sitting in a chair to speak because of her painful gout. She lectured until three weeks before her death. She died on March 26, 1916, and is buried in Bellefontaine Cemetery in the family plot.

MARGOT FORD MCMILLEN

Blow, Susan. *Educational Issues in the Kindergarten.* New York: D. Appleton, 1909.

Dains, Mary K., ed. *Show Me Missouri Women: Selected Biographies.* Kirksville, Mo.: Thomas Jefferson University Press, 1989.

Forbes, Cleon. "The St. Louis School of Thought." Master's thesis, Oklahoma University, 1929.

Menius, Joseph. *Susan Blow.* St. Clair, Mo.: Page One Publishing, 1993.

BODMER, KARL (1809–1893)

Among the early artists to explore the trans–Mississippi River frontier, Karl Bodmer's stay in St. Louis was perhaps the most brief. Yet, his extraordinary frontier images produced during a scientific expedition across North America from 1832 to 1834 are some of the most artistically accomplished images of western North America from the early nineteenth century.

The son of a cotton manufacturer, Karl Bodmer was born in Zurich, Switzerland, on February 2, 1809. At thirteen years of age his family apprenticed him to study art with his uncle, Johann Jacob Meier, from whom he learned drawing and painting. In 1828 Bodmer settled in Koblenz and engraved portfolios of picturesque views of the scenic Rhineland for which he became well known. In 1832 his popular prints attracted the attention of Prince Alexander Philipp Maximilian of Wied-Neuwied (1782–1867), a wealthy scientist and naturalist. Maximilian had explored South America in 1815 following the scientific theories of Alexander von Humboldt in search of the origins of mankind. Criticized for his own drawings of that expedition, Maximilian hired Bodmer to accompany him on his journey to North America to continue his study of "primitive" cultures.

Maximilian's party arrived in Boston in July 1832 to begin their expedition across North America. Along his journey to the West Maximilian stopped to study the human and natural history at the Peale Museum in Philadelphia, Charles Bird King's Indian Gallery in Washington, D.C., and with Charles Lesseur's scientific community in New Harmony, Indiana. Maximilian's group arrived in St. Louis in March 1833 where they prepared for the long journey into the West by gathering stores and studying maps under the guidance of the famed explorer **William Clark.** While in St. Louis Maximilian and Bodmer examined some of **George C. Catlin**'s paintings in a local collection, and it is speculated that they may have visited **Peter Rindisbacher** (1806–1834) before his premature death.

The expedition departed St. Louis in April for a yearlong journey up the Missouri River to the most distant Euramerican outpost, Fort Mackenzie, in present-day Montana. Bodmer's extensive body of sketches and watercolors portray the daily encounters of the expedition party and the prince's interest in "primitive" man, botanical specimens, and geology. Among the important images from the journey that Bodmer preserved were the images of the Mandan Indian Nation and their chief, Mato-Tope. In painstaking detail Bodmer recorded the culture of this nation (including the spectacular ritual presented in *Bison Dance*) prior to their almost total extermination by a smallpox epidemic in 1837.

Bodmer's watercolors of the upper Missouri River are among the earliest depictions of the distinctive geological formations that Maximilian coined the "white castle." In his journals the prince described the remarkable sandstone cliffs as "the most strange forms. . . . you may imagine that you see colonnades . . . little towers, pulpits, organs with their pipes, old ruins, fortresses, castles, churches with pointed towers." While camped at Fort Mackenzie, Bodmer witnessed a frightening attack of Assiniboine and Cree Indians upon a group of encamped Blackfeet outside the fort, which he re-created in the dramatic print *Fort Mackenzie, August 28th, 1833.*

After spending a bitterly cold winter at Fort Clark, Maximilian's expedition returned to St. Louis in the spring of 1834 and departed for Europe in August. Back in Germany Maximilian published the text of his journals in 1836 with plans to follow with an illustrated volume. In 1836 Bodmer moved to Paris to exhibit his gallery of Indian paintings and to promote the forthcoming volume. Beginning in 1839 the German edition of Maximilian's *Travels in the Interior of*

North America appeared, with prints after Bodmer's sketches, followed by the French and then English editions. Despite the tremendous investment by Maximilian, *Travels* was, unfortunately, a commercial failure and nearly bankrupted the prince. Perhaps because of the difficulty with the volumes on North America, Bodmer declined the prince's invitation to accompany him on an expedition to Egypt in 1846.

While in Paris promoting his gallery of Indian paintings, Bodmer became interested in contemporary French art. In 1849 he moved to Paris to study painting and joined French artists Jean-François Millet (1814–1875) and Charles Emile Jacque (1813–1894) at the artists' colony in nearby Barbizon. Under the influence of the Barbizon artists, Bodmer began to paint rural landscapes and animal pictures. In 1850 he won second prize at the annual Paris Salon and went on to work in this style for the next three decades, earning considerable distinction as a painter and engraver and receiving the Legion d'Honneur in 1876.

Bodmer's only other venture in North American subjects was a commission in 1851 from an American publisher for a portfolio, *Annals of the United States Illustrated.* Because he was overbooked for commissions, Bodmer recruited his new friend and colleague Jean-François Millet to assist by painting the landscapes. The publisher angrily canceled the commission when he discovered that Bodmer was not producing the images, and only four of these rare prints were pulled.

Late in life, Bodmer became very sickly. He withdrew from active participation in the Barbizon community in the 1860s. In 1884 his declining health forced him to sell his home in Barbizon and move to Paris where he died an unknown man on October 30, 1893. For North America his legacy rests in a single but extraordinary body of images of the trans-Mississippi frontier that preserves in exacting detail and with delicate beauty the plains landscape and native culture.

JOSEPH D. KETNER

Ewers, John C., et al. *Views of a Vanishing Frontier* Omaha: Center for Western Studies, Joslyn Art Museum, 1984.

Joslyn Art Museum. *Karl Bodmer's America.* Omaha: Joslyn Art Museum, 1984.

BOERNSTEIN, HENRY (1805–1892)

Henry Boernstein, a journalist and dramatist, was born Georg Christian Heinrich Börnstein, on November 4, 1805, in Hamburg, Germany, the son of Franz Sigmund Börnstein, a former actor turned merchant, and Ilse Sophie Hesse Börnstein. In 1813 his parents moved to Lemberg, Galizia, Austrian Poland

(now Lvov, Ukraine), where Boernstein was educated. With a Catholic father and a Protestant mother, Boernstein had to attend Catholic religious classes due to Austrian law, despite having been baptized a Protestant; this intensified what became a lifelong hostility toward the Catholic Church. From 1821 to 1826 he served in the Austrian army, after which he worked in Vienna as a journalist before joining a traveling company as an actor. In 1829 he took advantage of a peculiar Hungarian law to marry the actress Marie Steltzer (1814–1892), though she was only fifteen at the time. Boernstein served as theatrical director in the Austrian cities of St. Polten (in 1830–1831) and Linz (from 1832 to 1839) before leading a traveling company through Italy and Germany, arriving in Paris in 1842.

In the mid-1840s Boernstein settled in Paris, working as a translator, journalist, and theatrical director, in close contact with German radical émigrés. In 1844–1845 he published *Vorwärts!* an originally moderate cultural and political weekly that was transformed into a radical journal under the influence of Arnold Ruge, Heinrich Heine, Karl Ludwig Bernays, and Karl Marx. The Paris *Vorwärts!* was closed by the French government in early 1845, and Boernstein had to promise to abstain from political journalism to keep his French residency. This led to a definitive break between Boernstein and Marx, who went into exile. After the French Revolution of February 1848, Boernstein helped form a Paris-German Legion to support a revolution in Germany. After the French Republic was subverted by Louis-Napoléon, Boernstein emigrated to America in 1849.

Upon his arrival in the United States, Boernstein farmed in Highland, Illinois, until summoned by publisher Wilhelm Gempp to take over the editorship of the *Anzeiger des Westens* in March 1850. Although the *Anzeiger* was already one of the most important German-language newspapers in the Midwest, Boernstein used all his talents to boost circulation. He published his anti-Jesuit serial novel, *Die Geheimnisse von St. Louis,* in 1851, translated into English (as *The Mysteries of St. Louis*), French, and Czechoslovakian for St. Louis radical newspapers also published by Gempp. In book form the novel was the most widely read German American novel of the 1850s, and it would remain in print in Germany into the 1870s. This was only the first of many literary supplements designed by Boernstein to increase subscriptions. He eventually purchased the *Anzeiger* and became its publisher, with Karl Ludwig Bernays as editor.

Boernstein tried to mobilize the German-speaking population of St. Louis behind a political program inspired by the European revolutions of 1848, promoting hostility toward organized religion and direct confrontation with American nativism. He opposed those Germans who wanted to use the United States as a mere platform for launching revolutions in Europe, and he sought instead to turn immigrants' attention to their political situation in America. In 1852 Boernstein successfully supported former senator **Thomas Hart Benton** for a seat in the United States House of Representatives from St. Louis, launching an alliance between Benton Democrats and German radicals that would continue in the Missouri Republican Party of **Frank Blair** into the early 1860s.

When the Republican candidate for president in 1856, **John Charles Frémont,** was not placed on Missouri ballots, Boernstein distributed tickets with the name of the Know-Nothing candidate, Millard Fillmore, marked "Under Protest." Boernstein was the Republican candidate for superintendent of the common schools in the 1860 election.

In 1851 Boernstein helped establish a freethinker "League of Free Men" with the Silesian leftist Franz Schmidt, and he established several theatrical and cultural associations, culminating in the St. Louis German Opera in 1859. He composed several German-language plays to dramatize his causes, and he became a major owner of beer halls, breweries, and other enterprises.

Boernstein's confrontational tactics as a journalist helped drive many religious Missourians—both Catholic and Protestant—to support the secessionist position. The leader of the Missouri Synod Lutherans, C. F. W. Walther, regarded Boernstein as a major enemy of Christianity, as did Catholic archbishop **Peter Kenrick.** Boernstein even managed to alienate Germans of his own political orientation, so that in 1857 German radical opponents launched the *Westliche Post.*

At the time of the secession crisis in April 1861, Boernstein was elected colonel of the Second Missouri Volunteer regiment organized for three months' service at the St. Louis arsenal by Frank Blair and Gen. **Nathaniel Lyon** over the objections of Gov. **Claiborne Fox Jackson.** Boernstein's regiment participated in the seizure of Camp Jackson on May 10, 1861, as well as in the occupation of Jefferson City in June, expelling the elected government. Boernstein was placed in command of Jefferson City with a small detachment, and on July 4, 1861, he compelled those state officials in his custody to swear allegiance to the United States at a public ceremony. Although his reputation before the war had been as an uncompromising radical, Boernstein came to support the moderate policies of Lincoln and Blair against the German radicals he had once led, many of whom became fanatical supporters of Frémont and his program of immediate abolition.

After being mustered out of military service in July 1861, Boernstein was rewarded with the office of U.S. consul in Bremen, Germany. In Bremen, Boernstein waged a propaganda campaign on behalf of the Lincoln government to sway European opinion. Continued concern by Republican leaders about German radical hostility toward Frank Blair led to Boernstein being brought back to St. Louis in the fall of 1862 to resume control of the *Anzeiger des Westens* in support of Blair's campaign for reelection to the United States House of Representatives. Pro-Frémont Germans attacked Boernstein and his colleague Karl Ludwig Bernays (recalled from his own office as consul in Zurich), and the circulation of the *Anzeiger* was mortally injured in the controversy. The *Anzeiger* closed in early 1863 after Boernstein's return to Bremen, and his other business enterprises collapsed as well. In later years, Boernstein regretted ever having taken the consular post; he believed he could have kept the St. Louis Germans behind Lincoln and Blair, and his personal fortune could have been maintained, had he remained in St. Louis.

Boernstein never returned to the United States, though he retained American citizenship until his death on September 10, 1892. Following his replacement as consul in 1866, he went back to Vienna, where he resumed theatrical direction and the writing of plays. He continued to write for the U.S. German-language press, culminating in the serial publication of his memoirs in the years 1879 to 1881. By the early 1890s he was the last living representative of the Viennese journalistic tradition predating 1848. In his will he directed that a tombstone declare that he and his wife, Marie, died "Citizens of Missouri." A street is named after him in the Vienna district of Strebersdorf, but his grave at the Matzleindorfer Protestant Cemetery was obliterated by official action in 1941.

Henry Boernstein played a major role in the political and cultural development of St. Louis and Missouri in the 1850s, but the impact of his actions must continue to be in dispute. Did his sensationalism simply create more enemies for the Union, leading several religious groups to side with secession? Did his strident support for Lincoln and Blair split what could have been a solid radical front for Missouri Germans, eventually undermining the viability of a radical regime? It will remain a matter of perennial dispute whether Boernstein's clever, slippery personality influenced Missouri for better or for worse.

STEVEN ROWAN

Boernstein, Henry. *The Mysteries of St. Louis.* Ed. Steven Rowan and Elizabeth Sims. Trans. Friedrich Münch. Chicago: Kerr, 1990.

Börnstein, Heinrich. *Fünfundsiebzig Jahre in der Alten und Neuen Welt: Memoiren eines Unbedeutenden.* Ed. Patricia Herminghouse. 1881. Reprint, New York: Peter Lang, 1986.

Rowan, Steven, "Anticlericalism, Atheism, and Socialism in German St. Louis, 1850–1853: Heinrich Börnstein and Franz Schmidt." In *The German-American Press,* ed. Henry Geitz, 43–56. Madison, Wis.: Max Kade Institute for German-American Studies, 1992.

———. "Franz Schmidt and the Freie Blatter of St. Louis, 1851–1853." In *The German-American Radical Press: The Shaping of a Left Political Culture,* ed. Elliott Shore, Ken Fones-Wolf, and James P. Danky, 31–48. Urbana: University of Illinois Press, 1992.

———, trans. *Germans for a Free Missouri: Translations from the St. Louis Radical Press, 1857–1862.* Columbia: University of Missouri Press, 1983.

BOGGS, LILBURN W. (1792–1860)

Born in Lexington, Kentucky, on December 14, 1792, Lilburn W. Boggs became one of the most important and controversial politicians in Missouri in the antebellum era. As the state's sixth governor, serving from 1836 to 1840, Boggs's policies on two issues—Mormonism and the construction of a new capitol—aroused controversy. His administration was also plagued by the panic of 1837, one of the most serious national economic downturns in the first half of the nineteenth century, which effectively blocked his plans to expend state funds for internal improvements for railroads and waterways. He was successful, however, in chartering the Bank of the State of Missouri to help control the state's finances and in passing the Geyer Act, which laid the foundations of the state public school system and the creation of the University of Missouri.

Born and raised in Kentucky, Boggs enlisted in the military and served in the War of 1812. Afterward he became a bookkeeper in the Insurance Bank of Kentucky. In 1816, however, like so many other Kentuckians, he moved to the Missouri Territory to seek his fortune and make his place in the young nation. He opened a store in St. Louis in 1816 but within a year had become cashier of the newly created Bank of Missouri. In August 1817 he married Julia Anne Bent, daughter of Judge **Silas Bent,** a prominent jurist and political figure in the territory. This relationship helped Boggs gain entrée to the upper echelons of state leaders.

A year after his marriage, Boggs moved westward up the Missouri River to the booming community of Franklin, then a major outfitting point for the Rocky Mountain fur trade, and opened a general store. In 1820 his business success was ensured when he was appointed by the U.S. government as the assistant factor at Fort Osage, in the western part of the state, providing government trade goods to the Indians. His wife's health necessitated that he return to St. Louis in the fall of 1820, however, and she died within a short time due to medical complications following the birth of their second son. Boggs then returned to Fort Osage and remained in business there until the government abandoned the factory system associated with Indian affairs in 1822.

Boggs opened a regular shop in Sibley, near Fort Osage, in 1822, and operated a business in which he frequently traveled to other communities with his wares. Because of this type of trade, Boggs became one of the best-known men in western Missouri, a powerful advantage in his later political career. While involved in this trade, he also met and married, in July 1823, Panthea Boone, a granddaughter of **Daniel Boone.** Three years later Boggs moved his business to the newest Missouri boomtown, Independence, which soon supplanted virtually all other centers for outfitting traders going to the West.

Not long after moving to Independence, Boggs ran for the Missouri State Senate from the newly created Thirteenth District. Probably because of his wide acquaintance in the region, he was unopposed in the contest. In 1828 he ran for a second term, also winning handily. While in the state senate Boggs became closely identified with the Jacksonian Democrats then in control of the state. He was nearly always teamed with the senior U.S. senator from Missouri, **Thomas Hart Benton,** and the Democrats who ran the state.

Because of his loyalty to party, as well as his power base in the western part of the state, Boggs was chosen by the Democratic Party to run for lieutenant governor with the gubernatorial candidate **Daniel Dunklin** in 1832. Both were elected with comfortable majorities. As lieutenant governor Boggs had to be in Jefferson City only while the legislature was in session. Consequently, he spent much time while in office in Independence attending to his business and dealing with local political issues.

This began to change in January 1835 when Boggs and several other senior Democratic Party officials met in convention to nominate a slate of candidates for office. Boggs received the nod for governor and ran against the well-known St. Louis businessman **William Henry Ashley,** the Whig Party's candidate. The Democratic machine got behind Boggs's candidacy, and the party's entire ticket was elected. In the summer of 1836 Daniel Dunklin resigned the last few months of his gubernatorial term, and Boggs succeeded him.

The highest priority Boggs brought to the governor's office was the chartering of the Bank of the State of Missouri. He sponsored a law that incorporated a middle position between the Whig demand for a powerful state-owned bank and the Democratic emphasis on private banks without the power to issue currency. His proposal called for a bank with a rigidly circumscribed capital, one-half to be subscribed by the state and the remainder from private stockholders. The bank could issue bills of large denominations to meet the requirements of St. Louis business firms, with specie being reserved for most everyday transactions. With the mixture of public and private sectors in the bank, Boggs hoped to stabilize the state's economy, create monies for state projects, and satisfy a multitude of philosophical positions relative to banking in the state.

At the same time Boggs pressed for the passage of a bill to build a new capitol building in Jefferson City. He suggested selling several state-owned lots in the capital to raise the seventy-five thousand dollars he estimated as the cost of a new building. He also advocated the issuance of state bonds to raise funds for the project. In 1838 the new capitol was started, but was still incomplete in 1840 when the legislature began an investigation of possible malfeasance in the raising and disbursing of funds. Boggs was personally tarred by the investigators, mostly regarding the manner in which some of the money had been raised. Although he escaped formal censure, it affected his ability to accomplish other goals.

The most public scandal of Boggs's administration was the handling of the so-called Mormon war in western Missouri in the fall of 1838. Boggs, who personally disliked the Mormons as a clannish group of religious zealots who caused problems wherever they went, overreacted to difficulties in Gallatin, Missouri, in August 1838 when a riot broke out at the precinct during an election. A Mormon was prohibited from voting, probably unjustly, so a posse led by **Joseph Smith Jr.,** the Mormon prophet, responded by riding from their stronghold at Far West (the seat of government in Mormon-controlled Caldwell County) to Gallatin and confronting a local justice of the peace, Adam Black. Black and other non-Mormons sent alarming reports to Boggs and petitioned him for troops to put down a rebellion of the Mormons against state authority. As a result Boggs ordered the commanders of seven divisions of state militia to stand ready to march and deployed a small peacekeeping force to western Missouri.

Sustained trouble developed on October 25, 1838, when a Mormon military unit under David W. Patten, an apostle in the church, engaged a detachment of militia under Capt. Samuel Bogart at what has been christened the Battle of the Crooked River. Several casualties resulted, with three Mormons killed (one of whom was Patten) and one fatality in Bogart's ranks. The engagement of state troops, regardless of the circumstances surrounding it, and rumors that the Mormons were in open rebellion against the state were sufficient to prompt Boggs to call out reinforcements to restore order. He placed Gen. John B. Clark of Howard County in command, and gave him explicit instructions on October 28, 1838, for dealing with the Mormons. His instructions were an overreaction of the worst magnitude. He said, "The Mormons must be treated as enemies, and must be exterminated or driven from the State if necessary for the public peace—their outrages are beyond all description." This declaration led directly to the state militia's attack on several families of Mormons at Haun's Mill on October 30, killing eighteen and wounding another fifteen.

At the same time, in late October 1838, Boggs's state troops surrounded Far West, and demanded the surrender of Joseph Smith and his key lieutenants. They eventually surrendered on October 31. The militia commander had the Mormon leaders court-martialed and ordered their execution, but **Alexander W. Doniphan** of Clay County, apparently the only lawyer present, protested the decision and promised legal action against the militia commanders if they carried out the sentence. Instead, Smith and his associates were taken to Liberty and kept in jail over the winter of 1838–1839 to await a civil trial. Eventually, while being transported from Daviess to Boone County, the Mormons escaped and left the state. It was widely rumored that they were allowed to escape by civil authorities who viewed a trial as meaningless at that point. Smith went to Illinois, where most of his followers had migrated following the October war.

At the end of his gubernatorial term in 1840, Boggs returned to Independence and worked in his business. He did not emerge again in the public light until 1842 when he was shot and nearly killed by an unknown assassin while reading in his Independence home. Suspicion of the attack was laid at the feet of the Mormons, and one of Smith's followers was arrested, but no one was ever convicted of the crime. Perhaps because of the publicity associated with his attempted assassination, Boggs was readily elected to the state senate in the fall of 1842, serving four years before retiring from public office.

In 1846 Boggs's business fell apart, and he lost his home in an economic depression. He left with his family by wagon on May 10, 1846, for California, where he hoped to start anew. He reached Sutter's Fort in November, and within a short time had been appointed alcalde (chief civil authority) of California north of Sacramento. At the same time Boggs opened a general store and during the gold rush made a fortune outfitting miners. In 1852 he purchased a farm in Napa Valley and retired from business. He lived there in relative seclusion until his death on March 4, 1860.

ROGER D. LAUNIUS

Arrington, Leonard J., and Davis Bitton. *The Mormon Experience: A History of the Latter-Day Saints.* New York: Knopf, 1979.

Gordon, Joseph F. "The Political Career of Lilburn W. Boggs." *Missouri Historical Review* 52 (January 1958): 111–22.

LeSueur, Stephen C. *The 1838 Mormon War in Missouri.* Columbia: University of Missouri Press, 1987.

McCandless, Perry. *A History of Missouri: Volume II, 1820 to 1860.* Columbia: University of Missouri Press, 1972.

McLaws, Monte B. "The Attempted Assassination of Missouri's Ex Governor, Lilburn W. Boggs." *Missouri Historical Review* 60 (October 1965): 50–62.

BOGY, LEWIS VITAL (1818–1877)

Born in Ste. Genevieve on April 9, 1818, a descendant of early French pioneers who settled in that area, Lewis V. Bogy became the first native-born Missourian to serve the state as a U.S. senator.

After attending the local common schools, Bogy moved to Kaskaskia, Illinois, in 1832 to study law with Nathaniel Pope. He interrupted his legal studies to enlist as a private in the Black Hawk War. Following his stint in military service, Bogy entered the law school at Transylvania University in Lexington, Kentucky. Following his graduation from that institution in 1835, he opened a law office in St. Louis. He served one term in the Missouri House of Representatives before moving back to Ste. Genevieve in 1849. Shortly thereafter Bogy was elected again to the Missouri House.

In the practice of law Bogy specialized in the complicated and controversial land cases stemming from the pre-American Spanish and French grants and titles. Bogy also devoted considerable time, effort, and money to the development of the rich iron deposits in the Pilot Knob region, and was an important investor in the Iron Mountain and Pilot Knob Railroad. In his later years, Bogy served on the University of Missouri Board of Curators.

Throughout his life, Bogy remained active in civic and political affairs. Although his oratory lacked the eloquence of some of his contemporaries Bogy appears to have been a bold, fluent, and ardent speaker who expressed himself with an earnestness that conveyed a sense of honest conviction. Contemporaries considered him an eminently fair man who refrained from the vituperative personal attacks so characteristic of those years.

As an active Democrat, Bogy's sympathies were clearly with the South as sectional conflict came to engulf the state and nation. He did not, however, join with the extreme Southern secessionist wing of the Democratic Party, but opted instead to become a conditional Unionist. Bogy remained a moderate in politics who spoke out against the Radicals who gained control of the state. He joined forces with former Whigs such as **James Sidney Rollins** and old-line Democrats such as **Frank Blair** to support the Conservative Union Party movement, and he served on a St. Louis steering committee backing President Andrew Johnson. He informed Johnson about their determination to drive the Radicals from power in the state. As a reward for his role in the Conservative Union movement, the president appointed Bogy as commissioner of Indian affairs, a post he held in 1867 and 1868.

Some contemporaries who knew Bogy believed that he harbored a longtime ambition to become a U.S. senator. Immediately before the General Assembly convened for its 1872–1873 session, Bogy announced his candidacy as a Democrat for the United States Senate. Elected by the General Assembly with a large majority, Bogy took his place in the Senate on March 4, 1873.

The new senator carried no great reputation or well-known stance on major national issues with him to Washington, D.C. Nevertheless, Bogy took an active part in the work of the Senate. As might be expected, he demonstrated an interest in and knowledge of matters related to the operation of the Bureau of Indian Affairs. He reflected the prevailing views of most white Americans on Indian policies, but he did express some concern for Native American rights. Bogy also supported the growing popular demand to increase the nation's currency favored by the "Greenback" movement. The "want of money," Bogy stated, was one of the major problems of the nation's farmers.

In what may have been his major action in the Senate, Bogy vigorously and boldly opposed acceptance of the Louisiana electoral vote for presidential candidate Rutherford B. Hayes. He charged the Louisiana returning board with fraud, and declared that the Democratic candidate Samuel J. Tilden was the honest winner of the 1876 presidential election. Bogy, of course, lost that battle.

Some of Bogy's friends believed that his exertions during the heated senatorial debates over the controversial presidential electoral-vote returns adversely affected his health. Disappointed that a stay in Colorado did not improve his condition, Bogy returned to St. Louis where he died on September 20, 1877. He was buried in Calvary Cemetery in St. Louis.

PERRY McCANDLESS

Bay, W. V. N. *Reminiscences of the Bench and Bar of Missouri.* St. Louis: F. H. Thomas, 1878.

Congressional Record. 45th Cong., 2d sess., 1878.

BOLDUC, LOUIS (1739?–1815)

Louis Bolduc was born near Quebec City in the village of St. Joachim around 1739 (his baptismal record is not extant), son to Zacharie and Jeanne Meunier Bolduc. Young Louis fled the St. Lawrence River Valley as the French and Indian War of 1756 to 1763 turned decisively against the French. His native village of St. Joachim was one of the many villages in the valley that British troops burned during their approach to Quebec in 1759.

Bolduc settled in Ste. Genevieve during the early 1760s and married on January 28, 1765, Agathe Govreau, a native of Kaskaskia. The newcomer to the region therefore married into a firmly rooted local family. Louis and Agathe had four children over a seven-year period, three of whom—Elizabeth, Louis Jr., and Etienne—survived into adulthood.

Bolduc immediately plunged into the various economic activities that occupied enterprising men of colonial Ste. Genevieve: agriculture, lead mining, salt making, and commerce. Although Bolduc was illiterate, he was energetic, ambitious, and successful. He was soon a respected and influential man, frequently elected as church warden, which was an office reserved for the leading citizens of the parish.

Bolduc was in New Orleans on business when his first wife, Agathe, died in Ste. Genevieve in August 1773. She, as many women at that time, died of complications from childbirth. Her last child lived long enough to be baptized Jean-Baptiste but also died in infancy, as about one-third of the children did in colonial Ste. Genevieve. The inventory of the Bolduc estate (total appraised value 17,459 livres) as a consequence of Agathe's death reveals that in 1774 Louis was already well-to-do.

Within less than two years Bolduc had remarried, once again to a local woman, Marie Courtois, who was some fourteen years his junior. The new Bolduc couple had two children, Henri and Jean-Baptiste, both of whom died in infancy. The early deaths of three of Bolduc's six children by two wives was not extraordinary by contemporary standards, and Louis and Marie had no more children.

Whatever the misfortunes of his personal life, Bolduc's wealth continued to increase. His commercial activities expanded dramatically, as the American Revolution was a catalyst to commerce in the Mississippi Valley, and Bolduc shipped large amounts of foodstuffs out of Ste. Genevieve. Slaves were a good index of wealth in colonial Ste. Genevieve, and by 1791 Bolduc owned twenty-one.

Severe flooding during the 1780s (especially the major flood of 1785) persuaded the residents of Ste. Genevieve to move their community to higher ground. By 1793 Bolduc decided to relocate to the New Town, or Petites Cotes as it was then known.

He selected a choice residential plot at the southwest corner of La Grande Rue (Main Street) and Rue à l'Eglise (Church Street, now Market Street). His vertical-log residence, built in that year, still stands in the center of old Ste. Genevieve as one of the premier historic sites in the Midwest.

Bolduc had prospered mightily under the colonial regimes of both France and Spain, and he had little reason to welcome the coming of American sovereignty to Ste. Genevieve with the Louisiana Purchase. Yet, Bolduc entered the American era of his life in 1804 with many assets: he belonged to the upper stratum of society in Ste. Genevieve, and he and his wife, at ages sixty-eight and fifty-four respectively, were in robust health despite the fact that they had both already lived beyond their projected life expectancy, given the time and place. Bolduc, like many of his francophone compatriots in Ste. Genevieve, clung stubbornly to his old habits; for example, he never learned English, despite the fact that he was a resident of the United States.

Between 1810 and 1815 Bolduc dictated a number of wills and codicils, systematically preparing for the eventual distribution of his possessions. He died a wealthy man in 1815, owning taxable property, including his residence and twelve slaves, worth $3,030.00, in addition to $10,000 in cash. Three hundred piastres, or dollars, of this were to be deducted and distributed to the parish poor, after which widow Marie was to receive one-half of the total, in accordance with the Customary Law of Paris; the other half went to his one surviving child, Elizabeth, and various grandchildren, great-grandchildren, and his nephew Pierre Bolduc, who had recently arrived in Ste. Genevieve from Canada.

Bolduc was interred in the Roman Catholic cemetery of Ste. Genevieve on March 4, 1815, with his soul committed to the "Holy Trinity, under the protection of the Glorious Virgin Mary, . . . and all the saints of paradise." His widow, Marie, survived him by eleven years.

CARL J. EKBERG

Ekberg, Carl J. *Colonial Ste. Genevieve: An Adventure on the Mississippi Frontier.* Gerald, Mo.: Patrice Press, 1985.

Houck, Louis. *The Spanish Regime in Missouri: A Collection of Papers and Documents Relating to Upper Louisiana.* 2 vols. Chicago: R. R. Donnelley and Sons, 1909.

Papeles de Cuba, various legajos. Archivo General de Indias, Seville, Spain.

Ste. Genevieve Archives. Microfilm. Missouri Historical Society, St. Louis.

Ste. Genevieve Parish Records. Microfilm. State Historical Society of Missouri, Columbia.

BOLLING, RICHARD WALKER (1916–1991)

Richard Bolling was born in New York City on May 17, 1916, to Richard Walker Bolling, chief surgeon at St. Luke's Hospital, and Florence Easton Bolling. His mother educated young Richard at home until age ten, when he began formal schooling at Phillips Exeter Academy in Exeter, New Hampshire. Bolling was unhappy there, and at thirteen years of age, after his father's death, Bolling persuaded his mother to move to the paternal home in Huntsville, Alabama. He received a B.A. in English literature from the University of the South, in Sewanee, Tennessee, in 1937. He taught at the Sewanee Military Academy until starting postgraduate work in literature at Vanderbilt University in 1939. World War II intervened before he completed his doctoral studies, and in 1941 Bolling enlisted in the army. He spent five years in the Pacific, attached to MacArthur's command. He received the Legion of Merit and a Bronze Star before being discharged from the army with the rank of lieutenant colonel in 1946.

Richard Bolling married Barbara Stratton on June 7, 1945. They raised their only child, Andrea Walker, with Barbara's three children from a previous marriage. The family moved to Kansas City, Missouri, where Bolling had a position as director of student activities and veterans' affairs at the University of Kansas City.

Bolling's liberal ideals emerged early. He helped found the Americans for Democratic Action (ADA) in 1945, an organization he described as a political home for non-"Stalinist" liberals. In 1947 he became the ADA's midwestern director. In 1946 Bolling became the national vice chairman of a liberal veterans' organization, the American Veterans Committee, organized to counter what he saw as the extreme rightward tilt of the Veterans of Foreign Wars and the American Legion.

Bolling's political career began in the rough-and-tumble world of the Kansas City ward system. In 1946 he worked for Jerome Walsh's unsuccessful congressional campaign. After the machine candidate defeated incumbent Roger Slaughter, vote-fraud charges followed. By aligning with Walsh, Bolling had identified himself with clean government, anti-Pendergast groups. This experience led to an unofficial attachment with the *Kansas City Star* to investigate vote fraud.

Bolling won the congressional seat for Missouri's Fifth District in 1948. Defeat of the Pendergast machine's control over Kansas City's Democratic Party required a strange, but effective, coalition of gangster Charles Binaggio's faction, university people, and veterans. **Tom L. Evans,** one of **Harry S. Truman**'s oldest friends and the owner of the Crown Drug

Store chain, coordinated this effective group against the Pendergast-backed candidate, Emmet Scanlon (whom Truman had endorsed before Bolling filed).

A self-proclaimed liberal, Bolling came to Congress on Truman's coattails committed to the same New Deal principles as the president. Once elected Bolling made it his first order of business to cultivate Truman's friendship; two years later the president's support gave Bolling the boost he needed to again defeat the Pendergast group for reelection. In thirty-five years of service, he won seventeen successive congressional elections to become one of the most influential congressmen in the history of the United States House of Representatives.

Representative Bolling, his unwavering liberalism notwithstanding, was fervently anticommunist. He believed that communists represented a genuine danger to the United States, and, though later in life he did not hesitate to call this a mistake, he supported the activities of the House Un-American Activities Committee. Despite his anticommunist sentiments, Bolling voted to uphold Truman's veto of the McCarran Act of 1950. He was also one of the few legislators who denounced Sen. Joseph McCarthy on the floor of the House and criticized President Eisenhower for not controlling McCarthy.

He never changed his belief, however, that world communism represented a threat to the United States, its allies, and developing nations throughout the world. Thus, he embraced an activist American foreign policy and generally supported foreign aid. Congressman Bolling also believed that intervention in Vietnam, though handled poorly by the civilians and military alike, was a necessity.

Bolling became a protégé of Speaker of the House Sam Rayburn, who assigned him to the powerful Rules Committee in 1956. Under the leadership of conservative Howard W. Smith of Virginia, the committee had taken for itself the authority to accept or reject legislation before passing it to the floor for deliberation. Frustrated that a coalition of conservative Republicans and entrenched southern Democrats were strangling civil rights legislation and other progressive bills, Bolling turned his reform-minded activism upon the House itself. He referred to the Dixiecrat opposition to civil rights proposals as "the most backward part of the Democrat donkey leading the whole Republican elephant around by the nose." From his committee position, Bolling led a revolt against the legislative stranglehold of the Rules Committee and successfully guided the Civil Rights Act of 1957 through the House. Considered by Bolling to be his greatest accomplishment, this first civil rights legislation since Reconstruction eased the way for expanded legislation of the 1960s.

Using outside pressure from labor unions and civil rights organizations on the committee and on the

House as a whole, Bolling's behind-the-scenes leadership led to Rayburn's successful effort to recapture the Rules Committee by enlarging its membership from twelve to fifteen. In January 1961 the House approved the Rayburn plan, and finally the liberal leadership controlled the Rules Committee.

In addition to civil rights, and reflecting the concerns of his Kansas City constituents, Bolling championed most traditional liberal Democratic causes, especially those of labor and veterans' affairs. He routinely voted for public housing, increased unemployment-compensation payments, and a higher minimum wage. He also favored maintaining agricultural price supports and more generous Social Security benefits.

The years following Speaker Rayburn's death in 1961 were often frustrating for Bolling. His years of experience guaranteed him considerable influence in the workings of the House, yet he was no confidant of the new Speaker, John W. McCormack. Congressional watchers blamed Bolling's failure to secure the House majority leadership in 1962 and 1976 on his sometimes abrasive personality. His ill-disguised contempt for Rayburn's successor did nothing to further his cause among McCormack's supporters.

Bolling experienced personal difficulties about this same time. He received treatment for alcoholism, and after years of marital difficulty he and his wife divorced. He later married Nona Goddard Herndon, on February 29, 1984.

Despite personal and professional disappointments, Bolling continued as one of America's ablest legislators. Journalist William S. White described him as "an occupational, professional anticipator of difficulties; a smoother-out of ruffled feelings; an estimator of the human weaknesses and strengths of other Democrats; a worker of small and sometimes large miracles." During the last years of his tenure in the House, Bolling was instrumental in reforming the congressional budget process and helping to revive the Democratic caucus. In 1979 McCormack's successor to the Speaker's chair, Carl Albert of Oklahoma, appointed Bolling as Rules Committee chairman.

Bolling criticized the rules and mores of the House throughout his career. His book *House Out of Order,* published in 1965, called for fundamental changes in the seniority system, especially the election process for committee chairmen, and for open committee meetings. The House adopted these changes in the early 1970s, largely because of Bolling's influence with young House Democrats such as Morris Udall, Donald Fraser, and Thomas S. Foley. He wrote *Power in the House: A History of the Leadership of the House of Representatives,* published in 1968, from the same reformist perspective. Only an educated public, Bolling argued, could reclaim control over its government and make it genuinely work for the common good rather than for powerful special interests.

A leading Democratic spokesman during Ronald Reagan's first term, Bolling accused the president of trying to impose a "tyranny" on Congress through the budget process. Retiring in 1983 Bolling taught at the University of Missouri at Kansas City and elsewhere. Articles on politics and public policy authored by him appeared in magazines such as the *New Republic* and the *Bulletin of the Atomic Scientists.* He died of a heart attack in his Washington, D.C., home on April 21, 1991.

DEBORAH L. CRAMER

Biographical Dictionary of the United States Congress, 1774–1989. Bicentennial ed. S.v. "Bolling, Richard Walker." Washington, D.C.: U.S. Government Printing Office, 1989.

Bolling, Richard Walker. *House Out of Order.* New York: Dutton, 1965.

———. Oral History, by Niel M. Johnson, 1988–1989. Harry S. Truman Library, Independence, Mo.

———. *Power in the House: A History of the Leadership of the House of Representatives.* New York: Dutton, 1968.

New York Times, April 23, 1991.

White, William S. "The Invisible Gentleman from Kansas City." *Harpers* (May 1961): 84–87.

BOLLINGER, GEORGE FREDERICK (1771?–1842)

A group of German-Swiss immigrants landed in Philadelphia in 1710 and settled in southeast Pennsylvania. In 1768 some moved south to western North Carolina where George F. Bollinger was born in about 1771, one of twelve children. His father was a Revolutionary War veteran. As a young man in his midtwenties, Bollinger and a friend explored the trans-Mississippi in the Cape Girardeau District. He negotiated a Spanish land grant from **Louis Lorimier** upon the condition that he bring a colony of settlers to the Whitewater River.

In January 1800 Bollinger's group of twenty families, each receiving several hundred acres, moved to the Spanish territory, to what became known as the "Dutch Settlement" on the Whitewater River. Bollinger's land lay along the river near modern Burfordsville. His wife died before reaching the settlement; they had only one child, Sarah.

After the transfer of the territory to the U.S. government in 1804, Bollinger built a log dam, a log mill, and a blockhouse. He persuaded a German Reformed minister in North Carolina to join his group on the frontier. Bollinger's two slaves helped produce the agricultural crops and cared for the livestock. In 1806 Bollinger was one of the first assessors to levy taxes for the Cape Girardeau District.

When Missouri became a second-class territory in 1812, Bollinger was elected as a member of the new territorial assembly. He served multiple terms, helping to establish local governments, including judicial circuits, and founding new counties. Residents of newly created Madison County honored him in 1819 by naming the county seat Fredericktown. Territorial governor **William Clark** appointed him lieutenant colonel of the Fourth Regimental Militia, a position of leadership that he had earlier enjoyed as militia captain along the Whitewater.

Citizens elected Bollinger to the new Missouri State Senate in 1820, and again in 1828 and 1830; he was state representative in 1826, 1834, and 1838. Bollinger's political passion even led to a conviction for assault and battery upon a fellow politician from Cape Girardeau County in 1824.

Bollinger and his extended relations accumulated the substantial property holdings along the Whitewater. His success allowed him to send his daughter Sarah back to Salem, North Carolina, for schooling at the Moravian Academy.

In 1819 **Timothy Flint** visited Bollinger's Dutch Settlement and recorded his revulsion at so many domestic distilleries and at the prevalence of homemade liquors. Flint concluded, however, that the Germans worked hard, had productive orchards, built solid buildings and fences, and dramatically improved the land.

Bollinger's mill symbolized the community's success in processing grain, including the making of flour, and creating carding facilities for wool. To these he added a distillery and a blacksmith shop, and in 1825 he renovated and further improved the mill, which lay along a primary road from Jackson westward to Greenville. By 1830 Bollinger owned thirteen slaves, in addition to the six free blacks who resided in his household; during the 1830s he almost tripled his slave ownership. As his resources increased, so did his purchases of land in the region.

By the time of his death on September 23, 1842, Bollinger had achieved political and economic success as a frontier entrepreneur and had realized his goals of founding a new society with a promising future for his descendants. His Whitewater properties were flourishing, and he owned several hundred acres near his mill, on Hubble Creek, on Byrds Creek, and in three other Missouri counties. His livestock holdings in horses, cattle, and sheep were impressive. He left all this and more than thirty-five slaves in trust for his daughter, Sarah.

In 1851 Missourians honored him again with the organization of Bollinger County. George F. Bollinger and the efforts of his neighbors are today memorialized at the Bollinger Mill State Historic Site at Burfordville.

Lynn Morrow

Bollinger, Orenia, ed. *The Bollinger Connections.* Fredericktown, Mo.: McMinn Printing, 1984.

Douglas, Robert. *History of Southeast Missouri.* Reprint, Cape Girardeau, Mo.: Ramfre Press, 1961.

Hamilton, M. Colleen, Dennis Naglish, and Joseph M. Nixon. "Report of Phase I Cultural Resources Survey of Bollinger Mill State Historic Site, Cape Girardeau County, Missouri." *Research Report No. 95.* Archaeological Survey, University of Missouri–St. Louis, June 1989.

BONNEVILLE, BENJAMIN LOUIS EULALIE DE (1796–1878)

Benjamin Louis Eulalie de Bonneville was born in Paris, France, in 1796. His father, a publisher, was a close friend of Thomas Paine. When the elder de Bonneville criticized Napoléon's regime, he was arrested, his newspaper suppressed, and the family ruined. Paine brought Mme de Bonneville, Benjamin, and his younger brother Thomas to New York, and provided for their support. Appointed to West Point, Benjamin graduated in 1815.

After serving with the artillery in New England, Bonneville was sent to the Southwest in 1820. He served with the Seventh Infantry at Fort Smith, Arkansas, and Fort Gibson in the Indian Territory. Visiting New York in 1824 Bonneville met another of his father's friends, the Marquis de Lafayette. He accompanied the old general to France, serving for a year as his secretary.

On his return Bonneville resumed his post at Fort Gibson. The young captain's duties brought him into frequent contact with Indians, trappers, and traders whose colorful lives contrasted sharply with the dull routine of garrison duty. Bonneville planned an adventure of his own in the western mountains for scientific and military exploration, for fame, and for profit in the fur trade. He found financial backers in New York, and secured a two-year leave of absence.

In September 1831 Bonneville arrived in St. Louis. He spent the winter traveling, consulting traders, gathering men, and outfitting his expedition. On May 1, 1832, he left Fort Osage with 110 men and twenty wagons. For more than three years they ranged the Far West. In August 1832 the novice trader established Fort Bonneville on the Green River in the heart of prime trapping country. From this base he sent out exploring parties, the most important of which was Joseph Walker's expedition to the Great Salt Lake and California in 1833. Bonneville himself twice crossed the mountains to reconnoiter the Hudson Bay Company's posts on the Columbia River. Probably on his own initiative, possibly on secret orders from the War Department, he explored routes through the mountains, kept detailed journals, drew maps, tested British strength in the Northwest, and by dispatch reported his findings to the general-in-chief of the army.

Bonneville savored the adventure and freedom of mountain life, but failed as a businessman. He was too inexperienced, his resources too limited to compete with the established American companies of the Rocky Mountain fur trade. Although he caused his rivals some anxiety in the race for prime trapping areas and experienced trappers, ultimately the American companies drove Bonneville out of business. He returned to Missouri in late August 1835 and learned that he had been dropped from the army's rolls for overstaying his leave. Over the protests of fellow officers, but with Sen. **Thomas Hart Benton** supporting his claims, President Andrew Jackson reinstated Bonneville in April 1836.

The captain returned to duty with the Seventh Infantry in the Southwest, surveying roads and policing Indians and settlers. He served with his regiment against the Seminoles in Florida from 1839 to 1842. When the Mexican War began in 1846, Bonneville was promoted to major and transferred to the Sixth Infantry. He served in Mexico under Gen. Winfield Scott. During much of that campaign he was in active command of his regiment, and was brevetted lieutenant colonel for gallantry in the battles of Contreras and Churubusco.

After the war Bonneville served at various western posts. As colonel of the Third Infantry in 1857, he temporarily commanded the Department of New Mexico. Although much ridiculed by his junior officers, "Old Bonny Clabber" led a punitive expedition against the Mogollon Apache that won the praise of his commander and the territorial legislature.

Bonneville retired from active duty in 1861, but was immediately called back to service as recruiter and chief mustering and disbursing officer in Missouri during the war. Brevetted brigadier general in 1865, he again retired and moved to Fort Smith, Arkansas. His first wife and only child had died of fever in St. Louis some ten years earlier, and Bonneville married again in 1870 to Susan Neis of Fort Smith. He died on June 12, 1878.

Bonneville's reputation rests on his expedition to the Rocky Mountains. His maps and reports provided useful military intelligence, and he was the first to prove that wagons could be taken across the Continental Divide. Washington Irving's account of the expedition, drawn directly from Bonneville's journals, appeared in 1837. The book was eagerly received by a wide audience; it intensified a growing interest in the Far West, supported arguments for American expansion, and provided a reliable guide for travelers. Bonneville himself spent most of his later life attempting to recapture the spirit of adventure that moved him in 1832.

MARY ELLEN ROWE

Baumer, William, Jr. *Not All Warriors: Portraits of 19th Century West Pointers.* Reprint, Freeport, N.Y.: Books for Libraries Press, 1971.

Todd, Edgeley W., ed. *The Adventures of Captain Bonneville, U.S.A., by Washington Irving.* Norman: University of Oklahoma Press, 1961.

Utley, Robert. *Frontiersmen in Blue.* Lincoln: University of Nebraska Press, 1967.

BOONE, DANIEL (1734–1820)

Daniel Boone is most commonly known as a hunter, trapper, and frontier settler, but he also speculated in western lands, worked as a surveyor, owned stores where he traded furs (often in conjunction with a tavern), and led militia against Indians in Kentucky and Ohio. Boone gained national recognition for leading settlement parties to Kentucky and Missouri and for his skill in dealing with the Indians.

Born on a farm on the banks of Owatin Run in Oley township, Pennsylvania (present-day Exeter township, near Reading), on October 22, 1734, Boone was the son of English immigrant parents who were members of the Society of Friends. As a boy he helped his mother tend a herd of milk cows and roamed in the nearby fields and woods. By the age of thirteen Boone owned his first gun, and he often went into the woods alone for several days to provide game for the family table. Although he learned to read and write from Sarah Day, the wife of his brother Samuel, Boone never had more than a rudimentary, informal education, but he was considered as well, if not better, educated than most men on the frontier, especially because he liked to read.

In 1750 the Boone family left Pennsylvania for North Carolina, because Daniel's father, Squire, had been expelled from the Society of Friends in March 1748 for letting his son Israel marry a woman outside the Quaker faith. Thereafter, Daniel distrusted religious organizations, though he professed to be a Christian. Throughout his life, however, Boone retained his Quaker dislike for violence.

The Boone family moved first to a farm near Harrisonburg, Virginia, where they stayed for several years. While his parents, brothers, and sisters began life anew, Daniel went on the first of many extended hunts in the Shenandoah Mountains during the summer and autumn of 1750. Thereafter, much of his life would be spent away from home while he trapped and hunted deer for their skins, which he sold to help support his family.

When Boone's parents acquired 640 acres at the forks of the Yadkin River in North Carolina in October 1750 and moved there late in the year, Daniel went with them. Boone helped his father clear land and farm, but he preferred to hunt and trap in the woods. As a professional hunter who contributed to the deerskin trade, Boone played an important role in the local economy, and he soon acquired a well-known reputation for his marksmanship and hunting ability.

Indian hostility brought danger to isolated frontier settlements, and Boone joined the county militia by the summer of 1753. In 1755, when Great Britain and France engaged in a war to determine control of the trans-Appalachian frontier, Boone, at the age of twenty, joined a company of North Carolina volunteers as a teamster to accompany Gen. Edward Braddock's army in its attack on Fort Duquesne. When the French and their Indian allies ambushed and overwhelmed Braddock's force, Boone jumped on a horse from his wagon, cut the harness, and escaped to the rear, narrowly avoiding death.

Boone returned home during the summer of 1755 after visiting relatives in Exeter following his flight from the Battle of the Monongahela. A year later, on August 14, 1756, he married Rebecca Bryan, with his father, Justice of the Peace Squire Boone, presiding. Their first child, James, was born on May 3, 1757, followed by five sons and four daughters: Israel, January 25, 1759; Susannah, November 2, 1760; Jemima, October 4, 1762; Levina, March 23, 1766; Rebecca, May 26, 1768; Daniel Morgan, December 23, 1769; Jesse Bryan, May 2, 1773; William, June 20, 1775 (who died in infancy); and Nathan, March 2, 1781.

Soon after his marriage, Daniel and **Rebecca Bryan Boone** moved to a small farm along Sugartree Creek near present-day Farmington, North Carolina, where they lived for about ten years, until Cherokee hostilities forced them to flee to Culpeper County, Virginia, for safety in 1759. There Boone worked as a teamster, hauling tobacco to market. Thereafter, he gave most of his attention to hunting to support his family, and in 1760 he first crossed the Blue Ridge Mountains on a long winter hunt. In November 1762 Boone moved his family back to Rowan County, North Carolina. Four years later, he again relocated his family, this time to the mouth of Beaver Creek to escape the settlements and to be closer to his hunting grounds in the Blue Ridge Mountains.

In 1767 Boone crossed the mountains and made his first long hunt into Kentucky, passing through the Cumberland Gap in May 1769; he did not return home until the spring of 1771. Upon his return Boone felt increasingly crowded by the settlements, and his creditors often sued him for nonpayment of his debts. As a result he decided to move his family to Kentucky. On September 25, 1773, Boone led a party of about fifty men, women, and children west across the Appalachians. An Indian war party, however, blocked their path through the Cumberland Gap. Nevertheless, Boone continued to venture over the mountains, and, in March 1775, as an employee of the Transylvania Company, he led a party that cut the Wilderness Road to Kentucky and established the settlement of Boonesborough.

Boone moved his family to the settlement in September 1775, where land speculator Richard Henderson, who had organized the Transylvania Company to settle his western lands, promised him two thousand acres for his services. The American Revolution, however, soon changed the government structure in Virginia and North Carolina, and the company's land claims in Kentucky were not validated by the new government. Consequently, Boone never received title to those lands.

On May 20, 1775, the residents elected Boone to serve as representative to a convention charged with organizing a government for the settlements. At the convention, held in Boonesborough, Boone introduced two measures, which the delegates approved. One provided for hunting restrictions to preserve game, and the other encouraged horse breeding. Boone also became responsible for the defense of Boonesborough. Although he continued to supply his family and the settlement with meat by hunting and though he attempted to survey lands for himself and other settlers, when the American Revolution began hostile Indians, supported by the British, made the countryside more dangerous than ever before, and in April 1777 Boone was wounded in a Shawnee attack on Boonesborough.

During the American Revolution, the British urged the Shawnees to strike the American settlements south of the Ohio River, and Boonesborough became a major target. In January 1778 a large Shawnee war party under the leadership of Blackfish moved against the settlement and captured Boone, who had accompanied a group to make salt at a nearby spring. Boone convinced Blackfish to take him and his men to their village and to refrain from attacking Boonesborough. He would then convince the settlers to surrender to the British. The Shawnees agreed and took Boone north across the Ohio River, and in March Boone met with the British in Detroit. Boone convinced the British that the Kentuckians wanted to abandon the American cause, and they agreed to let Boone persuade the residents of Boonesborough to surrender.

Boone, however, escaped from Shawnee captivity in June and returned to Boonesborough to warn the settlement of Shawnee and British intentions to attack the town. Although he helped organize the defense of Boonesborough and foiled a Shawnee attack in

September, a few settlers remained convinced that he had betrayed them to the British. The stigma of a traitor marred his reputation among some frontier people for many years. He even suffered the humiliation of a court-martial for treason in October 1778, but he was quickly acquitted and promoted to the rank of major in the Kentucky militia.

In 1779 Boone settled a party of family members and newly arrived emigrants from North Carolina at Boone's Station, near present-day Athens, Kentucky. There he farmed and located and surveyed land for speculators, claiming a portion for his services, and he soon regained his reputation as an honest and trustworthy leader.

In November 1780 Virginia officials promoted him to the rank of lieutenant colonel in the Fayette County militia, and its citizens elected him as the county's representative to the Virginia assembly, where he took his seat in April 1781. While Boone served in Richmond, the British, under Cornwallis, captured him on June 4, after the assembly adjourned and fled to Charlottesville. He was soon released, and he returned to Richmond in the autumn for the second session of the assembly. In November 1782 Boone also participated in a raid across the Ohio against the Shawnees.

Boone moved his family to Limestone, Kentucky, in 1783, where he operated a tavern and trading house and continued his work as a surveyor for settlers and speculators who had land certificates and warrants from Virginia. Eventually, Boone claimed more than twelve thousand acres, making him one of the largest resident land speculators in Kentucky. He was, however, a bad businessman, and he sold most of his acreage for less than market value. Moreover, he made bad loans and posted bond for the debts of others. Between 1786 and 1789 creditors and landowners sued him at least ten times for faulty surveys, breaches of contract, and bad debts.

Despite his misfortune as a land speculator, the voters of Bourbon County elected Boone to the Virginia assembly in 1787, and he took his seat in the state legislature from October until January 1788, during which time he sponsored a bill for the establishment of ferries in Kentucky and supported a resolution that demanded Great Britain surrender its western posts.

After serving a second time in the Virginia assembly, Boone returned to Limestone, but he soon decided to move to Point Pleasant at the mouth of the Kanawha River in present-day West Virginia. There, in 1789, he opened a store, particularly to serve the fur and ginseng trade as well as to supply the local militia, and he continued to work as a surveyor. In October the justices of the newly organized Kanawha County court recommended Boone for the rank of lieutenant colonel in the militia, which made him the third-ranking officer in the county.

In April 1791 Boone was again elected to the Virginia assembly at Fort Lee, now Charleston, West Virginia, to represent Kanawha County. He sat for his third and last time in the Virginia assembly from October through December and usually voted with the majority. Although his constituents recognized him as a respectable leader, he was not wealthy. In 1792 Boone's taxable property included only two horses, one slave, and five hundred acres, and he lived in a cabin near present-day Charleston, supporting his family by hunting.

Boone remained in Virginia until the summer of 1796 when he moved his family to Brushy Fork, Kentucky, where he farmed and hunted. In November 1798 the depletion of game and pressing creditors forced him to move again, this time to the mouth of the Little Sandy on the Ohio River.

At that time Boone's son **Daniel Morgan Boone** had scouted lands for settlement in Missouri and had applied for a land grant along the Femme Osage River from the Spanish lieutenant governor **Zenon Trudeau** at St. Louis. Trudeau urged Morgan and his father to bring a party of settlers to Missouri, and he offered Boone 1,000 arpents (about 850 acres) plus 600 arpents for every family that he brought with him. Boone accepted the offer and, in September, led his family and a group of settlers to Missouri where they arrived during the first week in October. Lt. Gov. **Charles de Hault Delassus** welcomed Boone and appointed him the syndic, that is, chief administrative officer, for the Femme Osage District. The appointment became official on June 11, 1800. As the district's syndic Boone served as the justice of the peace and militia commander. He also supervised land surveys and recommended applicants for land concessions.

Boone, however, gave more attention to hunting and trapping than to his own administrative responsibilities and farming. When the Missouri country became a possession of the United States with the Louisiana Purchase in 1803, Boone's land claim became jeopardized. In 1809 a commission charged with the responsibility of sorting out conflicting claims held Boone's Spanish land grant invalid because he had not occupied, surveyed, and improved it as Spanish law required. By that time Boone had moved to a cabin on land owned by his son **Nathan Boone,** near present-day Defiance, Missouri. By 1805, however, Boone's health began to fail, and he was unable to spend long periods hunting in the woods during the winter months.

During the War of 1812 Boone often wanted to ride on patrols with the local militia company, but his age and infirmities kept him at home. His neighbors, however, often sought his advice when rumors circulated about a pending Indian attack. After Rebecca died on March 18, 1813, Boone spent most of his time with his daughter Jemima and her husband, Flanders Callaway, so that he could be near Rebecca's grave along Turque Creek. Although Congress confirmed his original Spanish land grant in 1814, Boone took little interest in daily affairs after Rebecca died, and he began to put his affairs in order in anticipation of his death, including paying his debts, reading the Bible, and buying a coffin.

As Boone grew more feeble, however, he still attempted to make brief hunting and trapping expeditions into the nearby countryside, but the cold weather further deteriorated his health. In late September 1820, one month shy of his eighty-sixth birthday, Boone became seriously ill at Nathan's home. Although the cause of his illness remains uncertain, it proved fatal, and Boone died on September 26, 1820. He was buried two days later next to Rebecca.

At the time of his death, Boone epitomized the frontiersman. He had the reputation of being an excellent hunter and trapper as well as a public servant who not only led men, women, and children to a dangerous frontier, but also helped protect them. Although he was not a good businessman and lost most of the lands that he claimed, Boone's reputation for prowess with his rifle, courage, and leadership grew after his death, and his life soon became part of American folklore.

R. DOUGLAS HURT

Bakeless, John. *Daniel Boone.* New York: William Morrow, 1939.

Faragher, John Mack. *Daniel Boone: The Life and Legend of an American Pioneer.* New York: Henry Holt, 1992.

BOONE, DANIEL MORGAN (1769–1839)

Daniel Morgan Boone was born on December 23, 1769, the seventh child of Daniel and **Rebecca Bryan Boone,** at their home in North Carolina along the banks of the Yadkin River. He moved to Kentucky with his parents in the autumn of 1773 and settled at the site of present-day Boonesborough.

During the autumn of 1787 Boone hunted with his father north of the Ohio River in Indian Territory. A decade later he traveled to Missouri in search of good lands and to call on the Spanish governor and inquire about land grants and restrictions on settlement. In Missouri he found the Femme Osage River valley appealing. Boone asked Lt. Gov. **Zenon Trudeau,** on behalf of his father, about the possibility of a land grant to settle a group of immigrants. The governor offered **Daniel Boone** a grant of 1,000 arpents (about 850 acres) and 600 arpents for each family that

migrated. Morgan Boone then built a cabin with his four slaves and began clearing land near the mouth of Femme Osage Creek at a location known as Darst's Bottom. He returned to Kentucky by the autumn of 1798. A year later, in September 1799, he left with his family for Missouri, embarking with his mother and other family members in a pirogue, while his father drove their livestock overland. They settled about twenty-five miles southwest of St. Charles.

On March 2, 1800, Boone married Sarah Griffin Lewis, a thirteen-year-old girl who had recently immigrated with her parents from Virginia. After the wedding in St. Charles, they returned to his farm. During the winter of 1800–1801, he trapped along the Niangua and Pomme de Terre Rivers and at the headwaters of the Grand Osage. The next winter he trapped with his brother **Nathan Boone,** William T. Lamme, and William Hayes Jr.

In January 1805 the voters in the St. Charles District elected Boone to the position of justice in the court of common pleas. He also joined Nathan in the manufacture of salt at Boone's Lick in Howard County until 1810. In 1814 he helped Nathan survey the road from St. Charles to Boone's Lick. Boone continued to live on his farm until 1821, and he owned two slaves. He also served on the commission that selected Jefferson City as the site for the capital.

In September and October 1812 Boone served as a spy for Gen. **Benjamin Howard.** He also built a stockade, called Boone's Fort, at Darst's Bottom at the mouth of Femme Osage Creek near the present-day town of Matson. During the War of 1812 the frontier people considered it the largest and strongest fort in St. Charles County. Boone also served as the captain of a company of local militia, known as Howard's Rangers, which formed part of the Missouri Rangers, from July 19, 1813, to June 21, 1814, after which he reenlisted. He was responsible for building fortified posts along the Missouri River. In 1816 he moved to Montgomery County where he worked as a surveyor for the government, and he also surveyed much of the land in St. Charles, Warren, and Lincoln Counties.

In 1825 Boone moved to the present-day site of Kansas City where he cleared land and built a cabin. The next year, however, Gen. **William Clark,** superintendent of Indian Affairs, appointed him to the position of farmer for the Kansa Indians. During the autumn of 1827 Boone settled about seven miles west of present-day Lawrence, Kansas, on the north bank of the Kansas River. He taught agricultural practices to the Kansa Indians for five years. On June 6, 1831, he also entered 80 acres and, on September 12, 1831, another 160 acres of government land in Jackson County, Missouri. He claimed an additional 80 acres on April 28, 1836, but sold 80 acres to Boone Hays on June 27, 1837.

In 1836 Boone was appointed as one of the commissioners to locate a county seat for Johnson County, Missouri, and they chose Warrensburg. Daniel Morgan Boone fathered nine children. He died of cholera in Jackson County on July 13, 1839, and is buried in an unmarked grave either in the Westport churchyard or on the property that he sold to Hays.

R. DOUGLAS HURT

Faragher, John Mack. *Daniel Boone: The Life and Legend of an American Pioneer.* New York: Henry Holt, 1992.

Foley, William E. *The Genesis of Missouri: From Wilderness Outpost to Statehood.* Columbia: University of Missouri Press, 1989.

BOONE, JOHN WILLIAM "BLIND" (1864–1927)

John William "Blind" Boone, a concert pianist and composer who played and wrote both classical and ragtime music, was born on May 17, 1864, in Miami, Missouri, where his mother, Rachel Boone, who had fled to freedom, worked as a cook in the camp of the Seventh Missouri Militia. Boone's father was a white bugler with whom Rachel formed a temporary liaison. Shortly after Boone's birth, mother and son moved to Warrensburg where Rachel worked as a domestic in a number of homes, including that of future U.S. senator **Francis Marion Cockrell.** At six months of age, Boone developed "brain fever" (probably some form of encephalitis or meningitis). His anxious mother was told by local doctors that his life could be saved only by removing his eyeballs to relieve the pressure on his brain—an operation that of course left him blind.

In spite of the handicap, Boone developed into a happy youngster who quickly displayed an inborn musical talent. His mother married Harrison Hendrix, a widower with five children, when John was eight, and the youngster fit readily into the larger family.

Recognizing the need to develop his ability, Rachel persuaded Cockrell and others to underwrite sending John to the Missouri School for the Blind in St. Louis in 1873 when he was nine years old. Boone did not take well to formal education but constantly gravitated toward the music room to listen to the older students practicing. One of these, Enoch Donley, befriended him and tried to give him piano lessons, only to have his pupil respond by playing by ear complicated pieces he had heard the senior students practicing. As word of Boone's talent spread, he was frequently called upon to entertain visitors to the school.

During his second year there, Boone became increasingly aware of racial prejudice as Missouri moved into a more conservative era. He began sneaking out of the dormitory at night to visit the "tenderloin" district of St. Louis where he could listen to the itinerant piano players grinding out wild but melodious tunes in the many dives in the area.

Eventually Boone ran away from school and returned to Warrensburg with the help of a train conductor who befriended him. He organized several children into a "tin whistle band," which played at fairs and picnics for whatever loose change they could pick up. On one such occasion he was kidnapped by a transient gambler, Mark Cromwell, who used Boone's talent to bring in money for his habit. Eventually rescued by his stepfather, Boone, nevertheless, had developed a wanderlust and soon struck out on his own, working the trains with the help of the railroad crews with whom he had developed friendships. He had also become acquainted with ministers at Glasgow and Fayette, who offered him board for playing the piano at their churches.

While thus engaged, Boone came to the attention of John Lange, a prominent black contractor and entrepreneur in Columbia, who recognized the possibilities in Boone's musical talent. In December 1879 Lange invited Boone to play in a local festival, billing him as "Blind John" who could produce "very fine music by intuition" and play "the most difficult pieces by ear." Three months later Boone matched talents with another virtuoso, "Blind Tom" Bethune, when the latter played a concert in Columbia. Lange decided, with the approval of Boone's mother, to launch him on the small-town midwestern concert circuit. Lange recruited a banjo picker, a violinist, and a ten-year-old vocalist named Stella May as his assistants, and thus began what eventually would be known as the Blind Boone Company.

Although crowds initially were sparse and profits low, Lange kept the company going, convinced that Boone had the talent to make a successful career. He arranged for several teachers to help Boone improve his technique and broaden his repertoire. The company had turned the corner financially by 1885 when Boone, at age twenty-one, became a full partner in the operation. By then the company was playing a ten-month tour, which included larger cities, usually performing six nights a week. By 1915 Boone had played eighty-four hundred concerts, traveled more than twenty thousand miles, and worn out sixteen pianos. The company usually played one- or two-night stands throughout the Midwest—Missouri, Kansas, Illinois, Iowa, and Oklahoma—staying in the homes of prominent black citizens in the small- and middle-size communities. They performed in both theaters and churches with mixed but segregated audiences in the former, while attendance in the latter depended upon whether it was a white or black church. Frequently in the larger cities the company would play a black church one night and a white church the next.

The typical Boone concert ran two hours without intermission. Opening with some hymn variations, which he played with great embellishment, Boone would move on to some classical pieces and even occasionally play imitations of other musical instruments on the keyboard. Adapting a ploy he had learned from the Blind Tom concert, Boone began inviting someone from the audience to come forward and play a difficult number, which he would repeat without missing a note. He would then move on to play a variety of black melodies, "plantation songs," the precursors of ragtime, using his own arrangements. He called this "putting cookies on the lower shelf so that everyone can get at them." He concluded most concerts with his own composition, "The Marshfield Tornado," which depicted a storm that visited that small southwestern Missouri town during the Sunday-evening church hour in the early 1880s.

Standing only five feet tall and weighing 250 pounds, the blind musician became a well-known figure in the midwestern communities to which he returned year after year during his heyday. As fame and wealth came his way, he loved to dress fashionably and was given to the ostentatious display of ornate jewelry. Yet, he also gave thousands of dollars to black churches for their special projects. He married Eugenia Lange, the youngest sister of his manager, in 1889, and maintained a large ten-room home near downtown Columbia as his summer headquarters; the couple had no children.

By the 1890s as Boone's fame spread and the popularity of black music increased, Lange began publishing a number of his compositions, ranging from sparkling waltzes, to classical descriptive pieces, to minstrel or "coon songs"—the forerunners of ragtime. Many of these are now long forgotten, and the remaining copies of his sheet music are collectors' items. Although he never made a phonograph recording, Boone was one of the first artists to cut piano rolls directly. He signed a contract with the QRS Company of Chicago, one of the leading piano-roll manufacturers, in 1912 to produce eleven rolls over the next five years, thereby becoming the first black pianist to make rolls for any company.

Boone's career went into decline after World War I. His last major tour took him to most eastern cities and universities, including Harvard and Yale, over eighteen months in 1919 and 1920. Thereafter he found himself playing primarily on the tank-town circuit. His longtime manager and friend John Lange died in 1916, and thereafter financial problems began to plague the company. His new manager, Wayne Allen of Columbia, found it increasingly difficult to book major concerts. America was entering the Jazz Age, which Boone deplored, and the development of radio and motion pictures began eating away at concert audiences. Boone continued playing through the spring of 1927 when ill health forced his retirement. He died of apoplexy at Warrensburg on October 4, 1927. Probate proceedings revealed that he had dissipated most of his wealth during the final decade.

Boone was certainly a musical genius. Contemporary reviews attest to his popularity. Although his compositions are largely forgotten today except for two rag medleys—"Strains from the Alleys" and "Strains from the Flat Branch," which occasionally appear in the repertoires of current ragtimers—Boone left behind a lively range of works from classical to popular. He was truly one of America's pioneer black artists, embracing both sides of the American style that emanated from black musical traditions at the turn of the century.

WILLIAM E. PARRISH

Batterson, Jack A. *Blind Boone: Missouri's Ragtime Pioneer.* Columbia: University of Missouri Press, 1998.

Blind Boone Memorial Foundation. Papers. Western Historical Manuscripts Collection, Columbia.

Fuell, Melissa. *Blind Boone: His Early Life and His Achievements.* Kansas City: Burton Publishing, 1915.

Hackley, E. Azalia. Collection. Detroit Public Library, Detroit.

Parrish, William E. " 'Blind' Boone's Ragtime." *Missouri Life* 7 (November–December 1979).

BOONE, NATHAN (1781–1856)

Nathan Boone was born on March 2, 1781, the youngest child of Daniel and **Rebecca Bryan Boone,** at Boone's Station, near present-day Athens, Kentucky. At the age of seven he moved with his parents to a farm near Point Pleasant at the mouth of the Kanawha River in what is now West Virginia. For eighteen months beginning in 1793, he attended a Baptist school near Lexington, Kentucky. The next year, at the age of thirteen, he accompanied his father on a hunting trip north of the Ohio River, and he began to learn the skills of a woodsman.

During the summer of 1795 the Boone family moved to Brushy Fork, Kentucky, about six miles east of present-day Millersburg, where **Daniel Boone** farmed and hunted for three years. Then the family relocated to the mouth of the Little Sandy on the Ohio River, where Nathan apparently had gone a short time before to break new land. His father, however, had difficulty living anywhere for a long period because of bad business ventures, debts, and a wanderlust.

In the autumn of 1799 Daniel Boone moved his family to Missouri, where he received a land grant from Spain. Before Nathan arrived, however, he married sixteen-year-old Olive Van Bibber at Little Sandy, Kentucky, on September 26, 1799. Boone and his wife traveled by horseback via Lexington, Louisville, and Vincennes. They reached St. Louis in late October and proceeded to his brother **Daniel Morgan Boone**'s grant in the Femme Osage District, about twenty-five miles southwest of St. Charles, where they spent the winter.

Boone built a cabin about four miles northwest of Morgan's settlement on the bank of the Femme Osage where he had received a Spanish land grant of approximately four hundred acres. He spent the next few years working as a contract surveyor for the federal government in St. Charles, Montgomery, and Warren Counties. He also engaged in extended hunting and trapping expeditions, and on several occasions lost his furs to the Indians.

In the spring of 1805 Nathan and Morgan traveled to Howard County where they developed a salt-making business by boiling water from a saline spring. This site soon became known as Boone's Lick. The brothers transported their salt by canoe downriver to St. Louis for sale, and they enlarged their operation and employed twenty men. Hostile Indians, however, forced them to abandon their saltworks, and they sold it in 1810.

While Nathan Boone operated the saltworks, he also began military service, which would become his life's work. In 1808 he served as a militia captain and guide for Capt. Eli B. Clemson and Brig. Gen. **William Clark,** and he helped build Fort Osage (first called Fort Clark) in September. Boone played a major role in convincing the Osage to negotiate a peace treaty that year.

During the War of 1812 Boone helped organize a group of mounted rangers for three months. In March 1812 he raised a company for one year, serving under Gen. **Benjamin Howard** as a captain. Boone's rangers patrolled a two-thousand-square-mile area known as the St. Charles District, which extended from the mouth of the Salt River on the Mississippi to Fort Clemson at the mouth of Loutre Creek on the Missouri River. The rangers also helped the army regulars, under Lt. John Campbell, build a host of blockhouses for defense, such as Fort Mason near present-day Hannibal.

On August 15, 1813, Boone led a seventeen-man expedition against the Indian towns near Peoria. Although a war party of Sauk and Foxes attacked his camp one night along the Illinois River, Boone and his men escaped. He also fought at the Battle of the Sink Hole near the Cuivre River. On December 10, 1813, he was promoted to the rank of major, and received an honorable discharge in June 1815. Most of his military service during the War of 1812 involved routine patrols in northern and western Missouri. When the rangers were not needed, Boone returned to his farming and surveying activities, and he completed the survey for the Boone's Lick Road

from St. Charles to Old Franklin in 1814. This road served as the major route to the Oregon and Santa Fe Trails.

In 1820 the voters in St. Charles County elected Boone to the Constitutional Convention that met in St. Louis from June 12 to July 19. He served on the committee in charge of the convention's printing, and he worked to have the capital located in St. Charles rather than St. Louis. After the convention, Boone returned to his farming and surveying work, and he became one of the wealthiest men in the county. The military, however, recalled him a dozen years later while he surveyed a boundary between the Sioux, Foxes, and Sauk for Gen. William Clark, who was superintendent of Indian Affairs. On June 16, 1832, Boone again became a captain of mounted rangers. His company enlisted at St. Charles on August 11, 1832, for duty with Col. Zachary Taylor in the Black Hawk War.

On November 22, 1832, the army transferred Boone to Fort Gibson in Indian Territory where he commanded a company of mounted rangers. The following spring he surveyed the boundary between the Creek and Cherokee Nations. On August 15, 1833, he received a captain's commission in the newly created federal regiment of dragoons.

Boone took part in the recruitment process while stationed at Franklin, Missouri, from October 15, 1833, to April 29, 1834. He joined his regiment in June 1834, and commanded Company H of the First Dragoons. In late September 1834 Boone led Company H, under Col. **Stephen Watts Kearny,** to Iowa, where they wintered at Fort Des Moines, located near the mouth of the Des Moines River at present-day Montrose, Iowa.

During the spring of 1835, Boone led a ten-week reconnaissance into Sioux country, which resulted in a sharp skirmish in the upper Des Moines River valley. Outnumbered, his men held the Sioux at bay and escaped under cover of darkness. On September 16, 1836, he attended the cession treaty council at Davenport, Iowa, where the Sauk and the Foxes agreed to removal. When the army abandoned Fort Des Moines on June 1, 1837, Boone departed with Company H for Fort Leavenworth, Kansas. During his three years of duty in Iowa, he explored much of the country, the details of which were later incorporated into the first map of the state, where a county and a river were named in his honor.

In 1837 Boone sold his home in St. Charles County to pay debts and moved his family to a farm two miles north of Ash Grove, Missouri. He had discovered this country during his trapping expeditions more than thirty years earlier, and he liked the look of the land. However, he did not leave the army. On September 5, 1837, Boone participated in an expedition that explored possible routes for a military road between Fort Leavenworth to Fort Gibson. In the spring of the next year, he directed the survey of the road from Fort Leavenworth to Fort Snelling, Minnesota. During 1839 Boone served as the first commander of the new Fort Wayne on Cherokee land at Spanvinaw Creek in present-day eastern Oklahoma. By early September he had returned to Fort Leavenworth and, along with Colonel Kearny, embarked on another reconnaissance to learn about a possible uprising of the Otoes and to hold a cession treaty council with the Potawatomi.

In late March 1840 Boone led two companies of dragoons to the Otoes' village along the Nishnabotna River in Iowa, where they had been threatening white settlers, and he ordered them to leave the territory. He then conducted more surveying work near Fort Gibson. On May 14, 1843, he took his dragoons west along the Arkansas River to the Santa Fe Trail and then south to the Canadian River to demonstrate to the Indians the military power of the United States. He returned to Fort Gibson on July 31. A month later, T. Hartley Crawford, commissioner of Indian Affairs, sent Boone to Texas where he joined Gen. Sam Houston for peace negations with the Comanche.

Boone led his company of dragoons on patrols in Indian Territory and Arkansas during 1844 and 1845. These expeditions were routine until November 20, 1845, when he was ordered to the Arkansas to end the lawlessness between the old settlers and the Treaty Cherokee. The army sent Boone to the vicinity of present-day Evansville, Arkansas, to keep the two factions apart, and he remained there until the federal government settled tribal differences during the summer of 1846.

Boone did not serve in the Mexican War because of his age. On February 16, 1847, he was promoted to major in the First Dragoons. He continued to serve at Fort Leavenworth until September 9, 1848, when he took a leave of absence because of poor health, and returned to his farm near Ash Grove. On July 25, 1850, he was promoted to lieutenant colonel of the Second Dragoons, apparently while on sick leave. He remained at home until he resigned from the army on July 15, 1853.

Boone fathered fourteen children. At the time of his death in Greene County on October 16, 1856, he owned twelve hundred acres and eleven slaves. He is buried in the cemetery north of Ash Grove.

R. DOUGLAS HURT

Faragher, John Mack. *Daniel Boone: The Life and Legend of an American Pioneer.* New York: Henry Holt, 1992.

Foley, William E. *The Genesis of Missouri: From Wilderness Outpost to Statehood.* Columbia: University of Missouri Press, 1989.

Hurt, R. Douglas. *Nathan Boone and the American Frontier.* Columbia: University of Missouri Press, 1998.

Walker, Wayne T. "Nathan Boone: The Forgotten Hero of Missouri." *Journal of the West* 18 (April 1979): 85–94.

BOONE, REBECCA BRYAN (1739–1813)

The granddaughter of Welsh Quakers who settled in Pennsylvania in the late seventeenth century, Rebecca Bryan moved to the Yadkin valley of North Carolina with her grandfather and parents at age ten. She was born in Virginia on January 9, 1739, into a large clan of Bryans. In 1751 Squire Boone and his extended multigenerational family settled nearby in the valley. A common heritage of Quakerism helped to bring the families together, and many intermarriages took place.

At a Boone-Bryan wedding in 1753, Rebecca and **Daniel Boone** began their courtship, leading to marriage in August 1756. Rebecca was seventeen, Daniel five years older. The marriage lasted fifty-six years until her death. She bore ten children, six sons and four daughters, over a period of twenty-five years. Throughout her marriage there were always children and, later, grandchildren in her home. At one time in the early 1780s she presided over a household of nineteen or twenty people on Marble Creek in Kentucky. Sometimes they owned a few slaves.

Boone created homes in North Carolina, Virginia, Kentucky, and Missouri, but at least twice she refused to move. Starting married life in North Carolina in a small cabin on her father-in-law's land, she established five more homes over the next twenty years in Yadkin valley; Culpeper County, Virginia; and Boonesborough, Kentucky. In the 1780s they lived in three towns in Kentucky and Virginia and several cabins in different locations in Kentucky. In 1799 they moved to Missouri and into their own home in 1803, where they lived for ten years, until her death, their longest residence. The houses ranged in size from single-room cabins to a tavern (in Limestone, Kentucky).

As head of her household, Boone had to feed and clothe her family. Feeding meant planting, cultivating, and harvesting a kitchen garden, providing most of the family's fruits and vegetables. She cared for chickens, pigs, and cows. Butter and cheese making were daily chores. Preservation of meat, domestic or game, also fell to her. Clothing began with flax and wool grown at home, spun, dyed, woven, and finally sewn. Since male family members wore buckskin when hunting, she was probably also proficient in tanning and preparing hides for clothing. She and the girls made candles and soap, and chopped firewood.

She was a competent hunter, providing meat during Daniel's long absences. Without her housework the family could not have survived, and her work freed Daniel to engage in his long hunts, his legislative duties, his surveying and land speculating, and his many trips to market ginseng and hides collected by family and neighbors.

Only one child, William, born in 1775, died in infancy. Oldest sons James and Israel were killed by Indians while still young and unmarried, but the other seven children married and had families, providing the Boones with sixty-eight grandchildren. In 1759 the threat of Indian attacks caused the Boones to move to Virginia to stay with friends. The next year Daniel departed to hunt in Kentucky and was gone about two years. Rebecca had no word from him during that time, and when he returned in 1762 she was pregnant, probably by Daniel's brother Ned. Jemima, born the fall of Daniel's return, after they had moved back to Yadkin, was the daughter closest to Daniel over the years.

Rebecca Boone is representative of the frontier wives of American history in her moves, her hard work, her many children, and her tolerance and patience with a restless husband. Like most women on the frontier, she left few records to document her life and feelings. Buried among the accounts of her husband's and children's exploits are references to her. Family tradition described her as tall and buxom, with black hair and dark eyes, and as a good, neat housekeeper. Her simplicity and mild speech reflected her Quaker background. The Boone children continued to live close to their parents, demonstrating their good relationships. The family's move to Missouri, for instance, involved almost one hundred people, and more Boones arrived later.

In February 1813 Rebecca Boone became ill while sugaring with family members. She died on March 18, surrounded by family. Daniel had a coffin made for her from local black walnut, and she was buried at the Boone-Bryan burying ground in the Charette community near the Femme Osage valley. Daniel missed her and had a duplicate coffin made for himself, which he kept clean and ready for his own use seven years later.

JO TICE BLOOM

Faragher, John Mack. *Daniel Boone: The Life and Legend of an American Pioneer.* New York: Henry Holt, 1992.

BOTHWELL, JOHN HOMER (1848–1929)

John Homer Bothwell, a capitalist, philanthropist, attorney, and state representative, was born in Maysville, in Clay County, Illinois, on November 20, 1848, the son of James K. and Marian Brissenden Bothwell. He attended the University of Indiana, and graduated in 1869 with a bachelor of science degree. After reading law at Springfield, Illinois, he entered Union University Law School, in Albany, New York, from which he graduated in 1871.

Bothwell came to Sedalia, Missouri, in 1871. At that time Sedalia was a rapidly growing community offering good prospects to able young men. He opened a law practice, handling mostly civil cases. Although his interest lay in banking and corporate law, from 1873 to 1876 he served as assistant prosecuting attorney for Pettis County, receiving recognition for his skill in criminal prosecution. In 1890 Bothwell served as acting judge of the circuit court.

Bothwell became active in local affairs shortly after his arrival in Sedalia. In 1880 and 1881, he was secretary to the Sedalia Exposition. He led the campaign to build a new courthouse in 1884, which resulted in the construction of the imposing Second Empire structure.

Bothwell was a principal stockholder in the Sedalia National Bank, and in 1896 he became its president. He owned large amounts of real estate, and platted the Bothwell and Weed addition to Sedalia. He was instrumental in establishing the Midland Savings and Loan Company.

In 1884 Bothwell married Hattie Ellen Jaynes, the daughter of Col. Anderson D. and Mary Jane Brown Jaynes. In 1886 the couple had a child who died at birth. Hattie died of unknown causes in 1887.

In 1902 Bothwell moved to St. Louis and organized the West St. Louis Water and Light Company, which created the first water system in St. Louis County. The company furnished water for the St. Louis World's Fair, as well as the towns of Clayton, Kirkwood, Webster Groves, Maplewood, and Wellston.

Bothwell was active in the Republican Party. In 1892 he was elected first vice president of the Missouri League of Republican Clubs, and later that year he chaired the Republican State Central Committee. He represented Missouri at the Republican National Convention in 1896, 1908, and 1928. He represented Pettis County in the Thirty-fifth, Thirty-eighth, Forty-first, and Forty-second General Assemblies, where he served on a variety of committees reflecting his interest in constitutional law, including the Judiciary Committee, the Criminal Fees and Costs Committee, the Rules Committee, and the Seat of Government Committee. His work on the 1889 revision of the Missouri statutes was praised, as was his careful study of election law. In 1889 he was instrumental in the passage of the reform-ballot law, and in 1895 he worked for the revision of election laws for large cities. Bothwell was a delegate to the 1922–1923 convention that drafted a series of proposed amendments to the Missouri Constitution submitted to the voters in 1924.

Bothwell, who served as president of the Sedalia Board of Trade, encouraged the growth of Sedalia partly by encouraging outside investment. In 1896 he prepared the proposal for a constitutional amendment that would move the state capital to Sedalia, a measure that was defeated by Missouri voters. His major contribution to Sedalia was his role in persuading the Missouri Pacific Railroad to locate its principal manufacturing and repair shops there, resulting in a $2 million investment that created eighteen hundred new jobs. He also led the efforts that culminated in the Missouri State Fair's being located in Sedalia.

Following the typical pattern of the nineteenth-century capitalist and philanthropist, Bothwell used his considerable skill to benefit his community as well as himself. During the 1920s he formed a corporation that established the Bothwell Hotel, which became Sedalia's premier hotel. He also helped organize Bothwell Hospital by mandating that fifty thousand dollars of his donation to the hospital trust be invested in the hotel company; he also donated one hundred thousand dollars in government bonds to the hospital. He built and donated to the community a rural school, Bothwell School, and a residence for its teacher, near the site of his rural home, Stony Ridge Farm.

The Bothwell Lodge at Stony Ridge Farm, now a state historic site, was begun as a retreat in 1898. Constructed in four sections, the large arts-and-crafts-style building was completed in 1928. Bothwell died on August 4, 1929. Following the death of Bothwell's niece in 1969, the lodge was given to the state, and in 1974 the Missouri Department of Natural Resources assumed responsibility for its development as a state park.

RHONDA CHALFANT

Bothwell, John Homer. Papers. Bothwell Lodge State Historic Site, Sedalia, Mo.

Ihrig, B. B. *The First One Hundred Years: A History of the City of Sedalia, Missouri, 1860–1960.* Sedalia, Mo.: Hurlbut Printing, 1960.

"John Homer Bothwell." In *Missouri: Mother of the West,* by Walter Williams and Floyd Shoemaker, vol. 4. Chicago: American Historical Society, 1930.

Portrait and Biographical Record of Johnson and Pettis Counties, Missouri. Chicago: Chapman Publishing, 1919.

Sedalia Democrat, August 5, 1929.

Sedalia Evening Sentinel, 1904.

BOTTOMLEY, JAMES LEROY (1900–1959)

James LeRoy Bottomley, a star first baseman for the St. Louis Cardinals of the National League from 1922 to 1932, was born in Oglesby, Illinois, on April 23, 1900. His father, a coal miner, soon moved the family to Nokamis, Illinois. Bottomley graduated from the local high school, and then worked as a blacksmith and machinist—though he still found time to play semipro ball in the area.

Bottomley's break came in 1920 when **Wesley Branch Rickey,** general manager of the Cardinals, gave him a tryout. Rickey signed Bottomley to a minor league contract with Sioux City, Iowa, of the Western League. He played three seasons in the minor leagues. He was the first homegrown Cardinal, "the man who started the farm system," according to Rickey.

Given a late-season job at first base with the Cardinals in 1922, Bottomley drove in thirty-five runs in thirty-seven games and made an unassisted double play, the first of fifty-five in his career. In 1923, his first full season, Bottomley hit .371 and drove in ninety-four runs. It was the first of several great seasons that played a key role in the Cardinals' ability to win pennants in 1926, 1928, 1930, and 1931 and World Series Championships in 1926 and 1931. Frank Frisch called him "the best clutch hitter I ever saw," and Bill Terry, the New York Giants' player-manager, called him "a winner who held St. Louis's championship clubs together," the man "we feared the most."

On September 6, 1924, Bottomley had six hits in six at bats and set a major league record, which still stands, by driving in twelve runs against Brooklyn, breaking the mark of Wilbert Robinson, the Dodger's manager that day. Bottomley's best season came in 1928 when he hit .325, a league-leading 31 homers, and drove in 136 runs (also tops in the league), and won the Most Valuable Player Award. For the latter he received one thousand dollars in gold. In 1931 Bottomley hit .3482, finishing behind teammate **Charles James "Chick" Hafey** (.3489) and Bill Terry (.3486) in the closest batting-championship race in major league history.

Hampered by injuries in 1932, Bottomley was traded to Cincinnati, who dealt him to the St. Louis Browns after the 1934 season. There he ended his major league career in 1937 as a player-manager. He managed the Syracuse club in the International League the following season.

Bottomley managed to save much of his baseball income, including twenty-two thousand dollars in World Series bonuses. He bought a farm near Bourbon, Missouri, but health problems caused him to move to nearby Sullivan where he was buried after an apparent heart attack in a downtown St. Louis parking lot caused his death on December 11, 1959. Shortly before he died he had returned to baseball as a scout for the Cubs and as a manager in the Appalachian League.

The well-liked Bottomley's constant smile resulted in his nickname "Sunny Jim." His swaggering stroll and habit of wearing his hat tilted to the left also made the six-foot, 180-pound left-hander a Ladies' Day favorite. He was so popular in St. Louis that his wedding made the front page of the St. Louis papers, even though by then he played for Cincinnati.

On the strength of his career .310 batting mark, 2,313 hits, 465 doubles, 1,177 runs scored, 1,422 runs batted in, and fine fielding, Bottomley was elected posthumously to the Baseball Hall of Fame in 1974.

JOHN E. MELTON

Broeg, Bob. *The Pilot Light and the Gashouse Gang: The Story of Frank Frisch and His Contemporaries.* St. Louis: Bethany Press, 1980.
Gershman, Michael. *1990 Baseball Card Engagement Book.* Dallas: Taylor Publishing, 1990.
New York Times, December 12, 1959.
Shatzin, Mike, ed. *The Ballplayers: Baseball's Ultimate Biographical Reference.* New York: William Morrow, 1990.

BOURGMONT, ETIENNE DE VÉNIARD SIEUR DE (1679–1734)

Etienne de Véniard sieur de Bourgmont was the first known white man to explore the lower and middle Missouri River and systematically record his observations. For years (approximately 1712 to 1719), he lived among the Missouri tribe, near the mouth of the Grand River, and used their village as a base for wide-ranging exploration and trading missions. He took the daughter of a Missouri chief as his wife, and their son was born in 1714. The journal of his expedition upriver that same year, *Routte qu'il faut tenir pour monter la rivière du Missoury* ("Route to Be Taken to Ascend the Missouri River"), enabled the French cartographer Guillaume Delisle to draw the first reasonably accurate map of the river, from its mouth on the Mississippi to the Platte in present-day southeastern Nebraska. In a separate report, *L'Exacte Description de la Louisiane,* the explorer described the flora, fauna, and Indian tribes along the route.

Bourgmont was born in April 1679 at Cerisy Belle-Etoile, in central Normandy. He left his native land around 1698 to serve in the French Troupes de la Marine in Canada, but deserted at Detroit in 1706 to live as a trader and explorer. In 1712 he moved from the Great Lakes region to the Missouri country, and there built a network of contacts and alliances among the river tribes pledging to support the French and each other against encroachments from Spanish and English rivals and from hostile tribes from the North, notably the Foxes.

In 1720 Bourgmont returned to France, preceded by glowing recommendations from the colonial administration in Louisiana. That same year he was commissioned as captain of the colonial troops, with the title of commandant of the Missouri River, and created a Knight of the Order of the Cross of Saint Louis. Armed with these new honors, he persuaded the French government to appoint him to lead still another expedition, this time into the uncharted lands of the "Padoucas" (that is, the Plains Apache) who, from their villages in present Kansas, were blocking French access to the gold mines of the Rocky Mountains and trade with New Mexico. A base, Fort d'Orleans, was to be established on the Missouri, near the village of the tribe of the same name.

Bourgmont arrived back in New Orleans in January 1723 to begin a long haggle with the colonial government to obtain boats, supplies, and a crew. Reluctant officials could provide only grudging and minimal support, and the expedition did not arrive at the site of the new fort on the Missouri until November. The winter of 1723–1724 was spent in building the fort and mobilizing allies among the river tribes. An advance base was established at the main village of the Kansa tribe, near the mouth of the Kansas River.

At dawn on July 24, 1724, a long column— French soldiers, Indian warriors, packhorses, bearers, and straggling women, children, and dogs—set off from the Kansas village, with flag flying and drum beating. However, progress was slow. Illness, heat, and humidity took a heavy toll. Bourgmont himself became seriously ill, and had to be taken back to Fort d'Orleans.

Bourgmont sent an emissary to the head chief of the Padoucas to explain what had happened and to promise he would try again after recovering from his illness. He kept his promise. On October 8, 1724, a small party of Frenchmen, with a picked escort of Indians, again set out from the Kansa village on their march across the prairies to the Plains Apache country, some 250 miles to the southwest. By an adroit combination of bribery, charm, and threats, Bourgmont persuaded the Padoucas to forsake their alliance with the Spaniards and to forge a new one with the French. In a solemn ceremony the Padouca chiefs agreed to trade with the tribes of the French alliance "without trouble or greed," and to allow the French unhindered access to New Mexico.

On his triumphant return to France, in September 1725, the explorer took with him a chief of the Missouri tribe, an Osage, an Oto, and the daughter of the head chief of the Missouris. In Paris and Versailles, they were feted by directors of the Compagnie des Indes and entertained at the Château de Fontainebleau by young King Louis XV himself. Burdened with gifts, the Indians were sent back to the Missouri country, where presumably they spread word of the might and glory of France. Bourgmont, now elevated to the French nobility with the rank of *écuyer* (squire), retired with his wife to the small estate of his family at Cerisy. All three of the children of this marriage died in infancy, and the noble title that had dearly cost Bourgmont lapsed. Bourgmont himself died at Cerisy in December 1734.

The achievements that had once been considered so important proved disappointing. Within a few years Fort d'Orleans was abandoned as unnecessary, and all traces of it disappeared. The expected trade with New Mexico never developed on any significant scale. The Padoucas were forced out of their lands by Comanches.

Nevertheless, in the "Route" document, in the "Exact Description," and perhaps in other writings no longer extant, Bourgmont opened the eyes of Europeans to a new world within the New World: the 433,000 fertile square miles of the Missouri River basin, twice as large as France, and readily accessible via navigable rivers. So far as is known, he did it with little, if any, official support.

FRANK NORALL

Dictionary of Canadian Biography. S.v. "Véniard de Bourgmond."

Michigan Historical Collections. 1888–1912. Vols. 33, 34. Lansing, Mich.

Nasatir, Abraham P. *Before Lewis and Clark: Documents Illustrating the History of the Missouri, 1785–1804.* Vol. 1. 1952. Reprint, Lincoln: University of Nebraska Press, 1990.

Norall, Frank. *Bourgmont Explorer of the Missouri, 1698–1725.* Lincoln: University of Nebraska Press, 1988.

Pratz, Le Page du. *Histoire de la Louisiane, Contenant la Decouverte de ce Vaste Pays, sa Description Geographique . . . Deux Voyages dans le nord du Nouveau Mexique, etc. . . . .* 3 vols. Paris, 1758.

BOYER, KENTON LLOYD (1931–1982)

Kenton Lloyd Boyer was born May 20, 1931, in Liberty, Missouri. He was the third-oldest son in a family of thirteen children of Vern and Mabel Boyer. Ken Boyer grew up in nearby Alba, Missouri, where his father operated a general store and service station.

Boyer began his baseball career as a pitcher, but by the time he entered high school he had moved to third base because of his hitting ability. During the summers, he and his brothers joined a semipro team directed by his high school coach, Eldon Mailes. The best hitter on the team, Boyer attracted the attention of Runt Marr, who signed him to a contract with the St. Louis Cardinals in 1949 for a six thousand dollar bonus.

Boyer made his professional debut with the Class D Lebanon, Pennsylvania, team in the North Atlantic League where he batted .455 over sixteen games. He moved to Hamilton, Ontario, in the Pony League the next year where he hit .342. In 1951 he advanced to Omaha, a Class A team in the Western League, where he again hit more than .300.

Boyer spent the next two years in military service, returning to professional baseball in 1954 with the AAA Houston team in the Texas League. His eye-popping statistics—a .319 batting average, 21 home runs, and 116 runs batted in (RBIs)—earned him a promotion to the major leagues in 1955, where he was to play for the next fifteen years.

Boyer was a regular from the day he joined the St. Louis Cardinals, who had so much confidence in him that they traded Ray Jablonski, their incumbent third baseman, during the off-season. For the next twelve years, with one exception, Boyer was the St. Louis Cardinal's best third baseman. In 1957 the Cardinals had to make room for an exceptional rookie, Eddie Kasko. To allow Kasko to play his natural position of third base, Boyer volunteered to play center field. But Kasko was injured the following year, and the Cardinals acquired Curt Flood from Cincinnati to play center field, so Boyer returned to third base, winning five consecutive Gold Glove awards.

Boyer's greatest year was 1964, when he played a major role in the Cardinals' first pennant in eighteen years. He was named the Most Valuable Player that year, hitting .295, leading the league in RBIs with 119, while hitting 24 homers. His grand-slam homer in the fourth game of the World Series turned the tide for the Cardinals, who were trailing two games to one. The Cardinals went on to win the game four to three, and the World Series in seven games.

After the 1965 season, the Cardinals' general manager, Bob Howsam, released all of his starting infielders. Boyer was traded to the New York Mets. He drifted to the White Sox and then to the Los Angeles Dodgers, retiring after the 1969 season.

Boyer returned to the Cardinal organization as a minor league manager at Arkansas, Sarasota, and Tulsa. Many felt that when Red Schoendienst stepped down as manager of the St. Louis Cardinals, Boyer would be his replacement. However, much to Boyer's dismay, in 1977 the Cardinals named Vernon Rapp as Schoendienst's successor. Boyer then accepted an offer from the Baltimore Orioles to manage their Rochester farm club. The Cardinals called him to replace Rapp on April 29, 1978, and he managed the team until June 1980 when he was replaced by Whitey Herzog.

Boyer remained in the Cardinals' organization as a scout through 1981. He was slated to manage their Class AAA team at Louisville, but had to decline when he was diagnosed with lung cancer. He died on September 7, 1982, at the age of fifty-one.

Boyer is easily the best third baseman in St. Louis Cardinals' history. He was a superb fielder and an excellent hitter, with a career average of .288, 282 home runs, 68 triples, 316 doubles, and 1,137 RBIs. In all-star play, Boyer batted .348, and received many all-star honors from the *Sporting News.*

Despite these credentials, Boyer was criticized by some fans as a casual player who did not hustle. However, he was so skilled that he made the game seem effortless. Aware of this criticism, Boyer shrugged it off, saying, "I can't change, that's the way I am."

Throughout his playing career, Boyer, Eddie Matthews of the Braves, and Brooks Robinson of the Orioles were considered the best third basemen in baseball. Both Matthews and Robinson are in the Baseball Hall of Fame; Boyer is not. However, in 1984, the Cardinals retired Boyer's uniform number, "14," and placed it in the St. Louis Hall of Fame in Busch Stadium.

BURTON A. BOXERMAN

Halberstam, David. *October 1964.* New York: Villard Books, 1994.
Raines, Rob. *The St. Louis Cardinals.* New York: St. Martin's, 1992.
Sporting News, archives.
St. Louis Post-Dispatch, archives.

BRACKENRIDGE, HENRY MARIE (1786–1871)

A lawyer, author, diplomat, and journalist in the early Federal and Jacksonian eras, Henry Marie Brackenridge used his western travels as the basis for books about frontier life and manners, distinguished by their wit, clarity, and powers of keen observation. Born in Pittsburgh, on May 11, 1786, he was the son of Hugh Henry Brackenridge, one of the earliest men of letters in the post-Revolutionary West. Young Henry received a thorough education in French, Spanish, political theory, and science, as well as English literature and the ancient classics.

Brackenridge's remarkably spartan schooling began early. By the time he was only seven, his father sent him into a virtual wilderness, to Ste. Genevieve, to learn French with the family of Vital St. Gemme Beauvais, and later to Gallipolis at the residence of **Antoine Saugrain.** Following his return, he studied at the Pittsburgh Academy, and then briefly at Jefferson College. He completed his education with the study of law, and subsequently practiced in Baltimore and elsewhere.

Brackenridge set out for the Missouri Territory in 1810 with the intention of becoming an attorney in St. Louis. His legal practice did not keep him from writing a number of descriptive regional sketches for **Joseph Charless**'s *Missouri Gazette,* the territory's first newspaper. Brackenridge first gained national attention through these early writings, destined to become the basis of his later published observations on the West. Brackenridge reported on such topics as the prehistoric mound sites surrounding St. Louis, the city's general topography, the Mississippi River, and the region's soil and climate. He also described the various towns, the people of the Mississippi Valley, and their manners and customs. Thomas Jefferson, an avid student of the West, appreciated Brackenridge's pieces.

While in St. Louis Brackenridge availed himself of the opportunity to go on a tour of the upper Missouri at the invitation of fur trader **Manuel Lisa** in 1811. The trip added even more to his store of knowledge about Missouri and the West.

Prior to 1815 Brackenridge enjoyed a moderately distinguished law career in Missouri and later in New Orleans. He aided in drafting the act for the territorial judiciary and served as a district judge in the Louisiana Territory. His observations on the preparations for war on the frontier in 1812 attracted favorable notice from President James Madison and helped launch his diplomatic career. His dispatches and letters led to his appointment as secretary to the American Commission on South American Affairs. His books, *The History of the Late War* in 1816 and *The Voyage to South America* in 1819, were widely read in Europe and America and were praised for their voluminous information.

Brackenridge's knowledge of French and Spanish, both learned in frontier towns, were useful in his life as a diplomat, writer, traveler, official secretary, and interpreter. He eventually came to work for Andrew Jackson when the latter was governor of Florida, assuming an active role in official matters as Jackson's secretary during the 1820s. He also served as a judge in Florida.

Brackenridge represented Pennsylvania as a Whig in Congress from October 13, 1840, to March 3, 1841, following the resignation of Richard Biddle. In his later years Brackenridge lived on a farm near Pittsburgh, writing and leading a scholarly life until his death on January 18, 1871.

Brackenridge's early writings reveal a sympathetic understanding of French-colonial culture and the manners and customs of the surging American frontier. He had a generally high level of understanding and sympathy about early Louisiana that was much appreciated in the young nation. His descriptions of people, places, nature, and geography were accurate and naturalistic, not bitingly satirical. His observations were stripped of embellishment, exaggerations, and the caustic preconceived cultural notions of superiority that marred so much of early American travel literature. His gifted prose added entertainment to his writings. His earliest books included the first editions of his *Views of Louisiana in 1811,* published by Zadok Cramer in 1814. The international success of *Views* encouraged Brackenridge to publish *Journal of a Voyage Up the River Missouri Performed in Eighteen Hundred and Eleven* in 1815.

In the 1830s Brackenridge published his third major work on Missouri and Louisiana, *Recollections of Persons and Places in the West.* Partly autobiographical, the book is valuable in depicting an analytical view of society in the early trans-Mississippi settlements.

Brackenridge practiced law in rude backcountry courts and large eastern cities, including Baltimore and Washington, D.C. His education was tempered by his wilderness schooling in the French language, and by the books and private tutoring he received from his father, a noted satirist and author of *Modern Chivalry.* Brackenridge's career in politics ranged from special commissions and international delegations on Pan-American issues to local politics of the frontier towns where he occasionally lived.

In less talented individuals this patchwork quilt of pieced-together vocations—writer, lawyer, diplomat, traveler, social commentator, historian, and judge—would have produced little more than a mediocre legacy. However, Brackenridge's true gift lay in his skilled writing, and in his excellent works that observed a frontier society in the progress of growth and development. Wherever he traveled, especially in the still exotic lands of the Old Northwest and Louisiana Territory, he created with his energetic pen valuable, sympathetic sketches that have become primary sources on the lands and society with which he came into contact.

JOHN NEAL HOOVER

Brackenridge, Henry Marie. *Recollections of Persons and Places in the West.* Philadelphia: James Kay, 1835.

———. *Views of Louisiana: Together with a Journal of a Voyage Up the Missouri River in 1811.* Pittsburgh: Cramer, Spears, and Eichbaum, 1814.

Brackenridge, Hugh Henry. *The Life and Writings of Hugh Henry Brackenridge.* Princeton: Princeton University Press, 1932.

Keller, William F. "A Glimpse of the Life and Letters of Henry Marie Brackenridge." *Western Pennsylvania Historical Magazine* 37:1 (March 1954): 1–17.

McDermott, John Francis. "Henry Marie Brackenridge and His Writings." *Western Historical Magazine* 20:3 (September 1937): 181–96.

BRADLEY, OMAR NELSON (1893–1981)

Missouri has produced many celebrated soldiers, but none, not even **John J. Pershing,** accomplished more than Omar Nelson Bradley. Born in Clark, Missouri, on February 12, 1893, Bradley's boyhood was marked by poverty, hard work, and personal loss. His mother, Sarah Hubbard Bradley, had to provide for the family as best she could after her husband, John S. Bradley, died when Omar was thirteen. Although he knew him for only a few years, the boy was greatly influenced by his father, a part-time schoolteacher who, apparently, was a man of exemplary character. He taught the boy to hunt and shoot and, more significantly, bequeathed him his own high standards of modest integrity. The family settled in Moberly, and there Omar grew up in the small-town atmosphere of northeast Missouri. Helping out by holding a number of part-time jobs, he developed into an outstanding athlete, and dreamed of the greater world.

After high school, promoted by a Sunday-school teacher, Omar applied for admission to West Point, not because he desired a military life but because it was the lowest-cost education available. Narrowly, he was nominated and joined the most famous class in the academy's history, the class of 1915, the class the "stars fell on." The class provided more than thirty generals in World War II, including Dwight D. Eisenhower and Bradley, both of whom eventually became five-star generals. "Brad," as he was known at the Point, was a steady, popular, if unremarkable, cadet, proficient in mathematics, but best known for his deadly baseball arm on the West Point team. He knew Eisenhower well, and this connection, among others made at the Point, did him no harm in later years. He finished 44th in a class of 164. He also met Mary Elizabeth Quayle and married her in 1916; she died in 1965. Less than a year later, he married Kitty Buhler. Mary gave him one daughter, Elizabeth.

Bradley was commissioned a second lieutenant of artillery upon his graduation and undertook a remarkable seventy-year career. With Europe at war in 1915, it seemed an excellent time for a cadet to enter the service, especially as the United States was likely to become a combatant. For some it was. Bradley, however, found himself assigned to a series of western outposts where he gained experience in soldiering but no significant advances in rank or status. Although stationed on the Mexican border, he did not take part in Pershing's pursuit of Pancho Villa. When, in 1917, America entered World War I, Bradley had the misfortune to be assigned to guard copper mines in Montana. He missed the American Expeditionary Force experience altogether. Others, such as George C. Marshall and Douglas MacArthur, gained valuable experience and reputations in France. Bradley gained nothing but a temporary promotion to major and anonymity. After the war Bradley remained in the sharply reduced army.

The interwar period was a lean time for the army, which translated into long periods in grade for career men such as Bradley. It also meant that most of his duty was directed toward extended tours in drab stateside camps, punctuated by instruction in the army's extensive officer schools.

In 1919 Bradley was assigned to teach military science at South Dakota State College and was called to instruct in mathematics at West Point the next year. In these years he cemented friendships, learned to go "by the book," and developed a quiet but outstanding competence in the fundamentals of command. A turning point came in 1925 when he graduated from the Army Infantry School at Fort Benning. He had proved himself an excellent prospect for higher command and was beginning to be noticed. He next completed the course at the Command and General Staff School at Fort Leavenworth, and by 1934 he had made it through the Army War College. By then he knew most of the army's principal officers personally and was known to them as a steady man to have around.

Of all the men Bradley impressed in these years, none was to affect his career more than George Marshall. With war threatening again, Marshall had become the key soldier in Washington. He appointed Bradley commandant of the Fort Benning Infantry School, after calling him to Washington to serve on the general staff in 1938. This put the Missourian in a position to help shape America's plans for the coming conflict. Bradley's thoroughness appealed to Marshall, and perhaps he liked Brad's view that one should never trust to intuition. In any case Bradley got his first star in 1941, going directly from lieutenant colonel to brigadier. After Pearl Harbor he moved on to major general in February 1942.

Bradley wanted a combat command, but the pressing need to train the expanding army meant that he first commanded the Eighty-second Infantry and then the Twenty-eighth Infantry divisions. In these assignments he gained his troops' affection and was on his way to becoming known as the "G.I. General." But with Marshall one of the Joint Chiefs and Eisenhower in command in North Africa, Bradley soon got into the war. Eisenhower called him to be his "eyes and ears" among American commanders in North Africa where Bradley began his complicated relationship with the aggressive Gen. George S. Patton. Among such colorful officers, Bradley was valued as a team player and a stable leader. Eventually, he was given command of the Second Corps, which ruptured the German lines in Tunisia and contributed directly to Axis defeat in the theater.

In 1943 Bradley rose to lieutenant general, and, while still subordinate to Patton in the Sicily campaign, was marked by Eisenhower, named European supreme commander, for a major role in the coming invasion of France. Sent back to England, he took over the U.S. First Army, comprising thirteen divisions. Thus began his long series of strategical disputes with British Field Marshal Bernard Montgomery and his mistrust of Eisenhower's apparent truckling to the British. On D day, June 6, 1944, Bradley was aboard the *Augusta* as his troops went ashore at Utah and Omaha Beaches. The near disaster at Omaha Beach, however, confirmed his view that only careful planning and execution can avert catastrophe. This approach facilitated the American breakout of Normandy in July and, except for Montgomery's caution, might have trapped the entire German army at Falaise.

After Normandy Eisenhower gave Bradley command of the Twelfth Army, a vast U.S. force composed of four armies of well over a million men, the largest force ever to serve under an American field commander. Cooperating with Eisenhower's broad front move toward the German frontier, Bradley nevertheless chafed under restrictions placed upon his armies by Montgomery's rival schemes and demands for supplies. Despite debates with Eisenhower, including one occasion when he briefly offered his resignation, he loyally served and proved a firm and competent leader when the United States Army was severely tested in the German winter counterattack at the Bulge in late 1944. Refusing to retreat even when the enemy was but ten miles away, Bradley was awarded the Bronze Star. In the new year, the Twelfth Army breached German lines in many places, and the First Army was the first Allied force across the Rhine. As victory approached, Bradley was promoted to four-star general. That spring his soldiers linked up with Russian troops at Torgau.

At war's end Bradley received high praise from Eisenhower, Churchill, **Maxwell Taylor,** and many others. He was decorated with, among many others, the Presidential Medal of Freedom, the Croix de Guerre, and the Knight Commander of Bath. He accepted President Truman's appointment to lead the Veterans Administration from 1945 to 1947, then moved on to become army chief of staff and then chairman of the Joint Chiefs for two terms. He supported Truman in the MacArthur controversy during the Korean War, believing that the Soviet Union was the true threat to U.S. security. In 1950 he was raised to the rarefied rank of five-star general, and followed with his memoir, *A Soldier's Story,* in 1951.

Bradley eventually became chairman of the board of Bulova Watch Company, but continued his intense interest in America's armed forces during his retirement. He even agreed to serve as an adviser for the popular film *Patton* in the 1970s. He spent his last years at Fort Bliss, Texas, and died in New York of a stroke on April 8, 1981. He was buried in Arlington National Cemetery. A loyal soldier to the end, he had attended President Reagan's inauguration in a wheelchair a few weeks earlier. A Missouri schoolmaster's influence had reached further than he could have dreamed. Omar Bradley, one of America's greatest generals, lived a long life, but did not outlive the lessons of a wise father.

C. DAVID RICE

Bradley, Omar N. *A Soldier's Story.* New York: Henry Holt, 1951.

Bradley, Omar N., and Clay Blair. *A General's Life.* New York: Simon and Schuster, 1983.

Mylander, Maureen. *The Generals.* New York: Dial Press, 1974.

Weigley, Russell F. *Eisenhower's Lieutenants.* Bloomington: Indiana University Press, 1977.

BRASHEAR, MINNIE M. (1874–1963)

Educator and **Mark Twain** scholar Minnie M. Brashear was born on October 17, 1874, in Brashear, Missouri, a town named by her father when it was only a railway station given to him for his help in establishing the new Quincy, Missouri, and Pacific Railroad. In 1882 the family moved twelve miles away to their permanent home on a large farm near Kirksville. Richard Brashear, a successful farmer and trader in livestock, so impressed Minnie with his passionate devotion to education, books, and community service that she chose to distinguish herself as a university professor, scholar, and activist citizen. When she published her first book, *Mark Twain: Son of Missouri* in 1934, Richard Brashear's influence was acknowledged in her dedication: "To the Memory of My Father."

In 1892 Brashear earned a bachelor of scientific didactics degree from the First District Normal School in Kirksville (later Northeast Missouri State University). She taught high school in Missouri and Montana while enriching her education; for example, she studied at the Harvard Annex (later Radcliffe) in 1897–1898. College teaching jobs followed: Beaver College in Pennsylvania from 1901 to 1904, the state teachers college in Kirksville from 1904 to 1914, the University of Idaho from 1914 to 1919, and the

University of Missouri at Columbia from 1919 to 1944. She continued her studies, acquiring an A.B. from Missouri in 1908, spending a summer term in 1910 at Oxford, completing an A.M. at Missouri with a thesis on Joseph Conrad in 1922, and earning a Ph.D. in 1930 at the University of North Carolina with a dissertation on Mark Twain.

Four years later the dissertation had become a book of major importance, *Mark Twain: Son of Missouri.* Brashear brought to the book a thorough knowledge of Twain's oeuvre, of Twain scholarship, and of the region in which he grew to manhood. But what gives special distinction to her book is that, as Fred Lorch observed in his review, she asked the right scholarly question at the right time: "How is Mark Twain to be accounted for?" Her convincing answers, emphasizing the biographical evidence of Twain's formative years in Missouri and the corroborating textual evidence of his works, prompted the noted scholar Edward Wagenknecht to conclude twenty-five years later that *Mark Twain: Son of Missouri* is "perhaps the earliest really scholarly book about Mark Twain. . . ."

Brashear was also a productive teacher and a conscientious faculty member. A survey of the theses and dissertations she directed, evaluated, or enriched with advice during her years at the University of Missouri records a common theme of thanks and appreciation by students for her comprehensive knowledge of Mark Twain and her many acts of generosity. Those postgraduate works also indicate an impressive scholarly relationship among distinguished faculty with whom she worked, including **H. M. Belden, Frank Luther Mott,** and young **Elmer Ellis.**

Brashear held traditional faculty memberships in the Association of University Professors, the Modern Language Association, and the Faculty Women's Club (serving as president in 1930–1931). She was especially active in promoting the interests of women through such organizations as the YWCA, the AAUW, the League of Women Voters, and the State Federation of Women.

Retirement from the university in 1944 brought Brashear greater freedom to pursue enduring interests, including more books: *The Art, Humor, and Humanity of Mark Twain,* coedited with Robert Rodney in 1959, and, three years after her death, *The Birds and Beasts of Mark Twain,* also coedited with Rodney. Retirement also brought her back to Kirksville (where the family home and Brashear Park still remain for townspeople to enjoy). There she continued her interest in educational societies and the college from which she had graduated in 1892. She also renewed her social participation in the community, joining the Monday Club and the Sojourners Club.

She again took her place in the Trinity Episcopal Church. She died at the age of eighty-eight on April 1, 1963.

CLYDE G. WADE

Brashear, Minnie M. "Mark Twain Juvenalia." *American Literature* 2 (1930): 25–53.

Conard, Howard L., ed. *Encyclopedia of the History of Missouri.* New York: Southern History, 1901.

Dains, Mary K., ed. *Show Me Missouri Women: Selected Biographies.* Kirksville, Mo.: Thomas Jefferson University Press, 1989.

Lorch, Fred W. "Mark Twain: Son of Missouri." *American Literature* 6 (1935): 460–63.

Wagenknecht, Edward. Introduction to *The Art, Humor, and Humanity of Mark Twain,* ed. Minnie M. Brashear and Robert M. Rodney. Norman: University of Oklahoma Press, 1959.

BRIDGE, HUDSON ERASTUS (1810–1875)

St. Louis's status as a commercial gateway of the American West is due in large part to New England entrepreneurs who immigrated to the city before the Civil War. Hudson Erastus Bridge ranked as one of the most successful of that group. He arrived in St. Louis as a salesman, became a wealthy manufacturer, and invested his profits into the local economy. He played a critical role in developing the city's transportation network, and he exercised his considerable influence to keep Missouri in the Union.

Bridge was born in Walpole, New Hampshire, on May 17, 1810, and was raised on the family farm in Bennington County, Vermont. At age twenty-one he struck out on his own as a salesman, moving to Troy, New York, and then to Columbus, Ohio. In 1835 he moved to Springfield, Illinois, to work for manufacturers of the popular Jewett plow. St. Louis impressed Bridge with its growth potential, and he moved there in 1837 to sell plows, tin plates, copper, sheet iron, and Franklin stoves for distributors Hale and Rayburn.

By 1838 the company became Bridge, Rayburn, and Company, and set about becoming a manufacturer of stoves. By 1842 it had developed a stove model that Bridge presented at an agricultural fair. He recruited his brother Harrison to join the firm, and within six years they created the Empire Stove Works and thereby secured their own wealth. In 1857 the company's name changed to Bridge, Beach, and Company following the death of Harrison in 1850 and the subsequent elevation of associate John H. Beach. As such, it remained in operation for seventy years.

Bridge was one of many St. Louisans who recognized that the city was too dependent upon river transportation and needed to create railroad networks with which to reach western markets and suppliers. He invested in several railroad companies, but was most actively involved with the Pacific Railroad (later the Missouri Pacific Railroad), serving as president of the company. Bridge is credited with completion of its line between St. Louis and Kansas City while overcoming obstacles such as corruption among fellow board members and a takeover attempt by the Union Pacific. Recognizing that Chicago had gained advantage over St. Louis during the Civil War by building its own railroad network into the West, Bridge and other business leaders realized that St. Louis needed a railroad bridge across the Mississippi River. They formed the St. Louis and Illinois Bridge Company, and hired **James Eads** to design and construct a bridge that opened for traffic in 1874 and still bears Eads name.

Bridge invested in the growth of his adopted city in many ways. He served on the boards of Boatmen's Savings Bank and Merchants Bank. He twice served as president of the St. Louis Railway Company, operator of a street-railway system. He invested in the cultural life of the community, too. In response to appeals from his church minister **William Greenleaf Eliot,** Bridge became one of the original incorporators and trustees of Washington University, and one of its largest early benefactors. He financially backed establishment of the Mary Institute, the Polytechnic Institute, and the St. Louis Mercantile Library Association.

Bridge exerted his influence to hold the state of Missouri in the Union during the Civil War. He had long been a supporter of Congressman **Frank Blair,** the leader of the St. Louis Republican Party who spearheaded the Unionists during the crisis of 1861. Blair placed Bridge on his Committee of Safety, a citizens group organized to help the federal forces retain control of the city. In his only instance of public office holding, Bridge agreed to serve as a Unionist delegate to the 1861 state convention.

An astute investor Bridge made money during the war in ventures that were new to him. He speculated in gold and in U.S. bonds, and profited from buying hogs and cattle in Missouri and selling them in Illinois and in the East. He formed H. E. Bridge and Company to trade in southern cotton, with his agents following the Union army south. Late in the war he bought army surplus clothing and resold it to wholesalers.

Bridge became a millionaire several times over. He owned a summer home in Newport, Rhode Island, and vacationed annually in Europe. In 1862 he established his home outside of St. Louis in Glendale. Bridge married Helen Agusta Holland, and they had six children, four of whom survived him. Bridge died on February 25, 1875, at Glendale.

VICKI JOHNSON

Adler, Jeffery S. *Yankee Merchants and the Making of the Urban West: The Rise and Fall of Antebellum St. Louis.* Cambridge: Cambridge University Press, 1991.

Bridge, Hudson. Collection. Missouri Historical Society, St. Louis.

Mahoney, Timothy R. *River Towns in the Great West: The Structure of Provincial Urbanization in the American Midwest, 1820–1870.* Cambridge: Cambridge University Press, 1990.

Primm, James Neal. *Lion of the Valley: St. Louis, Missouri, 1764–1980.* 3d ed. St. Louis: Missouri Historical Society Press, 1998.

Scharf, J. Thomas. *History of St. Louis City and County: From Earliest Periods to the Present Day.* Philadelphia: Everts, 1883.

BRIDGER, JAMES "JIM" (1804–1881)

Jim Bridger, a skilled hunter, fur trader, frontiersman, wilderness guide, and scout, was born on March 17, 1804, in Virginia. His mother, Chloe, and surveyor father, William, operated a tavern in Richmond. In 1812 the family moved to the Missouri Territory, settling near St. Louis. At the age of thirteen, with both parents already dead, James was apprenticed to Phil Creamer, a St. Louis blacksmith who became his mentor and foster father.

While Bridger's practical skills of horsemanship and marksmanship became legendary, he was an unlettered man. David Brown, a contemporary friend, once remarked that Bridger "was perfectly ignorant of all knowledge contained in books; not even knowing the letters of the alphabet."

In 1822 Bridger became aware of **William H. Ashley**'s advertisements in various frontier newspapers offering employment to "enterprising young men" who would engage in fur trapping for Ashley's firm. The ads promised two hundred dollars per annum plus other benefits. General Ashley and his partner, **Andrew Henry,** were organizing a new fur company and needed talented workers. Traditionally, fur companies of the period hired agents, built trading posts in the wilderness areas, and exchanged goods for the pelts secured by Indians. However, Ashley and Henry decided that the cost of building and maintaining trading posts, and the uncertainty of Indians as trappers, made the conventional methods undesirable. Instead, they were developing a relatively new concept, proposing to secure energetic young men as fur trappers and transport them to the upper-Missouri area. These "mountain men" (as they became known) operated somewhat as independent entrepreneurs. Instead of regular fixed frontier trading posts, Ashley and Henry brought supplies to an annual "rendezvous" point, and there the company exchanged pelts for money and supplies. With lowered costs, and individualized incentives for the young trappers, profits would be higher both for the company and for the mountain men.

Bridger was selected to be part of this pioneering 1822 venture. Although he was probably among the youngest of the initial group of mountain men (which included individuals such as **Jedediah Smith,** Milton Sublette, and Thomas Fitzpatrick), Bridger was an excellent choice. He was of good physique, tall (over six feet), and a quick learner of wilderness crafts and Indian ways.

For the next forty-six years, Bridger repeatedly traversed the western United States, learning about the West and making many useful discoveries. In the fall of 1824, for example, he traced the route of Bear River into the Great Salt Lake—reportedly the first white man to visit the lake. In 1825 he was among the earliest non-Indians to view and describe the many wonders of Yellowstone with its bubbling hot waters and painted hills and ravines.

In 1830 Bridger and four associates (Sublette, Fitzpatrick, Henry Fraeb, and Jean-Baptiste Gervais) purchased the old Ashley company. They continued to operate the Rocky Mountain Fur Company until 1834 when it was reorganized as part of John Jacob Astor's American Fur Company system. Soon the appearance of fashionable silk hats reduced the demand for beaver hats, and the fur industry declined.

As the fur business changed, the growing need of the frontier was for capable scouts and guides. Bridger became a favorite guide for the army and others.

In 1843 Bridger established a trading post, which he named Fort Bridger, on what was soon to be called the Oregon Trail. He sold supplies and provided repair services to emigrants going west. Among those who stopped at Fort Bridger, he developed a reputation as a master yarn spinner, earning the nickname "Old Gabe."

In 1868 Bridger returned to a farm he owned near Kansas City where the renowned trapper, explorer, and scout died on July 17, 1881. He is buried at the Mount Washington Memorial Cemetery. The large monument over Bridger's grave detailing some of his accomplishments was erected by a friend, Gen. G. M. Dodge. On the hundredth anniversary of Bridger's birth, General Dodge delivered the eulogy at Bridger's grave, commenting that Bridger was "one of the most expert hunters and trappers in the mountains . . . [and also] a Guide without equal."

J. Calvin Holsinger

Alter, Cecil J. *Jim Bridger.* Norman: University of Oklahoma Press, 1962.

Chittenden, Hiram Martin. *The American Fur Trade of the Far West.* Vol. 1. Stanford: Academic Reprints, 1954.

March, David D. *The History of Missouri.* Vol. 1. New York: Lewis Historical Publishing, 1967.

Missouri: The WPA Guide to the "Show Me" State. St. Louis: Missouri Historical Society Press, 1998.

Morgan, Dale. "Opening of the West: Explorers and Mountain Men." In *The Book of the American West,* ed. Jay Monahan. New York: Bonanza Books, 1963.

Phillips, Paul Chrisler. *The Fur Trade.* Vol. 2. Norman: University of Oklahoma Press, 1961.

BRIGGS, FRANK PARKS (1894–1992)

Frank Parks Briggs, a newspaper publisher, farmer, and Missouri state senator, was born on February 25, 1894, in Armstrong, in Howard County, Missouri. He attended public schools in Armstrong and Fayette, Missouri, before entering Central College in Fayette and earning his B.A. in journalism from the University of Missouri in 1915. Briggs married Catherine Ann Shull of St. Joseph, Missouri, on May 28, 1916.

Briggs edited papers in Shawnee and Oklahoma City, Oklahoma, and owned and edited newspapers in Fayette, Moberly, and Trenton before buying the *Macon Chronicle-Herald* in 1924. His colleagues in the newspaper business recognized his stature by electing him president of the Missouri Associated Dailies in 1937.

In 1930 Briggs was elected as the first Democratic mayor of Macon in fifty-two years and held that office until he resigned in 1932 when voters of the Ninth District elected him to the state senate. Briggs served actively in that body until 1945. He was elected president pro tempore of the Sixty-first Senate and served as chairman of several committees, including those on education, the University of Missouri, teachers colleges and libraries, agriculture, roads and highways, and municipal corporations, among others.

In 1945 Gov. **Phil M. Donnelly** chose Briggs to complete **Harry S. Truman**'s term in the United States Senate when Truman vacated the position to accept the vice presidency. Briggs served in the Senate from 1945 to 1946, but, according to his son, Tom, he clashed with the Democratic Party leadership: "He wasn't one of the guys to go with the flow like a lot of those senators. He was told what to do and he didn't like that." He ran for reelection against **James P. Kem,** losing in the Republican landslide of 1946.

Briggs returned to Macon to actively resume his newspaper-publishing business and became increasingly active in conservation. He was a member of the Missouri State Conservation Commission from 1947 to 1961, serving as chairman from 1955 to 1956. In 1961 President John. F. Kennedy appointed him assistant secretary of the interior for fish and wildlife, a position that he described as his "most satisfying government job" because he could "get more done." He returned to Macon in 1965 and continued as publisher of the *Chronicle-Herald* until its sale in 1973. Frank Parks Briggs died on September 23, 1992.

ERIKA K. NELSON

Briggs, Frank P. Papers. 1894–1992. Western Historical Manuscripts Collection, Columbia.

Columbia Daily Tribune, September 24, 1992.

Obituary. *Missouri Historical Review* 87 (January 1993).

Official Manual of the State of Missouri, 1943–1944. Jefferson City: Secretary of State, 1944.

BROADHEAD, JAMES OVERTON (1819–1898)

James Overton Broadhead was born on May 29, 1819, in Charlottesville, Virginia, the oldest child of Achilles and Mary Broadhead. His uncle, Frank Carr, tutored him in classical languages, and he attended high school in Albemarle County before taking courses at the University of Virginia for one year in 1835.

Broadhead accepted a teaching position at a private school in Baltimore for a year before deciding in 1837 to move to St. Charles County, Missouri. It was his good fortune at this time to be befriended by **Edward Bates,** who employed him as a tutor for three years in his home, a position that gave Broadhead the opportunity to read law in preparation for his acceptance into the bar in 1842.

After receiving his license to practice law, Broadhead moved to Bowling Green in Pike County, residing there until 1859. In 1845 he was elected to serve as a delegate to the state Constitutional Convention, and as a Whig he probably worked for the reapportionment of county representation in the General Assembly. Many Democrats also favored this change, which failed to become law when Missouri voters rejected the proposed new constitution.

After his service in the convention, the people of Pike County elected Broadhead to the Missouri House of Representatives, where he served in 1846 and 1847, and to the state senate, where he served from 1850 to 1853. In the General Assembly, Broadhead was a partisan politician, quick to take advantage of divisions in the Democratic Party. In 1851 he helped elect **Henry S. Geyer,** the first Whig from Missouri in the United States Senate. After the dissolution of the Whig Party in the mid-1850s, Broadhead first became a member of the nativist American Party and afterward a member of the Democratic Party.

After moving to St. Louis, Broadhead formed a law partnership with Fidelio C. Sharpe with whom he practiced for many years until Sharpe's death. In 1861 Broadhead was elected as a delegate to the state convention called by **Claiborne Fox Jackson** and his supporters for the purpose of removing Missouri from the Union. However, the secessionists miscalculated, and all of the delegates sent by the people of Missouri to the convention opposed secession. Broadhead vigorously opposed secession and chaired the committee that recommended that the governor, lieutenant governor, secretary of state, and members of the General Assembly be replaced with men loyal to the Union.

During wartime Broadhead was named to a committee of safety established to protect Union interests in St. Louis. Early in 1861 the committee organized six military regiments and maintained a correspondence with prominent Union men throughout the state to coordinate their efforts. The committee also supported Gen. **Nathaniel Lyon**'s breakup of Camp Jackson where state militia forces mostly sympathetic to the Southern cause were encamped on the outskirts of St. Louis. That same year Broadhead was appointed U.S. attorney for the eastern district of Missouri, a position that he resigned in 1863 when he was commissioned as a lieutenant colonel of volunteers and appointed provost marshal for Missouri, southern Iowa, Arkansas, Kansas, and the Indian Territory.

At the war's end Broadhead vigorously opposed the ratification of a constitution drafted largely under Radical Republican influences, believing that many of its measures were too harsh. Resuming the practice of law, he represented clients in cases stemming from the war, railroad issues, and corporate and commercial questions. Before the United States Supreme Court, Broadhead argued two important cases, one for the railroads and another for the Mormon Church against an act of Congress confiscating church property. He was successful in both cases.

In 1868 and 1872 Broadhead served as a delegate to the Democratic National Conventions. In 1875 he represented St. Louis County at a state Constitutional Convention that replaced the 1865 constitution with a more conservative one. In 1876 he was appointed as a special prosecutor against the Whiskey Ring conspirators, who had illegally retained revenues from the excise tax on distillers, defrauding the federal government of thousands of dollars. In 1878 Broadhead was chosen first president of the American Bar Association.

Broadhead served in the United States Congress between 1883 and 1885, during which time he was a member of a special commission to look into French spoliation claims against the U.S. government. In this capacity he delivered a speech on the floor of the House supporting some of the French claims. In 1893 he became minister to Switzerland, a post he held until his resignation in 1897, after which he returned to St. Louis where he died on August 7, 1898.

DENNIS K. BOMAN

Biographical Dictionary of the United States Congress, 1774–1989. Bicentennial ed. S.v. "Broadhead, James Overton." Washington D.C.: U.S. Government Printing Office, 1989.

Broadhead, James O. "Early Events of the War in Missouri." In *War Papers and Personal Reminiscences, 1861–1865: Read before the Commandery of the State of Missouri, Military Order of the Loyal Legion of the United States.* St. Louis: Becktold, 1892.

———. *Speech of Hon. James O. Broadhead, of Missouri in the House of Representatives, Wednesday, January 14, 1885.* Washington, 1885.

———. *Speech of James O. Broadhead Delivered before the Convention of 1861.* St. Louis: Continental Printing, 1861.

Hodge, J. W., ed. "Hon. James O. Broadhead, St. Louis." In *The United States Biographical Dictionary and Portrait Gallery of Eminent and Self-Made Men, Missouri Volume.* Kansas City: Ramsey, Millett, and Hudson, 1878.

BROKMEYER, HENRY CONRAD (1826–1906)

Henry Conrad Brokmeyer, a "mechanic," self-taught philosopher, and politician, was the founding, if often absent, genius of the St. Louis movement. He was born on August 12, 1826, near Minden, in the Prussian Rhineland. Between episodes of aggressive leadership of the so-called St. Louis Hegelians, and periods in which he renounced all human company in order to better study philosophy, Brokmeyer had an impressive career in Missouri politics, beginning with a term as representative for Warren County in the Missouri House of Representatives from 1862 to 1864 and ending as lieutenant governor from 1877 to 1881. Although Brokmeyer (who sometimes spelled his name "Brockmeyer") spoke at state and national Democratic conventions and was repeatedly solicited to run for the United States Congress, he retired from public life in 1879 to pass most of his remaining years in the Oklahoma Indian Territory. Even more so than **William Torrey Harris,** with whom he was closely associated, Brokmeyer saw himself as an apostle of the philosopher G. W. F. Hegel, and in pursuit of philosophical truth he did not hesitate to sacrifice fame, friendship, health, and (it might be argued) sanity.

Brokmeyer's career was an unlikely one for a man who saw himself primarily as a philosopher. He emigrated to the United States at the age of sixteen and arrived in St. Louis four years later. He was originally employed in the city as a tanner, and he pursued that and other trades in Memphis, Tennessee, and Columbus, Mississippi. Yearning for formal education, the German mechanic studied at Georgetown College in Kentucky and at Brown University, but his tendency to question authority managed to get him expelled from both institutions.

Brokmeyer returned to St. Louis in 1854 to work as an iron molder for the Excelsior Stove Works, and later with Bridge, Beach, and Company. He accumulated sufficient capital to engage in land speculation in and around the city, but after spectacular failure in that business retreated to a cabin in rural Warren County, Missouri. There he immersed himself in the study of philosophy. A compulsion to teach what he had learned brought Brokmeyer back to St. Louis in 1858, where he met William Torrey Harris and other young enthusiasts of German philosophy.

With the encouragement of his friends Harris, **Denton Jacques Snider,** and **John Gabriel Woerner,** Brokmeyer began translating major Hegelian texts into English. He was constantly revising these translations, some of which appeared in abridged installments, beginning in 1867, in the St. Louis–based *Journal of Speculative Philosophy.* Although Brokmeyer's rendering of Hegel's *Science of Logic* remained unpublished, it was circulated among Harris and other members of the St. Louis movement. When in 1890 Harris, as the dean of American educationalists and the chief proponent of Hegelianism in the country, published *Hegel's Logic: A Book on the Genesis of the Categories of the Mind,* he acknowledged Brokmeyer as his teacher and Brokmeyer's translation as his first guide to Hegel. To Brokmeyer, philosophy was more than simply a vocation or a tool: it was a way of life. As Harris observed,

> [Brokmeyer] could flash into the questions of the day, or even into the question of the moment, the highest insights of philosophy and solve their problems. Even the hunting of wild turkeys or squirrels was the occasion for the use of philosophy. Philosophy came to mean with us, therefore, the most practical of all species of knowledge. We used it to solve all problems connected with school teaching and school management. We studied the "dialectic" of politics and political parties and understood how measures and men might be combined by its light.

Some sense of Brokmeyer's "practical" view of philosophy can be gained from his semiautobiographical novel, *Mechanic's Diary,* which historian William Goetzmann deems "perhaps the strangest and most interesting of the writings left by the St. Louis Hegelians."

Brokmeyer was always adamant, and occasionally violent, in the expression of his philosophical and political views. His friends kindly indulged "Brok's" excesses, while recognizing that his dogmatism failed to help him in organizing his ideas. Brokmeyer's friend Woerner made him appear as "Professor Rauhenfels" (German for "rock-hard") in his Civil War novel, *The Rebel's Daughter.*

While it is often unfairly argued that Hegelians placed too much trust in established government as the rational reconciler of conflicting social interests (Hegel said that the state was the march of God in the world), in Brokmeyer's case this was true. In fact, he went through a striking political, philosophical transformation as a result of the Civil War, from a libertarian in the mold of Henry David Thoreau to an upholder of a strong federal government and the executive branch in particular. On January 16, 1864, Brokmeyer stood up before the Missouri House of Representatives to berate his fellow legislators for not giving their full support to federal policies and President Lincoln. He was undoubtedly ahead of his time—or at least ahead of contemporary public opinion—in acknowledging that Lincoln's authoritarian and even unconstitutional measures were justified in serving the Union cause.

A more flawed opinion, and one that Brokmeyer shared with some of his fellow St. Louis Hegelians, was that St. Louis was destined by virtue of an irresistible confluence of forces to be the greatest of American cities in an American-dominated world. Denton Snider, a historian of the St. Louis movement, testifies to the St. Louis Hegelians' anxiety in the 1870s and 1880s as they watched Chicago outstrip St. Louis in population and economic importance. More firmly in the grip of the "Great St. Louis Illusion" than the others, Brokmeyer, said Snider, "could on small provocation fall into profane if not obscene anti-Chicago paroxysms."

Despite, or perhaps because of, such eccentric views, Brokmeyer enjoyed considerable political popularity, which he exploited to lead a useful public life. During the Civil War he joined the Missouri State Militia, raised a regiment, and was promoted to lieutenant colonel. In defiance of the intimidation of the "Secesh" element in Warren County, he was elected state representative in 1862 (as a Union Democrat). He subsequently served as a St. Louis alderman in 1866, in the state senate from 1871 to 1875, where he chaired the judiciary and ways and means committees, and as a delegate to the state Constitutional Convention in 1875, where he authored restrictions on expenditures to the proportion of state revenues. He was elected lieutenant governor as a Democrat in 1876, and served briefly as acting governor in 1877.

Since few of Henry Brokmeyer's papers have survived, it is difficult to determine what precisely led him to abandon a promising political career in the late 1870s. Those who knew him well, like Snider and Harris, implied that Brokmeyer tired of politics and despaired of the country's future once events did not follow his elaborate and ambitious predictions. Like the other St. Louis Hegelians, he was dismayed by the laissez-faire atmosphere of postwar America. Although it is probably not true, as some have claimed, that Brokmeyer moved to Oklahoma Territory to preach Hegel to Native Americans, he clearly preferred the territory's relative peace to the social strife of Gilded Age America. He died on July 26, 1906.

DENYS P. LEIGHTON

Brokmeyer, Henry C. *A Mechanic's Diary.* Washington, D.C.: E. C. Brokmeyer, 1910.

Goetzmann, William. *The American Hegelians: An Intellectual Episode in the History of Western America.* New York: Knopf, 1973.

Hyde, William, and Howard L. Conard, eds. *Encyclopedia of the History of St. Louis.* New York: Southern History, 1899.

Leighton, Denys P. "William Torrey Harris, the St. Louis Hegelians, and the Meaning of the Civil War." *Gateway Heritage* 10 (fall 1989): 33–45.

Snider, Denton J. *The St. Louis Movement in Philosophy, Literature, Education, Psychology, with Chapters of Autobiography.* St. Louis: Sigma, 1920.

BROOKINGS, ROBERT SOMERS (1850–1932)

Robert Somers Brookings was born in rural Cecil County, Maryland, on January 22, 1850, son of Richard Brookings, a physician, and Mary Carter Brookings. His father died before he reached two years of age. His mother thereafter married her cousin, Henry Reynolds, a carpenter, and moved with her children to the latter's home in Baltimore. During the summers Brookings returned to his birthplace to live with a maternal uncle, physician Robert Carter. Depression in Baltimore during the Civil War compelled the Reynolds household to move to Hartford County, north of the city. In 1864 Brookings attended a boarding school near Rising Sun, Maryland, but left after less than a year. He resolved to enter the business world, and in preparation studied accounting for a brief time in Baltimore.

In 1866 Brookings moved to join his older brother Harry in St. Louis, and like him worked as a bookkeeper at Cupples and Marston, a wholesale household-implements and cordage firm headed by **Samuel Cupples.** In 1868 Cupples promoted Robert to be a traveling salesman (or "drummer") and assigned him territory extending from Montana and San Francisco to New Orleans. Brookings proved very adept at selling for the firm. While on the road he also strove to "improve" himself in ways not immediately related to sales, such as by reading (Plutarch's *Lives* was a favorite), learning German, and playing the fiddle.

In 1871 the Brookings brothers announced plans for their own business; Cupples instead offered them a partnership, as Samuel Cupples and Company, which they accepted. Throughout the 1870s Brookings continued his long sales expeditions, but also made executive policy decisions for Cupples, including the establishment of offices in other major cities. Although in many respects still a typical nineteenth-century businessman, Brookings persisted in educating himself beyond the needs of his business. Out of concern that he lacked manners befitting a gentleman, for example, he took lessons in deportment from Sarah Beaumont Keim, the elderly daughter of the pioneer physician **William Beaumont.** From Marshall Snow, dean of the college at Washington University, he received lists of readings in history, politics, and literature. One early expression of his acquired tastes was to become a leading supporter—and eventually president—of the Choral Society, a precursor of the St. Louis Symphony. He also joined the St. Louis Mercantile Library Association, and as president there too was instrumental in providing the association with a new building and endowment.

In 1882 Harry Brookings left the partnership, which now became known as the Samuel Cupples Wooden-Ware Company. The younger Brookings directed the firm in all but title. Briefly, he contemplated drawing back from his contentious business life to pursue new goals. He had already (in 1880) traveled in Europe, ostensibly to study model worker housing recently constructed in England, but more truly for pleasure and personal discovery. In 1884 he returned for an extended stay in Berlin, this time openly to savor artistic life. In Berlin he met the noted violinist Joseph Joachim, who is said to have gracefully convinced the young American that his musical talents were insufficient to launch a concert career.

After the European sabbatical, Brookings returned to his St. Louis commercial interests, for a time with renewed vigor. In meeting a particularly stiff challenge in the late 1880s he proved that he had not lost touch. The position of the Cupples Company as a leading supplier of rope and twine was threatened by formation of the National Cordage Company, which attempted to monopolize manufacture and distribution. Brookings countered by acquiring a small New York cordage factory and rapidly expanding its production capacity. The tactic succeeded dramatically, eventually leading to a collapse of the National Cordage Company, which in turn contributed to the outbreak of a nationwide business depression in 1893.

Arguably, Brooking's greatest achievement as a business executive entailed the design, financing, and construction of Cupples Station (the St. Louis Terminal Cupples Station and Property Company), a large warehouse complex of eighteen buildings adjacent to the railroad yards in downtown St. Louis, between 1893 and 1895. Its advanced design and strategic location consolidated and facilitated freight handling and storage operations of Cupples as well as other wholesale firms in the congested urban center, and proved a model for similar commercial developments in other U.S. cities.

In 1891 Brookings was appointed a director of the corporation, that is, trustee, of Washington University. Four years later, he became president of the board. Thereafter he dominated the university administration, orchestrating major decisions on finance and governance, while leaving academic details to the chancellors who reported to him. Among the major developments at Washington University that he oversaw in the 1890s included the absorption of two previously independent medical schools (St. Louis Medical and Missouri Medical Colleges), the purchase of land for a new campus at the western border of the city of St. Louis, and the initial planning of its buildings. Engaged in his new career as university executive, Brookings gradually withdrew from active management of the Cupples enterprises (he retired as head in 1909), but retained control over a variety of other commercial enterprises. He and Cupples transferred the ownership of Cupples Station to the university in 1900.

The opening of the new Washington University campus was delayed one year by the St. Louis World's Fair, located mostly on the large municipally owned Forest Park, adjoining the campus to the east. To provide extra space for the extravaganza of 1904, Brookings leased his institution's land and newly finished buildings to the Louisiana Purchase Exposition Company. The deal offered the university a windfall opportunity to recoup some of the immense costs of the relocation, and also served to attract donations from wealthy St. Louisans to build other campus structures only dreamed of in the original plans. In April 1905 the university finally occupied its "hilltop" overlooking the park, with its centerpiece a Tudor Gothic–style administration building that was the gift of Brookings himself (which since 1928 has been named Brookings Hall).

Other major changes in the university during Brookings's administration took place in the medical school. In the decade since taking control of the old proprietary colleges, Brookings had allocated substantial funds to improve facilities and training standards. A harsh review by Abraham Flexner in his national survey of medical colleges for the Carnegie Foundation for Advancement of Teaching in 1909, however, persuaded Brookings to undertake far more extensive reforms. With additional advice from Flexner and Carnegie Foundation president Henry Prichett (a former Washington University professor), plans were laid to hire and endow a new faculty, and to build a new campus for the school on the eastern edge of Forest Park in conjunction with two privately administered hospitals. Construction took place between 1912 and 1915, when the medical campus was dedicated. Brookings contributed substantially to the project from his own fortune.

Through Prichett, Brookings met Andrew Carnegie himself, who asked him to advise both the Carnegie Corporation and the Carnegie Peace Foundation in Washington, D.C., in 1910. That same year Brookings joined other Washington governing boards, including those of the Smithsonian Institution and the National Civic Federation. President William Howard Taft named him to a special Commission on Economy and Efficiency, charged with examining the financial practices of federal agencies. The commission was discontinued by President Woodrow Wilson, but Brookings and other business and academic leaders founded a private agency to continue its aims in 1916. This was the Institute for Government Research (IGR), and Brookings became its vice chairman.

After the United States entered World War I in 1917, President Wilson created the War Industries Board (WIB) to set priorities in the production of armaments and other goods. Wilson named Brookings to chair the board, and, to serve with him, the financier Bernard Baruch and the railroad executive Robert Lovett. The war effort rapidly led to sharp price increases and shortages of critical goods, in response to which the authority of the WIB was extended to include consideration of price controls. Brookings and Baruch clashed on this (the former favoring, the latter opposing) and on many other key issues before the WIB. At seeming variance with his background as a provincial, self-taught business leader, Brookings took positions that marked him as almost radical: for example, he advocated representation on the boards of directors of major corporations.

The armistice was reached before any major restructuring of the U.S. economy was deemed necessary. Nevertheless, Brookings argued for carrying on the study of major issues that he had grappled with as head of the WIB. In 1922, with assistance from the Carnegie Corporation, he established the Institute of Economics (IE) in Washington to "collect, interpret, and lay before the country in a coherent form the fundamental economic facts." At the same time Brookings called upon his old associates at Washington University to form a special graduate school, based in Washington and named for himself, to train high-level leaders within the government. The two new institutes were to operate in conjunction with the earlier IGR, although each was to have its own board of trustees and function according to its own mission.

From the start various complications troubled the operation of the three bodies. A technicality of Missouri law prevented Washington University from administering a program outside the state; nevertheless, a faculty was assembled and the curriculum begun at the Brookings School. More disruptive were recurrent disputes between the staffs of the three institutes over the philosophy and range of their respective programs. In 1926 Brookings ordered the preparation of a plan for consolidation. The plan was carried out the following year, creating the new Brookings Institution. The former IE director, Harold G. Moulton, was promoted to serve as the first Brookings president (a position that he held until 1952).

A bachelor until his midseventies, Brookings married a longtime friend, Isabel Vallé January of St. Louis, in 1927, and thereafter they made their principal home in Washington. He spent much time in his last years writing, and in all published three books: *Industrial Ownership* (1924), *Economic Democracy* (1929), and *The Way Forward* (1932). Isabel Brookings nursed him through periods of ill health in the late 1920s and early 1930s. A generous philanthropist in her own right, she donated money to construct a law school building at Washington University in 1923 and the headquarters of the Brookings Institution in Washington in 1931. Brookings died on November 15, 1932.

PAUL G. ANDERSON

Brookings, Robert S. Papers. Archives. Brookings Institution, Washington, D.C.
———. Papers. Archives. Olin Library, Washington University, St. Louis.
Critchlow, Donald T. *The Brookings Institution, 1916–1952: Expertise and the Public Interest in a Democratic Society.* De Kalb: Northern Illinois University Press, 1985.
Hagedorn, Hermann. *Brookings: A Biography.* New York: Macmillan, 1936.
Morrow, Ralph E. *Washington University in St. Louis: A History.* St. Louis: Missouri Historical Society Press, 1996.

BROWN, BENJAMIN GRATZ (1826–1885)

Benjamin Gratz Brown, a Missouri senator, governor, and U.S. vice presidential candidate, was born to politics. His Virginia-born paternal grandfather, John, served as the Marquis de Lafayette's aide-de-camp during the Revolution and read law with Thomas Jefferson before becoming Kentucky's first U.S. senator. His father, Mason Brown, was equally political and became a prominent Whig. His mother, Judith Bledsoe Brown, a member of another political family, was related to Henry Clay by marriage. But extending from the web of Whigs was a familial strand to Andrew Jackson's adviser and Democratic power broker, Francis Preston Blair Sr., to whom Gratz was related on both his father's and his mother's sides. It was the Blair family, particular Preston's two sons, **Frank** and **Montgomery Blair,** who had the most decisive influence on Gratz's life.

Brown was born on May 28, 1826, and named after his wealthy Jewish merchant uncle, Benjamin Gratz. Brown's family dropped the "Benjamin" during his childhood, and he was known ever after as "Gratz." After his mother's early death he grew up at his grandfather John's estate, Liberty Hall. He matriculated at Transylvania University in 1841, where he lived with his uncle Benjamin Gratz, a school trustee. As chance would have it his uncle was also boarding Brown's cousin, Frank Blair, who was attending law school, and two years later Benjamin opened his door to another Brown kinsman, **Joseph Shelby,** the future Confederate general. In 1845 Gratz left Transylvania for Yale College, from which he graduated in 1847. Returning to Kentucky he studied law with his father, and continued with a more formal stint at the Louisville Law School. Brown came to adulthood a committed young Whig, swept up in an upsurge of antislavery sentiment, and briefly espoused a moderate emancipationism, which was conventionally close to that advocated by Henry Clay.

In 1849 Brown's life underwent sharp change when he moved to St. Louis to join his cousins Montgomery and Frank Blair's law practice. The Blairs were lieutenants of **Thomas Hart Benton,** Missouri's longtime Democratic senator. The aging but fierce Benton was locked in a political death struggle with the Southern-sympathizing wing of Missouri's Democratic Party. While hostile to both blacks and abolitionism, Benton and the Blairs believed that following the Southern-style Democrats threatened to drag Missouri into the same sort of economic stagnation they saw in the South. Free-white immigrants, upon whose labor the North's dynamic market economy depended, would bypass the state to avoid degrading competition with slave labor, and the development of Missouri industry would be retarded. When Benton lost his Senate seat in 1850, it was considered a temporary setback. In 1852 the Bentonites founded the St. Louis newspaper the *Missouri Democrat* to serve as their voice. Brown, who had contributed editorials from its inception, became its editor in chief in 1854.

Brown's journalist work coincided with active involvement in formal politics. In 1852 he won election to Missouri's General Assembly and immediately became a controversial figure for his vigorous Bentonite partisanship and outspoken hostility to the Kansas-Nebraska bill, which would have allowed the possibility of extending slavery into what had been designated by the Missouri Compromise as free soil. Two turbulent years later, he won reelection to the House by only twelve votes. His seating in the Missouri House was hotly contested, and the investigating committee's decision to seat him came upon a single vote.

This close political shave, however, left Brown's partisanship unstinted. When **Robert M. Stewart,** a future governor, made unflattering remarks about Thomas Hart Benton during Benton's 1855 effort to regain his Senate seat, Brown challenged him to a duel. After terms were set Stewart withdrew his remark, and violence was avoided. Not so the following year. Brown's steady denunciation of rival politicians and their views was often personal. **Thomas C. Reynolds,** soon to become Missouri's lieutenant governor and subsequently exiled secessionist governor, was a particular target. When Reynolds responded with pointed abuse in a rival newspaper, he succeeded in provoking a challenge. The two men, who had nearly dueled once before, met on August 26, 1856. While Brown missed his shot, Reynolds wounded Brown in the knee. Brown walked with a limp the remainder of his life.

By the time of his duel with Reynolds, Brown was drifting toward the Republican Party. With Frank Blair's elevation to the United States Congress, Brown became the political leader of a growing number of similarly evolving Missouri politicians. He made clear his new political departure in a dramatic 1857 speech to the state legislature in which he forcefully called for the end of Missouri slavery. Far from attacking slavery on humane grounds, however, he set himself up as the champion of the aspirations of free-white labor and called slavery a barrier to economic progress. Much of his analysis began on old Bentonite grounds, however, and he no longer damned secessionism and abolitionism as twin evils. His speech was actually designed to work on several levels: the call for slavery's end was designed to appeal to German immigrants, most of whom were hostile to the institution; the call for economic progress was designed to appeal to moderate Whigs whose party had self-destructed over the slavery issue; and the emphasis on free labor was designed to appeal to the aspirations of ordinary farmers who had made up the backbone of Benton's followers.

Brown's views, helped by the panic of 1857, appealed to many Missourians but made him, perhaps, even more enemies. Thomas Hart Benton thought the speech a rank betrayal, while proslavery advocates denounced Brown as an abolitionist. In 1858 he was soundly defeated for reelection. His political troubles continued when he quarreled with Frank Blair, who forced him out of the job as editor in chief of the *Missouri Democrat* in 1859.

The time, Brown decided, was propitious for a vacation from politics. In August 1858 he married Mary Hansome Gunn, the daughter of a former mayor of Jefferson City and the official state printer. She was seventeen, while he was thirty-two. Together they would have six children. Following his departure from the *Democrat,* he began a new life and organized the Citizens Railway Company of St. Louis, the first effort to provide the city with a "street railroad."

Brown threw himself intensely into building his company, but events brought him back into politics. In 1860 he served as an **Edward Bates** delegate to the Republican National Convention in Chicago. Unlike the Blairs, however, Brown only tepidly supported Bates, whom he considered too conservative. When the rush of delegates began moving toward Lincoln he gladly brought the Missouri delegation into line.

With the outbreak of the Civil War in Missouri, Brown organized a regiment of volunteers, which, despite his complete absence of military training, he commanded as a colonel. The regiment's three-month career was lackluster, made up of patrolling St. Louis streets, a brief foray into southeastern Missouri, and reinforcing Gen. **Franz Siegel** after the Battle of Carthage. The work was dull, plagued with inefficiencies and shortages, and not to Brown's liking. When his brief term of service expired, he happily gave it up.

Brown found political battle far more exhilarating than military battle. **John C. Frémont**'s famous hundred days as Missouri's military commander stimulated Brown to the same degree that it appalled pro-Union moderates. When Lincoln removed Frémont from his post, Brown captured Frémont's constituency, many of whom were German immigrants. In so doing, he established himself as the leader of the radical wing of Missouri's Republican Party. Brown, in fact, began to think of himself as a revolutionary. He helped found the Missouri Emancipation Society and called for the immediate abolition of slavery, which he no longer tied to African deportation schemes. Rebels, he proclaimed, deserved "eternal" punishment, and safety required severe restrictions on the civil rights of Southern sympathizers. He openly opposed Gov. **Hamilton Gamble,** a moderate Unionist, as little better than a Copperhead; judged the conservative Missouri Republicans, led by his cousin Frank, as possessing inadequate militancy; and set himself and his followers up as monitors of Lincoln's conservative tendencies. While loathed by many, through his extremism Missouri's "Prince of the Radicals" had arrived atop state politics. In a grueling and bitter 1863 campaign Brown won selection by the state legislature to the United States Senate to fill the vacancy left by the expulsion of pro-Southerner **Waldo P. Johnson.**

In the Senate Brown was probably even more radical than he had been back home. Abolitionist William Lloyd Garrison marveled that a state like Missouri could send such a man to the Senate. But much of Brown's term was dedicated to the state's economic concerns: he helped obtain $6.7 million in reimbursements to the state for military expenditures; secured federal land grants to develop several railroad lines; and worked to improve navigation on the Mississippi River, along with a concession to build a bridge across it at St. Louis. Brown also advocated a number of reforms, such as limiting partisanship in government through the extension of the civil service, nationalizing the telegraph lines, and reducing the hours for federal employees as a prelude to a general reduction of working hours for nongovernment workers.

Yet, for all his overheated rhetoric, by the war's end Brown's radicalism was rapidly cooling. Radical leadership in Missouri had passed to St. Louis lawyer **Charles Drake,** who was the leading spirit behind Missouri's 1865 constitution, which contained harsh restrictions on the civil rights and liberties of those deemed Southern sympathizers. This was now too much for Brown. Backing away from earlier talk of eternal punishment of Rebels, he called for "Universal Suffrage and Universal Amnesty." Restrictions on civil rights could be justified only by wartime conditions. Those who had sided with the South deserved forgiveness and, along with the new freedmen, deserved the franchise—an enfranchisement, he announced, that should also be extended to women.

Talk of giving former Rebels the vote did little to endear Brown to Radicals controlling Missouri. When his term ended in 1867 he pleaded poor health, did not seek reelection, and was replaced by Drake. Back in Missouri he left politics behind and took up residence at his country home near Ironton. There he leased a quarry, from which he later provided granite for St. Louis's Eads Bridge, which was built over the Mississippi River with the concession he obtained as senator. (He would be the featured speaker at the bridge's dedication in 1874.)

If Brown's calls for universal suffrage and amnesty were too advanced for the political climate of 1865, the ground had rapidly shifted by 1869. A revolt within the Missouri Republican Party led to the so-called Liberal movement. Much like Brown, leading Liberals, such as Missouri senator **Carl Schurz** and *Missouri Democrat* editor William Grosvenor, had called for universal amnesty, civil service reform,

and tariff reduction. The Liberals' appeal, moreover, was greatly enhanced by their opposition to the Grant administration, which had matched corruption with ineptitude. To carry off their plans Schurz and Grosvenor turned to Brown, whom, they believed, as a southern-born former Radical, could make a convincing case for amnesty and an end to civil proscriptions on Southern sympathizers.

In 1870 the revolt became formalized with the formation of the Liberal Republican Party, which immediately made Brown its gubernatorial nominee. The campaign that followed was bitter, personal, and fully entered into by an alarmed Grant administration. Tales of Brown's excessive drinking, which had first circulated during his Senate campaign, were now given wide circulation. Although these tales—which included stories of Brown drunkenly buttering watermelon, vomiting in the Jefferson City streets, and delivering lengthy, incoherent speeches—had some basis in fact, they swayed few voters. While the race was considered tight, Democrats, who had not put up their own candidate, joined Liberal Party revolters, and Brown won a smashing victory.

During the course of Brown's governorship, restricted by the Missouri constitution to two years, he attempted to encourage the social healing of the wounds of war; he demonstrated strong support for education, with particular concern for women's education; worked to reform the criminal system, and took a special interest in judicial offenders; encouraged the development of a nonpartisan civil service system; and replaced the old, dilapidated governor's mansion with a handsome Second Empire–style mansion, which continues as the governor's residence today.

Despite these measures Brown's principal preoccupation during his governorship was running for president. Missouri's Liberal movement had encouraged imitators all across the country, taking strong root in key states such as Ohio, Illinois, and New York. In the process Brown became an important national figure. Unfortunately for his aspirations, Brown had become estranged from Schurz, the leading Liberal of the day. Some of the contention was personal, but some was Schurz's dislike of Brown's openhanded sharing of patronage with Democrats. This sharing had extended to Brown's help in making his, now Democratic, cousin Frank Blair, with whom he had reconciled, a U.S. senator. Instead of his fellow Missourian, Schurz supported Charles Francis Adams in the presidential race. At the Liberal Republican Party National Convention in Cincinnati, Schurz informed Brown he might have the vice presidential nomination on an Adams ticket if he bowed out, but Brown refused. Failing to obtain the nomination for himself, Brown threw his support to newspaper editor Horace Greeley, who went on to win the nomination, and rewarded Brown with the second spot. Nationally, the Democrats reluctantly followed the Liberal lead and adopted the Greeley-Brown ticket. The result was a disaster. Greeley was actually hostile to many tenets of the Liberal program, and Southern Democrats had never forgiven his wartime rhetoric. Many Americans, moreover, regarded Greeley as an eccentric for the many "isms" he had embraced over the years. As for Brown, descriptions of drinking habits now found a national audience. In the election Grant won by an even wider margin than in 1868. With the ticket's defeat the Liberal Republican movement was dead.

After the 1872 election Brown formally became a Democrat, as did many Liberals, but he retired from politics. Uncertain finances drove him from his various business enterprises back into legal practice. His health, never strong, was chronically poor. The free moments of his life were given over to his avocational interest in mathematics, writing two short books on the subject. He died at his home in Kirkwood, Missouri, on December 13, 1885.

KENNETH H. WINN

Carnahan, Jean. *If Walls Could Talk: The Story of Missouri's First Families.* Jefferson City, Mo.: MMPI, 1998.

Peterson, Norma L. *Freedom and Franchise: The Political Career of B. Gratz Brown.* Columbia: University of Missouri Press, 1965.

BROWN, MARGARET TOBIN "MOLLY" (1867–1932)

Out of the tragedy of the sinking of the White Star ocean liner *Titanic* came lasting fame and recognition for Margaret "Maggie" Brown, when she ably assisted in the aftermath of that disastrous night of April 14, 1912. With her command of many foreign languages, she translated for passengers on the rescue ship, many of them immigrant women who had lost their husbands, and created a roster of messages to send to relatives on arrival in New York. Hailed as a heroine of the tragedy, Brown replied to newspaper reporters that she was "unsinkable," and the nickname stuck. While she was never known as "Molly," that was the nickname given to the character in the stage play and musical *The Unsinkable Molly Brown,* based on her life.

Maggie Tobin, born in Hannibal, Missouri, on July 18, 1867, was the second child of Irish immigrant widower John Tobin and his second wife, widow Johanna Collins. Their combined family grew to a total of six children; they lived on John's wages as a laborer at the Hannibal Gas Company. Maggie completed her education at her aunt Mary O'Leary's private school around the age of thirteen. She went on to work at the Garth Tobacco Factory and later was a waitress at the Continental Hotel, and possibly the Park Hotel, both in Hannibal. In 1886 Maggie and her older brother, Dan, journeyed to Leadville, Colorado, to live with their half-sister, Mary Ann, and her husband, Jack Landrigan. It was in Leadville that Maggie met James Joseph "J. J." Brown. After a brief courtship, they were married in Leadville on September 1, 1886.

J. J. Brown was a mine superintendent at the Ibex Mining Company. He also owned a good deal of stock in the company, so when gold was discovered at the Little Johnny Mine in 1894, the Browns realized a fortune. With that wealth came eccentricity for Maggie, as her great social ambition began to govern her actions. The Browns moved from their Leadville log cabin to Denver, purchasing a home in the fashionable neighborhood of Pennsylvania Avenue, near the state capitol. Their children, Lawrence (called Larry, born in Hannibal in 1887) and Catherine Ellen (called Helen, born in Leadville in 1889), were enrolled in expensive boarding schools.

Brown lived her life conspicuously in the public eye, wearing glamorous clothes, hosting elaborate parties, and traveling extensively across Europe. She made sure her pursuits were chronicled in the society pages—the more outrageous and embellished the story was, the better she liked it. She soon became accepted by all but the very highest level of Denver society, who considered her a semi-illiterate, crude miner's wife. Her pursuit of social acceptance, though, came at the cost of her marriage, as well as the respect of her children, who were often embarrassed by her ostentatious activities.

Her flamboyant social life did not, however, prevent Brown from giving millions of dollars to charity. She made generous contributions to orphanages, hospitals, and Catholic charities. The preservation of poet **Eugene Field**'s Denver home was due to her efforts: she purchased and gave the home to the city as a historic landmark. She organized relief for miners' wives and children after the 1914 Ludlow massacre of the southern Colorado coal strike. It was this charitable Maggie Brown who was the heroine of the *Titanic* disaster. She enjoyed the excitement surrounding her heroism, particularly since it gained her entrée to the theretofore elusive upper level of Denver society.

In her unquenched desire for publicity, Brown ran unsuccessfully for a United States Senate seat in 1914. She became more and more outspoken, and found herself sued for slander at times. In 1922 J. J. Brown died. Although divorced, neither had remarried, and he had continued to support Maggie's activities. Upon his death, she received half of his $10 million fortune.

The last years of Brown's life were spent traveling between Colorado and New York, staying in luxury hotels. She died of a stroke in her Barbion-Plaza suite in New York on October 26, 1932, at the age of sixty-five. Her personal estate was left to charities.

Brown's Denver home is now maintained as a museum, after having served as the governor's mansion from 1902 to 1903, and as a home for wayward girls during the 1960s. A group called Historic Denver Incorporated purchased the home in 1970 and continues to maintain it today.

CHRISTYN L. ELLEY

Hagood, J. Hurley, and Roberta Roland. *Hannibal Yesterdays: Historic Stories of Events, People, Landmarks, and Happenings in and near Hannibal.* Marceline, Mo.: Jostens, 1992.

Kohl, Edith Eugenia. *Denver's Historic Mansions: Citadels to the Empire Builders.* Denver: Sage Books, 1957.

Priddy, Bob. *Across Our Wide Missouri.* Vol. 2. Independence, Mo.: Independence Press, 1984.

Whitacre, Christine. *Molly Brown: Denver's Unsinkable Lady.* Denver: Historic Denver, 1984.

BROWN, WILLIAM WELLS (1814?–1884)

William Wells Brown was a black abolitionist and author who spent his youth as a slave in Missouri. After escaping in 1834 Brown joined the abolitionist movement as an antislavery lecturer in the Northeast. His vivid description of slavery in St. Louis formed the basis of his lectures and a book, *Narrative of William W. Brown, a Fugitive Slave, Written by Himself,* published by the Massachusetts Anti-Slavery Society in 1847. The *Narrative* was a best-seller; several thousand copies sold in the first three months, and nine editions appeared over the next two years in the United States and England. Like Frederick Douglass's better-known slave narrative, Brown's story was only secondarily a biographical work. He wrote it to convince white readers that slavery was immoral and inhumane and should be abolished. His story is an underused resource for Missouri history, one that offers a unique perspective on St. Louis as a slave society during the years between 1827 and 1834.

William Wells Brown was born into slavery on a plantation near Lexington, Kentucky, about 1814. Although his mother named him William, Brown was called Sanford by his owners. His father was probably his master's brother. His mother, Elizabeth, and her seven children came to Missouri in 1816 with their master, Dr. John Young, when he purchased farmland on the Missouri River in what became Montgomery County. Brown worked as a servant in Young's home until he was about twelve years old. In 1827 Young moved to St. Louis and bought a farm four miles northwest of town. Although Brown intermittently lived and worked as a house servant on the farm, he spent most of the next six years hired out, either in St. Louis or on steamboats plying the Mississippi and lower Missouri Rivers.

Typical of urban areas, slave owners in St. Louis—about 40 percent of the white householders in 1830—treated their slaves as rental property. Young hired Brown out to local businessmen, and the teenager moved every few months. He worked a succession of unskilled jobs in Freeland's Tavern, on the steamboat *Missouri,* and at the Missouri Hotel. For a short time he was a printer's helper in the newspaper office of **Elijah Lovejoy,** who several years later was martyred for advocating abolition. According to his text Brown also spent a year in service to a slave trader, James Walker, accompanying him on three sales trips to New Orleans. Although he was usually separated from his family, Brown maintained an affectionate relationship with his mother and vowed to stay in St. Louis while she was in the city. He made plans to leave only after Young sold her downriver. Thirteen years after his escape, Brown published the narrative of his teenage years. No other sources are available with which to compare the details he gave of his experiences while living in Missouri.

In the *Narrative,* Brown portrayed a social system almost entirely controlled by slave owners, one in which slaves like himself were isolated individuals who resisted the system at their peril, and on their own. The Missouri Slave Code and local ordinances that defined slaves as chattel and denied them civil rights also restricted interactions between slaves and free persons, white or black. The urban hiring-out system, however, made it possible for Brown to move through the city and mingle with many different people. He was able to acquire the skills, sophistication, and money necessary for his eventual escape. Unlike the heroic slave stereotypes in other antislavery tracts, Brown's narrator was savvy and streetwise, and lived by his wits.

Although he must have known the local African American community well, Brown revealed almost nothing about it in the *Narrative,* which followed a literary formula already well established for abolitionist autobiographies. With few exceptions he characterized other slaves as stereotypical victims of oppression, which conformed to the genre, but also provided the cover of anonymity for the people he left behind, who, in 1847, still lived in a slave state. Years later, in 1861, he wrote of visiting in Canada former slaves and free people he had known in St. Louis. However, in the narrative he only rarely gave the reader a glimpse of his hidden life.

Although much of the story takes place in St. Louis, Brown provided little context for the events he described. As in most slave narratives, slave owners appeared as stereotypes: general enough to be universal, and specific enough to be believable. However, the slaveholders in Brown's narrative were all prominent St. Louisans, individuals well known to anyone familiar with the city in the early 1830s and easily verified in the standard sources. They included such prominent men as **John Darby,** Daniel Page, and **John O'Fallon.** The only major figure in the *Narrative* that has not been verified is the slave trader James Walker, who may have been a composite character.

When Brown did occasionally put his slave owners in context, it was always for a specific purpose. It was important to him to counter the prevailing belief that slavery in Missouri was "more benign" than slavery in the Deep South, that urban slavery was "milder" than plantation slavery. His narrative, like all slave narratives, followed a basic plot. He included descriptions of whippings and other sadistic punishments, delicate but unmistakable references to the rape of slave women, and scenes depicting the heartless separation of families. However, Brown took pains to tie these events directly to identifiable St. Louisans. Vivid descriptions of slave owners attacking slaves in public places reminded readers that a slave on the streets of St. Louis was always vulnerable to random attack and without legal recourse. Brown argued that while the city did not look or function like a plantation cotton field, the same omnipresent, oppressive social system prevailed.

Following an unsuccessful escape attempt with his mother in 1832, Brown was sold by Dr. Young to a St. Louis merchant, who several months later sold him again to a local steamboat captain, Enoch Price. On January 1, 1834, when Captain Price's boat docked on the Cincinnati levee, Brown, known until then as Sanford, escaped on foot and headed for northern Ohio. He took back the name William that his mother had given him at birth, added the name Wells Brown for his first benefactor in freedom, and created a new life for himself as William Wells Brown. He spent the next two years in Cleveland working on a Lake Erie steamboat and helping other fugitive slaves escape to Canada.

After moving to Buffalo, Brown lectured for the Western New York Anti-Slavery Society. He was so compelling a speaker that in 1847 the Massachusetts Anti-Slavery Society hired him as a circuit lecturer. He used his own experiences as his text. When the *Narrative* was published, Brown sent a copy to Capt. Enoch Price, his last master and still his legal owner. Price offered to sell his former slave, but Brown refused to negotiate with him. After the passage of the Fugitive Slave Law in 1850, however, he realized that he could be returned to slavery if not legally free and permitted the transaction, which was completed in 1854.

Although Brown always insisted he learned to read only after his escape, he quickly became a talented and prolific author. After publishing the *Narrative,* he lived for five years in England, where he wrote a travelogue and in 1853 a novel, *Clotelle; or, The President's Daughter.* He subsequently published two dramas and three volumes of black history. Throughout his life he preached against the doctrine of racial inferiority, urging black people to respect themselves and to strive for self-improvement through hard work. "All I demand for the black man," he asserted, "is that the white people shall take their heels off his neck, and let him have a chance to rise by his own efforts."

Brown rewrote his life story a number of times in his later books. In 1856 his daughter, Josephine, published a short authorized biography. All these versions were substantially the same, though dates and duration vary some. In these biographical writings Brown did not add more details of his life in slavery than he had in the original *Narrative.* Instead, he reworked the material in fictional form, no longer constrained by the structure and expectations of the slave narrative and the necessity to protect the people involved. His last book, *My Southern Home; or, The South and Its People,* appeared four years before his death on November 6, 1884. In the preface Brown explained that the incidents depicting slave life were based on his own recollections. Many of the stories were fictionalized accounts of events from the same period covered by the *Narrative.* Some were set on a plantation similar to Dr. Young's farms in Kentucky and Missouri. There in the slave quarters, far from the big house, a community of slaves functioned as an extended family, a setting far different from the city where Sanford, an alienated teenage slave, fought for survival and freedom in the early 1830s. These stories provide another perspective on his years in St. Louis and on how a much older Williams Wells Brown remembered and interpreted them to himself and his public.

KATHARINE T. CORBETT

Andrews, William L. *To Tell a Free Story: The First Century of Afro-American Autobiography, 1760–1865.* Urbana: University of Illinois Press, 1986.

———, ed. *From Fugitive Slave to Free Man: The Autobiographies of William Wells Brown.* New York: Penguin Books, 1993.

Brown, William Wells. *Narrative of William W. Brown, a Fugitive Slave, Written by Himself.* 2d ed. Boston: Massachusetts Anti-Slavery Society, 1848.

Farrison, William Edward. *William Wells Brown: Author and Reformer.* Chicago: University of Chicago Press, 1969.

Ripley, C. Peter, ed. *The Black Abolitionist Papers.* Chapel Hill: University of North Carolina Press, 1985–1986.

BROWNLEE, RICHARD S., II (1918–1990)

A fifth-generation Missourian, Richard S. Brownlee II spent more than a quarter century promoting and preserving the history of his native state. Born in Brookfield on March 12, 1918, he attended elementary and secondary schools there and in 1935 enrolled at the University of Missouri, the alma mater of his father and his paternal grandfather and grandmother.

While at the university Brownlee proved an excellent student, and, after graduation, received an honorary Phi Beta Kappa membership. He joined a number of university and social organizations, including the international relations club; the homecoming committee; Stirpes and Diamonds, the honorary organization for ROTC noncommissioned officers; and the Sigma Nu fraternity. Brownlee earned his A.B. degree from the university in 1939 and a bachelor of journalism degree the following year. He then accepted a position with the advertising department of the Coca-Cola Company.

Brownlee's civilian life was interrupted by World War II. In January 1941 he began his military service as a private in the United States Army. He served in the Asian Pacific and American theaters and ended his tour of duty as a special staff officer in the general staff of the Western Flying Training Command. Brownlee received a promotion to captain before his discharge. While on furlough in December 1942 he had married his Kappa Kappa Gamma sweetheart, Alice Rowley of New Haven, Missouri. Two children were born to this marriage, Richard S. Brownlee III and Margaret Ann.

After his discharge Brownlee worked brief stints with newspapers in Lebanon and Warrensburg, Missouri. His love of history, however, led him to enroll in graduate school at the University of Missouri in 1947. Three years later he obtained an M.A. degree in history. He earned his Ph.D. in history from the university in 1955 under the guidance of Prof. **Lewis Atherton.** Keenly interested in western military history, Brownlee chose military subjects for both his master's thesis and his doctoral dissertation.

In 1950 Brownlee became assistant director of adult education at the university and also taught in the statewide academic-extension program. In addition he served as a special assistant to University of Missouri president **Elmer Ellis,** while Ellis chaired the Missouri State Bond Building Drive during the mid-1950s.

With numerous demands on his time, Brownlee was still able to revise his doctoral dissertation into a book-length manuscript. The Louisiana State University Press published his *Gray Ghosts of the Confederacy* in 1958. Brownlee's study of guerrilla warfare on the western border during the Civil War became a best-seller in its field, and numerous reprintings since that time attest to its continued significance.

In May 1960 the State Historical Society of Missouri named Brownlee director, secretary, and librarian. During his twenty-five years as director, he oversaw the activities and expansion of the society's valuable reference, newspaper, and manuscript libraries; its fine arts collection; and its publication program. Brownlee supervised a move into new quarters and witnessed the tripling of library users of the society's growing collections. Besides administering the society's manuscript collection, in 1961 he was also named assistant director of the University of Missouri's Western Historical Manuscripts Collection. In 1963 the university's collection became integrated with the society's holdings, and Brownlee became director of the Joint Collection, which expanded into a four-campus collection in 1968. Constantly in demand as a speaker, he gave some nine hundred talks to local historical societies and fraternal, patriotic, and civic groups.

While director of the society and Joint Manuscript Collection, Brownlee provided valuable service to allied programs and projects. He assisted in the formation of the Missouri Museum Associates and served as the director of the Missouri Cultural Exhibit at the New York World's Fair. He was also a member of the State Historical Records Advisory Board, the Missouri State Records Commission, the Missouri Civil War Centennial Commission, and the Missouri Sesquicentennial Commission.

In addition to being one of the state's respected Missouri and Civil War historians, Brownlee earned an enviable reputation as an amateur archaeologist. He helped found the prestigious Missouri Archaeological Society and contributed articles to the *Missouri Archaeologist.*

The recipient of numerous awards, including the State Historical Society's Distinguished Service Award, Brownlee was also selected to the Missouri Academy of Squires, an elective academy of one hundred citizens who have rendered exceptional service to state and community.

Brownlee retired on August 31, 1985. While health problems limited his physical activity, he nevertheless enjoyed his early retirement years. He died as a result of a congenital heart problem on February 14, 1990.

JAMES W. GOODRICH

Brownlee, Richard S., James W. Goodrich, and Mary K. Dains. "The State Historical Society of Missouri, 1898–1973: A Brief History." *Missouri Historical Review* (October 1973): 1–27.

Goodrich, James W. "Richard S. Brownlee II (1918–1990)." *Missouri Historical Review* 84 (July 1990): 375–83.

Havig, Alan R. *A Centennial History of the State Historical Society of Missouri, 1898–1998.* Columbia: University of Missouri Press, 1998.

BRUCE, BLANCHE K. (1841–1898)

Blanche K. Bruce, a black political leader, was born into slavery in Farmville, in Prince Edward County, Virginia, on March 1, 1841. Although Bruce's early years are shrouded in mystery, some believed that he was brought to Chariton County, Missouri, during the early 1850s. Other sources claim Bruce was employed during childhood as a printer's devil at a shop in Brunswick, Missouri, shortly thereafter. This has not been verified, though it might explain his ability to read and write at an early age.

During and immediately after the chaos of the Civil War, Bruce found his way to Hannibal where he taught black children in an institution that may have been administered by the Freedmen's Bureau. Thereafter he enrolled at Oberlin College in Ohio, though sources do not indicate in what field. After receiving his degree Bruce decided to go south.

Bruce was part of a larger migration of Northerners who believed the Reconstruction in the South offered them opportunities for personal advancement and a chance to help other African Americans as well. Most accounts of this movement of northern capital and people to the South focus on the activities of white carpetbaggers, but Bruce's case shows that African Americans believed they could reconstruct themselves as well as Southern society.

Bruce settled in Floreyville, Mississippi, in 1868. Once there he engaged in a variety of occupations, including newspaper editor, planter, and teacher. He also became involved in the turbulent and sometimes violent field of Mississippi Reconstruction politics. Bruce was intelligent, proud, hardworking, and very popular among blacks and white Republicans in Mississippi. During the mid-1870s he successfully created a political machine, which eventually secured him a United States Senate seat. Along the way, in 1870, he was appointed sergeant of arms of the state senate by Gov. James L. Alcorn and named tax assessor and eventually sheriff of Bolivar County. In 1872 he also served as a member of the board of the Mississippi River Levee Commission that focused on future improvements in the river's navigation and safety. Bruce even somehow managed to control the office of superintendent of education.

In 1874 Bruce was elected to the United States Senate, a position that he held from 1875 to 1881, one of the most controversial and violent periods in U.S. history. In the Senate he became an outspoken defender of human rights. He introduced legislation to improve conditions for freedmen, denounced federal policy toward Native Americans in the West, argued against a bill restricting Chinese immigration, and investigated election fraud in Mississippi. Often critical of Republican indifference toward the freedmen, Bruce was assertive and aggressive as a politician. After 1876 he found his position as a Republican senator increasingly untenable as Mississippi Democrats redeemed the state for their party. In 1881 he found himself not only out of office but also unable to return to his home in Mississippi.

Still considered a valuable asset to the Republican Party, Bruce received the appointment of register of the Treasury, a post that he held until 1885. He established his permanent home in Washington, D.C., but continued ownership of a one-thousand-acre plantation in Mississippi, from which he became wealthy. In 1889 President Benjamin Harrison appointed him recorder of deeds of the federal city, then a position of high status, in gratitude for his long, faithful service to the U.S. government. Seven years later President William McKinley reappointed Bruce to his former office at the Treasury Department as register. On March 17, 1898, Bruce died, leaving behind his widow, Josephine B. Wilson, and his son, Roscoe Conkling Bruce.

CHRISTOPHER K. HAYS

Foner, Eric. *Reconstruction: America's Unfinished Revolution, 1863–1877.* New York: Harper and Row, 1988.

Gatewood, Willard B. *Aristocrats of Color: The Black Elite, 1880–1920.* Bloomington: Indiana University Press, 1990.

Woodward, C. Vann. *Origins of the New South, 1877–1913.* Baton Rouge: Louisiana University Press, 1980.

BRUCE, NATHANIEL C. (1868?–1942)

Although his date of birth remains uncertain, Bruce was probably born in 1868, on a farm near Danville, Virginia. He attended Halifax County Public Schools while helping his father, a former slave, on the family farm. Bruce left home at the age of fourteen to attend Shaw Normal and Industrial High School in Raleigh, North Carolina, and then Shaw University, where he received a bachelor of arts degree, graduating with honors. He continued his education, first at Bates College in Maine, then at Hampton Institute in Virginia, and, finally, at Tuskegee Institute in Alabama, where he received a master's degree *pro merito*. Bruce came to Missouri as a principal of a black high school in St. Joseph, and, after briefly serving in that position, he set out to establish his own school.

In 1907 Bruce established an agricultural school near Dalton, in Chariton County, Missouri, "to train negro youth 'back to the land' and for efficient service in the home and on the farm." Initially, the school had five students, three boys and two girls, each of whom spent half the day in a classroom and the other half working in the fields. In 1911 Bruce reorganized his school under a board of trustees as the Bartlett Agricultural and Industrial School after substantial contributions from white philanthropists, including Mr. and Mrs. Herschel Bartlett, Judge and Mrs. W. K. James, and Mr. and Mrs. **Adolphus Busch Sr.,** enabled him to purchase twelve acres of land and build classrooms and a dormitory.

A former student of Booker T. Washington, Bruce modeled his school after his mentor's Tuskegee Institute in Alabama, billing it as "the Tuskegee of the Midwest." While hundreds of thousands of blacks were leaving the rural South for northern cities, Bruce advocated vocational and agricultural training for blacks so that they could achieve economic independence as a means to political and social rights. By 1914 the hard work of Bruce, his staff, and their students began to pay off. In spite of a drought their entry in a statewide agricultural contest won the *Missouri Ruralist* first prize for the highest corn yield and finished second nationally in corn production at the Panama-Pacific International Exposition held in San Francisco. "Place Missouri black boys on the Missouri black land, behind the world-famed Missouri mule," Bruce boasted, "and nothing can beat the combination for raising corn or other crops."

By 1920 more than five hundred students had enrolled in the school since its inception. The teachers' salaries and the operating expenses during this period came almost exclusively from private donations supplemented by money earned from crops and livestock raised at the school. The Bartlett School also sponsored the annual Missouri–Mid-Western States Negro Farmers' and Farm Women's Conference, which sometimes attracted as many as fifteen hundred rural blacks to its farm and produce exhibits. As president of the organization, Bruce "carried the gospel of better farming" to thousands of rural Missouri blacks.

From 1918 until 1922 Bruce served as the first chairman of the Missouri Negro Industrial Commission, which Gov. **Frederick D. Gardner** had initially established for the purpose of organizing black Missourians, especially farmers, behind the war effort. Commission members, all of whom espoused Washington's self-help philosophy, traveled the state selling war bonds, encouraging blacks to plant gardens and conserve food, teaching them better methods of cultivation and crop production, and generally "urging and stimulating [the black] race's old time loyalty, fidelity, and hearty, persistent labor." From its beginning, the Missouri Negro Industrial Commission offered as one of its primary legislative recommendations the establishment of a state-supported agricultural school for black Missourians. Bruce, of course, hoped that the Bartlett School would become that institution, and, for the next several years, he and his fellow commissioners lobbied for funding for the school. Finally, in 1923, the Bartlett School was reorganized with a state appropriation as a demonstration farm and agricultural school for black youths. It was placed under the general control of the University of Missouri's College of Agriculture and renamed the Dalton Vocational School.

In 1924 Bruce was appointed state inspector of black schools by the state superintendent of schools, and later that year he left the principalship of the Dalton School to devote more time to his new position. As state inspector, Bruce traveled Missouri championing his program of vocational education. By the mid-1920s, however, his advocacy of such training for black students, to the exclusion of academic training, began to rankle more and more of his fellow African American leaders. In 1926, before the Moberly school board, Bruce proposed that black youth be trained "to take pride in any work they had to do whether cooking, washing, ironing, scrubbing or driving nails," rather than "high book learning." **Roy Wilkins,** a *Kansas City Call* columnist and future executive director of the National Association for the Advancement of Colored People, bitterly criticized Bruce's narrow-mindedness. "We can't get along without the higher book learning," Wilkins wrote, "and the man who says so is either playing to a 'cracker' 'hill billy' gallery for a mess of pottage or else he is woefully ignorant." Whether as a result of the controversy created by his comments or not, Bruce resigned the inspector position the next year.

After resigning as inspector Bruce occupied a number of educational and agricultural positions in state and federal government. During 1928 and 1929 he served as temporary U.S. farm agent for the flooded cotton counties of southeast Missouri, and was later appointed director of education for black inmates in the state's prison system. He died on June 27, 1942, in Chariton County, Missouri, within a short distance of the institution he had founded. The *Kansas City Call* mourned his passing: "[He] spent many of his best years at [the Dalton Vocational School] and inspired the lives of many young people."

PATRICK J. HUBER AND GARY R. KREMER

Dalton Vocational School. Papers. Inman E. Page Library, Lincoln University, Jefferson City, Mo.

Greene, Lorenzo J., Gary R. Kremer, and Antonio F. Holland. *Missouri's Black Heritage, Revised Edition.* Columbia: University of Missouri Press, 1993.

Huber, Patrick J., and Gary R. Kremer. "Nathaniel C. Bruce, Black Education and the 'Tuskegee of the Midwest.'" *Missouri Historical Review* 86:1 (October 1991): 37–54.

Kansas City Call, July 10, 1942.

BRUNS, ANNA ELISABETH HENRIETTE GEISBERG (1813–1899)

During her lifetime, Anna Elisabeth Henriette Bernadine Geisberg Bruns, known as "Jette," recorded a wealth of historical and personal information in her intimate correspondence and in her autobiography. Her writings present a remarkable record of an immigrant woman's life on the Missouri frontier in the nineteenth century.

Bruns was born on October 28, 1813, in Stromberg, Westphalia, to Max Friedrich Geisberg and Johanna Huffer. When Johanna died from complications after childbirth in 1827, Jette was sent for further education to the home of her uncle in Münster. In 1831 she returned to the family home in Oelde to care for her ill father and six younger siblings. Six months after her father's death, she married Dr. Johann Bernhard Bruns, on May 24, 1832.

Caught up by the emigration fever sweeping Germany and troubled by his own difficulties in collecting fees from his poverty-stricken patients, Dr. Bruns resolved to investigate America. He returned to Germany determined to emigrate, although Jette mustered little enthusiasm for the venture. After a two-month-long sea voyage and another six weeks' travel on land, she arrived in Westphalia, Missouri, on November 2, 1836. With her were her brothers, Franz and Bernhard Geisberg; her young son, Hermann; and Bruns's brother, David. Their small log cabin "with two bedsteads, one table, four chairs and one bench" quickly became constraining as winter descended, and she missed her comfortable home in Oelde.

During the first five years in Westphalia Bruns gave birth to three more children: Max, Johanna, and Rudolph. However, just before her twenty-eighth birthday in the fall of 1841, she lost all three of them within three weeks, from dysentery. After they were buried, she wrote in her autobiography, "his mother has had peace. Peace to nourish her grief, peace to capture resignation." However, the loss haunted her for many years.

The years in Westphalia were lonely, with Dr. Bruns traveling with his practice, and finding it as difficult to collect fees in Missouri as it had been in Germany. Jette's brother Bernhard developed a recurring fever that caused hallucinations and kept him from working. She became responsible for him and for Franz's children after his wife died from tuberculosis and Franz left to seek his fortune in the California gold mines. In 1851 Dr. Bruns moved his family across the Osage to Shipley's Ferry where they lost a fourth child to sunstroke.

Upon Franz's return from his unsuccessful trip, the family determined to move to Jefferson City. Bruns commented in a letter home, "I do not like farm life at all anymore. . . . It does not bring me anything but a great deal of trouble." Her husband, however, felt otherwise, struggling for months with severe depression and pneumonia before building a store with an apartment upstairs for the family. The business thrived, and in 1856 Bruns was able to return to Germany for a visit.

Following that visit, the family built a large home directly across from the capitol. In 1858 Franz died at age forty-two after a short illness, leaving his three children for Bruns to raise. She had five of her own as well. While she took great joy in the children, she sometimes felt crowded by them.

During the Civil War, Caspar, Franz's son, was wounded at Fort Donelson in March 1862 and died a few days after returning home. Bruns's son, Heinrich, was killed the following year at the battle of Iuka, Mississippi. Her husband became ill in 1864 while serving as a Union major. For a time he was cared for by Dr. Wilhelm Follenius, son of **Paul Follenius,** who was serving as a member of the Missouri House of Representatives. Shortly after the legislative session ended and Follenius departed, Dr. Bruns died.

Her husband's death left Bruns with four of her own children, two of Franz's, and few financial resources. She took in boarders, most often prominent German legislators, to support herself and her children. Her dining room was sometimes referred to as the "radical corner" or "the German Diet," with **Friedrich Muench** and others debating political issues over meals. Bruns's letters reveal her keen interest in politics, but her daily duties made it impossible for her to engage in the debates at her own table.

Late in her life Bruns resided with one or another of her children, always relating the joys and griefs of these years in her letters to her brother Heinrich. She wrote faithfully until failing eyesight made it impossible. She died November 7, 1899, at age eighty-six.

KENNETH LUEBBERING AND R. D. ANDERSON

Kremer, Gary. Review of *Hold Dear, as Always: Jette, a German Immigrant Life in Letters,* by Jette Bruns. *Ozarkswatch* 3 (summer 1989): 25.

Schroeder, Adolph E., and Carla Schulz-Geisberg, eds. *Hold Dear, as Always: Jette, a German Immigrant Life in Letters,* by Jette Bruns. Trans. Adolph E. Schroeder. Columbia: University of Missouri Press, 1988.

BRYANT, ARTHUR (1902–1982)

Arthur Bryant initiated a Kansas City tradition that earned him the title of "Barbecue King." His barbecue restaurant, which he proudly called a "grease house," is a storehouse of legends, a restaurant supported by presidents and plumbers that gave Kansas City its renown as a barbecue capital. Recognized internationally and a favorite stopping place for celebrities, blue-collar workers, politicians, entertainers, and presidents passing through the Kansas City area, Bryant's restaurant's popularity took off in the 1950s and 1960s when sports enthusiasts attending the old Municipal Stadium were drawn there. Former President **Harry S. Truman** ate there often, and in October 1979 President Jimmy Carter went there for lunch.

Bryant was born on a farm in east Texas on August 15, 1902. He went to Prairie View State Industrial College in Prairie View, Texas, where he studied teaching and economics. He received a degree in agriculture and a job offer at a local high school. After graduation he joined the navy for a tour of duty. In 1931 Bryant decided to travel before he settled down. His first stop was to visit his brother, Charlie Bryant, in Kansas City. He never left.

Bryant secured a job at the barbecue restaurant owned by Henry Perry where his brother was employed. After Perry's death, Charlie Bryant took over the business. When Charlie retired in 1946 Arthur became the proprietor. According to one local story, which is perhaps apocryphal, Charlie had always refused to share the secret of the barbecue sauce with anyone, including his brother. Thus, when Charlie left, Arthur Bryant had to concoct his own version. After having the sauce chemically analyzed, he adjusted it according to what he thought customers would like: cutting down on the cayenne pepper and altering the ratio of paprika and salt in the tomato-puree base so it was hot, but not incendiary. Bryant kept the redbrick restaurant as a simple diner with linoleum floors, Formica tables, and red plastic chairs.

Arthur Bryant's Restaurant became a local phenomenon as a result of Kansas City jazz musicians who traveled frequently and became skilled at distinguishing the finest of barbecue sauces. The crowds soon followed their lead. Then local writers and journalists aided Bryant's cause. Nationally, New York columnist Calvin Trillin proclaimed repeatedly that Bryant's "House of Good Eats" was simply "the single best restaurant in the world."

Generous to his small staff, Bryant customarily gave them paid vacations in Florida each January, the only time of the year that the restaurant's doors were shut.

Over the years the success of his barbecue made Bryant reasonably wealthy, but he never wavered from his spartan existence. He continued to cook more than two thousand pounds of U.S. choice beef per day for thirteen hours over a wood fire until he died of heart failure on December 28, 1982, at the age of eighty.

JULIE MAURER

Bryant, Daretha. Interview by author. Kansas City, Mo., April 30, 1996.

Kansas City Call, December 31, 1982–January 6, 1983.

Kansas City Times, February 10, 1981.

"The Man Who Outbarbecued Texas." *Southwest Airlines* (April 1982).

Springfield Daily News, December 29, 1982.

BUCKNER, ALEXANDER (1785–1833)

Although Alexander Buckner served in Missouri's 1820 Constitutional Convention, the state General Assembly, and the United States Senate, there is little in the historical record about his life. He was born in Jefferson County, Kentucky, in 1785. He studied law, and went to the Indiana Territory about 1812 and opened a law office in Clark County. He moved with his father, Nicholas, and his five sisters to Cape Girardeau County in the Missouri Territory in 1818. Upon his arrival in Cape Girardeau County, Buckner purchased a farm, and established a legal practice. His talents as a lawyer gave him public exposure and connections that enabled him to enter politics—a field that appealed to him more than the law.

In less than a year after arriving in Missouri, Buckner was appointed as a territorial circuit attorney. He was elected as one of five delegates from Cape Girardeau County to the convention that wrote the constitution under which Missouri was admitted into the Union. Following statehood, Buckner served in both the Missouri State Senate and the Missouri House of Representatives. In 1830 the General Assembly elected him to the seat in the United States Senate previously held by **David Barton.**

Buckner's election as a U.S. senator revealed the confused nature of Missouri politics at the time. In the absence of party organizations or platforms, contests for public office were personal and often bitter affairs.

After Andrew Jackson carried the state in the 1828 presidential election, his Missouri followers rallied around Sen. **Thomas Hart Benton**'s campaign to elect "true" Jackson men to public office. Most Jackson supporters in Missouri opposed the American System: the Bank of the United States, protective tariffs, and federally funded internal improvements. The anti-Jackson minority generally favored the American System and liked Barton.

Barton's intemperate personal habits doomed his chances for reelection, and the anti-Jackson forces had no candidate who could successfully challenge the rising tide of the Jackson-Benton forces. That set the stage for a bit of political intrigue. When the General Assembly met to elect a U.S. senator, the names of six prominent individuals were put forth as candidates for the position. Alexander Buckner was one of them. The *St. Louis Beacon* presented Buckner as a Jackson supporter. Benton called all six "true" Jackson men, but Buckner had not made his stand on the American System clear. Probably for that reason, the anti-Jackson men, as a matter of self-interest, made Buckner their choice.

With no announced opposition candidate in the field, the Jacksonian leaders planned to give complementary votes to each of the candidates in the first round, and then elect Gov. **John Miller** on the second ballot. The anti-Jackson men saw their chance, and, with their support and a share of the Jackson party votes, Buckner won the Senate seat on the first ballot. The Jackson-Benton men were angry, the opposition jubilant. The *Missouri Intelligencer* in central Missouri proclaimed Buckner's election a victory for the anti-Jackson party and the American System.

There is no evidence that Buckner was involved in the maneuvering of the anti-Jackson forces, and the *Missouri Intelligencer*'s assessment appears to have been correct. In the Senate Buckner voted to recharter the Bank of the United States, and he spoke in favor of the existing protective tariffs. Buckner's tenure in the Senate was cut short by his early death in 1833. How he might have aligned himself in the emerging two-party alignments would be conjecture, but it seems reasonable to assume that he would have joined the Whig Party and supported its platform.

There is little in the record about Buckner's personal life, aside from reports that he carried himself with great dignity, and was affable and respectful of others. Contemporaries appear to have considered him a fluent and persuasive speaker, an industrious worker, and one who could impress those with whom he came in contact. Throughout his life Buckner was an active Mason.

Buckner and his wife both died of cholera within hours of each other at their home south of Jackson on June 6, 1833. They were buried on their farm, and left no descendants. In 1897 Buckner's remains were removed from the farm grave and reinterred in the Cape Girardeau city cemetery.

PERRY McCANDLESS

Bay, W. V. N. *Reminiscences of the Bench and Bar of Missouri.* St. Louis: F. H. Thomas, 1878.
Conard, Howard L., ed. *Encyclopedia of the History of Missouri.* New York: Southern History, 1901.
McCandless, Perry. *A History of Missouri: Volume II, 1820 to 1860.* Columbia: University of Missouri Press, 1972.

BULGER, MILES (1877–1939)

Miles Bulger was a Kansas City and Jackson County Democratic politician of the Pendergast era. Determined, blunt, and seldom neutral about anything, he pursued power relentlessly, eventually overreaching in the cruel game of machine politics, the Kansas City model. Born into an Irish Roman Catholic family on June 10, 1877, in Kansas City, he was only five when his father died. Bulger received only a primary education and learned to use his fists almost as soon as he could double them. He went to work in his early teens, undertaking hard common laboring jobs, and by his seventeenth birthday he was a plumbing apprentice with much bigger aspirations.

A lifelong friend commented insightfully on how Bulger drove himself forward: "When I first saw him he was a kid, carrying a plumber's kit. He was strong and wiry, with more grit and get-up than the other Irish youngsters. Just to show how he handled himself, I recall that before he was 20 years old he had built a duplex on Summit Street near Twentieth, and because he was not yet of age his mother had to take title to the property. Nothing could down him. And even in those days he would crash through to his objectives."

From 1902 to 1914 Bulger was an alderman in the lower house of the Kansas City legislature, for years serving as presiding officer. He represented the Southwest Boulevard–Observation Park District on the west side in the Second Ward, which included the south side of downtown. He ruthlessly built his own little political empire in the Second Ward, earning the appellation of the "Little Czar." In 1912 he won election to the first of two consecutive terms as presiding judge of the three-judge administrative Jackson County Court. Bulger used patronage to construct his own county organization and claimed to favor minority rights, erecting a segregated county home for African American juvenile delinquents that he named after himself.

Bulger aspired to become the boss of closely intertwined Kansas City and Jackson County politics. He attempted to simultaneously work with and battle against two competing, yet more powerful, chieftains: **Thomas J. Pendergast,** the leader of the Goat faction; and his Rabbit-faction counterpart, **Joseph Shannon.** On July 28, 1913, the *Kansas City Journal* evaluated Bulger's endeavors: "He has labored in both the Shannon and Pendergast camps and in efforts to cater to both he has had some bad, but beneficial experiences." Enemies of Bulger, with some reason, accused him of corruption (**Harry S. Truman** wrote privately that as presiding judge, Bulger pocketed $500,000 in tainted money). At first Pendergast protected Bulger from possible grand-jury investigations, only to break violently with him. In 1920 a Pendergast, Shannon, and Republican coalition defeated a "Bulgerism" county ticket. In 1922 Bulger moved on to the first of three terms in the General Assembly, finding a legislative position unrewarding because there were few jobs to distribute.

On March 7, 1924, Pendergast, in the process of taking over Kansas City, launched a preemptive strike against Bulger. Pendergast-underworld ruffians disrupted and seized control of a Second Ward primary meeting, winning a pitched battle over Bulger's henchmen. Subsequently, Pendergast took complete charge in the Second Ward, relegating the erstwhile Little Czar to political oblivion. In 1923 the combative Bulger had slugged a Pendergast lackey, county administrative judge and later city manager **Henry F. McElroy,** before numerous witnesses in downtown Kansas City. But, after losing power, Bulger ran away from a fight with the burly, temper-prone Pendergast, purportedly a former saloon bouncer.

In 1930 Bulger sold his interests in the Bulger-Woolfe Cement Company and retired from politics, undergoing a dramatic character transformation. He lived quietly with his wife, the former Katherine Cotter, whom he had married in 1906, in a large mansion at a prestigious Ward Parkway address. He devoted time to playing bridge at the socially correct Kansas City Club and to becoming a patron of the arts. Back in 1907, while on the council, he had expressed outspoken criticism of municipal art, saying in a much quoted statement: "Art is on the bum in Kansas City." On January 3, 1939, Bulger died of a coronary ailment. Two weeks earlier he had suffered a heart attack walking outside his large mansion.

LAWRENCE H. LARSEN

Kansas City Star, January 3, 1939.
Reddig, William M. *Tom's Town: Kansas City and the Pendergast Legend.* 1947. Reprint, Columbia: University of Missouri Press, 1986.

BURGESS, ALBERT (1856–1932)

Albert Burgess, dean of St. Louis's black attorneys, whose legal career spanned fifty years, was born in Detroit, Michigan, on October 14, 1856. One of five children, Burgess attended an all-black school until age twelve, when the law was changed, permitting him to transfer to a previously all-white school. His father, Amos Burgess, a free black who had never been a slave, was a custodian at the Detroit City Hall, where Burgess worked during school vacations, earning spending money and acquiring the ambition to be a lawyer. In 1874 he graduated from high school and enrolled at the University of Michigan, in the literature department. In 1875 he enrolled in the University of Michigan Law School and received his diploma in March 1877.

Following graduation, Burgess returned to Detroit and became a clerk in the law office of Francis G. Russell, whose brother, W. H. H. Russell, practiced law in St. Louis. He then clerked briefly in the law office of Michener and Speed.

In November 1877, after reading a black newspaper published in St. Louis that revealed St. Louis blacks' need for a lawyer of their own race, Burgess decided to relocate. His father provided the funds, and on November 15, 1877, Burgess arrived in St. Louis with a letter of recommendation to W. H. H. Russell from his brother in Detroit. On New Year's Eve Burgess passed the law examination before the St. Louis Court of Appeals, becoming the first black lawyer admitted to the St. Louis bar.

Burgess opened a law office in the Hutchison Building on Fifth Street. Later he and John D. S. Ferrier, a black attorney from Jackson, Mississippi, became partners and established the law firm of Burgess and Ferrier, which continued until Ferrier's death from tuberculosis a few years later.

In September 1885 Burgess married Mary Thomas and fathered three children: Wilmont Amos, Elmer A., and Myrtle A. All three graduated from the University of Toronto, near the home of Burgess's sister in Windsor, Canada. Wilmont became principal of the Dessalines School in St. Louis; Elmer was the director of physical culture for the black schools of Baltimore, Maryland; and Myrtle taught music in St. Louis. Mary Burgess died in 1923.

Burgess was instrumental in founding the Emigration Aid Society in 1879 by filing its articles of incorporation and by serving as its secretary. He was the first treasurer of the Mound City Bar Association and, in private life, held memberships in the Anniversary Club and the Boule.

In 1894 Republican Mayor Cyrus Walbridge appointed Burgess assistant city attorney. He was reappointed by Republican Mayor Henry Ziegenhein, Walbridge's successor, in 1896, and served until the middle of Mayor **Rolla Wells**'s term in 1902, when Wells appointed a Democrat. During his tenure Burgess was a prosecutor in the Carondelet Police

Court and handled all south–St. Louis cases arising from the streetcar strike of 1900. Along with his patronage position, Burgess continued in private practice and toward the end of his career handled part of the city collector's legal work, which required travel to other Missouri towns.

Burgess's legal career paved the way for other black lawyers in St. Louis, and by 1927 there were thirty practicing in the city. On November 30, 1932, at the age of seventy-six, Burgess died in his home on Cook Avenue. His funeral was held at All Saints Episcopal Church, where he had been a senior warden and member of the bishop's council. He was interred in St. Peter's Cemetery in St. Louis.

SHARREN G. WOLFMAN

Demmon, I. N., ed. "University of Michigan General Catalogue of Officers and Students, 1837–1911." Ann Arbor: University of Michigan, 1912.

"First Negro Lawyer in St. Louis Completing Fifty Years of Practice." *St. Louis Globe-Democrat Magazine,* May 29, 1927.

Smith, J. Clay, Jr. *Emancipation: The Making of the Black Lawyer, 1844–1944.* Philadelphia: University of Pennsylvania Press, 1933.

St. Louis Argus, December 2, 1932.

BURNETT, PETER HARDEMAN (1807–1895)

Born on November 15, 1807, in Nashville, Tennessee, Peter Hardeman Burnett was the eldest son of George and Dorothy Hardeman Burnett, originally spelled Burnet. At the age of ten young Burnett moved with his family to Howard County, Missouri. In 1826 he returned to Tennessee where he worked as a clerk in hotels and stores around Nashville. While there he met and married Harriet W. Rogers, and they for a time ran a general store.

When the store did not succeed, however, Burnett brought his wife to the Missouri frontier and settled in Liberty, in Clay County, about 1828. For an enterprising young man in the Jacksonian era, no place in the United States was more inviting than the recently created state of Missouri, and Burnett made the most of the state's opportunities. In Liberty he founded the *Far West* newspaper, studied and later practiced law, and invested in several businesses. By the early 1830s he had built a fine law practice in western Missouri, had begun to establish political ties, and had made credible economic gains.

In one of his earliest political activities, Burnett became involved in the process of incorporating into Missouri the Platte country, a fertile tract located between the state's original western boundary and the Missouri River in present-day northwest Missouri. Originally reserved for Native Americans, many in the western part of the state viewed it as rich land that they wanted to use. In 1835 Burnett participated in a rally in Clay County advocating annexation of the Platte region, and served on a committee to prepare a memorial to Congress on the issue that included several other leading political figures, including **Alexander Doniphan** and **David Rice Atchison.** Within two years Congress had approved the annexation, ordered the removal of the Indians to the West, and opened the region to American settlement. When learning of the decision, Burnett supposedly rode "hell-bent-for-leather" from Liberty to the settlement of Barry, in what became western Platte County, with the news of annexation. After the announcement the townspeople adjourned to the local "grocery" to imbibe. In the commotion Burnett lost his tall hat, but according to one eyewitness "more than one hat went up, like the Hebrew children, on that occasion."

Burnett also found himself involved in the most sustained controversy in the state during the 1830s: the Mormon problem in the western part of the state. Significant numbers of the sect's members had settled in Jackson County beginning in 1831. In 1833 they had been forcibly expelled from the county, and had moved as refugees to other counties in the area. For a time Burnett, acting as state prosecutor in the western region, was involved in cases against several members of the church for bad debts and other charges. On at least one occasion he also represented a member of the church in a civil suit.

When violence erupted between the Mormons and the citizens of Daviess County, in northwestern Missouri, in August 1838, it appeared that general civil war could not be averted, and Gov. **Lilburn W. Boggs** called out the militia to restore the peace. Burnett was an officer in the Clay County militia and participated in the dramatic siege of the Mormon stronghold of Far West, in Caldwell County; the trial of several Mormon leaders, including the prophet **Joseph Smith Jr.;** and the eventual expulsion of the sect from the state in the winter of 1838–1839.

Burnett's business activities, never truly successful, took a turn for the worse in the early 1840s, and that, coupled with the failure of his wife's health, prompted him to consider making a new start farther west. The place that caught Burnett's attention was Oregon, for which he set out with a historic wagon train of 875 people that left Independence, Missouri, on May 22, 1843. As its captain for a time, he led the train on the epic trek to Oregon in the summer of 1843 and reached the mission of Marcus Whitman on October 14. Once the train disbanded Burnett and his family left their friends and journeyed on to Fort Vancouver where he took up farming near the mouth of the Willamette River. The farm failed, however, and he later established another farm near the present town of Hillsboro, Oregon.

Burnett quickly became prominent in territorial politics, serving on a legislative committee for the region in 1844, as a judge in the Oregon Supreme Court in 1845, and as a member of the territorial legislature in 1848. Even as his political fortunes in Oregon rose, in the fall of 1848 Burnett led a cadre of 150 men to California where the gold rush was just getting under way. There he continued a meteoric political career. In less than a year he had been appointed judge of the superior tribunal of California. He also lobbied for California statehood, and in the process attained the governorship on November 13, 1849, a post he held until January 6, 1851, when he resigned and began a highly successful law practice. In 1857 and 1858 Burnett served on the California Supreme Court, but that was his last public office.

For the rest of his long life, Burnett engaged in a variety of business activities, especially finance as the founder in 1863—with Sam Brannan and Joseph Winans—of Pacific Bank in San Francisco. He served as its president for many years, retiring only in 1880. Burnett died on May 17, 1895. H. H. Bancroft appropriately characterized Burnett's career as one of great success, due largely to his ability to be in the right place at the right time and to accommodate the circumstances of the situation.

ROGER D. LAUNIUS

Bancroft, Hubert Howe. *History of California.* Vol. 4. San Francisco: History Company, 1888.

Burnett, Peter H. *The American Theory of Government Considered with Reference to the Present Crisis.* New York: D. Appleton, 1861.

———. *The Path which Led a Protestant Lawyer to the Catholic Church.* New York: D. Appleton, 1860.

———. *Recollections and Opinions of an Old Pioneer.* 1880. Reprint, New York: Da Capo Press, 1969.

LeSueur, Stephen C. *The 1838 Mormon War in Missouri.* Columbia: University of Missouri Press, 1987.

McCandless, Perry. *A History of Missouri: Volume II, 1820 to 1860.* Columbia: University of Missouri Press, 1972.

BURNS, LULU W. (1868–1957)

Lulu W. Burns was the first woman from St. Clair County elected to the Missouri House of Representatives, in November 1940, ultimately serving four terms. She was born near Springfield, Illinois, on November 7, 1868, to William and Eva Eads White. The family moved to Missouri in 1871 and settled in Bates County. Lulu attended public schools and the

Butler Academy, where she received a B.S. degree in 1884. For several years she taught in area schools. On December 18, 1895, she married William E. Burns of Appleton City. They farmed for twelve years until he became postmaster in Appleton City; she served as his bookkeeper.

Burns became active in politics and club work. After her husband's death in 1935, she managed her farms and investments. In 1940 she chaired the Women's Republican Club of St. Clair County, was elected treasurer of the Republican Committee of St. Clair County that year, and served as an alternate delegate from Missouri at the Philadelphia Republican National Convention.

The Republican Party of St. Clair County had no candidate for representative on the ticket for the November 1940 election, and in September the Republican committee chose Burns to fill the vacancy. She accepted the challenge and began actively campaigning. The Republicans made a clean sweep of the county in the November election, and Burns defeated her opponent by less than six hundred votes. At seventy-two she became the oldest woman representative elected up to that time.

In the legislature, education became a prime concern of Burns, and she was appointed to the Education Committee, as well as to the Agriculture, Children's Code, Society Security, Old Age Assistance, and University Committees.

Burns ran for reelection in 1942, at a time when the country was at war and rationing in effect. She ran on her good record of the past session and promised again to work for measures to benefit the state. She was especially interested in the welfare of her county and its citizens. Missouri voters that year elected a record number of six women to the House of Representatives, including Burns.

In the Sixty-second General Assembly, Burns was elected secretary of the majority party. She chaired the University and Education Committees and served again as a member of the Agriculture, Social Security, and Children's Code Committees. In that session Burns supported the Civil Code Bill that simplified court procedure, making trials speedier and less expensive.

The Sixth Congressional District elected Burns as a delegate to the Republican National Convention in Chicago in 1944. Because of gas and tire restrictions that year, Burns did not campaign extensively for the legislature, but asked voters in newspaper ads to support her reelection if her services had been satisfactory. She had no family ties to interfere with her work, and she was willing to give her time and knowledge to the job.

In November 1944 Burns won her third term. One of the major bills for which she worked that session permitted the services of women jurors.

Burns appeared before a senate committee in her successful efforts to get the bill passed. She chaired the House University Committee, served as secretary of the majority party caucus, and held membership in the important Appropriations Committee as well as in the Agriculture, Children's Code, Education, and Social Security Committees. She also received national recognition by being appointed as a member to the advisory committee of the National Rivers and Harbors Congress in Washington, D.C.

Burns won reelection in 1946 and served her fourth term. In the November 1948 election, the Democrats swept the country with a surprising Truman victory for the presidency. Burns was the only Republican in her area who suffered defeat, however. She lost by nearly two hundred votes.

After retirement from the legislature, Burns married George E. Poling of Osceola on January 24, 1950. Lulu Burns Poling died October 30, 1957.

MARY K. DAINS

Appleton City Journal, 1940–1948, November 7, 1957.

Dains, Mary K. "Forty Years in the House: A Composite Portrait of Missouri Women Legislators." Missouri Historical Review 87 (January 1993): 150–67.

Official Manual of the State of Missouri, 1941–1942. Jefferson City: Secretary of State, 1942.

Official Manual of the State of Missouri, 1945–1946. Jefferson City: Secretary of State, 1946.

Official Manual of the State of Missouri, 1947–1948. Jefferson City: Secretary of State, 1948.

BUSCH, ADOLPHUS, SR. (1837–1913)

No family, except perhaps the **Chouteaus,** dominated St. Louis like the Busch family. The owners of the largest brewery in the world and for most of the last half of the twentieth century of the St. Louis Cardinals baseball team, the family lived on a scale far beyond even wealthy Missourians. Of the four Buschs to head the family between the 1860s and the 1980s, Adolphus, who founded the dynasty, and **August A. Busch Jr.,** known to everyone as "Gussie," influenced the beer industry and St. Louis the most.

Born in Germany on July 10, 1837, Adolphus Busch came to St. Louis in 1857. Educated at the gymnasium in his birthplace of Mayence, in the academy at Darnstadt, and in a high school at Brussels, Busch worked as a shipping clerk in a malt-and-hop storage facility in St. Louis. In 1859 he began a brewery supply business, but closed it after a few years. On March 7, 1861, he married Lilly Anheuser, daughter of Eberhard Anheuser, the owner of the Bavarian Brewery.

After serving a four-month tour with **Nathaniel Lyon** during the Civil War, Busch went to work for his father-in-law and by 1865 held controlling interest in the business. Anheuser died in 1880, and Busch changed the name of the brewery to the Anheuser-Busch Brewing Association. He also started the Adolphus Busch Glass Manufacturing Company. With profits from the brewery, Busch invested in the Laclede Gas Light Company, founded the Manufacturer's Railroad, and served as president of the Busch-Sulzer Brothers Diesel Engine Company, the Geyser Ice Company of Waco, Texas, and the Grand Pacific Hotel of Chicago. In addition, he became director of the South Side Bank in St. Louis and a number of other banks and corporations. His income reached an estimated $2 million per year—at a time before income taxes.

Peter Hernon and Terry Ganey, authors of a study of the Busch family, described Busch as "P. T. Barnum, Buffalo Bill and Cornelius Vanderbilt rolled into one." Only five-foot-five with "a fair, boyish complexion, long and wavy hair," Busch grew a mustache and goatee in his early twenties to look older. In his later years, he grew rotund, and his hair, which he wore long and "swept back, except for a small lock that was allowed to curl up over his forehead," thinned and turned gray. He spent his money with relish, noteworthy even in a time when others spent extravagantly. "A president called him a prince. His workers called him a king."

Busch's talents included identifying the southern United States as a good market for beer and devising the technology to exploit it. In 1873 his staff developed the process that led to pasteurized, bottled beer. Busch built icehouses along railroad tracks, which allowed him to ship beer to Texas. After the invention of the refrigerated railroad car, he perfected it in order to transport his product. At the same time he developed distribution networks and carefully guided the brewery in producing beer more efficiently. Adroit at public relations, Busch sought to "win the American people over to our side, to make them all lovers of beer." In 1905 he said, "I stand ready to sacrifice my annual profits for years to come if I can gain my point and make people look upon beer in the right light." He introduced the Budweiser brand in 1876, and in 1894 he purchased the rights to a painting of Custer's Last Stand, which adorned the taverns across the country with the Budweiser logo prominently displayed.

Busch described the secret of his success as a willingness "to work double the time I was paid for." Near the end of his life he offered his philosophy of labor relations. "All without exception from the lowest to the highest positions have been promoted on their merits. Moreover, all of my employees who hold positions of responsibility rose from labor's ranks, none of them from the ranks of the rich. That is so because the former have proven more intelligent, more readily schooled, and trained than the latter. That is to be expected, of course, because those from the labor ranks are more ambitious and industrious."

While undoubtedly one of the richest men in St. Louis, Busch never received acceptance by the city's old monied class. Restaurant owner Tony Faust became his closest friend, and when in St. Louis, Busch went to his restaurant every afternoon at four to play cards with businessmen, actors, boxers, and others. Busch played to win. Prominent lawyer Charles Nagel took care of the brewery's legal matters and became a loyal, influential friend. A Republican but inactive in politics, Busch committed himself against Prohibition, and became a national leader in opposing the effort to end the manufacture and sale of alcoholic beverages.

Busch spent a considerable amount of time at his estate in Germany, which he named Villa Lilly, after his wife. His grandson Gussie remembered wonderful long summer days with Busch in Germany, witnessing the lifestyle of the merchant prince. From that experience, Gussie learned "what it meant to be the head of one of the richest families in America—and one of the most powerful."

Busch was honored by his native country. Germany conferred upon him the Order of Red Eagle, the Order of Commercial Councilor, and the Order of Philip the Good. He contributed two hundred thousand dollars to Washington University, one hundred thousand dollars to San Francisco after the 1906 earthquake, and fifty thousand dollars to establish the Germania Museum at Harvard University.

In 1907 Busch contracted pneumonia and never fully recovered. He died at Villa Lilly on October 10, 1913, leaving a sizable estate and a reputation summarized by a *St. Louis Post-Dispatch* editorial: "What purpose can an obituary serve in the case of a man whose career and life are known to everybody? There was no citizen of St. Louis better known, in more than one sense, than Adolphus Busch. . . . The very human qualities of the man drew the public to him in an unusual intimacy. In his death the world has a singular example of successful enterprise coupled with high integrity. St. Louis has lost a big private citizen actively identified with a half-century of its growth, and thousands of men and women and children have lost a good friend."

LAWRENCE O. CHRISTENSEN

Brown, Mary Louise. "The Stark and Anheuser-Busch Imagery, 1913–1933." *Gateway Heritage* 9 (fall 1988): 18–23.

Busch, August A., Jr. "Budweiser: A Century of Character." *Newcomen Society in North America* (January 6, 1955): 5–21.

Hernon, Peter, and Terry Ganey. *Under the Influence: The Unauthorized Story of the Anheuser-Busch Dynasty.* New York: Simon and Schuster, 1991.

St. Louis Post-Dispatch, October 11, 1913.

BUSCH, AUGUST A., JR. (1899–1989)

August A. Busch Jr., who was called Gussie, assumed control of the Anheuser-Busch brewery in 1946. By then the company founded by his grandfather, **Adolphus Busch Sr.,** had survived the difficult years of Prohibition and the depression under the leadership of Gussie Busch's father, August Anheuser Busch Sr., and his older brother, Adolphus Busch III. Born in St. Louis on March 28, 1899, August A. Busch Jr. attended Fremont School and Smith Academy but showed little interest in formal education. Gussie enjoyed the pleasures of Grant's Farm, which his father acquired in 1903. The two-hundred-acre farm became the home to a menagerie of exotic animals. He spent his youth learning to ride well, shoot straight, and enjoying the life of wealth provided by a doting family. He learned to handle a team of horses like a professional and by age fourteen drove coaches competitively. During World War I he served for ten months "as a stable sergeant." Young Busch also enjoyed the sport of boxing.

Busch began his working life in a family-owned bank, then moved to another family enterprise, the Manufacturer's Railway Company, before beginning employment in the brewery at age twenty-four. At first he was assigned only menial tasks, but within four months his father made him general superintendent of brewing operations. Five years earlier Busch had married Marie Christy Church, a twenty-two-year-old graduate of Miss Wright's School in Bryn Mawr, Pennsylvania, who was a descendant of **William Clark.** Described as "beautiful and refined, and not at all like Gussie," she bore two children, Lilly and Carlota, before dying from pneumonia in 1930.

Busch's failure to win acceptance in St. Louis high society did not seem to bother him. When the prestigious St. Louis Country Club did not admit him, he started one of his own. He also established the Bridlespur Hunt Club in the mid-1920s and served as master of foxhounds for a decade. He kept a stable of horses that won prizes around the country, and his passion for the animals led him to acquire his famous Clydesdales. Horse enthusiasts credit him with saving the breed from extinction.

Busch's marriage to Elizabeth Overton Dozier on September 22, 1933, failed to produce tranquility in his life. The two had apparently had an affair before the death of his first wife, and their marriage occurred only two weeks after Dozier's divorce from her husband, Lewis. She gave birth to a daughter, Elizabeth, and a son, August A. Busch III. Busch volunteered for service in the army in June 1942 and received the rank of lieutenant colonel with an assignment to the Pentagon. He oversaw ammunition production, won promotion to colonel in 1944, and received the Legion of Merit medal for his service.

Following the death of his brother in 1946 Busch became president and chief operating officer of Anheuser-Busch. Over the next thirty years he developed the company into the largest brewery in the world. A consummate salesman and promoter of his beer, he successfully waged war with his rivals in the industry. His life centered on the business. Described as "generous and endearing but impatient with fools," Busch hired Al Fleishman to market his products and brought Frank Schwaiger from Germany to be his brew master. Schwaiger made certain that Budweiser retained its high standards. A scandal in the 1970s involving payments to coerce restaurants and wholesalers to stock Anheuser-Busch beer resulted in a substantial fine and indicated that Busch sometimes skirted the law in fighting the competition.

Meanwhile, Busch's personal life underwent significant change. In 1949 he met twenty-two-year-old Josephine Trudy Buhalzer in Switzerland. She regularly stayed at the Busch home at Grant's Farm, and when Busch's second marriage ended with a costly divorce settlement in 1952, he married Buhalzer. The following year Busch purchased the St. Louis Cardinals baseball team for $3.75 million, and his public-relations firm set out to create the image of Busch as savior of the Cardinals. Sportswriter Ted Schafters described Busch's reputation before the purchase as that of one "who chased women right and left . . . [was a] heavy, two-fisted drinker and was disliked by more polite society. . . . People just put up with him. He had no reputation at all as a civic leader."

The baseball team became "a traveling billboard for the brewery," and Busch became a celebrity. His picture adorned the cover of *Time,* and a feature story in *Life* called him "one of the most resplendent citizens in St. Louis history." He enhanced his reputation by helping organize St. Louis leaders into Civic Progress, a group committed to revitalizing the city's downtown. Busch Stadium, completed in 1965 as the new home of the St. Louis Cardinals, was a centerpiece of the city's Civic Center Redevelopment project.

Busch's personal life seemed to flourish along with his public image. He and Trudy produced seven children between 1954 and 1966. His baseball team won pennants and the World Series in 1964 and 1967. Tragedy struck, however, in December 1974, when a car accident killed Busch's youngest child, Christina. The next year his eldest son, August III, forced him out of the top post at the brewery. The "Big Eagle," as many called him, lost many of the perks of power, but retained control of the Cardinals, even though the

brewery owned them. In 1978 he and Trudy dissolved their marriage in a nasty divorce. In March 1981 he married Margaret Snyder, his secretary and a longtime Anheuser-Busch employee. She died in 1988.

A strong Democrat until 1972, when he supported Richard Nixon for president, Busch said that Franklin Roosevelt's efforts to end Prohibition had influenced his politics. He once observed, "I'll be damned if I bite the hand that fed me." He had been close to **Harry S. Truman,** John F. Kennedy, and Lyndon Johnson.

When Busch died on September 29, 1989, his personal fortune was estimated to be $1.5 billion. The death of the man who had been called "the most resplendent citizen in St. Louis history" occasioned an outpouring of tributes. Sen. John Danforth said: "Mr. Busch has left an indelible mark on America. He's given us the best beer in the world, the best baseball team in the world, and a stadium to go with it. His beloved city of St. Louis has a swagger and a style that he did so much to create." The *St. Louis Post-Dispatch* editorialized, "He was brash, profane, civic-minded and hot tempered." But the words of St. Louis County Prosecutor George "Buzz" Westfall captured St. Louis sentiment best: "This is one of the saddest days in St. Louis history. I grew up in north St. Louis near Sportsman's Park thinking that Mr. Busch owned St. Louis, and my opinion hasn't changed."

LAWRENCE O. CHRISTENSEN

Brown, Mary Louise. "The Stark and Anheuser-Busch Imagery, 1913–1933." *Gateway Heritage* 9 (fall 1988): 18–23.

Busch, August A., Jr. "Budweiser: A Century of Character." *Newcomen Society in North America* (January 6, 1955): 5–21.

Hernon, Peter, and Terry Ganey. *Under the Influence: The Unauthorized Story of the Anheuser-Busch Dynasty.* New York: Simon and Schuster, 1991.

"Kindly Caricatures: August A. Busch." *Mirror* (June 11, 1908): 4–5.

St. Louis Post-Dispatch, September 30, 1989.

BUSH, ISIDOR (1822–1898)

Isidor Bush—a journalist, businessman, civic leader, and abolitionist—ranks as probably the most prominent Jew in Missouri during the nineteenth century. He was born in the ghetto of Prague, Bohemia, on January 15, 1822, the great-grandson of Israel Honig Edler von Honigsberg, who was the first Jew raised to nobility in Austria. As a child, Isidor was pampered by his father, Jacob (his mother, Fredericka, had died when young Bush was only three years old), and he enjoyed a pleasant childhood. Educated by private tutors, he associated with many Austrian Jewish intellectuals of the time.

In 1837 Jacob Busch—the name was spelled "Busch" in Europe, but "Bush" in America—moved to Vienna, where he became a partner in Schimd's Oriental Printing Establishment. Although only fifteen, young Isidor became engrossed in his father's publishing business and turned zealously to the study of languages. Soon he spoke four languages fluently, and could read and write in Greek, Latin, and Hebrew as well as in his native German. Within a short time the firm of Schmid and Busch, in which Isidor became part owner, became one of Vienna's largest publishers of Hebrew books, including Bibles, prayer books, the Talmud, and various commentaries. Young Isidor also edited and published the *Kalendar und Jahrbuch für Israeliten,* the first popular annual of Jewish scholarly articles printed in the German language in Austria. Even before coming to America, then, he had established himself as a pioneer in journalism.

As did many other liberal intellectuals in the aftermath of the unsuccessful revolutions of 1848, Bush fled to America with his wife (he had married the former Theresa Taussig in 1844) and their son, Raphael, arriving in January 1849 in New York City. There he opened a small stationery and bookstore. Shortly thereafter, on March 30, 1849, the pioneering Bush published the first number of *Israel's Herold,* a weekly journal patterned after the one he had produced in Vienna. It began a new and distinguished phase of American journalism: the American Jewish press printed in German. Unfortunately, though, the effort failed financially, and Bush was forced to suspend operations after only three months. Strapped for funds, in July 1849 he moved to St. Louis where his wife's family, the Taussigs, had settled earlier.

The small Jewish population in St. Louis in the 1840s—no more than perhaps a hundred or so when Bush arrived—augured disaster should he attempt another enterprise in journalism, and so Bush undertook instead a career in business. It proved a wise choice, though for the rest of his life he continued to write numerous essays and articles for various journals, both local and national. He opened a general store in Carondelet with his brother-in-law Charles Taussig, and they continued profitably in that south–St. Louis location for many years.

More important to Bush financially, in 1851 he purchased land in Jefferson County south of St. Louis, at a place later called Bushberg, where he engaged successfully in the raising of grapes. Before long Bush earned the reputation as a leading authority in viticulture; in 1868, in fact, he published *The Bushberg Catalogue,* a manual for raising grapes for wines, which was translated into many languages and enjoyed international circulation and acclaim. In 1870 he organized the firm of Isidor Bush and Company, which grew into one of the most successful wine and liquor enterprises in St. Louis.

Bush's business ventures went beyond wine and liquor, though. During the 1850s the expanding St. Louis and Iron Mountain Railroad Company named him its general passenger agent and auditor; he later became a director of the railroad, serving until 1865 when the line was taken over from New York by financier Jay Gould. In 1857 Bush helped incorporate the Peoples' Savings Bank in St. Louis, serving for a while as its president. In the late 1860s he was also president of the Mechanics Savings Bank, and later he served as actuary for the German Mutual Life Insurance Company. Despite these many successes, Bush never became a wealthy person; he suffered his share of financial setbacks, but managed to endure them placidly, paying off all debts. Nevertheless, he prospered sufficiently to participate in many endeavors, within both the Jewish community and the larger body politic.

One of those associations was the B'nai B'rith, the famous national Jewish fraternal and philanthropic organization. Shortly after he arrived in the United States in 1849, Bush joined New York's Zion Lodge No. 2; after he moved to St. Louis he became a member of Missouri Lodge No. 22 when it was established in 1855. In 1863 he helped organize a new St. Louis chapter, Ebn Ezra Lodge No. 47, with which he affiliated for the remainder of his life and for which he served honorably for many years in various capacities in District Grand Lodge No. 2.

One of Bush's most rewarding accomplishments resulted from that affiliation: the B'nai B'rith Cleveland Orphans Home. Intended originally to care for children of immigrants and Civil War casualties, the nationally recognized home opened in 1868 and provided its services well into the twentieth century. Bush also framed several national insurance and endowment programs for B'nai B'rith, which many members adopted. Indeed, B'nai B'rith held Bush in such high esteem that it tendered him a testimonial dinner in Philadelphia in 1890 that was graced by dignitaries from all over the country.

In St. Louis Bush was one of the original members of B'nai El Congregation, the second permanent Jewish congregation in St. Louis, when it was formed in 1852. He served that congregation faithfully for the rest of his life, occasionally as an officer. He led in efforts to organize religious education for Jewish children in St. Louis. His devotion to Judaism and his loyalty to his adopted country both were well illustrated in an incident mentioned by his longtime friend and biographer Samuel Bowman: "I recall in 1863, when things looked darkest for the Union forces, attending a service at Temple B'nai El and listening to a patriotic sermon delivered by Isidor Bush from its pulpit, exhorting the members to stand loyally by and give their full support to the Government of Lincoln."

Bush's influence and impact extended considerably beyond the St. Louis Jewish and business communities. Becoming a naturalized citizen in 1854, he ardently opposed slavery and championed the Union cause. Physical disabilities suffered in a fire as a child precluded military service during the Civil War. He contributed, instead, in a civilian capacity—in one instance, at least, as secretary to flamboyant Gen. **John C. Frémont** when the latter, early in the war, commanded Union forces in Missouri. Bush also served on the St. Louis City Council and the board of education. The latter was especially meaningful to Bush, who always held education—especially public education—as a high priority.

Probably Bush's greatest mark on St. Louis and Missouri history resulted from his participation in several state conventions during the Civil War period. The first met in February and March 1861, with Bush an elected delegate from St. Louis, and culminated in a critical political victory of Missouri Unionists over secessionists. Succeeding conventions—actually a provisional government that replaced a secessionist legislature—kept Missouri in the Union.

Bush stood out in those state conventions not only as an ardent Unionist, but also as a vigorous advocate for the immediate and complete freedom of all slaves throughout Missouri. Despite strong abolitionist sentiment, however, emancipation remained a minority view in the state convention until the so-called Radical Republicans came into control toward the end of the Civil War. In 1865 the convention called to write a new constitution emancipated slaves throughout the state, a goal Bush had championed for years.

Bush lived until August 5, 1898, and was regarded with respect and admiration as one of St. Louis's finest citizens. He was, among other things, a vice president of the Missouri Historical Society in 1882; later his oil portrait graced in honor the walls of that organization's stately building in St. Louis's Forest Park. He was in constant demand as a speaker at civic functions, and his earlier journalist leanings led him to author numerous articles and essays in many publications.

Throughout a life filled with civic accomplishments and distinguished public service, Bush retained a strong and open attachment to Judaism. Indeed, wrote a biographer, "the dominant note of his life was his fidelity and loyalty to the Faith of his Fathers," as demonstrated by his lifelong devotion and service to B'nai El Temple and B'nai B'rith. Ironically, one of the greatest sorrows of Bush's life was "his inability to secure the sympathetic interest of his wife and only son in the noble work he was engaged in for the welfare of his co-religionists. . . . The Taussig family of St. Louis, of which his wife was a member, were not at all interested in Jewish affairs, and soon after their arrival in America became members of the

Christian Church. . . . In view of the strong influence of his wife's family, it was a source of wonder, as well as gratification to his friends, that Mr. Bush preserved his affection and interest in the people of his faith." Isidor Bush is buried in Bellefontaine Cemetery in St. Louis in the Bush family plot.

WALTER EHRLICH

Bowman, Samuel. "Isidor Bush." *Modern View* (September 19, 1924).

Furth, Jacob. "Sketch of Isidor Bush." *Jewish Voice* (January 1, 1915).

———. "Sketch of Isidor Bush." *Missouri Historical Society Collections* 4 (1914): 303–8.

Kisch, Guido. "*Israels Herold*: The First Jewish Weekly in New York." *Historia Judaica* 2 (October 1940): 63–84.

Peixotto, Benjamin F. "Isidor Bush." *Menorah* 9 (September 1890): 123–26.

Wax, James A. "Isidor Bush: American Patriot and Abolitionist." *Historia Judaica* 5 (October 1943): 183–203.

BUTLER, EDWARD (1838?–1911)

Historians and popular writers have often regarded Col. Edward Butler as the "boss" of late-nineteenth-century St. Louis politics. A survey of his career, however, reveals a political opportunist whose power was limited to controlling votes in his own wards. "What should I want to hold office for?" Butler asked. "I have always preferred to let the other fellow hold the office, and then get acquainted with him." Throughout his career Butler remained a Democratic ward and faction leader in a Republican city.

The "Village Blacksmith," as Butler was known, was born in Ireland around 1838 and came to New York at the age of twelve. He arrived in St. Louis in 1857 and quickly found work as a journeyman blacksmith. His participation in politics began after the Civil War with membership in an Irish temperance association that provided him with contacts and friends in the city's Democratic Party. In 1872 the board of police commissioners awarded Butler his first government contract to shoe the city's horses after his support for the reelection campaign of Mayor Joseph Brown. By the mid-1870s Butler controlled the Fifth Ward and could fix votes and help secure elections for the Democratic Party. His rising popularity in the party was first tested in the mayoral election of 1874–1875 and during the adoption of the 1876 city charter.

In the 1874 mayoral election, Butler supported Arthur Barret against independent **Henry Clemens Overstolz** and Republican Constantine Maguire. Barret died shortly after his election, and Butler successfully campaigned for James Britton against

Overstolz in the 1875 mayoral contest. According to the city council's election report, massive fraud, particularly in Butler's Fifth Ward, secured Britton's victory. The council awarded the election to Overstolz. Despite the council's decision, Butler proved his ability to engineer vote fraud in his ward.

A more significant test of Butler's power was the new home-rule city charter approved under the Missouri Constitution of 1875. The charter altered the city's ward boundaries and divided Butler's Fifth Ward into three wards: the First, the Seventeenth, and the Eighteenth. Butler's vote fixing in the 1876 charter referendum held the old ward boundaries, and originally helped defeat the charter. An investigation uncovered Butler's fraud, and a recount provided enough votes for approval of the charter. In a hallmark of his career, however, Butler salvaged some political reward by directing his own men to testify in the fraud investigation.

Butler retained control over only the First Ward created under the new charter (though he later extended his operations to the Nineteenth Ward). In the 1877 municipal election, the first held under the new ward boundaries, Butler reversed his earlier position and supported the incumbent mayor, Overstolz. The Overstolz-dominated board of health awarded Butler's brother-in-law, James Hardy, the city's garbage-collection contract. The *St. Louis Post-Dispatch* revealed that Butler was a silent partner in Hardy's business, and the House of Delegates voted to stop payment on the contract. In the new bidding, however, Overstolz's board passed a bill raising the fee out of the price range of competing companies. Hardy, with Butler behind him, retained the contract on his next bid.

Butler's role in the party was challenged at the 1881 Democratic convention. The Armory Hall Democrats, a group of business Democrats led by **Joseph Pulitzer,** attempted to nominate one of their own, Edward Simmons, as the party's mayoral candidate. Butler fought back and on the third ballot secured Overstolz's renomination by three votes. In the worst defeat in a municipal election to that time, however, Overstolz lost to Republican William Ewing by almost fourteen thousand votes, partly due to negative publicity from disaffected Democrats. In 1885 Butler's candidate for mayor, C. C. Rainwater, lost the nomination to dark-horse candidate **David R. Francis,** president of the city's Merchants' Exchange. Butler switched his allegiance to Francis and helped him win the 1885 election.

Reformers continually challenged Butler's influence within the party and the city government. He was indicted in 1883 for conspiring to obstruct the enforcement of laws against gambling and lotteries—though the prosecutor lost the case when much of their evidence was thrown out as hearsay. In the

summer of 1886 the city grand jury launched an investigation into corruption in the House of Delegates that charged Butler with undue influence over that body. No indictments resulted from the investigation, but it further tarnished Butler's image.

Despite strong opposition within the party, Butler arranged the entire 1887 Democratic ticket but lost badly in the April election. During the 1888 campaign Butler arranged the "Koetter's Hotel Caucus"—a secret organization within the Democratic Party that decided all nominations before the convention met. A vigorous campaign against Butler, led by the *Post-Dispatch* and reform Democrats upset over his control of the party, helped defeat the "Koetter's Hotel" slate. Butler was shouted down at the next party convention and had no role in the selection of a mayoral candidate. Despite Butler's predictions to the contrary, the Democratic nominee, Edward Noonan, defeated Col. James Butler (no relation) in 1889.

Butler's businesses expanded in the 1880s, though his political fortunes declined. In 1883 he opened the Standard Theater, featuring popular theater and burlesque shows, at a cost of more than ninety thousand dollars. He also expanded his blacksmithing business to seven shops, shoeing almost two thousand horses per week. By 1893 Butler had recovered his lost prestige in the Democracy and arranged James Bannerman's nomination as mayor. Although Butler positioned his own judges to count the ballots, Bannerman, tainted by his association with "Butlerism," lost to Republican Cyrus Walbridge by more than three thousand votes.

In 1896 Butler again helped to name the Democratic slate but lost the election by more than ten thousand votes. Butler's decline in the party was fully evident by 1897 when his candidates lost the election for precinct committee men in his home territory, the First and the Nineteenth Wards. Butler again switched his support and attended the party convention as an ally of former state labor commissioner Lee Meriwether. Two days of fighting subsided when Butler's opponents retained control of the convention and successfully nominated businessman Edwin Harrison. Harrison, because of the raucous convention, lost the election to popular Republican candidate Henry Zeigenhein. Even Butler's First and Nineteenth Wards overwhelmingly voted for Zeigenhein.

In order to avoid the fight that broke apart the party in 1897, Butler and the business Democrats arranged a deal to unify the party. Butler and the other ward leaders were given control over nominations to the lower house, while the business Democrats chose the nominees for the upper house and executive positions. In addition, Butler's son James was chosen as the Democratic candidate for the Fifty-seventh

Congress—a longtime goal for Butler. The strategy worked. James was elected to Congress in 1900, and businessman **Rolla Wells** was elected mayor in 1901.

Throughout the 1880s and 1890s Butler maintained his contracts with the city government; his business flourished under both Republican and Democratic administrations. The most famous arrangement, a streetlighting contract in 1900, was immortalized by Lincoln Steffens in his muckraking classic, *The Shame of the Cities*. Butler apparently bribed some members of the House of Delegates to pass a bill that required lighting gas lamps in certain sections of the city. While Butler and the politicians haggled over the price of the contract, the streets remained dark. St. Louis circuit attorney **Joseph W. Folk** indicted "Colonel Ed" for his role in the lighting scandal as well as for his attempt to bribe two members of the health board to renew his garbage contract. Folk won the garbage-contract trial, but the state supreme court reversed the jury's decision on a technicality. He lost the lighting-scandal trial because the jury did not believe the testimony of the prosecution's witnesses.

Butler still had little control over his own political fortune. The Republican candidate for the 1900 congressional election, William Horton, challenged his loss to James Butler in the House of Representatives. The House could not decide a winner because of the fraud on both sides and declared the seat vacant. James put his name in for both elections to fill the vacant seat of the Fifty-seventh Congress and the election for the Fifty-eighth Congress—both held on November 4, 1902. He won both elections, and the results were again challenged. In the election for the Fifty-seventh Congress, the house decided that James had been elected through vote fraud, engineered by himself and his father, and awarded the seat to his opponent, George C. R. Wagner. George Reynolds, the defeated Republican contender for the seat in the Fifty-eighth Congress, also challenged his loss. The house concluded that James had legitimately won that election, and allowed him to serve. After his son's election, Edward Butler finally retired from politics. He died on September 10, 1911, leaving a fortune worth millions to his wife, Ellen O'Neill Butler; his two surviving children, James Butler and Catherine V. Huey; and his thirteen grandchildren. Thousands attended his funeral, the fourth largest in the city at that time.

EDWARD C. RAFFERTY

Geiger, Louis. "Joseph Folk v. Edward Butler: St. Louis, 1902." *Journal of Southern History* 28 (November 1962): 438–49.

Harrison, Ann Croft. "Edward Butler: The Beginnings of a Boss." Master's thesis, Washington University, 1969.

Rafferty, Edward C. "The Boss Who Never Was: Colonel Ed Butler and the Limits of Practical Politics in St. Louis, 1875–1904." *Gateway Heritage* 12 (winter 1992): 54–73.

Steffens, Lincoln. *The Shame of the Cities.* Reprint, New York: Hill and Wang, 1957.

Teaford, Jon C. *The Unheralded Triumph: City Government in America, 1870–1900.* Baltimore: Johns Hopkins University Press, 1984.

Zink, Harold. *City Bosses in the United States: A Study of Twenty Municipal Bosses.* Reprint, New York: AMS Press, 1968.

CAIRNS, ANNA SNEED (1841–1930)

Educator and reformer Anna Sneed Cairns was born on March 18, 1841, in New Albany, Indiana, daughter of the Reverend Samuel K. and Rachel Crosby Sneed. She acquired a strong abolitionist sentiment from her father, a longtime minister of the Presbyterian church, and she was an avid reader of classics and world history.

After graduating from Monticello Female Seminary in Godfrey, Illinois, Cairns taught school one year in Lexington, Missouri. With the beginning of the Civil War in Missouri, she returned to her parents' home in St. Louis and opened her own school, Kirkwood Seminary, in 1861. Although she began the institution with no money, property, or equipment and only seven students in a small building, the school grew and prospered. In 1866 she built a school for one hundred children, chartered it two years later, and constructed a larger building in 1881. The curriculum offered a Christian and liberal arts education and college preparatory for young women. In 1891 Cairns purchased six acres in St. Louis, south of Forest Park, and relocated her school, then known as Forest Park College. Two years later it became Forest Park University for Women.

On April 7, 1884, Anna Sneed married John G. Cairns, a St. Louis architect. Because of her great admiration for her father, she retained her maiden name, calling herself Anna Sneed Cairns. Her husband designed the main building of Forest Park College.

Because of financial difficulties in the 1890s, Cairns realized no salary from her institution. In 1904 she leased one of her buildings to the Louisiana Purchase Exposition to help pay her debt.

Despite her busy schedule, Cairns had varied interests. In 1876 she attended Saturday classes at the St. Louis School of Design and resumed her interest in painting and drawing. Her work included china painting and wood carving. She later devoted time to two of her favorite causes: prohibition and woman suffrage.

Cairns joined the St. Louis Woman's Christian Temperance Union (WCTU) and helped to revive local interest in that work. She attended the national WCTU convention in 1882 in Louisville, Kentucky, and began to work actively in the national organization. The next year she became superintendent of the Missouri State WCTU Legislative Department.

In that position she collected statewide petitions calling for a prohibition amendment to be voted on by Missouri citizens. The Missouri House of Representatives passed the amendment in 1887, but it failed in the senate. In 1910 the legislature finally passed the amendment, but the voters rejected it.

Always concerned about equal education and women's rights, Cairns joined the Missouri Equal Suffrage Association. She helped organize local groups around the state, publicized the association's activities in local newspapers, and encouraged petition drives. In 1897 and 1899 she spoke at the state capitol in behalf of woman suffrage. Cairns also encouraged women to serve as school directors and superintendents.

After more than fifty years of teaching, Cairns experienced difficulty getting Forest Park University accredited by the state committee on accreditation. Evidently, the institution needed more modern leadership and better facilities. Enrollment had begun to decline, and Cairns sold the university in 1926. She died on September 1, 1930, and was buried at Oak Hill Cemetery in Kirkwood.

MARY K. DAINS

Bishop, Beverly D., and Deborah W. Bolas, eds. *In Her Own Write: Women's History Resources in the Library and Archives of the Missouri Historical Society.* St. Louis: Missouri Historical Society, 1983.

Conard, Howard L., ed. *Encyclopedia of the History of Missouri.* New York: Southern History, 1901.

Dains, Mary K., ed. *Show Me Missouri Women: Selected Biographies.* Kirksville, Mo.: Thomas Jefferson University Press, 1989.

Johnson, Anne. *Notable Women of St. Louis.* St. Louis: Woodward, 1914.

CALLISON, CHARLES H. (1913–1993)

Charles H. Callison, a conservationist and author, was a key leader, strategist, and chronicler of the environmental movement in Missouri and the nation for more than a half century.

Born on November 6, 1913, in Lousana, Alberta, Canada, to Guy and Dorinda Callison, Charles moved at age five with his parents to a farm in Monroe County in their native Missouri. Upon graduation in 1937 from the University of Missouri School of Journalism, he edited weekly newspapers in Garnett,

Kansas, and Boonville, Missouri. In 1941 he joined the staff of the Missouri Conservation Commission as information officer and editor of the *Missouri Conservationist*. In 1946 he became executive secretary of the Conservation Federation of Missouri, which he built into an effective citizen voice for conservation. He organized the Clean Streams Committee to win passage of Missouri's first effective water-pollution-control law and authored a historical work titled *Man and Wildlife in Missouri* (1953).

Callison left Missouri for Washington, D.C., in 1951 to become secretary and conservation director of the National Wildlife Federation, where he became a leading authority on conservation legislation. From 1957 to 1959 he also served as chairman of the Natural Resources Council of America and edited a book, *America's Natural Resources* (1957).

In 1960 Callison joined the New York staff of the National Audubon Society, becoming executive vice president in 1966. He oversaw the chartering of hundreds of new chapters and the transformation of a society of fifty thousand bird-watchers into an effective grassroots force of four hundred thousand organized for action at local, regional, and national levels. His "National Outlook" column appeared in ninety-eight consecutive issues of *Audubon* from 1961 to 1977, chronicling some of the most momentous years of conservation history.

Callison assisted in drafting the Wilderness Act, the Endangered Species Act, the Wild and Scenic Rivers Act, and other major bills; was instrumental in organizing the Environmental Defense Fund; and was appointed to resource-advisory committees by four presidents. He also won appointment to the New York State Environmental Board, helped organize a successful campaign for a billion-dollar state bond issue for water-pollution control, and wrote numerous unsigned editorials for the *New York Times*.

Callison retired from Audubon in 1977 to become president of the Public Lands Institute, which he founded to focus attention on the vast, neglected acreage of the Bureau of Land Management in the West. Returning with his wife, Amy, to Jefferson City, Missouri, he traveled widely and prepared a two-volume study, *Areas of Critical Environmental Concern on the Public Lands* (1984, 1986), calling for protection of more than a thousand critical areas. He also wrote the text for a photographic interpretation of the public lands, *Overlooked in America* (1991), and many other articles and reviews.

Although he lived in the East for more than a quarter century, Callison was always known as a Missourian, and he made some of his finest contributions to his home state. In 1970 he served on a blue-ribbon committee that proposed the "Design for Conservation," a program of institutional development and land acquisition for the Conservation Commission funded since 1976 by a dedicated sales tax. In 1982, at a time of crisis for state parks, he led in establishing the Missouri Parks Association, for which he served as president, editor, legislative leader, and coauthor of *Exploring Missouri's Legacy: State Parks and Historic Sites* (1992). He helped establish the Citizens Committee for Soil, Water, and State Parks to win passage of a dedicated tax by statewide referendum in 1984 and coordinated an initiative petition campaign for its renewal in 1988, providing the financial base for Missouri to become a leader among the states in park management and soil conservation. He served and advised numerous other state, local, and national groups. Active to the end, he died on February 23, 1993, leaving his wife, three children, and eight grandchildren.

Charles Callison was awarded the Audubon Medal, the highest honor of the National Audubon Society, in 1978, and in 1979 he was granted the honorary degree of doctor of science by the University of Missouri. He was an honorary life member of the Wildlife Society and received the Frances K. Hutchinson Medal of the Garden Club of America, the Department of Interior Conservation Award, the Distinguished Service Award of the American Forestry Association, and numerous state and local awards. Callison was admired for his sense of history and vision for the future, his unflagging faith in the potential of grassroots citizen action, and his lifelong habit of giving others the credit.

Susan Flader

Callison, Charles. *Man and Wildlife in Missouri: The History of One State's Treatment of Its Natural Resources.* Harrisburg, Pa.: Stackpole, 1953.
Flader, Susan. "Charles H. Callison, 1913–1993." *Heritage* 11:1 (February 24, 1993): 1–3.
Graham, Frank, Jr. *The Audubon Ark: A History of the National Audubon Society.* Austin: University of Texas Press, 1990.
New York Times, February 26, 1993.

CALLOWAY, DEVERNE LEE (1916–1993)

DeVerne Calloway was born in Memphis, Tennessee, on June 17, 1916. She attended LeMoyne-Owen College in Memphis and did graduate work at Atlanta University and Northwestern University in Evanston, Illinois. She taught school in Georgia and Mississippi before joining the American Red Cross and traveling to China, Burma, and India during World War II. While in India she led a protest against the segregation of black soldiers in Red Cross facilities.

DeVerne Lee moved to Chicago after the war and became a member of the Congress of Racial Equality in 1946. She later joined the staff of the

Jewish Welfare Fund and developed skills in fund-raising. In 1946 she married **Ernest Calloway,** a political activist and union organizer (he later became president of the St. Louis NAACP, research director of the Teamsters' Joint Council no. 3, and a professor of urban affairs at St. Louis University). In February 1961 the couple began publishing *Citizen Crusader,* later named *New Citizen,* a newspaper covering black politics and civil rights in St. Louis.

Calloway was elected to the Missouri House of Representatives on her first bid for public office in November 1962, becoming the first black woman elected to the state legislature. She served on the house committees on education, public health, safety, and social security. She also served on the elections committee and the accounts committee, as chairman of the Federal-State Relations Committee, as chairman of the State Institutions and Properties Committee, and as secretary of the legislature's Democratic caucus. During her career in the legislature, she worked actively to increase state aid to public education; to improve welfare grants and services for dependent children, the blind, the disabled, and the elderly; and to reform prisons.

In 1978 Calloway served on the education committee that presided over the transfer of administrative control of Harris-Stowe Teachers College from the St. Louis Board of Education to the state. She also served on many community boards, including the board of the Union-Sarah Economic Development Corporation, an organization incorporated to improve the economic, educational, and social opportunities in the north St. Louis area.

Calloway was elected to her tenth term in the Missouri House in November 1980, and she retired from public office at the conclusion of that term. Calloway died at age seventy-six at the home of her sister, Evelyn Iles, in Memphis, Tennessee, of an apparent heart attack on January 23, 1993.

KENN THOMAS

Calloway, DeVerne. Oral History Interview, February 23, 1983. Western Historical Manuscripts Collection, St. Louis.

———. Papers. 1929–1989. Western Historical Manuscript Collection. University of Missouri, St. Louis.

CALLOWAY, ERNEST ABNER (1909–1989)

Ernest Calloway was born in Herberton, West Virginia, on January 1, 1909. His family became one of the first black families in the coal-mining communities of eastern Kentucky when they moved to Letcher County in 1913. Calloway's father helped organize the county's first United Mine Workers local. Calloway attended high school in Lynchburg, Virginia.

Calloway quit school and ran away to Harlem in 1925, during the time of the Harlem Renaissance. He worked as a dishwasher in Harlem until his mother became ill, and he returned to Kentucky at age seventeen. Calloway worked in the mines of Consolidated Coal Company until 1930. During the early 1930s, he traveled around the United States and Mexico as a drifter. After a frightening hallucinatory experience in the mountains of Baja, California, in 1933, he returned to the Kentucky coal mines.

That same year Calloway submitted an article on marijuana use to *Opportunity,* the magazine of the National Urban League. *Opportunity* rejected Calloway's manuscript but asked him to write another article on the working conditions of blacks in the Kentucky coalfields. He submitted the second article, "The Negro in the Kentucky Coal Fields," and *Opportunity* published it in March 1934. The article resulted in a scholarship to Brookwood Labor College in New York, a training facility for labor organizers headed by the radical pacifist A. J. Muste.

From 1935 to 1936 Calloway worked in Virginia and helped organize the Virginia Workers' Alliance, a union of unemployed Works Progress Administration workers. In 1937 he moved to Chicago and organized railway-station porters (known as Redcaps) and other railroad employees into the United Transport Employee Union. Calloway helped write the resolution creating the 1942 Committee against Discrimination in the Congress of Industrial Organizations (CIO). When the first peacetime draft law took effect in 1940, Calloway was the first black to refuse military service because of race discrimination. The case received national publicity but was never officially settled. Calloway never served in the segregated army.

Calloway joined the national CIO news editorial staff in 1944. In 1946 he married DeVerne Lee, a teacher who led a protest against racial segregation in the Red Cross in India during World War II. The following year he received a scholarship from the British Trade Union Congress to attend Ruskin College at Oxford, England, but by the time it was granted, Calloway had returned to the United States and had started work with the CIO Southern Organizing Drive in North Carolina. Because of a dispute over organizing tactics in an attempt to unionize workers at R. J. Reynolds Tobacco Company, Calloway left the CIO in 1950 and returned to Chicago. There Harold Gibbons of the St. Louis Teamsters Union enlisted him to establish a research department for the Teamsters in St. Louis.

In 1951 Calloway advised the rank-and-file union committee that developed a plan to integrate public schools in St. Louis. The Teamsters presented it to the St. Louis Board of Education three years prior to the Supreme Court decision on integration. The board rejected the proposal.

In 1955 Calloway was elected president of the St. Louis NAACP. Within the first two years of his presidency, membership grew from two to eight thousand members. He led successful efforts to gain substantial increases in the number of blacks employed by St. Louis taxi services, department stores, the Coca-Cola Company, and Southwestern Bell. The NAACP opposed a proposed city charter in 1957 because it did not include civil service reforms, public accommodations sections, or support for civil rights. The charter was defeated.

In 1959 Calloway served as campaign director for the Reverend John J. Hicks, who became the first African American elected to the St. Louis Board of Education. Calloway also directed the campaign for **Theodore D. McNeal**'s 1960 senatorial race. McNeal won by a large margin, becoming the first African American elected to the Missouri State Senate. The following year Ernest and **DeVerne Lee Calloway** began publishing *Citizen Crusader* (later named *New Citizen*), a newspaper covering black politics and civil rights in St. Louis. Also in 1961 Calloway was the technical adviser for James Hurt Jr.'s successful campaign as the second African American to be elected to the St. Louis school board. DeVerne Calloway became the first black woman elected to the Missouri legislature in 1962 when she won a seat in the House of Representatives in her first bid for public office.

Calloway worked with the Committee of Fair Representation in 1967 to develop a new plan for congressional-district reapportionment. Supported by black representatives in the Missouri legislature and a coalition of white Republicans and Democrats, the plan created the First Congressional District, which proved more favorable to black interests. In 1968 Calloway filed as a candidate for Congress in the new district. He was defeated in the Democratic primary by William Clay, who became the first African American elected to Congress from Missouri.

In 1969 Calloway began lecturing part-time at the Center for Urban Programs at St. Louis University. He became an assistant professor when he retired as research director for the Teamsters in June 1973, and he later became professor emeritus of urban studies. Calloway suffered a disabling stroke in 1982. He died on December 31, 1989.

KENN THOMAS

Calloway, Ernest. *Architects of an Unfinished American Dream.* St. Louis: Marcus Albrecht, 1981.
———. Oral History Interview, July 31, 1970. Western Historical Manuscripts Collection, St. Louis.
———. Papers. 1932–1989. Western Historical Manuscripts Collection, St. Louis.

CAMPBELL, ROBERT (1804–1879)

Robert Campbell's lengthy life bridged the transition from fur trade to modern capitalistic agriculture in the trans-Mississippi expanses stretching westward from Missouri to the Rocky Mountains. Campbell's career was also illustrative of those intrepid frontier merchant-capitalists who made their homes in the thriving city of St. Louis in the mid-nineteenth century. It was easy for business leaders such as Campbell to pass from one type of venture to another as St. Louis evolved from frontier village to urban metropolis. His early business experiences in the West steeped him in knowledge of risk and fluctuating fortune.

Born in northern Ireland on February 12, 1804, Campbell came to the United States as a teenager. By the age of twenty, he was in St. Louis and had become involved in **William Henry Ashley**'s fur-trade activities. As a young man Campbell associated with many legendary frontier figures, including Ashley, **Pierre Jean De Smet, Jedediah Strong Smith,** Thomas Fitzpatrick, and **Jim Bridger.** Washington Irving and other writers immortalized Campbell as a courageous Indian fighter of great repute, of striking and prepossessing appearance, and as a great leader in the rough-and-tumble frontier wilderness.

Wishing to strike out on his own as a trader, trapper, and outfitter, Campbell sought to eliminate the middlemen in the fur trade. Within a short period he attempted to exploit the fur trade of the upper Missouri and Yellowstone regions. Early in life he suffered from numerous respiratory ailments, and he never wholeheartedly embraced the mountains, but in the 1820s and 1830s he resolutely went about earning his great wealth in that lonely and dangerous setting. That fortune became the base for his future ventures.

Campbell's shrewd partnerships and trading alliances made him a leading trader by the early 1830s, when he joined forces with his fellow trapper and trader **William Sublette.** That historic partnership challenged the well-established American Fur Company headed by John Jacob Astor and his western agent, **Pierre Chouteau Jr.** Competition was played out both in the Rockies through the construction of forts and rival trading posts and in the business houses of St. Louis.

Throughout the late 1830s and 1840s, the firm of Sublette and Campbell maintained its position as a fair-minded competitive outfitter for western fur-trading ventures. Campbell's success benefited from his earlier firsthand associations in the wilderness. Throughout the 1840s and even into the 1850s, Campbell financed fur-trading ventures and entrepreneurs. His word and handshake were said to have been as good as currency throughout the West.

In St. Louis, Campbell's banking and financial operations fueled his numerous western financial endeavors. They also helped develop the city's economy. His diversified interests included both dry goods and the familiar staples of western trade. He was president of the Merchants National Bank, as well as the owner of the famed Southern Hotel, a St. Louis landmark for many years. In such ventures Campbell was symbolic of those early St. Louisans who looked to urban progress for financial gain, along with the traditional commercial opportunities in markets across the Southwest, California, and the Pacific.

Campbell was respected as much by his rivals as by friends, and presidents, governors, and generals sought his advice. He was universally renowned for his knowledge and understanding of western affairs. For example, he was entrusted with the organization and outfitting of troops in St. Louis during the Mexican War, and his efforts proved especially beneficial to Missouri and its citizens.

Campbell's extensive knowledge of Native American affairs, and the deep respect numerous tribal leaders held for him, led to his appointment as one of the commissioners in the Fort Laramie Council of 1851, leading to the treaty by the same name, which outlined for the first time the concept of reserved lands for many of the Plains Indian tribes. At the height of the Indian wars, during the Grant administration, Campbell served once more as an Indian commissioner. He was one of the fairest-minded white diplomats available to Native tribespeople and contributed enormously as a stabilizing presence who carried profound weight with the chiefs.

Owing to the substantial wealth he had amassed by midcentury, Campbell became a philanthropist and a great civic booster of St. Louis. With his wife, Virginia Kyle Campbell, of Raleigh, North Carolina, he made his home in fashionable Lucas Place, just west of downtown, the city's first neighborhood of fine houses. They hosted a swirling array of parties, events, dinners, and important affairs. At the time of his death on October 16, 1879, Campbell could look back on a life well lived and symbolic of the greatest activities that helped settle the American West. Respected by virtually all in St. Louis and Missouri for his considerable achievements, he lived a life unblemished by scandal of any sort, becoming, truly, a favorite son of Missouri, symbolic of the earliest citizens' energies and enthusiasm toward making St. Louis a gateway to empire.

Campbell's sons continued in their father's tradition of banking and philanthropy. In the 1940s the Campbell House became a museum, a monument to the great mountain man's life and career, tangible evidence of St. Louis's earliest economy and its visionary westering inhabitants.

JOHN NEAL HOOVER

Brooks, George R., ed. "The Private Journal of Robert Campbell, 1833." Parts 1 and 2. *Bulletin of the Missouri Historical Society* 20:1 (1963): 3–24; 2 (1964): 107–18.

Campbell, Robert. Papers. Mercantile Library Association, St. Louis.

Hafen, LeRoy R., ed. *The Mountain Men and the Fur Trade of the Far West.* Glendale, Calif.: Arthur H. Clark, 1971.

Morgan, Dale L. *The West of William Ashley.* Denver: Rosenstock, 1964.

Nester, William. *From Mountain Man to Millionaire: The "Bold and Dashing Life" of Robert Campbell.* Columbia: University of Missouri Press, 1999.

Sunder, John E. *The Fur Trade on the Upper Missouri, 1840–1865.* Norman: University of Oklahoma Press, 1965.

CANARY, MARTHA JANE (CALAMITY JANE) (1856?–1903)

Martha Jane Canary, better known as Calamity Jane in the folklore of the American Wild West, was born near Princeton, a farm village in northwest Missouri near the Iowa line. The year of her birth is uncertain. Some believe it was 1848, while Calamity, in a diary whose authorship is highly suspect, allegedly wrote she was born on May 1, 1852. The federal census of 1860 recorded she was four years old at that time, making her birth year 1856. She was the oldest of six children. Presumably, she was a tomboy who did her chores, and learned to ride, to shoot, and to fend for herself in the harsh surroundings of frontier Missouri. She could read and write, which indicates some schooling, but the details are unknown.

Shortly after the Civil War the family left Missouri, apparently traveling the Mormon Trail to the gold and silver mines of Utah and Montana. Within a few years both parents died, leaving Calamity alone to survive in the masculine world of the untamed West. Dressed like a plainsman, she drifted from job to job throughout the West. She washed dishes at Fort Bridger, cooked for cowhands, nursed the sick, worked in saloons and brothels, and became a freighter (or mule whacker) who transported supplies to mining camps, Union Pacific Railroad construction sites, and army posts in Colorado, Montana, and the Dakota country. Her reputation as a gritty and boisterous woman who could outwork, outbrawl, outcarouse, and outtalk most men spread until even the Indians of the western Plains called her the "Crazy Woman who rode the devil's horse."

There are different versions of how she got her nickname, "Calamity." Some believe James Butler "Wild Bill" Hickok gave it to her after she warned him about a couple of angry cowboys who were coming to kill him and retrieve the money they had lost in a card game. However, the romantic account is that she rescued a wounded trooper about to be scalped in an Indian skirmish. Grateful she had saved him from a dire calamity, he said, "I name you Calamity Jane, the Heroine of the Plains." Like most nicknames, it probably evolved from those who knew her and sensed that wherever and whenever she was around, a calamity was about to happen.

In the early 1870s Calamity was with Gen. George Armstrong Custer's command on a scientific and military expedition into the Black Hills of the Dakota Territory. Custer's orderly observed that she trailed the regiment, dressed in male clothing, and covered with lice. She sometimes did a trooper's laundry for a shot of whiskey. During the Sioux and Cheyenne uprising that led to the massacre of Custer and 250 soldiers at the Battle of the Little Big Horn on June 25, 1876, Calamity worked as a freighter in the command of Gen. George Crook. It was said that she was so well disguised as a man that the troopers did not know she was a woman until they heard she could not cuss as well as a man. One of the legends of Calamity Jane casts her in the role of an army scout in the war against the Plains Indians. There is even a photograph of her dressed as a scout, with the caption "Gen. Crook's Scout." However, neither Custer nor Crook would have used a woman in the demanding and dangerous job of an army scout in the Indian country.

The most sentimental part of the legend of Calamity Jane is the love affair between her and Hickok. There is no historical documentation, however, that they ever courted, married, or had a daughter named Janie, whom Calamity allegedly gave to an English couple after Hickok spurned her for another woman. They were only acquaintances whom some say never saw one another more than three or four times. Calamity used Hickok's name, as she did those of other legendary figures, such as William "Buffalo Bill" Cody, E. C., "Teddy Blue" Abbott, and Belle Starr in exaggerated stories of their relationships, many of which became a part of the mythology of the American West.

In the late 1880s the Calamity Jane character appeared in a number of the popular dime novels. The plots varied from the standard one, in which the male hero saves the powerless woman and they live happily ever after, to the heroine who saves the man only to lose him to another woman. A couple of the titles were *The Beautiful White Devil of Yellowstone* and *Deadwood Dick in Leadville; or, Calamity Jane, the Heroine of Whoop-Up.* Nearly a century later, Larry McMurtry, a Pulitzer Prize–winning author, revived Calamity Jane in his novel *The Buffalo Girls* (1990). The author admits that the character of Calamity Jane in the book is based more on the legends rather than on the facts of her life.

By the early 1880s Buffalo Bill Cody had tamed the West and taken it to the American public in his spectacular Wild West show. Although Cody helped Calamity when she encountered hard times, he never hired her to perform in one of his extravaganzas. He may have been responsible for booking her in a small-time Wild West show that folded in Chicago in 1884, leaving the cast to sell their ponies for railroad tickets back to Montana. In the remaining years of her life, Calamity became a kind of sideshow attraction, appearing in dime museums and selling abbreviated autobiographies and pictures of herself to travelers in the upper Yellowstone area of Montana. A few years before her death, she was taken to the Pan American Exposition in Buffalo, New York, to portray a woman of the West, only to be placed in police custody for public drunkenness. Destitute and alcoholic, Calamity became dependent on friends and acquaintances for her livelihood until her death in Terry, South Dakota, on August 1, 1903. Even in death the legend of Calamity Jane lived on as friends buried her in Mount Moriah Cemetery, in Deadwood, South Dakota, next to the grave of Wild Bill Hickok.

CHARLES T. JONES JR.

Lamar, Howard R., ed. "Calamity Jane (1852–1903)." In *The Reader's Encyclopedia of the American West.* New York: Thomas Y. Crowell, 1977.

McMurtry, Larry. *The Buffalo Girls.* New York: Simon and Schuster, 1990.

Sollid, Roberta B. *Calamity Jane: A Study in Historical Criticism.* Helena, Mont.: Western Press, 1958.

Whithorn, Bill, and Doris Whithorn. *Calamity's in Town: The Town Was Livingston, Montana.* Livingston, Mont.: Livingston Enterprise, n.d.

CANNON, CLARENCE A. (1879–1964)

Clarence Andrew Cannon was born on April 11, 1879, on a farm just south of the tiny Protestant settlement soon to be incorporated as Elsberry, Missouri. Cannon developed his personality and his values in this small farming community where people took seriously both their faith in God and their politics. He brought these values to Washington and grew to be one of the most powerful men in the United States Congress, and, arguably, the world's foremost authority on parliamentary procedure.

After graduating from Elsberry High School, Cannon briefly attended Buchanan College, a Baptist school in Troy, Missouri, seeking the preparatory education that his small high school had not afforded him. He enrolled in La Grange Junior College in Hannibal, another Southern Baptist school, in the fall of 1896. Two years later Cannon put his education on hold to volunteer for the Spanish-American War. His company was transported to St. Louis en route to Cuba when Randolph Cannon learned of his son's plans. The elder Cannon quickly traveled to St. Louis to retrieve his son, thus postponing Clarence's military career.

Cannon returned to his studies at La Grange. Never content with simple class work, he played on the football team at La Grange and taught history during his final year. He also served as president of the Baptist Young People's Union and frequently spoke at church gatherings and student meetings in support of temperance. He graduated from La Grange in 1901, then moved back to Elsberry to teach history and Latin in the high school for two years, also serving as assistant superintendent.

In 1903 Cannon enrolled in William Jewell College in Liberty. He graduated first in his class, receiving his B.A. in 1904. The following year he worked on his master's thesis at William Jewell while teaching at Canton High School. He received his M.A. in 1905.

Cannon taught history at Stephens College in Columbia from 1905 until 1908 while attending the University of Missouri law school. While pursuing his law degree, Cannon courted Ida Dawson Wiggington, a native of Elsberry who was a student at Stephens College. On August 30, 1906, the two were married in a small private ceremony in the home of the bride's father. The Cannons had what their daughter described as "the love affair of the century." Ida Cannon was exceptionally involved in her husband's career, working in his law office, campaigning with him, even advising him on correspondence with his political colleagues. During a tribute to Cannon in Jefferson City in 1963, the speaker remarked, "It is impossible to talk about Mr. Cannon without also talking about Mrs. Cannon . . . [she] has been his counterpart in every endeavor."

When Cannon was admitted to the Missouri bar in 1908, the couple moved to Troy where he began the practice of law in the firm of Avery, Young, and Woolfolk. Less than six months later, Cannon and Woolfolk established their own firm.

While in Troy, Cannon generously contributed his time to the community and was in great demand as an orator for such events as high school graduations and meetings of community organizations. He devoted much of his time to religious causes. For six years, beginning in 1909, he served as clerk of the Cuivre River Baptist Association before being elected moderator, a position comparable to chairman. The Lin-

coln County Sunday School Association elected him its president in 1910, and at the same time he served as secretary of the Layman's Missionary Movement of Lincoln County.

Cannon's fervent involvement in the community combined with his education and ambition motivated him to pursue a political career. As his first venture into the political arena, he sought the 1910 Democratic nomination for Lincoln County state representative. He lost the primary but remained active, devoting his energy to the reelection campaign of Missouri congressman **Champ Clark.** Clark's Ninth District included Cannon's home county of Lincoln, and Clark had known Cannon's father for many years. Cannon sent out letters urging loyal Democrats to vote, and traveled throughout Lincoln County speaking on Clark's behalf. Overall, it was a successful election year for the Democratic Party, and Clark won by a heavy margin.

In April 1911 the United States House of Representatives elected Clark its Speaker. Remembering Cannon's loyalty and support, Clark offered him a position as the Speaker's clerk. Cannon left his law practice in Elsberry and moved to Washington. He quickly learned about the workings of the House and who wielded power. He continued to hone his skills as a congressional aide and gained expertise on the subject of parliamentary procedure. In March 1914 House leaders appointed him journal clerk. More important, in 1917 he succeeded Clark's son as House parliamentarian, a position he held until 1920.

Champ Clark lost his seat in the House during the Republican landslide of 1920. His death in early 1921 opened the Democratic nomination for the 1922 election. Because of his relationship with Clark, his carefully cultivated contacts in Lincoln County, and his reputation as a parliamentarian, Cannon presented himself as the logical choice for the Democratic slot.

In the 1922 election Cannon defeated Theodore Hukriede, the incumbent Republican representative who had defeated Clark in the previous election. Cannon offered himself as the candidate of the common people, primarily farmers and small businessmen, who were the majority in the Ninth District. Farmers had prospered during World War I due to the increased demand for agricultural products. The prospect of future profits lured them into going into debt to expand their operations. By 1922 the boom had ended; agricultural prices had fallen, and many farmers could not pay their debts, losing their machinery and their land. Since most small-town businesses depended on agriculture, many rural communities in Missouri and other agricultural states were economically depressed. Farm relief and other economic issues determined Cannon's election to office more than party affiliation. Hukriede's dubious voting record on farm issues and in favor of tax breaks for big business no doubt contributed to his defeat in November 1922.

Once in office Cannon diligently worked to accomplish the goals he had set during his campaign. He associated himself with the "Farm Bloc," a coalition of congressmen from agricultural states whose common goal was to pass crucial farm legislation through both houses. The Farm Bloc successfully passed the Capper-Volstead Act, which legalized farm cooperatives, and the Agricultural Credits Act, which supplied farmers with short- and long-term loans. Cannon first actively participated in the Farm Bloc by introducing the McNary-Haugen Bill in 1924, which aimed to attain parity between the selling price of farm products and the cost of living. The bill proposed to have the government set a fair price for farm commodities and market the surpluses abroad in exchange for a fee paid by the farmers. The Missouri Farmers Association and the Missouri Farm Bureau supported the bill and selected Cannon to be their spokesman in Congress. Cannon presented the bill to the House in May 1924 and spoke in its defense several times thereafter, often using his expertise on House rules to baffle opponents. Despite his efforts, the House voted down the bill in early June. However, in this battle Cannon had established himself as a champion of the farmer and a loyal representative of his district, characteristics that would secure reelection for the next forty years.

Cannon compiled the longest service record of any Missourian as a member of the House of Representatives. He was first elected as a Democrat to the House in 1922 and was reelected to the succeeding twenty Congresses until his death in 1964. He served as chairman of the Committee on Appropriations from 1941 until his death, except for the Eightieth and Eighty-third Congresses when the Republicans held the majority. He also served as parliamentarian of the Democratic National Convention from 1920 until 1960.

While in Congress, Cannon devoted much of his time to improving House procedures to make them more efficient. Through his efforts, House time spent on parliamentary procedure decreased by three-fourths, and obstructive tactics became difficult to implement. He became such an expert on House rules that he published several studies on the body's procedures. The House periodically published editions of "Cannon's Procedure (1928)" until 1963. The *Encyclopædia Britannica* and the *Americana Encyclopedia* published his work on parliamentary law in 1929 and 1940, respectively.

Throughout his career Cannon advocated veterans' benefits. He sponsored and guided through the Congress a $2.1 billion bonus bill for veterans of World War I. During the first year of the New Deal, Cannon voted against the "economy act" that cut veterans' benefits by $400 million a year, the only member of the Missouri delegation to do so.

Cannon consistently promoted the interests of farmers. He served as chair of the House Subcommittee on Agricultural Appropriations. From this powerful position, he staunchly supported the Rural Electrification Administration, and his influence obtained appropriations for the Joanna Dam and the Meramec River Project. He also exerted his influence to establish the U.S. Soil Conservation Nursery in Elsberry.

At the time of his death, Cannon was one of the oldest and most powerful members of the House of Representatives. As chairman of the House Appropriations Committee, he influenced the shape of every federal budget from the administration of Franklin Roosevelt to that of Lyndon B. Johnson. Always concerned about spending, Cannon became known as "the watchdog" of the budget. He died of a heart ailment on May 12, 1964, in Washington, D.C.

ERIKA K. NELSON

Biographical Dictionary of the United States Congress, 1774–1989. Bicentennial ed. S.v. "Cannon, Clarence A." Washington, D.C.: U.S. Government Printing Office, 1989.

Cannon, Clarence A. Papers. 1896–1964. Western Historical Manuscripts Collection, Columbia.

Lilley, Stephen R. "The Early Career of Clarence Cannon, 1879–1924." Master's thesis, Northeast Missouri State University, 1976.

———. "A Minuteman for Years: Clarence Cannon and the Spirit of Volunteerism." *Missouri Historical Review* (October 1983): 33–50.

New York Times, May 13, 1964.

Official Manual of the State of Missouri, 1957–1958. Jefferson City: Secretary of State, 1958.

CARNEGIE, DALE (1888–1955)

Dale Carnagey (later changed to Carnegie) was born in Maryville, Missouri, on November 24, 1888. He was the second son of James William and Amanda Elizabeth Harbison Carnagey. The family lived on a farm near a river that overflowed frequently and ruined their crops. From these humble beginnings Dale Carnegie became a pioneer of the self-development movement and a best-selling author with worldwide recognition and acclaim.

Young Carnegie liked to recite at local functions and Sunday school, and with the urging of Nicholas M. Souder, a teacher who boarded with the family, he joined the high school debate team. The family moved to a farm near Warrensburg, and at the age of sixteen, with his mother's encouragement, he enrolled in the State Normal School (later Central Missouri State University) in 1904. The family could not afford the fees for room and board in town, so he rode a horse the three miles to school each day.

Carnegie joined the debate team during his first year when he realized that athletics and debating were the two ways to gain prestige at the normal school. He lost every debate the first year but later achieved great success after observing a Chautauqua lecturer who visited Warrensburg. Carnegie copied his dialect, gestures, and vocabulary. By 1906 Carnegie was well known on campus for his speaking ability, and in 1907 he was elected president of the sophomore class. In 1908, during his junior year, Carnegie coached other students in debate and public speaking and also received a regent's certificate, which entitled him to teach in Missouri. When he left the school in 1908, he needed only one more year to complete a bachelor's degree.

At the age of twenty Carnegie traveled to Nebraska to sell correspondence courses for the International Correspondence Schools. He later took a job in Omaha with Armour and Company, selling meat in South Dakota. Although he was successful at sales, he quit his job with the intention of going to Boston to become a Chautauqua lecturer. Instead, however, he went to New York and enrolled in the American Academy of Dramatic Arts in 1911. After a brief period as an actor on tour and as a used–Packard truck salesman, Carnegie decided to become a public-speaking teacher.

Despite his previous success as a speaker, Carnegie knew that it would be impossible for him to teach at an established university without the proper credentials. Instead, he approached the manager of the YMCA on 125th Street with a proposal to teach adult night classes. There was no salary with the job, but he arranged to receive a percentage of the fees. His classes were very successful, and he invited the students to give speeches about their individual experiences. This technique drew a positive response. By 1914 he earned as much as five hundred dollars per week and opened courses at the YMCAs in Philadelphia, Baltimore, and Wilmington.

Carnegie began his career as an author in 1915, coauthoring *The Art of Public Speaking* with J. Berg Esenwein. In 1916 he sold out a one-night lecture at Carnegie Hall, named for Andrew Carnegie, the steel magnate. He then decided to change the spelling of his name to that of the famous industrialist since most journalists already spelled it that way.

Carnegie joined the army during World War I and spent eighteen months at Camp Upton on Long Island. During this period he met Lowell Thomas, an English instructor at Princeton University. After his discharge Carnegie became Thomas's business manager for his "With Allenby in Palestine and Lawrence of Arabia" lecture tour in Great Britain. Both men lectured and narrated, while the audiences viewed films. Thus began a lifelong friendship between the two men.

During the tour Carnegie observed the "orators" at London's Hyde Park. He noted that the speakers who were most enthusiastic drew the largest audiences. Carnegie realized that his earlier approach to teaching was wrong. His emphasis on voice control, diction, and gestures for effective public speaking did not have the emotional impact needed to reach the audience. Enthusiasm became the bedrock of the Dale Carnegie "technique" for the rest of his life. He kept thousands of note cards that contained personal and career information on historic figures and unusual events to make his presentations more interesting to his audiences.

In 1921 Carnegie received the status of fellow of the Royal Geographic Society. That same year he also met and married Lotitia Baucaire in Europe. Never a happy marriage, it ended in divorce in 1931. From 1923 to 1925 Carnegie traveled throughout the world visiting the Arctic, Africa, and Europe.

Carnegie returned to the United States and resumed his public-speaking classes. In 1926 he wrote a two-volume text titled *Public Speaking: A Practical Course for Businessmen,* which became the basic text for his courses. He also opened an office near Times Square in New York, and in 1932 published *Lincoln: The Unknown.* Other books reflecting his interest in famous people included *Little Known Facts about Well-Known People* (1934) and *Five-Minute Biographies* (1937).

In 1935 Carnegie gave a special lecture called "How to Win Friends and Influence People" as part of his course. Leon Shimkin of Simon and Schuster persuaded Carnegie to expand it into a book, which was completed and published in November 1936. The book was a great success, selling five thousand copies per day for two years, and it remained on the bestseller lists for ten years. By the end of 1937 the book had sold 750,000 copies and won international fame for Carnegie. *Time* named him author of the year in 1937. By the time of his death in 1955, sales had reached nearly 5 million copies, and increased to 15 million by 1980. The book was translated into more than thirty languages and remains a steady seller in the 1990s.

Although ignored by academic teachers of rhetoric and not considered a literary work, Carnegie's book was very popular and was considered among the best of self-help literature. Written in a plain style, it was practical and adopted the moralistic tradition of self-improvement at a time when Americans were looking for a new success formula during the Great Depression. The book made his name a household word.

The real key to the book was its ability to persuade the reader that the other person should be made to feel important. His checklist for getting along with people included not criticizing them. He felt criticism was dangerous because it could wound a person's pride, hurt their sense of importance, and arouse resentment. He urged genuine interest in other people and being a good listener. Much of modern industrial psychology seeks to encourage the same things in human relationships. Carnegie believed there was one all-important law of human conduct: "Always make the other person feel important."

Carnegie also wrote a second best-seller in 1948, *How to Stop Worrying and Start Living.* His training methods that worked to build self-confidence during the 1930s continue to be used in the 1990s. What the Carnegie courses taught fitted well with modern cultural and organizational changes that swept U.S. companies after World War II. By 1989 the Dale Carnegie courses had a worldwide enrollment of more than 170,000, a 60 percent increase since 1983. General Motors Corporation sent more than twenty thousand employees through the courses, and IBM more than nine thousand. Approximately 425 of the Fortune 500 companies used Carnegie courses.

Carnegie's later years were happy. In 1944 he married Dorothy Reeder Price Vanderpool of Tulsa, Oklahoma. She was his secretary and a former Carnegie-course student. A daughter, Donna Dale, was born in 1951. The family lived in a large, comfortable home in Forest Hills, New York. Carnegie also owned a ranching and farm operation south of Harrisonville, Missouri. Never reluctant to acknowledge his simple roots, Carnegie frequently returned to his family's farm at Belton, Missouri, and spoke at local clubs and social events.

In June 1938 Carnegie returned for summer commencement at his old school in Warrensburg, which honored him with "Dale Carnegie Day" activities, including a picnic on the school lawn and a lecture by Carnegie in the afternoon. In 1955 he again returned to the college and on July 29, 1955, was awarded an honorary degree of doctor of letters by Central Missouri State College.

On November 1, 1955, Carnegie died of uremia. After funeral rites were held in Forest Hills on November 3, he was returned to Belton, Missouri, for funeral rites in the Belton Methodist Church and buried in the family plot with his parents and grandmother at the Belton Cemetery.

In its fall 1990 issue, *Life* published its list of "The *Life* 100 Most Important Americans of the 20th Century." Dale Carnegie was among them.

ARTHUR F. MCCLURE AND VIVIAN RICHARDSON

Boorstin, Daniel J. *The Americans: The Democratic Experience.* New York: Random House, 1973.

Current Biography Yearbook. New York: H. W. Wilson, 1955.
Hobart, Stephen B. "Dale Carnegie: Missourian Who Made Good, 1888–1955." Master's research paper, Central Missouri State University, 1984.
Huber, Richard M. *The American Idea of Success.* New York: McGraw-Hill, 1971.
Kemp, Giles, and Edward Claflin. *Dale Carnegie: The Man Who Influenced Millions.* New York: St. Martin's, 1989.
"Old Grads Return for Carnegie Day." *Student* (July 5, 1938).

CARR, WILLIAM C. (1783–1851)

William C. Carr, one of the first attorneys to practice law in Missouri, was born in Albemarle County, Virginia, on April 15, 1783. He came to St. Louis in 1804, only three weeks after U.S. officials assumed control there, but a month later he moved to Ste. Genevieve and established a law office. The next year Carr returned his legal practice to the territorial capital. In 1807 he married Ann Maria Elliott, a "Yankee girl" from Connecticut, and they had three children. Three years after her death in 1826, he married Dorcas Bent, daughter of the prominent jurist **Silas Bent,** and the couple had several children.

Following his arrival in the Louisiana Territory, Carr took an immediate dislike to the French Creole inhabitants, declaring that "the French manner of living is not only extremely disagreeable to us but is really very low." He allied himself with other incoming Americans who shared his anti-French views and soon became embroiled in the political squabbles that divided territorial inhabitants. Carr was a bitter critic of Gov. **James Wilkinson** and took an active role in an attempt to block his confirmation in the United States Senate. When that effort failed, Carr complained that President Thomas Jefferson "appears to desire the conciliation of a minority of French demagogues even at the expense of a majority of the citizens of the United States."

Carr also waded into the Spanish land-claims controversy on the side of those opposing wholesale confirmations. Secy. of the Treasury Albert Gallatin had assigned him to investigate cases of suspected land fraud in the Louisiana Territory. In his capacity as territorial land agent, Carr joined land commissioner and territorial judge **John B. C. Lucas** in charging that the majority on the Board of Land Commissioners had injured the American government's interest with their extreme liberality. Carr's outspoken criticism of allegedly fraudulent land claims won him support among newly arriving American settlers.

Following Missouri's advancement to second-class territorial status in 1812, the voters in St. Louis County elected Carr to the territorial House of Representatives, and he became its first Speaker. He served in that leadership capacity only briefly, but completed two full terms as a member of the house. In 1815 Carr backed the establishment of the territory's second newspaper, the *Western Journal,* but when the short-lived publication failed, he withdrew from journalism and turned his attention to other matters. The territorial legislature named him to serve as a trustee for the St. Louis schools in 1817.

When Missouri governor **Frederick Bates** died in office in 1825, Carr was a candidate to succeed him. In the special election to fill the office, he finished second in a field of four. The victor, **John Miller,** subsequently appointed Carr to the St. Louis Circuit Court where he served from 1826 until 1834. Carr had to withstand an impeachment attempt in 1832. The Missouri House of Representatives formally charged Carr with showing favoritism in his court, inattention and neglect in discharging his duties, and lacking the natural capacity and legal attainments for the office. Carr, however, won an acquittal in a senate trial.

Carr resigned from the court in 1834 and returned to his private practice in St. Louis. He acquired extensive landholdings and also engaged in farming. He died on March 31, 1851, and left his heirs a substantial estate.

WILLIAM E. FOLEY

Carr, William C. Papers. Missouri Historical Society, St. Louis.

Foley, William E. "Territorial Politics in Frontier Missouri, 1804–1820." Ph.D. diss., University of Missouri, 1967.

CARSON, CHRISTOPHER "KIT" HOUSTON (1809–1868)

Born in Madison County, Kentucky, on December 24, 1809, famed frontiersman Christopher "Kit" Carson could trace his ancestry to Scotch-Irish immigrants who settled in Lancaster County, Pennsylvania, during the early eighteenth century. Lindsey Carson married his second wife and Kit's mother, Rebecca Robinson Carson, in 1795. When Kit's birth occurred fourteen years later, thirteen Carsons occupied their three-room log cabin on Tate's Creek. Hearing the tales of cheap land and plentiful game in the "Boon's Lick" area in the West, Lindsey Carson moved his large family to Missouri in 1811.

The area north of the Missouri River (named after **Daniel Boone**'s sons in present-day Howard County) epitomized the rugged American frontier. Frequent Indian attacks kept the settlers in a state of insecurity. After the War of 1812 called Kit's father into the militia, the family spent their first four years living in stockades in Fort Hempstead, Fort Kincaid, and Fort Cooper. Young Kit received little formal education. The threat of Indian attack and his father's death in 1818 further limited educational opportunities, leaving Kit basically illiterate. As he grew, he devoted most of his time to clearing land, farming, hunting, and developing a reputation as an outstanding marksman. Kit's stepfather, Joseph Martin, worried that his stepson might never learn a trade, and persuaded a saddler to apprentice the boy in 1824. Making saddles proved boring, however, so in 1826 Kit disobeyed his parents and followed his older brothers to Bent's Caravan, a wagon train headed west to Santa Fe. His great life's adventure had begun.

Kit's first trip on the Santa Fe Trail became a lesson in frontier survival. The young Missourian became a "cavvy boy" who helped the men running the wagon train. His duties ran the gamut of frontier chores, including caring for the mules, repairing wagons, and hunting for food. Water was scarce. In some regions the hot sun gave way to cold nights. Sickness, rattlesnakes, and Indians also contributed to the uneasy atmosphere.

Indians particularly worried the Carson brothers, who remembered the terrifying attacks upon their family in Missouri. Although the West had been U.S. territory for nearly a quarter century, it still "belonged" to the Plains tribes—the Kansa, Pawnee, Osage, Sioux, and Comanche. Farther west, the Mescalero Apaches and the Navajos fiercely defended their lands against the white man's encroachment. These were some of the most powerful tribes that roamed the region west of the Missouri River. With the exception of a serious injury inflicted by the Blackfeet in 1831, Carson's luck and skill as an Indian fighter kept him from injury during his many years of danger on the frontier.

In his early career, between 1826 and 1833, the young Missourian held numerous jobs, including Santa Fe Trail teamster and Gila River copper miner, but the activities that he enjoyed most were those that entailed hunting, trapping, and scouting. Following several expeditions between Franklin, Missouri, and Santa Fe, New Mexico, Carson moved farther west, joining a Taos, New Mexico, train headed across the Mojave Desert to California's San Joachin Valley in 1829. Taos became Carson's home base during the 1830s when he joined Thomas Fitzpatrick and **Jim Bridger,** trappers who imbued him with a great love for the West.

Not all Indians represented a threat. Kit learned to differentiate between hostile tribes and "friendlies" who greeted the men as they explored new territory. One of the friendlies was a young Arapaho girl named Alice whom Kit married in 1836. The marriage produced Kit's daughter, Adaline, whom he brought back to Missouri in 1842, following Alice's premature death. During this trip Carson became a scout with **John C. Frémont**'s famous western expedition, beginning a new chapter in his already exciting life.

On June 10, 1842, Carson and an Indian scout led the Frémont party on the first stage of a journey designed "to explore the country between the frontiers of Missouri and the South Pass in the Rocky Mountains and on the line of the Kansas and Great Platte Rivers." The trip greatly enhanced Carson's reputation as one of the West's finest scouts. Returning to the "Kawsmouth Region" near Independence, Missouri, Carson decided to trap his way back to the Southwest along the Rocky Mountains until he reached his home in Taos, where he married his second wife, Josefa Jaramillo, on February 6, 1843.

Carson also scouted for Frémont's second and third expeditions (in 1843–1844 and 1845–1846, respectively), and assisted in the "pathfinder's" liberation of California at the outbreak of the Mexican War. In October 1846 he joined Gen. **Stephen Watts Kearny**'s Army of the West that swept through New Mexico and recaptured Los Angeles. In June 1847 President James Polk appointed the western scout as lieutenant in the Mounted Riflemen. Although Frémont's political opponents in Congress later rejected the appointment, they did not seriously weaken Carson's reputation, which, by this time, had reached legendary proportions.

Tired of Indian fighting Carson eventually turned to more sedentary activities, such as farming. During the 1850s, however, new Indian uprisings intervened. In 1853 he left his farm to become the government's agent in charge of the Ute Nation. In this capacity he helped maintain peace between the tribe and the United States Army. At the outbreak of the Civil War, Carson resigned his agency and returned to the military as an officer in the New Mexico Volunteer Infantry.

Navajos and Mescalero Apaches provided the Confederate opposition. Although Kit argued that he could negotiate peace with the two hostile tribes, he received orders to kill "all Indian men of the Mescalero tribe. . . ." While Carson's troop did eliminate a number of warriors in the resulting battles, he was not an "Indian hater," and, despite his orders, spared the lives of five hundred Mescalero men, women, and children whom he transferred to Santa Fe.

White settlers, however, needed protecting, and Kit conducted his final military campaigns against the Kiowa and Comanche in 1864, breaking the power of those two tribes. Carson's spectacular successes resulted in his appointment as a general and commander of Fort Garland in 1866. In 1867 he resigned from the military, and a year later moved his family to Boggsville, Colorado. Suffering from a tumor that lodged in his throat, Carson died on May 23, 1868.

Although Kit Carson called Missouri home for about twenty of his fifty-eight years, he lived in no place long enough to be called a permanent resident after his first trip to Santa Fe at the age of fifteen. An American patriot, he was essentially a citizen of the West. This celebrated American frontiersman really belonged to the mountains, deserts, streams, and valleys of the land that stretched toward the Pacific, far beyond the outer bounds of Missouri that he roamed as a boy.

J. CHRISTOPHER SCHNELL

Burdett, Charles. *Life of Kit Carson: The Great Western Hunter and Guide: Comprising Wild and Romantic Exploits as a Hunter and Trapper in the Rocky Mountains . . . with an Account of Various Government Expeditions to the Far West.* Philadelphia: J. E. Potter, 1862.

Quaife, Milo Milton, ed. *Kit Carson's Autobiography.* Lincoln: University of Nebraska Press, 1966.

CARVER, GEORGE WASHINGTON (1865?–1943)

Historians have been unable to determine the exact date, or even year, of George Washington Carver's birth. Biographer Linda O. McMurry asserts that "it seems likely that he was born in the spring of 1865," and Carver himself often said that he was born "about 1865." Likewise, uncertainty surrounds the identity of Carver's father. When asked about his father, the future scientist usually named a slave on an adjoining farm who had been killed in an accident before George was even born.

Such uncertainty about Carver's birth serves to accentuate the lack of regard a slave society had for the personal value of people whom it refused to regard as anything other than property. What can be said for certain is that he was born near the end of the Civil War on the Newton County farm of Moses and Susan Carver and that he was born to a woman named Mary, then owned by the Carvers. If Carver was in fact born in 1865, he would have been born free, at least technically, since slavery was officially abolished in Missouri on January 11, 1865. When George was but a few months old, he and his mother were kidnapped by one of the many bands of bushwhackers who roamed western Missouri during the Civil War era. Moses Carver hired a neighbor to track down and rescue young George and his mother. The neighbor was partially successful: he recovered the infant slave. The return of George Carver to his master's farm cost Moses Carver one of his finest horses. George Carver never saw his mother again. Throughout his life he often spoke and wrote of the trauma that resulted from having been raised an orphan.

George Carver and his brother Jim were raised by Moses and Susan Carver in postemancipation Missouri. He was a frail, sickly child who, because of his poor health, spent much of his time assisting Susan Carver with domestic chores. While his brother Jim helped Moses Carver take care of the farm, George learned how to cook, mend, do laundry, embroider, and perform numerous similar tasks. Apparently, he was still very young when he developed a fascination for plants, probably as a result of helping Susan Carver take care of the garden.

Susan Carver taught George to read and write, there being no nearby school for blacks. At about the age of eleven, Carver was sent to Neosho to attend a school for blacks conducted by a teacher named Stephen Frost. While in Neosho he boarded with Andrew and Mariah Watkins, a childless black couple. He stayed in Neosho for at least two years until the late 1870s, when his desire for more education and a wanderlust of indeterminate origin drove him to hitch a ride with westward migrating blacks on their way to Kansas.

For the next decade Carver traveled from one midwestern community to another, often using the domestic skills he had learned from Susan Carver and Mariah Watkins to survive. By the late 1880s his travels took him to Winterset, Iowa, where a local white couple, John and Helen Milholland, befriended him and encouraged him to enroll in nearby Simpson College. After a year of studying piano and art at Simpson, Carver transferred to the State Agricultural College at Ames and changed his emphasis of study to agriculture. He earned a bachelor's degree in agriculture from that school in 1894 and served on its faculty while pursuing a graduate degree in agriculture, which he was awarded in 1896.

In that same year, Carver was recruited by Booker T. Washington to join the faculty at Tuskegee Institute in Alabama. Although Carver went to Tuskegee with high hopes, and he remained there until his death in 1943, he was often unhappy and at odds with both the Tuskegee administrators and his fellow workers. Much of the conflict he experienced stemmed from the fact that he had spent his entire life until 1896 outside of the South, whereas his coworkers were all southern born and bred.

Carver's research with peanuts, sweet potatoes, and other foodstuffs gained him regional notoriety. He was credited with making significant efforts to help the South escape its reliance upon the single crop of cotton and with supplementing the meager diets of poor southerners, black and white. National attention came in the wake of his testimony in support of a peanut tariff before the House Ways and Means Committee of Congress in 1921. He testified on behalf of the United Peanut Growers' Association. As biographer Linda McMurry has written, with this testimony he "won a tariff for the peanut industry and national fame for himself."

Over the course of the next two decades, Carver's fame grew, and he became widely known for his experiments. He was also enlisted by white liberals to serve in the cause of improving race relations. Throughout the 1920s and 1930s he traveled across the South speaking to groups of white youths in an effort to promote racial harmony. He did so primarily at the behest of the YMCA and an Atlanta-based group known as the Congress for Interracial Cooperation. Always a deeply religious man, Carver's belief in racial equality stemmed from his conviction that all people were created in God's image and were equal in his sight.

During the mid-1930s more attention was drawn to Carver when he began to offer treatment of peanut-oil massages to victims of infantile paralysis. Word of Carver's treatment spread, and the Tuskegee campus became a Lourdes-like sanctuary for people seeking relief from the effects of polio. Although there is no scientific basis to the claims, many people asserted that they had been "cured" by Carver's treatment.

The Great Depression provided additional opportunity for Carver's fame to grow. By the 1930s, he had gained an international reputation as someone who could make the maximum amount of products from a minimum amount of resources. Even the Soviet Union sought his agricultural expertise during the bleak 1930s, though he declined to leave "his people" in the South.

Over the course of his life, Carver became friends with a great many people, some of them quite rich and famous. One of the relationships he valued most was his friendship with automobile manufacturer Henry Ford. Indeed, in his later years, when he was often quite ill, Carver was frequently visited by Ford who had an elevator installed in the dormitory in which Carver lived so that the aging scientist could go from his room to his laboratory with a minimum amount of difficulty.

George Washington Carver died at Tuskegee Institute on January 5, 1943, after a lengthy illness. He is buried on the Tuskegee campus, not far from the burial site of Booker T. Washington. Barely six months after Carver's death, Congress passed legislation creating the George Washington Carver National Monument on the farm where he was born near Diamond, Missouri. The monument was the first national memorial to an African American. The Senate sponsor of the legislation was **Harry S. Truman.**

GARY R. KREMER

Holt, Rackham. *George Washington Carver.* Garden City, N.Y.: Doubleday, 1943.

Kremer, Gary R., ed. *George Washington Carver: In His Own Words.* Columbia: University of Missouri Press, 1987.

McMurry, Linda O. *George Washington Carver: Scientist and Symbol.* New York: Oxford University Press, 1981.

CATLIN, GEORGE C. (1796–1872)

Catlin is among the earliest artists to paint the Native Americans and the landscape of the Great Plains. His stated ambition was to "rescue" and preserve the appearance, costume, and customs of the Plains Indians, because in his opinion "they are 'doomed' and must perish." The publications and Indian Gallery that Catlin produced from his six years of touring Indian territory from 1830 to 1836 did more to disseminate information about and promote interest in Plains Indian culture than any previous efforts.

George Catlin was born on July 26, 1796, the son of Revolutionary War veteran Putnam Catlin and Polly Catlin. Prior to becoming an artist, Catlin started his career as an attorney. Raised on a Wilkes-Barre, Pennsylvania, farm, he was sent by his parents to a private academy for his education in 1810. Catlin then entered law school in 1817 and passed the Connecticut bar exam the following year. He returned to Montrose, Pennsylvania, to enter legal practice with his older brother. However, the law profession did not inspire Catlin. He claimed to be compelled to follow "another and a stronger passion . . . that for painting."

Distracted during his legal career by his constant sketching of judges, juries, and clients, Catlin had already acquired some facility in draftsmanship. In 1821 the Pennsylvania Academy of Fine Arts accepted four of Catlin's miniatures for its annual exhibition. Three years later the academy accepted him as a full member based upon his work as a miniaturist and portrait painter. Ambitiously seeking further academic accomplishment, in 1826 Catlin moved to New York City where he exhibited and earned membership in the National Academy of Design. His association with the National Academy, however, was short-lived. He resigned after a dispute over the poor hanging of three of his portraits in the annual exhibition of 1827. In fact, Catlin's portraiture did not achieve the technical accomplishment of his peers. William Dunlap, perhaps the first important chronicler of the arts and design in the United States, described Catlin as an "utterly incompetent" portrait painter.

While on a sketching trip in upstate New York in 1826, Catlin executed his first portrait of a Native American, the important Seneca chief Red Jacket. It was about this time that Catlin announced to his colleagues his ambition to record the Indian nations of North America and produce an extensive gallery of Indian portraits to preserve their history. In 1830, against the wishes of his family, Catlin embarked on a westward expedition. Arriving in St. Louis he solicited the advice of Gen. **William Clark** before heading to Fort Leavenworth to begin the ambitious project for which he would spend the next six years traveling through the West drawing, painting, and gathering artifacts. According to his *Letters and Notes,* Catlin visited forty-eight tribes and painted 310 portraits and more than 200 genre subjects, recording Native chiefs and the rituals of their people, some of which could not be subsequently witnessed by Euramericans. In the summer of 1832 he stayed at Fort Clark, close to the Mandan village where the Mandan chief Four Bears received the artist as a great medicine man because of the magic of his paintings. Four Bears entertained Catlin, related the lengthy history of his people, and introduced him to the O-Kee-pa, the Mandan torture ceremony. Catlin's images of the self-mutilation and ritual dance of the O-Kee-pa are the earliest images by whites to record this Indian rite.

Catlin professed that he wished to preserve the image of the ideal "primitive" man through his portraits, such as that of Keokuk on horseback. The romantic conception of the uncivilized "savage" developed from the eighteenth-century Enlightenment philosophy of the natural man as a more pure human, in closer contact with nature, from whom "civilized" men could learn about the origins of humanity. Yet, based upon his experiences with Native Americans, Catlin objected to the term "savage, as expressive of the most ferocious, cruel, and murderous character that can be described," while he found that the Native American has "been endowed by his maker with all the humane and noble traits that inhabit the heart of a tame man." Ironically, Catlin's Indian Gallery did perpetuate this stereotype of Native Americans and exploited their culture as a theatrical curiosity for Anglo-Americans and Europeans. Furthermore, Catlin proved quite the promoter and was prone to exaggerate Native life and customs through his words and paintings, leading one contemporary to accuse Catlin of "a great deal of humbug."

In the fall of 1837 Catlin opened his traveling Indian Gallery in New York. With this extensive body of paintings Catlin attempted to persuade Congress to acquire the complete set as a historical record of the Plains Indian nations. However, after years of futile efforts he abandoned hopes to make his work part of the nation's archives. Recognizing the European fascination with exotic western Americana, Catlin traveled to London in 1840 where his gallery was very popular. He added to his gallery a live production of Ojibwa Indians in a stage routine that prefigured the theatrical "Wild West Shows" later in the century. While in London he published his *Letters and Notes on the Manners, Customs, and Conditions of North American Indians* and followed with a set of twenty-five lithographs titled *North American Indian Portfolio.* Catlin moved his gallery and Indian show to Paris in 1845 where he experienced similar success and received the patronage of King Louis Philippe, who commissioned fifteen copies of his Indian Gallery. Unfortunately, Catlin's Paris days were difficult. His wife died, and he was forced by the 1848 rebellions to flee the city. Despite his considerable success in Europe, Catlin had not managed his money well and was sentenced to a debtors' prison in 1852. However, his debts were absolved through the benevolence of American Joseph Harrison, who bought the collection.

Seeking to revive his reputation and to create a new body of work, Catlin embarked on a series of three trips to South America between 1853 and 1860 to produce a historical record of Indian people there, but the works did not receive the popular response of his earlier work. Following his South American ventures he moved to Brussels in 1860 where he remained until 1870, when he returned to the United States. At the invitation of Joseph Henry, secretary and director of the Smithsonian Institution, Catlin installed his gallery at the Smithsonian where he lived in a small tower apartment. Quite ill, Catlin returned to Jersey City, New Jersey, where he died on December 12, 1872. Catlin was a forgotten man at his death. It was not until 1879 that the heirs of Joseph Harrison donated Catlin's Indian Gallery to the Smithsonian Institution in realization of the artist's lifelong ambition.

JOSEPH D. KETNER

Catlin, George. Archives. Gilcrease Museum, Tulsa.
———. Indian Gallery. National Museum of American Art, Smithsonian Institution, Washington, D.C.
———. *Letters and Notes on the Manners, Customs, and Conditions of North American Indians.* 1841. Reprint, New York: Dover, 1973.
Troccoli, Joan Carpenter. *First Artist of the West: George Catlin Paintings and Watercolors.* Tulsa: Gilcrease Museum, 1993.
Truettner, William G. *The Natural Man Observed: A Study of Catlin's Indian Gallery.* Washington, D.C.: Smithsonian Institution Press, 1979.

CAULFIELD, HENRY STEWART (1873–1966)

Congressman and governor of Missouri from 1929 to 1933, Henry S. Caulfield was born on December 9, 1873, in St. Louis, Missouri. He attended St. Charles College and Washington University, graduating from the latter with an LL.B. degree in 1895. He was admitted to the Missouri bar the same year. In 1902 Caulfield married Fannie Alice Delano of Cuba, Missouri, and their family came to include three daughters and a son.

Caulfield's successful law practice assisted his nomination and election on the Republican ticket in 1906 to the Sixtieth Congress from the Eleventh District. He did not seek renomination at the end of his term and returned to St. Louis where he combined the practice of law and public service. In succession Caulfield served as excise commissioner of St. Louis (1909–1910), judge of the St. Louis Court of Appeals (1910–1912), member of the St. Louis Public Library Board (1918–1921), city counselor (1921–1922), and member and chair of the Board of Freeholders (1925–1926).

In 1928 Caulfield won the Republican nomination for governor of Missouri and swept to victory over his Democratic opponent, Francis M. Wilson, in the national Republican landslide of that year. Caulfield's administration began with bright promise. He enjoyed the backing of his party on a joint ballot of the house and senate, and the state's economy shared in the seemingly durable national prosperity of the twenties. He drew upon the Lincoln heritage of the Republican Party in his inaugural address of January 1929, candidly acknowledging that the state had failed to provide its black citizens equal educational opportunities. He noted that four thousand black children in several Missouri counties had been denied admission to white schools, and were also unserved by black schools. He criticized the exclusion of blacks from the University of Missouri and the lack of financing for Lincoln University that kept the black school a university in name only. As a first step in addressing and correcting these and other needs, he called for a survey of the entire state government and the physical condition of the state's institutions.

The "State Survey Report," issued by a blue-ribbon commission of prominent citizens in November 1929, revealed that Missouri was failing to attain a proper standard in many areas due to its failure to tax the wealth of its taxpayers. Accordingly, the legislature increased the state income tax from 1 to 2 percent in 1931 as a step toward better financing of the state's various programs.

Unfortunately, the problems caused by the Great Depression of the 1930s and a severe drought at the beginning of the decade forced the Caulfield administration to reorder its priorities as general tax revenues declined and demands for state services increased. The legislature passed the School Law of 1931 to make underfinanced school districts eligible for state aid achieve a limited standard, but in practice this support lengthened the life of one-room schools and retarded the improvement of education that many Missourians believed would result from school consolidation. Highway safety, however, received a major boost in 1931 when the legislature created the State Highway Patrol to police the state's extensive system of highways. With Caulfield's backing, the legislature authorized funds for direct relief to the needy and made plans for an old-age pension program. Most of the funds for direct assistance, however, came from the federal government through the relief activities of the Reconstruction Finance Corporation. Caulfield, following the lead of President Herbert Hoover, rejected a still larger role for the state and federal government in combating the Great Depression. The governor's vigorous support of Hoover led to his choice as the keynote speaker at the 1932 Republican National Convention. "If you are not loyal to Hoover," he told the convention audience, "don't call yourself Republicans."

When his term as governor ended in January 1933, Caulfield returned to St. Louis for another three decades of public service. He served on the St. Louis Board of Election Commissioners from February 1937 until May 1938 when he announced his candidacy for the United States Senate. He won the nomination of his party, but was decisively defeated by the Democratic incumbent, **Bennett Champ Clark.** His compassionate nature and administrative abilities led to his appointment as director of public welfare of St. Louis from 1941 to 1949. He resumed the practice of law after leaving office and accepted one more public service assignment by serving on the State Reorganization Commission of Missouri in 1953, charged with rewriting the antiquated operations of the state government that had been initially addressed by the "State Survey Report" of Caulfield's gubernatorial term.

Caulfield died at the age of ninety-two on May 11, 1966, and was buried in Oak Grove Cemetery in St. Louis. As a Lincoln Republican, he had lived to see the desegregation of the state's system of public education and the onset of an era of civil rights.

FRANKLIN D. MITCHELL

Biographical Directory of the American Congress, 1774–1971. S.v. "Caulfield, Henry Stewart." Washington, D.C.: U.S. Government Printing Office, 1971.

Mitchell, Franklin D. *Embattled Democracy: Missouri Democratic Politics, 1919–1932.* Columbia: University of Missouri Press, 1968.

Shoemaker, Floyd Calvin. *Missouri and Missourians: Land of Contrasts and People of Achievements.* Vol. 3. Chicago: Lewis Publishing, 1943.

CELIA (?–1855)

Celia, the property of Robert Newsom, in 1855 stood trial in Fulton, Missouri, for the murder of her master, a prosperous Callaway County farmer. The events that led to her arrest, her trial, and her ultimate fate provide a fascinating case study of the significance of gender in the slaveholding South and the manner in which the southern legal system was manipulated to ensure the slaveholder's power over his human chattel while creating the illusion of a society that extended the protection of the law to it slaves.

Purchased a year after the death of his wife in 1849, Celia served as Robert Newsom's concubine for five years, during which time she bore him two children. She lived in a brick cabin that Newsom built for her behind the farmhouse that he shared with two adult daughters, one of whom had two children of her own. By 1850 Newsom's two sons had established their own farms near that of their father. Sometime in 1854 Celia began a relationship with George, another of Newsom's slaves. Upon Celia's becoming pregnant for a third time, George demanded that she cease to have sexual relations with their master. Celia appealed to the Newsom women to prevent their father from sexually abusing her. The daughters, however, were in no position to control the actions of their father, who continued to regard sexual relations with Celia as his privilege.

Although Celia warned her master that she would use force to prevent further sexual exploitation, on a June night in 1855 Newsom demanded sex. She responded by striking him with a club. Then, frightened that an angered Newsom would kill her, she beat him to death and disposed of his body by burning it in her fireplace. The family's search for the missing father led George, at first accused of harming Newsom, to implicate Celia in his disappearance. Under threat to her children, Celia confessed and was arrested and tried. Missouri law assigned her public council, led by John Jameson, a noted attorney and Democratic politician who had served as Speaker of the Missouri State House and three terms in the United States House of Representatives. To aid Jameson, who was renowned as a jury advocate rather than as a legal scholar, two young lawyers from well-established Callaway County families, Isaac M. Boulware and Nathan Chapman Kouns, were also assigned to Celia's defense.

Jameson based his defense on the premise that under Missouri law Celia possessed the same right to use deadly force to defend her honor as did white women. This defense not only recognized the crime of rape against slave women, something not acknowledged by the legal system of any antebellum southern state, but also threatened a slaveholder's control over the reproductive capabilities of female slaves.

For precisely these reasons it was disallowed by the presiding judge, who agreed with the prosecution's traditional contention that a female slave had no right to use deadly force to reject her master's sexual demands. A jury of local farmers convicted her, and Celia was sentenced to hang. Her defense attorneys immediately appealed the verdict, only to have the presiding judge refuse to allow a stay of execution for the appeal to be heard. After what appears to have been an escape arranged to ensure that Celia's appeal would be heard, she evidently hid in the woods near the Newsom farm in an effort to see her children. While there she was recaptured by Harry Newsom, Robert's oldest son, and returned to jail, but only after her original execution date had passed. The Missouri Supreme Court rejected her attorneys' appeal for a new trial. On December 23, 1855, Celia was hanged in Fulton.

MELTON A. MCLAURIN

McLaurin, Melton A. *Celia: A Slave.* Athens: University of Georgia Press, 1991.

Williamson, Hugh P. "Document: The State of Missouri against Celia, a Slave." *Midwest Journal* 8 (spring/fall 1956): 408–20.

CERVANTES, ALFONSO J. (1920–1983)

A prominent businessman and two-term mayor of St. Louis, Alfonso J. Cervantes dedicated much of his life to the economic and social improvement of the city. His most notable contributions to Missouri include the renovation of the riverfront and downtown St. Louis and his work for the improvement of social justice and human rights.

Born on August 27, 1920, to second-generation Spanish immigrants, Cervantes grew up in an impoverished neighborhood on the south side of St. Louis. With his father away from home during much of the Great Depression and his mother selling homemade mayonnaise and angel-food cakes to support the family, Cervantes began exploring means of earning his own money. As a young child, he charged the neighborhood kids a nickel admission into the miniature golf course he had created in his backyard. He also sold the *Saturday Evening Post* and *Ladies' Home Journal.*

Cervantes attended St. Louis University High School and Hadley Vocational School before dropping out and moving to California at age fifteen. He performed odd jobs in Hollywood before creating the Cervantes Rhumba Club, earning a comfortable living organizing rhumba lessons and holding dance contests. He remained in California until 1941, when he enlisted in the merchant marine and during World War II served as a radio officer on supply ships.

After the war Cervantes returned to St. Louis and began taking night classes at St. Louis University. He also opened an insurance business and shortly thereafter acquired part of a taxicab company whose owner could not afford to pay his insurance premium. Cervantes continued to prosper in the business community. Beginning in 1949 he served on the Board of Aldermen and was its president for four years. At the time of his election as mayor, he presided as chief executive of Group Underwriter Mutual Insurance Company and held controlling interest in ten other St. Louis corporations.

When Cervantes took the office of mayor of St. Louis on April 20, 1965, his agenda included an attack on racial discrimination, an elevation of the crime-control effort, and a physical and economic rejuvenation of the city. His interest in racial equality began during his service on the Board of Aldermen. Initially, he voted against the Public Accommodation Bill that required that the city's hotels, restaurants, and bars to be open to all races. By the time the bill reached the board for a second time, Cervantes's brother, the Reverend Lucius Cervantes, had convinced him of the atrocity of segregation, and Cervantes supported the bill. As one of his first achievements as mayor, he reorganized the Council on Human Rights to better deal with such issues as discrimination, the disadvantaged, and minority unemployment. Also, during the uproar following the assassination of Martin Luther King Jr., Cervantes worked alongside black leaders to avoid riots in St. Louis.

In 1969 Mayor Cervantes united St. Louis citizens and government officials on the Commission on Crime and Law Enforcement to lead an offensive against criminal elements in the city. Foot patrols and mounted police units patrolled city parks, the downtown area, and the riverfront. Ironically, in the midst of his efforts to stop criminal activity in St. Louis, an article in *Life* accused Cervantes of having business and personal associations with organized crime figures. The article, written by a former St. Louis journalist, claimed that attorney Morris Schenker, Cervantes's choice to head the newly formed Commission on Crime and Law Enforcement, provided substantial legal assistance to members of the Mafia in the United States. The article also pointed out that Anthony Sansone, another close colleague of Cervantes and son-in-law of Syrian Mafia leader Jimmy Michaels, ran gambling and bookie operations in south St. Louis. Cervantes responded to the accusations by requesting a full investigation by the St. Louis Board of Police Commissioners, the Task Force on Organized Crime and Racketeering in St. Louis, and the U.S. district attorney for the eastern district of Missouri. Cervantes sued *Life* for $12 million for libel. (The libel suit, however, went nowhere. Although the reporter's charges could not be substantiated, it could also not be proved that his attack on Cervantes, a public figure, had been maliciously inspired.)

In possibly his most enthusiastic venture, Cervantes worked to renovate the city and promote tourist activity in St. Louis. He encouraged local businessmen to invest in bringing to St. Louis two exhibits from the New York World's Fair for the purpose of attracting tourists. The Spanish Pavilion, refurbished to house a restaurant and theater, closed after only a year due to financial problems. The *Santa Maria* came loose from its berth on the Mississippi during a storm and sank. Cervantes did succeed in raising $25 million in bonds to build the Gateway Convention Center, projected to bring in $85 million annually to St. Louis. In 1978 Mayor James F. Conway suggested renaming the building the Alfonso J. Cervantes Convention and Exhibition Center to honor the former mayor's achievements, lending credence to supporting Cervantes's own assessment: "I like to believe I have turned the city around. I think I have sold St. Louis on itself."

After leaving the mayor's office, Cervantes engaged in a variety of business activities. He died on June 24, 1983, from cancer at the age of sixty-two.

ERIKA K. NELSON

Cervantes, Alfonso J. *Mr. Mayor.* Los Angeles: Nash Publishing, 1974.
———. Papers. 1920–1983. Western Historical Manuscripts Collection, Columbia.
St. Louis Post-Dispatch, June 24, 1983–1990.
Walsh, Denny. "Cervantes, Alfonso." *Life* 68:20 (May 29, 1970): 24–31.
Who's Who in American Politics. 5th ed. New York: R. R. Bowker, 1975.

CHAMBERS, JORDAN WEBSTER (1898–1962)

Jordan Webster Chambers Jr., born on December 24, 1898, in Nashville, Tennessee, was an African American politician. He was the son of Jordan Webster and Alice E. Chambers, and he had three sisters. He attended Sumner High School in St. Louis. He and his wife, Lenore Chambers, married when he was eighteen; they had no children.

Chambers became involved in Republican Party politics in the 1920s. Like most blacks he voted Republican out of loyalty to Abraham Lincoln. After Roosevelt's election in 1932 Chambers realized that the large black vote in St. Louis represented political power. He took demands of patronage jobs for African Americans to the Republicans. They only laughed. He took similar demands to the Democratic machine in St. Louis, and they promised help.

Chambers organized the Cooperative Civic Association, which later became the Nineteenth Ward Democratic Organization. In 1933 Chambers's organization helped elect Bernard Dickmann as the first Democratic mayor of St. Louis in twenty-four years. As soon as he was elected, Dickmann began helping the black community by building Homer G. Phillips Hospital and by hiring African Americans for better jobs at city hall.

Adam Clayton Powell, a U.S. congressman from New York, referred to Chambers as a political genius. Chambers's organizational leadership skills were extraordinary. In his ward he organized not only precinct captains but also captains for every block. Block captains knew everyone on their blocks and how they voted. When a new family moved in, the block captain called on them to ask about their politics and tell them how to register to vote. The block captain also knew who in his block needed a job, who needed help to go to school, and who needed welfare, food, or coal. Chambers and his Nineteenth Ward Democratic Organization took care of those needs, no matter what party the household supported.

Chambers organized the Young Democratic Club. Its members helped the Nineteenth Ward Democratic Organization report votes and drive people to the polls. By promoting new leaders within his organization, Chambers kept potential leaders loyal and the organization strong.

Chambers owned the Peoples Undertaking Company in St. Louis. He and his wife lived upstairs, and his political headquarters was next door. In 1936 he was elected constable and Democratic committeeman of the Nineteenth Ward, the first black Democratic committeeman in St. Louis. Chambers was credited with getting out the black vote for **Harry S. Truman** in several close elections.

Jordan "Pops" Chambers sported a large white hat and an ever present cigar. Blacks called him the Negro mayor of St. Louis. He influenced black voters in neighborhoods outside his ward, and advised politicians who had black constituents all over St. Louis. He traveled around the state, often to Kansas City, meeting with top officials, and was usually the only black present. Chambers refused to beg for favors. He simply stated the case for what he believed blacks deserved. He was able to get jobs for African Americans in places they had never worked before and political posts for which they had never been considered.

A typical example of his constant crusade for better jobs occurred when Mayor Joseph Darst called and offered Chambers ten patronage jobs at city hall. Chambers was not satisfied because the job openings were for porters. He told Darst to divide those jobs between all the wards, and, when good jobs became available, divide those among all wards, too. He said,

"My people are not all porters." Chambers's campaign for better jobs for blacks was good for African Americans all over the city, because politicians in other wards had to keep up with the progressive integration of jobs in order to please their black constituents.

Chambers helped integrate the police force in the late 1940s when H. Sam Priest was president of the St. Louis Police Board. Next Chambers pushed for new beats for blacks, then he wanted to integrate the beats, and finally he wanted black sergeants in uniforms riding in squad cars. Chambers and Priest worked together to hire blacks for important office jobs at police headquarters and to promote a black to the rank of lieutenant.

Chambers was instrumental in getting blacks appointed as circuit judges, members of the Human Relations Council, and members of the St. Louis Housing Authority. He pushed for low-income housing projects and housing for senior citizens in his ward.

Beginning in the early 1940s Chambers owned and operated the Club Riviera in St. Louis. For more than fifteen years the nightclub was one of the hottest spots in the country. Movie stars and politicians came, the audience was always integrated, and the tips were handsome. It was a large club filled with linen-covered tables and had a balcony with tables. The far end featured a stage for the orchestra and a large dance floor. There were two shows nightly and three on Sundays. Customers paid admission and brought their own liquor while the club sold setups, sodas, and food. Chambers booked performers at the peak of their careers. Popular entertainers at the Riviera included George Shearing, Cab Calloway, Duke Ellington, Louis Armstrong, **William "Count" Basie,** Frankie Lane, Nat King Cole, Louis Jordan, Cozy Cole, Earl Hines, Lionel Hampton, Dinah Washington, and Erskine Hawkins. In 1952 **Josephine Baker** performed at the Club Riviera after her big homecoming show at Kiel Auditorium to benefit the St. Louis School District and to promote integration.

Chambers remained active in politics and civil rights and continued to operate his nightclub for the remainder of his life. Each spring he sponsored special graduation nights at the Club Riviera, one for graduates of Sumner High School and their parents, and one for graduates of Vashon High School and their parents. During the summer college students visited the club, discussing politics and civil rights with Chambers into the wee hours of the morning.

Chambers died on August 11, 1962, right after a primary election. More than two thousand people attended his funeral, many of them politicians. Gov. **John Montgomery Dalton** gave the eulogy, while Atty. Gen. Tom Eagleton; H. Sam Priest, president of the Board of Police Commissioners; and J. Wesley McAfee, president of Union Electric Company attended. President John F. Kennedy and Vice President Lyndon B. Johnson sent telegrams of condolence.

ANN MORRIS

Calloway, Ernest. Papers. Western Historical Manuscripts Collection, St. Louis.

Farmer, Oscar. Oral History Interview, 1994. Western Historical Manuscripts Collection, St. Louis.

St. Louis Argus, August 17, 1962.

Welek, Mary. "Jordan Chambers: Black Politician and Boss." *Journal of Negro History* 57 (October 1972): 352–69.

CHAPMAN, CARL HALEY (1915–1987)

Carl Haley Chapman has appropriately been called the dean of Missouri archaeology, a title that addresses both his knowledge of the prehistory of the state and his tenure in carrying out studies of that prehistory. For more than four decades, Chapman and his students and colleagues at the University of Missouri surveyed thousands of acres for signs of prehistoric remains, excavated dozens of sites, and organized a loosely knit group of amateurs with an interest in archaeology into a coordinated workforce of sizable proportion. Over the course of his career, Chapman either wrote or helped write several books and monographs and well over a hundred articles on Missouri prehistory. Without doubt his most cited work is *The Archaeology of Missouri,* a two-volume set. The volumes represent the knowledge of Missouri prehistory as held by an individual who had seen more artifacts from the state than anyone else and thus was able to make specific correlations between objects found at widely separated locales.

Chapman was born in Steelville, in Crawford County, Missouri, on May 29, 1915. He apparently developed an interest in archaeology at an early age and soon began conducting informal surveys for archaeology sites around his home county. His actions caught the eye of Jesse Wrench, a professor of history at the University of Missouri, who loaned Chapman the money to attend the university. There were no formal courses in archaeology, though Wrench and others brought visitors in to supplement courses in sociology and history. Chapman graduated in 1939 and the following year was appointed the first director of American archaeology at the university. In 1941 he took a leave from his position to attend graduate school at the University of New Mexico. There he met and married Eleanor Finley. After Pearl Harbor was bombed in 1941, Chapman enlisted in the air force, becoming a bombardier, and was eventually captured and held in a German prison camp.

Following the war Chapman returned to the University of New Mexico, receiving his master's degree in 1946, the same year he took a position at the University of Missouri as assistant professor of sociology and anthropology and director of American archaeology. In 1949 he took a leave of absence to complete course work at the University of Michigan toward a doctorate in anthropology. He received the degree in 1959, submitting a dissertation titled "The Origin of the Osage Indian Tribe: An Ethnographical, Historical and Archaeological Study."

One of Chapman's great achievements was lobbying Congress to pass legislation aimed at increasing the funding for the examination of archaeological resources before they were destroyed by federal projects such as reservoir impoundment and road construction. The United States had long had legislation that provided protection for archaeological sites, but most of it, beginning with the Antiquities Act of 1906, applied to only a few sites rather than to all sites on federal lands. With the assistance of Charles R. McGeimsey of the University of Arkansas, Chapman in 1969 began an almost nonstop lobbying effort, in the process persuading the Society for American Archaeology—the largest professional archaeological organization in the United States—to join the effort, which resulted in a massive outpouring of support. A draft bill was jointly sponsored by Sen. Frank Moss of Idaho and Cong. Charles E. Bennett of Florida in 1969 and was signed into law in 1974. The final legislation was titled the Archaeological and Historic Preservation Act of 1974, though it has always been known simply as the Moss-Bennett Act.

In 1975 the Society for American Archaeology presented Chapman its Distinguished Service Award for his lobbying efforts, and in 1979 he was elected president of the newly formed Society of Professional Archaeologists, an organization that he helped form as a way to certify that archaeologists were competent to carry out federally funded projects. In 1984 the University of Missouri–Columbia recognized Chapman for his lifetime accomplishments by bestowing on him the Thomas Jefferson Award, signifying a lifelong commitment to the principles of the former president. Carl Chapman and Eleanor Chapman were killed on the evening of February 18, 1987, in an automobile accident near Kissimmee, Florida, leaving two sons, Richard and Stephen.

Michael J. O'Brien

Obituary. *Missouri Historical Review* 81 (July 1987): 512.

CHARLESS, JOSEPH (1772–1834)

Joseph Charless, the first printer in St. Louis and father of journalism west of the Mississippi River, witnessed the transformation of St. Louis from a rude frontier village to a cosmopolitan metropolis and business center. Charless was born in the village of Killucan in County Westmeath, Ireland, on July 16, 1772, the only child of Edward and Ann Chapman Charles. Joseph, who added an extra *s* to his name after he arrived in America to give clue to its proper bisyllabic Irish pronunciation, had worked as a printer in Dublin following an apprenticeship at the press of William Kidd in Mullingar.

Eighteenth-century Ireland was a troubled place, and problems with governmental censorship may have caused Charless to flee his native land in 1795 and travel to the United States in search of more promising business opportunities and greater freedom. Charless settled in Pennsylvania where he opened a bookstore, established a press, and began publishing the *Mifflin Gazette* in Lewistown. He next worked with his countryman Mathew Carey, a successful Philadelphia printer and publisher, who befriended many Irish expatriates. Charless began printing, selling, and distributing books in frontier towns in the Ohio Valley in association with Carey. He traveled from settlement to settlement selling religious books such as the quarto-size Rheims-Douay version of the Bible, which he had designed and printed in Philadelphia for Carey, along with an assortment of spellers, textbooks, children's books, and works of history.

In Lexington, Kentucky, Charless briefly published the *Independent Gazeteer* in 1803, and in 1807 he began printing the *Louisville Gazette*. While in Kentucky he produced numerous titles for himself and for others, the most successful being *Charless's Kentucky, Tennessee, and Ohio Gazeteer*, which went through four numbers before ceasing publication. Under a contract for the western territories, he also printed and distributed Noah Webster's famed "blue back" *Spelling Book*. In 1808 he moved to St. Louis where he became the city's first printer. The Ramage hand-printing press and several fonts of type he took with him were the first to reach the capital of the Louisiana Territory.

Many of the newly arriving Anglo-Americans who moved west of the Mississippi following the Louisiana Purchase considered the printing press an indispensable tool for building a new democratic order. As early as 1805 territorial governor **James Wilkinson** had decried the lack of a press in St. Louis, and three years later his successor **Meriwether Lewis** subsidized Charless's relocation to Missouri with a contract to print the territorial laws and official documents. The publication of the first issue of the *Missouri Gazette* on July 12, 1808, marked the beginning of printing in Missouri. Charless sensed that it was a historic moment, noting in the *Gazette*'s prospectus, "It is evident that in every country where the rays of the press are not clouded by despotic power, that the people have arrived to the highest grade of civilization." The *Missouri Gazette,* also known at various times as the *Louisiana Gazette,* served subscribers in St. Louis and eventually in communities as far-flung as Ste. Genevieve and Potosi in Missouri and Cahokia and Wood River in Illinois. Between 1808 and 1815 the *Gazette* was the sole printing establishment in St. Louis, and Charless truly was the "printer to the territory." For a brief time after his arrival in St. Louis, he had continued to publish the *Louisville Gazette,* but in 1809 he closed his Kentucky office in order to devote his full attention to his operations in Missouri.

Charless was responsible for other printing firsts in the Missouri Territory. In 1809 the new territorial printer published **Frederick Bates**'s compilation of *The Laws of the Territory of Louisiana, Comprising All Those which Are Now Actually in Force Within the Same,* the first book-length work published west of the Mississippi and probably the first Missouri publication bound between hardcovers. He had previously printed Bates's "Oration Delivered before the Saint Louis Lodge, No. 111. At the Town of Saint Louis in the Territory of Louisiana, Wednesday, the 9th Day of November, 1808," a short pamphlet much less imposing than its title. In 1812 Charless printed the St. Louis Missouri Fur Company's "Articles of Association," a broadside historic in the annals of the American fur trade. Six years later he published Missouri's first almanac, *Charless' Missouri and Illinois Almanac.*

In the *Gazette,* Charless occasionally included notices and other documents in French for the benefit of St. Louis's large Creole populace. He opened his columns to local "correspondents" and community leaders, published official documents and excerpts from eastern newspapers, and offered his readers selections from western travel narratives and poetry. The *Missouri Gazette* was a cultural linchpin that documented many aspects of territorial life.

Being a frontier editor was not without peril. On more than one occasion, the fiery, uncompromising Irishman discovered that his opinions could endanger both life and livelihood. His early experiences in Ireland prepared him for such occupational hazards. In St. Louis local toughs and critics unhappy with his stands on issues threatened him physically and pelted his house with brickbats. Charless ardently defended his views in an age when frontier folk sometimes held their emotions on their sleeves and occasionally preferred to resolve differences with duels and brawls rather than reasoned discourse. He had plenty of critics, including **Thomas Hart Benton,** who for a time edited the rival *St. Louis Enquirer,* established in 1818.

Having fled Ireland to escape oppression, Charless refused to condone what he considered injustices. He adopted the unpopular stance of advocating restrictions on the spread of slavery during the Missouri statehood crisis. He editorialized against what he considered elitist and aristocratic pretensions and routinely criticized the powerful St. Louis clique that he labeled the "Little Junto." After Benton killed Charless's friend **Charles Lucas** in a duel, he used the *Gazette*'s columns to condemn both the perpetrator and the practice. He also questioned the validity of Spanish land concessions in Louisiana, much to the consternation of many of St. Louis's largest land claimants.

The controversies that continually seemed to engulf him prompted Charless to sell his profitable enterprise to James C. Cummins in 1820. Cummins later resold the *Gazette,* renamed the *Missouri Republican,* to Charless's eldest son, Edward, who continued to publish the newspaper founded by his father. Missouri's first newspaper remained in existence under various names and publishers until it closed in 1921, thus making it one of the longest-running major daily newspapers in U.S. history.

Following his retirement from publishing in 1820, Joseph Charless remained active. He was a strong supporter of early St. Louis cultural institutions. A lover of books, Charless established a reading room adjacent to the *Gazette*'s offices, and he also worked to create a public library. To help make ends meet, he also operated a livery stable, a boardinghouse, a tavern, and an apothecary. Even those who disagreed with his views respected his entrepreneurial successes. When he died in St. Louis on July 28, 1834, Charless could claim an eventful life and distinguished career that had helped bring the gift of the printed word to St. Louis, which soon became a major nineteenth-century printing center. His publications encouraged public debate in the frontier territory, educated and entertained readers hungry for newspapers and books, and contributed handsomely to the historical memory of St. Louis's early days.

JOHN NEAL HOOVER

Kaser, David. *A Directory of the St. Louis Book and Printing Trades to 1850.* New York: New York Public Library, 1961.

———. *Joseph Charless, Printer in the Western Country.* Philadelphia: University of Pennsylvania Press, 1963.

McMurtrie, Douglas C. *The Early Career of Joseph Charless: The First Printer in Missouri.* Columbia: n.p., 1932.

———. *Early Missouri Book and Pamphlet Imprints, 1808–1830.* Chicago: n.p., 1937.

CHARLESS, JOSEPH, JR. (1804–1859)

Joseph Charless Jr. was a Missourian with big family shoes to fill. His father, **Joseph Charless,** an indomitable Irishman, had infused the family with a sense of community pride and spirit that carried on from generation to generation. Young Joseph was born on January 17, 1804, shortly before Joseph Sr. struck out for the wilds of Missouri. No doubt the son had been told the tales many times of his father's printing press that, when it arrived safely in St. Louis in 1808, became the first of its kind west of the Mississippi River.

In his formative years Charless was an avid worker, reader, and printer, working under the shadow of his father at the *Missouri Gazette.* Although the work was rewarding, it was mutually agreed that the boy should have the opportunity to obtain a formal education. Thus, he returned to the town of his birth, Lexington, Kentucky, to study at Transylvania University. Upon graduation he studied law under the tutelage of a prominent member of the St. Louis bar, Francis Spalding. This mentorship proved helpful as Charless returned to his alma mater and obtained a law degree.

Upon his return to St. Louis, Charless's professional goals became somewhat clouded when his father sold the *Missouri Gazette* in 1820 to James Cummins. Two years later, however, Charless again combined the practice of law with the power of the press when he repurchased the paper from Cummins. Nevertheless, the next few years were not personally rewarding, and it was at this juncture of his life that he finally decided to end his association with the printing business.

By 1828, now divorced from the newspaper profession, both Charlesses ventured into wholesale drugs. This, along with other business undertakings, proved highly remunerative. Soon Charless Jr. had established a reputation among St. Louisans for his business acumen. Even the death of his father in 1834 did not derail his worldly pursuits. Throughout this decade and the next he continued to amass a sizable fortune. By the 1840s Charless had diversified his holdings by branching out into banking and commerce. He was first appointed president of the State Bank of Missouri and later held the same title for the Mechanics' Bank of St. Louis. He was also named to the board of directors of the Pacific Railroad Company.

Although philosophically aligned with the Whig Party, Charless tried to remain above political and factional strife. Reminiscent of his father's sense of noblesse oblige, his public activities revolved mainly around municipal reform fund-raisers for charities, and aid to poorhouses, hospitals, and education. His first active involvement in this latter field of endeavor occurred when he became a director of the St. Louis public schools.

Charless was also intimately involved in the history of higher education in Missouri. In the decade of the 1850s, for example, more than twenty colleges were granted charters in the state. Some of these, such as Washington University, evolved into secular liberal-arts schools to which Charless generously contributed. Other institutions of higher learning were affiliated with religious denominations, and some were in fact seminaries. Most of the Protestant church leaders believed that it was necessary to disperse their schools throughout various parts of the state. The Presbyterian Church, of which Charless was a member, was no exception. The family had been intimately involved in religious affairs since his mother's early days when she, along with eight others, founded the first Presbyterian church in Missouri. The Presbyterians, no doubt with Charless's encouragement, sought a suitable location for a new college. After some investigation and financial enticement, the church leaders selected the town of Fulton. In 1853 a charter was obtained and a cornerstone laid for Westminster College.

Charless, however, did not live to see all his dreams of higher education fulfilled. His tragedy came at the hand of Joseph W. Thorton. The latter, an employee of a bank of which Charless served as director, was charged with fiduciary irregularities, and Charless's testimony helped convict him. Thorton sought revenge. On June 3, 1859, as Charless was organizing a new endowment drive for Westminster, his assailant shot him on Market Street in St. Louis. The public outcry over the murder nearly led to a public lynching. Only military intervention postponed Thorton's fate. The next day Charless expired, but not before he forgave Thorton his deed. He was buried in Bellefontaine Cemetery. Although his murderer pleaded not guilty by reason of insanity, he was hanged later the same year.

DICK STEWARD

Conard, Howard L., ed. *Encyclopedia of the History of Missouri.* New York: Southern History, 1901.

Hyde, William, and Howard L. Conard, eds. *Encyclopedia of the History of St. Louis.* New York: Southern History, 1899.

Scharf, J. Thomas. *History of St. Louis City and County: From Earliest Periods to the Present Day.* Vol. 2. Philadelphia: Everts, 1883.

Stevens, Walter B. *Centennial History of Missouri.* Vol. 2. Chicago: S. J. Clarke, 1921.

———. *Missouri: The Center State, 1821–1915.* Vols. 1 and 2. Chicago: S. J. Clarke, 1915.

CHOPIN, KATE (1850–1904)

Kate Chopin began and ended her life in St. Louis, with an interlude as a young wife and mother in New Orleans and rural Louisiana. Her stories of Creole life in Natchitoches Parish, Louisiana, established her as a talented local-color writer in the southern tradition. Some of her lesser-known stories explored the complexities of the emerging urban culture of the late nineteenth century. *The Awakening,* her second novel, won her a place in history, both as a writer and as a critic of women's roles in the family and the community. Her early life and her mature experience in St. Louis influenced her perception of the human condition. A community of writers and intellectuals in St. Louis supported and shaped her literary life. Louisiana provided the setting for much of her fiction, but St. Louis provided the environment in which she created an important body of work.

Biographer Emily Toth has convincingly argued that Catherine O'Flaherty was born on February 8, 1850, not 1851, as previous biographers believed. Her father, Thomas O'Flaherty, was a successful Irish-born businessman with a son from a previous marriage. Her mother, Eliza Faris O'Flaherty, was the daughter of a French family with a history dating back to the founding of St. Louis. A great-grandmother, Victoire Verdun Charleville, shared stories of Kate's Creole ancestors, which influenced Chopin's later Creole tales. The O'Flaherty family owned slaves and occupied a handsome Greek Revival–style home. A neighbor, Kitty Garesche, became a schoolmate and lifelong friend. Kitty and Kate attended Sacred Heart Academy, a convent school. Kate left school for two years after her father's death in November 1855 in the railroad disaster on the Gasconade Bridge that killed thirty prominent St. Louis citizens. Kate's half brother, George, and her beloved great-grandmother both passed away in 1863. While St. Louis seethed with divisions during the Civil War period, Kate O'Flaherty returned to school and graduated from the Sacred Heart Academy in 1868. As a student she read widely and began writing diary entries, poems, and short stories.

After her marriage to Oscar Chopin in 1870, Kate Chopin left St. Louis and began raising a family in Louisiana. Apparently, the couple spent several years in New Orleans before settling in Cloutierville, in Natchitoches Parish, where Oscar Chopin's family had long owned a plantation. There they lived in a spacious timber-frame home with front and rear verandas. The landscape and the people of central Louisiana deeply impressed Kate Chopin and inspired many of her later published stories. Her Creole ancestry helped her to understand and sympathize with her Louisiana neighbors. Scholars have speculated about the extent to which the author's own married life resembled the sad marriage in *The Awakening,* but there is no definitive answer to this question. Unlike Leonce Pontellier, Oscar Chopin suffered recurrent fevers, probably aggravated by the moist climate and lack of medical services in rural Louisiana. In December 1882 he died.

A widow and the mother of six children, Kate Chopin returned to St. Louis in 1884 and there began her writing career. In 1889 the Chicago magazine *America* introduced her to the public by printing her poem "If It Might Be." A local editor accepted her first published story that same year for the *St. Louis Post-Dispatch.* Other local journals, including **William Marion Reedy**'s *St. Louis Mirror* and the *St. Louis Criterion* carried her stories and essays. At her own expense she published her first novel, *At Fault,* in 1890. National magazines, including *Vogue* and *Atlantic,* carried her stories in the 1890s. Critics warmly praised the collection of Creole tales published as *Bayou Folk* in 1894. The stories in *Bayou Folk* and *A Night in Acadie,* published in 1897, established Chopin as a local-color writer with a gift for characterization.

Chopin's Creole stories found a ready audience, partly because they did not challenge accepted images of southern life. In the bayou landscape of these stories, husbands could be cruel, and wives could lead complex emotional lives, but they remained within social bonds defined by custom. Racial and class divisions limited interaction. In her famous story "Desiree's Baby," Chopin confronted the difficult issue of race, but failed to transcend common fears and stereotypes. Armand Aubigny accused his wife, Desiree, of being black and bearing him a black child. Desiree, distraught, ran away through fields, where black workers picked cotton. Unable to live with his rejection, she disappeared, presumably ending her own life. Armand then discovered that his forebears, not Desiree's, were black. Chopin presented the story as tragic irony, but did not clearly reject the racial ideology that caused Desiree's death.

At Fault, Chopin's first novel, took a more critical look at American life in the nineteenth century. Fanny Hosmer, an unattractive female character, exemplified the alienation and futility of some middle-class women's existence. Fanny was bored, shallow, and hopelessly alcoholic. Her husband, David, fled from her and her troubles to the world of Thérèse La Firme, a Creole widow in rural Louisiana. In contrast to the hard reality of St. Louis, the world of the bayou seemed dreamlike, idyllic. Fanny, who represented the complexities of the modern city, simplified matters for David and Thérèse by drowning in a flood. The bayou romance softened the novel. Nevertheless, the book offered a gritty portrait of an indolent middle-class woman, adrift in the city.

Publishers showed no interest. Critics generally disliked or dismissed the self-published book.

Chopin spent her most creative years in the heart of a modern industrial city. In 1886, the year after her mother's death, Chopin moved to a house on Morgan Street (now Delmar). Her neighbors included artists, musicians, tradesmen, and managers—people on the way up or down in a whirl of capitalistic enterprise. The David and Fanny Hosmers of the world passed by her doorstep. Robert E. Lee Gibson, a poet and the head clerk of the St. Louis Insane Asylum, became her ardent admirer. **Logan Uriah Reavis,** who wrote books promoting St. Louis as the future capital of the United States, wandered the streets in baggy clothes and dirty shirts. Chopin could ride the streetcar to every corner of her city or sit by her window and almost literally watch the city grow.

In stories with St. Louis settings, the author revealed a keen understanding of urban pretensions and reality. The central character in "A Pair of Silk Stockings" suddenly found fifteen dollars and squandered it on all the temptations of St. Louis in the 1890s: shopping in a department store, dining in a restaurant, attending a matinee, and riding a cable car for miles. She enjoyed her guilty pleasures, but her life seemed purposeless. The title character in "The Blind Man" ambled through the city selling pencils. As he turned a corner, a speeding streetcar screeched to a halt. A prominent businessman, who failed to see the car coming from the other direction, died under its wheels. The blind man wandered on, like the city itself, unaffected by the tragedy.

In "Miss McEnders" an affluent woman did charity work among poor factory laborers, but responded coldly to her dressmaker, who revealed that she had an illegitimate child. McEnders suffered a crisis of conscience when she learned some hard truths about the questionable source of her father's wealth. In these stories with urban settings, Chopin questions the materialism and moral blindness of modern society.

Chopin's second novel, *The Awakening,* published in 1899, portrayed the inner life of a woman who rejected her role as a businessman's ornamental wife, but failed to define a place for herself in a cruelly judgmental community. Edna Pontellier's closest friend was a woman who gloried in motherhood, devoting all her energies to raising her children. Another woman friend lived the solitary life of a dedicated musician, rejecting companionship and pouring all her emotions into her art. Edna admired both these women, but she could not be like them. Leonce, her husband, regarded her as a part of his household, one of his possessions, but not as a woman at the center of his life. Robert, the man she loved, drew away from her out of fear and conventionality. A third man, who became her lover, offered her no fulfillment.

A physician in the novel hinted that he had dealt with other troubled, rebellious women like Edna. But Edna failed to connect with any of these possibly sympathetic souls. She possessed the courage to defy society's rules, but she could not find a way to live in opposition to them. Feeling completely alone and finding no other path to liberation, Edna committed suicide. The novel challenged conventional values and shocked many critics.

Scathing reviews, condemning the novel as immoral, gave *The Awakening* the aura of a banned book. In fact, the book may never have been banned. Historians perpetuated the story, based on oral testimony, that the St. Louis Mercantile Library removed *The Awakening* from circulation. Per Seyersted, an important Chopin biographer, however, questioned the story of the book's banning. In twenty years of research, he found no documentation of the incident. Frequent retelling of the book-banning anecdote created an image of Chopin as a lonely iconoclast, rejected by her St. Louis neighbors—an image that distorted the truth.

Although she challenged accepted mores, Chopin was never as lonely as her heroine Edna Pontellier. Throughout her life she had numerous friends and supporters in her native city. Her connections with her mother's family, her girlhood associates, and her own children remained strong throughout her life. Dr. Frederick Kohlbenheyer, her personal physician and intellectual companion, read many of her manuscripts. Kohlbenheyer had connections to the St. Louis literary establishment through an association with publisher **Joseph Pulitzer.** John A. Dillon, editor of the *St. Louis Post-Dispatch,* supported women's rights and encouraged Chopin's literary efforts. William Marion Reedy, the eccentric editor of the *St. Louis Mirror,* befriended the author and publicly praised her talent. The *Mirror*'s reviewer vilified *The Awakening,* but a circle of close friends remained her champions to the end of her life. Sue V. Moore, a local editor, staunchly rebuffed the critics and came to the author's defense. Local editors continued to accept her writings. Kate Chopin became a charter member of the Wednesday Club in 1890 and continued to associate with the intelligent and affluent women who made up its membership. She read "Ti Demon," a Creole story, at a club meeting in November 1899, months after critics expressed shock at the content of *The Awakening.*

Sympathetic scholars have portrayed Kate Chopin in her final years as a tragic figure who failed to draw parallels between herself and Edna Pontellier, who chose death over life in a society that refused to let her grow. While Chopin produced no book-length work after *The Awakening,* she continued writing, publishing, and participating in the social life of her home city. The *St. Louis Mirror,* the *St. Louis Post-Dispatch,* and the *St. Louis Republic* published several of her stories and articles between 1899 and 1904. National magazines such as *Vogue* and *Youth's Companion* continued to print her work.

Chopin's death coincided with a celebration of progress, the St. Louis World's Fair. By all accounts, she had great enthusiasm for the fair, more properly, the Louisiana Purchase Exposition. She bought a season ticket and traveled the short distance from her home to the fairgrounds nearly every day. The fair offered a spectacle of electric lights, fantastic inventions, and artificial waterways. Bands played ragtime, a new music that challenged traditional rhythms and echoed the rapid cadence of city life. On August 20, 1904, a particularly hot day, Chopin returned from the fair and later suffered a hemorrhage of the brain. Two days later, with her children at her bedside, she died.

In the year of her death, St. Louisan Alexander De Menil praised *Bayou Folk,* slighted her novels, and defined Chopin as a Creole writer. For several decades this assessment of her work prevailed. In 1923 Fred Lewis Pattee identified her as a master of the American short story. Daniel Rankin, who published a full-length biography of Chopin in 1932, unearthed important information about her early life. Scholarly interest remained limited until the 1960s, when Larzer Ziff defined Chopin as an American realist with the stature of Theodore Dreiser. The Norwegian scholar Per Seyersted collected and published *The Complete Works of Kate Chopin* in 1969. His important biography of the author appeared in the same year. By the 1970s students of women's history, as well as American literary history, flocked to libraries to study Chopin's fiction. Dissertations and articles proliferated as the focus of critical attention shifted from her short stories to her 1899 novel. In the 1980s and 1990s, *The Awakening* became a popular text in college literature, women's studies, and American studies classes.

Chopin ultimately gained fame as a realist rather than a local-color writer, a novelist rather than a short story writer, a modernist rather than a teller of sentimental tales. She often chose rural settings for her fiction, but she lived in the city most of her life. The troubles of Edna Pontellier in *The Awakening* were the troubles of an affluent urban woman who spent her vacations on Grand Isle but lived in New Orleans. Her empty life resulted partially from traditional definitions of women's roles, but mostly from the fact that those definitions no longer had meaning in urban America at the end of the nineteenth century. Chopin observed this emerging society in St. Louis in the 1880s and 1890s, the most creative years of her life. St. Louis influenced her thinking and nurtured her talent, while local editors, publishers, mentors, and friends encouraged her efforts.

BONNIE STEPENOFF

Chopin, Kate. *The Complete Works of Kate Chopin.* 2 vols. Baton Rouge: Louisiana State University Press, 1969.

Rankin, Daniel. *Kate Chopin and Her Creole Stories.* Philadelphia: University of Pennsylvania Press, 1932.

Seyersted, Per. *Kate Chopin: A Critical Biography.* Baton Rouge: Louisiana State University Press, 1969.

Skaggs, Peggy. *Kate Chopin.* Boston: G. K. Hall, 1985.

Toth, Emily. *Kate Chopin.* New York: William Morrow, 1990.

Ziff, Larzer. *The American 1890s: Life and Times of a Lost Generation.* New York: Viking, 1966.

CHOUTEAU, AUGUSTE (1749?–1829)

In the early history of St. Louis and its trans-Mississippi hinterlands, Auguste Chouteau occupied a place of singular importance. His pivotal role in the unfolding story of the North American heartland truly made him Upper Louisiana's "First Citizen." A clever entrepreneur, Chouteau pioneered in the development of the trans-Mississippi fur trade, the establishment of commercial relations with key Missouri and Mississippi Rivers Indian tribes, and the initiation of varied business and financial enterprises west of the Mississippi. He also participated directly in the growth of St. Louis and Upper Louisiana as an adviser to governments, a public servant and office-holder, a civic benefactor, and a social and cultural leader.

Ambitious and calculating, Chouteau knew how to drive a hard bargain, but he was also a man of his word. That combination helped make him St. Louis's principal merchant and wealthiest citizen. The reserved and enigmatic Chouteau was a complex man sometimes difficult to fathom. Friends and admirers lauded his contributions and touted his achievements, but enemies and rivals resented his influence and feared his power. No one doubted his ability to get things done.

The exact month, day, and year of Auguste Chouteau's birth in New Orleans cannot be determined with certainty, but the best evidence points to September 7, 1749. In all matters regarding Auguste's early years, the surviving record is scant. His father, René Auguste Chouteau, was a New Orleans inn- and tavern keeper who had immigrated to North America from his native France sometime prior to his September 20, 1748, marriage in New Orleans to Marie Thérèse Bourgeois. The fifteen-year-old bride was a native of that city and ten years younger than her husband.

For unexplained reasons, sometime after Auguste's birth René Chouteau abandoned his wife and son and returned to France, leaving them to fend for themselves. During her husband's extended absence, Marie Thérèse Bourgeois Chouteau styled herself as Widow Chouteau, and formed a liaison with **Pierre de Laclède Liguest,** a well-born Frenchman who had come to New Orleans in 1755. The couple had four children who, like their mother, had to use the name Chouteau since neither French statutes nor church law sanctioned divorce and remarriage.

Laclède, a successful merchant, took a special interest in Auguste Chouteau and employed him as his clerk. Even at his young age, the lad thrived among the books and ledgers that Laclède considered so important. Taking full advantage of the opportunities afforded him, Chouteau had already gained a solid educational foundation and a healthy respect for learning when he joined Laclède on an expedition up the Mississippi in 1763.

Laclède's business partner, Antoine Maxent, had dispatched them upriver to oversee the establishment of a trading headquarters in Upper Louisiana. In December Chouteau, who was barely fourteen, accompanied Laclède during a reconnaissance of the region to search out a suitable place for the new trading post. Laclède selected a site on the west bank of the Mississippi a short distance below the mouth of the Missouri where he and Chouteau notched some trees to mark the spot before returning to nearby Fort de Chartres to await warmer weather.

As soon as the late-winter thaws made it possible to navigate the Mississippi, Laclède placed his young lieutenant in charge of a crew of thirty laborers and assigned them to initiate construction at the designated site. On February 14, 1764, Chouteau reached the location chosen by Laclède, and the next day the workforce began clearing the land under his direction. When Laclède arrived on the scene in early April, work was well under way on the new settlement that he named St. Louis.

Despite his relative youth and inexperience, Auguste Chouteau quickly proved his worth. Not only did he help Laclède found a new city, but he also spent a great deal of time overseeing the exchange of goods with the Indians who came to St. Louis to trade. In the early 1770s Laclède publicly acknowledged Auguste's contributions by making him a business partner. Laclède's endorsement suggested that by the time Chouteau was in his early twenties, he already had attained the business acumen and managerial skills that became hallmarks of his successful mercantile career.

The confident young trader established a strong rapport with many of the region's Native American inhabitants. Chouteau developed especially cordial ties with key segments of the powerful Osage tribe. Some influential leaders came to view him as an ambitious but fair-minded person whose word they could trust and whose connections they could use to their advantage. Their decision to invite him to join them for a conference with Spanish officials in St. Louis sometime around 1770 helped launch Chouteau's lifelong involvement in Indian diplomacy. In subsequent years Indians and Europeans alike frequently solicited his support and assistance. He readily obliged, but as with most things that he did, Chouteau remained ever mindful of his own interests.

Chouteau took advantage of his growing ascendancy among the Osages to build a thriving trade, often in partnership with his brother, **(Jean) Pierre Chouteau,** and other trusted relatives. These extended-family business arrangements were a complicated but integral feature of the Chouteau mercantile empire. Although the traffic in furs remained the mainstay of the family's business operations, Chouteau also ventured into retail merchandising, real estate, and banking.

Chouteau waited until 1786 to marry, and in selecting his mate he chose well. His bride, Thérèse Cerré, the daughter of a wealthy and successful merchant, brought a handsome dowry with her. The couple had nine children. The first two, Marie Thérèse and Catherine Emilie, died in infancy, but the remaining seven, Auguste Aristide, Gabriel Sylvestre (also known as Cerré), Marie Thérèse Eulalie, Marie Louise, Emilie Antoinette, Henry Pierre, and Edward René all lived to adulthood. To accommodate his growing family, Chouteau purchased Laclède's original stone trading headquarters in 1789 and transformed it into a stately residence befitting someone of his rising status. The elegant two-story mansion quickly became a focal point for business and social activity in early St. Louis.

Chouteau proved adept in cultivating the favor of the Spanish officials who governed Louisiana. His cordial hospitality rarely failed to impress, and with friends in high places he fared well under a paternalistic system that bestowed special favors on a select few. In 1794 Auguste persuaded the Baron de Carondelet to grant his family a six-year monopoly of the lucrative Osage trade in return for their agreement to construct, equip, and operate a fort in the heart of the Osage country. In making the offer Chouteau cast himself in the role of a public benefactor, but in effect the arrangement enabled the Chouteaus to capture a major portion of St. Louis's dwindling fur supply.

The agreement to establish Fort Carondelet pleased both Spanish officials who appreciated the declining number of Osage depredations directed against settlements in Upper Louisiana and the Osage factions residing on the Osage River who welcomed the opening of a permanent trading post near their villages. The principal objections to the deal came from disgruntled rival traders who found themselves shut out of the profitable Osage trade. Their protests fell upon deaf ears until near the end of the Spanish regime when the Chouteaus' equally audacious competitor **Manuel Lisa** took a page from their book and wrested the Osage monopoly from their control. But that surprising development came too late in the Spanish era to be of much consequence.

Auguste Chouteau consistently followed a conservative course in matters of business. He declined to participate in efforts by **Jacques Clamorgan** and others to penetrate the risky upper Missouri trade in the 1790s. Chouteau also turned aside business overtures from the powerful American fur merchant John Jacob Astor. He clearly preferred to keep business in the family.

The historic Louisiana Purchase in 1803 confronted Chouteau with new and unexpected challenges. Keenly aware of the probable effects of Louisiana's transfer to the United States, St. Louis's leading merchant determined to make the best of a situation not of his choosing. Desirous of maintaining his family's preeminent position and its well-established influence, he wasted little time in offering his services to the incoming American authorities. Chouteau exhibited remarkable adaptability in adjusting to the requirements of an alien government and culture.

Meriwether Lewis and **William Clark,** then preparing for their great expedition to the Pacific, were among the first Americans to take advantage of Chouteau's offer. The Chouteau brothers opened their homes to the American explorers and assisted them in outfitting and financing their expedition. Not only had Auguste Chouteau and his family successfully ingratiated themselves with representatives of the incoming government, but predictably they turned a profit to boot.

Following the departure of Lewis and Clark on their mission, Chouteau continued to build good relationships with American officials. He lavishly entertained **William Henry Harrison,** Upper Louisiana's first civilian territorial governor, who had appointed him as a justice of the peace and a judge of the court of quarter sessions for the St. Louis district. Governor Harrison was sufficiently impressed with his new appointee to commend him to President Thomas Jefferson as the most influential citizen of Upper Louisiana.

Despite this auspicious beginning, the transfer of authority presented the Chouteaus and their French Creole cohorts with serious new problems. They clearly would have preferred to retain a military government in place of the republican framework that Congress authorized for the territory. Reports that U.S. officials might not confirm the land titles granted by French and Spanish authorities greatly alarmed the Chouteaus and all other large land claimants. Auguste Chouteau responded by spearheading a series of public meetings to protest congressional attempts to limit confirmation of Spanish land claims and to seek a hearing for their concerns.

Chouteau's public activities did not prevent him from continuing to oversee his business operations. Although the volume of Chouteau's fur shipments slowly declined in the years following the American takeover, he continued to dispatch sizable quantities of furs and peltries from his St. Louis warehouse to firms in New Orleans, Canada, and Europe. He also entered the U.S. market for the first time.

The rising U.S. interest in the trans-Mississippi West caused British operatives in Canada to take steps to counter the growing American competition in the fur trade. Chouteau declined an invitation from a group of Michilimackinac-based merchants to join them in a venture intended to capture a greater share of the trade in the Old Northwest and in the region west of the Mississippi. Eager not to alienate U.S. officials, Chouteau turned down the proposed partnership but continued to do business with the northern traders.

Chouteau had other more pressing matters to ponder. Plans to open government-operated trading factories west of the Mississippi posed a threat to his well-established trade with tribes along the lower Missouri. He also kept a wary eye on Astor and his designs on the western fur market. But the most immediate threat came from rival trader Manuel Lisa. His efforts to initiate trade with tribes along the upper Missouri constituted the most serious challenge to the long-standing Chouteau hegemony in St. Louis trading circles.

In the case of Lisa, the always cautious Chouteau deferred to his more impetuous brother, Pierre, who laid aside past differences and joined forces with the family's old nemesis to form the St. Louis Missouri Fur Company in association with William Clark, William Morrison, Pierre Menard, and **Andrew Henry,** among others. Although Auguste allowed his brother to take the lead in that venture, he closely monitored its operations.

The unsettled times had not been propitious for the short-lived Missouri Fur Company or for the inhabitants of the remote and sparsely populated western territories. Angry Indian tribes sought to impede the white man's penetration of their lands, while Spanish and British agents continued to challenge U.S. authority west of the Mississippi. The situation steadily deteriorated as the European disorders unleashed by Napoléon Bonaparte's imperial ambitions further muddied western America's already troubled waters.

As U.S. officials hastily sought to improvise defensive arrangements for their exposed western territories, Chouteau responded to the call. In 1806 Gov. **James Wilkinson** appointed him as a lieutenant colonel in the territorial militia, and the next year acting governor **Frederick Bates** assigned him to command the territory's First Militia Regiment. Chouteau never saw active duty, but when an Indian attack on St. Louis seemed imminent following the U.S. declaration of war on Great Britain in 1812, he headed a Committee of Safety formed to organize the city's defenses.

When the war ended, Auguste embarked upon a belated but highly successful career as a diplomat and peacemaker for the United States. In 1815 President James Madison tapped him to serve as one of three commissioners assigned to conclude treaties with various western Indian nations. For the next six years Chouteau expended much of his time and energy negotiating with Native American tribal leaders.

In 1816 Auguste announced the closing of his mercantile establishment and his retirement from the fur trade, but after conducting business in St. Louis for nearly a half century, it took him years to settle his accounts. After closing his store, Chouteau continued the auxiliary enterprises at his gristmill and distillery. He also devoted considerable time to banking, serving as president of the Bank of Missouri, which had its offices in the basement of Chouteau's St. Louis mansion. He retained that post until shortly before the institution was forced to close its doors in 1821. Chouteau directed most of his remaining energies to the management of his vast real estate holdings. Through the years he had acquired extensive tracts in St. Louis and the surrounding regions. When he died in 1829, his confirmed holdings exceeded fifty thousand acres, making him one of Missouri's largest landowners.

Auguste Chouteau also made time during his lengthy career for elective and appointive office. In addition to his extended tenure on the St. Louis Court of Common Pleas, he served on many boards and councils, including Missouri's Territorial Legislative Council, the St. Louis Board of Trustees, and the St. Louis Public School Board. Chouteau always displayed a keen interest in the advancement of knowledge. His private library, the finest in Upper Louisiana, contained more than six hundred volumes at the time of his death.

Over the decades Auguste Chouteau had done many things to contribute to the public good. Undeniably, he was first and foremost a man of business, but he also maintained a sense of commitment to the public welfare throughout his long and useful life that ended in St. Louis on February 24, 1829.

WILLIAM E. FOLEY

Chouteau Collections. Missouri Historical Society, St. Louis.

Foley, William E., and C. David Rice. *The First Chouteaus: River Barons of Early St. Louis.* Urbana: University of Illinois Press, 1983.

CHOUTEAU, AUGUSTE PIERRE (1786–1837)

Those acquainted with the Chouteaus, the founders and principal family of St. Louis, considered Auguste Pierre the most gifted and brilliant of them all. He was tall and well built, and his face was ruddy from years on the frontier, yet he was noted for his ease and grace in St. Louis parlors. His family expected much of him, but his life was a disappointment. He neglected his responsibilities as husband and father, leaving his eldest son in a boarding school in Pennsylvania for three years without paying the boy's fees or writing the headmaster. His improvidence caused the eviction of his white wife and children from their St. Louis home, and confiscation of their belongings. His illegal dealings in Osage lands caused the impoverishment of his Indian family. He incurred enormous debts, and died crushed under obligations. Yet, he is remembered not as a failure but as one of the best-known and best-loved Indian traders. On a dangerous frontier where territory was disputed with bloodshed, his patience and wisdom maintained peace.

Chouteau was born on May 9, 1786, in St. Louis, the eldest son of Pelagie Kiersereau and **(Jean) Pierre Chouteau.** His father had built Fort Carondelet in 1794 to trade with the Osage Indians. In 1804 Auguste Pierre Chouteau and his cousin **Charles Gratiot** were appointed to the military academy at West Point, where they studied for two years and were introduced to eastern society. They graduated in 1806, Auguste ranking fourth and Charles sixth in a class of fifteen. Gratiot became a general; Chouteau served under Gen. **James Wilkinson** on the southwest frontier for six months, and was called "Colonel Chouteau" for the rest of his life.

Chouteau resigned from the army to enter the fur trade, the family business. His first assignment in 1807 was to establish a post among the Mandan Indians, high up the Missouri River, but his boats were turned back by an Arikara attack, and the expedition was an expensive failure. In the summer of 1808 young Chouteau again ascended the Missouri to trade with the Sioux, returning in the fall. During the winter of 1808–1809 he accompanied his Indian-agent father to the Mandan villages to return a chief to his people. In that same winter he became a founding partner of the St. Louis Missouri Fur Company, and ascended the Missouri beyond the Mandan to trade with other Indians until May 1810. Then he returned to St. Louis and never again traded on the Missouri.

On February 15, 1809, Chouteau married his first cousin, Sophie Labbadie, the daughter of Sylvestre Labbadie and Pelagie Chouteau Labbadie, who bore Auguste ten children. With his father's influence, Chouteau obtained the appointment of U.S. Osage subagent, which made his trade with those Indians illegal. It was his last appointment as agent, for he could not afford to give up his trade for the meager salary of a government agent. Nevertheless, he continued to aid the government in its Indian affairs, attending councils and negotiating treaties without any pay, but not without interest in the supply of Indian annuity goods and supplies.

In the summer of 1815 Chouteau and Jules DeMun took goods along the Arkansas River to the eastern slope of the Rocky Mountains to trade with new groups of Indians. The results were disastrous. The traders were captured by Spanish soldiers south of the Arkansas in Spanish territory, and the entire party was imprisoned in Santa Fe for forty-eight days. Their goods were confiscated, and they were sent home in rags with one miserable horse apiece. Later they filed a claim against the United States for thirty thousand dollars, but the claim was not allowed during their lifetimes.

Chouteau's next venture was an even worse catastrophe for his career and family relations. Late in 1817 he and DeMun bought goods on credit from his brother **Pierre Chouteau Jr.,** a partner in Berthold and Chouteau, to start a store in St. Louis. The business failed; by 1821 Chouteau had lost his new frame house and the brick store, and incurred a debt amounting to sixty-six thousand dollars as was claimed in his brother's lawsuit against him fifteen years later. His was a failure unprecedented among the vigorous and ambitious Chouteaus.

In 1822 Chouteau and his brother Paul Liguest Chouteau obtained a two-year license to trade with the Osages and Kickapoo on the Arkansas River, and bought goods on credit from their brother Pierre. Auguste left his home in St. Louis, his wife and children, his powerful relatives, and his immense debt and moved to the Osage country once and for all. On the Osage River he persuaded Chief **White Hair (Paw-Hiu-Skah)** to follow him south to Three Forks, the junction of the Verdigris, Neosho (Grand), and Arkansas Rivers, a beautiful country where ample water, grass, and salt attracted humans and their prey of fur-bearing animals. Here the brothers bought the trading house of Brand and Barbour on the banks of the Verdigris with its ten or twelve houses, thirty acres of farmland, and a ferry. They traded with the Osages; with emigrating Creeks, Cherokee, and Choctaw; and with white settlers on the move from Arkansas. In 1824 the government built Fort Gibson nearby as a military post located on the east side of the Neosho near its mouth. Chouteau used the fort not only as

a market for his goods but also for frequent social events with the officers.

Thirty-five miles north of the Verdigris post, at La Saline on the Neosho, Chouteau bought another property that became his family home. La Saline had a two-story double house with a surrounding veranda, formerly the house of the late Joseph Rivar, Paul Liguest Chouteau's partner in the Osage trade since 1817. Here Auguste lived in rough frontier luxury, like a feudal lord with his black and Indian retainers and his many children, some by his Osage wife, Rosalie, and others by Rosalie's sister and by the beautiful Mihanga ("Mo-hon-ga") whose portrait hung in the Indian Gallery of the Department of War in Washington.

By 1825 Colonel Chouteau was in charge of four Osage trading posts kept by relatives: his half brothers, François Gesseau Chouteau, Cyprien Chouteau, and Pharamond Chouteau; and his cousins Auguste Aristide Chouteau and Pierre Melicourt Papin. In addition, his brother Paul Liguest Chouteau ("Liguest" or "Major Chouteau") had been an Osage subagent since 1819 and became an agent in 1830. Until the Verdigris post was swept away by a flood in 1833, Liguest had his agency there.

In 1829 Sam Houston began to live at La Saline with the Cherokee, who, he claimed, had admitted him to their tribe. He discovered that the Cherokee had been cheated of their annuities, and succeeded in getting the dishonest agent dismissed and Paul Liguest Chouteau appointed as agent. He also became a fast friend of Auguste's, and the two men engaged in some dubious sales of land belonging to Chouteau's wife and children, which cost Rosalie and the children dearly after Chouteau's death.

Houston and Chouteau went to Washington together on this and other business. At Independence on his return, Chouteau met commissioners appointed to set aside lands for emigrating Indians by making treaties to deprive the Osages of their lands. Traveling with the commissioners were distinguished visitors—Washington Irving, Charles J. Latrobe, and young Count de Pourtales—who all wrote accounts of Chouteau's hunting lessons, camping craft, and hospitality at La Saline. They also experienced the power of Chouteau and his Osages, who demanded more land and larger annuities than the commissioners could grant them, and the commissioners went home frustrated.

In 1835 Chouteau built a new trading post in the form of a stockade post on the Canadian River a hundred miles west of Fort Gibson. At this post, called Camp Holmes, Colonel Chouteau, Colonel Arbuckle, and Sam Houston were commissioned to conduct a council to make peace between the sedentary Indians on the Arkansas and the nomadic

Plains Indians, and here Chouteau traded with the Comanche, Wichitas, Osages, and other Indians.

During the Texas revolution of 1837, both Texan and Mexican agents had tried to influence the Indians and had succeeded in raising their anger to the pitch of war. Chouteau was commissioned as a special agent to prevent hostilities and was visited by twenty-two chiefs of eight different nomadic tribes. During the summer of 1837 he achieved this most difficult peace with the usual presents and promises, one promise being to meet them again at Camp Holmes in October. He could not keep his promise; by October he was mortally ill, and died at Fort Gibson on Christmas Day 1837. He was given a military funeral by officers at Fort Gibson, and was buried in the fort cemetery with all honors.

JANET S. LECOMPTE

Chouteau Collections. Missouri Historical Society, St. Louis.

Foreman, Grant. *Indians and Pioneers.* New Haven: Yale University Press, 1930.

————. *Pioneer Days in the Southwest.* Cleveland: Arthur H. Clark, 1926.

Irving, Washington. *A Tour on the Prairies.* Norman: University of Oklahoma Press.

Lecompte, Janet. "Auguste Pierre Chouteau." In *The Mountain Men and the Fur Trade of the Far West,* ed. LeRoy R. Hafen. Glendale, Calif.: Arthur H. Clark, 1971.

CHOUTEAU, BERENICE (1801–1888)

Berenice Thérèse Menard Chouteau, the "Mother of Kansas City," was born on August 13, 1801, in Kaskaskia, Illinois. Her mother was Thérèse Godin Menard of Kaskaskia, and her father was Pierre Menard, a French Canadian who became the first governor of Illinois Territory.

Berenice's mother died in 1804, leaving three small daughters and one son. In 1806 Berenice's father married Angelique Saucier, who became "Mamma" to Berenice. Little is known of Berenice's childhood, but her father was affluent, and his house, still standing today, was well staffed with servants. As schools were remote and scarce, Berenice was probably tutored at home, a common practice among the French.

During the late eighteenth and early nineteenth centuries, the French communities along the Mississippi were close-knit, and it is almost certain that Berenice Menard and François Chouteau were acquainted at an early age. In addition, François's mother, Brigitte Saucier Chouteau, and Berenice's stepmother, Angelique Saucier Menard, were half sisters. François Chouteau and Berenice Menard were married July 12, 1819, the bride being seventeen years of age.

Berenice's husband, a member of the Chouteau fur business, was commissioned to establish a trading post west of the Missouri. On their wedding journey, the couple navigated up the Missouri River, probably as far as Council Bluffs. For their trading post and home, they chose a location on the riverbank east of present Kansas City.

By the spring of 1821 Berenice and François Chouteau were living in log buildings in western Missouri. Their establishment was destroyed by the Missouri River flood of 1826. They rebuilt on the south bank, farther west, closer to the present city center.

Chouteau's claim to the title "Mother of Kansas City" rests not so much on whether she was the first white woman in the area, a point of discussion, but on what she did upon her arrival. She was the first white woman to settle permanently, establish a home, and raise a family in the wilderness that became Kansas City.

As other families settled near the Chouteau trading post, a small French community developed. Chouteau set the tone of the community by emphasizing family values, religion, charitable works, and the joys of life: social gatherings, dancing, music, and flowers. The Chouteaus became the parents of nine children: Edmond François (1821–1853), Pierre Menard (1822–1885), Louis Amedee (1825–1827), Louis Sylvestre (1827–1829), Benjamin (1828–1871), Frederick (1831–?), Benedict Pharamond (1833–1834), Mary Bridgitte (1835–1864), and Thérèse Odile (1837–?). François Chouteau died suddenly, on April 18, 1838.

Chouteau was then obliged to support her five living children. She apparently accomplished this by operating the farm and the Chouteau merchandising business, then a retail store rather than a trading post. In 1844 the Missouri River flooded again and swept away the Chouteau enterprise. She never reopened the store and rebuilt her home atop the bluff.

During the Civil War and until 1867, Chouteau lived in Ste. Genevieve and then Kaskaskia. She then returned to Kansas City and lived with her son, Pierre Menard Chouteau, and his wife, Mary Polk Chouteau. By this time Chouteau was nearly blind and had suffered financial reverses. Letters to her brother, Edmond Menard, document her difficulties. She outlived her husband and all nine of her children.

Chouteau died on November 19, 1888. She had seen her wilderness home become a rough frontier town, then a bloody Civil War battlefield, and at last emerge as a thriving city. Already at the time of her death, Berenice Thérèse Menard Chouteau was called the "Mother of Kansas City."

DOROTHY B. MARRA

Foley, William E., and C. David Rice. *The First Chouteaus: River Barons of Early St. Louis.* Urbana: University of Illinois Press, 1983.

Guide to the Microfilm Edition of the Pierre Menard Collection. Springfield: Illinois State Historical Society, 1972.

Menard, Pierre. Collection. Illinois State Historical Society, Springfield.

Native Sons of Kansas City Collection. Western Manuscript Collection. University of Missouri, Kansas City.

CHOUTEAU, FRANÇOIS (1797–1838)

François Gesseau Chouteau, the "Father of Kansas City," was born in St. Louis on February 17, 1797. His parents, Brigitte Saucier and **(Jean) Pierre Chouteau,** were members of the French population that inhabited the Louisiana Territory. François was the grandson of **Pierre de Laclède Liguest** and nephew of **Auguste Chouteau,** the cofounders of St. Louis.

François grew up in St. Louis surrounded by family members engaged in a thriving fur business. His education probably consisted of tutoring at home, a common practice among the French. As a youth he may have lived at the Chouteau trading post among the Osage Indians on the Marais de Cygne.

On July 12, 1819, François Chouteau and Berenice Thérèse Menard of Kaskaskia, Illinois, were married. Their wedding journey was a boat trip up the Missouri River, looking for a site to build a trading post. They probably went as far as Council Bluffs, before choosing a location below the great bend in the Missouri and the mouth of the Kansas River. The young couple lived briefly in St. Louis while preparations were made for the move to western Missouri. François Chouteau and **Berenice Thérèse Menard Chouteau** became the parents of nine children.

François Chouteau's honorific title, the "Father of Kansas City," was assigned to him early in the history of Kansas City, recognizing that he established the first permanent business and home in what became metropolitan Kansas City. By the spring of 1821 the Chouteau complex was operating east of present downtown Kansas City. The river flooded in 1826, destroying the buildings. The Chouteaus rebuilt on the south bank on higher ground, farther west, putting them closer to the present city center. French fur traders camped near the post when they brought in pelts, and some settled and became farmers.

Chouteau traveled extensively in Kansas Territory, visiting Indian tribes, including Shawnee, Kansa, Kickapoo, Piankashaw, Peoria, Wea, Fish, and Loup. He encouraged them to hunt and trap animals and trade or sell the pelts at the Chouteau trading post where he stocked a large supply of trade goods.

Long-standing good relations and mutual trust between the extended Chouteau family and the Native Americans contributed to Chouteau's success. Ultimately, however, the fur business depended on fur supply and fashion whims. By the late 1830s the European clientele preferred silk rather than fur hats. This, in addition to thinning populations of fur-bearing animals, caused the fur industry to wane. Chouteau's business became less dependent on the barter of furs and more engaged in selling merchandise for cash to Indians and non-Indians. The enterprise became known as Chouteau's Emporium and Farm.

Letters written by Chouteau to his uncle and his father-in-law and business backer, Col. Pierre Menard of Kaskaskia, Illinois, document the kinds of problems faced by frontier businessmen early in the nineteenth century: slow and unreliable communication, the hazards of shipping goods on the Missouri, fluctuating prices of furs and pelts, and unreliable employees. While operating his business, Chouteau also bought and sold real estate along the Missouri River and on the bluffs to the south. His name appears on government land patent records as the original owner of much property that became the heart of Kansas City.

Chouteau died in Kansas City on April 18, 1838, at the age of forty-one, probably of a heart attack. He was buried in St. Louis. Chouteau was an Indian liaison, a pioneer businessman, and a realtor as well as a community leader of the small French settlement that evolved into Kansas City.

DOROTHY B. MARRA

Barry, Louise. *The Beginning of the West: Annals of the Kansas Gateway to the American West, 1540–1854.* Topeka: Kansas State Historical Society, 1971.

Foley, William E., and C. David Rice. *The First Chouteaus: River Barons of Early St. Louis.* Urbana: University of Illinois Press, 1983.

Hill, Edward. *The Office of Indian Affairs, 1824–1880.* New York: Clearwater Publishing, 1974.

Menard, Pierre. Collection. Illinois State Historical Society, Springfield.

Primm, James Neal. *Lion of the Valley: St. Louis, Missouri, 1764–1980.* 3d ed. St. Louis: Missouri Historical Society Press, 1998.

CHOUTEAU, JEAN PIERRE (1758–1849)

Jean Pierre Chouteau, known as Pierre, was a pioneer settler in St. Louis and the territory that was to become Missouri. The son of **Pierre de Laclède Liguest** and his common-law wife, **Marie Thérèse Bourgeois Chouteau,** Pierre and his half brother,

Auguste Chouteau, carved out a trading empire in the Mississippi and Missouri valleys and pioneered in the settlement of a vast portion of North America. First under the authority of Spain, and then the United States, Pierre and Auguste developed the fur trade among the Native American tribes in the trans-Mississippi region and helped establish Spanish and American authority over the people of the area. No man did more than the younger Chouteau to push the trade frontier up the wide Missouri, nor to negotiate understandings with tribal people.

When the American government acquired Louisiana in 1803, Chouteau overcame his misgivings concerning the democratic republic and became an effective, if controversial, Indian agent for the new government. He also contributed substantially to the outfitting of the Lewis and Clark expedition, sent by President Thomas Jefferson to explore the Louisiana Purchase lands. Accepting the permanence of the American presence, Chouteau persuaded the dangerous Osage nation to remain faithful to the United States during the War of 1812, an achievement of some importance on the western American frontier. Ever the entrepreneur, Chouteau enriched himself both as a merchant and as an official, played a significant part in the development of St. Louis's civic institutions, and sired many children, some of whom were to enlarge upon the financial and mercantile dynasty their father had helped create.

Pierre Chouteau was born in New Orleans on October 10, 1758, the oldest of four children produced by the Laclède-Chouteau union. His mother was married to René Chouteau, who abandoned her and their son, Auguste, sometime after 1752 and returned to his native France. She eventually assumed the title of "Widow" to gain property rights and custody rights under French law. Shortly after 1755 she formed a liaison with Laclède, which both considered to be a binding marriage. As a Catholic, and as her husband still lived, she could not remarry, and to retain their rights the children she bore Laclède received the Chouteau name.

At the end of the Seven Years' War, or the French and Indian War, in 1763, the territory of Louisiana was ceded by France to Spain. Laclède formed a partnership with Gilbert Antoine Maxent to exploit the fur trade with Native Americans of Upper Louisiana. Maxent had received exclusive trading rights in the area, and Laclède was to establish a trading post for the purpose. In August 1763 Laclède, along with Auguste Chouteau, began the voyage upstream. An outpost was established in February 1764 near the confluence of the Mississippi and the Missouri Rivers and was called St. Louis. By September Marie Thérèse Chouteau had arrived with Pierre and his three younger sisters, Marie Louise, Marie Pelagie, and Victoire. Pierre was not quite

six years old. Although he would visit New Orleans many times in later years, his true home was now St. Louis.

St. Louis's existence depended upon the fur trade with the Indian nations, especially the Osages. But Spanish officials made the town the administrative center for Upper Louisiana as well, and the village began to expand. French settlers from the eastern, or British, side of the Mississippi helped boost the population, and the hope of profits attracted other trappers, merchants, professionals, artisans, and drifters. Laclède and Auguste Chouteau sold goods to these settlers, sent out agents to the trapping grounds, carried on negotiations with the Indians, and enjoyed the Spanish system of restricted trade. As the years passed, their operations spread far and wide up the Mississippi and Missouri Rivers.

Despite his trade advantages, Laclède found it impossible to collect on many notes and died in debt in 1778. Auguste and Pierre had gained much business experience by then, however, and began to work to clear the family of obligations and make the trade a lucrative one. Growing up in a frontier town, Pierre was constantly in contact with Indians and often accompanied his father and brother to their villages. When he was seventeen he took up residence in an Osage village, as Auguste was needed in St. Louis to conduct business because Laclède's frequent trips to New Orleans and declining health absented him from the store. His almost continuous contact with the Osages allowed Pierre to master their language, learn their ways, and gain their friendship and confidence. It served him well, for the Osages were the largest and fiercest tribe in the region, and the Chouteaus' exclusive right to trade with them was the basis for the family fortune.

The Osage people loved Pierre Chouteau, and their affection was expressed in generosity. Not the least of their gifts to him was a large tract of land along the Lamine River during the period of Spanish rule. In return Chouteau obtained trade goods, weapons, and tokens of esteem for the chiefs from both the Spanish and the Americans. After the American annexation he also escorted a delegation of chiefs to Washington to meet with President Thomas Jefferson. Influential American officials in Washington mistrusted the Chouteaus, however, uncertain of their loyalty to the United States and resentful of Chouteau's request for a virtual trade monopoly with the Indians of Upper Louisiana. Even so, the Jefferson administration named Chouteau the American Indian agent in the area. In that post he did a fine job of administering Indian affairs, but, after leading a dangerous mission to return a chief of the Mandan to his village in 1809 following a visit to Washington, he was charged with misappropriation of War Department funds. Eventually, he cleared his name with federal officials, and performed outstanding service in maintaining the U.S. alliance with the Osages during the War of 1812.

Whether he was a government official or not, Pierre Chouteau never ceased in his primary role as an entrepreneur. Over the years he acquired real estate in St. Louis, large land grants in various locales, mills, stores, thousands of promissory notes, and interests in lead mining, and became a founding partner in the St. Louis Missouri Fur Company in 1808 with successful frontier traders such as **Manuel Lisa,** William Morrison, and Sylvestre Labbadie. This company began the organized exploitation of the fur trade far up the Missouri toward the Rocky Mountains.

Besides his activities in commerce, Chouteau was active in St. Louis political and civic life. A strong advocate of the maintenance of slavery in an American Missouri, he and his half brother were prominent in the debate over Missouri's statehood in 1820. He was also a justice of the peace, several times a member and chair of the St. Louis Board of Trustees, and, though failing to be elected mayor in 1826, he was elected to the Missouri State Senate in 1821 shortly after the territory achieved statehood. By then, however, the Chouteau political power was in decline as large numbers of Americans succeeded the old French families in positions of authority. Yet, the Chouteau brothers, and their expanding progeny, continued for many years as social and economic leaders in the new state. Few famous visitors to St. Louis refused the hospitality of their sumptuous homes or failed to remark upon their lively conversation and gracious hospitality.

Like his half brother, Auguste, Pierre Chouteau was a devoted father and husband and sired a large family. He married the wealthy Pelagie Kiersereau on July 26, 1783, and their union produced four children: **Auguste Pierre Chouteau,** later a West Point graduate and trader in the Indian territory of Oklahoma; **Pierre Chouteau Jr.,** who rose to become a partner and then owner of John Jacob Astor's American Fur Company and one of the richest men in the West; Pelagie Chouteau, who married into the influential Berthold trading family; and Paul Liguest Chouteau, who became an Osage Indian agent. After the older Pelagie died in 1793, Pierre married Brigitte Saucier in 1794. Together they produced five sons— François Gesseau, Cyprien, Pharamond, Charles, and Frederick—all of whom were involved in the family business operations.

Chouteau lived to an old age and died on July 9, 1849, full of honors and the rich experiences of a long and eventful life. Yet, though he lived and died a legendary figure, he was not a universally loved man. He antagonized many with his shrewd business practices, and he perturbed many American officials and businessmen after 1804 with his fierce defense of contested Spanish land grants. It is well established that he was admired and respected. He was undoubtedly a consummate merchant, and he was certainly a vital force in opening much of the western continent to trade and settlement. Pierre Chouteau stands with his half brother, Auguste Chouteau, as a patriarch of the "Royal Family of the Wilderness."

C. DAVID RICE

Foley, William E. *The Genesis of Missouri: From Wilderness Outpost to Statehood.* Columbia: University of Missouri Press, 1989.

Foley, William E., and C. David Rice. *The First Chouteaus: River Barons of Early St. Louis.* Urbana: University of Illinois Press, 1983.

McDermott, John Francis, ed. *The Spanish in the Mississippi Valley, 1762–1804.* Urbana: University of Illinois Press, 1974.

Nasatir, Abraham P. *Before Lewis and Clark: Documents Illustrating the History of the Missouri, 1785–1804.* 2 vols. 1952. Reprint, Lincoln: University of Nebraska Press, 1990.

Stoddard, Amos. *Sketches, Historical and Descriptive of Louisiana.* Philadelphia: Mathew Carey, 1812.

CHOUTEAU, MARIE THÉRÈSE BOURGEOIS (1733–1814)

Marie Thérèse Bourgeois Chouteau was born in New Orleans on January 14, 1733, but she was to become the matriarch of the founding family of St. Louis. As the mother of **Auguste Chouteau** and his half brother, **(Jean) Pierre Chouteau,** the men who established St. Louis as the commercial center of a vast western market in the fur trade, and as the grandmother and great-grandmother of countless other Labbadies, Gratiots, Prattes, and Papins, Chouteau, with her informal mate, **Pierre de Laclède Liguest,** established a French-speaking dynasty that powerfully shaped early Missouri history. Yet, her contribution to the settlement of Missouri was more than biological. She was a clever businesswoman in her own right and exerted considerable social influence in St. Louis for a half century.

Chouteau's father was Nicholas Bourgeois, who died when she was five years old. Her mother was Marie Joseph Tarare, a Spaniard, and Bourgeois's death left Marie Joseph with three young children and pregnant with another. Given the meager prospects for widows in eighteenth-century New Orleans, it was fortunate that she married Nicholas Pierre Carco the following year. Despite some accounts suggesting that young Marie was placed in an Ursaline nunnery for the remainder of her childhood, the careful research of **John Francis McDermott III** has rendered the proposition untenable. Indeed, there is every reason to suppose that she was raised in her stepfather's home until her arranged marriage at age fifteen with a baker and tavern keeper, René Auguste Chouteau, on September 20, 1748.

The facts of the marriage between René Chouteau and Marie Bourgeois do not indicate a happy union. At least one son, Auguste, the future cofounder of St. Louis, was born to the couple, probably in 1749. A second boy, René, is mentioned in New Orleans parish records as being baptized in September 1749, but as scarcely any other information is known concerning René Jr., it may well be that Auguste and René Jr. were one and the same. In any event, Marie's husband soon abandoned her and their son and sailed for France. The cause is unknown, but for Marie, a young mother with no connections, it meant shifting for herself. In those trying times, the resourcefulness and good sense that she would demonstrate in later years kept her and her boy afloat. Then, perhaps in 1755, she met Laclède.

Laclède was a polished merchant from an accomplished family in southern France. He was born in 1729 and had come to New Orleans in 1755 with his share of his father's legacy to start a career in business. Educated and attentive, Laclède impressed Marie, and a bond was forged between the two that was regarded as a marriage by both and by others. As Roman Catholics, Laclède and Chouteau could not officially wed because of her existing marriage to the truant René. Hence, Marie had to continue as Madame Chouteau, or, as she sometimes styled herself, Widow Chouteau, even though her legal husband still lived. As a widow she could acquire property and have legal custody of her children. With Laclède, Chouteau had four children: (Jean) Pierre Chouteau, born on October 10, 1758; Marie Pelagie Chouteau, born on October 6, 1760; Marie Louise Chouteau, born on December 4, 1762; and Victoire Chouteau, born on March 3, 1764. As René Chouteau was not to return to New Orleans until 1767, it is obvious that he was not the father of these children, but his wife gave her children the Chouteau name.

Wishing to improve relations and trade with Native American tribes in the vicinity of the confluence of the Mississippi and Missouri Rivers, as the French and Indian War ended in 1763, authorities in New Orleans granted Gilbert Antoine Maxent exclusive trading rights in the area. Maxent, in turn, formed a partnership with Laclède to organize a trading post to develop the fur trade in Upper Louisiana. In August 1763 Laclède, with Chouteau's son Auguste, began a three-month journey up the long river. After a stay at Fort Chartres, near Ste. Genevieve, Laclède moved on and selected a site for the post. In February 1764 Auguste, with a party of workers, began to clear the land and build cabins and storage facilities. St. Louis had come into existence.

September saw the arrival of Chouteau with her other children. She occupied a new building constructed as a trading post. Having left New Orleans in June, she passed some time at Fort Chartres, and then came to St. Louis to move into the new structure. For the next fifty years she would reside in the new city on the Mississippi. In that period she would see the village become a significant American town, the gateway to the West.

Chouteau moved her family again in 1768. In that year Laclède established the family in a new stone house. There he resided with Chouteau and the children until his death in 1778. In his will Laclède provided that the house and other properties would pass to Auguste Chouteau and the Laclède-Chouteau children but that Marie Chouteau would have use of the house as long as she lived. Meanwhile, the city grew as new residents arrived from French settlements on the eastern, or British, side of the river and as the developing fur trade stimulated economic growth. Spanish authorities supported commercial activity, and the Laclède-Chouteau enterprises expanded.

In her new community Chouteau presided over the operations of the busy household, acquired property (including at least several slaves), owned cattle, kept bees, and engaged in a number of business transactions. Her sons, Auguste and Pierre, as grown men, came to control the fur trade and were dominant in St. Louis business and political affairs for decades, but it appears that they did not dominate their mother. She also helped provide handsome dowries for her three daughters, which, no doubt, contributed to advantageous marriages. After Laclède died, moreover, Chouteau first bought and then sold his farm on Grand Prairie at a handsome profit; and when her son-in-law Joseph Papin, in pursuit of runaway Indian slaves, brought about the accidental death of her slave Baptiste, she sued him and won six hundred dollars in damages. Later, she participated in businesses operated from her house. As a businesswoman and as matriarch of the founding family, she became a powerful factor in the commercial and social life of the city.

Well before Laclède's death, however, Chouteau's lawful husband returned from France to New Orleans. In 1774 he initiated legal proceedings in New Orleans to compel the restitution of his wife from St. Louis to New Orleans. René Chouteau was never held in much regard in New Orleans, however, and had several brushes with the law and spent time in jail. Nevertheless, Gov. Luis de Unzaga ordered Lt. Gov. **Pedro Joseph Piernas** in St. Louis to send Marie Chouteau downriver. Piernas dragged his feet, however, unwilling to offend the territory's premier family and a woman of ability and property. By the time of René Chouteau's death in 1776, no action had been taken on the matter. Marie Chouteau remained in St. Louis but did not fail to press the authorities for possession of her legal husband's small estate. Predictably, she succeeded and divided a small sum of money between herself and the children who bore the Chouteau name.

Chouteau is best remembered for her role as matriarch. She had hundreds of descendants connected to the preeminent commercial and political families of St. Louis. Her grandson, **François Chouteau,** opened a trading post in 1821 on the Missouri, far to the west of St. Louis and thus became a founder of Missouri's second metropolis, Kansas City. Yet, she was also a capable and shrewd woman who made her way in a society not designed for independent women. Indisputably, Pierre Laclède was a vital agent in her rise to wealth and prominence, but the size of her estate by the time of her death, which exceeded two thousand dollars, proved Chouteau managed her affairs quite well in the four decades of her widowhood. When she died on August 14, 1814, St. Louis lost a hardy pioneer and a woman of substance. As late as 1825, Auguste and Pierre erected an iron cross on her tomb as a memorial and as a token of respect.

C. DAVID RICE

Corbett, Katherine T. "Veuve Chouteau, a 250th Anniversary." *Gateway Heritage* 3:4 (spring 1983): 42–48.

Cunningham, Mary B., and Jeanne C. Blythe. *The Founding Family of St. Louis.* St. Louis: Midwest Technical Publications, 1977.

Foley, William E. "The Laclède-Chouteau Puzzle: John Francis McDermott Supplies Some Missing Pieces." *Gateway Heritage* 4:2 (fall 1983): 18–25.

Foley, William E., and C. David Rice. *The First Chouteaus: River Barons of Early St. Louis.* Urbana: University of Illinois Press, 1983.

CHOUTEAU, PIERRE, JR. (1789–1865)

Pierre Chouteau Jr., scion of St. Louis's founding family and the most influential of its second-generation progeny, amassed a substantial fortune and attained considerable notoriety as a fur merchant, railroad builder, and financier. Chouteau, an amiable French Creole who could be as ruthless as the occasion required, subjugated his life to his business. In contrast with his father, **(Jean) Pierre Chouteau,** and his uncle, **Auguste Chouteau,** he eschewed involvement in public and community service, though he did represent St. Louis County in Missouri's 1820 Constitutional Convention. Aside from lending his unqualified support to the defense of slavery, however, he played no significant role in the

convention's proceedings. Afterward, he generally left such matters to others, preferring to concentrate on business affairs. In his later years the wealthy but aging entrepreneur confided to his daughter Julie that for reasons of "ambition or advantage or even perhaps a little vanity," he found himself unable to withdraw from business, noting that he could not remain stationary while everything around him appeared to move ahead. Drive, ambition, and audacity clearly were the hallmarks of the prominent merchant-capitalist whose life spanned an era that began when St. Louis was still a part of imperial Spain and ended shortly after the conclusion of the American Civil War.

Pierre Chouteau Jr., the son of (Jean) Pierre and Pelagie Kiersereau Chouteau, was born in St. Louis on January 19, 1789. Like his father, he was frequently called "Cadet," a nickname the French employed to designate a second-born son. He was schooled in St. Louis where he learned the essentials for a man of business along with an ability to read and speak English, even though to the consternation of his American correspondents he persisted in the practice of writing all his letters in French.

Chouteau began his career in the fur trade at about the age of fifteen as an apprentice in the office of his uncle Auguste. He accompanied his father on trading expeditions in the Indian country, and in 1807 was granted a license to trade with the Osages, a tribe that had long been the mainstay of his family's Indian business operations. He occasionally handled matters for his father when the latter was away from St. Louis, and by 1810 young Chouteau had proved himself sufficiently to be sent to the lead mines near present-day Dubuque, Iowa, to look after the Chouteau interests there. He attended to those duties until the onset of the War of 1812 forced him to return to St. Louis, where the following year he opened a store selling crockery and hardware in partnership with his sister Pelagie's husband, Bartholomew Berthold.

The Chouteaus had long favored keeping business in the family. A complex system of commercial partnerships, linking them with members of their extended family, enabled the Chouteaus to pool their assets, retain control of their trading operations, and avoid the pitfalls of working with strangers. Chouteau's 1813 marriage to his cousin Emilie Anne Gratiot continued that tradition and expanded the family network. Emilie's sister Julie was married to Jean P. Cabanné who later joined Chouteau in a business partnership. Another sister, Isabelle, was the wife of trader Jules DeMun, and Emilie's brother, **Charles Gratiot,** was an officer in the United States Army with valuable governmental contacts.

Pierre Chouteau Jr. and Emilie Chouteau had five children, three of whom lived to adulthood. He was a devoted husband and father, but he did not allow family responsibilities to interfere with his obligations to his company's expanding mercantile operations. The firm of Berthold and Chouteau had begun dispatching traders into the Indian country. Not all the ventures it outfitted were successful. Chouteau's brother, **Auguste Pierre Chouteau,** and his partners, brother-in-law Jules DeMun and cousin John B. Sarpy, sustained losses and found themselves deeply in debt to Berthold and Chouteau. Auguste Pierre Chouteau left St. Louis in 1822 and took up residence in present Oklahoma, where he oversaw Berthold and Chouteau's "Osage Outfit" staffed by a host of younger members of the Chouteau clan.

Berthold and Chouteau, sometimes called the French Company, struggled to hold its own in the increasingly competitive St. Louis fur market. It established additional trading posts, including the one operated by Cadet's brother **François Chouteau** near the junction of the Kaw and Missouri Rivers on the site that became Kansas City. In the 1820s **William H. Ashley**'s trading operations in the Rocky Mountains and John Jacob Astor's St. Louis–based western department of the American Fur Company (AFC) posed new threats to the French Company, which reorganized itself in 1822 when **Bernard Pratte,** who was married to Cadet's cousin Emilie Labbadie, became a partner. This was the first of many reorganizations for the firm that operated under several different names, including Berthold, Chouteau, and Pratte; Bernard Pratte and Company; Pratte, Chouteau, and Company; and eventually Pierre Chouteau Jr. and Company, but as the firm evolved it was Pierre Chouteau Jr. who took charge of directing its operations.

As the company battled to stave off its numerous competitors in the volatile fur business, Chouteau found it necessary to reassess his insistence on complete family autonomy. He cautiously began doing business with the powerful AFC and in 1826 signed an agreement with Astor designating Bernard Pratte and Company as the AFC's exclusive western agent. Following the merger of the two firms' western operations, Chouteau perhaps consoled himself with the knowledge that Ramsay Crooks, who headed the AFC's western department for Astor, had chosen Pratte's daughter Emilie as his wife. Under the terms of the agreement with the AFC, Chouteau was named to superintend business activities in the Indian country, for which he received a salary of two thousand dollars per year plus expenses.

The union proved beneficial for Chouteau and his St. Louis firm. He wasted little time in mastering the ruthless techniques that had made Astor the greatest American fur merchant. The strategy was simple: eliminate competitors by buying them out and putting them to work. With the AFC's backing, Chouteau was ready to challenge his principal rivals in the western trade. One by one they found themselves compelled to give way to the powerful new combine whose reach extended from the upper reaches of the Mississippi and Missouri Rivers to the Rockies. Chouteau played a key role in the introduction of steamboat traffic on the upper Missouri, and was a passenger along with artist **George C. Catlin** when the *Yellow Stone* completed the first successful steamboat voyage to the upper-Missouri country in 1832. Scientists, artists, and foreign dignitaries frequently traveled on AFC steamboats as guests of the company. It was good publicity, and their favorable reports helped offset the company's generally poor image.

Chouteau and his operatives had a not-wholly-undeserved reputation for utilizing questionable business practices in their pursuit of profits. Most notably, the firm employed numerous subterfuges to circumvent federal efforts to discourage the use of liquor in the Indian trade. The shrewd and crafty fur merchant was willing to do whatever was necessary to counter the opposition. Nor did he hesitate to use his money and influence to affect U.S. policies. He and his agents involved themselves in Indian treaty making in an effort to profit from the annuities that the government paid the tribes in return for the surrender of their lands. Chouteau frequently traveled to New York and Washington, D.C., where he conducted business and lobbied for favorable treatment for the company and its interests. He also served as a director for the short-lived St. Louis branch of the Bank of the United States.

When John Jacob Astor retired from the fur business in 1834, Chouteau and his partners had purchased the AFC's western department. Everything did not go smoothly for Chouteau once he was on his own in handling the company's western operations. He terminated the company's involvement in the mountain trade after silk hats had replaced the fashionable beaver tall hats, and made the traffic in buffalo robes the staple of Pierre Chouteau and Company's fur and hide business. He relied heavily on his son-in-law **John F. A. Sanford** (best known for his involvement in the *Dred Scott* case) and also began preparing his son Charles to take charge of managing the St. Louis fur business for him. The younger Chouteau officially took up those reins in 1849, an eventful year for the family that also saw the death of Chouteau's elderly father and the loss of some of the firm's business buildings in a catastrophic fire that devastated large sections of St. Louis.

Pierre Chouteau Jr. was not yet ready for retirement. Instead he turned his attention to new ways for making money in an America that was in the throes of industrializing: building railroads and making iron. In 1849 he founded a firm in New York—later known as Chouteau, Merle, and Sanford—that supplied railroads with iron. That same year, he joined **François**

Vallé and James Harrison in their iron-making ventures at Iron Mountain in St. François County, not far from Ste. Genevieve. The firm of Chouteau, Harrison, and Vallé subsequently developed extensive operations that included mines, smelting plants, and rolling mills. Following the construction of a railroad to Iron Mountain in the 1850s, Chouteau touted the locality as a summer resort for vacationing St. Louisans. The Iron Mountain and Southern Railroad was a branch of the Illinois Central in which Chouteau also had interests.

Chouteau's diverse financial holdings forced him to spend more of his time in New York than in St. Louis, but the powerful business magnate never forgot his French Creole origins. Failing health that rendered him completely blind during the last six years of his life eventually forced him to curtail his activities. When he died in St. Louis on September 6, 1865, Chouteau was a wealthy man who had succeeded in elevating the Chouteau family's fame and fortune to new heights. Not everyone approved of the way he had done it, but he was not unique in that regard. He was in most respects a man of his times, albeit a highly successful one.

WILLIAM E. FOLEY

Chouteau Collections and Fur Company Ledgers and Account Books. Missouri Historical Society, St. Louis.

Lecompte, Janet. "Pierre Chouteau, Junior." In *The Mountain Men and the Fur Trade of the Far West,* ed. LeRoy R. Hafen. Glendale, Calif.: Arthur H. Clark, 1971.

CHURCHILL, WINSTON (1871–1947)

Winston Churchill, editor, author, and sometime politician, emerged in the early decades of the twentieth century as one of America's most popular novelists. Born on November 10, 1871, in St. Louis, Missouri, to Edward S. and Emma Bell Blaine Churchill, he traced the beginning of his family in America to John Churchill, who came from England to the Plymouth Plantation in the early 1640s. Other distinguished ancestors included the Puritan clergyman Jonathan Edwards (1703–1758) and two presidents of Yale College, Timothy Dwight (1752–1817) and his grandson, Timothy Dwight (1828–1916). Churchill was not related to the well-known Englishman Winston S. Churchill. By 1900, however, both men had published a novel. So that the reading public on both sides of the Atlantic would be able to distinguish between them, the two men agreed that the American would retain the name Winston Churchill, while the Englishman would add the middle initial *S,* for Spencer.

Three weeks after Churchill's birth, his mother died. Reared in the home of her sister, Mrs. James B. Gazzams, he attended school in St. Louis, graduating from the Smith Academy in 1890. Appointed to the United States Naval Academy at Annapolis, he maintained an excellent academic record. He graduated fifth in his class in 1894, but resigned his commission to become the editor of the *Army and Navy Journal.* It was during this time that he encountered an assistant secretary of the navy, Theodore Roosevelt, who was most influential on his life and career.

Churchill married Mable Harlakenden Hall, the daughter of a wealthy St. Louis iron manufacturer, on October 22, 1895. They became the parents of three children.

With the rise of imperialism and the Spanish-American War in the 1890s, there was a resurgence of patriotism and interest in American history. Churchill once said that he wrote his historical novels at a time when "Patriotism was patriotism. Arms and the Man! Villains were villains. . . ." The young writer launched his literary career with the publication of his first historical novel, *The Celebrity* (1898). A year later he published *Richard Carvel,* a novel of the American Revolution that established him as a first-rate writer of historical fiction. In this book the historical John Paul Jones and the fictional Richard Carvel of Maryland joined in a series of adventures that led to the climatic naval engagement between the *Bon Homme Richard* and the British man-of-war *Serapis* on September 23, 1779. Churchill meticulously researched the American Revolutionary era, as well as the life of John Paul Jones. While writing the book he lived in London and Annapolis where much of the novel's action and romance take place.

The Crisis (1901) is regarded by many critics as the best of Churchill's historical works. In this book, he set the scene in St. Louis before and after the Civil War. It is the story of the love between a young New Englander and a proud daughter of the Old South who are torn apart by the war, but are at last reunited at the war's end. The two most important historical figures depicted are President Abraham Lincoln and Gen. **Ulysses S. Grant,** under whom the hero served in the Union army. Churchill said that much of the actual work on the book was done in an office in the Old Security Building in St. Louis. In his last historical novel, *The Crossing* (1904), he returned to the epoch of the American Revolution.

In 1898 Churchill moved to Cornish, a tiny community near the Connecticut River in western New Hampshire. There he built Harlakenden, a stately home on high ground that looked westward across a scenic valley toward the river. From 1913 to 1915 President Woodrow Wilson and his family vacationed in Cornish and rented Harlakenden for the summer White House. When fire destroyed the house in 1923, Churchill moved into a modest farmhouse nearby.

The move to Cornish marked a major turning point in Churchill's life and career. Inspired by Theodore Roosevelt and the causes of the Progressive movement, he became a political activist. Elected to the New Hampshire legislature in 1902, he served two terms and worked for improvement and conservation of state forests, reform of the election system, and regulation of the railroads. In 1906 he stumped for the Republican nomination for a two-year term as governor. Although he ran an effective campaign against the corrupt railroad monopoly in the state, the entrenched political forces defeated him. In 1912 he ran for governor of New Hampshire on the Bull Moose ticket (a member of Roosevelt's breakaway Progressive Party), but lost to the first Democrat to be elected governor since 1875. Despite a disappointing political track record, Churchill helped to lay the groundwork for a number of Progressive reforms that were later adopted in the state.

Involvement in Progressive politics and concern for the economic and social problems of the day changed the direction of Churchill's literary career. From writing novels filled with adventure and romance, he now concentrated on novels that dealt with current issues. One contemporary called him "the first of the literary reformers." In *Coniston* (1906) he wrote about the tumult in state politics of which he had firsthand experience. The theme of *Mr. Crewe's Career* (1908) was the railroad monopoly in the state. Marriage and divorce were the major concerns of *A Modern Chronicle* (1910). The Social Gospel movement that called the church to return to its ministry of victims of economic and social injustice became the subject of *The Inside of the Cup* (1913). In *The Far Country* (1915) he attacked the corrupt alliance between business and politics. Because Churchill made clear the source of his inspiration for reform and social justice, he was one of the most effective and popular apologists for the Progressive movement.

During World War I, Churchill served as a naval propagandist. Based on his wartime experiences, he published *A Traveller in War Time* (1918). After the war Churchill's career as a novelist ended. In poor health and depressed by marital and emotional problems, he again changed the direction of his life, turning to painting and carpentry. He also pursued his interests in history, archaeology, etymology, and philosophy. The study of the Bible became one of his chief preoccupations. He lived a quiet and simple life in the country far from the stress of deadlines and the pressures of politics. His first book after more than twenty years, *The Unchartered Way* (1940), which was a summary of his philosophical and religious thought, went largely unnoticed by the public.

Churchill died suddenly while on vacation in Winter Park, Florida, on March 12, 1947, of a heart attack. He was buried beside his wife on their property in Plainfield, New Hampshire.

CHARLES T. JONES JR.

Churchill, Winston. *The Crisis*. New York: Macmillan, 1901.
———. *The Inside of the Cup*. New York: Macmillan, 1913.
Dictionary of American Biography. Supplement 4. S.v. "Churchill, Winston."

CLAMORGAN, CYPRIAN (1830–?)

Grandson of **Jacques Clamorgan,** Cyprian Clamorgan wrote *The Colored Aristocracy of St. Louis* (1858), one of the most important pieces of literature on free African Americans living in a slave community. In this slim volume, readers are allowed to perceive free blacks as men and women with diverse personalities, aspirations, learning, and attitudes. In Clamorgan's pages, they become individuals rather than an undifferentiated mass. His elite achieved various levels of wealth, pursued a number of different occupations, came from free as well as slave states, and responded differently to the problems of being nominally free within a slave society. Clamorgan wrote about more than forty free African Americans living in St. Louis during the 1850s.

Clamorgan was the fourth child of Appoline Clamorgan, who died eight days after his birth in 1830. The youngest child of Jacques Clamorgan, Appoline never married, but, according to a black barber named Gabriel Helms, lived with a white man named Langham, and St. Louisans called her Mrs. Langham. Born in 1803 Appoline was Jacques's second child. Jacques fathered a son named St. Eutrope in 1799 by a free woman named Helen or Heleine; Appoline by a slave woman named Anna and sometimes called Susanne; a son named Cyprian Marial in 1803 by another slave woman named Judith; and another son by Judith named Maximin in 1807. Jacques wanted to ensure that his children by slave women received their freedom, so he penned three affidavits to establish their status in 1809. None of Jacques's children lived long: St. Eutrope died in 1822; Maximin "about 1825"; Cyprian Martial in 1827; and Appoline three years later.

Appoline's children included Louis, Henry, Louisa, and Cyprian. Little is known about their rearing, but two of them attended school in Illinois during 1832. Louisa died in 1833. Cyprian's book indicated that he received a good deal of formal education. Written with clarity, style, wit, and frequent literary allusions, Clamorgan's book suggests learning and uncommon talent. He revealed familiarity with the writings of Lord Byron, Miguel Cervantes, William Shakespeare, Alexandre Dumas, and even Count D'Orsay.

By the 1840s all Appoline's sons had become St. Louis barbers. A newspaper announced in 1845 that the "Splendid Hair Cutting and Shaving Saloon" of Iredell and Clamorgan had installed baths, with tubs of "the finest Italian marble, the rooms large, airy and elegantly furnished." Louis Clamorgan was Iredell's partner. The *St. Louis City Directory for 1848* listed Louis at the "Italian Baths," Henry as a barber without a specific place of employment, and Cyprian at the "American House."

During the 1850s Clamorgan's name disappeared from the St. Louis city directories. Louis died in 1851. Henry remained a barber and in 1859 owned the "Clamorgan Baths." According to the manuscript census of 1860 for St. Louis, Henry owned real estate valued at ten thousand dollars and personal property worth three thousand dollars. Besides his barbershop, he owned and rented houses.

Clamorgan appeared in the historical record as a participant in a series of court cases during the 1870s and in 1880. By that time he may have left St. Louis, for his name does not appear in the "Vital Statistics of the City of St. Louis," a record of St. Louis deaths dating from 1850. Henry died in 1883, and Julius, a son of Louis, died in 1881. All that can be discovered about Cyprian is that he was still alive in 1880.

LAWRENCE O. CHRISTENSEN

Christensen, Lawrence O., ed. "Cyprian Clamorgan: The Colored Aristocracy of St. Louis (1858)." *Bulletin of the Missouri Historical Society* 31 (October 1974): 3–31.

Circuit Court of St. Louis County. Series O, No. 29647, June 1874. "Cyprian Clamorgan v. Fanny Deaver and John Burke" and "Affidavits of Jacques Clamorgan, Sept. 16, 1809."

St. Louis Globe-Democrat, January 24, 1879.

St. Louis Missouri-Republican, June 10, 1845.

Supreme Court of the State of Missouri, Series O, No. 33079, 1880. "Henry Clamorgan, Cyprian Clamorgan, Leon A. Clamorgan and Julius Clamorgan v. The Baden and St. Louis Railway Company."

Winch, Julie, ed. *The Colored Aristocracy of St. Louis, by Cyprian Clamorgan.* Columbia: University of Missouri Press, 1999.

CLAMORGAN, JACQUES (1730?–1814)

Jacques Phillippe Clamorgan arrived on the Missouri frontier in the early 1780s and spent the rest of his long life as a trader, land speculator, merchant, financier, statesman, explorer, and promoter. Abraham P. Nasatir, his biographer, described Clamorgan as "endowed with a tremendous imagination, together with an illusive pen and glib tongue. His ability to put vast dreams onto paper and persuade all of their reality was envied by everyone." Respected by all who knew him, his background kept him from being socially accepted by the aristocratic French Creoles of the area. He kept a "well-stocked harem of colored beauties," and though he never married, Clamorgan fathered four children by three women. His amorous activities may explain his lack of social acceptance. Some contemporaries also wondered at his proclivity for intrigue and at times doubted his probity, but he maintained friendships with the most important merchants in New Orleans, Cahokia, Kaskaskia, and Montreal, as well as St. Louis.

Born about 1730 in the West Indies, Clamorgan could trace his ancestry to Welsh, French, Portuguese, and probably African antecedents. He became associated with Thompson and Company of Kingston, Jamaica, as early as 1780, "probably in the slave trade between that island and New Orleans." He also became associated with Marmillion and Company of New Orleans about the same time. By 1783 Clamorgan had arrived in Spanish Louisiana, and a year later appeared in Upper Louisiana in the company of St. Louis merchant François Marmillion. Court records disclose that he participated in litigation in 1787, and land records show him engaged in land speculation. At one point his unconfirmed claims reached 1 million arpents, equivalent to about 850,000 acres. He took an interest in civic affairs, contributing to and serving as warden in the Catholic church in Ste. Genevieve. Clamorgan's trading led him to travel extensively in the Missouri River valley. Nasatir called him "the precursor of Lewis and Clark." He traveled across Texas and engaged in trade with Santa Fe "long before his successors made those trails famous."

Clamorgan is best known for his involvement in the Missouri Company, a creation designed to remove the British from Spanish territory and to monopolize the Indian trade on the frontier during the 1790s. Clamorgan's plans included discovering a route to the Pacific and becoming rich as a result of the company. One of nine board members of the company, Clamorgan served as its director and "chief dreamer." The company sent three expeditions up the Missouri River in attempts to dislodge the British from the Indian trade, tried to make it to the Pacific, and failed in both efforts. Clamorgan manipulated the company's articles to gain more control, ingratiated himself with Gov. Gen. Baron de Carondelet to secure "exclusive trade of the Upper Missouri," and gained a paper monopoly on the Indian trade of the upper Mississippi Valley. Ironically, credit from Andrew Todd, a British subject, financed Clamorgan's activities, and when Todd died in the yellow fever epidemic in New Orleans in 1796, Clamorgan's empire and the Missouri Company collapsed. Most of the board members went bankrupt, and Clamorgan faced ruin too, but former enemies Daniel Clark and **Auguste Chouteau** of St. Louis saved him from bankruptcy in 1799.

When the United States acquired the territory, Clamorgan seemed to move easily with the change, receiving appointment "as one of the first judges of the common pleas and quarter sessions in St. Louis," from Gov. **William Henry Harrison.** He also rented his house to the government to use as a jail. In 1807 he received a license from the United States to trade with Santa Fe, arriving there with three other traders, a slave, and trade goods. Delayed by Spanish officials, he returned to Missouri in 1808, the first Missourian to trade in Santa Fe. By then almost eighty years old, Clamorgan lived another six years, dying in St. Louis on October 30, 1814.

LAWRENCE O. CHRISTENSEN

Christensen, Lawrence O., ed. "Cyprian Clamorgan: The Colored Aristocracy of St. Louis (1858)." *Bulletin of the Missouri Historical Society* 31 (October 1974): 3–31.

Nasatir, A. P. "Jacques Clamorgan: Colonial Promoter of the Northern Border of New Spain." *New Mexico Historical Review* 17 (April 1942): 101–12.

Tharp, Dan L. "Jacques Clamorgan." In *Encyclopedia of Frontier Biography*. Glendale, Calif.: Arthur H. Clark, 1988.

CLAPP, ANNA LANSING (1814–1889)

Anna Lansing Clapp, president of the Ladies' Union Aid Society (LUAS) of St. Louis, was born on August 28, 1814, at Cambridge, New York, to parents of Dutch ancestry, Harmanus Wendell and Catalina Hun Lansing. After completing her education at Albany, Clapp taught for three years in the school of the Reverend Nathaniel Prime in Newburgh, New York. In 1838 she married Alfred Clapp and moved to Brooklyn, where she joined several benevolent organizations and served as treasurer of the Industrial School Association. The couple relocated to St. Louis just before the outbreak of the Civil War, when her husband became president of the Missouri Mining Company.

Initially forced to maintain a low profile because of secessionist sentiment, the LUAS of St. Louis first met in the home of Mrs. Frank Holy on July 26, 1861. Clapp was elected president of the organization in the fall and served in that capacity until the group disbanded in 1869. Operating under her able leadership and working in concert with the Western Sanitary Commission (WSC), the LUAS provided ancillary care to the thousands of wounded soldiers shipped to St. Louis hospitals for medical treatment throughout the war.

The organization maintained office space, together with the WSC and the Army Medical Corps, at City General Hospital. As the wounded from battles waged in the western department flooded the city, society members organized visiting committees, wrote letters home to families, and supplied food and hospital stores. They also distributed religious materials under the auspices of the Christian Commission and sent nursing escorts onto the battlefields to accompany soldiers back to St. Louis on floating hospitals outfitted by the WSC.

Clapp's political prerogatives clearly shaped the society's constitution, for members were required to show "satisfactory proof" of Union loyalty and demonstrate a willingness to use their "influence in advancing the cause of the same." The preamble originally guaranteed aid only to soldiers in the United States Army, but because of the number of Confederate soldiers detained in St. Louis during the war, it was amended in November 1863 to include all "who suffer in the cause of the Union, and also sick and wounded prisoners of war." By 1863 LUAS members lent support to the WSC Refugee Home, the Gratiot Street Prison Hospital, a special diet kitchen at Benton Barracks Hospital, and 684 destitute soldiers' families.

Clapp's consummate administrative abilities also provided the necessary ingredients for corporate viability beyond the spheres customarily limited to nineteenth-century women, for LUAS members not only documented their contributions to the war effort by submitting daily visiting-committee summaries and publishing annual reports but also set an example for other aid societies around the country. The women staffing the special diet kitchen at Benton Barracks served 19,382 meals between May and October 1863 alone, and their operation became a model for similar enterprises elsewhere. The LUAS also secured a government contract for the manufacture of hospital garments in 1862, and Clapp went to Washington, D.C., to ensure its renewal in 1864.

All society goods and monies were either contributed or earned by such efforts or by participation in community fund-raisers such as the Mississippi Valley Sanitary Fair in 1864. Overall, the LUAS paid five hundred soldiers' wives to assemble hospital garments and otherwise supplemented their wages with a monthly appropriation from St. Louis County's War Relief Fund. Fund-raisers netted $17,675 during the 1863–1864 fiscal year, and the WSC donated $50,000 from the proceeds of the Sanitary Fair to the society. All funds were distributed to those in need.

In the aftermath of the war, Clapp continued to contribute to the social welfare of the St. Louis community as president of the Western Female Guardian Home (1865–1869) and director of both the Colored Orphans' Home of St. Louis (1868) and the St. Louis Protestant Orphan Asylum (n.d.). She also officiated at the first woman-suffrage meeting at Mercantile Library on May 8, 1867. Later tied to the national woman-suffrage movement, the group was thereafter called the Women's Suffrage Association of Missouri.

Buried at Bellefontaine Cemetery after her death on December 6, 1889, Clapp left both the example of a lifetime of community service and a spirited testimony of Union loyalty amounting to legend: when Clapp's secessionist neighbors attempted to seize her Union flag by force in April 1861, she stopped them immediately by declaring: "You can only reach that flag over my dead body!"

PAULA COALIER

Blair, Emily Newell. "Forward: History of Woman Suffrage in Missouri." *Missouri Historical Review* 14 (April–July 1920): 284–88.

Brockett, L. P., and Marcy C. Vaughn. *Woman's Work in the Civil War: A Record of Heroism, Patriotism, and Patience.* Philadelphia, 1867.

Coalier, Paula. "Beyond Sympathy: The St. Louis Ladies' Union Aid Society and the Civil War." *Gateway Heritage* 11 (summer 1990): 38–51.

Trowbridge, Prentiss Sabin. Papers. Missouri Historical Society, St. Louis.

CLARK, BENNETT CHAMP (1890–1954)

Born in Bowling Green, Missouri, on January 8, 1890, Bennett Champ Clark was the son of Genevieve Bennett and **James Beauchamp "Champ" Clark.** He spent his childhood years in Bowling Green and Washington, D.C., where his father served in the House of Representatives (1893–1895 and 1897–1921), including eight years as Speaker (1911–1919). As a child Clark often accompanied his father to the House of Representatives; by age fourteen he was a precinct captain in Bowling Green. At the Democratic National Convention in 1912, he participated in the effort to secure the party's presidential nomination for his father. Despite majority support Champ Clark's candidacy was defeated by the party's rule requiring a two-thirds majority for nomination. Woodrow Wilson emerged as the Democratic nominee, leaving young Bennett bitterly disappointed. In 1936, with the blessing of Franklin Roosevelt, Clark would lead a successful fight at the Democratic convention to repeal the two-thirds requirement.

Having graduated from the University of Missouri in 1912, Clark enrolled in George Washington University's law school, graduating in 1914. In 1913, while still in law school, he became the parliamentarian for the House of Representatives, a job his father offered to him only after two-thirds of the House members signed a petition supporting him. Clark resigned in 1917 to enlist in the armed forces following American entry into World War I.

After completing officers' training camp with a captain's commission, he transferred to the Missouri National Guard, where he was elected lieutenant colonel of the Sixth Missouri Infantry, which later became the Thirty-fifth Division, 140th Infantry. Despite his father's intervention, he was unable to receive a combat assignment. Instead, he served as a staff officer in France, where he first met **Harry S. Truman;** he completed his military service as assistant chief of staff, first for the Eighty-eighth Division and later for the Thirty-fifth Division. In 1919, while still overseas, he became the youngest colonel in the American Expeditionary Force. That same year he helped establish the American Legion and became its first national commander. After the war he also served a term as head of the Thirty-fifth Division Veterans Association and became a member of the Veterans of Foreign Wars.

Following the war Clark briefly practiced criminal law in Bowling Green. After losing the only criminal case he ever prosecuted, he joined the St. Louis law firm of Fordyce, Holliday, and White, specializing in corporate law and becoming a successful trial lawyer. In 1922 he married Miriam Marsh, whose father had been the Democratic National Committee's treasurer during the 1916 and 1920 presidential campaigns. They had three sons: Champ, Marsh, and Kimball.

Clark remained interested in politics, though he declined retiring senator **James A. Reed**'s support for a United States Senate race in 1928. He decided to forego that race because Democratic prospects seemed bleak amid persistent Republican prosperity of the 1920s. Instead, he began work that year on his book, *John Quincy Adams: Old Man Eloquent,* a biography of a politically famous son of a politically famous father.

In 1932 Clark announced his candidacy to replace retiring U.S. senator **Harry Bartow Hawes.** Having trusted Reed's promise to obtain Kansas City boss **Thomas J. Pendergast**'s consent for his candidacy, Clark soon learned that Pendergast had already agreed to support another candidate, Charles M. Howell. A third candidate, Prohibition supporter Charles Hay, seemed likely to carry the dry rural vote.

Short on funds, lacking previous experience in elected office, and facing the powerful Pendergast machine, Clark persisted, relying on his base of support in the American Legion and on the name recognition he enjoyed courtesy of his father. A vigorous campaign also helped. Using an old Ford equipped with a public address system, he spoke to crowds in 110 of Missouri's 114 counties, bluntly stating his positions. He advocated the repeal of Prohibition, even though this jeopardized his appeal to dry rural voters. In Joplin he criticized tariffs, acknowledging that local zinc-mining interests would disagree with him.

Clark's strategy proved effective. Although Howell received 82,000 more votes than Clark in Kansas City, Clark defeated Howell by 55,000 votes in St. Louis. He also triumphed in the rural areas of the state, where he carried 194,000 votes to Hay's 135,000 and Howell's 72,000. After defeating Republican Henry Kiel in the general election, Clark gained seniority over other incoming senators when Senator Hawes resigned one month before his term expired and Gov. **Guy Brasfield Park** appointed Clark to fill the vacancy.

Clark's maverick politics continued beyond his campaign. A firm believer in Jeffersonian ideology, he soon began to criticize the New Deal, objecting to bureaucratization and to the expansion of federal and presidential powers. He opposed the establishment of both the Agricultural Adjustment and the National Recovery Administrations and was among the first Democrats to raise objections to Franklin Roosevelt's "court-packing" plan.

Clark also challenged Roosevelt's foreign policy, in part to protect Congress's role in shaping foreign policy, but also because of his commitment to international neutrality. Although such a stance reflected the strong isolationist sentiments of his German American constituency, Clark's resentment toward Woodrow Wilson over the 1912 nomination fight also fueled his isolationism. He participated in the Nye Committee hearings and, together with Gerald Nye, cosponsored neutrality legislation designed to prevent a recurrence of the events that had drawn the United States into World War I.

Clark's relationship with the Roosevelt administration distinguished him from Missouri's junior senator, Harry Truman, a consistent Roosevelt supporter. The two had other differences as well. In 1934 Clark supported **Jacob Le Roy Milligan** against Truman, the Pendergast candidate, in the Democratic senatorial primary. In the following years the two senators frequently sparred over federal patronage. Roosevelt's appointment, on Clark's recommendation, of U.S. attorney **Maurice M. Milligan,** who prosecuted dozens of workers in the Pendergast machine, also complicated the relationship. Generally, however, the two senators learned to cooperate and supported each other's reelection bids despite earlier differences. In 1945 Truman was Clark's best man

when Clark, whose first wife had died in 1943, married British actress Violet Heming.

By the late 1930s Clark's political prospects looked good. In 1938 he easily won reelection to the Senate, and his name began to surface as a possible dark-horse candidate for the Democratic presidential nomination in 1940. By 1944, however, his good fortune had vanished; former Missouri attorney general Roy McKittrick defeated him by seventeen thousand votes in the primary. McKittrick would later lose the general election to Gov. **Forrest C. Donnell.**

Clark's problems began well before 1944. His attacks on the New Deal cost him Roosevelt's endorsement for a third term. His struggles against Gov. **Lloyd Stark** in 1940 had compromised his support within the Missouri Democratic Party. He had lost credibility through his persistent isolationism, which he maintained until Pearl Harbor, long after Missouri voters had begun to favor American intervention. Determined opposition from the CIO-PAC also hurt. More important was his neglect of his constituents. Finally, a serious drinking problem interfered with his senatorial duties and caused Democratic leaders to doubt his suitability for higher office.

Never wealthy, Clark asked President Harry Truman to appoint him to a federal judgeship in 1945. Truman agreed to help his colleague and friend. Clark served nine years on the Circuit Court of Appeals of the District of Columbia. While vacationing in Gloucester, Massachusetts, he suffered a cerebral hemorrhage and died on July 13, 1954.

MARK SONNTAG

Alexander, Jack. "Missouri Dark Mule." *Saturday Evening Post* 211:15 (October 8, 1938): 5–7, 32–39.

Dictionary of American Biography. Supplement 5. S.v. "Clark, "Bennett Champ."

Gilbert, Clinton W. "Bennett Champ Clark." *Collier's* 91 (March 11, 1933): 23.

Goodrich, James. "Bennett Champ Clark." In *The Harry S. Truman Encyclopedia,* ed. Richard S. Kirkendall. Boston: G. K. Hall, 1989.

McCormick, Robert. "Runnin' Scared." *Collier's* 102 (October 22, 1938): 22, 77.

St. Louis Post-Dispatch, July 14, 1954.

Tait, Samuel W., Jr. "Champ Clark's Boy." *American Mercury* 28 (January 1933): 70–77.

CLARK, CARRIE ROGERS (1868–1946)

Carrie Rogers Clark was born in 1868 at Ravanna, in Mercer County, Missouri, to Col. William Beals and Cynthia Buren Rogers. The next year the family moved to Trenton where Rogers established the

Trenton Republican-Times, later published by his daughter from 1924 to 1946.

Carrie Rogers attended the University of Kansas–Lawrence; Colorado College, in Colorado Springs; the College of Sisters of Bethany in Topeka, Kansas; the Armour Institute of Chicago; and the Cincinnati Conservatory of Music.

On February 10, 1892, Rogers married Frank Louis Clark, who died less than two years later. Their only child, Perry Joseph, died at birth.

For three years Clark taught kindergarten and then became a librarian at Jewett Norris Library in Trenton, where she remained for twelve years. When her brother, N. G. Rogers, died in 1913, she went to work with her father at the newspaper. Her father died in 1924, and she assumed complete charge of the daily publication.

Clark changed the appearance of the paper by adding new type and using eight columns instead of six. She also consolidated with another newspaper, giving her the only daily publication in the area. Clark remained committed to her father's high ideals, promoting projects that would be beneficial to the growth and development of the community. A strong supporter of the Eighteenth Amendment to the Constitution, she never allowed any liquor advertising or propaganda to appear in her newspaper.

Clark took an active role in civic affairs because she saw the need for something to be done. She, like her father, also assisted several young people in their educations. A member of the Daughters of the American Revolution and the Trenton Commercial Club, she served as the first president of the Business and Professional Women's Club at the time it was organized and two terms as president of the XCIX Club, a cultural organization. A member of the Baptist church, she taught a Sunday-school class and served as organist for twenty-five years.

At one time Clark was the only woman member of the Associated Press of Missouri. In addition, she served as treasurer of the Missouri Press Association. During Journalism Week at the University of Missouri–Columbia in 1929, Clark spoke to members of the press association, telling her audience that a "woman's newspaper has just the same problems to meet and the same public to serve as had a man produced paper." A newspaper is a big factor in community progress and high ideals. She insisted the *Trenton Republican-Times* was still run on the policies outlined by her father years before.

Convinced that women could and would make good in the business world, Clark proved it could be done. In November 1940 the Kansas City Board of Trade presented its annual award to the *Trenton Republican-Times* as the best small daily in the state. The award included a scholarship for a deserving young person, which gave Clark great joy.

Clark lived in the same family home in Trenton most of her life. She continued her work at the newspaper until a few weeks before her death on April 5, 1946.

MARY K. DAINS

Dains, Mary K., ed. *Show Me Missouri Women: Selected Biographies.* Kirksville, Mo.: Thomas Jefferson University Press, 1989.
Trenton (Mo.) Republican-Times, April 6, 1946.

CLARK, GENE (1944–1991)

Gene Clark was a cofounder of the seminal 1960s folk-rock group the Byrds. The band's first single, a recording of Bob Dylan's "Mr. Tambourine Man," rose to the top of the popular-music charts in 1965.

Harold Eugene Clark was born on November 17, 1944, in Tipton, Missouri, the son of Kelly and Jeanne Faherty Clark and the second oldest of thirteen children. His father was a sergeant stationed at Camp Bowie, Texas, at the time, and his mother and the children lived in Tipton with her parents until after World War II when the family moved to the Kansas City area.

Clark attended school in Raytown, a suburb of Kansas City. In the early 1960s he played in a local band called the Surf Riders until the New Christy Minstrels hired him on one of its passes through Kansas City.

Clark became one of the five founding members of the Byrds, playing with the band from 1964 until 1967. He played harmonica and tambourine, and assisted with the vocals. He wrote many of the group's early songs, music that broke new ground with its blend of folk and rock. Other band members were Jim McGuinn (who later used the name Roger), lead guitar and vocals; David Crosby, rhythm guitar and vocals; Mike Clarke, drums; and Chris Hillman, bass guitar and vocals. Clark wrote and sang "I Feel a Whole Lot Better," and contributed to arrangements for the group's first record and biggest hit in 1965, "Eight Miles High." The Byrds' version of Pete Seeger's "Turn! Turn! Turn!" also reached number one on the record charts.

Clark left the Byrds permanently in 1967, at least partly because of his fear of flying. He later led a tribute version of the Byrds for a short period of time during the 1980s. After he left the group he continued to make albums, either alone or with other performers, though none achieved the success of the original Byrds. Other performers attained hit records with Clark's songs, including the Turtles' rendition of "You Showed Me." Linda Ronstadt, the Eagles, and Tom Petty also recorded Clark's work.

In 1990 an extensive four-CD retrospective of the Byrds was released by Columbia Records. In 1991 the group was inducted into the Rock and Roll Hall of Fame. In 1993 *Entertainment Weekly* reminded readers that the Byrds were once called "America's answer to the Beatles" in terms of musical influence. The magazine also described them as "a band without whom rock and country rock wouldn't exist."

Clark died from natural causes on May 24, 1991, at his home in Sherman Oaks, California, a suburb of Los Angeles. In the 1980s Clark had undergone surgery to remove part of his stomach because of ulcers. His body was brought back to the place of his birth for burial in St. Andrew's Catholic Cemetery on a hill overlooking Tipton.

ARTHUR F. MCCLURE

New York Times, May 26, 1991.
Obituary. *People* (June 10, 1991).
Obituary. *Time* (June 10, 1991).
"100 Greatest CDs." *Entertainment Weekly* (November 5, 1993).
Tipton (Mo.) Times, June 6, 1991.
Variety, June 3, 1991.

CLARK, JAMES BEAUCHAMP "CHAMP" (1850–1921)

On March 7, 1850, Daniel Webster delivered the last great speech of his distinguished career in defense of the Compromise of 1850. By historical coincidence, a future orator-statesman, James Beauchamp "Champ" Clark, was born on that day in a poor cabin outside Lawrenceburg, Kentucky.

A Missouri congressman, the House minority leader, the Speaker of the House, and an unsuccessful candidate for the Democratic presidential nomination in 1912, Champ Clark was a political leader during the Progressive Era. Like Daniel Webster, Clark's oratorical skills furthered his career; like Webster, despite his party leadership, no major legislation bears his name; like Webster, the presidency eluded Clark. Unlike Webster, Champ Clark's political arena was the House of Representatives, where he led the Democrats in the 1910 fight to reduce the power of Speaker Joseph Cannon and, as Speaker, inaugurated a series of democratic reforms.

Clark moved to Missouri in 1875 after graduating with honors from Bethany College in West Virginia (1873) and from the Cincinnati Law School (1875). He taught school in Louisiana, Missouri, for a year before launching his legal career. He practiced law for most of the period from 1876 to 1897, usually combining a private practice with a political post. He served as a city attorney for both Louisiana and Bowling Green, Missouri, before becoming the assistant county attorney (1881–1884) and then the county attorney for Pike County, Missouri (1884–1888). He maintained his Bowling Green law office

during his service in the state legislature (1889) and for his first several terms in the United States House of Representatives.

Clark married Genevieve Davis Bennett in 1881. The couple had four children. Champ Clark and Anne Hamilton Clark were both born in the 1880s and died in infancy. Their surviving children were **Bennett Champ Clark,** born in 1890, and Genevieve Clark, born in 1894; she recalled in 1970 that her father was a reserved man who was not demonstrably affectionate. However, the written word freed him of his inhibitions. When he traveled the Chautauqua circuit, Clark sent daily cards and letters to Bennett and Genevieve as they were growing up. "You know now or will in the coming years how much I love you," he wrote to three-year-old Bennett. "Kiss Middy for me," he wrote frequently to his "dear Bab." Clark's correspondence with Bennett, while the younger man was in France during World War I, provides a poignant insight into the intense love between the two men. And when Genevieve's only child, Champ, died of pneumonia in 1919, she recalled, "My father quit living."

In his memoirs Clark tells about his father giving him a copy of William Wirt's *Life of Patrick Henry* when he was about ten years old: "that book determined me to be a lawyer and a congressman before I had ever seen a lawyer, a law-book, a courthouse, or a Congressman." Although the Speaker can be accused of exaggeration in his childhood remembrance, the evidence is clear that he consciously planned a political career. Born James Beauchamp Clark, while a law student he experimented with "Jamie," "Beauchamp," and "Beau" before settling upon "Champ" as an eye-catching and easily remembered name. He joined the Missouri Democratic Party in 1876 and thereafter worked conscientiously to begin his "life work proper," which meant a seat in the United States House of Representatives. His goal was "to achieve a name worthy of a place beside the best of the immortals."

Clark began his quest at the local level. He became a popular civic and religious leader, first in Louisiana and then in Bowling Green. In July 1876 he was elected a member of the Louisiana Fire Company. He helped organize the Louisiana Lyceum where he enjoyed debating such topics as: "That the Whipping Post Should Be Re-established as a Punishment for Petty Larceny." He taught a Sunday-school class for young men and was active in the Masons.

Clark was engaged in Democratic politics steadily from 1876 onward. After holding local and county prosecutor positions, he was elected to a term in the state legislature in 1888. He unsuccessfully sought the Democratic nomination to the House in 1890 for Missouri's Ninth District, but won both the nomination and the election in 1892. He failed reelection in

1894 due to the depression, but was reelected in 1896 and in each successive election until 1920, when he lost in the post–World War I Republican landslide. Clark's hold on the district's congressional seat was due not only to his popularity but also to the gerrymandering tactics of the Democratically controlled state legislature.

Although he wrote extensively during his career—first for local newspapers in Missouri and later as a congressman for national periodicals such as the *North American Review* and the *Saturday Evening Post*—Clark's forte was oratory. His ability furthered his career as an attorney and as a politician. He was a colorful, dramatic, and entertaining speaker. He "takes a five-gallon inspiration, . . ." said the *Louisiana Journal,* and "belches forth his pent-up effervescence. . . . The audience likes it." After his election to the House, Clark traveled the country as a Chautauqua speaker, delivering such speeches as "Richer than Golconda," "Aaron Burr," "The United States in the Twentieth Century," and "Daniel Webster."

Clark was a Jeffersonian and a southern Democrat, and his views reflected those biases. In 1912 he said of Jefferson, "So clear was his vision as a statesman, that after a century of legislation we have not attained his lofty standard of political conduct." Clark described people in Jeffersonian terms in an 1881 address: "In the aggregate, humanity is good, noble, honest, and patriotic." This philosophy caused Clark to support such democratic policies as the direct election of senators, the elimination of the electoral college ("a clumsy and cumbrous nuisance"), and primary elections for the selection of presidential and vice presidential candidates. The first recorded reference of his support for woman suffrage is a journal entry in 1882: "Wrote an article for *Vandalia Leader,* entitled 'Equality v. Mother Wiggins'—the latter having answered an article I had written in favor of Woman Suffrage."

Throughout his career Clark advocated party loyalty. As minority leader (1908–1911 and 1919–1921) and Speaker (1911–1919), he worked to unite the urban and rural segments of the party in the House. As a loyal Democrat he campaigned for both the conservative Grover Cleveland and the populist William Jennings Bryan in presidential races. Because the Ninth was "The rich Mesopotamia of our western world," he was an agrarian. To help farmers he supported the monetization of silver in the 1890s; after the turn of the century, he supported the party's shift to favoring a more flexible currency, and ultimately supported the Federal Reserve. Clark urged the reduction of tariff rates until the passage in 1913 of the Underwood-Simmons Tariff accomplished this goal. "My people cannot be protected," he said in 1897, "because their surplus must be sold in Liverpool." Later he modified his demand for free trade in order to appease Democrats from industrial states. Closely related to both monetary and tariff policies was Clark's support for an income tax.

Clark's southern perspective is most clearly seen in his views about race. "In Missouri," he said in a 1900 House speech, "every man, . . . white or black, has the right to vote . . . but I am a Southern man in feeling and in thought, and I know that what they do down there [is for] self-preservation. . . ." The representative's view about race combined racism and social Darwinism.

Clark followed the party leadership in supporting the Spanish-American War. Missourians favored intervention in Cuba, which Clark believed was consistent with the Monroe Doctrine. He also believed that Canada would become part of the United States. However, he opposed imperialistic expansion to Hawaii and the Philippines, and opposed Chinese immigration: "The Chinese problem is to the Pacific coast what the negro problem is to the Southern States. . . ."

Interestingly, Clark's Jeffersonian concept of justice and democracy also influenced his views about race and imperialism. After watching an 1876 trial in Louisiana, Missouri, he confided to his journal: "Learned that there is no justice for a negro in this country." His views about imperialism reflected a belief in the democratic process. As members of the United States, it was not proper for Hawaiians or Filipinos to be denied statehood, nor was it just to restrict Chinese voting in California. If these people were not "fit for citizenship," he argued, then they should not be made part of the country.

As the election of 1912 approached, Clark enjoyed support for the presidential nomination among party regulars from the West, the Midwest, and the South. At the Baltimore convention, he led the voting for twenty-seven ballots, holding a majority of nine. But William Jennings Bryan switched his support to Woodrow Wilson on the fourteenth ballot. In addition, Clark's florid rhetoric, his partisanship, and his cries for harmony obscured his progressive tendencies from the urban press and from progressive delegates. He was viewed by some as a timeserver who had never sponsored any important legislation. He failed to gain the required two-thirds majority, and on the forty-sixth ballot Wilson was nominated.

Clark's memoirs reveal that he regarded his loss of the presidential nomination as the central event of his career. Historically, however, he is more significant as a congressional leader. As minority leader after 1908, he unified the rural and urban factions of the House Democrats, leading them in their opposition to the Payne-Aldrich Tariff (1909) and in the removal of

Speaker Joseph Cannon from the Rules Committee (1910). As Speaker after 1911, Clark democratized House procedures at the expense of his own power; for example, he permitted a division of debate time between Democrats and Republicans. He also restored the caucus, and actively led the Democratic majority in the achievement of New Freedom legislation after 1913. Declaring that he refused to be "a rubber stamp Speaker," Clark spoke out in debate; for instance, he resisted until 1917 U.S. entry into World War I and the Selective Service Act. Clark's popularity as Speaker was so great that he was reelected in 1916 when the Republicans could have elected their own Speaker.

Clark suffered the second defeat of his congressional career in 1920. He died on March 2, 1921, one day before the end of his term, and five days before his seventy-first birthday.

Clark was a colorful and significant political leader. He is the only Speaker of the House in Missouri's history and was a major political leader during the Progressive Era. Further, he is representative of the political type at the turn of the century. Wearing a broad-brimmed slouch hat, a stand-up collar, and a cutaway coat, Clark defended America's farmers from industrial "Plutocrats." He was a "ring-tailed roarer" on behalf of America's past, even as he supported such policies as woman suffrage, the income tax, and the direct election of senators, which pushed the country into a new future.

GEOFFREY FAHY MORRISON

Cannon, Clarence. Papers. Western Historical Manuscripts Collection, Columbia.

Clark, Bennett Champ. Papers. Western Historical Manuscripts Collection, Columbia.

Clark, Champ. *My Quarter Century of American Politics.* 2 vols. New York: Harper and Brothers, 1920.

———. Papers. Western Historical Manuscripts Collection, Columbia.

Morrison, Geoffrey F. "A Political Biography of Champ Clark." Ph.D. diss., St. Louis University, 1971.

CLARK, MERIWETHER LEWIS (1809–1881)

Meriwether Lewis Clark was born in St. Louis on January 10, 1809, the eldest child of explorer and territorial governor **William Clark** and his first wife, Julia Hancock Clark. One of Meriwether's earliest memories was of sitting beside his illustrious father while he negotiated treaties with the Indians following the War of 1812. He never forgot the time when one of the chiefs laid his hand on Meriwether's

head while addressing Governor Clark and likened himself to the governor's son.

Meriwether Lewis Clark was admitted to the United States Military Academy on July 1, 1825, and graduated from West Point on July 1, 1830. Brevet Lieutenant Clark was assigned to the Sixth Infantry, then stationed at Jefferson Barracks just south of St. Louis. He saw active service in the Black Hawk War in 1832 and resigned from the United States Army on May 31, 1833. On January 9, 1834, he married Abigail Churchill of Louisville, Kentucky. Before her death in 1852, she gave birth to seven children: William Hancock (1839), Samuel Churchill (1843), Mary Eliza (1845), Meriwether Lewis II (1846), John O'Fallon II (1848), George Rogers II (1850), and Charles Jefferson (1852).

Benefiting from the superior technical education he received at West Point, Clark made his living as an architect and engineer in St. Louis. The Italianate Church of St. Vincent de Paul (still standing in south St. Louis) was among his designs. His professional accomplishments also extended to public service. In 1836 Clark was elected to represent St. Louis in the Missouri General Assembly. In 1840 he was appointed city engineer; later he served as recorder of the city court.

Clark resumed his military career in 1846, when, at the outset of the war with Mexico, he accepted appointment as major and commanding officer of a volunteer artillery battalion being raised in St. Louis. In July and August, Clark and his volunteers, including "many of the first young men of the town," moved via the Missouri River from St. Louis to Fort Leavenworth before following the Santa Fe Trail into northern New Mexico to join Gen. **Stephen Watts Kearny**'s small Army of the West assembling at Santa Fe. Clark later accompanied **Alexander Doniphan**'s column into Mexico, fighting at the Battle of Sacramento. In 1849, after his return to St. Louis, Clark was appointed federal surveyor general for Illinois and Missouri.

Clark briefly resumed martial duties in August 1854. After the St. Louis militia proved ineffective in stopping riots between native-born Know-Nothings and immigrants, the mayor called for the creation of a special volunteer citizen police. The distinguished soldier Clark was put in charge of "outdoor operations," supervising thirty-three prominent citizens serving as captains and seven hundred volunteers, more than ten times the normal police force. Clark's volunteers patrolled for several days, putting an end to disorder in the city.

Like many Missourians, the Clark family seems to have been initially reluctant to participate in civil war. On the eve of the secession crisis, Clark wrote to one of his sons to explain that "both the South and North are wrong and have gone too far in their abuse of each other." He recommended that Missouri and "the Great West" should deal with the troublemakers as if they were "two very naughty boys quarreling." First, they should be warned to desist. If that failed, the problem should be solved by "chucking their heads together" and sitting them down "for better behavior."

Clark was fifty-two years old and in semiretirement when war broke out in Missouri in 1861. Gov. **Claiborne Fox Jackson** appointed him to the rank of brigadier general in the pro-Confederate Missouri State Guard and gave him responsibility for raising troops in the St. Louis area. Unfortunately for Clark, his efforts were generally unproductive because of heavy Union control of his home territory. Clark left the state guard for the Confederate service in November 1861, accepting a position as a major of artillery. He was soon promoted to colonel. Colonel Clark held several staff positions in 1862, but late in the year the irascible general Braxton Bragg removed him from command in response to Clark's assertions that Bragg had made him a glorified clerk. Clark was subsequently assigned to the Ordnance Department in Richmond, and from November 1864 he commanded an infantry brigade in the Army of Northern Virginia until he was taken prisoner at Amelia Court House, Virginia, on April 5, 1865.

After the war Clark moved to Kentucky and on December 30, 1865, married Julia Davidson at Louisville. He served as the architect of the state buildings and later as the commandant of cadets at the Kentucky Military Institute. Meriwether Lewis Clark died in Frankfort, Kentucky, on October 28, 1881, at the age of seventy-two. He is buried at Bellefontaine Cemetery in St. Louis.

WILLIAM C. WINTER

Allardice, Bruce S. *More Generals in Gray.* Baton Rouge: Louisiana State University Press, 1995.

Coues, Elliott, ed. *The History of the Lewis and Clark Expedition.* New York: Francis P. Harper, 1893.

Kennerly, William C., and Elizabeth Russell. *Persimmon Hill: A Narrative of Old St. Louis and the Far West.* Norman: University of Oklahoma Press, 1949.

Schneider, John C. "Riot and Reaction in St. Louis, 1854–1856." *Missouri Historical Review* 68 (January 1974): 171–85.

Stadler, Frances H. "Letters from Minoma." *Bulletin of the Missouri Historical Society* 16 (April 1960): 237–59.

Winter, William C. "'Amidst Trials and Troubles': Captain Samuel Churchill Clark, C.S.A." *Missouri Historical Review* 92 (October 1997): 1–17.

CLARK, PETER HUMPHRIES (1829–1925)

Peter Humphries Clark provided leadership for African American communities in St. Louis and Cincinnati, Ohio. One biographer titled an article "In His Veins Coursed No Bootlicking Blood," and that line summarized Clark's personality. He consistently demanded respect and accepted the responsibilities of leadership. A teacher, journalist, and race leader, Clark deserved the accolades contemporaries heaped upon him.

Born in 1829, Clark spent almost sixty years in Cincinnati before moving to St. Louis in 1888. His father owned a barbershop in the Ohio city and had been a freedman since 1817. Peter attended a private black elementary school, graduating in 1844, and continued his education in Hiram S. Gilmore's private high school, graduating in 1848. His father died, leaving Peter the barbershop, but the young man bristled at his white clientele's demand that he refuse service to blacks, and he left the business. According to one authority, Clark proclaimed that he intended to shave not another white man, but if he did, "he would cut his throat."

In 1849 Ohio appropriated funding for black public schools, and Clark became the first black teacher hired in Cincinnati. Except for an interlude in the 1850s, during which he edited a newspaper and ran a grocery store and contemplated migrating to Liberia because of discrimination in Cincinnati, he remained in the Cincinnati school system until 1886. He became principal of the first black public high school in the city in 1866, retaining the position until a Republican-controlled school board fired him. By 1886 Clark had abandoned the Republican Party and become a nationally known Democrat. He accepted the job of principal of the black State Normal and Industrial School in Huntsville, Alabama, but stayed only one year. He could not tolerate the sycophancy required by local whites. St. Louis attracted Clark because his daughter Ernestine Nesbit taught there. Clark began teaching in Mound City in 1889 and continued until he retired in 1908. He remained in St. Louis until his death on June 21, 1925.

As a young man Clark had achieved some national recognition. In 1853 he attended the Colored National Convention in Rochester, New York, serving as one of the four secretaries at that antislavery convention. Later that same year, he drafted a constitution for the National Equal Rights League, an organization that led in promoting rights for blacks before and after the Civil War. Politically active for the remainder of his life, Clark moved from one party to the next seeking a political home that recognized the rights of African Americans to participate equally in the democratic process. During the Civil War he remained in Cincinnati, lambasting Lincoln for his reluctance to end slavery and commemorating the contributions of blacks to the Civil War effort in his booklet titled "The Black Brigade of Cincinnati," published in 1864.

Short, wiry, and bearded, Clark easily carried the title of "professor" that contemporaries gave him. Black historian George Washington Williams, who knew Clark, called him a "capital little fellow. He is sarcastic, industrious, earnest, nervous, and even practical at times."

A Republican during most of this era, in 1878 Clark became a member of the Socialist Labor Party. He served on the national executive committee of the party and won its nomination for a seat in Congress. Only 275 people voted for him, and he returned to the Republican Party in 1879. Receiving little incentive to stay in that party, by 1882 Clark had become a Democrat. From the late 1860s onward, Clark argued that blacks should divide their votes and support the party that best represented their interests. To remain in only one party would make them politically ineffective, he believed.

In 1888 Clark and **James Milton Turner** vied for chairmanship of a national meeting of black Democrats. Clark won the position, but he and Turner soon made peace, and in 1892 they originated and helped organize a mass black protest against lynching and other racial outrages. By then both men lived in St. Louis. They set aside May 31, 1892, as a day of "humiliation, fasting, and prayer." They asked all St. Louis blacks, regardless of party, to demonstrate to the nation their concern about lynching and racial injustice. Clark delivered the major speech of the day. He urged African Americans to protest wrongdoing whenever they saw it, and he refuted the claim that lynchings were caused by black men raping white women.

Clark's reputation peaked in the 1890s. As that decade opened, the *Freeman,* a black newspaper published in Indiana, asked its readers to identify the "Ten Greatest Negroes." They named Peter Clark, along with such other prominent blacks as Frederick Douglass, T. Thomas Fortune, and James Milton Turner. As Clark aged and continued to teach, he became a much venerated but less politically active personage in the St. Louis black community.

LAWRENCE O. CHRISTENSEN

Christensen, Lawrence O. "Peter Humphries Clark." *Missouri Historical Review* 88 (January 1994): 145–56.

Grossman, Lawrence. "In His Veins Coursed No Bootlicking Blood: The Career of Peter H. Clark." *Ohio History* 86 (spring 1977): 80–93.

Gutman, Herbert. "Peter H. Clark: Pioneer Negro Socialist, 1877." *Journal of Negro Education* 34 (fall 1965): 413–15.

Kremer, Gary R. *James Milton Turner and the Promise of America: The Public Life of a Post–Civil War Black Leader.* Columbia: University of Missouri Press, 1991.

CLARK, WILLIAM (1770–1838)

William Clark, the renowned American explorer who joined **Meriwether Lewis** in leading an overland expedition to the Pacific from 1804 to 1806, is an enduring national hero. The story of Lewis and Clark's daring trek across the North American continent is the stuff of high adventure that two centuries later still retains the power to fascinate and inspire. Clark's fame clearly rests on his role as coleader of the Corps of Discovery, but not to be overlooked is the prominent place that he occupies in Missouri's early history. Following his return from the Pacific, Clark moved to St. Louis where he achieved further distinction as a militia officer, territorial governor, and federal Indian agent. During his years in Missouri, he helped defend America's exposed western frontier, enhanced his reputation as an Indian diplomat, and successfully administered a burgeoning territory whose diverse cultures seemed perpetually in collision.

William Clark was born in Caroline County, Virginia, on August 1, 1770, the ninth of John and Ann Rogers Clark's ten children. Young William grew up amid the turmoil and uncertainties of the Revolutionary War. Five of his brothers fought in that conflict, and one of them, George Rogers Clark, won national acclaim for his role in wresting control of the trans-Appalachian West from the British. William had been too young to take up arms for the American cause, but the experiences of his family members undoubtedly contributed to his decision to become a soldier.

After the war members of the Clark family moved to Kentucky and settled on a farm south of Louisville, drawn to the region, no doubt, on the recommendation of George Rogers. Kentucky had much to offer new settlers, but educational opportunity was not among its enticements. As a consequence, young William was denied the kind of classical education that had been afforded his older brothers in Virginia. The Clarks did not, however, neglect his schooling. George Rogers Clark, who seemed especially determined that his little brother should receive a proper education, awakened in the lad a fascination for science and natural history. Thanks to his family's diligence, with the exception of his deficiencies in written language, especially his poor spelling and faulty grammar, William Clark was well prepared to make his way in the world.

In 1789 William Clark joined the militia and embarked upon the first of several expeditions that took him north of the Ohio to fight Indians. He found the military life to his liking, and in 1792 secured a commission as a lieutenant in the regular army. Clark fought under Gen. Anthony Wayne at the Battle of Fallen Timbers, but resigned a captain's commission in 1796 to return home to look after the family property, threatened by George Rogers Clark's mounting debts and periodic alcoholic binges. For the next eight years William Clark labored, as any respectable Virginia planter would have, to repair the family's estate and increase its land- and slaveholdings. Nonetheless, when an unexpected opportunity presented itself to Clark in 1803, he was quick to accept.

Meriwether Lewis, a fellow Virginian with whom Clark had served in the Ohio campaigns, invited him to become coleader of an expedition to the Pacific for President Thomas Jefferson. Clark's affirmative response launched a great friendship and one of the most successful partnerships in U.S. history. Confusion concerning Clark's military rank (Lewis had promised him a captain's rank, but he was commissioned as a lieutenant) never became an issue, and Lewis, who treated Clark as his equal, never bothered to tell the men under their command about the mixup. In history they would be forever known as the "Captains of Discovery."

During the fall and winter of 1803–1804 Lewis and Clark busied themselves recruiting members for the expedition, ordering the necessary equipment and supplies, and overseeing the arrangements required for such an ambitious undertaking. They established a winter camp on the Rivière à Dubois (Wood River), a small stream opposite the mouth of the Missouri. During their stay there, both men often traveled to St. Louis where they became fast friends with many of that city's leading traders. Those visits provided a welcome diversion from camp life, but the pleasant gatherings also allowed them to confer with the persons who knew most about the country that the American expedition was preparing to traverse.

With Clark in charge, the Corps of Discovery broke camp on May 14, 1804, and headed up the Missouri. Lewis joined them in St. Charles, where on May 21 the forty-some members of the expedition embarked on their historic journey. Lewis's choice of Clark as his coleader turned out to be a good one. The partners worked well together. Clark was an experienced woodsman and a seasoned soldier who knew how to command. His excellent cartographic skills, his abilities as a waterman, and his aptitude for Indian negotiations proved especially valuable. Even Clark's less polished writings serve as the primary source of information about the expedition's day-to-day activities, since in many instances only his daily journal entries survive.

After successfully completing their seven-thousand-mile, twenty-eight-month excursion, the Captains of Discovery received a rousing reception in St. Louis on September 23, 1806, followed by equally enthusiastic outpourings during a triumphant trip to the national capital. Their accomplishments far exceeded Jefferson's expectations, notwithstanding their failure to discover an all-water route to the Pacific. In gratitude, the president offered Lewis the governorship of the Louisiana Territory, and he invited Clark to serve as the principal U.S. Indian agent for tribes west of the Mississippi and as brigadier general of Louisiana's territorial militia. Clark's acceptance of those positions marked the beginning of his lengthy and fruitful association with Missouri.

When Clark arrived in St. Louis to take up his new duties in early May 1807 he immediately took steps to counter the growing British influence among the Indian tribes in the region and to shore up the territory's inadequate defenses. Among other things, he worked with local officials to improve the state of military readiness by revising territorial militia laws. However, he devoted most of his time to Indian matters. Like Jefferson and Lewis, Clark believed that trade was the crucial element in shaping relations between the United States and Native people. In 1808 Governor Lewis dispatched Clark to a high bluff overlooking the Missouri River, near the present town of Sibley in Jackson County, for the dual purposes of establishing a combined U.S. trading factory and military fort and securing an agreement with the Osages relinquishing control over an immense tract of land in the Louisiana Territory. With the assistance of a detachment of troops from Cantonment Belle Fontaine and a company of mounted dragoons, Clark supervised the construction of the new installation, sometimes referred to as Fort Clark but better known as Fort Osage. He also persuaded representatives of the Osage Nation to sign a treaty ceding their homeland in Missouri and Arkansas to the United States, thanks to the assistance of **White Hair (Paw-Hiu-Skah),** a compliant tribal leader. However, that treaty soon came under fire and had to be renegotiated when angry members of the fragmented Osage tribe rejected White Hair's claims to leadership and questioned his authority to represent them in negotiations. Clark placed the blame for the misunderstandings on the interference of the powerful Chouteau family. The disgruntled Indians successfully forced U.S. officials to revise the original agreement, but even with those changes the die had been cast and the Osage cession of lands to the United States had been accomplished.

Although Clark had been willing to do what was necessary to secure tribal acquiescence to the 1808 Osage land cession, on more than one occasion he came to the defense of beleaguered Native people. In 1810 he recommended a presidential pardon for a Sac Indian convicted of murdering a white trader, and later that year he characterized a band of transplanted Shawnee as "a peaceable and well disposed people . . . of great service to our frontier settlements." Such philanthropic sentiments did not meet with much approval in the western settlements and later proved detrimental when Clark unsuccessfully sought elective office.

Clark did not allow his public responsibilities to keep him from doing business on the side. In 1809 he joined forces with **Manuel Lisa** and other prominent traders to form the St. Louis Missouri Fur Company and promptly assisted his new partners in negotiating a contract with the U.S. government to facilitate the Mandan chief Sheheke's return to his village on the upper Missouri. Both as an Indian agent and later as a territorial governor, Clark was predisposed to favor family members with government appointments and contracts.

The outbreak of the War of 1812 presented Clark with new and more serious challenges, especially after he became governor of the Missouri Territory in 1813, a post he held until Missouri became a state. In 1814 the governor took personal charge of a military expedition to Prairie du Chien on the upper Mississippi in the heart of British country. Clark believed that the establishment of an American presence there would effectively isolate the Indians on the lower Mississippi from their British allies in Canada and forestall renewed Indian hostilities throughout the valley. Once the region had been secured, Clark returned to St. Louis, but by midsummer the British and their Indian allies had returned to capture the U.S. outpost at Prairie du Chien.

Although the Treaty of Ghent, signed in late 1814, marked an official end to the hostilities, violence persisted along much of the exposed western frontier. In an attempt to secure a cessation of fighting, President James Madison named Clark, along with Gov. Ninian Edwards of the Illinois Territory and St. Louis merchant **Auguste Chouteau,** to conduct negotiations with western Indian tribes. The peace commissioners summoned representatives of various tribes to meet at Portage des Sioux in the Missouri Territory in July 1815. Clark and the other commissioners spent the remainder of the summer concluding treaties with tribal representatives. In return for their agreement to submit to U.S. authority in the region, the tribes received promises of friendly commerce with American traders.

Although Indian affairs occupied much of Governor Clark's time, he also had to address the problems of governing a frontier territory where personal feuds and animosities frequently exacerbated disagreements over public policy. In the rough-and-tumble arena of Missouri territorial politics, Clark generally sided with members of the St. Louis junto

who had long dominated affairs in the territory. Influential French Creole fur merchants and powerful land claimants with substantial holdings in unconfirmed Spanish titles formed the junto's nucleus, but they could also count on the support of some powerful American allies, such as the governor.

Clark's open identification with the St. Louis clique made him a favorite target for the barbs of the antijunto faction, controlled by rival land speculators who objected to the confirmation of large unapproved Spanish grants. Rightly or wrongly, Clark's loyalty to longtime friends and members of the territorial establishment, coupled with his belief that their continuing support was in the national interest, guided his political choices. Ultimately, his close association with individuals representing the old order in a rapidly changing territory turned out to be a serious liability. Clark's political instincts may have been flawed, but his considerable talents as an Indian diplomat, territorial administrator, and military commander; his conscientious devotion to official duties; and his consistent commitment to the welfare of the territory and its inhabitants earned him the distinction of being Missouri's best territorial governor.

However, Clark's laudable record of service meant little in Missouri's changing political climate. When Missouri gained congressional authorization to enter the Union in 1820, Clark announced that he would be a candidate to become the new state's first elected governor. The death of his wife, Julia Hancock Clark, in Virginia kept him out of the state during the campaign. The absentee candidate mistakenly referred voters with questions about his suitability for the office to the old inhabitants and early settlers with whom he had long been on friendly terms. His close identification with that group and the unpopularity of his Indian policies sealed his fate among the legions of recently arrived American farmers in the new state's outlying regions. When the returns were in, **Alexander McNair** had defeated Clark handily.

Despite his loss in the gubernatorial contest, Clark continued to reside in St. Louis. After statehood he retained his position as U.S. Indian agent, and in 1822 federal officials gave him the title of superintendent of Indian affairs at St. Louis, a post that he occupied until his death. Notwithstanding his more elevated designation, Clark's power and influence were clearly on the wane, but his fame as an explorer had not diminished. Distinguished guests visiting St. Louis routinely called on him, and he delighted in showing them his museum filled with Indian artifacts and other miscellaneous curiosities, including animal and reptile skins, mineral samples, and mastodon bones. In his final years, William Clark shared honors with **(Jean) Pierre Chouteau** as the city's elder statesmen and its primary links to the past. Clark died in St. Louis on September 1, 1838.

Clark married twice. In 1808 he wed Julia Hancock in Virginia. The couple had five children, two of whom died in childhood. Julia died in 1820, and the following year he married her cousin, Harriet Kennerly Radford. They had two children prior to her death in 1831.

WILLIAM E. FOLEY

Bakeless, John. *Lewis and Clark: Partners in Discovery.* New York: William Morrow, 1947.
Clark, William. Papers. Missouri Historical Society, St. Louis.
Moulton, Gary E., ed. *Journals of the Lewis and Clark Expedition.* 11 vols. Lincoln: University of Nebraska Press, 1983– .
Steffen, Jerome O. *William Clark: Jeffersonian Man on the Frontier.* Norman: University of Oklahoma Press, 1977.

CLEMENS, SAMUEL LANGHORNE (MARK TWAIN) (1835–1910)

Samuel Langhorne Clemens was the sixth child of John Marshall and Jane Lampton Clemens. He was born on November 30, 1835, in Florida, Missouri. His father, believing that nearby Hannibal would prove a more prosperous place to conduct his business, moved the family some thirty miles to the port village in 1839, and it is with Hannibal and the Mississippi River that runs beside it that Clemens's youth is most closely associated. Sam Clemens was naturally frail and often sick as a child, and he was subjected to a number of home remedies, some of which he recalled in *Tom Sawyer* and elsewhere; at the age of four he first walked in his sleep and would continue to do so intermittently for the next several years. By the time he was nine or ten years old, however, Sam Clemens's health had sufficiently improved for him to enjoy swimming, fishing, and playing pirates with his friends, and he spent two or three months each year with his cousins on the farm of John Quarles.

Clemens's childhood experience was a mixture of simple and often mischievous pleasure combined with exposure to disturbing local violence and tragedy (he witnessed a shooting in the streets, stumbled upon a corpse in his father's office, and saw one of his friends drown). He was also probably nervous and confused by the family's reversal of fortunes. His father had some years before purchased seventy-five thousand acres of Tennessee land and believed that it would one day make them all wealthy, but by 1846 his mother was cooking meals for guests, and they sold their furniture to pay debts. The next year John Clemens died of pneumonia. Although he continued his schooling, Sam took on a number of odd jobs

in town, including that of a printer's devil for the *Missouri Courier.* In 1851 he became a typesetter and editorial assistant for his brother Orion's newspaper, the *Western Union;* it was in this paper that he published his first known sketch, "A Gallant Fireman." The next year he signed a sketch "W. Epaminondas Adrastus Perkins," the first of a number of pen names he adopted until in 1863 he settled on the name "Mark Twain."

By 1853 Clemens's childhood was effectively over, though all his life he would retain a boyish exuberance and fondness for mischief that would amuse and exasperate his friends and family. In June 1853 he left Hannibal for St. Louis to work as a typesetter, and later that summer he traveled to New York where he worked in a large print shop. By the end of the year he was employed in Philadelphia. During the next few years he traveled about working as a typesetter in St. Louis, Keokuk, and Cincinnati. At the age of twenty-two he boarded a steamboat with the intention of traveling to South America; instead, he became a cub riverboat pilot, apprenticing himself to Horace Bixby for five hundred dollars.

By April 1859 Clemens had received his piloting license and was making good money as a riverboat pilot, but the Civil War brought a halt to the prosperous river traffic, and Clemens joined the Marion Rangers, a group of Confederate volunteers. His stint as a soldier lasted only two weeks, however, and many years later he would recall his antic military adventures in "A Private History of the Campaign that Failed." Ill-suited for life as a soldier, Clemens traveled to Nevada with Orion, who had recently been appointed territorial secretary. In the West Clemens worked for his brother for a time, but also did some mining and speculated in silver- and gold-mining stocks. He found that work as a local reporter for the *Virginia City Territorial Enterprise* was steadier and more profitable, however.

In February 1863 Clemens sent three articles to the *Enterprise* from Carson City and signed them "Mark Twain," which was the first time he used this pseudonym. Forever after, Clemens and Mark Twain would be virtually indistinguishable fellow travelers; many of Clemens's closest friends would sometimes call him Mark, and he frequently signed his letters with that name. The literary persona he adopted during these years proved the most valuable property he would take with him when he left the Nevada Territory. Already he had acquired something of a reputation as a literary comedian, often publishing articles and sketches in New York newspapers, and he profited by his association with other humorists such as Artemus Ward and Bret Harte. The publication of "Jim Smiley and His Jumping Frog" in 1865, however, was the beginning of Twain's national reputation as a humorist. The story was intended for a collection of humorous sketches Ward was preparing, but the tale arrived too late to be included. Instead, it was published in the *Saturday Press* and was subsequently reprinted all over the country.

After serving as a traveling correspondent for the *Sacramento Union,* writing a series of letters about his experiences in the Hawaiian Islands, Clemens gave his first public lecture in October 1866 and shortly thereafter embarked on a lecture tour throughout California and Nevada. Although he generally disliked lecturing, he had a natural aptitude for taletelling and speech making and knew that the lecture circuit would put money in his pocket and promote his public reputation. Not long after that lecture tour, he became a traveling correspondent for the *San Francisco Alta California* and on June 8, 1867, sailed on the *Quaker City,* bound for Europe and the Holy Land. On board he met Mary Mason Fairbanks, who would become one of his closest friends and advisers, and a young man named Charles Jervis Langdon, who in a few years would become his brother-in-law.

Clemens fell in love with Olivia Langdon, so the story goes, the moment Charles Langdon showed him a photograph of her. The Langdons were a wealthy and well-respected New York family, socially far above the station of young Samuel Clemens. Undaunted by their differences and offering his own good moral character as his only collateral, Clemens proposed to the young woman known familiarly as "Livy." His courtship of Olivia was an ardent one. He divided his time in 1868–1869 between lecturing and preparing a book on his travels in Europe and the Holy Land to be called *Innocents Abroad,* but he still found time to write hundreds of love letters to Olivia, expressing his admiration for her and pledging to give up smoking and drinking and to attend church regularly. All three ventures were successful. His lecture tour was profitable, *Innocents Abroad* (1869) was well reviewed and sold well, and Clemens and Olivia were married on February 2, 1870. His efforts to reform himself resulted in only a temporary transformation, however.

Olivia's father, Jervis Langdon, generously supplied the capital for Clemens to buy one-third interest in the *Buffalo Express* and, to Clemens's surprise, also bought the newlywed couple a furnished house in Buffalo. Their first child was born in November 1870 and named after his grandfather, but Langdon Clemens would die of diphtheria eighteen months later. The Clemenses did not like living in Buffalo. They moved to Hartford, Connecticut, in 1871 and two years later bought a lot in the Nook Farm area of the city. They contracted to have a house built there and found it quite comfortable, though it was still unfinished when they moved in on September 19, 1874. For the next seventeen years, their Hartford house would be "home" for the Clemens family. Sam

and Livy also often made extended visits to Quarry Farm, the home of Livy's adopted sister, Susan Crane, in Elmira, New York. In fact, the Clemens's three daughters were born in Elmira: Olivia Susan (Susy) on March 19, 1872; Clara Langdon on June 8, 1874; and Jane Lampton (Jean) on July 26, 1880.

The next few years would prove the most productive and in many ways the happiest of Twain's career. In 1872 he published *Roughing It,* an account of his experience in Nevada, California, and the Sandwich Islands. That same year he began writing with his Hartford neighbor Charles Dudley Warner his first novel, *The Gilded Age* (1873). Twain's most original contribution to that novel was the character of Colonel Sellers, whom he had modeled after his mother's cousin James Lampton, and, in 1874, he wrote a play titled *Colonel Sellers* that proved a long-standing commercial success. That same year he returned to the manuscript of *The Adventures of Tom Sawyer* (1876) and began writing a series of articles about his experiences as a cub pilot for the *Atlantic Monthly.* "Old Times on the Mississippi" would appear in seven installments beginning January 1875 and later be incorporated into his book *Life on the Mississippi* (1883). A few months after he had seen *Tom Sawyer* through the press, Twain began writing what he would call in a letter to his friend William Dean Howells "Huck Finn's Autobiography." Clearly, during these years Twain was drawing upon his memories of Missouri and the Mississippi River for inspiration, and the result was some of his most original and memorable work.

The Adventures of Huckleberry Finn was Twain's masterpiece, but several times he put the manuscript away, unsure whether he would ever return to it. Between the time he began *Huck Finn* and its eventual publication in 1885, Twain involved himself in a number of other projects. He collaborated with Bret Harte on the play *Ah, Sin,* and published another travel book, *A Tramp Abroad,* in 1880 and the novel *The Prince and the Pauper* in 1881. The next year he traveled to St. Louis and Hannibal in order to gather material for *Life on the Mississippi.* After the book was published, he returned to the story of Huck Finn with a will and a purpose. Dissatisfied with his publisher, Twain decided to found his own publishing company, Charles Webster and Company, and *The Adventures of Huckleberry Finn* was the first volume the company published.

During the next few years Twain did relatively little writing, though he did attempt to continue the adventures of Huck Finn and Tom Sawyer in "Huck Finn and Tom Sawyer among the Indians" but was unable to finish it. He became more and more absorbed in several business projects and investments. In addition to his involvement with his publishing company, Clemens took a business interest in a perpetual calendar, a history game, and other inventions, but his largest and, it would eventually prove, his worst investment was in the Paige typesetter. For each of forty-four consecutive months, Clemens contributed three thousand dollars to the development of a working prototype of an automatic typesetting machine.

The investment was a disaster, but as late as August 1889 Clemens was confident enough that the device would be a financial success that he wrote to Howells that he would soon retire from literature and live off the profits of the Paige machine. He had long been a believer in progress and technological advancement, and some of that faith is reflected in his novel *A Connecticut Yankee in King Arthur's Court* (1889), but his optimism was severely tested by a series of failures. His publishing house was in debt and had cash-flow problems, and Clemens was having difficulty finding investors for the Paige machine. In 1891 he closed his Hartford house and moved his family to Europe, partly in the hope that the baths there would improve Livy's health and partly to live more cheaply. Even though rheumatism in his arm made writing difficult, Twain continued to contribute stories and articles to magazines and to work on two novels, *Pudd'nhead Wilson* (1894) and *Personal Recollections of Joan of Arc* (1895).

The financial panic of 1893 made Clemens's prospects even bleaker, and stories published during this period (such as "The Million Pound Bank-Note," "The Esquimau Maiden's Romance," and "Is He Living or Is He Dead?") express both his cynicism and his desperate hopes for a windfall. The windfall came, not in the form of actual cash, but in the person of Henry Huttleston Rogers, vice president of the Standard Oil Company. Rogers took an immediate and practical interest in Clemens's financial difficulties, and over the next several years advised the author on ways to relieve his indebtedness. In 1894, after assigning his property, including his copyrights, to his wife, Clemens declared his publishing company bankrupt. In an effort to repay his creditors, the next year he embarked on a round-the-world lecture tour, traveling first across the United States and then sailing from Vancouver to Australia, New Zealand, India, South Africa, and eventually arriving in England in July 1896. The lecture tour provided Clemens with much needed capital and the basis for another travel book, *Following the Equator* (1897). By early 1898 Clemens had repaid all his outstanding debts.

Only a month after arriving in England, the Clemenses learned that their daughter Susy was ill. On August 18, 1896, Clemens received a telegram that Susy had died; Livy and Clara were already on a ship bound for the United States. The death of their daughter caused a lingering sadness in the Clemens household: they did not celebrate birthdays or holidays for several years afterward. Twain threw himself into his work, as much for a relief from depression as anything else. Much of what he wrote during this period was, in the author's mind at least, too cynical and scandalous for the reading public. However, most of his unpublished (and often unfinished) manuscripts were no more toxic than his brilliant satire "The Man that Corrupted Hadleyburg," published in *Harper's Magazine* in 1899, or his venomous denunciation of imperialism in "To the Person Sitting in the Darkness," published in the *North American Review* in 1901.

In 1900 after living several years in Europe, Clemens returned to live in the United States and was greeted warmly by an adoring public. The family was glad to be home but found that the sad memories associated with their home in Nook Farm made it impossible for them to live there, and they rented a house in Riverdale, New York. Perhaps Clemens's sadness was somewhat relieved by the appreciative recognition he was receiving. In October 1901 he received an honorary doctor of letters from Yale University, and the next year he received an honorary doctor of laws degree from the University of Missouri–Columbia. He traveled to Columbia to receive the degree in June 1902. It would be the last time Clemens visited his native state, and he probably knew it, for he visited St. Louis and Hannibal and took a short trip on the Mississippi River with his old friend and teacher Horace Bixby.

Later that summer Livy became violently ill. For the next several months Clemens was allowed to see his wife for only five minutes on days that she was feeling well, and the whole family worried that she was dying. For the sake of her health, they moved to Florence, Italy, in 1903, and though she did improve for a time, Olivia Clemens died there on June 5, 1904. Something of the quality of love Clemens felt for Livy is conveyed in his moving piece "Eve's Diary," published the following year, but a sadder and more cynical side of the man is revealed in the three versions of *The Mysterious Stranger* manuscripts (unpublished at the time of his death) and the philosophical dialogue *What Is Man?* (published anonymously in 1906).

Samuel Clemens had received worldwide acclaim (he received a third honorary degree, from Oxford University, in 1907), but he was often bitter and lonely. Perhaps as an antidote to his depression, he spent much of his time dictating his autobiography; feeling the absence of grandchildren in his life, he also established a club for young girls he called his "angelfish" and corresponded with them often. In 1908 Clemens moved into his new house in Redding, Connecticut. He wanted to call the house "Innocents at Home" but his daughter Clara persuaded him to name it "Stormfield" after his fictional sea captain who sailed for heaven but entered at the wrong port.

Stormfield was an eighteen-room Italianate villa, a dramatic contrast to the two-room house Clemens had been born in seventy-three years earlier. His daughter Clara was married in the house in July 1909, and his daughter Jean died of an epileptic seizure there on the day before Christmas the same year. Clemens himself would die at Stormfield on April 21, 1910. He was buried in the family plot in Elmira, New York.

TOM QUIRK

Ferguson, J. DeLancey. *Mark Twain: Man and Legend.* Indianapolis: Bobbs-Merrill, 1943.

Hill, Hamlin. *Mark Twain: God's Fool.* New York: Harper and Row, 1975.

Kaplin, Justin. *Mr. Clemens and Mark Twain.* New York: Simon and Schuster, 1966.

Rasmussen, R. Kent. *Mark Twain, A to Z: The Essential Reference to His Life and Writings.* New York: Facts on File, 1995.

Tenney, Thomas Asa. *Mark Twain: A Reference Guide.* Boston: G. K. Hall, 1977.

Wecter, Dixon. *Sam Clemens of Hannibal.* Boston: Houghton, Mifflin, 1952.

CLERMONT (GRA MON OR "ARROW-GOING-HOME") (1720s?–1796?)

The name of this Osage chief is variously rendered Gra-Mon, Gra-moie, Gra-to-moh-se, and Gleh-mon. French orthography reduced the name to Clermont, which Americans anglicized as Claremore. He was probably born in the mid-1720s. By the mid-1760s he had assumed the hereditary office of peace chief (Tsi-zhu Gahige) of the main village of the Big Osage in present Vernon County. Because the duties of his office included diplomatic negotiations with foreigners, French and Spanish officials assumed Clermont was the head chief of the Osages. From at least 1767 through the 1780s, he used the prestige derived from European recognition and trade to strengthen his hand in Osage politics.

In the mid-eighteenth century, some Osages established new villages on the Verdigris and Arkansas Rivers, drawn by the abundance of game and access to trade and war routes southward. The "Arkansas band" became a haven for malcontents from the older villages and was perceived by Osage leaders as a threat to tribal unity. Clermont sought to reestablish the traditional chiefs' authority over the dissidents by isolating them from the French and Spanish traders and denying them access to the new wealth and weapons revolutionizing Osage life. By channeling

trade through his village, he attempted to create a monopoly that would strengthen his prestige and that of his clan.

Although he was a shrewd diplomat and trader, Clermont met his match in St. Louis traders **Auguste Chouteau** and **(Jean) Pierre Chouteau.** The Chouteaus built a trading post, Fort Carondelet, near the Big Osage villages in 1795, after the Spanish government granted them a monopoly of the Osage trade. While Auguste generally managed affairs in St. Louis, Pierre spent much of his time in the Osage villages, consolidating his power there. The Chouteaus' meddling in tribal politics angered Clermont, and he attempted to limit their influence. They in turn supported his rivals in factional disputes.

After 1796 Clermont seems to disappear from the documentary record; he probably died about that time, though neither the Chouteaus nor the Spanish government recorded the fact. **White Hair (Paw-Hiu-Skah),** Clermont's chief rival and the Chouteaus' chief ally, successfully claimed the office of Tsi-zhu Gahige of the Big Osage villages, though he had no hereditary right to the title.

MARY ELLEN ROWE

Burns, Louis F. *A History of the Osage People.* Fallbrook, Calif.: CIGA Press, 1989.

Din, Gilbert C., and Abraham Nasatir. *The Imperial Osages: Spanish-Indian Diplomacy in the Mississippi Valley.* Norman: University of Oklahoma Press, 1983.

Mathews, John Joseph. *The Osages: Children of the Middle Waters.* Norman: University of Oklahoma Press, 1961.

Rollings, Willard H. *The Osage: An Ethnohistorical Study of Hegemony on the Prairie-Plains.* Columbia: University of Missouri Press, 1992.

CLERMONT II (?–1828)

Following the death of **Clermont (Gra-Mon or "Arrow-Going-Home")** in 1796, his son, also known as Clermont, was denied the hereditary office of peace chief (Tsi-zhu Gahige) that he considered justly his. He left with many followers to join the dissident Osage factions on the Arkansas. They welcomed him: his hereditary claim to office gave their band a new legitimacy and prestige among the Osages and attracted more tribesmen from the other Osage villages.

The younger Clermont had opposed foreign trespass on Osage lands. He earned a reputation as a fearless warrior against traditional Native enemies and showed little mercy to French and Spanish hunters caught poaching in Osage territory. In 1792 he reportedly led raids near Ste. Genevieve. He steadfastly opposed the Chouteaus' influence in Osage affairs, and their support of the insurgent **White Hair (Paw-Hiu-Skah**) outraged him. He offered friendship to the new government when the United States assumed control of the Louisiana Territory, but haughtily refused to acknowledge the appointment of **Pierre Chouteau** as U.S. Indian agent for the Osages. Clermont II opposed any sale or alienation of Osage lands, and refused to participate in any negotiations involving the Chouteaus or Paw-Hiu-Skah. Gov. **Meriwether Lewis** regarded Clermont II's band as hostile to the United States. Lewis attempted to prohibit trade with them and invited their Native enemies to attack them. In response, Clermont II boycotted the 1808 treaty council at the new Fort Osage and refused to move his people to the fort. Government officials insisted, and he later agreed to the revised treaty of 1809, though he firmly denied approving any sale of Osage lands.

Although Clermont II maintained his village (near present Claremore, Oklahoma), the Osage people were weakening. Factional strife, epidemics, the decline of the fur trade, the loss of prime hunting grounds to settlers, and the whiskey trade all took a toll, but most devastating was the relentless pressure of eastern refugee tribes crowding into Osage territory. The more numerous Cherokee were particular foes of the Osages. In 1817 they and their allies raided Clermont II's village, killing at least thirty-eight people and carrying off one hundred captives. Despite such pressure Clermont championed his people's claim to their lands until his death in 1828. He was succeeded by his son, also known as Clermont, who attempted, even less successfully, to protect his people's rights. Pressure from the U.S. government and Cherokee aggression proved overwhelming, and his people agreed to removal in 1839.

M ARY E LLEN R OWE

Burns, Louis F. *A History of the Osage People.* Fallbrook, Calif.: CIGA Press, 1989.

Din, Gilbert C., and Abraham Nasatir. *The Imperial Osages: Spanish-Indian Diplomacy in the Mississippi Valley.* Norman: University of Oklahoma Press, 1983.

Mathews, John Joseph. *The Osages: Children of the Middle Waters.* Norman: University of Oklahoma Press, 1961.

Rollings, Willard H. *The Osage: An Ethnohistorical Study of Hegemony on the Prairie-Plains.* Columbia: University of Missouri Press, 1992.

COCKRELL, FRANCIS MARION (1834–1915)

Cockrell was one of the "Confederate brigadiers" who appeared in the United States Senate following the Civil War; the only difference in his case was that he came from a loyal state, albeit a divided one. He was a native Missourian, having been born in Johnson County on October 1, 1834, the son of Joseph and Mary Ellis Cockrell. He attended a rural school and Chapel Hill College in Lafayette County and taught school one term while he studied law. In 1855 he began to practice law in Warrensburg.

In May 1861 Cockrell enlisted as a private in the Missouri State Guard to oppose Federal efforts to hold Missouri in the Union. Despite his lack of military experience, he quickly advanced through the ranks, and in July 1863 was appointed brigadier general. Cockrell's unit fought in the western theater and participated in the battles at Carthage, Wilson's Creek, Elkhorn Tavern, Corinth, and Vicksburg. In the spring of 1864 General Cockrell led his brigade in the Atlanta campaign and then into Tennessee with General Hood. He was at Mobile in the spring of 1865 when the Confederate forces there surrendered. During the course of the war, Cockrell was wounded on five occasions and captured three times.

Following the war Cockrell returned to Warrensburg, resumed his law practice, and entered Democratic politics. In 1874 he was defeated in the gubernatorial race, but the next year the General Assembly named him to the Senate. He was reelected four times, becoming the second U.S. senator from Missouri to serve for thirty years—**Thomas Hart Benton** had been the first.

In the Senate Cockrell did little to distinguish himself. Although the Democratic Party was in the minority for twenty-six of Cockrell's thirty-year tenure, the role of the minority should be to offer alternative programs. However, Cockrell simply expressed opposition to anything the majority proposed. True to his southern identification, his outlook was parochial and bound to the past. He seemed the classic "Bourbon Democrat," harping on economy, meaning no federal services and low taxes. Yet, in a contradictory vein he avidly sought tidbits from the pork barrel for his constituents, which perhaps explains his long tenure in Washington.

The major bills proposed by Cockrell were private ones such as pension legislation and claims for small sums on the part of individuals against some government agency. Since the Pension Bureau had formal procedures for persons claiming the right to receive a pension for military duty, private pension bills were a waste of time for Congress and, all too often, meant acceptance of a claim rightfully denied by the bureau. Likewise, procedures existed to handle claims. Cockrell's course hardly lived up to the best idea for governmental economy.

Cockrell eagerly supported efforts to improve navigation of the Mississippi, Missouri, and Osage Rivers at the same time he opposed federal aid to build railroads. Here he misjudged the needs of his own state as railroads superseded rivers as the major arteries of transportation.

Cockrell strongly opposed all sorts of reforms. He voted against the Pendleton Civil Service Bill in 1883 in committee and spoke against it on the floor, claiming it would not be needed if Democratic administrations had alternated with Republican instead of the long period of Republican dominance since 1861. In other words, he supported the Jacksonian concept of rotation in office. Cockrell was singularly insensitive to the needs of the Indians, even opposing the guarantee of reservations against the intrusion of homesteaders. He denounced a bill to indemnify Oklahoma tribes for lands taken from them by squatters and expressed indignation at the idea of "taxpayers" reimbursing the tribes. Instead, he desired to see claims against Indians for supposed depredations paid from money somehow taken out of the Indian lands.

In company with the majority of Missouri Democrats in the 1890s, Cockrell favored the unlimited coinage of silver to inflate the currency, a position that caused his name to be raised in connection with the Democratic presidential nomination in 1904. When Alton B. Parker, a stalwart of the Democratic Party's gold faction, emerged that year as the leading presidential candidate, the rival silver faction was appalled. Not only had Parker opposed the policies of silver presidential candidate William Jennings Bryan in 1896, but he had also "traitorously" bolted from the party. Eight years later the silverites still had not forgiven him, and with his political ascent, Missouri senator **William Joel Stone** and others close to Bryan rallied behind Cockrell in an attempt to block Parker's nomination. After they failed Parker led the party to a crushing defeat magnified by the disaffection of large numbers of silver Democrats who either sat out the election or crossed party lines to vote for the popular incumbent, Theodore Roosevelt. In the national landslide Missouri went Republican for the first time since Reconstruction. The Missouri legislature consequently selected a Republican for the United States Senate seat, ending Cockrell's tenure. Clearly out of step with the changing times and new issues confronting the nation, his retirement brought only polite tributes to his lengthy service. Roosevelt, faced with a Democratic vacancy on the bipartisan Interstate Commerce Commission, appointed Cockrell to the six-year term. Cockrell died on December 13, 1915.

RUTH WARNER TOWNE

Baker, Mary Ellen Butler. "The Senatorial Career of Francis Marion Cockrell." Master's thesis, Central Missouri State College, 1961.

Dictionary of American Heritage Biography. Vol. 2. S.v. "Cockrell, Francis Marion."

Towne, Ruth Warner. *Senator William J. Stone and the Politics of Compromise.* Port Washington, N.Y.: Kennikat Press, 1979.

COLE, HANNAH (1770?–1843)

Hannah Cole was one of the earliest permanent settlers of Cooper County in the Boon's Lick region of central Missouri. She was born in Virginia in the early 1770s, the daughter of Holbert and Agnes Allison. She married William Temple Cole in 1789, and they moved to Kentucky about 1805 and then to Missouri in 1807 where they joined the Cooper family and others at Loutre Island (across from present-day Hermann, Missouri). In July 1810 Hannah's husband was killed by Sac and Potawatomi Indians in the vicinity of present-day Mexico, Missouri, while in pursuit of Indians who had stolen horses from the Loutre Island settlers.

During the winter of 1810–1811, the recently widowed Hannah Cole and her nine children left Loutre Island accompanied by her brother-in-law **Stephen Cole** and his family. They joined **Benjamin Cooper** in the Boon's Lick country. The Coopers chose to settle on the north bank of the Missouri River in the bottomlands, not far from Boone's salt lick, but the Coles elected to take up residence on the river hills along the south bank of the river.

When the Indian troubles associated with the War of 1812 broke out, Cole and her family erected a crude fortification around their cabin located where Boonville now stands, but later they were forced to retreat to the north side of the river where Forts Hempstead and Kincaid afforded better protection. After the war the Coles returned to their homes, and for a brief period Hannah Cole's fort became the county seat of Howard County. Indeed, the first circuit, county, and probate courts were held there. Several of Cole's sons operated a ferry across the Missouri River prior to 1816, the year that the Howard County court granted her the first ferry license.

When Cooper County was formed in 1818 out of the southern half of Howard County, Boonville was established as the county seat near Cole's fort, and she was convinced to sell for a paltry sum her preemption right to most of the land on which the town was platted. She then purchased land about fifteen miles south of Boonville and moved there with her family. Cole died in 1843, and was buried in the old Briscoe Cemetery twelve miles south of Boonville.

ROBERT L. DYER

Draper Manuscripts. State Historical Society of Wisconsin, Madison.

Dyer, Robert. *Boonville*. Boonville, Mo.: Pekitanoui Publications, 1987.

History of Howard and Cooper Counties, Missouri. St. Louis: National Historical Company, 1883.

Johnson, W. F. *History of Cooper County, Missouri*. Topeka, Kans.: Historical Publishing, 1919.

COLE, STEPHEN (1775?–1822)

Stephen Cole, for whom Cole County, Missouri, was named, was born in Virginia in about 1775, the son of William Temple and Nellie Bowends Cole. In 1799 Stephen Cole married Phoebe Allison, a sister of his brother William Temple Cole Jr.'s wife, Hannah. Both families settled in Kentucky about 1805, and two years later they went to Missouri where they joined other Kentuckians at Loutre Island. Following William Temple Cole's death at the hands of Indians in 1810, Stephen Cole, his family, his widowed sister-in-law, Hannah, and her children all moved to the Boon's Lick country in central Missouri. **Hannah Cole** settled on the site of present-day Boonville, and Stephen, his wife, and their five children chose a location about a mile and a half downriver from Hannah and her nine children. They were the earliest permanent settlers in what became Cooper County. Following the outbreak of the War of 1812, both Cole families fortified their dwellings, but they eventually retreated to the safety of Forts Hempstead and Kincaid on the north side of the river. After the war they returned to their homes in the future Cooper County.

Cole, along with his namesake nephew, Stephen, accompanied one of the early expeditions to Santa Fe in 1822 and was killed during the venture by the Navajo on the banks of the Rio del Norte.

ROBERT L. DYER

Draper Manuscripts. State Historical Society of Wisconsin, Madison.

Dyer, Robert. *Boonville*. Boonville, Mo.: Pekitanoui Publications, 1987.

History of Howard and Cooper Counties, Missouri. St. Louis: National Historical Company, 1883.

Johnson, W. F. *History of Cooper County, Missouri*. Topeka, Kans.: Historical Publishing, 1919.

COLMAN, NORMAN JAY (1827–1911)

Norman Jay Colman is best known as the country's first secretary of agriculture, but this is only one of the many honors that came to a man who was committed to the progressive improvement of American agriculture.

Colman's association with agriculture began at his birth on his parents' farm in Richfield Springs, New York, on May 16, 1827. There Colman was exposed to the intricacies and dynamics of an agricultural lifestyle. His interest in agriculture, however, was to remain secondary to his academic goal of becoming a lawyer. In 1847, at the age of twenty, he left New York for Kentucky to attend law school at the University of Louisville. He received his LL.B. degree in 1852, and then moved to New Albany, Indiana, to practice law. So impressive were his legal exploits that in 1855 he was elected to the district attorney's office. Colman, however, declined the position in order to pursue his agricultural interests in Missouri.

Upon his arrival in St. Louis, Colman became involved in city government and gained a position on the St. Louis Board of Aldermen. Three years later, at the age of thirty-one, Colman purchased the agricultural monthly magazine the *Valley Farmer* to develop and highlight his ideas on improving American agriculture. The Civil War placed a temporary check on Colman's agricultural interests, and he served proudly in the pro-Union Eighty-fifth Missouri Militia. Immediately following the war, he expanded his publishing interests through the establishment of a new agricultural journal titled *Colman's Rural World*. During its fifty-year run Colman continually hammered home the necessity of cooperation between government, academic researchers, and farmers to improve American crop production. Through his effort the magazine eventually became the nation's most influential proponent of the application of scientific ideas and management to agriculture.

Colman's message attracted the attention of many federal and state agriculture and political officials. His widespread popularity within Missouri, especially St. Louis, made him a prominent member of the Missouri Democratic Party. In 1865 Colman was elected to the Missouri State Board of Agriculture, a position he held until his death. He was also chosen to be president of the Missouri State Horticulture Society. He gained his first political experience by serving in the Twenty-fourth Missouri General Assembly from 1866 to 1867, a position in which he acquired the reputation as a people's politician. Coming off his successful service in the state legislature, Colman was nominated for lieutenant governor by the Missouri Democratic Party in 1868. That was not a good year to be a Democrat in Missouri. Triumphant Radical Republicans had disfranchised large numbers of Democrats whom they claimed either supported or sympathized with the South during the Civil War, and Colman was defeated. Defeat, however, did not mean the end of his political aspirations. By 1874 the Democrats had returned to power in Missouri, and Colman was elected to the lieutenant governor's office.

Colman's involvement with the Missouri State Board of Agriculture kept him abreast of the most progressive ideas about farming. As lieutenant governor, he had the power and influence to direct further attention and funds toward improvements in Missouri agriculture. His work in the lieutenant governor's office brought him praise from agricultural leaders and Democratic Party elites from across the nation. President Grover Cleveland was so impressed by Colman's agricultural efforts in Missouri that in 1885 he appointed Colman as the U.S. commissioner of agriculture. Colman was now able to fully develop and implement his ideas on a national basis, positively affecting agricultural production and methods in ways he could not have realized before. His progressive agricultural ideas were debated and implemented during a time when the nation was undergoing a period of dramatic change from a largely agrarian to an urban nation. Colman understood the effect of capitalism upon American agriculture and the increasing demand for fewer farmers to produce ever greater quantities of food for the American public and the world.

To demonstrate the value of his scientific ideas for agriculture, Colman maintained an experimental farm near St. Louis. He argued that his progressive ideas could best be implemented through the development of federally funded experimental farms or stations in cooperation with universities and land-grant institutions. His dream became law under what is known as the Hatch Act. Because of the success of these experimental farms, Colman was thereafter referred to commonly as the "Father of the Experiment Station." In recognition and appreciation of his work, President Cleveland elevated Colman's office to a cabinet-level position, making Colman in 1889 the nation's first secretary of agriculture.

Following his widely lauded tenure in Washington, Colman received the honor of "officier du meriter agricole" from the president of the French Republic in recognition of his work in agriculture. Colman returned to his St. Louis farm and again immersed himself in both the Missouri State Board of Agriculture and his ongoing duties on the University of Missouri Board of Curators. Praised both nationally and internationally, Colman's achievements did not go unrecognized at home. In 1905 the University of Missouri awarded him an honorary LL.D. degree, and the same year he also earned an honorary Ph.D. from the University of Illinois. During these same years Colman was also elected president of both the National Editorial Association and the Missouri Press Association.

Colman died on November 3, 1911, on a train near Centralia, while returning to St. Louis after reviewing horses in Kansas City to add to his much-prized stock. Immediately, word of his death spread throughout the state and nation. The *St. Louis Globe-Democrat* devoted two days of coverage to his death and funeral.

Today, many of Colman's agricultural ideas have become institutionalized and remain a testament to his beliefs and work.

PAT CURRAN

Dictionary of American Biography. Vol. 2. S.v. "Colman, Norman Jay."

Lemmer, George F. *Norman J. Colman and Colman's Rural World: A Study in Agricultural Leadership.* Columbia: University of Missouri Press, 1953.

Shoemaker, Floyd C., ed. *Missouri, Day by Day.* Vol. 1. Columbia: State Historical Society of Missouri, 1942.

St. Louis Globe-Democrat, November 3, 4, 1911.

Stevens, Walter B. *St. Louis: History of the Fourth City, 1763–1909.* Vol. 3. Chicago: S. J. Clarke, 1909.

Summers, Floyd G. "Norman J. Colman: First Secretary of Agriculture." *Missouri Historical Review* 19 (1925): 407–8.

COMBS, LOULA LONG (1881–1971)

Loula Long Combs was the tomboy daughter of the lumberman **Robert Alexander Long** and Pennsylvania Quaker Ella Wilson Long. Born in Columbus, Kansas, on January 30, 1881, Combs was the youngest of two daughters. Her sister, Sallie, became more like their mother, a fine lady, whereas Loula remained a sportswoman all her life.

Because of Robert Long's lumber business the family moved to Kansas City in 1891 where they built a fifty-room mansion known as Corinthian Hall in the city's northeastern district. Robert Long also built Longview Farm near Lee's Summit, Missouri. Longview Farm had 1,780 acres that contained forty buildings, a twenty-acre artificial lake, a half-mile racetrack, a grandstand, and a clubhouse. Whitewashed post and rail fencing enclosed the entire farm.

Loula Long loved horses, and her father supported her expensive interest. In 1893 she showed the Long family horses at the first American Royal in Kansas City, which promoters held in a tent. As soon as her father thought she was old enough, she began to ride competitively. In her first show, the Fairmont Park Horse Show, she won first place. Not only did she ride, but she also trained, bred, and showed horses.

Loula Long also competed in international shows. In 1910 in the Olympia Show in London she won the international roadster class against eighteen veteran male drivers. By 1920 she earned fifteen thousand dollars a year in prize money. That year also marked the start of her twenty years of showing horses at the Devon, Pennsylvania, horse show.

Robert Long indulged his talented daughter. At age fifteen Loula told her father that her studies gave her migraines and asked if she could stop them. Her father agreed and allowed her to devote all her time to horses. A charming young woman when things went her way, she exuded charm throughout her life.

Loula Long married Robert Pryor Combs on June 30, 1917, and in 1919, after his army discharge, they moved to Longview Farm. The son of the pastor of the Longs' church, Pryor Combs had known Loula Long since childhood. He worked as the treasurer of the Long-Bell Lumber Company.

Training, breeding, and showing horses required hard work and self-discipline, qualities that Combs manifested despite the great wealth of her family. Unlike some indulged children, she treated friends and family with respect. She became quite attached to her animals, and when she sold a favorite horse for twenty-five thousand dollars she wept as he was taken away.

Longview Farm became renowned for having the best saddle stallions and the finest harness-horse operation in the country. In 1920 the *Horse Show Chronicle* proclaimed Longview Farm the big money winner in the United States for that year. Combs's personal earnings amounted to $14,758. She exhibited 395 classes at 16 shows, winning 31 championships, 3 reserves, and 170 blue ribbons. In 1947 at the age of sixty-six, Combs wrote her autobiography, *My Revelation,* and three years later *Who's Who and Where in Horsedom* was dedicated to her.

Horse shows filled Combs's life. Illness kept her from showing in the 1956 American Royal, which marked only her second absence from the Royal in sixty-two years. With a wide-brimmed hat adorned with feathers and flowers (her trademark), she officially retired in 1961 to a standing ovation at the American Royal in Kansas City. In 1964 Combs and her sister, Sallie, donated 147 acres of Longview Farm to Longview Community College.

Combs's last triumph occurred in 1967 at the age of eighty-six. She became the only woman to be inducted by the horse-show world into the Hall of Fame in Madison Square Garden. Combs died in Kansas City on July 5, 1971.

CATHLIN MALONEY MAUER

Bradley, Lenore K. *Robert Alexander Long: A Lumberman of the Gilded Age.* Durham, N.C.: Forest History Society, 1989.

Combs, Loula Long. *My Revelation.* Lee's Summit, Mo.: Longview, 1947.

Dains, Mary K., ed. *Show Me Missouri Women: Selected Biographies.* Kirksville, Mo.: Thomas Jefferson University Press, 1989.

Jones, Linda Newcom. *The Longview We Remember.* [Independence, Mo.]: Storm Ridge Press, 1990.

COMBS, THOMAS SELBY (1898–1964)

Thomas Selby Combs was born in Lamar, Missouri, on March 25, 1898, where he attended the local public schools and Lamar Institute. In 1915–1916 he was a student at Marion Military Institute. He received an appointment to the United States Naval Academy in 1916 and was graduated in 1920. During the summer of 1918, he served aboard the USS *Kansas,* which was on escort duty in the Atlantic during World War I. Later education included graduate work at the Naval Academy in 1930–1931 and receipt of the S.M. degree from the Massachusetts Institute of Technology in 1932.

After service aboard the battleships *Florida, Minnesota, Connecticut,* and *Nevada* from 1919 until 1922, Combs was assigned to flight training at the Naval Air Station in Pensacola, Florida. Throughout most of the 1930s he served aboard the carrier *Saratoga,* was squadron commander aboard the carrier *Enterprise,* and was commanding officer of a bomber squadron in San Diego, California. Following the nation's entry into World War II, he was captain of a seaplane tender that saw action in the Aleutian Islands in 1942. He obtained the rank of rear admiral and became chief of staff for aircraft in the southwest Pacific in 1943, which later included command of two fleet air wings. In 1944–1945 he was commanding officer of the *Yorktown,* which participated in several campaigns against Japanese forces.

Between the end of World War II in 1945 and his retirement in 1960, Admiral Combs held several senior positions: chief of staff to the commander of the Seventh Fleet, 1945–1946; deputy chief, Bureau of Aeronautics, Department of the Navy, 1946–1948; commander of a carrier division, 1949–1950; chief of staff and aide to the commander in chief, Atlantic Fleet, 1950–1951; commander, Second Fleet, Atlantic, 1953–1954, during which time he became a vice admiral; commander, Sixth Fleet, Mediterranean, 1954–1955; member of the National Advisory Committee for Aeronautics, Department of the Navy, 1955–1956; deputy chief of Naval Operations for Air, 1956–1958; and successively commander of the Eastern Sea Frontier, commandant of the third Naval District, commander of the Atlantic Reserve Fleet, commander of the New York Naval Base, and naval adviser to the American military staff at the United Nations, 1958–1960.

Following retirement, Combs served as vice chairman and executive director of the Florida Judicial Council, which was established to investigate the state's judicial system. He remained in this position until his death in Tallahassee, Florida, on December 9, 1964.

Combs served the nation and the United States Navy with distinction during his forty-four years of active service. In recognition of his services, he was twice awarded the United States Distinguished Service Medal. He was also the recipient of the Legion of Merit with Oakleaf Cluster and the Silver Star. His foreign decorations included the Grand Cordon of Yun Hui and the Cloud Banner, Second Grade, from China, and the Order of Naval Merit from Spain.

As a senior naval officer Combs was very much involved in the Pacific conflict during World War II. Having entered naval aviation in 1922, he remained in this critical service throughout the war. American air power played a prominent role in turning the tide of war in the Pacific and ultimately contributed heavily to Japan's military collapse in 1945. Likewise, Combs held senior commands during the first fifteen years of the cold-war era between the United States and the Soviet Union and their respective coalitions.

JOSEPH T. HATFIELD

The National Cyclopedia of American Biography. S.v. "Combs, Thomas Selby."

New York Times, December 11, 1964.

Who Was Who in America with World Notables. Vol. 4. Chicago: A. N. Marquis, 1968.

COMPTON, ARTHUR HOLLY (1892–1962)

Arthur Holly Compton earned international recognition for his research in X rays by sharing the 1927 Nobel Prize for physics with British scientist Charles T. R. Wilson. Compton contributed the "Compton Effect" to the scientific vocabulary. In 1941 Compton chaired the National Academy of Sciences Committee, which was established to evaluate the military possibilities of atomic energy, and in 1942 became head of the University of Chicago's Metallurgical Laboratory, under whose auspices Enrico Fermi and his group created the first nuclear chain reaction. Compton contributed significantly to the research that produced the atomic bomb, and joined a select few involved in deciding to use the bomb against the Japanese to end World War II. Washington University in St. Louis hired him to become chancellor in 1945, and he headed the team of administrators that began the transformation of that institution into a major research university.

Born in Wooster, Ohio, on September 10, 1892, Compton earned a bachelor's degree at the College of Wooster in 1913, where his father served as a professor of philosophy and dean. He earned an M.A. in 1914 and a Ph.D. in 1916 from Princeton University. His two older brothers also earned Ph.D.s from Princeton. Brother Karl, also a physicist, held the

presidency of the Massachusetts Institute of Technology from 1930 to 1948, and brother Wilson, an economist, became president of Washington State University in 1944. Arthur did research for Westinghouse on aircraft instruments during World War I, and after the war taught at the University of Minnesota. In 1919 the National Research Council chose him as a member of the first class of fellows. He went to Cambridge University where he worked in Ernest Rutherford's laboratory on radiation research. Upon his return to the United States, Compton was hired by Washington University in St. Louis as the head of the department of physics. He stayed in St. Louis until 1923, when the University of Chicago attracted him. He taught there until 1945, when he became chancellor at Washington University. He remained as chancellor until April 10, 1953, when he received appointment as distinguished service professor of natural philosophy, a position he held until 1961. That year he announced that he would become a professor-at-large, dividing his time between Washington University, the University of California–Berkeley, and the College of Wooster. While at Berkeley the next year, he died suddenly on March 15, 1962.

While Compton's importance as a contributor to atomic energy research is well recorded, his significance in changing Washington University is less well known. As Ralph Morrow, the historian of Washington University, wrote, "There is remarkable agreement that Compton began the process that transformed Washington University from a local college into a research university of international standing." He restructured the administration by delegating authority to capable people who agreed with his view that "The primary strength of the University is its faculty." He attracted well-known people to join the faculty, bringing some of them from the Manhattan Project. Compton formalized tenure procedures and put in place greater opportunities for faculty governance. He proved effective in involving the St. Louis business community in the life of the university, and he understood the new environment of government financing of university research. He sought to make enrollment more selective, emphasized quality teaching, and encouraged the highest standards of research. Finally, albeit too slowly for some, he oversaw the racial integration of the university. Racial tests for admission ended on May 9, 1952, "with a whimper rather than a bang." As Morrow summarized his approach to desegregation, "Compton was the careful commander whose makeup would not let him storm the citadel until all of its guns had fallen silent."

Besides making such educational and scientific contributions to American life, Compton served as a member of the National Cancer Advisory Board from 1937 to 1944 and as general chair of the Laymen's Missionary Movement from 1934 to 1948. His work with the latter organization reflected Compton's deeply religious views. Twenty institutions awarded him honorary degrees. His wife, Betty Charity McClosky Compton, and two sons, Arthur Allen Compton and John Joseph Compton, survived him.

LAWRENCE O. CHRISTENSEN

Chancellor's Records. Compton Series. Olin Library, Washington University, St. Louis.

Compton, Arthur Holly. *Atomic Quest: A Personal Narrative.* New York: Oxford University Press, 1956.

Morrow, Ralph. *Washington University in St. Louis: A History.* St. Louis: Missouri Historical Society Press, 1996.

New York Times, March 16, 1962.

Pfeffenberger, Amy M. "Democracy at Home: The Struggle to Desegregate Washington University in the Postwar Era." *Gateway Heritage* 10:3 (1989): 15–25.

Williams, Robert Chadwell. "From the Hill to the Hilltop: Washington University and the Manhattan Project, 1940–1946." *Gateway Heritage* 9:3 (1988): 14–27.

CONROY, JACK (1898–1990)

The son of Irish immigrants (his father was a miner and local union leader), Jack Conroy was born on December 5, 1898, in a coal-mining camp near Moberly, Missouri. His childhood in the "Monkey Nest" coal camp left a deep, lasting impression on him, with its communal and oral traditions, periodic labor strife, and domestic tragedy, including the deaths of his father, two half brothers, and a brother in work accidents. Like Jack London's Martin Eden, Conroy was a working-class lad with a thirst for learning, despite his lack of formal education. At thirteen he entered an apprenticeship in Moberly's Wabash Railroad shops, where he was soon elected recording secretary of the union local and saw his first publication in the union's journal.

When the great railroad strike of 1922 was broken, Conroy joined thousands of uprooted workers searching for work in factory cities. He abandoned his correspondence-school studies and hopes of gaining a college education, and with his nephew, Fred Harrison, hopped freight cars in desperate search of work to support his family. During the course of the next fifteen years, Conroy migrated from a Des Moines steel mill to a Hannibal rubber-heel factory, to auto plants in Toledo and Detroit, returning, after the crash in 1929, to the Monkey Nest coal camp, long since abandoned. During the all-too-brief "proletarian nights" between shifts of day labor building brick roads, digging ditches, or working on construction jobs, Conroy created an astonishing variety of sketches and short stories while founding and editing literary magazines.

Conroy's life and work raise interesting questions about the role of orality and literacy, the nature of literary authorship, and the circumstances of gaining access to learning, writing skills, and publication among working-class people. His first novel, *The Disinherited* (1933), a great part of which was first published by H. L. Mencken in the *American Mercury,* gathers together workers' voices overheard in the mines, mills, and factories of Conroy's own experience. Critics—conservative and radical alike—hailed the book as something very new in American literature, a testimony of working-class existence written from within the experience of factory work. To one critic, Conroy was an "American Gorky" (the Russian author whose work contains vivid scenes of working-class life and tales of downtrodden, ignored, homeless people). John Dos Passos called *The Disinherited* "an absolutely solid, unfaked piece of narrative as good as the best of Jack London." Erskine Caldwell wrote to Conroy shortly after the book's publication: "That's the way to write . . . what counts is the increasing value as it slowly penetrates the mind and lives of the people." When in May 1935 Conroy delivered one of the main addresses at the First American Writers' Congress in New York City, it seemed a worker-writer had finally claimed a small piece of American literary territory. His second novel, *A World to Win,* was less successful. On the strength of having written *The Disinherited* (Conroy still supported his family as a manual laborer), Conroy received Guggenheim funding in 1935 to document the migration of southern blacks to northern industrial cities such as Detroit and Toledo.

As a founder and editor of several literary magazines, Conroy attempted to create circuits of communication as alternatives to the dominant systems of literary production. Like his mentor, H. L. Mencken, Conroy was interested in finding and encouraging new talent. He gained his early editorial experience with the *Rebel Poet* (1931–1932). The year 1933 was a signal time for Conroy's burgeoning literary career. In addition to the publication of *The Disinherited,* he founded the *Anvil,* whose purpose, Conroy wrote, was to find and publish "stories for workers." As editor of the acclaimed *Anvil* (1933–1935) in Moberly, and later the *New Anvil* (1939–1940) in Chicago, Conroy was involved in furthering the early literary careers of writers such as Nelson Algren, Meridel Le Sueur, James T. Farrell, Richard Wright, Willard Motley, Erskine Caldwell, **Langston Hughes,** Kenneth Patchen, Joseph Vogel, Sanora Babb, William Carlos Williams, and Norman Macleod. Richard

Wright's first publication in a magazine of national circulation appeared in the *Anvil.* Conroy printed two of Erskine Caldwell's short stories when other editors refused them for their daring exposure of racism and intolerance.

The focus of literary politics and cultural prerogatives shifted abruptly with the ascendancy of the Popular Front after 1935, followed by diminishing interest in critical realism and worker writing. The *Anvil* lasted longer than most of the "little magazines" that sprang up across the American landscape in the 1930s (thirteen issues) and had a larger circulation than any other journal of its kind (five thousand at its peak). In a coup engineered by the cultural doyens of the left's cultural movement, however, the journal was taken from Conroy's control and absorbed into the New York–based *Partisan Review,* which, under its editors, Philip Rahv and William Phillips, later abandoned its commitment to literary radicalism in favor of modernism.

In 1938, with little income from his writing and the Guggenheim stipend ended, Conroy moved to Chicago where he joined the Federal Writers' Project (FWP). A participant in an industrial folklore project, he was later assigned to a black history project where he met novelist and scholar Arna Bontemps. Conroy's assignment owed in part to his earlier studies of worker migration. Conroy and Bontemps's collaborative efforts resulted in an acclaimed study, *They Seek a City* (1945), perhaps the earliest instance of interracial literary collaboration. The phrase *racial equality,* which had been used and abused in the politics of the 1930s, acquired significant meaning in this joining, for common literary purpose, of a coal miner's son and a university-educated novelist. Novelist and critic Dorothy Canfield called *They Seek a City* "one of the remedies we Americans need to take as part of the treatment for a malady of heart and soul and mind which is a great danger of our nation." A new version of *They Seek a City,* reflecting the civil rights era, appeared in 1965 as *Anyplace but Here,* which won the James L. Dow Award offered by the Society of Midland Authors.

A pioneer in the study of occupational folklore, Conroy made numerous contributions to the FWP's special project under Benjamin A. Botkin's direction, drawing upon tales he recalled from the Monkey Nest coal camp, the Wabash shops, and various factory settings. Botkin published six of these tales in his *Treasury of American Folklore* (1944). As Conroy's literary contacts grew, along with his literary reputation, he became a book reviewer for the *Chicago Sun-Times* and editor for the *New Standard Encyclopedia* in Chicago. (The FWP lost its funding in 1943.)

Following World War II, literary radicals such as Conroy slipped into obscurity when publishers were no longer willing to take risks with their work, thus exercising a kind of self-censorship. Many former *Anvil* contributors were silenced in the cold-war climate of fear and repression. Conroy himself was investigated by the FBI, but nothing came of it.

In 1947 Conroy put together a collection called *Midland Humor.* Literary collaboration fit the temperament and talent of Conroy, with his trove of tall tales, and Bontemps, who had already written several successful children's books before meeting Conroy on the Illinois Writers' Project in Chicago. Their joint authorship resulted in the publication of three very successful juveniles, *The Fast Sooner Hound, Slappy Hooper,* and *Sam Patch,* based largely on folk material Conroy had gathered on the Illinois Writers' Project.

Following his retirement to Moberly in 1966, Conroy gleaned from memories of his earliest days in Monkey Nest coal camp a series of autobiographical "Monkey Nest tales," published in literary magazines such as *New Letters,* and gathered together in *The Weed King and Other Stories* (1985). Selecting *The Weed King* for a list of outstanding new books, Russell Banks wrote that "this collection of stories and re-told folk tales is a buried treasure. Conroy, an 86 year old giant of a man, still writing proletarian narratives and author of the 1930s classic, *The Disinherited,* brings us the sense and the passionate sensibility we are too much without these greedy days."

The social climate of the 1960s, with its renewed interest in civil rights, disenchantment with "the establishment," and desire to seek a fair appraisal of writers maligned during the cold-war era, inspired a reassessment of the radical literary legacy of the 1930s. Conducted by scholars such as Daniel Aaron, whose sensitive introduction to the new edition of *The Disinherited* (1962), and the publication of *Anyplace but Here,* led to invitations for Conroy and other former literary colleagues from the 1930s to speak to younger generations of students and scholars in symposia and forums. Granted the State of Illinois's Literary Times Award in 1967, Conroy received an NEA writers' grant and an honorary doctorate from the University of Missouri–Kansas City in the late 1970s and in 1980 the first Mark Twain Award bestowed by the Society for the Study of Midwestern Literature. In his hometown Conroy was honored with a special Jack Conroy Day, on May 22, 1984. In his last years, Conroy welcomed to his home "pilgrims," as he called old friends and scholars who came to Moberly to interview him for their dissertations and books. He died on February 28, 1990, at age ninety-one and is buried in Sugar Creek Cemetery, the miners' graveyard near Monkey Nest.

DOUGLAS WIXSON

Bontemps, Arna, and Conroy, Jack. *Anyplace but Here.* Reprint, Columbia: University of Missouri Press, 1997.

Conroy, Jack. *The Disinherited: A Novel of the 1930s.* Introduction by Douglas Wixson. Columbia: University of Missouri Press, 1990.

———. *The Jack Conroy Reader.* Ed. Jack Salzman and David Ray. New York: Burt Franklin, 1979.

Conroy, Jack, and Curt Johnson. *Writer in Revolt: The Anvil Anthology, 1933–1940.* New York: Lawrence Hill, 1973.

Wixson, Douglas. *Worker-Writer in America: Jack Conroy and the Tradition of Midwestern Literary Radicalism, 1898–1990.* Champaign: University of Illinois Press, 1994.

COOK, FANNIE FRANK (1893–1949)

Fannie Frank Cook had a distinguished career as an activist and author whose efforts received local, state, and national recognition. She was born on October 3, 1893, the second of three children and the only daughter of Julius and Jennie Michael Frank of St. Charles, Missouri. Julius Frank was a German Jewish immigrant who came to the United States shortly after the Civil War, and his wife was the sister of Elias Michael who became president of Rice Stix Dry Goods Company, which later became the Famous Barr department stores, now owned by the May Company. The family moved to St Louis when Fannie Frank was five, and Julius Frank joined his brother-in-law at the dry-goods company. In 1890 Julius Frank became a partner in Frank and Meyer Neckwear Company, which later became Fishlowitz and Frank, the largest neckwear company in the country. His sons, Simon and William, joined him in the business in 1900.

When Fannie Frank was a child she won a writing contest. Years later she recalled: "As a matter of fact, my undoing was having a piece accepted by *St. Nicholas Magazine* when I was seven. My father was proud of me." Julius Frank's pride in his daughter's accomplishments no doubt contributed to Fannie Frank's healthy self-esteem and her belief that it was acceptable for a woman to use her talents and abilities. Jennie Frank's sister-in-law, Rachel Stix Michael, was also an important family influence. Rachel Michael, a respected St. Louis humanitarian, introduced young Fannie to social activism and to leaders such as Jane Addams, a pioneer social worker.

Fannie Frank attended Hamilton Grade School and Soldan High School from which she graduated in 1911. In 1914 she completed her undergraduate education at the University of Missouri–Columbia. She married Jerome Cook, a St. Louis physician, on October 28, 1915. The couple had two children, Robert and Howard.

In 1916 Fannie Frank Cook, perhaps unwittingly, declared a pattern for her life. She completed her master's in English at Washington University. In her thesis she identified her concern for social justice and her belief that literature must be purposeful and reflect the social concerns of the times. "The question of social betterment is the big question of today," she wrote. "The fight between labor and capital is on. Our lives reflect these things, and so our drama must also reflect them in portraying the spirit of our times." In many ways Cook was a traditional homemaker of her time, married to a young physician, expecting her first child, and active in organizations such as the League of Women Voters. Yet, her education, her family background, her artistic energy, and her social sensitivity were a remarkable combination that empowered her career as an activist and an author.

Initially, Cook began her career as a part-time lecturer in English at Washington University. Her activist efforts focused on improving the quality of education for black Americans by removing the barriers of segregation and promoting integration, and creating opportunities for better working conditions and economic improvement for all working-class people. During the years between the completion of her master's thesis in 1916 and her death in 1949, Cook lived and wrote as a social activist.

In 1924 Cook was appointed chairman of the Education Committee of the St. Louis League of Women Voters, and her appointment to that office no doubt allowed her to participate in improving the conditions of minority education. Along with other members of the league, she was responsible for implementing better training for black educators.

In 1930 Cook was appointed chairman of the Race Relations Committee of the Community Council of St. Louis. In that capacity she addressed many significant issues, one of which was the segregation of St. Louis theaters.

Along with Josephine Johnson Cannon, who won the Pulitzer Prize for her novel depicting rural poverty, *Now in November* (1934), Cook formed the St. Louis Committee for the Rehabilitation of the Sharecroppers in 1939, a project to purchase land and establish homes and schools for dislocated sharecroppers in the Missouri Bootheel. The committee purchased ninety-three acres of land and established a self-governing camp and school for black sharecroppers. In her search for federal assistance Cook managed to attract the sympathetic attention of Eleanor Roosevelt. A fictional record of Roosevelt's experience with the camp members survives in Cook's short story "Zorella's Hat," published in the December 23, 1943, issue of the *New Republic*.

Cook was appointed to the St. Louis mayor's Race Relations Commission in 1943, and in that same year she joined others in founding the St. Louis

People's Art Center. This project was an outgrowth of a Works Progress Administration art project of 1942 and was a learning environment where black and white adults and children could work in an integrated artistic environment. This project is believed to be the first integrated art project in St. Louis. Cook was a member of the project's board of directors and served as a dedicated volunteer until her death.

Cook had been interested in writing since childhood and was a prolific author. She wrote short fiction, journalism, oratory, and poetry. Her personal papers, now in the possession of the Missouri Historical Society at St. Louis, include a large volume of carefully preserved correspondence with political leaders of the time such as Henry Wallace and Eleanor Roosevelt, and with literary figures such as Robert Penn Warren, **Jack Conroy,** and Ann Petry.

Cook wrote five novels that are direct reflections of her own activist experience and her personal understandings of racial and religious prejudice. Her third novel, *Mrs. Palmer's Honey,* was published in 1946 and received the first Doubleday Dorna Award as "An outstanding work dealing with the American Negroes." The story of Honey Hoop, a young black maid employed by the Palmer family, the novel describes Honey's rise from a menial position with the Palmers to a position of prominence as a union organizer in a factory in St. Louis. Realities of racial discrimination in St. Louis housing also appear in the novel. As an activist, Cook had helped St. Louis domestic workers organize a union, and she was actively involved in efforts to abolish segregation in housing in St. Louis. One of her most courageous activist statements was her testimony in case of *Shelley v. Kraemer.* After the Missouri Supreme Court upheld the legality of restrictive racial covenants in housing, they were overturned by the United States Supreme Court on May 3, 1948, which declared them as nonreinforceable in a court of law. Speaking to fellow St. Louisans about her inspiration for *Mrs. Palmer's Honey,* Cook explained: "St. Louis is a rich field for any writer. Many have taken the historical aspect of the city. I felt that the subject was ready and waiting. St. Louis is a dramatic stage for writing. I see its failures, its fascinations. I feel too that I know the interracial St. Louis. I am challenged by feelings of the people, the drama of the change of the domestic worker into the industrial."

Cook died on August 25, 1949, of an apparent heart attack; she was fifty-six years old. Her novels are little remembered, yet her contributions to the welfare of black Americans are significant. She is best remembered as a progressive Missourian whose writing was an expression of her activist experience and her sense of moral mission.

HELEN GOLDMAN

Cook, Fannie. *Boot Heel Doctor.* New York: Dodd, 1941.

———. *Mrs. Palmer's Honey.* Garden City, N.Y.: Doubleday, 1946.

———. Papers. Missouri Historical Society Archives, St. Louis.

Goldman, Helen. "Parallel Portraits: An Exploration of Racial Issues in the Art and Activism of Fannie Frank Cook." Ph.D. diss., St. Louis University, 1992.

Rabinowitz, Paula. *Labor and Desire.* Chapel Hill: University of North Carolina Press, 1991.

COOKINGHAM, L. PERRY (1896–1992)

Perhaps L. Perry Cookingham had more influence in the physical patterning of twentieth-century metropolitan Kansas City than anyone else. While he served as city manager of Kansas City, Missouri, from 1940 to 1959, the city grew from 60 to 130 square miles. That growth included expansion of the city north of the Missouri River, the establishment of the Kansas City International Airport, the planning and partial construction of the beltways encircling the downtown area, and the beginning of the extensive urban redevelopment in the downtown area and elsewhere.

At the age of forty-four, Cookingham came to Kansas City as a person with considerable previous urban governmental experience. Laurie Perry Cookingham was born in Chicago, Illinois, on October 6, 1896, the son of a railroad official and his wife. He grew up in Danville, Illinois, served in the army during World War I, and earned a civil engineering degree from the Detroit Institute of Technology. By the mid-1920s he worked in the public-works department of Flint, Michigan, where he met his wife, Harriette West.

In 1926 Cookingham became the first city manager of Clawson, Michigan, a small Detroit suburb. There he began to learn a great deal about administering a city. In 1931 he became the city manager of Plymouth, Michigan. At the same time he worked as the deputy administrator of a federal area–relief commission. Cookingham subsequently became the director of the work division of the Federal Emergency Relief Administration for Wayne County, Michigan.

In 1936 Cookingham became the city manager of Saginaw, Michigan, a city of ninety thousand. He served Saginaw for more than four years, until May 1940. During that time he became the president of the International City Managers Association.

In 1939, after thirteen years of exercising almost total political domination over Kansas City, the **Thomas J. Pendergast** machine collapsed. Pendergast had run the city's government through the city manager. From the inception of the city manager form of government in 1926, **Henry F. McElroy** had held the post. Pendergast appointed and controlled him, which he accomplished by controlling a majority of the members of the elective city council. When the reformers took power, they looked at the city manager's office as a key to wholesale administrative reform. They sought the best professional city manager they could find, and hired L. Perry Cookingham.

Cookingham, athletically built, with gold-rimmed glasses and a small, thin mustache, brought to Kansas City a high capacity for work, which was sometimes accompanied by what one observer has described as "a determined, almost ominous gaze." But he also brought a sense of humor.

Upon taking the city manager's position, Cookingham found gross inefficiency and fraud. The city was $20 million in debt. Patronage jobs abounded. City contracts had been made without competitive bidding. He quickly began to rectify the situation. After six months, two thousand employees had been terminated. Within a year, half of the deficit had been eliminated. He instituted modern budgetary and accounting systems.

Comprehensive and metropolitan planning held Cookingham's interest the most. At the end of World War II he encouraged the city leaders to consider annexation, and in 1946 the electorate approved the addition of nineteen square miles north of the Missouri River to the city. Studies of traffic needs followed. Kansas City won an All-American City Award in 1950. In 1953 the city bought land for an airport that could accommodate jet aircraft, and thus evolved Kansas City International Airport. Cookingham also led an effort to redevelop parts of the downtown district, and in the process implemented his belief that "a progressive city does not just happen."

In 1959 the city council forced Cookingham to resign. A coalition of Democrats defeated the nonpartisan Citizens' Association. Kansas City had nine city managers during the next four years.

Cookingham had no trouble finding another position. He became the city manager of Fort Worth, Texas, where he worked for four years. He then retired and returned to Kansas City. For the next three years he administered the People to People Program, an organization created by President Dwight D. Eisenhower to encourage international cultural understanding. He became a board member of the local redevelopment authority. For nine years he worked as a consultant for Howard, Needles, Tammen, and Bergendoff, an internationally known consulting firm.

In the 1970s Cookingham received several local honors. In 1976 a new traffic way to the airport was named Cookingham Drive. Harriette Cookingham

died in 1987. L. Perry Cookingham died on July 22, 1992, at the age of ninety-five.

Donald B. Oster

Brown, Theodore A., and Lyle W. Dorsett. *K. C.: A History of Kansas City, Missouri.* Boulder, Colo.: Pruett, 1978.

Gilbert, Bill. *This City, This Man: The Cookingham Era in Kansas City, Missouri.* Washington, D.C.: International City Management Association, 1978.

Haskell, Henry C., Jr., and Richard B. Fowler. *City of the Future.* Kansas City: Frank Glen, 1950.

COONTZ, ROBERT EDWARD (1864–1935)

Robert Edward Coontz, whose naval career encompassed nearly a half century, was born in Hannibal, Missouri, on June 11, 1864. Attending local public and private schools, he began his preparatory education at Inglesile College in 1878–1879 and continued at Hannibal College in 1879–1880. Given the nickname "Senator" while studying at Annapolis, he was commissioned an ensign upon graduation from the Naval Academy in 1885. Promotions through grades followed, with Coontz advancing to rear admiral in 1917 and admiral two years later.

Assigned initially to the *Mohican* on the West Coast, Coontz was later transferred to the gunboat *Pinta,* which operated from the naval station at Sitka, Alaska. During his six years of duty in the Alaskan waters, he became a qualified pilot.

When the Spanish-American War erupted in 1898, Coontz was aboard the *Charleston,* which took possession of Guam, and later joined in the expulsion of Spanish forces from the Philippines. The officers and crew of the *Charleston* also joined in the suppression of the ensuing Filipino insurrection against the American authority in the Philippine Islands. This was followed by service as executive officer aboard a training ship in 1899–1901, and later as senior watch officer aboard the *Philadelphia* during a disturbance in Panama in 1902. When the American battleship fleet, then second in size only to the British navy, made its well-publicized world voyage, beginning in late 1907 and lasting until 1909, it included the *Nebraska,* with Coontz as executive officer. Next, he was commandant of midshipmen at the United States Naval Academy in 1910–1911. Holding the rank of captain, Coontz was appointed governor of Guam in 1912, the United States having acquired the island under the Treaty of Paris that ended the Spanish-American War. Guam was beset by a wave of violence and murder at the time, a problem that the "hanging governor" dealt with decisively.

From 1913 to 1915 Coontz was commanding officer of the battleship *Georgia.* The ship was in Mexican waters and became involved in the Vera Cruz incident in which American forces momentarily occupied the city in 1914. From July 1915 until the summer of 1918 Coontz was commandant of the Thirteenth Naval District and the Puget Sound Navy Yard.

World War I had erupted in Europe during the summer of 1914, and the United States clung to an uneasy neutrality as the war accelerated and ultimately attained global proportions. On August 31, 1918, the United States having joined the Allied war effort in early April of the preceding year, Coontz was given command of the Seventh Division of the Atlantic Fleet. For a brief time after the armistice of November 11, 1918, was proclaimed, Coontz served as acting chief of naval operations while his superior was abroad with President Woodrow Wilson's peace delegation. Coontz resumed his regular command briefly, followed by a transfer to the Pacific fleet, where he was second in command. Appointed chief of naval operations in October 1919, he served in that capacity until July 1923. On August 4, 1923, he was appointed commander in chief of the U.S. fleet, serving aboard the flagship *Seattle* from August 1923 until October 1925.

From late 1925 until his retirement in June 1928, Coontz was commandant of the Fifth Naval District at Norfolk, Virginia. He was recalled briefly to active duty in 1930 to assist in the investigation of the Alaskan railroads, and then to head up a special court to investigate an explosion at the Naval Ammunition Depot in Lake Denmark, New Jersey.

Active in retirement, Coontz was a delegate from Alaska to the Democratic National Convention in 1928, and an active supporter of Franklin D. Roosevelt in 1932. During these years Coontz wrote his autobiography, *From the Mississippi to the Sea* (1920), and *True Anecdotes of an Admiral* (1934). Both during his naval career and in retirement, he was active in veterans' organizations, including service as commanding general of the Military Order of Foreign Wars (1920–1923) and commander in chief of the Veterans of Foreign Wars (1932–1933). Seventy years old and suffering from heart disease, with complications, he died in Bremerton, Washington, on January 26, 1935.

Admiral Coontz received several awards for his naval service, which had been about equally divided between sea and shore duty, including medals from the Spanish-American War, the Philippine insurrection, the Vera Cruz incident, and World War I, including the Distinguished Service Medal. He was also designated a commander in the French Legion of Honor. Moreover, he was the recipient of honorary LL.D. and doctor of naval science degrees from the University of Missouri (1926) and the Pennsylvania Military Academy (1931), respectively.

During his naval career, Coontz played a broadly influential role, both in terms of the navy and for the United States during an expansive and eventful period of the nation's history. A strong advocate of a large and efficient modern navy, he nonetheless worked with senior leaders to make reductions in force in the immediate postwar period, which included major naval reductions and limitations required under an international agreement concluded in the Washington Conference of 1921–1922. He strengthened the power and authority of the office of naval operations, which both resulted in the creation of a more efficient, cohesive, and unified national fleet and enabled the office to formulate and implement naval policies. Naval maneuvers and cruises were expanded to international levels, as was evident in the Hawaii–Australia–New Zealand crisis in the summer of 1925, which involved forty-five ships and forty-three thousand men. The largest concentration of American naval power ever assembled up to that time, such cruises provided significant experience for the navy while also serving as a symbol of America's rapidly expanding global interests. While adhering to the navy's traditional emphasis upon capital ships, Coontz conducted tests to determine the effectiveness of aircraft against warships. As a result, he advocated construction of aircraft carriers as an integral element of the navy's overall fighting capabilities. He also called repeatedly for the addition of submarines, cruisers, and destroyers to the fleet, as well as the development of a merchant marine to carry a majority of the world trade.

In effect, Coontz was both a product of and a spokesman for the emerging American economic, industrial, and political colossus of the twentieth century.

JOSEPH T. HATFIELD

Dictionary of American Biography. Vol. 2, supplement 1. S.v. "Coontz, Robert Edward."
The National Cyclopedia of American Biography. S.v. "Coontz, Robert Edward."
New York Times, January 27, 1935.
Who Was Who in America: A Companion to Who's Who in America. Vol. 1. Chicago: A. N. Marquis, 1942.

COOPER, BENJAMIN ABBOTT (1756–1840)

Benjamin Cooper, a member of one of the most important pioneering families of the Boon's Lick region, was born in Virginia in 1756, the son of

Francis and Ann Abbott Cooper. He married Anna Fullerton. Cooper was a large man, more than six feet tall, and weighed about two hundred pounds. He was a natural leader, noted for his courage and for his quick and fiery temper. He served as a ranger in a Virginia militia company during the Revolutionary War and also fought against the Indians in Kentucky where he became acquainted with **Daniel Boone.** In fact, Boone's move to what would later become the Missouri Territory may have prompted Benjamin and the other Coopers to follow him a few years later.

Cooper and his family came to St. Charles County from Madison County, Kentucky, in 1806. In 1808 he made an initial attempt to establish a settlement near Boone's salt lick in central Missouri, but territorial governor **Meriwether Lewis** ordered his party to return downriver until such time as Indian claims to the area could be extinguished. Cooper settled in the area of Loutre Island (across from present-day Hermann, Missouri) where the families of his younger brothers Sarshel and Braxton joined them. In the spring of 1810 Benjamin Cooper and his brothers returned to the Boon's Lick region along with members of the Cole families and the other Kentuckians at Loutre Island. The Coopers established a settlement not far from Boon's Lick.

During the War of 1812 settlers on both sides of the river constructed forts, the largest being Cooper's Fort at the bottomland site of the Cooper settlement on the north side of the Missouri. Three other forts were built north of the river—Fort Hempstead, Fort Kincaid, and Fort Head—and at least three forts were also built south of the river: **Stephen Cole**'s fort, **Hannah Cole**'s Fort and Fort McMahan. But as the period of unrest continued into 1814 most of the settlers congregated in the northern forts.

Benjamin Cooper was appointed a colonel in the ranger militia during the War of 1812, and his brother Sarshel was appointed captain. Fighting with the Indians continued in the Boon's Lick region into the spring of 1815, when someone opened a hole in the chinking of Sarshel Cooper's fortified cabin and shot him as he held his youngest child on his lap.

Benjamin Cooper died in 1840 and was buried beside his wife, Anna, in a cemetery on a hill southeast of the present hamlet of Petersburg, overlooking the bottom where Cooper's Fort once stood. They left behind seven sons and three daughters.

ROBERT L. DYER

Draper, Lyman C. Manuscripts. State Historical Society of Wisconsin, Madison. Microfilm copy, Western Manuscripts Collection, State Historical Society of Missouri, Columbia.
History of Howard and Cooper Counties, Missouri. St. Louis: National Historical Company, 1883.

Johnson, W. F. *History of Cooper County, Missouri.* Topeka, Kans.: Historical Publishing, 1919.
Sketches from the Life of Major Stephen Cooper. Oakland, Calif., 1888.

CORI, GERTRUDE T. (1896–1957)

Gertrude "Gerty" Theresa Cori was born August 15, 1896, in Prague, Germany, the eldest daughter of Otto and Martha Meustadt Radnitz. After studying with local tutors and attending private schools, she entered the medical school of the German University of Prague in 1914, receiving her M.D. in 1920.

That same year Gerty Radnitz married Dr. Carl Ferdinand Cori, whom she met in medical school and who shared her interests in outdoor sports. They both desired to do biochemical laboratory research instead of practicing medicine. After working in postwar Vienna the Coris welcomed an opportunity to come to the United States, and by 1922 they were working in Buffalo, New York, at the New York State Institute for the Study of Malignant Diseases. The Coris became naturalized citizens of the United States in 1928.

In 1931 Carl Cori became chairman of the department of pharmacology at Washington University School of Medicine in St. Louis, but Gerty Cori was given only a token research position in the same department even though they had previously collaborated in research and published jointly. Carl Cori later moved to the department of biochemistry within Washington University, and Gerty Cori was made professor of biochemistry in 1947. That same year the Coris and Bernardo Houssay of Argentina shared the Nobel Prize in medicine and physiology. Cori was the third woman and the first American woman to receive this honor.

The Nobel Prize was awarded the Coris and Houssay for their discovery and isolation of glucose-1-phosphate, an intermediate in the conversion of glycogen to glucose and subsequently energy that was later called the "Cori ester." In later years, Cori studied glycogen-storage diseases of children, demonstrating that a human heritable disease can stem from a defect in an enzyme, and was researching actively until her untimely death in 1957 of myelofibrosis. The Coris had only one son, Thomas, born in 1936, the same year they isolated the Cori ester.

Besides the joint Nobel Prize the Coris shared the Midwest Award from the American Chemical Society (1946) and the Squibb Award in Endocrinology in 1947. Gerty Cori received the Garvan Medal (1948), the St. Louis Award (1948), the Sugar Research Prize (1950), the Borden Award (1951), and honorary doctor of science degrees from Boston University (1948), Smith College (1949), Yale University

(1951), Columbia University (1954), and the University of Rochester (1955). In 1947 Cori was one of twelve women honored at Hobart and William Smith College in Geneva, New York, during ceremonies marking the centennial of the first medical degree conferred on a woman. Cori was appointed by President **Harry S. Truman** to the board of the National Science Foundation in 1952. She was a member of the U.S. National Academy of Sciences, the American Philosophical Society, the American Society of Biological Chemists, the Harvey Society, the American Chemical Society, the American Society of Arts and Sciences, and Sigma Xi.

After fighting a brave ten-year battle against the disease for which there was no cure, Cori died in St. Louis on October 26, 1957.

ELIZABETH J. BAILEY

Dains, Mary K., ed. *Show Me Missouri Women: Selected Biographies.* Kirksville, Mo.: Thomas Jefferson University Press, 1989.

Houssay, Bernardo A. "Carl F. and Gerty T. Cori." *Biochimica et Biophysica Acta* 20 (1956): 11–15.

Ochoa, Severo. "Gerty T. Cori, Biochemist." *Science* 128 (July 4, 1958): 16.

Opfell, Oglas S. *The Lady Laureates: Women Who Have Won the Nobel Prize.* Metuchen, N.J.: Scarecrow Press, 1988.

Parascandola, John. "Cori, Gertrude Theresa Radnitz." In *Notable American Women, the Modern Period: A Biographical Dictionary,* ed. Barbara Sicherman et al. Cambridge: Harvard University Press, Belknap Press, 1980.

COUZINS, ADALINE WESTON (1815–1892)

Adaline Weston Couzins, a volunteer nursing escort and relief worker during the Civil War, was born in Brighton, England, on August 12, 1815. She was brought to the United States at the age of eight and eloped with John Edward Decker Couzins in 1834. A carpenter and builder by trade, her husband served as chief of police in St. Louis throughout the Civil War and as U.S. marshal of the eastern district of Missouri from 1884 to 1887. The couple headed the relief corps in the cholera epidemic of 1849, setting the tone for their later contributions as tireless public servants.

When news of war reached St. Louis in April 1861, Couzins volunteered her services to one of the city's leading surgeons, Charles Pope. She and her husband later met the first train transporting wounded soldiers to St. Louis from the battlefield after **Nathaniel Lyon**'s defeat at Wilson's Creek on August 10. They helped carry the men into the New House of Refuge Hospital, and Couzins "washed and dressed them with the appliances of hospital stores she had gathered together when news came of the battle."

Thereafter, Couzins contributed her services to the Union cause as a member of the Ladies' Union Aid Society (LUAS) of St. Louis. She and another society member, Arethusa L. Forbes, volunteered to inspect and report the conditions and number of casualties lying in the wake of Gen. **John C. Frémont**'s disastrous march into southwest Missouri during the winter of 1862. Within twenty-four hours of their return to St. Louis, a "long line" of hospital cars was sent to retrieve the wounded. Both women were severely frostbitten on the trip, and Forbes never again attempted such a dangerous venture.

Undaunted, Couzins recovered and, together with other society members and supplies provided by the LUAS, proceeded to the front to attend to the wounded after the Battles of Shiloh; Donaldson; Corinth; Pillow; Vicksburg; Red, White, and Yazoo Rivers; and others. In a letter to Couzins's daughter, Phoebe, years later Forbes recalled a time when her mother briefly took charge of patient care on one sanitary boat because the "regular male doctors lay drunk in their cabins on liquors furnished by the Ladies Union Aid for the wounded soldiers." Phoebe later noted the grisly reality of serving on the battlefields and hospital steamers, remembering the "maimed, bleeding, dying soldiers by the hundreds" on a single boat and the attendant boxes of amputated limbs.

Although some women proved temperamentally unsuited for battlefield or steamer duty, the chief surgeon for the Western Sanitary Commission, Simon Pollack, claimed Couzins to be "conspicuous" among the female volunteers for her "native intelligence, great experience, and untiring activity," since she "did not mince matters, nor do work by halves." Unlike the sanitary commission or regular-army nurses, Couzins received no remuneration for her services and paid for her own passage to the battlefields and occasionally for that of others.

Wounded in the knee by a minié-ball fragment at the siege of Vicksburg in 1863, Couzins became increasingly immobile and finally bedridden and destitute in her old age. In 1888 Sen. T. W. Palmer of Michigan lobbied for a government pension in her behalf, citing her unrelenting efforts as a relief worker during the war. **James Overton Broadhead** went to Washington, D.C., to second Palmer's request, and numerous other St. Louisans prepared testimonials to Couzins's contributions. On March 27 Senate Bill 2356 was passed without debate.

A founder of the Female Guardian Home of St. Louis, Couzins headed the Ladies' Sanitary Corps of the Special Health Department of St. Louis after the war and campaigned actively for woman suffrage. She also applied to **Edward Bates,** Lincoln's attorney general, for the position of head of the St. Louis post office. Bates claimed his eyes sparkled with animation and pleasure as he read her petition, and he said, "Yes, yes, Mrs. Couzins, you should have that office; no one in our country deserves it more, and I know you *well,* and I know you will do the office justice."

Although she did not get the job, Bates's confidence in her abilities clearly reflected not only Couzins's record as a nursing escort and relief worker during the war but also her impeccable character, for by all accounts she possessed the "quiet temperament and greater courage to perform the hardest parts" and performed them with a philanthropic spirit and love of country. A lifelong member of the Second Baptist Church, Couzins died on May 9, 1892, and was buried at Bellefontaine Cemetery.

PAULA COALIER

Coalier, Paula. "Beyond Sympathy: The St. Louis Ladies' Union Aid Society and the Civil War." *Gateway Heritage* 11 (summer 1990): 38–51.

Couzins, J. E. D. Papers. Missouri Historical Society Archives, St. Louis.

Hanaford, Phebe A. *Daughter of America: Or, Women of the Century.* Augusta, Maine: True, 1882.

COUZINS, PHOEBE WILSON (1842–1913)

Phoebe Wilson Couzins, a lawyer and suffragist, was born on September 8, 1842, to John Edward Decker and **Adaline Weston Couzins.** She graduated from the St. Louis public high school at fifteen and taught Sunday school at the Second Baptist Church. Her father was chief of police in the city during the Civil War, and her mother served as a nursing volunteer for the Ladies' Union Aid Society, escorting wounded soldiers back to St. Louis after battles in the western department. An ardent Union supporter and always a notably striking woman, Couzins served as the queen of flowers at a fund-raiser given to aid the Western Sanitary Commission in June 1863, leading her flower maidens through their dances with "great vivacity and ability."

In 1869 Washington University Law School admitted Couzins, becoming one of the first schools in the country to offer a woman an education in jurisprudence. She graduated in 1871 and, in the course of her life, was admitted to the bar associations of Missouri, Arkansas, Utah, and Kansas, and the Dakota Territory federal courts. Although Couzins never practiced law professionally beyond a two-month period in 1884, she was the second woman in the United States to graduate from law school, the second admitted to a bar association, and the third allowed to practice law nationwide. At her graduation celebration, she explained her motivation for earning a law degree, claiming to be spurred "solely by a desire to open new paths for women, enlarge her usefulness, widen her responsibilities and to plead her case in a struggle which [she] believed surely was coming. . . ."

Couzins's motivation also rested on her mother's relief efforts during the war, a fact she forcefully attested to in a speech at Independence Square in Philadelphia during America's centennial celebration on July 4, 1876. A member of the Woman Suffrage Association of Missouri until she resigned when it aligned itself with the American Woman Suffrage Association in 1871, Couzins served as a delegate to the American Equal Rights Association convention held in St. Louis in October 1869. Susan B. Anthony was present, and after the convention Couzins joined with Anthony and Elizabeth Cady Stanton to form the more radical National Woman Suffrage Association, lecturing extensively to full houses around the country and serving as an association delegate at both the Democratic National Convention in St. Louis in June 1876 and the centennial celebration.

After the American and national associations merged in 1890, Couzins's participation in the suffrage movement effectively declined, owing not only to her earlier censure of the American organization but also to her resentment of the wealth and social position of the new wave of feminists. Couzins's increasing intractability also contributed to her decline. As one of two delegates to the Board of Lady Managers of the World's Columbian Exposition at Chicago in 1890, she was summarily dismissed from her paid job as secretary after she attempted to control the chair and others on the board. By the late 1890s Couzins's disillusionment with suffrage and its attendant priority, temperance, was complete, and she briefly renounced both causes and accepted a position as a lobbyist and lecturer for the United Brewers' Association in 1897.

Although the brewers did not drop her from their payroll until 1908, Couzins retracted her renunciation of women's rights activities at the Church of the West in Kansas City in 1902. She confessed her feeling of "shame" for "slurring" those "noble women" in the movement and added a comment of portentous significance for twentieth-century women: "Until we are large enough to think of mind, of genius, of ability without the consciousness of sex, we are yet in the infancy of our development, we belong in kindergarten." Couzins delivered this speech on crutches, suffering from yet another bout of the debilitating arthritis that eventually forced her to solicit financial assistance from St. Louis friends such as I. H. Lionberger and **William Bixby**.

Couzins continuously maintained close ties with St. Louis and attended her father on his deathbed, cooling him with five hundred pounds of ice, in August 1887. After he died she succeeded him for two months as the first female U.S. marshal. Despite her national reputation as a suffragist, many years on the lyceum circuit, and numerous articles published in St. Louis newspapers, Couzins died penniless on December 6, 1913. A friend paid for her funeral, and she was buried at Bellefontaine Cemetery with her U.S. marshal's badge pinned to her chest. In June 1950 Missouri's women lawyers acknowledged Couzins's many groundbreaking contributions by erecting a simple stone monument on her previously unmarked grave.

PAULA COALIER

Couzins, J. E. D. Papers. Missouri Historical Society Archives, St. Louis.
Dains, Mary K., ed. *Show Me Missouri Women: Selected Biographies.* Kirksville, Mo.: Thomas Jefferson University Press, 1989.
Hill, Sarah Jane Full. *Mrs. Hill's Journal: Civil War Reminiscences.* Ed. Mark M. Krung. Chicago: R. R. Donnelley, 1980.
The National Cyclopedia of American Biography. S.v. "Couzins, Phoebe."
Rice, Patricia. "Golden-Tongued Champion of Equal Rights." *St. Louis Post-Dispatch,* August 8, 1976.
Stanton, Elizabeth Cady, Susan B. Anthony, and Matilda Joslyn Gage. *History of Women Suffrage (1861–1876).* 1882. Reprint, New York: Arno and the *New York Times,* 1969.

COWDEN, HOWARD A. (1893–1972)

The founder of the Consumers Cooperative Association (CCA) (now Farmland Industries) and the original field man for the Missouri Farmers Association (MFA), Howard A. Cowden affected the lives of Missouri and midwestern farmers as much as anyone in the twentieth century.

Born on May 18, 1893, in Pleasant Hope just north of Springfield, Cowden grew up as a southwest Missouri farm boy at the turn of the century. His postsecondary education consisted of short courses in agriculture at the University of Missouri–Columbia, and one semester at Missouri State Normal School (now Southwest Missouri State University) at Springfield. He taught school for four years near or in his hometown of Pleasant Hope.

After the end of World War I, Cowden took the position of secretary for the newly formed Polk County Farmers Association, which was affiliated with the MFA (organized in Columbia in January 1917). Cowden's Polk County work attracted the attention of **William Henry Hirth,** founder of the *Missouri Farmer* and originator of the MFA.

Cowden's involvement in cooperative business ventures resulted from a law change by the Missouri legislature in 1919 that enabled farm cooperatives to function properly. This led to his employment by the MFA as its first field man in January 1920. Continuing in that position until 1927, Cowden greatly expanded membership and cooperative ventures within the MFA.

After a falling-out with his former sponsor, Hirth, Cowden organized the Cowden Oil Company in January 1928 to sell petroleum and lubricants to farm cooperatives in Missouri and elsewhere. The following year he was able to interest representatives from six midwestern cooperatives in the idea of forming a cooperatives' cooperative to supply such products on a broad scale. The company took over the assets of Cowden Oil Company and emerged as the Union Oil Company (renamed Consumers Cooperative Association in 1935). Cowden established company headquarters in North Kansas City, Missouri.

Initially organized to supply petroleum products to cooperatives in the region, the CCA launched a diversification program in the mid-1930s. By 1936 the company manufactured its own brand of paint and began distribution of groceries to member cooperatives for resale. Never successful as a business venture, the grocery department of the CCA ceased distribution in 1953. Cowden led the CCA to enter the tractor-manufacturing business in 1935, but the effort ceased in 1940.

Beginning in 1938 Cowden organized a transportation department for the CCA as a means of distributing its products. On the eve of World War II, Cowden's CCA provided merchandise bearing the "Co-Op" label to 121 cooperatively owned stores in seven midwestern states, but mostly in Kansas and Missouri.

During World War II the demand for increased meat and food output prompted Cowden to promote expansion into livestock-feed manufacturing and fertilizer production. In the post–World War II era these became high-volume products for the cooperatives.

The overall significance of the success of Cowden's CCA is that it boosted the activities of hundreds of farmer-owned cooperatives in the Midwest. These companies charged their members retail prices on the products purchased and returned dividends in "patronage checks" at the end of the financial year. Thus, stock in the cooperative ventures did not pay dividends; the only way to get patronage benefits was to buy at the "Co-Op." The CCA operated on the same principle with regard to its member cooperatives as well.

Cowden retired as president and chief executive officer of the CCA at age sixty-eight in 1961. For a brief period he served as chairman of the board of the organization. Beginning in late 1961, however, he assumed the role of consultant to Nationwide Mutual Insurance Companies, which enabled him to continue his advocacy for all types of cooperative ventures across the country and even in other nations.

During his lifetime Cowden served as first president of the National Cooperative Refinery Association; first elected chairman of the Board of Governors for the Agricultural Hall of Fame in Bonner Springs, Kansas; and president of the International Cooperative Petroleum Association, among other responsibilities.

Cowden died at his home in Oakwood, Missouri, in suburban Kansas City, on December 22, 1972. His beloved CCA became Farmland Industries in September 1966, after he was no longer associated with the venture. In 1995 Farmland Industries was the largest cooperatively owned company in the United States.

WILLIAM S. WORLEY

Cowden, Howard A. Clipping File. Missouri Valley Room, Kansas City Public Library, Kansas City.

Fite, Gilbert. *Beyond the Fence Rows: A History of Farmland Industries, Inc., 1929–1978.* Columbia: University of Missouri Press, 1978.

Fowler, Dick. *Leaders in Our Town.* Kansas City: Burd and Fletcher, 1952.

COX, LESTER EDMUND (1895–1968)

Lester Edmund Cox, a businessman and philanthropist, was born in Republic, Missouri, on August 22, 1895, and spent his adult life in nearby Springfield, where he became widely known for his varied business interests and for leadership in community affairs. He married Mildred Belle Lee in 1918; they had three children: Virginia Belle "Ginny" Cox Bussey, Lester L. "Bud" Cox, and Catherine Lee "Kitty" Cox Lipscomb. Lester E. Cox learned the importance of community service from his mother, Amanda Belle Britain Cox, who tended garden produce and stitched quilts to give to the Burge Deaconess Hospital in north Springfield. A self-made millionaire at the time of his death, Cox thrived on challenges, and based his business priorities on the slogan "Find a need and fill it."

Cox's business interests ranged widely. Of rural roots, concern for the soil and agricultural pursuits remained the keystone of his interests, with a primary business based upon what became the largest tractor and farm equipment distributorship in the United States. He originally sold Ford/Dearborn equipment;

later, when Ford changed company organization policies, Cox sold English-built David Brown equipment over a nine-state Midwest region.

Cox also developed companies and investments, including radio and television stations, airlines, mining, oil, advertising, furniture manufacturing, building construction, warehousing, and insurance.

Cox is perhaps most vividly remembered in Springfield, Missouri, for his willingness in 1949 to rescue the financially plagued Burge Hospital, renamed Lester E. Cox Medical Center after his death. Although Cox wanted even his hobbies to earn money, he believed there were two chief benefits of money—after achieving financial independence: to create opportunity for others and to bring them happiness. Rescuing Burge Hospital from bankruptcy, which kept the doors open to countless Ozark residents needing medical care, became the avenue for Cox to live up to that two-part creed.

Cox helped Springfield's Burge Hospital by becoming a hardworking president of the board of directors, and by giving the institution outright financial gifts. He convinced others of the need to keep the hospital open; he persuaded the staff doctors to contribute heavily to the hospital's rescue, and Cox personally matched the amount they raised. Initially, Cox contributed $150,000; in a later phase when a crippled-children's wing and a nurses' dormitory were added, he contributed another $100,000. He also persuaded Floyd Jones, the founder of several regional bus lines and Ozark Airlines, to contribute generously to the hospital. Cox took his duties as president of the board seriously, devoting his Saturday mornings to meticulous inspections of the hospital, insisting on "clean floors, smiling nurses, and good food."

During his career, Cox actively worked as a "booster" for the Ozarks, for Missouri, and for the nation. Eschewing corporate decisions when possible in favor of personal responsibility, Cox often ruminated that "had Moses been a committee he could never have brought the Hebrews out of . . . slavery to the Promised Land." Notwithstanding this philosophy, much of his civic service was in league with others. Cox served twelve years on the Board of Curators for the University of Missouri, and nine years on the Board of Curators of Southern Methodist University. He also served as president of the Springfield Chamber of Commerce, organized a USO War Dads' servicemen's canteen during World War II, served on the board of directors of the St. Louis–San Francisco Railway, obtained tax-free status from the Federal Communications Commission for the University of Missouri's television station, KOMU-TV, was responsible for the University of Missouri's acquisition of a power plant from private sources when the state legislature proved niggardly on the matter, and served on the board of directors of Ozark Airlines. Cox died on August 14, 1968.

EDGAR D. McKINNEY

Hulston, John K. *Lester E. Cox, 1895–1968: He Found Needs and Filled Them.* Cassville, Mo.: Litho Printers and Bindery, 1992.
Joplin Globe, December 3, 1961.
Springfield Leader and Press, December 24, 1968.
Springfield News and Leader, August 21, 1968.
St. Louis Globe-Democrat, February 12, 1961.

COX, OLIVER CROMWELL (1901–1974)

Oliver Cromwell Cox was arguably one of the most controversial of mid-twentieth-century social scientists. Born on August 24, 1901, in Port-of-Spain, Trinidad, in the West Indies, Cox was one of six children born to William and Mary Blake Cox. He came to the United States in his late teens, hoping for a career in medicine. He completed his secondary education at the Central YMCA High School in Chicago. Later, he earned a bachelor of science degree in law in 1928 from Northwestern University, in Evanston, Illinois. Cox was stricken with polio in 1929, and he walked with great difficulty for the remainder of his life. The illness seems to have caused him to abandon his hope for a career in law, switching instead to the social sciences; he thought that his disability would impede his career as a lawyer. He earned a master of arts degree in economics in 1932 and a Ph.D. in sociology in 1938 from the University of Chicago. His dissertation was titled "Factors Affecting Marital Status among Negroes." In a letter to a former student written in 1971, Cox explained that "[t]he depression caused me to change to sociology."

Upon completion of his Ph.D., Cox embarked on an academic career, teaching first at Wiley College in Marshall, Texas, and later at the Tuskegee Institute in Alabama. At Wiley College, Cox developed a lifelong friendship with the distinguished African American poet **Melvin B. Tolson.** In 1949 Cox moved to Jefferson City, Missouri, and took a job teaching sociology at the state's all-black public institution of higher education, Lincoln University.

Cox was an original thinker and a prolific scholar. During the early 1940s he began exploring and writing about race and class in a series of articles in the *Journal of Negro Education.* His work culminated in the publication of *Caste, Class and Race: A Study in Social Dynamics,* the book for which he is best known. In his book Cox traced the rise of racial prejudice to the emergence of capitalism and the effort of capitalists to exercise control over the workers they exploited.

Such ideas resulted in Cox being labeled a Marxist, a designation he denied. Cox's criticism of capitalism and of institutional racism resulted in attacks on his work from a variety of sources. As early as 1944, while Cox was teaching at Wiley College, an FBI informant reported that Cox had "questionable tendencies." Although the FBI alleged that it never considered Cox a serious threat to national security, it continued to gather information on him into the 1960s. Much of this information remains classified and unavailable to researchers.

Cox retired from Lincoln University in 1970. Subsequently, he moved to Detroit where he taught for a few more years at Wayne State University. Always a loner, Cox never married and spent his more than twenty-year tenure at Lincoln University living in a dormitory room. He died on September 4, 1974. Among the awards he received was the W. E. B. DuBois Award (1968), given by the Association of Social and Behavioral Scientists, and the DuBois-Johnson-Frazier Award (1971), sponsored by the Caucus of Black Sociologists.

GARY R. KREMER

Cox, Oliver Cromwell. File, Lincoln Collection. Inman E. Page Library, Lincoln University, Jefferson City, Mo.
Hunter, Herbert M. "The Life and Work of Oliver C. Cox." Ph.D. diss., Boston University, 1981.
Hunter, Herbert M., and Sameer Y. Abraham. *Caste, Class, and the World System: The Sociology of Oliver C. Cox.* New York: Monthly Review Press, 1988.
Morgan, Gordon D. "In Memoriam: Oliver C. Cox, 1901–1974." *Monthly Review* 28 (May 1976): 34–40.

CRAIGHEAD, ALEXANDER (1792–1848)

Alexander Craighead was a Missouri pioneer businessman of southeast Missouri who platted and named the village of Caledonia, in Washington County.

Born in 1792, Craighead came to Ste. Genevieve about 1810 from Nashville, Tennessee, when he was eighteen years old. He was descended from Scotch-Irish Presbyterians of some distinction. His father, grandfather, great-grandfather, and great-great-grandfather were all Presbyterian ministers. In 1715 Craighead's forebears began to tread the great Scotch-Irish immigration route from Ulster to Pennsylvania, then to Virginia, Carolina, and Tennessee. In the 1740s his grandfather Alexander was leader of an anti-British faction of Reformed Presbyterian "Covenanters" in Mecklenberg County, North Carolina.

Craighead's father, Thomas Brown Craighead, was the founder of Nashville's Davidson Academy. Thomas Craighead's six sons were all cultivated and ambitious. The youngest, Thomas Brown Craighead Jr., moved through Missouri to pioneer in northeast Arkansas, where he became the namesake of Craighead County.

In Ste. Genevieve young Alexander Craighead opened a general store with a partner named Wilson in 1810. A year later he went inland to Potosi, the new raw-lead mining town soon to be the seat of Washington County (created in 1814). He opened another store and gained interest in, or ownership of, the newly discovered Mine à Shibboleth. A title dispute embroiled him in a lawsuit with the notorious adventurer **John Smith T.** Meanwhile, Craighead and Wilson gained a third partner, one of the Ste. Genevieve Dodges of the family of **Henry Dodge,** subsequently governor of and U.S. senator from Wisconsin. During the War of 1812 Craighead became a major, and doubtless made money in the lead business. By 1817 he had moved twelve miles south of Potosi, into the Bellevue Valley and opened another store, this time in partnership with **Andrew Henry** who had helped establish the Missouri Fur Company in 1809 and who later became a partner of **William H. Ashley.**

Bellevue Valley, first entered in 1798, was probably the earliest settlement of Americans in Missouri away from the rivers. Pious Presbyterians and Methodists, such as Craighead, with Scotch-Irish roots were its residents. The congregations that greeted Craighead were among the earliest of those denominations west of the Mississippi. The churches, located near each other in the valley's north end, signaled the possibility of a town. Craighead seized the opportunity to secure land, plat it, and name it "Caledonia," Latin for "Scotland." Craighead knew not only Latin but also French, a language in which he often corresponded. Surely "Caledonia" suited the local inhabitants who both respected learning and remembered their Scottish roots.

Craighead may well have chosen the Bellevue Valley for religious and cultural reasons, following sojourns in Catholic Ste. Genevieve and rough-and-tumble Potosi. The valley's high Scotch-Irish population and healthful Ozark climate were congenial. The combination of fertile farmland and rich mines were propitious for business.

Craighead and Henry built a log store building and residence that survives to the present in a good state of preservation. Built around 1816 it is one of Missouri's significant pioneer-period structures. The 1818 town plat was straightforward, fifty-four lots in six files of nine ranks each. The axis was some eight degrees off true north because it followed the boundary between two Spanish land grants not oriented to the compass.

Subsequent development of the town followed the plan exactly.

Four lots were retained for the notable Washington County pioneer **John Rice Jones,** a veteran of George Rogers Clark's Vincennes campaign of the Revolution, Washington County delegate to the 1820 Missouri Constitutional Convention, and later justice of the Missouri Supreme Court. The town would surely attract other important, well-connected people. Craighead and Henry reserved lots for themselves, doubtless depending upon an increment of value to support their investments.

The panic of 1819 overtook all, however, driving neighboring pioneer miner **Moses Austin** from Potosi to secure a land grant in Texas, though he died in Missouri before taking it up. Austin's Texas venture, as well as the financial reverses that triggered it, drew many other Washington County citizens away, depleting the society and economy in ways that can only be surmised. In February 1819 Craighead was sued for recovery of a $7,200 debt, which was a bad sign. He obtained the Caledonia postmaster's appointment, but soon lost it. Henry left in 1822 for a second fur-trading trip to the Rockies, his most famous exploit. He returned in 1824 to the status of a prominent and good citizen, including election to the county court. Craighead, however, disappeared from public record, last noted as a county property owner on the 1825 tax rolls. A Craighead family genealogy says of him: "died, Mo., 1848, unmarried."

ROBERT FLANDERS

Bellevue-Beautiful View: The History of the Bellevue Valley and Surrounding Area. Caledonia: Bellevue Valley Historical Society, 1983.

Flanders, Robert. "Caledonia: Ozarks Heritage of the High Scotch-Irish." *Gateway Heritage* 4 (spring 1986): 34–52.

CRAWFORD, JOAN (1908–1977)

Joan Crawford was born Lucille LeSueur on March 23, 1908, in San Antonio, Texas, as she described, "in a drab little place on the wrong side of the tracks." A chorus girl by way of Kansas City, she would later live in a twenty-seven-room Hollywood mansion and become one of the great film stars. Her mother was Anna Johnson LeSueur, but Crawford did not meet her biological father until she was an established star. Her parents separated shortly after her birth, and her mother subsequently married Henry Cassin, a theater owner in Lawton, Oklahoma. She used the names LeSueur and Cassin interchangeably until she started work in Hollywood and received her professional name, which was selected in a magazine contest.

When Crawford was still a child her family moved to Kansas City where she was known as

Billie Cassin. Her mother and stepfather separated, and Crawford paid her way through school at the St. Agnes Academy and Rockingham School by working in the kitchen and dining room. She won her first dancing contest at the Jack O'Lantern Cafe in Kansas City. She once told an interviewer that she never really went beyond the sixth grade and that she "began working when I was nine years old scrubbing floors."

In the fall of 1922 Crawford went to Stephens College in Columbia, Missouri, and worked in the school dining room. She faked her birth date as 1906 when she registered and forged a high school record. She left Stephens after three months, realizing she was unprepared for college, and went back to Kansas City determined to be a dancer. On her return she entered a training program with the Bell Telephone Company but disliked being a telephone operator and soon quit the job. She next accepted a position wrapping packages at Woolf Brothers Clothing Store for twelve dollars per week, then moved to Rothschild's for slightly more money. She finally worked for fifteen dollars a week at Emery, Bird, and Thayer selling women's wear.

After she accumulated enough money to buy a wardrobe, Crawford applied to a theatrical agent, who found a job for her in a chorus in Springfield, Missouri. While en route to Springfield she decided to use Lucille LeSueur as her stage name. The show closed in two weeks, and she returned to Kansas City and then landed a job in Chicago. She attracted the attention of J. J. Shubert, and he invited her to join the chorus of his revue, *Innocent Eyes,* which opened in New York and played for three months. In 1924 she was in the chorus of *The Passing Show.* Eight months later, a Metro-Goldwyn-Mayer talent scout discovered Crawford and offered her a five-year contract. She immediately left her mother's Kansas City apartment bound for Hollywood.

In 1926 Crawford played a chorus girl in her first movie, *Pretty Ladies,* starring Zasu Pitts and Lillian Tashman. It was the Roaring Twenties, a high-living era of short skirts and hip flasks marked by the excesses of the so-called flaming youth. No one epitomized the decade more than Joan Crawford. She went on to star in *Our Dancing Daughters,* and became one of Hollywood's most glamorous stars in the 1930s and 1940s.

In 1945, with the 1920s long behind her, Crawford displayed her great acting versatility in the movie *Mildred Pierce,* a serious dramatic film with none of the wild overtones of her earlier movie roles. Her selection for an Academy Award as best actress was widely popular. In private life she was realistic and down-to-earth. She was genuinely well liked both on and off the set in the film industry.

Crawford returned to Kansas City several times after she found fame in Hollywood. In 1933 about eight hundred people swarmed around a train that stopped at Union Station while she was en route from New York to Hollywood. In 1935 Crawford made another brief stopover in Kansas City. She last visited Kansas City in May 1960 when she attended a ribbon-cutting ceremony for the opening of a Pepsi-Cola bottling plant. On that occasion Crawford commented that riding past the old Rockingham school "brought back a lot of memories." "I scrubbed floors there to earn money for school."

On May 10, 1977, Crawford died of a heart attack in New York City. She married four times. Her husbands were Douglas Fairbanks Jr., Franchot Tone, Phillip Terry, and businessman Alfred Steele. Steele, her last husband, was board chairman of Pepsi-Cola and died in 1959. Crawford became a director of the firm and frequently made personal appearances for the corporation.

At the time of Crawford's death, the *Kansas City Times* editorialized that she "built a classic American success story and formidable motion picture career on the talent and determination of a Kansas City youngster who pursued her dream."

ARTHUR F. McCLURE AND VIVIAN RICHARDSON

Current Biography. New York: H. W. Wilson, 1946.
"Hollywood's Once and Only Star." *Time* (May 23, 1977): 97.
Kansas City Times, May 13, 1977.
Quirk, Lawrence J. *The Films of Joan Crawford.* New York: Citadel Press, 1968.
Thomas, Bob. *Joan Crawford.* New York: Bantam, 1979.
Variety, May 18, 1977.

CREEL, GEORGE (1876–1953)

George Creel was a government administrator, political adviser, journalist, author, and politician. The son of Henry and Virginia Creel, George was born on December 1, 1876, in Lafayette County, Missouri. Virginia Creel supported her three sons and alcoholic husband by operating a boardinghouse in Kansas City. Eventually, the family moved to Odessa, Missouri, where George received some formal education. Dropping out of high school after one year, he returned to Kansas City and became a cub reporter for the *Kansas City World* until a quarrel with his city editor prompted him to board a cattle train to New York City to seek his fortune. Instead, he sold a few jokes to magazines and shoveled snow.

In 1899 Creel returned to Kansas City to publish, for a decade, the small *Kansas City Independent.* As a journalist he advocated political progressivism and sought the destruction of the Boss **Tom Pendergast**'s machine. Having failed to achieve this lofty objective, Creel moved westward to Denver in 1909 where he worked for the *Denver Post* and the *Rocky Mountain News*. He took his progressive political ideas with him, using his editorials to advocate social reform and to combat special interests and political chicanery.

When the United States entered World War I in 1917, President Woodrow Wilson recognized Creel's party loyalty and journalistic prowess by appointing him chairman of the Committee on Public Information. As head of this pioneering agency, Creel made his most significant contribution by successfully managing the news at home and cultivating America abroad.

As "Uncle Sam's Press Agent," Creel inundated a global audience with drawings, film footage, pamphlets, and press releases. He organized a nationwide speakers' bureau, the "Four Minute Men," who gave thousands of patriotic speeches at public meetings, theatrical performances, and wherever else they could be heard. The bureau deserves credit for much of the success of the government-sponsored "Liberty Loan" drives. Creel's role as censor earned him the enmity of critics such as H. L. Mencken and I. F. Stone who accused him of unfair scrutiny and censorship before releasing news for public consumption. Scholars have rejected that criticism, praising him for his restraint and sound judgment.

Creel defended President Wilson's objectives at the Peace of Paris, and when the United States Senate rejected the Treaty of Versailles an embittered Creel temporarily retired from the political arena. During the 1920s he wrote books defending the work of the Committee on Public Information and several popular biographies of what he thought were misunderstood characters in American history, including George Custer, Sam Houston, and Thomas Paine. The flamboyant, restless self-styled rebel moved to California, dabbled in silent films as both a screenwriter and a onetime actor, and married actress Blanche Bates.

The Great Depression and Franklin Roosevelt's election to the presidency lured Creel back into active political life. During Roosevelt's first term, Creel enthusiastically accepted appointment as chairman of the National Advisory Board for the Works Progress Administration. In 1934 he unsuccessfully challenged Upton Sinclair in the Democratic primary for California governor. As the depression continued, Creel's loyalty to New Deal politics waned. In spite of his political activity, he remained active as a journalist by writing a regular column for *Collier's*.

The Roosevelt administration's handling of the war caused Creel to renounce his political liberalism and to move to the right wing of the Republican Party.

Big government, he concluded, stifled individualism and exuded inefficiency. Moreover, Roosevelt had been too compassionate to the vanquished as well as to the Soviet Union at Yalta. The presidency of fellow Missourian **Harry S. Truman** did not cause Creel to reconsider his political defection, for though he considered Truman an honest man, he could not forgive him for his loyalty to the Pendergast machine.

Creel remained active in state and local politics in California during the final years of his life. In 1949 the United Mine Workers' president, John L. Lewis, asked Creel to prepare a report on the union's welfare and retirement fund.

A prolific author, Creel wrote fifteen books and more than three hundred articles. In his autobiography he argued that if his public life appeared to have been erratic at times, he had been consistent in one important respect: "My whole adult life had been devoted to criticism of the barnacled faults of the American system; yet never once have I doubted the wisdom and rightness of the system itself."

Creel died in San Francisco on October 2, 1953. His second wife and two children survived him.

JACK B. RIDLEY

Bean, Walton E. "George Creel and His Critics: A Study of the Attacks on the Committee on Public Information." Ph.D. diss., University of California, Berkeley, 1941.

Creel, George. *How We Advertised America.* New York: Harper and Brothers, 1920.

———. *Rebel at Large: Recollections of Fifty Crowded Years.* New York: G. P. Putnam's Sons, 1947.

Dictionary of American Biography. Supplement 5. S.v. "Creel, George."

Mock, James R., and Cedric Larson. *Words That Won the War: The Story of the Committee on Public Information, 1917–1919.* New York: Russell and Russell, 1939.

Stone, I. F. "Creel's Crusade." *Nation* (December 9, 1939): 647–49.

CRITTENDEN, THOMAS THEODORE (1832–1909)

At five o'clock on October 5, 1882, a man "armed to the teeth" walked into the capitol office of Gov. Thomas Theodore Crittenden. "I surrender to you, Governor Crittenden, my arms, this pistol, which no man has put his hand upon since 1864." With his dramatic surrender, **Frank James** wrote the final chapter of the marauding James Gang and secured Crittenden's place in history as the man who brought them to justice.

Thomas Crittenden was born on New Year's Day 1832, in Shelbyville, Kentucky, where he joined a prominent political family (one uncle served the state both as a governor and as a senator). At age twenty-three, Crittenden graduated from Centre College in Danville, Kentucky, and immediately began studying law in his uncle's firm. The following year he received his license to practice law.

On November 13, 1856, Crittenden married Caroline Jackson. The next summer they moved to Lexington, Missouri, where he established a law practice. With the onset of the Civil War, Crittenden, a strong Union man, helped organize the Seventh Cavalry of the Missouri State Militia. He served with the cavalry throughout the war, obtaining the rank of colonel. Shortly before the war ended, Gov. **Willard Preble Hall** appointed Crittenden attorney general when Aikeman Welch died in midterm. Following the war Crittenden relocated his family and his law practice to Warrensburg, Missouri.

In 1872 voters in the Seventh Congressional District elected Crittenden to the United States Congress. Two years later he failed to win the Democratic nomination when delegates balloted 690 times before choosing Col. **John Finis Philips** as their nominee for Crittenden's congressional slot. In 1876, however, voters returned Crittenden to Congress. Upon completing the term he returned to Missouri and began focusing on the 1880 gubernatorial election. After securing the Democratic nomination, he won the general election by more than fifty-four thousand votes. On January 10, 1881, Crittenden became the twenty-fourth governor of Missouri.

Crittenden outlined his three major goals for the state: "First, the elevation of its financial standing. Second, the strengthening of its school funds, giving a higher education to its boys and girls of all classes. Third, the suppression of outlawry."

To improve state finances, Crittenden sought to collect on loans extended to the Hannibal and St. Joseph Railroad. A battle and several suits followed before the railroad paid the millions of dollars it owed. He also placed great importance on education. Missouri schools, which were flourishing before his term, continued to do so with his leadership.

The governor's third goal, the "suppression of outlawry," proved the most daunting task of Crittenden's administration. In the wake of the Civil War, gangs swept across the state terrorizing people, robbing both banks and trains. None was more notorious than the James Gang. Previous governors attempted but failed to stop them. However, Crittenden launched a new and controversial strategy. Limited by law to offering only a three-hundred-dollar reward from the state treasury, Crittenden secured fifty thousand dollars in pledges from railroads to offer larger rewards. Then he issued a proclamation offering five thousand dollars for the arrest and conviction of each member of the gang except the James brothers, for which he offered five thousand for the capture and an additional five thousand for the conviction of either Frank or **Jesse James.** The strategy proved successful. Robert Ford, a member of the James Gang, shot and killed Jesse on April 3, 1882. Frank surrendered the following autumn in the governor's office. Through surrender, capture, and death, the gang disintegrated. Crittenden had secured the demise of the James Gang with twenty thousand dollars, none of which came from the state treasury. Many applauded Crittenden for ending what they described as a curse against the state, while others expressed dismay at the way it was accomplished.

After leaving office Crittenden settled in Kansas City where he opened a new law firm. In 1893 President Grover Cleveland appointed him as the United States consul general to Mexico. Crittenden served for four years before returning to Kansas City, where he passed away on May 29, 1909. Crittenden left behind his wife of more than fifty years and three sons (Caroline, his daughter, had died of diphtheria while living in the Governor's Mansion). Shortly before his death he wrote of his governorship, "I did my duty before God and man, as I saw it, and now believe my views and actions have resulted in great good to the state."

LISA HEFFERNAN WEIL

Avery, Grace Gilmore, and Floyd C. Shoemaker. "Governor Thomas T. Crittenden." In *The Messages and Proclamations of the Governors of the State of Missouri,* vol. 6. Columbia: State Historical Society of Missouri, 1924.

Crittenden, H. H. *The Crittenden Memoirs.* New York: G. P. Putnam's Sons, 1936.

Crittenden, Thomas Theodore. Papers. Western Historical Manuscripts Collection, Columbia.

Shoemaker, Floyd Calvin. "Administration of Thomas T. Crittenden, 1881–1885." In *Missouri and Missourians: Land of Contrasts and People of Achievements,* vol. 2. Chicago: Lewis Publishing, 1943.

CROSS, ASA BEEBE (1826–1894)

Asa Beebe Cross moved to Kansas City, Missouri, in the spring of 1858, where he opened a lumberyard and offered his services as an architect, but he had to wait until 1871 before he could devote himself full-time to architecture. Although there were other architects in the city, Cross attracted so much business that he can be called Kansas City's first architect of consequence, even though he proved a rather derivative designer.

Born in southern New Jersey on December 6, 1826, Cross followed in his father's craft and became a house carpenter. Family tradition holds that early on he briefly received some form of architectural instruction, possibly in Philadelphia. Sometime between 1850 and 1855 he moved to St. Louis, presumably as a carpenter-builder, and there he received the additional training that enabled him, by 1857, to become a partner of the architect John Johnson.

Family tradition also holds that in the mid-1850s Cross became involved in the Minnesota lumber industry, which sent most of its product to St. Louis. Better documented is his association with the St. Louis lumber merchant Matthew Rippey, who helped him establish, in April 1858, the A. B. Cross Company, with the aim of marketing Minnesota pine lumber in Kansas City. Before he left St. Louis, Cross married a young widow, Rachel Code.

When he arrived in Kansas City, Cross encountered a city still young and rather raw with perhaps a population as large as four thousand. More important, the community held the promise of continued growth, since much of the immigration entering the Kansas Territory, and traffic on the trails to the west and southwest, came through Kansas City. Although the Cross lumber company faced considerable competition, it prospered until the severe drought of 1860 and the onset of the Civil War the following year. By then Cross had demonstrated his ability as an architect, most notably in his Mechanic's Bank (1860). However, with the region's economy seriously depressed, both the lumber trade and the need for architectural service declined precipitously.

The Cross lumber business somehow managed to survive, possibly by receiving help from his St. Louis partner, Rippey, until a recovery of sorts began in 1863. By then Cross had gained a reputation as a solid businessman, and was elected city treasurer that year. In 1864 he was urged to stand for mayor, but he refused.

Between 1860 and 1867 Rachel Cross gave birth to two daughters and two sons. The last son died while quite young. Rachel's child from her first marriage, William E. Code (born in 1856), became an assistant in the lumberyard at age twelve, and Cross later provided him with architectural instruction.

Cross had good reason to be optimistic about being an architect in Kansas City. The first railroad had arrived in 1865, and in 1866 the federal government authorized the first bridge for the Missouri River, to cross at Kansas City. The city did indeed prosper, and as construction increased so did Cross's architectural practice. By 1867 he limited his lumber business to wholesale operations and finally closed it in 1871. By then he had established himself as the city's major architect. He designed the city's first public school (1867), and he produced Kansas City's first impressive office building, Vaughan's Diamond (1869). Selected as the architect for a large hotel, Cross was then asked to complete it as a satellite courthouse for Jackson County (1869–1872).

Cross had demonstrated his preparation to take on any type of architectural project. In 1872, for example, in addition to various commercial and residential structures, he produced the German community's Turner Hall, and buildings for the Kansas City Industrial Exposition. Cross also designed several religious buildings, including the city's first synagogue (1874).

The commission for the city's Union Depot came to Cross in 1877, which the architect made sure would be credited to his stepson, William Code, thereby identifying Code as a specialist in railroad design. With the completion of the depot in 1878, Cross made Code his partner, and they quickly gained other railroad projects, including depots in Kansas, Colorado, and Illinois. The firm, through Code, opened a Chicago office in 1882, but Code became ill and soon returned to Kansas City, where he died early in 1883. Thereafter, Cross had no partners and simply employed draftsmen whenever he needed assistance. Major projects continued to come his way, such as the large but stolid Gillis Opera House (1881–1883) and the Commerce Bank (1883–1885), the latter executed in the highly individual style of Frank Furness.

By the mid-1880s Kansas City's growth had encouraged more architects to open offices, including representatives of major firms headquartered elsewhere. Thus, while Cross remained well situated in his profession, competitors such as Van Brunt and Howe, who had moved their office from Boston to Kansas City in 1887, were rapidly rising in favor. A number of the newcomers clearly were better educated and certainly more sophisticated as designers. Competition may account for Cross's acceptance of the chance to become the county's supervising architect in 1888, in addition to his private practice. His new duties focused on helping county officials in the task of replacing the Kansas City courthouse, which had received severe damage from a tornado in 1886.

Those responsible for the new courthouse project quickly attracted accusations of malfeasance, even before Cross received his appointment. The project suffered various delays, the first relating to site selection. Then a curiously conducted architectural competition generated charges that Cross and county officials had rigged the process, since the officials chose the design submitted by a person whom the city directory identified as merely a draftsman in Cross's private practice.

Documents retained by Cross's family tell little about the competition but do indicate his intimate involvement with all aspects of the construction process. Cross most likely gained his appointment as the county's supervising architect through longtime political connections and his many years of accomplishment as an architect. Despite the complaints about the competition, the new courthouse, when completed in 1892, was large and substantial, and it contained many modern structural and mechanical features.

In 1885 a group of Kansas City architects named Cross chairman of the delegates that went to St. Louis to help establish the Missouri Association of Architects, which sought to make clear the significance of the professionally qualified architect in contrast to the self-proclaimed builder-architect. The association named Cross as one of its trustees. Soon the association affiliated with the Western Association of Architects, which in turn merged with the American Institute of Architects in 1889. By then, of course, Cross was deeply immersed in the contentious courthouse project, and though he retained the respect of his peers he no longer held a leadership role in his profession.

Rachel Cross died in 1890 after a long illness, and Cross also had health problems. Upon completion of the courthouse in 1892, Cross concentrated on his general practice, but he no longer received the sizable commissions he once enjoyed. Ill in the fall of 1893, he later suffered another bout of "nervous prostration" (perhaps a stroke) and died on August 18, 1894, several months short of his sixty-eighth birthday.

Obituaries in several newspapers stressed Cross's role as a major shaper of Kansas City in its formative years, and indicated the respect that the pioneer architect had earned. Asa Beebe Cross achieved his professional status by being in the right place at the right time, and having an additional source of income in the lumber trade until the city needed him as a full-time architect. As an architect, he was good enough to earn commissions from distant places, and fortunate in having enough work locally to keep quite busy until the last years of his life, when a new generation of professionals gained their ascendancy.

The number of buildings constructed from Cross's designs may well have exceeded one thousand. Most were commercial buildings and residential structures, but his production also included examples of nearly every other building type. By the 1970s, however, only a few of his buildings remained, hardly enough to explain the true significance of Kansas City's pioneer architect. They include Old St. Patrick's Church (1875) and the remodeled Bent-Ward House (1871), both in Kansas City, and the Vaile Mansion in Independence, Missouri (1881).

GEORGE EHRLICH

Ehrlich, George. "The Bank of Commerce by Asa Beebe Cross: 'A Building of the Latest Architecture.'" *Journal of the Society of Architectural Historians* 43:2 (May 1984): 168–72.

Ehrlich, George, and Peggy Schrock. "The A. B. Cross Lumber Company, 1858–1871." *Missouri Historical Review* 80:1 (October 1985): 14–32.

CROW, WAYMAN (1808–1885)

Wayman Crow, a merchant, philanthropist, and civic leader in St. Louis for a half century, was born on March 7, 1808, in Hartford, Kentucky, the youngest of eight children. His parents, Joshua and Mary Wayman Crow, had migrated from Maryland to Kentucky where Joshua practiced law until his death in 1830. Mary was an exceptional woman endowed with business acumen and abundant energy, a legacy passed on to her son Wayman. His formal education at the Hopkinsville, Kentucky, country school was over when he was twelve years old, and he became an apprentice to a storekeeper who sold dry goods, groceries, and hardware. Young Wayman received his food and clothing and slept on a cot in the store where he learned bookkeeping and business practices, as well as the humbler cleanup tasks. When the store owner, Strother J. Hawkins, retired, Crow, not yet fifteen, was transferred to the firm of Anderson and Atterbury, who soon entrusted him with the running of the business. When his apprenticeship was over, he took complete charge of a branch store in the town of Cadiz. Before moving to Pittsburgh, his employers made it possible for Crow to buy the business on credit. In 1835, when he sold out in order to broaden his enterprises, he had accumulated more than twenty thousand dollars, a fortune for so young a person.

In search of a new home farther north, Crow was detained in St. Louis by an illness. He decided to look no further for the next location of his business and his home. St. Louis had a population of eight thousand in 1835 and was growing rapidly in its prime position in command of the Mississippi River system. Crow formed a partnership with his cousin Joshua Tevis of Philadelphia to be known as Crow and Tevis. Later, the firm became Crow, McCreery, and Company, then Crow, Hagardine, and Company. Crow remained the head of the firm until his death. He quickly became involved in community affairs and in Missouri politics. He was elected to the Missouri State Senate as a Whig in 1840 and again in 1850. He was also elected president of the St. Louis Chamber of Commerce in 1840, a position he held for ten years. He assisted in getting charters for the Hannibal and St. Joseph and the Missouri Pacific Railroads, as well as the Mercantile Library of St. Louis and the St. Louis Asylum for the Blind. In 1844 he became president of the Marine Insurance Company and the Perpetual Insurance Company.

Undoubtedly, Crow's greatest contribution to his city, state, and far beyond was the founding of Washington University. In 1853, while attending a session of the legislature in Jefferson City, by candlelight, he drafted an act of incorporation for an institution of higher education. He called it Eliot Seminary, to honor his friend and pastor, **William Greenleaf Eliot.** He named himself and the surprised Eliot as incorporators, along with fifteen other members of the Unitarian congregation. The following year steps were taken to rename the school Washington Institute; in 1857 the state legislature incorporated the school as Washington University. Over the years Crow liberally donated monies designated for scholarships, a chair of physics (1875), and real estate estimated at worth more than two hundred thousand dollars. After the death of his son, Wayman Crow Jr., in England in 1878, Crow built a museum at Nineteenth and Locust as a memorial. In 1881 he deeded it to Washington University as a fine arts school and museum. Later, the St. Louis Museum of Fine Arts became a separate institution.

Wayman Crow married Isabella Conn of Union County, Kentucky, in 1829. (Coincidentally, her sister Maria was married to Crow's brother Phillips Crow.) Five of their children lived to maturity: Cornelia Carr, Mary Emmons, Emma Cushman, Wayman Crow Jr., and Isabella Kealhofer. The family lived in a spacious house for many years, but moved after the children had grown up. Wayman Crow remained active in business until his death on May 10, 1885; Isabella Crow died in 1892. They are buried in Bellefontaine Cemetery in St. Louis.

Although Wayman Crow made an enormous contribution to the social and cultural development of both St. Louis and the state of Missouri, he has not received the attention that he deserves. While his public career is well documented, to date no body of personal correspondence has emerged to illuminate his life and character. The correspondence of sculptor **Harriet Goodhue Hosmer** is the best index extant to Crow's public career and his family life. He emerges as a giant of nineteenth-century achievement and a devoted father, husband, and friend, recognized for these characteristics in his own time, if not in ours.

DOLLY SHERWOOD

Langsdorf, Alexander S. "The Washington University Story, 1853–1953." St. Louis: Washington University, 1953.

Monnig, Eugene G. "Washington University: The First One Hundred Years, 1853–1953." Slide lecture prepared for the Engineering Century Club Breakfast Forum, March 15, 1984.

"My Dearest Mr. Crow." *Washington University Magazine* 51:3 (fall 1981).

Sherwood, Dolly. *Harriet Hosmer, American Sculptor, 1830–1908.* Columbia: University of Missouri Press, 1991.

CROWDER, ENOCH HERBERT (1859–1932)

Enoch Herbert Crowder was born on April 11, 1859, at Edinburg, Missouri, the youngest of seven children. Enoch and his family suffered hardships during the Civil War when his father, John Herbert Crowder, was serving in the Union army. After the war Enoch worked on the family farm while attending Grand River College in Edinburg. He finished a college preparatory course of study in 1875 and taught in a rural school near Chillicothe, Missouri. In 1877 Crowder received an appointment to the United States Military Academy at West Point and graduated thirty-first in a class of fifty-four in 1881.

The army commissioned Crowder a second lieutenant in the Eighth Cavalry Regiment and posted him to Fort Brown, Texas. While there Crowder studied law and was licensed as an attorney in 1884. Later that year the army transferred him to Jefferson Barracks, outside St. Louis, and the following year detailed him at the University of Missouri–Columbia as a professor of military science and tactics, a post he held until 1889. While at the university Crowder improved the military standards of the student battalion, gained acceptance of academic credit for military training, introduced summer camps for cadets, convinced the Missouri General Assembly to make the cadet corps part of the state militia with commissions for the officers, and shocked many by offering military instruction to a separate company of female students. Crowder also continued his legal training, earning an LL.B. from the University of Missouri in 1886 and giving lectures on constitutional and international law as an instructor in the law school.

In 1886 and 1889 Crowder participated in campaigns against Geronimo and Sitting Bull. Aside from these two periods when he was away from Missouri, Crowder spent his time reading law at the offices of Crittenden, MacDougal, and Stiles in Kansas City and teaching. In 1891 the army promoted Crowder to captain and assigned him to the Department of the Platte at Omaha, Nebraska, as acting judge advocate. On January 11, 1895, he received a promotion to major in the judge advocate general's department, where he served for the rest of his career.

During the Spanish-American War, Crowder went to the Philippines as judge advocate on Gen. Wesley Meritt's staff. After the war he served as civil adviser and administrator during the governorships of both Gen. E. S. Otis and Gen. Arthur MacArthur and worked in a wide variety of legal capacities, including as president of the Board of Claims, member of the Board to Revise Basic Laws, and associate justice of the Philippine Supreme Court.

Upon returning to the United States in 1901, Crowder performed general duties in the judge advocate general's office. In 1904 he became a military observer on the staff of General Kuroki's Japanese First Army in Manchuria during the Russo-Japanese War. Between 1906 and 1909 Crowder served in Cuba on the executive staff of provisional governor Charles E. Magoon and became, in effect, the minister of state and justice. In this post Crowder supervised the 1908 Cuban elections and headed the commission that drafted most of the organic laws for the new Cuban Republic.

On February 15, 1911, the army promoted Crowder to brigadier general and appointed him judge advocate general. He served in that post for three consecutive terms. During his tenure Crowder revised the Articles of War, rewrote the *Manual for Court-Martial,* modernized military prisons, and reformed the penal system. With American involvement in World War I a possibility early in 1917, Secy. of War Newton D. Baker asked Crowder to draft a selective-service law. Recognizing the American public's hostility to military conscription in the past, Crowder consulted with congressional leaders and the general staff before drawing up a law that, with few changes, Congress enacted on May 18, 1917. An important provision of the law placed responsibility for conscription on local draft boards, which could set exemptions for local circumstances, and reinforced the concept of "friends and neighbors" calling young men to national service. On May 22, President Woodrow Wilson appointed Crowder provost marshal general to supervise the Selective Service Act. On July 20, 1917, the first lottery numbers were drawn. That October the army promoted Crowder to major general. In December 1918 Crowder received the Distinguished Service Medal "for especially meritorious and conspicuous service" in organizing the United States Army for war. He also received awards from England, France, Italy, and Japan.

In 1919 the president reappointed Crowder judge advocate general, a position he held until his retirement from military service in 1923. President Warren G. Harding next appointed Crowder as U.S. ambassador to Cuba, where he had been invited in 1919 by the government to help revise election laws and resolve disputed elections. In 1927 Crowder retired from government service and set up a private law practice in Chicago. Poor health forced his retirement from legal practice in 1931, and on May 7, 1932, he died at Walter Reed Hospital in Washington, D.C. Crowder never married and had no children.

LAURENCE R. CARVER II

Chambers, John W., II. *To Raise an Army: The Draft Comes to Modern America.* New York: Free Press, 1987.

Dictionary of American Biography. Vol. 21, supplement 1. S.v. "Crowder, Enoch Herbert."

Pérez, Louis A., Jr. *Cuba under the Platt Amendment, 1901–1934.* Pittsburgh: University of Pittsburgh Press, 1986.

Stanley, Peter W. *A Nation in the Making: The Philippines and the United States, 1899–1921.* Cambridge: Harvard University Press, 1974.

Who's Who in America. Vol. 17. Chicago: A. N. Marquis, 1932.

Wooster, Robert. *The Military and United States Indian Policy, 1865–1903.* New Haven: Yale University Press, 1988.

CROY, HOMER (1883–1965)

Homer Croy, a newspaperman, novelist, and humorist, was born on March 11, 1883, on a farm six miles northwest of Maryville, Missouri. He attended Maryville High School and later the University of Missouri where he was a member of the first class in the first school of journalism in the world. Croy worked his way through school, digging postholes for a farmer near Columbia, writing for the local newspapers, and becoming the *Kansas City Star*'s correspondent in Columbia. He never graduated, however, because he failed his advanced Shakespeare class in his senior year. However, on June 6, 1956, he received from the University of Missouri an honorary degree of doctor of literature.

Croy wrote almost exclusively about Missouri and characters from the northwest Missouri area. Although he was primarily a humorist, *West of the Water Tower* (1923) is a serious, realistic novel, reflecting the influence of Theodore Dreiser and Thomas Hardy. The book, about a boy and a girl "in difficulty," was first published anonymously with apprehension that the reading public was not ready for such themes. A best-seller, it sold 103,000 copies. Jesse L. Lasky, a Hollywood movie magnate, paid twenty-five thousand dollars for the book's movie rights, the highest price ever paid for an American novel at that time.

Croy wrote many books on American folklore and frontier history, including *Wonderful Neighbor* (1945), *Jesse James Was My Neighbor* (1949), *He Hanged Them High* (1952), *Wheels West: The Story of the Donner Party* (1955), and *Last of the Great Outlaws: The Story of Cole Younger* (1956).

One of Croy's principal works, *Our Will Rogers* (1953), is regarded as a highly fitting biography of America's beloved humorist. His other key works include *How Motion Pictures Are Made* (1918); *They Had to See Paris* (1926), which became Will Rogers's first talking picture; *Fancy Lady* (1927); *Caught* (1928); *Coney Island* (1929); *Headed for Hollywood* (1932); *Sixteen Hands* (1938); *Mr. Meek Marches On*

(1941); *Family Honeymoon* (1942); *Corn Country* (1947); *What Grandpa Laughed At* (1948); *Lady from Colorado* (1957); *Trigger Marshall* (1958); and *The Star Maker: TV Story of D. W. Griffith* (1959).

Croy's autobiography, *Country Cured,* was published in 1942. One follows his life from his birth on his father's farm through his days in high school and at the University of Missouri–Columbia, his first newspaper jobs, his breaking ties with home, and then his days in New York. One also sees his gullibility in selling his stories, his timidity in seeking his first job, and his awkwardness in dealing with success that caused him to flee from a meeting of important authors. Many of his self-effacing characteristics come forth in his work.

Croy died on May 25, 1965, at his home in New York City. His ashes were scattered, as he requested, on the Croy farm near Maryville. There could be no more fitting epitaph to this kindly Missourian than the title of the book *How to Win Friends and Influence People,* the book **Dale Carnegie** dedicated to him. The United States Postal Service honored Croy's memory with a stamp cancellation (his picture and a water-tower sketch) on March 11, 1991, his 108th birthday celebration.

VIRGIL ALBERTINI

Croy, Homer. *Country Cured.* New York: Duell, Sloan, and Pearce, 1943.

————. *Wonderful Neighbor.* New York: Duell, Sloan, and Pearce, 1945.

Kansas City Star, January 9, 1944.

Shipp, Cameron. "About the Author." In *What Grandpa Laughed At,* by Homer Croy, 249–50. New York: Duell, Sloan, and Pearce, 1948.

Tootle, Harry King. "Harry King Tootle Gives Inside Dope on Homer Croy, Northwest Missouri's Author." *St. Joseph News-Press,* August 28, 1949.

CRUZAT, FRANCISCO (1739–1790)

Francisco Cruzat, the only Spanish lieutenant governor of Upper Louisiana to occupy that office twice, was born in Navarre, Spain, on March 10, 1739. He came to Louisiana with Lt. Gen. Alejandro O'Reilly in 1769 as a captain of grenadiers. In 1775 Gov. Luis de Unzaga named Cruzat to succeed **Pedro Joseph Piernas** as lieutenant governor in St. Louis. Cruzat, who was less restrained and more outgoing than Piernas, was a good choice to administer the sprawling borderland region. Upper Louisiana's French inhabitants liked him, and under his tutelage they became more comfortable with the ways of the Spanish regime. Although his initial term as lieutenant governor was short, it came at the critical moment when the outbreak of the American Revolution threatened to intensify the Anglo-Spanish conflict throughout the Mississippi Valley. Louisiana's staunchly pro-American new governor, Bernardo de Gálvez, recalled Cruzat in 1778 and appointed Capt. **Fernando de Leyba** to replace him in St. Louis.

Following his return to New Orleans, Captain Cruzat participated in the campaign Gálvez led against the British. He took part in the conquest of Baton Rouge in 1779, and early the next year he gained a promotion to the rank of lieutenant colonel. Lieutenant Governor Leyba's sudden death in St. Louis in June 1780 prompted Gálvez to reassign Cruzat to his former post. The decision to return the well-liked Cruzat to St. Louis was popular. When Cruzat took charge there in September 1780 the situation was precarious. Shortly before Leyba's death, three hundred hastily assembled defenders had successfully repulsed an assault against the town by a force of British soldiers, Canadian traders, and Indian warriors.

Following Cruzat's arrival in St. Louis, a local delegation came to his headquarters demanding compensation for the services they had rendered in defense of Upper Louisiana's capital. Cruzat was unable to grant their request, but his actions during the ensuing months enabled the Spaniards to regain the confidence of their French-speaking subjects. He called upon his diplomatic skills to negotiate agreements with several Indian tribes and persuaded them to surrender British medals and banners in return for promises of Spanish replacements. Cruzat did complain that a chronic scarcity of trade goods limited his effectiveness and compelled him to make purchases from local merchants at inflated prices.

Persistent rumors of a new spring offensive against St. Louis prompted Cruzat to order the construction of a ten-foot-high stockade for protection. Unlike Leyba, Cruzat did not hesitate to draw upon the royal treasury for essential supplies and equipment as workers hurriedly erected a wooden palisade on all sides of the village except for its naturally fortified stretches along the river.

Acting on his own initiative, Cruzat dispatched a military expedition up the Illinois River in January 1781, commanded by Eugene Pouree, captain of St. Louis's Second Militia Company. The force, with assistance from friendly Indian tribes, launched a surprise attack that destroyed the British fort at St. Joseph, Michigan. Cruzat intended the Spanish show of force to forestall another attack on St. Louis and to prevent wavering Indian allies from reverting to the British. At the very least, the successful operation provided the beleaguered residents of Upper Louisiana with a badly needed boost in morale.

Although Cruzat's actions prevented further attacks against St. Louis, they failed to check British influence among the tribes in the upper Mississippi Valley. However, with only limited resources at his disposal, there was little else that Cruzat could do to reverse Spain's declining fortunes.

Items needed for the Indian trade were still in short supply in New Orleans, where a partial British blockade of the gulf had disrupted trade. Even when the scarce goods could be procured, there was no assurance that the shipments would reach St. Louis. British fugitives driven out of Natchez following the Spanish conquest of that post frequently joined with itinerant traders and Indians to pilfer boats attempting to travel up the Mississippi.

Not even the lieutenant governor's family was immune from the fugitives' mischief. Cruzat was married to Nicanora Ramos, a native of Cartegena, Spain, and the couple had two sons, Antonio and José. When Madame Cruzat and the two boys were en route to St. Louis in May 1782, a roving British band seized them near present-day Memphis, Tennessee. The freebooters released them but kept the forty-five hundred pesos in cash intended for government expenses and the precious cargo of Indian goods consigned to Upper Louisiana's merchants. Nicanora Cruzat died in St. Louis in April 1786, but both sons lived to enjoy distinguished careers in the service of Spain.

In 1787 Cruzat relinquished his post at St. Louis to **Manuel Pérez.** The well-liked Cruzat had secured a promotion and been assigned to command the newly created Third Battalion at Pensacola, where he died in 1790.

WILLIAM E. FOLEY

Dinn, Gilbert C., and Abraham P. Nasatir. *The Imperial Osages: Spanish-Indian Diplomacy in the Mississippi Valley.* Norman: University of Oklahoma Press, 1983.

Foley, William E. *The Genesis of Missouri: From Wilderness Outpost to Statehood.* Columbia: University of Missouri Press, 1989.

Nasatir, Abraham P. *Borderland in Retreat.* Albuquerque: University of New Mexico Press, 1976.

CUMMINGS, JOHN A. (1840–1873)

John Cummings, a Catholic clergyman and defendant in a major nineteenth-century civil rights case, was born in 1840. Records fail to indicate the place of his birth. In 1858 he began studies for the Catholic priesthood at St. Vincent's Seminary in Cape Girardeau, Missouri. Ordained in 1863, he served a year at St. Malachy's Church in St. Louis. Archbishop **Peter Richard Kenrick** of St. Louis named him pastor of St. Joseph's Church in Louisiana, Missouri, the following year.

Many slaveholders lived in the Louisiana area, but Cummings's parishioners were mainly Irish railroad workers, not planters. He never put on record his views on the Civil War then still raging. Shortly after the close of the war in 1865, Missouri drew up a new constitution. Article 2, Section 3, demanded a loyalty oath of clergymen, requiring them to deny eighty-six specific acts that stretched from outright treason to expressing sympathy for either an individual Confederate or the Southern cause.

Following the guidance of Kenrick, who claimed the oath demanded a sacrifice of religious liberty, Cummings refused to take the oath. He preached on September 3, 1865. A grand jury at Bowling Green, twelve miles west of Louisiana, indicted him on September 5. A Methodist church served as a temporary courthouse. On the following Friday, Judge Thomas Jefferson Fagg, a former slaveholder, sentenced Cummings to a fine of five hundred dollars or a term in jail. Cummings refused to pay the fine and went to jail. His railroad-worker parishioners camped around the lockup in support of their pastor.

The Missouri Supreme Court justices, all appointees under the new constitution, upheld Fagg's decision. With the financial support of Kenrick, Cummings appealed his case to the United States Supreme Court. He happened to meet **Frank Blair,** a former congressman and major general on **William T. Sherman**'s staff. Blair had worked to keep Missouri in the Union and now saw extremists in his own party causing disorder. With Cummings's consent Blair asked his brother, the lawyer **Montgomery Blair,** once a member of Lincoln's cabinet, to represent Cummings before the Supreme Court. Montgomery, in turn, enlisted the aid of another outstanding lawyer, David Dudley Field, a nationally prominent attorney and the brother of Supreme Court justice Stephen Field.

In March 1866 attorneys Blair and Field offered two main arguments on behalf of Cummings before the Supreme Court: first, proscriptive sections of the Missouri Constitution were ex post facto because they defined, as criminal, acts that were not criminal at the time of the commission; and second, they assumed that clergymen were guilty of treason until proved innocent. Thus, it was "a bill of attainder" prohibited by the Constitution of the United States.

The court delayed ten months. On January 14, 1867, Justice Field delivered the opinion of the court and reversed the judgment of the Missouri Supreme Court in a five-to-four decision. The Radical Reconstructionists in Congress responded angrily to the decision. They harassed Justice Field, a Lincoln appointee, who sided with four justices who had served on the court at the time of the *Dred Scott* decision ten years earlier.

In the meantime, Kenrick had moved Cummings to St. Stephen's Parish, in Indian Creek, Missouri, a rural community forty miles from the Mississippi River. Cummings remained as pastor of that parish only until September 1870, when he became ill. He died three years later in a St. Louis hospital conducted by the Sisters of Charity.

When Cummings died no local newspaper, religious or secular, published an obituary of his short life. However, he left his own obituary, sunk deep in the records of the Supreme Court. The Cummings case, to quote Justice Hugo Black, stands as "one more of the Constitution's great guarantees of individual liberty."

WILLIAM B. FAHERTY

Bradley, Harold C. "In Defense of John Cummings." *Missouri Historical Review* 58 (October 1962): 10–15.

———. "John A. Cummings and the Missouri Test Oath, 1865." Master's thesis, Saint Louis University, 1965.

Faherty, William Barnaby. "The Ironclad Oath: John Cummings, 1840–1843." In *Rebels or Reformers: Dissenting Priests in American Life*. Chicago: Loyola University Press, 1987.

CUMMINGS, ROBERT (1908–1990)

Born in Joplin, Missouri, on June 9, 1908, Charles Clarence Robert Orville Cummings was a successful movie and television actor. His mother, Ruth Kraft Cummings, was an ordained minister, and his father, Charles C. Cummings, was a physician who helped form the original medical staff at St. John's Hospital in Joplin in 1921.

After treating Orville Wright for a facial rash, the elder Cummings passed his interest in aviation, along with the name of Orville, to his son. Robert became a pilot while still a student at Joplin High School. After graduation in 1928 he attended Drury College in Springfield, Missouri, and then transferred to the Carnegie Institute of Technology to study aeronautical engineering.

In need of money after the crash of 1929, Cummings enrolled in the American Academy of Dramatic Arts in New York, which paid male actors fourteen dollars a week. British actors were in fashion on Broadway, so Cummings went to London in 1931 to acquire a British accent. He returned as "Blade Stanhope" and immediately received a part in the play *The Roof.* He went on to act in several other Broadway plays and was given the lead in the Ziegfeld's Follies opposite Fanny Brice.

In 1935 Cummings made his film debut in *The Virginia Judge,* using a southern accent and the name "Brice Hutchens." He began acting under his true name in the film *So Red the Rose.* He became a popular leading man and went on to act in more than one hundred films, mostly light romantic comedies. His characters were usually one-dimensional, affable, inept young men in such films as *Three Cheers for Love* (1936), *College Swing* (1938), *Three Smart Girls Grow Up* (1939), *The Devil and Miss Jones* and *It Started with Eve* (1940), *Princess O'Rourke* (1943), *You Came Along* (1945), *The Bride Wore Boots* (1946), *The Pretty Girl* (1950), *My Geisha* (1962), and *What a Way to Go, Promise Her Anything,* and *The Carpetbaggers* (1964). He showed more depth and received critical praise for his dramatic roles in *The Saboteur* and *King's Row* (1942), *The Lost Moment* (1947), and *Dial M for Murder* (1954).

In the 1950s Cummings switched his focus to television, where he achieved his greatest success and popularity. He continued his lighthearted, limp, youthful characters in four situation comedies: *My Hero* (1952–1953), *The Bob Cummings Show* (1955–1959 and 1961–1962), and *My Living Doll* (1964–1965). He is most famous for his role as a swinging-bachelor photographer, Bob Collins, on the first *Bob Cummings Show,* which was later syndicated as *Love That Bob.* He won an Emmy in 1954 for his work in the Studio One production of *Twelve Angry Men.*

Cummings was married five times and fathered three sons and four daughters. Besides his career and family, he made time for his two other passions: flying and health fitness. In 1938 he became the first certified flight instructor, and during World War II he trained dozens of military pilots. Reflecting originally his father's influence, Cummings held a lifetime commitment to exercise and nutrition. He employed a personal trainer and took between one and five hundred health supplements a day, which he believed maintained the youthful appearance necessary for his roles. He wrote a book on this subject in 1960 called *Stay Young and Vital.* He died in California on December 2, 1990.

FRANCES T. GIGLIO

"Bob Cummings Visits Home in Joplin." *Missouri News Magazine* (September 1956): 8–9.

Current Biography Yearbook. New York: H. W. Wilson, 1956.

Eells, George. "Bob Cummings: The Life and Times of a Perennial Juvenile." *Look* (October 14, 1958): 110–14.

Inman, David. "Bob Cummings." In *The TV Encyclopedia.* New York: Perigree Press, 1991.

International Dictionary of Film and Filmmakers. Vol. 3. S.v. "Cummings, Robert (Bob)."

New York Times, December 4, 1990.

CUPPLES, SAMUEL (1831–1912)

Samuel Cupples was born the thirteenth child of James and Elizabeth Bigham Cupples on September 13, 1831. The Cupples emigrated from County Down, Ireland, to Harrisburg, Pennsylvania, in 1814.

At the age of fifteen Samuel Cupples left for Cincinnati where he worked for a pioneer dealer in woodenware. Cupples was such a success in business details that the company decided to send him to St. Louis to set up a branch office. He loaded a flatboat with ax and broom handles and butter churns and started down the Ohio River. By the time he reached Cairo, he had sold the entire shipment. He went back to Cincinnati, got another load of the material, and started a business of his own. He opened a store on the levee of St. Louis in 1851, the day after he arrived.

Settlers all over the country needed the woodenware objects that Cupples sold, and he developed an efficient method of distributing them. At this juncture, brothers Robert and Harry Brookings came West seeking their fortunes. Cupples engaged the young men and put them to work selling his products. They were so successful that they decided to leave the Cupples Company and go into business for themselves. When Cupples heard this, he offered to make them partners. **Robert Brookings** showed creative genius in merchandising. He decided to build warehouses next to the rail tracks to cut down handling. This saved so much time that the Cupples Warehouses became the depot for everything that came to the city, and at that time everything came to the city by railroad. Eventually, Cupples and Brookings gave the Cupples Center to Washington University, and for years it was the main source of that institution's endowment.

Cupples amassed a fortune. He was extraordinarily generous and civic-minded in the use of his wealth. He often said that he had enjoyed earning his fortune and that he intended to enjoy dispensing it while he was alive. He managed to give most of it away before his death. He established a technical school in St. Louis and with the help of his partner, Robert Brookings, built two engineering buildings at Washington University.

Cupples's other substantial benefactions included the building of an orphanage, a Methodist chapel, and a library at Central Methodist College in Fayette, Missouri. He was a devout Methodist, and from his earliest days in St. Louis taught Sunday school at his church. His deep religious convictions were also expressed in his charitable work for the needy. For many years he was head of the St. Louis Provident Association to which he contributed generously.

His wife, Martha Kells Cupples, was well known as a gracious hostess and also a philanthropist. She was especially interested in the Girls' Industrial Home and the welfare of orphans. After her death Cupples built a Methodist orphanage as a memorial to her.

Samuel Cupples's life was punctuated with great personal sorrows. He married Margaret Amelia Kells in 1854, but she died just four years later. In 1860 he married her sister Martha Sophia Kells. They had three daughters, all of whom died as young children, one in 1871 and two within a week of each other in 1874. The Cupples then adopted Amelia, the daughter of the third Kells sister, Harriet.

Cupples died on January 7, 1912, and is interred in the family mausoleum in Bellefontaine Cemetery.

M. B. McNamee

Hyde, William, and Howard L. Conard, eds. *Encyclopedia of the History of St. Louis.* New York: Southern History, 1899.

CURTIS, SAMUEL RYAN (1805–1866)

Samuel Ryan Curtis figured largely in Missouri's Civil War history from August 1861 through October 1864. Born in New York on February 3, 1805, Curtis grew up in Ohio, where he received an appointment to West Point. He graduated in 1831 and served one year as a lieutenant in the Seventh Infantry. He resigned to become a civil engineer and attorney in Ohio. During the Mexican War he served as the adjutant general of Ohio and, later, as colonel of the Third Ohio Infantry. His year of service included appointments as a military governor in Mexico and to the staff of Gen. John E. Wool.

Following the war Curtis was chief engineer at both Keokuk and St. Louis, distinguishing himself in river improvements and railroad promotion. In the spring of 1856 he was elected mayor of Keokuk, and in the fall won election as the Republican candidate for Iowa's First Congressional District. He was reelected in 1858 and 1860. In Congress he chaired a committee planning the Pacific Railroad.

At the outbreak of the Civil War, Curtis received a commission as colonel of the Second Iowa Infantry, which guarded railroads in northern Missouri. He returned for a special session of Congress in July 1861. Appointed brigadier general, he resigned his seat and took charge of Jefferson Barracks and Benton Barracks at St. Louis. In December 1861 Curtis gained command of the Army of Southwest Missouri, leading it to victory on the battlefield at Pea Ridge, Arkansas, in March 1862, and winning promotion to major general. Logistics foiled his attempt to capture Little Rock, Arkansas, and he led his army to Helena, on the west bank of the Mississippi River. Critics argued that he had left Missouri open to attacks by guerrilla forces, and he was also accused, but exonerated, of charges of malfeasance at Helena regarding cotton speculation and "contrabands."

Curtis took leave in August 1862 to become one of the incorporators of the Pacific Railroad. In September he received command of the Department of the Missouri, encompassing Missouri, Arkansas, Kansas, and Indian Territory. Departmental command brought with it vexatious political problems that ultimately diminished the luster of his military reputation. Curtis found little common ground with Gov. **Hamilton Rowan Gamble** concerning the employment of the state's militia, assessment of secession sympathizers, and emancipation of slaves. Instead, Curtis often seemed to be a tool of the Radical faction in Missouri.

Continuing political and military controversy in Missouri led President Lincoln to remove Curtis from command in the spring of 1863. There was no fault with Curtis, Lincoln told his successor, but in Missouri's political quarrel he had no power to remove the governor. In January 1864 Curtis received command of the Department of Kansas, including Kansas, the Territories of Colorado and Nebraska, and Indian Territory. He directed much of his attention to dealing with Indians, but the most climactic event of his tenure came during **Sterling Price**'s Missouri expedition. In October 1864 Curtis led an army of Kansans to victory over Price at Westport, in what was the largest battle in Missouri. Although outside of his own department and despite problems with logistics and questions of jurisdiction, Curtis directed pursuit of Price's army as far south as the Arkansas River. He received little credit for his success. Appointed to the Department of the Northwest, including Iowa, Wisconsin, and adjacent territories, he finished the war in that quiet post. He then served on commissions to negotiate with Indian tribes on the upper Missouri and to inspect construction of the Union Pacific Railroad. Curtis died following an inspection trip on December 26, 1866, at Council Bluffs, Iowa.

Despite Curtis's victories in two critical campaigns affecting Missouri, and his long tenure as departmental commander, Curtis is not well known. Historians generally consider him a capable and underrated military leader. He reached the pinnacle of his success at Pea Ridge, but later experienced personal misfortune and political controversy. His promotion to major general arrived on the same day as news of his daughter's death in 1862, and he lost his son, Maj. Henry Z. Curtis, to **William Clarke Quantrill**'s guerrillas at Baxter Springs, Kansas, in 1863. Curtis tended to become involved in disputes and carried on corrosive quarrels with Governor Gamble and **John Schofield.** He became embroiled in Kansas politics during Price's expedition, and displeased **Ulysses S. Grant** when pursuit of the Rebel army was interrupted short of the Arkansas River. These disputes and the relative historiographical neglect of the trans-Mississippi theater have contributed to Curtis's obscurity.

JOHN F. BRADBURY JR.

Burkard, Dick J. "The Edge of Glory: The Civil War Career of Samuel Ryan Curtis." Master's thesis, Southern Illinois University, Edwardsville, 1984.

Duffus, Gerald R. "A Study of the Military Career of Samuel R. Curtis, 1861–1865." Master's thesis, Drake University, 1966.

Gallaher, Ruth A. "Samuel Ryan Curtis." *Iowa Journal of History and Politics* 25 (July 1927): 331–58.

Holst, David L. "General Samuel Curtis and the Civil War in the West." Master's thesis, Illinois State Normal University, 1974.

Monnett, Howard N. *Action before Westport, 1864.* Boulder: University Press of Colorado, 1995.

Shea, William L., and Earl J. Hess. *Pea Ridge: Civil War Campaign in the West.* Chapel Hill: University of North Carolina Press, 1992.

D

DALTON, JOHN MONTGOMERY (1900–1972)

In the years after his governorship, John Montgomery Dalton did not fit the glitzy, slick political image. The forty-fifth governor of Missouri drove a beige Buick Wildcat with cloth seats, four doors, and four dented fenders. A collection of ten to twenty-five rubber bands hung from both the volume and the tuner dials of the radio. Match sticks, paper clips, pens, and a trash can were neatly organized in a plastic tray that fit over the center hump. Two working compasses sat on the dash, pointing in opposite directions, allowing him to choose his course. The wide, well-worn Wildcat was Dalton's rolling desk—a cultivated habit from years of stumping the campaign trail.

Dalton was born to Frederick Andrew and Ida Jane Poage Dalton, on November 9, 1900, in Walker, Vernon County, Missouri, the sixth of seven children. The family moved to Columbia in 1914 so the children might have access to the schools in the university town. Dalton graduated from high school there and from the University of Missouri where he received a law degree in 1923.

That same year Dalton began practicing law in Kennett, Missouri. Later, he moved his practice to Senath, Missouri, where on November 22, 1925, he married Geraldine "Jerry" Hall of Cardwell. The couple moved back to Kennett in 1929. In addition to practicing law, Dalton served on numerous committees. He was president of the Kennett Chamber of Commerce, the Dunklin County Bar Association, the Kennett Board of Education, and the Lions Club, rising to district governor in 1932. He was elected as an elder in the First Presbyterian Church of Kennett and became a thirty-third-degree Mason.

Dalton stepped into the political arena in 1930, but his fascination with political life had begun twenty-five years earlier when he was allowed to accompany his father, steward of the state asylum at Nevada, Missouri, and Missouri governor **Joseph W. Folk** during a buggy-ride inspection of the facility. He ran for Dunklin County prosecuting attorney in 1930 and lost by less than two hundred votes. The next year he was appointed marshal of the Missouri Supreme Court in Jefferson City, a position he held until 1937, when he returned to Kennett to practice law.

To aid his legal practice he organized four rural electric cooperatives in southeast Missouri and acted as their attorney. He was city counselor of Kennett from 1944 to 1953 and legislative counsel for the Missouri Rural Electrification Association in 1951–1952. He served eight years as chairman of the Dunklin County Central Democratic Committee. He was also chairman of the Democratic State Speakers Bureau and a member of the Democratic State Committee. The experiences honed his people skills.

Nicknamed "Scrubby" by his youngest grandson, Dalton fit the physical description: short and round. He was also balding; but his modest looks, strong moral character, and vivacious personality made him a man of the people. The civic-minded, energetic man launched a grassroots campaign to become attorney general in the dust of small Missouri farm towns. He accepted invitations to speak, to dedicate buildings, to ride in parades, to kiss babies, to eat, and to drink. He spoke people's names while greeting them with a warm smile, a direct gaze, and a strong handshake.

In 1952 Missouri's rural voters elected Dalton attorney general. He was the first candidate in forty years to win the Democratic nomination for statewide office without carrying either Kansas City or St. Louis. Reelected in 1956 he secured the greatest majority of votes of any candidate on the state ticket. In 1959 he received the Wayman Memorial Award as outstanding attorney general of the year, presented by the National Association of Attorney Generals. The following year Dalton was elected governor of Missouri. He was the first Missouri governor to receive 1 million votes. (Democratic presidential nominee John F. Kennedy only narrowly carried the state.)

When Dalton took office, Missouri's financial coffers stood empty, despite a postwar reserve fund and a 1956 $75 million state bond issue. In his inaugural address he proposed to finance vital programs for education, highway, mental health, and industry by reforming "Missouri's jerry-built tax structure." During his sixteen-hour workdays, he built strong working relationships and friendships by inviting members of the General Assembly to breakfast and lunch at the executive mansion. When those tactics proved insufficient to sway a majority of legislators, he looked to the press and to the general public for support in the politically unpopular task of tax reform.

In 1961 Dalton proposed and won approval for a withholding system to collect state income taxes, and an increase in beer, liquor, and cigarette taxes. In 1962 he obtained a gasoline-tax increase of two cents per gallon, and he persuaded the legislature to increase the state sales tax by one cent in 1963.

When space-age technology accelerated the demand for well-educated workers, Dalton successfully pressed for the creation of a four-campus system for the University of Missouri at Columbia, St. Louis, Kansas City, and Rolla and a state-financed junior college system. During his administration the School Foundation Program for public schools was fully financed for the first time and a state commission on higher education was established.

As part of a comprehensive highway program, Dalton signed a law that made drunken driving a graduated felony, established a point system for driver's license revocation, required seat belts in all new cars beginning in 1965, and authorized construction of 294 miles of interstate highway.

Dalton established new intensive-treatment mental health centers in St. Louis, Kansas City, and Columbia. He also signed legislation endorsing the principle of equal pay for women.

In industrial development, Dalton reorganized the Division of Resources and Development into the Division of Commerce and Industrial Development and conducted tours in the United States and a trade mission abroad to attract industry to Missouri. Those efforts produced results when the state experienced a record increase in new plant construction.

Dalton lived by the principle that "nothing is politically right that is morally wrong," and encouraged others toward faithful and scrupulous behavior. At the end of his administration, a surplus balance of all state funds totaled more than $122 million.

Following his governorship Dalton opened a law practice in Jefferson City and served on the Board of Trustees of Stephens College, the Board of Trustees of the School of the Ozarks, the Board of Visitors of the University of Missouri, and as president of both the Des Moines Federal Home Loan Bank and the Board of Trustees of Westminster College. He died of cancer in Jefferson City, Missouri, on July 7, 1972.

FRAN DALTON-COOPER

Cloud, Tilghman R. *The Messages and Proclamations of the Governors of the State of Missouri.* Ed. Marcia M. Moss and Richard S. Brownlee. Vol. 20. Columbia: State Historical Society of Missouri, 1965.
Daily Dunklin Democrat, January 21, 1964–April 25, 1991.
Official Manual of the State of Missouri, 1963–1964. Jefferson City: Secretary of State, 1964.

DARBY, JOHN F. (1803–1882)

John Darby was a highly accomplished and distinguished lawyer, banker, philanthropist, and public official in early St. Louis. Attaining the office of mayor in 1835, he was subsequently elected to that post four times. His achievements on behalf of the city rank him among the most important individuals to have been mayor in antebellum St. Louis.

Darby was born in Person County, North Carolina, on December 10, 1803. The son of a prosperous southern planter, the young boy was groomed to farm the land that his father bought in St. Louis County in 1818. Darby's insatiable thirst for knowledge was instilled first in the rudimentary schoolhouse, and next through self-instruction in Latin, classical literature, and mathematics. In his early twenties, while still farming for his father, he resolved to return to North Carolina to be tutored by his clergyman grandfather. Subsequently, the young man studied law in John J. Crittenden's law offices in Frankfort, Kentucky, and by 1827 he was an attorney in Missouri.

The new lawyer quickly distinguished himself not only in law but also in St. Louis politics and civic affairs. In 1835 he landed his first term as mayor, running under the Whig banner. He embraced the office with skill and energy, and launched far-reaching improvements for the city. During his second term, Darby promoted completion of the National Road to St. Louis and planned for a railroad convention to bring rail development to Missouri. These initial steps proved premature, but later, as a delegate to the 1849 Pacific Railroad Convention in St. Louis, Darby again urged a transcontinental route through the city. He had invited **Thomas Hart Benton** to keynote the great affair, and the senator's impressive oratory ensured that St. Louis would not be bypassed by the iron horse.

Darby envisioned the city's need to own land for various municipal purposes. He secured the early commons and drill grounds for the city's first public park, which later became Lafayette Park. He planned for other parks and squares and hastened the process of improving vacant lots and tracts with city funding. His controversial decision to purchase land for a city hall was a bold and dramatic move. Most important, he sought federal help to rescue the St. Louis harbor from silting, a problem first noted in the 1830s. Darby recognized that rechanneling the Mississippi would ensure St. Louis's commercial future, and he was instrumental in securing the assistance of the army engineers and young Lt. Robert E. Lee for this important project.

Between his terms as mayor, Darby served in the Missouri House of Representatives where he helped to initiate the chartering of the St. Louis Law Library, one of the city's oldest public libraries. Darby won election to Congress in 1850, and as a Missouri representative he continued to back projects supportive of St. Louis, particularly those related to rail development. After serving one term in Congress, he returned to St. Louis and established a banking concern. He also continued to practice law and distinguished himself in his handling of many Spanish land-grant cases.

When he died on May 11, 1882, John Darby was one of the most respected leaders of St. Louis. He was a link to the city's territorial past and its founding generation. He and young Americans like him who settled in St. Louis in the 1820s tempered a respect and understanding for the old St. Louis with fresh outlooks and insights. Darby's successes spawned a succession of energetic civic leaders and high-thinking public officials who promoted and developed St. Louis to its best advantage during the mid-to late nineteenth century. In an era when civic corporations and chambers of commerce, known merely as commercial exchanges, were in their infancy, it fell to an aspiring, conscientious mayor to exert the leadership needed to build consensus for the massive projects that helped build a great city. Darby's work signaled the rise of mayoral leadership based on strong advocacy and vision. He and his successors lived to see St. Louis rise from an outpost to one of the largest cities in the United States.

JOHN NEAL HOOVER

Darby, John F. *Personal Recollections.* St. Louis: Jones, 1880.

Primm, James Neal. *Lion of the Valley: St. Louis, Missouri, 1764–1980.* 3d ed. St. Louis: Missouri Historical Society Press, 1998.

Scharf, J. Thomas. *History of St. Louis City and County: From Earliest Periods to the Present Day.* Philadelphia: Everts, 1883.

Stewart, A. J. D., ed. *The History of the Bench and Bar of Missouri.* St. Louis: Legal Publishing, 1898.

Van Ravenswaay, Charles. *Saint Louis: An Informal History of the City and Its People, 1764–1865.* St. Louis: Missouri Historical Society Press, 1991.

DARWELL, JANE (1879–1967)

Jane Darwell, a pioneer film actress whose career spanned more than sixty years, was born Patti Woodward on October 15, 1879, in Palmyra, Missouri, where her family maintained a summer home. Her father, W. R. Woodward, served at various times as president of the Louisville and Southern Railroad and the Toronto Hamilton and Buffalo Railroads, and her mother, Ellen Booth Woodward, was the daughter of a Presbyterian minister in Seymour, Indiana. Darwell had two older brothers.

Darwell's family moved from Louisville to Chicago when she was four years of age. She went to Douglas Public School, Miss Loring's private school, Miss Annie Nell's school in Louisville and graduated from the exclusive Dana Hall in Boston where she studied voice and piano.

Darwell joined a stock company at the Chicago Opera House in 1906, and at the end of her engagement she went to Europe on a trip with her father. Upon her return she played with various stock companies throughout the country, and assumed the stage name of Jane Darwell. She entered motion pictures in the early silent days in 1914 and appeared in several Cecil B. DeMille productions. In 1915 she accepted an offer from the Bert Lytell and Evelyn Vaughn stock company and appeared at Alcazar Theater in San Francisco in *The Only Son.* The company later traveled to Hawaii.

Darwell appeared in more than two hundred feature films, but her best-known role was that of Ma Joad in John Ford's screen version of John Steinbeck's *Grapes of Wrath,* for which she won the 1940 Academy Award for best supporting actress. She always contended that it was her favorite role. She once commented that she nearly always played grandmothers and housekeepers and that "I've played Henry Fonda's mother so many times that he calls me 'Ma' and I call him 'son.' " Her last movie role was as the "Bird Woman" in *Mary Poppins* in 1963. Some of her best films were *The Ox-Bow Incident, Jesse James, Gone with the Wind, Huckleberry Finn, Back Street, Tender Comrade,* and *Sunday Dinner for a Soldier.*

Darwell died of a heart attack at the Motion Picture Country Hospital in Woodland Hills, California, on August 13, 1967, at the age of eighty-seven.

ARTHUR F. MCCLURE AND VIVIAN RICHARDSON

Kansas City Times, August 15, 1967.

McClure, Arthur F., Alfred E. Twomey, and Ken Jones. *More Character People.* Secaucus, N.J.: Citadel Press, 1982.

Variety, August 16, 1967.

DATCHURUT, ELIZABETH
(dates unknown)

Among the Spanish documents in the Ste. Genevieve Archives is a lengthy 1798 court proceeding in French, titled "Elizabeth Datchurutt [*sic*], Free Negress (Claiming that Antoine Aubuchon Is the Father of Her Ten Children) v. The Heirs of Antoine Aubuchon." The story is one of interracial love, betrayal, and a quest for justice.

Elizabeth Datchurut was a free African American woman, apparently of some substance, who settled in Ste. Genevieve sometime before 1770. Handsome and spirited, she attracted the attention of a married French planter, Antoine Aubuchon. Unable—or at least unwilling—to leave his wife, Aubuchon began a lifelong affair with Datchurut, farming at least some of his land in partnership with her and treating her with affection and respect. Their loving relationship produced ten children on whom he doted and for whom he promised to provide support until they were grown.

Unfortunately, Aubuchon died suddenly in 1798 without a written will, leaving his French wife and children as his only legal heirs and Datchurut and her children with nothing. A less assertive woman would have given up in despair, but Datchurut was determined to salvage at least something from their relationship. Lacking any standing in court as an heir, she sued the estate essentially as a creditor, and demanded part of the crop she had helped raise and several items of personal property. The most important part of the suit, however, was symbolic: a request that Aubuchon's family acknowledge him as the father of her children and allow them to carry his name.

Datchurut recovered part of the crop, a small amount of personal property, and grudging acknowledgment of her children's paternity. Shortly afterward she moved to St. Louis, buying a house on Church Street where her mixed-race children mingled freely with both blacks and whites. Her death is unrecorded, and her children and grandchildren for the most part disappeared among a mass of Aubuchons of both races who spread out across Missouri. An exception is a grandson Pierre, nicknamed "Conan," who used the surnames Aubuchon and Datchurut interchangeably, as if proud of both parts of his ancestry. Pierre accumulated considerable real estate in and around St. Louis, married another propertied free black, Celeste Morin, great-granddaughter of the early settler Flore, and sired a large and distinguished black St. Louis family.

JUDITH A. GILBERT

"Agreement and Arrangement between Elizabeth Dacherutte, Free Negro, and the Heirs of the Late Sr. Antoine Aubuchon, Resident of Ste. Genevieve." March 3, 1799. Ste. Genevieve Archives (Litigations, no. 80). St. Louis: Missouri Historical Society.

Collet, Oscar W. *Grantor Index to St. Louis Deeds.* S.v. "Aubuchon, Pierre."

"Elizabeth Datchurutt [*sic*], Free Negress (Claiming that Antoine Aubuchon Is the Father of Her Ten Children v. The Heirs of Antoine Aubuchon." March 3, 1799. Ste. Genevieve Archives (Litigations, no. 80). St. Louis: Missouri Historical Society.

St. Louis Archives. Vol. 2. St. Louis: Missouri Historical Society.

DAUBIN, FREELAND ALLEN (1886–1959)

Freeland Allen Daubin was born in Lamar, Missouri, a small town in the southwestern part of the state, on February 6, 1886. He received his early education in the local public schools. Recipient of an appointment to the United States Naval Academy, he was graduated in 1909 and commissioned an ensign. A lieutenant commander at the end of World War I, he continued to advance professionally, achieving the rank of rear admiral in late 1941.

A submariner, Daubin was assigned to the surface fleet, serving aboard battleships and destroyers, during the 1920s and 1930s. He returned to submarine duty in early 1941 as commander of a submarine squadron at Pearl Harbor. At the time of the Japanese attack on Pearl Harbor on December 7, 1941, Captain Daubin was commander of the submarine base at Pearl Harbor. The base provided berthing, overhaul and repair, supply stores, and training facilities for the twenty-two American submarines assigned to the base at the time. Appointed commander of submarines of the Atlantic Fleet in March 1942, he remained in that position until November 1944. Among his many duties in this position, he was responsible for the procurement and training of submarine officers and men for both the Atlantic and the Pacific submarine forces.

Daubin received a number of administrative assignments as well during his active naval career. These included a tour of duty of the United States Naval Headquarters in London, and an assignment in the office of the chief of Naval Operations in Washington, D.C. Following his Atlantic submarine command, he served as commandant of the New York Naval Shipyard in Brooklyn, from December 1944 until March 1946. While there he supervised the launching of several aircraft carriers, including the commissioning of the USS *Franklin D. Roosevelt.* In 1946 he became commandant of the Seventeenth Naval District, which included the Alaskan Sea Frontier and the North Pacific, with headquarters in Kodiak, Alaska. Admiral Daubin, whose navy career spanned some four decades, retired in 1948. He died at Bethesda Naval Hospital on October 24, 1959, and was buried at Fort Rosecrans National Cemetery, in San Diego, California.

Admiral Daubin, **Thomas Selby Combs,** and **Charles Andrews Lockwood Jr.** were contemporaries and the "Lamar triumvirate" of admirals who amassed records of distinctive national service. Daubin was awarded the Distinguished Service Medal in 1945. With many years of experience and knowledge of submarines and submarine warfare, he was cited for "exceptionally meritorious service" as commander of the Atlantic Fleet. He was praised for his contributions to the "splendid results of our submarine operations against the enemy," as well as for the training of officers and crews for submarine service. He, like Admiral Lockwood, had been a pioneer in the U.S. submarine service. As a young lieutenant he had been widely acclaimed in naval circles for an article he published in the *Journal of the United States Naval Institute* in early 1917, two months before the United States officially entered World War I. The primary thrust of the article was that submarines should be used as units of the fleet. Fleet war games, he pointed out, had demonstrated the "tremendous value" of submarines as an integral part of the fleet in carrying out its responsibility to defend the nation's coastlines. A lieutenant commander at the end of World War I, he commanded a crew that transported a German submarine to the United States for study, chiefly because it had an impressive cruising radius of seven thousand miles. Also, following the Japanese aerial assault on Pearl Harbor in 1941, he interceded to prevent a grounded Japanese midget submarine from being destroyed, because he believed that an assessment of its characteristics and capabilities could be significant in the protracted struggle that lay ahead. As commander of the Atlantic submarine force, he had the daunting task of fulfilling the enormous demands of wartime expansion in the submarine service while prosecuting the war-against-enemy forces plying the North Atlantic and waters along the Atlantic seaboard. Overall, his most abiding contribution was in the "development and use of procedures and weapons of submarine warfare."

JOSEPH T. HATFIELD

New York Times, October 25, 1959.

Roscoe, Theodore. *United States Submarine Operations in World War II*. Annapolis, Md.: United States Naval Institute, 1949.

Who Was Who in America with World Notables. Vol. 3. Chicago: A. N. Marquis, 1960.

DAVIS, CHARLES BLEVINS (1903–1971)

Charles Blevins Davis created and almost totally financed the first international post–World War II cultural exchange. He was, for the early years of the cold war, a one-man cultural division of the State Department.

Born in 1903 in Osceola, Missouri, Davis grew up comfortably in Independence where he attended school with Fred Wallace, younger brother of **Bess Truman.** He often visited the Trumans' home, played piano duets with Harry, and teased little Margaret.

Davis attended Kansas City Junior College and briefly studied at Princeton until he returned home when the family suffered financial reverses. He graduated from the University of Missouri in 1925 and taught high school English and was a junior high school principal in Independence. During these years Davis spent summers traveling and winters directing local productions. He consulted with Bess Truman on these projects, which included the first play presented at the University of Kansas City and a pageant for the dedication of the Jackson County Courthouse. Presiding judge **Harry S. Truman** subsequently wrote a recommendation for Davis.

While attending Yale Drama School on a fellowship, Davis met William Randolph Hearst at a 1937 luncheon at the Yale Club. Before lunch was over Hearst commissioned Davis to write a series of articles on the upcoming English coronation. The articles attracted the attention of producers at NBC, who asked Davis to write a coronation drama for radio. He was then hired by NBC and directed the *Great Play* series, which facilitated his meeting, selecting, and directing many Broadway personalities.

During World War II Davis utilized his connection with his neighbor, Senator Truman, to produce large-scale patriotic shows throughout the country. He became nationally known as a personal friend of the Truman family, and was invited to observe Margaret Truman commission the battleship *Missouri* and served as her escort at the inauguration of her father as vice president.

On October 2, 1946, Davis and Marguerite Hill were secretly married at the Mayflower Hotel in Washington with Bess Truman in attendance. The couple was then invited to dinner at the White House. The wedding was not announced until the couple sailed six weeks later. "Mrs. James N. Hill Weds Truman Friend" was typical of the headlines that proclaimed the wedding. Davis had married a well-known social leader and philanthropist who was one of the richest women in the country. She was in her sixties and the widow of the son of the founder of the Great Northern Railroad.

The honeymooning couple stopped in London, where Davis served as a delegate to UNESCO's Drama Association Conference. Back home Davis purchased the Swinney estate in Independence and had it extensively renovated. He also produced his first successful Broadway play and donated the profits to the American National Theatre and Academy (ANTA). The couple then returned to London, where Davis broadcast the wedding of Princess Elizabeth, and, at the request of Bess Truman, was honored at a reception at the American Embassy.

By early 1948 the couple was in Beverly Hills, where Marguerite Davis's ill health had been reported to her New York trustee, George Sloan. Davis wrote to Sloan: "In case of dire necessity we will contact Dr." Ten days later she died, apparently suffering a heart attack while traveling by train from California to New York. Davis telephoned his physician cousin, Frederick Liebolt, from Albuquerque. Liebolt flew to Kansas City where he met the train and pronounced Marguerite Davis dead. After the funeral Davis returned to Independence, moved into his new estate, and prepared to spend his inheritance.

To help counteract the increasingly bitter Soviet propaganda attacks during the cold war, the United States Information and Educational Exchange Act of 1948 was passed. It authorized a program within the State Department that minimized government restrictions and maximized the power of private capital. By this time multimillionaire Davis, a generous contributor to the reelection campaign of President Truman, was again escorting Margaret Truman to social events. This association helped to propel Davis onto the board of the ANTA and into the presidency of the American Ballet Theatre. Davis sponsored a production of *Hamlet* to Europe with the help of Bess Truman. He also financed a European tour of Ibsen's *Wild Duck* performed by African American actors. However, it was Davis's production of *Porgy and Bess* that reached the zenith of U.S. cultural diplomacy in December 1955 when it was presented in Leningrad with unprecedented global press coverage.

It was impossible for Davis to make a profit on the worldwide *Porgy and Bess* tours, as he paid American salaries and charged local prices. It is estimated that he lost $3.5 million on the show. In deep financial trouble, Davis mortgaged his Independence estate more than once and gave incorrect financial statements. He was eventually brought to trial, his estate was auctioned, and he subsequently moved to Peru. Davis died in London on July 16, 1971, and was buried in Independence. A local paper pointed out that few men of the twentieth century "can say that they both invented and financed an American foreign policy."

SHARON BAGG

Community Observer, July 29, 1971.
Davis, Blevins. Papers. University of Missouri, Kansas City.
Kansas City Star, January 16, 1955.
Wolfert, Ira. "Porgy and Bess: Ambassadors at Large." *Nation* (May 19, 1956): 429.

DAVIS, DWIGHT FILLEY (1879–1945)

Dwight Filley Davis never became a professional athlete, nor a professional soldier. With a single exception, he never held elective office. Nevertheless, during his lifetime he excelled in athletics, the military, and public service. He used the combination of intelligence, education, and family wealth to propel himself into a life of effective public leadership.

Born on July 5, 1879, in St. Louis, Davis was the son of John Tilden Davis, a prominent wholesale-dry-goods merchant and banker, and Maria Jeanette Davis, the daughter of a mayor of St. Louis, **Oliver Dwight Filley.**

Davis graduated from the local Smith Academy in 1895, and from Harvard University in 1900. While at Harvard he became an excellent tennis player. He and his partner, Holcomb Ward, won the U.S. national doubles championship in 1899, 1900, and 1901. In 1900 he donated a silver cup, which would become known as the "Davis Cup," to the winners of international lawn-tennis competition. He participated in the 1900 and 1902 competitions.

In 1903 Davis graduated from the Washington University School of Law. He never practiced law, nor did he ever become actively involved in his family's mercantile interests. Instead, he became an energetic and able public servant for the St. Louis community. From his 1905 marriage to Helen Brooks of Boston, Massachusetts, until his active involvement in World War I, Davis served his city in a variety of ways. He served in an appointive capacity within the St. Louis municipal government, and he became involved in private civic enterprises. His affiliations placed him in the mainstream of American progressivism.

Davis started his public service in 1903 when he became the city's public-baths commissioner. He became a member of the board of the St. Louis Public Library, and he belonged to the Civic League, the Playgrounds Association, the Tenement House Association, and the National Municipal League. Elected to the St. Louis House of Delegates in 1907 as a Republican, he served only a single term. He subsequently worked for the community through appointive and advisory positions. From 1911 to 1915 he chaired the City Planning Commission. During that same period he worked as the commissioner of the city's Department of Parks and Recreation. While park commissioner, he placed tennis courts in several of the city's parks. Those public courts were the first of their kind in America. Indeed, Davis wanted to democratize recreation, thereby placing it within the reach of average Americans. He also actively supported the 1914 St. Louis Pageant and Masque, an event created by reformers who wanted to combine increased awareness of the city's history with a participatory exercise that would increase the area's sense of community.

Davis became involved in World War I even before the United States entered the war. In 1916 he served as a member of the War Relief Commission. A captain in the Missouri National Guard, Davis served with valor during the war. At the war's conclusion he held the rank of lieutenant colonel, and earned the Distinguished Service Cross.

In 1920 Davis attempted, unsuccessfully, to obtain the Republican nomination for election to the U.S. Senate, but President Warren G. Harding appointed him director of the War Finance Corporation. Appointed assistant secretary of war in 1923, Davis became the secretary of war in 1925. He approved the court-martial of airpower advocate Gen. William "Billy" Mitchell, but he also urged the army to modernize. Davis established the Army Industrial College for the purpose of educating officers in the problems of mobilizing industry in time of war.

In 1929 President Herbert Hoover appointed Davis governor general of the Philippines. He resigned from that position in 1932 after his wife became seriously ill, and she died that same year. Their marriage produced four children. Davis remarried in 1936, to Pauline Morton Sabin.

In 1935 Davis was placed on the board of trustees of the Brookings Institution, a nonpartisan, nonprofit corporation devoted to public service through research and training in economics and government. He became the institution's chairman in 1937.

Davis held one last public position. A Republican who had been critical of President Franklin D. Roosevelt, nevertheless, in 1942 Davis accepted the president's offer of heading the new Army Specialist Corps, a unit that commissioned men who could not meet the army's physical requirements but who had special expertise that would be helpful in the war effort. He became a major general.

Davis died on November 28, 1945. Appropriately, he was buried at Arlington National Cemetery.

DONALD B. OSTER

Dictionary of American Biography. Supplement 3, 1941–1945. S.v. "Davis, Dwight Filley."
Oster, Donald B. "Nights of Fantasy: The St. Louis Pageant and Masque of 1914." *Missouri Historical Society Bulletin* 31 (April 1975): 175–205.

DEAN, JAY HANNA "DIZZY" (1911–1974)

It was the fourth game of the 1934 World Series in Detroit on October 6. The visiting St. Louis Cardinals, who had overcome an eight-game deficit with the Giants in September to get to the series, were slight favorites to beat the Tigers.

Cardinals ace pitcher Dizzy Dean stood on first base as a pinch runner. Dean charged down the base path toward second base, trying to break up a double play. Billy Rogell tagged second base and turned to throw to first, but the ball instead hit Dean in the temple. The pitching ace was down. Despite his insistence that he had not been injured, they carried

him off the field and sent him to a Detroit hospital to be examined for a concussion. The next day a Detroit newspaper reported the now famous headline: "Dean's Head Examined: X-rays Revealed Nothing."

Jay Hanna Dean (later changed to Jerome Herman Dean) was born in Lucas, Arkansas, on January 16, 1911, into a family of poor sharecroppers. Dean's schooling extended only to the fourth grade. Two Dean children died in infancy. Elmer was born in 1908, followed by Jay three years later in 1911, and Paul two years after that. Dean's mother died when Paul was an infant, the family frequently moved around.

Dean got his start in organized baseball in the United States Army. He reported at Fort Sam Houston in 1926, later recalling that he enlisted because "I didn't figure on spendin' my life pickin' cotton, so I joined the army. You got your shoes free and all the grub you wanted and the pay was $19 a month and that was more money than I'd ever seen or was gonna make on a farm somewhere. And I'd heard they could use smart fellas like me."

Disruptive and irresponsible but at the same time friendly and likable, Dean was less than the ideal soldier until his pitching abilities came to light. James Brought had him moved to the Twelfth Field Artillery in 1927 so he could play ball there. Brought is credited with giving Dean the nickname he carried the rest of his life, "Dizzy," after finding him pitching potatoes at trash-can lids instead of preparing them in the kitchen, and hollering, "You dizzy son of a bitch." Once a San Antonio newspaper account used the nickname in describing a game in which Dean struck out seventeen hitters against the St. Mary's Rattlers, he was forever known as Dizzy Dean.

Dean signed with the St. Louis Cardinals organization in 1930 and was sent to its Class A farm team at St. Joseph, Missouri. He won his first professional game on April 20, four to three. Halfway through the season, the St. Joseph Saints were struggling despite Dean's seventeen-and-eight record, so he was called up to help the Houston Buffaloes who were contending for the Texas League title. At the end of the season in early September, the Cardinals called Dean up to the majors to help in a heated pennant race. Two days after clinching the National League title, the Cardinals gave this brash new pitcher a chance to pitch his first big-league game, in which he beat the Pittsburgh Pirates three to one. Dean bragged through the off-season that he was the only pitcher who had never lost a major-league game. Unable to get along with Cardinals manager Gabby Street, Dean found himself pitching in the minors again in 1931, where he posted a twenty-six-and-ten record at Houston with a 1.53 earned run average.

Dean and the Cardinals management made peace before the 1932 season. Dean had a respectable year for a rookie, winning eighteen and losing fifteen games, and went twenty-and-eighteen in 1933. However, it was during the 1934 season that twenty-four-year-old Dean blossomed.

Dean's younger brother, Paul, pitched for the Cardinals that year too. Never one to be humble, Dizzy claimed that he and his brother—"Me 'n Paul," he said—would win forty-five games between them and lead the Cardinals to the World Series. Then they did exactly that.

The Deans won forty-nine games (more than half the Cardinals total for the season), and appeared in almost a third of the 154 games in the season. With the Cardinals eight games behind the New York Giants in early September, the Deans led the Gashouse Gang to a championship in an incredible final month. Dizzy won three games in the last week, as the Cards passed the Giants in the final two games of the season. Dean posted a thirty-and-seven record, the first pitcher to win thirty games since **Grover Cleveland Alexander** in 1917; only one other, Denny McLain in 1968, has won thirty games since.

Dizzy and Paul (nicknamed by the press "Daffy," which he detested) combined to win all four games in the seven-game World Series against the Detroit Tigers. Some argued that Detroit manager Mickey Cochrane lost the series before it started, at least mentally, with his decision that Tiger ace Schoolboy Rowe would not start against Dizzy Dean.

Dean was well on the way to a stellar career as a pitcher, with records of twenty-eight-and-twelve and twenty-four-and-thirteen in the next two years. Midway through another outstanding season, Dean pitched in the 1937 All-Star game, where a line drive off the bat of Earl Averill broke his toe. Dean tried to return to the lineup before fully healed, and changed his once fluid delivery to compensate for the toe, thus injuring his arm—an injury from which he never recovered. St. Louis traded Dean in the off-season to the Chicago Cubs for three players and $185,000, but his pitching days were really over; he won only sixteen games over the next three seasons with the Cubs. He retired in 1941.

Dean quickly found his way to the radio booth, announcing games for the two St. Louis teams, the Cardinals and the Browns. He gained a reputation for lively and entertaining broadcasts. In a way, it was a perfect match: a medium utterly reliant upon sound and a man never at a loss for words. In early 1947 the Cardinals created a new radio network of six stations spanning two states; on January 11 Cards owner Sam Breadon introduced the station, and announced that games would be covered by the up-and-coming Harry Caray (the future Hall of Fame broadcaster) and former manager Gabby Street to

offer a more "dignified" broadcast. Dean announced Browns games only.

New York Yankees owner Dan Topping offered Dean a contract as part of the television announcing team in 1950. He canceled his only pending commitment—speaking about "Radio Announcing I Have Did" at Southern Methodist University—to go to work for New York.

Dean returned to St. Louis in 1952 as a broadcaster for Bill Veeck's Browns. The following year, he started broadcasting television's new *Game of the Week* on ABC, sponsored by Falstaff. He was the first national baseball television announcer in the United States. He continued to use his down-home aphorisms with newly created words and butchered grammar that made his broadcasts so distinctive. Soon New York viewers heard about runners who "slud" into base, some of whom were "throwed" out, hitters who "swang" at pitches, and hurlers who were never as good as the self-proclaimed "Great Dean."

When the *Game of the Week* switched to NBC in 1965, Curt Gowdy replaced Dean as the lead announcer. Dean retired to Mississippi in 1966; he died after two heart attacks on July 17, 1974.

Despite winning only 150 games in his career, Dean stands among the great pitchers of his generation. He was a Most Valuable Player in 1934, one of only two thirty-game winners since World War I, and set a record for striking out seventeen batters in one game (against the Cubs in 1933). He was inducted into the Baseball Hall of Fame in Cooperstown in 1953. His antics on and off the field contributed to baseball's popularity, and his work as a pioneer television announcer introduced a homespun, lively style of broadcasting baseball games that endeared the game to an entire generation of young baseball fans. Former Cardinal teammate Joe Medwick offered an epitaph of sorts at the end of Dean's funeral: "Well, that's the ball game."

JEFFREY E. SMITH

Devaney, John. *The Greatest Cardinals of Them All.* New York: G. P. Putnam's Sons, 1968.

Gregory, Robert. *Diz: Dizzy Dean and Baseball during the Great Depression.* New York: Penguin Books, 1992.

Staten, Vince. *Ol' Diz: A Biography of Dizzy Dean.* New York: HarperCollins, 1992.

DEAS, CHARLES (1818–1867)

Charles Deas, one of the first frontier painters, lived and worked in St. Louis in the late 1840s, using the city as a base for trips west. His paintings of western-genre scenes were well received during his lifetime, and he experienced success both in St. Louis and nationally. After his death in an asylum in 1867, Deas slipped into obscurity; few of his works survive in museum collections today.

Born in Philadelphia on December 22, 1818, Deas studied art as a boy. He had hoped to enter West Point to pursue a military career as his older brother had done, but when denied admission to the academy, he decided to try art as a profession. He moved to New York City where he studied at the National Academy of Design. The academy elected him an associate member in 1839, and Deas exhibited several works in its gallery over the following years.

In the spring of 1839 Deas left New York to travel west, in search of adventure and subjects for his artwork. He may have been inspired by the New York exhibit of **George C. Catlin**'s Indian Gallery, which contained hundreds of portraits and scenes of the "vanishing race" painted by Catlin during his travels in the 1830s.

Deas traveled to Fort Crawford at Prairie du Chien, in Wisconsin Territory, where his brother, a lieutenant in the army, was stationed. From there Deas made his first forays into the frontier, accompanying army expeditions along the upper Mississippi. He began to sketch and paint the Indians he encountered: the Chippewa, Sac, Fox, and Winnebago tribes. Deas became fascinated with the dress and customs of the Indians, and soon made paintings of Indians and the West his specialty.

By the fall of 1841 Deas moved to St. Louis, establishing a studio and portrait-painting practice to support himself. An 1847 biographer wrote: "He is now established at St. Louis, and it is gratifying to add, from his own testimony, that he has there found all that a painter can desire in the patronage of friends and general sympathy and appreciation." While living in St. Louis, Deas continued to make regular trips from the city to find inspiration for his work, most notably in 1844 on a trip to Kansas to accompany a party from Fort Leavenworth traveling to meet the Pawnee on the Platte River. On his return Deas used his frontier sketches to compose paintings in his St. Louis studio. He exhibited his works at the Mechanics Fairs in St. Louis in the 1840s, receiving complimentary notices in the local press.

In addition to his St. Louis exhibitions, Deas sent paintings regularly to the Pennsylvania Academy of Fine Arts and the American Art Union in New York. Works distributed and sold through the art union included titles such as *The Indian Guide, One of the Shawnee Tribe, Oregon Pioneers, The Mountain Pass, Wounded Pawnee, Western Scenery,* and *Sioux Ball Playing.* Through the union, Deas's paintings reached an appreciative eastern audience eager for images of the wild frontier. Praised for his ability to depict details of Indian clothing and customs, Deas favored scenes of Indian life and the mountain men and trappers who interacted with them on the western frontier. As his career progressed, Deas began to paint scenes high in drama, perhaps hinting at a growing inner emotional turmoil. Two later paintings, *Death Struggle* and *Prairie Fire,* portray the danger of life on the frontier.

In 1847, with the backing of Missouri senator **Thomas Hart Benton,** Deas became a finalist to complete the murals in the U.S. Capitol; unfortunately, he lost the commission to an artist with more political clout.

Deas left St. Louis in 1848 to return to New York City. In 1849, suffering from "melancholia," he was admitted to an asylum, where he died in obscurity on March 23, 1867. Although he apparently continued to paint (his later works were described as "wild pictures"), his artistic career was essentially over at age thirty.

Although few of Deas's works survive and he is little known today, he was an artist who received much acclaim during his lifetime. Had illness not shortened his career, he may have achieved even greater success. Traveler and author Charles Lanman, who stopped in St. Louis on a trip west in 1846, summarized the artist's career: "The bright particular star who uses the pencil here, is Charles Deas. . . . he makes this city his headquarters, but annually spends a few months among the Indian tribes, familiarizing himself with their manners and customs, and he is honorably identifying himself with the history and scenery of a most interesting portion of the continent."

BETH RUBIN

Clark, Carol. "Charles Deas." *American History Illustrated* 12 (April 1987): 19–33.

———. "Charles Deas." In *American Frontier Life: Early Western Painting and Prints.* New York: Abbeville Press, 1987.

Lanman, Charles. *A Summer in the Wilderness.* New York: D. Appleton, 1847.

McDermott, John Francis. "Charles Deas: Painter of the Frontier." *Art Quarterly* 13 (autumn 1950): 293–311.

Tuckerman, Henry T. *Artist-Life; or, Sketches of American Painters.* New York: D. Appleton, 1847.

DEGUIRE, MARIE-JOSEPH (?–1788)

During the first half of the eighteenth century mixed-race marriages were common throughout French Louisiana, including the Illinois country. In 1721 an observer at Kaskaskia remarked, "The French habitants, even the substantial ones, marry Indian women, and they get along very well together." Although by midcentury there were progressively fewer marriages between white Creole men and full-blooded Indian women, there was enough Indian ancestry among Ste. Genevieve's citizens to make the very issue meaningless. Marie-Joseph (sometimes Josette) Deguire Larose, whose birth date is unknown, was the natural daughter of Jean-Baptiste Larose, a master tailor from Kaskaskia, and an Indian slave woman belonging to Joseph Buchet, a longtime notary at Fort de Chartres. In the autumn of 1747 Deguire paid Buchet one hundred livres "to redeem" two of his natural children borne by one of Buchet's slaves. Apparently, Deguire took it upon himself to raise his children from that time on, and simply ignored the wishes of their Indian mother.

In 1759 Deguire's daughter Marie-Joseph married Louis Tirat (also known as Louis St. Jean) in Kaskaskia, and shortly thereafter the couple moved to Ste. Genevieve. By 1774 Tirat had died, but Marie-Joseph, now Widow Tirat, vouched for her daughter and namesake when the latter married Joseph Joubert. Three years later Joubert returned the favor by witnessing her marriage to Pierre Verrau of Ste. Genevieve.

When Marie-Joseph Deguire Verrau's father died in Ste. Genevieve in 1781, she petitioned, as his natural daughter, the government for his estate. Since Deguire had no other living children, Marie-Joseph received his entire estate. There is some question, however, of what would have happened if Deguire had had legitimate children. Probably, Marie-Joseph as a mixed-blood child would have been entirely excluded from the distribution of his property. In 1786 Marie-Joseph's second husband, Pierre Verrau, died in Ste. Genevieve, leaving her as his sole heiress. Thus, she outlived her father and two husbands, and inherited the estates of all three. She then went on to a third marriage, with François Bernier, before she died in 1788, having done well for herself in colonial Ste. Genevieve society.

CARL J. EKBERG

Belting, Natalia M. *Kaskaskia under the French Regime.* Urbana: University of Illinois Press, 1948.

Ekberg, Carl J. *Colonial Ste. Genevieve: An Adventure on the Mississippi Frontier.* Gerald, Mo.: Patrice Press, 1985.

DELASSUS, CHARLES DE HAULT (1767–1843)

Following the Louisiana Purchase, Charles de Hault Delassus, Upper Louisiana's last Spanish lieutenant governor, had the unenviable task of dismantling the Spanish regime and transferring authority to the incoming U.S. officials. However, disappointment and embarrassment were nothing new to this well-born son of French nobility, who more than once found himself forced to take a path not of his choosing. His journey began in Bouchain in the province of Flanders where he was born on November 17, 1767, the eldest son of **Pierre-Charles Delassus de Luzières** and Domitilde-Josephe Dumont. When he was fifteen the young Frenchman joined the Spanish army as a second lieutenant, a not uncommon occurrence since members of the Bourbon dynasty ruled both France and Spain. The military life suited Delassus, who by 1794 had attained the rank of lieutenant colonel and a much coveted assignment with the king's personal battalion, the Royal Walloon Guards.

But while Delassus's military career flourished in Spain, events in Revolutionary France forced members of his family to leave their native land and flee to North America in 1791. Unfortunately, they did not fare well in their new surroundings, notwithstanding the assistance they received from the governor of Spanish Louisiana, the Baron de Carondelet. By 1794 Delassus's parents, who had settled in Upper Louisiana at a place they named New Bourbon, found themselves nearly destitute. Unaccustomed to a life of poverty, they appealed to their eldest son for assistance. With regret Delassus relinquished his promising new post with the Royal Walloon Guards and asked for a transfer to Louisiana so that he could be near his family. His superiors granted his request and reassigned him to the Louisiana Regiment. In 1796 Carondelet appointed him commandant at New Madrid, Spain's commercial point of entry for river traffic on the upper Mississippi. Three years later Delassus replaced **Zenon Trudeau** as lieutenant governor in Upper Louisiana, a post he retained until Spain relinquished its control of the province in 1804.

During his tenure in Upper Louisiana, Delassus labored to maintain Spanish authority against all challengers in the sprawling, sparsely populated region. Indian affairs frequently required his attention, as in 1802 when he personally took command of the militia expedition that he dispatched to New Madrid to demand satisfaction from a party of Mascoutens responsible for killing a trader. Meanwhile, the lieutenant governor's personal debts mounted as he struggled to look after parents who found it difficult to forsake their profligate ways. Delassus used the prerogatives of his office and his ability to grant favors to forestall the consequences of his burgeoning obligations. He took special advantage of his authority to convey land grants, and by the end of the Spanish era Delassus had become one of Upper Louisiana's largest land claimants.

When rumors of the pending transfer of the Louisiana Territory to the United States reached St. Louis in the summer of 1803, Delassus found it increasingly difficult to shield himself from his creditors and to uphold the authority of his office. Once his superiors confirmed that Spain had retroceded

Louisiana to France and that the French in turn had sold the territory to the United States, it fell to him to oversee the formal transfer of authority in Upper Louisiana. Delassus dutifully completed the necessary arrangements and presided over the final lowering of the Spanish flag during ceremonies held in St. Louis on March 9 and 10, 1804. Spain's loyal servant handled his difficult role with dignity and aplomb even though the experience left him increasingly embittered as onetime friends and allies turned away during his final days in office. Delassus revealed his mounting frustration when he scrawled "the Devil take all" as his final entry in one official ledger.

Following his departure from St. Louis in 1804, Delassus remained in Spanish service. He rejoined the Louisiana Regiment in Pensacola and stayed there until he resigned from the army in 1811. Delassus had continued to look after his parents until their deaths in 1806, but their passing merely compounded his already precarious financial situation as he inherited responsibility for their hefty debts. After retiring from military service, Delassus divided his time between St. Louis and New Orleans, frequently pressing for confirmation of the vast landholdings that he claimed under Spanish title. The litigation in those cases dragged on for years, and most of his claims were rejected. Those that were confirmed proved insufficient to satisfy the demands against him. Delassus died in New Orleans on May 1, 1843, largely forgotten and with little to show for his years of loyal service.

WILLIAM E. FOLEY

Archibald, Robert R. "Honor and Family: The Career of Lt. Gov. Carlos de Hault de Lassus." *Gateway Heritage* 12 (spring 1992): 32–41.

Delassus–St. Vrain. Papers. Missouri Historical Society Archives, St. Louis.

Houck, Louis. *The Spanish Regime in Missouri: A Collection of Papers and Documents Relating to Upper Louisiana.* 2 vols. Chicago: R. R. Donnelley and Sons, 1909.

DEMPSEY, TIMOTHY (1867–1936)

Known to St. Louisans as "Father Tim," the Monsignor Timothy Dempsey was born in the diocese of Killoloe at Cadamstown, in County Offaly, Ireland, on October 21, 1867. The eldest of twelve children, eight boys and four girls, born to Thomas H. and Bridget Ryan Dempsey, Timothy was baptized the day after his birth. As he grew, he gained a reputation for mischief. He first attended the local national school and then studied at St. Mary's Seminary at Mullinger, in County Meath. On June 14, 1891, he was ordained a priest for service in the Archdiocese of St. Louis by Bishop Comerford. The ordination

took place at St. Patrick's Foreign Mission College in Carlow, Ireland, where Dempsey had completed his preparation for the priesthood.

On September 17, 1891, Father Dempsey was appointed assistant pastor at Indian Creek in Monroe County, Missouri. In quick succession he became associate pastor at St. Patrick's Church near Moberly, Missouri, and at St. John's Church in Moberly. In 1893 he was assigned to Holy Angels Church on the south side of St. Louis. Three years later he moved to the Church of the Assumption in St. Louis. On July 11, 1898, he was appointed to the church where he would serve the remaining thirty-eight years of his life: "Old" St. Patrick's in the heart of St. Louis's "Kerry Patch." The neighborhood was in transition, but full of life and trouble. "There are just enough Irish to make things interesting," Dempsey noted, "but for the most part my charges are Poles, Lithuanians, Italians and Czecho-Slovaks."

Dempsey became known for his work with "men who didn't get the breaks." He opened a hotel that offered clean rooms for workingmen in 1906. During the bitter winter of 1907 the hotel is said to have accommodated nearly ten thousand guests. In 1910 the needs of working families were met by St. Patrick's day nursery, and in 1911 Dempsey started a hotel for working women. In 1922 he opened a home for working African American workers. He initiated a free labor agency in 1906, and the White Cross Crusade in 1922, to provide food for tubercular and undernourished children and clothing and furniture for their parents. His response to the Great Depression was "Father Tim's Free Lunch Room." In 1931, the year it opened, the lunchroom served 82,455 meals, and during the first eleven years it averaged eight thousand meals daily.

Labor violence affecting his parishioners moved Father Dempsey to intervene in a 1910 strike. His efforts were so successful that he was frequently asked to mediate labor disputes. He won the respect of both management and labor; it is estimated that he "amicably adjusted at least fifty strikes."

Through Dempsey's efforts some peace was achieved among the gangs that brought violence to the streets around St. Patrick's. In 1923 leaders of both the Eagan and the Hogan gangs attended ceremonies at St. Patrick's celebrating Dempsey's being honored as monsignor for his work among the poor. The presence of both men was possible because Dempsey had negotiated an armistice between the rivals.

In 1909 Dempsey purchased a large section of ground in Calvary Cemetery, in St. Louis, so that the "boys," who had no one, could be buried in consecrated ground. He called it "Exiles Rest" after his first hotel. When he died of a heart attack on April

6, 1936, he was buried there among 226 of his "boys." Father Dempsey's charities continue today.

Donald F. Molitor

Doyle, Francis M. "Father Tim Dempsey: A St. Louis Institution." Monsignor Timothy Dempsey File. Archives of the Archdiocese of St. Louis, Kenrick Pastoral Center. Shrewsbury, Mo.

Faherty, William B. *Dream by the River: Two Centuries of St. Louis Catholicism, 1766–1967.* St. Louis: Piraeus, 1973.

The New Catholic Encyclopedia. S.v. "Dempsey, Timothy."

———. S.v. "Father Tim."

Rothensteiner, John E. *History of the Archdiocese of St. Louis in Its Various Stages of Development from* A.D. *1637 to* A.D. *1928.* Vol. 2. St. Louis: Blackwell Wielandy, 1928.

DE SMET, PIERRE JEAN (1801–1873)

Pierre Jean De Smet was born in Dendermonde, Belgium, on January 30, 1801. When he died on May 23, 1873, he was one of St. Louis's most widely known residents. "The funeral," the *St. Louis Globe-Democrat* predicted, "will be one of the largest ever witnessed in the city."

In 1821 De Smet had joined a small company of Belgian youths heading for the New World. Following their landing in Philadelphia, these young men entered the novitiate of the Society of Jesus, a Roman Catholic religious order at White Marsh, Maryland. In the spring of 1823 this group of young Jesuits was sent westward. "We left home and Country for the Indians," De Smet explained later; "the Indians are in the West; to the West let us go." Bishop **Louis William DuBourg,** whose episcopal territory included Missouri, only recently admitted to the Union, had requested the Jesuits to conduct an Indian school on the frontier outskirts of St. Louis.

The 1820s, however, initiated a half century of drastic change in the Indian West. Beginning in 1824 Superintendent of Indian Affairs **William Clark** negotiated twelve additional land-cession treaties, removing the tribes from Missouri and relocating the Native American frontier from Missouri's eastern boundary to its western boundary. With their St. Regis Indian Seminary relocated in 1829 to a campus within the heart of St. Louis, the Jesuits' main apostolate changed from educating Indians to educating the sons of the pioneers. It was, accordingly, exceptional that Father De Smet—ordained in 1827 at St. Ferdinand's Church in Florissant by DuBourg's successor, Bishop **Joseph Rosati**—kept a lifelong commitment to "my beloved Indians."

On September 23, 1833, before the Honorable **William C. Carr** of the Third Judicial District, De Smet completed his naturalization process, renouncing "all allegiance and fidelity to any foreign power." In appreciation of his new homeland, De Smet also anglicized his signature on the process papers: thereafter he would be "Peter John" De Smet. He later served his new country in various government positions. As an army chaplain in the late 1850s he completed tours of duty in both the Kansas Territory and the Pacific Northwest. In the 1860s, as part of his special concern for Native Americans, De Smet served as a government field agent among the tribes along the middle stretches of the Missouri River.

In 1840 De Smet headed westward along the Oregon Trail to begin his work among the Indians. That summer Chief Big Face accorded him a special welcome. During his stay in the Flathead hunting camp in southwestern Montana, De Smet became "Blackrobe." This new name—descriptive, by Indian custom—noted the formal priestly garb that De Smet wore. "Blackrobe" was also indicative of an official role and office: De Smet had been chosen by the Indians as a spiritual leader to serve a religious-minded people. De Smet was awarded such status not only by all the Sioux bands but by all the tribes he encountered, and two successive generations of Indian leaders likewise sought Blackrobe's counsel. By midcentury De Smet had become "the most influential white man" among the Indians of the Great Plains and the Pacific Northwest.

Keeping a promise to Big Face, De Smet returned in 1841 as the leader of a group of six Jesuit missionaries. On the banks of the Bitterroot River, De Smet and his missionaries began their so-called Reduction Program. Their gospel message was accommodated and adjusted to the Native culture: the sole function of the missionaries was to Christianize. "The Cross" was not used as "a promotional tool for the Crown." Just as the biblical "Christians" of Antioch remained Greek, so the Native Americans baptized at St. Mary's became and remained "Christian Indians."

By 1846, however, the widespread invasions of even the remote Indian areas were seriously affecting the traditional lifestyle of the Native Americans. The increased numbers of emigrants passing along the Oregon and other trails had altered the ecology in these areas. In 1851 De Smet, along with knowledgeable Indian leaders summoned to Fort Laramie, agreed to a federal treaty proposing "peaceful coexistence." But within a few years the plan had failed the tribes. The two cultures had proved so disparate as to be incompatible. The extermination of the buffalo herds in many parts of the Great Plains caused the native economies to collapse in numerous areas. By the mid-1860s only the uninformed Sioux leaders, secluded in remote southeastern Montana, could continue to believe they still held control of their future.

In 1868 a number of knowledgeable tribal leaders formed a "Peace Ride" to escort their Blackrobe to the camp of the militant Sitting Bull. These chiefs believed, as did De Smet, that their people faced utter destitution, and they were ready to agree to federal promises: secured reservations along with supplies and "adjustment programs" by which the current threat of Indian extinction might be avoided. Through their effort Sitting Bull joined the debate on the possible signing of the Second Fort Laramie Treaty.

De Smet's prominence was based upon his unique relationship with the Indians. Accordingly, Blackrobe's intercessory powers were sought by Washington politicians, by St. Louis merchants involved in the fur trade, by officials and field agents administering the Indian policy, and by military figures directing the Army of the West. However, De Smet not only became an outstanding figure on the streets of St. Louis but also gained renown across the United States and Western Europe. In 1872 Missouri governor **B. Gratz Brown** called Father De Smet "one of our most distinguished citizens . . . perhaps more esteemed than any other."

Many factors, in addition to the pressing concerns about the "Indian Question," contributed to De Smet's prominence. His service as both "explorer and reporter" played a major role. His books on his experiences among Native Americans and his widely circulated correspondence gave him fame on both sides of the Atlantic. De Smet traveled extensively across the West, making more than twenty extended journeys, mostly by way of "my very own Missouri." Additionally, there were trips to other Jesuit institutions in various cities of the United States, and nine trips back to Europe on missionary business. While St. Louis had served as headquarters for De Smet during many of these years, he was actually present in the Gateway City for less than a third of them.

Even the last of De Smet's work as a Jesuit was exceptional. He was an activist in a period when many of his religious brethren were moving to a semimonasticism. In addition to his Indian apostolate, De Smet filled a number of service assignments for his fellow Jesuits—activities in the marketplace, rather than the cloister. From the termination of the Reduction Program in 1847 until his final days, De Smet was the procurator, or financial supervisor, of the Missouri Jesuits, working as treasurer and fund-raiser, public relations director and vocation promoter. In brief fashion De Smet described his many activities for both his Indian missions and his religious brethren as "an endless search for Men and Means."

JOHN J. KILLOREN

Carriker, Robert C. *Father Peter John De Smet: Jesuit in the West.* Norman: University of Oklahoma Press, 1998.

Chittenden, Hiram M., and Alfred T. Richardson. *Life, Letters, and Travels of Father De Smet, S.J.* 4 vols. New York: Kraus Reprint, 1969.

Garraghan, Gilbert J. *The Jesuits of the Middle United States.* 3 vols. 1938. Reprint, Chicago: Loyola University Press, 1990.

Jesuit Records and Archives. Missouri Province. St. Louis, Mo.

Killoren, John J., S.J. *"Come, Black Robe": De Smet and the Indian Tragedy.* Norman: University of Oklahoma Press, 1994.

Laveille, Eugene. *The Life of Father De Smet, S.J.* Trans. M. Lindsay. 1913. Reprint, Chicago: Loyola University Press, 1981.

DICKSON, MOSES (1824–1901)

Moses Dickson was born in Cincinnati, Ohio, on April 5, 1824, three months after his parents, Robert and Hannah Dickson, moved there from Virginia. He had five sisters and three brothers.

As a young man Dickson became a barber. At sixteen he traveled by steamboat to the South where he toured for three years. He vowed to work toward the end of slavery. He left New Orleans in May 1844 for St. Louis. For the next two years he traveled throughout Iowa, Illinois, and Wisconsin. He met twelve others in St. Louis on August 12, 1846, and presented a plan for ending slavery in the United States. The group formed a secret organization known as the Knights of Liberty. In ten years they hoped to be ready to begin a national insurrection to abolish slavery in the United States.

Dickson married widow Mary Elisabeth Butcher Peters (born in Ste. Genevieve, Missouri, on August 18, 1818) at Galena, Illinois, on October 5, 1848. They had one daughter, Mamie Augusta. The Dicksons moved permanently to St. Louis in 1849.

According to Dickson by 1856 some 47,240 members of the Knights of Liberty throughout the South stood ready to fight for their freedom. In August of that year another organization, the Order of Twelve, was organized in Galena, Illinois. This group was not told of the existence of the secret Knights of Liberty.

By July 1857 Dickson stated that many stood ready to revolt. However, the group postponed their revolt, and when war broke out the membership joined the Union army. In 1866 Dickson, who had been active in the Underground Railroad, joined the AME church and became a minister. In 1871 Dickson, grand master of the black Missouri Masons, a supporter of the "Lincoln Institute" (later Lincoln University) in Jefferson City, and lobbyist for black education in Missouri, organized a group known as the Knights and Daughters of Tabor, an African American organization dedicated to self-improvement that had its beginnings in the earlier Knights of Liberty and Order of Twelve. The first meeting of the Knights and Daughters of Tabor was held in Independence in 1871. The following year an additional meeting was held at Independence, founding the National Grand Temple and Tabernacle of the Order of Twelve, of the Knights and Daughters of Tabor. The society was neomasonic and devoted to African American advancement, encouraging Christian demeanor, the "getting of homes and acquiring of wealth," and "man's responsibility to the Supreme Being."

Mary Dickson died on February 18, 1891, at the age of seventy-two. The Reverend Moses Dickson died on November 28, 1901, and is buried in St. Louis.

WILLIAM PATRICK O'BRIEN

Dickson, Reverend Moses. *Manual of the International Order of Twelve of Knights and Daughters of Tabor.* 3d ed. St. Louis: A. R. Fleming Printing, 1900.

————. *Why You Should Become a Knight and Daughter of Tabor.* N.p., n.d.

Muraskin, William A. *Middle-Class Blacks in a White Society: Prince Hall Freemasonry in America.* Berkeley and Los Angeles: University of California Press, 1975.

DISNEY, WALT (1901–1966)

While Walt Disney's success as an entrepreneur is undeniable, his status and significance as an artist are open to question. Ironically, the same traits that are praised for bringing about Disney's financial success are those that are cited as the cause of his artistic limitations.

Born in Chicago on December 5, 1901, Walter Elias Disney was the fourth of five children. In 1906 his father, Elias, ever searching for better economic situations, moved the family to a small farm in Marceline, Missouri, about one hundred miles northeast of Kansas City. Although life with Elias Disney on the farm seems to have been harsh and even brutal, Walt Disney always remembered it fondly in later life, and it was on the farm that he began to draw. When the farm failed in 1910, Elias moved his family to Kansas City, Missouri, where he bought a *Kansas City Star* newspaper route and put Walter and his brother Roy to work helping deliver newspapers, at no pay.

At the age of fourteen Walt Disney began attending Saturday classes at the Kansas City Art Institute. After graduating from Benton Elementary School,

Disney enlisted in the Red Cross Ambulance Corps, and eventually shipped out to France, where he delivered supplies after the armistice, and where he also first made money with his drawings.

Returning to Kansas City in 1919, he failed to land a job with the *Star,* but he did find employment with a commercial art studio, where he met Ub Iwerks, and the two soon started their own commercial studio. Struggling financially, Disney decided to take a job with the Kansas City Film Ad Company, which made one-minute animated spots for local movie theaters, allowing Iwerks to take over their small enterprise.

Disney began experimenting with his own camera, and soon thereafter formed his own corporation, Laugh-O-Gram, which created seven-minute animated fairy tales. Disney hired a New York distributor for those shorts who failed to return any profits to him. Disney had to let his staff go, and after some desperate times (living for days on food he could scrounge) he went bankrupt. Disney decided he could not succeed as an animator in Kansas City, and in 1923, with borrowed money and the proceeds of the sale of his camera, he took the train to Los Angeles.

In Hollywood Disney soon found a distributor for his *Alice in Cartoonland* series, which was so successful that he was able to send for Iwerks and other Kansas City animators. With a five-hundred-dollar loan from an uncle, he began the Disney Company. During this period he met Lillian Bounds, and in July 1925 they were married; they had two daughters.

In 1927 Disney created Oswald the Lucky Rabbit, for which he again found a New York distributor who, however, managed not only to copyright Oswald but also to lure away four of Disney's best animators. Although stunned by this betrayal, Disney recovered immediately by creating Mickey Mouse, whose worldwide appeal began with his appearance in *Steamboat Willie* (1928), the first sound cartoon and a film that is still admired for its remarkable fusion of sound and image. Disney himself, incidentally, did not draw Mickey Mouse (Iwerks did), but he was Mickey's voice for most of his life. Learning from his past experiences, Disney copyrighted Mickey Mouse, and he also began the uncustomary but provident practice of refusing to sell the rights to any of his films. Disney next created the *Silly Symphonies* series, which included the first color cartoon, *Flowers and Trees* (1932), the extraordinarily popular *Three Little Pigs* (1933), and *Band Concert* (1935), which some critics consider Disney's finest cartoon. By the mid-thirties Disney's studio had become established, profitable, and dominant.

By then Disney no longer did the drawing himself, leaving that task to his large staff (750 workers by 1937), which he carefully supervised. He did involve himself directly in the storyboarding of his films, at which, by all accounts, he excelled. Disney's unwavering demand for richer backgrounds and more realistic detail led to the development by his technicians of a multiplane camera, which made it possible to create a more realistic three-dimensional image. Disney also realized in the early 1930s that he should diversify, and hence he began to merchandize his cartoon characters, a development that soon created one-third of the company's profits while at the same time rescuing from financial ruin companies such as the Ingersoll Watch Company and the Lionel Train Company.

Disney's most significant creation in the 1930s was *Snow White and the Seven Dwarfs* (1937), the first feature-length animated film, which Disney made in spite of the reservations of bankers, critics, and family (his wife thought dwarfs were "nasty"). Although *Snow White* was a major critical and financial success, Disney's next features—*Pinocchio* (1940), *Fantasia* (1940), *Dumbo* (1941), and *Bambi* (1942)—did not fare as well, and by 1940 Disney owed his bankers $4.5 million, forcing him to begin offering public stock in his company. Further trouble came that year when the company moved into new but more impersonal offices in Burbank, a move that exacerbated lingering discontent among the staff (Disney's pay scale was quite low). In May 1941 the Disney animators went on strike, which, as *Time* put it, Disney "handled badly" and "lost . . . gracelessly" (as late as 1947 he was still blaming the strike on communist agitators). Although his profits suffered from the loss of foreign markets during the war, the company remained solvent by making training and propaganda films for the government and the armed forces.

Due to the cultural changes after the war, public interest in animated films declined, so Disney, while still making a few animated films (*Cinderella* in 1950 and *Sleeping Beauty* in 1959), branched out into other extremely successful ventures. He began making animal documentaries, such as *The Living Desert* (1953) and *The African Lion* (1955), and live-action films such as *Treasure Island* (1950) and *The Absent-Minded Professor* (1961). In 1953 Disney established his own distribution company, Buena Vista, which meant that he now had total control of all his films, and all their profits. Disney was one of the first movie producers to embrace television. In 1954 he introduced his own program on ABC; it was an immediate hit. With financial backing from the ABC Network, Disney ignored the scorn and disapproval of his critics and created Disneyland, which opened in 1955 to enthusiastic crowds.

Disneyland's enormous success led to Disney's 1964 purchase of twenty-seven thousand acres of Orlando swampland where he planned to build Disney World. That same year saw the release of his most profitable movie, *Mary Poppins,* which grossed $45 million in its initial release. The following year Disney, suffering from cancer, began to fail quickly, and he died on December 15, 1966.

While there is no question that Walt Disney, his creations, and the company that he founded are culturally important, assessments of the man and his work vary greatly. As an entrepreneur Disney had the right mixture of determination, savvy, vision, inventiveness, and timing to succeed. He seemed to feel more pride in his financial kingdom than in his cultural empire. When asked by a reporter what his most rewarding experience had been, Disney responded: "The whole damn thing. The fact that I was able to build an organization and hold it." His innovations and quest for perfection made his films dominant in the 1930s and '40s, and without Disney animated films might never have become the art or the profession they are today. A major attraction of Disney's animated features is their music, which, beginning with *Snow White and the Seven Dwarfs* and continuing to the present, includes a long list of popular hits. From *Steamboat Willie* onward, his animation cleverly and often humorously synchronized sound and image. In the use of new technologies he was often ahead of his time. After a few unsuccessful attempts at repeating popular cartoons, Disney avoided sequels to his hits. The extent of his successes vindicates Disney's conviction that he best knew the kind of entertainment that people craved. During his lifetime, Disney was honored with more than seven hundred awards, citations, and honorary degrees, including thirty-one Oscars, five Emmys, and the presidential Medal of Freedom. In the year of his death, the company he started with a five-hundred-dollar loan grossed $116 million.

"We make the pictures," Disney was fond of repeating, "and then let the professors tell us what they mean." The professors, however, as well as many reviewers and journalists, have often found disturbing meanings in Disney's productions. According to his critics, in order to achieve his goals, Disney exercised such total control over his company that he effectively destroyed individuality; many young artists, like Walt Kelly, left Disney early on. For Disney there was only one way to draw, and that way was realistic, but merely a surface realism. His use of folk tales was reductive, distorted, sexist, racist, or patriarchal; these faults were only compounded when the popular Disney book versions of the tales began to replace the originals. His portrayal of animals, both in documentaries and in animated films, was condescending and false, since he invariably made them anthropomorphic and mostly cute or adorable. His wholesome and sanitized creations (including the theme parks) have been criticized as obsessive, idealized, and a pretentious form of escapism. His drive for perfection focused on lovely appearances and technological innovations rather than on substantive meanings. Disney's attempts at high art were often scorned; Stravinsky felt that the use of "The Rite of Spring" in *Fantasia* was "execrable" and the visuals accompanying his music "an unresisting imbecility."

Disney's American values have been deemed exclusively bourgeois and right-wing (when President Johnson presented him with the Medal of Freedom, Disney wore a conspicuous Goldwater button), but at the same time he seems not to have been aware of or sensitive to important political issues (he was the only film producer to meet with Nazi filmmaker Leni Reifenstahl during her visit to Hollywood). It has also recently been alleged that from 1940 until his death Disney was an informant for the FBI. These allegations and assessments have thus led some to view Disney's extraordinary popularity as an ominous development. He has, his detractors argue, diminished rather than expanded or deepened American culture.

After his death in 1966, Disney's company went through a long period of struggle. Internal conflicts as well as profound cultural changes due to phenomena such as Vietnam, Watergate, and a more permissive society caused the company to struggle in the 1970s; the notable exception was the opening of Walt Disney World in 1971. The company, with new management headed by Michael Eisner, regained its sense of direction in the 1980s with a number of highly successful developments. In 1983 it launched the successful Disney Channel. A full thirty years after the release of its last feature-length animated film, the studio offered *The Little Mermaid* (1989), and its success has been followed with a steady flow of feature hits, including the first completely computerized feature-length animated film, *Toy Story* (1995). The company has also acquired several smaller independent studios, which have produced such non-Disney but highly successful films as *Pretty Woman* (1990), *The Hand That Rocks the Cradle* (1992), and *Pulp Fiction* (1995).

The company has expanded and improved its profitable theme parks, and it has developed or franchised new ones, notably Euro Disney and Tokyo Disneyland. It has recently built an actual city, Celebration, Florida, for twenty thousand inhabitants. In 1996 Disney made its largest acquisition, Capital Cities/ABC. With its taking on of the restoration of the New Amsterdam Theater in New York City, the company has been praised as the primary catalyst for the restoration of the Times Square area in Manhattan.

The company has increased its merchandizing of Disney products; in fiscal 1995 it opened 105 new Disney stores around the world, including one next to the New Amsterdam Theater. Its diversified holdings now include professional sports teams, cruise lines, newspapers (including the *Kansas City Star*), ice shows, magazine and book publishing, and theatrical productions, plus tie-ins with high-profile food and drink companies.

Disney has been aggressive in implementing social actions, such as recycling and a camping program for inner-city youths, and it now grants equal health benefits to the gay partners of its employees. Disney's refusal to accede to China's threats if it did not drop its backing of a film about the Dalai Lama was a principled and highly praised decision. The company's present financial strength must surely exceed Walt Disney's grandest dreams: its gross revenues currently top $12 billion a year.

The Walt Disney Company, which is still closely and jealously identified with its founder, has more than continued Disney's dream of influence, control, and diversification, and it is now a major conglomerate or, to some, an empire. Some observers, understandably, view these developments as being in step with the necessary commercialization of all entertainment and with the inexorable displacement of traditional industries with the entertainment business. Others, also understandably, regard this encroachment of the Disney ethos as an indication of cultural shrinkage, and thus they view the swelling corporate ghost of Disney as something of a Monstro that is swallowing America, perhaps never to release it.

THOMAS D. COOKE

Bell, Elizabeth, Lynda Haas, and Laura Sells, eds. *From Mouse to Mermaid: The Politics of Film, Gender, and Culture.* Bloomington: Indiana University Press, 1995.

Eliot, Marc. *Walt Disney: Hollywood's Dark Prince.* Rev. ed. New York: HarperCollins, 1994.

Leebron, Elizabeth, and Lynn Gartley. *Walt Disney: A Guide to References and Resources.* Boston: G. K. Hall, 1979.

Maltin, Leonard. *Of Mice and Men: A History of American Animated Cartoons.* New York: McGraw Hill, 1980.

Schickel, Richard. *The Disney Version: The Life, Times, Art, and Commerce of Walt Disney.* Rev. ed. New York: Simon and Schuster, 1985.

Watts, Stephen. *The Magic Kingdom: Walt Disney and the American Way of Life.* Boston: Houghton Mifflin, 1997.

DOCKERY, ALEXANDER MONROE (1845–1926)

Alexander Monroe Dockery, Missouri's first governor in the twentieth century, was an old guard Democrat who presided over an administration more evocative of the past than of the future. A practitioner of traditional politics, a believer in limited government, and a fiscal conservative, Dockery generally disdained the progressive-reform impulses that were in ascendancy at the dawn of the new century.

Dockery was born near Gallatin, Missouri, on February 11, 1845, the only child of Willis E. and Sarah Ellen Dockery. Alexander attended public schools and briefly studied at the Macon Academy prior to enrolling at the St. Louis Medical College where he graduated in 1865. Following a year of postgraduate work at Bellevue Hospital in New York City, Dockery established a medical practice at Linneus, Missouri, before moving to Chillicothe where in 1869 he married Mary E. Bird.

In addition to his work as a physician, Dockery found time to serve on the local board of education, and in 1872 he began a ten-year stint as a curator of the University of Missouri. While still living in Chillicothe, Dockery formed a partnership with a local druggist, Thomas Bootin Yates, to purchase a bank in Gallatin. Dockery, who apparently found banking more to his liking than medicine, moved to Gallatin and proved an adept money manager, a talent that he subsequently put to good use during his political career.

Dockery served on the Gallatin City Council and in 1881 was elected mayor. He also assumed an active role in Democratic politics. In 1882 he won a seat in the United States House of Representatives where he served for sixteen years. For ten of those years he was a member of the powerful House Appropriations Committee, and his work on that panel earned him the title of "Watchdog of the Treasury." Among other things he was instrumental in modifying the accounting methods used by the Treasury Department. He also served on the committee on post offices and post roads. Always attentive to the interests of his constituents, Dockery opposed high tariffs because he considered them harmful to American farmers.

In 1900 Dockery announced his intention to run for governor. He was unopposed for the Democratic nomination and defeated Republican Joseph Flory in the general election. Dockery took office as Missouri's thirtieth chief executive on January 14, 1901. He offered no sweeping legislative agenda and preferred to concentrate his attention on ensuring efficient fiscal management of the state government. During his term growing state revenues did permit increased appropriations for state institutions and for public schools and also made it possible to entirely liquidate the state's bonded indebtedness. Dockery also helped direct the state's participation in the 1904 Louisiana Purchase Exposition, better known as the St. Louis World's Fair.

An old-line Democratic partisan, Dockery was slow to address the charges of cronyism and corruption that threatened members of his party. He had little sympathy for the actions of St. Louis's reform-minded circuit attorney **Joseph W. Folk,** and questioned his loyalty to the party. Dockery unsuccessfully opposed Folk's bid to become the Democratic gubernatorial candidate in 1904. Folk secured the nomination and triumphed in the general election, and Dockery's departure from office in 1905 marked the passing of a political era in Missouri.

Following the expiration of his term, Dockery returned to Gallatin where he devoted his energies to civic affairs and to the oversight of local road building and maintenance. In 1913 President Woodrow Wilson appointed him an assistant postmaster general with responsibility for managing the postal department's financial operations. He subsequently went back to Gallatin where he died on December 26, 1926.

STEPHEN MAIDMENT

Shoemaker, Floyd Calvin. *Missouri and Missourians: Land of Contrasts and People of Achievements.* Chicago: Lewis Publishing, 1943.

Shoemaker, Floyd, and Sara Guitar, eds. *The Messages and Proclamations of the Governors of the State of Missouri.* Vol. 9. Columbia: State Historical Society of Missouri, 1926.

DODGE, HENRY (1782–1867)

Henry Dodge served his nation in a long and prosperous life on the nineteenth-century frontier. At an early age he established himself as a strong military leader and skillful negotiator. He served with distinction during the War of 1812, the Winnebago and Black Hawk Wars, and led the first regiment of mounted United States Dragoons. Although renowned for his military exploits, Dodge also possessed adept political skills and served as the first territorial, later state, governor of Wisconsin, and held office in the United States House of Representatives and Senate during the fractious 1850s. Dodge lived most of his life in Wisconsin, but learned important economic and political lessons as a young adult in Missouri.

Nancy Hunter Dodge gave birth to Henry in the area of Vincennes, Indiana, on October 12, 1782. He remained with her until the age of fourteen, when legend recounts that he fled for his life after interceding in an Indian attack upon a young woman. By 1796 Dodge had joined his father, **Israel Dodge,** and his uncle John in Missouri's Ste. Genevieve district. He received little formal education, but worked in various family businesses, including salt production, lead mining, whiskey distillation, and trade.

Henry Dodge married Christina McDonald in 1800 and together they raised nine children during their long marriage. He earned valuable experience in both commerce and politics during this period, serving as deputy sheriff before succeeding his father as district sheriff in 1806. Dodge subsequently served as lieutenant and adjutant in the district militia, and first lieutenant and captain in the Ste. Genevieve cavalry. Despite such positions of civil and military authority, he became involved in various questionable intrigues during this period. In 1804 he and his friend **John Smith T.** set off down the Mississippi to join Aaron Burr's conspiracy to seize land in the Southwest, but were intercepted in New Madrid and indicted for treason against the United States. The government later dropped charges against the two, and they resumed their lives in Ste. Genevieve.

The Missouri Territory organized in 1812, and one year later Dodge was appointed as its marshal. Soon thereafter, he received a commission of brigadier general and led five military units during the War of 1812 against Native populations in the western theater, gaining treaty concessions with the Miami, the Teton, and the Yankton Sioux. Dodge remained active in military and political affairs after the war and, in 1820, served as a delegate to the Missouri Constitutional Convention. The lead-industry boom surpassed public duty, however, and led him, in 1827, to Michigan Territory. Dodge moved his large family and slaves first to Galena, Illinois, then to the present site of Dodgeville, Wisconsin.

Dodge discovered the largest viable lode of iron ore in the region and erected two smelting furnaces that formed the core of a small community. The mining boom brought many settlers to the Michigan Territory, which extended westward to present-day North Dakota and southward into Iowa. Friction resulted with the Native population, erupting in the Winnebago War in 1827 and the Black Hawk War in 1832. Dodge participated in both, thereby enhancing his military reputation, political connections, and negotiation skills. President Andrew Jackson established the United States Dragoons in 1833 to monitor Native American activities on the frontier and engaged Henry Dodge to lead its first regiment.

Dodge's ensuing return to Wisconsin initiated a thirty-year political career in that state. The territory officially split from Michigan in 1836, and its new voters elected Dodge to lead them. He served as territorial governor and superintendent of Indian affairs from 1836 to 1841, helped establish the legislative assembly and judiciary, acquired thousands of acres via treaty from Native people, worked for safe inland waterways and harbors on Lake Michigan, and protected landowner rights. Dodge served as territorial delegate in the House of Representatives from 1841 to 1845 when he returned to the territorial governorship. Wisconsin entered the Union in 1848 during Dodge's second gubernatorial term, and he facilitated the transition to statehood. His political career culminated with a return to Congress, where he served as U.S. senator from Wisconsin between 1848 and 1857.

Henry Dodge retired from public office in his seventy-fifth year and died ten years later, on June 19, 1867, in Burlington, Iowa. During his lifetime the United States had grown from a young republic hugging the Atlantic Coast to an expansive nation stretching across the continent. He contributed to its development through private economic endeavors and public service. As a soldier, Indian agent, and statesman, Dodge applied lessons from his experiences in Missouri to the new state of Wisconsin—helping to fashion viable communities for those who followed.

RACHEL FRANKLIN WEEKLEY

Fisher, Kathy. "Fathers and Sons: The Dodges on the Frontier." Des Moines: Collections of the Iowa State Historical Library, 1969.

Gregg, Kate L. "The War of 1812 on the Missouri Frontier." Parts 1 and 2. *Missouri Historical Review* 33 (October 1938): 3–22; (January 1939): 184–202.

Hempstead, Stephen, Sr. "I at Home: Part III." *Bulletin of the Missouri Historical Society* 14 (October 1957): 59–96.

Houck, Louis. *A History of Missouri, from the Earliest Explorations and Settlements until the Admission of the State into the Union.* Vol. 2. Chicago: R. R. Donnelley and Sons, 1908.

McCarty, Dwight G. *The Territorial Governors of the Old Northwest: A Study in Territorial Administration.* Iowa City: State Historical Society of Iowa, 1910.

Pelzer, Louis. *Henry Dodge.* Iowa City: State Historical Society of Iowa, 1911.

DODGE, ISRAEL (1760–1806)

Israel Dodge exemplified the adventurous spirit of a young, expanding United States at the turn of the nineteenth century. He carried forth the traditions and legacy of the renowned American branch of the Dodge family, descended from Tristram Dodge, an English immigrant who reached Massachusetts in 1661. Israel, along with his brother, John, transplanted cultural mores of both family and country to the western frontier in their varied roles as soldiers, farmers, merchants, traders, and public servants.

Born in Canterbury, Connecticut, on September 3, 1760, Israel Dodge matured quickly in colonial America. He traveled to Africa aboard a slave ship when only fifteen years old and fought with the Connecticut militia in the American Revolution two years later. He was wounded in 1777 at the Battle of Brandywine during a hand-to-hand fight with a British regular and earned the rank of second lieutenant in the Continental army by the war's end. Afterward, he followed his brother, John, to the newly acquired U.S. territories in the Ohio and Mississippi Valleys.

Israel Dodge met his future wife, Nancy Hunter, while transporting supplies between Kaskaskia and Clark's Colony, a fortified settlement on the Mississippi River below the mouth of the Ohio. They married by 1781, and Nancy moved briefly to Kaskaskia. The young Nancy Dodge gave birth to Henry, the couple's only child, a year later. Israel settled his family at Spring Station, near present-day Louisville, Kentucky, and later at Bardstown. In the early 1790s he left his family and sought a more prosperous livelihood on the frontier of Spain's Upper Louisiana.

Dodge joined his brother, John, in the young settlement of New Bourbon by 1793. They pledged loyalty to the king of Spain and established a prosperous life through a variety of endeavors. The census of Spanish Illinois listed Israel as an agriculturalist, but he also engaged in lead mining, produced salt on the Saline River, and operated a prosperous distillery, breweries, and a mill on Dodge Creek. In 1799 he petitioned the region's lieutenant governor, **Charles de Hault Delassus,** for a land grant of one thousand arpents, which Dodge had already improved. The concession was granted a mere ten days later after the endorsement of New Bourbon's founder, the lieutenant governor's father, **Pierre-Charles Delassus de Luzières,** who proclaimed the beneficence of Israel Dodge and the value of his business endeavors to the people of Spanish Louisiana. Dodge prospered both personally and professionally in his new home, for he remarried in 1804, taking Catherine Camp as his wife. Dodge's business interests flourished through multiple ventures within the region and through trade via New Orleans.

Despite his loyalty to the Spanish crown, Dodge retained good standing as a patriotic American after the transfer of Louisiana to the United States and, in fact, raised the U.S. flag in Ste. Genevieve on the occasion of the American takeover in 1804. **William Henry Harrison,** governor of Indiana Territory and the Louisiana Territory, appointed Dodge as sheriff of the Ste. Genevieve district in that same year, an appointment that he carried throughout the rest of his life. **Henry Dodge,** who had joined his father and uncle in 1796, contributed to the family's frontier enterprises and served as deputy sheriff in Ste. Genevieve. Israel Dodge lived the remaining two years of his life in the Ste. Genevieve district, dying in 1806 at the age of forty-six.

Dodge represented the entrepreneurial zeal that contributed to the settlement of early Missouri. As an American he brought cultural traditions from the eastern United States to its newest territorial addition at the turn of the nineteenth century and participated in the transplantation of political institutions as well. He provided much needed agricultural products, minerals, milling services, and trade to the inhabitants of the Louisiana territory. Although reputedly known as an undisciplined rabble-rouser in his youth, he facilitated the development of both capitalist and democratic European traditions in the Upper Louisiana during the tenuous transitional period in the early nineteenth century.

RACHEL FRANKLIN WEEKLEY

Douglass, Robert Sidney. *History of Southeast Missouri: A Narrative Account of Its Historical Progress, Its People, and Its Principal Interests.* New York: Lewis Publishing, 1912.

Fisher, Kathy. "Fathers and Sons: The Dodges on the Frontier." Des Moines: Collections of the Iowa State Historical Library, 1969.

Houck, Louis. *A History of Missouri, from the Earliest Explorations and Settlements until the Admission of the State into the Union.* Vol. 2. Chicago: R. R. Donnelley and Sons, 1908.

Pelzer, Louis. *Henry Dodge.* Iowa Biographical Series. Iowa City: State Historical Society of Iowa, 1911.

DONIPHAN, ALEXANDER W. (1808–1887)

Born on July 9, 1808, in Mason County, Kentucky, Alexander William Doniphan was the son of Joseph and Anne Smith Doniphan, both from Virginia. After training as an attorney in Kentucky, Doniphan moved westward and settled in Lexington, Missouri, in March 1830 where he began practicing law. In May 1833 he moved to Liberty, Missouri, a boomtown in the far western part of the state.

In Liberty Doniphan continued to build his law practice, acquiring as a client an unpopular group, the Mormons, who had been physically run out of Jackson County. Doniphan began legal action against Jackson County to place the Mormons back on their land and to obtain damages for losses from anti-Mormon violence. He also filed criminal charges against those accused of mob actions. He did not have much success. In February 1834 Missouri Atty. Gen. **Robert William Wells** informed the Mormons after preliminary hearings "that all hope of criminal prosecutions were at an end." Civil charges were no more satisfactorily dealt with, and in the end the Mormons were unable to return to Jackson County. Doniphan, however, helped establish the especially created county of Caldwell in western Missouri as a haven for them.

In 1838 Doniphan entered the Missouri State Militia, accepting a commission as brigadier general of the Western Division. Although this marked the beginning of his military career, he did not know that he would soon cross paths with the Mormons once again. The rapid growth of Caldwell County, and the Mormons' movement into surrounding counties, had brought tension to the western part of the state. A series of incidents, in which both sides were at fault, erupted violently in August 1838 during an election at Gallatin, in Daviess County, north of the Mormon-controlled Caldwell County. By early September the countryside was ablaze with anti-Mormon sentiment.

Sustained trouble came on October 25, 1838, when a Mormon military unit under David W. Patten, an apostle in the church, engaged a detachment of militia under Capt. Samuel Bogart at what has been christened the Battle of the Crooked River. Several casualties resulted, with three Mormons being killed (one of whom was Patten) and one fatality in Bogart's ranks. The engagement of state troops, regardless of the circumstances surrounding it, and rumors that the Mormons were in open rebellion against the state were sufficient to prompt Gov. **Lilburn W. Boggs** to call out reinforcements to restore order.

Doniphan's troops arrived at Far West, Missouri, the seat of government in Mormon-controlled Caldwell County, late in October 1838 and linked up with militia from other locations. Their task was to gain the surrender of Mormon weapons and the turning over of key Mormon leaders for which they possessed arrest warrants. Doniphan served as a mediator in these negotiations, eventually securing the surrender of the Mormon leaders on October 31.

The next day Gen. Samuel Lucas convened a court-martial, found **Joseph Smith Jr.** and other Mormon leaders guilty of treason, and ordered their execution by firing squad. Doniphan, apparently the only lawyer present, protested that the court-martial had been "illegal as hell" because civilians were not subject to military law and because the judges sitting for the court-martial were not all members of the military. Despite his pleas, on the morning of November 2 Doniphan received orders to execute the prisoners. He refused to carry out the order and wrote to General Lucas: "It is cold-blooded murder. I will not obey your order. My brigade shall march for Liberty tomorrow morning, at 8 o'clock; and if you execute these men, I will hold you responsible before an earthly tribunal, so help me God."

Doniphan's stand prompted Lucas to bring the prisoners to Richmond for trial during the week of November 12, 1838. Once again Doniphan served as the Mormons' legal counsel. After a preliminary court of inquiry the majority of the prisoners were released, but the Mormon prophet Smith and a few other key leaders were placed in the Liberty jail over the winter of 1838–1839 to await trial. Eventually, Doniphan was able to get a change of venue for them from Daviess to Boone County. While en route to the county seat at Columbia, they were allowed to escape and leave the state.

Doniphan's identification with the unpopular Mormons in Missouri during the 1830s did not hurt his personal career in the 1840s. His legal career escalated after the Mormon War, and he was showered with important and lucrative cases. In 1840 he was also elected to his second term in the state legislature by an overwhelming majority. By the early 1840s, therefore, Doniphan had demonstrated his capabilities in three career endeavors: the law, politics, and the military. He was not yet forty years old at the time.

When the United States entered the war with Mexico in 1846 Doniphan commanded the First Missouri Volunteers. Part of the Army of the West under the command of **Stephen Watts Kearny,** Doniphan's Missourians made up nearly half of the 1,650-man army. Departing Fort Leavenworth in June 1846 for the Southwest, by August the army had reached Santa Fe, where the Mexican government surrendered without a battle. While other parts of the army pushed on toward California, Doniphan's men remained in Santa Fe with orders to pacify or defeat hostile Indians and establish a government acceptable to Congress, and only then to push southward into Chihuahua, Mexico.

Doniphan quickly created a code of organic laws for the new territory and began actions to pacify the Indians of the region. In late 1846 he campaigned against the Navajo north of Santa Fe, hounding the Navajo and Zuni chieftains and their people until they were willing to meet at treaty tables. By December 1846 his efforts had brought at least a temporary peace among the southwestern Indians.

Late in the year Doniphan's men marched for El Paso and on Christmas Day camped near the city at a place called El Brazito. They soon learned that a Mexican army was approaching; by the time the Mexicans attacked, Doniphan's men had moved into defensive positions. After a short fight the Mexicans had lost 40 to 50 killed and 150 wounded. Doniphan's casualties were 7 wounded.

A few days later Doniphan's column marched into El Paso, where they rested before moving on to Chihuahua. On February 28, 1847, Doniphan was nearing Chihuahua when he encountered a sizable Mexican force of about three thousand regular troops supported by another thousand ranchers and peasant farmers near the Sacramento River. Doniphan's Missourians began a flanking action, which the Mexicans countered with a cavalry charge into the American center. They were driven back by artillery, dispersing the tightly concentrated Mexican forces. Throughout this action Doniphan sat serenely on his horse and at one point remarked sarcastically, "Well, they're giving us hell now boys." At a key moment Doniphan ordered his troops to advance across the field. The battle secured the province for the United States.

After this action, Doniphan's force joined Zachary Taylor's army at Buena Vista. Soon, with the First Missouri's enlistment expiring, Doniphan marched them to Port Isabel, near Matamoros, and they sailed for New Orleans and then on to St. Louis where the men were mustered out. In one year his men had traveled more than thirty-five hundred miles by land and another thousand by water, fought two major battles in Mexico, established an Anglo-American–based government in New Mexico, subdued southwestern Indians, and paved the way for the annexation of the territory that became New Mexico and Arizona.

After the war Doniphan continued his business, legal, and political activities. His most significant political activity took place in 1860–1861 when he worked to prevent Missouri's secession from the Union and as a delegate to the Washington Peace Conference. Thereafter he continued private pursuits until his death on August 8, 1887, at his home in Richmond, Missouri.

ROGER D. LAUNIUS

Bauer, K. Jack. *The Mexican War, 1846–1848.* New York: Macmillan, 1974.

Clark, Kimball. "The Epic March of Doniphan's Missourians." *Missouri Historical Review* 80 (January 1986): 134–55.

Duchateau, Andre Paul. "Missouri Colossus: Alexander W. Doniphan, 1808–1887." Ph.D. diss., University of Oklahoma, 1973.

Launius, Roger D. *Alexander William Doniphan: Portrait of a Missouri Moderate.* Columbia: University of Missouri Press, 1997.

LeSueur, Stephen C. *The 1838 Mormon War in Missouri.* Columbia: University of Missouri Press, 1987.

Maynard, Gregory P. "Alexander W. Doniphan: Man of Justice." *Brigham Young University Studies* 13 (summer 1973): 462–72.

DONNELL, FORREST C. (1884–1980)

Born in Quitman, Missouri, on August 20, 1884, the only child of dry-goods operator John Cary and Barbara Lee Waggoner Donnell, Forrest C. Donnell attended private school at Cameron before graduating from Maryville High School in 1900. He then earned a B.A. (1904) and an LL.B. (1907) from the University of Missouri–Columbia. A child prodigy encouraged by his mother, he excelled as the valedictorian of each of his graduating classes and became a member of Phi Beta Kappa, the Order of the Coif, and the Missouri bar. From 1907 until 1940, save for an appointment as the attorney for Webster Groves, he practiced law as a partner in a succession of St. Louis

firms and served on several American Bar Association committees. He appeared every bit a barrister: dignified in manner and dress, nearly six feet tall, of medium build, with slightly curly, reddish hair.

On January 29, 1913, Donnell wed Hilda Hays of St. Louis, who gave birth to a daughter, Ruth, the following year and a son, John Lanier, in 1918. Raised a Presbyterian, Donnell deferred to his wife's faith and taught Sunday school at Grace Methodist Church. He presided over the Missouri Sunday School Council of Religious Education, as well as a local evangelistic union, and served as a state delegate to the General Conference of the Methodist Church. His secular commitments included service to the Missouri School for the Blind and the State Historical Society. Later, as a thirty-third-degree Mason, he led the state lodge.

Perhaps because his father served as mayor of Maryville, Donnell showed an interest in politics. Instead of following the family's southern Democratic heritage, however, he actively campaigned for **Herbert S. Hadley** in 1908, the Republican Party's first post-Reconstruction governor of Missouri, and led the state's Young Republicans eight years later. Originally influenced by Theodore Roosevelt, Donnell eventually became more conservative. His Republicanism was reinforced by **Seldon Palmer Spencer,** who recruited him out of law school, became his first partner, and was elected a U.S. senator in 1918.

Throughout the 1920s and 1930s, Donnell succeeded in the boom-bust economy and, particularly during the depression, served the community. Suddenly, in 1940, he became the Republican Party's gubernatorial nominee opposing his former Sunday school pupil and Democratic machine–backed candidate Lawrence McDaniel. Equally ironic, according to his daughter, Donnell had been recommended for the candidacy by another catechism student and friend: baseball entrepreneur **Wesley Branch Rickey.** As significant, given his widely known public service, Donnell defeated three primary candidates easily.

Although few gave him much chance of beating the party of Franklin D. Roosevelt in a perennially Democratic state and in a presidential election year, Donnell stunned McDaniel. He won by only 3,613 votes, benefiting from an antimachine campaign that divided the Democratic Party and brought him statewide support. Democratic leaders, fearful of a Republican Party rebirth through gubernatorial patronage, charged voting irregularities and moved to deny—the press said "steal"—Donnell's victory. Hence, the Democratic Speaker refused to announce Donnell's election officially, and the Democratic majority in joint session voted to investigate the election, despite opposition from their own outgoing governor, **Lloyd Stark.** Donnell, in turn, requested that the Missouri Supreme Court order the Speaker to fulfill his constitutional duty, which it did unanimously. Despite this verdict by Democratic judges, McDaniel conceded only after a recount disclosed that the governor-elect had received even more votes than officially recorded.

Throughout these proceedings, which seemed especially repugnant because Democrats had won all other state executive offices and retained control of the state legislature, Donnell acted the statesman. Inaugurated on February 26, 1941, more than six weeks after the official date, he presented an ambitious program. Ironically, he failed to pass much of it even after fellow Republicans took control of the house and an equal share of the senate in 1942. He advanced a state merit system, a secret-ballot measure, and a bipartisan administration for the liquor-control department; he brought state unemployment compensation in line with federal social security regulations; and he backed higher salaries for legislators. He also supported marriage laws requiring blood tests and waiting periods. However, Donnell failed to convince lawmakers of benefits derived from infusing the state social security system with matching federal dollars; his initiatives for civil service reform and public disclosure of committee votes also languished.

Nor did Donnell actively promote the history-making Missouri Constitutional Convention, which occurred during the second half of his administration and became law shortly after his departure from the governorship in 1945. Like other incumbents of both parties, including U.S. Senator **Harry S. Truman,** Donnell questioned its partisan impact. Politically, he drew his core support from rural voters opposing constitutional revision and, philosophically, he challenged prospects of enlarged governmental power.

Donnell's record revealed problems wrought by World War II, personal philosophy, and party politics. He spent much time on the international crisis, creating a state defense council that he chaired. He benefited from a boom economy that stimulated military production and created surplus revenues, yet limited the building of much needed public projects. And, amid these concerns, he reacted forthrightly to both the lynching of **Cleo Wright** in Sikeston and the efforts to defuse racial tension in St. Louis. As significant, Donnell's legalistic, meticulous style and opposition to patronage slowed legislative and party-building initiatives, while Barak Mattingly, state leader of the Republican Party, advanced his own personal power at the expense of party unity.

Still, in 1944, Donnell's popularity and voter dissatisfaction with his opponent carried him into the United States Senate. Unable to succeed himself as state executive, Donnell campaigned against Roy A. McKittrick, who as attorney general had endeavored

to deny Donnell the governorship four years earlier; Donnell benefited from voters remembering the "steal" and his tempered response to it, and from a series of gambling-house raids that hinted at the persistent corruption of machine politics. Again he triumphed by a minuscule margin, despite opposition from Mattingly in the primary and token support from party workers in the election.

Perhaps surprising to those aware of Donnell's more liberal gubernatorial positions, he identified with "conservative" Republicans on national issues. He admired Robert A. Taft, whose father he voted for in 1912 and whose own presidential candidacy he supported in 1948 and 1952. In the younger Taft, he found an influential statesman and shrewd political leader who shared his own beliefs in "equal justice under the law," equal opportunity, and individual freedom.

Hence, Donnell voted for the Taft-Hartley Act (1947) and similar antilabor measures, while supporting lower income taxes and opposing an excess-profits tax. He, like Taft, proved moderate on social issues, endorsing public housing and federal aid to education (excluding parochial and private schools). Similarly, while initially and privately struggling with Joseph McCarthy, Donnell soft-pedaled McCarthyism (though on one occasion he reportedly permitted sponsors of a rival bill to be labeled communists). He shared further the Ohio senator's unilateralism in foreign affairs, which dated back to his opposition in the League of Nations. Small wonder that Donnell joined Taft to oppose the North Atlantic Treaty Organization (1949) and most foreign aid.

Donnell continued his lifelong opposition to patronage and voted against President Harry S. Truman's appointment of cronies such as Democratic National Committee Chairman **Robert Emmet Hannegan** for postmaster general. Doubtlessly, he delighted in casting one of only two dissenting ballots—the other being Taft's—against the former St. Louis party leader who had been involved in the "governorship steal."

Nonetheless, Truman Democrats had the last laugh: **Thomas C. Hennings Jr.** defeated Donnell by 92,593 ballots in 1950. Despite the campaign appearance of Senator McCarthy, Donnell became the only incumbent Republican senator to lose that year. He refused to press the anticommunist issue to his advantage, perchance because he—like Hennings, who attacked McCarthyism—respected civil liberties. His other beliefs were out of step with numerous voters—often union or black—who recalled his antilabor positions, forgot his housing-education commitment, and disagreed with his unilateral position in the cold war. Nor did his refusal to perform individual favors or indulge visiting delegations ingratiate him with constituents. Unwilling to leave Washington before the Senate adjourned, he never overcame the campaign lead that Hennings mounted or the charge of being too conservative. Equally important, Donnell again lacked strong backing from his own divided party and neglected to exploit the reform that brought him into office.

Donnell was a capable executive and hardworking senator. Yet, he never sought control of the party apparatus, and he failed, like most Missouri Republicans, to cultivate urban voters or address changes wrought by the depression and war—a major reason he was the party's last governor and U.S. senator until the 1970s. Donnell was more a constitutional lawyer and public servant than a political leader or party regular. A man of "relentless integrity," he followed his conscience; an outsider, he symbolized political honesty and the hope of Republican Party resurgence. Donnell, who neither drank, smoked, nor swore, practiced law almost until he died from pneumonia, on March 3, 1980, at the age of ninety-five.

DOMINIC J. CAPECI JR.

Current Biography. New York: H. W. Wilson, 1950.
Donnell, Forrest C. Papers. Missouri Historical Society, St. Louis.
———. Papers. State Historical Society of Missouri Manuscripts. University of Missouri–Columbia.
———. Papers. Western Historical Manuscripts Collection, Columbia.
March, David D. *The History of Missouri.* Vol. 2. New York: Lewis Historical Publishing, 1967.
Soapes, Thomas F. "Republican Leadership and the New Deal Coalition: Missouri Republican Politics, 1937–1952." Ph.D. diss., University of Missouri–Columbia, 1973.

DONNELLY, PHIL M. (1891–1961)

Phil M. Donnelly was born in Lebanon, Missouri, on March 6, 1891. He was educated in Missouri schools, eventually receiving an LL.B. degree from St. Louis University in 1913. During his career he received honorary degrees from Culver-Stockton College, Westminster College, and William Jewell College.

In 1913 Donnelly entered private law practice in his hometown of Lebanon, Missouri, where he served as the city attorney and as the prosecuting attorney for Laclede County. In 1922 Donnelly entered state politics and was elected to the Missouri House of Representatives. In 1924 he won a seat in the Missouri State Senate, where he served until 1944. As a member of the state senate, Donnelly served in several leadership posts, including party leader of Senate Democrats and president pro tempore.

On November 7, 1944, voters elected Donnelly governor of Missouri. One of the first tasks confronting the new governor was the naming of a successor to Sen. **Harry S. Truman. Thomas C. Hennings Jr.,** a Democrat from St. Louis, was interested in securing the Missouri Senate seat. Hennings lobbied for the position, trying to convince Franklin D. Roosevelt and Truman to intervene on his behalf. However, Donnelly refused Henning's candidacy, selecting **Frank Parks Briggs** instead.

During his first term, Governor Donnelly became embroiled in a conflict with Missouri labor. In 1947 the legislature passed the King-Thompson Anti-Strike Law, and Donnelly signed it. The legislation prohibited strikes against utility companies, and Donnelly enthusiastically supported it. He also opposed efforts of organized labor to unionize the St. Louis Police Department. Both of these actions revealed Donnelly's conservative political philosophy, and his willingness to oppose powerful factions in his own party.

Donnelly left office in 1948, but his involvement in Missouri politics continued. Supporters mentioned him as a candidate for the United States Senate in 1950. Party leaders thought that he would be a strong candidate against Republican **Forrest C. Donnell,** despite his poor relationship with organized labor. But instead of running for the Senate, Donnelly decided to try for a second term as Missouri governor.

In 1952 voters reelected Donnelly. In winning his election, though, he had to overcome some substantial obstacles. First, labor unions opposed his nomination. Second, a national political trend favored the Republican Party. Although Donnelly won, his party lost control of the Missouri House of Representatives and had only a small majority in the state senate. Consequently, during his second term, Governor Donnelly dealt with an opposition party in control of the state house.

Education became an important issue during Governor Donnelly's second term. His relationship with Missouri educators started poorly, however. In 1953 he vetoed an appropriation for Missouri schools that he viewed as excessive, which precipitated a strong reaction from teachers and administrators. Missouri educators filed a lawsuit against the governor, questioning the legality of his veto. The Missouri Supreme Court refused to hear the case. Despite the difficult beginning, Governor Donnelly's second term did see major education reforms. To increase state revenues for education, the legislature enacted a higher sales tax on cigarettes. In 1956 the voters of the state approved a bond issue of $75 million for the construction of buildings at state colleges and universities.

Donnelly left office in 1957. He had been a memorable chief executive for the state, demonstrating in each of his two terms a willingness to challenge interests within the state and his own political party. A conservative Democrat, he achieved important reforms. He returned to his hometown of Lebanon where he practiced law until his death on September 12, 1961.

MICHAEL E. MEAGHER

Gille, Frank H. *Encyclopedia of Missouri.* St. Clair Shores, Mich.: Somerset, 1985.

The History of Laclede County, Missouri. Tulsa, Okla.: Heritage, Publishing, 1979.

Kemper, Donald J. *Decade of Fear: Senator Hennings and Civil Liberties.* Columbia: University of Missouri Press, 1965.

Meyer, Duane G. *The Heritage of Missouri.* St. Louis: River City Publishers, 1982.

Official Manual of the State of Missouri, 1947–1948. Jefferson City: Secretary of State, 1948.

"Phil M. Donnelly." *Missouri Historical Review* (January 1962): 179–81.

DOOLEY, THOMAS A., III (1927–1961)

Thomas A. Dooley III was born in St. Louis on January 17, 1927. His father, Thomas A. Dooley Jr., was general manager of the American Car and Foundry Company, a major producer of railcars with plants in St. Louis and St. Charles. His mother, Agnes Wise Dooley, came from a prominent Pennsylvania family with roots in colonial America. The Dooleys were a leading Irish-Catholic family in St. Louis. Thomas A. Dooley Sr. was a captain of industry who designed the first all-steel railroad boxcar produced in North America, an invention that greatly enhanced American Car and Foundry's business when the United States entered World War I.

Thomas A. Dooley III was the first of three sons born into the Dooley family (he had an older half brother from his mother's first marriage to an army officer who was killed in an airplane crash). The Dooleys lived in several homes in the city's west end, where Tom Dooley was educated in the grammar school of St. Roch's Church, and at Barat Hall, a private school operated by the Sisters of the Sacred Heart at City House, a convent located behind the "new Cathedral" in the central west end. In 1939 the family moved to an estate at Fair Oaks in Ladue, a wealthy suburban community in St. Louis County. In 1944 Tom Dooley graduated from St. Louis University High School, a Jesuit institution and the oldest school west of the Mississippi. He attended the University of Notre Dame between 1944 and 1948, though he completed but five semesters of course work. In November 1944 Dooley enlisted in a navy corpsman program and served in naval hospitals in New York and California before returning to Notre Dame in the fall of 1947. Although he never earned his undergraduate degree, Dooley gained admission to St. Louis University School of Medicine in 1948, at a time when three years of premedical study was often considered sufficient preparation.

Dooley was a controversial and erratic medical student: he was required to complete his final year before finally receiving his degree in 1953. His stern father had died shortly after Dooley began his medical studies, and he soon began missing classes and evading responsibilities. With few prospects for a medical career in St. Louis, Dooley reenlisted as a lieutenant (junior grade) in the navy's medical corps following a residency at Camp Pendleton in California. Shortly after being stationed at the U.S. Naval Hospital at Yokusuka, Japan, Dooley was assigned to a special task force aiding in the evacuation of nearly 1 million North Vietnamese fleeing that new nation in the wake of the communist Viet Minh's victory over the French at Dien Bien Phu in April 1954. Dooley (who had studied briefly at the Sorbonne in Paris) was responsible for translating orders between French and American naval landing craft as refugees were loaded aboard.

In October 1954 Dooley was reassigned to a medical intelligence task force sponsored by the Military Advisory and Assistance Group, whose leader, Lt. Gen. John W. O'Daniel, was a staunch supporter of Ngo Dinh Diem, the newly appointed premier of the fledgling state of South Vietnam. Dooley's official duties entailed collecting samples for epidemiological research, but his primary role was as a liaison between the refugee campaign, dubbed the "Passage to Freedom," and American reporters and politicians with an interest in Southeast Asia. Dooley was so effective as a spokesman for the cause of Diem that in May 1955 he was awarded the highest honor the new nation could bestow upon a foreigner. In later years it was revealed that the award ceremony, like many of the events surrounding the Passage to Freedom, was orchestrated for publicity purposes by Edward G. Lansdale, a "freelance" CIA agent assigned for cover to the United States Air Force.

Dooley returned to Yokusuka in June 1955 and was urged by a naval physician and by friends to write an account of his experiences in Vietnam. With the aid of Capt. William J. Lederer, a navy public information officer and friend of Lansdale, Dooley produced "Deliver Us from Evil," a firsthand account of the Passage to Freedom that was quickly acquired by *Reader's Digest* and published as a condensed book, excerpts of which appeared in the magazine's April 1956 edition. A longer version was then published under the same title by Farrar, Straus, and Cudahy. The book was a best-seller and won great acclaim for its author. *Deliver Us from Evil* introduced millions of readers in the United States and abroad to the emerging struggle in Southeast Asia between communism and the forces of pro-Western democracy.

In early 1956 Dooley embarked on a lengthy publicity tour on behalf of *Deliver Us from Evil.* Amid glowing reviews for the book, Dooley was suddenly forced to quietly resign from the navy because of homosexual activities that had been observed by agents of the Office of Naval Intelligence who had tailed Dooley throughout the winter. Just as suddenly, Dooley announced in April that he was returning to Southeast Asia as a private citizen to launch nongovernmental, nonsectarian medical missions in northern Laos. This new program, Operation Laos, was sponsored by the International Rescue Committee (IRC), a voluntary international relief agency headquartered in New York City. In 1955 the IRC had similarly promoted Operation Brotherhood, a program launched by Lansdale and funded in part by the CIA that sent Filipino medical professionals and political operatives to Vietnam to work on behalf of the Diem regime.

Dooley established his first clinic at Vang Vieng, Laos, in September 1956. The following January he was authorized to move Operation Laos to Nam Tha, a strategically important town just miles from the Chinese border in northwestern Laos. Along with three young American corpsmen, Dooley brought Western medicine to rural Laos for the first time; although by his own admission the level of care he provided was rather primitive, it still represented an important gesture in a politically volatile environment. The Lao communist (Pathet Lao), clients of North Vietnam and beholden to the dictates of Ho Chi Minh, sought to undermine any neutralist or pro-American regime in the country. In response, the U.S. State Department lavished tens of million of dollars in economic aid to Laos, while covert intelligence operations substituted for open military support, which was banned by the Geneva Accords of 1954.

Throughout his tenure in Laos, Dooley maintained an arrangement with KMOX radio in St. Louis to provide weekly audiotapes for broadcast on a weekend program, *That Free Men May Live.* The broadcast described Dooley's clinical work while promoting the vision of foreign aid that inspired his mission: small-scale, "person to person" programs that would win the propaganda war with Soviet communism in the region.

Dooley returned to the United States in the autumn of 1957 to write a book about his experience in Laos and to raise funds for an ambitious new project known as MEDICO (Medical International Cooperation). MEDICO was a greatly expanded version of Operation Laos, formed to establish private medical missions under the auspices of the IRC throughout the developing world. Dooley was placed in charge of a clinic in Muong Sing, Laos, that he established

with the help of two young American corpsmen, Dwight Davis and Earl Rhine. MEDICO flourished in the early months of its existence, largely due to the publicity generated by Dooley's public appearances and the success of his second book, *The Edge of Tomorrow.* His cause also benefited from the great success of the controversial 1958 novel *The Ugly American,* coauthored by William J. Lederer. The book repeated many of the same charges Dooley had leveled against the U.S. foreign aid program.

Dooley's triumph was short-lived. In August 1959 he was diagnosed with malignant melanoma and returned to New York for radical surgery, which was filmed for an award-winning *CBS Reports* documentary, "Biography of a Cancer." Just weeks after the surgery, Dooley embarked on a fund-raising tour that netted more than $1 million for MEDICO and brought "the jungle doctor to Laos" greater fame than ever.

In December 1959 he returned to Laos, though MEDICO was no longer associated with the IRC. It soon became apparent that MEDICO was too dependent on Dooley's personal charisma to take firm root in developing nations where he was not personally involved. Dooley published his third and final book, *The Night They Burned the Mountain,* in the spring of 1960, when his cancer appeared to be in remission. By the end of the summer, however, his illness had spread, while the political situation in Laos rapidly deteriorated. A coup d'état led by an officer of the Royal Lao Army resulted in a countercoup by an American-backed Lao general. Dooley's mission of peaceful medical service was obliterated in the struggle just as his own health deteriorated. He returned to New York for treatment in late December 1960 and died there on January 18, 1961. While MEDICO quickly floundered, President John F. Kennedy cited Dooley's example when launching the Peace Corps in 1961. For many years after his death Dooley continued to inspire others toward a life of service, as the controversial aspects of his own life receded into the past.

James T. Fisher

Dooley, Agnes W. *Promises to Keep: The Life of Doctor Thomas A. Dooley.* New York: Farrar, Straus, 1962.

Dooley, Thomas A. *Deliver Us from Evil.* New York: Farrar, Straus, and Cudahy, 1956.

———. *Edge of Tomorrow.* New York: Farrar, Straus, and Cudahy, 1958.

———. *The Night They Burned the Mountain.* New York: Farrar, Straus, and Cudahy, 1960.

Fischer, James T. *Dr. America: The Lives of Thomas A. Dooley, 1927–1962.* Amherst: University of Massachusetts Press, 1997.

DOW, BLANCHE HINMAN
(1893–1973)

Born on February 9, 1893, in Louisiana, Missouri, Blanche Hinman Dow grew up in a college environment. Her father, Ernest Wentworth Dow, was a Baptist minister who was a Colgate College graduate. He held a number of pastorates in the East before coming to Missouri, where he was president of Southwest Baptist College, Pierce City Baptist College, and Grand River College.

Blanche Dow's elementary education was in a private school in Missouri, and her secondary education was pursued in a Canton, Massachusetts, private school. She received her B.A. degree from Smith College in 1913. Later she earned M.A. and Ph.D. degrees in French from Columbia University. Her doctoral dissertation, "The Varying Attitude toward Women in French Literature of the Fifteenth Century," was published by the Institute of French Studies. She had earlier earned a diploma from the Boston School of Expression and studied at the Sorbonne.

Dow was a speech instructor at Milwaukee-Downer Seminary and an instructor in French and dramatics at Grand River College. However, the most significant years of her work in higher education were spent at Northwest Missouri State Teachers College, in Maryville, and at Cottey Junior College, in Nevada, Missouri. At Northwest Missouri State, she taught French and drama and eventually became chairman of the department of romance languages.

In 1949 Dow became the sixth president of Cottey Junior College and served in that position for sixteen years. She had developed a strong interest in international relations and as a representative of the American Association of University Women (AAUW) had attended the 1932 Disarmament Conference at Geneva. Under Dow's leadership at Cottey, the college initiated a program of a third year of language study in France for Cottey graduates. During her presidency Cottey College became an international campus, for she led the college in the development of its policy of accepting international students.

Dow played an active role in the AAUW. She served as president of the Missouri division in 1937–1939 and rose through various appointments and offices to be national president from 1963 to 1967. Other offices besides those in the AAUW included participation in a White House meeting on racial unrest, 1963; membership on the steering committee of the National Women's Committee for Civil Rights, 1963–1965; chairman of the First Missouri Commission on the Status of Women, 1964; and member of the U.S. commission to UNESCO, 1965–1968. During the Lyndon B. Johnson presidency she received appointments to citizens' committees for community relations and the employment of the handicapped,

and was a member of the National Advisory Council on Poverty, for the Office of Economic Opportunity.

During her lifetime Dow received numerous honors and awards, including the Medal of St. Louis, the highest award of the Federation of French Alliances, and the Distinguished Women in America Award from Christian College in Columbia, Missouri. In addition, the Southwest Central Region of the AAUW established the Blanche Hinman Dow International Fellowship in her honor. Honorary doctorates were awarded to her by Culver-Stockton College, Iowa Wesleyan College, Missouri Valley College, Western College for Women, and the University of Missouri.

In 1965 the Cottey Junior College Board of Trustees awarded the title of president emerita to Dow. Upon her death on May 24, 1973, the editor of the *Nevada Daily Mail* wrote, "she was an explorer by nature and never displayed any qualms about poking into new and unknown fields."

WILMA LEONARD TURNER

Clapp, Stella. *Out of the Heart: A Century of PEO, 1869–1969*. Des Moines: PEO Sisterhood, 1969.

Oldfather, C. H. "President Elect, Cottey Junior College." *PEO Record* (May 1949).

Postlewaite, Ken. "Blanche Hinman Dow." *Nevada Daily Mail,* May 24, 1973.

Stockard, Orpha. *The First Seventy-Five Years*. Nevada, Mo.: Cottey College, 1961.

Wallace, Edith Markham. "Inauguration of Dr. Blanche Hinman Dow." *PEO Record* (January 1950).

DRAKE, CHARLES DANIEL
(1811–1892)

Seldom, if ever, has a Missouri politician been hated so intensely by so many Missourians as was Charles Daniel Drake, an attorney, author, state legislator and constitutionalist, U.S. senator, and, finally, chief justice of the United States Court of Claims. He was long an anathema to many because of his role as a Radical Republican during the extremely turbulent 1860s, culminating in the adoption and ratification of the short-lived Missouri Constitution of 1865, which included a loyalty test oath, or "kocklebur oath," requiring all voters, officeholders, attorneys, clergymen, directors of corporations, jurors, and teachers to swear that they had never given aid or comfort to any person engaged in hostility against the United States or Missouri.

Charles Drake, the only son of Daniel Drake, a nationally known medical scholar and practitioner, was born in Cincinnati, Ohio, on April 11, 1811. After his stormy youthful years under the misguided supervision of his father, Drake served as a midshipman in the United States Navy, and subsequently studied law in the Cincinnati office of his uncle Benjamin Drake, earning admission to the bar in 1833. When the fledgling lawyer's practice did not meet his expectations, he decided to go farther west. After a month's stay in Jacksonville, Illinois, he went to St. Louis.

Young Drake quickly struck up acquaintances with St. Louis lawyers, among them Wilson Primm, with whom he formed a partnership, and **Hamilton Rowan Gamble,** who remained his intimate friend and mentor until their paths diverged during the Civil War. Although Drake had little or no money, his father's reputation gave him entrée to gatherings of the societal upper crust. Hence, at a wedding of two socially prominent St. Louisans, Drake had the opportunity to meet his future wife, Martha Ella Taylor Blow, youngest daughter of Capt. Peter Blow and sister of **Henry Taylor Blow,** a St. Louis industrialist.

The law firm of Primm and Drake specialized in the collection of debts owed eastern creditors by St. Louis entrepreneurs. Drake seemed to be doing well. Indeed, in 1838 he initiated what proved the most enduring achievement of his life: the founding of the present Law Library in St. Louis. Moreover, his legal experience during these years may well have been the germ of his "Treatise on the Law of Suits by Attachment in the United States," first published in 1854, which became a standard work on that subject and was cited by the United States Supreme Court and many state courts.

Drake's good fortune proved short-lived. The depression following the panic of 1837 seriously hurt the collection business, though it was probably Drake's cantankerous disposition, a fault evident throughout his public life, that may have ended his partnership with Primm and precipitated the decline in the number seeking his services. At any rate, this marked the onset of hard times and misfortune that dogged him throughout the 1840s. Not only was his income too meager to support his family, but his wife and two of his children died.

In the hope of financial reward and possible political preferment Drake worked energetically in 1844 for the election of Henry Clay, the Whig presidential candidate. He helped to organize Clay clubs and conducted the publication of the *Mill Boy,* issued weekly during the campaign from the office of the *Missouri Republican.* Clay's defeat was more than a bitter disappointment, for Drake's dire financial straits forced him to undergo the humiliation of taking his second wife, Margaret Austin Cross, and the children to Cincinnati where they had to live off his father's bounty. Again, desperate to find some means of earning a livelihood, Drake threw himself into the presidential campaign of 1848 in support of Zachary Taylor, only to learn after the Whig victory

that others had a firmer grasp on the political plums than he.

After a stint in Washington, D.C., as treasurer of the Presbyterian Board of Foreign Missions, Drake decided in 1850 to return to St. Louis, where he followed his father's advice to abjure politics and devote his time to the practice of law. During the next few years he established a reputation as an earnest, hardworking attorney. At the same time he helped, as a ruling elder, to promote the work of the Second Presbyterian Church, published his "Treatise on Suits by Attachment," became president of the Law Library Association, and in recognition of his strong advocacy of secondary education was chosen to deliver the principal address at the dedication of the first public high school building erected in St. Louis, on March 24, 1856.

In 1859 Drake, by then a Democrat, reentered politics when he was elected to fill a vacancy in the Missouri House of Representatives. There his arrogance and supercilious treatment of his colleagues endeared him to none. More important, in his fight for the passage of his Sunday blue laws he earned the lasting enmity of ethnic Germans by charging them with wantonly desecrating the Sabbath, "a curse imported from foreign lands." Noting the antislavery sentiment among Germans, he scorned "the imported infidelity of the Red Republicanism of Europe" that had become the "Black Republicanism of Missouri." He did not stand for reelection.

During the years of growing tension between the South and the North, which culminated in the Civil War, Drake moved by degrees from a defender in 1859 of the slave system and the castigation of abolitionists to rabid attacks on the South and slavery. In this he was hardly less consistent than any other Missourian. Once he had convinced himself that slavery was the cause of the "crime of secession," it was but a short step to contending that those who opposed the emancipation of slaves were likely to be disloyal as far as they dared.

For a number of reasons emancipation sentiment was growing by the spring of 1862. That fall the election of state legislators showed Union men favoring emancipation in some form. The form, however, soon became an issue between those who advocated gradual and conditional emancipation (Conservatives or Claybanks) and men who demanded the slaves be freed immediately and unconditionally (Radicals or Charcoals). Such was the situation when Drake became a candidate to fill a vacancy in the state convention, nearly all of whose members had been elected in 1861. Although he was not a pronounced immediate emancipationist, Drake, with the support of the Charcoals, won easily. That he was a well-known Union man and, of late, a vociferous opponent of slavery was enough for most voters.

When provisional governor Gamble called the convention into its fifth session, he said the time had come to pass an ordinance of emancipation, but he did not recommend any plan. He had been reluctant to deal with the matter, but the national administration, as well as public opinion, forced his hand. About all he and the Conservatives, who controlled the convention, could do was to try to slow the pace. Drake and the Radicals wanted the convention to end slavery as soon as possible, to submit to popular vote whatever emancipation ordinance was passed, and to provide for elections to replace the executive officers chosen by the convention in 1861. None of these was passed. The emancipation ordinance, as passed after much wrangling, would not end slavery until July 4, 1870, and after that date the freedmen would remain as servants, the length of servitude depending upon the age of the black at the time he was freed. Thus, the stage was set for Drake and the Radicals to contend that Gamble and the Conservatives had passed a "bogus" emancipation ordinance, a charge they used as a political spearhead to attack the administration.

Soon after the state convention adjourned, Drake and a number of St. Louis Radical Union men called for a mass convention in Jefferson City on September 1, 1863, to lay the foundation for a statewide organization. Drake made the keynote speech in which he denounced the Gamble administration, called for a new state convention that would end slavery immediately and unconditionally, permit the people to elect their own rulers, and disfranchise every man who had ever taken any part in support of "this damnable rebellion." Before it adjourned the convention provided for a Committee of Seventy "true Union men" led by Drake to lay the Radical grievances before President Abraham Lincoln.

When the president met with the delegation on September 30, Drake read an address in which he charged that Governor Gamble and Gen. **John Schofield,** commander of the Military District of Missouri, were allowing Rebels to endanger the lives and property of Union men. He demanded that Schofield be replaced, federal military forces replace the state militia, and men not truly loyal be kept from the polls. Lincoln talked seriously with the Radicals for about three hours, but he indicated no intention of changing course in Missouri.

Drake remained in Washington for several days after the meeting and may have tried to see Lincoln again. At any rate, on October 5 Lincoln wrote a letter to "Honorable Charles D. Drake and Others, Committee" in which he explained his refusal to bow to Radical demands. He did agree, however, that General Schofield must try to ensure that only those eligible to vote under the laws of the state participate in elections. Drake held up publication of the letter until October 23 in order to publish his own comments along with it.

Drake immediately turned his attention to the campaign for the election of three judges to the Missouri Supreme Court. Much to the surprise and chagrin of the Radicals, all three Conservative candidates won. Doubtless the vehemence with which Drake and other Radicals attacked the Gamble administration cost them votes, for they seemed to suggest the possible use of force to overthrow it. Drake himself was adept at using words and phrases inciting in their effect, but ones that were so carefully qualified that he could deny what he seemed to have said.

Soon Drake had to face another problem, namely, keeping the Radicals united. Starting early in 1864 Republicans in state after state called for the president's renomination, so it was clear long before the Republican Party (called the Union Party to attract War Democrats) convened in Baltimore that Lincoln would be the nominee. Drake and nearly all the Missouri Radicals were opposed. He and other Radical leaders realized, however, that a victory in the state depended upon the party's being united and cooperating with the national Union Party. Hence, even though the delegates to the Radical Union convention in Jefferson City knew that Lincoln would be the presidential nominee, the Radical leaders persuaded the convention to send delegates to Baltimore, all the while severely criticizing Lincoln's policies and pretending this was an anti-Lincoln move. Drake was named one of the delegates at large, but he did not go to Baltimore. He wrote years later that he could not afford the expense of attending. Probably the real reason was that he, a well-known vociferous and articulate critic of Lincoln, was willing to keep quiet, but could not bring himself to attend a convention he knew was controlled by the administration.

Drake gave scant support publicly to the party during the 1864 presidential campaign. He made only three speeches, none of them in Missouri. He never said anything that could be construed as an endorsement of Lincoln, except in a backhanded way. It is likely that Radical political strategists, including Drake himself, believed his playing a prominent role would be divisive, not unifying, for the party. Perhaps, too, he simply could not enthusiastically work for the Radical gubernatorial candidate, Col. **Thomas Clement Fletcher,** who had defeated him for the nomination.

The Radical Republican victory in November was accompanied by popular approval of a new state convention and the election of delegates thereto for the purpose of considering amending the 1820 Missouri Constitution so as to abolish slavery immediately, limit the elective franchise to loyal men, and promote the public good. Drake, one of twenty candidates for the ten seats awarded St. Louis, won easily. Other

Radicals were elected to almost three-fourths of the sixty-six seats.

It soon became clear after the delegates assembled on January 6, 1865, in the Mercantile Library in St. Louis that most of them looked to Drake for leadership. Long before the convention met, he planned for the delegates to draft a new constitution, though many people inside and outside the convention hall did not believe either the General Assembly or the people intended that. His perseverance, strategic maneuvers, and skill as a debater, however, carried the day, though Radical distrust of the General Assembly no doubt helped him. The work was finished and the proposed new constitution adopted on April 8. On June 6, 1865, the document was ratified by the voters, each of whom had to take the loyalty test oath.

The new constitution was called the "Drake Constitution," a "Draconian Code," and by more than a few "Drake's Abomination." It was indeed Drake's Constitution, not that all provisions were products of his mind, but had it not been for him the convention would very likely have passed ordinances freeing the slaves, which it did on January 11, prescribed a loyalty test oath for voters and officeholders, vacated certain offices, and then adjourned sine die. His input during the convention proceedings was greater than that of any other delegate, and, moreover, during the ratification process Drake took upon himself defense of the convention's handiwork and outlined the strategy adopted by the Radicals, thus subjecting himself to a torrent of abuse and ridicule by opponents.

The term *Draconian Code* linked Drake's name with the Athenian lawgiver as opponents of the new constitution attacked the loyalty oath. Drake, who probably wrote the entire section, said he copied it from the Maryland Constitution, which included the denial under oath of a long list of acts in order for a person to escape disqualification. The General Assembly would repeal the oath, but not until 1871. Actually, Radicals who had suffered at the hands of guerrillas wished to punish disloyalists further, including the confiscation of their property. Drake sternly opposed confiscation other than property held in slaves, unless the accused was found guilty of treason. The oath did catch in its net some loyal Union men and persons not involved in political affairs. Drake unsuccessfully opposed the oath of the clergy; later, the application of the oath to them was declared unconstitutional by the United States Supreme Court.

The convention did not produce an "abominable constitution." Thanks in great measure to Drake it improved the 1820 constitution in a number of ways, namely, the evils inherent in special legislation and the granting of special charters were curtailed; it sought to guard against hasty and ill-considered legislative action; the state was forbidden to grant money or credit to private persons or corporations; it laid the basis for the establishment of a sound public school policy for all between the ages of five and twenty-one, though it permitted separate schools for blacks; and it made approval by the people an integral part of the process for amending the constitution. Indeed, after passions stirred by the war had subsided and the loyalty test oath had been repealed, no great popular demand existed for the new Constitutional Convention that nonetheless met in 1874.

Drake stumped the state in 1866 to help the Radical Republicans get control of the General Assembly. Many of them, especially those in rural Missouri, looked to him as the oracle of Radicalism. Hence, a grateful party elected him to the United States Senate in 1867. The following year he campaigned hard for the Radical Republican gubernatorial candidate, **Joseph McClurg,** and in behalf of "pure undefiled Radicalism." He made a strong plea for the enfranchisement of blacks, a position opposite to that which he had taken at the Constitutional Convention. The proposition was soundly defeated, but the election of candidates marked the high point of the Radical movement in Missouri.

Time soon showed that Drake could not maintain an important role in Missouri politics from his position in Washington. As soon as issues other than those growing directly out of the war became important, as business and social contacts between erstwhile Rebels and Union men weakened the barriers of hatred and suspicion, Drake's leadership was weighed and found wanting. The rebuilding of courthouses, schools, and churches, as well as the construction of roads and railroads, seemed more important than fidelity to a party that appeared anything but progressive and a leader who insisted on preaching "a dogma of eternal hate."

The first major test of Drake's leadership came early in 1869 when **Carl Schurz,** editor of the *Westliche Post* in St. Louis, became a candidate for the United States Senate. Drake, whose candidate was Benjamin F. Loan of St. Joseph, correctly saw the Schurz candidacy as a scheme to reduce his influence and divide the Radical Republicans. Consequently, he went to Jefferson City to lead in person the fight against Schurz. There he made the mistake of engaging the wily German in debate at the Radical Republican caucus. Much to the delight of the audience, Schurz goaded Drake into losing his temper and launching an attack on ethnic Germans, who made up fully one-third of the Radical legislators. Drake, suffering from a humiliating blow to his prestige, left Jefferson City before the balloting resulted in a Schurz victory, which marked the beginning of the end of Drake's hectic political career. In the following November the Radical Republican Party went down to ignominious defeat, never again to take part in a political campaign.

Soon after it became clear that Drake had no political future in Missouri, President **Ulysses S. Grant** appointed him chief justice of the court of claims, a position he held until he retired in 1885. Drake died on April 1, 1892. His remains were cremated and the ashes interred at Bellefontaine Cemetery in St. Louis.

DAVID D. MARCH

Drake, Charles D. Autobiography. Manuscripts. State Historical Society of Missouri, Columbia.

March, David D. "Charles D. Drake and the Constitutional Convention of 1865." *Missouri Historical Review* 47 (January 1953): 110–23.

———. "Charles D. Drake of St. Louis." *Missouri Historical Society Bulletin* (April 1953): 291–310.

———. "The Missouri Radicals and the Re-Election of Lincoln." *Mid-America* 34 (July 1952): 172–87.

Parrish, William E. "Reconstruction Politics in Missouri, 1865–1870." In *Radicalism, Racism, and Party Realignment,* ed. Richard O. Curry, 1–36. Baltimore: Johns Hopkins University Press, 1969.

———. *Turbulent Partnership: Missouri and the Union, 1861–1865.* Columbia: University of Missouri Press, 1963.

DREER, HERMAN (1889–1981)

Herman Dreer, a respected black St. Louis educator and scholar, was born on September 12, 1889, in Washington, D.C. Following his graduation from high school, Dreer continued his education at Bowdoin College in Brunswick, Maine. Ultimately, he earned his master's degree in Latin theology from the Virginia Theological Seminary in Lynchburg, Virginia, where he was also employed as an instructor. In 1912 he married Mary Thomas, one of his students. In 1955 he received a Ph.D. in sociology from the University of Chicago.

In 1914 Dreer and his family settled in St. Louis where he instructed black students in a variety of subjects, including history, English, Greek, and sociology, at Sumner High School. Troubled that St. Louis blacks were denied an opportunity to continue their education, Dreer became a key figure in the establishment of Douglas University in 1935 and Stowe Teachers College in 1940. He also fought for the integration of Washington University during the 1940s. In addition, Dreer assisted the Shelley family in their legal struggle against restrictive housing covenants in 1947 (the landmark civil rights case *Shelley v. Kraemer*) by conducting legal and historical research and offering financial support. After retiring from Sumner High School, he continued teaching at Stowe Teachers College and Harris-Stowe College.

As a scholar Dreer, who was appalled at the lack of attention accorded African American history, dedicated his career to broadening Americans' understanding of race relations and black culture. His Ph.D. dissertation, "Negro Leadership in St. Louis: A Study in Race Relations," continues to provide a valuable window into the city's black community. Dreer also edited *American Literature by Negro Authors* in 1950, as well as writing two works of fiction, *The Immediate Jewel of His Soul* in 1919 and *The Tie That Binds* in 1958. He was a weekly columnist for the *St. Louis Argus* between 1967 and 1975, focusing upon African American history. Finally, Dreer, a deeply religious individual, was the minister of the King's Way Baptist Church from 1950 to 1970. He died on August 7, 1981.

CHRISTOPHER K. HAYS

Dreer, Herman. "Negro Leadership in St. Louis: A Study in Race Relations." Ph.D. diss., University of Chicago, 1955.

———. Papers. 1933–1976. Western Historical Manuscripts Collection, St. Louis.

DREW, CAROLINE (1893–1980)

Caroline Drew, the director of the equitation program at Columbia's Christian College for thirty-five years, was born March 6, 1893, at Calleo, Missouri, to Julian Freeman and Jessie Maud Hurt Reed. Her father trained workhorses, and as a teenager Caroline began assisting him. She also exhibited horses, and despite the lack of formal riding lessons she won more than one hundred horsemanship classes.

On December 23, 1913, Caroline Reed married Claud H. Drew, a professional horseman; they had two children, James Howard and Shirley, who later directed the equitation program at Stephens College in Columbia. The Drews made their home on a farm near Fayette, and both worked together training and showing horses. One of the most famous horses they trained, Stonewall King, was a national champion that won every class a five-gaited stallion could enter. Caroline Drew exhibited him in several ladies' classes.

In 1927 Drew became director of horsemanship at Christian College, now Columbia College. There she managed a large budget, along with the horses and equipment; recruited and supervised teachers and other staff; trained students in the riding program and guarded their safety; and organized horse shows sponsored by the college. Her work brought national recognition, and she enjoyed a special student-teacher relationship with the Christian College women, who called her "Mom Drew." The college curriculum included shows, sales, and other horse-related events. In the class work Drew stressed that even though her students worked with horses, they could remain ladies. She and her students traveled around the country, attending shows and meeting riders and trainers. She had strict rules for their travels, but her students gave few problems.

Claud Drew assisted his wife at the college, supplying horses and managing the college farm. After his death in the 1940s, Caroline continued to live and work with her son, James Howard, until his death in 1978.

Despite her busy schedule at Christian College, Drew found time for other activities. In 1947 and 1948 she chaired the Boone County Horse Show and served as steward in 1957. She was the superintendent of the Missouri State Fair Horse Show in Sedalia from 1957 through 1960, the first woman to hold that position.

Drew retired from Christian College in 1962, but remained active working with horses and horse shows. She was a member of the American Saddle Bred Pleasure Horse Association, a director of the Missouri Horse Shows Association, and a registered judge for the American Horse Shows Association.

After suffering from a broken hip, Caroline Drew died on February 25, 1980, at the Lenoir Convalescent Center in Columbia, Missouri. She was buried at Memorial Park Cemetery in Columbia.

MARY K. DAINS

Columbia Daily Tribune, February 26, 1980.
Columbia Missourian, February 27, 1980.
Dains, Mary K., ed. *Show Me Missouri Women: Selected Biographies.* Kirksville, Mo.: Thomas Jefferson University Press, 1989.
Harrison, Jack. "Famous Horses and Horsemen." *National Horseman* (April 1980).

DUBOURG, LOUIS WILLIAM (1766–1833)

William DuBourg was a formidable force for Catholicism and for education in the early republican period of American history. A soldier of the faith in a faithless age, DuBourg believed and practiced the proverb that, if trained properly, the young will in their maturity return to the honest teachings of their parents. Before and after Missouri was separated from the Louisiana Territory, Father DuBourg touched many hearts and established several institutions that would continue to influence the territory for many years after it matured into statehood.

Late in his life, which spanned the turbulent period of 1766–1833, DuBourg was named bishop of Montauban and archbishop of Besançon in France, but his most productive years were in America. Born on February 16, 1766, in Santo Domingo of a mercantile family originally from the Bordeaux area, he was educated by the Sulpicians in Paris, a clerical order committed to the education of priests. The influence of this order, and especially of its longtime leader, Jacques-Andree Emery, profoundly shaped DuBourg's life and ministry.

Throughout a career characterized by both success and failure, DuBourg's passion was education, especially of seminarians. Few individuals could lay claim to establishing more educational centers. St. Mary's of Baltimore, Mount St. Mary's, Georgetown University, St. Louis University, and St. Mary's of the Barrens were academies either directly founded by DuBourg or considerably enhanced by his efforts. Other schools in New Orleans and in France profited as well from his dedicated labors. DuBourg also affected the development of American Catholicism by his lasting influence on such critical religious leaders as Mother Elizabeth Seton, Mother **Rose Philippine Duchesne,** Bishop **Joseph Rosati,** and Bishop Benedict Flaget.

In 1792 DuBourg fled the persecutions of the French Revolution. Journeying to Spain, he learned the Spanish language before sailing for America in 1794. In Baltimore he experienced the good luck that often advanced his career by being befriended by the influential Bishop John Carroll. Tutoring French and Spanish exiles allowed the immigrant to master English, and his ability and enthusiasm brought him an invitation to join the Company of Saint-Sulpice. In his new tongue, the gifted cleric stirred faithful congregations with his brilliant preaching and inspired students with memorable lessons.

By 1796 Carroll had named DuBourg president of Georgetown College. Soon the curriculum was revised and expanded, the student body grew, and the energetic president had even established a new women's academy for the Poor Clares. Rising anti-French sentiment in the United States probably led to DuBourg's departure from Georgetown in 1798, but that did not prevent his transforming Baltimore's St. Mary's seminary into St. Mary's College for foreign Catholics. As in many ventures in his life, however, DuBourg's single-minded determination to reach his goal alienated others. In trying to create the best school in America, he provoked opposition from his old colleagues at Georgetown, especially when St. Mary's was opened to American students. Still, between 1799 and 1812, the year DuBourg left the institution, St. Mary's flourished and in 1806 received authority from the state of Maryland to confer degrees.

In 1806 DuBourg also met Elizabeth Seton. The conjunction of these two formidable forces was to have profound consequences. Together they organized the Sisters of Charity of St. Joseph's at Emmitsburg, Maryland. DuBourg's characteristic impetuosity generated storms at Emmitsburg, but he did launch one of the Church's finest enterprises, and in the years to follow Mother Seton was to become renowned for her piety and her inspiration of countless American Catholics.

The United States went to war with Great Britain in 1812, and Father DuBourg, at the age of forty-six, went to Louisiana as apostolic administrator of New Orleans. This was an especially interesting period of DuBourg's ministry. Initially, his mission was to serve as the overall clerical authority of the diocese. The vice of New Orleans, however, coupled with the insubordination of the popular Spanish Capuchin, Father Antonio de Sedella, the pliable pastor of New Orleans's lukewarm Catholics, determined DuBourg to request a new bishopric for Louisiana. A triumphal visit to France and Rome secured this prize for DuBourg and many clerical recruits for Louisiana, but not control in New Orleans. Despite a symbolic role in Jackson's victory over the British in January 1815, followed by his appointment as bishop of Louisiana and the Two Floridas, DuBourg found he could not safely reside in New Orleans.

To avoid an outright schism, DuBourg left his diocesan seat in 1817 and removed to St. Louis in Upper Louisiana. Although in his fifties, DuBourg came to St. Louis brimming with energy and projects. By now a man of considerable influence in Europe, and despite his difficulties in New Orleans, the bishop entertained no doubts that the Church could achieve great things in the trans-Mississippi territory.

Dedication aside, the overland journey from Annapolis to St. Louis brought home to DuBourg the untamed nature of the land he was entering. When his coach overturned on a rugged road, he almost suffered a fractured skull. In January 1818, however, he arrived safely in St. Louis and found a city commanding many advantages that, unlike New Orleans, extended a warm welcome to the anxious prelate. For the next five years, DuBourg would repay the inhabitants' devotion with unstinting service.

The devotion of the St. Louis Catholic community, mostly French, but some Irish too, did not mean that there was a proclivity to support the Church financially. DuBourg spent much of his time trying to raise funds for church construction and to provide priests for the outlying parishes. He soon had a modest cathedral under way, yet his passion for education of seminarians could not be set aside. By the spring of 1818 he had already established St. Mary's of the Barrens near Perryville. Equally important was the arrival in August of Philippine Duchesne and her Religious of the Sacred Heart. Their mission was to educate Catholic girls on the frontier, still another of the projects DuBourg had helped set in motion while in Europe. Shortly, they were installed in St. Charles and began a long and fruitful intellectual mission.

The bishop tackled these projects with his usual vigor and disregard for financial and political problems. Naturally, he often found himself embroiled in controversy because his commitment to the faith outdistanced the means to fulfill the commitment. It did not deter him. Instead, he cultivated the influential families of the area, such as the Prattes and the Chouteaus, brought priests from Europe, visited his far-flung parishes, fought off dangerous illnesses, conferred with Osage chiefs, tried to obtain federal funds for Indian education, and introduced the Jesuit Order to Missouri in 1823. Among others, DuBourg imported and inspired the indefatigable Father **Pierre Jean De Smet,** the most celebrated Catholic missionary of the American West. These same Jesuits would eventually institute St. Louis University.

The last year DuBourg was in St. Louis was 1823. The episcopacy of Louisiana had expanded, and he felt the need to return to New Orleans to administer his see. Although he was in St. Louis but five years, and though he left the Missouri Church in considerable debt, his ministry, particularly his work in Catholic education, left a permanent imprint. DuBourg's return to New Orleans lasted only until 1826; then he returned to his native France, believing his career to be at an end. Instead, he was to gain new offices and launch still more projects.

DuBourg's homecoming in France was successful but less dramatic than his earlier achievements. He died at Besançon, the seat of his archbishopric, on December 12, 1833. Archbishop DuBourg's contributions overshadow his faults, but he was no saint. He was often a poor judge of character, he antagonized respectable colleagues with his cavalier attitude toward finances, and he was not above self-advertisement. Always, he seems to have left unresolved crises in his wake. A more cautious man, however, would have been valued more but achieved less.

C. DAVID RICE

Kunkel, F. W. "Life and Times of the Most Rev. William DuBourg, S.S." Parts 1 and 2. *Voice* 28 (March 1951): 14, 30; (June 1951): 8–9, 31–32.

Melville, Annabelle M. *Louis William DuBourg, Bishop of Louisiana and the Floridas, Bishop of Montauban, and Archbishop of Besançon, 1766–1833.* Chicago: Loyola University Press, 1986.

The New Catholic Encyclopedia. S.v. "DuBourg, Louis William Valentine."

DUCHESNE, ROSE PHILIPPINE (1769–1852)

Rose Philippine Duchesne, a French pioneer missionary on the American frontier, was born on August 29, 1769, in Grenoble, France. She was the eldest of five children. Her mother, Rose-Euphrosine Périer, came from an enormously wealthy family that had made its fortune in commerce and banking. Her father, Pierre-François Duchesne, was a prominent lawyer, civic leader, and politician.

At age twelve Duchesne's parents enrolled her as a boarding student in Sainte-Marie d'en Haut, a cloistered Visitation monastery on an Alpine mountain overlooking the Duchesne mansion. There she conceived her lifelong desire to work among Native Americans and cultivated an already notable tendency toward self-sacrifice and physical austerity. Her resolve to become a nun caused her parents to withdraw her from the school in 1783. Despite their disapproval Duchesne continued her penitential practices, refused to marry, and returned to Sainte-Marie d'en Haut in September 1788 to become a novice. The outbreak of the French Revolution delayed her religious vows, however, and in 1792, when monastic houses were outlawed, she was forced to leave Sainte-Marie.

Duchesne grasped little of the Revolution's meaning within French society. Her wealthy relatives, deeply committed to the Revolution when it served their own political and financial interests, turned reactionary as soon as it began to extend rights to a broader cross section of the French populace. Like many aristocratic Catholic women, Duchesne was shocked at the enforced closure of convents, the exile of priests, and the eventual prohibition of public Catholic worship, drawing no connection between these actions and the hierarchial Church's aristocratic lineage, vast lands, wealth, and privileges. Unaware of the social and institutional structures that perpetuated inequities, she was nonetheless, in contrast to most members of her class, profoundly moved by the suffering of others and willing to dedicate her life and fortune to alleviate it.

Duchesne proved her extraordinary determination, creativity, and courage repeatedly in the years following her expulsion from the monastery. Thwarted in her attempts to be a nun, she experimented with a variety of religious lifestyles and engaged in numerous charitable activities, often in defiance of Revolutionary-government strictures. She attempted a self-styled religious life at her family's country home, but that proved too irritating to her family and too sedentary for her energetic temperament. In 1793 she began charitable works in Grenoble, caring principally for priests imprisoned or in hiding, in addition to attending the poor, the sick, and the dying. She organized the "Ladies of Mercy," a group forcibly disbanded for almost a year during the Reign of Terror for their aid to priests who had refused to submit to legislation regulating the clergy. Finding her niche in a society that proscribed virtually all religious orders proved impossible. She fulfilled

some family duties, caring for her dying mother in the mid-1790s and, later, living briefly with a quirky and self-indulgent grandmother who threw her frank granddaughter out.

In another interlude punctuating her charitable work in Grenoble, Duchesne joined some former Visitation nuns who had regrouped in the convent of Saint-Marcellin. The women, however, found her austere interpretation of religious life too harsh. She returned once more to Grenoble, this time to offer religious instruction to poor boys. Her charitable work during these years was both conservative, given its focus on aiding priests and ministering spiritually to the poor and the sick, and revolutionary because the caring respect she showed the poor defied the then culturally dominant view that poverty, sin, and vice were inextricably bound.

In 1801, with antireligious sentiment easing, Duchesne used her wealth to lease the monastery of Sainte-Marie d'en Haut. The enthusiasm of the women who joined her, including some former Visitation sisters and their superior, quickly vanished: they found her ideals regarding religious life too demanding. By August 1802 all but three had moved out. Despite gossip regarding her uncompromising character, Duchesne's foundation prospered. In 1804 she met Father Joseph Varin and his charismatic friend Madeleine-Sophie Barat, the young leader of a fledgling group of women religious who would eventually take the name of the Society of the Sacred Heart of Jesus. Devotion to the Sacred Heart in Barat's nineteenth-century religious idiom referred to the cultivation of the sentiments symbolized by the heart: love, generosity, compassion, and forgiveness. At thirty-five Duchesne ended her association with the Visitation order and placed herself under the tutelage of Barat.

The new order opened schools for young girls, one of the few works available to nuns. Narrow religious and social conventions of the time imposed cloister upon them and considered women naturally suited to religious education. Their work both reflected and challenged assumptions dominant within nineteenth-century society. Class bias is evident, for example, in both the order's organization and its educational ideals. Women from "respectable" or aristocratic backgrounds were designated "choir religious" who handled the teaching responsibilities and all governance. Those from humbler backgrounds were "coadjutrix sisters" in charge of the domestic chores and service work for the convent and school. Similarly, wealthy girls received a superb boarding-school education, while poor girls attended a separate day school that provided minimal academic training and emphasized manual labor.

These unsurprising social discrepancies were accompanied by striking innovations. The boarders were taught subjects formerly reserved for boys: the nuns rejected the notion that girls were inherently less capable. That poor girls were even considered educable, that they were treated with the "tenderest love" and dignity, challenged the prevailing sentiment. In both schools the nuns emphasized religion above all, aiming to reshape the religious fabric of French society through the future influence their students would have as the moral educators of their families. Duchesne remained at Sainte-Marie from 1805 to 1815, variously directing the boarding school, teaching, and overseeing the material necessities of the school and convent. Her excessive workload suited her penchant for severe self-denial and corporal austerity.

In 1815 Duchesne went to Paris for a meeting of the rapidly growing order and there remained as Barat's secretary. She began to labor in earnest to expand the order's mission to the New World, with work among Native Americans. In 1818 Duchesne, now forty-eight, and four other religious embarked on the rough 110-day journey to St. Louis, a frontier trading post of about forty-five hundred. The bishop of Louisiana, **Louis William DuBourg,** had assured Duchesne that they would work among the Indians but reneged on this promise, compelling them instead to start schools for English- and French-speaking children.

DuBourg sent the religious to St. Charles, Missouri, a small village about twenty miles northwest of St. Louis that he predicted would be an international crossroads; Duchesne deemed it "a tomb" where their work would surely fail. The nuns opened a boarding school for wealthy St. Louis girls, DuBourg's preferred project; a modest day school; and, reflecting Duchesne's preference, the first free school west of the Mississippi. Although no abolitionist, Duchesne opposed DuBourg by admitting mestizo children into school.

In another departure from convention, Duchesne tried, to no avail, to form a type of religious order for women of color. The schools foundered financially, and in 1819 the nuns moved to Florissant, another small town near St. Louis forced upon them by DuBourg. Financial difficulties beset these schools, too. They would have closed but for Duchesne's protests on behalf of the flourishing free school.

In 1825, encouraged by the Jesuits, Duchesne opened a boarding school for Native American girls. The school failed when the U.S. government pressured the Native Americans to move west. A more promising foundation was made in the wealthier town of St. Louis in 1827. The nuns' work included care of orphans and a Sunday school for mulatto girls in addition to the schools for white settlers. Typical of all Duchesne's endeavors, the free school flourished while the paying schools languished. Her difficulties were compounded by her poor mastery of English

and her decided lack of interest in cultivating the friendship of wealthy St. Louisans.

By contrast, convents and schools founded by the order at Opelousas in lower Louisiana (1821) and St. Michael's near New Orleans (1825) under the direction of Eugénie Audé, one of Duchesne's companions, proved spectacular successes of refined French education, as did the short-lived foundation at La Fourche near St. Michael's under another religious. A struggle pitting these flourishing southern foundations against the poorer Missouri foundations was aggravated by Audé's attempts to circumvent Duchesne's authority as titular head of all the U.S. foundations.

Other religious wrote letters to Barat complaining of Duchesne's lack of administrative savvy, her inattention to the outward appearance of the order's properties, her disinterest in cultivating ties with the wealthy, and her tendency to accumulate debts even as she continued to give money to the needy. Barat recognized Duchesne's failings, but chose to keep her as superior over all the foundations, deeming her unswerving commitment to the poor, a quality lacking in some of the other religious, essential to the order's mission.

In 1832 the foundation at St. Charles was re-opened, in part due to Duchesne's predilection for serving poorer populations. Barat, citing Duchesne's age and increasing difficulty managing the growing order, finally relieved her as superior of all the U.S. foundations. Until 1840 Duchesne served as superior first of the St. Louis convent and then the languishing Florissant foundation, which she defended against repeated attempts to close it. Her transition into old age was beset by trials, including scrupulosity, intense anxiety, a sense of isolation, and severe doubts about her self-worth. In 1840 her lifelong wish to become a simple member of a community was finally granted.

Now seventy-one, Duchesne reinitiated her pleas to live and work among the Native Americans. Despite Duchesne's failing health, Barat felt she could no longer refuse her old friend's request. In 1841 Duchesne and three other religious moved to Sugar Creek in present-day Kansas where they lived among the Potawatomi, a group that had lost most of its land in the preceding fifty years to the U.S. government. Although too frail to do much work, Duchesne earned the intense admiration of the Potawatomi, who called her "Quah-kah-ka-num-ad," meaning "woman who prays always." She felt rejuvenated: she even wrote to friends of founding new missions in the Rockies. A crushing trial came, however, within a year: her companions considered her health too precarious, and she was forced to leave.

Duchesne lived ten more years in St. Charles, Missouri, suffering often from loneliness and a sense of uselessness. She continued to write letters, to send donations to priests working among Native Americans, to help in the free school, and to speak vociferously on behalf of the order's poorer foundations and against the external show of the more prosperous foundations. Her extreme self-abnegation and low self-esteem stood in stark contrast to the opinions of those around her who were awed by her unyielding allegiance to the least fortunate. The Jesuit **Pierre Jean De Smet,** noted for his work among Native Americans, wrote to her shortly before her death thanking her for her charity to him and to the Native people.

Duchesne died in St. Charles, Missouri, on November 18, 1852. She was beatified by the Roman Catholic Church on May 12, 1940, and canonized on July 3, 1988. Her remains lie in a simple, austere chapel in St. Charles, Missouri. Once planned as a magnificent shrine, it was then redesigned to reflect better her own commitments to the poor.

CATHERINE M. MOONEY

Baunard, Louis. *Life of Mother Duchesne.* Trans. Lady Georgianna Fullerton. Roehampton, England: n.p., 1879.

Callan, Louise. *Philippine Duchesne: Frontier Missionary of the Sacred Heart, 1769–1852.* Westminster, Md.: Newman Press, 1957.

Mooney, Catherine M. *Philippine Duchesne: A Woman with the Poor.* New York: Paulist Press, 1990.

DUDEN, GOTTFRIED (1789–1856)

In 1860 Missouri's foreign-born German population totaled 88,487, ranking the state sixth in the number of transplanted Germans in the United States. Promotional literature, which prompted foreigners to settle in Missouri and other midwestern states, contributed significantly to this German influx. Gottfried Duden's *Report of a Journey to the Western States of North America and a Stay of Several Years along the Missouri (during the Years 1824, '25, '26, and 1827),* first printed in 1829, proved one of the most influential titles in emigration literature.

Duden was born in Remscheid, in Duchy of Berg, on May 19, 1789. His parents were members of the Remscheid professional class. Their professional and financial positions allowed Duden to pursue an education that groomed him for government service. He attended the Universities of Düsseldorf, Heidelberg, and Göttingen, earning a degree in law from the latter institution in 1810.

In 1811 Duden was appointed as an attorney in the Prussian civil service. He then served as an auditor for Düsseldorf courts until 1813 when he obtained a lieutenancy in the Second Bergian Infantry and took part in the Napoleonic Wars. In 1814 he returned to the civil service.

Since his youth Duden had been worried about the dismal political, social, and economic conditions that created Germany's discontented and disillusioned masses. The disastrous effects of the Napoleonic Wars and the Napoleonic codes, Prussian rule, and increased population made Duden acutely aware of the lessening economic opportunities for the poverty-stricken people of his homeland. Reeling from the postwar depression and crop failures in 1816–1817, Germans faced higher unemployment, overcrowded housing, and increased crime.

Duden was convinced that the governments of the German states and their reactionary policies would not solve the problems confronting the people. In 1816 he began to assess the relationship between the political German states and the individual. He published his views in 1822 under the title *Concerning the Significant Differences of the States and the Ambition of Human Nature.* Duden believed that emigration to America would solve his countrymen's problems. The available land in the United States and its democratic form of government fostered his opinion, and he decided to travel to America to find out if his conclusions were true.

Duden resigned from the civil service in 1823. With Ludwig Eversmann, he left Europe and sailed to the United States. During the voyage he wrote letters about the transatlantic experience that would emulate the format he chose for writing the remainder of his *Report.*

Disembarking at Baltimore the two Germans traveled overland to St. Louis. Duden looked at land in both Illinois and Missouri as possible sites for German emigrants. He decided upon the interior of Missouri. On February 20, 1825, he wrote that he had settled about fifty miles above the mouth of the Missouri River, near Lake Creek in present-day Warren County. He had paid for some 270 acres of land; Eversmann had purchased 180 acres nearby.

Duden penned romantic descriptions of the Missouri land. He believed that the life of a Missouri farmer would be ideal for emigrating Germans. He carefully described the labor involved in clearing, fencing, cultivating, and harvesting the land. He thought these tasks to be less arduous than in his homeland. Since Duden hired what he needed done, exemplifying the gentleman farmer, he did not experience the grueling work required of the yeoman farmer.

Duden thought that between $775 and $990 in American money would be needed for a family of five to travel to the United States, buy eighty acres of land, purchase some farm animals, construct a log cabin, and obtain essential home furnishings. He suggested that emigrants bring tools and other implements from their homeland. Traveling in groups and establishing farming communities would be the least costly approach to emigration.

Once in the United States, and in particular in Missouri, the transplanted Germans would find an absence of thievery (common in their homeland) and a much safer place to live. The emigrant, Duden idealistically recounted, would find no poverty.

In the appendix to his *Report,* Duden provided a more workmanlike but still positive description of American institutions. Stability, he stated, personified American democracy. The country's abundance satisfied the physical, emotional, and ethical needs of the people. Rural surroundings produced a pleasant social environment, and because the vast majority of the citizens were farmers, agrarians would always provide a consensus for the structure of national policies and legislation.

In all Duden wrote thirty-six letters, an appendix about the "nature" of the United States, and postscripts for emigrating farmers. First published in 1829, revised in 1834, and especially published by the Swiss Emigration Society in 1832 and 1835, Duden's *Report* became a major piece of promotional literature. Most historians of German emigration point to this work as being the most important treatise to entice thousands of emigrants to leave the Rhineland for Missouri.

Duden's promotional piece, however, was not always well received. His optimistic view failed to account for many of his countrymen who were unable to live the life of gentlemen farmers. Disgusted by the hard work required to farm, or thwarted by the fickleness of nature, some German emigrants became angry at Duden and his *Report.* The volume became known to some as "Duden's Eden." His Warren County farm was labeled as Duden's "castle in the sky." Words like *shallow* and *exaggerated* appeared in critiques. Many believed that the emigrants' misfortunes were due to Duden's unrealistic appraisal.

Unconcerned at first by the negative attacks, Duden by 1832 tried to answer and refute his critics. He defended his beliefs and his writings in his revised edition of the *Report,* as well as in his two-volume work *Europe and Germany as Viewed from North America* (1833–1835) and his *De Tocqueville's Work* (1837). Embittered, the disillusioned Duden returned to Remscheid by the late 1830s and concentrated on studying jurisprudence. In the early 1840s he stopped advocating emigration. Duden died in Remscheid on October 29, 1856.

JAMES W. GOODRICH

Bek, William, ed. and trans. "Gottfried Duden's 'Report,' 1824–1827." Parts 1–7. *Missouri Historical Review* 12 (October 1917): 1–21; (January 1918): 81–89; (April 1918): 163–79; (July 1918): 258–70; 13 (October 1918): 44–56; (January 1919): 157–81; (April 1919): 251–81.

Finckh, Alice H., ed. and trans. "Gottfried Duden Views Missouri." Parts 1 and 2. *Missouri Historical Review* 43 (July 1949): 334–43; 44 (October 1949): 21–30.

Goodrich, James W. "Gottfried Duden: A Nineteenth-Century Missouri Promoter." *Missouri Historical Review* 75 (January 1981): 131–46.

———, ed. *Report on a Journey to the Western States of North America and a Stay of Several Years along the Missouri (during the Years 1824, '25, '26, and 1827),* by Gottfried Duden. Columbia: State Historical Society of Missouri and University of Missouri Press, 1980.

DUGAN, ELIZABETH JANE (ROSA PEARLE) (1848?–1911)

Elizabeth Jane Dugan, better known by her pseudonym "Rosa Pearle," was the founder, editor, and principal writer of *Rosa Pearle's Paper,* a Saturday-evening society weekly published in Sedalia, Missouri, from 1894 until 1911. Questions remain as to whether she was born in Warren County, Ohio, in 1848 or Bridgewater, Pennsylvania, in May 1849. Dugan came to Sedalia with her parents Talbot and Elizabeth McLean Dugan in the early 1870s. She did not marry, and her writing suggests she believed marriage robbed a woman of her spirit. She lived with her brother Emmett, and helped raise Alice, Oscar, and Frank, the children of their brother Alonzo, who had died in 1864. Dugan died on January 10, 1911, of kidney disease.

At a time when "scribbling women" were frequently viewed with patronizing contempt, Dugan was recognized by the *Kansas City Journal* as "one of Missouri's brightest newspaper women." Between 1890 and 1900, fewer than twenty-five Missouri women edited newspapers; most of these women had assisted husbands or fathers and assumed management of their papers upon their deaths. Only a few founded the papers they edited.

Dugan began her writing career as a poet; her works were printed in the *New York Post,* the *New York Sentinel,* and the *New York World.* She continued to write poetry throughout her life. She began her journalistic career with the *Sedalia Bazoo,* edited by J. West Goodwin. Serving as a news writer, society editor, and general editor, she wrote news and editorial essays for the *Bazoo.* Her outspoken commentary matched the flamboyant Goodwin's trenchant social criticism; it is likely that she was influenced by Goodwin's view of the journalist as social reformer. At her death Goodwin eulogized Dugan by saying that "her aim was to make Sedalia a better city, socially and morally."

Dugan wrote briefly for a short-lived Sedalia paper called the *Earth,* which was billed as "the original family, literary and society paper." After working for the *Chicago Tribune* for a time, she was offered a job on the *New York Tribune,* which she refused because of poor health.

In 1894 Dugan and her niece Alice, or "Allie," began *Rosa Pearle's Paper,* a society paper described by one Sedalia matron as "very pretty." The eight-page Saturday-evening weekly, devoted to "society, literature, drama, and music," was praised by the *Sedalia Morning Gazette,* the *Sedalia Weekly Bazoo,* and the *Sedalia Sunday Democrat.* The *Kansas City Journal* referred to *Rosa Pearle's Paper* as "handsomely printed and in every way creditable to the publisher."

The front page of *Rosa Pearle's Paper* noted the affairs of "Sedalia Society." Dugan described musicales, teas, weddings, and receptions with detailed accounts of ladies' gowns, table decorations, flower arrangements, and entertainment. She named eligible young ladies and provided a list of bachelors. Regular columns included "Fashion Notes" and "Music Notes," as well as editorial comments from "Your Aunt Fuller" (another of Dugan's pseudonyms). Theater was particularly popular in Sedalia at that time, and she regularly reviewed the performances.

Dugan moved beyond news of tea parties and church sociables, however, to confront issues of the day. She lamented the lack of courtesy of men who smoked, but she also questioned the propriety of women's smoking. She castigated men who would not work to support their families. Critical of inequities, she denounced the low wages paid most working women. While she deplored the tactics of the Knights of Labor, she recognized the lack of fairness in the treatment of the working class. She raised questions about woman suffrage and about temperance. In doing so, Dugan continued the tradition of journalist as social critic, and promoted the rights of women and the poor. Her work addressed issues of interest to the so-called new woman of the early twentieth century, presaging a time when women would be active in all aspects of journalism.

RHONDA CHALFANT

Dains, Mary K., ed. *Show Me Missouri Women: Selected Biographies.* Kirksville, Mo.: Thomas Jefferson University Press, 1989.
Kansas City Star, September 11, 1910.
McGruder, Mark A. *History of Pettis County, Missouri.* Topeka, Kans.: Historical Publishing, 1919.
Rosa Pearle's Paper, May 19, 1894–June 16, 1901.
Sedalia Democrat-Sentinel, January 10, 1911.
Vaughn, Alma. "Pioneer Women of the Missouri Press." *Missouri Historical Review* 64 (April 1970): 289–305.

DUKE, BASIL WILSON (1838–1916)

In early 1861 the fate of St. Louis and, with it, probably Missouri itself rested in the hands of a few individuals. The Union narrowly won the brief but intense struggle for the city because the Union's twin "Missouri Saviors," **Nathaniel Lyon** and **Frank Blair,** harnessed the superior material and manpower assets available to Unionists in St. Louis just in time to foil the plans of Missouri's pro-Confederate governor **Claiborne Fox Jackson** and his militia general **Daniel Marsh Frost** to seize the U.S. arsenal in St. Louis. Until Lyon snatched victory for the Union by his capture of Frost and his militia units at Camp Jackson in St. Louis on May 10, 1861, the struggle for St. Louis nearly resulted in a victory for the pro-Confederate forces, not because of any abilities of the inept Jackson or the overly cautious Frost but because of the talents and spirits of the younger pro-Confederate St. Louisans such as militia captain and "Minuteman" Basil Duke.

Basil Wilson Duke was born on May 28, 1838, in Scott County, Kentucky, the only child of United States Navy captain Nathaniel Wilson and Mary Pickett Currie Duke. After attending private academies, Basil Duke enrolled at Centre College in Danville, Kentucky, and then Georgetown College in Georgetown, Kentucky. He next studied law at Transylvania University in Lexington, Kentucky, from which he graduated in 1858. That same year Duke moved to St. Louis to practice law.

Law was not the primary focus of attention for the young Duke but rather politics. In the presidential election of 1860, Duke, like Missouri governor Claiborne Fox Jackson, supported moderate Stephen A. Douglas, though both Jackson and Duke were much closer philosophically to southern Democrat candidate John C. Breckinridge. Stephen Douglas's young brother-in-law (and later Union army officer), James Madison Cutts Jr., would briefly join Duke's St. Louis law practice after graduating from Harvard Law School in 1860.

Even before the election returns reflecting the detested Lincoln's election as president were known, Duke helped to raise five companies of secessionist-minded St. Louisans known as "Minutemen" and was elected captain of one of the companies. In early 1861 these units were incorporated into the Missouri Militia. Duke correctly sensed that the best chance of seizing St. Louis and its valuable federal arsenal was to provoke an incident that would compel the St. Louis police force and the state militia, both of which were heavily dominated by Southern sympathizers, to intervene on the side of the Minutemen. On March 3, 1861, the eve of the meeting of the Missouri State Convention in St. Louis to decide the issue of secession, the Minutemen raised a crude secessionist flag over the courthouse and another in front of their headquarters at the nearby Berthold mansion. They were soon confronted with an angry pro-Unionist mob. Sadly, for Duke's carefully calculated plans, the Unionists dispersed before attacking. Duke lamented that "the opportunity we had hoped and striven for did not occur; and we could not afford to attack the arsenal without having been ourselves assailed."

Shortly after the flag-raising incident, Duke was appointed to the St. Louis Board of Police Commissioners pursuant to hastily enacted legislation intended to place ultimate control of the St. Louis police in the hands of the pro-Confederate governor, Jackson. Duke and his three other police commissioners, however, were thwarted by United States army captain (soon to be general) Nathaniel Lyon in their attempts to block the arming of pro-Union (and largely German American) "Home Guard" units. Duke attributed this new failure to the same "fatal policy of irresolution and delay" by the governor and the more conservative St. Louis secessionists that had doomed the earlier attempts to seize the arsenal.

Governor Jackson next sent Duke and fellow minuteman captain Colton Greene to the then Confederate capital in Montgomery, Alabama, on a secret mission to obtain a cannon from Confederate president Jefferson Davis to bombard the arsenal into submission. The two captains succeeded in obtaining some cannons, muskets, and ammunition that they brought to St. Louis by steamboat in boxes marked "Tamaroa Marble." The arms and munitions arrived in St. Louis on May 9, 1861, but were captured the next day by Union forces at Camp Jackson. Although Duke would warn militia general Daniel Frost of information that he had received as police commissioner that Lyon intended to march on Camp Jackson the next day, Frost chose to ignore the warnings of his young captain.

Disgusted by numerous lost opportunities in Missouri, Duke soon made his way back to his native Kentucky where, on June 18, 1861, he married the sister of soon-to-be-famous Confederate cavalryman John Hunt Morgan. Duke enlisted in Morgan's rifle company and was elected first lieutenant. After Morgan's company became part of the Second Kentucky Cavalry, Duke was appointed its lieutenant colonel and later colonel. Duke, like Morgan, distinguished himself in several cavalry engagements in the fighting in Kentucky and Tennessee.

Wounded in April 1862 at the Battle of Shiloh, Duke was captured in the summer of 1863 after the failure of Morgan's spectacular raid into Indiana and Ohio. Eventually exchanged, Duke was appointed a brigadier general in the fall of 1864, and, for the balance of the war, commanded a cavalry brigade that operated in eastern Kentucky and western Virginia. Duke surrendered to Union forces in Washington, Georgia, on May 10, 1865, the fourth anniversary of the Camp Jackson affair.

Duke only briefly visited St. Louis in 1865 and then moved to Louisville, Kentucky, where he resumed the practice of law. In 1869 he was elected to the Kentucky House of Representatives. From 1875 to 1880 he served as the commonwealth attorney for the Fifth Judicial Circuit and for the next twenty years as counsel for the Louisville and Nashville Railroads.

Apart from his distinguished professional career as a soldier and an attorney, Basil Duke proved a gifted historian. He was editor at various times of the *Southern Bivouac,* the *Mid-Continent Magazine,* and the *Southern Magazine.* His *Morgan's Cavalry* (1876) and *Reminiscences* (1911) are superb accounts of his Civil War experiences. Duke died on September 16, 1916, in New York City and was buried in Lexington, Kentucky.

MARSHALL D. HIER

Dictionary of American Biography. Vol. 5. S.v. "Duke, Basil Wilson."

Duke, Basil W. *Morgan's Cavalry.* 1867. Reprint, New York: Neal Publishing, 1906.

———. *Reminiscences of General Basil W. Duke, C.S.A.* Garden City, N.Y.: Doubleday, Page, 1911.

Henning, James. "Basil W. Duke, 1839–1916." *Filson Club Quarterly* 14 (April 1940): 59–64.

Snead, Thomas L. *The Fight for Missouri.* New York: Charles Scribner's Sons, 1888.

Winter, William C. *The Civil War in St. Louis: A Guided Tour.* St. Louis: Missouri Historical Society Press, 1994.

DUNKLIN, DANIEL (1790–1844)

Missouri's fifth governor, Daniel Dunklin, was born on January 14, 1790, in the Greenville district of South Carolina, where he attended public school. Upon the death of his father, Daniel's older brother moved the family to Kentucky in 1806. With dreams of becoming a lawyer, young Daniel read Blackstone while working in an unsuccessful farming operation. In 1810 Dunklin moved with his mother to a small farm near Potosi in Missouri Territory.

During the War of 1812 Dunklin joined the volunteer rangers for campaigns in Missouri and Illinois Territories. After the war he served as Washington County sheriff for four years. He was admitted to the bar but seldom practiced law.

In 1815 Dunklin married his childhood sweetheart, and they operated a small tavern in Potosi, which became a common meeting place. Dunklin gained a reputation as a wise man, well informed on public issues, and took a leading role in founding the Potosi Academy. As his interest in politics grew, the voters of Washington County elected Dunklin to the state legislature where he distinguished himself with his knowledge of parliamentary law during the 1822–1823 term.

Following his stint in the General Assembly, Dunklin devoted his primary attention to his business operation, especially his mining interests. But the lure of politics drew him into an active role in the party of Andrew Jackson. Under a Jackson Party label, he was elected lieutenant governor in 1828. To consolidate "true" Jackson men on a single ticket, the Democratic Party held a state convention in late 1831 that named Dunklin as the party's candidate for governor. Dunklin won the election, and the Democratic Party carried the state in 1832.

An ardent states' rights advocate, Dunklin feared national encroachment upon state sovereignty. Like other Jacksonian Democrats, he opposed the Bank of the United States, protective tariffs, and nationally sponsored internal improvements, and favored selling public lands to actual settlers at cheap prices.

Dunklin did not, however, support South Carolina in its effort to nullify the Tariff of 1832. In a confused attempt to explain his position, he stated that he could support nullification in a case of clear usurpation of power by the federal government, but he could not support the right of a state to nullify a federal law it deemed only a misuse of national power.

Reflecting his party's general position, Dunklin did not view the state government as an agency for promoting economic development. As governor, Dunklin, who is sometimes called the father of Missouri's public school system, worked to increase the state's role in public education. Speaking to the General Assembly he referred to education as "the best safeguard to our republican institutions," and he asked for and received authority to appoint a commission to make recommendations for a statewide public school system. He even suggested that tax revenues might be used to fund schools. Although the commission's extensive recommendations were not accepted, the General Assembly did enact a much improved school code in 1835.

Governor Dunklin did call for state action to deal with some social problems. He recommended that the General Assembly establish a state institution for the deaf and dumb, and he also proposed to reduce the cruel and revengeful aspects of criminal punishment. The General Assembly did not respond to these recommendations.

The arrival of the Mormons in Missouri confronted Dunklin with some problems. When **Joseph Smith Jr.** petitioned the governor to protect his followers against hostile Missourians who had violently expelled church members from their land in Jackson County, Dunklin expressed his sympathy for their plight but suggested that legal redress was available through the judicial system. Such was not the case, and more serious problems involving the Mormons developed after Dunklin left office.

Three months before his term as governor expired, Dunklin resigned his office to accept President Jackson's appointment as surveyor general of Missouri, Illinois, and Arkansas, but he held the post only a short time.

After 1838 Dunklin devoted most of his time to his business and farming interests. In 1840 he moved to a large farm he purchased near Herculaneum. After being caught in a severe storm, he developed pneumonia and died on July 25, 1844. Daniel Dunklin was buried with full Masonic honors in a field near his home in Jefferson County.

PERRY McCANDLESS

Fitzgerald, Fred. "Daniel Dunklin." *Missouri Historical Review* 21 (April 1927): 395–403.

McCandless, Perry. *A History of Missouri: Volume II, 1820 to 1860.* Columbia: University of Missouri Press, 1972.

Stephens, F. F. "Daniel Dunklin." In *The Messages and Proclamations of the Governors of the State of Missouri,* ed. Buel Leopard and Floyd C. Shoemaker. Vol. 1. Columbia: State Historical Society of Missouri, 1922.

EADS, JAMES BUCHANAN
(1820–1887)

Born in Lawrenceburg, Indiana, on May 23, 1820, James Buchanan Eads became an engineer of great renown, remarkable for the variety of his accomplishments. This controversial "nonengineer" became a vice president of the American Society of Civil Engineers and a leader in creating civil works in the latter half of the nineteenth century. In recent years historians have found a renewed interest in this unusual and intensely dedicated man.

At the age of twenty-two Eads persuaded two St. Louis boatbuilders, Calvin Case and William Nelson, to enter into partnership with him in the salvage business. The new company constructed a diving bell designed by Eads, a variety of mechanical equipment, and a twin-hulled salvage boat known as a "submarine." Eads was his own diver much of the time. Salvage operations provided him with many opportunities to stress metal and machinery to its limits. His "testing laboratory" was a full-scale enterprise designed to raise and salvage cargo and hulls from the scouring currents, whirlpools, and water boils of the sediment-laden Mississippi.

A specialist in the salvage of boats sunk in the Mississippi River, Eads also built some of the first "ironclad" steamboats used in battling the Confederacy during the Civil War. These jobs gave him experience in working underwater and with iron and steel, talents that proved invaluable in building the nation's first major steel bridge across the Mississippi at St. Louis. Many of Eads's accomplishments were thought impossible by his well-educated contemporaries. Although he was not formally educated, Eads was very knowledgeable, and he read everything available on machinery, materials, and hydraulics.

Two of Eads's Mississippi River works are still functioning today, serving people and commerce. The first project is Eads Bridge at St. Louis, which has carried rail and vehicular traffic since 1874. The beauty and grace of its design continues to delight artists and photographers.

The second project is the jetties at South Pass, one hundred miles beyond New Orleans, at the end of the Mississippi delta. Following a great controversy with the Army Corps of Engineers, the jetties were constructed so that the flow of the river keeps the channel from filling with silt. Ships continue to travel daily through this deep channel.

Early in the Civil War, Eads became convinced that ironclad gunboats would be essential to the Union war effort in controlling the rivers. Although his initial efforts were rebuffed, the government finally advertised for bids. Taking the contract at a low price, Eads organized a workforce of four thousand men and delivered the first boat in four months. In the course of building more boats, he invented a steam-actuated rotating gun turret.

Eads foresaw that railroads would be the main transportation system for the latter half of the nineteenth century, just as canals had been for the first half. To make St. Louis the major East-West rail center, a bridge was needed across the 1500-foot fast-flowing Mississippi. There was no precedent for such a bridge.

Business and political disputes loomed as the bridge concept became imminent. The Wiggins Ferry Company stood to lose its monopoly on moving freight and people across the river. Powerful railroad financiers were less than enthusiastic. Chicagoans believed that such a bridge would cut into their city's increasing importance as a rail center. Political opponents mustered enough force for a congressional bill in 1865 that would limit the authorization to a bridge that "spans no less than five hundred feet and minimum clearance of fifty feet." They were confident such requirements would doom the project.

Eads announced his unprecedented plans: ribbed arches with spans of 502, 520, and 502 feet made from a recently invented but as yet unproved alloy called steel were to be the main superstructure. Foundations were to be based on bedrock to ensure stability during spring floods and winter ice jams. On the basis of those preliminary plans, Eads was elected chief engineer of the St. Louis and Illinois Bridge Company.

"Impossible and impractical" was the opinion of many citizens and the engineering establishment. Eads, aware of his own limitations, had the mathematical theory and calculations checked by a nationally prominent mathematician, William Chauvenet at Washington University.

Less than fourteen months after erection of the superstructure began, the strength of the bridge was dramatically demonstrated to the public on July 2, 1874. Fourteen locomotives with their tenders full of coal and water were coupled together, seven on each track. They moved back and forth across the bridge, stopping at the middle of each span. A tremendous citywide celebration was held on dedication day, July 4, with a five-hour parade followed by a fireworks display.

The railroad companies chose to boycott Eads Bridge and continue transferring freight across the Mississippi by ferryboat, which ultimately forced Eads's company into bankruptcy only four years after the bridge opened to traffic. The $10 million structure was bought at auction for only $2 million by English bondholders, who formed a new company. In 1881 Jay Gould's Missouri Pacific became the sole lessee of the bridge and assumed all its debts; the lease was transferred in 1889 to the Terminal Railroad Association of St. Louis.

Eads died on March 8, 1887, at the age of sixty-six in Nassau, in the Bahama Islands.

DAVID P. BILLINGTON AND
J. WAYMAN WILLIAMS

Belcher, Wyatt Winton. *The Economic Rivalry between St. Louis and Chicago, 1850–1880.* New York: Columbia University Press, 1947.
Kouwenhoven, John A. "Eads Bridge: The Celebration." In *The Eads Bridge.* Princeton: Art Museum, Princeton University, 1974.
Scott, Quinta, and Howard S. Miller. *The Eads Bridge.* St. Louis: Missouri Historical Society Press, 1999.
Williams, J. Wayman. "James B. Eads and His St. Louis Bridge." *Civil Engineering* 47:10 (October 1977): 102–6.
Woodward, Calvin. *A History of the St. Louis Bridge.* St. Louis, 1881.

EAGELS, JEANNE (1894–1929)

Jeanne Eagels was born in Boston, Massachusetts, on June 26, 1894, and moved to Kansas City with her parents when she was two years old. She rose to international fame on the stage and in films, and in her short life she probably met with more than the normal amount of success, failure, happiness, and sorrow. She died in a doctor's office at Park Avenue Hospital, in New York City, at the age of thirty-five from an overdose of sleeping pills.

The family name was spelled "Eagles," but Jeanne changed it when she became an actress. She had less than two years of formal education. She attended the Georgia Brown Dramatic School in Kansas City, and with her earnings as a stock clerk at Emery, Bird, and Thayer Department Store she bought gallery seats for theatrical productions in Kansas City.

Eagels appeared in road shows and played small parts in a stock company whose leading lady, Eva Lang, she idolized. Eagels became a chorus girl in shows in the Midwest presented by the Dubinsky brothers. She was a featured dancer, an ingenue, and a leading lady for the Dubinskys. She had a love affair with the oldest brother, Maurice, and may have married him, but the historical record is unclear.

Eagels left Kansas City for New York while still a teenager and won a small part in *Mind-the-Paint-Girl,* and later worked her way into the chorus of Ziegfeld's Follies. She secured dramatic parts on Broadway and first attracted attention when she appeared in 1911 as Miss Ranault in *Jumping Jupiter.* She toured with Julian Eltinge in *The Crinoline Girl,* played Kate Merryweather in *The Great Pursuit,* and toured with George Arliss as Lady Clarissa in *Disraeli.* She also had leading roles in *The Professor's Love Story* and *In the Night Watch.* But her best-known role was as Sadie Thompson in *Rain,* which opened in 1923 and ran for two years in New York. The play was based on Somerset Maugham's short story "Sadie Thompson."

In 1925 Eagels married Edward Harris "Ted" Coy and divorced him three years later. She once said that Coy was the only man she had ever loved. He was married when they first met in 1924 in Pittsburgh where she was appearing in *Rain.* He obtained a divorce shortly afterward, and his wife retained custody of their five children. A former captain of the Yale football team and an All-American Team selectee, Coy inherited three hundred thousand dollars upon the death of his mother and was a banker.

Eagels always regarded Kansas City as her home and expressed a strong desire to return. One of her dearest wishes was to let Kansas City see her in her great success, *Rain.* She announced during the two-year run in New York:

I'm going home. . . . There is no place like the one in which I was reared. . . . I want to go back to Kansas City. . . . I suppose that's foolish. . . . Nobody will remember the girl who used to ride the streetcar from the Georgia Brown Dramatic School to her home out northeast with her make-up on to impress people with the fact that she was an actress. Kansas City wasn't even aware of my existence. But I'd like to stand on its front doorstep some fine morning and say to the old town: "Well, see who's here! Little Jeanne Eagels has come back home to show you what she can do!" I hope they'd like me.

They certainly did, and *Rain* was a sellout for two weeks at the Kansas City's Shubert Theater.

Eagels made several silent films, including *Man, Woman and Sin,* with John Gilbert. However, silent films failed to catch her elusive charm, and she appeared somewhat hard and unglamorous. In 1928 her health, which was never robust, began to deteriorate.

The frequent drenchings with water that she sustained while performing in *Rain* may have weakened her, and she suffered constantly from chills and fevers.

After her death on October 3, 1929, Eagels's body was brought to Kansas City for burial. A large crowd attended the services that were held at St. Vincent's Catholic Church. Steady rain fell as the funeral cortege drove slowly toward Cavalry Cemetery. Frederic March, Eagels's leading man in *Jealousy,* described her as "one of the most gifted actresses of our generation."

ARTHUR F. MCCLURE AND VIVIAN RICHARDSON

Kansas City Star, July 22, 1930–May 25, 1981.
New York Times, October 4, 1929.

EASTER, LUKE (1915–1979)

When Luke Easter joined the Cleveland Indians in 1949, he became the first African American from St. Louis to play major league baseball outside the Negro National League. Born on August 4, 1915, in Jonestown, Mississippi, Easter and his family moved to St. Louis in 1924 two years after his mother, Maude, died. Easter's father, James, a Tuskegee Institute graduate, found work shoveling sand in a glass factory in St. Louis. Young Luke dropped out of school in the ninth grade, finding work shining shoes, blocking hats, and pressing suits at a dry cleaners.

Easter developed his batting eye by swinging a broomstick at hard-thrown bottle caps. Soon after, he played outfield and first base for the Titanium Giants, a semiprofessional team of African Americans from the National Lead Company. His weekly pay of twenty dollars was increased by an additional ten to twenty dollars for participating in weekend games.

Easter loved baseball and softball as both a player and a spectator. Just before joining the U.S. Army in 1941, Easter and two friends drove to Memphis to watch a tournament. Future major leaguer Sam Jethroe fell asleep at the wheel on the return trip, causing an accident. Easter was hospitalized with two broken ankles, an injury that plagued him for the rest of his playing career.

In 1945 two Negro National League teams denied Easter a chance to try out: the Kansas City Monarchs and the Chicago American Giants. Both said that Easter, at six-foot-four and 225 pounds, was too big and awkward to play baseball.

Easter joined a traveling team briefly when Abe Saperstein recruited him for the Cincinnati Crescents in 1946. In 1948 he jumped to the Homestead Grays in the Negro National League for an additional hundred dollars' pay. The Grays were interested in acquiring Easter as a home run hitter to take over the slugging job left vacant by the untimely death of catcher Josh Gibson.

Like many African American players in the period, Easter played baseball in Latin America in the off-season. The integrated Latin American leagues provided black ballplayers an additional outlet unavailable to them in the United States. When Bill Veeck purchased the Cleveland Indians and enlisted Saperstein as a scout, **Satchel Paige** and Luke Easter were among the first players he recruited. Easter played briefly with San Diego in the Pacific Coast League before being called up to Cleveland.

Knee problems and subsequent surgery meant Easter's career started off badly. In 1950 he developed into a crowd-pleasing, long-ball hitter. He played first base for the Indians through 1954 and is credited with hitting the longest home run in Cleveland Municipal Stadium—a 477-foot shot into the right-center-field upper deck on June 30, 1950.

In 1949 Dodgers catcher Roy Campanella overheard some teammates saying that no one had ever hit a baseball into the center-field bleachers in the Polo Grounds—the home of the Giants. Campanella, who had played with Easter in the Negro National League, corrected them: Easter hit a 500-foot home run into the center-field bleachers in a game between the Homestead Grays and the New York Cubans.

Easter played with various minor league teams between 1955 and 1963 in Charleston, Buffalo, and Rochester. Carrying a lifetime batting average of .274, he hit ninety-three home runs during his brief major league career. During his time with the Indians, many hailed him as "a hitter with the talent of Babe Ruth."

After his playing career, Easter returned to Cleveland, where he became a steward for the Air Craft Workers Alliance at TRW. In 1979 two men accosted him in the parking lot outside a Cleveland Trust Company branch. Easter was carrying about forty thousand dollars from payroll checks he had cashed. The two men shot him in the chest on March 29, 1979, and he was pronounced dead on arrival at the hospital.

JEFFREY E. SMITH

Cattau, Daniel J. "Luke Easter: The First Black Major Leaguer from St. Louis." *St. Louis Post-Dispatch Magazine* (April 5, 1992): 8–13.
———. "So, Maybe There Really Is Such a Thing as 'The Natural.'" *Smithsonian* 22 (July 1991): 117–27.
Moffi, Larry, and Jonathan Kronstadt. *Crossing the Line: Black Major Leaguers, 1947–1959.* Jefferson, N.C.: McFarland, 1994.
New York Times, March 30, 1979.
Young, A. S. "Doc." In *Great Negro Baseball Stars, and How They Made the Major Leagues.* New York: A. S. Barnes, 1953.

EASTERLY, THOMAS MARTIN (1809–1882)

Thomas Martin Easterly, who settled in St. Louis in 1848, operated one of Missouri's first permanent galleries. He worked in the daguerreotype process, the first practical and widely used technique for making pictures with a camera. Introduced in France in 1839, the technique produced one-of-a-kind pictures on silvered copper plates.

In the early 1860s when the collodion process popularized tintype and duplicate paper prints made from glass negatives, Easterly ignored the developments, firmly believing that the highly detailed daguerreotype pictures could never be surpassed for beauty or permanence. His 1865 broadside urged the public to "save your old daguerreotypes for you will never see their like again." By the 1870s he was America's only photographer working exclusively in the outmoded daguerreotype process.

Easterly was born in Guilford, Vermont, on October 3, 1809, the second of five children born to Tunis and Philomela Richardson Easterly. His father, a native of New York, was a farmer and part-time shoemaker. Little is known about Easterly's early life. During the 1830s and early 1840s, he worked as an itinerant calligrapher and teacher of penmanship, traveling in Vermont, New Hampshire, and New York. By 1844 he was practicing the art of photography.

Easterly's earliest known daguerreotypes, made more than a decade before outdoor photography was popular or profitable, picture architectural landmarks and scenic sites in Vermont. Taken in the mid-1840s, his picturesque views of the Winooski and Connecticut Rivers are the only known examples of daguerreotypes that self-consciously emulate the romantic landscape paintings of the Hudson River school artists. He is also the only American daguerreotypist who routinely identified his work with engraved signatures and descriptive captions. While millions of daguerreotypes survive, the majority bear no clues to identify their makers.

Easterly first traveled west in the fall of 1845. Working for brief periods in various towns along the Mississippi, he and a partner, Frederick Webb, advertised their services as representatives of the Daguerreotype Art Union. In October of that year, Iowa newspapers reported that Easterly and Webb had secured a "splendid likeness" of the murderers of Col. George Davenport shortly before their execution in Rock Island, Illinois. After months of travel on the Mississippi and Missouri Rivers, the partners spent the winter of 1846–1847 in Liberty, Missouri. Their partnership was apparently dissolved by early spring, when Easterly traveled alone to St. Louis, where he made portraits of residents and visiting celebrities in a temporary gallery on Glasgow Row. His now famous portrait of Chief Keokuk, the leader of the Mississippi Sac and Fox, was taken in St. Louis in March 1847. Easterly's daguerreotype of a streak of lightening, one of the first successful attempts to record an "instantaneous" photographic image, was also made during this six-month stay in St. Louis. The *Iowa Sentinel* described this novel effort as an "Astonishing Achievement in Art." Before Easterly left for the East in August 1847, the *St. Louis Reveille* declared him the "unrivaled daguerreotypist."

John Ostrander, the operator of St. Louis's first daguerreotype gallery, brought Easterly back to Missouri in early 1848. Preparing for an extended "tour of the south," Ostrander recruited Easterly to take over the operation of his portrait gallery during his absence. When Ostrander died during his travels, Easterly continued the practice. Many of his unique streetscapes recording midcentury urban life were taken from his gallery windows. In June 1850 he married Anna Miriam Bailey, a St. Louis schoolteacher.

During the heyday of the daguerreotype in the early 1850s, Easterly's artfully crafted portraits ensured him a steady clientele that ranged from boot makers to millionaires. He also attracted customers by advertising his "rich and rare collection" of "Distinguished Statesmen, Eminent Divines, Indian Chiefs, and Notorious Robbers and Murderers." Many of these portraits survive in the Missouri Historical Society's extensive Easterly Collection. **Sterling Price, William Greenleaf Eliot, Charles Keemle,** and Ethan Allen Hitchcock are among Easterly's many sitters who played prominent roles in the cultural or economic development of Missouri.

While many daguerreotypists promoted their talents as "likeness makers," Easterly took greater pride in his accomplishments outside the gallery. He demonstrated those talents—and his unusual ambitions—with "beautiful landscapes, perfect clouds," and his "collection of illustrative views" of St. Louis and its environs. George Rockwell, another St. Louis photographer, expressed amazement at seeing "thousands" of beautiful views in Easterly's gallery in the late 1850s. On the basis of this work, many scholars now regard Easterly as the first American photographer to fully recognize and explore the potential of on-site photography. His surviving inventory of more than 180 views represents the only large body of outdoor work to survive intact from a daguerreotype studio. In addition, his many scenes documenting the rapidly changing landscape of St. Louis during the 1850s provide our only photographic record of the process of urbanization in mid-nineteenth-century America. His scenes made outside the city include a view of the Missouri State Capitol, which was reproduced in 1852 as an engraving in the *Western Journal and Civilian*.

As the daguerreotype fell out of fashion, Easterly suffered the practical consequences of his steadfast loyalty to that process. His income and health declined from the late 1850s onward. Despite the diminishing market for pictures on silver, he maintained his gallery until 1865, when a fire that destroyed much of his work forced him to move his practice to a smaller location. City directories listed him as a "Daguerrean Artist" until 1880. He died in St. Louis on March 12, 1882. An announcement of his death in the *Practical Photographer* noted the difficulties that Easterly had endured in refusing to bend to popular taste or financial necessities: "Mr. Easterly, strange to say, never was a photographer, . . . but stuck to Daguerreotyping until the last. In fact, we may say that he was starved out of the business, for it left him in poor health and pocket." The long illness and partial paralysis that preceded Easterly's death may have been related to his years of exposure to mercury, a key ingredient in the daguerreotype process.

After Easterly's death, his wife sold the bulk of his personal collection to John Scholten, a St. Louis photographer. Scholten's family gave the plates to the Missouri Historical Society, where they remained essentially forgotten for nearly a century. The rediscovery of Easterly's work occurred in the 1980s, when scholars began to give more serious attention to the study of pre–Civil War photography.

DOLORES A. KILGO

Davidson, Carla. "The View from Fourth and Olive." *American Heritage* 13 (December 1971): 76–91.

Guidrey, Gail R. "Long, Fitzgibbon, Easterly, Outley: St. Louis Daguerreans." *St. Louis Literary Supplement* 1 (November–December 1977): 6–8.

Kilgo, Dolores A. *Likeness and Landscape: Thomas M. Easterly and the Art of the Daguerreotype.* St. Louis: Missouri Historical Society Press, 1994.

Van Ravenswaay, Charles. "Pioneer Photographers of St. Louis." *Missouri Historical Society Bulletin* 10 (October 1953): 49–71.

EASTON, RUFUS (1774–1835)

Born in Litchfield, Connecticut, on May 4, 1774, Rufus Easton grew up there and studied law from 1791 to 1793 under Ephraim Kirby, who conducted one of the famous law schools in the early Republic. Admitted to the bar in Rome, New York, Easton practiced there until leaving for the West.

In 1804 Easton moved to Vincennes, in Indiana Territory, and met other young men heading west, such as **Edward Hempstead** and **John Scott,** most of whom accompanied Gov. **William Henry Harrison**

to Missouri in late 1804 to establish the territorial government. Easton settled in St. Louis and lived the rest of his life in the vicinity. He married Abial Abby Smith, a New Yorker, by whom he had seven daughters and four sons.

Appointed prothonotary of the St. Louis district court in 1804, Easton also served short terms as U.S. attorney for the same district. In March 1805 he accepted a presidential appointment as a judge of the territorial superior court. By late 1805 the judges were embroiled in a dispute with Gov. **James Wilkinson** over the timing of a legislative meeting of the governor and judges to provide laws for the territory. During the political maneuvering Easton was charged with fraud but was later acquitted. However, the controversy was instrumental in President Jefferson's decision against reappointing him.

No longer a judge, Easton busied himself in his law practice and land-agency business, serving clients in both Missouri and Illinois Territories. At one point he became incensed about remarks made by James Donaldson of the Board of Land Commissioners. Charging into a meeting of the board, he caned Donaldson. The commissioners promptly charged Easton with assault and battery and sentenced him to two weeks in jail. The record is silent about whether or not he served the sentence, but he continued his work as postmaster of St. Louis, a position he accepted in 1805 while a judge and held for more than six years.

In November 1812 the residents of the territory went to the polls for the first time, electing a legislature and a nonvoting delegate to Congress. Easton ran against Edward Hempstead and lost. The next year Easton became a commissioner of the new Bank of St. Louis and solicited subscribers to the bank. In December 1818 he became a director of the bank, which failed the next summer.

The 1814 delegate election brought out four candidates, including Easton. His support came chiefly from southern districts and from new American residents. Successful in the voting, he went to Washington, D.C., and worked hard for his constituents.

The 1816 nonvoting-delegate campaign was furiously fought between Easton and John Scott. Easton represented the political faction that included **Joseph Charless,** William Russell, Judge **John B. C. Lucas,** and **David Barton.** The election resulted in victory for Scott by a margin of only fifteen votes. When Governor Clark certified Scott's election, Easton announced his intention to contest the election. Scott and Easton both went to Washington.

Easton petitioned the United States House of Representatives to unseat Scott, and the Committee on Elections collected information. Both men produced depositions and letters of support that the committee considered. Within four weeks the committee recommended that Easton should be seated. When the full House debated the matter, both Scott and Easton spoke on the floor, but the House declared the seat vacant on January 13, 1817, and called for a new election. The 1817 election campaign continued discussions of the previous year with renewed vigor. The largest number of voters in the territory's history returned John Scott to Congress with a large majority.

Easton continued to practice law, speculate in land, and serve the people. By 1818 he operated a land agency with Rufus Pettibone in St. Louis. Elected as state attorney general for the new state of Missouri in 1821, Easton served until 1826. He moved to St. Charles, where he died on July 5, 1835, leaving his family an estate of less than two thousand dollars.

JO TICE BLOOM

Easton, Rufus. Papers. Missouri Historical Society, St. Louis.

Foley, William E. *The Genesis of Missouri: From Wilderness Outpost to Statehood.* Columbia: University of Missouri Press, 1989.

Tice, Nancy Jo. "The Territorial Delegate, 1794–1820." Ph.D. diss., University of Wisconsin, 1967.

ECKEL, EDMOND JACQUES (1845–1934)

Born on June 22, 1845, in Strasbourg, France, Edmond Jacques Eckel demonstrated an early interest in architecture through mechanical drawings he created at age twelve and apprenticeships he served as an adolescent in his native city. At the age of fourteen, Eckel developed a general knowledge of construction through practical experience with his father's relative, a building contractor. His work with the city architect offered an introduction to the profession and helped prepare him for admission to the world's most famed school of architecture, the École des Beaux-Arts, in Paris.

At the École Eckel followed the usual academic progression, first joining a studio, or atelier, as an *aspirant* in 1863. During his years in the Atelier Paccard and later the Atelier Vaudoyer, Eckel practiced his skills in a fraternal setting where members exchanged ideas and offered assistance to one another. *Aspirants* were not admitted to the institution as students until they had passed the demanding entrance examinations—a feat Eckel accomplished at age twenty-one. Upon successful examination results, Eckel simultaneously progressed to the second class, as was customary at the École; advancement to the first class was determined by points received from judges at competitions. Because no graduation marked the culmination of the program at the time,

students simply left the institution when they desired. In 1868 Eckel, who had achieved respectable scores but never advanced to the first class, departed the École, as well as his homeland. Exposure to construction projects in Strasbourg, combined with his academic background and exercises at the École, provided Eckel with an exceptional understanding of architecture—one to be unrivaled in mid-America.

Considering that the only two schools of architecture in the United States were still in their infancy, Eckel's migration to the country was timely: formally educated architects were in short supply when postwar reconstruction, western expansion, and technological advancements provided tremendous building opportunities. With this awareness Eckel intended to establish himself in Kansas City, but an altered railroad itinerary instead brought him to St. Joseph on July 3, 1869, marking the start of a career and residency that spanned sixty-five years. As the second largest city in the state, St. Joseph was burgeoning with wealth derived from trade networks afforded by its ideal proximity to rail and river transportation; it was ripe for the proliferation of Gilded Age architecture in both public buildings and dwellings.

First employed as a draftsman with P. E. Meagher and the firm of Stigers and Boettner, Eckel soon forged a series of partnerships, punctuated by periods of independent practice in St. Joseph: Eckel and Meier (1873–1874); Stigers, Boettner, and Company (1875–1877); Boettner and Eckel (1878–1880); Eckel and Mann (1880–1885, 1887–1891, and 1903–1905); Eckel and Van Brunt (1892); Eckel and Boschen (1908–1910); and finally, Eckel and Aldrich (1910–1959), a firm sustained by Eckel's partner and son, George, until his death in 1959. Schooled in the traditions of the École, Eckel trained numerous draftsmen under his employ in an atmosphere much like the French ateliers. His professionalism enticed promising colleagues to St. Joseph where they became his partners and were influenced by his tutelage.

Due to the popularity of revival styles during the extended period in which Eckel worked, his portfolio of more than four hundred projects represents his mastery of a wide range of building types and architectural styles, a diversity and architectural significance supported by more than twenty-five Eckel-associated properties listed in the National Register of Historic Places. Some of his most exuberant work was created in high-Victorian styles during the late nineteenth century, including the storefronts of Wholesale Row, residences in the Hall Street and Museum Hill districts, and buildings in the Richardsonian Romanesque style that evolved when the enigmatic draftsman Harvey Ellis worked with Eckel and Mann from about 1888 to 1893. In contrast to these buildings, the St. Joseph Public Library (1900) and the city hall (1927) reveal classical influences Eckel internalized at the École and habitually applied to his student designs.

Eckel secured most of his work from local clients who were prominent figures among affluent social and business circles. He enhanced these contacts through his memberships in the Benton Club, the Chamber of Commerce, the Elks, the Odd Fellows, the Scottish Rite, and the St. Joseph Country Club. Yet, Eckel's commissions occasionally extended to other areas of the state, such as the city hall for St. Louis (1890–1904) and the designs he developed for patrons in California, Iowa, Kansas, Pennsylvania, Texas, and elsewhere. As a long-standing member of the Western Association of Architects, Eckel became a fellow of the American Institute of Architects when the two organizations merged in 1889.

Eckel's physical stamina matched his professional passion: rather than retire at age sixty-five, he organized a new partnership and remained active in the practice until his death on December 12, 1934, at the age of eighty-nine. Near the close of Eckel's career, architect John Albury Bryan recognized him as "the outstanding man in the history of the profession in the western section of the State." Historic streetscapes and skylines attest to Eckel's influence on the built environment of St. Joseph, a city he shaped perhaps more than any other architect.

TONI M. PRAWL

Bryan, John Albury. *Missouri's Contribution to American Architecture.* St. Louis: St. Louis Architectural Club, 1928.

"Contemporary Architects and Their Works: E. J. Eckel, F.A.I.A." *Western Architect* 17 (September 1911): 79–106.

Eaton, Leonard K. *Gateway Cities and Other Essays.* Ames: Iowa State University Press, 1989.

Eckel, Edmond J. Papers. 1860–1952. Western Historical Manuscripts Collection, Kansas City.

Mann, George R. *Selections from an Architect's Portfolio.* St. Louis: I. Haas, 1893.

Prawl, Toni M. "E. J. Eckel (1845–1934): A Beaux-Arts Architect at Practice in Missouri." Ph.D. diss., University of Missouri, 1994.

EDOM, CLIFTON C. (1907–1991)

Clifton Cedric Edom, called the father of photojournalism, founded the University of Missouri–Columbia photojournalism department in 1943, and served as the director until his retirement in 1972. He was born on February 12, 1907, in Baylis, Illinois, the son of Harry N. Edom, a railway-station agent, and Myrtle Hubbs Edom. He attended grade school in Baylis and Pittsfield, Illinois, and high school in Pittsfield, graduating in 1924.

After a year at Western Illinois State Teachers College (now Western Illinois University), Edom taught school in Pike County, Illinois. Concurrently, he attended Milo Bennett Linotype School in Ohio in the spring of 1925. He set type for the *Pike County Democrat* and the *Pike County Times* in Pittsfield. He then worked in the proof room of R. R. Donnelley and Sons Company in Chicago from 1927 to 1929. He married Vilia C. Patefield in Yorkville, Illinois, on June 30, 1928, and moved to Edgar, Wisconsin, in 1929 where he and his wife purchased the weekly *Edgar News.*

While running the newspaper Edom became interested in photography. In 1930 the Edoms moved to Wausau, Wisconsin, where for five years he worked on the daily *Record-Herald.* The next move brought them to Missouri. Edom served as a teacher and educational director of Tasope', the Aurora School of Photo-Engraving. In Aurora, Missouri, he edited the *Tasope 'News* and the *Pix,* monthly publications devoted to photography and photoengraving on zinc plates for weekly and small daily newspapers. Because of his experience in Aurora, Edom was hired in 1943 by University of Missouri dean **Frank Luther Mott** to replace Earl McPeak, who had left for military service in the navy. Making the zinc engravings for the *Missourian* was an important part of the job. Edom also taught McPeak's beginning photography class and the advanced class that provided the photographs used by the *Missourian.* He attended university classes while teaching, and received his bachelor of journalism degree in 1946.

During World War II, University of Missouri journalism students were mostly women, supplies were minimal, and old equipment was not replaced. Edom was not content with the style of photography then in vogue, and contacted, among others, Roy Stryker, who directed photographers for the Farm Security Administration. Edom asked Stryker how he could raise standards in his classes and make more worthwhile and honest photographs that would contribute more to publications. He was influenced by the work of the photographers who documented the harsh conditions of rural America during the depression, and wanted to move newspaper photography away from the posed, manipulated picture to one that was more truthful. He also wanted to make photographers equal to reporters in status.

Edom and Mott coined the word *photojournalism,* and in 1943 Edom started the Fifty Print Competition and Exhibition, which evolved into the internationally renowned Pictures of the Year Competition and Exhibition after a merger with the *Encyclopædia Britannica* photo competition in 1947. In 1944 Edom founded Kappa Alpha Mu, a national photography honorary fraternity.

In 1949 Edom created the annual Missouri Photo Workshop, in which a different Missouri town is documented during one week by a group of professional and student photojournalists. Workshop director Bill Kuykendall stated: "He helped establish a meeting place for professionals and students. . . . He had great instincts and worked to help photographers distinguish between the real and the superficial." Edom said about the workshop, "We believe that documentary photography is the background—the roots, if you please—of modern photojournalism. In an effort to echo and reecho the Roy Stryker concepts of picture communication, the Missouri Photo Workshop was begun. The serious in-depth approach to a picture story at a workshop adds to the spontaneity, the integrity, and the believability of the pictures. It is truth with a camera." The Missouri Photo Workshop has been active for more than four decades, and continues to influence aspiring photographers. By documenting small Missouri towns, a fragment of the history of the state has been recorded, and through the publication of the photographs that history is shared. Although Edom retired in 1972, he continued to direct the annual Pictures of the Year Competition and Exhibition until 1983 and the Photo Workshop until 1986.

Edom's many honors and awards include, in 1955, the Joseph Sprague Award from the National Press Photographers Association (NPPA) "for devoted service in advancing photojournalism as author, editor, and teacher. . . ." He was named professor emeritus in 1973 by the University of Missouri Board of Curators, and that same year was given an award for twenty-five years of service to the Photo Workshop. (The award was designed by former University of Missouri students and members of the *National Geographic* staff.) In 1974 he received the first Robin F. Garland Educators Award given by the NPPA (which also presented a special citation for thirty years of work on the annual picture contest in 1980). The University of Missouri Medal of Honor for Distinguished Service in Journalism was given to him in 1977. The Missouri government also honored him in 1977 with two separate Congratulatory Resolutions from the Missouri State Senate—one from the Columbia area, and one from the Forsyth area. In 1982 the Education in Photography Award from Photographic Administrators Inc. in New York City was awarded to Edom for his lifetime dedication to teaching. In 1984 he was the recipient of the Progress Award, the highest award given by the Photographic Society of America.

After retiring the Edoms moved to the Forsyth area, and Edom died on January 30, 1991, in Branson. In 1993 the Missouri Press Association in Columbia inducted both Edoms into their hall of fame. Vilia Edom was the national executive secretary of Kappa Alpha Mu and assistant manager of the Missouri Press Association, and she assisted with the workshops. A former student, Bill Epperidge, said, "She was a second teacher to us." In 1984 the University of Missouri approved a permanent scholarship, the Cliff and Vi Edom Scholarship. The Edoms' daughter, Verna Mae Edom Smith, coauthored in 1991 a publication with her parents that documents the Missouri Photo Workshops from 1949 to 1991.

CAROLYN K. COLLINGS

Edom, Clifton C. Papers. 1943–1978. University of Missouri–Columbia School of Journalism. University Archives, Columbia.

Edom, Clifton Cedric. *Missouri Sketch Book: A Collection of Words and Pictures of the Civil War.* Columbia, Mo.: Lucas Brothers, 1963.

———. *Photojournalism: Principles and Practices.* Dubuque, Iowa: W. C. Brown, 1976.

———. *Twice Told Tales and an Ozark Photo Album, with Emphasis on Taney County, Missouri.* Republic, Mo.: Western Print, 1983.

Edom, Clifton Cedric, Vilia C. Edom, and Verna Mae Edom Smith. *Small Town America: The Missouri Photo Workshops, 1949–1991.* Golden, Colo.: Fulcrum Publishing, 1993.

Kalish, Stanley E., and Clifton C. Edom. *Picture Editing.* New York: Rinehart, 1951.

EDWARDS, CLIFF "UKULELE IKE" (1895–1971)

Singer-actor Cliff "Ukulele Ike" Edwards was born in Hannibal, Missouri, on June 14, 1895, and is best remembered for his voice portrayal of "Jiminy Cricket" in Walt Disney's 1940 animated film *Pinocchio,* in which he sang the unforgettable "When You Wish upon a Star." To older generations he was known as "Ukulele Ike" and was possibly the best-known player of that stringed instrument.

Edwards started his show business career in St. Louis saloons, using his trick voice and talent on the ukulele to become a vaudeville headliner. In Chicago he teamed with pianist Bobby Carleton, who wrote the tune "Ja Da," which became one of the biggest hits of the 1920s and made Edwards a top figure on the vaudeville circuits.

Edwards's success led to work with comedian Joe Frisco, and a role in George Gershwin's Broadway musical *Lady Be Good,* with Fred Astaire. Edwards began his Hollywood career under contract with Metro-Goldwyn-Mayer, introducing the classic song "Singing in the Rain" in the *Hollywood Review of 1929.* In the 1920s and 1930s he made several recordings, of which four—"June Night," "Sleepy Time Gal," "I Cried for You," and "Toot, Toot, Tootsie Goodbye"—sold nearly 8 million copies. Edwards appeared in more than one hundred films and was credited with selling more than seventy-four million records during his lifetime. Late in his career he recorded an album titled *Ukulele Ike Sings Again* for Disneyland Records.

Walt Disney cast Edwards for the voice of Jiminy Cricket, Pinocchio's conscientious companion who was always just a whistle away. Edwards's experience as a radio singer with a smooth delivery and easygoing manner were perfect for the part. Over the years he continued to voice Jiminy, in the 1947 Disney feature film *Fun and Fancy Free* and for segments of *The Mickey Mouse Club* and other miscellaneous film and television assignments.

Universally acclaimed since its release in 1940, *Pinocchio* won Academy Awards for best original score and best song, "When You Wish upon a Star." The song not only set the film's theme but also provided a recurring melody and unifying element for the rest of the film. The musical number has since become a world-famous Disney theme. Edwards also sang "Give a Little Whistle," a song tailor-made for the crooning cricket that allowed him to strut while expounding on his duties as Pinocchio's conscience.

Edwards was twice married and divorced, first to Broadway singer Irene Wiley and later to actress Nancy Dover. Although the Disney studio continued his small salary for years after he left their employ, Edwards was almost destitute at the time of his death, and his burial was paid for by the Actors Fund. Both organizations quietly helped Edwards meet his hospital and other expenses in his later years. Edwards died on July 17, 1971, in a Hollywood convalescent home and left no next of kin. Residents of Hannibal, Missouri, offered to bury him in that community after they learned he died penniless. He was buried, however, in a special actors' plot in Valhalla Cemetery in North Hollywood. About thirty-five of his friends attended the funeral.

ARTHUR F. MCCLURE AND VIVIAN RICHARDSON

New York Times, July 23, 1971.
St. Louis Post-Dispatch, July 22, 1971.
Variety, July 28, 1971.

EDWARDS, JOHN CUMMINS (1806–1888)

Born on June 24, 1806, in Frankfort, Kentucky, John Cummins Edwards was raised near Murfreesboro, Tennessee, and educated at a local academy. He was admitted to the Tennessee bar but moved to Missouri in 1828 and immediately became involved in local politics. In 1830 Democratic governor **John Miller** appointed the twenty-four-year-old Edwards to the post of secretary of state, a position he held until 1835, and again briefly in 1837. For seventeen of

the next nineteen years Edwards remained active in Missouri politics.

In 1836 Edwards was elected to the General Assembly, where he became embroiled in the monetary-policy question. He associated himself with the **Thomas Hart Benton** "hard" camp, opposing privately held banks and small-denomination bills. Edwards's stand connected him to the powerful Central Clique, earning him a seat on the Missouri State Supreme Court from 1837 to 1839, and a nomination to Congress.

Edwards served in the United States House of Representatives from 1841 to 1843, but did not seek reelection. While in the House, he showed his western Jacksonian colors, favoring free land for the unemployed and opposing tariffs. While in Congress Edwards worked on two popular land issues: helping settlers in the Platte country clarify the registration of landownership, and helping block federal settlement of the border dispute between Missouri and Iowa.

Edwards's moderate and conciliatory views, along with the backing of the Central Clique, led to his nomination as the Democratic candidate for governor, and his narrow electoral victory over Democrat-turned-Whig Charles H. Allen. In his inaugural address Edwards outlined his view of government, stating, "The government has nothing to give except what it first takes from the people; and to take away to give back again would only be robbing with one hand and restoring with the other." Edwards was not opposed to governmental action, only to those actions that seemed to benefit a few at the expense of many.

During Edwards's tenure as governor, nineteen new counties were formed, telegraph communication was completed to St. Louis, the voters rejected the proposed new constitution of 1845, and Missouri's first railroad, the Hannibal and St. Joseph, was chartered. For his part Edwards instituted a new tax-collection system, which helped the state treasury go from a deficit to a surplus. He succeeded in passing a conservative but improved incorporation law. To give the common man a chance at higher education, he secured approval of a tax to establish a free normal school at the University of Missouri, though funding was never sufficient to see its fruition. Edwards succeeded in creating the state hospital at Fulton, and initiated a debate on prison reform. He began the process of resolving the Iowa border dispute by agreeing to arbitration by the United States Supreme Court. During the Mexican War he raised a volunteer regiment, commanded by **Alexander W. Doniphan** and **Sterling Price,** that subsequently played a conspicuous role in the war.

Edwards's administration was not without its troubles. The legislature refused to reimburse him for the refurbishing of the Governor's Mansion, citing excessive expenses. He was also criticized by the legislature for personally traveling to New Orleans to sell state bonds. Others attacked him for naming the inexperienced congressman Price as a commander of the Missouri regiment. Moreover, the peaceful Edwards was nearly drawn into a duel over the scolding of a boy who had hit him with a rock. Finally, a St. Louis grand jury publicly protested his "too free use of the pardoning power," granting freedom to more than fifty criminals, including three abolitionists who had attempted to lead Missouri slaves to freedom.

Edwards's frustration showed in his valedictory message. "The governorship is a despicable office for any man to be condemned to hold. Two of my predecessors have resigned before their terms were out, and a third committed suicide. I have been compelled to go armed to protect myself against assassins." Public life had taken its toll on Edwards. Shortly after leaving office, he caught "gold fever." In 1849 he outfitted a stock train and set out for California. He settled in Stockton, married, fathered eleven children, and became a merchant and rancher. He returned to politics only once, as the mayor of Stockton. He died on September 17, 1888.

KEITH D. SWANSON

Larkin, Lew. "No Coddling." *Missouri Historical Review* 45 (January 1951): 212–13.

McCandless, Perry. *A History of Missouri: Volume II, 1820 to 1860.* Columbia: University of Missouri Press, 1972.

Park, Eleanor G., and Kate S. Morrow. *Women of the Mansion, 1821–1836.* Jefferson City, Mo.: Midland Printing, 1936.

Primm, James Neal. *Economic Policy in the Development of a Western State, Missouri, 1820–1860.* Cambridge: Harvard University Press, 1954.

Shoemaker, Floyd Calvin. *Missouri and Missourians: Land of Contrasts and People of Achievements.* Vol. 1. Chicago: Lewis Publishing, 1943.

EDWARDS, JOHN NEWMAN (1839–1889)

John Newman Edwards was born in Warren County, Virginia, on January 4, 1839. He moved to Lexington, Missouri, in either 1854 or 1855. Soon after his arrival in Missouri, he began what would be his lifelong career writing for newspapers, working as a printer with the *Lexington Expositor.* A short time later, as both border strife and the Civil War came to the state, he became involved in the struggles that would be at the center of his colorful career as a soldier and journalist.

Early in the war Edwards joined the Confederate forces of **Joseph Orville Shelby.** Edwards fought in many battles and skirmishes, but his most important task was his ghostwriting of Shelby's military reports and in the process earning an unwarranted reputation for Shelby as a great writer. Very much the prose poet, Edwards took his cue from such writers as Victor Hugo and Sir Walter Scott. His sentences are elaborate, and his allusions are grand and excessive. Edwards's bushwhackers and soldiers are either warriors of the stature of Achilles and Hector, or they are needlessly compared to historical or contemporary rebels of note, but none, according to Edwards, made of sterner stuff than his own heroes.

Edwards's career can be grouped around his involvement with three men: Shelby, **William Clarke Quantrill,** and **Jesse James.** The involvement with Shelby is the basis for Edwards's devotion to the Confederate cause and two of his three books. The first book, *Shelby and His Men; or, The War in the West* (1867), reports the events of the war under Shelby. The book is unabashedly pro-Confederate— Union forces are always large and vicious, while Confederate forces are small and valiant—as historical accuracy is sacrificed in favor of romantic myth.

Edwards's second book, *Shelby's Expedition to Mexico: An Unwritten Leaf of the War* (1872), recounts the adventures of Shelby and the thousand or so men who, refusing to accept the Southern loss, fled to Mexico. Their trip was a failure, and their motives remain unclear to this day. Edwards's story does nothing to solve the mysteries, but it does provide pages of colorful prose and heroes of epic proportions.

In Edwards's third and final book, *Noted Guerrillas; or, The Warfare on the Border* (1875), the figure that emerges is the border warrior and bushwhacker Quantrill. In this account Quantrill takes on the heroic image of the avenger. His wrongs, according to Edwards, were meted out only under the most extreme provocation. It was indeed a time of great wrongs, and Edwards's stories recall the period with such vivid detail that he, as much as anyone else, is responsible for the legacy, for both good and ill, of Quantrill and his followers.

A more important contribution to American history and legend is Edwards's treatment of Jesse and **Frank James**. Without Edwards it is doubtful there would have been a legend of the James brothers. In 1868 Edwards and John C. Moore established the *Kansas City Times.* With his position at the newspaper and his writings that appeared elsewhere, Edwards launched a barrage of editorials, articles, and letters, many reputedly from Jesse James, but in all probability written by Edwards himself, geared toward nurturing the image of James as a good-hearted victim of a vindictive and unforgiving society.

Edwards led an active life as a soldier, journalist, and writer of books. His were "lost causes": first the war, then the doomed world of Missouri's outlaw period, and finally his long personal battle with the bottle. He died, surely in part because of alcoholism, on May 4, 1889, in Jefferson City, Missouri. The state seems to have mourned his death in an outburst of eulogy, and then he was largely forgotten, though it is difficult to imagine why, given his many accomplishments. A romantic figure, Edwards remains inextricably tied to the most often romanticized period of Missouri history.

LARRY OLPIN

Castel, Albert E. *William Clarke Quantrill: His Life and Times.* New York: Frederick Fell, 1962.

Connelley, William E. *Quantrill and the Border Wars.* Cedar Rapids: Torch Press, 1910.

Edwards, Jennie, ed. *John N. Edwards: His Life, Writing, and Tributes.* Kansas City: Jennie Edwards, 1889.

O'Flaherty, Daniel. *General Jo Shelby: Undefeated Rebel.* Chapel Hill: University of North Carolina Press, 1954.

Saults, Dan. "Missouri's Forgotten Quixote." *Focus Midwest* 1 (October 1962): 20–23.

Settle, William A., Jr. *Jesse James Was His Name.* Columbia: University of Missouri Press, 1966.

ELIOT, THOMAS STEARNS (1888–1965)

T. S. Eliot—a poet, playwright, literary theorist, and critic—is the only Nobel Prize winner to have been born in Missouri. Numerous words from Eliot are familiar even to those who have no idea of their authorship—the phrase "the waste land," for instance; the lines "This is the way the world ends / Not with a bang but a whimper"; the songs from *Cats,* the Andrew Lloyd Webber musical with lyrics from Eliot's *Old Possum's Book of Practical Cats.* Although he lived more than half his life in England, Eliot's affection for his native state and his appreciation of its influence on him were lifelong.

Thomas Stearns Eliot was born on September 26, 1888, in St. Louis. The Eliot family, noted in Burke's *Distinguished Families of America,* had already contributed much to the city's life. In 1834 **William Greenleaf Eliot,** the poet's grandfather, had moved from Boston to St. Louis to found the city's first Unitarian congregation; in 1857 he founded Smith Academy, a boys' preparatory school, and Mary Institute, a school for girls. He was chancellor of Washington University from 1872 until his death in 1887, the year before T. S. Eliot was born.

T. S. Eliot, called "Tom" by family and friends, was the seventh and last child of Henry Ware and Charlotte Champe Stearns Eliot, a native New Englander. Henry Ware Eliot was president of the Hydraulic Press Brick Company. Charlotte Eliot, a teacher and reformer, wrote of her father-in-law's life and nurtured a lifelong desire to write poetry. Besides his parents Eliot remembered as his "earliest personal influence" Annie Dunne, the Irish Catholic woman who was his nurse.

Eliot was schooled at Miss Lockwood's, a primary school "a little way out beyond Vandeventer Place," and at Smith Academy, where he was an outstanding student who wrote stories and verses for the school paper. His summers were spent in the family's large house overlooking the ocean at Gloucester, Massachusetts. In 1905 he was sent to Milton Academy in Massachusetts to prepare for entering Harvard the next year. He was never to live in St. Louis again. In 1953, however, in an address delivered at Washington University, Eliot made clear his debt to the city of his birth: "St. Louis affected me more deeply than any other environment."

After receiving his bachelor's degree in three years, Eliot stayed at Harvard to begin graduate studies that he would continue at Oxford and the Sorbonne and in Germany. His Ph.D. thesis on the philosophy of Francis Herbert Bradley was accepted at Harvard, though Eliot never returned to receive the degree.

Eliot earned his living as other-than-poet for almost all his life. As a young man he taught first at High Wycombe Grammar School, near London, and then at London's Highgate Junior School, where he taught a wide range of subjects, including art and baseball, with varying degrees of success. From 1917 to 1920 he worked at Lloyd's Bank in London, principally in the Colonial and Foreign Department. He edited the *Criterion,* a significant literary magazine. In 1925 he became an editor at the London firm of Faber and Faber, a position he held for most of the rest of his life.

The start of World War I interrupted Eliot's traveling fellowship in Germany, and he went to Merton College, at Oxford. England was to become his permanent home. In 1927, when he was thirty-nine, Eliot was received into the Church of England and became a British citizen. In a preface to "For Lancelot Andrewes" (1928) he called himself "classicist in literature, royalist in politics, and Anglo-Catholic in religion." He became a daily communicant of St. Stephen's Church in London, a parish in which he served as warden for twenty-five years. Eliot had not so much rejected the United States as he had found in England a spiritual and intellectual home.

Several publishers deal with the question of whether Eliot is to be considered "American" or

"English" by including his work in both their British and their American anthologies. A. D. Moody, a noted British scholar speaking in St. Louis on the hundredth anniversary of Eliot's birth, indicated the complexity of the question. Most of Eliot's poems are not "conspicuously American," though they are American in much of their language, speech rhythms, and "habit of skepticism." At the same time, Moody said, "Eliot's is an English and European poetry that only an American could have written."

Eliot started "The Love Song of J. Alfred Prufrock" while at Harvard, finished it in Munich, and published it in *Poetry* in June 1915; his career as a poet had begun. *Prufrock and Other Observations* appeared two years later, and "The Waste Land" in 1922.

Although much of Eliot's poetry depicts a secular world, one may argue that all his poetry is spiritual in its quest, and the late works are realized in a profoundly spiritual way. "The Waste Land" describes a spiritually sterile land thirsting for life-renewing water. The speaker in "The Hollow Men" (1925) gropes haltingly toward truth; the speaker in "Ash Wednesday" (1930) voices the agony of one who longs "to turn" yet "sit still." With "Four Quartets" (1935–1942), a meditative poem on time and timelessness and the meaning of the Incarnation, Eliot's movement toward a thoroughly Christian poetry is complete. He arrives at "a condition of complete simplicity / (Costing not less than everything)."

The poet John Berryman once remarked of the opening of "Prufrock" (with its well-known image of the evening "spread out against the sky / Like a patient etherised upon a table"): "With this line, modern poetry begins." From the first, reactions to Eliot's poetry have been greatly mixed. Many readers and writers find in Eliot's sometimes startling juxtapositions a perfect expression of the discontinuities of modern life and hail him as a revitalizer of language and sensibility. Readers with more traditionalist tastes denounce his poetry for the very qualities that others praise. On one point both admirers and detractors are generally agreed: it is not necessary to like Eliot, but to understand modern poetry it is necessary to read him. No writer of the twentieth century has prompted a larger amount of critical commentary, and Eliot's works have engaged many of the best literary minds throughout the world. Furthermore, as Dame Helen Gardner has observed, Eliot "created the taste by which he is enjoyed."

Eliot's five plays continue his spiritual themes and have prompted a reexamination of the concept "poetic drama." His first play, *Murder in the Cathedral* (1935), commissioned for a festival at Canterbury Cathedral, has transcended the limited audience for which it was written. It was followed by *The Family Reunion* (1939), Eliot's most difficult play; *The Cocktail Party* (1950), his greatest commercial success; and *The Confidential Clerk* (1954), the least often performed of the plays. Admiration for Eliot's last play, *The Elder Statesman* (1959), has focused on its testimony to the power of love.

Muriel Bradbrook's judgment that "had he not become the most famous poet of his time, Eliot would have been known as its most distinguished critic" is widely shared. His essays set forth a theory of literature, redirected attention to a number of Elizabethan dramatists, and helped create a twentieth-century audience for the metaphysical poets, notably John Donne.

Finding fulfillment in his personal life took even longer for Eliot than the rest of his spiritual journey. In June 1915, the month of the publication of "Prufrock," Eliot married Vivien Haigh-Wood, whom he had known for only a few months. That the Eliots' relationship was complex is an understatement, but all observers agree that, almost from the beginning, the marriage caused grievous pain to both husband and wife. Not until after they were married did Eliot discover that his wife had suffered from various illnesses, emotional and otherwise, since her childhood. She was in mental institutions for much of the last thirty years of her life. The Eliots were separated in 1935, and Vivien Eliot died in 1947. In 1950 Valerie Fletcher became Eliot's secretary at Faber and Faber, and in 1957 she and Eliot were married. All indications are that in the seven years remaining to him, T. S. Eliot found with Valerie a life of joy.

T. S. Eliot died in London on January 4, 1965. His ashes were taken to St. Michel's Church, in East Coker, the village from which his ancestors had set out for America. At his death commentators on both sides of the Atlantic called him the most important poet writing in English in the twentieth century. His obituary in the *Times* (London) was titled "The Most Influential English Poet of His Time," and an obituary in *Life* asserted that "our age beyond any doubt has been, and will continue to be, the Age of Eliot."

Eliot received a multitude of awards and honorary degrees, including some of the highest honors available to writers. In 1948 he received both the Nobel Prize for literature and the Order of Merit. On the second anniversary of his death, Valerie Eliot unveiled a stone in her husband's memory in Westminster Abbey. Finding no memorial to Eliot in St. Louis, Leslie Konnyu, a Hungarian American man of letters living in that city, commissioned a plaque to be sculpted by Andrew Osze and had it installed at his own residence. The plaque now hangs in the St. Louis Public Library. A memorial to Eliot may also be found in St. Louis's Walk of Fame.

In 1980 Konnyu founded the T. S. Eliot Society as a literary discussion group. By 1988 the society had grown into an international organization strong enough to summon many leading Eliot scholars to St. Louis for a four-day celebration of the centennial of the poet's birth. Today, though the society's membership reaches to ten countries on four continents, its annual meeting continues to be held in St. Louis on the weekend nearest Eliot's birthday.

LINDA WYMAN

Ackroyd, Peter. *T. S. Eliot.* New York: Simon and Schuster, 1984.

Bradbrook, M. C. *T. S. Eliot.* London: Longman, Green, 1963.

Gardner, Helen. *The Art of T. S. Eliot.* New York: E. P. Dutton, 1949.

Sencourt, Robert. *T. S. Eliot: A Memoir.* New York: Dodd, Mead, 1971.

Smith, Grover. *T. S. Eliot's Poetry and Plays.* 2d ed. Chicago: University of Chicago Press, 1974.

ELIOT, WILLIAM GREENLEAF (1811–1887)

William Greenleaf Eliot was born on August 5, 1811, in New Bedford, Massachusetts, and died on January 23, 1887, in Pass Christian, Mississippi. He was the first pastor of the Church of the Messiah (now the First Unitarian Church of St. Louis) and the founder (along with **Wayman Crow**) of Washington University in St. Louis. A graduate of Columbian College in Washington, D.C., and Harvard Divinity School (from which he received an honorary doctor of divinity degree in 1854), Eliot was ordained in Boston as a Unitarian evangelist and arrived in St. Louis in November 1834, dedicated to a lifetime of religious and public service and ready, in his words, "to lay my aches in the Valley of the Mississippi." He married his first cousin, Abigail Adams Cranch (1817–1908), in 1837. Fourteen children were born to them, only five of whom survived to adulthood.

From modest beginnings the Church of the Messiah grew to be one of the largest and most influential churches in the city. Its minister and members were prominent in the organization of numerous cultural and civic institutions, including the Mission Free School, the Academy of Science, the Art Museum, and the Missouri Historical Society. The church occupied three buildings during Eliot's lifetime, including a magnificent edifice at Ninth and Olive built in 1851, where Ralph Waldo Emerson heard Eliot preach and dubbed him the "Saint of the West."

Eliot's most notable contributions were in the area of education. As president of the city school board, he was instrumental in obtaining the first public school taxes in 1850. Soon afterward he embarked on his most ambitious undertaking. Originally named "Eliot Seminary," Washington University was incorporated in 1853 by seventeen members of the Church of the Messiah. Although its charter was remarkably liberal and explicitly nonsectarian, in its formative years the university was financed mainly by Unitarians. Eliot traveled broadly to appeal for support, and his fund-raising abilities were legendary, causing a prominent businessman to remark that if he could have had Eliot for a partner, "together we would have made most of the money west of the Alleghenies." Eliot was the first president of the board of directors of Washington University and continued in that role until his death, even after being named the school's third chancellor in 1870. He resigned his pulpit at that time and was named pastor emeritus.

Mary Institute (1859), a preparatory school for women, was named for Eliot's beloved eldest daughter, who died of an unnamed illness at age sixteen. A parallel school for boys, Smith Academy, closed its doors in 1917, its most famous graduate being the poet **T. S. Eliot,** grandson of the founder.

Besides his civic work Eliot traveled extensively as a Unitarian missionary, helping establish new churches throughout the Midwest, from New Orleans to Milwaukee. He was a lifelong director of the American Unitarian Association, headquartered in Boston, and in 1847 turned down an invitation to head the national denomination because of his sense of duty to his church and his original intention to devote his life to St. Louis. During the Civil War Eliot founded and served as a member of the Western Sanitary Commission for aid of the wounded of both armies and their widows and children. He was an early advocate of prohibition and woman suffrage.

Eliot's published works include several collections of sermons, his popular *Lectures to Young Women* and *Lectures to Young Men,* and *The Discipline of Sorrow,* which he wrote following the death of his daughter Mary in 1855. In 1855 he also published *The Life of Archer Alexander,* which chronicles the story of a slave whom Eliot helped to free; **Archer Alexander**'s likeness is featured in a sculpture by Thomas Ball called Freedom's Memorial in Lincoln Park, in Washington, D.C.

A man of great achievement and extreme modesty of character Eliot requested there be no monuments to his own memory. A simple circular plaque was placed in 1853 at Washington University, honoring the "Unitarian Minister, Educator, Philanthropist," along with a quotation from his inaugural address: "Those who come nearest to Truth come nearest to God." An older memorial, located in Eliot Hall of the First Unitarian Church of St. Louis, reads: "His best monument is to be found in the many educational and philanthropic institutions of St. Louis, to which he gave the disinterested labor of his life. The whole city was his parish and every soul needing him a parishioner." He is buried in Bellefontaine Cemetery under a simple marker, inscribed at his request, "Looking Unto Jesus."

EARL K. HOLT III

Eliot, Charlotte C. *William Greenleaf Eliot: Minister, Educator, Philanthropist.* New York: Houghton, Mifflin, 1904.

Holt, Earl K., III. *William Greenleaf Eliot: Conservative Radical.* St. Louis: First Unitarian Church of St. Louis, 1985.

Howarth, Herbert. *Notes on Some Figures behind T. S. Eliot.* Boston: Houghton Mifflin, 1964.

ELLIOTT, GORDON "WILD BILL" (1905–1965)

Gordon "Wild Bill" Elliott was one of the screen's top western moneymakers during the 1940s and 1950s and was voted one of the ten best "Money Making Stars" in the *Motion Picture Herald* Poll from 1942 to 1952. Elliott reversed the general pattern by abandoning "straight" acting for the western field. His nickname was acquired in 1938 when he played in a Columbia serial called *The Great Adventures of Wild Bill Hickok.*

Elliott was born Gordon Nance on October 16, 1905, on a ranch near Pattonsburg, Missouri, where he learned the cowboy arts of riding, roping, and shooting. He moved to Kansas City with his parents when he was ten years old. As a boy he tamed horses in his father's stockyard and was exposed briefly to the rodeo circuit.

Elliott attended Rockhurst College but left for Hollywood where he gained acting experience at the Pasadena Playhouse and changed his name to Gordon Elliott. Most of his early films were nonwesterns, including his debut in *Wonder Bar* in 1934. After his appearance in *The Great Adventures of Wild Bill Hickok,* Elliott made a series of westerns, including several in which he re-created his role as Wild Bill Hickok and a fifteen-episode serial called *Overland with Kit Carson.*

Elliott next teamed up with Tex Ritter in several western films, and in 1942 made his last serial, *Valley of Vanishing Men,* with Slim Summerville. Afterward, Elliott starred in eight "Wild Bill Elliott" films for Republic Pictures, followed by the "Red Ryder" series of sixteen films beginning in 1943.

After the "Red Ryder" series, Republic featured Elliott in several "major" westerns, the first of which was *In Old Sacramento.* He later appeared in several westerns for Allied Artists and was a television spokesman for a national cigarette manufacturer.

Elliott was married twice and had one daughter, Barbara. He retired to his Nevada ranch in 1957, and on November 26, 1965, he died of cancer at his Las Vegas home at the age of sixty.

ARTHUR F. MCCLURE AND VIVIAN RICHARDSON

Holland, Ted. *B Western Actors Encyclopedia.* Jefferson, N.C.: McFarland, 1989.

McClure, Arthur F., and Ken D. Jones. *Heroes, Heavies and Sagebrush of the "B" Genre.* Cranbury, N.J.: A. S. Barnes, 1972.

Parish, James Robert. *Great Western Stars.* New York: Ace Books, 1976.

Variety, December 1, 1965.

ELLIS, ELMER (1901–1989)

One of the most prominent and successful administrators in Missouri's higher education history was Elmer Ellis. Born in McHenry County, North Dakota, on July 27, 1901, Ellis attended his native state's university from which he received an A.B. degree in 1924 and an A.M. degree in 1925. During the latter year he began teaching at North Dakota State Teachers College, at Mayville, and he also married his high school sweetheart, Ruth Clapper. In 1928 Ellis began his Ph.D. program in American history at the University of Iowa. He completed the degree requirements in 1930, the same year that he accepted an assistant professorship in the history department of the University of Missouri.

By the time Ellis became a full professor in 1940, he had already earned a fine reputation as a teacher. He had also edited *Mr. Dooley at His Best* (1938) and had become involved in college administration, serving as assistant dean of the University of Missouri graduate school during the summers of 1936, 1939, and 1941. A Fulbright scholar and a Guggenheim fellow, Ellis published two more books in 1941: *Henry Moore Teller: Defender of the West* and *Mr. Dooley's America: A Life of Finley Peter Dunne.* Ellis provided the impetus for the establishment of the university's Western Historical Manuscripts Collection in 1943 and set it on a course to become one of the finest research collections in the Midwest.

During World War II the United States Army commissioned Ellis as a captain in 1943. He reported to Jefferson Barracks and then spent the majority of his military career as a major in the army's historical branch. He received an early discharge at the request of the university's president, **Frederick A. Middlebush,** who wanted Ellis to become the vice president for extradivisional activities, a newly created administrative position.

In January 1946 Ellis became the dean of arts and science for the University of Missouri. His achievements in that position convinced the university's board of curators to appoint him as the "acting" president of the institution in 1954. A year later the board removed "acting" from Ellis's title. As president of the university, Ellis was known as a man of integrity. His openness with faculty, staff, and students provided for excellent morale on the campuses at Columbia and Rolla. He successfully worked to improve salary and benefits for the employees, as well as to improve and expand research facilities.

In 1951 Ellis was elected president of the Mississippi Valley Historical Association. The respect he received in educational circles mirrored his favorable reputation with the elected officials of the state. From 1955 through 1959 the governors and General Assemblies doubled funding for the Columbia campus and tripled investment in the Rolla campus. Ellis's success in securing increased appropriations occurred in a state that he often said "always had northern ideas of education and southern ideas of taxation." Gov. **Phil M. Donnelly** called upon Ellis in 1956 to help lead a $75 million capital-improvement campaign. A skilled politician, Ellis played an important part in securing voter approval of the bond issue from which the university received some $22 million for the building of needed facilities.

During Ellis's presidency, the establishment of the university's four-campus system proved the most challenging and important event. With Gov. **John Montgomery Dalton**'s support, Ellis helped persuade Missourians that the university should establish campuses in the state's major metropolitan areas, St. Louis and Kansas City. The expansion of the university system required the approval of leaders in education, agriculture, business, and labor, as well as the support of the state's political leaders. Ellis proved adept at working with all these segments, and in the spring of 1963 the four-campus system became a reality. He provided his own recollection of this major accomplishment in Missouri's educational history when he wrote *My Road to Emeritus,* which was published in 1989.

Ellis retired as president of the university system in 1966, though he maintained an office in Jesse Hall on the Columbia campus. His years at the helm of the university prompted one student of the institution's history to write: "No president . . . has had such an important impact. . . . Ellis should rank first as the most influential president."

Ellis spent part of his retirement years as a consultant. His first consultation, at the behest of the Rockefeller Foundation, took place at the Universidad del Valle in Cali, Colombia. Asked to assist with specific educational or state-agency problems, Ellis later consulted in the states of Kentucky, North Carolina, Tennessee, Virginia, Arkansas, and Texas.

A member of the State Historical Society of Missouri since 1931, and a trustee since 1965, Ellis, after his retirement, devoted more time to its interests. Besides serving on the society's finance committee,

he spent three years as its president beginning in 1974. He received the society's Distinguished Service Award in 1978, only one of many awards bestowed upon him during his lifetime, including the University of Missouri Curators' Award for Outstanding Service in 1988. In 1972 the university renamed the main library on the Columbia campus Elmer Ellis Library.

President Emeritus Ellis died August 27, 1989. Just prior to his death, he had reviewed and corrected the page proof of his autobiography, a book that briefly preserves the accomplishments of one of Missouri's foremost educators.

JAMES W. GOODRICH

Christensen, Lawrence O. "Presidents and the Presidency." *Missouri Historical Review* 84 (October 1989): 23–41.

Ellis, Elmer. *My Road to Emeritus.* Columbia: State Historical Society of Missouri, 1989.

Fite, Gilbert C., ed. *Elmer Ellis: Teacher, Scholar, Administrator.* Columbia: University of Missouri Press, 1961.

Smith, Rowland H. "The Ellis Years." *Missouri Alumnus* 47 (September 1959): 3–5, 32–33.

ELLIS, JOHN BRECKENRIDGE (1870–1956)

John Breckenridge Ellis wrote more than twenty-five books during his long life. At eighteen months, he contracted spinal meningitis, which left him without the use of his legs. When nineteen years old, his eyesight began to fail, and he taught himself braille. His eyes remained weak for a number of years, but he never lost his sight. Confined to a wheelchair and to a hand-operated tricycle, Ellis nevertheless taught for a number of years, maintained an ambitious writing schedule, and helped organize the Missouri Writers Guild, serving as its president for five terms.

Born on February 11, 1870, near Hannibal, Missouri, Ellis spent his early youth in St. Louis, where his father was a preacher and practiced law. Apparently dissatisfied or finding conflict in those two callings, the senior Ellis accepted the presidency of Woodland College in Independence before establishing Plattsburg College in Clinton County in 1880. The younger Ellis graduated from his father's school in 1886 and began teaching English and literature there. His father installed a hand-operated elevator so his son could get from the family's living quarters on the lower level of the college building to the classrooms on the upper floor. Ellis earned an M.A. degree in 1897. Culver Stockton College awarded him an honorary doctorate for his literary accomplishments. He taught at Plattsburg College until 1899, when it closed. He taught at Central Christian College in

Albany, Missouri, from 1900 to 1902. Afterward, he devoted himself to writing.

Ellis's mother and father encouraged him to become a writer. A member of the Kentucky aristocracy, Ellis's mother wrote poetry under the name of Pauline C. Ewing. She also worked with **Susan Elizabeth Blow** in the kindergarten movement in St. Louis. Ellis's father published learned tracts on linguistics under his own name, John William Ellis, and poetry under the name of Henry C. Blount. At the age of fifteen, John Breckenridge Ellis decided to become a writer and at nineteen sold his first work to the *Louisville Courier Journal,* a well-known Kentucky newspaper.

Ellis's most famous book was *Fran,* which appeared in 1912 and remained on the best-seller list for two years. It and five other stories were made into movies, and *Fran* and three other pieces became stage plays. Other titles included *In the Days of Jehu* (1898), *King Saul* (1898), *Shem: A Story of Captivity* (1899), *Adnah: A Tale of the Time of Christ* (1902), *The Holland Wolves* (1902), *The Red Box Clew: For the Young from Seven to Seventy* (1902), *Stork's Nest* (1905), *Arkinsaw Cousins: A Story of the Ozarks* (1908), *Twin Stars: A Novel* (1908), *The Soul of a Serf: A Romance of Love and Valor among the Angles and Saxons* (1910), *The Story of a Life* (1910), *Something Else: A Novel* (1911), *The Little Fiddler of the Ozarks: A Novel* (1913), *Lahoma* (1913), *The Third Diamond* (1913), *The Woodneys: An American Family* (1914), *His Dear Unintended* (1917), and *The Mysterious Dr. Oliver: A Mystery Story* (1929). His autobiography, which primarily traces his literary efforts, records the first forty-two years of his life. Titled *Adventure of Living,* it was published in 1933. Ellis averaged almost a book a year between 1933 and 1940, publishing six volumes. He maintained that production until 1943.

After the success of *Fran,* Ellis wintered in California and Oklahoma, while returning to Plattsburg for the summer. He lived briefly in Arkansas. He died in Cordell, Oklahoma, on April 2, 1956.

LAWRENCE O. CHRISTENSEN

Ellis, J. Breckenridge. *Adventure in Living.* Cedar Rapids: Torch Press, Bookfellow Book, 1933.

McIntyre, O. O. "Happily Ever After." *Hearst's International-Cosmopolitan* (March 1934): 56–69.

"Missouri Writer's Guild Fiftieth Anniversary." *Missouri Historical Review* 60 (October 1965): 78–79.

Who Was Who in America. Chicago: A. N. Marquis, 1960.

ELLIS, ROY (1888–1972)

Roy Ellis completed his term as president of Southwest Missouri State College on August 31, 1961. At the time of his retirement, he had served as the chief executive of a Missouri state-supported college or university longer than anyone else in the history of the state, having begun his presidency on February 2, 1926.

Born on March 9, 1888, Ellis was the son of David Franklin and Cornelia Pyatt Ellis, who resided on a farm near Seymour, Missouri. As was often the case with early settlers of the Ozarks, the parents of Roy Ellis migrated from far-western North Carolina to make their home on the Webster County–Wright County line in Missouri. These transplanted residents of the Carolina Appalachians found the less mountainous Ozarks a pleasant place to live. Ellis enthusiastically shared his parents' appreciation for the Ozarks and spent most of his life in the region, except for his years away at college. After his death in Springfield, Missouri, on January 9, 1972, he was buried in the Seymour cemetery.

For his elementary education, Ellis attended the New Grove School in rural Wright County. His high school studies were also in Wright County at the Hartville School where he graduated in 1908. The next school year, Ellis matriculated at Missouri State Normal School, Fourth District, in Springfield. He received a junior-college degree, a bachelor of pedagogy, from the school in 1911. Missouri State Normal School, Fourth District, became Southwest Missouri State Teachers College in 1919 and Southwest Missouri State College in 1945.

In 1912 Ellis continued his undergraduate education at the University of Missouri in Columbia, where he earned a bachelor of arts and a bachelor of science in education in 1914. His graduate education was conducted at Harvard University and at Columbia University in New York City. Ellis was awarded a master of arts degree in political science and public law at Harvard in 1917. Columbia University conferred his Ph.D. degree in political science and public law in 1930.

Ellis's entire career was associated with education. As early as 1906—before he graduated from high school—he began teaching in the rural elementary schools of Wright County. In 1911–1912 he acted as the principal of a Texarkana, Arkansas, grammar school. From 1914 to 1916 he was employed as the superintendent of the Greenfield, Missouri, schools. Ellis was first hired at Missouri State Normal School in 1917 as the head of the department of sociology and economics. Nine years later he became the president of his alma mater.

Ellis was an accomplished speaker and writer. From 1908 to 1910 he served as a member of the first intercollegiate debate team at Missouri State Normal School. He delighted audiences with his tongue-in-cheek essays regarding the importance of college administrators.

Ellis was recognized for having written two scholarly histories. The first, *A Civic History of Kansas City, Missouri,* was his Ph.D. dissertation at Columbia University. Printed in 1930, it was distributed by the press of Elkins-Swyers Company of Springfield, Missouri. A second book penned by Ellis was titled *Shrine of the Ozarks: A History of Southwest Missouri State College, 1905–1965,* and was published by the college in 1968. The latter was written, following his retirement, at the request of the board of regents. The governing board recognized that, in view of his having served for more than forty years as a staff member of the institution, Ellis was eminently qualified for the assignment. The book proved to be a comprehensive and thoughtful history of the school; Ellis commented only briefly and modestly about his own accomplishments as president of the college.

In 1923 Ellis married Frances Nations. Their only child, David Owen Ellis, was born in 1925. In 1960 Ellis was granted an honorary doctor of laws degree from the University of Missouri. The Southwest Missouri State College Alumni Association presented to him the Outstanding Alumnus Award at homecoming ceremonies in the fall of 1961.

DUANE G. MEYER

Ellis, Roy. *A Civic History of Kansas City, Missouri.* Springfield, Mo.: Elkins-Swyers, 1930.
————. *Shrine of the Ozarks: A History of Southwest Missouri State College, 1905–1965.* Springfield, Mo.: Southwest Missouri State College, 1968.
March, David D. *The History of Missouri.* Vol. 4. New York: Lewis Historical Publishing, 1967.
Springfield News and Leader, January 10, 1972.

EMERSON, JOHN WESLEY (1830–1899)

John Emerson, a lawyer in Ironton, Missouri, became a small-town Victorian gentleman who lived a significant public life in southeast Missouri and St. Louis. His cosmopolitan interests included the law, poetry, literature, philosophy, public speaking and education, building and landscape design, and wilderness sporting and conservation. He devoted much energy to land, timber and mineral speculation, local and state Democratic politics, and researching the life of Gen. **Ulysses S. Grant.** Emerson was the financial founder of Emerson Electric Company in St. Louis.

John Emerson descended from the famous Emerson family of New England. His father, William Emerson, was a professor of mathematics and literature while the family lived in Massachusetts, New York, and Canada. Both parents, however, were dead by the time Emerson reached age eighteen. He worked his way through college, graduating from the University of Michigan. He studied law in Pennsylvania, married, and took his wife and younger brother, George, to the Arcadia valley in Missouri in 1857. His legal talents quickly earned him a judicial seat in the Fifteenth District.

In 1862 the young judge began his military career by enlisting in the Sixty-eighth Regiment Enrolled Missouri Militia, but later paid the three-hundred-dollar commutation tax to continue his legal work. In early 1864 Gov. **Willard Preble Hall** appointed Emerson as colonel of the Sixty-eighth Regiment, and he resigned his judgeship. By spring 1864 he began to lobby the adjutant general to form a new volunteer regiment and received permission by late summer to develop the Forty-seventh Missouri Infantry; the colonel became a major in the new militia. He spent most of his time, however, guarding communications in middle Tennessee, mustering out at St. Louis in March 1865.

The war veteran returned home and resumed his duties on the judicial bench. Emerson inherited some money, and made investments in land, commercial farms, and timber while purchasing numerous delinquent-tax lands. By 1871 the judge had become the landlord of the local newspaper (the *Ironton Register*), completed a new Gothic frame house in Ironton, promoted many commercial enterprises with his pen and on the podium in southeast Missouri, and traveled the St. Louis Iron Mountain Railway looking after his investments. Plagued with ill health throughout his life, perhaps recurring malaria, Emerson announced his retirement from the law in June 1871 to attend Berkeley Divinity School in Middleton, Connecticut. In March 1873 he withdrew his name as a candidate for the Episcopalian Orders, again citing ill health. John Emerson and his wife, Sarah, left for Colorado, where he had mineral investments, and traveled the Pacific Coast in quest of restored health.

The Emersons always retained investments in southeast Missouri and property in Ironton. For the rest of their lives they traveled extensively throughout the United States and Canada while Emerson enjoyed writing romantic, florid narratives that described the sublime wonders of nature, which were popular in Victorian America, published as travelogues in the *Ironton Register.* When riding the rails in southeast Missouri, he wrote about former Irontonians who had become business people throughout the region. In June 1875 he reopened his law practice in Ironton.

At age forty-five Emerson assumed the mantle of a small-town aristocrat. Throughout southeast

Missouri he delivered keynote addresses at civic, fraternal, and Democratic political meetings. He was always on the stage at Independence Day rallies, spoke at educational exercises in private and public schools, delivered eulogies, and gave popular law lectures at Arcadia College. Eli Ake, the *Ironton Register*'s editor, often printed his speeches, even his legal briefs, for public circulation.

In late 1876 Emerson decided his ill health demanded liquidation of many Missouri properties and a move to Colorado. He sold his sawmill, and businessmen gave him a farewell supper in January 1877. The Emersons spent months traveling, lived with John's brother, George, in Pennsylvania, but the unsettled and indecisive Emersons found themselves back in Ironton by September.

Emerson was about to renew his efforts in the Ozarks. He still owned thousands of acres in Butler County and immediately challenged all southeast Missouri newspaper editors to "go to work and write up the country, and try to get a share of immigration to the Southeast." By late fall the promoter had purchased the old Lindsay-Grandhomme estate in Ironton, the grandest house in the county. The Emersons finally made a long-term commitment and made the property into a model that was soon imitated by a number of St. Louisans who began building summer estates in the Arcadia valley during the 1880s.

The couple poured their wealth into creating a landscape that became known throughout southeast Missouri and in St. Louis. The brick Italianate house sat in a terrain designed for public view. Guests stayed in summer cottages, fished in the trout-stocked ponds, walked about Sylvan Lake, and enjoyed yard lanterns and all the handsome appointments that adorned a great estate. St. Louis designers and tradesmen worked on the grounds, completing it in five years. Emerson used his estate to promote the area for recreation and the embryonic conservation movement. Neighbors imitated his experiments in fish ponds and in stocking creeks and rivers.

The Emerson estate almost became a personality itself in efforts to celebrate patriotism and General Grant. In 1882 Civil War veterans held a Blue and Gray reunion at Pilot Knob. The occasion began efforts to locate a statue of Grant on Emerson's grounds, the place where Grant first assumed duties as a brigadier general under the "Grant Oak." Emerson regularly made his spacious grounds available for militia encampments. In 1886 the gentleman promoter and the Twenty-first Illinois veterans proudly witnessed the unveiling of a bronze statue on the historic site. Public calls for Emerson's entry into Democratic politics came regularly to the Ironton counselor, but he declined them all until offered a post in 1887 as a U.S. marshal in St. Louis. The presidential appointment allowed Emerson to maintain an office in St. Louis, where he already spent considerable time and had numerous business and social connections.

Emerson required a staff in his St. Louis office. He hired a law clerk, Alexander Metson, to handle much of his business. At night Metson and his brother experimented in electricity. When the marshalship ended in 1890, Emerson staked the Metson brothers with twenty-five thousand dollars to begin an infant manufacturing business in electric lighting and "railway specialties," and called it Emerson Electric. For a couple of years Emerson maintained a St. Louis law office, riding the train back and forth to Ironton. In 1892 he returned full-time to Sylvan Lake, leaving the business of Emerson Electric to others.

Emerson continued to travel, write for the newspaper, and entertain frequent ecclesiastical, political, and business elites. In 1894 he received Grant's widow, their son, Col. Frederick Grant, and a group of distinguished St. Louisans. At lakeside Emerson presented **Julia Dent Grant** with a pencil sketch of the "Grant Oak," the spring, and the memorial monument. He published magazine articles about Grant and made annual pilgrimages to famous Civil War battle sites to collect information on the general. He intended to write a Grant biography in Ironton, but a final illness overcame him, and he died on June 20, 1899.

Ironically, the fastidious Emerson died intestate, his wife passing away in 1904. Canadian and Massachusetts heirs began a battle for his assets. By 1911 Emerson's former law partner, W. R. Edgar, was representing him in the settlement before the Missouri Supreme Court. By then heirs had sold or appropriated for themselves all personal properties at the estate, leaving the house to be sold to new owners.

LYNN MORROW

Dyer, Davis, and Jeffrey L. Cruikshank. *Emerson Electric Co.: A Century of Manufacturing, 1890–1990*. St. Louis: Emerson Electric, 1989.

Morrow, Lynn. "Estate Building in the Missouri Ozarks: Establishing a St. Louis Tradition." *Gateway Heritage* 2 (winter 1981–1982): 42–48.

———. "John Wesley Emerson." St. Louis: Missouri Historical Society.

ENGELMANN, GEORGE (1809–1884)

George Engelmann, a physician and scientist, was born in Frankfurt am Main, Germany, on February 2, 1809. His parents, Julius Bernhard and Julie Antoinette May Engelmann, ran a private boarding school for girls in Frankfurt where they accepted a young niece, Dorothea Horstmann, into their household. Over the years George and Dora shared an interest in plants and each other, which led in the 1820s to their secret engagement.

Engelmann furthered his botanical studies at the Senckenberg Institute in Frankfurt, and in 1827 enrolled at the University of Heidelberg, but left a year later during student protests to study at Berlin and then the University of Würzburg. He received a medical degree on July 19, 1831, and his dissertation on plant monstrosities, which he illustrated, received praise from the dying Goethe. In the summer of 1832 the fledgling physician traveled to Paris with university friends Louis Agassiz and Alexander Braun for further study and in search of professional prospects outside Germany. That autumn Engelmann sailed to the United States.

For the next two years Engelmann lived frugally on an uncle's Illinois farm twenty miles east of St. Louis. He explored Illinois and Missouri as a scientist, collecting plant and animal specimens and recording daily temperatures—making him one of the area's first reliable meteorologists. Despite lingering thoughts of returning to Germany, he resumed his travels in 1835, exploring southern Missouri and Arkansas for several months before a series of physical ailments finally forced him back to St. Louis.

Recovered in health and ambition, Engelmann opened a medical practice in the city, which soon flourished, transcending the city's ethnic barriers. In 1836 he joined the Medical Society of Missouri and also helped to found the Western Academy of Natural Science. His growing success in obstetrics allowed him by 1840 to travel to Germany and marry Dora, who had waited for him for eight years. The couple then returned to St. Louis where in 1847 they had a son, George, who later became a doctor.

Despite a grueling medical practice, Engelmann still found time to conduct important scientific work, especially in his favorite subject, botany. Throughout the 1840s he collaborated with Harvard botanist Asa Gray in promoting western plant collection. Engelmann often helped equip these collectors with scientific instruments and instruction, and frequently received their western plant specimens for study and further distribution. Engelmann thus became an authority on dodders (parasitic plants), as well as cacti, agaves, mistletoe, grapes, oaks, and pines. His scientific articles on these plants earned him international attention.

The delays of publishing in the East frustrated Engelmann. In 1856 he and several other men established the Academy of Science of St. Louis. The new academy published scientific papers in its journal, *Transactions,* and Engelmann, its first president (a position he would hold for fifteen terms), rarely lost an opportunity to promote science in his adopted city.

A special opportunity came the same year of the academy's founding when businessman **Henry Shaw** consulted Engelmann about creating a large garden in St. Louis. Engelmann persuaded Shaw to make his garden botanical as well as horticultural, which required a library and an herbarium. Engelmann spent nearly two years in Europe visiting gardens, buying books, and obtaining the prized Bernhard herbarium (an immense collection of plant specimens) for Shaw. When Shaw opened his Missouri Botanical Garden in 1859 he continued to rely on Engelmann as his chief scientific adviser, and would continue to do so for the next twenty-five years.

By 1869 Engelmann was able to partially retire from medicine and travel more extensively to study plants in the field. With Dora Engelmann, his lifelong botanical collaborator, he made extensive trips to Michigan, the Carolinas, and Colorado. In 1872 he helped the Missouri state entomologist Charles V. Riley determine which native grapevines best resisted the phylloxera plant louse then ravaging European vineyards. The information proved crucial in saving the French wine industry.

Engelmann temporarily lost interest in his scientific pursuits in 1879 when Dora died. Only a long journey to the Pacific Coast with Charles S. Sargent in 1880 rekindled his pleasure in botany and life. In California he met the naturalist John Muir, who later sent Engelmann acorn specimens and his thanks for his "hard good work."

However, the work was nearly done. A trip to Europe in 1883 ended when Engelmann fell ill; he returned to Missouri where he died on February 4, 1884. He was buried next to Dora Engelmann in Bellefontaine Cemetery in St. Louis. As a memorial his friends collected his scattered botanical writings into one volume. His library, herbarium, and worldwide correspondence were given to the Missouri Botanical Garden.

MICHAEL LONG

Dictionary of Scientific Biography. Supplement 1. S.v. "Engelmann, George."

[Gray, Asa]. "George Engelmann." *Proceedings of the American Academy of Arts and Sciences* 19 (1884): 516–22.

Long, Michael. "George Engelmann and the Lure of Frontier Science." *Missouri Historical Review* 89 (April 1995): 251–68.

Sander, Enno. "George Engelmann." *Academy of Science of St. Louis Transactions* 4 (1878–1886): 1–18.

Shaw, Elizabeth A. "Changing Botany in North America, 1835–1860: The Role of George Engelmann." *Missouri Botanical Garden Annals* 73 (1986): 508–19.

Timberlake, Patricia P. "George Engelmann: Scientist at the Gateway to the American West, 1809–1869." Master's thesis, University of Missouri–Columbia, 1984.

ESTHER (?–1833)

One of the largest property owners in early St. Louis was a woman identified in court records simply as "Esther, a free mulatto." Born into slavery in Virginia, Esther (along with her young daughter, Sile) came to Kaskaskia, Illinois, in 1779 with an owner who shortly fell into debt and lost her to one of his creditors, the St. Louis merchant and fur trader **Jacques Clamorgan.**

When Clamorgan took Esther into his house in 1782, he was already one of the most powerful men in St. Louis, a friend of the Spanish commandant and proprietor of a vast expanse of land in Upper Louisiana. Esther, whose strong will and ambition matched Clamorgan's, quickly became not only his mistress but an indispensable business assistant as well. She impressed merchant Gabriel Cerré as a formidable presence "who seemed to have the control within the premises when Clamorgan was absent—and very much so when he was at home."

Under Clamorgan's tutelage Esther plunged into speculations of her own and soon assembled an impressive portfolio of St. Louis real estate: two houses and their lots, an entire city block, and the forty-arpent "Dodier Tract" west of town and the eighty-arpent "Mound Tract" to the north (about thirty-four and sixty-eight acres, respectively). An astute businesswoman, she made a tidy living raising crops and livestock on these properties.

Esther's relationship with Clamorgan did not remain happy. Although he emancipated her and made a gift to her of Sile, he had a violent temper and at times abused her physically. When he began a series of affairs in 1797 with other women (with whom he eventually fathered four children), Esther left him. She moved with Sile into one of her houses, where she supported the two of them and eventually four grandchildren with the income from her property.

In 1809, however, Esther's fortunes took a turn for the worse; she discovered that Clamorgan, who had suffered financial ruin under American rule, had filed forged deeds, claiming her real estate as his own. For the rest of her life, Esther fought in the courts trying to reclaim the property. In the end she was only partly successful, holding onto her own house and the Mound Tract but losing the rest to Clamorgan and his heirs (he died in 1814) and to the chicanery of her own lawyer. She was saved from poverty by the Mound Tract, which proved her shrewdest investment, as it lay directly in the path of the city's expansion to the north and was of enormous interest to speculators. Esther was able to support herself by selling shares to speculators, living in comfort until she died in 1833 and bequeathed the remainder as a loving legacy to her grandchildren.

JUDITH A. GILBERT

Gilbert, Judith A. "Esther and Her Sisters." *Gateway Heritage* 17 (summer 1996): 14–23.

EVANS, JOHN THOMAS (1770–1799)

John Thomas Evans, an explorer, surveyor, and mapmaker, was born in 1770 in Waunfawr, near Caernarvon in northwest Wales, the son of a well-known Methodist preacher. After completing his studies, Evans went to London in 1791 in search of work. While there he associated with a Welsh literary society whose members believed that a tribe of North American Indians were descendants of legendary Welsh explorers who had visited the New World in the twelfth century. The London society decided to send Evans to America in search of Welsh Indians along the upper Missouri River.

Evans arrived in Baltimore on October 10, 1792, and briefly worked as a clerk in a countinghouse. Ignoring attempts by acquaintances in Baltimore and Philadelphia to dissuade him from undertaking his proposed journey into the wilderness, Evans set out for Spanish Louisiana in March 1793. Two months later he arrived in New Madrid, and from there he headed for St. Louis. While en route to Upper Louisiana's capital, the young traveler lost his way, but **John Rice Jones,** a fellow Welshman in the Illinois country, heard about his plight and offered him assistance.

Evans had learned that the Company of Explorers of the Upper Missouri (known as the Missouri Company), based in St. Louis, had initiated plans to send its third major expedition up the Missouri River under the direction of the firm's new principal explorer and director of affairs in the Indian country, **James MacKay.** That news reinforced Evans's decision to go to St. Louis.

It was not an opportune time for a Welshman to journey to Upper Louisiana. War between Spain and England seemed imminent, and Evans's attempts to explain to Lt. Gov. **Zenon Trudeau,** through an interpreter, his quest for a tribe of Welsh Indians must have seemed preposterous. Suspicious of British spies seeking to enter the Spanish country, Trudeau ordered Evans to prison. Eventually, influential intercessors persuaded the Spanish official to release the young Welshman. James MacKay, who had learned about Evans's plans, was among those who interceded in his behalf.

In preparation for his upcoming voyage upriver for the Missouri Company, MacKay "sent for & engaged for my assistant Mr. Evans who spoke and wrote the Welch language with facility. . . ." In late August 1795 the MacKay expedition, with Evans as second in command, left St. Louis. Three months later they reached an Omaha village in today's northeastern Nebraska, where they constructed Fort Charles. That winter MacKay sent Evans to explore the upper reaches of the Missouri and to search for a passage from the river's sources to the Pacific. Evans and his party made it as far as present-day South Dakota, where they encountered a hostile Sioux band that forced them to retreat to Fort Charles.

When spring arrived Evans started upriver again, and in September 1796 he reached the Mandan villages in North Dakota. He occupied a nearby fort belonging to Canadian-based British traders whom he directed to leave Spanish soil. The British operatives in the region challenged the claims Evans asserted in Spain's behalf, and in one dramatic encounter the Mandan foiled a trader's attempt to murder Evans. Evans remained on the upper Missouri until May 1797 when he headed downriver for St. Louis. Following his return there in July, Evans reported his failure to locate the Welsh Indians whom he now concluded did not exist.

The Spaniards employed Evans as a surveyor at Cape Girardeau. He also collaborated with MacKay, who had preceded him back to St. Louis, in the preparation of a large-scale map showing the Missouri River from St. Charles, Missouri, to the Mandan villages. **Meriwether Lewis** and **William Clark** carried a copy of that map during their celebrated expedition to the Pacific.

In 1798 Evans traveled to New Orleans where he was a guest in the residence of Gov. Manuel Gayoso de Lemos. Evans became ill and died there sometime in 1799. Upon learning of his death, MacKay observed, "Mr. Evans was a virtuous young man of promising talents, undaunted courage & perseverance." Although Evans had failed to find any Welsh Indians or to reach the Pacific shores, the youthful explorer did provide valuable new information about the upper Missouri River and its Indian inhabitants.

THOMAS DANISI

Nasatir, Abraham P. *Before Lewis and Clark: Documents Illustrating the History of the Missouri, 1785–1804.* 2 vols. 1952. Reprint, Lincoln: University of Nebraska Press, 1990.

———. "John Evans, Explorer and Surveyor." *Missouri Historical Review* 25 (January 1931): 219–39; (April 1931): 432–60; (July 1931): 585–608.

Williams, David. "John Evans' Strange Journey." *American Historical Review* 54 (January 1949): 277–95; (April 1949): 508–29.

Williams, Gwyn A. *Madoc: The Making of a Myth.* Oxford: Oxford University Press, 1987.

Wood, W. Raymond. "Nicholas de Finiels: Mapping the Mississippi and Missouri Rivers, 1797–1798." *Missouri Historical Review* 81 (July 1987): 387–402.

EVANS, TOM L. (1896–1970)

Tom L. Evans of Kansas City was a successful Missouri businessman and friend of Missouri politicians of national rank. He was born on September 1, 1896, in Larned, Kansas, and died on September 1, 1970, in Kansas City, Missouri. His family moved to the Kansas City area at the turn of the century, and he resided there for the rest of his life. He worked in a drugstore as a young man and organized the Crown Drug Store Company in Kansas City, which expanded into a successful midwestern operation. His business philosophy emphasized consumer satisfaction and service.

Evans also developed a Kansas City radio station into KCMO Broadcasting. Upon the acquisition of a television license, the company became one of the Midwest's largest communication operations. He also held interests in the Hotel President in Kansas City and the Gallop Map and Stationery Company. He was a founder of the Advertising and Sales Executive Club of Kansas City and a charter member of the Saddle and Sirloin Club. He served on many boards, including the American Royal and the Kansas City chapter of the American Red Cross.

Evans met **Harry S. Truman** as a young man at the Tenth Ward Democratic Club, and they remained friends for the rest of their lives. Evans had no desire to run for public office; his interest was in helping those who were already serving in elected positions. Evans assisted Truman with numerous campaign-related activities. He was widely recognized for his fund-raising successes and often traveled with candidate Truman. At times he served as Truman's campaign manager. He was even a stand-in for the president during the "Whistle Stop" campaign. Evans refused to accept any political office except the chairmanship of the local Democratic Club in Kansas City.

Evans continued to assist President Truman following his retirement to Independence. He helped oversee an effort to establish a facility to house the Truman Papers. Through fund-raising and direction, he took an active role in the formation of an organization that constructed the Truman Library and established an endowment for the study of the Truman presidency. Since Evans was the only individual on the board of directors from Kansas City, it became his responsibility to oversee the construction and to pay the bills. He organized the dedication ceremonies and proudly watched his friend receive the recognition. During Truman's retirement Evans was actively involved with the former president's daily activities and special events such as his birthday recognitions.

Evans's friendship and political activities also included helping the Missouri congressman **Richard Walker Bolling,** for whom Evans served as campaign manager from 1949 to 1970. Evans served as a fund-raiser and helped the congressman win re-election in successive contests. Kansas City charities and Truman supporters often called upon Evans for financial assistance and for help in gaining access to the former president.

Truman mentioned Evans in his *Memoirs* and in *Mr. Citizen,* but respected his friend's desire to maintain his privacy. As Tom Evans lived his life helping others from the sidelines, so his legacy remains within the shadows, as he probably would have wanted.

LOUIS A. RENFROW

Evans, Tom L. Oral History. Harry S. Truman Library, Independence, Mo.
———. Papers. Harry S. Truman Library, Independence, Mo.
Renfrow, Louis A. "Tom L. Evans, 1896–1970: A Biographical Study of a Kansas City Businessman, Civic and Political Leader." Master's thesis, Central Missouri State University, 1973.

EVANS, WALKER (1903–1975)

Walker Evans's career as an outstanding twentieth-century documentary photographer owes much to his eye for form and to his friends who were themselves artists. Born in St. Louis on November 2, 1903, Evans grew up in the Midwest. In 1919, when his parents separated, he moved with his mother and sister to New York City. He graduated from Phillips Exeter Academy in Andover, Massachusetts, in 1922 and spent a year at Williams College. His most significant education, however, came from the friends he made in New York when he returned in 1927 from a year in Paris.

Ben Shahn, Paul Grotz, Ralph Steiner, and Berenice Abbott helped Evans learn the techniques of photography. Abbott also introduced him to the photographs of Eugene Atget that became models for Evans's own work. He became acquainted with Hart Crane, and three of Evans's photographs of the Brooklyn Bridge illustrated Crane's poem "The Bridge" (1930). But Evans's career began to take shape only when Lincoln Kirstein championed his work.

A Harvard graduate, the editor of the important literary quarterly *Hound and Horn,* and a member of the Museum of Modern Art's first advisory council, Kirstein helped Evans get his first gallery showing, involved him in photographing Victorian buildings in Boston that led, in 1933, to his first museum exhibition, and was instrumental in Evans being the first photographer to have a one-person show at the Museum of Modern Art. Kirstein also wrote the essay for the catalog of that show, *American Photographs* (1938). As the title suggests, Evans wanted his exhibit to represent a photographic portrait of the America he had seen in his travels.

Prior to this exhibition Evans had photographed African sculpture for the Museum of Modern Art and made a trip to Havana, Cuba, to shoot photographs to illustrate Carleton Beals's *Crime of Cuba* (1933). Between 1935 and 1937 Evans made photographs for the federal government's Farm Security Administration. In the summer of 1936, on loan to *Fortune,* Evans went to Alabama with James Agee to illustrate a story about tenant families working in the cotton industry. *Fortune* never used the material, though Evans published some of the photographs in *American Photographs.*

Evans won Guggenheim fellowships in both 1940 and 1941 to continue his "portrait of America." Because of illness and other reasons, Evans never completed the project. However, the work that for many epitomizes Walker Evans's supreme achievement appeared in 1941. Houghton Mifflin published *Let Us Now Praise Famous Men,* Agee's eloquent story of three tenant families accompanied by thirty-one of Evans's photographs. The collaborative work would later become recognized as one of the twentieth century's American classics. However, in the short term World War II rather than the depression took center stage, and Evans became a writer.

From 1943 to 1945 Evans worked at *Time,* writing movie, art, and book reviews, and in 1945 he became *Fortune*'s only staff photographer. He continued at *Fortune* for the next twenty years in various photographic and editorial positions, producing portfolios on such topics as street scenes in Chicago, historic resorts north of Boston, vintage office furniture, and the "Beauties of the Common Tool." Although Evans's work at *Fortune* continued the standards he had established in his earlier work, it did not advance those standards.

In 1960, however, Evans saw a renewed interest in his earlier work. In the wake of popularity for James Agee's Pulitzer Prize–winning posthumous novel, *A Death in the Family* (1957), Houghton Mifflin issued a second edition of *Let Us Now Praise Famous Men,* which attracted wide recognition. For this edition Evans wrote a preface, "Agee in 1936," and doubled the number of his photographs. In 1962 the Museum of Modern Art mounted another exhibition of Evans's work and reissued *American Photographs*. In 1966 Evans had two photographic books published: *Many Are Called* (photographs made secretly in the late 1930s on New York's subways) and *Message from the Interior* (photographs of domestic interiors).

When he retired from *Fortune* in 1965, Evans entered the academic world, becoming a visiting professor at the Yale School of Graphic Design. In 1968 Williams College awarded him an honorary doctorate of letters degree. After his retirement from Yale, Evans served as artist-in-residence at Dartmouth College in the fall of 1972. Although he ended his career as a teacher, his strongest influence was on younger photographers, particularly Helen Levitt, Robert Frank, Diane Arbus, Chauncey Hare, and William Christenberry. Evans died in Connecticut on April 10, 1975.

LARRY VONALT

Evans, Walker. Photographic Collection. J. Paul Getty Museum, Los Angeles.

Mora, Gillis, and John T. Hill. *Walker Evans: The Hungry Eye*. New York: H. N. Abrams, 1993.

Papageorge, Tod. *Walker Evans and Robert Frank: An Essay on Influence*. New Haven: Yale University Art Gallery, 1981.

Rathone, Belinda. *Walker Evans: A Biography*. Boston: Houghton Mifflin, 1995.

Thompson, Jerry L. *The Last Years of Walker Evans: A First-hand Account*. New York: Thames and Hudson, 1997.

EWING, THOMAS, JR. (1829–1896)

Thomas Ewing Jr., a jurist, politician, and soldier, was born in Lancaster, Ohio, on August 7, 1829. His father, Thomas Sr., had been a U.S. senator and served in the cabinets of three presidents. In 1848 at the age of nineteen, young Ewing served as a private secretary to President Zachary Taylor. He later graduated from Brown University and studied law in Cincinnati. He was admitted to the bar in the winter of 1856 and married Ellen Cox, the daughter of a Lancaster Presbyterian minister.

In 1856 Ewing joined the law and real estate firm of his brother, Hugh; his foster brother and brother-in-law, **William T. Sherman;** and Daniel McCook in Leavenworth, Kansas. Ewing became active during this period in the struggle to prevent Kansas from joining the Union as a slave state. He was a leader in the conservative faction of the Free-State Party and was appointed the first chief justice of the Kansas Supreme Court in 1861. He resigned the same year, at the request of **James Henry Lane,** to raise a regiment, the Eleventh Kansas Cavalry, and

was elected colonel. In 1862 Ewing helped organize a body of scouts called the "Red Legs" to protect the border with Missouri. He was promoted to the rank of brigadier general in the United States Volunteers on March 13, 1863. In fact, all four members of his law firm joined and eventually became generals in the Union army.

In June General Ewing was appointed to command the District of the Border with headquarters in Kansas City, Missouri. It was in this capacity that he issued General Order No. 11 following **William Clarke Quantrill**'s infamous raid on Lawrence, Kansas, in August 1863. The viciousness of the raid drew national attention and caused many to demand revenge and justice. The raid placed considerable pressure on Ewing, not only to track down and punish the irregulars but also to respond to the far more immediate and serious problem of keeping revenge-seeking Kansans out of Missouri.

Order No. 11, issued on August 25, 1863, required that all persons residing in Bates, Cass, Jackson, and upper Vernon Counties, except those living within one mile of a military post, vacate their homes by September 9, 1863. The forced evacuation of twenty thousand Missourians outraged most, and in particular artist and state treasurer **George Caleb Bingham,** who promised to destroy Ewing with pen and brush if the order was not rescinded. Bingham kept his promise and painted two identical paintings titled *Martial Law* or *Order No. 11*. The paintings depicted the forced evacuation at gun point of a Missouri family from their home.

The political pressure was so severe that Ewing was transferred to command the St. Louis District. In 1864 Gen. **Sterling Price** and his Confederate Army of Missouri entered southeast Missouri from Arkansas. Ewing, who had traveled to Pilot Knob to reconnoiter Price's army, entered Fort Davidson on September 27, 1864, and found himself surrounded. With only nine hundred troops confronted by nine thousand Confederates, Ewing refused to surrender.

Col. Lauchlan A. Maclean, Price's adjutant and a personal enemy of Ewing in Kansas, urged a frontal assault. Ewing's forces, who were outnumbered but protected by the earthen walls of the fort, humiliated the Confederate troops and caused more than one thousand casualties. Ewing realized he could not continue to defend the fort against Price's numbers and evacuated the fort in the darkness of the early morning. He moved his troops through the loosely formed Confederate line without being recognized or challenged. For his unbelievable victory and escape, he was rewarded with a brevet promotion to the rank of major general. He resigned from the service a few months later, in February 1865.

Order No. 11 destroyed any political future Ewing might have had in Kansas, so he moved to Washington, D.C., to practice law. Controversy again entered his life when he took a courageous but unpopular case and defended Elman "Edward" Spangler and helped in the defense of Samuel A. Mudd and Samuel Arnold during the Lincoln murder-conspiracies trial.

Ewing returned to Ohio to enter the political arena again. Bingham, learning of Ewing's plans, forwarded his "address to the Public" and copies of Order No. 11 to Ewing's enemies in Ohio, which helped to defeat him in his bid for state office in 1871. Ewing was elected in 1877 and 1879 to the United States House of Representatives and was the favorite to win the governorship in Ohio in 1880. However, his enemies again used the pen and brush of the deceased artist Bingham to defeat him in a close race. Ending his quest for political office, Ewing moved to New York City. There he successfully practiced law until his death, at the age of sixty-six, on January 20, 1896.

CHARLES R. MINK

Brownlee, Richard S. "The Battle of Pilot Knob, Iron County, Missouri, September 27, 1864." *Missouri Historical Review* 59 (October 1964): 1–30.

Ewing, Thomas. Family Papers. Manuscript Division. Library of Congress, Washington, D.C.

Ewing, Thomas, Jr. "The Struggle for Freedom in Kansas." *Cosmopolitan* 17 (May 1894).

Larkin, Lew. *Bingham, Fighting Artist: The Story of Missouri's Immortal Painter, Patriot, Soldier, and Statesman.* Kansas City: Burton Publishing, 1954.

Mink, Charles R. "General Orders, No. 11: The Forced Evacuation of Civilians during the Civil War." *Military Affairs* 34 (December 1970): 132–36.

FAIR, EUGENE (1877–1937)

Eugene Fair served as president of Northeast Missouri State Teachers College from 1925 until his death on August 13, 1937. He was regarded as a progressive educator who, as a teacher, was "deeply interested in his subject" and whose "sympathies were with the student." He supported the Missouri State Teachers Association, and in 1927 was elected its president. At the time of his death he was president of the American Association of Teachers Colleges. Fair also represented Adair County in the Fifty-first General Assembly. He was survived by his wife, Alta Mona Lorenz Fair, and three children.

One of eight children, Eugene Fair was born on October 19, 1877, near Gilman City in northwest Missouri. His father, Joel Fair, was a farmer who, for "relaxation and diversion," made fine furniture and when necessary helped construct coffins for neighbors. Contemporaries described Joel as sunny, jovial, and religious. Although Eugene's mother, Sarah Jane Brown Fair, "could barely write her name" and "had difficulty in reading books and newspapers," she and her husband believed strongly in education. Eugene Fair's early education took place in the rural schools of Harrison County.

Fair attended Avalon College in Trenton, Missouri, from 1895 to 1896. In the fall of 1896 he entered the State Normal School in Kirksville, Missouri, from which he earned a certificate to teach elementary school in 1898. During the next two years he taught in rural schools in Harrison and Jefferson Counties. Fair returned to the State Normal School in the fall of 1900 and at the end of the school year received a life certificate and a bachelor of science degree.

Fair attended the University of Missouri at Columbia from 1901 to 1904, earning a bachelor of arts degree and then taught in the Murphysboro, Illinois, township high school for one year. He returned to the State Normal School in Kirksville as an assistant professor of American history, a position he held until 1908. The next year he accepted an appointment as a student instructor at the University of Missouri and received a master of arts degree. He returned to Kirksville as a professor of American history and government.

In 1915 Fair received a leave of absence from the normal school to enter Columbia University. The following summer he taught at George Peabody College in Nashville, Tennessee, and then returned to Kirksville as a professor of political science from 1916 to 1925. He completed his doctor of philosophy degree from Columbia University in 1923.

During his tenure at the State Normal School, Fair established the department of political science. When the junior high school was initiated, Fair voluntarily taught a ninth-grade class under the supervision of the school's director because he believed those enrolled in a teachers college should know how to teach children as well as college students. He thought that elementary and secondary education was unsatisfactory and introduced extension and correspondence courses for teachers to improve their skills. He had a "great interest in the academic freedom of faculty members" and led a movement to "secure faculty committee participation in certain phases of administration."

During World War I, Fair assisted in the organization of a Student Army Training Corps on the normal school campus and headed the war-savings certificate drive for Adair County. He was "overwhelmingly elected" to serve in the Fifty-first General Assembly from 1921 to 1922. As a legislator he served on several committees, including the Committee on Education and Public Schools; as chairman he succeeded in making into law nine of the ten measures he proposed.

In February 1925 the Board of Regents elected Fair president of the college, and he assumed his duties in September of that year. He promptly set up a system of laboratory schools that included the elementary and junior high schools on campus as well as, with the cooperation of local school boards, area schools. Besides Kirksville, six area schools participated. A "cadet teaching" experiment followed. Instead of merely observing in the classroom, students served as regular teachers for one quarter, with no pay; they received ten hours of credit and then resumed their studies. One grade, or room, had three teachers per year. Fair inaugurated a new system of organization of the entire college, reorganized student government, "systematized facilities for scientific measurement of student abilities," and initiated the Council of the Faculty.

On August 8, 1937, Fair "was stricken by cerebral hemorrhage" while attending a meeting of Alpha Phi Sigma, an honorary fraternity, in St. Louis. Earlier that day he had met with an architect to discuss "plans for a campus building program." A few weeks earlier Gov. **Lloyd Stark** had released $300,000 for construction to replace Baldwin Hall, which had been destroyed by a fire in 1924. Fair was also attempting to obtain $250,000 from the federal government's Public Works Administration and hoped to build a total of three buildings on campus.

Fair "was a joking, fighting educator" and enjoyed "participating in the scraps which developed over some proposals." He was a Republican, a Presbyterian, a Rotarian, a trustee of the State Historical Society, and a member of Phi Beta Kappa, Kappa Delta Pi, and Phi Delta Kappa. His scholarly works include *An Introduction to the Study of Oriental History* (1908), *Government and Politics in Missouri* (1922), and *Public Administration in Missouri* (1923).

MAXINE J. CHRISTENSEN

Kirksville Daily Express, August 13, 1937.

Obituary. *Missouri Historical Review* 32 (October 1937): 114.

Simmons, Lucy. *The Contributions of Eugene Fair to Education.* Kirksville, Mo., 1935.

———. *History of Northeast Missouri State Teachers College.* Kirksville, Mo.: Auten Printing and Publishing, 1927.

FIELD, EUGENE (1850–1895)

Eugene Field's parents left Vermont and moved to St. Louis, where they were married and where Eugene was born on September 13, 1850. The New England legacy might have atrophied in the boy had it not been for his mother's death, which meant he spent much of his early life with relatives in the Northeast. Eugene's father—who played a significant part in the *Dred Scott* case—orchestrated the boy's upbringing. **Roswell M. Field** may well have wondered how fully in charge he was when Eugene, verging upon manhood, put in a brief and inconsequential stint at Williams College. After the senior Field died, Eugene, then under the guardianship of John W. Burgess, moved west to Knox College in Galesburg, Illinois, in 1869.

Rankling under the direction of Burgess, a man who would become one of the nation's foremost political scientists, Field excelled in extracurricular endeavors, as he did after relocating to the University of Missouri. After his father's estate was settled, Field embarked on a few months of European travel and study, which gave rise to some arresting stories and gave him an opportunity to write an impressive amount of letters. The object of those missives, Julia Comstock of St. Joseph, became Field's wife in 1873, shortly after his return to America. They had many children, not all of whom survived to adulthood. Although often childlike and a spendthrift, Field worked

exceedingly hard. The pace would take its toll, and Julia outlived him by more than four decades.

Aside from his European diversion, Field spent almost all of the 1870s in Missouri, and there he laid the base for his reputation for inspired high jinks and fine writing. His work for newspapers in three Missouri cities—the *St. Louis Journal* in 1873–1875, the *St. Joseph Gazette* in 1875–1876, the *St. Louis Times-Journal* in 1876–1880 and the *Kansas City Times* in 1880–1881—did not allow much of his material to be identified. Before long, however, Field's opinions and verse came to be widely recognized. Before earning his own titled column in the 1880s, he came to enjoy, in St. Louis and Kansas City, a subsection of the editorial page. Informed readers knew when they were reading Field's copy.

Field's verse was notoriously humorous. Relentlessly, he practiced and parodied the form. In "The Little Peach," which developed something of a life of its own, Field fashioned a hallmark of the lugubrious, dyspeptic, and mordant mode into which the verse of that time frequently veered. Perhaps understandably, he allowed the world to believe that he was innocent of poetry until the end of the 1870s, but he had been widely known for his sorties into metered form several years earlier, thus serving in 1874 as poet of the Missouri Press Association.

Field's involvement with the press association reflects some of his interests that are sometimes overlooked. As an energetic and aspiring journalist, he had no aversion to the organizational obligations of the trade, and he served the association accordingly. His bohemian bent deserves mention, but it can all-too-readily be exaggerated. Another quasi-organizational aspect of Field's activities in Missouri and later involved politics, that is, Republican politics. It could hardly have been otherwise, given his connections and the tensions of the times. He came to the world's attention first as a political commentator—puckish, poetic, and Republican. In Missouri he regularly covered sessions of the state legislature. In 1874 he took on the special assignment of reporting the campaign of the Republican gubernatorial candidate, a task he relished. Day after day, his barbs and witticisms, rhymed or not, had partisan purposes and targets.

In the summer of 1881 Field left Kansas City and the *Times* for the *Denver Tribune.* He returned to Missouri only as a visitor, but he and his native state remembered one another. He mercilessly assailed Missouri for harboring Democrats and outlaws, often insisting that they were interchangeable categories. While continuing his assaults on Democrats, Field honed some new, or undeveloped, forms. He now made the parodied primer a central ingredient. *The Tribune Primer* of 1882, a compilation of some of Field's newspaper items, supposedly designed for the "nursery brigade," was his first separately published work.

Two other enduring elements of Field's subject matter became manifest in Denver. At that time Missouri figured as part of the West, but Colorado gave Field the occasion and the awareness to dramatize the western dimension. His fictive mining camp on "Red Hoss Mountain" became a featured location for much of his remaining work, and there one could find "Casey's Table d'Hote," where Professor Vere De Blaw played the piano and "Three-Fingered Hoover" typified the simple manhood of the setting. "Red Hoss Mountain," the epicenter of what Field vaunted in "The Red, Red West," was engagingly unrestrained, but it was shot through with poignancy and melancholy as well. Field's primer items often had a sardonic quality, but from the Colorado experience and the deaths of two of his children he refined the sentimentalism regarding childhood, which would become his most lasting claim.

After two years in Denver, Field heeded the call of Melville Stone and the *Chicago Daily News* (later the *Record*), and there he remained for the last twelve years of his life. Sometimes referred to as America's first columnist, Field had clear authorial identification, and in his columns he embellished themes already established. His West now included Chicago—brash, upstart, and gauche. That sort of impish material yielded his first full-length book, *Culture's Garland,* in 1887. The sentimental stories and poems grew into something of a stock-in-trade, most notably "Little Boy Blue." He again contributed humorous commentary on the politics of Chicago, Illinois, and the nation in general; in fact, he wrote about politics as much as anything else, and continued his staunch allegiance to the Republican Party.

In cultural rather than political terms, Field's writing aided in the nation's final accommodation with things theatrical. In youth he had contemplated an acting career, and the very name of his column through the Chicago years, "Sharps and Flats," registered not only a musical motif but a theatrical one as well. That was the title of a popular play of the time, one coauthored by his colleague, friend, and, in time, biographer, Slason Thompson. Field made friends of many prominent actors, including Sol Smith Russell, Francis Wilson, Emma Abbott, and Helena Modjeska. He offered whimsical accounts of these and other friends. For example, he made mock serious appraisals of Emma Abbott's baby, a child that had not gone through the formality of coming into existence, and he specialized in stories of Modjeska, to whom he had ascribed in Denver a touching poem, "The Wanderer," taken by many to have been Modjeska's own.

America's love affair with its actors would have been consummated without Field, but his exceedingly popular column rendered those thespians more lovable and interesting, if not always more authentic. He did something of the same for the national pastime. Here again, a long-held interest bloomed in the presence of the great White Sox teams of A. G. Spalding in the mid-1880s. Field gained the reputation of being baseball's foremost fan, and he did his part in heading the game toward its zenith in the years after the turn of the century.

A final noteworthy emphasis involved arcane and classical letters. Here too, Field intensified interest into something of an obsession. In one form it appeared in such items as "A Proper Trewe Idyll of Camelot," or Field's favorite self-designation, "ye gentle knight sans peur et sans monnaie." In a related form it surfaced in the book on which he was at work when he died, *The Love Affairs of a Bibliomaniac.* It also emerged in retranslations of odes of Horace, which were fashionable in the late nineteenth century.

All these forms and emphases reside in the dozen volumes of Field's collected works (1896, 1900), nearly all the items of which appeared first in "Sharps and Flats" and then in individually published volumes from 1889 to 1895, the year of Field's death.

Immensely popular from the 1880s to the 1920s, Field's work has not done well since. The most recent book-length publication, Robert Conrow's *Field Days* (1974), added little to what Slason Thompson and Charles Dennis did in their biographical ventures of 1901, 1924, and 1927. In fact, the basis for the intensely fond regard for the "poet of childhood" has been undermined. His support for the Republican Party, even as the party of reform, can do little more than puzzle people with scant awareness of party postures prior to the 1930s. Sentimentalism flourishes, but it has veered into channels different from those of Field. Even his celebrations of the West, both playful and poignant, no longer resonate positively. In his own time, however, and for three or four decades thereafter, Field helped shape and beautifully represent some vital ingredients of the American ethos. Eugene Field died on November 4, 1895.

LEWIS O. SAUM

Conrow, Robert. *Field Days: The Life, Times, and Reputation of Eugene Field.* New York: Charles Scribner's Sons, 1974.

Dennis, Charles Henry. *Eugene Field's Creative Years.* Garden City, N.Y.: Doubleday, 1924.

Thompson, Slason. *Eugene Field: A Study in Heredity and Contradictions.* 2 vols. New York: Charles Scribner's Sons, 1901.

———. *Life of Eugene Field: The Poet of Childhood.* New York: D. Appleton, 1927.

FIELD, MARY KATHERINE KEEMLE (1838–1896)

By any standard applied today, Kate Field would qualify as a feminist. A journalist, lecturer, actress, author, and businesswoman, she traveled widely and championed many causes, including woman suffrage, Hawaiian annexation, and the abolition of Mormon polygamy. Never married, she channeled her abundant energy into her varied occupations, her travel, and her friendships. Her vivacity and charm commanded the attention of thousands of loyal readers as well as those who flocked to her lectures.

Mary Katherine Keemle Field, "Kate" to her family, friends, and those who came to know her through her lectures and writings, was born in St. Louis on October 1, 1838. She came by her love of theatricality, oratory, and writing naturally. Her father was Joseph M. Field, a well-known St. Louis actor, dramatic critic, theatrical manager, editor, and journalist. Her mother, Eliza Field, was an accomplished actress, with nearly one thousand roles to her credit. In 1844 Joseph Field, along with his brother Matthew Field and Charles Keemle, both experienced newspapermen, founded the *St. Louis Reveille,* a paper that gained a national reputation and flourished until its offices were destroyed by the Great Fire of 1849. The Fields continued their theatrical careers, touring as well as performing as regulars at playhouses in Mobile, New Orleans, and St. Louis. In 1851 Joseph Field invested in the construction of a new theater on Market Street in St. Louis. Serving as both manager and actor, he named it the Varieties Theater. In addition, he managed the Royal Street Theater in Mobile, performing there with his wife during winter seasons. In 1856 he died suddenly of a bronchial infection. His wife eventually moved to Boston to join her millionaire brother-in-law and sister.

Kate Field had by this time also left St. Louis for Boston to continue her education at an exclusive girls' school at her uncle's expense. Hyde and Conard, in their *Encyclopedia of the History of St. Louis,* relate that when Field was sixteen her family sent her to Europe to "finish" her education through travel. A story that appears to have been widely circulated and reported as truth during her lifetime holds that, while traveling in Sicily, she was abducted and held for ransom. In the March 2, 1887, issue of the *Kentucky Gazette,* an article profiling Field prior to her delivery of a lecture narrated that while in Sicily she was abducted by brigands who demanded seven thousand livres for her release. According to the *Gazette,* though her family paid the ransom, Field remained a captive for six weeks, during which time she thoroughly learned the Italian language. While she was his prisoner, Manrico Bolero, chief of the bandits, fell in love with Field and proposed; she refused. The story, however, did not end there, the *Gazette* contended. After she was ransomed, "her goodness and wit so preyed upon [Bolero's] mind that he forsook his evil occupations, distributed his ill-gotten gains among the poor, and joined a Benedictine monastery."

While this romantic narrative is in some dispute, the fact that Field traveled widely in Europe is not. At age twenty she went to Florence to study voice. During that time, she began her career as a journalist, sending travel articles to American newspapers. She also met and became well acquainted with members of a group of literary personages who were then residing in Florence. Robert Browning, Elizabeth Browning, Walter Savage Landor, George Eliot, and Anthony Trollope were among the literati who welcomed the young, aspiring journalist into their inner circle.

Returning to Boston in 1861, Field advanced her reputation as a journalist through articles written for the *Atlantic Monthly* about the famous friends she had made in Europe. She also reported for the *Springfield (Mass.) Republican* on Charles Dickens's 1867–1868 American Reading Tour, and it was largely these articles that cemented her fame. She later expanded her Dickens pieces into a book, *Pen Photographs of Charles Dickens's Readings.*

Other interests engaged Field's attention as well. Hoping to follow in the footsteps of her mother and father, she mounted the stage at Booth's Theater in New York in 1874 as Peg Woffington in Charles Reade's *Masks and Faces.* But criticism of her work was sharp, and thespian success eluded her. Nevertheless, she continued to pursue what she once called "the desire of her childhood," acting in dramatic productions almost constantly until 1878. She did have one notable success, singing and dancing in a musical monologue she had written, titled *Eyes and Ears in London.* The *Boston Journal* pronounced the piece "one of the most brilliant and sparkling that has been introduced in Boston in a long time," and the *Boston Transcript* judged her singing "quite exceptional, not only that it is dramatic and forcible, but that every word is distinctly audible."

This clarity of diction was no doubt honed in another of Field's pursuits, that of lecturer on the several topics that consumed her interest. One such topic was Mormonism, a subject she chanced upon when, as she describes, "I had become ashamed of sailing east year after year, and determined to hitch my wagon to the star of empire and learn something of my own great country." In typical Kate Field fashion, she set out to cross the mountains on horseback. When snow blocked her way, she stopped at Salt

Lake City for what she supposed would be a wait of approximately one week. Interest and indignation kept her there many months, researching the topic of Mormonism, which she subsequently adopted as one of her causes célèbres.

Field's energetic assault on the Church of Jesus Christ of Latter-day Saints manifested itself in lectures given after her return from Utah. "Mormonism," she told a packed house at Music Hall in Kansas City, "makes serfs of its followers . . . brutalizes humanity . . . [and] becomes inchoate treason." Her contempt for the religion was due in large part to its validation of polygamy, a practice that was anathema to Field's sensibilities as it demonstrated the contempt in which, she believed, the Mormon religion held women.

Field's passion and eloquence were not reserved for one subject alone. With the founding in 1890 of a journal called *Kate Field's Washington,* she provided herself with a platform from which to sound forth weekly on art, education, music, drama, and the various reforms she supported. The publication was a success in every way except financial, and it folded in five years.

Financial success eluded Field in another quarter as well. In 1882 she invested in the Co-operative Dress Association, a commercial venture that began auspiciously but ended a few short years later in bankruptcy. Her monetary losses were great, and her bitterness even greater. To another female investor she wrote, "I have lost $3,500 in stock and $5,000 in money loaned, the association was managed by me and killed by them."

Field's several occupations kept her busy, and thus she was not often able to return to her hometown of St. Louis. When she did, it was to give a lecture or to attend an event. During one such visit in 1891, the *St. Louis Post-Dispatch* noted: "[Kate Field] has achieved decided eminence in journalism and the lecture field, and is possessed of such bold and original powers of observation and expression that her views on subjects of public interest have never failed to command interested attention." Well pleased with this assessment, Field returned the favor by praising the city of her birth in *Kate Field's Washington,* citing its streets, which were "far better paved and infinitely more attractive than [those of] New York or Philadelphia," and its "residential parks . . . unique on this side of the water."

The encomiums of the *Post-Dispatch* and other reviewers aside, Field was not always as convinced of her talents and worth. "All our lives are failures," she wrote to a friend in 1891. "I'm sure mine is but I do the best I can." Doing her best included penning no fewer than eight books in addition to the countless articles she contributed to the nation's leading newspapers. At a time when women did not often venture far from the home fires, she traveled, wrote, acted, lectured, and, in her own words, lost "none of my womanliness in the effort." She was indeed a pioneer feminist.

Field's last venture led her to the Hawaiian Islands as a roving correspondent for the *Chicago Times-Herald.* While there, she contracted pneumonia and died on May 19, 1896. Friends eulogized her as "peculiar because it is peculiar to be plain-spoken," "a curious admixture of sentiment and assurance," and "an indefatigable worker, quick and ready with her pen and her tongue . . . the soul of honesty and honor." These final assessments would have pleased Kate Field.

DEBORAH STEWARD

Hyde, William, and Howard L. Conard, eds. *Encyclopedia of the History of St. Louis.* 4 vols. New York: Southern History, 1899.

Ludlow-Field-Maury Papers. Missouri Historical Society, St. Louis.

Moss, Carolyn J. "Kate Field: The Story of a Once-Famous St. Louisan." *Missouri Historical Review* 88 (January 1994): 157–75.

Shoemaker, Floyd C., ed. *Missouri, Day by Day.* Columbia: State Historical Society of Missouri, 1942–1943.

Theatrical Collection. Missouri Historical Society, St. Louis.

FIELD, ROSWELL M. (1807–1869)

Roswell Martin Field, a prominent lawyer in antebellum St. Louis and father of the poet **Eugene Field,** was born in Newfane, in Windham County, Vermont, on February 22, 1807. His father, Martin Field, a graduate of Williams College, was an attorney. His mother was Esther Kellogg Field, a devout Congregationalist of Puritan lineage.

As a child Field attended the academy at Newfane, and at age nine was placed under the tutelage of the Reverend Luke Whitcomb of Townsend, Vermont, to prepare for college. In 1818 Roswell Field and his older brother Charles enrolled at Middlebury College from which Roswell graduated in 1822 at age fifteen, having acquired a proficiency in five languages: Latin, Greek, German, Spanish, and French. After college, along with his brother, he chose to practice law and for three years studied under his uncle Daniel Kellogg. On September 22, 1825, at age eighteen, Field was admitted to the bar of Windham County and practiced law with his father at Newfane. During this period he became active in politics, and from 1835 to 1836 served in the Vermont General Assembly. As a legislator his most notable effort was a bill to abrogate the common law requiring religious oaths of witnesses in the Vermont courts.

In 1832 while practicing law in Newfane, Field formed an attachment for a young lady from Windsor, Vermont, and after a whirlwind courtship, they were married. The lady's mother viewed the daughter's civil marriage to Field invalid, and a series of legal suits in the Vermont courts followed. Three of the suits eventually reached the Vermont Supreme Court, which later ruled the marriage null and void. Several of Field's pleadings in these suits came to the attention of Justice Joseph Story of the United States Supreme Court who pronounced them "masterpieces of special pleading."

Embittered by the outcome of the cases, Field in 1839, at age thirty-two, moved west to St. Louis where he entered into law practice with Myron Leslie, also of Vermont. The partnership lasted only a few years. Field then went into practice for himself, specializing in real estate law. Here his knowledge of Spanish and French was immensely useful in handling land controversies involving early French and Spanish claims in Missouri, and he soon achieved a reputation as one of Missouri's foremost real estate attorneys. During this period Field also served as attorney for the St. Louis school board.

However, Field is best remembered as the attorney for the slave **Dred Scott,** whose suit for freedom (*Dred Scott v. John F. A. Sandford*) Field filed in 1853 in the federal court following six years of futile litigation by the slave in the Missouri courts. Serving without compensation, Field in 1854 took the case to the United States Supreme Court where it soon became immersed in the controversy over the extension of slavery into the territories. On March 6, 1857, the Supreme Court, in a landmark decision, denied Scott his freedom, ruling that African Americans were not citizens and that Congress lacked the power to prohibit slavery in the territories.

In 1848 Field married Frances Maria Reed, also of Vermont, and by her had six children, four of whom died in childhood. The two surviving sons, Eugene and Roswell, were sent to New England to be raised by Field's sister after the death of their mother in 1856. Eugene, trained as a journalist, later achieved fame as a poet.

During the Civil War, Field was a strong supporter of the Union, along with **Frank Blair** and others. Field refused all positions of public office in Missouri, and in 1869, at age sixty-two, died of cancer in St. Louis.

KENNETH C. KAUFMAN

Bay, W. V. N. *Reminiscences of the Bench and Bar of Missouri.* St. Louis: F. H. Thomas, 1878.

Fish, Judge Frank L. "Roswell M. Field." *Proceedings of the Vermont Historical Society.* St. Albans, Vt.: The Society, 1923.

Gray, Melvin L. "Recollections of Judge Roswell M. Field." In *The History of the Bench and Bar of Missouri,* ed. A. J. D. Stewart. St. Louis: Legal Publishing, 1898.

Kaufman, Kenneth C. *Dred Scott's Advocate: A Biography of Roswell M. Field.* Columbia: University of Missouri Press, 1996.

FILLEY, CHAUNCEY IVES (1829–1923); FILLEY, GILES FRANKLIN (1815–1900); FILLEY, OLIVER DWIGHT (1806–1881)

In the three decades prior to the Civil War the burgeoning western economy attracted thousands of New Englanders to St. Louis. Many of them came to operate commercial houses, either on their own or as western branches of eastern establishments, intending to eventually return to the East. Others, however, were looking for a more permanent home, and frequently those New Englanders turned to manufacturing rather than commerce. The most successful of this group were entrepreneurs who recognized the opportunities presented by the explosive growth of the West. Their success helped establish St. Louis as the leading antebellum trade and shipping center of the Mississippi Valley, and their northern attitudes and preferences shaped cultural and political developments within their adopted community. When the sectional crisis of the 1850s erupted into war in 1861, these St. Louis New Englanders proved critical in helping Unionist forces keep Missouri in federal hands. The experiences of the Filley family help illustrate this history.

Giles Franklin Filley and Oliver Dwight Filley were brothers who came to the West to practice the trade of their father, a tinner. Oliver, born on May 23, 1806, in Bloomfield, Connecticut, was the first to arrive, coming to St. Louis in 1829 with another brother, Marcus. Within a year of their arrival they owned a tinner shop, and in 1834 their younger brother, Giles, born on February 15, 1815, in Wintonbury, Connecticut, joined the enterprise.

Soon, however, Giles Filley left the business to pursue a new venture. He thought that the rich clay deposits in Missouri would make earthenware manufacturing profitable, and in 1844 he traveled to London to investigate the process. He hired skilled workers who returned with him to St. Louis. His pottery manufacturing venture succeeded, until the workers decided to strike out on their own. By 1849 he gave up on the project and sold his remaining china importing business to his cousins, Edward A. Filley and Samuel R. Filley.

Giles Filley rejoined Oliver, and they concentrated their efforts on manufacturing cookstoves for the western market. They soon developed a new model, the Charter Oak stove, which, after its introduction in 1852, eventually catapulted the Filleys' Excelsior Stove Company to its position as one of the largest manufacturer of stoves in the United States.

Chauncey Ives Filley was Oliver and Giles's younger cousin, and it was to Chauncey's brothers that Giles had sold his earthenware business. Chauncey was born on October 17, 1829, in Lansingburg, New York. He had planned a legal career and had trained for it in New York, but he changed his mind when he visited St. Louis in 1850 and saw the bustling wharf. Chauncey joined his brothers, Samuel and Edward, in the earthenware sales business, but eight years later they dissolved their enterprise. Chauncey opted to import china products on his own. He traveled to London to secure suppliers and purchase his initial stock, and returned to St. Louis where he operated a profitable supply house until his retirement in 1873. Unlike Giles and Oliver, Chauncey did not become wealthy, but he was a respected businessman and a community leader in his own right.

Perhaps the most enduring contributions made by Chauncey, Giles, and Oliver Filley were not in business, but in politics. They were Benton Democrats who became Free Soilers, and they helped organize the Republican Party in Missouri. They also played key roles in securing St. Louis for the Union.

Oliver became the first Filley to hold public office in St. Louis. Once a Democrat and a friend of Sen. **Thomas Hart Benton,** Oliver moved into the Free-Soil Party over the issue of the Wilmot Proviso. He was a manufacturer, not a politician, but in 1858 his friends persuaded him to run for election as mayor on the Free-Soil ticket. He won the election, and reelection in 1859 for a two-year term. During his three years in office he worked to reduce the city's public debt, and he supported several major reforms: the change from a bicameral to a unicameral city government, prohibition of Sunday liquor sales, and the establishment of a nonpolitical board of control for the city's largest charity, the Mullanphy Trust. He oversaw important improvements in public services, including introduction of a city fire alarm system, and organization of the city's first paid fire department. He chose not to run for reelection in 1861, but he remained a member of the inner circle of Missouri Republicans.

The state of Missouri and the city of St. Louis divided over the secession crisis of 1861, and all three Filleys staked their future with the Union. In the early stage of the crisis the state's voters rejected secession, but the pro-Southern governor, **Claiborne Fox Jackson,** hoped to force Missouri into the Confederacy. He assembled state militia forces into camps, and planned to seize the federal arsenal in St. Louis.

By May 1861, when the militia arrived in St. Louis, Oliver Filley no longer held public office, but he and the other Republican leaders recognized that civilians had to take initiatives to support the federal army if St. Louis was to remain in the Union. Oliver joined Cong. **Frank Blair** in organizing a Committee of Safety, and they quickly recruited volunteers to help the army maintain control of the city and capture the state forces.

Giles Filley did his part by organizing a body of men from the Excelsior Stove Company to help defend the arsenal. He would later serve on the St. Louis County Board of Assessors, which was charged with extracting fines from pro-Confederate St. Louisans. He also helped underwrite publications of the Union newspaper, which was established during the war to support the president.

Oliver and Giles Filley were unconditional Unionists who supported the Lincoln administration as it waged war to restore the Union. However, like many Unionists, they did not support converting the war effort into a drive to secure abolition of slavery. Missouri Republicans broke into two factions, the emancipationist Charcoals and the conservative Claybanks. Conservatives objected to more than the antislavery policy of the Lincoln administration: they also opposed the president's policy of arming African American soldiers, and they believed that martial law should be revoked in St. Louis. Oliver and Giles, along with Frank Blair, were leaders of the Claybanks.

Chauncey Filley had moved into the Republican Party from the Free Soilers as well. He rose to prominence within the state organization, and represented Missouri at the party's 1860 national convention. He supported the president as the war advanced. However, unlike Oliver and Giles, Chauncey moved into the radical emancipationist wing of the party, and became a leader within the Charcoal faction.

In the St. Louis mayoral contest of 1863 the two Republican factions vied for control of the city, and each side nominated a Filley as their candidate: Oliver Filley from the Claybanks, and Chauncey Filley from the Charcoals. Chauncey won, and his victory signaled the ascendancy of the radical faction within the Republican Party. While he was forced to resign after serving only half of his two-year term due to ill health, his faction remained in control of the state government long enough to engineer the abolition of slavery in Missouri and the implementation of a new state constitution.

Chauncey Filley was ultimately the most politically active Filley, and he influenced state politics for more than six decades. He represented Missouri at each Republican National Convention from 1860 to 1896. Three times he served as state party chairman, and from 1876 to 1892 he sat on the Republican

National Committee. He won election as a delegate to the 1865 state Constitutional Convention, and a grateful Republican administration appointed him postmaster of St. Louis in 1873. Chauncey Filley believed he represented the common person against the "silk-stocking" members of his party, and he moved from the antislavery wing to the Progressive wing of his party. He founded a local Good Government Republican Club, and he supported Theodore Roosevelt's 1912 challenge to the reelection bid of President William H. Taft. In explaining that decision, Filley said that he had "been a progressive ever since he became a Republican in 1856." His views were revealed in two collections of his speeches and writings published at the turn of the century.

Chauncey Filley was an influential politician, and he was also a popular civic leader and booster. The Board of Trade, formed after the Civil War to promote St. Louis, elected Chauncey as its president three times. In 1869 he presided over the Mississippi Valley Commercial Convention in New Orleans, where he publicized the trade advantages of St. Louis over Chicago. He led the drive to build a railroad bridge across the Mississippi River and was one of the incorporators of the St. Louis and Illinois Bridge Company, which hired **James Buchanan Eads** and financed the ten-year project to complete construction. Chauncey headed the effort to organize the big public celebration on the day that the Eads Bridge finally opened, July 4, 1874.

Each of the three Filley men married women from their home states. Oliver wed Chloe Veline Brown in Bloomfield, Connecticut, in 1835. Their grandson **Dwight F. Davis** became the secretary of war and the governor-general of the Philippines, and established the Davis Cup tennis competition. Giles married Maria M. Farrington of Hartford, Connecticut. Chauncey's wife, Anna Elizabeth Adams, came from his hometown of Lansingburg, New York.

All three Filley cousins enjoyed long lives. Oliver lived to age seventy-five, and died August 21, 1881, in New Hampshire. Giles survived him until February 27, 1900. Chauncey lived to be ninety-three, and died in St. Louis on September 24, 1923.

VICKI JOHNSON

Adler, Jeffrey S. *Yankee Merchants and the Making of the Urban West: The Rise and Fall of Antebellum St. Louis.* Cambridge: Cambridge University Press, 1991.

Filley, Chauncey Ives. *Some More Republican History of Missouri.* St. Louis: Chrismann Printing, 1902.

———. *Some Republican History of Missouri.* St. Louis, 1898.

Filley Family. Papers. Missouri Historical Society, St. Louis.

Primm, James Neal. *Lion of the Valley: St. Louis, Missouri, 1764–1980.* 3d ed. St. Louis: Missouri Historical Society Press, 1998.

Scharf, J. Thomas. *History of St. Louis City and County: From Earliest Periods to the Present Day.* Philadelphia: Everts, 1883.

FILLMORE, CHARLES (1854–1948); FILLMORE, MYRTLE (1845–1931)

In 1886 Charles Fillmore and Myrtle Fillmore, who until then had lived rather unremarkable Victorian middle-class lives in Kansas City, Missouri, embraced the New Thought movement's promise of a healthy and self-determined life. Three years later they founded the Unity School of Christianity, which from modest beginnings went on to become a worldwide organization.

Prior to their conversion to New Thought, life for the Fillmores had been hard, with cycles of poverty and prosperity and unflagging aspiration. Charles was born on August 22, 1854, on the Minnesota frontier, the son of an Indian trader. He had endured a spartan upbringing made more burdensome by a childhood skating accident that left him in chronic pain and in need of braces to support a weakened and shortened leg for much of his adult life. Deprived of a formal education, Charles was tutored by the mother of a friend who introduced him to Shakespeare, Shelley, Emerson, Tennyson, and Robert Ingersoll. At the age of twenty he left Minnesota, moving first to Caddo, Oklahoma, and then to Denison, Texas, where he found work as a railroad clerk. Somewhat self-taught, Charles sought like-minded company in Denison and found a literary circle that he attended regularly. His faithfulness was rewarded when he met his future wife, Myrtle Page. He later recalled that when he saw Myrtle reciting a poem, he heard a voice tell him, "Charles, that's your wife."

Born in Page, Ohio, on August 6, 1845, as Mary Lee Page, a name for which she bore no fondness, Myrtle adopted a variation of her father's pet name for her, Myrtiles. Her upbringing was more refined than her husband's, and she was afforded a formal education at Oberlin's Literary Course for Ladies. However, even more than Charles, Myrtle struggled with her health, having been diagnosed with incipient tuberculosis in her childhood. Yet, she was no less adventurous or ambitious than her husband. Leaving home after completing the course at Oberlin, she ventured to Clinton, Missouri, to live with her brother and teach school. She later moved to Denison to accept a teaching appointment in 1874.

Charles's and Myrtle's paths separated for a few years beginning in 1878, when they both lost their jobs in Denison. Myrtle moved back to Clinton, while Charles moved to Colorado, where he eventually found some success in real estate speculation. Finally in 1881 Charles felt financially secure enough for marriage and brought Myrtle to Gunnison, Colorado, where they prospered for a time and began a family. Two sons, Lowell Page (1882) and Waldo Rickert (1884), were born in Colorado, while a third, Royal (1889), was born in Kansas City. Two of the sons were destined to play important roles in the Unity empire, while Lowell died tragically in 1923. After successive business failures, Charles moved the family to Kansas City where he again tried his hand at real estate.

The Fillmores fit the profile of many middle-class Protestants attracted to the teachings of New Thought and Christian Science during the end of the nineteenth century. They were both well read in the fashion of the day, generally religious, and very familiar with Scripture. They viewed themselves as freethinkers and shared in the commonsense appreciation of the authority of science, and their respectable Protestant orientation influenced their freethinking. They joined Methodist or Episcopal congregations in the various cities in which they lived and played an active role in the temperance movement. They found in New Thought a compatibility of science and faith and the unity of experience and knowledge, an approach to spiritual longing that honored their Christian heritage but also promised that faith could be reasonable and scientific yet powerful.

Moreover, the freethinking piety of the Fillmores had been leavened by a tough-minded yet quixotic economic pragmatism as they struggled with uneven success to climb the slippery pole of upward mobility. Charles's real estate career gave evidence of a midwestern mix of savvy and naïveté. Beginning in Gunnison he exhibited a pattern that repeated itself in Pueblo, Colorado, and on a more spectacular level in Kansas City. In each city he entered land booms at the bottom of the curve with little in the way of liquid assets and quickly assembled an impressive portfolio. At the peak of his success in Kansas City in 1885, he had amassed an estate worth approximately $150,000, but he was left with large tracts of unsalable land when the markets collapsed.

In addition to the mercurial uncertainty of their financial aspirations, the Fillmores struggled increasingly with unsatisfactory health, though despite their frustrations concerning their physical infirmities they did lead aggressively energetic lives. Myrtle gave birth to three children between 1882 and 1889. Nevertheless in 1886, the year that his real estate empire collapsed, Charles's eyesight deteriorated and Myrtle's strength was tested by a bout with malaria. Searching for a way to make sense of, and to overcome, the circumstances that besieged their lives, Myrtle attended a lecture series held by E. B. Weeks, a disciple of New Thought–guru Emma Curtis Hopkins. She came away from the lecture transformed, repeating what would become her mantra: "I am a child of God and I do not inherit sickness."

Persuaded by his wife's enthusiasm and improvement in health, Charles began a self-study course in metaphysics that concentrated on New Thought writings, and quickly became an apostle of the movement, publishing at his own expense a metaphysical periodical, *Modern Thought,* in 1889. From the modest success of the paper, the Fillmores began a correspondence school and a broad-based publishing operation that printed several periodicals on New Thought and faith living, including one for children titled *Wee Wisdom,* edited by Myrtle Fillmore. The name for the ministry came as an inspiration to Charles in a prayer and meditation gathering of New Thought fellow travelers. It carried two meanings: the unity of all faiths and, more important, the unity of life.

Heavily influenced by Emma Curtis Hopkins, a former associate of Mary Baker Eddy and a leading light in New Thought's firmament, the Fillmores learned to intellectually nibble from many theological plates, and their theology evolved as a compilation of New Thought, Christian Science, and traditional Protestantism. Like the New Thought writers, the Fillmores taught that life was one—a unity of spirit, mind, and body—and that health and prosperity were governed by both spiritual and scientific eternal laws. They emphasized the value of all spiritual experience, teaching that the search for spiritual truth should draw lessons from the experience of all faiths. This emphasis on the universality of inspiration gave the Unity teaching a rather eclectic and protean character.

Thus, on the one hand, Charles Fillmore could teach that reincarnation was a scientific spiritual truth or that there were many Christs in many faiths. Yet, on the other hand, he insisted that Unity should be understood as part of the Christian tradition. He was sufficiently concerned about this last point to publicly break from New Thought in 1905, declaring that it no longer fit his standard of faith and that he preferred to think of Unity as an expression of "practical Christianity."

The emphasis on the practical spirituality of healing and prayer gave Unity its popular appeal. Although never as absolutist as the Christian Scientists, the Fillmores taught that healing and prosperity were the natural state of the unified spiritual life. They drew this lesson first from their own experiences, believing that their health and prosperity had been found in the spiritual wholeness offered in the teachings of New Thought. Charles rarely spoke about his own condition, except to comment that the chronic pain of his early life no longer afflicted him. However, his followers claimed that his withered leg gained strength over the years until it appeared to be almost normal. Myrtle, by contrast, was more direct when speaking about the change in her physical condition. She saw herself almost as a new creation, claiming that in her pre-Unity days she had been "an emaciated woman upon whom doctors and relatives had placed the stamp of tuberculosis."

The Fillmores even flirted with the idea that death might be avoided or at least controlled. Unity chroniclers recorded that prior to her death on October 6, 1931, Myrtle intimated that it was time for her to move on to the "invisible plane of existence," implying that in effect she controlled the timing of her own departure.

The teachings on healing and spiritual power transformed Unity from a family operation run out of Charles's real estate office into a national ministry. In 1890 Myrtle announced in the pages of *Modern Thought* that a small group of the faithful would gather every evening at ten to pray in "silent soul communion" for "all those who are in trouble, sickness or poverty." She invited readers to participate in the moment of transcendent spiritual unity by setting aside at least fifteen minutes during the appointed hour and agreeing to meditate and pray over the words provided each month in her column. Known first as the Society of Silent Help and later simply as Silent Unity, this ministry of mediation and meditation proved consistently popular, providing Unity with a steady stream of correspondence and support leading to a gradual increase in subscriptions and contributions.

Building on this base Unity evolved into an even larger institutional structure, leading to the purchase in 1919 of Unity Farm, which later, in an expanded form, became the retreat center and metaphysical school known as Unity Village. By the end of World War I, Unity had become what the Fillmores had explicitly set out to avoid: a denomination with facilities in many of America's major metropolitan areas and an international correspondence outreach.

Following the death of Myrtle in 1931, Charles married Cora G. Dedrick, who had been the Fillmores' private secretary for a number of years. He gradually turned operations of the organization over to his sons and devoted the remainder of his life to lecturing and writing. He died at Unity Village in the presence of his sons on July 5, 1948.

RICHARD COTNER

Braden, Charles Samuel. *Spirits in Rebellion: The Rise and Development of New Thought.* Dallas: Southern Methodist University Press, 1963.

Freeman, James Dillett. *The Story of Unity.* Lees Summit, Mo.: Unity School of Christianity, 1954.

Meyer, Donald B. *The Positive Thinkers: Popular Religious Psychology from Mary Baker Eddy to Norman Vincent Peale and Ronald Reagan.* Rev. ed. Middletown, Conn.: Wesleyan University Press, 1988.

FINIELS, NICOLAS DE
(dates unknown)

Nicolas de Finiels, an expatriate French engineer who served the Spanish monarchy during the late colonial era, remains little known. Yet, he enjoys the distinction of having prepared two of the most valuable source documents pertaining to Upper Louisiana in colonial times: a lengthy memoir titled *An Account of Upper Louisiana* and a meticulously drawn map of the central Mississippi River valley. The forty-thousand-word *Account* provides important information about Upper Louisiana in the late 1790s on subjects ranging from geopolitics to details of domestic life. The map, undeniably the best ever created of the eighteenth-century Illinois country, complements Finiels's text with a careful rendering of both physical and cultural features of the Mississippi Valley from the mouth of the Illinois River south to the outpost of New Madrid.

There is no direct evidence concerning Finiels's exact place and date of birth, his education, or the circumstances that prompted him to leave France. The best guess is that Finiels, a sharp critic of the French Revolution, was one of the numerous political refugees who came to the United States during the early 1790s. The earliest documented account places him in Philadelphia in 1797, where he made the acquaintance of Carlos Martinez de Irujo, the Spanish minister to the United States. Irujo was, at the time, actively seeking to strengthen Spain's position in its North American borderlands. So too was Louisiana's governor-general, Don Francisco Luis Hector de Carondelet, who had launched a major campaign to improve the dilapidated military fortifications in St. Louis. The French agent-general Georges-Victor Collot met Finiels and Irujo in Philadelphia and shared with them impressions about Louisiana gained during his recent travels. Seeking to pass himself off as a friend of the Spanish regime, he offered suggestions for improving St. Louis's faulty defenses and suggested that Finiels be appointed to oversee such a project.

Without authorization from his superiors, Irujo retained Finiels as an engineer for the Spanish service and dispatched him to St. Louis. Finiels's hostility to the French Revolutionaries and his open sympathy for the royal house of Bourbon evidently persuaded Irujo that he could be trusted with the assignment. Finiels arrived in St. Louis in early June 1797, accompanied by his wife and mother-in-law. During his stay in Philadelphia he had apparently met and married Marianne Rivière, a Creole from St. Domingue. Officials in Upper Louisiana received Finiels cautiously. Lt. Col. Carlos Howard, the newly appointed Spanish military commander, was understandably hesitant to involve a stranger in the sensitive task of constructing military fortifications. Finiels suggested changes, but he was powerless to effect them without more explicit authorization from the Spanish government.

While he awaited a decision on his official status from Spanish administrators, Finiels reconnoitered Upper Louisiana's settlements, gathered information about the region and its people, and put his talents as a draftsman to work. **James MacKay,** a prominent trader recently returned from the upper Missouri country, employed him to prepare a final draft of the famed Evans-MacKay map that **Meriwether Lewis** and **William Clark** later found so helpful. Finiels also struck up a friendship with Lt. Gov. **Zenon Trudeau,** another French Creole in Spanish service. During this time Finiels drafted a map of the central Mississippi valley. Despite his frustrations, he was prepared to remain in St. Louis, but his plans were dashed in 1798 when he received word that authorities in Madrid had rejected his appointment.

Finiels departed for New Orleans, where, despite the government's pronouncement, Louisiana's new governor, Manuel Gayoso de Lemos, decided to reemploy him. Finiels remained in New Orleans for the duration of the Spanish regime, working under Governor Gayoso and his successors on a vast array of projects, including drawing maps, repairing levees, planning fortifications, and even designing fire engines.

In 1800 Spain ceded Louisiana to France, and the French government named Pierre-Clement de Laussat to take charge of the province. Following his arrival in New Orleans in 1803, Laussat needed someone who was intelligent and literate, and who was knowledgeable about Upper Louisiana and willing to serve France. Nicolas de Finiels qualified on all counts. He was a royalist and a Roman Catholic, but his chronic financial problems and a lingering loyalty to France may have persuaded him to work for Laussat, even though he represented a revolutionary despot, Napoléon Bonaparte. It is unclear whether Laussat in fact hired Finiels to write his *Account* or whether the observant French engineer merely hoped to position himself for possible employment with the French regime by obliging Laussat. According to the notation on the manuscript, Finiels wrote his *Account of Upper Louisiana* in June 1803. A short time later the astounding news that France had agreed to sell Louisiana to the United States reached New Orleans, and the disappointed Laussat packed his bags and returned to France, taking along his copy of Finiels's

Account and the original manuscript map of the Mississippi Valley that Finiels had also prepared.

Following Louisiana's transfer to the United States, Finiels cast his lot with Spain and remained in Spanish service. He participated in the 1805–1806 Spanish expedition into east Texas and drew an excellent map of that region. He was stationed successively at Havana and Pensacola. He bought property at the latter place and was wounded there during Andrew Jackson's controversial 1818 raid into Spanish Florida. Finiels's four sons followed their father into the Spanish army. The date of Finiels's death is unknown.

CARL J. EKBERG AND WILLIAM E. FOLEY

Ekberg, Carl J., and William E. Foley, eds. *An Account of Upper Louisiana by Nicolas de Finiels.* Columbia: University of Missouri Press, 1989.

Wood, W. Raymond. "Nicolas de Finiels: Mapping the Mississippi and Missouri Rivers, 1797–1798." *Missouri Historical Review* 81 (July 1987): 387–402.

FITZGIBBON, JOHN (1817–1882)

John Fitzgibbon was Missouri's most widely known pioneer photographer. On trips throughout the state in the early 1850s, he introduced many rural Missouri patrons to portraits made with a camera. From the outset of his career, Fitzgibbon maintained a high national profile. He was a key figure in the formation of America's first national photographic societies and a prolific writer on technical improvements and on photography in Missouri. These activities helped to establish St. Louis's early reputation as a center for progressive development on photography.

Fitzgibbon was born in London in 1817. At an early age he emigrated to America with his family. His father, Michael Fitzgibbon, a native of Dublin, worked in New York City as a ship chandler. By his early teens John Fitzgibbon was apprenticed to a saddle maker in Philadelphia, where he married Amelia Wright, who died in St. Louis during the Civil War. By the late 1830s he found a more appropriate outlet for his gregarious personality as an innkeeper in Lynchburg, Virginia. In 1841, inspired by America's immediate enthusiasm for the new daguerreotype "likeness," Fitzgibbon learned to make pictures with the camera. Five years later, when itinerant photographers were serving most patrons in western states, he opened St. Louis's second permanent photographic establishment.

During the years before the Civil War, Fitzgibbon was Missouri's most colorful and entrepreneurial photographer. A masterful and energetic self-promoter, his creative marketing strategies epitomized the intensely competitive nature of the business during this early era. By 1858 his advertisements promoted his "princely," thirteen-room establishment as the largest portrait gallery in America. Like successful operators in the East, he competed for patrons by featuring a large gallery display of celebrity portraits. In the early 1850s his now-lost daguerreotype exhibit of citizens, politicians, and performers reportedly exceeded one thousand images. In 1854 when progressive eastern galleries began to make paper photographs, Fitzgibbon imported assistants from New York to introduce the technology in Missouri.

Fitzgibbon first gained national attention through his many articles and letters that appeared in the *Daguerrean Journal* and the *Photographic Art Journal,* America's first publications devoted to photography. He was also Missouri's most faithful contributor to eastern photography competitions during the 1850s. *Leslie's Illustrated Newspaper* furthered his reputation in 1856 when it published a series of St. Louis views based on Fitzgibbon's photographs. *Leslie's* concluded the series with an article on Fitzgibbon that accompanied an engraved portrait of the photographer.

Restless by nature, Fitzgibbon traveled frequently to maintain his connections with eastern editors and suppliers or to make portraits in less populated areas of Missouri. Despite his claims as the proprietor of the most successful gallery in the West, he struggled continuously to support his wife and five children. To supplement his income he made an extensive professional tour through Missouri, Arkansas, and into Indian Territory in 1854, and in 1857 he traveled to compile a collection of views in Central America and South America.

For reasons unknown, Fitzgibbon sold his St. Louis gallery in 1861 to move to Vicksburg, Mississippi. During the Civil War, when he attempted to return north through a Confederate blockade, he was captured and imprisoned briefly, possibly in Cuba. Following his release he went to New York City where he opened a gallery backed by his son-in-law, Dan Bryant, a successful actor.

In 1869 Fitzgibbon returned to practice in St. Louis with his new wife and accomplished photographer, Maria Dennis. In 1876, when he became the founder-editor of the *St. Louis Practical Photographer,* his wife took over the operation of their gallery. Fitzgibbon died on a train passing through Xenia, Ohio, on August 12, 1882. After her husband's death, Maria Fitzgibbon became the editor of his journal, which was renamed the *St. Louis Photographer* in 1883 and the *St. Louis and Canadian Photographer* in 1888.

DOLORES A. KILGO

"J. H. Fitzgibbon, Esq., Daguerrean Artist, of St. Louis." *Frank Leslie's Illustrated Newspaper* 4 (September 5, 1857): 213.

Obituary. *Philadelphia Photographer* 19 (October 1882): 315–16.

Van Ravenswaay, Charles. "Pioneer Photographers of St. Louis." *Missouri Historical Society Bulletin* 10 (October 1953): 49–71.

Wright, Bonnie. " 'This Perpetual Shadow-Taking': The Lively Art of John Fitzgibbon." *Missouri Historical Review* 91 (October 1981): 22–30.

FLETCHER, THOMAS CLEMENT (1827–1899)

Thomas Clement Fletcher was born in Herculaneum, Missouri, on January 22, 1827, the son of Clement B. Fletcher, a merchant, and Margaret Byrd Fletcher. As there were no public schools in Jefferson County at the time, young Fletcher attended the subscription school of Willard Frissell, who had come there from Massachusetts. At age seventeen Fletcher secured employment in the circuit clerk's office, advancing to the position of deputy two years later and being elected to that office in 1849. He married Mary Clara Honey, his childhood sweetheart, in 1851.

Fletcher studied law and was admitted to the bar in the mid-1850s. In 1856 he was appointed land agent for the southwest branch of the Pacific Railroad and moved with his family to St. Louis. Although he came from a slaveholding family, Fletcher followed the lead of Sen. **Thomas Hart Benton** in opposing slavery's extension. He campaigned actively for Benton in the gubernatorial race in 1856; following Benton's defeat, Fletcher joined **Frank Blair, B. Gratz Brown,** and other former Benton Democrats in organizing the Republican Party in Missouri.

During the late 1850s Fletcher formed a partnership with his brother-in-law, Louis J. Rankin, to purchase the site and lay out the town of DeSoto in Jefferson County. He built a home there and moved his family to the new town in 1860. That same year he served as a delegate to the Republican National Convention in Chicago, which nominated Abraham Lincoln for the presidency, and he took an active role in the ensuing campaign.

With the outbreak of the Civil War, Fletcher was appointed assistant provost marshal general at St. Louis by Gen. **Nathaniel Lyon** and continued in that post for the next year. During the summer of 1862 he recruited the Thirty-first Missouri Volunteers as part of a larger recruitment effort headed by his friend Frank Blair. Most of those volunteering for the Thirty-first were from Jefferson County and included his brothers, William and Carroll. Fletcher became their colonel, receiving his commission in October 1862.

Fletcher saw action with Blair's brigade at Chickasaw Bayou, north of Vicksburg, on December 19, 1862, where he was wounded and captured. He spent the next five months in Libby Prison at Richmond. Exchanged in May 1863 he rejoined his regiment in time to be present at the surrender of Vicksburg on July 4. He later participated with his regiment in the struggle for Lookout Mountain at the battle of Chattanooga in December and commanded a brigade in the Atlanta campaign the following spring. While engaged in the latter, he contracted a severe cold, which settled in his back, making it impossible for him to mount his horse. On the recommendation of the regimental surgeon, he returned home to recuperate.

Upon his recovery Fletcher was asked by Gen. William S. Rosecrans to raise two volunteer regiments (the Forty-seventh and the Fiftieth Missouri) to resist the Confederate invasion of Gen. **Sterling Price** in September 1864. Fletcher led these forces at the Battle of Pilot Knob where their efforts did much to halt Price's push toward St. Louis. His services in this campaign were rewarded by President Lincoln with a brevet promotion to brigadier general of volunteers. Thereafter, he rejoined Gen. **William T. Sherman**'s army on the March to the Sea, during which he received word of his nomination as the Radical Union candidate for governor.

Fletcher was chosen as governor over Democrat **Thomas Lawson Price** by a majority of forty thousand in a contest that saw some fifty-two thousand fewer voters go to the polls than had four years earlier. Racked by four long years of intense guerrilla warfare, Missouri had seen many of its citizens leave the state, while others were disfranchised by the test oath imposed by the provisional government. In many areas of the state, conditions were still too turbulent to allow a peaceful election. Those who did vote turned overwhelmingly to the new Radical Union Party, which was demanding immediate emancipation of Missouri's slaves. In addition to Fletcher's election, a full slate of Radical state officeholders was swept into office while the Radicals carried both houses of the legislature and secured a mandate for a new constitutional convention.

Governor Fletcher was inaugurated on January 2, 1865. In his inaugural address, he took a moderate stance toward Reconstruction: "Being victorious everywhere, let magnanimity now distinguish our actions and, having nothing more to ask for party, let us, forgetful of past differences, seek only to promote the general good of the people of the whole commonwealth." Five days later the new convention met in St. Louis and promptly passed an emancipation ordinance freeing all of Missouri's slaves, a measure that the governor heartily endorsed.

Thereafter governor and convention parted company as the latter, under the leadership of **Charles**

Daniel Drake, proceeded to draw up a new and highly prescriptive constitution. Governor Fletcher believed that the new document usurped too much legislative authority by placing the needs of the time into a structure that might be too inflexible for the future. He particularly opposed the stringent test oath for voting, officeholding, and the practice of certain professions adopted by the convention while hinting that he would like to see the newly freed slaves enfranchised. The convention rejected the latter move for fear that it would cause the new constitution to fail when put to a popular referendum. As it was, the constitution was approved only narrowly, primarily with the help of the soldier vote.

In spite of these differences, Governor Fletcher joined with other Radical leaders in seeking to promote a progressive image for postwar Missouri. He supported the establishment of a strong public school system for both whites and blacks and saw significant progress made toward that end during his administration. While seeking the enhancement of the University of Missouri through the use of the Morrill Act land-grant funds to place the agricultural college there, he also supported the establishment of Lincoln Institute (later University) to train black teachers, which was underwritten by funds raised from two black regiments. Realizing the need for trained teachers generally, he also pushed through legislation requiring regular teacher institutes in each county. He also called for the establishment of state-supported normal schools, though they did not come into existence until after he left office.

Concerned about rebuilding the state's population, which had been diminished by the war, Governor Fletcher urged the legislature to establish a state board of immigration that could promote the wonders of Missouri. The legislature responded positively, and Fletcher quickly dispatched agents to the eastern states and Europe to attract those who were interested in emigrating. He also realized the need to complete the state's meager rail system and worked hard to place the roads into the hands of various companies that could accomplish the task after those previously responsible had defaulted on their bonds. This was done only at great cost to Missouri taxpayers. Fletcher came under intense suspicion of collusion in the process, but a legislative committee exonerated him of any wrongdoing, and nothing of this nature has ever been proved against him.

Among Governor Fletcher's more difficult tasks was the enforcement of the prescriptive test oath and registry laws designed to disfranchise former Confederates and Southern sympathizers. While not personally sympathetic to these measures, he did not hesitate to call out the militia as needed to enforce them in conservative counties and to prosecute violators vigorously in the courts. With regard to the

Ouster Ordinance passed by the state convention in 1865, which vacated all state and local offices, Fletcher tended increasingly to leave patronage in the hands of his subordinates and department heads, which led to large-scale rumors of nepotism and corruption.

Governor Fletcher remains something of an enigma. Elected to office on his record as a war hero, he never appears to have been really comfortable in that post. While proving himself a staunch friend of Missouri's blacks and counting many admirers and supporters among the liberal German element, he found himself increasingly at odds over proscription and patronage with the more ardent Radicals led by Charles D. Drake. By midterm Fletcher openly despised public office and claimed that only considerable property holdings, accumulated before the war, against which he drew frequently, made it possible for him to live comfortably as governor.

At the close of his term in January 1869, Fletcher returned to St. Louis to practice law. He moved to Washington, D.C., in 1890 where he continued in legal practice until his death on March 25, 1899.

WILLIAM E. PARRISH

Barclay, Thomas S. *The Liberal Republican Movement in Missouri, 1865–1871*. Columbia: State Historical Society of Missouri, 1926.

Parrish, William E. *A History of Missouri: Volume III, 1860 to 1875*. Columbia: University of Missouri Press, 1973.

Reppy, John H. "Thomas Clement Fletcher." In *The Messages and Proclamations of the Governors of the State of Missouri,* ed. Grace G. Avery and Floyd C. Shoemaker, vol. 4. Columbia: State Historical Society of Missouri, 1924.

FLINT, TIMOTHY (1780–1840)

Frontier missionary Timothy Flint is remembered as much today for his literary, social, and geographical writings as for his religious pursuits. The son of William and Martha Kimball Flint, Timothy was born near Reading, Massachusetts, on July 11, 1780. He graduated from Phillips Exeter Academy and Harvard College, after which he read for the ministry. Upon the conclusion of his studies he briefly taught school at Cohasset, Massachusetts, and then preached at Marblehead, where he met and married Abigail Hubbard, a relative of the famous merchant Peabody. Together they would have three children, one of whom, Micah, became a credible poet.

In 1802 Flint became pastor of the Congregational Church in Lunenburg, Massachusetts. His ministry was a contentious one, however, and in 1814 he resigned when his request for a salary increase was denied by his parishioners, many of whom clearly wished for a separation from their pastor. Part of Flint's problem was political. He was a conspicuous Federalist with a Republican congregation. However, these differences were greatly exacerbated by Flint's forceful and often impolitic manner. Years later the British writer Fanny Trollope (mother of novelist Anthony Trollope) described Flint in glowing terms in her reminiscences of life in America: "He is the only person I remember to have known [in America] with first-rate powers of satire, and even sarcasm, whose kindness of nature and of manners remained perfectly unimpaired." Perhaps, but Trollope herself clearly shared many of Flint's strong opinions.

After his separation from his Lunenburg congregation, Flint served a short time as a missionary within New England. In 1815 he was accepted as an agent for the Connecticut Missionary Society for service in Kentucky and Ohio. While in Cincinnati he read Samuel J. Mills and Daniel Smith's book describing the missionary possibilities in Missouri Territory, which prompted Flint to write the prominent St. Louis Presbyterian layman **Stephen Hempstead,** who apparently encouraged him to come.

Flint's desire to Christianize the West was conceived in the broadest cultural terms. Westerners would not merely accept Jesus but also embrace New England culture. He intended to effect this change as much by literary means as by preaching. In seeking an appointment from the Connecticut Missionary Society he declared: "An object, which I have had more especially in view, has been to establish in some central place a religious publication, like our own monthly papers; except that it should more particularly vindicate our literature, charities, and institutions." As things worked out, Flint would actually write nothing in Missouri, but his most important work would be based, or partly based, on his experiences there. This is especially true for his best book, *Recollections of the Last Ten Years in the Valley of the Mississippi,* but also for his *Condensed Geography and History of the Western States,* his highly popular biography of **Daniel Boone,** and a number of didactic and sentimental novels.

Flint's arrival in St. Louis in May 1816 proved controversial. He would soon turn to teaching to support his income, which was traditional and considered appropriately complementary to a missionary's religious duty. However, when he first arrived it was in a flatboat laden with seven thousand dollars of merchandise, which he, with his cousin, intended to resell—and his prices were not cheap. Flint had brought his large and extended family to the frontier with him and hoped for no more than its respectable support, but his pecuniary interests quickly aroused suspicion. Instead of a Yankee minister, St. Louis residents saw, or thought they saw, a price-gouging Yankee peddler. Things did not get better. At various times during the course of his missionary sojourn, Flint engaged not only in business but also in land speculation, or various building enterprises, all of which did much to harm his reputation.

Unfortunately, things were little better for Flint inside the religious community. Despite his troubles he began preaching immediately upon his arrival in the city, and became the first Protestant minister to celebrate communion in St. Louis. His presence disturbed fellow missionary **Salmon Giddings.** Flint had come to St. Louis of his own volition, whereas Giddings had been specifically chosen by the Connecticut Missionary Society to minister to the Missouri-Illinois region. Giddings dismissed most of the charges lodged against Flint as unfair, but Flint's desire to settle permanently with his family in St. Louis led Giddings to complain to the society that his fellow missionary was neglecting his charge. What was sorely needed on the frontier were itinerant missionaries, not settled clergy.

Conflict with Giddings was joined with a great distaste for St. Louis. The "wickedness of the place," Flint wrote, "threw a continual gloom" over his mind. In St. Louis, he said, "even the sentiment of a God was universally erased." "Duels," he lamented, "were continuously occurring and all was confusion and uproar. Although there was a general attendance upon my meeting it was of thoughtless young men and women, upon whom instruction and exhortation seemed lost." In late August 1816 Flint sought relief in moving to St. Charles, but found none. His first Sunday services were marked by the noisy conduct of a horse race outside his door.

In late 1819 Flint accepted the principalship of a Presbyterian academy in Rapide, Louisiana, on the Red River near New Orleans. After a disastrous attempt to move to Louisiana brought him back to St. Charles in 1821, he tried again and this time succeeded in establishing the school as a Yankee outpost in the South. While happy in this work, the climate did not agree with him, and his health deteriorated.

After a restorative visit to New England, he returned to Cincinnati in 1827 where he began his climb to literary fame. His most important works include *Francis Berrian; or, The Mexican Patriot* (1826); *Recollections of the Last Ten Years, Passed in Occasional Residences and Journeyings in the Valley of the Mississippi* (1826); *A Condensed Geography and History of the Western States* (1828; revised in 1832 as *The History and Geography of the Mississippi Valley*); *The Adventures of Arthur Clenning* (1828); *George Mason, the Young Backwoodsman; or, Don't Give Up the Ship* (1829); *The Shoshonee Valley* (1830); *The Biographical Memoir of Daniel Boone, the First Settler of Kentucky* (1833); and *Indian Wars of the West* (1833).

In addition to the publication of his own works Flint became an editor of note. Between 1827 and 1830 he served as the editor of the well-respected, if profitless, *Western Monthly Review,* which was followed by a brief stint as the editor of the *Knickerbocker; or, The New-York Monthly Magazine.* He also edited the frontier classic *The Personal Narrative of James O. Pattie* (1831).

In 1833 Flint left Cincinnati to resume his principalship in Louisiana, where he, despite frequent travels, at last remained. Seven years later, on August 16, 1840, Flint died unexpectedly on a return trip to visit relatives in Salem, Massachusetts.

KENNETH H. WINN

Cannon, Thomas C. "Founders of Missouri Presbyterianism." *Journal of the Presbyterian Historical Society* 46 (1968): 197–218.

Ellinwood, DeWitt, Jr. "Protestantism Enters St. Louis: The Presbyterians." *Bulletin of the Missouri Historical Society* 12 (1956): 253–73.

Flint, Timothy. *Recollections of the Last Ten Years, Passed in Occasional Residences and Journeyings in the Valley of the Mississippi.* Ed. George Brooks. 1826. Reprint, Carbondale: Southern Illinois University Press, 1968.

Kirkpatrick, John Ervin. *Timothy Flint: Pioneer, Missionary, Author, Editor, 1780–1840.* Cleveland: Arthur H. Clark, 1911.

FLOWER, JOSEPH ROSWELL (1888–1970)

In 1907 a young Joseph Roswell Flower committed his life to Pentecostalism, a fledgling movement that had emerged from an interracial revival the year before and emphasized the availability and importance of "spiritual gifts" such as speaking in tongues. Before his thirtieth birthday, Flower had helped to found Pentecostalism's second-largest denomination, the Assemblies of God (AG), and he quickly emerged as one of its most powerful figures. During the next forty years he used his influence to guide Pentecostalism into mainstream American culture.

Flower was born in Bellville, Canada, on June 17, 1888, into a tradition of revivalism and a family of spiritual sojourners who traversed down a number of the subcultural streams that eventually combined to become Pentecostalism. In 1902 his family emigrated to Zion, Illinois, to join the faith community of Alexander Dowie, a faith-healing evangelist and theological precursor of Pentecostalism. Dowie taught that Christ's atoning death liberated believers from sickness, as well as from sin. While Dowie's teachings influenced Flower's worldview by preparing him for the Pentecostal movement, the Flower family's immediate experience in Zion, where they encountered scandal and factional infighting, was one of disillusionment. Chastened, the Flowers moved to Indianapolis, where they found spiritual relief in a Christian Missionary Alliance (CMA) congregation, and young Flower entertained plans for a career in law.

Flower came of age intellectually and spiritually in Indianapolis through the teachings of the CMA, an evangelical fellowship formed in the urban revivals of the late nineteenth century. Reflecting the frustration of its middle-class constituency with the liturgical dryness of urban churches and the absence of biblical conviction on the part of seminary-trained clergy, the CMA combined biblical fundamentalism with an equally strong emphasis on vibrant, inner-spiritual piety. Accordingly, CMA leaders, anticipating later Pentecostal teachings, emphasized the importance of the Holy Spirit for spiritual empowerment. Thus for Flower and for many other founding AG patriarchs, the CMA was, in effect, a school for Pentecost.

In 1907 Pentecostalism came to Indianapolis in separate revivals conducted by Glen Cook and Thomas Hezmalhalch, both fresh from the Los Angeles revivals that had given birth to Pentecostalism. While young J. Roswell Flower found the revivalists' exhortations compelling, the promised "infilling" of the Holy Spirit—the spiritual experience that Pentecostals believed prepared believers to receive the supernatural gifts of the Spirit—and the accompanying experience of speaking in tongues eluded him. Nevertheless, he committed his life to full-time ministry, and the following year ventured to Kansas City to join the ministry of A. S. Copley. While en route he stayed at a faith home operated by two Holiness women who had converted to Pentecostalism. After lingering there for a month, he received the much desired experience, though without the accompanying manifestation of speaking in tongues, which did not present itself for several months.

Following a two-year apprenticeship in Kansas City, Flower returned to Indiana and in 1911 married Alice Reynolds, whose family also attended the Alliance church in Indianapolis. The Flowers then embarked on a series of Pentecostal ministries in the Indiana and Western Ohio region, ranging from itinerant evangelism to assisting in establishing a Bible school. In 1913 Flower, having already established solid connections with Pentecostalism's nascent leadership, began publishing a regional newsletter with the aid of his wife, thus strengthening his own claim to leadership. During Pentecostalism's formative moment, the publishers of newsletters, along with Bible school directors, acted as an ex officio bureaucratic network for a movement still ripe

with anticipation of the Second Coming of Christ, and resistant to any formal organization.

As the world marched toward World War I, this incipient hierarchy became increasingly concerned about the institutional flimsiness of the movement, and in 1913 a handful of nationally prominent leaders issued a call for an organizing convention to establish a national Pentecostal fellowship. The convention, held the following year in Hot Springs, Arkansas, formally established the Assemblies of God, and elected Arkansas evangelist and editor E. N. Bell as the new denomination's first chairman and chose Flower as the first secretary-treasurer. Bell and Flower established a denominational headquarters in a storefront in Findlay, Ohio. The headquarters was later transferred to St. Louis and in 1918 was moved one final time, partly at the impetus of Flower, to Springfield, Missouri.

Flower's first two-year term in office initiated a forty-year career of administrative ministry in the AG. In 1919 the AG General Council, the fellowship's governing body of ordained ministers and congregational representatives, selected Flower as its first foreign missions' secretary. In 1923, after the post's responsibilities were divided, Flower became foreign missions' treasurer. Then in a rare setback in 1925, Flower was voted out of office, and he moved to Pennsylvania to pastor a church in Scranton. He did not linger long from the center of denominational polity, though, and was elected as superintendent of the AG northeastern district in 1929, and in 1931 as a nonresident assistant general superintendent. Finally, in 1935 Flower returned to Springfield as general secretary-treasurer, a position he held until the post was divided in 1947 when he assumed the role of general secretary, which he retained until his retirement in 1959.

In each of his various tenures, Flower strove to spread the Pentecostal movement and to build rational and permanent institutional foundations for the AG. His willingness to balance pragmatic action against dogmatic belief frequently brought him into conflict with those in the organization who were less practically inclined. Flower's innate understanding of his constituency allowed him to win more battles than he lost. On occasion, however, his sense of timing betrayed him. In 1925, for example, his failure to win reelection resulted in part from his attempt to persuade the AG General Council to adopt a constitution and bylaws.

Flower's most important battle came during the most divisive controversy in Pentecostalism's history, which was referred to in classic Victorian understatement as the "new issue." From 1913 to 1915 the Oneness, or Jesus Only, movement threatened to surmount Pentecostalism. This movement, which quickly evolved an explicit anti-Trinitarian doctrine, initially taught that all Pentecostal converts should be baptized in the name of only Jesus in strict adherence to New Testament formulas. The new doctrine appealed to the Pentecostal impulse to return to the pure practices of the New Testament and to the anti-intellectual and populist instincts of many Pentecostals who desired a priesthood of all believers intellectually leveled by the revelation of the Holy Spirit.

Flower, while sympathetic to the emphasis on spiritual openness that had helped give birth to the Oneness movement, feared that the emphasis on special revelation would devalue scriptural authority and lead to continuing fragmentation. Accordingly, he used his position as a denominational editor to disseminate a Trinitarian message and worked behind the scenes to sustain a pro-Trinitarian majority among the AG leadership. His position appealed to northeastern Pentecostals who, like Flower, had been nurtured on the teachings of the CMA. By 1916 Flower's efforts bore fruit when the AG General Council endorsed Trinitarian orthodoxy.

Flower's crowning achievement came in 1942 when he led, with General Superintendent E. S. Williams, a delegation to the organizing convention of the National Association of Evangelicals (NAE). The following year Flower, Williams, and the leadership persuaded delegates to the 1943 general council to authorize affiliation with the NAE. In the following years Flower acted as a liaison between the AG and the NAE and served on the latter's executive committee.

The decision to join the NAE was only one element in a broader process of cultural mainstreaming that defined the history of the Assemblies of God from the mid-thirties to the mid-sixties. Flower welcomed this process and used his position to expedite it. He supported the Assemblies' shift away from a position of official pacifism just prior to World War II and secured political support from the NAE to persuade the War Department to commission Pentecostal chaplains. Partly inspired by the difficulty in finding qualified chaplains, the Assemblies' leadership determined to upgrade the educational credentials of its ministers and introduced resolutions to improve the curricula at AG Bible colleges and sought the sanction of evangelical accrediting associations. Flower played a critical role both in arriving at that decision and in guiding the resolution through contentious debates at the AG General Council.

The process of mainstreaming, however, created resistance and resentment from many within the denomination who feared the authentic Pentecostal message was being compromised. Thus, during Flower's last years in office he alternately worked to calm the fears of denominational conservatives and zealously guarded the reputation of the AG against

the enthusiasm of a new wave of Pentecostal movements that sought to recapture the intensity of the movement's early days. The extravagant claims of Pentecostal healing evangelists were of particular concern to Flower, and he used his authority to keep the activities of healing evangelists within the boundaries of common sense and respectability.

In 1959 Flower, along with several other AG leaders, retired and turned the reigns of power over to a second generation of Pentecostal leaders, most of whom had been born in the twentieth century. Flower lived the remainder of his years as a Pentecostal elder statesman, residing in Springfield. He died on July 23, 1970.

RICHARD COTNER

Anderson, Robert Mapes. *A Vision of the Disinherited: The Making of American Pentecostalism.* New York: Oxford University Press, 1979.

Blumhofer, Edith. *The Assemblies of God: A Chapter in the Story of American Pentecostalism.* Springfield, Mo.: Gospel Publishing House, 1989.

Dictionary of Pentecostal and Charismatic Movements. S.v. "Flower, Alice Reynolds."

Flower, J. Roswell. Interview by William Menzies. 1967. Assemblies of God Archives, Springfield, Mo.

———. Personal correspondence. NAE Collection. Assemblies of God Archives, Springfield, Mo.

McGee, Gary B. *The Gospel Shall Be Preached: A History of Assemblies of God Missions.* Springfield, Mo.: Gospel Publishing House, 1986.

FOLK, JOSEPH W. (1869–1923)

Born on October 29, 1869, in Brownsville, Tennessee, Joseph Wingate Folk was the son of Henry Bate and Martha Estes Folk. After migrating to west Tennessee from North Carolina, Henry Folk taught school, studied law, and started a law practice in Brownsville in 1866. Joseph Folk attended the public and private schools of his hometown, and finished his early education at the Brownsville Academy at the age of sixteen.

After graduating Folk worked as a clerk for the Southern Express Company in Memphis, Tennessee, and then as a bookkeeper for a grocery concern. Returning to Brownsville he read law for a year in his father's office. Deciding to pursue the law as a career, he entered the Vanderbilt University Law School in Nashville (from which he earned an LL.B. in 1890) and was admitted to the bar in 1890.

Folk became a partner in his father's law office and concentrated his attention on the study of criminal law. He quickly became active in the Democratic Club in Brownsville, and made an unsuccessful run for the office of state representative in the Tennessee legislature in 1892. As he continued his legal career, he also contributed articles to newspapers, gave speeches on special occasions, and became an active member of the Knights of Pythias.

In the fall of 1893 Folk moved to St. Louis, Missouri, to join his uncle, Judge Frank M. Estes, in a law partnership. He soon began to establish himself as an attorney and continued his interest in politics. He was one of the organizers of the Jefferson Club, a local but powerful organization of young Democrats. Folk made a name for himself by leading a successful fight to get the Jefferson Club to support William Jennings Bryan in 1896, and served as president of that body in 1898–1899.

After a transit strike paralyzed the city of St. Louis for forty-five days during the summer of 1900, Folk offered his services as a mediator and worked out a settlement that was acceptable to both management and labor. He received a great deal of publicity for helping end the strike, and his efforts at persuading the company to negotiate a settlement made him popular with organized labor. With his support in the Jefferson Club, his success in the transit strike, and the approval of Boss **Ed Butler** and the Democratic political machine who concluded he was "safe," Folk won nomination as the Democratic Party's candidate for the office of circuit attorney in 1900. He defeated his Republican opponent, Judge Eugene Mcquillen, and began a four-year term as the city's chief law-enforcement officer.

Once in office Folk let it be known that he would strictly enforce the law. He immediately prosecuted ten individuals for election fraud and began an investigation of possible corruption in the St. Louis municipal assembly. The latter investigation centered on allegations that a so-called combine, referred to by some as the "Big Cinch," controlled the assembly and operated illegally by selling municipal franchises, licenses, and garbage contracts to the highest bidder, and by providing tax breaks or other special privileges for money. Although many had suspected such a combine before, it was Folk's investigation that substantiated those suspicions.

Folk's first prosecution involved the Suburban Railway Company. He charged that officers of that corporation had agreed to pay (bribe) members of the assembly combine to secure a franchise extension in 1900. Folk eventually obtained thirteen convictions in the case, seven on charges of bribery and six on charges of perjury. The case became even more sensational when two agents for the combine jumped bail and fled to Mexico. When only one of the fugitives could be persuaded to return and stand trial, Folk went to Washington and convinced President Theodore Roosevelt and Secretary of State John Hay that bribery should be included in the extradition treaty with Mexico. The treaty was revised, the revision was made retroactive, and the second escaped felon returned to St. Louis for trial.

Three other bribery cases grew out of the Suburban scandal and soon shocked St. Louisans who learned a new term, *boodle,* that described the degenerative influence of bribery on municipal governance. A second investigation involving the Central Traction Company revealed that the company's president had paid $250,000 to the assembly combine to obtain permission to consolidate the street railway lines in St. Louis. A third investigation into the way in which the city contracted to have its garbage collected led to charges that Boss Butler had offered $2,500 to two members of the city's board of health in exchange for a garbage contract. A fourth investigation into the manner in which the assembly granted a ten-year street lighting contract for the city revealed that approximately $50,000 had been paid to the combine to ensure approval of a measure granting the franchise.

Folk was able to push most of his prosecutions to successful conclusions despite bitter opposition from many businessmen and most "organization" politicians. Many in St. Louis thought that Folk's zealous actions and self-righteous manner hurt business, damaged the city's reputation, and betrayed the Democratic Party. His enemies, and more than a few of his friends, even tagged him with the nickname "Holy Joe." But for the most part the revelations shocked the public conscience by proving that the corrupt actual government of the city was directed by an alliance between corrupt businessmen and corrupt politicians. The investigations resulted in thirty-nine indictments, including twenty-four for bribery and thirteen for perjury, and involved twenty-one members of the municipal assembly, Boss Butler, and several prominent men of wealth. Many of the indictments, however, were later overturned by the state supreme court on legal technicalities.

Regardless, Folk's investigations had lasting historical significance. They attracted national attention to the problem of municipal corruption, and gave people a thorough look at the nature and extent of the problem. He also helped give impetus to what was becoming known nationally as the progressive reform movement. During the course of his investigations Folk shared his findings with journalist Lincoln Steffens whom he encouraged to aid his efforts in the national press. The two articles that Steffens wrote for *McClure's,* "Tweed Days in St. Louis" and "The Shamelessness of St. Louis" in 1903 and 1904, signaled the start of the movement in American journalism known as "muckraking."

The boodle trials were not Folk's only accomplishments as circuit attorney, merely the most sensational. He also closed gambling operations, crusaded against graft in the police department, made war on phony investment firms, and cooperated with Missouri attorney general Edward C. Crow in the investigation of the baking-powder trust in which the lieutenant governor and several legislators were arrested for bribery. For his overall record as a crusading attorney, Folk won fame and placed himself in a position for higher public office at either the state or the national level.

In 1904 the Missouri Democratic Party nominated Folk as its candidate for governor. His campaign emphasized honesty in government, a theme that had taken on new urgency after allegations of bribery and graft in the state legislature surfaced in 1903. Even though many Democratic Party leaders in St. Louis opposed his nomination, Folk was popular with most voters and won a convincing victory over Republican Cyrus P. Walbridge, winning by thirty thousand votes even though all other Democratic state candidates went down to defeat in the Roosevelt Republican landslide.

As governor, Folk insisted on the strict enforcement of the law and advocated a new kind of public morality that equated bribery with treason and labeled bribers and bribees as traitors. Before his term in office ended in 1908, the national press had picked up on this new theme. Folk became known as the champion of the "Missouri Idea": the conviction that Missouri could set an example in civic righteousness by reclaiming popular control of the law and enforcing it.

Hampered by Republican control of the lower house of the legislature during his first two years in office, Folk concentrated his early legislative efforts on law enforcement. Successes included vigorous antitrust prosecutions, the end of free railroad passes for state officials and legislators, extension of the statute on bribery from three to five years, improved election laws, reform of the St. Louis police department, repeal of the law legalizing racetrack gambling, and enforcement of the Sunday-closing law. Other legislative proposals—requiring that franchises be sold at auction and that witnesses in bribery cases be compelled to testify—were rejected. One other related measure, an antilobby law requiring formal registration of lobbyists, gained legislative approval in 1907.

During his final two years in office, with Democratic control of both houses of the legislature, Governor Folk was more successful. This was due in no small part to his willingness to be less the prosecutor and more the administrator, and to his own expanding vision of progressivism. The result was the successful enactment of a broad program of political, social, and economic reform as well as an expansion of the state's regulatory powers. Achievements included passage of an initiative and referendum amendment to the state constitution, a statewide direct primary

law, a child-labor and compulsory-school-attendance law, an eight-hour law in mines and smelters, and a pure-food bill. In addition, the legislature enhanced the regulation of railroads (including the setting of maximum freight and passenger rates), private corporations, and public utilities. The state also established boards of law examiners, dental examiners, and veterinary examiners as well as horticulture, dairy, and poultry commissions. A related accomplishment was the creation of the Missouri library commission, which worked to coordinate and expand the public library services of the state.

Folk had demonstrated considerable skills as a prosecutor, advocate, and administrator. However, his unwillingness to compromise principles, his moralistic approach to politics, and his unflinching commitment to honest government cost him the support of the machine elements within his party and prevented him from developing the political coalition that was ultimately necessary for success at the next political level. As a result his ambitions for higher public office were constantly thwarted. Folk lost the Democratic senatorial primary in 1908 to incumbent **William Joel Stone,** who had the strong support of Democratic political organizations in St. Louis and Kansas City. He failed in a second try for a senate nomination in 1910.

Stymied on the political front, Folk returned to private law practice and toured as a Chautauqua speaker on topics relating to political reform and civic righteousness. He returned to politics in 1912 to campaign for Woodrow Wilson, and President Wilson rewarded him with an appointment as solicitor for the State Department. Folk resigned his position in 1914 to become chief counsel for the Interstate Commerce Commission. In that capacity he conducted several important investigations involving the business affairs of several major railroad companies, including the New York, New Haven and Hartford, and Rock Island lines.

After Senator Stone's death in 1918, Folk again became a candidate for the United States Senate. This time he won the Democratic nomination, but lost the election. Leaving politics he worked briefly as a counselor for the St. Louis Chamber of Commerce (1918–1919) before opening a private law office in Washington, D.C. As the chamber's counselor, Folk led the city's unsuccessful legal battle against the Terminal Railroad Association for excessive freight charges stemming from its virtual monopoly of rail and bridge traffic entering St. Louis from the East.

During World War I, Folk made many patriotic speeches and became an ardent Wilsonian internationalist. In 1919 he became the American counsel for the Egyptian National Committee in its successful effort to end British rule and establish Egyptian autonomy. In 1922 he represented the government of Peru in negotiations with Chile over a boundary dispute, and was instrumental in persuading the U.S. government to act as arbitrator.

Folk received honorary LL.D. degrees from the University of Missouri (1905), William Jewell College (1906), Drury College (1907), Westminster College (1907), Southwestern Baptist University (1908), and Baylor University (1919). He was a member of the American Bar Association, the Society of International Law, and the National Press Association. He was also a member of the Baptist Church.

Folk had married Gertrude Glass on November 10, 1896; they had no children. He suffered a nervous breakdown, evidently from overwork, in March 1922. He died of a heart attack in New York City on May 28, 1923.

STEVEN L. PIOTT

Burckel, Nicholas Clare. "Progressive Governors in the Border States: Reform Governors of Missouri, Kentucky, West Virginia, and Maryland, 1900–1918." Ph.D. diss., University of Wisconsin, 1971.

Geiger, Louis G. "The Public Career of Joseph W. Folk." Ph.D. diss., University of Missouri, 1948.

Piott, Steven L. *Holy Joe: Joseph W. Folk and the Missouri Idea.* Columbia: University of Missouri Press, 1997.

Thelen, David. *Paths of Resistance: Tradition and Dignity in Industrializing Missouri.* New York: Oxford University Press, 1986.

Thurman, A. L. "Joseph Wingate Folk: The Politician as Speaker and Public Servant." *Missouri Historical Review* 59 (January 1965): 173–91.

White, William Allen. "Folk." *McClure's* 26 (December 1905): 115–32.

FOLLENIUS, PAUL (1799–1844)

Paul Follenius, the cofounder with **Friedrich Muench** of the Giessen Emigration Society and the third son of a lawyer at the Hessian Ducal Court, was born in Giessen (Grand Duchy of Hesse) on May 5, 1799. His mother died a few days after his birth, and he was taken to live with his father's parents in the little village of Romrod on the Vogelsberg, where his grandfather was a forester. After his father remarried, Follenius rejoined the family in Giessen.

At the age of fifteen Follenius interrupted his schooling at the gymnasium to participate in the 1814 campaign against Napoléon, in which he distinguished himself for bravery and was wounded. He thought of following a military career but concluded he would become only a tool of the ruling princes as a soldier. Deciding instead to study law, he quickly made up the time lost in the military, and in the spring

of 1817 enrolled at the University of Giessen, where Münch and his brothers were students.

Follenius soon joined the *Burschenschaft*, the "League of Black Brothers," a fraternity distinguished by the black clothing its members wore and their advocation of wide sociopolitical reforms and the creation of more democratic government within a unified Germany. A disagreement with university authorities led to a half-year suspension for not showing the required submissiveness to the administration. The assassination of the Russian diplomat August von Kotzebue in Mannheim in March 1819 by Jena theology student Karl Sand and the attempt on the life of the Hessian minister of state in Wiesbaden resulted in the *Karlsbader Beschlusse* of September 1819, government decrees aimed at the suppression of student activities at the university by strict censorship measures and police surveillance of students suspected of possible revolutionary tendencies. Instead of achieving the popular uprising against the reactionary governments they had hoped to inspire, the students and other revolutionaries had been met by inertia and indifference from the people whose lives they were hoping to improve. However, harassment by police, arrests, and the threat of imprisonment haunted them for years after they had graduated and become teachers, lawyers, pastors, or businessmen.

After concluding his studies, Follenius practiced law and developed a growing practice in Giessen. In December 1825 he married Maria Münch, in Niedergemunden, acquired a home at the edge of the city of Giessen, and seemed to have accepted the political realities of the time, though his brother Karl Follenius had fled the country and lived in exile in America. An attempt on April 3, 1833, to capture the main guardhouse of the Frankfurt police by a group of their former fraternity brothers who still hoped to trigger a popular uprising failed, and, though neither Follenius nor Münch had taken part, led to renewed harassment by Hessian police, the military of Prussia, and the Federation of German States. Realizing that the reactionary forces had succeeded in suppressing any hope of political and social reforms, Follenius and Münch decided to emigrate and, in March 1833, issued *A Call and Explanation with Regard to an Emigration on a Large Scale from Germany to the American Free States.* In July 1833 they circulated a second edition of the *Call* with a detailed constitution of the Giessen Emigration Society. They planned to create a model German republic in the Arkansas Territory and from there work for a rejuvenated Germany.

Before the group departed, scouts returned with an unfavorable report on conditions in Arkansas, and leaders changed the destination to Gottfried Duden's settlement in Warren County, Missouri. With about five hundred persons waiting to emigrate,

Follenius left from Bremen with the first contingent of about seventy families on the *Olbers* on March 31, 1834, bound for New Orleans, where they arrived on June 4.

On the trip up the Mississippi, Follenius became ill and had to leave the boat in Paducah. Upon reaching St. Louis, his group decided to disband, and the treasurer mistakenly distributed all the common funds of the society. The second group of 350 members, sixty families, led by Münch, set sail for Baltimore on July 24 after a seven-week voyage. After learning in St. Louis that their common funds had been disbursed, this group also disbanded.

Only the leaders and a half dozen families settled at their destination in Warren County. In July 1834 Follenius bought the log cabin and farm near Dutzow formerly owned by Duden, and with Münch set out to repay members of the society who had lost their funds. According to Münch, Follenius "learned to swing an axe as well as any man" as a pioneer farmer, but times were hard. In 1844 Follenius made an attempt to resettle in St. Louis to work with Wilhelm Weber of the *Anzeiger des Westens* and publish a journal, *Die Waage.* He lacked the necessary capital for the venture, and the journal collapsed after the first three issues. In the fall of 1844 Follenius moved back to Warren County, where he died on October 3, 1844, of typhoid fever. His grave, protected by a wrought-iron fence, lies in a field in the shadow of Duden's Hill.

ADOLF E. SCHROEDER

Aufforderung und Erklärung in Betreff einer Aus-
wanderung im Grossen aus Teutschland in die
nordamerikanischen Freistaaten. Zweite, mit den Statuten der Giessener Auswanderergesellschaft vermehrte Auflage. Giessen: J. Ricker, Juli, 1833.

Bek, William G. "The Followers of Duden." *Missouri Historical Review* 18 (April 1924): 92–106.

Cunz, Dieter. "Karl Follen: In Commemoration of the Hundredth Anniversary of His Death." *American-German Review* 7 (October 1940): 25–27, 32.

Finckh, Alice H., ed. "Three Latin Farmers: Paul Follenius, Frederick Muench, George Muench." For the Reunion of Muench and Follenius Descendants, Augusta, Mo., October 6, 1984.

Münch, Friedrich. "Das Leben von Paul Follenius." In *Gesammelte Schriften von Friedrich Münch,* ed. Konrad Nies. St. Louis: C. Witter, 1902.

FOSTER, RICHARD BAXTER (1826–1901)

Richard Baxter Foster, a teacher, minister, soldier, principal, and abolitionist, was born in Hanover, New Hampshire, on October 25, 1826, to Richard and Irene Burroughs Foster. He was the descendant of a distinguished New England family that had come from Ipswich, England, in 1634. His grandfather had served in the Continental army during the American Revolution. Growing up around Hanover, Foster was well steeped in the Congregationalist tradition, and entered nearby Dartmouth College, from which he graduated in 1851. (Much later, in 1891, Howard University of Washington, D.C., awarded Foster an honorary doctor of divinity degree.) After Dartmouth, Foster moved west to Illinois and then to Iowa, where he taught at a school for African American youths.

On October 23, 1851, Foster married Jemine Ewing, and they had one son. Jemine Foster died on October 3, 1853, and on May 8, 1855, Foster married Lucy Reed. The second Mrs. Foster was ten years younger than her husband, and she bore him ten children, eight boys and two girls. Two of the children died of diphtheria in November 1875 in Osborne, Kansas.

During the summer of 1856, the abolitionist-minded Foster campaigned with John Brown in the Kansas border disputes. He later moved to Nebraska, and in 1862 enlisted in the First Nebraska Regiment. After the passage of General Order No. 143 in 1863, which authorized the enlistment of African American troops, Foster volunteered for service with a black regiment. He was commissioned as a first lieutenant and served the remainder of the war with the Sixty-second U.S. Colored Infantry Regiment (formerly the First Missouri Volunteers of African Descent). Foster was assigned to Company One of the Sixty-second, and acted as regimental adjutant for most of the war.

The regiment was first organized in December 1863 at Benton Barracks in St. Louis. There the Western Sanitary Commission, a benevolent association, began organizing classes for black soldiers. The classes, in reading and writing, continued in the black regiments, as the former slaves were taught around the campfires by their white officers. Some of these officers, including Foster, were college-educated men who were inspired by a sense of mission to help uplift their black brothers. As the war continued, members of the black regiments became increasingly aware of the lack of educational opportunities for them in Missouri.

The Sixty-second Colored Infantry served in Louisiana and Texas until 1866. The troops dug trenches and built fortifications in the most unhealthy areas of those states. Under such conditions the regiment lost four hundred men. The men of the Sixty-second saw their first action at the end of the war in the Battle of Palmetto Ranch, Texas, where the Second Texas Confederate cavalry had cannons and superior rifles. After the first day of battle, May 12, 1865, the Union commander learned that the war was over, and ordered a withdrawal. Foster, who commanded the rear guard, proudly noted that while a white regiment broke into chaos and ran from the battlefield in disorder, the men of the Sixty-second maintained their ranks. In January 1866 at Fort McIntosh, Texas, the regiment was ordered into four companies and excess officers and noncommissioned officers were released from service. Foster was one of those to go home.

At home a conversation between Foster and another officer centered on the absence of a school for former slaves in Missouri where the soldiers could continue their education. Foster was asked if he would establish such a school if the regiment raised the money. A movement began and resulted in the men and officers of the Sixty-second raising $5,000. Foster agreed to lead the venture, and a committee was formed to aid in the effort. Foster went to the Sixty-fifth U.S. Colored Infantry Regiment to seek more funds. Stationed at Baton Rouge this sister regiment had seen the same type of duty as the Sixty-second, but had lost seven hundred men. They raised $1,379.50. While their contribution was smaller, Foster noted that a private, Samuel Saxton, gave $100, though he earned only $13 a month.

Foster headed for St. Louis where he hoped to open the school and gain greater financial support. The organizing committee was replaced by a board of trustees, adding a couple of prominent men from St. Louis. In St. Louis Foster learned the Methodist church was planning to create Central University. A meeting was arranged between the two boards. Foster offered the $6,300 raised by the regiments if Central University would admit black students and open at once. The offer was refused, and Foster headed for Jefferson City where he hoped for better fortunes.

In seeking a schoolhouse, however, Foster met prejudice. He asked the local black Methodist church for help, but was refused by the pastor because the teacher would be white. He then turned to the white Methodist church, but the pastor refused because the students would be black. Finally, Foster was allowed to use an abandoned schoolhouse on "Hobo Hill." The condition of the school was deplorable. However, on September 17, 1866, Foster opened Lincoln Institute with two students. One, Henry Brown, was a former member of the Sixty-second. Later he was joined by John Jefferies of the regiment, but most of the former soldiers were from other regiments. The school became filled with students, though teachers remained scarce. Foster's father-in-law, Festus Reed, offered his services as an assistant teacher for no salary, but at the end of the school year the board compensated him with $200.

The school constantly struggled for adequate financing. From 1866 to 1868 Foster was both principal and teacher of Lincoln Institute. In 1868 he was able to retain the services of a black teacher, W. H. Payne, whose $400 annual salary was paid by the American Missionary Association. Upon the recommendation of Governor Chalin of Massachusetts, Frederick Douglass, Henry Ward Beecher, and Charles A. Beal were employed as the school's national agents and fund-raisers. Foster was also to raise his salary. Fortunately, he was successful and raised $6,000 in his first year. Because of the institute's continued shortage of funds, Foster requested that the Jefferson City Board of Education hire him to provide instruction to the black children of the community as provided by law, and that he be allowed to charge nonresident blacks $1.00 per month. The board agreed. He was also employed to take a census of black children during the summer holidays.

The state superintendent of schools praised the instruction at Lincoln Institute and recommended that the state give assistance to the school and make it the center for training black teachers. Foster had put forth the idea that Lincoln should share in the 1862 Morrill Act land-grant monies. The proposal was backed by a petition from outstanding black citizens of the state under the leadership of **James Milton Turner** and **Moses Dickson.** While the legislature rejected Lincoln's sharing the land-grant monies, in 1870 it approved of Lincoln Institute receiving $5,000 annually for providing teacher training. The school had to raise several thousands of dollars to receive the aid, but it managed with contributions from the Freedmen's Bureau and others.

Between 1870 and 1871 W. H. Payne served as principal of Lincoln Institute, while Foster secured more funds by teaching in the public schools of Jefferson City. In 1871 Foster returned to Lincoln as the principal. In this same year Lincoln Institute, with the aid of a Jefferson City black businessman, Howard Barnes, secured the finances to erect its first building on the site of today's campus. At the end of the 1871 school year Foster was denied reappointment by the board for failing to support one of the candidates for governor in the previous election. He did accept reemployment as a fund-raiser for the institute, and continued to be a supporter of the school for the remainder of his life.

Foster was sent to Osborne, Kansas, in May 1872 by the American Home Missionary Society, where he was ordained as a minister in August 1872. He was pastor of the First Congregational Church there for ten years. He settled his family in a farmhouse just outside of Osborne, and his religious activities prospered. Within a year his nondenominational membership had built a church, and he provided religious services to several remote communities. In July 1879 Foster wrote to his former regiment members that he was on a committee of the Kansas Congregational Association "to see to the interests of the colored people brought there by the exodus. [Maj. Joseph

K.] Hudson is on a state central committee for the same purpose, so you see we are at our old work. Kansas welcomes the Negro, her patron saint is John Brown." Between 1882 and 1884 Foster took charge of the Congregational church in Red Cliff, Colorado. He then returned to Kansas and served at churches in Milford (1884–1886) and Cheney (1886–1890).

In 1890 Foster went to Oklahoma and organized a church at Stillwater, where he served for four years. In 1894 he assumed his next pastorate at Perkins, Oklahoma, for two years, and then, because of his advancing age, went to a smaller church in Okarche, Oklahoma. He also lectured once a week at nearby Kingfisher College on the subject of Bible and church history. In 1898 Foster's health failed, and he resigned his pastorate. After serving thirty years in the ministry, Foster died at Okarche, Oklahoma, on March 30, 1901, at the age of seventy-four.

ANTONIO F. HOLLAND

Foster, Richard B. File. Lincoln Collection. Inman E. Page Library, Lincoln University, Jefferson City, Mo.
Holland, Antonio F., Timothy R. Roberts, and Dennis White. *The Soldiers' Dream Continued: A Pictorial History of Lincoln University of Missouri.* Ed. Rosemary Hearn. Jefferson City, Mo.: Lincoln University, 1991.
Savage, W. Sherman. *History of Lincoln University.* Jefferson City, Mo.: New Day Press, 1939.

FOURCHET, JEANNETTE (?–1803)

In 1763, seeing his French outpost in Illinois on the verge of falling into Protestant hands, the Catholic priest at Cahokia freed his church's slaves and sent them on their way. After a period of wandering, many of the refugees made their way to the newly founded village of St. Louis, among them a woman named Jeannette Fourchet.

Fourchet holds the distinction of being one of the first lot owners in St. Louis and the founding mother of one of the city's most prominent African American families. In 1765 she received from **Pierre de Laclède Liguest** a 120-by-150-foot lot. Fourchet had married a former slave named Gregory, a blacksmith, and together they built a French "house of posts in the ground" on their lot. In 1770 Gregory died, leaving Jeannette with four small children, the house, and a few tools of his trade.

Dependent on her own resources, Fourchet supported her family with a home laundry business, and in 1773 began farming forty arpents (about thirty-four acres) given her by the Spanish government. When her assets were inventoried later that year, it was obvious that she had not only survived but also prospered; her household boasted such luxuries

as feather beds, linen bedcovers, pewter tableware, copper candlesticks, and a crystal saltcellar.

The occasion for the inventory was Fourchet's marriage to the black gunsmith Valentine. In keeping with French custom, the couple entered a prenuptial agreement, keeping their existing assets in their own names. Significantly, though Valentine was a successful tradesman, Jeannette brought more wealth to their union than he did, and probably contributed at least as much to their success over the next few years. In 1788 they received another land grant, eighty arpents (about sixty-eight acres) in the Prairie Desnoyers, and began farming it along with the forty-arpent tract in the Grand Prairie. When Valentine died two years later, his estate inventory hinted at their prosperity. The "house of posts" was now covered with shingles, filled with fine walnut furniture, and flanked by two substantial outbuildings.

Fourchet lived until 1803, supporting herself with the farms and then, after her health began to fail, with a mortgage on her house. She left the estate to her daughter, Susanne; a son, Augustin; and a grandson, Jean Baptiste Marly. Augustin died soon afterward, but Susanne and Jean Baptiste lived well by gradually selling their increasingly valuable properties. Jean Baptiste remained a bachelor, dabbling in real estate and listing his occupation in the 1850 census as "gentleman." Susanne married a well-to-do Frenchman named Jean Baptiste Irbour, with whom she had a daughter, Julie, who married the butcher and cattle dealer Antoine Labadie; together they founded one of the city's largest and most prominent black families.

JUDITH A. GILBERT

Gilbert, Judith A. "Esther and Her Sisters." *Gateway Heritage* 17 (summer 1996): 14–23.
Williams, Christine. "Prosperity in the Face of Prejudice: The Life of a Free Black Woman in Frontier St. Louis." *Gateway Heritage* 19 (fall 1998): 4–11.

FOXX, REDD. *See* Sanford, John Elroy.

FRANCIS, DAVID ROWLAND (1850–1927)

Mayor of St. Louis, governor of Missouri, secretary of the interior, president of the Louisiana Purchase Exposition, and ambassador to Russia, David R. Francis played an important role in the political life of the state and nation for almost forty years. A member of St. Louis's "Big Cinch," a group of economic and political leaders, Francis made a fortune as a grain dealer and as an officer of the Mississippi Valley Trust Company, the Terminal Railway Association, Union

Electric Company, and three different street railway companies.

Born in Richmond, Kentucky, on October 1, 1850, Francis attended Robert Breck's academy for girls, because the owner wanted a companion for his son. Because he had an uncle in St. Louis, Francis entered Washington University, graduating in 1870 with a B.A. degree. He wanted to earn a law degree, but he could not finance further education. His St. Louis uncle, David Pitt Rowland, employed him in his grain commission house. In six years Francis learned the business, paid off college debts, and saved enough to open his own firm in 1877. Seven years later he reorganized the business under the name David R. Francis and Brother.

Francis's reputation grew quickly. In 1884 he became president of the St. Louis Merchants' Exchange, the youngest person ever to hold that position. In 1885 St. Louisans elected him mayor by twelve hundred votes. Four years earlier voters had given his Republican opponent in the election a majority of fourteen thousand votes. As mayor, Francis used business techniques to cut city expenses and to institute efficient administrative practices. He vetoed legislation that he deemed corrupt.

In 1888 the Democratic Party nominated Francis as its candidate for governor, and he defeated his Republican opponent, E. E. Kimball, by more than thirteen thousand votes. Relatively unfamiliar with state government, Francis cultivated committee chairmen and other legislators by hosting dinners and holding receptions in which he made clear his vision of what the state needed. He succeeded in passing laws that tightened regulations on railroads and provided for a state grain inspector. He secured passage of the state's first antitrust law, and increased appropriations for the state university. In 1892, when Academic Hall burned on the Columbia campus, he withstood efforts to change the school's location and pushed through the legislature a $250,000 appropriation for a new building. He also secured passage of the first secret-ballot law, a uniform-textbook law for the public schools, and appointment of a geological survey commission.

After leaving the governor's office, Francis remained active in Democratic politics. In the controversy over the free coinage of silver, he voiced strong support for the gold standard and President Grover Cleveland. In 1896 Cleveland appointed Francis secretary of the interior, a position he held until Cleveland left office in 1897. During the rest of the 1890s and early 1900s, Francis devoted himself to the Louisiana Purchase Exposition in St. Louis. He lobbied for the city to be the location of the celebration of the one-hundredth anniversary of the purchase, he organized the fund-raising campaign to finance the celebration, and he served as president of the board of directors that oversaw the celebration. Certainly no one devoted more of his time and energy to the World's Fair than Francis. At one point he explained at least one motive for his work:

> St. Louis has needed something like this. We are a peculiarly self-centered people. We own our own city. We have always stood ready to furnish capital to others. We are strong and prosperous financially. But we are perhaps too independent. We need to be brought more closely into contact with the outside world. We need to learn something of our own merits and possibilities, so that many of our own people will realize a little better than they do that St. Louis is, in its own way, as great a city as any on the continent.

In 1916 Francis left the United States for his last political adventure. President Woodrow Wilson appointed him as ambassador to Russia. With the world at war and the United States still neutral, Francis could hardly foretell what challenges he faced. As he left St. Louis on March 23, he made a strong statement urging the nation to prepare militarily for war, while praying for peace.

> I have lived three-score and five years, and sometimes ask myself the question propounded to me by many whom I have met, that is, why at my age, after rounding out half a century of activity, should I assume an onerous responsibility in an untried field, why take upon myself the stupendous task of such proportions as to tax the ability, if not to appall a diplomat of experience and distinguished service.
>
> The reply made to myself is that I consider this call one of duty, to which it would be recreant not to respond. . . . If my government, in its wisdom, calls me to an important post, which it thinks I am competent to fill on account of my years or my experience in domestic government, or in national or international commerce, I would be a poor citizen indeed if I permitted personal interests, or friendly associations, or love of ease, or even ties of consanguinity, to interfere or to prevent a favorable response on my part.

During Francis's time as ambassador he saw the Russian monarchy of Nicholas II overthrown and the establishment of a provisional government under Alexander Kerensky and the overthrow of that government by Vladimir I. Lenin and his Bolsheviks. The United States led all other governments in recognizing the Kerensky government. The Bolshevik revolution presented Francis with great difficulties. Officials refused to allow his reports to go to Washington, and he received communications from the State Department sporadically. He confronted mobs set on destroying the embassy in Petrograd, with pistol in hand, and eventually fled the capital when the approach of German troops made it unsafe for a representative of the United States to stay. By then, of course, the United States had declared war against Germany, and Russia had withdrawn from the war, signing the Brest-Litovsk Treaty with Germany. Francis moved the embassy from place to place by train until settling in Vologda, and he became dean of the diplomatic corps that remained in Russia. Many diplomats fled the country. Consistently, Francis urged the Russian people to stay with the allies and protested against the Brest-Litovsk Treaty, warning the Russians against German intrigue.

Francis's health gave way under these tough circumstances, and on November 6, 1918, attendants carried him on a stretcher aboard a U.S. warship. In London he underwent an operation. He returned to St. Louis without ever recapturing his health and died on January 15, 1927. His wife of almost fifty years, Jane Perry, preceded him in death in 1925. The couple had six sons.

LAWRENCE O. CHRISTENSEN

Cockfield, James H., ed. *Dollars and Diplomacy: Ambassador David Rowland Francis and the Fall of Tsarism, 1916–1917.* Durham: Duke University Press, 1981.

Dictionary of American Biography. S.v. "Francis, David Rowland."

Francis, David R. Papers. Missouri Historical Society, St. Louis.

St. Louis Globe-Democrat, January 16, 1927.

Stevens, Walter B. "Missourians, David R. Francis' Best Speech." *Missouri Historical Review* 21 (April 1927): 347–52.

———. "Missourians Abroad: David R. Francis, Ambassador Extraordinary and Plenipotentiary to Russia." *Missouri Historical Review* 13 (April 1919): 195–225.

FRANK, NATHAN (1852–1931)

Nathan Frank, a St. Louis political, civic, and business leader, was born in Peoria, Illinois, on February 23, 1852. He attended the public schools of Peoria and St. Louis, and Washington University in St. Louis. He graduated from Harvard Law School in 1871. The following year he was admitted to the Missouri bar, devoting his practice to commercial and bankruptcy law. Frank became so thoroughly familiar with the laws governing those cases that in 1874 he compiled and edited *Frank's Bankruptcy Law,* which went through four editions and is still in use today.

During his early years as an attorney, Frank became active in the Republican Party and lost a close race for Congress in 1886 after unsuccessfully contesting the election of his opponent, John M. Glover. Two years later Frank ran again on the Republican and Union Labor tickets and was elected to Congress from Missouri's Ninth District, becoming the only Jew to serve in Congress from the state of Missouri. He declined to be a candidate for reelection in 1890.

During his single term in Congress, Frank gave almost unswerving support to his party and to his president, Benjamin Harrison, and accomplished much, on both the national and the local levels. Nationally, he made use of his knowledge of bankruptcy law. He was also responsible for the passage of a federal reapportionment bill that fixed the House membership at 356—the only such measure to be passed unanimously. Locally, he was responsive to the needs of his constituents and successfully sponsored many bills for the physical improvement of his district and for private pensions for St. Louis Civil War veterans. Frank also successfully amended a tariff bill to include a provision to protect the hide dealers of his district by banning duties on hides.

Although Frank retired from the House of Representatives, he did not lose his interest in politics. He sought the Republican senatorial nomination from Missouri in 1910, 1916, and 1928, but was unsuccessful on all three occasions.

Frank also devoted much time to business and civic interests in St. Louis. In 1904 he served on the executive committee for the Louisiana Purchase Exposition in St. Louis, and played an important role in bringing the World's Fair to St. Louis. The following year he founded a daily newspaper called the *St. Louis Star.* In 1924 Frank developed plans for a bandstand in Pagoda Lake in St. Louis's Forest Park, and donated the fifty thousand dollars needed for the project. The completely renovated and refurbished bandstand still stands today across from the entrance to the Muny Opera. In addition, Frank was one of the city's most active real estate traders and investors. Among his holdings were large tracts of downtown properties and midtown apartment buildings.

Frank was extremely active in the St. Louis Jewish community, generously donating both his time and his money to nearly every local and national Jewish cause, including the Jewish War Relief Committee, the St. Louis Jewish Orphans' Home, the Jewish Hospital of St. Louis, the St. Louis Jewish Old Folks' Home, and the St. Louis Federation of Jewish Charities, the forerunner of today's Jewish Federation.

Nathan Frank died on April 6, 1931. He was one of St. Louis's most distinguished citizens, but far less influential than he might have been because he skimmed the surface of too many activities. Had he remained in Congress, historians think he could have been more effective for his district and the city. Had he devoted his time exclusively to his law practice, he might have received a judicial appointment. Had he devoted more of his time to his newspaper, it might still be in existence today. Had he been involved only in real estate, his contributions in that field might have been greater. However, his inability to find one field and devote his time to it should not minimize Frank's contribution to St. Louis. Both the Jewish and the sectarian populace of the city benefited from his works, and few people have equaled his generosity or prominence.

BURTON A. BOXERMAN

Biographical Directory of the American Congress, 1774–1971. S.v. "Frank, Nathan." Washington, D.C.: U.S. Government Printing Office, 1971.

Boxerman, Burton A. "The Honorable Nathan Frank." *Missouri Historical Review* 67 (October 1972): 52–74.

The National Cyclopedia of American Biography. S.v. "Frank, Nathan."

FRANKLIN, CHESTER ARTHUR (1880–1955)

Chester Arthur Franklin, the publisher and editor of the *Kansas City Call* from 1919 to 1955, was born on June 7, 1880, in Denison, Texas. The only child of George F. Franklin, a barber, and Clara Williams Franklin, a teacher, Franklin moved with his family to Omaha, Nebraska, in 1887. Shortly after arriving in Omaha, George Franklin founded the *Enterprise,* a successful African American weekly. C. A., as his friends called him, graduated from high school in 1896 and attended the University of Nebraska at Lincoln for two years before returning home to help his ailing father with his newspaper. In 1898 the Franklins moved to Denver, where George purchased the *Colorado Statesman,* a weekly that he renamed the *Star.* The elder Franklin died in 1901, but his widow and son continued to publish the paper.

In 1913 C. A. Franklin moved to Kansas City, Missouri, where he opened a printing shop. His business prospered, and on May 6, 1919, he published the first issue of the *Kansas City Call.* The paper rarely used sensational headlines to increase sales. Instead, Franklin focused his rapidly growing paper on race issues and politics. He only hired journalists with college degrees, and in fact selected a young University of Minnesota graduate named **Roy O. Wilkins** as the *Call*'s first full-time news editor in 1923. When Wilkins left the paper in 1931, Franklin hired Lucile Bluford, a University of Kansas graduate, as his replacement.

Franklin met Ada Crogman, a young actress, in 1922, and they married in 1925. Under her guidance he curbed his manic work habits and moderated his sometimes volatile temper. With a reliable staff and an established reputation, Franklin curtailed his hours at the *Call,* and the couple became leaders of Kansas City's African American community. They organized charitable functions for Jackson County's various African American institutions, and Ada Franklin often hosted local theatrical productions.

By 1930 the *Call,* with nearly fifteen thousand subscribers in more than a dozen states, offered Franklin a large audience for his opinions on economics and race, and on local, state, and national politics. In 1933 it became the first black paper in the country to secure verification of its subscription lists from the Audit Bureau of Circulations, an organization that validated circulation reports for advertisers. By the mid-1940s the *Call* had more than forty thousand subscribers, making it one of the most prosperous African American weeklies in the nation.

As a member of the National Negro Business League, Franklin frequently reminded his readers to patronize African American businesses, and as a member of the Republican Party, he regularly endorsed GOP candidates in municipal, county, state, and national elections. He reserved his strongest editorials, however, for the evils of **Thomas J. Pendergast**'s Democratic machine. Franklin had little patience for bossism, and he frequently used the *Call* to demand various municipal and county reforms.

Ironically, one Pendergast man won Franklin's trust. **Harry S. Truman,** the presiding judge of the Jackson County Court from 1927 to 1934, actively supported the county's African American institutions and earned a reputation as an honest administrator. Franklin's paper endorsed Truman for reelection to the county court in 1930 and supported his successful bid for the United States Senate in 1934. Perhaps more important, the two men remained close during the senator's first term, and they worked together during Truman's reelection campaign. Without the support of Missouri's African American voters, Truman's political career might have ended in 1940. The two parted ways politically in 1941. In his second term Truman remained committed to the New Deal and to the dying Pendergast machine, both of which Franklin opposed. Nevertheless, they corresponded sporadically until Franklin's death in 1955.

In addition to his business ventures, which included the Colored Mail Order Corporation and a cooking school, Franklin became increasingly involved in the early civil rights movement. He organized rallies to protest discrimination in defense industries, joined the NAACP in supporting Lucile Bluford's failed 1940 lawsuit against segregation at the University of Missouri, and became more openly hostile to discrimination of all types. In 1947 Sam Houston University of Austin, Texas, awarded

Franklin an honorary doctor of law degree in recognition of his contributions to civil rights. C. A. Franklin died on May 7, 1955.

Thomas D. Wilson

Grothaus, Larry. "Kansas City Blacks, Harry Truman, and the Pendergast Machine." *Missouri Historical Review* 68 (October 1974): 65–82.

————. "The Negro in Missouri Politics, 1890–1941." Ph.D. diss., University of Missouri–Columbia, 1970.

Wilson, Noel. "The *Kansas City Call* and the Negro Market." Ph.D. diss., University of Illinois, 1971.

Wilson, Thomas D. "Chester A. Franklin and Harry S. Truman: An African-American Conservative and the 'Conversion' of the Future President." *Missouri Historical Review* 87 (October 1993): 48–77.

FRAZER, JEAN TOMLINSON (1894–1969)

Jean Tomlinson Frazer, a talented Missouri photographer, brought smiles to pictures. She was born on March 2, 1894, in Hannibal, Missouri, to Herbert and Minnietta Campbell Tomlinson. Herbert Tomlinson came to Hannibal in 1884. Both he and his brother Porter were photographers, and they owned Tomlinson Brothers Studio in Hannibal. Jean Tomlinson quit school at age fourteen to help her father in his photography business. Her brother, Ralph, also worked in their father's studio, as a film retoucher.

Tomlinson hoped to change the type of visage seen on most studio photos. She wanted her patrons to be happy and to show a happy face on their portraits. Traditionally, clients had to sit perfectly still, and the photographer advised them not to attempt a smile but sit quietly, lips closed, and eyes straight ahead. It was nerve-racking experience for the subject to sit or stand without moving a hand or foot, resist all desires to scratch, or shift weight, or close his or her eyes. Photographers considered it frivolous to smile in a photo or portrait. However, young Jean Tomlinson wanted everyone to smile, and thus the idea of "the Jean Smile" was born. Good cameras were available at that time, and their speed was practically instantaneous compared to the first one her father owned. Tomlinson won her first international award certificate for a portrait of a baby with an impish smile.

Tomlinson married Edward Harold (Hal) Frazer on April 8, 1919, and she renamed the business the Frazer Studio. Hal, also an excellent photographer, took a picture of Jean in fishing clothes holding a large catfish she had caught. Not only was she smiling, but they had manipulated the mouth of the fish so that it, too, was smiling. The smiling portraits had started a trend that never waned. An examination of the hundreds of available portraits prove Frazer's artistic talent.

The Frazer Studio had no Victorian gimmicks of canvas backdrops and props. The background of classic simplicity usually consisted of a wall with pleated drapes from ceiling to floor or painted walls. Lighting, used in various ways, highlighted the smiling subjects. Persons sat on simple chairs and benches. Upon request, Frazer photographed women with unusual hairdos, holding flowers, or displaying bared shoulders by means of a satin drape with a rose tucked in the bosom. Her bridal portraits appeared carefully posed, with everyone comfortable and pleasant looking. Frazer's photos were known for their careful retouching and for tinting. She used the sepia developing process, and her hand-tinted portraits had a more natural look.

The Frazers sold their business in 1937, but Jean Frazer continued to retouch and tint portraits for other studios. She also served as a volunteer office worker in the Marion County Red Cross. She died on August 30, 1969. Interment was at the Frazer lot in Barkley Cemetery, in New London, Missouri.

Petra DeWitt

Dains, Mary K., ed. *Show Me Missouri Women: Selected Biographies.* Kirksville, Mo.: Thomas Jefferson University Press, 1989.

Howard, Goldena Roland. *Ralls County, Missouri.* Marceline, Mo.: Walsworth, 1980.

FRÉMON DE LAURIÈRE, AUGUSTIN CHARLES (dates unknown)

The French Revolution induced many royalists to emigrate to the Louisiana Territory in the late eighteenth century. Augustin Charles Frémon de Laurière made his way in July 1794 to New Bourbon, an immigrant enclave in the North American backcountry. A native of St. Pere Curet, near Nantes in the Breton region, Frémon retained royalist loyalties as well as his status as Lord du Bouffray and des Crois. He had fought in the counterrevolutionary Vendée, but found asylum in Upper Louisiana and quickly adapted to life there. Frémon pledged loyalty to the Spanish crown soon after his arrival and in 1795 commanded a militia unit engaged in an expedition along the Mississippi River.

New Bourbon's founder, **Pierre-Charles Delassus de Luzières,** encouraged Frémon to establish a school providing formal instruction in nearby Ste. Genevieve. Frémon submitted an educational plan to Lieutenant Governor Carondelet titled "An Education Program Suitable to the Youth of Illinois," which received the government's endorsement. Frémon based his plan on French educational theory, which called for a rational approach adhering to principles of virtue and the liberal arts. He adapted theory, however, to suit the practical needs of his students in Ste. Genevieve. The curriculum was made up of eight components, including instruction in language arts, mathematics, geography, agriculture, Catholicism, deportment, recreation, and art. He conducted his classes in French, relying on motivational strategies to maintain order rather than firm discipline. Students fell within three aptitude levels in each class, received grades monthly, and competed in public examinations every three months. Although highly successful, Frémon's school lasted only two years. District residents contributed books and materials, but without government funding the project came to an end in 1798.

Charles Frémon remained in Ste. Genevieve for the next few years before moving farther west. After the school closed, he served as the town's *greffier,* or notary, functioning as an official witness and legal administrator for the commandant. He drafted wills, deeds, and contracts; conducted inventories; held public sales; and settled estates in this capacity. He received a grant of ten thousand arpents near the Prairie à Rondo in 1797, but made few improvements to the property.

Frémon married Josephine Celest Chauvet Dubreuil in St. Louis on May 21, 1799. They joined Louis Labeaume a year later in an entrepreneurial venture to produce salt. The two families established a large saltworks with four or five furnaces along La Saline Ensanglantee, located one day's travel west of St. Louis on the frontier of Spanish Louisiana. In March 1801 Frémon asked Lt. Gov. **Charles de Hault Delassus** for a grant of ten thousand arpents at this location and provided a sample of his product to demonstrate his skills. Delassus approved the grant, extolling the quality of Frémon's salt over all others. Frémon formally ended his residence in the Ste. Genevieve district, sold his land, and moved to the frontier. The salt operation was beset, however, with problems: Indians attacked settlements on the fringe of the backcountry, its location far from markets made distribution difficult, the partners repeatedly lost cargo in the Saline and Mississippi Rivers, and the high salt tax restricted profits. Despite the high quality and large quantity of its product, the business failed by 1805.

Frémon de Laurière then adopted a third profession, that of deputy surveyor for the St. Charles District of Upper Louisiana. Documentation shows that he worked in this capacity through 1806, but thereafter he disappears from the written record until 1833. He testified in that year regarding Spanish civil procedures for granting, surveying, and recording land concessions in the territory. Even though his own concession on La Saline Ensanglantee had been surveyed and recorded, U.S. legislation in 1807 disallowed any prior grant that included a salt spring or mine. This was remedied by 1832, however, when a more liberal law approved the original claims. Frémon's grant received final certification in 1836, but little is known about his life at that point. The date and place of his death are unknown.

Augustin Charles Frémon de Laurière found asylum in Upper Louisiana and expressed his gratitude through his service to the community. He served as an educator, notary, entrepreneur, and surveyor during his time in North America. His most important contribution, however, was the establishment of arguably the finest school in Ste. Genevieve for two brief years in the late eighteenth century. Its curriculum stressed adaptability, which Frémon demonstrated in his own life. Although brief in tenure, his educational program provided a cultural foundation for liberal arts and practical craft on the Missouri frontier.

RACHEL FRANKLIN WEEKLEY

Ekberg, Carl J. *Colonial Ste. Genevieve: An Adventure on the Mississippi Frontier.* Gerald, Mo.: Patrice Press, 1985.

Foley, William E. *A History of Missouri: Volume I, 1673 to 1820.* Columbia: University of Missouri Press, 1971.

Houck, Louis. *A History of Missouri, from the Earliest Explorations and Settlements until the Admission of the State into the Union.* Vol. 2. Chicago: R. R. Donnelley and Sons, 1908.

Liljegren, Ernest R. "Frontier Education in Spanish Louisiana." *Missouri Historical Review* 35 (April 1941): 345–72.

FRÉMONT, JESSIE BENTON (1824–1902)

Jessie Benton Frémont, the daughter of Sen. **Thomas Hart Benton** of Missouri and Elizabeth Preston McDowell Benton, was born on May 31, 1824, at Cherry Grove, her maternal grandparents' estate in Rockbridge County, Virginia. A lively, quick-witted girl, the second of five children, she became her father's favorite. "I think I came into father's life like a breath of his own compelling nature," she wrote, "strong, resolute, but open to all tender and gracious influences, and above all loving him." The Benton family lived mainly in Washington, D.C., but throughout Jessie's childhood they spent long periods in St. Louis, Thomas Benton's political base. Both in Missouri and in Washington, the senator closely supervised his daughter's education, emphasizing history, literature, and languages. In St. Louis she attended a French primary school and studied

Spanish with a tutor. More informally, she acquired a shrewd knowledge of politics and a fascination with the West.

While reluctantly attending Miss English's Female Seminary near Washington, D.C., Jessie Benton met **John Charles Frémont,** a dashing army explorer of illegitimate birth. Despite her parents' opposition, "there was no room for reason" in their romance, and on October 19, 1841, when Jessie Benton was seventeen, they secretly married. Although Thomas Benton was predictably furious, within months he had accepted his favorite daughter's marriage and begun to promote her husband's western career.

In 1842 while John Frémont journeyed west from St. Louis to the Rocky Mountains as the head of his first major expedition, Jessie Frémont remained in Washington, pregnant with the first of their five children (two of whom would die in infancy). A year later, when John set out on a far bolder expedition that would take him to Oregon and Mexican-held California, Jessie stayed in St. Louis during his fourteen-month absence. Waiting was always difficult for a woman of her vigorous temperament, but when he returned she assumed a more active role in collaborating with him on the expedition reports. Enlivened by her sense of drama and vivid narrative style, these richly detailed accounts, now classics in the literature of exploration, made John Frémont and his scout, **Christopher "Kit" Houston Carson,** national heroes, and influenced thousands to go west.

During his third expedition (1845–1847), John Frémont became involved in the conquest of California, but when United States Army and Navy authorities quarreled over supreme authority there, he rashly sided with the navy and was court-martialed. His sensational trial, conviction, and partial pardon by President James Polk only increased his fame, but the Frémonts, embittered, decided to begin a new life in California.

In March 1849, while John traveled overland on a privately financed expedition to locate an all-weather railroad route from St. Louis to the Pacific, Jessie Frémont set out via Panama to join him in San Francisco. Accompanied by her young daughter, she crossed the isthmus by dugout and mule, and nearly died of a dangerous tropical fever. Reunited in California, the Frémonts found their fortunes abruptly reversed when immense gold deposits were discovered at their Sierra Nevada ranch and John was elected as California's first senator.

In 1856 when her husband became the first presidential candidate of the newly formed Republican Party on the platform opposing the extension of slavery, Jessie Frémont played an active though necessarily half-hidden role in what many enthusiasts called the "Frémont and Jessie" campaign. Former Washington newspaper editor Francis Preston Blair and his two sons, **Frank** and **Montgomery Blair,** who had both apprenticed in Thomas Benton's St. Louis law office, were among Frémont's most important supporters. Benton, however, convinced that the election of a sectional candidate would lead to civil war, opposed his son-in-law's presidential bid. Benton's stand created a painful family rift that Jessie Frémont, unhappily caught between husband and father, was only partially able to heal before Benton's death in 1858.

Although John Frémont gained the majority of northern votes, he was defeated nationwide. The Frémonts retreated to California, but four years later, when Abraham Lincoln's election brought Civil War, the new president named John Frémont as commander of the Department of the West with headquarters in St. Louis. Jessie Frémont eagerly joined her husband in "this noble chance in a great cause." Arriving in St. Louis on July 25, 1861, she found it "a hostile city," tenuously held by a small Union force. She soon wrote to the Blair family in Washington, including Postmaster Gen. Montgomery Blair, her conduit to the president, describing the difficulties they faced: inadequate troops, supplies, and funds as well as the constant harassment of Confederate sympathizers, "thick and unremitting as mosquitoes."

Over the next months, Frémont served as her husband's aide and confidante, attending to his secret correspondence, joining staff meetings, seeing visitors, and arranging for his views and actions to be favorably presented in the press. She also worked closely with **William Greenleaf Eliot,** a Unitarian minister and founder of Washington University, to establish the Western Sanitary Commission, and brought an old friend, superintendent of army nursing Dorothea Dix, to St. Louis to advise on hospitals and the care of the wounded. Never so alive as when she could channel her energy into action, Frémont found it the "Most wearing and most welcome work of my life." Some, however, shocked that a woman would play such an active role, branded her "General Jessie."

On August 30, 1861, with Jessie Frémont's full support, John Frémont issued a decree freeing the slaves of Missouri rebels. Northern abolitionists hailed this first, albeit limited, emancipation proclamation, but Lincoln, still attempting by a moderate stance to retain border-state loyalty, directed Frémont to revoke the decree. Jessie Frémont rushed to Washington where, in a dramatic meeting with the president, she argued for the immediate emancipation of the slaves. Responding to her in what she felt was a "sneering" tone, Lincoln called her "quite a female politician."

Meanwhile, St. Louis congressman and longtime ally Frank Blair, motivated by rivalry as well as genuine concern, informed Lincoln through his brother, Montgomery, that Frémont was proving an inadequate commander. Over the next two months, the Blairs' attacks as well as Union defeats in Missouri, the discovery of profiteering among Frémont's staff, and opposition to his emancipation decree all combined to convince Lincoln to relieve Frémont of his command on November 2, 1861. Writing bitterly afterward to friends, Jessie Frémont called Lincoln a "sly, slimy" man and condemned his "tenderness toward slavery." In 1863 she published *The Story of the Guard,* a skillfully indirect defense of her husband's Missouri command.

After the war Jessie Frémont immersed herself in domesticity, but when the Frémonts lost the remains of their gold-rush fortune in the financial panic of 1873, she began to write professionally to help support the family. In such books as *A Year of American Travel* (1878) and *Souvenirs of My Time* (1887), she included accounts of the Missouri she had known in her youth as well as during the Civil War. Despite her efforts the Frémonts lived the remainder of their lives in genteel poverty. John Frémont's business schemes inevitably failed, his term as territorial governor of Arizona ended with his forced resignation, and even his memoirs, written with his wife, never achieved the success they hoped for.

In 1888 the Frémonts settled in Los Angeles, but John soon returned east on business, a pattern of separation begun in their first years of marriage. Although her husband's restlessness, emotional remoteness, and rumored infidelities pained her through the years, Jessie Frémont remained fiercely devoted. When he unexpectedly died in July 1890 in a New York boardinghouse, her children feared she might kill herself. Nonetheless, she lived twelve more years in increasing serenity, her finances augmented by a small government pension and a house donated by a group of California women. She died in Los Angeles on December 27, 1902.

During Frémont's lifetime, many observed that in character she resembled her father: John Frémont himself wrote that she had Benton's "grasp of mind, comprehending with a tenacious memory." But while Thomas Hart Benton could exercise his talents directly, his daughter, as a nineteenth-century woman with more limited options, channeled much of her energy and ambition into her husband's career. Nevertheless, she managed to carve out a place for herself as a writer and opponent of slavery. Perhaps most important in her own eyes, she was the vital "connecting link" between her father's vision of a transcontinental nation and her husband's part in achieving this goal. One of her proudest moments came in May 1868 when, before a large crowd in St. Louis's Lafayette Park, she unveiled **Harriet Goodhue Hosmer**'s bronze statue of Thomas Hart Benton, holding a map in his hand and facing west.

PAMELA HERR

Blair Family. Papers. Library of Congress, Washington, D.C.

Blair-Lee Family. Papers. Firestone Library, Princeton University, Princeton, N.J.

Frémont Papers. Bancroft Library, University of California, Berkeley.

Herr, Pamela. *Jessie Benton Frémont: A Biography.* New York: Franklin Watts, 1987.

Herr, Pamela, and Mary Lee Spence. *The Letters of Jessie Benton Frémont.* Urbana: University of Illinois Press, 1993.

FRÉMONT, JOHN CHARLES (1813–1890)

Neither born in Missouri nor residing in the state for a prolonged period, John Charles Frémont nonetheless played a significant role in the foundation of modern Missouri. A formidable western hero, Frémont emerged as a prominent antislavery Republican in the 1850s. During the ensuing Civil War he assumed command of the Union's Western Department based in St. Louis. In that capacity he issued a famous order suppressing rebel elements and attempting to free the slaves of disloyal Missourians. This effort intensified the internecine warfare already disrupting the state, but it also paved the way for the eventual abolition of slavery in the state.

Frémont's parents, Charles Frémont and Ann Beverly Whiting Pryor, apparently never married. In 1811 Ann fled her elderly husband, John Pryor, in Virginia to join Frémont, a young French dancing instructor. On January 21, 1813, John Charles was born in Savannah, Georgia. After his father died John grew to maturity in Charleston, South Carolina, where he attended the College of Charleston. However, a lack of diligence prompted his dismissal in 1831, just three months short of his graduation.

Frémont's relationship to Missouri grew primarily from family connections: he became the son-in-law of Missouri's legendary Democratic senator **Thomas Hart Benton**. At first the powerful senator did not sanction the union between his young daughter Jessie and the unproved Frémont. Following his aborted college career Frémont had served briefly as a mathematics instructor on naval vessels and as an assistant on two surveying missions in the South. In 1838 the support of secretary of war Joel Poinsett brought an appointment as a second lieutenant in the army's Bureau of Topographical Engineers. Frémont gained valuable experience in scientific exploration by assisting a respected French scientist, Joseph Nicollet, in mapping the region between the Mississippi and Missouri Rivers.

In 1841 Frémont received his first independent assignment to survey the Des Moines River region; upon his return he secretly married Jessie Benton, on October 19, 1841. The senator gradually accepted the marriage and became an important patron of John's exploring career. St. Louis thereupon became the family's base of operations; along with Westport, Missouri, St. Louis would serve as the staging point for Frémont's western expeditions.

Following Nicollet's death the task of completing the scientist's systematic exploration of the western domain fell to his protégé, Frémont. Although the topographical engineers had devised plans to survey the western trails, Senator Benton's involvement transformed the primarily scientific objectives of the expeditions into political ones as well. In June 1842, after organizing his first major expedition (and securing **Kit Carson** as a guide) in Missouri, Frémont followed the Kansas River to the Platte and finally the Sweetwater River in today's Wyoming. He and Benton had interpreted his orders to allow him to visit the strategic South Pass in the Wind River Mountains. Frémont reported that this opening in the Rocky Mountains was easily passed by settlers in wagons, thus helping to encourage further American emigration to the Oregon country. A second expedition in 1843–1844 completed the explorer's path along the Oregon Trail and culminated in a risky but successful winter crossing of the Sierra Nevada into Mexican California.

Prepared with **Jessie Benton Frémont**'s valuable help, John Frémont's reports of his first two expeditions did more than just provide prospective travelers with useful information about the overland trail. Beyond clarifying the nature of the Continental Divide, Frémont's journals challenged the notion that the Plains were a barren wasteland, revealed the existence of the Great Basin, and downplayed the risks of the overland journey to the fertile valleys of Oregon and California. Not the least important, the report elevated Frémont to the level of national hero.

During Frémont's third expedition of 1845–1846 the brevet captain assumed command of the "Bear Flag" revolt of American settlers against Mexican authority in California. Joining American naval forces, Frémont formed the "California Battalion" to help secure the province. After a brief revolt by Californians of Spanish descent, Frémont accepted their final surrender at Cahuenga and was appointed in January 1847 as the temporary military governor of California.

The appointment brought the inexperienced army officer into conflict with Gen. **Stephen Watts Kearny.** Believing his appointment by Commodore Robert Stockton to be legitimate, Frémont refused Kearny's contrary orders and was arrested. In a celebrated court-martial in Washington, Frémont won much public sympathy (and the support of Senator Benton), but in January 1848 was found guilty of disobedience. Rejecting President James K. Polk's offer of clemency, the miffed explorer instead resigned his commission.

With Senator Benton's backing, Frémont subsequently led two privately financed expeditions designed to prove the feasibility of an all-weather "central route" for a railroad to the Pacific. While such a route would have benefited Benton's Missouri backers, Frémont's journeys in 1848–1849 and 1853–1854 proved unsuccessful; other transcontinental routes would later be selected.

California now became the adopted home of John Frémont and Jessie Frémont. A large area known as the Mariposa proved to hold immense wealth in gold. In December 1849 Frémont had been selected as one of California's first U.S. senators. He served a short term from 1850 to 1851 as an antislavery Democrat. Failing to win reelection, Frémont returned to private life until growing controversy over slavery in the western territories opened a new phase in his public career.

Both parties sought the heroic and celebrated figure, but Frémont's antislavery predilections prevented him from responding to Democratic overtures. Instead, in 1856 he accepted the first presidential nomination of the Republican Party, and pledged to prevent the spread of slavery to western territories such as Kansas. Although he did not win the support of Missouri (or the endorsement of his Democratic father-in-law), he did manage to carry most of the free states. However, organizational problems in key states such as Pennsylvania prevented an electoral triumph. Frémont's image had appealed to new young voters and helped to establish the new party, which went on to elect Abraham Lincoln as president four years later.

When Civil War erupted in 1861 Frémont supported the Union without hesitation, despite his southern origins. His reputation and personal connections (although Senator Benton had died, the powerful Blair family supported Frémont at this point) made him the logical choice to head the Western Department, whose primary responsibility was the divided state of Missouri. Assuming command in July 1861 Frémont found himself instantly overwhelmed by the disorder in the state, and by the lack of men and materials. He received little direction from authorities in Washington. Although Gen. **Nathaniel Lyon** had done much to secure the Union position in Missouri, he also stirred up rebel resentments. While Lyon's troops pursued rebel forces in the southwestern corner of the state near Springfield, Frémont allowed the irascible General Lyon the discretion to attack superior rebel forces at Wilson's Creek on August 10, 1861. Lyon's defeat and death shocked the North and brought scrutiny to Frémont's command.

Reacting to the setback with characteristic impetuosity, Frémont first placed St. Louis and then the entire state under martial law. (This directive would remain effective for the virtual remainder of the war.) Then on August 30 he issued a sudden order stating that captured rebel guerrillas could be shot. Most significantly, he directed that the slaves of rebel masters be freed. While antislavery elements cheered Frémont's emancipation edict (and a few Missouri slaves won their freedom), it worried President Lincoln who sought to retain the loyalty of border-state slaveholders. Although the directive had won the support of the St. Louis press, it antagonized other elements within Missouri who resisted any interference with slavery. Associates of Gov. **Hamilton Rowan Gamble** marked Frémont for removal. When President Lincoln directed him to modify the order, Frémont instead dispatched his wife to Washington to plead for support. Confronting the president on this issue proved counterproductive, and she returned to Missouri defeated. The president publicly directed Frémont to reverse the order.

In the meantime charges of corruption and incompetence, motivated by Frémont's political enemies (which now included the Blair family), beset the general's command. Investigations failed to demonstrate serious wrongdoing but tarnished Frémont's reputation enough to allow Lincoln to remove what had become a political liability. Another defeat at Lexington was not offset by a minor victory by Frémont's cavalry guard at Springfield. While seeking battle with the enemy in southern Missouri, Frémont was removed from command in November 1861.

The Frémont emancipation edict opened a new chapter in the war that originally sought only to restore the Union to its original form. Especially in Missouri, the man known as the "Pathfinder" had staked out a position that heretofore had been politically unacceptable. His removal from command could have been predicted. Nonetheless, fierce strife continued to plague the state; federal authorities would later adopt even more severe measures than Frémont had contemplated. Yet, Frémont's order had inspired "radical" elements in the state and elsewhere that desired more forceful steps against slavery. Congress passed a new confiscation act (like Frémont's decree, it sought to free the slaves of rebel masters), Lincoln issued his own emancipation decree in September 1862, and in Missouri radicals were successful in eliminating slavery (in January 1865) before the adoption of the Thirteenth Amendment in December 1865.

Frémont's career never recovered from the political attacks he sustained after his emancipation decree.

In March 1862 Lincoln appointed him to command the Mountain Department, but he found defeat in the Battle of Cross Keys in Virginia on June 8, 1862. Following another dispute over command Frémont asked to be relieved. His military service was at an end, but during the 1864 presidential campaign antislavery elements considered him as a replacement for Lincoln. Frémont eventually withdrew from the race, helping to ensure Lincoln's reelection.

Union victory in the war led by Gen. **Ulysses S. Grant** and Gen. **William T. Sherman,** along with Lincoln's assassination, left General Frémont's efforts largely forgotten. Poor business decisions resulted in the loss of his beloved Mariposa and financial distress for the rest of his life. Hopes to revive his dreams of a Pacific railroad originating in Missouri proved illusory. From 1878 to 1883 Frémont served as governor of Arizona Territory. Jessie Frémont helped him to pen his memoirs, published in 1887. Not completely forgotten by the continental nation he had helped to create, he was restored to the rank of major general and placed on the retired list with pay in April 1890. A sudden attack of peritonitis claimed the elderly hero in New York on July 13, 1890.

The legendary Frémont name dots the American landscape from Ohio to California, though no county or city in Missouri bears it. Yet, Frémont fought to keep Missouri part of the American Union and sought to free the state of the shackles of slavery. He led exploring parties to the west from Missouri's river towns and hoped to build a transcontinental railroad westward from its borders. His exploits helped point the state toward the growth and promise of modern statehood.

VERNON L. VOLPE

Herr, Pamela. *Jessie Benton Frémont: A Biography.* New York: Franklin Watts, 1987.

Nevins, Allan. *Frémont, Pathmaker of the West.* 2 vols. New York: Longman, Green, 1955.

Parrish, William E. *Turbulent Partnership: Missouri and the Union, 1861–1865.* Columbia: University of Missouri Press, 1963.

Volpe, Vernon L. "The Frémonts and Emancipation in Missouri." *Historian* 56 (winter 1994): 339–54.

FROMAN, JANE (1907–1980)

Asked to name the ten best female singers of the day, famed musical producer Billy Rose replied, "There is Jane Froman and nine others."

Froman, born on November 10, 1907, in University City, Missouri, spent her childhood in Clinton and adolescence in Columbia. Her parents separated when she was five. Afterward, she began to stutter, which she endured all her life except when she sang.

After graduating from Christian (later Columbia) College and attending the University of Missouri, Froman entered the Cincinnati Conservatory of Music in 1928. Subsequently, she auditioned as a vocalist for a radio station, and within a few years her career skyrocketed. She was honored in 1934 as the most outstanding female radio artist in America.

At the peak of her profession on radio, Broadway, and in nightclubs, Froman volunteered to travel for the USO. "It never occurred to me," she wrote, "to ignore the request from FDR to depart for overseas. . . . The boys at the front needed a lift." On February 22, 1943, the plane carrying Froman and thirty-eight others crashed into the Tagus River in Lisbon, Portugal. One of fifteen survivors, Froman sustained horrible injuries: a cut below the left knee nearly severed her leg, she had multiple fractures of her right arm, and a compound fracture of her right leg led doctors to consider amputation. She underwent thirty-nine operations over the years as a consequence of the accident. She stubbornly fought amputation, but wore a leg brace the remainder of her life. Although unable to walk, Froman appeared briefly on Broadway eight months after the accident and later, with indomitable willpower, regained her career despite lifelong medical problems from the crash.

In 1945, on crutches, Froman toured Europe, performing ninety-five shows for the troops. Her courageous appearances were an inspiration to all. Returning to New York she continued performing, had her own television show on CBS from 1952 to 1955, and recorded for Capitol Records. The 1952 movie *With a Song in My Heart* depicted her life; it starred Susan Hayward, but Froman's voice was dubbed in for the musical numbers.

In May 1961, after a thirty-four-year career, Froman retired to Columbia, Missouri. Previously divorced from Donald M. Ross, an entertainer, and John C. Burn, the pilot who rescued her in 1943, Froman happily married newspaperman Rowland H. Smith on June 20, 1962. Although retired, she remained active, believing in giving "something back" to society.

Froman's numerous charitable and community activities included Easter Seal Campaigns, serving on boards of civic groups, and being a trustee for Columbia College. Her favorite cause was the Jane Froman Foundation, which supported psychiatric programs for children at the famed Menninger Clinic, where in 1949 she sought treatment for postcrash emotional trauma.

In 1969 Froman abandoned retirement. She sang in a Christmas program at Arrow Rock, Missouri, that benefited the Jane Froman Music Camp, a project that was created to help youngsters develop their musical potential, with Froman serving as its consultant. In her final public performance, she sang at the 150th anniversary commemoration of Missouri statehood. She was part of a troupe that entertained in Washington, D.C., at the National Press Club on October 28, 1971. She captivated the audience and received standing ovations.

Throughout her life Froman accepted many awards, but two were especially meaningful. One was a Gold Medallion from the USO in 1968 thanking her for her devotion to the armed forces. The other was her election to the Missouri Academy of Squires in 1971. She did not believe she deserved this "beautiful honor," but it meant much to her because it came from "fellow Missourians."

Froman treasured life, enjoying such pastimes as sporting events, dancing despite the heavy leg brace, playing bridge, gardening, knitting, needlepoint, and visiting with friends. Occasionally, precarious health limited her activities, but she handled discouraging times with an inner strength that others admired.

Everyone who met Froman remembers her as a gracious lady. A close friend recalls her as "a highly talented individual, a very special person, and a great Missourian." Clinton, Missouri, agreed, honoring her on July 25, 1973, with "Jane Froman Day," declaring her "a symbol of courage and unselfishness."

On April 22, 1980, Jane Froman Smith died of cardiac arrest. The next day the Missouri State Senate passed a resolution recognizing her accomplishments.

With songs in her heart and a marvelous voice that shared them with the world, with a spirit of determination and courage that made her an inspiration, and with a compassion that put the needs of others first, Jane Froman brought honor to Missouri, the state she loved.

ILENE STONE

Froman, Jane. Papers. Western Historical Manuscripts Collection, Columbia.
———. "The Woman I Have Become." *Good Housekeeping* (November 1952): 57, 134–36.
Meiner, Deena. "Aunt Jane, with Love." *Missouri Life* (September–October 1983): 35–39.
Priddy, Bob. "Across Our Wide Missouri, Jane Froman: With a Song in Her Heart." *Missouri Life* (July–August 1980): 27–30.
Taves, Isbella. "Jane Froman: Courage Unlimited." *McCall's* (May 1952): 30–31, 56, 61, 66.

FROST, DANIEL MARSH (1823–1900)

Daniel Marsh Frost, a Confederate army officer, was born on August 9, 1823, in Mariaville, in Schenectady County, New York. He graduated from West Point in 1844, fourth of twenty-five cadets in his class, and was assigned initially to the First Regiment Artillery before transferring to the cavalry. He served on the staff of Gen. Winfield Scott in the Mexican

War, seeing action at Vera Cruz and winning a brevet for gallantry at Cerro Gordo. After the war, Frost was wounded while serving on the frontier as an Indian scout. He studied cavalry tactics in Europe for a year before returning to the First Regiment Mounted Rifles. In 1853 he resigned his army commission and returned to St. Louis, the home of his wife, Eliza Brown Graham, daughter of Maj. Richard Graham and granddaughter of **John Mullanphy.** There he engaged in the fur trade and lumber business and also practiced law.

Frost was appointed to the Board of Visitors of the U.S. Military Academy and in 1854 won election as a Democrat to the Missouri State Senate. He served one term, during which he framed an act creating the state's militia. Gov. **Robert Marcellus Stewart** appointed Frost brigadier general in that militia, and in the fall of 1860 he led a brigade to southwestern Missouri to suppress border hostilities created by antislavery guerrilla "Jayhawkers" from Kansas.

At the outbreak of the war in 1861, Frost sympathized with the South and openly favored the secession of Missouri. He urged the state's governor, **Claiborne Fox Jackson,** to convene the General Assembly and to send agents to the Confederate government to obtain mortars and siege guns in preparation for an attack on the federal arsenal in St. Louis (which held the largest store of munitions in the slave states). Frost also suggested that the governor order him to mobilize the state militia to oppose federal troops stationed in the city. On May 2 Jackson ordered all state militia district commanders, including Frost, to convene military camps of instruction. Frost commanded the First District, which included St. Louis and its environs, and soon received four pieces of artillery from the Baton Rouge arsenal (captured by Louisiana Confederates) to aid in his proposed attack on the St. Louis arsenal. Unknown to Frost and Jackson, on the night of April 25, arsenal commander **Nathaniel Lyon** had secreted all of its arms and ammunition to Illinois, thus rendering the arsenal inert as a military target.

On May 10 Lyon surrounded the St. Louis encampment, named Camp Jackson in honor of the governor and located in Lindell Grove at the city limits, forcing Frost to surrender it. While Lyon marched the prisoners through the city's streets to the arsenal, shooting erupted, killing twenty-eight and precipitating two days of rioting in St. Louis. In the summer of 1861, upon receiving his parole and exchange after the Camp Jackson incident, Frost left the state, urging Confederate commanders in Arkansas and Kentucky to invade Missouri. His earnestness gained him an appointment as brigadier general in Confederate service.

Given command of the Seventh and Ninth Divisions of the Missouri State Guard, in March 1862 Frost led the troops at the Battle of Pea Ridge, Arkansas. Confederate general Earl Van Dorn appointed Frost as commanding officer of the artillery brigade of the Army of the West. Frost then acted briefly as inspector general of the Army of the Mississippi under Braxton Bragg before assuming brigade command again in the Army of the West. He fought at the Battle of Prairie Grove in Arkansas, serving under Thomas C. Hindman and succeeding him temporarily as division commander. After participating in the campaigns of Helena and Little Rock, Frost received news of his wife's banishment from their home near St. Louis in April 1863, which caused him to leave the army that fall to care for her.

Requesting a sixty-day leave of absence, approved by **Sterling Price,** Frost took his family first to Mexico, then to Cuba, and finally to Canada. Theophilus Holmes, commanding the District of Arkansas, protested and ordered Frost to return at once to his brigade. Enraged, Frost resigned his commission in November 1863, though it was widely publicized that he deserted. Believing that his northern birth and the surrender of Camp Jackson had besmirched his reputation, Frost refused to return to the army. Following the war he returned to his home in St. Louis and spent much of his remaining life trying to clear his name. He died on October 29, 1900, and is buried in Calvary Cemetery in St. Louis.

CHRISTOPHER PHILLIPS

Knapp, Joseph G. *The Presence of the Past.* St. Louis: St. Louis University Publications, 1979.

Miller, Robert E. "Daniel Marsh Frost, C.S.A." *Missouri Historical Review* 85 (July 1991): 381–401.

Phillips, Christopher. *Damned Yankee: The Life of General Nathaniel Lyon.* Columbia: University of Missouri Press, 1990.

Shea, William L., and Earl J. Hess. *Pea Ridge: Civil War Campaign in the West.* Chapel Hill: University of North Carolina Press, 1992.

Snead, Thomas L. *The Fight for Missouri from the Election of Lincoln to the Death of Lyon.* New York: Charles Scribner's Sons, 1886.

Warner, Ezra J. *Generals in Gray: Lives of the Confederate Commanders.* Baton Rouge: Louisiana State University Press, 1959.

FULLER, OSCAR ANDERSON (1904–1989)

Oscar Anderson Fuller was the first African American to earn a doctor of philosophy degree in music in America. He was Lincoln University's department of music chairman from 1942 to 1974, and he and his wife continued to live in Jefferson City upon his retirement. A brief listing of his many awards and citations includes Pioneers in Education for the State of Missouri, Missouri Music Educators Hall of Fame, Missouri American Choral Director Association—Choral Director of the Year, Academy of Musical Recorded Arts and Sciences Award, Missouri Arts Council Award, Olaf Christiansen Choral School Award, and the Lincoln University Board of Curators Award of Recognition.

Fuller was born in Roanoke, Virginia, on September 20, 1904. He was a third-generation teacher; his father was dean of Bishop College, in Marshall, Texas. Fuller's father's family had a rather extraordinary educational background. The family consisted of six brothers and one sister. The brothers all earned doctoral degrees in their areas of study; the sister earned her master's degree from Columbia University.

Oscar Fuller's childhood was influenced by educational goals and the higher-education environment at Bishop College. He earned his bachelor of arts degree at Bishop and then left, as he said, "to better himself" at the New England Conservatory. He had met several people at Bishop who had attended the conservatory and they gave him very positive comments about the school. New England Conservatory president George W. Chadwick encouraged Fuller to continue his studies at the University of Iowa.

Chadwick wanted Fuller to meet two legendary people in music study and educational theory development: Phillip Greeley Clapp, a nephew of Horace Greeley, and Carl Emil Seashore. Clapp was considered a prodigy on piano; Seashore was an eminent psychologist who was developing a test of musical ability. Fuller went to Iowa and earned his master of arts degree in 1934.

As a student-scholarship worker Fuller served as a piano accompanist and for two semesters wrote radio programs for the university radio station. The programs were a mixture of solo and group performances, with music written by African American composers. In 1940 Fuller returned to the University of Iowa to begin his doctoral work, with an emphasis on composition. He graduated with a doctor of philosophy degree in music in 1942.

As graduation approached Fuller had many teaching offers. Two Lincoln University faculty members were also working on their doctoral degrees at Iowa. Milton Hardiman, in the foreign-languages department, and James D. Parks, in the art department, told Lincoln University president Sherman Scruggs about Fuller and his work at Iowa. Scruggs asked Fuller to come for an interview.

And so I came here. I had them [other college offers] when I came for the interview. I had a letter and a check in my pocket to move to another institution and I wasn't thinking of accepting Lincoln's offer. I liked it, Lincoln University, and

I went back and told Mama, Mrs. Fuller. She said, "We can go anywhere for a year to two because for a little while you are going to continue to get offers." I am not one who runs around, you know, from pillar to post, so I said, let's see if we can do something for Lincoln's program.

Scruggs promised to be supportive of Fuller's efforts. The music program did not offer any degrees in music when Fuller started. However, by 1954, through Fuller's vision, the music department had developed three music degree programs: a bachelor of music degree, a bachelor in music education degree, and a music therapy degree. A significant certification process was finally achieved when the Lincoln music program was approved by both the National Association of the Schools of Music and the State of Missouri Department of Education.

Fuller's childhood academic environment at Bishop College and his previous employment experiences were the foundations for his success at Lincoln. From 1924 to 1929 he was the music department chairman at North Carolina Agricultural and Technical University, and from 1929 to 1942 he was the music department chairman at Prairie View State University.

Fuller's continuing vision and diplomatic personality, and the quality musical performances given by his students, attracted the attention of the Missouri legislature. Thus, Lincoln University was awarded state financing for a 1,500-seat auditorium and fine arts center; the cornerstone was laid in 1954.

Prior to 1954 Lincoln University was an undergraduate institution primarily for African American students; after 1954 the school became integrated. Fuller guided the music department through this difficult era. To both the African American freshmen and the white freshmen, Fuller was the person who could fill their minds with music knowledge and wonderful performance opportunities while diminishing racial concerns.

A single example, from his many successful community music projects, was his collaboration with Stephens College, which was an internationally known women's college with a successful music program. When the yearly full-scale opera productions were presented, the Lincoln male choral students participated, which provided not only a wonderful music opportunity but also an opportunity for people, from diverse ethnic and cultural backgrounds, to successfully work together toward common goals. The Detroit Chapter of the Lincoln Alumni Association presented to Fuller upon his retirement an award that bears this inscription: "The touch of your life has been an endless source of love and strength to humanity." This is certainly an appropriate tribute for this Missouri scholar, teacher, and humanitarian who died on July 15, 1989.

STEVEN HOUSER

Fuller, O. Anderson. Papers. Lincoln Collection. Inman E. Page Library, Lincoln University, Jefferson City, Mo.

Houser, Steven D. "O. Anderson Fuller: The First Black Doctor of Philosophy in America, and His Development of the Music Education Curriculum at Lincoln University." Ph.D. diss., University of Missouri–Columbia, 1982.

Marshall, Albert P. *Soldiers' Dream: A Centennial History of Lincoln University of Missouri.* Jefferson City: Lincoln University, 1966.

G

GAGE, JOHN BAILEY (1887–1970)

John Bailey "Jake" Gage, Kansas City "clean-up" mayor, lawyer, and civic leader, the son of John Culter and Ida Gage, was born on February 24, 1887, on an eighty-acre farm on the outskirts of Kansas City. Gage spent his early years on the farm, leading to a lifelong interest in agribusiness. He considered his farming experience and a summer he spent in 1906 with a joint American-Canadian survey team in Alaska as fundamental in molding his character, teaching self-reliance, and instilling a love of the outdoors. Gage's father, a wealthy landholder, lawyer, and Harvard College graduate, was a Union Democrat who served as city attorney of Kansas City and as a member of the General Assembly.

At age sixteen Gage matriculated at the University of Kansas, graduating in 1907. Active in student affairs, he joined the campus debating team and Sigma Alpha Epsilon fraternity. Following the completion of his undergraduate studies, he enrolled in the Kansas City School of Law, graduating in 1909 and gaining admission to the bar. For the next two decades he taught night courses at the school, numbering among his students future president **Harry S. Truman** and Supreme Court justice **Charles Evans Whittaker.**

Gage, inheriting a great deal of money and extensive properties following his father's death in 1915, began raising cattle near Eudora, Kansas, and building a law practice in Kansas City. He married Constance Lane in 1916, the union ending in tragedy in 1919 with her death from influenza. In 1922 he married Marjorie Hines, a social activist who encouraged him to participate in civic affairs. In 1934 he supported the National Youth Movement, a reform organization that mounted an unsuccessful effort in the March city election to defeat the notorious political machine headed by **Thomas J. Pendergast,** kept in power by fraudulent voting practices and underworld enforcers. The state of affairs deteriorated to the point that Gage considered moving away from Kansas City, its reputation badly tarnished by rampant racketeering, commercial vice, gangsterism, and public corruption. However, he stayed and spoke out against the Pendergast machine.

After federal vote-fraud trials in 1937 and 1938 resulted in the conviction of 259 machine officials and Pendergast going to jail for income tax evasion in 1939, Gage spearheaded a new broadly based nonpartisan reform movement. In early 1940 he stood for mayor as the candidate of the United Campaign Committee. Hal Luhnow, a top organizer of the anti-Pendergast campaign, recalled: "Most people go into politics to feather their own nest. But Jack Gage was in there for only one purpose, the good of the city. . . . He was the right man for the spot. We certainly picked the right man." Gage had told his wife, "Well, you and I have both been talking better government and a better city and they seem to think that I'm the only one they can agree on. I don't know why. It's the silliest thing in the world."

Gage easily won a two-year term, repeating his triumph in 1942 and again in 1946, both times under the banner of the Citizens Association. Under Kansas City's 1925 city charter the mayor had only one vote in the city council, which appointed a city manager by a majority vote. Gage and a new city manager, **L. Perry Cookingham,** worked well together in successfully guiding Kansas City through World War II. The Gage administration initiated a merit hiring program and drastically cut the size of the city government. Without a large tax increase, Gage announced in 1946 the retirement of nearly $20 million in Pendergast-era debt, the largest up to that time accumulated by an American city. Gage's greatest accomplishment was in demonstrating that honest government had a chance of working in Kansas City. He retired from office leaving the Citizens Association in firm control and the Pendergast machine ruined and discredited at the municipal level.

Gage rejected overtures to run for governor and never again sought public office. He returned to his law firm, managed his farm properties, and remained active in civic affairs. He served terms as president of the American Shorthorn Breeders Association, the American Milking Shorthorn Breeders Association, the Saddle and Sirloin Club, and the American Royal, Kansas City's primary livestock show. He was active in the Citizens Association, was regional vice president of the National Municipal League, and from 1949 to 1956 was a vice chairman of the Midwest Research Institute. He belonged to numerous organizations, including the Kansas City Posse of the Westerners, sat on corporate and bank boards, promoted various city bond issues, and championed flood control. In short, he embodied all the best virtues expected of a civic leader in Kansas City.

On December 12, 1969, a delivery truck hit and seriously injured Gage as he crossed a downtown street en route to his law office. He never fully regained consciousness and died on January 15, 1970, leaving his wife, four children (two boys and two girls), and eleven grandchildren.

Historian Joseph L. Adams Jr., the biographer of Gage, aptly delineated his contribution to the life of Kansas City: "He saw city government as a system to serve the people, not to fulfill his personal ambition. Gage stood as a symbol in Kansas City, a symbol of honest government with the fiery will to fight for it. He was the heart of his community and his public service stands as an example of reform government." Adams concluded that Gage was a man of "courage, persistence, and integrity."

LAWRENCE H. LARSEN

Adams, Joseph L., Jr. "Reformer: Kansas City Style." Master's thesis, University of Missouri–Kansas City, 1971.

Gage, John Bailey. Papers. Western Historical Manuscripts Collection, Columbia.

Haskell, Henry C., Jr., and Richard B. Fowler. *City of the Future: A Narrative History of Kansas City, 1850–1950.* Kansas City: F. Glenn Publishing, 1950.

Kansas City Star, January 15, 1970.

Spletstoser, Frederick M. "A City at War: The Impact of World War II on Kansas City." Master's thesis, University of Missouri–Kansas City, 1971.

GAINES, LLOYD (1912–?)

Lloyd Gaines's efforts to obtain a legal education in Missouri resulted in a Supreme Court decision that marked the beginning of the end of state-sponsored racial segregation. Gaines was born in Mississippi on March 10, 1912. When he was fourteen years old, the family moved from Oxford, Mississippi, to St. Louis. Gaines attended public schools in St. Louis and graduated first in a class of fifty from Vashon High School in 1926. He won a $250 scholarship in an essay contest and later enrolled as a freshman at Stowe Teachers College in St. Louis. After a year at Stowe, Gaines transferred to Lincoln University in Jefferson City, Missouri. During his senior year he was elected class president. He graduated with honors from Lincoln in 1935.

Gaines wanted to become a lawyer, but in 1935 state laws prohibited the University of Missouri from admitting black students. Gaines decided to challenge the state's segregation policies. His efforts were aided by Sydney Redmond, a St. Louis lawyer who was one of several black attorneys in various cities who served as cooperating attorneys with the NAACP. Redmond contacted Charles Houston at the NAACP's headquarters in New York, suggesting that Gaines might be the ideal candidate to test the state's segregation laws.

Houston, a Harvard graduate and a former dean of Howard University Law School, was hired by the NAACP in 1935. The organization had previously decided to mount a litigation campaign in which state laws requiring racial segregation would be challenged as violations of the Equal Protection Clause of the United States Constitution. After joining the NAACP, Houston devised a litigation strategy that involved filing suits insisting that facilities provided for black students be physically and otherwise equal to those accorded to white students. This "equalization" strategy focused initially on graduate schools because none of the states that practiced segregation had established graduate schools for black students. The separate and demonstrably unequal facilities that had been established were limited to primary and secondary schools and a few undergraduate institutions.

A few months before Gaines decided to test Missouri's laws, a successful desegregation suit had been brought against the University of Maryland. In that case a trial judge had ordered the law school at the University of Maryland to admit a black student since the university had failed to provide graduate educational opportunities for African Americans. The judge's decision was later upheld by the Maryland Supreme Court. Gaines was probably aware of the Maryland decision when he decided to challenge Missouri's policies.

Houston eventually agreed to represent Gaines. After the University of Missouri denied Gaines's application, Houston filed suit in state court against the university. At the conclusion of the trial, the judge issued a decision upholding the state's segregation laws. The case was later appealed to the Missouri Supreme Court.

It must first be noted that the state provided scholarship assistance to black students who were barred from graduate schools in Missouri. Relying on the policy of providing out-of-state scholarships, the Missouri Supreme Court held that the state's actions did not violate the Equal Protection Clause of the Constitution. It found that the state complied with the Fourteenth Amendment as long as the educational opportunities afforded to black students were "substantially equal" to those provided to white citizens. The out-of-state scholarships, the court found, satisfied this requirement.

When the case reached the United States Supreme Court in 1938, the court held that the provision of financial assistance for educational opportunities in other states did not satisfy Missouri's obligation under the Fourteenth Amendment. It ruled that the right to equal protection was a "personal one." Each state had a constitutional obligation to provide equal educational opportunities within its borders. Since the state of Missouri had not done so, it was obligated to admit Gaines to the University of Missouri.

While the case was pending, Gaines enrolled in graduate school at the University of Michigan. He received a master's degree in economics in 1937. He later worked briefly as a clerk in the Michigan Civil Service in Lansing. He returned to St. Louis in December 1938 and told friends and news reporters that he expected to enter the University of Missouri in September.

In January 1939 Gaines addressed an NAACP meeting in St. Louis, stating that he was "ready, willing and able to enroll in the law department at the University in September and had the fullest intention of doing so." In April 1939 Gaines traveled to Kansas City to speak at an NAACP meeting. On April 27 he traveled to Chicago. Before leaving, Gaines told an acquaintance that he intended to spend a few days in Chicago and return to St. Louis. However, Gaines abruptly dropped out of sight. Numerous efforts were made to locate him. Photographs were published in newspapers across the nation to no avail. Speculation concerning his whereabouts ranged from sightings in Mexico to reports of his death. Gaines was last seen leaving a fraternity house in Chicago.

Although he did not enjoy the fruits of his victory, Lloyd Gaines made an immeasurable contribution to the struggle of African Americans to eliminate state-sanctioned segregation. His case, *Missouri ex rel. Gaines v. Canada*, was the first in a long line of United States Supreme Court decisions that eventually lead to *Brown v. Board of Education*, which declared segregation in public education to be a violation of the United States Constitution.

LELAND WARE

Bluford, Lucille H. "The Lloyd Gaines Story." *Journal of Educational Sociology* 32 (February 1959): 242–43.

Grothaus, Larry. "The Inevitable Mr. Gaines." *Arizona and the West* 26 (1984): 21–42.

Kelleher, D. T. "Case of Lloyd Gaines: The Demise of the Separate but Equal Doctrine." *Journal of Negro History* 56 (October 1971): 262–71.

Sawyer, R. McLaran. "The Gaines Case: The Human Side." *Negro Educational Review* 38 (January 1987): 4–14.

"Strange Disappearance of Lloyd Gaines." *Ebony* 6 (May 1951): 26–28.

GAMBLE, HAMILTON ROWAN (1798–1864)

Born on November 29, 1798, Hamilton R. Gamble was the youngest son of Joseph and Anne Hamilton Gamble. He was a Winchester, Virginia, native and received his education at Hampden-Sidney College. By 1816 Gamble earned licenses to practice law in three states: Virginia, Tennessee, and Missouri. He moved to Howard County, Missouri, two years later. His brother, Archibald, was a clerk on the Missouri Circuit Court and appointed Hamilton to a deputy clerk position. Gamble soon became a prominent St. Louis attorney by arguing land litigation cases. He married Caroline J. Coalter of Columbia, South Carolina, in 1827. During the next three decades, Gamble increasingly allied himself with the Whig Party. He served one term in the state legislature by the mid-1840s. In 1851 he had been appointed to the Missouri Supreme Court but resigned after four years and semiretired.

Gamble resided in Pennsylvania shortly before the outbreak of the Civil War in 1861. At the insistence of his brother-in-law, Atty. Gen. **Edward Bates,** Gamble returned to Jefferson City in late February to run for a seat in the state convention convened to decide whether Missouri should leave the Union. Missouri was a crucial border state for the Union and a major cause of concern for President Abraham Lincoln's administration because of its noted Southern sympathies. At the meeting Gamble emerged as the dominant pro-Unionist spokesman after delivering an impassioned speech that persuaded conditional Unionists to vote against secession. His peers selected him as chairman of the Committee on Federal Regulations. The committee's final report rejected any notions of secession and gave its full support to the Unionist position.

Once war erupted in April 1861 Gamble realized that the state government could be torn apart by partisan politics and differing loyalties. In early summer moderate Unionists organized a provisional government in order to restore peace after Gov. **Claiborne Fox Jackson** and his pro-Confederate supporters fled from Jefferson City. Gamble emerged as the leader of the moderates and became provisional governor in mid-July. Over the next three years, he tried to achieve conservative Unionist goals despite increasing obstacles from officials in Washington, D.C., military personnel, and Radical Republican opponents.

The question of emancipating Missouri's slaves became the first issue on Gamble's agenda when the General Assembly convened at Jefferson City on December 29, 1862. He endorsed a gradual system of emancipation, but he confronted opposition from the Radicals who wanted an immediate end to slavery in Missouri. That disagreement prevented the enactment of any emancipation measure. By the summer of 1863 the Radical Union Party was gaining strength under the leadership of **Charles Daniel Drake.**

Gamble's relationship with the military also proved less than amicable at times. He clashed repeatedly with Gen. **John Charles Frémont,** appointed by President Lincoln as head of the Department of the West. Gamble tried to reorganize the militia under his direct supervision and control, but Frémont viewed his actions as undermining military authority. A compromise was finally reached between the governor and the Lincoln administration when Frémont was replaced with Maj. Gen. **Samuel Ryan Curtis.** However, military and civil relations continued to worsen. Gamble considered Curtis's leadership dictatorial, especially after the commander issued General Order No. 30 in 1863, which allowed military courts to issue death sentences to those suspected of traitorous activities. Lincoln eventually transferred Curtis, and chose Gen. **John McAllister Schofield** as a replacement. Schofield and Gamble managed to establish a cordial relationship.

Gamble received another blow to his administration shortly after Schofield assumed command. The *Missouri Democrat* reprinted a letter from Lincoln to Schofield warning him to avoid the factionalism that caused his predecessor's removal. Gamble believed the letter was a negative appraisal of his abilities as governor. Upset by the personal attack, he wrote a letter of resignation but later withdrew it.

The pressures of office began to take a physical toll on Gamble's health by 1863. The governor had been plagued by illness throughout the war and sustained a devastating injury to his elbow after slipping on a patch of ice on the capitol steps. In his weakened state, he contracted pneumonia and died on January 31, 1864. With his death, the moderate position dwindled as the Radicals gained absolute control in Missouri.

Perhaps William Parrish best summarized Gamble's importance to the state in his *History of Missouri: Volume III, 1860 to 1875:*

> The state stood much in debt to the departed leader. Although in the end he was too conservative for many Missourians, he had inherited an exceedingly difficult situation in 1861 and performed a highly creditable job in dealing with it. . . . he was pushed by events rather than leading them as time went on. But he had followed his conscience, and, in the long run, his steady hand made possible a smooth transition of political power.

GAYLA KOERTING

Cain, Marvin R. *Lincoln's Attorney General: Edward Bates of Missouri.* Columbia: University of Missouri Press, 1965.

Meyer, Duane G. *The Heritage of Missouri.* St. Louis: River City Publishers, 1982.

Nagel, Paul C. *Missouri: A Bicentennial History.* New York: W. W. Norton, 1977.

Parrish, William E. *A History of Missouri: Volume III, 1860 to 1875.* Columbia: University of Missouri Press, 1973.

———. *Turbulent Partnership: Missouri and the Union, 1861–1865.* Columbia: University of Missouri Press, 1963.

GARDNER, FREDERICK D. (1869–1933)

A successful businessman and Missouri's wartime governor, Frederick Gardner led the state through World War I by supporting vital organizations such as the Missouri Council of Defense and the selective service. He also presented and carried out a plan to balance the state budget, reformed the state penal system, and acquired funding to improve the state highway system.

Born on November 6, 1869, in Hickman, Kentucky, Frederick Dozier Gardner attended public schools in Kentucky and Tennessee. In 1887 he moved to St. Louis to begin his business career, taking a job as an office boy for the St. Louis Casket Company. His hard work and reliability paid off with his promotion to bookkeeper. At the age of twenty-four Gardner owned stock in the company, and eventually acquired a controlling interest to become president. He married Jeanette Vosburgh of St. Louis on October 10, 1894. In 1898 he created the Memphis Casket Company, acting as chairman of the board of directors. Around the same time he became involved in casket manufacturing plants in Texarkana and Dallas, Texas.

Primarily a businessman, Gardner served in only one public office before becoming a candidate for the governorship, but he demonstrated a genuine interest in the welfare of the public. His membership on the St. Louis Board of Freeholders, a group established to create a charter for the city, prompted him to write a series of articles explaining its provisions and potential impact on the growth of the city. In 1893 Gardner visited nations of the Old World, evaluating their land credit systems, and subsequently, as a private citizen, presented to the Missouri legislature a concept that would evolve into the state's land-bank plan.

Gardner's reputation as a businessman and public servant earned him the Democratic gubernatorial nomination in 1916. His campaign focused on four major issues: an agricultural land-credit system, a balanced budget, reform of the penal system, and improvement of the road system. Gardner's promise to "devote the four best years of my life wholly and unreservedly to the service of the people of Missouri" convinced voters to elect him to office. He narrowly defeated the Republican nominee, Judge Henry Lamm, a ten-year veteran of the Missouri Supreme Court.

Inaugurated on January 9, 1917, Governor Gardner moved quickly to fulfill his campaign pledges and his responsibilities as leader of the state. He arranged short-term, low-interest loans with St. Louis banks in order to pay off the $2.5 million budget deficit that had accumulated over many years. He then implemented his plan for rehabilitation of state finances by enacting three tax laws to replenish state coffers. The corporation franchise tax, the inheritance tax, and the income tax enacted under Gardner's administration proposed to equalize and make impartial the collection of taxes. The reorganization of the state's financial system during Gardner's administration also aimed to cut spending and to improve the economic status of Missouri.

A champion of prison reform, Governor Gardner asked the General Assembly to consolidate the management of the state penal system under one bipartisan body. He aimed to improve the efficiency of the system by putting inmates to work within the state prisons. By the end of his term the penal system not only became self-supportive but also boasted an unprecedented net profit of nearly two hundred thousand dollars. Gardner also supported the existence of educational opportunities for Missouri inmates.

During his second year in office, Gardner followed through on his campaign pledge to improve the highway system. He created a bipartisan state highway commission and proposed a $60 million bond issue to be funded by automobile license fees. In the fall of 1918 Gardner presented an original plan to the Missouri legislature that would, after its adoption as a constitutional amendment, provide thousands of miles of paved roads to Missouri counties, regardless of their financial strength. Gardner accomplished these changes while mobilizing Missourians to fight World War I. He asked the state's citizens to sacrifice for the war effort and condemned those who questioned U.S. participation in the conflict.

At the end of his term Gardner's supporters urged him to run for U.S. senator, but he declined and instead returned to St. Louis to resume his business interests. More than once after leaving office his fellow Democrats encouraged him to pursue the Democratic nomination for president or vice president, but Gardner opted not to resume his public career. He remained active in the Democratic Party and even wrote a liquor plank that was presented at the 1932 Democratic National Convention. Gardner died on December 18, 1933, in St. Louis.

ERIKA K. NELSON

Christensen, Lawrence O., and Gary R. Kremer. *A History of Missouri: Volume IV, 1875 to 1919.* Columbia: University of Missouri Press, 1997.

Jackson, William Rufus. *Missouri Democracy: A History of the Party and Its Representative Members, Past and Present.* Vol. 2. Chicago: S. J. Clarke, 1935.

Official Manual of the State of Missouri, 1917–1918. Jefferson City: Secretary of State, 1918.

GELLHORN, EDNA FISCHEL (1878–1970)

Edna Fischel Gellhorn, a social reformer and civic leader, was born in St. Louis, Missouri, on December 18, 1878. Her socially prominent parents were leaders in the city's Ethical Culture movement. Washington E. Fischel taught clinical medicine at Washington University. Martha Ellis Fischel was a founding member of the Wednesday Club, an elite women's club concerned with civic improvement, and an early advocate for women's social service. She later directed the St. Louis School of Philanthropy, forerunner of the George Warren School of Social Work. Their daughter, Edna, received her education at private women's schools where she impressed her classmates with her energy and leadership ability. They elected her president of the Mary Institute high school class of 1896 and lifetime president of the class of 1900 at Bryn Mawr College. In 1903 Edna Fischel married George Gellhorn, a gynecologist and recent German immigrant. They had a daughter and three sons, all of whom pursued successful professional careers.

Edna Gellhorn was a classic example of the women of her class at the turn of the century who defined their civic work as "municipal housekeeping." As a young matron she organized charity events, but worked equally hard for the passage of clean-water and pure-milk legislation, the first of many crusades in a lifetime spent challenging the status quo. Throughout periods of reform and reaction, she steadfastly pursued a vision of social justice formed as a young woman during the Progressive Era. Gellhorn always acknowledged that it was because she had a supportive husband who could afford household help that she was able to combine a career of civic activism with the responsibilities of home and family.

In 1910 Gellhorn joined the recently revived St. Louis woman suffrage movement. She held office in both the St. Louis and the Missouri Equal Suffrage Leagues, and helped organize the dramatic "Walkless-Talkless Parade" at the 1916 Democratic National Convention in St. Louis. There suffragists silently lined the streets between the delegates' hotel and the convention hall to demonstrate support for a suffrage plank in the party platform. As one of the organizers of the 1919 national suffrage convention, also held in St. Louis, Gellhorn answered the call to "raise up a league of women voters" when it appeared that suffrage victory was in sight. Elected the first president of the Missouri League of Women Voters, she traveled the state in the caboose of a milk train to hold classes for first-time voters. Gellhorn was three times president of the St. Louis League of Women Voters and served on the national board. During those years the league successfully lobbied for legislation on child welfare, women's property rights, and joint guardianship of children.

A friend once said that Gellhorn belonged to "almost all the white-hat organizations." Through her work with civic groups, she played a leading role in most of the progressive reform movements of her lifetime. Commitment, expertise, and organizational skills earned her positions of responsibility and influence seldom accorded women who made volunteerism their careers. She was regional director of Herbert Hoover's World War I food program, and his World War II food-rationing program. In the 1930s she led the League of Women Voters' effort to institute the merit system in Missouri government hiring. Gellhorn also worked for passage of a new Missouri Constitution in 1945. After World War II she promoted slum clearance and smoke abatement. She led the league to becoming one of the first racially integrated civic groups in St. Louis. She served on a citizens' committee for Homer G. Phillips Hospital for African Americans, and always regretted she had not been able to attend the 1963 March on Washington. Gellhorn was active in the Missouri Social Hygiene Association and the Social Security Commission. In 1964 she served on the Missouri Commission on the Status of Women. The National Municipal League awarded her its Distinguished Citizen Award in 1965.

During the cold war Gellhorn became increasingly concerned with the state of international relations and the direction of U.S. foreign policy. She organized a local chapter of the American Association for the United Nations in 1955 and was a founder of the Citizens Committee on Nuclear Information.

Next to helping women become informed social activists and voters, Edna Gellhorn cared most about education. She served on personnel policy committees for the St. Louis public schools and helped to found the John Burroughs School, a private preparatory school. She received honorary LL.D. degrees from Lindenwood College in 1956 and from Washington University in 1964, which also honored her in 1964 by endowing the Edna Fischel Gellhorn Professorship of Public Affairs.

In 1953, when she was seventy-five, Edna Gellhorn said, "I'm glad I was born in a time of stress. And I have infinite faith in the future." Involved and forward-looking until the end, she died in St. Louis on September 24, 1970, at the age of ninety-one.

KATHARINE T. CORBETT

Carlson, Mrs. Harry. "The First Decade of the St. Louis League of Women Voters." *Missouri Historical Society Bulletin* 26 (October 1969): 32–52.

Dains, Mary K., ed. *Show Me Missouri Women: Selected Biographies.* Kirksville, Mo.: Thomas Jefferson University Press, 1989.

Gellhorn, Edna. Collection. Washington University Archives, St. Louis.

———. "Ramification, Schools, and League of Women Voters." In "History of the Woman Suffrage Movement in Missouri," ed. Mary Semple Scott. *Missouri Historical Review* 14 (April/July 1920): 349–61.

Missouri Woman. Vols. 1–5. March 17, 1915–August/September 1919.

Sabrin, Susan. "Edna Fischel Gellhorn." In *Notable American Women, the Modern Period: A Biographical Dictionary,* ed. Barbara Sicherman et al. Cambridge: Harvard University Press, Belknap Press, 1986.

GENTRY, ANN HAWKINS (1791–1870)

Ann Hawkins Gentry, the second woman to receive an appointment as U.S. postmaster, served in that position in Columbia, Missouri, from 1838 to 1865. She was born on January 21, 1791, in Madison County, Kentucky. She married **Richard Gentry** on February 10, 1810. The Gentrys' first child was born while Richard served in the War of 1812. Three other children had arrived by 1816 when the family moved to the Missouri Territory. Ann Gentry made the journey riding a thoroughbred mare and holding her infant daughter on her lap. After first settling in St. Louis County, they moved to Franklin on the Missouri River in 1818.

In 1820 Richard Gentry and others founded the settlement of Smithton, a forerunner of Columbia. Ann Gentry began housekeeping in a log cabin that also served as Columbia's first tavern. There she raised thirteen children and operated the business while her husband served in the Missouri State Militia, traded in Santa Fe, and held the office of state senator (from 1826 to 1830). When Richard served as postmaster in Columbia from 1830 to 1837, Ann assisted him during his absences, handling the mail from their new two-story brick home.

In 1837 Richard Gentry was commissioned as colonel of a volunteer regiment for service in the Seminole War. He co-signed notes so that his men could buy horses for the campaign. He died in battle on Christmas Day 1837. When Ann Gentry received the tragic news, she replied: "I'd rather be a brave man's widow than a coward's wife." She continued alone to operate the business and rear her large family. Sen. **Thomas Hart Benton,** a friend of the family, helped obtain the postmaster appointment for Gentry in addition to a widow's pension of thirty dollars per month. Colonel Gentry left only a modest estate, but as the notes he co-signed came due, Ann Gentry paid them in full.

Gentry conducted her duties as postmaster with efficiency and courtesy. Although a Democratic president appointed her to the position, each succeeding chief executive reappointed her until her retirement in 1865. By that time she had accumulated and invested a sizable fortune for that day—twenty thousand dollars.

In addition to her work in the post office and as manager of the tavern, Gentry had many family responsibilities. She reared not only her children, but several grandchildren as well. When her daughter Martha died in childbirth, she cared for the grandchild as her own.

The Civil War years were sad for Gentry. Although a strong Unionist herself, her family became divided. Some fought for the North, others for the South. Her youngest son, Nicholas Hawkins Gentry, fought with the Confederacy and died of wounds suffered at the Battle of Wilson's Creek in southern Missouri. A grandson deserted both the Union and the Confederate armies and hid from authorities in his grandmother's home.

A longtime member of the Columbia Presbyterian Church, Gentry died on January 18, 1870, and was buried in the Columbia Cemetery.

MARY K. DAINS

Crighton, John C. *A History of Columbia and Boone County.* Columbia, Mo.: Computer Color-Graphics, 1987.

Dains, Mary K., ed. *Show Me Missouri Women: Selected Biographies.* Kirksville, Mo.: Thomas Jefferson University Press, 1989.

GENTRY, RICHARD (1788–1837)

Richard Gentry distinguished himself as a soldier, civic leader, merchant, and pioneer settler in Missouri. Born in Madison County, Kentucky, on August 21, 1788, he was the son of Richard Gentry Sr., a Revolutionary War veteran who was reportedly present when British general Lord Cornwallis surrendered to Gen. George Washington at Yorktown in 1781. From his father, young Richard undoubtedly developed a desire to serve in the military.

At age nineteen Richard Gentry received a commission from the governor of Kentucky to serve as a lieutenant in the Nineteenth Regiment of the Kentucky State Militia. He was promoted to the rank of captain in 1811 and ensign of volunteers in 1813. He served in that capacity during the War of 1812, fighting under the command of Gen. **William Henry Harrison** on the northern border of the United States.

Gentry married Ann Hawkins in February 1810. They packed up their belongings in 1816 and moved from Madison County, Kentucky, to a frontier home in the Missouri Territory. After farming for a year in St. Louis County, they moved up the Missouri River to Franklin, in Howard County. While at Franklin, Gentry was involved in land speculation and became a member of the Smithton Company in 1818.

Through the Smithton Company Gentry purchased land in what is now Boone County. In 1820 he moved to the town site of Smithton, where he briefly operated a tavern before Smithton was abandoned as a county seat in favor of the new town of Columbia, less than a mile to the east. In Columbia Gentry resumed the operations of the tavern and became immersed in local and state politics.

Gentry was elected the first mayor of Columbia, defeating **William Jewell,** with whom he maintained a spirited political rivalry. Gentry was also elected to the state senate in 1826 and served until 1830. Through his involvement in the Jacksonian wing of the Democratic Party, as well as his friendship with Sen. **Thomas Hart Benton,** Gentry was able to secure an appointment as postmaster of Columbia by President Andrew Jackson in 1830.

While serving in the state senate, Gentry became involved in the thriving overland trade occurring by way of the Santa Fe Trail. In 1827 and 1830 he led trading expeditions from Missouri to Santa Fe. On his return trip in 1830 Gentry drove forty mules from Santa Fe to Independence, Missouri. These were among the first mules to be introduced to the state.

As in Kentucky, Gentry served in the militia in Missouri. With political allies and demonstrated leadership, he rose through the military ranks. He was appointed captain in 1821, colonel in 1822, and major general in 1832. During the Black Hawk War of 1832, Gentry commanded the Missouri troops sent to defend the northeast border of Missouri.

In 1835 the United States went to war against the Seminole Indians in Florida. To back up Senator Benton's claim that Missouri volunteers could handle the Seminoles better than the regular troops, Gentry recruited more than a regiment of troops for service in Florida. Most of the troops came from Boone County and other central Missouri counties. They were placed under the command of Major General Gentry.

Following a ceremony in Columbia, Gentry and his troops departed from Columbia on October 15, 1837. They traveled overland to St. Louis, steamed down the Mississippi River to New Orleans, and sailed across the Gulf of Mexico to Tampa, Florida. Desertion, sickness, and military discharge reduced Gentry's regiment to slightly more than two hundred men. Once in Florida the Missouri volunteers were placed under the command of Col. Zachary Taylor and dispatched to southern Florida to aid in flushing the Seminoles from the Everglades.

On Christmas Day 1837 Gentry and the Missouri volunteers engaged the Seminoles at the Battle of Lake Okeechobee. During the fighting Gentry was mortally wounded in the abdomen, but continued to rally his men. He died later that day. Despite criticizing the Missouri regiment for its performance in battle, Colonel Taylor praised Gentry's leadership and bravery.

Gentry's body was returned to Missouri, and he was buried at Jefferson Barracks. In recognition of his service, a lake in southern Florida was named in his honor. In 1841 the Missouri legislature named a county for him.

Richard Gentry and **Ann Hawkins Gentry** had thirteen children, nine of whom survived into adulthood. Following Richard's death, Ann was appointed postmaster of Columbia. She was only the second woman in the country to hold that position and served until 1865.

MARK S. HUDSON

Crighton, John C. "The History of the Gentry Family Was an Epic of Courage." *A History of Columbia and Boone County.* Columbia, Mo.: Computer Color-Graphics, 1987.

Gentry, North Todd. Papers. Western Historical Manuscripts Collection, Columbia.

Mahon, John K. *History of the Second Seminole War, 1835–1842.* Gainesville: University of Florida Press, 1967.

Shoemaker, Floyd Calvin. *Missouri and Missourians: Land of Contrasts and People of Achievements.* Chicago: Lewis Publishing, 1943.

Switzler, William. *A History of Boone County, Missouri.* 1882. Reprint, Columbia: Boone County Historical Society, 1994.

Williams, Walter, ed. *The History of Northwest Missouri.* Chicago: Lewis Publishing, 1913.

GENTRY, WILLIAM (1818–1890)

William Gentry, a livestock farmer, railroad executive, and candidate for governor, was born on April 14, 1818, in Howard County, Missouri, the son of Reuben Estes and Elizabeth White Gentry. Reuben Gentry, a native of Madison County, Kentucky, settled in Missouri's Boonslick region in 1809. In 1824 he moved to a farm in what would (in 1833) become Pettis County, and it was there that William Gentry was reared with his three older brothers and one sister. In 1840 William Gentry married Ann Redd Major of Pettis County by whom he had five daughters and three sons.

Before the Civil War Gentry dealt heavily in livestock and land, eventually accumulating fifty-seven hundred acres in Pettis County. After the war he pursued other business interests, but remained primarily a farmer until his death. Always interested in promoting and improving agriculture, Gentry helped organize the Pettis County Agricultural and Mechanical Association in 1857, and invited the association to hold its annual fairs at Oak Dale, his showplace farm southwest of Georgetown.

Although slave owners, Gentry and his relatives were Unionists. On September 10, 1862, Gov. **Hamilton Rowan Gamble** appointed Gentry major of the Fortieth Regiment Enrolled Missouri Militia (EMM). He was later major of the Fifth Provisional Regiment EMM. His activities were confined to Pettis County and surrounding counties, and his duties were "home guard" in nature. The most action he saw was during Confederate cavalry commander **Joseph Orville Shelby**'s raid of September 22–October 26, 1863, when Gentry unsuccessfully pursued part of Shelby's command around west-central Missouri.

In the decade after the war, Major Gentry (as he was known the rest of his life) became identified with railroad interests. He assisted in organizing the Tebo and Neosho Railroad from Sedalia, Missouri, to Fort Scott, Kansas, in 1866, and when it became part of the Missouri, Kansas, and Texas Railroad, he was elected a director of the latter. He also served as president of the Sedalia, Warsaw, and Southern Railroad (the so-called Narrow Gauge Railroad), and the Lexington and Saint Louis Railroad Company (the Lexington Branch). Both the Narrow Gauge and the Lexington Branch were absorbed by the Missouri Pacific Railroad.

Prior to 1874 Gentry had sought no public office other than judge of the Pettis County Court, an office he held for several years before and during the Civil War, and again in the 1880s. On September 2, 1874, the newly organized People's Party unanimously nominated him to be its candidate for governor of Missouri. The farm-oriented People's Party was an outgrowth of the Granger movement that had come to Missouri in 1870. After a slow start, by 1875 Missouri boasted 2,009 local Granges out of a national total of 21,697. The panic of 1873 and the subsequent farm depression, and the perception that unregulated and unscrupulous railroads were levying freight and passenger rates based upon "all that the traffic would bear," made farmers receptive to a reform-minded political party. Although the National Grange discouraged involvement in politics, Missouri Grangers joined the People's Party with the hope of electing some of their own to state office. Of the party's ten candidates, five were Grangers, including Gentry.

Gentry's platform called for, among other things, suppression of lawlessness and mob violence, equal justice and rights for all law-abiding citizens regardless of former "differences," no further increase in the state debt, enough regulation of the railroads "to protect the people from extortion without impairing the rights" of the railroads, and the election to Congress of men sympathetic to the "true interests of the producers of the West."

At their convention the Democrats nominated state senator **Charles Henry Hardin** for governor. The Republicans, divided as they were into Liberal and Radical factions, met and decided not to run anyone for state office, but stopped short of endorsing the People's ticket.

Gentry's call for railroad regulation is ironic considering his own active involvement in building three and serving as president of two of them. His career, with one exception, seems not to have been an issue, however. Political opponents instead accused him of being unqualified for high office, of mistreating prisoners of war in 1861, of promising his slaves freedom before selling them back into slavery in 1863, and of self-serving behavior and fraud in the murky affairs of the Lexington Branch Railroad, which crossed Oak Dale. Gentry's friends and supporters publicly refuted the charges and defended his character. Meanwhile, Gentry campaigned around the state with Liberal Republican senator **Carl Schurz,** at the time a lame duck. Despite Senator Schurz's vigorous efforts, Hardin defeated Gentry on November 3 by a 14 percent margin. Gentry carried thirty-four counties and received between 40 and 50 percent of the vote in thirty-two more. But he was unable to carry any of the important former slaveholding counties in "Little Dixie," the western Missouri River valley, and southeast Missouri. On the positive side, several of the People's planks were either adopted by the General Assembly or incorporated into the new 1875 constitution, including regulation of the railroads.

Major Gentry resumed his busy private life. His wife had died in 1873, and late in 1874 he married her sister, Evelyn Witcher. Gentry died on May 22, 1890, and was buried in Crown Hill Cemetery in Sedalia.

WILLIAM B. CLAYCOMB

Jefferson City People's Tribune, September 30–October 7, 1874.

North, F. A., ed. *History of Pettis County, Missouri.* N.p., 1882.

Sedalia Daily Bazoo, August 27–October 15, 1874.

Shoemaker, Floyd Calvin. *Missouri and Missourians: Land of Contrasts and People of Achievements.* Vol. 2. Chicago: Lewis Publishing, 1943.

St. Louis Democrat, September 6–November 2, 1874.

U.S. War Department. *The War of the Rebellion: A Compilation of the Official Records of the Union and Confederate Armies.* Vol. 22. Reprint, Gettysburg: National Historical Society, 1971–1972.

GEYER, HENRY S. (1790–1859)

Henry S. Geyer was born in Frederick, Maryland, on December 9, 1790. He received a private education at home and additional instruction from his maternal uncle, Daniel Sheffie, a prominent lawyer and member of Congress from Virginia. After studying in his uncle's law office, Geyer returned to Maryland in 1811 to practice law. In 1812 he enlisted as a first lieutenant in the Thirty-sixth Regiment, Maryland Infantry, and served until 1815, attaining the rank of captain. In August 1815 he moved to St. Louis, Missouri, where he resumed the practice of law.

Soon after his arrival Geyer challenged George Kennery to a duel that was fought at Bloody Island on the Mississippi River. The disagreement, the nature of which is unknown today, was settled at ten paces with pistols. Kennery was wounded in the leg and was unable to stand. Both parties agreed to await his recovery before finishing the contest. Later, however, the men reconciled and became good friends.

In 1818 Geyer was elected to the territorial assembly, and in that year he published a compilation of Missouri's territorial laws, popularly known as "Geyer's Digest." Following statehood he served in the Missouri House of Representatives and was elected Speaker of that body in 1821, 1822, and 1824. In 1822 he and Rufus Pettibone were chosen to revise the state's laws. Their work, which entailed compiling, revising, and eliminating inconsistencies in the state law code, was completed by November 1824. Failure to provide funding for the establishment of new schools prevented implementation of the code's educational provisions. However, by the mid-1830s growing public interest in state support for schools motivated the legislature to reassess the state's educational system. Geyer once again shouldered this task, and in 1839 the General Assembly approved the Geyer Act, which authorized the creation of a comprehensive system of public schools at the elementary, secondary, college, and university levels. The complicated plan was never put into effect, but the legislature did vote to establish a state university at Columbia.

Geyer's compilation of Missouri's territorial law in 1818 and his work in the state legislature greatly enhanced his reputation as a lawyer, ensuring a lucrative practice. According to a contemporary, William Van Ness Bay, Geyer often made use of "sarcasm, invective, irony, and ridicule" in his legal arguments. His oratory was not flowery, like many lawyers of the period; instead he presented his cases cogently and concisely. His forte was the cross-examination of witnesses. According to Bay these talents, coupled with his great knowledge of the law, made Geyer Missouri's most able lawyer.

In 1824 Geyer supported Henry Clay's presidential bid and endorsed his American System, which sought to promote manufactures and trade through protective tariffs, internal improvements, and a national bank. When President Andrew Jackson vetoed the bill to recharter the Bank of the United States in 1832, Geyer helped compose a set of protest resolutions, stating that the bank had been "highly beneficial" to Missouri and the country. In the mid-1830s he also helped form and take a leadership role in Missouri's Whig Party.

In 1850 Millard Fillmore offered Geyer the position of secretary of war, which he declined. In 1851 **Thomas Hart Benton**'s insistence that Congress had the power to restrict slavery in the federal territories helped end his career as a U.S. senator. Divisions in both the Democratic and the Whig Parties made finding a successor to Benton very difficult. Geyer, who was a replacement candidate, failed to put forth a clear-cut opinion concerning Congress's power to restrict slavery; this ambiguity enabled him to gain enough support from Whigs and Democrats to secure election. He served one term in the United States Senate, from 1851 to 1857. His vote for the Kansas-Nebraska bill, which repealed the Missouri Compromise, demonstrated his strong proslavery views. At the end of his senatorial term, he did not seek reelection, but he did continue to practice law.

Because of his knowledge of Missouri law, his demonstrated ability before the United States Supreme Court (as a senator he pleaded cases in Washington), and his strong southern views, Geyer was recruited to aid Reverdy Johnson in representing **John F. A. Sanford,** the slave-owner defendant in the landmark *Dred Scott* case. In writing his decision, Chief Justice Roger B. Taney, also a Marylander, borrowed from Geyer's brief that cited important legal precedents on the questions of federal jurisdiction over state cases and the citizenship status of blacks. Geyer argued for limited federal oversight of state supreme court decisions, against Scott's right to bring suit in federal court, and stated that the Missouri Compromise was unconstitutional.

Geyer died in St. Louis, Missouri, on March 5, 1859, at the age of sixty-eight, and was interred at Bellefontaine Cemetery.

DENNIS K. BOMAN

Bay, W. V. N. *Reminiscences of the Bench and Bar of Missouri.* St. Louis: F. H. Thomas, 1878.

Biographical Dictionary of the United States Congress, 1774–1989. Bicentennial ed. S.v. "Geyer, Henry S." Washington, D.C.: U.S. Government Printing Office, 1989.

Colton, David L. "Lawyers, Legislation, and Educational Localism: The Missouri School Code of 1825." *Missouri Historical Review* 69 (January 1975): 121–46.

Fehrenbacher, Don E. *The Dred Scott Case: Its Significance in American Law and Politics.* New York: Oxford University Press, 1978.

Gantt, Thomas T. *Henry Sheffie Geyer: An Address before the Law Library Association of St. Louis, December 7, 1885.* St. Louis: Nixon-Jones Printing, 1885.

McCandless, Perry. *A History of Missouri: Volume II, 1820 to 1860.* Columbia: University of Missouri Press, 1972.

GIDDINGS, SALMON (1782–1828)

During the Second Great Awakening, from 1798 to 1837, Americans became increasingly interested in the salvation of unchurched souls on the frontier. This was especially true of New Englanders, who organized missionary groups to Christianize the Indians, check the spread of Catholicism, and minister to the spiritual needs of those who had fallen away from the religion of their forebears. Among the most zealous, as well as effective, of the small army of missionaries who went west was Salmon Giddings, who became the father of Presbyterianism in the Mississippi River Valley of Missouri and Illinois.

Giddings was born in Hartland, Connecticut, in 1782. He attended Williams College and, in 1811, entered staunchly Calvinist Andover Theological Seminary in Massachusetts, from which he received his license to preach in 1814. The following year the Missionary Society of Connecticut commissioned the thirty-three-year-old bachelor to undertake the arduous duty of taking the Gospel to the frontier, choosing for him the region that had composed Upper Louisiana, where it was thought his good facility with the French language would prove useful to the society's work among the Creole population.

Giddings arrived in St. Louis on April 6, 1816. His initial appearance in the area brought suspicion as to his motives. Many frontiersmen viewed New Englanders as hostile to republicanism, and their ministers as apostles for the union of church and state. Giddings's behavior soon put these fears to rest, but hidden behind his quiet and circumspect manner lay an intense evangelical zeal that spurred him into indefatigable travel throughout the region to spread Christ's Gospel. Before his untimely death Giddings would take the lead in organizing more than a dozen congregations in eastern Missouri and western Illinois, including the Concord Church in Bellevue—Missouri's first Presbyterian church (1816), the Bonhomme Presbyterian Church in what is now Chesterfield (1816), the First Presbyterian Church of St. Louis (1817), the St. Charles Presbyterian Church (1818), the Edwardsville Presbyterian

Church (1818), the Kaskaskia Presbyterian Church (1821), and the Collinsville Presbyterian Church (1823). Giddings's success in building congregations led to the founding of the Presbytery of Missouri on December 18, 1817. Located in St. Louis, it became the first presbytery west of the Mississippi River.

During the course of his travels, St. Louis remained Giddings's home base, from which he operated a school. His organization of the First Presbyterian Church of St. Louis in 1817 gave the town its first regularly organized Protestant church, which became the leading Protestant body of the era. His St. Louis congregation included those immigrants from the nation's middle border who would soon dominate Missouri society and politics, the best remembered of whom today are **Alexander McNair,** who would soon become Missouri's first governor; **Thomas Hart Benton,** soon to be Missouri's first senator; and jurist Nathaniel Beverly Tucker. In 1825, with help from eastern sympathizers, Giddings's parishioners were, at last, able to construct their first church building.

The following year Giddings brought his missionary work to an end and resigned from the Connecticut Missionary Society to become the official pastor of the First Presbyterian Church of St. Louis. A few weeks later, on December 4, 1826, he married Almira Collins, the daughter of the founding family of Collinsville, Illinois. Sometime during the late winter of 1828, she bore a son whom Salmon did not live to see. Probably with the help of liberal medicinal bleeding, Giddings died from the effects of a fall from a horse on January 31, 1828. The great Baptist missionary **John Mason Peck,** Giddings's friend, conducted the funeral service before an audience of two thousand mourners. When the Presbyterian Church (U.S.) and the United Presbyterian Church (USA) rejoined in 1983, the newly reorganized presbytery for eastern Missouri and western Illinois was named Giddings-Lovejoy, in tribute to Giddings's pioneering missionary work, along with that of abolitionist-martyr **Elijah Parish Lovejoy.**

KENNETH H. WINN

Cannon, Thomas C. "Founders of Missouri Presbyterianism." *Journal of the Presbyterian Historical Society* 46 (1968): 197–218.
Ellinwood, DeWitt, Jr. "Protestantism Enters St. Louis: The Presbyterians." *Bulletin of the Missouri Historical Society* 12 (1956): 253–73.

GILES, GWEN (1932–1986)

The distinction of becoming the first black woman elected to the Missouri State Senate belongs to Gwen Giles of St. Louis. She was born on May 14, 1932, in Atlanta, Georgia. She attended St. Liguori and St. Alphonso Rock High Schools, and took courses at St. Louis and Washington Universities. Giles and her first husband, Eddie E. Giles, had a son, Karl, and a daughter, Carla.

Giles's early political activities included managing campaigns for Ruth C. Porter and for William L. Clay, the first black congressman from Missouri. An excellent cook, Giles was known for "bringing the pots" to the congressman's meetings in St. Louis and to other community gatherings.

Beginning in the 1960s Giles promoted involvement of St. Louis religious leaders in the civil rights movement. She was a member of the Archdiocesan Commission on Human Rights, the Black Catholic Association of the Archdiocese, and the St. Louis Conference on Religion and Race.

In 1970 Mayor **Alfonso J. Cervantes** appointed Giles executive secretary of the St. Louis Council on Human Relations. In 1973 Mayor John Poelker appointed her commissioner of human relations, in which position she updated a city ordinance to protect women, the elderly, and the handicapped, and promoted passage of the 1976 Comprehensive Civil Rights Ordinance.

Appointed to fill an unexpired term as senator from the Fourth District, Giles was elected to the office in 1977. During that term she chaired the Interstate Cooperation Committee and was vice chair of Industrial Development. Committees on which she served included Apportionment, Elections, Military and Veterans Affairs, Labor and Management Relations, and Public Health, Mental Health, Developmental Disabilities, Welfare, Medicaid, and Consumer Protection.

Cochair of the Legislative Black Caucus, Giles examined the Bi-State Development Agency for racial discrimination in hiring policies. Bills she sponsored included ratification of the Equal Rights Amendment, direct bank deposits of public assistance payments, change in the blue law to allow shopping on Sundays, compensation of personal injury–type crime victims, and Aid to Dependent Children for unemployed parents. In 1980 she worked with state representative Billie Boykin, vice chair of the House Congressional Reapportionment Committee, in redrawing congressional district lines.

Nationally, Giles was a member of the Order of Women Legislators and twice a delegate to the Democratic National Convention. As chair of the West End Community Conference in St. Louis, she worked on school desegregation issues. Through her leadership the conference received $30 million for housing rehabilitation.

Giles's memberships included the International Consultation on Human Rights; the Missouri Black Leadership Conference, of which she was cofounder; the Missouri Committee-International Women's Year

Commission; the National Association for the Advancement of Colored People; the National Association of Christians and Jews; the National Association of Human Rights Workers; the National Council of Negro Women; the Region Seven Executive Council of Civil Rights; and St. Rose's Catholic Church.

Among Giles's recognitions was appointment by President Jimmy Carter to a task force to assist in selecting talented women for positions in the federal government. Just before her death, she was awarded the Commitment to Justice Award by the Greater St. Louis Committee for Freedom of Residence. Harris-Stowe State College of St. Louis has established a scholarship fund in her name. Catalpa Park in the West End and Wellston Post Office have been renamed for her.

The first woman and the first black to hold the position of St. Louis city assessor, Giles died while in that office on March 15, 1986. As assessor she "guided St. Louis through the difficult state-mandated reassessment fairly and efficiently," said Mayor Vincent Schoemehl. "She was a pioneer whose life of public service will serve as a model for generations to come."

BETTY COOK ROTTMAN

Boykin, Billie. Interview by author. August 1992.

Evans, Pearlie. Interview by author. August 1992.

Morgan, Thelma Wood, ed. *Profiles in Silhouette: The Contributions of Black Women of Missouri.* Comp. Projects Committee of the St. Louis Alumnae Chapter of Delta Sigma Theta, 1980.

Official Manual of the State of Missouri, 1980–1981. Jefferson City: Secretary of State, 1981.

Shepherd, Delores. Interview by author. August 1992.

St. Louis Globe-Democrat, March 28–April 1, 1986.

GILLISS, WILLIAM (1788–1869)

Later in life William Gilliss would be a successful Indian trader, real estate speculator, and businessman, and one of Kansas City's founding fathers, but in 1802 he was simply a fourteen-year-old Baltimore runaway headed out to sea. Aboard ship he gained a reputation for physical strength and carpentry skills and acquired a rudimentary education in reading and writing. Gilliss, who was born in Maryland in 1788, left the sea in 1806 at New Orleans and traveled to Cincinnati where he began business as a carpenter and builder with some assistance from **William Henry Harrison,** who befriended him. During the War of 1812 Gilliss enlisted and served under Harrison's command.

After the war Gilliss moved to the frontier Illinois town of Kaskaskia, where he soon became a prominent citizen. There he speculated in land, built the hotel where the first Illinois legislature met in 1818, and engaged in trade with the Indians moving westward. More important, given his ensuing career, a group of Delawares adopted him into their tribe in 1819.

By 1820 Gilliss had merchant friends across the Mississippi River in Ste. Genevieve and St. Louis, as well as Kaskaskia, and subsequently became an agent of the trading company Menard and Vallé. The lucrative mobile trading markets lured Gilliss, on their behalf, into following the tribes into the Ozarks interior, where Indians settled prior to political decisions that organized the Kansas reservations. His usual customers were the Delawares, but he traded with the Shawnee, the Peoria, the Piankashaw, the Weas, the Creek, and the Kickapoo as well.

By 1822 the Delaware nation of some twenty-five hundred congregated on James River (now in Christian County, Missouri) where Gilliss built his largest trading emporium. He had another at the mouth of Swan Creek (now in Taney County, Missouri) and several rendezvous points across the Ozarks where he marketed manufactured goods for shares of federal annuity payments furnished to the tribes in treaty arrangements. The gathering of Indians at Delaware Town on the James River represented the largest concentration of population in southwest Missouri until Civil War Springfield. The James River post at the western end of the Ste. Genevieve–based trade network caused the development of a "great interior highway," which would one day become Route 66 and, still later, Interstate 44, running from southwest Missouri toward St. Louis.

In the early 1830s Gilliss moved to Jackson County, where he multiplied his fortune in the Kansas Indian reservation trade and in real estate investments. The first of these investments were made in Westport, but in 1838 he joined a new company, which founded a new town they named Kansas. This promotion proved successful, and Gilliss successfully sold a great number of lots in the 1840s. In 1849–1850 he and **Benoist Troost** built Kansas City's "first real hotel," the Gilliss House. The famous stopover greeted city guests and thousands of travelers headed west. By 1857 the hotel had registered twenty-seven thousand guests, and would continue as the center of Kansas City's social life until the end of the Civil War. In 1854 Gilliss aided in the establishment of the town's first permanent newspaper, the *Kansas City Enterprise,* later the *Journal.* Three years later he helped incorporate the chamber of commerce, and two years after that he became a director in a branch bank of the Mechanics' Bank of St. Louis. In 1867 he drove the last spike in the rail of the Cameron Railroad. William Gilliss died on July 18, 1869, but his name is kept current in Kansas City at the Gilliss Orphan's Home, which he founded.

Much of our knowledge about Gilliss's career comes from his extraordinary probate case, litigated in 1869–1872, that eventually landed in the Missouri Supreme Court. The case began when two of his Piankashaw grandsons sued his half-million-dollar estate. The verdict of the case depended on whether Gilliss and his Indian wife, Kahketoqua (the boys' grandmother), were legally married. The court heard testimony from Indians and traders who had lived across the Ozarks, had known Gilliss, and had lived among the Indians, and it included details of Gilliss's family life and about Indian consorts who played important political roles in Gilliss's successful economic fortunes.

Kahketoqua, the daughter of a Piankashaw chief, was much sought by the traders. Gilliss finally won her and lived with his bride at the James River trading post. Witnesses in the lawsuit testified to the courtesies and congenial treatment that Gilliss accorded Kahketoqua. Together they had a daughter, Nancy. In the years to come Gilliss sent clothes to Nancy and kept an open store account for her near her Kansas reservation. On the basis of this evidence the Piankashaw grandchildren were victorious in court, winning a third of Gilliss's estate. Upon their success other suits were filed, but apparently none were successful.

LYNN MORROW

Morrow, Lynn. "Trader William Gilliss and Delaware Migration in Southern Missouri." *Missouri Historical Review* 75 (January 1981): 147–67.

GILPIN, WILLIAM (1815–1894)

"The untransacted destiny of the American people is to subdue the continent," William Gilpin declared in 1846. An apostle of Manifest Destiny, Gilpin was at various times in his life a soldier, explorer, editor, lawyer, politician, territorial governor, and land speculator. In the course of his multifaceted career he became deeply involved in the great dramas of his era, including western expansion, the conflict over slavery, and the Civil War.

Gilpin was born on October 4, 1815, to a prosperous Pennsylvania merchant family. Educated at the University of Pennsylvania, he won appointment to West Point in 1834. He left the military academy after one term, but in 1836 enlisted in the army and served in campaigns against the Seminoles. Gilpin first visited Missouri in 1837 when the army sent him west.

Gilpin left the army in 1838, settled in St. Louis, and joined the Missouri bar. In 1839, however, he set his law practice aside to become editor of the *Missouri Daily Argus,* a Democratic newspaper allied with **Thomas Hart Benton.** For most of the next

two decades Gilpin was deeply involved in Missouri politics. In 1840 he left the *Argus* to become clerk of the Missouri legislature, a position he held until the end of the 1841 session.

Gilpin soon moved to the frontier town of Independence where he made his home until 1861. In 1843 he joined **John Charles Frémont**'s expedition to the Oregon country where he helped foment efforts at territorial organization. Gilpin's journey through the West convinced him of the region's future as the heart of an American continental empire. He became an ardent advocate of western settlement, predicting in speeches, articles, and books that an army of settlers would carry American power to the Pacific and beyond. In the spirit of Manifest Destiny, anticipating the ideas of Frederick Jackson Turner, Gilpin maintained that the conquest of North America would be the result of historical progress that began with European exploration and settlement of the New World. The westward movement of Europeans and Americans, he believed, was the foundation of their superior democratic culture.

Gilpin resumed his military career in 1846, serving in the Mexican War with **Stephen Watts Kearny**'s army until June 1847. In 1847 and 1848 Gilpin commanded a unit of Missouri troops, suppressing Indian raiding along the Santa Fe Trail.

Illness sidelined Gilpin through most of 1849 and 1850, but by the end of 1850 he was once again active in Missouri politics. He ran unsuccessfully for Congress in 1850 and for governor in 1852.

Gilpin also forayed into town promotion during the 1850s. His first venture, Gilpintown, near Independence, failed, but he later helped to plat the site of Kansas City.

Gilpin's return to political life in the 1850s coincided with the social and political upheavals caused by the growing tide of migration westward and the increasingly explosive issue of slavery. By the mid-1850s, as the conflict in Kansas demonstrated, territorial expansion became embroiled in the slavery issue. Gilpin maintained a proslavery position through much of the decade, largely because most Missouri Democrats held that view and because he believed that slavery should not be an obstacle to western settlement. However, "Bleeding Kansas" and the rising sectional anger over slavery proved that belief futile, and by the late 1850s Gilpin adopted the popular sovereignty position advocated by Stephen A. Douglas. However, he was now at odds with the majority of Missouri Democrats, and in 1859 he joined the Republican Party.

Gilpin's new party and president soon rewarded his service. On March 22, 1861, Lincoln appointed him governor of Colorado Territory. Gilpin arrived in Denver in May 1861, quickly organized the new government, and, fearing a threat from Confederate forces operating in Texas and New Mexico, formed the First Colorado Volunteers. The Colorado unit played a key role in stopping the Confederate advance in New Mexico at the Battle of Glorieta Pass in March 1862.

By that time, however, Gilpin was in serious political trouble. He had financed the Colorado troops with drafts issued on his own authority, but came under harsh criticism when the Treasury Department initially refused to honor them. Gilpin compounded his critics' anger by labeling them as Confederate sympathizers. On March 18, 1862, President Lincoln removed him as governor.

Gilpin remained in Colorado and continued his career as a western booster. In 1863 he purchased control of the Beaubien land grant in southern Colorado and for the next three decades promoted land sales and settlement there.

William Gilpin died in Denver on January 20, 1894.

JAMES WHITESIDE

Bancroft, Hubert Howe. *History of the Life of William Gilpin.* San Francisco: History Company, 1889.

Gilpin, William. *Mission of the North American People: Geographical, Social, and Political.* New York: Da Capo Press, 1974.

Kearns, Thomas L. *William Gilpin: Western Nationalist.* Austin: University of Texas Press, 1970.

Lamm, Richard D., and Duane A. Smith. *Pioneers and Politicians: Ten Colorado Governors in Profile.* Boulder, Colo.: Pruett Publishing, 1984.

Smith, Henry Nash. "The Untransacted Destiny: William Gilpin." In *Virgin Land: The American West as Symbol and Myth,* 35–43. 1950. Reprint, Cambridge: Harvard University Press, 1978.

GLASGOW, EDWARD JAMES (1820–1908); GLASGOW, WILLIAM HENRY (1822–1897)

In 1846 a group of Missouri traders had the misfortune to become involved in the Mexican War while on an annual spring trek down the Santa Fe and Chihuahua Trails. Their fascinating firsthand accounts of their adventures over the nearly two years they were away survive in a series of letters that James Glasgow and William Glasgow wrote to family members in St. Louis as well as a journal kept by William.

The Glasgow brothers came by their business acumen and sense of adventure naturally. Their Delaware-born father, William Glasgow Sr., arrived in the St. Louis area in 1816 to work in the mercantile business. Settling in Belleville, Illinois, after his marriage to a local girl, Sarah Mitchell, he fathered two sons—Edward James, born on June 7, 1820, and

William Henry, born on February 19, 1822—before moving his family and business to Herculaneum, Missouri, in 1823 and then to St. Louis in 1827. By then the boys had a sister, Eleanor Ann, born in 1824. Mary Susan, born in 1829, completed the family. The Glasgow boys were educated locally, concluding their education at St. Charles College and St. Louis University before joining family enterprises. Both their father and their uncle, James Glasgow, were involved in various importing and dry goods businesses over the years.

The sedentary life of a commercial clerk apparently suited neither brother, for after learning the local end of the mercantile business, each left the city before age twenty-one to learn the Mexican end of the Santa Fe and Chihuahua trade. James Glasgow made his first trip in 1840, sailing around the Cape of Good Hope to reach Mexico's west coast where he handled his family's business interests in the port of Mazatlán. William Glasgow took a different route, landing on Mexico's east coast from New Orleans, then heading overland to Mazatlán. He celebrated his twenty-first birthday en route. By the time William arrived, James had already returned to the States, leaving a business partner in charge of operations. William, meanwhile, was supposed to bring a consignment of spices back to St. Louis via the Chihuahua and Santa Fe Trails.

James Glasgow continued in the Southwest trade for the next three years, while William stayed in St. Louis, taking a job on a Missouri River steamboat and presumably working again for his father or uncle. In May 1846 the brothers, each with his own stock of goods for the Mexican trade, left Independence, Missouri, with other traders heading for Mexico. It was to be the longest, most frustrating, yet most exciting trip of their careers.

On May 11, 1846, the United States declared war on Mexico. The merchants' wagon train had not been able to leave in time to avoid being detained by the United States Army as it crossed Kansas. The merchants were ordered to halt while the troops assembled and then were allowed to follow as the army took control of the Santa Fe. Detained again, they finally received permission to leave, only to stop again at Valverde, 150 miles south. There they awaited the arrival of **Alexander W. Doniphan**'s First Missouri Volunteers, who were to lead the way into Mexico.

The merchants became alarmed when weeks turned into months, as they had neither provisions for the men nor means to feed their livestock for such a prolonged stay. Finally, just before Christmas, Doniphan arrived and the merchants were again under way. Hearing that the Mexicans planned to make a stand at Chihuahua, Doniphan pressed the traders into temporary military service, ordering them to form two battalions. Both James and William were elected officers. The army, with the merchants behind them, entered Chihuahua following a minor skirmish on the outskirts of town. When Doniphan was ordered to move on, many of the merchants, fearful without the army's protection, left. They sold their stock to a handful of merchants who decided to remain and try to negotiate with local officials on their own. The Glasgows were among this group.

The Glasgows had maintained regular correspondence with family members from the time they left Independence, documenting the excitement as well as the frustrations of their venture. They sent their letters with anyone they met who was heading to Missouri. The letters ceased, however, when Doniphan left. The brothers were detained, though not imprisoned, in Mexico for nearly a year, and had no way to dispatch a letter until **Sterling Price**'s Second Missouri Volunteers arrived in Chihuahua in March 1848. The remaining Americans lost little time in closing their businesses and returning to the States. William Glasgow returned in May, taking a steamer from the port of Brazos to New Orleans and up the Mississippi River. James Glasgow returned via the Santa Fe Trail, arriving in early July.

Neither brother ever returned to Mexico. Both eventually married and raised families in St. Louis. They jointly operated a wholesale grocery business in town for more than twenty years, providing supplies for the Southwest trade. William Glasgow later became president of the St. Charles Car Company. He died on August 29, 1897, while visiting a daughter in Colorado and was buried in Bellefontaine Cemetery in St. Louis. James Glasgow, less successful in business, was nonetheless widely respected in the community and served as director of several banks. He was often sought in his old age by writers and historians seeking firsthand information about southwestern trade and the Mexican War. He died on December 7, 1908, and is buried in Calvary Cemetery in St. Louis.

MARY E. SEEMATTER

Gardner, Mark L., ed. *Brothers on the Santa Fe and Chihuahua Trails: Edward James Glasgow and William Henry Glasgow, 1846–1848.* Niwot: Colorado University Press, 1993.

Seematter, Mary E. "Merchants in the Middle: The Glasgow Brothers and the Mexican War." *Gateway Heritage* 9 (fall 1988): 34–43.

GLENNON, JOHN JOSEPH CARDINAL (1862–1946)

John Joseph Cardinal Glennon was born at Hardwood, Ireland, on June 14, 1862. In 1878, when he was sixteen, he entered All Hallows College in Dublin to prepare for the priesthood. Four years later Bishop John Hogan of Kansas City, Missouri, visited the college to enlist seminarians for his newly established diocese in the American Midwest, and John Glennon volunteered to join him. Hogan ordained his recruit in the sacristy of his nearly completed cathedral on December 20, 1884, after receiving word from Rome that Glennon could become a priest at the age of twenty-two.

Glennon spent two years at St. Patrick's Parish in Kansas City before returning to Europe to further his studies. After several months at the University of Bonn he asked permission of Hogan to enroll in a Roman theologate, but Hogan called him home and made him the cathedral rector and vicar general of the diocese. In 1896 Pope Leo XIII appointed Glennon a bishop to succeed Hogan when he chose to retire; he was consecrated by Archbishop Kain of St. Louis on June 29, making him, at the age of thirty-four, one of the youngest bishops in the world. Six years later the same pope named him to succeed Kain in St. Louis, making him the youngest archbishop in the world.

Glennon took residence in St. Louis at the time of the 1904 World's Fair and entered easily into its spirit while developing friendships with many prominent leaders of the St. Louis community. From then on he was included in every important project the city promoted.

The new archbishop quickly saw that St. Louis needed a new cathedral and a new seminary. Glennon tackled the cathedral first, breaking ground in May 1907. Seven and a half years later the building was dedicated for use; the cost had reached $1.73 million. World War I interrupted work, but it was completed by 1926 except for many of the mosaics that continued to be added until the late 1980s. Glennon's cathedral stands as one of the great church buildings of the Western Hemisphere to this day. The new Kenrick Seminary opened its doors in September 1915. It was followed sixteen years later by another seminary for college students. Both were designed to prepare priests for several midwestern states.

Archbishop Glennon was the premier preacher in the American Catholic Church from 1905 until 1935, when his health began to decline. He spoke monthly at the cathedral, accepted invitations to preach both in the United States and abroad, and dealt with social issues as well as church matters. He was magnificently equipped for oratory: tall and dignified, exceptionally handsome, facile in rhetoric, poetic in phraseology, and blessed with a rich voice further enhanced by a slight touch of Irish brogue.

Glennon's position as archbishop gave him a seat at the table with the other archbishops of the country who made the major American Church decisions prior to 1919 when Rome suggested that the bishops of the country also be included in the annual meetings. Glennon was secretary of the archbishops from 1904 until 1919 and served on numerous committees through those years dealing with matters as diverse as Catholic colonization, government census work, anti-Catholic bias, and the creation of a national Catholic university in Washington, D.C.

Good citizenship was second nature to Glennon. He supported American war efforts during both world wars and lent his prestige to the leaders of the Easter Rebellion in Ireland in their actions of April 24–29, 1916, by calling for Ireland's freedom from England. Glennon was equally active as a leader in his St. Louis Archdiocese. He served for thirty years before requesting of Rome his first auxiliary bishop. His record of concern for black Catholics was not good, but he did encourage progressive steps in church worship, orphan care, and programs for the poor, as well as the establishment of new parishes and schools.

Rome finally acknowledged Glennon's accomplishments when Pope Pius XII named him a cardinal in December 1945. Glennon was then eighty-three years old. He thought first of not going to Rome to receive the red hat but changed his mind and traveled there by way of Ireland. After a long series of ceremonies complicated by a severe cold he had developed before leaving St. Louis, he arrived back in Ireland on his way home but died there on March 9, 1946, before he could complete the trip. His body was returned to the city he had served so long and well; it was interred in his cathedral, and the red hat hung from the ceiling in the chapel over his grave.

The archdiocese Glennon left behind had an auxiliary bishop, 899 diocesan and religious-order priests, 500,000 Catholics, 277 parishes, 280 educational institutions of all levels attended by more than 47,000 students, and 17 hospitals with a 1945 care list of 67,000 patients. The only diocesan hospital for children was raised in Glennon's memory several years later, a living epitaph honoring his life and achievements.

NICHOLAS SCHNEIDER

Code, Joseph Bernard. *Dictionary of the American Hierarchy.* New York: Joseph F. Wagner, 1964.

Morgan, Thomas P. *Speaking of Cardinals.* New York: G. P. Putnam's Sons, 1946.

Rothensteiner, John E. *History of the Archdiocese of St. Louis in Its Various Stages of Development from* A.D. *1637 to* A.D. *1928.* 2 vols. St. Louis: Blackwell Wielandy, 1928.

Schneider, Nicholas. *The Life of John Cardinal Glennon.* Liguori, Mo.: Liguori Publications, 1971.

GRABLE, BETTY (1916–1973)

Betty Grable will always be remembered as the World War II pinup girl with the beautiful legs. She was one of those cultural icons who always managed to "summarize the bounds of a generation's youth." After 1944 her famous pose in a white swimming suit decorated barracks' walls and ships' bulkheads throughout the world and became an unofficial symbol of the wives and sweethearts on the American home front.

On December 18, 1916, Betty was born Ruth Elizabeth to Conn and Lillian Hoffman Grable in St. Louis's predominantly German south side. Conn Grable was a bookkeeper who attained success in the 1920s in the stock and investment business. With their affluence the Grables moved to Forest Park Apartment Hotel in one of St. Louis's better neighborhoods. As a child Grable and her older sister, Marjorie, lived a hotel life and entered the exclusive St. Louis girls' school, Mary Institute. Grable, whose mother arranged for her to study toe, tap, ballet, and acrobatic dancing, as well as saxophone and voice, began performing on local stages.

The Grables usually vacationed at a Michigan lake resort, but in the summer of 1928 Conn Grable decided to drive the family to Los Angeles in a touring car. Lillian Grable was enthralled with the movie colony, and the following spring she took Betty out of Mary Institute and moved to Los Angeles permanently, leaving Conn Grable in St. Louis.

Fox Studio put out a call for sixty girls who could sing and dance, and Betty was one of five hundred who showed up. She was hired, and in 1930 she appeared in a specialty dance number in her first film, *Let's Go Places.* The same year she was a Goldwyn Girl in Eddie Cantor's *Whoopee.*

During the next few years Grable played bit parts in comedies, toured with a Frank Fay–Barbara Stanwyck stage show, and appeared as a torch singer with Ted Fio Rito's band. She married her costar in *College Swing,* Jackie Coogan, "the Kid" of silent movie fame, on November 11, 1939. That same year she went to Broadway for a supporting role in the musical *DuBarry Was a Lady* and ended up stealing the show from its star, Ethel Merman.

Grable's forty-two movies during the 1930s and 1940s were financial successes, and for a record-setting twelve years she was listed as one of the top ten box office stars. The Treasury Department reported that she was the highest salaried American woman in 1946–1947.

The modest Grable always maintained that her acting, singing, and dancing were average, and admitted that "my legs saved me." When the *Harvard Lampoon* called her the worst actress of the year, she wired back: "You're so right." People wanted to see her in tights, which they did as she danced in her own style to the public's delight.

When Alice Fay became ill, Grable received an offer to costar with Don Ameche in the film *Down Argentine Way.* The movie was a smash hit and became the format for a dozen other Grable movies such as *Pin-Up Girl, Moon over Miami,* and *Mother Wore Tights.* She married band leader Harry James on July 5, 1943, and the couple had two daughters, Victoria and Jessica. She and James were horse-racing fans and owned several horses. When her career faded in the 1950s, they moved to Las Vegas where she occasionally performed. Grable divorced James in 1965. Afterward, she starred for several months in the musical *Hello Dolly* in Las Vegas.

In September 1971 Grable returned to St. Louis to close out the Municipal Opera season in *This Is Show Business,* a nostalgic musical that also starred Don Ameche and Rudy Vallee. Grable made both personal and professional visits to Kansas City. Her sister, Marjorie, was the wife of David T. Arnold, a Kansas City native who worked for the *Kansas City Star.* Grable also appeared in downtown Kansas City in 1936 with Jackie Coogan in *Hollywood Secrets,* a stage revue at the Mainstreet Theater.

In 1972 Grable presented an Academy Award for Best Musical Score, but it was clear that she was ill. Doctors diagnosed that she was suffering from lung cancer, and she died on July 2, 1973.

ARTHUR F. McCLURE AND VIVIAN RICHARDSON

Martin, Pete. "The World's Most Popular Blonde." *Saturday Evening Post* (April 15, 1950): 26–27.
Pastos, Spero. *Pin-Up: The Tragedy of Betty Grable.* New York: Berkeley Books, 1986.
St. Louis Post-Dispatch, July 3, 1973.
Warren, Doug. *Betty Grable: The Reluctant Movie Queen.* New York: St. Martin's, 1981.
Williams, Whitney. "Betty Grable's $3,000,000 Legs." *Variety* (July 11, 1973).

GRANT, DAVID M. (1903–1985)

David Marshall Grant, an African American lawyer and civil rights leader, was born in the Mill Creek valley area of St. Louis on January 1, 1903. His parents were William Samuel and Elizabeth Margaret Holliday Grant, both chiropodists. He had an older sister and two older brothers, all of whom were born at home because there was no maternity hospital for blacks in St. Louis at that time.

The Grant children commuted two and a half miles across town to attend the segregated Wheatley Grade School and Sumner High School. David graduated from Sumner in 1918. Upon graduating, he worked as a waiter on Great Lakes steamers out of Detroit, and in 1920 he played the cello for his brother William's jazz orchestra on the steamboat *Majestic* out of New Orleans.

Grant attended the University of Michigan in Ann Arbor from 1920 to 1923. From 1923 to 1927 he worked as a waiter at fashionable resorts in Hot Springs, Mackinac Island, French Lick, and West Palm Beach. He also served as a club car porter and a private car porter on railroads out of St. Louis.

In 1927 Grant entered Howard University Law School in Washington, D.C., from which he graduated in 1930. He was admitted to the Missouri bar in 1930, the federal bar in 1938, and to the bar of the United States Supreme Court in 1948.

Returning to St. Louis in 1930, Grant became active in Democratic politics. In those days most blacks voted Republican out of loyalty to Abraham Lincoln. Grant realized that the black vote guaranteed the success of Republican candidates in St. Louis, yet blacks received nothing in return except a few mop and broom jobs at city hall. He urged blacks not to guarantee their votes to any party.

In 1931 when the Woolworth Company opened a new dime store in a black community in north St. Louis without a single black clerk, Grant organized the first black picket for economic justice in St. Louis. The effort led to the hiring of black clerks. Following that success Grant helped organize the Colored Clerks' Circle, a union that picketed stores in black neighborhoods that refused to hire black help.

In 1932 and 1933 Grant publicized the fact that the citizens of St. Louis had passed a large bond issue in 1923, including more than $1 million for a black hospital, yet blacks were still being treated in the small, old, rented City Hospital Number 2. At ward meetings Grant showed slides of the inside of the hospital, graphically illustrating the appalling, overcrowded, unsanitary conditions. His campaign caused blacks to throw their votes to the Democratic Party and elect Bernard Dickmann as the first Democratic mayor of St. Louis in twenty-four years. Mayor Dickmann initiated construction of Homer G. Phillips Hospital as soon as he took office.

Dickmann appointed Grant as assistant city counselor in 1933, and he served in that office until 1941. Grant became the leading dispenser of patronage to black Democrats in St. Louis. In 1941 he was appointed assistant circuit attorney, but he was fired in 1942 when he went to Jefferson City to represent the NAACP in a protest against a lynching in Sikeston, Missouri. Grant went into private practice, opening an office in a building where many prominent black lawyers, doctors, and businessmen had offices.

During the late 1930s and early 1940s Grant served with Thurgood Marshall on the Legal Redress Committee of the NAACP. In 1939, when the state of Missouri hastily established Lincoln Law School in St. Louis to comply with the United States Supreme Court's *Missouri ex rel. Gaines v. Canada* decision in the **Lloyd Gaines** case mandating separate but equal public higher education, Grant picketed the law school and was promptly arrested. In 1942 he litigated and won a case against the statewide practice of paying black teachers lower salaries than white teachers.

From 1941 to 1943 Grant and **Theodore D. McNeal** led the St. Louis chapter of the March on Washington Movement. The movement, organized by A. Philip Randolph, sought to end discrimination in the hiring practices of defense industries during World War II. To avoid a march by thousands of blacks, President Roosevelt issued Executive Order 8802 in July 1941, ending such discrimination and creating the Fair Employment Practice Commission. The St. Louis March on Washington Committee brought Randolph to St. Louis for a huge rally at Kiel Auditorium on August 21, 1942, at which Randolph and Grant spoke eloquently. The committee picketed and successfully integrated the Small Arms Plant and the Carter Carburetor Company.

In 1943 Grant helped organize a picket of Southwestern Bell Telephone Company, which led the company to open offices with black employees in black neighborhoods. After serious riots in Detroit and Harlem in 1943, Mayor Alois Kaufmann established an Interracial Commission for the city of St. Louis. He appointed Grant to the commission, but Grant later admitted that the commission had been largely ineffective.

From 1943 to 1945 black women conducted sit-ins to integrate the lunch counters at downtown department stores. Grant acted as their lawyer each time they were arrested. He served as president of the St. Louis NAACP from 1945 to 1948.

In 1945 Grant brought suit against Washington University, requesting that the university open to blacks or lose its tax-exempt status. He took the case all the way to the United States Supreme Court, but dropped the suit when Washington University integrated in 1948. Grant also successfully picketed the American Theater.

In 1950 Grant became the first black appointed to the St. Louis Police Retirement Board. In 1952 he was instrumental in bringing **Josephine Baker** to St. Louis to give a benefit homecoming performance at Kiel Auditorium on behalf of the committee protesting overcrowding in the St. Louis black schools. Because Baker could not stay at the Chase Hotel she stayed at the Grants' home.

Grant was elected as one of thirteen members of the Board of Freeholders to rewrite the St. Louis City Charter in 1956, and served as chairman of the Committee on Legislation. However, in 1957, when last-minute changes to the new charter threatened to reduce black representation on the St. Louis Board of Aldermen, Grant refused to sign the new charter, and he launched a successful campaign among black voters to defeat it. In 1957 the St. Louis Board of Aldermen appointed Grant their director of

legislative research, a part-time position he held until the end of his life.

In 1960 Grant served with Eleanor Roosevelt on the National Democratic Platform Committee and helped write the civil rights plank for the Kennedy-Johnson campaign. In 1961 he was appointed as a member of the Missouri State Advisory Committee to the U.S. Commission on Civil Rights. In 1962 President John Kennedy appointed Grant as a delegate to represent the United States at the celebration of Uganda's independence. President Lyndon Johnson appointed Grant to his Committee on Government Employment Policy.

In 1980 the Missouri Bar Association honored David Grant as a senior counselor in recognition of his fifty years as a practicing lawyer.

Grant married Mildred Hughes, and they had two children, David Wesley and Gail Melissa. David Grant died in St. Louis on August 12, 1985. His life was a tribute to civil rights. To carry on his mission, St. Louis University Law School established the David M. Grant Fellowship in 1989, an annual award to a third-year law student who has shown interest in civil rights and working with indigent clients.

ANN MORRIS

Adams, Patricia L. "Fighting for Democracy in St. Louis: Civil Rights during World War II." *Missouri Historical Review* 80 (October 1985): 58–75.

Grant, David. Oral history interview. 1970. Western Historical Manuscripts Collection, St. Louis.

———. Papers. Western Historical Manuscripts Collection, St. Louis.

GRANT, JULIA DENT (1826–1902)

Although best known as a general's wife and a first lady, Julia Dent Grant left an important legacy in her own right. She shared in the mixed fortunes of **Ulysses S. Grant,** promoted her husband's welfare, served her family, and fulfilled her patriotic duty, capturing much of these experiences in *The Personal Memoirs of Julia Dent Grant.*

Julia Dent was born in St. Louis, Missouri, on January 26, 1826, the daughter of "Colonel" Frederick and Ellen Wrenshall Dent. Julia, the fifth of seven children and the first girl, grew up at White Haven, the family farm and estate, where she fished, rode horseback, and played in the woods. As a schoolgirl she declared that she would marry "a soldier, a gallant, brave, dashing soldier." Upon returning home from boarding school, she met that soldier in Ulysses S. Grant. Invited to White Haven by her brother Frederick Dent, who had been Grant's West Point roommate, Ulysses became a frequent visitor. He and Julia enjoyed walks and horseback rides, often dodging her siblings and slaves to be alone. Ulysses proposed in the summer of 1844, but delayed their marriage until August 22, 1848, due to his service in the war with Mexico.

The Grants had four children: Frederick, Ulysses Jr. "Buck," Nellie "Ellen," and Jesse. In 1850, while Ulysses was posted to army duty in Detroit, Julia returned home to White Haven for the birth of their first child. Their second child, Ulysses Jr., was born in Ohio, and their last two children were born at the White Haven estate after Ulysses Grant's resignation from the army in 1854.

By 1855 the Grants farmed eighty acres of land given to Julia as a wedding present by her father, while Ulysses managed the rest of the White Haven estate. Although these were financially trying times for the Grants, Julia remained supportive and considered herself "a splendid farmer's wife," raising chickens and occasionally churning butter, leaving the rest of the domestic chores to the slaves. In her husband's absence during the Civil War she served as financial manager and agent, leasing sections of the farm, collecting rent from tenants, and consolidating land titles.

Throughout the war letters helped to ease the pain of separation, but Grant often traveled to meet her husband at various encampments. Ironically, when she brought the children to see the Union generals, her slave Jule assisted with the children's care. Grant continued to be her husband's trusted confidante, and often offered political advice, as in inviting President Lincoln and the first lady to visit them at the front.

During Ulysses Grant's two terms as president of the United States, from 1869 to 1877, Julia Grant was an active participant in official matters. She attended Senate hearings, read through the president's mail, and met with cabinet members, senators, justices, and diplomats. She reveled in her role as hostess, and held an elaborate wedding in the White House East Room for her daughter Nellie in 1874. She enjoyed her time so completely at the White House that she felt like a "waif" when they departed in 1877.

That same year the Grants embarked on a world tour in which they visited many countries. Being treated as American celebrities proved a welcome break from the political turmoil of the presidency. Nearly one-third of Grant's memoir is devoted to recalling this trip, clearly a high point in her life.

A short time after their return to the States, doctors diagnosed Ulysses with throat cancer. In a last effort to provide for his family, he wrote his memoirs in 1885 and died quietly at Mount McGregor, New York, surrounded by his family. The profits from Ulysses's memoirs left Julia a wealthy woman, and she chose to live in New York and Washington, D.C. For the last seventeen years of her life, Grant worked to promote the memory of her beloved husband. In 1897 she attended the dedication of Grant's Tomb in New York City with President McKinley at her side.

Grant also planned to leave her memoirs for the world. Completing them in 1897, she had difficulty finding an editor with whom she could agree, and it was not until 1975 that they were published. She died from heart and kidney complications on December 14, 1902, at the age of seventy-six, and is buried next to her husband in Grant's Tomb. All four of her children outlived her, producing thirteen grandchildren.

SHARRA VOSTRAL

Casey, Emma Dent. "When Grant Went A'Courtin." Grant Collection. Missouri Historical Society, St. Louis.

Ross, Ishbel. *The General's Wife: The Life of Mrs. Ulysses S. Grant.* New York: Dodd, Mead, 1959.

Simon, John Y., ed. *The Personal Memoirs of Julia Dent Grant.* New York: G. P. Putnam's Sons, 1975.

GRANT, ULYSSES S. (1822–1885)

"Whoever hears of me in ten years will hear of a well-to-do old Missouri farmer," said Capt. Ulysses S. Grant when he resigned from the army in 1854. In ten years, of course, everybody knew Grant as commanding general of the Union army.

Born at Point Pleasant, in Clermont County, Ohio, on April 27, 1822, the son of Jesse R. and Hannah Simpson Grant, the oldest of six children, he was named Hiram Ulysses Grant after a family conference concluded with a name drawn from a hat. Jesse preferred "Ulysses," insisted on using that name, and in his son's boyhood "Hiram" was virtually forgotten. An enterprising and thrifty tanner, Jesse soon moved his family to Georgetown, Ohio, where the family lived comfortably but across the street from the noxious tannery. Ulysses had a normal boyhood, preferring farming and activity involving horses to tannery work. He received an education at the Georgetown school, then attended for one year each academies in Maysville, Kentucky, and Ripley, Ohio.

At age seventeen Grant entered the United States Military Academy at West Point. His father had arranged the appointment over Ulysses's protest. Preparing to leave, he worried that fellow cadets would tease him about the initials "H. U. G." and decided to reverse his first and middle names. Arriving at West Point he learned that somehow he had received an appointment as Ulysses S. Grant, either through the appointing congressman's assumption that he bore his mother's maiden name as a middle name or through confusion with a younger brother named Simpson. Eventually he acquiesced to bureaucracy and retained his army name for the rest of his life, insisting that his middle initial stood for "nothing." At West Point Grant took to both studies and military life with similar reluctance. He graduated twenty-first in a class of thirty-nine, buoyed by an aptitude for mathematics that led him to consider teaching as a career.

Grant first came to St. Louis in 1843 as a recent graduate of West Point assigned to Jefferson Barracks, then the largest military base in the nation. His West Point roommate, Frederick T. Dent, encouraged him to visit the Dent family at its country home, White Haven, about five miles from the Barracks. Grant found the Dents congenial, and after their seventeen-year-old daughter, Julia, returned from spending the winter social season in St. Louis, he visited more often: in Julia, he had found the love of a lifetime. So had Julia, but the army sent Grant to Louisiana, to Texas, and into the Mexican War. He served under Gen. Zachary Taylor at the Battles of Resaca de la Palma, Molino del Rey, and Monterrey. Assigned as a quartermaster in Gen. Winfield Scott's advance from Vera Cruz to Mexico City, Grant saw little action until the closing battles but won commendation from all and promotion to brevet captain. Four years passed before Grant married Julia Dent in 1848 in the Dent town house in St. Louis.

Col. Frederick Dent had come to St. Louis as a pioneer merchant. Born in Cumberland, Maryland, he brought southern attitudes to Missouri, reflected in the title "colonel" that was achieved without military service. Tiring of commercial life, he lived at White Haven, a country estate in south St. Louis County where slaves did the work and the master did hardly anything. Involved in land disputes originating in conflict between Spanish and American land grants, his fortunes ebbed but not his pride. He first objected to his daughter's courtship by a junior officer; after they married he clashed with his "Yankee" son-in-law, whose father was an antislavery Whig.

Again the army sent Grant away, this time with **Julia Dent Grant.** But she returned to her family home to give birth to their first child, Frederick Dent Grant. Later, in 1852, assigned to the Pacific Coast when Julia was again pregnant, Grant went without her, and for two lonely years she waited in Missouri for her husband, who was even lonelier in Oregon and California. Prevented by low pay from bringing his wife and two boys to join him, afflicted with migraines and malaria, assigned to a small and lonely post commanded by a martinet, Grant finally resigned and rejoined Julia in St. Louis.

Grant spent six years in St. Louis, where he first farmed land given to Julia by her father and also managed the Dent family estate. Two more children were born in St. Louis County. Grant,

aided by neighbors, built his own log house, named Hardscrabble, in which the family lived for a few months before moving to White Haven to assist Julia's father after her mother died.

To raise cash Grant cut mining timbers and sold cordwood in St. Louis. Hard times during the depression of 1857 and a recurrence of Grant's malaria in 1858 drove him off the farm and into St. Louis to look for work. He became an unsuccessful real estate agent and lost an appointment as county engineer when members of the county court rejected him as a Democrat. Unable to locate a good job in St. Louis, he reluctantly moved to Galena to work in his father's leather goods store. Grant's St. Louis years were marked by poverty but not unhappiness, and he dreamed of returning to the farm.

Grant lived in Galena for one year before the Civil War began. He drilled local volunteers, accompanied them to Springfield, and served as an aide and mustering officer to Illinois governor Richard Yates, who remembered him when an unruly regiment drove its colonel into premature retirement.

Grant led the Twenty-first Illinois into Missouri to protect the North Missouri Railroad. He had not yet encountered an enemy when promotion to brigadier general brought him assignments to Ironton, Cape Girardeau, and Cairo, Illinois. He fought his first battle at Belmont, Missouri, on November 7, 1861, after taking his force downriver on transports from Cairo. He overran a Confederate camp, then retreated in some disorder when Confederate reinforcements crossed the Mississippi from Columbus, Kentucky. Both sides claimed victory, but neither deserved credit.

Grant's next expedition to Fort Henry on the Tennessee River led to victory when the fort surrendered to gunboats even before troops arrived. He then pursued the fleeing garrison to Fort Donelson on the Cumberland River, besieging the far stronger position. When Fort Donelson surrendered on February 16, Grant had won the first major Union victory of the Civil War, captured an entire army, and acquired a nickname, "Unconditional Surrender," taken from his crisp demand to Gen. Simon B. Buckner.

Campaigning on the Tennessee River, Grant was surprised at Shiloh on April 6, and his troops were driven back to the riverbank. Reinforced the next day, Grant counterattacked and was more than redeemed. Late in the year he began an overland campaign against the Confederate citadel of Vicksburg, Mississippi, that turned into a winter of frustration. In the spring he ran transports below the city, crossed the river, turned east to capture the state capital of Jackson, then drove Confederates back to Vicksburg, which surrendered on July 4 after a prolonged siege. Grant had captured a second army. In November he won the Battle of Chattanooga, driving Confederates from Lookout Mountain and Missionary Ridge.

Promoted to lieutenant general and given command of all U.S. forces in March 1864, Grant accompanied the Army of the Potomac through a bloody spring campaign, including the Battles of the Wilderness, of Spotsylvania, and of Cold Harbor. At its conclusion Grant besieged Petersburg below Richmond, a siege that lasted until late March 1865, when he launched an offensive that drove Gen. Robert E. Lee from Petersburg and Richmond to surrender at Appomattox Courthouse on April 9.

After the war Grant continued to command the army and to administer Reconstruction. As congressional Republicans quarreled with President Andrew Johnson, Grant stood between them. Johnson tried to use Grant's enormous popularity to bolster his cause by appointing him secretary of war ad interim to replace radical favorite Edwin M. Stanton. When Congress insisted on Stanton's reinstatement, Grant resigned and broke with Johnson. In the process Grant strengthened his Republican ties and received their nomination for president in 1868.

Grant entered the White House as the youngest man yet elected and inexperienced in politics. He supported black civil rights and amnesty for Confederate leaders, placed religious leaders in charge of Indian affairs, and backed the recommendations of the Civil Service Commission. Gradually, however, his support for Reconstruction waned in the face of southern white persistence, his Indian "peace policy" foundered amid religious bickering, and his support for civil service reform fell victim to congressional intransigence. He was more persistent, but equally unsuccessful, in attempting to annex Santo Domingo. Nonetheless, he easily won reelection in 1872 over Horace Greeley and might have received a third nomination had he not adamantly declined to consider the prospect. In retrospect, scandals are the best-remembered aspect of the Grant presidency. None touched him personally, though several came close. At the end of his second term he assured Congress that "Failures have been errors of judgment, not of intent."

After the war grateful countrymen gave Grant houses in Philadelphia, Washington, and Galena. He lived in Galena only during the 1868 presidential campaign when he sought to avoid the public. After he began to receive pay as a general, he reclaimed his Hardscrabble farm and the estate of his wife's family in St. Louis County, planning to retire there, a place he thought of as home. In 1867 he sent an Ohio relative to manage his property. From Washington he dispatched a steady stream of letters to St. Louis, directing the rebuilding of the farm and the management of the horses at his personal expense. Genuinely fond of horses from his childhood, he aimed ultimately to make his estate a breeding farm.

In the summer of 1875 Grant received disturbing news from a trusted St. Louis friend that local culprits in the Whiskey Rebellion—a scheme to defraud the government of liquor taxes—had attempted to misuse the president's name and friendship to avoid prosecution. "Let no guilty man escape," Grant wrote. The prosecution disclosed that many of Grant's St. Louis friends had participated in fraud. The ring even included one of Grant's own White House staff. Outraged that friends had abused his trust, he decided to end his long ties to St. Louis. He had his agent dispose of personal property on the Missouri farm, then lease the land.

After leaving the White House, Grant toured the world for more than two years, nearly secured the Republican nomination in 1880, then settled in New York City. He invested heavily in the firm of Grant and Ward in which his son Ulysses Jr. was a partner, and the other partner, Ferdinand Ward, was a swindler. When the firm collapsed in 1884 Grant was impoverished and humiliated. To repair his finances he began to write reminiscences that he soon converted to full-scale memoirs. Despite the onset of throat cancer, he grimly determined to finish his work and did so before he died on July 23, 1885, at Mount McGregor, New York. Posthumously published, *The Personal Memoirs of U. S. Grant,* modest and incisive, capped the career of an American hero.

JOHN Y. SIMON

Lewis, Lloyd. *Captain Sam Grant.* Boston: Little, Brown, 1950.

Little, Kimberly Scott. *Ulysses S. Grant's White Haven.* St. Louis: National Park Service, 1993.

McFeely, William S. *Grant: A Biography.* New York: W. W. Norton, 1981.

Simon, John Y., ed. *The Papers of Ulysses S. Grant.* Carbondale: Southern Illinois University Press, 1967– .

———. *The Personal Memoirs of Julia Dent Grant.* New York: G. P. Putnam's Sons, 1975.

Stevens, Walter B. *Grant in St. Louis.* St. Louis: Franklin Club, 1916.

GRATIOT, CHARLES (1752–1817)

At the time of the Louisiana Purchase, Charles Gratiot's outspoken support for the incoming American regime set him apart from Upper Louisiana's other French Creole leaders. The Swiss-born Frenchman was well suited for the task of persuading his French-speaking compatriots to welcome their new American rulers. He spoke English fluently, had sided with the Americans during the Revolutionary War, and had traveled extensively in the United States in the 1780s and 1790s.

Gratiot was born in Lausanne, Switzerland, in 1752, a descendant of French Huguenots who had fled Normandy to escape religious persecution. He was educated in Lausanne, prior to being sent to London to secure a mercantile education under the tutelage of an uncle. In 1769 he journeyed to Canada and served as an apprentice to another uncle who was a fur merchant in Montreal. While in his uncle's employ Gratiot traveled to Michilimackinac and Detroit and visited Spanish Illinois.

After terminating his business relationship with his uncle, Gratiot moved to Cahokia in 1777 where he opened a store in partnership with a firm based in Michilimackinac. Following the outbreak of the Revolutionary War, he rendered assistance to George Rogers Clark and his western forces. The conflict disrupted Gratiot's trading operations and probably contributed to his decision to move across the river to St. Louis in 1781.

Gratiot married Victoire Chouteau, sister of the influential St. Louis fur merchants **Auguste Chouteau** and **(Jean) Pierre Chouteau,** on June 26, 1781. The Gratiots had thirteen children, nine of whom survived infancy. Marriage into the Chouteau family afforded Gratiot powerful new business connections, but as an established trader he brought valuable commercial contacts of his own to St. Louis.

Although the peripatetic merchant now called St. Louis home, business frequently took him away from the city. In 1783–1784 he traveled to Virginia in an unsuccessful effort to press his claims for repayment of Revolutionary War debts, and on his return he paid a visit to Philadelphia where he conferred with suppliers. He went to Europe in 1791 seeking financial support for a proposed trading house in New Orleans. His fourteen-month journey took him to France, Switzerland, and England, and finally to Canada. He failed in his efforts to secure funding for the New Orleans venture but did manage to secure London fur merchant John Henry Schneider's backing for an establishment at Michilimackinac. After returning to St. Louis briefly in late 1792, Gratiot went to Michilimackinac where he conducted business and acted as an agent for the Chouteau brothers.

Back in London in the fall of 1793, Gratiot momentarily flirted with the idea of remaining permanently in Europe to manage a trading house in St. Petersburg, Russia, in association with Schneider. When that scheme failed to materialize, Gratiot headed back to North America in mid-1794. Following a sojourn that included stops in several U.S. cities, he rejoined his family in St. Louis and opened a retail store. He continued to dabble in the fur business and corresponded regularly with American fur dealer John Jacob Astor to whom he owed money. Astor unsuccessfully attempted to use his connection with

Gratiot to facilitate his entry into the St. Louis market. Gratiot also engaged in farming, milling, distilling, tanning, salt making, mining, and land speculating. The substantial real estate holdings he accumulated proved his most tangible assets.

When the U.S. authorities arrived to take possession of Upper Louisiana in 1804, Gratiot signed the official transfer documents as a witness during ceremonies marking the occasion in St. Louis. Shortly thereafter he journeyed to St. Charles to see off members of the Lewis and Clark expedition then on their way to the Pacific. He also participated in numerous public meetings intended to air local concerns about new U.S. policies. When some of his French Creole friends and associates responded angrily to a proposed new framework of government for Upper Louisiana, Gratiot persuaded them to adopt a more conciliatory tone in their remonstrances.

Gratiot held a number of local offices, including judge of the court of common pleas, justice of the peace, clerk of the board of land commissioners, and member of the St. Louis Board of Trustees prior to his death in St. Louis on April 20, 1817.

WILLIAM E. FOLEY

Barnhart, Warren Lynn. "The Letterbooks of Charles Gratiot, Fur Trader: The Nomadic Years, 1769–1797." Ph.D. diss., St. Louis University, 1971.

Gratiot, Charles. Papers. Charles Gratiot Letterbook. Missouri Historical Society, St. Louis.

GREEN, A. P. (1875–1956)

Allen Percival Green bought a small brick plant in Mexico, Missouri, in 1910 and built it into a multimillion-dollar firm with branches all over the world. He managed and was president of the A. P. Green Fire Brick Company for more than thirty years and was also active in many charitable and public service causes during his lifetime.

A. P. Green was born in Jefferson City, Missouri, on July 22, 1875, the son of Joseph Henry and Eliza Homan McHenry Green. His father was a real estate investor. Green attended public schools in Jefferson City and graduated from high school there. He attended the Missouri School of Mines and Metallurgy at Rolla as a student for one year in 1894–1895. He left school to become assistant city engineer in Sedalia for three years. In 1900 he became a salesman for the Harbison-Walker Refractories Company in Pittsburgh, Pennsylvania. In four years he became general manager. With this valuable experience he returned to St. Louis in 1904 to become vice president and general manager of the Evans and Howard Fire Brick Company. In 1910 he purchased the Mexico Brick and Fire Clay Company for eighty-five thousand dollars.

On June 17, 1903, at Sedalia, Green married Sara Josephine Brown whose father was a local physician. The Greens were the parents of five children. Their three daughters—Josephine, Elizabeth, and Martha—married, respectively, Neal S. Wood, Arthur D. Bond, and Walter G. Staley. They also had twin sons, Allen P. Jr. and Robert S. Green.

Arthur Bond became a vice president of the A. P. Green Companies. He was an All-American football player at the University of Missouri and later a Rhodes scholar. The Greens' grandson Christopher S. "Kit" Bond became governor of Missouri in 1973 and a U.S. senator in 1987.

A. P. Green Industries was a pioneering company in refractories manufacture and distribution, and a leading innovator in product development. The company was the leader in open-pit mining of raw materials and in the use of tunnel kilns for firing refractories. It was founded in 1910 and incorporated under Missouri law as the A. P. Green Fire Brick Company on December 4, 1915. In 1965 the name of the company was changed to A. P. Green Refractories Company (APG). In 1967 the company was acquired by U.S. Gypsum (USG). In 1987 as a result of the transfer of APG Lime from USG to A. P. Green, the name of the company was changed to A. P. Green Industries. Between 1950 and 1980 A. P. Green acquired several domestic refractory plants, and the company has been active internationally with wholly owned manufacturing, sales, and installation operations in Canada. In 1931 A. P. Green Refractories (Canada) Limited was formed and located in Weston, Ontario. In 1954 A. P. Green Refractories Limited was acquired in the United Kingdom and located in Bromborough, England. The company also has partial ownership of a refractory operation in the country of Mexico and technical and sales licensing agreements in many other foreign countries.

The Allen P. and Josephine B. Green Foundation was established in 1941. The foundation makes grants in a variety of fields, but with a primary focus on medical research. During a twenty-year period in the 1950s and 1960s, the foundation contributed more than nine hundred thousand dollars to research on Parkinson's disease and related diseases of the nervous system and more than six hundred thousand dollars for pediatric neurology research. The Greens established the foundation with the welfare of children as a major interest.

The Greens were Presbyterians and were deeply interested in education with a particular interest in Westminster College and the University of Missouri. The A. P. Green Chapel was dedicated on October 11, 1959, on the campus of the University of Missouri in Columbia. The chapel was constructed so that it would function as an integrated part of the Memorial Student Union on campus.

In 1946 A. P. Green was in attendance at Westminster College when Winston Churchill delivered his famous Iron Curtain speech. As a member of the Westminster College Board of Trustees, Green also served that day as a member of the reception committee along with his son-in-law Neal Wood.

Green was interested in service to the young, and served as a member of the national boards of directors of the Boy Scouts of America and the Young Men's Christian Association.

Green died in St. Louis on June 9, 1956.

ARTHUR F. McCLURE

Read, Orville H. *The Refractories People: A History of the A. P. Green Refractories Co.* [St. Louis]: A. P. Green Refractories, 1978.
Who Was Who in America. Vol. 3. Chicago: A. N. Marquis, 1960.
"World Spotlight Turns on Westminster." *Westminster College Bulletin* ser. 46, no. 1 (April 1946).

GREEN, DUFF (1791–1875)

Born near Versailles, Kentucky, on August 15, 1791, politician, publisher, and businessman Duff Green lived a long and eventful life. Although contemporary opinion of Green was sharply divided, he was undeniably a self-made man. His early education was sound if rudimentary, much of it informal and learned from his mother. His first profession was teaching, but he left the classroom to enlist in the War of 1812. In that conflict he distinguished himself while fighting Indians at Fort Harrison where he met then-captain Zachary Taylor, who later as president remembered Green.

Following the war Green returned to Kentucky where he married Lucretia Maria Edwards on November 26, 1813. They had eleven children, five of whom survived to adulthood. Green tried his hand at shop keeping, which he disliked. In the autumn of 1816 he received a commission to survey lands in Howard County, Missouri, then on the edge of the American frontier. Territorial governor **William Clark** appointed him as a colonel in the Missouri State Militia. After coming to Missouri Green studied law, and by late 1818 he had established a legal practice.

Local tradition attributes the founding of the town of Chariton, about two miles above Glasgow, to Duff Green even though he failed to mention it in his autobiography, perhaps because an outbreak of malaria forced the settlement's abandonment by 1837. Green was heavily involved in land speculation, served as the first postmaster at Chariton, and started the first stagecoach line west of the Mississippi. He was also active in Howard (and later Chariton) County politics. Politically prominent, a good organizer, and skillful in settling local Indian problems, he was elected as a brigadier general of the First Division of the Missouri Militia, and for the rest of his life he was addressed as General Green.

Howard County voters elected Green in 1820 to the Missouri Constitutional Convention as a proslavery delegate who opposed congressional control, or "dictation." Green had previously revealed his ardent support for states' rights in the toast he gave on the occasion of the arrival of the first steamboat at Franklin: "The Union—It is dear to us, but liberty is dearer." His friend John C. Calhoun later used a version of that toast in his famous 1830 encounter with Andrew Jackson. Following his service in the Missouri Constitutional Convention, Green served first in the state house and subsequently in the state senate. As a member of the General Assembly he supported a state-backed loan office to help mitigate the financial disaster caused by the panic of 1819.

In December 1823 Green purchased the *St. Louis Enquirer,* which, ironically, had belonged to **Thomas Hart Benton,** an individual whom he personally detested. Green used the newspaper to promote Calhoun's presidential candidacy, and when the South Carolinian opted to seek the vice presidency, Green supported Andrew Jackson.

Determined to carry his campaign to the national level, Green decided in 1826 that the *Enquirer* did not reach a sufficiently broad audience. That year he sold most of his property in Missouri (at a loss) in order to purchase the *U.S. Telegraph* in Washington, D.C. Drawing upon the example of Missouri's factional struggles, he helped keep public focus on the charges that a corrupt bargain between John Quincy Adams and Henry Clay had wrongfully prevented Jackson from becoming president in 1824. Despite Green's strong advocacy for the election of Jackson in 1828, he subsequently joined Calhoun in withdrawing support from the president, whom they believed had failed to champion states' rights sufficiently. In 1832 Green used the *U.S. Telegraph* to oppose Jackson's reelection. He failed in that effort, and the *Telegraph*'s readership declined rapidly, forcing Green to cease its publication in 1837. Although periodically he published other newspapers, none ever commanded the prestige or power that the *Telegraph* had wielded at its peak.

After 1837 Green turned his attention to business. He tried unsuccessfully for twenty years to exploit coal and iron ore deposits in Maryland and Virginia and also sought to promote the construction of canals and railroads. The outbreak of the Civil War in 1861 destroyed his business dealings in the North and nearly overwhelmed him financially. He personally appealed to Lincoln to issue a statement promising not to interfere with slavery, but after failing in that effort Green headed south to join the Confederate cause. During the war he purchased an ironworks near Jonesboro, Tennessee, and directed his efforts to supplying the South with iron. When the war ended, he lost that business and spent the rest of his life trying to recover his fortune until his death in Dalton, Georgia, on June 10, 1875.

MARSHALL TED PHELPS

Green, Duff. *Facts and Suggestions, Biographical, Financial, and Political: Addressed to the People of the United States.* New York: Richardson, 1866.
———. Papers. Library of Congress, Washington, D.C.
———. Papers. University of North Carolina Library, Chapel Hill.
Green, Fletcher. "Duff Green: Militant Journalist of the Old School." *American Historical Review* 52 (January 1947): 247–64.

GREEN, JAMES S. (1817–1870)

James S. Green was born in Fauquier County, Virginia, on February 28, 1817, and settled in Lewis County, Missouri, in 1838. Without benefit of a formal education, he studied law and was admitted to the Missouri bar at Monticello in 1840. After establishing his legal practice, Green actively involved himself in Missouri politics as a supporter of **Thomas Hart Benton,** the state's powerful Democratic U.S. senator.

Green appears to have been one of the ablest members in the 1845 Missouri Constitutional Convention. Despite his lack of formal training, he impressed others with his knowledge of constitutional law. In 1846, running as a Benton Democrat, he won election to the United States House of Representatives from Missouri's Third District. He won reelection to Congress in 1848, but a breach opened between Benton and himself as he became an increasingly ardent advocate of the South's most extreme proslavery and states' rights positions. A staunch racist, he spoke out in strong and derogatory terms to justify slavery on the grounds that whites were inherently superior to blacks. During the controversial and heated congressional debates over the expansion of slavery into new territories, leading to the Compromise of 1850, Green was the only member of the Missouri delegation in the House of Representatives who consistently voted with the Southern ultras. He had become more in tune with Missouri's pro-Southern senator **David Rice Atchison** than with the Union-minded Benton.

In January 1850 Green stood, as an anti-Benton Democrat, for election by the Missouri General Assembly to a seat in the United States Senate. He lost in his bid for office, but so did Benton, who, after thirty years of service in the Senate, was replaced by **Henry S. Geyer,** a Whig.

President Franklin Pierce appointed Green as chargé d'affaires to Colombia, South America, in 1853. That position proved too monotonous and too far from home for Green, who returned to Missouri in 1854 suffering from the ill effects of an unhealthy climate.

Back in his home state Green renewed his role in politics as an uncompromising spokesman for the South and as a determined opponent of Benton. He became a leading Missouri advocate of the doctrines of John C. Calhoun, a senator from South Carolina. Throughout Benton's effort to regain a Senate seat, and in his 1856 campaign for the governorship, Green followed him around the state making every effort to bring about his defeat. James G. Blaine wrote that no other man did as much to break Benton's power in Missouri as Green. While this is an overstatement, it is an indication of Green's political passion.

Green was elected again to the United States House of Representatives in 1856, but before his term began the Missouri General Assembly selected him to fill the state's vacant United States Senate seat. In 1855 none of the three senatorial candidates—Benton, Atchison, and **Alexander W. Doniphan**—had been able to muster a majority in the General Assembly. In 1857, with Atchison no longer in the race, Green (as a member of the ultra-Southern faction) easily won election to complete the remaining four years of the senatorial term.

In the Senate Green devoted his major efforts to championing the Southern cause during the great sectional controversies of those years. An able orator he spoke out in support of slavery, its expansion, and the right of a state to secede from the Union. One disappointed contemporary, believing that Green had been led astray by Calhoun, observed that he had become one of the most active supporters of the rebellion.

When his senatorial term ended on March 3, 1861, Green returned to Missouri and made his home in St. Louis. He worked with Missourians such as Gov. **Claiborne Fox Jackson** and Lt. Gov. **Thomas Caute Reynolds** in the unsuccessful effort to move Missouri out of the Union and into the Confederate States of America.

During the 1860s Green practiced law in St. Louis, but his declining health reduced the amount of work he could do. He died on January 19, 1870, just before his fifty-third birthday. He was buried at Canton in Lewis County.

PERRY MCCANDLESS

Bay, W. V. N. *Reminiscences of the Bench and Bar of Missouri.* St. Louis: F. H. Thomas, 1897.
March, David D. *The History of Missouri.* New York: Lewis Historical Publishing, 1967.

GREENE, LORENZO JOHNSTON (1899–1988)

Lorenzo Johnston Greene was born on November 16, 1899, in Ansonia, Connecticut. In 1917 he became the first African American to graduate from Ansonia High School. He received his B.A. degree from Howard University in 1924. He earned his M.A. degree in history from Columbia University in 1926 and immediately began work toward his doctorate.

In 1928 Greene began a long association with Carter G. Woodson, the "Father of African American History." From March 1928 to February 1930 he helped Woodson and Charles H. Wesley in surveying African American churches in Baltimore, Maryland, and Suffolk, Virginia. When the survey ended he continued to work for Woodson, researching *The Negro Wage Earner,* which was published in 1930 and coauthored with Woodson.

In June 1930 Greene and Woodson planned a campaign to sell books published by Woodson's Associated Publishers. Greene led a team of four other young men through the South and Midwest on this book-selling expedition. He returned to Washington in 1931 to help in studying black employment in the District of Columbia. Greene coauthored the results of this study, *Negro Employment in the District of Columbia* (1932), with Myra Colson Callis. In 1932 Greene also served on the Committee on Negro Housing of President Herbert Hoover's Conference on Home Building and Home Ownership. He worked with Charles S. Johnson in editing the committee's report, *Negro Housing* (1932).

In the fall of 1933 Greene joined the faculty of Lincoln University in Jefferson City, Missouri. He completed requirements for his doctorate at Columbia University in 1942. His dissertation, "The Negro in Colonial New England, 1620–1776," became part of the Columbia University Studies in History, Economics, and Public Law.

Throughout his years at Lincoln University, Greene was active in promoting scholarship in African American history and in advancing human rights in Missouri. He edited the *Midwest Journal* from 1947 until its end in 1956. This journal supplemented the *Journal of Negro History* and offered additional publishing opportunities to scholars in African American history and related fields.

In 1939 Greene helped to solicit aid and to spread the word about the plight of the sharecroppers camped along the highways in southeast Missouri to protest the conditions in that area. Through his membership in the Missouri Association for Social Welfare he worked to end segregation in public accommodations. He was also a leader in the successful effort to secure the establishment of the Missouri Human Rights Commission. Beginning in 1957 he served as a member of the Missouri State Advisory Committee to the U.S. Commission on Civil Rights. He surveyed school desegregation in Missouri and wrote *Desegregation of Missouri Schools, 1954–1959* (1959, 1961).

Greene's other publications include *Missouri's Black Heritage,* with Gary R. Kremer and Antonio F. Holland (1980; revised by Kremer and Holland, 1993). In 1971 the University of Missouri–Columbia awarded him the doctor of humane letters degree. Greene retired from the faculty of Lincoln University in 1972. He died on January 24, 1988, in Jefferson City, Missouri.

Greene ranks among the pioneers who shaped and established African American history as an academic discipline and research field. He devoted his life to teaching and to furthering the work of the Association for the Study of Afro-American Life and History. He left a lasting legacy in the quality of his work.

ARVARH E. STRICKLAND

Greene, Lorenzo J. "Lincoln University's Involvement with the Sharecropper Demonstration in Southeast Missouri, 1939–1940." *Missouri Historical Review* 82 (October 1987): 24–50.

———. *Selling Black History for Carter G. Woodson: A Diary, 1930–1933.* Ed. Arvarh E. Strickland. Columbia: University of Missouri Press, 1996.

———. *Working with Carter G. Woodson, the Father of Black History: A Diary, 1928–1930.* Ed. Arvarh E. Strickland. Baton Rouge: Louisiana State University Press, 1989.

Meier, August, and Elliott Rudwick. *Black History and the Historical Profession, 1915–1980.* Blacks in the New World Series, ed. August Meier. Urbana: University of Illinois Press, 1986.

Strickland, Arvarh E. "The Plight of the People in the Sharecroppers' Demonstration in Southeast Missouri." *Missouri Historical Review* 81 (July 1987): 403–16.

GREENWELL, GUY A. (1917–1990)

Guy A. Greenwell, who served as curator of birds at the National Zoological Park from 1972 until 1985, was born on August 10, 1917, near Joplin, Missouri, the son of Kelly E. and Leola B. Greenwell.

Guy Greenwell's interest in birds was sparked by his father who owned and operated Greenwell's Poultry Company in Joplin. By age three, Guy had a phenomenal knowledge of birds and their habits. This intense interest led him to study bird life from books and in the wild. As a teenager he gave bird lectures to hundreds of students in public schools throughout the lower Midwest. Often addressing people many years his senior, he spoke to civic clubs, served as a summer camp counselor, and, at age twelve, hosted his own weekly radio nature show. He became widely known as the "Birdboy of the Ozarks."

In 1925, at age eight, Greenwell became the youngest person elected to the Izaak Walton League, and in 1927 he became the youngest member of the American Ornithologist Union. In 1933 he began collecting birds for Rudolf Bennitt, an associate professor of zoology at the University of Missouri. After graduation from Joplin High School in 1934, Greenwell studied two semesters at the University of Missouri but left school for financial reasons.

From 1944 to 1949 Greenwell worked for the Missouri Conservation Commission, supervising the establishment of a major wildlife refuge near Chillicothe. He later married Kathryn Jane Carmichael and returned to Joplin to serve as the office manager for a roofing company. He and his wife established their own nationally recognized wildlife refuge at Robin's Roost, their farm near Redings Mill in northern Newton County.

In 1972 the Smithsonian Institution named Greenwell curator of birds at the National Zoo. Shortly after his arrival in Washington, D.C., he oversaw the removal of birds to a new facility at Front Royal, Virginia. He chose to remain at Front Royal to head the new Conservation and Research Center rather than return to Washington. He remained there until his retirement in 1985.

While serving as national curator of birds, Greenwell directed the center's bird life research, visited zoos and wildlife refuges on every continent, wrote extensively on birds and bird management, and assisted many nations with the establishment or management of their zoos and wildlife refuges. He wrote portions of two famous wildlife books, *A Thinking Man's Guide to Rearing Wild Waterfowl* and *Home Grown Honkers.*

Greenwell was active in wildlife organizations, serving as a member or on the board of directors of nearly every state and national wildlife federation. He was a founding member and director of the International Wildlife Waterfowl Association. In 1969 he was named Missouri Wildlife Conservationist of the Year, the highest honor given by that statewide organization.

After retiring from the National Zoo, Guy Greenwell returned to Missouri to live near his stepson, Larry Gindling. In retirement at his rural Neosho home, he continued his study of bird life, corresponded with birders around the world, and took special interest in the ruby-throated hummingbirds in his backyard. Guy Greenwell died in Joplin, at age seventy-two, on January 9, 1990.

KAY HIVELY

Greenwell, Guy A. Personal Papers and Interviews. In possession of Kay Hively, Neosho, Mo.

GREGG, JOSIAH (1806–1850)

From his father, Wheelwright Harmon Gregg, Josiah Gregg inherited a roving spirit that shaped his character and his life. The elder Gregg had already moved his family from Pennsylvania to Kentucky to North Carolina to Overton County, Tennessee, when Josiah was born on July 19, 1806. In 1809 the family moved to Illinois and in 1812 to Cooper's Fort, in Howard County, Missouri. Four years later the Greggs moved again, and in 1825 finally settled near the future site of Independence.

While his brothers followed the usual pursuits of boys growing up on the Missouri frontier, Josiah's frail health and aptitude for learning seemed to destine him for a professional career. Largely self-educated, he displayed a talent for mathematics and a vigorous scientific curiosity early in life. After a year of teaching school in 1824, he considered medicine as a profession, but instead took up the study of law. The drudgery of law books was not to his taste, however. Boredom, frustration, uncertainty, and chronic ill health laid the young man low in 1830. His doctor diagnosed the condition as chronic dyspepsia and consumption, and prescribed a trip to the prairies, where pure air, healthful activities, and a change of scenery would restore his health. Gregg's brothers, Jacob and John, had both traveled with traders' caravans to Santa Fe in the 1820s. Drawing on their knowledge and connections, the family arranged passage for Josiah with a caravan leaving Independence for Santa Fe in May 1831. Although an invalid at the journey's beginning, Gregg quickly recovered his health, paid his way by working as a bookkeeper, and taught himself Spanish on the trip.

The traveling life of a Santa Fe trader appealed to Gregg's restless nature and insatiable curiosity. He spent the next nine years in the trade, completing four trips from Missouri to Santa Fe and back again. On his fourth trip in spring 1839, he blazed a new trail from Van Buren, Arkansas, to reach Santa Fe ahead of rivals.

Although Gregg had some financial success as a trader, his trips were far more than moneymaking ventures. He claimed to enjoy good health only when living the free-ranging life of the caravans. He wanted to know everything about the prairies and all that lived upon them. He drew maps and kept careful records of his observations on the long trips. Returning to Missouri in 1840, Gregg began to fashion a book from his maps and notes. Accustomed to a roving life, he found it hard to stay in one place even to work on his book, however. To earn a living he sold mules and bought land in Texas, worked at various odd jobs in Missouri, worked as a surveyor in Van Buren, Arkansas, and opened a store there with his brother and another partner.

In 1843 Gregg traveled to Philadelphia and New York to find a publisher for his book. After many frustrations and false starts, he finally secured a contract with Henry G. Langley in New York. The first edition of his book, *Commerce of the Prairies,* rolled off the press in the summer of 1844, and immediately became a best-seller. By fall a second edition was in progress; within a year British and German editions appeared, and by 1854 there would be five reprints in the United States.

The book's success was due in part to some fortunate connections with good publicists in the East. The timing was right as well: interest in the Far West was rapidly growing in the United States and abroad in these years of the Oregon Trail, Polk's election on an expansionist platform, and disputes with Britain and Mexico over U.S. expansion. Gregg's book deserved its success on its own merits as well. Plain but elegant and sensitive language captured the romance of the prairie and the strange lands beyond, yet provided practical advice for the traveler. With a new map prepared by Gregg, his book was the most complete and reliable guide then available to the Santa Fe Trail. His careful descriptions of life on the trail and in New Mexico quickly established the book as a classic of western literature. Although the success of *Commerce of the Prairies* might have initiated a career as a writer, the drudgery of desk work was not to Gregg's taste. He continued to keep journals of his travels, worked intermittently on manuscripts, and occasionally wrote for newspapers, but he never published another book.

Still searching for a niche in life, Gregg returned to the study of medicine. He may have had some formal training in his youth, but more likely taught himself enough to acquire a reputation as a doctor among the fraternity of Santa Fe traders. In the fall of 1845 he entered medical school at the University of Louisville, and in March 1846 received an honorary degree in medicine. Again, Gregg could not discipline himself to routine study and practice. Instead, he returned to Missouri to join another caravan bound for Santa Fe. War with Mexico interrupted his trip, and he left the traders' caravan en route to join the Arkansas volunteers bound for Mexico. Gregg served as a civilian aide, guide, interpreter, and mapmaker on Gen. John Wool's staff, as well as war correspondent for the *Louisville Gazette.* He quickly tired of the discipline of military life, the soldiers' coarse behavior, and General Wool's difficult temperament, however. After witnessing the Battle of Buena Vista in February 1847, Gregg left to seek adventure for a short time with Col. **Alexander W. Doniphan**'s Missouri volunteers. Next, a proposed business venture with

Santa Fe trader Samuel McGoffin failed. Gregg then cast about unsuccessfully for a government job, and finally set himself up as a doctor in private practice serving the army of occupation and other Americans in Saltillo, Mexico.

Since 1846, if not earlier, Gregg had been collecting botanical specimens for **George Engelmann,** the founder of a collection that would become the St. Louis Botanical Gardens. In the spring of 1848 Gregg's restless nature got the better of him again. He abandoned his medical practice and set off on a scientific expedition through central Mexico to collect for Engelmann and indulge his own fascination with botany, ornithology, and geology.

Arriving at Mazatlán in time to hear of the gold strike in California, Gregg boarded a ship for San Francisco, more from the drive of his relentless curiosity than expectations of a fortune. In California he encountered former business partner Jesse Sutton, and considered another attempt at the mercantile business, but continued his scientific collecting and exploring. In October 1849 the men of a small mining camp on Trinity River elected him to lead an expedition across the mountains to the coast in search of the river's mouth, a good port, and direct access to the sea. Although bad weather and rugged terrain discouraged most of the party, Gregg and seven men struggled through the mountains in November and December 1849. They named the Mad River, followed it to the coast, and discovered and named Trinity Bay. (A later expedition by sea would rediscover the bay and rename it Humboldt Bay.) On the point of starvation, suffering from exhaustion and exposure, and quarreling bitterly among themselves, the party did not tarry to make further discoveries, but turned back to the settlements. During the return trip a fall from his horse exacerbated the effects of hardship and hunger for Gregg. He died and was buried by his comrades in the California wilderness in late February 1850.

Gregg's life epitomized the restless spirit of adventure and quest for opportunity that drove nineteenth-century American expansion. His book, *Commerce of the Prairies,* remains a masterpiece in the literature of the West.

MARY ELLEN ROWE

Fulton, Maurice Garland. *Diary and Letters of Josiah Gregg.* 2 vols. Norman: University of Oklahoma Press, 1944.

Gregg, Josiah. *Commerce of the Prairies.* Ed. Max L. Moorhead. Norman: University of Oklahoma Press, 1954.

Horgan, Paul. *Josiah Gregg and His Vision of the Early West.* 1941. Reprint, New York: Farrar, Straus, and Giroux, 1972.

GREGG, KATE LEILA (1883–1954)

Kate Leila Gregg, a professor of English at Lindenwood College in St. Charles and a noted editor of materials documenting the exploration of Missouri and the West, was born in Chehalis, Washington, on March 18, 1883. Her parents, Charles Carrol and Mary Adelia Phillips Gregg, moved with their family to Clarkston, Washington, in 1890, and Kate attended Yale University in 1911–1912, and was awarded a Ph.D. from the University of Washington in 1916. Her dissertation, "Thomas Dekker: A Study in Economic and Social Backgrounds," was published in 1924.

Interspersed with her college attendance, Gregg taught in Idaho and Washington public schools for six years and headed the English department at the University of Idaho in 1912–1913. She served as a teaching fellow at the University of Washington from 1913 to 1915, as a Denny fellow in 1915–1916, and, following the receipt of her doctorate, as an instructor in English from 1916 to 1920.

In 1920 Gregg moved to Minneapolis, where she engaged in women's club work. She returned to teaching in 1922 as an associate professor of English at Elmira College, in Elmira, New York. She began her long-term association with Lindenwood College in 1924 as a member of the English faculty and retired from teaching in 1946. Not long after her arrival in St. Charles, she became interested in the early history of the West.

Although Gregg's academic training was in English, she became most well known as an editor of primary source materials describing exploration in Missouri and the West during the first half of the nineteenth century. *Westward with Dragoons,* her first effort in this field, which was published in 1937, presented the journal kept by **William Clark** on his trip to establish Fort Osage in 1808. Reviewers acclaimed Gregg's detailed annotations and appended materials.

In 1952 Gregg edited **George Champlin Sibley**'s journal and diaries kept by Joseph Davis and Benjamin H. Reeves while they mapped the route between Missouri and New Mexico from 1825 to 1827. This volume, *The Road to Santa Fe,* which included an extensive introduction by Gregg, was probably her best-known work.

At the time of her death in 1954, Gregg had largely completed the transcription and annotation of journalist Matthew Field's diaries, letters, and newspaper articles chronicling his 1843 trip to the Rocky Mountains with a party headed by Sir William Drummond Stewart. **John Francis McDermott III** completed the work begun by Gregg, and the volume, titled *Prairie and Mountain Sketches,* appeared in 1957. In addition to these volumes, Gregg published several articles about Missouri history in the *Missouri Historical Review* and wrote a pageant, *The Spirit of Blanchette,* for the 1938 St. Charles Pageant of Progress.

Gregg was a member of Phi Beta Kappa and Pi Lambda Theta, a professional education sorority. She helped establish the St. Charles Historical Society in 1937, served as the organization's first historian, and held the office of president in 1939. She also served as the first woman president of the Historical Association of Greater St. Louis, an organization of history teachers in area high schools, colleges, and universities.

In 1946, following her retirement from Lindenwood, Gregg campaigned for the office of state representative from St. Charles County. She ran unopposed in the Democratic primary but was defeated by Ben Borgelt in the November general election. Gregg continued research on various projects throughout her retirement years, dividing her time between her home in Chehalis and St. Charles.

Following a heart attack, Gregg died in Chehalis on July 9, 1954. Although not trained as a historian, Gregg, a meticulous documentary editor, made widely available important sources on the exploration of Missouri and the West.

LYNN WOLF GENTZLER

Dains, Mary K., ed. *Show Me Missouri Women: Selected Biographies.* Kirksville, Mo.: Thomas Jefferson University Press, 1989.

"Dr. Kate L. Gregg." *Lindenwood College Bulletin* 128 (October 1954): 3.

"Kate L. Gregg." *Missouri Historical Society Bulletin* 11 (October 1954): 88–90.

"Kate Leila Gregg." In *Missouri and Missourians: Land of Contrasts and People of Achievements,* by Floyd Calvin Shoemaker, vol. 5. Chicago: Lewis Publishing, 1943.

GRIMES, ABSALOM (1834–1911)

Missouri residents, like those of other border states during the Civil War, had sharply divided loyalties. While most supported the pro-Union government, others sent their sons to fight in the Confederate army. Surrounded by the enemy, these families could not keep in touch with their loved ones unless someone smuggled their contraband letters across the Union lines.

Absalom Carlisle Grimes, a daring young Confederate captain, volunteered for this dangerous job. From 1862 to 1864 he defied increasingly heavy federal surveillance to deliver mail to the South—and to spy on Union troops. Six times he was captured and imprisoned; five times he managed to escape. The last time, under sentence to be hanged, he finally won a pardon from President Abraham Lincoln, who was apparently impressed by his courage.

Born in Kentucky on August 22, 1834, Grimes grew up in St. Louis where his father, William Leander Grimes, was a riverboat pilot. As a boy Grimes worked as a messenger for the Morse Telegraph Company and once delivered a telegram to the hotel suite of famous singer Jenny Lind, then performing in St. Louis. Lind was so pleased by the young Grimes that she gave him a free pass to her concert.

Trained by his father, Grimes earned his pilot's license in 1852, and for the next nine years he plied the river between St. Louis and St. Paul. When he tried to renew his license in 1861 a German-born inspector asked him to swear allegiance to the government; indignantly refusing to take such an oath from an "alien," Grimes and two friends— one of them **Samuel Langhorne Clemens (Mark Twain)**—stalked out of the office.

The men joined the Missouri Confederate militia, but Clemens quickly got his fill of war. Grimes became a member of Company K, First Missouri Cavalry, and then an infantryman, but his capture and quick escape from federal troops near Springfield gave him an inkling of his finest talent. Captured a few days later in the Battle of Pea Ridge, he helped sixty Confederates escape, then did so himself on his way to the Alton prison.

Named a mail runner by Gen. **Sterling Price,** Grimes quickly organized a ring of Missouri women who gathered Southern-bound mail and delivered it to him, sometimes sewn in their petticoats. Then he dodged federal police, traveling by steamboat or on foot and taking assumed names as he went. Some trips were successful, while others ended in arrest.

In his most spectacularly successful adventure, Grimes and a bold partner soldered metal boxes filled with letters to the bottom of a small skiff painted light gray to match the fog. Then they floated down the Yazoo River, past federal sentries and a gunboat blockade, to deliver mail to the Confederate army at Vicksburg.

When captured, Grimes was ingenious at escaping. At the Gratiot Street prison in St. Louis, he once slipped out of handcuffs in front of the warden, who angrily ordered that a thirty-two-pound cannonball be chained to his ankle. At his court-martial, Grimes appeared—carrying the cannonball. Next he was sentenced to be shot, but he managed to tunnel his way out of the jail and walk away wearing a federal artillery officer's epaulets, cleverly fashioned from a yellow envelope.

Grimes's closest call came in 1863, when he was again locked up at the Gratiot Street prison. As punishment for an attempted escape, Grimes and another prisoner were handcuffed each morning to a post in the jail yard. But on December 31 the weather turned suddenly fierce; snow drifted around Grimes, who was dressed in thin clothing. He lost consciousness and would have frozen to death if some Southern-sympathizing women next door had not seen him and asked a judge to intervene.

Shot in the leg and neck during another foiled escape, Grimes was sent to the prison hospital; as soon as his condition improved, he was to be executed. He did begin to get better, and some officials were due to assess his condition. However, a sympathetic doctor slipped him syrup of ipecac, which made him so ill that his hanging was postponed.

A few days later President Lincoln responded to a plea from Grimes's friends and commuted his sentence to imprisonment until December 1. But a villainous warden ignored the order, held Grimes past his release date, and administered a savage whipping of 161 lashes, scarring him for life.

At last Grimes was released; he married his long-time sweetheart and resumed his life as a riverboat captain. As an old man, at his daughter's prodding, he wrote a long reminiscence of his days as a Confederate spy. He died in St. Louis on March 27, 1911, at age seventy-six and was buried in Barclay Cemetery in New London, Missouri.

CANDACE O'CONNOR

Grimes, Absalom C. *Absalom C. Grimes, Confederate Mail Runner: Edited from Captain Grimes's Own Story by M. M. Quaife, of the Burton Historical Collection.* New Haven: Yale University Press, 1926.
Missouri Republican, March 28, 1911.
St. Louis Post-Dispatch, October 16, 1960.

GRIMSLEY, THORNTON (1798–1861)

St. Louis developed as a major supply center for U.S. expansion into the trans-Mississippi West. This expansion began in advance of railroads and depended upon horse travel. Demand arose for new kinds of long-distance saddles, and St. Louis saddlers responded. They had been exposed to various styles of saddlery, such as Spanish-style saddles used in the Southwest. The city soon gained a reputation for its quality saddlery, in large part due to Thornton Grimsley. He was an inventive saddler who developed a saddle well suited for the American West. Furthermore, he was an entrepreneur who translated a smart idea into a successful business. Grimsley played an important role in the story of how St. Louis came to become the leading trade and shipping center to the West in the years before the Civil War.

Born on August 20, 1798, in Bourbon County, Kentucky, Grimsley lost both parents when he was seven years old. He was apprenticed to saddler John Jacoby, who became his foster father. When his apprenticeship ended in 1816 Grimsley journeyed to St. Louis on a business trip for his employer. He determined to settle there, but first returned home to attend school for a year. By 1822 he had moved to St. Louis, married fellow Kentuckian Susan Stark, and opened his own saddlery store. Grimsley would remain in the saddlery business there for the rest of his life. For a time he operated in partnership with his own apprentice John Young in the firm of Grimsley and Young. Later he formed a partnership with his son John J. Grimsley and son-in-law George L. Stansbury as Thornton Grimsley and Company.

Grimsley's first big success came when he designed a saddle for use by those engaged in the fur trade, a key industry in the St. Louis economy. He sold hundreds of saddles to the American Fur Company, thus launching his business. By 1833 Grimsley had designed a saddle for use by the military, and he secured a contract with the United States Army to adopt the Grimsley Saddle as its regulation saddle. It remained the official army saddle for twenty-six years. Members of **Stephen Watts Kearny**'s expedition of 1846 rode on Grimsley Saddles, as did dragoons who fought in the Mexican War. In 1859 the army switched to a different saddle, the McClellan Saddle, but many who rode in the armies of the Civil War kept their Grimsley Saddles, including St. Louisans **Ulysses S. Grant** and **William T. Sherman.**

Grimsley experienced limited military activities, though he remained a civilian. In 1832 he raised a company and volunteered in the Black Hawk War in Illinois. In 1836 he declined the offer of a captain's commission in the United States Army dragoons, unwilling to leave his home in St. Louis. He raised a volunteer regiment for the Mexican War, but for political reasons his unit was not called for service. He belonged to local St. Louis militia companies, and as a colonel he led many ceremonial drills and parades.

Grimsley played a role in the political life of his community. He served as a St. Louis alderman twice, in 1826 and again in 1835. Voters sent him to the Missouri House of Representatives in 1828, and to the state senate in 1838. He favored the concept of publicly financed internal improvements, and joined the Whig Party. In his first term as alderman he sought to improve the city's wharf. As a state legislator he championed construction of a national road as far as Jefferson City. In his second term as alderman he led a movement to create the city's first public park and parade ground in an area that had formerly been the old southwest commons. Some in St. Louis ridiculed the project as "Grimsley's Folly," but he succeeded, and in 1851 the area was dedicated as Lafayette Park. In the state senate Grimsley worked on behalf of the St. Louis and Iron Mountain Railroad, and led the drive to build a public workhouse in St. Louis. His party nominated him for a seat in Congress in 1839, but he failed to win election. Still, it is a measure of his popularity that he served as grand marshal when the city celebrated the groundbreaking of the Pacific Railroad on July 4, 1851.

Grimsley and Susan Stark had ten children. His daughter Minerva married **Henry Taylor Blow,** and their daughter **Susan Elizabeth Blow** was a pioneer in establishing public kindergartens in the city's school system. Thornton Grimsley died on December 22, 1861, in St. Louis.

VICKI JOHNSON

Ahlborn, Richard E., ed. *Man Made Mobile: Early Saddles of Western North America.* Washington, D.C.: Smithsonian Institution Press, 1980.

Edwards, Richard, and M. Hopewell. *Edwards's Great West and Her Commercial Metropolis.* St. Louis, 1860.

Hyde, William, and Howard L. Conard, eds. *Encyclopedia of the History of St. Louis.* New York: Southern History, 1899.

Primm, James Neal. *Lion of the Valley: St. Louis, Missouri, 1764–1980.* 3d ed. St. Louis: Missouri Historical Society Press, 1998.

Scharf, J. Thomas. *History of St. Louis City and County: From Earliest Periods to the Present Day.* Philadelphia: Everts, 1883.

Steffen, Randy. *United States Military Saddles, 1812–1943.* Norman: University of Oklahoma Press, 1973.

GUITAR, ODON (1825–1908)

Odon Guitar was born on August 31, 1825, in Madison County, Kentucky, to John and Emily Gordon Guitar. John Guitar, a native of Bordeaux, France, immigrated to America in 1818. He worked in New York City before moving to Kentucky around 1820, where he met and married Emily Gordon. In 1827 they moved to Boone County, Missouri.

Community members characterized Odon Guitar as possessing an "adventurous disposition . . . and a bold and daring spirit." He was a "roystering young man . . . at intervals addicted to 'sprees' and carousing, and a lover of card-playing and cockfighting." Despite his adventures, Guitar ranked high throughout school.

Guitar enrolled in the first session of the University of Missouri in 1842 and graduated in 1846 with an A.B. degree. At the moment he should have been reading his prize-winning commencement speech, Guitar was marching to the Mexican War with **Alexander W. Doniphan**'s First Missouri Mounted Volunteers. Guitar returned in July 1847 after serving with distinction and traveling thirty-five

hundred miles by land and twenty-five hundred miles by water.

Guitar began studying law with his uncle, John B. Gordon, a widely respected attorney and orator, and in 1848 he was admitted to the bar. Two years later, however, adventure beckoned again, and Guitar was swept from his law practice to the fields of California in the gold rush. He panned enough gold to have a watch made, which he carried throughout his life. He resumed his Columbia law practice in October 1851.

In 1852 Guitar became secretary for the Boone County Whigs. The following year the citizens of Boone County elected him to the General Assembly. He served from 1854 to 1856 and from 1858 to 1860.

In an 1856 speech to the University Alumni Association, of which he was the first president, Guitar warned of the impending dangers of the slavery conflict, an address that reportedly caught the attention of Abraham Lincoln.

In May 1861 a Union meeting was held in Columbia. In what many witnesses reported was his finest speech, Guitar stated that though he had owned slaves and had been taught that slavery was of divine origin, he would gladly give up any and all benefits of it in order to preserve the Union. He predicted that a war would pit brother against brother, father against son, and neighbor against neighbor. Soldiers and bushwhackers would plunder and burn homes, farms, schools, churches, and bridges. "If the glorious old ship of State shall be dismasted by the storm, deserted by her crew, and left to flounder and sink amid the waves of anarchy which will engulf her, it would be glory enough for him to go down with the wreck." This stand led **George Caleb Bingham** to write to **James Sidney Rollins,** "Guitar is the truest man you have among you, all honor to him."

In May 1862 Gov. **Hamilton Rowan Gamble** asked Guitar to form a regiment of volunteers, known as the Ninth Cavalry Missouri State Militia. In August Guitar received a promotion to brigadier general for victories over Confederate colonels J. A. Poindexter and John Porter. These victories earned the regiment the nickname of the "Bloody Ninth." In July 1863 Guitar took charge of the District of North Missouri, formed by the counties north of the Missouri River.

When Guitar resigned from the militia in 1864, he again devoted himself to law. North Todd Gentry described Guitar as "known far and wide as a lawyer who could speak, entertain and convince." His oratory was once described as having a "torrential quality." Legend holds that in 140 homicide cases, Guitar defended only one person who was put to death, and only five clients were sentenced to serve time. "His zeal, enthusiasm and aggressiveness made him dreaded by some and respected by all," Gentry said. Guitar served as president of the Boone County

Bar Association from 1860 to 1878, as the county attorney from 1852 to 1863, and also as the city attorney. He strongly supported education, serving as a curator of the university and as president of the Columbia Board of Education.

On December 26, 1865, Guitar married Kate Leonard, the youngest daughter of Judge **Abiel Leonard.** They moved into Guitar's home, called Eagle's Nest, and raised seven children.

In 1882, at the age of fifty-seven, Guitar retired from his law practice and devoted himself to business deals, which proved financially draining, and his farm, which boasted the first modern dairy herd. Politically, he participated in the state Republican Party.

The community still called on Guitar late in his life, once to keep the university in Columbia after the legislature threatened to move it following a fire, and another time to fight a legal battle for the Columbia waterworks. In 1907 he fought for the building of a new county courthouse and won.

Guitar died on March 13, 1908. In a tribute North Todd Gentry wrote, "As a lawyer, a political leader, a citizen, and a soldier in two wars, he had no superiors; and few, if any, equals."

LISA HEFFERNAN WEIL

Gentry, North Todd. *The Bench and Bar of Boone County, Missouri.* Columbia, Mo.: n.p., 1916.

———. "General Odon Guitar." *Missouri Historical Review* 22 (1928): 419–45.

Guitar, Nancy. "A Biographical Portrait of Odon Guitar: Man of Honor in Turbulent Times." Master's thesis, University of Missouri–Columbia, 1976.

Guitar, Odon. Collection. Western Historical Manuscripts Collection, Columbia.

Zimmermann, Mark J. "Odon Guitar: Travails of a Nineteenth-Century Missouri Conservative." Master's thesis, University of Missouri–Columbia, 1972.

GUNDLACH, JOHN H. (1861–1926)

John H. Gundlach effectively blended the potentially disharmonious careers of businessman, politician, and civic reformer. He stands as a major practitioner of early-twentieth-century progressivism in St. Louis, Missouri.

Born on October 6, 1861, John was the son of Peter and Elizabeth Reiff Gundlach. His father had emigrated from Germany in order to manufacture shoes.

Gundlach graduated from high school in 1877 and attended Grier's Commercial College. He first worked for Boehl and Koenig Photography and then another business establishment before going to Chicago in 1882. In 1883 he returned to St. Louis to work as a bookkeeper. In 1884 he married St.

Louisan Emma D. Dreyer. They had two daughters, Alice and Ruth.

In 1885 Gundlach started working for the Wabash Railroad, rising to the position of chief clerk. However, in 1892, at the age of thirty-one, he started his own realty company, the John H. Gundlach Company, and specialized in north–St. Louis residential property.

In 1901 Gundlach was elected to the St. Louis City Council as a Republican. Reelected several times, he served as the president of that body between 1909 and 1913. In the American urban experience, reformers have often worked from outside formal political office, at least initially. In contrast Gundlach became a major reform progressive while serving in elective office.

When the Civic League was founded in 1902, the Progressive movement started in St. Louis. Made up mostly of successful business- and professional men, the league had the financial backing of the Business Men's League. The Civic League's goals centered on promoting municipal charter reform and public improvements. Gundlach, desirous of creating a better physical and governmental St. Louis, joined the league. Both he and the league in general became increasingly supportive of comprehensive city planning.

Landscape architect **George Kessler,** who had come to St. Louis to help build the 1904 Louisiana Purchase Exposition, gained Gundlach's and the Civic League's attention, for he had created the highly praised park and boulevard system of Kansas City, Missouri. It was hoped that he could bring that kind of planned integrative beauty to St. Louis. Reflecting the ideas of Kessler, the league published the *City Plan for St. Louis* in 1907. In 1908 the league created a charter-reform committee.

In 1908 Gundlach publicly expressed his philosophy and his specific hopes regarding the improvement of St. Louis. He exemplified both structural and social justice progressivism. He both supported the comprehensive, integrated boulevard system so cherished by Kessler and advanced a riverfront project and a central trafficway in front of Union Station. Gundlach also advocated the creation of an official city plan that would enhance "rational" life. He spoke of the city's obligation to provide clean and sanitary habitations for all its citizens, which he thought could be accomplished through indirect means—through private investment in new housing.

In 1909 Gundlach continued his highly activistic political and civic presence as president of both the city council and the Civic League. In 1910 the City Plan Association was formed, but a bond issue that would have implemented some of the dreams of the City Beautiful advocates failed at the polls. In 1911 Gundlach guided a city-plan commission ordinance through the city council. Both he and Kessler became members of that commission.

In 1913 Gundlach tried another approach. He and others formed the St. Louis Pageant Drama Association, and he chaired the executive committee. The highly successful St. Louis Pageant and Masque followed in 1914. Gundlach hoped that such extravaganzas would increase citizens' sense of community and thus enhance the chances of revising the city charter and passing bond proposals for public improvements. The voters did create a new city charter in 1914, but no physical improvements occurred.

Gundlach lived a rich and varied life. As of 1921 he belonged to the St. Louis YMCA, the St. Louis Academy of Science, the Horticultural Society, the Mercantile Library, and the St. Louis Riding Club. He also continued to be a civic reformer. He saw his civic dreams partially fulfilled in 1923 when the voters approved an $87 million bond package that included construction of the central trafficway. That same year he chaired the chamber of commerce's Committee on Smoke Abatement, and the city passed an ordinance in 1924.

Gundlach died on April 8, 1926, at the age of sixty-four. A civic reformer to the end, he worked earlier that year to get the smoke-abatement ordinance implemented.

DONALD B. OSTER

Gundlach, John H. Collection. 1888–1926. Missouri Historical Society, St. Louis.

Muraskin, Jack. "Municipal Reform in Two Missouri Cities." *Missouri Historical Society Bulletin* 25 (April 1969): 213–28.

Oglesby, Richard E. "Smoke Gets in Your Eyes." *Missouri Historical Society Bulletin* 26 (April 1970): 180–99.

Oster, Donald B. "Community Image in the History of St. Louis and Kansas City." Ph.D. diss., University of Missouri–Columbia, 1969.

———. "Nights of Fantasy: The St. Louis Pageant and Masque of 1914." *Missouri Historical Society Bulletin* 31 (April 1975): 175–205.

Rafferty, Edward C. "Orderly City, Orderly Lives: The City Beautiful Movement in St. Louis." *Gateway Heritage* 11 (spring 1991): 40–62.

GUNN, RAYMOND (1904–1931)

Raymond Gunn, a twenty-seven-year-old black ex-convict, was burned to death by a lynch mob in 1931 near Maryville, a thriving farming and college town of fifty-two hundred in northwest Missouri, one of at least twenty-two men (seventeen of whom were African Americans) who have been lynched in the state since the turn of the twentieth century. The calculated barbarity with which the mob murdered Gunn made the incident one of the most sensational and well-publicized lynchings of the thirties.

Raymond Gunn was born in Maryville on January 10, 1904, the son of a black working-class couple later described as "hard-working and law-abiding" and "highly respected in the community." After completing the seventh grade, Gunn worked as a cook and houseman for various white businesses in the city until 1925 when he was convicted of assault with intent to rape a white female student from the Northwest Missouri State Teachers College (now Northwest Missouri State University) and sentenced to four years in the state penitentiary at Jefferson City. A model prisoner, he gained an early release from prison in 1928. Some Maryville residents believed that Gunn harbored "a grudge against college girls," and he fell under suspicion for two similar assault cases against white coeds in the year following his release from prison. Neither case went to trial, however.

In 1929 Gunn married a local woman, and the couple moved to Omaha, Nebraska, where a short time later Gunn's wife died of pneumonia. Sensational rumors circulated in Maryville that Gunn had not only beaten her to death but also committed a series of infamous ax murders in Omaha. Around 1930 Gunn returned to Maryville and began earning a living as a commercial hunter and trapper, but his prison record and long-standing bad reputation, fueled by contemporary racist stereotypes of black criminality, made him a marked man in Maryville.

On December 18, 1930, police arrested Gunn for the murder of Velma Colter, a twenty-one-year-old schoolteacher at Garret School and the daughter of a Nodaway County farm couple. Two days earlier a farmer had discovered her partially nude body, her skull fractured in several places, in a one-room schoolhouse three miles southwest of Maryville. The evidence compiled against Gunn appeared damning. After being interrogated by the county prosecuting attorney and three detectives, Gunn made a full confession to beating the teacher to death with a club that he carried to kill small game. He told investigators that he had intended to rape Colter but had become frightened and fled before he could commit the act.

After Gunn's confession Nodaway County sheriff Harve England and two deputies transported the prisoner to St. Joseph for his protection. Two days later a mob of 150 Nodaway County residents came to lynch Gunn, but the Buchanan County sheriff, with the aid of local National Guardsmen, repelled the mob. That night authorities moved Gunn to Kansas City for safekeeping. Two weeks later, on his twenty-seventh birthday, Gunn returned to Maryville in the custody of sheriff's deputies to await arraignment for Colter's murder on the opening day of circuit court,

Monday, January 12. That same day the editor of the *Maryville Daily Forum* advised against extralegal violence in an editorial titled "Time for Cool Heads."

A crowd began gathering in downtown Maryville around four on the cold, wintery morning of January 12. A few hours later hundreds of men milled about the courthouse square, joined by dozens of newspaper reporters and photographers sent to cover the expected lynching. Around nine a mob composed of a dozen unmasked men overpowered Sheriff England and two deputies and seized Gunn from an automobile while he was being transported to the courthouse for his preliminary trial. The only defense the sheriff reportedly offered consisted of an order to the mob to "Stand back." Sheriff England refused to request the assistance of a National Guard unit, which was mobilized and waiting for his call in the Maryville armory one block away from the courthouse.

The mob led Gunn to the Garret School where twelve ringleaders extracted a signed confession from a weary Gunn, his face lacerated and bloodied from abuses suffered during the three-mile death march. Two men then climbed to the roof of the schoolhouse on a makeshift ladder and forced Gunn to follow them. They ordered Gunn to lie prone across the ridge of the roof, chained his legs and arms to the ridgepole, and poured gasoline over his outstretched body. Other men on the ground doused the inside walls and floor of the school. Then one of the leaders lit a torch and tossed it inside the structure, and in a flash the interior of the school was ablaze. Seconds later the roof burst into flames. Gunn shrieked and writhed in agony as his trousers burned away from his body. For five minutes an inferno of flames and billowing smoke raged and then died down a little after the gasoline was burned out, providing a better view of the grisly spectacle to the thousands of spectators amassed around the schoolhouse. A reporter from the *St. Joseph Gazette* later gave this graphic eyewitness account of Gunn's final moments: "He twisted and revealed a huge blister ballooning on his left upper arm. Pieces of his skin blew away to the wind as the blistering heat became more intense and soon his torso was splotched with white patches of exposed flesh. His hair burned like a torch for a moment[;] then his head sagged. His body writhed. It took on the appearance of a mummy." Eleven minutes after the fire reached him, Gunn was dead.

A crowd of three thousand watched Gunn burn to death, including nearly one thousand women and hundreds of children. A Maryville policeman directed traffic at the scene, and it reportedly took three hours for the jammed cars to clear the country road. Many of the spectators had come from ten, fifteen, and forty miles away to witness the lynching. Among the cars were dozens of license plates from Iowa, Kansas, Nebraska, and even one from Louisiana. All afternoon crowds poked about the smoldering ashes for teeth and bone fragments. Gunn's charred remains were carried away in the pockets of souvenir hunters.

Gunn's lynching prompted investigations and calls for action from state officials. Gov. **Henry Stewart Caulfield** ordered the state attorney and the adjutant general to investigate the incident. In the General Assembly, Representative Gil P. Bourk, a Kansas City Democrat, introduced a house resolution condemning the lynching and calling for an investigation.

Orland Kay Armstrong, a professor at Drury College in Springfield, Missouri, also conducted a carefully researched investigation into the lynching for the Commission on Interracial Cooperation, an antilynching organization headed by Will Alexander. Armstrong's findings provided the basis for one chapter in sociologist Arthur F. Raper's classic study, *The Tragedy of Lynching,* published in 1933. The region's major newspapers, including the *Kansas City Star,* the *Kansas City Times,* and the *St. Joseph News-Press,* strongly condemned the lynching, as did other national dailies. The *Atlanta Constitution,* for example, published an editorial cartoon featuring a raised arm holding a lighted torch, labeled "Maryville Lyncher," and the smoldering remains of a schoolhouse on the distant horizon. It was captioned "The Torch of Civilization in Missouri."

Black Missourians responded with predictable outrage to the Gunn lynching. In St. Joseph, for example, where Gunn family members moved in mid-January, a group of ministers and laymen met to denounce local and state officials for "idly standing by" while Gunn was lynched. The committee drafted an angry letter to Governor Caulfield that not only demanded that "the sheriff and his deputies be discharged and tried for criminal neglect" but also "that Nodaway County be forced to pay an exceedingly large damage to relatives of Gunn." No one was ever charged with the Gunn lynching, despite the fact that Sheriff England told reporters that if asked by a grand jury he "could give names" of the participants in the lynching. Newspaper accounts of the incident agreed that all the mob's leaders, except for one, were local men.

On the day following Gunn's murder, the *Kansas City Times* reported that "news of the lynching caused twenty-two of the about 100 Negroes living in Maryville to leave town." Over the next several days more black residents followed, including the Gunn family, who had lived in Maryville for four generations. After arsonists torched their home, the Gunns moved fifty miles south to St. Joseph. According to one investigator, the Maryville mayor and a committee of businessmen presented the pastor of a local black church with "a list of about 10 Negroes that were branded as undesirable, and [he] was requested to ask these to leave town and not return." White business owners also received threatening letters, warning them to fire their black employees.

All this pressure on African Americans had the desired effect. The 1930 census reveals that there were eighty-four blacks living in Maryville in that year; however, by 1940, despite substantial decennial growth in the white population, the city's black population had declined to thirty-one. Writing in 1986 local historian Martha L. Cooper summarized the far-reaching effects of the 1931 lynching: "Raymond Gunn died without a trial to determine his guilt or innocence. A way of life for the black population of Maryville died with him."

PATRICK J. HUBER AND GARY R. KREMER

Armstrong, Orland K. Papers. Western Historical Manuscripts Collection, Columbia.

Cooper, Martha L. *Life, Liberty, and the Pursuit of Happiness: Nodaway County, Missouri, a Black History, 1840–1940.* Maryville, Mo.: n.p., 1986.

Greene, Lorenzo J., Gary R. Kremer, and Antonio F. Holland. *Missouri's Black Heritage, Revised Edition.* Columbia: University of Missouri Press, 1993.

National Association for the Advancement of Colored People. Papers. Administrative Files. Library of Congress, Washington, D.C.

Raper, Arthur F. *The Tragedy of Lynching.* Chapel Hill: University of North Carolina Press, 1933.

Woods, Howard B. "Thirty-one Lynching Spectre Still in Mo. Town." *St. Louis Argus* (October 10, 1958): 1.

H

HADLEY, HERBERT SPENCER (1872–1927)

Born on February 20, 1872, in Olathe, Kansas, Herbert Spencer Hadley was the son of John Milton and Harriet Beach Hadley. His father served as a major in the Ninth Kansas Cavalry during the Civil War, and then worked as sheriff of Johnson County and clerk of the district court before serving one term (from 1877 to 1879) as a Kansas state senator. Later in life he operated a milling business in De Soto, Kansas.

Herbert Hadley gained his education in the public schools of Olathe, at the University of Kansas (A.B., 1892), and at Northwestern University Law School (LL.B., 1894). While at Northwestern, Hadley honed his speaking skills as a collegiate debater and helped establish the *Northwestern Law Review*. He entered private legal practice in Kansas City, Missouri, immediately after graduating from law school.

Continuing his father's interest in politics, Hadley gained public office in 1898 as assistant city counselor for Kansas City. The position involved trial work for the city. He joined the Missouri Republican Club of Kansas City and soon became its vice president. With his experience as a trial lawyer and his connections in the Republican Club, Hadley successfully ran for the office of prosecuting attorney of Jackson County in 1900. He served in the position for two years and established a reputation as a vigorous prosecutor. He won special acclaim for his investigation of jury tampering in the civil court system and for a successful campaign to suppress public gambling. Defeated for reelection in 1902, Hadley accepted a position as legal counsel for the Metropolitan Street Railway of Kansas City. He reversed his political fortunes in 1904, taking advantage of the Roosevelt Republican landslide in Missouri to win election for a four-year term as state attorney general.

Hadley proved just as vigorous in his new state office as he had been as prosecuting attorney, focusing his attention on possible violations of both state and federal laws regulating corporations. During his term as attorney general, Hadley either began or continued suits against the Standard Oil Corporation, the International Harvester Corporation, and the Association of Lumber Manufacturers as well as numerous insurance and meat-packing companies for violations of antitrust statutes.

Hadley's prosecution of Standard Oil for violation of Missouri's antitrust law proved an especially significant legal victory. After uncovering evidence that the Standard Oil Corporation of New Jersey, operating through three subsidiaries, had arbitrarily divided Missouri into trading zones for anticompetitive purposes, Hadley prosecuted the three companies involved in quo warranto proceedings begun on March 29, 1905. He eventually took the case to five different states and called 119 witnesses, including the highest officials in the Standard Oil Corporation. The supreme court of Missouri finally ruled in favor of Hadley on December 23, 1908. The court required the three corporations to forfeit their right to conduct business in Missouri and levied a fine of fifty thousand dollars on each. Hadley's investigation established a body of evidence that was later used in similar prosecutions against Standard Oil in other states as well as in a federal suit for violation of the Sherman Anti-Trust Act. The case brought national acclaim to Hadley, established him as a progressive reformer, and marked him for future political prominence in Missouri.

As attorney general Hadley also conducted successful legal contests against railroad companies for violations of Missouri's maximum freight rate and passenger fare laws. Information gained in these cases concerning the cost and value of railroad properties in the state was later used by the state board of equalization to increase the tax assessments of those companies. Hadley also assisted Gov. **Joseph W. Folk** in his crusade to enforce provocative Sunday-closing laws in St. Louis and in ousting the Delmar Jockey Club at the St. Louis County Racetrack. Hadley's reform record, the publicity gained from the Standard Oil case, and his position as the highest ranking elected Republican official in the state helped gain him election as governor of Missouri in 1908, after defeating Democrat William Cowherd by 15,879 votes.

Voters identified Hadley with progressive ideals and a reform agenda, but the Democratic Party's control of the senate in 1909 to 1910 and the house in 1911 to 1912 precluded enactment of all that the new governor envisioned. The Forty-fifth General Assembly declined to follow his suggestions for ways to enhance state revenues, for granting home rule to larger cities, for creating a public service commission, and for establishing a state immigration commission. Nonetheless, Hadley's first administration was not without its accomplishments. The legislature expanded the duties of the state board of health, created the office of state food and drug commissioner, regulated the hours of women workers, expanded safety inspection of mines, and established a board of nurse examiners. His administration also made headway in the area of conservation. A fish and game commission was created and a game protection board established. The legislature also approved legislation for a Missouri waterways commission and appropriated fifty thousand dollars to study waterways, land drainage, and reclamation.

Partisan divisions plagued Hadley's last two years in office as well. One success, however, was in the area of penal reform, a cause Governor Hadley enthusiastically promoted. The legislature enacted a new penal code law that included a supervised prisoner-release program aimed at prisoner rehabilitation and less-crowded prisons. Steps were also taken to abolish the convict labor system for state prisoners. A special commission of the Missouri Supreme Court, the creation of which had been strongly endorsed by Hadley, successfully recommended the establishment of special juvenile courts in counties with populations greater than fifty thousand. In the larger view, the Hadley administration not only promoted progressive legislation that improved public health and safety but also expanded the bureaucratic and regulatory nature of progressive reform in general.

Identified with the Theodore Roosevelt wing of the national Republican Party, Hadley served as floor leader of the Roosevelt forces at the Republican National Convention in 1912. After William Howard Taft won the nomination, Hadley declined to follow Roosevelt into the new Progressive Party and remained a loyal Republican.

After leaving the governor's office in 1913, Hadley joined a Kansas City law firm. He also served as special counsel to the Interstate Commerce Commission, from 1913 to 1916. In 1917 he moved to Colorado for health reasons, and assumed a teaching position in the law school at the University of Colorado. He also acted as special counsel for the Colorado state railway commission, from 1919–1921. Hadley returned to Missouri in 1923 to become chancellor of Washington University in St. Louis.

Hadley's most important work in his later years was as an advocate of legal reform. A member of both the council on legal education of the American Bar Association and the council of the American Law Institute, Hadley helped the latter organization write a model code of criminal procedure. He was also among a prestigious group of legal scholars selected to submit articles to *The New Federalist*. The volume, published by the American Bar Association, was designed to update the original *Federalist Papers* of Alexander Hamilton, James Madison, and John Jay. Hadley also served as chairman of the committee on criminal procedures of the National Crime Commission, and was one of the authors of the *Missouri Crime Survey* (1926). Recommendations that came out of these studies led to the establishment of an intermediate reformatory and the creation of a parole board that came to be important elements in Missouri's penal reform efforts.

Hadley received honorary degrees from Northwestern University (1909), the University of Missouri (1910), and Harvard University (1925). He was a leading organizer of the Knife and Fork Club of Kansas City, the Young Republican Association of Missouri, and the National Association of Attorneys-General.

Hadley married Agnes Lee on October 8, 1901. The couple had three children. Continually hampered by pulmonary disorders and a weak heart, Hadley died from complications in St. Louis on December 1, 1927.

STEVEN L. PIOTT

Burckel, Nicholas Clare. "Progressive Governors in the Border States: Reform Governors of Missouri, Kentucky, West Virginia, and Maryland, 1900–1918." Ph.D. diss., University of Wisconsin, 1971.

Hahn, Harlan. "The Republican Party Convention of 1912 and the Role of Herbert S. Hadley in National Politics." *Missouri Historical Review* 59 (July 1965): 407–23.

Miller, William T. "The Progressive Movement in Missouri." *Missouri Historical Review* 22 (July 1928): 456–501.

Piott, Steven L. *Holy Joe: Joseph W. Folk and the Missouri Idea.* Columbia: University of Missouri Press, 1997.

Thelen, David. *Paths of Resistance: Tradition and Dignity in Industrializing Missouri.* New York: Oxford University Press, 1986.

Worner, Lloyd Edson. "The Public Career of Herbert Spencer Hadley." Ph.D. diss., University of Missouri, 1946.

HAFEY, CHARLES JAMES "CHICK" (1903–1973)

Considered by contemporaries of the hard-hitting 1920s as a top right-handed hitter, "Chick" Hafey put fear into pitchers and third basemen because of his line-drive hitting. The tall, rangy outfielder achieved all-star status despite a career jeopardized by ill health and poor eyesight.

A native of Berkeley, California, Hafey was born on February 12, 1903, to Charles and Mary Hafey.

He starred for St. Mary's High School as a football halfback and a baseball pitcher. Following graduation and after pitching in a semiprofessional league, he attended a Cardinals tryout camp in 1923. Vice president and manager **Wesley Branch Rickey,** who eagerly sought young players for his fledgling farm system, signed Hafey. Although a wild pitcher, Hafey impressed Rickey enough as a hitter that Rickey commented, "You're an outfielder now."

Following two impressive seasons in the minor leagues, the six-foot, 185-pound Hafey attracted the attention of other major league teams. One team offered thirty-five thousand dollars for the twenty-one-year-old outfielder, but the Cardinals quickly matched it and promoted Hafey to the major leagues in 1924 as one of the first products of Rickey's famed farm system.

Early in the 1925 season **Rogers Hornsby,** recently appointed player-manager, installed Hafey as the regular left fielder. The rifle-armed rookie produced a solid year for the fourth-place Cardinals, hitting .302 and contributing fifty-seven RBIs.

Hafey started only fifty-four games for the 1926 world champion Cardinals because of serious sinus problems. He underwent several operations over the years, but his condition persisted. Getting hit in the head with pitches had also sidelined him. After studying Hafey's slow reaction to inside pitches, the team doctor theorized that Chick had impaired vision. After holding a card over each eye Hafey found his left eye blurred. He made no attempt to correct his vision until 1929 when he became the first major league outfielder to wear glasses full-time. That decision led to the greatest season of his career, and in 1931 he became the first batting champion to use spectacles. General manager Rickey believed, "If Chick Hafey had been blessed with normal eyesight and good health, he might have been the greatest righthanded hitter the game has ever known."

In 1927 Hafey began five years as a premier hitter for the Cardinals. He ripped line drives down the third-base line so frequently he compiled a .317 lifetime batting average and batted .329 or better in six consecutive years. Following the 1927 season Rickey shrewdly signed the blossoming Hafey to a three-year contract for an average of eight thousand dollars per year.

Shy and soft-spoken, Hafey played a crucial role for the 1928 pennant winners. He started the most games in his career (133) and was a league leader in slugging average (.604). However, he had an unproductive World Series, collecting only three singles against the victorious New York Yankees. Playing in four World Series, in which he hit only .205, Hafey attributed his postseason shortcomings to the cool autumn air, which adversely affected his sinuses and produced headaches.

Hafey became the Cardinals' strongest hitter during the 1929 and 1930 seasons, leading the team in home runs both years. Following the 1930 season he expected a pay increase and stubbornly held out for $15,000. He had to settle for $12,500 and a fine of $2,100 for reporting ten days late to spring training. He refused to allow this dispute to affect his play as he narrowly beat teammate **James LeRoy Bottomley** and New York Giants–great Bill Terry to win the 1931 batting title, while the Cardinals captured the World Series.

Hafey demanded $15,000 for the 1932 season, and Rickey responded by trading the star to Cincinnati for two players and $50,000. Hafey, a fan favorite, considered the trade the saddest day of his career, but he did receive his long-sought $15,000. To characterize Hafey's play and personality, Rickey said: "Everything he hit was a line drive and everything he threw was a line drive. And every time he argued with you, it was on the line. He knew exactly what he wanted."

Although Hafey's health problems persisted in Cincinnati, his selection to the first National League All-Star team in 1933 proved he still had the respect of his peers. Throughout his career he maintained a prankster's sense of humor. He once tied the hands and feet of teammate Ernie Lombardi to the bedposts while he slept and yelled, "Fire, Lom! Fire!"

Hafey retired early in the 1935 season but made a one-season comeback in 1937 to compile a career .317 average with 341 doubles, 164 home runs, and 833 RBIs. He retired for good with his wife, Bernice, to their five-hundred-acre sheep and cattle ranch near Calistoga, California, where he achieved the financial independence baseball could not give him.

For five years (1927–1931) Hafey proved he was one of the finest outfielders ever to play the game. Due to his short career he did not receive immediate Hall of Fame consideration. In 1971 the Veterans Committee recognized Hafey's contributions and immortalized him with other baseball greats. Emphysema and a stroke caused Hafey's death on July 2, 1973.

MICHAEL R. SNODGRASS

Borst, William A. *Biographical Dictionary of American Sport: Baseball.* Ed. David L. Porter. Westport, Conn.: Greenwood Press, 1987.

James, Bill. *Historical Baseball Abstract.* New York: Villard Books, 1988.

Rains, Rob. *The St. Louis Cardinals: The 100th Anniversary History.* New York: St. Martin's, 1992.

St. Louis Globe-Democrat, July 6, 1973.

St. Louis Post-Dispatch, July 8, 1973.

HALL, JOYCE C. (1891–1982)

Joyce C. Hall organized a company known as Hall Brothers (later restyled as Hallmark Cards, Inc.) in Kansas City, Missouri, in 1912. His older brother Rollie was the other brother in the business title.

Born on August 29, 1891, in David City, Nebraska, Joyce Hall received his middle name of "Clyde" from Rollie some time in early childhood. Selling products became Hall's early vocation. At age nine he began to sell cosmetics, soaps, and lemon extract door-to-door for the California Perfume Company (which later became part of Avon). In 1902 his older brothers, William and Rollie, bought a bookstore in Norfolk, Nebraska, some sixty miles away. Moving with the rest of his family to Norfolk, Joyce sold books and postcards at the store before and after school.

At age sixteen Hall learned of the potential for wholesaling postcards from traveling salesmen. Investing $180 saved from his bookstore job, and convincing his brothers to make a similar investment, young Hall organized what became the Norfolk Post Card Company. Convinced that he needed a central location to sell cards more successfully, Hall moved to Kansas City, Missouri, in 1910. He convinced his mother, Rollie, and sister Marie to join him in Kansas City the following year. By 1912 they were marketing greeting cards and postcards with Kansas City scenes under the "Hall Brothers" logo.

The company added Valentine cards in 1913. Before World War I they opened retail shops in Kansas City and Chicago. By the 1920s the company's logo, a torch and shield, found its way onto a wide variety of greeting cards and postcards. The company moved from merchandising to printing, though Hall considered himself a salesman first throughout his life.

Hall married Elizabeth Ann Dilday in 1921. Three children were born over the next ten years: Elizabeth Ann, Barbara Louise, and Donald Joyce. Hall established the family home on acreage purchased along Indian Creek, south of Kansas City.

With the coming of the depression, Hall Brothers suffered sharp declines in sales as families in the Midwest slowed in their purchases of the company's products. Faced with the necessity of reducing expenses, Hall twice asked employees to vote on whether to accept pay cuts for all or layoffs for some. The employees agreed to 10 percent pay cuts each time; by the end of the 1930s Hall Brothers was back to full pay.

During the 1950s Hall developed a close friendship with President Dwight D. Eisenhower. Together with other influential businessmen from across the nation, Hall chaired an effort to establish the People-to-People program. The goal was to foster personal contact among ordinary citizens around the world.

In 1971 Hall received the Eisenhower Medal for his work with this organization.

Hall's business prowess did not go unrecognized. In 1974 the Association of Greeting Card Publishers recognized him for his contributions to the industry. The following year the Kansas City Press Club honored him as "Kansas Citian of the Year." In 1977 *Fortune Magazine* elected him to their hall of fame for business leadership.

Possibly one of Hall's greatest contributions to Kansas City and the region came in 1968 when he announced the Crown Center redevelopment plan. While the company operated branch manufacturing and shipping facilities in outlying towns, Hallmark Cards had always maintained its creative center and main printing facility near downtown Kansas City. The Crown Center plan demonstrated that Hall's choice was permanent. Additionally, the company indicated that it would construct hotels, office buildings, retail sales space, and apartment and condominium sites to help anchor economic and social life in the center of Kansas City.

One national contribution of the company over the decades has been the sponsorship of the Hallmark Hall of Fame, featuring the highest quality television dramas. Through this medium the company's slogan, "When You Care Enough to Send the Very Best," has gained national and international attention. In recognition of Hall's longtime advocacy (and financial support) for quality television, the National Academy of Television Arts and Sciences awarded its first Emmy given to a sponsor to Joyce Hall in 1961.

Joyce C. Hall died in Kansas City on October 29, 1982, at age ninety-one.

WILLIAM S. WORLEY

Fowler, Dick. "Joyce C. Hall." In *Leaders in Our Town*. Kansas City: Burd and Fletcher, 1952.

Hall, Joyce C., and Curtiss Anderson. *When You Care Enough*. Kansas City: Hallmark, 1979.

Jones, Jack M. "O.K., J. C.: A Salute to Joyce C. Hall, Founder of Hallmark Cards." *Missouri Business* 26:9 (October–November 1976): 2–11.

HALL, URIEL SEBREE (1852–1932)

Born on a farm in Randolph County, Missouri, on April 12, 1852, Uriel Sebree Hall was the son of William Augustus Hall, a circuit court judge, and Octavia Sebree Hall. He earned a bachelor of arts degree from Mount Pleasant College in Huntsville in 1873. He passed the Missouri bar in 1879 and entered into practice with his father and Thomas B. Reed in Moberly. In 1880 he married Maggie E. Hollins, and the couple had two daughters, Margaret and Octavia. Hall served as Moberly's city attorney from 1880 to 1882 and as superintendent of schools, holding the latter position from 1882 to 1888. He left education in 1889 to devote himself to the growing agricultural reform movement in Missouri.

Hall earned a reputation as a gifted speaker, attracting attention as a delegate to the state Democratic convention in 1880. Representatives from farmers' organizations selected him as state lecturer for the Missouri chapter of the Farmers' and Laborers' Union, also known as the Missouri Alliance, in 1889. Lecturers were responsible for directing the educational programs of the alliance and creating a united constituency among farmers. As an educator, lawyer, and superb orator, Hall excelled at his post. Membership in the organization doubled during his year as lecturer. The following year the organization elected Hall its president.

During Hall's presidency membership in the union peaked, and Missouri farmers were successful in pressing their demands that could be achieved through state action. Among these were tighter restrictions on foreign corporations operating in Missouri, a reduction in interest rates on contracts, and a secret ballot for municipal elections. Hall, a staunch Democrat, advocated working within the existing political structure for reform. He ardently opposed the formation of a third party. All state chapters of the Missouri Alliance remained officially nonpartisan during his presidency.

In two important areas Hall differed greatly from fellow alliance members. He opposed the subtreasury plan of national leader C. W. Macune and the free coinage of silver, fearing their inflationary effects upon the national economy. Many of the organization's members embraced these measures as solutions to their troubles. In December 1890 Hall headed the Missouri delegation to the national convention of the Farmers' Alliance at Ocala, Florida, where he worked to have the subtreasury plank removed from the national platform. By 1891 disaffection increased with Hall's leadership in the Missouri Alliance. Many agitated for a third party, and Hall came under increasing attack for his conservative policies. On August 17, 1891, Leverett Leonard of Saline County defeated Hall for president of the alliance.

Hall remained dedicated to the same principles when he embarked upon a career in national politics the following year. As a Democratic representative from Missouri's Second District to the Fifty-third and Fifty-fourth Congresses (1893–1897), Hall continued to work for the interests of small producers and the agricultural community. He actively participated in debates about regulation of railroad rates, agricultural reform legislation, tax regulation, and, once again, the silver issue. The latter brought about the end of Hall's political career. In 1895 he got the best of **Richard Parks Bland** ("Silver Dick") of Lebanon in a debate on the silver issue in Huntsville. Inspired

by this success he challenged the opposition to bring in an outsider to debate the silver issue with him. William Jennings Bryan, the best-known prosilver advocate of the era, accepted the challenge and won the debate. Following his loss to Bryan, Hall chose not to seek reelection to Congress in 1896.

Hall returned to education, founding Prairie Hill Academy in 1897 and serving as its president until accepting the presidency of Pritchett College in Glasgow, in 1904. Hall remained at Pritchett until 1917 when low attendance led the board of trustees to ask for his resignation.

Hall next opened the U.S. Hall West Point and Annapolis Coaching School. Beginning in 1902 he operated the school from his farm, but moved it to Columbia in 1917 at the request of the Commercial Club of Columbia. It was the only such school west of the Allegheny Mountains, developing a national reputation for preparing young men for the entrance examinations at the nation's military academies. Hall retired in 1932 when operations were turned over to his daughter Octavia. Finally, Hall opened Hall Theater in Columbia in 1932, running it until his death on December 31, 1932.

CATHERINE L. MARCRUM-PHELPS

Clevenger, Homer. "The Farmers' Alliance in Missouri." *Missouri Historical Review* 39:1 (October 1944): 24–44.

Conard, Howard L., ed. *Encyclopedia of the History of Missouri.* New York: Southern History, 1901.

History of Randolph and Macon Counties, Missouri. St. Louis: National Historical Company, 1884.

"Pritchett College Board of Trustees Proceedings, 1896–1926." Vol. 2. Western Historical Manuscripts Collection, Columbia.

University of Missouri President's Office Papers. Folder 1958, Collection 2582. Western Historical Manuscripts Collection, Columbia.

HALL, WILLARD PREBLE (1820–1882)

Willard Preble Hall, Missouri's Unionist governor in 1864–1865, was born at Harper's Ferry, Virginia, on May 9, 1820. Upon graduation from Yale College in 1839, he gained admission to the Missouri bar and joined his brother, Judge William A. Hall, in the practice of law in Buchanan County.

In 1844 Hall traveled to Washington, D.C., as a presidential elector for Democrat James K. Polk, and by 1846 the people of northwest Missouri elected Hall to the United States House of Representatives. His quick rise to prominence is a clear illustration of the confidence and esteem the people of the region developed for him.

Hall learned of his election while serving in the First Missouri Volunteers commanded by Col. **Alexander W. Doniphan** during the war with Mexico. At the time, Hall was engaged in developing a code of laws by which the conquered territory of New Mexico would be governed. This code, nicknamed the "Kearny Code" after Gen. **Stephen Watts Kearny,** the leader of the American forces, remained the fundamental law of the territory for forty-five years. Doniphan explained why he chose Hall to draft the code by saying, "System and order and logical arrangement were natural for him."

After taking his seat in Congress in 1847, Hall was reelected to two more terms before declining further election. In Congress he vigorously advocated the expansion of U.S. territory and the passage of acts aiding the improvement of railroads and schools in Missouri. He introduced a bill into the House in December 1851 to organize the Territory of Platte and open the region west of Missouri to settlement. The measure failed, but a reworked version served as the basis for Stephen Douglas's bill creating the Kansas and Nebraska Territories. Early in the development of this legislation, Hall was said to be "the only Missourian in the Congress who took an active interest" in its passage. Residents of Hall's congressional district strongly supported his efforts to authorize settlement in the adjacent territory because the anticipated growth and development promised to benefit northwest Missouri greatly.

At the end of his service in the House, Hall returned to his law practice in St. Joseph, turning his attention away from it briefly in an unsuccessful bid for a United States Senate seat in 1856.

Following the outbreak of the Civil War, Hall served as a pro-Union delegate in the 1861 state convention called to consider the issue of secession. After Gov. **Claiborne Fox Jackson** fled the capital and proclaimed his support for the Confederacy, the state convention declared the state's executive offices vacant, created a provisional government, and elected **Hamilton Rowan Gamble** governor and Hall lieutenant governor. Because Hall had supported the moderate Stephen Douglas during the 1850s and had been a conciliatory force in the state convention, he seemed a good choice. When Gamble died in 1864, Hall, who had been carrying out many of the governor's duties for some time because of Gamble's frail health, assumed the office. Through the turbulent times of the Civil War, Hall did a commendable job until **Thomas Clement Fletcher** replaced him in 1865.

After leaving office Hall returned to his law practice. For nearly twenty years he provided wise legal counsel and guidance in planning and carrying out public improvements in northwestern Missouri. His election as the first president of the Missouri Bar Association in 1880 demonstrated the respect he enjoyed among his peers.

In addition to his public service, Hall carried out agricultural experiments on his farm in St. Joseph until his death on November 2, 1882. Throughout his lengthy forty-three-year career, Hall held the esteem of his contemporaries and maintained an untarnished reputation.

JERRY E. WILSON

Bay, W. V. N. *Reminiscences of the Bench and Bar of Missouri.* St. Louis: F. H. Thomas, 1878.

Goodrich, James W. "In the Earnest Pursuit of Wealth: David Waldo in Missouri and the Southwest, 1820–1878." *Missouri Historical Review* 66 (January 1972): 155–84.

Stewart, A. J. D., ed. *The History of the Bench and Bar of Missouri.* St. Louis: Legal Publishing, 1898.

HAMMOND, SAMUEL (1757–1842)

Samuel Hammond's lengthy career as a soldier, businessman, and public official earned him mention in the histories of at least three states: Georgia, Missouri, and South Carolina. He was born in Richmond County, Virginia, on September 21, 1757. At the age of seventeen he volunteered for the militia when Virginia's governor, Lord Dunmore, sent troops to the Ohio country to quell an Indian uprising. During the Revolutionary War Hammond joined the army and participated in campaigns in Virginia, Pennsylvania, New Jersey, and South Carolina. By war's end he had attained the rank of lieutenant colonel.

Hammond married Rebecca Rae in 1783, and they settled in Savannah, Georgia, where he and his brother Abner established a mercantile business. During the 1790s the Hammonds involved themselves in French diplomat Edmond-Charles Genêt's schemes to launch a military assault against Spanish East Florida, but their association ended when Spanish authorities arrested Abner Hammond in St. Augustine. While in Georgia Samuel Hammond also commanded a militia campaign against the Creek Indians and served as state legislator, surveyor general, Indian commissioner, and U.S. congressman. Following the death of his first wife, Hammond married Eliza O'Keefe in 1802.

After Congress created a government for the newly acquired Louisiana Territory in 1804, President Thomas Jefferson appointed Colonel Hammond as the civil and military commandant of Upper Louisiana's St. Louis subdistrict. He moved to St. Louis with his family in the fall of 1804, bringing with him an impressive record in military service and politics that enabled him to become an important player in territorial affairs during the next two decades.

When Gen. **James Wilkinson** arrived in St. Louis the following year to take up his duties as territorial governor, the two men started on friendly terms, but they later found themselves on opposing sides in the battle over confirmation of old Spanish land grants. Wilkinson supported the claims of the powerful but declining French Creoles, while Hammond sided with the growing number of Americans who questioned the validity of their Spanish titles. As a result of this disagreement Hammond declined to sign a petition urging the United States Senate to confirm Wilkinson's gubernatorial appointment. Wilkinson retaliated by pressing for murder charges against Hammond's nephew, Samuel Hammond Jr., who had killed a drunken Kickapoo Indian in St. Louis. Wilkinson clearly sought to use the incident to embarrass the elder Hammond. When the coroner declared young Hammond had acted in self-defense, all charges were dropped, but by then Samuel Hammond was firmly in the anti-Wilkinson camp. Jefferson subsequently heeded the growing complaints about Governor Wilkinson's conduct and ordered his removal from the territory. Many of the governor's critics urged the president to name Hammond as Wilkinson's successor, but the post eventually went to **Meriwether Lewis.**

In 1812 Hammond was an unsuccessful candidate for territorial delegate to Congress, but the following year President James Madison appointed him to serve as a member of territorial Missouri's legislative council. The president later named him as U.S. receiver of public monies in St. Louis.

When Missourians prepared to enter the Union, the voters in Jefferson County selected Hammond to represent them in the 1820 Constitutional Convention. He was actively involved in land speculation, lead mining, and banking. In 1808 he and **Moses Austin** founded the city of Herculaneum to serve as a river depot for lead shipments from nearby Mine à Breton. He acquired substantial property holdings in St. Louis and was elected president of the Bank of St. Louis, which opened its doors in 1816. Poor management and the aftereffects of the panic of 1819 forced the bank's closure in 1820, and the failure of that venture left Hammond deeply in debt.

Hammond and his wife left Missouri in 1824 and returned to South Carolina where his creditors had him arrested for nonpayment of debts. Their action forced him to sell his remaining St. Louis properties to satisfy the claims against him. Although Colonel Hammond was in his late sixties when he moved to South Carolina, he sought a position in government service, undoubtedly for the financial remuneration that it would provide. In 1827 South

Carolina's governor named him surveyor general, and four years later the state's voters elected him secretary of state. After serving his term, Colonel Hammond retired to his farm near Hamburg, South Carolina, where he died on September 11, 1842.

MICHAEL BRENNAN

Drumm, Stella M. "Samuel Hammond." *Missouri Historical Society Collections* 4:4 (1923): 402–22.

HANDY, WILLIAM CHRISTOPHER (1873–1958)

Although William Christopher Handy spent relatively little of his long life in Missouri, his "St. Louis Blues" (1914) secured a place for him in the state's musical history. Handy's second important published composition, "St. Louis Blues" grew out of melodies he heard there and of memories of his troubles in the depression years of the 1890s. The songs "Memphis Blues" (1912) and "The Beale Street Blues" (1917) and others earned Handy the title of "Father of the Blues," and maintained for St. Louis its reputation as an important musical center in the early twentieth century.

W. C. Handy was born on November 16, 1873, in Florence, Alabama. His father, a Methodist Episcopal minister, had high hopes for the bright, talented child, but opposed his musical aspirations. As a youngster Handy studied the organ and voice, which his father believed would help him if he became a minister, but he also taught himself to play the cornet, which led to open conflict between father and son.

After completing high school, Handy taught school for a short time, and then worked at the Bessemer pipe works in Birmingham, Alabama. In the 1890s, when economic times became more difficult, Handy turned to music for a living. He joined a quartet and in 1892 headed for Chicago, hoping to perform at the World's Columbian Exposition, which, unbeknownst to Handy, had been postponed for a year. He traveled to St. Louis in search of work as an entertainer but found the city overrun with unemployed musicians who gathered in the district near the levee. He remained in the city, discouraged and impoverished but alert to the music and people around him. In spite of his trials in St. Louis, Handy clung to his dream of becoming a musician, and in the next several years he rose to national prominence.

After leaving St. Louis Handy traveled to Henderson, Kentucky, where he began playing with local black orchestras, and where he met his future wife. In 1896 he joined W. A. Mahara's Minstrels as a cornet player, and a year later he was promoted to bandleader. Except for a brief hiatus between 1900 and 1902 when he served as bandmaster at Alabama

A&M College, Handy remained with Mahara's Minstrels until 1903. Between 1903 and 1908 he organized and led military and dance bands in the area around Clarksdale, Mississippi, and then moved to Memphis, Tennessee.

While living in Memphis Handy began to develop a distinct variety of African American music that eventually became part of the blues craze of the 1920s. His initial publication, "Memphis Blues" in 1912, has been described by some scholars as more of a cakewalk than a blues composition. Handy himself wanted his second song, "St. Louis Blues," to "go beyond its predecessor and break new ground," but he also hoped to combine the appealing syncopation of ragtime with the melodic tradition of spirituals. The song became a popular hit almost immediately, and its composer, at age forty, entered a new phase of national celebrity.

Handy promoted the blues as well as other African American genres through a music company he established with Harry Pace in Memphis in 1908. Ten years later Pace and Handy Music Company moved its headquarters to New York, where it became a leading publisher of songs by black artists. When the company broke up two years later, Pace founded Pace Phonograph Company and Black Swan Records, and Handy formed Handy Music Company. In 1917 Handy and his orchestra began making recordings for Columbia Phonograph Company, becoming black pioneers in that field of entertainment.

In the 1920s and 1930s Handy became a prominent advocate for African American music. In 1928 he produced an all-black program at Carnegie Hall. He issued an anthology of blues in 1926, a compilation of black songwriters and composers in 1936, *Book of Negro Spirituals* in 1938, and *Unsung Americans Sung* in 1944. Handy also served as a musical consultant for World's Fairs in Chicago (1933), San Francisco (1939), and New York (1939). In 1940 NBC Radio featured an all-Handy program, marking the first time it had honored a black artist in that way.

In 1958 Nat "King" Cole portrayed Handy in a biographical film titled *St. Louis Blues,* but Handy himself never saw the finished product. On March 28, 1958, W. C. Handy died in New York. By the end of his life, he had become an honored entertainer and had succeeded in making African American folk music popular and accessible to a wider American audience.

SUSAN CURTIS

Biographical Dictionary of Afro-American and African Musicians. S.v. "Handy, William Christopher."

Ferris, William. *Blues from the Delta.* Garden City, N.Y.: Anchor Press, 1978.

Goldberg, Isaac. *Tin Pan Alley: A Chronicle of the American Popular Music Racket.* New York: John Day, 1930.

Handy, W. C. *Father of the Blues: An Autobiography.* New York: Macmillan, 1941.

Schuller, Gunther. *Early Jazz: Its Roots and Musical Development.* New York: Oxford University Press, 1968.

HANNEGAN, ROBERT EMMET (1903–1949)

Born on June 30, 1903, in St. Louis, Missouri, Robert Emmet Hannegan attended public schools and enrolled at St. Louis University where he excelled in all sports, organized a young Democrats club, and received his law degree in 1925. His early career focused on sports rather than the legal profession. He managed to earn a living coaching swimming and football at St. Louis University while also playing professional football and baseball.

Hannegan helped found the "Knights of the Cauliflower Ear," a business group based on the proposition that St. Louis would become the "sports mecca for America." His early fascination with sports almost derailed a political career that developed during the 1920s.

Hannegan's marriage to childhood sweetheart Irma Protzmann restored priority to the law since it brought the responsibility of caring for his wife and four small children. As an attorney he also returned to a promising future in the equally competitive world of St. Louis politics, dominated by the increasingly powerful Democratic machine developed by William Igoe and Bernard "Barney" Dickmann.

Hannegan learned considerable political technique from his father who, while serving as a captain in the St. Louis Police Department, also doubled as a ward heeler for the Igoe-Dickmann machine. In 1933 newly elected Mayor Dickmann persuaded the genial young Irishman to take charge of St. Louis's Twenty-first Ward. Within a year he was the Democratic Central Committee chairman presiding over the largest city in the state and coboss of what political analysts now called the Dickmann-Hannegan machine.

Hannegan's quick ascendancy within the St. Louis Democratic Party set a pattern he duplicated at all levels of political competition. It also coincided with the growing statewide hegemony wielded by **Thomas J. Pendergast**'s Kansas City Democratic machine. When a local revolt resulted in Hannegan's transfer to the state capital as the machine's legislative representative, he formed a friendly relationship with Gov. **Guy Brasfield Park** and other Pendergast representatives.

During Hannegan's Jefferson City experience, he met one of the machine's most effective rural politicians who understood and manipulated the tremendous advantages offered by a St. Louis–Kansas City alliance: **Harry S. Truman.** The "man from Independence" became Hannegan's closest Pendergast ally in a relationship that, starting with Truman's election to the United States Senate in 1934, lasted the duration of their careers.

Although the two machines competed for the spoils of office, Hannegan, unlike Dickmann, saw the need to cooperate and divide patronage rather than risk losing it. While he organized Dickmann's three successful mayoral campaigns, the St. Louis politico never forgot Truman's importance in maintaining his Kansas City connections. This alliance proved decisive in Truman's 1940 primary victory over Gov. **Lloyd Stark** (whom Mayor Dickmann supported) and federal prosecutor **Maurice M. Milligan,** who was still enjoying a hero's adulation from his successful prosecution of boss Tom Pendergast. A grateful Senator Truman gave Hannegan credit for the St. Louis votes that ensured his victory.

In 1942 Truman persuaded Sen. **Bennett Champ Clark** (whose own debt to the St. Louis machine was not inconsiderable) to support Hannegan for the position of collector of internal revenue for the Eastern District of Missouri. Even though the St. Louis press, remembering Hannegan's role in the attempted 1940 "Governorship Steal," unanimously opposed the appointment, President Franklin D. Roosevelt made it official.

Hannegan's tenure as eastern Missouri's IRS collector proved so successful that, within a year, Roosevelt promoted him to commissioner of internal revenue for the entire nation. Employing the formula that worked so well in St. Louis, Hannegan quickly gained access to the president's inner circle and especially the Democratic urban bosses who formed a crucial component in the New Deal coalition. In fact, Hannegan moved up so rapidly that, on January 22, 1944, Roosevelt nominated him to succeed Frank C. Walker as chairman of the Democratic National Committee.

Resigning his post as IRS commissioner, Hannegan now subtly exploited his natural affinities with the other bosses who desired a fourth term for Roosevelt. He also rebuilt the national Democratic organization, which had deteriorated following James A. Farley's departure as chairman. During the six months following his appointment, Hannegan traveled ten thousand miles, mending intraparty schisms, promoting the New Deal's domestic achievements, and, most important, stressing the importance of continuing Roosevelt's leadership during the emerging Allied victory over the Axis powers.

By the time the Democratic convention met in Chicago in July 1944, the key question did not involve Roosevelt's renomination (which was a fore-gone conclusion) but focused on his vice presidential choice. Undoubtedly, historians will best remember Hannegan for his role in securing the nomination for his close friend Sen. Harry S. Truman. Twice, on July 11 and again on July 19, he secured letters from Roosevelt approving Truman's selection by the party bosses who controlled the convention. Although Roosevelt's secretary, Grace Tully, remembered in her memoirs that Hannegan insisted that she reverse the president's original memorandum that listed William O. Douglas first and Harry Truman second, the shrewd St. Louis boss denied this allegation until his death. Equally important was his role at the convention wherein he deftly turned the delegates Truman's way after a first ballot produced no nominee.

Following Roosevelt's death Hannegan served the new president in the dual positions of Democratic national chairman and postmaster general until criticisms following the Republican victories of November 1946 forced his quiet withdrawal from national politics. Suffering from ill health, Hannegan returned to St. Louis where he pursued his first love: sports. Forming a syndicate with Fred M. Saigh Jr., he briefly owned the St. Louis Cardinals before a heart ailment forced his permanent retirement in January 1949.

Truman never forgot the invaluable assistance his old friend rendered on the road to the presidency. Shortly before Hannegan's death, the president, addressing a large gathering in Kansas City, turned to his compatriot and said: "He had something to do with getting me into these spots where I am now, and I don't know whether to spank him or thank him." One week later, on October 7, 1949, Hannegan died of a heart attack at the age of forty-six.

J. CHRISTOPHER SCHNELL

Current Biography. New York: H. W. Wilson, 1945.

Hamby, Alonzo L. *Beyond the New Deal: Harry S. Truman and American Liberalism.* New York: Columbia University Press, 1973.

Larsen, Lawrence H., and Nancy J. Hulston. *Pendergast!* Columbia: University of Missouri Press, 1997.

New York Times, October 7, 1949.

Truman, Margaret. *Harry S. Truman.* New York: William Morrow, 1973.

HARDEMAN, JOHN (1776–1829)

John Hardeman, best remembered for the botanical showplace he created on the banks of the Missouri River in the 1820s, was born in Virginia's Dan River region, not far from the North Carolina border, in 1776. The second son of Thomas and Mary Perkins Hardeman, John followed his peripatetic father from

Virginia to North Carolina, to Tennessee, and eventually to Missouri. He came from hardy stock and inherited from his parents a westering impulse that he shared with successive generations of pioneering Hardemans. At the same time, though, he often stood apart from his kinfolk and backwoods neighbors. A man of many talents and diverse interests, John Hardeman was a prosperous merchant who wrote poetry, a successful farmer who collected Indian artifacts and read great books, an amateur botanist who searched for unusual plants to cultivate in his experimental garden, an attorney who seldom practiced law, and an agnostic who questioned the beliefs of his Christian friends.

Hardeman was well schooled in many subjects. For a time he studied mathematics, most likely at the Davidson Academy in Nashville, but by 1802 he had entered the world of business and farming. In that year he and his older brother opened a country store in Franklin, Tennessee. The Hardeman brothers acted as buyers and marketing agents for local producers of cotton, tobacco, pork, whiskey, and peltries. They regularly shipped those commodities to Natchez, Baton Rouge, and New Orleans and also provided ginning services for local farmers. When an aspiring young attorney named **Thomas Hart Benton** moved to Tennessee in 1804, Hardeman extended him credit to obtain the books he needed for his legal studies, and that assistance initiated their lifelong friendship. By the time the Hardemans sold their thriving mercantile establishment in 1806, John had acquired sufficient funds to allow him to devote his primary attention to looking after his farm and conducting agricultural experiments.

After gaining admittance to the Tennessee bar in 1810, Hardeman dabbled briefly in politics, but following an unsuccessful campaign for the state senate in 1812, he withdrew permanently from the political arena. He was well on his way to becoming a prosperous Tennessee planter, but in 1817 he headed for the famed Boonslick country in the Missouri Territory where he joined his wanderlust father, who had moved there a year earlier. John Hardeman purchased land along the north bank of the Missouri River in Howard County, five miles above the new settlement of Franklin. The slaves Hardeman brought with him cleared the wilderness property for his new plantation that he called Fruitage Farm. Those same slaves also produced the cotton, corn, tobacco, hemp, and livestock that helped Hardeman finance agricultural experiments that produced such wonders as three-foot radishes, turnips thirty inches in circumference, and 672 pounds of citron melons on a single vine. His friend Senator Benton helped publicize his efforts to develop improved plant and animal species.

Hardeman's Garden, an elaborate nine-acre English garden filled with exotic plants, ornamental shrubs, and fruit that Hardeman had obtained from many parts of the world, made Fruitage Farm one of central Missouri's major attractions. **Henry Shaw** visited it long before he established his famed botanical garden in St. Louis. Tragically, the 1826 flood that destroyed much of nearby Franklin also swept away the showplace garden and claimed more than half of Fruitage Farm.

In addition to his agricultural pursuits, Hardeman held part interest in a Franklin general store and operated a ferry between his farm and Arrow Rock on the other side of the river, but it was the lure of profits from the newly opened Santa Fe trade that caught Hardeman's eye in the 1820s. Two years after the rampaging Missouri had ravaged his farm, Hardeman organized a trading expedition and set out for the Southwest. He traveled all the way to Sonora where he sold his wares. After completing his business, he chose to return home via New Orleans, but while passing through that city he contracted yellow fever and died there on September 2, 1829.

Hardeman married twice. In 1805 he wed Lucretia Nash in Baton Rouge, and they had two children. Lucretia died in 1812, and Hardeman waited until 1823 to remarry. His second wife, Nancy Knox of Boonville, bore him three children.

WILLIAM E. FOLEY

Hardeman, Nicholas Perkins. *Wilderness Calling: The Hardeman Family in the American Westward Movement, 1750–1900.* Knoxville: University of Tennessee Press, 1977.

HARDIN, CHARLES HENRY (1820–1892)

Four days before his twentieth birthday, Charles Henry Hardin received a letter from his uncle **William Jewell**. "It becomes you, having the fire of an honorable ambition burning in your bosom," wrote the highly respected Missouri physician. "Are you striving with almost agonizing efforts to lay deep and broad the foundation for future respectability and usefulness?" Through his ambition and effort, Hardin would in fact become a great philanthropist, a respected statesman, and governor of Missouri.

Within several months of his July 15, 1820, birth, Hardin's family moved from Trimble County, Kentucky, to Missouri. The following summer they established their permanent home in Columbia, where Hardin attended primary school. When his father died in 1830, he worked with his mother in the family's tanning business. In 1837 he attended the University of Indiana at Bloomington. Two years later Hardin transferred to the University of Miami in Oxford, Ohio, where he and seven friends founded Beta Theta Pi fraternity. After graduation he returned to Columbia and obtained his license to practice law. With his admission to the bar, he moved to Fulton and established his own law firm.

On May 16, 1844, Hardin married Mary Barr Jenkins, a graduate of Bonne Femme College. Throughout their lives she was his most trusted advisor and friend. Four years after their wedding, Hardin entered public service for the first time as an attorney in the Second Judicial Circuit. Voters rewarded his efforts by electing him to serve as a Whig state representative in 1852, 1854, and 1858. He entered the state senate as a conservative Unionist in 1860. While there he drafted a resolution calling for a state convention to decide Missouri's stance in the Civil War, but he also included a provision that required voter approval for secession. When Gov. **Claiborne Fox Jackson,** who hoped to secede from the Union, called a legislative meeting in Neosho, Missouri, while fleeing federal troops in October 1861, Hardin attended but was the only senator present who voted against secession. Despite his vote, the following year Hardin, like one-third of the Missouri voting population, was considered a Southern sympathizer and was disfranchised.

With the outbreak of war Hardin returned to Audrain County where he and his wife had established a farm. Following the war the Hardins moved closer to Mexico, Missouri, where they built a home and Hardin established a new law firm. He also cofounded the Mexico Southern Bank, where he served as president.

Voters, now all reenfranchised, returned Hardin to the state senate in 1872, where he served as the chair of the Judiciary Committee for the second time. Two years later, when the Democrats met in Jefferson City to select their candidates, Hardin won the nomination for governor. He needed 159 votes to secure the nomination; he received 159 1/6. That fall he won the election with a more sizable margin. On January 12, 1875, he entered office as Missouri's twenty-second governor.

Hardin faced a considerable state debt left from Civil War expenditures and funding for railroad construction. Using the skills he learned as a small boy in his family's business, Hardin reduced the debt by eliminating wasteful practices and by refinancing bonds. During his administration grasshoppers ravaged the state, stripping vegetation and "eating everything but the mortgages" as one farmer reported. In the hope of ending the plague, a woman wrote to the governor pleading that he set aside a day for prayer. Hardin shared the letter with his devout wife, who readily agreed. On May 17, 1875, the governor issued the "Grasshopper Proclamation." On the appointed day, people gathered in their churches. Within days it began to rain, and the grasshoppers moved northward out of Missouri.

After the governor's term the Hardins returned to Audrain County and took up their favorite causes, in particular Mexico's Hardin Female College, which they had founded four years earlier. Hardin also established a city park and supported the Mexico Military Academy. Many friends credited him with being one of the state's greatest philanthropists. Hardin died on July 29, 1892. In loving memory, Mary Hardin published his biography in 1896, hoping it would inspire others. She died eight years later.

LISA HEFFERNAN WEIL

Avery, Grace Gilmore, and Floyd C. Shoemaker. "Governor Charles Henry Hardin." In *The Messages and Proclamations of the Governors of the State of Missouri,* vol. 5. Columbia: State Historical Society of Missouri, 1924.

Hardin, Charles H., and Mary J. Hardin. Papers. Western Historical Manuscripts Collection, Columbia.

Hardin, Mary Barr. *Life and Writings of Governor Charles Henry Hardin.* St. Louis: Buschart Brothers, 1896.

Shoemaker, Floyd Calvin. "The Administration of Charles H. Hardin, 1875–1877." In *Missouri and Missourians: Land of Contrasts and People of Achievements,* vol. 2. Chicago: Lewis Publishing, 1943.

HARDING, CHESTER (1792–1866)

Chester Harding was one of the first professional artists to visit St. Louis. An untrained itinerant artist who began his career traveling the frontier, Harding went on to realize tremendous success on the East Coast and abroad. He became one of the most successful portrait painters in America, painting many of the most prominent men and women of his day, and traveled to England, where he received portrait commissions from British nobility. Yet, even at the pinnacle of his success, Harding continued to travel to earn commissions, frequently stopping in St. Louis where he found early acclaim.

Born on September 1, 1792, in Conway, Massachusetts, Chester Harding grew up on small farms in Massachusetts and New York. He received little formal education and held a series of unsuccessful jobs as a young man, including chair turner, traveling peddler, cabinetmaker, and tavern keeper. In 1816, with his debts mounting, Harding headed west to escape creditors and found work as a house and sign painter in Pittsburgh. After meeting a portrait painter there, Harding decided to try his hand at painting and discovered that he had some ability to capture likenesses on canvas. His brother, a chair maker and artist in Paris, Kentucky, convinced him to leave Pittsburgh and try his luck as an artist in the West.

After stops in Paris and Cincinnati, Harding moved to St. Louis with his wife and children in the spring of 1820. A letter of introduction to Gov. **William Clark** produced Harding's first St. Louis client. Harding wrote that Clark "kindly helped me about getting a suitable room for a studio, and then offered himself as a sitter. This was an auspicious and cheerful beginning." Few other artists were working in St. Louis in the early 1820s, and orders for portraits began to pour in from wealthy St. Louisans who wished to have their likenesses preserved.

Perhaps Harding's best-known portrait was of the frontiersman **Daniel Boone**—apparently the only image of the man painted from life. Harding traveled some one hundred miles west of St. Louis to find the eighty-six-year-old Boone, making several sketches that he later turned into finished portraits. While at work on his Boone portraits at a Franklin, Missouri, inn, he employed the innkeeper's son, **George Caleb Bingham,** to assist in his studio; it was Bingham's first exposure to the art of portraiture. Bingham, who later achieved national prominence painting genre scenes of the rivers and people of Missouri, began his career, like Harding, as an itinerant portrait painter traveling to Missouri river towns, and Harding served as an important early influence.

Harding left St. Louis in July 1821 to work in Washington and Boston, where his success continued unabated. In 1823 Harding traveled to Europe, spending three successful and busy years there, painting portraits for wealthy British patrons. The shift from nomadic frontier artist to portrait painter of British nobility was not easy. Harding wrote, "[H]ere I saw a great deal of high life; and it requires but little imagination to see, that the transition from the back woods of Missouri to this seat of luxury and elegance, was most imposing, and in some respects, embarrassing." Yet, Harding also recognized the appeal that his rugged manner and naive charm held for his wealthy clients. He capitalized on his lack of education, promoting himself as a self-taught frontier artist. Regaling his sitters with stories of his experiences in the Wild West, Harding provided an afternoon of entertainment along with a portrait.

Harding returned to the United States in 1826, settling with his family in Springfield, Massachusetts, where he spent his remaining years. However, he continued to spend much of each year traveling, seeking portrait commissions. He made regular trips to St. Louis (usually during the winter months), announcing his arrival with newspaper advertisements. Two of Harding's children settled in St. Louis, increasing his attachment to the city. While visiting in the winter of 1865–1866, Harding began his last work, a full-length portrait of Gen. **William T. Sherman.** He returned to Boston to complete the portrait but died shortly thereafter, on April 1, 1866.

As one of the first artists to reside in St. Louis, and a frequent visitor throughout his life, Chester Harding left a lasting impression on the artistic heritage of Missouri. He introduced the art of portraiture to many St. Louisans, painted the city's prominent citizens, and influenced later artists such as George Caleb Bingham who were encouraged by Harding's success on the frontier and beyond.

BETH RUBIN

Harding, William P. G. *A Sketch of Chester Harding, Artist.* Boston: Houghton Mifflin, 1929.

Lipton, Leah. "Chester Harding and the Life Portraits of Daniel Boone." *American Art Journal* 16 (summer 1984): 4–19.

———. *A Truthful Likeness: Chester Harding and His Portraits.* Washington, D.C.: Smithsonian Institution Press, 1985.

McDermott, John Francis. "How Goes the Harding Fever?" *Missouri Historical Society Bulletin* 8 (October 1951): 52–59.

Rubin, Beth. "The Backwoodsman Newly Caught: The Missouri Apprenticeship of Portraitist Chester Harding." *Gateway Heritage* 12 (summer 1991): 64–73.

HARKNESS, REBEKAH (1915–1982)

Composer and philanthropist Rebekah Harkness was born on April 17, 1915, to wealthy St. Louis parents Allen Tarwater West and Rebekah Semple West. She grew up in a world of luxury, attending the Rossman and John Burroughs private schools in St. Louis and a finishing school, Fermata, in Aiken, South Carolina. She also traveled with her family around the world and spent her summers in the resort town of Watch Hill, Rhode Island. However, Rebekah became a rebellious teenager and sought adventure, especially after a 1935 trip around the world with her brother in which they managed to survive a number of harrowing escapades. During this adventure she acquired a taste for world travel and exotic places.

Rebekah began to take ballet lessons to lose weight; she also studied sculpting. In 1938 she married Dickson Pierce, and they became the parents of two children. The marriage ended in divorce six years later, and Rebekah moved to New York. In 1947 she married William Hale Harkness, a Standard Oil Company heir and New York attorney. He became the father of her third child. This happy marriage was cut short by the death of Bill Harkness in 1954. Rebekah inherited his fortune, estimated at between one quarter and one half billion dollars, along with the presidency of the William Hale Harkness Foundation.

As a young widowed heiress, Harkness donated millions of dollars to medical research and constructed the William Hale Harkness Medical Research Building at New York Hospital.

After her second marriage Harkness began to refine her talent for sculpture. She also renewed her interest in music, studying musical composition in Fontainebleau, France, with Nadia Boulanger; in the Dalcroze School of Geneva, Switzerland; and the Mannes College of Music in New York. She also studied orchestration with Lee Holby and received a D.F.A. degree from Franklin Pierce College, in Rindge, New Hampshire, in 1968. She composed more than one hundred musical compositions, including "Mediterranean Moods" (1956), "Music with a Heartbeat" (1957), "Gift to the Magi" (1959), "Letters to Japan" (1961), and "Macumba" (1965).

In 1957 Marquis de Cuevas commissioned Harkness to score a ballet for his Grand Ballet, which was performed the following year at the Brussels World's Fair. Her score, *Voyage vers l'Amour,* received twelve curtain calls.

In 1959 Harkness formed the Rebekah Harkness Foundation, which was devoted to dance. The foundation helped several projects aimed at increasing dance in public schools, a winter season of modern dance at Hunter College, and a free, open-air summer dance festival as part of the New York Shakespeare Festival at Central Park's Delacorte Theater. The foundation also sponsored Jerome Robbins's Ballets U.S.A. (1961), Pearl Primus's tour to Africa (1962), the Robert Joffrey Ballet (1962–1964), the Harkness Ballet (1964), and the Harkness Youth Dancers (1968). With the Harkness Ballet she sought to create a uniquely American style of ballet combining adagio, jazz, and ethnic forms with the traditional dance.

To house her new company, Harkness purchased and remodeled in grand style the Watson town house in New York, which became the Harkness House for Ballet Arts. She also purchased and remodeled the Colonial Theater in New York City and opened it as the Harkness Theater, the first theater in the city designed only for dance, in 1974.

Harkness received many awards, including the Bronze Medal of Appreciation, New York City (1965); the Congressional Record Citation (1965–1966); a citation from the White House (1968); the Two Thousand Women of Achievement Award (1970); and the Annual Award Ballet des Jeunes, Philadelphia (1975). She served on the board of directors of the President's Council Youth Opportunity and was a trustee of the John F. Kennedy Center for Performing Arts.

In 1961 Harkness married her third husband, Benjamin Harrison Kean, a physician. The marriage lasted only four years. Rebekah Harkness died of cancer in New York City on June 17, 1982.

MARY K. DAINS

Current Biography. New York: H. W. Wilson, 1982.

Dains, Mary K., ed. *Show Me Missouri Women: Selected Biographies.* Kirksville, Mo.: Thomas Jefferson University Press, 1989.

The Good Housekeeping Woman's Almanac. New York: Newspaper Enterprise Association, 1977.

Who's Who in America. Chicago: A. N. Marquis, 1984.

Who's Who of American Women, 1972–1973. Chicago: A. N. Marquis, 1974.

HARLOW, JEAN (1911–1937)

Jean Harlow was born Harlean Carpenter in Kansas City, Missouri, on March 3, 1911. Her father, Mont Clair Carpenter, was a successful dentist who first worked out of the home, and then later had an office downtown. Harlow's early childhood was spent in comfortable circumstances in Kansas City, Missouri; in Kansas City, Kansas; and in another suburb, Bonner Springs, Kansas.

Harlow's father was born in Joplin, Missouri, and attended dental school in Kansas City. Her maternal grandfather, Samuel D. Harlow, was a real estate agent in Kansas City, Kansas. His wife was Ella Williams Harlow, and their only child was Jean J. Harlow, Harlean's mother, from whom she took her stage name. Harlow spent at least some of her childhood years with her grandparents. When she was five, she entered Miss Barstow's school.

After her parents divorced in 1921, Harlow and her mother left Kansas City for Los Angeles. She eloped at sixteen with a young banker, Charles F. McGrew II, and the young couple lived in a Spanish bungalow in Beverly Hills. However, the young bride yearned for a career in films, which her husband opposed.

Harlean Carpenter eventually registered with Central Casting as Jean Harlow, and made a brief appearance in a movie with star Lois Moran. When her grandfather joined her husband in opposition to her film career, she stopped her acting efforts. Shortly thereafter, she separated from her husband and was reported to have been awarded a sizable settlement, which she later claimed was never accepted.

Instead, Harlow worked as a fifteen-dollar-a-day film extra. The eccentric millionaire Howard Hughes then cast her to play the lead in a movie about aviation, *Hell's Angels,* in 1930. That film and a skillful press agent, who labeled her "the Platinum Blonde" started her on a seven-year career in which she earned as much as four thousand dollars per week. Other roles followed quickly, including *The Public Enemy* (with James Cagney), *Red Dust, Iron Man, The Secret Six, Hold Your Man, Bombshell,* and *Dinner at Eight.*

In 1932 Harlow entered into an improbable second marriage with German-born Metro-Goldwyn-Mayer (MGM) executive Paul Bern, who was twenty years her senior. It concluded tragically on September 5, 1932, two months after their marriage, when Bern was found shot to death under mysterious circumstances. Months later the death was ruled a suicide. In September 1933 Harlow married a cameraman, Harold Rosson, but the union ended in divorce in 1934.

Harlow began filming *Saratoga* in 1937 with Clark Gable, but near the picture's completion she developed a mysterious malady. Not wanting to delay production, she continued to work until the pain became too severe. After one week in Good Samaritan Hospital, she died of uremic poisoning on June 7, 1937, at the age of twenty-six. Her funeral was pure Hollywood lore, with only 250 people allowed to attend the services in Wee Kirk o' the Heather. Thousands looked on from a distance, and the lawn was carpeted with flowers. She was buried in Forrest Lawn Memorial Park Cemetery.

The final years of Harlow's life were satisfying both professionally and personally. She signed a lucrative contract with MGM and was engaged to actor **William Powell,** another actor with Kansas City roots, at the time of her death.

In her short career Jean Harlow, the world's first "Blonde Bombshell" with the "platinum" hair, embodied all-American sex. Depression audiences adored her roles as the wise-cracking tart in films such as *Red Dust* and *Dinner at Eight*. Offscreen, Harlow was the original troubled sex goddess. Her legendary life and career still evoke curiosity. As she once said, "No matter what I do, I always end up on page one."

ARTHUR F. McCLURE AND VIVIAN RICHARDSON

Brown, Curtis F. *Jean Harlow*. New York: Pyramid, 1977.
Kansas City Star, June 13, 1937.
Los Angeles Examiner, June 8, 1937.
Pascal, John. *The Jean Harlow Story.* New York: Popular Library, 1964.

HARNEY, WILLIAM SELBY
(1800–1889)

Born in the village of Haysboro, near Nashville, Tennessee, on August 22, 1800, William Selby Harney spent his adult life as an officer in the United States Army. Commissioned a second lieutenant in the First Infantry Regiment by order of President James Monroe on February 13, 1818, Harney accompanied Gen. Henry Atkinson on the Missouri River expedition of 1824–1825, served in the Black Hawk War of 1832, and fought in the Second Seminole War of 1836–1841. During these years he met men of future prominence, including Jefferson Davis, Zachary Taylor, and Abraham Lincoln.

The army promoted Harney quickly during his fifty-four years of service. He received the rank of major on May 1, 1833, and, with the aid of family friend President Andrew Jackson, a position in the office of paymaster. Harney's paymaster duties took him to the frontier garrisons of the 1830s, from Jefferson Barracks near St. Louis to Fort Gibson in the Indian Territory, and to old friends such as Jefferson Davis and Sam Houston.

The massacre of Maj. Francis Dade's command by the Seminoles in 1836 caused Harney to accept a field command in the Second Dragoons. On August 15, 1836, he received a promotion to lieutenant colonel from President Andrew Jackson. After the war Harney turned his Indian fighting skills against the Comanche of western Texas.

During the Mexican War in 1846, Harney served in the armies of Gens. John E. Wool, Zachary Taylor, and Winfield Scott. On June 30, 1846, Harney advanced to the rank of colonel and command of the dragoon forces. His service with General Scott had a shaky start: a court-martial for refusing to relinquish his command to a junior officer, Maj. Edwin V. Sumner. He was convicted of insubordination but maintained his command. Scott subsequently received a letter of reprimand for his action against Harney from President James K. Polk.

Harney served with distinction in Scott's Vera Cruz campaign. At the battle of Cerro Gordo on April 18, 1847, he led a brilliant charge to capture El Telegrafo, a steep hill, and captured part of General Santa Anna's artillery command. For this action General Scott promoted Harney to the rank of brevet brigadier general, and later the city of New Orleans presented him with a black stallion for his bravery, while the city of St. Louis held a parade in his honor.

The 1850s marked the return of General Harney to the Indian campaigns, this time on the upper Great Plains. President Franklin Pierce requested that Harney lead a punitive expedition against the Brule Sioux who had committed several massacres in the Fort Laramie area. In the summer of 1855 Harney gathered a force of some six hundred men from frontier garrisons, and on September 3 engaged the Brule Sioux at Ash Hollow in Nebraska. Harney's forces virtually exterminated his Indian opponents. The Indians suffered eighty-six dead, and fifty women and children captured, while Harney lost only six men. The Sioux remained peaceful the rest of the summer along the Oregon Trail, with Harney spending the winter of 1855–1856 in southern Dakota. The next spring he built Fort Randall to keep a watchful eye on the Indians of the region.

During the rest of the 1850s Harney saw service in "Bleeding Kansas," the Utah expedition (that is, the Mormon crisis), and the Departments of Oregon and the West. The army promoted him on May 14, 1858, to brigadier general, making him the fourth-ranking officer in the army.

As commander of the Department of Oregon Harney almost involved the United States in a war, the Pig War, with Great Britain over the Puget Sound island of San Juan, but diplomacy resolved the problem. Later, as commander of the Department of the West, Harney faced a critical dilemma: control of the St. Louis arsenal. A conflict with Capt. **Nathaniel Lyon** and Cong. **Frank Blair** quickly developed. In April 1861 Blair and Lyon engineered Harney's recall by President Lincoln to Washington, D.C., so they could muster the four regiments of the St. Louis home guard into the service of the Union cause. As Harney returned to Washington, Confederate authorities detained him and took him to Richmond, Virginia, where Jefferson Davis, Robert E. Lee, and others sought unsuccessfully to convince him to join the Southern cause.

On May 10, 1861, the day before Harney was to return to command in St. Louis, Blair and Lyon captured Camp Jackson, a state militia camp on the edge of St. Louis. Harney attempted to secure peace for Missouri in an agreement with the state guard commander, **Sterling Price.** President Lincoln dismissed Harney at Blair's request, and because of Blair's enmity Harney left the service.

President Andrew Johnson recalled Harney to active duty with the rank of brevet major general on March 13, 1865, to serve as one of the original seven Indian commissioners. The Indian commission sought to force the Plains Indians onto reservations.

Harney listened to the Indians' concerns at the councils held at Medicine Lodge Creek in 1867 and at Fort Laramie in 1868, and encouraged a peaceful solution to the growing tensions on the frontier. He succeeded in establishing reservations for the Sioux, the Cheyenne, and the Crow in the territories of Montana and the Dakotas in 1868. In April 1872 Harney officially retired from the army, but not from military life.

On May 9, 1889, Harney died in Orlando, Florida, and was buried at Arlington National Cemetery.

BERNARD M. BROWN

Adams, George Rollie. "General William Selby Harney: Frontier Soldier, 1800–1889." Ph.D. diss., University of Arizona, 1983.

Hutton, Paul Andrew. *Soldiers West: Biographies from the Military Frontier.* Lincoln: University of Nebraska Press, 1987.

Johnston, Charles H. L. *Famous Scouts, Including Trappers, Pioneers, and Soldiers of the Frontier.* Boston: Page, 1910.

Reavis, Logan U. *The Life and Military Service of General William S. Harney.* St. Louis: Bryan, Brand, 1878.

HARRINGTON, EDWARD MICHAEL, JR. (1928–1989)

Edward Michael Harrington Jr. was born in St. Louis on February 24, 1928. While he was known as Ned to friends in St. Louis and Ed to his classmates at the College of the Holy Cross, it was as Michael Harrington that he would gain recognition as the preeminent democratic socialist in America.

Harrington's mother, Catherine Fitzgibbon Harrington, grew up in the Irish American neighborhood known as Kerry Patch northwest of downtown St. Louis, where her immigrant father had established himself as a businessman and a local leader of the Jacksonian Democratic Club. In 1922, two years after receiving a teaching degree from Harris Teachers College in St. Louis, she married Edward Michael Harrington Sr., an Irish American attorney.

Michael Harrington attended a parish grammar school, St. Rose's, until the fourth grade, when his devoutly Catholic parents enrolled him in Chaminade College Prep School, a prestigious school occupying a large campus in suburban St. Louis County. Harrington was so gifted academically that in 1940 his parents decided to enroll him at St. Louis University High School, bypassing his eighth grade year at Chaminade. He excelled in high school and at the College of the Holy Cross in Worcester, Massachusetts, which, like his high school, was operated by the Jesuits. At Holy Cross he cultivated a passionate interest in literature and was elected president of the debating society. Ironically, he "rebelled" against his parent's staunch Democratic loyalties by flirting with conservative Republicanism as an editorial writer on the college newspaper. He also began to speak out against racism at a time when American Catholic institutions were just beginning to reexamine the legacy of racial segregation.

Harrington had decided to become a poet while at Holy Cross, but in deference to his parents' wishes, he enrolled in Yale University's Law School in 1947. He left Yale after one year and later claimed, "The day I left law school I switched from Taft Republicanism to democratic socialism without even bothering to tarry while in the liberal camp between." He enrolled in the graduate literature program at the University of Chicago, earning an M.A. degree in 1949.

The roots of Harrington's vocation to eradicate poverty grew out of an experience in St. Louis shortly after he completed his graduate degree. He had become fascinated with the "bohemian" subculture of New York's Greenwich Village and was working in the Pupil Welfare Department of the St. Louis Public School System to finance a move to New York City. One rainy afternoon he entered a decaying house near the Mississippi River that "stank of stopped-up toilets, dead rats, and human misery. It was a terrible shock to my privileged, middle-class nostrils. . . . An hour or so later, riding the Grand Avenue streetcar, it dawned on me that I should spend the rest of my life putting an end to that house and all that it symbolized."

After moving to New York City Harrington combined his bohemian and radical interests by embracing voluntary poverty and taking up residency at the Catholic Worker community in Lower Manhattan. He helped edit the *Catholic Worker*, a newspaper that promoted the pacifist, anarchist, and communitarian mission of the radical Catholic movement founded by Dorothy Day and Peter Maurin in 1933. He spent many evenings at the nearby White Horse Tavern where he shared company not only with fellow Catholic Workers but also with such renowned literary figures as Dylan Thomas and Norman Mailer.

In 1952, while traveling to a communion breakfast in Pennsylvania where he had been scheduled to speak, Harrington "decided I could not go to communion since I no longer believed in the faith, not even by way of an existential leap." He now ardently embraced a strictly secular brand of socialism, becoming active in the Young Socialist League, an organization closely linked with an anticommunist wing of the fragmented left led by Max Schachtman. Harrington's writing and speaking abilities and his gift for translating Marxian abstractions into the American vernacular resulted in a rapid ascent to the upper echelons of American democratic socialism, where he forged enduring relationships with such influential figures as A. J. Muste, Bayard Rustin, Norman Thomas, and others who were "both my inspiration and my postgraduate university."

In 1958 Schachtman and Harrington led their constituents into the mainstream Socialist Party as a unified bloc, enabling Harrington to widen his influence among young leftists. By 1962, when a group of student radicals met in Port Huron, Michigan, to formalize the transformation of the Student League for Industrial Democracy (SLID) into Students for a Democratic Society (SDS), Harrington was invited to participate, both because SLID was sponsored by the Socialist Party and because he was, as Tom Hayden of SDS later wrote, one of the few people over the age of thirty trusted by members of the younger generation. But while the "Port Huron Statement" was a watershed for the burgeoning New Left, it represented a personal setback for Harrington, who was dismissed as an Old Leftist for arguing fervently

that the Soviet Union continued to represent a great menace to authentic socialist movements.

At precisely the moment his influence began to wane among student radicals, Harrington was thrust into national attention as the author of *The Other America*, the most sustained analysis of poverty to appear in the postwar era. He argued that in the midst of great affluence, "somewhere between 20 and 25 percent of the American people are poor. They have inadequate housing, medicine, food, and opportunity." Using the tools of advocacy journalism he showed how structural changes in the U.S. economy had created a culture of poverty for those who fell outside the purview of welfare-state liberalism, including residents of inner cities being hindered by the interstate highway system and agricultural workers rendered obsolete by mechanization. As in all his political writings, Harrington insisted in *The Other America* that a just society would not only ensure full employment but promote humane values as well. This existential dimension distinguished his work from that of more orthodox Marxists, but he struggled to convince readers that socialism in practice could offer more than a bureaucratic collectivism.

The Other America inspired Presidents John F. Kennedy and Lyndon B. Johnson to seek means to end poverty in America. Many of Johnson's Great Society programs, especially the War on Poverty, addressed the sources of inequality first exposed by Harrington, who suddenly found himself a celebrity expert on poverty, in great demand as a public speaker. During one such engagement in 1965 he experienced an anxiety attack he described as the first symptom of a "nervous breakdown" that was linked, he believed, to the irony of a socialist author becoming highly successful for writing about the poor. He concluded that his preoccupation with ideological purity was counterproductive at a time when "one did not have to be a socialist to be outraged by the existence of poverty in the wealthiest society in human history."

In books such as *The Accidental Century* (1965), and *Socialism* (1970), Harrington explored the philosophical origins of his convictions, arguing that in the modern era "man has socialized everything except himself." He wrote, "The question is not, therefore, Will the future be collectivist? It is, rather, Can the collectivist future be made humane and democratic and libertarian? There is no choice but to be as revolutionary as the revolution that is taking place."

In 1971, weary from the internecine struggles of the Socialist Party, Harrington resigned as party cochair to found the Democratic Socialist Organizing Committee (DSOC), a group that sought to influence the left wing of the Democratic Party. Harrington pursued "the creation of a viable, relevant socialist center for thought and action—a center geared to the everyday experiences of activists in the trade unions, in the women's movement, in the struggle for minority rights, and in all the movements of the democratic left." He now embraced the New Left and joined its leaders in demanding the unconditional withdrawal of American forces in Vietnam. In 1982 the DSOC merged with the New American Movement—a successor to SDS—to form the Democratic Socialists of America (DSA). Harrington, who became the group's first chairman, noted: "In terms of the United States of America, we had either created an important bridge to a future Left or mobilized an ineffective remnant. Only time will tell."

In 1973 Michael Harrington became a professor of political science at Queens College in New York. He became active in the Socialist International, a group with ties to such prominent figures as Willy Brandt of West Germany and Olaf Palme of Sweden.

Harrington tirelessly continued to write, lecture, and organize on behalf of the democratic socialist movement. In 1984 he was stricken with cancer of the neck, which later spread to his esophagus. He died on July 31, 1989.

JAMES T. FISHER

Gorman, Robert A. *Michael Harrington: Speaking American.* New York: Routledge, 1995.

Harrington, Michael. *The Accidental Century.* New York: Macmillan, 1965.

———. *Fragments of the Century.* New York: Simon and Schuster, 1972.

———. *The Long Distance Runner: An Autobiography.* New York: Henry Holt, 1988.

———. *The Other America: Poverty in the United States.* New York: Macmillan, 1962.

———. *The Politics at God's Funeral: The Spiritual Crisis of Western Civilization.* New York: Holt, Rinehart, and Winston, 1983.

HARRIS, JOHN WOODS (1816–1877)

In 1817 Mary Woods Harris carried one-year-old John Woods Harris into the future Boone County, Missouri, as her husband, Overton Harris, led the family horse along the Boone's Lick Road. They settled in northwestern Boone County on Thrall's Prairie. John Woods Harris had been born the previous August 31 in Madison County, Kentucky.

Throughout Harris's boyhood and early adulthood, many people active in establishing early community organizations surrounded him, including his father who served as the first county sheriff and his first employer, William Cornelius, the president pro tempore of the state senate. They each instilled in Harris a deep sense of community responsibility.

At fourteen Harris worked in a Columbia mercantile establishment. Before the age of twenty he established a mercantile business in Monroe County and later one in Rocheport. By the 1850s his businesses flourished.

On February 27, 1854, Harris married Annie Mary McClure, the daughter of William McClure, who had previously purchased a farm ten miles northwest of Columbia on which he built a home. Two years after their marriage, the Harrises purchased his farm. They added buildings and restored others, including a log cabin that stood within a stone's throw of the mansion. The small cabin had been Harris's first home in Boone County. He devoted himself to this land for the rest of his life.

Harris worked to establish roads, railroads, banks, and schools. He participated in numerous road and railroad meetings, serving as a delegate to a national railroad convention in St. Louis at twenty-five. He served as a member of the board of directors and as president of many banks, including Rocheport Savings Bank, Boone County National Bank, and the State Bank of Missouri.

Harris actively participated in the Whig Party in Boone County. In 1860 and 1864 voters elected him to the General Assembly. Although he owned slaves, Harris stood with the Union. As a reward the secretary of the navy appointed him to the board of examiners for the United States Naval Academy.

Harris sincerely believed in the value of education. He served as a trustee for a local school and accepted an appointment to the University of Missouri Board of Curators, a position he held for many years.

The link between the many business, political, and educational commitments Harris embraced was found in his progressive view of agriculture. He saw beyond the subsistence farming of his time to the opportunities provided by developing technologies and markets. As a merchant Harris learned of the new farm machinery available and utilized it on his farm. As a politician he fought to establish the railroads and then hauled the first load of cattle. As an educator he encouraged experimentation and sought to position his farm as a model for emerging possibilities.

Harris served on the first State Board of Agriculture and later became its president. He helped establish the agricultural college at the university in Columbia. He continued to support the college by awarding a gold medal each year to the student who wrote the best paper on innovative farming practices. The college later presented Harris with an honorary master's degree in agriculture.

Harris's farm grew from the original six hundred acres to eighteen hundred. He stocked it with more than one thousand head of livestock, including new breeds of cattle, sheep, and hogs. He experimented with seed varieties in his garden, vineyard, and orchard. Reporters from rural publications visited the farm, and all returned to their papers to write about "one of the state's best farms."

In 1872 this widely acknowledged consensus received official validation when the State Board of Agriculture sponsored a contest to select the model farm of the state. Harris's farm won; from then on, it was known as the Model Farm of the State of Missouri, the only farm ever to receive the title. The *Columbia Herald* wrote, "Indeed, this farm is the sermon of his life, and will, for years to come, be a speaking model to every farmer, illustrating what it is possible for taste, energy, and good judgement to perform in that vocation of life."

John Woods Harris died on his farm on May 3, 1877, at the age of sixty, less than a year after the death of his wife. He left four children. In its final tribute *Colman's Rural World* wrote, "He held many high positions in this State, but his best efforts were made in improving and elevating the noble profession to which he gave his life's work. In farming, he displayed preeminent ability, great practical skill, and excellent taste."

LISA HEFFERNAN WEIL

Crighton, John C. "John Harris's Estate near Roche-port Seen as Model Farm of State." In *A History of Columbia and Boone County.* Columbia, Mo.: Computer Color-Graphics, 1987.

Rogers, Jane Harris. "The Model Farm of Missouri and Its Owner." *Missouri Historical Review* 18 (January 1924): 146–57.

Switzler, William F. *A History of Boone County, Missouri.* St. Louis: Western Historical, 1882.

HARRIS, WILLIAM TORREY (1835–1909)

Born on September 10, 1835, in North Killington, Connecticut, William Torrey Harris was a philosopher and educator active in St. Louis between 1857 and 1880, and during that time he was perhaps Missouri's most influential intellectual. He cofounded the St. Louis Philosophical Society (1866), established the *Journal of Speculative Philosophy* (1867), headed the administration of the St. Louis public schools (1866–1880), and provided the organizing force behind the St. Louis Movement in philosophy, education, and civic activism. He left Missouri in 1880 to direct a private "school" of philosophy in Concord, Massachusetts, and later served as U.S. commissioner of education (1889–1906). During the last two decades of his life, he wrote and lectured widely as an educational authority and engaged in extensive editing projects, including *Johnson's New*

Universal Cyclopedia and *Webster's New International Dictionary.* He died on November 5, 1909, in Providence, Rhode Island.

At no point was Harris's impact so great as during his St. Louis period when his activities achieved a remarkable ripple effect in Missouri, in the United States, and internationally. His chief legacy to St. Louis was a tradition of innovation in educational philosophy and of competent school administration. Disciples included **Susan Elizabeth Blow,** founder of the American kindergarten movement, and Louis Soldan, Harris's successor as superintendent of the public schools and eventual president of the National Education Association.

Harris devoted much of his immense energy to expounding the philosophy of G. W. F. Hegel (1770–1831), translating it into acceptable American terms—as one historian describes it, "making Hegel talk English"—and defending Hegelianism against the Anglo-Scottish empiricism of Locke, Hume, John Stuart Mill, and William Hamilton and the evolutionary materialism of Herbert Spencer and G. H. Lewes. It is according to the success or failure of this self-appointed task that Harris has been subsequently judged. Because the Hegelian philosophical system was so quickly superseded by technical developments in Western philosophy, it is tempting to dismiss Harris as a failure; however, to do so would ignore his many important contributions as well as miss the significance of St. Louis Hegelianism for American intellectual history.

During his first decade in St. Louis (1857–1867) Harris formed his mature views, and it is in the context of his career in St. Louis that his thought and practice should be examined. A native of Connecticut, Harris's formal education was acquired haphazardly in rural and city schools, in no less than five private academies, and during three unhappy years at Yale College (he left without earning a degree). Although his own schooling had been disorganized, as an educational authority he advocated a strict system of age grading and promotion through academic accomplishment. His self-education was heavily skewed toward "metaphysical" authors and subjects, notably, the works of Coleridge, Carlyle, Goethe, Kant, and the American transcendentalists.

Harris found the Germanized cultural atmosphere of antebellum St. Louis congenial. He came to regard his acquaintance with **Henry Conrad Brokmeyer** (1826–1906) at the Mercantile Library in 1858 as one of the turning points of his life, because the eccentric and rebellious German guided him through the morass of post-Kantian German philosophy. Meanwhile, Harris had secured a teaching position at Clay School and brought his New England bride, Sarah T. Bugbee, to St. Louis. He returned Brokmeyer's intellectual favor by joining other local enthusiasts in commissioning "Brok" to translate Hegel's *Science of Logic* into English. This arrangement, in fact, was the origin of both the Philosophical Society and the *Journal of Speculative Philosophy.*

As important as Brokmeyer's tutelage to the development of Harris and the other St. Louis Hegelians (most notably at this time, **Denton Jacques Snider** and **John Gabriel Woerner**) was the shared experience of the Civil War in a border state traumatized by conflicting loyalties. Although Harris was honorably exempted from military service (the leadership of the public schools thought him indispensable), he was not slow to draw from the spectacle of the war a political-philosophical lesson that coincided with the conclusions he simultaneously drew from his study of idealist philosophy.

Harris believed in the Hegelian dialectic, in the action of ideas combining and transcending each other in the formation of higher syntheses. Two ideas that had been in conflict since the founding of the American Republic were liberty (expressed as political democracy) and property (including slavery). In Harris's view, the Union "cause" in 1861 represented a "world-historical" attempt to reconcile the contradiction between democracy and slavery. The Union stood for individual liberty, while the agrarian-capitalist aristocracy of the Confederacy denied the same to African American slaves. The persistence of the Southern slave system was to Harris a clear example of a society within American society resisting the evolution of its fundamental idea. Harris wrote to his uncle in Connecticut explaining his view of the war: "We are finding the rational internal limit to the freedom which we had secured externally before. Every world-historical nation has an idea posited as the basis of its consciousness that it must develop and bring out in all its forms."

The outcome of the Civil War was to Harris and his fellows decisive proof of the validity of the Hegelian philosophy of history and of the truth of Hegelianism in general. The St. Louis Hegelians saw the war as a vindication of strong government, since it was through effective state-directed institutions (namely, state militias, the Union army, and Lincoln's presidency) that the United States became reconciled to its national idea.

Harris regarded Hegelianism as a means of maximizing the potential for reconciliation between individuals and society, and as, in fact, the only philosophy through which to achieve the coexistence of individual wills with a tolerable degree of social harmony. The larger goal of Harris and his Hegelians, however, was to spread a democratic gospel of "speculative philosophy" that they insisted was an activity open to all with inquiring and critical minds and not merely to "professionals" and applied to fields as diverse as politics, historical thought, and education.

Self-education or self-cultivation was to support formal schooling as an essential process in the education of the individual toward citizenship in a democratic society. Speculative philosophy widely practiced, according to Harris, would encourage the rational and cooperative qualities of human nature, and Hegelian thought, with its insistence on the role of the state as the great harmonizer of individual wills, seemed to offer a promising recipe of national unity for postwar America.

Harris was no proponent of an authoritarian state. Rather, he envisioned key roles for intermediate institutions—such as democratic local governments, public schools, and voluntary organizations like the St. Louis Philosophical Society—in curbing individual egotism and establishing norms for rational behavior. Historians have consequently described St. Louis Hegelianism, in contrast to some of its European varieties, as a liberal philosophy of progress well suited to what was still an undisciplined frontier society.

Harris and St. Louis Hegelianism never made an impact upon American philosophy equivalent to that of the pragmatism of John Dewey. Nevertheless, Hegelianism and other forms of absolute idealism did have their day in the American academy, particularly at Princeton, Cornell, and the University of California (whose philosophy department was established by George Howison, a St. Louis Hegelian). This was due in no small part to Harris and the *Journal of Speculative Philosophy,* in which some of the most important early essays of Dewey, C. S. Peirce, and Josiah Royce appeared. As for Harris's independent philosophical work, *Hegel's Logic: A Book on the Genesis of the Categories of the Mind* (1890) did not go beyond exposition of Hegel's system.

Harris's less than decisive impact on American philosophy might be explained by his lack of focus; he simply spread himself too thin. Yet, his failure as a general philosopher obscures the more enduring impact of his educational philosophy and practice, both locally and nationally. Prominent educators of the first half of the twentieth century such as Nicholas Murray Butler of Columbia University continued to speak of Harris's contributions with great respect. As superintendent of the St. Louis public schools, Harris provided firm direction during a period of growth and social change for the city. He demonstrated political tact in negotiating with the German population of St. Louis over the use of the German language in the schools, though the legitimate claims of black St. Louisans for better educational provisions were largely ignored. Harris left the public school administration in the able care of Soldan and others, his essays on pedagogy and school organization were read around the world, and he was the obvious choice for the education commissionership. He was awarded many honorary degrees by American and European universities. One acknowledgment of his service to education in Missouri is Harris-Stowe College in St. Louis, named for him.

Although Harris remained confident in the ability of formal and continuing education to make Americans—including the inhabitants of newly acquired territories and protectorates—responsible citizens, he lost some of his faith in the Hegelian philosophy of history. Looking back in 1906 on the four decades following the Civil War, he detected no "hieroglyph of reason" revealing America's national purpose, and he regarded the monopolizing tendency of American industry, trade unionism, and socialism as growing threats to liberty and property. His conservative style of reform was adopted by the majority of the St. Louis Movement during the last quarter of the nineteenth century, when the movement merged with other campaigns for social reform and municipal renovation.

DENYS P. LEIGHTON

Dictionary of American Biography. Vol. 8. S.v. "Harris, William Torrey."

Goetzmann, William H. *The American Hegelians: An Intellectual Episode in the History of the American West.* New York: Knopf, 1973.

Kucklick, Bruce. *Churchmen and Philosophers: From Jonathan Edwards to John Dewey.* New Haven: Yale University Press, 1985.

Leighton, Denys P. "William Torrey Harris, the St. Louis Hegelians, and the Meaning of the Civil War." *Gateway Heritage* 10:2 (fall 1989): 33–45.

Primm, James Neal. *Lion of the Valley: St. Louis, Missouri, 1764–1980.* 3d ed. St. Louis: Missouri Historical Society Press, 1998.

Watson, David. "Social Theory and National Culture: The Case of British and American Absolute Idealism, 1860–1900." *Social Science History* 5:3 (summer 1981): 251–74.

HARRISON, WILLIAM HENRY (1773–1841)

William Henry Harrison, a soldier, territorial governor, and the ninth president of the United States, was born at Berkeley plantation in Charles City County, Virginia, on February 9, 1773. His father, Benjamin Harrison, was a prominent planter, member of the Continental Congress, signer of the Declaration of Independence, and governor of Virginia. After being educated at home by private tutors, Harrison attended Hampden-Sydney College. He studied medicine in Richmond and Philadelphia, but abandoned his pursuit of a medical career to join the army. In 1791 he secured a commission as an ensign and was assigned to the Tenth U.S. Infantry Regiment at Fort Washington in the Northwest Territory.

Within a year Harrison attained the rank of lieutenant and became aide-de-camp to Gen. Anthony Wayne. He participated in the Battle of Fallen Timbers and was a signer of the Treaty of Greenville. On November 25, 1795, Harrison married Anna Symmes, the daughter of judge and land speculator John Cleves Symmes. They had ten children, including John Scott Harrison, who served in Congress and fathered Benjamin Harrison, the twenty-third president of the United States. In 1797 Harrison earned a promotion to captain, but the following year he resigned his commission to accept an appointment as secretary of the Northwest Territory. With the territory's advancement to the second grade of government in 1799, the voters elected him as the territory's first delegate to the United States Congress.

While serving as territorial delegate, Harrison chaired the House Public Lands Committee and initiated the Harrison Land Act of 1800 that reformed public land policies. He also spearheaded the initiative for dividing the Northwest Territory into the Indiana and Ohio Territories. In 1800 President John Adams appointed him the first governor of the Indiana Territory.

Following the Louisiana Purchase, Congress attached the region north of the thirty-third parallel, known as Upper Louisiana, to the Indiana Territory for administrative purposes. Harrison exercised his powers to establish laws, appoint territorial judges, and reorganize the court and militia system for the newly formed District of Louisiana, which included all of present-day Missouri. The notion of an absentee government caused genuine concern in the region, particularly among a clique of influential French Creole residents and land claimants. They feared that Harrison and Indiana's other territorial officials, ignorant of Upper Louisiana's specific needs and problems, could not govern the region effectively. The failure of Congress to specifically sanction slavery in Upper Louisiana added to the local discontent. The district's inhabitants also objected to congressional plans to relocate eastern Indian tribes in the area and to limit confirmation of Spanish land titles.

Despite their defiant opposition to the annexation, Upper Louisiana's Creole leaders greeted Harrison warmly when he arrived in St. Louis in October 1804. He won their approval by appointing some of them to newly created territorial offices. His visit turned out to be a cordial affair, especially after he lent his support to their efforts to petition Congress to grant the District of Louisiana territorial status with a government of its own. When Congress consented and established the Louisiana Territory on March 3, 1805, Harrison's brief administration of Upper

Louisiana officially ended, but he had earned the gratitude and respect of the region's inhabitants.

Harrison's responsibilities as territorial governor and superintendent of Indian affairs included the contradictory tasks of maintaining cordial relations with the various tribes while persuading them to surrender vast tracts of land to the U.S. government. He sought to win Indian confidence and cooperation by inoculating them against smallpox, regulating fur traders, and prohibiting the sale of liquor, but his relentless efforts to secure their acquiescence to huge land cessions inevitably spawned a hostile relationship.

In November 1804 Governor Harrison held a council in St. Louis with leaders of the Sac and Fox tribes and concluded a treaty in which they surrendered fifteen thousand acres in what is now southern Wisconsin and western Illinois. As governor, Harrison negotiated twelve treaties with various tribes, transferring about seventy-five thousand square miles of land to the United States.

Angered by the white man's endless encroachment on their lands, several tribes in the region formed a confederacy under the leadership of the Shawnee warrior Tecumseh and his half brother Tenskwatawa, also known as the Prophet. In 1810 Harrison met with Tecumseh in Vincennes to negotiate a peace, but the Shawnee leader threatened the governor with war if he permitted further white settlement in the territory. Harrison refused to yield, and the council ended in an impasse, with both sides expecting war. Fearing an attack on Vincennes, Harrison marched his forces to the village of Prophetstown in northwestern Indiana in 1811. On November 11 a Shawnee band led by Tenskwatawa attacked Harrison's army encampment near the confluence of the Wabash and Tippecanoe Rivers. Harrison's forces repelled the assault, dispersed the Indians, and burned Prophetstown to the ground. The Battle of Tippecanoe was a bittersweet victory for Harrison, whose army sustained 188 casualties without engaging their nemesis Tecumseh who was away seeking to persuade the Creek and Cherokee to join his confederacy. Following the engagement at Tippecanoe, Harrison's critics charged that he had conducted a haphazard campaign. The governor's supporters countered with a version celebrating his heroism and extolling the virtues of "Old Tippecanoe."

Continuing Indian hostilities and growing tension with the British forced Harrison to concentrate on territorial defenses. Following the declaration of war against Great Britain in 1812, he badgered President James Madison for a military command. Frustrated with Madison's inaction, he journeyed to Frankfort, Kentucky, to assemble volunteers to assist with the defense of Vincennes. News that the British were besieging Gen. William Hull's army at Detroit prompted Harrison's appointment as a brevet major general in the Kentucky militia. He traveled to Cincinnati and assumed provisional command of Gen. William Winchester's army with the intention of assisting Hull, but he arrived too late to be of service.

On August 22, 1812, President Madison made Harrison a brigadier general in the regular army and appointed him commander in chief of the Northwestern army on September 17. Upon his promotion to major general the next year, Harrison resigned as governor of the Indiana Territory. In the fall of 1813 his army marched into Canada and defeated a combined British and Indian force at the Battle of Thames. Harrison's victory and Tecumseh's death in that engagement effectively halted the offensive against the United States in the Northwest.

After the war an army contractor charged Harrison with improprieties involving army supply contracts. Although his accuser failed to substantiate the charges, Harrison's ensuing disagreement over the matter with Secy. of War John Armstrong prompted him to resign his military commission in May 1814.

Harrison returned to North Bend, Ohio, to pursue a political career. He served in Congress from 1816 to 1819, and in the Ohio State Senate from 1819 to 1821. He lost contests for the United States Senate in 1821 and the House in 1822. Three years later the Ohio legislature elected Harrison to the Senate where he served as chairman of the Military Affairs Committee. He resigned in 1828 to accept an appointment as the U.S. minister to Colombia. President Andrew Jackson recalled him the following year in response to Simón Bolívar's charges that Harrison had plotted his overthrow. Harrison admitted his dislike for Bolívar but vehemently denied complicity in any conspiracy.

Harrison returned to Ohio where financial difficulties forced him to accept the menial position of clerk of the Cincinnati Court of Common Pleas. In 1836 he ran as the Whig Party's presidential candidate against Democrat Martin Van Buren. Although he lost the contest, the election catapulted Harrison to national prominence and positioned him as a major presidential contender. With Daniel Webster's support, Harrison defeated Henry Clay for the right to head the Whig presidential ticket in 1840.

Harrison's age, sixty-seven, and his alleged lack of political ability became campaign issues. Referring to his age, an editor of the *Baltimore Republican* wrote: "Give [Harrison] a barrel of hard-cider and a pension of two thousand a year . . . and he will sit the remainder of his days in a log cabin . . . and study moral philosophy." Missouri's Democratic senator **Thomas Hart Benton** scoffed at Harrison's candidacy, saying, "availability was the only ability sought by the Whigs."

The Whigs turned such criticism to their advantage and waged a successful presidential contest known as the log cabin and hard-cider campaign. Although the Whigs did not adopt a formal platform, they borrowed a page from Andrew Jackson's successful 1828 campaign by touting Harrison's military exploits. The decision by the Whigs to use popular songs and such slogans as "Tippecanoe and Tyler Too" ushered in modern political campaign techniques that helped Harrison defeat Van Buren.

Following his election as president, Harrison called a special session of Congress to address the nation's failing economy and to seek reestablishment of the Bank of the United States, but his death on April 4, 1841, occurred before Congress could assemble. Harrison was the first president to die in office, and his presidency of thirty-one days was the shortest in U.S. history.

Nonetheless, Harrison left a substantial legacy. As governor of the Indiana Territory he had been instrumental in opening the frontier to white settlement. His brief, but methodical, administration of Upper Louisiana created a framework of law and order for the new territorial government. Harrison also played a significant role in the conduct of Indian-white relations. Like Thomas Jefferson, he admired the Indians and at the same time regarded them as obstacles to national progress. Unable to reconcile his philanthropic views of Native Americans with frontier realities and public policy goals, he resorted to his political and military instincts in carrying out his official duties.

Harrison attained the highest office in the land, but did not have time to establish a presidential record. Regardless, his innovative campaign in 1840, with its ballyhoo and festive appeal, was the first truly popular presidential race in American history.

GARY W. POND

Cleaves, Freeman. *Old Tippecanoe: William Henry Harrison and His Time.* New York: Charles Scribner's Sons, 1939.

Esarey, Logan, ed. *Governors' Messages and Letters: Messages and Letters of William Henry Harrison, 1800–1816.* 2 vols. Indianapolis: Indiana History Commission, 1922.

Goebel, Dorothy B. *William Henry Harrison: A Political Biography.* Indianapolis: Historical Bureau of the Indiana Library and Historical Department, 1926.

Pond, Gary W. "William Henry Harrison and United States Indian Policy in the Northwest and Indiana Territories, 1783–1813." Master's thesis, Central Missouri State University, 1995.

HARVEY, MARIE TURNER
(1866–1952)

Although she gained world fame as an educator, Marie Turner Harvey's own formal schooling was in a rural school. She was born on a farm near St. Louis to Franklin and Anna Zimpelann Turner on May 13, 1866. When she was fifteen she visited an aunt in Kansas where she met teachers who encouraged her to take the county teachers' examination and teach at a rural school.

After teaching in Kansas, Turner returned to Missouri in 1889 to become principal of two elementary schools in Clayton, a suburb of St. Louis. In 1901, while attending the summer session at the State Normal School in Kirksville, she met H. Clay Harvey, a mathematics professor. They were married a year later.

As a faculty wife, Harvey joined the school's president, John R. Kirk, in promoting the rural life movement, an aspect of progressivism. One of Kirk's efforts was the erection in 1907 of a model rural school on the campus. He had designed it with a furnace and a dynamo for generating electricity and pumping water into the schoolhouse. There were facilities for new courses—such as domestic science for the girls and manual training for the boys—and a garden plot. Pupils from nearby farms were brought to the campus in a horse-drawn bus. What the school lacked was a teacher who agreed with Kirk's philosophy. Marie Harvey did, so he offered her the position in 1910; she eagerly accepted and began an experiment in the latest style of progressive education.

After two years Harvey had only begun to execute many of her ideas that developed as she worked. However, at that point her tenure as instructor came to an end along with her marriage. In April 1912 Clay Harvey filed a petition of divorce, and Marie countered. Each charged the other with various misconduct, and the case became front-page news for the Kirksville daily paper. Two months later lawyers worked out a settlement by which Marie Harvey received the divorce and a handsome share of the property in return for withdrawing the worst of her charges. Because of the scandal, the normal school dismissed them both.

Harvey quickly turned adversity into opportunity. She prevailed upon the board of directors of Porter School, northwest of Kirksville, to offer her the position of teacher and to renovate the building in accordance with the design of the model school. The board also agreed to permit her to implement curricular changes and to provide a cottage where she and her mother could live. Amid protests about lack of funds, she offered the solution of community donations of time, labor, and equipment. As soon as the board agreed, she cajoled patrons, older pupils, and anyone available to join the work.

The second phase brought changes in the classroom. Older girls in the domestic science class learned how to prepare and serve meals and practiced by providing lunches for other pupils. Everyone washed hands at the sink and dried on individual towels, then took seats at a long table with Harvey at the head. She oversaw behavior and directed the conversation about school and community projects.

Harvey followed John Dewey's philosophy in her teaching. She wove farm experiences into all basic subjects. For example, a poultry club in which the children raised chickens and kept detailed records served as material for arithmetic problems, essays, and speeches. In recognition of Harvey's progressive methods, Dewey sent his daughter Evelyn to spend a month observing the Porter School. The result was a book titled *New Schools for Old.*

Harvey publicized the school by traveling to teachers' conventions and other meetings to lecture on her achievements. Visitors from all parts of the nation and many foreign countries came to Porter to observe. Several metropolitan papers and major periodicals dispatched writers for stories, and Harvey wrote others herself that she sent to various journals.

Harvey's work at Porter School ended in 1924 when she returned to Kirksville to become an instructor in rural education at what had become Northeast Missouri State Teachers College. In any event, the rural life movement and progressive enthusiasm for reforms of all kinds had waned. Harvey's deeper goals of bringing urban amenities to the rural home and thereby keeping the farm population stable proved impossible in the face of societal changes. However, these things became apparent only in retrospect. In her time Harvey and Porter School seemed to offer a solution to many problems. Harvey died on June 28, 1952, in Kirksville.

RUTH WARNER TOWNE

Harvey, Marie Turner. Papers. Archives. Pickler Memorial Library, Northeast Missouri State University, Kirksville, Mo.

Ryle, Walter H. *Centennial History of Northeast Missouri State Teachers College.* Kirksville, Mo.: Board of Regents, 1979.

Towne, Ruth Warner. "Marie Turner Harvey and the Rural Life Movement." *Missouri Historical Review* 84 (July 1990): 384–403.

HATCH, WILLIAM HENRY (1833–1896)

Born near Georgetown, Kentucky, on September 11, 1833, to Quaker parents, the Reverend William and Mary Adams Hatch, William Henry attended public schools in Lexington, Kentucky, and read law in an office at Richmond. He gained admission to the bar in 1854. Soon thereafter he moved to Hannibal, Missouri, and began a law practice, but he wanted a political career and became a leader in the Democratic Party, gaining election as circuit attorney for the Sixteenth District in 1858, with reelection two years later.

Hatch supported John Bell and Edward Everett on the Constitutional Union Party ticket in 1860. As a Southern sympathizer he refused to take the loyalty oath required of public servants and lost his office in 1862. Hatch joined the Confederate army and advanced in rank from captain to lieutenant colonel. Although he returned to Missouri after the war, the Radical Republicans prevented him from voting or holding office until 1871. He unsuccessfully sought the Democratic nomination for governor in 1872, but in 1878 he was elected to Congress from the First District; he served eight terms.

In Congress Hatch primarily concerned himself with agricultural affairs. He served as chairman of the Committee on Agriculture during which time he sponsored a bill to establish agricultural experiment stations with federal support. Although the idea of federal aid for agricultural research through a system of state experiment stations did not originate with Hatch, he favored support to increase the research base that would help farmers improve their productivity, and he introduced the bill in 1886. Congress approved it, and President Grover Cleveland signed it on March 2, 1887. Known as the Hatch Act, it is one of the most important pieces of legislation passed by Congress because the research conducted at the stations affects every resident in the United States.

Hatch also proposed and sponsored a bill to create the Bureau of Animal Industry (1884), an act to regulate the sale of oleomargarine (1884), and a meat inspection act (1890). He also succeeded in elevating the Department of Agriculture to cabinet status in 1889. Congress had considered a bill to raise the status of the department in 1876, but it did not pass. In 1881 as a member of the Agriculture Committee, Hatch supported the principle of such legislation and urged that a cabinet post be created under the "general welfare" clause of the Constitution. He argued that every other interest had organized representation in the federal government except agriculture, and he believed the size and diversity of the agricultural community deserved such representation. Although the House of Representatives passed such bills in 1882 and 1884, the Senate did not vote on them. On March 7, 1888, Hatch reported a bill from the Committee on Agriculture that gave the department the higher rank. This time the bill passed the House and the Senate, and President Cleveland signed the act, elevating the Department of Agriculture to cabinet status on February 9, 1889.

Hatch's flirtation with Populism during the early 1890s cost him support in the Democratic Party, and he lost influence in Congress and his district. In 1894 he was defeated for reelection. He retired to his farm, but served as president of the National Dairy Union. He married twice. His first wife, Jennie L. Smith, died in 1858. Three years later he married Thetis C. Hawkins; they had one child, Sara Rodes. Hatch died on December 23, 1896.

R. DOUGLAS HURT

Baker, Gladys L. *Century of Service: The First 100 Years of the United States Department of Agriculture.* Washington, D.C.: United States Department of Agriculture, 1963.

Cyclopedia of American Agriculture. Vol. 4. S.v. "Hatch, William Henry."

Mumford, F. B. "William H. Hatch: His Great Contribution to Agriculture." *Missouri Historical Review* 18 (July 1924): 503–6.

HAWES, HARRY BARTOW (1869–1947)

A Missouri legislator, congressman, and U.S. senator, Harry B. Hawes was born in Covington, Kentucky, on November 15, 1869. Educated in the public schools of Covington, he graduated with an LL.B. degree from St. Louis Law School (later incorporated into Washington University) in 1896. He was admitted to the bar of Missouri the same year.

Throughout his long legal career Hawes combined the practice of corporation and international law. His early clients included the St. Louis Merchants Exchange, the Territory of Hawaii, and private individuals. His representation of Mrs. Adolphus Busch of the Busch brewing family on behalf of her safe return to the United States from imperial Germany during World War I became an issue in Missouri politics during the war and in the Prohibition era. Hawes, a lifelong Democrat, defended the right of private citizens to travel abroad and even to lend money and provide arms to belligerents in time of war.

After serving a four-year term as the president of the St. Louis Board of Police Commissioners at the turn of the century, Hawes gained election to the Missouri House of Representatives in 1916. During the legislative term of 1916–1917, he chaired the Good Roads Committee and authored the bills that revised the state's road laws and created the State Highway Department. He also spearheaded the drive for passage of a $60 million bond issue that, along with funds provided by the Federal Highway Act of 1916, provided for the construction of Missouri's first highway system. At the same time Hawes helped to organize and advocate the Lakes-to-the-Gulf Water-

ways Association and the improvement of shipping on the Mississippi River.

During World War I Hawes was commissioned a captain in the United States Army with service in the psychological section of the Military Intelligence Department. His assignments included work in France and Spain in 1918, leading to his appointment to the post of assistant military attaché at the United States Embassy in Madrid. He was honorably discharged from the army with the rank of major in 1919.

Hawes won election from Missouri's Eleventh Congressional District of the St. Louis area to the United States House of Representatives in 1920, and he served in Congress for three successive terms. With Republicans in control of the Congress and the White House throughout the twenties, Hawes and his fellow Democrats waged an uphill battle to secure the enactment of programs on their agenda. His personal popularity and acceptance by both wings of the badly divided rural and urban Missouri Democratic Party led to his nomination and election as a U.S. senator in 1926 to fulfill the remaining months of the unexpired term of the late **Seldon Palmer Spencer** and a full term commencing in 1927.

Hawes's senatorial term was distinguished by his work in behalf of flood control, wildlife, and independence for the Philippines. His "Missouri Plan" for the construction of levees along the Mississippi River was adopted by Congress two years after the devastating flood of 1927. His interest in wild-life management led to his appointment to the Migratory Bird Conservation Commission in 1929. He coauthored the Hawes-Cutting Bill of 1932 that pledged the United States would end its colonial control of the Philippines. His advocacy of this measure reflected the original anti-imperialist position taken by the Democratic Party at the turn of the century when the nation first established its control over the Philippines.

Hawes did not seek reelection in 1932. Following his return to private life, he resumed the practice of law and the pursuit of his lifelong interest in wild-life conservation. In Washington, D.C., where he maintained his permanent residence, he provided legal counsel to the sugar and cordage interests, among others, of the Philippines Commonwealth in the United States. His game-conservation activities often brought him back to his adopted state where he became a spokesman for the propagation and stocking of black bass in the rivers and streams of Missouri.

Hawes's active membership in various organizations reflected a wide range of recreational and intellectual interests, including hunting, kennel, fishing, and yachting clubs. He was a member of numerous professional organizations and social clubs in Washington and president of the Jefferson Club of

St. Louis, a Democratic organization that exercised some influence in the politics of the city and the state. He was well liked by **Harry S. Truman,** and when he died in Washington on July 31, 1947, the president designated their mutual friend, presidential press secretary **Charles G. Ross,** to attend the funeral. Hawes's cremated remains were returned to Missouri for scattering on the waters of the Doniphan River.

Despite the fact that the tenure of Hawes in the Missouri legislature and the United States Senate was limited in years of service, he authored important enduring legislation in both bodies. His authorship of the Hawes Road Law of 1916 and the federal legislation for levee construction along the Mississippi River, as well as his advocacy of an internal water transportation system from the Great Lakes to the Gulf of Mexico, contributed to the modernization of the transportation system of twentieth-century Missouri and the nation. His notable work in behalf of wild life and conservation rivaled the achievements of other prominent conservationists of his era. His advocacy of individual rights, civil liberties, and anti-imperialism placed him among the great Jeffersonians of his generation.

FRANKLIN D. MITCHELL

Hawes, Harry B. *My Friend the Black Bass.* New York: Frederick A. Stokes, 1930.

————. *Philippine Uncertainty: An American Problem.* New York: Century, 1932.

Mitchell, Franklin D. *Embattled Democracy: Missouri Democratic Politics, 1919–1932.* Columbia: University of Missouri Press, 1968.

National Cyclopedia of American Biography. S.v. "Hawes, Harry Bartow."

HAWKEN, JACOB (1786–1849); HAWKEN, SAMUEL (1792–1884)

Christian Hawken, a respected gunsmith of Hagerstown, Maryland, taught his six sons and several grandsons the craft of rifle making. The eldest son, Jacob (born in 1786), completed his apprenticeship and ventured west to establish his own business in 1807. By 1815 he had opened a gun shop in St. Louis.

Jacob's brother Samuel (born on October 26, 1792) served in the Maryland militia during the War of 1812, moved to Ohio after the war, and finally joined Jacob in St. Louis in 1822. Their partnership flourished.

Although J & S Hawken offered a complete line of firearms for the local trade, the firm became famous for a distinctive rifle developed for westering traders, explorers, and hunters. The Hawken Rocky Mountain Rifle was compact, sturdy, accurate, and reliable. It was light enough to carry on a long ride, but of heavy caliber—sufficient to bring down a buffalo with one shot.

The brothers outdistanced their competition by employing the latest technology to produce quality weapons. They were among the first western gun makers to adopt the new percussion lock in place of the old flintlock. They continually updated equipment and standardized parts and production. By the late 1830s their gun shop had grown into a small factory where they experimented with assembly-line production and marketing techniques usually associated with early-twentieth-century American industry. Several workmen from the Hawken shop went on to open gun shops of their own. At least one of these, Christian Hoffman and Tristam Campbell's shop in St. Louis, apparently operated as a subsidiary of J & S Hawken in the 1840s.

Jacob Hawken died of cholera on May 8, 1849, during the epidemic that struck St. Louis in that year. Samuel Hawken became ill but recovered in time to help St. Louis rebuild after fire devastated the business district that same year. The California gold rush helped the city and the Hawken gun shop back to prosperity, and Samuel continued to operate the business until his health failed in 1859. Hoping a trip west might restore him, he left his son William in charge of the St. Louis shop and joined the mining rush to Colorado. Finding prospects encouraging, he opened a gun shop in Denver in 1860; his son promptly sold the St. Louis business and joined him there.

In 1861 Hawken returned to St. Louis, where he had some property and many friends. "Uncle Sammy" was known throughout the city for his involvement in volunteer fire companies and other civic projects. He died in St. Louis on May 9, 1884. J. P. Gemmer (1838–1919), who had taken over the St. Louis gun shop, continued to trade on the Hawken name until he retired in 1915. Jacob's son Christopher abandoned gun making after his father's death, tried his luck in the California gold rush, and then returned to St. Louis and opened a livery stable. In 1857 he married and built a home on the outskirts of St. Louis, the only building associated with the Hawken family still standing today.

Although the Hawken Rifle has entered western legend as the mountain man's weapon of choice, trappers of the 1820s and 1830s generally preferred the old-style flintlocks. Although renowned for its quality, the Hawken Rifle was expensive, and its percussion lock and large caliber required a nearby source for caps, powder, and lead. Traders with ready access to such supplies did prefer Hawken Rifles. **William Henry Ashley** carried a prized custom-made Hawken, as did Lucien Fontenelle, Andrew Drips, John Sarpy, and other leading figures of the Missouri fur trade. Hawken Rifles were popular among the Santa Fe traders, and frontier scouts, guides, and hunters eagerly acquired them when they could afford them. **Jim Bridger** in his later years, **Kit Carson,** and others celebrated in western literature popularized the Hawken Rifle.

The full significance of the Hawken brothers has yet to be appreciated, however. Their innovative production and marketing methods deserve further study as precedents for later American industrial development.

MARY ELLEN ROWE

Baird, John D. *Hawken Rifles: The Mountain Man's Choice.* Big Timber, Mont.: Buckskin Press, 1968.
Hanson, Charles, Jr. *The Hawken Rifle: Its Place in History.* Chadron, Nebr.: Fur Press, 1979.

HAZARD, REBECCA NAYLOR (1826–1912)

Although her name is not well known, Rebecca Naylor Hazard deserves to be listed with such company as Henry Ward Beecher, Thomas Wentworth Higginson, and Julia Ward Howe. In 1878 Hazard succeeded these notables as the elected president of the American Woman's Suffrage Association, the first president of that organization to reside west of the Mississippi River. Her road to this office was one of ever increasing hard work, activism, and philanthropy.

Rebecca Naylor was born on November 10, 1826, in Woodsfield, Ohio. Her mother, Mary Archbold Naylor, numbered among her relatives nephew John D. Archbold, who became one of the multimillionaires of the Standard Oil Company. This fact caused the Archbold family some consternation, as overall it was not a family known for its prowess in accumulating wealth.

Rebecca's father, Robert F. Naylor, a member of an old Virginia family, married Mary Archbold in 1823 and moved to Woodsfield. There Rebecca, their eldest daughter, attended first the Monroe Institute and then the Marietta Female Seminary until the age of fourteen. Had this been her only education, she might not have developed her skills and talents to the extent that she did. Her true education, however, came in the form of books; she was an avid and passionate reader.

When she was fourteen, Rebecca's family moved first to Cincinnati and from there to Quincy, Illinois. It was in Quincy that she met and married William T. Hazard in 1844. In 1850 the couple moved to St. Louis, and soon thereafter Rebecca Hazard began to take an interest in destitute young girls. As director of the Girls' Industrial Home, she invested both time and money in an institution that eventually sheltered thousands of homeless children.

When the Civil War began, Hazard turned her attention to sick and wounded soldiers, first by joining a group of women who sewed items needed by the soldiers, and then as one of the organizers of the Ladies' Union Aid Society (LUAS), an association dedicated to hospital service.

Hazard's next project grew from the fact that a great number of former slaves, mainly women and children, flooded into St. Louis as the war progressed. Poor and homeless, they often did not live long. Touched by their plight, Hazard and a few other women formed a new society dedicated to bringing aid and succor to this group of sufferers. Money to fund the effort was slow in coming, however. To fill the treasury, Hazard wrote an appeal that was first published in a St. Louis newspaper and eventually sent to papers in the eastern states. Donations soon began pouring in, and the society amassed three thousand dollars to fund its operations.

Word of Hazard's abilities spread, and in 1863 she, along with five other women, was appointed by the LUAS to help organize the Sanitary Fair, an event held to raise money to aid sick and wounded soldiers. The fair was an overwhelming success, bringing in more than a half million dollars. At the close of the war, Hazard assisted in the founding of the Guardian Home for unfortunate women.

In 1867 Hazard helped form the Woman-Suffrage Association of Missouri, which she served for the next twenty years. Her organizational skills and her tireless activism were recognized in 1878 with her election as president of the American Woman's Suffrage Association.

Continuing in her efforts to advance the cause of women, she assisted in forming the School of Design in St. Louis, an institute that afforded women the opportunity to learn the various fields of decorative art. She also became an active member of the Women's Christian Temperance Union.

In later years Hazard was able to indulge her love of books and literature when she opened her home near Kirkwood to a group of women who devoted themselves to the study of poets and philosophers. She wrote two papers collectively titled "Two Views of Dante" in which she advanced her theory that Dante had used "man's physical form in exemplification of his theme . . . a body deranged by disease to illustrate the wretched condition of a soul disordered by sin." Her explication was praised by several noted Dante scholars. For more than sixteen years, Hazard's literary society met weekly in her home.

Hazard and her husband had five children, two of whom died in infancy. Rebecca Hazard died in Kirkwood on March 1, 1912, and was buried in Bellefontaine Cemetery.

DEBORAH STEWARD

Conard, Howard L., ed. *Encyclopedia of the History of Missouri*. New York: Southern History, 1901.

Hazard, Rebecca N. *A New View of Dante*. St. Louis, 1891.

———. *A View of Dante*. Kirkwood, Mo., 1887.

Shoemaker, Floyd C., ed. *Missouri, Day by Day*. Columbia: State Historical Society of Missouri, 1942–1943.

HEARST, PHOEBE APPERSON (1842–1919)

When she was a little girl in pigtails, Phoebe Elizabeth Apperson sometimes rode on the shoulders of neighbor George Hearst. Then he caught gold fever and left for California. A dozen years later he returned to Missouri a rich man. He came to tend to his dying mother and stayed in the Meramec Valley for several months while trying to resolve a land dispute. While there, he discovered that the little girl in pigtails had grown up and was teaching school. Despite the twenty-two-year difference in their ages, he began to court her.

Phoebe's parents thought Hearst crude. But the independent, strong-willed couple overcame her family's opposition and married on June 15, 1862. She was only nineteen but was shrewd enough to take the unusual step of signing a prenuptial contract that guaranteed her a good living if he died before she did. Her marriage to the uncultivated miner eventually lifted this extraordinary woman from her life as a small-town Missouri schoolteacher and enabled her to become an education pioneer, a philanthropist of enormous goodwill, and one of the most influential American women in the early twentieth century.

Phoebe Apperson Hearst was born a farm girl in the Whitmire settlement near St. Clair, Missouri, on December 3, 1842, the eldest of three children. Not until her later years did she spell her first name with an "o." She attended the Salem log school, south of the present town of Anaconda, as well as schools in Steelville, St. James, and, briefly, a boarding school in St. Louis. At the age of seventeen, she was a teacher at the Reeder school in present-day Meramec State Park.

By the time Phoebe and George returned to San Francisco following their marriage, she was pregnant with their only child, William Randolph. Phoebe spoiled him, taking him to Europe for an extensive tour at age ten. In later years she built a playhouse big enough for her grandchildren to ride their bicycles in. When William felt he had conquered the newspaper publishing world on the West Coast, she gave him $7.5 million to buy the *New York World*.

However, there was within this doting mother a constitution of steel. In the early years of her marriage to Hearst, she accompanied him on horseback to his mining operations in Idaho, Montana, Nevada, Utah, and the Dakotas. While visiting the Hearst mines in New Mexico, she was astonished to find only a single church in the village of Pinos Altos, and it was Catholic, prompting her to donate money for a Methodist church.

Hearst soaked up culture and lavishly supported the arts. At one time she was the sole sponsor of efforts to keep a series of symphony concerts in San Francisco. She built, and for several years supported, free libraries in Lead, South Dakota, and Anaconda, Montana.

When George Hearst became a U.S. senator in 1886, Phoebe Hearst took her philanthropic efforts to Washington, D.C., where she gave one quarter million dollars to construct the National Cathedral School for Girls. She provided thousands of dollars for St. Albans School, established a special school that trained 90 percent of Washington's kindergarten teachers, and was a major contributor to the restoration of George Washington's home at Mount Vernon.

George Hearst died in 1891, leaving his widow an estate worth $17 million. For several years Phoebe Hearst divided her attention between her interests in Washington and the family's holdings in California, but eventually she centered her life on the West Coast. On February 17, 1897, she and Alice McClellan Birney founded the National Congress of Mothers, and for many years Hearst underwrote most of the group's expenses. In 1924, five years after Hearst's death, the organization became the National Congress of Parents and Teachers.

During the 1890s Hearst became interested in the University of California, where she established several scholarships. In 1896 she gave almost two hundred thousand dollars to fund an international contest to develop a master plan for the Berkeley campus. In the mid-1890s her interest in archaeology and anthropology prompted her to finance a study of an ancient civilization in Florida. She supported archaeological expeditions in Russia, Italy, and Egypt, requiring that all the artifacts they found be sent to the University of California, which was then building a special museum to house them.

Each spring Hearst took the university's graduating class by special train to the private railroad station at her hacienda near Pleasanton for an all-day picnic, where she treated them to the unique experience of riding in an automobile. She became a regent of the university in 1897 and served in that role until her death. Through her efforts the University of California recruited its first women professors for the Berkeley campus.

Prior to America's entry in World War I, Hearst participated in a War Preparedness Day Parade in the summer of 1916, despite receiving a note threatening her life if she marched. She later said there was nothing for her to do but march, and she did—at the head of the women's brigade. Moments after her group passed one particular street corner, a bomb went off, exacting a high toll among the bystanders. During World War I the United States christened a 10,500-ton liberty ship in her name.

Hearst understood that wealth is having money, and richness is using it to benefit others. In this sense she was both wealthy and rich, especially when compared with her pampered son, who is widely remembered only as the former. She remained vigorous in her support of education and culture until she died of influenza at her Spanish-style villa, La Hacienda del Pozo de Verona, near Pleasanton, on April 13, 1919. W. A. Swanberg, a biographer of her son, called the Missouri-born philanthropist, "California's greatest lady, and one of the nation's most remarkable women."

BOB PRIDDY

Procter, Ben. *William Randolph Hearst: The Early Years, 1863–1910.* New York: Oxford University Press, 1998.

Robinson, Judith. *The Hearsts: An American Dynasty.* Newark: University of Delaware Press, 1991.

Swanbery, W. A. *Citizen Hearst.* New York: Scribner's, 1961.

HEINKEL, FRED VICTOR
(1897–1990)

A champion for the American farmer, Fred V. Heinkel lived with a passion for advancing agriculture. This devotion became his lifeline and the Missouri Farmers Association (MFA) the vehicle through which it flowed.

Fred Victor Heinkel, whose grandfather migrated to Missouri from Germany, was born to William G. and Cora Belle McDaniel Heinkel on September 22, 1897, on a farm near Oermann in Jefferson County, Missouri. In 1904 he moved with his parents to Franklin County where he attended school through the sixth grade. His formal education ended there, and he then devoted his time to the family farm.

However, lack of formal education did not hinder this man who, throughout his career, received a number of citations and honorary degrees. Heinkel often expressed pride about his accomplishments in business, but was equally proud that he had passed high school equivalency and teacher certification exams.

Heinkel was fond of saying he walked out of the corn rows and into the office. He had a small farm in Franklin County when he became vice president of the MFA in 1936, a nonsalaried position requiring oversight at meetings and office functions. In a mere four years he became president of the

MFA when **William Henry Hirth,** the organization's founder, died.

Under Heinkel's direction the MFA moved from being a simple brokerage and commission house to a business organization that bought and sold commodities. He assumed responsibility for speaking on behalf of the farm membership of the MFA, and for a variety of other organizations he served. Considered a liberal on farm policy, Heinkel aggressively advocated programs that provided opportunities for farmers to receive fair incomes. He succeeded in securing a number of improvements in farm and rural programs.

Assuming the association presidency in 1940, Heinkel won reelection to that office each year until 1979. Fostering an organization of granitelike financial solvency and an impeccable reputation produced many rewards for Fred Heinkel and his organization. His political sagacity made the MFA an important force in the local, as well as the national, farming scene.

Heinkel made clear what he believed and did not waver from those beliefs. In the first decade of his presidency, he began his political involvement by ramrodding the King Road Bill through the Missouri General Assembly, providing for state-maintained all-weather country roads. Heinkel's drive to develop a unified voice for agriculture led him, with leaders of five other national farm groups (both conservative and liberal), to formulate the National Farm Coalition. He served as its first president.

During the 1940s the legislative programs initiated and promoted by the MFA represented one of the most credible performances of any farm group in the history of the farm movement. Heinkel campaigned for better rural telephone service, improved rural roads, and extended Rural Electrification Association benefits for farm families. During World War II the U.S. Department of Agriculture appointed him to its advisory committee.

Heinkel also gave strong support to a $9 million appropriation for a four-year medical school. Due in large part to the support and effort of the MFA, the legislature located the medical school and teaching hospital in Columbia.

Further political involvement came with President **Harry S. Truman**'s appointment of Heinkel as a member of a committee to study the Missouri valley flood problem. Heinkel, in conjunction with two senators, **William Stuart Symington** and **Thomas C. Hennings Jr.,** fought to prevent destruction of the Rural Electrification Association in the Senate and to have Table Rock Dam completed. Heinkel's MFA was instrumental in obtaining relief for drought-stricken Missouri farmers in late 1953 and early 1954.

In 1961 President John F. Kennedy summoned Heinkel to the White House. He had narrowed to two the number of candidates for the position of U.S. secretary of agriculture: Heinkel and a young and recently defeated governor from Minnesota, Orville Freeman. Kennedy chose Freeman, though Heinkel surpassed him in experience. Allegedly, the president preferred Heinkel, but Robert Kennedy expressed concern about Heinkel's age, sixty-four, and his lack of formal education. Although not chosen, Heinkel remained a staunch supporter of Kennedy's farm program, in part because he contributed to its formulation.

Heinkel served as president of the MFA for thirty-nine years, as well as president and chairman of the board of MFA subsidiary companies. He served on the University of Missouri Board of Curators (1953) and was one of the founders of MFA Insurance Companies, later renamed Shelter Insurance Company.

During most of his adult life Heinkel resided in Columbia, Missouri, with his wife, the former Dorothy Hart, whom he married in 1946. Fred Heinkel died on October 31, 1990, at the age of ninety-three.

DONNA K. COGELL

Heinkel, Fred V. Papers. Western Historical Manuscripts Collection, Columbia.

Kirkendall, Richard. *A History of Missouri: Volume V, 1919 to 1953.* Columbia: University of Missouri Press, 1986.

Lay, Chuck. "Fred Heinkel, 1897–1990." *Today's Farmer* (February 1991): 7–11.

March, David D. "Fred Victor Heinkel." In *The History of Missouri.* New York: Lewis Historical Publishing, 1967.

Wood, Maggie. "Starting an Insurance Company." *Shield* 6:8 (August 1983): 33–37.

Young, Raymond A. *Cultivating Cooperation: A History of the Missouri Farmers Association.* Columbia: University of Missouri Press, 1995.

HELIAS, FERDINAND (1796–1874)

Ferdinand Benedict Marie Guislain Helias d'Huddeghem, a Jesuit priest, was the first resident Catholic pastor of central Missouri. He described himself as a "cosmopolitan priest," which indeed he was. His story is a fascinating one of a man born of nobility in Ghent, Belgium, who decided as a youth to become a missionary among the Native Americans of the New World and ended up as the "apostle of the Catholic Church in Central Missouri."

Ferdinand Helias was born on August 3, 1796, in Ghent, the capital of Flanders, Belgium, in the same house where the Emperor Charles V, count of Flanders, was born. His grandfather and later his father, Emmanuel Francis (b. 1762), were the chief lawyers for the city of Flanders, and his father was also on the faculty of the law school in Louvain, Belgium.

Helias's mother, Marie Charlotte Guislaine of Lens (b. 1769), was the daughter of Charles, the count of Lens. Her mother was a baroness. There was also some spiritual royalty in the family. One brother was named for a Blessed (the step below a formal declaration of sainthood in the Catholic Church) Idisbald Van der Gacht, an abbot who was a relative on his mother's side.

Helias was the third of eleven children. His brother Idisbald, eight years younger, became a diocesan priest. One sister, Pauline Marie, became an Augustinian nun. Several children died in infancy, and one was stillborn. Ferdinand was his father's favorite and was a very devout child.

Helias became a Jesuit novice on October 9, 1817. His call to come to the United States as a missionary to the Native Americans came from a sermon by Father Charles Nerinckx, a famous Jesuit missionary to Kentucky, but his father would not approve. Helias volunteered to come study in the United States but was told to wait.

Helias's classmates went to Switzerland while he went to Paris, then to Fribourg, Switzerland, and Namur, Belgium, for his studies. He was ordained a priest at Pentecost in 1825. Eight years later his old prayer was granted: he received permission to go to the United States.

Helias arrived in New York in May 1833 and went to the Jesuits' Georgetown College in Maryland. He became assistant to the novice master, and an instructor for the German-speaking children in the area, including Pennsylvania.

On August 6, 1835, Helias received permission to go to Missouri and arrived in St. Louis on August 22. St. Louis University had been founded by the Jesuits six years earlier; they had come to establish the St. Louis province in 1823, two years after Missouri's statehood. While awaiting an official assignment, Helias taught moral theology (that is, ethics), calligraphy, and Italian at the college and served as the community "minister," or house administrator.

St. Charles succeeded Florissant as the center from which the Catholic settlements along the Missouri River were served by the Jesuits. Helias cared for the German-speaking parishioners at St. Joseph Church and also traveled to Illinois, in addition to his other teaching and administrative duties. His intense pastoral zeal was combined with a brilliant and curious mind as shown in his unpublished memoirs and "History of the Central Missouri Mission."

One of the most touching stories in his memoirs is of an Iroquois father, a native of Canada, and his two sons who came all the way from California, across the Rockies, to find the "black robes" (the Native

American name for the Jesuits) to baptize his two sons and hear his confession.

In 1838 Helias was sent to establish the first permanent residence in Westphalia to serve the eighteen "stations" (centers where the Catholic community gathered) along the Missouri, Gasconade, Osage, and Moreau Rivers. He arrived on May 11, and celebrated mass in a home in Bonnots Mill. Helias eventually founded several churches: St. Joseph in Westphalia; Sacred Heart in Rich Fountain; Immaculate Conception in Loose Creek; St. Francis Xavier in Taos, which later became his residence; St. Ignatius (renamed St. Peter) in Jefferson City; St. Thomas the Apostle in St. Thomas; and Assumption in Cedron. He tells of putting these parishes far enough apart to keep the peace between people from different kingdoms in the Old Country: Bavarians in Rich Fountain (originally New Bavaria, renamed for the abundant water supply), Rhinelanders in Loose (which he called Louis) Creek, and Prussians in Westphalia. The settlers of Taos included Belgians of his own Germanic ethnic background. Helias celebrated mass once a month in some of his parishes and made occasional visits to his other stations.

Helias's memoirs and his "History" give detailed and sometimes emotional accounts of his experiences and opinions, ranging from ecstatic praise of the United States to his spirited defense of his fellow Germans against prejudice and his dislike of "Americans" (that is, northern Protestants) who targeted his Catholic flock and their doctrines. They are balanced by his nineteenth-century-style ecumenism, which included attendance by government officials from Jefferson City at a solemn religious service in Taos, and the troubles caused by his attempts to minister without partisanship during the Civil War.

Helias died at Taos on August 11, 1874. His body was kept there because the glass on the casket broke in the heat and was therefore prevented from being sent by train to St. Louis for burial, as was Jesuit custom. It was a fortuitous accident. There is a Helias museum at Taos today.

Hugh F. Behan

Helias, Ferdinand. "History of the Central Missouri Mission." Jesuit Archives. St. Louis Provincialate, St. Louis.

———. Memoirs. Jesuit Archives. St. Louis Provincialate, St. Louis.

Rothensteiner, John E. *History of the Archdiocese of St. Louis in Its Various Stages of Development from A.D. 1637 to A.D. 1928.* 2 vols. St. Louis: Blackwell Wielandy, 1928.

Schmidt, Daniel A. *The Heritage of St. Thomas.* Jefferson City, Mo.: Bob Dew Printing, 1974.

Welschmeyer, Joe. *Sacred Heart Sesquicentennial, 1838–1988.* N.p., 1988.

HEMPSTEAD, EDWARD (1780–1817)

Edward Hempstead, a prominent early Missouri attorney and politician, was born in New London, Connecticut, on June 3, 1780. He studied law, gained admission to the bar in 1801, and practiced his profession for three years in Rhode Island before deciding to seek new opportunities in the rapidly developing western American territories. Hempstead stopped briefly in Vincennes, in Indiana Territory, but soon determined to go on to the recently acquired Louisiana Territory. According to one account, the eager young attorney walked from Vincennes to St. Louis, carrying his belongings in a bundle slung over his back.

Not long after his arrival in Upper Louisiana in 1804, Hempstead secured an appointment as deputy attorney general for the districts of St. Charles and St. Louis. He initially took up residence in St. Charles, where he devoted much of his time to studying French, but in 1805 he moved his law practice to St. Louis. Although he opposed the political machinations of the pro-French governor, **James Wilkinson,** Hempstead somehow managed not to alienate prominent local French Creole leaders. He was, in fact, one of the first American lawyers in the territory to appreciate the profitability of handling land adjudication cases for French clients unfamiliar with American legal practices. Following Wilkinson's departure, Hempstead became a champion of the Spanish land claimants' cause.

Hempstead quickly emerged as a rising star in the fledgling trans-Mississippi legal community. His courtroom oratory was so successful that other lawyers attempted to imitate his sharp, preemptory speaking style. Gov. **Meriwether Lewis** appointed him attorney general for the territory in 1809. Hempstead's legal practice flourished, and in 1812 he formed a brief partnership with **David Barton,** another up-and-coming member of the territorial bar.

Other members of the Hempstead clan soon followed Edward from their native New England to St. Louis. His father, **Stephen Hempstead,** became an ardent backer of efforts to organize Presbyterian churches in the trans-Mississippi territory, and his widowed sister, Mary Hempstead Keeney, married the renowned Spanish trader **Manuel Lisa.** Edward's 1808 marriage to Clarissa Dubreuil helped cement his relationship with the St. Louis Creoles, who increasingly looked to him for assistance in litigating land claims cases.

When Congress approved the creation of Missouri as a second-class territory in 1812, Hempstead declared as a candidate for territorial delegate. With backing from a coalition of French Creoles and long-established Americans, he defeated the three other contenders in the race and became Missouri's first representative in the United States Congress.

Hempstead compiled an impressive record during his brief tenure as the territory's nonvoting congressional delegate. He successfully lobbied for added federal military assistance to protect the exposed territory against the increased threats caused by the declaration of war against Great Britain in 1812. His announcement early in 1813 that Congress had agreed to authorize the raising of ten companies of rangers, including three for the Missouri Territory, was especially welcomed by his anxious constituents. Hempstead also helped secure congressional approval for a more liberal land-confirmation policy that included an agreement to rescind a previous decision to deny all grants issued by Spanish authorities after 1800.

Despite his successes as territorial delegate, Hempstead declined to seek reelection in 1814. Following the completion of his term in Congress, he returned to St. Louis and resumed his thriving legal practice.

A tragic accident cut short Hempstead's promising career. He died in St. Louis on August 9, 1817, from complications of injuries he sustained when he was thrown from his horse. Many mourned his premature passing, including his good friend **Thomas Hart Benton** who insisted on attending his funeral services before going to meet **Charles Lucas** on the dueling ground.

WILLIAM E. FOLEY

Foley, William E. *The Genesis of Missouri: From Wilderness Outpost to Statehood.* Columbia: University of Missouri Press, 1989.

Hempstead Papers. Missouri Historical Society, St. Louis.

Tice, Nancy Jo. "The Territorial Delegate, 1794–1820." Ph.D. diss., University of Wisconsin, 1967.

HEMPSTEAD, STEPHEN (1754–1831)

Stephen Hempstead was born on May 6, 1754, in New London, Connecticut. As a young man he fought in the Revolutionary War, earning the nickname "Fighting Stephen." He was twice wounded, and his home was burned by British troops. As a veteran he received a lifetime pension of thirty-six dollars per year. He married Mary Lewis of New London in 1777. They had seven sons and three daughters.

The second son, **Edward Hempstead,** came to the Louisiana Territory in 1804, settling in St. Louis, where he was appointed deputy attorney general for the districts of St. Charles and St. Louis. His brothers Stephen Jr. and Thomas soon joined him, and in 1811

Stephen Sr. brought his wife, his widowed daughter, Mary Keeney, and her son Christopher to St. Louis, taking up residence on a large farm north of the city, on land now partly occupied by Bellefontaine Cemetery.

Although he held no appointed or elected office in St. Louis County, Stephen Hempstead functioned in a number of official capacities. He performed marriages, oversaw the repair and building of roads and bridges, and served as a judge at local elections. In short, he served as a kind of "Mr. Fixit" for the entire county. He was often called on to tend the sick, usually employing either bleeding or blistering to effect a cure. His advice was sought for all kinds of family emergencies. In addition, he operated his large farm with the help of a cadre of slaves.

From 1813 to 1831 Hempstead kept a detailed diary in which he recorded the events of his life and the lives of his children and neighbors, a narrative that was, in effect, a register of the residents of the entire county in its early days. From this multivolume work we learn of many operations of daily farm life in Missouri. He mentions sheep killed by wolves, harvesting pumpkins, retting flax, the death of a cow from eating white lead at Christian Wilt's lead factory, butchering hogs, the death of a newborn lamb, and other routine events.

Deeply religious, Hempstead never missed an opportunity to attend worship services, wherever and whenever they were held. He was instrumental in bringing to St. Louis ministers of the Presbyterian faith, and in forming the first Presbyterian church in the St. Louis area, Bonhomme, whose pastor, the Reverend **Salmon Giddings,** arrived in 1816 and was made welcome in the Hempstead household. Hempstead made frequent visits to St. Louis to solicit funds for the building of a meetinghouse in the city, and noted in March 1817 the first Presbyterian baptism in St. Louis.

The Hempstead farm afforded a large burying ground where interments were many and frequent. One funeral was that of Edward Hempstead, who died following a fall from his horse. The Reverend Mr. Giddings preached the funeral oration. On the following day it was back to threshing and "chopped weeds." When Hempstead's wife became ill, the rather grisly aspects of her cure were detailed. First she was given sulphur water as a cure; then, short of breath, she was blistered and given laudanum; and after a dose of mercury she died in September 1820. Blistering was a favorite remedy for almost any ailment; one Lewis, a slave, underwent several blisterings and twenty-four bleedings before beginning to improve.

Needy families could count on Hempstead for help. He took in several families who had come to

St. Louis without funds, and canvassed the neighborhood for donations of money and clothing. He arranged the purchase of a hearse for the city and purchased lots at auction for a Presbyterian church. He is best remembered for his many benevolent acts and his determination to see Protestantism established in Missouri, where it had been said that "when we cross the Mississippi, we travel beyond the Sabbath."

In 1831, at the age of seventy-seven, he began to lose strength. He made his last diary entry on September 24 of that year, and died quietly on October 3 at his farm outside St. Louis.

FRANCES H. STADLER

Hempstead Papers. Missouri Historical Society, St. Louis.

Jensen, Dana O., ed. "I At Home: The Diary of Stephen S. Hempstead, Sr." *Bulletin of the Missouri Historical Society* 13 (October 1956): 30–56.

HENDERSON, JOHN B. (1824–1913)

John Henderson, the son of James and Jane Dawson Henderson, was born in Pittsylvania County, Virginia, on November 16, 1824. Hard times forced his family, including two sisters and a brother, to move in 1832 to Lincoln County, Missouri, where both parents died in 1836. Henderson's education was meager. In 1842 he attended school at Prairieville, in Pike County, studied a short time at the Norville school, and returned to the Prairieville school as its teacher in 1843. While teaching he read law and was admitted to the bar in 1847, and moved to Clarksville, Missouri.

Henderson's political activity emerged at the same time as his move to Clarksville. In 1848 he was a Democratic candidate for state representative of Pike County, on a platform supporting the Independent Treasury system, national internal improvements, the Mexican War, and self-determination for each state regarding slavery. The election was a party victory, and marked Henderson's first elected office. The highlight of his term was his offering moderate resolutions based on squatter sovereignty for the organization of the territories acquired from Mexico. Although his resolutions were not adopted, he subsequently voted for the more extreme Jackson-Napton Resolutions that divided the Democratic Party, and cost Sen. **Thomas Hart Benton** his seat and Henderson's election to the United States House of Representatives. Henderson did not advocate disruption of the Union, and his vote for the Jackson-Napton Resolutions did not support that view.

Following adjournment of the legislature Henderson moved to Louisiana, Missouri, the largest community in Pike County. In 1850 he withdrew his candidacy for reelection as state representative to accept the Democratic nomination for the United States House of Representatives—which was a mistake. Henderson's virtual anonymity outside Pike County, the division of the Democratic Party, and the slavery question combined to defeat him.

Between 1850 and 1856 Henderson's concentration on his legal practice and real estate transactions provided him with financial security. From 1853 to 1855 he served as judge of the court of common pleas in Louisiana, but resigned to resume political activities.

In 1856 he was the Pike County anti-Benton Democratic candidate for state representative. Not only was his campaign successful, but the state Democratic committee appointed him as a James Buchanan presidential elector as well. His 1856–1857 term in the House was politically uneventful, though he was appointed by Gov. **Robert Marcellus Stewart** to serve as division inspector for the Second Military District with the rank of colonel. Henderson tried again in 1858 for the House of Representatives, but was defeated by incumbent Thomas L. Anderson.

Henderson's conviction that popular sovereignty was the solution for "Bleeding Kansas" led him to support and campaign for Illinois senator Stephen A. Douglas in the 1860 presidential election, becoming a Douglas delegate to the Democratic National Convention in Charleston, South Carolina. Upon his return to Missouri Henderson received the Second Congressional District's nomination for Congress. The 1860 campaign focused on three issues: abolition, slavery expansion into the territories, and the split in the Democratic Party. This last issue cost Henderson the election. Following his unsuccessful campaign, he actively worked for Douglas in Missouri, was subsequently chosen as a Douglas presidential elector from the First Electoral District, and was appointed to the Democratic State Central Committee.

Between January 1860 and the summer of 1861, Henderson became recognized as an influential Missouri political figure. Throughout this period he maintained his moderate, conservative attitude for the Union and the Constitution.

In January 1861 Henderson was elected from the First Senatorial District to attend the Missouri state convention that was to determine secession or union. A measure of his stature within the strife-torn Democratic Party was his election by fellow delegates to represent the Second District at the border-state convention in Frankfort, Kentucky. Throughout the early summer of 1861 Henderson spoke at public rallies in northeast Missouri on behalf of the Union. Gov. **Hamilton Rowan Gamble** appointed Henderson brigadier general for northeast Missouri in August 1861 because of his unwavering support of the Union. When the two U.S. senators from Missouri did not take an oath of loyalty, their seats were declared vacant, and Lt. Gov. **Willard Preble Hall,** in Gamble's absence, appointed Henderson to fill the vacancy of **Trusten W. Polk** in 1862. Henderson's appointment was received with general satisfaction by the newspapers and Union supporters.

Henderson's terms in Washington, D.C., were dominated by three events that had national impact: his leadership in the adoption of emancipation, his search for a permanent solution to the Indian wars, and the impeachment trial of President Andrew Johnson.

Senator Henderson supported Lincoln's call for gradual, compensated emancipation for loyal slave owners in the border states. He did not believe the federal government had the constitutional authority to free the slaves of loyal men. He authored a bill to pay Missourians for their slaves, but it was defeated in the House because there were no Missouri senators in Washington, D.C., from March to November 1863 to support the legislation. On January 11, 1864, after his election to a six-year term, Henderson introduced a constitutional amendment for the immediate abolition of slavery in the United States, which subsequently became the Thirteenth Amendment to the Constitution.

As the chairman of the Senate Indian Affairs Committee, Henderson sought a solution to the continuing friction between Indians and whites. In July 1867 he sponsored a bill establishing a special peace commission to meet with the Indians. Signed by President Johnson, the law authorized the commission to restore peace to the Plains, secure a right-of-way for Pacific railroads, protect frontier settlements, and recommend a permanent Indian policy. The commission traveled to the Great Plains in the summer of 1867. Their subsequent recommendations were not carried out, and peace for the Plains was lost. However, Henderson's involvement does indicate his interest in finding a solution to the long-standing problem. When his leadership was needed to win approval of the work of the peace commission in the spring of 1868, he was diverted by the impeachment trial of President Johnson.

Following a long struggle between the president and Congress, the House of Representatives passed eleven articles of impeachment and presented them to the United States Senate. The trial began on March 13, 1868. For conviction, a two-thirds majority was required; there were twelve Democrats and forty-two Republican senators. On the basis of party loyalty the Republicans had the necessary thirty-six votes to impeach. To avoid conviction the president had to gain the votes of seven Republican senators. On May 16, 1868, in spite of intense public

and political pressure, Henderson joined six other Republicans and the twelve Democrats voting "not guilty," and President Johnson avoided conviction. Henderson believed the evidence did not support a guilty vote. He was not reelected to the Senate by the Radicals who controlled Missouri's legislature, as they were not pleased with his "not guilty" vote. Thus ended Henderson's national legislative career.

Henderson married in 1868 and returned to Louisiana, Missouri, after his defeat for reelection in 1869. He remained in Louisiana and was active in the Liberal Republican movement in 1870, and in 1871 accepted the Republican Party's nomination for the United States Senate but was defeated. In 1872 the party nominated him to run for governor, but the Democratic tide overwhelmed his campaign. In 1873 the Republican caucus selected him again for the Senate, but the General Assembly chose a Democrat. Henderson never sought elective office again, but he did remain active in party politics.

President **Ulysses S. Grant** appointed Henderson as special U.S. prosecuting attorney in 1875 to prosecute the Whiskey Ring defendants in St. Louis. When Henderson attempted to prosecute Orville E. Babcock, Grant's private secretary, he was fired.

By the early 1880s Henderson had moved to St. Louis to continue his law practice and was instrumental in organizing the movement against a third term for former President Grant. By the late 1880s he had moved to Washington, D.C., where he built a house known in Washington society as "Henderson's Castle."

In 1884 Henderson attended the Republican National Convention in Chicago, and was chosen as the permanent chairman of the convention.

President Benjamin Harrison considered Henderson for nomination to his cabinet, and was supported by several national newspapers, but instead nominated him to serve as head of the U.S. delegation to the first Pan-American conference in Washington in 1889. In 1892 Henderson was appointed by President Harrison to the board of regents of the Smithsonian Institution, a position he held until just before his death in Washington, D.C., on April 12, 1913.

ARTHUR H. MATTINGLY

Henderson, John B. "Emancipation and Impeachment." *Century* 85 (December 1912): 206–10.
Lincoln, Abraham. Papers. Library of Congress, Washington, D.C.
Mattingly, Arthur H. "Senator John Brooks Henderson, U.S. Senator from Missouri." Ph.D. diss., Kansas State University, 1971.

HENNINGS, THOMAS C., JR.
(1903–1960)

Thomas C. Hennings Jr., a lawyer, politician, and U.S. senator, was born in St. Louis, Missouri, on June 25, 1903. His father, a lawyer and onetime St. Louis Circuit Court judge, was an active player in Democratic politics in St. Louis. Young Thomas was close to his father and adopted his passion for both law and politics. He graduated from Soldan High School in St. Louis and continued his education at Cornell University, graduating in 1924 with a bachelor of arts degree. Upon his return to St. Louis, he completed his law degree at Washington University.

Hennings practiced law until 1928 when he became an assistant circuit attorney in charge of felony cases. In this capacity as a prosecutor, he won more than 90 percent of the twenty-five hundred cases he handled. His success not only earned him a reputation as an excellent prosecutor but also caught the attention of the Democratic leaders who were looking for a candidate for the United States House of Representatives seat in the newly created Eleventh District. He ran unopposed in the Democratic primary in 1934 and then defeated Leonidas C. Dyer, a twenty-two-year House veteran from the old Twelfth District.

The new district, which encompassed a large African American population, gave Hennings an easy victory because of his outspoken support of civil rights and Franklin D. Roosevelt's New Deal. As a strong supporter of civil rights, he worked to advance equality for African Americans in the administration's relief and recovery programs. The district rewarded him for his efforts by reelecting him in 1936 and 1938. At the urging of the city's Democratic Party, he withdrew from the race in 1940 to run for the office of circuit attorney, which he won easily. In 1941 Hennings received a leave of absence to enter the navy. Upon his discharge in 1943, he returned to St. Louis to practice law.

Hennings's political aspirations now included the Senate seat of former Missouri governor **Forrest C. Donnell.** In 1949 he openly began his quest for the seat. After a meeting with President **Harry S. Truman,** who told him he would not oppose his candidacy, Hennings told friends he planned to announce his intention to run for the Senate that summer. His belief that Truman would not play an active hand in the selection of a candidate in the Democratic primary was strengthened when both James M. Pendergast and John Nangle, in separate meetings with Truman, confirmed this view.

In November Sen. Forrest C. Donnell announced his bid for reelection. Donnell, a conservative Republican, was a proven vote getter in the rural areas of the state. Hennings, planning to announce his candidacy, was shocked to learn that Truman had publicly supported state senator Emery W. Allison of Rolla in the primary. Determined to continue, Hennings announced his bid for the Senate seat. His announcement split the Democratic Party. He now faced seemingly insurmountable odds: the president of the United States, Gov. **Forrest Smith,** the hierarchy of the Democratic Party, and St. Louis mayor Joseph M. Darst all opposed his nomination. But Hennings won the primary in a close race, thanks to a sixty-thousand-vote plurality he accumulated in St. Louis. Many St. Louis Democrats resented Truman's interference in the state primary election and his ties with the Kansas City machine and threw their support to Hennings. In the general election Hennings had little difficulty defeating incumbent Donnell. Thus, he became the first native St. Louisan elected to the United States Senate.

Returning to Washington, Hennings soon gained a reputation as an outstanding lawyer and one of the foremost experts on the Constitution. His liberal views were well known, yet he was respected by his conservative colleagues.

Hennings became a leader of his fellow senators who were strong advocates of civil rights. He was outraged at Joseph C. McCarthy's unsubstantiated charges against individuals, and in 1952, as chairman of a subcommittee, submitted findings that helped lead to a vote of censure against the Wisconsin senator.

During his political career, Hennings earned the respect of both liberals and conservatives. He was a staunch defender of the Warren court's decisions on civil liberties and was instrumental in killing the Bricker amendment in 1954, which would have limited the treaty-making power of President Dwight D. Eisenhower. He had a tendency to support unpopular causes that he believed in and won the reputation as "watchdog for individual rights."

There is little doubt Hennings was an exceptional politician and a party man, serving a term as Democratic conference secretary. The one constant during his fifty-seven years was his uncompromising passion for the law, the Constitution, and individual rights. This champion of civil liberties succumbed to abdominal cancer on September 13, 1960, in Washington, D.C.

CHARLES R. MINK

Hennings, Thomas C., Jr. Papers. Missouri Historical Society, St. Louis.

———. Papers. Western Historical Manuscripts Collection, Columbia.

Kemper, Donald J. *Decade of Fear: Senator Hennings and Civil Liberties.* Columbia: University of Missouri Press, 1965.

HENRY, ANDREW (1775?–1833)

Andrew Henry, a mountain man whose innovations revolutionized the modi operandi of the American fur business, was a partner in both the St. Louis Missouri Fur Company and the firm of Ashley and Henry. Although largely forgotten today, it was Henry, more than anyone else, who redirected the fur industry's focus from trading with the Indians to relying on independent trappers.

Henry was born in York County, Pennsylvania, around 1775. He left home as a young man after a disagreement with family members over his plans for marriage, and eventually landed in Nashville, Tennessee, where he resided between 1798 and 1800. In the latter year, he settled at Ste. Genevieve in Upper Louisiana but returned to Nashville briefly in 1802. The following year he was back in Ste. Genevieve seeking to engage in lead mining. He formed a partnership with **William Henry Ashley,** and they purchased a 640-acre tract, subsequently known as "Henry's Diggings," in the mining district of Washington County.

As a rising man of business, Henry also involved himself in civic affairs, serving as a justice of the peace, a militia officer, and a trustee for the Ste. Genevieve Academy. In 1805 he married Marie Villars, the French Creole daughter of a former commandant at Ste. Genevieve, but, mysteriously, the marriage lasted only three weeks. Their brief union did produce a daughter. In 1807 Henry bought out Ashley's half interest in the mine, which he continued to work.

By 1809 Henry had done sufficiently well to enable him to join the newly formed St. Louis Missouri Fur Company as a partner, in association with **Manuel Lisa, (Jean) Pierre Chouteau, William Clark,** and several other noteworthy individuals. Although Henry was the least known of the firm's partners, he became one of its ablest field captains. He traveled up the Missouri with the company's 1809 expedition, and spent the next two years in the wilderness in pursuit of furs. A skilled woodsman, liked and respected by his men, Henry accompanied a contingent to the Three Forks area of the Missouri where they encountered stiff opposition from hostile Blackfeet Indians.

In the fall of 1810 Henry set out in search of a friendlier environment for trading. He led an expedition across the Continental Divide to winter and trade among the more peaceful tribes beyond the Rockies. After a difficult winter on the Snake River, where he and his men were forced to subsist on roots and dress themselves in skins, Henry returned to the upper Missouri with enough beaver pelts to show a modest profit for the venture. Following his return to St. Louis in the fall of 1811, Henry withdrew

from the fur trade, discouraged perhaps by the dissension among his partners, the growing likelihood of war with Britain, and his displeasure with company operations.

Following the outbreak of the War of 1812, Henry enlisted in the territorial militia, serving as a major in a regiment commanded by his friend and former partner William H. Ashley. He resumed mining for a time, but he was deeply in debt and perpetually hounded by creditors. Operations had ceased at his mine by 1816, and he apparently turned to farming after acquiring a promising spread on the Black River in Washington County, Missouri. In 1819 he married Mary Fleming, and in contrast with his first marriage this one lasted until Henry's death fourteen years later. The couple had four children.

With his debts mounting and a new wife and child to support, Henry was ready to return to the fur trade. In 1821 he entered discussions with Ashley, and the former partners formed a new venture known as the Ashley and Henry Company. They agreed that Henry would be the firm's principal agent in the field and that Ashley would handle the business end of the operations. Largely at Henry's instigation, they planned to introduce three significant innovations. First, the company intended to place its primary emphasis on trapping rather than trading. Second, the firm would no longer seek to maintain a fortified trading post as the hub of its field operations. Third, the trappers in the field would be independent businessmen, not company employees.

In the spring of 1822 the firm dispatched an expedition upriver with Henry in command. Their intended destination was the fur-rich Three Forks area, but after losing many of their horses to an Assiniboine raiding party, Henry decided to proceed only as far as the mouth of the Yellowstone. From there he dispatched trappers up the Missouri and the Yellowstone to winter in the beaver country.

When Henry ventured into Blackfeet territory in the spring of 1823, members of the hostile tribe attacked and once again inflicted casualties. He retreated to the mouth of the Yellowstone to await word from Ashley, who was expected to arrive upriver from St. Louis. However, **Jedediah Strong Smith** brought news that the Ashley expedition had been ambushed by the Arikara. Henry left a small force at the Yellowstone camp, and took the remainder of his men downriver to assist Ashley's beleaguered band.

With the upper Missouri now effectively closed by the Arikara and the Blackfeet, Henry subsequently decided to vacate the Yellowstone post and head west to the Bighorn River and the friendlier Crow territory. After wintering there, he returned to St. Louis in the summer of 1824 with the furs that his parties had collected. He intended to return to the mountains but never did, choosing to remain with his family in Missouri.

Henry withdrew from the business before he and Ashley turned a profit, leaving him destitute and ignored. He died at his Washington County farm on June 10, 1833, with little to show for his labors. Consigned to live in Ashley's shadow, it was, in fact, Andrew Henry who had been responsible for many of the innovations that had helped make his partner both rich and famous.

WILLIAM E. FOLEY

Clokey, Richard M. *William H. Ashley: Enterprise and Politics in the Trans-Mississippi West.* Norman: University of Oklahoma Press, 1980.

Oglesby, Richard E. *Manuel Lisa and the Opening of the Missouri Fur Trade.* Norman: University of Oklahoma Press, 1963.

White, Linda, and Fred R. Gowans. "Traders to Trappers: Andrew Henry and the Rocky Mountain Fur Trade." Parts 1 and 2. *Montana: The Magazine of Western History* 43 (winter 1993): 58–65; (summer 1993): 54–63.

HIMES, CHESTER BOMAR (1909–1984)

Chester Bomar Himes began writing while serving a prison sentence for armed robbery and went on to become one of the most popular American authors in France on the basis of his series of crime novels set in Harlem. His dark and cynical view of the effects of racism on the American psyche, both black and white, did not fit well with the movement for integration in the post–World War II period, and he achieved only sporadic success in the United States, though his work was extremely influential on a later generation of African American artists who began working in the 1960s and 1970s.

Himes was born on July 29, 1909, in Jefferson City, Missouri, where his father taught blacksmithing and wheelwrighting as the head of Lincoln Institute's mechanical department. In 1914 the family moved to Alcorn, Mississippi, where the elder Himes taught at Alcorn A&M, and a few years later to Pine Bluff, Arkansas, where he taught at Branch Normal Institute. After Chester's brother Joseph was blinded in an accident in 1922, the family moved to St. Louis so that Joseph could be treated at Barnes Hospital. While in St. Louis, Chester attended Wendell Phillips High School.

In 1925 the family moved to Cleveland, Ohio, where Himes graduated from high school the next year. He entered Ohio State University in the fall of 1926, but left the following year because of failing grades and disciplinary problems. He returned to Cleveland where he was arrested in 1928, having robbed the house of a rich white couple at gunpoint and stolen their car. Sentenced to twenty-five years, he ended up serving seven and a half years in the Ohio State Penitentiary before being paroled in 1936.

Himes began publishing short stories in *Abbott's Monthly* and the *Atlanta Daily World* in 1933. In 1934 his two short stories of prison life, "Crazy in the Stir" and "To What Red Hell," were printed in *Esquire,* which published several of his stories over the next twelve years. After being paroled in May 1936, Himes returned to Cleveland where he worked for the Works Progress Administration as a library research assistant and then as a member of the Ohio Writer's Project. Moving to California in 1940 he worked at numerous war-industry jobs, primarily as an unskilled laborer, while also publishing stories in *Crisis, Opportunity,* and *Negro Story.* He was appalled by the level of racism he encountered in wartime Los Angeles, writing later in his autobiography, "Los Angeles hurt me racially as much as any city I have ever known—much more than any city I remember from the South."

Himes moved to New York in 1944, but Los Angeles provided the setting for his first two novels, *If He Hollers Let Him Go* (1945) and *Lonely Crusade* (1947). *If He Hollers* was a moderate success, but the failure of *Lonely Crusade* left Himes embittered for years and determined to leave the country as soon as possible. Both works focus on racial and class tensions among workers in the booming war industries. Seeking to explore racism in all its subtleties and nuances, Himes argued that not only did racism have a debilitating effect on whites, but it also had severe consequences for black consciousness. In a 1947 speech at the University of Chicago, he stated: "If this plumbing for the truth reveals within the Negro personality homicidal mania, lust for white women, a pathetic sense of inferiority, paradoxical anti-Semitism, arrogance, uncle tomism, hate and fear and self-hate, this then is the effect of oppression on the human personality. These are the daily horrors, the daily realities, the daily experiences of an oppressed minority."

In 1953, with the money from the advance for his autobiographical novel *The Third Generation,* Himes left the United States for Europe where, except for a few brief periods, he spent the rest of his life. Living in Majorca, Spain, in 1954, he wrote *The Primitive,* a sensational novel of the love-hate relationship between a black man and a white woman, which Himes considered his finest work. However, he constantly had trouble with his publishers, both American and European, and for most of his life he made little profit from his writing. Strapped for money while living in Paris in 1956, he began writing crime fiction for Gallimard's "La série noire." His first crime novel, *For Love of Imabelle* (1957), won the prestigious French Grand Prix for the year's best detective story.

Between 1957 and 1969 Himes published nine crime novels set in Harlem, most of them based on the exploits of his two fictional detectives, Coffin Ed Johnson and Grave Digger Jones. These novels are marked by grotesque characters, graphic violence, an atmosphere of barely controlled chaos, and a grim sense of humor. As Himes wrote in his autobiography:

Some time before, I didn't know when, my mind had rejected all reality as I had known it and I had begun to see the world as a cesspool of buffoonery. Even the violence was funny. A man gets his throat cut. He shakes his head to say you missed me and it falls off. Damn reality, I thought. All of reality was absurd, contradictory, violent and hurting. It was funny, really, if I could just get the joke. And I got the handle, by some miracle.

Toward the end of his life Himes began to be recognized by a younger generation of black writers and artists—notably John A. Williams, Ishmael Reed, and Melvin van Peebles—as a major influence on the generation that came of age after World War II. Himes also, for the first time in his life, attained a degree of financial security. After the publication of *Blind Man with a Pistol* (1969), the last in his crime series, he moved to Cabo de Moraira, Spain, and wrote the two volumes of his autobiography, *The Quality of Hurt* (1972) and *My Life of Absurdity* (1976). He died in Moraira on November 12, 1984.

DAVID COCHRAN

Fuller, Hoyt W. "Traveller on the Long, Rough, Lonely Old Road: An Interview with Chester Himes." *Black World* 21 (March 1972): 4–22, 87–98.

Lundquist, James. *Chester Himes.* New York: Frederick Ungar, 1976.

Milliken, Stephen F. *Chester Himes: A Critical Appraisal.* Columbia: University of Missouri Press, 1976.

Muller, Gilbert H. *Chester Himes.* Boston: Twayne, 1989.

Williams, John A. "Chester Himes: My Man Himes." In *Flashbacks: A Twenty-Year Diary of Article Writing,* 292–352. Garden City, N.Y.: Doubleday, 1974.

HIRTH, WILLIAM HENRY (1875–1940)

Born in Tarrytown, New York, on May 28, 1875, William Henry Hirth moved to Missouri with his parents three years later, where they farmed near Lead Creek in Pike County. Later, his family farmed in Audrain County. Hirth became interested in solving the economic problems of farmers and, at the age of sixteen, joined the Farmers' Alliance. Despite his youth the Audrain County Alliance elected him secretary and lecturer. In 1896 he supported William Jennings Bryan on the Democratic ticket for the presidency.

Hirth attended McGee College in Macon County from 1894 to 1895, followed by two years at Central Methodist College in Fayette. He did not graduate and took a job as a salesman for the New York Life Insurance Company to polish his skills in dealing with the public. He then studied law and gained admittance to the bar about 1901. Hirth did not practice law but instead purchased the *Columbia Statesman* in 1906, selling it in 1911 because in 1908 he had bought the *Missouri Farmer and Breeder* and devoted his attention to it. In 1914 he changed the name of the agricultural paper to the *Missouri Farmer.* Hirth used his position as a journalist to advocate cost-of-production prices plus a small profit, cooperative marketing, and leadership by farmers to gain economic change in agriculture.

In 1914 Hirth began organizing agricultural-marketing and purchasing clubs at the county level to help farmers solve their economic problems. These local clubs then joined for the purpose of cooperative buying at wholesale prices. Hirth believed that several hundred farmers who acted collectively could gain lower prices for farm and home necessities—such as fertilizer, coal, and flour—if they purchased in carload lots. These farm clubs also operated exchanges through which farmers could market their commodities and save commission fees. In early January 1917 the farm clubs, with Hirth's direction, established the Missouri Farmers Association (MFA), which served as the state organization. Soon, the MFA became the largest independent agricultural organization in the United States. Hirth used the *Missouri Farmer* to disseminate organizational information and to support the MFA.

Hirth believed that farmers could wield considerable power if they acted collectively. In 1923 he launched a "producer's contract" program in which farmers contracted to market their crops, livestock, poultry, and dairy products through only the MFA. Hirth wanted to bind at least 75 percent of the farmers in every community to collective buying and selling through the organization. By doing so, he contended, farmers could control sales to central markets and agricultural prices. Few members participated in this contract-marketing system, but they actively supported the business agencies of the MFA. By 1920 the MFA controlled 75 grain elevators, 125 produce exchanges, and approximately 100 livestock-shipping associations. In 1924 the MFA operated livestock commissions at the stockyards in Kansas City, St. Joseph, and Chicago.

During the 1920s Hirth supported the McNary-Haugen plan to enable the federal government to sell price-depressing surplus agricultural commodities, at a loss if necessary, on the world market. He believed that domestic prices would then increase behind the protective tariff. As chairman of the midwestern lobbying organization known as the Corn Belt Committee, Hirth sought congressional approval for the McNary-Haugen Bill.

Hirth opposed the agricultural policies of the Coolidge and Hoover administrations, particularly the creation of the Federal Farm Board, because the government did not effectively address the problems of surplus production and low prices. Although he was a Democrat, he did not support the Agricultural Adjustment Act (1933) of the Roosevelt administration because it emphasized reductions in production rather than guaranteed and protected domestic prices. In 1936 Hirth became a Democrat candidate for governor, but **Lloyd Stark** defeated him in the primary.

Hirth's personal commitment to improving the economic lives of farmers and his business and organization skills won him many friends, but his abrasive personality also earned him many enemies. He married Lillian Vincent in 1900. They had one son, William Vincent. Hirth died in Columbia, Missouri, on October 24, 1940.

R. Douglas Hurt

Meyer, Duane G. *The Heritage of Missouri*. St. Louis: River City Publishers, 1982.

Saloutos, Theodore. "William A. Hirth: Middle Western Agrarian." *Mississippi Valley Historical Review* 38 (September 1951): 215–32.

———. "William Hirth and the Missouri Farmers Association." *Missouri Historical Review* 44 (October 1949): 1–20.

Young, Raymond A. *Cultivating Cooperation: A History of the Missouri Farmers Association*. Columbia: University of Missouri Press, 1995.

HODGEN, JOHN THOMPSON (1826–1882)

John Thompson Hodgen, one of Missouri's most outstanding physicians, was born in Hodgenville, in Larue County, Kentucky, on January 19, 1826, and died in St. Louis on April 28, 1882, when he was in the prime of his career. His parents, Jacob and Francis Park Brown Hodgen, were both intelligent and eager to educate their son to the best of their ability. The family moved to Pittsfield, Illinois, where young Hodgen attended the lower grades. He later graduated from Bethany College in West Virginia. At age twenty he enrolled as a student in the medical department of the University of Missouri, located, at that time, in St. Louis. After graduation in 1848 he served what later was referred to as an internship at the then-new St. Louis City Hospital. Hodgen and his classmate Ellsworth Smith were the hospital's first interns. On completion of that year Hodgen was appointed as demonstrator in anatomy at the Missouri Medical College. In 1854 he was elevated to professor of anatomy, and in 1858 his subjects were expanded to include both anatomy and physiology.

The era of the Civil War was a catastrophe, not only to St. Louis and its citizens, both Unionists and Confederates, but also to medical facilities. The buildings of the Missouri Medical College—better known as McDowell Medical College—were arrogated and converted into the Gratiot Street federal military prison. Hodgen moved his large medical and surgical practice and teaching expertise to the St. Louis Medical College, which a decade after Hodgen's death became part of Washington University Medical School.

Many positions were bestowed on Hodgen during and after the war. He was surgeon general for the state of Missouri until the end of the war, consulting surgeon to St. Louis City Hospital from 1862 to 1882, president of the St. Louis Medical Society in 1872, chairman of the surgical section of the American Medical Association in 1873, president of the Missouri State Medical Society in 1876, and president of the American Medical Association in 1880. For a midwestern medical school professor and general surgeon to receive all those honors was truly remarkable.

On a local level, for twenty years, from 1862 to 1882, Hodgen was a consulting surgeon at St. Louis City Hospital, and he was a member of the St. Louis Board of Health for many years and president of that group in 1867–1868. During his long tenure as a professor and clinical instructor in surgery he trained and nurtured many budding surgeons in the St. Louis area.

In addition to the many honors he received, Hodgen had one more important forte. He invented a number of surgical instruments, particularly orthopedic appliances; some were so widely accepted that they were used throughout the medical world. Among his inventions included a wire splint for a fracture of the thigh; a suspension cord and pulleys that would allow flexion, extension, and rotation in leg fractures; and many other splints for other types of fractures. A forceps dilator to remove foreign bodies from the trachea was perfected by Hodgen; when successful, it eliminated the need for a tracheotomy. Another of his inventions was a double-action syringe used as a stomach pump not only to neutralize stomach contents in accidental poisoning but also to flush out noxious gastric material.

Like most eminent physicians, Hodgen contributed to the leading medical journals of his era. He submitted informative articles of interest to both the specialists, who were usually surgeons, and the general practitioners. Usually, general practitioners treated all but the most critical cases, either in their offices, in the patient's home, or, occasionally in rural areas, in a large house converted to a makeshift hospital for obstetrical cases and minor surgery. Some of the medical articles contributed by Hodgen include: "Wiring the Clavicle and Acromion for Dislocation of the Scapular End of the Clavicle," "Modification of the Operation for Lacerated Perineum," "Two Deaths Following the Use of Chloroform," "Use of Atropine in Collapse from Cholera," "Three Cases of Extra-Uterine Pregnancy," "Skin Grafting," and "Report on Antiseptic Surgery."

Many articles reflected Hodgen's specialty and his interest in orthopedics and surgery, while some of the articles were of concern to the general practitioner. The article on the repair of the lacerated perineum should have also appealed to the general practitioner since this group of doctors did most of the obstetrics at that time, and perineal lacerations were not uncommon.

The use of chloroform was becoming popular. It was used as an anesthetic for childbirth and surgery, and was used particularly in the homes since it was not flammable, pleasant to inhale, and easy to administer, but potentially dangerous. The purpose of articles such as those by Hodgen was to caution the medical community of chloroform's potentially lethal complications.

The "Use of Atropine in Collapse from Cholera" was a timely article. In 1849, 4,557 persons died in St. Louis from Asiatic cholera, a sizable number by any accounting, but in a city with a population of about seventy thousand the percentage of deaths was truly catastrophic.

Because of these many accomplishments, John T. Hodgen ranked high among outstanding Missouri physicians.

LAWRENCE E. GIFFEN SR.

Costello, Cyril. "Medicine in the Time of John T. Hodgen." *Missouri Medicine* 69 (1972).

Hyde, William, and Howard L. Conard, eds. *Encyclopedia of the History of St. Louis.* New York: Southern History, 1899.

Scharf, J. Thomas. *History of St. Louis City and County: From Earliest Periods to the Present Day.* Philadelphia: Everts, 1883.

Schleuter, R. E. "John T. Hodgen, 1826–1882." In *Centennial Volume,* by St. Louis Medical Society. St. Louis, 1939.

HOFFMAN, CLARA CLEGHORN (1831–1908)

Clara Cleghorn Hoffman was born in De Kalb County, New York, on January 18, 1831. She attended schools in New York and Massachusetts and later moved to Iowa and then to Columbia, Illinois, where she taught school. She met her husband, Goswin Hoffman, a German physician, while in Columbia, and they married in 1862.

Hoffman is perhaps best known for her service as the president of the Missouri Women's Christian Temperance Union (WCTU) for twenty-five years, beginning in 1883. The WCTU, which had a national chapter as well as representation in each state, opposed the manufacture and distribution of all liquor.

The Missouri WCTU was a controversial organization not only because of its mission but also because its leadership and members were women. "White Ribbon Workers," as they were called, asserted a political position in an era when such actions from women were not readily considered appropriate. On the contrary, many did not think such a cause was proper for a group of ladies to address, and often churches even refused the Missouri WCTU the opportunity to speak to their congregations. While some Missourians supported prohibition, others adamantly opposed it, believing that saloons and taverns were rightly and permanently woven into American culture. Some Missourians, of course, were indifferent.

Hoffman and her hundreds of Missouri "White Ribbon Workers" (named for their white ribbon badges) spent years in pursuit of prohibition. Gradually, they saw progress as first towns and then counties went "dry."

In addition to serving as president of the Missouri WCTU for many years, Hoffman was the recording secretary of the national organization for twelve of those same years. After her election as president of the Missouri chapter, she became a well-known and widely traveled lecturer. In 1895 she was sent as a delegate to the world's convention of the union held in London. On that trip she spoke in Great Britain, Germany, France, and Switzerland. Reports of her speeches described her as presenting her cause with passion and force in a voice that was rich and melodious. She was considered by many to be a talented and gifted speaker.

What may not be so well known of Hoffman is that she was an educator before she became a noted public speaker. She taught school in Warrensburg, Missouri, and in 1871 moved to Kansas City where she continued teaching. She served as principal of the Lathrop school in Kansas City for twelve years before taking the position as WCTU president. Her position as school principal paid twelve hundred dollars per year; the WCTU paid no salary. While principal,

Hoffman organized a night school to educate newspaper boys. She worked to help poor children and for other charitable causes in Kansas City.

Clara Hoffman died of pneumonia in Kansas City at a home she shared with her only surviving son, Guy, and his family on February 13, 1908. Her husband had preceded her in death in August 1893, and her other son, Harry, died in May 1896.

Frances E. Willard, who shared Hoffman's deep belief in the temperance movement, referred to her friend and colleague as "the Thomas H. Benton of the prohibition movement. She is every whit as able as was the great senator from Missouri and brings to her plea for protection of the Christian fireside a logic as powerful, a pathos far more tender, and a personality vastly more home-like." Willard called Hoffman "Missouri's Great Heart."

LISA A. KREMER

Dains, Mary K., ed. *Show Me Missouri Women: Selected Biographies.* Kirksville, Mo.: Thomas Jefferson University Press, 1989.
Kansas City Journal, May 28, 1899.
Kansas City Post, January 18, 1908–January 18, 1927.
Kansas City Star, January 17, 1915.
Kansas City Times, February 14, 1908–April 3, 1925.
"Necrology." *Missouri Historical Review* 2 (April 1908): 251.

HOLLAND, LOUIS E. (1878–1960)

More than any other person, Louis Edward Holland brought commercial aviation to Kansas City, Missouri. He was born in Parma, New York, on June 29, 1878, the son of Edward and Capitola Woodams Holland. He completed his formal education at an elementary school in Rochester, New York. He worked in a bicycle factory and then opened his own bicycle shop, which he operated until 1900, when he began working for the *Rochester Democrat Chronicle* newspaper as an engraver. That same year he married Adelia Ward Garratt, a native of Ontario, Canada.

Holland soon became an accomplished photoengraver. In 1902, looking for more opportunity, he moved to Kansas City, Missouri, and went to work for the Thompson and Slaughter Engraving Company. In 1905 he became the superintendent of Kansas City's largest engraving company, Teachenor and Bartberger.

In 1916 Holland contemplated going into business with a young Kansas City manufacturer of automotive accessories, but advertising agencies that appreciated his photography skills helped him finance the establishment of his own company, Holland Engraving.

Holland soon had a thriving business. By 1921 his firm had become the largest engraving company west of the Mississippi River. An inventor and engineer, Holland also created a commercial-grade lawn sprinkler that he manufactured under the name of Double Rotary Sprinkler Company. He also invented an electrical etcher, which he manufactured through another company, Holland Corporation.

Holland's technical acumen and business successes deserve recognition, but they were important primarily because they provided the financial resources that enabled him to accomplish even more significant things.

From 1922 to 1925 Holland served as president of the Advertising Clubs of the World. The American advertising industry had recognized both his organizational and his technical talents. His position led him to travel in Europe, where he used the continent's budding commercial aviation facilities. Perceiving commercial aviation's importance for the future, he wanted it for Kansas City.

In 1925 Holland became the vice president and then president of the Kansas City Chamber of Commerce. He used those offices to advance his commercial aviation dreams. He convinced Kansas City's city manager, **Henry F. McElroy,** that a public airport would be advantageous for the city. In May 1927 McElroy authorized the lease of a tract of land at the bend of the Missouri River, just north of the downtown. The recently acclaimed national hero **Charles A. Lindbergh** flew the *Spirit of St. Louis* onto the new airstrip on August 17, 1927. Following a parade and a reception, Lindbergh dedicated the field.

In 1928 Holland became the executive manager of the chamber of commerce. From that office he worked to achieve the passage of a bond proposal that would allow the city to buy the new airfield. A $1 million bond issue passed in August 1928. Without hesitation, Holland pressured Kansas City's government to develop its new airfield. As a result, on December 8, 1929, officials dedicated a passenger terminal and turned it over to air transportation companies.

Holland did not stop there. He thought that Kansas City could become the headquarters of Transcontinental and Western Air, the predecessor of Trans World Airlines (TWA), if the city provided them with financial aid. Working through chamber of commerce president Conrad Mann, who had ties with the **Thomas J. Pendergast** political machine, Holland received $500,000 of the 1931 "Ten-year Plan" public-improvements bond proposal designated for municipal airport improvements. After the bond issue passed, Holland convinced city manager McElroy to spend $280,000 to build airport facilities for Transcontinental and Western Air. The airline then announced it would base its headquarters and operations in Kansas City. From 1931 to 1944 the company spent $40 million in wages and materials in Kansas City.

A friend of Sen. **Harry S. Truman,** Holland received an appointment in the Roosevelt administration during World War II. He served as deputy chairman of the Smaller War Plants Division of the War Production Board, and he became the first chairman of the Smaller War Plants Corporation. After the war he became president of the American Automobile Association.

In 1935 Holland's wife, Adelia, died. The marriage had produced four children: Vera, Norma, Garratt, and Helen. Holland later remarried. Louis Holland died on May 25, 1960.

DONALD B. OSTER

Fowler, Dick. *Leaders in Our Town.* Kansas City: Burd and Fletcher, 1952.

Heath, Jim F. "Frustrations of a Missouri Small Businessman: Lou E. Holland in Wartime Washington." *Missouri Historical Review* 68 (April 1974): 299–316.

Holland, Lou E. Papers. Harry S. Truman Library, Independence, Mo.

Leyerzapf, James W. "Aviation Promotion in Kansas City, 1925–1931." *Missouri Historical Review* 66 (January 1972): 246–67.

———. "The Public Life of Lou E. Holland." Ph.D. diss., University of Missouri–Columbia, 1972.

HOLLIDAY, HAROLD L., SR. (1918–1985)

Harold L. Holliday devoted his career to advancing the cause of civil rights in Missouri. He spent twenty-five years as either a member of the executive committee or as an officer in the Kansas City chapter of the Missouri National Association for the Advancement of Colored People, including president. For ten years he served as an officer or as a member of the board of directors of the Urban League. He served twelve years in the Missouri House of Representatives, and he was a magistrate judge in Kansas City. His political strength came from his association with Freedom, Inc., an important Jackson County black political organization.

Born on June 28, 1918, in Muskogee, Oklahoma, Holliday moved to Kansas City with his mother and sister in 1920. He attended segregated public schools in Kansas City, graduating from Lincoln High School in 1935. He earned a B.A. degree from Lincoln University in 1939 and an M.A. degree in economics from the University of Michigan in 1941. Drafted into the United States Army in September 1942, Holliday gained the rank of second lieutenant before his honorable discharge in 1945. He applied for admission to the University of Kansas City Law School but was rejected because of his race. Working with an organization called the American Veterans Committee, Holliday gained admission in 1948 and graduated with honors in 1952, the first black to receive a law degree from the school (which became the University of Missouri–Kansas City in 1964). He became a practicing lawyer when he passed the bar in September 1952.

Holliday quickly challenged segregation in the Kansas City schools. Success came when he and attorney Lewis W. Clymer won a suit to allow black students to attend Benton school, which later became D. A. Holmes school. In 1957 Holliday served as the general counsel for the Community Committee for Social Action in a suit to desegregate eating establishments in downtown Kansas City stores. When Bruce Watkins Jr. and **Leon Jordan** founded Freedom, Inc., in 1961, Holliday became a charter member and later became chairman of the board of directors.

Running on the Democratic ticket with the support of Freedom, Inc., Holliday won a seat in the Missouri House of Representatives in 1964. Kansas City voters returned him to the house in each election through 1976, and he became known as an articulate voice for the poor and oppressed citizens of Missouri. He authored a number of laws, including one that ended the ban on interracial marriages in Missouri. In 1976 Holliday lost a Democratic primary race for a state senate seat. After leaving the legislature, he served as a magistrate judge in Kansas City and then as associate regional counsel in the U.S. Department of Housing and Urban Development. He retired from that position in 1983.

Holliday died after a lingering battle with prostate cancer on March 21, 1985. At a service attended by more than five hundred people, Robert Wheeler asked the mourners to "look deeper and beyond into Holly and his personality. If we look deeper and beyond, our vision will yield not only a portrait of a man of many accomplishments, it will also reveal the legacy he has bequeathed to us. He has blazed trails for us. He has accelerated the speed of the wheels of justice which turn so disappointingly ponderously. And, even in his death, Harold Holliday, characteristically, throws down a challenge to us."

LAWRENCE O. CHRISTENSEN

Holliday Papers. Black Archives of Mid-America, Kansas City, Mo.

Kansas City Call, March 22–April 4, 1985.

Official Manual of the State of Missouri, 1967–1968. Jefferson City: Secretary of State, 1968.

Wheeler, Robert R. "A Look Deeper-Look Beyond: A Tribute to Harold Holliday, Sr., March 26, 1985." Black Archives of Mid-America, Kansas City, Mo.

HORNSBY, ROGERS (1896–1963)

Born on April 27, 1896, at Winters, Texas, Rogers Hornsby began his professional baseball career in 1914 when he and his brother, Everett, walked into a tryout in Dallas. The St. Louis Cardinals bought Hornsby's contract in 1915 for five hundred dollars. Later that season the nineteen-year-old shortstop played his first major league game for the Cardinals. After struggling at the plate, he received help from manager Miller Huggins who corrected a flaw in the young player's stance; as a result he had a .316 batting average in 1916.

During the 1920s Hornsby ranked among the finest hitters ever to play the game. His .424 batting average in 1924 is the highest in modern major league history. He holds the National League lifetime records for slugging percentage at .578, most years leading the league in slugging percentage at nine, and most home runs by a second baseman at 263. He led the National League in batting for six consecutive seasons, from 1920 through 1925.

Hornsby attributed his hitting prowess to his personal habits. He claimed that a player could not hit with power without eleven hours' sleep and eating plenty of juicy steaks. To preserve his sharp batting eye, he never read and never went to the movies.

Hornsby spent most of his career as a player-manager. His reputation for a turbulent personality marked him as a troublemaker in the major leagues. His first managing assignment came in St. Louis where he succeeded **Wesley Branch Rickey** in 1925—the same year he won the Most Valuable Player Award. In 1926 Hornsby led the Cardinals to their first world championship season. At the end of the year, he was traded to the New York Giants for Frankie Frisch and Jimmy Ring, after Cards owner Sam Breadon became fed up with the constant battles with his manager. A year later, in January 1928, Hornsby was traded to the Boston Braves; in May he became manager. In November he was traded to the Chicago Cubs for two hundred thousand dollars and five players. The following year he was again voted the National League's Most Valuable Player.

Hornsby replaced Cubs manager Joe McCarthy in September 1930 and was fired in mid-1932. At the end of the season he signed with the St. Louis Cardinals and the following year went crosstown to the Browns. There he stayed until fired as manager in 1937.

Press coverage for the period is filled with accusations that Hornsby drummed managers off the teams for which he played. He wore a Braves uniform less than two months before becoming the team's manager, and played almost two seasons with the Cubs before taking the helm at Chicago. In 1933 he was hired as the Browns' manager. Hornsby was elected to the Baseball Hall of Fame in 1942. After a year managing in the Mexican League and a sabbatical from organized baseball, he joined the St. Louis Browns as manager in 1952. He lasted part of the season, but joined the Cincinnati Reds as manager, staying throughout the 1953 season.

After scouting for the soon-to-be New York Mets in 1961, Hornsby became a coach for the expansion team the following year. Hornsby died on January 5, 1963, in Chicago.

JEFFREY E. SMITH

Alexander, Charles C. *Rogers Hornsby: A Biography.* New York: Holt, 1995.

Devaney, John. *The Greatest Cardinals of Them All.* New York: G. P. Putnam's Sons, 1968.

Rains, Rob. *The St. Louis Cardinals: The 100th Anniversary History.* New York: St. Martin's, 1992.

HOSMER, HARRIET GOODHUE (1830–1908)

Harriet Goodhue Hosmer, the most renowned woman sculptor of the nineteenth century, was born on October 9, 1830, in Watertown, Massachusetts. Her mother died of tuberculosis when Harriet was not yet six; two infant brothers and an older sister succumbed to the same disease. Ahead of his time, her physician father, Hiram Hosmer, insisted on rigorous physical training for his surviving child, but he found himself helpless in controlling her unruly behavior. He finally sent her to Elizabeth Sedgwick's school in Lenox, Massachusetts, an important turning point in Hosmer's life. There she met Cornelia Crow, a student from St. Louis. She formed a lifelong bond with the Crow family, especially with St. Louis businessman and civic leader **Wayman Crow,** Cornelia's father.

When she had completed her education, Hosmer returned home certain that she wanted to be a sculptor. Unable to gain admission to anatomy classes in Boston because she was female, she went to St. Louis to visit the Crow family. Wayman Crow helped open the door to Joseph Nash McDowell's Missouri Medical College where Hosmer began her studies in anatomy in November 1850. She stayed with the Crow family, walking the mile or more to the medical college and taking part in the social life of the family. She also took time to travel down the Mississippi by steamboat, then up the river to its source, before returning to Watertown with her diploma in anatomy after a stay of nearly a year in St. Louis.

In November 1852 Hosmer began her studies in Rome with the English sculptor John Gibson. She sent her first original work, a bust of the mythic Daphne, to the Crow family as a gift of appreciation. Wayman Crow commissioned her first full-length statue, a marble Oenone, the shepherdess abandoned by Paris, prince of Troy. Both pieces are in the collection of Steinberg Gallery at Washington University, along with a portrait bust of Wayman Crow, modeled by Hosmer in Rome and presented to him as a surprise at the Washington University commencement in 1868.

When Dr. Hosmer withdrew his financial support from his daughter, Wayman Crow became her official patron. He advanced money to meet her needs, advised her on all matters, and was her dear friend and confidant. His influence was apparent in the commission for the Mercantile Library, though the donor was Alfred Vinton. The recumbent marble image of Beatrice Cenci was exhibited at the Royal Academy in London before it was shipped to its permanent home at the Mercantile Library in St. Louis.

Called home in 1860 by the serious illness of her father, Hosmer received the news from a jubilant Crow that she had captured the commission for the statue of Sen. **Thomas Hart Benton,** Missouri's first public sculpture. When she accepted the coveted commission, she expressed her appreciation to the people of Missouri for giving her a chance. She asked to be judged only as an artist, not as a *female* artist. The bronze image of Benton now stands in Lafayette Park, St. Louis, where it was dedicated on May 27, 1868, before a huge crowd.

Hosmer was highly successful in her chosen career. In addition to the works associated with St. Louis and the Crow family, Hosmer produced *Medusa,* a companion bust to *Daphne;* a sarcophagus monument to Judith Falconnet in the Church of Sant' Andrea della Fratte in Rome; *Puck,* a mischievous marble sprite replicated many times; *Zenobis,* the captive queen of Palmyra; *The Sleeping Faun* and its companion, *The Walking Faun;* as well as bas-relief medallions and fountains.

Hosmer was known internationally as an artist as well as for her independent lifestyle. She had a circle of interesting friends that included Nathaniel Hawthorne, who visited her in her studio, and Robert Browning and Elizabeth Barrett Browning, whom she persuaded to sit for the *Clasped Hands of the Brownings.* Her clients were members of the English aristocracy, including the Prince of Wales, who later became Edward VII. Nonetheless, she never forgot her Missouri connections and took a keen interest in news of St. Louis. Familiar names such as **William Greenleaf Eliot,** George Partridge, and

James Erwin Yeatman are included in her letters to Crow, along with mention of Washington University, Shaw's Garden (the Missouri Botanical Garden), and Tower Grove Park. Hosmer continued to write to Crow until his death in 1885, a great loss to her. St. Louisans, in turn, took a proprietary interest in her and her international acclaim.

Although most of her best-known works were done in the 1850s and 1860s, Harriet Hosmer had a long career and kept her studio in Rome even while she spent prolonged periods of time in Britain. In her later years, she returned to her native Watertown, where she died on February 12, 1908.

DOLLY SHERWOOD

Curran, Joseph Leo, ed. "Harriet Goodhue Hosmer: Collected Sources." 7 vols. Watertown Free Public Library Collection, Watertown, Mass.; 1974 Microfilm Archives of American Art. Smithsonian Institution, Washington, D.C.

Kasson, Joy S. *Marble Queens and Captives: Women in Nineteenth-Century American Sculpture.* New Haven: Yale University Press, 1990.

Rubenstein, Charlotte Streifer. *American Women Sculptors: A History of Women Working in Three Dimensions.* Boston: G. K. Hall, 1990.

Sherwood, Dolly. *Harriet Hosmer, American Sculptor, 1830–1908.* Columbia: University of Missouri Press, 1991.

HOUCK, LOUIS (1840–1925)

Louis Houck was born on April 1, 1840, in Mascoutah, Illinois. His father, a native of Bavaria, was a journalist who published German-language newspapers in Illinois, Kansas, and Missouri during the 1840s and 1850s. Houck occasionally attended private schools, and he studied for a year at the University of Wisconsin. His education during those years was focused on mastering his father's occupation.

During the Civil War, the young Houck published a German-language newspaper in Illinois that criticized Abraham Lincoln. The criticism led to mob violence against the newspaper office. Although later Houck occasionally wrote for the *Missouri Republican,* his publishing career was essentially over.

Through self-study, Houck became a lawyer, and he soon moved to St. Louis, where, during the final year of Andrew Johnson's presidency, he served as an assistant U.S. district attorney. In 1869 he moved to Cape Girardeau, where he practiced law and wrote favorable articles about southeast Missouri for the *Missouri Republican.*

Houck's marriage in 1872 to Mary Hunter Giboney gave him increased social status as well as substantial real estate holdings. The Giboneys had received large land grants when Spain ruled the area.

After his marriage Houck sought to increase the value of Giboney land by promoting economic development of the city and local area.

Thus, Houck became a railroad developer, his chief significance to southeast Missouri. His first railroad, built in 1880–1881, connected Cape Girardeau to the important Iron Mountain Railroad, fourteen miles away. During the next three decades, Houck built a series of small railroad systems that traversed much of southeast Missouri's lowlands.

Although variations existed, the railroads had many common characteristics: they were poorly constructed and poorly maintained. The reports of the state railroad commissioners were replete with examples of such weaknesses. Houck's short lines were built for three major reasons: to serve large landowners or lumber companies; to satisfy small towns anxious to obtain a railroad; or to create connections with through lines such as the Iron Mountain and Cotton Belt Railroads. It is likely that Houck hoped to sell them to major lines. Certainly, his disposal in 1902 of his most successful railroads, those in the Bootheel, to the Frisco Railroad for $1.33 million gave him financial security.

Among the myths of the area is that Louis Houck won a legal battle with Jay Gould over control of one of Houck's railroads. Supposedly, after Gould failed to have a pro-Gould receiver named to run the railroad, he said to Houck: "You are the first man that ever beat me in a railroad fight. I have seen your railroads. . . . I have heard you conduct your cases . . . and I want to say, sir, that you are a d___ poor railroad man, but a d___ fine lawyer." The story must be apocryphal since Jay Gould died in 1892 and the receivership battle occurred between 1893 and 1896.

Even more important than railroads in the development of the southeast Missouri lowlands were the land reclamation projects that Houck opposed in the early 1900s. As a landowner in the largest reclamation district, Little River Drainage District, he fought its legality all the way to the United States Supreme Court—but lost.

Houck was on the board of regents of Southeast Missouri Normal from 1886 to 1925, and from 1889 to his death he was the board's president. He donated land to the college and closely observed its activities. He championed the cause of state colleges as opposed to the University of Missouri.

In the early twentieth century, Houck gained a reputation as a historian of early Missouri. Although he expressed an interest in history, he wrote relatively little on the subject until after he sold his major rail lines to the Frisco Railroad. His significant historical works were a three-volume *History of Missouri* (1908) and a two-volume set of documents, *The Spanish Regime in Missouri* (1909). His studies did not extend beyond the territorial period. While subsequent historical treatment has greater analysis, Houck deserves much credit as an early pioneer in the field of Missouri history.

Houck died on February 18, 1925, at the family estate near Cape Girardeau.

LEON P. OGILVIE

Doherty, William T., Jr. *Louis Houck: Missouri Historian and Entrepreneur.* Columbia: University of Missouri Press, 1961.
———. "The Missouri Interests of Louis Houck." Ph.D. diss., University of Missouri, 1951.
Houck, Louis. *A History of Missouri, from the Earliest Explorations and Settlements until the Admission of the State into the Union.* 3 vols. Chicago: R. R. Donnelley and Sons, 1908.
———. *The Spanish Regime in Missouri: A Collection of Papers and Documents Relating to Upper Louisiana.* 2 vols. Chicago: R. R. Donnelley and Sons, 1909.
Ogilvie, Leon Parker. "The Development of the Southeast Missouri Lowlands." Ph.D. diss., University of Missouri–Columbia, 1967.

HOUSTON, DAVID FRANKLIN (1866–1940)

David Franklin Houston distinguished himself in three careers: academic, political, and business. A political scientist by training, he rose to the chancellorship of Washington University in St. Louis. In 1913 President Woodrow Wilson appointed him secretary of agriculture, a position he held until 1920 when he became secretary of the treasury for a brief period. Leaving government in 1921, he eventually became chairman of the board of the Mutual Life Insurance Company.

Born in Monroe, North Carolina, on February 17, 1866, Houston went to South Carolina College and earned a B.A. degree in 1887. At only twenty-two years of age, he became superintendent of the Spartanburg, South Carolina, schools, serving the district until 1891. From Spartanburg, he went to Harvard University, earning an M.A. degree in 1892.

An opportunity to teach at the university level came in 1894 when Houston became adjunct professor of political science at the University of Texas. He published *A Critical Study of Nullification in South Carolina* as volume 3 in the Harvard Historical Studies Series in 1896, and Texas promoted him to associate professor in 1897. He remained at Texas until 1900, when Texas A&M selected him as its president. He continued in that position for eight years before moving to Washington University as chancellor, a position he held officially until 1917, but in reality until only 1913, when he moved to Washington, D.C., as secretary of agriculture.

Col. Edward House served as Houston's connection to Wilson. Houston had become acquainted with House while in Texas, and according to his memoirs, House approached him about a cabinet post not long after Wilson's election to the presidency. Houston admired Wilson as a fellow academic and as a "principled" man in government. When House asked him about a cabinet position, Houston chose secretary of agriculture because of the importance of farming to the nation.

U.S. entrance into World War I made agriculture even more significant, and Houston and the nation moved quickly to meet the agricultural needs of the Allies. Congress appropriated more than $11 million and directed the Department of Agriculture to improve the health and to increase the production, conservation, and utilization of livestock and plants. This charge included a provision to supply seeds to farmers and to extend and enlarge the availability of market news to them. Both Congress and Houston sought to further develop the cooperative agricultural extension service. Houston's department made surveys of the country's food supply, gathered and disseminated information about farm products, and conserved food by preventing loss in storage and transit. The Agriculture Department provided farmers with advice about market conditions and the distribution of perishable foods, sought to maintain the quality of agricultural products by investigating and certifying their condition, helped farmers secure an adequate labor force, and increased its research role. The department administered control of stockyards and supervised producers of ammonia, other fertilizers, and farm-equipment industries.

While Houston's department worked with production, Herbert Hoover and his Food Administration controlled and regulated the commercial distribution of food, promoting conservation and eliminating waste. The two agencies worked well together. Houston praised the administration and faculties of agricultural colleges for their support of his department's work. Finally, a national advisory committee, created by Houston and Hoover, provided the perspective and advice of farmers and their organizations. In addition, five thousand extension workers linked this elaborate federal machinery to individual farmers. Houston wrote that these agents "constituted the . . . intimate touch with the millions of people in the farming districts."

Houston's career in government ended with Wilson's departure from office. For the next twenty years he pursued a business career, achieving significant success. Houston died in New York on September 2, 1940.

LAWRENCE O. CHRISTENSEN

Houston, David. *A Critical Study of Nullification in South Carolina.* Harvard Historical Studies Series, vol. 3. New York: Longman, Green, 1896.
————. *Eight Years with Wilson's Cabinet, 1913–1920: With a Personal Estimate of the President.* 2 vols. Garden City, N.Y.: Doubleday, 1926.
Selby, P. O. "David F. Houston." In *Missouri College Presidents: Past and Present.* Kirksville: Northeast Missouri State University, 1971.
Shoemaker, Floyd C. "Hon. David F. Houston." In *Official Manual of the State of Missouri, 1919–1920.* Jefferson City: Secretary of State, 1920.

HOWARD, BENJAMIN (1760–1814)

Benjamin Howard, a lawyer by vocation, a politician by obligation, and a soldier by preference, served as governor of the Louisiana (and later Missouri) Territory between 1810 and 1813. He was born in Virginia in 1760 and moved to Boonesboro, Kentucky, in the 1770s when his father, John Howard, acquired sizable land tracts there. During the early 1790s Benjamin fought in the Indian wars in the Northwest Territory as a soldier and officer. When those hostilities ended in 1795 with the signing of the Treaty of Greenville, Howard returned to Kentucky where he studied law and established a legal practice in Lexington. He married Mary T. Mason in Virginia in 1811; they had no children.

Howard was a member of the Kentucky legislature from 1800 until 1802, and Kentucky voters twice elected him to the United States House of Representatives, where he served from 1807 until 1810. As a member of Congress, Howard lobbied to increase U.S. military strength before he resigned to become governor of the Louisiana Territory. President James Madison had selected him to succeed **Meriwether Lewis** in that post.

Howard considered his new office a step forward politically but apparently later regretted his decision. He always preferred his native state over St. Louis as a place of residence. Madison appointed Howard governor in April 1810, but he did not go to the territory until September. Despite his tardiness in arriving in St. Louis and his subsequent lengthy absences from the territory, local residents considered him a good choice for the post. They welcomed his military experience because of the growing threat of Indian hostilities.

In 1811 Governor Howard directed the organization of additional militia companies and superintended the construction of several blockhouses in remote sections of the territory with the assistance of **William Clark,** then serving as brigadier general of the territorial militia. In the aftermath of Gen. **William Henry Harrison**'s bloody encounter with the Shawnee and their allies at Tippecanoe in the Indiana Territory, Howard recommended a series of military campaigns directed against hostile tribes along the Louisiana Territory's northern frontier. On his own initiative he organized a company of mounted riflemen to act as rangers and then sought approval from federal authorities. Congress subsequently authorized the new unit that patrolled the territory's exposed regions under the command of **Nathan Boone.**

Howard also lent his support to efforts to advance Louisiana's status to a second-class territory. Congress authorized the change on June 4, 1812, and renamed the territory Missouri to avoid confusion with the new state of Louisiana, formerly known as the Territory of Orleans.

When Congress declared war on Great Britain in June 1812, Governor Howard again recommended a major offensive campaign against the belligerent western tribes, but Secy. of War John Armstrong declined to sanction the ambitious plan. Fearing an attack on St. Louis, residents made plans to fortify the city in early 1813. In the governor's absence, acting governor **Frederick Bates** mustered the militia and ordered it to stand ready for immediate action.

Notwithstanding his frequent absences from the territory, Governor Howard continued to oversee its defenses. In the spring of 1813 he ordered the evacuation of Fort Osage, which he considered indefensible because of its remote location and the small number of troops stationed there. When the War Department reorganized the army command structure in an effort to improve the general conduct of military operations, President Madison issued Howard a special commission, making him a brigadier general in the United States Army and placing him in charge of all forces in the territories of Missouri and Illinois. Madison had given Howard the option of either taking the new military position or continuing his current post as governor of the Missouri Territory. Having already decided not to seek reappointment as governor, Howard accepted the military commission and surrendered his office as territorial chief executive in March 1813. The president named William Clark as his successor.

Following his appointment as brigadier general, Howard organized an expedition to chastise warring tribes in the Illinois Territory. He returned to St. Louis after completing a successful campaign, but in January 1814 Gen. William Henry Harrison ordered him to report to Cincinnati. Harrison planned to send Howard to Detroit as a replacement for Gen. Lewis Cass, but federal officials countermanded that directive when residents of the exposed western territories strenuously objected to General Howard's removal. They ordered him to return to St. Louis with his command, where he died on September 18, 1814. The popular official's death came as a severe blow to the war-weary residents of the Missouri Territory who had respected his military savvy. Howard County, Missouri, formed in 1816, was named for him.

MARK MORASCH

Biographical Dictionary of the United States Congress, 1774–1989. Bicentennial ed. S.v. "Howard, Benjamin." Washington, D.C.: U.S. Government Printing Office, 1989.

Carter, Clarence E., ed. *Territorial Papers of the United States.* Vol. 14. Washington, D.C.: U.S. Government Printing Office, 1949.

Foley, William E. *The Genesis of Missouri: From Wilderness Outpost to Statehood.* Columbia: University of Missouri Press, 1989.

HOWARD, ELSTON (1929–1980)

Born in St. Louis on February 23, 1929, Elston Howard became one of the finest catchers in major league baseball during the years he played. He began his professional career in 1950, only three years after Jackie Robinson took the field for the Brooklyn Dodgers, becoming the first African American in the major leagues.

After graduating from Vashon High School in St. Louis, Howard joined the Kansas City Monarchs in the Negro National League. He played in the formerly segregated minor leagues from 1950 to 1954 before joining the New York Yankees in 1955. He was the first African American to play for the Yankees, placing him among the pioneers in integrating the majors. Howard saw little action behind the plate in his early years with the Yankees. Baseball Hall of Fame catcher and fellow St. Louisan Yogi Berra was ensconced there, winning the Most Valuable Player Award in 1961.

Howard began his career as an outfielder in 1948 with the St. Louis Braves, a semiprofessional team in a local all-black league. He joined the Monarchs the following year, and they in turn sold his contract to the New York Yankees. He completed the 1950 season with the Muskegon, Michigan, team in the class A Central League as an outfielder. After two years in the U.S. military, Howard worked a season with Toronto in the International League. He joined the Yankees at the start of the 1955 season. By then he was already learning his new position behind the plate.

While Howard good-naturedly said that he did not mind catching and was happy just to play major league ball, not everyone agreed. In a March 1954 article in the *Afro-American,* Sam Lacey wrote that Howard had been mistreated and was unhappy as a player. Lacey argued that Howard did not like playing as a catcher and did not receive adequate help from coach (and former catcher) Bill Dickey. He asserted that the Yankees were trying to sabotage the talented young player's career because of his race.

As with most black players in the 1950s and early 1960s, Howard's race was the subject of public comment in interview questions. The Yankees had investigated Howard's personal life before signing him, determined that their first African American player be of impeccable moral character. The Howards of St. Louis were above reproach. Elston's father, Travis Howard, was an educator.

Howard was often quoted as saying the Yankees treated him like any other player, yet *Afro-American* sportswriter Lacey suggested otherwise, asserting that official scorers and sportswriters were unduly harsh on the young catcher. "The crusade extends to the Press Box, too," wrote Lacey.

> For example, in the first inning of the game with the Nates, Elston over-ran a ball which Tom Umphlett had popped and couldn't pick up. Many times in my Press Box career, I have heard the play scored as a hit. The "Yankee" newsman promptly called out Error 2 as they do in baseball, denoting the number of the catcher. In the third inning, pitcher Jim McDonald threw a curve which dug into the dirt and skidded past Howard, allowing a runner to advance a base. Wild pitch? No, it was ruled a passed ball— the latter goes against the catcher. Yes, friends, this boy's plight here is one that would prove intolerable for many of us.

Howard played twelve seasons with the Yankees, assuming full-time catching duties in 1962. He was the 1963 Most Valuable Player in the American League, the first black to win the league's coveted award and only the third catcher to receive it, preceded by Mickey Cochran in 1934 and Yogi Berra in 1951, 1954, and 1955.

Yankee manager **Casey Stengel** claimed in 1959 that New York was converting Howard to a catcher because he was not a fast runner, which Stengel considered a requirement for outfielders. Sports magazine writer Joe Trimbell reported that "Howard isn't really slow, but he doesn't have the leg speed that most Negro athletes possess. It was the electrifying speed of Jackie Robinson, Larry Doby, Junior Gilliam, Willie Mays, and most of the other original Negro players who first attracted them to big league scouts." Stengel agreed, noting that "he has a better arm than Berra, and handles the pitchers about as good."

In 1967 Howard was sold to the Boston Red Sox for cash along with minor league pitchers Ron Klimkowksi and Pete Magrini. The Red Sox released him in 1968.

Elston Howard died on December 15, 1980, of heart disease, a year after being named administrative aid to the Yankee owner, George Steinbrenner.

JEFFREY E. SMITH

Grossinger, Richard, and Lisa Conrad, eds. *Baseball, I Gave You All of the Best Years of My Life*. Berkeley, Calif.: North Atlantic Books, 1992.

Halberstam, David. *October 1964*. New York: Villard Books, 1994.

Hollander, Phyllis, and Zander Hollander, eds. *The Masked Marvels: Baseball's Great Catchers*. New York: Random House, 1982.

New York Times, December 15–17, 1980.

HUBBLE, EDWIN POWELL (1889–1953)

Edwin Powell Hubble became one of the world's leading astronomers. He was born on November 20, 1889, in Marshfield, Missouri, at the home of his maternal grandparents, the third of eight children born to John and Virginia Lee Hubble. His father attended Drury College in Springfield and Washington University Law School before becoming an insurance salesman. The Hubbles owned 640 acres in the Ozark Township, and Edwin spent his first few years growing up among the fruit trees that provided the family with additional income. His father's job made it necessary for the family to move extensively throughout the Midwest. They lived briefly in Kansas City and St. Louis, but finally settled in Wheaton, Illinois.

In Wheaton, Edwin Hubble began attending the Central School in September 1901. During his first few years he made good grades but did not have many friends. His popularity grew in high school when he participated in basketball and football and was the captain of the track team. In addition to his academic excellence and athletic participation, Hubble also held jobs delivering newspapers and ice. He even worked one summer with a surveying crew in Wisconsin. He graduated from high school in June 1906, and won a scholarship to the University of Chicago.

Hubble had an interest in astronomy and hoped to major in it at the university. His interest in the subject may have begun when his grandfather built him a crude telescope for his eighth birthday. His father opposed his pursuit of a degree in astronomy, thinking it an impractical occupation. Instead, John Hubble wished for his son to become a lawyer. Accordingly, Edwin took courses to satisfy his prerequisites for law school, while also taking courses in mathematics and astronomy. He took up boxing and soon won a reputation on campus as an excellent heavyweight boxer. He was later offered the opportunity to train to fight the world champion, Jack Johnson.

Hubble became a member of the Kappa Sigma fraternity, and the Blackfriars, a group of campus actors, invited him to become a member of their troupe. In June 1908 Hubble received his two-year associate in science degree and won a junior college scholarship in physics. The scholarship allowed him to become the future Nobel laureate Robert Millikan's laboratory assistant. Popular with other students and the professors, Hubble became a student marshal of the university, which required him to represent the student body at all convocations. His fellow students elected him vice president of the senior class.

Upon graduation Hubble's academic and extracurricular excellence led him to become a Rhodes scholar. For the next three years he studied law at Queen's College. After completing his law degree in 1913, Hubble joined his family in Louisville, Kentucky, and opened a law office. Although he prospered, he closed his office after only one year. He went to work in New Albany, Indiana, as a high school teacher of Spanish, physics, and mathematics. He also coached the basketball team through an undefeated season. Yet, he could not forget his passion for astronomy.

After his father died Hubble wrote to the University of Chicago, hoping to receive funding to pursue his interest in astronomy. The assistantships in astronomy had already been given out for the year, but officials suggested he contact Edwin B. Frost. Frost served as the director of the University of Chicago's Yerkes Observatory at William's Bay, Wisconsin, and Hubble became his assistant from October 1914 to May 1916. During this time he taught a class in introductory astronomy and worked as graduate head of Snell Hall. After he presented his dissertation, "Photographic Investigations of Faint Nebulae," Chicago awarded him a Ph.D. in astronomy. He graduated magna cum laude. His dissertation had needed revisions, but the committee overlooked them so he could graduate in time to join the army.

Hubble reported for duty in May 1917 and was stationed at Camp Grant as a member of the Eighty-sixth Division; they left for Europe in July 1918. In Europe he served as both a field officer and a line officer in the trenches. In November a bursting shell hit him. He awoke in a field hospital behind enemy lines. He later claimed that he quietly left the hospital and found his way back across the lines. The shell injured his right elbow, and he could never straighten it again. After the armistice Hubble served four months with the occupation forces in France and Germany, where he dealt with reparations claims and court-martials.

After returning to the United States, Hubble took a position at Mount Wilson Observatory, where he used the new Hooker one-hundred-inch telescope to study stellar objects lying beyond our solar system. In 1925 he presented the first significant classification system for galaxies at a meeting of the International Astronomical Union at Cambridge, England. This system is still used by astronomers today.

In the late 1920s Hubble concentrated on developing a reliable extragalactic distance scale. By 1929 he had discovered that radial velocities of receding galaxies are proportional to their distance. Hubble's Law, as it came to be known, proved that the universe was expanding as suggested earlier by Alexander Friedmann and George Lemaitre.

Hubble was also concerned with international affairs and served as the chairman of the Southern California Joint Flight for Freedom Committee. He left Mount Wilson during World War II to work as the chief of ballistics and director of the Supersonic Wind Tunnel Laboratory at Aberdeen Proving Ground in Maryland, and received the Medal of Merit for his work. In 1946 he became the chairman of the research committee at Mount Wilson and Palomar Observatories. He was instrumental in the planning and construction of the Hale two-hundred-inch reflector telescope on Palomar Mountain. When the construction was completed in 1949, he was given the honor of being the first astronomer to use it.

Always active in his community, Hubble served on the board of trustees of the Henry E. Huntington Library and Art Gallery and as president of the Pure Air Council of Southern California. He won several prestigious awards for his work, including the Barnard Medal, the Bruce Gold Medal, the Franklin Gold Medal, and the Royal Astronomical Society Gold Medal. In 1948 he was elected as an honorary fellow of Queen's College.

Hubble died on September 28, 1953, in San Marino, California. In April 1990 a satellite was launched containing a telescope that had a magnitude twenty-five times better than the best earth-based telescope. This telescope, the Hubble Space Telescope, can gather light as far as 14 billion light-years into space.

CYNTHIA HEIMBERGER

Bezzi, Tom. *Hubble Time.* San Francisco: Mercury House, 1987.

Christianson, Gale E. *Edwin Hubble: Mariner of the Nebulae.* New York: Farrar, Straus, and Giroux, 1995.

Dictionary of Scientific Biography. S.v. "Hubble, Edwin Powell."

HUGHES, LANGSTON (1902–1967)

James Mercer Langston Hughes was a descendant of arguably one of the more prominent black families in nineteenth-century America. His maternal grandfather was Charles Langston (1817–1892), the Ohio abolitionist and half brother of the better-known John Mercer Langston (1829–1897), an educator, diplomat, and politician. In 1869 Charles Langston married Mary Sampson Patterson Leary, the widow of Lewis Sheridan Leary, who died in John Brown's raid on Harper's Ferry, West Virginia, in 1859. Carrie, their second child, Hughes's mother, was born in Lawrence, Kansas, in January 1873.

Born on February 1, 1902, in Joplin, the county seat of Jasper County, Missouri, Langston was the second child of James Nathaniel and Carrie Mercer Langston Hughes. As a result of James Hughes being denied the right to practice law in Guthrie, in the township of Langston, in the Indian Territory, the star-crossed couple, shortly after their marriage, moved in the summer of 1899 to the lead-mining town of Joplin, where James worked as "a stenographer and bookkeeper for a mining firm." Two years before his birth, Hughes's bereaved parents buried his brother on February 8, in an unmarked grave in Joplin's Fairview Cemetery. After four years of marriage, James abandoned his family and moved first to Cuba, and then to Mexico. Langston Hughes made his only return trip to Joplin as an adult in 1958.

Of African, Scottish, English, French, and Indian ancestry, Hughes traced his roots back to Indiana and Kentucky on his paternal side and to Louisa County, Virginia, on his maternal side. Arnold Rampersad, his biographer, reminds us that Hughes was raised with the idea that "he had a messianic obligation to the Afro-American people, and through them to America." The mature Hughes came to realize that art "did more than resist social injustice: it reaffirmed a higher moral principle." This awareness enabled him to withstand social pressures that tested his creative imagination, especially during the Great Depression of the 1930s and the withering backlash of the 1960s.

Hughes spent most of the first thirteen years of his life with his maternal grandmother. They lived in a quiet neighborhood that bordered the University of Kansas. He joined his mother and stepfather, Homer Clarke, in Lincoln, Illinois, in 1914, where he finished grammar school in 1916. The family moved to Cleveland, Ohio, where he graduated from the multiethnic Central High School in 1920. As a senior there, he was elected president of the class yearbook. By the time he entered Columbia University in 1922, he had unsuccessfully tried two reconciliations with his estranged father, who lived in Mexico. He graduated from Lincoln University in Pennsylvania with a B.A. in 1929.

Langston Hughes is one of the best-known and most versatile American writers of the twentieth century. He wrote more than forty books. His creative range—poetry, essays, autobiography, fiction, drama, columns, translations, gospel song-plays, libretto, juvenile fiction, radio and television scripts, history and biography, anthology, and humor—is dazzling. His influence on writers such as Leopold Senghor, Aime Cesaire, Jacques Roumain, Nicolas Guillen, and Gabriela Mistral testify to his humanism and his vision. Hughes's manifesto, "The Negro Artist and the Racial Mountain" (1926), still resonates in the work of black writers. He wore gracefully the title "Poet Laureate of Harlem."

Closely identified with the Harlem Renaissance, Hughes, an indefatigable world traveler, lived through World War I, the Great Depression, World War II, the Korean War, the cold war, and the rise of the modern civil rights movement. He witnessed the building civil unrest sweeping across America; his writings were prophetic scripture for leaders of the civil rights movement with his recurring theme of the "dream deferred," a mantra for the "freedom now" generation.

In the 1920s Hughes showed early promise of his talent by having several of his poems published in the *Crisis, Opportunity, Vanity Fair,* and a special Harlem issue of *Survey Graphic,* as well as other journals by the end of the decade. Grounded in the blues and jazz aesthetics, Hughes was in sync with the longings and aspirations of black people as is evident in his signature collection, *The Weary Blues* (1926).

In his autobiography, *The Big Sea* (1940), Hughes tells of the composition of his most anthologized poem, "The Negro Speaks of Rivers" (1921), which was written "just outside of St. Louis, as the train rolled toward Texas." Having graduated from high school, he was on his way to Toluca, Mexico, to see his father when the great muddy Mississippi River jarred his imagination. Rampersad notes that "the sense of beauty and death, of hope and despair, fused in his imagination," and the adolescent Hughes became one with the ages. In his benchmark poem, Hughes depicts the timeless dignity of Africans and tells the heroic story of black people in the promised land with the American dream before them but just beyond their reach.

Alain Locke, America's first black Rhodes scholar and a distinguished professor of philosophy at Howard University, grasped the genius of Hughes, who incorporates blues and jazz forms into his art. For him Hughes represented "not the ragged provincialism of a minstrel but the descriptive detachment of a Vachel Lindsay and Sandburg . . . the democratic sweep of a Whitman."

Hughes combines an optimistic vision with a fidelity to African American sensibility to comment on our common humanity. The recurring threads that inform his art and imagination center on black people's gift of song, story, and laughter. Hughes shows us how the discourse of black America informs and alters our understanding of cultural history and our understanding of aesthetic value.

Like Whitman, Hughes was a bard of the open road. He sang heroic sagas of common people across the globe in their fight for social justice and human dignity. From an inauspicious beginning in Joplin, Missouri, Langston Hughes rose to become the bard of black America.

The "charming, ever smiling" Hughes cultivated the image of the boy next door, jovial, gentlemanly, and unassuming. Although he never married, he adopted black America as his family. He unflinchingly records the trials and triumphs of African Americans and brings their voices out of the silences that have marginalized them. As such, he places blacks at the center of the American experience. For example, he gave us the feisty Alberta K. Johnson and the redoubtable Jesse B. Simple. He deftly revised American letters and saw strength in diversity. In spite of "the adulation of thousands of readers," Hughes spent his life in "nomadic loneliness."

Two of Hughes's last public appearances had Show-Me State connections. In the midst of the turbulent 1960s, he spoke at New York's Plaza Hotel at the fifty-seventh annual dinner of the Poetry Society of America in April 1967. The guest of honor was the Missouri-born **Marianne Moore** (1887–1972), a dear friend who received the Gold Medal for Distinguished Achievement from the society. In early May Hughes attended the annual dinner of the Missouri Society of New York.

On May 22, 1967, Langston Hughes, black America's most original and beloved writer, died in New York City.

DOLAN HUBBARD

Barksdale, Richard K. *Langston Hughes: The Poet and His Critics.* Chicago: American Library, 1977.

Berry, Faith. *Langston Hughes: Before and Beyond Harlem.* Westport, Conn.: Lawrence Hill, 1983.

Hughes, Langston. *The Big Sea: An Autobiography.* 1940. Reprint, New York: Hill and Wang, 1963.

Miller, R. Baxter. *The Art and Imagination of Langston Hughes.* Lexington: University Press of Kentucky, 1989.

———. *Langston Hughes and Gwendolyn Brooks: A Reference Guide.* Boston: G. K. Hall, 1978.

Rampersad, Arnold. *The Life of Langston Hughes.* 2 vols. New York: Oxford University Press, 1986–1988.

HUGHES, RUPERT (1872–1956)

Rupert Hughes, a versatile popular writer, was born in Lancaster, Missouri, on January 31, 1872. When he was seven years old his family moved to Keokuk, Iowa, where his father, Felix, practiced law and his mother, Jean, raised a brood of talented children. Rupert's siblings included Howard, later a noted inventor and father of Howard Hughes, the eccentric billionaire. Hughes earned a B.A. in 1892 and an M.A. in 1894 from Adelbert College (which later became part of Western Reserve University), and an M.A. from Yale in 1899. By that year Hughes had already abandoned plans to teach English literature in favor of a writing career.

As a playwright, short story writer, novelist, biographer, poet, composer of popular songs, music historian, and screenwriter, Hughes created a bewildering mix of scholarship and ephemeral entertainment, of fiction and nonfiction. His first book, *The Lakerim Athletic Club* (1898), was first a serialized magazine story for boys. Hughes was briefly a reporter for the *New York Journal,* and then served, during the late 1890s until 1901, as assistant editor of several magazines, including *Current Literature,* all the while writing short stories, poetry, and plays in his spare time. For eighteen months in 1901 and 1902, he worked in London on the editorial staff of the *Historian's History of the World,* and in New York from 1902 to 1905 he helped edit the *Encyclopædia Britannica.* From 1905 until his death Hughes sustained a comfortable life with earnings from his pen.

Hughes's stage productions include *All for a Girl* (1908), which starred his second wife, Adelaide Manola Mould. His many volumes of fiction include a number of historical novels and *The Old Nest* (1912), a novel that Hughes based on his family. He adapted this story as a successful motion picture in 1921. Increasingly employed as a movie screenwriter and director, Hughes moved to Hollywood in 1923. His film *The Patent Leather Kid* received an Academy Award nomination in 1927. Several books about music, notably *American Composers* (1900) and the *Music Lovers' Cyclopedia* (1914; rev. ed., 1939), are among his nonfiction titles.

Hughes's most important work was a well-researched and controversial three-volume biography of George Washington (1926–1930). Although more enduring scholarly works have superseded it, the Hughes biography broke new ground at a time when Parson Weems's Washington myths masqueraded as fact. Hughes's *Washington* appeared during an age of debunking, but its author argued that a search for truth, not iconoclasm, was his motive. Since Hughes's better books, like the Washington biography, are little used today, he is likely to be remembered for works of shallow sensationalism such as *Souls for Sale* (1922), which exploited current Hollywood scandals, and for the *New Yorker*'s 1950 evaluation of his prose style as "rather primitive."

While he became a successful writer, Hughes also sustained a career as a citizen-soldier. He entered the

New York National Guard in 1897 as a private and left the California State Guard in 1943 as a colonel.

Hughes's three marriages ended unhappily. He was divorced from Agnes Wheeler in 1903, and two wives, Adelaide Manola Mould and Elizabeth Patterson Dial, committed suicide, in 1923 and 1945, respectively. Rupert Hughes died on September 9, 1956, in Los Angeles at the age of eighty-four.

ALAN R. HAVIG

Dictionary of American Biography. Supplement 6, 1956–1960. S.v. "Hughes, Rupert."

Hughes, Rupert. "My Father." *American Magazine* 98 (August 1924): 34–35, 66–70.

————. "My Mother." *American Magazine* 98 (September 1924): 16–17, 118–24.

New York Times, September 10, 1956.

Shoemaker, Floyd Calvin. *Missouri and Missourians: Land of Contrasts and People of Achievements.* Vol. 5. Chicago: Lewis Publishing, 1943.

Twentieth-Century Authors: A Biographical Dictionary of Modern Literature. S.v. "Hughes, Rupert."

HUNT, ANNE LUCAS (1796–1879)

We can guess the character of Anne Lucas Hunt by the good she did during her life and by the legacies she left at her death; altogether she gave more than a million dollars in money and real estate to various charitable institutions. With quiet generosity she founded the House of the Good Shepherd, as well as the church and school of St. Mary's, and gave to the Little Sisters of the Poor.

The facts of Hunt's life, though, come largely from an undated memoir she wrote as an old woman, recalling her early days in St. Louis. She was born, she wrote, on September 23, 1796, in Montpelier, Pennsylvania, six miles from Pittsburgh. Her father was **John B. C. Lucas,** an attorney and later a U.S. congressman who had emigrated from Normandy, France; her mother was Anne Sebin Lucas, handsome, well educated, with a shrewd business sense. Anne Lucas Hunt was the only daughter in the family, which grew to include eight sons.

When Anne Lucas was eight years old, the family left Pennsylvania for St. Louis because they were "desirous of having the benefit of French society." In a journey that took three months, they traveled by flatboat, horse, and keelboat to their new home, where her father was appointed judge of the Louisiana Superior Court and a member of the board of land commissioners.

On his wife's advice, John B. C. Lucas also began investing in St. Louis real estate. "By purchasing a lot at a time," wrote Hunt, "he at length came to own all the land from Market Street to St. Charles, and from Fourth Street to Jefferson Avenue. He did not buy it as a speculation, but for what it would produce; it turned out, however, to be an immense speculation, for the whole seven arpents front did not cost him over $700.00, and that property is now worth, I suppose, seventy millions!"

As the daughter of a prominent family, Anne Lucas lived a privileged life. After her mother's death in 1811, Anne must have also had to manage their large household. Soon her father built a home in the country. "I remember that people told my father that he was not doing a prudent thing in taking me, a fourteen-year-old girl, so far away; that the Indians might carry me off some time when he was down town attending to his business."

In 1814 Anne Lucas married Capt. Theodore Hunt, a former U.S. naval officer who went into partnership with fur trader **Manuel Lisa.** The couple had eight children, three of whom survived to adulthood. Captain Hunt died in 1832.

By 1832 most of Hunt's brothers had also died, but the death of her brother **Charles Lucas** in 1817 was a particularly painful blow. Wounded in his first duel with **Thomas Hart Benton,** a political rival, Lucas was killed when his opponent demanded a second encounter. Hunt became so fearful of meeting Benton that she and her husband moved to a country home, which they sold in 1820 to Frederick Dent, father-in-law of Gen. **Ulysses S. Grant.** Next they moved to what is now Normandy; Hunt christened her home there "the 'shelter,' because I kept it as a shelter in my old age in case I should need it."

Four years after the death of her first husband, Hunt married his cousin, **Wilson Price Hunt;** as chief American partner of John Jacob Astor's Pacific Fur Company, he had headed an 1811 fur-trading expedition to Astoria, a tiny outpost at the mouth of the Columbia River, and had returned to St. Louis in 1813. There he became a real estate investor and mill owner. He died in 1842.

Twice widowed, Hunt devoted herself to her family, her charities, and the considerable estate she had inherited from her father, who died in 1842. However, the St. Louis of her youth was also in her thoughts. In her memoirs she recalled wistfully its old forts, Indian mounds, and handsome Chouteau's Pond. "Around where the Court House now is, prairie chickens, quails and other game were trapped in abundance," she wrote.

Hunt died at her Lucas Place home on April 13, 1879. Her obituary in the *Missouri Republican* attested to her generosity of spirit: "Her children and most intimate friends unhesitatingly assert that they never heard her speak slightingly of any person, and when others did so in her presence she invariably reproved them and became herself the defender of the person so spoken of."

At Hunt's request, her funeral was devoid of ostentation, with no high mass or drapery around the church. Her coffin was a simple black, with only a silver cross on the lid. Instead of a personal eulogy, she requested that her funeral sermon consist of a warning to the living.

CANDACE O'CONNOR

Hunt, Anne L. "Early Recollections." *Glimpses of the Past* 1:6 (May 1934): 41–51.
Lucas Papers. Missouri Historical Society, St. Louis.
Missouri Republic, April 14, 1879.

HUNT, CHARLES LUCAS (1820–1885)

In his excellent eyewitness depiction of life in Civil War St. Louis, *The Story of a Border City during the Civil War,* the pro-Union pastor of the Second Baptist Church, **Galusha Anderson,** waxed sensationalistic only in describing the activities of a secret pro-Confederate organization behind Union lines known variously as the "Knights of the Golden Circle" and the "Order of American Knights." Anderson claimed that the Knights, with reportedly hundreds of thousands of members from Missouri to New York, constituted probably the most formidable secret organization that ever existed in the United States. In support of this claim, he cited their audacious plan to capture St. Louis for the Confederacy in coordination with Confederate general **Sterling Price**'s invasion of Missouri in the summer of 1864.

Anderson's alarm was essentially groundless because long before they could rise up to aid Price's invasion, the Knights and their plans were well known to the Union commander of the Department of the Missouri, Maj. Gen. William Rosecrans, and his provost marshal, John Sanderson, who planted Union agents in their ranks.

Prominent among those ensnared by this Union counterespionage was Charles Lucas Hunt, the Knights' forty-four-year-old grand commander of the state of Missouri. Hunt had earlier purchased revolvers for his St. Louis followers and had even traveled to Canada to meet secretly with the exiled leader of the most extreme "Peace Democrats" or "Copperheads," former U.S. congressman from Ohio Clement L. Vallandigham, to whom Hunt proposed armed resistance against the Union. Vallandigham refused Hunt's bold suggestion as treasonous. Once in federal custody, however, Hunt soon lost his courage, and in July 1864 he managed to buy his release from his squalid prison quarters in the Gratiot Street prison in St. Louis, thanks to his signed confession and (according to Hunt family tradition) a gift of a silver service to a key Union official. In 1865 Hunt further distanced himself from his former Rebel companions

by enrolling in a unit of the Missouri State Militia, a Union military organization.

Charles Lucas Hunt was born in St. Louis on April 6, 1820, to Theodore and **Anne Lucas Hunt.** Theodore Hunt (1778–1832), a New Jersey native, had moved to St. Louis in 1814 after a relatively brief career as a naval officer and an even briefer one as a captain of a merchant ship. In St. Louis he met and married Anne Lucas, and pursued, with mixed success, various business ventures, including a tanyard, a store, and a bank. He also served as the recorder of land titles in Missouri from 1824 until his removal for political reasons early in President Andrew Jackson's first term.

The mother of Charles Lucas Hunt, Anne Lucas Hunt (1796–1879) was the daughter of French-born Missouri territorial judge **John B. C. Lucas** and the younger sister of attorney **Charles Lucas,** killed in an infamous 1817 duel with **Thomas Hart Benton,** who later became a U.S. senator. Charles Lucas Hunt was doubtless named in honor of this "martyred" uncle. Widowed by Theodore Hunt in 1832, four years later Anne married a relative of Theodore, **Wilson Price Hunt,** an important St. Louis fur merchant, but was again widowed in 1842. As a result of inheritances from her two husbands, her brother, and her father, as well as her own prudent real estate investments, Anne Lucas Hunt became very wealthy. She was a noted benefactor of various Catholic charities. Another frequent object of her bestowals was her son Charles, who desperately needed them after repeated business failures.

Educated at the Dominican College in Bardstown, Kentucky, as well as St. Louis University, Charles Lucas Hunt left college to pursue a series of largely unsuccessful business ventures. One early such enterprise was an apothecary shop in downtown St. Louis. After the failure of the shop and other ventures, Hunt became the principal investor in the *St. Louis Leader,* an elegant newspaper that was both Catholic and proslavery in its editorial policy. The newspaper boasted of its "long, long purse" (namely, Hunt's) and its large staff. Such extravagance cost Hunt nearly $150,000 by the time he sold his interest in the failing paper in the late 1850s.

For the rest of his life, Hunt would turn to real-estate investments and animal breeding with somewhat greater success. However, his sporting-instructor instincts often interfered with his business judgment. Early in his career as a real estate investor, for example, he parted with a most valuable downtown St. Louis property for a fraction of its eventual worth just to obtain funds for a trotting horse that had caught his eye.

On an 1850 visit to Europe in the company of the famed Jesuit missionary and explorer **Pierre Jean De Smet,** Hunt was introduced to the king of Belgium and received an appointment as the Belgian counsel in St. Louis, a largely honorary position that Hunt prized. During the Civil War he was able to use his position as counsel to temporarily evade Union conscription. Union authorities began to regard Hunt's position as counselor for a foreign government as particularly sinister, however, when they discovered that his Missouri Knights occasionally used the name of the "Corps de Belgique."

Following the Civil War, Hunt wisely concentrated his remaining energies on raising horses, dogs, and chickens. At his death on February 9, 1885, his obituaries especially noted his nationally known racehorses, John Davis and April Fool, and his many rare breeds of poultry. Thanks largely to his inheritance upon the death of his mother six years earlier, the free-spending Hunt was worth more than eight hundred thousand dollars at his own death.

MARSHALL D. HIER

Hunt, Theodore. Papers. Missouri Historical Society, St. Louis.

John Sanderson Report. Missouri Historical Society, St. Louis.

Klement, Frank L. *The Copperheads of the Middle West.* Chicago: University of Chicago Press, 1960.

Reavis, L. V. *St. Louis: The Future Great City of the World.* St. Louis: C. R. Barns, 1876.

St. Louis Globe-Democrat, February 10, 1885.

"Theodore Hunt." *Bulletin of the Missouri Historical Society* 4 (July 1948): 272–73.

HUNT, WILSON PRICE (1783–1842)

Wilson Price Hunt was born to a prosperous merchant family in Asbury, New Jersey, on March 20, 1783. As a young man he journeyed west. A cousin, John Wesley Hunt, was a successful merchant in Lexington, Kentucky, but Wilson Price Hunt's quest for opportunity and adventure drew him farther west. In 1804 he opened a general mercantile business in St. Louis with partner John Hankinson, and explored opportunities beyond the Missouri settlements. He considered, but ultimately declined, joining **Manuel Lisa** in a risky trading expedition to Santa Fe in 1806. That same year Hunt met the returning explorers **Meriwether Lewis** and **William Clark** in St. Louis, sold them supplies, and garnered valuable information about their discoveries.

In 1809 the aggressive and enterprising young merchant attracted the notice of New York fur magnate John Jacob Astor, who was seeking just such a man for a new project. Astor envisioned a transcontinental American fur company controlling the trade across the center of North America. He invited Hunt to join him in organizing the Pacific Fur Company. As part of Astor's plan, Hunt was to establish a base of operations on the Northwest coast, open overland communications between that post and St. Louis, and manage Astor's trade with China and the monopoly on trade with the Russian settlements in Alaska that he had just won.

To initiate the project Astor launched two expeditions in 1810. One, led by Duncan McDougal, was to travel by sea to the mouth of the Columbia River and establish a trading post there. The group arrived in March and built Fort Astoria in April 1811. Wilson Price Hunt was to lead the second, overland, opening a trail from St. Louis to the Columbia, and selecting sites for the network of trading posts Astor intended to build along the route. Delayed by the problems of recruiting men and gathering supplies from the fur-trade centers of Montreal, Michilimackinac, and St. Louis, Hunt's expedition finally left St. Louis on October 21, 1810. After spending the winter at the mouth of the Nodaway River, the party started for the Columbia in April 1811.

Searching for a more direct route than that of Lewis and Clark, the Astorians struck out overland, following native trails along the Bighorn and Wind Rivers, into the Wind River Mountains. West of the Continental Divide they lost their way, and suffered bitterly from hunger, harsh weather, and difficult terrain. After a disastrous attempt to navigate the wild Snake River in dugouts, Hunt split his force into smaller parties to forage for food and the best route to the Columbia. The overland group straggled into Fort Astoria through January and February 1812.

Hunt assumed overall command of the operations at the new post. When the ship *Beaver* arrived loaded with men and supplies in May 1812, the Astorians felt secure enough to expand their operations. Hunt left for Sitka to complete Astor's business arrangements with the Russians. There he traded his cargo for a large shipment of sealskins that he dispatched to China, then continued to the Hawaiian Islands to meet another long-overdue supply ship from Astor.

During Hunt's absence the junior partners left in charge at Astoria learned that the United States and Great Britain were at war, that a Northwest Company expedition was coming down the Columbia to take Fort Astoria, and that a British warship was momentarily expected off the coast to secure the capture. By the time Hunt returned in February 1814, his partners had agreed to sell the fort and its contents to the Nor'Westers before all was taken by force. Although Hunt was outraged by the agreement, he had little choice but to conclude the transaction. While other Astorians returned to the United States or entered the employ of the Northwest Company, Hunt salvaged what he could of the assets and spent the next two years in the Pacific Coast trade, hoping to bring Astor some profit on his investment. He arrived in New

York with a cargo of luxury goods from China in October 1816.

Hunt returned to St. Louis in 1817. He bought a large tract of land on Gravois Creek southwest of the city, developed a farm, and built a gristmill. He remained a prominent St. Louis businessman, dealing primarily in furs and peltries. In 1822 he was appointed postmaster for St. Louis.

During Hunt's absence in 1814, a cousin, retired naval officer Theodore Hunt, moved to St. Louis and established himself as a tanner and furrier. He joined Manuel Lisa in a trading venture up the Missouri River from 1814 to 1817, then returned to his former business until 1824, when he was appointed U.S. recorder of land titles for the St. Louis District. He died in 1832, leaving his wife, Anne (the daughter of Judge **John B. C. Lucas**), and three children. In 1836 Wilson Price Hunt married **Anne Lucas Hunt;** they had no children. Hunt remained a close associate of John Jacob Astor, occasionally serving as his western representative in legal and business matters. Wilson Price Hunt died in St. Louis on April 13, 1842.

MARY ELLEN ROWE

Brandon, William. "Wilson Price Hunt." In *The Mountain Men and the Fur Trade of the Far West,* ed. LeRoy R. Hafen, 6:186–206. Glendale, Calif.: Arthur H. Clark, 1968.

Irving, Washington. *Astoria.* Norman: University of Oklahoma Press, 1964.

Ronda, James P. *Astoria and Empire.* Lincoln: University of Nebraska Press, 1990.

HURST, FANNY (1889–1968)

Fanny Hurst, the daughter of Rose Koppel and Samuel Hurst, was born at the home of her maternal grandparents in Hamilton, Ohio, on October 19, 1889. A short time later she was taken to St. Louis, her home for the next twenty years. The family was, in Hurst's words, "well-fixed" for the era, with her father drawing about ten thousand dollars annually from his shoe factory. Although sources often refer to Hurst as an only child, she had a sister, Edna, eleven months younger, who died from diphtheria at age three. Hurst described her home life as "arid" with "little fun" other than her mother's "flashes of wit," and stated that she "adored" her dramatic, verbal, but long-suffering mother, and "liked" her intelligent, judgmental father. The tone of her autobiography suggests, however, that she craved her father's affection most and that she enjoyed a happy childhood; her parents, by indulgence rather than by knowledge of progressive education, allowed her to learn what she wished as she wished. She depicted her parents and most of the events of her childhood with the warm, sympathetic touch that marks her fiction.

Hurst, whose teachers recognized and encouraged her talents, succeeded in almost every endeavor. She excelled in drama and athletics—especially tennis—primarily in an attempt to be "special." Her natural abilities lay in literature and writing, and she pursued both with fervor. By the age of thirteen she was reading writers such as Coleridge, Tolstoy, Howells, Pushkin, and Hardy. For one semester she attended a private St. Louis school, Harperly Hall, but, unhappy, transferred to Central, the single white public high school in St. Louis at that time, with an enrollment of fourteen hundred and known for its "innovations." There her essays were read aloud at teachers' meetings. She felt particularly indebted to William Schuyler, the assistant principal, a man "with his head in the clouds," who encouraged her thinking and writing. A prolific writer, Hurst wrote essays for other students (for which she lost the honor of having her essay read at graduation).

With great confidence, Hurst submitted her poems, stories, and essays to major publishers. Sources credit her with submitting a verse masque to the *Saturday Evening Post* at the age of fourteen; her autobiography indicates she was older, a freshman in college. By the age of eighteen she had so many rejection slips that her parents used them to discourage her from writing.

While studying at Washington University, Hurst had her first publications, "Ain't Life Wonderful" and "Home," in the St. Louis weekly *Reedy's Mirror;* she also wrote a few freelance assignments for the city's newspapers. She graduated with a B.A. in 1909, and in 1910 moved to New York, ostensibly to work on a graduate degree at Columbia, but really to immerse herself in writing. In New York she experienced the kind of life she would write about: she worked as a waitress in Child's restaurant, as a salesclerk "behind the ribbon counter of Hearns," and as an actress. "For a stretch of twenty-six months, without even meeting an editor, writer or publisher, I wrote, peddled, rewrote, repeddled, without so much as one acceptance or word of encouragement." Her career took shape when she was encouraged by Robert H. Davis, editor of *Munsey's,* who said to her, "Girl, you are a writer!" Two years later her first book, *Just Around the Corner,* appeared.

Hurst married Jacques S. Danielson, a Russian-born pianist, in 1915. The marriage was in the independent vein that Hurst had followed and would follow all her life. Kept secret for five years, the marriage when announced created a sensation since the couple had separate residences and separate careers. By all accounts, and particularly Hurst's autobiography, the marriage was happy and enduring, though the couple had no children. Danielson died in 1952.

Hurst was highly successful by most standards. In her twenties she was sought by major publications such as the *Saturday Evening Post, Metropolitan Magazine,* the *Delineator, Century, Red Book,* and *Cosmopolitan.* She was acquainted with many of the top writers of the era—Sinclair Lewis, Willa Cather, Rebecca West, F. Scott Fitzgerald, and Theodore Dreiser, for example—but said she mingled with them only slightly, if at all, feeling "awe" in their presence; she preferred the "surge" of the common people. These claims probably sprang from modesty, since Hurst's circle of friends was far from common. A close friend of Eleanor Roosevelt, Hurst was a frequent guest at the White House, and mixed with prominent political and social figures of the time.

Sources disagree as to which publication established Hurst's success. Contenders for that position are *Lummox* (Hurst's favorite), *Every Soul Hath Its Song,* and *Humoresque.* A number of her books were best-sellers, and some were translated into sixteen languages and made into plays or movies. *Back Street* and *Imitation of Life,* for example, still appear as American movie classics. She dealt with current and sensitive issues such as class struggle, sexual liberation, and racism—she "wrote against the second-class status of Negroes"—but primarily her works are of the experiences of women in a male-dominated society. Her heroines are often abandoned, abused, or destroyed; if they happen to attain professional success, but without male companionship, they are unfulfilled. Hurst wanted to write the "history of woman in four or five volumes," and, as Kunitz and Haycraft noted, may have been doing so all along.

Critics agree that Hurst's writing never attained the level of quality that makes for literary greatness. At her worst, she overwrote, exercised poor taste, and descended into sentimentality. Nonetheless, critics agree on the strengths of her work: rich with detail, vigorous, and always warm and sympathetic. One must remember that Hurst wrote during the years of high modernism, when the division between popular and literary writing widened, and when the sentimental novel was excluded from serious consideration as art. Hurst herself questioned the division, wondering why a work could not be of literary merit just because it was popular. She recalled with chagrin the then current judgment: better to be a classical failure than a popular success.

The energy Hurst brought to her writing, she brought to other concerns as well. She lectured at universities, appeared often on radio and television programs, and served for various periods with numerous civic and national organizations, including the Women's National Housing Commission and the New York World's Fair Commission. During the war she campaigned for war bonds—her group of campaigners included **Charles A. Lindbergh** and Albert Einstein. In 1952 she was appointed by the president as a U.S. delegate to the United Nations World Health Assembly in Geneva. She was given the "key" to Versailles, and traveled to Canada and Israel at the invitations of their governments.

Hurst, though not noted among the great literary writers of her era, was one of the most popular, well paid, and prolific. She was a handsome woman, a gracious hostess, and admirably surprised by and grateful for her success, though she obviously earned it with perseverance and talent. Twenty-five years after first leaving St. Louis, she was invited, along with **T. S. Eliot** and Judge Learned Hand, to receive an honorary degree from Washington University. She visited Cates Avenue and found it "remarkably" free of change. It was as she earlier described it, "a dream street but still a real street." Hurst died on February 23, 1968.

ROSE MARIE KINDER

Buck, Claire, ed. *The Bloomsbury Guide to Women's Literature.* New York: Prentice Hall, 1992.

Herzberg, Max J., ed. *Reader's Encyclopedia of American Literature.* New York: Thomas Y. Crowell, 1962.

Hurst, Fannie. *Anatomy of Me.* Garden City, N.Y.: Doubleday, 1958.

Kunitz, Stanley J., and Howard Haycraft, eds. *Twentieth-Century Authors.* New York: Wilson, 1942.

Tante, Dilly, ed. *Living Authors.* New York: H. W. Wilson, 1931.

Uffen, Ellen Serlen. "Fannie Hurst." *American Women Writers.* New York: Fredrick Ungar, 1980.

HUSMANN, GEORGE (1827–1902)

George Husmann was born on November 4, 1827, in Meyenburg, Prussia, the son of J. H. Martin and Louise Charlotte Wesselhoeft Husmann. The elder Husmann, a justice of the peace and the village schoolmaster, was an avid gardener who undoubtedly inspired his son's future career. Young George attended school for eighteen months in Meyenburg; in later years his older brother Frederick tutored him in English, French, German, and the classics.

In 1837 the Husmanns emigrated to America. Arriving in Philadelphia, the family bought shares in the German Settlement Society, which pledged to found a "New German Fatherland" in America. In the winter of 1838–1839 the Husmanns journeyed to Hermann, Missouri, a colony established in 1837 to promote the society's ideals.

Hermann's colonists harvested a grape crop in 1845 and began bottling wine in 1846. By 1847 George Husmann—ultimately the "father" of commercial grape growing in Missouri—had planted the first vineyard on his father's farm. Little is known, however, of these initial efforts, and in 1850 Husmann left Missouri and grape growing for the California mines.

Upon the death of his brother-in-law in 1852, Husmann returned to Hermann to help his widowed sister manage her farm. With her death he inherited the property and began planting vineyards and orchards on what became a model fruit farm in Missouri. In 1854 he married Louise Caroline Keilmann.

During the 1850s Husmann's fame as a viticulturist spread throughout the state. Initially successful with the Norton's Virginia, he introduced the Concord variety into Missouri in 1855. In 1859 he built a winery in Hermann and helped found the Missouri Fruit Growers' Association, which became the Missouri Horticultural Society in 1861. In 1862 he published his first of several works on grape growing.

Like most Missouri Germans, Husmann sided with the Union during the Civil War. He saw eighteen months' service, primarily with the Fourth Infantry Missouri Volunteers, and was mustered out in February 1863. He served as a member of the state's Constitutional Convention of 1865, voting against the constitution because it denied black men suffrage.

In 1865 Husmann became a charter member of the Missouri State Board of Agriculture, serving as vice president from 1867 to 1868. In 1866 he produced his influential *Cultivation of the Native Grape and Manufacture of American Wines,* a work published in four editions. The following year he became one of the directors of Hermann's first bank. During the presidential election of 1868 he served as an elector for Grant and Colfax from Missouri's Second District.

In 1869 Husmann again severed his ties with Hermann, moving to Bluffton and serving as president of the Bluffton Wine Company from 1869 to 1872. During this period he became a member of the board of curators of the University of Missouri and continued his advocacy of viticulture and wine making. From 1869 to 1873 he published the monthly *Grape Culturist,* the only contemporary American journal devoted to the subject. In February 1869 he held a "universal trial of native wines" in his St. Louis cellars, the purpose of which was "to convince the public that good wines can be produced in America." Clearly, his interest was expanding beyond its Missouri roots. Indeed, he and other Missouri grape growers achieved international renown in the late 1870s and 1880s when they helped save French vineyards from the devastation of phylloxera (root louse) by shipping resistant American stock to replace French vines.

The depression year 1871 presented Husmann with challenges, as the price of grapes and wine plummeted. His winery a failure, he moved to Sedalia in 1872 and began Husmann Nurseries, which struggled. From 1878 to 1881 he turned to academia,

becoming a professor and the superintendent of pomology and forestry at the University of Missouri in Columbia. Responsible for extensive new plantings at the university, he used the campus as a laboratory for students whom he employed as laborers. He continued to publish, and in 1880 he helped found the Mississippi Valley Horticultural Society, which became the American Horticultural Society in 1885.

In 1881 Husmann was invited to become manager of Talcoa Vineyards in Napa, California, and thus returned to viticulture and wine making. In California his career flourished, and his wines attained acclaim. He wrote extensively until the end of his life, in 1888 publishing *Grape Culture and Wine Making in California,* a standard authority for many years. Husmann died on November 5, 1902, in Napa, California.

CAROL HEMING

Dictionary of American Biography. S.v. "Husmann, George."

Hooker, H. D. "George Husmann." *Missouri Historical Review* 23 (April 1929): 353–60.

The Standard Cyclopedia of Horticulture. S.v. "Husmann, George."

"Vignettes of Famous Missourians." *Missouri Historical Review* 50 (October 1955–July 1956): 405–7.

HUSTON, JOHN (1906–1987)

Remarkably complicated or even contradictory as both a man and a filmmaker, John Huston lived a life and made films both noted for a mix of good and bad qualities, of successes and failures. As Huston himself remarked: "I've lived a number of lives."

Huston was born on August 5, 1906, in Nevada, Missouri. His parents were both itinerant tradespeople. His mother, Rhea Gore Huston, was a newspaperwoman, and his father, Walter, was an actor. Later moving around the country alternately with his separated parents, Huston's education was unremarkable, and he left high school before graduating. Incorrectly diagnosed as having an enlarged heart and nephritis, he was restricted in diet and activities for two years, finally escaping his confinement by a daring midnight swim in a dangerous canal.

As a young man Huston easily mixed his love of the physical and the aesthetic. He boxed his way to a twenty-three and two record as an amateur lightweight in California, and as a horseman he rode and consorted with Mexican cavalrymen for a considerable period in the mid-1920s. Later in life he loved to hunt, but he also had a passion and flair for painting, which he pursued all his life. He was also a voracious and extensive reader, an interest that became essential to his filmmaking. He spent time studying painting in Paris, where he supported himself by etching portraits on street corners or singing for coins. Early jobs included newspaper reporting, editing, writing short stories, and, finally, initially with his father's help, writing screenplays.

Accounts of Huston's life and character suggest some inconsistencies. He was enormously charming, witty, generous, a great storyteller (especially with his "hypnotic voice"), fiercely independent, and adventurous. At the same time, he was a gambler, drinker, and heavy smoker, suffering from emphysema during his last decades. To some he was a "grown-up bully" and unpredictable, and his charm was offset by a "prehistoric monkey face." The failure of all five of his marriages has been attributed in large part to Huston's constant adventures with other women.

Huston's output as a filmmaker is equally strewn with alternating successes and failures. His first directed film, *The Maltese Falcon* (1941), is praised as a minor masterpiece and as the American film that initiated the film-noir style. Indeed, the one universally praised trait in Huston's films is their careful and elaborate visual sense, which is attributed to his interest in painting. Most of his approximately forty films are cinematic renditions of significant or famous literary works, which Huston approached boldly but with a respect that forced him to adapt his style to the demands of each work, a flexibility of which he was reportedly proud: hence, the lack of the kind of consistent style that would earn him the lofty designation of auteur.

Huston is also noted for the respect he showed most actors, allowing them to develop their own talents and insights in a particular role. Given his challenging literary interests, his changing styles, the varying temperaments and talents of actors, as well as the demands and limitations of Hollywood film production, the diversity and mixed receptions of Huston's best-known films after *The Maltese Falcon* are understandable: *The Treasure of the Sierra Madre* (1948; Oscar for directing and writing), *The Asphalt Jungle* (1950), *The Red Badge of Courage* (1951), *The African Queen* (1952), *Moby Dick* (1956), *The Misfits* (1961), *Freud* (1962), *The Night of the Iguana* (1964), *Reflections in a Golden Eye* (1967), *Fat City* (1972), *Wise Blood* (1979), *Annie* (1982), *Prizzi's Honor* (1985), and *The Dead* (1987). Although his films often depict men on adventurous quests, they usually show those protagonists as doomed failures.

While in the army during World War II, Huston made two service films that emphasized the futility and grim results of war. One film was drastically shortened and the other suppressed until 1980.

Huston appeared in many films as a narrator or in minor but memorable roles; in Roman Polanski's *Chinatown* (1974) he is chilling as the incestuous, greedy, and successful Noah Cross.

Huston maintained residences in numerous places, including an estate in Ireland during the 1960s, where he became a citizen. In his later years he lived in a modest and remote Mexican home.

In 1983 Huston received a Lifetime Achievement Award from the American Film Institute, and the next year he received a similar tribute at Cannes. He died on August 28, 1987, in Newport, Rhode Island.

THOMAS D. COOKE

Allen, Cohen, and Harry Lawton. *John Huston: A Guide to References and Resources.* New York: G. K. Hall, 1997.

Brill, Lesley. *John Huston's Filmmaking.* New York: Cambridge University Press, 1997.

Cooper, Stephen, ed. *Perspectives on John Huston.* New York: G. K. Hall, 1994.

"The Films of John Huston." *Proteus* 7:2 (fall 1990).

Huston, John. *An Open Book.* New York: Knopf, 1980.

Studlar, Gaylyn, and David Desser, eds. *Reflections in a Male Eye: John Huston and the American Experience.* Washington, D.C.: Smithsonian Institution Press, 1993.

HYDE, ARTHUR MASTICK (1877–1947)

Born in Princeton, Missouri, on July 12, 1877, Arthur Mastick Hyde was educated in the public schools of Princeton and at Oberlin Academy in Ohio. He received his undergraduate education at the University of Michigan, graduating with a B.A. degree in 1899. He studied law at the University of Iowa, earning an LL.B. degree in 1900. Upon admission to the Missouri bar, he began the practice of law in his father's Princeton law firm in 1900.

Hyde's association with the law firm continued until 1915 when he moved to nearby Trenton to establish a practice with Judge Sam Hill and to begin a number of business enterprises. He held the distributorship of Buick automobiles for several northern Missouri counties, represented numerous insurance companies, operated a loan and investment service, and held farming and lumber interests. These enterprises of the prosperous years of the early twentieth century made Hyde a modestly wealthy man.

Following in the footsteps of his father, former U.S. congressman Ira Barnes Hyde, Arthur Hyde became interested in politics upon graduation from law school. He served two terms as the mayor of Princeton, from 1908 to 1912. He followed Theodore Roosevelt into the Progressive Party in 1912, gaining the nomination on the Progressive ticket as state attorney general. He lost this first bid for statewide office, and by 1916 he had returned to the Republican Party.

In 1920 the electorate in Missouri and around the nation produced the Republican landslide that carried Hyde into the Governor's Mansion and Warren G. Harding into the White House. Hyde became the second Republican to hold the governorship since the end of Reconstruction. Similarly, Republicans gained control of both houses of the legislature for the first time in fifty years. The 1920 election, in addition to inaugurating a dozen years of Republican ascendancy in Missouri and in the federal government, also found the voters approving a Prohibition enforcement act by a substantial margin.

Hyde pledged to give all Missourians, regardless of creed, race, or color, "a fair hearing and a square deal." In that spirit the voters approved a referendum in 1921 that enabled women, recently enfranchised in Missouri and the nation, to hold any office in the state. While the state still clung to segregation of the races in public education, counties with a population of more than one hundred thousand were authorized to establish high schools for blacks, and the state's school of higher education for blacks, Lincoln Institute in Jefferson City, was designated as Lincoln University in 1921.

Hyde's promise to give the state an efficient, businesslike administration accomplished with fewer tax dollars was quite popular. Accordingly, the Hyde administration in 1921 secured the lowering of the general property evaluation from fifteen to seven cents per hundred-dollar valuation. The state income tax was cut from 1.5 to 1 percent, and the corporation franchise tax was reduced by half. A state bond issue permitted the expansion of the state highway system by almost eight thousand miles of paved roads.

The Hyde administration also invested substantially in the state's public education system, with increased spending for schools at all levels. The state's school for the blind and the school for the deaf were designated as educational institutions. Governor Hyde also worked to assist the agricultural extension service and the University of Missouri School of Agriculture in the dissemination of scientific agricultural information to the farmers of Missouri.

Hyde's interest in agriculture, as well as his keen business skills acquired before and during his tenure as president of the Sentinel Life Insurance Company in 1927–1928, led to his appointment as secretary of agriculture in the Herbert Hoover administration. The passage of the Agricultural Marketing Act in 1929 made Hyde an ex-officio member of the Farm Loan Board, the lending and marketing mechanism designed to deal with two chronic problems in American agriculture: overproduction and the marketing of crops at harvest time. Farmers were urged to reduce crop acreage voluntarily and to form cooperatives for the orderly marketing of crops with credit provided by the Farm Loan Board. Ironically, the Department of Agriculture under Hyde also promoted practices to make the farmer more efficient and more productive through the utilization of power equipment, pest control, and business practices. By 1933, when Hyde left office at the end of the Hoover administration, it was apparent that the voluntary business-efficiency approach to agriculture's distress was not working and presaged a new method when the Franklin D. Roosevelt administration came into office that year.

Hyde practiced law in Kansas City for a year before he returned to Trenton in 1934 to supervise his extensive farm holdings and pursue his many other private and public interests. He opposed the New Deal's agricultural policies and, in defense of Hoover's policies, collaborated with Ray Lynam Wilbur, the former secretary of the interior in the Hoover administration, in compiling the speeches and state papers of the former president.

Hyde also served as a trustee of Missouri Wesleyan College and Southern Methodist University. Earlier he had received honorary LL.D. degrees from Park College in 1922; Drury, Marshall, and Westminster Colleges in 1923; and from his alma mater, the University of Michigan, in 1929. A member of the Methodist Episcopal Church of Princeton since 1909, he served his church as a leader of men's Bible classes and as one of the conveners of the 1935–1936 Conference of Methodist Laymen. He belonged to the Sons of the American Revolution and various fraternal organizations, achieving the rank of thirty-third degree in the Masonic order. He and his wife, the former Hortense Cullers, were the parents of one daughter, Caroline.

Hyde's political philosophy echoed the programs of the national Republican Party of the 1920s and 1930s. Tax cutting, application of business principles to government, voluntary associations for producers and manufacturers, private charity, and individual responsibility with equality for all were values that Hyde championed in and out of office. These policies had served him well during his term as governor, but his Republican successors struggled to make dwindling state revenues match growing state needs. When the Great Depression engulfed the entire nation, a majority of Missourians cast their future with the Democratic liberalism of the New Deal.

Hyde died of cancer in New York City on October 17, 1947, at the age of seventy and was buried in the IOOF cemetery at Trenton.

FRANKLIN D. MITCHELL

Dictionary of American Biography. Supplement 4, 1946–1950. S.v. "Hyde, Arthur Mastick."

Hyde, Arthur M. Papers. Western Historical Manuscripts Collection, Columbia.

Kirkendall, Richard S. *A History of Missouri: Volume*

V, 1919 to 1953. Columbia: University of Missouri Press, 1986.

Shoemaker, Floyd Calvin. *Missouri and Missourians: Land of Contrasts and People of Achievements.* Vol. 2. Chicago: Lewis Publishing, 1943.

HYLAND, ROBERT FRANCIS, JR. (1920–1992)

A civic leader and broadcasting executive, Robert Francis Hyland Jr. is remembered as the "voice behind the voice of KMOX." The son of Robert F. and Genevieve Burks Hyland, Robert was born on March 25, 1920. Robert spent his youth in the shadow of his successful father, a pioneer in the field of sports medicine. An orthopedic surgeon, the elder Hyland was nicknamed the "Surgeon General of Baseball."

A lifelong resident of St. Louis, Robert Hyland's formal education also took place within the city. He attended Baret Hall (a private Catholic school for boys), St. Louis High, and earned a baccalaureate in business from St. Louis University in 1940. Soon after graduation, Hyland entered the navy but allergies plagued him, and officials granted him a medical discharge.

In 1951 Hyland went to work at radio station KMOX as the general sales manager. In less than a decade he achieved national prominence in broadcasting. In 1955 he became the general manager of KMOX, and in 1959 CBS made him a network vice president. Three times the network invited him to become president of CBS. The first time, Hyland recounted, his first wife was dying; the second and third times, he was too busy to leave St. Louis.

For thirty-seven years Hyland applied his innovative and entrepreneurial skills at KMOX. Described by his employees simply as "the boss," this meticulous and hardworking manager typically arrived at the station about three in the morning and rarely left before six at night.

As the general manager of KMOX, Hyland sought to elevate his station to national prominence. His recruits included Jack Buck, Harry Caray, Jack Carney, Bob Costas, Joe Garagiola, Bob Hardy, and Anne Keefe, all of whom enjoyed at least local notoriety as broadcast journalists. Bob Costas once said that Hyland assembled a concentration of talent at KMOX worthy of launching a new network.

From the 1960s through the 1980s Hyland led KMOX into regional prominence by introducing call-in programs (he took special pride in *At Your Service*); editorials (Hyland read his own editorials); and blanket sports coverage. KMOX became the first commercial station to broadcast a college course for credit, live coverage from both houses of the Missouri legislature, and football games from the sidelines.

From 1989 to 1991 KMOX achieved the "triple crown of radio": the News Talk Station of the Year award (1989), the Station of the Year award (1990), and the National Association of Broadcasters' Legendary Station award (1991). In a 1990 address to a group of broadcast journalists, Hyland summarized his vision: "[U]se your creativity and journalistic know-how to attract the public interest while turning out top-level journalism."

In addition to his role in broadcasting, Hyland demonstrated his devotion to St. Louis by a lifetime of civic service. He belonged to fifty-two civic groups, thirteen professional organizations, eight social clubs, and two academic societies. This torrent of civic activity earned him "St. Louis Man of the Year" honors in 1988.

A devoted Catholic, Hyland was called a "visible Catholic layman" by diplomatic observers, while his critics called him a "tireless papal flag waver." His most memorable project involved St. Anthony's hospital. He led the drive to save the hospital from financial ruin and to move it to south St. Louis County. His fund-raising efforts resulted in the creation of the Hyland Center at St. Anthony's for chemical dependency and psychiatric care. As Archbishop John L. May said, "He saved St. Anthony's Hospital and kept it Catholic."

Hyland took special pride in his involvement with "the Muny," which imported Broadway shows to the outdoor theater in St. Louis. As chairman of the Missouri–St. Louis Metropolitan Airport Authority, Hyland became embroiled in public debate regarding the expansion of Lambert Field.

Many admired Hyland for his tireless, meticulous devotion to his job and his city. Others characterized him as "insular, conservative [and] a caretaker of the cocoon."

Hyland died of cancer in St. Louis on March 5, 1992. His second wife and two of three children survived him. Hyland continued to inspire controversy after his death. Claims amounting to millions of dollars were filed against the Hyland estate by a variety of individuals and groups, including Mercantile Bank, the St. Louis Symphony, and the former president of Lindenwood College.

JACK B. RIDLEY

Hyland, Robert. Vertical file. Missouri Historical Society Library, St. Louis.

Kimbrough, Mary. *Movers and Shakers: Men Who Have Shaped St. Louis.* Tucson, Ariz.: Patrice Press, 1992.

March, David D. *The History of Missouri.* Vol. 3. New York: Lewis Historical Publishing, 1967.

St. Louis Post-Dispatch, March 2, 1990–July 23, 1992.

I

ICHORD, RICHARD (1926–1992)

Richard Howard Ichord II was born on June 27, 1926, in Licking, in Texas County, Missouri. He attended public schools, graduating valedictorian of his senior class at Licking High School. He enlisted in the United States Naval Air Corps and served in the Naval Transport Service in the Pacific theater during World War II until receiving an honorable discharge in 1946. In 1947, while attending the University of Missouri, he married Vera Rodgers of Licking. Ichord received his B.S. in accounting in 1949 and taught accounting and business while pursuing his law degree at the university. He received his J.D. in 1952 and was admitted to the Missouri bar.

Immediately after completing his degree, Ichord began the practice of law in Houston, Missouri. At the same time, he began campaigning for a seat in the Missouri House of Representatives. He impressed the voters in Texas County with his enthusiasm and desire to be a state representative and won the election easily. In the Missouri House, Ichord proved a competent legislator and worthy adversary to Republican opponents. In 1953 he served as commissioner of the State Reorganization Committee that studied the economy and efficiency of state executive offices. The same year he served as chairman of the Committee on Penal Institutions. He continued working in the state legislature for eight years, maintaining the support of his constituents and earning the respect of his colleagues. In 1957 his fellow legislators elected him Speaker pro tempore, and two years later elected him Missouri's youngest-ever Speaker of the House of Representatives.

In 1960 Ichord once again threw himself into an intense campaign, this time vying for a seat in the United States House of Representatives. In "the upset of the decade," Ichord defeated the well-supported incumbent, A. S. J. Carnahan, to win his position in Congress. On January 3, 1961, he began what would be a twenty-year tenure in the United States House of Representatives.

Once in Washington, Ichord quickly established contacts and moved up through the ranks. His ambition and energy seemed endless. He earned his reputation through diligence and hard work. However, as his status in Washington heightened, his connection with his home district and the people who had supported him in his early elections weakened. He and his wife divorced during his early years in Congress. He married his second wife, Milicent M. Koch, in 1967.

As his prominence in Congress increased, Ichord focused his energy less on the needs of his Missouri district and began to concentrate on national and international affairs. The alleged spread of communism in the United States and abroad seriously distressed Ichord. He campaigned against the Communist Party throughout his years in the House and from his experience coauthored the book *Behind Every Bush*. Ichord served on the House Un-American Activities Committee, later know as the Internal Security Committee, for many years, acting as its chairman from 1969 until its termination in 1975. The committee investigated student protests on college campuses, unrest in the U.S. prison system, riots in U.S. cities, and the movements of special-interest groups such as the Ku Klux Klan, the Students for a Democratic Society, the Black Panther Party, the Christian Youth Corps, and the New Mobilization Committee. His ceaseless crusade against communism drew a considerable amount of both admiration and criticism. His supporters praised him for his patriotism, while his opponents accused him of suppressing the freedoms guaranteed by the Constitution.

Ichord's concern over the spread of communism translated into his backing for U.S. military participation in world affairs involving communist countries. He ardently supported the war in Vietnam and conducted inquiries into anti-Vietnam activities. He also introduced legislation banning travel to nations with whom the United States was at war. He consistently advocated increased military budgets, saying, "Military weakness does not promote peace. It breeds war." He served as the second-ranking member of the House Armed Services Committee, chairing the Defense Industrial Base Panel, the Research and Development Subcommittee, and the Military Installations and Facilities Subcommittee.

Ichord retired from the House on January 3, 1981, after serving ten consecutive terms. Frustrated by his colleagues' devotion to regional and special-interest legislation, and perhaps feeling that his own power and importance in the House was diminishing, he decided to pursue other interests. He continued to practice law and make use of his expertise in military affairs.

The Washington Industrial Team, Inc., which counseled the government on its military-industrial problems, appointed Ichord its president from 1980 to 1984. He also served as cochairman of the American Freedom Coalition and president of Legislative Associates International, a group that advised international clients on an array of issues. In June 1992 he led an American delegation on a peace mission to North Korea, the first meeting of its kind with the president and high-ranking officials of that communist country.

At the height of his career, Richard Ichord was a prominent and influential member of the United States House of Representatives. He was known nationally for his anticommunism crusade and his support for greater U.S. military strength. In 1980 he said, "You can't be a leader with diplomacy alone. Diplomatic power doesn't mean anything without the military power to back it up." After retiring, the Pentagon awarded him the Distinguished Civilian Service Award, the highest honor bestowed on civilians. Closer to home, his influence in Congress ensured the establishment of the National Scenic Riverways, Missouri's first national park. He was also a key benefactor of Fort Leonard Wood. He died on December 25, 1992, in Nevada, Missouri, after suffering a heart attack.

ERIKA K. NELSON

Biographical Dictionary of the United States Congress, 1774–1989. Bicentennial ed. S.v. "Ichord, Richard." Washington, D.C.: U.S. Government Printing Office, 1989.

Houston Herald, December 31, 1992.

Ichord, Richard H. Papers. Western Historical Manuscripts Collection, Columbia.

Licking News, December 31, 1992.

New York Times, December 26, 1992.

Official Manual of the State of Missouri, 1979–1980. Jefferson City: Secretary of State, 1980.

J

JACKSON, CLAIBORNE FOX (1806–1862)

Claiborne Fox Jackson was born in rural Fleming County, in northeastern Kentucky, on April 4, 1806. The son of Dempsey and Mary Pickett Jackson, prosperous tobacco farmers and slaveholders, Claiborne was one of ten children and received only slight formal education before emigrating in 1826 with several older brothers to Franklin, Missouri, a small Howard County trading village located just north of the Missouri River. Driven by ambition, he worked there briefly in the older brothers' mercantile establishment before taking partnership in the business.

In 1832 Jackson organized and was elected captain of a company of Howard County volunteers to serve in the Black Hawk War. Upon his return to Missouri, he gave up his share of the brothers' store and moved across the Missouri River to Saline County, where he purchased and operated a similar establishment. While there he met and married the daughter of **John S. Sappington,** a local physician who gained national prominence for his promotion of the use of quinine as a treatment for malarial fevers. Sappington, a wealthy slave owner, proved an influential and well-connected presence, having personal acquaintances with such luminaries as Andrew Jackson and **Thomas Hart Benton.** By both his status and his efforts on his ambitious son-in-law's behalf, Sappington provided Jackson with an important ingress into both the elite circles of central Missouri and, ultimately, the rough-and-tumble world of frontier Missouri politics. Twice widowed, Jackson would wed three of Sappington's daughters.

Elected to the Missouri General Assembly as a Democrat in 1836, Jackson served one term before retiring to semiprivate life in Fayette, in Howard County, which was well known as a locus of power in Missouri state politics. During the next four years he worked at the State Bank of Missouri's Fayette branch, making valuable personal connections and party alliances, as well as honing his political skills. In 1842, campaigning as an ardent supporter of Sen. Thomas Hart Benton, he was again elected to the state legislature and within two years was chosen Speaker of the House, an obvious position of influence that he would hold for two successive terms. Ultimately, he would serve with distinction in both houses of the Missouri legislature.

While leader of the General Assembly, Jackson allied with a powerful group of proslavery politicians known as the "Central Clique," which was made up of delegates from the dense slaveholding counties around Fayette that exerted great influence over Missouri's political fortunes. When Benton, the state's Democratic bellwether, showed strong opposition to slavery's extension into the western territories following the Mexican War, Jackson broke with him, publicly renouncing his Free-Soil efforts. In part, Benton's opposition to Jackson's candidacy for governor in 1848 promoted his openly hostile stance against "Old Bullion." Jackson forced the issue when he was elected to the state senate in that same year.

Young and aggressive, Jackson and the other members of the Central Clique saw the emotional issue of slavery's extension as a potential watershed for their own political careers. Seeing a chance to overturn the power structure of the Democratic Party—traditionally dominated by more moderate Bentonians—they leveraged the issue in the General Assembly. In 1848, led by Jackson, the anti-Benton faction introduced what became known as the Jackson Resolutions, which asserted that Congress had no authority to limit slavery in the territories, upholding the doctrine of popular sovereignty yet sanctioning the extension of a compromise line through the new territories in order to maintain future peace between slave and free states. The resolutions further included a set of instructions to the state's senators (elected by the state legislature) and representatives in Washington to vote in favor of slavery's extension into the territories.

Jackson, as spokesman for the Central Clique, condemned Benton's failure to support the United States Senate's "Calhoun Resolutions," introduced by South Carolina senator John C. Calhoun in 1847, asserting that the territories belonged to all the states and that the federal government could not enact laws that would deprive any state of their rights—specifically those prohibiting slavery. Although the Missouri General Assembly passed the Jackson Resolutions overwhelmingly, Benton refused to heed them, which forced him to defend his controversial stance. The furor cost Benton his reelection in 1850, ending his thirty-year tenure in the United States Senate, but greatly enhanced Jackson's own political standing. Benton's influence was nevertheless strong enough to prevent Jackson's nomination for Congress both in 1853 and in 1855.

As a result, Jackson held no elected office during the 1850s, yet he maintained ample political ties within the Democratic Party. Despite his once ardent defense of Southern rights, Jackson appears to have played politics in order to curry favor from all sides. In 1852, as chairman of the state Democratic Central Committee, he helped to arrange both Southern and Benton Democrats alternately on the party's campaign slate. In 1857 he managed the campaign of gubernatorial candidate **Robert Marcellus Stewart,** who won the election as a moderate Democrat. In 1858 Jackson supported a moderate Whig in his campaign for Congress. His strategy appears to have succeeded in gaining his appointment as Missouri's first state bank commissioner in 1857. While orchestrating the reorganization of the state's banking system in response to the national panic, Jackson used the position as a rostrum from which to posture himself for various unsuccessful bids for public office. Generally supporting hard-money policy, he condemned the "bankable fund" system by which Missouri banks hoarded gold and circulated paper and vowed a return to specie payments. Yet, during the panic of 1857, he supported paper money, drawing criticism from Jacksonian Democrats. One charged that "C. F. Jackson has dabbled with banks until he has made a fortune."

Judging by the census returns, one can little doubt that Jackson's personal fortunes did indeed grow during the 1850s, though probably not from graft as his critics charged. In 1850, with a family of seven, including five children between the ages of six and sixteen, he already boasted real property holdings in Howard County worth $10,000 and owned twenty slaves. In 1856, at the death of his father-in-law, John Sappington, Jackson inherited a large portion of the estate, including the Sappington home in the Arrow Rock district of Saline County. As a result, in 1860 he owned real estate worth nearly $49,900 and thirty-eight slaves, and held personal property valued at $71,500. Living now at Fox Castle, the Sappington plantation, Jackson listed himself for the first time as a farmer, as did two of his three adult sons who still resided with the family. Fourteen of his slaves were males between the ages of thirteen and fifty-three, indicating that they were field hands, which suggests that Jackson operated a substantial plantation and had advanced into the ranks of the planter elite. His actions in the ensuing years demonstrate that he intended to preserve his newfound status.

Stymied in his attempts to gain election to Congress, Jackson began actively campaigning for the Democratic nomination for the gubernatorial election of 1860. Although he remained staunchly supportive of Southern rights, his recent moderate stance earned him more broad-based support, and though he was viewed as a dark horse among the nine declared candidates at the outset of the April 1860 convention, Jackson drew strength from uninstructed delegates, many of whom were sympathetic to the Southern cause. Winning the nomination on the fourth ballot he sought to achieve the unity of a long-divided party by not declaring for either of the Democratic presidential candidates, Stephen A. Douglas and John C. Breckinridge.

As Jackson stumped the state, leaders of the state's two Democratic factions confronted him about his nonsupport of either presidential candidate. Forced to declare one or the other or lose the support of both, Jackson again sought neutral ground. At Fayette (the final stop on his canvass), he claimed personal support of Breckinridge but conceded that Douglas was the party's best hope for the presidency, and though he strongly disagreed with the Illinoisan's stance on slavery in the territories, he came out for Douglas. In August Jackson won a narrow victory over Constitutional Unionist Sample Orr and two other candidates, receiving 74,446 votes to Orr's 66,583. The two "moderate" candidates polled nearly 90 percent of the state's popular vote. Similarly, in November, in the presidential election, Douglas won a narrow victory over John C. Bell; again, Missouri supported moderate candidates rather than those viewed as being either secessionist or "Black Republican."

With Abraham Lincoln's presidential victory in 1860, Jackson's moderate stance changed abruptly. Believing the new federal government to be firmly opposed to slavery's extension and hostile to Southern rights, Jackson in his January 1861 inaugural address defended the actions of the seceded states, labeled Northern states as aggressors, and called on Missouri to "best consult her own interest, and the interest of the whole country, by a timely declaration of her determination to stand by her sister slaveholding states, in whose wrongs she participates, and with whose institutions and people she sympathizes."

Politically, Jackson was too savvy to ignore the recent elections' mandates for moderation, yet in his address he proposed a state convention, ostensibly to consider the issue of secession. Recognizing the unlikelihood of withdrawal, however, Jackson probably had other motives in calling for the convention. An astute judge of popular sentiment, he believed that most Missourians—even the delegates to the convention—would be so adamantly opposed to coercive measures that efforts on the part of the Lincoln administration to bring the seceded states back into the Union would play into his hands. Jackson probably intended for the convention to frame a debate on the issue of coercion—an issue that, by the very nature of the ensuing conflict, the federal, not the

Confederate, government stood most likely to lose. As expected the convention, which met in February (and to which not even one avowed secessionist delegate was elected), decided against seceding. Rather, after a long debate, it adopted resolutions calling for state neutrality, asserting that "at present, there was no adequate cause to impel Missouri to dissolve her connection with the Federal Union." As Jackson had hoped, the convention made it clear that this stance could change if either of the belligerent governments should in any way use coercion on Missouri.

With secession not yet a dead issue, Jackson set about making clandestine preparations. At the same time that he called the state convention, he called for a general pro-Southern convention to determine a united course of action. He began organizing the state militia as authorized by the militia act of 1858, asked the legislature to pass a military bill designed to give the governor sweeping powers to arm the state, sent agents to the Confederate government to procure arms, and arranged for some of the militia to raid the federal arsenal at Liberty. The real prize, however, lay in St. Louis, where the state's other arsenal housed the largest number of arms of any such storehouse in the slave states. Lincoln's call for seventy-five thousand volunteers on April 15 in response to the firing on Fort Sumter bolstered Jackson's efforts, and he fashioned a ringing retort to cull public support: "Your requisition in my judgment, is illegal, unconstitutional and revolutionary in its object, inhuman and diabolical, and cannot be complied with. Not one man will the state of Missouri furnish to carry on such an unholy crusade." Collectively, he hoped that the call and response would rejuvenate the secession issue, and wrote privately to the president of Arkansas's state convention that Missouri would be ready to secede in thirty days.

Buoyed by the recent events, Jackson ordered the state militia to assemble on May 3 in encampments throughout Missouri. One such assemblage, located on the outskirts of St. Louis and named "Camp Jackson" in his honor, received a shipment of ordnance (without carriages) confiscated by Confederates from the Baton Rouge arsenal and sent to St. Louis's secessionists by authorities in Richmond. Although the guns were sent to assist in taking the arsenal, the gesture was now moot; radical Unionist **Francis Preston Blair Jr.,** a U.S. congressman, and **Nathaniel Lyon,** a volatile army captain in command at the arsenal, had already removed its large cache of weaponry to Illinois. On May 10 Lyon used federal troops to break up the encampment, capturing the militia and its officers and precipitating two days of rioting in St. Louis. In response the legislature immediately passed Jackson's long-debated military bill, dividing the state into military districts and authorizing enlistments for a State Guard. Jackson named **Sterling Price,** a military hero and former governor, as the commander of the state militia.

Reacting to Lyon and Blair's strong moves in St. Louis, Jackson sent Price to St. Louis in late May to meet with the federal commander of the Department of the West, **William Selby Harney,** in an attempt to maintain peace in the agitated state. Jackson knew Price to be a moderate (he had chaired the state's secession convention), and depended upon such temperance to present federal authority in the state as being coercive and thus move Missouri toward secession. The Price-Harney agreement, which stipulated that Harney would keep federal troops in St. Louis while Price preserved order in the interior counties, seemed to avoid conflict between state and federal troops. Jackson only reaffirmed the agreement by issuing a public letter appealing to the citizens of the state to respect civil authorities and refrain from hostile activities. When Harney was relieved of command on May 30, leaving Blair and Lyon in charge of more than ten thousand well-armed troops in St. Louis, as compared with just one thousand poorly armed State Guardsmen, an anxious Jackson sought to buy some time in order to avert potential hostilities. He issued another public letter upholding his personal commitment to neutrality and condemning the arming of troops in St. Louis as a violation of the Harney-Price agreement that should be opposed by the citizenry of the state. Secretly, he advised the district commanders of the State Guard to step up their recruitment and mobilization, hoping to renew the effort for Missouri's secession now that radicals represented federal authority in the state.

At the urging of several of the state's leading moderates, Jackson and Price requested a meeting with Blair and Lyon. Held on June 11, at the sumptuous Planters' House hotel in St. Louis, the conference failed to effect any compromise. After four hours of heated debate, Lyon peremptorily ended the meeting by declaring war on the state. Believing that Missourians would now see the federal government as coercive aggressors and that a new secession convention would authorize withdrawal from the Union, Jackson hastened back to Jefferson City. On June 12 he issued a proclamation calling for fifty thousand men to defend the state and reminding the Missouri citizenry that though the state was still part of the Union, "the power to disturb that relation . . . has been wisely vested in a Convention which will, at the proper time, express your sovereign will. . . ." However, Jackson was unprepared for the swiftness of the federal commanders' next move. Within twenty-four hours of Jackson's proclamation, Lyon had launched a river campaign that on June 16 captured Jefferson City, forcing Jackson and other pro-Southern legislators to flee the capital to nearby Boonville, where a large encampment of State Guardsmen had organized. When Lyon pursued, Jackson ordered the troops to give battle, against the advice of their commander, **John Sappington Marmaduke.** In a brief engagement the federal troops easily routed the State Guard, sending them, led by Jackson, into headlong flight toward the southwestern corner of the state, pushing back a host of federals under **Franz Sigel** near Carthage before encamping at Cowskin Prairie.

Jackson soon left Missouri to secure support from the Confederate army and government. He convinced Leonidas Polk to send an "army of liberation" into southeastern Missouri, then hastened to Richmond where he met with Jefferson Davis. When Davis promised financial aid for Missouri troops, Jackson returned to Missouri and on August 5 issued a proclamation from New Madrid declaring Missouri an independent and sovereign state—an act of doubtful legal validity. After the Battle of Wilson's Creek, Jackson accompanied Price and his troops to Lexington, where he called the General Assembly to convene in special session in Neosho in October 1861. Bringing his family with him, Jackson led this remnant legislature, made up of those who had by now been deposed by the provisional state government (and who probably never achieved a quorum), which passed a provisional ordinance of secession and authorized relations with the Confederacy. In November the Confederate government formally recognized Missouri as its twelfth state, though it remained in Union control for the remainder of the war.

In the spring of 1862 Jackson accompanied Price and the Missouri army into Arkansas, where they fought at the Battle of Pea Ridge. The Confederate defeat ended the chance of reclaiming Missouri, and Jackson retreated. Soon his health began to fail, and he and his family retired to Little Rock, where he died of cancer on December 6, 1862. He is buried in the Sappington family cemetery at Arrow Rock, Missouri.

CHRISTOPHER PHILLIPS

Kirkpatrick, Arthur Roy. "The Admission of Missouri to the Confederacy." *Missouri Historical Review* 55 (July 1961): 366–86.

———. "Missouri in the Early Months of the Civil War." *Missouri Historical Review* 55 (January 1961): 99–108.

Lyon, William H. "Claiborne Fox Jackson and the Secession Crisis in Missouri." *Missouri Historical Review* 58 (July 1964): 422–41.

Parrish, William E. *Turbulent Partnership: Missouri and the Union, 1861–1865.* Columbia: University of Missouri Press, 1963.

Phillips, Christopher. *Damned Yankee: The Life of General Nathaniel Lyon.* Columbia: University of Missouri Press, 1990.

Snead, Thomas L. *The Fight for Missouri from the Election of Lincoln to the Death of Lyon.* New York: Charles Scribner's Sons, 1886.

JACKSON, HANCOCK LEE (1796–1876)

Hancock Lee Jackson was born in Madison County, Kentucky, on May 12, 1796. He married Ursula Oldham in the spring of 1821, and the following fall the couple moved to Missouri. They first made their home in Howard County, but the next year they moved to a farm in the still unorganized area that became Randolph County. The Jacksons had eleven children.

When Randolph County was formed in 1829, Jackson was elected as its first sheriff. He served as a member of the 1845 Missouri Constitutional Convention, but he did not play an important role in the deliberations that produced a document subsequently rejected by Missouri voters.

Following the U.S. declaration of war against Mexico in 1846, Jackson raised a company of Missouri volunteers, who elected him as their captain. Serving under Brig. Gen. **Sterling Price,** Jackson and his company fought in at least two engagements during the Mexican War. His military service in the popular war undoubtedly helped him advance his political career in Missouri.

Jackson's first major venture into state politics resulted in his election to the state senate in 1850 as a Democrat. Two years later he won reelection, but appears to have been an inactive participant in the General Assembly's proceedings. When the Democratic Party's internal differences widened, Jackson aligned himself with its pro-Southern, states' rights wing.

When Democrats at the 1856 state party convention in Jefferson City failed to reach an agreement on a state platform or on a candidate for governor, they split into two groups. Meeting separately, one faction composed of old Jacksonians nominated **Thomas Hart Benton.** The other faction, representing a majority of the original convention members, nominated the strong pro-Southern, proslavery, states' rights team of **Trusten W. Polk** for governor and Hancock Lee Jackson for lieutenant governor. The Polk-Jackson wing emerged from the meetings carrying the regular Democratic Party label, and won the election.

Like many lieutenant governors, Jackson was not much involved in the governing process. But Polk's service proved short. Early in 1857 the General Assembly elected him to become one of the state's U.S. senators, and on February 27 Jackson assumed office as the acting governor. His stint was also brief because the constitution required officials to call a special election to choose a new governor. The following August Missouri voters elected **Robert Marcellus Stewart,** who took office as governor on October 22, 1857.

During his abbreviated term Jackson made only one major address to the General Assembly. In his message he called attention to the ongoing depression and the hardships that it created. He placed much of the blame on a credit and banking system that, he asserted, had exceeded its lawful limits. He called upon the General Assembly to remedy the questionable practices involving railroad construction, especially the state's heavy reliance on bonded indebtedness to promote and build railroads. Jackson emphasized the paramount importance of upholding the honor and credit of the state. He recommended a tax to pay interest on the bonds, state representation on railroad boards, and stricter regulation of banking operations and currency issues. His few months as acting governor gave him little chance to secure passage of his recommendations. Although Jackson recognized the serious nature and widespread effects of the depression, he did not recommend any direct state action to stimulate economic recovery or bring relief in cases of individual hardships.

The divisive slavery question and the resulting sectional tensions that threatened to disrupt the Union dominated the elections of 1860 in Missouri and produced a split in the Democratic Party. **Claiborne Fox Jackson,** Hancock's cousin, ran for governor on the regular Democratic ticket. An extreme pro-Southern faction nominated Hancock to run against Claiborne, but he made a poor showing in the contest as the great majority of Missourians voted for candidates they considered moderates.

Just prior to the 1860 presidential election, President James Buchanan appointed Jackson as U.S. marshal for the Western District of Missouri. Following Abraham Lincoln's election, Jackson resigned the post and returned to private life. Moving to Salem, Oregon, in 1865, he died on March 19, 1876.

PERRY MCCANDLESS

Leopard, Buel, and Floyd C. Shoemaker, eds. *The Messages and Proclamations of the Governors of the State of Missouri.* Vol. 3. Columbia: State Historical Society of Missouri, 1922.

JAEGER, HERMAN (1844–?)

Herman Jaeger was born in Brugg, Switzerland, on March 23, 1844, the sixth of seven children of Charles and Mary Custer Jaeger. His father was a farmer and merchant, and his mother was the granddaughter of educator Johann Pestalozzi. Jaeger attended school in Switzerland until he reached age sixteen. From 1860 to 1863 he served an apprenticeship in a dry

goods house, and from 1863 to 1864 he worked in a wine house near Lake Geneva. In addition, he almost certainly received some training in viticulture before leaving Switzerland.

In 1864 Jaeger emigrated to the United States, arriving in Norfolk, Virginia, proceeding to St. Louis, and settling near Neosho, in Newton County, Missouri, in 1865. His farm originally consisted of forty acres; when his brother John arrived and bought the adjoining forty acres, the two merged their properties and their skills. In 1866 Jaeger planted his first vines. Having brought cuttings of East Coast varieties to Missouri, he was able to graft the Concord and the Virginia onto root stock of the hardy (but sour) grapes that grew wild in the Ozarks. From this modest beginning, Jaeger went on to originate around one hundred varieties of grapes before his disappearance in 1895.

The early grafting experiments, however ultimately successful, nearly led to initial disaster. Jaeger's eastern cuttings imported into the Ozarks a blight, downy mildew, which threatened to destroy his vineyards. He responded to the crisis by concocting a blend of sulphur, iron sulfate, and copper sulfate. Using this mixture, he was eventually successful not only in combating the blight but also in pioneering experiments in spraying to control crop disease.

Jaeger's major concern throughout his life was the development of increasingly hardy varieties of American grapes. His work received international recognition during the late 1870s and the 1880s. In this period, as vineyards in France became increasingly infested with phylloxera, or root louse, the French government sought assistance from experts around the globe. French growers reluctantly concluded that the best way to combat the problem was to import disease-resistant American vines, which saved their vineyards from total devastation. Although other Missouri growers contributed hardy stock as well—notably, **George Husmann** from Columbia and **Isidor Bush** from St. Louis—the French apparently saw Herman Jaeger's contribution as especially significant: on January 1, 1889, they awarded him the cross of the Legion of Honor for his efforts.

In 1872 Jaeger married Elise Wagenrieden from St. Louis; the couple had one daughter. His wife died in 1873, and the following year he married Elise Grosse, also from St. Louis. This marriage produced three or four children.

Most accounts claim that Jaeger was something of a recluse, though he apparently maintained contact with other horticulturists and published in American and European journals. In 1895, however, the disappearance of this slightly eccentric grower rendered him the subject of Ozark folklore. Some concluded that he suffered ill health, others believed he was mentally unbalanced or had met with an unfortunate accident, and still others thought he fled financial difficulties. Perhaps most reliable is the speculation that he was despondent over the successes of prohibitionists in Newton County. Whatever the reason, in July 1895 Herman Jaeger left home, ostensibly to attend to some business affairs; he never returned to his family or vineyards. Elise Jaeger later received a letter from her husband, undated, but postmarked Kansas City, Kansas, in which he told her he wanted to "make an end to it, before I get crazy." A police investigation revealed nothing of Jaeger's fate, and the question of what became of him remains unanswered.

CAROL HEMING

History of Newton, Lawrence, Barry, and McDonald Counties, Missouri. Chicago: Goodspeed, 1888.

Ladwig, Tom. "Herman Jaegar's [*sic*] Legacy." *Missouri Life* (November–December 1982): 47–48.

The Standard Cyclopedia of Horticulture. S.v. "Jaeger, Herman."

"This Week in Missouri History." *Missouri Historical Review* 49 (October 1954–July 1955): 154–55.

JAMES, ALEXANDER FRANKLIN (1843–1915); JAMES, JESSE WOODSON (1847–1882)

Jesse James was America's self-proclaimed Robin Hood. What is most remarkable about his mythic stature as a man who robbed the rich and gave to the poor is that he earned that status during his own lifetime, long before that "dirty little coward," Bob Ford, "laid poor Jesse in his grave." The legacy of Jesse James and his brother, Frank, was more than an avalanche of dime novels and cheap western movies that mythologized their murderous careers. They were the inspiration of countless western outlaws who tried to emulate them, and they somehow won the grudging respect of many who should have known better. The mantle of myth deified the facts of their violent lives and somehow made them men to be admired rather than despised. For sixteen years they plundered and murdered in a half-dozen states, and when Jesse died and Frank surrendered, the public seemed to mourn the one and to forgive the other.

The remarkable story of the James brothers began simply, on the Clay County farm of a respectable Baptist minister, the Reverend Robert James, and his wife, Zerelda Cole James. Frank James was born on January 10, 1843, and Jesse followed three and a half years later, on September 4, 1847. In 1850 Robert James departed for California. He did not seem the type to be lured by gold, but leave he did, promising to return. Instead, he died in the gold country. After a brief and unsuccessful second marriage, the resourceful and determined Zerelda

James married Reuben Samuel, a physician, in 1855. The two stood by each other through the difficult years that followed.

The James boys grew up on the farm, though neither was especially fond of farm labor. Frank was quiet and bookish, spending far more time reading than working the farm. Jesse was popular in the community and notably religious. Some even thought he would follow his father into the ministry. However, Missouri lay at the center of the events that were pushing the nation toward civil war. "Bleeding Kansas" was not far from Clay County, and Zerelda Samuel, a slaveholder, left no doubt about her sympathies. In 1861, when Missouri's citizens voted to stay with the Union, many, like the James family, backed Gov. **Claiborne Fox Jackson,** who refused to provide troops for the cause and mobilized the State Guard with the intent of supporting the Confederacy. Frank James joined a unit of the Home Guard on May 4, 1861.

A brutal and vicious conflict with few redeeming moments followed. Guerrilla outrages were matched by federal ineptitude and flagrant disregard for the rights of citizens. Union volunteers were not regular army either, and they took their prejudices and personal animosities into the conflict as well. By the summer of 1861 federal troops were looting, stealing, and killing with reckless abandon, driving still more of the local population into the arms of the guerrillas.

In the early phases of the conflict, Frank James fought at the Battle of Wilson's Creek under the command of Gen. **Sterling Price.** Left behind with the measles, he was captured and allowed to go home. He took the oath of allegiance to the United States, but within months he was again with the guerrillas. Legend credits him with being one of a small group that rescued Gen. **Joseph Orville Shelby** from Union troops prior to the Battle of Prairie Grove, but more reliable sources suggest that he was with the bushwhackers of Fernando Scott in the winter of 1862–1863. On August 7, 1863, the *Liberty Tribune* identified Frank as one of the three men who robbed a man near the town.

Frank James had joined **William Clarke Quantrill**'s raiders, and he was present at the assault on Lawrence, Kansas, in which 150 Union troops died in one of the worst atrocities of the war. Frank wintered with Quantrill in Texas in 1863–1864, rode with **William "Bloody Bill" Anderson** in the summer of 1864, and then followed Quantrill east late in the year. In May 1865, after pillaging the Kentucky countryside, Quantrill was killed, and on July 26, 1865, Frank James surrendered and was paroled.

In the meantime young Jesse James was apprenticed to guerrilla warfare as well. It is unclear when he joined the Confederate partisans, but it may have been as early as the autumn of 1863, before Quantrill's raiders went to Texas, though some sources report he was initiated under the command of Fletcher Taylor, one of Anderson's lieutenants. In either case, tradition holds that his service was preceded by an incident at the James farm during which Union militia put a rope around Reuben Samuel's neck and pulled him off the ground several times, threatened Zerelda Samuel, and whipped young Jesse in an attempt to gain information about guerrillas for whom he and his mother were carrying messages. Later, Jesse's mother and at least one of her other children were arrested and held at St. Joseph. Embittered by these experiences, according to the legend, Jesse joined the guerrillas.

Whatever the truth about his motivation, Jesse James was riding with Anderson by the summer of 1864. In mid-August he was shot in the chest. He survived what his associates believed was a mortal wound and was back in the saddle before the end of September. On the morning of September 27, 1864, thirty of Anderson's men, Jesse and Frank among them, struck Centralia, Missouri, terrorized the town, and murdered twenty-four Union soldiers. In a sharp action later that day, the guerrillas routed a Union force that pursued them, and Jesse killed the Union commander, Major Johnson.

Afterward, Jesse James apparently wintered in Texas with George Shepard's irregulars, returning to Missouri in midspring of 1865, unaware of the Confederate surrender at Appomattox. The guerrillas were regarded as outlaws, and Jesse was shot in the chest under a flag of truce when he attempted to surrender.

Somehow both Frank James and Jesse James managed to survive the war, but they still faced troubled times. Postwar Missouri was a divided land where fear and hate ruled, and violence persisted. Revenge became a way of life for former Unionists and former guerrillas alike, and the Union men seemed to have the upper hand. Still, the suggestion that "Buck" and "Dingus," as Frank and Jesse were called by their friends, were "driven" to a life of crime simply was not true. They returned to the farm. Jesse joined the Baptist Church at Kearney. The only complaint about them was that Frank spent more time with Shakespeare than his crops and that Jesse took a long time to recover from his war wounds.

Nonetheless, the war had changed the James boys. They had learned to take what they wanted during the war, and their skills with guns and horses were unmistakable. Of course, many veterans had the same abilities and went on to live constructive lives. For Jesse and Frank, things would be different.

On February 13, 1866, the first daylight robbery of a bank in peacetime in American history occurred at Liberty, Missouri. Robbers took more than sixty thousand dollars from the Clay County Savings Bank and killed a college student named George Wymore in their escape. Frank James and Jesse James were not immediately named as suspects in that robbery or in others that followed. The James boys were not implicated until the gang struck the bank in Russellville, Kentucky, and they were not accused outright until the robbery of the Daviess County Savings Bank at Gallatin, Missouri, on December 7, 1869. The Gallatin bank job was accompanied by the murder of John W. Sheets, the bank owner and cashier whom the robbers believed had been involved in the death of Bloody Bill Anderson. A series of leads brought a posse to the Samuel farm where Frank and Jesse made a desperate escape.

The suspicions of the past now gave way to open accusations and active pursuit. Jesse James protested his innocence in letters to the press as he would many times in later years. The ploy, combined with their sheer bravado, drew attention to the gang. Their method was simple—and familiar. It was the old guerrilla tactic: strike fast and hard with surprise, scatter and hide, and re-form later to strike again. The James gang was made up mostly of former bushwhackers, notably the Youngers: Cole, Bob, Jim, and John. On June 3, 1871, the James brothers and the Youngers robbed the bank at Corydon, Iowa, and stopped at a political rally on the edge of town to announce that they had just cleaned out the bank. Months later they struck a bank in Columbia, Kentucky, and killed a man in the process, but on September 26, 1872, Jesse and Frank sealed their reputations as daring desperadoes when they robbed the box office at the Kansas City fair in the midst of a crowd of ten thousand people. Although less than one thousand dollars was taken, and a small girl was shot in the leg, the legend of the James gang took a giant leap.

John Newman Edwards, the editor of the *Kansas City Times* who championed Missouri's Confederate guerrillas, wrote an article in which he praised the daring of the outlaws with such gushing adulation that his condemnation of the robbery was scarcely noticed. Edwards became the chief apologist for the James boys in the ensuing years. His column was followed by a letter from one of the gang, probably Jesse, signed, "Jack Shephard, Dick Turpin, Claude Duval." If readers failed to recognize the names of three of England's most famous social bandits, they could not have missed the significance of the statement, "we rob the rich and give to the poor."

The premises of the legend of Jesse and Frank James were now in place. The brothers were heroic guerrillas who had been driven to violence in retribution for wrongs they and their family had endured. They had been branded as outlaws and forced into a life of crime. It was not an original idea, but it resonated well with pro-Southern Missourians, and it gave a certain moral stature to common criminals. As Edwards and others promoted the theme, the James gang came to symbolize all the frustrations of Southern sympathizers who saw themselves wronged by an unjust system.

Bankers and other businessmen in the region did not buy the image, but they unwittingly contributed to it when they retained the Pinkerton Detective Agency to find the boys. These "Yankee mercenaries" had little success, but their reputation as tools of business against labor and their record as Union spies won more sympathy for the James gang. Even after a Pinkerton agent was murdered near the Samuel farm, and two more were shot by the Youngers in a gunfight that also left John Younger dead, much of the public still saw the outlaws as the victims.

More robberies followed. On May 27, 1873, the gang robbed the bank at Ste. Genevieve, Missouri. On July 21, 1873, they wrecked a train near Council Bluffs, Iowa, killing the engineer and getting away with a paltry sum compared to the gold shipment they expected to find. On January 31, 1874, they robbed another train, at Gad's Hill, south of St. Louis. The bandits made a great show of checking the hands of passengers, not wanting to rob workingmen, they said, and brought smiles to the faces of the victims with inquiries about "Mr. Pinkerton."

By then the James-Younger gang had gained national notoriety. In November 1873 Edwards had penned a lengthy and lurid account of the suffering of Frank and Jesse at the hands of the authorities, and thereafter virtually every robbery in a half-dozen states from Kansas to Mississippi was attributed to the James boys. In the midst of their growing fame, Jesse married Zerelda Mimms on April 24, 1874, and within the year Frank eloped with Ann Ralston. The brothers dropped out of sight for a time, but in the fall of 1874 lawlessness, and the James-Younger gang in particular, became issues in the state elections.

On the night of January 26, 1875, the legend took another leap when Pinkerton agents tossed a flare into the Samuel home that exploded, killing the nine-year-old half brother of Jesse and Frank and mangling their mother's hand so badly it had to be amputated. The Pinkertons were indicted, and a movement was launched to pardon the James and Younger brothers that fell just short of the two-thirds vote required in the legislature.

The gang was suspected of still more robberies in 1875, but on September 7, 1876, they made their first serious mistake. They attempted to rob the First National Bank of Northfield, Minnesota. The robbery turned into a debacle. Two of the gang, William Stiles (alias Bill Chadwell) and Clell Miller, were killed by townsmen, and Samuel Wells (known as Charlie

Pitt) was killed later by the pursuing posse. Frank James and Jesse James escaped with the Youngers, but Bob Younger was seriously wounded. Jesse and Cole quarreled after Jesse proposed that Bob be left behind or killed. When Cole refused, Frank and Jesse abandoned the Youngers, who were soon caught and later went to prison. The James brothers fled west into Dakota Territory, and during the following months were reported to have robbed banks and trains from Montana to Texas.

The Northfield disaster had cost the James boys dearly, not only in lost friends but also in public support. Jesse James and Frank James quietly slipped away, while officials in several states chased rumors. The brothers settled in Nashville, Tennessee, where Jesse lived under the name "Thomas Howard" and Frank called himself "B. J. Woodson." During this interlude they apparently kept out of trouble, though the papers were full of tales of imagined exploits from Missouri to Mexico. In the summer of 1879 Jesse went west to Las Vegas, New Mexico, apparently to investigate ranching opportunities, and allegedly met William H. Bonney ("Billy the Kid") in the process. The trip failed to produce results, however, and on October 8, 1879, Jesse and five or six others robbed the Glendale train in Missouri.

Frank was still uninvolved in crime at the time, raising prize-winning Poland-China hogs and racing horses. On March 11, 1881, he succumbed to the pressure of his brother and robbed a man of five thousand dollars at Muscle Shoals, Alabama. When their accomplice, Bill Ryan, was captured shortly thereafter, the brothers decided it was time to leave Nashville. Jesse put together a new gang, but it was not the same. The new men were not comrades from bushwacker days but common thugs with no real loyalties. The gang struck trains at Winston and Blue Cut, Missouri. Both were botched affairs. Increasingly suspicious of his gang members, Jesse killed Ed Miller, the brother of Clell Miller.

Eventually, Jesse James moved his family to St. Joseph where he passed himself off as a cattle buyer. He fell in with Robert Ford and Charlie Ford and scouted banks for future jobs. Jesse was suspicious of Bob Ford, but was unaware that Bob had killed the James's cousin Wood Hite and had already talked privately with Gov. **Thomas Theodore Crittenden** concerning rewards for Frank and Jesse. On April 3, 1882, Bob Ford killed Jesse as he stood on a chair straightening a picture. The Ford brothers were tried for murder and found guilty, but the governor pardoned them.

Frank James, who seemed genuinely committed to putting his old life behind him, made inquiries about his safety in the event he came in, and six months after Jesse died, accompanied by John

Edwards, Frank surrendered to Governor Crittenden in Jefferson City. He was tried both in Missouri and in Alabama, but each time he was found not guilty. He lived the rest of his life struggling with his notoriety, never finding satisfying work, and pursuing a long list of menial jobs. For a time he and **Cole Younger** had a "Wild West Show," but it soon failed. Oddly, he rarely talked about the early days. He died on February 18, 1915, of a stroke.

GARY L. ROBERTS

Edwards, John Newman. *Noted Guerrillas; or, The Warfare of the Border.* St. Louis: Bryan, Brand, 1877.

Fellman, Michael. *Inside War: The Guerrilla Conflict in Missouri during the American Civil War.* New York: Oxford University Press, 1989.

Prassel, Frank Richard. *The Great American Outlaw: A Legacy of Fact and Fiction.* Norman: University of Oklahoma Press, 1993.

Settle, William A. *Jesse James Was His Name.* Columbia: University of Missouri Press, 1966.

Wellman, Paul I. *A Dynasty of Western Outlaws.* Garden City, N.Y.: Doubleday, 1961.

White, Richard. "Outlaw Gangs of the Middle Border: American Social Bandits." *Western Historical Quarterly* 12 (1981): 387–408.

JAMES, LUCY WORTHAM (1880–1938)

Lucy Wortham James was born in St. James, Missouri, on September 13, 1880. Her mother was Octavia Bowles James, the daughter of a doctor. Her father, Thomas, was the son of "the iron king of Missouri," William James, and the namesake and grandson of Maramec Iron Works's founder.

The collapse of the ironworks by 1884 sent Thomas James to the Dakota hills and elsewhere attempting to make a living in real estate and fur trading. Octavia James contracted tuberculosis and had to relocate to the milder climate of El Paso, Texas. With her fourteen-year-old daughter by her side, she died in 1894.

After her mother's death, Lucy James's great-uncle Richard G. Dunn invited her to live with him in New York. A wealthy man, Dunn offered many opportunities to the young James. She attended the Spence School and was introduced to such things as opera, art, music, and literature. She even traveled to Vienna to study piano. Her exposure to tuberculosis, however, made her dreams of becoming a concert pianist impossible.

Giving up the piano, James returned to America in 1903. Her father was leaving for Japan, and she begged to accompany him. Upon their arrival, Lucy James encountered the U.S. chargé d'affaires,

Huntington Wilson. After pursuing James throughout her stay in Japan, Wilson proposed, and the two were married in Baltimore, Maryland, in 1904. The newlyweds then returned to Tokyo so that Wilson could fulfill his new duties as the first secretary of the American legation.

At the time of their marriage, the social qualities of a wife helped determine the political progress of her husband. James handled such responsibility with great success. Hosting magnificent parties and gatherings, she was well liked and admired by many in Washington, D.C.

Despite the individual successes of Lucy James and her husband, their marriage was a failure. Upon return from a diplomatic trip to South America in 1915, the two divorced. The former Mrs. Wilson retained her maiden name and was known thereafter as Lucy Wortham James.

The death of her father in 1912 left James with a sizable inheritance, including a share of the Dunn fortune. She eventually became owner of R. G. Dunn and Company, which later became Dunn and Bradstreet, Inc. With a high aptitude for business, James reformed the company and established a pension plan for elderly employees.

Regardless of where she lived at the time, James returned to St. James, Missouri, every spring. She held fond memories of her childhood there and was well liked by the residents. She was always willing to help others and showed a friendly interest in the concerns of the locals. James used her fortune to help those in need, setting up programs for social services and funding grants to send children to school. She also gave money for medical research. She even moved to St. James during the depression and used her own money to protect residents from bankruptcy.

James did not want the projects she had started to end. She wanted her funding to remain flexible enough to adapt to the changing needs of society and people. With that in mind, she put the New York Community Trust in charge of her funds so that charities in need could receive financial assistance. She established the Lucy Wortham James Trust to continue her philanthropic work while she was living and the Lucy Wortham James Memorial for the distribution of funds after her death. She bought the land of the long-abandoned Maramec Iron Works in the 1920s in order to beautify the area and to create a park for the public to enjoy. In another project she funded, trees were planted in St. James to replace those killed by disease. A library was also established in the town after her death.

James helped many people during her lifetime. In a show of appreciation for her deeds, the people in St. James sent a Christmas gift to the bedridden philanthropist in 1938. Only nine days after completing her letter of thanks, on January 19, 1938, Lucy Wortham James died in New York.

SHELLY L. LEMONS

Genet, Nancy. *Lucy Wortham James.* St. James, Mo.: James Foundation, 1971.

March, David D. *The History of Missouri.* New York: Lewis Historical Publishing, 1967.

Norris, James D. *Frontier Iron: The Maramec Iron Works, 1826–1876.* Madison: State Historical Society of Wisconsin, 1964.

JAMES, THOMAS (1776–1856)

Thomas James spent little of his life in Missouri, but he significantly influenced the state. With a strong background in iron making, he largely financed and organized the Maramec Iron Works during the 1820s. He and his partner, Samuel Massey, opened south-central Missouri to increased settlement. The ironworks supplied needed material for the growth of industries in St. Louis and the eastern United States. James D. Norris summarized the importance of James's contribution: "The Maramec Iron Works, as the first successful large-scale foundry west of the Mississippi River, proved that high profits were to be made from the exploitation of Missouri's iron and timber resources, and it encouraged other entrepreneurs to invest in the state's developing economy."

Born on November 5, 1776, Thomas James came from a family of experienced iron makers. His father died at sea in the winter of 1784–1785, and James went to live with his grandparents in Jefferson County, Virginia. He later lived with an uncle on his mother's side of the family in Harpers Ferry, Virginia, and attended Charlestown Academy. He moved to Chillicothe, Ohio, in 1798 and engaged in a variety of commercial activities. He and John McCoy traded for Indian furs and ginseng and marketed them in Asia through a New Orleans agent. Later, the partners slaughtered, pickled, and packed hogs for resale in the West Indies. James opened a store to sell iron products and invested in the Scioto Salt Works, controlling a readily available supply of the necessity. He sold the works when competition began to cut into profits. He also invested in a number of iron furnaces to secure a certain supply for his iron store. He owned an interest in the Brush Creek Furnace, the Marble Furnace, the Buckhorn Furnace, and Rapid Forge, all in Ohio. James took an active role in managing these facilities and "rapidly accumulated a sizable capital resource base." By the mid-1820s he had become one of the wealthiest men in Ohio, with a sizable interest in both of Chillicothe's banks. Norris described James as the embodiment of the entrepreneur: a risk taker who exploited opportunities for their potential profits.

James and Massey arrived in Missouri in 1826, traveling to Maramec spring. They immediately grasped the possibilities offered by this impressive source of waterpower; the readily available ore, flux, and timber; plus the stone needed to build the furnace and to make iron. James and Massey formed a partnership that called for James to invest the bulk of the money with Massey supplying the remainder and providing the day-to-day management of the operation. Massey received six hundred dollars per year as salary and one-third of the profits. To build the works, they transported a large community of skilled artisans some six hundred miles from Ohio to the Missouri wilderness. They purchased the initial land at the federal land office in Jackson, Missouri, and within a decade owned more than ten thousand acres. Workmen completed the furnace in 1829. An estimated seven hundred skilled artisans came to the area to work in the ironworks. James and Massey also owned and hired slaves to do a variety of tasks. They came from as far away as Columbia, Fulton, and Fayette, Missouri.

Massey managed the works until he sold his interest in 1847 to Thomas. Thomas's son, William, became the manager in that year and continued to operate Maramec Iron Works until August 1875. He also built the Ozark Iron Works some miles away in Phelps County, but economic difficulties caused the closure of both operations and bankruptcy for William James in December 1877. Thomas James failed to see the demise of his Missouri investment. He died on June 14, 1856.

LAWRENCE O. CHRISTENSEN

James, Lucy Wortham. Papers. Western Historical Manuscripts Collection, Columbia.

James and Dun Papers. Ross County Historical Society, Chillicothe, Ohio.

Norris, James D. *Frontier Iron: The Maramec Iron Works, 1826–1876.* Madison: State Historical Society of Wisconsin, 1964.

JENKINS, BURRIS ATKINS (1869–1945)

Born on October 2, 1869, ten miles from Independence, Missouri, on a small farm near the Santa Fe Trail, Burris Atkins Jenkins in the early twentieth century was one of America's preeminent liberal Protestant clergymen. For thirty-five years, 1907 to 1942, he was the minister of the Linwood Boulevard Christian Church (Campbellite or Disciples of Christ), a large and influential congregation in Kansas City. While he excelled as a preacher, he also wrote sixteen books that included scholarly works on the

New Testament and Protestantism, sermon collections, six novels, and his autobiography, *Where My Caravan Has Rested* (1939).

Burris Jenkins's father, Andrew Jenkins, died of consumption when Burris was nine years old. Concerned about her children's education, Burris's mother, Sarah Jenkins, moved to Kansas City where they attended school. Influenced by his devout mother and the venerable Alexander Proctor, the minister of the Christian Church in Independence, Jenkins enrolled in Bethany College, in Bethany, West Virginia, a Campbellite institution founded in 1844. He graduated in 1891 with a bachelor of arts degree and as an ordained minister in the Christian Church.

After a short time in California, Jenkins resumed his religious studies at Yale and Harvard, receiving a bachelor of sacred theology degree in 1895 and a master of arts degree in 1896 from Harvard. From 1896 to 1900 he served a Christian Church in Indianapolis, Indiana, and taught a course in the New Testament at the University of Indianapolis. In 1901 he became president of Kentucky University in Lexington.

In 1907 Jenkins accepted a request by the congregation of the Linwood Boulevard Christian Church to become their minister. During his tenure church membership and attendance grew. Innovative programs were added to the traditional services that increased lay participation and involved the congregation more in the life of the community. It was one of the first churches to show movies, to open the parish hall to recreational events for young people and families, to establish a psychiatric clinic, and to provide a prekindergarten school. The Sunday Evening Forum that replaced the traditional evening evangelistic service presented programs on a variety of subjects. Well-known personalities such as Jane Adams, Upton Close, Vachel Lindsey, and Sinclair Lewis spoke to the forum.

When the United States intervened in World War I in 1917, Jenkins joined the War Service Group of the YMCA. While overseas he served as a correspondent for the *Kansas City Star*. On the basis of his wartime experiences he wrote *Facing the Hindenburg Line* and *It Happened "Over There."* As an editor he strongly supported President Woodrow Wilson's campaign to make the United States a member of the League of Nations. Overworked and discouraged by the defeat of the league, Jenkins left the newspaper to devote his full attention to his preaching and writing.

In 1926 Jenkins participated in "Sinclair Lewis' Sunday School Class," a group of liberal Protestant clergymen and Catholic priests of Kansas City who met regularly with the popular American author while he was in Kansas City researching his novel on the fake Fundamentalist preacher Elmer Gantry.

Lewis created headlines when at a Sunday Evening Forum at Linwood Church he challenged God to prove his existence by striking him dead in the next fifteen minutes. Jenkins denied the published accounts of the incident. When he did not denounce Lewis, however, his critics branded him a heretic and chided him for being the master of a three-ring circus at the Linwood Church.

During the 1930s Jenkins and other Kansas City clergy joined **Samuel S. Mayerberg,** the Reform rabbi of Temple B'Nai Jehudah, in the crusade against **Thomas J. Pendergast**'s corrupt domination of city government. The Kansas City Ministerial Alliance was one of the first groups to call for reform and the breakup of the Pendergast political machine.

Fire destroyed the Linwood Church (now Community Christian Church) on November 1, 1939. Although Jenkins suffered from osteomyelitis and was about to retire, he agreed to remain as minister until the first phase of a rebuilding program had been completed. The church purchased property in Kansas City's Country Club Plaza area and commissioned the internationally famous architect Frank Lloyd Wright to design the new structure. Completed in 1942 the church auditorium was considered by many as too radical in design and a Plaza eyesore. Now, however, the church is one of the city's architectural treasures.

Following the dedication service of the auditorium, Jenkins and his wife, Martha, retired to El Centro, California. He died on March 13, 1945. He was survived by his wife and three sons, Burris Jr., Logan, and Paul.

Charles T. Jones Jr.

Durrett, Sue, and Fran Collins, eds. *Community Christian Church: A Centennial History, 1890–1990.* Kansas City, Mo.: Community Christian Church, 1990.

Jenkins, Burris A. *Where My Caravan Has Rested.* New York: Willett Clark, 1939.

JESSE, RICHARD HENRY (1853–1921)

Richard Henry Jesse, eighth president of the University of Missouri, was born on March 1, 1853, at Epping Forest, Virginia. He was educated in the public schools, in Hanover Academy, and at the University of Virginia, where he received a bachelor's degree. He continued his education in Europe, studying at the University of Munich and the University of Berlin. Before coming to the University of Missouri, he taught Greek, Latin, and English at Louisiana State University and at Tulane. He married Addie Henry Polk in 1882; they had six children.

Jesse served as president of the University of Missouri from 1891 to 1908. His presidency saw one of the greatest crises in the university's history as well as some of its greatest growth. On January 9, 1892, just six months after Jesse's inauguration, fire destroyed Academic Hall, the university's main building. All that remained were the six majestic Ionic columns that, at Jesse's insistence, were left standing. He moved quickly to keep the university open, utilizing churches and the county courthouse for classes. Some politicians used the fire as an excuse to try to remove the university from Columbia, but with strong support from Gov. **David Rowland Francis,** the institution was able to rebuild Academic Hall and to construct six additional buildings—a manual training building; the law building (soon to be known as the "Law Barn"); a chemistry laboratory; a biology, geology, and museum building; a physics and engineering building; and a power plant—which, with Academic Hall, formed the nucleus of what later came to be known as Francis Quadrangle, one of the most impressive campus spaces in the Midwest.

Jesse's administration brought both growth and organizational change, as well as substantial improvements in quality. By 1900 enrollment passed one thousand for the first time, and in 1902 the student body numbered two thousand, and there were two hundred in the School of Mines and Metallurgy at Rolla, where Jesse urged concentration upon the mining curriculum rather than expansion into other fields. He placed great emphasis on graduate education and research, recruiting young Ph.D.'s who built the university's reputation for scholarship. Among them were George LeFevre in biology, **Isidor Loeb** in history, John Pickard in art and art history, Herman Schlundt in chemistry, and Frank Thilly in philosophy. The College of Agriculture enjoyed one of its greatest periods of development during Jesse's administration. He appointed Henry J. Waters as dean, and M. F. Miller, **Frederick B. Mumford,** and J. C. Whitten as professors. In 1908 Missouri's reputation for scholarship and graduate education was recognized when the university became the twenty-second member of the prestigious Association of American Universities.

Organizationally, the university established a summer school, primarily for the benefit of teachers, and began to offer extension courses in all parts of the state. At Jesse's retirement, plans for the School of Journalism (established in 1908) neared completion.

Jesse was not particularly popular with the students—he seemed aloof and remote—but many positive developments in student life occurred during his administration. The curators built a second men's dormitory and a dormitory for women (appropriately named Read Hall, after **Daniel Read,** the university's sixth president, who was responsible for the admission of women). Parker Memorial Hospital, opened in 1901, greatly benefited students. Student organizations proliferated, a number of new publications, including the *Savitar,* were inaugurated, and intercollegiate athletics, especially football, greatly expanded. The engineers began St. Pat's Day, and the Aggies started the Farmers' Fair. Bleachers were built at Rollins Field, and the university helped form the Missouri Valley Conference. Additional facilities included Rothwell Gymnasium, a golf course, and tennis courts.

Jesse worked hard to develop alumni associations in various parts of the state. He traveled extensively, speaking to alumni and other organizations. He accomplished all this while administering a growing and changing university with little help—during the early part of his administration he did not even have a secretary. As a result, his health, once robust, declined to the point that in December 1907, on the advice of his physician, he submitted his resignation to take effect at the end of the school year. He continued to live in Columbia until his death on January 22, 1921. In that year the curators renamed Academic Hall in his honor.

JAMES C. OLSON

Olson, James C., and Vera Olson. *The University of Missouri: An Illustrated History.* Columbia: University of Missouri Press, 1988.

Selby, P. O. "Richard Henry Jesse." In *Missouri College Presidents: Past and Present.* Kirksville: Northeast Missouri State University, 1971.

Severance, Henry O. *Richard Henry Jesse: President of the University of Missouri, 1891–1908.* Mimeographed. Columbia: privately printed, 1937.

Stephens, Frank F. *A History of the University of Missouri.* Columbia: University of Missouri Press, 1962.

Viles, Jonas. *The University of Missouri: A Centennial History.* Columbia: University of Missouri, 1939.

JEWELL, WILLIAM (1789–1852)

In some respects, William Jewell's story is similar to those of thousands of others who settled in Missouri between the War of 1812 and the 1830s. He was born in Loudion County, Virginia, on January 1, 1789, to George and Mary Jewell. The family moved to Kentucky sometime after 1812 and stayed there long enough for William to grow up and attend Transylvania College where he studied medicine. He also became involved in politics, and the voters of his district elected him to one term in the Kentucky legislature.

In the early decades of the nineteenth century, thousands of migrants from Kentucky, Tennessee, and Virginia followed the trails first established by

Daniel Boone and his sons and settled in the Missouri River valley in central Missouri. In 1820 William, his parents, and his three sisters moved to Howard County, Missouri, in the heart of the Boone's Lick region. In this rapidly growing area, an ambitious man like William Jewell had ample opportunities to make an impression. In 1821 he relocated to the village of Columbia in what was soon to be Boone County.

Almost immediately Jewell entered politics and obtained a position on the committee in charge of surveying Columbia's streets. As a member of this committee, later as mayor, and eventually as a member of the state legislature, Jewell emphasized a rational, organized plan for economic expansion. He insisted that the streets in Columbia be wide, straight, and flat. As mayor he antagonized some members of the fledgling community by instituting inspections for slaughterhouses, pigpens, and stables. He represented a class of men determined to establish orderly, self-regulating communities in the frontier world they inhabited.

Jewell's efforts to bring "civilization" to Missouri can be illustrated on several levels. In 1823 he established the Columbia Baptist Church, the first congregation of any denomination in the town. He opposed gambling and horse racing and joined the first temperance society in Columbia. He volunteered as an army surgeon for the Black Hawk War in 1831–1832. When several towns in central Missouri were vying to be the seat of the state university in the late 1830s, Jewell gave eighteen hundred dollars to help secure its location in Columbia. As a state legislator he supported a number of progressive measures, including the abolition of whipping and pillory as punishment for nonslaves, the establishment of a public hospital in St. Louis, and support for the St. Louis public schools and library association. A Whig, Jewell's politics transcended pure party loyalty. He supported Democrat **Thomas Hart Benton** for U.S. senator at least once, but voted for Whig Henry Clay in the election of 1844.

Jewell's interest in seeing Missouri and Columbia grow was not completely altruistic. He was a businessman as well as a public servant. He actively practiced medicine, and while he earned a reputation for braving harsh weather and bad roads in order to see patients, he did not hesitate to sue those who failed to pay him. Among other business ventures, he became a stockholder in the Columbia and Missouri River Plank Road Company. He owned at least six slaves, some of whom he freed in 1836. He emancipated the remainder of them in his will. Jewell's political influence and financial success, along with his strong personality, made him a respected, if not always liked, figure in Columbia.

In 1843, seeking to further his vision of progress through education and religion, Jewell offered the Baptist General Association of Missouri ten thousand dollars to build an institution dedicated to the training of Baptist ministers. The association initially failed to raise matching funds, but Jewell left his offer on the table. Finally, on February 27, 1849, the Baptist General Association chartered what would become William Jewell College in Liberty, Missouri. Jewell, a self-taught architect, personally oversaw the construction of the early college buildings he had helped finance. While in Liberty he suffered a heat stroke and died of complications on August 7, 1852. He was buried in Boone County.

ROBERT FAUST

Gentry, North Todd. "Dr. William Jewell." Address delivered at William Jewell College, Liberty, Mo., December 6, 1932.

Lawson, L. M. *Founding and Location of William Jewell College.* Columbia: State Historical Society of Missouri, 1914.

Parrish, William E., Charles T. Jones Jr., and Lawrence O. Christensen. *Missouri: The Heart of the Nation.* 2d ed. Arlington Heights, Ill.: Harlan Davidson, 1992.

JOHNSON, ALONZO "LONNIE" (1889?–1970)

Alonzo "Lonnie" Johnson was an extraordinarily gifted blues guitarist and talented singer who pioneered a sophisticated, jazz-inflected urban blues guitar style. Although the year of his birth remains disputed, Johnson was born probably on February 8, 1889, in New Orleans, Louisiana. He grew up hearing an eclectic mixture of musical styles ranging from jazz, ragtime, and country blues to old-time country, European classical, and Tin Pan Alley. His father, a violinist, led a string band, and Johnson's six brothers and five sisters all played instruments.

Johnson dropped out of school and went to work in a lumberyard as a teenager. In 1910 he began performing as a violinist and guitarist in the brothels, saloons, and cabarets of Storyville, the red-light district of New Orleans. In his mid- to late twenties, Johnson also played with his father's band at weddings and festivals and on street corners around the city, and performed in local theaters with his brother James "Steady Roll" Johnson, who played piano and violin.

Between 1917 and 1919 Johnson toured England and continental Europe with a musical revue company. While abroad all of his family, except James, died when the Spanish influenza epidemic swept through New Orleans. Deeply saddened by this crushing loss, Johnson took his music on the road, first to Texas and then, in 1920, to St. Louis,

Missouri. He settled in the city and, according to blues historian William Barlow, eventually established himself as the "most influential musician in St. Louis blues circles during the 1920s." Between 1920 and 1922 Johnson and his brother, James, worked professionally in St. Louis as violinists in Charlie Creath's band, the Jazz-O-Maniacs; aboard the SS *St. Paul;* and later with the Fate Marable Band, another Mississippi-riverboat orchestra. "I played every excursion boat out there for five years," Johnson later recalled. In 1925 he married blues singer Mary Smith; they had six children, including the musician Clarence Johnson. That same year Johnson won a musical talent contest at the Booker T. Washington Theater sponsored by OKeh Records, and he received as first prize a phonograph recording contract.

Johnson made his first recording on November 2, 1925, as a singer and violinist on the Jazz-O-Maniac's "Won't Don't Blues." That same week he inaugurated his own recording career on the OKeh label with his guitar instrumental "Mr. Johnson's Blues," and its flip side, "Falling Rain Blues," on which he sang and played violin. Over the next seven years Johnson recorded more than 130 selections for OKeh and various other phonograph companies, including "Ball and Chain Blues" (1926), "Roaming Rambler Blues" (1927), "Away Down in the Alley Blues" (1928), "She's Making Whoopee in Hell Tonight" (1927), "There Is No Justice" (1932), and "Racketeer's Blues" (1932), making him one of the most extensively recorded bluesmen of his generation. His music often addressed the daily experiences and hard times of urban, working-class African Americans, especially recently arrived southern migrants. "My blues is built on human beings on land," he once explained. "See how they live, see their heartaches and the shifts they go through with love affairs and things like that—that's what I write about and that's the way I make my living."

An extremely versatile musician who played several stringed instruments, Johnson worked extensively for OKeh Records as a studio musician between 1925 and 1932. He not only played guitar on the recordings of such blues musicians as Alger "Texas" Alexander, Victoria Spivey, and Clara Smith, but also accompanied jazz bands: in 1927 he recorded with Louis Armstrong's Hot Five ("I'm Not Rough," "Hotter than That," and "Savoy Blues") and the following year with Duke Ellington and His Orchestra ("The Mooche" and "Misty Morning"). Of particular note is the series of spectacular guitar duets that Johnson recorded in the late 1920s with famed jazz guitarist Eddie Lang, including such classics as "A Handful of Riffs," "Hot Fingers, " and "Bull Frog Moan," all of which were recorded in 1929.

After slumping record sales during the early years of the depression prematurely derailed his recording career, Johnson drifted in and out of the musical profession. In 1929 he toured southern theaters on the black vaudeville circuit as a member of blues singer Bessie Smith's Midnight Steppers Revue. During the early 1930s he lived briefly in New York City, where he played in nightclubs and at house parties and hosted a blues show at a local radio station. After divorcing his wife in 1932, Johnson settled in Chicago, where he worked solo and with small bands in nightclubs throughout most of the 1930s. He toured extensively in St. Louis, Kansas City, Detroit, and West Coast cities during World War II.

After his initial stardom Johnson sought to revive his musical career on several occasions with comeback recording sessions, including with Decca in 1937, Bluebird in 1939, and King in 1947, with whom he scored a number-one hit on the rhythm and blues charts the following year with "Tomorrow Night." Johnson worked extensively outside the music business later in life, including employment stints as a steel mill worker, a coal miner, and in the late 1950s as a janitor at the Ben Franklin Hotel in Philadelphia, Pennsylvania.

In 1963, at the age of seventy-four, Johnson toured with the American Folk Blues Festival in England and in continental Europe. By the mid-1960s he had settled in Toronto, Ontario, where he continued to play local blues clubs and concert festivals until around 1969 when poor health forced him into retirement. "I've lived a very beautiful life," he told an interviewer near the end of his life. "I've seen it sweet and I've seen it very hard. . . . But somehow or other I managed to make it." He died of a stroke on June 16, 1970, in Toronto at the age of eighty-one and was buried in Philadelphia. A brilliant instrumentalist whose jazzy guitar playing was both highly innovative and technically dazzling, Johnson made more than five hundred recordings during his career and deeply influenced such legendary jazz and blues guitarists as Charlie Christian, Django Reinhardt, Robert Johnson, Aaron "T-Bone" Walker, and B. B. King.

PATRICK J. HUBER

Barlow, William. *"Looking Up at Down": The Emergence of Blues Culture.* Philadelphia: Temple University Press, 1989.

Blues Who's Who: A Biographical Dictionary of Blues Singers. S.v. "Johnson, Lonnie."

Humphrey, Mark A. "Bright Lights, Big City: Urban Blues." In *Nothing but the Blues: The Music and the Musicians,* ed. Lawrence Cohn, 151–203. New York: Abbeville Press, 1993.

The New Grove Dictionary of American Music. Vol. 2. S.v. "Johnson, Lonnie."

JOHNSON, JOSEPHINE W. (1910–1990)

A Missouri modernist author and naturalist, Josephine Winslow Johnson gained national acclaim as the recipient of the 1935 Pulitzer Prize for literature. Born on June 20, 1910, in Kirkwood, Missouri, Johnson spent most of her formative years at Hillbrook, a one-hundred-acre gentleman's farm on the outskirts of St. Louis. The Edwardian propriety of her parents, Benjamin Hughes Johnson (1867–1926) and Ethel Franklin Johnson (1879–1964), molded much of the young woman's persona and resultant literary themes. With her father's early death, Johnson, her three sisters, and their mother carved a life for themselves at Hillbrook, at times opening their home to such pacifist groups as the Fellowship of Reconciliation.

The young Johnson early immersed herself in nature, learning to chronicle adolescent pain and reflections in her Hillbrook nature diaries. She attended Washington University in St. Louis from 1927 to 1932 where she initially majored in art, then English, never completing a degree. During her college years she wrote and published short stories and poetry, winning the 1934 St. Louis Writer's Guild award for her poem "Ice Winter." In the process she gained the attention of the esteemed editors Ellery Sedgwick of the Atlantic Press and Clifton Fadiman of Simon and Schuster. Upon Sedgwick's recommendation, Johnson was nominated to the prestigious Bread Loaf Writers' Conference in Middlebury, Vermont, in 1934. Two years later she served as one of Bread Loaf's fiction staff members.

Johnson's Pulitzer Prize–winning novel, *Now in November,* is a modernist work about Missouri farm life during the Great Depression, and is undoubtedly her best work of fiction. Her success compelled the shy but compassionate Johnson into the sociopolitical situation of the day, where she was courted by both the Communist and the Socialist Parties, ultimately becoming a member of the Norman Thomas Party. *Jordanstown,* Johnson's second novel, is a paean to equality and the less fortunate, but its subsumption to the proletarian agenda rendered it totally unsuccessful. She would later term *Jordanstown* "her greatest embarrassment."

Johnson involved herself as a journalist in the 1935 St. Louis Gas House Strikes, the Scottsboro case, and the Southern Tenant Farmers Union. Putting action to words, she volunteered to paint murals for the St. Louis Mission Free and Turner Schools (1935), was arrested in Arkansas for investigating injustices against sharecroppers in the Delta area (1936), and volunteered at rehabilitation farms near Sikeston, Missouri (1938). Her personal connections in the thirties included Missouri historian **Charles Van Ravenswaay,** novelist Bernard DeVoto, and fellow writer William Saroyan.

Soon after winning the Pulitzer, Johnson published a collection of short stories, *Winter Orchard* (1935); a well-reviewed book of poetry, *Year's End* (1937); and a self-illustrated children's book, *Paulina* (1937). Her short stories "Dark" and "John the Six" won, respectively, the 1934 and the 1935 O'Henry Short Story Memorial Awards.

Johnson married twice. Her first marriage, from 1939 to 1941, to Thurlow Smoot gave her a son, Terrence, but it soon ended in divorce. The following year she married an arbitrator for the National Labor Relations Board, Grant Cannon, in retrospect defining the years of their marriage, 1942 to 1969, as the happiest of her life. In the spring of 1942 Johnson taught at the University of Iowa Writers' Workshop, but her discomfort with large groups curtailed her tenure there. That same year the couple's first child, Annie, was born. In 1947, when Cannon accepted a position with the *Farm Quarterly* in Cincinnati, the couple moved to what Johnson would affectionately call "the Old House" in Newtown, eventually moving to the Summerside area of Clermont County in 1956. In 1952 the Cannons' last child, Carol, was born. During her marriage to Cannon, Johnson published three books: *Wildwood* (1945) and *The Dark Traveler* (1963)—both novels—and her second short story collection, *The Sorcerer's Son* (1965). In Cincinnati the couple became involved with the local Friends Group and worked together on both local and national humanitarian issues until Cannon's death from cancer in 1969.

In 1970 Johnson was awarded an honorary doctorate of humane letters from Washington University. Before her death she published three more books: *Inland Island* (1969), a collection of nature essays that she termed her favorite work; *Seven Houses,* her autobiography (1973); and *Circle of Seasons* (1974), a series of poetic vignettes accompanied by nature photographs. Johnson died on February 27, 1990, and in accordance with her wishes, her body was donated to the University Hospital Medical Center of Cincinnati.

Johnson's writing at its best sits alongside that of Willa Cather, Mari Sandoz, and Marjorie Kinnan Rawlings. Many of her themes derive from a feeling of powerlessness, agnosticism, and a perennial quest for elusive security. Her literary styles range from a modernistic poetic fluidity in her youth to a postmodernist unvarnished terseness in later years. Her images, generative but implacable, create metaphors from roots, potatoes, owls, and the rounded stone. Unusually prescient, Johnson predicted global overpopulation but, ever humanitarian, devoted much of her life to raising awareness of the plight of the downtrodden and the disadvantaged. A naturalistic naturalist, the dialectic paradox of Johnson's life and writing was that she metabolized the tincture of disease and the specter of solace from the same source, the rural Missouri and Ohio landscapes.

QUENTIN R. CARTER

Carter, Quentin R. "Josephine W. Johnson and the Pulitzer." Ph.D. diss., University of Denver, 1995.

Hoffman, Nancy. Afterword to *Now in November,* by Josephine W. Johnson. New York: Feminist Press, 1991.

Johnson, Josephine W. Papers. Olin Library Manuscript Collection. Washington University, St. Louis.

———. *Seven Houses: A Memoir of Time and Places.* New York: Simon and Schuster, 1973.

Mcfadden-Gerber, Margaret. "Josephine Winslow Johnson." In *American Women Writers,* ed. Lina Mainiero. New York: Frederick Ungar, 1980.

Wilk, Mary Beth. "The Inland Woman: A Study of the Life and Major Works of Josephine W. Johnson." Ph.D. diss., University of Massachusetts, 1978.

JOHNSON, WALDO PORTER (1817–1885)

Waldo Porter Johnson was born in Bridgeport, now West Virginia, on September 16, 1817. His father, William, a prosperous farmer and merchant, and his mother, Olive Waldo, were descendants of early settlers in the area. The couple raised nine children. After a private school education, Waldo attended Rector College in Pruntytown, Virginia. He graduated in 1839 and then studied law, and in 1842 started to practice in the Virginia courts.

Johnson did not stay long in Virginia. Six of his mother's brothers had emigrated to Missouri, and Johnson left his native state in March 1843 to join them. He chose to settle in Osceola, near two of his uncles. Besides practicing law, he speculated in land and began to accumulate large holdings.

At the beginning of the Mexican War, Johnson served in a company captained by his uncle **David Waldo.** His military service, however, was brief. Elected to the 1846 Missouri legislature while he rode with **Alexander W. Doniphan**'s Missouri mounted volunteers, Johnson resigned from the army to fulfill his legislative duties. In the fall of 1847 he traveled to his native state and married Emily Moore, who bore him five children. After the legislative term ended in 1848, Johnson became a circuit attorney. Three years later he won election as judge of the Seventh Judicial Circuit.

Johnson resigned his judgeship in 1852 so he could devote more time to his business interests and resume his law practice. By the end of the decade he was considered a wealthy man as well as one of the most prominent lawyers in the state.

An advocate of peace instead of civil war, Johnson was selected by Missouri's General Assembly as one of five commissioners to attend a peace conference held in Washington, D.C., in early February 1861. On March 18, 1861, the General Assembly elected Johnson, a Democrat, to replace **James S. Green** as one of Missouri's U.S. senators.

Johnson went to Washington for a special session of Congress called by Abraham Lincoln to convene on July 4, 1861. He opposed secession but also believed in states' rights. While he desired peace, he decided to join the Southern cause if war became a reality. After the Union defeat at Manassas, Johnson offered an amendment to a bill asking that governors convene legislatures to select two representatives from each congressional district to attend a convention in Louisville, Kentucky. The delegates would be charged to find ways to bring the war to a peaceful resolution. When the amendment failed twenty-nine to nine, Johnson, who would be expelled from Congress, left Washington and spent a brief time in Virginia with relatives before returning to Missouri to join the Confederate forces.

A lieutenant colonel in the Fourth Missouri Infantry, Johnson saw action at Pea Ridge and suffered two wounds during the battle. He also participated in the Battle of Corinth, Mississippi. Afterward, he returned to Missouri and recruited a cavalry regiment and six infantry companies to fight for the Confederacy. When Confederate senator R. L. Y. Peyton died, Gov. **Thomas Caute Reynolds** appointed Johnson to take his place. A champion of western interests and usually a staunch supporter of Jefferson Davis's policies, Johnson, nevertheless, eventually favored taking control of the war effort away from Davis and Braxton Bragg and transferring it to Robert E. Lee, Joseph E. Johnston, and P. G. T. Beauregard. He served in the Confederate senate until it was dissolved.

Johnson escaped arrest for his part in the rebellion, making his way to Hamilton, Canada, where his family joined him. They stayed in Canada until April 1866, when Johnson went back to Washington, D.C., and obtained a parole from the federal government.

Fearful of postwar conditions around Osceola, Johnson settled in Sedalia, resumed his law practice, and immersed himself in his business affairs. Public office held no interest for him after the war. However, in 1875 he won election to the Democratically controlled Constitutional Convention, which selected Johnson as its president. It met for about three months, drafting a lengthy, detailed document that placed numerous restrictions upon the powers of the state and other Missouri governmental units. The restrictions resulted from reactions to unhealthy political and business conditions and practices that had festered in the state. Passed unanimously by the convention members in early August, the constitution of 1875 was ratified by voters at a special election on October 30. It became law a month later.

In 1876 Johnson moved to St. Louis to practice law, though he spent much time in Osceola, where he died on August 14, 1885. He was buried at Forest Hill cemetery in Kansas City.

JAMES W. GOODRICH

Encyclopedia of the Confederacy. S.v. "Johnson, Waldo."

Johnson, Waldo Porter, III. *Johnson Letters.* N.p., 1960.

March, David D. *The History of Missouri.* New York: Lewis Historical Publishing, 1967.

Stevens, Walter B. *Missouri: The Center State, 1821–1915.* Chicago: S. J. Clarke, 1915.

Stewart, A. J. D., ed. *The History of the Bench and Bar of Missouri.* St. Louis: Legal Publishing, 1898.

Warner, Ezra J., and W. Buck Yearns. *Biographical Register of the Confederate Congress.* Baton Rouge: Louisiana State University Press, 1975.

JONES, EDWARD D., JR. (1925–1990)

Edward D. "Ted" Jones Jr., a business and financial leader, conservationist, and philanthropist, was born in St. Louis on December 18, 1925. He attended the University of Missouri prior to entering the United States Army in 1944. After leaving military service, Jones worked as a page at the New York Stock Exchange and subsequently acquired his securities license. He married Pat Young in 1950, and became a salesman for Edward D. Jones and Company, a firm his father had founded in St. Louis in 1871.

Initially, the younger Jones traveled through small towns selling securities door-to-door. In 1957 he opened a branch office of Edward D. Jones and Company in Mexico, Missouri. During the 1960s the younger Jones pioneered the strategy of bringing Wall Street to Main Street. While other investment companies concentrated their activities in metropolitan areas, Jones located offices for his firm in rural towns and suburban areas. After twenty years as a salesman, he became a senior partner. Under his guidance the company experienced continued growth. At the time of his death in 1990, Edward D. Jones and Company operated more than fifteen hundred offices in forty-four states with gross annual revenues of more than $300 million.

Jones loved the rural countryside, and following his retirement in 1980 he located his residence on a 740-acre wildlife refuge he owned in Callaway County, Missouri. Upon learning in 1986 that the Missouri-Kansas-Texas Railroad planned to abandon its line between St. Charles County and Sedalia, Jones suggested transforming the abandoned roadbed into a hiking and biking trail. In an effort to launch the proposed project, he donated two hundred thousand dollars in 1987 to purchase the old Katy right-of-way. For the next two years he lobbied members of the Missouri General Assembly for state funds to assist with the development of Missouri's longest biking trail, and agreed to contribute an additional $2 million to further the trail's development. His determined efforts eventually bore fruit when state legislators agreed to provide funding for the scenic trail that extended across two-thirds of the state.

Jones and the Katy Trail's other supporters had to overcome a determined effort to prevent its construction, but the trail proved immensely popular and even gained acceptance among some of its earlier critics. Among other things the trail's heavy use helped revitalize some smaller towns along its route, a development that its principal benefactor would have appreciated. Edward D. Jones died in Columbia, Missouri, on October 3, 1990.

LISA FISCHER

Lindholm, Bob. "Something of Value." *Missouri Conservationist* (April 1990): 7–9.

St. Louis Post-Dispatch, October 4–8, 1990.

JONES, JOHN BEAUCHAMP (1810–1866)

A journalist and author, John Beauchamp Jones was born on March 6, 1810, in Baltimore, Maryland. His childhood, spent in Kentucky and Missouri, became the basis for much of his fiction. Settling in Arrow Rock, Missouri, in 1835, he opened one of the first mercantile stores in Saline County. In 1840 he married Frances T. Custis of Accomack County, Virginia. He left Arrow Rock around this time as well, though the exact date is not known.

Stories and books written by Jones drew upon his experiences as an early settler in Missouri's Boonslick region and as a business owner in Arrow Rock. For example, prominent local residents such as **John S. Sappington,** a wealthy landowner and physician who had become famous for his quinine-based antimalarial medicine, and the artist **George Caleb Bingham,** who displayed a preliminary sketch of the "County Election," are mentioned in Jones's *Life and Adventures of a Country Merchant* (1854).

In 1841 Jones was editor of the *Baltimore Sunday Visitor.* When he could not find a publisher for his novel *Wild Western Scenes* (1841), he published it as a series in the *Visitor.* The book was later published by J. B. Lippincott and Company of Philadelphia and soon found great success: by 1856 the fortieth edition was published, and over the next twenty years one hundred thousand copies were sold. The popularity of Jones's books can be attributed to their humor and local color. Although the books were not great literature, readers enjoyed Jones's style and the personal experiences that came through his books about frontier life in Missouri.

In 1842 Jones became editor of the *Madisonian,* which served as a voice for the Tyler administration. His party labors were subsequently rewarded when he received the consulate to Naples in the Polk administration.

In 1857 Jones established the *Southern Monitor* in Philadelphia, which, staunchly devoted to Southern interests, helped to fuel the growing sectional crisis. He edited the *Monitor* until the outbreak of the Civil War caused him to leave Philadelphia for the South.

At the beginning of the war Jones went to Montgomery and found clerical work in the Confederate War Department. During his service he kept a diary, which he subsequently published in two volumes under the title *A Rebel War Clerk's Diary* (1866). These books reveal important aspects of the Confederacy's inner history, and offer special insight into the society and economics of Richmond during 1864–1865.

The hardship of the war, combined with debilitating disease, exhausted Jones's vigor. He died in Burlington, New Jersey, on February 4, 1866, while the diary was in press.

MISTY CATES

Bradford, Gamaliel. *Biography of the Human Heart.* Boston: Houghton Mifflin, 1932.

Dictionary of American Biography. Vol. 10. S.v. "Jones, John Beauchamp."

Missouri: The WPA Guide to the "Show Me" State. St. Louis: Missouri Historical Society Press, 1998.

Orr, A. H., ed. *History of Saline County, Missouri.* Marceline, Mo.: Walsworth, 1967.

Spott, Carle Brooks. "Development of Fiction on the Missouri Frontier, 1830–1860." *Missouri Historical Review* 29 (1935): 279–94.

JONES, JOHN RICE (1759–1824)

John Rice Jones, a pioneering jurist renowned for his erudition, was one of the principal framers of Missouri's 1820 constitution and a member of the state's first supreme court. He was born in Wales on February 10, 1759, attended Oxford University, and practiced law in London before immigrating to the United States in 1784. After residing briefly in Philadelphia, Jones headed west in 1785 and settled at Vincennes, in present-day Indiana. The following year he joined a force, led by George Rogers Clark, enlisted to defend Vincennes against

an anticipated assault from the Wabash Indians. Once that threat subsided, Jones traveled farther west to Kaskaskia, located on the east bank of the Mississippi, and from there in 1789 he warned the military commander at Vincennes that the Spaniards in Upper Louisiana were making every effort to depopulate the settlements on the American side of the river.

Jones, who was fluent in English, French, and Spanish, soon made himself well known throughout the region. In 1795 the peripatetic attorney went to New Orleans to confer with Louisiana's governor-general, the Baron de Carondelet, concerning the claims of a group of Michilimackinac merchants he represented. He sought compensation for property that Spanish authorities in Upper Louisiana had seized from his clients in 1793. Lt. Gov. **Zenon Trudeau** wrote Carondelet from St. Louis that the "caustic character of the lawyer Jones whom you have seen, aside from his wranglings, has a talent destined to trouble us." Jones also accompanied **Moses Austin** during his 1797 visit to Upper Louisiana's lead mines and served as his interpreter. He subsequently joined Austin, in partnership with **François Vallé II** and Lt. Gov. **Charles de Hault Delassus,** for the purpose of conducting mining operations at Mine à Breton, located in the hinterlands west of Ste. Genevieve.

Jones returned to Vincennes, where his legal skills and his friendship with territorial governor **William Henry Harrison** helped him secure appointment in 1801 as Indiana Territory's first attorney general. The following year he acted as secretary of a convention that unsuccessfully petitioned Congress to repeal the antislavery article of the Northwest Ordinance of 1787. Governor Harrison, acting in behalf of President Thomas Jefferson, selected Jones in 1805 to serve as a member of the territory's Legislative Council. Jones's proslavery views, in all likelihood, doomed his attempt in 1808 to become Indiana's territorial delegate to Congress. Shortly after losing that contest, he returned to Kaskaskia, where he championed the cause of separating the Illinois counties from Indiana Territory.

In 1810 Jones moved across the Mississippi to Ste. Genevieve and from there to St. Louis, before settling at Mine à Breton where he engaged in lead mining. He continued the partnership he had formed earlier with Moses Austin, and they each conveyed land for the creation of Potosi, which was selected to serve as the county seat for Washington County. A series of disagreements and misunderstandings between the two men gradually took their toll, and in 1814 Austin and Jones parted company and dissolved their remaining joint interests at Mine à Breton.

Notwithstanding his squabbles with Austin, Jones found time to dabble in territorial politics. He served one term as a representative in Missouri's territorial assembly, and then as a member and president of the Legislative Council. In 1820 the voters selected him as one of three delegates representing Washington County in the Missouri Constitutional Convention. Jones, dubbed by historian **Floyd Calvin Shoemaker** as the convention's "most learned member," assumed an active role in drafting Missouri's first constitution. He chaired several key committees whose reports helped shape the final document.

When the new state's House of Representatives convened in 1820, its members selected Jones as clerk. Later that year, however, the respected jurist failed in his bid to represent Missouri in the United States Senate, even though he apparently enjoyed the backing of influential members of the St. Louis junto. Missouri's newly elected governor, **Alexander McNair,** who had served with Jones at the Constitutional Convention, promptly appointed his well-schooled colleague to a seat on the Missouri Supreme Court. As a member of the high court, Jones frequently disagreed with his fellow justices, and his dissenting opinions still enliven the otherwise staid early state reports.

Jones married twice. His first wife, Eliza Powell, who was born in London, bore him three children. His union with Mary Barger, whom he wed in Vincennes, produced eight children. When Jones died in St. Louis on February 1, 1824, he had attained renown in the legal profession, success in business, and considerable personal wealth. He was highly respected, though not particularly well liked, but his failure to win popularity should not obscure his substantial contributions as a distinguished member of the bar in Indiana, Illinois, and Missouri.

WILLIAM E. FOLEY

Barnhart, John D., and Dorothy L. Riker. *Indiana to 1816: The Colonial Period.* Indianapolis: Indiana Historical Bureau and Indiana Historical Society, 1971.

Gracy, David B. *Moses Austin: His Life.* San Antonio: Trinity University Press, 1987.

Nasatir, Abraham P. *Before Lewis and Clark: Documents Illustrating the History of the Missouri, 1785–1804.* 2 vols. 1952. Reprint, Lincoln: University of Nebraska Press, 1990.

Shoemaker, Floyd C. "David Barton, John Rice Jones, and Edward Bates: Three Missouri State and Statehood Founders." *Missouri Historical Review* 65 (July 1971): 527–43.

JONES, JOSEPH JAMES (1909–1963)

The biography of Joseph James Jones is both the story of the life of an American artist and a chronicle of the changing times in which he lived. Rising to prominence at the height of the depression, Jones became a nationally recognized painter, producing images that reflected the social and physical conditions around him. In his art and politics he fashioned himself into a working-class hero who was eagerly embraced by a disillusioned America struggling to hold on to its idealism.

Jones was born in St. Louis on April 7, 1909, the grandson of a stonemason and the son of a house painter. By the time he was twenty he had joined his father as a full-time member of the House Painters' Union. However, the young man was practicing his painting techniques on canvases as well as the sides of houses. Without formal training he began to make a name for himself in local art circles with his portraits and still lifes.

In February 1933 ten local businessmen and art lovers formed the Cooperative Art Society, pledging the struggling artist a monthly stipend in return for his paintings. However, as Jones's art and activities became increasingly political his middle-class supporters withdrew their patronage. Announcing he had become a communist, he painted scenes of social protest that depicted lynchings and the plight of the poor. His became a familiar name in the local press for his progressive activities as well as his art, participating in public protests and displaying Soviet art.

In trouble with the local authorities, Jones left St. Louis for New York. In the spring of 1935 his one-man show at the American Contemporary Art Gallery received rave reviews. While his protest paintings garnered the most attention, a single rural landscape in the exhibit hinted at the direction Jones's work would take. In 1936 his *Painting of Wheatfields* exhibition opened at the Walker Gallery in New York, confirming his status as a rising star.

Between 1937 and the beginning of World War II, Jones was awarded a Guggenheim Fellowship to record conditions in the dust bowl and received a number of prestigious federal contracts for murals in post offices throughout the Midwest. When his show in the social-realist style in October 1937 was poorly received, Jones focused his attention on the American landscape. His political activities gradually ceased, but his personal life brought him once again to the media's attention. Divorced from his first wife in 1935, his relationship with Grace Adams Mallinckrodt, whom he married in the fall of 1940, was highly publicized.

Settling permanently in Morristown, New Jersey, Jones was hired to make a pictorial record of World War II as a part of the government's War Art Unit. When the program was dismantled, he became a correspondent for *Life.* Sent to chronicle army life in Alaska, he instead produced fragile watercolor landscapes of the unusual terrain. He became increasingly involved with the corporate businesses replacing the government agencies as patrons for art. For Gimbel Brothers department stores he produced views of the industrial face of Philadelphia. His other clients included Standard Oil in New Jersey, *Fortune,* and *Time.* By this time his style had changed drastically: his landscape scenes rendered in delicate line with watercolor washes were in stark contrast to the bold oil compositions of his early career.

Living quietly with his wife and four children in New Jersey, Jones continued to have local shows with generally favorable reviews. When he died of a heart attack on April 9, 1963, his obituary in the *New York Times* indicated his controversial past was all but forgotten. Joe Jones, the established artist of a thriving corporate America, had replaced the young, outspoken activist of another time.

Jones has been accused of being superficial in his early radicalism, as he seemed to have abandoned politics when it was no longer fashionable. However, his change of heart was symptomatic of the time. The heyday of social realism in art passed with the depression. Joe Jones, the working-class hero, was a product of a unique time and place. Whether for personal gain or with true conviction, as a young artist he added his voice to the discordant chorus of social unrest. As he matured and achieved success, his view of his country grew less critical. Although his style and politics may have changed, Jones's preoccupation with the American landscape remained constant. In the images that he created and the life that he lived, the house painter from Missouri left us an enduring document of the face of a changing America.

LOUISA IAROCCI

Marling, Karal Ann. "Joe Jones: Regionalist, Communist, Capitalist." *Journal of the Decorative and Propaganda Arts, 1875–1945* (spring 1987): 46–58.

———. "Workers, Capitalists, and Booze: The Story of the 905 Murals." In *Joe Jones and J. B. Turnbull: Visions of the Midwest in the 1930s.* Milwaukee: Patrick and Beatrice Haggerty Museum of Art, Marquette University, 1987.

JOPLIN, SCOTT (1868–1917)

Known during his lifetime as the "King of Ragtime Writers," Scott Joplin was an African American musician and the foremost contributor to a "Missouri style" of ragtime music in the 1890s and early 1900s. He wrote two operas, one ragtime ballet, and forty-four original pieces, seven of which were in collaboration with other composers.

Joplin was born on November 24, 1868, in Cass County, Texas, the second son of Jiles and Florence Joplin. During his early childhood, the Joplin family lived on a plantation owned by William Caves, but in the 1870s they moved to the recently founded town of Texarkana, where Jiles Joplin began working for the railroad.

While in Texarkana, the younger Joplin learned how to play piano, partly through his own efforts on an instrument owned by one of his mother's employers and partly through lessons from a German music teacher, Julius Weiss. His parents, both of whom were talented musicians, encouraged the boy, and eventually the family acquired a used square piano for his use.

As a teenager Joplin began performing at various local events. After refusing to give up piano playing for more steady employment as a railroad laborer, he left Texarkana sometime in the 1880s and supported himself as an itinerant musician. Like many African American entertainers in the Mississippi Valley in this period, Joplin improvised music that combined elements of the western musical tradition—adopting such forms as the waltz, schottische, and the march—with melodies and rhythms derived from African American musical culture.

In 1893 Joplin made his way to Chicago to perform for the throngs who visited the World's Fair Columbian Exposition. Although he did not perform as part of the official program of the fair, Joplin, like other black entertainers, found work in the cafés that lined the Midway Plaisance—the entertainment center of the fair—as well as the city's tenderloin district.

While in Chicago Joplin formed his first band, which consisted of a cornet, a clarinet, a tuba, and a baritone horn, and began arranging music for the group to perform. At the fair he met Otis Saunders, with whom he traveled for a time and who eventually brought him to Missouri. The Columbian Exposition was not particularly congenial to African Americans, as it featured few exhibits pertaining to black life and culture: official literature offered insulting stereotypical depictions of African Americans, and none of the U.S. commissioners, committee members, guides, or guards were black. Nevertheless, Joplin and other African American musicians found that visitors to the fair clamored to hear their music. In the years following the World's Fair, Joplin found increasing numbers of opportunities to perform his music for white as well as black audiences.

In 1894 Joplin and Saunders arrived in Sedalia, Missouri, where both found work in various downtown businesses. As an important railhead, Sedalia had attracted a large number of workers, businessmen, and entertainers—both black and white—in the decades since its founding just before the Civil War. By the 1890s the bustling railhead offered a wide range of employment opportunities, from common labor in the Missouri-Kansas-Texas Railroad shops to service-oriented positions in the downtown hotels, saloons, barbershops, and restaurants. While many African Americans worked in jobs that required manual labor, men such as G. T. Ireland, W. H. Carter, Dailey Steele, Tony Williams, and R. O. Henderson enjoyed communitywide prominence as professionals, property owners, or entertainers, and they formed the core of leadership within the black community. When Joplin came to Sedalia, he became friends with many of these individuals, joined their Queen City Concert Band, and performed in clubs of which they were the proprietors.

For the first couple of years in Sedalia, Joplin and Saunders divided their time between playing regular engagements in town and taking their acts on the road. In 1895 Joplin placed two songs, "Please Say You Will" and "A Picture of Her Face," with publishers in Syracuse, New York, while on a tour with the Medley Quartette. The following year a publisher in Temple, Texas, issued his "Great Crush Collision March." These early compositions represented Joplin's efforts at this stage in his career to make a permanent record of his music, but they also betray his lack of compositional sophistication and offer no evidence of the peculiar syncopated rhythms that marked his later work.

In part to redeem his deficiencies as a composer, Joplin took the advice of Otis Saunders and Tony Williams and enrolled in music courses at the George R. Smith College for Negroes, which had opened in Sedalia in 1893. There he undoubtedly built upon the foundation of musical knowledge he had gained from his first music teacher in Texarkana and learned more about music theory and notation. By 1897 he had learned how to replicate in sheet music the complicated rhythms he and his friends had been improvising for many years. In addition to writing his own compositions, Joplin also began collaborating with two younger musicians, Arthur Marshall and Scott Hayden. Through Hayden he met Belle Jones, who eventually became his wife.

By 1899 Joplin enjoyed the respect and affection of musicians and leaders in Sedalia's black community as well as considerable fame as an entertainer in white society. His local celebrity gave way to national attention in 1899 after the publication of "Maple Leaf Rag," which featured the rollicking syncopation, octave chord progressions, and lively melody that would mark much of the rest of his music. According to one of Joplin's contemporaries, "Maple Leaf Rag" initiated a musical revolution. Although not the first to do so, he had succeeded in capturing on the printed page the ragged rhythm Americans had found increasingly appealing in the 1890s. The song took the country by storm, and not only propelled Joplin into the national spotlight but also set the standard for the ragtime compositions that followed. By

the dawn of the new century, Joplin was known as the "King of Ragtime Writers," an appellation invented by John Stark, the white music-store proprietor who had published "Maple Leaf Rag."

In 1900, because of the tremendous success of "Maple Leaf Rag," Stark moved his business from Sedalia to St. Louis, where he established himself as one of the most important publishers of piano rags. Within a year Joplin followed him to St. Louis, and eventually Hayden and Marshall joined their older friend. All had high hopes of penetrating a larger, more lucrative urban market with both compositions and performances. Their presence, along with firmly established clubs such as Tom Turpin's Rosebud Café, confirmed St. Louis's reputation as a center for ragtime music.

Within the first two years of moving to St. Louis, Joplin published nine new pieces, including "The Easy Winners" (1901), "Elite Syncopations" (1902), and "The Entertainer" (1902). This proliferation of popular piano compositions attracted critical attention to Joplin as a composer. In 1909 Alfred Ernst, the director of the St. Louis Choral Symphony, reported in the *St. Louis Post-Dispatch* that he considered Joplin a remarkable musician who had succeeded in melding African American and classical European elements into a unique musical form. Ernst called Joplin "an extraordinary genius as a composer of ragtime," but looked forward to the King of Ragtime Writers turning his considerable talent to the field of serious composition.

By the time the music critic Monroe Rosenfield hailed Joplin as the King of Ragtime in an article that appeared in the *St. Louis Globe-Democrat* in 1903, Joplin had published *A Ragtime Dance* (1902), an extensive and innovative ragtime ballet, and he had nearly completed an opera called *A Guest of Honor.* Like Ernst and Rosenfield, Joplin believed that ragtime was capable of invigorating serious composition and that he was capable of writing more ambitious works. He organized a drama company and held rehearsals for the opera in an East St. Louis theater in 1903. In spite of the praise lavished by Ernst and Rosenfield, however, Joplin had trouble securing financial backing for the production. According to Arthur Marshall, the opera was staged only once as little more than a dress rehearsal. Joplin may have issued some of the individual compositions as discrete works, but if so he never indicated which had come from *A Guest of Honor,* and the opera itself disappeared as a coherent work.

In addition to the ballet and opera, Joplin continued to write popular piano rags. Between 1903 and his departure from St. Louis in 1907, Joplin published more than a dozen ragtime marches, waltzes, and two-steps, including "The Cascades" (1904), which was written as a tribute to the fountain featured in the Louisiana Purchase Exposition held in St. Louis in 1904. Like many of the ragtime musicians in the city, Joplin performed on the Pike, the entertainment district of the World's Fair, even though the fair itself did little to welcome African American visitors. Like other black entertainers in the early twentieth century, Joplin felt profoundly the conflict between the popularity of his music and the disdain for his race displayed by white society. His decision to perform at the fair in spite of discrimination against blacks represented a common conviction among African American entertainers that performing the music of their race and generation was essential to undermining prejudice against their community.

As the years passed Joplin's early hopes for success and advancement gave way to discouragement. Financial backing for serious composition was ever hard to find. A number of musical publishers in addition to John Stark eagerly published his short pieces, but that popular acclaim did not translate into social advancement.

On a personal level as well, Joplin faced disappointments. Belle Joplin had never adjusted to the life of a musician's wife. In 1905 she gave birth to a child who lived only a few months, and afterward the tension between the Joplins intensified. In spite of efforts by Arthur Marshall and Scott Hayden to intercede with Belle Joplin on behalf of her husband, the couple parted, and it is believed that within a couple of years she died.

Joplin went to Chicago to visit former students and to spend time with Louis Chauvin, an old friend. Together they composed "Heliotrope Bouquet," which was published in 1907, but within eighteen months of Joplin's visit, Chauvin died from the effects of advanced syphilis.

Joplin seems to have foundered under the weight of these personal and professional difficulties. He produced little new work in 1906 and 1907. He wanted to leave St. Louis, but was not sure where to go. In late 1907 he decided to try his luck in New York City, one of the nation's most important musical centers. He began performing with Percy G. Williams's vaudeville show and made some tours as well. In 1908 and 1909 Joplin began once again to issue new work, notably, "Pine Apple Rag" (1908), "Euphonic Sounds" (1909), "Solace: A Mexican Serenade" (1909), and "Wall Street Rag" (1909).

Shortly after arriving in New York, Joplin met Lottie Stokes, whom he eventually married. They settled into a house where Joplin taught and worked on his own music while his wife ran a boardinghouse. The Joplins lived relatively close to John Stark's new office in the district known as Tin Pan Alley. Joplin continued to publish with Stark as well as with a number of other prominent New York publishers.

While in New York Joplin became an active member of the Colored Vaudevillian Benevolent Association (CVBA), an organization created to monitor and maintain the quality of vaudeville shows. His participation in the association brought him into contact with several prominent African American entertainers and the drama critic for the *New York Age,* **Lester Walton**. In 1912 Joplin was named to the executive committee of the CVBA and became one of its most active members.

Sometime in the early twentieth century, Joplin began working on a second opera, *Treemonisha.* Set on a plantation outside of Texarkana after the Civil War, the opera tells of a young black woman who helps to free her people from ignorance and superstition. Although they were humble working people, her parents offer their labor to a white woman in exchange for lessons for their daughter, and as time passes the girl helps her neighbors learn to read, to rely on their intelligence, and to abandon conjuring, superstition, and magic. A group of conjurers conspire to punish the girl, but one of her friends uses his wits to frighten them away and bring Treemonisha to safety. In the end, *Treemonisha* offered a celebration of literacy, learning, hard work, and community solidarity as the best formula for advancing the race.

Treemonisha incorporated syncopation in many of the songs, but it would be inaccurate to characterize it as a ragtime opera. Joplin insisted it featured "strictly Negro" music and was grand opera, not ragtime. By 1911, when Joplin completed this opera, many music critics had denounced ragtime as vulgar, insubstantial music. Joplin continued to believe that his syncopated compositions could contribute to an emerging American school of music, but he, too, had become scornful of ragtime lyrics that relied on lewd language. The one critic who commented on the opera in the *American Musician* thought Joplin had succeeded in incorporating the best of African American music into a serious opera and called *Treemonisha* "an interesting and potent achievement."

Like most of Joplin's other serious efforts in these years *Treemonisha* faced obstacles to production. He could find no financial backing. After agreeing to stage the opera in the fall of 1913, managers of the Lafayette Theater in Harlem sold their establishment to new owners who backed out of the agreement. Joplin eventually staged the opera in the Lincoln Theater in 1915, but because of his limited resources he could afford no costumes, props, or orchestral accompaniment. The opera failed utterly to attract any critical comment.

By 1915 Joplin, like his friend Louis Chauvin, began to display the terminal symptoms of advanced syphilis. His behavior became unfocused and erratic, and he lost physical dexterity. Having invested most of his money in *Treemonisha* and finding it increasingly difficult to complete projects, he and his wife moved to less expensive quarters and were forced to run a less-than-respectable boardinghouse. In February 1917 Lottie Joplin hospitalized her husband for dementia. On April 1, 1917, Scott Joplin died.

Although he was penniless and disappointed at the end of his life, Joplin set the standard for ragtime compositions and played a key role in developing a Missouri style of ragtime. As a pioneer composer and performer, he helped pave the way for young black artists to reach American audiences of both races.

SUSAN CURTIS

Blesh, Rudi, and Harriet Janis. *They All Played Ragtime: The True Story of an American Music.* New York: Norton, 1950.

Curtis, Susan. *Dancing to a Black Man's Tune: A Life of Scott Joplin.* Columbia: University of Missouri Press, 1994.

Gammond, Peter. *Scott Joplin and the Ragtime Era.* New York: St. Martin's, 1975.

Haskins, James, and Kathleen Benson. *Scott Joplin.* Garden City, N.Y.: Doubleday, 1978.

Jasen, David A., and Trebor Jay Tichenor. *Rags and Ragtime: A Musical History.* New York: Seabury Press, 1978.

Reed, W. Addison. "The Life and Works of Scott Joplin." Ph.D. diss., University of North Carolina, 1973.

JORDAN, LEON (1905–1970)

Leon Jordan became one of the most influential African Americans in Kansas City's history. A tavern keeper and politician, Jordan also taught, was a social worker, and served in the United States Army. He joined the Kansas City police force and received promotion to lieutenant before resigning. He and Bruce Watkins Jr. organized Freedom Inc., a black political organization that greatly influenced Kansas City and Missouri politics. Jordan won election to the Missouri House of Representatives in 1964 and served three terms. He received the Legion of Honor from France and the Black Star of Africa and the Knights of African Redemption from the Liberian government. He served a number of civic organizations in Kansas City. He held the office of president of Freedom Inc. at the time of his death.

A third-generation Kansas Citian, Jordan was born on May 6, 1905. He attended the segregated public schools of Kansas City, Washburn University in Topeka for a year, and graduated from Wilberforce University in Ohio. He later attended Howard University Law School. He taught in the Kansas City public schools and at Western Baptist College.

Jordan joined the United States Army and served in the Twenty-fourth Infantry before joining the Kansas City police force in 1936. Promoted to detective sergeant, he went to Liberia in 1947 under a leave of absence to organize that country's police force. A pilot, Jordan had his own plane as he traveled across Liberia, successfully establishing up-to-date police procedures and creating a national police force. He returned to Kansas City in February 1952 and received a promotion to lieutenant. However, he soon discovered that his new position carried little responsibility and resigned from the force. He spent another three years in Liberia working on police matters.

In August 1955 Jordan purchased the Green Duck Tavern in Kansas City. His political involvement secured his election as Democratic committeeman for the Fourteenth Ward in 1958. Three years later he and Watkins created Freedom Inc., which helped place Watkins on the city council and was instrumental in Jordan's election to the General Assembly in 1964.

More than six feet tall and weighing more than two hundred pounds, Jordan revealed his political muscle in the 1968 election. Warren Hearnes sought a second term as governor in that year, and Jordan and he quarreled. Jordan's heavily Democratic ward followed its leader in opposing Hearnes. Lawrence K. Roos, Hearnes's Republican opponent, received 3,196 votes to the incumbent's 1,035. In the same election, the Democratic candidate for U.S. senator, Thomas F. Eagleton, received 4,779 votes to his Republican opponent's 328. Leon Jordan controlled the votes in the Fourteenth Ward of Kansas City. In 1968 Democrats in the Fifth Congressional District elected Jordan as their chairman. He became the first African American in Missouri to hold that position in a congressional district.

At just past one on the morning of July 15, 1970, gunmen killed Jordan with three shotgun blasts as he left the Green Duck to go to his car. His death shocked Missouri's leading politicians. George Lehr, a white man and rising star in Missouri's Democratic Party, said of Jordan: "Politically, he was almost a father to me. I don't know what to say. There's no way I can communicate what a loss this is. He was the Martin Luther King of this community. The number of kids he sent through school—paid their way through, no one will ever know."

LAWRENCE O. CHRISTENSEN

Archives. Bruce Watkins Center, Kansas City, Mo.

Black Archives of Mid-America, Kansas City, Mo.

Greene, Lorenzo J., Gary R. Kremer, and Antonio F. Holland. *Missouri's Black Heritage, Revised Edition.* Columbia: University of Missouri Press, 1993.

Kansas City Star, July 15, 1970.

Official Manual of the State of Missouri, 1967–1968. Jefferson City: Secretary of State, 1968.

KAYSER, HENRY (1811–1884)

Henry Kayser was a key figure in the intertwined worlds of politics and public improvements in mid-nineteenth-century St. Louis. In his long tenure as the city engineer, he oversaw the challenge of improving the urban landscape to meet the needs of an exploding population, while recognizing the limits of a public treasury that grew at a far slower rate.

Born in 1811 near the city of Koblenz, in western Germany, Kayser was apprenticed to an architect at the age of seventeen. Four years later, under the spell of the writings of **Gottfried Duden,** he left Europe with a sister and brother (his brother, Alexander, became an influential land attorney and Democratic politician in St. Louis) for Missouri. Arriving in the area in June 1833, the Kaysers initially tried their hands at farming outside the city. By his own account, Henry proved unsuited for farm life, and moved to the city a year and a half later.

Kayser returned to his areas of professional expertise, establishing himself as a drafting instructor and preparing maps for the Bureau of Indian Affairs and the surveyor general of public lands. In 1838 he was appointed to assist Capt. Robert E. Lee of the Army Corps of Engineers; over the following three years, as Lee traveled back and forth from his home in Virginia, Kayser supervised his plans for a levee to close the channel between Bloody Island and the Illinois shore of the Mississippi River. The levee, when completed, helped ensure a deeper channel—and thereby encouraged commerce—along the St. Louis waterfront.

Concurrent with his work on the harbor, Kayser was appointed as the first city engineer. In this post, which he held from 1839 to 1857 (with the exception of the years 1850–1853 and 1855–1856), he oversaw some of the most visible and most problematic functions of municipal government: street construction and repair, water supply, sewerage, harbor maintenance, and public buildings construction. Despite his later professed intention "to keep the City as much as possible out of debt and rest its progress, by the exercise of economy upon its own resources," he was forced to confront the multiplying demands of a city expanding in both size and population.

The expansion of the city limits, first in 1841 and again in 1855, saw St. Louis's area mushroom from less than five to seventeen square miles. During the same period, the city's population grew from sixteen thousand to more than one hundred thousand. Faced with low legal limits on public debt, the engineer's office confronted the task of stretching municipal tax revenues to supply adequate streets, sewers, and drinking water across the city. Special laws mandating street improvements in the "New Limits" areas further drained funding needed to complete and repair impassable roadways in the denser center of the city. St. Louisans, however, were not inclined to forgive their public officials. Kayser, like others who served as city engineer, protested that the continually poor repair of the city's streets "must be ascribed to want of means, and not of attention and management on the part of this office." Insufficient funds and continuous expansion forced him to rely on cheaply quarried macadam pavement, a surface of crushed limestone that turned either to dust, in a dry spell, or to mud, after a day of rain.

In the matter of sewers, Kayser was similarly burdened by political and financial exigency. The sinkhole that stagnated at the intersection of Ninth and Biddle Streets (only the most offensive of dozens throughout the city) was known to St. Louisans as "Kayser's Pond" until he ventured to drain it through the simplest, most expedient method available: opening it from underneath. In the 1840s such simple solutions (as well as the use of streets themselves as rudimentary sewers) constituted Kayser's response to the drainage problem.

Finally, in 1849, the city's cholera epidemic spurred passage of a state act providing for a general sewer system for the city. The two principal sewers designed in the wake of the sewerage act, beneath Biddle Street and Poplar Street (the latter, the city's largest, drained the Mill Creek valley through a complex culvert that bypassed the meandering bed of the creek itself), were initiated by Kayser's successor, **Samuel Ryan Curtis,** in the early 1850s. Nevertheless, Kayser supervised subsequent work on the projects, and he was instrumental in designing the overall sewerage system.

Kayser's skills and political acumen kept him in demand for a variety of public duties. He applied his engineering expertise to expanding the city reservoir's capacity in the 1850s, and he served on the board that investigated the collapse of the Gasconade Bridge in 1855. He served two terms as a Democratic representative in the city council, from 1858 to 1862, then retired from public office to devote his attention to land speculation. He returned to city hall for two years as city comptroller, from 1871 to 1873, but was slowed by failing health, including the progressively profound deafness that plagued him from 1874. Kayser died in Hoboken, New Jersey, in 1884, on his return from a family trip to Europe.

ERIC SANDWEISS

German Engineers of Early St. Louis and Their Works. St. Louis, 1915.

Hyde, William, and Howard Conard, eds. *Encyclopedia of the History of St. Louis.* New York: Southern History, 1899.

"Letters of Robert E. Lee to Henry Kayser, 1838–1846." *Glimpses of the Past* 3 (January–February 1936): 1–44.

KEARNY, STEPHEN WATTS (1794–1848)

Stephen Watts Kearny was born on August 30, 1794, in Newark, New Jersey. He was the youngest child of a large and prosperous Tory family whose fortunes suffered only temporary setbacks during the Revolutionary War. Raised in comparative comfort, he attended Columbia University as a young man. Discovering an aptitude for military command in militia service, he won a lieutenant's commission in the U.S. infantry in March 1812. He distinguished himself in the Battle of Queenstown Heights in 1813, and was later promoted to captain.

Kearny's western career began in 1819, when he accompanied Col. Henry Atkinson's Yellowstone expedition. He served at various western posts from Fort Detroit to Baton Rouge, and led four infantry companies on Atkinson's second Yellowstone expedition in 1824–1825. Kearny's men began the construction of Jefferson Barracks near St. Louis in the summer of 1826. The new post became the army's command and supply depot for the entire Mississippi Valley.

Kearny's promotion to full major in 1829 was celebrated in St. Louis, where he had forged warm friendships among the city's leading families. In September 1830 he married **William Clark**'s stepdaughter Mary Radford, forming a union that withstood the rigors and enforced separations of frontier army life. The couple raised nine children.

In 1833 Congress authorized the organization of the First Regiment, U.S. Dragoons, with Col. **Henry Dodge** commanding. Kearny, now a lieutenant colonel, was named second in command, with extensive responsibilities for recruiting and training. When Dodge resigned in 1836, Kearny was promoted to colonel and assumed command of the regiment. The assignment was due in part to his St. Louis connections: his friend Sen. **Thomas Hart Benton**

led the fight for the new regiment. However, Kearny's promotion was also largely based on his reputation for efficiency, for the discipline, training, and morale of the soldiers in his command, and for his diplomatic skill and experience in dealing with Indians and frontier settlers.

Kearny was an early spokesman for the strategy of concentrating the army's limited manpower at a few permanent posts, from which mobile units might patrol roads and trouble spots. Creation of the First Dragoons, who would be stationed at Fort Leavenworth, Kansas, but would patrol a thousand miles of frontier, was a step in implementing the strategy, and Kearny was the logical choice as commander.

From 1837 to 1841 Kearny's dragoons patrolled the frontier, escorted displaced eastern Indians to their assigned lands in Indian Territory, and policed the Oregon and Santa Fe Trails. When they were not on duty in the field, Kearny kept the men busy at drill and training exercises, and made the First Dragoons the army's model unit. In 1837 he published the first training manual for U.S. dragoons. More than any other man Kearny was responsible for creating this new branch of the service, forerunner of the U.S. cavalry. He also assisted younger men, Philip St. George Cooke and Philip Kearny among them, in establishing military careers that would later be of great importance to the United States.

In 1842 Kearny assumed command of the Third Military Department, headquartered at St. Louis. In 1845 he led an expedition to South Pass along the Oregon Trail to patrol, show the flag, and treat with tribes along the route. His were the first U.S. troops to reach South Pass. He concluded his remarkable march with a long swing southward along the New Mexico border, to Arkansas Fort and Bent's Fort. The march conditioned his men to the rigors of desert campaigning, and provided crucial reconnaissance when war with Mexico commenced in 1846.

At the declaration of war with Mexico, Kearny was ordered to organize an expedition that would secure the Santa Fe Trail, seize New Mexico and establish a temporary government, and then continue west to conquer California. The federal government requested two thousand Missouri volunteers and authorized raising companies of Mormon volunteers from the parties then on their way west from Nauvoo, Illinois. Kearny had no trouble recruiting men. The war was a popular cause in Missouri; the idea of taking New Mexico and the Santa Fe trade, with California in the bargain, fired patriotic ardor. Kearny had useful connections with leading St. Louis families, and was widely respected as a brave and capable leader who looked after his men's welfare. Volunteers flocked to his banner.

The training, discipline, and spirit that Kearny drilled into his dragoons carried them through the grueling march to Santa Fe. The regulars provided a valuable example to the Missouri volunteers, disgruntled by the rigors of campaigning. Kearny's Army of the West walked the 856 miles to Santa Fe in less than two months. They encountered no serious resistance; the Mexican governor and his troops retreated without giving battle. The Americans entered Santa Fe on August 18, 1846.

For the next six months Kearny acted as the military governor of New Mexico. On his orders, four Missouri lawyers serving with the volunteers wrote a code of laws for the province, which Kearny proclaimed with a bill of rights on September 22, 1846. He was later reprimanded for an unconstitutional assumption of civil authority, though his orders seemed to require such action. The administration of conquered provinces was a new problem for a federal government not yet prepared to deal with the constitutional implications of Kearny's success. Nevertheless, the so-called Kearny Code remained the basis of New Mexican law when the territory was incorporated into the United States. Kearny remained at Santa Fe long enough to build Fort Marcy, further strengthening the American position. Then, having appointed Charles Bent as governor and **Frank Blair** as district attorney for the territory, he continued on to California to complete his mission.

Col. **Alexander W. Doniphan** and most of the volunteers were left behind to hold Santa Fe and Taos, with orders to join the American armies south of the Rio Grande when relieved by Col. **Sterling Price** and a fresh contingent of Missourians. Meanwhile, as Kearny and about three hundred men on mules blazed a trail to California, Lt. Col. Philip St. George Cooke and the Mormon battalion followed, cutting a wagon road through the rugged desert country: Kearny intended to create the necessary support system to secure his conquest.

En route to California, Kearny's command intercepted dispatches from Commo. Robert Stockton of the United States Navy, announcing that he had landed with marines and pacified California. Now assured that his route lay open, and already encountering difficulty in finding sufficient food and water for men and animals, Kearny again split his command, sending all back to Santa Fe except for a guard of 110 men and two mountain howitzers. As they approached California the exhausted Americans learned that Stockton's assurance had been premature, that the Californians had rallied against him, and that the war was on again.

In early December Kearny's command encountered an enemy force directly in their path. The Americans were badly outnumbered, but they desperately needed the fresh mounts and supplies in the Californians' camp. Counting on the element of surprise to provide a quick victory and a much needed boost of morale for his men, Kearny attacked. In this Battle of San Pasqual, on December 6–7, 1846, the Americans held the field, but more than one-third of the command was killed or wounded, and Kearny himself was seriously wounded by enemy lances.

Kearny's battered force struggled to join Stockton's men at Monterey. The two officers led a joint expedition in January 1847, and dispersed the Californians at the Battle of the Mesa on the San Gabriel on January 9. When they disagreed on further action, however, Kearny demanded Stockton recognize his authority; Stockton refused. Lt. Col. **John Charles Frémont,** who had previously entered northern California with a small force and joined in the Bear Flag Revolt in June 1846, sided with Stockton. New orders arrived from Washington in February, clearly sustaining Kearny's authority. For the next three months he acted as military governor of California, consolidating the American position and establishing a temporary government. He returned to the United States in the summer of 1847.

Frémont's continued defiance forced the general to take action against the young officer, despite his regard for the family, particularly Frémont's father-in-law and Kearny's friend, Thomas Hart Benton. After a long and bitter court-martial, Frémont was found guilty of all charges and sentenced to dismissal from the army. Although President Polk restored him to duty, Frémont resigned rather than accept the verdict. He and his powerful father-in-law launched a relentless vendetta to discredit Kearny.

Meanwhile, Kearny was sent to Mexico to assist in concluding military operations. He arrived in April 1848, as military governor of the key port city of Veracruz. Almost immediately he became sick with malaria, and never fully regained his health. He managed to serve competently as military governor of Mexico City in May and June, supervising the final evacuation of U.S. troops.

Kearny returned to the United States in July, and resumed command of the Sixth Military District, headquartered at Jefferson Barracks. On September 7, 1848, he was appointed brevet major general, despite Benton's vigorous opposition, but the victory was hollow. Worn out by years of hard campaigning, he could not withstand the ravages of the fever contracted in Mexico. Kearny died on October 31, 1848, at the country house of his old friend **Meriwether Lewis Clark,** near St. Louis. His enemies, Benton and Frémont, survived to have the last word, obscuring the contributions of a dedicated soldier.

With his dragoon regiment, Kearny helped shape the army of the trans-Mississippi West. More than any other individual, he was responsible for securing the Southwest for the United States in 1846–1847. Contemporary Missourians remembered him as a brave and efficient soldier who for years stood guard over their western border.

MARY ELLEN ROWE

Bauer, K. Jack. *The Mexican War, 1846–1848.* Lincoln: University of Nebraska Press, 1992.

Clarke, Dwight L. *Stephen Watts Kearny: Soldier of the West.* Norman: University of Oklahoma Press, 1961.

Harlow, Neal. *California Conquered: The Annexation of a Mexican Province.* Berkeley and Los Angeles: University of California Press, 1982.

KECKLEY, ELIZABETH (1818?–1907)

Elizabeth Keckley is best known for her 1868 memoir, *Behind the Scenes; or, Thirty Years a Slave and Four Years in the White House,* published by G. W. Carlton of New York. A seamstress, Keckley served as Mary Todd Lincoln's personal dress designer, nurse, and confidante during the difficult war years and following President Lincoln's assassination. In her memoir Keckley revealed some of the intimate details of life in the White House as well as the details of the "Old Clothes Scandal," the result of Mary Todd Lincoln's 1867 attempt to sell part of her wardrobe to relieve herself of debt.

Although Keckley claimed to have written *Behind the Scenes* to aid Lincoln—and promised to donate the book's profits to her upkeep—many considered the book an exposé of the former first lady, particularly as it contained an appendix of personal letters from Lincoln, which Keckley's editor, James Redpath, probably included without her permission. The backlash against the memoir was swift. Robert Lincoln convinced the publisher to suppress Keckley's book but could not stop the publication of a cruel parody: *Behind the Seams, by a Nigger Woman Who Took in Work from Mrs. Lincoln and Mrs. Davis.* Mary Todd Lincoln broke her connection with Keckley, and Keckley's business failed as she lost many of her dressmaking clients and friends in the wake of the controversy.

Originally read primarily for its revelations about the former president's family, today *Behind the Scenes* is read as the memoir of a remarkable black woman. Keckley was born a slave on the Burwell plantation in Dinwiddie, Virginia, in approximately 1818 to slaves Agnes Hobbs, a seamstress, and George Pleasant, a literate man whose master took him west when Elizabeth was a child.

Keckley learned to sew by helping her mother, who made the clothes for the seventy slaves on the Burwell plantation as well as for the twelve members of the Burwell family. At fourteen Elizabeth Keckley went to work as the only servant of her master's eldest son, a Presbyterian minister, who brought her to Hillsboro, North Carolina. A determined woman, she fought back when a local schoolteacher and then her master beat her. Eventually, both men repented their efforts to subdue her spirit. She was less successful at resisting the sexual advances of a white neighbor, Alexander Kirkland, who "persecuted me for four years" and by whom she became pregnant with her only child, George Kirkland.

Keckley escaped her sexual enslavement when she joined the household of another of the Burwell children, Ann Burwell Garland. To serve the Garlands, she moved first to Virginia and then to St. Louis, where Ann Garland's husband had gone to try, unsuccessfully, to improve his fortune. With the Garland family in financial distress, Keckley "kept bread in the mouths of seventeen persons for two years and five months" through her work as a seamstress. During this time she married fellow slave James Keckley, who had misrepresented himself to her as a free man. Their marriage, which lasted eight years, was not happy.

Determined to secure freedom for herself and her son, Keckley arranged to purchase their freedom for twelve hundred dollars. However, she was unable to save such a sum, as all her income went to support her owners. Eventually, she borrowed the money from her wealthy clients, and she and her son were freed on November 15, 1855.

Keckley remained in St. Louis until 1860, by which time she had repaid her benefactors. Once relieved of that obligation, she moved to Washington, D.C., sending her son to Wilberforce University in Xenia, Ohio. He soon left Wilberforce to join the Union army, enlisting as a white man in the First Regiment of Missouri; he died in the Battle of Wilson's Creek, in Springfield, Missouri, on August 10, 1861.

As a free woman in Washington, D.C., Keckley proved herself a capable businesswoman. She established a dressmaking business and eventually employed twenty seamstresses. A prominent member of the Washington, D.C., African American community, Keckley involved herself in charity work on behalf of her race. She founded the Contraband Relief Association in 1862, helped found the National Association for the Relief of Destitute Women and Children, and was a liberal contributor to the Fifteenth Street Presbyterian Church. She briefly taught domestic art at Wilberforce University in the 1890s, but she lived out the end of her life in Washington, in the Home for Destitute Women and Children.

Her business ruined by the scandal surrounding the publication of *Behind the Scenes,* Keckley paid her room and board from the small pension she received from the War Department after the death of her son. She died of a stroke on May 24, 1907, and was buried in the Harmony Cemetery in Washington, D.C. Although her acquaintances remembered her as a woman of culture and refinement, Keckley had faded from prominence by the time of her death.

MARTHA KOHL

Andrews, William L. "The Changing Moral Discourse of Nineteenth-Century African American Woman's Autobiography: Harriet Jacobs and Elizabeth Keckley." In *Decolonizing the Subject: The Politics of Gender in Woman's Autobiography,* ed. Sidonie Smith and Julia Watson. Minneapolis: University of Minnesota Press, 1992.

Foster, Frances Smith. "Autobiography after Emancipation: The Example of Elizabeth Keckley." In *Multicultural Autobiography: American Lives,* ed. James Robert Payne. Knoxville: University of Tennessee Press, 1992.

Keckley, Elizabeth. *Behind the Scenes; or, Thirty Years a Slave and Four Years in the White House.* New York: Oxford University Press, 1988.

"Modiste Elizabeth Keckley: From Slavery to the White House." Exhibition at the Black Fashion Museum, New York, n.d.

KEEMLE, CHARLES (1800–1865)

"Colonel" Charles Keemle (the title was honorific, dating from a stint as a fur trader and frontiersman in the 1820s) was by any standard one of the most colorful and most influential figures in the public life of St. Louis in the first half of the nineteenth century. As a journalist he had a hand in the editing, printing, or management of nine newspapers, including the *Reveille* from 1845 to 1850, the most important literary journal of the antebellum frontier. As a businessman, he operated the city's most successful printing firm. As a patron of the arts, he nurtured friendships and business relationships with writers and theatrical artists, and financed the building of St. Louis's first important theater. As a public official, he served the city as recorder of deeds, having turned down more prestigious appointments at the state and federal levels.

Keemle was born in Philadelphia in October 1800, the son of a ship's captain. The family was living in Norfolk, Virginia, when his mother died in 1806. Taken in by an uncle, Keemle was apprenticed on the *Norfolk Herald;* at sixteen, he traveled west by foot and flatboat to start a new journal, the *Indiana Sentinel,* in Vincennes.

Keemle's tenure there was brief. In August 1817 he arrived in St. Louis to work on the second paper west of the Mississippi, the *Emigrant.* That paper became the *St. Louis Enquirer,* edited by **Thomas Hart Benton,** whom Keemle served diligently for three years, making a powerful ally in the process.

In 1820 Keemle accepted a position as a clerk with the American Fur Company, and spent the winter trading with the Kansas tribe. In 1821 he traveled with a large party to the base of the Rocky Mountains, in the territory of the Crow tribe, where he spent three years as an agent and clerk. His work was successful, though not without adventure. Accounts of a skirmish involving his band of adventurers and members of the Blackfeet tribe vary, but suggest that Keemle's leadership and pluck were instrumental in avoiding the loss of most of his men.

By 1825 Keemle was back in St. Louis, where he established the printing house that made his fortune. Over the next seven years he was involved in the founding or the operation of several newspapers, most of them partisan organs for the Democratic Party of Senator Benton. Keemle and Benton eventually parted company over the issue of slavery, but for more than twenty years they enjoyed a close and mutually beneficial association.

In the 1830s Keemle made the acquaintance of both Joseph M. Field, a writer and journalist, and the actor and theatrical manager **Noah Miller Ludlow.** Keemle contributed heavily to the thirty-thousand-dollar cost of building Ludlow's New St. Louis Theater in 1837, and even acted in a benefit performance. In the late 1830s, he married Mary Oliver, the daughter of a prominent Philadelphia family. Their friendship with the Ludlows, the Fields, and writer and actor **Solomon Franklin Smith** ripened into a lifelong affection. Joseph Field was married in the Keemle's parlor, and Keemle was godfather to Field's daughter, **Mary Katherine Keemle Field,** who, as Kate Field, became one of the most widely celebrated writers and platform lecturers of the nineteenth century.

In 1838 Keemle entered into a partnership with **Alphonso Wetmore** and his son Leonidas to publish the first literary weekly in St. Louis, the *Missouri Saturday News.* This ephemeral journal lasted only a year, but was of great significance in the development of the short story as a literary form. Five years later, Keemle began a similar but more successful venture, the *Reveille,* with Joseph Field and his brother Matthew Field, a widely known poet and travel writer. The paper quickly earned a national reputation; during its five years of existence, its contributors included William Cullen Bryant, John S. Robb, Sol Smith, and Joe Miller.

The *Reveille* was Keemle's last and greatest contribution to the literary and journalistic history of St. Louis. He had been sought as a candidate for public office, but refused all offers, including a nomination to run for mayor, an appointment as secretary of state of Missouri, and a post as Indian agent for the Platte River district. In 1853 he accepted the relatively undemanding position of recorder of deeds for St. Louis County, which he held until 1861. Thereafter, he lived in quiet retirement with his wife and three daughters in their home in Compton Heights until his death on September 28, 1865.

Robert C. Boyd

Edwards, Richard, and M. Hopewell. *Edwards's Great West.* St. Louis: Edwards's Monthly, 1860.
Scharf, J. Thomas. *History of St. Louis City and County: From Earliest Periods to the Present Day.* Philadelphia: Everts, 1883.

KEIL, WILLIAM (1811?–1877)

William Keil was born on March 6, 1811, or 1812, in Bleicherode, Erfurt, Prussia. His education was undoubtedly rudimentary. He served an apprenticeship as a tailor at Kolleda, Merseburg, Prussia, where he married Louisa Reiter. During his youth he apparently became involved with unconventional religion and medicine, attending illegal pietistic conventicles and practicing folk healing. Most sources claim he was influenced by the ideas of mystic Jakob Boehme (1575–1624) and alchemist and physician Paracelsus (1493–1541); because of his minimal education, however, Keil's knowledge of their work was surely limited.

A journeyman tailor, Keil arrived with his wife in New York City in 1835 or 1836. He soon moved west to Pittsburgh where he continued to dabble in mysticism and folk medicine and where he assumed the title of "Doctor." In 1838 he was converted to Methodism by Wilhelm Nast, the founder of the German Methodist movement. Keil worked for a time as a Methodist class leader and preacher but ultimately renounced organized religion, and founded a cult.

Keil's reputation as a charismatic preacher spread throughout western Pennsylvania and into surrounding regions. In the early 1840s a group of schismatic Harmonists—disaffected followers of German utopian George Rapp—became attracted to Keil's message and almost certainly contributed to plans to establish a Keilite religious utopia in the American West. In early 1844 three "spies" entered the wilderness and found a 2,500-acre location on the North River in Shelby County, Missouri, suitable for their purposes. That fall Keil, his family, and a small group of faithful arrived at the site of Bethel; in the spring of 1845 large numbers of colonists followed. Within a few years Bethel's population had climbed to more than six hundred.

Helping Keil gather followers and disseminate an increasingly apocalyptic message were several lay exhorters, among them Carl Koch, who left a memoir. Initially a loyal supporter, Koch reveals growing dismay as Keil identified himself first as a prophet and finally as an incarnation of Christ. Referring to himself as the *Centralsonne* (Central Sun) and to his flock as *Lichtfursten* and *Lichtfurstinnen* (princes and princesses of light), Keil came to promote "self-deification" and the deification of his family. Indeed, his birthday became a major colony holiday along with Easter, Pentecost, Harvestfest, and Christmas.

Koch eventually left the fold, but most other followers appeared satisfied with their patriarchal leader and their lives in Bethel. Keil's avowed purpose was to return his flock to the communal ways of the primitive Christian church in order to prepare for the final days. Although a few residents pursued private enterprise, the majority surrendered all assets to a common treasury. Colonists satisfied their needs from a communal warehouse; as children attended school, parents worked in small commonly owned workshops or in the fields and pastures. Yet, equality extended only so far. While each family received a modest home, members built a mansion for the Keils. Although he was the father of eight or nine children, Keil frequently recommended celibacy for members of his flock. By all accounts he ruled with the firm hand of an autocrat.

With Bethel thriving, Keil began to experiment with satellite colonies in the surrounding area. He established the settlements Hebron, Elim, and Mamri nearby; in 1850 twenty-five Bethelites founded Nineveh (now Connelsville) in Adair County, constructing a second residence to accommodate the doctor during visits.

By 1854, however, Keil seemed concerned that the outside world was contaminating his colonies. Evidence suggests he may also have been losing his grip as autocrat. Again "spies" went west to seek greater isolation, selecting Washington's Willapa Valley as the location for a new colony. Ironically, when Keil arrived in 1855, he deemed the site unsuitable because "there is no market for the things produced; . . . no prospect for the development of such market; [and] no way by which one can earn his livelihood." Moving on, he found the less remote Willamette Valley in Oregon a more amenable location for the new colony, Aurora.

Several wagon trains from Missouri proceeded to Oregon during the 1850s and 1860s, but Bethel and Nineveh remained viable, if deteriorating, communities despite the loss of population. Keil attempted—with mixed results—to maintain autocratic hold on both his eastern and his western settlements. While the Oregon experiment flourished for a time, none of Keil's utopias survived his death in Aurora on December 30, 1877. Two years later the colonies formally disbanded, and the remaining residents divided up the properties.

Carol Heming

Bek, William G. "A German Communistic Society in Missouri." *Missouri Historical Review* 3 (1908–1909): 52–74, 99–125.

Grant, H. Roger. "Missouri's Utopian Communities." *Missouri Historical Review* 66 (1971–1972): 23–31.

———. "The Society of Bethel: A Visitor's Account." *Missouri Historical Review* 68 (1973–1974): 223–31.

Heming, Carol Piper. " 'Temples Stand, Temples Fall': The Utopian Vision of Wilhelm Keil." *Missouri Historical Review* 85 (October 1990): 21–39.

Hendricks, Robert J. *Bethel and Aurora: An Experiment in Communism and Practical Christianity.* New York: Press of the Pioneers, 1933.

Koch, Carl G. *Lebenserfahrungen.* Cleveland: Verlagshaus der Evangelischen Geneinschaft, 1871.

KELLY, EMMETT LEO (1898–1979)

Contrast is the word that best describes the key to Emmett Leo Kelly's success as the modern American clown Weary Willie. The early American clown world involved groomed characters wearing starched shirts and white face paint, while performing highly active skits. Weary Willie, the famous hobo clown developed by Emmett Kelly, appeared shabbily dressed, withdrawn, depressed, and paralyzed by bad luck and depression. Moving as if in slow motion, Kelly's character when performing the simplest of tasks evoked roaring laughter from the audience.

In the 1930s, when Kelly began promoting his hobo clown character, the depression had sent a new wave of tramps and hoboes hitchhiking and hopping freight trains across the United States. Eventually, almost every circus had at least one hobo clown. Kelly's unique character, Weary Willie, came to stand for all hoboes "in the popular imagination and indeed, the clown who would come to stand for all modern clowns."

Emmett was born on December 9, 1898, to Thomas Kelly, a railroad worker, and Mollie Schimick Kelly in Sedan, Kansas. His family moved to Houston, Missouri, when he was four. Kelly called Houston home, and the town annually celebrates its favorite son with "Emmett Kelly Days."

By following Kelly's life the evolution of the outcast, depressed character of Weary Willie becomes clear. He first tried to earn a living as a cartoonist in Kansas City in 1917. His attempt was unsuccessful, but one of his cartoon characters was a sad-faced hobo called Weary Willie.

Always attracted to the vagabond circus environment, during the 1920s and 1930s Kelly earned a living by performing odd jobs, usually as a trapeze artist, with a variety of circuses. During a stint with the Hagenbeck-Wallace Circus, he gradually developed the makeup for the character of Weary Willie and brought him to life in the arena.

After touring with several circuses in the 1930s and performing in nightclubs during World War II, Kelly joined the Ringling Brothers and Barnum and Bailey Circus in 1942. During his fifteen-year relationship with that circus, the character of Weary Willie became fully developed, and Kelly became a star attraction.

In 1957 a labor dispute caused Kelly to leave Ringling Brothers and move to another entertainment arena. He was hired by the Brooklyn Dodgers to entertain the crowds prior to games at Ebbets Field. The following year he performed the same routine for the St. Louis Hawks basketball team.

During the 1950s Kelly brought his act to film and television. He appeared in several films, including *The Greatest Show on Earth, The Fat Man,* and *Wind across the Everglades.* Television appearances were plentiful, and included the *Jackie Gleason Show, Captain Kangaroo,* the *Ed Sullivan Show,* and *Person to Person.* He also filmed the *Emmett Kelly Show,* a television series.

Kelly married Eva More on July 23, 1923, a union that produced two sons, Emmett and Thomas Patrick. Circus life and traveling caused difficulties in the marriage, which eventually ended in divorce. On April 20, 1954, Kelly married Elvira Gebhardt. To this marriage two daughters were born, Stasia and Monika.

Kelly confessed that his family experiences contributed significantly to his professional development as a clown. In his autobiography, *Clown,* he explained how he first began to understand and enter into the character of Weary Willie. During a bout of depression around 1935, when his first marriage was ending, Kelly believed that he and his character became indistinguishable.

Kelly worked as a clown until his death on March 28, 1979.

DONNA K. COGELL

Ballantine, Bill. *Clown Alley.* Boston: Little, Brown, 1982.

The Cambridge Dictionary of American Biography. S.v. "Kelly, Emmett Leo."

Kelly, Emmett, and Beverly F. Kelly. *Clown.* New York: Prentice Hall, 1954.

Kelly, Francis Beverly. "The Land of Sawdust and Spangles." *National Geographic Magazine* (October 1931): 463–516.

Webster's American Biographies. S.v. "Kelly, Emmett Leo."

Who Was Who in America. Vol. 2. London: George Prior Associates, 1981.

KEM, JAMES PRESTON (1890–1965)

Known for his conservatism, his isolationist philosophies, and his consistent opposition to the policies of fellow Missourian **Harry S. Truman,** James Preston Kem won election to the United States Senate in 1946 by riding the wave of discontent surrounding the Democratic Party and the Truman presidency. A prosperous Kansas City lawyer, he returned to his lucrative private practice six years later after losing reelection to Democrat **William Stuart Symington.**

Born in Macon, Missouri, on April 2, 1890, Kem attended Blees Military Academy, graduated from the University of Missouri in 1910, and received his law degree from Harvard University in 1913. After passing the Missouri bar, he began what would become a prosperous career in law as a junior lawyer in Kansas City. In 1917 he entered the armed services and remained in the United States Army infantry for two years during World War I. In 1920, a year after leaving the service, he married Mary Elizabeth Carroll of Bullit County, Kentucky.

Undoubtedly, Kem's success as a corporate lawyer provided him with the visibility and respect that allowed him to step into the political arena. In 1943, the same year he served as president of the Lawyers Association of Kansas City, he chaired the Jackson County Republican Committee. The following year he served as delegate to the Republican National Convention, evidence of his growing support in the Kansas City area. As the 1946 election drew near, widespread displeasure with Truman's performance as president as well as the expansion of the federal government and the growing influence of organized labor caused a large number of Democratic voters to absent themselves from the polls, allowing the Republicans to increase their numbers in Congress. Kem defeated **Frank Parks Briggs,** also of Macon, who was an associate and supporter of President Truman, to win his first and only term in the United States Senate.

While in office Kem proved an across-the-board opponent of Truman and his policies. He accused Truman of political corruptibility, charging him with having ties to the Kansas City underworld, namely the **Thomas J. Pendergast** machine. Kem prompted the Kefauver Committee, a group established by Congress to investigate organized crime, to visit Kansas City. The committee uncovered evidence that suggested an ongoing relationship between Missouri politicians and the multimillion-dollar gambling industry in Kansas City. These findings and their publication contradicted the image of Kansas City as the "Heart of America" and in turn damaged the reputations of Missouri and Harry Truman.

During his term in the Senate, Kem clashed with Truman and the Democratic Party over foreign policy and the extent of the federal government's participation in domestic affairs. On June 27, 1950, Kem questioned President Truman's order to send American troops to Korea, asking if the president had "arrogated to himself the authority to declare war." He accumulated a record as one of the two lowest-ranking supporters of the administration's foreign policy in terms of senatorial roll-call votes with a support rate of 3 percent. One of thirteen senators who voted against the creation of the North Atlantic Treaty Organization, Kem called the program "a sinkhole for untold billions of the money of American taxpayers." As a consistent critic of foreign aid programs, he attempted to ban aid to countries that traded with communist regimes and proposed that countries receiving aid from the United States be required to send written acknowledgment of compliance.

With respect to domestic policy, Kem favored limited government activity. He opposed legislation supporting public housing programs and federal aid to education. He also opposed the creation of the Missouri Valley Authority. At a time when Missouri received federal funding for flood control as well as farm subsidy programs, Kem's stance on these issues likely led to his election loss in 1952. Running on a strong Democratic ticket, Symington defeated Kem by a large margin. Kem's mudslinging and other McCarthy-like tactics, and his constituents' shifting opinions concerning the political issues of the day, contributed to his demise.

After stepping down, Kem moved his law practice to Washington, D.C., and continued his career until 1957. After retirement he resided in Virginia. In July 1964 an auto accident left him injured. On February 24, 1965, a weakened James P. Kem died in the University of Virginia Hospital after a long illness stemming from those injuries.

Erika K. Nelson

Biographical Directory of the American Congress, 1774–1971. S.v. "Kem, James P." Washington, D.C.: U.S. Government Printing Office, 1971.

Congressional Directory, 82nd Congress, Second Session. Washington, D.C.: U.S. Government Printing Office, 1971.

Dillard, Irving. "Farewell to Mr. Kem." *New Republic* (October 27, 1952): 16–17.

Kem, James P. Papers. Western Historical Manuscripts Collection, Columbia.

Kirkendall, Richard S. *A History of Missouri: Volume V, 1919 to 1953.* Columbia: University of Missouri Press, 1986.

Official Manual of the State of Missouri, 1947–1948. Jefferson City: Secretary of State, 1948.

KEMPER, FREDERICK T. (1816–1881)

Frederick Thomas Kemper was an educator and the founder of Kemper Military School and College. Born at Madison Courthouse, Virginia, to William and Maria E. Allison Kemper on October 12, 1816, Kemper received his early education at home. In 1836 he went to Marion College in Palmyra, Missouri, from which he graduated in 1841. He then taught there for three years. In Philadelphia, Missouri, he tried to set up a school, before moving to Boonville in 1844.

On June 3, 1844, Frederick Kemper opened a school, the New Boonville Male Academy. The school began with only five students but quickly grew to thirty-three by the end of the first session. The *Boonville Observer* noted on November 5, 1844, that "Mr. Kemper is said to be (and we doubt not, is) a thorough scholar, his capacities for teaching are of a high order and we hope he will meet with a liberal patronage." One of his students noted: "[H]is studies were of quite an extensive sweep. . . . He was not, however, in any department a specialist." The second session saw enrollment reach sixty-five, and the school began a series of name changes that ended in 1854 when it became the Kemper Family School. According to Kemper he was drawing students from throughout the state, generally from wealthy families.

On July 17, 1854, Kemper married Susan Holten Taylor with whom he had eleven children. In the fall of 1856 Kemper sold the school and accepted a position at Westminster College in Fulton, where he would stay for the next five years. He held the chair of physical science and managed administrative duties for the school in the absence of President Samuel Laws. He eventually became the professor of Greek. The departure of President Laws and the crisis of the Civil War led Kemper to leave Fulton and return to Boonville in 1861.

On September 16, 1861, Kemper reopened his school in Boonville, but he realized the need to become more than a boarding school during the war. The school reopened with about 70 students, including girls, most of whom were day students, but enrollment reached 135 in 1862–1863. The school developed three divisions: the Primary School (which focused on spelling, writing, math, geography, and penmanship), the Grammar School (in which students were taught English, Latin, and Greek), and the Collegiate School (which offered college preparatory work).

Kemper was an advocate of strict family discipline and Christian morals. As an early memorialist described him, he "sought to be an earnest, intelligent, useful, cheerful Christian . . . because of the important souls intrusted to his care." A former student, L. M. Lawson, said of Kemper: "I know but few men in any position in life so thoroughly imbued with the importance of his calling, and so earnestly devoted to his profession. . . . His students show that he does good work."

In 1864 the Primary School was eliminated, the beginning of a number of changes. Kemper decided to reduce the size of the school in order to give it more of a family atmosphere. He limited enrollment to only a dozen boarding students and less than forty day students. With the opening of a public school in Boonville in 1867, Kemper returned to his original concept of a boarding school, and by the 1871–1872 school year he had accomplished that goal. By 1872 the outline of a military-type discipline was beginning to appear, and in 1873–1874 the school adopted a cadet-gray uniform, similar to the ones at West Point. The school grew not only in enrollment but also in physical size. Kemper bought three lots in 1866 to add to his holdings and in 1876–1877 purchased thirty additional acres.

On March 9, 1881, Frederick Kemper died at his school after a short illness. The next day a large number of local citizens turned out to mourn his passing. As emblazoned on a plaque on the front door of the Kemper Military School and College, he had successfully built an institution that does "not make mere scholars but men."

DONALD E. HEIDENREICH JR.

Quarles, James Addison. *The Life of Prof. F. T. Kemper A.M., a Christian Educator.* New York: Burr Printing, 1884.

KEMPER, RUFUS CROSBY, SR. (1892–1972)

Onetime grain company executive and longtime banker in Kansas City, Rufus Crosby Kemper Sr. transformed a tiny, struggling bank into a regional power. Born on February 23, 1892, in Valley Falls, Kansas, Kemper pursued a career that his grandfather, Rufus Crosby, had followed. His father, **William T. Kemper,** also entered banking by becoming cashier for the bank owned by Crosby and married the boss's daughter.

One year after Rufus Crosby Kemper's birth, the Kemper family moved to Kansas City, Missouri, where W. T. Kemper invested in grain companies and the mercantile business. Unlike his father, who was already a shoe salesman when many boys were finishing high school, Crosby Kemper graduated from Kansas City's Central High School and the University of Missouri. He attended the Wharton School of Finance at the University of Pennsylvania for one year.

Returning to Kansas City in 1915, Kemper worked briefly in his father's Commerce Trust Bank.

In 1916 he moved to Kemper Mill and Elevator Company (essentially a grain trading company owned by his father) and intended to build a career in that field. World War I intervened, however, and Kemper served in a supply division in France. During his absence, W. T. Kemper sold the grain business because of the death of the manager. Upon his return Crosby Kemper found that his former position had disappeared. Although W. T. Kemper headed Commerce Trust, Crosby's older brother, James, was being groomed for leadership there.

Kemper borrowed twenty-five thousand dollars and purchased 20 percent of the stock in the City Center Bank in Kansas City, Missouri, and assumed control of its management. Changing the name to City National Bank and Trust, and moving it from a downtown location to a new building well south, Kemper established a degree of independence from Commerce Trust.

City Bank weathered the "runs" of the early depression, though deposits fell from $10 million in 1929 to $4 million in 1933. Kemper later claimed that the bank met all demands for deposits without borrowing any money from the Federal Reserve. Other large Kansas City banks, such as Fidelity Trust, were not able to and had to close their doors.

At the time of W. T. Kemper's death in 1938, Crosby Kemper was vice chairman of the Commerce Trust board of directors while James Kemper served as president. However, federal banking regulations that took effect in 1939 prohibited Crosby from holding official positions with both City National and Commerce Trust. Thus, he resigned from Commerce Trust and concentrated on the growth of City National Bank.

Kemper engaged in several endeavors in addition to banking. He led a group of investors who successfully returned control of Kansas City Southern Railway to local management. Much later in life he led an effort that brought the headquarters of United Utilities to the Kansas City region. The company later renamed itself United Telecommunications and then Sprint Inc. At the time, Kemper served as board chairman for United Utilities. He and company management successfully fended off takeover bids by both General Telephone and International Telephone and Telegraph, because either would have removed the company headquarters from Kansas City.

Kemper held directorship in many Kansas City businesses such as Business Men's Assurance, Kansas City Life, Kansas City Southern, and Kansas City Fire and Marine Insurance. His civic interests included the American Royal, which resulted in his family's donation of a sizable sum for the construction of Kemper Arena, primarily as the principal site for the livestock show. He also served on the board of regents for Rockhurst College.

Kemper died on October 24, 1972, in Kansas City after a brief period of heart problems.

WILLIAM S. WORLEY

Fowler, Dick. *Leaders in Our Town.* Kansas City: Burd and Fletcher, 1952.

Kemper, William T. Clipping File. Missouri Valley Room, Kansas City Public Library, Kansas City.

Schondelmeyer, Brent. *Building a First-Class Bank: The Story of United Missouri Bank.* Kansas City: United Missouri Bancshares, 1986.

KEMPER, WILLIAM T. (1866–1938)

Progenitor of two of Missouri's most prominent banking families, William T. Kemper also headed companies involved in grain and railroad transportation. Born on November 3, 1866, in Gallatin, Missouri, he retained a Kentucky heritage from both his parents. He once referred to his family as "old-time Rebels."

Kemper's entry into the business world came as a salesman for Noyes, Norman, and Kemper, a St. Joseph company in which his father held part interest. His introduction into banking came in Valley Falls, Kansas, where he had already established a mercantile business before he was twenty-one years of age. Marrying the bank owner's daughter, he also assumed the position of cashier for the Valley Falls Bank of Deposit. His father-in-law, Rufus Crosby, also served as a cattle rancher and merchant in the northeast Kansas community.

Kemper and his young bride sold their interest in the Valley Falls mercantile and bank in the depression year of 1893, and moved to Kansas City, Missouri. Kemper organized the Kemper Mill and Elevator Company, the Kemper Investment Company, and the Kemper Mercantile Company with sale profits from Valley Falls. By 1900 he served as the youngest elected president of the Kansas City Board of Trade.

Kemper involved himself in politics during this period as well. Selected as one of three Kansas City police commissioners in 1902, he attempted to succeed his fellow commissioner **James A. Reed** as mayor in 1904 on the Democratic ticket. Kemper allied himself with alderman **Jim Pendergast**'s Democratic faction. They were defeated by the **Joseph B. Shannon** Democrats, who in turn lost to the Republicans in the general election of 1904. Kemper also ran unsuccessfully as an independent Democrat for mayor in 1906.

When **Thomas Hart Benton** painted his famous mural in the Missouri capitol, he portrayed Kemper sitting next to **J. C. Nichols.** Both listened intently to a speaker standing next to **Tom Pendergast,** the longtime Kansas City political boss from 1910 to 1939.

Kemper reentered the banking business in 1906 through a stock purchase. He bought into Commerce Trust, a new affiliate of the National Bank of Commerce controlled by physician **William Stone Woods** (whose donations helped to underwrite William Woods College in Fulton, Missouri). Both banks reorganized in the bank panic of 1907, and Kemper emerged from the crisis as the active president of the companies.

In 1917, while still involved at Commerce Trust, he became the receiver for the bankrupt Kansas City, Mexico, and Orient Railroad. By 1923 he had sold his Commerce Trust stock to devote his full attention to operating the Orient Railroad as its president. That venture ended with the profitable sale of Orient's assets to the Santa Fe Railroad in 1927.

In 1925 Kemper's oldest son, James, assumed the presidency of Commerce Trust. His middle son, **Rufus Crosby Kemper,** bought a small bank in 1919, which he soon renamed City Bank and Trust. Between 1927 and 1933 W. T. Kemper worked with Crosby at the smaller bank. In 1933 W. T. and Crosby, together with James, bought out the other investors in Commerce Trust, and W. T. resumed his position as board chairman. He held that office until his death on January 19, 1938. At that time his son James was president of Commerce Trust, and his son R. Crosby served as president and chairman of City Bank. The latter also served as vice chairman of the board of Commerce Trust.

Federal banking legislation prohibited the holding of officer positions in more than one bank after January 1, 1939. Crosby resigned his position at Commerce Trust, and remained chairman of City National Bank. James assumed the Commerce Trust chairmanship upon W. T. Kemper's death.

William T. Kemper held various posts in the national banking structure. He unsuccessfully sought the chairmanship of the Reconstruction Finance Commission during the New Deal. He long served as the Tenth Federal Reserve District representative on the Federal Reserve Council. At his death he chaired the Missouri Social Security Commission, which oversaw social security at the state level.

Since the passing of Kemper, Commerce Trust has evolved into Commerce Bancshares, and City Bank has been transformed into UMB Bancshares. These two interstate banking companies ranked among the largest in Missouri in the 1990s.

WILLIAM S. WORLEY

Fowler, Dick. *Leaders in Our Town.* Kansas City: Burd and Fletcher, 1952.

Kemper, William T. Clipping File. Missouri Valley Room. Kansas City Public Library, Kansas City, Mo.

Schondelmeyer, Brent. *Building a First-Class Bank: The Story of United Missouri Bank.* Kansas City: United Missouri Bancshares, 1986.

KENRICK, PETER RICHARD (1806–1896)

Peter Richard Kenrick, the first Catholic archbishop in the Midwest, was born on August 17, 1806, in Dublin, Ireland, was educated there, and was ordained to the priesthood in 1832. He came to America the following year to work with his older brother, Bishop Francis Patrick Kenrick of Philadelphia.

The younger Kenrick wrote works of theology and church history. The most noted of these, *The Validity of the Anglican Ordinations* (1841), was to go unchallenged for more than a century. In spite of his scholarly inclinations and success, Kenrick held several posts in the church in Philadelphia. In 1841 he became coadjutor bishop of St. Louis.

Upon Kenrick's arrival the diocese included all of Louisiana Territory except the state of Louisiana and the future states of Iowa and Minnesota. The city of St. Louis would grow from 16,469 in 1840 to 77,860 in 1850. Before Kenrick died, the population would exceed 450,000.

The diocese boasted a cathedral, a seminary and college at Perryville, a university that would welcome faculties of law and medicine, a hospital under the Sisters of Charity, four societies of women religious teachers, a large Catholic population that spread from richest to poorest, and a tradition of Catholicism that stemmed from colonial days. Kenrick saw problems, too: a heavy debt on the cathedral, people unaccustomed to supporting a free church in a free society, few clergy whose native language was English, and no German priest to shepherd a growing German Catholic population. Beyond the city lay a territory of seemingly endless extent, the home of many nomadic people, some of whom wished to learn more about Christianity.

During his early years in St. Louis, Kenrick visited many parts of the state. An immigrant himself, he welcomed newcomers and sought priests who could speak their languages. He appointed a German-speaking vicar-general and urged him to recruit priests from Europe. He wanted priests to participate in the choice of the bishop of the diocese. While autocratic in outlook, he let his subordinates handle their own affairs without interference.

Kenrick began a Catholic journal, opened a seminary in Carondelet, and invited sisterhoods to come to the diocese. He approved the founding of the initial St. Vincent de Paul Society in America. When Ambrose Heim, a young priest who had begun a bank for poor people, died, Kenrick ran the bank successfully.

During the Civil War Kenrick preserved an Olympian neutrality in a divided diocese. At the close of the conflict, he urged his priests to refuse the ironclad oath and supported those who would not take it, such as **John A. Cummings,** who carried his case to the United States Supreme Court.

At the Council of Baltimore in 1866, Archbishop Martin Spalding of Baltimore wanted to defer to Rome regularly; Kenrick wanted American affairs handled locally. At times he seemed pigheaded in defending his position. At the Council of the Vatican four years later, he joined with a group of bishops from non-Latin countries in opposing Roman centralization and the declaration of papal infallibility. On this latter question, he saw no compelling arguments in Scriptures or tradition and refrained from voting. However, he accepted the decision of the majority since he had always held that a universal Council of Bishops had the guidance of the Holy Spirit.

Badgered by Roman authorities because of his stand at the council, Kenrick handed over the administration of the archdiocese to his coadjutor archbishop, Patrick Ryan, in 1871. When the extremely popular Ryan became archbishop of Philadelphia thirteen years later, Kenrick resumed control in St. Louis.

When strikes of the western railroad turned to violence in 1887, Kenrick opposed the Knights of Labor, America's first national labor union. The organization had not called the strike but strongly supported it. Kenrick's opposition to the Knights broke the unanimity of the archbishops and sent the issue to Rome for decision. However, James Cardinal Gibbons of Baltimore upheld the cause of the Knights of Labor.

Shortly after his fiftieth jubilee as a bishop in 1891, Kenrick made another serious mistake. Even though he had recommended many able priests as bishops, he suggested a less able young man as his coadjutor. Lacking the confidence of his peers among the priests of the archdiocese, the young man failed to win the approval of the bishops. Kenrick's last years were clouded by misunderstandings with his coadjutor and eventual successor, John J. Kain, a man his priests wanted but whom he had not chosen. By that time, the once huge archdiocese covered merely the eastern half of Missouri.

Kenrick died on March 4, 1896. He had towered over the Catholic people of the Midwest for a half century, and they revered and stood in awe of him. With justification, his friend Archbishop Patrick Ryan of Philadelphia called him "in many ways the greatest of her [the American Catholic Church's] bishops." History would seem to validate this judgment. Many of the issues Kenrick fought for at Vatican I won acceptance at Vatican II, one hundred years later.

WILLIAM B. FAHERTY

Faherty, William B. *Dream by the River: Two Centuries of St. Louis Catholicism, 1766–1967.* St. Louis: Piraeus, 1973.

Hennesey, James. *The First Council of the Vatican: The American Experience.* New York: Herder and Herder, 1963.

Kenrick, Peter Richard. Business Papers. Archdiocesan archives. Kenrick Seminary, St. Louis.

———. Personal Papers. Archives. University of Notre Dame, South Bend, Ind.

Miller, S. J. "Peter Richard Kenrick: Bishop and Archbishop of St. Louis, 1806–1896." Parts 1–3. *Records of the American Catholic Historical Society of Philadelphia* 84 (March 1973); (June 1973); (September 1973).

Rothensteiner, John E. *History of the Archdiocese of St. Louis in Its Various Stages of Development from* A.D. *1637 to* A.D. *1928.* Vol. 1. St. Louis: Blackwell Wielandy, 1928.

KESSLER, GEORGE E. (1862–1923)

Although regarded by contemporaries as one of the leading landscape architects and city planners of the turn-of-the-century City Beautiful movement, George Edward Kessler has since been forgotten by historians. He firmly believed in the Progressive faith that the environment could transform the decayed condition of American cities. He spent his life trying to realize what he called the ideal city and the ideal citizenship: an urban social order that "devoted itself to solving . . . the civic problems of the community; with a consciousness awakened to community service . . . not just to the tangible things of wood and stone, but to civic beautification and the recreational as well."

Kessler was born in Frankausen, Schwarzburg-Rudolstadt, Germany, on July 16, 1862. His parents emigrated to the United States in 1865, arriving in Hoboken, New Jersey, and eventually settling in Dallas, Texas. His father, Edward, was an unsuccessful and unhappy merchant and importer with an artistic temperament. After his father's death in 1878, his mother, Antoine Zetzshe, returned to Germany and decided to find a profession that better suited her son's artistic interests than the business world. She settled on landscape architecture as a suitable career that combined both the practical goals of engineering and the artistic goals of reshaping the land.

Kessler began his study of landscape architecture in the Grand Ducal gardens at Weimar, where he received instruction in forestry, botany, and landscape design. He concluded his formal education with studies at the Charlottenburg Polytechnicum and a course in civil engineering at the University of Jena. He spent his last year in Europe studying civic design in cities from Paris to Moscow.

By 1882 Kessler returned to the United States, spending his first few months in the country as a gardener in New York City's Central Park, designed by famed landscape architect Frederick Law Olmsted. Friends helped Kessler secure a job in Fort Scott, Kansas, laying out Merriam Park, a resort eight miles from Kansas City, Missouri. Within months he turned the rugged landscape of Merriam into a remarkably beautiful pleasure ground. His work on Kansas City's 1893 park and boulevard plan, prepared with the help of August Meyer and **William Rockhill Nelson,** gained him national recognition. The centerpiece of Kessler's design was the Paseo, a system of parks and streets that combined the City Beautiful goals of functional purpose and landscape theory.

Kessler remained an adviser to the Kansas City Park Board and maintained an office in the city for the rest of his life. His national prominence, however, soon brought offers from around the country. He was hired in 1902 as the landscape architect for the St. Louis Louisiana Purchase Exposition held in 1904. Kessler placed more than 10 million flowers throughout the fairgrounds and designed the magnificent Sunken Garden and Cascade Gardens that delighted Exposition visitors. More important, however, was the impression his design gave to St. Louis's reformers and leaders. Kessler's work on the fair convinced him to open an office in the city in 1903 and brought him two planning jobs: the improvement and expansion of Kingshighway Boulevard and the post-Exposition restoration of Forest Park.

The Kingshighway Boulevard Commission, formed in 1902, hired Kessler to draft plans to improve and expand the road to link the city's parks. Kessler's proposal included extensions of the roads from Chain of Rocks in the city's northern section to Carondelet Park in the city's southern section. The plan proposed to establish the Chain of Rocks as a park area, upgrade the roads leading to Kingshighway (providing better access to the central business district), and expand the entrances to Forest Park, Tower Grove Park, and Carondelet Park. The improved boulevard, lined entirely with trees, would become a continuous park throughout the city and increase access to recreation and nature for the city's population.

Kessler began the restoration of Forest Park in 1906. He replaced thousands of trees destroyed in preparation for the Exposition, added a water drainage system and a network of five lakes (including the lake in front of the park's Art Hill), paved and improved roads throughout the park, and laid plans for building the World's Fair Pavilion of Government Hill. He also suggested covering the River Des Peres, which presented a health risk since it served as a sewer for the city's western region. Retained from the fair were the Art Building (now the St. Louis Art Museum) and the famous statue of St. Louis. His design greatly improved Forest Park and made it an enduring symbol of civic pride and urban beauty.

Kessler also recommended changing park management by removing it from politics. He urged that only experts with training and knowledge in park design be appointed to govern the park. His vision of urban space and park management formed the center of the St. Louis Civic League's comprehensive plan to redesign the city, *City Plan for St. Louis, 1907.*

Kessler's proposals for Kingshighway and the park and boulevard system became embroiled in St. Louis's class politics: both were opposed by the city's working-class residents. They argued that the plans benefited only the city's automobile- and property-owning class, derisively nicknamed the "Big Cinch," and unfairly taxed the class that least benefited from the alterations. The Kingshighway proposal, originally defeated in a 1905 bond issue, finally passed in 1906 when it was attached to the proposition for a municipally controlled toll-free bridge—a popular issue for the city's working class. In 1910 the bond issue for the park and boulevard system failed.

Kessler moved to St. Louis in 1910. From 1909 to 1914 he served on the St. Louis Park Board, improving the design of all city parks, and also built the massive amphitheater (880 feet wide and 200 feet deep) used for the St. Louis Pageant and Masque of 1914. In 1911 he was appointed to the City Plan Commission and began work on the plan for a Central Traffic Parkway. The commission recommended a parkway between Twelfth Street and Jefferson Avenue, extending from the Municipal Courts Building, past Union Station, to a proposed group of public buildings at Grand Avenue. The plan included three separate but connected roads: a trafficway for business vehicles, a boulevard for light residential traffic, and tree-lined walkways for pedestrians. The area to be destroyed by the parkway, however, housed a large number of African Americans. St. Louis's segregationists, attempting to pass a residential segregation ordinance and fearful of the specter of black dispersal, successfully campaigned against the parkway.

By the time he moved to St. Louis Kessler was the leading landscape architect and city planner of the early twentieth century. He designed park and boulevard systems and improved a host of cities across the country, including Memphis, Cincinnati, Dallas, Syracuse, Houston, Salt Lake City, and Indianapolis. **August A. Busch, William Keeney Bixby, Robert Somers Brookings, David R. Francis,** and other prominent St. Louisans retained Kessler for landscape work on their homes. He designed gardens and tree-lined walkways for colleges and universities from Washington University in St. Louis to Baptist

College in Shanghai, China. During World War I he laid out improvements for camps in San Antonio, Texas; Little Rock, Arkansas; and Deming, New Mexico. For a quarter of a century, his extensive work throughout the United States and Europe carried him an estimated fifty thousand miles per year.

George Kessler died in Indianapolis on March 19, 1923, and was buried in St. Louis's Bellefontaine Cemetery. Historians and planners have criticized his vision of beauty, order, and harmony in urban space as either quixotic fantasy or a reflection of naïveté and class bias. As blight and decay increasingly seem the destiny of urban America, however, it might be time to reevaluate Kessler's vision. After his death, the Kansas City Park Board eulogized Kessler for his love of beauty and his commitment to improving the urban landscape: "To that goal he consecrated his life. And in that line of work he played the part of both pioneer and prophet."

EDWARD C. RAFFERTY

Kessler, George Edward. Papers. Missouri Historical Society, St. Louis.

McConachie, Alexander Scot. "The 'Big Cinch': A Business Elite in the Life of a City, St. Louis, 1895–1915." Ph.D. diss., Washington University, 1976.

Rafferty, Edward C. "Orderly City, Orderly Lives: The City Beautiful Movement in St. Louis." *Gateway Heritage* 11 (spring 1991): 40–65.

Scott, Mellier G. *American City Planning since 1890.* Berkeley and Los Angeles: University of California Press, 1969.

Wilson, William H. *The City Beautiful Movement in Kansas City.* Columbia: University of Missouri Press, 1964.

———. *The City Beautiful Movement.* Baltimore: Johns Hopkins University Press, 1989.

KING, AUSTIN A. (1802–1870)

Born in Sullivan County, Tennessee, on September 21, 1802, Austin A. King was educated in the local common schools and read "in a country law office." Admitted to the bar in 1822, he practiced law in Tennessee until 1830 when he emigrated to Columbia, Missouri, where he formed a partnership with John B. Gordon and became involved in Democratic politics. His legal and political career was long and distinguished, serving two terms as Boone County's representative to the General Assembly (1834 and 1836), as the first circuit judge in Caldwell County beginning in 1837, as governor from 1848 to 1853, and as a U.S. congressman from 1863 to 1865.

During his first years in Missouri, King "rode the circuit," representing clients before Judge David Todd's court. In 1832 King served as colonel of the First Regiment, Third Division, of the Missouri militia during the Black Hawk War in Illinois, where he met a young captain of the Illinois militia named Abraham Lincoln. After returning to Missouri, King served as judge advocate in the court-martial proceedings against Gen. Benjamin Means, commander of the Seventh Brigade, Seventh Division, of the militia. Means was indicted for disobedience of orders and mutiny, and was found not guilty on December 19.

From his early years in Missouri, King exhibited a deep interest in the promotion of education. He supported the establishment of Columbia College, the Columbia Female Academy (later renamed Stephens College), and Richmond College. He also served as a school board member of Ray County, and on November 25, 1836, he introduced resolutions in the General Assembly to establish a "seminary of learning" to instruct teachers of common schools. While governor he unsuccessfully sought to found a department of education headed by a state superintendent of schools, and advocated "the permanent endowment of the state university."

In 1838 armed bands of Missourians and Mormons clashed in the northwestern part of the state. Gov. **Lilburn W. Boggs** sent the state militia under the command of Maj. Gen. Samuel Lucas, who surrounded the Mormon forces at Far West, Missouri, in Caldwell County, forcing them to surrender. More than fifty men were charged with several crimes, including treason and murder, and were brought before Judge King in Richmond, Missouri. Ten of the prisoners were held over for trial and the rest were given their unconditional release or made to post bond.

During his years as a circuit judge, King remained active in Democratic politics, supporting Martin Van Buren for president in 1840. During the 1844 gubernatorial convention, he lost the nomination to **John Cummins Edwards.** In 1848, however, King received the gubernatorial nomination, in large part because he had avoided the factionalism of the 1844 state convention. His candidacy brought together the different factions of the Democratic Party, enabling him to defeat the Whig candidate, **James Sidney Rollins.**

During the 1848 campaign Rollins accused the Democrats of moving too slowly "to aid private internal improvement companies." King responded that the Democratic Party had correctly avoided a large public debt that might have harmed the state's credit. Nevertheless, during the 1848–1849 legislative session 142 companies were chartered, while only 32 companies had received charters in the previous session. In 1850 King recommended that state credit be used to help finance railroad construction. A total of $3.5 million in state bonds was issued to two railroads that year. Working with the legislature, he also advocated or acquiesced in the promotion of road-building projects, commerce, factories, swampland drainage, and a geological survey of the southeastern and southwestern portions of the state. Additionally, he secured the passage of bills establishing an asylum for the insane, a school for the deaf and dumb, and a state home for the blind.

The issue of slavery complicated King's duties as governor. Although he signed the Jackson Resolutions—passed by a large majority—he also vetoed a fugitive slave law, stating that it was unconstitutional. Over the next few years, he opposed Missourians voting on the Lecompton Constitution in Kansas, and at the Democratic National Convention in 1860 he supported Stephen A. Douglas for president, believing that his election would preserve the Union. At the convention King participated in the debates and denounced secession. In 1861 he supported both **Hamilton Rowan Gamble**'s provisional government and Lincoln's administration, and in February 1865, while serving in the United States Congress, he voted for a constitutional amendment to abolish slavery.

After the Civil War, King returned to the practice of law until his death in St. Louis on April 22, 1870. He was buried in Richmond, Missouri.

DENNIS K. BOMAN

Biographical Dictionary of the United States Congress, 1774–1989. Bicentennial ed. S.v. "King, Austin A." Washington, D.C.: U.S. Government Printing Office, 1989.

Dictionary of American Biography. Vol. 10. S.v. "King, Austin A."

History of Caldwell and Livingston Counties, Missouri. St. Louis: National Historical Company, 1886.

Leopard, Buel, and Floyd C. Shoemaker, eds. *The Messages and Proclamations of the Governors of the State of Missouri.* Vol. 2. Columbia: State Historical Society of Missouri, 1922.

McCandless, Perry. *A History of Missouri: Volume II, 1820 to 1860.* Columbia: University of Missouri Press, 1972.

Switzler, William F. *History of Boone County, Missouri.* St. Louis: Western Historical Company, 1882.

KINNEY, NATHANIEL N. (1839–1888)

Nathaniel "Nat" N. Kinney has a popular image of a romantic, violent, swashbuckling westerner, a champion leader of Baldknobber vigilantes in Taney County who knew how to harness both men and horses. His image, like that of the vigilance committee he helped organize, is often exaggerated and partly fabricated.

Kinney was an imposing figure variously described as six-foot-two to six-foot-five, weighing some 220 or 250 pounds (accounts of his size are smaller in Kansas newspapers because he did not have the legendary persona there that emerged in Missouri's sensationalized press). Writers have emphasized his "dual personality." Negative descriptions of him came from political opponents and victims of violence associated with Kinney and the Baldknobbers; Baldknobber apologists, principally the descendants of the Alonzo Prather family and journalists who interviewed them, have portrayed Kinney's better qualities.

Kinney was born in New York in 1839, lived in Virginia, spent time as a Union soldier in the Civil War, emigrated to Indiana, apparently spent a brief time in Colorado, and moved to Neosho Falls, Kansas, by 1875. He farmed on a modest scale, but in 1877, at age thirty-eight, he decided to move to Topeka, which was undergoing tremendous economic and population growth. While there, he worked as a teamster and became manager for a public hack service.

In Kinney's spare time he led a ruffian's life in Topeka, remembered locally in many public episodes. However, an old militia mate from Kansas recalled Kinney as a helpful person with travelers at the Topeka train depot, giving directions and aid. In Missouri his contemporaries witnessed his passionate rhetoric devoted to a pursuit of vigilante leadership and political power. According to neighbors, though, he knew the quiet of family life, was proud of his children, and loved fine horses.

In Kansas Kinney joined the Topeka Rifles, a local militia, to side with merchants and the Atchison, Topeka, and Santa Fe Railway to combat public unrest and maintain the public peace following violent labor strikes in 1877. These nationally reported strikes were the first major railroad strikes in American history. A local newspaper referred to Kinney and three other large men in the militia group as the "Big Four" who presented a conspicuous physical threat to any opposition.

Because of his exceptional height, comrades chose Kinney as color sergeant to carry the flag, and the Topeka Rifles became known as the Capitol Guards. In militia meetings Kinney exhorted his peers with emotion and was recognized among the local men as an orator. He also developed considerable skill as a marksman and horseman, winning local competitions. In fact, he had several racehorses quartered at the local fairgrounds.

Kansas newspapers reported that Kinney left Topeka in 1880, the year that voters approved a prohibition amendment. The *Topeka Daily Commonwealth* said, "Kinney left Kansas with that rough and rowdy element that went when the open saloon disappeared." Kansans labeled him a drunken brawler and even a coward who picked fights with men his physical inferior. One journalist recalled that a prominent Kansas legislator knocked Kinney unconscious with a billiard cue in a local saloon. The press said Kinney headed for southwest Missouri where, by March 1882, he was working on the public square in Springfield as an employee in a saloon.

By the summer of 1882 citizens in Springfield organized a local militia, the Springfield Light Guards. Anxious to serve, Kinney titled himself "captain," but, as in both the Civil War and Kansas, his peers denied his election as an officer. In December 1882 a fight in Kinney's saloon left a man mortally wounded. In January 1883 he relocated north of Kirbyville, in Taney County.

Kinney began speaking for the agricultural reform of the Grange, a populist movement that agitated for fencing livestock. Local Democrats soon drafted him as their candidate for state representative in 1884, but he lost.

Kinney's defeat did not restrain his ardor for becoming a local leader. He organized a neighborhood Sunday school where he sometimes preached. Seeking the high moral ground he soon became inextricably enmeshed in a local regulator movement called the Baldknobbers. This group desired capitalist modernization and called for law and order. They advocated swift punishment for crime, churches and evangelical morality, and literacy and education, and wanted squatters to legally enter their land and become tax-paying citizens. They selectively whipped and beat members of the opposition, and hanged two of them. Some anticipated new railroads and boomtowns at Forsyth and Kirbyville.

Kinney became chairman of the local Democratic Party in 1886 and ran again for state representative. Taney was the only county in the "Keep-Sake" district of Republican-dominated southwest Missouri that wavered in its control of the local courthouse. Party workers imported a well-known Republican from Boone County, Arkansas, to oppose Kinney and another from Greene County, Missouri, to run for prosecutor. Kinney narrowly lost by forty-nine votes, and Republicans kept local control.

Kinney returned to third-party politics, speaking for the Agricultural Wheel at local public celebrations and Civil War encampments. Old hatreds from vigilante conflict followed him, and on August 20, 1888, a member of the opposition killed him at Forsyth.

LYNN MORROW

Hartman, Mary, and Elmo Ingenthron. *Bald Knobbers: Vigilantes on the Ozarks Frontier.* Gretna, La.: Pelican Publishing, 1988.

Kalen, Kristen, and Lynn Morrow. "A Bald Knobber Sues Springfield!" *White River Valley Historical Quarterly* 32 (spring 1993): 12–15.

Morrow, Lynn. "Nathaniel N. Kinney." *White River Valley Historical Quarterly* 32 (fall 1993).

Upton, Lucile Morris. *Bald Knobbers.* Caldwell, Idaho: Caxton Printers, 1939.

KIRK, JOHN R. (1851–1937)

John R. Kirk, born on January 23, 1851, was the son of George and Mary Jane Ried Kirk. While still a boy he acquired a keen interest in the professional aspects of teaching and determined to devote his life to education. He first taught school at the age of nineteen. Three years later he attended the First District Normal School in Kirksville where he became an admirer of its president, **Joseph Baldwin,** and his views of what teacher education should be. In 1878 Kirk received a baccalaureate, but he did not earn a master's degree until 1930, after his retirement.

After serving one term as state superintendent of schools, Kirk was chosen in 1899 to head the First District Normal School. He worked diligently to restore Baldwin's standards in terms of curriculum and faculty: both were increased in number and strengthened in depth of scholarship.

Long concerned about raising the standards of rural education, Kirk developed a design for a rural school building that would offer all the amenities of urban schools plus facilities for courses in agriculture, domestic science, and industrial science. Shortly after assuming the presidency of the normal school, he instructed the carpenters to build a model drawn to scale, which he took with him to meetings of state and national education groups to illustrate his ideas. To make the First District Normal School a center for improving rural education, he persuaded the governing board in 1906 to build a rural schoolhouse on the campus using his model for its design. Known as the Model Rural School, it opened in 1907 with a teacher employed by the board and twenty-eight pupils transported by a horse-drawn hack to the campus from nearby farms. The curriculum featured Kirk's ideas about what rural children needed to learn in addition to the standard common-school courses. Interest in rural education led Kirk into the National Rural Life Movement, and he spearheaded in 1911 the formation of the Missouri Rural Life Conference. Both it and the Model Rural School were casualties of World War I.

Catastrophe and controversy marked the last years of Kirk's presidency. In January 1924 fire destroyed Baldwin Hall, the original administration and classroom building, and the library. For a time the future of the college was in doubt, but Kirk and the faculty, students, and citizens of Kirksville rallied to donate books, money, and other gifts to supplement the insurance and construct a new library.

Meanwhile, Kirk came under attack for a variety of reasons. His autocratic methods and his mid-nineteenth-century morals, which led him to ban dancing, card playing, and smoking by students, became increasingly intolerable to many young people of the 1920s. Some regents, faculty, and townspeople thought that Kirk had outlived his usefulness as president. A triumvirate of faculty eager for administrative positions engaged in a letter-writing campaign urging board members to "retire" Kirk. Although he had loyal friends among both the faculty and the board, Kirk apparently decided that it would be better if he did resign. In a meeting of the board in February 1925, a series of face-saving actions, to which all parties agreed, took place. Kirk was reelected president, promptly resigned, was granted the title "President Emeritus," given a year's leave of absence, and elected to teach one course on educational psychology upon his return. Until his death on November 7, 1937, citizens of Missouri recalled only his quarter century of service to the college, not the controversy that ended his tenure as president.

RUTH WARNER TOWNE

Kirk, John R. Papers. Archives. Pickler Memorial Library, Kirksville, Mo.

Minutes of Board of Regents of First District Normal School and Northeast Missouri State Teachers College. Archives. Pickler Memorial Library, Kirksville, Mo.

Ryle, Walter H. *Centennial History of Northeast Missouri State Teachers College.* Kirksville, Mo.: Board of Regents, 1972.

KNELL, EMMA R. (1877–1963)

Emma R. Knell, a businesswoman and politician, was born in Moline, Illinois, on October 21, 1877, and moved with her family to southwest Missouri in the early 1880s. She was educated in the Carthage public schools, graduating from high school in 1897. In the fall of 1897, Knell enrolled in a course in embalming at the National School of Embalming in St. Louis. She graduated the next year. She also studied music under E. R. Kroeger at Forest Park University.

Knell's father had established the Knell Mortuary soon after the family arrived in Carthage. Emma Knell began handling the business's finances and correspondence while she was still in high school. Her father, however, wanted her to join the business as an embalmer because he "always entertained the belief that it was a delicate thing to turn the remains of a beloved mother or sister over to a man." In 1899 Emma Knell became one of the first Missouri women to be licensed as an embalmer.

In 1902 Knell joined her father as a founder of the Knell Fair, later called the Southwest Missouri Fair and, still later, the Ozark District Fair. Knell served as the secretary of the fair from its inception, and in 1911 she also assumed the duties of general manager when her father resigned from that position.

Throughout the first two decades of the twentieth century, Knell worked quietly and efficiently in the family mortuary business, apparently giving little or no thought to politics. Indeed, on more than one occasion she expressed a lack of interest in politics.

During the 1924 primary election, southwest Missouri residents became concerned about the prospect that a tuberculosis hospital at Webb City would be closed because of a lack of state funding. The hospital was of special interest to the many miners and their families of the region. Knell was approached by J. F. Lee, presiding judge of the Jasper County Court and a Democrat, who urged her to run for the state legislature. Knell reacted with surprise and disbelief, telling Lee that she was uninterested in the position and that she was a Republican. Lee and other supporters persisted in their effort to get the well-known and popular Knell to run for public office, and she finally relented. She conducted a low-key campaign and, in the end, won both the primary and the general elections with ease, thereby becoming the first Republican woman elected to the Missouri General Assembly.

Once in office Knell introduced a bill that would double the state appropriation allowed for tuberculosis patients confined in state hospitals. Sen. A. L. McCawley, a Jasper County Democrat, persuaded the senate to increase the appropriation even more. Thanks largely to Knell's intense lobbying, the Knell-McCawley Bill was passed by both houses and signed into law by Republican governor **Sam Baker** after Knell visited him. The Webb City hospital was saved. In addition to her activities in support of the Knell-McCawley Bill, she also served as chairman of the Children's Code Committee and as a member of the Appropriations, Official Salaries and Fees, and Roads and Highways Committees.

Knell was elected to the General Assembly again in 1926, but chose not to run in 1928. In 1930 she ran again and won a close race. Among the bills she helped enact during her final term was one that created the Missouri State Highway Patrol. She retired from the legislature after completing her third term in 1932.

After leaving the legislature, Knell returned to the family business. She became president in 1943, after her brother's death. She was also active in a host of local organizations, including the First Baptist Church, the PEO Sisterhood, and the Pythian Sisters. She served for several years as a director of the

Missouri Funeral Directors Association and of the National Funeral Directors Association.

Emma Knell died in Carthage on September 19, 1963.

GARY R. KREMER

Dains, Mary K. "Women Pioneers in the Missouri Legislature." *Missouri Historical Review* 85 (October 1990): 40–52.

———, ed. *Show Me Missouri Women: Selected Biographies.* Kirksville, Mo.: Thomas Jefferson University Press, 1989.

KOCHTITZKY, OTTO L. (1855–1935)

Otto L. Kochtitzky was born in South Bend, Indiana, on May 4, 1855. In 1870, three years after the family moved to Lebanon, Missouri, Kochtitzky's father, Oscar, became Laclede County's state representative. Later, the elder Kochtitzky became the chief clerk for Missouri's registrar of lands.

In 1850 a federal law had given to the states all land classified as swampland. Missouri donated such land to each county. In his capacity in the land registrar's office, Oscar Kochtitzky sent his two sons, John and Otto, to southeast Missouri to prepare another survey of the state's swampland.

While working on the survey, Otto Kochtitzky learned of an uncompleted plank road in New Madrid County. As authorized by the county court, the plank road company was to receive nearly one hundred thousand acres upon the completion of the road, but the company had dissolved. The young Kochtitzky saw an opportunity for his father. Together with Missouri's state auditor and two Ohio entrepreneurs, the elder Kochtitzky formed a partnership to complete the road. The partners decided that plank roads were outmoded and, with the approval of the county court, built a railroad instead. Otto Kochtitzky, a self-taught "engineer" with only a high school education, was in charge of the road's construction. After three years of operation, the railroad was sold to the Cotton Belt Railroad. The Kochtitzky group retained the land rights, until Charles L. Luce, one of their major partners, bought them out.

Whether the county court had acted properly remained unclear. Under state law, swampland was to be given only when drainage improvements had been made. In 1885 Luce, in an attempt to meet that requirement, began dredging the Little River, with Otto Kochtitzky in charge. Luce died in 1886, but the operation continued until 1889, when fire destroyed the dredging machine. After the fire, and in spite of Kochtitzky's pleas, the work stopped. In 1892 New Madrid officials sought to recover the land. A compromise was reached in which the company secured more time to complete the dredging. Once again Kochtitzky took charge, and he completed the work before the 1899 deadline.

By this time Kochtitzky believed that mere dredging of the principal streams in the area was insufficient. He asserted that except for the extraction of lumber, less than 5 percent of the swampland had value. He emphasized the need for more aggressive reclamation projects. The first formal drainage districts authorized under state law were small and confined to one county. If water was removed from one district, it increased drainage problems in adjacent areas. Kochtitzky became the major proponent of an integrated drainage system. He studied the topography and existing drainage ditches in the seven counties of the lowlands and prepared detailed topographical maps of each county. It appears that he had to cajole some of the large landowners for their continued support of large districts. In 1907 the Little River drainage district was organized. The district included nearly five hundred thousand acres, of which only twenty-two thousand were improved.

When construction began, Kochtitzky refused an offer to become the engineer. He later regretted that decision. At that time he owned seven steam-powered dredges and thought that he had more to gain financially through his private drainage endeavors, but his machine soon became obsolete with the rapid improvement of the internal combustion engine.

The Little River project was completed in 1916. The transformation of "swampeast" Missouri into an excellent agricultural area took longer and was more expensive than Kochtitzky had envisioned. Nevertheless, his long-range prediction proved accurate: the lowlands are among the nation's most productive agricultural areas.

Kochtitzky died June 23, 1935, in Cape Girardeau, Missouri.

LEON P. OGILVIE

Kochtitzky, Otto. *The Story of a Busy Life.* Cape Girardeau, Mo.: Ramfre Press, 1957.

McDowell, Gary Lane. "Local Agencies and Land Development by Drainage: The Case of 'Swampeast' Missouri." Ph.D. diss., Columbia University, 1965.

Ogilvie, Leon Parker. "The Development of the Southeast Missouri Lowlands." Ph.D. diss., University of Missouri–Columbia, 1967.

KREKEL, ARNOLD (1815–1888)

Arnold Krekel, who served from 1865 to 1888 as a U.S. judge for the Western District of Missouri, was born on March 12, 1815, in Langenfeld, near Düsseldorf, in Prussia. In 1832 he emigrated to the United States with his parents, two sisters, and three brothers. On the journey from New York to Missouri, his mother became ill and died in Louisville, where the family had stopped to get medical help.

Francis Krekel settled near Augusta in St. Charles County, and Arnold worked as a farmhand and split rails to pay for his schooling. Learning English from neighbors, he studied Latin, French, and mathematics under Julius Mallinckrodt. At age twenty-six Krekel was elected justice of the peace, and two years later entered St. Charles College to study surveying. Upon completing his studies, he served as the St. Charles County and U.S. deputy surveyor. In 1843 he married Ida Krug, a native of Bavaria, and in 1844 began the study of law.

Although from a Catholic family, Krekel's liberal views and intellectual interests drew him to the company of the German "Latin farmers" and former revolutionaries who had settled in St. Charles and Warren Counties in the early 1830s. When the *Verein der Vernunftglaübigen,* the Association of Rationalists, was founded in Augusta on April 9, 1844, Krekel was one of the thirty-six charter members.

Krekel was admitted to the bar in 1845, and from 1846 to 1852 he served as the prosecuting county and city attorney of St. Charles. In 1852 he established the *St. Charles Demokrat,* a German-language weekly reviewing literature and the arts, as well as politics and business. Elected to the Missouri House of Representatives in 1852, he was an advocate of railroad development, voting for the first railroad appropriation granted by the state. In 1854, having acquired considerable landholdings in St. Charles County, he sold the North Missouri Railroad (later the Norfolk and Western) rights-of-way through his property in Dardenne Township. He laid out the original town of O'Fallon in 1855, naming it for **John O'Fallon,** the St. Louis businessman who was president of the North Missouri Railroad.

A **Thomas Hart Benton** Democrat of considerable influence among his German compatriots, Krekel was nominated as attorney general in 1856. Later, his opposition to slavery led him to join the Republican Party, and in 1860 he was one of the delegates to the Chicago convention that nominated Abraham Lincoln for the presidency.

After the May 10, 1861, capture of Camp Jackson in St. Louis, Krekel organized Home Guards in St. Charles County and neighboring counties made up almost entirely of German immigrants. Serving as provost marshal of St. Charles, Lincoln, and Warren Counties in 1861–1862, he proved an able administrator in dealing with civilians and former Confederates. "Krekel's Dutch," encamped near Cottleville, were credited with effectively discouraging Confederate enlistment in the counties north of the Missouri River. The unit was officially accepted into the Union army in July 1861, and though not involved in any of the major battles of the war, they protected vital communication lines and safeguarded lives and property in the area against guerrilla attacks.

Krekel was elected as a member of the 1865 Missouri State Constitutional Convention, and as president of the convention united the members in their deliberations. On January 11 "An Ordinance Abolishing Slavery in Missouri" was signed, making Missouri the first border state to abolish slavery. On March 31, 1865, President Lincoln appointed Krekel as U.S. district judge for the Western District of Missouri.

Throughout his public career Krekel was a strong proponent of education. He served on the first St. Charles School Board, and as a member of the Missouri House of Representatives, he supported the bill setting aside 25 percent of state revenue for the support of organized schools, which became law in 1853. After the Civil War he joined Lt. **Richard Baxter Foster** in efforts to found a school for blacks in Jefferson City. Lincoln Institute was opened on September 17, 1866, and for more than ten years Krekel lectured without charge to the students, served as a member of the executive committee of the board of trustees, and in 1883 was elected president of the board. From 1872 through 1887 he taught at the newly established School of Law at the University of Missouri, delivering an annual series of lectures on federal courts and federal law, including bankruptcy and maritime law. Bankruptcy became his specialty, and his rulings in this area had a substantial impact.

Krekel's twenty-three years as a federal judge covered the period when Missouri was evolving from a pioneer to an industrial state. Almost one-third of his cases from 1867 to 1878 dealt with defaults on municipal bonds and private bankruptcies. Other cases involved Civil War pension claims, theft from the mails, extortion by tax collectors, tax evasion, and in 1885 one of the earliest cases in the area of labor law.

In poor health Krekel resigned from the court on June 9, 1888, and on July 14 he died in Kansas City of Bright's disease. He was buried in Oak Grove Cemetery in St. Charles County, eulogized in German and English by his colleagues and compatriots.

ADOLF E. SCHROEDER

Arndt, Karl J. R., and May E. Olson. *German-American Newspapers and Periodicals, 1732–1955.* Heidelberg: Quelle and Meyer, 1961.

History of St. Charles, Montgomery, and Warren Counties, Missouri. St. Louis: National Historical Company, 1885.

Larsen, Lawrence H. *Federal Justice in Western Missouri: The Judges, the Cases, the Times.* Columbia: University of Missouri Press, 1994.

Sachs, Howard F. "Missouri's Gilded Age, as Viewed by Judge Arnold Krekel." *Kansas City Bar Journal* (June 30, 1955): 13.

Savage, W. Sherman. *The History of Lincoln University.* Jefferson City: Lincoln University, 1939.

Westhoff, Mary J. "Nicholas Krekel." In *O'Fallon Centennial, 1856–1956.* Warrenton, Mo.: Bilmac Press, 1956.

KUHLMAN, KATHRYN J. (1907–1976)

Kathryn Johanna Kuhlman, born in Concordia, Missouri, on May 9, 1907, became Missouri's most famous independent deliverance evangelist of the twentieth century. When she died in Tulsa, Oklahoma, on February 20, 1976, millions counted her as their minister and thousands claimed that they had experienced her healing powers.

Kuhlman was one of the early pioneers of radio with a Denver show in 1933 called *Smiling Through.* She created the Christian talk-show format with her long-running series on CBS, *I Believe in Miracles.* Beginning in 1965 she taped more than five hundred nationally syndicated television programs that featured people who had been healed through her ministry. She denied that she was a "faith healer," claiming that healing was produced by the Holy Spirit; her gift was in recognizing the healing.

Kuhlman's career in evangelism began at the age of seventeen while visiting her sister Myrtle Parrot, wife of the Sedalia-born Everette Parrot. Both Myrtle and Everette had attended Moody Bible Institute and were evangelizing the West. Myrtle persuaded her mother, Emma Walkenhorst Kuhlman, to allow Kathryn to travel with them for a short period. When the time came for Kathryn to return home, she chose to stay with her sister and brother-in-law and soon found herself at the altar giving her testimony and ministering to those who responded to Everette's message.

At the age of twenty-one, in 1928, Kuhlman began her own ministry in Boise, Idaho. Together with her highly educated pianist friend Helen Gulliford, she traveled to towns in the West that no one else would evangelize. Often staying in turkey houses or outbuildings, they begged local communities for the opportunity to preach. Their travels took them through Idaho, Utah, Colorado, and elsewhere. Luck was with them when they came to Denver, Colorado, in 1933 to begin a ministry that would last more than five years.

Kuhlman defended her call to the ministry by claiming that God could find no man that was able and willing to pay the price of a servant of God, so he called her, a woman. Throughout her later career in Franklin and Pittsburgh, Pennsylvania, she testified fervently that if she had a choice she would be married with children. In reality she had married Burroughs Waltrip in 1938, a recently divorced, itinerant minister. By 1944 their marriage was in ruins.

Kuhlman met Waltrip shortly after the accidental death of her father, Joseph Adolph Kuhlman, in 1934. She was at the height of her early career, having established with Helen Gulliford the Denver Revival Tabernacle. The handsome Waltrip visited the tabernacle and fell in love with Kuhlman. Their relationship caused a scandal that eventually destroyed both of their careers. In 1944, after years of soul-searching and rejection by communities, Kuhlman bought a one-way ticket heading east. She never saw Waltrip again.

Kuhlman came to Franklin, Pennsylvania, in 1944 where she built an evangelistic radio ministry on WKRZ in Oil City that reached all the surrounding states. She was preaching at the Gospel Tabernacle in Franklin when people began to experience healing. Eventually, Kuhlman moved to Carnegie Hall to conduct her famous "Miracle Services." When she died in 1976 she held regular services at the Shrine Auditorium in Los Angeles and in Pittsburgh and also made guest appearances all over the world, including one at Kiel Auditorium in St. Louis in 1972.

Kuhlman accepted an honorary doctorate in humane letters from Oral Roberts University in 1973 even though she consistently preached disdain for educated clergy or theologians. Having dropped out of school at the age of fourteen, she never found the time to complete a high school or college degree. She claimed her education came directly from the Holy Spirit. There is some evidence to suggest that she was influenced by Charles Price, Phil Kerr, and Aimee Semple McPhereson as well as Norman Vincent Peale's *Power of Positive Thinking.* A recent biography by Wayne Warner claims that Kuhlman did enroll for two years at the Simpson Bible Institute but was suspended in 1926 "after being caught in a midnight rendezvous."

Success necessitated the creation of the Kathryn Kuhlman Foundation. Millions of dollars poured into her foundation that supported twenty-two mission stations around the globe. Substantial sums of money were also donated to higher education, including Evangel College in Springfield.

Kuhlman's down-home preaching style and simple message brought comfort to millions of people as they listened to her on the radio or watched her on television. In an age of increasing religious polarities, her message and ministry were both Pentecostal, that is, charismatic, and ecumenical. She brought Christians (Protestants and Catholics), Jews, Muslims, and atheists together under one roof to attend her services.

MARLA J. SELVIDGE

Buckingham, Jamie. *Daughter of Destiny: Kathryn Kuhlman, Her Story.* New York: Pocketbooks, 1976.

Hosier, Helen Kooiman. *Kathryn Kuhlman: The Life She Led, the Legacy She Left.* Old Tappan, N.J.: Fleming H. Revell, 1976.

Leisering, Katherine Jane. "An Historical and Critical Study of the Pittsburgh Preaching Career of Kathryn Kuhlman." Ph.D. diss., Ohio University, 1981.

Warner, Wayne. *Kathryn Kuhlman: The Woman behind the Miracles.* Ann Arbor: Servant Publications, 1993.

L

LACLÈDE, PIERRE DE (1729–1778)

The founder of St. Louis, Pierre de Laclède, frequently signed himself Laclède Liguest. Since men customarily signed only their last name, Pierre had been given the additional name Liguest—after a meadow owned by the Laclèdes—to help distinguish him from other family members. Years later puzzlement about Laclède's signature was one of many uncertainties that confounded St. Louisans writing about their city's founder and its early history.

Laclède was born in Bedous, France, on November 22, 1729. Little is known about his early years aside from the fact that he was well educated and that he received an award for his fencing skills at the Military Academy of Toulouse in 1748. Members of his family had achieved recognition in their native province as attorneys, officeholders, and scholars, and he seemed determined to follow their examples. The Laclède family home contained a large library that no doubt contributed to his lifelong habit of collecting books. At the time of his death his personal library contained more than two hundred titles, including some that in all likelihood he had acquired in his youth.

On June 7, 1755, Laclède Liguest departed from La Rochelle on a ship bound for the West Indies. Later that year he settled in New Orleans where he established himself as a successful wholesaler and a rising man of business. Like so many younger sons of successful European families, Laclède had taken his inheritance and come to North America with the intent of building his own fortune.

Sometime after his arrival in New Orleans, Laclède met **Marie Thérèse Bourgeois Chouteau,** whose husband, René Chouteau, had abandoned her and their son Auguste and returned to his native France. The polished and self-assured Laclède apparently wooed and won *Veuve* (Widow) Chouteau (as she styled herself following her husband's departure). The couple formed a liaison that lasted until Laclède's death in 1778, notwithstanding René Chouteau's attempts to reassert his marital rights following his return to Louisiana in 1767.

The Laclède-Chouteau union produced four children: **(Jean) Pierre Chouteau,** born on October 10, 1758; Marie Pelagie Chouteau, born on October 6, 1760; Marie Louise Chouteau, born on December 4, 1762; and Victoire Chouteau, born on March 3, 1764. The children were all born in New Orleans, and since

neither French statutes nor church law sanctioned divorce and remarriage, the circumstances dictated that Marie Thérèse retain the name Chouteau. Likewise, each of her four children by Laclède was christened Chouteau, and the absent René Chouteau's name was entered in the church baptismal register as that of their legitimate father.

Along with looking after his own children, Laclède also served as a mentor for **Auguste Chouteau,** whom he employed as his clerk. Laclède was well qualified to instruct his youthful charge about the vagaries of the New World marketplace. He had arrived in New Orleans not long after the outbreak of the French and Indian War in North America, and despite the vicissitudes of a wartime economy he pressed ahead with his mercantile ventures.

An unexpected opportunity presented itself to Laclède when Louisiana's governor, Jean Jacques D'Abbadie, granted New Orleans merchant Gilbert Antoine Maxent exclusive trading rights for six years with Indian tribes along the Missouri River and the west bank of the upper Mississippi River. Laclède formed a partnership with Maxent and agreed to take charge of the firm's fur-trading operations in Upper Louisiana.

A hastily organized trading expedition set out from New Orleans under Laclède's command in August 1763 and reached Ste. Genevieve, a small French village on the west bank of the Mississippi, on November 3. When Laclède failed to find a building large enough to house the supplies and equipment he brought with him, he readily accepted an offer from the commandant of nearby Fort de Chartres to store his merchandise there until a better place could be located.

Once the goods were safely under cover, Laclède established a temporary trading camp in the adjacent village of Ste. Anne de Fort Chartres. As news of his presence reached nearby Indian tribes, delegations eager to exchange furs for merchandise began arriving at the camp. Encouraged by his favorable reception, Laclède set out in early December to look for a more accessible spot for permanent company headquarters. He confined his search to the region west of the Mississippi, because shortly before he left New Orleans officials had informed him that France had agreed to cede all its territory east of the river to Great Britain. He settled upon a location on a bluff overlooking the Mississippi, south of the mouth of the Missouri. Afterward, Laclède boasted that he had found "a situation where he was going to form a settlement which might become, hereafter, one of the finest cities in America—so many advantages were embraced in this site by its locality and its central position for forming settlements."

As soon as the late-winter thaws made it possible to navigate the Mississippi, Laclède dispatched Auguste Chouteau and a party of thirty laborers to the site he had designated, and in mid-February they began clearing the land. By the time Laclède arrived in early April to inspect the project, work was well under way. During his visit he directed that the town be laid out in a gridiron pattern similar to the one in New Orleans. After unveiling the city's design, the enterprising Frenchman announced that he intended to call the settlement St. Louis, after King Louis XV's patron saint, Louis IX.

Laclède capitalized on the uncertainties created by the expected British takeover and invited the French-speaking inhabitants on the east side of the Mississippi to move across the river to his new settlement where he had taken up residence with Marie Thérèse Chouteau and their children in September 1764. Thanks to his aggressive promotion, the town was already well established when word arrived in late 1764 that France had secretly agreed to surrender New Orleans and all the territories west of the Mississippi to Spain. The news surprised Laclède and could scarcely have been welcomed by St. Louis's French Creole inhabitants, who suddenly found themselves about to become Spanish subjects. Although they could only speculate about the long-term effects of these sudden and unexpected developments, neither Laclède nor the other settlers were disposed to leave their growing community.

British captain Harry Gordon visited St. Louis in 1766 and advised his superiors that Laclède, the town's principal Indian trader, might well gain control of the entire trade along the Missouri and upper Mississippi. According to Gordon, "he appears to be sensible, clever, and has been very well educated; is very active and will give us some Trouble before we get the Parts of this Trade that belong to us out of his hands." Gordon's account made clear that under Laclède's guidance, St. Louis was quickly emerging as a hub for fur-trading operations in the region.

Not all Indians had to travel to St. Louis. Laclède hired and outfitted agents who went to the villages of tribes in the surrounding territory to purchase their furs, but he failed in his efforts to maintain Maxent, Laclède, and Company's absolute control over the traffic in furs. French officials had canceled D'Abbadie's exclusive grants on the grounds that they were detrimental to commerce. The loss of the trading monopoly was a severe blow to Laclède's

fortunes, but he continued to participate actively in the fur trade.

A few months after the Spanish officials took charge in St. Louis, Laclède moved his family into a new stone dwelling he had constructed. He resided there with Marie Thérèse Chouteau until his death, but residents of the close-knit frontier community do not appear to have ever seriously questioned the unmarried couple's living arrangements. The nature of their relationship remained a matter so private that even the pair's four children could never bring themselves to acknowledge Laclède publicly as their father.

In 1769 Maxent terminated his partnership with Laclède and agreed to sell him the firm's assets in St. Louis. Since he did not have sufficient cash on hand to pay for his purchase, Laclède had to give Maxent a series of notes to cover the transaction. Once Laclède was on his own, he made Auguste Chouteau a partner in his reorganized business operations and later invited his son-in-law Sylvestre Labbadie to join them. Unfortunately, Laclède accumulated many uncollectible notes that threatened him with bankruptcy. He owed Maxent money and had to borrow to meet his current expenses. In 1777 Maxent foreclosed and forced Laclède to relinquish ownership of his St. Louis properties.

An ailing Laclède informed Auguste Chouteau of the sad state of his affairs on the final day of 1777. In the melancholy letter penned from New Orleans, Laclède worried that he would likely die in debt. His lamentation proved ominously prophetic. While en route back to St. Louis on May 27, 1778, he died on board his boat about two leagues below the Arkansas Post. Officials determined that he had died of natural causes and ordered him buried at a site long since forgotten. Many in St. Louis mourned his passing, but following his death the city's founder sank into obscurity and was for a time all but forgotten.

Factual errors, historical misrepresentations, and feuding descendants complicated subsequent efforts to rescue Laclède from the margins of history and write about his role in the founding of St. Louis and his relationships with the Chouteaus. Much of the confusion persisted until historian **John Francis McDermott,** a Laclède descendant, undertook the methodical research that finally made it possible to separate fact from fancy in the saga of St. Louis's founder.

WILLIAM E. FOLEY

Chouteau Collection. Missouri Historical Society, St. Louis.
Foley, William E. "The Laclède-Chouteau Puzzle: John Francis McDermott Supplies Some Missing Pieces." *Gateway Heritage* 4 (fall 1983): 18–25.

Foley, William E., and C. David Rice. *The First Chouteaus: River Barons of Early St. Louis.* Urbana: University of Illinois Press, 1983.

Laclède, Pierre. Collection. Missouri Historical Society, St. Louis.

McDermott, John Francis. "The Exclusive Trading Privileges of Maxent, Laclède, and Company." *Missouri Historical Review* 29 (July 1935): 272–78.

———. "Myths and Realities Concerning the Founding of St. Louis." In *The French in the Mississippi Valley,* ed. John Francis McDermott, 1–15. Urbana: University of Illinois Press, 1965.

LAMBERT, ALBERT BOND
(1875–1946)

Important in the history of business in Missouri, Albert Bond Lambert made even larger contributions to the development of aviation. Benefiting from his father's accomplishments, he enjoyed the business success that enabled him to play his other role.

Lambert was born in St. Louis on December 6, 1875, the son of Jordan W. Lambert, the founder of the Lambert Pharmaceutical Company. In 1896 young Albert put aside his studies at the University of Virginia to become president of the company, best known for an antiseptic called Listerine. He expanded the company's operations, establishing factories in France and Germany. A profitable enterprise, it soared in the 1920s when a new advertising campaign generated fears about halitosis and portrayed Listerine as the best means of avoiding or curing this malady that left one a social failure. He stepped down as president in 1923, becoming chairman of the board of directors, and retired from business in 1926 when his firm became a division of a larger corporation.

By then Lambert was heavily involved in his other career, aviation. Focusing first on balloons, he had joined with other St. Louisans in 1907, many of them millionaires like himself, to found the St. Louis Aero Club and build an airfield, the first in the city. He soon became a balloon pilot and participated in races. Balloons had uses for national defense, and Lambert became a champion of military preparedness as an officer of the Navy League. After the United States declared war in 1917, he organized and financed a training school in St. Louis for balloonists; it was assimilated into the Army Signal Corps and moved to Texas, and Lambert, commissioned a major, served as its commanding officer.

After the war Lambert organized the National Balloon Race but soon shifted his focus to airplanes. He had become an airplane pilot before the war, and in 1920 he purchased land northwest of the city and developed it into a multipurpose airfield, superior to the one the city had constructed in Forest Park. In 1927 a flyer, **Charles A. Lindbergh,** working for the major firm based at the field, turned to Lambert for support for a plan to demonstrate what aircraft could do by flying nonstop across the Atlantic. Lambert made the first pledge, and his prestige helped the young man get additional support. The backers called themselves the Spirit of St. Louis Organization, and Lindbergh, upon his return from Paris, hailed them in his book *We* as the "Men Whose Confidence and Foresight Made Possible the Flight of the 'Spirit of St. Louis.' "

As Lindbergh and his backers had hoped, the pilot's accomplishments gave a big boost to aviation in St. Louis. To Lambert, it seemed that the flight to Paris had enhanced the city's reputation and that a follow-up flight to Latin America would hasten the establishment of airmail service between the United States and Mexico. In 1928, still under Lindbergh's spell, St. Louis voters overwhelmingly endorsed a bond issue that enabled the city to purchase and develop Lambert's field into one of the nation's most important airports. Lambert sold it at a low price.

After these exciting and important events, Lambert and Lindbergh remained in touch with one another. When it was rumored in 1937 that the flyer and his family planned to settle permanently in England, it was Lambert who reported that he had received a letter from his friend expressing a desire to return home. After he returned, Lindbergh visited with Lambert and admired his ongoing efforts to improve St. Louis.

Lambert did not limit his life to business and aviation. He contributed to the Louisiana Purchase Exposition of 1904, was a member of the city council from 1907 to 1911, and served effectively on the St. Louis police board from 1933 to 1941. A man of many interests, he spent some of his time focusing on music, science, and travel. He was a husband, the father of four children, and an Episcopalian; he was also an athlete, playing football in college and winning golf championships in later years. He joined a number of clubs, where he often played leadership roles.

However, Lambert gained historical significance chiefly in aviation. Highly regarded around the world as well as at home, he helped make St. Louis a major aviation center. In the last years before his death in his mansion near Forest Park on November 12, 1946, he developed plans for further expansion of the city's airport. It continues to be known as Lambert Field.

RICHARD S. KIRKENDALL

Crouch, Tom D. *The Eagle Aloft: Two Centuries of the Balloon in America.* Washington, D.C.: Smithsonian Institution Press, 1983.

Fox, Stephen. *The Mirror Makers: A History of Amer-*

ican *Advertising and Its Creators.* New York: William Morrow, 1984.

Horgan, James J. "City of Flight: The History of Aviation in St. Louis." Ph.D. diss., St. Louis University, 1965.

New York Times, March 24, 1927–November 13, 1946.

The Wartime Journals of Charles A. Lindbergh. New York: Harcourt Brace Jovanovich, 1970.

"The Wings of the Eagle." *Everybody's Magazine* 33 (September 1915): 257–70.

LANE, JAMES HENRY (1814–1866)

James Henry Lane, a soldier, Kansas politician, and U.S. senator, was born on June 22, 1814, probably in Lawrenceburg, Indiana. His father, Amos, a native of New York State, was a lawyer who served in the Indiana legislature and the United States House of Representatives. His mother, Mary Foote Howes Lane, of a distinguished Connecticut family, "a woman of culture," opened a school for her children and others.

As a young man Lane operated a store with a brother-in-law until 1836, studied law in his father's office, and in 1840 was admitted to the Indiana bar. The next year he married Mary E. Baldridge of Youngstown, Ohio, a granddaughter of Gen. Arthur St. Clair. The marriage became stressful because of their removal to frontier Kansas and Lane's infidelity. A divorce in 1856 was followed by their remarriage in 1857.

Throughout his dramatic life Lane was a leader. His vaulting ambition, his charismatic public speaking, and his tendency to trim "his sails to catch the favoring breeze" help explain his success. When war with Mexico broke out in 1846, he organized a force, and within a short time he won election as a colonel. During the war, though without military training, he earned a favorable reputation as a soldier.

On his return to Indiana, Lane skillfully exploited his military glory and served as lieutenant governor from 1849 to 1853. Success in this post led to election to the United States House of Representatives in 1852. An ardent Democrat, he voted for the unpopular Kansas-Nebraska Act that reopened the Louisiana Territory to slavery. He declined renomination, and in April 1855, driving a ramshackle buggy, he arrived with his family in Lawrence, Kansas. The next day he opened a law office and was soon scanning opportunities to rise in politics. He observed slaveholding Missouri's influence in shaping Kansas affairs: Missouri "Border Ruffians" had illegally voted in Kansas, electing a proslavery legislature and sending a proslavery delegate to Washington.

Frustrated by Missouri Democrats in his effort to organize a Kansas Democratic Party, Lane joined the Free State movement. In October—six months after arrival—he maneuvered his election as president of the Topeka convention that drafted a Free State constitution, which Free State voters ratified.

During the so-called Wakarusa War, when twelve hundred Missourians invaded Kansas, Lane became a brigadier general commanding forces defending Lawrence. He was dissuaded from attacking the invaders, who outnumbered his men, and acquiesced to an arrangement effecting an exodus by the Missourians. His impetuosity and radicalism had come to the fore; these traits characterized the remainder of his career. While he fought to make Kansas a free state, he emerged as a leading Kansan.

Acting under the unauthorized Topeka constitution, the Free State legislature elected Lane to the United States Senate. In Washington he failed to win acceptance of a crudely prepared petition for admission of Kansas to the Union under the Topeka document. By May events in Kansas commanded his attention. Missouri "Border Ruffians" "sacked" Lawrence, and John Brown and his associates murdered five proslavery men at Pottawatomie Creek. Further invasions, skirmishes, and killings occurred in "Bleeding Kansas," to the nation's dismay.

Lane launched a speaking tour in behalf of a free Kansas. When Missourians closed the Missouri River route to Kansas—the usual gateway to the territory—Lane organized a new route through Iowa and Nebraska. By way of the "Jim Lane Trail" passed countless Free State emigrants as well as "Lane's Army of the North." His activities alarmed Missourians, who formed a force of about twelve hundred who entered Kansas under the leadership of U.S. senator **David Rice Atchison** and others. They collided with Lane's army at Bull Creek, sending the invaders back to Missouri.

For nearly two years Lane was relatively inactive, but upon admission of Kansas as a free state in 1861 he won election as U.S. senator. Guerrilla warfare and possible secession in Missouri engaged his attention. Winning the favor of President Lincoln he headed the "Kansas Brigade." The threatening activities of Confederate general **Sterling Price** in Missouri incited Lane and his men to invade the state in September, destroying property, setting the torch to Osceola, plundering, and freeing slaves.

Price retreated to the south, and Lane, after failing to win command of the Missouri-Kansas border, resigned his commission. In August 1863 **William Clarke Quantrill**'s band, partly to avenge Lane's burning of Osceola, raided Lawrence, killing 180 men and destroying the town. Lane called on Kansans to make a retaliatory attack. Gen. **John M. Schofield,** commanding the Missouri department, prevented this move.

In the Senate Lane portrayed himself as a radical Republican. He urged emancipation and arming the blacks, and advanced a scheme to colonize freedmen in western Texas, where they could "demonstrate to the world capacity for self-improvement and self-government." Opposed for reelection by rivals and critics, he escaped defeat by the timely advance of Price's cavalry toward Kansas. Lane helped Union general **Samuel R. Curtis**—serving as an aide experienced in border warfare—turn Price toward Arkansas.

Reelected to the Senate in 1865, Lane at first supported Andrew Johnson's policies. Voting to uphold the vetoes of the Freedmen's Bureau and Civil Rights Bill, he was out of touch with the radical sentiment that consumed his state. His resulting unpopularity, poor health, and charges of financial wrongdoing added to his unstable temperament and impelled him to suicide on July 11, 1866. An exotic figure, wild in physical appearance, intense in his passions, and gifted in leadership, Lane figured prominently in saving Kansas from proslavery and pro-Confederate influences.

JAMES A. RAWLEY

Castel, Albert. "Jim Lane of Kansas." *Civil War Times Illustrated* 12 (April 1973): 22–29.
Stephenson, Wendell Holmes. *The Political Career of James H. Lane.* Topeka: Kansas Printing Plant, 1930.

LANE, ROSE WILDER (1886–1968)

Rose Wilder Lane was born on December 5, 1886, in Dakota Territory to Almanzo and **Laura Ingalls Wilder.** Repeated crop failures drove the Wilders from their homestead claim, and after brief sojourns in Minnesota and Florida the family left De Smet, South Dakota, for Mansfield, Missouri, where they settled in 1894. Lane's rudimentary formal education in Mansfield was supplemented by a year of high school in Crowley, Louisiana, where she lived with an aunt until graduation in 1904.

Lane learned telegraphy and left home at seventeen to work in Kansas City. Eventually her work took her to San Francisco, where she married newspaperman Gillette Lane in 1909. They were divorced in 1918. During this period Lane began work as a feature writer for the *San Francisco Bulletin* and as a freelance writer. She published popular biographies of Henry Ford, Charlie Chaplin, Jack London, and Herbert Hoover. In 1920 she went to Europe as a traveling correspondent for the *San Francisco Call and Post* and as a publicity writer for the Red Cross and the Near East Relief. For four years she traveled throughout Europe, the Caucasus, and the Middle East. During these travels she developed her lifelong fascination with Albania.

Lane returned to her parents' Missouri farm until 1926, when she traveled again to Albania with the hope of living there permanently. However, she felt obliged to return to care for her aging parents, and from 1928 to 1935 she remained with them. The stock-market crash and the depression destroyed her small fortune and the hope that she could establish sufficient savings to support her parents and free herself to travel again. Nonetheless, these years also saw the beginning of the collaborative writing between Lane and her mother that resulted in the enormously popular *Little House* books by Laura Ingalls Wilder. Lane's silent hand in these books was never acknowledged; essentially, she rewrote her mother's amateurish narratives, providing the professional art that made the stories compelling. As the income from the books grew, Lane felt free to leave home again. After brief stays in Columbia, Missouri, and New York City, she bought a home in Danbury, Connecticut, in 1938.

During her early years as a freelance writer, Lane published several novels and many stories and articles of no great consequence. The depression and the Roosevelt administration, however, focused her thoughts on a few essential beliefs, and she became a vigorous opponent of the New Deal and a proponent of civil liberties and self-reliance. Her best novels, *Let the Hurricane Roar* (1933) and *Free Land* (1938), developed these themes and brought her substantial recognition, as did her similar articles in the *Saturday Evening Post.* She penned a summary of her political beliefs in *The Discovery of Freedom* (1943). During World War II she drew national attention for her refusal to accept a food-ration card, while her opposition to social security resulted in an ill-founded and much publicized investigation by the FBI, much to the bureau's embarrassment. In 1965, at age seventy-eight, Lane went to Vietnam to report on the conflict for *Woman's Day.* She died on October 30, 1968, in her Danbury home on the eve of another trip to Europe.

WILLIAM HOLTZ

Holtz, William. *The Ghost in the Little House: A Life of Rose Wilder Lane.* Columbia: University of Missouri Press, 1993.

LANE, WILLIAM CARR (1789–1863)

Born on December 1, 1789, in Fayette County, Pennsylvania, William Carr Lane spent the majority of his adult life west of the Mississippi as a physician and a politician. The army offered Lane his first opportunity to practice medicine and introduced him to the city of St. Louis, where he made his home. His lengthy political career in Missouri was highlighted by his election as St. Louis's first mayor. Late in his life Lane accepted the post of governor of the territory of New Mexico. After serving for less than a year in that capacity he returned to St. Louis where he resided until his death in 1863.

One of eleven children of Presley Carr and Sarah Stephenson Lane, William Carr Lane received his initial education in Pennsylvania. In 1811 he left Pennsylvania to study medicine in Louisville, Kentucky. After two years his mentor left for New Orleans, leaving Lane behind without immediate prospects. Looking for adventure, he joined the United States Infantry in 1813 to fight the Indians led by Tecumseh and the Shawnee Prophet in the Northwest Territory. While Lane was at Fort Harrison the Indians made themselves scarce, but bilious fever flourished. As a result of his earlier training in medicine Lane was appointed surgeon's mate and went to work fighting the fever. He spent the next six years alternately pursuing his medical education at the University of Pennsylvania and serving in the army.

On February 26, 1818, Lane married Mary Ewing of Vincennes, Indiana, whom he had met during his frequent assignments at Fort Harrison. A year later, probably at Mary's request, he resigned his commission in the army and settled in St. Louis. The couple subsequently produced eight children; unfortunately, only the two eldest daughters survived to adulthood and outlived their parents.

In addition to practicing medicine, Lane almost immediately involved himself in Missouri politics. In 1819 he was elected as one of five trustees of the "borough," as St. Louis was then called. By 1821 he was quartermaster general for the state of Missouri. He held this post until 1823, when St. Louisans elected him as the city's first mayor. Lane proved such a popular choice that he served five consecutive annual terms before focusing his attention on state politics. In 1826, while still mayor, he ran for and won one of St. Louis's four seats in the Missouri House of Representatives. St. Louisans reelected him to this office again in 1830 and 1832. In 1837 he resumed his position as mayor of St. Louis. Lane maintained this post for the next two terms. During his time as mayor Lane was credited with the initial planning of St. Louis city government. In 1839, after serving nine terms as mayor and three terms in the state House, Lane declared himself finished with politics and retired to his medical practice and his family for the next thirteen years.

Following the premature death of his favorite son, Victor, Lane grew discontented with St. Louis life and readily accepted President Millard Fillmore's invitation to serve as New Mexico's second territorial governor. Despite the protestations of family and friends who feared for his health and safety, the sixty-three-year-old Lane embarked on the arduous journey to the western territory. On September 13, 1852, he was inaugurated as governor but held the post for only ten months. At the end of his term he ran for New Mexico's lone seat in the United States House of Representatives, but lost to a native New Mexican. Although he contested the election, Lane ultimately returned to his home and family in St. Louis.

With the coming of the Civil War Lane showed himself to be an ardent states' righter and a secessionist. This position put him at odds with many of his neighbors, friends, and family members. Because he was so outspoken about his beliefs Lane feared he might be arrested by the Unionist forces running St. Louis during the war, though this never came to pass. After several weeks of illness William Carr Lane died in his home in St. Louis on January 6, 1863.

KRISTA CAMENZIND

Darby, John F. *Personal Recollections of Many Prominent People Whom I Have Known and of Events—Especially of Those Relating to the History of St. Louis—during the First Half of the Present Century*. St. Louis: G. I. Jones, 1880.

Historical Society of New Mexico. "Historical Sketch of Governor William Carr Lane, Together with the Diary of His Journey from St. Louis, Missouri to Santa Fe, New Mexico, July 31, to September 9, 1852." No. 20 (November 1, 1917): 5–21.

Horn, Calvin. "Governor Lane: 'Bold and Brave.'" *New Mexico Magazine* 35 (October 1957): 24, 54–57.

"Letters of William Carr Lane, 1819–1831." *Glimpses of the Past* (January–June 1940): 47–118.

LATHROP, JOHN HIRAM (1799–1866)

John Hiram Lathrop, the first president of the University of Missouri, was born in Sherbourne, New York, on January 22, 1799. The difficult task of establishing a state university in the Missouri frontier rested on his capabilities, and he proved equal to it. A graduate of Yale University, Lathrop was serving as professor of law, civil polity, and political economy at New York's Hamilton College when the call to Missouri came; he accepted the challenge on November 16, 1840.

In 1839 the Boone County seat of Columbia, with its population of nine hundred citizens, was selected as the site for the University of Missouri. The selection process was competitive, generating bitterness in the surrounding communities of Callaway, Cole, Cooper, Saline, and Howard Counties. The final selection of Boone County created disinterest in the institution as a site for higher learning in Missouri; it was up to Lathrop and the board of curators to turn that negativity around and develop an institution that would be distinguished for its role in higher education. Since the Missouri General Assembly did not appropriate any money toward this endeavor, it was Lathrop's tenacity that fulfilled the university goals.

"*I accept,* gentlemen," read Lathrop's 1840 letter to the board of curators, "the place offered me by the Board of Curators whom you represent, with a mind open to the greatness of the trust I thereby assume, and with the full determination to pursue, with zeal, fidelity, and the ability which God has given me, the high and valuable ends for the accomplishment of which the appointment has been made." Lathrop did not know that the zeal and determination of which he wrote would be practically his only assets in his enterprise. When he arrived in Columbia in 1841, there was no faculty, only a handful of students from the already established Columbia College, and no university buildings to speak of, save the seventy-five-thousand-dollar building under construction.

Despite these seeming adversities, Lathrop issued a handbill in March 1841 announcing that university classes would begin on April 14, 1841. In those early years, Lathrop and the other three instructors often went without pay in order to keep the doors open to the seventy-some students enrolled. It was not until two years later, in June 1843, that the university moved into its new building. Six months earlier, understanding the financial difficulties that continued to stalk the fledgling institution, Lathrop voluntarily reduced his salary from $2,500 per year to $1,250 per year; the curators immediately accepted his offer. Despite the monetary hardships, the first commencement exercises in the university's history were held on November 28, 1843; two cousins, Robert L. Todd and Robert B. Todd, were the focus of the three-hour and ten-speech ceremony.

The university offered the traditional four-year liberal arts course, and, while course offerings were sometimes limited due to financial constraints, many graduates went on to professional careers, particularly in law. Looking to expand the curriculum in 1846, Lathrop proposed establishing a connection with the Missouri Medical College in St. Louis, which was approved by the board of curators. He also suggested the adoption of the two-term session (twenty-one weeks each) and the establishment of a university normal school for the instruction of teachers. A program of civil engineering was added in 1849. Extracurricular intellectual activities were not slighted at the campus; with President Lathrop's encouragement, two literary societies were established: the Union Literary Society and the Athenaean Society.

While these slow strides forward proved Lathrop's tenacity in establishing the university, other decisions were out of his hands. In 1845 the General Assembly rewrote the university statute, increasing the number of curators from fifteen to twenty, possibly in an effort to obtain quorums at meetings. These additional five members were to be the governor, the state treasurer, the secretary of state, the state auditor, and the university president. The inclusion of the four state officials increased the influence of politics in the university's affairs; the years of progress came to include years of partisan politics as national events leading to the Civil War divided Missourians and the university. The new (primarily Democratic) board of curators, elected in 1849, criticized Lathrop's eight-year administration and, suspicious that the New England Yankee who was closely affiliated with Boone County Whig leaders was not actively proslavery, forced him to resign. Lathrop's "unhesitating reliance on the co-operation and indulgent support of the curators," expressed in his 1840 acceptance letter, made him disheartened by the events leading to his resignation in July 1849. He left the university, having visibly strengthened its internal organization.

Lathrop accepted a position as the first chancellor of the University of Wisconsin; from 1859 to 1860 he served as president of Indiana University. In 1862 he returned to the University of Missouri as a professor of English; a month later he was named chairman of the faculty. After the Civil War he was once again chosen president of the university, this time to lead the postwar campus to higher educational ambitions. He remained in this position until his death by typhoid fever on August 2, 1866. His widow, Frances, and at least three children survived him; his son Gardiner later became a leading Kansas City attorney. The "learning, talents, integrity, and upright moral character" of John Hiram Lathrop, expressed in resolution at his resignation dinner, served him well as founder of the oldest state university west of the Mississippi River.

CHRISTYN L. ELLEY

Gentry, North Todd. *Bench and Bar of Boone County, Missouri.* Columbia, Mo.: E. W. Stephens, 1916.

Lathrop, John Hiram. Papers. Western Historical Manuscripts Collection, Columbia.

Olson, James C., and Vera Olson. *The University of Missouri: An Illustrated History.* Columbia: University of Missouri Press, 1988.

Stephens, Frank F. *A History of the University of Missouri.* Columbia: University of Missouri Press, 1962.

Viles, Jonas. *The University of Missouri: A Centennial History.* Columbia: University of Missouri, 1939.

Weaver, John C. "Footsteps in the Corridors behind Us." *Missouri Historical Review* 62 (1968): 213–34.

LAWLESS, LUKE (1781–1846)

Luke Lawless was an able, erratic, and scholarly lawyer and jurist of early Missouri. A slender five-foot-ten Irishman of military bearing, he was very reserved, had few intimates, and seldom mixed socially. He was an impressive speaker, however, having a quick wit and facility for repartee, and was adept at irony and sarcasm. An accomplished linguist and skilled in judicial analysis, he appeared absentminded and frequently arrived late or missed appointments. He had an excessive fondness for potatoes, eating large quantities at just about every meal. At times he displayed a quick temper, once losing a fistfight to a sheriff of St. Louis County. A practical man, Lawless asserted, "When your head is under an ass's heel there is but one thing to be done—that is, to lie perfectly still."

Lawless's background was both interesting and cosmopolitan. Born in Dublin in 1781 into a prominent Roman Catholic family with strong republican leanings, he entered the British navy at an early age and mustered out following the peace of Amiens of 1802. As an ardent Irish patriot, he was a sympathetic supporter of the rising of 1798 against English rule in Ireland. He read for the bar in Dublin, gaining admittance during the Michaelmas term of 1805. Five years later, feeling discriminated against on religious grounds and for his republican tendencies, he fled to France to fight the British in an Irish regiment in the army of Napoléon Bonaparte. Lawless distinguished himself as a military secretary (a form of staff officer), rising to the rank of colonel. After Waterloo he emigrated to the United States and settled in St. Louis where he opened a law office.

Lawless became a friend of **Thomas Hart Benton** and served as his second in his 1817 duel with **Charles Lucas.** Lawless frequently represented claimants against the federal government in the complex litigation regarding the validity of land titles granted in Missouri under Spanish rule. An estimated twenty-five hundred land grant cases remained unsettled in 1824 when Congress passed special legislation giving primary jurisdiction to the United States District Court of Missouri, presided by Judge **James Peck.** Lawless, who had taken some seventy land grant cases on a contingent-fee basis, became enraged when Peck ruled against him in 1826 in the test case of *Soulard v. United States.* After Lawless wrote a letter published in a St. Louis newspaper attacking the reasoning behind the decision and charging eighteen errors of fact, Peck cited him for contempt, sentencing him to jail for twenty-four hours and suspending him from federal practice for eighteen months.

Lawless retaliated by launching a four-year campaign to impeach Peck. "By God, I will have him before the Senate," Lawless exclaimed. The con-troversy raised questions about the use of judicial power, and in 1830, in only the fourth such action under the Constitution, the House of Representatives impeached Peck. Lawless helped the House managers prepare their case against Peck, but after a trial of several weeks, on January 31, 1831, the Senate found him not guilty by a vote of twenty-two to twenty-one, far short of the two-thirds majority required for conviction. Peck, his reputation tarnished, suffered the further indignity of seeing *Soulard* reversed by the Supreme Court a year prior to his death in 1836.

Gov. **Daniel Dunklin** appointed Lawless as a judge of the St. Louis Circuit Court following the resignation of Judge **William C. Carr** in 1834. Lawless's tenure on the court was controversial. Accounts in local newspapers ridiculed his conduct on the bench, and sixteen members of the St. Louis bar urged the governor not to reappoint him. Lawless's handling of a grand jury, summoned to investigate the 1836 lynching of Francis McIntosh, added to his notoriety. McIntosh, a free black riverboatman, had stabbed a deputy sheriff to death while attempting to escape his custody. After the authorities placed the accused murderer in the St. Louis jail, a mob stormed the building and removed the prisoner to the edge of town where they chained him to a tree and lit a fire beneath him. McIntosh died a slow and agonizing death, but during the subsequent inquest Lawless advised the grand jurors that spontaneous mob action transcended their jurisdiction and was beyond the reach of human law. He attempted to place blame for the affair on the abolitionists, by suggesting that their inflammatory writings had incited McIntosh to attack the deputy. Lawless was undoubtedly aiming his remarks at **Elijah Lovejoy,** editor of the *St. Louis Observer* and one of the judge's severest critics. Lovejoy, who responded by calling Lawless a foreigner and a papist whose notions of government had been formed amid the turbulent agitations of Ireland when anarchy and illegal violence prevailed, subsequently fled from St. Louis to Alton, Illinois, where he died at the hands of an antiabolitionist mob.

After serving on the St. Louis Circuit Court for three years, Lawless returned to private practice. He died on September 3, 1846, at the age of sixty-five, leaving his wife, Virginia de Greuhm Lawless, a baroness whose first husband had been the Prussian minister to the United States. A memorial resolution of the bar of St. Louis praised Lawless's attributes: "Gifted in intellect, of the highest culture, steady in his attainments, of kindly disposition, and with an instructive relish for all that was elegant and refined, he was happily adapted to teach and delight, in that polished society of which he was the chief ornament." Left unsaid was any mention of the Peck affair, the most important aspect of Lawless's experience in Missouri.

LAWRENCE H. LARSEN

Bay, W. V. N. *Reminiscences of the Bench and Bar of Missouri*. St. Louis: F. H. Thomas, 1878.
Bushnell, Eleanore. "The Impeachment and Trial of James H. Peck." *Missouri Historical Review* 74 (January 1980): 137–67.
Larsen, Lawrence H. *Federal Justice in Western Missouri: The Judges, the Cases, the Times*. Columbia: University of Missouri Press, 1994.
Van Ravenswaay, Charles. *St. Louis: An Informal History of the City and Its People, 1764–1865*. St. Louis: Missouri Historical Society Press, 1991.

LAZIA, JOHN F. (1896–1934)

John Lazia, originally John Lazzio, was born in the "Little Italy" section of Kansas City in 1896, the son of Italian immigrants. Little is known about his early life, except that his formal education ended after the eighth grade. A bright and popular child, he impressed adults enough to be asked to clerk in a law office and eventually to be given the opportunity to study law.

However, in 1914, at the age of eighteen, Lazia committed an armed robbery, which brought him $250, a diamond stickpin, a watch, and a quick arrest. Even then he had a following and supporters. The police discovered a plot to disrupt the court where he was arraigned. Purportedly, supporters planned to break him out of jail, and the jury that convicted him received death threats. A judge sentenced him to fifteen years in the Missouri Penitentiary. He served less than a year.

Upon his release from prison, Lazia began his Kansas City career, both in business and in politics. An amiable, soft-spoken, well-dressed young man of moderate size and height, a wearer of rimless glasses, the intelligent and articulate Lazia engaged in legitimate business enterprises, including real estate, soft drink manufacturing, and a carnival company. He and his associates were also involved in illegal gambling and the bootleg liquor industry. "Brother John," the name some of his associates called him, had a financial interest in a dog racetrack at Riverside, north of the Missouri River. He also owned Cuban Gardens, a nearby roadhouse. A natural leader who had considerable organizational and executive ability, Lazia saw his businesses grow.

Lazia became more politically active in 1928, when his subordinates used strong-arm tactics to take control of the North Side Democratic Club, the longtime headquarters of the Democratic Party in the area known as Little Italy. Lazia deposed Mike Ross, an Irish American who had worked with **Jim Pendergast** since the turn of the century and who by 1928 was closely associated with **Tom Pendergast**'s Democratic organization. Ross and Pendergast also shared business interests. Despite moving his residence to the more southern part of the city, Ross had hoped to maintain his control of the North Side Club. Lazia destroyed that plan.

Initially, the ouster of his colleague incensed Tom Pendergast, but, being a political pragmatist, he soon came to an agreement with Lazia. Thereafter, the North Side Democratic Club could be counted on to deliver seventy-five hundred votes for the Pendergast machine. Pendergast soon called Lazia "one of my chief lieutenants."

Through his political connections, Lazia had influence within the Kansas City Police Department. Having connections with both the underworld and the police department, he could sometimes provide a bridge between the two. In 1931 he was instrumental in obtaining the release of Kansas City dress manufacturer **Nell Donnelly (Reed)** after she was kidnapped. He also helped obtain the release of Mary McElroy, the daughter of city manager **Henry F. McElroy,** after she was kidnapped in 1933.

A federal grand jury investigated Lazia for possible income tax evasion in 1933. He had failed to report some $125,000 of his recent income. His extravagant lifestyle had drawn attention: he had placed large bets on horse races, he had a second home at stylish Lake Lotawana in rural Jackson County, and his wife, Marie, had expensive tastes. Convicted and sentenced to a year in jail in February 1934, Lazia remained free while his case was being appealed.

Lazia knew he had enemies. For good reason, a bodyguard drove his bulletproof car. Yet, he was not expecting what happened to him in the early hours of July 10, 1934. Having probably obstructed someone's illegal activities in Kansas City, Lazia was marked for death. After he and his wife had spent an evening visiting nightspots in downtown Kansas City, they arrived at their midtown apartment well after midnight. As they got out of the car, Lazia was hit by several bullets. He died a few hours later. He was thirty-eight years old.

At Lazia's wake several thousand people viewed his body. The official funeral procession included 120 cars and four trucks filled with flowers. The funeral was held at Holy Rosary Church, a block from Lazia's boyhood home.

DONALD B. OSTER

Dorsett, Lyle W. *The Pendergast Machine*. New York: Oxford University Press, 1968.
Larsen, Lawrence H., and Nancy J. Hulston. *Pen-

dergast! Columbia: University of Missouri Press, 1997.

Miller, Richard Lawrence. *Truman: The Rise to Power.* New York: McGraw-Hill, 1986.

Reddig, William M. *Tom's Town: Kansas City and the Pendergast Legend.* 1947. Reprint, Columbia: University of Missouri Press, 1986.

LEAKE, DOROTHY VAN DYKE (1893–1990)

Dorothy Van Dyke Leake, an educator noted for her ecological work and her efforts to preserve Crane Creek in Stone County, was born on September 6, 1893, in Columbus Junction, Iowa. Her parents, Benjamin Franklin and Fannie Fern Van Dyke, moved their family to Granite, Oklahoma, in 1900. After spending her childhood and adolescent years in Oklahoma, Van Dyke came to Missouri in 1910 to attend Drury College in Springfield. She received a B.A. in biology in 1914, followed by an M.A. a year later.

Van Dyke taught in public schools in Missouri and Oklahoma from 1915 until 1918, when she moved to Enid, Oklahoma, to head the biology department at Phillips University for a year.

In June 1919 Van Dyke married Harold Henderson Leake, whom she had met while a student at Drury College. The couple made their home on property purchased for them by Benjamin Van Dyke in 1920. These 131 acres, which included the headwaters of Crane Creek in the northwest corner of Stone County, became the focal point of the Leakes' lives. They spent the first seven years of their married life on the Crane Creek property, and their two children were born there.

In 1927 and 1928 Leake attended summer classes in chemistry, first at the University of Missouri and then at Columbia University. She resumed her teaching career in 1928 when she became head of the chemistry and biology department at Monett Junior College. In 1933 she left Missouri to accept a professorship of biology at Southeastern State College in Durant, Oklahoma. With the exception of one year, 1944–1945, Leake spent the remainder of her academic career in Oklahoma.

About 1937 Leake began work on her Ph.D. at the University of Oklahoma. While teaching at least part-time either in the Norman public schools or at Oklahoma A&M College in Stillwater, she eventually completed the degree in 1944. She spent 1945–1947 teaching botany at the University of Oklahoma; a two-year stint in Oklahoma A & M College's botany department followed. In 1949 she returned to Southeastern State College as a professor and then head of the department of biology, where she remained until her retirement from academic life in 1959.

Leake specialized in the study of algae and published several articles on species found in Oklahoma and the Ozark Mountains in the *Proceedings of the Oklahoma Academy of Science.* Another article on algae appeared in the *American Midland Naturalist.*

Leake always retained a close interest in the Crane Creek property, and following her retirement she focused her professional work on "the ecology, physiology and taxonomy of algae" in the vicinity. In a time of increasing stream pollution, she became dedicated to preserving "Crane Creek at its ecological peak." The creek had been stocked with rainbow trout from California's McCloud River in the 1880s and remained one of the few midwestern streams with a "self-sustaining population" of the species. Leake and her husband's dedication to the stream's ecology proved instrumental in the survival of the fish. Always eager to share their ecological interests, they made their property into an outdoor classroom for use by youth groups and students of all ages.

In addition to her ecological work, Leake was an accomplished illustrator, primarily of plants. Her pen-and-ink drawings appeared in *The Handbook of Rocky Mountain Plants,* published by Ruth Ashton Nelson in 1969, and in 1972 the Hunt Institute for Botanical Documentation at Carnegie-Mellon University chose her illustrations for inclusion in the Third International Exhibition of Botanical Art and Illustration. She and her husband respectively illustrated and wrote *Wildflowers of the Ozarks,* which appeared in 1981. *Desert and Mountain Plants of the Southwest,* published posthumously in 1993, featured Leake's illustrations and text written by her children, John Benjamin Leake and Marcelotte Leake Roeder.

Drury College recognized Leake's ecological and botanical work in 1989 by awarding her an honorary doctorate degree. The Oklahoma Academy of Science make her an honorary life member in 1961, noting that she had "served science with honor and distinction." Other awards included Drury College's Distinguished Alumni Award and the Ellen Swallow Richard Award from the Living Water Center, in Eureka Springs, Arkansas, for work in ecology.

Following a distinguished career as an educator, a botanical illustrator, and a nationally known environmental activist, Leake died in Aurora, Missouri, on July 23, 1990.

LYNN WOLF GENTZLER

Broyles, Carmen, ed. "I'm Making Every Effort to Preserve": Dorothy Leake's Love for the Ozarks." *Bittersweet* 7 (summer 1980): 4–13.

Dains, Mary K., ed. *Show Me Missouri Women: Selected Biographies.* Kirksville, Mo.: Thomas Jefferson University Press, 1989.

Henderson, Harold, and Dorothy Van Dyke Leake. Papers. Western Historical Manuscripts Collection, Columbia.

Lemons, Marcia Lee. "Dorothy Leake: Biologist, Artist, and Defender of Crane Creek." *Springfield! Magazine* 7 (September 1985): 42–43.

Love, Kathy. "To Cherish and Protect: Dorothy Leake's One Woman Crusade to Control Pollution." *Missouri Conservationist* 49 (August 1988): 4–7.

LEAR, WILLIAM POWELL
(1902–1978)

William Powell Lear, an engineer, entrepreneur, and inventor, pioneered the small corporate jet plane that bears his name and developed the automobile radio, the automatic pilot for aircraft, and the eight-track stereo cartridge.

The son of Reuben Marion and Gertrude Elizabeth Powell Lear, Bill Lear was born in Hannibal, Missouri, on June 26, 1902. His parents' marriage soon dissolved, and Gertrude and son Bill moved to Dubuque, Iowa, then to Chicago where Lear spent his formative years. His mother, a fundamentalist Christian and strict disciplinarian, expected her maverick son to adopt her values.

A bright, imaginative, and headstrong student, Lear sometimes contradicted and embarrassed his science and vocational teachers. As a result, the sixteen year old withdrew from school, lied about his age, and joined the navy, where he illustrated a special talent for electronics and became an instructor in "wireless receivers."

Following his term in the navy, this "wizard with the wireless" returned to Illinois and launched his entrepreneurial career by developing the first practical automobile radio. He served as president of Quincy Radio Lab (1922–1924) and the Lear Radio Lab in Tulsa (1924–1928) before returning to Chicago to work for Radio Coil and Wire Company (1928–1931).

Lear sold his car-radio patent (the first of 150 patents in his career) to Motorola and directed his attention to a new passion: airplanes. In 1931 the newly licensed pilot flew to New York City and plunged headlong into the aircraft components industry. Before leaving New York in 1934, Lear sold his idea for an aircraft radio to the Radio Corporation of America.

In 1934 Lear moved to Dayton, Ohio, to found Lear Aviation. He developed a navigational direction finder for aircraft, but had difficulty in marketing it. He found it frustrating to compete with major corporations in the sale of technical equipment. Moreover, his acerbic personality did not appeal to air force officials who elected not to purchase Lear's allegedly superior direction finder.

In 1939 World War II began in Europe, and Lear moved to Grand Rapids, Michigan, and formed Lear, Inc. He channeled his energies toward the development of aircraft instruments, including his most famous invention: a lightweight automatic pilot. The autopilot used electronic impulses to enable an aircraft to fly automatically on a fixed course. Ultimately, his autopilot set new performance standards and earned him aviation's highest honor: the Collier Trophy. The technological requirements of war had catapulted Lear into the forefront of the aviation industry. By 1945 Lear, Inc., had supplied $100 million worth of spare parts to the armed services.

In the decade following World War II, Lear sold his Grand Rapids plant and moved to Wichita, Kansas, to build a jet plane. Developing a small corporate jet became an obsession, and he struggled to convince financiers and engineers that his idea would work. From 1963 to 1967 this "hands-on" executive could be found day and night in his shirtsleeves on the assembly line at his Lear Jet Corporation plant.

Overcoming many financial and design problems, the intrepid industrialist developed the Learstar. In an effort to expand sales of his corporate jets abroad, he became the first American to fly a private plane to the Soviet Union. This self-promotion had the intended effect, and Lear Jets became a familiar profile in the world's air corridors. However, several crashes marred Lear's success in aircraft design. Critics pointed to icing problems on the exterior surfaces, and sales plummeted. Accordingly, in 1967 Lear sold his company to the Gates Rubber Company whose engineers modified the plane's design, corrected the icing problem, and restored its popularity.

Lear had temporarily lost his passion for aircraft design, so he devoted his energy to a scheme to develop a steam-powered automobile. Even before it became evident that his efforts would be his most colossal blunder, Lear once again succumbed to the magnetism of flight. In 1969 he unveiled plans to design and develop a faster and more efficient Learfan business jet.

By early 1978 Lear knew that leukemia would soon claim his life. Completing work on a turboprop business jet consumed the last few weeks of his life. Survived by his fourth wife and six children, Lear died in Reno, Nevada, on May 14, 1978.

JACK B. RIDLEY

Boesen, Victor. *They Said It Couldn't Be Done: The Incredible Story of Bill Lear.* Garden City, N.Y.: Doubleday, 1971.

New York Times, May 15, 1978.

Who Was Who in America. Vol. 7. London: George Prior Associates, 1981.

LEE, CHARLES ALBERT (1891–1984)

A biographer notes that the accomplishments of Charles Albert Lee as an educator show that he "entered the field of usefulness for which nature intended him."

Lee was active as an educator for sixty-two years before his retirement as a college professor in 1971 at the age of eighty. His teaching appointments took him into rural schoolrooms near Rolla in Phelps County; to California, Missouri, where he was a high school science teacher; and to Lamar and Butler where he was superintendent. He filled all these positions before he won the Democratic primary in 1922 and was elected state superintendent of schools, defeating the incumbent, **Sam Baker,** a Republican who was later elected governor of Missouri.

Lee was born on July 18, 1891, on a farm near Rolla, the son of G. B. and Susan Green Lee. He received his elementary education in the rural schools of Phelps County and attended high school in St. James and Rolla. In 1916 he completed studies at Central Missouri State Teachers College, and in the summer of 1917 he received a master of arts degree from the School of Education at the University of Missouri–Columbia.

Shortly before his graduation in May 1917, Lee was married to Inez Long, the daughter of Lemuel L. Long and Medora Adams Long of Independence. The couple had four children: Charles Albert Jr., Robert Edward, Loyd Lemuel, and Gerald B.

After his first election as state superintendent in 1922, Lee won reelection in 1926 and 1930. It was noted that at thirty-one he was the youngest person to be elected to that state office and, subsequently, the first person to be elected to three terms. After he lost his bid for a fourth term, Lee attended Teachers College at Columbia University, later receiving his Ph.D. He accepted an appointment in the department of education at Washington University in St. Louis, retiring in 1969. His last teaching assignment was on the faculty of Southern Illinois University in Edwardsville.

A biographical sketch published by W. T. Carrington, who also was a lifelong educator, noted that Lee "tightened up all the screws" when he was state superintendent. "He wisely assigned his inspectors to districts and kept them away from the office. . . . Others may advocate state activities. He does it." Lee's major concerns as state superintendent were directed toward the consolidation of rural schools, advancing the establishment of kindergarten and high school classes, and stressing the importance of equality in opportunities for students and in financing of schools, large and small, urban and rural.

In his efforts to consolidate small schools, Lee wrote that in 1925, 2,652 districts in Missouri had an average daily attendance of fewer than fifteen pupils, 952 had fewer than ten pupils, and 35 districts had terms less than four months long. He observed, "The little old red schoolhouse has served its mission. . . . In the one-room schoolhouse, so common in rural communities, effective and rational teaching is almost impossible."

Lee's efforts for equality in financing resulted in passage of a revised apportionment law by the Missouri General Assembly in 1931. The legislation replaced a system under which 2,500 of the 9,000 school districts received "almost all school moneys as priority claims, the remaining 6,500 getting what was left." The new law established the principle of a minimum guarantee of state aid, based on a minimum levy by a school district.

As state superintendent Lee was an ex-officio member of several state boards, including the boards of regents of the five teachers colleges and Lincoln University in Jefferson City, the state's institution of higher learning for African Americans. In 1926, as a member of the Lincoln board, Lee appeared before a meeting of the North Central Association to support Lincoln's applications for admission as a teachers college and a liberal arts college. The school had already been inspected for admission, and the applications were granted shortly after Lee's appearance before the association's meeting in Chicago.

In a move extremely rare in political annals, Lee wrote in a report on public schools during the 1928–1929 term that his elective office should be abolished. He argued that the superintendent should be appointed by members of a state board of education who in turn were appointed by the governor, observing, "Service of this quality will not often be secured by means of a popular election."

Lee's interest in elections was not restricted to educational positions. In 1954 he ran for the St. Louis County Council, and two years later, at the age of sixty-five, he renewed his bid for statewide office as a candidate for governor. He took leave from Washington University to launch his campaign, but was defeated in the Democratic primary by **James T. Blair Jr.** of Jefferson City, who was elected in November. Lee's campaign platform called for increased funding for public schools and revision of the state income tax law to provide aid to the schools of Missouri.

Lee made his home in Webster Groves, Missouri, after his final retirement. He was active in the Congregational Church and in his garden, tending to his dahlias and winning ribbons for his efforts. He died on October 10, 1984, at the age of ninety-three and was buried in Paddlewheel Cemetery at Licking, Missouri.

JERENA E. GIFFEN

Carrington, William Thomas. *History of Education in Missouri, Autobiographical.* N.p., 1931.
Jackson, W. R. *Missouri Democracy.* 3 vols. Chicago: S. J. Clarke, 1935.
Missouri Report of Public Schools. Jefferson City: State Department of Education, 1923–1934.
Official Manual of the State of Missouri, 1923–1924. Jefferson City: Secretary of State, 1924.
Official Manual of the State of Missouri, 1927–1928. Jefferson City: Secretary of State, 1928.
Official Manual of the State of Missouri, 1933–1934. Jefferson City: Secretary of State, 1934.

LEMP, ADAM (1798–1862)

Adam Lemp, patriarch of what was destined to become one of America's great brewing families, was born in 1798 in Eschwege, in central Germany. He emigrated to the United States in 1836 to escape the political and social upheaval in his homeland.

After a two-year stay in Cincinnati, Lemp made his way to St. Louis, where he settled permanently in 1838 and established a small grocery business. Shortly thereafter he branched out into the manufacture and sale of vinegar and, using skills he had mastered in Germany, brewed beer as well.

As the city's population grew, so did the sales of Lemp's beer (especially among the beer-loving German citizenry). The popularity of his product convinced Lemp to abandon the grocery business and devote his full energies to brewing. In 1840 he established the Western Brewery. Initially, the total output of his establishment was only about one hundred barrels per year. In his crude and modest plant, he made excellent beer, as evidenced by the large crowds that gathered nightly at Lemp's Hall, a saloon located on the same premises as his brewery.

Lemp's brewery was not the first in the city, but it quickly became the largest and most popular such operation. His success can largely be attributed to the fact that he was the first brewer in the Midwest to offer a German-style lager beer in a city that attracted some forty-five thousand new German settlers between 1835 and 1860. In fact, Lemp was the first brewer west of Philadelphia to produce lager, which is still the most popular style of beer consumed in America.

Lemp's beer used a type of yeast and a brewing process that differed from those used in making the traditional English-style ales and porters found in the Midwest in the 1830s. Because lager required a long period of aging before it was ready for consumption, Lemp found the naturally cool conditions in St. Louis's vast network of underground caves perfectly suited to this purpose in the days before refrigeration. He discovered and outfitted a large cavern in south St. Louis with twenty thirty-barrel oak casks for aging his fine brew.

By 1850 Lemp's revolutionary product had won the hearts and palates of the natives as well as those of their immigrant neighbors. Together they helped to make Western Brewery the largest of twenty-four such facilities in St. Louis and set into motion one of St. Louis's most prosperous and powerful brewing dynasties.

Adam Lemp died in St. Louis on August 23, 1862.

STEPHEN P. WALKER

Baron, Stanley Wade. *Brewed in America: A History of Beer and Ale in the United States.* Boston: Little, Brown, 1962.
Primm, James Neal. *Lion of the Valley: St. Louis, Missouri, 1764–1980.* 3d ed. St. Louis: Missouri Historical Society Press, 1998.

LEMP, WILLIAM J. (1836–1904)

William J. Lemp, one of the most prominent brewers in the history of St. Louis, was born in Germany in 1836. The son of brewing great **Adam Lemp,** William spent his early childhood in Germany, and was brought to St. Louis by his father at the age of twelve. He was educated in the St. Louis public schools and St. Louis University. A gifted brewer and businessman, his talents and training fully qualified him for a career in his father's brewery, where he quickly rose to the position of superintendent.

Naturalized in 1858, Lemp took an active role in the affairs of his adopted land. Upon the outbreak of the Civil War, he enlisted in the Third Regiment of the United States Reserve Corps, being mustered out with the rank of orderly sergeant. Shortly thereafter he married Julia Feickert on December 3, 1861.

Upon the death of his father in 1862, Lemp assumed full control of the Western Brewery. The progressive businessman realized early that his father's modest brewing facilities would be inadequate to satisfy the growing demand for the family's famous recipe. Thus, in 1864 he commenced with plans for a larger brewery—still in existence—at the site of his father's lager cave in south St. Louis. The brewery's new location minimized the time and labor involved in handling the beer, which Adam Lemp had hauled to the cave by horse-drawn wagons, and also offered room for expansion.

The brewing plant Lemp built was a marvel of efficiency, and was one of the largest and best-equipped such facilities in the nation. He strived to keep abreast of the latest technology, and the machinery in his plant was of the latest construction. His was one of the first breweries to employ artificial refrigeration and automated bottling machines. Lemp was also one of the first to make use of the recently perfected pasteurization process to ensure the safe shipment of beer over long distances.

The latter process enabled Lemp to become one of the first of a handful of so-called national brewers: those who embarked on large-scale promotional efforts to sell their brands to an ever growing audience. Eventually, Lemp opened dozens of branch offices to support his nationwide marketing efforts. He even set up his own railway, the Western Cable Railway Company, so he could maintain control over all aspects of the shipment of his product. Over his vast network, Lemp marketed six brands of beer. In addition to the flagship label, Falstaff, the William J. Lemp Brewing Company produced Tally, Tip Top, Standard, Culmbacher, and Extra Pale (a forerunner of modern "light" beers). He shipped his beer to South America, Mexico, Cuba, India, Japan, the Hawaiian Islands, China, the Philippines, Australia, and all the major cities of Europe. By the end of the nineteenth century, the company's annual output of five hundred thousand barrels of beer made it the eighth largest American brewery, with annual sales surpassing $3.5 million.

For many years the William J. Lemp Brewing Company enjoyed a position of dominance in the St. Louis brewing industry. Lemp's beer won awards at every state fair in the Union along with silver medals at the Centennial Exposition in Philadelphia and the Paris Exposition of 1878. In addition, Lemp's was the only American beer served at the U.S. Pavilion during the Paris Exposition of 1900, and the only bottled beer served by the official caterers at the 1901 Pan American Exposition. In 1904, at the Louisiana Purchase Exposition, Lemp sold more bottled beer than any other brewer.

As an active participant in civic affairs, Lemp held a seat on the board of directors of the First National Bank, and a similar position on the board of the German Savings Institution. A member of the Merchants' Exchange, he served as its vice president and on numerous important committees. Lemp's far-reaching business holdings also placed him on the boards of several other brewing and ice plants, mostly in Texas and other parts of the South. In addition to his business interests, Lemp served on the board of the Louisiana Purchase Exposition, and was chairman of the agriculture committee. As one of the city's leading and most wealthy citizens, he was also a member of several important and prestigious social clubs, including the Concordia Turnverein and the Liederkranz Club.

Of Lemp's five sons and three daughters, several achieved notable success in their own rights. When Lemp's brewery was incorporated as the William J. Lemp Brewing Company in 1892, sons William Jr.,

Louis, Charles, and Frederick held the positions of vice president, superintendent, treasurer, and assistant superintendent, respectively. The marriage of his daughter Hilda to Gustav Pabst in 1897 united two great brewing dynasties of the day.

Although Lemp had groomed Frederick to take over the family business, his son met an untimely death in 1901 at the age of twenty-eight. Frederick's passing, coupled with the loss of his best friend and fellow brewer, Frederick Pabst, in 1904, caused Lemp to sink into a depression that culminated in his suicide at the family mansion on February 13, 1904.

On the day of his funeral, the brewery's telegraph office received messages of condolence from around the world. Fellow brewer **Adolphus Busch** was among the pallbearers who carried Lemp to his final resting place in the large family mausoleum in St. Louis's Bellefontaine Cemetery.

Throughout his career, William J. Lemp earned the highest praise and admiration of not only his associates but also the citizens of St. Louis. He was recognized as a man of outstanding executive ability, as attested by the success of his brewing operations. By the time of his death, he had built his father's humble family trade into a colossal business covering several city blocks, along with rail and shipping facilities on the riverfront. In all, the great brewing plant was valued at some $6 million in 1904.

STEPHEN P. WALKER

Baron, Stanley Wade. *Brewed in America: A History of Beer and Ale in the United States.* Boston: Little, Brown, 1962.

Hyde, William, and Howard L. Conard, eds. *Encyclopedia of the History of St. Louis.* New York: Southern History, 1899.

Reavis, L. V. *St. Louis: Future Great City of the World.* St. Louis: Gray, Baker, 1875.

Reedy, William Marion, ed. *The Makers of St. Louis.* St. Louis: The Mirror, 1906.

LEONARD, ABIEL (1797–1863)

Abiel Leonard, a lawyer, jurist, and political leader, was born in Windsor, Vermont, on May 16, 1797, the product of a long New England line going back to the early days of the Massachusetts Bay Colony. He studied at Dartmouth for two years, 1813–1815, and then read law in at least two New York law offices.

Upon the completion of his studies, Leonard decided to head west to launch his legal career. In 1819 he arrived, without funds or connections, at Franklin, the fabled frontier boomtown in central Missouri's Boonslick country, founded at the conclusion of the War of 1812. While he initially taught school, by 1823 Leonard had established a legal practice covering several central Missouri counties.

In 1824 Leonard was appointed to succeed **Hamilton Rowan Gamble** as the prosecuting attorney for the First Judicial District of Missouri. While in that position he fought a duel with Taylor Berry, who had tested Leonard's mettle by publicly humiliating him. Although Leonard was a short, slight man, he summoned his strong resolve and mortally wounded Berry at first fire. He was briefly deprived of his civil rights for his action, but a sympathetic General Assembly quickly restored them.

Following the duel, Leonard's practice began to flourish. While the duel established his courage and strong sense of honor in a southern society that valued such qualities, his success as a lawyer and judge was due to his brilliant and logical mind, intellectual honesty, and profound knowledge of the law. During his lifetime he was widely regarded as one of the most capable lawyers of his day. He demanded the highest fees for his services, and carried on his practice statewide.

Leonard was also politically active as a leader of the Whig Party. In 1834 he was elected to the state legislature. In 1838 political friends unsuccessfully entered his name to oppose **Thomas Hart Benton** for the United States Senate, an action that won neither Leonard's approval nor his pleasure. In 1839 he was chosen as chairman of the central committee in the state's first Whig convention.

Leonard strongly supported such Whig programs as the American System, but where Unionism was concerned, he was more independent. He supported Andrew Jackson's stand against nullification and later refused to join pro-Southern Whig plots to unseat Senator Benton. When the Whig Party in Missouri finally split over the question of congressional control of the spread of slavery, Leonard adopted the conservative stance of favoring both slavery and the Union, and placed himself in opposition to the Southern Party movement forged by Whig leader John B. Clark and Democrat **Claiborne Fox Jackson.** Once Governor Jackson's secessionist government had been driven from Jefferson City by federal military forces, Leonard lent the prestige and weight of his legal learning to the proposition that the state convention had the authority to remove Jackson and his cohorts from power and establish a provisional Unionist state government.

By 1855 Leonard's reputation had become so firmly established that his colleagues, in an unusual gesture, transcended the volatile partisan divisions to urge, with near unanimity, his candidacy for the seat on the Missouri Supreme Court that had been vacated by Hamilton Gamble. He served only one two-year term on the bench, but during that brief time he enhanced his reputation for great legal learning and exhaustive research in the opinions he wrote.

In 1830 Abiel Leonard married Jeanette Reeves, a daughter of Benjamin Reeves, former lieutenant governor of Kentucky and surveyor of the Santa Fe Trail. Their union produced seven children. By 1850 their household also included nine slaves. In 1833 the Leonards moved from New Franklin to Fayette, the county seat of Howard County. There, in 1835–1836, they built their beloved home, Oakwood: a stately Federal-style brick house that was enlarged and improved over the years and has now been placed on the National Register of Historic Places.

Abiel Leonard died at his home on March 28, 1863.

JAMES M. DENNY

Culmer, Frederick A. "Abiel Leonard." Parts 1 and 2. *Missouri Historical Review* 27 (1933): 113–31, 217–39, 315–36; 28 (1933–1934): 17–37, 103–29.

Leonard, Abiel. Papers. Western Historical Manuscripts Collection, Columbia.

LEONARD, NATHANIEL (1799–1876)

A prominent farmer and stock raiser of Cooper County and the founder of Ravenswood Farm, Nathaniel Leonard was born in Windsor, Vermont, on June 13, 1799, and grew up on a farm near Lewistown, New York. After a brief engagement with the American Fur Company in Chicago, he moved to Missouri in 1824, where his older brother, **Abiel Leonard,** had established himself as a lawyer. With Abiel's financial backing, Nathaniel purchased eighty acres of land in Cooper County. From this modest beginning, he founded Ravenswood Farm. This celebrated farm eventually grew to encompass nineteen hundred acres. In 1832 Nathaniel married Margaret Hutchinson, and their union produced six children.

Leonard is best remembered as a leader in the establishment of the purebred cattle industry in Missouri. In 1839 he purchased a purebred shorthorn bull named Comet Star and a purebred heifer called Queen for six hundred and five hundred dollars, respectively; these purchases formed the foundation for the Ravenswood herd that went on to earn an international reputation and produce some of the highest priced cattle of the nineteenth century. Leonard also enjoyed considerable success in jack-stock and mule breeding, and was an acknowledged leader in Missouri's lucrative mule industry. At the time of his death on December 30, 1876, Leonard was able to pass on to his heirs the Ravenswood Farm and four nine-hundred-acre farms in Saline County in addition to cash and livestock.

Leonard's fourth child, Charles E. Leonard, inherited Ravenswood and continued to improve its celebrated shorthorn herd. In 1872 he married Nadine

Nelson, the daughter of wealthy Boonville banker James M. Nelson. In 1880 Nelson financed the construction of the brick Ravenswood house, a spacious mansion built in the Italianate style. The house is listed in the National Register of Historic Places and has been photographed by the Historic American Buildings Survey.

JAMES M. DENNY

Ashton, John. *Historic Ravenswood: Its Founders and Its Cattle.* Columbia: E. W. Stephens, 1926.

Culmer, Frederick. "Selling Mules Down South in 1835." *Missouri Historical Review* 24 (July 1930): 537–49.

Denny, James M. "Vernacular Building Process in Missouri: Nathaniel Leonard's Activities, 1825–1870." *Missouri Historical Review* 78 (October 1983): 23–50.

Dyer, Robert L. *Ravenswood.* Columbia: Tiger Press, 1969.

Gall, Jeffery L. "A Search for the Rising Tide: The Letters of Nathaniel Leonard, 1820–1824." *Missouri Historical Review* 76 (April 1982): 282–301.

Leonard, Nathaniel. Papers. 1800–1896. Western Historical Manuscripts Collection, Columbia.

LEONARD, ZENAS (1809–1857)

Zenas Leonard, a fur trapper best known as the author of *Adventures of a Mountain Man,* a classic work in the literature of the Rocky Mountain fur trade, was born in Clearfield County, Pennsylvania, on March 19, 1809. In 1830 he joined a mercantile firm in Pittsburgh as a clerk, but the lure of western adventure drew him to a fur-trapping expedition bound for the Rocky Mountains. The party of seventy men led by Capt. John Gant of the short-lived firm of Gant and Blackwell left the Missouri settlements in April 1831. Upon reaching the confluence of the Laramie and Platte Rivers in late August, they divided into trapping parties of fifteen to twenty men for the winter hunt. Leonard's group soon lost contact with the others, lost their horses to starvation over the winter, and lost most of their pelts and supplies to Indian raiders. Struggling back to the appointed rendezvous in the spring, Leonard and his men learned that their employers were bankrupt and could offer them no assistance. They trapped the next season for Thomas Fitzpatrick of the Rocky Mountain Fur Company, finding high adventure but little monetary gain.

In July 1833 the party signed on with Capt. **Benjamin Louis Eulalie de Bonneville,** who had established a fort on Green River the summer before and was now recruiting men for a second season's hunt. Bonneville sent a party under Joseph R. Walker to explore the region beyond the Great Salt Lake, search for beaver streams, and scout the activities of Spanish, British, and American rivals there. Leonard accompanied Walker as a clerk, traveled with him to the Pacific Ocean, wintered in the Spanish settlements, and returned with the party to rendezvous with Bonneville in July 1834. He spent one more winter trapping in the Rocky Mountains for Bonneville, then accompanied his employer back to the States in 1835. While most of his comrades remained in the mountains, in hopes of yet making a little money or simply for the adventure and freedom of the trapper's life, Leonard chose to return "lest I should also forget the blessings of civilized society."

Leonard returned to an amazed family in Pennsylvania, who had long since decided he was dead. He began to write a narrative of his experiences, based on the journal he kept during his travels. The editor of the *Clearfield Republican* published the early chapters in his paper, then published the entire narrative in book form in 1839. Leonard's narrative became more than a story of the adventure and hardships of a trapper's life. It was also a revelation of the potential value of exotic California to the Union and a warning of the threat to U.S. interests in the West posed by the British, the Spanish, and the Russians. Through his book, Leonard joined a small but growing number of voices demanding the effective U.S. occupation of the Pacific Coast.

By the time the book was published, Leonard had again left Pennsylvania. He intended to return to the Rocky Mountains, but found the comforts of civilization too enticing to abandon entirely, and so stopped at Missouri's western border. Fort Osage, near present Independence, Missouri, was established in 1808 as a U.S. military post and factory, that is, Indian trading post. The factory was closed in 1822, and the military abandoned the post in 1827, but a small civilian settlement had already grown up around it. For a few years the settlement was the staging site for westering expeditions such as those of Gant and Blackwell or Bonneville. Early in 1836 Archibald Gamble and William Russell gained control of the site and laid out the town of Sibley (named after the former government factor and first civilian resident, **George C. Sibley**). Later that year Leonard settled in Sibley and opened one of the first general merchandise stores in the area. He sold to the local farmers, dealt in furs and merchandise for the Indian trade, and operated a steamboat between Sibley and St. Louis.

Leonard married Isabel Harrelson, and the couple eventually had three children. Leonard died on July 14, 1857, and is buried in the Sibley cemetery.

MARY ELLEN ROWE

Leonard, Zenas. *Adventures of a Mountain Man.* 1839. Reprint, Lincoln: University of Nebraska Press, 1978.

LeSIEUR, FRANÇOIS (?–1826); LeSIEUR, JOSEPH (?–1796)

François and Joseph LeSieur migrated southward through the Illinois country and into present-day Missouri in the late eighteenth century from the Canadian community of Machiche, St. Ann Parish, in Three Rivers, Canada. Their father, Charles, had emigrated there from the south of France.

In 1785 François and Joseph entered the employ of Gabriel Cerré, one of St. Louis's most prominent fur traders and merchants. They established a fur trade post for Cerré in 1793 at a bend in the Mississippi River just south of the confluence of the Ohio, called L'Anse à la Graisse. For years, Native Americans had prepared furs and melted animal fat that had saturated the soil, so it was dubbed "Greasy Cove," or "the Cove of Grease." The area was a well-established rendezvous point for hunters and traders because of its abundant supplies of bear and buffalo.

Cerré's trading post enjoyed considerable success in the mid-1790s because of its prime location and good management by the LeSieurs. It led to the development of a more permanent settlement, on the east bank of the Chapoosa Creek, or St. John's Bayou, fed initially by migration from Vincennes. In 1789 Col. **George Morgan** established an American colony there, named New Madrid, to serve as a buffer between Anglo-European and Native communities. The town's population base and Euramerican origin date to the LeSieurs, however, and for this reason they are credited with the initial settlement of the New Madrid district.

François LeSieur organized another trading post and initial settlement near Carruthersville in present-day Pemiscot County in 1794, known as La Petite Prairie (Little Prairie). The town was platted on a grant of land measuring approximately two hundred arpents, subdivided into individual one-arpent lots. Little Prairie was situated atop a high ridge overlooking the Mississippi River, with abundant natural resources and trade opportunities. Fort St. Fernando, constructed nearby, provided some measure of protection for the town's growing population, reported as 78 persons in 1799 and 103 in 1803. François served as a lieutenant in the Second Company of the local militia, functioning as the town's syndic, or civil and military commandant, until 1797. By 1801 he owned the area's first flour mill, and had become a prosperous merchant in Little Prairie. The community flourished until the great earthquakes of December 1811 virtually destroyed the town. The remaining population quickly dispersed after the disaster, with many returning to New Madrid. François LeSieur founded Point Pleasant, located a few miles north, four years later. He lived there until his death in 1826. Joseph had remained in New Madrid, where he died in 1796.

Although Joseph LeSieur had married and had two sons in Canada prior to moving into the Illinois country, all had died, and so he left no heirs. He bears mention only once separately from his brother in published accounts, as a messenger to the Loup Indians in 1794 for **Louis Lorimier,** the commandant at Cape Girardeau.

In 1791 François LeSieur had married Cecile Guibault (or Guilbeaut), a Vincennes native who bore him seven children. After her death François married Miss Bonneau, another Vincennes native, and they had one son together. He married a third time in 1820, to the widow of Little Prairie's Charles Loignon.

RACHEL FRANKLIN WEEKLEY

Douglass, Robert Sidney. *History of Southeast Missouri: A Narrative Account of Its Historical Progress, Its People, and Its Principal Interests.* Chicago: Lewis Publishing, 1912.

Foley, William E. *A History of Missouri: Volume I, 1673 to 1820.* Columbia: University of Missouri Press, 1971.

Goodspeed's History of Southeast Missouri. 1888. Reprint, Independence, Mo.: BNL Library Service, 1978.

Houck, Louis. *A History of Missouri, from the Earliest Explorations and Settlements until the Admission of the State into the Union.* Vol. 2. Chicago: R. R. Donnelley and Sons, 1908.

Morrow, Lynn. "New Madrid and Its Hinterland, 1783–1826." *Bulletin of the Missouri Historical Society* 36 (July 1980): 241–50.

Postlethwaite, Samuel. "Journal of a Voyage from Louisville to Natchez, 1800." *Bulletin of the Missouri Historical Society* 7 (April 1951): 312–29.

LEWIS, HENRY (1821–1904)

Henry Lewis, a landscape painter who resided in St. Louis from 1836 to 1850, is best known as the artist of two ambitious Mississippi River projects: a large panorama of the entire length of the river and a book, *Das Illustrirte Mississippithal* (The Mississippi Valley illustrated), containing lithographs of his paintings of the Mississippi Valley.

Lewis, born in England on January 12, 1821, came to the United States in 1829, serving as an apprentice mechanic and carpenter in Boston before moving to St. Louis with his father in 1836. In St. Louis he worked as a carpenter and scene painter in a theater, and began to paint landscapes professionally.

Although self-taught, his works received favorable notices in local exhibits. An 1845 *Missouri Republican* article described him as "a landscape painter of more than ordinary merit."

While working at the theater, Lewis began to make plans for a large-scale panoramic painting of the entire length of the Mississippi River. These enormous paintings on yards of canvas that unrolled before an audience became a fad in mid-nineteenth-century America, and the relatively unexplored regions along the Mississippi River provided ideal subject matter for several panoramic painters. St. Louis in the 1840s was home to four such artists, each trying to top the others' Mississippi canvas. Lewis claimed to have the idea first.

To complete his panorama, Lewis traveled along the river by boat in the summers of 1846–1848, sketching sights along the way. Seated atop the cabin of his specially built boat, the *Mene-Ha-Ha,* Lewis sketched scenes on both sides of the river as they "floated downstream quietly and safely, never rocking, so that there was no difficulty in making sketches on board."

With the help of several artists, Lewis completed his panorama—reportedly 1,325 yards of canvas—in the fall of 1849, exhibiting it not only in St. Louis but also across the Midwest, the East Coast, and Canada. Audiences paid twenty-five or fifty cents to view the "mammoth panorama," admiring Lewis's depictions of life along the river, from the Falls of St. Anthony to New Orleans. A pamphlet, with effusive descriptions of the scenes presented, accompanied showings of the panorama. In 1851 Lewis took his giant canvas to Europe. Competition among traveling panoramas was stiff, however, and he never earned much money on the project. He eventually sold the panorama to a Dutch planter who supposedly took it with him to Java where it disappeared.

After touring Europe with his panorama, Lewis settled in Düsseldorf, Germany, a vibrant international art center that attracted many Americans, including Western artists **George Caleb Bingham,** Albert Bierstadt, and **Charles "Carl" Ferdinand Wimar.** In Düsseldorf, Lewis studied art seriously for the first time, and embarked on the second major project of his career.

Using his panoramic sketches and notes, Lewis published *Das Illustrirte Mississippithal* with descriptive text in German and seventy-eight color lithographs of the region. The text was mainly a compilation from various sources that he had translated into German; the book's main attraction was his illustrations. The beautifully colored lithographs depicted scenes from the entire length of the river, from Minnesota to Louisiana, including river towns, forts, and Indian encampments along the way.

The book, originally designed to appeal to Germans considering emigrating to the United States, was issued in installments from 1854 to 1857. The venture was a commercial flop; few copies were sold, and a planned English version was never executed. Complete copies of the book are extremely rare today. Although the public paid little attention to the book in Lewis's lifetime, the volume has since become an important source for information and images of the Mississippi Valley region before later development changed many of the sites Lewis depicted.

Lewis remained in Düsseldorf for the rest of his life, but continued to paint scenes of the Mississippi Valley, frequently sending paintings back to his brother in St. Louis, who exhibited and sold them for him. Henry Lewis served as a U.S. consular and commercial agent from 1867 to 1884, returning to the United States only once, in 1881 to visit relatives. He died in Düsseldorf on September 16, 1904.

Although he spent the last fifty years of his life in Europe, Lewis remains an important artist in the history of Missouri. His depictions of the Mississippi River and the surrounding towns continue to serve as rich artistic and historic resources of the region.

BETH RUBIN

Heilbron, Bertha, ed. *Making a Motion Picture in 1848: Henry Lewis's Journal of a Canoe Voyage from the Falls of St. Anthony to St. Louis.* St. Paul: Minnesota Historical Society, 1936.

Lewis, Henry. *The Valley of the Mississippi Illustrated.* Ed. Bertha Heilbron. Trans. A. Hermina Poatgieter. St. Paul: Minnesota Historical Society, 1967.

McDermott, John Francis. "Henry Lewis's 'Great National Work.' " In *The Lost Panoramas of the Mississippi,* by John Francis McDermott. Chicago: University of Chicago Press, 1958.

Schmitz, Marie. "Henry Lewis: Panorama Maker." *Gateway Heritage* 5 (winter 1982–1983): 36–48.

LEWIS, MERIWETHER (1774–1809)

Meriwether Lewis, of the Lewis and Clark expedition, was born on August 18, 1774, in Albermarle County, Virginia, on the family's Ivy Creek plantation, Locust Hill. The home was near Thomas Jefferson's Monticello and closer still to the town of Charlottesville. Lewis's first name, odd to modern ears, was his mother Lucy's maiden name. When only five years old Lewis suffered the loss of his father, William, and the next year his mother married John Marks. Seeking better circumstances, Marks moved the family to Georgia, but was himself dead by 1791. In the meantime, young Lewis had returned to Virginia and, under an uncle's care, began attending private Latin schools. During these years he received a rudimentary education and seems to have developed a keen interest in natural history and a love of the outdoors. His mother returned to Virginia in 1792 with her children, and Lewis joined them.

At the age of twenty Lewis entered military service in the Virginia militia during the Whiskey Rebellion, but soon joined the regular army and was eventually assigned to the First Infantry Regiment. By 1800, at the age of twenty-six, he had risen to the rank of captain and probably saw for himself a career in military service. During these years he moved about on various assignments, with no apparent combat experience, but with exposure to command, the frontier, and Indians. It was also during this period that he met fellow soldier **William Clark,** four years his senior and his superior officer for a time. Little is known of that encounter, but it is certain that they struck a deep friendship, and it lasted their lifetimes. Their names have become inseparable in history.

Shortly before assuming the presidency in 1801 Jefferson called Lewis from military duty to become his private secretary while allowing the captain to retain his army rank. It now seems possible that Jefferson selected the young officer not only to groom him for western exploration but also to use Lewis's knowledge of military personnel in order to remove weak links and political opponents from the officer ranks. More important, perhaps, he knew that Lewis's military experience had equipped him for leading the expedition he envisioned. During his stay with Jefferson, Lewis had the president's magnificent library at his disposal, and he used the opportunity to prepare himself. There must have also been lengthy discussions about the western country, with the president playing a mentoring role.

The popular conception of the expedition is that of heroic achievement, but Jefferson planned the endeavor as a venture in scientific inquiry. To that end he instructed Lewis carefully. In a detailed letter to the captain in June 1803, Jefferson laid out his intentions for the expedition. Lewis was to be involved in investigations in three large categories: studies of the land, of indigenous people, and of native plant and animal species. What Jefferson wanted was someone skilled in the sciences but also a person who could stand up to the rigors of wilderness travel and the demands of Indian diplomacy. He knew that no such person existed at the time but that Lewis came as close to meeting his requirements as anyone on the continent. Furthermore, he knew that Lewis could be trained for the scientific aspects of the work. In this regard, Lewis spent about six weeks in the spring of 1803 in and around Philadelphia on crash courses in the sciences. There he learned the latest in medicine, astronomy, botany, and zoology, and he outfitted the expedition with modern scientific equipment, including sextants, octants, and compasses, and also

requisitioned the necessary camp equipment and a good supply of Indian presents.

During this time Lewis asked Clark to join him as co-commander of the expedition, to which Clark enthusiastically agreed. As Lewis headed west in the summer of 1803 to meet Clark near Louisville, Kentucky, the Louisiana Purchase was completed, and the transaction made the expedition all the more important. Now they would be exploring U.S. territory as well as investigating new terrain. After wintering in Illinois across from St. Louis, the Corps of Discovery, as they styled themselves, started up the Missouri River on May 14, 1804.

Lewis and Clark initially commanded a force of about forty men, including regular army enlistees and French boatmen. The summer's trip, across Missouri and through Kansas, Nebraska, and Iowa, was laborious but exhilarating. It was marked by friendly relations with Indians except for one tense encounter with Teton Sioux. Lewis stood firm in the face of demands for excessive payments for the right of passage through Sioux territory, and the Tetons backed down. During the summer one of the men, Charles Floyd, died, apparently of a ruptured appendix. No other such loss occurred during the trip. By late fall the explorers reached the Mandan and Hidatsa Indians living near present-day Bismarck, North Dakota, and they settled in for the winter.

In the spring of 1805 the corps, now numbering thirty-three, including the Shoshone woman Sacagawea, continued up the Missouri. They crossed the Rocky Mountains in late summer with the help of Sacagawea's people and found streams that carried them to the coast. Along the way they met Natives who had never seen white people, most notably Nez Percé Indians, with whom they made friendly contact. They spent the winter of 1805–1806 on the Oregon coast among Clatsop Indians and began their return trip in March 1806.

The captains split the command in July on the crest of the Rockies. Lewis and a small detachment followed a shortcut to the Missouri River and explored its northern tributaries, while Clark descended the Yellowstone River with the main party. On Lewis's excursion the corps had its only deadly engagement with Natives, when Lewis and his men killed two Piegan Blackfeet who were stealing horses and guns. Later Lewis was accidentally shot in the hip by one of his men, but he mended quickly under Clark's care. The reunited corps reached St. Louis in September 1806.

Lewis was the nominal leader of the expedition, though Clark was given equal authority. Lewis served as the party's naturalist and astronomer and performed most of the scientific tasks. He took careful notice of the land's prospects for future agricultural use, while also studying plant and animal life, noting mineral deposits, and recording the country's climate. His accomplishments in the biological sciences are particularly noteworthy. He was the first to describe in detail a host of plant and animal species that were new to science and to provide better understanding of the range, habits, and physical characteristics of many known species. He, along with Clark, wrote at length of the seasonal changes and range of plant life, of the extent and habits of animals, and of the migrations of birds and mammals. Lewis has been universally praised for his ecological descriptions and is credited with a host of natural history discoveries.

As compensation for his work on the expedition Lewis was appointed governor of Louisiana Territory in 1807. The governorship was to be the just reward of a national hero; however, to lead a westering expedition is one thing, and to guide a politically fractious territory quite another. Lewis's biggest mistake was trying to govern from Washington—an impossible task and incredible folly on his part. He received his appointment in March 1807, but it was fully a year before he actually arrived again in St. Louis. His procrastinating seems inexcusable, especially since the man in charge had little knowledge of Indian affairs, a responsibility essential to the effective administration of the office, and he was openly critical of Lewis. **Frederick Bates** loomed large in Lewis's coming problems. He was territorial secretary and acting governor in Lewis's absence, and he became Lewis's enemy almost immediately, perhaps because he desired the governorship for himself or maybe because Lewis was chosen over Bates's father as Jefferson's private secretary. Bates thought Lewis was too much of a military man and unsuited to the office of governor.

One immediate problem after Lewis's arrival was the return of Big White, a Mandan Indian chief who had returned with the exploring party and had visited Jefferson in Washington. The first attempt to take him back had turned into a debacle when the small party was attacked by Arikara Indians and retreated. Fearing larger Indian problems, Jefferson insisted that Big White be returned to his people as quickly as possible. To accomplish this Lewis commissioned a military and commercial expedition under **(Jean) Pierre Chouteau** to return the chief to the Mandan. A total of $7,000 was allotted by Lewis for the trip, plus an additional $940 for gifts to be given to the Arikara in order to ensure safe passage and bring the recalcitrant tribe back into the American fold.

Lewis showed poor judgment in this decision. It was bad enough that he engaged a private company for service and paid for it with government funds without authorization, but it was a more serious mistake that members of his family and some close friends would share in the profits of the venture. Moreover, the administration in Washington had changed, and Lewis did not enjoy his former influence. President James Madison and his cabinet were not as obliging as the previous executive. The government agreed to go along with the $7,000 expenditure but protested the other bills of exchange, principally the $940. When Lewis's creditors learned of his problems they began to call in their notes, and Lewis was nearly at the point of financial ruin. He owed several thousand dollars on land purchases and on a mining enterprise. All the while, Bates was reporting Lewis's difficulties and faulty management to Washington officials.

Lewis concluded to go east with his unaccepted accounts and clear up the difficulties. He left St. Louis by boat on September 4, 1809, and arrived at Chickasaw Bluffs and Fort Pickering (modern-day Memphis, Tennessee) by the middle of the month. There he decided to go overland instead of by boat, fearing that the British might steal his expedition journals and the papers he carried to clear his accounts. On September 29 he resumed his journey. During his time at the Bluffs he was observed by Capt. Gilbert C. Russell, commander of the fort, who considered him in a state of "mental derangement" and worried that he was drinking too heavily. He also learned that Lewis had made attempts to kill himself. Russell thought, however, that Lewis had regained his composure if not his complete health by the time he departed.

Lewis traveled northeast from Fort Pickering along the Natchez Trace. With him were Maj. James Neely, two servants, and perhaps a third slave. The group reached Robert Grinder's stand (southwest of modern Nashville, Tennessee) about sunset on October 10, 1809. Mr. Grinder was not there, but Mrs. Grinder put the group up for the night, Lewis in a cabin by himself and the servants in a nearby stable, since Neely had stayed behind to hunt for lost horses. During the night Mrs. Grinder heard pistol shots but was afraid to investigate and apparently heard Lewis crying out and ranting. At daybreak the servants found Lewis dead in his cabin and bloody from the bullet wound in his head and chest and razor cuts on his body. Apparently they did not hear the shots or his cries during the night. He died just at daybreak, and his last words heard by Mrs. Grinder apparently were: "I am no coward, but I am so strong. It is so hard to die."

Neely came up later that day to bury Lewis and then went on to Nashville where he wrote Jefferson of the events. Jefferson accepted the suicide story without hesitation, as did Clark when he learned of it later. The strongest evidence for suicide may be in the ready acceptance of the act by the people who knew Lewis best. There are some, however, who believe that he was murdered. Ironically, three years after his death a Washington official decided to allow the protested bills, and the money was paid to Lewis's estate.

Jefferson had expected Lewis to write a report of the expedition, but not one word had been written before his death in Tennessee. Lewis had all the expedition journals with him at that time. Fortunately, they were saved and were given to Jefferson, who passed them on to Clark with the idea that he would publish the expedition's story. In 1810 Clark convinced Nicholas Biddle of Philadelphia to paraphrase the men's diaries, and they were finally published in 1814. Published numerous times since then, the journals are now being edited in their entirety at the University of Nebraska. The journals themselves were deposited for the most part in the American Philosophical Society in Philadelphia, where they remain today. A national treasure, these diaries stand as the lasting legacy of Lewis's greatness.

GARY E. MOULTON

Ambrose, Stephen E. *Undaunted Courage: Meriwether Lewis, Thomas Jefferson, and the Opening of the American West.* New York: Simon and Schuster, 1996.

Bakeless, John. *Lewis and Clark: Partners in Discovery.* New York: William Morrow, 1947.

Dillon, Richard. *Meriwether Lewis: A Biography.* New York: Coward-McCann, 1965.

Lavender, David. *The Way to the Western Sea: Lewis and Clark across the Continent.* New York: Harper and Row, 1988.

Moulton, Gary E., ed. *Journals of the Lewis and Clark Expedition.* 11 vols. Lincoln: University of Nebraska Press, 1983.

LEYBA, FERNANDO DE (?–1780)

Controversy swirled around Upper Louisiana's third lieutenant governor in life and in death. Virtually nothing is known about Fernando de Leyba's early life aside from the fact that he was born in Barcelona, Spain, and came to Louisiana where he served as a captain in the Stationary Regiment. In 1778 Gov. Bernardo de Gálvez appointed him to replace the popular **Francisco Cruzat** as lieutenant governor in St. Louis. He assumed command of his new post at a time when worsening relations with the British pushed Spain ever closer to open warfare.

Soon after arriving in Upper Louisiana, Leyba established contact with George Rogers Clark, the leader of the successful American military campaign in British Illinois. When Clark's fighters occupied Kaskaskia in July, Leyba hurriedly wrote a note congratulating them on their victory.

A short time later Leyba welcomed the victorious Clark to St. Louis with military salutes and a round of festivities. The two men became fast friends, and

Clark, who informed the Continental Congress that he was "proud and pleased at the fine reception he had been given by the Spanish commandant," returned to St. Louis on several occasions to purchase supplies from the local merchants.

Leyba faced formidable challenges in defending his exposed domains. Time and the elements had taken their toll on the wooden fortifications the Spaniards had constructed at the mouth of the Missouri in 1768. Leyba recommended replacing them and requested that two hundred regular troops be sent to Upper Louisiana. Gálvez declined to approve Leyba's recommendations, noting that he had no authority to authorize such large expenditures from the royal treasury.

Conditions were understandably precarious. Leyba reported that the unprecedented number of Indians descending upon him seeking advice and assistance had exhausted his supplies of food and merchandise. He warned his superiors that the chronic shortages of goods in St. Louis would cause the Indians to turn to the British. His attempts to regulate the fur trade also elicited protests from some traders who complained that he sold trading licenses to the highest bidders.

Word that Spain had gone to war against Great Britain reached St. Louis in February 1780. Upon hearing that news, Leyba promptly accelerated his efforts to secure Upper Louisiana's settlements against attack. St. Louis was especially vulnerable. Its strategic location and its use by the American rebels as an unofficial supply base made it a prime target for a British assault, but there were fewer than forty regular Spanish troops in all of Upper Louisiana. Even before Leyba had learned of the state of war, he had authorized the construction of a public road linking Ste. Genevieve and St. Louis for use in the event that ice blocked travel on the Mississippi during the winter months. He also took steps to reorganize the local militia into a more viable fighting force.

The peril became clear in late March when reports reached St. Louis warning of an imminent Indian attack from the north. Since Leyba's requests for additional support from New Orleans had been denied, he was forced to secure the funds needed for fortifying St. Louis through a public subscription. He intended to construct four stone towers, but only the one known as Fort San Carlos was built. It played an important role in repelling the subsequent assault against the city, thanks in part to the installation of the five cannons Leyba had rescued from the abandoned fort on the Missouri. When insufficient funds forced Leyba to scale back his plans for fortification, he resorted to digging trenches around the village's perimeter.

On May 9, 1780, Leyba learned that a large British and Indian war party had begun moving down the Mississippi. To augment his meager forces, he ordered the regular soldiers and militia at Ste. Genevieve to report to St. Louis. He also summoned all hunters and trappers within seventy-five miles of the capital to return immediately. With a total defensive force of slightly more than three hundred, he prepared to defend the city.

The attack on St. Louis came on May 26, 1780, when a band of British soldiers, Canadian traders, and Indian warriors, numbering perhaps as many as one thousand, swooped down upon the city from the northwest. Leyba's defensive measures paid off, and the outnumbered defenders managed to fend off the attackers, but the costs of victory had been high. The fifty-three St. Louisans killed or taken prisoner represented a substantial loss for a village with only seven hundred inhabitants.

Local critics denounced Leyba for having failed to do more. Some resented his use of forced requisitions in constructing fortifications. Reports of an impending second attack upon St. Louis renewed the sense of despair.

Personal problems added to Leyba's woes. His wife died unexpectedly in St. Louis, leaving him with two young daughters. A lingering illness made matters worse for the beleaguered official. All of this proved too much for Leyba, who died in St. Louis on June 28, 1780.

Long after his death, local tradition perpetuated the myth of Leyba as a traitorous and incompetent official whose neglect nearly led to the destruction of St. Louis. He clearly deserved better. His record was no worse than most. He had successfully managed a difficult assignment and done as much as could have been reasonably expected with the limited resources available to him. Ironically, in gratitude for Leyba's successful defense of St. Louis, his superiors in New Orleans promoted him to the rank of lieutenant colonel, but he did not live to receive the news.

WILLIAM E. FOLEY

McDermott, John Francis. "The Myth of the 'Imbecile Governor': Captain Fernando de Leyba and the Defense of St. Louis in 1780." In *The Spanish in the Mississippi Valley, 1762–1804,* ed. John Francis McDermott. Urbana: University of Illinois Press, 1974.

LINDBERGH, CHARLES A.
(1902–1974)

Charles A. Lindbergh was not really a Missourian. In fact, he lived in the state only briefly. Nevertheless, that short period was a crucial time in his life. It was the time during which he became a national hero. Furthermore, his accomplishments then testified and contributed to the rise of St. Louis as a center of American aviation.

Although Lindbergh began life in Detroit, he was a Minnesotan in his early years. Within a few days of his birth on February 4, 1902, his parents took him to their Minnesota farm on the banks of the Mississippi River, near Little Falls. In 1906 the voters elected his father, an immigrant from Sweden and a progressive Republican, to Congress, and for the next ten years the boy divided his time between the nation's capital, which he did not like, and Minnesota, which he loved. The elder Lindbergh's opposition to American involvement in World War I destroyed his political career.

Disliking school, young Lindbergh devoted little time to it and obtained his education in other ways. He loved the outdoors and developed strong interests in science, engineering, automobiles, farm machinery, and motorcycles. He dropped out of the University of Wisconsin in his sophomore year but obtained an honorary degree from that institution after he became a hero.

By the early twenties, Lindbergh had found the focus of his life. He learned to fly in 1922–1923, joined the Army Air Service in 1924, and became a commissioned officer the following year. Flying, including the constant threat of death, and aviation's prospects filled his life with excitement and purpose.

In 1926 Lindbergh moved to St. Louis to work for the city's leading aviation firm, Robertson Aircraft Corporation. When they obtained a contract to fly the mail, the Robertsons hired Lindbergh as their chief pilot. He also became an officer in the Missouri National Guard. On flights between St. Louis and Chicago, the young flyer thought of crossing the Atlantic, nonstop and alone, from New York City to Paris.

Lindbergh soon obtained the resources needed to make the trip. He focused his appeals on St. Louis business people, recognized that the city's location gave it great potential, and argued that the flight would enlarge interest in aviation and advertise the city as an aviation center. Most airplane manufacturers and O. K. Bovard of the *St. Louis Post-Dispatch* lacked confidence in the enterprise and declined to help. Others, however, responded positively, including **Albert Bond Lambert,** a pharmaceutical manufacturer, promoter of air travel, and developer of a flying field; Lindbergh's employers, William Robertson and Frank Robertson; Harry Hall Knight, a local stockbroker and president of the city's Flying Club; Harold M. Bixby, president of the State National Bank and head of the chamber of commerce; E. Lansing Ray, the publisher of the *Globe-Democrat;* and Earl Thompson, an insurance executive and civic leader with an active interest in flying.

The name given to Lindbergh's plane testified to the Missouri connection. His backers were called the Spirit of St. Louis Organization; his plane, a single-engine monoplane constructed by the Ryan firm in San Diego, became the *Spirit of St. Louis*. After acquiring the plane, Lindbergh flew it nonstop from San Diego to St. Louis and then to New York City.

Plane and pilot, "We," according to the title of a book Lindbergh would write, triumphed over the odds. On May 20, 1927, with experts regarding the flight as dangerous and predicting failure, Lindbergh and the *Spirit of St. Louis* took off from New York; on May 21 they landed in Paris. Never before had one person flown so far.

The huge crowd that greeted Lindbergh was but a preview. He immediately became a hero on both sides of the Atlantic, nowhere more than in St. Louis where he was given a large, enthusiastic welcome upon his return and commissioned a colonel in the National Guard. The Missouri Historical Society exhibited to large crowds the thousands of items that admirers gave to him. The chamber of commerce, which changed the name of its magazine to the *Spirit of St. Louis*, proclaimed that the feat typified "the same spirit of enterprise that has animated St. Louis in the past and has become a foremost factor in its present progress." Also expressing a spirit of enterprise, four thousand people competed in a Spirit of St. Louis poetry contest.

Lindbergh's accomplishment stimulated a boom in American aviation. The pilot and his plane toured the nation, sponsored by the Guggenheim Fund and the Department of Commerce. Although uncomfortable in his new relations with crowds and the press, he tolerated them because of his eagerness to give flying a boost. The tour, though it may have done even more to demonstrate the attractiveness of the man than the virtues of aviation, was highly successful. The number of pilots and airports, the airline business, and airline stocks soared.

In Missouri the flyer enjoyed success in Kansas City as well as in St. Louis. In the west-side city, **Louis E. Holland,** the president of the chamber of commerce, was busily promoting economic growth. Viewing aviation as an economic enterprise of great potential and Kansas City as especially well suited to capitalize on that, he had taken the lead in a battle to persuade the city administration to build a municipal airport. Aided by Lindbergh's prestige, Holland succeeded, and the hero dedicated the airport.

In St. Louis Lindbergh's backers felt good about what had been accomplished. The people had become more interested in aviation, and passed a bond issue in 1928 by a large margin. The funds enabled the city to purchase the airfield from Lambert, enlarge it, and construct additional facilities on it, and these developments made St. Louis more important in air travel.

In the new circumstances of his life, Lindbergh became wealthy. He received financial rewards from the transatlantic trip itself and went to work for Transcontinental Air Transport (later TWA) and Pan American Airways. The wealthy American ambassador to Mexico, Dwight Morrow, a former partner in the J. P. Morgan empire, promoted a goodwill tour of Latin America by the attractive hero. That gave him an opportunity to get to know the Morrow family, including daughter Anne. They married in 1929.

As a consequence of the marriage, St. Louis lost its place as the base for Lindbergh's continually widening activities. He conducted global explorations, with Anne as his partner, that benefited commercial aviation, and he clashed with President Franklin Roosevelt in the airmail controversy of 1934. He also contributed to medical research and aided Robert Goddard's work on rockets.

Tragedy struck the young couple in 1932. A kidnapper seized and murdered their first son, and the press gave these events and the trial and execution that followed enormous publicity. Even earlier, Anne and Charles had resented the intrusions of the press into their lives, and now their resentment grew. Thus, in 1935 they moved to England to gain privacy for themselves and their growing family.

Spending three years as an expatriate had a powerful impact on Lindbergh's thinking. Already convinced that the United States was in decline, he grew equally critical of Great Britain and France and harsh in his appraisal of the Soviet Union. Germany, on the other hand, impressed him more favorably. Permitted to observe its air force closely, he concluded that Hitler's regime far outranked its rivals in this new form of power.

Returning home, Lindbergh soon lost his status as a national hero. Fearing a destructive air war, he fought against American intervention much as his father had during World War I and clashed with Roosevelt once again. Administration spokesmen and others, focusing on Lindbergh more than any other foe of intervention, denounced him as pro-German, the "No. 1 Nazi fellow traveler" in the United States, and anti-Semitic. Despite the vilification Lindbergh pressed forward just as he had in the *Spirit of St. Louis*. In 1941 he participated in an America First rally in St. Louis. However, Missouri, like most of the nation, moved by events in Europe and Asia, rejected his point of view.

After Pearl Harbor, Lindbergh dropped out of the spotlight. Although distrusted by some people, he contributed quietly to the war effort in several aviation projects, including combat missions against the Japanese. More acceptable during the cold war, he participated in the development of the anti-Soviet military policy. Once again he promoted commercial aviation. In 1954 he won a Pulitzer Prize for a book on the most spectacular episode in his life. *The Spirit of St. Louis* became a film with Jimmy Stewart in the leading role. Then, in his last years, this amazing man became a critic of technology and an environmentalist.

On August 26, 1974, Charles Lindbergh died in Maui in one of the three homes he shared with Anne. For a time the American people had embraced him as a hero. Missouri participated in that part of his life, and he, in turn, made contributions to the state. A model of his famous plane in the terminal at Lambert Field reminds us of the connection between the man and the place.

RICHARD S. KIRKENDALL

Cole, Wayne S. *Charles A. Lindbergh and the Battle against American Intervention in World War II.* New York: Harcourt Brace Jovanovich, 1974.

Davis, Kenneth S. *The Hero: Charles A. Lindbergh and the American Dream.* Garden City, N.Y.: Doubleday, 1959.

Hixson, Walter L. *Charles A. Lindbergh: Lone Eagle.* New York: HarperCollins College Publishers, 1996.

Horgan, James J. "City of Flight: The History of Aviation in St. Louis." Ph.D. diss., St. Louis University, 1965.

Leyerzapf, James W. "Aviation Promotion in Kansas City, 1925–1931." *Missouri Historical Review* 66 (January 1972): 246–67.

Oster, Donald B. "Community Image in the History of St. Louis and Kansas City." Ph.D. diss., University of Missouri, 1969.

LINK, THEODORE CARL (1850–1923)

Theodore Carl Link is best known as the architect of St. Louis's Union Station, but if he had never worked on the massive structure he would still have been a major Missouri architect. His many homes and churches, as well as his monumental gateways to St. Louis's most exclusive neighborhoods and his original ideas for the design of Forest Park, were enduring contributions to the character of his adopted home city. Equally significant are other accomplishments such as the Mississippi State Capitol in Jackson; Monticello Seminary in Godfrey, Illinois; and the Louisiana State University campus in Baton Rouge, which distinguish him as one of America's most important turn-of-the-century architects.

Link was born in Wimpfen, Germany, on March 17, 1850, and received his early education in Heidelberg. He trained in architecture and engineering in London and at the École des Arts et Métiers in Paris before emigrating to the United States in 1870. He worked in New York and Philadelphia for two years, then was hired as a civil engineer for the Texas Pacific Railroad. He moved to St. Louis in 1873 and continued his railroad work in the bridges and buildings department of the Atlantic and Pacific Railroad Company. Sometime around 1874 he began designing the new Forest Park for the city of St. Louis, first as chief engineer and then as superintendent of public parks. It was also about this time that he married Annie Fuller of Detroit, Michigan, with whom he eventually had five children.

City directories for 1876 list Link as a civil engineer for the St. Louis and San Francisco Railway Company, but it was also about this time that he moved back East. Contemporary sources indicate that he worked in Pittsburgh, Philadelphia, and New York until his return to St. Louis in 1883, but, unfortunately, few records remain of his activities during these formative years. Upon his return he began work for the engineering company of his old friend Julius Pitzman, former chief city surveyor and civil engineer with whom he had worked on the Forest Park design. After two years, and following a trip to Europe, Link finally opened his own architectural firm in 1885, just as St. Louis was undergoing a building boom.

Link is best known for his monumental stone buildings designed in the manner of the leading architect of the period, Henry Hobson Richardson, who died in 1886. Richardson had built a number of highly influential buildings, and his "Romanesque Revival" predominated in the building styles of the next two decades, largely through the efforts of younger architects, the "Richardsonians" who sought to emulate the master's powerful designs. Link was undoubtedly one of these, but unlike some of his contemporaries who slavishly copied Richardson's designs, he more often adapted forms and materials sensitively and with originality, earning himself the descriptive title of "Utilitarian Eclectic" by a recent scholar. Many of Link's creations, such as the Second Presbyterian Church (1898–1899), the gates of Portland and Westmoreland Places (ca. 1891), and certainly his masterpiece, Union Station (1892–1894), reveal strong Richardsonian influences in their dependence upon ponderous, blocklike forms constructed from rough-hewn limestone or granite adorned with delicately carved details, dominant tower formations, rounded arches, and red-tile roofs. At the same time, though, each is a response to specific purposes, circumstances, and Link's own vision. While he was competing with the legacy of Richardson and with architects who also saw themselves as his heirs (especially Richardson's own firm of Shepley, Rutan, and Coolidge, which established a St. Louis branch in 1890), Link managed to win the St. Louis Union Station commission with his innovative design.

During the course of his career Link had several partnerships, the most important of which may have been with Edward Cameron who joined him in 1891. Cameron had worked in Richardson's Boston office and in 1885 had moved to Chicago to supervise the construction of Richardson's MacVeagh and Glessner Houses and the famous Marshall Field department store. Upon their completion and following Richardson's death, he returned to his hometown of St. Louis and joined Link's firm. His participation in the planning and construction of Union Station must have been considerable, and the building is properly attributed to the firm of Cameron and Link, even though the two men dissolved their partnership just as the great structure was nearing completion in 1894.

For the next decade Link continued his successful practice, building homes and churches for the most prominent St. Louisans, even contributing to the Louisiana Purchase Exposition in 1904 with his Mines and Metallurgy Building. About the same time, though, his attention began to turn south where he had received a major commission for the Mississippi State Capitol in Jackson (1900–1903). Clearly one of his most important commissions, this and the later plan for the Louisiana State University campus in Baton Rouge (1923) would conclude his career. Link died while supervising the construction of Louisiana State University on November 12, 1923, at the age of seventy-three.

JONI L. KINSEY

Cox, James. *Old and New St. Louis.* St. Louis: Central Biographical Publishing, 1894.

Hyde, William, and Howard L. Conard, eds. *Encyclopedia of the History of St. Louis.* New York: Southern History, 1899.

Kinsey, Joni L. "Prairie Monuments: Henry Hobson Richardson and the Architecture of Mid-America." *Gateway Heritage* 10 (winter 1989–1990): 26–35.

Lowic, Lawrence. *The Architectural Heritage of St. Louis, 1803–1891: From the Louisiana Purchase to the Wainwright Building.* St. Louis: Washington University Gallery of Art, 1982.

LINK, THEODORE CARL "TED" (1904–1974)

Theodore Carl "Ted" Link was born in St. Louis on September 22, 1904, the namesake of his famous grandfather, architect **Theodore Carl Link,** a German immigrant who designed Union Station and more than one hundred other St. Louis buildings. Ted wanted to follow in his grandfather's and father's career, but took only a few night courses in architecture at Washington University.

Link began his journalism career at the *St. Louis Star* where he worked from 1924 to 1933. He began to focus on organized crime with his reporting on the Cuckoo gang wars and violent clashes involving the Ku Klux Klan in Illinois. In his colorful style he compared the Klan shootouts with the gunfight at the O.K. Corral. Link discovered the existence of the Green Ones, a gang responsible for "almost a killing a day . . . in 1926–27."

After leaving the *Star* Link investigated a health-fraud racket for the National Lead Company before working briefly for both the *Globe-Democrat* and the *Times.* When he joined the *Post-Dispatch* staff in 1938 he became one of a handful of men to have worked for all four St. Louis newspapers.

During World War II Link joined the marines, working as a correspondent and as editor of *Chevron.* He served in the Pacific, and was wounded on Bougainville in 1943. He was discharged in 1945 after receiving a Purple Heart and a citation for service.

Link resumed his investigations into organized crime upon his return to the *Post-Dispatch.* A probe into gambling brought a discovery of vote fraud in Kansas City and bribery involving a prosecutor and a sheriff and gave Link a growing realization that close ties existed among criminal organizations around the country.

Through Link's ties to the Shelton gang he learned of connections to the Capone gang in Chicago and of both groups' involvement in political corruption in Illinois. His reports led to indictments against Republican officials during the 1948 campaign. Link himself was indicted in return, but Illinois voters defeated the machine of Gov. Dwight Green, replacing him with Adlai Stevenson. A new state's attorney dismissed the indictments against Link, and he later received the American Newspaper Guild's special award for distinguished public service.

In 1949 Link exposed additional connections between organized crime in St. Louis and gangs in other major cities. His 1950 articles on Miami as the national capital of organized crime brought him to the attention of Sen. Estes Kefauver's committee investigating underworld activities. Link not only covered the committee hearings for the *Post-Dispatch* but also provided leads to committee staff. At the conclusion of the hearings, Kefauver wrote, "In numerous instances, the first leads of the connections among the underworld, conniving politicians and corrupt law enforcement officials were supplied to the committee . . . out of Ted Link's voluminous files."

Link played no party favorites in his probes of political corruption. In 1951 he went after Democratic national chair William Boyle Jr., who had accepted payments from a St. Louis company that obtained more than five hundred thousand dollars in government loans. Boyle also had ties to the local Internal Revenue Bureau (IRB), now the Internal Revenue Service, which Link exposed, resulting in Boyle's resignation, the conviction of the revenue director, and the reform of the IRB. Link's articles won a Pulitzer Prize for the *Post-Dispatch.*

Link continued to investigate political corruption and organized crime for the rest of his career. His later work included articles disclosing how Sen. Richard M. Nixon attempted to fix a financial supporter's Cuban gambling debts and lauding President Dwight D. Eisenhower's intervention when Republican senators and IRB officials attempted to block reforms in the IRB's St. Louis office. Link covered union corruption and renewed gang violence in the 1950s, while in the next decade he wrote long series on the living conditions in the slums and on the Garrison investigation into the Kennedy assassination.

While Link was described as "a bold reporter but a quiet man," in 1960 stories about his life briefly overshadowed his reporting. He was indicted and tried for the shooting death of an intruder at his home. Although the story was front-page news for several months and drew at least one irate editor to call for him to be "muzzled," he was acquitted.

Link's work over his long career resulted in important public actions to curb corruption and greed in public life and exposed the workings of organized crime to the public eye. Upon his death on February 14, 1974, the *Post-Dispatch* called him "persistent, incorruptible and unintimidated," a high compliment indeed for this quiet man.

KENNETH LUEBBERING

New York Times, February 15, 1974.
St. Louis Post-Dispatch, February 15–28, 1974.

LINN, LEWIS F. (1795–1843)

A frontier doctor, Jacksonian Democrat, and U.S. senator, Lewis F. Linn has been called both "Missouri's model senator" and the "Father of Oregon." At the time of his death the *St. Louis Missouri Reporter* editorialized that "No man in Missouri ever commanded more general and sincere respect, . . . [nor] possessed a more wide-spread or deserved popularity."

Born near Louisville, Kentucky, on November 5, 1795, Lewis was orphaned at the age of twelve. **Henry Dodge,** his stepbrother then living in Ste. Genevieve, became his guardian.

At an early age Linn started the study of medicine under Dr. William Craig Galt of Louisville. Linn was visiting in Ste. Genevieve when the War of 1812 broke out, and he entered military service as a surgeon to Missouri troops commanded by his

guardian, General Dodge. Following his military service, Linn completed his study of medicine in a medical college in Philadelphia. He opened a practice in Ste. Genevieve, and soon established himself as one of the area's most popular, caring, and respected physicians.

Linn's active interest in public affairs helped make him a recognized leader of the Democratic followers of Andrew Jackson and **Thomas Hart Benton** in southeast Missouri. He served one term in the state General Assembly. When **Alexander Buckner** died in 1833, Gov. **Daniel Dunklin,** a Jackson-Benton Democrat, appointed Linn to fill Buckner's United States Senate seat. In 1834 the General Assembly elected him to complete Buckner's term. Gaining quick popularity and respect, he won reelection in 1836 without opposition. The General Assembly reelected him in 1842 for a second full term with an overwhelming majority.

In his early senatorial years, Linn spent a great deal of time working to settle disputed old Spanish land claims—still a matter of concern to some influential Missourians. He soon shifted his primary attention to matters of broader statewide interest and to efforts to encourage national westward expansion. Among other things, he worked for federal support of internal improvements, improved frontier defenses—including military posts and roads—and western expansion, and for a liberal disposition of public lands to settlers.

Working with Missouri's senior senator, Benton, Linn helped push through Congress legislation authorizing the Platte Purchase. This measure, enacted in 1837, added Indian lands to Missouri by extending the state's northwestern boundary westward to the Missouri River and forcing the removal of several Indian tribes residing in that area. Like most westerners, Linn viewed the Indians as warlike savages and a hinderance to western expansion.

Linn made his major mark in the Senate with his persistent drive to organize the Oregon territory and to promote American settlement there. Under an 1818 agreement with Great Britain, the Oregon country was open to occupation by both British and U.S. citizens. In 1838 Linn introduced a bill to organize the Oregon territory under American law. To encourage Americans to go there, he proposed to offer each settler a 640-acre grant of land. The bill failed to win congressional approval, at least in part because some members feared it might upset other ongoing negotiations with Britain. Linn had little such diplomatic concern. He believed the American title to Oregon was indisputable, and he wanted the British out. As a part of his continuing attempts to press for American occupation and organization of the Oregon country, he put measures before the Senate calling for military occupation of the region, construction of a U.S. fort on the Columbia River, and military protection for settlers en route to Oregon.

Linn set forth a glowing picture of the wealth and importance of the Oregon country. He spoke and wrote of its valuable fur-bearing animals, its prodigious fisheries, its virgin forests, its mineral resources, and its productive soil. The acquisition of Oregon, he asserted, would facilitate direct and profitable trade with the Orient.

Linn, who died unexpectedly on October 3, 1843, did not live to see the fulfillment of his Oregon dream. Even so, he played a major role in creating the Oregon "fever" that propelled the migration of Americans to the Northwest in the late 1830s and early 1840s. That migration, along with his aggressive senatorial advocacy, contributed much to the final attainment of his goals for Oregon.

During his public career Linn remained somewhat in the shadow of Missouri's senior senator, Thomas Hart Benton, the powerful and aggressive leader of the Jacksonian Democrats. However, in his own right Linn won a strong following in Missouri and the respect of his fellow senators.

PERRY MCCANDLESS

Husband, Michael B. "Senator Lewis F. Linn and the Oregon Question." *Missouri Historical Review* 66 (October 1971): 1–19.

Linn, E. A., and N. Sargent. *The Life and Public Service of Dr. Lewis F. Linn.* New York: D. Appleton, 1857.

LISA, MANUEL (1772–1820)

Manual Lisa, a bold St. Louis merchant who spearheaded the opening of the northern and far-western fur trade following the Louisiana Purchase, was born on September 8, 1772, in New Orleans. His father, Christobal de Lisa of Murcia, Spain, was an employee of the Spanish government, and his mother, Maria Ignacia Rodriguez Lisa, was from St. Augustine, Florida. Little is known about Lisa's childhood, but his experiences on the New Orleans waterfront must have affected his decision to become a river trader.

By 1796 Lisa owned a boat that he operated on the Mississippi River. That year he married his first wife, a widow named Polly Charles Chew. Lisa arrived in St. Louis in the late 1790s with the intention of transferring his business operations to the Missouri River. The sly, swarthy Lisa successfully petitioned Spanish officials in 1799 to grant him land in Upper Louisiana suitable for raising cattle. He had no intention of farming, but he recognized that Spaniards were more likely to grant land requested for agricultural purposes.

When Lisa arrived in St. Louis, **Auguste Chouteau** and **(Jean) Pierre Chouteau** dominated fur-trading operations along the lower Missouri with the benefit of a monopoly of the Osage trade awarded by Spanish authorities. The daring and aggressive Lisa challenged the influential Chouteaus and the monopoly system that made them powerful. He refused to settle for a small share of the market. Instead, he advocated a competitive and open trade policy with the Indians. Although he failed in his efforts to introduce free trade, he did manage to wrest the Osage monopoly from the Chouteaus in 1802. His victory came too near the end of the Spanish period in Louisiana to be of much value, but he had succeeded in capturing the attention of the St. Louis trading community.

The American acquisition of the Louisiana Territory ushered in a new era, and Lisa rushed to take advantage of the change in governments. He helped supply **Meriwether Lewis** and **William Clark** for their epic journey to the Pacific, and following the expedition's return in 1806 he drew upon the information they had gathered to prepare for his first trip up the Missouri. In 1807 Lisa led such a trading and trapping expedition in partnership with Kaskaskia merchants Pierre Menard and William Morrison. Early in his career, Lisa recognized the necessity of developing mutual trust and respect in order to ensure friendly relations between fur traders and Indians, and while traveling upriver he continued his practice of giving gifts and peace offerings to the Indians. His close ties with the Indians caused his enemies to complain that he had turned the Missouri River tribes against all other traders and trappers. After establishing Fort Raymond as a fur-trading headquarters at the junction of the Yellowstone and Bighorn Rivers, Lisa left his crew in the mountains and returned to St. Louis in 1808.

Lisa dreamed of further exploring the great Northwest. To that end he established the St. Louis Missouri Fur Company in 1809 in partnership with William Clark, Pierre Chouteau, **Auguste Pierre Chouteau,** Reuben Lewis, Benjamin Wilkinson, Sylvestre Labbadie, and **Andrew Henry.** They wanted to gain sole control of the upper Missouri fur trade. The new firm sent a major trading expedition upriver in the spring of 1809, but the enterprise encountered opposition from the hostile Blackfeet Indians and also experienced many financial and supply problems. When the business was not as profitable as they expected, the partners reorganized the company in 1812.

Lisa led every expedition up the Missouri for the company. He knew each Indian tribe along the river well enough to predict which goods each would buy or trade. Despite his efforts, company profits again declined. With Lisa deeply in debt, the Missouri Fur

Company folded in 1814. That same year William Clark, governor of the Missouri Territory and Lisa's former partner, appointed him subagent for the Missouri River tribes. With the War of 1812 raging, Clark instructed Lisa to seek peaceful relations with those tribes. Lisa's efforts proved successful and helped calm the fears of St. Louis's war-weary residents.

While living and working among the Omaha Indians, Lisa took an Indian wife, Mitain, notwithstanding Polly Lisa, his wife in St. Louis. Following Polly's death in 1818, Lisa married Mary Hempstead Keeney. When she subsequently accompanied him up the Missouri, Lisa hurriedly arranged to have Mitain sent into the wilderness to avoid any embarrassment.

In 1819 Lisa formed another Missouri Fur Company, this time with new partners Joshua Pilcher, Andrew Woods, Moses B. Carson, John B. Zenoni, Joseph Perkins, Thomas Hempstead, and Andrew Drips. That venture also failed, but Lisa did not live to see its demise. He had returned to St. Louis in 1820, and by late summer his health was failing. After preparing his will and attempting to clear his debts, he died on August 12, 1820.

Despite his business failures, Manuel Lisa left his mark on the fur trade. In addition to opening the Northwest trade to the United States, he promoted the connection between business success and good relations with the Indians. Through his successes and his travels, the highly respected and sometimes feared Lisa earned the title "the king of the Missouri."

SHELLY L. LEMONS

Oglesby, Richard E. *Manuel Lisa and the Opening of the Missouri Fur Trade.* Norman: University of Oklahoma Press, 1963.

Phillips, Paul C. *The Fur Trade.* Norman: University of Oklahoma Press, 1961.

LITTON, JERRY L. (1937–1976)

In his four years in the United States House of Representatives, Jerry L. Litton accomplished as much as many congressmen do in their extended careers. A successful cattle rancher, he advocated the rights of farmers and all hardworking citizens. Often referred to as a "breath of fresh air in Washington," Litton impressed his colleagues with his honesty and his political incorruptibility. House majority leader Thomas P. "Tip" O'Neal claimed that in his twenty-two years in Congress he had never been more impressed by a freshman congressman than by Jerry Litton.

Litton was born in a farmhouse without plumbing or electricity near Locke Springs, Missouri, on May 12, 1937. During his youth, an accident crippled his father, forcing his mother to support the family

by selling milk from the family's eleven cows. One tragedy followed another. The family's house burned in 1945, and the following year a respiratory disease killed all their hogs.

The economic struggles of Litton's family apparently did not detract from his success in the classroom. He attended a small country school in Locke Springs and graduated from Chillicothe High School in 1955. While in high school, Litton served as president of both the National Honor Society and the Chillicothe chapter of Future Farmers of America (FFA). In 1956–1957 the FFA elected him as national secretary. After graduating from high school, Litton spent two years traveling across the United States giving speeches on behalf of the FFA.

A hard worker, Litton earned money during high school and college as a part-time newscaster for radio stations and as an agricultural writer for the *Columbia Missourian,* becoming the newspaper's farm director. He also farmed during the summers on land that he leased himself. He saved his money, graduating from high school with a bank account of fifteen thousand dollars. He also served in the United States Army National Guard from 1955 until 1962.

Litton's political inclinations became evident during his formative years. In 1954 the Livingston County Young Democrats elected him as its president. He attributed an increased interest in politics to a meeting with former U.S. president **Harry S. Truman** in 1957. The student body of the University of Missouri elected him its vice president during his sophomore year of college, and in 1960 he served as president of the University of Missouri Young Democrats and chair of the National Youth for Symington for President. While studying at the university, Litton also served as the youngest-ever president of his fraternity, Alpha Gamma Rho.

Litton majored in agricultural journalism at the university, receiving the Citation of Merit from the College of Agriculture in recognition of his academic achievements. In 1959 he married Sharon Summerville of Chillicothe. She helped support the family by working full-time as a secretary. Litton graduated from the University of Missouri in 1961 with a B.S. in agricultural journalism and a minor in economics. After graduation the Littons moved back to Chillicothe to join Jerry's parents in a cattle-breeding business.

During the 1950s Litton had persuaded his father to borrow twenty thousand dollars to begin breeding Charolais cattle, a variety imported from France. By 1961 the Litton Charolais Ranch had grown to more than five hundred acres. The family hung wood paneling on the walls of the barn and covered the floors with Astroturf. The cattle stood in carpeted stalls and listened to soft music while being monitored by closed-circuit television. A computer system determined genetic superiority by recording the vital statistics of each animal. The Charolais cattle bred in this scientific manner set new records for weight, progeny, and beef quality. Experts hailed the Littons' advanced system of breeding and evaluation as being "the most sophisticated program ever instituted in the beef breeding industry." The success of their state-of-the-art breeding techniques brought in buyers from all over the world and made the Littons millionaires. Aside from managing the ranch, Jerry Litton edited the *Charolais Bull-O-Gram,* a newsletter published by the ranch and sent to customers and later circulated around the world.

Litton's accomplishments in the cattle-breeding business brought him respect as well as wealth. In 1967 he was chosen as the youngest member of the Governor's Advisory Council on Agriculture. He also served as president of the Performance Registry International, a worldwide cattle organization.

In 1972 the voters of Missouri's Sixth District elected Litton to replace W. R. Hull in the United States House of Representatives. Litton's first election to public office merely continued a long history of political activity that began in high school and continued in the 1960s. As a stepping-stone for his political career, he raised money in 1970 for Sen. **Stuart Symington**'s reelection as finance chairman for the Sixth Congressional District. Litton's 1972 campaign emphasized his agricultural background. His appeal to rural voters in the district allowed him to upset the incumbent by a narrow margin.

Taking office on January 3, 1973, Litton quickly earned the respect of his colleagues. "I made it very clear to the Democratic leadership when I arrived that I didn't intend to be told how to vote and, consequently, few people ever try to tell me how to vote." As a freshman congressman from a rural district, he received a coveted appointment to the Agriculture Committee. He also served as chair of the Forestry Subcommittee during the Ninety-fourth Congress. Other appointments included membership on the Committees on Education, Labor, and Social Services; Commerce, Housing, and Transportation; and Government Operations.

Not surprisingly, Litton focused much of his energy on the interests of farmers. He proposed legislation that would provide funding for agricultural research and technology. In 1973 he fought President Nixon's executive order allowing the Department of Agriculture to inspect the tax returns of the country's 3 million farmers. Nixon rescinded the order soon after Litton presented the matter before Congress. Litton coauthored the Litton-Weicker Bill that would protect all taxpayers by prohibiting the IRS from disclosing tax return information for reasons other than tax collection or enforcement. He chided President Nixon, saying, "The IRS is there to gather taxes to run our country and not to serve as a gestapo type agency gathering information on private citizens. . . ."

Litton believed in uniting the urban and rural communities, saying, "What is good for the consumer is good for the farmer and vice versa." On June 18, 1973, Litton gathered the leaders of American agriculture in Washington for Farm Summit, a meeting aimed at bringing producers and consumers together. His work in this area led to his selection as Agriculture Spokesman of the Year for 1975 by Chevron Chemical Company and *Farm Chemicals Magazine.*

Litton firmly supported economy in the government and reduction of the national debt. To gain attention for his concerns, he suggested cutting the number of limousines used by the executive branch from eight hundred to twenty-seven. He also cosponsored a bill that would have prohibited incumbent congressmen from voting themselves pay increases. When Litton received a raise in his second term, he turned it over to the clerk of the House to reduce the national debt. He wanted to eliminate lengthy congressional recesses such as the "lame duck" period of a departing congressman between the election of his or her successor in November and the inauguration in January.

Litton believed that the government spent an inordinate amount of money on foreign policy and wanted to reduce foreign aid. He supported a bill to cut U.S. funding of the United Nations from one-fourth to one-sixth of its operating budget, believing that the organization no longer defended the principles it was created to protect. He opposed U.S. appropriations for the reconstruction of North Vietnam, saying, "I do not approve of Nixon's scrapping approximately one hundred domestic programs in order to aid a country which has cost us 46,000 lives and $135 billion."

Outside of Washington, Litton stayed in touch with the needs and interests of his constituents. Beginning in March 1974 the Congressional Club in his district sponsored a monthly television program, *Dialogue with Litton,* that aired statewide. Open to the public, these meetings offered voters a chance to ask questions and state their concerns about political issues. For each show Litton invited a guest, including such prominent political figures as Vice President Gerald Ford, Majority Leader "Tip" O'Neal, Georgia governor Jimmy Carter, and Sen. Hubert H. Humphrey. The guests offered their views and responded to questions. Surprisingly, when aired on prime time *Dialogue with Litton* attracted a 16 percent larger share of the television audience than *Monday Night Football.*

Rather than running for reelection to the House in 1976, Litton decided to seek the seat of retiring U.S. senator Stuart Symington. He defeated the incumbent's son, James Symington, and former governor Warren Hearnes in the Democratic primary on August 3, 1976. The same evening, Litton, his wife, and two children died in a plane crash just after takeoff from Chillicothe Airport en route to a victory celebration in Kansas City.

ERIKA K. NELSON

Biographical Dictionary of the United States Congress, 1774–1989. Bicentennial ed. S.v. "Litton, Jerry L." Washington, D.C.: U.S. Government Printing Office, 1989.

Congressional Directory 1974. 94th Congress, 2d sess., 1974.

Litton, Jerry L. Papers. 1937–1976. Western Historical Manuscripts Collection, Columbia.

Litton, Mildre. Telephone interview by author, August 30, 1994.

New York Times, August 4, 1976.

Official Manual of the State of Missouri, 1973–1974. Jefferson City: Secretary of State, 1974.

LOCKWOOD, CHARLES ANDREWS, JR. (1890–1967)

Charles Andrews Lockwood Jr. was born in Fauquier County, Virginia, on May 6, 1890, but was raised in Missouri. After attending high school in Lamar, Missouri, he enrolled in the Wertz Preparatory School in Annapolis, Maryland. Recipient of an appointment to the United States Naval Academy in 1908, he was graduated with a B.S. degree four years later and commissioned an ensign. He was promoted through grades to the rank of vice admiral in late 1943.

Lockwood was assigned successively to the *Mississippi* and the *Arkansas,* followed by a tour of duty at the Great Lakes Naval Training Station in Illinois in 1913–1914. In the summer of 1914, he began his underwater career, where he would spend most of his time in military service. Given his first submarine command in late 1914, he directed a submarine division of the Pacific Fleet in 1917, at the age of twenty-seven. Following a brief trip to Japan to purchase ships for the Emergency Fleet Corporation, he returned to a succession of submarine commands. Subsequent assignments included the Yangtze Patrol, 1922–1923; navy yard repair officer, 1924–1925; membership on the United States Naval Mission to Brazil, 1929–1931; first lieutenant aboard the *California* and executive officer of the *Concord,* 1932–1933; instructor in navigation and seamanship at the Naval Academy, 1934–1937; submarine desk officer under the chief of naval operations, 1937–1939; chief of staff and aide to the commander of the fleet's submarine force, 1939–1941; and naval attaché to the American embassy in London, 1941–1942. Promoted to the rank of rear admiral in late 1941, he served as commander of submarines in the southwest Pacific from May 1942 until February 1943 when he became leader of the Pacific Fleet's submarine force. His advancement to vice admiral followed in October 1943. Upon completion of his assignment in December 1945, he returned to the United States Navy until his retirement in July 1947.

A contemporary and friend of Adm. **Freeland Allen Daubin,** Lockwood quickly grasped the significance and potential of submarines as devastating weapons of warfare and became an American pioneer in the field. Like his fellow Missourian, he knew and understood submarines and submarine warfare and used such knowledge and experience effectively.

Known respectfully by staff and crew members as "the Boss," Lockwood amassed an enviable record of achievement. Within six months of the Japanese aerial assault on Pearl Harbor, he was given command of the fleet's submarine force in the southwest Pacific. Less than a year later, he was commander of the fleet's Pacific submarine force, a position he held for the remainder of the war. American submarine forces in the Pacific took a crippling toll on enemy shipping during World War II. They claimed an estimated two-thirds of Japan's merchant tonnage and one-third of its combatant ships. Lockwood's submarine forces also sealed off Japan from its widely dispersed forces, including the Asian mainland, during the closing stages of the war. Moreover, the submarines were used effectively for other war-related purposes, including the rescue of downed air crews and seamen, scouting in advance of the landing of American troops on the atolls and islands, survival and salvage operations, and communications with resistance forces in the Philippines and elsewhere in the Pacific theater.

Lockwood also had a reputation for practicality as well as inspiration. His submarine crews were admonished to "take what comes rather than wait for something better." He also played an active role in the elimination of functional flaws and in improving the accuracy of torpedoes used by his crews, slashing much of the red tape in the process to overcome the problem. The achievements resulting from the Lockwood "watch" were indeed singularly impressive.

Lockwood was the recipient of numerous awards and honors, including the Distinguished Service Medal with two stars, and the Legion of Merit. He was also named to the Order of Orange-Nassau by the Netherlands, and was named a knight commander of the Order of Bath by Great Britain.

Lockwood served as a technical consultant with the motion picture industry on films about submarines following his retirement. He, with coauthor Hans Christian Adamson, also wrote several books related to his experiences while on active duty, including *Sink 'Em All* (1951), *Hellcats at Sea* (1955), *Zoomies, Subs, and Zeroes* (1956), *Through Hell and Deep Water* (1956), *Tragedy at Honda* (1960), and *Battles of the Philippine Sea* (1967).

Lockwood's autobiography was called *Down to the Sea in Subs* (1967).

Having served on active naval duty for thirty-five years, Lockwood died in Monte Sereno, California, on June 7, 1967, and was buried at the Golden Gate National Cemetery.

JOSEPH T. HATFIELD

Ethridge, James M., and Barbara Kopala, eds. *Contemporary Authors: A Bio-Biographical Guide to Current Authors and Their Works.* Vols. 1–4. Detroit: Gale Research Company, 1967.

Morison, Samuel Eliot. *History of the United States Naval Operations in World War II.* 15 vols. Boston: Little, Brown, 1947–1963.

———. *The Two Ocean War: A Short History of the United States Navy.* Boston: Little, Brown, 1963.

LOEB, ISIDOR (1868–1954)

Isidor Loeb, a longtime Missouri educator and authority on state government and taxation, was born on November 5, 1868, in the Howard County village of Roanoke. One of twelve children born to Bernhard and Bertha Myer Loeb, young Isidor entered the University of Missouri at Columbia in 1881. He received a bachelor of science degree in 1887 and master of science and bachelor of laws degrees from the institution in 1893. Loeb continued his education at Columbia University in New York, where he earned a doctor of philosophy degree in 1901. He also studied at the University of Berlin in 1899–1900.

Loeb began his thirty-three-year tenure on the faculty of the University of Missouri as a tutor in history in 1892. He was named assistant professor of history in 1895 and professor of political science and public law in 1902, a title he held until 1925. From 1910 to 1916 he served as dean of the faculty; in the latter year he became dean of the School of Business and Public Administration. In 1923 he served a brief term as acting president of the university.

In 1925 Loeb resigned from the University of Missouri and assumed similar positions at Washington University. He served as a professor of political science and dean of the School of Business and Public Administration at the St. Louis school until 1940. That year he retired and was named dean emeritus. In 1933 Loeb was elected president of the American Political Science Association. Both the University of Missouri and Washington University presented him with honorary degrees, the former in 1933 and the latter in 1953.

Loeb's influence extended beyond his work as a university professor and administrator. Throughout Missouri he became recognized for his expertise in state government issues, particularly taxation. He served as a member of the Missouri State Tax Commission in 1906, and the next year published a speech calling for a new state constitution. During the Constitutional Convention of 1922–1923, Loeb wrote for the *St. Louis Post-Dispatch* a series of articles about the constitution's history and the need for revisions. The series was reprinted and distributed to the convention's delegates. Twenty years later, Loeb actively participated in the movement to call the 1943–1944 Constitutional Convention. He served as an adviser to members of that convention, particularly on tax matters.

Interested in his native state and its history, Loeb helped found the State Historical Society of Missouri in 1898; he served as the organization's first secretary, resigning in 1901. He remained involved in the society throughout his life, serving as a trustee from 1901 to 1944, then as a life trustee from 1944 to 1954, and as president from 1944 to 1947.

Following his retirement from Washington University in 1940, Loeb maintained his interest in public affairs. During World War II he served as a regional director of the Office of Price Administration in St. Louis and as a special investigator for the War Labor Board.

Isidor Loeb died in St. Louis on June 4, 1954. His wife, Carrie Lengsfield Loeb, whom he had married in 1915, had died in 1951. A son and two daughters survived him. Loeb's work as an educator and his profound knowledge of state government had a significant impact on Missouri throughout the first half of the twentieth century.

LYNN WOLF GENTZLER

McReynolds, Allen. "Dr. Isidor Loeb." *Missouri Historical Review* 36 (July 1942): 430–34.

Shoemaker, Floyd Calvin. *Missouri and Missourians: Land of Contrasts and People of Achievements.* 5 vols. Chicago: Lewis Publishing, 1943.

Viles, Jonas. *The University of Missouri: A Centennial History.* Columbia: University of Missouri, 1939.

LOISEL, REGIS (1773?–1804)

Regis (Registre) Loisel was born near Montreal, Canada, about 1773, and at an early age he entered the fur trade. He worked on the Des Moines River, perhaps for the Canadian-based merchant Andrew Todd, whose interest stretched from Michilimackinac south and westward into Spanish territory. Loisel first appeared in St. Louis in 1793, about the time a large shipment of Todd's merchandise was confiscated as smuggled contraband by Spanish authorities there.

Todd supplied several St. Louis traders, among them **Jacques Clamorgan.** As director of the Missouri Company, Clamorgan acquired a controlling interest and the company's monopoly on the Missouri River fur trade. Through Clamorgan's influence, the Spanish government in 1795 granted Todd a monopoly on the Indian trade north of the river. To legitimate their clandestine alliance and facilitate their various projects, the two tapped young Loisel in 1796, and organized the firm of Clamorgan, Loisel, and Company. Using Loisel as his agent, Todd bought heavily into the Missouri Company. The partners had nearly achieved their trading empire when Todd's sudden death in the New Orleans yellow fever epidemic of 1796 shattered the project. Both the Missouri Company and Clamorgan, Loisel, and Company were heavily in debt to Todd. In the years of litigation that followed, Todd's heirs destroyed both companies and nearly bankrupted Clamorgan in their efforts to recover the debt.

Clamorgan and Loisel continued cooperating informally to control the Missouri River trade. When Clamorgan secured the government monopoly on trade with the Otos, Omaha, and Poncas, Loisel asked for the river tribes above Clamorgan's grant. The intricate and shifting business alliances of St. Louis required wide connections, however. In May 1800 Loisel married Helene Chauvin, daughter of Jacques Chauvin, one of the lesser St. Louis traders who had repeatedly joined his peers in attempts to break Clamorgan and the Missouri Company.

Soon after the wedding, Loisel returned upriver to explore the potential of his grant. He traveled far into present-day South Dakota, and may have begun construction of a trading post on Cedar Island, about thirty-five miles downriver from the modern city of Pierre. Business prospects in the neighborhood were poor: the Teton Sioux favored the Montreal-based Northwest Company and strongly opposed the St. Louis traders' efforts to contact tribes farther upriver, a connection that would supply their enemies and cut their profits as middlemen in a lucrative river trade.

To strengthen his position, Loisel entered a two-year partnership in July 1801 with Hugh Heney, a Canadian of old Northwest Company connections, now working for Clamorgan and **Auguste Chouteau.** While Clamorgan and Loisel cooperated in protecting the Oto-Ponca-Omaha trade from interlopers, Clamorgan acquired an interest in the new Loisel-Heney partnership, and Chouteau outfitted the partners for another trading venture on the upper Missouri.

In 1802 they ascended the river, and Loisel completed his trading post, Fort aux Cedres, on Cedar Island. Again, however, trade was frustrated by the Sioux blockade and serious competition from the Northwest Company. The trader returned to St. Louis early in 1803 and so impressed Lt. Gov. **Charles de Hault Delassus** that he commissioned Loisel to undertake a formal investigation of conditions on the upper Missouri for the Spanish government. Loisel again ascended the river, stationed one trading party above his fort at the mouth of the Cheyenne River and another below among the Arikara, while he spent the winter of 1803–1804 at his fort. Old problems plagued him: the Sioux demanded extravagant presents and refused to allow his men to visit other tribes or to resupply the party upriver. Loisel's protests and alarm at British incursions may have been sincere, but Heney openly returned to his old associates in the Northwest Company.

His venture failing, Loisel returned to St. Louis in May 1804. On the way downriver he encountered the Lewis and Clark expedition, and shared information, advice, and maps with the officers. In his formal report Loisel warned of British and American designs on the upper Missouri and Spanish possessions to the south. He asked for a commission as Indian agent to the upper Missouri tribes. Spanish officials in St. Louis and New Orleans strongly approved both the report and the request, but before they could act Loisel fell seriously ill. He died in New Orleans in October 1804.

Loisel was among the first to challenge the Sioux blockade on the river trade. His Fort aux Cedres was probably the earliest establishment on the upper river. Clamorgan hoped to continue the project, and tried unsuccessfully to claim the fort after Loisel's death. The fort was soon abandoned, however, and burned, probably in early 1810. In St. Louis Loisel left a wife, two daughters, and a son. Both girls married into the Papin family, St. Louis traders related to the Chouteaus. The son, Regis Jr., was said to be the first St. Louis native ordained to the priesthood.

MARY ELLEN ROWE

Abel, Annie Heloise, ed. *Tabeau's Narrative of Loisel's Expedition to the Upper Missouri.* 1939. Reprint, Norman: University of Oklahoma Press, 1968.

Nasatir, Abraham P. *Before Lewis and Clark: Documents Illustrating the History of Missouri, 1785–1804.* 1952. Reprint, Lincoln: University of Nebraska Press, 1990.

LONG, EDWARD V. (1908–1972)

Edward V. Long was born on July 18, 1908, in Lincoln County, Missouri. He received his undergraduate degree from Culver-Stockton College and attended law school at the University of Missouri. After completing his education, he settled in Bowling Green, Missouri, and accepted a teaching position. He taught until 1935, when he began a private law practice, apparently with ambition to pursue a career in politics. In 1937, barely a year after beginning his practice, he won election as prosecuting attorney of

Pike County. In addition, he became Bowling Green's city attorney.

In 1945 Edward Long sought and won a seat in the Missouri Senate, where he served for more than a decade, eventually becoming the majority leader of the senate Democrats. After serving as majority leader from 1949 to 1954, his fellow senators elected him president pro tempore. In 1956 Long won election as lieutenant governor. He undoubtedly had every expectation of completing his four-year term, but on September 13, 1960, U.S. senator **Thomas C. Hennings Jr.** died. To name a successor to Hennings the Missouri Democratic Party held a special convention, with Rep. Charles H. Brown and Gov. **James Thomas Blair Jr.** as the two leading candidates for the nomination. The convention deadlocked, with both Brown and Blair having strong support among the delegates, and Long emerged as a compromise candidate. On September 21, 1960, the State Democratic Convention named Edward Long as its choice for the Democratic nomination for the United States Senate, and Governor Blair had no choice but to accept the decision. He named Long to the post on September 23, 1960, and Long served as Missouri's temporary senator until November 8, 1960, when voters elected him to complete the remaining two years of the Hennings term. In 1962 he was elected to a full six-year term.

In succeeding Hennings, Long had large shoes to fill. Hennings, a liberal from St. Louis, was popular in the state, and he earned a national reputation in the area of civil liberties, having attacked the red-scare tactics of Sen. Joseph McCarthy. Undoubtedly, Hennings's legacy influenced Long's political career.

Long served as chairman of the Senate Subcommittee on Administrative Practice and Procedure, which studied the surveillance activities of federal law enforcement agencies. Long published several articles about President John F. Kennedy's proposed wire-tap legislation. On March 26, 1962, Carey McWilliams, the editor of the *Nation* sent a letter to Long asking him to write an article identifying the disadvantages of President Kennedy's proposed legislation. The article appeared in the July 14, 1962, issue. Long argued that Kennedy's legislation would give too much authority to law enforcement officials.

Long followed the *Nation* piece with another in the July 1962 issue of *Focus Midwest* under the title "Big Brother Is Listening." On August 6, 1962, Robert L. Bevan, Long's legislative assistant, sent a letter to St. Louis attorney Thomas J. Guilfoil requesting his help in getting the *Focus Midwest* article republished in the *St. Louis Post-Dispatch*.

In 1966 Long published a book titled *The Intruders: The Invasion of Privacy by Government and Industry.* He warned readers that the individual zone of privacy was being threatened by technological

advances and advocated that legislation be passed to prevent this dangerous erosion of civil liberties. In the Senate he proposed legislation designed to strengthen individual civil liberties, including a bill making postal surveillance of mail a violation of federal law.

Long's voting record leaned in the moderate to liberal direction. Besides a liberal record on civil liberties, he supported the civil rights reforms of both Kennedy and Johnson. In February 1963 he voted for a change in Senate Rule 22 that would have revised the guidelines for cloture, requiring sixty votes instead of a two-thirds majority. Civil rights activists saw the change in Rule 22 as an important step in gaining Senate approval for civil rights legislation. Although the February 1963 attempt proved unsuccessful, it nonetheless indicated Long's strong support of the civil rights cause. At the 1964 Democratic National Convention, he expressed support for the delegation representing the Mississippi Freedom Democratic Party, and was supportive of party reforms designed to increase black representation at future party conventions. He also voted in favor of the Medicare insurance program for elderly Americans.

Long's record of support for civil liberties eventually caused immense difficulty for his political career. In its May 26, 1967, issue, *Life* charged Long with having sinister motives for his record on civil liberties. According to the author, William Lambert, Long conducted hearings and criticized federal law enforcement agencies because of his ties to the Teamsters and its embattled president, Jimmy Hoffa. Lambert accused Long of trying to prevent Hoffa's prosecution, and later, after Hoffa's conviction, of trying to get the decision overturned. In substantiating its argument, the *Life* article traced Long's ties to the Teamsters back to his days as Missouri's lieutenant governor. Long reportedly had connections to Morris Shenker, Hoffa's chief attorney. However, the *Life* story did more than identify connections between Long and the Teamsters and Hoffa. According to Lambert, Shenker had paid Long forty-eight thousand dollars, though Long had not practiced law since the 1950s. In addition to these accusations, *Life* asserted that Long used federal money to pay the salary of his housekeeper and to pay the rent on his law office in Bowling Green. The charges led the Senate to conduct an investigation, which cleared Long of the charges of illegal or improper activities. However, the magazine stood by its story, and in its November 10, 1967, issue restated the charges and, in fact, delved into the alleged relationship between Long and individuals whom the magazine called "gangsters" and "gamblers."

The *Life* articles had a substantial impact on Long's political standing in Missouri. With Long up for reelection in 1968, Republican opponents became optimistic about their chances of defeating him if he succeeded in getting the Democratic nomination. Missouri governor Warren Hearnes did not support Long's renomination. Consequently, with encouragement from Hearnes, Lt. Gov. Thomas F. Eagleton challenged Long for the Democratic nomination and defeated him in the Democratic primary. Long died on November 6, 1972.

MICHAEL E. MEAGHER

Kemper, Donald J. *Decade of Fear: Senator Hennings and Civil Liberties.* Columbia: University of Missouri Press, 1965.

Lambert, William. "A Deeper Debt of Gratitude to the Mob." *Life* (November 10, 1967): 38–38b.

———. "Strange Help: Hoffa Campaign of the U.S. Senator from Missouri." *Life* (May 26, 1967): 26–31, 76.

Long, Edward V. *The Intruders: The Invasion of Privacy by Government and Industry.* New York: Frederick A. Praeger, 1966.

———. Papers. Western Historical Manuscripts Collection, Columbia.

LONG, ROBERT ALEXANDER (1850–1934)

Missouri's most famous lumber entrepreneur—past, present and, arguably, future—was Robert Alexander Long. He was the founder and, until shortly before he died, the chief engine that drove the monolithic Long-Bell Lumber Company that for nearly three decades could rightfully boast of its consistent stature in the top tier of lumber-manufacturing companies in the United States.

Born on December 17, 1850, in Kentucky, the lumber magnate made his most powerful mark in southern lumber. Long carved a fortune out of the Louisiana pineries in the 1880s, 1890s, and early 1900s, then moved on to the Pacific Northwest where he began his venture in ponderosa pines and Douglas firs in 1918 with an initial purchase of an 87,000-acre tract in Klamath and Lake Counties in southern Oregon. He founded and built a model city, Longview, Washington, at the confluence of the Columbia and Cowlitz Rivers; its centerpiece, at the time of construction in 1924, was the largest sawmill in the world. When Long-Bell purchased its last big tract in 1923, the company owned nearly 270,000 acres of timberland in the Pacific Northwest.

In 1920 Long-Bell was the nation's largest lumber producer. The company's corporate umbrella covered ten sawmills, principally in Louisiana, with a combined annual lumber cut of 560 million board feet, and 121 retail lumberyards in Oklahoma, Kansas, and Arkansas. It employed twelve thousand people, and

its sales from wholesale and retail lumber stood at $43.6 million.

Long's company reached this pinnacle within a relatively short period of forty-five years. He had opened a lumberyard in 1875 in Columbia, Kansas, with two partners: Victor Bell and Long's first cousin Robert White. None of the three young men knew anything about lumber. The common lumber term SISE ("Surface One Side and Edge") eluded them. Bell and White went to Kansas City and to college at the end of the summer. Long was left to wear all the hats: handyman, lumberyard man, bookkeeper, and salesman. He had never heard of lumber brokers or mill salesmen and bought his opening stock from a retail lumber firm. Predictably, the venture failed, but Long secured a bank loan and reopened the yard. It was onward and upward from then on. By 1900 the company was so successful it had outgrown its small-town headquarters and was moved to Kansas City.

Long's life makes an exciting story: the boy from the farm who rose from obscurity to national prominence in the lumber industry within thirty years. He was a leader within the industry's trade associations: the Southern Lumber Operators' Association, the Yellow Pine Manufacturers Association, and the National Wholesale Lumber Dealers' Association. Because of Long's stature, Theodore Roosevelt invited him to represent the industry at a conference for conservation held at the White House in 1908.

Long liked to give the impression that he came from a far more impoverished background than he actually did. He was brought up on a 300-acre farm outside Shelbyville, Kentucky, near Lexington in the state's bluegrass country. His parents, Samuel and Margaret White Long, held piety and hard work in high esteem. As soon as Robert and his eight brothers and sisters could walk, they were given chores. However, the family never wanted for the basic necessities, and one early history of Shelby County describes Samuel Long as "a prosperous farmer of the neighborhood, interested in all public enterprises, and [who] reared a large family of reputable citizens."

Robert's education went two years beyond the primary grades. His father had ambitions for his son and sent him to a college preparatory school for boys where he boarded for fifteen months, from ages fourteen to sixteen.

The countryside near Shelbyville and Lexington, with its beautiful, old plantation-style homes, its green pastures, its purebred livestock and especially horses, fueled Long's ambition. He determined that he, too, would live in a columned mansion on a hill, ride in fine carriages, and own the fastest and best saddle horses. He eventually accomplished these goals. He owned one of the most imposing mansions ever built in Kansas City, which since 1941 has housed the Kansas City Museum. He founded one of the Midwest's finest farms, a 1,680-acre gentleman's farming estate known as Longview Farm in Lee's Summit, Missouri, whose saddle horses put Missouri on the map in that industry. His passion for building philanthropy was realized in the construction of churches out of cut limestone, and schools and libraries in Longview, Washington. He spearheaded the drive to build Kansas City's Liberty Memorial with a seventy-five-thousand-dollar donation and directed its whirlwind building campaign.

Long was dedicated to philanthropic giving. All his adult life he contributed freely to his church, the Disciples of Christ (later the Christian Church), even in his last decade when his great company was foundering. By the time he died he had given much of his wealth away.

Long married Martha Ellen "Ella" Wilson in 1875. They had two daughters, Sallie America Long, born in 1879, and **Loula Long Combs,** born in 1880, who became a well-known show-ring personality, famous for her Hackney-breed horses and ponies. The man who at one time had been the wealthiest man in Kansas City, worth an estimated $30 to $40 million in 1920, left a personal estate of less than one hundred thousand dollars at the time of his death on March 15, 1934.

LENORE K. BRADLEY

Bradley, Lenore K. *Robert Alexander Long: A Lumberman of the Gilded Age.* Durham, N.C.: Forest History Society, 1989.

McClelland, John M., Jr. *R. A. Long's Planned City.* Longview, Wash.: Longview Publishing, 1976.

"Robert A. Long." In *Kansas City and Its One Hundred Foremost Men,* comp. Walter P. Tracy. Kansas City: Walter P. Tracy, 1924.

LORIMIER, LOUIS (1748–1812)

Louis Lorimier was born a French Canadian and became a British subject after Great Britain's conquest of Canada, a Spanish subject by allegiance after crossing the Mississippi River, and, finally, an American citizen through the Louisiana Purchase. Although early in life he fought against Americans, through his assistance in acquiring grants of land, he influenced those with pioneering spirits to move across the Mississippi River and settle in the Cape Girardeau District. It became the most American of Upper Louisiana districts. The entire area of southeast Missouri developed and prospered early because Lorimier was successful in bringing about harmonious relations between the Indians under his influence, the new American colonists, and the earlier French and Spanish settlers.

Pierre Louis Lorimier, known generally as Louis, was born at Lachiene, on Island of Montreal, in 1748.

He was a descendant of Capt. Guillaume de Lorimier who came to Canada from Paris in 1695 and was appointed commandant at Fort Rolland in 1705. His parents were Capt. Claude-Nicholas-Guillaume de Lorimier and Marie-Louise Lepallier dit Laferte. He reached his fifteenth birthday in 1763, the same year Great Britain gained control of Canada.

By 1769 Lorimier had joined and later succeeded his father in trade with Indians at "Laramie's Station," portage of the Miami and Maumee Rivers at Pickawillany in Ohio. (The French pronunciation of "Lorimier" sounded like "Laramie.") During the Revolutionary War the trading post became a center for Indians and British Tories.

Lorimier accompanied D'Aubin in 1778 on a raid into Kentucky. They attacked Boonesborough, captured **Daniel Boone,** and took him to the Shawnee Indian village on the Little Miami River. A few years later, in 1782, Lorimier barely escaped when Gen. George Rogers Clark captured and plundered Lorimier's store. That year Lorimier compiled his "Memoir de Service" in hopes of receiving some restitution from the British government, though apparently he never did. He was unable to reestablish the store and may have lived at Vincennes for a time to escape his creditors. He moved west of the Mississippi by 1787.

Lorimier took the oath of allegiance to the Spanish monarch and settled in the Ste. Genevieve District with many of his Indian followers. Through the marriage to his first wife, Charlotte Pemanpieh Bougainville Lorimier, a half-blood Shawnee, Lorimier had acquired great influence over those Indians. He established a trade center on Saline Creek at Big Shawnee Spring, about five miles from the present town of St. Mary's. He continued his trade with the Indians in association with the firm of Menard and Peyroux and received exclusive rights to trade with the Delaware and Shawnee Indians between the Mississippi and Arkansas Rivers.

Lorimier was of service to the Spanish government in warding off attacks by the hostile Osage Indians living to the north and west. For his assistance during a threatened invasion of Spanish territory by the French and Americans in 1792, he was granted a large area of land and given authority to establish a post between Ste. Genevieve and New Madrid. He chose an area just south of a big bend of the Mississippi River. Thus, Cape Girardeau was established as an independent post in 1793 with Lorimier as commandant. He petitioned Governor-General Carondelet in September 1795 and was awarded a grant in October. The first area was forty arpents in front and eighty arpents deep where the city of Cape Girardeau now stands. He was granted other lands making a total of eight thousand arpents. He then traveled to Indiana and Ohio in 1796 to induce displaced Indians to move into the area. By 1799 he had constructed a large building as a store and residence, which became known as the Red House. Lorimier altered his attitude toward Americans and began aiding them with their petitions for Spanish land grants in the vicinity of his establishment. Perhaps he saw financial gain by having a larger population to make use of his commercial enterprises.

After the Louisiana Purchase, Lorimier became a U.S. citizen. He donated land and money for the construction of public buildings to be used as the seat of justice and for educational purposes. Lorimier Cemetery was also established on land donated by him. He built primitive roads into Cape Girardeau that provided the means for travel and trade. He developed two mills, one on Cape la Cruz Creek and one on Hubble Creek. He ran a ferry service across the Mississippi before and after the Louisiana Purchase.

Lorimier's children by his first wife included sons Louis Jr., who established a farm on the fork of Cape la Cruz Creek and died by 1832; August Bougainville, who received an appointment to West Point, but died by 1822 without marrying; Verneuil Raphael, who moved to the South, probably Texas; and Victor, who married Sally Sheppard. His daughters, Marie Louise and Agatha, married locally, and their descendants remain in the area. Lorimier also fathered a son named William, born in 1781, who became an early farmer in the district. Lorimier's first wife, Charlotte, died in 1808. He married a second time to Marie Bethiaume. Lorimier died in 1812 and was buried next to his first wife in the Lorimier Cemetery.

MARGARET BEGGS

Cape Girardeau County, Records of the Various Courts. 1799–1839. Cape Girardeau County Courthouse, Jackson, Mo.

Foley, William E. *The Genesis of Missouri: From Wilderness Outpost to Statehood.* Columbia: University of Missouri Press, 1989.

Houck, Louis. *A History of Missouri, from the Earliest Explorations and Settlements until the Admission of the State into the Union.* Chicago: R. R. Donnelley and Sons, 1908.

———. *The Spanish Regime in Missouri: A Collection of Papers and Documents Relating to Upper Louisiana.* 2 vols. Chicago: R. R. Donnelley and Sons, 1909.

LOUISE (?–1773) AND MARIANNE (DATES UNKNOWN)

A curious judicial inquest, recorded at Ste. Genevieve in 1773–1774, reveals a good deal about the condition of North American Indian slave women and children in colonial Missouri. This inquest constitutes one of the most touching series of documents contained in the civil records of colonial Ste. Genevieve.

Céledon, a mixed-blood huntsman, lived off and on in the home of Jean-Baptiste Deguire Larose in Ste. Genevieve. He was wanted for having stolen Louise, an Indian slave woman from Kaskaskia, and perhaps also for her murder. Her body had been found south of Ste. Genevieve near the Rivière aux Vases in March 1773. Céledon disappeared, but he struck again the next month. On April 24, civil judge **François Vallé I** and two witnesses went to the residence of Widow Aubuchon (or Lasource) to collect information about the theft of her Indian slave Marianne. Widow Aubuchon recounted that on the night of April 20–21, Marianne was tethered with a chain in a locked and barred room at the Aubuchon residence, where she slept with her nine-year-old son, Baptiste. On the morning of April 21 the widow discovered that the bars on the window of Marianne's room had been cut. Marianne was gone, though both of her sons remained.

Baptiste told Vallé that during the night when he was sleeping, Céledon (the boy recognized his voice) came to the window and called to his mother, begging her to come with him, for he had good horses. Marianne had asked Baptiste to accompany them, but he said he refused to go without his younger brother, six-year-old Louis. His mother replied that Louis could not come because he would encumber them and slow their flight from Ste. Genevieve. She, however, would flee to "her country" but promised to return with Indian warriors the following winter to take her boys. She then cast off her chains with tools that Céledon must have provided, slipped out of the window, and raced for her freedom on the back of an Indian pony with Céledon. A detachment of ten militiamen later pursued them in vain. As skillful as the townsmen might have been, they proved no match in the bush for an Indian woman and her mixed-blood companion.

However, the case of Marianne and Céledon remained open, for François Vallé persisted in gathering information from other hunters and trappers who had encountered the two fugitives in winter camps or on traplines. According to their accounts, Céledon repeatedly insisted that the Indian woman Louise had killed herself accidentally when she seized the muzzle of a flintlock that had a "tender" action. Although the precise truth of the matter will never be known, Céledon's account appeared plausible. Louise was probably unaccustomed to handling firearms; moreover, Céledon had no motive for killing her after he had gone to the trouble of stealing her out of Kaskaskia. Other woodsmen from Ste. Genevieve clearly did not consider Céledon a murderer and did not hesitate to make camp with him on the Black River, which became his stamping ground.

Jean-Baptiste Bequet Jr. from Ste. Genevieve frequently associated with Marianne and Céledon and provided the fugitives with provisions from town. Céledon also claimed that if he were not a fugitive, he would gladly work to pay for Marianne, for he understood she had belonged to Widow Aubuchon. Although he was unaware of it, Céledon's notion that he might purchase Marianne was illegal, for Spanish governor Alejandro O'Reilly's decree of 1769 had absolutely forbidden commerce in Indian slaves.

Commandant Vallé's deponents informed him that Marianne lived with Céledon on the Black River and that both carried fusils, that is, light muskets. Charles Boyer of Ste. Genevieve had conversed with Marianne at a hunting camp and reported she wept as she asked about her two sons. Boyer told her that one remained with Widow Aubuchon and the other had been placed at the home of Antoine Aubuchon, the widow's brother. No evidence exists that Marianne tried to retrieve her sons, who remained slaves in Ste. Genevieve in 1778. Such a rescue mission would have been virtually assured of failure.

Jean-Baptiste Bequet reported from the Black River that Marianne prayed for her children to be raised with the fear of God in their hearts, which suggests that though she must have hated white civilization, she accepted its religion. In any event, she told Mathieu Lafitte she had made her choice and would not, even for her children, return to Ste. Genevieve. The Creole practice of Indian slavery had created for Marianne a heartrending dilemma, forcing her to make an anguishing moral choice.

In March 1774 François Vallé closed the Marianne-Céledon case. He almost certainly realized Céledon had not murdered Louise and that her death had in fact been accidental. Thus, the fugitive remained guilty merely of stealing an Indian slave whose bondage the Spanish colonial government questioned in any case. Given the honorable status that Marianne and Céledon enjoyed in the confraternity of the coureurs de bois, any chance to apprehend them appeared unlikely. Vallé prudently dropped the issue, and Marianne and Céledon, a gallant couple caught between two cultures, disappeared from the historical record.

CARL J. EKBERG

Ekberg, Carl J. *Colonial Ste. Genevieve: An Adventure on the Mississippi Frontier.* Gerald, Mo.: Patrice Press, 1985.

LOVEJOY, ELIJAH PARISH (1802–1837)

Elijah Parish Lovejoy, an antislavery clergyman and editor, was born near Albion, Maine, on November 9, 1802, the eldest child of the Reverend Daniel Lovejoy, a Congregational minister and farmer, and Elizabeth Patee Lovejoy, parents who instilled in their children stern religious and moral principles. Elijah graduated from Waterville (now Colby) College in 1826 and in 1827 moved to St. Louis, where he embarked on what he at first intended to be a secular career. However, he never neglected his lifelong conviction that he bore a moral responsibility to direct and improve society. From the time of his arrival in St. Louis, he perceived a gulf between himself, a pious New Englander, and what he construed to be the immoral, materialistic condition of the rapidly growing city.

In the spring of 1828 Lovejoy founded a private classical high school designed in part to imbue western youth with New England values but relinquished it in August 1830 when he joined T. J. Miller in publishing the *St. Louis Times* to advocate the presidential candidacy of Henry Clay. In that political enterprise, Lovejoy displayed a flair for the biting, outspoken expression that would characterize most of his later writing.

In 1832 when a religious revival swept St. Louis, Lovejoy, influenced by two reverends, William S. Potts and David Nelson, underwent the conversion experience that had previously eluded him and subsequently decided to follow his father's example of entering the ministry. After study at Princeton he was ordained a Presbyterian clergyman and with financial support from the American Home Missionary Association returned to St. Louis in November 1833. He organized a Presbyterian church to the west of the city and spent long hours traveling in the vicinity as an evangelist and advocate of such reform causes as temperance. On March 4, 1835, he married Celia Ann French of St. Charles, Missouri. They had two children.

Lovejoy had been induced to return to St. Louis partly because a group of Presbyterian clergymen and reformers, having decided to launch a newspaper to expound their evangelical reform cause, offered the editorial post to him. On November 27, 1833, five days after returning to the city, he issued the first number of the *St. Louis Observer.*

Apart from its strictly religious advocacy, the newspaper focused on two particularly controversial themes: anti-Catholicism and antislavery. In unrestrained language Lovejoy condemned the Catholic Church and its communicants, a Protestant concern that was then receiving revived attention from several prominent eastern evangelicals, among them Lyman Beecher and George Bourne. Locally, Lovejoy was encouraged in his campaign by his fellow Protestant clergymen, especially the Reverend Edwin F. Hatfield, pastor of the Second Presbyterian Church. The issue was especially sensitive and, from Lovejoy's point of view, especially pertinent in St. Louis, where one-third of the population was said to be Catholic and where Catholic influence appeared to be growing. On that account his strictures were certain to arouse resentment.

Unlike his opposition to Catholicism, Lovejoy's critique of slavery seemed, at first, relatively moderate and, for the period, inoffensive. He expressed approval of the American Colonization Society, a conservative organization that advocated removal of freed slaves to Africa, and criticized both the rhetoric and the program of the adherents of William Lloyd Garrison, who condemned slavery in the most vigorous language and called for its immediate end. Yet, as Lovejoy would soon discover, even restrained discussion of the subject was likely to meet an unfavorable reception in a slave state.

Like many other Presbyterian clergymen at the time, Lovejoy's moderation on slavery rapidly waned as popular hostility to discussion took the form of mob action. Advocates of the antislavery cause were soon defending their own rights as well as the rights of slaves. Accordingly, Lovejoy reassessed his position, and in the summer of 1835 his expression of strong antislavery sentiment began to appear regularly in the *Observer*. In October and November 1835 opposition to such views heightened in St. Louis as slaveholders there, as elsewhere throughout the South, mobilized to halt the subversion of their institutions. Extralegal organizations were formed in the city to identify and expose abolitionists and to expel free blacks who had moved there from other states. In that way the slavery issue in St. Louis was transformed from being a contest only over slavery into one also over the civil rights of its opponents.

Much of the local apprehension about the spread of abolitionism focused on the *Observer*, the only antislavery newspaper in the region. Lovejoy made his situation still more perilous, but also more problematic, by offering his opinion that the "real origin of the cry 'Down with the Observer' is to be looked for in its opposition to Popery. The fire that is now blazing and crackling through this city, was kindled on Popish altars and has been assiduously blowed up by Jesuit breath." Despite such injudicious statements, he found enough support from civic leaders to continue his course until the summer of 1836. However, as his antislavery views grew ever more unrestrained and local tolerance for them correspondingly declined, his situation became untenable. On the night of July 21, after a particularly offensive article had appeared in the *Observer*, the newspaper's offices were broken into and some of its printing materials were destroyed.

Lovejoy had already concluded that St. Louis could no longer be the scene of his activities. The next day he crated his press and sent it across the river to Alton, Illinois, where he assumed it would

be safe, and prepared to move there himself. He also packed his furniture for shipment, but before it could be dispatched it was destroyed by a mob.

Alton proved little more receptive to abolitionist activity than St. Louis. A mob, allegedly from St. Louis, destroyed Lovejoy's press before he could remove it from the wharf where it had been delivered. He ordered a replacement at once. At a public meeting convened shortly after his arrival in Alton, he promised that his newspaper would henceforth eschew abolitionist doctrine, but the pledge was severely compromised when he also affirmed his intention to "hold myself at liberty to speak, to write, and to publish whatever I please on any subject." In turn, city leaders declared their intention "in all lawful ways to prevent the publication" of an abolitionist newspaper in the city. Thus, the route toward confrontation was prepared.

Despite his apparent pledge, Lovejoy had not significantly altered his opinions or retreated from his claimed right to publish them, as was made clear in the first regular issue of the *Observer* to appear in Alton: "The system of American Negro Slavery is an awful evil and sin . . . , and it is the duty of us all . . . to effect the speedy and entire emancipation of that portion of our fellow-men in bondage amongst us. . . ." Never, he declared, would he yield to mob pressure against "the rights of conscience, the freedom of opinion, and of the press." As might have been expected, and to the disapproval of most, Lovejoy's antislavery stance remained as it had been in St. Louis.

Accompanying his unwelcome opinions on this vexed subject were expressions suggesting an attitude of self-righteousness and moral superiority at which many took offense. He criticized the citizens of Alton for what he considered their easy morality, their intemperance, their blasphemy, and their disregard for the Sabbath. Most irritating of all, when the city began to suffer effects of the financial panic of 1837, he blamed the residents' toleration of slavery and their faulty values and materialism for their plight.

The denouement of Lovejoy's career was not long in coming. Antagonism to his presence in Alton greatly deepened in the summer of 1837 when he endorsed plans to hold a convention in the city for the purpose of organizing a state auxiliary to the American Antislavery Society. Most of his remaining local support then evaporated, for few citizens welcomed the prospect of Alton's acquiring the reputation of being an abolitionist center. On August 21 a mob wrecked the *Observer*'s press. A new one was destroyed before it could be placed in operation. A fourth press was then ordered. This time Lovejoy and a small band of supporters determined to defend it by force. On the evening of November 7, 1837, a mob besieged the warehouse where the press was stored, and one of its members mounted a ladder to set fire to the roof. When Lovejoy came out to deter the arsonist, he was shot and killed. No one was ever punished for the murder.

Lovejoy's death precipitated a controversy among abolitionists throughout the country over the morality of the use of force, even in self-defense. However, in the long run the fact that Lovejoy died while defending freedom of the press—the right of an editor to express opinions even when they defy majority opinion—overshadowed all other considerations and accounts for his continued, distinguished historical reputation.

MERTON L. DILLON

Dillon, Merton L. *Elijah P. Lovejoy: Abolitionist Editor.* Urbana: University of Illinois Press, 1961.

Gill, John G. *Tide without Turning: Elijah P. Lovejoy and Freedom of the Press.* Boston: Beacon Press, 1958.

Lovejoy Papers. Wickett-Wiswall Collection, Southwest Collection. Texas Tech University, Lubbock.

LUCAS, CHARLES (1792–1817)

Charles Lucas seemed destined for a promising career in law and politics in the Missouri Territory until an 1817 duel with **Thomas Hart Benton** cost him his life. The second of six children, Lucas was born on a farm near Pittsburgh, Pennsylvania, on September 25, 1792, the son of John B. C. and Anne Sebin Lucas. In 1805 he accompanied his family to St. Louis where his father had accepted positions as a judge of the Superior Court of the Louisiana Territory and as a member of the territorial land claims commission. The next year Charles went to Philadelphia for schooling, and after the completion of his education studied law in Litchfield, Connecticut.

Lucas returned to St. Louis in 1811 and joined a territorial militia unit sent to patrol along the Illinois River. He subsequently transferred to a St. Louis volunteer artillery company led by his brother Robert. When Robert resigned his command in 1813, the St. Louis volunteers elected Charles to replace him. He was given the rank of captain, and for the duration of the War of 1812, the artillery company he commanded periodically reported for duty at the nearby military installation at Portage des Sioux.

In 1814 Lucas was admitted to the territorial bar, and that same year he won a seat in the territorial assembly as a representative from St. Louis County. Three years later President James Madison appointed him U.S. attorney for the Missouri Territory. Lucas dabbled in land speculation, and in 1816 he and Asa Morgan purchased a tract of land in present-day Cooper County that they had chosen for a new town.

They drew up plans and laid out a plat for Boonville, Missouri, which they filed in 1817.

The popular and well-liked young Lucas soon found himself at odds with Thomas Hart Benton, another rising member of the St. Louis bar. Benton had allied himself with a political faction highly critical of Lucas's father who had become a staunch foe of the territory's Spanish land claimants. Charles Lucas and Benton first clashed publicly while representing opposing parties in a case argued in the St. Louis Circuit Court in October 1816. They exchanged insults in their closing statements, and after losing the case Benton alleged that Lucas had defamed him. He demanded satisfaction in a duel, but Lucas declined the challenge.

Their paths crossed again on election day in August 1817 when Lucas questioned Benton's eligibility to vote on grounds that he had failed to pay his taxes. Benton's derisive dismissal of his detractor as a "puppy" provoked Lucas to respond by demanding to settle the affront with a duel. Benton accepted, and they faced off on Bloody Island near St. Louis on August 12 using smoothbore pistols at a distance of thirty feet. Benton escaped from the encounter with a bruised knee, but Lucas sustained more serious injuries from a bullet that cut the artery in his neck.

Initially both men pronounced themselves satisfied. Benton subsequently reconsidered and demanded a second meeting after declaring that Lucas's friends had questioned his conduct in the affair. Their second meeting took place on September 27, 1817, and in that encounter Lucas died after a bullet hit near his heart.

Charles Lucas's untimely death cast a pall over the territory and left its mark on all who had been involved in the affair, but most especially on **John B. C. Lucas,** who devoted his remaining days to defending his son's reputation, while vilifying Benton, whom he labeled an assassin.

BIANCA ADAIR

Hier, Marshall D. "Lawyer Benton's Last Duel." *St. Louis Bar Journal* 36 (summer 1989): 45–46.

Lucas Collection. Missouri Historical Society, St. Louis.

Van Ravenswaay, Charles. "Bloody Island: Honor and Violence in Early Nineteenth-Century St. Louis." *Gateway Heritage* 10 (spring 1990): 4–21.

LUCAS, JOHN B. C. (1758–1842)

When John B. C. Lucas died in St. Louis in 1842 at the age of eighty-four, his obituary described him as "peculiar in some of his traits of character, but in point of intelligence, in the honesty of his purposes, purity of his intentions and philanthropy of his feelings, he was all a man should have been." It was a remarkably apt characterization of Lucas who had been a key player in the rough-and-tumble of territorial politics and one of the more distinctive public figures in early Missouri history. He was sharp tongued, ill tempered, prone to passionate outbursts, and disposed to carry grudges. However, he was also intelligent, talented, witty, satirical, politically incorruptible, and unbending in his republican principles. It was hardly surprising that someone who could be alternately so charming and so obstinate spent the greater part of his lengthy life embroiled in controversy.

Jean Baptiste Charles Lucas (later shortened and Americanized to John B. C. Lucas) was born in Pont-Audemer, France, on August 14, 1758. The son of a distinguished and prosperous family, Lucas received an excellent education. He attended the Honfleur and Paris law schools and was graduated from the law department of the University of Caen in 1782. He married Anne Sebin, whom he had met in Honfleur, and returned to the city of his birth to practice law.

Following the American Revolution, Lucas turned his thoughts to the possibility of emigrating to the United States. He admired the new nation's republican form of government and drew additional inspiration from Benjamin Franklin, the U.S. minister to France, who encouraged him to move to America. Armed with a letter of introduction from Franklin, Lucas and his wife set sail for Philadelphia in 1784. They settled in western Pennsylvania and purchased a small farm on the banks of the Monongahela, six miles from Pittsburgh, where Lucas took up farming and worked to improve his English. During the 1790s he also participated in occasional trading expeditions that took him as far west as Upper Louisiana's French settlements on the Mississippi River.

In Pennsylvania Lucas ventured into politics and participated in meetings associated with the Whiskey Rebellion. He also helped wage a battle against land speculation companies. He served in the Pennsylvania Assembly and later as an associate judge in Allegheny County. In 1802 the voters elected him to represent western Pennsylvania in the United States House of Representatives, where among other things he chaired the committee handling legislation dividing Louisiana into the territories of Louisiana and Orleans. His constituents reelected him to a second term in 1804, but before he could take his seat in the Ninth Congress he resigned to accept the dual appointments President Thomas Jefferson offered him as a justice of the territorial superior court and as a member of the board of land commissioners in the newly created Louisiana Territory. Albert Gallatin, Lucas's close friend and his predecessor in the House of Representatives, had recommended him for the posts.

Lucas arrived in St. Louis with his family in September 1805. Ironically, the French-born American official proved no friend to Upper Louisiana's French-speaking Creoles, whom he considered unprepared for republican government. After taking up residence in St. Louis, Judge Lucas became a central figure in a bitter political feud swirling about Gov. **James Wilkinson.**

As a member of the board of land commissioners, Lucas angered the governor by taking vigorous exception to some decisions rendered by the board's pro-Wilkinson majority favoring the holders of large concessions. Lucas's determined opposition to the wholesale confirmation of Spanish land titles in Missouri earned him the universal contempt of Louisiana's larger land claimants. The rigid and doctrinaire Lucas scorned all pleas for leniency in the land-claims cases. His earlier encounters with Pennsylvania land jobbers made the irascible commissioner naturally suspicious of large-scale speculators, and his reading of the evidence in Upper Louisiana convinced him that the majority of the biggest claims were fraudulent. Although Lucas's stand probably embodied too narrow an interpretation, the judge did have legitimate cause for opposing the indiscriminate confirmation of titles, especially in cases involving extremely large claims.

Wilkinson's subsequent removal as governor diminished political infighting in the territory, but Lucas continued to stand firm against the proponents of a more liberal confirmation policy. In 1809 Lucas's political opponents launched an all-out campaign to have him removed from the board of land commissioners, but the president chose to continue him in that office until the board completed its work in 1812. Meanwhile, Lucas retained his post on the territorial superior court until Missouri became a state.

In the highly charged and intensely personal political culture of early Missouri, Judge Lucas was never far from the whirl of individual feuds and personal grudges. That was especially true in the tragic 1817 episode involving his son Charles and **Thomas Hart Benton.** The Benton-Lucas imbroglio ended when **Charles Lucas** lay dead from a mortal wound inflicted by Benton on the infamous dueling ground known as Bloody Island. For the rest of his life the elder Lucas devoted himself to defending his deceased son's reputation and to discrediting Benton, whom he considered an assassin.

This was not the only tragedy that the Lucas family faced. One son had drowned, another died during the War of 1812, yet another appears to have committed suicide, and at least two others died when they were quite young. Of the nine Lucas children, only two outlived their father: a daughter, **Anne Lucas Hunt,** and a son, James.

In 1820 John B. C. Lucas announced as a candidate for the Missouri Constitutional Convention. Although he had owned slaves, Lucas declared himself in favor of restricting the further introduction of slavery in Missouri. For him and for most others supporting eventual restriction, the issue was economic, not moral. He touted the advantages of free labor over slave labor in promoting the new state's long-term economic development. Lucas, like all other restrictionists, was soundly defeated.

Despite his loss Lucas made one final try for elective office when he put forward his name for election to the United States Senate in 1820. His hatred for Benton, who had announced as a candidate, may have prompted Lucas's decision to enter the race. The General Assembly chose **David Barton** and Benton as the state's first two U.S. senators. Although Lucas managed a respectable third-place finish in the six-man field, Benton's election was a bitter pill for him to swallow.

Having failed in his bid for elective office, Lucas unsuccessfully solicited appointment as a federal district judge for the new state of Missouri. President James Monroe did nominate him to serve on the Florida Land Claims Commission in 1823, but he declined the post. Lucas retired to private life and devoted his time to the development of his extensive real estate holdings in St. Louis and surrounding areas and to the oversight of his other business interests. When he died in St. Louis on August 29, 1842, Lucas bequeathed a substantial estate to his heirs.

WILLIAM E. FOLEY

Cleland, Hugh C. "John B. C. Lucas: Physiocrat on the Frontier." Parts 1–3. *Western Pennsylvania Historical Magazine* 36 (March 1953): 1–15; (June 1953): 87–100; (September–December 1953): 141–68.

Foley, William E. *The Genesis of Missouri: From Wilderness Outpost to Statehood.* Columbia: University of Missouri Press, 1989.

Lucas Collection. Missouri Historical Society, St. Louis.

McDermott, John Francis. "John B. C. Lucas in Pennsylvania." *Western Pennsylvania Historical Magazine* 21 (September 1938): 209–30.

LUDLOW, NOAH MILLER (1795–1886)

Noah Miller Ludlow, a pioneer of theatrical life and art on the frontier, played comic roles for his entire career but remained, by nature and by fortune, "a very unhappy man," in the words of historian Willam G. B. Carson. Ludlow was born in New York City in 1795; his attraction to the stage was early and intense, but his career did not begin until he was eighteen, when he moved to Albany to live with his brother. His first role was in a melodrama, *The Two Thieves;* his work attracted the attention of the leader of the first company to tour the West, and in 1815 he started down the Allegheny with the Drake Company.

After stops in Pittsburgh and Frankfort the players arrived in Nashville. There Ludlow formed a new company, taking on the role of impresario for the first time. In September 1817 he married; by December he and his company and his new wife were in New Orleans, where he gave, according to his own recollection, the first professional performances in English. He first came to St. Louis in 1819, bringing the first professional company the city had seen. The footloose Ludlows toured widely through the South during the following years, in the theater as well as in other ventures, including Brown's Circus. In 1826 Ludlow made his New York stage debut, and his company appeared there in 1828 at the Chatham Theater.

In 1835 Ludlow formed a partnership with **Solomon Franklin Smith** that, though often acrimonious and finally openly antagonistic, lasted for eighteen years and resulted in the creation of the most powerful and significant theatrical enterprise in the West. Their firm developed a reputation for dealing fairly with actors—a rarity in the day—and for maintaining the highest standards of probity in their choices and presentations of plays. Their geographic reach extended from Missouri and Ohio to Mobile and New Orleans, and their artistic reach from Shakespeare and Sheridan to the most popular low comedies of the day. In 1837, with the political and financial support of **Charles Keemle** and other prominent citizens, the partners built the New St. Louis Theater, the first structure in the American West built expressly as a theater. For the following decade and a half it was a focal point for drama in the Mississippi Valley and beyond.

After 1837 the Ludlows made their headquarters in St. Louis, typically wintering in Mobile. Much of the theatrical business was managed at a distance; stock companies in cities such as Cincinnati established a local presence and were joined by touring performers with national reputations. The enterprise was often financially shaky, however, and Ludlow, who was an adroit manager of people, was notoriously poor at managing money. Disputes over financing led to increasing tension with Smith, and the firm of Ludlow and Smith was dissolved in 1853.

Although he was handsome, with a high forehead and a fine nose, Ludlow was often stiff and ill at ease and made an ungainly first impression; one actress described him as "looking as if he had swallowed a poker." Even Matthew Field, who became his son-in-law, was put off at first, though Field grew so fond of

Ludlow that he split with his old friend Smith when the partnership broke apart.

For thirty-three years Ludlow lived in retirement in St. Louis, making occasional stage appearances (the last, according to one source, when he was in his eighties) and writing. His memoir, *Dramatic Life As I Found It,* appeared in 1880. Unfortunately, his antagonism toward Smith did not diminish with age, though his memory had begun to slip; the result, Carson shows, is an unfairly vindictive account of their relationship, which actually reached its nadir in 1860, when Smith's support for the Union cause ended any chance for reconciliation.

Late in life Ludlow completed *A Genealogical History of the Ludlow Family* (1884), and an overwrought work of fiction called *Mantua; or, The Spirit of the Glen.* He died of infirmities on January 9, 1886. As a performer he was skilled; as a manager he was dedicated, if inept in some ways; as a father and family man he was fiercely loyal; and as a pioneer he was instrumental in bringing the theater and its culture to the people of the frontier.

ROBERT C. BOYD

Carson, William G. B. *Managers in Distress: The St. Louis Stage, 1840–1844.* St. Louis: St. Louis Historical Documents Foundation, 1949.

Ludlow-Field-Maury Papers. Missouri Historical Society, St. Louis.

LUZIÈRES, PIERRE-CHARLES DELASSUS DE (1739–1806)

Pierre-Charles Delassus de Luzières played an important role in the history of Upper Louisiana during the decade preceding the Louisiana Purchase. He was born in Bouchain in the province of Flanders on March 9, 1739. His father, Charles-Philippe de Hault Delassus, was mayor of Bouchain, as well as a councillor to Louis XVI; his mother was Anne-Marguerite d'Arlot.

Pierre-Charles followed in his father's footsteps, becoming a councillor to Louis XVI, and with the coming of the French Revolution he, not surprisingly, cast his lot with the king. In 1790 he fled Revolutionary France for North America, and, passing through Philadelphia, settled briefly in Pittsburgh. Luzières's entourage in America included his wife, Domitilde-Josephe Dumont, whom he had married on May 13, 1765; three of their five children, Charles-Auguste (b. 1767), Jeanne-Felicite-Odile (b. 1773), and Philippe-François-Camille (b. 1778); and Jeanne-Felicite's husband, Pierre-Augustin Derbigny, who later served briefly as governor of the state of Louisiana.

Traveling via the Ohio and Mississippi Rivers, Luzières first visited Ste. Genevieve in Spanish Upper Louisiana in 1792. He reconnoitered the region, probably staying with **François Vallé II,** and in the spring of 1793 descended the Mississippi to New Orleans to lay out his grandiose plans to the governor-general of Louisiana, Francisco Luis Hector de Carondelet. Luzières proposed to found a new community in Upper Louisiana adjacent to Ste. Genevieve and to name it New Bourbon in honor of the Bourbon king of France, Louis XVI, who had recently been guillotined in Paris. Governor Carondelet approved of the plan, and by the summer of 1793 Luzières was back in Upper Louisiana designing his settlement, arranging to have his house built high on the hills above the floodplain of the Mississippi, and waiting for his family to arrive from the East.

Despite bouts of malarial fever in the autumn of 1793, Luzières's hopes for success in the New World started to materialize. His family arrived safely in Spanish Illinois; his large vertical-log house was soon completed; and the settlement of New Bourbon began to take shape. In 1797 Governor Carondelet appointed Luzières commandant of the newly created New Bourbon District of Upper Louisiana, and his first major task was to conduct a comprehensive census of the district. The document he created constitutes the single most important source on the settlement at New Bourbon, whose 270 people included whites and both free and enslaved blacks. A majority of the thirty-eight heads of household enumerated on the census were Creoles from the Illinois country, but New Bourbon also had a significant number of American families (such as those of John Dodge and his brother **Israel Dodge**) who had migrated to Spanish Illinois from the east side of the Mississippi.

To the New Bourbon census of 1797 Luzières included a lengthy appendix titled "Observations on the Character, Qualities, and Occupations of the Inhabitants of the New Bourbon District." This document, together with his extended correspondence with Governor Carondelet, reveals that the politically conservative French aristocrat had remarkably progressive ideas about improving the economy and modernizing the society of the New Bourbon District. He planned to exploit the natural resources of the area more efficiently, build levees to control the Mississippi River, and introduce a medical doctor and a trained midwife.

Luzières's plans met with sporadic success for a few years, and his son **Charles de Hault Delassus** rose in the Spanish colonial bureaucracy, serving as commandant at New Madrid (1796–1799) and then as lieutenant governor of Upper Louisiana (1799–1804). However, the alien environment, the river-valley fevers, his wife's profound unhappiness, and mounting debts gradually ground down Luzières's body and spirits. His letters to Carondelet became a jeremiad of grievances. With the Louisiana Purchase

Luzières became an American citizen, which did not please him, and in his last years he presented a pathetic figure who found some solace in wine and whiskey. Luzières's wife died in July 1806, and he died in December. Both were buried in the Roman Catholic cemetery in Ste. Genevieve, but their insubstantial gravestones have long since disappeared, and the whereabouts of their graves are unknown. The Missouri frontier did not treat these gentle folks gently. Within fifty years the entire community of New Bourbon had disappeared, and the site of the once flourishing village is now occupied by a supplier of building materials.

CARL J. EKBERG

Archibald, Robert R. "The Career of Lt. Gov. Carlos de Hault de Lassus." *Gateway Heritage* 12 (spring 1992): 32–41.
Delassus–St. Vrain Papers. Missouri Historical Society, St. Louis.
Ekberg, Carl J. *Colonial Ste. Genevieve: An Adventure on the Mississippi Frontier.* Gerald, Mo.: Patrice Press, 1985.
Houck, Louis. *The Spanish Regime in Missouri: A Collection of Papers and Documents Relating to Upper Louisiana.* 2 vols. Chicago: R. R. Donnelley and Sons, 1909.
McDermott, John Francis. "The Career of Lt. Gov. Charles de Hault de Lassus." *Louisiana Historical Quarterly* 30 (April 1947): 359–438.
Papeles de Cuba, various legajos. Archivo General de Indias, Seville, Spain.

LYON, NATHANIEL (1818–1861)

Nathaniel Lyon, a United States Army officer from 1841 to 1861, was born in rural Ashford (later Eastford), Connecticut, on July 14, 1818, the son of Amasa Lyon, a farmer and local lawyer, and Kezia Knowlton Lyon. The seventh of nine children, Nathaniel received a common school education and in 1837 gained entrance to West Point, from which he graduated in 1841, eleventh in his class of fifty-two. Choosing the infantry over more prestigious branches of military services, Lyon was assigned to the Second U.S. Infantry in Florida. After participating in campaigns against the Seminoles, he was transferred in 1842 to Sackets Harbor, New York.

Possessing a violent, hair-trigger temper, Lyon received a court-martial for the brutal beating and torture of an unruly enlisted man. A sworn bachelor, he was fiercely independent and throughout his career proved a contentious and nearly unpromotable subordinate in peacetime. However, during the Mexican War he showed himself an able leader in battle, participated at Contreras and Churubusco, was wounded, and received promotion to brevet captain for gallantry.

Lyon's unique beliefs about religion caused him to believe himself the Creator's chosen instrument for meting out punishment. Always rigid, after returning from Mexico he began to demonstrate an appetite for inflicting pain. Transferred to California, Lyon led an expedition in 1850 to seek and punish local Indians accused of murdering three white residents. The action resulted in the extermination of two complete tribes. Moreover, Lyon's draconian punishments of enlisted men became notorious. Convinced of his own moral righteousness, Lyon questioned authority at all levels, and upon being transferred to Kansas in 1854 caused the court-martial of a superior officer and the removal from office of the territory's first governor by exposing a fraudulent land sale involving government property near the first territorial capital of Pawnee and involving a land company for which Lyon himself served as trustee.

In Kansas Lyon witnessed firsthand the violence that erupted over the government's attempt to settle the issue of slavery by means of the Kansas-Nebraska Act. He attributed the territory's bitter strife to the "contemptible arrogance" of its proslavery faction. Accusing the federal government of "subserviency to the slave interest," Lyon resolved to use all means to thwart the "Slavocracy," which he regarded as the source of the nation's woes. He allowed soldiers at Fort Riley to vote illegally in a territorial election, assisted Free State Jayhawkers to escape arrest, and, though not an abolitionist, used government horses to assist fugitive slaves. By 1860 Lyon had become a strident adherent to the Republican Party, and wrote newspaper editorials supporting candidate Abraham Lincoln and condemning the Democratic Party, which he had formerly supported.

In January 1861 Lyon and two companies of infantry were transferred to St. Louis to bolster the defenses of the city's federal arsenal. Although Missouri remained in the Union, it boasted an active secessionist minority, which included the governor and much of the legislature. Arriving on February 6, Lyon believed the city's military leadership to be of dubious loyalty, and feared an attack upon the arsenal from the city's secessionists. He quickly acquainted himself with Congressman **Frank Blair,** leader of St. Louis's radical Republicans, brother to one of Lincoln's cabinet members, and son of one of the party's founders. In return for rifles with which to arm the city's large German element, which ardently supported the federal government, Blair offered Lyon immunity from the administration for any actions he might take in attempting to protect the arsenal. Together they forced the removal of Lyon's moderate department commander, Gen. **William S. Harney.** Lyon then assumed charge of both the department and the arsenal. He enlisted into federal service several thousand Home Guard militia, mostly Germans, and on May 10 captured the state militia encampment, located on the city's outskirts, many of whose members were secessionists. While returning to the arsenal, Lyon's untrained Home Guards fired upon a civilian mob, killing at least twenty-eight, most of whom were unarmed. Several days of riots ensued, causing thousands to flee the city. Lyon's actions hastened thousands of recruits to flock to State Guard camps around the state and caused a jittery state legislature to pass a military bill providing Gov. **Claiborne Fox Jackson** with unprecedented power to arm the state for war.

The day after the fracas, Harney was reinstated as commander of the department. In an effort to preserve peace, he and former governor **Sterling Price,** commander of the State Guard, drafted and published an agreement stating that the state forces would assume responsibility for keeping order in Missouri. Believing the Harney-Price agreement a mere subterfuge to afford the governor time to arm the state troops, Lyon—a newly commissioned brigadier general of volunteers—and Blair obtained an order from Lincoln that relieved Harney of command for the second time. Again Lyon assumed temporary command of the department.

On June 11 Jackson and Price met with Lyon and Blair at the Planters' House Hotel in St. Louis. After four hours Lyon abruptly ended the conference by declaring, "This means war." Within forty-eight hours he launched an expedition up the Missouri River toward Jefferson City, causing the governor and the secessionist legislators to flee. After occupying the state capital, Lyon pressed on toward Boonville, where State Guard forces were concentrated. On June 16 his troops easily scattered the Guardsmen, who joined with Confederate forces in Arkansas under Brig. Gen. Ben McCulloch to form a force more than double the size of Lyon's. When Price

learned that Lyon was at Springfield, he convinced McCulloch to move north into Missouri. Continuing south, Lyon skirmished with the Confederates at Dug Springs, then withdrew to Springfield. McCulloch and Price encamped on Wilson's Creek south of the city.

Losing troops daily to enlistment expirations, most of whom were St. Louis Home Guardsmen, Lyon feared the loss of his entire force without giving battle. He agreed to a rash plan by one of his subordinates, Col. **Franz Sigel,** the popular leader of Lyon's German troops, and divided his force for a surprise pincer attack. At dawn on August 10 Lyon and Sigel struck the encamped Confederates. At the battle's height, Lyon was shot in the heart and killed. After four hours of pitched fighting, the federal force withdrew.

In defeat, Lyon became the North's first battlefield hero, and its first general to fall. After a whistle-stop procession, he was buried in Phoenixville, Connecticut.

CHRISTOPHER PHILLIPS

Adamson, Hans Christian. *Rebellion in Missouri, 1861: Nathaniel Lyon and His Army of the West.* New York: Chilton, 1961.

Oates, Stephen B. "Nathaniel Lyon: A Personality Profile." *Civil War Times Illustrated* 6 (October 1968): 15–25.

Peckham, James. *General Nathaniel Lyon and Missouri in 1861.* New York: American News, 1866.

Phillips, Christopher. *Damned Yankee: The Life of General Nathaniel Lyon.* Columbia: University of Missouri Press, 1990.

Price, Richard Scott. *Nathaniel Lyon: Harbinger from Kansas.* Springfield, Mo.: Wilson's Creek National Battlefield Foundation, 1990.

Woodward, Ashbel. *Life of General Nathaniel Lyon.* Hartford, Conn.: Case, Lockwood, 1862.

MacKAY, JAMES (1759–1822)

James MacKay, a Scotsman renowned for his talent, zeal, and industry, won high marks in colonial and territorial Missouri for his accomplishments as a fur trader, explorer, Spanish civil servant, militia officer, and American governmental official. He was born in 1759, four miles north of the parish of Kildonan, in the County of Sutherland, in Scotland's northern highlands.

Sometime before 1776 MacKay traveled to North America to join the numerous members of the MacKay clan who had preceded him across the Atlantic. He went to Canada where he engaged in the fur trade in the employ of British traders for whom he made voyages of discovery in the American interior. He journeyed to the Mandan villages on the upper Missouri in 1787, making him one of the earliest European traders to visit those settlements.

In June 1789 MacKay conferred in New York City with Diego de Gardoqui, Spain's minister to the United States, paving the way for his eventual decision to transfer his allegiance to the Spaniards. On this occasion the Scottish trader presented Gardoqui with a map charting his travels up the Saskatchewan to the Rockies and his trip to the Mandan. In the meantime, MacKay established a trading partnership with John Robertson in Cincinnati, and in 1792–1793 he took part in public meetings at Cahokia, across from St. Louis. On May 20, 1793, **Zenon Trudeau,** the lieutenant governor of Upper Louisiana, wrote that he was meeting "a well informed Canadian *mozo*," who had been to the Mandan nation and possessed information concerning the British trade.

That fall MacKay traveled to New York and Montreal, and in August 1794 he dissolved his partnership with Robertson and went to St. Louis where the Company of Explorers of the Upper Missouri (the Missouri Company) selected him to succeed Jean Baptiste Truteau as principal explorer and director of the firm's operations in the Indian country. MacKay's knowledge and previous experiences made him an ideal candidate for the assignment. The company's backers instructed him to lead an expedition upriver, oversee the construction of a chain of forts to protect Spanish trade from British encroachments, and discover a route to the Pacific Ocean.

In August 1795 MacKay and his second in command, **John Thomas Evans,** left St. Louis with a party of thirty-three and headed up the Missouri.

MacKay traveled as far as an Omaha village in today's northeastern Nebraska, where he constructed a post known as Fort Charles. He remained in the Indian country until the spring of 1797 when he went back to St. Louis. Following his return, Mackay requested a land concession, worked as a surveyor, and helped draft a large-scale map illustrating the Missouri River from St. Charles, Missouri, to the Mandan villages, using the important geographical information that he and Evans had obtained during their expedition.

In 1798 MacKay traveled to New Orleans seeking employment in the Spanish service. On May 1, 1798, Louisiana's governor, Manuel Gayoso de Lemos, appointed him as captain of the militia and commandant at the post of St. Andrews, located on the Bonhomme bottoms of the Missouri River, twenty-four miles west of St. Louis.

MacKay returned to Upper Louisiana to take up his new duties at St. Andrews where he oversaw operations until a flood destroyed the settlement. He also solicited and received land concessions amounting to more than fifty-five thousand arpents as compensation for various services rendered to the Spanish crown.

In 1800 MacKay married Isabella Long in St. Louis, and the couple had nine children. The following year he was named commandant of the district of St. Charles, encompassing all the country north of the Missouri River. Following the Louisiana Purchase, MacKay transferred his loyalties to the incoming American regime. He provided **Meriwether Lewis** and **William Clark** with valuable information prior to their departure for the Pacific in 1804. That year territorial governor **William Henry Harrison** appointed MacKay to serve as a judge on the Court of Common Pleas and Quarter Sessions. He later held other minor judicial appointments, and in 1816 the voters of St. Louis County elected him as a member of Missouri's territorial legislature.

In 1808 MacKay moved his family to the Gravois District, near present-day White Haven, and in 1819 he built a handsome brick home in St. Louis where he died on March 16, 1822. After MacKay's death, his family continued to press for confirmation of land patents that had been denied as fraudulent, and in 1833 his survivors won approval for their claims.

THOMAS DANISI

Duckworth, Henry. "Hudson's Bay Company of Manitoba, Winnipeg." *Beaver* 68 (June–July 1988): 25–42.

Jackson, John C. "Brandon House and the Manitoba Connection." *North Dakota History Journal of the Northern Plains* 49 (winter 1982): 11–19.

Nasatir, Abraham P. *Before Lewis and Clark: Documents Illustrating the History of the Missouri, 1785–1804.* 2 vols. 1952. Reprint, Lincoln: University of Nebraska Press, 1990.

MAGOFFIN, SUSAN SHELBY (1827–1855)

Susan Shelby Magoffin was born on July 30, 1827, at Arcasia, her father's estate near Danville, Kentucky. She enjoyed a life of privilege and comfort as the daughter of one of Kentucky's wealthiest and most prominent families. The Shelby family included soldiers, pioneers, and politicians, most notably Susan's grandfather, Revolutionary War–hero Isaac Shelby, first governor of the state.

Perhaps Susan Shelby also longed for a life of adventure and distinction. A well-bred young woman of her time and place, she expressed her desire by accepting the most romantic and enterprising of her suitors, Santa Fe trader Samuel Magoffin, who was also the child of Kentucky pioneers, as her future husband. His father came from Ireland in the 1790s, married into a prominent Kentucky family, and prospered. His eldest brother, James Wiley Magoffin, ventured farther west and established himself in the Santa Fe trade by 1825; Samuel joined him by 1828. The Magoffins grew wealthy from the trade and traveled widely from the United States to Santa Fe, to their stores in Chihuahua and Saltillo, and to as far away as Mexico City. In 1828 James was appointed U.S. consul at Saltillo and subsequently carried out a variety of missions for the U.S. and Mexican governments. In 1830 he married into a prominent and well-connected Chihuahua merchant family. The brothers retained their ties to Kentucky, however. In 1840 another Magoffin brother married Susan Shelby's elder sister, and Samuel visited the Shelby household whenever he passed through on business trips to the East. Although twenty-seven years his junior, Susan fell deeply in love with the debonair merchant. On November 25, 1845, they were married.

In June 1846 the couple left James Magoffin's house near Independence, Missouri, with a caravan of merchandise for Santa Fe and Chihuahua. Susan Magoffin is chiefly remembered today for the journal she kept on this trip. Although she modeled her journal on **Josiah Gregg**'s *Commerce of the Prairies,* it became a lively and original record of her own experiences and impressions of the land and its inhabitants. She believed she was the first "American lady" to travel the Santa Fe Trail, and is the first whose record of the experience is known. She made the trip at a particularly critical time: the United States had declared war on Mexico in May 1846.

Enjoying the adventure of her new life, Magoffin at first seemed oblivious to the international situation, but events soon overtook her. She and her husband followed Gen. **Stephen Watts Kearny**'s army to Santa Fe, and later followed Col. **Alexander W. Doniphan**'s force to Chihuahua. Her journal vividly describes wartime conditions, the army officers who paid her court, and the Mexican people she encountered. Indirectly she offers much evidence of the American merchants' role in the war and the American acquisition of New Mexico.

Samuel and Susan Magoffin returned to Kentucky in 1848, then in 1852 moved to Barrett's Station, near Kirkwood, Missouri. Samuel bought a large estate there and proceeded to enlarge his fortune through land speculation.

The experience in Mexico had ruined Susan Magoffin's health. She had suffered a miscarriage on the way to Santa Fe, and on the return trip a nearly fatal bout of yellow fever and the premature birth of another child who died a few days later weakened her further. A daughter, Jane, was born in Kentucky in 1851, and another, Susan, in Missouri in 1855. This last birth overtaxed the mother's strength, and she died on October 26, 1855. She was buried in Bellefontaine Cemetery in St. Louis.

MARY ELLEN ROWE

Drumm, Stella M., ed. *Down the Santa Fe Trail and into Mexico: The Diary of Susan Shelby Magoffin.* 1926. Reprint, Lincoln: University of Nebraska Press, 1962.

MAHNKEY, MARY ELIZABETH (1877–1948)

Mary Elizabeth Mahnkey was a lifelong newspaper and magazine journalist, and a regional poet. Born in Boone County, Arkansas, on August 16, 1877, but reared in Taney County, Missouri, she began writing for the public at age fourteen. She wrote local columns for county newspapers for forty years before widening her audience in 1930 by writing for Springfield newspapers and statewide magazines for the rest of her life. The depression tourist trade and market for regional journalism significantly enhanced her opportunities and notoriety. Some have called her a "backwoods philosopher" and others the "poet laureate of the Ozarks."

Mahnkey was reared in a progressive family devoted to education and promotion of local society. Her father, Alonzo Prather, was a five-term state representative, a local orator, and a journalist. He founded a Springfield newspaper in 1880, but soon moved to Taney County where he was proprietor and editor of *Home and Farm*. Daughter Mary Elizabeth began writing for her father's paper and continued for the next fifty-seven years while living in Taney County. She had a brother who became a career newspaper journalist and her son Douglas has authored numerous stories and two books.

Mahnkey attended subscription schools, never graduating from a high school, but obtained a teacher's certificate in 1893, and taught a few terms at Ridgedale (1894), Union Flat (1896), and Branson (1898). Between teaching assignments she attended a local academy at Bradleyville, Missouri, where she was active in the literary society and edited the school newspaper.

In 1899 Mary Elizabeth Prather and Charles Preston Mahnkey married. They were farmers and country merchants operating mercantile establishments in several hamlets, including Mincy, Melva, and Oasis. Charles managed cotton gins and water mills, while Mary Elizabeth was the postmistress and the clerk in the stores. While at Oasis on Long Creek, improved transportation and the attraction of Lake Taneycomo brought tourists and journalists from Springfield who provided trade and discussions about local society and changes in the countryside.

In 1930 Mahnkey began a monthly column called "In the Hills" for Springfield newspapers, which she continued until 1948. She received much regional acclaim for her serial, "When Roseville Was Young," a historical remembrance of Kirbyville, Missouri, in the *Branson White River Leader* in 1933–1934. Monthly magazines such as *Game and Fish News, Missouri Magazine*, folklore serials, and the *Arcadian Magazine* carried her poems and short stories. Occasionally, she placed stories in the *St. Louis Post-Dispatch* and *Country Home Magazine*. A few of her writings were used by radio journalists. The only collected work published during her lifetime was a pamphlet of poetry titled *Ozark Lyrics*. It began as a successful money-raising event sponsored by a women's civic group, the Taneyhills Study Club, and was published in 1934. Her "In the Hills" columns and the Roseville story are significant cultural and historical writings.

In 1935 *Country Home Magazine* sponsored a rural-correspondent contest. Forsyth editor-publisher W. E. Freeland encouraged Mahnkey and helped her select a number of her columns. The Crowell Publishing Company in New York chose her from a field of sixteen hundred to receive the national award as the best rural correspondent.

Mahnkey's family background and paternal direction encouraged her creative writing, but she later noted that she felt compelled to write. She dedicated one of her poems to the question, "My Poems?"

implying that the exercise was routine, as the poems came to her when she churned butter, made bread, hung clothes, and they just "danced 'round my head." She also said she wrote her stories to counter the negative stereotypes of the Ozarks prevalent in the sensationalized urban press, and for the old people who enjoyed memories of times past. Her writings have a distinctly feminine point of view and have probably had a wider audience among women than men.

Mahnkey wrote sentimentally of life and death, music, dancing, laughter, school, love, common domestic chores, and natural environments. She maintained a literary reverence for neighbors and nature, and a fondness and pride in the common work and joys of life. Her poems vary in quality as some are more polished than others.

Poet **John G. Neihardt** wrote in the preface of Mahnkey's *Ozark Lyrics* of her warmth that "grows out of the womanly heart of one who is truly a good neighbor to her fellows and to everything that lives." *St. Louis Post-Dispatch* correspondent F. A. Behymer said in 1948, "She wrote to make the best of things, making the best of things when life has grown weary and life's fabric has grown thin."

In 1975 Mahnkey became one of the first six inductees into the Ozark Hall of Fame at the School of the Ozarks, in Point Lookout, Missouri. She died on August 13, 1948.

LYNN MORROW

Mahnkey, Mary Elizabeth. *Marigold Gold: Verses of the Ozarks*. Ed. Ellen Gray Massey. Lebanon, Mo.: Bittersweet, 1990.
———. *Ozark Lyrics*. Reprint, Forsyth, Mo.: Little Photo Gallery, 1985.
White River Leader, July 27, 1933–March 22, 1934.

MAIER, WALTER A. (1893–1950)

Walter Arthur Maier was born on October 4, 1893, in Boston, Massachusetts, the son of German immigrants Emil and Anna Schad Maier. He grew up in Boston and received his education at Concordia Collegiate Institute in Bronxville, New York, graduating in 1912, and Concordia Seminary in St. Louis, graduating in 1916. He also received a B.A. from Boston University (1913) and an M.A. (1920) and Ph.D. (1929) from Harvard Divinity School.

Maier was ordained into the Lutheran ministry and served briefly as an assistant pastor in Boston. During World War I he worked at a prisoner-of-war camp for Germans on Gallup Island, Massachusetts, and as a chaplain at Camp Gordon, near Atlanta.

In 1920 Maier became the executive secretary of the Walther League, a Lutheran youth organization, and edited the *Walther League Messenger* until 1945.

The publication provided Maier with an outlet for his religious, political, and personal views. He vigorously attacked communism, the Catholic Church, intervention in European power struggles, atheism, and lodges in his effort to uphold the ideals of Christian morality and the Scriptures.

Maier met his future wife, Hulda Eickhoff, at the Walther League; she was secretary of its junior department. They were married in 1924 and had two sons, Walter A. Maier II and Paul L. Maier.

Maier moved to St. Louis in 1922 to become a professor of the Old Testament at Concordia Seminary. There he became interested in the developing technology of radio, sensing its possibilities as a medium for proclaiming the Christian Gospel. He helped organize the religious radio station KFUO, which first broadcast from the seminary building in south St. Louis. In 1926 the seminary moved to a new campus in suburban Clayton, and the Lutheran Laymen's League financed new facilities for the radio station on the campus.

Maier's early career reflected his boundless energy. In addition to his teaching, radio, and editorial activities, he organized and developed a mission congregation in the central west end of St. Louis and spent his summer vacations preaching at a Lutheran resort in Pennsylvania, attracting a considerable following from around the country.

Maier saw the potential for religious radio broadcasting beyond KFUO. On October 2, 1930, he began to preach the Gospel to the nation with the first broadcast of *The Lutheran Hour* from station WHK in Cleveland. Financial problems brought that effort to an end after nine months, but the program continued to generate mail, and a book of radio sermons titled *The Lutheran Hour* was published by the Concordia Publishing House.

Maier kept busy with his teaching and speaking engagements. He also produced *Truth Triumphant,* a pageant to celebrate the four-hundredth anniversary of the Augsburg Confession. Held at the St. Louis Arena, the production involved a cast of more than four thousand and played to almost twenty thousand people.

In 1936 *The Lutheran Hour* returned to the air, carried by the Mutual Broadcasting System. This time the program generated enough support to survive. By the fall of 1937 it was heard on sixty-two stations, and when World War II began it expanded overseas. More than one thousand stations carried the program by its fifteenth season. In 1950 ten international offices had been opened, and the program was being produced in twenty-five languages.

Maier received a large volume of mail in response to the broadcasts. People sought his help with religious and personal problems, and also sent contributions to support the program. Seminary students were recruited to help with the work. The staff directed listeners to churches, offered spiritual guidance, and provided free devotional materials and mementos.

In the 1930s Maier began a heavy schedule of *Lutheran Hour* rallies throughout the country that attracted standing-room-only crowds. Several national magazines, such as the *Saturday Evening Post,* took note of his work in major features. After World War II Maier was asked to serve on a commission advising the Allied Military Government on educational and religious issues in Germany, and in 1948 he served as a chaplain at the Republican National Convention in Philadelphia.

Not all the attention was positive. Some criticized Maier's message and approach. Efforts were made to link him with anti-Semitic preachers and to launch a Federal Communications Commission investigation of his views and political associations. Some within his own church considered him a problem, but despite the opposition his popularity never waned.

Maier died on January 11, 1950, after a series of heart attacks. His funeral was televised from the Concordia Seminary chapel by NBC affiliate KSD in St. Louis, the first televised funeral in the nation.

MARVIN A. HUGGINS

Anderson, James L. "An Evaluation of the Communicative Factors in the Radio Preaching of Walter A. Maier of the Tenth Lutheran Hour Series in 1942–1943." Ph.D. diss., Southwestern Baptist Theological Seminary, 1976.

Lambing, Jamie. *A Guide and Inventory of the Papers of Walter A. Maier: First Speaker of "The Lutheran Hour."* St. Louis: Concordia Historical Institute, 1993.

Maier, Paul L. *A Man Spoke, a World Listened.* 1963. Reprint, St. Louis: Concordia Publishing, 1980.

Rudnick, Milton L. "Fundamentalism and the Missouri Synod." Ph.D. diss., Concordia Seminary, 1963.

Sulston, Kenneth Hartley. "A Rhetorical Criticism of the Radio Preaching of Walter Arthur Maier." Ph.D. diss., Northwestern University, 1958.

Zeitler, Lester Erwin. "An Investigation of the Factors of Persuasion in the Sermons of Dr. Walter A. Maier." S.T.M. thesis, Concordia Seminary, 1956.

MAJOR, ELLIOTT WOOLFOLK (1864–1949)

Elliott Woolfolk Major was born in Lincoln County, Missouri, on October 20, 1864, the son of James Reed and Sarah Ann Taylor Woolfolk Major. His father was a farmer and part-time gold prospector. Major gained his education in the public schools of Pike County, Missouri, and at the Watson Seminary in Ashley, Missouri.

Major started his professional career as a teacher, but soon turned his attention to the study of law. He began his training in the law office of noted Missouri politician **James Beauchamp "Champ" Clark** in Bowling Green, Missouri, and gained admission to the Missouri bar in 1885. Major served as Clark's clerk in the Missouri legislature in 1889, and for a brief time became Clark's law partner.

Major quickly established a reputation as a successful trial lawyer, and began to cultivate an active interest in politics. Elected to the state senate from Missouri's Eleventh District (composed of Pike, Lincoln, and Audrain Counties) in 1896, Major served during the 1897 and 1899 sessions of the legislature. His recognized abilities as a legalist undoubtedly contributed to his selection as editor of the *Revised Statutes of Missouri* in 1899.

Major's legal career reached its peak in 1908 with election to the office of Missouri attorney general on the Democratic Party ticket. As attorney general he argued a number of cases before the Supreme Court of the United States. One significant decision upheld the constitutionality of Missouri's two-cent passenger fare and maximum freight-rate laws. Another important decision involved the state's suit against Standard Oil for antitrust violations; the court unanimously upheld Missouri's law. During his term as attorney general Major brought to successful conclusion several suits begun by his predecessor, **Herbert Hadley,** against the lumber, beef, and harvester combines. Under Major's direction his department compiled a vigorous record of law enforcement, arguing more than one thousand cases before the Missouri Supreme Court and writing nearly twelve hundred opinions concerning Missouri statutes.

At the request of George Chamberlain, a U.S. senator from Oregon, Major also wrote a brief and argument for the state of Oregon in its successful case against the Pacific Telephone and Telegraph Company The company had challenged the 1899 initiative and referendum amendment to the Oregon Constitution as violating provisions guaranteeing a republican form of government. The decision was important not only for the future of direct democracy in Oregon (and in Missouri, which enacted a virtually identical statute in 1908) but also for sustaining the principle that voters could create their own laws and veto legislative statutes.

Upon completion of his term as attorney general (1909–1912), Major won election as governor on the Democratic ticket in 1912. He received 337,019 votes to 217,819 for his Republican opponent, John C. McKinley, and 109,146 for Progressive candidate Albert D. Nortoni. Major had campaigned as a moderate reformer recommending the creation of a state public service commission, the passage of a workmen's compensation law, simplified court procedures, and municipal and presidential primaries.

As governor Major continued to compile a record of achievement. With his endorsement the Democratically controlled legislature passed a law granting married women equal legal rights with husbands in cases involving the care of underage children. He also supported the so-called Orr Law, which prohibited insurance companies from quoting noncompetitive fire insurance rates and aimed at curtailing the practice by which the larger insurance companies conducted what amounted to a rate-fixing arrangement. A number of these companies suspended business in Missouri rather than comply with the law, and businessmen felt threatened. Despite demands from the leading commercial organizations for the governor to call a special session of the legislature to confront the problem, Major refused and continued to support the Orr Law. When the state supreme court formally upheld the Orr Law, the companies returned to the state.

Major was also instrumental in promoting construction of the new state capitol building, in authorizing cities to adopt the commission form of government, in overseeing compliance with the Federal Reserve Banking Act of 1913, in passing an absentee voting law, and in establishing a public service commission, a highway department, a board of pardons and paroles, a commission for the blind, and an insurance bureau. He successfully resisted the imposition of new state taxes, but left the next governor with little money to support the new state agencies. Major also actively supported education. During his administration the rural school year was lengthened, rural secondary schools were established, teachers training programs were created, state assistance was increased, and agricultural schools were encouraged to take advantage of the Smith Lever Act that provided federal funding for farm demonstration agents.

Major was a passionate advocate of the good-roads movement. To promote road improvements in Missouri, he proclaimed August 20–21, 1913, as public holidays to be known as "Good Roads Days." This public-spirited, volunteer effort resulted in hundreds of miles of new or improved roads. Major pursued this interest at the federal level, and provided testimony at federal hearings in which he advocated using federal funds to support highway maintenance.

The Democratic state convention endorsed Major as a vice presidential candidate with Woodrow Wilson in 1916, but the national convention selected Thomas R. Marshall instead. After leaving public office in 1917, Major resumed his private law practice in St. Louis. He continued an active legal career until his retirement in 1945.

Major received an honorary B.S. degree from Wesleyan College in Warrenton, Missouri. He held memberships in the American, Missouri, and St. Louis Bar Associations, and in numerous fraternal orders, such as the Odd Fellows, the Knights of Pythias, the Elks, the Moose, and the Masons. He attended the Methodist Episcopal Church. He married Elizabeth Terrill in Bowling Green, Missouri, on June 14, 1887; they had three children. Elliott Major died on July 9, 1949.

STEVEN L. PIOTT

Christensen, Lawrence O., and Gary R. Kremer. *A History of Missouri: Volume IV, 1875 to 1919.* Columbia: University of Missouri Press, 1997.

Guitar, Sarah, and Shoemaker, Floyd C., eds. *The Messages and Proclamations of the Governors of the State of Missouri.* Columbia: State Historical Society of Missouri, 1926.

Shoemaker, Floyd Calvin. *Missouri and Missourians: Land of Contrasts and People of Achievements.* Vol. 2. Chicago: Lewis Publishing, 1943.

Stevens, Walter B. *Missouri: The Center State, 1821–1915.* Vol. 3. Chicago: S. J. Clarke, 1915.

Thelen, David. *Paths of Resistance: Tradition and Dignity in Industrializing Missouri.* New York: Oxford University Press, 1986.

MAJORS, ALEXANDER (1814–1900)

Those familiar with the Pony Express recognize Russell, Majors, and Waddell as the entrepreneurs behind the famous, if short-lived, venture. Overshadowed by his flamboyant partners, Alexander Majors conducted the firm's overland freighting business. His activities placed him at the forefront of westward expansion, as witness and participant in some of the most celebrated events of the nineteenth century. He endured the rigors of the environment, but fared less well in the world of commerce.

Laurania Kelly Majors, daughter of Revolutionary War–veteran Beil Kelly, bore her first child in Franklin, in Simpson County, Kentucky, on October 4, 1814. She and her husband, Benjamin, named their son after his paternal grandfather, Alexander, who had farmed in North Carolina before moving his family to Kentucky.

In 1818 Benjamin Majors moved his young family of two boys and a girl to richer lands in the Missouri Territory. The following year they settled near Sni-A-Bar Creek, approximately thirty miles south of the Kaw River near Fort Osage. Laurania Majors died in 1820, when Alexander was only six years old, from injuries sustained during the journey. The boy worked on the family farm throughout his youth, and by age twenty established his farm in Cass County, near the headwaters of the South Grand River.

On November 6, 1834, Majors married Catherine Stalcup, of Jackson County, Missouri. The Majors family grew quickly, and farming failed to provide a sufficient income. In the summer of 1846 Majors supplemented his income by trading goods on the Potawatomi Indian Reservation in what later became Kansas Territory. Two years later he tried his luck on the Santa Fe Trail. He set out in August 1848 with six wagons and six bullwhackers who pledged to conduct themselves as gentlemen while in his employ. The troupe made the journey in record time, just ninety-two days, and made a tidy profit.

In 1850 Majors expanded his business to ten wagons and accepted his first government contract to transport military supplies from Fort Leavenworth to Fort McKay in Kansas Territory. With the exception of 1852 he engaged in the freighting business from 1848 to 1867. His success, which in 1854 included a carrying capacity of one hundred wagons, attracted the attention of William H. Russell, who offered partnership rather than competition.

Majors and Russell established their headquarters in Leavenworth, Kansas, two miles south of the federal supply depot. Russell engaged separately in a variety of entrepreneurial ventures with various partners, including **William B. Waddell.** Many of these undertakings saddled the partnership with additional debt, but engagements with Waddell merged smoothly with the freighting business. The trio conducted transactions under the name of Majors and Russell from 1855 to 1858, then operated as Russell, Majors, and Waddell through 1861.

Operations required the establishment of a second office, in Nebraska City, in Nebraska Territory, which Majors staffed. His wife had died on January 14, 1856, so in 1858 he moved from Westport to Nebraska with second wife, Susan Wetzel, whom he had married on March 23, 1857. Military efforts to subdue Native Americans and Mormons fed a steady demand for supplies, which the firm sometimes had trouble satisfying.

The business thrived, despite an increasing debt load and delivery problems. Russell expanded operations to include passenger service—with acquisition of a bankrupt stage line—and mail delivery through the Pony Express. By 1861 debt and technology ended the viability of Russell, Majors, and Waddell. The partners quickly separated, each struggling to salvage personal assets and shield themselves from ruin.

By then forty-seven years of age, Majors tried to reestablish his personal freighting business, but the task proved too great. He sold his business to Edward Creighton, champion of the telegraph, and took his family to Salt Lake City, where he lived from 1867 to 1879.

In Utah Majors worked briefly on the transcontinental railroad and tried his hand at silver mining, with little success. He then moved to St. Louis for one year and settled in Denver for a brief period, from 1887 to 1891. While in Denver he wrote his memoirs, *Seventy Years on the Frontier* (1893), hoping to recoup some of his lost fortune. William "Buffalo Bill" Cody, a former Pony Express rider, found his past employer in poverty, funded the autobiography, and supported Majors through his final years.

Alexander Majors died in Chicago on January 13, 1900. By all accounts he was an honorable and compassionate man of deep religious conviction. Although fame came through the Pony Express, Majors merits greater recognition by virtue of his hard work, skill, and ambition. He saw the United States blossom from a fledgling republic to a burgeoning world power and aided its transformation by braving the American frontier.

RACHEL FRANKLIN WEEKLEY

Bloss, Roy S. *Pony Express: The Great Gamble.* Berkeley, Calif.: Howell North Press, 1959.

Kansas City Star, January 15, 1900.

Majors, Alexander. *Seventy Years on the Frontier: Alexander Majors's Memoirs of a Lifetime on the Border.* Ed. Prentiss Ingraham. Chicago: Rand, McNally, 1893.

Settle, Raymond W., and Mary Lund Settle. *Empire on Wheels.* Stanford: Stanford University Press, 1949.

———. *Saddles and Spurs: The Pony Express Saga.* Harrisburg, Pa.: Stackpole, 1955.

Smith, Waddell F., ed. *The Story of the Pony Express.* San Francisco: Hesperian House, 1960.

MALONE, ANNIE MINERVA TURNBO POPE (1869–1957)

Annie Minerva Turnbo Pope Malone was born in Metropolis, Illinois, on August 9, 1869, to Robert and Isabella Cook Turnbo. Orphaned at an early age, Malone lived with her older brothers and sisters in Metropolis and Peoria, Illinois. She was a sickly child and attended school sporadically during her teens. She attended high school briefly in Peoria, and discovered an affinity for chemistry.

In 1900 Malone moved to Lovejoy, Illinois, with an older sister. Recognizing the largely untapped market for beauty products for African American women, she launched a successful hair care business. Her skill with chemical compounds played a critical role in the development of her hair-straightening formula. A keen businesswoman, she quickly looked for larger markets for her products. The St. Louis economy was booming as plans for the upcoming 1904 Louisiana Purchase Exposition unfolded. Following a move to St. Louis in 1902, Malone patented the trade name of her product line, Poro, in 1906.

She entered marriage to a man named Pope in 1903; divorce quickly followed.

Malone married her second husband, St. Louis school principal Aaron E. Malone, in 1914. By 1918 she was worth well over a million dollars and opened Poro College, a multipurpose facility featuring a beauty operators' training school, a five-hundred-seat auditorium, a roof garden, committee rooms, and an elegant dining room. Conscious of her role in promoting a positive image of the black community to white St. Louisans, Malone brought prominent African American entertainers and community leaders to St. Louis. In 1920 Marian Anderson, Roland Hayes, and Ethel Waters performed on the stage of the Poro College Auditorium.

A generous philanthropist, Malone donated regularly to the Howard University Medical School and the St. Louis Colored Orphans Home, which was renamed the Annie Malone Children's Home in 1946 in appreciation of her generosity and years of service on the board of directors. Always active in the National Association of Colored Women, she served as president of the St. Louis chapter in 1922.

Malone established branches of Poro College in fifteen cities from New York City to Los Angeles by 1922. Considered one of the richest women in St. Louis, she paid $38,498 in Missouri state income tax in 1924, marking her as a multimillionaire. She drove one of the first Rolls-Royces in St. Louis and made headlines when her daughter and niece arrived at a charity function in similar luxury vehicles.

A stormy divorce from Aaron Malone jeopardized the financial empire in 1927. Annie Malone called prominent African Americans from across the country as character witnesses. Black newspapers across the country ran editorials, cartoons, and banner headlines attacking her husband. She ultimately settled with him for two hundred thousand dollars.

In 1930 Malone moved the Poro headquarters to Chicago. Although she continued her generous contributions to St. Louis charities, she essentially abandoned her St. Louis facility. It was sold under foreclosure in 1937. Her business profits continued to increase, though, and she had thirty-two branches by the mid-1950s. Annie Minerva Turnbo Pope Malone died in Chicago on May 10, 1957.

SUZANNA MAUPIN LONG

Baldwin, Helen I., et al. *Heritage of St. Louis.* St. Louis: St. Louis Public Schools, 1964.

Long, Suzanna Maupin. " 'I Made It Mine Tho' the Queen Waz Always Fair': The St. Louis Black Clubwoman Movement, 1931–1946." Master's thesis, University of Missouri–St. Louis, 1988.

Necrologies. Vol. 29. Missouri Historical Society, St. Louis.

Tinling, Marion. *Women Remembered: A Guide to Landmarks of Women's History in the United States.* New York: Greenwood Press, 1986.

MARBUT, CURTIS FLETCHER (1863–1935)

Curtis Fletcher Marbut revolutionized American thinking in soil science and had an international influence on the study of the geography of soils. He was a professor of geology at the University of Missouri (1895–1910), a leading scientist for the Bureau of Soils at the United States Department of Agriculture in Washington, D.C. (1910–1935), and his writings make up much of the foundation for modern American geography and agricultural advancement.

Marbut's Palatine German ancestors, the Meerboldts, emigrated to Philadelphia in 1784. Their pioneering experiences took them to South Carolina, Tennessee, and, by 1841, to Barry County, Missouri. There, in the Little Flat Creek valley, parents Nathan and Jane Marbut reared a large family, naming the future scientist for two Unionist officers, Gen. **Samuel R. Curtis** and Col. **Thomas Clement Fletcher.**

Curtis Marbut was born in 1863 and attended the local Marbut school with twenty-four cousins and was instructed by another cousin. He became a teacher at age seventeen, but later enrolled in an academy in Cassville. Subsequently, he recalled that the local professor's field trips around Barry County in the early 1880s inspired his desire to learn of the natural world. Curtis raised cattle on his father's farm, sold all his animals in 1885, and journeyed to Columbia to begin collegiate studies at age twenty-two.

University life suited the young scholar. Curtis graduated with a degree in geology in 1889, and borrowed money to attend Harvard University where he earned a master's degree in geology in 1894. He completed a residency, course work, and a thesis, published as *Physical Features of Missouri,* but he never returned to take the oral exam for his doctorate: he was in Missouri teaching and had begun his long and distinguished publishing career.

Marbut never lost sight of home. In 1900 he purchased land adjacent to his grandfather's Barry County property. The following year he and 425 other Marbuts attended a family reunion in the neighborhood. Thirty years later, as he planned for a retirement of writing at Orchard Farm, he designed his house in the New England Cape Cod style with interiors from a home-builders magazine. He supervised the construction by letter while relatives and workmen carried out his wishes along Little Flat Creek.

While Marbut taught at the university, he was a member of the Missouri Geological Survey doing extensive fieldwork from 1890 to 1904. In 1899–1900 he bicycled across much of Europe, and he was director of the Soil Survey of Missouri from 1905 to 1910. During these youthful years he became a charter member of two fraternities, a member of another, and won a gold medal for the first comprehensive "Soil Survey Map of the United States," which was displayed at the 1904 World's Fair in St. Louis.

In 1909 Marbut's wife died. Their eldest daughter, Louise, assumed the role of surrogate mother for the other four children. Curtis Marbut never remarried.

In 1910 Marbut took a leave of absence from the university, a leave that continued for the rest of his life. He became a special agent for the federal Bureau of Soils; by 1913 he was the scientist in charge and later the chief scientist. He accelerated his extensive field investigations by traveling in nearly every county in the United States. His worldwide study of soils included work and directing field trips in Canada, Western Europe, Russia, the Balkans, the interior of Brazil, Argentina, and the West Indies. He lectured at many universities, including several summers at Clark University in Worcester, Massachusetts, and served on numerous committees and commissions.

In 1920 Marbut introduced Soviet soil science to Americans by translating from German into English K. D. Glinka's *Great Soil Groups of the World and Their Development.* This work laid the foundation for the international study of soils, with Marbut often serving as chair of international delegations devoted to global research. During his tenure in Washington, D.C., soil surveys were conducted across half of America, and his monumental works in the *Bureau of Soils Bulletin* in 1913 and in the *Atlas of American Agriculture* in 1935 became foundational for textbooks and teaching in American education.

Marbut's many honors included honorary doctorates from the University of Missouri in 1916, and Rutgers University in 1930. He was president of the Association of American Geographers in 1924, and received the profession's highest award, the Cullum Medal, in 1930. A permanent display of Marbut's life and work may by viewed in Temple Hall on the campus of Southwest Missouri State University in Springfield.

When Marbut reached seventy, President Franklin D. Roosevelt twice waived Marbut's mandatory retirement from civil service. Marbut was in great demand by international scientific circles. Following a conference in Oxford, England, he traveled the trans-Siberian railroad on his way to organize soil surveys in China and contracted pneumonia. He died in Harbin, China, on August 25, 1935.

LYNN MORROW

Krusekopf, H. H., ed. *Life and Work of C. F. Marbut.* Memorial vol. Columbia: Soil Science Society of America, 1942.

Marbut, Curtis Fletcher. Papers. Western Historical Manuscripts Collection, Columbia.

MAREST, PIERRE GABRIEL (1662–1714)

Pierre Gabriel Marest, a Roman Catholic missionary priest in the Illinois country, was born on October 14, 1662, in Laval, a town in France's old province of Maine. His family was religious; both Pierre Gabriel and his brother Joseph became Jesuit priests.

On October 1, 1681, young Pierre Gabriel Marest entered the Jesuit novitiate in Paris. Two years later he was sent to teach at the Jesuit college in Vannes where he spent five years. In 1688 he returned to his own studies, taking a year of philosophy at La Flèche, studying his first year of theology at Bourges, and completing his seminary training at the College Louis-le-Grand in Paris. He was then ordained a priest and completed the "tertianship," or third year, of Jesuit training.

In 1694, at the age of thirty-two, Marest was sent to New France. At that time France was just beginning its seventy-five-year struggle with England for control of the North American continent. Marest was assigned as a chaplain on one of two ships sailing from Quebec to the Hudson Bay in August 1694 under the command of the famous Canadian Pierre le Moyne, Sieur d'Iberville. Since at this time Marest knew no Indian languages, his superiors believed that he could better serve as a chaplain to the French Canadians than to the Indians.

Marest's time as a chaplain in the Hudson Bay region was filled with adventure. He witnessed the French attack on an English fort and the fort's surrender and also had his first encounter with North American Indians. Eventually, in September 1695, he was captured by the English and taken as a prisoner back to England.

Marest was soon released, and he returned to France where he immediately asked his Jesuit superiors to send him back to America, hoping this time to serve as a missionary. His request was granted, and he arrived again at Quebec in 1698. He was soon dispatched by the famous priest Jacques Gravier to assist at a village of Illinois Indians near present-day Peoria, Illinois. After two years of missionary service at this village, Marest accompanied one group of the Illinois Indians, the Kaskaskia, as they moved to the South. The Kaskaskia were determined to move because of fears of raids by the Iroquois from the Northeast. The Kaskaskia and Father Marest first stopped on the west bank of the Mississippi River at the mouth of the River des Peres, now within the boundaries of the city of St. Louis.

The mission on the River des Peres lasted only until 1703 when the Kaskaskia decided to recross the Mississippi into the Illinois country and move approximately fifty miles farther south near the mouth of the Michigamea, now the Kaskaskia, River. There they laid out their new village, and it was there that Father Marest spent the remaining eleven years of his life, ministering to the Kaskaskia. He was able to make two trips back to the Peoria mission, and on the second of these visits he unexpectedly encountered his brother Father Joseph Marest and was able to spend several weeks with him.

Pierre Gabriel Marest was an outstanding missionary, respected by both Native Americans and the French. His mission at Kaskaskia was one of the most successful in North America. He became a superb Indian linguist, but none of his Indian transcriptions have been found. Besides his spiritual work, he taught the Indians agriculture and cattle raising, making the Kaskaskia among the most peaceable and industrious of the Indian tribes of the midcontinent. Marest died at Kaskaskia on September 15, 1714, during an epidemic.

JOHN WAIDE

Bannon, John Francis. "Black-Robe Frontiersman: Gabriel Marest, S.J." *Bulletin of the Missouri Historical Society* 10 (April 1954): 351–66.

Campbell, Thomas Joseph. *Pioneer Priests of North America*. Vol. 3. New York: America Press, 1911–1913.

Garaghan, Gilbert J. "Earliest Settlements of the Illinois Country." *Catholic Historical Review*, n.s., 9 (January 1930): 351–62.

Thwaites, Reuben Gold, ed. *The Jesuit Relations and Allied Documents*. Vols. 64–66, 71. Cleveland: Burrows Brothers, 1896–1901.

MARMADUKE, JOHN SAPPINGTON (1833–1887)

Born on March 14, 1833, near Arrow Rock, Missouri, John Sappington Marmaduke is the only Missouri governor whose father held the same position. Son of **Meredith Miles Marmaduke** and grandson of Dr. **John S. Sappington,** John grew up in one of Missouri's most famous political families.

Young Marmaduke attended local subscription schools in Saline County, Masonic College in nearby Lexington, and in 1850 went to New Haven, Connecticut, for schooling at Yale. In 1852 he moved to Cambridge, Massachusetts, where he attended classes at Harvard for a year. Finally, his father, through Congressman **John S. Phelps**—a longtime political friend in southwest Missouri—managed to gain an appointment for Marmaduke to the United States Military Academy at West Point. He remained there until his graduation in 1857. The young second lieutenant soon saw action in the Far West, including service in Utah during the Mormon War and duty in New Mexico.

In 1861 Marmaduke returned home to his family in Saline County to consider his choice in the upcoming war. His father supported the Union, but John and brothers Vincent and Henry chose to serve the Confederacy. John resigned his commission with the United States Army and accepted another as colonel in the Missouri State Guard. Against Marmaduke's advice, his superiors ordered him to take a stand at Boonville in June 1861, with poorly armed troops facing fully outfitted Unionists; Marmaduke and the State Guard suffered quick defeat. The retreat of Marmaduke's militia became known as the "Boonville Races," and the humiliated Colonel Marmaduke angrily resigned from his uncle **Claiborne Fox Jackson**'s State Guard. The disillusioned soldier returned home, consulted with his father, and left for his father's homeland in Virginia where he received a commission as a lieutenant colonel in the Confederate Army.

Marmaduke became known as a duty-bound and capable officer in Arkansas and Tennessee. He survived a wound at Shiloh and received a promotion to brigadier general. In 1862 the military transferred him to the trans-Mississippi theater where he commanded troops in Arkansas and Missouri.

In Arkansas in 1863 a growing dispute between Marmaduke and Gen. Lucien Walker resulted in the most notable Civil War duel between Confederate officers. Commanding officer Gen. **Sterling Price** was informed of the impending duel and sent orders to Marmaduke to remain at headquarters; he ignored the order, and mortally wounded Walker. General Price placed Marmaduke under arrest, but pressing needs on the battlefield led to his release. No charges were ever brought against him.

Marmaduke commanded an important part of General Price's forces in the fall 1864 Confederate invasion of southeast Missouri. Marmaduke advanced through several towns, including Pilot Knob, before reaching Hermann, where his forces inflicted considerable damage. Then his troops joined a general westward retreat from Union forces. At Westport Marmaduke miraculously survived after two horses were shot from under him, but during retreat in a rearguard fight the Unionists captured him. He spent the rest of the war in prison at Fort Warren, Massachusetts, where he remained until his release in August 1865. While incarcerated, Confederate officials raised his rank to major general, making him the last Confederate soldier to achieve such distinction. The

promotion acknowledged his earlier leadership and valor in Arkansas.

Given his freedom, the thirty-two-year-old former Confederate took a six-month tour of Europe. He returned to St. Louis in the spring of 1866, and successively established a commission house, entered the insurance business, edited an agricultural journal for three years, and served as secretary of the Missouri State Board of Agriculture in 1873–1874.

In 1875 Missouri created the state railroad commission and Gov. **Charles Henry Hardin** appointed Marmaduke as a commissioner. He served five years, later using his experience and interest in railroad regulation to good advantage as governor.

In 1880 Marmaduke's friends belatedly backed him for the gubernatorial nomination, but **Thomas Theodore Crittenden** easily became the Democratic choice. Gen. **Joseph Orville Shelby** and other influential former Confederates continued to push for Marmaduke's election.

In 1884 Marmaduke won the nomination and the governor's post amid great political turmoil in Missouri. With at least six parties or coalitions seeking power, he won a close election. The factionalism among Missourians soon manifested itself in the growing dissent over railroad management.

Marmaduke's term was marked by labor conflict in two railway strikes that seriously affected Missouri. In the early spring of 1885 and again in 1886 commerce on Missouri's rails was stalled. In 1885 Missouri Pacific workers launched a major strike over wages, affecting the traffic in Missouri and Kansas. The Missouri governor initiated arbitration among the dissenting parties that resulted in a bloodless, successful resolution permitting the resumption of rail operations.

In 1886 labor-related disputes closed rail traffic from Missouri to Texas. Violence erupted, with property damage and personal injury. Again, Marmaduke played a mediator's role, and after a modest show of force by the Missouri adjutant general, a few troops, and locally armed deputies, the rail trade resumed. The public clamored for legislative reform of rail rates, and the governor took the lead in securing new regulations to curtail collusion in establishing rates.

Marmaduke's experience with railroad strikes and consultations with the adjutant general about the state militia exposed the exceedingly poor condition of Missouri's militia. He and his adjutant general, James Jamison, bolstered morale in the militia through their efforts to enlist men rather than just officers, who then recruited troops. However, a basic problem was the absence of an appropriate budget for provisions and funds to pay soldiers when they were on duty in service of the state. Marmaduke unsuccessfully urged major legislative reform, but his efforts brought attention to the problems that the state addressed in future years. Local militias honored him in name with the Marmaduke Guards, the Marmaduke Rifles, Camp Marmaduke, and so on. Missouri folk musicians remember him in a favored melody, "Marmaduke's Hornpipe."

The governor visited several of Missouri's institutions, including the university, the school of mines, insane asylums, and the penitentiary in an attempt to understand their needs. During his administration the state began the tradition of allocating one-third of the state general revenue for public education. He laid the groundwork for a new state hospital at Nevada, a juvenile reform school for boys at Boonville, and an industrial home for girls at Chillicothe. In the climate of a surging temperance movement Marmaduke's administration passed a "local option" law in 1887. Dozens of counties and towns began to create "dry" districts throughout the state.

John Marmaduke, a bachelor who retained the services of two nieces as hostesses at the mansion, served three years of his term before dying of pneumonia in Jefferson City on December 28, 1887. Lt. Gov. **Albert Pickett Morehouse** served the remainder of the term and promoted many of the same causes advocated by Marmaduke. The governor was a talented man who exhibited his father's interest in progressive agriculture, his grandfather's concern for education, and his family's interest in public service.

LYNN MORROW

Huff, Leo. "The Last Duel in Arkansas: The Marmaduke-Walker Duel." *Arkansas Historical Quarterly* 23 (spring 1964): 36–49.

Lee, John F. "John Sappington Marmaduke." *Missouri Historical Society Collections* 2:6 (July 1906): 26–40.

Sharp, Grace Marmaduke. "The Marmadukes and Some Allied Families." *William and Mary Quarterly* 15 (April 1935): 151–72.

Shoemaker, Floyd Calvin. *Missouri and Missourians: Land of Contrasts and People of Achievements.* Chicago: Lewis Publishing, 1943.

MARMADUKE, MEREDITH MILES (1791–1864)

Meredith Miles Marmaduke, Missouri's eighth governor, was a native of Westmoreland County, Virginia, born on August 28, 1791, to Vincent and Sarah Porter Marmaduke. His chosen profession in civil engineering halted abruptly in 1812 with his selection as colonel of a Virginia frontier-defense regiment during the War of 1812. President James Madison made him a U.S. marshal for the Tidewater District after the war, but following a term as Westmoreland County's circuit clerk, Marmaduke moved in 1823 to Franklin, Missouri, "for health reasons."

The newcomer prospered in his adopted state. In Franklin's lively business atmosphere Marmaduke enthusiastically exploited the Santa Fe Trail's commercial opportunities. In 1824 he made the first of several trips to Santa Fe and kept a hand in this venture until the mid-1830s. Meanwhile, on January 4, 1826, he married Lavinia Sappington, the daughter of Arrow Rock's famed Dr. **John S. Sappington.** In so doing he benefited both professionally and politically. Appointed surveyor of Saline County, he platted the town site for Arrow Rock in 1829, and soon after joined Sappington in operating a general store at nearby Jonesboro.

About 1835 Marmaduke established himself on the large farm five miles west of Arrow Rock where his seven sons and three daughters grew to maturity. Involving himself with the Central Clique that was rising to dominate Missouri's Democracy, he secured his party's nomination for lieutenant governor in 1840 and swept into office on a ticket headed by Gov. **Thomas Reynolds.** Then, on February 9, 1844, Reynolds committed suicide, leaving Marmaduke to finish the final months of his term.

Marmaduke's brief tenure was hardly routine. His vigorous advocacy of mental–health care reforms led to early improvements in Missouri's handling of this problem. Also, auguring public tragedies to come was the issue of pardoning Alanson Work from the state penitentiary. Work and two associates from Connecticut had recently entered confinement for a heinous grand larceny: "enticing a slave out of the state. . . ." Abolitionist clamor for the inmates' release drew from Governor Marmaduke a firm refusal to pardon because of the disorderly furor such an act would generate.

Such conduct was not enough to win Marmaduke the nomination for a full term at the Democratic state convention that year. Instead, the party chose a "unity" candidate, John D. Edwards, who succeeded Marmaduke on November 20, 1844. This did not end Marmaduke's political career, however, for in 1845 he was elected as Saline County's delegate to a constitutional convention that vainly tried to reform the constitution of 1820. In 1848, as a firm ally of U.S. senator **Thomas Hart Benton** and with **Frank Blair** as his campaign manager, Marmaduke again sought the gubernatorial nomination. Again he was brushed aside for a compromise candidate, **Austin A. King,** at a convention torn again by the growing rift between Benton's "Hard" adherents and those "Soft" elements increasingly offended by Benton's antislavery inclinations.

Marmaduke might well thereafter have been content with a role as president of Saline County's first agricultural society and of the district fair association, but the deadly sectional crisis of 1860 propelled him onto the political stage one last time. His son

Vincent stood for election as a "firm Union" man to the Constitutional Convention chosen in early 1861 to debate secession. In the furor following the Camp Jackson affair on May 10, Vincent joined those bolting to the Confederate cause. His brother **John Sappington Marmaduke,** an 1857 graduate of West Point and future governor of Missouri, rose to major general in the Southern armies, and Vincent became a colonel after Union authorities "deported" him for "treasonous conduct."

Not so their father, whose judgments faithfully mirrored the complexities of Missouri's public opinion in that tormented hour. A Bentonite to the end, Marmaduke openly condemned secession. Emulating Gov. Sam Houston of Texas, he warned fellow citizens of the calamities awaiting them in their contemplation of civil strife. The contending parties treated Governor Marmaduke with profound respect, though he frankly and evenhandedly despised "thieving" Unionist militiamen and Confederate partisan "bushwhackers." By the time of his death on March 26, 1864, at his Saline County farmstead, his friends and neighbors had reason enough to regard him as prophetically "inspired."

R. LESLIE ANDERS

History of Saline County, Missouri. St. Louis: Missouri Historical Company, 1881.

Marmaduke, M. M. Manuscript Collection. Missouri State Historical Society, Columbia.

McCandless, Perry. *A History of Missouri: Volume II, 1820 to 1860.* Columbia: University of Missouri Press, 1972.

Napton, William Barclay. *Past and Present of Saline County, Missouri.* Indianapolis: B. F. Bowen, 1910.

MASSIE, GERALD R. (1911–1989)

Missouri's first official state photographer, Gerald R. Massie, preserved the beauty and the history of the state through his photographs from 1945 to 1974. He was born on September 22, 1911, in Clinton, Missouri, to William R. and Hazel Witt Massie.

Massie's interest in photography developed early in life when, at the age of ten, he won his first camera, a $1.98 Brownie. While attending Clinton High School, he became the first editor of the school paper, the *Cardinal.* Later, he was employed as a printer's devil at the *Clinton Eye,* learning Linotype operation. After graduation he joined the International Typographical Union, which enabled him to apply for a night position with the *Kansas City Star* as a journeyman Linotype operator. During the day he began a second career as a freelance photographer.

Massie's strong interest in photography followed him into the military. On March 10, 1942, he was drafted into the United States Strategic Air Force as an aerial photographer, technical sergeant. In this position he operated photographic equipment from aircraft in flight for the purpose of determining the effect of bombing missions for the Intelligence Office and News Releases. He assisted in the laboratory processing of still and motion pictures, and also took ground news pictures. After two years of service, he was promoted to master sergeant, photographic laboratory chief, and was in charge of a heavy bombardment–group photographic laboratory. While in the European theater, from September 5, 1942, to July 13, 1945, one of his bombing mission assignments included the first mass daylight raid on Berlin. When a bomber returning from the Continent to England crashed, three men were killed, and Massie was hospitalized. For his service he was awarded many medals, including Bronze Stars and a Good Conduct Medal.

Massie's first goal, after leaving the air force, was to marry Henrietta Hendrich, and the second was to think about a job in civilian life. He married Henrietta on September 22, 1945, in Clinton, and then sought employment in Jefferson City. He wanted to expand his military experience by using his photographic skills to serve and promote his state. He thought that Missouri could have its own photographer at a cheaper rate than hiring commercial cameramen to take scenic pictures. He was introduced to the director of the newly formed Resources and Development Commission (later called Commerce and Industrial Development), which was created by the General Assembly to publicize the state. Massie was hired by the commission to secure photos for their publications and to supply prints to publicize the state in the nation's newspapers and magazines.

The commission published pictorial booklets on areas of Missouri that were divided along watershed and recreational lines. According to Massie, this method of covering small areas in detail had never been attempted by any state. His responsibility was to document these areas fully, and photograph everything of interest therein. He covered his assignment thoroughly, by traveling fifteen to twenty thousand miles and by producing about two thousand photographs a year. He once climbed 1,771 feet for a photograph of Tom Sauk Mountain Falls, and descended 1,630 feet to document the first iron ore removed from a mine near Sullivan, Missouri. He produced sixteen pictorial booklets on Missouri regions.

In a 1948 interview in *U.S. Camera,* Massie said, "Imagination is seventy-five percent of photography. The idea must be firmly fixed before composition and balance are established. Every picture should tell a story, and the photographer must see his actors and props in their proper places on the ground glass before he releases the shutter."

Massie was an expert technician in the darkroom. He experimented with double-negative composites, time exposures, bas-relief, and infrared film for aerial photographs. He claimed artistic license for the composites, and said, "I have as much right to add certain elements to a photograph as a writer has to use adjectives." His images appeared in national magazines and newspapers, as well as Missouri state publications, encyclopedias, and school textbooks; they were also used to advertise Missouri in foreign countries, and reproduced on cake-box tins, china plates, silver spoons, silk scarves, glass, postcards, and puzzles.

In 1947 two of Massie's photographs, "Missouri Dragon" and "Sunset on the Lake of the Ozarks," were selected from one hundred best news shots in a national contest sponsored by the University of Missouri School of Journalism and the *Encyclopædia Britannica*. Massie said he derived his greatest satisfaction from the "Missouri Dragon," an aerial view of the Lake of the Ozarks taken on infrared film at ten thousand feet. Other popular images include the "Missouri Mules" and images of the mansion and the capitol. Massie photographed famous personalities such as Sir Winston Churchill, President **Harry S. Truman,** and **Thomas Hart Benton.**

Massie's period of state service stretched across the governorships of **Forrest C. Donnell, Phil M. Donnelly, Forrest Smith, John Montgomery Dalton, James Thomas Blair Jr.,** Warren Hearnes, and Christopher "Kit" Bond. In his more than twenty-eight years with the state, Massie served as acting director of his division three times, and at various intervals directed the Industrial, Tourism, Information, and Museum sections. The recipient of many professional awards, he was appointed to the Missouri Academy of Squires in 1961 by Governor Blair for his photographic achievements.

Massie's daughter, Kathleen, and son, Dan Thomas, were both born in Jefferson City where Massie served as an elder and deacon for the First United Presbyterian Church. He retired in 1974, and focused on his hobby of fine furniture construction until his death on May 11, 1989, in Jefferson City. In 1991 Massie's widow, Henrietta, donated thirty-five hundred photographs and negatives to the Missouri State Archives. Her gift allows the art of Gerald R. Massie to further enrich the lives of Missouri residents. The images he discovered through the camera lens tell the story of our state.

CAROLYN K. COLLINGS

Massie, Gerald R. Collection. Missouri State Archives, Jefferson City.

MAXWELL, JAMES (?–1814)

James Maxwell, the vicar-general of Spanish Illinois, Catholic pastor of Ste. Genevieve, and religious and civic leader in territorial Missouri, was born in Ireland in the early 1740s, and completed studies for the Catholic priesthood at the Irish College of the University of Salamanca in Spain. In 1794 the Spanish government sent him to Upper Louisiana Territory as vicar-general to newly appointed bishop Penalver y Cardenas of New Orleans.

Maxwell succeeded Paul Von Heilgenstien as pastor of Ste. Genevieve. Since the log rectory was in poor condition, Maxwell resided at the nearby village of New Bourbon. Bishop Penalver asked Maxwell to make a report about the religious situation in St. Louis. Maxwell determined that the settlement had no resident pastor and the small log church was dilapidated. Church records show that Maxwell also visited other parishes over the years, such as Florissant, Fredericktown, New Madrid, Cape Girardeau, Potosi, Old Mines, and Perryville. Eventually, he built a substantial residence in New Bourbon.

At the turn of the century, many Anglo-Americans from east of the Mississippi were crossing into Spanish territory. The Spanish government presumably thought that an English-speaking priest could deal effectively with these people, and could perhaps bring some of them into the Catholic Church. In this capacity the priest performed the weddings of many Protestant newcomers.

Father Maxwell looked upon the area as a refuge for his fellow Irish suffering under the English Penal Laws. He applied for and won extensive land grants of slightly more than one hundred thousand acres, roughly a hundred miles west of Ste. Genevieve between the Current and the Black Rivers. He opened a general store there and visited regularly, occasionally staying for weeks. Like many other settlers, Maxwell owned slaves.

Maxwell's nephew Hugh Maxwell came from Ireland and married Odile, a daughter of merchant-trader Pierre Menard of Kaskaskia, a friend of the priest. Unfortunately, not enough other Irish immigrants were able to settle on the granted lands. Years later, since the purpose had not been carried out, Father Maxwell's heirs could not sustain claim to the property.

At the end of the Spanish regime, Missouri was temporarily under the jurisdiction of the bishop of Baltimore. While Bishop Penalver and many priests of Spanish Illinois left for other assignments, Father Maxwell stayed. His facility with the English language gave him an opportunity to show his interest in public and political affairs.

In 1807 the citizens of Ste. Genevieve planned an academy and pledged three thousand dollars for that purpose. They elected Maxwell as chairman of the board of trustees. The territorial legislature chartered the school in 1808, but offered no further inducement. The federal government refused a land grant. Nonetheless, the board built a fine school building, and classes began in French and English with poor children and Indians educated free of charge. Unfortunately, a shortage of funds brought the school to a close in a few years.

In May 1810 Archbishop John Carroll of Baltimore wrote Father Maxwell in regard to complaints he had received about the Irish priest from forty-three heads of Anglo-American families and their Kentucky missionary, Father Stephen Badin. The archbishop did not list the complaints. Maxwell replied in November. He severely criticized French priests as "a jealous, meddling and troublesome set of men." His French parishioners, on the other hand, were good people. Not one French name appeared among the forty-three laymen who signed the letter of complaint.

Following the creation of the Missouri Territory in 1812, President James Madison appointed Maxwell to the legislative council. The newly formed body met on January 19, 1814, and elected Maxwell as its presiding officer. Before the second session, though, he had a fatal accident. As he returned on May 28, 1814, to his home in New Bourbon after services at the church in Ste. Genevieve, his horse shied unexpectedly and threw him against a fence. He died that night. A hill in Ste. Genevieve bears his name and recalls his memory.

WILLIAM B. FAHERTY

Rothensteiner, John. "Father James Maxwell of Ste. Genevieve." *St. Louis Catholic Historical Review* 4 (July 1922): 142–54.

MAYERBERG, SAMUEL S. (1892–1964)

Samuel S. Mayerberg, a Kansas City religious and civic leader, was born on May 8, 1892, in Goldsboro, North Carolina, the son of a rabbi, Julius L. Mayerberg. Samuel's parents encouraged his early interest in becoming a rabbi, but, by his own admission, he spent more time as a youth in pursuits other than Jewish studies. Following his graduation from high school in 1908, he went on to obtain bachelor and master of arts degrees from the University of Cincinnati. In 1917 he received a rabbinical degree from Hebrew Union College in Cincinnati, a center in the United States of Reform Judaism and his father's alma mater. The same year Samuel Mayerberg married Gertrude Rothschild of Cleveland, Ohio.

Prior to coming to Kansas City in 1925 as rabbi of Temple B'nai Jehudah, Mayerberg served for three years as assistant rabbi of Temple Beth-El in Detroit, Michigan, and for eight as rabbi of Congregation B'nai Jeshurun in Dayton, Ohio. Especially in Dayton, he engaged in a variety of activities, setting a pattern for the rest of his career. He was president of the Montgomery County chapter of the Red Cross, a member of a court-appointed board to construct a county orphanage, and an organizer of the Ohio Society for the Welfare of the Mentally Ill.

In Kansas City Mayerberg increasingly felt a religious obligation to speak out on public questions, despite warnings from important Jewish businessmen that he remain in the background. "This fearsome attitude of some prominent Jews always sickens me, and I am praying for the day when all Jews will be so completely filled with the spirit of American liberty, that they will not hesitate to fulfill public responsibility without fear of reaction or the pain of bigots and fanatics," he told students at Hebrew Union College in 1942. "I warn you that, when you are in active rabbinical service, situations will confront you which will require you to speak out as free men. Be sure you know the facts and that the facts are right; then speak honestly and courageously." His creed caused him in 1930 to attack a University of Missouri president for what he considered meddling in faculty affairs and in 1931 to accuse state officials of inadequately protecting an African American prisoner, **Raymond Gunn,** lynched by a large mob in Maryville, Missouri.

On May 21, 1932, in a lecture before a good-government club, Mayerberg launched a crusade for honest government in Kansas City, denouncing the practices of the all-powerful and notorious political organization headed by **Thomas J. Pendergast.** Mayerberg, later stating he believed ministers should never engage in partisan politics, said he unswervingly accepted the premise that when "depraved and selfish men" preyed upon a community, a religious leader had not only the "right" but also the "compelling duty" to lead a movement to eradicate "such fell powers." Given a climate of terror in Kansas City, Mayerberg's opposition, which made headlines in the *Kansas City Star,* carried considerable risk. Unknown parties tried to assassinate him in 1932, and machine propagandists embarked on a long-running campaign of slander and ridicule, depicting him as a fuzzy-headed do-gooder from out of town.

Mayerberg helped form the anti-Pendergast Charter League and, after declining to run for mayor, played a major role in organizing the National Youth Association, which in 1934 ran a slate of reform candidates in a bloody and fraudulent nonpartisan city election. Pendergast henchmen killed four people and injured dozens of others at the polls, and machine functionaries certified that an estimated sixty-five thousand illegal votes ensured victories by improbably large margins for most machine candidates. However, Mayerberg's leadership emboldened cleanup forces. After Pendergast went to jail in 1939, in honest elections reformers routed and destroyed the Pendergast machine at the municipal level and, as the Citizens Association, dominated Kansas City's municipal government in ensuing decades.

Mayerberg, throughout his thirty-two years as head rabbi of Temple B'nai Jehudah, remained active in Kansas City educational, religious, and civic life. He taught religious history at the University of Kansas and the University of Kansas City, discussed current literature before large public audiences, and lectured on a wide variety of subjects before organizations and university convocations. He adopted a modernist approach toward some aspects of the Jewish religion that sometimes caused controversy; for example, many rabbis objected to his proposal before the Central Conference of American Rabbis to abandon the observance of the Seventh Day of Passover. In 1957 Gov. **James T. Blair Jr.** appointed Mayerberg to the Kansas City Board of Police Commissioners, where he championed better wages for police- and firemen.

Mayerberg received many honors over the years, including a doctor of divinity degree from Hebrew Union College and an honorary doctorate in law from Park College. Fifty Protestant ministers honored him as a prophet of God. He was rabbi emeritus of Temple B'nai Jehudah at the time of his death from a heart attack on November 21, 1964.

In a nonreligious context, Mayerberg's most important contribution was his role in bringing down the Pendergast machine. An obituary writer in a Kansas City newspaper emphasized the controversial crusading side of the slightly built, intellectual, and courtly rabbi: "Outspoken in his convictions and always articulate in expressing them, Dr. Mayerberg earned many friends and followers at the same time he was making bitter enemies, many of whom even sought to kill him." Mayerberg compressed his own philosophy of life into a few words: "The end of the matter is this: to revere God and to follow all his commandments. This is the whole of the man."

LAWRENCE H. LARSON

Kansas City Times, November 22, 1964.

Mayerberg, Samuel. *Chronicle of an American Crusader.* New York: Block Publishing, 1944.

Reddig, William M. *Tom's Town: Kansas City and the Pendergast Legend.* 1947. Reprint, Columbia: University of Missouri Press, 1986.

McBRIDE, MARY MARGARET (1899–1976)

Described as neurotic and ample, Mary Margaret McBride became a great success on network radio while disclosing to the world her insecurity and guilt. Her accessible personality delighted "millions of American housewives, five days a week for more than 20 years. . . ."

Mary Margaret McBride was born in Paris, Missouri, on November 16, 1899. She once said her father, Thomas Walker McBride, was "a farmer with itchy feet, and no sooner would he get a run-down place in shape, then we'd move to another spread that needed fixing up." Her "warm and loving mother," Elizabeth Craig McBride, was the daughter of a Baptist minister. Mary Margaret attended Paris public schools until her great-aunt Albina sent her to William Woods in Fulton, Missouri, then a preparatory school, and the University of Missouri with the understanding that Mary Margaret would eventually "become associated" with William Woods. (Her great-aunt had given the school a large gift.) After one year at the university, Mary Margaret informed Albina that she wanted to be a writer. The money stopped, and Mary Margaret took a job on a Columbia newspaper at ten dollars per week to finance her education. She graduated from the School of Journalism in 1919.

McBride's ambition was to work for a newspaper in New York City and write a great novel. In her first job she went as far as Washington, D.C., where Douglas Meng, an old family friend who was assistant sergeant at arms of the United States Senate, desired to start "a news service, as a sideline, to supply small Missouri newspapers with on-the-spot Washington news." McBride stayed in Washington for less than a year.

During the next decade McBride held a variety of jobs, moving first to Cleveland to work as a general reporter at the *Cleveland Press,* which after a year led to a publicity job in New York City at the Interfaith Council headquarters. When the council had financial difficulties, McBride secured a job with the *New York Evening Mail,* where for the first year she worked as a "sob sister," reporting heartrending stories. Her first "front-page splash with a by-line" was an interview with two old ladies who had lost everything in a fire. In 1924 when the *Mail* was sold, McBride lost her job but was paid one hundred dollars per week for a year to complete her contract.

Stella Karn, a freelance publicity agent, persuaded McBride to take advantage of the situation and write freelance magazine articles, and from 1924 to 1929 McBride wrote for the *Saturday Evening Post, Cosmopolitan,* and several other publications. She also wrote books as a ghostwriter, as a collaborator, and on her own. During this time, she invested in the stock market, rented an apartment on Park Avenue, had an agent and a secretary, and vacationed in Europe.

McBride lost her investments because of the stock market crash, but the depression did not affect the magazine market until 1931. She earned forty thousand dollars in 1930, but during the next four years she experienced the most difficult times in her life.

In 1934 McBride auditioned for a possible women's program on station WOR and became Martha Deane, a kindly grandmother devoted to her large family. In fewer than three weeks on the air she became confused about "her family" and told her audience: "Look, I'm not a grandma, nor a mother, nor am I married. Why don't I just be myself?" She continued to use the name Martha Deane as long as she worked for WOR. McBride refused to advertise products in which she did not believe and either tested them herself or paid a laboratory to do the testing. She visited plants, met executives and workers, and told stories in her commercials about her experiences. Because of her Baptist training she refused to advertise tobacco products and alcohol. Listeners believed she "would only recommend the best." While still at WOR, she also edited the women's page of the *Newspaper Enterprise Association Syndicate* from 1934 to 1935 and in 1937 began appearing on a weekly fifteen-minute CBS program using her own name.

In 1938 the University of Missouri School of Journalism awarded McBride its honor medal. Two years later Missouri's governor, **Lloyd Stark,** proclaimed November 22 as Mary Margaret McBride Day in Missouri, and she returned to Mexico, Missouri, for the event. That same year she left WOR. She did not like the fifteen-minute format at CBS and in 1941 took a position with NBC for a weekly forty-five-minute program. There she secured an audience of millions with her half-hour interviews, fifteen minutes of homemaking tips, and ad-lib commercials.

McBride interviewed a great variety of people, from Eleanor Roosevelt to **Sally Rand,** and Gen. **Omar Bradley** to a flagpole sitter. "Experts regard[ed] her as a genius at making celebrities 'give' before the microphone." Once when she was late for a show she explained to her audience that she "had got caught in [her] corset zipper." It required the building janitor to disengage her and her physician to patch her up. She received one thousand letters a week, and if one of her shows contained controversy, she received as many as five thousand letters.

Stella Karn arranged the celebration of McBride's tenth anniversary on the radio at Madison Square Garden. On her fifteenth-year celebration she broadcast from Yankee Stadium with sixty-five thousand people in attendance. William Woods honored her twice, first by asking her to give the graduation address (the first woman to do so) at the fiftieth anniversary of the college and then by awarding her an honorary degree of letters at the school's centennial.

McBride retired from network radio on her twentieth anniversary and moved to her home in the Catskill Mountains. She broadcast three times a week from her living room and continued to write books as well as a daily newspaper column for the Associated Press. On April 7, 1976, Mary Margaret McBride died at her home after a long illness.

MAXINE J. CHRISTENSEN

Dains, Mary K., ed. *Show Me Missouri Women: Selected Biographies.* Kirksville, Mo.: Thomas Jefferson University Press, 1989.

McBride, Mary Margaret. *A Long Way from Missouri.* New York: G. P. Putnam's Sons, 1959.

———. *Out of the Air.* Garden City, N.Y.: Doubleday, 1960.

Missouri Authors File. State Historical Society of Missouri, Columbia.

New York Times, April 8, 1976.

Obituary. *Missouri Historical Review* 71 (October 1976): 126.

McCANSE, KEITH (1885–1964)

Gov. **Sam Baker**'s appointment of Keith McCanse as game and fish commissioner in 1925 made him the first professional conservationist named to fill an administrative and policy-making position in Missouri. He was the first commissioner with previous experience in the department, and in four years he utilized his skills as an administrator, conservationist, and publicist to move the agency from the realm of political patronage and make it a part of the governmental bureaucracy. During his one term, McCanse doubled the income of the Game and Fish Department and inaugurated a professional bookkeeping system, with detailed budget accounting and periodic inventories of department assets. Missouri increased the number of its state parks from four to fourteen and its fish hatcheries from two to seven. His work as a publicist has rarely been equaled. Shortly after his resignation in 1929, McCanse headed a group of St. Louis sportsmen who became the first to propose that the Game and Fish Department be placed under the control of a commissioner, thereby anticipating the 1936 constitutional amendment that created the modern Department of Conservation.

The Scotch-Irish McCanse family hailed from east Tennessee and migrated to the Ozarks about 1840. Grandfather William McCanse located in Mount Vernon in 1844, became a merchant, a multiple-term county treasurer, and the cofounder of the Farmers Bank. Keith's father, George, became the bank's largest stockholder and actively supported Republican gubernatorial candidates, a tradition that Keith emulated. George and Keith participated in the famous Galena-to-Branson float trips in the early twentieth century, and Keith became fast friends with Jesse Tolerton of Taney County, the game and fish commissioner in Gov. **Herbert Hadley**'s administration of 1908 to 1912.

McCanse was born on May 10, 1885, and was schooled in accounting, banking, and insurance. Beginning in 1908 he worked for financial institutions in Springfield and Joplin and for the Missouri secretary of state before assuming a position with the St. Louis Southern Surety Company in 1914. Later he moved to Kansas City where he became a successful stockbroker.

In 1919, however, McCanse suffered from multiple physical ailments and at age thirty-four moved to Taney County with his wife and two small children to regain his health. He survived the dreaded flu epidemic, but lost sight in his left eye.

The new Lake Taneycomo district on White River had become a haven for outdoorsmen and journalists and, in an unforeseen development, had created an outdoor laboratory for the exchange of ideas concerning conservation. In 1921 McCanse assumed the position of local game warden, and his speaking engagements throughout southwest Missouri made him one of the most effective proponents of conservation in the state. He was co-organizer of the local Sportsman's League that lobbied for innovative legislation, and with the founding of the Izaak Walton League in 1923 he became a well-known Waltonian.

In 1925 as commissioner of the Game and Fish Department, McCanse revolutionized the agency. He established three divisions: Fish Hatcheries, State Parks and Game Refuges, and Enforcement. He created professional positions, including chief clerk, attorney, and director of public information. He favored the public relations section and gave his personal attention to the creation of the monthly *Missouri Game and Fish News,* forerunner to the *Missouri Conservationist.* By 1927 he began using radio to promote departmental goals. Soon, McCanse ventured into film and by 1929 had commissioned six reels of motion pictures to spread his "gospel of conservation."

McCanse expanded the number of locations where citizens could purchase hunting and fishing licenses by allowing banks, hardware stores, drugstores, and other cooperative businesses to sell them. The increase in sales enlarged revenue and enabled McCanse to implement summer training seminars for members of the department. The increased income also permitted him to hire more than one hundred additional deputies for the field. With widening audiences, McCanse used the *Game and Fish News* to

publish rosters of float-fishing outfitters statewide, another commencement in outdoor promotion.

While McCanse's Republican connections proved useful, his hard work earned him influence in state and national game and wildlife associations. He was a member of an eleven-man committee that successfully lobbied for congressional passage of the Migratory Bird Refuge Bill, and in 1927 he spent several weeks in Pennsylvania, a leading state in the conservation movement, to acquire new ideas for Missouri.

In 1929 McCanse began working for KMOX radio in St. Louis, doubling his salary. He promoted conservation and Ozarks recreation as a public speaker and spokesman for the Ozarks Playgrounds Association and the Missouri Ozarks Chamber of Commerce. He also published his family-produced annual, *Where to Go in the Ozarks,* as the first comprehensive guide to Ozarks tourism.

After failing as a Republican candidate for lieutenant governor in 1932 and in his speculative Sunrise Beach promotion on the newly created Lake of the Ozarks, McCanse returned to financial management. His work took him to Texas where he remained active in real estate promotion and Republican politics for the rest of his life. Keith McCanse died on October 2, 1964.

LYNN MORROW

Game and Fish News, 1925–1929.

Morrow, Lynn. "Keith McCanse: Missouri's First Professional Conservationist." *White River Valley Historical Quarterly* 31 (winter 1992): 3–12.

McCLURG, JOSEPH WASHINGTON (1818–1900)

Joseph Washington McClurg was Missouri's second and final Radical Republican governor, serving from 1869 to 1871. His one term represented the brief zenith and quick demise of Radical political power in the state. Both before and after his gubernatorial years, McClurg engaged in frontier trading and industry, along with promoting the Union cause. He was also known as an honest Presbyterian who consistently acted upon the dictates of his conscience.

McClurg's grandfather migrated from Ulster, Ireland, to Pittsburgh, Pennsylvania, arriving with enough resources to commence a mercantile business and a foundry. His father, also named Joseph, owned an iron business in Ohio. In 1814 the elder McClurg married St. Louisan Mary Brotherton. The future Missouri governor was born four years later on February 22, 1818. He attended Ohio academies, taught school in Mississippi during 1835–1836, and became a St. Louis County deputy sheriff in 1837–1838, working for his uncle, Sheriff James Brotherton.

Young Joseph continued exploring new horizons. He traveled to Texas, studied law and passed the bar, and served as clerk of a circuit court from 1839 to 1841. All the while he corresponded with Mary Johnson, a lady whom he had met in Farmington. He returned to Missouri in 1841 to marry her. Mary McClurg's stepfather, William Murphy, was a frontier entrepreneur, and following his marriage Joseph entered a decades-long association with Murphy and other relatives in merchandising throughout the interior counties of the Ozarks.

McClurg mined lead and managed a country mercantile in southwest Missouri before joining the '49ers gold rush to California. He stayed in the Golden State two years, selling goods in a store. He returned to Missouri in June 1851, and within a year he joined relatives on the Osage River in a wholesale and retail business, known as McClurg, Murphy, and Jones. By 1855 the firm influenced the creation of a new county seat at Linn Creek, which was superior to Erie in Camden County as a steamboat landing. By 1861 McClurg's partners had died, and new family members, E. B. Torbert and Marshall Johnson, took their places.

At the beginning of the Civil War, McClurg immediately took up the cause of the Union and organized the Osage Regiment of Missouri Volunteers and the Hickory County Battalion. Now Colonel McClurg, he suffered the loss of his wife, Mary, in October 1861. After assigning the care of his children to family and friends, he turned his energies toward the war. He attended the emancipation convention in Jefferson City in June 1862, and the following November voters in the Fifth District elected him to the first of three congressional terms. In the explosive years of the 1860s McClurg joined storekeepers, country doctors, and other nonprofessional politicians who assumed leadership roles.

The Rebels retaliated against McClurg for his role as a catalyst for Unionists in the Osage country. Southern sympathizers burned his mercantile store in Linn Creek twice; the losses totaled more than $150,000 in goods by March 1863. The congressman wrote letters comforting his children who were in Ohio attending school, and by the fall of 1863 he more forcefully established his support for abolition by freeing his own slaves. During the summer of that fateful year, McClurg's business partner Torbert fled to St. Louis with the firm's remaining resources from Linn Creek. McClurg subsequently labored for a generation to methodically retire his debts and interest payments, and to satisfy former partner Torbert's financial demands for merchandise McClurg had given to the Union cause.

In July 1868 Missouri's Radicals nominated McClurg for governor. At the height of Radical political power, he defeated the Democratic nominee, Congressman **John S. Phelps** of Springfield. As a result of the "Drake Constitution" of 1865, McClurg became the first two-year-term governor. McClurg's devotion to the intransigent **Charles Daniel Drake** caused his own political fortunes to wane with those of Missouri's "truest" Radical.

McClurg was not an orator, but his term was free of scandal, and he followed a conservative fiscal policy that cut the state debt in half. His eldest daughter, Fannie McClurg, was hostess at the Governor's Mansion where polite society heard the governor's lectures against the use of alcoholic beverages, a sentiment not favored by the heavy German population along the Missouri River. Noteworthy in his administration were the foundings of the Rolla School of Mines, the Agriculture School at the University of Missouri, and state teachers colleges at Warrensburg and Kirksville.

McClurg's tenure, however, was known more as a time of growing dissatisfaction with disfranchisement and party strife. The governor pleased Drake by purging dissidents among state employees and requiring that 5 percent of the remaining employees' annual salaries be donated to the Radical campaign fund. Other voices in Missouri, however, called for an end to Radical-sponsored restrictions on voting and the rights of citizenship. This sentiment eventually led to the establishment of the Liberal Republican Party, which brought about the end of Radicalism in Missouri. Postwar society and business relations between former combatants demanded full political participation by all, according to the Liberal Republicans. Although the Radicals nominated McClurg again, Liberal Republican **B. Gratz Brown,** with Democratic support, defeated him in 1870 in a landslide victory.

In 1871 the fifty-two-year-old McClurg returned to Linn Creek to again take up his varied business enterprises of merchandising, mining, steamboats, and land speculation. Once again, family members, sons-in-law Charles Draper and Marshall Johnson, formed a company: Draper, McClurg, and Company. Profits in merchandising fueled exploration and excavation of surface lead and iron in Missouri's Central Lead District near the Osage River. The company operated as many as four steamboats on the Osage and Missouri Rivers. Their shipping points became trade centers for railroad ties more than for metals as the depression in the 1870s spelled an end to their prospecting for minerals.

The former governor did succeed in gaining government contracts for improvements on the Osage River. Removal of sandbars and channeling revived the lower Osage traffic. Men who worked for the

Presbyterian McClurg remembered his intolerance of profanity and his insistence on resting by the riverside on Sundays, regardless of the urgency of their work.

By 1885 profits were low, and creditors and the courts seized McClurg's steamer, *Emma.* Within the year he sold his Camden County lands, Linn Creek town lots, and his 1850s country mansion. In 1886, instead of retirement, the entrepreneur and family members headed for a new homestead on the high plains of South Dakota. A year later Charles Draper brought them back to Lebanon.

In 1889 McClurg received an appointment as government land-office receiver in Springfield, Missouri. For four years the registrar worked in what would be his final political job. In 1893 he returned to Lebanon, where he taught Sunday school, visited the public schools, and took an active village elder's role in local society. On December 2, 1900, he died at the Charles Draper farm north of Lebanon.

LYNN MORROW

McClurg-Draper Papers. Western Historical Manuscripts Collection, Columbia.

Morrow, Lynn. "Joseph Washington McClurg: Entrepreneur, Politician, Citizen." *Missouri Historical Review* 78 (January 1984): 168–201.

Shoemaker, Floyd Calvin. *Missouri and Missourians: Land of Contrasts and People of Achievements.* Chicago: Lewis Publishing, 1943.

McCOY, ISAAC (1784–1846)

Isaac McCoy was born on June 13, 1784, in Fayette County, Pennsylvania. At the age of six, he traveled with his family to the vicinity of Louisville, Kentucky, where his father, William, served as an itinerant preacher. The younger McCoy received no formal education, but wishing to become a minister like his father, he learned to read and write through religious instruction at home. In 1803 he married Christiana Polke and moved to Vincennes, Indiana. For several years he had no opportunity to preach and served as the town's jailer until he received his first call in 1810 from the Maria Creek Baptist Church.

In 1816 McCoy gained a one-year appointment from the Baptist Board of Foreign Missions to minister to both whites and Indians in the West. Focusing most of his efforts on the region's Indians, he founded a mission and school among the Miami tribe in western Indiana. His purpose was to provide Indian children free instruction in agriculture, religion, and other "civilizing" customs. While engaged in this enterprise, McCoy observed firsthand the destructive consequences of whiskey and disease and the decimation of wildlife that accompanied the westward movement of whites into frontier regions. He noted similar conditions at missions that he founded near

Fort Wayne, Indiana, and at Niles and Grand Rapids, Michigan.

These observations led McCoy to conclude that the federal government must take action to protect the Indians by removing the tribes from the bad influence of whites. Always short of cash, he raised money locally and gained the support of Michigan's governor, Lewis Cass. McCoy also made frequent trips to the East and to Washington, D.C., to raise funds and promote his plans.

In 1827 McCoy published *Remarks on the Practicability of Indian Reform Embracing Their Colonization,* in which he detailed his plans for Indian removal as an expedient to prevent the continued disintegration of the tribes. Believing the Indians held legal title to their traditional lands, he argued that the United States should pay a fair price for them. With this money the government could establish interest-accruing trusts from which the tribes could receive annuities and other benefits. The lands west of Iowa, Missouri, and Arkansas would be set aside permanently for Indian habitation. By settling in territories isolated from whites, McCoy asserted that missionaries could then properly Christianize and civilize the Indians at mission schools.

In 1828 Congress appropriated money to find suitable sites for Indian relocation. As one of the commissioners appointed to travel with Indian delegations into the West, McCoy inspected lands that Congress proposed to exchange for Native homelands. From August through October the commissioners and delegations traveled along the Osage, Neosho, and Kansas Rivers, inspecting the land bordering these waterways.

The following year McCoy investigated the Kansas River valley region looking for a suitable home for the Potawatomi and Ottawa Indians. In November he traveled to Washington and participated in the Indian-removal debate, appearing before the House Committee on Indian Affairs. While McCoy recognized the problems of Jackson's Indian policy, he was certain that without removal the eastern tribes could not survive.

In 1830 McCoy accepted an appointment to survey the new Indian territory and soon became involved in work on the Shawnee reservation near present-day Kansas City. He was sufficiently committed to this work to purchase a nearby tract of land. During this time he also sought to reduce tensions between Missourians and Mormons who were rapidly filling Missouri's Jackson County, which their leader, **Joseph Smith Jr.,** had designated as the location for Zion.

In 1832 McCoy established a mission seven miles from the juncture of the Kansas and Missouri Rivers and three miles west of the state line. He acquired a printing press and published a newspaper, the *Shawanoe Sun,* edited by Johnston Lykins, McCoy's son-in-law. They also printed a translation of part of the New Testament in the Shawnee language. However, McCoy's vision of a separate Indian country had no chance for fulfillment because the force of white migration had already brought settlers into the territory reserved for the Indians.

During his final years McCoy continued his beneficent work for the Indians, despite many difficulties and disappointments. He accepted a position in Louisville, Kentucky, as corresponding secretary of the American Indian Mission Association and wrote *The History of Baptist Indian Missions* and several numbers of the *Annual Register of Indian Affairs within the Indian Territory.* On June 21, 1846, McCoy died in Louisville, Kentucky.

DENNIS K. BOMAN

Annals of Kansas City. Kansas City: Missouri Valley Historical Society, 1921.

McCoy, Isaac. *Remarks on the Practicability of Indian Reform Embracing Their Colonization.* New York: Gray and Bunce, 1829.

Schultz, George A. *An Indian Canaan: Isaac McCoy and the Vision of an Indian State.* Norman: University of Oklahoma Press, 1972.

Shoemaker, Floyd C., ed. *Missouri, Day by Day.* Vol. 1. Columbia: State Historical Society of Missouri, 1942.

McCOY, JOHN CALVIN (1811–1889)

John Calvin McCoy is a prominent figure in the history of early Kansas City. He came to the Kawsmouth region in 1830 when it was still a frontier settlement of French and Indian fur traders and a few Anglo pioneers. He spent a lifetime there, founding the town of Westport in 1833 and watching the region change from a raw wilderness to a metropolis of belching smokestacks, iron bridges, and fast-moving cable cars. He played a pivotal role in the birth of Kansas City, but looked on his efforts in later years with a bittersweet pride, not at all certain the change was for the better.

McCoy, born at Vincennes, Indiana, on September 28, 1811, was the son of the prominent Baptist missionaries Isaac and Christiana Polke McCoy, remembered for their work on behalf of American Indians. Like his father, John C. McCoy (known to friends as Calvin) was high-principled, generous, and intelligent, yet he owned slaves. He so sympathized with the Southern cause that he temporarily fled Kansas City during the Civil War. His son, Spencer Cone McCoy, was a Confederate soldier, killed in 1861 at the Battle of Wilson's Creek.

A man who loved mathematics, McCoy worked as a surveyor, building contractor, and realtor. Yet, he possessed a poetic vein that led, perhaps, to his most important work: a rich body of reminiscences that he wrote over a number of years for the *Kansas City Journal,* signing himself "An Old-Timer." His writings are a delightful and vital contribution to Kansas City's early history, especially as they diverge from the formal tradition first recorded by the city's 1850s boosters who promoted Kansas City as a "place of destiny," blessed by geography and visionary, enterprising businessmen. While the town boosters fashioned a story of unbridled success, McCoy snickered and spoke of the town's first history, Charles Spalding's 1858 *Annals of the City of Kansas,* "as puff for the young town" and a "stereotyped fraud" that became history.

When McCoy spoke of the high bluffs on which Kansas City was built, he spoke of "those unpromising hills." Far from envisioning a great metropolis at the confluence of the Kansas and Missouri Rivers, McCoy said the town's fourteen founders, himself among them, wanted only "to make a few dollars each." In 1838 they formed the Town of Kansas Company, a speculative land venture that included a steamboat landing at the site of what is now Kansas City. The landing served as a gateway to Westport, a town four miles south that McCoy had founded in 1833. Hoping to tap into the nearby Indian and Santa Fe trades, he opened Westport's first store but soon sold it. "He was not fitted by nature or inclination for a mercantile life," his daughter Nellie McCoy Harris later said.

McCoy first came to the Kawsmouth region in August 1830 as part of a surveying party led by his father, who had long championed legislation to remove eastern Indian tribes west of the Mississippi River where he thought they could be free from the negative influences, such as whiskey, brought on by contact with white frontiersmen. Soon after Congress passed the Indian Removal Act of 1830, **Isaac McCoy** was commissioned to survey a boundary for the soon-to-emigrate Delaware Indians. He took two of his sons along: Rice McCoy, as assistant surveyor, and John Calvin, just nineteen years old, as "baggage master."

Years later, John McCoy recalled how the party, which also included two white men as chain carriers and a black man as cook, passed single file through the public square in Independence, which then was a town of about 150 people. They stopped to buy provisions and then headed "across the stump-covered ground" toward the western Missouri border.

"The picture as I first saw it," McCoy wrote, was of "precipitous hills, deep, impassable gorges and of the dense forests." The Kansas River bottoms, which later teemed with stockyards and railroad tracks, were so thick with vines, brushwood, and fallen timber as to be "almost impenetrable." Here and there, "the cabin of a settler peeped from the wilderness and now and then a canoe, with an Indian at the paddle." Mostly, however, he remembered "the still, quiet solitude interrupted only by the barking squirrel, the howl of the wolf, the distant baying of the hunter's dog."

Years later when the high bluffs had been leveled and the city's population had mushroomed, McCoy longed "for the good old days of genuine disinterested honesty . . . when one might lie down to sleep without fear of having his throat cut, his pockets picked, or the socks stolen off his feet."

McCoy acquired much property in Kansas City, operated a ferry, and served as a Jackson County surveyor in 1836, as a director of Mechanic's Bank, and as a deacon at Central Presbyterian Church. He built one of the first brick houses in the city, owned a farm south of town, planted trees, and built and rented property.

McCoy married twice. His first wife, Virginia Chick, died on May 28, 1849, during a cholera epidemic. He remarried, on April 17, 1850, to Elizabeth Woodson Lee, a widow. McCoy died at his home on September 2, 1889, just shy of his seventy-eighth birthday. He left his widow and seven surviving children. He is buried in Kansas City's Union Cemetery.

Kansas City newspapers eulogized him as "the last of the historic 14," the "great patriarch of Kansas City," and the "veteran pioneer" who was recognized as an authority on all matters pertaining to the town's early history.

SHIRL KASPER

Kansas City Journal, September 3, 1889.
Kansas City Star, September 2, 1889.
Kansas City Times, September 3, 1889.
McCoy, Isaac. Papers. John C. McCoy Collection. Kansas State Historical Society, Topeka.
McCoy, John C. File. Special Collections Department. Kansas City Public Library, Kansas City.
McCoy, John Calvin. Scrapbooks. Native Sons Collection. Western Historical Manuscripts Collection, Kansas City.

McCOY, JOSEPH GEITING (1837–1915)

Joseph Geiting McCoy was born in Sangamon County, Illinois, on December 21, 1837, the son of David and Mary Kilpatrick McCoy. He spent his early life on a farm about ten miles west of Springfield, Illinois. He attended a local rural school for his elementary education and enrolled at Knox College in Galesburg for the 1857–1858 school year. He married Sarah Epler of Pleasant Plains, Illinois,

on October 22, 1861. The union produced seven children.

Joseph McCoy began a career as a livestock trader in 1861. By the end of the Civil War he was purchasing, feeding, transporting, and selling large numbers of cattle, mules, hogs, and sheep. By the late 1860s he joined a trading firm operated by his brothers, William and James, known as "William K. McCoy and Brothers." It was apparently also during this period that Joseph decided on a plan to find a suitable place in the North to which Texas cattle could be driven for shipment to packers in northern and eastern states. The deadly splenic fever, or "Texas fever," carried by the Texas longhorns had hindered the transport of Texas cattle to new markets. While the Texas stock was largely resistant to the disease, the fever was lethal to domestic stock. In 1867 the Kansas legislature passed a quarantine law that permitted the driving of longhorns through limited, unsettled parts of the state. The statue also authorized the shipment of Texas cattle through Kansas by rail.

Although McCoy was not the first to propose a scheme for transporting Texas cattle to urban markets, he managed to persuade Texas ranchers to drive their cattle to Abilene. He had already secured a deal with the eastern division of the Union Pacific for the transport of the cattle. In addition, he built the three-story Drovers Cottage hotel with a livery stable, constructed his own stockyards, and established a bank. Yet, all this was done at great financial risk because the law did not allow Texas cattle across land leading to Abilene. McCoy was able to procure Gov. Samuel Crawford's " 'semi-official' endorsement of the Abilene location" for a market. This, coupled with the reluctance of Dickinson County officials to enforce the quarantine law, made way for the first cattle drive to Abilene in September 1867.

Over the next four years, Abilene grew from a community of "about one dozen loghuts" into the main shipping point for Texas cattle. In 1871 McCoy was elected mayor of Abilene. During his tenure he appointed "Wild Bill" Hickok as town marshal. McCoy appeased his supporters by creating a "covert assessment of gamblers and prostitutes" instead of raising the town's liquor-license fees. Political infighting and McCoy's "recklessly overbearing administrative style" prevented him from serving another term. However, by this time Abilene had reached its apex as the center of the cattle drives. Punitive shipping rates and the encroachment of settlers purchasing land in Dickinson County led to the creation of new cattle towns down the line.

In 1872 McCoy moved to Wichita where he promoted the Chisholm Trail and engaged in the sale of wrought-iron fencing. He then moved to Kansas City, Missouri, in 1873 and established the livestock commission firm of Joseph G. McCoy. He also helped organize the Live Stock Men's National Association in Kansas City, serving as its first corresponding secretary. McCoy believed that this organization would help cattlemen make better marketing decisions. By acting in concert, they would be protected from "oppression and outrage at the hands of strong monopolies."

McCoy later worked for the United States Census Bureau, gathering statistics about livestock. He found employment as an agent for the Cherokee Nation, collecting taxes on the cattle that grazed on their land. McCoy moved back to Wichita where he drifted between various occupations. He then moved to Oklahoma and actively encouraged white settlement in the territory. In 1890 he lost an election to become a territorial representative in Congress. Three years later he was appointed by the Treasury Department to deter the opium traffic in the Pacific Northwest. With failing health, McCoy returned to Kansas City in 1914, where he died on October 19, 1915.

For all McCoy's accomplishments, he is best remembered for his description of the Texas longhorn cattle drives. *Historic Sketches of the Cattle Trade of the West and Southwest,* published in 1874, is the only account written by "an eyewitness and a participant." It is considered to be one of the most important works written on the subject.

KRISTINE STILWELL AND GARY R. KREMER

Atherton, Lewis. *The Cattle Kings.* Bloomington: Indiana University Press, 1961.

Dictionary of American Biography. Vol. 11. S.v. "McCoy, Joseph Geiting."

Dykstra, Robert R. *The Cattle Towns.* New York: Knopf, 1968.

McCoy, Joseph G. *Historic Sketches of the Cattle Trade of the West and Southwest.* Ed. Ralph P. Bieber. 1874. Reprint, Glendale, Calif.: Arthur Clark, 1940.

McCOY, WILLIAM (1813–1900)

William McCoy, considered "one of the most influential residents of western Missouri," was born in Chillicothe, Ohio, on May 14, 1813. He was one of seven children born to John McCoy, a dry goods merchant. After attending the local academy, William was afforded the opportunity to pursue a higher education. After graduating in 1831 from a college in Athens, Ohio, he studied medicine but decided not to enter the profession.

In 1838 McCoy, his brother John, and a business partner, Carey A. Lee, were outfitted with the stock from the senior McCoy's operation. For about six years they did business in Ohio. Then they moved to Missouri, their destination supposedly determined

by the toss of a coin. When the young men arrived in Independence, they established their dry goods store on Liberty Street. There they sold merchandise to local settlers and outfitted pioneers heading west on the overland trails. The trade proved quite lucrative, but the duties of maintaining the store also occasioned minor regrets for McCoy. In 1841 he wrote a letter to his brother Samuel, saying, "We are pushing the frontier 2000 miles beyond us. Nothing will stop the westward march but the eternal barrier of the Pacific. I should like to take the journey to enlarge my observations of the world but of course cannot. . . . Years have come upon me so fast that I cannot spare the time."

By 1848 the McCoys expanded the scope of their business ventures. The brothers, in cooperation with **David Waldo, Silas Woodson,** and James Brown, formed a company to transport supplies to United States Army outposts in the West. Two years later William McCoy, David Waldo, and Jacob Hall successfully secured the first government contract for delivering the U.S. mail from Independence to Santa Fe. The mail contract did not generate the desired profits, and it was not renewed when it expired in 1854. On the heels of this venture, McCoy, Waldo, and others created a coal company that seemed to promise a profitable return. However, the Civil War interfered with operations and led to the termination of the enterprise. When the war broke out, the community of Independence was divided in its sympathies. McCoy spoke publicly in support of the federal government and tried to minimize the hostilities among his neighbors.

McCoy found his final calling in finance. In 1857 he assisted in the formation of the Independence Savings Institution, the first private bank in Independence. During the Civil War he was a member of the banking firm of Stone, McCoy, and Company. Later he worked for the First National Bank, where he had the dubious distinction of being briefly locked in the bank vault after an armed robbery. By 1880 his son, A. L. McCoy, joined him in the banking business. By 1886 William McCoy was president of the McCoy Banking Company and his son served as cashier. He retired from banking entirely in 1898.

During his lifetime McCoy was actively involved in civic affairs and assisted in the development of Independence. He was elected the first mayor in 1849, fulfilling a one-year term. He helped to organize the Independence public schools and was treasurer on the first board of directors. He was a member of the first board of trustees for the First Presbyterian Church in Independence and served as an elder in the church for many years. He was one of the petitioners and board members for the Independence Female College, established in 1871 and subsequently known as the Kansas City Ladies' College until its closing in 1905.

On September 13, 1900, McCoy died in Independence, Missouri. His wife, Eleanor Waddle McCoy, preceded him in death. The couple had two children, A. L. McCoy and Nannie McCoy Miner, both of Independence.

KRISTINE STILWELL

Conard, Howard L., ed. *Encyclopedia of the History of Missouri.* New York: Southern History, 1901.

Goodrich, James W. "In the Earnest Pursuit of Wealth: David Waldo in Missouri and the Southwest." *Missouri Historical Review* 66 (January 1972): 173–77.

The History of Jackson County, Missouri. Index ed. Kansas City, Mo.: Union Historical Company, 1881.

McCoy, Alexander. *Pioneering on the Plains, Journey to Mexico in 1848, the Overland Trip to California.* Kankauna, Wis.: privately printed, 1924.

Wilcox, Pearl. *Jackson County Pioneers.* Independence, Mo.: privately published, ca. 1975.

McDERMOTT, JOHN FRANCIS, III (1902–1981)

One of the foremost authorities on the early history of culture, art, and society in the Mississippi Valley from colonial times to the mid-nineteenth century, John Francis McDermott III produced many seminal monographs and trenchant articles that focused both scholarly and popular attention on the contributions of St. Louis and the state of Missouri to national development. As an Americanist of the first rank in his generation, McDermott has long been appreciated as a pioneering figure in the interdisciplinary American-studies movement.

Born in St. Louis on April 18, 1902, McDermott was the son of John F. and Mary Steber McDermott. His father practiced law in St. Louis. The young McDermott attended Price School and, later, Clayton High School. Graduating from Washington University in 1923, he received a master of arts degree in English from that institution in 1924, the same year in which he married Mary Stephanie Kendrick. The marriage produced one child, John Francis McDermott IV.

From 1924 to 1936 McDermott was an instructor in English at Washington University. He became an assistant professor in 1936 and an associate professor in 1949, a position he held until 1961, when he became associate professor of American cultural history. In 1963 he became a research professor of the humanities at Southern Illinois University at Edwardsville. He retired in 1971, becoming research professor emeritus.

During his nearly fifty years of service at two universities, McDermott enjoyed a productive career in writing, research, teaching, and speaking. As a young instructor of English he edited a trade edition of *The Collected Verse of Lewis Carroll.* He also coauthored with Kendall Taft and Dana Jensen the popular textbook *The Technique of Composition,* which went through several editions.

By the mid-1930s McDermott translated his general love of writing and textual editing into a lifelong study of the cultural growth of his native Missouri. Beginning with such short pieces as "Paincourt and Poverty" in *Mid-America* and "The Confines of a Wilderness" in the *Missouri Historical Review,* he examined the region's local story within the national and international context of French colonial history.

In 1938 McDermott published *Private Libraries in Creole St. Louis.* By this time he was regularly producing published papers about the history of printing, books, journalism, and settled institutions of the early Mississippi Valley. A strong theme developed in all his subsequent work that celebrated what he felt was the neglected record of steady cultural growth, sophistication, and progress in the region. He also began producing editions of early pioneers' journals, diaries, and rare printed or manuscript accounts and letters by the keenest observers of the frontier period, including Washington Irving, John Treat Irving, Alfred S. Waugh, Matthew C. Field, and **Henry Marie Brackenridge.** McDermott began a long association with the University of Oklahoma Press when he edited such works as *Tixier's Travels on the Osage Prairies* (1940) as well as *The Western Journals of Washington Irving* (1944) and Irving's *Tour on the Prairies* (1956).

McDermott's best-known works nationally were his major contributions as an art historian for the painters of St. Louis and the trans-Mississippi West, many of whom at various times had maintained studios in the old frontier river town. Monographs and shorter pieces included important studies about **George Caleb Bingham,** Seth Eastman, John James Audubon, **Charles Deas, John Casper Wild,** Nicolas Point, Titian Peale, **Peter Rindisbacher,** Samuel Seymour, Leon Pomarede, John Banvard, and **Henry Lewis.** Often McDermott produced the first major, modern data on his subjects, rescuing them from near oblivion and paving the way for further research.

In Missouri McDermott is perhaps best known for his unflagging interest in the founding families of St. Louis, especially the lives of **Pierre de Laclède Liguest** and **Auguste Chouteau.** Through an important series of published symposia in the 1960s and 1970s, McDermott brought together his and his colleagues' best writing connecting the history of St. Louis with the history of the Mississippi Valley and the trans-Mississippi West. These edited collections include *Research Opportunities in American Cultural History* (1961), *The French in the Mississippi*

Valley (1965), *The Frontier Re-examined* (1967), *Frenchmen and French Ways in the Mississippi Valley* (1969), *Travelers on the Western Frontier* (1970), and *The Spanish in the Mississippi Valley, 1762–1804* (1974).

McDermott promoted the publication of the primary documents and basic texts of St. Louis history. He founded the St. Louis Historical Documents Foundation, which published under his specific or general editorship *The Early Histories of St. Louis* (1952), *Old Cahokia* (1949), and *Before Lewis and Clark: Documents Illustrating the History of the Missouri, 1785–1804,* by Abraham P. Nasatir (1952). He was the general editor of a noted series of works long out of print and other primary sources, *Travels on the Western Waters,* for Southern Illinois University Press. He also produced important reference works, including *A Glossary of Mississippi Valley French* (1941).

McDermott held numerous professional memberships and was the associate editor for the *French-American Review.* He served on the editorial board of the *Old Northwest,* and was a trustee of the Missouri Historical Society, the William Clark Society, and a founder of the St. Louis chapter of the Westerners International.

McDermott received many academic honors, including awards from the French and Spanish governments and from academic societies in those countries. He was awarded honorary doctorates in humane letters from the University of Missouri–St. Louis and from Southern Illinois University at Edwardsville. He was the recipient of numerous research grants and fellowships, including a Guggenheim Fellowship in 1954, a Newberry Library Fellowship in Midwestern Studies in 1947, and many grants from the American Philosophical Society from 1939 to 1964. At the time of his death on April 23, 1981, John Francis McDermott was involved in a number of unfinished research projects, including a long-intended biography of his famous ancestor **Pierre de Laclède.**

JOHN NEAL HOOVER

Foley, William E. "The Laclède-Chouteau Puzzle: John Francis McDermott Supplies Some Missing Pieces." *Gateway Heritage* 4 (fall 1983): 18–25.

McDermott, John Francis. Research Collection. Southern Illinois University at Edwardsville.

St. Louis Globe. Research Collection. St. Louis Mercantile Library. University of Missouri–St. Louis.

McDONALD, JOHN (1832–1912)

John McDonald's name was well known in St. Louis in the late 1870s for his involvement in the infamous Whiskey Ring scandal of 1875. Through the workings of the ring, he exercised a considerable amount of influence on national politics during the Grant administration.

Born in Rochester, New York, in 1832, McDonald was orphaned before he was ten years old and forced to make his own way in life. He reportedly worked his way west, picking up whatever odd jobs he could along the inland waterways—the canals, lakes, and rivers—eventually arriving in St. Louis at about age fifteen. Although lacking formal education he moved into successively more responsible and better-paid positions within the river trade. By the 1850s he was a passenger agent for steamboat companies in St. Louis and later owned and operated his own steamer, carrying freight and passengers on the Missouri River.

At the outbreak of the Civil War McDonald, a strong Union supporter, raised and outfitted the Eighth Missouri Regiment, sworn in by **Nathaniel Lyon** at the arsenal at the beginning of the war. The Eighth Missouri saw action in many of the western campaigns, fighting in the Battles of Fort Henry, Fort Donelson, and Shiloh. Elected major of his unit, McDonald was later appointed a brigadier general by President Lincoln and served under Gen. **William T. Sherman.** He was known as "General McDonald" for the rest of his life.

Not long after the war ended, McDonald married Addie Hayes of Memphis, Tennessee. The wedding was among the first postwar nuptials between a federal officer and a belle of an old southern family. Compounding the irony, this friend of Lincoln, Grant, and Sherman was also related by marriage to Confederate leader Jefferson Davis.

After the war McDonald earned his living as a claims agent, working on commission for clients who hired him to pursue their past-due claims against the federal government. His work often took him to Washington, D.C., where he renewed old friendships and forged new ones among incumbent Republican bureaucrats and politicians.

When Congress created a new federal position of inspector of internal revenue in 1868, McDonald's friends urged him to apply. Few were surprised when he received his commission to head the Missouri District in October 1869, over the strong objections of two leading Missouri Republicans, Sen. **Carl Schurz** and Radical Republican leader **Charles Daniel Drake.** In a highly unusual arrangement, McDonald, a relatively minor federal bureaucrat, wielded an extraordinary amount of power. Since Missouri's two senators, Schurz and Democrat **Frank Blair,** who succeeded Drake, were out of favor with President Grant, and McDonald was Grant's friend and ally, McDonald and his colleagues controlled federal patronage in the area.

To show his appreciation for the appointment and on the pretext of building a "war chest" for Grant's 1872 reelection campaign, McDonald and his friends devised a scheme to defraud the government of a percentage of the taxes he was responsible for collecting. What the president knew of this scheme is a matter of speculation. Some of the money did go to support Republican reelection efforts, but a good deal of it lined the pockets of the coconspirators. The plan involved underreporting the amount of whiskey produced and reusing legitimate federal tax stamps that had been carefully affixed for easy removal. It required collusion among local businessmen and some minor federal officials. While some distillers willingly participated, others were coerced. Eventually, the government estimated that it had lost $3.5 million while the ring operated.

When Grant was reelected in 1872 the original stated reason for the ring's existence was realized. By then, however, its operations were functioning so smoothly and the graft so rampant that ending its operations seemed highly unlikely. None of its leaders seemed concerned about the possibility of exposure and openly boasted of their influence in Washington. Periodic attempts to expose suspected fraud were unsuccessful: ring members always seemed to have advance warning and operated as they should when inspectors appeared.

The demise of John McDonald and the Whiskey Ring began in June 1874 when reform-minded Benjamin Bristow took over the Treasury Department and instituted his own secret investigation. The undercover investigators provided irrefutable evidence of the ring's operation. McDonald and his colleagues went to trial. He was convicted and sentenced to three years in the state penitentiary and ordered to pay a five-thousand-dollar fine, while his coconspirators received sentences proportionate to their level of involvement. Few served their full sentences. McDonald received a presidential pardon on Grant's last day in office, later writing his version of how the ring operated and who was involved in a volume titled *Secrets of the Great Whiskey Ring*. After his term in prison he returned to St. Louis but later lived in Greenlake, Wisconsin, and in Chicago, where he died in 1912.

MARY E. SEEMATTER

Guese, Lucius E. "St. Louis and the Great Whiskey Ring." *Missouri Historical Review* 36 (January 1942): 160–83.

McDonald, John. *Scrapbook of Clippings Concerning the Activities of John McDonald, 1876–1877.* Scrapbook File. Missouri Historical Society, St. Louis.

———. *Secrets of the Great Whiskey Ring: And Eighteen Months in the Penitentiary.* St. Louis: W. S. Bryan, 1880.

Seematter, Mary E. "The St. Louis Whiskey Ring." *Gateway Heritage* 8 (spring 1988): 33–42.

McDONNELL, JAMES SMITH, JR. (1899–1980)

James Smith McDonnell Jr. was born in Denver, Colorado, on April 9, 1899, to James S. and Susan Belle Hunter McDonnell. He earned a B.A. from Princeton in 1921 and an M.A. in aeronautical engineering from the Massachusetts Institute of Technology in 1925. He alternated graduate studies with pilot training at the Army Air Corps Flying School in San Antonio, Texas, during 1923–1924. McDonnell married Mary Elizabeth Finnely in 1934, and the couple had two sons, James S. McDonnell III and John F. McDonnell. Mary Elizabeth died in 1949, and McDonnell married Priscilla Brush Forney in 1956.

From 1924 to 1928 McDonnell held engineering positions with several aircraft manufacturers, including Consolidated Aircraft Company, Stout Metal Airplane Company, and Hamilton Aerospace Manufacturing Company. In 1928 he formed his own aircraft company, McDonnell and Associates. He developed the Doodlebug, a monoplane for private pilots, as his first plane, hoping to capitalize on America's fascination with flight. The firm quickly fell victim to the poor economy of the late 1920s and folded in 1929. Lacking the capital to form another company immediately, McDonnell worked for better-established aircraft firms during the next ten years. From 1933 to 1938 he served as chief project engineer for the Glenn L. Martin Company in California.

By 1939 McDonnell had sufficient funds and contacts to form McDonnell Aircraft Company in St. Louis. With the U.S. entry into World War II, McDonnell shifted the firm's emphasis heavily into military research. "McAir," as the company was known, began missile research in 1943. It won its first navy contract in 1944 and delivered the Gargoyle missile in 1945. More contracts were awarded for military aircraft, and McDonnell expanded production facilities. In 1946 McDonnell Aircraft delivered the first carrier-based jet fighter, the FH-1 Phantom, to the navy. Later jets included the Banshee, the Demon, and the Voodoo. (McDonnell maintained an interest in animism dating back to his Princeton days and named his early jets after spirits or spirit elements.)

McDonnell possessed a keen business sense and rapidly integrated key government programs into the company's research. In 1959 NASA awarded McDonnell Aircraft the prime contract to develop the Mercury manned orbital craft. Based on the success of the Mercury Project, NASA awarded McDonnell Aircraft the contract to develop the two-man Gemini craft in December 1961.

In 1967 McDonnell completed the largest aerospace merger in history when his firm acquired Douglas Aircraft, another manufacturing giant. The merger brought a lucrative commercial aircraft business, as well as additional combat aircraft, under McDonnell's control. The corporate conglomerate, named McDonnell Douglas Corporation, quickly became the nation's largest government contractor, replacing Lockheed by 1968. McDonnell served as chairman and chief executive officer (CEO) of the corporation. Donald Douglas, former president of Douglas Aircraft, effectively retired following the merger. McDonnell stepped down as CEO of McDonnell Douglas Corporation in 1972. Although he remained chairman of the firm, his nephew Sanford N. McDonnell assumed the duties of CEO.

Throughout his business career, McDonnell received many noteworthy honors. Washington University awarded him an honorary doctorate in 1958. Princeton, Clarkson College, the University of Missouri–Rolla, and the University of Arkansas also awarded him honorary degrees. He received the Daniel Guggenheim Medal in 1963, the Robert J. Collier Trophy in 1966, the Founders Medal of the National Academy of Engineers in 1967, the Forrestal Award in 1972, was named to the National Aviation Hall of Fame, and was an honorary fellow of the American Institute of Aeronautics and Astronautics.

James Smith McDonnell Jr. died on August 22, 1980.

SUZANNA MAUPIN LONG

Francillon, Rene J. *McDonnell Douglas Aircraft since 1920.* London: Putnam, 1979.

"Scotsmen Caught Young: The Founders of McDonnell Douglas." St. Louis: McDonnell Douglas Corporation, n.d.

Yenne, Bill. *McDonnell Douglas: A Tale of Two Giants.* New York: Crescent Books, 1988.

McELROY, HENRY F. (1865–1939)

Henry F. McElroy was born on August 17, 1865, at Amboy, Illinois, the son of B. E. and Anne Ferren McElroy. His schooling stopped when he was fifteen. In 1882, at age seventeen, he clerked in a store in Dunlap, Iowa, and helped keep the store's accounts. He worked in Chicago for a time. In 1895 he moved to Kansas City, Missouri, where he entered the real estate field and became a respected, well-liked businessman.

McElroy married Marie Oribison, a native of Kansas City, Kansas. They had two children: Mary, born in 1907, and Henry, born in 1909. Marie McElroy died in 1915, and Henry McElroy never remarried. His daughter, Mary, lived with him after she finished her education.

McElroy acquired a variety of Kansas City acquaintances and friends. Politically, he became a member of the Pendergast faction of Jackson County and Kansas City Democrats known as the "Goats," and he established a good business relationship with **J. C. Nichols,** an emerging leader in real estate development.

In 1922 factional leader **Thomas J. Pendergast** needed attractive candidates for two important Jackson County positions, those of western and eastern judges, or administrators, of the county court. For the eastern, more rural, area of the county, he selected former farmer, World War I veteran, and Kansas City businessman, **Harry S. Truman** of Independence and Grandview. For the western district, the area encompassing Kansas City, he selected Henry F. McElroy. Both were elected. In 1924, however, neither was reelected, when Pendergast's Democratic factional rivals **Joseph B. Shannon** and **Miles Bulger,** who had been denied a share of county patronage jobs, instructed their supporters to vote Republican.

Both Truman and McElroy rebounded, Truman becoming the presiding judge of the Jackson County Court in 1926, and McElroy becoming Pendergast's choice to be the first city manager of Kansas City. Pendergast had obtained the power to select the city manager when, in November 1925, five of his supporters were elected to the city council authorized to hire the manager. A city charter, approved by the Kansas City voters earlier that year, had created the city manager's position.

Thanks to Pendergast, McElroy, at the age of sixty, became one of the most powerful public officials in the state. He also had the support of many individuals within the Kansas City business community who viewed him as a successful, self-made businessman who understood the value of a dollar.

Upon becoming the city manager in 1926, McElroy bluntly said he would run the city's business in a partisan way. Totally loyal to Pendergast, he initiated centralized administrative methods that the city needed. In 1930 the reform-minded *Kansas City Star* even praised his administrative efficiency. However, some Republicans spoke negatively of "McElroyism."

Improvements did occur in Kansas City. After being encouraged by chamber of commerce officials, McElroy worked successfully to obtain the Kansas City Municipal Airport in 1927. Two Missouri River toll bridges became free bridges. Most important, as the national economic depression deepened, the city government launched a ten-year plan for public improvements. Conrad Mann, president of the chamber of commerce, even though a Republican, had a working relationship with the Pendergast machine. He led the Civic Improvement Committee of One Hundred that created the campaign to get the $32 million bond issue approved. The voters passed the bond package in 1931. It provided funds for a new police station, a city hall, a courthouse, a municipal auditorium, the paving of Brush Creek, and improvements to the city's minor league baseball stadium. When the various construction projects started, McElroy had workers use picks and shovels in order to maximize the number of jobs during the depression. He also made sure those workers were Democrats.

McElroy made enemies as well as friends. In 1933 Mary McElroy was kidnapped and held for ransom for thirty hours. The thirty-thousand-dollar ransom was paid, and she was released unharmed. In 1934 someone shot a bullet through the front door of the McElroy residence. The *Kansas City Star* also began to criticize the Pendergast regime. There were rumors and suspicions, later confirmed, that McElroy's celebrated "country bookkeeping" was sloppy at best and illegal at worst. There was talk of secret slush funds, deficit spending, payroll padding, and irregular contract procedures.

The indictment of Thomas J. Pendergast for income tax evasion on April 7, 1939, initiated the machine's fall. McElroy resigned from the city manager's position on April 13. On May 22 Pendergast pleaded guilty, and on May 29 he entered the federal prison at Leavenworth, Kansas. McElroy, dispirited, experienced rapid physical decline. At the age of seventy-four, on September 15, 1939, he died. Mary McElroy committed suicide on January 20, 1940.

DONALD B. OSTER

Brown, A. Theodore, and Lyle W. Dorsett. *K. C.: A History of Kansas City, Missouri*. Boulder: Pruett Publishing, 1978.

Dorsett, Lyle W. *The Pendergast Machine*. New York: Oxford University Press, 1968.

Larsen, Lawrence H., and Nancy J. Hulston. *Pendergast!* Columbia: University of Missouri Press, 1997.

Miller, Richard Lawrence. *Truman: The Rise to Power*. New York: McGraw-Hill, 1986.

Reddig, William M. *Tom's Town: Kansas City and the Pendergast Legend*. 1947. Reprint, Columbia: University of Missouri Press, 1986.

McKENDREE, WILLIAM (1757–1835)

William McKendree was the first American-born bishop of the Methodist Episcopal Church and the first bishop to have close ties with Missouri Methodism. Born in Virginia on July 6, 1757, the eighth child of John and Mary McKendree, he received little formal education. His biographers report that he served as a volunteer in the Revolutionary War.

As a young man, the son of a small planter, McKendree forsook his parents' Anglicanism and joined a Methodist society on probation. After a decade of wavering, he became a convert to Methodism. In 1788 he began his itinerant ministry in Virginia. Bishop Francis Asbury appointed him as a deacon in 1790 and an elder of the church in 1791. At the age of forty-three, he rode with Bishop Asbury and Bishop Richard Whatcoat through the Cumberland Gap to Kentucky. There he began his life as a preacher on horseback in the new western conference of the church. In 1808, wearing frontier garb, he preached a sermon at the general conference of the church in Baltimore, where he was elected a bishop. After that conference, he returned to the West.

Official histories say that McKendree rode through Missouri in 1807, crossing the Mississippi River near Herculaneum, preaching at Coldwater (forty miles north of Herculaneum) and in St. Charles County near Fort Zumwalt.

Despite ill health and heavy administrative responsibilities, McKendree worked hard to bring Methodism to the Missouri Territory. In frontier areas such as Missouri, ministers rode from cabin to cabin, preaching the Gospel. Evangelists conducted camp meetings that lasted from five to ten days. These outdoor meetings, at which ministers spoke from wooden platforms surrounded by tents and wagons, produced high levels of emotion and many converts.

As a bishop of the church, McKendree presided over conferences all over the United States, but the West remained his stronghold. On his recommendation, the general conference of the Methodist Church approved the establishment of the Missouri conference in 1816, encompassing all of Illinois, western Indiana, Missouri, and Arkansas, with no western boundaries.

Nearly two centuries later, the oldest extant Methodist building west of the Mississippi bears McKendree's name. Old McKendree Chapel, a national Methodist shrine, three miles east of Jackson in Cape Girardeau County, was the second meetinghouse constructed by the Methodists in Missouri. The first, called Shiloh, was constructed before 1814 in the Bellevue valley near Caledonia. Believers held camp meetings on the site of old McKendree Chapel as early as 1806 when McKendree was the presiding elder of the Cumberland district of the western conference of Methodism. Some scholars say, but not all agree, that he preached at a camp meeting on the site in 1818 when he traveled through eastern Missouri from Cape Girardeau to the confluence of the Missouri and Mississippi Rivers. Local farmers built the log chapel on the property of William Williams in 1818–1819 before a meeting of the Missouri conference in September 1819. Old McKendree Chapel was still occasionally used for services when it won listing on the National Register of Historic Places in 1987.

An eloquent preacher, a talented administrator, and a rugged traveler, McKendree played an important role in the spread of Methodism in Missouri. His sermons at camp meetings reached frontier farmers and their families who came seeking fellowship, inspiration, and a sense of community.

In the tradition of the circuit rider, McKendree visited campsites and cabins throughout the Mississippi and Missouri Valleys during the great westward migration of the early nineteenth century. After 1816 he oversaw the development of Methodism as an organized religion, with churches and Sunday schools, in Missouri. He never married, but lived the hard life of a saddlebag preacher. Despite worsening health after 1820, he continued traveling in the West until his death at the home of his brother James McKendree in Sumner County, Tennessee, on March 5, 1835.

BONNIE STEPENOFF

Billhartz, Terry D., ed. *Francis Asbury's America: An Album of Early American Methodism.* Grand Rapids, Mich.: Francis Asbury Press, 1984.

Dictionary of American Biography. Vol. 12. S.v. "McKendree, William."

History of the United Methodist Churches of Missouri. St. Louis: Methodist Historical Society, 1984.

Luccock, Halford, and Paul Hutchinson. *The Story of Methodism.* New York: Abingdon Press, 1949.

Tucker, Frank C. *The Methodist Church in Missouri, 1798–1939: A Brief History.* Nashville: Parthenon, 1966.

———. *Old McKendree Chapel.* Cape Girardeau, Mo.: Concord Publishing, 1984.

McNAIR, ALEXANDER (1775–1826)

Alexander McNair, the first governor of the state of Missouri, was born in what was then Cumberland County, in central Pennsylvania, on May 5, 1775, the seventh and youngest child of David and Ann Dunning McNair. Alexander's letters suggest that he received only a rudimentary education in his early years, and the oft-cited claim that he studied at Philadelphia College, later the University of Pennsylvania, seems somewhat dubious. He volunteered for a military company raised to suppress the 1794 Whiskey Rebellion, and five years later when war with France threatened, he was commissioned as an ensign in the United States Tenth Infantry. Those experiences gave him a penchant for military life that he carried with him to Missouri.

The McNairs were Federalists actively involved in Pennsylvania politics and land speculation. They also sold merchandise, especially ironware, in settlements along the Ohio River. Alexander McNair traveled to Ohio and Kentucky to peddle wares in

1801–1802, and the next year he expressed an interest in securing a government contract to supply western U.S. military posts. There is no evidence that his bid was successful, but in the fall of 1804 McNair accompanied Indiana's territorial governor, **William Henry Harrison,** when he went to St. Louis to establish a new government for the Louisiana Territory. McNair decided to stay in St. Louis, and Governor Harrison helped him secure appointments there as both an adjutant in the Louisiana territorial militia and a justice on the Court of Common Pleas and Quarter Sessions. McNair's appointment to the bench was somewhat surprising in view of his family's strong Federalist leanings, but those past connections apparently mattered less in the remote frontier territory.

When St. Louis was incorporated as a town, McNair became one of its five elected trustees. He helped reorganize the St. Louis Police Department, and in recognition for those efforts he was named sheriff of St. Louis County in 1810.

Given his land-speculation activities in Pennsylvania, it was no surprise that McNair quickly championed the cause of Louisiana's Spanish land claimants. His support for confirming the Spanish land titles made him popular among St. Louis's influential French Creole leaders, and he soon became associated with the "little junto," a powerful clique of St. Louis businessmen, lawyers, and land claimants. McNair's 1805 marriage to Marguerite Reihle further cemented his ties with the city's leading Creole families. His defense of the Spanish claimants rekindled a feud with Judge **John B. C. Lucas,** an outspoken foe of a liberal confirmation policy in the Louisiana Territory. Lucas had previously clashed with McNair over speculative land dealings when both men resided in western Pennsylvania.

McNair took special interest in his militia duties. In 1808 he advised his brother of the dangers of an Indian attack and noted that if hostilities erupted, "I am so much of a military man that I must have a hand in the war." Following the outbreak of the War of 1812, McNair was named adjutant and inspector general of the territorial militia with the rank of colonel. He commanded the First Regiment, and at war's end the popular officer traveled to the national capital to urge federal officials to compensate unpaid territorial rangers and militiamen.

However, business appears to have been the primary purpose for that journey. While en route to Washington, D.C., McNair stopped in Baltimore to purchase goods for his firm, McNair, Thompson, and Company, and in Washington he lobbied U.S. officials for government contracts. He apparently succeeded because he secured a contract to supply the military post at Prairie du Chien, and in 1816 he claimed to be the leading sutler in the Missouri country.

With so much business to look after, McNair declined President James Madison's nomination to serve as a commissioner charged with negotiating treaties with western Indian tribes. He did accept an appointment to the newly created position of federal register of lands in St. Louis when it was offered to him in 1816. The lucrative post made him one of the highest paid officials in the territory, and he relinquished it only after he was elected governor in 1820.

McNair began to gradually distance himself from the St. Louis clique. As register of lands he championed squatters' rights and supported the small claims of newer American settlers. He also voiced his support for statehood and joined **Thomas Hart Benton** in condemning Congress for its delay in admitting Missouri into the Union. He still retained enough support among members of the St. Louis caucus to secure their backing for a seat in the 1820 Constitutional Convention. He won election as a delegate on an antirestrictionist platform that pledged to oppose placing any limits on slavery.

McNair played a relatively minor role in the convention's proceedings, but his positions on many issues placed him at odds with former political associates. He opposed life tenure for judges and criticized the high salaries set for the governor and the judges. One of Missouri's first territorial politicians to capture a glimpse of the future Jacksonian vision of American democracy, McNair was already positioning himself to run for governor by championing the interests of the growing ranks of American settlers in Missouri's out-state regions.

In the absence of well-organized political parties, Missouri's established leaders supported territorial governor **William Clark** as their candidate to become the new state's first governor. McNair announced his intention to oppose Clark. The former explorer, who was out of the state attending to his sick wife, did little campaigning, but his powerful friends in St. Louis waged a vigorous effort on his behalf.

The race for governor was bitterly contested. McNair campaigned by appealing to rural voters throughout the state for support against his former allies in the St. Louis clique. He criticized members of the state Constitutional Convention for keeping its procedures secret and denounced the new constitution's undemocratic features. He also took exception to the high salaries the constitution provided for state officials, while conveniently overlooking the handsome sums he had been paid as federal register of lands.

Clark's supporters countered by questioning McNair's ability to hold such a high office and claiming that he had made no contribution in the Constitutional Convention. They accused him of doing too much campaigning in the tippling shops and backstreets among the dirtiest blackguards. McNair clearly benefited from the new constitution's provision granting universal white manhood suffrage, and with the support of out-state voters he easily defeated Clark. The death of two of McNair's children from typhoid shortly after the election tempered the joy of his victory.

As Missouri's first governor, McNair initially declined to call for state action to promote economic growth or social improvements. He seemed concerned that governmental power might be misused to serve a privileged few. When he addressed the General Assembly in the summer of 1821, Governor McNair took note of the great public and private distress caused by the state's depressed economic conditions, but he cautioned the legislators to act to provide relief only "if it can be done without trenching out the fundamental principles of the Constitution." He offered no specific recommendations for legislative action.

On its own initiative the General Assembly enacted a series of laws intended to relieve debtors and to guard against property foreclosures. The legislators also created a state loan office and authorized the issuance of banknotes in an effort to stimulate the economy. These highly controversial actions proved generally unsuccessful and were soon repealed or found unconstitutional.

In November 1821 McNair told the General Assembly that it had a "destiny" to awaken the slumbering energies of the state with a well-planned program to encourage the development of its internal resources. Once again, however, he made no specific recommendations, and the legislators took no action. McNair did propose the establishment of agricultural societies to promote improved farming methods and to conduct meat and grain inspections. He recommended the use of federal land grants to support public schools and internal improvements. The General Assembly authorized the establishment of only a tobacco warehouse to facilitate tobacco sales in the state. It also adopted a design for the state seal.

Although McNair's term as governor was not marked by significant legislative enactments, his administration should not be judged a failure. His actions probably reflected the wishes of the majority of Missourians at the time. A constitutional provision prohibited McNair from seeking reelection, so the voters had no chance to register formally their views on his administration.

The economic downturn that followed the panic of 1819 had ruined McNair financially. With a large family to support, the hard-pressed former governor gratefully accepted a U.S. government appointment as Osage Indian agent. While serving in that capacity he contracted influenza and died on March 18, 1826, leaving his family—including a two-week-old tenth child—nearly destitute. McNair was buried in the Old Military Graveyard in St. Louis but later reinterred in Calvary Cemetery.

PERRY McCANDLESS

Keller, Kenneth W. "Alexander McNair and John B. C. Lucas: The Background of Early Missouri Politics." *Bulletin of the Missouri Historical Society* 33 (July 1977): 231–45.

McCandless, Perry. *A History of Missouri: Volume II, 1820 to 1860.* Columbia: University of Missouri Press, 1972.

Stevens, Walter B. "Alexander McNair." *Missouri Historical Review* 17 (October 1922): 3–21.

———. "McNair." In *The Messages and Proclamations of the Governors of the State of Missouri,* ed. Buel Leopard and Floyd C. Shoemaker, 1:3–14. Columbia: State Historical Society of Missouri, 1922.

McNEAL, THEODORE D. (1905–1982)

A politician, labor organizer, and civil rights advocate, Theodore D. McNeal had the distinction of being the first African American elected to the Missouri Senate. He also served as the first black member on the University of Missouri Board of Curators, and was the first black president of the St. Louis Board of Police Commissioners.

McNeal was born on November 5, 1905, in Helena, Arkansas. After graduating from high school in his hometown, he stopped in St. Louis en route to Seattle, where he planned to contact a relative who had promised to help him attend college. Instead, he remained in St. Louis, obtaining a job at a ceramics and brick plant. A few years later, while on vacation from his regular job, he took a temporary position working on a Pullman car. E. J. Bradley, a local leader of the fledgling International Brotherhood of Sleeping Car Porters, urged McNeal to accept a permanent job as a porter and to help organize the union in St. Louis. In 1930 McNeal joined the union. At that time, only seven of approximately eight hundred St. Louis–area Pullman-car workers belonged to the union.

Seven years later, McNeal and other union officials succeeded in signing a hard-earned contract between the Pullman Company and the brotherhood, a hallmark agreement between a large American company and a predominantly black union. Now recognized as a tough negotiator and an efficient organizer, McNeal joined the national staff of the union as a field representative and chief negotiator. In 1950 he became national vice president of the union.

Meanwhile, during World War II, McNeal became involved in promoting fair-employment practices for blacks in St. Louis. In 1942 he helped organize a rally at Kiel Auditorium to protest job discrimination in war industries because defense plants had refused to put blacks in higher-paying production-line jobs. The rally attracted twelve thousand people. In 1944 he led a series of lunch counter sit-ins in downtown department stores in search of more equitable employment opportunities for blacks.

McNeal had earned national recognition within his union and achieved some local recognition as a civil rights leader when he decided, at the age of fifty-four, to enter politics. In 1960 he challenged incumbent senator Edward J. "Jellyroll" Hogan for his Seventh District senate seat. He defeated Hogan in the Democratic Party primary by a six-to-one ratio and became the first black elected to the Missouri Senate.

For the next ten years McNeal served with distinction in the state senate. He led the passage of the Fair Employment Practices Act (1961), the first meaningful civil rights measure enacted by the Missouri legislature. He strongly supported the creation of the University of Missouri–St. Louis (1964) and helped in the passage of the state Civil Rights Code (1965). As chairman of the Senate Appropriations Committee, he became the first African American in the nation to be named to such a powerful position in a state legislature. Senator McNeal's peers regarded him as a skilled, meticulous, and fair political leader.

In 1970 McNeal chose to retire from politics, but not from public life. Missouri governor Warren Hearnes immediately appointed the former senator to serve as the first black on the University of Missouri's governing board. In 1973 McNeal resigned from the board of curators to accept an appointment from Governor Christopher S. Bond as president of the St. Louis Board of Police Commissioners. His three-year term as leader proved challenging and tumultuous. The rigors of the job, combined with a sincere desire to retire from public life, prompted the seventy-one-year-old McNeal to announce in 1973 that he would not accept reappointment as president of the police board. He wanted time to relax and travel.

McNeal received a number of awards and honors, including the Urban League Award of Merit (1961), the National Conference of Christians and Jews Award (1968), and the St. Louis Civil Liberties Award (1972). He received honorary degrees from the University of Missouri, Lincoln University, and Lindenwood College. He also served as a trustee of Washington University. Chancellor William H. Danforth praised McNeal for his interest in integrating black students into student government and campus life rather than calling for the expansion of black studies programs.

McNeal died on October 25, 1982, in Jewish Hospital in St. Louis following a lengthy illness.

JACK B. RIDLEY

Greene, Lorenzo J., Gary R. Kremer, and Antonio F. Holland. *Missouri's Black Heritage, Revised Edition.* Columbia: University of Missouri Press, 1993.

Official Manual of the State of Missouri, 1969–1970. Jefferson City: Secretary of State, 1970.

St. Louis Argus, June 23, 1977.

St. Louis Post-Dispatch, October 25–November 5, 1982.

St. Louis Sentinel, June 23, 1977.

McNUTT, AMY SHELTON (1889–1983)

Amy Shelton McNutt was born near Paris, Missouri, on August 24, 1889. Orphaned at an early age, she was reared by her grandmother. Following graduation from the high school in Paris, she enrolled in nearby William Woods College in Fulton, where in 1907 she received a degree in liberal arts and in 1908 a degree in domestic science.

In 1912, after a brief stint of teaching school, Amy Shelton married Vachel H. McNutt, a graduate student in geology at the Missouri School of Mines and Metallurgy (now the University of Missouri–Rolla). McNutt received two graduate degrees from the school, was an instructor in geology, and organized the first course in petroleum geology in any university or college west of the Alleghenies. In 1913 he embarked on a career as a consulting geologist that led him and his family into the oil fields of many western states. Joining her husband in his work, Amy McNutt made a home for him and their two children in undeveloped areas of the West.

In 1927 the McNutt family and a friend purchased the historic Gallagher Ranch, a ten-thousand-acre spread near San Antonio, Texas. In 1833 the founder of the ranch, Peter Gallagher, had received a large land grant from the Mexican government to establish a military depot to supply the troops of General Santa Anna. The McNutts turned it into the first dude ranch in Texas. After a long illness, Vachel McNutt died in 1936. Amy McNutt then moved to Texas to become the sole owner and manager of the ranch. Under her supervision it grew into a popular vacation resort, as well as a successful working cattle ranch.

In 1952 Amy McNutt married Robert Emmett Dye, a mining engineer, who had been Vachel McNutt's roommate while they were students at the Missouri School of Mines and Metallurgy. After Dye's death in 1956 McNutt established a $1 million V. H. McNutt Memorial Foundation. She also funded Robert Emmett Dye Scholarships for mining engineering students in the department of geology at the school. In recognition of her commitment to helping students acquire a good education, the school awarded her the first Distinguished Service Citation in 1964 and, in 1967, the honorary degree of doctor of humane letters.

Another Missouri institution of higher education, Westminster College in Fulton, shared in her generosity. When the ruins of the historic London church of St. Mary the Virgin, Aldermanbury, designed by Sir Christopher Wren, was moved and reconstructed on the college campus to commemorate Winston Churchill's prophetic lecture called "The Sinews of Peace" (popularly known as "the Iron Curtain Address") at Westminster, McNutt gave the bell tower and bells in memory of her father-in-law, W. B. A. McNutt, an alumnus of the college.

In 1960 Randall B. Cutlip became president of William Woods College, then a small two-year liberal arts college for women. Through the years McNutt had shown little interest in her alma mater, until Cutlip aroused her curiosity and enlisted her support for upgrading the academic program and expanding the campus facilities. She was elected to the board of trustees in 1966 and in 1971 became the board's vice chairman. In 1968 William Woods College awarded her the school's first honorary degree.

Under Cutlip's leadership the college entered the 1970s with McNutt providing funds for the Campus Center that housed the student union, the college store, and the post office. She made possible the completion of the Fine Arts Center, the Centennial Hall (a dormitory), the Burton Business Building, the college maintenance building, and the Virginia Cutlip Residence Center. In addition, she left more than $1 million in trust to the college at the time of her death. William Woods College was the largest single beneficiary of her philanthropy.

In 1983 McNutt made available to the University of Missouri–Rolla sufficient funds to ensure the construction of the V. H. McNutt Engineering and Earth Science Building. In early October of that year she flew to Rolla to participate in a groundbreaking ceremony. Ten days later, on October 14, 1983, she died in San Antonio, Texas. It was fitting that her memorial service was held in the chapel of the Southwest Craft Center, a beautiful arts and crafts facility above the San Antonio River, to which she had contributed generously.

CHARLES T. JONES JR.

Christensen, Lawrence O., and Jack B. Ridley. *UM–Rolla: A History of MSM/UMR.* Columbia: University of Missouri Printing Services, 1983.

Hamlin, Griffith A. *"Moma Mac" of Texas: The Life and Works of Mrs. Amy Shelton McNutt.* Fulton, Mo.: William Woods College, 1981.

———. *William Woods College: The Cutlip Years, 1960–1980.* Fulton, Mo.: William Woods College, 1980.

McQUEEN, TERRENCE STEVEN (STEVE) (1930–1980)

Terrence Steven McQueen, one of the 1960s top box-office draws and one of the highest-paid actors of the 1970s, was born in Indianapolis, Indiana, on March 24, 1930, to William and Julian Crawford McQueen. His father deserted the family when Steve was only three months old, and his mother returned to live with her uncle, Claude W. Thompson, on a farm outside Slater, Missouri. She soon returned to Indianapolis with Steve and then two years later left him with her uncle for six years when she moved to California.

Young Steve enjoyed farm life, and it was in Missouri that his love for racing began when his great-uncle gave him a red tricycle for his fourth birthday. He enjoyed racing other children on a dirt bluff near the farm. He disliked school and was often absent from the one-room schoolhouse he attended, preferring the outdoors instead. Discipline problems in town gave him a reputation as a troublemaker. A mastoid infection at age five also left him partially deaf the rest of his life. McQueen came back to the farm outside Slater a few times after he became a star to visit his great-uncle but never went into town.

McQueen's mother, having remarried, returned to Missouri when he was nine and moved him to Indianapolis. Never adjusting well to city life, he joined a street gang and spent time playing pool and stealing hubcaps. At age twelve he and his mother moved to California where she remarried again. Steve and his new stepfather had a stormy relationship that often became physically violent. He joined another street gang and was arrested for fighting and stealing. In 1944 his parents sent him to a reform school, Boys Republic in Chino, California.

Three months later McQueen ran away. After he returned, a school counselor befriended him. Through long talks and counseling McQueen finally responded with good work habits and remained at the school. He gained his release in 1946 after completing the ninth grade, and he then moved to New York where his mother lived. He joined the merchant marines, worked odd jobs, and eventually entered the United States Marine Corps. Although he was demoted several times and spent forty-one days in the brig for going AWOL, he was honorably discharged in 1950 and returned to New York City.

McQueen lived in Greenwich Village and absorbed the bohemian culture. An actress girlfriend introduced him to Sanford Meisner, who accepted him as a student in the Neighborhood Playhouse. He played small roles in summer stock and at the Actors Studio until 1956 when he replaced Ben Gazzara on Broadway in *A Hatful of Rain.*

McQueen gained a reputation as a fighter and carried this trait into his relationships with costars in an attempt to earn their respect. Throughout his career he remained an enigma to the public and to his fellow actors. His explosive temperament often showed on-screen, and films with physical action appealed to him. He enjoyed racing cars and motorcycles and was an avid collector of cars, motorcycles, and vintage airplanes.

McQueen became known for his tough-guy roles in films such as *The Magnificent Seven, Hell Is for Heroes, The Great Escape, Nevada Smith, Bullitt, The Getaway, Papillion,* and *The Towering Inferno.* Ironically, in his last film, *The Hunter,* he played a bounty hunter, a role he made popular in the 1950s television series *Wanted Dead or Alive.* He received an Academy Award nomination in 1967 for *The Sand Pebbles,* in which he brilliantly portrayed his trademark role of a bitter outsider.

McQueen was first married to actress and dancer Neile Adams in 1956 and had two children, a son, Chad, and a daughter, Terri. His second wife was actress Ali MacGraw. His third wife, Barbara Minty, was with him when he died in Juarez, Mexico, from a heart attack after surgery for a cancerous tumor on November 7, 1980.

ARTHUR F. McCLURE AND VIVIAN RICHARDSON

Kansas City Times, November 12, 1980.

Moses, Robert. "Hard and Fast." *American Movie Classics* (October 1993): 4–6.

Nolan, William F. *McQueen.* New York: Berkeley Books, 1984.

Variety, November 12, 1980.

McREYNOLDS, ALLEN, SR. (1877–1960)

Allen McReynolds Sr. had a long and distinguished career in law, in public affairs, and in state government and politics. He was born in Carthage, Missouri, on November 7, 1877, and lived there until his death. His parents, Samuel and Helen Halliburton McReynolds, were both descended from families of lawyers. In fact, his maternal grandfather, Judge Wesley Halliburton, took part in the Constitutional Convention that produced the Missouri Constitution of 1875. Allen McReynolds was a leader in the Constitutional Convention of 1945 that produced a new state constitution to replace the 1875 document.

After completing high school in Carthage, McReynolds matriculated at the University of Missouri in Columbia and completed his undergraduate work in 1901. He then read and studied law in his father's firm and was admitted to the Missouri bar in 1903. He continued his legal practice in the family firm of McReynolds and Flanagan until his death.

In 1906, when McReynolds was still establishing his law practice, he married Maude Atwood Clarke of Carthage. Born in Canada, she moved to Jasper County with her family when she was only eight years old. The couple had two children: Helen Elizabeth, who married state senator George Rozier of Jefferson City, and Allen McReynolds Jr., who became a prosperous farmer, a manager, part owner of the Joplin stockyards, and a banker in several southwest Missouri communities.

McReynolds began his political career in the state legislature in 1934 when he was elected as a state senator. A Democrat, he served for two terms, for a total of eight years. Once in the senate, he became more and more involved in statewide issues.

Of the hundreds of issues that McReynolds faced during his public life, four were of special concern to him and proved of particular historical significance. First, he served as an influential delegate to the Constitutional Convention in 1943–1944. He was outspoken in his desire to protect a nonpartisan court plan. He was worried that a provision called the Parker substitute would undermine the effectiveness of the nonpartisan court plan and the use of merit in evaluation of public employees. Attending a meeting of the State Historical Society of Missouri in Columbia, he heard of the adoption of the Parker substitute. McReynolds returned to Jefferson City where the Constitutional Convention was in session and successfully led the opposition to the plan.

Second, in 1940 McReynolds was a candidate for the Democratic gubernatorial nomination. He entered the race primarily because of his concern over the influence of urban bosses within the Democratic Party. Both Kansas City and St. Louis had such bosses who exercised great power over the state party as well as over political events in their cities. In the primary campaign McReynolds ran against Lawrence V. McDaniel, a St. Louis liquor excise commissioner. It was a close race, but McDaniel narrowly won the nomination. By raising the issue of boss or machine control in the Democratic Party, McReynolds contributed to the defeat of McDaniel in the 1940 general election.

Third, McReynolds supported the New Deal as proposed by President Franklin Delano Roosevelt. McReynolds chaired the Senate Committee on Social Security that wrote the legislation needed in Missouri to provide state cooperation with the federal social security system. The legislation passed in 1937.

Fourth, McReynolds became a curator of the University of Missouri in 1945 and served for five years, four of them as board president. Under his leadership the medical school at Columbia was authorized.

Of course, there were many other state activities that received McReynolds's support and leadership. For twenty-five years he was a member of the board of the State Historical Society of Missouri and president

of the group from 1937 to 1941. He wrote articles for the *Missouri Historical Review* in addition to participating in the society's administration. From 1951 to 1956 he served on the board of Stephens College in Columbia.

McReynolds was an outstanding citizen and leader in Carthage, in Jasper County, and in the state of Missouri. He died on September 29, 1960, in Carthage, Missouri.

DUANE G. MEYER

Carthage Evening Press, September 29–October 1, 1960.
Dunn, Gerald. "The Great Governorship 'Steal.'" *Missouri Supreme Court Historical Journal* (summer 1989): 7–11.
March, David D. *The History of Missouri.* New York: Lewis Historical Publishing, 1967.

MEACHUM, JOHN BERRY (1789–1854)

John Berry Meachum, best known for his important roles as a spiritual leader, educator, and abolitionist, was born into slavery in Virginia on May 3, 1789. The son of a Baptist preacher, he was apprenticed as a youth to a white carpenter under whose tutelage he learned the craft of cabinetmaking and coopering. Of unusual talent and with a complying master, Meachum eventually saved enough money to purchase his freedom and that of his father. The Meachums then resettled in Kentucky where John married and began a family. However, it was not long before Meachum, attracted by the promise of new opportunities for self-advancement, moved to the booming river town of St. Louis in 1815, where he quickly discovered a demand for his carpentry skills. Following several years of hard work, he saved enough money to open his own modest cooperage shop.

Meachum became active in St. Louis's antebellum black community. In 1822, with the assistance of a group of northern missionaries dispatched by the Baptist Triennial Missionary Convention of Philadelphia, he organized religious services for St. Louis's African American residents. In February 1825 Meachum, a profoundly religious man, was ordained. Afterward, he and his followers founded the First African Baptist Church, one of the first black Protestant churches west of the Mississippi River. This institution and others like it provided blacks, both slave and free, with a measure of hope and solace in a society that increasingly devalued and exploited them. Meachum, a charismatic individual, gained a large and loyal following of both free blacks and slaves who had received permission from their owners to attend his services. In recognition of his years of service and experience, in March 1853, a year before his death, Meachum was honored by being elected as the first vice president of the Western Colored Baptist Convention at a regional convention in Alton, Illinois.

Besides his church activities, Meachum also conducted, with the assistance of several white missionaries, a school in the basement of his church, where he taught the fundamentals of reading and writing to black men, women, and children. Unfortunately, white resistance to black education made it impossible for him to continue classes at his church. An 1847 Missouri statute outlawed education for blacks, slave or free. As a result, Meachum and his followers created a "floating school" on a steamboat anchored in the center of the federally regulated Mississippi River. Here he continued to prepare black residents for freedom. According to a number of sources, one of Meachum's most famous students was the black civil rights leader **James Milton Turner,** who became the minister resident and consul general to Liberia in 1871 and Missouri's most prominent black political figure of the post–Civil War era. Consequently, Meachum's floating school became an important symbol of African American defiance and independence throughout the antebellum period.

Meachum was well known for his dedication to black freedom and self-reliance. Throughout the 1830s and 1840s, he purchased at least twenty slaves from their white masters. Transforming his barrel factory into a training ground for freedom, he hoped to prepare African Americans for life after slavery by teaching them practical skills such as carpentry and coopering. Once a slave was purchased, Meachum maintained legal ownership of the individual until he or she had earned enough money laboring in his establishment to reimburse him. According to a number of historians, this was a common practice among "benevolent free men of color at the time." In so doing, Meachum hoped to instill in his charges a sense of discipline, hard work, and self-respect. Sadly, Meachum did not live to witness the emancipation of his people. On February 19, 1854, he died while speaking to his congregation during church services.

CHRISTOPHER K. HAYS

Babcok, Rufus, ed. *John Mason Peck: Forty Years of Pioneer Life.* Philadelphia, 1864.

Moore, N. Webster. "John Berry Meachum (1789–1854): St. Louis Pioneer, Black Abolitionist, Educator, and Preacher." *Missouri Historical Society Bulletin* 29:2 (January 1973): 96–103.

MEADOR, LEWIS ELBERN (1881–1975)

Lewis Elbern Meador was born on a Barry County, Missouri, farm on September 9, 1881. During the Civil War his grandfather joined the Union Home Guards and was killed in the Battle of Pea Ridge. Meador attended the University of Chicago where he earned an A.B. degree in 1910. He entered law school at Chicago but disliked the emphasis on controversy and elected to pursue studies in history, philosophy, and political science. He enrolled at Columbia University and earned his M.A. there in 1913. Franklin Goodnow, later president of Johns Hopkins University, and historian Charles A. Beard were among his favorite teachers because, he said, they taught students to base decisions on established principles. While at Columbia University, Meador shared an office with Robert Moses, a fellow student who later gained fame as an urban planner in New York City.

Following the completion of his studies, Meador began a forty-year career teaching political science, history, and economics at Drury College in Springfield, Missouri. In 1917, following America's entry in World War I, Meador went to the Great Lakes Naval Training Station for naval aviation training and continued to pursue flying until the end of the war. In 1931 Meadow nearly became blind from glaucoma and cataracts. With student readers and Leeson Hay Cook Meador, his wife of fifty-four years, to assist him, he continued a full teaching schedule and fulfilled extensive civic duties during the following twenty-three years, including twenty summer sessions at the University of Colorado, Boulder.

Meador played an especially important role as a member of the Missouri Constitutional Convention that met in 1943 and 1944. He was well prepared for his duties in the convention. He had written a thesis detailing the weaknesses of Missouri's 1875 Constitution, which was then in effect, and his long years of teaching state and local government had provided him with additional insights. Meador and the other members of the Constitutional Convention drafted a proposed new constitution to replace the outdated 1875 document, and Missouri voters overwhelmingly approved its ratification in February 1945. The new constitution was considerably shorter than its predecessor, but Meador insisted that its length could have been reduced even further. At the conclusion of the convention, members of the press selected Meador as the outstanding delegate. Kim Duval, a reporter for the *St. Louis Globe-Democrat,* wrote, "This man Meador, because of his knowledge of politics, of education, of taxation and many other subjects, is invaluable on the work of this convention." The University of Missouri awarded him an honorary LL.D. in recognition of his work at the convention.

Meador also assumed an active role in community affairs, serving as president of the Springfield Chamber of Commerce and as a member of the original Wilson's Creek National Battlefield–project steering committee and the committee that initiated the movement to dam the White River to form Table Rock Lake. He chaired the thirteen-member commission elected in 1952 to write a new Springfield city charter that was approved the following year. He received numerous honors, including election to the Greater Ozarks Hall of Fame at the College of the Ozarks, the naming of Meador Park in Springfield in his honor, election as a member of the Missouri Academy of Squires, and the awarding of honorary degrees by Drury College and by Westminster College in Fulton, Missouri.

Above all Meador was a teacher. Occasionally, he spoke of his teaching objectives. When Drury College established the L. E. Meador Chair of Political Science in 1968, he responded, "I had in mind my chief objective to impress upon my students the importance of solving the many perplexing problems and questions that they will meet in the society in which they live. They should take a constructive and active part in trying to bring about a more democratic and more hopeful world in which future generations can live." Meador died in Springfield on November 15, 1975.

JOHN K. HULSTON

Hulston, John K. *An Ozark Boy's Story, 1815–1945.* Point Lookout, Mo.: School of the Ozarks Press, 1971.

Meador, Lewis E. Vertical Files. Drury College Library Archives, Springfield, Mo.

Official Manual of the State of Missouri, 1945–1946. Jefferson City: Secretary of State, 1946.

MIDDLEBUSH, FREDERICK A. (1890–1971)

Frederick A. Middlebush, the twelfth president of the University of Missouri, was born on October 13, 1890, in Grand Rapids, Michigan. He received undergraduate and graduate degrees from the University of Michigan, and taught at Knox College before coming to the University of Missouri in 1922 as an associate professor of political science. In 1917 he married Catherine Sofie Paine; they had no children.

Middlebush rose rapidly at the University of Missouri: he was promoted to professor in 1923 and appointed dean of the School of Business and Public Administration in 1925. He became acting president in 1934, and because of **Walter Williams**'s illness assumed the responsibilities of the presidency. The

board of curators appointed him president on July 1, 1935, a position he held for the next nineteen years.

During Middlebush's administration the university emerged from the Great Depression, underwent the trials of World War II, and experienced the greatest period of growth in its history, as veterans by the thousands sought to take advantage of the G.I. Bill of Rights to gain a college education.

As Missouri recovered from the depression, Middlebush was able to secure appropriations for salary improvements, increased equipment, and a substantial building program. All forms of growth ceased during the war, but resumed and accelerated with the advent of peace. Enrollment, which had fallen to 1,500 during the war, reached 11,452 by 1947–1948. A substantial building program accompanied the increase in enrollment, including new dormitory complexes. Similar development occurred at the Missouri School of Mines and Metallurgy, where postwar enrollment reached 3,025 in 1948–1949, and additional buildings were added. Curtis Wilson, appointed dean by Middlebush, effectively administered the School of Mines during the war and the immediate postwar years.

Under Middlebush's leadership the university rebuilt its reputation as a research institution after having suffered a period of decline in the twenties and early thirties. By its centennial in 1939 the University of Missouri had secured its place as one of the country's major universities.

Middlebush was popular with the students, and student life flourished during his administration. Fraternities and sororities continued to dominate student social life, though with the expansion of the dormitory system, nonaffiliated students assumed a larger role in the life of the campus. Football generated great enthusiasm, as Don Faurot led the Tigers to successive conference championships.

Middlebush and the board of curators resisted efforts of African American students to gain admission to the university, arguing that Lincoln University provided adequate opportunity. The university admitted black students to programs not available at Lincoln only under court orders. It was not until the 1954 Supreme Court decision *Brown v. Board of Education* that black students were admitted in large numbers.

In addition to participating extensively in statewide educational activities, Middlebush extended his reach well beyond Missouri, serving as president of the Carnegie Foundation and the National Association of State Universities and Land-Grant Colleges. He served on the Hoover Commission on the Reorganization of the Executive Branch of the United States Government, and on the National Science Board. Always interested in the educational programs of the armed services, he served as a member of the Board of Visitors of the United States Naval Academy and the Air University.

It was widely assumed that Middlebush would serve as university president until 1955, when he would reach the mandatory retirement age of sixty-five. Because of failing health, however, he resigned in 1954. He had served as president of the university longer than any of his predecessors, and had compiled an impressive record of achievement. He continued to live in Columbia until his death on June 8, 1971.

JAMES C. OLSON

Olson, James C., and Vera Olson. *The University of Missouri: An Illustrated History*. Columbia: University of Missouri Press, 1988.

Selby, P. O. "Frederick Arnold Middlebush." In *Missouri College Presidents: Past and Present*. Kirksville, Mo.: Northeast Missouri State University, 1971.

Stephens, Frank F. *A History of the University of Missouri*. Columbia: University of Missouri Press, 1962.

Viles, Jonas. *The University of Missouri: A Centennial History*. Columbia: University of Missouri, 1939.

Who Was Who in America. Vol. 5. New Providence, N.J.: A. N. Marquis, 1973.

MILLER, JOHN (1781–1846)

John Miller, a staunch advocate of the Democratic policies of Andrew Jackson and Sen. **Thomas Hart Benton,** served as governor of Missouri for seven years and as a representative in the United States Congress for six years. Born in Berkeley County, Virginia (now West Virginia), on November 25, 1781, Miller moved in about 1803 to Steubenville, Ohio, where with his brother he edited and published the *Steubenville Gazette*.

Miller served in the Ohio militia, and after the outbreak of the War of 1812 he received a commission as a colonel in the Nineteenth Infantry of the United States Army. Colonel Miller was in charge at Fort Meigs in Ohio, when in 1813 a combined British-Indian force unsuccessfully placed the installation under siege; after August 1814 Miller was in command of the entire northern frontier.

At the war's end Miller chose to remain in the army and was stationed at Fort Bellefontaine in the Missouri Territory. During the summer of 1815 he commanded the troops summoned to patrol at the great assemblage of Indians gathered to confer with U.S. officials at nearby Portage des Sioux. Colonel Miller resigned from the army in 1817, and accepted an appointment as register of the land office at Franklin. He made Howard County his home until near the end of his life.

The resignation of Lt. Gov. Benjamin Reeves and the subsequent death of Gov. **Frederick Bates** in mid-1825 created a vacancy in the state's top office that necessitated a special gubernatorial election at the year's end. John Miller was one of four candidates who filed to seek the empty post. In the absence of clearly identified parties in the state, two competing political factions were contesting for primacy. A nationalist, commercially oriented group supported Missouri's popular U.S. senator **David Barton** and President John Quincy Adams, while an opposing agrarian, states' rights faction favored Missouri's second senator, Thomas Hart Benton, and Andrew Jackson, who was certain to be the Democratic candidate for the presidency in 1828.

Sensing some public resistance to the growing political factionalism in Missouri, Miller, with good reason, attempted to remain aloof from the partisan squabbles. His St. Louis friends still viewed him as an independent with nationalist leanings, but his new central-Missouri neighbors considered him one of their own. Senator Benton worked hard for Miller's election, and when the results were in the *St. Louis Missouri Advocate* gleefully proclaimed Miller's victory as a popular endorsement for Jackson and Benton.

As governor, Miller moved to embrace Benton and the Boonslick Democrats, who came to control Missouri politics during the next two decades under the banner of Andrew Jackson and the Democratic Party. When the popular governor sought reelection in 1828 no one came forth to oppose him.

As an adherent of Jeffersonian principles, Governor Miller generally favored a limited governmental role in social and economic affairs. He did call upon the General Assembly to make effective use of national land grants to support public schools, which he praised as the cornerstone of a free republican government. In 1832 the governor recommended that the General Assembly establish a conservative, republican-style state bank, with the state acting as a guardian and trustee of the bank's funds. Like Jackson and Benton, Miller favored hard money, opposed paper currency, and detested the Bank of the United States. As governor, Miller, the old Indian fighter, frequently mobilized the militia to police Indian incursions, thereby demonstrating his determination to maintain control over Indian affairs within Missouri's borders.

Miller called upon the General Assembly to memorialize Congress to support actions he deemed important for Missouri. He urged Congress to enact Benton's plan to graduate downward the price of public lands, though in time he came to favor the transfer of all public lands, including the salt springs and lead mines, to the state. Miller also called for federal protection along the Santa Fe Trail, an important trade route for Missourians. As a good Jacksonian Democrat, Miller urged adoption of Benton's proposed constitutional amendment calling for the abolition of the electoral college and the direct election of the president.

When his term as governor expired in 1832, Miller returned to Howard County. In 1836 the voters handily elected him to serve in the United States House of Representatives. He won reelection in 1838 and 1840. As a congressman he regularly voted to support the same Democratic policies and programs he had favored as governor. He voted against protective tariffs and the rechartering of the Bank of the United States. He never proposed new or special programs, nor did he take a lead in congressional proceedings. Miller, who was neither combative by nature nor unduly partisan, refused to debate questions that he feared might increase sectional hostility. As political partisanship and sectional disagreements intensified, he chose not to seek reelection in 1842. After his term in Congress ended, Miller, who had never married, took up residence at Florissant in St. Louis County, where he died on March 18, 1846.

Perry McCandless

Leopard, Buel, and Floyd C. Shoemaker, eds. *The Messages and Proclamations of the Governors of the State of Missouri.* Vol. 1. Columbia: State Historical Society of Missouri, 1922.

McCandless, Perry. *A History of Missouri: Volume II, 1820 to 1860.* Columbia: University of Missouri Press, 1972.

MILLER, LOUIS (1853–1933)

Louis Miller was an influential builder-architect who lived in Arcadia, in Iron County, and was a builder for fifty years in the southeast Missouri Ozarks and the Bootheel. His projects included commercial, governmental, and private buildings; country seats; model farms; water towers; and cobblestone bungalows, all of which were worthy of promotion and imitation.

Born in Jefferson County, Missouri, on October 13, 1853, Miller moved to Arcadia Valley in 1860 with his widowed mother, Joanna, and two siblings. Little is known about his childhood except that Joanna Miller reared her children with the help of another German-born lady, Mary Ernst. Young Louis demonstrated a precociousness for mechanical ability. Perhaps encouraged by his mother's teachings and the example of a German grandfather who was an architect, Louis attended subscription school for a few years and the Methodist Arcadia high school for eight months.

As a young man Miller apprenticed under a master builder. As he matured in the business, he subscribed

to trade journals; took correspondence courses; developed his own clientele; worked as a subcontractor to famous St. Louis architects William Eames, Thomas Young, and **Theodore Link;** and published designs in the *Journal of Carpentry and Building, Building Age,* and the *Craftsman.* He combined academic blueprints and pattern-book plans with his own notions of natural materials.

Miller represented the craftsman movement in American architecture in southeast Missouri. He promoted environmentally compatible buildings for "village improvement," constructed naturally textured exteriors and interiors, was concerned that the whole house—front and back—have aesthetic appearances to the viewer, made decorative urns and fences of natural materials (especially cobblestone), employed Japanese design qualities in roof pitch and in gardens, and pleaded in the newspaper for conservative approaches toward management of local natural resources while applauding the moral value of handwork. All these craftsman qualities remain today at his splendid Bethesda Springs bungalow park in Arcadia.

The St. Louis and Iron Mountain Railroad passed through Arcadia southward to the Bootheel and into Arkansas. Miller practiced his trade in the towns along the railroad, often having dozens of men busy in multiple locations. His greatest distinction, though, was as a builder for wealthy St. Louisans who desired summer homes in Arcadia valley. From the 1880s into the 1920s, this late-Victorian resort society traveled less than ninety miles down the rails on a special "Arcadia Accommodation" train to vacation in fashionable homes there.

During the 1880s Miller built three estates in Arcadia that made him a prominent contractor and builder-architect for summer homes. First, in 1884, he constructed a two-story frame house for his future in-laws, Joseph and Fredonia Ringo, a Mississippi County planter family with large mercantile and agricultural investments. Second, in 1886, he built his own country seat as a model estate with a great stone water tower. At the corner of his property he built an office and a carpenter's finishing shop that faced east toward the railroad depot and St. Louis Lane, which led past farms that would become summer estates. Third, in 1887, Gen. John W. Turner hired Eames and Young to develop his estate; Miller executed the fashionable shingle-style addition to the standing Italianate house. At this latter site, Miller designed a number of outbuildings that served as a model complex imitated throughout the valley. For the next twenty years he built expensive summer homes for the St. Louis trade.

The successful builder-architect was active in the Methodist Church South, became a Sunday school teacher, served as director of the Arcadia school board in 1887, was selected as a Mason in 1892, and was chosen as director of the new Iron County Bank in 1896. Miller built extensively in Farmington, Fredericktown, Bonne Terre, Bismarck, Piedmont, Des Arc, Doniphan, Greenville, Sligo, and nearby Ironton. He consumed enough manufactured brick at those projects to establish his own brickyard in Mount Vernon, Illinois.

In 1903 Miller built one of the most monumental log buildings in Missouri at Sligo for the American Steel and Sligo Furnace Company. The great clubhouse was a hotel, restaurant, and community building. In Arcadia he developed a clubhouse for Clarence Jones on his Maples model farm, including a picturesque stone and wood water tower that remains today as a primary symbol of Miller's achievements. He joined others to promote Rainbow Dam and Lake Killarney, to secure the Jefferson Barracks Rifle Range, and to advance the purchase and development of the Epworth Methodist Assembly grounds.

In 1916 Miller combined his business with that of his talented builder-engineer son, Louis Miller Jr. The elder Miller retired in 1924 and died on October 21, 1933. Louis Miller Jr. continued his father's tradition of building craftsman bungalows that give the Arcadia valley a distinctive cultural landscape.

LYNN MORROW

Morrow, Lynn. "Estate Builders in the Missouri Ozarks: Establishing a St. Louis Tradition." *Gateway Heritage* 2 (winter 1981–1982): 42–48.
———. "Louis Miller: Master Craftsman and Folk Artisan of Southeast Missouri." *Gateway Heritage* 4 (summer 1983): 26–37.

MILLER, RICHARD E. (1875–1943)

Richard Edward Miller was born on March 22, 1875, in St. Louis, the son of Richard Levy Miller (an engineer and bridge builder, originally from West Virginia) and Esmeralda Miller. He attended the St. Louis School of Fine Arts from 1893 to 1897, winning academic prizes for his drawing and painting of the figure. While a student he became a member of the newly founded Society of Western Artists and the St. Louis Association of Painters and Sculptors, exhibiting in their annual shows.

In 1899, after two years as an illustrator for the *St. Louis Post-Dispatch,* Miller left St. Louis for Paris to continue his art training. He enrolled at the Académie Julian, studying with the well-known French academicians Jean-Paul Laurens and Benjamin Constant. Miller specialized in portraiture and figure painting: initially dark, academic paintings primarily of old peasant women, in the French realist tradition still popular at the time, later shifting to the subject he is most identified with, fashionable women in the intimacy of their boudoirs, painted with a bright and lively postimpressionist palette and brushwork.

Miller's star rose rapidly. In 1900 he won a third-place medal for *At Her Devotions,* his first Paris Salon entry. In 1904 he won a silver medal at the Louisiana Purchase Exposition in St. Louis, where he exhibited five paintings. He sold paintings to the French government in 1904 and again in 1907. In 1908 he was made a knight of the French Legion of Honor, and in 1909 he was given a gallery of his own at the Venice Biennale, where his work was critically acclaimed. He was also an instructor at the École Colarossi in Paris, and had private students, many of them American. By 1912 Miller was at the pinnacle of his European career.

Miller exhibited his work internationally, though his primary market remained America, where he was represented by the Macbeth Gallery in New York City. He exhibited regularly at the Salon des Artistes Français in Paris (where, after 1905, his submissions were no longer subject to jury review, a mark of high distinction) and in important annual and biennial exhibitions of American art at such museums as the Carnegie Institute, the Corcoran Gallery of Art, the Chicago Art Institute, and the Pennsylvania Academy of the Fine Arts (for which he also served on the Paris jury), among others. Many of these museums purchased his work for their permanent collections.

While residing in France Miller was an active member of the Paris Society of American Painters, which promoted the works of American artists living and working in France. He and his close friend and colleague Frederick Frieseke were admired by the art community for their ready willingness to help young artists. Both men were frequently found at the Dome café at the aperitif hour, where fellow artist Abel Warshawsky described Miller as "blond, nervous, and bespectacled," noticeable from afar for the wide-brimmed Stetson hat he regularly wore.

Miller painted both in Paris—he had a studio on the Left Bank—and, in summer, in the French countryside. Like many compatriots before him and along with his close friend and colleague Frieseke, Miller was drawn to the French village of Giverny, where he painted and taught during several summers. There he met the giant of French impressionism, Monet, who had established his home in Giverny; he also met his future wife, Harriette Adams, from Providence, Rhode Island. She was part of a group of young American women who had come to Giverny with educator Mary C. Wheeler for summer art instruction provided by Miller. The two were married in 1907 in London; their only child, Elsbeth, was born in Giverny in 1909.

It was during summers in the countryside that Miller's paintings became lighter, brighter, and more loosely painted, as he and several other American artists, known as the "Giverny Group" (which included Karl Anderson, Frederick Frieseke, Lawton Parker, Louis Ritman, and Guy Rose), experimented with color, light, and brushwork to create a highly distinctive and decorative postimpressionist aesthetic.

Although Miller's travels are poorly documented, it is known that he went to Holland at least once before 1905 and to England during his sojourn in France. In 1912 he began summering in St. Jean du Doigt in Brittany, where he remodeled an old house and enthusiastically made plans to settle there more permanently. These plans were cut short by the outbreak of World War I in 1914.

By January 1915, the year he was elected to the National Academy of Design, Miller was back in the United States. He spent part of 1916 and 1917 in Pasadena, California (where his Giverny colleague and friend Guy Rose had already become an established artist), painting and teaching at the Stickney Memorial School of Fine Art, focusing his instruction on painting the model outdoors. The art press welcomed Miller and his "modern" tendencies, calling him "a godsend for California."

However, California did not attract Miller permanently. With his hope of returning to France extinguished by the war, Miller turned to the East Coast. By the late summer of 1917 he had moved to Provincetown, Massachusetts, a fishing-village-turned-art-colony then attracting a number of expatriate artists back from Europe. Miller was no doubt encouraged in this move by Charles Hawthorne, a leading painter and influential teacher who founded the Cape Cod School of Art in Provincetown in 1899. There can be no doubt that Miller and Hawthorne knew each other in France. Miller also knew artists Max Bohm and John Noble in France, and all three moved to Provincetown within two years of one another, quickly becoming leading artists in the community.

Miller's career continued to flourish. He traveled regularly to St. Louis, Boston, New York, and periodically to Europe. He painted portraits, including many prominent St. Louisans such as Monsanto founder John F. Queeny, Gov. **David Rowland Francis,** Washington University president **Robert Somers Brookings,** and Mississippi Trust Company chairman Julius S. Walsh, among others.

In 1919 and 1921 Miller was commissioned to paint four murals for the Senate chamber of the state capitol in Jefferson City, Missouri. The murals, which are still in place, depict four scenes of state history: *Daniel Boone at the Judgment Tree; President Jefferson Greeting Lewis and Clark at the White House; Benton's Speech at St. Louis, 1849;* and *Blair's Speech at Louisiana, Missouri, 1866.*

Miller taught and developed the genre for which he is best known: highly decorative, vigorously brushed images of women in colorful, sun-dappled interiors. He painted female nudes and, late in his career, Provincetown landscapes and marines.

Provincetown became Miller's home. The family lived in a renovated carriage barn, a project that received much of Miller's personal attention and came to be featured in the magazine *American Home Journal.* Behind the house Miller erected a spacious studio overlooking a garden that he and his wife had created, referred to as "an American Giverny garden." Miller was a founding member of the Beachcombers Club, an association of Provincetown artists more social than artistic, known for its high-spirited and humorous activities. He was also an active member of the fledgling Provincetown Art Association, founded in 1914, serving for years as an honorary vice president and also exhibiting and jurying the work of others.

Miller was an outspoken critic of early-twentieth-century modernism as it gathered momentum in the United States after the groundbreaking New York Armory Show of 1913. Himself once considered modern for his progressive blend of traditional and impressionist painting, which combined strong draftsmanship and composition with rich color and surface texture, Miller came to be viewed as artistically conservative as abstraction gained currency. Nevertheless, he retained a solid artistic presence both locally and nationally, based on a successful career, the continued demand for his paintings, his outspoken personality, and his respected teaching. He continued exhibiting in all the important American art annuals, garnering sales, prizes (including the Walter L. Clark Prize at the Grand Central Art Galleries in New York in 1928 and the Gold Medal by Allied Artists of America in 1933), and favorable reviews; at the same time he served on prestigious awards and selection juries.

Miller's artistic renown and activity did not prevent him from being quite civic minded. During the depression he served as director of local Works Progress Administration art projects. He also worked to attract artists to Provincetown year-round.

Miller in the last years of his life participated less in local and national exhibitions, and returned, to some extent, to painting the kinds of simple, hard-working people that were the subjects of his first Paris canvases. Instead of French peasant women, he now painted the Portuguese fishermen of Provincetown: gray, sober canvases expressive of quiet human dignity.

Miller began traveling to the South during the winters, spending seasons in Fort Lauderdale, Sarasota, and St. Augustine, Florida. He favored the latter town for his winter retirement, and had hoped to buy a small house and garden there. He never did: he died in St. Augustine on January 23, 1943, at the age of sixty-seven.

MARIE LOUISE KANE

Ball, Robert, and Max W. Gottschalk. *Richard E. Miller, N.A.: An Impression and Appreciation*. St. Louis: Longmire Fund, 1968.

Burrage, Mildred Giddings. "Art and Artists at Giverny." *World Today* 20 (March 1911): 344–51.

Pica, Vittorio. "Artisti contemporanei: Richard Emile Miller." *Emporium* 39 (March 1914): 162–77.

Seares, Mabel Urmy. "Richard Miller in a California Garden." *California Southland* 38 (February 1923): 10–11.

Thompson, Wallace. "Richard Miller: A Parisian-American Artist." *Fine Arts Journal* 27 (November 1912): 709–14.

Warshawsky, Abel G. *The Memories of an American Impressionist*. Ed. Ben L. Bassham. Kent, Ohio: Kent State University Press, 1980.

MILLES, CARL (1875–1955)

Carl Milles, an internationally known sculptor, never lived in Missouri, but his illustrious career received its American debut in St. Louis. From that introduction he significantly altered the urban landscape of St. Louis and Kansas City with his whimsical, monumental sculpture fountains.

Carl Milles was born Carl Emil Wilhelm Anderson in Lagga, Sweden, on June 23, 1875. At the age of ten he was sent to boarding school in Stockholm where he became more interested in the waterfront and the tales of the sailors than in his academic studies. In 1892 he left school and became apprenticed to a cabinetmaker. While working in Stockholm he attended the technical school and after graduation in 1897 set out for a position in South America. He got as far as Paris. He stayed there until 1904, working as a coffin maker, an ornamental woodcarver, and finally as a sculptor.

Although heavily influenced by Rodin, Milles took an independent path after World War I, bringing medieval, classical, and Swedish folk themes and forms into his art. In his highly personal interpretations he began to produce a unique sculpture that won both critical acclaim and condemnation.

By the time Milles came to the attention of the cultural community in the United States he had established himself as the preeminent sculptor of Sweden. In 1931 he became professor of sculpture at the prestigious Cranbrook Academy in Bloomfield Hills, Michigan. That same year he was invited by the St. Louis art community, led by the director of the St. Louis Art Museum, Meyric Rogers, to lecture and show some of his works for a modern-arts festival. The success of this event led Rogers and others to arrange that summer for the first showing of Milles's works by an art museum in America. The show at the St. Louis Art Museum was a great success.

Once introduced in St. Louis, and with the active backing of Rogers, Milles's name became linked with the proposal to create a civic memorial fountain in Aloe Plaza across from the massive, romanesque Union Station. An Aloe Plaza Commission was appointed to choose a sculptor for the fountain, and Milles was selected.

The Milles design was to commemorate the meeting of the Missouri and Mississippi Rivers. His design included nineteen figures, the most important being the male nude "Mississippi" and the female nude "Missouri." Christened as the *Marriage of the Waters* the design created an uproar in St. Louis. The nudity of the figures rushing toward each other was seen by some citizens of the city as pornographic. Calmer minds finally prevailed, and in 1938 the Municipal Arts Commission voted to approve the fountain.

The figures are in a basin two hundred feet long and thirty-five feet wide. Ninety jets of water constantly spray and veil the figures of "Mississippi" and "Missouri" and their companions of tritons and naiads. The fountain was finally dedicated in 1940, with a new more chaste title, the *Meeting of the Waters*.

The *Meeting of the Waters* was the first of more than two dozen sculpture fountains Milles created in the United States. In 1945 he became an American citizen and established his permanent home in Bloomfield Hills.

In 1947 William Volker, a millionaire philanthropist, died in Kansas City, and the city fathers appointed a memorial committee to commemorate Volker's contributions to their community. The committee decided a fountain would be the most fitting memorial and upon the recommendation of the American Academy of Sculptors chose Carl Milles to execute their wishes.

Milles was seventy-five years old when he was sought by the Kansas City group. At first he was reluctant to accept their commission, but after visiting the city he accepted the contract. In consultation with Milles the committee chose a site on the mall, south of the Nelson-Atkins Gallery of Art. Volker had been a benefactor, a "good Samaritan" to the city, and Milles developed his design around that theme. His design used the legend of the fourth-century Saint Martin, bishop of Tours, who had cut his cloak in half to help a freezing beggar. This selfless act was rewarded by a vision of Christ and Martin's conversion to Christianity.

Milles's design created a series of interconnected pools with jets of water shooting up around the figures. The focus of the fountain was a fourteen-foot-tall mounted Saint Martin in the act of cutting his cloak in half. At his feet the nude figure of the beggar reaches up to receive the gift. Watching over the scene is a flute-playing angel held aloft by a bronze pole, while a centaur and a seated angel watch from a distance. The seated angel has caused a great deal of comment over the years since it appears to be scratching its leg and is wearing a wristwatch.

Although the commission was awarded Milles in 1950, the project ran into a number of delays. Sadly, he was not able to see its final placement, having died at Millesgarden, Sweden, on September 19, 1955. In his absence the project was carried on by his chief assistant, Peter Berthold Schiwetz, and in September 1958 the fountain was dedicated as the *Volker Memorial Fountain*. Ironically, as the *Meeting of the Waters* was Milles's first sculpture fountain in the United States, the *Volker Memorial Fountain* was his last.

In 1988 the Missouri Botanical Garden installed seven copied works by Milles in its water-lily ponds. The result was a water-lily sculpture garden that served as a retrospective study of Milles's figures. Included were figures from the *Meeting of the Waters* and the *Volker Memorial Fountain*.

Carl Milles had a positive impact on the arts and the urban landscape of Missouri. His interpretative use of folklore, humor, and classical design brought to the people of Missouri two artistically significant sculpture fountains. His fountains became center-pieces for the arts in both St. Louis and Kansas City. The detail of the "Mississippi" figure, the fantasy of the naiads, the selfless devotion of Saint Martin, and the humor of the little angel with the wristwatch glorify life and the joy of living.

THEODORE FINKELSTON

Hardy, Hathaway. "Sweden's Millesgarden." *Architectural Digest* (October 1988): 86–90.

McCue, George. *Sculpture City: St. Louis*. New York: Hudson Hills Press, 1988.

Piland, Sherry, and Ellen J. Uguccioni. *Fountains of Kansas City*. Kansas City, Mo.: City of Fountains Foundation, 1985.

Rogers, Meyric R. *Carl Milles: An Interpretation of His Work*. New Haven: Yale University Press, 1940.

St. Louis Globe-Democrat, September 20, 1955.

MILLIGAN, JACOB LE ROY (1889–1951)

Jacob Le Roy "Tuck" Milligan was born on March 9, 1889, in Richmond, in Ray County, Missouri. He attended public school and went to the University of Missouri in Columbia, earning a law degree. In 1913 he passed the Missouri bar and the following year began the practice of law in Richmond with his older brother, **Maurice M. Milligan.**

World War I interrupted Jacob Milligan's legal career. On April 8, 1917, two days after the United States entered the conflict, he enlisted in the Sixth Regiment, Missouri Infantry. From August 4, 1917, until May 23, 1919, he was a captain of Company G, 140th Infantry Regiment, Thirty-fifth Division. He embarked for France in April 1918 and saw considerable action on the western front. He distinguished himself in action, receiving two citations, the Purple Heart and the Silver Star.

Following his release from service and his return to Richmond in 1919, Milligan entered politics as a Democrat. He won a special election to fill a vacancy from the Third Congressional District of Missouri to the Sixty-sixth Congress, serving from February 14, 1920, to March 3, 1921. He lost the election for a full term in the Harding sweep of 1920. He regained the seat in 1922 and triumphed in the next five congressional elections. During his career as a congressman he championed Missouri River improvement projects, sought economy in government, and supported early New Deal legislation. He was assistant Democratic whip and sat on many committees. In 1928 he was an elected delegate to the Democratic National Convention in Houston.

In 1934 Milligan, with help from his friend and fellow Democrat Sen. **Bennett Champ Clark** of Missouri, ran for the United States Senate nomination in the August Democratic primary. He lost, running behind Rep. John J. C. Cochran of St. Louis and the winner, presiding judge **Harry S. Truman** of Jackson County. Truman's margin of victory came from Kansas City, where the political machine headed by **Thomas J. Pendergast** delivered more than one hundred thousand votes, many of which were fraudulent.

Jacob's brother, Maurice Milligan, the U.S. attorney for the Western District of Missouri, successfully prosecuted sensational vote-fraud cases in Kansas City in 1936 and 1937 and sent Pendergast to jail for income tax evasion in 1939, effectively destroying the machine. In 1940 Maurice Milligan ran, and he too lost to Truman in a three-way Democratic primary for the nomination. The two Milligans, both of whom had distinguished public careers, are probably best remembered for losing to Harry Truman.

Jacob Milligan, following his 1934 defeat, left elective politics and returned to the practice of law. From May 3, 1949, until April 27, 1950, he held the appointed position of president of the Kansas City Police Board. He resigned following allegations of criminal penetration of the police department, later defending his actions on national television during the Kefauver hearings that investigated organized crime.

Milligan died in Kansas City of an apparent heart attack on March 9, 1951. He was survived by his wife, Mary Kate Milligan, and a stepson.

LAWRENCE H. LARSEN

Kansas City Star, March 9, 1951.

Larsen, Lawrence H., and Nancy J. Hulston. *Pendergast!* Columbia: University of Missouri Press, 1997.

New York Times, March 11, 1951.

MILLIGAN, MAURICE M. (1884–1959)

Maurice Milligan was born on November 23, 1884, in Richmond, in Ray County, Missouri. While a student at Richmond High School, he studied law on the side. He secured admittance to the Missouri bar only a couple of days after his high school graduation. He earned a bachelor's degree from the University of Missouri and received a law degree in 1908 from the same institution. He married Sue McDonald, raised a son and daughter, and practiced law in Richmond with his younger brother, **Jacob Le Roy Milligan,** who eventually served as a member of Congress for thirteen years. Maurice Milligan saw service in World War I.

By his own account Milligan became "a victim of the virus of politics" in his teens when he was a clerk in the Missouri State Senate. As a Democrat he won election in 1909 as city attorney in Richmond and in 1915 as judge of the probate court in Ray County, a post he held for more than fifteen years. In February 1934 President Franklin D. Roosevelt appointed him to a four-year term as the U.S. attorney for the Western District of Missouri. Milligan obtained the prosecutor's position chiefly through the efforts of his brother and Democratic senator **Bennett Champ Clark** of Missouri.

In the course of his duties as U.S. attorney, Milligan received considerable national attention for his battle against the powerful Pendergast machine in Kansas City. In the vote-fraud trials of 1936 and 1937 federal juries brought in 259 guilty verdicts for conspiracy to interfere with the rights of citizens to vote. Nineteen defendants were dismissed, but none of the 270 persons named in thirty-nine indictments were acquitted. More important, the trials and investigations resulted in the striking of more than 60,000 of 270,000 names from the voter-registration lists in Kansas City, severely hurting the machine.

In 1938 Sen. **Harry S. Truman** unsuccessfully opposed Milligan's reappointment to a second term,

charging he had unconscionably accepted large fees in bankruptcy-receivership cases and engaged in other unethical practices. Undeterred by Truman's assault, Milligan then went after bigger game, and in 1939 he and his small staff, with the help of other federal agencies, built a tax evasion case against machine leader **Thomas J. Pendergast.** Indicted in April 1939 Pendergast pleaded guilty and went to the United States Penitentiary in Leavenworth, Kansas, ending the domination of his notorious organization at the municipal level.

Milligan and Gov. **Lloyd Stark** both ran and lost to Truman in the August 1940 Missouri Democratic Senate primary, splitting the antimachine vote. Milligan, who had resigned to run for the Senate, was reappointed as U.S. attorney in September 1940 and appointed to still another four-year term in 1942, both times without opposition from Senator Truman. On a leave of absence as a special assistant to the attorney general, Milligan conducted an investigation into possible election fraud in the 1940 elections that resulted in the closing of loopholes in the federal election laws.

In 1946 Milligan returned to the practice of law. Truman refused to appoint him to another term as U.S. attorney on the grounds that he had held the job far too long. In 1948 Milligan wrote a controversial book about his experiences, *Missouri Waltz: The Inside Story of the Pendergast Machine by the Man Who Smashed It.* Detractors, including President Truman, saw the book as a rather open attempt to link Truman to the criminality of the Pendergast machine. Milligan never again sought public office and died in Kansas City on June 19, 1959.

LAWRENCE H. LARSEN

Dorsett, Lyle W. *The Pendergast Machine.* Lincoln: University of Nebraska Press, 1980.

Larsen, Lawrence H., and Nancy J. Hulston. *Pendergast!* Columbia: University of Missouri Press, 1997.

Milligan, Maurice M. *Missouri Waltz: The Inside Story of the Pendergast Machine by the Man Who Smashed It.* New York: Scribner's, 1948.

Reddig, William M. *Tom's Town: Kansas City and the Pendergast Legend.* 1947. Reprint, Columbia: University of Missouri Press, 1986.

MINOR, VIRGINIA LOUISA (1824–1894)

Virginia Louisa Minor was born on March 27, 1824, in Caroline County, Virginia, the second of seven children of Warner and Maria Timberlake Minor. She was descended from a long line of distinguished Virginia planters. On August 31, 1843, she married Francis Minor of Orange, Virginia, who was a distant cousin, a graduate of Princeton and the University of Virginia Law School, and a practicing attorney. In 1845 they moved to St. Louis where they continued to live for the remainder of their lives. They had one child, Francis Gilmer, who was born in 1852 and died in 1866 in a shooting accident.

The Minors were avid supporters of the Union during the Civil War, despite their southern planter–class background. Virginia Minor participated in the Ladies' Union Aid Society, first founded in 1861 to assist wounded soldiers and their families, but eventually expanded to become the principal auxiliary of the Western Sanitary Commission. At the close of the war Minor and other women who had labored in support of the cause turned their energies toward securing rights for women. They assumed that their public demonstration of citizenship during the war, along with Republican Party support for the expansion of citizenship to the freed people in the war's aftermath, would facilitate the acquisition of similar rights for women.

Both Minor and her husband worked actively for the suffrage cause in Missouri for the remainder of their lives. Virginia Minor is credited with being the first person to take a public stand for woman suffrage in the state, when in 1867 she circulated a petition to the state legislature asking that a proposed amendment to the state constitution permitting African American men to vote be extended to include women. This petition was overwhelmingly rejected by the state legislature, and Minor and her husband turned their energies toward the courts.

In 1872 Minor attempted to register to vote, and when denied this right she and her husband filed a test case against the St. Louis registrar who had rejected her. According to the Minors, women already had the right to vote as citizens under the Constitution, a right that the recent passage of the Fourteenth Amendment and the enfranchisement of the freedmen served only to reinforce. After losing their case in the lower courts, the Minors appealed to the Supreme Court of the United States. In 1874 the court ruled unanimously to uphold the lower courts, stating that citizenship for women did not necessarily include suffrage, and that the right to regulate woman suffrage resided properly with the states and not with the federal government.

The strategy of claiming that women already had the franchise under the Constitution, as presented by the Minors to the Supreme Court in 1874, was initially endorsed in 1869 by the National Woman Suffrage Association, of which Virginia Minor was a member. With the failure of this strategy, woman suffragists split into two organizations, the National Woman Suffrage Association and the American Woman Suffrage Association. The former argued for the necessity of a federal amendment to the Constitution; the latter supported legislation by individual states. Virginia Minor, who was a founding member of the Woman's Suffrage Association in Missouri in 1867, and its first president, resigned from that organization when the majority of its membership voted to affiliate with the American Woman Suffrage Association. Minor remained an avid supporter of the National Woman Suffrage Association and the federal strategy.

In 1879 Minor once again became president of a suffrage organization when a St. Louis branch of the National Woman Suffrage Association was formed. When the two associations finally reunited in 1890, Minor was once again elected as president of the organization. She held this position until 1892, when she was forced to retire because of ill health. She died two years later, on August 14, 1894, and was buried at Bellefontaine Cemetery in St. Louis.

LeeAnn Whites

Morris, Monia Cook. "The History of Woman Suffrage in Missouri, 1867–1901." *Missouri Historical Review* 25 (October 1930–July 1931): 67–82.

Scott, Mary Semple, ed. "History of the Woman Suffrage Movement in Missouri." *Missouri Historical Review* 14 (April–July 1920): 281–384.

Staley, Laura. "Suffrage Movement in St. Louis during the 1870s." *Gateway Heritage* 3 (spring 1983): 34–41.

Stanton, Elizabeth Cady, Susan B. Anthony, and Ida Husted Harper, eds. *History of Woman Suffrage.* 1881. Reprint, New York: Arno Press, 1969.

MITCHELL, EWING Y. (1873–1954)

Born on June 5, 1873, in Springfield, Missouri, one of fourteen children born to Confederate general Ewing Y. Mitchell, young Ewing became enamored with politics while living with his brother-in-law, Missouri congressman **Richard P. Bland,** known as "Silver Dick." Following a brief period as a page in the United States Senate, Mitchell graduated with a law degree from National University in 1894.

The law did not interest Mitchell. His real affection was Democratic politics, which he practiced with a zeal bordering on fanaticism. During the 1890s he fell under the spell of the fiery populism practiced by William Jennings Bryan. Next came the Progressive Era, with its code of ethics that appealed to the young Missourian who preached a "politics of morality," emphasizing honor, frankness, efficiency, fairness, and righteousness. President Woodrow Wilson and Missouri governor **Joseph W. Folk** were Mitchell's heroes. Political machines that corrupted the democracy were his enemies.

Following a hiatus during the Republican ascendancy of the 1920s, Mitchell in 1932 seized upon the presidential candidacy of New York's governor, Franklin D. Roosevelt, whom he perceived as a personal reincarnation of Progressivism. Fighting against **Thomas J. Pendergast**'s Kansas City machine that supported **James A. Reed,** Mitchell organized "FDR delegates" at both the State and the National Democratic Conventions. He also served as the state chairman of the Roosevelt Business and Professional League. When FDR defeated President Herbert Hoover, he angered Pendergast by appointing Mitchell as assistant secretary of commerce.

When Mitchell assumed his new office, he began a campaign aimed at eliminating all forms of corruption in the Department of Commerce and in Missouri politics. Remembering FDR's promise to the "forgotten man," Mitchell launched a miniature crusade against waste and inefficiency in the Commerce Department and against Pendergast's corruption and vote fraud in Missouri.

Mitchell's cleanup campaign ran counter to FDR's policies of interest-group liberalism, legislative experimentalism, and ideological planning. Since fighting the depression, not cleaning up government, was the New Deal's top priority, Mitchell's cries of corruption fell on deaf ears. When Mitchell persisted, Roosevelt dismissed him in June 1935.

Cast out by the New Deal, Mitchell became an ardent critic, then a Republican. Like other old Progressives, he pursued a brand of reform that belonged to an earlier era. Still, he represented many of the positive aspects of this code of ethics in his uncompromising sense of honesty, integrity, and morality. Unfortunately, like his mentor Woodrow Wilson, Mitchell was naive and sacrificed a national career for an ideal. However, like Governor Folk, he equated bribery with treason.

In one sense, Mitchell's disgust with FDR and the New Deal's Machiavellian tactics served as a microcosmic symbol of Progressivism's unethical relationship with interest-group liberalism. However, in another, it showed the narrow limitations of Progressive ideology. In either case, Mitchell never compromised. He died in Springfield, Missouri, on August 28, 1954.

J. CHRISTOPHER SCHNELL

Mitchell, Ewing Y. *Kicked In and Kicked Out of the President's Little Cabinet.* Washington, D.C.: Andrew Jackson Press, 1936.
———. Papers. Western Historical Manuscripts Collection, Columbia.
Schnell, J. Christopher. "New Deal Scandals: FDR's Commerce Department." *Missouri Historical Review* 69 (July 1975): 357–75.
———. "Progressivism versus Interest Group Liberalism: A Political Biography of Missouri's Ewing Young Mitchell." Ph.D. diss., Kansas State University, 1972.

MONSEES, LOUIS M. (1858–1947)

Louis M. Monsees, a livestock breeder, is recognized for his contributions to the breeding of Missouri mules. He was born on November 20, 1858, the son of John H. and Lucinda Momberg Monsees, near Smithton, in Pettis County. As a youth he attended local schools while working with his father on the family farm.

In 1880 Monsees married Rickey Kastens, and in 1886 the couple purchased one hundred acres, which became the core of Limestone Valley Farm. By 1919 the farm had increased to seven hundred acres, with seven barns and three houses. Monsees was joined by his sons Nicholas, Deo, and Kalo in the management of the farm.

Monsees's career as a breeder of jacks and jennets had begun in 1870; at the age of twelve, he traded two pocketknives, a small pistol, and four dollars to a westbound traveler for a jack named Toby. His first annual sale of mules brought a total of $8,490. In the years that followed, the annual sale at his Limestone Valley Farm became the nation's leading auction of mules, often setting the year's market price. In 1910 total sales were $67,750. Individual jacks frequently brought more than $500; an occasional animal brought up to $5,000.

The Missouri mule developed as a result of many years of selective breeding for qualities such as large size, stamina, longevity, and spirited temperament. The mule is a hybrid of a male jackass and a female horse. European jacks were imported into the United States, especially into Kentucky and Tennessee, in the late 1820s. Two of these animals—Imported Warrior, of Maltese stock owned by Henry Clay, and Imported Mammoth, a Catalonian jack—were large beasts credited with improving the quality and increasing the size of American mules.

During the mid-nineteenth century, stockmen began importing draft horses, especially Percherons, into the United States in an attempt to improve the size and quality of farm horses. At the same time, breeders of racehorses were refining the thoroughbred. Early Missouri mule breeders bred thoroughbreds and Percherons to produce a large, spirited draft horse. When these mares were bred to large Kentucky jacks, the offspring were superior mules.

In the years following the Civil War, Missouri became recognized as the nation's leading producer of young mules, both because of the quality of the stock and because Missouri breeders won awards for their superior animals. The Limestone Valley Farm herd produced many prize-winning animals, including the St. Louis Exposition's grand champion, Orphan Boy, and the two-time Missouri State Fair grand champion and the 1915 San Francisco Panama-Pacific Exposition reserve grand champion, Limestone Monarch. Limestone Mammoth, of Imported Warrior and Imported Mammoth bloodlines, won all exhibitions in his ten-year show career. Monsees was the highest money winner at the St. Louis Exposition; his mules garnered more prizes than all other exhibitors combined: fifty out of fifty-three at St. Louis. At the 1915 San Francisco Panama-Pacific Exposition, his herd won thirty-three out of thirty-six prizes.

Monsees, believing that the quality of the jack was dominant in influencing the quality of the offspring, bred jacks with the bloodlines of both Imported Warrior and Imported Mammoth. By the early years of the twentieth century, most of the mules in the United States had bloodlines traceable to Limestone Valley Farm mules.

Monsees was also active in local agricultural and community organizations. A firm believer in scientific methods of farming, he actively supported Pettis County's efforts to secure a county extension agent. He was influential in establishing the mule show at the Missouri State Fair in 1911, and served as president of the Pettis County Bureau of Agriculture, which was organized in 1912. He was president of the Pettis County Wolf and Fox Hunters Association, and a member of Woodmen of the World, the Benevolent and Protective Order of Elks, and the Smithton Methodist Church. He also served as vice president of the American Jack Stud Association.

In the early twentieth century, mules were replaced by tractors, and Missouri's position as a leading producer of mules declined. Monsees retired in 1935, and spent his remaining years at Limestone Valley Farm, providing advice to breeders and dealers. He died at his home in Smithton on March 10, 1947.

RHONDA CHALFANT

"L. M. Monsees and Sons." In *Souvenir: Missouri State Fair, 1917,* ed. J. D. Smith. Sedalia, Mo.: Sedalia Printing, 1917.

"Limestone Valley Farm." In *Sedalia, Missouri,* ed. George Scruton. Sedalia, Mo.: Sedalia Evening Sentinel, 1904.

McGruder, Mark A. *History of Pettis County, Missouri.* Topeka, Kans.: Historical Publishing Company, 1919.

Renner, G. K. "The Mule in Missouri Agriculture, 1821–1950." *Missouri Historical Review* 74 (July 1980): 433–57.

Sedalia Democrat, March 10, 1947.

MOORE, MARIANNE (1887–1972)

Although Marianne Moore is probably the most original of the modernist poets born in the United States, her career shares important parallels with that of **T. S. Eliot,** her fellow native Missourian. Both grandchildren of ministers, Moore and Eliot were born within less than a year of each other—Moore in 1887, Eliot in 1888—and within a few miles of each other. Moore was born in Kirkwood, a suburb of St. Louis, and Eliot in St. Louis. Both attended college in the East; Moore graduated from Bryn Mawr in 1909, the same year Eliot graduated from Harvard.

In 1915 they began to publish their poetry professionally; Eliot, however, was the first to publish a book of poems, *Prufrock and Other Observations* (1917). Moore echoed Eliot's title when she published *Observations* (1924), her first book in the United States. In that book she provided notes for her poems as Eliot had done when he published his famous poem "The Waste Land" (1922). Each served as editor of an important literary journal; for more than a decade Eliot edited the *Criterion;* Moore edited the *Dial* from 1925 to 1929. Their careers intersected in 1935 when Eliot edited and wrote an introduction for Moore's *Selected Poems.*

Both won major literary awards early and late in their literary careers. Eliot won the *Dial* Award for poetry for "The Waste Land" and Moore for *Observations.* Moore won the Pulitzer Prize for poetry, the National Book Award, and the Bollingen Prize for her *Collected Poems* (1951) and Eliot the Nobel Prize for literature in 1948. Eliot achieved his literary fame earlier and on a much broader scale than Moore gained hers. Still, late in her career, Moore became a celebrity in her own right.

Finally, Moore and Eliot shared, perhaps because of their ministerial grandfathers in Missouri, a belief in Christianity. Their belief distinguished them from other modernist poets such as Wallace Stevens and William Carlos Williams, but the nature of their beliefs sharply delineates the major differences between their poetry. From the beginning Moore's poetry exhibits what she would call "a steadfastness" of belief. Apparently, she did not experience, as Eliot's early poetry suggests he did, the uncertainty of belief, "the dark night of the soul," what Moore in her 1936 review of Eliot's *Collected Poems* called the "Horror, which is unbelief." In that same review Moore acknowledged that the certainty of faith her poetry reveals is a condition gained only through struggle. She observed, "One who attains equilibrium in spite of opposition to himself from within, is stronger than if there had been no opposition to overcome; and, in art, freedom evolving from a liberated constraint is more significant than if it had not by nature been cramped."

The "steadfastness" of Moore's belief provided a solid foundation for the originality of her vision. It was the constraint that provided the buoyancy to her poems, as she acknowledged in a 1948 essay, "Humility, Concentration, and Gusto," when she wrote, "gusto thrives on freedom, and freedom in art, as in life, is the result of a discipline imposed by ourselves." The confidence provided by her belief permitted her to never compromise her vision, to go on doing, as she wrote of another artist, what idiosyncrasy told her to do. Consequently, her poems often seem to have peculiarly "unpoetic" subjects such as steamrollers, quartz clocks, or animals such as the pangolin and the jerboa.

Because she shaped her poems on the design of the poem's first stanza—a design determined intuitively rather than traditionally—they do not look and sound like traditional poems. Other modernist poets developed an interplay between the old and new way of writing poems, as Eliot called for them to do in his famous essay "Tradition and the Individual Talent," but none developed that interplay as singularly as did Marianne Moore.

The daughter of Mary Warner Moore and John Milton Moore, Marianne Craig Moore was born on November 15, 1887, in the home of her grandfather, John R. Warner, pastor of the Kirkwood Presbyterian Church. Pregnant with her daughter, Mary Warner Moore and her one-year-old son, John Warner, had come to live with her father because her husband, an engineer, had suffered a nervous breakdown when his plans to manufacture a smokeless furnace failed. Marianne Moore would never see her father. His absence knotted the bond of mother, brother, and sister that formed so much of Moore's sense of steadfastness and affection.

When the Reverend John Warner died in 1894, Mary Moore moved her family to live with relatives in Pennsylvania, settling eventually in Carlisle. Mary Moore taught at the Metzger Institute, where Marianne earned her preparatory education. As a single mother without family support, Mary Moore proved exceptional. She provided her children with college educations: Warner at Yale and Marianne at Bryn Mawr. After earning her A.B., Marianne returned to Carlisle, where in 1910 she graduated from Carlisle Commercial College. From 1911 through 1915 she taught commercial subjects at the U.S. Indian School in Carlisle. Jim Thorpe, the famous athlete, was one of her students.

While teaching in Carlisle, Moore began to submit her poems to literary journals, and, in 1915, after numerous rejections, she found success first in England, when Richard Aldington published seven of her poems in the *Egoist*. In that same year she also published poems in Alfred Kreymborg's *Others* and Harriet Monroe's *Poetry*. In 1915 she made her first journey, at the invitation of Kreymborg, to New York where she experienced, at Alfred Stieglitz's Studio 291, her introduction to modern art. When she returned to Carlisle, she knew that one day she would have to live in New York.

In 1916 Marianne Moore and her mother moved from Carlisle to Chatham, New Jersey, to keep house for her brother, who had accepted a position as minister of a Presbyterian church. Mary Moore and her two children developed an intense closeness and exclusiveness, including pet names for each other taken from Kenneth Grahame's *Wind in the Willows*. Their closeness seemed to have constructed, in the words of Donald Hall, "a single ego three times stronger than an ordinary human ego." Their extraordinary relationship, Hall continues, was marked by "scrupulosity, kindness, ambition, reticence, relentlessness, eccentricity, modesty, and egotism," and it survived Warner Moore's career in the navy and his marriage. It also provided Marianne Moore with the character and the steadfastness that helped make her the poet she became.

In 1918, when Warner Moore went to sea as a navy chaplain, Marianne Moore and her mother moved to metropolitan New York where Marianne would live the rest of her life. There she worked at a branch of the New York Public Library and continued to publish in the modernist literary journals. Her poems and her personality attracted a wide range of friends. Friendship led to the publication in 1921 of her first book, *Poems,* when H. D. (Hilda Doolittle) and Bryher (Winifred Ellerman) published it without Moore's knowledge or consent. Her editorship of the *Dial* led to a lifelong friendship with Hildegarde and James Sibley Watson, one of the journal's copublishers.

During her editorship, Moore wrote many reviews and essays but no poetry. Not until some time after the *Dial* ceased publication in mid-1929 did Moore, then living in Brooklyn with her mother, begin again to write poetry. Some of those poems such as "The Steeple-Jack," "The Jeroboa," "The Plumet Basilisk," and "Nine Nectarines" are among her best known because, in part, they appeared first, at the suggestion of T. S. Eliot, in her *Selected Poems* (1935), and would continue to appear first in the collected and "complete" editions of her works. In the mid-1930s, Moore began another important and abiding literary friendship when she became a mentor to the young poet Elizabeth Bishop.

On July 9, 1947, Mary Warner Moore died, and her daughter suffered the loss of not only her mother, but also her dearest friend, her most severe critic, and her lifelong companion. To lessen her sorrow, Moore immersed herself in translating La Fontaine's *Fables* and in preparing her *Collected Poems,* which appeared in 1951 and won the Pulitzer Prize, the National Book Award, the Bollingen Prize, and the

Gold Medal of the National Institute of Arts and Letters. These awards and the publication of her translation of *The Fables of La Fontaine* (1954) and a selection of her prose pieces, *Predilections* (1955), thrust Moore, then in her midsixties, into celebrity.

Network television interviewed her; the *New Yorker* "profiled" her; George Pratt Lynes and Richard Avedon photographed portraits of her; *Esquire* and *Saturday Review* featured her on their covers; and the Ford Motor Company asked her to name an automobile for them. Although she provided Ford with a plethora of exotic names, the company decided finally to keep the name in the family and called the car Edsel.

Moore's celebrity troubled some of her admirers and led them to consider her later poems inferior. Similarly, some readers were disappointed at her reduction in *The Complete Poems of Marianne Moore* (1967) of her well-known poem "Poetry" to only its first three lines. (The older original version with the line about poetry containing "imaginary gardens with real toads in them" she relegated to the notes.) Yet, as Margaret Holley has remarked, these late poems represent a shift from the private to the public, from the analytic to the celebratory. They also demonstrate the "steadfastness" of belief and advocacy of moral value that characterize this remarkable artist's work and person. Like the work of a magician, her poems transform the ordinary so that we see the world and ourselves anew. Marianne Moore died on February 5, 1972.

LARRY VONALT

Hall, Donald. *Marianne Moore: The Cage and the Animal.* New York: Pegasus, 1970.

Holley, Margaret. *The Poetry of Marianne Moore: A Study in Voice and Value.* Cambridge: Cambridge University Press, 1987.

Molesworth, Charles. *Marianne Moore: A Literary Life.* New York: Atheneum, 1990.

Moore, Marianne. Collection. Rosenbach Museum and Library, Philadelphia.

Stapelton, Laurence. *Marianne Moore: The Poet's Advance.* Princeton: Princeton University Press, 1978.

Willis, Patricia C., ed. *Marianne Moore: Vision into Verse.* Philadelphia: Rosenbach Museum and Library, 1987.

MOORE, WALTHALL, SR. (1886–1960)

Walthall Moore Sr. was born on May 1, 1886, in Marion, Alabama, the son of John and Sarah Moore. His family moved to St. Louis later that same year. He was educated in the city's segregated elementary and secondary schools. Following his secondary education, he enrolled in Howard University in Washington, D.C.

Upon completion of his education at Howard University, Moore returned to Missouri and helped incorporate Missouri's first African American–owned steam laundry. He also worked as a clerk in the St. Louis post office and, later, in the Railway Mail Service. He became active in politics during the late teens, and he ran for the state legislature as a Republican in 1920. He was elected to represent the Sixth District of Missouri (a part of the city of St. Louis). Thus, in 1921, Moore became the first African American in Missouri history to serve in the General Assembly.

Moore's greatest contribution to his state came in the form of a bill he introduced to upgrade Lincoln Institute in Jefferson City to a state university. Up to this point, Lincoln had served the state's black population primarily as a normal and vocational training school. Although the bill designating Lincoln as the state university for Missouri's African American population passed, Moore's request for a $1 million appropriation for the school was rejected.

Moore failed in his bid for reelection in 1922, but won election in 1924 to represent St. Louis's Third District. He served in the legislature from 1925 through 1930, completing four terms as a state representative. During his tenure he served on the following committees: Workmen's Compensation, Municipal Corporations, and Appropriations. He became one of Missouri's delegates-at-large to the 1928 Republican National Convention.

Moore also became a symbol of social progress. Along with his political standing, he held great popularity as a public figure, and his speaking engagements spanned the state. His eloquence and sincerity won over both black and white audiences. He was fond of voicing his dedication not only to black causes, but to the traditional obligations of his office.

Moore died in St. Louis on April 8, 1960. He is buried in Oakdale Cemetery in St. Louis. His wife, F. A. Ferguson of Marion, Indiana, preceded him in death. Moore was survived by a son, Walthall Moore Jr.

GARY R. KREMER

Official Manual of the State of Missouri, 1929–1930. Jefferson City: Secretary of State, 1930.

St. Louis Argus, April 15, 1960.

St. Louis Globe-Democrat, September 14, 1958.

MOREHOUSE, ALBERT PICKETT (1835–1891)

Albert P. Morehouse was born on July 11, 1835, in Delaware County, Ohio, the son of Stephen Morehouse, a native of Newark County, New Jersey, and Harriett Wood Morehouse, a native of New York and the daughter of Russell Wood, who also later settled in Delaware County, Ohio. Albert's education was limited, but at age eighteen he began teaching school in Ohio, and in 1856 moved to Nodaway County, Missouri, where he continued teaching and studied law. In 1860 he was admitted to the bar, beginning practice in Montgomery County, Iowa.

When the Civil War began Morehouse moved back to Nodaway County and was a schoolteacher in the Graham area. In November 1861 he enlisted in Colonel Kimball's Six-Month Militia for the Union side and was elected as first lieutenant of Company E, made up of Nodaway County men. After the six-month period expired, Morehouse enrolled in the Thirty-sixth Enrolled Missouri Militia, Company G, and was promoted to assistant provost marshal in 1862, and finally to quartermaster sergeant.

While the militia was camped in Lafayette County, Missouri, Morehouse and his men visited the McFadden farmhouse where the daughter provided the soldiers with food and even made tea for them. Morehouse was struck by the beauty of Mattie McFadden, and she, in turn, was attracted to the tall, handsome lieutenant. The couple corresponded, kept in touch during the war, and were married in 1865 in Lexington, Missouri. They had three children: Nannie, Anna, and Edwin.

Enrollment in the Thirty-sixth Militia permitted Morehouse to remain in Maryville, where he joined Amos Graham in law practice. By 1871 Morehouse had a full-fledged real estate business in Nodaway County, plus he was actively engaged in politics, especially through his newspaper, the *Nodaway Democrat.* In 1872 he was delegate to the Democratic National Convention in Baltimore, and in 1876 to the Democratic National Convention in St. Louis.

In 1876 Morehouse ran for the state legislature and won, unseating H. M. Jackson by 197 votes. During the January 1877 session, he sent a letter to his newspaper stating that the "legislative mill grinds slow," and Jefferson City was dull and gloomy.

Again, in 1882, Morehouse ran a successful campaign for representative. His public service and contacts in Jefferson City were groundwork for the next step, lieutenant governor. He shared the 1884 Democratic ticket with **John S. Marmaduke,** and they readily carried the state. As lieutenant governor, Morehouse became the presiding officer of the Senate in January 1885. Governor Marmaduke died in office in December 1887, and Morehouse became the governor of Missouri on January 3, 1888, serving out the remainder of the term.

In 1888 Morehouse became a candidate for governor and had strong support in northwest Missouri. However, **David R. Francis** received the Democratic nomination. Morehouse left Jefferson City and returned to Maryville where he again entered the real estate business, this time with Nat Sission.

The county was shocked on September 23, 1891, when they learned of the death of Morehouse. He had just assisted in driving some cattle from near Ravenwood to his Barnard farm, and became overheated. The next day he was ill and was so delirious that watchers were called in. When daughter Nannie left her father alone for just a brief moment, he took his own life. Dr. Koch listed the death as delirium caused by sunstroke and compounded by typhoid fever. A. P. Morehouse is buried in Oak Hill Cemetery in Maryville, with a "governor" marker for a headstone.

THOMAS W. CARNEAL

Cooper, Martha. *The Civil War and Nodaway County.* Parts 1 and 2. Signal Mountain, Tenn.: Mountain Press, 1989.

———. *Life, Liberty, and the Pursuit of Happiness: Black History of Nodaway County.* Maryville, Mo.: Accent Printing, 1986.

Guitar, Sarah, and Floyd C. Shoemaker, eds. *The Messages and Proclamations of the Governors of the State of Missouri.* Vol. 7. Columbia: State Historical Society of Missouri, 1926.

The History of Nodaway County, Missouri. St. Joseph, Mo.: National Historical Company, 1882.

MORGAN, GEORGE (1743–1810)

George Morgan, a merchant, government official, and land speculator, and the founder of New Madrid, Missouri, was born in Philadelphia, Pennsylvania, on February 14, 1743, the youngest of Evan and Joanna Biles Morgan's nine children. Orphaned at an early age, George lived with a great-aunt until the age of thirteen when he was apprenticed to merchant John Baynton. At the firm of Baynton and Wharton, Morgan advanced from apprentice to clerk and finally to full partner. In 1764 he married Baynton's daughter Mary, and their forty-six-year marriage produced eleven children.

When Baynton and Wharton expanded its operations into the Illinois Country, the partners placed Morgan in charge of the firm's headquarters at Kaskaskia, where he quickly rose to prominence. However, the company lost money, and in the early 1770s it went out of business. After returning to Philadelphia, Morgan spearheaded a lengthy campaign to secure compensation for merchants who had sustained losses during Pontiac's Rebellion. His tenacious and protracted efforts all came to naught when the Continental Congress, the Virginia legislature and courts, and eventually the United States Congress and Supreme Court all rejected the claims.

In 1775 Morgan enlisted in a light infantry company, with the rank of first lieutenant and later captain, but shortly thereafter he left the unit to accept an appointment from the Continental Congress as an Indian agent. His previous experience in the western country had led to his selection. Early in 1777 he was given the rank of colonel and named deputy commissary general of purchases in the Western Department. He held that post until he resigned in 1779 to pursue various speculative ventures.

When the Continental Congress rejected one of his projects in 1788, Morgan conferred with the Spanish minister to the United States, Don Diego Gardoqui, about a plan for recruiting Americans to settle in Spain's sparsely populated domains on the west bank of the Mississippi. Morgan enthusiastically endorsed the idea and quickly presented the Spanish official with an ambitious proposal for the establishment of a colony near the mouth of the Ohio River in present-day Missouri. In return for his services, Morgan asked to be placed in charge of the colony with the rank of colonel in the Spanish army. In addition, he requested a salary and land grants for himself and members of his family. He also suggested that the Spaniards grant the colony's inhabitants religious freedom and permit them self-government, subject to the king's veto. Morgan contended that such liberal terms would be essential to ensure that the Anglo-American settlers would remain loyal to Spain.

Gardoqui gave the American promoter letters of reference and promises of financial support, and on the strength of those assurances Morgan pressed ahead without first securing royal approval for the scheme. On October 3, 1788, he issued a handbill announcing his plans for the settlement of New Madrid and recruiting volunteers to join him in the venture. He selected approximately seventy individuals who accompanied him to Upper Louisiana, but following their arrival local Spanish officials warned Morgan that the site he had selected for the settlement opposite the mouth of the Ohio was prone to flooding. He promptly chose an alternate location forty miles further south and drew up an elaborate plan for New Madrid, which was to be the centerpiece of his colony. It provided for wide streets, public parks, schools, and churches of various denominations. Morgan also displayed an uncommon concern for the environmental quality of the settlement. He initiated a land survey, authorized preliminary land sales subject to final royal approbation, and put his crews to work clearing land and constructing buildings in anticipation of an influx of American settlers. With work under way at New Madrid, Morgan headed for New Orleans to secure final approval for the project from Spanish officials.

Morgan's grand design came to an abrupt end in May 1789 when Louisiana's governor-general, Esteban Miró, rejected many elements of the plan. Miró feared that the conditions that Morgan proposed would create an essentially American set-tlement that would cause Spain problems. Morgan was not the only American interested in collaborating with the Spaniards to promote immigration, and Miró apparently concluded that an alternative proposal submitted by Gen. **James Wilkinson** was preferable.

Having failed to secure the terms that he desired, Morgan returned to Philadelphia in 1789 and quickly lost interest in the settlement. He turned his attention to the development of an estate in western Pennsylvania that he had inherited from his brother, and died there on March 10, 1810.

JAMES W. PAGE III

Houck, Louis. *The Spanish Regime in Missouri: A Collection of Papers and Documents Relating to Upper Louisiana.* Vol. 2. Chicago: R. R. Donnelley and Sons, 1909.

Savelle, Max. *George Morgan: Colony Builder.* New York: Columbia University Press, 1932.

MOSS, LUELLA ST. CLAIR (1865–1947)

Luella St. Clair Moss, an educator and community activist, was born in Virden, Illinois, to Symour and Julia McLynn Wilcox on June 25, 1865. Educated in the public schools, Moss was the first female graduate of Virden High School and the valedictorian of her class. In 1865 she received a B.S. degree from Hamilton College in Lexington, Kentucky. The following year she married Franklin P. St. Clair, a mathematics instructor at Hamilton. Because of his illness, they left Lexington and lived for short periods in West Virginia, Pennsylvania, and Illinois. For about four years they resided in Colorado, where Luella St. Clair taught school in a rural area. Their only child, Annilee, was born in 1889.

In the summer of 1893 Franklin St. Clair became the president of Christian College, a school for women in Columbia, Missouri; however, a few months later, on November 21, he died. The trustees of Christian College then offered the presidency to his young widow, who became one of the first women in the United States to hold such a position.

Because of St. Clair's innovations during her first tenure at Christian College, enrollment increased, and she was able to double the number of faculty members. However, illness forced her to resign the presidency in 1897. A friend, Emma Moore, replaced her. By April 1899 St. Clair had recovered her health, and she and Moore became copresidents. Together they began to expand the college's facilities. During this second presidential tenure, however, St. Clair suffered the loss of her child: in January 1900, a month before her eleventh birthday, Annilee St. Clair died of rheumatic fever.

From 1903 to 1909 Luella St. Clair served as the first female president of Hamilton College, her alma mater. There, too, she made many improvements and doubled enrollment. Then, in 1909, when Moore resigned as president of Christian College, the school's trustees asked St. Clair to resume that position. During her third presidency at Christian, St. Clair continued its expansion: a total of eight new buildings were added during her three administrations. Two years after returning to Columbia, in 1911, Luella St. Clair married Woodson Moss, a physician teaching at the University of Missouri's medical school. Upon his death in 1920, Luella St. Clair Moss retired as president of Christian College.

Retirement allowed Moss time to pursue other interests she had developed over the years. She was one of the founders in 1899 of the Tuesday Club, a women's group in Columbia. This organization, active in furthering civic projects, developed the city's public library. Moss, an officer of the Equal Suffrage League in Columbia, helped to establish the League of Women Voters after ratification of the Nineteenth Amendment and to organize sessions to educate women about citizenship. From 1925 to 1927 she served as president of the Missouri League of Women Voters and began its first statewide bulletin, the *Missouri Woman Citizen.* In 1922 she won the Democratic primary as a candidate for the Eighth Congressional District, the first woman ever nominated in the state to run for Congress. However, Moss lost the general election.

Numerous other distinctions came to Moss over the years: she was the first woman on the Columbia Board of Education (1922–1925), president of the Missouri Federation of Women's Clubs (1929–1931), and the first woman appointed to the Missouri Library Commission (1933) and then its president (1935). In 1930 she was the first woman to be a vice president of the Disciples of Christ's international convention held in Washington, D.C. On three other occasions she went to Washington as a delegate to the Conference on the Cause and Cure of War. She served on the national board of the League of Women Voters and on the New York World's Fair Committee. She received membership in Delta Kappa Gamma, an international honor society for women in education. In 1937 Culver-Stockton College awarded Moss an honorary LL.D. degree.

Along with other Missouri women who campaigned for woman suffrage, Moss's name appears on a plaque in the state capitol under an inscription honoring those "whose courageous work opened the opportunities for complete citizenship to all the women in the state." The national office of the League of Women Voters in Washington also recognized her contributions to woman suffrage by including her name on a National Roll of Honor. Moss died on August 18, 1947, in Columbia, Missouri, where she is buried.

PATRICIA ASHMAN

Dains, Mary K., ed. *Show Me Missouri Women: Selected Biographies.* Kirksville, Mo.: Thomas Jefferson University Press, 1989.

Hale, Allean Lemmon. *Petticoat Pioneer: The Story of Christian College, Oldest College for Women West of the Mississippi.* St. Paul, Minn.: North Central Publishing, 1968.

Moss, Luella St. Clair. Manuscripts Collection. Western Historical Manuscripts Collection, Columbia.

MOTEN, BENNIE (1894–1935)

"We called it the Kansas City beat, . . . and I think the man responsible for this more than anyone else was Bennie Moten," recalled guitarist Charles Goodwin.

Benjamin "Bennie" Moten was born on November 13, 1894, in Kansas City, Missouri. At age twelve he played baritone horn in Blackburn's Juvenile Brass Band. A year later he switched to piano and studied with Charlie Watts and Scrap Harris, local teachers who were former students of **Scott Joplin.**

Moten organized his first band in 1918, which was known as "B. B. & D." for its members Bennie Moten, Bailey Hancock, and Dude Lankford. By 1921 the band had grown to six pieces and was playing at the Panama Club and Street's Hotel Lounge in Kansas City. Okeh Records recorded Moten's "Elephant Wobble" and "Crawdad Blues" in 1923 in their St. Louis studio. Moten's was the first Kansas City band and only the third jazz group anywhere to be recorded. He recorded with Okeh again in 1924 and 1925, for a total of twenty titles.

In 1926 Moten signed with Victor Records. His was the only band in the Southwest to hold a recording contract at that time; he eventually recorded seventy-seven titles with Victor. His orchestra, now consisting of ten pieces, dominated the Kansas City jazz scene. They toured widely in the Midwest and, beginning in 1928, on the East Coast as well. Along with recording trips to Camden, New Jersey, they booked engagements in ballrooms in New York and Philadelphia.

In 1929 Moten raided several members from the Blue Devils, including **William "Count" Basie,** Jimmy Rushing, Hot Lips Page, and Eddie Durham. In 1931 Walter Page, leader of the Blue Devils, also joined the band. In December 1932 the Bennie Moten Orchestra made its last recording with Victor. Titles from that session include "Moten Swing," "Prince of Wails," "Toby," and "Lafayette," and are regarded by many as the finest expressions of the Kansas City style. Because of the worsening depression, Victor did not record Moten's orchestra after 1932, and there is no documentation for how the band evolved over the next three years.

Beginning in the mid-1920s and through the 1930s, jazz musicians from throughout the Southwest were "goin' to Kansas City" for jobs. Kansas City was a wide-open town under **Thomas J. Pendergast**'s political machine, and gambling halls and cabarets provided steady employment for jazz bands. Elements of ragtime, brass bands, and blues came together to form a distinctive Kansas City sound. One historian states that the "discography of the Bennie Moten Orchestra . . . is by itself a capsule history of Kansas City style."

Moten began as a ragtime pianist. The riff—a repeated rhythmic phrase—is borrowed from ragtime and forms the foundation of Kansas City jazz. His early recordings reflect a crude, "stomping" style based on a 2/4 beat because Moten was still using a tuba in the rhythm section, a carryover from brass bands. When Walter Page joined Moten in 1931, he brought the string bass to the rhythm section, which allowed the band to use a flexible 4/4 rhythm and play hard swing. Moten is widely credited with popularizing this distinctive sound that became known as the Kansas City style.

Moten had a strong musical sense and hired the best musicians for his band. Other alumni of the Moten band include Lester Young, Ben Webster, Buster Smith, Eddie Barefield, Dan Minor, Harlan Leonard, and Woodie Walder. Moten was a good but unremarkable pianist. After hiring Basie he devoted more of his time to the business side. A shrewd promoter, Moten scheduled his band in cities around payday, renting a hall and holding a dance when people were flush with money.

In 1935 Moten scheduled an engagement for his band in Denver. He stayed behind in Kansas City for a tonsillectomy he had long postponed. Dr. Bruce, a prominent local surgeon and a friend of Moten's, performed the operation. Whether the doctor was hungover from the previous night out with Moten or whether Moten flinched at the wrong moment will never be known. In any case, an artery was cut, and Moten died of heart failure on April 2, 1935.

Nephew Buster Moten took over the band, but he lacked Bennie's personality and leadership. The band split in two, with most of the members going with Buster Smith and Count Basie. Known as the Barons of Rhythm, this band carried on the Moten heritage of the Kansas City sound.

JANET BRUCE CAMPBELL

Driggs, Franklin S. "Kansas City and the Southwest." In *Jazz,* ed. Nat Hentoff and Albert J. McCarthy. New York: Rinehart, 1959.

Pearson, Nathan W., Jr. *Goin' to Kansas City.* Urbana: University of Illinois Press, 1987.
Russell, Ross. *Jazz Style in Kansas City and the Southwest.* Berkeley and Los Angeles: University of California Press, 1971.

MOTT, FRANK LUTHER (1886–1964)

Frank Luther Mott was a journalism historian and educator and the third dean of the Missouri School of Journalism. He was born in Keokuk County, Iowa, on April 4, 1886, the son of David Charles Mott, a weekly newspaper editor and publisher, and Mary E. Tipton Mott. His early education involved learning by newspaper reporting and studying literature and philosophy in college. He began at Simpson College at Indianola, Iowa, and then transferred his senior year to the University of Chicago to complete his bachelor of philosophy degree in 1907. After spending ten years as a newspaper publisher and editor in Iowa, he decided to become an academic. Mott received his M.A. (1919) and a Ph.D. (1928) in English at Columbia University.

While Mott began his academic career as a professor of English, he was appointed professor of journalism and director of the Iowa School of Journalism in 1927 before moving to Missouri in 1942. As the third dean of the Missouri School of Journalism, he built the graduate program and taught until his retirement as professor emeritus and dean emeritus in 1956. Known by students for his histrionics as a lecturer in the famed required undergraduate course, History and Principles, he began by explaining, "history throws light on the growth and meaning of principles, and the principles give meaning to history." One session nearly always included his dramatic recitation of "The Face on the Barroom Floor," a lesson in colorful reporting.

Mott's contributions to scholarship are legendary. He wrote more than a dozen books and edited or coedited a dozen more and authored more than one hundred scholarly articles. His best-known work was the award-winning five-volume series *A History of American Magazines* (1928, 1938, 1957, 1968), a detailed chronology of the great editors, their influence, and their salaries. In 1939 he received a Pulitzer Prize for volumes 2 and 3. After publishing volume 4 in 1957, he received the Bancroft Prize and the 1958 National Research Award of Kappa Tau Alpha, a journalism scholastic fraternity. His fifth volume was published posthumously (1968).

Concerning his vast scholarship, Mott once wrote that "the profession and business of journalism, to which most of my life has been dedicated, suffers more than most occupations under the tyranny of the clock." He began the race against time with fiction, *Six Prophets Out of the Middle West* (1917), and short stories such as "The Man with the Good Face" (1921), which was reprinted the next year in *O'Brien's Best Short Stories*. He collaborated with artist Grant Wood on the monograph *Revolt against the City* (1935).

For decades, American journalism students used Mott's history text, *American Journalism: A History of Newspapers in the United States through 250 Years, 1690 to 1940* (1941, 1950, 1962). He defined his focus as follows: "The whole history of American journalism is a history of the leadership of great editors and publishers. And it is a mistake to assert, as some do, that the day of the great paper, the great editor, the great newspaper writer and the great publisher is past."

In "A Free Press" (1958), written on the anniversary of the fiftieth year of the Missouri School of Journalism, Mott stressed the importance of mass communication in a democracy: "if those decisions are to be made intelligently, they must be based upon adequate knowledge possessed by people concerning events and conditions." He recorded in his diary, "It is a public service that the journalist performs and should be looked upon as such by the laws and by legislature."

Mott also wrote *Jefferson and the Press* (1943) and *Golden Multitudes* (1947), a history of best-sellers in America. In 1962 he publicly reminisced in *Time Enough: Essays in Autobiography* that anything "a person wants to do, if he wants hard enough to do it and if it is within his power, he will find time for."

Just before his death, Mott found time to complete *The Missouri Reader* (1964). He wrote about his adopted state, "Missouri is a state of extraordinary variety—in its topography, its population, its culture, its activities, its history." His edited collection showed Missouri's versatility through stories, such as **Mark Twain**'s "Steamboats at Hannibal"; essays, such as **Mary Margaret McBride**'s "Country Fair"; songs, such as "The Ballad of Jesse James"; poems, such as **Sara Teasdale**'s "Sunset (St. Louis)"; sketches, such as William Allen White's "The Man Who Made the Star" and **Langston Hughes**'s "I Remember the Blues"; and folktales, such as **Vance Randolph**'s "Who Blowed Up the Church House?"

Mott had his critics, and some of Missouri's editors and publishers would have agreed with Iowa colleague George Gallup's assertion that "he did not qualify as a real newspaperman." Yet, as an educator and scholar, he had universal respect. Beloved by graduate students, his Literature of Journalism weekly seminar was legendary. Held in his book-lined home study, ideas fed the soul, and tea, coffee, and cookies fed the body.

Mott's peers recognized his vast scholarship and leadership. Right after World War II he assisted the U.S. military in France and Japan in the special training of journalists. He served as the editor in chief of *Journalism Quarterly*, the first scholarly journal in the field, and as chair of the National Council for Research in Journalism. Twice he was elected president of the American Association of Schools and Departments of Journalism. With George Gallup, he founded *Quill and Scroll*.

During the growing pains of journalism education, Mott was one of the founding giants. He wrote, "No matter how burdened or harried we are, there is always time for what we want most if we make it. . . . There is time enough in a life." For his "time enough," he received honorary degrees from Simpson College and Boston, Temple, and Marquette Universities.

Mott married Vera H. Ingram in 1910, and they had one daughter, Mildred Mott Wedel. Mott died on October 23, 1964.

BETTY HOUCHIN WINFIELD

Columbia Missourian, October 23, 1964.

Kansas City Star, October 23, 1964.

Marshall, Max Lawrence. "Frank Luther Mott: Journalism Educator." Ph.D. diss., University of Missouri–Columbia, 1968.

Mott, Frank Luther. Papers. Western Historical Manuscripts Collection, Columbia.

———. *Time Enough: Essays in Autobiography.* Chapel Hill: University of North Carolina Press, 1962.

New York Times, October 24, 1964.

MUENCH, FRIEDRICH (1799–1881)

Friedrich Muench was born on June 25, 1799, the son of a Lutheran pastor in Niedergemuenden in the German state of Hesse. While studying theology at the University of Giessen (1816–1819) he was exposed to rationalist religion and radical democratic political movements—influences that would stay with him for the rest of his life. He returned to a pastorate in his hometown as assistant and then successor to his father. In 1826 he married Marianna Borberg, with whom he had two children before her early death in 1830. One and one-half years later he entered a second marriage with Louise Fritz that was to last nearly half a century.

Disillusioned by renewed political repression and the failed revolutionary efforts of the early 1830s, Muench and his university friend and brother-in-law **Paul Follenius** formed the Giessen Emigration Society. In 1834, influenced by Gottfried Duden's guidebook, they led a party of five hundred to Missouri, where they hoped to found a model German republic. The society broke up and scattered almost immediately upon arrival, but Muench, Follenius, and several other families settled on farms near Dutzow in Warren County. Having been exposed to agriculture in his youth, Muench was among the more successful of the so-called Latin Farmers, and supported his growing family largely through farming, though he never became wealthy from his 120 acres.

Muench never formally held a pulpit in America, but did deliver an occasional rationalist sermon or lecture, and in 1844 he helped found a rationalist religious society in eastern Missouri. He also contributed frequently to a local rationalist journal, the *Hermann Licht-Freund* (Friend of Light). In 1847 his *Treatise on Religion and Christianity, Orthodoxy and Rationalism,* which had previously appeared in German, was published in Boston through the efforts of Theodore Parker.

Under the pen name "Far West," Muench became a well-known and frequent contributor to German newspapers in Philadelphia, New York, Cincinnati, St. Louis, and rural Missouri, as well as several papers in Germany. On the topic of agriculture, he became editor in 1860 of the short-lived *Farmer-Zeitung* of St. Louis, and for twenty-five years contributed to and then coedited the German edition of the *American Agriculturist.* He was one of the pioneers of viticulture in Missouri, and his treatise on the subject appeared in various German editions between 1859 and 1877 and in an 1865 English translation under the title *School for American Grape Culture.*

Muench was solicited to write an immigrant guidebook on the state of Missouri, and upon its appearance in 1859 he made his only visit back to Germany, promoting his book and his adopted state. During and after the Civil War he served without pay under three governors on the state board of immigration.

Although the 1850 Census shows him owning a black female domestic, Muench firmly opposed slavery in his political and journalistic career. Like most Missouri Germans, he initially associated with the Democratic Party, giving his first speech on its behalf in 1840. However, he followed its Free-Soil Benton wing and eventually broke with it entirely. Even before the Republican Party was organized in Missouri, Muench campaigned in 1856 for presidential candidate **John Charles Frémont** among the Germans of New York, Pennsylvania, Ohio, and Indiana. In 1860 he served as a delegate to the Republican convention that nominated Lincoln, ran on the party's statewide ticket in Missouri, and campaigned among Illinois Germans as well. In 1862 he was elected to a four-year term in the state senate, where he distinguished himself as an uncompromising member of the "Charcoal" radical emancipationist faction.

Muench never held elective office thereafter but continued his journalistic efforts, writing in favor of black suffrage in 1868. Disillusioned by the corruption under President **Ulysses S. Grant,** he supported the Liberal Republicans in 1872 but was disappointed

with the nomination of Horace Greeley, and subsequently returned to the Republican fold.

Muench died at his farm near Dutzow on December 15, 1881, survived by his wife, six children, thirty-three grandchildren, and eight great-grandchildren.

Because of the early demise of the Giessen Society, Muench played a relatively minor role in attracting immigrants to Missouri. However, a St. Louis paper did report an upsurge of immigration from areas that he had visited in 1859. Muench's efforts on behalf of rationalist religion also bore little fruit among the peasant-stock rank and file. He was probably more successful in promoting viticulture and more progressive techniques of agriculture. Above all, though, the firm Unionist and emancipationist stand of Missouri Germans, not only in St. Louis but equally among rural residents, owes much to the decisive leadership of Friedrich Muench.

WALTER D. KAMPHOEFNER

Bek, Wilhelm G. "Followers of Duden." Parts 1–3. *Missouri Historical Review* 18 (April 1924): 415–37; 19 (October 1924): 114–29; (February 1925): 338–42.

Muench, Friedrich. *Gesammelte Schriften.* St. Louis, 1902.

Muench, Gerd Alfred. "Friends of Light *(Lichtfreunde):* Friedrich Münch, Paul Follenius, and the Rise of German-American Rationalism on the Missouri Frontier." *Yearbook of German-American Studies* 23 (1988): 119–39.

Muench, Julius Thamer. "A Sketch of the Life and Work of Friedrich Muench." *Missouri Historical Society Collections* 3 (April 1908): 132–44.

Rowan, Steven, trans. *Germans for a Free Missouri: Translations from the St. Louis Radical Press, 1857–1862.* Columbia: University of Missouri Press, 1983.

MULLANPHY, JOHN (1758–1833)

John Mullanphy, a merchant and philanthropist, was born in 1758 near Enniskillen, in County Fermanagh, in northern Ireland. His mother died at a young age, and after his father's second marriage, he moved in with his uncle. At the age of twenty he joined the Irish Brigade in the French Army. Following his service in the army, he returned to his native country and in 1789 married Elizabeth Brown of Youghal, in County Waterford.

In 1792 Mullanphy emigrated to Philadelphia with his wife and young child. He spent his first several years in Philadelphia and Baltimore, where he established himself as a prosperous merchant, and formed a close friendship with Bishop John Carroll. Soon, however, he was lured by the opportunities of the western frontier, and in 1799 he set out for the wilderness of Kentucky. He built a brick house and store in Frankfort, and was noted for laying the first pavement in that town. As one of the few Catholics in Frankfort, he regularly hosted missionary priests who held mass at his home. Each year he traveled to Baltimore and Philadelphia, returning with wagon loads of goods for his Frankfort store. In 1803 he fitted a schooner for the West India trade that made several successful trips before being lost at sea in a storm.

In 1804 Mullanphy made the acquaintance of **Charles Gratiot,** who soon convinced him of the prospects of a move to St. Louis. That same year, Mullanphy along with his wife, five children, several servants, and the goods from his store set out by boat for St. Louis. Benefited by his fluency in French in this territory that had only recently been added to the United States via the Louisiana Purchase, he quickly rose to a position of prominence and respect in the community. He was named justice of the peace and officiated many marriages, one of which was the marriage of **Alexander McNair,** who later became the first governor of Missouri. After a few years in St. Louis, Mullanphy moved his family downriver to Natchez where he established a store, and then to Baltimore. Each year he transported goods to his establishments in the West, and came to be called the great western merchant.

However, while Mullanphy's business enterprises continued to turn a profit, it was his successful corner of the cotton market during the War of 1812 that made his fortune. He was in New Orleans when the British troops attacked the American forces in January 1815, and his stores of cotton were used as breastworks in the famous defense of the city. When he went to Gen. Andrew Jackson to protest the seizure of his cotton, the general provided him with a musket and sent him to the lines to defend his investment. Following the battle, Mullanphy, believing that peace was soon at hand, traveled upriver to Natchez to await the news. When the news of peace arrived, he hastened by river to New Orleans, arriving a few days ahead of the overland mail. He hurriedly bought and stockpiled large stores of cotton at three and four cents per pound. When the news reached New Orleans and free trade resumed, he loaded his cotton on a ship for Liverpool where he sold it for thirty cents per pound, thus reaping an enormous profit.

Soon after the war Mullanphy returned to St. Louis where he invested heavily and wisely in real estate. His numerous land and financial transactions often embroiled him in lawsuits, and he was known to remark that he would rather lose one thousand dollars in legal fees than get cheated out of one dollar that was rightfully his. Mullanphy also invested his wealth in a host of charitable ventures to the lasting benefit of St. Louis. He donated a parcel of land and provided financial backing for the city's first hospital, and brought the Sisters of Charity to St. Louis to tend to the sick. He also provided land to the Sisters of the Sacred Heart for a school to educate orphans. When a cholera epidemic hit the city in 1832, he hired a Philadelphia doctor, Julian Henry, to care for victims at his own expense.

Upon Mullanphy's death on August 29, 1833, one newspaper obituary read, "the orphan and afflicted have lost a most liberal benefactor and literature a firm supporter." His philanthropic endeavors were carried on by his children, most notably his son Bryan Mullanphy and his daughter **Ann Mullanphy Biddle.** Onetime mayor of St. Louis, Bryan Mullanphy upon his death willed one-third of his estate to the establishment of a fund to furnish relief to all poor emigrants traveling to the West, while Ann Biddle donated much of her inherited wealth to the relief of widows and orphans.

In his *Recollections,* longtime mayor of St. Louis **John F. Darby** wrote, "Amongst the distinguished men engaged in laying the foundation of this city and building up the same, no one was more prominent than John Mullanphy . . . at the time of his death, [he] was said to be the wealthiest man in the Valley of the Mississippi, his estate being reckoned by millions. He was a most worthy and good man. In charitable deeds he never had a superior in the city of St. Louis."

DENNIS NORTHCOTT

Cochran, Alice Lida. "The Saga of an Irish Immigrant Family: The Descendants of John Mullanphy." Ph.D. diss., St. Louis University, 1958.

Darby, John F. *Personal Recollections of Many Prominent People Whom I Have Known, and of Events—Especially Those Relating to the History of St. Louis—during the First Half of the Present Century.* St. Louis: G. I. Jones, 1880.

Hyde, William, and Howard L. Conard, eds. *Encyclopedia of the History of St. Louis.* New York: Southern History, 1899.

Kenny, Laurence. "The Mullanphys of St. Louis." *United States Catholic Historical Society Historical Records and Studies* 14 (May 1920).

MUMFORD, FREDERICK B. (1868–1946)

A pioneer in agricultural education in Missouri during the early 1900s, Frederick B. Mumford made a name for himself as dean of the College of Agriculture at the University of Missouri and as a leading authority on agriculture at the state and national levels.

Mumford was born on a farm near Moscow, Michigan, on May 28, 1868. He attended Albion

College in Albion, Michigan, for three years before transferring to Michigan Agricultural College (MAC) where he received his B.S. in 1891. Enrolling in graduate school there, he showed great promise as an animal scientist and helped strengthen the already prestigious MAC animal-science research program. After receiving his M.S. in 1893, he remained at MAC for two years, serving as an assistant professor. In 1895 the University of Missouri College of Agriculture offered him a position as an associate professor in the department of animal husbandry. Mumford accepted the offer and became only the fifth faculty member in Missouri's College of Agriculture.

Mumford quickly became an integral part of the teaching staff at Missouri, and the College of Agriculture awarded him a full professorship in 1904. Five years later he became dean of the College of Agriculture, a position he held until his retirement. His rapid advancement came as a result of hard work and achievement within the university as well as outside of it.

Mumford's accomplishments and his leadership helped establish a strong reputation for the College of Agriculture. During his early years at Missouri, he authored *Animal Husbandry,* a textbook commonly used in agricultural curricula. He spent the 1900–1901 academic year studying European farming methods at the University of Leipzig and at the University of Zurich.

Outside of his work at the university, Mumford stressed the importance of scientific agriculture to farmers across Missouri. In 1912, at Mumford's recommendation, the university's board of curators voted to create an agricultural extension service that would provide farmers and their families with valuable knowledge gained at the college's Agricultural Experiment Station. The success of the extension program set the stage for establishment of the Missouri Cooperative Extension Service under the Smith-Lever Act in 1914.

Throughout his career Mumford provided invaluable leadership in times of crisis. In 1917 Gov. **Frederick D. Gardner** selected him to head the Missouri Council of Defense created to encourage the production and conservation of food during World War I. A tribute to Mumford's administrative talents, the council organized county, township, and town councils and coordinated the efforts of more than twelve thousand people by the time of its disbandment in 1919.

The council, in conjunction with the College of Agriculture Extension Service, distributed to Missouri farmers ninety-two war-propaganda pamphlets with titles such as "The New Patriotism" and "Farming on a War Basis." These pamphlets served a dual purpose of encouraging a positive attitude toward the war and of motivating increased food production to support the war effort. After the war Mumford assisted in the Mission Américaine de Rapprochement to France, which appraised the necessity of postwar U.S. aid to that country. During the Great Depression, Mumford served on the Missouri Commission on Reconstruction and Relief, the State Board of Agriculture, the State Farm Debt Adjustment Committee, and the State Planning Board.

During Mumford's forty-two years at the University of Missouri, the College of Agriculture grew impressively. At the time of his arrival, there were two seniors in the college; at the time of his retirement, the College of Agriculture boasted more than nine hundred students. The faculty rose to seventy-five, and the departmental library expanded from four volumes to twenty-five thousand. Mumford played a significant role in transforming Missouri's College of Agriculture from a struggling school to one of the top programs in the country.

Mumford retired from the College of Agriculture in 1938 at the age of seventy, but continued working in his profession. In 1940 the National Association of State Universities and Land Grant Colleges elected him as its president. During his early years with the association, Mumford helped draft the Purnell Bill of 1925 and the Bankhead-Jones Bill, both of which Congress enacted, providing additional funds for the research programs of agricultural colleges. During World War II Mumford volunteered his administrative services to the war effort.

After World War II Mumford and his wife spent their winters in Florida. On October 14, 1946, en route from Columbia to St. Louis on the first leg of their journey to their southern home, they were in a one-car accident that took the life of Mrs. Mumford. Frederick Mumford died on November 16, 1946, from injuries sustained in that accident.

ERIKA K. NELSON

Christensen, Lawrence O. "Missouri's Response to World War I: The Missouri Council of Defense." *Midwest Review* 12 (1990): 34–44.

———. "Popular Reaction to World War I in Missouri." *Missouri Historical Review* 86 (July 1992): 386–95.

Lee, Richard L. "Frederick Blackmar Mumford, 1868–1946: A Brief Biography." *Journal of Animal Science* (July 1992): 1989–93.

Mumford, Frederick Blackmar. Papers. 1868–1946. Western Historical Manuscripts Collection, Columbia.

MURPHY, JOSEPH (1805–1901)

Joseph Murphy, a renowned St. Louis wagon maker, gained fame and fortune as a leading practitioner of his trade. His sturdy, well-constructed wagons facilitated the rapid American movement into the trans-Mississippi West during the second and third quarters of the nineteenth century.

Murphy was born in Thornogs, in County Louth, Ireland, to James and Mary Murphy in 1805. To escape the harsh conditions in their homeland in 1818, the Murphys sent thirteen-year-old Joseph to America with his aunt Brigid. They were to travel to Creve Coeur, Missouri, where three of his uncles owned a sizable farm. Unfortunately, upon their arrival Joseph and his aunt discovered that the farm had been lost to creditors and the relatives were nowhere to be found. To support themselves they moved to St. Louis where Brigid eventually married, and Joseph was apprenticed to the wagon shop of Daniel Caster. During this time he learned how to attend to customers' needs and how to judge the quality of lumber—talents that would prove extremely useful in later years.

On Christmas Day 1825 the apprenticeship ended, and Murphy opened his first wagon shop by renting space from Daniel Caster. The Murphy Wagon Company moved several times before Murphy settled on a site for his business and his home in St. Louis.

Initially, business was slow, and Murphy constructed and repaired not only wagons but also plows, wheelbarrows, ox yokes, carts, and drays. In the early years he seldom had more than one order for a wagon at a time, but as emigrant, merchandising, and military interests in the land west of the Mississippi River increased, so did his orders.

Murphy's reputation for impeccable workmanship carried far, and travelers of all types clamored for his sturdy wagons specially designed to stand jolting over roadless prairies. Murphy often traveled sixty to seventy miles to secure suitable seasoned timber, split by hand. Instead of boring bolt holes into the wood, he burned them with a heated iron one size smaller than the bolt. In this way, the wood around the bolt would not crack or decay. Contrary to popular practices of the day, he refused to use generous coats of paint to hide poor workmanship. Nothing left the shop until Murphy was satisfied with its quality. Many families bound for California and Oregon acquired Murphy wagons for the journey, hoping to avoid the delays caused by breakdowns and accidents common in less well-built wagons.

The Santa Fe trade, however, allowed Murphy to show his wagon-making expertise. In 1839 Gov. Manuel Armijo sought to discourage American merchants from entering Mexico by imposing a tax of five hundred dollars on each wagon load of merchandise imported from the United States. American traders could not afford such a stiff tariff, and it appeared that Armijo would succeed in keeping them out. Murphy responded by creating a larger wagon, capable of carrying enough materials to make the long, tiring, and often life-threatening journey to Santa Fe more profitable.

Murphy's new wagon was huge, larger than any of its predecessors. The wheels alone were seven feet high, the tongue fifty feet long, and it could carry four to five thousand pounds of merchandise compared to the ordinary one thousand. It took four pairs of oxen to pull the behemoth, but pull it they did, and the new wagon cut the tax by 75 to 80 percent, thus ensuring the successful operation of the Santa Fe trade for several more years.

The Mexican War of 1846 and the gold rush of '49 made Murphy rich. On March 21, 1901, the *St. Louis Globe Democrat* claimed, "During the rush for gold in 1849 Mr. Murphy made all the wagons that left this city for the coast, and travelers returning would meet one caravan after another that was made up exclusively of the Murphy wagons."

The arrival of the railroad spelled the end of the wagon era, and the Murphy Wagon Company ceased operation in 1894. During its sixty-nine years of business, Murphy's company sold wagons to farmers, immigrants, traders, miners, and the military. The West could not have been settled without the talents of Joseph Murphy and others like him. Murphy died on March 20, 1901.

MARY VOGT

Bott, Emily Ann O'Neil. "Joseph Murphy's Contribution to the Development of the West." *Missouri Historical Review* 47 (October 1952–July 1953): 18–28.

Cox, James. *Old and New St. Louis.* St. Louis: Central Biographical Publishing, 1894.

Van Ravenswaay, Charles. *St. Louis: An Informal History of the City and Its People, 1764–1865.* St. Louis: Missouri Historical Society Press, 1991.

MURRAY, MATTHEW S. (?–1951)

Born in Dayton, Ohio, Matthew S. Murray graduated from the University of Dayton and arrived in Clinton, Missouri, in 1902. The Frisco Railroad hired him as an engineer in charge of maintenance in 1906, and two years later he moved to Sikeston, Missouri, where he became enmeshed in Bootheel Democratic politics.

In Sikeston Murray quickly entered the power structure when local voters elected him to the first of two terms as Scott County land surveyor. His engineering expertise, combined with a natural affinity for political manipulation, enabled the transplanted Ohioan to earn a reputation as a leading southeast Missouri Democrat.

This combination of politics and engineering paid Murray great dividends during his residence in Sikeston from 1908 until 1922. His work for the Missouri

Department of Highways brought him into contact with the political machinations of the state bureaucracy, resulting in his move to the state capital in 1922. Rising in the ranks, he became Missouri's chief engineer, specializing in the field of "highway studies."

Murray lived in Jefferson City from 1922 until 1926, and he met **Thomas J. Pendergast,** then just a local boss who owned the Ready-Mixed Concrete Company, which was already beginning to pave many of the poorly maintained roads throughout Jackson County. Murray also became acquainted with other members of the Pendergast machine who showed an interest in road building, particularly the newly elected commissioners on the county court, **Harry S. Truman** and **Henry F. McElroy.**

Sensing Pendergast's power, Murray quickly won the boss's trust by bestowing contracts on the machine's companies and padding state highway rolls with "Goats"—the name given to members of Pendergast's Kansas City Democratic organization. The Pendergast connection became an essential element in Murray's rise to power—and, ultimately, in his downfall.

On February 15, 1926, Pendergast secured Murray's appointment as Kansas City's first director of public works, a position he held until his arrest in 1939. During this period he demonstrated a blatant favoritism toward the boss in the awarding of local contracts. Although the projects frequently served vital needs in the metropolitan area, Murray immersed himself in machine politics, padding the public work rolls, accepting "no-bid contracts" from Pendergast's companies, and taking bribes from grateful benefactors.

In 1928 Murray played an instrumental role in creating the Committee of One Hundred, local leaders who outlined the Ten-Year Plan, a $49,950,000 bond issue voters approved on February 5, 1931. Faced with a worsening depression, the Kansas City program sanctioned public works projects that beautified and modernized the metropolis and, through the New Deal, became a model for the nation.

In 1933 Murray and other local officials demonstrated the inherent economic and political benefits resulting from their plan to Harry L. Hopkins,

Franklin D. Roosevelt's federal emergency relief administrator, who used it as a blueprint for the Civilian Works Administration. In June 1935 Hopkins appointed Murray as Works Progress Administration (WPA) director in Missouri.

Murray directed one of the largest public works projects in the nation. While continuing to draw a salary as director of Kansas City's work relief, he also controlled $250 million in federal patronage. In this way, Murray spread the tentacles of the Pendergast machine into every Missouri county. The WPA became a powerful political machine. Although reformers complained, President Roosevelt, through Hopkins, allowed Pendergast to run the organization.

Murray's demise occurred during the struggle between Pendergast and Gov. **Lloyd Stark** over state and federal patronage in 1937 and 1938. When Governor Stark used state workers to campaign for his handpicked candidate for the Missouri Supreme Court, James M. Douglas, Murray commanded his WPA machine to boost Pendergast's choice, James V. Billings. Billings's defeat brought about Pendergast's (and Murray's) decline. In the investigation and prosecution that followed, a federal court convicted Murray of five counts of income tax evasion in 1939.

Following two years' incarceration at the Leavenworth, Kansas, federal penitentiary, Murray moved to Tulsa, Oklahoma, where he completed his engineering career for a road-building company. He died on April 28, 1951.

J. CHRISTOPHER SCHNELL

Dorsett, Lyle W. *The Pendergast Machine.* New York: Oxford University Press, 1968.

Evans, Timothy K. " 'This Certainly Is Relief!': Matthew S. Murray and Missouri Politics during the Depression." *Bulletin of the Missouri Historical Society* 28 (July 1972): 219–33.

Kirkendall, Richard S. *A History of Missouri: Volume V, 1919 to 1953.* Columbia: University of Missouri Press, 1986.

Larsen, Lawrence H., and Nancy J. Hulston. *Pendergast!* Columbia: University of Missouri Press, 1997.

NAPTON, WILLIAM BARCLAY (1808–1883)

William Barclay Napton, a lawyer and state supreme court judge, was born in Princeton, New Jersey, on March 23, 1808, the son of a merchant tailor. He entered Princeton College in 1822 at the age of fourteen and graduated in 1826. He spent the following two years as a tutor in the Virginia home of Gen. W. F. Gordon, a tobacco planter and lawyer in Albermarle County. Gordon would soon serve his district in Congress (1829–1835), and it was in General Gordon's household that Napton took his first lesson in politics, listening to the well-formed opinions of such venerable Old Republican houseguests as Philip Babour and William C. Rives. As General Gordon prepared to enter Congress, Napton entered the University of Virginia where he studied law and modern languages. He finished his studies in 1830, entered the Virginia bar in 1831, and in 1832 moved to Missouri, settling first in Columbia and shortly afterward in Fayette, in Howard County, where he edited the *Boonslick Democrat.* In 1840 he acquired his Elk Hill estate in Saline County.

In 1836 Napton won election as secretary of the state senate. Later that year he was appointed attorney general of Missouri. First appointed to the state supreme court by Gov. **Lilburn W. Boggs** in 1838, Napton served on the bench for nearly thirty years. His tenure on the court was long and influential, but it was not continuous. He was not reappointed in 1852 following a split in the Democratic Party between the Free-Soil wing led by former Missouri senator **Thomas Hart Benton** and the proslavery faction favored by Napton. Napton had authored the Jackson Resolutions (1849), adopted by the Missouri legislature and named for state senator **Claiborne Fox Jackson,** a leading sponsor of the measure. The resolutions attacked Benton and other Free-Soil Democrats and declared that slavery was the concern only of the people of the states and territories. The resolutions also promised to seek "mutual protection" among the slave states "against the encroachments of northern fanaticism."

By 1854 Napton had embraced a proslavery analysis of American society that reached well beyond John C. Calhoun's concurrent-rights doctrine and may have been influenced by George Fitzhugh's *Sociology for the South,* published in that year. "I can only account for the great diversities between society here and that to be found in our free states," he wrote, "by the fact that we have no free white laboring population in our midst." Clearly excluding St. Louis from his analysis, Napton described the positive influence slavery had on class and gender relations. It seemed "to be the tendency of society in the free states to discard modesty from the list of female virtues—to break down all distinctions of sexes." In the North, "men, women, and Negroes are indiscriminately blended" in reform societies that championed women's rights, abolitionism, and temperance. By contrast, slaveholding communities in Missouri and throughout the South remained "untouched by such disastrous monomaniacs." "To slavery," Napton declared, "we owe this distinction."

Like other proslavery Democrats, Napton identified slavery with social stability. Whether Northerners acknowledged it or not, democracy and republican institutions required slavery. "Where slavery is not permitted to set foot," he wrote in 1856, society is "subjected to sudden outbursts of popular excitement growing out of ignorance, bigotry, and envy, themselves the natural offspring of an oppressed and starved labouring class." Slavery muted the "contest between capital and labor in the free states of the North," Napton continued. "Slavery has extracted the sting from universal suffrage." The "strange" truth was that "the hopes of our experiment in democratic institutions depend on the southern states, who have hitherto unquestionably . . . taken the lead in governmental policy and action."

Napton returned to the Missouri Supreme Court in 1856 when proslavery Democrats held sway, but he was ousted a second time, in 1861, when Republicans and the Union army controlled the state and when Napton refused to take the prescribed loyalty oath. His sentiments during the Civil War lay entirely with the South (one son, Thomas L. Napton, fought with Nathan Bedford Forrest), but, following the dictates of prudence amid guerrilla warfare, he moved his family and law practice to the Unionist bastion of St. Louis in 1863.

Napton returned to the supreme court in 1872 when Liberal Republicans joined forces with Democrats to unseat the Republican regime in Missouri, and he remained on the bench until 1880. He held fast to his Old Republican principles. In 1881, two years before his death, he observed that "time alone" would determine "whether or not the conversion of the Federal government into a national one, which the Civil war effected, will result in ultimate benefit." His preference remained strongly on the side of a limited federal government, founded on "the principles of state sovereignty as defined by Jefferson and Madison."

In 1838 Napton married Malinda Williams, the daughter of Thomas L. Williams, a judge on the supreme court of Tennessee. She died in 1862, leaving him with eight surviving sons and one daughter. William Napton died on January 8, 1883.

LOUIS S. GERTEIS

History of Saline County, Missouri. St. Louis: Missouri Historical Company, 1881.

Napton, William Barclay. Papers. Missouri Historical Society, St. Louis.

————. *The Past and the Present of Saline County, Missouri.* Chicago: B. F. Boner, 1910.

NATION, CARRY AMELIA MOORE (1846–1911)

Carry Amelia Moore Nation, an internationally known temperance crusader, was born on November 25, 1846, to George and Mary Campbell Moore. Her father, a prosperous stock trader and farmer, moved his family to numerous counties in Kentucky before migrating to Missouri when Carry was nine years old. Various accounts have attributed these and subsequent relocations either to his roving nature or to his wife's insanity, since Mary Moore believed herself to be Queen Victoria. Others in her Campbell family were also mentally ill, which has led some to question Carry Nation's sanity when she began her saloon smashing in the early 1900s.

In 1854 the Moores settled on a farm in Cass County, Missouri, near the town of Belton. In 1862, with Civil War battles close to their farm, Moore moved his family to Texas, where his fortunes dwindled. After a year they returned to their Missouri property. However, the area's Union military commander ordered all residents of that western region to relocate to Kansas City, in order to undercut support of Confererate guerrillas. In nearby Liberty, Missouri, Carry attended school for about one year. The close of the war brought the Moores back to their farm.

On November 21, 1867, Carry Moore married Charles Gloyd, a young physician who once boarded with the Moores and who practiced medicine in Holden, Missouri. Her parents, having discovered that Gloyd drank heavily, had counseled her against the union. Carry soon learned for herself that her husband was an alcoholic, and, though pregnant, she agreed to return to her parents' home. Her only child, Charlien, was born on September 27, 1868; six months later Gloyd died of alcoholism.

Carry Moore, deciding it was her responsibility to care for Gloyd's widowed mother, moved back to Holden. After selling Gloyd's medical instruments, his books, and some property her father had given her, she built a small house for her daughter, her mother-in-law, and herself.

From May 1871 to July 1872 Carry Moore attended the recently opened Normal Institute in Warrensburg, Missouri, and received a teacher's certificate. For four years she taught in Holden but lost her job when a school board member wanted the position for his niece. Having no way to provide for her family, she prayed for a new husband to support them. When shortly afterward she met David Nation, a widower with a small daughter, she assumed God had sent him to her. Although he was nineteen years older than she, and they had little in common, Carry Moore married David Nation on December 30, 1874.

At the time David Nation, a lawyer, preacher, and journalist, was editing a newspaper in Warrensburg, and the family lived there until he decided to move to Texas in 1877. While her husband tried to practice law, Carry Nation undertook the arduous work of operating a run-down hotel in Columbia, Texas. In 1879 she moved to Richmond, Texas, and purchased a hotel there. From the time of her baptism as a young girl in Missouri, Nation was deeply religious; during these years in Texas, she became convinced that she had prophetic dreams and visions.

In 1889 the Nations moved to Medicine Lodge, Kansas, where David Nation accepted a ministerial position. Carry Nation soon became known as "Mother Nation" because of her charitable and religious work. In 1892 she helped organize a local chapter of the Women's Christian Temperance Union (WCTU), and she served as the jail evangelist. Convinced that alcohol was the basic cause of the inmates' crimes, and remembering that her own life had been disrupted by an alcoholic husband, Nation decided to take action against the illegal "joints" in Medicine Lodge that openly flaunted Kansas's prohibition against alcohol—a rarely enforced statute since 1881. In 1899 Nation and Mrs. Wesley Cain closed their first joint by praying and singing hymns inside the saloon, and soon they rid Medicine Lodge of all such enterprises.

On June 7, 1900, believing that she heard a divine voice telling her to "go to Kiowa," Nation headed for that town. There for the first time she used violent tactics to close the saloons: she hurled bricks at barroom fixtures. In December 1900 she destroyed much of the bar and what she considered a risqué picture in the Carry Hotel in Wichita. The next month in Topeka she began using a hatchet to destroy saloons. Her hatchet wielding quickly brought nationwide attention, but these forays often proved dangerous. She received numerous beatings, and by her own account she was jailed on twenty-three occasions.

In the summer of 1901 Nation undertook a lecture tour. She also published at various times antialcohol papers such as the *Smasher's Mail,* the *Hatchet,* and the *Home Defender* (a title she gave herself). In 1902 she began her autobiography, which was published in 1904. Perhaps irritated that his wife allowed him no important role in managing her affairs, David Nation divorced her in November 1901.

To support herself Nation sold miniature pewter hatchets and continued her lectures across the United States. She spoke at universities, where the students, especially at Yale, ridiculed her. She appeared at Coney Island, New York; in New Jersey she even performed in a play titled *Hatchetation.* In 1908 Nation toured the British Isles with her prohibition message.

In January 1911, while lecturing in Eureka Springs, Arkansas, Nation collapsed onstage. Taken to a hospital in Leavenworth, Kansas, she stayed there until her death on June 2, 1911. As she requested, she was buried next to her mother's grave in Belton, Missouri. Not until 1924 was a tombstone erected with the following inscription: "Faithful to the Cause of Prohibition. 'She Hath Done What She Could.' "

Carry Nation's notoriety created controversy within the WCTU and among other prohibition supporters, who denounced her tactics for bringing ridicule to their cause. However, no other single individual publicized that cause as did Carry Nation. In her self-styled role as the Home Defender, she vividly depicted the ravages of alcoholism. Although she died eight years before Prohibition succeeded, she surely helped pave the way for the ratification of the Eighteenth Amendment.

PATRICIA ASHMAN

Asbury, Herbert. *Carry Nation: The Woman with the Hatchet.* New York: Knopf, 1929.

Caldwell, Dorothy J. "Carry Nation, a Missouri Woman, Won Fame in Kansas." *Missouri Historical Review* 63 (July 1969): 461–88.

Day, Robert. "Carry from Kansas Became a Nation All unto Herself." *Smithsonian* 20 (April 1989): 147–64.

Madison, Arnold. *Carry Nation.* Nashville: Thomas Nelson, 1977.

Nation, Carry A. *The Use and Need of the Life of Carry A. Nation.* Rev. ed. Topeka, Kans.: F. M. Steves and Sons, 1905.

Taylor, Robert Lewis. *Vessel of Wrath: The Life and Times of Carry Nation.* New York: New American Library, 1966.

NEIHARDT, JOHN G. (1881–1973)

Ironically, John Gneisenau Neihardt, who at age twelve dedicated his life to the writing of poetry, became best known for a collaborative work of nonfiction, *Black Elk Speaks* (1932). This is not to say Neihardt was not a good poet. The passion of his first collection of lyrics so attracted Mona Marinsen, an American student of Auguste Rodin, in Paris that her correspondence with Neihardt resulted in their marriage.

The Quest (1916), Neihardt's collected lyric poetry, and *The Song of Hugh Glass* (1915), the first of his five epic poems that form *A Cycle of the West* (1949), won him, in 1917, an honorary degree from the University of Nebraska. Public schools began teaching *Hugh Glass* and *The Song of Three Friends* (1919), the second of Neihardt's epic poems, and in 1921 the Nebraska legislature made him state poet laureate in perpetuity.

Neihardt was long fascinated by western matters. Born on January 8, 1881, near Sharpsburg, Illinois, he soon moved west, eventually settling in Wayne, Nebraska. There, at thirteen, he entered Nebraska Normal College and in two years earned a bachelor of science degree. His college readings fed his desire to write poetry. This desire rose out of a dream vision he had in 1892 in which a great voice drove him, flying through the air, toward a spiritual goal.

At nineteen Neihardt attempted to achieve that goal. He paid a New York firm to publish *The Divine Enchantment* (1900), a long, mystical poem. Most of its five hundred copies became fuel for Neihardt's stove. His first collection of lyrics, *A Bundle of Myrrh* (1907), paid better rewards. It attracted the notice of Mona Marinsen, who in 1908 became Neihardt's wife. Their marriage lasted until her death in 1958.

Neihardt stopped writing lyrics in 1912 and began his lifework, an epic poem about the conquest of the Missouri River Valley from 1822 to 1890 that he completed thirty-seven years later. *A Cycle of the West* consists of five epic poems—more than sixteen thousand lines of rhymed couplets—that detail both the adventures of fur trappers and traders who "opened" the West to white settlement and the confrontation (the wars and their results) between the settlers and the Native Americans. These five poems in order in *A Cycle of the West* are *The Song of Three Friends* (1919), *The Song of Hugh Glass* (1915), *The Song of Jed Smith* (1941), *The Song of the Indian Wars* (1925), and *The Song of the Messiah* (1935).

Some of these same materials also became books of prose. *The River and I* (1910) followed from a boat trip Neihardt made in 1908 down the Missouri

River. Much of his prose narrative *The Splendid Wayfaring* (1920) reappeared in *The Song of Jed Smith*. However, the material he gathered on the Pine Ridge Reservation in early 1930 for *The Song of Messiah* eventually brought Neihardt renown.

Neihardt had gone to Pine Ridge hoping to learn about the Ghost Dance religion. There he met Black Elk, an elder Lakota holy man whose life story Neihardt transformed into *Black Elk Speaks*. He saw this work as a collaboration in which his "function was both creative and editorial." His success in so effectively telling Black Elk's story came from both his considerable writing skills and from his own spiritual experiences that enabled him to empathize with Black Elk. N. Scott Momaday calls the book "one of the truly fortunate collaborations in our American heritage, bridging times, places, and cultures." Neihardt's novel *When the Tree Flowered* (1951) recounts, like *Black Elk Speaks,* the life of a Lakota holy man. Although the novel uses some incidents from Black Elk's life, it focuses mostly on events in the life of Eagle Elk.

Despite favorable reviews, *Black Elk Speaks* failed commercially, and Neihardt continued to support his family and his poetry through journalism and teaching. Early in his career he owned the newspaper in Bancroft, Nebraska. From 1926 to 1948 he worked as a literary editor for the *St. Louis Post-Dispatch*. He became poet-in-residence and lecturer at the University of Missouri in 1948 and taught until 1961. In that year the governor of Nebraska named the first Sunday in August an annual holiday in honor of Neihardt.

In "retirement" Neihardt wrote his autobiography, *All Is but a Beginning* (1972) and *Patterns and Coincidences* (1978). Finally, international recognition came to him in the late 1960s when the spirituality and authentic view of Lakota life in *Black Elk Speaks* appealed to college readers. Neihardt's appearance on the *Dick Cavett Show* in 1970 charmed an even larger audience of readers. John G. Neihardt died November 4, 1973.

LARRY VONALT

Deloria, Vine, Jr., ed. *A Sender of Words: Essays in Memory of John G. Neihardt.* Salt Lake City: Howe Brothers, 1984.

Neihardt, John G. *All Is but a Beginning.* New York: Harcourt Brace Jovanovich, 1972.

———. Papers. Western Historical Manuscripts Collection, Columbia.

———. *Patterns and Coincidences: A Sequel to "All Is but a Beginning."* Columbia: University of Missouri Press, 1978.

Petri, Hilda Neihardt. *Black Elk and Flaming Rainbow: Personal Memories of the Lakota Holy Man and John Neihardt.* Lincoln: University of Nebraska Press, 1995.

Whitney, Blair. *John G. Neihardt.* Boston: Twayne, 1976.

NELSON, WILLIAM ROCKHILL (1841–1915)

William Rockhill Nelson, of British, Quaker, and Huguenot heritage, was born five miles west of Fort Wayne, Indiana, on March 7, 1841, to the aristocrat Isaac DeGroff and Elizabeth Nelson. Nelson's forebears' names are in American Revolutionary city charters and regimental rosters.

Explosive and impatient in nature, William Rockhill Nelson, the second son of five children, was named for his maternal grandfather, had thin hair, a rotund build, and an odd gait. An intelligent child, he learned to read by age five. He had a quick mind, but society's strict rules of behavior conflicted with his freedom-loving spirit. Even as a child he yearned to be unrestricted so he could behave as he pleased.

In later life Nelson remarked, "I always resented parental restraint—not for lack of affection for my father, but because I never enjoyed being bossed." Discipline annoyed him. He never missed an opportunity to participate in a rebellion, and he considered himself a law unto himself: "It was my disposition to think that no one had any rights over me." These tendencies culminated in his lifelong tendency to oppose the status quo and to champion reform activities.

Nelson obtained his early education in Fort Wayne's public schools. He remarked, "I recall that my chief end in life before I was sent to Notre Dame was to break up whatever school I was attending." In order to instill discipline and to curb his rebellious nature, his father sent him, on September 2, 1856, to Notre Dame College because "it was the Botany Bay of Indiana where all bad boys were sent." Nelson persisted in his insurgent nature at Notre Dame. At the completion of one year, in which he was enrolled in history, grammar, composition, bookkeeping, Latin, and algebra, college authorities expelled him. Only eighteen years old, he next began to study law as a deputy to the clerk of the Allen County Circuit Court and was admitted to the bar before he reached the statutory age of twenty-one.

Although a resident of the Northern state of Indiana, Nelson expressed compassion toward the Southern cause and was a Democrat when the Civil War broke out. When President Abraham Lincoln called for volunteers, Nelson's father, a true Democrat who did not find slavery offensive, but was not a secessionist, did not encourage his son to respond. Nelson and his father opposed Lincoln's election in both 1860 and 1864. The Nelsons were instrumental in

Allen County's support of Stephen Douglas in 1860 and George McClellan in 1864.

In 1876 Nelson immersed himself in the Democratic presidential campaign of New York governor Samuel Tilden. Recognizing Tilden as a reformer who viewed politics as a means to achieve the common good, Nelson became Tilden's Indiana campaign manager. The American judicial system profoundly shocked Nelson when the disputed 1876 presidential election and presidency was awarded to Gov. Rutherford B. Hayes. Further disillusionment plagued him when the Democratic Party, in 1880, failed to renominate Tilden. Following these political rebuffs, Nelson renounced the Democratic Party and became a mugwump.

On April 16, 1879, Nelson and Samuel Morss purchased the *Fort Wayne Sentinel*. They promptly established a journalistic policy of crusading for community improvements. Nelson based his reforms and reformist ideology "on the theory that he knew what people should have and was determined to provide it to readers as he thought they should have it." Fort Wayne citizens failed to respond to their reporting, so the owners considered Brooklyn, Seattle, Liberty, and Kansas City as more promising locations for establishing an independent, progressive newspaper. Finally, in 1880, the owners selected Kansas City.

Nelson and Morss established the *Kansas City Star* as an evangelical newspaper, and no person was exempt from their crusading: Jay Gould and his national telegraph syndicate; Col. Kersey Coates and the Coates Opera House; and the proposed selection of **Frank James** as chief doorkeeper of the Missouri legislature all received attention.

Nelson's individualistic style of journalism distinguished his youth. He revolted against the oppressive business practices of the period. The publisher publicly supported what he often referred to as the middle class, people who were owners of small businesses and property, supporters of families, and promoters of their communities. Although he adhered to the eight-hour day and higher wages for labor, he conceived of countless reasons for not advancing wages in his plants. A developer of real estate, he at no time granted leases on his one hundred houses because he desired the privilege to evict any tenant who incurred his disapproval.

In his promotion and support of political candidates, Nelson advocated that the middle class take political action against urban political machines. His uncompromising attitude ill-fitted him for the role of a stump speaker. He preferred to persuade through his newspapers, away from the public eye. Nelson was too autocratic to be a real liberal. A nonpartisan, he promoted some Republican causes, advocated Democratic liberalism mixed with capitalistic philosophy, and supported Bull Moose Progressivism at various times.

Upon the assassination of President William McKinley in 1901, Nelson sent a telegram to Theodore Roosevelt expressing his and the *Kansas City Star*'s wholehearted support. This established a relationship that existed over the next fourteen years. Writing to Roosevelt in 1910, he stated, "I have wondered whether sooner or later there would not have to be a new party of the Square Deal." Two years later Roosevelt organized the Progressive Party.

By late July 1912 Nelson had succeeded in creating Progressive Party organizations in almost all of Missouri's counties. His role in the entire Progressive movement is significant for two reasons: First, he made a national statement when he resigned his post as Republican National Committeeman. Second, he ardently devoted himself to direct participation in politics. Nelson embraced the triad philosophy of the Progressive movement: to drive money out of the voting booth and out of the courthouse, to provide free justice, and to provide minimum-wage standards.

Nelson's reforming zeal ranged from support for municipal proprietorship of public utilities to running water in farm women's kitchens and to establishing parks and boulevards as enrichments of the urban environment. The park movement in Kansas City gathered impetus through the 1880s and 1890s. Although not the architect of the City Beautiful Movement, Nelson served as its foremost proponent and as a pivotal contributor. He had a habit of placing exotic squirrels in the parks. In order to acquire assistance for the park movement, he organized the Hammer and Padlock Club.

William Rockhill Nelson died on April 13, 1915, at his residence, Oak Hall, in Kansas City, Missouri. He was dedicated to the full and inclusive reforms of service to humanity and democratic government. He is buried at Mount Washington Cemetery in Independence, Missouri. His estate helped fund the famous Nelson-Atkins Museum of Art in Kansas City.

TIMOTHY C. WESTCOTT

Garwood, Darrell. *Crossroads of America: The Story of Kansas City.* New York: W. W. Norton, 1948.

Johnson, Icie F. *William Rockhill Nelson and the Kansas City Star: Their Relation to the Development of the Beauty and Culture of Kansas City and the Middle West.* Kansas City, Mo.: Burton, 1935.

Kansas City Star. *William Rockhill Nelson: The Story of a Man, a Newspaper, and a City.* Cambridge: Riverside Press, 1915.

Wilson, William H. *The City Beautiful Movement in Kansas City.* Kansas City, Mo.: Lowell Press, 1990.

Wolferman, Kristie C. *The Nelson-Atkins Museum of Art: Culture Comes to Kansas City.* Columbia: University of Missouri Press, 1993.

Worley, William S. *J. C. Nichols and the Shaping of Kansas City: Innovation in Planned Residential Communities.* Columbia: University of Missouri Press, 1990.

NEMEROV, HOWARD (1920–1991)

Howard Nemerov was born on February 29, 1920, in New York City, and died on July 5, 1991, at his home in St. Louis. In 1941 he was awarded a B.A. from Harvard University, where he wrote an honors thesis on the works of Thomas Mann, thereby earning a university prize as well as the praise of Mann himself. After serving as a pilot in the Royal Canadian and United States Air Forces during World War II, Nemerov published his first book of poetry, *The Image and the Law,* in 1947, and during the next forty-four years he published more than three dozen works of fiction, poetry, and criticism. He served for two years (1988–1990) as poet laureate of the United States, and was the recipient of the first Theodore Roethke Memorial Award (1968), the National Book Award (1978), the Pulitzer Prize for poetry (1978), the Bollingen Prize for poetry (1981), the National Medal for the Arts in poetry (1987), and the first Aiken/Taylor Prize for poetry from the *Sewanee Review* and the University of the South (1987). He was the subject of two documentaries broadcast on PBS and elsewhere: "Howard Nemerov: Collected Sentences" and "Nemerov, Too." During his forty-five-year career as a teacher, he taught at Hamilton College, Bennington College, Brandeis University, Hollins College, and Washington University.

Upon joining the faculty at Washington University in 1969, Nemerov and his wife, Margaret, moved to University City in St. Louis. There he became a part of a writing community that was to include Stanley Elkin, Mona Van Duyn, John Morris, and many others. "The End of the Opera," dedicated to Mona Van Duyn, explores the relationship between life and art. "Remembering Ford Madox Ford and Parade's End" was written for Sondra Stang, a Ford scholar who taught at Washington University. His last book-length collection of new poems, *War Stories,* is dedicated to St. Louis residents and writers Albert Lebowitz and Naomi Lebowitz.

St. Louis honored Nemerov in a variety of ways: in addition to the two documentaries, he was awarded a star on the St. Louis Walk of Fame sponsored by the restaurant Blueberry Hill, and in 1990 he won the St. Louis Award "for the honor he has brought to the St. Louis Community through outstanding literary achievement."

Nemerov gleaned much of the material for his later poetry from various sites throughout Missouri—especially St. Louis. Weekend walks with his neighbor to the St. Louis Zoo and daily walks to and from Washington University were the impetus for poems such as "Wolves in the Zoo," "Walking Down Westgate in the Fall," "The Consent," and "Ginkgoes in Fall." Visits to the St. Louis Museum of Art inspired him to write poems in *Sentences* (1980) such as "Monet," "Museum," and "At an Exhibition of Muslim Calligraphy," which describes how writing becomes art for those forbidden to make images and was inspired by another 1978 exhibit, Calligraphy and the Arts of the Muslim World.

"Fish Swimming amid Falling Flowers," in *Inside the Onion* (1984), describes a picture in the St. Louis Art Museum attributed to the northern Sung painter Liu Ts'ai. Nemerov's note recommends "Readers interested to check out Liu Ts'ai's vision against current carp going about their business will do well to look down from the bridge over the lake at the Japanese garden called Sei-wa En at Shaw's Garden in St. Louis. Between life and art there are differences, but only the ones you would expect; ink is thicker than water, not by much."

As Nemerov implies in the passage above, Missouri settings provide more than superficial details; from them emerge the themes that were his enduring preoccupations. Intrigued by the relation between art and life, he sought to reach the essence beyond the power of speech, which he saw embodied in the "silent work" of a picture. He held that poems about paintings do not or should not speak about the paintings they refer to but "about the silence of the paintings; and where a poet was lucky his poem will speak the silence of the painting." When Nemerov wrote about paintings, he deliberately maintained the stance of the beholder, never leading us to assume that we are facing real life, but rather a single and limited perspective of reality. Thus, his "Fish Swimming among Flowers" renders art's ability to capture a process: the artist captures the process of fish swimming, and Nemerov captures the process of the artist capturing the process of fish swimming. His technique is itself a challenge to the very notion that there is an "objective" reality independent of the observer.

Nemerov likewise challenges the boundary between order and chaos, suggesting that the corresponding Western dichotomies of culture and nature, art and nature, subject and object, are false. Wyatt Prunty observes that Nemerov regards "the mind's determination to find order as just as much a fact as the world's resistance to order." Nemerov therefore builds his poetry "upon the mutual dependence of these apparent opposites, and his accomplished plumbing of this central riddle makes his work a permanent part of our literature."

Nemerov was also intent on capturing the intimate relationship between nature and human nature, which he believed was the artist's responsibility to render. In his essay "The Protean Encounter," he uses Menelaus's encounter with Proteus in *The Odyssey* as the analogy for the role of the artist: "The grasping and hanging on to the powerful and refractory spirit in its slippery transformations of a single force flowing through clock, day, violet, greying hair, trees dropping their leaves, the harvest in which by a peculiarly ceremonial transmutation the grain by which we live is seen without contradiction as the corpse we come to." The final poem in *War Stories,* "Landscape with Self-Portrait," renders this relationship beautifully: the lawn that has been "won from the meadow" corresponds to the self, which is just as tentatively linked to time and being.

Nemerov's portrayal of nature is the means by which he addresses human mortality. In a moving tribute published in the *Sewanee Review* only two months after the poet's death from cancer, his friend and former Hollins colleague Louis Rubin recalled, "He had figured out, a long time back, long before any illness, that because he was going to *die,* everything he or anyone could say or think or do was to that extent a compromised, crucially-limited activity, that was of qualified significance—that if he was going to write anything really meaningful about the human experience he had to *start* with that assumption."

The final sequence of poems in *The Western Approaches* (1975) explores mortality by means of the transience of the natural world. In "The Dependencies" he finds an analogy for life in the intricate and unfathomable pattern of a spider's web. In "The Consent" he addresses the universal human frustration that the length of our lives is ultimately not our decision but fate's. He describes a night in late November, when the ginkgo trees along the walk at Washington University suddenly drop all their leaves "in one consent." The leaves that had "spread aloft their fluttering fans of light" so beautifully the day before are analogous to lives that are suddenly and unjustifiably lost before their prime.

DONNA L. POTTS

Bartholomay, Julia. *The Shield of Perseus: The Vision and Imagination of Howard Nemerov.* Gainesville, Fla.: University of Gainesville Press, 1972.

Mills, William. *The Stillness in Moving Things.* Memphis, Tenn.: Memphis State University Press, 1975.

Nemerov, Howard. *The Collected Poems of Howard Nemerov.* Chicago: University of Chicago Press, 1977.

———. *Figures of Thought: Speculations on the Meaning of Poetry and Other Essays.* Boston: David R. Godine, 1978.

———. *A Howard Nemerov Reader.* Columbia: University of Missouri Press, 1991.

———. *Reflexions on Poetry and Poetics.* New Brunswick, N.J.: Rutgers University Press, 1972.

NICHOLS, J. C. (1880–1950)

Born on August 23, 1880, in Olathe, Kansas, Jesse Clyde Nichols became a salesman early in life. He huckstered Johnson County produce in Kansas City, Kansas; sold maps to westerners in Utah; and managed to organize his college fraternity into a break-even operation—all while completing both high school and University of Kansas diploma requirements at valedictorian levels.

After graduating from Kansas, Nichols spent one year on scholarship at Harvard University where he was awarded a second B.A. degree in 1903. His Harvard experience turned his sales interest toward land development. Nichols joined with two older fraternity brothers to form Reed, Nichols, and Company in 1903. They spent two years developing land and building houses to sell to 1903 flood victims in northwest Kansas City, Kansas.

By 1905 Nichols persuaded farmer friends of his father from near Olathe to invest in land just south of the Kansas City, Missouri, city limits. Within three years the young entrepreneur and his assistant, John C. Taylor, established enough of a record to gain the financial backing of some of the wealthier people in Kansas City. In April 1908 Nichols announced that he was ending his association with the Reed brothers in order to launch the J. C. Nichols Company that controlled through purchase or sales agreement the disposition of approximately 1,000 acres of potential residential property.

Nichols and his backers employed **George Kessler,** the designer of the St. Louis World's Fair of 1904 and of the Kansas City park and boulevard system, as the landscape architect. Nichols led the group in underwriting the cost of electrifying an old steam commuter railway on the east side of the property and in donating more than 100 acres to Kansas City for a wide parkway on the west side. Included in the 1,000 acres in 1908 were 237 acres next to the state line in Johnson County, Kansas. This land became the heart of Mission Hills—Nichols's most prestigious development.

The size of Nichols's land development meant that he could provide attractive home sites for a wide range of the Kansas City population, from middle-income families to the wealthy. The east side (with the exception of a few mansions now part of the University of Missouri–Kansas City) became essentially a middle-class haven using the new streetcar service. The more affluent west side encouraged mansion building along and near Ward Parkway (land donated by Vassie James Ward in memory of Nichols's early investment partner, Hugh Ward).

Before World War I Nichols began to provide small shopping areas for his residents since they were located so far from downtown and other streetcar-based shops. He also moved quietly to acquire land in the Brush Creek valley, which he would begin to transform in the 1920s into the Country Club Plaza shopping area and apartment district. Unlike other outlying shopping centers (including his own, such as Colonial and Brookside shops), the Plaza was not directly connected to streetcar access and always provided abundant free parking for automobiles. It became a model for other upscale shopping facilities around the nation until the rise of the enclosed mall in the 1960s.

Nichols engaged in a wide range of professional activities. He served as a vice president of the National Board of Realtors and was a founder of the Urban Land Institute, a land development association. He also helped form the American Institute of City Planners and the National Association of Homebuilders. Locally, Nichols promoted river transportation on the Missouri River and the formation of the Midwest Research Institute to serve as a research and development laboratory for regional industry. The latter project resulted from the efforts of Nichols and several other Kansas City business leaders to attract World War II industry between 1940 and 1942.

By the time of Nichols's death on February 16, 1950, the J. C. Nichols Company had developed more than 3,500 acres of residential and retail property, built hundreds of houses, and started the residential land boom in northeast Johnson County, Kansas, which continued into the 1990s. An estimated fifty thousand people lived or had lived in houses on land developed by J. C. Nichols in the Kansas City region.

In a city where changing real estate values have been the norm since the nineteenth century, Nichols's residential areas have held or have increased in value and attractiveness steadily, for more than ninety years in some cases. The "Country Club District" continues to be the most desirable place to live in the Kansas City metropolitan region.

WILLIAM S. WORLEY

Fowler, Dick. "J. C. Nichols." In *Leaders in Our Town*. Kansas City: Burd and Fletcher, 1952.

Nichols, J. C. *Real Estate Subdivisions: The Best Manner of Handling Them*. Washington, D.C.: American Civic Association, 1912.

Molyneaux, Gary O. A. "Planned Land-Use Change in an Urban Setting: The J. C. Nichols Company and the Country Club District of Kansas City." Ph.D. diss., University of Illinois at Urbana–Champaign, 1979.

Worley, William S. *J. C. Nichols and the Shaping of Kansas City: Innovation in Planned Residential Communities*. Columbia: University of Missouri Press, 1990.

NIEBUHR, KARL PAUL REINHOLD (1892–1971)

Karl Paul Reinhold Niebuhr was born in Wright City, Missouri, on June 21, 1892, the second son of an immigrant German pastor in the German Evangelical and Reformed Church. By the time Reinhold was ten years of age, the family had moved to Lincoln, Illinois, where his father pastored a church. A brother, two years younger, Helmut Richard Niebuhr, would follow Reinhold into the study and adoption of the profession of minister and, later, theologian and teacher. Niebuhr's father was authoritarian in the German tradition of the paterfamilias and had a poor relationship with the first-born son, Walter, but a better, more approving relationship with Reinhold.

Niebuhr attended his church's college, Elmhurst in Illinois, and seminary, Eden in St. Louis. After a year in seminary, he was accepted at Yale University where he came into contact with modern liberal Protestant theology. Niebuhr's father blended an evangelical emphasis on the divinity of Christ, the supernatural inspiration for the Bible, and the importance of prayer with liberal concerns for social improvement, ecumenicism, and a disinterest in doctrinal precision. Niebuhr came naturally to much of the liberal agenda for social welfare, though he spent much of his life resisting the temptation to reduce theological speculation to philosophy and regard for Jesus as the ideal human.

Niebuhr was less concerned with the abstract and more concerned with the practical affairs of a pastor's life. After the death of his father, he left Yale and took up his father's pastorate in Illinois briefly, until he accepted a position at Bethel Evangelical Church in Detroit. He moved to Detroit with his mother and a sister and remained there for thirteen years. His education at Yale, which introduced him to liberal theology as well as secular American progressive causes and ideas, was as important for Niebuhr's development as were his years in the gritty industrial city of Detroit, where he engaged himself in the lives of his parishioners and the day-to-day reality of living in Henry Ford's town.

For most of his life, Niebuhr strived to make the connection between theological abstractions and the daily challenges of social and political engagement.

He regarded Ford with ambivalence, unsure whether he was an exploitative genius who could engineer speedups and pay reductions and still convince people he was giving them a holiday, or whether Ford was naive and sentimental in his vision of industrial capitalism.

Niebuhr's biggest concern, and one to which he returned again and again with a variety of popular and unpopular applications, was the question of the relationship of Christianity to culture. As pastor, not as theologian, he wrestled with the question of how the church addressed the problems of an industrial society, or racial division, or the labor movement. When his liberalism encountered the hard lives of the industrial workers and the ravages of World War I, Niebuhr declared himself (at various times) a pacifist, a Socialist, a trade unionist, and an integrationist in his effort to develop a Christian response. Yet, he was equally careful to avoid identifying Christianity with national culture or a particular political solution.

While serving as pastor in Detroit, Niebuhr also became a regular contributor to the *Christian Century.* Much of what he wrote was contained in one of his first books, *Does Civilization Need Religion?* He rejected the liberal belief in a society getting better and better on its own efforts, but embraced the liberal appeal to reason and its rejection of superstition and magic. Niebuhr followed the example of Kant and James in his analysis: he granted the primacy of reason in its own sphere and then outlined another sphere—that of morality and personality. In this sphere, the reason of religious experience operated as the standard of truth, not scientific reasoning. The truth of Jesus Christ was not propositional but dramatic and liberating. Civilization needed religion, Niebuhr argued, because religion posed ultimate ethical goals as well as the experiences of love and self-sacrifice necessary to achieve those goals. He invoked Alfred North Whitehead to buttress his belief in a sphere of spirit. His work gained attention for Niebuhr as well as an invitation to teach applied ethics at Union Theological Seminary in New York.

In 1928 Niebuhr moved to New York to teach. Initially, he combined his part-time teaching position with work as a journalist for the *Christian Century,* the *New Republic,* and *World Tomorrow.* He had already gained a reputation as a radical by his 1924 support of Robert LaFollette's Progressive candidacy for president, and he perpetuated this reputation in New York by supporting the Socialist candidate for president in 1928, running on the Socialist ticket himself later, and founding the Fellowship of Socialists Christians in 1930. Niebuhr was less concerned about theology proper than with moral applications and the ethical dimension of how a Christian could live in the world. His forays into politics illustrate this concern. For Niebuhr, socialism was the perfect middle ground

between ineffective reformist tinkering and the romantic revolution of the Communists, who were too dogmatic for his taste.

By this time Protestantism had developed in several directions, none of which provided Niebuhr with a comfortable footing for his religious beliefs and his interest in politics. In the liberal tradition, the Social Gospel had declined and was succeeded by an emphasis on church and belief that built character. From this tradition evolved the secular civil religion of the humanistic theist John Dewey, whose primary focus was to consider how beliefs function (not if they corresponded to absolute truth in the real world). Dewey proposed in 1934 in *A Common Faith* a set of humanistic values that united religious traditions, promoted ideals such as community and justice, and was transmitted through schools that produced democratic character. The Fundamentalists rejected modernism and its openness to free inquiry that undermined their notion of absolute truth. Their emphasis on biblical inerrancy created a hostility to intellectual development and led them to reject modern material values. Niebuhr was uncomfortable with all these positions.

In 1929 Niebuhr read the first English translation of the neoorthodox Swiss theologian Karl Barth. Although he approved of Barth's repudiation of the bankruptcy of liberal theology, Niebuhr initially feared Barth's neoorthodoxy as a "new kind of fundamentalism." Niebuhr was much more influenced by his own brother, H. Richard Niebuhr, whose critique of American Protestantism charged that the churches had sold themselves out to a corrupt civilization of humanism, materialism, capitalism, and human-centered doctrines. These churches preached "a God without wrath that brought men without sin into a kingdom without judgments through the ministration of a Christ without a cross." Niebuhr wrestled with these ideas in his increasingly popular classes, his political work with the Socialist cause, and his articles for the *Christian Century* and *World Tomorrow.* As the economy tumbled into the Great Depression and the Nazis came to power in Germany, preaching their politics of division, Niebuhr could not help but contrast the social evils afoot with the limits of a faith in reason and the innate goodness of people.

In 1932 Niebuhr produced his classic and principal contribution to Christian social thought, *Moral Man and Immoral Society,* which marked a new territory that he called Christian realism. He argued that social and political institutions are self-serving, always less than ideal, and cannot produce the moral standards by which individuals live. Niebuhr would argue later that Dewey's vision was too tepid to address the real evils abiding in social and political institutions. The goal of Christian action should be justice rather than love. Only an admission of the limits of human effort would provide a realism that was both Christian enough and muscular enough to address injustice.

The features of Christian realism can be found in *Moral Man and Immoral Society,* as well as in the more theoretical work *The Nature and Destiny of Man* (1941). Christian realism (or American neoorthodoxy, as it is also called) has several features. First, it has a renewed emphasis on the sovereignty of God: Niebuhr points to the ravages of the depression to illustrate the insufficiency of native goodness and the necessity for people to turn to God. Second, a respect for Revelation: since one can know nothing about God by one's own efforts, one can know God only as revealed in the Word. Third, the rejection of an optimistic anthropology: Niebuhr resurrects the idea of original sin, reintroduces the reality and seriousness of sin, and argues that group evil is more difficult to bring under control than individual evil. Fourth, a new Christology: revelations about who God is are to be found in Christ, and it is not the historical Jesus to whom one looks for revelations about God. And fifth, a cross-denominational view of church: Niebuhr proposed a view of Church that transcends denominational boundaries and sparks renewed interest in ecumenicism. The Church is the first sign of the Kingdom and it should reveal a kingdom of God's making, not man's. In general, these ideas would dominate seminaries for the next twenty years.

In the fall of 1930, Niebuhr met an English woman who had come to Union to study for the year. By the time she left in 1931, she and Niebuhr were engaged. Ursula Keppel-Compton was a devout Anglican, extremely intelligent, and attractive as well. They married in December 1931 at Winchester Cathedral in England; they had two children, Christopher and Elizabeth, and eventually Ursula began to teach in the department of religion at Barnard.

Marriage was not the only change Niebuhr underwent. As the Nazi threat increased and Japan invaded Manchuria, Niebuhr began to relinquish his claim on absolute pacifism that he had espoused for some years, and withdrew from Socialist politics. By 1940 he supported Roosevelt's candidacy for president, and in 1941 he endorsed the U.S. entry into World War II. During and after the war he became involved in Democratic politics, and after the war he helped found the liberal Americans for Democratic Action. In 1940 he helped create and served as editor of a new magazine on religion, *Christianity and Crisis,*

in which he continued to press for the application of Christianity to political, economic, and social dimensions.

Niebuhr's political views, like most Democrats and Republicans as well, took a turn toward the right amid the anti-Communism frenzy after World War II. He was still a fervent Democrat, but was caught up in the red scare like many others. By the end of the 1940s, Niebuhr had acquired the status of the country's public theologian. "The Serenity Prayer" was first used by Niebuhr during World War II, printed in one of his columns in 1951, and adopted by Alcoholics Anonymous as their official prayer and used by many other groups, card companies, and religious goods manufacturers:

> God, give us the serenity to accept what cannot be changed;
> Give us the courage to change what should be changed,
> Give us the wisdom to distinguish one from the other.

In 1952, at the age of fifty-nine, Niebuhr suffered the first of many small strokes that left him partially paralyzed and with impaired speech. For the next twenty years he maintained a more restricted level of activity and relied increasingly upon his wife, Ursula, for physical maintenance. He remained close to his brother Richard, a professor at Yale and a respected theologian in his own right, until Richard's death in 1962. Although he continued to write, publish, and speak (after 1963 he no longer held a teaching post), Niebuhr declined in importance in theological circles. He died on June 1, 1971.

JANICE BRANDON-FALCONE

Ahstrom, Sydney E. *A Religious History of the American People.* New Haven: Yale University Press, 1972.

Fox, Richard W. *Reinhold Niebuhr.* New York: Pantheon Books, 1985.

Lovin, Robin. *Reinhold Niebuhr and Christian Realism.* New York: Cambridge University Press, 1995.

Marsden, George. *Religion and American Culture.* New York: Harcourt Brace Jovanovich, 1990.

Noll, Mark. *A History of Christianity in the United States and Canada.* Grand Rapids, Mich.: William B. Eerdmans, 1992.

OAKIE, JACK (1903–1978)

Jack Oakie was long considered one of the screen's most notorious scene-stealers. He had a unique brand of comedy and was the master of the double and triple take. He was born Lewis Delaney Offield on November 12, 1903, in Sedalia, Missouri. His father was a grain dealer, and his mother was a psychology teacher. Oakie took his stage surname from the move that his family made to Muskogee, Oklahoma, when he was five.

In the 1920s Oakie landed a job as a dancer in George M. Cohan's *Little Nelly Kelly* on Broadway. He went from Broadway to vaudeville, with Lulu McConnell as his partner, before landing roles in *Artists and Models, Innocent Eyes,* and others. In 1927 Oakie went to Hollywood, and in his first film he was cast as a comedian in director Wesley Ruggles's *Finders Keepers.* He was under contract to Paramount for nine years where he played the perennial freshman at "Paramount U." He appeared in many of the big musicals of the day with Bing Crosby, Lanny Ross, Lily Pons, Burns and Allen, Maurice Chevalier, and Alice Faye, all making their first pictures with the cherubic Oakie in the cast. His characterization of Benito Mussolini in Charlie Chaplin's *Great Dictator* won him an Oscar nomination for best supporting actor in 1940. His pictures included *Chinatown Nights, Paramount on Parade, Touchdown, Once in a Lifetime, Sailor Be Good, College Rhythm, Call of the Wild, Big Broadcast of 1936, Thanks for Everything, Hello Frisco Hello, The Merry Monahans, When My Baby Smiles at Me, Around the World in Eighty Days,* and *Lover Come Back.*

Oakie spent part of his boyhood in Kansas City with his grandmother and attended Woodland School. He sold papers for the *Kansas City Star.* He later recalled that he made good money selling "extras" on the night Woodrow Wilson was reelected as president in 1916. He also appreciated the good press the *Star* gave him during his acting career.

In 1960 Oakie and his wife arrived at Union Station in Kansas City on their way to Sedalia to mark his birthplace during the town's centennial celebration. He was quick to ask in Kansas City about Woodland School, stating proudly, "I graduated from there."

In his later years, Oakie made some television appearances and lived in baronial style on a ten-acre estate in Northridge, at the northern end of the San Fernando Valley. He died on January 23, 1978, at the age of seventy-four. Oakie is still considered one of the best of the wisecracking comedians during the golden age of Hollywood, a consummate ogler who could steal a scene simply by looking at a girl's legs.

ARTHUR F. MCCLURE AND VIVIAN RICHARDSON

Kansas City Times, January 24, 1978.

McClure, Arthur F., and Ken D. Jones. *Star Quality: Screen Actors from the Golden Age of Films.* Cranbury, N.J.: A. S. Barnes, 1974.

Oakie, Jack. *Jack Oakie's Double Takes.* San Francisco: Strawberry Hill, 1980.

Obituary. *Time* (February 6, 1978): 93.

O'FALLON, BENJAMIN (1793–1842)

Prominent in Missouri as an Indian agent and advocate of the American fur-trade interests in the 1820s, Benjamin O'Fallon was generally forgotten after his retirement from public life. He was born in Lexington, Kentucky, on September 20, 1793. His mother, Frances "Fanny" Clark O'Fallon, was the youngest sister of George Rogers Clark and **William Clark.** His father, James, came from Ireland in 1774 and served through the Revolutionary War as a surgeon in Washington's army. In 1789 the senior O'Fallon came west as a general agent for the South Carolina Yazoo Land Company, and lived in St. Louis for a time while pursuing schemes with Spanish officials, French agents, and Kentucky and Carolina adventurers. Moving to Kentucky, he allied himself through marriage to the prestigious Clark family in 1791. His first son, **John O'Fallon,** was born that November. When James O'Fallon died a few months after the birth of his second child, Benjamin, the two boys remained with their mother's family. By 1807 William Clark had assumed formal guardianship of his nephews.

In 1808 Clark brought Benjamin to live with him in St. Louis. Undisciplined and volatile, with chronic ill health, the boy showed little promise for a future career despite the aid of his powerful uncle, then an Indian agent and soon the territorial governor of Missouri. Clark hoped to establish his nephew as a merchant in St. Louis.

In 1813 O'Fallon and James Kennerly (cousin of Clark's first wife, brother to the second Mrs. Clark) joined in a short-lived partnership selling pork, beef, and flour in the city. In 1814 Clark appointed

O'Fallon as contractor to supply his military expedition to Prairie du Chien.

In 1815, with Clark's assistance, O'Fallon built saw and gristmills north of St. Louis. He quickly tired of his new career, however, and sold his mills in 1816 to try his luck as an Indian trader on the upper Mississippi. Hoping for the best, Clark appointed his nephew as special agent for the Sioux and neighboring tribes. Clark's continuing efforts finally won O'Fallon a regular appointment as subagent for the upper Missouri River in 1818. In 1819 O'Fallon was confirmed as an Indian agent for the Missouri River tribes, to accompany Gen. Henry Atkinson's Yellowstone expedition.

Through 1819 and 1820 O'Fallon held councils with the Kansa, Missouri, Oto, Omaha, Iowa, and Pawnee tribes. He quarreled with Atkinson over policy in dealing with the Indians and the relative authority of military commander and Indian agent. O'Fallon's own policy was clearly defined: he believed it necessary to impress the independent tribes with the power of the U.S. government through a show of force and firmness in negotiations. He was preoccupied with countering the British threat, real or perceived, to the northern frontier, and was a particular foe of British fur traders found on the American side of the border. The fur trade, in his view, would be the agent of national sovereignty along the upper Missouri.

O'Fallon's quarrel with the military broke out afresh after Col. Henry Leavenworth's 1823 Arikara campaign, and he freely aired his case in the public press. Earlier support for the efforts of **Thomas Hart Benton** and others to abolish the factory system of government-operated trading posts had enhanced O'Fallon's standing among the St. Louis traders: he was now widely recognized as a leading advocate of American traders' rights, and of aggressive measures against British infiltration of the northern frontier.

In 1825 O'Fallon accompanied Atkinson's second Yellowstone expedition to meet with the tribes between Council Bluffs and the mouth of the Yellowstone. For some bands this was the first contact with representatives of the U.S. government. The councils asserted American control of the region, bolstered the confidence of American fur traders, and weakened the position of the British traders among the tribes. Again, however, O'Fallon and Atkinson quarreled violently over policy and respective authority.

In the end O'Fallon had to abandon the field. Since youth, chronic problems with spleen, liver, and bowels had plagued him. Bad health incapacitated him through much of 1824. The arduous 1825 trip further undermined his health, and he returned to St. Louis dangerously ill. To the burden of poor health was added growing family responsibilities. For years relatives had urged him to marry, hoping a good wife would steady and calm his temper. In 1823 he finally took their advice and married Sophia Lee, the daughter of St. Louis auctioneer Patrick Lee. Eventually the couple had eight children, too large a family to support adequately on an Indian agent's salary.

O'Fallon resigned his commission in December 1826, and retired to a small plantation near St. Louis. He built a gristmill and erratically pursued other sources of income, but unlike his wealthy brother, John, Benjamin O'Fallon had no talent for making money. He continued to write letters and work for government action on his favorite causes: a hard line against British influence from Canada and support for American fur interests. He maintained close ties with the American Fur Company, and though poor health precluded seeking office for himself, he was active in politics. Befriended by Andrew Jackson during a trip to Washington, D.C., in 1819, O'Fallon remained an ardent supporter of Jackson throughout his life. O'Fallon's health declined steadily through the 1830s; he died on December 17, 1842.

Benjamin's brother, John, was also prominent in Missouri affairs, and the two were often confused by later writers. Contemporaries normally referred to Benjamin as "Mr. O'Fallon" until 1819, when appointment as an Indian agent conferred the honorary rank of major. Thereafter he was always "Major O'Fallon." John came to Missouri as "Captain O'Fallon" in 1817. In December 1820 he awarded himself the title of colonel, and was addressed as "Colonel O'Fallon" from that time onward.

MARY ELLEN ROWE

Carter, Clarence Edwin, ed. *The Territorial Papers of the United States.* Washington, D.C.: U.S. Government Printing Office, 1951.

O'Fallon, John. Papers. Missouri Historical Society, St. Louis.

Steiger, John W. "Benjamin O'Fallon." In *The Mountain Men and the Fur Trade of the Far West,* ed. LeRoy R. Hafen. Glendale, Calif.: Arthur H. Clark, 1968.

O'FALLON, JOHN (1791–1865)

John O'Fallon, a St. Louis merchant, banker, and philanthropist, was widely praised after his death as a model of business success and civic spirit, the ideal "self-made man." It was a reputation he had spent his life building. His father, Irish-born Dr. James O'Fallon, came west in 1789, dodging a tangle of bad debts, political intrigue, and land speculation gone awry in the Carolinas, to launch new schemes as a general agent of the South Carolina Yazoo Land Company. To strengthen his hand against his rival Gen. **James Wilkinson**, O'Fallon sought an alliance with Kentucky war hero George Rogers Clark. He married Clark's sister Frances in 1791; on November 17, 1791, John O'Fallon was born. James died soon after the birth of their second child, **Benjamin O'Fallon,** in 1793, and the Clark family raised the two boys. By 1807 **William Clark,** then an Indian agent and later the territorial governor of Missouri, had assumed their formal guardianship.

Clark planned a career practicing law in Missouri for O'Fallon, and sent him to good preparatory schools in Kentucky. By 1811, however, O'Fallon abandoned the plan and his studies. He experimented with his stepfather's trade of merchant, then joined Col. Joseph Daviess's Kentucky volunteers in **William Henry Harrison**'s 1811 Indian campaign. During the War of 1812 he served as Harrison's secretary and aide-de-camp, but by war's end had attained only the regular commission of captain in the Second Rifle Regiment.

Frustrated with his lagging military career, O'Fallon explored other options. While stationed at Fort Bellefontaine near St. Louis in 1817, he decided that Missouri's expanding economy offered the quickest route to the wealth and status he so ardently desired. An energetic but fruitless campaign for a federal job in 1818 convinced him that his uncle William Clark could or would do little to further his prospects. O'Fallon then proceeded to build a network of his own influential contacts among high-ranking military officers, government officials, and the merchants in his stepfather's family and their business associates. His efforts won him the lucrative contracts of sutler and paymaster to the 1818–1819 military expedition up the Missouri River.

O'Fallon held the joint appointment of sutler and paymaster to the upriver posts until 1823, engaged in the Indian trade and real estate investment on the side, and prospered through the hard depression years of the early 1820s. After 1823 his activities centered primarily in St. Louis, and reflect the range of the city's commercial life. Besides real estate investments, he bankrolled the mercantile firm of O'Fallon and Keyte, developed a large farm and orchard, sold lead and other local products to the East, distilled whiskey for the local market, engaged in banking, served in both houses of the state legislature to get favorable monetary legislation passed, served as an adjutant general of the state militia (primarily for the salary, his letters seem to indicate), and acted as the St. Louis agent for several eastern commercial houses, most notably the Philadelphia firm of Comegys and Company.

By the early 1830s O'Fallon was wealthy and so highly respected in St. Louis that not even business failure could tarnish his image. Appointed president of the St. Louis branch of the Bank of the United States in 1829, he managed the bank skillfully and profitably. He could not forestall closure when his branch fell victim to Andrew Jackson's crusade against the bank, but his conservative policies kept losses to a minimum and preserved the bank's reputation in Missouri. He remained closely associated with St. Louis banking for the rest of his life, serving as a director of the State Bank of Missouri and associating with various private banks over the years.

O'Fallon took an active role in Whig politics in the 1840s, hoping to repair the fiscal damage done by Jacksonians to Missouri and the nation. After the disintegration of the Whig Party, he generally retired from politics, but continued his efforts to bring railroads to Missouri. In the 1850s he served as president of two railroad companies, the Ohio Mississippi and the North Missouri. The railroad towns of O'Fallon, Missouri, and O'Fallon, Illinois, are named for him.

O'Fallon's sense of status required more than merely the accumulation of wealth. By the 1860s, when his personal fortune reportedly reached $8 million, he had given away perhaps as much more in charitable donations and civic and philanthropic projects. Besides large contributions to churches and private charities and aid to individuals, he built St. Louis Medical College, endowed O'Fallon Polytechnic Institute, donated a fortune in real estate to St. Louis and Washington Universities and the city of St. Louis, and engaged in numerous civic projects over the years.

O'Fallon married twice, first in 1820 to Harriet Stokes, a wealthy English emigrant. Her brother William Stokes was involved in a notorious St. Louis divorce case in 1821–1822, but the impact of this scandal was more than balanced by the value of the Stokes fortune to a fledgling businessman. The two daughters of that marriage died in childhood, and Harriet O'Fallon died in 1826. In 1827 O'Fallon married Caroline Sheets, the daughter of a wealthy Baltimore merchant family with a sizable fortune of her own. After John O'Fallon's death on December 17, 1865, she continued his philanthropic projects in St. Louis. The couple had four sons—James, Benjamin, Henry, and John Julius—and a daughter, Caroline, who married the noted St. Louis physician and teacher Charles A. Pope.

MARY ELLEN ROWE

O'Fallon, John. Papers. Missouri Historical Society, St. Louis.

Rowe, Mary Ellen. " 'A Respectable Independence': The Early Career of John O'Fallon." *Missouri Historical Review* 90 (July 1996): 393–409.

Smith, Thomas A. Papers. Western Historical Manuscripts Collection, Columbia.

O'HARE, CARRIE KATHLEEN RICHARDS (1876–1948)

Carrie Kathleen "Kate" Richards was born on March 26, 1876, in Ottawa County in central Kansas, and achieved fame as a social critic and Socialist activist. The most noteworthy years of her public life were spent in Missouri, especially St. Louis. She was the daughter of homesteaders Andrew and Lucy Sullivan Richards who were forced off the land by economic and natural disasters as were other farmers of that era.

In 1887 the Richards family moved to Kansas City, Missouri, where young Kate finished her public education, graduating from Central High School in 1892. After one year at Pawnee City Academy in southeast Nebraska, she taught school briefly in Nebraska. Deciding against a teaching career, she moved back to her family in Kansas City in 1895.

Considering some type of a religious commitment within the Disciples of Christ, Richards was drawn to combating the social problems she observed in the urban-industrial environment. She joined many other young women in the temperance movement, and then worked for the Kansas City branch of a national chain of missions, the Florence Crittenden Mission and Home. That institution sought to bring middle-class virtues to prostitutes and alcoholics, and Richards's task was to encourage them to attend mission programs.

However, Richards came to question the efficacy of such activities, and abandoned the cause. Next she worked as a clerk in the office of the machine shop her father operated, and soon was employed in the shop itself, despite the taunts of the male workers. Becoming one of the first women members of the International Order of Machinists, Richards immersed herself in labor issues. She happened to hear a speech by the legendary labor organizer Mary Harris "Mother" Jones, and became interested in radical solutions to contemporary economic issues. She then met J. A. Wayland, publisher of the most widely read Socialist newspaper in the country, the *Appeal to Reason.* At the end of the century, she joined the small but dynamic Socialist movement that was emerging throughout the United States.

Kate Richards enrolled in the International School of Social Economy in 1901 in Kansas where she was trained as a Socialist organizer. There she met and married another student, **Francis Peter "Frank" O'Hare** of St. Louis. After their marriage on January 1, 1902, the couple honeymooned while touring for the Socialist Party of America in Missouri and Kansas. They spent much of the next few years on the road speaking for their cause, with Kate O'Hare also starting her career as a columnist for the Socialist press. She addressed topics such as decent working conditions and an end to child labor, as well as other economic and social issues from a Socialist perspective. In those years, she bore four children, Richard in 1903, Kathleen in 1905, and Eugene and Victor in 1908.

From 1904 to 1909 the O'Hares homesteaded in Oklahoma while engaged in Socialist Party activities. Kate O'Hare soon eclipsed her husband in party fame, and became a popular public speaker on the Socialist hustings, drawing huge crowds. She also became an increasingly well-known journalist in Socialist circles. Leaving Oklahoma because of Frank's poor health, they moved briefly to Kansas City, Kansas, in 1909, where Kate ran for the United States House of Representatives on the Socialist ticket in 1910. The next year the O'Hares established their most permanent home when they moved to St. Louis.

When Kate O'Hare settled in St. Louis, she was one of the most significant leaders in the Socialist Party west of the Mississippi River. She worked as a columnist and editor for a regional Socialist monthly called the *National Rip-Saw,* while also undertaking constant speaking trips across the country on behalf of the Socialist Party. She became nationally prominent in her party, serving on its executive committee as well as in other major positions, and was a nominee for its vice presidential candidate in the general election of 1916. She also represented her party abroad to the international Socialist movement, and when she went to England to participate in its meetings she became only the second woman to do so. In 1916 she was the party's nominee for the United States Senate from Missouri, the first woman to run for the Senate. She was also nominated for the St. Louis Board of Education, and addressed crowds in and around St. Louis as a party speaker.

O'Hare became well known in St. Louis civic affairs. She worked for woman suffrage with groups such as the Equal Suffrage League of St. Louis and the local branch of the National American Woman Suffrage Association, and was an avid debater with representatives of the antisuffrage forces. In addition, she was active in the St. Louis branch of the Woman's Trade Union League. O'Hare accepted a mayoral appointment to a municipal committee on unemployment, and she was involved as an investigative reporter in hearings in St. Louis of the state senate Minimum Wage Committee. In her involvement in civic affairs, she brought a Socialist point of view to the public dialogue where she cooperated with middle-class reformers such as **Roger Nash Baldwin,** but was often a gadfly to civic leaders with whom she battled constantly, such as the influential archbishop **John Joseph Glennon.**

In 1914 O'Hare turned her attention to World War I, and her speeches and writings offered an ideological interpretation of the war as an imperialist adventure. She was a committed foe of the preparedness movement, locally and nationally, and determined to discourage American intervention in the war. In April 1917 O'Hare was a delegate to a hastily called convention of the Socialist Party that met in St. Louis during the same week that the United States declared war on Germany. She was elected chair of the major policy-making committee of the convention that condemned American involvement in the war in favor of the international solidarity of workers.

Following the convention O'Hare resumed her national speaking tour in which she continued to emphasize the economic roots of the war. After delivering virtually the same speech at least seventy-five times in various states—always with agents of the Justice Department in her audiences—she was arrested under the Espionage Act following her talk in Bowman, North Dakota, in July 1917. She was convicted in a highly politicized atmosphere by a jury of twelve businessmen, and was sentenced by a hostile judge to five years in the Missouri State Penitentiary in Jefferson City.

After losing an appeal to the United States Supreme Court, O'Hare began to serve her sentence in April 1919. She worked in one of the facility's industrial shops at what she called scab labor. She was appalled by the prison conditions, which in fact were considered at the time as among the most congested and retrogressive in the country, and she successfully pressured introduction of a number of changes. Diseased prisoners began to be segregated from the larger population of inmates, prisoners were served warm meals and given access to the library, and the dining room was painted. O'Hare conducted case studies of her fellow inmates that she hoped would have value in the field of criminology, but in this effort she was thwarted by the prison administration, and her field notes were destroyed. She tried to help her fellow inmates by distributing foodstuffs and reading materials to them, and assisting in their legal proceedings and in establishing themselves in society once their terms were completed. For a few months of her own prison term, she was housed in a cell adjacent to another famous radical, anarchist Emma Goldman, and the two became lifelong friends despite their conflicting ideologies.

An energetic campaign was waged across the country by Frank O'Hare to win Kate's early release from prison. Support came from Socialists, pacifists, and other sympathizers, and in May 1920 President Woodrow Wilson commuted her sentence. Kate O'Hare returned to St. Louis and resumed her national speaking tours, this time focused on the release of prisoners still held under the Espionage and Sedition Acts. She and Frank revived the *National Rip-Saw,* which, like many radical periodicals, had been forced to cease publication during the war. They published the monthly at first in Girard, Kansas, and then in St. Louis.

The Socialist Party had fragmented at the end of the war, and O'Hare, who still believed in its tenets while opposing the new Communist movement, devoted the bulk of her energies to prison reform, especially the prohibition of contract labor. In the meantime, the O'Hare family left St. Louis, and Kate O'Hare, long interested in education, became a founder of a workers' school in rural Arkansas, Commonwealth College. She worked for the college for several years as a trustee, administrator, instructor, and fund-raiser. In 1928 she was divorced, remarried that same year, and settled in California with her second husband, Charles C. Cunningham, an engineer and businessman.

For the remaining twenty years of her life, O'Hare—the name she continued to use in her public activities—while intermittently retired, worked in the Upton Sinclair End Poverty in California movement during the depression, served briefly on the staff of a Progressive Party member of the United States House of Representatives, and worked for the director of penology for the state of California in a program to reform conditions in San Quentin Prison. Active to the end as a public speaker on civic issues, she died in Benicia, California, on January 10, 1948.

SALLY M. MILLER

Basen, Neil K. "Kate Richards O'Hare: The 'First Lady' of American Socialism, 1901–1917." *Labor History* 21 (spring 1980): 165–99.

Foner, Philip S., and Sally M. Miller. *Kate Richards O'Hare: Selected Writings and Speeches.* Baton Rouge: Louisiana State University Press, 1982.

Miller, Sally M. *From Prairie to Prison: The Life of Social Activist Kate Richards O'Hare.* Columbia: University of Missouri Press, 1993.

———. "Kate Richards O'Hare: Progression toward Feminism." *Kansas History* 7 (winter 1984–1985): 263–79.

O'Hare, Frank P. Papers. Missouri Historical Society, St. Louis.

O'Hare, Kate Richards. *Dear Sweethearts: Letters from Kate Richards O'Hare to Her Family.* St. Louis: Missouri Historical Society.

O'HARE, FRANCIS PETER (1877–1960)

Francis Peter "Frank" O'Hare was born in New Hampton, Iowa, on April 23, 1877, to Peter Paul O'Hare, an Irish immigrant from Belfast, and Elizabeth Weijers O'Hare, a Dutch immigrant. In 1881, following Peter O'Hare's abandonment of his family, Elizabeth and her four children moved to St. Louis, where they lived in the notorious Kerry Patch slum.

Frank O'Hare dropped out of high school in the eleventh grade to take a job with an electric company that helped build Union Station. He worked as a pricing clerk at Simmons Hardware and then at Emerson Electric for Thomas Meston, who became O'Hare's intellectual mentor for several years. In 1900 O'Hare became a Socialist and began to espouse a political creed that was part midwestern Populism and part Americanized Marxism. The next year he met his future wife, Kate Richards, at a school for Socialist agitators in Girard, Kansas. The couple began their calling as itinerant lecturers with a honeymoon tour of Missouri towns and eventually became two of the most popular speakers on the Socialist Chautauqua.

In 1911 Frank O'Hare returned to St. Louis to serve as circulation manager and de facto editor of the *National Rip-Saw*. Through a combination of hard-hitting investigative forays into the underside of capitalism, aggressive sales tactics, and revenue from advertisements for sleazy products, O'Hare made the *Rip-Saw* into the most popular Socialist monthly in American history. He coordinated the itineraries and edited the copy of his "star" writers, including his hero and friend Eugene Debs, Oscar Ameringer, and **Kate Richards O'Hare.** Although he identified emotionally with the left wing of the Socialist Party and looked upon foreign-born, urban party leaders as his sworn enemies, O'Hare often found himself in agreement with the evolutionary Socialists of the center and right on theoretical and tactical questions.

In early 1917 O'Hare resigned from the *Rip-Saw* and moved his family to Ruskin Commune in Florida. Following his wife's imprisonment for violating the Espionage Act during World War I, he returned to St. Louis to edit *Frank O'Hare's Bulletin* and to publish Kate O'Hare's prison letters to raise money and publicize her case. In his spare time he invented the first accounting machine with a mechanical memory, though he failed to seek a patent on the device until it was too late.

Once his wife's release had been won in 1920, O'Hare restarted the *Rip-Saw,* this time as the publisher. The O'Hares launched the Children's Crusade to dramatize the plight of the families of leftists still languishing in prison after the war. The publicity campaign speeded the release of political prisoners, but brought the *Rip-Saw* to the brink of bankruptcy and caused the O'Hares to be expelled from the Socialist Party. Subsequently, they moved their magazine to New Llano Cooperative Colony in Louisiana, only to be caught in a bitter factional fight that led to the collapse of their publication and, ultimately, of their marriage; the O'Hares' divorce became final in 1928. Later in the year Frank married Irene Reynolds, a pious young woman who doted on him for the rest of his life.

In the late 1920s O'Hare had begun a second career in business in St. Louis, acting as an efficiency expert for a hat manufacturer. Losing his job in the aftermath of the stock market crash, he worked for a labor-press syndicate in New York and wrote freelance articles for labor magazines and the *St. Louis Post-Dispatch.*

In 1937 O'Hare returned to St. Louis for good, teaming up with other prewar radicals to publicize a Socialist-style cure for the depression that they called "Abundance for All." During World War II he became a regular book reviewer for the *Post-Dispatch* and contributed occasional features. O'Hare also continued his amateur career as an inventor, creating, among other things, an automatic mapmaking device (another creation that he waited too long to patent) and more practical moneymaking schemes such as a slide-rule instruction book.

O'Hare also founded a luncheon club, the Dunkers, and published a newsletter that featured club activities, book reviews, and essays reflecting O'Hare's continuing faith in democratic socialism. He insisted that the Dunkers reach across lines of race, class, and gender. During the heyday of McCarthyism, the club became a refuge for free speech, where liberal businessmen and politicians, labor leaders, women, and African Americans met on equal terms to discuss common civic concerns. Eventually, the Dunkers evolved into a freewheeling intellectual salon, while O'Hare continued to be a gadfly against the St. Louis establishment and a revered role model for a new generation of radicals and community activists.

O'Hare died in St. Louis on July 16, 1960. **Roger Nash Baldwin,** founder of the American Civil Liberties Union, neatly summarized his friend's contribution to the history of Missouri: "The strength of our democracy lies largely with its dissenters, its rebels, its optimists and prophets. Frank O'Hare was all of these."

PETER H. BUCKINGHAM

Buckingham, Peter H. *Rebel against Injustice: The Life of Frank P. O'Hare.* Columbia: University of Missouri Press, 1996.

Miller, Sally M. *From Prairie to Prison: The Life of Social Activist Kate Richards O'Hare.* Columbia: University of Missouri Press, 1993.

O'Hare, Frank P. Papers. Missouri Historical Society, St. Louis.

St. Louis Post-Dispatch, October 23, 1960.

OLIVER, MARIE ELIZABETH WATKINS (1854–1944)

Marie Elizabeth Watkins Oliver, creator of the Missouri state flag, was born on January 11, 1854, in

Ray County, Missouri, the daughter of Charles Allen and Henrietta Rives Watkins. She was educated by governesses, in private schools, and at Richmond College. On December 10, 1879, she married Robert Burett Oliver. The marriage ceremony was held at Westover, the home of the bride's mother. The couple lived at the groom's home in Jackson, Missouri, until 1896 when they moved to Cape Girardeau. Robert Oliver practiced law and Mary Elizabeth Oliver raised her family and participated in many civic activities. The union produced five sons and one daughter: Robert Burett Jr., John Byrd, Allen Laws, William Palmer, Charles Watkins, and Marie Marguerite.

In 1904 Oliver joined the Nancy Hunter Chapter of the Daughters of the American Revolution (DAR) in Cape Girardeau, and in 1907 was elected state DAR vice regent. Mrs. Samuel McKnight Green appointed a committee to determine whether the state of Missouri had a flag and, if not, to design one and secure passage of a bill in the legislature to make it the state's official flag.

After corresponding with secretaries of state in every state and territory, Oliver designed what would become the flag of the state of Missouri. To create the design she had envisioned, she asked Mary Kochtitzky, a Cape Girardeau artist, to assist in the project. The flag has a tricolor background, featuring a red stripe at the top, a white stripe in the center, and a blue stripe at the bottom. The center of the flag has a blue circle enclosing the Missouri coat of arms. Around the coat of arms, within the blue circle, are twenty-four stars, denoting Missouri as the twenty-fourth state to enter the Union.

Oliver's husband, a former state senator, drafted a bill that Sen. Arthur L. Oliver, a nephew of the flag's creator, introduced in the Missouri Senate on March 17, 1909. The bill passed the Senate twenty-four to one, but failed to pass in the House of Representatives. Senator Oliver reintroduced the bill in the Senate in 1911 and it passed twenty-three to two, but failed again in the House of Representatives.

In 1911 the Missouri State Capitol burned, destroying the original flag painted by Kochtitzky. Oliver and Mrs. S. D. MacFarland made a duplicate flag out of silk. On January 21, 1913, Charles C. Oliver, a state representative from Cape Girardeau County, introduced the Oliver Flag Bill in the House of Representatives, and it passed on March 7. The Senate quickly passed the same bill. Gov. **Elliott Woolfolk Major** signed it on March 22, 1913.

Marie Elizabeth Watkins Oliver, who served as state regent of the Missouri DAR in 1910–1911, died on October 18, 1944.

KAY HIVELY

Leach, Blanche Shaeffer. *Missouri State History of the Daughters of the American Revolution.* Kansas City: Smith-Grieves, 1929.

Oliver, Allen L. "The Missouri State Flag." *Missouri Historical Review* 52 (October 1952): 35–39.

Shoemaker, Floyd C., ed. *Missouri Historical Review* 39 (January 1945): 281.

Waal, Carla, and Barbara Oliver Korner, eds. *Hardship and Hope: Missouri Women Writing about Their Lives.* Columbia: University of Missouri Press, 1997.

O'NEILL, ROSE CECIL (1874–1947)

Rose O'Neill is as important a figure in the history of illustration, popular culture, and American art as the more famous Charles Dana Gibson, Norman Rockwell, and J. C. Leyendecker. Born in Wilkes-Barre, Pennsylvania, on June 25, 1874, she began publishing her work at age thirteen when she won a drawing contest for the *Omaha World Herald.* By her early twenties, she was established as a popular illustrator, and during the golden age of illustration published numerous illustrations in *Truth, Life, Ladies' Home Journal, Cosmopolitan, Collier's, Harper's Bazaar, Everybody's,* and *Good Housekeeping,* including more than seven hundred cartoons in an eight-year period for the most notable humor magazine of the day, *Puck.* Her career spanned five decades during which she was equally prodigious in the creation of advertising art, book illustrations, and fine art. A novelist and poet, she nevertheless remains best known today as the creator of the Kewpie doll.

A self-taught artist, O'Neill learned from her artistically inclined family. Her Irish-born father, William P. O'Neill, loved the English language, quoting from Shakespeare, Byron, Cowper, and Moore to his children and providing, through his itinerant book business, classics in literature and the arts. A dreamer and romantic who moved his family to a homestead in Nebraska, then Omaha, and finally the Ozarks of Missouri near what is now Branson, William O'Neill and his more pragmatic wife, Aseneth Ceceilia Smith O'Neill, encouraged the artistic and independent intellectual lives of three daughters and two sons. Arranging for audiences with Edwin Booth and Madame Modjeska, William wanted Rose to be an actress. However, after short runs in *A Pair of Kids* and *The Southerner,* she managed to leave Omaha for New York City, where she began to sell her works to magazines while lodging with the Sisters of St. Regis.

By 1898 O'Neill had married a dashing Virginian, Gray Latham, often a model for urbane males in her cartoons and illustrations. This marriage and her second in 1902 to Puck editor Harry Leon Wilson both ended painfully in divorce. Nevertheless, by 1914 O'Neill was one of the wealthiest artists in America, making $1.4 million on her cartoons, illustrations, and Kewpie dolls.

Derived from the decorative magazine characters encouraged by *Ladies' Home Journal* editor Edward Bok as a departure from her ethnic, social, and gender cartoons from the 1890s, the Kewpies (baby talk for Cupid) were chubby elves whose bumbling good nature made them popular with children and adults. For the next thirty years O'Neill drew them for *Ladies' Home Journal, Woman's Home Companion, Good Housekeeping,* and the *Delineator,* syndicating a comic strip in the 1930s for Sunday newspapers nationwide.

On March 4, 1913, O'Neill patented a doll based on the Kewpies, overseeing the bisque original in Germany. Manufactured in various sizes and materials from bisque to plush, the dolls even drew critical attention. As a dizzying array of Kewpie spin-offs ensued—nursery china, glassware, napkin rings, fabrics, inkwells, vases, and ice cream molds—Alexander King irreverently christened the phenomenon "a dimpled bonanza," and the Kewpies "an ossified hunk of peach ice cream." Americans loved the Kewpies, persisting from that time in calling Rose O'Neill the "Mother of the Kewpies," and ironically denying the seriousness and accomplishment of her other art.

However her popular public characterized her, Rose O'Neill consistently created fine art that was accomplished and original throughout her life. Just as she had been inspired in her early illustrative technique by the masters Gustave Doré, Michelangelo, Leonardo da Vinci, and Greek sculptors represented in her father's library, she was a quick study of Toulouse-Lautrec, Vidu, Vargas, Charles Dana Gibson, Gordon Grant, Louis Glackens, and others. Her book illustrations of her own novels, beginning in 1904 with *The Loves of Edwy,* demonstrate a daunting mastery of styles and techniques. By 1929, when she published *The Goblin Woman,* a melodramatic novel of deep psychological overtones, she had experimented with Pre-Raphaelite and symbolist imagery, developing through word and image the recurring theme of androgyny. The juxtaposition of four children's books and four adult novels from 1904 to 1936 demonstrates her artistic and experimental fluency concurrently in the popular and the fine arts.

A critically successful exhibit at the Galerie Devambez in Paris in 1922 signals an important creative benchmark in O'Neill's accomplishments as a serious artist. She commingled Kewpie and so-called monster imagery, referencing psychological and social themes signaled in art, religion, and philosophy. Often displaying blended male and female characteristics in brooding figures she called her "sweet monsters," the exhibit capped a European art career she shared with her popular reputation in New York and Bonniebrook, Missouri. Later she revealed that the monster drawings were inspired by the "enchanted woods" of her Missouri retreats, which suggested to her a vital primitive, or Old World, quality of Ozark people and places.

In 1914 O'Neill shocked her American Kewpie public by depicting "woman" as "Sheepwoman" in the *New York Post.* Arguing visually in this commingled imagery of a sheep head and female torso of the unliberated condition of women, O'Neill overtly addressed the issues of suffrage and the woman artist. Earlier she had drawn Kewpies marching in an illustration for votes for women, and though not politically active espoused a feminist theme throughout her work.

By the mid-1930s O'Neill enjoyed a reputation as a fanciful, bohemian, eccentric artist who created salons in the 1920s at her estate in Connecticut. She had met and entertained the noble, the famous, and the obscure, from "fishermen, laborers, and taxi-drivers" to European nobility and writers such as Kahlil Gibran. "Keeping perpetual open house," however, along with the lifetime support of her Missouri family, particularly her brother "Clink" and mother, "Memmie," ironically left her a virtual pauper by the late 1930s. She retired in her last years to Bonniebrook, the family estate in the Ozarks that had remained a home place for her since 1896. Although isolated from the creative and social life of New York and Europe, she developed a friendship with **Vance Randolph,** the Ozark folklorist, and continued to draw and write. Her memoirs of this period, unpublished during her life, ended on a hauntingly lonely note:

Ah, few there are who live, alas
And they are far from here
Who know how young and dear I was
When I was young and dear.

Although O'Neill's excessive generosity to people who largely did not reciprocate resulted in her impoverishment at the time of her death, she ranks among the most talented and versatile women of her era. Accomplished in a dazzling number of artistic forms and genres, she provocatively addressed social, cultural, and aesthetic issues throughout her career, often as covertly and complexly as our best artists have. Rose O'Neill died at Bonniebrook on January 7, 1947.

SHELLEY S. ARMITAGE

Armitage, Shelley. *Kewpies and Beyond: The World of Rose O'Neill.* Jackson: University of Mississippi Press, 1995.

Formanek-Brunell, Miriam, ed. *The Story of Rose O'Neill: An Autobiography.* Columbia: University of Missouri Press, 1997.

Goodman, Helen. *The Art of Rose O'Neill.* Chadds Ford, Pa.: Brandywine River Museum, 1989.

McCanse, Ralph Alan. *Titans and Kewpies: The Life and Art of Rose O'Neill.* New York: Vantage Press, 1968.

OTIS, MERRILL E. (1884–1944)

Merrill E. Otis, born outside the village of Hopkins in Nodaway County in northwestern Missouri on July 7, 1884, grew up on a farm. He attended high school in Hopkins and nearby Maryville. In 1902 he matriculated at the University of Missouri, receiving a bachelor's degree in 1906, a master's in 1907, and a law degree in 1910. Active in campus organizations, he was the Class of 1906 orator and belonged to both the prestigious legal Order of the Coif and Phi Beta Kappa.

Starting in 1911 Otis practiced law in northwestern Missouri. Entering Republican politics, he lost political races for Congress and for prosecuting attorney of Sullivan County. He received patronage jobs in St. Joseph as first assistant city counselor and then as city counselor. From 1921 to 1923 he served as assistant attorney general of Missouri and in 1923–1924 as chair of the Missouri Public Service Commission. In mid-1924 he became assistant to the solicitor general of the United States. During the October 1924 term of the Supreme Court he argued twenty-three cases for the government. In 1925 Republican congressman Charles Faust of St. Joseph was instrumental in helping Otis secure an appointment as one of two judges of the United States District Court for the Western District of Missouri. Otis married Sophie Hersch on October 8, 1916, and they had a daughter, Dorothy.

During the New Deal Otis became one of the better-known members of the federal judiciary. A conscientious man, he seldom took vacations. His custom was to spend long hours on the bench and to take work home at night. He taught courses at the Kansas City School of Law, becoming the institution's honorary president. Much sought for his oratorical ability, he had a reputation as a colorful after-dinner speaker. Critics thought he favored big business. Indeed, Otis vigorously struck down or tried to restrict early New Deal legislation, following a pattern generally consistent with the rulings of the Supreme Court. He launched a series of thinly veiled public attacks on President Franklin D. Roosevelt. Skirting an overt violation of legal ethics, he spoke obliquely, talking in parables about the flag and the soundness of the Constitution. When he really wanted to lash out, he lectured in classical terms about the Greeks and the Romans, what knowledgeable listeners called his "Trial of Socrates" speech.

Otis aspired to a higher bench, even the Supreme Court. He wrote many articles for law journals, mainly on idealistic legal themes, and he compiled what he considered his important opinions and speeches into a 1937 book, *In the Day's Work of a Federal Judge.* Because of a combination of his controversial views and Democratic control of the national government, Otis remained a federal district judge.

Otis stood strongly for law and order during the crisis created in Kansas City in the 1930s by the excesses of the Pendergast machine. In 1936 and 1937, along with colleague Judge **Albert L. Reeves,** Otis presided over vote-fraud trials that led to the conviction of 259 machine functionaries. More fundamentally, after the leader of the political organization, **Thomas J. Pendergast,** pleaded guilty to tax evasion in May 1939, Judge Otis sentenced him to fifteen months in the state penitentiary, imposing a heavy fine, five years' probation, and other restrictions. Otis's sentence effectively ended Pendergast's rule, and his machine collapsed. Many observers thought the sentence overly lenient, but Pendergast was a sixty-seven-year-old first-time offender.

In 1944 Otis was elected president of the prestigious six-thousand-member American Judicature Society. The honor was his last. He fell seriously ill and died at age sixty on December 23, 1944. The brand of conservatism based on "rugged individualism" that Judge Otis supported ebbed in the Roosevelt years, though to the end he remained true to his cherished principles.

LAWRENCE H. LARSEN

Flannigan, John H. "Judge Merrill E. Otis, 1884–1944." *Journal of the Missouri Bar* 2 (December 1946): 182–84.

Larsen, Lawrence H. *Federal Justice in Western Missouri: The Judges, the Cases, the Times.* Columbia: University of Missouri Press, 1994.

Otis, Merrill E. *In the Day's Work of a Federal Judge: A Miscellany of Opinions, Addresses, and Extracts.* Ed. Alexander M. Meyer. Kansas City: Brown-White, 1937.

OUSLEY, MAYME (1887–1970)

Citizens of St. James elected Mayme Ousley as the first woman mayor in Missouri on April 5, 1921. Born on January 2, 1887, to Thomas and Rebecca Dunham Hanrahan of Edgar Springs in Phelps County, Mayme attended school in Rolla. There she met and married Edward William Ousley, a student of Washington University Dental School in St. Louis. The wedding occurred on September 24, 1905. After graduation

Dr. Ousley set up his dental practice in St. James, and the couple lived there the rest of their lives.

Dr. Ousley joined the St. James semiprofessional baseball team. Mayme Ousley followed the team as they traveled from town to town and often scolded them about their appearance. The players nicknamed her "Granny" Ousley, and the name remained with her.

Ousley became active in the local Republican Party and announced her candidacy for mayor in February 1921, less than two years after Missouri women received the right to vote in the Nineteenth Amendment. She promised to draw a salary of only one dollar a month and spent six weeks in door-to-door campaigning asking all the women for their votes. The turnout was so large on election day that more ballots had to be printed. Ousley won by eight votes. The incumbent mayor, J. J. Forester, was so upset because of his defeat by a woman that he did not attend the meeting of the town council to administer to her the oath of office on May 2, 1921.

Ousley vowed to clean up the city and the city hall. She threw out the cuspidors from the hall, painted the small frame building inside and out, and partitioned the interior, making a small office for herself, one for the councilmen, and one for a jail. She cleaned up the streets and sidewalks and ordered landlords to install indoor plumbing. Signs at the edge of town warned: "Drive slow and see our beautiful city, drive fast and see our jail." The mayor, however, proved compassionate to the underprivileged and those needing advice and a helping hand.

Soon after her election, Ousley found herself in great demand as a speaker. She addressed chambers of commerce and League of Women Voters chapters around the state. In January 1922 she was elected secretary-treasurer of the Ozark Trail Association of Missouri. That same year she appeared before the highway commission urging construction of a highway between St. Louis and Springfield.

During her term as mayor Ousley promoted a bond issue to build a new power plant and advocated a city water system. She worked actively to encourage industrial firms to locate in the city.

After her successful term as mayor, Ousley ran for the Missouri House of Representatives in 1924 and for state senator from the Twenty-fourth District in 1926, but she suffered defeats in both races. Unfortunately, she ran as a Republican candidate in a Democratic county, and her popularity could not overcome the handicap.

Ousley ran for St. James mayor again in 1927, but was not elected. In 1930 she was drafted as a last-minute candidate for mayor without her knowledge or consent. She did not have time to campaign and lost by two votes. Nine years later she ran unopposed for the office of mayor. The town by this time showed financial improvement with railroad construction and a new high school building in progress. Ousley campaigned for a new sewer system.

In 1941 Ousley was elected for her third term as mayor with a margin of nearly four hundred votes over her opponent. She suffered defeats in 1943 and 1947, but in 1955 she won again for her fourth and final term. By this time she was nearly seventy years of age.

Ousley also served as a trustee of the State Board of Training Schools and the Odd Fellows Retirement Home in Liberty, was a president of the State Assembly of Rebekah Lodge of Missouri, a member of the Trinity Episcopal Church of St. James, an officer of the Phelps County Historical Society and the Order of Eastern Star, and a member and officer of the National Good Roads Association.

Mayme Ousley died on October 29, 1970. Her portrait hangs in the St. James City Hall.

MARY K. DAINS

Dains, Mary K., ed. *Show Me Missouri Women: Selected Biographies.* Kirksville, Mo.: Thomas Jefferson University Press, 1989.

March, David D. *The History of Missouri.* Vol. 4. New York: Lewis Historical Publishing, 1967.

Ousley, Mayme H. Papers. 1889–1967. Western Historical Manuscripts Collection, Rolla.

Smith, Wallace. "Missouri's First Woman Mayor." *Missouri Life* 12 (August 1984).

St. James Leader-Journal, November 5, 1970.

OVERSTOLZ, HENRY CLEMENS (1822–1887)

Henry Clemens Overstolz was a St. Louis businessman and politician. He was born on July 7, 1822, in Münster, Prussian Westphalia, Germany, one of five children of Wilhelm Overstolz, who was descended from a noted family of Cologne patricians, and Thérèse Duse Overstolz. He settled in St. Louis as a general merchant in 1846, and had prosperous successive careers in merchandising, lumber, and banking. In 1875 he married Philippine Espenschied of St. Louis, who bore him six children and survived him to marry Otto E. Forster.

In 1847 Overstolz was elected as a member of the St. Louis City Council. In 1853 he was elected as comptroller (the first German-born person elected to citywide office), reelected in 1854, but defeated in 1855 in the Know-Nothing sweep. In 1856 he was elected to the Missouri State Board of Public Works, and during the secession crisis he openly aligned himself with the Constitutional Unionists who supported the continuation of slavery and other Southern interests but opposed secession.

Overstolz withdrew from public life during the Civil War and its immediate aftermath, and he did not return to the city council until 1871, becoming president of the council in 1873. In 1875 he was an independent candidate for mayor, losing to Arthur B. Barrett, a Democrat. On Barrett's death there was a second election in May 1875, after which Overstolz successfully contested the announced victory of Democrat James H. Britton and was inaugurated on February 9, 1876.

Overstolz supported the separation of the city of St. Louis from St. Louis County, and in 1877 he was elected as the first mayor to serve a four-year term under the new charter of St. Louis as an autonomous city. He was nominated by both the Democratic and the Republican Parties for that mayoral election.

Much of Overstolz's political correspondence deals with supporting petitioners to the Republican administration of President Rutherford B. Hayes for positions in federal service. As the first mayor under the new charter, Overstolz had an opportunity to set precedents for later officeholders.

As mayor in 1877 Overstolz was celebrated for showing restraint in the face of the general strike (lasting a week, starting on July 21) called by labor leaders during the national railway strike. By the time he had completed his four-year term, political reformers regarded Overstolz with hostility. In April 1881 Peter L. Foy wrote **John F. Darby** that they had done good work in defeating Overstolz's bid for reelection, since "in defeating him we defeated the rings and the corruptionists generally." Overstolz was succeeded by William L. Ewing, a Republican.

Henry Overstolz was one of the most successful German political figures in St. Louis in the nineteenth century, but he achieved that success by becoming an integral part of the prevailing system without challenging it or overstressing his ethnic origins. In this sense, he was the epitome of a "crossover" politician. He died on November 29, 1887.

STEVEN ROWAN

Burbank, David T. *The Reign of the Rabble: The St. Louis General Strike of 1877.* New York: Augustus M. Kelley, 1966.

Darby Papers. Missouri Historical Society, St. Louis.

Moehle, Odon F. "The History of St. Louis, 1878–1882." Master's thesis, Washington University, 1954.

Overstolz, Henry. Papers. Missouri Historical Society, St. Louis.

OWEN, JAMES M. (1903–1972)

James M. Owen, a young advertising and insurance professional in Jefferson City, left mid-Missouri in the early depression for Branson to help his father open a new business. The White River and the Ozarks immediately captured his imagination, and he remained in Taney County for the rest of his life. The young entrepreneur became central in Branson's civic and governmental affairs while founding the famous Jim Owen Boat Line and many other local businesses. His promotions for the Galena-to-Branson float-fishing trip made him the most prominent figure in Ozarks tourism in the mid-twentieth century.

The skilled publicist was born on September 11, 1903, in Elkland, in Webster County, graduated from Marshfield High School, and during the 1920s attended the College of Agriculture at the University of Missouri–Columbia for three years. Owen spent time in advertising for a Jefferson City newspaper, but joined his father in 1933 to open a new drugstore in Branson. That same year, Owen, famous for his witty personality, acquired financial backing to establish the successful Hillbilly Theater in Branson. Later, he created a traveling theater with a portable generator, projector, screen, popcorn, and folding seats to present entertainment at country crossroads on the weekends.

In 1935 the portly Owen founded his float-fishing business with a half-dozen guides, johnboats, a truck, and showmanship. He catered to business and corporate clients who eagerly sought the sport of smallmouth-bass fishing while enjoying deluxe overnight trips and a selection of over one hundred amenities from the commissary. Tourists could have portable toilet seats, floating-bar boats iced for the thirsty, seating in director's chairs, and dining enjoyment of steaks, chicken, fish, and all the trimmings each night.

Owen's guides, including the already well-known boatbuilder Charley Barnes and yarn-spinner Tom Yocum joined others tutored by Owen on how to talk "hillbilly." They established the noon and evening camps, told tales and legends at the campsite, served as fishing and hunting guides, and secretly managed trotlines at night to ensure enough catfish for dinner. Eventually, Owen's fleet included three dozen guides and forty boats, and after World War II only affluent sportsmen could afford his catered tour. Owen even met his wife, Barbara, on one of his floats, an opportune match with an outdoors woman from Oklahoma who became an effective business partner.

Almost overnight Jim Owen became a success on the waters of the White River from Galena, Missouri, to Cotter, Arkansas. Corporate guests brought filmmakers and journalists for the experience. *Life, Look,* the *American,* the *Saturday Evening Post, Outdoor Life, Field and Stream, Sports Afield,* travel serials, major urban newspapers, and film and radio programs ran features about Owen's attractions. Ralph Foster, the media giant in Springfield, became one of Owen's best friends, and later Paul Henning, producer of the

Beverly Hillbillies television program, promoted the 1970 book *Jim Owen's Hillbilly Humor* and called Owen "the best friend the Ozarks ever had."

Owen is credited with bringing many celebrities to the Ozarks, including actors Gene Autry, Forrest Tucker, and Charlton Heston, comedian Smiley Burnette, artist **Thomas Hart Benton,** and outdoors writer Robert Page Lincoln, all of whom gave recognition and credibility to Owen.

Businessman Owen kept a card file on everyone who floated with him. He recorded their tastes in liquor, food, and sport, and which guides pleased them the most; he sent hundreds of birthday letters annually. His float business expanded to other regional rivers, especially the Buffalo River in Arkansas where Benton sketched his famous Ozark river scenes.

Owen's meteoric rise in tourism also led to twelve years as mayor of Branson (1935–1939, 1941–1943, and 1945–1949) and the opportunity to invest in an array of businesses. As a local politician he hired taxis and introduced free transportation to the polls. In addition to his theater, float-fishing business, and the Owen Drug Store, he was a nationally known dog breeder with his Owen kennels, and served as president of the National Fox and Fox Hound Protective Association. He was the first president of a local bank, a prosperous real estate salesman, and a local columnist. He bred prize gamecocks; was a landlord; operated a mule-powered merry-go-round for picnics and fairs, a bowling alley, an archery range, and a hamburger stand; and raised dairy cattle and ponies.

Always courting visibility, Owen aided in the founding of the Branson Silver Cornet Band and beat the bass drum himself during their march performances. He led all these pursuits in the guise of "hillbilly culture," which became significant in state history as Owen, perhaps more than any other individual, eroded the negative implications of the stereotypical term *hillbilly* into positive capital gains for tourism. Only after his death did other family names replace his at the top of the tourist industry, such as the Trimbles at the Shepherd of the Hills Farm and the Herschends at Silver Dollar City.

Owen's float business yielded to the federal reservoirs of Bulls Shoals and Table Rock dams with his last float conducted in 1958. In 1966 he suffered a stroke, becoming partially paralyzed. The legendary businessman spent the remainder of his years occupied with the Jim Owen Realty Company, appearances as a celebrity, writing for magazines, and traveling. He died on July 12, 1972.

LYNN MORROW

Godsey, Townsend. "The King of the Floaters." *Missouri Life* (March–June 1977): 67–74.
Saults, Dan. "Gently Down the Stream." *Sports Afield* (May 1974): 78–79, 184–85.

PAGE, GERALDINE (1924–1987)

Geraldine Page was born in Kirksville, Missouri, on November 22, 1924, to Leon Elwin Page, an osteopathic physician, and Edna Pearl Maize Page. A strong proponent of the Method approach to acting, she was best known for her portrayal of tormented Tennessee Williams heroines. Most notable were the stage and film productions of *Summer and Smoke* and *Sweet Bird of Youth.*

Page's family moved to Chicago when she was five years old, and her first stage appearance, at age seventeen, was at the Englewood Methodist Church in *Excuse My Dust.* After graduation from Englewood High School, she studied at the Goodman Theater School from 1942 to 1945 and then spent the next five years in Midwest summer stock theater. In 1950 she moved to New York City in search of an acting career.

Page worked many odd jobs, including hat-check girl, theater usher, sales clerk, lingerie model, and factory worker before landing a role in an off-Broadway production of Tennessee Williams's play *Summer and Smoke* in 1952. The rave reviews she received led to other acting roles and also to her first film, *Hondo,* opposite John Wayne in 1953. Her first Broadway role was in Vina Delmar's play *Mid-Summer* in 1953.

Blacklisted in Hollywood during the McCarthy era because she had studied under Uta Hagen, an actress and teacher with liberal beliefs, Page did not make another film until *Summer and Smoke* in 1961. In the interim she returned to New York where she had two stage triumphs, *The Immoralist* and *The Rainmaker.*

Page starred in many films, plays, and television productions for the next three decades and was nominated for eight Academy Awards. She finally won an Oscar for best actress in *The Trip to Bountiful* in 1987. Her other Academy Award nominations were for roles in *Summer and Smoke, Sweet Bird of Youth, Interiors, Hondo, You're a Big Boy Now, Pete and Tillie,* and *The Pope of Greenwich Village.* Other films included *Toys in the Attic, Happiest Millionaire, Monday's Child, The Beguiled, Day of the Locust, White Knights,* and *Whatever Happened to Aunt Alice?* Page won Emmys for her television roles in adaptations of Truman Capote's "Christmas Memory" and for "Thanksgiving Visitor." She performed in several Broadway plays, including *The Three Sis-*

ters, Strange Interlude, P.S. I Love You,* and *The Great Indoors.* She received a Tony nomination for *Agnes of God* and for the Broadway revival of *Blithe Spirit.*

Page was known as an "actor's actor" who projected a pained vulnerability in her performances. She will always be remembered for her masterful portrayal in *The Trip to Bountiful* of an elderly woman who desperately wants to visit her hometown one last time before she dies.

Page was married three times, including to Alexander Schneider, a violinist; and actor and director Rip Torn, with whom she had two sons and a daughter. She died in New York on June 13, 1987, of a heart attack.

ARTHUR F. MCCLURE AND VIVIAN RICHARDSON

Current Biography. New York: H. W. Wilson, 1953.
Kansas City Star, February 23, 1986.
New York Times, June 15, 1987.
Obituary. *Newsweek* (June 22, 1987).
Variety, June 17, 1987.

PAGE, INMAN EDWARD (1853–1935)

Inman Edward Page was born a slave in Warrenton, Virginia, on December 29, 1853, to Horace and Elizabeth Page. His father, a livery stable operator, was able to purchase freedom for himself and his family, and, in 1862, they moved to Washington, D.C., where Inman attended the private school of George F. T. Cook. Economic problems forced Inman to leave the school and seek employment to help his family. During this time, he attended a night school taught by George B. Vashon, and acquired an elementary knowledge of Latin. After the opening of Howard University, he resolved to enroll there. He sought employment as an ordinary laborer at fifteen cents per hour, grading the university's grounds. That enabled him to attend Howard University, and he later served as a clerk for Gen. O. O. Howard, the school's founder and the commissioner of the Freedmen's Bureau.

In the fall of 1873, Inman Page and George W. Milford became the first black students to enter Brown University in Providence, Rhode Island. Page faced a great deal of prejudice but reversed his lot by winning a prize in a school oratorical contest. He was unanimously picked for the signal honor of giving the oration at the graduation exercise of the senior class.

In the fall of 1877, with an A.B. degree in hand, Page began his duties at the Natchez Seminary in Natchez, Mississippi. After a successful school year, he returned to Providence, Rhode Island, to marry Zelia R. Ball, who had graduated in 1875 from Wilberforce University. Three children were born to this union: Zelia, Mary, and Inman E. Page Jr., who died at age seven.

Page went to Jefferson City, Missouri, in 1878 to teach at Lincoln Institute as professor of ethics and assistant principal. In 1880 officials put him in charge of the school and of the institute's high school; he was the first to use the title "president." Page served as president of Lincoln Institute for eighteen years. In 1880 Brown University awarded him a master of arts degree. Later, Wilberforce and Howard Universities awarded him honorary degrees of doctor of laws.

Upon assuming the presidency, Page began a campaign to build the public image of Lincoln Institute throughout the state. His efforts resulted in greatly increased enrollments and new support from the state legislature, and brought him statewide recognition.

Under Page Lincoln Institute continued to grow and develop. In 1887 college work was added to the curriculum, and in 1891 the school was designated as a land-grant institution. In that year the state also appropriated ten thousand dollars for an industrial arts building and an additional nine thousand dollars for tools, machinery, and apparatuses. In addition, the legislature provided one thousand dollars to build a residence for the president on the campus. In 1895 Memorial Hall, dedicated to the school's founders, was built with forty thousand dollars from the state.

In 1898 state political leaders forced Page out as president of Lincoln Institute. He then became the first head of the Colored Agricultural and Normal University at Langston, in Oklahoma Territory. He hoped to do for the new Langston University and the black citizens of Oklahoma what he had done for Lincoln Institute over the previous eighteen years. During his eighteen-year tenure at Langston, he was elected head of the Oklahoma Association of Negro Teachers. With the coming of statehood for Oklahoma, though, Page, a lifelong Republican, was forced out of the presidency because of partisan politics.

From 1916 to 1918 Page served as president of the Colored Baptist College of Macon, Missouri, which later became Western University and was moved to Kansas City, Missouri. Later, Page went to Nashville, Tennessee, where he served as president of a larger Baptist institution, Roger Williams University. However, his health failed, and he returned to Oklahoma City in 1920. From 1921 to 1922 Page was supervising principal of the city's black elementary school and principal of Douglass High School. In 1922 he was

recalled to Lincoln Institute, recently renamed Lincoln University of Missouri, but in August 1923, on leave from the Oklahoma City Schools, he tendered his resignation and resumed his duties at Douglass High School.

Page spent his remaining twelve years as an administrator in Oklahoma City's public schools. In June 1935 he retired and was given the title "principal emeritus." On December 21, 1935, he died at the age of eighty-one in the home of his daughter Zelia in Oklahoma City. He was buried on the campus of Langston University.

Four buildings in Oklahoma were named in Page's honor. On May 19, 1950, Lincoln University named its recently constructed library in memory of Inman E. Page, who had brought statewide recognition to the institution he had served so well.

ANTONIO F. HOLLAND

Breaux, Elwyn E., and Thelma D. Perry. "Inman E. Page, Outstanding Educator." *Negro History Bulletin* 32 (May 1969): 8–12.

Holland, Antonio F., Timothy R. Roberts, and Dennis White. *The Soldiers' Dream Continued: A Pictorial History of Lincoln University of Missouri.* Ed. Rosemary Hearn. Jefferson City, Mo.: Lincoln University, 1991.

Marshall, Albert P. *Soldiers' Dream: A Centennial History of Lincoln University.* Jefferson City, Mo.: Lincoln University, 1966.

Patterson, Zella J. Black. *Langston University: A History.* Norman: University of Oklahoma Press, 1979.

Savage, W. Sherman. *History of Lincoln University.* Jefferson City, Mo.: New Day Press, 1939.

Simmons, William J. *Men of Mark.* 1887. Reprint, New York: Arno Press, 1968.

PAIGE, SATCHEL (1906–1982)

"That skinny old Satchel Paige with those long arms is my idea of the pitcher with the greatest stuff I ever saw," remarked Hall of Fame pitcher **Dizzy Dean.** By his own count Paige won two thousand of the twenty-five hundred games he pitched for about 250 different teams. In a career that stretched from 1924 until 1967, he claimed three hundred shutouts and fifty-five no-hitters. His best strike-out record in a single game was twenty-two, a figure he reached several times, once in a game against Babe Ruth's All-Stars. His phenomenal speed, control, stamina, and showmanship made Satchel Paige a folk hero of baseball.

Leroy Robert Paige was born on July 7, 1906, in Mobile, Alabama, the son of John (a gardener) and Lula (a domestic worker) Paige. He earned his nickname at the age of seven while carrying passengers' suitcases, or satchels, at the train depot. He rigged up a pole and rope so that he could carry more bags at a time. His coworkers said he looked like a walking satchel tree, and Leroy became "Satchel."

When he was twelve, Paige was arrested for shoplifting and sent to the state Industrial School for Negro Children in Mount Meigs, Alabama. During his five years in reform school, he honed his pitching skills. In 1924 the tall, lanky right-hander joined the black semiprofessional Mobile Tigers. Paige played with several similar teams around Mobile until he received an offer in 1926 to play for the Chattanooga Black Lookouts of the Negro Southern League.

Because they were excluded from playing in the major leagues, blacks organized their own league structure in the 1920s. As the black population grew in urban areas and with the resulting prosperity of World War I, black teams and leagues experienced a new level of stability. The Negro National League and the Eastern Colored League formed the "majors." Leagues such as the Negro Southern League functioned as the minors, providing a training ground for new talent.

From Chattanooga, Paige began his nomadic practice of jumping to the larger paycheck. He played for the New Orleans Black Pelicans, the Baltimore Black Sox, the Birmingham Black Barons, and the Nashville Elite Giants. Finally he joined Gus Greenlee's Pittsburgh Crawfords in 1931, a team Paige called the best he ever saw, black or white. With the Crawfords, Paige's fame spread nationwide.

The financial instability of the Great Depression forced the leagues and many teams to disband. The teams that survived did so by barnstorming, crisscrossing the country to play wherever they could draw a crowd. Teams used novelties and gimmicks to lure paying fans: portable lighting systems, celebrities such as track stars Jesse Owens and Babe Didrickson, donkey ball, and clowning.

In this atmosphere Paige began to advertise himself as the "World's Greatest Pitcher—Guaranteed to Strike Out the First Nine Men!" He claimed a variety of unique pitches, including "bloopers, loopers and droopers . . . jump ball, bee ball, screw ball, woobly ball, whipsy-dipsy-do, a hurry-up ball, a nothin' ball and a bat dodger." By whatever name, Paige's mainstay was his fastball with pinpoint control. Opposing hitters said in dismay, "You can't hit what you can't see." Paige resurrected old tricks, such as calling in the outfielders and striking out the next batter. He also added his own crowd pleasers, such as never revealing his age and making grand entrances at stadiums. Newspapers were filled with stories about his buying sprees, flashy cars and women, and trips to exotic countries.

With his talent and reputation, Paige played by his own rules. Although signed with one team, he pitched for numerous others on a per-game basis. Having him pitch even a few innings was guaranteed to attract a large crowd, and owners borrowed him to help them make payroll. "Anytime a team got in trouble, it sent for Satchel to pitch," remembered a teammate. "So you're talking about your bread and butter when you talk about Satchel."

Paige pitched for the Crawfords through the 1934 season. In the fall of 1934 and in 1935 he pitched for an integrated semiprofessional club in Bismarck, North Dakota. He also anchored the pitching staff for a group of Negro League all-stars who barnstormed against Dizzy Dean's major league all-stars in the early 1930s.

Paige returned to the Crawfords in 1936, but the next summer he jumped to the Dominican Republic to pitch for dictator Rafael Trujillo's team. Hoping to enhance his political career by winning the Dominican pennant, Trujillo lured nine Crawfords south by offering salaries far in excess of what the Negro Leagues could pay. Returning to the States after winning the pennant, they barnstormed briefly as the Trujillo All-Stars.

Greenlee was furious with Paige for jumping his contract and sold him to the Newark Eagles. Paige refused to recognize the sale and went to Mexico in 1938. He pitched winter and summer, sometimes every day for a month, in the Mexican League. By the end of the summer his arm was so sore he could not raise it above his head. He had been pitching year-round since 1929 but instead blamed the spicy Mexican food for his "miseries."

J. L. Wilkinson, owner of the Kansas City Monarchs, realized that Paige could still draw a crowd. He signed him to a contract with the Monarchs' farm club and named it Satchel Paige's All-Stars. Paige coached the team and pitched an inning or two in games across the Midwest. Although told by several doctors that he would never pitch again, Paige did regain strength in his arm and was called up to the Monarchs' main team by 1941. He led them to a World Series victory in 1942, winning three of the four games against the Homestead Grays.

Paige pitched for the Monarchs and for independent clubs between 1939 and 1947. He also barnstormed against Bob Feller's major league all-stars after the regular season ended. It is estimated that he made as much as forty thousand dollars a year, three to four times more than any other player in black baseball.

As the most heralded pitcher in the country, Paige chipped away at the color barrier even before **Branch Rickey** signed Monarchs teammate Jackie Robinson to a contract with the Dodgers. Paige refused to play in any town where he could not get a meal or a room.

In 1948 Paige joined the major leagues and helped the Cleveland Indians win the American League pennant. With a six-and-one record, the forty-two-year-old Paige was selected rookie of the year. The Indians released him in 1949. He played two more years with the St. Louis Browns, beginning in 1951, and was selected for the American League All-Star team in 1952. After he was released, Paige barnstormed and played with Miami from 1956 to 1958 and Portland in 1961. He went to Hollywood to play a cavalry sergeant in the 1958 motion picture *The Wonderful Country*. He last pitched in the majors for the Kansas City Athletics in 1965. He closed his long pitching career barnstorming with the Indianapolis Clowns in 1967. He coached for the Atlanta Braves in 1968 in order to be eligible for his major league pension.

Throughout his career Paige charmed reporters with his wit and homespun philosophy. As the oldest player in the major leagues, he offered six maxims for a long life: (1) Avoid fried meats, which angry up the blood. (2) If your stomach disputes you, lie down and pacify it with cool thoughts. (3) Keep the juices flowing by jangling around gently as you move. (4) Go very light on the vices, such as carrying on in society. The social rumble ain't restful. (5) Avoid running at all times. (6) Don't look back. Something might be gaining on you.

For more than thirty years, Paige called Kansas City home, where he and wife, LaHoma, raised eight children. Paige served as deputy sheriff before an unsuccessful run for state legislature in 1968. Three days before his death the city honored him by dedicating the Satchel Paige Memorial Stadium. Paige died of a heart attack on June 8, 1982, and was buried in the Forest Hill Cemetery in Kansas City.

Paige was the first player from the Negro Leagues elected to the Baseball Hall of Fame, in 1971. The inscription on his plaque summed up his life: "His pitching was a legend among major league hitters."

JANET BRUCE CAMPBELL

Bruce, Janet. *The Kansas City Monarchs: Champions of Black Baseball.* Lawrence: University Press of Kansas, 1985.

Paige, Leroy. *Maybe I'll Pitch Forever.* Ed. David Lipman. Garden City, N.Y.: Doubleday, 1962.

———. *Pitchin' Man.* Ed. Hal Lebovitz. N.p., 1948.

Peterson, Robert. *Only the Ball Was White.* Englewood Cliffs, N.J.: Prentice Hall, 1970.

Rogosin, Donn. *Invisible Men: Life in Baseball's Negro Leagues.* New York: Atheneum, 1983.

PAPIN, GRACE (GRACE ASHLEY) (1889–1989)

Grace Ashley Papin, creator of the Grace Ashley "shirt-stud" dress, reached national prominence in the 1930s by designing a shirtwaist dress (and a blouse cut on the same lines) offered in many fabrics and with interchangeable jeweled studs. The dress was grounded in simplicity: it was altogether adaptable to the mood and occasion by changing its jeweled studs or accessories (low heels for golf, a smart hat for lunch, diamond clips for cocktails) and was promoted for its democratic style—"worn by the Sloans and the Vanderbilts, as well as the saleswoman behind the counter, the housewives around the bridge table." For her design, Ashley was touted as "a sort of Henry Ford of dressmaking, engaged in the mass production of one model."

Details about Ashley's early years are sketchy, but she was reportedly born in St. Louis to Frank and Bertha Romyne on February 17, 1889. In 1921 she married Mark Ingram Ashley, and she worked in the custom dressmaking business with her mother before setting off on her own following her divorce from Ashley. Even after her divorce and remarriage, she continued to use the name "Ashley" professionally.

The story of Ashley's entry into the business is recounted with slight variations in many newspaper and magazine articles. The popular legend has it that in 1934 she designed a blouse for a customer using jeweled studs as closures and on a whim showed it to a buyer at the Marshall Field department store in Chicago, who placed an order for several dozen. By 1937 she had established a large business, selling four thousand Grace Ashley blouses and dresses each week to carefully selected retail stores in cities throughout the country.

A shrewd businesswoman, Ashley built a prosperous business during the height of the depression and achieved unusual prominence in the male-dominated business world by designing, manufacturing, selling, and promoting her dresses. She frequently appeared in *Vogue* and *Harper's Bazaar* during the late 1930s and early 1940s as her own model. Her retail shop and showroom in St. Louis were outgrowths of her custom business, and for years she lived in a flat in the same building. In 1936 she opened a second location, in New York. She incorporated in 1946, and her business flourished for well over two decades.

Over the years Ashley received several recognitions, and in 1936 the Women's Advertising Club of St. Louis named her one of twelve outstanding women of achievement. Honored for her business acumen she won the advertising award "for designing and selling a style (the Shirt-Stud Frock) which has received national acclaim and already become a fashion classic." In 1942 the Group Action Council of Metropolitan St. Louis named Ashley as one of forty-eight women of achievement.

Ashley's success allowed her to maintain a lavish lifestyle. In 1937 she purchased Greystone, an English Victorian river estate overlooking the Illinois lowlands near Pevely, Missouri. On August 31, 1940, she married Harry E. Papin Jr., a descendant of a prominent St. Louis family.

Although Ashley changed details of the dress and blouse over the years and offered several variations of the shirtwaist style, her name became synonymous with the original shirt-stud dress. Others tried to emulate her success. Shortly after she trademarked the name "Grace Ashley" for use in clothing labels in 1937, she sued Gimbel Brothers department store in New York for trying to sell a cheaper blouse as an original "Grace Ashley." The New York Supreme Court found that Gimbel Brothers had infringed her trademark, and the case was settled for an undisclosed sum.

One of Ashley's great passions was the Campbell House Museum in St. Louis, the pre–Civil War home of fur trader **Robert Campbell.** In 1941 Ashley boosted the William Clark Society's campaign to preserve the mansion by purchasing the contents of the drawing room for the Campbell House Foundation. As the president of the foundation recalled in 1961, "it was [Ashley Papin's] timely offer, back in February 1941, that really gave the William Clark Society the needed courage to go ahead with the campaign." Ashley Papin continued her involvement with the foundation as vice president, president, and board member. In 1961 she was made an honorary member for life of the Campbell House Foundation.

Grace Ashley Papin died in St. Louis on August 20, 1989, at the age of ninety.

SHARON FIVEL

Ashley, Grace. Scrapbook. 1936–1947. Missouri Historical Society Archives, St. Louis.

Campbell House Scrapbook. Campbell House Museum Archives, St. Louis.

Letter. John Bryan to Grace Ashley Papin, August 29, 1961. Grace Ashley Scrapbook. Campbell House Museum Archives, St. Louis.

Shoemaker, Floyd Calvin. *Missouri and Missourians: Land of Contrasts and People of Achievements.* Vol. 5. Chicago: Lewis Publishing, 1943.

Supreme Court of the State of New York, County of New York. "Grace Ashley against Gimbel Bros., Inc." Index no. 29011, 1937–1938.

PARK, GEORGE S. (1811–1890)

George S. Park, a businessman, newspaper editor, educator, and college founder, was born near Grafton, Vermont, on October 28, 1811, the son of a farmer. In 1825 he moved to Ohio where he taught school for a year. In 1828 he traveled to Illinois and bought land in Putnam County. He also taught school in Sangamon County, Illinois.

Early in 1832 Park entered Illinois College at Jacksonville, Illinois, but poor health forced him to drop out of school in his junior year. In 1834 he moved to Callaway County, Missouri, where he again taught school. In the fall of 1835 he went to Texas, which was then seeking independence from Mexico. He enlisted in the army on December 9, 1835, and served under Col. James Fannin. Early the following year, when Fannin's troops were besieged at the Goliad, Park was allegedly one of three survivors of the massacre. After escaping he continued to serve in the Texas army and was honorably discharged on December 9, 1836. He returned to Jackson County, Missouri, where for a time he taught school.

Park next undertook endeavors that were to mark him as a frontier entrepreneur, leader, and educator. Following the settlement of the Platte Purchase, which opened land to white settlements in northwest Missouri, Park made a claim in what is now Platte County. He purchased a steamboat landing site from David and Stephen English. In 1839 he built a home on the river bluffs and began to plat the town that was to bear his name. He filed a plat for the town of Parkville in 1844, and worked steadily at acquiring land and encouraging settlement, local business, and riverboat trade.

Park maintained a lifelong interest in religion and education. His religious interest first manifested itself in 1845 when he helped organize the Parkville Presbyterian Church. In 1847 he married Eliza Ann Vore of Clear Creek, Illinois. From this union three children were born, none of whom lived beyond childhood. Eliza Park died in 1854 and was buried in the Old Parkville Cemetery.

Park established a business district in Parkville and built a stone hotel next to the river to encourage business. In 1853 he started a newspaper known as the *Industrial Luminary.* In the bitter debates over slavery in Kansas and the resulting tension between Kansas and Missouri, Park took a position that Kansas should be allowed to decide its own affairs without interference from Missourians. His antislavery views incurred the enmity of Platte County's proslavery proponents. On April 14, 1855, they raided his newspaper office, threw his printing press into the Missouri River, and warned him to leave Missouri and not to return. Subsequently, local supporters rallied to Park's defense, and he continued to be prominent locally and to maintain a residence in Parkville.

Park had been in Manhattan, Kansas, when the raid on the *Industrial Luminary* occurred. He had acquired a land claim there with a group of New Englanders interested in starting an institution of higher education. In 1858 he contributed five hundred dollars for the school, and for the next five years he promoted the establishment and operation of Bluemont College, the antecedent of Kansas State University.

During this time Park was involved in a variety of enterprises. In 1855, following the destruction of his press, he returned to Illinois where he invested in real estate and acquired substantial landholdings. On July 12, 1855, he married Marie Louis Holmes in Magnolia, Illinois. From this union a daughter, Ella Park, was born and grew to adulthood.

Returning to Parkville in the fall of 1855 Park continued to be involved in his business interests and church affairs. In 1859 he promoted plans for a railroad between Parkville and Cameron, Missouri, to be called the Parkville and Grand River Railroad. The Civil War halted this project, and eventually the railroads crossed the Missouri River at Kansas City, which built the Hannibal Bridge. His railroad plans were eventually enfolded in the Chicago, Burlington, and Quincy Railroad line that passed through Parkville.

Park divided his time intermittently between his landholdings in Illinois and Platte County, Missouri, for the rest of his life. Following the Civil War he ran for the Missouri legislature. In November 1866, in a contested election against Daniel Burns, Park was declared the winner of a seat in the state senate. As a member of the Senate he introduced a bill to found a state industrial university, but the proposed legislation failed. After the war Park was founder and first president of the Missouri Horticultural Society, which he headed for many years.

In 1874 Park moved his family to the Park homestead near Magnolia, Illinois, where he spent much of the remainder of his life. Nevertheless, he remained interested in establishing a religious college on his extensive Parkville landholdings, and he continued to be active in church affairs. On March 29, 1875, Elisha Sherwood, a clergyman friend, introduced Park to John A. McAfee, then president of Highland College in Highland, Kansas. As a result of their discussion, McAfee and sixteen students and faculty members migrated in April to Parkville and established Park College in Park's hotel, which he donated to the enterprise. Park College, which proved to be George Shepherd Park's principal legacy, opened its doors to students in May 1875.

In succeeding years Park left the operation of the college to McAfee, but he took a firm hand in shaping the institution's educational thrust through his stipulations for grants of buildings, money, and land. He desired for the new institution to emphasize Christian training for missionary service. Student work programs and self-help were to become hallmarks of the college. New buildings were constructed largely with student labor, and agricultural and maintenance work were essential to the institution's survival. When the college began to thrive, a board of trustees was appointed in 1879. During the last decade of his life, Park shaped and supported the college with donations of money and land for specific programs.

Park lived his last years on the family farm in Illinois, where he died on June 6, 1890. He and his wife, who survived him, are buried in the Park College plot of the Walnut Grove Cemetery in Parkville, Missouri.

HAROLD F. SMITH

Park, S. George. General Files. Park College Archives, Parkville, Mo.

Paxton, W. M. *Annals of Platte County, Missouri.* Kansas City, Mo.: Hudson-Kimberly Publishing, 1897.

Sanders, Walter F. *A History of Park College, 1875–1945.* Parkville, Mo., n.d.

PARK, GUY BRASFIELD (1872–1946)

Elected thirty-eighth governor of Missouri in 1932, Guy Brasfield Park took office at a time of economic crisis and social unrest in the state and the nation. During his four-year term he strongly supported Franklin D. Roosevelt's New Deal and pressed for full state compliance with the president's programs for dealing with the Great Depression.

Park's father, Thomas Woodson, came to Missouri from Kentucky in 1857 and served under Gen. Sterling Price during the Civil War. In 1866 the elder Park married Margaret E. Baxter, a music teacher at Gaylord Institute, an academy for young ladies in Platte City, Missouri. They had six children, but only two reached adulthood. The younger of their surviving sons, Guy B. Park, was born in Platte City on June 10, 1872.

Guy Park received most of his education at Gaylord Institute and often said he was the only male ever to graduate from a female institution. He also attended the University of Missouri and received an LL.B. degree from the law department in 1896. The same year he was admitted to the Missouri bar. After spending two years in Denver, Colorado, he returned to his hometown and opened a law office. Shortly thereafter he entered politics and was elected city attorney. He later served two terms as county prosecuting attorney, and in 1922 he was elected circuit court judge of the Fifth Judicial District, which included the counties of Platte, Clinton, DeKalb, Andrew, and Holt. His reputation as a capable judge and a loyal Democrat led to his reelection in 1928.

Park married Eleanora A. Gabbert of Weston, Missouri, on November 16, 1909. In 1933 their only child, Henrietta Park Krause, became the first governor's daughter to be married in the Governor's Mansion. While serving as first lady, Eleanora Park collaborated with Kate S. Morrow in writing *Women of the Mansion, Missouri, 1821–1936,* a compilation of biographical sketches of women who had acted as hostesses at the mansion.

Park's ascendancy to the governor's office came as a surprise. In the 1932 general election, Park's longtime friend and political ally Francis Murray Wilson was the Democratic gubernatorial candidate. Wilson became ill during the campaign and died three weeks before election day. Encouraged by a warm endorsement from Wilson's family and the backing of Kansas City's powerful Pendergast machine, the Democratic Party's central committee nominated Park to replace Wilson on the ticket. Park defeated his Republican opponent, Edward H. Winter, by 338,123 votes, at that time the largest plurality ever received by a Missouri gubernatorial candidate. In the Democratic landslide in Missouri, presidential candidate Franklin Roosevelt doubled his vote in the state over the Republican incumbent, Herbert Hoover. The decisive Democratic victory ended twelve years of Republican control of the governor's office and mandated that the governor-elect and the General Assembly cooperate fully with Roosevelt and the New Deal.

In his inaugural address on January 9, 1933, Park pledged to relieve the distressed conditions of the people of Missouri. Following Roosevelt's inauguration in March, Park and the General Assembly moved to bring Missouri in line with the federal programs and agencies created to overcome the depression. The state amended old laws and enacted new ones to prepare the way for aid to farmers, public works programs, banking reforms, and direct emergency aid to the poor. Park rehabilitated the state penal and eleemosynary institutions, consolidated state boards and bureaus to reduce costs and streamline operations, and inaugurated a general sales tax to raise revenue. The Park administration increased funds for public education and enacted a state social security law and an old-age pension law. By the close of his term, the federal Works Progress Administration, the Rural Resettlement Administration, the Civilian Conservation Corps, and the National Youth Administration were all operating in Missouri.

After leaving office Park returned to Platte City and resumed his law practice. In 1943–1944 he served as a member of the Missouri State Constitutional Convention. Park died in Jefferson City of a heart attack on October 1, 1946. He was buried in the family plot in the Marshall section of the Platte City Cemeteries.

CHARLES T. JONES JR.

Clark, Albert M. "Guy Brasfield Park." In *The Messages and Proclamations of the Governors of the State of Missouri,* ed. Dorothy Penn and Floyd C. Shoemaker, vol. 18. Columbia: State Historical Society of Missouri, 1947.

Park, Eleanora G., and Kate S. Morrow. *Women of the Mansion, Missouri, 1821–1936.* Jefferson City, Mo.: Midland Press, 1936.

Park, Guy Brasfield. Papers. 1932–1937. Western Historical Manuscripts Collection, Columbia.

Schnell, J. Christopher, Richard J. Collings, and David W. Dillard. "The Political Impact of the Depression on Missouri, 1929–1940." *Missouri Historical Review* 85 (January 1991): 131–57.

PARKER, CHARLES CHRISTOPHER, JR., "BIRD" (1920–1955)

Charlie Parker died in New York City on March 12, 1955, at the age of thirty-four. His death ended a meteoric career that changed the course of American jazz music, bringing it to levels of artistry rarely seen before or since. In the process jazz became recognized as one of America's most significant contributions to world culture.

Parker was born in Kansas City, Kansas, on August 29, 1920, during a pivotal era in the city's history. The passage of Prohibition had occurred one year earlier. By Parker's tenth birthday the country was "dry" and mired in the Great Depression. However, Kansas City, Missouri, was in full vigor. Booze, gambling, and prostitution were freely available under the rule of political boss **Tom Pendergast.** This wide-open atmosphere helped give rise to a thriving nightclub scene where scores of jazz musicians played the night away. This unique time and place proved fertile ground for young Charlie Parker.

In early childhood Parker showed little interest in music. When he was about eight his family moved from Kansas City, Kansas, to Kansas City, Missouri—just a few blocks from the jazz clubs. His mother wanted her son to be a doctor. However, by the age of thirteen Parker had become a saxophone player and joined a high school dance band. From this point he gave up all thoughts of becoming a high school graduate, much less a doctor.

By all accounts Parker became obsessed with the saxophone and jazz. He spent as much time as he could at the clubs listening and learning. By 1935 he was "a high school dropout, professional musician, dabbler in drugs," married, and, as his wife soon told him, "the father of a child-to-be."

Parker was only an average musician until 1937. The turning point came one spring night that year as he tried to play in a club jam session with several seasoned jazz musicians. When his playing failed to measure up, they kicked him offstage. He left the club, vowing to return.

Parker spent the summer playing with a resort dance band in Taney County, Missouri. He performed with the band in the evening, and during the day he studied harmony with the band's pianist. In the fall

Parker returned to the scene of his earlier humiliation in Kansas City, where he now gained acceptance by some of the town's established performers.

During the next eight years Parker helped reinvent jazz. Bored with the musical style known as "swing," he began experimenting. With the help of several key musicians, including Dizzy Gillespie and Thelonious Monk, he developed the style known as "bebop." Bebop revolted against the congruent, flowing phrases of swing, instead using unusual harmonies and complex rhythms. It featured long improvised solos that sometimes lasted ten minutes. In this new style Parker was the undisputed king.

Bebop brought Parker world fame and became an anthem for the beat generation. However, his intense lifestyle, marked by drug, sex, and alcohol abuse, brought him nothing but trouble. The last ten years of his life were miserable. His indulgences made him unreliable and volatile. He was in and out of psychiatric wards, and battled peptic ulcers brought on by alcohol abuse.

Parker died in a friend's apartment while watching the *Tommy Dorsey* show on television. The attending doctor noted the cause of death as pneumonia, cirrhosis of the liver, ulcers, and a possible heart attack; he estimated Parker's age, based on his condition and appearance, at between fifty and sixty—he was only thirty-four.

Parker's life quickly became part of beat-generation folklore. For the beatniks his life and death symbolized their indifference and contempt for post–World War II society, but today he is best remembered as one of the most influential musicians of the twentieth century.

KENT C. BOYD

Albertson, Chris. *Charlie Parker: The Verve Years, 1950–1951.* Verve VE-2–2512, liner notes from the recording.

Berendt, Joachim E. *The Story of Jazz.* Englewood Cliffs, N.J.: Prentice Hall, 1978.

Blumenthal, Bob. *Charlie Parker: The Verve Years, 1952–1954.* Verve VE-2–2523, liner notes from the recording.

Charlie Parker in Sweden, 1950. Alamac QSR 2431, liner notes from the recording.

Reisner, Robert George. *The Jazz Titans.* Garden City, N.Y.: Doubleday, 1960.

Russell, Ross. *Bird Lives!* New York: Charterhouse, 1973.

PATTEN, NATHANIEL, JR.
(1793–1837)

Nathaniel Patten Jr. could be characterized as Missouri's quintessential pioneer country editor. As proprietor of the first newspaper published west of St. Louis and north of the Missouri River, he has taken his place as the father of journalism for a vast portion of the trans-Mississippi West. His stubborn, uncompromising tenacity in establishing the press in the wilderness, against strong obstacles, allowed his newspapers to reflect the independent Missouri spirit.

Born in Massachusetts on September 9, 1793, Patten apprenticed in the printing trades in Boston while still in his teens. Patten moved to Kentucky, where in 1814 he established his first independent newspaper, the *Winchester Advertiser.* He used this paper as a training ground to learn the business of editing and printing a small newspaper with a tiny circulation for a rural audience. This short-lived venture was only minimally successful, and in 1819 Patten moved to Franklin in the Missouri Territory. In that settlement more than one hundred miles west of St. Louis, Patten launched the *Missouri Intelligencer and Boon's Lick Advertiser.*

Prior to printing the prospectus for the new journal, Patten apparently formed a sketchy partnership with Benjamin Holliday. Their names appear in the earliest numbers of the *Intelligencer* as co-owners, but the weight of evidence supports Patten's claim as the newspaper's founder. For the next decade and a half, Patten was the guiding light of the tabloid-size *Missouri Intelligencer,* which became one of the most respected papers in early Missouri.

While adhering to the traditional journalistic principles of truthful and fair reporting intended to enlighten and entertain all readers, Pattern also supported a policy offering his subscribers opposing viewpoints on national and local political issues. He used his own progressive attitudes and Whiggish persuasion to make endorsements rather than to attack the political opposition. He faithfully filled his columns with news of interest to mid-Missouri settlers.

The exigencies of managing a newspaper on the frontier may have dictated this cautious stance. Never in good health, Patten's frail constitution required him to conserve his energy. The uncertainties of supply sources for ink, paper, and equipment to keep his old ramage press in working order, and the unreliability of the mails that brought news from the East, occupied many of his waking hours. Subscribers often paid him in goods and services, and to augment his meager income he assumed the added burden of serving as the local postmaster. Patten, who insisted on staying at the editorial helm with the help of a few well-trained assistants, ran a stable operation.

Patten published the *Intelligencer* in Franklin for seven years, but dwindling subscriptions and decline in the town's fortunes led him to move the paper to Fayette, the seat of Howard County. He prospered in Fayette despite the competition from a rural Jacksonian publication, the *Western Monitor,* edited by **James H. Birch.**

When the prospect of dramatically increased subscriptions prompted Patten to move his paper to the growing community of Columbia in 1830, the *Missouri Intelligencer* enjoyed a reputation as a solid journal that offered extensive news coverage in each issue. Patten ranked first among his editorial peers, and his paper was recognized throughout the state for its good management, its typographical appearance and readability, and its editorial and literary style. In Columbia the *Intelligencer* served as a resource not only for news but also for commentary on a wide array of cultural and educational topics, including literature and the arts.

Ill health caused Patten to enter semiretirement by 1835. After selling his interests in the *Missouri Intelligencer* to a group of citizens in Columbia, where it continued to appear under various names until the 1930s, Patten established the *St. Charles Clarion and Missouri Commercial and Agricultural Register* in 1836, his final journalistic effort. His death on November 24, 1837, cut short another highly promising venture, but Nathaniel Patten left a remarkable journalistic legacy in early Missouri as an editorial exemplar who set a high standard for subsequent newspaper publishers.

JOHN NEAL HOOVER

Brownlee, W. E. "The Literary Editing of Nathaniel Patten Jr., from 1822–1835 in the *Missouri Intelligencer.*" Master's thesis, University of Missouri, 1953.

Lyon, William H. *The Pioneer Editor in Missouri, 1808–1860.* Columbia: University of Missouri Press, 1965.

Scroggins, Albert T., Jr. "Nathaniel Patten Jr. and the *Missouri Intelligencer and Boon's Lick Advertiser.*" Ph.D. diss., University of Missouri, 1961.

Shoemaker, Floyd Calvin. *Missouri and Missourians: Land of Contrasts and People of Achievements.* Chicago: Lewis Publishing, 1943.

Taft, William H. *Missouri Newspapers, When and Where, 1808–1963.* Columbia: State Historical Society of Missouri, 1964.

PATTERSON, ROSCOE CONKLING (1876–1954)

Born in Springfield, Missouri, on September 15, 1876, Roscoe Conkling Patterson attended private and public schools as well as Drury College and the University of Missouri before receiving his law degree from Washington University in 1897. He simultaneously launched careers in law and politics in Springfield at the age of twenty-one.

Following in the footsteps of his rock-ribbed conservative Republican father, John A. Patterson, and his grandfather Joseph A. Patterson, who served as prominent lawyers, judges, and political leaders in Greene County, Missouri, Roscoe Patterson won election as the local prosecuting attorney, holding office from 1903 to 1907. In 1912 he began his political ascension when southwestern Missouri Republicans selected him as their representative to the state committee. He held that position until 1920, when he won election to the United States House of Representatives as Missouri's Seventh District congressman.

After failing to win reelection in 1922, Patterson returned to his Springfield law practice until 1925 when President Calvin Coolidge appointed him U.S. attorney for the Western District of Missouri. He served in that position until he defeated Charles M. Hay in the 1928 campaign for the United States Senate. The senatorial campaign focused on Prohibition. Since both Patterson and Hay assumed steadfast "dry" positions, the 1928 Republican landslide that swept Herbert Hoover, the entire state ticket, and ten of sixteen congressional candidates also carried Patterson to the Senate.

Once in the United States Senate, Patterson exhibited an extremely conservative posture and defended President Herbert Hoover's philosophy of rugged individualism and laissez-faire economics. He served on the commerce, military affairs, mines and mining, and pension committees during his relatively undistinguished freshman term from 1929 to 1935. His most notable achievement occurred when he sponsored the Lindbergh Law, stemming from the kidnapping of the son of the famed aviator **Charles A. Lindbergh.**

As the depression deepened, Patterson's rigid opposition to public-works projects and other liberal proposals made him "fair game" for ambitious Democrats who aspired to his seat. In 1934 he faced his greatest challenge when **Thomas J. Pendergast,** the Kansas City political boss, nominated **Harry S. Truman** (then one of the machine's Jackson County commissioners) in the Democratic senatorial primary. When Truman won the primary, he challenged Patterson in the general election.

Patterson made several serious mistakes in defending his Senate seat against Truman. Probably his chief miscue was his steadfast rejection of the New Deal's relief measures. When Patterson accused Roosevelt of dictatorial actions against business, Truman and Pendergast noted that large corporations supported agencies such as the National Recovery Administration. Another crucial error occurred when Patterson supported segregationist southern Republicans, a position that cost him badly needed black votes. Furthermore, many farmers (left out of the 1920s prosperity) and organized labor also supported

Truman. In brief, the New Deal coalition defeated Patterson's effort at reelection.

Swept aside in the New Deal landslide, Senator Patterson returned to Springfield in 1935 where he resumed his law practice. Proud of his legal ability, he once said that out of forty men he prosecuted for murder, juries convicted "nearly all," while "not one" among another forty he defended against the same charge received more than a light sentence.

Following a stroke in July 1954 Patterson's health rapidly deteriorated. He died on October 22, 1954.

J. CHRISTOPHER SCHNELL

New York Times, October 23, 1954.

Patterson, Roscoe C. Papers. Western Historical Manuscripts Collection, Columbia.

Schmidtlein, Gene. "Truman's First Senatorial Election." *Missouri Historical Review* 57 (January 1963): 128–55.

Shoemaker, Floyd C., ed. *Missouri, Day by Day.* Vol. 2. Columbia: State Historical Society of Missouri, 1943.

St. Louis Post-Dispatch, October 23, 1954.

PECK, JAMES HAWKINS (1785?–1836)

James Hawkins Peck was the first federal judge in Missouri. Born in rural Jefferson County, Tennessee, sometime between 1785 and 1790, he was one of twelve children of Revolutionary War veteran Adam Peck and his wife, Elizabeth. James, a strapping six-footer, after serving in the army in the War of 1812 and probably practicing law in Tennessee, moved to Missouri in 1817. He soon embarked on a public career as U.S. attorney of the Missouri Territory. Although he never married, he had at least one close woman companion and fought in the streets over another. He gained a reputation as a "polished gentleman" in frontier St. Louis.

Through political connections, especially those of his friend Sen. **David Barton** of Missouri, Peck in 1822 received an appointment as the U.S. district judge of the District of Missouri, the primary federal judiciary office in the state. (No circuit justice was assigned to Missouri until 1837.) Consequently, Judge Peck had greater authority than most other federal trial judges, especially in major criminal cases.

Peck experienced serious problems over complex Spanish land-grant litigation. Legal questions abounded over the validity of grants given by Spanish colonial officials. After the American occupation, acts of Congress and various legal procedures failed to resolve matters. In 1824 Congress allowed Peck's court extraordinary powers over certain Spanish land cases, with direct appeal possible to the Supreme Court. While there were many cases, a single one,

Soulard v. United States, epitomized the great economic and political implications of the cases in Missouri. It was, in a sense, a battle between "new rising economic interests" and the "old colonial establishment." In 1826 Peck ruled against Soulard, holding that no Spanish law or usage governed "incomplete" concessions made prior to the cession of Louisiana to the United States. In the aftermath Peck cited Soulard's lead counsel, **Luke Lawless,** for contempt for writing a letter published by a newspaper attacking the legal and factual basis of the decision.

Lawless responded by sending a petition to Congress claiming Peck had exceeded his authority. After much delay, the House of Representatives voted 129 to 49 on April 21, 1830, to impeach Peck. By then the Jacksonians were firmly in control, and it suited their purposes to challenge judicial authority. A six-week impeachment trial, only the fourth in the nation's history, consumed the greater part of the 1830–1831 second session of the Twenty-first Congress. Sensational evidence arose related to Peck's perceived eye troubles. Prosecution witnesses claimed he sometimes held court with a white handkerchief bound around his eyes, but they failed to relate the practice to his judicial performance. Peck's lawyer, former U.S. attorney general William Wirt, built his case on the proposition that English and American precedents supported the authority of a judge to punish contentious behavior by contempt. On January 31, 1831, twenty-two senators voted Peck not guilty and twenty-one guilty, far short of the two-thirds majority required to convict. In general, northeastern senators voted to acquit and southern ones to convict. Afterward, James Buchanan pushed through Congress a bill developed as a guideline for the federal courts to forbid all constructive contempts.

Judge Peck's postimpeachment experience was mixed. Friends considered him the near victim of a political removal by Jacksonians. Enemies viewed him as an abuser of judicial power and of individual liberty. The realities of a Jacksonian ascendancy in Missouri dashed any hopes that Peck might have entertained of further advancement or a restored reputation. In January 1836, after deferring the question for years, the Supreme Court reversed Peck in *Soulard* on the grounds he should have admitted certain oral evidence. Peck, who had come to believe that the Soulard and many other claims were fraudulent, severely criticized the Supreme Court in a rambling statement that seemed to mirror a deteriorating physical condition. The judge, isolated from the main currents of Missouri political life, lived alone in modest quarters in St. Louis, surrounded by few material possessions.

On April 29, 1836, after an illness of seven weeks, Peck died of what physicians diagnosed as "common pneumonia." In *Soulard* he had challenged the claims of powerful old colonial interests, which was not enough to leave him with a reputation as a towering figure in early Missouri history or as an able interpreter of federal law.

LAWRENCE H. LARSEN

Bay, W. V. N. *Reminiscences of the Bench and Bar of Missouri.* St. Louis: F. H. Thomas, 1878.

Bushnell, Eleanore. "The Impeachment and Trial of James H. Peck." *Missouri Historical Review* 74 (January 1980): 137–67.

Davis, Charles B. "Judge James Hawkins Peck." *Missouri Historical Review* 27 (October 1932): 3–20.

"James Hawkins Peck, Missouri's First Federal Judge, 1788–1836." *Missouri Bar Journal* 3 (June 1932): 92–93.

PECK, JOHN MASON (1787–1858)

John Mason Peck, a pioneer, Baptist missionary, noted preacher, author, and journalist on the early Missouri and Illinois frontiers, produced important writings that promoted settlement and settled institutions in the Mississippi Valley. As one of the first American historians to write about the region, he offered a pioneering sociological analysis of its prospects for growth and progress. Peck's emigrant guides and his *Gazetteer of Illinois* form a cornerstone of the primary printed literature of the midwestern region where he labored for forty years; his many travels from hamlet to hamlet in Missouri and the Old Northwest familiarized him with frontier life and the pioneer history of these areas.

Born in Litchfield, Connecticut, on October 31, 1787, Peck was the son of Asa and Hannah Farnum Peck, a farming family with deep New England roots. His growing conviction as a young man that Baptist missionary work was his true calling led to Peck's ordination as a preacher in New York in 1813. By 1817, after further study and preparation, he and James Welsh established the Western Baptist Mission, one of the first Protestant churches in St. Louis.

Peck, who maintained constant communication with religious, educational, and benevolent societies in New England, New York, and Philadelphia, became convinced early in his career that schooling was woefully inadequate in the rapidly developing territories of the trans-Appalachians. Traveling, preaching, and writing "indefatigably," Peck founded Rock Spring Seminary some eighteen miles from St. Louis in St. Clair County, Illinois. After moving to Upper Alton, Illinois, the school, one of the first colleges in the state, eventually grew to become Shurtleff College thanks to bequests Peck solicited personally from Benjamin Shurtleff of Boston.

Peck encouraged the gathering of primary accounts and descriptive materials that he knew would be lost otherwise. Students of history in his own time and later appreciated his gifted understanding of the past and his historical analysis. Jared Sparks, the early biographer of prominent figures in the new American Republic and, later, president of Harvard College, published Peck's important biography *Daniel Boone* (1847), an account of the famed frontiersman's life based on interviews that Peck conducted at Boone's home on the Missouri frontier. Peck was concerned with the pioneering spirit exemplified by **Daniel Boone** and was one of the first serious writers to recognize that he was a powerful symbol for the unimpeded growth of America.

In 1852 Harvard bestowed upon Peck an honorary doctorate (in systematic theology), at the same time it conferred an honorary doctorate of law on Alexis de Tocqueville. This was no mere coincidence. Peck's admirers had in fact likened him to de Tocqueville. As the quintessential pioneer intellectual, he was a keen student and observer of the western lands as a laboratory for civilization's eventual triumph.

Peck ceaselessly promoted frontier settlement. He routinely made journeys on horseback through Missouri and the Ohio Valley shoring up fragile missions, schools, and charitable societies he had helped establish. His books encouraged internal improvements of all kinds in the West to promote settlement. He studied prospects for missions among Native Americans, and he collected anything he could about the Indian tribes. By inclination he was a political moderate, an abolitionist worried about the effects of nonviolent dissent in slaveholding areas. However, Peck's vocal antislavery views were important rallying cries in keeping Illinois united as a free state during the dangerous political controversies of the early 1820s.

When Peck came to St. Louis, he immediately began to preach to slaves. He had, in fact, ordained **John Berry Meachum,** a former slave, and he regularly preached to Meachum's African American congregations.

Peck was a friend of numerous influential figures, including Illinois governors Edward Coles, John Reynolds, and Ninian Edwards; religious leaders Peter Cartwright and **Elijah P. Lovejoy;** and politicians **Thomas Hart Benton** and Abraham Lincoln. Peck marshaled them into service in promoting the western states and territories.

As a journalist Peck edited several periodicals, including the *Western Watchman* in the late 1840s. His writings included *Guide for Emigrants* (1831) and *The Travelers' Directory for Illinois* (1840). He edited James Perkins's *Annals of the West* (1850), a work that was as close as Peck came to completing his own proposed magnum opus, "The Moral Progress of the Great Central Valley of the Western World," for which he had gathered notes and sketches for many years. Peck also wrote *The Principles and Tendencies of Democracy* (1839), a bibliographical work; *The Death of Eminent Men a National Calamity* (1834); "Historical References for the Valley of the Mississippi" in *The American Pioneer* (1843); and sketches on western cities for Charles A. Dana's *The United States Illustrated in Views of City and Country* (1853).

Peck optimistically believed that continued emigration and settlement would ensure the growth of civilized institutions and society in the western territories. To this end he spoke out constantly for the establishment of schools and churches to receive the new settlers. He clearly expected churches to be leaders in promoting western settlement.

Peck's influence was gradually recognized, and he was honored as one of the first men of letters in the Mississippi Valley. He worked to unite isolated communities and families on the frontier into a large, productive commonwealth. His eloquence and zealous belief in social progress helped create a sense of pride and destiny in the areas he served. Peck is representative of those individuals of genius in the early West who helped ensure its rapid rise to prominence in national affairs. He died on March 14, 1858.

JOHN NEAL HOOVER

Babcock, Rufus, ed. *The Memoirs of John Mason Peck.* 1864. Reprint, Carbondale: Southern Illinois University Press, 1965.

Bartee, Wayne. "John Mason Peck: A Pioneer in Advancing the Gospel." Liberty: Missouri Baptist Historical Commission, n.d.

Harrison, Paul M. "John Mason Peck: American Baptist de Tocqueville." *American Baptist Quarterly* 3 (September 1984): 215–24.

Hoover, John Neal. "A Man of Letters on the Frontier and His Library." In *A Guide to the John Mason Peck Collection in the St. Louis Mercantile Library.* St. Louis: St. Louis Mercantile Library Association, 1989.

Jennings, Helen L. *John Mason Peck and the Impact of New England on the Old Northwest.* Ann Arbor, Mich.: University Microfilms, 1961.

PENDERGAST, JAMES FRANCIS (1856–1911)

The second of nine children, James Pendergast was born in the little town of Gallipolis, Ohio, on January 27, 1856. Soon after his birth, however, the Pendergast family moved to St. Joseph, Missouri. After attending public schools there, Jim, propelled by the ambition that would later fuel his rise to power, moved to Kansas City in 1876.

Pendergast settled in the West Bottoms, an industrial center known for its preponderance of railroad yards, packing houses, and shanties, as well as houses that maintained and propagated the underground and red-light activities of the region. The adjacent North End offered a similar cultural climate. Ethnically and racially diverse, this area represented a motley collection of people thrust together by common occupation and low social standing.

Although Pendergast worked as a manual laborer for a time, his unquenchable ambition pushed him to seek greater things, and when a horse named Climax won big for him at the track, he purchased a joint hotel and saloon in the heart of the West Bottoms. A popular spot from the start, the saloon became a universal gathering place where Pendergast made contacts and formed friendships with the diverse population of the region.

Pendergast rose from virtual obscurity to the heights of local political power because of his ability to form political ties with leaders of all factions. He was also able to win the support of many residents of the West Bottoms and the North End. In 1892 this large support block paid off as he easily won the nomination for alderman and then crushed his Republican opponent by a five-to-one majority in the ensuing election.

Although Pendergast soon became a prominent political figure, he never forgot the loyalty of his working-class friends. He continually fought for legislation that would benefit the working citizens of Kansas City in general. He opposed salary cuts for already underpaid firemen, and he put up bond for several African Americans living in his territory, an act that immediately won him the favor of that sector of the community and solidified his dominance in the First Ward. This kind of political kinsmanship earned Pendergast the trust and respect of the many citizens of this region—citizens who would, in turn, come out in large numbers on election day to show their support.

As alderman, Pendergast demonstrated the backing he possessed when, in 1894, he and only one other Democrat won election as Republicans swept in a landslide victory. After another smashing victory in 1896, "Big Jim," as he was now called, began to explore means of expanding his political domination beyond the First Ward. Making the most of a second saloon purchase in the North End, Pendergast began to surround himself with the powerful men involved in liquor and gambling interests. Ironically, opposition to these very interests by the newly elected prosecuting attorney Frank Lowe propelled the alderman's rise as a political force. By attacking the gambling interests, the reform-minded Lowe threatened the very core of business in the North End. Thus, when Pendergast decided to confront the reformer and organized opposition to Lowe's reelection, he found himself in command of a powerful and aroused constituency.

With this backing, "Big Jim" easily elected his own man, **James A. Reed,** as prosecuting attorney in the following election. By forming alliances with two powerful industrial leaders in the next election, Pendergast engineered Reed's nomination for mayor of Kansas City. In order to defeat a Republican ticket that had marched uncontested to six straight mayoral victories, the alderman organized a large-scale Democratic campaign that appealed to each interest group individually. He held citywide rallies and provided free lunches for voters. The outcasts of society, those the Republicans had dismissed as riffraff, turned out in large numbers to support the man who listened to their stories and assisted them with their needs. When officials tallied the votes, Reed held a narrow margin of victory. The results showed that the deciding votes had been cast, not surprisingly, in the lower-income areas of the West Bottoms and the North End.

Failing health began to curtail further opportunities for Pendergast's advancement. Although he again ran for office and won reelection, his weakened condition forced him to begin delegating responsibilities to the heir apparent to the Pendergast throne, his younger brother Tom.

In 1910 Pendergast retired officially from the city council and from all political responsibility. Soon after, on November 10, 1911, he died from kidney failure at the age of fifty-five. In his will he left his family about one hundred thousand dollars, but he bequeathed to Kansas City a much greater legacy. He took a chaotic and ineffective Democratic Party and transformed it into a well-oiled machine. He bettered the lives of many lower-class workingmen who had previously failed to receive even the smallest consideration of those in the higher offices. Probably the most important contribution, however, was the personal grooming of the younger **Thomas J. Pendergast** to run the machine that he had so ably constructed. This tutelage would mold the shape of Kansas City and Missouri politics for many years to come.

LYLE W. DORSETT AND DAVID P. SETRAN

Dorsett, Lyle W. "Alderman Jim Pendergast." *Bulletin of the Missouri Historical Society* 21 (October 1964): 3–16.

———. *The Pendergast Machine.* New York: Oxford University Press, 1968.

Larsen, Lawrence H., and Nancy J. Hulston. *Pendergast!* Columbia: University of Missouri Press, 1997.

Reddig, William M. *Tom's Town: Kansas City and the Pendergast Legend.* 1947. Reprint, Columbia: University of Missouri Press, 1986.

PENDERGAST, THOMAS J. (1872–1945)

Sixteen years younger than his politically oriented brother James, Thomas J. Pendergast was born in St. Joseph, Missouri, on July 22, 1872. Following in "Big Jim's" footsteps, Tom, together with two of his brothers, made his way to Kansas City in 1890. With a stocky frame and a massive mustache, Tom did not immediately earn the respect of those who so admired his brother. Starting as a bookkeeper in one of Jim's saloons, however, he learned about politics under the direct supervision and watchful eye of his older brother.

Pendergast's advancement into politics was rapid. He received an appointment as deputy county marshal for Jackson County in 1896. Four years later Mayor **James A. Reed** appointed him superintendent of streets, a job rich in political value because of the heavy patronage involved. Pendergast became even more enmeshed in Kansas City politics when he won election as county marshal in 1902, supported heavily by both the Pendergast "Goats" and the "Rabbits" under the control of **Joseph B. Shannon.** Although he lost the position in 1904 and failed at election again in 1906, Pendergast remained politically active, assuming many of the aldermanic responsibilities of his ailing brother Jim. By the time Jim died in 1911, Tom had acquired a thorough knowledge of the colorful world of Kansas City politics.

Although many assumed that **Jim Pendergast**'s death would end his faction's influence and result in the rise to power of the Shannon faction, nothing could have been further from the truth. Tom immediately won the aldermanic post his brother had held since 1892. Republican majorities throughout the city, however, made Democratic expansion nearly impossible. The two politicians, Pendergast and Shannon, pooled their resources and, with the help of newly formed Democratic clubs, defeated the Republicans soundly in the ensuing election.

Pendergast expressed displeasure at "dividing the spoils" with Shannon, and with victory in hand sought to wield power on his own terms. His party won elections during the teens, but in 1920 Republicans swept the state and county races. To counter this development, in 1922 Pendergast made one of the best tactical moves of his illustrious political career. To gain influence in Jackson County, he stood behind **Harry S. Truman** in his bid for the county judgeship. Once elected Truman refused to take part in the graft of the Pendergast machine and offered no preferential treatment to friends of the machine who had previously received important favors. Truman made an exceedingly popular judge and an expert administrator. Thus, he bolstered the machine's reputation at a crucial time, increasing needed patronage in rural Jackson County. Through his alliance with the upright Truman, Boss Tom secured dominance in the region.

Although Pendergast achieved his goal of becoming the undisputed leader of the Kansas City Democratic Party, opposition remained strong. In 1924 reformers initiated a movement to establish a nonpartisan council-run government in Kansas City. Supporters offered a vision of deliverance for Kansas City politics from graft and corruption. So many citizens accepted this view that the plan seemed certain of victory. Pendergast, never one to admit defeat, cleverly decided to support the nonpartisan plan. When the new charter passed, it soon became clear what the nature of this "nonpartisan" government would be. Officials soon lined up against each other along party lines. Although the Republicans took the mayorship, the Democratic "Goats" took the majority of the council seats.

This was the beginning of a new phase of political involvement for Boss Tom. During the reign of Big Jim and in the early years of Tom's political power, Pendergast influence found its locus in the lower-income industrial neighborhoods of the city. Pendergast provided turkey dinners for more than twenty-five hundred needy people every Christmas in these impoverished areas. He assisted the citizens of "Little Italy" by giving them government jobs. He even provided opportunities for African Americans in the community, once throwing his support behind one of them in a confrontation with a white Democrat. These activities and handouts ensured him the support of the low-income community. However, by the 1920s Kansas City demographics had changed dramatically, with a new majority of native-born, middle-class constituents.

Pendergast adapted to these new circumstances. He revealed a tremendous "sixth sense" regarding the needs, desires, and trends of the community. The "ward healer" of the West Bottoms and North End now discovered a new image to promote his increased expansion: middle-class respectability. The *Missouri Democrat,* a machine newspaper, ran pictures of Pendergast "the family man" and "world traveler." Rather than providing middle-class residential citizens with the necessities of life, which they did not need, he addressed their social needs. Lieutenants organized political clubs that sponsored dinners, dances, and parties for men and women. Pendergast sponsored baseball and bowling leagues to suit the interests of the younger, more active members. He also provided benefits to local businesses and community groups. Some received preferential treatment in hiring procedures, while others, like the Kansas City Power and Light Company, gained large tax abatements. Predictably, Pendergast's favors resulted in business support for his organization, which also controlled the police department. Kansas City during these years looked increasingly like "Tom's town."

Pendergast achieved statewide power when his handpicked associate **Guy Brasfield Park** won the governor's race in 1932. The Park administration offered Pendergast the opportunity to extend his influence statewide and provide countless favors for individuals of all interest groups. When Franklin Roosevelt and his New Deal policies came to power in the White House, Pendergast was able to capitalize on the opportunity. Although apparently backing James Reed, an old Pendergast associate and a challenger to Roosevelt for the 1932 presidential nomination, Tom actually favored Roosevelt from the start. The Roosevelt administration knew this and thus rewarded him with their favors. He often approached James Farley, the chairman of the Democratic state committee of New York and later postmaster general, with requests for favors that were quickly granted. More important, the Roosevelt administration gave Pendergast needed patronage and control of federal relief in Missouri.

When Pendergast secured for his man Truman the nomination for senator, things were looking good for the boss. He tightly controlled Kansas City and Jackson County, as well as the state capitol and the federal relief program. From this pinnacle of power, however, Pendergast soon tumbled. **Lloyd Stark,** running for Missouri governor in 1936, sought and received Pendergast's endorsement for nomination. After winning the election Stark aided prosecutors in bringing election-fraud charges against the boss, and the case dragged through the courts for two years, leaching power from the machine.

To strengthen himself politically, in 1938 Stark decided to oppose the boss at the polls. When Stark's man won election to the state supreme court over Pendergast's in 1938, the erosion of the boss's political power was evident to all. President Roosevelt, well aware of the important political ramifications of the events taking place in Missouri, chose political expediency over loyalty and began backing Stark. Concurrently, district attorney **Maurice M. Milligan,** an anti-Pendergast Democrat, charged the boss with income tax evasion in 1939. Pendergast had apparently received undeclared earnings in an insurance scandal and had also failed to declare more than $1 million of his income.

Boss Tom lost his case in federal court and received a sentence of fifteen months in federal prison and a fine of ten thousand dollars on the first count. The judge gave Pendergast five years' probation on the second. As it turned out, Pendergast died on January 26, 1945, before he had finished the probationary period and seemingly just before he would have received a presidential pardon from Truman.

Pendergast created a machine in Kansas City the likes of which has not been equaled in that area. Soon after his demise, the Democratic Party began to falter. Attempts to revitalize the sputtering machine failed. The factionalism of the pre-Pendergast era returned and has remained dominant ever since. Boss Tom, the big Irishman from St. Joseph, lived and died by the power politics for which he was famous. He constructed a potent political machine that extended his influence throughout Missouri, and, indeed, throughout the nation.

LYLE W. DORSETT AND DAVID P. SETRAN

Dorsett, Lyle W. *Franklin D. Roosevelt and the City Bosses.* Port Washington, N.Y.: Kennikat Press, 1977.

———. *The Pendergast Machine.* New York: Oxford University Press, 1968.

Ferrell, Robert H. *Truman and Pendergast.* Columbia: University of Missouri Press, 1999.

———, ed. *The Kansas City Investigation: Pendergast's Downfall, 1938–1939.* Columbia: University of Missouri Press, 1999.

Larsen, Lawrence H., and Nancy J. Hulston. *Pendergast!* Columbia: University of Missouri Press, 1997.

Reddig, William M. *Tom's Town: Kansas City and the Pendergast Legend.* 1947. Reprint, Columbia: University of Missouri Press, 1986.

PENNEY, JAMES CASH (1875–1971)

One of the more remarkable American success stories began on a farm in Caldwell County, Missouri, on September 16, 1875, when James Cash "J. C." Penney was born, the seventh of twelve children of James Cash and Fannie Pazton Penney. The elder Penney, whose family was from Kentucky, continued a family tradition and became a Primitive Baptist preacher. The elder Penney also operated a farm near Hamilton, Missouri.

Raised on a formula of Christian love and hard work, J. C. Penney wanted to be a lawyer, but after graduating from Hamilton High School, he worked on the family farm for two years. After his father died, Penney became a clerk at the J. M. Hale and Brother store in Hamilton in 1895 in order to contribute more directly to the family's income.

In 1897 Penney's doctor advised him to move to the West in order to improve his health. He found a job in Denver, Colorado, but soon took his three hundred dollars of accumulated savings and purchased a butcher shop in Longmont, Colorado. When that business failed, he began clerking at T. M. Callahan's dry goods store.

In 1899 Callahan sent Penney to Evanston, Wyoming, to operate a second store. That same year Penney married Berta A. Hess of Salt Lake City, a young woman he had met in Longmont. By 1902 Penney had so impressed his employer Callahan that he sent him to open a store at another mining center, Kemmerer, Wyoming. Callahan also sold Penney a one-third interest in that store. Reflecting his own religious values, Penney named it the Golden Rule Store. Gross sales amounted to nineteen thousand dollars the first year.

In 1903 Penney, Callahan, and another investor established a second store. Profits from their joint ventures allowed Penney to open his first wholly owned store in 1904. He soon had another second store at Cumberland, Wyoming. In 1907 he bought out his partners for thirty thousand dollars. At the same time he acquired a new partner, Earl Corder Sams of Simpson, Kansas, who had started with Penney as a clerk in the Kemmerer store.

Penney followed Callahan's practice: store managers could become part owners of subsequent stores if they provided one-third of the money needed to start the new store. Manager-owners then created additional stores by giving their valuable employees the same opportunity. In that way Penney's Golden Rule Stores became a budding chain utilizing central auditing and buying. Penney moved company headquarters from Kemmerer to Salt Lake City. By 1911 the chain included twenty-two Golden Rule Stores, and sales topped $1 million. Penney had not invented the American chain store, but Penney's became one of the more successful chains in the early years of the twentieth century.

Family tragedy muted Penney's economic success. In 1910 Berta Penney contracted pneumonia and died, leaving two children, Roswell Kemper Penney and James Cash Penney Jr. Later, in 1919, Penney married Mary Hortense Kimball, a native of Salt Lake City. They had one child, Kimball Penney. Mary Penney died in 1923.

In 1912 the Golden Rule Stores became the J. C. Penney Stores, and the next year the business became a full corporation, J. C. Penney Company. Penney moved corporate headquarters to New York City, the nation's dry goods center.

Through Penney's leadership, and that of Earl Corder Sams, the company grew rapidly. By 1916 the company had 127 stores, all located in smaller towns and cities. Twenty-two of those stores had annual gross sales of at least $1 million. In 1917 Penney became chairman of the board, and Sams became the company's president.

Ever the moralizer, Penney began to express the principles upon which he was building his empire. Claiming that success was a matter of the spirit, he offered six axioms: preparation, hard work, honesty, having confidence in people, appealing to the human spirit, and applying the Golden Rule, which he said constituted "a law of love."

In the 1920s the J. C. Penney Company grew to more than one thousand stores, and Penney became a multimillionaire. He used some of his wealth to memorialize what he considered valuable parts of his early life. His childhood spent on a Missouri farm stimulated him to establish Emmadine Farm at Hopewell, New York. The farm specialized in pure-bred Guernsey cattle, and Penney became a leader in the American Guernsey Cattle Club and the New York State Guernsey Breeders Association. He also began purchasing farmland in Caldwell, Daviess, Grundy, and Livingston Counties in north Missouri, including the farm that had once belonged to his family. He established six agricultural and livestock model farms there for the purpose of demonstrating advanced scientific farming and breeding. At his horse farm he made a conscious effort to revitalize Missouri's declining horse and mule industry by concentrating on the development of thoroughbred workhorses and jacks.

Significantly, in 1923 Penney established the five hundredth store in his chain at Hamilton, Missouri, where he had started clerking twenty-eight years before. However, he waited until his first employer, J. M. Hale, had retired and closed his own store.

Penney flourished in the late 1920s, both professionally and personally. In 1926 he married Caroline B. Authenrieth of Phoenix, Arizona. They had two children, Mary Frances and Caroline Marie. He received honorary degrees from Kansas Wesleyan University, Boston University, and Rollins College. He honored his parents by constructing a residential community at Penney Farms, near Jacksonville, Florida; he called it Memorial Home Community. The complex provided housing for retired ministers and their spouses, and in 1946 Penney gave it to the *Christian Herald* along with an endowment.

The 1929 stock market crash and subsequent depression greatly diminished Penney's fortune. He had invested too heavily in Florida real estate. When land values collapsed, much of his $40 million fortune disappeared. A nervous and physical wreck, he entered a sanitarium in 1931. He recovered his health, and at the age of fifty-six he started to rebuild. His company survived the depression. Having reduced the prices of its merchandise in order to increase volume, the chain actually grew.

In 1946 Penney became the company's honorary chairman; he resigned from that position in 1958. In 1948 he wrote the autobiographical *Main Street Merchant.* That was followed by *Fifty Years with the Golden Rule* in 1950 and *View from the Ninth Decade* in 1960. In an address given at Stephens College in Columbia, Missouri, in 1949, he expressed his philosophy when he said, "the secret of business success is that there are no secrets." He said that all one needed was "knowledge of your fellow human beings," "creative insight," and "the ability to sacrifice a temporary advantage for the sake of a permanent one."

At the age of ninety-five, Penney died on February 12, 1971, in New York City. At that moment the J. C. Penney Company was the second-largest nonfood retailer in the United States.

DONALD B. OSTER

Beasley, Norman. *Main Street Merchant: The Story of the J. C. Penney Company.* New York: Whittlesey House, 1948.

Lebhar, Godfrey M. *Chain Stores in America, 1859–1962.* New York: Chain Store Publishing, 1963.

Penney, James Cash. "A Guide to Youth." *Missouri News Magazine* (October 1956): 10–11.

———. "Of Thoroughbreds." *Missouri Magazine* (April 1938): 9–10.

Segar, Eva. "Missouri's 'Good' Penney." *Missouri Life Magazine* (March–April 1976): 31–37.

PÉREZ, MANUEL (1735–1819)

Manuel Pérez, Spanish lieutenant governor in St. Louis from 1787 to 1792, was born in Zomora, Spain, in 1735. He joined the Spanish army at the age of eighteen and saw service in Spain and Portugal before coming to New Orleans with Lt. Gen. Alejandro O'Reilly in 1769. He married Jeanne Catherine Dubois in New Orleans in 1776, and the couple had five children. After Spain entered the American Revolutionary War in 1779, Pérez participated in campaigns against the British at Mobile and Pensacola that earned him a promotion to the rank of captain in 1780.

Following his arrival in St. Louis in November 1787 to take up his duties as lieutenant governor, Pérez reported that the city's fortifications were in a dilapidated state. He had the north bastion rebuilt with stone but lacked sufficient funds to do anything more. In his new post Pérez faced the daunting challenges of improving Upper Louisiana's defenses and fending off a growing number of British and American incursions into Spanish territory.

Pérez had to devote much of his time to matters involving the Osage Indians. Recurring Osage depredations produced demands for action against the powerful tribe, but Pérez favored a cautious course as he struggled to balance the conflicting demands of

Indians, traders, settlers, and his Spanish superiors. The chronic fear of Osage attacks prompted Spanish authorities to encourage emigrant Indian tribes from east of the Mississippi to move to Upper Louisiana so they could act as a buffer between the hostile Osages and the region's exposed settlements. Pérez became an ardent proponent of Indian colonization. He fully supported trader **Louis Lorimier**'s efforts to persuade members of the Shawnee and Delaware tribes to join him at a settlement south of Ste. Genevieve.

Pérez sought other ways to diminish the Osage threat. As an alternative to suspending trade with them, he suggested the construction of a fort near the principal Osage villages on the Osage River, no doubt with encouragement from St. Louis's principal merchant **Auguste Chouteau.** Spanish officials in New Orleans ignored his proposal, but during the administration of his successor **Zenon Trudeau** they belatedly heeded Pérez's advice and Chouteau's lobbying and contracted with the Chouteau family to build and maintain an installation at a location somewhere in present-day Vernon County, Missouri, known as Fort Carondelet.

To counter the growing British influence among Indian tribes west of the Mississippi, Pérez also recommended the construction of forts at the mouths of the Des Moines and the St. Peters Rivers, but in this instance the governor-general in New Orleans declined on the grounds that the proposed installations would be too remote and isolated to be effective.

As the Spaniards searched for ways to strengthen their hold on the sparsely populated province, they invited Americans to settle in Upper Louisiana and become Spanish subjects. With the encouragement of the Spanish minister to the United States, Col. **George Morgan** developed an elaborate plan for a large American settlement on the west bank of the Mississippi. When Morgan and members of his advance party arrived in St. Louis in 1789, Pérez cordially welcomed them with offers of horses, guides, and provisions. The American promoter soon lost interest in the ambitious venture and returned to the United States, but the settlement known as New Madrid remained.

Pérez labored diligently to administer the remote frontier province with the limited resources at his disposal. The task took its toll on the veteran soldier who asked to be relieved of his duties in St. Louis on account of advanced age and poor health. Trudeau replaced him as lieutenant governor in 1792, and the following year Pérez officially retired after thirty-nine years in Spanish service. He resided in New Orleans where he held minor civil offices until his death there in November 1819.

WILLIAM E. FOLEY

Foley, William E. *The Genesis of Missouri: From Wilderness Outpost to Statehood.* Columbia: University of Missouri Press, 1989.

Houck, Louis, ed. *The Spanish Regime in Missouri: A Collection of Papers and Documents Relating to Upper Louisiana.* 2 vols. Chicago: R. R. Donnelley and Sons, 1909.

Nasatir, Abraham P. *Borderland in Retreat.* Albuquerque: University of New Mexico Press, 1976.

PERKINS, RICHARD MARLIN (1905–1986)

Marlin Perkins served as director at three zoos during his career: the Zoological Gardens in Buffalo, New York; the Lincoln Park Zoo in Chicago; and the St. Louis Zoo. During his tenure in Chicago he first appeared on WBKB, an experimental television station broadcasting to three hundred receivers in the Chicago area and then on network television. For twenty-three years Perkins hosted *Mutual of Omaha's Wild Kingdom,* an Emmy-award-winning television program reaching 35 million people in forty countries. Through this program he "became one of the nation's best known zoologists."

Richard Marlin Perkins was born in Carthage, Missouri, on March 28, 1905, the third son of Joseph Dudley and Mynta Mae Miller Perkins. After "trying railroading, farming, and carpentry," Joseph Perkins decided to become a layer and eventually was "elected judge of the circuit court, division 1, of Jasper County," a position he held for twenty years. Mynta Perkins died of pneumonia when Marlin was nearly seven years old, and he was sent to Pittsburg, Kansas, to live with his mother's sister and her husband. Perkins enrolled in the third grade of the Pittsburg Normal School, and it was there he became interested in snakes when a professor of the zoology department brought one to class. Soon "snake catching became a favorite occupation."

In 1919 Perkins entered Wentworth Military Academy in Lexington, Missouri. Two years later his father married Laura Gashweiler, a widow, and Marlin returned to Carthage. After he completed high school in 1923 he took a year off to visit his brothers in California. The next fall he entered the University of Missouri in the College of Agriculture, taking courses in zoology and animal husbandry. For the annual agricultural fair Perkins wrote a pamphlet and arranged an "educational exhibit to show farmers the value of snakes." As a result of a zoology class, he became interested in wild animals and transferred to the College of Arts and Sciences. He decided he needed to be sure that he wanted to work with wild animals before he continued his education, and after his sophomore year took his first job with the St. Louis Zoo in 1926.

The zoo hired him as a laborer sweeping sidewalks, trimming hedges, and mowing grass for $3.75 per day. Two weeks later he was made a relief animal keeper, which took him all over the zoo raking animal yards, scrubbing walls, and cleaning cages. After two months he was placed in charge of the reptiles, all six of them, which were housed in a basement and not on display.

George Vierheller, the zoo's director, authorized a temporary exhibit in an effort to demonstrate to the governing board public interest in a reptile house. After two weeks lines on Sundays were a block long waiting to see the exhibit. The board soon sanctioned the design and construction of a reptile house. In the spring of 1927 while the reptile house was under construction, Perkins spent six weeks studying under Raymond L. Ditmars, curator of reptiles at the Bronx Zoo, who encouraged him to go on a snake-hunting expedition both to acquire snakes and to generate publicity.

In 1928 Perkins suffered a life-threatening bite from a forty-five-inch Gaboon viper. The snake bit him on his left index finger as he cleaned mites from its face. Perkins was rushed to a hospital, and since there was no Gaboon-viper antivenom available, he received North American antisnakebite serum, cobra antivenom, serum made from the venom of the fer-de-lance, as well as several blood transfusions. He remained in the hospital for three weeks, and it took him six months to recuperate. Ironically, the viper died the day Perkins left the hospital. Undeterred and following Ditmars's advice, during the latter part of 1929 Perkins made a trip to Panama, Guatemala, and Honduras where he collected snakes, crocodiles, iguanas, turtles, and an armadillo. During the next eleven years he built the zoo's collection to five hundred specimens.

In 1930 when Perkins was twenty-five years old and earning thirty-three hundred dollars per year, he married Elise More. Their daughter, Suzanne, was born in 1937, and the following year Perkins accepted the directorship of the zoo in Buffalo, New York. The Works Progress Administration was in the process of building a new zoo that was in various stages of construction when Perkins arrived. The only available space for his office was in an old, stinking building, so bad that Perkins threw up the first time he entered it. He spent little time in his office. The Buffalo Zoological Gardens was funded by the city government. It was regarded as a nonessential service, and as a result was always short of funds. Perkins therefore jumped at the chance to become director of the Lincoln Park Zoo in Chicago where he served from 1944 to 1962.

In an effort to educate visitors Perkins revised the identifying labels of the animals and provided a children's zoo and zoo nursery. In order to publicize the zoo he appeared on experimental television from 1945 to 1949 when twenty-eight NBC stations picked up the program and carried it as *Zoo Parade.* In a continuous effort to improve the program, in 1955 Perkins traveled to Africa to film on location. During the summer of 1957 he filmed the show along the Amazon River for two months and returned to learn that *Zoo Parade* had been canceled.

In 1953 Perkins and his wife divorced, and on August 13, 1960, he married Carol Morse Cotsworth who had three children. Two weeks after the wedding he left for Nepal with Edmund Hillary on an expedition to look for the Abominable Snowman. In 1962 Perkins began negotiations with Mutual of Omaha to develop *Wild Kingdom.* That summer he was offered the job of director of the St. Louis Zoo. To allow for Perkins's continued television work the *Wild Kingdom* production company worked out an agreement with the Zoological Board of Control to "pay the zoo $25,000 per year," and at the end of September Perkins moved to St. Louis.

Perkins increased the staff, built a large parking lot, fenced the zoo, constructed a miniature railroad and a central plaza, reconstructed the waterfowl ponds and the 1904 World's Fair birdcage, and developed an educational department. In 1970 he reached the mandatory retirement age of sixty-five and became director emeritus.

Perkins received an American Education Award in 1974 and was granted honorary doctoral degrees from the University of Missouri–Columbia; Northland College in Ashland, Wisconsin; Rockhurst College in Kansas City, Missouri; McMurray College in Jacksonville, Illinois; and the College of St. Mary in Omaha, Nebraska. He received the Criss Award for meritorious service and in 1978 was given a special award from the American Association of Zoological Parks and Aquariums when the board "created a Marlin Perkins Award, to be presented to a member of AAZPA who made a special, outstanding contribution to the zoo profession." Perkins authored four books, including an autobiography.

After retirement Perkins gave more time to *Wild Kingdom* and continued as host until, after twenty-three seasons, illness forced him to retire in 1985. He died of cancer at his home on June 14, 1986.

MAXINE J. CHRISTENSEN

Forsyth, Patricia. "That Awful Perkins Boy." *Missouri Life* 6 (October 1978): 23–27.
New York Times, June 15, 1986.
Perkins, Marlin. *My Wild Kingdom: An Autobiography.* New York: E. P. Dutton, 1982.
———. Papers. Western Historical Manuscripts Collection, St. Louis.
St. Louis Post-Dispatch, June 15, 1986.

PERRY, IVORY (1930–1989)

A community organizer, civil rights campaigner, housing specialist, and antipoverty activist, Ivory Perry spent many years channeling the needs and aspirations of the African American community in St. Louis into remedial and corrective action.

Born on May 5, 1930, to a sharecropping family in Desha County, Arkansas, Perry worked in the fields picking cotton as soon as he was old enough to walk. He dropped out of high school to help support his mother and sisters, and enlisted in the army in 1948 after his mother's death. Perry saw combat during the Korean War as a member of the Twenty-fourth Infantry Regiment of the Twenty-fifth Division, the last all-black unit in the U.S. military. Discrimination within the army overseas and incidents in which he was denied service at lunch counters while home on leave moved Perry toward an activist stance, and he joined civil rights protests shortly after leaving the military in 1954.

Perry became active in the St. Louis chapter of the Congress of Racial Equality in the early 1960s. He participated in many nonviolent direct-action protests in St. Louis, at the opening of the New York World's Fair in 1964, and in actions organized by the Civic and Voters League in Bogalusa, Louisiana. In 1965 the Human Development Corporation of the Office of Economic Opportunity hired Perry to work as an outreach worker specializing in housing as part of the federal government's War on Poverty. In that capacity he organized demonstrations calling for the enforcement of housing codes and the prosecution of slumlords. In the late 1960s he helped organize a rent strike in St. Louis public housing that kept rents affordable for tenants, and he helped establish local chapters of the National Tenants Organization and the National Welfare Rights Organization.

Perry's greatest triumph came in the 1970s when his ceaseless agitation made St. Louisans aware of a lead-poisoning epidemic that threatened the health of many children living in older buildings that had lead-based paint on the inside walls. Perry organized community residents, medical technicians, and physicians to set up lead-poisoning screening and treatment programs, and his activism proved decisive in persuading the city government to pass legislation banning the use of lead-based paints for building interiors and playground equipment.

Ivory Perry remained active during the 1970s and 1980s, organizing senior citizens and tenants against high utility rates and shutoffs of service for those unable to pay their bills. He fought to keep Homer G. Phillips Hospital open as a full-service health care center for the black community, and he helped workers at the Morgan Linen and Supply Company pressure their employer for better treatment.

When budget cuts eliminated his job with the Human Development Corporation, Perry secured low-level positions within the city government that enabled him to remain active in protests and demonstrations. He announced his first bid for elective office in 1989 when he offered himself as a candidate for a position on the St. Louis Board of Aldermen. However, on February 15, 1989, just a few weeks before the election, he came home from work to find one of his sons attempting to commit suicide with a kitchen knife. As he tried to wrestle the knife from his son's grasp he was stabbed in the chest and died. In 1990 the city of St. Louis named a neighborhood park in his honor.

GEORGE LIPSITZ

Cummings, Charles Kimball. "Rent Strike in St. Louis." Ph.D. diss., Washington University, 1975.
Lipsitz, George. *A Life in the Struggle: Ivory Perry and the Culture of Opposition.* Philadelphia: Temple University Press, 1988.
St. Louis American, February 23–March 1, 1989.
St. Louis Post-Dispatch, February 16, 1989.
St. Louis Sentinel, October 19, 1989.

PERRY, JOHN EDWARD (1870–1962)

John Edward Perry was born on April 2, 1870, at Clarksville, Texas, the son of former slaves Anderson and Louise White Perry. He attended local segregated schools in Clarksville before enrolling at Bishop College in Marshall, Texas. After completing his course of study, Perry returned to Clarksville where he taught school for one year. Subsequently, he enrolled at Meharry Medical College in Nashville, Tennessee, graduating with a degree in medicine in 1895.

Perry moved to Joplin, Missouri, shortly thereafter. He had intended to open up a medical practice, but found the black population of Joplin too small to sustain a physician. Subsequently, he traveled to central Missouri in the hope of establishing a practice. He settled for a time in Jefferson City and in Mexico, before finally moving to Columbia. His practice in Columbia allowed him to continue medical studies at the Chicago Post-Graduate Medical School for six months.

During the Spanish American War, Perry served as a physician with the Seventh U.S. Volunteer Infantry. After the war he returned to Columbia, where he remained until 1903.

Perry's experiences as a physician, combined with a growing awareness of the inability of African Americans to gain advanced medical training at facilities for whites, convinced him of the need for a black-owned and -operated hospital where African American men and women could be trained. He moved to Kansas City in 1903, committed to the goal of establishing such a facility. In November 1910 Perry began construction of the Perry Sanitarium, a fifteen-bed facility in Kansas City.

In 1916, having outgrown the facility, Perry spearheaded an effort to purchase a larger complex that he converted into a community hospital. This facility became known later as the Wheatley-Providence Hospital. Perry continued to practice medicine at this facility until February 1945. He also helped establish and practiced at a second Kansas City hospital for blacks known as City Hospital No. 2.

After his retirement Perry moved to Houston, Texas, to assist in the reorganization of that city's black hospital. While there he married Ora Brown Stokes, a national field secretary for the Women's Christian Temperance Union. Perry's first wife, Fredericka Douglass Sprague, who was the granddaughter of Frederick Douglass, had died in 1943. The first marriage produced one child, Eugene Boone Perry, who also became a physician.

Perry returned with his wife to Kansas City in 1947 where he continued to care for some of his former patients in his home. In March 1947 his memoir, *Forty Cords of Wood,* was published by Lincoln University, a school on whose governing body he served for twenty-five years. Perry also served for twenty-five years as a medical examiner for the Santa Fe Railroad, for the Yellow Cab Company, and for the Public Service Company. He was also president of the National Medical Association. He was active in civic affairs, including the building campaign for the Paseo YMCA, and he served for many years on the executive board of the Kansas City Urban League.

J. Edward Perry died in Houston on May 15, 1962. Funeral services were held at the Second Baptist Church, to which he had belonged for much of his life. Perry was buried in the Highland Cemetery.

GARY R. KREMER

Kansas City Call, May 25, 1962.

Perry, J. Edward. *Forty Cords of Wood.* Jefferson City, Mo.: Lincoln University, 1947.

Young, William H., and Nathan B. Young Jr. *Your Kansas City and Mine.* Kansas City, Mo.: n.p., 1950.

PERSHING, JOHN J. (1860–1948)

John J. Pershing ranks as one of America's premier soldiers and one of Missouri's proudest contributions to the nation. Commander of the American Expeditionary Force (AEF) in World War I, Pershing personified Kipling's ideal of the individual who could keep his head when all around him were losing theirs. On the western frontier, in Cuba, in the Philippines, in Mexico, and especially in France in 1917–1918, Pershing's calm assurance in the midst of peril secured American victory.

Pershing was born in a Missouri braced for civil war. On September 13, 1860, Ann Thompson Pershing gave birth to her first child, John, in Linn County, near Laclede, Missouri. Eight more children followed in subsequent years. The father, John Fletcher Pershing, a settler of Alsatian descent, stood for the Union in a divided Missouri. It almost cost him his life because, when John was only three, **William Clarke Quantrill**'s raiders stormed Laclede and, had they found him, would have killed the elder Pershing.

The war began a harsh childhood for the boy. Three of Pershing's siblings died early, and his father lost his store and his land in the depression of 1873. When his father became a traveling salesman, young Pershing hired out on various farms. Hard work made him strong, while Methodism and adversity made him quiet, determined, and sober. Law appealed to him, but lacking funds he took work as a janitor and then as a teacher in the public schools; it was at this time that he discovered a natural ease with African Americans that contributed to his later nickname, "Black Jack."

By 1880 Pershing had saved enough money to attend Kirksville Normal School and earned his degree in elementary didactics in 1882. He then applied for a nomination to West Point, a school that had the advantage of offering a free education and an invaluable circle of friends and acquaintances. Resolute study and a brilliant examination paper brought him the nomination over eighteen competitors, and a memorable career was launched.

Ironically, Pershing did not intend to be a soldier. West Point would be but a step toward his chosen profession of law. However, at the academy his ability and maturity brought him the class presidency four years running, and he smoothly fit into the hard discipline and merciless hazing of the corps. Devoid of the flair of a MacArthur or a Lee, Pershing became captain of the corps through discipline and intelligence.

Still expecting limited service, Lieutenant Pershing accepted an assignment at Fort Bayard, New Mexico, in 1886. After tedious garrison duty and brief combat with the Apache, he participated in suppressing the Sioux on the northern Plains, and his "limited service" was settling in as a career. A break came when he was named commandant of the languishing military science program at the University of Nebraska in 1891. At Lincoln he reformed instructional policies and so inspired the cadets that an elite fraternity was created that would become the Pershing Rifles. The young officer also found time to fulfill a dream: he earned his law degree in 1893.

A significant assignment came to Pershing in 1895 when he took command of D Troop of the Tenth Cavalry, a unit of black "buffalo soldiers" in Montana. Fair play and discipline won their confidence, an achievement few white officers could match. Meanwhile, Pershing, more stoic than ever, honed his command skills and toughened his constitution for the hard campaigns of the future. He was evolving into "Black Jack."

It was fortunate that Pershing was prepared, for he soon found himself in the war with Spain in Cuba. The Spanish-American War of 1898 was not the army's finest hour, but Pershing's seasoned Tenth Cavalry performed well at San Juan Hill, winning him the Silver Star and a promotion to captain. The campaign also brought him important connections, including the friendship of Theodore Roosevelt. Roosevelt and others intervened at key points in Pershing's life; it is unlikely he would have encountered such momentous opportunities otherwise.

After Cuba Pershing was sent to the Philippines to help secure that new American possession. Many tribal and religious groups on the islands resisted America's new dominion as they had Spain's before, but Pershing did not doubt his country's mission. In a brilliant campaign around Lake Lanao, Pershing combined force and diplomacy to crush Moro resistance on Mindanao. Back in the States his fame won him promotion, and courtship won him the hand of Helen Francis Warren, twenty-one years his junior and the daughter of Sen. Francis E. Warren of Wyoming, the chair of the Military Affairs Committee.

Sent to Japan as a military observer in 1905, Pershing journeyed to Manchuria to witness action in the Russo-Japanese War, a preview of World War I. His informative reports impressed Theodore Roosevelt, and in 1906 the president raised Pershing to brigadier general, bypassing more than eight hundred officers. Ignoring the expected complaints, Roosevelt then sent his favorite general back to the Philippines. In the next few years the Pershing family expanded with the addition of Helen, Anne, and Warren. The general continued his successful pacification campaign in the Moro province and traveled in Asia and Europe. These were the happiest days of his life.

In 1914 Pershing received the prestigious command of the Presidio in San Francisco. However, the developing confrontation with revolutionary Mexico along the Rio Grande border led Pershing to El Paso. As he awaited events there, word arrived of the shocking death of his wife and two daughters in a domestic fire at the Presidio. Warren survived, but the blow wounded Pershing beyond help. Always the soldier, however, he accepted his most demanding assignment to date: to chase down the Mexican bandit-revolutionary Pancho Villa who had raided Columbus, New Mexico, and fled into the wilderness beyond the Rio Grande.

In the spring of 1916 Mexico was a volcano of revolutionary intrigue and violence. President Woodrow Wilson sought to walk a tightrope between neutrality in the Great War in Europe, raging since 1914, and upholding American prestige and interests in Mexico. Pershing, commanding a small punitive force in hostile territory, without a declaration of war, and with uncertain logistical and diplomatic support, pursued Villa with grim resolution, enduring with his men the trials of occasional combat and endless filth and discomfort. Diplomacy ended the campaign short of its goal, but Pershing could take pride in his conduct and in his promotion to major general.

In April 1917 the United States entered World War I against Germany and her allies. Wilson, who disliked the army's favorite general, Leonard Wood, selected Pershing to lead the AEF to France. Some were surprised; others were outraged. Nonetheless, Pershing began the daunting task of building an American army that could fight on equal terms with the huge European forces. With a draft law in place, the army grew rapidly, but in Europe Pershing struggled to prevent the piecemeal use of his troops as replacements in units of America's allies, Britain and France. Pershing doggedly trained his army, envisioning a force of 3 million men, and stood down the threats of Allied leaders impatient with his aims. Demanding a sector in the line for American units, he meant to take the offensive when they were ready. Backed by his government, General Pershing prevailed.

American troops did join Allied units to help stem the last great German offensives of the war in the spring of 1918. At Belleau Wood and Château-Thierry, the doughboys' gallant defense was decisive, and at Cantigny a small American offensive succeeded. Then, under a new unified Allied command, Pershing activated the First Army for the proposed Saint-Mihiel offensive in August. The French supreme commander, Foch, wanted to cancel the attack, but Pershing refused and won certain, if limited, success. With Germany weakened, the Allies prepared for a major war-winning offensive in September.

On September 25, 1918, the AEF began a vast assault along the Meuse River into the Argonne forest. It dwarfed any American military operation in history. Both the First and the Second Army, more than six hundred thousand men, smashed into German lines. Pershing's patience, determination, and planning paid off. Desperate, the heroic German defense could not stop the AEF. By November the Americans had ruptured the German supply lines. On November 11, 1918, the armistice ended the war, and Black Jack Pershing's AEF had contributed momentously to victory.

Pershing, raised to general of the armies in 1919, and burdened with decorations, won the Pulitzer Prize in 1931 for his book *My Experiences in the World War.* He also served as army chief of staff. He lived to see another American victory in Europe in 1945 and died in Washington on July 15, 1948. He was interred, a national hero, in Arlington National Cemetery. In a life spanning the Civil War to World War II, Pershing had done his duty, and much more.

C. DAVID RICE

Goldhurst, Richard. *Pipe Clay and Drill: John J. Pershing, the Classic American Soldier.* New York: Reader's Digest Press, 1977.

Pershing, John J. *My Experiences in the World War.* New York: Frederick A. Stokes, 1931.

Smythe, Donald. *Pershing: General of the Armies.* Bloomington: Indiana University Press, 1986.

Vandiver, Frank E. *Black Jack: The Life and Times of John J. Pershing.* College Station: Texas A&M University Press, 1977.

PETERS, NELLE E. (1884–1974)

The architect Nelle Elizabeth Nichols Peters worked in Kansas City, Missouri, from 1909 to 1967, at a time when few women were active in that profession. Her success as an architect came from her work as a designer of apartment buildings and hotels, particularly in the 1920s.

Born in South Dakota on December 11, 1884, Peters attended Buena Vista College at Storm Lake, Iowa, from approximately 1899 to 1903. Interested in both mathematics and art, she determined to become an architect, and gained employment in 1903 as a "draftslady" with an architectural firm in Sioux City, Iowa. In addition to her on-the-job training, she studied through correspondence courses.

In 1909 Peters's employer sent her to their Kansas City office, but she received less work than expected. Consequently, she decided in 1910 to set up an independent practice, which was easy to do in Missouri since the state did not impose any requirements on those wishing to be architects.

In 1911 Nelle Nichols married William H. Peters, a railroad architect. During the twelve years of their marriage she retained her independent practice, which consisted mostly of small apartment buildings. After becoming associated with the developer Charles E. Phillips in 1913, her career flourished. Phillips preferred to develop rows of similar houses, or, more important, apartment buildings on larger tracts of land. Why he chose Peters to be one of his principal designers is not known, but her proved competency as a designer of multiunit housing may have been a factor.

During World War I government restrictions on private construction hampered developers and architects, but by 1920 matters had improved considerably. Phillips became one of the city's most prolific developers, now emphasizing larger apartment buildings. Once again he employed Peters, and her practice flourished through 1927 when the residential market became quite saturated. By then she had established herself not only as a major architect in Kansas City but also as one with a national reputation for hotel and apartment-building work.

Peters proved particularly adept at fitting several apartment buildings onto a lot in a "court group," which enhanced their residential character, and she became noted for her design of large apartment buildings containing compact yet livable units, including the then-popular kitchenette type. One of the most important of her designs, Kansas City's Ambassador Hotel, designed in 1924, had eight stories plus a roof garden and contained 105 apartment units and 108 hotel rooms, along with retail shops.

Peters's architectural practice extended well beyond Kansas City, and she did commercial as well as residential work, but her close association with hotel and apartment design meant that once market forces reduced the demand for such work, her career began to decline. The onset of the Great Depression of the 1930s, followed by World War II, virtually ended her architectural practice during that period. Concurrently, she also suffered a serious illness and had to support herself in part through work as a seamstress.

With the return of a peacetime economy, and the renewal of privately funded construction, Peters could once again work as an architect, but she no longer received large-scale commissions. Her last major project was completed in 1959, an educational wing for a church in Butler, Missouri. In her final years of practice she worked out of her apartment, doing projects that required little or no direct supervision, such as remodeling. She retired in 1967, and her last years were spent in a nursing home, where she died on October 7, 1974. By then few people remembered her extraordinary achievements in the 1920s when she became a successful woman architect in a "man's profession."

Nelle Peters produced a large number of buildings, many of which still stand in Kansas City. For the most part they exhibit her tendency toward conservative style and ornament, with her innovative skills reserved for the physical arrangement of the buildings and the units they contained. That her reputation eroded so quickly is a fate shared by many other architects, despite the fact that they were instrumental in the shaping of their communities. In Nelle Peters's case, the tenacious efforts of architectural historian Sherry Piland succeeded in reassembling the facts of her career, enabling scholars to again recognize her pioneering achievement.

GEORGE EHRLICH

Ehrlich, George, and Sherry Piland. "The Architectural Career of Nelle Peters." *Missouri Historical Review* 83 (January 1989): 161–76.
Flynn, Jane Fifield. "Nelle Nichols Peters." In *Kansas City Women of Independent Minds*. Kansas City, Mo.: Fifield Publishing, 1992.

PETTIS, SPENCER DARWIN (1802–1831)

Spencer Darwin Pettis never saw his thirtieth birthday. Like **Joshua Barton, Charles Lucas,** and far too many other young Missourians of talent and ambition, his life was cut short in a duel.

Pettis, who was born in Culpepper County, Virginia, in 1802, came to believe the West held the key to fame and fortune, and he set his sights on the newly admitted state of Missouri. Sometime in 1821 he arrived in central Missouri's Boonslick region, a popular destination for new immigrants. He began to practice law in the frontier town of Fayette in Howard County. In 1824 the Boonslick voters elected Pettis to the Missouri General Assembly. His selection came in spite of his youth and the fact that he did not meet the minimum age of twenty-four years required by the 1820 constitution for membership in the lower house.

Pettis did not retain his legislative position for long. On July 22, 1826, Gov. **John Miller** appointed him as Missouri's fourth secretary of state. During this time he cultivated the friendship of Sen. **Thomas Hart Benton** and laid the political groundwork for his successful election in 1828 as Missouri's sole delegate in the United States House of Representatives. Benton also considered Pettis a leading candidate to replace Missouri's other U.S. senator, **David Barton.** Yet, politics, as Barton knew all too well, could be fraught with physical danger: he had recently lost his younger brother Joshua in an affair of honor.

Missouri's transition from politics based upon personal and factional loyalty to party identification was not smooth. As the second decade of statehood dawned, the air was charged with political violence. Western gentlemen had not yet learned how to resolve their differences without frequently resorting to force and intimidation.

As a loyal Bentonite and Jacksonian, Pettis staked out positions on banking, tariffs, land policy, and currency compatible with the view of leaders in the emerging state Democratic Party. During Pettis's bid for reelection in 1831, his rhetoric at times became both personal and polemical. Maj. **Thomas Biddle,** an army paymaster stationed at Jefferson Barracks and brother of Nicholas who was president of the Bank of the United States, took particular umbrage with Pettis's remarks. Opposition to the national bank was the hallmark of a good Jacksonian, and the issue was especially acute in St. Louis, the location of a branch of that bank. When Pettis's verbal assaults cast aspersions on the character of Nicholas Biddle, Thomas quickly came to the defense of his brother. He and Pettis waged a bitter and personal feud in the columns of the *St. Louis Times* and the *St. Louis Beacon.* Believing that he had to defend the honor of his family name, Biddle learned that Pettis, a bachelor, was ill and virtually incapacitated in his room at the City Hotel in St. Louis. He entered the ailing congressman's room, and repeatedly struck him with a rawhide whip.

Pettis did not hesitate to seek legal action against his assailant. On two occasions he had Biddle arrested, but still believed that the code of honor required him to issue a challenge to redress the physical humiliation he had suffered. However, acting on the advice of his mentor, Senator Benton, Pettis, who was seeking reelection to Congress, postponed taking that step until the election returns were in. Following his victory at the polls, Pettis sent his second, Capt. Martin Thomas, with the challenge and awaited the terms. The response astonished Pettis. Because of Biddle's nearsightedness, he called for pistols at five feet with both principals turning on the count of "one" and firing. The terms, tantamount to a suicide pact, were so outrageous and barbarous that Pettis could have refused to duel without any imputation of cowardice, but he felt duty bound to proceed.

On August 27, 1831, the principals, their seconds, and surgeons took their positions on an island sandbar in the Mississippi. As the moment of truth drew near, Pettis clung to a faint hope that he might be able to survive the ordeal. On the word he suddenly stooped, hoping to inflict a mortal wound in Biddle's abdomen while dodging his fire. The tactic failed. While Pettis's bullet found its mark and lodged in Biddle's stomach, his adversary's ball was also on target and passed entirely through the congressman's body. Both men had been mortally wounded. As they were carried from the field, each expressed remorse over the affair.

Back in St. Louis, as Pettis lay dying, he asked **James Hawkins Peck,** a federal judge, if he believed he had vindicated his honor. According to **John F. Darby,** a onetime mayor of St. Louis and a witness to the event, Peck told the expiring young congressman that he had fought bravely in defense of his honor. He then exhorted him to die, as he had fought, like a man. Senator Benton, Pettis's chief adviser in this affair, also paid his final respects. The following day, August 28, 1831, Spencer Pettis died. The funerals of both combatants were said to be among the largest in the city's history. Pettis was honored posthumously by having a county named in his honor.

More than any other duel, this one forever destined the island sandbar in the Mississippi to bear the epithet "Bloody Island." Although it was not Missouri's last such encounter, the Pettis-Biddle affair had a numbing effect on the code duello, by dispelling the aura of romance and chivalry surrounding it.

DICK STEWARD

Darby, John. *Personal Recollections of Many Prominent People Whom I Have Known, and of Events—Especially Those Relating to the History of St. Louis—during the First Half of the Present Century.* St. Louis: G. I. Jones, 1880.

Hyde, William, and Howard I. Conard, eds. *Encyclopedia of the History of St. Louis.* New York: Southern History, 1899.

Scharf, J. Thomas. *History of St. Louis City and County: From Earliest Periods to the Present Day.* Vol. 2. Philadelphia: Everts, 1883.

"Spencer Darwin Pettis, 1826–1828." Biography Series. Missouri State Archives, Jefferson City.

PEYROUX DE LA COUDRENIÈRE, HENRI (1743?–?)

Henri Peyroux de la Coudrenière was born in France around 1743, the son of Marguerite-Suzanne Peyroux; the identity of his father is unknown. Peyroux married a Portuguese woman née Rodriguez, but they apparently had no children.

Peyroux and his wife emigrated to Louisiana in 1783, where he at first occupied himself recruiting Acadians to settle in Louisiana. Although born a Frenchman, he, like many other cosmopolitan persons in colonial Louisiana, had no qualms about serving the Spanish Bourbon colonial regime. Peyroux also participated in Robert Cavelier de La Salle's prophetic vision that Louisiana possessed a boundless future, if only European colonizers would make the necessary commitment to recruiting settlers and developing the region.

In 1787 Gov-Gen. Esteban Miró appointed Peyroux to succeed Antonio de Oro as commandant of Ste. Genevieve in Upper Louisiana. Peyroux moved to town with his wife, his mother, and his brother Pierre. He was manifestly energetic and conscientious in performing the duties of this post, but almost immediately he became engaged in a power struggle with **François Vallé II** and **Jean-Baptiste Vallé,** who were the leaders of the wealthiest and most influential family in Ste. Genevieve. This struggle was a classic confrontation between a local power elite and an outside official imposed from above.

Peyroux and the Vallés disagreed about virtually everything, and their disputes were exacerbated by personal enmity. During the early 1790s it became evident that the old town of Ste. Genevieve, located immediately on the banks of the Mississippi, was doomed and that a new locus of settlement would have to be established. Peyroux advocated resettlement at the Saline, and the Vallés supported a move to Petites Cotes. The Vallés, who understood the sentiments of their community better, triumphed in this dispute, and Petites Cotes became the new town of Ste. Genevieve, whose historic center is now a tourist attraction.

In 1792–1793 Peyroux undertook a prolonged trip to Philadelphia via New Orleans. His purpose in the American capital was to find "honorable German, Flemish, Dutch, or French families" and induce them to emigrate to Spanish Louisiana. Peyroux met Thomas Jefferson, the U.S. secretary of state, while he was in Philadelphia, but his plans for recruiting settlers came to naught. His lengthy visit to the capital of the American Republic, however, created problems for him in Louisiana, for it was rumored that he had imbibed republican revolutionary political ideas that were abhorrent to the Spanish monarchy.

In 1794, when officials in Spanish Louisiana feared an attack by American or French republican revolutionaries, Peyroux was accused of disloyalty to the Spanish regime. Likely the Vallés, with support from their friend Lt. Gov. **Zenon Trudeau** in St. Louis, were behind these accusations. Peyroux was dispatched for investigation to New Orleans, where he was eventually cleared of all charges.

In 1798 Manuel Gayoso de Lemos appointed Peyroux commandant at the recently founded settlement of New Madrid, where he served until 1803. In that year the lieutenant governor of Upper Louisiana, **Charles de Hault Delassus,** dismissed him for insubordination, which charge, given Delassus's friendship with the Vallé family, may have been trumped up. Peyroux was quintessentially a European colonizer, and rather than face a future in American Louisiana he returned to France, where he was swallowed up in the Napoleonic imperium. The date and place of his death are unknown.

CARL J. EKBERG

Ekberg, Carl J. *Colonial Ste. Genevieve: An Adventure on the Mississippi Frontier.* Gerald, Mo.: Patrice Press, 1985.

Houck, Louis. *A History of Missouri, from the Earliest Explorations and Settlements until the Admission of the State into the Union.* 3 vols. Chicago: R. R. Donnelley and Sons, 1908.

Nasatir, Abraham Phineas. *Spanish War Vessels on*

the Mississippi, 1792–1796. New Haven: Yale University Press, 1968.

Winzerling, Oscar William. *Acadian Odyssey.* Baton Rouge: Louisiana State University Press, 1955.

PHELPS, JOHN S. (1814–1886)

In 1903 **Walter Williams** asked four hundred distinguished Missourians to name leaders who had done the most for Missouri in various fields. Only eight individuals were included in his hall of fame for statesmen. They were the giants of Missouri's history in the nineteenth century: men such as **Thomas Hart Benton, Frank Blair, B. Gratz Brown,** and John S. Phelps.

Phelps was better known and more acclaimed in Missouri a century ago than he is today. Born on December 22, 1814, in Simsbury, Connecticut, he was educated at Trinity College (formerly Washington College) and was admitted to the Connecticut bar at the age of twenty-one. In 1837 he moved to Springfield with his wife, **Mary Whitney Phelps,** with the intention of practicing law in southwest Missouri.

Phelps immediately began to accumulate a wealth of honors and achievements that earned him nationwide respect. He quickly established himself as one of the foremost lawyers in the West. Perhaps his best-known legal achievement was gaining the acquittal of Wild Bill Hickok who killed Dave Tutt in a duel on the public square in Springfield on July 21, 1865.

In 1840 Phelps's political career began with his election to the Missouri legislature. In 1844 he was elected to the United States House of Representatives, where he represented southwest Missouri for eighteen years. Although he was a representative from one of the least-developed regions in the nation—a large area with no bridges, telegraph lines, or railroads—Phelps rose to a position of national prominence as chairman of the Ways and Means Committee. Then as now, little legislation could pass Congress without the imprint of the chairman of this powerful committee.

Phelps's national stature reached its peak in 1860 when he was known as the "Father of the House." He was in line to become Speaker of the House, but failed to win that post. The Northerners feared he was pro-Southern because he represented a slave state, while the Southerners feared he was pro-Union because of his Connecticut roots.

In 1861 Phelps began his most important, and best-recognized, service to the state of Missouri. Between 1861 and 1870 Missouri endured a period of agony and chaos difficult to comprehend today. Missouri was a slave state at the time of the secession crisis. Phelps, who owned seventeen slaves that he used to farm the 1,050-acre plantation he owned just south of Springfield, opposed secession. He and his Unionist allies successfully resisted attempts by the legally elected government of Missouri to lead the state into secession.

Phelps did not confine his actions to politics. He organized a regiment that he actively commanded in the federal victory at Pea Ridge in March 1862. More than 30 percent of his badly outnumbered regiment died while awaiting federal reinforcements. In the words of a member of the regiment, Phelps "walked up and down the line as if he were on dress parade." His coolness inspired his men to victory.

In July 1862 President Abraham Lincoln appointed Phelps as military governor of Arkansas for the purpose of establishing a loyal civil government. However, Lincoln's efforts at Reconstruction were premature. Confederate opposition was so intense that Phelps had little chance of success, and Lincoln terminated his commission in early 1863.

The conclusion of the Civil War did not end Missouri's turmoil. While guerrilla warfare flared, the Radical wing of the Republican Party controlled Missouri elections from 1866 to 1870. In effect, Democrats who sympathized with the South were disfranchised by the constitution of 1865 and by the Radicals' heavy-handed enforcement at the polls. In 1868 Phelps, who was the Democratic Party's nominee for governor, lost the election because many of his fellow Democrats were forced to remain at home.

Eight years later, by which time the franchise had been restored to former Confederate supporters, Missouri voters elected Phelps governor. During his term from 1877 to 1881 Phelps advocated economical government, reduced state expenditures, and low taxes. When a railroad strike in St. Louis and other parts of the state threatened to produce major disruptions in the summer of 1877, Governor Phelps supported a show of force to end the disturbances.

Phelps's numerous accomplishments suggest that he was a strong and persuasive individual. Once widely renowned as a leader, he gradually sank into obscurity following his death in St. Louis on November 20, 1886.

HERBERT R. COHEN

Avery, Grace, and Floyd C. Shoemaker. *The Messages and Proclamations of the Governors of the State of Missouri.* Columbia: State Historical Society of Missouri, 1924.

Phelps, John S. Papers. Shepard Room. Missouri Public Library, Springfield.

PHELPS, MARY WHITNEY (1813–1878)

Although Mary Whitney Phelps lived in an era when the "woman's place was in the kitchen," she embodied the free-spirited, goal-oriented woman of the late twentieth century.

Mary Whitney was orphaned soon after her birth in Portland, Maine, on January 8, 1813. When she married **John S. Phelps** in 1837, she and her husband began a new life in the village of Springfield in the Missouri Ozarks. Because John was a young circuit-riding judge, he was absent for extended periods of time. During one of those early absences Mary had a log cabin built on a lot that John had purchased in Springfield.

In 1844 John Phelps was elected to represent the southwest Missouri district in Congress, where he served for eighteen years. The Phelpses purchased a 1,050-acre plantation in an area of present-day Springfield called Phelps Grove. There were separate houses for the family, and five cabins to accommodate their seventeen slaves. The plantation included other structures, such as several barns and stables, an icehouse, and a smokehouse.

Through necessity, Phelps was forced to demonstrate her business acumen and executive ability by managing this plantation during her husband's long absences in Washington. She had responsibility for the care of her family and the seventeen slaves. In addition, as the wife of a congressman, she made several trips to Washington. In later years she enjoyed the personal friendship of President Abraham Lincoln not only because of her social attributes but also because of her determination to relieve wartime suffering.

In wartime women often assume the burdens of caring for the dead, wounded, and homeless, but Phelps's efforts merit special comment. When the Union army retreated following its defeat at the Battle of Wilson's Creek, the body of Gen. **Nathaniel Lyon,** who had been killed in that engagement, was brought to a Springfield home belonging to the Phelpses, where Mary Phelps maintained a nightlong vigil before removing the body to an outdoor cellar on the plantation. By then the Confederates had arrived from Wilson's Creek, and were rumored to be prepared to mutilate the general's body. Phelps prepared a coffin and had the body temporarily buried. Relatives of Lyon arrived shortly after the burial to claim the body, and began a triumphant train procession to Connecticut. General Lyon was the North's first hero. Mary Phelps's role in protecting his body was central to providing the North with an opportunity to energize its effort in the war's early months.

During the Battle of Pea Ridge in March 1862, Phelps arrived on the scene to care for the wounded of the regiment commanded by her husband. The unit, which had been involved in key actions of the battle, had sustained heavy casualties. A wounded member wrote, "Regardless of all impending danger, with that indomitable will, which ever characterized her, Mrs.

Phelps set to work to bring systems out of chaos. She at once constituted herself medical supervisor, nurse, quartermaster, and commissary." Searching for words to pay the highest compliment, he finally said, "The court of heaven has no seat too high for Mary Phelps."

In 1865 Congress awarded Phelps twenty thousand dollars in recognition of her care of General Lyon's body and her many other meritorious acts. She used these funds to establish in Springfield a Soldiers' Orphan Home for children whose fathers were killed in action. When the congressional funds were exhausted, Phelps conducted other fund-raising activities to continue the orphanage for as long as it was needed.

After the war Phelps received national attention as a vice president of the National Woman's Suffrage Association in 1870. In this capacity she appeared before Congress to support giving women the right to vote.

Phelps died on January 25, 1878, of pneumonia. Her death occurred only a few days before her husband was inaugurated as governor of Missouri.

HERBERT R. COHEN

Dains, Mary K., ed. *Show Me Missouri Women: Selected Biographies.* Kirksville, Mo.: Thomas Jefferson University Press, 1989.

Escott, George S. *History and Directory of Springfield and North Springfield.* Springfield, Mo.: Patriot-Advertiser, 1878.

Phelps, Mary Whitney. Papers. Shepard Room. Missouri Public Library, Springfield.

PHILIPS, JOHN FINIS (1834–1919)

John Finis Philips was a jurist, politician, and soldier. Steadfast and resolute in his views, he physically resembled the German leader Otto von Bismarck. Philips was born on December 31, 1834, the last of eleven children of John G. and Mary Copeland Philips, in Thrall's Prairie, in Boone County, Missouri. He attended the University of Missouri from 1851 to 1853, and graduated from Centre College in 1855. He read for the law in Fayette, Missouri, and joined the bar in 1857. The same year he married Fleecie Batterton, beginning a long wedded life that produced a son, Emmet, and a daughter, Hortense. Philips developed a large and lucrative practice in Georgetown, Missouri. A nominal Whig, during the secession crisis he supported the Union and gained election to the state convention that established a provisional government.

Unionist governor **Hamilton Rowan Gamble** commissioned Philips as a colonel in the Seventh Regiment State Militia and Cavalry, organized at large in Missouri in 1862. Philips commanded his troops through several bitter campaigns, displaying characteristic determination and considerable courage. His most memorable moment in combat came in October 1864 during the Battle of Westport in Jackson County. At a crucial juncture at Byram's Ford, a key river crossing, Philips mounted a counterattack that routed a Confederate assault force. He was nominated as a brigadier general of volunteers by Gov. **Willard Preble Hall,** but was never confirmed by the General Assembly. At the end of the Civil War, Philips commanded the District of Missouri.

In 1865 Philips moved to Sedalia, forming a law partnership with former Confederate senator and future U.S. senator **George Graham Vest** and joining the Democratic Party. Philips gained a reputation as one of the most able legal practitioners and stirring orators in Missouri. He was a delegate to the 1868 Democratic National Convention, ran unsuccessfully for Congress, and served a term as mayor of Sedalia. He won election to the Forty-fourth Congress in 1874, but did not stand for reelection. In 1877 he was a delegate to a Pan-Presbyterian Convention in Edinburgh, Scotland. In 1878 he ran successfully in a special election for a seat in the Forty-sixth Congress. During his congressional career, Philips followed the dictates of the Democratic leadership. His finest moment came when he authored a subcommittee report that detailed Republican vote fraud in South Carolina. He believed Republican President Rutherford B. Hayes's election was "grounded and steeped in fraud and perjury."

Defeated for reelection to Congress in 1880, Philips started to think in terms of using his considerable connections to obtain judicial positions. Inside Missouri he was a member of a powerful statewide Democratic faction called the "Big Four." In 1882 Philips became a commissioner of the Missouri Supreme Court, an important appointed appellate position. During 1883 he temporarily vacated his position with the court to defend **Frank James** on a murder charge. A controversial move, Philips claimed he had promised to defend the notorious James long before becoming a state official.

In 1884 Gov. **Thomas Crittenden,** a friend and Democratic political ally, appointed Philips as one of three judges of a new Kansas City court of appeals, a position he held when he became the judge of the United States District Court for the Western District of Missouri in 1888. Philips the politician and his close political associates combined to make Philips the lawyer a federal judge.

Throughout his twenty-two years on the federal bench, Philips, while following his model of "Find a way or make one," compiled a conservative probusiness record. Business enterprises frequently received more than the benefit of a doubt, and he called strike leaders "professional agitators." Railroads usually won when they were parties in litigation before his court. In an Elkins Act rate case, for example, he took a one-sided position on rebates, claiming that shippers rather than railroad companies were the true offenders. He placed a number of railroads in receivership, despite charges that receiverships protected the railroads instead of punishing them for gross mismanagement. Railroad lawyers, well aware of his position, filed many cases of national importance in the Western District. Despite criticism, Philips resolutely went ahead making prorailroad decisions, on the basis of the commerce clause that undermined state transportation laws, while broadening the scope of federal jurisdiction, a necessary part of creating a national system not subject to restrictive statutes. Philips further solidified his reputation as a probusiness judge by following a policy of imprisoning local Missouri county officials for failing to raise tax money to make full payment of railroad bond issues.

Philips retired on June 25, 1910, at age seventy-five. He opened a law office in Kansas City, participated in the affairs of the State Historical Society of Missouri, and remained much in demand as a speaker. On March 13, 1919, he died on vacation in Hot Springs, Arkansas. In recognition of his distinguished career, he received honorary degrees from Centre College, the University of Missouri, and Central College of Fayette, Missouri.

LAWRENCE H. LARSEN

Kansas City Star, March 13, 1919.

Larsen, Lawrence H. *Federal Justice in Western Missouri: The Judges, the Cases, the Times.* Columbia: University of Missouri Press, 1994.

Lopata, Edwin. *Local Aid to Railroads in Missouri.* New York: Arno Press, 1981.

Shoemaker, Floyd C. "In Memoriam: Judge John F. Philips." *Missouri Historical Review* 13 (October 1918–July 1919): 284–85.

PHILLIPS, HOMER G. (1880–1931)

Homer G. Phillips was born in Sedalia, Missouri, on April 1, 1880. He was raised by an aunt after his parents died. From these humble beginnings he rose to a position of national prominence. Phillips was able to obtain an education that culminated at Howard University Law School in Washington, D.C. While he was a student at Howard, he lived in the home of Paul Lawrence Dunbar, a well-known black poet. After graduating from Howard, Phillips returned to Missouri and established a thriving law practice in St. Louis.

Phillips became active in St. Louis politics after joining the Republican Party. During the 1920s he ran unsuccessfully against the popular L. C. Dyer for the United States Congress. Phillips was also a crusader for civil rights causes. When the city of St. Louis enacted an ordinance that limited areas in which African Americans were allowed to reside, he brought a suit that resulted in the invalidation of the segregation ordinance.

After the 1917 race riots in East St. Louis, Illinois, Phillips defended African Americans in several criminal prosecutions. During the early 1920s he was one of the founding members of the St. Louis Negro Bar Association, which later became the Mound City Bar Association. His activities and reputation extended beyond St. Louis and the Midwest. In 1927 he was elected president of the National Bar Association, a national organization of black attorneys.

In 1922 Phillips joined with other black leaders in an effort to persuade the city of St. Louis to issue bonds for the construction of a hospital that would serve the black community. Although he did not live to see the fruition of this endeavor, a hospital that was named to honor his memory was completed in 1937. From the late 1930s until the early 1980s, the Homer G. Phillips Hospital provided medical services to the black residents of St. Louis. The facility also served as a teaching hospital for black physicians and nurses.

The circumstances of Phillips's death are a haunting episode in the history of St. Louis. On the morning of June 18, 1931, Phillips, who was then fifty-one years old, left his home. He waited for the streetcar that he regularly rode to his office. After purchasing a newspaper, he rested on a window ledge. According to the account of a witness, Phillips was approached by two black males who struck him in his face and fired six pistol shots into his body. The assailants fled as Phillips lay dying on the sidewalk. Two black youths were later arrested and tried for the murder, but the jury found them not guilty. Several rumors circulated concerning the circumstances of the crime. At the time of his death, Phillips was representing a black labor official who reported receiving a threatening telephone call that day. He was also scheduled to appear as the chief witness in a perjury case that was pending against another lawyer. The actual circumstances of his death were never determined.

Phillips was a tireless crusader for civil rights and the interests of the black citizens of St. Louis. The hospital that bore his name stood as a testament to the high esteem in which he was held.

LELAND WARE

Clayton, Edward T. "Strange Murder of Homer G. Phillips." *Ebony* 32 (September 1977): 160.
Richardson, Stanley, Jr. "Homer G. Phillips: The Man and the Hospital." *St. Louis Bar Journal* 30 (spring 1984): 26.

Smith, J. Clay. *Emancipation: The Making of the Black Lawyer, 1844–1944*. Philadelphia: University of Pennsylvania Press, 1993.

PIERNAS, PEDRO JOSEPH (1728?–?)

Pedro Joseph Piernas, the first Spanish lieutenant governor in St. Louis, occupied that post between 1770 and 1775. He was born in San Sebastian, Spain, in either 1728 or 1729 and came to Louisiana with Gov. Antonio de Ulloa in 1766 as a captain in the Spanish army. The following year Ulloa sent Capt. Francisco Ríu and a contingent of Spanish soldiers to the Illinois country with instructions to build military fortifications at the junction of the Missouri and Mississippi Rivers. When trouble erupted at the outpost on the Missouri and some of Ríu's men deserted, Ulloa named Piernas to replace Ríu as commandant of Upper Louisiana.

Ulloa dispatched Piernas to take charge of Fort Don Carlos, but late in 1768 rebels seeking to reinstate French authority in New Orleans forced Ulloa to flee to Cuba. Before Ulloa departed he sent new orders to Piernas, instructing him to withdraw from Upper Louisiana after delivering Fort Don Carlos to the former French commandant in St. Louis. Piernas reached the Missouri River installation in March 1769 only thirteen days before he received Ulloa's directive to evacuate. He withdrew from the fort immediately but tarried in nearby St. Louis for nearly a month while attempting to settle disputed government accounts with local merchants. Piernas headed downriver in late April and arrived in New Orleans in May. He and his men sailed for Havana in July, the last Spanish soldiers to leave the province in the aftermath of the uprising.

The next year a military expedition headed by Lt. Gen. Alejandro O'Reilly reestablished Spanish authority in Louisiana. After taking charge in New Orleans, O'Reilly solicited information about conditions in Upper Louisiana from Captain Piernas who had returned from Cuba. Although Piernas had been in Upper Louisiana only briefly, his detailed report offered an optimistic assessment of the region's potential. In early 1770 O'Reilly took steps to place Upper Louisiana under full Spanish control by appointing a lieutenant governor to direct operations in St. Louis. He selected Piernas for the newly created post and granted him broad powers for maintaining order, administering justice, regulating trade, and managing Indian affairs.

In New Orleans Piernas had married Fecilite Robineau de Portneuf, and she joined him in St. Louis where she gave birth to at least two children. After he assumed control in St. Louis in May 1770, the new lieutenant governor moved quickly to solidify popular support behind the Spanish regime. Among other things he allayed local anxieties by publicly affirming the land titles granted by his French predecessor.

Piernas also solicited advice from influential French residents, especially concerning the management of Indian affairs, a task that he quickly discovered commanded a disproportionate share of his time. Piernas was a quick learner. When the Indians initially misinterpreted his reserved and dignified bearing as a sign of unfriendliness, he wisely copied the French practices of feasting and giving gifts to help win them over.

Piernas found the Osages especially vexing. He favored trade sanctions for bringing errant tribes to terms but soon discovered the shortcomings of that strategy. When Piernas refused to send Spanish-licensed traders to their villages, the Indians simply sought British replacements. In 1772 Canadian trader Jean Marie Ducharme secretly crossed the Mississippi and headed up the Missouri with merchandise for the Indian trade. Piernas learned of Ducharme's illicit activities and dispatched a militia company, under the command of St. Louis's founder **Pierre de Laclède,** to capture the trading party and seize its goods. They managed to intercept the expedition, but Ducharme escaped his captors and fled to Canada. Even so, Piernas had acted decisively to uphold Spanish authority in the region.

By all accounts, during his five-year stint as Upper Louisiana's lieutenant governor, Piernas proved a good soldier and a competent administrator who served his king well. On April 24, 1775, he relinquished control in St. Louis to his successor, **Francisco Cruzat.**

Piernas returned to New Orleans and was assigned to the headquarters staff where he steadily advanced in rank. In subsequent years when the governor-general was away from the capital Piernas occasionally served as Louisiana's acting governor. In 1785 he attained the rank of colonel and was named commander of the Louisiana Regiment, a fitting climax to a distinguished career in Spanish service. The date and place of his death are unknown.

WILLIAM E. FOLEY

Din, Gilbert C., and Abraham P. Nasatir. *The Imperial Osages: Spanish-Indian Diplomacy in the Mississippi Valley.* Norman: University of Oklahoma Press, 1983.

Foley, William E. *The Genesis of Missouri: From Wilderness Outpost to Statehood.* Columbia: University of Missouri Press, 1989.

POLK, TRUSTEN W. (1811–1876)

Trusten W. Polk, governor of Missouri and a U.S. senator, was born in Sussex County, Delaware, on May 29, 1811. His parents, William Nutter and Levinia Causey Polk, were both members of politically prominent families. Polk attended the common schools in Delaware, Cambridge Academy on Maryland's eastern shore, and Yale College in New Haven, Connecticut, from which he graduated with honors in 1831. He wanted to enter the ministry, but at his father's urging he read law with James Rogers, Delaware's longtime attorney general. After two additional years of study at the Yale Law School, he returned briefly to his native state.

In 1835 Polk moved to St. Louis where he established a successful legal practice. Although he had been thwarted in his desire to become a minister, he retained strong religious convictions. In St. Louis he embraced the temperance movement, and in 1836 the local Young Men's Temperance Society elected him president. Polk met Elizabeth Skinner in St. Louis, where they were married on December 26, 1837. The couple had five children.

Polk took an active interest in education. He assisted with the creation of the Missouri Medical College in St. Louis and joined early discussions organized by **Henry S. Geyer** to win support for the establishment of a state university. He served briefly as St. Louis's city counselor until poor health forced him to resign. In an effort to recuperate he left Missouri and embarked upon a lengthy trip that took him to Cuba, the eastern United States, and Canada. He used his sabbatical to study educational systems in the states he visited.

Polk returned to Missouri in the fall of 1845, following his selection as a delegate to the Missouri Constitutional Convention. As chair of the Committee on Education he urged the delegates to include an article in the proposed constitution mandating state support for free public schools. He also assumed an active role in the debates about banks and corporations.

Although he was an urban Democrat, Polk embraced the hard currency and proslavery doctrines favored by his party's outstate agrarian factions. In 1854 he ran unsuccessfully for a seat in the United States House of Representatives, but two years later the anti-Benton Democrats chose him as their gubernatorial nominee. Polk defeated **Thomas Hart Benton** and American Party candidate R. C. Ewing with a plurality of 41 percent in the three-way race. His election marked an important victory for members of the influential Central Clique.

Polk took the oath of office as governor of Missouri on January 5, 1857, but eight days later members of the General Assembly chose him to succeed Geyer in the United States Senate. On February 27, after serving less than two months of his term as governor, Polk resigned to take his seat in the Senate.

Polk's strong pro-Southern convictions became apparent during the emerging national crisis. In 1858 he spoke out strongly in defense of slavery and the admission of Kansas under the Lecompton Constitution. During the secession crisis in early 1861 Polk called for "irrepealable" constitutional amendments to protect slavery and solemnly proclaimed that Missouri would take its position with the South if the federal government insisted on forcing the abolition issue.

Polk's Southern sympathies caused him to absent himself from the session of Congress that began on December 2, 1861. In January 1862 the Senate expelled Polk and Missouri's other senator, **Waldo P. Johnson,** on grounds of disloyalty and engaging in rebellion against the U.S. government. By then Polk had cast his lot with the Confederate cause.

Following his departure from the national capital, Polk returned briefly to St. Louis before heading to New Madrid and possibly Memphis. By mid-December he had joined **Sterling Price** and the Missouri State Guard. He served under Price's command until Jefferson Davis named him presiding judge of the Trans-Mississippi Department and ordered him to report to Little Rock, Arkansas.

When Polk learned that federal authorities had banished his family from St. Louis, he set out to find them. Sometime in 1863 Union forces captured Polk and sent him to the Johnson's Island prison camp in Sandusky, Ohio, where his health rapidly deteriorated. This prompted an agreement to parole him to St. Louis, reportedly in exchange for a Union prisoner in Mississippi.

Following his release Polk eventually found his way back to Arkansas where he joined Price and participated in his 1864 Missouri campaign. After they retreated to Arkansas, Polk resumed his duties there as presiding judge. When the war ended he fled to Mexico in search of Price. They traveled together for a short time, but Polk decided to return to the United States to rejoin his family.

The Polks moved back to St. Louis, and Trusten Polk reopened his law practice as soon as the United States Supreme Court declared Missouri's test oath for lawyers unconstitutional. He also continued his lifelong commitment to the work of the Methodist Episcopal Church South until his death in St. Louis on April 16, 1876.

DAVID C. AAMODT

Aamodt, David C. " 'Conviction of Duty': The Life of Senator Trusten Polk." Master's thesis, Central Missouri State University, 1994.

Polk, Trusten. Diary and Papers. Southern Historical Collection. University of North Carolina, Chapel Hill.

POPE, JOHN (1822–1892)

Although best known for his military debacle in Virginia at the hands of Confederate general Robert E. Lee at the Second Battle of Manassas, or Second Bull Run, on August 27–30, 1862, Union general John Pope's Civil War career was preordained by his easy successes and their resulting hubris gained during his earlier Missouri campaigns in 1861 and 1862. Most significantly, Pope owed his command of Union forces at Second Manassas to his April 1862 capture of fortified Island No. 10 in the Mississippi River a few miles from New Madrid, Missouri. In January 1865 a chastened Pope came back to Missouri to command the new Military Division of the Missouri, consisting of the Missouri and Kansas areas, and, following his death in Sandusky, Ohio, in 1892, his body was returned to St. Louis, Missouri, for burial in Bellefontaine Cemetery.

John Pope was born on March 16, 1822, in Louisville, Kentucky, the birthplace of his lawyer father, Nathaniel (1784–1850), a former secretary and congressional delegate of the Illinois Territory and later U.S. judge for the state of Illinois. Abraham Lincoln practiced law before the elder Pope and was later accused of promoting the judge's son as repayment for earlier judicial favors. The younger Pope secured an appointment to the United States Military Academy at West Point, from which he graduated in 1842, a respectable seventeenth in his class of sixty-two that included James Longstreet, who later became a Confederate general.

Unlike fellow Union Civil War generals and West Point graduates **Ulysses S. Grant, William T. Sherman,** and George McClellan, who resigned their commissions to pursue private business interests prior to the war, Pope steadfastly followed a military career his entire life. During the Mexican War the second lieutenant was twice breveted for his services at the Battles of Monterey and Buena Vista. By the outset of the Civil War he had achieved the permanent rank of captain and was serving on lighthouse duty. In the early spring of 1861 he was appointed mustering officer at Chicago and, effective May 17, 1861, was given the rank of brigadier general of volunteers.

In the summer of 1861 Pope was ordered to report to Missouri under the command of Gen. **John C. Frémont,** a man who would be under Pope's command one year later in Virginia. One of Pope's first actions in reaching his post in northern Missouri in July 1861 was to issue an order proclaiming that any partisans who took up arms against the Union would be dealt with summarily "without awaiting civil process." Although his blunt warning helped to reduce guerrilla activity in northern Missouri, similar orders issued a year later in Virginia met only defiance and derision.

In late February 1862 Pope assumed command of the Army of the Mississippi and proceeded to besiege Confederate-held New Madrid, Missouri, which fell on March 14. Next, in cooperation with naval forces under Flag Officer Andrew Hull Foote, Pope cut off and forced Confederate forces guarding Island No. 10 in the Mississippi River to surrender on April 8, 1862. Pope's achievement in capturing the approximately seven thousand Confederate troops, twenty-five field guns, small arms, and various emplaced cannons on Island No. 10, at minimal cost in Union casualties, while battling the swamps of the Missouri Bootheel, deserves high praise. Despite greater attention given to the Battle of Shiloh that took place at the same time, the capture of Island No. 10 won Pope recognition from Washington.

Following participation in General Halleck's campaign to capture Corinth, Mississippi, Pope was transferred to the East in June 1862 to take command of the Army of Virginia. That army had only recently been formed by the hasty combining of various demoralized Union commands that shared the dubious distinction of having been beaten in detail over the preceding weeks in Stonewall Jackson's famed "Valley Campaign."

Despite his handsome soldierly appearance and recent record of success in the West, Pope failed to inspire his new troops, many of whom resented not only his pomposity but also his having temporarily eclipsed Gen. George McClellan, who despite his failures remained popular with his troops. After being only narrowly checked by Stonewall Jackson and superior numbers at Cedar Mountain, Virginia, Pope permitted himself to be outmaneuvered by Lee and Jackson and defeated at Second Manassas in August 1862. He was then replaced in command by McClellan, whom Pope accused of having withheld vital troops from him at critical times during the battle.

Notwithstanding Pope's own failings at Second Manassas, which were considerable, even Lincoln believed that part of the Union defeat was attributable to the failure of McClellan and his generals in the Army of the Potomac to support Pope, one of whom declared that he did not care "one pinch of owl dung" for Pope. Despite his sympathy for Pope, Lincoln permitted him to be transferred to Minnesota to put down a Sioux uprising and then to other secondary commands in the West.

Pope remained in the army after the Civil War until retiring in 1886, having served creditably in various commands and eventually rising to the rank of major general in 1882. He died on September 23, 1892.

MARSHALL D. HIER

Dictionary of American Biography. Vol. 15. S.v. "Pope, John."

Glatther, Joseph T. *Partners in Command.* New York: Free Press, 1994.

Long, E. B. *The Civil War Day by Day.* Garden City, N.Y.: Doubleday, 1971.

Sandburg, Carl. *Abraham Lincoln: The War Years.* Vol. 1. New York: Harcourt, Brace, 1939.

Warner, Ezra J. *Generals in Blue.* Baton Rouge: Louisiana State University Press, 1959.

POST, JUSTUS (1780–1846)

Col. Justus Post, an extensive landowner, founder of Chesterfield in St. Louis County, a founder of the Bank of St. Louis, a Missouri state senator, and judge of the St. Louis County Court, was a speculator who amassed more than twenty-one thousand arpents within a few years of his arrival in Missouri in 1815. By 1820, though, the land bubble had burst.

Post's Yankee smugness and naïveté prevented him from gauging the shrewd trading skills of the French elite who controlled frontier St. Louis. His struggle to hold on to his dream of fortune and boundless opportunity failed in the next decade. In 1830 he retreated to the more Anglo territory of Illinois where he laid out the town of America and was buried in Caledonia, Illinois, in 1846.

A large collection of letters from Justus Post to his brother John in Addison County, Vermont, provide vivid descriptions of early St. Louis and St. Louis County and chronicle the evolution of Justus's determination to possess the fertile land of the Mississippi and Missouri River Valleys. He boasted, "I calculate we shall be immensely rich and reside in the center of the greatest Empire in the world."

Post was born in Morris County, New Jersey, on November 18, 1780, the youngest of eight children of John and Lois Post. The family moved to Addison County, Vermont, when Justus was young. He graduated from Middlebury College and then from the United States Military Academy in 1806 where he was the head of his class of five. As a second lieutenant of artillery, he was posted at Fort Columbus in New York Harbor. He was promoted to colonel at the outbreak of the War of 1812. As agent of fortifications he was put in charge of strengthening the defenses of the harbor.

Post resigned from the regular army at the end of the war and on August 14, 1815, started his three-month journey with his family and carriages bound for St. Louis, which they reached on November 6. He advised his brother, "We have arrived, after a long and tedious journey. We traveled 400 miles by carriage, 1000 miles on the Ohio, and another 150 by carriage."

St. Louis was a boomtown. The population had grown from 3,149 to 7,395 in just twelve months.

Word traveled quickly about the arrival of the prosperous Yankee with assets of seventeen thousand dollars, mostly in cash. His wife, Eliza Post, noted in her memorandum book the names of the rich and famous who called at their home in the first few months: **Auguste Chouteau, (Jean) Pierre Chouteau, Thomas Hart Benton, Charles Gratiot, Joseph Charless, William C. Carr,** and others, including Indian leaders.

Post found the French city too "gay and dashy" and complained constantly about the laziness of the habitants and their lack of barns that left cattle out to pasture all winter. He also included other Yankee observations about this alien culture. He did, however, send his three sons to the French school in town, assimilated socially with his power peers, and eventually bought slaves.

In 1816 Post bought land in Bonhomme, adjoining the Missouri River. He enthusiastically described the peach orchards, the abundant crops of corn, wheat, tobacco, hemp, sweet potatoes, even cotton, and the "dense growth of walnut, hickory, sycamore, elm, cottonwoods with trunks six feet through." By 1819 he referred to "my town of Chesterfield" where he had installed a blacksmith, a wagon maker, and a tutor for his sons. Masons started his two-story brick home, stable, corn house, and schoolroom. He also built a gristmill, a sawmill, a blacksmith shop, and a brick store. From this modest beginning, suburban Chesterfield now boasts a substantial population, and the streets surrounding the sprawling Chesterfield Mall bear the names of Justus Post and his relatives.

Post, who became one of the first directors of the Bank of St. Louis, smugly referred to the desire of the opposition bank headed by Auguste Chouteau to join forces with his: "It must not be done yet; they must do penance for a while. These lads must be tutored." The Bank of St. Louis folded in 1819. The Bank of Missouri held on two years longer.

Because he financed each new investment from the last, Post quickly became cash-poor in a decade when cash became so scarce that borrowing was not an option. Among his diverse investments were "salted" lead and copper mines. He even expected to find "gold and silver stowed away in these hills up here on the border of Mexico." His education in Latin, the classics, math, and astronomy had not prepared him well for business. The threat of bankruptcy sent him on an unsuccessful search for funds in New York City in 1821, and he repeatedly petitioned brother John for cash that was not forthcoming.

In Chesterfield Post started his public service career as judge of the St. Louis County Court and then as a state senator. Restless and plagued by financial difficulties, he decided at the expiration of his senatorial term in 1830 to move to his new town of America near the mouth of the Ohio River in Illinois.

While Chesterfield was to enjoy vigorous expansion in the next century, America has all but disappeared. Justus Post died on March 14, 1846.

Historian William E. Foley summed up this dreamer's role in the expansion of the West: "Justus Post and the thousands of others like him were the organizers, persuaders, discoverers of opportunities and risk takers who became the prototype of the American businessman."

ELIZABETH GENTRY SAYAD

Foley, William E. "Justice Post: Portrait of a Frontier Land Speculator." *Missouri Historical Society Bulletin* 36 (October 1979): 19–26.
Gentry, William R., Jr. "Foreword to the Justus Post Letters." Missouri Historical Society, St. Louis.
Post, Justus. Collection. Missouri Historical Society, St. Louis.

POST, TRUMAN MARCELLUS (1810–1886)

Truman Marcellus Post, a religious and cultural leader of St. Louis, was born in Middlebury, Vermont, on June 3, 1810, to Martin and Sarah Hulburd Post. He entered Middlebury College in 1824, delivering the valedictory address at his graduation in 1829, and thereafter studied law, supporting himself by working in various schools in Vermont. An illness briefly diverted Post from the law, and he spent five months attending Andover Theological Seminary. During the 1832–1833 winter he resumed his studies in Washington, D.C., learning the principles of American jurisprudence "amid the contests of the elder and younger Titans of political debate in their struggle over constitutional questions which were to convulse the country through an era of agitation that was to close with the arbitrament of civil arms."

At the urging of Congressman Joseph Duncan of Illinois, who later became the state's governor, Post moved to Jacksonville, Illinois, in the spring of 1833. In March President Edward Beecher of Illinois College invited Post to assist in the school's classics department. He was subsequently appointed professor of ancient languages and ancient history, holding both posts for fourteen years. He was admitted to the Illinois bar in June 1833, married Frances A. Henshaw in 1835, and was ordained in October 1840, after he assumed the pastorate of a small Congregational church in Jacksonville.

The Lovejoy riot at Alton in 1837 provided the impetus Post needed to articulate his antislavery sentiments and hone his prodigious talent for public debate. In a scathing letter to the *American Emancipator* titled "An Address to the People of Alton," Post proclaimed **Elijah P. Lovejoy**'s murder and the seizure of his printing press a violation of constitutional law, denouncing Alton as the city where "freedom of speech found its first American martyr" and calling for justice.

Post freely expressed his abolitionist sympathies in St. Louis after 1847. In that year he accepted an invitation to officiate as pastor for four years at the Third Presbyterian Church in St. Louis, reserving the right to freedom of religious and political expression, for "he did not want to add another to the slaves in Missouri." Between 1851 and 1852 the church reorganized as the First Trinitarian Congregational Church with Post as pastor and by 1860 enjoyed a singular prosperity and counted among its parishioners many influential St. Louisans. The outbreak of the Civil War divided the church and consequently reduced its membership and financial base, for Post's vocal support of Union prerogatives and active participation in local relief efforts estranged secessionist parishioners and friends alike.

After the church reorganized a second time, Post removed to a sister congregation called the Pilgrim Church, where he served as pastor until he retired in 1882. Given his independent spirit and long record of service, he has been rightfully called the "father" of Congregationalism in St. Louis, even as he advanced the prerogatives of the denomination on a national level. Post served as the vice president of the Congregational Union from its inception in 1853 and addressed its membership in New York and wrote a history of Congregationalism in Missouri in 1854, thereby establishing a vital link between his own parishioners and both the powerful and the poor churches in other localities.

Post also substantially broadened the cultural scope of St. Louisans after 1847. Maintaining his ties with the eastern academic establishment throughout his life, he lectured extensively on literary and historical topics and welcomed Ralph Waldo Emerson as a friend when the writer spoke at Mercantile Library in 1852. Post delivered the dedication address at Bellefontaine Cemetery in 1850, anticipating the moral and social roles rural cemeteries played in the life of nineteenth-century communities. He also wrote more than a hundred book reviews for the *St. Louis Intelligencer* and published his *Skeptical Era in Modern History* (1856) and numerous articles and addresses, including "Voices of History" (1851), "Religion and Education" (1856), "Palingenesy: National Regeneration" (1864), and "The Things which Cannot Be Shaken" (1886). In August 1855 Middlebury College awarded Post the degree of doctor of divinity, and he served as a board member and lecturer at Chicago and Andover Theological Seminaries and as a trustee of the Missouri School for the Education of the Blind and the Monticello Seminary of Godfrey, Illinois.

Still recognized by St. Louisans as both a national figure and a consummate public speaker late in his life, Post delivered his final address in May 1885 at the unveiling of the monument to **Frank Blair** in Forest Park. He was buried, appropriately, at Bellefontaine Cemetery after his death on December 31, 1886.

PAULA COALIER

Corbett, Katharine T. "Bellefontaine Cemetery: St. Louis City of the Dead." *Gateway Heritage* 12 (fall 1991): 58–67.

Hyde, William, and Howard L. Conard, eds. *Encyclopedia of the History of St. Louis.* New York: Southern History, 1899.

Luckingham, Brad. "The Pioneer Lecturer in the West: A Note on the Appearance of Ralph Waldo Emerson in St. Louis, 1852–1853." *Missouri Historical Review* 58 (October 1963): 70–88.

Post, T. A. *Truman Marcellus Post, D.D.: A Biography Personal and Literary.* Chicago: Congregational Sunday-School and Publishing Society, 1891.

POWELL, WILLIAM (1882–1984)

William Horatio Powell was the epitome of the suave, urbane leading man throughout his stage and film career. His most famous role was the sophisticated detective Nick Charles in Dashiell Hammett's *Thin Man* series.

Powell was born in Pittsburgh, Pennsylvania, on July 29, 1882, but the family moved to Kansas City in 1907. His accountant father, Horatio Warren, and his mother, Nettie Manila Brady Powell, hoped that he would become a lawyer. Young William, however, was drawn to the theater and worked as an usher at an opera house in order to be around professionals. Powell was active in theater at Central High School where he landed a supporting role in a school production of *The Rivals* and was also a cheerleader. He was already determined to become an actor.

Powell attended the University of Kansas for a short time in 1911, but returned home with the intention of earning enough money to study acting in New York. He worked for a local telephone company and persuaded a wealthy aunt to loan him seven hundred dollars so that he could attend the American Academy of Dramatic Arts in New York City. He was a classmate of Edward G. Robinson and Joseph Schildkraut at the school, until his money ran out six months later.

In September 1912, however, Powell was given a walk-on part in *The Ne'er-Do-Well*. In 1913 he won a supporting role in *Within the Law* and toured with the play for nearly two years. In 1915 he married Eileen Wilson, a cast member, and they had a son, William David, before they divorced in 1931.

In the 1930s Powell was one of the movie industry's leading romantic male performers. He married Carole Lombard, the greatest of the female screwball comedians. Two years later that marriage ended, and he began a much rumored relationship with **Jean Harlow.** Lombard in turn married Clark Gable. Powell and Harlow were engaged when she died in 1937. Powell's last marriage, to Diana Lewis in 1940, lasted until his death in 1984.

Although he was a master of romantic comedy, Powell was no stranger to dramatic roles. He won Academy Award nominations for the original *Thin Man* (1934), *My Man Godfrey* (1936), and *Life with Father* (1947). He was one of the few actors to make a successful transition from silent movies to the talkies. In his last film, made in 1955, he starred with Henry Fonda in *Mister Roberts.* Most moviegoers, however, remember him best for his classic profile, gazing comically at Myrna Loy with a highball glass in his hand while uttering a wisecrack.

When Powell died in Palm Springs on March 5, 1984, his hometown newspaper, the *Kansas City Times,* reminded its readers that this fine actor's "very first role" was at Central High School. An editorial remembered with "what elegant grace Nick Charles, super sleuth, grasped his highball glass as he crisply explained to the assembled suspects the facts of the case, preparing to unmask the guilty party." William Powell was one of the "distinctive" actors of Hollywood's golden era.

ARTHUR F. MCCLURE AND VIVIAN RICHARDSON

Current Biography. New York: H. W. Wilson, 1947.
Lamparski, Richard. *Whatever Became Of . . . ?* 2d series. New York: Crown Publishing, 1968.
Obituary. *Newsweek* (March 19, 1984): 90.
Variety, March 14, 1984.

PRATTE, BERNARD (1771–1836)

Bernard Pratte's father, Jean Baptiste, settled first on the east bank of the Mississippi. When France ceded that territory to England, he moved across the river to Ste. Genevieve, where he married Marie Ann Lalumandiere and established himself as a merchant, grain grower, and salt maker. Bernard Pratte, who was born on June 11, 1771, was well educated and trained to take over his father's mercantile interests. Expanding the family's business to include fur trading, he was licensed to trade with the Omaha in 1790 and with the Osage in 1794. By 1801 he was trading on the Des Moines River.

In 1794 Pratte married Emilie Sauver, daughter of Silvestre and Pelagie Chouteau Labbadie, thus allying himself with the powerful Chouteau family. Over the next few years he opened a dry goods and grocery store in St. Louis and moved his primary business interests and residence to that town. Active in civic affairs, he held a variety of public offices, including trustee of the town of St. Louis, commissioner of rates and levies for the St. Louis district, militia captain, school board member, and judge of the court of common pleas. In 1815 he was commissioned brigadier general of the territorial militia. He was a member of the 1820 Constitutional Convention, and appointed U.S. receiver of public monies for St. Louis in 1825.

Pratte continued both his mercantile and his fur-trading activities. The various realignments of the St. Louis traders to protect their interests on the Missouri River from American and Canadian interlopers produced in 1823 the firm of Bernard Pratte and Company, popularly known as the "French Company." This alliance of Pratte, Jean Baptiste Cabanné, **Pierre Chouteau Jr.,** Bartholomew Berthold, John B. Sarpy, and others united old rivals in an aggressive company that drove its opponents from the river. The partners, however, suffered some setbacks, as when at Cabanné's urging they attempted to break into the southwestern fur trade.

Pratte's eldest son, Sylvestre (born in 1799), who had been trading on the Missouri River perhaps as early as 1816, was sent to New Mexico in 1825 to establish company operations there. Chronic trouble with Mexican officials and depredations by hostile Indians and rival trappers in the mountains, combined with Sylvestre Pratte's poor management, doomed the project. Completing the disaster, the younger Pratte died in 1827 while leading a trapping party near the headwaters of the Platte.

On the Missouri River, by contrast, Bernard Pratte and Company proved so successful that John Jacob Astor's American Fur Company could not force the partners out, and so was forced to buy them in. After years of negotiations (during which Ramsey Crooks of the American Fur Company married Bernard Pratte's daughter Emilie), the two companies merged in 1827, with Bernard Pratte and Company thereafter acting as Astor's agent on the Missouri. When Astor retired from the fur trade in 1834, the company bought his Western Department and reorganized as Pratte, Chouteau, and Company.

By this time Pratte's second son, Bernard Pratte Jr. (1803–1896), was well established in the family business. He strongly supported innovations proposed by Pierre Chouteau Jr., such as replacing the company's keelboats with the new steamboats or hosting notable travelers such as the artist **George C. Catlin** as a public relations gesture, over the objections of his more cautious father. When the elder Pratte gradually retired from active involvement in company business, the younger took over as captain of the company's second steamboat in 1833.

The elder Bernard Pratte died on April 1, 1836, and under the partnership agreement Pratte, Chouteau, and Company terminated with the peltry return of 1839. The new firm of Pierre Chouteau Jr. and Company was organized without a Pratte among the partners: Bernard Jr. had withdrawn from the company in 1838 to serve in the Missouri legislature. In 1841 he and Jean Charles Cabanné (son of Jean Baptiste Cabanné) organized a rival company, which Chouteau drove off the river by 1845.

Bernard Pratte Jr. thereafter devoted his attention to his business interests in St. Louis. He was twice elected mayor of the city (1844 and 1845) on the Whig slogan "Henry Clay and Protection of American Industries." Characteristically, he advocated modern improvements: gas streetlights were installed, and the levee was paved with stone during his administration. He served as a director of the Bank of the State of Missouri, and like his father held various civic offices over the years. In 1850 he turned his St. Louis business over to the eldest of his seven children, a son also named Bernard Pratte, and retired to his farm in Montgomery County with his wife of twenty-six years, Louise Chenie Pratte.

MARY ELLEN ROWE

Billon, Frederic L. *Annals of St. Louis in Its Early Days under the French and Spanish Dominations, 1764–1804.* St. Louis, 1886.

Hyde, William, and Howard L. Conard, eds. *Encyclopedia of the History of St. Louis.* New York: Southern History, 1899.

Lecompte, Janet. "Pierre Chouteau Jr." In *The Mountain Men and the Fur Trade of the Far West,* ed. LeRoy R. Hafen, 9:91–124. Glendale, Calif.: Arthur H. Clark, 1965.

Nasatir, Abraham P. *Before Lewis and Clark: Documents Illustrating the History of the Missouri, 1785–1804.* 2 vols. 1952. Reprint, Lincoln: University of Nebraska Press, 1990.

Weber, David J. "Sylvestre S. Pratte." In *The Mountain Men and the Fur Trade of the Far West,* ed. LeRoy R. Hafen, 6:359–70. Glendale, Calif.: Arthur H. Clark, 1968.

PREETORIUS, EMIL (1827–1905)

Emil Preetorius was a German-language journalist in St. Louis. Born in Alzey, Rheinhessen, Germany, on March 15, 1827, he received a doctorate of laws at Giessen, also studying at Heidelberg. Although he was sympathetic to the 1848 revolutions, he reached St. Louis only in 1853. A leather merchant on arrival, Preetorius participated actively in the Freie Gemeinde von Nord–St. Louis, a freethinker congregation located in north St. Louis. He became one of the most important speakers on behalf of anticlerical atheism in the American Midwest.

An important campaigner for the Republican Party in 1860, Preetorius entered the Missouri legislature as an emancipationist in 1862. He worked as an editor of the leftist weekly *Neue Zeit* beginning in 1862, and he was with both the *Westliche Post* and the *Neue Zeit* during 1864 before becoming editor in chief of the *Westliche Post* on November 30, 1864.

The *Westliche Post* supported **John Charles Frémont** against Lincoln in the 1864 campaign, and after Lincoln's assassination in 1864 it severely attacked the moderate Reconstruction policies of Andrew Johnson. In Missouri Preetorius opposed the disfranchisement of noncombatant supporters of the South, a measure proposed by the Radical government. Preetorius invited Gen. **Carl Schurz** to join him in managing the paper in May 1867. In 1868 he hired **Joseph Pulitzer.** Schurz and Preetorius came to oppose **Charles Drake** and the Radical government of Missouri. Although Preetorius advocated the abolition of slavery, he opposed equality for blacks in civil or social life. After a bitter campaign, Schurz was elected U.S. senator by the Missouri legislature in 1868. The *Westliche Post* supported the Liberal Republican movement in 1872 led by Schurz and **B. Gratz Brown.** Schurz would continue as editor of the *Westliche Post* until he became U.S. secretary of the interior in March 1877, when Preetorius once more became the sole chief editor. During the general strike in July 1877, the *Westliche Post* opposed the demands of radical organized labor. The paper became the principal voice of German Republicans in the region and remained so for the remainder of Preetorius's life.

Emil Preetorius was regarded as a major civic leader of St. Louis in the 1890s, serving as president of the Missouri Historical Society in 1892–1893. He retired from his position of publisher of the *Westliche Post* on June 1, 1898, after the takeover of its major rival, the Democratic *Anziger des Westens,* passing his position to his son, Edward L. Preetorius (1866–1915). In 1913 a monument to St. Louis German journalism called *Naked Truth* was erected in Compton Hills Reservoir Park, bearing the names of Preetorius as well as Carl Schurz and the founder of the *Westliche Post* in 1857, Carl Danzer.

Preetorius was regarded during his lifetime as the leader of the German progressive community in St. Louis, and his career encompassed the years of its greatest successes. He died on November 19, 1905.

STEVEN ROWAN

Gemeinde, Freie. Papers. Western Historical Manuscripts Collection, St. Louis.

Nagler, Jorg A. *Frémont contra Lincoln. Die deutsch amerikanische Opposition in der Republikanischen Parteiwahrend des amerikanischen Burgerkriegs.* Frankfurt am Main and Burn, N.Y.: Peter Lang, 1984.

Saalberg, Harvey. "The *Westliche Post* of St. Louis: A Daily Newspaper for German-Americans, 1857–1938." Ph.D. diss., University of Missouri–Columbia, 1967.

PRICE, STERLING (1809–1867)

Born in Prince Edward County, Virginia, on September 11, 1809, Sterling Price was the son of a tobacco planter of middling status who provided a comfortable home and a good education for his five children. In 1830 the Price family joined the growing numbers of Virginia planters seeking new lands in Missouri.

Sterling Price tried his hand at storekeeping and the tobacco commission business, investing his profits in land around his father's extensive holdings near Keytesville. A handsome and personable young man, he mixed easily in local society and politics. Within two years of his arrival, Price was elected colonel of the Chariton County militia regiment. In May 1833 he married Martha Head, daughter of Judge Walter Head, a wealthy planter who came from Orange County, Virginia, in 1830. The couple eventually had seven children, five of whom survived to adulthood.

Early in his political career, Price allied himself with the powerful "Boonslick Democracy," a group of wealthy southern planters and merchants who settled Boone, Howard, and Chariton Counties, and who, in uneasy alliance with Sen. **Thomas Hart Benton,** dominated Missouri politics in the 1830s and 1840s. Price's tact, persuasive skills, and powerful presence made him an effective politician. He easily won election to the General Assembly in 1838. Returned in 1840 he was unanimously elected Speaker of the House. By this time he was an established political leader, planter, and entrepreneur. With partner Lisbon Applegate he operated a general mercantile business in Keytesville. He was building one of the finest tobacco plantations in the state, and in 1843 he built a tobacco warehouse at Keytesville Landing to expand his commission business. In 1844 he was elected to the United States House of Representatives. When the United States declared war on Mexico, Senator Benton secured Price a commission as colonel of volunteers to raise and lead a regiment of Missourians in Gen. **Stephen Watts Kearny**'s Army of the West.

Despite a severe illness, Price led his regiment to Santa Fe in September 1846, where he assumed command of the American army of occupation. In January 1847 he crushed a rebellion against the Americans, marching from Santa Fe with 350 men, driving the insurgents back to Taos, storming the town, and forcing their surrender. Price was promoted to brigadier general for this action, though political enemies and professional soldiers alike characterized the promotion as due more to political influence than merit.

The war was ending, and Price needed a smashing victory to silence his critics. In late February 1848 he reported rumors of another insurrection being planned to the south. Ignoring War Department orders to remain in his own district, he pushed his men on a grueling march southward until he located a Mexican army unit at Santa Cruz de Rosales. Although the peace treaty between the United States and Mexico had just been signed, Price attacked, killing more than two hundred Mexicans and losing four of his own men before accepting the Mexican surrender. Back in the United States the Democratic press celebrated his victory, and Price served briefly as military governor of Chihuahua. By October 1848 he was back home, enjoying the praise of supporters from President James Polk to the local press.

In 1852 Price was elected governor of Missouri. In national politics he was a Douglas Democrat, a nationalist who supported a transcontinental railroad on a central route to unify the nation, and who regarded popular sovereignty as the only constitutional solution to the question of slavery in the territories. Within the state Price favored a conservative policy of funding major railroad lines through equal contributions from state and private funds. He saw public support of local lines as a dangerous overextension of the state's credit, and considered the governor's role that of watchdog over the legislature. He relentlessly vetoed pork-barrel legislation, which secured him the respect and affection of Missouri voters while alienating the state's political leadership.

Price supported the 1854 Kansas-Nebraska Act, hoping for a peaceful resolution to the question of slavery in the territories. As opposing forces massed to claim Kansas, the Boonslick Democrats supplied the initial proslavery leadership and much of its rank and file. Price sympathized with them, but regarded their methods as a threat to national unity. He feared the abolitionists even more, believing their ultimate goal to be the subversion of the Constitution and the destruction of the American government and institutions. Consequently, while he declined to aid the Missourians then moving into Kansas, he did nothing to hinder them or to suppress the ensuing violence along the border.

During this time state political leadership fell increasingly into extremists' hands, and moderates such as Price were shunted aside. In January 1857 he gladly relinquished the governorship, returning to his neglected tobacco business and a project to prove that local railroad lines could be built with local funds. As president of the Chariton and Randolph County Railroad Company, he threw his resources and prestige into raising private capital to build the line. As a result, he neglected his own financial affairs, and the economic depression following the panic of 1857 nearly ruined him. Friends secured him an appointment as state bank commissioner, and the salary eased his financial difficulties and allowed him to take again an active role in state affairs.

In January 1861, as Southern states seceded from the Union, Gov. **Claiborne Fox Jackson** called for a state convention to determine Missouri's position. Voters overwhelmingly elected Unionists to the convention. Conditional Unionists, such as Sterling Price, hoped for compromise to prevent war, and regarded secession as a desperate last resort, to be employed only after all other remedies to preserve the Union while protecting the constitutional rights of the states had failed. Price was easily elected president of the convention meeting in St. Louis through February and March 1861. He presided over the passage of resolutions calling for union, peace, and compromise between North and South, and constitutional amendments to protect the rights of minority states.

St. Louis politician **Frank Blair,** determined to force Missouri into active support for the Union, organized a paramilitary unit he called the Home Guards, drawing primarily on pro-Union Germans in St. Louis. He convinced Capt. **Nathaniel Lyon** to muster these men into federal service. On May 10, 1861, Blair and Lyon used the Home Guards to arrest Missouri militiamen then gathered for their annual spring training at Camp Jackson, a bivouac near St. Louis. The Home Guards marched their prisoners through the streets of St. Louis, provoking a riot in which Guardsmen shot and killed at least twenty-eight unarmed civilians.

The event outraged pro-Southern Missourians. Price, who witnessed the disaster, hurried to Jefferson City to offer the governor his services. Although secessionists within the state government distrusted Price's moderate stance, they recognized his tremendous prestige and popularity. Somewhat reluctantly, Governor Jackson appointed him major general in command of the militia, or State Guard. Price immediately met with federal commander Maj. Gen. **William S. Harney** to draft a truce between Unionist and state forces. Blair used his Washington connections to have the conservative Harney replaced by the radical Lyon. State and federal officers met again in St. Louis on June 11; the meeting ended when Lyon declared war on the state of Missouri.

On June 15 Lyon captured Jefferson City, forcing the government to flee the capital. On June 18 he scattered state forces at Boonville. Price rallied the State Guard at Lexington, where he was attempting to repel Kansas raiders. Federal forces from Kansas, Iowa, and St. Louis converged on his position, but Price and his men slipped their trap. While Governor Jackson led the State Guard's withdrawal southward, Price rode to Arkansas and won the support of Confederate forces under Brig. Gen. Ben McCulloch. When Lyon rashly attacked the combined Missouri-Confederate forces at Wilson's Creek (Oak Hills) on August 10, 1861, the federals were routed, leaving their commander dead on the battlefield. The victorious allies briefly occupied nearby Springfield, then McCulloch returned to Arkansas, and Price struck north to clear the western counties of Kansas marauders, gather recruits, and secure the Missouri River. He trapped a federal army at Lexington and forced the surrender of thirty-five hundred men. Federal forces massed against him, and Price's outnumbered State Guard was once again forced to retreat southward.

Meanwhile, Governor Jackson convened the state legislature at Neosho on October 20, 1861, where it quickly passed an ordinance of secession. On November 28 the Confederate Congress admitted Missouri as the twelfth member of the Confederate States of America. Price's victories and skillful retreats were widely publicized throughout the South, bringing him considerable popular acclaim. He was praised as another George Washington, whose leadership sprang from natural ability, good sense, and personal courage rather than the paper degree of a military academy. At odds with popular sentiment, President Jefferson Davis and the West Point–trained officers on whom he relied disdained such amateur soldiers and showed little interest in defending Missouri or the critical Mississippi Valley. When Price was forced from Missouri to Arkansas in February 1862 by overwhelming federal numbers and the lack of Confederate support, he became a symbol for Davis's political opponents of all that was wrong with the president's conduct of the war.

In early March, McCulloch and Price joined forces under Maj. Gen. Earl Van Dorn to attack federal forces at Pea Ridge (Elkhorn Tavern), Arkansas. The Confederates were defeated and again retreated southward. As in his previous battles, Price's reckless courage in battle and his concern for his men (though himself shot in the arm, Price personally looked after his wounded during the retreat) intensified the soldiers' admiration for the fatherly leader they affectionately called "Old Pap."

Before Van Dorn could regroup to resume the offensive, the Davis administration virtually abandoned the trans-Mississippi states, concentrating all western units on the east side of the river. Price was commissioned a major general in the Confederate army and ordered to Memphis with his men. He promised his "boys" that they would soon return, pledging that their government would not ask them to sacrifice their lives far from home while their beloved state fell prey to an army of occupation.

Davis, however, had apparently given up the struggle for Missouri. In June 1862 Price met the president in Richmond. The two men quarreled violently; Price offered his resignation, but Davis could not let Price leave the army. There was talk in Richmond of making the popular Missourian the next president, or the head of a military junta to replace Davis. There were rumors of Price's interest in a proposed "Northwestern Confederacy" independent of either Confederate or federal governments. Davis made enough concessions to pacify Price and keep his Missourians east of the Mississippi.

In September 1862 Price captured a large federal supply depot at Iuka, Mississippi. The federals moved quickly to encircle him, but, as Gen. William Rosecrans warned, Price was "an old woodpecker" impossible to trap. The Missourian escaped with his men and the stockpiled supplies. He rejoined Van Dorn for an assault on Corinth, where the Confederates were defeated with terrible losses. Price's Missouri Brigade was celebrated as one of the finest units to serve in either army during the war, but the men's lives were squandered in fierce and hopeless assaults on impregnable enemy positions. Time and again they nearly carried the day, charging headlong against overwhelming odds, only to be thrown back at the last when promised support never came. After the bloody fight at Corinth, Price wept openly for the hundreds of "his boys" who lay dead or dying on the Mississippi battlefield.

In March 1863 Price was sent to Arkansas to command a division under Maj. Gen. Theophilus Holmes while his men remained in Mississippi. Davis relied on Price's popularity to raise another army in Arkansas and Missouri. Federal officials also recognized the power of his leadership, and offered him a full pardon if he returned to Missouri and took an oath of loyalty to the Union. Instead, Price went to work recruiting men and improving the living conditions of those already in service.

In early July Price and his recruits joined Holmes's ill-conceived attack on the federal stronghold at Helena, Arkansas, where the Confederates were repulsed with heavy losses. In March and April 1864 Price rallied and drove the enemy from Camden, pursued them to a hard fight at Jenkins Ferry, and pushed them back to Little Rock.

Price then launched his long-awaited offensive. On September 19, 1864, he crossed into Missouri with twelve thousand men, mostly raw recruits, and many unarmed. After a bitter fight to take Fort Davidson at Pilot Knob, Price lacked the manpower to seize his main objective, St. Louis, and so turned toward Jefferson City. As federal troops massed against him, he again diverted his march westward along the river.

With federal armies converging on him from all directions, Price fought his way across the Little Blue on October 20–21, 1864. After a hard fight his army crossed the Big Blue at Byram's Ford on October 22. Federal troops closed in at Westport on October 23, and the subsequent battle was the largest of the trans-Mississippi war, engaging forty-five thousand men. Although heavily outnumbered, Price saved the bulk of his army and supply train, retreating through Kansas and Indian Territory to Arkansas. The 1864 raid achieved Confederate military objectives in diverting federal troops and relieving pressure on other sectors, but failed to reestablish a Confederate state government in Missouri. There would be no second chance: a treaty terminating hostilities in the trans-Mississippi department was signed at Shreveport on May 26, 1865. In early June Price and other Missouri Confederates set out for Mexico rather than accept surrender.

Price led in establishing the largest Confederate colony in Mexico. As Emperor Maximilian's regime weakened, this progovernment settlement situated in the Cordova valley west of Vera Cruz made an easy target for rebels and outlaws, and could not be sustained. Broken in health and fortune, Price returned to Missouri in January 1867. As a gesture of reconciliation, his old enemy Frank Blair offered him a presidential pardon. Price replied simply, "I have no pardon to ask."

Price and his family settled in a house purchased by friends with the donations of thousands of Missourians, a token of their devotion to their former leader. In the spring he opened a commission business with his sons in St. Louis, but the old soldier's health steadily declined. On September 29, 1867, General Price died. He was buried in Bellefontaine Cemetery, with the largest funeral procession St. Louis had ever seen.

To many Missourians, Price represented heroism, a reluctant secession forced by Northern aggression, and self-sacrificing patriotism through all the hardship of war. In 1911 his admirers petitioned the state legislature for five thousand dollars, part of the governor's salary that Price never collected. That sum with private donations was spent in erecting a monument to the general's memory in his old hometown of Keytesville.

MARY ELLEN ROWE

Castel, Albert. *General Sterling Price and the Civil War in the West.* Baton Rouge: Louisiana State University Press, 1968.

Rea, Ralph R. *Sterling Price: The Lee of the West.* Little Rock: Pioneer Press, 1959.

Shalhope, Robert E. *Sterling Price: Portrait of a*

Southerner. Columbia: University of Missouri Press, 1971.

PRICE, THOMAS LAWSON
(1809–1870)

Thomas Lawson Price was born on January 19, 1809, near Danville, Virginia. Although he was the son of a wealthy plantation owner, he received only a rudimentary education. At the age of twenty he inherited a large estate and many slaves, a large part of which he sold. In 1830 he was married to Lydia Bolton and moved to Missouri the following year. Traveling with Price and his wife were several relatives and slaves. Originally, he had intended to settle in St. Louis but changed his plans to avoid the Asiatic cholera epidemic plaguing that city. This circumstance prompted him to continue his migration up the Missouri River to Jefferson City where he lived the remainder of his life.

Wisely investing capital from the sale of his Virginia lands, Price purchased both the City and the Central Hotels. In 1838 he received the mail contract to St. Louis, founding a stage line between there and Jefferson City. Later, he promoted stage lines to other parts of the state. While much engaged in his business ventures, Price, a member of the Democratic Party, ran for the office of state treasurer in 1838. Although defeated, he was not deterred from running for mayor in Jefferson City. In this effort he was successful and became Jefferson City's first mayor, a position that he held from 1839 to 1842.

In 1847 Price was commissioned major general of the Sixth Division of the Missouri militia and in 1849 was elected lieutenant governor, serving during the administration of **Austin A. King.** Price was an enthusiastic supporter of Sen. **Thomas Hart Benton,** who was then unpopular with many Missouri Democrats for his opposition to the spread of slavery to the western territories. One of Price's duties as lieutenant governor was to preside over the state senate. In this position he exerted his influence in favor of Benton's stand against the Jackson Resolutions, named after their chief proponent, **Claiborne Fox Jackson.** These measures proclaimed Missouri's support of the South in its determination to maintain slavery and its right to extend the institution into the federal territories. Benton feared that this policy would ultimately lead to Southern secession.

In 1851 Price presided over a joint session of the General Assembly when Benton ran for reelection to the United States Senate. Because of the Democratic Party split, **Henry S. Geyer,** a Whig, was elected after forty ballots. During this volatile election, Price impartially maintained order, though he was deeply disappointed by the legislature's decision.

In 1856 the Democratic Party sent separate delegations representing the Benton and the anti-Benton factions to the Democratic National Convention in Cincinnati. Price headed the Benton delegation and led them into the convention hall despite attempts to bar them from entering. On the convention floor he exchanged blows with those trying to keep him and other Benton delegates out and demanded to be heard. The president of the convention agreed to give them a hearing to determine which Missouri delegation should properly represent the state. A committee on credentials was established for that purpose, but Price and his fellow Benton delegates were not allowed back into the convention hall.

Before the Civil War Price expanded his business activities into manufacturing and mercantile pursuits. In addition, he was one of the incorporators of the Capital City Bank and president of the Jefferson Land Company. While serving as lieutenant governor he supported state aid for the building of railroads. He also participated as a large contractor on the Missouri and Kansas Pacific Railroads. As one of the fund commissioners of the Missouri Pacific, he participated in the extension of the railroad from Denver to Cheyenne.

In 1861 Price was appointed brigadier general of volunteers and was placed in command of Jefferson City, serving in that capacity until 1862. He resigned that position after his election to the United States Congress, filling the seat left vacant by John W. Reid's expulsion from the House of Representatives.

Price ran for governor in 1864 largely to protest the usurpation of citizens' civil and political rights by the military authorities. One such measure, the voter registration law, disfranchised much of the public, especially Democrats, and prevented his election. In 1868 Price was elected as a delegate to the Democratic National Convention supporting New York's governor, Horatio Seymour, and served as one of the convention's vice presidents.

Until his death on July 15, 1870, in Jefferson City, Price continued to manage his many business ventures, leaving behind a large estate to his second wife, Caroline V. Long, whom he had married in 1854 after the death of his first wife in 1849.

DENNIS K. BOMAN

Biographical Dictionary of the United States Congress, 1774–1989. Bicentennial ed. S.v. "Price, Thomas Lawson." Washington, D.C.: U.S. Government Printing Office, 1989.

Ford, James E. *A History of Jefferson City, Missouri's State Capital, and of Cole County.* Jefferson City, Mo.: New Day Press, 1938.

Hodge, J. W., Jr. *The United States Biographical Dictionary and Portrait Gallery of Eminent and*

Self-Made Men, Missouri Volume. Kansas City, Mo.: Ramsey, Millett, and Hudson, 1878.

Price, Thomas Lawson. *Valedictory of Lieut. Gov. T. L. Price, Delivered to the Senate January 3, 1853.* Jefferson City, Mo.: James Lusk, 1853.

PRICE, VINCENT (1911–1993)

Vincent Price, a versatile actor of stage, screen, and television, was born in St. Louis, Missouri, on May 27, 1911. One of four children born to Vincent Leonard and Margaret Cobb Price, he had a pedigree that included being the descendant of Peregrine White, the first colonial child born in Massachusetts. His father, a wealthy candy maker, was the president of the National Candy Company. The family wealth shaped young Vincent's life and future career. He was able to attend private schools, travel to Europe at age sixteen, and in 1933 graduate from Yale University with a B.A. degree in fine arts and English.

Convinced from an early age that he would like to be an actor, Price sought theater work in New York following his graduation from Yale. Unsuccessful, he took a position as an apprentice teacher at the Riverdale Country Day School. With financial assistance from his family he decided to go to London for further study. In England he studied fine arts at London University and the Courtauld Institute. Although he had failed to launch his acting career in New York, Price was still a theater buff. He was able to secure a small part in a production of *Chicago* at the Gate Theater and made his stage debut on March 13, 1935. He then won the role of Prince Albert in the West End production of *Victoria Regina* and was such a hit that the play's producer retained him for the same role on Broadway opposite Helen Hayes. The play ran at the Broadhurst Theater until June 1937.

Price had begun an acting career that would span more than fifty years. In 1938 he accepted his first Hollywood offer to appear in a film, *Service DeLuxe,* with Constance Bennett. In December 1938 he returned to Broadway in *Outward Bound.* Gathering further stage experience with Orson Welles's *Mercury Theatre* and in summer stock, he continued playing a variety of parts. In 1940 he was called back to Broadway to star in *Angel Street.*

From Broadway Price moved again to Hollywood where he established a permanent residence. Under contract to Twentieth Century Fox he appeared in many films, including *Song of Bernadette, Wilson, Leave Her to Heaven, Dragonwyck,* and, most notably, *Laura,* in the role of Shelby Carpenter. As a freelance actor he also appeared in *Up in Central Park, The Three Musketeers,* and *Son of Sinbad.* During this period he also worked for RKO and Republic Pictures.

In 1947 Universal-International signed Price to a long-term contract. With his six-foot-four frame, well-spoken English, and highly bred demeanor, he gave performances that were always singled out favorably by the critics, though the films themselves were not. Price's reputation as a master of the macabre was established in 1953 with his appearance in the three-dimensional horror movie *House of Wax.* Although he subsequently appeared in a variety of films, numerous New York stage productions, and summer-stock theaters, his name would always be synonymous with a lengthy roster of villains.

Along with his acting career, Price never lost his lifelong interest in art. He bought his first work, a Rembrandt etching, at age twelve for $37.50. He became an authentic art expert and appeared as a legitimate finalist on television's *$64,000 Challenge.* An avid collector, his private art collection came to be valued at more than $5 million. As an art expert he served as an art-buying consultant for the Sears Company during the 1960s. For more than forty years Price donated works to the Vincent Price Gallery of East Los Angeles College.

In film Price's most fruitful union was with Roger Corman, who starred him in a series of Gothic tales inspired by Edgar Allan Poe. Appearing with Price were such great horror-film stars as Boris Karloff, Peter Lorre, and Lon Chaney Jr. *The House of Usher, The Pit and the Pendulum,* and *The Raven* would all become classics of the genre. Villainy became Price's destiny, and though some may have been critical of his film roles, he said, "I'm not the least bit disappointed that I'm remembered primarily for my horror roles."

Throughout his later years Price appeared in television commercials, as a panel member of *Hollywood Squares,* and as one of the voices in the Disney feature *The Great Mouse Detective.* Between film and television appearances he toured in a one-man show portraying Oscar Wilde and made frequent appearances on the lecture platform, which made him familiar to college audiences. Away from acting Price wrote several books on his other two loves, art and cooking. One on art, *I Like What I Know,* was very popular, and his *Treasury of Great Recipes* sold more than 350,000 copies.

In an acting career that spanned fifty years he worked with artists as diverse as Cecil B. DeMille and Elvis Presley. His willingness to work with teen idols from Frankie Avalon to Michael Jackson won him a new generation of fans, as did his appearance as a regular on the *Batman* series on television. Toward the end of his life he exploited his reputation as the "Gable of Gothic" by contributing a ghostly voice on Michael Jackson's hit record *Thriller* and playing in his last film in 1990 as the creator in *Edward Scissorhands.*

Once described as a modern Renaissance man who dedicated his life to the arts, in 1990 Price was honored by the American Cinematheque with a retrospective of his work. For many years Price served on the board of directors of the Los Angeles Museum of Art and also the Latin Arts and Crafts Board. He was a member of the Elizabethan Club, the Yale Club, the Board of the Archives of American Art, the Whitney Museum Friends of American Art, the Royal Academy of Arts, the Fine Arts Commission for the White House, and numerous other organizations.

Price savored acting and dismissed people who looked down on his horror-film roles. In 1986 he observed, "People remember you as someone who is working for their pleasure. A man came up to me and said, 'Thank you for all the nice times you've given me.' That's really what it's all about." Price added, "I feel that I've had a good life. I haven't been as successful as some people, but I've certainly had more fun."

In 1974 Price wed the actress Coral Browne and remained with her until her death in 1991. Price's previous marriages to actress Edith Barrett from 1938 to 1948 and to designer Mary Grant from 1949 to 1973 ended in divorce. The veteran of more than one hundred films, two thousand television shows, and one thousand radio programs died at his Hollywood Hills home on October 25, 1993, from lung cancer.

ALFRED E. TWOMEY

Current Biography Yearbook. New York: H. W. Wilson, 1956.

Katz, Ephraim. *Film Encyclopedia.* New York: G. P. Putnam's Sons, 1979.

Parish, James Robert, and Steven Whitney. *Vincent Price Unmasked.* New York: Drake, 1947.

PULITZER, JOSEPH (1847–1911)

Born in Mako, Hungary, on April 10, 1847, to a Jewish grain merchant, Philip Pulitzer (born Politzer), and a Roman Catholic mother, Louise Berger, Joseph spent his formative years in Budapest. At the age of seventeen, he left home to realize his childhood dream of becoming a professional soldier. Like **Harry S. Truman,** Pulitzer suffered from weak eyes and an underdeveloped body that caused French and Austrian officers to reject him before an American agent recruited the young Hungarian into the Union army in 1864 to fight in the Civil War.

That fall Pulitzer sailed for the United States where he enlisted in the First Cavalry unit organized by **Carl Schurz,** named after Abraham Lincoln, and staffed mostly by Germans. Leaving the army in July 1865 after fighting in four brief skirmishes, he emigrated to St. Louis, Missouri's growing German community on the Mississippi River.

St. Louis was a city in turmoil and experienced several damaging setbacks just as Pulitzer arrived. Its chief rival for urban supremacy in the Midwest, Chicago, was cutting railroads into St. Louis's northern market area. Second, the Civil War severed river traffic to and from its potentially lucrative but now devastated southern hinterland. Finally, St. Louis seemed to lack entrepreneurial and political leadership as businessmen and politicians wallowed in corruption, crime, and vice, while the masses suffered in poverty.

In 1867 Pulitzer became a naturalized citizen and one year later obtained a position reporting the news for the *Westliche Post* following three years of manual labor. He immediately seized the opportunity to promote his new hometown and expose "evil" wherever it existed. Pulitzer's writing became a harbinger of the muckraking symbolic of the later Progressive movement as he excoriated St. Louis's pretentious upper class, revealed governmental and political corruption, and lamented the hopelessness of life in the slums.

Reforming the city proved more difficult than pulling himself out of poverty. Eventually, Pulitzer's knack for sensational writing would make him a millionaire—one of America's "nouveau riche," but never a robber baron. Noblesse oblige eventually became his credo: he would serve and protect the masses not only from "predatory plutocracy" but also from "predatory poverty."

Pulitzer was not content merely to describe the news. His reputation as a journalistic tribune enabled him to win a seat in the Missouri legislature as a member of Carl Schurz's Liberal Republicans in 1869. The Liberal Republicans named Pulitzer secretary of their 1872 national convention that nominated Horace Greeley. In 1875 Pulitzer became a key figure in the convention that rewrote the Missouri Constitution. Disappointed with the scandals that permeated the administration of President **Ulysses S. Grant** and conservative trends within the Republican Party, Pulitzer became a Democrat and campaigned for Samuel J. Tilden in 1876.

During the late 1870s Pulitzer combined two of the city's dailies, the *St. Louis Post* and the nearly defunct *St. Louis Dispatch.* In the first issue of the *Post and Dispatch* (he renamed it the *Post-Dispatch* a short time later), Pulitzer announced that his newspaper would support only "the people . . . will oppose all frauds and shams . . . will advocate principles and ideas rather than prejudices and partisanship . . . true, genuine, real democracy . . . true local government . . . hard money, home rule and revenue reform." Within three years his sensationalistic approach to muckraking journalism transformed the *Post-Dispatch* into a profitable enterprise making $85,000 annually.

Five years later Pulitzer duplicated his feat in an even more competitive market when he purchased the *New York World* from Jay Gould for $346,000 on May 10, 1883. Three years later it turned a $500,000 profit. Not content, he created the *Evening World* in 1887, which also became a highly lucrative enterprise. In New York, as in St. Louis, Pulitzer advocated the "aristocracy of labor" while attacking luxuries, inheritances, monopolies, and special interests and pushing civil service reform and the elimination of corrupt urban machines. Eventually, he developed a style one critic termed *yellow journalism* in order to compete with his rising young rival, William Randolph Hearst. This struggle for supremacy resulted in the escalating rhetoric that contributed to the U.S. declaration of war against Spain in 1898.

Pulitzer's controversial political writing and analysis continued to the end of his life. He feared no governmental leader, no matter how powerful—not even a president as popular as Theodore Roosevelt, whom he criticized for instigating Panama's uprising against Colombia. During the ensuing controversy, Pulitzer held fast to his position as Roosevelt blasted the newspaperman for his muckraking.

Gradually the years of doing battle with the political giants took their toll as Pulitzer slowly withdrew from journalism. Never in good health, he steadily declined after the age of forty. Nearly blind, he died on his yacht just off the South Carolina coast on October 29, 1911. His will stipulated that the two newspapers, the *New York World* and the *St. Louis Post-Dispatch*, always remain family property. Unfortunately, his sons mismanaged the *World* and succeeded in breaking the judicial order that forbade them from selling the paper. The *Post-Dispatch*, however, has continued under family control throughout the twentieth century. Although right-wing critics have attacked the paper as a bastion of liberalism, it began printing conservative as well as liberal analyses after the fall of its principal rival, the *St. Louis Globe-Democrat*, in the 1980s. Generally, however, the *Post-Dispatch* carefully adhered to the ideology Pulitzer placed in its "platform" on April 10, 1907:

I know that my retirement will make no difference in its cardinal principles, that it will always fight for progress and reform, never tolerate injustice or corruption, always fight demagogues of all parties, never belong to any party, always oppose privileged classes and public plunderers. Never lack sympathy with the poor, always remain devoted to the public welfare, never be satisfied with merely printing news, always be drastically independent, never be afraid to attack wrong, whether by predatory plutocracy or predatory poverty.

Joseph Pulitzer was one of America's greatest journalists who founded the concept of the modern American newspaper. His sustained crusades for honest government and against corruption in all forms established a model for all newspapers to follow. Although Pulitzer's historical reputation suffered because he allowed his competitive instincts to descend into "yellow journalism," his philosophy that the first rule of American journalism is to ensure the survival of American democracy remains his principal legacy. He also endowed the Columbia University Journalism School and the esteemed Pulitzer Prize in journalism, letters, drama, and music.

J. CHRISTOPHER SCHNELL

Barrett, James W. *Joseph Pulitzer and His World.* New York: Vanguard Press, 1941.
Noble, Iris. *Joseph Pulitzer: Front-Page Pioneer.* New York: Messner, 1957.
Swanberg, W. A. *Pulitzer.* New York: Scribner's, 1967.

PULITZER, JOSEPH, II (1885–1955)

Editor and publisher of the *St. Louis Post-Dispatch*, Joseph Pulitzer II, a communications pioneer, was born in New York City on March 21, 1885, the second child of Joseph and Kate Pulitzer. The elder Pulitzer (his children referred to him as "Old J. P."), a Hungarian immigrant, became a successful journalist by purchasing several newspapers and creating the awards that bear his name.

"Young Joe" Pulitzer attended Harvard, but a poor academic record prompted his father to insist that he withdraw from the university during his sophomore year to begin an apprenticeship at the *World*, a New York newspaper owned by the family. Subsequently, the elder Pulitzer sent his son to St. Louis in 1906 with a note to the editor of the *Post-Dispatch:* "This is my son Joseph. Will you try to knock some newspaper sense into his head?"

From 1906 to 1911 Pulitzer served an apprenticeship at the *Post-Dispatch*. Although the apprentice often antagonized the elder Pulitzer, he won his father's approval by punching Randolph Hearst in the stomach because the renowned publisher had been critical of "Old J. P."

In 1912, following the death of his father, Joseph Pulitzer became president of the Pulitzer Publishing Company, and he remained in St. Louis to publish the *Post-Dispatch* for the next forty-three years. During his tenure the *Post-Dispatch* became one of the nation's most highly regarded newspapers.

As a journalist Pulitzer adopted his father's credo: "never tolerate injustice or corruption, always fight demagogues of all parties . . . always be drastically independent." As Daniel Pfaff, author of *Joseph Pulitzer and the "Post-Dispatch"* stated: "he saw the purpose of his professional life as a continuity of commitment to liberal, independent journalism in a constitutional democracy." This commitment sometimes resulted in disputes between the publisher and his staff. Pulitzer usually sought objective, dignified, and hard-hitting coverage, but he occasionally restrained staff members who wanted to take positions more radical than he could support. Accordingly, four of his editors resigned in the 1930s and 1940s because of disagreements with Pulitzer. The publisher usually supported Democratic Party candidates for national office, though he endorsed Republicans Alf Landon in 1936 and Thomas Dewey in 1948 for the presidency.

In the 1920s the *Post-Dispatch* demonstrated its commitment to investigative journalism, prompting the U.S. Senate to reopen its inquiry of the Teapot Dome scandals of the Harding administration. In 1929 Pulitzer took the initiative in launching a campaign against fraudulent or misleading medical and health-care advertising. The *Post-Dispatch* rejected millions of dollars of questionable advertising and pioneered in advertising censorship in the public interest.

The *Post-Dispatch* won five Pulitzer Prizes for meritorious public service, and six staff members received the prize for individual achievements. Although he was a member of the advisory board on Pulitzer Prizes, Joseph always withdrew temporarily from the board when his newspaper became a candidate for an award.

Pulitzer also demonstrated his innovative spirit by anticipating a trend toward electronic journalism. Beginning in 1922 he invested company funds in radio station KSD. In 1947 his firm purchased a television station, KSD-TV, making the Pulitzer Publishing Company a major force across the entire communications spectrum.

In April 1945 Gen. Dwight Eisenhower invited Pulitzer to join a team of journalists to inspect the newly liberated Nazi concentration camps. Deeply disturbed by what he saw, Pulitzer returned to exhibit photographs of the camps and their victims and called for swift justice for those responsible for the atrocities.

Pulitzer usually shunned personal publicity, though he occasionally sought the limelight when he believed freedom of the press was threatened. For example, when the court fined and jailed two members of his staff for printing editorials and a cartoon critical of a St. Louis judge, Pulitzer, with considerable fanfare, successfully appealed to the Missouri Supreme Court.

Pulitzer inherited his father's impaired vision. Ultimately, he lost vision in his left eye and had only 20 percent vision in his right eye. He coped by having secretaries read to him several hours each day. In spite of his visual handicap, he devoted his leisure time to family outdoor activities, including yachting, swimming, fishing, and hiking.

Pulitzer died of a ruptured abdominal blood vessel on March 31, 1955. His second wife, two sons, and two daughters survived him. His ashes were scattered over Frenchman's Bay, near the family home at Bar Harbor, Maine.

JACK B. RIDLEY

Dictionary of American Biography. Supp. 5, 1951–1955. S.v. "Pulitzer, Joseph, II."

New York Times, April 3, 1955.

Pfaff, Daniel W. *Joseph Pulitzer II and Advertising Censorship, 1929–1939.* Journalism Monographs Series 77. Columbia, S.C.: Association for Education in Journalism, 1982.

———. *Joseph Pulitzer II and the "Post-Dispatch":* *A Newspaperman's Life.* University Park: Pennsylvania State University Press, 1991.

St. Louis Post-Dispatch, March 31, 1955.

QUANTRILL, WILLIAM CLARKE (1837–1865)

William Clarke Quantrill, a Confederate guerrilla, was born in Dover, Ohio, on July 31, 1837, to Thomas Henry Quantrill, a school principal, and Caroline Clarke Quantrill. At sixteen he graduated from high school and began teaching in the Dover school. Some months later, on December 7, 1854, his father died of consumption, plunging the family into poverty. Wishing to "make his fortune" so he could help his mother and siblings, Quantrill journeyed to Illinois and Indiana but found employment only as a bookkeeper and a teacher. Discouraged, he returned home, taught school again, and then went to Kansas Territory, where he eked out a living. He was a keen observer of the conflict between abolitionists, Free State advocates, and Southerners over whether the territory would enter the Union as a slave or a free state; although he sympathized with the Free Staters, he did not become involved.

In the spring of 1858 Quantrill signed on as a teamster for an expedition to resupply federal troops in Utah Territory fighting the Mormons. Many of the other teamsters were Southern fanatics who had come to Kansas from the Deep South to join in the struggle. Some would become Quantrill's lifelong friends and members of his guerrilla band. During the year he spent in their company traveling to Utah and back to Kansas, he was converted to their point of view.

Quantrill next taught school in eastern Kansas, but in the spring of 1860, dejected and poor, he gave up the dream of making his fortune in the West and decided to return to Dover. However, he first went to Lawrence where he encountered "border ruffians." Perhaps because they were like the teamsters who had befriended him on the Utah expedition and they shared his newfound political beliefs—and knew how to get their hands on money, albeit disreputably or illegally—he joined their band. Over the next eight months he stole livestock and participated in the returning of one runaway slave to his owner for the reward, the selling of another runaway, and an attempt to capture a number of others.

After a Douglas County grand jury indicted him on several charges, Quantrill was forced into hiding. In December 1860 he led a party of five white abolitionists to the Jackson County, Missouri, farm of wealthy slave owner Morgan Walker. The abolitionists intended to liberate Walker's slaves and steal his horses, but Quantrill surreptitiously arranged an ambush with Walker's son, Andrew, and then led the abolitionists into it. One was killed outright; the other four escaped, but two were subsequently hunted down and killed by Quantrill, Morgan Walker, and some neighbors. In setting the treacherous "Morgan Walker ambush," Quantrill was undoubtedly motivated by the five-thousand-dollar reward said to be offered for one of the abolitionists and may have wanted to ingratiate himself with Jackson County Southerners with whom he cast his lot.

After the war began Quantrill joined a Confederate company of Cherokee Indians who served under Gen. Benjamin McCulloch, notably at the Battle of Wilson's Creek. Quantrill subsequently enlisted as a private in Gen. **Sterling Price**'s army. He is said to have fought with "conspicuous daring" at the Battle of Lexington.

As Price retreated to Neosho, Quantrill returned to the Blue Springs area of Jackson County. He helped organize a Home Guard company of teenagers who sought to protect their neighborhood from raids by Kansas Jayhawkers; by the end of 1861 it had evolved into a fifteen-member guerrilla band with Quantrill as its leader.

As the band's reputation grew, new recruits were drawn to it, among them **Cole Younger** and **Frank James,** and at times it numbered a hundred men or more. Most recruits were teenagers, and Quantrill particularly wanted those who were single and motivated by revenge as the result of the harsh treatment meted out to themselves and their families by Jayhawkers and the federal militia. These attributes—extreme youth, lack of family responsibilities, and vengefulness—might make for reckless courage in battle, but they would seem to increase the likelihood of outrages.

In his early days as a guerrilla chieftain, Quantrill conducted himself honorably: he accepted surrenders, paroled prisoners, and forbade rape. He expected that he and his men would be treated as soldiers if captured until Gen. Henry W. Halleck, Union commander of the Department of Missouri, issued an order outlawing "bushwhackers," or guerrillas, and the federal military began summarily executing Quantrill's men. Quantrill immediately retaliated by killing prisoners and would later say that he felt "forced" into a "no quarter" type of warfare.

During 1862 "Quantrill's raiders" plundered

towns, skirmished with Union detachments, and waylaid the mails. Quantrill was formally commissioned as a captain under the Partisan Ranger Act of 1862, following the capture of Independence on August 11, 1862, for which victory he shared the credit with Confederate colonels Upton Hays and John T. Hughes.

Quantrill's activities during most of the summer of 1863 remain largely a mystery except for his planning of the audacious raid on Lawrence, Kansas, and his ongoing involvement with a beautiful Jackson County girl, Sarah "Kate" King. (In later years she said they were married, but others claimed she was his mistress.)

On August 13 a house in Kansas City that was being used by the federal military as a temporary prison for Southern girls, some of whom were relatives of Quantrill's raiders, collapsed, killing five and seriously injuring the rest. The guerrillas' conviction that the building had been undermined at the order of the military commander to murder the girls was one cause for the savagery of the Lawrence raid a week later. Among the others was that Lawrence was the headquarters for the Jayhawking bands that had made raids into western Missouri for years.

After snaking forty miles inside Kansas past patrols and garrisons, Quantrill struck Lawrence at dawn on August 21, leading a 450-man column: members of his own band and other guerrilla bands, Confederate army recruits, and Missouri civilians. Over the next four hours the raiders murdered approximately 200 men and teenage boys; nearly all were unarmed and unresisting, and often their womenfolk were pleading for their lives when the bullets struck. (On the other hand, in obedience to Quantrill's order issued just before the raid's commencement, no woman was raped or harmed. Quantrill killed no one and actually intervened to save some individuals.) The entire business district was burned as well as perhaps a hundred houses, resulting in a property loss estimated at $2 million in Civil War–era money. The massacre is considered the greatest atrocity of the Civil War.

During the raid Quantrill had remarked to Lawrencians that he had lost control of his men because so many had gotten drunk on looted liquor. Over the next six months some of his earliest followers would become disgusted with the degeneration of the band and leave; they were generally replaced by those attracted more by the prospects of plunder and violence than by loftier motives.

On October 6, while leading another amalgamated column to Texas, Quantrill routed the command of Gen. James G. Blunt, killing ninety-eight. Some who tried to surrender were murdered, and most of the wounded were dispatched.

In Sherman, Texas, during the winter of 1863–1864, Quantrill had an increasingly difficult time controlling his followers: they got drunk and shot up the town, and robbed storekeepers and even Confederate soldiers and sympathizers. Several robbery victims were murdered. On the journey back to Missouri, Quantrill was deposed at gunpoint by his lieutenant, George Todd, and left the band.

During the summer and fall of 1864, Todd and **William "Bloody Bill" Anderson** warred in western and central Missouri. Their escalating brutality culminated on September 27 in the "Centralia massacre": twenty-three unarmed soldiers were taken off a train, stripped to their underwear, and shot, and then their bodies were beaten with rifle butts and sabres; later in the day approximately one hundred recruits led by Maj. A. V. E. Johnston were routed and slaughtered, many after surrendering. Corpses were mutilated or decapitated, and at least one of the wounded was castrated.

After Todd and Anderson were killed in separate engagements, Quantrill emerged from seclusion, rallied the shattered remnant of his band, and, in December, took it south out of Missouri. The best evidence indicates he was headed for Virginia to fight under Robert E. Lee, but he became entangled in the guerrilla war being waged in north-central Kentucky. In mid-February 1865, after less than a month's sporadic fighting, he was driven into hiding.

Gen. John M. Palmer, the federal military commander of Kentucky, hired Edwin Terrell, a disreputable Union guerrilla, to hunt down Quantrill. Terrell ambushed Quantrill and his men on May 10, 1865, near Taylorsville, ironically while they were on their way to Louisville to surrender. Quantrill, shot in the back, was paralyzed. He died on June 6, 1865, at age twenty-seven. He was buried in Louisville's St. Mary's Catholic Cemetery.

In 1887 W. W. Scott, Quantrill's boyhood friend, robbed his grave. During the next 104 years the skull and various arm and leg bones were bartered, displayed in glass museum cases, and used in fraternity rituals. Today Quantrill's remains are buried in three graves in three states.

EDWARD E. LESLIE

Connelley, William E. Papers. Kansas State Historical Society, Topeka.
———. Papers. Western Historical Manuscript Collection, Denver Public Library, Denver.
Leslie, Edward E. *The Devil Knows How to Ride: The True Story of William Clarke Quantrill and His Confederate Raiders.* New York: Random House, 1996.

QUEENY, EDGAR MONSANTO (1897–1968)

Edgar Monsanto Queeny, a business executive, industrialist, and wildlife conservationist, served the

Monsanto Corporation as president from 1928 to 1943 and as chairman of the board from 1943 until 1960.

The son of John Francis and Olga Monsanto Queeny, Edgar was born in St. Louis on September 29, 1897, where he continued to reside for the remainder of his life. Four years after Edgar's birth, his father founded the Monsanto Chemical Company, the business Edgar would ultimately mold into a huge corporation.

When the United States entered World War I, Queeny interrupted his undergraduate studies at Cornell and joined the navy. Initially assigned to an overseas unit in Plymouth, England, Lieutenant Queeny completed his term of service as an instructor at a naval officers' training school at Mare Island, California.

After the war Queeny returned to Cornell University where he earned an A.B. degree in chemistry in 1919. Following graduation he married Ethel Schneider and began working at his father's establishment, the Monsanto Chemical Company. A five-year apprenticeship allowed Queeny to demonstrate his ample financial talents, and in 1924 he became vice president of the company.

In 1928 Queeny assumed the office of president of Monsanto. His father expressed concern about his son's penchant for innovation: "Edgar wants to change everything. He's going to ruin Monsanto." On the contrary, under Queeny's capable leadership for the next thirty-two years, the Monsanto Corporation became the third-largest chemical company in the United States and the fifth largest in the world. When Queeny retired in 1960 Monsanto produced chemicals, plastics, petroleum products, and man-made fibers in forty-four U.S. plants.

During World War II Queeny, alarmed by the federal government's increasing control over American business and industry, felt obliged to write a defense of private enterprise, *The Spirit of Enterprise.* Queeny saw himself as a crusader fighting against the intrusion of government policy into the private sector: "Thus I recognized my two selves: a crusading idealist and a cold, granitic believer in the law of the jungle." He delivered a salvo against the Roosevelt administration's drift toward "big government." Defending private enterprise, he called for a return to those laissez-faire principles he believed had provided America's historic business-industrial success. Sales of *The Spirit of Enterprise* elevated it to the nonfiction best-seller list for a few weeks in 1943, but its popularity was short-lived. As one reviewer put it, "this little book may one day serve as a document of the nineteenth-century . . . still flickering in the 1940s. . . . What is lacking in this book is any kind of solution."

Other than a commitment to private enterprise, Queeny maintained a lifelong passion for nature and its creatures. A recognized authority on wildlife, he wrote *Cheechako,* an account of an Alaskan bear hunt in 1941. In 1947 he published *Prairie Wings,* which is now recognized as a classic study of American wildfowl in flight.

In 1949 and 1952 Queeny, sponsored by the American Museum of Natural History, conducted safaris to Africa to film animals in their natural habitats. These journeys resulted in the production of six documentary films, including two theater releases, *Latuko* and *Wakamba.* Subsequently, Queeny produced films on Atlantic salmon, *Silver Lightning,* and on Alaskan wildlife, *The Great Country.* His interest in animals in their natural habitats led him to serve as a trustee of the American Museum of Natural History.

Although he was an active and influential member of Missouri's Republican Party, Queeny did not hesitate to attack party leaders when he felt they deserved criticism. For example, he openly scolded the Eisenhower administration for its materialist approach to American foreign policy, accusing State Department personnel of assuming that money could buy anything.

After retiring from the Monsanto Corporation, Queeny devoted much time to civic projects in St. Louis, serving as a director of the United Fund of Greater St. Louis, as chairman of the board of trustees of Barnes Hospital (the Queenys donated funds for construction of Queeny Tower at the hospital), and as a member the St. Louis Symphony Society. Queeny died in St. Louis on July 7, 1968, and is buried in Bellefontaine Cemetery in St. Louis.

JACK B. RIDLEY

New York Times, July 8, 1968.

Queeny, Edgar Monsanto. *Cheechako: The Story of an Alaskan Bear Hunt.* New York: Charles Scribner's Sons, 1941.

———. *Prairie Wings: Pen and Camera Flight Studies.* Philadelphia: Lippincott, 1947.

———. *The Spirit of Enterprise.* New York: Charles Scribner's Sons, 1943.

St. Louis Globe-Democrat, July 8, 1968.

R

RAMSAY, ROBERT LEE (1880–1953)

Robert Lee Ramsay, author of *Our Storehouse of Missouri Place Names,* born in Sumter, South Carolina, on December 14, 1880, was a professor of English at the University of Missouri in Columbia from 1907 to 1952 and a founding member of the American Name Society. With an A.B. from Fredericksburg College in Virginia in 1899 and a Ph.D. in English from Johns Hopkins University in 1905, he taught a variety of courses and published articles and books on literature, pedagogy, and place-name research.

As Ramsay developed a plan for a dictionary of Missouri place-names in the mid-1920s, he established a set of procedures for collecting information and classifying and describing the names of Missouri's towns, counties, and geographical features. Between 1928 and 1950 he directed seventeen M.A. theses and a preliminary doctoral study of place-names in the 114 Missouri counties and an M.A. thesis on the pronunciation of Missouri place-names. He also published monographs on the names in Boone and Franklin Counties.

Although Ramsay's plan for a dictionary has not been fulfilled, the results of his work on Missouri place-names is available to researchers. In 1945–1947 he prepared in quadruplicate four-by-six-inch card files, which are now located in the U.S. Geological Survey offices in Reston, Virginia, the Missouri State Archives in Jefferson City, the Western Historical Manuscripts Collection in Columbia, and the State Historical Society of Missouri in Columbia. Ramsay's correspondence and manuscripts are also deposited in the Western Historical Manuscripts Collection in Columbia. In 1988–1991 Ramsay's files, among other sources, were used in updating the Geographic Names Information System of the U.S. Geological Survey, a project that more than doubled the number of Missouri place-names in the survey's computerized files.

Robert Lee Ramsay died on December 14, 1953, in Columbia, Missouri.

Donald M. Lance

Ramsay, Robert L. *Our Storehouse of Missouri Place Names.* Columbia: University of Missouri Press, 1973.

———. "The Place-Names of Boone County, Missouri." *Publication of the American Dialect Society* 18 (1952).

———. "The Place-Names of Franklin County, Missouri." *University of Missouri Studies* 26:3 (1954).

Ramsay, Robert L., Allen Walker Read, and Esther Gladys Leech. "Introduction to a Survey of Missouri Place-Names." *University of Missouri Studies* 9:1 (January 1, 1934).

Schroeder, Walter A. *Bibliography of Missouri Geography.* Columbia: Extension Division, University of Missouri, 1977.

RAND, SALLY. *See* Beck, Helen Gould

RANDOLPH, VANCE (1892–1980)

Born in Pittsburg, Kansas, on February 23, 1892, Vance Randolph became an astute observer and recorder of Ozarkian folk culture. He moved to the vicinity of Pineville, Missouri, about 1923, and lived for most of his life in the Ozarks region bounded by Pineville; Galena, Missouri; Eureka Springs, Arkansas; and Fayetteville, Arkansas. Somewhat a maverick, Randolph personally sought ideas and functions outside the norm of his society, quickly observing differences among members of various social groups. This tendency would serve him in good stead as he noted the cultural characteristics of the Ozarkers of southwest Missouri among whom he lived.

Vance Randolph's economic mainstay was writing. While a graduate student working toward a Ph.D. in psychology at the University of Kansas, he wrote articles for the *Appeal to Reason,* a Socialist newspaper published in Girard, near his hometown of Pittsburg. He was a friend of Eugene V. Debs, and explored the range of Socialist thought during much of his life. In the same era, Randolph wrote articles on a variety of subjects that were published under pseudonyms. However, his writings on Ozarkian culture, beginning in the 1930s, composed his most important and most enduring legacy to folklore and cultural scholarship.

While Randolph's published accounts of Ozarkers are of inestimable value to folk culturists because he was among the first and certainly the most prolific of collectors and writers about Ozarkian culture, it is a fact that he preferred the unusual in his accounts. He chose to write about that segment of society living outside the mainstream of Ozarkian economic activity, the ridge dwellers; he had little to say about the relatively prosperous river-bottom farmers or town citizens. Therefore, his books, while entertaining, enlightening, and informative, are not always completely accurate and portray only segments of Ozarkian culture.

Books about the unusual sell better than those chronicling a more exact verbal portrait of society, and there is a certain air of "man bites dog" uniqueness in some of what Randolph wrote about Ozarkers. He always retained a keen interest in the way they lived, but the decades from 1930 to 1960 were financially lean years for him, and he apparently tailored his work to whatever book format sold best. While he was concerned about making a profit, he wrote largely about Ozark people who neither expected nor attained financial reward. These considerations aside, Randolph's body of published material about the culture of Ozarks mountain people is greater in scope and importance than that compiled by any of his regional contemporaries.

Randolph ranged widely over the Ozarks, collecting all aspects of folk culture. He was particularly interested in ballads and stories handed down from one generation to another in the typical oral tradition of relatively isolated Ozarkers of the early twentieth century. These collections of folklore became the basis for his best-known books. In all he authored 133 books and articles. Some of the works have a thin veneer of fiction making up their plots, but the incidents were generally true, or at least had been told to Randolph as truth.

Vance Randolph's background, observational skills, and natural inquisitiveness served him well. Although he never finished high school, his scholarly career included university studies in biology and philosophy, culminating with a master's degree in psychology from Clark University in Worcester, Massachusetts, in 1915. He later spent three years in graduate study in psychology at the University of Kansas, but did not complete his Ph.D. His lack of a terminal degree at times seemed to limit his opportunities for publication. During his most active years he never received a grant sufficient to allow full-time devotion to research and writing, nor did he enjoy assistance provided by student help. Folklorist William K. McNeil considers this as perhaps a blessing in disguise: Randolph personally collected every ballad, saying, and story in his publications, and therefore knew more about the region and its people than more scholarly writers might have. His work was eminently readable. His writing stood on its own merit, and had no traces of academic "dullness."

A proud man who traced his roots to the Virginia Randolphs, Vance occasionally showed flashes of temper. Before he established his national reputation as an expert on Ozarkian culture he worked briefly as a dialect adviser to a Hollywood film producer.

When told he was wrong on a point of dialect (by the producer who had never been to the Ozarks), Randolph angrily spat a great splotch of tobacco juice on the expensive office carpet and stalked out, never to return.

During most of his adult life, Randolph lived in and around Pineville, Missouri; in his later years he lived in Fayetteville, Arkansas. In 1930 he married Marie Wilbur, daughter of a Pineville, Missouri, physician. She died in 1938. During the 1940s Randolph lived for two years at Bonniebrook, home of Kewpie-doll creator **Rose O'Neill,** while collaborating on her autobiography. (The work was belatedly published in 1997.) Randolph married Mary Celeste Parler, a noted folklorist and English professor at the University of Arkansas in Fayetteville, in 1962.

Despite his impressive achievements in literary endeavors, Randolph received relatively few honors from the academic community. The University of Arkansas at Fayetteville awarded him an honorary doctorate in the late 1950s, and in 1978 the American Folklore Society elected him as a fellow. Ill and practically bedridden by that time, Randolph prized this honor above all others. With puckish humor he wrote to his friend Herbert Halpert, "This Fellow business has perked me up considerably, and Mary and I are truly grateful. If there is a ribbon goes with it, I'll sew it on my pajamas." Randolph would live two more years; he died on November 1, 1980.

Randolph's penchant for the unusual in society served him well as he observed natives in his adopted community. He clearly saw the unusual facets of Ozarkian lifestyle as a native of the region perhaps never could. His fascination for the irregular in life is probably best revealed in his handwritten notes on the back of a photograph in the Vance Randolph Collection of Lyon Library at the College of the Ozarks in Point Lookout, Missouri: "Uncle Jack Short, Galena, Missouri, 1940. One of his sons was **Dewey Short**, a Congressman. Another was Leonard Short, a bank-robber. I knew 'em and I liked Leonard best. I think Uncle Jack did too."

EDGAR D. McKINNEY

Cochran, Robert. *Vance Randolph: An Ozarks Life.* Urbana: University of Illinois Press, 1985.

Cochran, Robert, and Michael Luster. *For Love and for Money: The Writings of Vance Randolph, an Annotated Bibliography.* Batesville: Arkansas College Folklore Archive Publications, 1979.

Dorson, Richard M. "A Visit with Vance Randolph." *Journal of American Folklore* 67 (July 1954): 260.

Halpert, Herbert. "Obituary: Vance Randolph." *Journal of American Folklore* 94 (July–September 1981): 345–50.

Springfield Daily News, November 3, 1980.
Springfield News and Leader, November 9, 1980.

READ, DANIEL (1805–1878)

Daniel Read, sixth president of the University of Missouri, was born on June 24, 1805, in Marietta, Ohio. He attended private academies in Ohio and then went to Ohio University in Athens, graduating in 1824 with high honors. Immediately after graduation he began to teach at his alma mater, and for the next forty-two years he taught at the state universities of Ohio, Indiana, and Wisconsin. At Wisconsin he occupied the chair of mental philosophy, logic, rhetoric, and English literature. He served as president of Indiana University from 1853 to 1854.

After the death of **John Hiram Lathrop** (who served as the first and fifth presidents of the University of Missouri) in 1866, the board of curators offered the presidency to Read. Before accepting he visited Columbia to assess the university's prospects. He was discouraged by the general state of disrepair in which he found the institution and by the lack of public support—the legislature had yet to appropriate its first dollar for university operations. Even though he had not yet accepted the curators' offer, he taught Lathrop's courses during the fall semester and busied himself with preparing a report on the state of the university. He addressed the legislature, by invitation, in January 1867, urging support for the university's operations and expansion. He then returned to Wisconsin to await legislative action.

The legislature responded to Read's challenge by appropriating funds to rebuild the president's house (which had been destroyed by fire), repair the main building, and establish a normal school; the legislators also agreed to provide an annual appropriation from the general funds of the state. With these assurances, Read accepted the presidency and was inaugurated at the June 1867 commencement.

Read served as president until 1876, and transformed the institution from a college to a university. Under his leadership (and that of **James Sidney Rollins,** president of the board) the curators organized a normal school, a College of Law, and a School of Medicine. The College of Agriculture, established in response to the Morrill Act of 1862, was located in Columbia as a part of the university, an action that "saved" the university for Columbia. As part of the compromises that made this possible, the curators established a School of Mines and Metallurgy in Rolla. The legislature provided funds for the construction of a science building, and the improvement of the campus. Substantial improvements were made to the library, and Read recruited a number of outstanding faculty members, including Paul Schweitzer, who for thirty years devoted himself to teaching and research in chemistry.

One of Read's leading interests was the education of women, and during his administration women were first admitted to the university, initially to the normal school (Read argued, "Women are better teachers of children than men"), and then to all courses.

Despite Read's substantial contributions to the improvement and expansion of the university, the board of curators failed to renew his appointment when his term expired in 1876. Some argued that at seventy-one he was too old for the position, but as was true of a number of the early presidents of the university he was terminated in part for political reasons. At the time he was appointed his strong pro-Union views appealed to many legislators, but by the midseventies conservative Democrats, many of whom had supported slavery during the Civil War, were in control and they insisted that he be relieved.

Read died on October 3, 1878, in Keokuk, Iowa. Alice Brice, whom he had married in 1826, had died in 1874, but four of his children survived him. In recognition of Read's efforts to provide educational opportunities for women, the university named its first dormitory for women, completed in 1903, Read Hall.

JAMES C. OLSON

Olson, James C., and Vera Olson. *The University of Missouri: An Illustrated History.* Columbia: University of Missouri Press, 1988.

Read, Daniel. Papers. Western Historical Manuscripts Collection, Columbia.

Selby, P. O. "Daniel Read." In *Missouri College Presidents: Past and Present.* Kirksville: Northeast Missouri State University, 1971.

Stephens, Frank F. *A History of the University of Missouri.* Columbia: University of Missouri Press, 1962.

Viles, Jonas. *The University of Missouri: A Centennial History.* Columbia: University of Missouri, 1939.

REAM, VINNIE (1847–1914)

Vinnie Ream, sculptor and femme fatale, was born near Madison, Wisconsin, on September 25, 1847, the youngest of the three children of Robert and Lavinia Ream. Her father was a government surveyor who kept the family on the move throughout the antebellum West.

In 1854 Robert Ream was sent to survey land in Kansas, during which time he sent Vinnie to school in St. Joseph, Missouri, and, in 1857, to Christian College's academy in Columbia. A precocious student of pleasing personality, she displayed an unusual talent for art and music. These talents attracted the interest of the college president who brought her to the attention of **James Sidney Rollins,** an important Whig politician who had helped to found the school. Rollins would later prove an important patron.

Toward the end of 1858 Ream left the school to join her parents who had moved to Fort Smith, Arkansas. By the time she was twelve she had attracted a number of notable suitors, the most important of whom was Elias Cornelius Boudinot, a well-connected Democratic lawyer-journalist. An anglicized Cherokee Indian, Boudinot would win fame in his own right, and he became a leader of Cherokee Confederates during the Civil War. His passion for Ream proved lifelong. In 1871 he named the town of Vinita in what would become Oklahoma for her.

In Arkansas Robert Ream had left government service for private business, but without much success. In poor health, he moved to Washington, D.C., in early 1861 in search of new government employment. What he found was meager, and to help make ends meet Vinnie went to work at the post office. She also reestablished contact with James Rollins, now a Missouri congressman. Knowing of her ambition to become a sculptor, Rollins in 1863 took Ream to visit his friend Clark Mills, one of the most successful sculptors of the era. Like many others soon to follow, Ream quickly charmed Mills, and he offered to take her on as his assistant-pupil. Soon Mills began arranging minor commissions for Ream, and through these she met a number of powerful people within the Washington community.

Ream was ambitious and quickly set her sights high, indicating to others her desire to have President Lincoln sit for a bust. Again Rollins came to her assistance. Taking advantage of their old Whig Party acquaintanceship, and with the assistance of Illinois senator Orville Browning, he got Lincoln to agree. Thus, in late 1864 Ream began early-morning sculpting sessions as Lincoln worked quietly at his desk. She had essentially completed her work when Lincoln was assassinated on April 14, 1865.

In the wake of the canonization that followed Lincoln's death, Congress decided to offer a ten-thousand-dollar commission for the sculpting of an official statue of the martyred president. Given the climate, the money, and the project's high profile, America's best sculptors, including Hiram Powers, **Harriet Hosmer,** and Clark Mills, entered the competition. Another competitor was Vinnie Ream, who initiated a campaign of remarkable sophistication to win the commission. The key to her eventual success was the support of Radical Republican politician Thaddeus Stevens, who had previously sat for her for his own bust. Stevens, at the peak of his power, easily ramrodded her selection through the House of Representatives. Ream, however, had more trouble in the Senate due to the determined opposition of Charles Sumner. However, watching the proceedings on the arm of **William T. Sherman** from the visitors' gallery, she eventually found the necessary champions to secure the commission on July 28, 1866. The award made her not only the first woman to receive a federal art commission, but also, at eighteen, the youngest person.

That the most prestigious commission of the time went to an eighteen-year-old girl, whose artistic experience barely transcended that of a beginning apprentice, caused a great sensation. The *St. Louis News* demanded what everyone wanted to know: "WHO IS VINNIE REAM?" Feminist journalist Jane Swisshelm, soon a persistent Ream critic, suggested that in selecting Ream, legislators were swayed more by her womanly skills than her artistic ones. Disgusted by her selection, Hiram Powers would later dismiss Ream as having "no more talent for art than the carver of weeping willows on tombstones." The controversy over her selection, however, turned Ream into a national celebrity, and for all of her detractors she scarcely suffered for a want of admirers. Her Capitol-basement studio was constantly thronged with visitors—most typically with love-struck young men who besieged her with marriage proposals—but the famous came too, including **Ulysses S. Grant,** Matthew Brady, Robert Lincoln, and Elizabeth Cady Stanton, among others.

Ream had made it to dizzying heights, but it almost all came crashing down when she became involved in the intrigue over the impeachment of Andrew Johnson. The famously wavering Republican Kansas senator Edmund Ross was the Ream family's boarder, and she not only allegedly urged him to vote for Johnson's acquittal but also allowed her studio to serve as a meeting place for those opposed to Johnson's impeachment. Eventually her supposed activities on behalf of Johnson became widely rumored, and furious Radical Republicans obtained a vote ousting her from her Capitol studio. Fortunately for Ream, a tearful appeal to the faithful Thaddeus Stevens, then near death, proved effective, and he put an end to the effort to have her removed.

The following year Orville Browning, now secretary of the interior, judged Ream's clay model of Lincoln satisfactory. She accordingly received a five-thousand-dollar payment on her contract, which she used to finance a trip to Europe, eventually settling in Rome. In Europe she sought the famous, and when she did not they sought her. She had a romantic encounter with **John C. Frémont;** she enjoyed a whirlwind romance with Georg Brandes, leaving a lifelong mark on the great literary theorist; Franz Liszt posed for her and later composed a piece of music in her honor; she became a companion of Pre-Raphaelite painter Dante Gabriel Rossetti; the formidable Gia-coma Cardinal Antonelli gave his "little friend" gold medallions and took her to meet the pope; and she befriended American expatriate George Healy, who painted her as well.

In 1871 Ream returned to Washington in triumph. With General Sherman as her escort, she was present as her statue of Lincoln was unveiled on January 25 at an elaborate ceremony before President Grant and the assembled members of Congress and the Supreme Court. Ream resumed her residence in Washington, her life becoming a mix of society activities and minor sculpture commissions. She became close to George Armstrong Custer, and the infatuated **George Caleb Bingham** painted her twice.

Ream would never again repeat the success of the Lincoln commission, but she did obtain one other prestigious commission when in 1872 she was awarded twenty-five thousand dollars to sculpt a large memorial statue for Civil War admiral David Farragut. Once again her selection came amid disap-proving gossip when her victory in the competition came from a jury headed by Sherman, who had be-come her lover. On the day of its dedication, April 25, 1881, Congress adjourned and business shut down, as Ream came with President James Garfield to unveil her bronze statue.

In 1878 Ream married a society military officer, Richard Hoxie. General Sherman graciously gave the bride away. At her husband's urging she ceased paid artistic work after her completion of the Farragut statue, as unbecoming to her station, and they subse-quently had a son. The artistic urge remained, how-ever, and after a twenty-year artistic absence, Vinnie, with her husband's agreement, began to sculpt pro-fessionally again. When she died of uremic poisoning on November 20, 1914, Hoxie spoke for her many ad-mirers when he had carved on her tombstone: "Words that would praise thee are impotent."

KENNETH H. WINN

Griffen, Maude E. "Vinnie Ream: Portrait of a Sculp-tor." *Missouri Historical Review* 56 (1962): 231–43.

Hall, Gordon Langley. *Vinnie Ream: The Story of the Girl Who Sculptured Lincoln.* New York: Holt, Rinehart, and Winston, 1963.

Lemp, Joan. "Vinnie Ream and Abraham Lincoln." *Woman's Art Journal* 6 (1985–1986): 24–29.

Price, Joan Elliot. "Vinnie Ream Hoxie: The Early Sculptures." *American Art Review* 9 (1997): 140–43.

Prioli, Carmine. " 'Wonder Girl from the West': Vinnie Ream and the Congressional Statue of Abraham Lincoln." *Journal of American Culture* 12 (1989): 1–20.

REAVIS, LOGAN URIAH (1831–1889)

Born in the small village of Sangamon Bottom, Illi-nois, on March 26, 1831, Logan Uriah Reavis became perhaps St. Louis's greatest promoter during the river city's formative stages. He overcame tremendous obstacles because his physical deformities (a hunch-back and disproportionate hips) made him the butt of cruel jokes. His attempt at teaching in 1851 ended in failure when students also subjected him to ridicule and scorn.

Reavis's unsuccessful foray into teaching led to a career in journalism that began in 1855 with the *Beardstown (Ill.) Gazette* where he exhibited a natu-ral talent for promoting the village's "potential great-ness." Eventually he became one of the country's "promoter-intellectuals" who elevated their philoso-phies to a higher level than those advanced by typical small-town boosters. Reavis developed an outstand-ing reputation in Illinois (1855–1857), Nebraska (1857–1860), and again Illinois (1860–1866) before finally settling in St. Louis, where he lived from 1866 to 1889.

Reavis became a promoter par excellence during his formative years under the tutelage of Horace Greeley, the editor of the *New York Tribune,* who educated him in the ways of financing and operat-ing a newspaper. Greeley urged him to "speak of towns now rising but do nothing that will look like favoritism or puffing." Reavis determinedly accus-tomed himself to the ways of sophisticated big-city promotion. Like other promoter-intellectuals, Reavis learned to expostulate on such esoteric subjects as location theory, climatical patterns, and economic development. In 1866 he turned his attention to St. Louis, the "Gateway to the West."

At the time of Reavis's arrival, St. Louis desper-ately needed promotion. The river city had suffered grievously from economic deterioration inflicted dur-ing the Civil War. Its once prosperous ties to the South had suddenly disappeared. Chicago, its primary rival for midwestern economic primacy, had already con-quered the lucrative markets by spreading railroads to the north, east, and west. Local entrepreneurs backed Reavis's schemes because they promised parity with Chicago. Although he advanced many strategies, his major approach involved moving the national capital from Washington, D.C., to a central location on the Mississippi River.

In 1871 Reavis published *The Capital Is Movable; or, Facts and Arguments in Favor of the Removal of the National Capital to the Mississippi Valley.* The St. Louis promoter essentially argued that his metropolis was more "representative" of the nation geographi-cally, economically, and politically than Washington. He employed a quasi-scientific "centrality location doctrine" featuring a "concentric circle theory" introduced by Cincinnati's S. H. Goodin. He also emphasized St. Louis's position within the "Isothermal Zodiac," a concept advanced by **William Gilpin** who simplified it from a more complex formula conceived by the German geopolitician Alexander Von Humboldt. These ideas became the essential philosophy asserted in Reavis's subsequent work, *St. Louis: The Future Great City of the World* (1875).

Although Reavis attracted both national and international attention to St. Louis, he unfortunately earned few profits. Unlike other promoters, he neither capitalized upon his books nor sought political office but instead contented himself with small returns from his many articles.

It was a frustrated, poverty-stricken Reavis who, late in life, desperately turned to lecturing, a moneymaking device employed by other promoters. He emphasized St. Louis's attractiveness as an emigration transhipment place. Although it is impossible to state how many immigrants Reavis may have attracted, his speeches and literature became the major promotional source for St. Louis throughout the latter half of the nineteenth century.

As the city prospered, however, its promoter suffered. Reavis was primarily a writer and a lecturer—not an entrepreneur. Income produced by his tracts and biographies brought little satisfaction. Near the end of his life he was reduced to begging for money, prompting the *St. Louis Daily Times* to request contributions from wealthy businessmen to buy a house for the man who did "more to call the attention of the whole country to St. Louis than any other one person." This attempt also failed, and Reavis died bankrupt on April 25, 1889. Obituaries noted that the promoter who helped resurrect one of the "future great metropolises of the world" could not do the same for himself.

J. CHRISTOPHER SCHNELL

Reavis, Logan Uriah. Papers. Chicago Historical Society, Chicago.

———. Papers. Missouri Historical Society, St. Louis.

Schnell, J. Christopher, and Katherine B. Clinton. "The New West: Themes in Nineteenth-Century Urban Promotion, 1815–1880." *Bulletin of the Missouri Historical Society* (January 1974): 75–88.

Share, Allen J. "Logan Uriah Reavis: A Study in Prophecy and Promotion in Late-Nineteenth-Century St. Louis." Master's thesis, University of Missouri–Kansas City, 1966.

Snider, Denton J. *The St. Louis Movement in Philosophy, Literature, Education, Psychology, with Chapters of Autobiography.* St. Louis: Sigma Publishing, 1920.

REED, JAMES A. (1861–1944)

A U.S. senator, presidential aspirant, and conservative Democrat, James A. Reed was born near Mansfield, Ohio, on November 9, 1861. A few years later the Reed family moved from Ohio to a farm on the outskirts of Cedar Rapids, Iowa. Reed's father died when James was eight, leaving his mother and a family of six children with a mortgage-burdened farm. For the next several years Reed combined work on the family farm with the task of acquiring a formal education.

Reed demonstrated his bent for independent thought and action early in life. When he completed the course of study at Cedar Rapids High School in 1880, the principal directed Reed to rewrite his graduation speech on the grounds that its topic, "free thought," advocated atheism. Reed firmly rejected both the principal's interpretation of his speech and the order to rewrite it. The principal refused to award a diploma to the young scholar, giving hint of future conflicts between authority figures and the independent Reed.

For a brief time Reed studied at Coe College of Cedar Rapids and, in the fashion of the day, read law at one of the law firms of the city. In 1885 he was admitted to the Iowa bar and began the practice of law while still helping with the work on the family farm. He also made two unconventional personal decisions during his early adulthood. First, he changed his political affiliation from the dominant Republican Party of Iowa to the Democratic Party, motivated largely by his belief that the low tariff advocated by Democrats benefited agricultural producers. Second, he courted a married woman several years his senior. Reed and Lura Mansfield Olmstead were married upon her divorce in 1887, and the same year the couple began a new life in Kansas City, Missouri.

Reed's early years in Kansas City coincided with the rise of the house of Pendergast, the Democratic machine organized by **Jim Pendergast** from his West Bottoms saloon. Later **Tom Pendergast** succeeded his brother Jim as the boss of Kansas City. Reed forged a friendship and political alliance with Tom Pendergast that lasted through all his political campaigns.

In Kansas City Reed established a reputation for himself as an able lawyer, adding to that reputation as Kansas City counselor (1897–1898) and Jackson County attorney (1899–1900). His record as a prosecutor contributed to his election in 1900 and reelection in 1902 as mayor of Kansas City.

Despite his impressive achievements as a reform mayor, winning public control over the street railways, electric utilities, and telephone companies, Reed lost his bid for the Democratic nomination for governor to an even more popular progressive reformer, **Joseph W. Folk** of St. Louis. While Folk served his term as governor, Reed practiced law and bode his time until the state legislature elected him to the United States Senate in 1910. This election marked the beginning of an eighteen-year senatorial career for Reed and the last time that the legislature was empowered to elect a senator. The Sixteenth Amendment to the Constitution, ratified in 1913 and providing for the direct election of U.S. senators, brought Reed before the voters of the entire state in his subsequent races of 1916 and 1922.

During his first senatorial term Reed supported President Woodrow Wilson's New Freedom. He broke with his Democratic colleague, Sen. **William Joel Stone,** in voting for the congressional declaration of war in 1917. He parted company with President Wilson, however, over the centralizing and compulsive features of the war effort. He favored a volunteer defense force, but when his plan was rejected he supported the conscription of men and their deployment overseas. He criticized the Lever Food Act with its provisions for conservation as "vicious and unconstitutional."

Reed's break with Wilson became complete over the president's advocacy of U.S. membership in the League of Nations. The senator's strident opposition to the league, based on his conviction that the internationalist organization compromised the nation's independent foreign policy, earned for him and his like-minded colleagues the name of "Irreconcilable" and the implacable opposition of Missouri Wilson supporters. Democrats loyal to Wilson and the league denied Reed a seat in the Missouri delegation to the 1920 Democratic National Convention, an action that many believed would force Reed into retirement when his term ended two years later.

Despite the odds against his renomination, Reed announced his candidacy for a third term in 1922. Wilson supporters were confident that Breckenridge Long, third assistant secretary of state in the Wilson administration, would ride to victory on his advocacy of the league issue alone. Women voters, relative newcomers to electoral politics, organized their opposition to the staunch nationalist through a "Rid-Us-of-Reed" club. These internationally minded women were incensed that Reed had opposed the woman-suffrage amendment despite a majority of support for it in the state. According to the *Woman's Citizen,* Reed's five-hour-long speech against woman suffrage when it came before the Senate in June 1919 had cost the taxpayers six thousand dollars by prolonging the legislative session. Reed also alienated social reformers of both sexes who favored the Sheppard-Towner Maternity Act of 1922. Reed ridiculed this measure, which provided federal aid to the states to improve maternal and infant care, as an effort of maiden ladies in Washington telling mothers how

to care for their children. He railed, as well, against Prohibition as an unwise act of a democratic majority.

In defying the apparent majority views on these various issues, Reed also rejected the doctrine of responsible party government. That doctrine, advocated by President Wilson and his followers in Missouri, would have bound Reed to the will of the president and the Democratic Party as expressed in caucuses, platforms, and primary elections. Instead, Reed championed the conservative doctrine of the independent legislator who voted on issues according to his individual conscience and judgment. This philosophy guided Reed throughout his political career and life.

To the despair of his foes, Reed won the Democratic primary by six thousand votes, aided by Republicans who shared his antileague, pro-wet sentiments. In the general election he led the state Democratic ticket to victory with a convincing margin of forty-four thousand votes.

In 1928 Reed decided not to run for a fourth Senate term, seeking instead the Democratic presidential nomination. With William MacAdoo, the 1924 choice of the rural dry, old-stock wing of the Democratic Party out of the race on his own volition, Reed pinned his hopes on the belief that the delegates to the party's 1928 Democratic National Convention would be unwilling to nominate the urban, wet, Roman Catholic governor of New York, Alfred E. Smith. Reed's own stature had grown in the Senate during his third term as a ranking member of the judiciary and foreign relations committees. He was also appointed to a special committee in 1926 to investigate election scandals in two Senate races. He accepted the constitutionality of the Prohibition Amendment, but he castigated the Anti-Saloon League for its stubborn defense of Prohibition as an abuse of individual rights by a democratic majority. Although he had the unanimous backing of the Missouri delegation in his presidential bid, a national groundswell for Reed failed to materialize, and Smith carried the Democratic presidential banner, albeit to defeat, in 1928.

Reed returned to private life and the practice of law in Kansas City when his Senate term ended in 1929, but he had not abandoned his presidential aspirations. Accordingly, he allowed his name to go forward as Missouri's favorite-son candidate for president in 1932; anti-Reed and pro–Franklin D. Roosevelt forces in the Missouri delegation to the Democratic National Convention, however, contributed to the nomination of the New York governor.

Reed supported Roosevelt's election to the presidency in 1932, but as the liberal New Deal unfolded he assailed what he perceived as the abandonment of the Democratic Party's Jeffersonian opposition to the centralized power of the federal government. In 1936 he organized the National Jeffersonian Democrats to oppose the reelection of FDR, and the group took the same course in 1940 and 1944. Joining him in opposing FDR was his second wife, **Nell Donnelly Reed,** a highly successful dress manufacturer who married Reed in 1933 following the death of his first wife the previous year.

Reed's love of hunting kept him physically active all his life, as his love of law kept his mind sharp and focused. He was en route to Oklahoma to argue a case a few years before his death when the light plane in which he was riding crashed on landing. He broke his leg in the accident and required a cane or a crutch to walk afterward. He continued to hunt but from the backseat of an open car; he was on a hunting vacation at his upper Michigan ranch when he died on September 8, 1944, at the age of eighty-two. His funeral in Kansas City, followed by burial in Mount Washington Cemetery, was witnessed by a large crowd of admirers and public officials.

Reed was eulogized in the House of Representatives by fellow Missourian **Clarence Cannon** as one of the most eloquent men in an impressive list of congressional orators. Not only were his speeches models of judicial logic, Cannon concluded, but "they were genuine contributions to American literature" as well. The larger significance of Reed lies in his stout defense of the conservative philosophy of the independent legislator who believes that he represents democracy best not by relying upon the popular will but by acting according to the dictates of his conscience and his intellect.

FRANKLIN D. MITCHELL

Dictionary of American Biography. Supp. 3, 1941–1945. S.v. "Reed, James A."

Hults, Jan A. "The Senatorial Career of James Alexander Reed." Ph.D. diss., University of Kansas, 1986.

Meriwether, Lee A. *Jim Reed, "Senatorial Immortal."* Webster Groves, Mo.: n.p., 1948.

Mitchell, Franklin D. "The Reelection of Irreconcilable James A. Reed." *Missouri Historical Review* 60 (July 1966): 416–35.

REED, NELL DONNELLY (1889–1991)

Ellen Quinlan was born at Parsons, Kansas, on March 6, 1889, the twelfth of thirteen children. Her father, a native of County Cork, Ireland, worked on the railroad. The family called Ellen "Nell."

Upon graduation from high school, Nell Quinlan moved to Kansas City and worked as a stenographer. At the age of seventeen she married Paul Donnelly, also a stenographer, who lived at her rooming house. Then something unusual for those times occurred. Paul Donnelly, realizing that his wife had an above-average mind, supported her while she left Kansas

City and attended Lindenwood College at St. Charles, Missouri. She graduated in 1909. Only then did she return to Kansas City and resume her role as a housewife.

In 1916 Nell Donnelly made herself an attractive, ruffled, pink-and-white gingham housedress. She had tired of wearing the shapeless, male-designed housedresses of her time. In making that dress she had innocently begun an enterprise that would eventually make her one of the more successful businesswomen of twentieth-century America.

Friends and acquaintances asked Donnelly to make them similar housedresses. The demand became so great that she hired two neighbors to help her. She manufactured and delivered within two months eighteen dozen dresses at the request of Kansas City's George B. Peck Dry Goods Company. The Peck store subsequently sold the dresses for one dollar each, whereas the current price for other housedresses was sixty-seven cents. Those sales proved that women were willing to pay for style. With less than fifteen hundred dollars in start-up money, Donnelly set up a small factory in downtown Kansas City. During his spare time Paul Donnelly kept the enterprise's business records; when he returned home after serving in World War I, he and Nell created the Donnelly Garment Company. The business began to grow.

From the beginning, Donnelly was a shrewd and successful businessperson. She had a flair for stylish fashion. At a time when little division of labor and few assembly-line techniques existed in the ready-to-wear clothing industry, she introduced mass production efficiency. Gross sales amounted to $3.5 million by 1930. The company made a substantial profit while offering its employees good pay. Always close to her workers, Donnelly provided superior working conditions, a medical program that included hospitalization benefits, social programs, and even tuition aid for her employees and scholarships for their children. During the Great Depression the company continued to grow and employed more than one thousand persons.

Perhaps the Donnellys' success in the economically distressed 1930s made them a target. In 1931 Nell Donnelly and her chauffeur were kidnapped and held for seventy-five thousand dollars ransom. They were released unharmed, without the ransom being paid, after the family's lawyer and personal friend, former Kansas City mayor and U.S. senator **James A. Reed,** became involved. He contacted **Johnny Lazia,** a lieutenant of Kansas City political boss **Tom Pendergast.** Lazia had underground contacts, and evidently he placed pressure in the right places.

Donnelly experienced another eventful year in 1932. That summer James A. Reed received the Missouri Democrats' "favorite son" vote for president at the Democratic National Convention, before

Franklin D. Roosevelt received the nomination. Later that year Reed's wife of forty-five years died. On November 15 Donnelly started divorce proceedings against her husband, and she bought his 50 percent interest in the garment company. Then in December 1933 she married James A. Reed, who subsequently adopted her infant son, David.

The marriage brought happiness to both partners. Twenty-eight years older than Nell, James Reed provided the stability that she sought. He taught her to hunt and fish. Summers were spent at their seven-thousand-acre ranch in Michigan. By 1935 company sales exceeded $6 million. World War II military contracts allowed the company to continue to grow.

In 1944 James Reed died. As a memorial to her husband, in 1952 Nell Reed donated 731 acres of southern Jackson County land to the Missouri Department of Conservation. It became the James A. Reed Memorial Wildlife Area.

In the 1950s Reed continued to guide the company. The "Nelly Don" label became one of the largest in the nation, and her company's generous benefits caused the firm's workers to reject an attempt to unionize them. During the 1950s the company earned more than $14 million a year. In 1956 Reed sold the company. It became Nelly Don Inc. When asked about the secret of her success, she replied, "I just did what came naturally."

After retirement, Reed became involved in local civic affairs. She served on the Kansas City, Missouri, school board, and she became a trustee of the Midwest Research Institute. Nell Donnelly Reed died on September 8, 1991, at the age of 102.

DONALD B. OSTER

Bird, Caroline. *Enterprising Women, 1976.* New York: Norton, 1976.

Dains, Mary K., ed. *Show Me Missouri Women: Selected Biographies.* Kirksville, Mo.: Thomas Jefferson University Press, 1989.

Flynn, Jane Fifield. *Kansas City Women of Independent Minds.* Kansas City, Mo.: Fifield Publishing, 1992.

Wilson, Suzanne. "Nell." *Missouri Conservationist* 54 (April 1993): 4–8.

REEDY, WILLIAM MARION
(1862–1920)

William Marion Reedy discovered, promoted, and nurtured some of America's most important writers during his almost thirty years as the owner and editor of *Reedy's Mirror.* Founded in 1891 as a gossip sheet named the *Sunday Mirror,* it reached a circulation of 32,250 by 1898, when the *Dial*'s circulation stood at 5,000, the *Nation*'s at 12,000, and the *Atlantic*'s at 7,000. In his weekly magazine, Reedy published offerings by Edgar Lee Masters, Carl Sandburg, **Zoë Byrd Akins, Sara Teasdale, Fannie Hurst,** and Theodore Dreiser to name only some of the better-known writers of the period. In more than one instance, Reedy discovered these talents and unstintingly encouraged them to continue their work. He also introduced to American readers a number of European authors. Masters called him the "Boss of the Literary West." Reedy's accomplishments made him welcome on the East and West Coasts and in the White House of Theodore Roosevelt. He spent his entire career in St. Louis, the place of his birth.

Born on December 11, 1862, in the Irish neighborhood of Kerry Patch, Reedy attended public schools before enrolling in Christian Brothers College. After graduation he continued his education with another group of Jesuits by completing a business degree at St. Louis University at the age of eighteen. With the assistance of his policeman father who worked the Bloody Third District, Reedy found employment on the *Missouri Republican.* During the next decade he worked sporadically for the *Globe-Democrat* and sought a political post as commissioner of parks.

A large man with huge appetites for food and liquor, Reedy frequently felt the ire of the *Globe*'s editor, Joseph McCullagh, for missing work because of his drinking. After one binge, Reedy awoke to find himself married to a prostitute. A quick divorce and a successful marriage in 1897 to Eulalie Bauduy, the daughter of a physician, helped turn Reedy's life around. She died in 1901, causing Reedy to sink into a deep depression. In 1909 he married Margie Rhodes, a former madam who in 1907 had helped save the *Mirror* from bankruptcy. The marriage survived until Reedy's death on July 28, 1920, though the editor received a good amount of criticism for his choice of a wife.

While known for its publication of fiction and poetry, the *Mirror* also served as the vehicle for Reedy's political commentary and his well-known humor. He often combined the two to promote the single tax ideas of Henry George, to oppose Prohibition, to advocate woman suffrage, and to promote individual liberty. His literary criticism entertained and enlightened and reflected an extraordinary depth and breadth of reading. His chief biographer, Max Putzel, summarized Reedy's approach as follows: "His function as critic and editor was to bring life and letter into phase with one another, and he never lost the local, the common touch. This trait won him the admiration of a generation of writers through whom he became internationally influential."

In Reedy's obituary the *Globe-Democrat* called him "the greatest literary figure produced by his generation." A raconteur, Reedy became a speaker in such demand that "It was not unusual for him to deliver the main address at the funeral services of friends who had made last requests for him to speak." He died from heart disease in San Francisco after attending the Democratic National Convention. The *Mirror* ceased publication five weeks later.

LAWRENCE O. CHRISTENSEN

Dictionary of American Biography. Vol. 15. S.v. "Reedy, William Marion."

King, Ethel M. *Reflections of Reedy: A Biography of William Marion Reedy of "Reedy's Mirror."* Brooklyn: Gerald J. Rickard, 1961.

Putzel, Max. *The Man in the Mirror: William Marion Reedy and His Magazine.* 1963. Reprint, Columbia: University of Missouri Press, 1998.

St. Louis Globe-Democrat, July 29, 1920.

REEVES, ALBERT L. (1873–1971)

Albert L. Reeves was born on a farm near Steelville, in Crawford County, on the Ozarks Plateau in eastern Missouri, on December 21, 1873. He was one of six sons and a daughter of Benjamin Franklin Reeves, a farmer and Union veteran, and Margaret Isgrig Reeves. Albert attended rural public primary school and obtained a secondary education at the Franklin Institute in Sullivan, Missouri. He taught rural school in Spring Creek, in Franklin County, for the 1891 and 1892 terms. He matriculated at Steelville College, graduating with a B.A. degree in 1895. For the next three years he taught foreign languages at his alma mater and studied for the law in a Union, Missouri, law office. Admitted to the bar in 1899 he practiced law in Steelville for the following nine years. In 1900, running as a Republican, he won election from Crawford County to the Forty-first Missouri General Assembly, serving one term. From 1909 to 1913 he was the counsel for the Missouri Insurance Department.

Reeves married Mattie L. Ferguson on September 26, 1900. She bore him five children, three of whom lived to adulthood: Elizabeth, Ruth, and Albert Jr. Mattie Reeves died in 1911. Two years later, on March 10, 1913, Reeves married Blanche Armstrong. (In 1946 Albert Jr. would serve one term in Congress as a Republican from the Fifth Congressional District of Missouri.)

Following his second marriage, Reeves moved to Kansas City to practice law and further his fortunes. He held a minor appointed position on the Kansas City Civil Service Commission and in 1918 ran unsuccessfully for Congress as a Republican in a race probably decided by illegal ballots cast by the Pendergast machine.

Reeves, slightly built and stern faced, taught Bible studies at a large Baptist church, joined all the right clubs and lodges, and gained a reputation as upright and austere. From 1921 to 1923 he was an appointed commissioner of the Missouri Supreme Court, an appellate position. On January 24, 1923, President Warren G. Harding appointed Reeves as one of the two judges of the United States District Court for the Western District of Missouri. He was the choice of Republican leaders in the Kansas City legal and business community.

In his long tenure on the federal bench, Reeves gained a reputation as being scrupulously fair in civil cases and hard on lawbreakers in criminal proceedings. Some critics considered him a second prosecutor for the government. To many observers, he appeared overly zealous in handing out harsh sentences during Prohibition. Despite his reputation he received praise for judicial fairness in 1949 when he presided as a visiting judge in Washington, D.C., over the sensational Judith Coplon spy trial. Reeves forced the government to produce certain secret evidence collected against the defendant. In 1953 he lived up to his prosecutorial reputation in his handling of the Robert "Bobby" Greenlease kidnapping case, giving little doubt about where he stood in influencing the jury to recommend the death penalty in the penalty phase of the trial of the two defendants.

What may have been Judge Reeves's finest hour occurred during the Kansas City vote-fraud trials of 1936 and 1937. Defying veiled threats by representatives of the all-powerful **Tom Pendergast** political organization that worked closely with criminal elements, Reeves empaneled a grand jury to investigate widespread allegations of vote fraud in Kansas City. In a highly quoted statement the judge said: "Reach for all, even if you find them in high authority. Move on them." Ultimately, federal juries convicted 259 men and women for conspiracy to interfere with the right of citizens to vote. Authorities struck more than sixty thousand names from the voter registration lists in Kansas City, and the Pendergast machine received a blow from which it never recovered.

Reeves took senior status in the spring of 1954, capping thirty-one years of active service as a U.S. district judge. After retiring he remained on duty, working until 1964 as a visiting federal judge in many states, including Alaska. He was active in upholding school integration orders in the South. In 1961 he moved to Dunedin, Florida, where he lived until his death on March 24, 1971, at the age of ninety-seven.

LAWRENCE H. LARSEN

Kansas City Star, March 26, 1971.

Larsen, Lawrence H. *Federal Justice in Western Missouri: The Judges, the Cases, the Times.* Columbia: University of Missouri Press, 1994.

Larsen, Lawrence H., and Nancy J. Hulston. *Pendergast!* Columbia: University of Missouri Press, 1997.

New York Times, March 26, 1971.

Reddig, William M. *Tom's Town: Kansas City and the Pendergast Legend.* 1947. Reprint, Columbia: University of Missouri Press, 1986.

REID, MILDRED SANDISON FENNER (1910–1985)

Mildred Sandison Fenner Reid, editor of the *NEA Journal* for more than twenty years, was born on July 9, 1910, in Huntsville, Missouri, the oldest child of John Forte and Minnielee Holiday Sandison. In 1931 she received her B.S. degree from Northwest Missouri State Teachers College in Maryville. At the time of her graduation, she had been offered a teaching position in Kansas City. The college president, Uel W. Lamkin, however, told her about a position with the National Education Association (NEA) in Washington, D.C. The salary was less, but she thought the position offered greater opportunities, so she applied. She began as a staff member with the *NEA Journal* in 1931, moving quickly to assistant editor, then managing editor. In 1954 she became the first woman editor of the publication, later titled *Today's Education.*

Despite her busy schedule, Sandison continued her education, receiving an M.A. degree in 1938 and an Ed.D. from George Washington University in Washington, D.C., in 1942.

Mildred Sandison married H. Wolcott Fenner on February 1, 1940. A vice president of Ringling Bros. and Barnum and Bailey Circus, he died in 1972. Three years later she married Ernest G. Reid, a retired teacher, high school superintendent, and former colleague at Northwest Missouri State Teachers College. They made their home in Washington, D.C.

In addition to her work at the NEA, Reid wrote a number of scholarly works. With Eleanor C. Fishburn she coauthored *Pioneer American Educators* in 1944. The next year she published *NEA History.* She edited *Future Teachers of America, Source Book,* and *Schools Are People.* She and H. Wolcott Fenner wrote *The Circus: Lure and Legend.* A book of fiction for teenagers, *Twelve Going on Fifteen,* was published in 1985, and she had finished writing *Circus Times Five* at the time of her death in 1985. She published hundreds of articles in her field, presented many speeches, and participated in conferences and symposia around the world.

Reid held memberships in a number of organizations, including the National Federation of Press Women, the Education Press Association, as a board member of Senior Citizens of America, the National Council of Administrators, Women in Education, and as the first woman member of the Horace Mann League. She participated in editorial workshops throughout the world, including Manila in 1956 and Amsterdam in 1961. An active member of the Methodist Church, she taught a Sunday-school class for several years.

After working for forty-four years with NEA, Reid retired in 1975. At that time, the president of Ringling Bros. and Barnum and Bailey Circus invited her to establish a Department of Education service for the circus. As director of this department, she initiated and directed the program.

Mildred Fenner Reid received many honors and awards. In 1962 she received a Litt.D. degree from Glassboro State College in New Jersey. Northwest Missouri State Teachers College awarded her its first Distinguished Alumni Award in 1970. The next year the *Ladies' Home Journal* recognized her as one of the "Seventy-five Most Important Women in America." Reid died on November 8, 1985, in Washington, D.C.

MARY K. DAINS

Dains, Mary K., ed. *Show Me Missouri Women: Selected Biographies.* Kirksville, Mo.: Thomas Jefferson University Press, 1989.

Who's Who in America. Chicago: A. N. Marquis, 1965.

Who's Who in American Education. Vol. 1. Hattiesburg, Miss.: Who's Who in American Education, 1967–1968.

REYNOLDS, THOMAS (1796–1844)

Elected in 1840, Thomas Reynolds became the seventh Missouri governor. There are few records to document his early life. He was born in Bracken County, Kentucky, on March 12, 1796. He appears to have been well educated and gained admission to the Kentucky bar. Around 1820 he married Eliza Ann Young. Probably within the next two years, the young couple moved to Springfield, Illinois, with their son, an only child.

Reynolds quickly won a place for himself in that growing frontier community. He practiced law and served in the Illinois General Assembly (including one term as Speaker of the House of Representatives), as the state's attorney general, as judge of a circuit court, and finally as chief justice of the state supreme court. These public offices marked Reynolds as a man of ability, with prospects for a successful political career in Illinois. However, for reasons unknown, he moved to Missouri in 1829 and settled at Fayette in Howard County.

In his new home, Reynolds opened a law practice, entered into politics, and for a time edited the *Boonslick Democrat.* In politics he was an ardent Democrat and a loyal party man. He became one of the leaders of an influential and powerful group of central Missouri politicians known across the state as the Central Clique. Like Reynolds, members of the Central Clique were, for the most part, landowners and slaveholders with southern backgrounds. They supported Andrew Jackson nationally and idolized U.S. Sen. **Thomas Hart Benton.** Members of the Central Clique preached Benton's hard-money doctrine and supported his attacks against corporations and paper-issuing banks.

With this power base, Reynolds won election to the state legislature as the representative from Howard County in 1832. That body promptly elected him Speaker of the House. After serving one term, he was appointed judge of the second judicial circuit. In 1840 the Central Clique dominated the Democratic Party's state convention, and almost by acclamation that body nominated Reynolds as the party's candidate for governor. He won the gubernatorial election by a substantial margin.

In his inaugural address Reynolds voiced the agrarian, states' rights, and limited-government doctrines of the old-line Democrats. His was a clear stand against the emerging Whig Party with its platform calling for a national bank, paper currency, and internal improvements—a platform that appealed to the growing commercial and mercantile interests of the state and nation.

During the early 1840s political controversy in Missouri became increasingly intense, bitter, and often personal. As governor, Reynolds generally continued to hold to the Benton, hard-money line, and some spokesmen with opposing views attacked him with passion and vindictiveness. During his term of office, Governor Reynolds became deeply depressed. On February 9, 1844, he shot and killed himself in his office in the executive mansion. He left a note stating that the "slanders and abuse" of his political enemies "has rendered my life a burden to me."

Reynolds held a strong aversion to the longstanding practice of sending debtors to prison. In large part because of his efforts, the General Assembly enacted a law in January 1843 abolishing imprisonment for debt. That principle has been retained in each successive state constitution.

Contemporaries have described Reynolds as a man of considerable ability, with a clear mind and great powers of analysis. Demonstrating a sound knowledge of the law, he was recognized as an outstanding jurist. Despite the bitterness directed against him while governor, a friend recalled his genial habits, pleasant demeanor, integrity, and honesty of purpose. Perhaps because of these traits, the bitter barbs hurled at him compounded his depression. Gov. Thomas Reynolds was buried in Jefferson City.

PERRY MCCANDLESS

Bay, W. V. N. *Reminiscences of the Bench and Bar of Missouri.* St. Louis: F. H. Thomas, 1878.

Leopard, Buel, and Floyd C. Shoemaker, eds. *The Messages and Proclamations of the Governors of the State of Missouri.* Vol. 1. Columbia: State Historical Society of Missouri, 1922.

REYNOLDS, THOMAS CAUTE (1821–1887)

Elected lieutenant governor of Missouri in 1860, Thomas Caute Reynolds worked diligently to separate Missouri from the Union in 1861, and upon **Claiborne Fox Jackson**'s death maintained a Confederate Missouri government in exile in various places, including Marshall, Texas, until the end of the war. Rather than stay in the United States after the Confederate loss, Reynolds fled to Mexico with Gen. **Joseph Orville Shelby,** returning in 1868.

Born on October 11, 1821, in South Carolina, Reynolds graduated from the University of Virginia, studied in Germany at Heidelberg University, and served in the diplomatic corps as secretary to the U.S. legation in Madrid, Spain, before settling in St. Louis in 1850. A lawyer and a Democrat, Reynolds received an appointment as U.S. district attorney in St. Louis in 1853.

Quickly, Reynolds entered the contentious fray of 1850s Missouri politics. Strongly proslavery, he became an anti-Benton Democrat and began exchanging barbed notes in the city's newspapers with **B. Gratz Brown,** one of **Thomas Hart Benton**'s chief supporters. The combatants settled one near-duel amicably, but in 1856, with Reynolds a candidate for Congress and an outspoken opponent of the Bentonites, he and Brown faced each other with pistols at twenty paces. Reynolds wounded Brown in the knee, an injury that caused the future governor to limp for the remainder of his life. Reynolds escaped uninjured. He lost his race for Congress.

As a supporter of Missouri secession, Reynolds probably surpassed even Governor Jackson. Historian **Floyd Calvin Shoemaker** called him the driving force behind the secessionist movement. Both before and after Jackson's death in 1862, Reynolds spent time in the Confederate capital legitimating Missouri's status within the seceding states. Called brilliant by historian William Parrish, Reynolds apparently liked warfare, traveling with **Sterling Price**'s forces from time to time, and, near the close of the war, serving on General Shelby's staff. His connection with Shelby helped him make the decision to join the exodus to Mexico after the war.

Reynolds returned to St. Louis in 1868 carrying with him the seal of the state of Missouri, which had been removed when Jackson fled the capital city in 1861. Reynolds returned the seal to Gov.

Joseph Washington McClurg in 1869. In part as a result of the policies of his old antagonist B. Gratz Brown, Reynolds regained his civil rights and won a seat in the state legislature in 1874. Later, President Chester A. Arthur appointed him as a member of a commission to investigate relations with Latin America. His linguistic ability partly recommended him for the post: Reynolds spoke Spanish, French, and German fluently. In that decade of the 1880s, he suffered the death of his first wife when her dress caught fire from a spark from the fireplace. His health declined, and he came to fear becoming a burden to his second wife.

On March 30, 1887, Reynolds's body was found at the bottom of an elevator shaft in the Federal Building in St. Louis. Investigators never established whether his death resulted from accident or suicide, but not long before it occurred he wrote:

> I am troubled by insomnia and frequent nervous-ness. I suffer from persistent melancholy. My mind is beginning to wander. I have hallucina-tions and even visions, when I am awake, of materialized spirits of deceased ancestors, urging me to join them in another world. Life has become a burden to me. I am now still sound of mind and I write down this statement so that should I do anything rash, my friends may feel assured it was done in some temporary disorder of mind. . . .

These comments have led most writers to conclude that he committed suicide.

About the most important experience in his life and in the lives of many others in his generation, he observed to a group of former Confederate soldiers, "We have played at the grand game of Civil War, and so ably as to gain the admiration of the world, and the respect of magnanimous opponents. We lost it for want of trumps, but we drew at least our fair share of honor."

Lawrence O. Christensen

Hunter, Lloyd A. "Missouri's Confederate Leaders after the War." *Missouri Historical Review* 67 (April 1973): 371–96.

Kirkpatrick, Arthur R. "Missouri, the Twelfth Con-federate State." Ph.D. diss., University of Mis-souri–Columbia, 1954.

Miller, Robert E. "One of the Ruling Class, Thomas Caute Reynolds: Second Confederate Governor of Missouri." *Missouri Historical Review* 80 (July 1986): 422–48.

Parrish, William E. *A History of Missouri: Volume III, 1860 to 1875.* Columbia: University of Missouri Press, 1973.

Reynolds, Thomas C. Papers. Missouri Historical Society, St. Louis.

St. Louis Globe-Democrat, April 16, 1911.

RICHARDSON, KATHERINE BERRY (1858–1933)

Katherine Berry Richardson founded the highly re-spected Children's Mercy Hospital in Kansas City, Missouri. She was born on September 28, 1858, in Flat Rock, Kentucky, to Stephen Paine and Harriett Benson Berry. She was the younger of two girls. A farmer and grain-mill operator, Stephen raised his daughters after their mother's death in 1861. He later worked in the oil industry in Pennsylvania and man-aged to send his daughters through high school at a time when girls usually did not attend high school.

Katherine Berry attended Mount Union College in Alliance, Ohio, and received her bachelor of phi-losophy degree in 1882 and her master of philosophy degree in 1887. She continued her education at the Pennsylvania Women's College of Philadelphia and earned an M.D. degree in 1887. Berry became a teacher to help her sister, Alice, through Philadel-phia Dental College. After Alice Berry graduated as a dentist in late 1887, the sisters started a medical practice in La Crosse, Wisconsin.

In 1893 Katherine Berry married James Ira Rich-ardson of Eau Clair, Wisconsin. The couple had no children, and James died in 1903. The Richardsons moved to Kansas City in 1897, where Alice Berry Graham, recently widowed, joined them. The sisters established a medical practice in the downtown area and maintained living quarters above their office.

Richardson was a surgeon without a place to operate as no hospital allowed a woman on its staff. The sisters rented beds in a hospital for women and children and brought a number of their patients to this facility. The building was an old house in need of repair and stood beside a brick factory on a dusty, rutted road. In 1899 Richardson and Graham decided to purchase the hospital to keep it out of bankruptcy and named it the Free Bed Fund Association for Crippled, Deformed, and Ruptured Children.

Women doctors were generally not accepted in the late 1800s, and newspapers printed unkind arti-cles, ridiculing the sisters. Both women were totally dedicated to the care of children and through their frugality were able to care for and feed a child for ninety cents a day. They spoke to church groups and women's clubs to raise funds for the children, and, gradually, male doctors began to give their time and knowledge to the hospital.

Richardson wanted to help the black children of Kansas City and established a separate hospital for them, Mercy Wheatley Hospital for Negroes, and encouraged black doctors and nurses to treat the black children. In 1904 the sisters changed the name of the hospital to the Children's Mercy Hospital. Patient numbers increased over the years, and the sisters decided to build a new facility. In 1915 Richardson, with the aid of lawyer R. R Brewster, had raised enough money to start the building. The cornerstone, a memorial to her sister, Alice, who had died in 1913, read: "In 1897, Dr. Alice Berry Graham founded this hospital for sick and crippled children—to be forever nonsectarian, nonlocal, and for those who cannot pay." Richardson refused to admit that it was her idea to build Mercy, insisting that the credit belonged to her sister.

Richardson treated paying patients but did not turn away those who could not pay. Children at Mercy received kind but firm treatment. The hospital had a playroom, a schoolroom, and a playground. Richardson believed in sun and fresh air as aids to healing ill children. She specialized in plastic surgery of the face, including harelips and cleft palates. Children also received speech therapy after surgery so that they could lead normal lives. The hospital had a small laboratory to study children's diseases. Richardson dreamed of a large laboratory at Mercy for the discovery of the cure for infantile paralysis, but she was unable to fulfill her wish.

Richardson, a suffragist and a believer in woman's rights, was brash and demanding, and her rules for doctors and nurses appeared strict. She expected no less from her staff than from herself. She never retired and operated until a few days before her death on June 3, 1933. During her lifetime women were in charge of the hospital. Soon after her death, however, men took over executive positions.

Richardson made a lasting impression on the children of Kansas City and the surrounding towns. Mercy Hospital still accepts children from birth to sixteen years of age, and those who cannot pay for needed care are not turned away. Other hospitals in Kansas City, along with the Kansas City School of Dentistry, have accepted the highly regarded Children's Mercy Hospital as an affiliate.

PETRA DEWITT

Dains, Mary K., ed. *Show Me Missouri Women: Selected Biographies.* Kirksville, Mo.: Thomas Jefferson University Press, 1989.
Kansas City Star, June 3–5, 1933.
Who's Who in America. Vol. 17. Chicago: A. N. Marquis, 1933.

RICKEY, WESLEY BRANCH (1881–1965)

Wesley Branch Rickey, the famed baseball executive whose innovations left an indelible imprint on America's national pastime, was born on a farm in Stockdale, Ohio, on December 20, 1881. As a youth he was an outstanding athlete who excelled in football and baseball. His devout Methodist parents reared him in a strict Christian environment, and Rickey worked his way through Ohio Wesleyan University by playing semiprofessional baseball and football and by coaching the school's baseball team.

Rickey struggled to break into major league baseball as a catcher. The Cincinnati Reds acquired him from Dallas in 1903, but the National League team released him when he refused to play on Sunday. He returned to Dallas before being acquired by the St. Louis Browns in the American League. He caught only one game in 1905 for the Browns, but the next year he appeared in sixty-four games and batted .284. The Browns traded him to the New York Highlanders in the same league, but an injury to his arm caused him to have a poor season in 1907, hitting only .182.

During the off-season in 1908, Rickey toured as a prohibition lecturer, and later that year he entered the University of Michigan law school. During his law school days, he also coached the university's baseball team, and while there he discovered **George Sisler,** who later became a star for Rickey's St. Louis Browns team. Rickey practiced law and scouted for the Browns before his superb organizational skills landed him a full-time job in 1913 as an assistant to the president of the Browns. He later advanced to become the team's general manager and finally its field manager. Because of his religious convictions, Rickey turned his managerial duties over to a coaching assistant on Sundays.

In 1917 Rickey joined a group of St. Louis businessmen who had organized the Cardinals, a new National League team to play in their city. They selected Rickey as the organization's president, and he worked with the legendary manager Miller Huggins. The Cardinals finished third their first year in the league.

After serving as a major in the United States Army's chemical warfare unit during World War I, Rickey rejoined the financially strapped Cardinal organization. Because the Cardinals were unable to compete with other major league clubs for seasoned players, Rickey organized in 1919 a system of minor league affiliates to serve as a training ground for new talent for the Cardinals. His innovative "farm system" helped transform the St. Louis team into a serious contender in the 1920s and 1930s.

Rickey, whom the sportswriters dubbed "the Mahatma," had an eye for talent. He discovered and recruited many great stars, including George Sisler, **"Sunny Jim" Bottomley, Rogers Hornsby, Dizzy Dean,** and Joe "Duckey" Medwick. During Rickey's tenure with the Cardinals the team won six National League pennants (in 1926, 1928, 1930, 1931, 1934, and 1942) and four World Championships (in 1926, 1931, 1934, and 1942). The Cardinals' enormously popular "Gashouse Gang" was one of the more colorful teams in baseball history.

In 1942 after a disagreement with club owner Sam Breadon, Rickey left the Cardinals organization and became president and general manager of the Brooklyn Dodgers. Although he aroused the ire of some Brooklyn fans by selling favorite players, he made the team more disciplined and competitive. He developed a superb Dodger farm system, and by 1945 the team had climbed to third place in the National League.

Rickey made history with his bold and dramatic decision in 1947 to make Jackie Robinson the first black baseball player in the major leagues. His signing of African American players such as Robinson, Don Newcombe, Roy Campanella, and Jim "Junior" Gilliam helped lead the Dodgers to numerous pennants.

Walter O'Malley's desire for full ownership of the Dodgers forced Rickey out of the organization in 1950. The Pittsburgh Pirates employed him as the general manager from 1950 to 1959, and his leadership in that organization laid the foundation for the team's 1960 World Championship.

Rickey's final venture was a proposal to create a new Continental League. The third league never materialized, but his scheme forced both of the existing leagues to expand by adding new clubs.

Rickey was not especially beloved by many who knew and worked with him. The parsimonious executive was notorious for his tightfisted negotiations and alleged double-dealing. Nonetheless, no one questioned his genius as a baseball executive. His numerous innovations, including the farm system, the integration of the sport, and major league expansion, all did much to shape modern baseball.

Rickey, who suffered from heart disease, died on December 9, 1965, in Columbia, Missouri, where he had gone to attend his induction into the Missouri State Sports Hall of Fame. Two years later he was elected to the National Baseball Hall of Fame. The Branch Rickey Collection at the Library of Congress is one of the most comprehensive manuscript collections on major league baseball.

ARTHUR F. MCCLURE AND VIVIAN RICHARDSON

Biographical Dictionary of American Sports: Baseball. S.v. "Rickey, Wesley Branch."

New York Times, December 10, 1965.

Who's Who in America. Chicago: A. N. Marquis, 1945.

RIGDON, SIDNEY (1793–1876)

Born on February 17, 1793, on a farm near St. Clair Township, in Allegheny County, Pennsylvania, Sidney Rigdon was the fourth child of William and Nancy Rigdon. He became famous as a Mormon leader and was a central figure in the Mormon conflict in Missouri in the 1830s. As a boy he manifested a strong interest in religion, studied the Bible, developed excellent oratorical skills, and in 1817 entered the ministry as a Baptist preacher. Although enormously successful as a preacher who could attract and hold large congregations, his career as a Baptist pastor was controversial, largely because of his lifelong quest for what he called the Gospel in its fullness.

Working in the Mohoning Baptist Association of east-central Ohio, Rigdon came into contact with the work of Alexander Campbell, and in 1821 he affiliated with his efforts. Campbell's Disciples of Christ organization was part of a larger "restoration" concept then present in American Christianity, as several religious reformers sought to restore the Gospel to its "ancient purity." Rigdon remained a part of the Campbellite group through most of the 1820s, but split from it in 1830 over communalism (which Rigdon wanted to experiment with) and other ideas. Not long after this period, Rigdon learned of **Joseph Smith Jr.** and the rise of the Mormon religion in upstate New York from one of his former parishioners who had converted.

Perhaps the most important convert to early Mormonism, Rigdon was enticed to the church by missionaries traveling in the fall of 1830. Living in Kirtland, a suburb of Cleveland in Ohio's Western Reserve, Rigdon brought his parishioners into Mormonism and almost instantly created a sizable organization. Within months Joseph Smith and his New York followers had relocated to Kirtland, and the community was closely identified with Mormonism until 1838. Rigdon quickly became Smith's chief lieutenant and spokesman. From Kirtland, Smith sent followers to found Mormon communities around Independence, Missouri, proclaimed by the church as the center place of "Zion," the place for a utopian gathering of believers.

Rigdon was especially attracted to Mormonism because of its authoritative answers to religious issues, settling for him and other members several theological debates underway in the first part of the nineteenth century. In so doing, Mormonism reacted against an emerging American pluralism and secularism present in Jacksonian America. The early Mormon attempts to develop utopian communities under theocratic control during the 1830s and 1840s, therefore, were partially means of combating the increasing importance of democratic, competitive, secular tendencies and the overall decline of religion in American life. These efforts brought the church into conflict with the otherwise-minded established order.

Throughout most of the 1830s Rigdon lived in Kirtland, Ohio, but after a series of incidents that prompted the Mormons to abandon it in 1838, he moved to the church's stronghold of Far West, in Caldwell County, Missouri. As Smith's chief spokesman, Rigdon was in large measure responsible for creating in Far West the public attitudes that led to the "Mormon War" in Missouri in the fall of 1838. Two speeches in the summer, the "Salt Sermon" and his Fourth of July sermon, set the community on notice that the Mormons would brook no internal dissent and would not be pushed around by external forces. Rigdon became one of the "hard-liners" in the conflict that followed in the fall of 1838. In this last confrontation Gov. **Lilburn W. Boggs** issued an "extermination order" that essentially gave Missourians a license to kill Mormons.

Rigdon was arrested at Far West, along with several other Mormons, in November 1838, and bound over for trial on charges ranging from treason to riot. He spent part of the winter of 1838–1839 in the Liberty jail, but when his health failed he was brought to trial and—acting in his own defense—persuaded the court to dismiss the case. He then settled at the new Mormon community of Nauvoo, Illinois, and at the death of Joseph Smith Jr. in 1844 asserted his authority to lead the church. This was rejected by the members, and Rigdon founded his own Mormon splinter group in western Pennsylvania, where he was living at the time of his death on July 14, 1876.

ROGER D. LAUNIUS

Arrington, Leonard J., and Davis Bitton. *The Mormon Experience: A History of the Latter-day Saints.* New York: Knopf, 1979.

LeSueur, Stephen C. *The 1838 Mormon War in Missouri.* Columbia: University of Missouri Press, 1987.

McKiernan, F. Mark. *The Voice of One Crying in the Wilderness: Sidney Rigdon, 1793–1876, Mormon Reformer.* Lawrence, Kans.: Coronado Press, 1971.

RINDISBACHER, PETER (1806–1834)

Peter Rindisbacher's paintings and watercolors are among the earliest images of Native Americans and the frontier in western Canada and the United States. Unlike his successors, the artist-explorers **Karl Bodmer** and **George C. Catlin,** Rindisbacher did not come to the West to explore and record the frontier only to leave it. As a young boy he emigrated to Canada with his family from Switzerland and illustrated his experiences as a pioneering European settler on the frontier. In 1829 he moved to St. Louis, where he spent the final five years of his life and experienced the height of his artistic success. Recognized in his youth as "the boy artist," Rindisbacher, unfortunately, would not outlive his appellation, dying at twenty-eight years of age.

The Rindisbacher family lived in the valley of the Emme River in the Canton of Berne, Switzerland, when Peter was born on April 12, 1806. He demonstrated a prodigious interest in drawing as a boy, prompting his family to send him on an Alpine sketching tour with the Bernese miniature painter Jacob S. Weibel. This experience may have provided the young artist with his only formal instruction.

In 1821 the Rindisbachers joined a group of Swiss emigrants settling in the Hudson Bay Company's Red River Colony in western Canada. Arriving in the fall of 1821, the Swiss immigrants found depleted stores and faced severely cold weather and starvation during their first Canadian winter. Rindisbacher earned extra money for his family by selling his drawings and watercolors of the colony, its inhabitants, and the surrounding Native Americans. With his pictures he earned the respect of the other settlers and the officers in nearby Fort Garry. Capt. Andrew Bulger, governor of the colony, commissioned Rindisbacher to illustrate various scenes of life in the Red River Colony and became the artist's first patron. After Bulger's departure in 1823, subsequent governors and officers engaged "the boy artist" to record life in this remote colony, nurturing a connection to the military that Rindisbacher cultivated throughout his career. The original watercolors that he produced on-site provided him with the source material for the many copies that he made to order.

The Hudson Bay Company had misrepresented the climate and conditions when they recruited the Swiss settlers to emigrate to the Red River Colony. After successive years of poor crop yields, harsh winters, and spring floods, the Swiss settlers began to move south to St. Louis and what is now Illinois. In 1826 the Rindisbacher family finally abandoned the ill-fated Red River Colony and moved to a lead-mining colony at Gratiot's Grove (in northwestern Illinois) established by previous Swiss settlers on their exodus from the Red River Colony. They emigrated to the United States despite the threat of Indian attack, most notably the David Tully family massacre of 1823 that Peter Rindisbacher illustrated in one of his best-known paintings.

At Gratiot's Grove Rindisbacher immediately established contact with nearby United States Army officers who provided numerous commissions. As opposed to the Chippewa, Cree, and Assiniboine whom Rindisbacher had painted in Canada, here he encountered the Winnebago, Sauk, and Fox. In 1829 he accompanied a government expedition and recorded the negotiations at Prairie du Chien to purchase land rights from the Sauk and the Fox for the rapidly expanding settlements.

By the time of the treaty negotiations in 1829, Rindisbacher had acquired a considerable reputation as an illustrator of western life. Following the treaty he moved to St. Louis where he set up a studio as a painter of Native Americans and portrait miniatures. Here he experienced his greatest success with his pictures being printed in a number of popular magazines and books. Beginning in October 1829 with the publication of the unsigned lithograph *Sioux Warrior Charging* in the *American Turf Register,* a popular sporting magazine, Rindisbacher's images of life on the frontier appeared regularly in periodicals and helped to define the American conception of the West. He continued to produce copies of his original watercolors on order and served as an important resource for later artist-explorers such as Karl Bodmer, who may have visited Rindisbacher in March 1833 prior to traveling further west on his expedition with Prince Maximilian.

In St. Louis the artist expanded his practice to produce portrait miniatures for St. Louis citizens. By the early 1830s Rindisbacher's reputation was firmly established upon his popular frontier images and his portraits. His patrons prized the accuracy of his drawing and the realism of his images. Unfortunately, he died from unknown causes on August 12, 1834, just as his career was making tremendous progress. At the time of his death his paintings of western life were widely regarded. Posthumously, his paintings of a Sauk and Fox war dance and a buffalo hunt appeared as the frontispieces to two volumes of Thomas L. McKenney and James Hall's *Indian Tribes of North America* (1837).

Shortly after publication of the volumes, western frontier images by Catlin and Bodmer eclipsed Rindisbacher's work and obscured his accomplishments. Only in the mid-twentieth century have historians recognized the significance of his watercolors, and his works remain rare. Among the group of early frontier painters, Peter Rindisbacher created important documents of Canada and the Mississippi River Valley in the early-nineteenth-century frontier and shaped our conception of the West with such images as the interior of a tepee and a buffalo hunt. Although his time in Missouri was short, it was the most productive phase of his career, and he played an important role in establishing St. Louis as an early center for subsequent artist-explorers of the trans-Mississippi West.

JOSEPH D. KETNER

Josephy, Alvin M., Jr. *The Artist Was a Young Man: The Life and Story of Peter Rindisbacher.* Fort Worth, Tex.: Amon Carter Museum, 1970.

Nute, Grace Lee. "Notes and Documents: A Rindisbacher Watercolor." *Minnesota History* 23 (spring 1942): 154–56.

———. "Peter Rindisbacher, Artist." *Minnesota History* 14 (September 1933): 283–87.

RITTER, JOSEPH ELMER (1892–1967)

Joseph Elmer Ritter, the fourth archbishop of St. Louis, a civil rights leader, and an ecumenist, was born on July 20, 1892, in New Albany, Indiana, the son of Nicholas and Bertha Luette Ritter. Educated at St. Meinrad's Seminary in Indiana, he was ordained to the priesthood of the Catholic Church on May 30, 1917, and engaged in pastoral work, eventually becoming rector of the unfinished Cathedral of Sts. Peter and Paul in Indianapolis.

Consecrated auxiliary bishop of Indianapolis on March 28, 1933, Ritter succeeded Bishop Joseph Chartrand the following year. He reorganized the city's Catholic Charities Bureau, introduced the Catholic Youth Organization, and completed the cathedral. On December 19, 1944, Indianapolis became an archdiocese with Ritter its archbishop.

Two years later, on July 20, 1946, Pope Pius XII named Ritter archbishop of St. Louis, as successor of **John J. Glennon,** the recently named cardinal of the Church who had died on his return journey from Rome a few months before. The new archbishop of St. Louis and his predecessor contrasted sharply. Glennon, a tall, stately man of magnificent presence, and lofty and growingly aloof manner, spoke eloquently on major Church occasions. Ritter, of moderate height and unimpressive presence, unostentatious and approachable, lacked oratorical flair. Glennon had kept major decisions to himself but gave his pastors leeway. Ritter favored a highly controlled bureaucratic structure. He spent his first months in St. Louis getting acquainted and organizing his administrative team.

During the previous eighty years, the Church had done little for the small segregated black Catholic community that dated back to the colonial days. The new archbishop indicated early that a change would come. He announced before the fall school term of 1947 that segregation would end at Catholic churches and schools. Presuming that state segregation laws applied to parochial schools, a group of Catholics threatened to take the archbishop to court. Ritter called attention to a law of the Church: anyone hauling his bishop before a secular court when acting in his capacity as bishop incurred automatic excommunication. The Catholic community accepted his decision without further public discussion.

In this action, as in the integration of many Catholic hospitals over the succeeding years, Ritter saw himself as an administrator, not as a social reformer. Nonetheless, his firm stand on the parochial schools, seven years before the United States Supreme Court outlawed segregation in public schools, made him a symbol of racial reform. Later, he set up an archdiocesan human-rights office.

In the immediate post–World War II period, a building boom had set in. Ritter was faced with the need to open an average of three new parishes each year, mostly in St. Louis County. He began six high schools. All were coed, while earlier Catholic schools had been exclusively for boys or for girls. The archdiocese also planned a hospital for children to bear the name of John Cardinal Glennon.

Religious congregations staffed most Catholic missions throughout the world. Ritter changed this pattern by launching an archdiocesan mission in La Paz, Bolivia. Matching the generosity of the priests who volunteered for work in Latin America, the people of St. Louis regularly contributed more money to the foreign missions than any archdiocese of its size.

On December 16, 1960, Pope John XXIII named Ritter a cardinal of the Church. The newly named cardinal took an active part in the Second Vatican Council that Pope John called for the fall of 1962. Ritter startled his colleagues at the first session by successfully denouncing a document on "Revelation" sponsored by the Roman Curia. Returning to St. Louis between sessions, he promoted ecumenical discussions with members of other denominations. He took part in the reform of liturgical worship and the promotion of religious liberty. A highly regarded observer noted, "The cheerful, dynamic Archbishop of St. Louis, for all the simplicity of his approach, turned out to be the outstanding American prelate at the Council."

Ritter came back to St. Louis amid universal euphoria. Many Catholics expected administrative changes that would give a more substantial voice to the priests and the laity. Before he could establish priorities for bringing into daily Church practice the changes recommended by the council, Ritter died on June 10, 1967.

A mosaic in the St. Louis Central West-End Cathedral singles out two facets of Ritter's career: his strong stand in favor of civil rights for blacks and his ecumenical outlook in dealing with other denominations.

WILLIAM B. FAHERTY

Ellis, John Tracy. *Catholic Bishops: A Memoir.* Wilmington, Del.: Michael Glazier, 1983.

Faherty, William B. *Dream by the River: Two Centuries of St. Louis Catholicism, 1766–1967.* St. Louis: Piraeus, 1973.

Johnson, James. *Joseph Cardinal Ritter.* South Bend, Ind.: University of Notre Dame Press, 1964.

Rynne, Xavier. *Letters from Vatican City.* New York: Farrar, Strauss, 1963.

ROBIDOUX, JOSEPH, III (1783–1868)

Joseph Robidoux III, the eldest son of a large family, was born in St. Louis on August 10, 1783, to Joseph and Catherine Rollette Robidoux. The senior Robidoux was active in the trade of the Missouri River in the 1790s and early 1800s, concentrating his energies in the vicinity of Council Bluffs among the Iowa, Pawnee, Otoe, Omaha, and Missouri tribes. At sixteen, young Joseph apprenticed to his father and embarked upriver to winter in the general area of northwestern Missouri, probably with the Missouri tribe. He married Eugenie Deslisle of St. Louis in 1800, but was soon widowed after a son, Joseph IV, was born. Robidoux returned to "La Post du Serpent Noir" built in 1803, which was the Blacksnake Hills post later named St. Joseph, Missouri, a locality closely associated with the Robidoux clan for the next half century. Here in 1805 Joseph Robidoux fathered a child, Mary, by an Indian woman. This daughter would marry chief White Cloud of the Ioway.

When the senior Robidoux died in 1809, most of his estate was sold to pay the debts incurred in the fur trade. Joseph Robidoux III now assumed responsibility as the family's patriarch, directing and supporting the far-flung commercial activities of his young siblings: François, Antoine, Louis, Michel, and Isidor. As head of this adventurous, ambitious, entrepreneurial, and resourceful clan, he has aptly been described as the "kingpin of the prolific and energetic Robidoux family" by his biographer Merrill Mattes.

Like their contemporaries, the sons of other leading merchant-trader families of St. Louis, such as the Papins and the Chouteaus, the Robidoux brothers were displaced by incoming Anglo-Americans in the years after the War of 1812 and were drawn westward to seek their fortunes. These French Creoles were highly mobile and often polygamous. Joseph Robidoux remarried in 1814 to a St. Louis woman, Angelique Vaudry, by whom he had eight children, while simultaneously engaging in multiple "country marriages" to Indian women, primarily Otoes and Ioways. Six mixed-blood children received allotments on the Nemaha Half-Breed Reserve according to the terms of the 1830 Treaty of Prairie du Chien.

A vigorous contender in the Council Bluffs trade, Robidoux was in partnership with Alexander La-Force Papin in 1818 and in 1819 was the resident trader (or factor) for Pratte, Chouteau, and Company, also known as the French Company, at their Otoe post. Simultaneously, he and younger brother François operated a store in St. Louis, a partnership that dissolved in 1820.

Robidoux was one of the first to realize the commercial possibilities of the Santa Fe trade after Mexico won independence from Spain in 1821. He launched an expedition from the Otoe post in 1822 following a change in Mexican trade policies. Jean Baptiste Cabanné replaced Robidoux at the Otoe post in 1823. Historians have often been confused about this period in Robidoux's life because his relationship to the French Company after 1823 is unclear. Apparently, French Company officials initially regretted becoming involved in his profit- and risk-sharing western venture and criticized his actions. Robidoux persisted, finding other financial backing with which to outfit his brothers for expeditions to Mexican territory and to the Rocky Mountains for beaver hunting between 1823 and 1825, thus challenging the French Company's pretense to monopoly. Meanwhile, he cut into Cabanné's share of the Council Bluffs trade. Robidoux's initiative and obstinacy, along with his familiarity with Indian languages, his experience, his kin connections, and his willingness to traffic in contraband alcohol, gave him advantages over the better-capitalized French Company. As historian Annie Abel has aptly described this era of fur-trading activities on the Missouri River, "keenness of competition [was] measured by the amount of liquor distributed." Robidoux outmatched his rival, the hard-pressed Cabanné, who wrote to **Pierre Chouteau Jr.** repeatedly accusing Robidoux of unethical business practices, moral debasement, and perfidy. In one letter he said that Robidoux was "truly wicked, cunning, cheating, and a rogue."

When the French Company temporarily merged with the Western Department of Astor's American Fur Company from 1826 to 1834, Robidoux with brother Michel and Jean Baptiste Roy conducted a successful opposition from 1826 to 1828, getting licenses to trade along the Missouri River from Council Bluffs to the Blacksnake Hills. In the fall of 1828, the French Company came to a financial settlement, paying Robidoux thirty-five hundred dollars for his outfit and a salary of one thousand dollars for two years to stay out of the Indian country. In a brief period of retirement, Robidoux devoted himself to the family's bakery business in St. Louis while supporting his younger siblings' entrepreneurial endeavors, such as Antoine's construction of the Uncompahgre trading post in southwestern Colorado.

By the early 1830s Robidoux was back in the Council Bluffs trade, stationing himself once again in the Blacksnake Hills post, which he bought rights to for five hundred dollars. He rejoined the French Company and faced the opposition of his former partner, Jean Baptiste Roy. Unquestionably, Robidoux and Roy contributed a share of the lethal volumes of alcohol that debauched local and emigrant tribes at the Bluffs, the "whiskey capital of the East" in the 1830s and 1840s.

Robidoux's Blacksnake Hills post, a substantial log structure, was a staging area for western fur-trading expeditions, and he employed several traders and trappers in the 1830s and 1840s. As the fur and whiskey trade collapsed, Robidoux, like other former merchant-traders, resourcefully availed himself of newer opportunities and reaped profits in the sale of town lots.

Following the Platte Purchase, the Robidoux post became the nucleus for the multiethnic community of St. Joseph, Missouri. After gold was discovered in 1848, St. Joseph became the jumping-off place for overlanders going to California. It also served as a home base and staging area for the family trading ventures along the Platte River in the Scott's Bluff and Fort Laramie trading zones of Wyoming in the 1840s and 1850s.

St. Joseph prospered, and Joseph Robidoux was its leading citizen in civic and financial affairs, but visiting missionaries left disapproving reports of polygamy, gambling, and excessive drinking at his establishment. William McClurg Paxton, a visitor to Robidoux's home in November 1839, said that behind the trading house were five scaffolds on which the bones of Robidoux's many children by Indian wives were laid. In 1850 Rudolph Kurz claimed Robidoux was living with his sixty "papooses." (Many of these mixed-blood children were likely progeny of his brothers or sons.)

Little is known about Robidoux's declining years. According to one report he faced financial hardship because of his many dependents and because of his gambling debts in St. Joseph; he reputedly locked his alcoholic son Joseph Robidoux IV in a cellar until he deeded over the fortune in St. Louis town lots that he had inherited from his mother.

Joseph Robidoux died on May 27, 1868, at age eighty-four at the family home in St. Louis and was buried there.

TANIS C. THORNE

Chardon, Francis. *Chardon's Journal at Fort Clark, 1834–1839.* Ed. Annie H. Abel. Pierre: South Dakota Department of History, 1932.

Kurz, Rudolph. *Journal of Rudolph Friederich Kurz.* Ed. J. N. B. Hewitt. Smithsonian Institution, Bureau of American Ethnology Bulletin 115. Washington, D.C.: U.S. Government Printing Office, 1937.

Mattes, Merrill J. "Joseph Robidoux." In *The Mountain Men and the Fur Trade of the Far West,* ed. LeRoy R. Hafen. 10 vols. Glendale, Calif.: Arthur H. Clark, 1965–1972.

Robidoux, Orral Messmore. *Memorial to the Robidoux Brothers.* Kansas City, Mo.: Smith-Grieves, 1924.

Thorne, Tanis C. *The Many Hands of My Relations: French and Indians on the Lower Missouri.* Columbia: University of Missouri Press, 1996.

Wallace, William Swilling. *Antoine Robidoux, 1794–1860.* Los Angeles: Glen Dawson, 1953.

RODMAN, FRANCIS A. (1829–1888)

Francis A. Rodman, a Missouri secretary of state, was born in 1829 in Germany. Little is known of his early life, but he is believed to have emigrated to the United States in the wake of the German revolutions in 1848. He married Marie Magdalena Eberwine at Terre Haute, Indiana, on October 12, 1852. They had three children.

After living for a time in Cincinnati, Rodman emigrated to St. Joseph in 1858 to become the editor of the *St. Joseph Volksblatt.* A skillful orator, he served as president of the German Turner Society and played a prominent role in encouraging German enlistments during the Civil War. Strongly antislavery, he became an early adherent of the Missouri Radical Union Party when it was formed in the fall of 1863. Rodman helped organize the Forty-third Missouri Infantry on August 5, 1864, at Camp Rosecrans near St. Joseph and was commissioned as first lieutenant and quartermaster. Captured at Glasgow by **Sterling Price**'s Confederates during their raid into the state that fall, he was released a month later and returned to St. Joseph to learn of his election as secretary of state on the Radical ticket.

In that office, Rodman proved himself one of the most ardent adherents to the Radical cause. In the aftermath of the referendum on the constitution of 1865, a rumor circulated that the secretary had declined a $150,000 bribe to throw the election. When the constitution's opponents sought to inspect the canvass, Rodman indignantly refused them admission to his office. In the election of 1866 he refused to certify the votes from the conservative Callaway County on the grounds that fraud and intimidation had been used at the polls there. This reversed the results in the Ninth District congressional race from a 1,122 majority for the Conservative candidate to a 178-vote deficit in favor of the Radical incumbent. It also caused the Callaway seat in the Missouri House of Representatives to remain vacant for two years.

In the election of 1868 Rodman manipulated the canvass to an even greater extent, throwing out the votes in eight counties, affecting not only local and legislative races but also the results in two congressional districts. Although the Democrats secured a unanimous decision from the Radical state supreme court that Rodman had exceeded his authority, the Radical majority in the legislature accepted the secretary's canvass report and ordered new elections in those counties. Contests by the two Democratic congressional candidates before the Republican-dominated United States House of Representatives proved equally futile. This high-handed behavior earned him the sobriquet "Count" Rodman from disgruntled Democrats.

Rodman was the only Radical officeholder renominated in 1868. Rumor had it that he retained his post because of his threat to reveal the "real means" by which the constitution of 1865 had been adopted. Reelected that year, he served until 1871.

William F. Switzler of Columbia, who had been denied a congressional seat in both 1866 and 1868 because of Rodman's manipulations, sued the secretary for two thousand dollars in damages in July 1869. By the time Switzler obtained a judgment three years later, Rodman had declared bankruptcy and left the state. He spent the last fifteen years of his life in Chicago where he worked as a journalist and held a number of positions in city government. He died of apoplexy on July 1, 1888, and was buried in Graceland Cemetery in Chicago.

WILLIAM E. PARRISH

Parrish, William E. *Missouri under Radical Rule, 1865–1870.* Columbia: University of Missouri Press, 1965.

Selby, Paul O. *Missouri's Secretaries of State and Attorneys General.* Kirksville: Northeast Missouri State University, 1968.

ROLLINS, JAMES SIDNEY (1812–1888)

Missouri Whig Party leader, father of the University of Missouri, and patron and friend of painter **George Caleb Bingham,** James Sidney Rollins was born at Richmond in Madison County, Kentucky, on April 19, 1812. The eldest of the seven children of Dr. Anthony Wayne and Sarah Harris Rollins, James attended Richmond Academy, then Washington College in Pennsylvania, before graduating from Indiana University in 1830. Upon graduation he moved to Boone County, Missouri, to join his parents who had settled there earlier that year. For two years he studied law with **Abiel Leonard,** a future chief justice of the Missouri Supreme Court. In 1832 Rollins served as an aide-de-camp to Gen. **Richard Gentry** in the Black Hawk War, and was called "Major" Rollins ever after. He then completed his legal education at Transylvania University in Lexington, Kentucky, graduating in 1834. Returning to Missouri, he formed a law partnership in Columbia with Thomas Miller, a college friend. In 1837 he married Mary Elizabeth

Hickman. The marriage proved long and happy, producing eleven children, seven of whom survived to adulthood.

A man of diverse interests, Rollins was never sufficiently enthused by the law to make it more than a sideline. In 1835 Miller and Rollins purchased the *Missouri Intelligencer and Boon's Lick Advertiser,* changing the name to the *Columbia Patriot.* Rollins sold his interest in 1840. An astute businessman, he invested wisely in railroads and proved a successful land speculator. The most important of his holdings was his large estate, LaGrange, located just southwest of Columbia. By 1860 he farmed the plantation through the labor of twenty-four slaves.

As much as he loved his land, it was Whig politics that attracted Rollins's main interest. Like his father, Rollins began his political career as an ardent admirer of Henry Clay. He was a relentless champion of Missouri's economic development, promoting efforts to improve the navigability of Missouri's rivers. He was an early and ardent proponent of railroad building, serving at the age of twenty-four as president of Missouri's first railroad convention in 1836. Later, in the United States Congress he was a sponsor of the 1862 bill that led to the creation of the Union, Central, and Kansas Pacific Railroads. An emotional nationalist, he wanted to help transform America into a mighty civilization of prosperity and culture. As his first biographer put it, to Rollins statistics detailing America's material progress were as sublime as the words of the poet.

An important leader of the Whig Party until its dissolution in the mid-1850s, Rollins's political career began in 1838 when he won election to the Missouri House. Politically doomed to the minority as a Whig in an overwhelmingly Democratic state, Rollins, an uncommonly talented speaker, was more popular than his party. Although no Whig would ever be elected governor in Missouri, late in life Rollins freely admitted this had been his most desired goal. Nominated by the Whigs in 1848, he lost to **Austin A. King** in what was a decided improvement over his party's nominees' past standards.

After the collapse of the Whigs in the wake of the Kansas-Nebraska Act, Rollins briefly joined the anti-immigrant American Party, or "Know-Nothings," which served him, as it did many Whigs, as a flag of convenience for his opposition to a Missouri Democratic Party increasingly dominated by pro-Southern politicians. In 1857 he ran for governor as an independent. This time he came within a hair of securing his dream. Making common cause with the Democratic followers of **Thomas Hart Benton** and **Frank Blair** (who had large immigrant support), the Know-Nothings, and a Whig remnant, which refused to give up the party name, he lost, amid charges of Democratic fraud, to **Robert M. Stewart** by 334 votes.

As a Whig politician in a Democratic state, Rollins was by necessity as well as by temperament a consensus politician. The Civil War undercut the politics of moderation. While he was a slaveholder, he disliked slavery, thought it was immoral, and cherished and honored free labor. He did not believe that slavery was essential to Missouri's economy, nor to his own livelihood. Rollins despised the moral fanaticism of the abolitionists, but hated dis-Unionism more. For fire-eating Southerners to destroy America's rising glory to protect slavery was anathema to him. He was greatly distraught by the nation's growing polarization during the 1850s, and desperately sought a middle ground. Agitation on the subject by both sides hurt Missouri's economic development, scaring away investors and immigrants. Still, for Rollins, as for many others, if slavery was a moral evil it was also an intractable practical problem. Although he disliked it, he could not see how the two races could live freely side by side without violence. For all his caution, or perhaps because of it, he was considered "unsound" by proslavery Missourians, who attacked him fiercely as a free soiler.

In 1860 Rollins ran successfully for the United States Congress as a Constitutional Unionist. Many years before, in the course of Whig Party politics, he had made friends with Abraham Lincoln and enjoyed easy access to the White House, where the president relied on him for advice concerning Missouri and the border states. While he came to favor a gradual, compensated emancipation, Rollins initially voted against the Thirteenth Amendment to the Constitution as a member of Congress. When it failed to gain the necessary two-thirds margin in the House, he was one of the handful of congressmen who changed their vote to secure its passage.

Repelled by Republican measures in Missouri during the Civil War, Rollins returned to private life, joined the Democratic Party, and won election to the Missouri House of Representatives in 1866 and the Missouri Senate in 1868 and 1870. Like many Democrats, he made common cause with the Liberal Republican revolt against the Grant Republicans in 1870, and in 1872 he narrowly lost the Democratic nomination for governor. Perhaps rightly so. Rollins was, in fact, a weak Democrat, having joined the party largely in reaction to the viciousness of Missouri's Civil War. As those circumstances receded Rollins found himself out of sympathy with many Democratic policies, and decided that the Republican Party more clearly embodied his lifelong support of economic development and the "higher" concerns of state. In 1876 he joined the Republicans and remained a party member for the rest of his life.

As materialistic as Rollins's social views were, material progress was important to him principally as the means to a more humane civilization. He was conspicuously active in creating and promoting those things that he thought softened the hardness of life, such as an asylum for the insane, a school for the blind, the encouragement of art—even the laying out of rural cemeteries. In a speech in 1873 before a national convention of businessmen and government officials concerning the commercial uses of the country's waterways, he declared: "The culture and development of mind—that is the true 'internal improvement' without which all other is vain and empty. . . . Great is the Hoosac [Railroad], great the Michigan Central—but Harvard and Ann Arbor are infinitely greater."

Of all his humanistic enterprises little meant more to Rollins than the public support of education, and, in the end, nothing—not even his political career— meant more to him than the building up of the University of Missouri. In 1839, when he was just twenty-six and newly elected to the state legislature, the first bill he drafted was to establish the location of a state university. Only six centrally located counties were permitted to compete, and through his energetic efforts he secured such generous donations from Boone Countians (both he and his father gave liberally) that he ensured Columbia's selection as the new university's site. He would remain actively involved with the university for the remainder of his life.

Despite Rollins's early ambitions, the "University" of Missouri was never much more than a local community college during the first decades of its existence. The school suffered greatly during the Civil War—only one hundred students, six teachers, and some half-ruined buildings survived at its end. Many Republicans who believed Columbia was a hotbed of Confederate disloyalty called for the university's removal to a different location. During the next two decades Rollins not only fought off the challenge of those who would remove the university from Columbia but virtually refounded the school, securing its rerecognition as *the* state university and winning greatly increased support from the Missouri legislature. One of his bills created a normal school within the university, which not only added to its financial support but also helped ensure that there would be teachers to raise a badly needed crop of students to attend the school. More important, as a U.S. congressman Rollins helped sponsor the 1862 Morrill Act, giving large tracts of federal land to the states to support the creation of agricultural and mechanical colleges. After the war he began a protracted struggle, amid heated competition, to have the university designated as Missouri's federal land-grant school. His struggle finally came to a successful conclusion in 1870 when the university received 330,000 acres of federal land, the sale of which would be used to support the university.

In 1869 Gov. **Joseph McClurg** had put Rollins on the University of Missouri Board of Curators, and the curators immediately made him their board's president. Always close to university events, he was ever after in almost daily contact with the school administration. Significantly for his political career, though he detested the so-called Drake Constitution of 1865 for its harsh repression of Southern sympathizers and Democratic political opponents, Rollins found in Radical ranks the strong support for his lifelong desire to improve both higher and secondary education. Accordingly, despite forceful solicitation, he refused to denounce the repressive Radical measures as fervently as many wished because he feared it would jeopardize Radical support for the University of Missouri and its Columbia location. His willingness to compromise with the Radicals, however, came back to haunt him when doubts about his party partisanship cost him the Democratic nomination for governor in 1872. That same year the university, mindful of its debt to Rollins, formally named him "pater universitatis Missouriensis." His "fatherhood" of the University of Missouri continued another fourteen years, until on April 19, 1886, his seventy-fourth birthday, he resigned from the board of curators, ending his seventeen years as its president.

Rollins had an often-remarked talent for friendship. Curiously, for all his various activities, he is remembered best nationally for his friendship with George Caleb Bingham. Rollins met Bingham in Columbia in 1834 when the artist had his studio in the same building as Rollins's law office. Convinced of Bingham's genius, Rollins helped support the struggling painter by arranging for him to paint Rollins's relations and friends; by underwriting the costs of engraving Bingham's paintings, even after Bingham had become famous; by orchestrating lucrative commissions from the state legislature; and by arranging Bingham's appointment as the University of Missouri's first professor of art. Rollins's support, however, went far beyond money, for it was to Rollins that Bingham turned in good times and bad for direction and support, and it is through Rollins's preservation of Bingham's many letters that we have our best insight into the character and personality of the artist. For his part, Bingham returned Rollins's friendship in equal measure and enthusiastically took up Rollins's politics, much of which can be seen in the artist's paintings. Both named a son for the other man. Their close friendship endured until Bingham's death in 1879; Rollins delivered a funeral eulogy widely noted for its eloquence.

Rollins outlived his friend by nearly a decade. Yet, in 1874 Rollins's lifelong robust health had been permanently damaged when the train he was riding to St. Louis derailed. Through a determined force of will he eventually resumed his energetic round of activities, but through a progressively enfeebled body. He died in Columbia on January 9, 1888.

KENNETH H. WINN

Grissom, Daniel M. "Personal Recollections of Distinguished Missourians: James S. Rollins." *Missouri Historical Review* 18 (1924): 547–52.

Mering, John. "The Political Transition of James S. Rollins." *Missouri Historical Review* 53 (1959): 217–26.

Smith, William Benjamin. *James Sidney Rollins.* New York, 1891.

ROSATI, JOSEPH (1789–1843)

Joseph Rosati, first bishop of the Catholic diocese of St. Louis, was born in Sora in southern Italy on January 30, 1789. He attended a school in Rome conducted by the Congregation of the Mission, a religious brotherhood founded in seventeenth-century France by Saint Vincent de Paul.

Rosati entered this brotherhood, commonly known as the Vincentians, at the age of eighteen. Ordained to the priesthood in 1811, he served as a traveling missionary in small towns in central Italy until 1816 when Bishop **Louis William DuBourg** of the Louisiana Territory invited him and other Vincentians to work in the American West. Rosati landed in Baltimore in July 1816 and spent two years in Bardstown, Kentucky, learning English and becoming acquainted with frontier ways. In 1818 he arrived in Missouri where he opened a college and seminary in Perryville, and at the death of **Felix de Andreis** in 1820 became superior of the Congregation of the Missions in America.

On July 14, 1823, Pope Leo XII appointed the thirty-four-year-old Rosati as coadjutor bishop of Louisiana and Florida Territories to assist Bishop DuBourg. A man given to constantly changing enthusiasm, DuBourg took up residence in New Orleans and wanted Rosati to move the seminary from Perryville to the bayou country of west-central Louisiana in 1825. The coadjutor wisely urged delay.

The following year DuBourg went to France, presumably to get help for the work in the Mississippi Valley. He did send help but stayed in France, accepting a bishopric in the Pyrenees. Rosati succeeded to the double post of bishop of St. Louis and administrator of the diocese of New Orleans. At that time the diocese of St. Louis included the entire state of Missouri, the western two-thirds of Illinois, and all of the Louisiana Territory north of the state of Louisiana.

The new bishop invited Mother **Rose Philippine Duchesne,** who had opened a school in St. Charles, to St. Louis. He ordained to the priesthood six Belgian Jesuit seminarians who had conducted school for Native American boys near Florissant. In 1828 he invited the Jesuits to man St. Louis college, a school that Bishop DuBourg had started in 1818, and put under the direction of Father François Niel. During the same year Rosati ordained the son of a Creole merchant, John Francis Regis Loisel, the first priest born in St. Louis. At the invitation of Bishop Rosati and with the financial assistance of **John Mullanphy,** the Sisters of Charity of Emmitsburg, Maryland, opened a hospital in St. Louis.

In 1830 a Vincentian colleague, Leo De Neckere, accepted the bishopric of New Orleans, and Rosati was able to give complete attention to the St. Louis area.

A systematic man, Rosati left a daily journal that gives a clear picture of his busy days. His reports to the Leopoldine Foundation in Vienna, a society that assisted church activities in America, show a general's grasp of the geography of the area and an organizer's comprehension of the social patterns. He knew where the immigrants were locating and from whence they came.

DuBourg had commissioned a hastily built and small "cathedral." Pledges went uncollected, and the deed to the property remained in the hands of wealthy merchants who had not yet learned what a church in a free society required of its members. When gifts from Europe finally lifted the burden, Rosati planned a fitting cathedral in federal style. It was completed in 1834 in spite of heavy debts.

Rosati attended a conference of bishops in Baltimore in 1831, and so impressed his fellow prelates that they came to recognize him "as one of the most remarkable bishops in Christendom."

Rosati invited the Sisters of St. Joseph to come from France to open a school for the deaf. Six nun educators came, two trained for deaf education. They undertook schools in Carondelet and in Cahokia, Illinois.

Three times during the 1830s delegations from the Salish or Flathead tribes of western Montana came to St. Louis seeking a "Blackrobe." With the approval of Bishop Rosati, the Jesuit missionary **Pierre Jean De Smet** went to their villages in 1840.

In 1841 Pope Gregory XVI sent Rosati on a special mission to Haiti. Rosati sought Father **Peter Richard Kenrick,** chancellor of the diocese of Philadelphia, as his coadjutor. When Rosati died in Rome on September 25, 1843, after reporting on his official visitation of the church in Haiti, Kenrick succeeded him.

The "Old Cathedral" stands alongside the Arch as a living memorial to St. Louis's first bishop.

Even more credit goes to him for his tireless work in remaining close to his people, encouraging his coworkers, and organizing one of the great dioceses of America.

WILLIAM B. FAHERTY

Easterly, Frederick John. *The Life of Joseph Rosati, C.M., First Bishop of St. Louis, 1789–1843.* Washington, D.C.: Catholic University of America Press, 1942.

Faherty, William B. *Dream by the River: Two Centuries of St. Louis Catholicism, 1766–1967.* St. Louis: Piraeus, 1973.

Guilday, Peter. *A History of the Councils of Baltimore, 1791–1884.* 1932. Reprint, New York: Arno Press, 1969.

Rosati, Joseph. Papers. Archives of the St. Louis Archdiocese. Kenrick Seminary, St. Louis.

Rothensteiner, John E. *History of the Archdiocese of St. Louis in Its Various Stages of Development from* A.D. *1637 to* A.D. *1928.* St. Louis: Blackwell Wielandy, 1928.

ROSS, CHARLES G. (1885–1950)

Born in Independence, Missouri, on November 9, 1885, Charles G. Ross attended his town's public schools and graduated with the high school class of 1901, first among forty-one seniors including **Harry S. Truman.** That autumn young "Charlie" Ross—he was only sixteen—enrolled at the University of Missouri in Columbia, where he graduated Phi Beta Kappa in 1905. In college he interested himself in social science and English, the latter with some attention to writing. A few of his compositions have survived, including a long poem about a young lady who needed encouragement, perhaps exaggeration, from a suitor:

All the concentrated blisses
    of a life are in your kisses.
(So it ran for several pages
    Gaining eloquence by stages.)

This the maiden comprehended,
    Then her former note amended.
Getting daft and ever dafter,
    they were married shortly after.

Upon graduation Ross went to work full-time on the weekly *Columbia Herald,* and the next year joined the *St. Louis Post-Dispatch,* with which (save for two intervals) he associated himself until near the end of his life. The first of the intervals occurred when he was dismissed during the economic recession of 1906, after which he was rehired. The second, for a much longer time, began when he was offered a higher salary at a rival paper, the *St. Louis Republic,*

where he was a copyreader, and then in 1908 he joined the new School of Journalism at the University of Missouri; he was the second faculty member engaged for the opening of the school in the fall. Rising to the rank of full professor, he seems to have enjoyed his work, and went so far as to publish a textbook, *The Writing of News,* that enjoyed a modest sales in journalism schools around the country. At the end of World War I in 1918, apparently because he had tired of teaching the wartime journalism students who were mostly women, he again returned to the *Post-Dispatch,* this time as its Washington bureau chief.

Ross's professional life with the *Post-Dispatch* beginning with the Washington assignment brought him prominence nationally, in part because his paper was one of the best in the country, having been brought to a high level by **Joseph Pulitzer,** who died in 1911, and by his son, **Joseph Pulitzer II,** and partly because the owners gathered an extraordinary group of reporters and editors, possibly the best in the nation. In Washington Ross reported on the presidency and became well acquainted with Harding, Coolidge, Hoover, and Franklin D. Roosevelt. He met many members of Congress. As he made his way around the reportorial circuit, it was perhaps his fair-mindedness that made him stand out. When he secured a laudatory two-thousand-word statement from President Coolidge on his paper's fiftieth anniversary, and other members of the White House press corps protested this favoritism, the president explained: "I know where the *Post-Dispatch* stands," Coolidge snapped. "They don't praise me one day and stick a knife in me the next."

When the younger Pulitzer in 1934 decided to bring the *Post-Dispatch* into a more central, perhaps less Democratic, editorial position, he called Ross back to St. Louis to take charge of the editorial page. That year the paper opposed the Democratic candidate for U.S. senator, Truman, "an obscure man scarcely known outside the confines of Jackson County." The paper editorialized acidulously about Truman's connection to Boss **Tom Pendergast** of Kansas City. In 1936 it came out for Gov. Alf Landon of Kansas as the better candidate for president of the United States. When the New Deal's initiatives diminished during the next years, Pulitzer, reassured, sent Ross back to Washington in 1939, where he reported until 1945.

Upon the death of Roosevelt the new Missouri president of the United States overlooked the editorials of preceding years and insisted that Ross become his press secretary. Unfortunately, this new appointment was to mark an anticlimax to Ross's career, which had reached its height in 1931 when he won a Pulitzer Prize for a series of articles titled "The Country's Plight: What Can Be Done about It?" As press secretary he was close to the president, but ventured opinions only when asked, notably during the dismissal of Secy. of Commerce Henry A. Wallace in 1946. During these years Ross's physical condition deteriorated rapidly; he suffered two mild heart attacks, and in 1948 his personal physician gave him at best four years to live. On December 5, 1950, he died at his White House desk.

ROBERT H. FERRELL

Farrar, Ronald T. *Reluctant Servant: The Story of Charles G. Ross.* Columbia: University of Missouri Press, 1969.
Ross, Charles G. Papers. Harry S. Truman Library, Independence, Mo.
———. *The Writing of News.* New York: Henry Holt, 1911.

ROSS, NELLIE TAYLOE (1876–1977)

Nellie Tayloe Ross was the first woman in the United States to serve as a state governor and also the first woman appointed as director of the United States Mint. She was born on November 29, 1876, near St. Joseph, Missouri, to James Wynne and Elizabeth Blair Green Tayloe. While she was still a young girl, the family moved to Omaha, Nebraska, where she received her education in public and private schools. After studying for two years to become a kindergarten teacher, she taught in Omaha for a brief time. In 1902 she married William Bradford Ross, a lawyer whom she had met while visiting relatives in Tennessee, and moved with him to Cheyenne, Wyoming, where he had settled in 1901. The couple had four sons, three of whom lived to adulthood.

While her husband became involved in politics in Wyoming, Nellie Ross was happy, as she later related, being a wife and mother. (Long after she herself became politically active, she always insisted that a woman's fulfillment came primarily from her domestic role.) William Ross's career led him to the governorship of Wyoming in January 1923. However, on October 2, 1924, he died from complications following an appendectomy. Since Wyoming's constitution did not provide for a lieutenant governor, Secy. of State Franklin Lucas became acting governor until an election for a new governor could be held. Both the Republicans and the Democrats quickly held conventions to nominate their candidates for the November election. The Democrats unanimously chose the governor's widow to run against a Republican candidate, Eugene J. Sullivan, who had ties to the oil industry. Although Nellie Ross had not involved herself directly in politics, she had always been her husband's confidante, and she was convinced that she could carry out his programs. Her victory by more than eight thousand votes was due in large part to voters' sympathy for the widow and in part to their distrust of the oil interests since the recent Teapot Dome scandal. Then, too, some voters felt that the first state to give women the vote should be the first to have a woman as governor. On the same election day in November 1924, Miriam A. "Ma" Ferguson won Texas's gubernatorial race. However, the inauguration for Ross was on January 5, 1925, while Ferguson's came on January 20, thus giving Ross the distinction as first woman governor.

During her administration Ross sought stiffer regulations for mine safety, tax relief for the poor, more state loans for farmers, revision of state banking laws, fewer working hours for women, and ratification of the federal amendment to abolish child labor. Some of these measures passed in the Republican-controlled legislature, though not primarily because of her efforts. Historians have judged Ross as a capable and efficient administrator during her two years as governor. In 1926 she ran for reelection, but lost to Republican Frank C. Emerson by 1,365 votes.

Ross, an effective speaker, then became involved in the Democratic Party's national organization. She seconded the nomination of Al Smith at the Houston convention in 1928, and, while helping organize the women's division of the party, she served as vice chairman of the Democratic National Committee from 1929 to 1933. Because of her work for the party, President Franklin D. Roosevelt appointed her director of the United States Mint in 1933, a position she held until 1953. During her tenure, the operation of the mint increased dramatically as the demand for more coins began with the recovery from the depression and accelerated even more with the coming of World War II. The war years brought Ross the problem of reducing the amount of copper, zinc, and nickel in newly minted coins. She also oversaw the doubling of the Denver mint's capacity, and she supervised the construction of a new mint in San Francisco, a new gold depository at Fort Knox, and a silver depository at West Point. Her name is inscribed on the cornerstone of the latter three structures. As the first female director of the mint, she is therefore the first woman to have a mint medal with her likeness on it. Ross conducted her office as director so efficiently that in 1950 she returned about 20 percent of her department's appropriation. Ross, whose tenure ended with the coming of the Eisenhower administration, died on December 19, 1977, at 101 years of age.

PATRICIA ASHMAN

Aslakson, Barbara Jean. "Nellie Tayloe Ross, First Woman Governor." Master's thesis, University of Wyoming, 1960.
Biographical Directory of the Governors of the

United States, 1789–1978. Vol. 4. Westport, Conn.: Meckler Books, 1978.

Larson, T. A. *History of Wyoming.* Lincoln: University of Nebraska Press, 1965.

Priddy, Bob. "The First Woman Governor Hailed from Missouri." *Missouri Life* 12 (January–February 1985): 15–18.

Ross, Nellie Tayloe. "The Governor Lady." Parts 1–3. *Good Housekeeping* 85 (August 1927): 30–31, 118–24; (September 1927): 36–37, 206–18; (October 1927): 72–73, 180–97.

ROZIER, FERDINAND (1777–1864)

Ferdinand Rozier was an early resident of historic Ste. Genevieve and contributed to the development of an area considered the western frontier during the early 1800s. As a practical and successful businessman he helped establish the economy, and as a civic-minded individual he contributed to the development of local government, as did his descendants.

Rozier was born in Nantes, France, on November 9, 1777. His father, François Claude Rozier, was a partner in a prosperous import-export business that traded with merchants in New York and Philadelphia. The respect and admiration shown the senior Rozier is evident from his obituary. Ferdinand Rozier's grandfather was a lawyer in the Parlement of Paris.

After having attained a college education, Rozier served in the French navy from 1802 to 1805. While in the navy he visited the U.S. ports of Philadelphia and Baltimore in 1804. In 1805 Rozier's father and Capt. James Audubon planned a business venture in America. With articles of association drawn up, their sons Ferdinand Rozier (age twenty-eight) and John James Audubon (age twenty-one) sailed for America in April 1806.

Rozier and Audubon arrived in New York, but soon traveled to Audubon Sr.'s property, Mill Grove, thirty miles northwest of Philadelphia. By late summer of 1807 they traveled overland to Pittsburgh, then floated down the Ohio River to Kentucky. They engaged in the mercantile business there for three years. By the fall of 1810 the two friends decided to move farther west in hopes of establishing a more profitable business in Ste. Genevieve, which was a hub of commerce at that time. They purchased a keelboat and loaded it with merchandise, including dry goods, gunpowder, whiskey, and provisions for the trip. After spending part of the winter with Shawnee Indians at Tywappity Bottom, south of Cape Girardeau, Rozier and Audubon continued upriver to Ste. Genevieve.

There Rozier and Audubon found a ready market for the whiskey, and the business succeeded due to the efforts of Rozier. Audubon preferred to spend his time hunting and painting birds. In 1811 he sold his interest to Rozier and returned to Kentucky. They remained friends for life through correspondence and several visits. Rozier continued to succeed in business, making six long and dangerous trips to the East to purchase goods. The family occasionally accompanied him on purchasing trips to New Orleans. The business prospered, and branch stores were established at Perryville, St. Mary, and Potosi.

Rozier married Constance Roy of Fort Charters, Illinois, on October 8, 1813. They had ten children, eight sons and two daughters. Having received a college education, Rozier understood the importance of learning. His five oldest sons were tutored or attended school at St. Mary of the Barrens near Perryville; his three youngest sons studied at St. Vincent's in Cape Girardeau. His two oldest sons, Ferdinand Roy and Francis Claude, were taken to France to live with relatives and complete their education. They became merchants like their father. Joseph Adolphe studied law in Ste. Genevieve and France, and then returned to practice in New Orleans. Firmin Andrew, Charles Constant, and Amable Edward also studied and practiced law. Son Firmin established an academy for young men in 1854. It continued until the outbreak of the Civil War. Firmin also wrote a history of the early settlements in the Ste. Genevieve area. Charles was appointed to the board of regents of the state normal school in Cape Girardeau in 1872. Daughters Mary Lucile and Felicite attended the Visitation Convent at Kaskaskia, Illinois.

Three of Rozier's sons (Felix, Francis, and Firmin) married three daughters of **Jean-Baptiste Vallé,** the original owner of Vallé Mining Company, and in doing so became associated with the mining business. This company began in 1825 and grew to include the Perry mine. Felix became one of the principal owners and served as president of the company in the 1880s.

When the city of Ste. Genevieve was incorporated in 1827, Rozier served as mayor. Later, his sons Francis, Firmin, Felix, and Charles held that position. Joseph served a short term as mayor of New Orleans. Rozier's sons held numerous other county and city offices in Ste. Genevieve and Perry Counties. Firmin was elected to the state legislature for two terms beginning in 1850, then to the state senate for four years beginning in 1872.

Rozier continued in business until a few years before his death on January 1, 1864. He lived to be eighty-six and his wife eighty-three. Besides his ten children, at the time of his death he had 110 grandchildren and great-grandchildren.

Many Rozier descendants continue to live in the historic homes of Ste. Genevieve and are considered among the prominent citizens in Ste. Genevieve or Perry Counties and other areas of the state.

LYLE W. DORSETT

Basler, Lucille Seitz. *The District of Ste. Genevieve, 1725–1980.* Greenfield, Mo.: Vedette Printing, 1980.

Douglas, Robert Sidney. *History of Southeast Missouri.* Reprint, Cape Girardeau, Mo.: Ramfre Press, 1961.

Franzwa, Gregory M. *The Story of Ste. Genevieve.* St. Louis: Patrice Press, 1967.

Goodspeed's History of Southeast Missouri. Reprint, Cape Girardeau, Mo.: Ramfre Press, 1964.

Sharp, Mary Rozier. *Between the Gabouri.* Ste. Genevieve, Mo.: Histoire de Rozier, 1981.

RUSSELL, CHARLES MARION (1864–1926)

Charles Marion Russell was born on March 19, 1864, in Oak Hill, Missouri, which was at the time a suburb just west of St. Louis and is now in the Tower Grove Park area of the city. He grew up in an upper-middle-class family of six children, and it was expected that he would assume a place in the world of business after the appropriate years of education. Such prospects were not much to young Russell's liking. His imagination and love of the outdoors were nurtured by an uncle who had been a rider for the Pony Express, other family connections to explorers and travelers, as well as the romantic imagery of western folklore. This imagery was already fixed and focused on the disappearing Indian, the cowboy, the mountain man, and the wilderness. It was illustrated by such well-known Missouri artists as **George Caleb Bingham** and **Carl Wimar,** whose vision and work inspired Charles Russell.

As a boy Russell was not a good student, and, after an unsuccessful venture at a military school in New Jersey when he was fifteen, his parents arranged a trip to Montana in hopes that a summer working outdoors would settle the young man. He did not come back for two years, settling into the life for which he longed—outdoors, in the West, as a workingman. He worked briefly with a sheepherder but found it distasteful and moved on to take up a position for the next two years as a helper and apprentice to a trapper and hunter who sold meat to the ranchers and miners near Helena.

After two years of such work, and a brief visit home, Russell found employment near Billings as a night wrangler on several of the better cattle operations. From 1882 to 1893 he worked at night and on roundups in the spring and fall. He claimed later that this left his days free to observe the life of the cowboy and draw, sketch, and paint scenes of western life.

In 1885 Russell completed his first major oil painting, *Breaking Camp,* which he shipped back to Missouri where it was included in the St. Louis Exposition of 1886. He gained recognition in Montana the following year when he illustrated the bitter and disastrous winter of 1886–1887. The foreman of the ranch where he worked was asked for a report on the condition of a herd of five thousand cattle at winter's end. Russell included a small watercolor of an emaciated steer surrounded by wolves that he titled *Waiting for a Chinook,* though it also came to be known as *The Last of the Five Thousand.* By the age of twenty-two, Charles Russell was becoming known as an artist and illustrator of the West.

Eschewing formal training in art, Russell continued to work as a night wrangler while producing more and more drawings and paintings. By 1889 he was working only on the spring and fall roundups and painting summers and winters. Although he lived his adult life in Montana, mostly in or near Great Falls and Helena, he made frequent trips to Missouri to visit family and acquire art supplies. By 1893 he gave up working cattle operations to devote himself exclusively to art.

In 1896 Russell married Nancy Cooper, who began to manage his business affairs. Under her able management, Russell became one of the most successful artists of the West. She arranged that he met and was noticed by influential people in eastern cities, that his work was displayed in prestigious galleries, and that he had one-man shows in places where people had the money to buy art. He exhibited in St. Louis frequently, having his first one-man show there in 1903; he also exhibited the following year at the World's Fair. He showed his paintings and watercolors in New York and London, as well as Chicago, Minneapolis, and Washington, D.C.

Russell was always acutely aware that the West he chronicled was being overwhelmed by the progress that supported his work as a painter. He was often compared with Frederic Remington, a contemporary. Remington is usually regarded as the better artist—perhaps because of his formal training at Yale and his life in the East. Russell preferred to remain the rough, self-taught westerner. Additionally, he resisted the role of illustrator of Manifest Destiny. He was just as interested in chronicling the life of the Indian, as well as the cowboy, and lived for a time with the Blood Indians in northern Montana. His portrayal of Indians reflected a more sympathetic vision than that of Remington, who usually portrayed them as villains. Russell presented them as victims, impoverished by the move of progress, or set them as romantic heroes of the natural world.

By the 1920s Russell was spending most of his winters in southern California and was ambivalent about the transition he had witnessed and portrayed. He was granted an honorary doctor of laws degree by the University of Montana in 1925, and on October 24, 1926, Charles Russell died at the age of sixty-two in Great Falls, Montana.

JANICE BRANDON-FALCONE

Adams, Ramon F., and Homer E. Britzman. *Charles Russell: The Cowboy Artist*. Pasadena, Calif.: Trail's End, 1948.

Dippie, Brian W., ed. *Charles Russell, Word Painter: Letters, 1887–1926*. Fort Worth, Tex.: Amon Carter Museum; New York: Harry N. Abrams, 1993.

Hassrick, Peter H. *Charles M. Russell*. New York: Harry N. Abrams, 1989.

RUSSELL, THEODORE PEASE (1820–1899)

Born in 1820, Theodore Russell was the third son of Cyrus and Rebecca Russell, who emigrated with a large family from the Connecticut River valley to Missouri's Arcadia valley in 1838. Lured by a kinsman's land speculation in Missouri's famous iron deposits, they were minor shareholders and participants in a model urban dream named Missouri City that was projected to be a great new industrial town. Missouri City failed, but the Russells decided to stay.

Theodore Russell, like the other men of the family, had a classical education and a vision for social and institutional progress on the frontier. During the 1850s and 1860s he worked in the woods at the family sawmill, contracted for agricultural products sold to the Pilot Knob iron mine, managed his commercial orchard, and became a county official. Like all his siblings, he lived on a farm given to him by his parents, enjoying the luxury of never working for wages and priding himself on being a "book farmer." To the chagrin of his father, Russell never busily pursued profits to invest in land speculation, writing that "the opportunity of earning more was less attractive than that of working less."

Russell gained a great reputation as a storyteller, eventually writing a local newspaper column titled "Old Times" from 1884 until his death on February 26, 1899. He wrote of his boyhood in the East, late antebellum society in southeast Missouri, hunting in the great Ozarks outdoors, and timber and landscape, and completed a travelogue of his railroad trips to St. Louis during the late nineteenth century. His writings comprise an important account of frontier society, institutions, and material culture, as well as reflections upon the evolution of a preindustrial world into an industrial one that had significant economic ties to St. Louis.

Russell was a sickly child and grew up skilled in domestic arts such as cooking and sewing. Ever cognizant of his "boy-girl childhood," he took a doctor's advice to "rough it" in the outdoors rather than risk "never becoming a man." As a member of a family secure in land and the leisure it provided, Russell pursued the remedy for his poor health by developing a passion for hunting and the natural environment.

Describing himself as a "naturalist," Russell claimed that his goals in an outdoor life included education, moral self-improvement, recreation, and market hunting. He was the family hunter and proudly sported the nickname "Old Boone." He sought the wisdom of older, experienced hunters and spent large amounts of time in the hills and valleys surrounding Arcadia valley. He reveled in hunting exploits, especially during the 1870s after the extension of the St. Louis and Iron Mountain Railroad. Modern rail transportation opened an unprecedented game harvest, an opportunity not lost on Russell. He recorded killing as many as eighty deer in one week and, while admiring the new innovation of repeating Winchester rifles, boasted that if only he could have had one he would not have left many deer in the woods.

Russell's experience as a naturalist challenged him to reflect upon the dramatic environmental changes that he witnessed. While he was a romantic champion of open range, stock herding, and market hunting he was a vocal supporter of modernity. While musing about an Edenic Ozarks, he called for an active government that regulated the natural world to support hunting for sport and large game populations for naturalists.

Russell advocated self-sufficiency and small-town culture. He felt that the railroad offered great opportunity in independence and new economies for the working class. While he extolled modernity's virtues, he criticized labor-saving agricultural machinery as it began to reduce seasonal work and brought poverty upon squatters conditioned to open-range lifestyles. He bemoaned the circumstance as youths migrated to the cities to find factory work. His anxiety about the erosion of past lifestyles while accepting much of the new was typical of many of his era, but was rarely reflected upon so much in personal writings.

LYNN MORROW

Keefe, James F., and Lynn Morrow, eds. *A Connecticut Yankee in the Frontier Ozarks: The Writings of Theodore Pease Russell*. Columbia: University of Missouri Press, 1988.

Morrow, Lynn. "Theodore Pease Russell: Connecticut Yankee to Missouri Jeffersonian." *Missouri Historical Review* 84 (July 1990): 428–46.

Russell Family Papers. Western Historical Manuscripts Collection, Rolla.

RYLE, WALTER HARRINGTON, III (1896–1978)

While politics was his avocation and law his intended vocation as an avenue to a political career, Walter Harrington Ryle III became a teacher, public school administrator, college professor, and president for thirty years of Missouri's oldest teachers college. He was born on June 1, 1896, on a farm near Yates, to Walter Harrington, known as Harry, and Kate Stark Ryle.

After completing the courses offered in the Ryle School, Ryle enrolled in September 1913 in the First District Normal School in Kirksville. There he fell under the sway of **Eugene Morrow Violette,** a history professor, and **John R. Kirk,** the school's president. In what seemed a conversion experience akin to his acceptance of the Baptist faith, Ryle determined to become a teacher.

In 1927 Ryle, superintendent of schools at Holden, was appointed to the faculty of what was by then Northeast Missouri State Teachers College, provided he spend a year in graduate study. He transferred credits earned at the University of Chicago and the University of Wisconsin to George Peabody where he received a Ph.D. in history in 1930. His dissertation, published in 1930 and titled *Missouri: Union or Secession,* is considered the definitive work on the subject.

When the president of the teachers college died in August 1937, the board of regents quickly named Ryle the school's seventh president, a position he held until retirement in 1967. Growth marked his presidency. A campus of four buildings on fifteen acres enlarged to twenty-five buildings on sixty acres while enrollment went from 755 to 5,350, and the size of the faculty kept pace. Many fine trees, velvety grass, and a profusion of flowers for each season created a truly beautiful campus. Ryle's forte for politics and his meticulous accounting for funds and lean administration enabled him to gain ever increasing appropriations.

Curriculum revision and the addition of new programs paralleled physical growth. Ryle guided and directed faculty councils in implementing his educational philosophy. The first two years of college study contained required courses in general education, that is, basic liberal arts and sciences. In the junior and senior years students majored in a specific discipline and took professional courses such as the psychology of learning and the philosophy of education. In 1947 the college began to offer a master of arts degree, which Ryle anticipated would become a requirement for teacher certification, the fifth year of college work.

However, he insisted it not be a master of education degree but instead would require research, writing, and wide reading in the literature of the discipline. Thus it would prepare recipients for doctoral study.

The basis of Ryle's style of administration was the responsibility placed by the board of regents on him for the operation of the college. Therefore, he had to know what was transpiring. All chairmen of collegewide councils and committees reported to him, and he approved or vetoed their recommendations. At the same time he shared with the faculty the progress of negotiations with the legislature, budgetary considerations, plans for expenditures, and similar matters. He firmly upheld academic freedom and encouraged faculty members with problems to tell him their concerns. "The latch string to my office door is on the outside," he would say in closing a faculty meeting.

Although his presidential duties occupied most of his time, Ryle engaged in a variety of outside activities. He remained a participant in Democratic politics, taught a Sunday-school class at the First Baptist Church, and served as a Boy Scout executive, which led to his receipt of the Silver Beaver Award. Prior to Pearl Harbor he joined the Committee to Defend America by Aiding the Allies and gave speeches on the dangers of isolationism throughout northeastern Missouri. In 1942 he accepted the chairmanship of the Adair County Defense Council.

Ryle died on October 30, 1978, following a heart attack suffered on his way to attend a college committee meeting. As his funeral cortege left the First Baptist Church, a giant bell on the portico of Kirk Memorial mournfully tolled eighty-two times for each year of his life, marking the end of an era for Northeast Missouri State University.

RUTH WARNER TOWNE

Ryle, Walter H. Papers. Archives of Northeast Missouri State University. Pickler Memorial Library, Kirksville, Mo.

Towne, Ruth Warner. *A Winner Never Quits: The Life and Times of Walter Harrington Ryle.* Kirksville, Mo.: Simpson Publishing, 1970.

S

SANFORD, JOHN ELROY (REDD FOXX) (1922–1991)

Comedian John Elroy Sanford, best known to American audiences by his stage name "Redd Foxx," was born in St. Louis on December 9, 1922. His father, an electrician, abandoned his family and left them destitute when John was only four years old. Initially, John lived with his grandmother and attended Banneker School in St. Louis. During those years he often listened to radio comedy shows and determined that he wanted to enter show business. At the age of thirteen, Sanford moved with his mother to Chicago where he briefly attended DuSable High School. Sanford dropped out of school and joined two friends in a band called the Bon-Bons. In the summer of 1939 they hopped on a freight train bound for New York City. At about that time Sanford began using the name Redd Foxx, which he apparently developed by combining the nickname "Chicago Red," given him because of his hair color, with the surname of the baseball great Jimmy Foxx.

During the 1940s and 1950s Foxx performed in black clubs and music halls throughout the country. Occasionally he had to resort to sign painting to supplement his income. While working at the Brass Rail, a Los Angeles nightclub, Foxx recorded a comedy album, *Laff of the Party,* one of fifty-five such albums that he made during his career. The success of his albums led to invitations to perform at the top Las Vegas nightclubs and to guest appearances on nationally televised shows, including *Today* and the *Tonight Show.* Foxx, long noted for his risqué brand of humor, found it necessary to revise his routines for television audiences.

After viewing Foxx's performance in the 1970 movie *Cotton Comes to Harlem,* producers Norman Lear and Bud Yorken selected him to star in a new television situation comedy that they intended to produce. *Sanford and Son,* which featured Foxx in the role of an elderly junk dealer, first aired on the NBC network in 1972. Although it was a hit with American television audiences, it was a far cry from the off-color comedy that Foxx delivered in his nightclub act. Following a contract dispute, Foxx left the popular show in 1977 and returned to Las Vegas as a featured performer. He consented to play a role that Eddie Murphy wrote especially for him in the film *Harlem Nights.* Younger comics such as Murphy and Richard Pryor considered Foxx a comedic role model.

Despite his success as a performer who commanded impressive salaries, Foxx's personal finances were in shambles. The Internal Revenue Service confiscated many of his personal possessions when he failed to pay more than three-quarters of a million dollars in delinquent taxes. In an effort to repair his finances, Foxx agreed to return to the television screen in 1989 in a new series, *The Royal Family,* created especially for him by Eddie Murphy. On October 11, 1991, Foxx suffered a heart attack and died while filming an episode for the series. He was married four times.

DAWN FRY

Current Biography 33 (December 1972): 154–56.
Lyons, Douglas C. "Still Foxxy and Going Strong." *Ebony* 43 (June 1988): 52–58.
Robinson, Louie. "Redd Foxx: Prince of Clowns." *Ebony* 22 (April 1967): 91–94.

SANFORD, JOHN F. A. (1806–1857)

John F. A. Sanford, born in Winchester, Virginia, in 1806, was one of three children of Alexander and Mary Sanford, of English ancestry. Reared in Virginia, he graduated from West Point and went to St. Louis in 1832 as a U.S. Indian agent. His parents and sister joined him there. In St. Louis Sanford met and married, on November 22, 1832, Emilie Chouteau, the eldest daughter of **Pierre Chouteau Jr.** and scion of the prominent founding family of St. Louis. Sanford became a partner in his father-in-law's firm, Pierre Chouteau Jr. and Company, and eventually amassed a fortune in the fur industry, in mining, and in railroading. He was one of the founding directors of the Illinois Central Railroad Company. In 1836 Sanford moved to New York as the representative of the house of Pierre Chouteau Jr. and Company and of the American Fur Company. He returned often to St. Louis, though, for both business and family reasons.

John F. A. and Emilie Sanford had one child, Benjamin Chouteau Sanford, born in St. Louis on May 6, 1835. Emilie Sanford died shortly thereafter, on April 23, 1836. After he moved to New York, Sanford married again, to Isabella Davis of that city. They had two children, John F. A. and Emily Sanford.

In addition to great success in his commercial endeavors that contributed much to Missouri's economic growth and development, Sanford played a prominent role in Missouri and American legal and constitutional history through his association with the famous *Dred Scott* case.

Dred Scott's owner, Dr. John Emerson, had taken the slave into free territory, which became the basis for the slave's litigation for freedom. The suit was instituted in 1846 against the doctor's widow, Irene Sanford Emerson, John F. A. Sanford's sister. When she remarried and moved to Massachusetts, Sanford handled his sister's business affairs for her in Missouri, which included the pending slave litigation. Scott was duly freed by the Missouri lower court. When Sanford appealed on his sister's behalf to the Missouri Supreme Court, the latter reversed the freedom judgment in a singularly partisan and vitriolic decision clearly influenced by the broadening and divisive conflict over slavery.

Seeking clarification of long-standing "once free always free" principles that the Missouri Supreme Court had overthrown, St. Louis lawyers on both sides of the slavery issue brought a new case into the federal court system, anticipating it would eventually go to the United States Supreme Court. To expedite a hearing in the federal courts as a diversity suit, both sides stipulated in an "Agreed Statement of Facts" that Sanford owned Dred Scott—a signal oversimplification of the actual relationship, which was only that Sanford resided in New York and Dred Scott in Missouri.

Dred Scott v. John F. A. Sanford (the name was misspelled "Sandford" in official records) duly reached the Supreme Court. In the process, however, additional divisive issues became involved. On March 6, 1857, Chief Justice Roger B. Taney delivered the opinion of the Court and declared the following as the law of the land: "Negroes of African descent" were not and could not be citizens of the United States; slaves were property protected by the Constitution, and any law abolishing slavery in the territories (as in the Missouri Compromise) was unconstitutional; and regardless of his or her status elsewhere in the United States, when a person entered a slave state his or her status depended upon the law of that state as interpreted by its own courts. These extreme proslavery doctrines exacerbated already heated and volatile sectional controversies raging through the country and contributed substantially to bringing on the Civil War.

Although he was the nominal defendant in the case, Sanford did not play an active role in its progress. Like those who instituted the federal case, he sought only clarification of "once free always free." No known evidence linked him to the introduction of additional volatile issues that attorneys raised later.

Sanford probably never knew the outcome of the famous litigation and endeavors in which he engaged that had "made demands upon [his] mental resources that few men could have responded to as long as he." His mental faculties deteriorated a few months before the Supreme Court announced its decision, and Sanford was institutionalized in a New York insane asylum. He died there on May 5, 1857. Dred Scott died a little over a year later, on September 17, 1858. Neither lived to witness the outbreak of the bloody sectional strife precipitated by their famous litigation.

WALTER EHRLICH

Creoles of St. Louis. St. Louis: Nixon-Jones Printing, 1893.

Cunningham, Mary B., and Jeanne C. Blythe, eds. *The Founding Families of St. Louis.* St. Louis: Midwest Technical Publications, 1977.

Ehrlich, Walter. *They Have No Rights: Dred Scott's Struggle for Freedom.* Westport, Conn.: Greenwood Press, 1979.

Fehrenbacher, Don E. *The Dred Scott Case: Its Significance in American Law and Politics.* New York: Oxford University Press, 1978.

SAPPINGTON, JOHN S. (1776–1856)

John S. Sappington was a frontier physician in Tennessee and Missouri who became wealthy and famous as the creator and dispenser of "Sappington's Anti-Fever Pills," a quinine-based patent medicine for malaria and for fevers in general.

Sappington's family hailed from Maryland where he was born on May 15, 1776. Several family members were early American doctors. An uncle received a political appointment as justice in the new town of Nashville, and in 1785 brought brother Dr. Mark B. Sappington's family to middle Tennessee. The extended family engaged in land speculation and commercial agriculture, and Mark trained all four of his sons in the medical arts. About 1802 his son John removed to Franklin, Tennessee, where he became a successful planter, village leader, and physician.

In 1817, acting upon the advice of his friend **Thomas Hart Benton,** John Sappington scouted Missouri Territory looking for opportunities in land speculation. With a significant loan from Benton, Sappington moved his family to Howard County, Missouri, investing in several thousand acres in modern Saline County. In 1819 he located a few miles west of Arrow Rock where he remained for the rest of his life.

The doctor became a source of intelligence for new immigrants to the Boonslick region, advising on lands to purchase and acting as a money lender to many. Sappington continued his commercial agriculture business, exporting cotton, tobacco, livestock, and lumber to New Orleans, while marketing his own medical services throughout Boonslick counties and into northwest Missouri. By 1824 he and his family established a company business, Pearson and Sappington, at Jonesborough (now Napton), in Saline County, as a center for their commercial businesses and opened another store in Arrow Rock. They engaged in the Santa Fe trade, continued land speculation, managed tenant contracts for commercial agriculture, loaned money, milled grain and lumber, and manufactured salt. The business demanded the hiring of collection agents and the retention of lawyers for litigation. Profits encouraged Sappington to consider retiring from medicine in 1828.

Instead, Sappington continued what family members sometimes referred to as "his hobby" and hired others to work for him. In 1826 trader and planter **Meredith Miles Marmaduke** married a daughter, and eventually became the family business manager, and in 1830 Dr. George Penn became a major business and Jacksonian political ally.

By 1832 Sappington had discovered a workable chemical formula that included quinine and packaged it as a patent medicine that he marketed across Missouri. Within three years his success prompted him to create another family company, Sappington and Sons, to distribute his product nationally, becoming the first proprietary in the United States to use quinine to treat malaria. He assigned Missouri and Tennessee relatives to oversee sales in particular geographic regions, and they, in turn, hired additional route salesmen to travel the country from the Great Lakes to the East Coast, and especially to the Deep South. Sappington also added Dr. William Price to his business. Price's own marketing ideas helped open markets further as merchants throughout the country became agents for the antifever patent medicine.

In a time when most entrepreneurs had extreme difficulty, Sappington generated a large cash flow during the panics of 1837 and 1839. Expanding their land speculation, the family purchased thousands of acres in the Osage River valley. Sappington hired another physician, C. M. Bradford, into the company, and as the accounts grew they hired more lawyers to collect them. The most troublesome issue during this period became counterfeit pills manufactured by pharmacists and doctors from Michigan to Mississippi. Some imitations led to patient deaths, and severe criticism toward Sappington erupted from the professional medical establishment in the Ohio River valley.

In 1844 Sappington published his *Theory and Treatment of Fevers,* much to the chagrin of family members. The book revealed that Sappington used quinine, a much feared drug, and recommended that the general population manufacture their own pills using his formula. By now, due to the successful use of quinine in the Seminole Indian Wars of 1835–1842, many physicians were experimenting with large doses of quinine and publishing articles in debates over its efficacy. In 1844 Sappington also divided his national business into four separate companies, allocating all business assets to his children, grandchildren, and in-laws.

The sixty-eight-year-old doctor then turned his attention to agricultural estate building and by 1850 managed some seventy-four tenant farms in Saline County. His own Pilot Hickory seat became a leading stock farm in the Boonslick area. He continued lending significant amounts of money, including loans to the Cooper County court to build a bridge and to the new State Agricultural Society to capitalize the fairgrounds at Boonville. He established the Sappington School Fund that later attracted Missouri Valley College to Saline County, and distributed some $120,000 in resources to his children.

Through all of Sappington's economic success he remained a close ally and friend to Thomas H. Benton and the Boonslick Democracy. His sons-in-law Miles Marmaduke and **Claiborne Fox Jackson** and grandson **John Sappington Marmaduke** all became Missouri governors. **George Caleb Bingham** painted his portrait three times, and his family cemetery at Pilot Hickory is currently a state historic site. Sappington's career as an entrepreneurial physician is unique in American frontier history. He died on September 7, 1856.

LYNN MORROW

Hall, Thomas B., Jr., and Thomas B. Hall III. *Dr. Sappington of Saline County, Missouri, 1776–1856.* Arrow Rock, Mo.: Friends of Arrow Rock, 1975.

Morrow, Lynn. "Dr. John Sappington: Southern Patriarch in the New West." Jefferson City: Lynn Morrow, 1985/1988.

Terry, Robert J. "Dr. John Sappington: Pioneer in the Use of Quinine in the Mississippi Valley." *Proceedings of the Tercentenary Celebration of Cinchona* (1931): 164–80.

Young, James Harvey. "Patent Medicines: An Element in Southern Distinctiveness?" In *Disease and Distinctiveness in the American South,* ed. Todd L. Savitt and James Harvey Young. Knoxville: University of Tennessee Press, 1988.

SAUCIER, FRANÇOIS (1740–1821)

Known as "the pioneer of St. Charles," François Saucier was born in 1740 in the Illinois country near Fort de Chartres, the third of three sons to Jean Baptiste and Adelaide Lepage Saucier. Jean Baptiste also used the name François and became renowned during his military career as the civil engineer who designed the second Fort de Chartres. The younger

François Saucier also served in the military in the late eighteenth century, under both French and Spanish authority. He commanded Fort Massac at the time of its surrender to the English in 1765 at the end of the Seven Years' War. Saucier then moved to St. Charles, on the western side of the Mississippi, and married Angelique Roy dit Lapensee by 1787.

In 1799 **Zenon Trudeau,** lieutenant governor of the Upper Louisiana, asked Saucier to found a military post and settlement on the Mississippi River approximately fourteen miles northeast of St. Louis on a narrow neck of land defined by the convergence of the Missouri and Mississippi Rivers. Officials considered the location, called Portage des Sioux, to be a weak spot in the defense of Spanish Territory in the Upper Louisiana. It had earned its name after a band of Sioux had trekked across the point and attacked a group of Missouris. The Sioux caught the Natives by surprise because they had cut across this small peninsula at a point above the Missouri encampment, rather than traveling along the slower and more defensible water route, as expected. After hearing of plans to build a U.S. post on the eastern side of the Mississippi at Paysa, near the present site of Alton, Illinois, Spanish authorities feared that Americans would follow the Sioux example and ambush their hold on the area. Trudeau wanted Saucier to stem the American settlement by acting first. A fort in this location would help control trade on the Missouri River and provide a buffer against invaders.

Saucier accepted the commission and established a small village at Portage des Sioux in the St. Charles district of the Upper Louisiana. He encouraged many ethnic French settlers in the Illinois country to relocate on the western side of the Mississippi. He served as captain of the local militia and commandant of the community until 1804, when the Louisiana Territory became part of the United States.

Although political control had changed hands, Saucier continued to serve in prominent civil positions at Portage des Sioux through most of his life. In 1805 he became the presiding justice of the Court of Common Pleas and Quarter Sessions for the St. Charles District. The United States built a new fort there during the War of 1812, noted as the site of peace negotiations conducted between federal representatives and Native Americans following the war. Portage des Sioux remained the most important settlement in the district well into the nineteenth century, with Saucier as one of its leading citizens.

Trudeau had initially promised Saucier an annual salary of one hundred pesos for his services as commandant at Portage des Sioux. His successor, **Charles de Hault Delassus,** compensated Saucier with eighty-eight hundred arpents of land on the La Saline Ensanglantee (Bloody Saline River). Unfortunately, the salary was never paid, and the area's first board of land commissioners refused all but one thousand arpents to Saucier. He later sought recourse from the U.S. government for the lack of compensation for his services.

Saucier served as a delegate to a convention in St. Louis that protested American land policies, taxation, military service without compensation, the movement of Native Americans into the territory, and the attachment of the Louisiana District to the territory of Indiana. The convention produced a document attesting to these grievances, which Saucier signed on September 29, 1804.

Saucier lived in Portage des Sioux the remaining years of his life, in poverty for many of them. He again petitioned the government for relief in 1817, claiming only the one-thousand-arpent concession granted in 1799 and a small plot of the common field. The remaining balance of the original land grant was finally paid to his heirs on November 1, 1833.

François Saucier died on August 6, 1821, at the age of eighty-one, leaving twenty-two children and his second wife, Françoise Nicolle Les Bois.

RACHEL FRANKLIN WEEKLEY

Conard, Howard L., ed. *Encyclopedia of the History of Missouri.* New York: Southern History, 1901.

Foley, William E. *The Genesis of Missouri: From Frontier Outpost to Statehood.* Columbia: University of Missouri Press, 1989.

Houck, Louis. *A History of Missouri, from the Earliest Explorations and Settlements until the Admission of the State into the Union.* Vol. 2. Chicago: R. R. Donnelley and Sons, 1908.

Nasatir, Abraham P. *Before Lewis and Clark: Documents Illustrating the History of the Missouri, 1785–1804.* Vol. 2. 1952. Reprint, Lincoln: University of Nebraska Press, 1990.

Snyder, John F. "Captain John Baptiste Saucier at Fort Chartres in the Illinois, 1751–1763." *Transactions of the Illinois State Historical Society* 26 (1919): 215–63.

Snyder, Robert McClure, Jr. Papers. Collection 3524, folder 85. Western Historical Manuscripts Collection, Columbia.

SAUER, CARL ORTWIN (1889–1975)

Carl Sauer has probably had a more profound effect on American geographic thought than any other American geographer of the twentieth century. His work did much to bring respect to the academic field of geography and to elevate it to its present status as a fundamental research discipline in American universities.

Carl Ortwin Sauer was born on December 24, 1889, in Warrenton, Missouri, to William Albert and Rosetta J. Vosholl Sauer. His immigrant father was a professor of music and French at Central Wesleyan College, a German Methodist college in Warrenton. When Sauer was nine years old he was sent to Calw, Germany, for three years for a rigorous early education. He graduated from Central Wesleyan in 1908. In 1913 he married Lorena Schowengerdt, also of Warrenton. In 1915 he received a Ph.D. in geography from the University of Chicago, which had recently established the first department of geography in the United States.

In 1923 Sauer joined the department of geography at the University of California at Berkeley and later became its chairman, a position he held until 1954. The Berkeley or Sauer school of geography developed into one of the most distinctive approaches to geographic study in the United States. He retired in 1957, though his scholarly contributions continued until his death on July 18, 1975, in Berkeley.

Sauer received numerous honorary degrees and other honors, including the Daly Medal of the American Geographical Society, the Victoria Medal of the Royal Geographical Society of London, and the Humboldt Medal of the Berlin Geographical Society.

Throughout his long career in geography and as a contributor to humane scholarship in general, Sauer carried the indelible imprint of the German community of Warrenton. The Germans who settled the area were mostly Westphalians who had left a repressive Germany of the 1840s and had come to America for liberty and freedom of thought. People who valued education, they established a homogeneous community and supported a college based upon avowedly German ideas and values. Central Wesleyan embodied the philosophy of Johann Goethe, which permeated German intellectual culture in the nineteenth century. Among its marks were the value of historical study, which contrasted strongly with the progressivism of an American society with little use for the past, emphasis on understanding through personal experience as opposed to laws and principles of behavior, and the interactive role of humans and nature as opposed to separate analysis of them. From this classical Goethian worldview, Sauer learned that history and geography were inseparable, two parts of a whole. He also gained a global view that underpinned his entire professional career. Sauer's early years in a German-culture community in Missouri and his subsequent rise to prominence in American professional geography are primary reasons that American geography contains a strong German-classical tradition.

Sauer's primary theme throughout his career was the transformation of the natural landscape into a cultural landscape. He studied humans in their cultural contexts as agents of change in nature, a field sometimes known as human ecology. He was especially impressed with how human use of the land left it in worse condition. He spoke of "destructive land use" and a "robber economy" of the land. "We keep going," he said, "by deficit spending of nature's capital." *Sustainability* later became the word for the harmonious relations of people with the land they occupy and produce from. Ecologists have come to regard Sauer as a prophet who began writing on this theme around 1920, when it was little articulated.

Sauer insisted that geographers learn by field observation and study in the Goethian tradition of individual experience in nature. His own fieldwork was concentrated in the American Southwest and Mexico, but his numerous students and followers have worked in all parts of the world and always among "common folk." Sauer was appreciative of the wisdom of rural folk. He valued their understanding of their surroundings and natural processes. He spoke and wrote frequently of "homefolks" and was most comfortable among them, whether in Mexico or in Missouri during trips to visit family and friends.

Sauer's published works include several on Missouri. Foremost is his dissertation, published in 1920 as *The Geography of the Ozark Highland of Missouri*. It remains the unparalleled interpretation of the settlement of the Ozarks, including separate analyses of French, American, and German systems of land occupation. Other publications include "Homestead and Community on the Middle Border" (1962) and "Status and Change in the Rural Midwest: A Retrospect" (1963), both short essays on how the Missouri Sauer knew at the turn of the century had changed, usually not for the better.

A major accomplishment was the organization of an international symposium in 1955, "Man's Role in Changing the Face of the Earth." This gathering of scholars helped to lay the intellectual foundation for the environmental movement that blossomed in the 1970s. Sauer wrote the lead essay, "The Agency of Man on Earth," for the published collection of papers. Other publications probe the years of encounter between Europeans and Native Americans. A book of great influence is *Agricultural Origins and Dispersals* (1952), a stimulating reflection on the origin of plant and animal domestication throughout the world. A complete bibliography of Sauer's publications is in his obituary by John Leighly in the *Annals of the Association of American Geographers*.

WALTER A. SCHROEDER

Kenzer, Martin S. "Like Father, Like Son: William Albert and Carl Ortwin Sauer." In *Carl O. Sauer: A Tribute.* Corvallis: Oregon State University Press, 1987.

Leighly, John. "Carl Ortwin Sauer, 1889–1975." *An-*

nals of the Association of American Geographers 66 (September 1976): 337–48.

————, ed. *Land and Life: A Selection from the Writings of Carl Ortwin Sauer.* Berkeley and Los Angeles: University of California Press, 1963.

Sauer, Carl O. *The Early Spanish Main.* Berkeley and Los Angeles: University of California Press, 1966.

————. "The Geography of the Ozark Highland of Missouri." *Geographic Society of Chicago Bulletin* 7 (1920).

————. *Northern Mists.* Berkeley and Los Angeles: University of California Press, 1968.

SAUGRAIN DE VIGNY, ANTOINE FRANÇOIS (1763–1820)

Antoine François Saugrain de Vigny, born on February 17, 1763, was a scientist and physician trained in France who practiced medicine in St. Louis from 1799 until his death. He was descended from a family of booksellers and publishers and was related to numerous famous Frenchmen, including Joseph Guillotin, regent of the Faculty of Medicine in Paris, and Jean François Chalgrin, architect of the Arc de Triomphe.

Saugrain had an early classical education and by the age of ten was a laboratory assistant. He attended lectures in the Jardin du Roi and had courses in anatomy, surgery, chemistry, natural history, and physics from such leading scientists as Antoine François Fourcroy and Mathurin-Jacques Brisson.

Saugrain had practiced surgery at the Hotel-Dieu and, at the age of nineteen, was placed by Guillotin with Gilbert Antoine de St. Maxent, a wealthy merchant-official in Louisiana. He was admitted to the practice of surgery at New Orleans in 1783, at the age of twenty, and practiced there for about three years. Maxent's son-in-law, Bernardo de Gálvez, governor of Louisiana, requested his services after becoming viceroy of Mexico. Gálvez sent Saugrain to Paris to purchase a supply of laboratory materials, but died before Saugrain returned.

Saugrain joined Guillotin's project to found a French settlement in North America and came to Benjamin Franklin's home in Philadelphia in 1787 with letters of introduction and with a letter from Thomas Jefferson, Franklin's successor in Paris, to Gen. George Rogers Clark. He carried a hydrostatic balance and recorded measurements of plants and minerals in the Pittsburgh area. Because the Ohio River had frozen he did not leave for Louisville until the following March. His party of four was attacked and robbed; only Saugrain, who was wounded, and one other reached Louisville. Although he made scientific observations and tested minerals brought to him, this ended Guillotin's dream.

Saugrain returned to France in 1789, and the next year joined other Frenchmen in forming the village of Gallipolis on the Ohio River. There he manufactured thermometers, barometers, and other items, including the "pocket luminary," a small bottle lined with phosphorous oxide against which a sulphur-tipped piece of wood would ignite when rubbed and withdrawn. He also produced "phosphoric candles," or "ethereal matches." Papers, tipped with phosphorus, were sealed in a glass tube and would ignite when the tube was broken and the paper exposed to the air.

Saugrain married Genevieve Rosalle Michau on March 20, 1793, in Gallipolis. In 1796 or 1797 he and his family moved to Lexington, Kentucky, where he had been invited to improve the quality of iron bars.

Saugrain was invited by Lt. Gov. **Zenon Trudeau** to St. Louis in 1797. He was probably attracted by land grants he received near St. Charles. Saugrain moved his family to St. Louis late in 1799 or in 1800. He was appointed surgeon of the Spanish army post at St. Louis and also pursued his medical practice. He was the last of a line of French physicians dating back to 1765 and was the only resident physician from his arrival until 1807.

President Jefferson appointed Saugrain army surgeon at Fort Bellefontaine in 1805; he resigned the appointment in 1811. (The tradition, which originated in Eva Emery Dye's *Conquest,* that Saugrain supplied **Meriwether Lewis** and **William Clark** with thermometers or barometers is not true, but he was among a group of St. Louisans who journeyed with the expedition as far as St. Charles.) Family records indicated he mainly practiced medicine and also sold medicine as was common for physicians of that era.

Saugrain was the first physician to use the new Jenner cowpox vaccine for smallpox west of the Mississippi. He advertised in the *Missouri Gazette* in June 1809 that he had the vaccine, and indicated that he had already been using it and would make it available free to those who could not pay.

At his death Saugrain left a library of 450 volumes, of which 320 remain. These volumes reflect contemporary scientific developments, especially in botany and chemistry. His library holdings also suggest he had little interest in history, theater, gardening, or the writings of Voltaire or other philosophers.

The products of Saugrain's laboratory, his services as a physician, and his introduction of the smallpox vaccine all lessened the hardships of others. As the foremost Missouri scientist of his age, he has a unique place in the history of science and medicine in early St. Louis. Saugrain died in St. Louis on March 5, 1820.

SAMUEL E. DICKS

Dicks, Samuel E. "Antoine Saugrain, 1763–1820: A French Scientist on the American Frontier." *Emporia State Research Studies* 25 (summer 1976).

McDermott, John Francis. "Guillotin Thinks of America." *Ohio State Archaeological and Historical Quarterly* 48 (1938).

———. *Private Libraries in Creole St. Louis.* Baltimore: Johns Hopkins University Press, 1938.

Saugrain Library and Saugrain-Michau Collection. Missouri Historical Society, St. Louis.

Selter, Hélène Marie Fouré. *L'odyssée Américaine d'une famille française: Le docteur Saugrain.* Baltimore: Johns Hopkins University Press, 1936.

SAULTS, DAN (1911–1985)

Charles Daniel Saults was a leading voice in Missouri conservation for forty years. Trained as a journalist, he was a newspaperman, soldier in World War II, state and later federal bureaucrat, essayist, and popular speaker at national, state, and regional forums. He became an outdoor writer of national reputation.

Dan Saults was born in Knob Noster, Missouri, on May 20, 1911, the eldest son of a local businessman. After high school he attended Central Missouri State University for two years and transferred to the University of Missouri–Columbia, where he majored in journalism. He returned to Johnson County where his father and the local bank financed the purchase of the weekly newspaper, the *Knob Noster Gem,* in 1935.

The following year Saults editorially supported Proposition No. 4, the constitutional amendment that would establish the modern Missouri Department of Conservation. E. Sydney Stephens, the prime mover in the campaign, came personally to encourage the young editor, and Saults increased his published support while giving public speeches. The experience made the editor a convert to conservation. Saults continued to work in his hometown until enlisting in the army in March 1942.

Saults's communication skills were recognized by the army, which made him an intelligence officer and later captain of an infantry company that saw duty in North Africa and Italy. After the war he returned to civilian life in June 1946, and "sort of hating the world" he went to Brownsville, Texas, to write fiction. However, he soon learned that he needed a steady job.

James Kirkpatrick, managing editor of the *Jefferson City News-Tribune,* offered Saults a position with the morning *Capitol-News.* By chance, however, Saults learned that the Conservation Commission was conducting interviews for an editor of its *Conservationist* magazine. Unannounced, Saults asked for an audience. Sydney Stephens, a commissioner, "rather insisted I be hired," Saults recollected.

In April 1947 Saults began his influential tenure with the Department of Conservation where his primary clients were biologists. Bill Nunn later wrote of Saults's journalistic accomplishment, "Seeking to make arid research data palatable with a flavoring of entertainment, Saults added color and life to the magazine stories. And emotion." His favorite outdoors activities became turkey hunting and float fishing. In two years the department promoted him to chief of information while he retained the editorship.

Saults, the public voice for the department, traveled extensively throughout Missouri. He took particular interest in combating and helping defeat the proposed Corps of Engineer dams on Current River, a major achievement in environmental strategy used later on the Buffalo River in Arkansas. Although Saults loved the Ozarks rivers, he recognized that compromises must be made and led the Department of Conservation in public support for Table Rock dam. He visited the Irish Wilderness, a forested area in southeast Missouri, for which he maintained a lifelong romantic passion. A generation later he led proponents seeking an official wilderness designation for the Irish Wilderness in the Mark Twain National Forest.

During the 1950s Saults established professional and personal friendships with the leading conservationists in Missouri and became part of an influential group that made the Missouri Department of Conservation a national model. Under Saults's editorship the circulation of the *Conservationist* climbed from eight to eighty thousand. In 1957 he became deputy director of the department, continuing to write the lead editorial for the magazine and participate in freelance outdoor writing. He edited more than a dozen books for the department while writing two dozen articles a year.

In 1964 Saults left Missouri for a federal appointment as an information officer in the U.S. Department of the Interior, first with the Bureau of Land Management and in 1966 with the Fish and Wildlife Service. He maintained a vigorous schedule with the Conservation Roundtable in Washington, D.C., increased his visibility with the Outdoor Writers Association of America (OWAA) for which he became a leader, and continued to write conservation essays for federal publications. During the fight for the free-flowing Buffalo River in Arkansas, he hosted and arranged political meetings in Washington for Neil Compton and his Ozarks supporters. In 1970 Saults wrote the script for *So Little Time,* an award-winning film recognized by the North American Wildlife Conference and the OWAA. In late 1973 he retired to Branson, Missouri.

In retirement Saults kept himself in the public eye as a regional journalist while holding national offices with the OWAA. He coedited their popular bicentennial project, *America's Great Outdoors,* a study of two centuries of nature writing. From 1974 until his death on September 23, 1985, Saults delivered some fifteen speeches per year. His writing included a weekly column for the *Springfield News and Leader* and a monthly environmental report for the *Ozarks Mountaineer,* and he expanded his commentaries to include book and film reviews. His provocative prose struck a responsive cord in the Ozarks as readers wrote letters to the editor and sought him out with phone calls.

A self-professed romantic, Saults considered it essential that conservation become a way of life for Americans. He came to love the Ozarks for what it had been and its promise for what it could be in its exceptional biodiversity. He wanted readers to engage their imagination in the possibilities of the future and consider conservation as a state of mind.

LYNN MORROW

Bashline, L. James, and Dan Saults, eds. *America's Great Outdoors: The Story of the Eternal Romance between Man and Nature.* Chicago: J. G. Ferguson Publishing, 1976.

Nunn, Bill. "Saults Added a Touch of Himself to State Conservation Magazine." *Missouri Times* (December 19, 1983).

Saults, Dan. Papers. Western Historical Manuscripts Collection, Rolla.

SAVAGE, WILLIAM SHERMAN (1890–1980)

William Sherman Savage was born in Wattsville, Virginia, on March 7, 1890. The eldest of twelve children in his family, he attended grammar school until the age of eleven when he left to start work. Six years later he reentered school and was finally able to complete his elementary and secondary education at Virginia Union in Richmond, Virginia, and Morgan College in Baltimore, Maryland. Savage earned his A.B. at Howard University in 1917 and became a school administrator.

Savage's career in education was interrupted by World War I. He served in Europe but "in only the menial capacities that prejudice then allotted members of his race." Upon returning to the United States, he made the decision to pursue a graduate degree at the University of Kansas. A few years later Savage transferred to the University of Oregon and completed his M.A. in 1925. While at Oregon he was first encouraged to study the role of African Americans in the frontier of the trans-Mississippi West. He then attended Ohio State University, earning his Ph.D. in 1934. Savage was the first African American at the university to write a dissertation in the field of history;

it was later published by the Association for the Study of Negro Life and History (ASNLH).

While pursuing higher education Sherman Savage continued to work in the classroom. Serving first as principal of Oklahoma Industrial School in Mississippi, he later taught at Carolina A & T in Greensboro, North Carolina, and the Manual Training High School in Muskogee, Oklahoma. In 1921 Savage took a position at Lincoln University in Jefferson City, Missouri, where he would remain for thirty-nine years. Unable to truly retire at the age of seventy, he then taught at Jarvis Christian College in Hawkins, Texas, in 1960. In 1966 he was a visiting professor of history at California State University in Los Angeles.

Throughout his academic tenure Savage researched and wrote about African American history. His early work focused upon abolition literature, but by the late 1920s he was investigating the role of blacks in the American West. During this time he was a core member of an outstanding band of African American scholars in the ASNLH, directed by Carter Woodson. Savage's articles were published primarily in the *Journal of Negro History* and included: "Legal Provisions for Negro Schools in Missouri from 1865 to 1890" (1931); "The Negro in the Westward Movement" (1940); "The Contest over Slavery between Illinois and Missouri" (1943); "The Negro on the Mining Frontier" (1945); "The Role of Negro Soldiers in Protecting the Indian Frontier from Intruders" (1951); and "The Influence of William Alexander Leidesdorff on the History of California" (1953). Among the books authored by Savage were *The Controversy over the Distribution of Abolitionist Literature, 1830–1860; The History of Lincoln University; The History of Phi Beta Psi;* and, perhaps most important, *Blacks in the West.* For five years Savage also penned the column "Know Your History" in the *Kansas City Call.*

Savage received grants from the American Philosophical Society and the Social Science Research Council. He belonged to numerous organizations, including the American Historical Association, the American Association of University Professors, the Organization of American Historians, and the Southern Historical Association. He served as president of the Association of Teachers of Social Science in Black Colleges and was a member of the board of awards for the ASNLH.

In the last years of his life, Savage conducted research at the Henry E. Huntington Library. Ray Allen Billington, the senior historian at the Huntington Library, reflected on the legacy of Sherman Savage's work: "He was, in the truest sense, a pioneer, blazing a path into an aspect of the past that had been too long neglected but that his successors were to follow. No prospector or cattle rancher or mountain man was more fully a frontiersman than Sherman Savage as he labored alone and selflessly to bring recognition to the blacks who had played such a significant role in the westering process." Savage died on June 5, 1980.

KRISTINE STILWELL

Meier, August, and Elliott Rudwick. *Black History and the Historical Profession, 1915–1980.* Blacks in the New World Series, ed. August Meier. Urbana: University of Illinois Press, 1986.

Savage, W. Sherman. File. Lincoln Collection. Inman E. Page Library, Lincoln University, Jefferson City, Mo.

SCHAEFFER, FRANCIS AUGUST (1912–1984)

Although few Americans would recognize his name, Francis Schaeffer profoundly affected the development of American political culture during the 1970s and 1980s. His polemical writings helped to energize the prolife movement and inspired a generation of evangelicals to embrace an antisecular political activism.

Schaeffer was born to working-class parents in Philadelphia on January 30, 1912, and reared as a Lutheran. Religion, however, played only a minor role in his upbringing, and for a time during adolescence he fancied himself an agnostic. At the age of eighteen Schaeffer attended an engineering school and embraced a Fundamentalist understanding of Christianity after a six-month self-study program of the Bible. At the urging of evangelical friends he transferred to the Presbyterian Hampden Sydney College. In 1935 he began graduate school at Westminster Seminary, which had just been established by conservative and Fundamentalist Presbyterian scholars frustrated with what they perceived as modernist trends within Presbyterianism.

The time Schaeffer spent at Westminster defined the direction the rest of his life would take. In July 1935 before his first fall term at Westminster, he married Edith Rachel Seville, the daughter of missionaries to China. She became an important intellectual associate as well as a prodigious author. While attending Westminster Schaeffer gravitated, as did most of the school's students, to the Calvinist Scholasticism of Cornelius Van Till, a professor of theology at the seminary. Schaeffer took from Van Till two lessons: first, faith should not be restricted to salvation but must also expand to encompass all aspects of intellectual life; second, Christian faith, while derived from the revelation of a rational God, could not be dependent on human reason because reason, like all human attributes, was subject to the contingencies of sin and desire. The great folly of

modernist humanism, Schaeffer later argued, was its insistence on the viability of autonomous reason.

In addition to Van Till, Westminster's president and founder, J. Gresham Machen, profoundly shaped Schaeffer's intellectual development. Machen had founded Westminster with the hope of sustaining a conservative voice within the increasingly liberal Presbyterian church. However, during Schaeffer's first year at Westminster, Machen's decision to establish a conservative-oriented independent missions board that appealed to individual Presbyterian churches for both funds and candidates ruptured his relationship permanently with church bureaucracy and led to his expulsion. Machen's stand and the price that it exacted from him persuaded Schaeffer to reject compromise with secular culture as undesirable.

In 1937 Machen's followers split along moderate-conservative and Fundamentalist lines, with the Fundamentalists insisting on a premillennial interpretation of eschatology and a strict standard of personal holiness. Schaeffer sided with the Fundamentalists led by Carl McIntire and transferred to McIntire's newly established Faith Seminary. The following year he became the first ordained minister in McIntire's Bible Presbyterian Church.

During the next ten years Schaeffer pastored churches in Pennsylvania and Missouri, coming to St. Louis in 1943. He worked at the local level for the American Council of Christian Churches (ACCC), a confederation of small Fundamentalist denominations and independent churches formed by McIntire in order to counteract the influence of the far larger mainline Federal Council of Christian Churches. Schaeffer's zealousness on behalf of the ACCC generated some controversy during his tenure in St. Louis. As a board member of the local chapter of the Child Evangelism Association, he attempted to stack the organization's staff and board with fellow Fundamentalists from ACCC-affiliated churches, and later resigned rather than adhere to instructions from the national organization to follow a more inclusive policy.

In 1948 Schaeffer accepted an appointment for Europe with the Independent Board for Presbyterian Missions and moved his family to Switzerland. In part he hoped to be able to lay the groundwork for an international version of the ACCC. However, his work in Europe brought him into contact with the main currents of modernist culture, an exposure that initially precipitated a crisis of faith, then inspired him to deepen his own intellectual foundation through an informal but intensive reading regimen in philosophy and theology.

As Schaeffer evolved intellectually, he did not back away from his basic conservative orthodoxy but became convinced that evangelicals needed to confront modernism on its own terms. However, he found himself increasingly uncomfortable with the extreme separatism of McIntire. By 1956 he had become sufficiently disenchanted with McIntire to align himself with a splinter faction, and he established Covenant Seminary in St. Louis, the current home of the Francis Schaeffer Center.

Schaeffer's role as a public advocate of a confrontational evangelical orthodoxy began with the founding of L'Abri (or the "Shelter"), an intellectual and spiritual hostel that sprang up almost spontaneously in 1955 at his rural Swiss chalet. Beginning literally at Schaeffer's kitchen table, L'Abri grew along with Schaeffer's reputation through word of mouth into a community of evangelical seekers, with Schaeffer acting as the guru. By 1960 L'Abri's rising popularity had created a demand for Schaeffer as a speaker on the evangelical lecture circuit where he sharpened his critique of the evangelical tendency toward philosophical softness and cultural accommodation.

In 1967 Schaeffer transcribed a series of lectures given at Wheaton College into his first published book, *The God Who Is There: Speaking Historic Christianity into the Twentieth Century,* which he quickly followed with *Escape from Reason* and *He Is There and He Is Not Silent.* In these works, which established Schaeffer as an intellectual and cultural force within evangelicalism, he argued that Western culture had been corroding since the mid-nineteenth century because of a shift in philosophy and theology, beginning with Hegel, from a classical-Christian belief in rational-based moral certainty to a modernist dialectal relativism.

Schaeffer also argued that modernist relativism had seeped into evangelicalism. He pointed to the flirtation of many young evangelical scholars with Søren Kierkegaard. While these neo-evangelical scholars saw Kierkegaard's leap of faith as a bridge that would allow them to relate their faith to the alienation of modern experience, Schaeffer saw Kierkegaard's philosophy as a Gospel of despair. Schaeffer believed in a rational God who had created a comprehensible universe and could be understood through revelation verified by reason and experience.

Even among evangelicals Schaeffer's writings drew mixed reviews. A generation of college-bound evangelicals coming of age during the cultural ferment of the 1960s grouped his ideas as intellectual rocks to which they could hold fast. However, many who had come of age in the quieter fifties viewed his writings as simplistic, unnecessarily divisive, and lacking in scholarly rigor. Schaeffer's supporters responded that he never presented himself as an ivory-tower scholar but understood his role as a kind of intellectual prophet, one who clarified issues and called evangelicals to act on their faith both intellectually and politically.

The culmination of Schaeffer's polemical efforts came in the late 1970s with the release of two film series produced with the assistance of his son, Franky Schaeffer, which were widely shown in evangelical churches and on college campuses. The first of these series, *How Should We Then Live* (1977), recapitulated the historical themes of his books. The second series, *Whatever Happened to the Human Race* (1979), which featured the future surgeon general C. Everett Koop, drew parallels between the political and moral climate of contemporary America and Wiemar Germany. The film argued that the increasing acceptance of abortion as a contraceptive procedure was a clear indicator of a moral decadence that would lead to an inevitable devaluation of human life and ultimately result in the validation of social practices contemptuous of life, such as infanticide and euthanasia.

The presidential election of Ronald Reagan and the corresponding rise of the Christian New Right transformed Schaeffer from a prophet in the cultural wilderness to one of the priests at the temple of power. By the time of his death on May 15, 1984, he had become one of the New Right's most celebrated figures.

RICHARD COTNER

Dennis, Lane T. *Francis Schaeffer: Portraits of the Man and His Work.* Westchester, Ill.: Crossway, 1986.
Reugseger, Ronald. *Reflections on Francis Schaeffer.* Grand Rapids, Mich.: Zondervan, 1986.

SCHOFIELD, JOHN McALLISTER (1831–1906)

John McAllister Schofield was born in Gerry, in Chautauqua County, New York, on September 2, 1831, the son of James and Caroline McAllister Schofield. His father was a Baptist minister, and in 1843 the family moved to Freeport, Illinois. Schofield taught school briefly and considered law studies, but instead accepted a cadetship at the United States Military Academy in 1849, from which he graduated in 1853, seventh of fifty-two in his class. After serving briefly in Florida with the First Regiment of Artillery, in 1855 he was appointed first lieutenant and returned to West Point to teach natural philosophy. In 1857 he married Harriet Bartlett, the daughter of the chair of the philosophy department. In 1860, without resigning his army commission, Schofield left West Point on a year's leave of absence and became a professor of physics at Washington University in St. Louis.

This civilian position placed Schofield at the center of the secession crisis in St. Louis. On April 15, 1861, the day President Abraham Lincoln issued a call for seventy-five thousand volunteers to put down the Southern rebellion, the War Department contacted Schofield, detailing him to act as mustering officer for the state of Missouri. Schofield quickly notified Gov. **Claiborne Fox Jackson** of his presence in the state, but as Jackson had no intention of enlisting Missourians in a war that its populace had opted to avoid, Schofield received no reply.

Within a week Cong. **Frank Blair,** leader of the radical Unionists in St. Louis, learned of Schofield's presence in the city and secured his authority to enlist volunteers into federal service, which the moderate department commander **William S. Harney** had heretofore refused. With Schofield's aid, Blair and arsenal commandant **Nathaniel Lyon,** a regular army captain, enlisted four volunteer regiments and a reserve corps consisting of two more "Home Guard" regiments, totaling more than six thousand troops, into the federal ranks. Lyon, now a brigadier general of volunteers, commissioned Schofield a major in the First Missouri Volunteer Infantry regiment.

Schofield participated in the Camp Jackson affair in St. Louis in May 1861, and in June was named chief of staff of Lyon's Army of the West. In the summer of 1861 he assisted in the campaign to Jefferson City, the skirmish at Boonville, and the march to Springfield. He participated in the Battle of Wilson's Creek, and personally informed Gen. Samuel Sturgis of his accession to command upon Lyon's death. Following the battle, Schofield was offered a captaincy in the regular army, but he declined, opting to remain with his own regiment, which he had organized as artillery. In November 1861 he became a brigadier general of volunteers and headed the Missouri State Militia, organizing the force to suppress pro-Confederate guerrilla activity in the state.

In the fall of 1862 department commander **Samuel Ryan Curtis** named Schofield to command all federal troops in the Southwest, with headquarters at St. Louis. He supervised Union operations in Missouri and northern Arkansas, and took an active role in the controversy surrounding the emancipation of slaves in Missouri.

Although he was nominated for a major generalship in the volunteer army in November, political opposition by Radicals, resulting from his involvement in the factionalism in Missouri, blocked Schofield's Senate confirmation, and he reverted to his original rank. Embarrassed by the incident, in the spring of 1863 he applied for a new adjustment and was transferred to the Fourteenth Army Corps stationed in Tennessee. In May he received his appointment as major general, and returned briefly to St. Louis to command the Department of the Missouri.

In February 1864 Schofield assumed command of the Twenty-third Corps and led it through the rest of the war, serving in Georgia, Tennessee, and the Carolinas. Following the war he served briefly as secretary of war under **Ulysses S. Grant,** was promoted to major general in the regular army, and from 1876 to 1881 served as superintendent of West Point. In 1888 Schofield was named commanding general of the army. He retired in 1895 with the rank of lieutenant general. He died in St. Augustine, Florida, on March 4, 1906, and is buried in Arlington National Cemetery.

CHRISTOPHER PHILLIPS

McDonough, James L. *Schofield: Union General in the Civil War and Reconstruction.* Tallahassee: Florida State University Press, 1972.

Parrish, William E. *Turbulent Partnership: Missouri and the Union, 1861–1865.* Columbia: University of Missouri Press, 1963.

Phillips, Christopher. *Damned Yankee: The Life of General Nathaniel Lyon.* Columbia: University of Missouri Press, 1990.

Schofield, John M. *Forty-six Years in the Army.* New York: Century, 1897.

Warner, Ezra J. *Generals in Blue: Lives of the Union Commanders.* Baton Rouge: Louisiana State University Press, 1964.

SCHOOLCRAFT, HENRY ROWE (1793–1864)

Henry Rowe Schoolcraft has a deserved reputation as an accomplished scientist-explorer who began his career in the Ozarks. He made an epic journey through the interior Ozark region and published the first book-length descriptions of the environment and early settlement.

Schoolcraft was born near Albany, New York, on March 28, 1793, and at an early age embraced the literary arts. He wrote poetry and magazine articles, sought intellectual society, and cultivated a reserved, reflective, somewhat humorless personality. He attended college in Vermont, enthusiastically studying mineralogy and geology. His father was superintendent of a glassworks in New York where Henry learned the trade and became part of the management. Over the next eight years, he worked for New England glasswork companies, but by 1817 he was bankrupt.

In March 1818 Schoolcraft left New York, seeking work in his trade in Pittsburgh and Cincinnati, but in August landed in Missouri Territory where he met **Moses Austin** in Potosi. Before long Schoolcraft began to draft a scientific survey of Missouri lead mining, and Austin provided space at Durham Hall for him to store minerals and conduct experiments. His months of work convinced him to explore the southwestern hinterlands to authenticate mineral legends and offer a scientific survey to the federal government.

Levi Pettibone, a former acquaintance in New York, accompanied Schoolcraft on the survey that lasted from November 1818 to February 1819. Their many misadventures—becoming lost, going without food, and suffering injuries—were a testament to the unmapped lands and their own inexperience as outdoorsmen. Once back in Potosi Schoolcraft finished his manuscript, collected his mineral specimens, and went back to New York where he advertised his Mississippi Valley ore samples for sale and concluded plans for *A View of the Mines,* published in December 1819.

Anxious over his debts in Missouri and New York, Schoolcraft suggested that new legislation be passed to reorganize the mining industry to correct widespread injustices. The author proposed a new superintendent of mines in Missouri as part of the solution. Contemporary scholars praised his new scientific work, and in Washington, D.C., Schoolcraft sought government employment, including possibly the proposed Missouri superintendency.

Instead, Secy. of War John C. Calhoun rewarded Schoolcraft with an explorer's post on a new expedition to explore Lake Superior and the upper Mississippi regions. In 1820 Schoolcraft accompanied Lewis Cass, governor of Michigan Territory, to gather scientific knowledge about the Great Lakes region. For the next twenty years he worked feverishly, establishing himself as a pioneering scholar on the frontier. The scientist-explorer described mining techniques, flora and fauna, geography and geology, and Native American culture. Eventually, he authored thirty books of scientific and anthropological value. Practically all his book ventures, however, were financial failures. His security came from his government appointments.

The young Schoolcraft, whether in the Ozarks or the Great Lakes, denigrated white hunters and Indians as illiterate savages and drunkards, while ignoring farmers, merchants, and entrepreneurs. He serialized his second travel work, *Journal of a Tour into the Interior of Missouri and Arkansaw,* in an eastern publication and printed it as a book in 1821. By then, however, he was deeply involved in the northern territories.

In 1822 Schoolcraft received an appointment in the new Indian agency at Sault Ste. Marie serving tribes in modern Michigan, Wisconsin, and Minnesota. Once there he began to meet Anglicized Indians who farmed and lived in log houses. More important, he met and, in 1823, married an Indian woman who had a European education and her own literary talent, and Schoolcraft began to change his view of aboriginal people. The young couple began a family as Schoolcraft intensified his lifelong interest in religion. The loss of his son in 1827 devastated him, and he sought comfort in religious studies. By

1831 the potential for evangelical work among the Indians dominated his thinking as it would his work for the rest of his life.

In 1832 a Schoolcraft expedition discovered the Lake Itasca region, the source of the Mississippi River. Unfortunately, some questionable administrative decisions Schoolcraft made during the journey overshadowed this most famous accomplishment of his career. Schoolcraft continued his work, however, moving to the Island of Mackinac in 1833. He served four years in the territorial legislature, and when Michigan became a state in 1837 the federal government appointed him as state superintendent of Indian affairs.

Schoolcraft retained government employment on the frontier until the 1840 Whig presidential victory led to his dismissal the following year. He left the Island of Mackinac for New York, traveled extensively in Europe, and moved to Washington, D.C., to devote the rest of his life to literary pursuits. In 1839 he had published *Algic Researches,* which influenced Henry W. Longfellow's writings, and during the 1850s Schoolcraft finished his famous six-volume work, *Historical and Statistical Information Respecting the History, Condition, and Prospects of the Indian Tribes of the United States.* These books secured a lasting reputation for him as a pioneer in American ethnography. Schoolcraft's fieldwork in documenting Indian myths and tales made him the "father" of American folklore.

Schoolcraft's national significance lies in his work in the Great Lakes region. His writings on the Ozarks, his first work, were highly selective and prejudicial, responsible, in part, for the negative stereotyping of an American region. His published work about the settlements in southern Missouri and northern Arkansas, some lying along the international boundary of the United States and the Cherokee Nation, needs to be reissued with a scholarly commentary about his observations of the cultural and natural worlds he encountered in 1818–1819. Schoolcraft died on December 10, 1864.

LYNN MORROW

Bremer, Richard G. "Henry Rowe Schoolcraft: Explorer in the Mississippi Valley." *Wisconsin Magazine of History* 66 (1982): 40–59.

Lankford, George E. " 'Beyond the Pale': Frontier Folk in the Southern Ozarks." In *The Folk: Identity, Landscapes, and Lores,* ed. Robert J. Smith and Jerry Stannard, 53–70. Lawrence: Department of Anthropology, University of Kansas, 1989.

Schoolcraft, Henry Rowe. *Journal of a Tour into the Interior of Missouri and Arkansaw from Potosi, or*

Mine à Burton, in Missouri Territory, in a South-West Direction, toward the Rocky Mountains: Performed in the Years 1818 and 1819. London: Sir Richard Phillips, 1821.

————. *Scenes and Adventures in the Semi-Alpine Region of the Ozark Mountains of Missouri and Arkansas which Were First Traversed by DeSoto in 1541.* Philadelphia: Lippincott, Grambo, 1853.

————. *A View of the Lead Mines of Missouri: Including Some Observations on the Mineralogy, Geology, Geography, Antiquities, and Soil, Climate, Population, and Productions of Missouri and Arkansaw, and Other Sections of the Western Country.* New York: Charles Wiley, 1819.

SCHURZ, CARL (1829–1906)

Carl Schurz, a German American immigrant leader, major general, senator from Missouri, and secretary of the interior, was born in Liblar, near Cologne, Germany, on March 2, 1829. The son of the schoolteacher Christian Schurz and his wife, Marianne Jussen, Schurz was educated at the Marcellen Gymnasium in Cologne and at the University of Bonn, where he fell under the influence of the radical professor Gottfried Kinkel.

An enthusiastic nationalist, democrat, and republican, Schurz joined Kinkel at the time of the revolution of 1848 in advocating the professor's then-extreme principles. After participating in a failed expedition against the armory at Siegen, he joined the revolutionary army in the Palatinate and Beden as a lieutenant. Almost captured when the Prussians besieged and then took the fortress of Rastatt, he escaped through a sewer and succeeded in reaching safety across the Rhine in France.

Schurz soon returned to Germany incognito in order to liberate Kinkel, who had been captured and condemned to life imprisonment and was serving his sentence in a prison at Spandau, near Berlin. Schurz established contact with the professor's wife, was given money, and succeeded in bribing a prison guard, who lowered Kinkel from the roof so that Schurz could convey the professor to the sea and flee to Scotland, a feat that made him famous at the age of twenty-one.

After a brief stay in Great Britain and France, Schurz decided to emigrate to America. He had married Maragrethe Meyer, the daughter of a wealthy Hamburg merchant, so he had sufficient funds during his first years in the new country, which after a brief stay in New York he spent in Philadelphia. However, he soon decided to move to Wisconsin, where a large German population might enable him to enter politics. Settling in Watertown, he engaged in journalism and real estate speculations and soon joined the Republican Party, for which he delivered speeches in both German and English. So successful was his campaigning that in 1857, before he had even earned his final citizenship papers, he was nominated for lieutenant governor. Disappointed by his defeat in spite of the success of the Republican ticket, he nevertheless remained faithful to the party and sought the nomination for governor two years later. He failed again, but in 1860 became chairman of the Wisconsin delegation to the Republican National Convention in Chicago. Insisting on an antinativist plank in the platform, he was elected to the Republican National Committee, for which he undertook to win over immigrant groups in general and German Americans in particular for Abraham Lincoln.

The success of the Republicans' campaign was at the time widely believed to have been due to German support. Although this thesis has been disproved by modern historians, Schurz believed it and sought a reward for his services, which turned out to be an appointment as minister to Spain. After the outbreak of the Civil War, he raised some German regiments in New York and left for Madrid in June 1861. From there he urged Lincoln to inaugurate a policy of emancipation, but returned in December to enter the army as a brigadier general. He took part in the engagements leading to the Second Battle of Bull Run and in early 1863 was appointed major general.

Schurz's military career after his promotion was a disappointment. A commander of a division of the Eleventh Corps at Chancellorsville, he was overrun by Stonewall Jackson, and though he had warned his superiors of the danger of his position, he and his German troops suffered derision afterward. The Eleventh Corps again suffered a reverse at Gettysburg, where it was overrun on the first day, and no matter how well Schurz and his troops performed at Cemetery Hill afterward, they could not erase their unfavorable reputation. Transferred to the vicinity of Chattanooga, they were wrongly accused by Hooker of tardiness at Wauhatchie. Schurz was cleared by a court of inquiry; his military career with the Eleventh Corps, however, was at an end. After campaigning for Lincoln in 1864, he finished the war as chief of staff of the Army of Georgia.

Generally on good terms with Lincoln, Schurz soon quarreled with the president's successor. On a trip to the South for Andrew Johnson, he found the president's policies detrimental to the blacks and the Unionists. Johnson broke with him, and Schurz's report became a radical campaign document.

Schurz had always been a journalist, and after the war he became the Washington correspondent for the *New York Tribune,* editor of the *Detroit Post,* and in 1867 coeditor with **Emil Preetorius** and co-owner of the *St. Louis Westliche Post.* He moved to St. Louis, where he soon engaged in Republican politics. After serving as temporary chairman of the Chicago convention that nominated **Ulysses S. Grant,** he crisscrossed Missouri to rally the Germans for the general, and after the Republican victory challenged the political machine of Sen. **Charles Daniel Drake** to run for the United States Senate. Appealing to his German American fellow citizens and securing the support of the *Missouri Democrat,* in January 1869 Schurz obtained the nomination and was elected to the upper house.

Schurz's tenure as a loyal follower of President Grant did not last long. Dissatisfied with the president's handling of civil service reform and the effort to buy the Dominican Republic, he also began to oppose his party's radical Reconstruction policies. He favored the repeal of the former Confederates' disabilities in Missouri, and in August 1870, when the St. Louis Republican state convention refused to endorse his program, he, Gen. John McNeil, and Lt. Gov. Edwin O. Stanard bolted and presided over the new convention that nominated **B. Gratz Brown** for governor. With the aid of William M. Grosvenor and his antiprotectionist following, as well as Schurz's appeal to his compatriots, Brown defeated Gov. **Joseph W. McClurg,** the incumbent, and Democrats, who had collaborated with the liberals, captured the lower house of the legislature. Schurz, undaunted by this threat to his own reelection, sought to extend the liberal movement to the country at large and in 1872 presided over the Liberal Republican Convention in Cincinnati. Disappointed by the nomination of the protectionist Horace Greeley, he nevertheless campaigned faithfully for the ticket, which, as he had foreseen, was defeated in the fall.

Schurz's power in Missouri was now nearing its end. Defeated in 1875 by the Democrats for reelection, in 1876 he supported Rutherford B. Hayes, who appointed him secretary of the interior. In this position he introduced civil service reform, conservation of natural resources, and a liberal treatment of the Indians, though at first he continued the policy of concentrating Native nations in the Indian Territory, which subjected him to severe criticism.

At the end of Hayes's term, Schurz moved to New York to become one of the editors of the *Evening Post* but withdrew from the paper in 1883 after a dispute about his liberal labor policies. More and more insistent upon civil service reform, he was active in the National Civil Service Reform League, the presidency of which he eventually assumed. He continued his support of reform politics and in 1884 was one of the leading Mugwumps who backed Grover Cleveland against the Republican James G. Blaine.

Soon afterward Schurz joined the Hamburg-American Steamship Company as its American representative. He wrote books and articles, including columns for *Harper's Weekly,* of which he became an editor, and in 1896 he returned to the Republican Party to support William McKinley. Because of his opposition to imperialism, however, he later broke with the president. As a prominent member of the Anti-Imperialist League, in 1900 he even backed William Jennings Bryan, whose inflationary policies he detested. To emphasize his opposition to Theodore Roosevelt's imperialist adventures, he also favored Alton B. Parker in 1904. After completing most of his memoirs, he died in New York on May 14, 1906.

Schurz's importance lay in his success in showing his German American fellow citizens, for many of whom he served as a role model, how to integrate into American society while yet preserving their German heritage. Although his stay in Missouri was comparatively brief, it marked the high point of his career and contributed to the end of radicalism in the state.

HANS L. TREFOUSSE

Easum, Chester V. *The Americanization of Carl Schurz.* Chicago: University of Chicago Press, 1982.

Puess, Claude Moore. *Carl Schurz, Reformer, 1829–1906.* New York: Dodd, Mead, 1932.

Schurz, Carl. *The Reminiscences of Carl Schurz.* 3 vols. New York: McClure, 1907–1908.

Trefousse, Hans L. *Carl Schurz: A Biography.* Knoxville: University of Tennessee Press, 1982.

SCHWARTZ, CHARLES W. (1914–1991)

When asked who is Missouri's most famous twentieth-century wildlife artist, those knowledgeable immediately name Charlie Schwartz. However, his prominence and importance go beyond even that illustrious recognition. His life was synonymous not only with wildlife art but also with conservation education. Not only did Missourians learn from his biological research, writings, lectures, motion pictures, paintings, bronzes, drawings, and photography, but people throughout the nation and the world benefited from his commitment to nature and its creatures.

Charles W. Schwartz was born in St. Louis on June 2, 1914, the son of Frederick O. Schwartz, a physician, and Clara Walsh Schwartz. After graduating from McBride High School, where he starred on the football field, Schwartz enrolled at the University of Missouri.

The young St. Louisan's football career at the university was short-lived because of injury. A good student, Schwartz also developed his interest in art and photography while an undergraduate. Earning an A.B. degree from the university in 1938, he applied for graduate school, wanting to obtain an A.M. degree in zoology. He accepted a graduate assistantship to work with a young Ph.D. candidate, Elizabeth Reeder, a Phi Beta Kappa who taught in the zoology department. The Ph.D. candidate and her assistant discovered that they enjoyed each other as much as their field of study. She completed her doctorate in 1938; the couple married on December 22 of that year. A daughter, Barbara, and two sons, Bruce and John, were born of the marriage.

Schwartz completed his A.M. in 1940 and took a position as a biologist with the Missouri Conservation Commission. In 1945 the commission published his illustrated study, *The Prairie Chicken in Missouri*. Four years later it became the subject of his first movie.

The Schwartzes left Missouri in 1946 when Hawaii's Board of Agriculture and Forestry asked both to study wildlife conditions there. The couple, and by then two children, spent 1946–1947 in Hawaii. In 1949 their *Game Birds of Hawaii* was published. The Wildlife Society judged it the best publication in wildlife management and ecology during 1949–1950. The Schwartzes wrote and produced some two dozen conservation and wildlife films, a number of which won awards. The 1952 CONI Grand Medal was presented to them for *Bobwhite through the Year*. The American Association for Conservation Information picked their *Story of the Mourning Dove* as the best North American wildlife movie for 1959.

Holiday House published six collaborations by the Schwartzes between 1957 and 1973. *When Water Animals Are Babies*, completed in 1970, became a Junior Literary Guild selection. Studies of the three-toed box turtle were the subjects of two publications by the Missouri Department of Conservation. In 1959 the Conservation Department and the University of Missouri Press copublished one of the most important works by the Schwartzes, *Wild Mammals of Missouri*. The American Association for Conservation Information judged it the outstanding wildlife book in 1959. Because of its enduring popularity, *Wild Mammals* was published in a revised edition in 1981, a year after Schwartz's *Wildlife Drawings* was printed.

In 1961 the Conservation Department selected Schwartz as the artist for its first trout stamp. He would execute other Missouri trout stamps, as well as the first state duck stamp issued in 1979. The artist's depiction of three Canada geese preparing to set down on Missouri farmland remains popular with collectors throughout the nation. His artwork raised more than eighty thousand dollars to promote the passage of a conservation tax that Missouri voters approved in 1976. Besides contributing his own work to periodicals, Schwartz illustrated the publications of other Missouri wildlife writers. For a number of years he executed signed and numbered limited-edition prints for the Conservation Federation of Missouri to use in its fund-raising activities.

In 1965 when the Missouri Department of Conservation moved into new quarters in Jefferson City, Schwartz's first four panels for the mural *A Man and Wildlife in Missouri: The Conservation Effort* were unveiled. On the occasion of the department's fiftieth anniversary in 1987, the last four panels of this inspiring and impressive visual history were shown for the first time.

Schwartz, who received an honorary doctorate in science from the University of Missouri and was elected to the Governor's Academy of Missouri Squires, retired from the Missouri Department of Conservation in 1981. His career with the department had lasted forty years.

With houses in Jefferson City and Coeur d'Alene, Idaho, Schwartz did not act the retiree. He continued to work at his art, particularly wildlife sculpture, and to enjoy with his wife the outdoor activities they shared throughout the years, such as duck and turkey hunting, floating, and camping. They would continue to share adventures until pancreatic cancer slowed the feisty conservationist. He died at his home in Coeur d'Alene on July 4, 1991.

At the time of his death, Schwartz was at work on illustrations for a book that he and his wife were writing, *About Mammals and How They Live*, which would include all wild land-dwelling mammals of North America north of Mexico. Determined to complete the volume, Libby Schwartz, with the assistance of friends and repositories that owned Charlie's artwork, was able to bring the profusely illustrated book to publication in 1993. The Wildlife Society picked the book for its Conservation Education Award in 1994.

JAMES W. GOODRICH

Columbia Daily Tribune, January 23, 1977.

Keefe, Jim. *The First Fifty Years.* Jefferson City: Conservation Commission of the State of Missouri, 1987.

———. "The Schwartzes Live with the World." *Missouri Alumnus* 58 (November 1968): 32–35.

Missouri Wildlife 52 (August–September 1991).

Schwartz, Charles W. Vertical File. State Historical Society of Missouri, Columbia.

SCOTT, DRED (1800?–1858)

Dred Scott, a slave born in Virginia around 1800, was the property of Peter Blow. In 1830 the Blow family settled in St. Louis, where Blow sold Scott to Dr. John Emerson. In 1833 Emerson's career as an army surgeon took him and his slave to Illinois and the Wisconsin Territory. While at Fort Snelling in the Wisconsin Territory, Scott married Harriet Robinson, whose master, Maj. Lawrence Taliaferro, transferred her ownership to Emerson. Dred and

Harriet Scott subsequently had two daughters, Eliza and Lizzie. Posted in 1842 to the Seminole War in Florida, Emerson left his wife, infant daughter, and slaves in St. Louis. He returned the following year, but died shortly thereafter. The slaves were hired out to various people in St. Louis, and they also reestablished relations with the Blow family, Scott's former owners.

On April 6, 1846, Dred and Harriet Scott sued their mistress, Irene Emerson, for freedom in a Missouri state court. No political motivation was attached to the suit; it was instituted only to secure freedom for Dred Scott and his family. Unable to read or write, Scott may have learned of his right to freedom from white abolitionist lawyer Francis B. Murdoch, who had moved to St. Louis from Alton, Illinois, where he had prosecuted criminal offenders in the **Elijah P. Lovejoy** affair. Another possible instigator was the Reverend John P. Anderson, a former slave who was pastor of the Second African Baptist Church in St. Louis, to which Harriet Scott belonged. Murdoch provided the necessary bonds and legal papers to institute the suit; he shortly thereafter moved to California.

Based upon Missouri law and legal precedents, Scott's case for freedom seemed incontrovertible. Perhaps that explains why members of the Blow family readily backed the slave's cause when Murdoch left. Even as the litigation dragged on beyond what had promised to be a quick solution, they provided necessary legal and financial support.

Unanticipated developments converted an open-and-shut freedom suit into a cause célèbre. In the trial of June 10, 1847, in St. Louis, the court rejected one piece of vital evidence on a legal technicality, and the slave's freedom had to await a second trial. That took three years—until January 12, 1850—a delay caused by events over which none of the litigants had any control. The earlier technicality now corrected, the court unhesitatingly granted Scott his freedom.

During that delay, however, money earned by the slaves had been held in custody by the local sheriff to turn over to either the master or the freed slaves, depending upon the outcome of the case. Those accrued wages made ownership of the slaves more worthwhile in 1850 than in 1847. Meanwhile, Irene Emerson had remarried, to Dr. Calvin Clifford Chaffee, a Massachusetts abolitionist who was unaware of the litigation involving his wife. She left her St. Louis affairs in the hands of her businessman-brother **John F. A. Sanford.** Hoping to secure the accumulated Scott family wages, Sanford appealed the freedom decision to the Missouri Supreme Court.

Meanwhile, slavery had become a burning and divisive issue in Missouri politics, including in the elections of judges to the state supreme court. In due course, then, in a singularly partisan two-to-one decision, the Missouri Supreme Court on March 22, 1850, blatantly endorsed extreme proslavery tenets, overturned the long-standing "once free always free" precedent, reversed the lower court, and remanded Dred Scott to slavery.

To clarify the "once free always free" doctrine, friends of Dred Scott instituted a new case in the federal courts, *Dred Scott v. John F. A. Sanford.* (Court records erroneously misspelled the name as "Sandford.") Although he was often in St. Louis on business, Sanford was a legal resident of New York. Scott, as a citizen of Missouri suing Sanford, made possible a "diversity" case that could be litigated in the federal courts. However, it also created a new issue when Sanford's attorney claimed that Scott was not a citizen because he was "a Negro of African descent" and therefore lacked the right to sue in federal courts. The court found for Sanford, and the case was appealed to the United States Supreme Court.

Such nationally known legal figures as **Montgomery Blair** and George T. Curtis for Scott, and Reverdy Johnson and **Henry S. Geyer** for Sanford, argued the case—twice, in February 1856 and in December 1856. Virtually unknown until then, the litigation now aroused nationwide publicity and deep partisan interest. At first the Court sought to avoid controversial slavery matters. Prodded by proslavery Chief Justice Roger B. Taney and Associate Justices Peter V. Daniel and James M. Wayne, and by antislavery Associate Justice John McLean, the Court changed direction and decided to deal with those explosive issues.

The decision was announced on March 6, 1857, with Chief Justice Taney delivering the opinion of the Court that remanded Dred Scott to slavery. Each of the justices delivered a separate concurring or dissenting opinion. Extreme proslavery and antislavery views were expressed. According to the Court, blacks were not considered citizens of the United States. Slaves were property protected by the Constitution, and any law prohibiting slavery in the territories (such as the Missouri Compromise) was unconstitutional. Regardless of prior free or slave condition, the status of a person entering a slave state depended upon the laws of that state.

The decision triggered violent reactions in an already tense, sectional-ridden atmosphere. Fearing it pushed American law close to legalizing slavery throughout the entire country, antislavery forces mounted unprecedented assaults upon the decision and upon the majority members of the Court. Proslavery forces responded with equal fervor to defend their cause. The tragic result was to split a divided country even more and push it closer to civil war.

Throughout all this litigation, Dred Scott and his family remained in St. Louis, working at various jobs. Shortly after the decision, Chaffee transferred ownership to Taylor Blow in St. Louis, where, on May 27, 1857, he emancipated the slaves.

Scott lived only a year and a half longer, working most of that time as a porter in Branum's Hotel in St. Louis. He died on September 17, 1858, of tuberculosis. His remains are interred in St. Louis.

WALTER EHRLICH

Ehrlich, Walter. "Dred Scott in History." In *Annual Editions: American History,* ed. Robert J. Maddox, vol. 1. 12th ed. Guilford, Conn.: Dushkin Publishing, 1993.

———. *They Have No Rights: Dred Scott's Struggle for Freedom.* Westport, Conn.: Greenwood Press, 1979.

Fehrenbacher, Don E. *The Dred Scott Case: Its Significance in American Law and Politics.* New York: Oxford University Press, 1978.

Finkelman, Paul. *Slavery, Federalism, and Comity.* Chapel Hill: University of North Carolina Press, 1981.

Hyman, Harold M., and William M. Wiecek. *Equal Justice under Law: Constitutional Development, 1835–1875.* New York: Harper and Row, 1982.

SCOTT, JAMES SYLVESTER (1885–1938)

Music historians generally consider James Sylvester Scott the second greatest ragtime composer and pianist after **Scott Joplin.** Scott was born on February 12, 1885, in Neosho, Missouri, the son of former North Carolina slaves. He grew up in a large musical family; his mother played piano, as did his five brothers and sisters. A child prodigy, Scott played the instrument by ear, exhibiting an exceptional talent and an uncanny sense of absolute pitch, and later took lessons and learned to read music from John Coleman, a Neosho musician.

Around 1899, when Scott was about fourteen, his family relocated to Ottawa, Kansas, where he wrote his first composition. Two years later the family returned to Missouri and settled in Carthage. Over the next few years Scott occasionally performed in saloons and at a nearby amusement park, where he chiefly played ragtime, the syncopated style of American music popularized by Scott Joplin and other African American piano players around the turn of the century.

Scott went to work to help support his family while in his teens, first as a shoe-shine boy in a Carthage barbershop and then, in 1902, as a handyman for Dumars Music Company, one of the city's music stores. His job with Dumars proved Scott's big break. Not only did he receive a promotion to sales clerk and sheet-music demonstrator after Dumars

heard him play the piano, but in 1903 Dumars also issued two of Scott's ragtime compositions, *A Summer Breeze: March and Two Step* and *The Fascinator: March.* Scott was then only eighteen. *On the Pike: March and Two Step,* a song written in commemoration of the St. Louis World's Fair, appeared the following year. According to ragtime historians Rudi Blesh and Harriet Janis, Scott's earliest compositions, though clearly influenced by Joplin's widely popular *Maple Leaf Rag* (1899), demonstrate a "marked independence and originality," with a "flowing melodic content of strong Missouri country feeling."

In 1906, on a visit to St. Louis, Scott met John Stark, the owner of John Stark and Son, one of the nation's leading ragtime publishing firms. Stark, who had issued Joplin's *Maple Leaf Rag, The Entertainer* (1902), and several other works, published Scott's *Frog Legs Rag* later that year. Over the next sixteen years Stark's firm marketed the sheet music for more than two dozen of Scott's piano rags, songs, and waltzes, including his masterpieces *Grace and Beauty* (1909), *Quality: A High Class Rag* (1911), and *Climax Rag* (1914), which Jelly Roll Morton later recorded.

Scott left Carthage in 1914 after a twelve-year association with the Dumars Music Company, and settled in Kansas City, Missouri, where he began working as a music teacher and later opened a music studio in his home. Sometime in the late teens, he married a woman named Nora (maiden name unknown); they had no children. A short, slight man known locally as the "Little Professor," Scott supplemented his income from teaching music by working, beginning in 1916, as an organist and musical arranger at the Panama Theater, where he provided musical accompaniment for silent films.

Scott was not only an exceptionally accomplished piano player but also a prolific ragtime composer whose series of published rags reflected, according to Blesh and Janis, "an ever increasing complexity," characterized by "four- and five-note treble chords and varied bass construction." As one of his cousins recalled, "Jimmy never talked about his music, just wrote, wrote, wrote, and played it for anyone who would listen. He wrote music as fluently as writing a letter, humming and writing all at the same time." Scott's last published composition, *Broadway Rag: A Classic,* appeared in 1922, by which time jazz had already eclipsed ragtime as America's most popular music. He continued to work in Kansas City movie theaters, performing with large pit orchestras at the Lincoln and Eblon Theaters until around 1929, when he lost his job with the advent of sound films.

Throughout most of the 1930s, Scott taught music and also led an eight-piece dance band that played at social functions in the Kansas City area. After his wife's death he moved across the border to Kansas

City, Kansas, where, afflicted with what was then known as chronic "dropsy," or edema, his health declined. "Even then," another cousin remembered, "he kept on composing and playing, although his fingers were swollen and very painful."

Scott died on August 30, 1938, in Kansas City, Kansas, at the age of fifty-three. Although the publication of Blesh and Janis's *They All Played Ragtime* (1950) spawned a renewed interest in his music and one posthumously published composition, *Calliope Rag,* appeared in 1966, James Scott remains an obscure figure in the history of ragtime, overshadowed by the widely known Scott Joplin.

PATRICK J. HUBER

Blesh, Rudi, and Harriet Janis. *They All Played Ragtime.* 4th ed. New York: Oak Publications, 1971.

The New Grove Dictionary of American Music. Vol. 4. S.v. "Scott, James Sylvester."

Southern, Eileen. *The Music of Black Americans: A History.* New York: W. W. Norton, 1971.

SCOTT, JAMES T. (1887–1923)

James T. Scott, a thirty-five-year-old black janitor, was hanged by a lynch mob in Columbia, Missouri, in late April 1923, one of twenty-two men—seventeen of whom were African Americans—lynched in the state between 1900 and 1931.

Like most victims of extralegal violence, few details are known about Scott's life. He was born in New Mexico Territory on October 5, 1887, the son of James and Sarah Scott. A longtime resident of Chicago, he served overseas with the Eighth Illinois Infantry of the United States Army during World War I, and received a decoration for valor. It remains unclear when Scott settled in Columbia, but he moved there probably sometime in late 1918 or 1919. In 1921 he married Gertrude Carter, a local schoolteacher who taught at Frederick Douglass School, the city's segregated black school. Scott was the father of three children from a previous marriage, and was employed as a janitor at the medical building on the University of Missouri campus.

At the time of his murder Scott was being held without bond in the Boone County jail, charged with assaulting the fourteen-year-old daughter of a university German professor. The assault occurred near Stewart Bridge, an automobile overpass a quarter of a mile from the school's campus. The day before the lynching, the *Columbia Daily Tribune* reported that the white girl had "positively identified" Scott as her assailant, and its editor also published an editorial demanding "swift justice." Perhaps stirred by the newspaper's inflammatory remarks, a mob of approximately fifty unmasked men stormed the jail at eleven o'clock on Saturday night, April 28, and forced their way into Scott's cell using a sledgehammer and an acetylene torch.

Realizing that the local authorities had no intention of preventing the lynching, George L. Vaughn, a black St. Louis attorney who was visiting Columbia, telephoned Gov. **Arthur M. Hyde** in Jefferson City around midnight, and urged him to call out the National Guard. Fifteen minutes later the governor ordered the commanding officer of Battery B, 128th Field Artillery of the Missouri National Guard, which was headquartered in Columbia, to mobilize his troops and disperse the mob. However, the guard never arrived to prevent the lynching.

Two thousand spectators, some of whom were university students, witnessed the mob hang Scott from Stewart Bridge at 1:40 A.M. on Sunday morning, April 29, 1923, within sight of the dome of Jesse Hall, the university's administration building. Scott had maintained his innocence to the end, pleading unsuccessfully with those nearby to spare his life. His funeral was held on May 2 at the Second Baptist Church, and his body was interred in the Columbia Cemetery.

The lynching attracted front-page headlines from newspapers across the nation because of the University of Missouri's presence, and because of allegations that students actively participated in it. The *New York Times* headlined its front-page story of the lynching, "Missouri Students See Negro Lynched: Co-Eds Join Crowd which Cheers the Storming of the Columbia Jail." The *Chicago Defender,* a black weekly, captioned its account: "College Students Lead Missouri Lynch Mob." Acting university president **Isidor Loeb,** however, publicly denied such reports, calling them "absolutely false." Scott's murder, which occurred during one of the National Association for the Advancement of Colored People's most intensive campaigns to pass a federal antilynching bill, prompted an outraged W. E. B. DuBois, the editor of the *Crisis,* the organizations's magazine, to sarcastically proclaim in his editorial, "A University Course in Lynching": "We are glad to note that the University of Missouri has opened a course in Applied Lynching. . . . We are glad that the future fathers and mothers of the West saw [the lynching], and we are expecting great results from this course of study at one of the most eminent of our State Universities."

Subsequently, a Boone County grand jury indicted five white men, including a National Guard sergeant, for their participation in the lynching. On July 12, 1923, a jury acquitted George W. Barkwell, a Columbia contractor and former city councilman, of charges of first-degree murder after only eleven minutes of deliberation. The other four defendants were never prosecuted.

PATRICK J. HUBER AND GARY R. KREMER

Columbia Daily Tribune, April 21–July 17, 1923.

DuBois, W. E. B. "A University Course in Lynching." *Crisis* 26 (June 1923): 55.

Greene, Lorenzo J., Gary R. Kremer, and Antonio F. Holland. *Missouri's Black Heritage, Revised Edition.* Columbia: University of Missouri Press, 1993.

Huber, Patrick. "The Lynching of James T. Scott: The Underside of a College Town." *Gateway Heritage* 12 (summer 1991): 18–37.

Hyde, Arthur M. Governor's Papers. Western Historical Manuscripts Collection, Columbia.

National Association for the Advancement of Colored People. Papers. Administrative Files. Library of Congress, Washington, D.C.

SCOTT, JOHN (1785–1861)

Born in eastern Virginia on May 18, 1785, John Scott attended Princeton University, graduating about 1803. He moved with his family to Vincennes, Indiana Territory, and then in 1804 to Ste. Genevieve, Missouri Territory. He had made the acquaintance of men such as **Edward Hempstead,** Gov. **William Henry Harrison,** and **Rufus Easton** while in Vincennes. Scott, Hempstead, and Easton became colleagues quickly in the typical lawyering, land speculating, and politicking activities of the new territory. Like them, Scott served clients in both Missouri and Illinois Territories, working especially with the politicians in Illinois. It was in Illinois that he met and married Harriet Jones Brady, the widowed daughter of prominent politician **John Rice Jones.**

In 1808 and 1809 Scott was the attorney general for Missouri Territory, and he was the U.S. attorney for the territory from 1813 to 1817. He served on the legislative council in the upper house from 1814 to 1816.

Until his election as a territorial delegate in 1816, Scott remained out of the limelight of the intensely personal territorial politics. Hempstead and Scott led the successful movement to secure second-grade government, which meant an elected legislature and a nonvoting delegate to Congress.

By 1816 Scott was part of the powerful political group that included former delegate Hempstead, Gov. **William Clark, Thomas Hart Benton, Auguste Chouteau, Bernard Pratte,** and **Charles Gratiot.** They chose Scott to run for Congress against the incumbent, Rufus Easton. Scott's platform advocated private ownership of salt licks and lead mines, private entrepreneurs in the Indian trade, and faster surveying and sale of public lands. The 1816 delegate campaign was heated, and Scott won by a margin of only fifteen votes. Easton contested the election, and the United States House of Representatives referred the case to their Committee on Elections, which decided for Easton. After considerable debate, the House decided that the seat was vacant, and called for a new election. The next summer the voters sent Scott to Congress with a secure majority.

Scott's most important contribution lay ahead: securing an enabling act for the territory's statehood. The Missouri statehood debate continued for three years, foreshadowing the impending national struggle over slavery. Scott initiated the debate when he presented the first petition in February 1818.

In December 1819 a three-week debate covered all aspects of the slavery controversy from constitutional rights to the morality of slavery, but the House would not act. When the Senate bill came down, Scott spoke earnestly for the rights of Missouri residents derived from the Ordinance of 1787, the Constitution, and the American-French Treaty of 1803. Finally, the House acquiesced, and the enabling act was passed in the spring of 1820.

John Scott returned to St. Louis, having accomplished little for the territory besides the enabling act. However, he helped write the new state constitution, and was elected unopposed as Missouri's first representative in Congress following statehood.

Returning to Congress with Missouri's constitution, Scott refused recognition as the delegate, insisting instead that he be seated as a representative. The House recognized him only as a nonvoting delegate. The constitution's restrictions on free blacks and emancipation led to defeat of the admission act. Scott and others reworked the constitution and resubmitted it to Congress, where debate continued. Finally passed, President James Monroe signed Missouri's admission act on March 2, 1821.

John Scott continued to serve as a U.S. representative until 1826. In 1825, favoring John Quincy Adams over Andrew Jackson for president when the election went to the House, Scott voted for Adams without instructions from the state legislature, knowing that Missouri's electoral college members had voted for Henry Clay. This decision led to political defeat, since Missourians generally preferred Jackson. In the next election Scott defended his vote for Adams unsuccessfully.

Scott retired from politics to his law practice, which encompassed the whole state with special emphasis upon Ste. Genevieve, Cape Girardeau, and St. Louis. He lived to see the slavery controversy revived and the nation plunged into civil war, dying on October 1, 1861, at his home in Ste. Genevieve.

JO TICE BLOOM

Foley, William E. *A History of Missouri: Volume I, 1673 to 1820.* Columbia: University of Missouri Press, 1971.

SCYPION, MARIE JEAN (?–1802)

An unheralded Afro-Indian slave woman's dreams of freedom propelled one of the most protracted legal battles over slavery in Missouri history. Marie Jean Scypion, the central figure in the case, was born sometime during the 1740s in the vicinity of Fort de Chartres, a French military installation on the east bank of the Mississippi in the Illinois country. Her mother, a Natchez Indian woman known as Marie or Mariette, had been taken captive during an Indian conflict and sold into slavery. Her father was an African American slave named Scypion about whom little else can be determined with certainty.

Originally owned by a French priest, Marie Jean Scypion subsequently became the property of the Joseph Tayon family. The Tayons took her with them to St. Louis not long after the city's founding in 1764. In St. Louis Scypion bore three daughters, Celeste, Catiche, and Marguerite. Following their births, Madame Tayon removed Celeste and Catiche from Scypion's care and placed them in the custody of the two eldest Tayon daughters.

Even in the face of such personal adversity, Scypion remained, by all accounts, a fiercely determined individual who refused to allow the rigors of slavery to destroy her dignity and pride. After the Spaniards took possession of Louisiana, she questioned the legality of her enslavement because of her Indian ancestry. Spanish law specifically outlawed Indian slavery, but officials in St. Louis succumbed to local pressures and declined to fully enforce the controversial statute.

Scypion appears to have enjoyed the run of the Tayon household where she served as a cook and housekeeper. In fact, despite Joseph Tayon's repeated insistence that she was and always had been his slave, some of her acquaintances in St. Louis remained uncertain about her status. Not only did she retain her sense of independence, but somehow she also managed to instill that same defiant spirit in her children, notwithstanding the forced separations that kept them apart much of the time.

In 1799 Joseph Tayon unexpectedly decided to sell Scypion and her three daughters. Only a major row, provoked by Tayon's attempts to repossess Celeste and Catiche from his daughters, saved Scypion and her offspring from the St. Louis auction block. Insisting that their mother had given them the two slave women many years earlier, Tayon's daughters refused to return them to their father's custody. Feuding members of the Tayon family appeared before the Spanish magistrate in St. Louis on at least three occasions in 1799 and 1800. The matter of the slaves' maternal Indian heritage complicated the efforts to resolve the squabble. Tayon seemed hesitant to force the issue with his daughters after Lt.

Gov. **Zenon Trudeau** suggested that the slaves could not be legally sold because of their Indian ancestry.

When combined with years of toil, these added uncertainties took their toll on the aging Scypion. Her health had so deteriorated by January 1801 that one of Tayon's daughters took the ailing slave woman into her own home, where she died in June 1802. Marie Jean Scypion had set an example for her progeny, and that legacy reinforced their unremitting determination to be free.

Celeste, Catiche, and Marguerite had to endure the agonies of jury trials in 1806, 1827, and 1836 and countless legal appeals along with verbal threats and physical abuse, but in the end they triumphed. With assistance from a small cadre of sympathetic attorneys, jurists, and friends, Marie Jean Scypion's surviving children and grandchildren eventually secured a favorable verdict. In 1836 a Jefferson County, Missouri, jury awarded them their freedom on the very grounds that Marie Jean Scypion had first raised so many years before. Tragically, Marie Jean, who by then had been deceased for more than three decades, never experienced the freedom she longed for, but the lengthy legal odyssey she helped launch stands as a tribute to her courage and perseverance.

WILLIAM E. FOLEY

Foley, William E. "Slave Freedom Suits before Dred Scott: The Case of Marie Jean Scypion's Descendants." *Missouri Historical Review* 79 (October 1984): 1–23.
Jefferson County, Missouri, Circuit Court Records, November 5, 1835, March 7, 8, and November 8, 1836, in Minute Book 2. Trial notes and supporting documents are in Files 273 and 274.

SEIFERT, ELIZABETH (1897–1983)

Elizabeth Seifert published her first book in 1938 when she was forty-one years old. One of thirteen hundred entries, Seifert's *Young Doctor Halahad* won the ten-thousand-dollar Dodd, Mead, and Company–*Redbook* magazine prize for a first novel, and she continued to write two books a year until 1979 when illness forced her to slow down. Her last novel, *Two Doctors, Two Lives,* was published in November 1982.

Seifert was born in Washington, Missouri, on June 19, 1897. Her father, Richard C. Seifert, emigrated from Hanover, Germany, when he was seventeen. Her mother, Anna Sandford Seifert, could trace her family back to 1634 in Massachusetts. Two of Elizabeth's four sisters, Shirley and Adele, were also writers.

Seifert attended public schools in St. Louis, graduated from Soldan High School, and attended medical school at Washington University. Authorities requested that she withdraw because during World War I medical students were required to serve in army hospitals as part of their training. The base hospital unit for Washington University was in France, and since Seifert could not serve there because she was a woman, she became ineligible to receive a medical degree at the school. She did enroll in courses in anatomy, physiology, and medical dietetics and also audited a creative writing course. She earned an A.B. degree in 1918.

In 1920 Seifert married John J. Gasparotti, a World War I veteran. Sometime later the family, which then included four children, moved to Moberly, Missouri, when Gasparotti's company transferred him there to build and operate an ice plant. In 1925 the deadline for injured war veterans to claim benefits passed, and in 1926 Gasparotti's health began to fail. In 1937 he became totally disabled, forcing Seifert to secure employment as a clinical secretary in a Moberly hospital.

At the same time, Seifert intensified her interest in writing fiction, a practice she began at the age of ten. Her sister **Shirley Seifert** was a published author of historical novels, and Elizabeth asked her to critique her first novel. The older sister sent the manuscript to her agent, hoping he would discourage Elizabeth from writing. Instead he praised it as one of the best novels he had read. Elizabeth's mother asked her to stop writing so she would not compete with her older sister. When Elizabeth refused to comply with her mother's wishes, her mother excluded Elizabeth from her will.

Seifert kept to a schedule of writing from 7:00 A.M. until 1:00 P.M., with a break at 10:30 A.M. for a walk. During the walk she would sort out plots and characters. After lunch she read several newspapers and looked through technical medical journals for recent discoveries and obscure tidbits she might use in her novels. In 1976, on one of her morning walks, Seifert fell and broke her left arm and shoulder. Having temporarily lost the use of that arm, she taught herself to type with one hand.

On the publication of her fifty-first novel, Seifert's American publisher "entertained with a luncheon at the Waldorf Astoria," attended by her English publisher. When the English honored her with a dinner in London in 1960, Seifert, whose books were sold in more than thirty countries, had published more books in England than any other American writer. Early in her career she was asked to write soap operas, and motion picture companies expressed interest in her novels and in hiring her as a scriptwriter. She refused to leave Moberly to live in New York or Hollywood. When aspiring authors asked for her advice, Seifert told them to "Read, read, read. Start with the back of cereal boxes and continue straight through the Book of Revelations."

A Republican and active in the Episcopal Church, Seifert became the first woman in ninety years to serve on her church's vestry. She was a member of the State Historical Society of Missouri, the American Association of University Women, the Sorosis Club, Beta Sigma Phi, the Authors' League of America, the Ozark Folk Lore Society, and the Parent Teachers Association. She died on June 17, 1983, and was survived by her sister Adele, sons John III, Richard, and Paul, her daughter Anna, twelve grandchildren, and six great-grandchildren. She was buried at Jefferson Barracks National Cemetery in St. Louis beside her husband, who died in 1958.

MAXINE J. CHRISTENSEN

Columbia Daily Tribune, April 16, 1978.

Dains, Mary K., ed. *Show Me Missouri Women: Selected Biographies.* Kirksville, Mo.: Thomas Jefferson University Press, 1989.

Mallory, Charles Lloyd. "Voices: She Lives a Doctor's Life in Her Books." *Missouri Life* (December 1981).

Missouri Authors' File. State Historical Society of Missouri, Columbia.

Moberly Monitor-Index and Evening Democrat, June 19–20, 1983.

St. Louis Post-Dispatch, June 19, 1983.

SEIFERT, SHIRLEY LOUISE (1888–1971)

Born in St. Peters, Missouri, on May 22, 1888, Shirley Seifert became best known as the author of seventeen historical novels. An avid reader as a child, she told stories to her four younger sisters. Seifert attended high school in Washington, Missouri, for two years, and when her family moved to St. Louis she completed her high school education at Central High School. She studied classical and modern languages at Washington University in St. Louis, earned an A.B. degree in 1909, and graduated Phi Beta Kappa.

From 1917 to 1919 Seifert taught high school Latin and English in the St. Louis public schools. She did not like teaching, though, and in 1919 took a job as a secretary in the publicity division of the Liberty Loan office in St. Louis. That same year she sold her first short story, "The Girl Who Was Too Good Looking," to *American Magazine* for one hundred dollars, and began writing full-time. Seifert worked as a freelance writer for several years, and her short stories appeared in the *Saturday Evening Post, Ladies' Home Journal, Scribner's,* the *Delineator,* and other well-known periodicals.

In 1937 Seifert published her first novel, *Land of Tomorrow,* a story about life in Kentucky. She did extensive research for her novels, using diaries, early documents, newspapers, and letters, and produced a book about every two years. In 1938 *The Wayfarers,* the story of a soldier in the Civil War, received a Pulitzer Prize nomination. *The Proud Way,* a romantic story of Jefferson Davis, a choice of the People's Book Club, was dramatized on *The Cavalcade of America* and published in Braille. Critics said that Seifert's books were competent and well researched, but she "failed to elicit the readers' interest in her characters due largely to her own lack of investment of feelings in her creations."

Seifert taught fiction-writing classes in St. Louis and lectured on historical novel writing at writers' conferences. She was a member of Theta Sigma Phi, a society of women journalists. In 1948 the St. Louis Group Action Council named her the St. Louis Woman of Achievement, and in 1961 at the Missouri Historical Society annual meeting and dinner she received a citation for her "use of original historical materials in her many novels and for her co-authorship of the Grace Church history." In 1963 she wrote a guide book to St. Louis, *Key to St. Louis.*

Seifert lived in Charcot with her sister Adele for many years. She died on September 1, 1971, at the age of eighty-three. Her last novel, *The Medicine Man,* the story of Dr. **Antoine Saugrain,** was published shortly after her death.

MAXINE J. CHRISTENSEN

Current Biography. New York: H. W. Wilson, 1951.

Dains, Mary K., ed. *Show Me Missouri Women: Selected Biographies.* Kirksville, Mo.: Thomas Jefferson University Press, 1989.

Encyclopedia of Frontier and Western Fiction. S.v. "Seifert, Shirley Louise."

Obituary. *Bulletin of the Missouri Historical Society* 28 (January 1972): 136–37.

St. Louis Globe-Democrat, September 3, 1971.

St. Louis Post-Dispatch, September 5, 1971.

SERMON, ROGER T. (1890–1950)

Onetime Missouri gubernatorial candidate and twenty-six-year mayor of the city of Independence, Roger T. Sermon built a strong political base in the eastern half of Jackson County. Sermon maintained close ties with **Harry S. Truman** throughout his life, and his Independence political organization was closely allied with the Pendergast faction in Kansas City during most of that period.

Born in Independence on November 2, 1890, Sermon was a member of the third generation of his family to participate in the municipal government of his hometown. His education, like that of his friend and neighbor Truman, was essentially high school. He did attend one year at Spalding Business College in Kansas City, in 1908–1909. After serving a stint as a postman from 1910 to 1916, Sermon went

to Mexico with Independence Company, Battery C, Missouri National Guard.

Upon returning to Independence and his postal position, Sermon quickly found himself caught up in the mobilization for World War I. Serving with him in Battery C in France were Harry Truman, Eddie Jacobson, and James M. Pendergast, **Tom Pendergast**'s nephew. All these men were significant in local or national politics later in their lives.

With the demobilization following the armistice in November 1918, Sermon returned to Independence to stay. The following year he opened a grocery store near downtown Independence in partnership with R. Powell Cook. This business relationship lasted until Sermon's death in 1950. During the twenty-six years of his mayoralty, he tried to work mornings at the grocery store and afternoons at city hall. To facilitate the conduct of city business, Sermon in later years installed an extension of his city hall telephone at his store. He also took a midmorning coffee break during which he walked a block east to the Independence courthouse square to chat with friends and fellow politicians at the Woolworths lunch counter. In these informal ways, the eastern Jackson County political machine conducted business under Sermon's watchful eye.

As mayor, Sermon gained recognition for several accomplishments. He supervised the reconstruction of the city's aging electrical plant and used the new, more efficient plant's revenues to reduce taxes. By the 1940s the property assessment in Independence dropped to twenty cents per one hundred dollars of evaluation. Independence also eliminated its community chest campaign after the city's regular budget supplied funds to support local charitable organizations. Several capital campaigns for street paving and public buildings increased the services to citizens.

Possibly the most intriguing aspect of Sermon's career was his relationship with the Pendergast forces that included his friends James Pendergast and Harry Truman. Sermon based his political appeal on understanding the needs and thinking of his fellow Independence citizens. Clearly, the move to take political control of the city's welfare and charitable efforts can be interpreted as an effort to utilize those activities for political purposes, a tactic similar to that employed by the Pendergast organization.

Like Truman, Sermon remained faithful to the Pendergast faction in the days following the indictment, guilty plea, and imprisonment of its leader Tom Pendergast. Sermon worked tirelessly on Truman's behalf in the uphill 1940 senatorial reelection campaign. In 1942, however, he broke with James M. Pendergast–backed candidates to support the successful courthouse-cleanup campaign of that year. **Phillip M. Donnelly,** the successful 1944 Democratic candidate for governor whom

Sermon challenged in the statewide primary, was a Pendergast-endorsed figure.

Nevertheless, in 1945, Sermon attended Tom Pendergast's funeral, along with Vice President Truman, who flew in from Washington. Further, in 1946, when Truman asked for the defeat of Democratic congressman Roger T. Slaughter, Sermon took part in the successful effort along with James Pendergast. Possibly the best summary came from Sermon in a 1938 *Kansas City Star* interview: "We have very friendly relations with the Kansas City Democratic organization. The organization does not attempt to interfere with our city affairs."

Roger T. Sermon died of a heart attack on January 23, 1950. He had just been nominated in the Democratic primary election to serve another four-year term as mayor.

WILLIAM S. WORLEY

Kansas City Star, April 7, 1938.
Kansas City Times, January 24, 1950.

SHANNON, JAMES (1799–1859)

James Shannon, a clergyman, political activist, and university president who seemed to arouse controversy and opposition wherever he went, was born in County Monaghan, in the province of Ulster, Ireland, on April 23, 1799. The future president of the University of Missouri attended the University of Belfast where he earned degrees and became an avid student of ancient and modern languages. He emigrated to the United States and accepted a position at Sunbury Academy, a Presbyterian school in Georgia. Although he had prepared in Ireland to become a Presbyterian minister, he declined ordination by that denomination following his arrival in the United States because of his disagreement with their practice of infant baptism.

Shannon joined the Baptist Church and in 1826 became pastor of the First Baptist Church in Augusta, Georgia. Four years later he accepted an appointment as professor of languages at the University of Georgia, following a clamor from Baptists, the state's largest denomination, demanding the appointment of one of their members to the university's predominantly Presbyterian faculty. In 1835 he left the university to assume the presidency of Louisiana College, later Centenary College. During his tenure at the Louisiana school, Shannon shifted his religious affiliation to the Disciples of Christ, a denomination formed when some alienated Presbyterians, led by Ulsterman Alexander Campbell, joined the followers of Barton Stone, a "reforming Christian" from Kentucky.

At Campbell's urging, Shannon moved to Harrodsburg, Kentucky, in 1840 to become president of Bacon College, an institution operated by the Disciples, commonly called the Christian Church. Shannon, a staunch defender of slavery and an ardent champion of white supremacy, had his share of critics, including members of his denomination who accused him of prostituting Scriptures to uphold the peculiar institution and called for his resignation as president of the financially troubled school.

Shannon left Bacon College in 1850 to become the second president of the University of Missouri, a post he was tendered following the departure of **John Hiram Lathrop** for the University of Wisconsin. Proslavery Democrats in the Missouri General Assembly, who had disliked the Whiggish Lathrop, applauded Shannon's appointment. Before accepting the presidency at Missouri, Shannon insisted that he be permitted to continue to preach. His intemperate religious and political pronouncements soon embroiled the new president in controversy with both Benton Democrats and Whigs.

Shannon's outspoken support for the introduction of slavery in Kansas following the enactment of the Kansas-Nebraska Act in 1854 further angered his detractors who accused him of teaching politics in the university, delivering extremist proslavery speeches, and spending too much of his time preaching. He responded by pointing to the university's growth during his tenure, "notwithstanding the partisan war of unexampled fierceness which has been waged against me from my first appointment." The embattled president was not without defenders, but he declined reappointment as president of the University of Missouri in 1856 to become the first president of the newly formed Christian University in Canton, Missouri, later known as Culver-Stockton College. He held that post until his death on June 14, 1859.

HUGH F. BEHAN

Harrell, David E., Jr. "James Shannon: Preacher, Educator, and Fire-Eater." *Missouri Historical Review* 63 (January 1969): 135–70.
Olson, James C., and Vera Olson. *The University of Missouri: An Illustrated History.* Columbia: University of Missouri Press, 1988.
Shannon, James. Papers. Western Historical Manuscripts Collection, Columbia.

SHANNON, JOSEPH B. (1867–1943)

Joseph B. Shannon was born in St. Louis on March 17, 1867, one of eight children of Francis P. and Mary McKenna Shannon. The family lived in St. Louis until 1879 when a train accident killed Shannon's father. The family moved to Kansas City, Missouri, in order to make a fresh start. Joseph attended school for only a brief time, going to work at twelve years of age to help support his family.

The family lived southeast of downtown Kansas City, an area that would eventually become known as Shannonville and would be the base of Joseph Shannon's Ninth Ward.

Shannon became politically active even before he could vote and eventually headed a faction known as the Rabbits because Shannon allegedly once boasted that he had rabbits on every corner prepared to inform him whenever the governor arrived in town. In 1892 a Democratic Party patronage appointment placed him on the city's payroll as market master. That same year he married Cecelia Hutawa. They subsequently had three children: Joseph, Helen, and Frank.

Physically handsome and full of energy, Shannon also possessed a strong mind. It did not take him long to become a force in Kansas City Democratic Party circles. Having lost his patronage job because of a Republican victory in the municipal election of 1894, Shannon dedicated himself to the task of establishing a more permanent political presence. In order to gain political clout within Kansas City and Jackson County Democratic circles, he had to, depending on the circumstances, compete against or cooperate with another Democratic organization first run by **Jim Pendergast** and then by **Tom Pendergast.**

Shannon started his rise in 1896. At the Democratic county convention he threw the Ninth Ward's support to Frank Lowe, a young reform-minded lawyer who wanted the Jackson County prosecuting attorney's position in order to get rid of illegal gambling. Jim Pendergast did not want Lowe. Pendergast had saloon and gambling interests, and in the previous year he had aligned with the leader of another Jackson County Democratic faction, March K. Brown, in order to arrange for police protection of organized gambling. Shannon, with no gambling ties, could support Lowe. Lowe won both the Democratic nomination and the general election. His victory did not seriously threaten the well-entrenched Pendergast, but it did hurt Brown's credibility. Shannon took Brown's place as a political power broker.

At the 1898 Democratic county convention, Pendergast managed to derail Lowe by getting **James A. Reed** nominated for prosecuting attorney, a position Reed won. Pendergast added to his considerable power in 1900 by getting Reed nominated and then elected mayor of Kansas City. However, Pendergast's attempt to flex his political muscle by not supporting the Democratic Jackson County slate of candidates resulted in a Republican victory. In an effort to avoid another act of political self-destruction, Pendergast and Shannon realized they needed to work together. By 1902 Shannon had proposed "fifty-fifty," an agreement between Shannon and Pendergast that divided the county patronage jobs equally, regardless of which faction's candidates won.

The fifty-fifty agreement represented a setback for Pendergast. Even though he had aspired to assert political power beyond the First Ward and the North End, he could not, and he never did. In 1910, when he turned over his organization to his younger brother Tom, Jim Pendergast still held the same ground that he had a decade before.

From 1902 onward, "fifty-fifty" was used, not used, and used shakily. In 1908 Shannon became involved in the Democratic Party beyond the local and state level. He served as a delegate to the Democratic National Convention, as he would five additional times. In 1910 he became the chairman of the Missouri Democratic State Committee. In Jackson County, however, the talented and aggressive Thomas J. Pendergast still agreed to "fifty-fifty" in the 1912 elections, but after that he became increasingly restless over the arrangement.

In 1915 Pendergast changed "fifty-fifty" to "seventy-thirty." The next year Shannon succeeded in getting his protégé, Kansas City mayor Henry L. Jost, nominated again. To reduce Shannon's hold on the Kansas City municipal government, Pendergast instructed his supporters to vote for the Republican candidate for mayor, George H. Edwards, who won. The political knife had been wielded, and Shannon had been the victim. In addition, Pendergast supported **Frederick D. Gardner** for Missouri's governor, and Gardner won. Gardner proceeded to appoint police commissioners who were lenient toward the Kansas City liquor interests, which included Pendergast.

Yet, the fragile "fifty-fifty" was once again restored in 1918. Pendergast, Shannon, and an emerging Jackson County Democratic leader, **Miles Bulger,** worked together and shared patronage. In 1920 circumstances once again forced Pendergast to agree to "fifty-fifty" because Bulger, the presiding judge and administrator of the Jackson County Court, sought more power by making a deal with Shannon.

In 1922 Shannon supported Pendergast nominees **Harry S. Truman** and **Henry F. McElroy** as eastern and western judges of the county court. Truman and McElroy both won. However, Pendergast did not subsequently share the county patronage jobs with Shannon. Already unhappy, and a loser in the primary election, Shannon, with Bulger, returned the political knife to Pendergast in 1924. They instructed their followers to vote for the Republican candidates for the county court. The Republicans won. That episode removed any chance for the continuation of "fifty-fifty."

In 1925 Shannon and Pendergast met on a downtown Kansas City street and nominally patched up their differences. In effect, however, Shannon had to admit defeat. Later that year, in one last gasp of pride, he asked the voters of the Ninth Ward to vote against the proposed Kansas City municipal charter that would institute the city-manager form of government. Shannon knew that if Pendergast controlled the new smaller city council, he could turn the reformers' enlightened governmental structure back against them and, as a result, be an even stronger political force. The Ninth Ward voters followed Shannon's wishes, but all the other wards in the city voted in favor of the proposal. As a token, Pendergast granted Shannon two of the eight department directorships. The directors, however, worked under Pendergast's handpicked city manager, **Henry F. McElroy.**

In 1930 Pendergast asked Shannon if he would like to be the U.S. congressman from the Fifth District of Missouri. Shannon agreed, and he went to Washington. He was reelected five times.

Unlike his service as a political boss in Kansas City, as a congressman Shannon had little impact. He ran against popular currents. He espoused old-time Jeffersonian small government at a time when New Deal big government was in vogue. A longtime student of Thomas Jefferson, Shannon worked, unsuccessfully, to eliminate government's competition with business. He also failed to make Jefferson's birthday a national holiday.

Shannon died on March 28, 1943, at the age of seventy-six. To the end he remained a stately, silver-haired, benevolent figure, ready and willing to articulate the ideas of Thomas Jefferson, and able to offer humor and practical wisdom.

DONALD B. OSTER

Blackmore, Charles P. "Joseph B. Shannon: Political Boss and Twentieth-Century Jeffersonian." Ph.D. diss., Columbia University, 1954.

Brown, A. Theodore, and Lyle W. Dorsett. *K. C.: A History of Kansas City, Missouri.* Boulder, Colo.: Pruett Publishing, 1978.

Dorsett, Lyle W. *The Pendergast Machine.* New York: Oxford University Press, 1968.

Oster, Donald B. "Reformers, Factionalists, and Kansas City's 1925 City Manager Charter." *Missouri Historical Review* 72 (April 1978): 296–327.

Reddig, William M. *Tom's Town: Kansas City and the Pendergast Legend.* 1947. Reprint, Columbia: University of Missouri Press, 1986.

SHAPLEY, HARLOW (1885–1972)

Described by scholars and friends as a Renaissance man, Harlow Shapley was born on November 2, 1885, to Willis and Sarah Stowell Shapley. Willis, who died early in Harlow's childhood, taught school and farmed. Harlow grew up on a farm outside of Nashville, Missouri, with his fraternal twin Horace, younger brother John, and older sister Lillian. He attended a rural school in Jasper, Missouri, until the fifth grade and then taught himself at home. His lack of formal education kept him out of the prestigious Carthage High School. Instead, he attended the Presbyterian Carthage College Institute, graduating in a year and a half as valedictorian of his class.

During his teenage years, Shapley worked as a crime reporter for the *Daily Sun* in Chanute, Kansas, and briefly as a police reporter at the *Joplin Times.* When he was twenty-one years old, he enrolled at the University of Missouri with the intention of majoring in journalism, but he became a math and science major with an emphasis in astronomy. In his autobiography, *Through Rugged Ways to the Stars,* he described how he ended up in the field of astronomy: "I opened the catalogue of courses. . . . The very first course offered was archaeology, and I couldn't pronounce it . . . I turned over a page and saw astronomy: I could pronounce that and here I am." Officials recognized his talent and appointed him assistant director of the Law Observatory during his sophomore year and offered him a teaching assistantship during his junior year. In 1910 he graduated from the University of Missouri with high honors in mathematics and physics, and a year later earned an M.A. degree from the same institution.

Princeton University awarded Shapley the Thaw Fellowship. There he studied under noted astronomers Henry Norris Russell and Raymond Smith Dugan, beginning his first astronomical work on eclipsing binaries, which consist of two stars that revolve around each other, causing one or both stars to appear eclipsed. He tediously computed rough distances of more than ninety of them. Meanwhile, he also studied a supposed type of binary stars known as Cepheid variable stars, a class of pulsating stars whose light variations occur usually in periods of two months. He made the important discovery that they were not binary, but changed their brightness as they changed their size because of internal or surface pulsations. In 1913 he received a doctor of philosophy degree from Princeton University. The next year, Shapley began work at the Mount Wilson Observatory where he focused on studying variable stars in globular clusters.

Mount Wilson's sixty-inch telescope made Shapley's tedious task of measuring distances and estimating properties of variable stars in globular clusters successful. By 1918 he published a paper called "Remarks on the Arrangement of the Sidereal Universe" that created a new picture of the Milky Way. He believed the galaxy to be a convex lens–shaped disc, three hundred thousand light-years in diameter and thirty thousand light-years thick. He also came to the revolutionary conclusion that Earth's solar system was not the center of the Milky Way but actually fifty thousand light-years away from the center in the direction of Sagittarius. In April 1920 Shapley debated his view of the Milky Way with Hebert D. Curtis of the Lick Observatory at the annual meeting of the National Academy of Sciences. The "Great Debate," as it is often called, addressed the differences in their measurements of the universe. In 1930 Shapley revised his description of the universe because he had overestimated its diameter by one hundred thousand light-years.

In 1921 Shapley succeeded Edward Charles Pickering as director of the Harvard College Observatory and as Paine Professor of Practical Astronomy. By the 1930s, through Shapley's efforts, the Harvard Observatory had become a major research center, and the newly created graduate program in astronomy attracted students from around the world.

While director of the Harvard Observatory, Shapley became increasingly involved in national and international politics. During and after World War II, he spoke out against ultranationalism and urged peaceful coexistence among nations. At the onset of World War II, he helped hundreds of Jewish scientists escape persecution. One scientist, Richard Prager of the Berlin Observatory, commented that "every night at least a thousand Jewish scientists were saying a prayer of thanks for Harlow Shapley's humanitarian efforts, which had helped save them and their families."

In 1945 Shapley participated in shaping the United Nations Educational, Scientific, and Cultural Organization. During the same year he attended the annual Academy of Science meeting in Moscow where he spoke for cooperation between the Soviets and the United States. The House Un-American Activities Committee (HUAC) believed he spoke too passionately in favor of friendly relations with the Soviets and subpoenaed him in November 1946. A Democratic representative from Mississippi, John E. Rankin, a member of HUAC, commented, "I have never seen a witness treat a committee with more contempt." To be called a Communist offended Shapley, and he said of Rankin, "That man had the nerve to tell me that I am un-American." In 1949 Shapley became acting chairman of the Committee of One Thousand, an organization committed "to protect the freedoms guaranteed in the First Amendment against the House Committee on Un-American Activities." Even after being exonerated by the HUAC, in 1950 Shapley fell victim to the charges of Sen. Joseph McCarthy, who forced him to appear before a subcommittee as one of five alleged Communists connected with the State Department. These charges, of course, proved false, and a month after his appearance the American Association for the Advancement of Science elected Shapley its president, in support of his stance. Shapley called his fight against the "Red Hunters" his most significant contribution outside of astronomy.

In 1952 Shapley retired as director of the Harvard College Observatory. He spent the rest of his life at his home in Sharon, New Hampshire, with his wife, Martha, whom he had met in a mathematics class at the University of Missouri. They married on April 15, 1914, and had five children, Mildred, Willis, Alan, Lloyd, and Carl. He continued to live a busy life, lecturing on astronomy and writing. Harlow Shapley died on October 20, 1972, in Boulder, Colorado.

Cynthia Heimberger

A Biographical Encyclopedia of Scientists. S.v. "Shapley, Harlow."

Bok, Bart Jan. Harlow Shapley, 1885–1972: A Biographical Memoir. Washington, D.C.: National Academy of Sciences of the United States, 1978.

A Dictionary of Scientific Biography. S.v. "Shapley, Harlow."

New York Times, October 21, 1972.

Parker, Sybil. Modern Scientists and Engineers. New York: McGraw-Hill, 1980.

World Who's Who in Science. Chicago: A. N. Marquis, 1968.

SHAW, HENRY (1800–1889)

Among individuals whose public contributions improved the quality of life in Missouri, Henry Shaw holds a high place for giving to the public an outstanding botanical garden and a magnificent Victorian strolling park. He also endowed the School of Botany at Washington University.

Born on July 24, 1800, in the English industrial town of Sheffield, Shaw attended Mill Hill School near London. There he learned French, developed a lifelong concern for literature, and showed a slight interest in trees and flowers. The campus had been the home of botanist Peter Collinson. After six years young Shaw returned to Sheffield, presumably to help his father, Joseph, in business. Instead, the two embarked for Canada in 1818. The senior Shaw had previously enjoyed success in the manufacture of grates. However, he had borrowed money from his sister's husband to finance an American associate in selling Sheffield ware in the New World. The partner neglected his side of the arrangement, and the valuable cutlery lay unsold in a New Orleans warehouse.

Shortly after arriving in Canada, young Henry Shaw went to Louisiana to recoup his father's property. With sales depressed in the South, he went upriver to take advantage of the expanding economy of the St. Louis region. Shaw had an amazing capacity for keeping records, as his extensive business papers show. He did not pay for his English goods in coin, but sent in exchange tobacco, cotton, furs, and other American goods. He enlisted his mother's brother

James Hoole as his agent in London. Another uncle manufactured superb cutlery. Only later did Shaw learn that his father had debts to a brother-in-law.

Shaw did not like St. Louis at first because the state allowed slavery. When he brought his mother and sisters to the United States several years later, Mrs. Shaw would not move to Missouri because it was a slave state. Henry came to like the city, settled down, and eventually purchased slaves himself.

By the time the American market for Sheffield ware declined dramatically in 1840, forty-year-old Shaw, still unmarried, was relatively rich. He loaned money with property as backing and began to pick up many acres southwest of St. Louis at sheriffs' sales and foreclosures. He put his affairs in the hands of Peter Lindell, a partner in several business enterprises, and set out to visit his family in upstate New York before touring Europe. He kept a journal and all his hotel bills so that one can easily trace his itinerary. He returned to St. Louis in 1843 and became an American citizen on July 4 of that year. Then he went on a three-year tour. He enjoyed the company of several French girls and at least one young lady in Vienna, but never married.

In 1849 Shaw asked architect George I. Barnett to design a house in town and an Italianate villa on his property southwest of the city. Two years later he made a will, providing generously for his household servants and for his relatives in England, but leaving most of his property to his two sisters.

During 1851, while visiting Chatsworth, the estate of the duke of Devonshire, Shaw decided to open a public garden in St. Louis. He enlisted the advice of Sir William Jackson Hooker, director of the Royal Kew Gardens; Asa Gray of Harvard, American's leading botanist; and St. Louis's own **George Engelmann,** a gynecologist and amateur botanist.

On a trip to Europe in 1858, Engelmann purchased for Shaw books on botany and the herbarium of Jacob Bernhardi. These purchases later made possible the development of botanical research and an excellent library. Shaw called on architect Barnett again, this time to develop plans for a library, museum, and herbarium. Shaw directed the planting of countless trees of many varieties. On March 14, 1859, the Missouri state legislature authorized the opening of the Missouri Botanical Garden. Later that same year the *Magazine of Horticulture* called national attention to Shaw's gift.

When the residents of St. Louis voted down a proposal for a large city park, Shaw decided to give a 276-acre tract adjacent to the garden for a Victorian strolling park. The city government agreed to an annual budget to support the project. The state supreme court appointed a board to guide the park.

Shaw sought no public office and remained a notably private citizen. Among his few close friends,

perhaps the closest was his ward, Joseph Monell, whose education he financed. Shaw urged the preservation of forests. He wrote extensively on birds and trees but published only two short books, *The Rose* and *The Wine and Civilization.*

In 1885 Shaw established the School of Botany at Washington University in St. Louis, and invited William Trelease of the University of Wisconsin to head it. After Shaw's death on August 25, 1889, this outstanding botanist became director of the Missouri Botanical Garden and gave a splendid display garden international recognition as a center of botanical study and research.

In his will Henry Shaw left to his trustees of the garden, as a permanent endowment, the bulk of his estate valued at $2.5 million. The Missouri Botanical Garden gained a high place among the world's great gardens.

WILLIAM B. FAHERTY

Faherty, William Barnaby. *Henry Shaw: His Life and Legacies.* Columbia: University of Missouri Press, 1987.

Harris, NiNi. *Grand Heritage.* St. Louis: De Sales Community Corporation, 1984.

———. *Henry Shaw's Living Legacy.* St. Louis: Tower Grove Park, 1986.

MacAdam, David. *Tower Grove Park.* St. Louis: R. P. Studley, 1883.

Primm, James Neal. "Henry Shaw: Merchant Capitalist." *Gateway Heritage* 5 (summer 1984): 2–9.

Raven, Peter H. "The Missouri Botanical Garden in the World's Service." *Gateway Heritage* 5 (summer 1984): 40–48.

SHELBY, JOSEPH ORVILLE (1830–1897)

Joseph Orville Shelby has been hailed by a biographer as "the Jeb Stuart of the West," while contemporaries likened him to Nathan Bedford Forrest. The nobility of Stuart's mind-set may resemble Shelby's, but most military historians consider Shelby like Forrest, an untutored genius of leadership, organization, and tactics.

Born in Lexington, Kentucky, on December 12, 1830, "Jo" Shelby was the child of Orville and Anna Boswell Shelby. Descended of noted planters and rope manufacturers in Kentucky and Tennessee, he was also related to Kentucky's first governor, Isaac Shelby. Orville died when Jo was five, and in 1843 his mother married Benjamin Gratz. Jo's stepfather was a wealthy Pennsylvanian who took pains to educate his stepson, sending him to Transylvania University.

In 1852, with his paternal inheritance, Shelby entered Waverly, Missouri's busy commercial scene. Following his forebears' example, the young man developed a hemp factory in Waverly, a sawmill at Dover, and a seven-hundred-acre farm where slaves tended livestock, hemp, and wheat. On a bluff overlooking Waverly he built a mansion, and became a man of substance and a confidant of such politically prominent figures as his second cousin **Frank Blair, David Rice Atchison,** and **Claiborne Fox Jackson.** On July 22, 1858, Shelby joined a second cousin, Elizabeth N. Shelby, in a marriage blessed by seven children.

This was the decade of "Bleeding Kansas" and its border war, resulting from Missourians' attempts to prevent another abolitionist bastion on their frontiers. Among the "ruffians" abusing the territory's electoral processes was Shelby, acutely fearful he was living beyond his means and that abolition threatened his early ruin. As federal forces tipped the scales against pro-Southern Missourians, the turbulence was crippling western Missouri's economy.

When the Civil War erupted, Shelby recruited at his own expense a cavalry troop for the Missouri State Guard, and as hostilities shifted southward his troops followed, scrapping at Carthage and Wilson's Creek before facing the Yankees at Pea Ridge, Arkansas, in March 1862.

The following summer Shelby returned to Lafayette County and recruited the Fifth Missouri Cavalry. This made him a colonel, but he spent little time with his regiment. In September 1862 he rose to command the celebrated Iron Brigade, and led it until September 1864. Confederate officials in Richmond promoted him to brigadier general in early 1863.

The Iron Brigade swept across many western battlefields, and even waged a campaign, that included the Battle of Corinth, Mississippi, in October 1862. It participated in raids across Missouri, including **John S. Marmaduke**'s thrust at Springfield during the second winter of the war, terminating with the clash at Hartville in January 1863. The brigade joined Marmaduke's ill-fated drive on Cape Girardeau that spring, and the following autumn Shelby led it on a daring foray northward to Waverly. When **Sterling Price** undertook to "liberate" Missouri in the final autumn of the war, Shelby, commanding a division, proved a daring leader for the campaign that came to grief at Westport in October.

The Confederacy disintegrating, Shelby refused to surrender. Burying battle flags in the Rio Grande, his six hundred militants entered Mexico. Shelby was soon involved with Price in creating the "gringo" colony of "Carlota" near Vera Cruz. When the project failed, Shelby returned to the States in 1867.

Penniless, Shelby came back to Lafayette County, and with financial aid from kinsmen took up a farmstead near Aullville. His farming prospered, and he was sufficiently well off by 1885 to move to a farm more to his liking in Bates County.

Although his charisma was political "dynamite," Shelby refused to stand for office. Passing years tempered his youthful militancy, and the resentful adherent of the "Lost Cause" gradually came to champion a renewed American national spirit. In the election crisis of 1876–1877, he endorsed whatever disposition **Ulysses S. Grant** proposed to make of it. Later, with encouragement from Unionists led by former governor **Thomas Clement Fletcher,** President Grover Cleveland in 1893 appointed Shelby U.S. marshal for Missouri's western district. His handling of the Pullman strikers in 1894 was soon hailed as a model for fellow marshals.

When Gov. **William Joel Stone** chastised Shelby for exerting federal muscle in Missouri's affairs, Shelby retorted that Stone's problem had been settled at Appomattox. Although he voted for William McKinley in 1896, Shelby was a "gold Democrat" who disdained the inflationary silver schemes of William Jennings Bryan and the Populists. The truth was that he had learned how important sound currency was.

Shelby died at his home near Adrian on February 13, 1897, and was buried in the Forest Hill Cemetery in Kansas City, Missouri.

R. Leslie Anders

Edwards, John N. *Shelby and His Men; or, The War in the West.* Cincinnati: Miami Printing and Publishing, 1867.

Oates, Stephen B. *Confederate Cavalry West of the River.* Austin: University of Texas Press, 1961.

O'Flaherty, Daniel. *General Jo Shelby.* Chapel Hill: University of North Carolina Press, 1954.

SHERMAN, WILLIAM T. (1820–1891)

William T. Sherman was born in Lancaster, Ohio, on February 8, 1820. One of the major figures in American military history, he had strong ties to St. Louis. It was his favorite city, he lived many years there, and he lies buried in one of its largest cemeteries.

The death of Sherman's father in 1829 and his entry as a foster son into the family of Thomas Ewing were defining moments in the young boy's life. His graduation from the United States Military Academy in 1840 was another. His first visit to St. Louis in November 1843 was similarly important. At this time, he developed his lifelong affection for the city.

After army tours of duty in Florida, Alabama, South Carolina, and California, Sherman returned in September 1850 to the Third Artillery Regiment at Jefferson Barracks. Although he had married his foster sister Ellen Ewing that May, he came to Missouri alone. She remained in Lancaster, Ohio, to prepare for the birth of their first child. In October Sherman received promotion to captain in the Commissary Department and moved to a St. Louis boardinghouse. His wife and newborn daughter joined him in March 1851, and they bought a house. In addition to his army duties, Sherman oversaw property transactions for Thomas Ewing, who, with Henry Stoddard, had recently completed one of the largest land litigations in American history.

In October 1852 Sherman was transferred to commissary duty in New Orleans and there followed a decade of repeated failure. He left the army in the spring of 1853 and became manager of the San Francisco and later the New York branches of the Lucas and Turner Bank of St. Louis. He handled the jobs well, but financial conditions out of his control doomed both institutions. He failed as a lawyer and entrepreneur in Kansas but successfully founded the Louisiana Military Seminary in Alexandria, only to have secession cause him to return north.

Sherman refused to rejoin the army, however, and, in March 1861 he accepted the offer of St. Louis friends to become president of a street railroad company. It was in this capacity that he witnessed the Camp Jackson affair in May. Soon after, he responded to the pressure of relatives and went to Washington where he accepted command of the Thirteenth Regular Army Regiment. He was quickly transferred to division command in Irvin McDowell's army and distinguished himself in the July 1861 Union debacle at Bull Run. Soon after, he became second in command of Union forces in Kentucky.

It was because of events in the Blue Grass State that Sherman returned to Missouri. In late August 1861 he conferred with **John Charles Frémont** in an unsuccessful attempt to receive troops and supplies for Kentucky. When he was unfairly labeled as insane in December 1861 for his eccentric worry about the imminence of Kentucky's fall to the Confederates, he was sent to Sedalia on an inspection trip for Henry W. Halleck. He soon found himself in command of St. Louis's Benton Barracks, a recruit training camp. Beginning his historic friendship with **Ulysses S. Grant** at this time, he distinguished himself at Shiloh in April 1862.

Throughout the war, whether in Memphis, Vicksburg, Chattanooga, or Atlanta, on the way to the sea, or through the Carolinas, Sherman always had Missouri soldiers under his command. **Frank Blair,** the leading Missouri political leader, was among a coterie of Missouri officers who served under him.

Once the war was successfully completed and Sherman was universally acknowledged as one of the heroes of the Union war effort, he returned to St. Louis as commander of the Military Division of the Missouri. Leading St. Louis citizens raised thirty thousand dollars to purchase him a house at 912 N. Garrison Street. In this house his last child was born in 1867. When he became commanding general of the entire army in 1869, he moved to Washington, but in 1874 he returned to St. Louis in a pique over disagreements with the secretary of war, and wrote his famous memoirs in his St. Louis house. He and his family did not go back to Washington until 1876.

When he retired from the army in 1883, Sherman came back to St. Louis again and made his famous "I will not accept if nominated and will not serve if elected" statement in response to pressure from the 1884 Republican National Convention. He enjoyed retirement in his favorite city, but when his children grew up and went east, he and his wife moved to New York in 1886 to be near them. He enjoyed the New York theater, and he continued his vigorous defense of the Union war effort in spoken and written word.

On February 14, 1891, Sherman died in New York from complications of his lifelong asthma. His body was taken, according to his wishes, for final burial in Calvary Cemetery in St. Louis.

JOHN F. MARSZALEK

Marszalek, John F. *Sherman: A Soldier's Passion for Order.* New York: Free Press, 1993.

Sherman, William T. *Memoirs of General W. T. Sherman.* 1875. Reprint, New York: Library of America, 1990.

———. Papers. Ohio Historical Society, Columbus.

Sherman Family Papers. University of Notre Dame, South Bend, Ind.

Sherman Papers. Missouri Historical Society, St. Louis.

Winter, William C. *The Civil War in St. Louis: A Guided Tour.* St. Louis: Missouri Historical Society Press, 1994.

SHIELDS, JAMES (1810–1879)

James Shields holds the distinction of being the only person to be elected to the United States Senate from three different states. The peripatetic Irish Democrat represented Illinois, Minnesota, and Missouri in the Senate. Born in Altimore, in County Tyrone, Ireland, on May 10, 1810, Shields received a classical education before emigrating to the United States in 1826. He settled in Kaskaskia, Illinois, where he took up the study of law. Following his admission to the bar in 1832, he established a legal practice in Kaskaskia.

In 1836 Shields won a seat in the Illinois House of Representatives, and in 1839 he became the state auditor. He served as a judge on the Illinois Supreme Court from 1843 to 1845 prior to accepting an appointment as commissioner of the general land office.

Shields secured a commission as a brigadier general during the Mexican War and was wounded during the Battle of Cerro Gordo. President James K. Polk named him governor of the Oregon Territory in 1849, but he resigned that post upon learning that he had been elected to represent Illinois in the United States Senate.

Following the completion of his senatorial term in 1855, Shields moved to the Minnesota Territory. When Minnesota became a state three years later, he returned to the Senate following his election to fill a two-year term. After failing to win reelection, he headed for California where he met his future wife, Mary Ann Carr. They married in 1861 and had three children.

After the outbreak of the American Civil War, Shields secured an appointment as a brigadier general in the Union army and was placed in command of a division. In 1863 President Abraham Lincoln recommended the former senator for promotion to the rank of major general, but Congress failed to confirm his advancement. Shields resigned from the army in disgust, returned to California, and served as the railroad commissioner until 1866.

In 1866 he moved to Missouri and purchased a small farm near Carrollton where he established a law practice. He won a seat in the Missouri House of Representatives in 1874. In 1877 he became the railroad commissioner. The General Assembly chose Shields to serve in the United States Senate in January 1879 following the death of **Lewis Vital Bogy,** but he declined reelection in March of that year. His abbreviated term as Missouri's U.S. senator secured for him the distinction of being the only person to represent three different states in the upper house.

On June 1, 1879, Shields died in Ottumwa, Iowa, while on a lecture tour. His body was returned to Carrollton for burial in St. Mary's Cemetery. Statues of Shields were placed in Statuary Hall in the United States Capitol and on the courthouse square in Carrollton.

CHARLES MACHON

O'Meara, John B. "James Shields: An Appreciation." *Journal of the American Irish* 14 (1915): 140–45.

Onahan, William J. "General James Shields: Hero of the Mexican and Civil Wars and United States Senator from Three Different States." *Journal of the American Irish Historical Society* 9 (1900): 409–16.

Shoemaker, Floyd Calvin. *Missouri and Missourians: Land of Contrasts and People of Achievements.* Chicago: Lewis Publishing, 1943.

SHOEMAKER, FLOYD CALVIN (1886–1972)

When Floyd Calvin Shoemaker retired as secretary, librarian, and editor of publications of the State Historical Society of Missouri in 1960, he left behind a distinguished record of service as a collector, disseminator, and advocate of Missouri history. Born in Kissimmee, Florida, on May 7, 1886, Shoemaker was the only child of Frank C. and Emma Dreyer Shoemaker and moved with his parents to Bucklin, Missouri, in 1893. He attended the Bucklin public schools and, for one year, Brookfield High School.

A debater, violinist, and president of his senior class, Shoemaker received a bachelor of pedagogy degree from Northeast Missouri State Teachers College in Kirksville in 1906. He then transferred to the University of Missouri, where he earned a B.A. in 1909. After teaching history and Latin for a few months in early 1909 in the Gallatin High School, he returned to the university and pursued a master's degree while serving as an assistant professor of political science and public law. In 1910 he was appointed as assistant secretary and assistant librarian for the State Historical Society. He received his M.A. degree in 1911. Shoemaker later received two honorary doctorate of laws degrees, from Central College in Fayette in 1942 and from the University of Missouri in 1954.

In 1915 Shoemaker was named to head the State Historical Society, a position he retained for forty-five years. During his tenure he worked tirelessly to collect, preserve, and make available to scholars and the public the primary and secondary sources necessary to document the rich history of the state. Not content with merely augmenting the society's collections, Shoemaker also touted their availability and promoted their use through publications and innumerable speaking engagements. "One of my main objectives was to popularize Missouri history," he told an interviewer in 1968.

As the society's editor, Shoemaker supervised the publication of forty-five volumes of the *Missouri Historical Review,* the organization's quarterly journal, and edited or coedited thirty-five other diverse volumes. Included among these were two volumes of the *Journal of the Missouri Constitutional Convention of 1875,* twelve volumes of *Debates of the Missouri Constitutional Convention of 1875,* eighteen volumes of *The Messages and Proclamations of the Governors of the State of Missouri,* and four volumes of *Ozark Folksongs.* To promote widespread knowledge of Missouri history, Shoemaker edited a long-term series of articles for the state's newspapers titled "This Week in Missouri History." These short vignettes on historic events and prominent people appeared in newspapers throughout the state from

1925 until 1951. Many of the earlier sketches were included in *Missouri, Day by Day,* published by the society in 1942 and 1943.

Shoemaker contributed to scholarship on the state's history as a writer as well as an editor. His *Missouri's Struggle for Statehood, 1804–1821,* published in 1916, was the product of exhaustive research spanning some five years. Other of Shoemaker's writings focused on the overall history of the state: *A History of Missouri and Missourians,* volume two of *Missouri: Mother of the West,* and two volumes of *Missouri and Missourians: Land of Contrasts and People of Achievements.* Shoemaker wrote, edited, or supervised more than ninety publications during his long career.

Under Shoemaker's direction the State Historical Society of Missouri accomplished two projects of particular importance for the state. Beginning in 1951 and in conjunction with the State Highway Commission, the agency erected historic markers in every county and in the city of St. Louis. Designed to highlight events or sites of historical significance, these markers were prominently placed in turnouts or roadside parks. In 1957 the society undertook the first comprehensive inventory of historic sites in the state. Volunteers in every county evaluated local sites based on guidelines formulated by the society, and the results of the survey appeared in 1963 in the *Missouri Historic Sites Catalogue.*

As secretary of the society, Shoemaker concentrated on increasing membership. By 1937 the organization had the largest membership of any state historical society in the nation, a distinction that it retained throughout the remainder of his tenure. Shoemaker promoted the society and the study of state and local history throughout Missouri, helping to organize numerous local historical societies, speaking before civic and professional organizations, and officiating at the dedication of markers and historic sites. By 1955 his activities had earned him a statewide reputation, and the Missouri State Senate honored him on his fortieth anniversary as head of the society with a resolution naming him "Mr. Missouri."

Shoemaker was a founding member of the Missouri Writers Guild in 1915 and served as its first secretary and treasurer through 1920. He served as chairman of the Centennial Committee of One Thousand for the Missouri Centennial Celebration in 1916–1921, and chaired the Missouri subcommittee of the Butterfield Overland Mail Service Centennial in 1958. From 1941 to 1949 he was chairman of Sigma Delta Chi's National Historic Sites in Journalism Committee. Elected to Phi Beta Kappa while a student at the University of Missouri, Shoemaker became president of the university's chapter in 1960. In 1961 he was named to the Missouri Academy of Squires. The American Association for State and Local History honored him with two Awards of Merit for his role in promoting and popularizing the study of the state's history.

Shoemaker married Caroline Tull in 1911; they were the parents of one daughter, Evelyn. This first marriage ended in divorce. In 1944 he married L. Pearle McCowan. Shoemaker died in Columbia, Missouri, on August 6, 1972. His legacy endures in his publications and the rich resources available for the study of local and state history in the agency he served for fifty years.

LYNN WOLF GENTZLER

"Floyd Calvin Shoemaker, 1886–1972." *Missouri Historical Review* 67 (October 1972): 1–6.

March, David D. *The History of Missouri.* 4 vols. New York: Lewis Historical Publishing, 1967.

Shoemaker, Floyd Calvin. Collection. Western Historical Manuscripts Collection, Columbia.

SHORT, DEWEY JACKSON (1898–1979)

Dewey Jackson Short was born on April 7, 1898, in Galena, in Stone County, Missouri, to Jackson Grant and Permelia Cordelia Long Short. After graduating as valedictorian from Galena High School in 1915, he attended Marionville College at Marionville, Missouri, from 1915 to 1917. He earned an A.B. from Baker University in Baldwin City, Kansas, in 1919 and an S.T.B. from the Boston University School of Theology in 1922. He studied in Europe on a Frank D. Howard Fellowship at the Universities of Berlin, Heidelberg, and Oxford in 1922–1923. He was professor of philosophy and psychology at Southwestern College in Winfield, Kansas, for three years in the mid-1920s. A Methodist minister, Short occupied the pulpit at Grace Methodist Church in Springfield, Missouri, before choosing politics as a career.

Known as the "Silver Tongued Orator of the Ozarks" for his eloquent speaking ability, Short gained a statewide reputation because of his address to the Lincoln Day Banquet at Springfield, Missouri, in 1926. A Republican, he was elected to Congress in 1928 from the Fourteenth District of Missouri, a Democratic district. Defeated in 1930, he traveled to Europe and the Soviet Union in 1931. He ran unsuccessfully for the Republican nomination to the United States Senate in the at-large race in 1932, losing to Henry W. Keil. After redistricting was completed using the 1930 census, Short was elected to Congress in 1934 from the newly drawn Seventh District of Missouri and served in Congress until his defeat by Charles Brown in 1956.

Short spoke forcefully against the New Deal policies of President Franklin Roosevelt, predicting a massive federal government that would erode the liberties of the people. Because of his gift for oratory, Short was in demand throughout the country as a political speaker in the 1930s and 1940s.

In 1939 Short was a delegate to the thirty-fifth Interparliamentary Union at Olso, Norway, and was in Europe when World War II began. An isolationist, he spoke against America's entry in the war until the Japanese attack on Pearl Harbor made America's involvement imperative. A member of the Armed Services Committee (formerly named the Committee on Military Affairs) for twenty-four years, Short became chairman of the committee when the Republicans gained control of the House of Representatives under President Eisenhower in 1953–1955.

After leaving Congress in 1957 Short was appointed by President Eisenhower as assistant secretary of the army for civil-military affairs, and he served in that position from 1957 to 1960.

Short presided over the dedication of Table Rock dam in southwest Missouri in 1959, and in 1984 the Dewey Short Table Rock Lake Visitor Center was named in honor of his efforts in making Table Rock Lake a reality.

Short married Helen Gladys Hughes of Washington, D.C., in 1937. He was named to the Ozark Hall of Fame in June 1979. He died on November 19, 1979, at his home in Washington, D.C., and is buried at the Galena Community Cemetery in Galena, Missouri.

ROBERT S. WILEY

Current Biography. New York: H. W. Wilson, 1951.

Wiley, Robert S. *Dewey Short: Orator of the Ozarks.* Cassville, Mo.: Litho Printers, 1985.

Williams, Walter, and Floyd C. Shoemaker. *Missouri: Mother of the West.* Vol. 6. Chicago: American Historical Society, 1930.

SHREVE, HENRY MILLER (1785–1851)

Henry Miller Shreve was the designer of the Mississippi River steamboat and an inventor of a snag boat for clearing riverbeds of hazards. Born in New Jersey on October 21, 1785, to Col. Israel and Mary Shreve, he moved with his parents in 1788 to a large tract of farmland in western Pennsylvania purchased from George Washington. At fourteen, upon the death of his father, young Henry left home to begin his lifelong career as a riverman.

At age twenty-one, Shreve purchased a keelboat with which he pioneered in establishing trade between St. Louis, in the newly acquired Louisiana Territory, and Pittsburgh. In 1810 "Captain" Shreve ventured farther up the Mississippi to open trade in lead from Julien Dubuque's mines in Iowa. Successful in this and other trading ventures, Shreve married Mary Blair early in 1811 and established a home in

Brownsville, Pennsylvania. Two daughters, Harriet and Rebecca, and one son, Hampden, were born to this marriage; the son died in infancy. Late in life, after he had been widowed and remarried, Henry had a third daughter, Mary Shreve.

The human labor involved in bringing a loaded keelboat up a river was untenable; steam power offered an alternative that intrigued Shreve. Fulton steamboats were operating successfully in the East, and in 1811 one named the *New Orleans,* for the city of its destination, was nearing completion at Pittsburgh, intended for the Ohio and Mississippi Rivers. She made her maiden voyage safely despite an encounter with the New Madrid earthquakes in mid-December 1811. However, Fulton steamboats used low-pressure steam power, and the *New Orleans* lacked the power to master the currents above Natchez when a return voyage was attempted.

Shreve's first experience as master of a steamboat was on the *Enterprise,* built at Brownsville, Pennsylvania. The *Enterprise* had more steam power than the Fulton boat, and Shreve took it to New Orleans in time for it to serve Gen. Andrew Jackson in strengthening New Orleans against British attack in the War of 1812.

Fulton and his associates had obtained a monopoly on the use of steam power in New Orleans to prevent other entrepreneurs from operating on the Mississippi. Nevertheless, Shreve was determined to be in command of a steamboat for his own operations to New Orleans. After hiring a lawyer, he headed back to Brownsville, inspired to design a boat even better than the *Enterprise,* which had made the upriver voyage but with great difficulty. In 1817 a court decision invalidated the Fulton monopoly—an expensive battle for Shreve, but one finally brought to a satisfactory close.

In the meantime Captain Shreve had designed and constructed a completely new type of steamboat. His plans were for a higher-powered steam engine, set horizontally on a lower deck, over a hull similar to those of keelboats built for inland rivers. Above the engine deck he constructed another deck, a completely new concept in riverboat design, but one that became, with modifications, the plan for almost all steamboats that succeeded this first Shreve steamboat, the *Washington.*

Unfortunately, when the *Washington* was starting on her maiden voyage in July 1816, there was an explosion. Despite the ridicule and public denigration that followed, Shreve corrected the faulty safety valve and rebuilt his *Washington.* In 1817 he made a successful round-trip voyage to New Orleans. Shreve soon operated a fleet of vessels.

As steamboats increased in numbers, so did disastrous collisions with ancient trees, sometimes whole and rooted in the muddy river bottom. The government solicited suggestions for removing the hazardous snags, and Shreve's idea was accepted. He invented a double-hulled steam-driven "snag boat," and was asked to work with it in river clearance as an employee of the United States Corps of Engineers. When much clearance had been done, he was assigned to the Red River to destroy the centuries-old Great Raft that made the river impossible to navigate. Shreve and his crews worked for years on this project. Shreveport was founded in 1836 when the Red was navigable that far, and the end of the Great Raft was reached in 1839. Shreve was in the employ of the U.S. government from 1827 to 1841.

When in 1841 Shreve retired to Missouri farmland (now in the heart of St. Louis), Congress had approved payment of government money for Shreve's invention of the steam-powered snag boat, but none was received until after his death on March 6, 1851. A monument marks the grave of Henry Miller Shreve in St. Louis's Bellefontaine Cemetery, near the ever flowing true monument to his work, the busy Mississippi River.

EDITH McCALL

Hunter, Louis C. *Steamboats on the Western Rivers.* Cambridge: Harvard University Press, 1949.

McCall, Edith. *Conquering the Rivers: Henry Miller Shreve and the Navigation of America's Inland Waterways.* Baton Rouge: Louisiana State University Press, 1984.

SIBLEY, GEORGE CHAMPLIN (1782–1863)

George Champlin Sibley was born on April 1, 1782, in Great Barrington, a town near the Appalachian Trail in the Berkshire Hills of southwestern Massachusetts. He was the elder son of Dr. John and Elizabeth Sibley. His mother died in 1790, shortly after the family moved to North Carolina. Dr. Sibley had a varied career in medicine and later as a newspaper editor in Fayetteville. Before the Louisiana Purchase in 1803, Dr. Sibley moved to Louisiana, where President Thomas Jefferson appointed him U.S. Indian agent at Natchitoches, Louisiana, a post he held until 1814. As a friend and correspondent of Jefferson, he may have influenced the appointment of his son that same year as the assistant factor at Fort Bellefontaine near St. Louis. In that position Sibley learned the rudiments of the fur trade, as well as the operation within the government's Indian factory system.

In 1808 the government decided to establish a fort and factory to serve the Osage Indians at a place on the Missouri River about three hundred miles upstream from St. Louis, first sighted by **Meriwether Lewis** and **William Clark** on their expedition into Upper Louisiana in 1804. Appointed chief factor, Sibley joined Clark, the superintendent of Indian affairs at St. Louis, in erecting the complex that was christened Fort Osage in November 1808. It was, at the time, the westernmost frontier military and Indian trading outpost of the United States. As chief factor, Sibley engaged in the Indian fur trade, prepared the hides for transportation downriver to St. Louis, and served as a diplomatic liaison between the government and the Indians.

In May 1811 Sibley embarked on a three-month journey to the Grand Saline and Rock Saline (in northwestern Oklahoma) to explore the region, and to pacify the Kansa, Pawnee, and Osage Indians. On his return he shared his experiences with his father and other frontiersmen, including the legendary **Daniel Boone.** Now housed in the archives of the Missouri Historical Society his detailed account of the trip became an important historical source in America's frontier history.

During the War of 1812 the threat of Indian warfare led to the evacuation of Fort Osage and its relocation downriver at Arrow Rock. Since the crisis curtailed trade with the Indians, Sibley had time to find a wife. In 1815 he married Mary Smith Easton, the fifteen-year-old daughter of **Rufus Easton,** a prominent lawyer and the postmaster of St. Louis. The couple returned to Fort Osage, reopened the factory, and remained there until Sibley's retirement from government service in 1822. Western expansionists and private fur traders saw the factory system as a deterrent to national growth and economic freedom, and successfully lobbied the United States Congress to terminate the government-operated trading system in 1822. A treaty with the Osage in 1825 relieved the government of the need to keep the fort, and it was finally abandoned in 1827.

Appointed in 1825 as one of the three commissioners to survey and mark the road from the Missouri frontier to Santa Fe, Sibley completed the task and compiled the final report in 1827. In his report he recommended that the United States and Mexico cooperate to increase trade and protect traders and travelers from white renegades and hostile Indians on the trail. Although the survey was a remarkable achievement, the United States Congress largely ignored it, as did the Santa Fe traders, who preferred to follow the earlier trail.

In 1828 Sibley decided to dispose of his farm near Fort Osage and move to St. Charles, Missouri, where he owned 280 acres. He cleared the land for cultivation, built a log house, and named the farm Linden Wood for the large grove of trees that grew there. In December 1829 the Sibleys settled at Linden Wood, where they remained for the rest of their lives.

The Sibleys, in order to raise funds to pay their debts, started a boarding school for daughters of

St. Louis families. The school grew under their supervision. In 1853 it became Linden Wood Female College (now Lindenwood College), and was later endowed by the Sibleys' estate. Placed under the auspices of the Presbyterian Church, Lindenwood College became the first four-year women's college west of the Mississippi River.

From the time he served as a government worker on the frontier, Sibley favored political leaders who advocated a strong national government that defended the interests of the United States at home and abroad. He affiliated with the Whig Party, ran for public office three times without success, and attended the Whig National Convention in 1844, where he cast his vote for Henry Clay. By the outbreak of the Civil War, the former slaveholder had freed his few slaves and declared his allegiance to the Union.

Sibley died in his sleep on January 31, 1863, and was buried in the family plot on the Lindenwood College campus not far from the building named in his honor, Sibley Hall.

CHARLES T. JONES JR.

Brooks, George R., ed. "George C. Sibley's Journal of a Trip to the Salines in 1811." *Missouri Historical Society Bulletin* 21 (April 1965): 167–207.
Foley, William E. *The Genesis of Missouri: From Wilderness Outpost to Statehood.* Columbia: University of Missouri Press, 1989.
Gregg, Kate L. "The History of Fort Osage." *Missouri Historical Review* 34 (July 1940): 439–88.
———, ed. *The Road to Santa Fe: The Journal and Diaries of George Champlin Sibley and Others Pertaining to the Surveying and Marking of a Road from the Missouri Frontier to Settlements of New Mexico, 1825–1827.* Albuquerque: University of New Mexico Press, 1952.
Jones, Charles T., Jr. *George Champlin Sibley: The Prairie Puritan, 1782–1863.* Independence, Mo.: Jackson County Historical Society, 1970.

SIBLEY, MARY EASTON (1800–1878)

A pioneer woman in western Missouri and a regional leader in women's education, Mary Easton Sibley was born on January 24, 1800, in Rome, New York. The oldest child of Rufus and Abial Abby Easton, she came with her family to St. Louis in 1804, after President Thomas Jefferson appointed her father a judge in the new territory. Later **Rufus Easton** served as the first postmaster of St. Louis, as well as a territorial delegate to the United States Congress.

Mary Easton was an intelligent, good-looking, and outgoing young woman, who was properly educated in Mrs. Tevis's boarding school in Shellbyville, Kentucky. A skilled horsewoman, she and her father rode horseback to Washington, D.C., when she was only thirteen years old. In 1815 a family friend, **George Champlin Sibley,** and Mary began their courtship. Sibley, the factor at Fort Osage, on leave because of the threat of Indian uprisings in that area, had first met the Easton family when he was the assistant factor at Fort Bellefontaine near St. Louis. They were married on August 19. When the thirty-three-year-old George Sibley and his fifteen-year-old wife left St. Louis on their three-hundred-mile journey upriver to Fort Osage, Mary took her saddle, horse, organ with a drum and fife attachment, some furniture, and her library. As her husband well knew, she was determined to have "a very comfortable establishment . . . in the howling wilderness."

While they lived there, Sibley adjusted well to the primitive conditions on the Missouri frontier, according to her husband's commonplace book. Life among the Indians, fur traders, boatmen, and backwoodsmen may have toughened her physically, but there is no indication that it diminished her moral values, religious beliefs, or intellectual interests. George Sibley took pride in his young wife's independent spirit, her manner with the Indians, and the hospitality she showed to travelers on the Missouri River, including the legendary **Daniel Boone.** Mary Sibley, who was childless, had great affection for the Indian women and their children. She and George did their part to help educate Indian children at Harmony Mission not far from Fort Osage.

George Sibley retired from government service in 1822 at the time Congress closed the Indian factory system. He and Mary Sibley continued to live on a farm near the fort until a disastrous venture in the fur trade left them on the verge of bankruptcy. Following George Sibley's return from surveying the road to Santa Fe in 1827, they moved to St. Charles, across the Missouri from St. Louis. Not far from the village they owned a farm that they called Linden Wood. Presumably to help discharge their debts, Mary Sibley opened a boarding school for the daughters of local and St. Louis families. This was the beginning of what became the first four-year college for women west of the Mississippi River.

In 1831 the first building, a log structure that housed twenty students, was constructed. At first Sibley was the only instructor, while her husband kept a watchful eye on the finances. The school slowly increased in faculty and students, but retained a family atmosphere. Although there were hard times and it appeared that "Mrs. Sibley's School" would fail, as many other schools and academies did in the 1840s and 1850s, Linden Wood managed to survive. Toward the end of the 1840s the Sibleys envisioned a college for women wherein "female youth . . . may be properly educated, and qualified for the important duties of Christian mothers and school teachers."

In 1852 the Sibleys gave the land to Linden Wood

Female College. The St. Louis Presbytery took over the direction and care of the proposed college, though the boarding school continued. On February 24, 1853, the Missouri General Assembly incorporated Lindenwood College, and by 1870 it was placed under the Presbyterian Synod of Missouri.

After George Sibley died in 1863, Mary Sibley continued to live at Linden Wood. When she was seventy-one years old she left the Presbyterian Church to join the Second Adventists, a religious sect that proclaimed the Second Coming of Christ and the end of the world. Zealous in her newfound religion, she volunteered for missionary work in Japan, but by the time she reached California the rigors of the journey and ill health forced her return to St. Charles.

In time both faculty and students called Sibley "Aunt Mary," in respect for her devotion to the cause of women's education. She died on June 20, 1878, and was interred beside her husband in the family plot on the college campus.

CHARLES T. JONES JR.

Kansas City Times, January 5, 1862.

Jones, Charles T., Jr. *George Champlin Sibley: The Prairie Puritan, 1782–1863.* Independence, Mo.: Jackson County Historical Society, 1970.

Templin, Lucinda de Leftwich. *Two Illustrious Pioneers in the Education of Women in Missouri.* St. Charles, Mo.: Lindenwood College, 1926.

Woody, Thomas. *A History of Women's Education in the United States.* 2 vols. New York: Science Press, 1929.

SIGEL, FRANZ (1824–1902)

Franz Sigel, a soldier, editor, and public official, was born in Sinsheim, Baden, on November 18, 1824. He was a leader in the failed German revolution of 1848–1849 and was forced into exile. In May 1852 he moved to the United States and settled in New York City, where he worked as a tobacconist, surveyor, teacher, and musician. In 1855, with his father-in-law, Rudolf Dulan, Sigel formed the German-American Institute where he taught mathematics, history, and languages. He also taught in the public schools and the German Turner Society, belonged to the Fifth New York Militia, and wrote for the *New Yorker Staats-Zeitung* and the *New York Times.* In 1857 he moved to St. Louis to teach at the German-American Institute.

When the Civil War broke out Sigel was instrumental in rallying Germans to join the Union army and was commissioned a colonel of the Third Missouri Infantry. He played a prominent but undistinguished part in the Battle of Wilson's Creek on August 10, 1861. His bold but ill-fated flanking maneuver in this battle, however, became synonymous with Union failure. When Henry Halleck, commander of the Missouri Department, replaced him with **Samuel Ryan Curtis** in the winter of 1861, Sigel resigned from the army, which caused considerable uproar in the German American community. In early 1862 he returned to the army and partially redeemed himself by playing a prominent role in the Union victory at the Battle of Pea Ridge on March 7–8, for which he was promoted to major general. In May he was transferred to the eastern theater and took command of a division of Nathaniel P. Banks's troops at Harpers Ferry and fought in the Shenandoah Valley against Thomas J. "Stonewall" Jackson.

When the war department created the Army of Virginia in the summer of 1862, Sigel received his first significant command. He was ordered to take charge of the newly designated First Corps of the new army, composed of troops from **John Charles Frémont**'s Mountain Department. Sigel fought in the Battle of Second Bul! Run and later operated in and around the Shenandoah Valley. In January 1863 the war department disbanded the Army of Virginia, and Sigel's First Corps was reintegrated back into the Army of the Potomac as the Eleventh Corps.

In February Sigel took an extended leave of absence from the army and traveled to New York City where he gave numerous political speeches in support of the Republican Party. Although he wanted to return to the army to participate in the upcoming campaign, he lobbied to increase the size of his corps. Henry Halleck, then President Lincoln's chief of staff, refused Sigel's demands, and Sigel resigned from the army for the second time. He remained in New York City and continued to lobby for a more prominent command. Finally, in April, at the urging of several friends, Sigel rescinded his resignation and planned to return to his old command in Washington. Frustrated over Sigel's pettiness, Halleck had no use for him. Thus, Sigel missed the opportunity to command the Eleventh Corps at Chancellorsville in May. He eventually returned to the army in the summer of 1863 and was assigned to the District of Lehigh, Pennsylvania, in the Department of the Susquehanna.

More political lobbying won Sigel a more significant command in February 1864 with the Department of West Virginia, which included the lower Shenandoah Valley. On May 15, 1864, he fought John C. Breckinridge's Confederates at the Battle of New Market and was defeated. He was then assigned to the defense of Harpers Ferry and the Baltimore and Ohio Railroad, but was unable to keep the Confederates from inflicting serious damage to either. He was relieved of command on July 8, 1864, and spent the last year of the war in Baltimore and Washington hoping for another command. On May 4, 1865, he resigned his commission in the Union army.

Sigel returned to New York City after the Civil War and in 1869 worked for the Brooklyn Steamship and Emigration Company and the Metropolitan Railway. In June 1870 he was appointed internal revenue collector for the New York Ninth District by President **Ulysses S. Grant.** Elected to one term as register of the city in 1871, he served during Grover Cleveland's presidency as chief clerk in the county clerk's office from May 1885 to June 1886, and as pension agent for the New York District from March 1886 to May 1889. After retiring from politics Sigel published the *New Yorker Deutsches Volksblatt* and edited the *New York Monthly* from 1897 to 1900. He died in New York City on August 22, 1902.

In 1906 an equestrian statue of Sigel was dedicated in Forest Park in St. Louis. That same year, the Franz Sigel School was dedicated in Lafayette Square in his honor. In New York City a bronze equestrian statue of Sigel was erected in 1907 and a park in the Bronx was named for him. More recently, he was one of thirty-three Missourians honored in World War II by having a Liberty ship named for him. In 1998 Sigel, along with other Forty-eighters, was honored at the 150th anniversary of the German Revolution at the Badisches Landesmuseum in Karlsruhe, Germany.

STEPHEN D. ENGLE

Engle, Stephen D. *Yankee Dutchman: The Life of Franz Sigel.* Fayetteville: University of Arkansas Press, 1993.

Griffen, Lawrence E. "The Strange Story of Major General Franz Sigel: Leader and Retreater." *Missouri Historical Review* 84 (July 1990): 404–27.

Hess, Earl J. "Sigel's Resignation: A Study in German-Americans and the Civil War." *Civil War History* 26 (1980): 5–17.

SISLER, GEORGE (1893–1973)

George Sisler ranks among baseball's finest hitters. His longtime manager and lifetime friend **Branch Rickey** described him as "the smartest hitter who ever lived. He never stopped thinking. And in the field he was the picture player, the acme of grace and fluency."

"Gorgeous George," as he came to be known, was born on March 24, 1893, in Nimisila on the fringe of Ohio's coal country, where his father supervised a mine. At age fourteen he moved north to nearby Akron to live with his older brother who later played baseball for the Goodyear Wingfoots in the local industrial league.

Originally a pitcher on local semiprofessional teams, Sisler turned down college scholarships to Western Reserve and the University of Pennsylvania in favor of the University of Michigan. He graduated in 1915 with a B.S. in mechanical engineering and married his college sweetheart, Kathleen Holznagle, the day after the 1916 baseball season ended.

By then, Sisler had already played two seasons in the major leagues, having come up as a pitcher in 1915. Branch Rickey, his coach at Michigan and a scout for the St. Louis Browns, had convinced that club to sign him. Earlier, he had signed with Akron, a minor league team in the Ohio-Pennsylvania League. Akron transferred the contract to its parent team in Columbus, Ohio, which in turn sold it to Pittsburgh Pirates–owner Barney Dreyfuss. Under two contracts, Sisler's fate was decided on June 10, 1915. A national commission (the two major league presidents plus one team owner, at the time Garry Herrmann for Cincinnati) declared the Pittsburgh contract void, since young George signed it as a minor. Sisler went immediately to St. Louis to play for Rickey, who was then managing the Browns.

In his first major league game, pitching against the Washington Senators, Sisler made a dramatic double play. Roger Peckinpaugh bunted while Joe Judge started running from third base. Sisler fielded the bunt fifteen feet from the plate, tagged out Peckinpaugh, and threw the ball to catcher Hank Severeid for the second out.

Gorgeous George and fellow slugger Babe Ruth both began their careers as left-handed pitchers, but converted to other positions so they could play daily. Rickey switched Sisler to the outfield briefly, then to first base permanently in 1916 so he could have him bat in every game. Sisler won five games and lost seven in his pitching career, with a 2.13 earned run average. Two of his victories were complete games pitched against Washington fastballer Walter Johnson.

Sisler won the Most Valuable Player Award in 1918, hitting .341. His 1920, 1921, and 1922 seasons rank among the finest in baseball history—he batted .407, .371, and .420. However, he always considered 1920 his best season: he led the league in batting with a .407 average, games with 154, at-bats with 631, and hits with 257.

Eye problems kept Sisler out of the 1923 season, but he returned as the Browns player-manager in 1924, hitting only .305. He managed the team until 1927, when he turned managing duties over to Dan Howley. In 1928 the Browns sold Sisler's contract to Washington. After twenty games the Senators sold him to the Boston Braves in the National League where he played through 1930, his last major league season. He completed his playing career in the minors, with a year at Rochester in the International League and in 1932 with Shreveport-Tyler in the Texas League.

Sisler's lifetime performance statistics—batting average of .340, 2,812 hits, and .987 fielding average—rank him among the game's finest first base-men. He was in the first group of players inducted into the Baseball Hall of Fame in 1937 with past opponents such as Babe Ruth, Ty Cobb, Honus Wagner, and Walter Johnson.

Sisler endorsed St. Louis sporting goods after his career until 1943, when he joined the Browns as a scout and special hitting instructor. Sisler died on March 26, 1973, in St. Louis.

JEFFREY E. SMITH

James, Bill. *The Bill James Historical Baseball Abstract.* New York: Villard Books, 1986.
Light, Jonathan Fraser. *The Cultural Encyclopedia of Baseball.* Jefferson, N.C.: McFarland, 1997.
New York Times, March 27, 1963.

SMITH, FORREST (1886–1962)

During his political career that spanned nearly half a century and culminated in his election to the governorship of Missouri, Forrest Smith gained recognition for being a tax authority, a staunch supporter of an improved highway system, and an advocate of increased educational spending.

Born on February 14, 1886, on a farm in Ray County, Missouri, Smith grew up in Richmond, the county seat. He attended public schools and the Woodson Institute in Richmond, and Westminster College in Fulton. After graduation from college, he taught four years as principal of the Richmond grammar school. He married Mildred Williams of Richmond on October 12, 1915. The couple raised two daughters, Forrestine and Mary Josephine.

Smith began his political career in 1910, serving four years as deputy assessor for Ray County. In 1914 the voters elected him to the office of county clerk. Reelected in 1918, he served as president of the County Clerks' Association in Missouri. He first gained statewide recognition as a member of the bipartisan State Tax Commission in 1925. He served on the commission for seven years.

A Democrat, Smith ran unsuccessfully for the office of state auditor in 1928, the year of the Republican landslide, but won that position in 1932, 1936, 1940, and 1944, the first Missourian ever elected to a state office for four consecutive terms. During his sixteen years as state auditor Smith received national attention as a tax authority, serving as president and as one of the original organizers of the National Association of Tax Administrators; as president of the National Association of State Auditors, Comptrollers, and Treasurers; and as a member of the executive committee of the National Tax Association. Often referred to as the "Daddy" of the Sales Tax Act, Smith was an early advocate, and is generally credited with the adoption, of the retail sales tax in Missouri in the 1930s.

In 1948 Smith ran for governor of Missouri. In his campaign he promised improvement of Missouri's highway system, increased revenue for education, and improvement of the state health and medical systems. He defeated Murray E. Thompson by a wide margin, but accusations concerning his ties with organized labor and city political bosses clouded his ascent to office. A report produced by U.S. senator Estes Kefauver's subcommittee investigating organized crime in Missouri declared that the state narrowly escaped falling into the hands of the underworld. The murder of Charles Binaggio, a Kansas City politician and former Pendergast associate, in the First Democratic Club shortly after the election allegedly resulted from Binaggio's failure to deliver Missouri to the underworld. Reportedly, Binaggio had secured between one and two hundred thousand dollars for Smith's gubernatorial campaign from a Chicago-based syndicate in return for promises that the tight police control in St. Louis and Kansas City would be relaxed after the election, but no such lessening of control occurred. Further investigations uncovered no evidence of organized ties linking state government to mob activity in the state, and the allegations concerning Smith were dispelled.

Possibly the most important piece of legislation passed during Smith's term as governor, House Bill 185 proposed to increase the gasoline tax by four cents per gallon in order to fund a state highway program that would provide all-weather roads within two miles of every farm home in Missouri. Faced with heavy opposition from Missouri's auto clubs and trucking organizations, Smith argued that the improved highway system would "lift farmers out of the mud," encourage forward movement of the school-consolidation program, and facilitate the use of regional hospitals by rural residents who could not otherwise access medical care. In 1951 the gasoline tax rose from two to three cents per gallon. The following year, with additional revenues in sight, the State Highway Commission announced a ten-year improvement program that proposed to increase the miles of state roads from 19,675 to 32,000 at a cost of more than $5.5 million.

As governor, Smith advocated the extension of social security benefits to all state employees. He also supported the creation of a four-year state-supported medical school in Missouri.

After stepping down from the governor's office, Smith kept his residence in Jefferson City. He died in Gulfport, Mississippi, on March 8, 1962.

ERIKA K. NELSON

New York Times, March 9, 1962.

Obituary. *Missouri Historical Review* 56 (December 1962): 386–87.

Official Manual of the State of Missouri, 1947–1948. Jefferson City: Secretary of State, 1948.

Parrish, William E., Charles T. Jones Jr., and Lawrence O. Christensen. *Missouri: The Heart of the Nation.* 2d ed. Arlington Heights, Ill.: Harlan Davidson, 1992.

Smith, Forrest. Papers. 1940–1953. Western Historical Manuscripts Collection, Columbia.

SMITH, GEORGE RAPPEEN (1804–1879)

Born on August 17, 1804, in Powhatan County, Virginia, but reared in Kentucky, George Smith attended an academy in Georgetown, Kentucky, while a teenager, and afterward studied law in Frankfort. He married Melita Thomson, the daughter of Gen. David Thomson, and the couple produced three children in Kentucky: a son, David Thomson, who died at six months; and two daughters, Martha Elizabeth and Sarah "Sed" Elvira.

The Thomson extended family, including the Smiths and seventy-five slaves, moved to Missouri in 1833. Before and after the migration, Smith pursued various business ventures and political ambitions to escape the farming life he loathed. He quickly rose to prominence in the newly created Pettis County, receiving the honor of naming the new county seat, which he called Georgetown for his home in Kentucky.

During the Mormon war of 1838 Smith volunteered as a private in the state militia and afterward was commissioned as a brigadier general, commanding troops in four counties. Although he was elected justice of the peace in 1836, Smith failed in his bids for the state legislature in 1836 and 1840 and also failed to secure federal appointive office despite the victory of his Whig Party. After repeated frustrations he was ultimately named receiver of public moneys at Springfield in 1843, only to lose office with the victory of Polk and the Democrats the next year.

Frustrated with his political endeavors, Smith secured government contracts for delivering pork to Fort Gibson in Indian Territory, for mail transportation in west-central Missouri, and for delivering freight to Santa Fe. However, his energy was especially focused on the Pacific Railroad as it made its way, at least in theory, across the state. Smith championed the plan for the railroad to move south of the Missouri River, and became the official agent and promoter of the railroad for the region as well as a director. He sought support—and a commitment of funds—from his neighbors for the venture. After winning election to the legislature in 1854 by capitalizing on the split between the Benton and the anti-Benton factions of the Democratic Party, he similarly promoted the interests of the railroad, but to little avail. In fact, in Pettis County opposition to the railroad and the changes it would bring mounted, and eventually the citizens of Georgetown rejected his proposal to bring the railroad through town. Spurned, Smith began buying land along the proposed route. He also filed a plat for a new town situated on the railroad that would compete with Georgetown. Within a decade Georgetown withered, and Sedalia, the new community named for one of Smith's daughters, flourished.

An outspoken Whig, Smith retained his party affiliation longer than many Whig partisans who left the fold because of its association with Free-Soil sentiment. Smith, though, became more skeptical of the institution of slavery, even though he owned slaves. Ultimately he condemned slavery and switched to the American Party and then to the Republican Party.

During the war Smith fled briefly with his family and returned alone when Sedalia was occupied by the Union army. Appointed adjutant general, he resigned the position because he thought Gov. **Hamilton Rowan Gamble** was not prosecuting the war vigorously enough. With the Union army headquarters in his own house, Smith sometimes rode with troops to point out Rebel sympathizers. He visited President Lincoln seeking more aggressive political action, became a leader in the Republican Party, was elected in 1864 to the state senate and served as president pro tempore, became an elector for Lincoln, and was named mayor of Sedalia. This was the pinnacle of General Smith's public career.

The end of the war saw Smith leave his new position in the Missouri Senate to become an assistant U.S. assessor, only to lose that position at the hand of President Andrew Johnson. Afterward, he continued his activities promoting railroads, boosting the growth of Sedalia, and tending to his own varied and successful investments. He ran for Congress in 1870 as a Liberal Republican, rejoined the Republican Party in 1872 as a candidate for the legislature, and failed in both attempts. He served as city alderman, though, in 1874 and 1875.

George Smith was a proud and powerful individual but also a severe person whose warmth was known by only a few intimates. He died at his home in Sedalia on July 11, 1879.

MICHAEL CASSITY

Cassity, Michael. *Defending a Way of Life: An American Community in the Nineteenth Century.* Albany: State University of New York Press, 1989.

Harding, Samuel Bannister. *Life of George R. Smith, Founder of Sedalia, Mo.* Sedalia, Mo.: n.p., 1904.

The History of Pettis County, Missouri. N.p., 1882.

SMITH, JEDEDIAH STRONG (1799–1831)

To classify Jedediah Strong Smith as merely a mountain man understates the importance of his contributions. The deeply religious and literate trapper and trader earned the respect and admiration of the leading figures of the western fur trade. He also won acclaim as an explorer, cartographer, diplomat, and businessman whose travels did much to kindle American interest in California and the Oregon country.

A man of humble beginnings, Smith was born in Jericho (now Bainbridge), New York, on January 6, 1799, the sixth of the fourteen children of Jedediah and Sally Strong Smith. In 1810 his family began a westward trek that by 1817 had taken them to Ohio. The Smiths had little money, and that may have pushed the younger Jedediah on to St. Louis. There he got his first taste of the life of a trapper and hunter when he answered an advertisement in the *Missouri Gazette and Public Advertiser* in February 1822. Gen. **William H. Ashley** and his partner Maj. **Andrew Henry** were looking for "100 men to ascend the river Missouri to its source, there to be employed for one, two, or three years."

Smith signed on as a hunter and accompanied an expedition led by Ashley that in October reached the mouth of the Yellowstone River where Henry had constructed a company fort. Ashley returned to St. Louis, but Smith remained at Fort Henry to participate in the winter hunt. When spring came Henry dispatched young Smith back downriver to advise Ashley that he had been unable to secure horses to replace the ones that an Assiniboine raiding party had seized the previous summer. In May 1823 Smith delivered the message to Ashley who was then making his way up the Missouri with a trading party. Smith was present shortly thereafter when the Arikara (also known as the Rees) unexpectedly opened fire on the Ashley expedition. Ashley immediately sent Smith back to the Yellowstone to inform Henry of the ambush and to seek his assistance. Both partners had already identified Smith as a man they could depend upon. Later that summer at Ashley's urging, Col. Henry Leavenworth placed Smith in command of one of the companies that had been enlisted for the purpose of punishing the errant Rees.

After their difficulties with the river tribes, Ashley and Henry opted to send their parties to the Rockies overland. That fall they assigned Smith to lead a brigade westward through the Black Hills and to winter in the Crow country in present-day Wyoming. Along the way a grizzly bear nearly mauled Smith to death, ripping off his left ear in the process. Jim Clyman, a well-known trapper and a member of Smith's party, used a needle and thread to stitch up the cuts and sew Smith's ear back on. The bear's attack left Smith badly scarred, and from that point on he covered his ears with long hair.

In 1824 Smith's brigade rediscovered South Pass, the gently sloping route that made crossing the Continental Divide much easier. The returning Astorians had used it in 1811–1812, but thanks to Smith it became the primary gateway into the West. Smith was back in St. Louis in 1825 to outfit another trapping party destined for the Rockies, but this time not as a hunter but as a full-fledged partner of Ashley. At the summer rendezvous the following year Ashley sold out to Smith, David Jackson, and **William Sublette** who formed the company of Smith, Jackson, and Sublette.

That fall Smith set out from the beautiful Cache valley in present-day Utah on what was perhaps his greatest adventure. Always on the lookout for new beaver-rich territory, he went in search of the nonexistent Buenaventura River alleged to flow uninterrupted from the Great Salt Lake to the Pacific Ocean. Smith and the men who accompanied him, on what later became known as the South West Expedition, were the first Americans to travel overland to California through the Southwest. After turning northward, Smith and two companions crossed the Sierras eastward and traveled through the arid Great Basin to attend the 1827 rendezvous. Smith then headed back to the Southwest with a new party that eventually joined forces with some of the men he had left in California the year before. They trapped in northern California, reached the Pacific Ocean, and traveled up the Oregon coast. Along the way, Smith and his men managed to survive severe shortages of food and water, the stupefying heat of the Mojave Desert, incarceration by Mexican authorities, and two Indian attacks (one by the Mojave in Arizona and the other by the Umpqua in Oregon). Only Smith and three others escaped the Oregon massacre.

Smith and his partners decided to abandon the trade in the Rockies in 1829, but his stories of the wonders of California and the Oregon country along with the valuable geographic information that he provided later helped draw scores of others to the Far West. Smith returned to St. Louis with the intent to retire to the mercantile business, but in 1831 he agreed to join a trading expedition to Santa Fe. While he searched alone for water in the dry bed of the Cimarron River, a band of Comanche Indians attacked and killed him. Although his life had been short in duration, Jedediah Smith had made significant contributions to western exploration.

MARY VOGT

Brooks, George R., ed. *The Southwest Expedition of Jedediah S. Smith.* Lincoln: University of Nebraska Press, 1977.

Morgan, Dale L. *Jedediah Smith and the Opening of the West*. Lincoln: University of Nebraska Press, 1953.

Smith, Alson J. *Men against the Mountains*. New York: John Day, 1965.

SMITH, JOSEPH, JR. (1805–1844)

Born on December 23, 1805, in Sharon, Vermont, Joseph Smith Jr. was the son of Joseph and Lucy Mack Smith, both from longtime New England stock. As a youth in upstate New York during the 1820s, Smith claimed angelic visitations and delivery of a set of goldlike plates upon which was engraved the religious history of Hebraic peoples who came to America. Smith translated these plates through, he said, "the gift and power of God," and they were published as the Book of Mormon in March 1830. In part because of the excitement generated by the advent of the Book of Mormon as a history of certain tribes of Indians, Smith gathered around him a small group of followers and with their support organized a separate religious organization on April 6, 1830, in Fayette, New York.

In 1831 Smith sent the first Mormon converts to Jackson County, Missouri, near the reservations of Indians in Kansas whom the Mormons wanted to convert with their Book of Mormon scripture. He declared that Independence was the center of Zion, the capital of a theocracy envisioned to emerge with Christ's return to Earth and the advent of the millennial reign. From the outset Smith's followers were viewed by other Americans as suspect for these and other beliefs. This led to tension and in some instances brutality. Non-Mormons violently expelled the Mormons from Jackson County in 1833. In an effort to return the Mormon refugees to their homes, Smith formed a paramilitary expedition called "Zion's Camp" in the summer of 1834 and marched from Ohio to Missouri, threatening war. When he realized that the Missourians could not be bullied and after his troops contracted cholera, he abandoned this effort and returned to Ohio.

Smith's followers in Missouri settled in Caldwell County, which was especially created for their benefit in 1835, and founded a strong set of settlements anchored by the county seat at Far West. Smith moved there permanently in early 1838, but soon after his arrival internal divisions and external tensions combined to create a series of incidents that led to the eruption of violence in August 1838 during an election at Gallatin, in Daviess County, north of the Mormon-controlled Caldwell County. By early September the countryside was ablaze with anti-Mormon sentiment.

Sustained trouble came on October 25, 1838, when a Mormon military unit engaged a detachment of militia at the Battle of the Crooked River. The engagement of state troops, regardless of the circumstances, and rumors that the Mormons were in open rebellion against the state were sufficient to prompt Gov. **Lilburn W. Boggs** to call out reinforcements to restore order. They surrounded Joseph Smith at Far West, laying siege to the community while negotiating for the surrender of Smith and his chief lieutenants on October 31.

The next day the militia commander court-martialed Smith and other Mormon leaders for treason, and ordered their execution by firing squad. Clay Countian **Alexander W. Doniphan** protested this action, and instead the militia took the prisoners to Richmond, Missouri, and incarcerated Smith and four other Mormons after preliminary court proceedings. They were placed in the Liberty jail over the winter of 1838–1839 to await trial. Eventually, Doniphan was able to change the venue from Daviess to Boone County. While en route to the county seat at Columbia, Smith and his associates were allowed to escape and leave the state.

The experience in Missouri prompted Smith to erect a strong bulwark against larger society when he founded Nauvoo, Illinois, on the banks of the Mississippi River, in 1839. The Nauvoo city charter provided for a strong municipal court system, a Nauvoo Legion to protect the community, and a largely autonomous civil government. Coupled with the strong theocratic tendencies of the Mormons, the charter gave Joseph Smith control of virtually every aspect of Nauvoo government and society. The city became the most significant expression of Mormon culture and religion during Smith's lifetime, rivaling Chicago as the largest city in the state by 1845. It was there, furthermore, where Smith's unique religious teachings reached their most elaborate expression. These provocative religious ideas and the community's theocratic tendencies excited the ire of non-Mormons. When Smith used his power to quash dissent in Nauvoo in May 1844, he was arrested for violating civil liberties. However, he was murdered by a mob while a prisoner at Carthage, Illinois, on June 27, 1844, before he could be brought to trial.

ROGER D. LAUNIUS

Arrington, Leonard J., and Davis Bitton. *The Mormon Experience: A History of the Latter-day Saints*. New York: Knopf, 1979.

Brodie, Fawn M. *No Man Knows My History: The Life of Joseph Smith*. New York: Knopf, 1971.

Hill, Donna. *Joseph Smith: The First Mormon*. Garden City, N.Y.: Doubleday, 1977.

LeSueur, Stephen C. *The 1838 Mormon War in Missouri*. Columbia: University of Missouri Press, 1987.

SMITH, LUTHER ELY (1873–1951)

Generally speaking, the present icon of St. Louis, the Gateway Arch, had its origin in the mind of Luther Ely Smith.

Smith was born at Downer's Grove, Illinois, on June 11, 1873, the son of Luther R. and Adaline Ely Smith. In 1890 he graduated from Williston Seminary, in East Hampton, Massachusetts, and in 1894 he graduated Phi Beta Kappa from Amherst College. Smith then enrolled in the law school of Washington University, St. Louis, where he earned a degree in 1897. In 1898–1899 he participated in the Spanish-American War as a lieutenant in the Third U.S. Volunteer Engineers before returning to St. Louis, which he then made his home.

The young lawyer became a local leader in the American Progressive-reform movement. An independent Republican and a Christian, Smith believed that government could be the instrument of a better life, in St. Louis and in America. Throughout the Progressive Era and beyond, Smith advanced both social justice and structural reform. In 1902 he helped organize the Open-Air Playground Committee within the League for Civic Improvement. He became a vital member of the Civic League, an organization of professionals and businesspeople who worked for physical and governmental improvements in St. Louis. The league supported city planning and beautification.

Smith's civic activism developed while he built his law practice. He became a member of the St. Louis, Missouri, and American Bar Associations. From 1908 to 1913 he lectured on contracts at St. Louis University Law School. In 1909 Smith married SaLees Kennard. They had three children: Adaline, Luther, and SaLees.

In 1913 Smith again expressed his social-justice reform propensities. He served as the executive secretary of the St. Louis Pageant Drama Association, an organization of reformers who created the 1914 St. Louis Pageant and Masque in the belief that the giant civic drama would contribute to an enhanced sense of community that would, in turn, stimulate civic improvements. From 1916 to 1922 he chaired the Citizens City Plan Commission. He also rejoined the United States Army as a captain during World War I.

Returning to St. Louis after the war, Smith again immersed himself in reform activities during the early 1920s. A member of the Civic Development Bureau of the St. Louis Chamber of Commerce and chairman of the chamber's General Council on Civic Needs, he helped orchestrate the passage of the 1923 municipal bonds that brought physical improvements to the city. However, those bonds did not finance one of Smith's favorite projects, the redevelopment of the riverfront area of downtown St. Louis.

Smith's involvement in another project gave him the idea that eventually resulted in the construction of the Jefferson National Expansion Memorial complex. Between 1928 and 1940 he was a member of the George Rogers Clark Federal Sesquicentennial Commission that placed a memorial on the banks of the Wabash River at Vincennes, Indiana. He decided to try to use the federal-memorial concept both to honor St. Louis's role in American history and to achieve his goal of riverfront development. In 1933 Smith took his idea to Mayor Bernard Dickmann, who liked it, and their efforts led to the creation of the Jefferson National Expansion Memorial Association. In June 1934 the federal government endorsed the concept. A congressional resolution created the United States Territorial Expansion Memorial Commission, and Smith became the commission's executive secretary.

Even though St. Louis voters passed a bond proposal that would provide some local funds for the project, and even though the project's directors—the National Park Service—established a local office in 1936, the memorial languished, slowed by federal lassitude and by World War II. By 1942 the site had been cleared, but it served as only a giant parking lot.

Smith tried to keep the project alive. He also remained involved in other reforms. In 1939 he chaired the organization that successfully advocated a state nonpartisan court plan. In 1941 he became the vice chairman of the Civil Service Commission of St. Louis.

The St. Louis community granted Smith the 1941 St. Louis Award, given for outstanding citizenship. In 1942 Amherst College presented him with an honorary degree. After World War II Smith worked to complete the Jefferson National Expansion Memorial project. He and James L. Ford, an Amherst College friend, were instrumental in raising $250,000 as a prize in the architectural competition connected to the memorial. In 1948 it was announced that Eero Saarinen had submitted the winning Gateway Arch design. Smith did not live to see his dream come true. He died on April 2, 1951, eleven years before construction of the Gateway Arch began.

DONALD B. OSTER

Brown, Sharon. "Jefferson National Expansion Memorial: The 1947–1948 Competition." *Gateway Heritage* 1 (winter 1980): 40–48.

Kirschten, Ernest. *Catfish and Crystal.* 3d ed. St. Louis: Patrice Press, 1989.

Oster, Donald B. "Community Image in the History of St. Louis and Kansas City." Ph.D. diss., University of Missouri–Columbia, 1969.

Primm, James Neal. *Lion of the Valley: St. Louis, Missouri, 1764–1980.* 3d ed. St. Louis: Missouri Historical Society Press, 1998.

Raub, Patricia. "The Making of an Urban Landmark: Media Images of the St. Louis Gateway Arch." *Gateway Heritage* 8 (winter 1987–1988): 40–46.

SMITH, MELLCENE THURMAN (1872?–1957)

One of the first two women elected to the Missouri House of Representatives, Democrat Mellcene Smith represented the Second District of St. Louis in the Fifty-second General Assembly. She won election in November 1922 on the ticket of the Clean Election League, an organization that encouraged voters of both parties to elect honest citizens.

Smith was born in Buchanan County, Missouri, to John William and Cecelia Marion Thurman. Although she carefully concealed her birth date, it is believed to be 1872. She attended public and private schools in St. Joseph and Kansas City and studied voice with hopes of going onstage. Then she met and married Edward T. Smith of St. Louis. After moving to St. Louis, she worked as secretary-treasurer in her husband's St. Louis Law Printing Company. The couple had no children.

Smith became active in numerous civic, historical, and political organizations. She held memberships in the League of Women Voters (serving as president of the University City League), the Daughters of the American Revolution, the Women's Democratic State Committee, and the Twentieth-Century Art Club. She was an honorary state regent for the Daughters of the American Colonists, an honorary state president for the U.S. Daughters of 1812, and state vice president of the League of American Penwomen.

Long a member of the Christian Church, Smith played an active role in church affairs, including the State Board of Temperance League, the Church Peace Union, the World Alliance for Peace, and the Federal Council of Churches. At the Union Avenue Christian Church she taught a Sunday-school class of boys from the Masonic home. She contributed financially to the church and related institutions. The Smiths provided scholarships for students to attend the School of the Ozarks at Point Lookout.

Smith received two Victory Liberty Loan Medals, served as a Red Cross volunteer, worked in a movement to establish local libraries, and became an ardent supporter of Prohibition. She also worked for woman suffrage and participated in a victory parade celebrating the passage of the woman-suffrage amendment in 1919. The next year she was a delegate to the Democratic state convention.

The primary election of 1922 approached, and friends urged Smith to run for office. As a Democrat in Republican St. Louis County, she doubted that she had a chance. However, under strong pressure from the St. Louis League of Women Voters, she decided to file for representative and ran unopposed in the primary. A scandal erupted over the machine-controlled primary, and concerned citizens organized the Clean Election League. All but one candidate on the league slate won in a landslide election in November, upsetting the usually strong Republican machine.

Smith took her new office seriously and sponsored eleven bills. Six of them became laws, including House Bill 1, which made registration mandatory for voters in St. Louis County. She chaired the Committee on State Libraries and served on the Banks and Banking, the Children's Code, and the Eleemosynary Institutions Committees. A hard-working representative, Smith worked long hours and attended Democratic caucuses. She won many friends who admired her vast knowledge of current affairs. With a sense of humor and an amiable personality, she could present an interesting, logical, and convincing speech.

In 1924 Smith sought reelection for her second term of office, but was defeated in the Republican landslide in the November general election. She resumed her busy life with civic responsibilities, club work, and her hobby of genealogy. She later published a book on her family's history.

After her husband's death in 1954, Smith served as president of the St. Louis Law Printing Company. She died of cancer in St. Louis on June 21, 1957.

MARY K. DAINS

Dains, Mary K. "Women Pioneers in the Missouri Legislature." *Missouri Historical Review* 85 (October 1990): 40–52.
———, ed. *Show Me Missouri Women: Selected Biographies.* Kirksville, Mo: Thomas Jefferson University Press, 1989.
Official Manual of the State of Missouri, 1923–1924. Jefferson City: Secretary of State, 1924.
St. Louis Globe-Democrat, January 14, 1923–June 22, 1957.
St. Louis Post-Dispatch, September 24, 1950–June 21, 1957.

SMITH, SOLOMON FRANKLIN (1801–1869)

In honoring Solomon, his eighth son, with the name of Franklin, Levi Smith of New York was prescient. Like his great namesake, Sol Smith not only engaged in but also excelled at a daunting array of tasks, intellectual as well as physical. He was a successful actor and theater manager; in partnership with **Noah Miller Ludlow** he founded the firm that dominated commercial theater in the South and West for nearly twenty years. As a writer he played a key role in the development of the literary movement known as

"Southwest humor," and was one of the best of the "literary journalists" of the frontier. As a lawyer and statesman he was a central figure in the formation of a provisional government at the Missouri State Convention in 1861, an act that was the key to keeping the state firmly in the Union camp.

Born on April 20, 1801, Smith had little formal education. He was sent away from home at the age of eight to work on a farm; by age twelve he was in Boston, working in a store owned by one of his brothers. He moved from there to Albany in 1814 where he worked as a clerk and made the acquaintance of a theatrical troupe headed by Samuel Drake. It is likely that he first encountered Ludlow, his future partner and later his enemy, in Albany in 1814 or 1815. He tried to join Ludlow and the Drake company when they set off in 1815 on their western journey, but was compelled to return to Albany. In 1818 Smith did cut loose from his moorings, and drifted down the Allegheny to Pittsburgh, then to Ohio, and finally from town to town through Indiana and Kentucky, appearing on stage intermittently with the Drakes.

Smith was briefly apprenticed to a printer in Louisville and worked on a newspaper in Vincennes before settling for a time in Cincinnati, where he was employed by the Collins and Jones theatrical company as a prompter and set about the study of law. By 1822 he was managing the Globe Theater and editing a Jacksonian newspaper, the *Independent Press and Freedom's Advocate.* In that year he married Martha Therese Mathews and, having bought out Collins and Jones, established his own theatrical company with which he toured through the Ohio and Mississippi Valleys. In 1827 Smith and his wife joined the Caldwell company in New Orleans, traveling for the first time to St. Louis. In 1831 they were part of a company playing the Mississippi River towns under the direction of Noah Ludlow. The connection with Ludlow resulted in wider travels; by the summer of 1835 Sol Smith had made his debuts in New York and Philadelphia, and could legitimately claim star billing. As a performer his strength was in physical comedy; he was, a contemporary said, "tall and ungainly, with a large head and glaring gray eyes and an exceedingly big mouth," but he had the capacity to delight his audiences.

It was in 1835 that Smith became the junior partner in the firm of Ludlow and Smith, the dominant force in the western theater for the next decade and a half. Throughout his long, often acrimonious relationship with Ludlow, Smith was the active partner, traveling to all corners of their far-flung empire, conducting skirmishes with rivals in Mobile and New Orleans, and staying involved as a performer. Until much later in life, Smith managed to remain on speaking terms with Ludlow, despite a painful dispute over money. It was the issue of slavery and secession that drove the final wedge between them. When he came to write the ultimate version of his memoirs in 1868, Smith, an ardent Unionist, could not bring himself to mention the name of his erstwhile partner.

For several years in the late 1840s, Smith was a close associate and friend of **Charles Keemle** and the Field brothers, Joseph and Matthew, and a frequent and distinguished contributor to their literary newspaper, the *Reveille.* His sketches of river life, such as "Breaking a Bank," are among the most significant and most polished examples of Southwest humor, the movement that gave impetus to the career of **Mark Twain.** In 1846 Smith published *The Theatrical Apprenticeship,* his first autobiographical volume; this was followed by *The Theatrical Journey-Work* in 1854 and a revised and updated combination of the two, *Theatrical Management in the West and South,* in 1868.

After the breakup of Ludlow and Smith in 1853, Smith retired from the stage and devoted himself to the practice of law. An acquaintance describes him in the late 1860s as "looking like an undertaker in an extremely healthy season," yet he was wealthy and successful. As a lawyer he was active in the effort to hold Missouri for the Union, and his work at the state convention in 1861 may well be his most significant contribution to the history of the state.

Smith died of a stroke on February 14, 1869, mourned by many friends and admirers. In his epitaph, which he composed in the mid-1860s, he described himself as a "retired actor," included two quotes from Shakespeare, and concluded: "exit Sol."

ROBERT C. BOYD

Arnold, Wayne W. *Sol Smith: Chapters for a Biography.* Master's thesis, Washington University, 1939.

Carson, William G. B. *Managers in Distress: The St. Louis Stage, 1840–1844.* St. Louis: St. Louis Historical Documents Foundation, 1949.

SMITH T, JOHN (1770?–1836)

Pioneer, gunfighter, filibuster, man of letters, entrepreneur, land speculator, militia colonel, duelist, miner, judge, philanthropist, and folk hero—these and many more descriptions, all true yet all exaggerated, could be applied to one man: John Smith T. No early pioneer captivated Missouri audiences quite like this remarkable figure. His weapons, reportedly the truest in the western country, became icons of the age, and his tales of derring-do spawned myths and legends that survived well into the twentieth century. During his lifetime no Missourian represented the most extreme traits of southern convention and western individualism better than Smith T.

John Smith T was born sometime around 1770 in all likelihood on a small plantation in Essex County, Virginia. His father, Francis, was a fourth generation Virginian, and his mother, Lucy Wilkinson Smith, was a member of the same family as **James A. Wilkinson.** In late 1771 Francis Smith moved his family to Wilkes County, Georgia, even before that area was officially open to settlement. Following the outbreak of the Revolutionary War, Smith T's father went off to fight for the patriot cause. Smith T later returned to Virginia and studied briefly at the College of William and Mary before launching his own turbulent career in the wilds of the Tennessee frontier. It was there that he added the "T" to his name so as to distinguish his land titles and other enterprises from those belonging to hosts of other men, many of whom had taken refuge in the name John Smith. By the late 1790s Smith T had acquired a sizable reputation as both a land speculator and a gunfighter. At one juncture he owned or laid claim to more than a quarter-million acres in Tennessee and northern Alabama. His accuracy with both pistol and rifle, as well as his apparent readiness to use them, worked to his advantage as few squatters or land sharks ventured onto his property.

Smith T arrived in Spanish Missouri in approximately 1797. His purpose in this western endeavor was twofold. First, he hoped to obtain sizable Spanish land grant titles, especially on property with lead deposits. Second, he intended to use these resources as a springboard for future filibustering activities in the Southwest. His schemes were abetted after the Louisiana Purchase by the territorial governor, Gen. James Wilkinson, himself a coconspirator of Aaron Burr. To gain control of the lead-mining district in Missouri, Smith T and Wilkinson first sought to displace the most powerful American in the region, **Moses Austin.** The latter was stripped of his official positions. Next, these and other offices were given to Smith T. He became judge of the court of common pleas, commissioner of weights and levies, and lieutenant colonel of the militia. He used these positions to mount a spirited assault on Austin's virtual monopoly of the lead mines. This contest produced the first full-scale conflict in Missouri, the mineral war. Neither side emerged from the contest, which lasted roughly from 1805 to 1815, an undisputed winner.

Nevertheless, it was during this time that Smith T's fame as a gunfighter and duelist spread across the West. Folklorists claimed then and later that he was the most dangerous man in Missouri. His reputation notwithstanding, there was no one in the territory who elicited more opinionated responses than the colonel. On the one hand, his admirers claimed that his violent nature was more than equaled by his charitable side. They pointed to the lands donated for churches and schools as well as his generosity to the poor and downtrodden. On the other hand, one adversary, Moses Austin, claimed that Smith T was a god of darkness capable of wracking more havoc than forty men.

Although some of his contemporaries claimed that he killed fourteen men in duels, historians can record only one man who fell before Smith T's unerring aim. This protagonist was Lionel Browne, sheriff of Washington County. On the word, Smith T instantaneously fired, putting a bullet through Browne's forehead. If the colonel's dueling skills were more legendary than real, it was not for want of trying. Over the course of two decades he challenged such notables as Sam Houston, **Frederick Bates,** Samuel Perry, Andrew Jackson, Ste. Genevieve commandant Seth Hunt, and special agent for the Department of State John H. Robinson. All declined. Nevertheless, Smith T was not averse to other less institutionalized forms of violence. He was the prototype of western swashbuckling, killing at least four or five other men in individual frays while in Missouri.

The colonel, however, was more than just another frontier killer. Smith T epitomized the opening of the West. He developed towns, built roads and canals, and represented Missouri miners and settlers as a lobbyist in the halls of the United States Congress. In 1809 he launched one of the first trading expeditions to open up the Santa Fe Trail. In 1811 he led a military expedition against the Indians along the Mississippi River near Dubuque, Iowa, and Galena, Illinois. Two years later he commanded a filibustering expedition to Texas to wrest the territory from Spain. He died in 1836 attempting to open up new cotton lands in western Tennessee, but his body was returned to Missouri for burial.

DICK STEWARD

Brackenridge, Henry M. *Recollecting of Persons and Places in the West.* 2d ed. Philadelphia: J. B. Lippincott, 1868.

Darby, John F. *Personal Recollections of Many Prominent People Whom I Have Known, and of Events—Especially Those Relating to the History of St. Louis—during the First Half of the Present Century.* St. Louis: G. I. Jones, 1880.

History of Southeast Missouri. Chicago: Goodspeed Publishing, 1888.

Rozier, Firmin. *History of the Early Settlement of the Mississippi Valley.* St. Louis: G. A. Pierrot and Son, 1890.

Steward, Dick. *Frontier Swashbuckler: The Life and Legend of John Smith T.* Columbia: University of Missouri Press, 1999.

———. "John Smith T and the Way West: Filibustering and Expansion on the Missouri Frontier." *Missouri Historical Review* 89 (October 1994): 48–74.

SNIDER, DENTON JACQUES (1841–1925)

Denton Jacques Snider (born on January 9, 1841, in Mount Gilead, Ohio) was a literary critic and essayist, as well as the self-appointed historian of the St. Louis movement in philosophy. He collaborated with **William Torrey Harris, Henry Conrad Brokmeyer,** and other "St. Louis Hegelians" to establish the St. Louis Philosophical Society in 1866. During the 1860s and 1870s he was a frequent contributor to the St. Louis–based *Journal of Speculative Philosophy,* which made a wide impact as the first American professional journal of philosophy. Taking his own idealist and Hegelian interpretation of history seriously, Snider left St. Louis for Chicago in the late 1880s as he convinced himself that the world-historical moment of St. Louis had passed and that more rapidly expanding Chicago had displaced St. Louis as the city of America's (and the world's) future. He remained, however, on intimate terms with Harris and other leaders of the St. Louis movement, and his *St. Louis Movement in Philosophy, Literature, Education, Psychology, with Chapters of Autobiography* remains perhaps the best single source for understanding the outlook of the St. Louis Hegelians.

In 1864, following graduation from Oberlin College and a short period of service in the state militia, Snider settled in St. Louis to teach at Christian Brothers' College. Like Harris, Brokmeyer, and **John Gabriel Woerner,** Snider experienced the outbreak of the Civil War as an acute intellectual crisis: he regarded the secession and war as a conflict between the idea of law (since slavery as a form of property was upheld by the Constitution) and the rule of conscience (since the abolitionists regarded slavery as a violation of individual liberty and the socioeconomic system it undergirded as morally corrupt). At Oberlin, a major stop on the Underground Railroad of escaped slaves, Snider was disturbed by the abolitionists' blatant violations of the Fugitive Slave Law, but he saw the slave states' secession as a reprehensible breach of political contract and came to regard President Lincoln's emancipation policy as both morally and constitutionally necessary. Snider's book *The American Ten Years' War,* a Hegelian presentation of American constitutional history from the struggle over "Bleeding Kansas" to the reestablishment of federal union in 1865, epitomizes the St. Louis Hegelians' view of the American Civil War as marking "the elimination of the dualism introduced into the Union at its birth."

Snider's historical vision made the city of St. Louis and the state of Missouri during the 1860s into a locus of world-historical forces: evidence of Missouri's status was the range of conflicting opinions that had survived throughout the war regarding the appropriate direction for national development. Missouri's ambivalent experience as a border state and its strategic military role were portents of the great role the state would supposedly play in the nation's future.

Like their intellectual and generational counterparts in the Northeast, Snider and the St. Louis Hegelians regarded the war's mobilization of soldiers and civilians as a harbinger of greater national discipline and social cooperation, and of more effective integration of individuals into society through institutions, be they state militias, public schools, or philosophical societies. The mission of the St. Louis movement, then, was to train people to look beyond merely individual goals to serve a collective purpose; social service was the necessary complement of self-cultivation.

Snider participated in the St. Louis movement during its years of greatest accomplishment between 1866 and about 1880. He lent intellectual support to William Torrey Harris in the latter's task (as superintendent) of turning the St. Louis public school system into one of the best organized and best served in the United States. In addition to delivering many well-attended courses of public lectures in both St. Louis and Chicago and establishing literary "schools," Snider published more than a dozen books on literary, artistic, and historical topics, specializing in ancient Greek and Shakespearean drama and in the work of Goethe. Later in life he recanted certain of his more fanciful Hegelian opinions, admitting to having been "pretty badly poisoned" with "the Great St. Louis Illusion" of that city's special cosmic significance. Snider died on November 25, 1925, having outlived most of his St. Louis Hegelian friends.

DENYS P. LEIGHTON

Hyde, William, and Howard L. Conard, eds. *Encyclopedia of the History of St. Louis.* New York: Southern History, 1899.

Leighton, Denys P. "William Torrey Harris, the St. Louis Hegelians, and the Meaning of the Civil War." *Gateway Heritage* 10 (fall 1989): 32–45.

Snider, Denton J. *The American Ten Years' War.* St. Louis: Sigma Publishing, 1906.

―――. *The St. Louis Movement in Philosophy, Literature, Education, Psychology, with Chapters of Autobiography.* St. Louis: Sigma Publishing, 1920.

SNOW, EDGAR (1905–1972)

Edgar Snow grew up in Kansas City, Missouri, where he was born on July 17, 1905. After a year at Kansas City Junior College he moved to New York in 1924 to begin a new career in advertising with the Medley Scovil Company. He attended the University of Missouri Journalism School in 1925–1926 to enhance his credentials for his advertising work. Late in 1927, frustrated with advertising, he decided to take a year to work his way around the world and test his ability to market whatever writing he might produce.

In February 1928 Snow sailed for the South Seas as a deckhand on board the SS *Radnor.* The *Radnor*'s engine broke down, stranding him not too unhappily in Hawaii, where he wrote his first salable article. Low on funds and unaware of his sale, he stowed away on a Japanese ship to Yokohama. An account of that venture, published after he hurriedly left Japan for Shanghai, became his second success.

In Shanghai Snow walked into a job as assistant advertising manager for the *China Weekly Review,* which became the key to his future career. J. B. Powell, the *Review*'s editor and owner, and Thomas Fairfax Millard, its previous owner, both alumni of the University of Missouri School of Journalism, became Snow's mentors through the extraordinary political events then unfolding in China. His intended stay of a few weeks turned into a demanding, but productive, thirteen years with one significant interruption: ten months from September 1930 to July 1931, when he resumed his round-the-world journey only to decide after reaching India to return to China and write a book about an adventurous caravan journey from Kunming into Burma.

The Japanese changed Snow's writing plans in September 1931 by invading Manchuria. His account of the Japanese invasion preempted the story of his caravan journey. His first book became *Far Eastern Front.* He sold his first article about the invasion to the *Saturday Evening Post* just before his book came out. For the next twenty years the *Post* became a cornerstone of his career, providing him with a large and diverse American readership.

Snow married Helen Foster on December 25, 1932. Settled in Beijing, they collaborated on a collection of contemporary Chinese writing, *Living China,* featuring the modern master Lu Xun. In June 1936 Snow finally realized a long-sought opportunity to visit the then obscure Chinese Communist forces. *Red Star over China,* the story of his discovery, has since become a journalistic classic, still in print with close to 2 million copies released. Before returning to the United States in early 1941, he completed a sequel to *Red Star,* called *Battle for Asia,* challenging his American audience to square its stand on colonialism in Asia with its own democratic traditions before entering an increasingly inevitable war with Japan.

After Pearl Harbor, Snow became the *Saturday Evening Post*'s first foreign correspondent. He twice visited Russia for extended periods and published *People on Our Side* (1944), *The Pattern of Soviet Power* (1945), and *Stalin Must Have Peace* (1947).

In 1949 his first marriage ended in divorce, and he began a second with American actress Lois Wheeler. It lasted the rest of his life, and he became the father of two children, Xian and Christopher.

American cold-war policy left Snow professionally frustrated and sidelined. In 1951 he resigned as associate editor of the *Saturday Evening Post.* He reluctantly tried to revive public interest in his views with his autobiography, *Journey to the Beginning* (1958). In 1959 he and his family moved to Switzerland. In 1960, overcoming significant cold-war barriers, he became the first American journalist to enter Communist China. *The Other Side of the River* reminded the world of his long-empathetic, but objective, experience with the Communist movement in China.

Snow returned to China again in 1964 and 1970. His interviews with Mao Tse-tung, Chou En-lai, and other Red leaders made him a significant liaison between two politically disparate worlds. By 1970 the United States had already begun the long and delicate process of establishing diplomatic relations with the People's Republic. Mao used Snow's visit to send messages to America, only some of which were accurately read.

After Snow's last China trip he became increasingly ill. He died of pancreatic cancer on February 15, 1972, just three days before Nixon flew to Beijing to meet with Mao Tse-tung. The *Kansas City Star* editorialized, "Edgar Snow had at last become a prophet of great honor in his own country." The *New York Times* described his predictions on Japanese aggression leading to world war in the 1930s, on the decolonization that followed, and on the Chinese Communist Revolution as "prescient." Lois Wheeler Snow published his uncompleted final manuscript, *The Long Revolution,* with editorial help.

ROBERT M. FARNSWORTH

Farnsworth, Robert M., ed. *Edgar Snow's Journey South of the Clouds.* Columbia: University of Missouri Press, 1991.

Hamilton, John Maxwell. *Edgar Snow.* Bloomington: University of Indiana Press, 1988.

Snow, Lois Wheeler. *A Death with Dignity.* New York: Random House, 1974.

SNOW, THAD (1881–1955)

Thad Snow was born in Greenfield, Indiana, on November 1, 1881. According to Snow, his parents were moderately well-to-do. Although he did not complete high school, he first attended a private college and then transferred to the University of Michigan. In his senior year he had a physical breakdown and left the university.

When Snow returned to Greenfield, a physician uncle suggested farming as a way for him to regain his health. Snow's father had just bought a forty-acre farm, and turned it over to his young son. Snow wrote later that he "took to farming like a duck takes to water." In his newfound occupation, Snow did quite well in both corn and alfalfa farming. He soon wanted more land, but his attempts to buy additional land were unsuccessful. By 1910 he decided to find "new" country where he could spread out and be a pioneer.

Snow found that "new" country in what he called "Swampeast Missouri." That area had been settled quite early in Missouri's history, but the frequent floods, swamps, and a negative reputation as a result of the New Madrid earthquake had left the lowlands less settled than most other areas of the state. In 1910 Snow bought approximately one thousand acres of bottomland, most of which was unimproved. The farm was in Mississippi County, and the purchase was largely on credit. In his own mind he and his family had become pioneers. In both 1912 and 1913 the Mississippi River flooded his land. In spite of such obstacles, within a few years Snow was successfully growing corn, wheat, and alfalfa. Except for the open range, the farm scene appeared little different from his Indiana background. However, the high cost of land clearance and a drainage tax for reclamation projects made real profits impossible.

As a result of the high cost of reclamation, Thad Snow in particular and southeast Missouri in general were in a serious economic crisis. They needed more farmers to share the cost of reclamation projects. In an attempt to promote land development, the Southeast Missouri Agricultural Bureau was organized in 1919. Snow became its first president. He and other prominent citizens believed the answer was to attract farmers from midwestern states where land prices were much higher. Unfortunately, not many came.

Snow was an early advocate of good, that is, concrete, roads as a means of improving the area's economic status. He convinced several districts in Mississippi County to build concrete roads, half of which were paid for by the federal government. Later, when the Missouri Highway Department received funds to finance road building, these districts were reimbursed. A case can be made that these were the first truly rural concrete roads in Missouri.

After 1921 the area's effort to attract farmers switched from the Midwest to the South and from wheat and corn production to cotton. Cotton fever struck Snow. In 1924 he converted to cotton production and the tenant-sharecropping system. Within a few years he had twenty-three tenant and sharecropping families on his home farm, and still others on another farm he had bought on credit. For several years some semblance of prosperity came. However, that soon ended with the Great Depression. Snow came close to losing all his land. He declared bankruptcy, but through friendship with the person who held title to the land it was deeded back to Snow. Snow paid off the last debts in 1935.

During the 1930s and 1940s, Snow attracted attention beyond the Bootheel. New Deal administrators became aware of him when he claimed the existing cotton-parity payments discriminated against new cotton-growing areas of the country such as southeast Missouri. Snow became even more prominent as a result of the 1939 sharecropper highway-protest movement. It is not entirely clear whether Snow aided **Owen Whitfield** in organizing the demonstration, but he certainly helped publicize it. For at least two decades, many in the area felt that Snow was responsible for the sharecropper discontent.

It is true that from the early 1920s Snow sympathized with the farm laborers. In 1940 and 1941, at the request of then–Secy. of Agriculture Henry A. Wallace, Snow spent considerable time in Washington, D.C., in an effort to draft legislation that would guarantee farm laborers a share of any subsidy given to farm owners who grew cotton. He failed to accomplish that goal.

During the early 1940s Snow battled the Farm Security Administration (FSA) in its Bootheel activities. The FSA's purpose was to assist tenant, sharecropper, and agricultural laborers. In the context of large farm owners, Snow was one of its principal advocates. However, as it operated, he soon became a major critic. He charged that the FSA thwarted efforts of its clients to become independent.

Much of Snow's fame was due to his long and informal association with the *St. Louis Post-Dispatch.* For approximately two decades, he was a regular contributor. Today, he is best remembered for his autobiographical work, *From Missouri,* which shows him as an iconoclast who was quite capable of writing with tongue in cheek. *From Missouri* was published a few months before Snow's death on January 15, 1955.

Leon P. Ogilvie

Charleston Enterprise-Courier, January 20, 1955.

Ogilvie, Leon Parker. "The Development of the Southeast Missouri Lowlands." Ph.D. diss., University of Missouri–Columbia, 1967.

Snow, Thad. *From Missouri.* Boston: Houghton Mifflin, 1954.

St. Louis Post-Dispatch, January 16–17, 1955.

SOULARD, ANTOINE PIERRE (1766–1825)

Antoine Pierre Soulard was born in Rochefort, France, in 1766. Like his father he became an officer in the French Royal Navy, but in 1794 he was forced to leave France because of the Revolution. He sailed from France to Marblehead, Massachusetts, traveling to Pittsburgh on horseback, then by boat down the Ohio to the Mississippi. By February 1794 he had arrived in Ste. Genevieve, where he supervised the construction of a fort erected in response to rumors of a Franco-American invasion of Upper Louisiana. In a letter to the governor-general of Louisiana, Manuel Gayoso de Lemos, Soulard stated: "Shortly after, my good friend M. Zenon [Trudeau], took me in hand, and since then I have lived in St. Louis."

On February 3, 1795, Soulard was appointed as the first surveyor general of Spanish Upper Louisiana, at which point the first system for official surveys of this land was made possible—a necessity due to the increasing number of immigrants to the area. By the time of his appointment, Soulard had already drawn the prototype for an important Spanish version of a map of the Missouri River for use by Jean-Baptiste Truteaus's expedition up that river in 1794; a later version of the map was probably translated into French by Soulard in August 1795. He probably got much of his information on northern rivers from **James MacKay.** An English version of Soulard's map was carried by **Meriwether Lewis** and **William Clark** on the 1804–1806 expedition.

On October 30, 1795, **Zenon Trudeau** added to Soulard's duties the position of "adjutant protem of the Lt. Governor of these establishments of Illinois." A few weeks later, on November 16, Soulard married Julie Cerré, daughter of the influential merchant Gabriel Cerré. A portion of the land acquired through this marriage became the Soulard Market area of St. Louis.

In the process of changing governments after the United States purchased the Louisiana Territory, Spanish lieutenant governor **Charles de Hault Delassus** reported to captain of the United States Army **Amos Stoddard** that Soulard, "in his character of surveyor of this Upper Louisiana . . . can furnish you the most reliable information in regard to all the titles of grants." In 1805 **James Wilkinson,** the newly appointed governor of Louisiana Territory, kept Soulard on as surveyor general; at the time Wilkinson's decision seemed warranted since the Spaniards had removed all their plat books before the U.S. authorities could examine them. However, Surveyor General Soulard had received large tracts of land as payment for his services for the Spaniards. Just before leaving office in 1799, Trudeau "reportedly signed a series of blank concessions" that were distributed after he left by his successor Delassus to family and friends, including Soulard. These controversial land claims, as well as Soulard's previous loyalties to the Spanish government, prompted U.S. officials to oust him from office in 1806 and place the territory of Louisiana within the jurisdiction of the U.S. surveyor general.

Silas Bent, who replaced Soulard as surveyor of Louisiana, reported numerous mistakes in his work. Soulard defended himself against these accusations by suggesting that Bent was looking at field notes, not official documents, and that they were not meant for official use. Official surveys of portions of Soulard's own land had apparently been lost or destroyed between 1804 and 1806, so he himself experienced many difficulties in securing confirmation from the U.S. government for his personal land claims. From this point on, Soulard spent his life defending his work as surveyor general to the board of land commissioners in St. Louis.

Soulard died on March 10, 1825, at his home in St. Louis, leaving as heirs James Gaston, Henry Gustave, Eliza, and Benjamin Antoine. Julie Cerré Soulard died May 9, 1845, nine years after she finally regained from the city of St. Louis the title to her family's estate at what is now Soulard Market.

KAIA A. KNUTSON

Foley, William E. *The Genesis of Missouri: From Wilderness Outpost to Statehood.* Columbia: University of Missouri Press, 1989.

———. *A History of Missouri: Volume I, 1673 to 1820.* Columbia: University of Missouri Press, 1971.

March, David D. *The History of Missouri.* Vol. 1. New York: Lewis Historical Publishing, 1967.

Wheat, Carl I. *Mapping the Transmississippi West, 1540–1861.* Vol. 1. San Francisco: Institute of Historical Cartography, 1957.

SPENCER, SELDON PALMER (1862–1925)

A Republican U.S. senator, Seldon Spencer combined the practice of law with politics. While in his thirties he represented St. Louis in the Missouri House of Representatives in 1895–1896. He served as a circuit court judge in St. Louis from 1897 to 1903, and defeated **Joseph W. Folk** to fill the unexpired term of U.S. senator **William Joel Stone** when Stone died in 1918. Spencer won a full term in the Senate in 1920 by defeating Breckenridge Long by more than 120,000 votes and served until his death in 1925.

Born in Erie, Pennsylvania, on September 16, 1862, Spencer attended public schools until he entered Hopkins School in New Haven, Connecticut, in preparation for attending Yale University. He graduated from Yale in 1884, seventh in a class of 150. He came to St. Louis to study law at Washington University, completing his degree and passing his bar exam in 1886. He established a practice in St. Louis, while continuing to study at Washington University and teaching medical jurisprudence. Missouri Medical College recognized his work with an honorary M.D. degree, and Westminster College conferred both Ph.D. and LL.D. degrees on him.

Spencer won a seat in the Missouri House in 1894 and two years later won election for a six-year term as circuit judge. He returned to private practice and took an active interest in the Missouri Bar Association. He became president of that organization in 1908. The American Bar Association honored him with its vice presidency in 1914 and with membership on its executive committee from 1915 to 1917. In 1914 he also served as vice chair of the Board of Freeholders in St. Louis, which framed a new city charter. Other honors included president of the St. Louis chapter of the Sons of the American Revolution and president of the General Sons of the Revolution in 1923. Members of the New England Society elected him their president in 1905.

During his tenure in the United States Senate, Spencer at first favored ratification of the Versailles Treaty with reservations added. In 1919 he changed his position by signing the "round robin" of Senate Republicans that called the treaty simply "unacceptable." He worked with Senate Foreign Affairs Committee chairman Henry Cabot Lodge in defeating the treaty and made speeches against it during political campaigns in 1920, 1922, and 1924. On the Prohibition question, he usually voted dry.

An active Presbyterian and at one time state president of the YMCA, Spencer took his religion seriously. He married Susan M. Brooks, the daughter of James H. Brooks, a leading Presbyterian minister in St. Louis, and fathered three sons. His law partner, **Forrest C. Donnell,** a future governor, called him "a man of remarkable ability, noble character, and profound religious conviction." He died after a hernia operation in Walter Reed Hospital on May 16, 1925.

LAWRENCE O. CHRISTENSEN

Hyde, Arthur. Papers. Western Historical Manuscripts Collection, Columbia.

Obituary. *Missouri Historical Review* 19 (July 1926): 714–15.

Official Manual of the State of Missouri, 1919–1920. Jefferson City: Secretary of State, 1920.

St. Louis Post-Dispatch, May 17, 1925.

STANLEY, LOUISE (1883–1954)

Louise Stanley, an internationally known home economist and nutritionist, is credited with helping lay the foundation for the development of home-economics education throughout the world. She was born on June 8, 1883, in Nashville, Tennessee, the daughter of Gustavus Augustus and Eliza Munro Winston Stanley. She received a B.S. degree from Peabody College in Nashville in 1903, a B.S. in education from the University of Chicago in 1905, an M.A. from Columbia University in 1907, and a Ph.D. in biochemistry from Yale University in 1911.

Stanley became an instructor in the University of Missouri Home Economics Department in 1907. Two years later she started the first research program in home economics. In 1911 she advanced to professor and chairman of the department, a position she held until 1923. The second chairman of the department, she served during the construction of Gwynn Hall, the university's home-economics building, in 1919. During a leave of absence in 1918 she worked as a home-economics agent for the Federal Bureau of Vocation Education. Stanley wrote numerous articles for publication in academic, scientific, and popular journals.

In 1923 Stanley resigned from the university when President Calvin Coolidge offered her the position of chief of the new National Bureau of Home Economics in the U.S. Department of Agriculture. For the next twenty years she directed work in food, nutrition, clothing, textiles, housing, equipment, home economics, and social relationships. She applied the science of home economics to the improvement of rural conditions and to the promotion of more nutritionally adequate diets for all Americans.

After her term as the first bureau chief, Stanley became a special assistant to the research administrator of the Department of Agriculture in 1943. In this position she worked with food-research problems in overseas countries and advised foreign representatives. She attended international conferences as a representative of the United States. A member of the international committee of the American Home Economics Association (AHEA), she chaired the committee in 1949–1951. Although she retired in 1950, she continued as a consultant for the Agriculture Research Service.

Stanley received many honors and awards for her work in home economics. She was voted one of four most outstanding women in education in national balloting in 1934–1935. In 1940 she became the first woman to receive an LL.D. degree from the University of Missouri.

In recognition for her work the AHEA named one of its international scholarships the Louise Stanley Latin-American scholarship in 1953. The University of Missouri honored her in 1961 with the dedication of Stanley Hall, a building for the School of Home Economics. Her photograph is among twenty-seven famous agriculturalists hanging on the wall in the House Agriculture Committee room in Washington, D.C.

Stanley was the first woman member of the American Standards Association and a life member of the AHEA. She also held memberships in the American Chemical Society, the American Association of University Women, and Pi Lambda Theta.

Louise Stanley died on July 15, 1954, in Washington, D.C.

MARY K. DAINS

Dains, Mary K., ed. *Show Me Missouri Women: Selected Biographies.* Kirksville, Mo.: Thomas Jefferson University Press, 1989.

"Missouri Women in History: Louise Stanley." *Missouri Historical Review* 63 (July 1969): inside back cover.

Who's Who in America. Vol. 20. Chicago: A. N. Marquis, 1938.

STARK, JAMES HART (1792–1873)

James Hart Stark and the company he founded, now known as Stark Brothers Nurseries and Orchards Company, have brought worldwide acclaim to Missouri in the field of horticulture. Not only is Stark Brothers one of Missouri's oldest businesses, but it is also the oldest agricultural supplier in continuous service in the United States, and the largest fruit nursery in the world. Innovation has marked the Stark family's work in the development and improvement of many fruits, vegetables, roses, and other plants.

James Hart Stark was born on July 30, 1792, the son of a Revolutionary War soldier who served under Gen. George Washington. He fought in the War of 1812 and then left Bourbon County, Kentucky, in 1816 to move to Pike County, Missouri. Stark's father had experience in fruit growing, having operated nurseries in Virginia and Kentucky. James Hart, who was trained as a surveyor, brought a bundle of cuttings from his father's orchard to Missouri and grafted them onto native crab-apple trees, producing some of the first cultivated fruit west of the Mississippi River. Word of Stark's fruit spread throughout the region, and settlers were soon buying trees from him. He became known as "Missouri's Johnny Appleseed."

Stark practiced scientific horticulture. He carefully selected and grafted stock to create the most adaptable and strongest varieties of apples. In 1927 his grandson described a trip to the Stark Orchards in Louisiana, Missouri:

> As I remember it, was in the spring of 1857 that I went with our farm man—Uncle Math—to my grandfather's farm. . . . We went to get trees for ourselves and neighbors.
>
> As the mud was deep and the road very bad, we drove two yoke of oxen to a very high-wheeled, scooped-bed wagon. . . . When we arrived at Grandpa's there were a great many people there from the surrounding country, some coming from as far as Boonville over on the Missouri River.
>
> All stayed all night or for dinner and helped dig the trees. There was no railroad then and I don't think any river transportation. I don't recall that the trees were labeled, so each one had to remember the variety he got. I remember such names as Jeniton, Bellflower, Winesap, Rambo, Pryor's Red, Red June, Spitzenberg, Early Harvest, Golden Russet, and a little red apple they called a Milan. Oh Boy, I can taste them yet.

Besides developing his orchard, Stark took a strong interest in the growth of Missouri. He ran for the General Assembly as a Whig in 1836 on a platform that advocated a sound currency. He spoke in favor of the systematic development of public roads, promoted the building of railroads, and urged improvement of public education. His efforts on behalf of railroads did not result in success until after the Civil War, when Louisiana finally became connected to the rail system. Failing at election, he ran for county judge in 1840 and won. Once he acquired the title of judge, he continued to use it for the rest of his life.

Stark took a deep interest in horses, and his handsome stallion General John Stark was one of the ancestors of Rex McDonald, perhaps the most famous five-gaited horse in history.

James Hart Stark died on May 22, 1873. His son, William, entered the business before the Civil War. The only one of the founder's seventeen children to show an interest in horticulture, William consistently preached the importance of improving the quality of Stark trees and fruit. He passed on his enthusiasm for the enterprise to his own sons, Clarence, W. P., and Edgar. They associated the business with the plant-breeding expertise of Luther Burbank. Stark Brothers purchased and introduced many of Burbank's fruit and plant varieties. This working partnership resulted in Burbank's designation of the Starks as his exclusive partners in carrying on his work.

The Starks recognized early the importance of advertising their products. They promoted their stock in newspapers and magazines and were one of the first national advertisers in the United States. Clarence Stark possessed exceptional promotional skills; he created fruit fairs and contests for naming fruits, and developed the company's first catalog in 1894. Stark Brothers catalogs made use of new techniques in printing such as color and photographic illustration. Their slogan, "Stark Trees Bear Fruit," became known throughout the country.

Breakthroughs took place in 1893 and 1914, when the company introduced to the world the Red Delicious and the Golden Delicious apples, respectively. James Hart Stark would have been proud that those discoveries are now the most popular apples in the United States and are planted on every continent. Almost 60 percent of the world's apples are direct descendants of these Red and Golden Delicious apples.

MADELINE MATSON

Bowling Green Times, September 4, 1991.

Guttentag, Shirley. "Stark Bro's: Horticultural Pioneers." *Rural Missouri* 32 (April 1979): 21–23.

Louisiana Press-Journal, September 4, 1991.

"Stark Brothers Nurseries: Wondrous Place of Miracles." *Missouri Highways* 4 (October–November 1971): 25–30.

Terry, Dickson. *The Stark Story: Stark Nurseries 150th Anniversary.* St. Louis: Missouri Historical Society, 1966.

STARK, LLOYD CROW (1886–1972)

Born on a farm in Pike County, Missouri, on November 23, 1886, Lloyd Stark attended the United States Naval Academy and served in the United States Navy following his graduation in 1908. After military service he returned to his hometown, Louisiana, Missouri, where he took a position in the family business, Stark Brothers Nursery, founded as the first such operation west of the Mississippi by **James Hart Stark** in 1816.

Lloyd Stark used the nursery to display his considerable political talents within the business community. In 1914 he became president of the Mississippi Valley Apple Growers Association and later served as president of the Louisiana, Missouri, Chamber of Commerce and the American Association of Nurserymen before enlisting in the United States Army in 1917. During World War I he commanded the Second Battalion, 315th Field Artillery, and eventually led the entire regiment before the war was over.

Following the war Stark again returned to Louisiana and expanded the family operation in his new role as general manager. Simultaneously he developed

a statewide reputation as one of Missouri's rising new generation of potential political leaders. Stark's presidency of the Missouri-Illinois Bridge Company introduced him to the politics of highway construction as well as leaders such as **Tom Pendergast,** the Kansas City political boss who coincidentally owned one of the largest road-building concerns in the state, the Ready Mixed Concrete Company. In 1928 Stark chaired the Citizens' Road Committee, successfully promoting voter approval for a $75 million highway bond issue, unprecedented at the time. Both Pendergast and Stark saw the value in cultivating a mutually beneficial political alliance, which developed during the late twenties.

While Stark built his political career, he also expanded the family business, which grew to international proportions. Talking business as well as politics everywhere he went, the Missouri apple grower quadrupled profits in the 4,500-acre family corporation. During the 1930s Stark Brothers Nursery employed more than twenty-two thousand employees and served nearly a quarter of a million customers throughout the world. By 1936, when Stark captured the governorship, he had become one of the most powerful businessmen in the entire state.

Stark's drive for the governorship began as a cautious draft that failed in 1928. Four years later a second Stark boom failed when Pendergast picked state senator Francis M. Wilson. When Wilson died unexpectedly, Pendergast again ignored Stark in favor of **Guy Brasfield Park.** By the end of Park's term, however, Stark had developed a large rural constituency based on his promotion of paved "farm to market roads." Faced with a choice between a candidate whose position regarding the Kansas City machine was unknown and one who was his avowed enemy—**William Hirth**—Pendergast picked Stark, virtually ensuring his victory in the primary and in the general election over his Republican opponent, Jesse W. Barrett.

Stark, who had seemed friendly to Pendergast from 1928 to 1936, now portrayed himself as a reformer. Actually, he was more of a rival boss who sought to replace Pendergast in Missouri's pinnacle of power. Shortly after his election Stark pledged to reform Missouri politics, starting with his support of federal district attorney **Maurice M. Milligan,** who uncovered at least fifty thousand fraudulent Pendergast-machine votes.

In 1937 Stark appointed two antimachine commissioners to the Kansas City election board and intensified his attack by removing R. Emmett O'Malley, a Pendergast appointee, as superintendent of the Missouri Insurance Department. When the election removed the "ghost votes," Pendergast lost as the balance of power shifted.

The final stage of the machine's destruction occurred during the Democratic primary for the Missouri Supreme Court in 1938. The battle pitted James M. Douglas, Stark's candidate, against James V. Billings, who represented the boss's final attempt at controlling state politics. Rather than a classic struggle between a boss and a reformer, the Stark-Pendergast contest more closely resembled a clash between two rival machines. While Pendergast's handpicked Works Progress Administrator **Matthew S. Murray** coerced thousands of his employees to vote for Billings, Stark marshaled as many state workers for his candidate.

When Douglas won, President Franklin D. Roosevelt allowed federal patronage to flow into Stark's organization while the prosecution of Pendergast proceeded. The governor gained power over the Kansas City Police Board in April 1939, the same month a federal court indicted Pendergast for income tax evasion.

Aside from his destruction of the Pendergast machine, Stark could claim other achievements during his term in office. Working closely with FDR's New Deal, the governor initiated many state programs based on Roosevelt's blueprint for relief, recovery, and reform such as successfully closing county poorhouses throughout the state. Stark's legislative victories in the area of social welfare, public works, and education compared favorably with other "little New Deals" throughout the nation.

Stark's accomplishments in public health, education, and labor seemed especially noteworthy. He was the first Missouri governor to launch a major crusade against cancer resulting in the establishment of "a state-wide . . . clinic [Ellis Fischel Hospital] for the study and treatment of this dreaded disease." Under Stark, statewide appropriations for public schools nearly doubled, from $7.4 million in 1935 to $13.5 million in 1939. Faculty salaries at the University of Missouri and the state colleges gradually increased, and construction projects, delayed because of the depression, were initiated with increasing frequency. Stark's endorsement of collective bargaining won him the support of Missouri's labor unions.

Bolstering his political hopes on these solid achievements and limited by law to one term as governor, Stark set his sights on national office in 1940: the United States Senate seat held by **Harry S. Truman.** Since Pendergast's defeat in 1939, Truman seemed vulnerable. Unfortunately for Stark, several unforeseen factors combined to crush his senatorial hopes. First, federal prosecutor Maurice Milligan entered the Democratic primary, splitting the "reform vote." Second, Stark's educational achievements neglected Missouri's black electorate, which Truman effectively cultivated. Third, labor unions felt closer to Truman than Stark. Finally, Truman used his contacts with "courthouse gangs," independent farmers, Masons, and Baptists to his advantage, thus cutting into Stark's appeal to rural Missouri. Still, Stark lost to Truman by only 7,977 votes and carried more counties than Truman and Milligan combined.

Following his defeat in 1940, Stark returned to the rural life he loved. He operated three farms in northeast Missouri in addition to his worldwide apple-growing corporation. In semiretirement he also began a profitable career as a breeder of saddle and Percheron horses, Hereford cattle, Hampshire hogs, sheep, and hunting dogs. Maintaining homes in Eolia and St. Louis, Missouri, as well as Phoenix, Arizona, Stark died on September 17, 1972.

J. CHRISTOPHER SCHNELL

Kirkendall, Richard S. *A History of Missouri: Volume V, 1919 to 1953*. Columbia: University of Missouri Press, 1986.

Ryle, Walter H. "Biographical Sketch of Lloyd C. Stark." In *The Messages and Proclamations of the Governors of the State of Missouri,* ed. Sarah Guitar and Floyd C. Shoemaker, vol. 14. Columbia: State Historical Society of Missouri, 1949.

Slavens, George E. "Lloyd C. Stark as a Political Reformer, 1936–1941." Master's thesis, University of Missouri, 1957.

St. Louis Post-Dispatch, September 18, 1972.

STENGEL, CHARLES DILLON "CASEY" (1890–1975)

Charles Dillon "Casey" Stengel was born in Kansas City, Missouri, on July 30, 1890, and was Kansas City's most famous baseball player-manager. The son of Irish-German parents, he starred in baseball, football, and basketball at Central High School. He was nicknamed "Dutch" and later "Casey," for the initials "K. C." of his hometown.

Stengel spent three years studying dentistry at the Western Dental College, now the University of Missouri at Kansas City. To earn money for school he played baseball for a team sponsored by the Parisian Cloak Company, later Harzfeld's. In 1910 he quit his studies and signed for seventy-five dollars a month as an outfielder for Kankakee, Illinois, in the Northern Association, a minor league that soon disbanded. The reason he often offered for giving up his dental career was that he was left-handed, "and all the equipment of the period was for right-handed drillers."

Stengel then played with Maysville, Kentucky, in the Blue Grass League, batting .223 and fielding .987. For Aurora, Illinois, in the Wisconsin-Illinois League, in 1911, he won the batting championship with a .352 average and led the league in stolen bases. In 1912 he played 136 games in Montgomery,

Alabama, in the Southern League, and was drafted by the major league Brooklyn Dodgers, who paid three hundred dollars for him.

Stengel played seventeen games with Brooklyn that year, after getting four hits in as many times at bat during his first game. He was not noted for his batting but was a hitter who had a knack for connecting in the clutch. He batted .316 during that short season and compiled a .284 mark over a fourteen-year major league career as an outfielder with the Dodgers, the Pittsburgh Pirates, the Philadelphia Phillies, the New York Giants, and the Boston Braves. He hit .316 in 126 games in 1914, and achieved personal bests in 1917 with seventy-three runs batted in and sixty-nine runs scored with the Dodgers. In 1916 he played in his first World Series.

After being traded in January 1918 to Pittsburgh, Stengel hit .246 and fielded .957. He was traded in September 1919 to Philadelphia, where his option was taken in early 1921 by John McGraw's New York Giants. His 1921 batting average for the two teams reached .368, a career high, and .339 in 1923. He started in both the 1922 and the 1923 World Series by hitting .400 and fielding 1.000 in the 1922 classic and batting .417 and fielding 1.000 in the 1923 series. In the 1923 World Series he won two games with crucial home runs and outhit Babe Ruth. Stengel was traded to Boston in November 1923. He played his last two major league seasons there.

Stengel began his managerial career in 1925 with Worcester, Massachusetts, in the Eastern League. He managed the Toledo Mud Hens of the American Association from 1926 to 1931 and coached at Brooklyn in 1932 and 1933. When the Dodgers fired manager Max Carey in 1934, Stengel began his long major league managerial career. He endured nine bare years with Brooklyn and the Boston Braves. After 1936 the Dodgers paid him to sit out the fourth year of his contract. Hired by the Braves in 1938, he compiled six unenviable years. The Braves finished fifth in 1938, seventh the next three seasons, and sixth in 1942. Stengel, who resigned in 1943, was hired the next year by Bill Veeck as manager of the Milwaukee Brewers of the American Association. He finished first, then managed his hometown Kansas City Blues in 1945, and later managed Oakland in the Pacific Coast League.

On October 13, 1948, Stengel was signed to manage the New York Yankees by general manager George Weiss, who had tried for years to bring Stengel to the Yankees. There Stengel recorded an unprecedented ten pennants in twelve years and seven World Series championships. From 1949 to 1953 the Yankees won five straight pennants in Stengel's first five years, a standard by which other managers will always be measured.

In many unorthodox ways, Stengel rewrote managing rules. Although the Yankees suffered eleven injuries in 1949, he skillfully platooned his players, followed his intuition, and gambled on percentages. Derided previously as a clown manager, Stengel abruptly became "the Old Perfesser."

After being released in 1960 by the Yankees, Stengel returned to Oakland as a millionaire and served as a bank director. He and his wife, Edna Lawson, were married on August 16, 1924, and remained so for more than fifty years, but had no children.

From 1963 to 1965 Stengel managed the expansionist New York Mets. He was elected to the Baseball Hall of Fame in 1966 and saw his uniform number "37" retired by the Yankees. Stengel, who died of cancer on September 29, 1975, may have inspired more public affection than any other baseball figure since Babe Ruth.

ARTHUR F. MCCLURE AND VIVIAN RICHARDSON

Creamer, Robert W. "Casey Stengel: An Appreciation." *Sports Illustrated* (October 13, 1975): 41.
———. *Stengel: His Life and Times.* New York: Simon and Schuster, 1984.
New York Times, January 18, 1981.
The Yankee Encyclopedia. S.v. "Stengel, Casey."

STEPHAN, MARTIN (1777–1846)

Martin Stephan was born into poverty in Stramberg, Moravia, on August 13, 1777, and was orphaned at an early age. Trained in his father's trade of weaving, he went to Breslau as a journeyman linen weaver in 1797 or 1799. There a clergyman of the conservative Pietists took an interest in him and assisted him with obtaining a formal education. He studied at the universities in Halle and Leipzig, but discontinued his studies in 1809 without taking the examination.

Stephan was pastor of the Bohemian congregation at St. John's in Dresden from 1810 to 1837 where he developed a large and loyal following among conservative Lutherans. In 1837 he was suspended from his office after repeated confrontations with civil authorities and officials of the Lutheran church. The charges against him included literalism in interpretation of the Scriptures and the Lutheran Confessions, his followers' undue veneration of him, and mysticism.

His followers, however, saw in Stephan a champion of orthodoxy. Several hundred of them joined the emigration society he established, pooled their resources into its credit fund, and left their homes to establish a colony in Missouri. Stephan's wife and seven daughters chose to stay in Dresden.

In November 1838, 665 people left Bremen in five chartered ships, one of which was lost at sea. During the Atlantic crossing a formal hierarchy was established, with Stephan as bishop. Before they reached St. Louis, Stephan's authority was further strengthened when fellow travelers signed a declaration of obedience to him.

Resentment against Stephan within the group had begun even before they sailed, but it grew and spread in St. Louis. The bishop lived in "splendid seclusion" in lavish quarters, while the rank and file of his followers led a miserable existence. Many of the immigrants were ill, poorly housed, and meagerly fed. To make matters worse, Stephan, fearing that those who had good positions in the city might not follow him to the new colony, decreed that no one should be permitted to accept work that bound him for more than a single day.

The credit fund was badly mismanaged by Stephan and his advisers during this time, and there were many instances of excesses. At the end of several weeks the fund was nearly depleted. Using virtually the last available funds, the group purchased about forty-five hundred acres of land along the Mississippi River in Perry County for the site of their community. On April 26, 1839, Stephan and the first detachment of colonists left St. Louis for the settlement.

On May 5 two women confessed to improper relations with Stephan. Several more confessions were made in the following days. There was actually nothing new in such charges against Stephan, which were similar to allegations that had been made in Dresden. What was different now was that the leaders of the group were ready to believe them.

The pastors, still in St. Louis, decided to remove the bishop from office. They arrived in Perry County with two to three hundred additional colonists on May 29, and a council of pastors and laymen voted Stephan's removal from office and excommunication. He was charged with fornication and adultery, prodigal maladministration of the funds of others, false doctrine, and rejecting the Word of God, the church, the office of the ministry, and all divine order.

Stephan was given the choice of returning to Germany, facing trial, or being transported across the river to Illinois. He chose Illinois. Several days later he was followed by his maid, Louise Guenther, who admitted to being his mistress for the past seven or eight years. She remained in his employ until her death.

The expulsion of Stephan marked the beginning of a difficult period for the Saxon immigrants. Their funds depleted, they were ill-prepared for the demands of providing food and shelter in the colonies. A controversy over the administration of the group threatened the very existence of the Perry County settlements and the St. Louis congregation. Under the leadership of Pastor C. F. W. Walther, the group recovered, and though they gave up their hopes for an exclusive, autonomous community, their legacy includes the Missouri Synod, the largest association of Lutheran churches in the United States. Several communities that were part of the original settlement remain in Perry County.

Stephan spent the remainder of his life in relative seclusion in Illinois, plagued by illness and poverty. By 1841 he was preaching in the courthouse in Kaskaskia, Illinois, every two weeks. Later he organized a congregation in Horse Prairie, near Red Bud, Illinois. He died on February 22, 1846.

ROBYN BURNETT

Forster, Walter O. *Zion on the Mississippi: The Settlement of the Saxon Lutherans in Missouri, 1839–1841.* St. Louis: Concordia Publishing, 1953.

Kretzmann, P. E. "The Saxon Immigration to Missouri, 1838–1839." *Missouri Historical Review* 33 (January 1939): 157–70.

Vehse, Carl Eduard. *The Stephanite Emigration to America.* Translated by Rudolph Fiehler. Dresden: n.p., 1840; Tucson, Ariz.: Marion R. Winkler, n.d.

STEPHENS, LAWRENCE "LON" VEST (1858–1923)

Early in the nineteenth century the pioneer settlement at Boonville began flourishing; its strategic location on the Missouri River made it a significant port of entry for central and south-central areas of the state. A few entrepreneurs became wealthy through adeptly managed businesses, accumulation of real estate, and wise financial investments. From this cluster of preeminent Boonville families came Missouri's twenty-ninth governor, Lawrence Vest Stephens, called "Lon" from an early age, and his wife, Margaret "Maggie" Nelson. Their wedding on October 5, 1880, brought together two of central Missouri's notable families.

Lon was born on December 1, 1858, and attended schools in Boonville before completing his formal education at Washington and Lee University in Lexington, Virginia, where he graduated in 1878. Margaret completed her education at Mrs. Reid's finishing school in New York City.

In 1877 Stephens's father, Col. Joseph Lafayette Stephens, held controlling stock in a newspaper, the *Boonville Weekly Advertiser.* Lon briefly edited it in 1877–1878 and wrote a column in which he expressed opinions that other Missouri newspapers sometimes reprinted. His lively commentary aroused public interest and discussion. Such exposure helped establish his reputation, and facilitated his entry into politics.

Financial management, too, intrigued young Stephens, and in 1880 he began work in the Central

National Bank, the Boonville bank his father had established in 1865. Upon the death of his father in 1881, ownership passed to Lon and his older brother, W. Speed Stephens. The brothers were financial advisers for Cooper and Morgan Counties for a number of years. Bankers across the state acknowledged Stephens's expertise, and when the Fifth National Bank of St. Louis declared insolvency in 1887, Missouri bankers recommended his name to the U.S. comptroller of currency as receiver. In spite of his youthful age of twenty-nine, he handled the liquidation so capably that it secured his reputation as a financial wizard. In 1890 the state treasurer resigned amid scandal of mismanaged state funds; Gov. **David R. Francis** beckoned Stephens to replace him. Two years later voters elected Stephens to the office for a four-year term. Whether or not silver should be part of the federal monetary system was a raging issue through much of the latter years of the nineteenth century. Stephens aligned with and campaigned for the "silver" Democrats.

In August 1896 the Democratic nominating convention by acclamation chose Stephens as the party's candidate for governor. No greater honor could befall him, he said, than to be governor of his beloved state. He was elected on November 4, 1896.

Stringent economic measures characterized Stephens's administration; he reduced the state budget to less than $2 million, and to thwart loan sharks interest rates were limited to no more than 2 percent per month by law. He advocated a self-supporting penitentiary by contracting prisoners for labor; not only would this be a source of revenue, he noted, but it would also teach the men a useful trade.

Compassion also guided the Stephens administration, as the state assumed a greater role in providing and monitoring social services. The General Assembly authorized funding for upgrading facilities for two Civil War veterans homes, for creating a state hospital for the insane at Farmington, and for establishing an institution for retarded children at Marshall.

Under Stephens's administration the Missouri State Fair at Sedalia became a yearly event, the State Historical Society became a reality, and the planning initiated under the previous administration for the St. Louis World's Fair went forward. A collateral inheritance tax brought revenue to the University of Missouri.

With Stephens's sophisticated wife as first lady, the mansion in Jefferson City became the scene for some of the most glittering social events ever associated with Missouri state government. Margaret was an active first lady, though some perceived her role as inappropriate and were particularly alarmed about the influence she might exert on the governor in pardoning prisoners.

Even staunch admirers of Stephens described his administration as "politically stormy." Critics were especially harsh in their condemnation of his failure to use the state militia to curb the violence and destruction in St. Louis during a strike of streetcar workers after management refused to recognize the employees' union. Stephens maintained that it was St. Louis's responsibility. Stephens's slow response to Missouri's participation in the Spanish-American War also came under fire. While he regarded with apparent pride his expenditure of only about one-third of the allocation authorized by the General Assembly, others viewed it as draconian frugality.

Unfortunately, Stephens's expertise in finance did not always translate into political skills, and he sometimes angered entrenched politicians. His principal support had always come from small towns and rural areas; it was the major urban areas that produced the most condemning attacks on his administration and personal life. Stephens coped with flagrant, unparalleled corruption in both Kansas City and St. Louis.

Honors did come Stephens's way. The University of Missouri awarded him an honorary LL.D. in 1898. In appreciation for serving on their board and his special interest in their science program, one of the museums at Central Methodist College in Fayette bears his name. He was one of the trustees who judiciously managed the endowment fund for Barnes Hospital in St. Louis.

In the course of his vigorous career Stephens served as vice president and director of the Central National Bank in Boonville, and as director of the Bank of Versailles. He founded both the Bank of Bunceton and the Central Missouri Trust in Jefferson City. Many corporations counted him among their stockholders.

Religion played a significant role in the Stephenses' lives. Always active members of the Methodist Episcopal Church, South, they were major contributors to the church building fund in Jefferson City and assisted in sponsoring many fund-raising projects for the church as well as other charitable organizations.

Missouri's constitution prohibited Stephens from succeeding himself, and though his name was subsequently suggested for public office he vowed never again to seek or hold public office. He moved to St. Louis, and though he continued pursuing customary interests and extensive travel, his final decades were scarred by family problems and the failure of the family bank. Health disorders plagued Stephens much of his life, and a chronic eye condition finally culminated in virtual blindness. He died on January 10, 1923, in St. Louis, and is buried in Walnut Grove Cemetery in Boonville.

Marian M. Ohman

Guitar, Sarah, and Floyd C. Shoemaker, eds. *The Messages and Proclamations of the Governors of the State of Missouri.* Vol. 8. Columbia: State Historical Society of Missouri, 1926.

Jefferson City Daily Tribune, September 19, 1894.

Reedy, William M. "Lawrence V. Stephens." *Reedy's Mirror* 23 (December 18, 1914): 49–50.

Stephens, Lon Vest. *Sharps and Flats, by Ex-Gov. Lon V. Stephens.* Comp. M. V. Carroll. Sedalia: Sedalia Printing, 1902.

STEWART, ROBERT MARCELLUS (1815–1871)

Robert Marcellus Stewart, a railroad promoter, politician, and governor of Missouri, was born in Truxton, New York, on March 12, 1815. After attending schools in Truxton, he began teaching at the age of seventeen. He studied law and gained admittance to the New York bar in 1836. The next year he moved to Louisville, Kentucky, where he practiced law and worked for a newspaper. In 1839 he traveled to western Missouri and opened a law office at Bloomington, since renamed DeKalb. He subsequently moved his legal practice to St. Joseph and involved himself in Democratic politics. He was elected a delegate in the 1845 Missouri Constitutional Convention, and the following year he won a seat in the state senate where he served for ten years.

Following the outbreak of the Mexican War, Stewart organized a company for the Oregon Battalion and was elected captain. He accompanied the outfit as far as Fort Kearny, but failing health forced him to return to St. Joseph. In 1848 he accepted an appointment as register of the land office in Savannah, Missouri, but he soon resigned to initiate at his own expense a preliminary survey for a railroad linking Hannibal and St. Joseph. He anticipated that it would become a part of the Pacific Railway system and make St. Joseph a major railroad hub.

In the Missouri Senate, Stewart sponsored railroad legislation and supported state funding for public improvement projects. After securing financial backing from the state for the Hannibal and St. Joseph line, he traveled to Washington, D.C., and obtained a federal land grant. As the company's first president, Stewart oversaw the initial phases of construction.

When the Missouri General Assembly selected Gov. **Trusten W. Polk** to fill a vacant seat in the United States Senate in 1857, the Democrats chose Stewart to oppose Whig **James S. Rollins** in a special gubernatorial election. Stewart narrowly defeated Rollins and was sworn in on October 22. As governor, he continued to stress state improvements, but the escalating national crisis that threatened to disrupt the Union demanded much of his attention. He defended slavery and attacked abolitionism, but vetoed a bill that would have forced free people of color to leave the state or be sold into slavery.

Stewart was more moderate on the question of the Union than many members of his party. When violence erupted along the Kansas border in 1858, he temporarily helped restore order by sending state troops to patrol the region. In his final message to the General Assembly, he stated that "Missouri will . . . hold to the Union so long as it is worth the effort to preserve it. . . . She cannot be frightened . . . by the past unfriendly legislation of the North nor dragooned into secession by the restrictive legislation of the extreme South."

Following his retirement as governor, Stewart was elected as a delegate to the state convention convened to decide Missouri's future relationship with the Union. During those deliberations he declared himself an unconditional Unionist. In 1863 Gov. **Hamilton Rowan Gamble** commissioned Stewart to organize a brigade of Union soldiers, but later that year Gen. Henry Halleck relieved him of command because of his chronic drunkenness.

As a politician Stewart had managed to build a reputation as a talented and hardworking public official in spite of his legendary bouts with the bottle that sometimes impaired his judgment and led to public embarrassment. His condition steadily deteriorated until he died in St. Joseph on September 21, 1871.

PAUL A. WHITE

McCandless, Perry. *A History of Missouri: Volume II, 1820 to 1860.* Columbia: University of Missouri Press, 1972.

Shoemaker, Floyd C., ed. *The Messages and Proclamations of the Governors of the State of Missouri.* Vol. 3. Columbia: State Historical Society of Missouri, 1922.

STEYERMARK, JULIAN (1909–1988)

Perhaps no one knew the haunts of Missouri better than Julian Steyermark. For thirty-four years he searched every nook and cranny of Missouri's terrain, studying birds, amphibians, insects, and, above all, plants. Even while working as a botanist for the Field Museum of Natural History in Chicago—where he was employed to study the flora of Central and South America—he managed to find time to travel to Missouri with his wife and field partner, Cora, and continue his study of the state's flora. This work culminated with the publication in 1963 of his *Flora of Missouri,* a classic work that is widely regarded as one of the finest books on state floras ever written. He also worked tirelessly to promote conservation in Missouri, and it was his hope that through such work he could encourage others to enjoy and protect Missouri's natural resources.

Steyermark was born a short distance from the Missouri Botanical Garden in St. Louis on January 27, 1909. As a teen he frequented the garden and began painting watercolors of its orchid collection. His science teacher at Soldan High School encouraged him to pursue his interest in biology, and he entered Washington University in the fall of 1925, where he earned a B.A. in botany in 1929 and an M.S. in 1930. After taking an M.A. in biology at Harvard in 1931, he returned to Washington University for a Ph.D. from the Henry Shaw School of Botany in 1933.

Although from the beginning he focused mostly on plants—his still useful *Spring Flora of Missouri* appeared in 1940—Steyermark's first years in biology were characterized by the study of a wide range of organisms. In fact, one of his earliest publications was on the discovery of a new location for a freshwater jellyfish in Missouri.

Steyermark was a naturalist's naturalist; he liked nothing more than to be in what he called the "virgin" areas of Missouri—those areas where human activity had not significantly altered the natural communities—exploring and noting everything he found interesting. His early field notebooks are full of observations on various natural phenomena, and these descriptions reveal an enthusiasm for field study that would characterize his and Cora's work throughout their lives. Not surprisingly, his professional focus within biology—plant taxonomy—was the one area where he could devote most of his career to fieldwork. His field studies also prepared him for his role in conservation, with which he had been concerned since his undergraduate days at Washington University.

As a nature counselor at a summer camp in Maine during 1928–1930 Steyermark gave talks on the importance of conserving natural resources in Maine and elsewhere. Later, while collecting plants for his *Flora in Missouri* during the 1930s, 1940s, and 1950s, he lamented the construction of various dams in the Ozarks that he realized would destroy unique communities. Steyermark welcomed the arrival of both the U.S. Forest Service and the Missouri Conservation Commission in the 1930s, hoping that these organizations could effectively protect Missouri's natural resources. A number of outstanding examples of Missouri's natural communities now protected by various conservation organizations were first recognized and noted by Steyermark, and his meticulous method of documenting the location of rare and uncommon plant species has been invaluable for generations of workers trying to conserve Missouri's natural heritage.

Steyermark published at least seventy-five articles covering a wide range of topics on Missouri's natural communities. The Missouri Department of Conservation officially recognized his contribution to the state's conservation efforts in 1979 by naming a tract of forest in Marion County the Julian Steyermark Woods Conservation Area, and during the same year the Missouri Botanical Garden presented him with the rarely awarded Henry Shaw Medal.

In 1959 Steyermark accepted a position as a botanist at the Instituto Botánico in Caracas, Venezuela, where he contributed scientific publications on the country's flora, helped to create nature preserves, and was a leader in documenting the biodiversity of the American tropics.

In 1984 Steyermark returned to St. Louis as head curator of the Missouri Botanical Garden. There he continued his work on the flora of Venezuela and offered advice to those working on a revision of his classic *Flora of Missouri*. When he died at his home in St. Louis on October 15, 1988, Missouri lost one of its most accomplished scientists and ardent conservationists.

JOHN HAYS

Annals of the Missouri Botanical Garden 76 (fall 1989): 627–780.

Steyermark, Cora. *Behind the Scenes.* St. Louis: Missouri Botanical Garden, 1984.

Steyermark, Julian. *Flora of Missouri.* Ames: Iowa State University Press, 1963.

———. Papers. Missouri Botanical Garden Archives. Missouri Botanical Garden, St. Louis.

———. *Spring Flora of Missouri.* St. Louis: Missouri Botanical Garden, 1940.

Steyermark, Julian A., Paul E. Berry, and Bruce K. Holst, eds. *Flora of the Venezuelan Guayana.* Vol. 1. Portland: Timber Press, 1995.

STILL, ANDREW TAYLOR (1828–1917)

Andrew Taylor Still, the founder of an alternate system of medicine that he called "osteopathy," was born in Lee County, Virginia, on August 6, 1828, the son of Martha Moore and the Reverend Abram Still, a physician as well as circuit rider of the western-expanding Methodist Church. He provided medical care for his church members, administering not only to their souls but also to their bodies when needed.

When Andrew was nine years old, his family moved to northern Missouri. He attended school whenever it was available; at other times he was instructed by his parents. His father was a stalwart abolitionist, and the Missouri slaveholding Methodists in Macon County did not look favorably on his abolitionist sermons.

The Methodist Church North eventually transferred Reverend Still to Indian Territory in eastern Kansas. In 1853 Andrew with his wife and family followed his father to Kansas, where Andrew farmed and continued to study medicine under his father's tutelage. Father and son took care of the medical needs of the Shawnee Indians; Reverend Still continued in his missionary work on the reservation.

Andrew Still's first wife, Mary Margaret Vaughn, died about six weeks following the birth of their fifth child, on September 29, 1859. His future second wife, Mary Elvira Turner, moved from New York to Kansas to live with her sister and brother-in-law and teach in a primitive rural school. Still met Turner while he was on a house call to administer to the children of her sister; after a short courtship they were married on November 25, 1860.

War clouds were gathering over Kansas. On September 6, 1861, Still enlisted in the Ninth Kansas Cavalry, serving as a hospital steward. He was discharged at Harrisonville, Missouri, on February 2, 1862, when his unit was mustered out, and he returned home to organize a company of militia. On May 15, 1862, he was commissioned a captain and soon thereafter a major. He again volunteered during the Price raid; he and his Kansas forces were placed under the command of Maj.-Gen. **Samuel Ryan Curtis.** This was the last effort of Gen. **Sterling Price** as he attempted to divert Union troops from the East by making a desperate foray through Missouri in October 1864. An incident during that incursion almost ended the osteopathic profession before it was established. According to Still, "during the hottest period of the fight, a musket ball passed through the lapels of my vest; another passed through the back of my coat making an entry and exit about six inches apart."

Still developed a strong aversion to the use of drugs while practicing with his father on the Kansas Indian reservation. Many physicians' therapeutic armamentarium, including Still's father's, encompassed bleeding, purging, and heroic toxic doses of calomel; this experience and his familiarity with Civil War military medicine did little to allay Still's therapeutic nihilism.

However, less severe treatments for various illnesses were beginning to permeate the West, attracting the attention of the more educated citizens and some physicians, including Still. These panaceas included phrenology, mesmerism, lightening bone-setting, and spiritualism. Still also became obsessed with the human skeleton and its anatomic bony relationship. He theorized that if the bones of the skeleton were not in normal alignment, there would be an obstruction of the blood or the nerves that would result in disease; conversely, health would result if the blood and nerve supply were released from this obstruction by manipulation of the skeletal system. Ancient Indian burial grounds supplied Still with a sufficient supply of bones for anatomic study and

frequent demonstrations of his theories to anyone who would listen.

Still considered all medications poison and tolerated none for his patients. It was not long before the local townspeople in Palmyra, later renamed Baldwin, Kansas, became aware of his complete abandonment of drugs and his total reliance upon the laying on of hands and manipulation. Many of his patients considered Still's behavior eccentric; some were convinced he had a mental problem.

Still's practice diminished to the extent that his family at times lived in poverty. Through extreme parsimonious planning, his wife managed to keep the family intact. During this critical period, Still decided to visit his brother Edward in Macon, Missouri, with the intention of relocating to Missouri. He visited with his brother for several months, and again encountered opposition, particularly from the Methodist church, and so he moved to Kirksville, Missouri, some thirty miles north of Macon. Still believed that Kirksville was his mecca. Here he met a few people who befriended him; at least they were not derisive toward his unusual medical concepts.

Still opened an office on the south side of the square in Kirksville. In the local newspaper, the *North American Register,* he advertised himself as a magnetic healer. He sent for his wife and children, and they arrived in Kirksville in May. Still continued his practice of drugless medicine, incorporating phrenomagnetic healing, along with his obsession for anatomic manipulation. In 1883 he added into his therapeutic armamentarium the ancient art of "bone-setting," and advertised himself in the local newspaper as a "lightening bonesetter." During this period he traveled from town to town, usually accompanied by one or more of his sons and his bag of Indian bones, teaching and explaining his type of manipulation to whomever would listen.

The work of this drugless doctor who cured people by "laying on of the hands" without medicine spread by word of mouth throughout Adair and surrounding counties; the number of patients increased to such a degree that Still was unable to manipulate all of them. Patients from not only Missouri but also surrounding states descended on Kirksville, making a boomtown out of the community, and resulting in a bonanza for the merchants.

By successfully imparting the knowledge of anatomy and the practice of manipulation to his sons and three family friends, Still felt more confident in starting a school and being able to teach the practice of medicine he named "osteopathy." Fortunately, Dr. William Smith, a recent graduate of Edinburgh and now a surgical-supply salesman for A. S. Aloe of St. Louis, was visiting Kirksville and in the course of his business heard many stories about the miraculous cures by Still, and decided to visit him. Smith was impressed with Still's knowledge, particularly in anatomy. Still prevailed upon Smith to remain in Kirksville and help him open a school of osteopathy.

The first class of the new osteopathic school was held in a newly constructed frame structure, sixteen by twenty-two feet, too small even for the initial group of students. On October 3, 1892, the first osteopathic school opened with seventeen students, including five members of Still's family, and two instructors, Still and Smith. In the fall of 1893 the second class of about thirty enrolled, including several from the first class who wanted more training. More space was needed. In rapid succession, a three-story infirmary, forty-eight by eighty-eight feet, was built. This space was inadequate by 1896, and an addition to double the capacity was added. In several more months a second addition was added that tripled the size of the facility and could accommodate one thousand patients and five hundred students. The completed structure contained sixty-seven rooms and thirty thousand square feet. In 1895 a maternity unit was opened in a twelve-room house near the new infirmary. The next structure completed in 1905 was the American School of Osteopathy (ASO) hospital that had a capacity for seventy-five patients, and was essentially a surgical hospital. The next year a training school for nurses was established. By 1900 the ASO claimed to offer all subjects taught by the average western medical school.

The Kirksville institution continued to expand under the watchful eye of Andrew Still. He permitted a medical curriculum simulating the courses taught in the average midwestern medical school. One subject that he absolutely forbade was instruction in the use of drugs. In its place manipulation was used for all diseases. This strict policy caused a rift within the faculty for a number of years. The medical community as a group found Still objectionable, partly for economic reasons since he was attracting a large number of their patients.

One medical physician, F. A. Grove, like Still was from Virginia, and the two became friends, though they argued frequently over the cause and treatment of disease. They met quite often at a local Kirksville drugstore. Grove enjoyed heckling Still, and the reverse was true. For example, during a typhoid epidemic in Kirksville, Grove asked Still what bone he was going to set to cure typhoid-fever cases.

Andrew Still was never against surgery—only what he considered unnecessary surgery. Throughout his career he performed minor surgeries, usually as a result of farm accidents. During the Civil War there were anecdotal references to his having removed bullets and other foreign objects and performing surgery on injured military personnel.

William Smith was in charge of the new surgery department at the ASO hospital. He was assisted by J. B. Littlejohn, a graduate of the University of Glasgow who like Smith took training at the ASO while he was in Kirksville and received a D.O. degree.

The "Old Doctor," as Still was lovingly known by faculty, students, and townspeople, died on December 12, 1917, at the age of eighty-nine. His legacy, in addition to the introduction of manipulation into the field of medicine, extends to the start of an osteopathic school a little more than one hundred years ago with seventeen students. From that beginning developed the second-largest field of alternate medicine in the United States.

LAWRENCE E. GIFFEN SR.

Gevitz, Norman. *The D.O.'s: Osteopathic Medicine in America.* Baltimore: Johns Hopkins University Press, 1982.

———, ed. *Other Healers: Unorthodox Medicine in America.* Baltimore: Johns Hopkins University Press, 1988.

Still, Andrew T. *Autobiography of Andrew T. Still.* Kirksville, Mo.: n.p., 1908.

Still, Charles E., Jr. *Frontier Doctor: Medical Pioneer.* Kirksville, Mo.: Thomas Jefferson University Press, 1991.

Trowbridge, Carol. *Andrew Taylor Still, 1828–1917.* Kirksville, Mo.: Thomas Jefferson University Press, 1991.

Walter, Georgia Warner. *The First School of Osteopathic Medicine, 1892–1992.* Kirksville, Mo.: Thomas Jefferson University Press, 1992.

STOCKARD, VIRGINIA ALICE COTTEY (1848–1940)

Originally called the Vernon Seminary, Cottey Junior College in Nevada, Missouri, was the dream and lifework of Virginia Alice Cottey Stockard. One of eleven children, Alice Cottey was born on March 27, 1848, near Edina. Although her parents encouraged all their children to read and to write, formal education was provided for only their sons.

Largely self-educated, Alice Cottey found most of her reading material in a Sunday-school library in her rural community. She was profoundly impressed by the biography of Mary Lyon, the founder of Mount Holyoke College, and dreamed of enrolling there. Since that was impossible, she attended a convent school in Edina, after which she was enrolled in a school for girls in Newark. In both instances she expressed impatience with the fact that education for girls concentrated on homemaking skills and social graces, with little attention given to the academics provided in schools for young men.

Cottey taught in a number of rural Missouri schools until 1875; then she joined the faculty of

Central College for Women in Lexington, Missouri. She had never given up her thoughts of starting a "midwestern Mount Holyoke." With the encouragement of her sister who offered her savings, Cottey sent out appeals for help to several Missouri communities. In 1884 she came to Nevada, Missouri, where a leading merchant had offered a cornfield on the outskirts of town. She came with three thousand dollars of her own savings and twenty-five hundred dollars from her family. On the seven acres donated by the community, a single brick building was completed; and Vernon Seminary opened on September 8, 1884. Twenty-eight students were enrolled on the first day, twelve of them boarding students. At the end of the first year, the enrollment had reached seventy-two.

In 1886 the name of the school was changed to Cottey Junior College for Women, and in 1887 it was chartered by the state of Missouri. With a steadily increasing enrollment, additional facilities were required. There was seldom a shortage of students, only a lack of the funds needed for expansion. Through these years the college continued to survive largely because of the indomitable will of Alice Cottey and a small faculty, which included her sisters.

On March 6, 1890, Virginia Alice Cottey was married to Samuel M. Stockard of Springfield, who was a widower with three children. He died six years later, and Alice Stockard reared and educated his children.

As Stockard grew old, she faced the possible dissolution of the college if she could not find a suitable custodian for it. She first offered the college to the Methodist Church, South, which was willing to accept it. However, when Stockard learned that the college would likely be merged with another school, she declined the denomination's offer. Next she turned to the Protect Each Other Sisterhood (PEO), an organization she had recently joined. PEO accepted the college in 1927. Since then, Cottey Junior College has been supported by the International Chapter of the PEO Sisterhood and is the only college administered by a women's organization. In 1929 Stockard retired from the presidency of Cottey Junior College at the age of eighty-one.

Stockard was awarded the honorary degree of LL.D. by Iowa Wesleyan College in 1930. This was the only academic degree ever received by this pioneer in women's education. It was reported that she commented on that occasion, "I've always wanted a hood." She continued to reside in Nevada and died there on July 16, 1940.

WILMA LEONARD TURNER

Campbell, Elizabeth McClure. *The Cottey Sisters of Missouri*. Parkville, Mo.: Park College Press, 1970.

Clapp, Stella. *Out of the Heart: A Century of PEO, 1869–1969*. Des Moines: PEO Sisterhood, 1969.

Cottrell, Debbie Mauldin. "Mount Holyoke of the Midwest: Virginia Alice Cottey, Mary Lyon, and the Founding of the Vernon Seminary for Young Ladies." *Missouri Historical Review* 90 (January 1996): 187–98.

Stockard, Orpha. *The First Seventy-Five Years*. Nevada, Mo.: Cottey College, 1961.

Troesch, Helen DeRusha. *The Life of Virginia Alice Cottey Stockard*. Des Moines: PEO Sisterhood, 1955.

STODDARD, AMOS (1762–1813)

Amos Stoddard, the first American commandant of Upper Louisiana, presided over the ceremonies in St. Louis marking the transfer of the Louisiana Territory to the United States. The eldest son of a Congregational minister, he was born in Woodbury, Connecticut, on October 26, 1762. The Stoddard family moved to Massachusetts, and in 1779 Amos enlisted as a private in the Twelfth Massachusetts Regiment of the Continental army. He reenlisted in an artillery unit and rose to the rank of noncommissioned officer while serving at Constitution Island, Stony Point, West Point, and Yorktown during the Revolutionary War.

In 1784 Stoddard went to Boston where he studied law while working as an assistant clerk for the Massachusetts Supreme Court. Two years later he interrupted his legal studies to accept a commission in the Massachusetts State Militia, which had been summoned to quell Shays's Rebellion. Stoddard attained the rank of captain and command of an artillery company, but resigned in 1788 to return to his clerkship with the supreme court. The next year he moved to Tauton, Massachusetts, to continue his legal education. After completing his studies, Stoddard was admitted to the bar and settled in Hallowell (in present-day Maine) where he served as a town barrister. His passion for military service prompted him to reenter the Massachusetts State Militia in 1796 as a brigade major and inspector of the Second Brigade. Stoddard served briefly in the Massachusetts legislature, but in 1798 he accepted a commission as a captain in the regular army.

Following the Louisiana Purchase, President Thomas Jefferson assigned Captain Stoddard to oversee the transfer of Upper Louisiana to the United States and to act as the military and civil commandant until a formal government could be established for the region. Stoddard arrived in St. Louis on February 24, 1804, and began making arrangements with Spanish lieutenant governor **Charles de Hault Delassus** for the formal transfer. Since Spain had not yet relinquished control of Upper Louisiana to France, Pierre

Clement Laussat, the French prefect of Louisiana, empowered Stoddard to represent the French government for protocol purposes during the transfer ceremonies in St. Louis. On March 9 Delassus formally transferred Upper Louisiana to Stoddard, acting for the French government, and the following day in his capacity as the American commandant Stoddard took possession of the territory for the United States.

During the ceremonies held in front of the government house in St. Louis, Stoddard sought to reassure the inhabitants of the region by promising to retain most Spanish governmental practices. They welcomed his decision to reappoint local commandants who had served under the Spanish regime, but remained concerned about the U.S. government's intentions regarding Spanish land titles. Other matters that competed for Stoddard's attention included Indian affairs, the organization of a militia, and the local slave code. On the whole his deft handling of his official duties greatly facilitated an orderly transfer of authority to the United States in Upper Louisiana. Maj. James Bruff replaced him as military commandant on July 1, 1804, but Stoddard continued his duties as civil commandant until October 1, 1804, when territorial governor **William Henry Harrison** took charge.

Following the completion of his assignment in St. Louis, Stoddard was sent to the territory of Orleans where he continued his military service. In 1807 he was promoted to major, and later, while posted at Fort Columbus in New York, he authored *Sketches, Historical and Descriptive, of Upper Louisiana.* The book, which was published in Philadelphia in 1812, provided a valuable account of the region and its people.

Stoddard next served with the First Artillery in Pittsburgh. In 1812 he briefly served as deputy quartermaster general, but the War of 1812 prompted his reassignment to the western frontier at Fort Meigs on the Maumee River in Ohio. On April 2, 1813, Stoddard was placed in command there, and during an assault on that installation he was mortally wounded and died on May 11, 1813.

Stoddard never married. A disciplined man, well adjusted to military life, he served his nation well. Stoddard County, Missouri, was named in his honor.

LAWRENCE HAVIRD

Hibbert, Wilfrid. "Major Amos Stoddard: First Governor of Upper Louisiana and Hero of Fort Meigs." *Historical Society of Northwestern Ohio Quarterly Bulletin* 2 (April 1930).

Stoddard, Amos. Papers. Missouri Historical Society, St. Louis.

———. *Sketches, Historical and Descriptive, of Upper Louisiana.* Philadelphia, 1812.

STONE, WILLIAM JOEL (1848–1918)

William Joel Stone has the distinction of being the only Missourian to serve the state as a representative in Congress, governor, and senator. He was three times elected to the House of Representatives (1884, 1886, 1888) and declined to seek a fourth term in order to run for governor. Elected governor in 1892, he was prevented from a likely reelection by the prohibition contained in the Missouri constitution at that time. He died in his third senatorial term having never lost an election. He was undeniably popular with the voters, and was both a consummate politician and an able statesman. He grew in stature as he matured in years and in understanding of the complex issues facing the nation.

Stone was born in Kentucky on May 7, 1848, the son of William Stone, a farmer. His mother died when he was four, and a stepmother soon appeared in the home followed by a succession of half brothers and sisters. There seemed to be too many mouths to feed when the farm did not yield well. The outbreak of the Civil War brought guerrilla fighting to the area where the Stone family lived. These things led William, at fifteen, to leave home and make his way on foot to Columbia, Missouri, where his sister, Matilda Turner, lived. She and her husband, an attorney, not only gave him a home but also sent him to the University of Missouri and then encouraged him to read law in Turner's office. After being admitted to the bar in 1869, he began practice in Nevada, Missouri. In 1874 Stone married Sarah Louise Winston of Jefferson City, and they had three children, a son, Kimbrough, and two daughters, Mabel and Mildred.

Stone's three terms in the House were not noteworthy, but as governor he gave the state an able administration, and he gained national attention. During the railroad strike of 1894, he refused to use the state militia to protect strike breakers, assigning the troops to only a few troubled spots to prevent looting or property destruction by any group or individual taking advantage of the strike.

Stone pushed for an employers' liability law in the 1895 legislative term to make it easier for workmen or their dependents to win damages from employers in work-related accidents, a forerunner of workmen's compensation. When the powerful railroad lobbyists used their influence to prevent passage of the measure, Stone attempted to get the General Assembly to adopt antilobbying and election-reform laws by addressing a letter to each member of the legislature. Nonetheless, they failed to adopt either measure. After Stone's term as governor expired, the chief lobbyist, William Phelps of the Missouri Pacific and allied railroads, counterattacked by charging that Stone was a lobbyist also. "We both suck eggs, but Stone hides the shells," Phelps quipped in 1900 at the Jasper County Democratic convention, a comment so comical that it haunted Stone for the rest of his life.

Meanwhile, Stone had joined with the governor of Illinois and three U.S. senators in designing the strategy by which advocates of unlimited coinage of silver gained control of the Democratic Party and nominated William Jennings Bryan on a silver platform. Stone's activities led the *St. Louis Republic,* owned by a "gold Democrat," to editorialize that Stone's way of "tiptoeing" into a community to "fix a little scheme" without attracting attention "had won for him the sobriquet of 'Gum-shoe Bill.' " Stone's loyal followers adopted this nickname as a term that stressed his skill in compromising conflicting views and gaining consensus on major Democratic programs, an ability he exemplified throughout his career.

In recognition of Stone's skills, Bryan requested that Stone be named to the Democratic National Committee and given a prominent role in the 1896 campaign. Stone became vice chairman and acted for the chairman when he left the country to recover from an illness. By 1900 Stone was high in Bryan's advisory group.

Stone devoted the years following his gubernatorial term to building a lucrative law practice for his son to take over and to making money to finance a senatorial campaign and provide a good income to support himself, his wife, and their daughters in Washington. Unfortunately, these laudable goals led him to accept legal fees from firms interested chiefly in his political connections. While this smacked of lobbying, it did not necessarily mean corrupt practices, as the muckrakers were to claim on the basis of outrageous charges by Phelps and the gold Democrats during the senatorial campaign of 1902. Despite their attacks, the state legislature elected Stone to the Senate in January 1903, for he clearly was the choice of the voters as expressed during the fall campaign. Although the charges were never substantiated and some were even proved false, Stone entered the Senate under something of a cloud. He ignored the allegations and concentrated on proving his ability as a lawmaker.

As a member of the minority party, Stone could accomplish little, but he studied major foreign policy issues facing the nation and visited the Philippines, paying his own way, to gain firsthand information about conditions in the Pacific. In his second term progressivism had become the mood of the nation, with tariff reduction a key issue. Stone, fierce partisan that he was, cooperated with leading Republican progressives and became the "Democratic conscience" with respect to tariff reform. President William Howard Taft relied on Stone for assistance in passing the Canadian Reciprocity Treaty.

In 1912 Stone served as **Champ Clark**'s manager at the Democratic convention. When it became apparent that Clark could not gain the necessary two-thirds majority for the nomination and Bryan threatened to bolt the party if Clark were the nominee, Stone became worried. He feared that a second split within sixteen years would bring an end to the party, and he concluded that Woodrow Wilson was the only man who could lead the Democrats to victory. Therefore, Stone quietly moved for an adjournment, which allowed Wilson's managers to make the deals required to bring about his nomination and foiled Clark's plan to confront Bryan face-to-face. Stone then campaigned enthusiastically for Wilson and a Democratic majority in Congress.

In the Sixty-third Congress, 1913–1914, Stone became one of the most influential senators, the one on whom Wilson depended to use the caucus and other compromising tactics to hold the slim Democratic majority in line and enact the major items in the Wilsonian reform program. Wilson listened to Stone's advice on appointments, though it sometimes contradicted the president's desire to avoid spoilsmanship, which, Stone stressed, had to be used to achieve the greater goal of accomplishing reform. Stone, as ranking majority member on the Finance Committee, handled some of the crucial aspects of the tariff bill in 1913 that did accomplish genuine reduction of rates. He also worked hard to perfect the Federal Reserve bill. In March 1914 he became chairman of the Foreign Relations Committee.

With the outbreak of the world war, Stone gained greater prominence. His statements, frequently quoted by the press, were often enigmatic, reflecting not only his habitual caution but also an uncertainty in his reaction to some of Wilson's policies. Stone feared that insisting that Germany adhere to accepted rules of blockade when using its new weapon, the submarine, would lead the United States into the war, a war in which it had no vital interest. At the same time he felt confident of Wilson's peaceful intentions and fully supported the president's repeated offers of mediation and espousal of a league of nations. As chairman of the resolutions committee at the Democratic nominating convention, Stone served as Wilson's emissary in placing a plank endorsing a league in the 1916 platform. When, following his reelection, Wilson outlined in some detail what should be the outcome of the war, Stone became enthusiastic. A "peace without victory" was precisely what the world needed, Stone decided.

Unfortunately, events in Europe destroyed the hope of a negotiated peace, to which the president and the senator reacted differently. When Germany announced the resumption of submarine warfare against neutral as well as enemy shipping, Stone agreed that Wilson had to carry out his threat of April

18, 1916, to sever diplomatic relations; however, he wanted to await German action before taking any other steps. Wilson agreed, but he moved rapidly when the sinkings began. With no prior consultation he asked Stone to push an armed-ship bill through the Senate. Stone was aghast after reading the proposal; he protested sharply, but Wilson was adamant and they parted angrily.

The measure probably had no chance in the few days remaining before automatic adjournment of the short session of Congress. In addition, the Republicans had undertaken a filibuster against major appropriation bills. Nevertheless, Stone presented the bill to his committee, while announcing that he would not sponsor it and would speak and vote against it. He gave a lengthy, well-prepared, carefully documented address in which he branded the measure unconstitutional because it handed to the executive the power to determine war or peace. Expressing repeatedly his faith in Wilson's integrity and wisdom, Stone nonetheless believed that the concept of arming merchant ships and taking other measures as the president saw fit was a dangerous power to hand any executive; it created a precedent that could bring disaster to the nation in the hands of some lesser president.

When the session expired without passage of the bill, Wilson denounced its opponents as filibusters whom he termed a "little group of willful men." The metropolitan papers included Stone in this category, though he neither joined nor condoned the filibuster. He compounded his infamy in the opinion of the press by voting against the war resolution in the special session of April 1917. He was one of six senators so voting, but the press singled out Stone for the greatest vilification. He was accused of "treason" for refusing to accept in its entirety the presidential position, an indication of how far the progressive idea of strong presidential leadership had gone. Stone had assisted in furthering that position, and now paid the price.

Once war was declared by Congress, Stone returned to his earlier stance and supported all the war measures presented by the president, including the draft, bond sales to the average citizen, and controls over all important aspects of the economy. He even handled and voted for the resolution of war against Austria-Hungary in December on the grounds that the logic of war with Germany called for treating its ally as an enemy.

When Wilson spoke to Congress in January 1918 to present the fourteen points upon which peace should be based, Stone accepted them fully. On that occasion he served as the president's official escort to the podium, and they shook hands pleasantly if not as cordially as in the past. Stone died before the war he had so dreaded had come to an end.

Stone has frequently been misjudged by historians; he was neither a conservative "bourbon" Democrat nor a corruptionist; he was not a Germanophile or an isolationist. He did not flaunt his progressive stance, preferring to work quietly to accomplish more, he felt, than a lot of talk could achieve. This he did, including genuine tariff reform, an improved banking and currency system, and better conditions for industrial workers. In foreign affairs he became a convert to the Wilsonian view of a new world order of peace and justice in which the United States would lead others. In respect to the immediate situation of World War I, Stone believed the president should wait until the belligerents were so exhausted that they would be forced to accept both his mediation and the peace terms he desired. After converting Stone, the president abandoned the liberal peace program. Stone felt the president had betrayed his own vision of a new world order and destroyed its chance. Lasting peace could not come from a war in which impartial leadership no longer existed.

Stone was a hardworking senator; he seldom missed a day of a session and always took care to be properly paired with another member if a committee meeting prevented him from voting. He was a favorite of reporters regardless of the position of their editors or publishers because he made good copy. He might not answer the queries posed by members of the press, but he told them a few stories or gave them some interesting comments about life in general if not the situation in particular. He did the same for young politicians. His sage and pithy advice was often couched in a tale, but the junior lawmaker, when he thought about it later, realized he had been given a gentle rebuke or a nudge of encouragement to work a bit more cautiously and not expect to "hit a homer every time at bat," as Stone sometimes phrased it.

Even his final illness illustrated Stone's conscientious conduct. He suffered a stroke while riding on a streetcar to the Capitol on the morning of April 10, 1918. Although he had fallen out of his seat, he was conscious and insisted on being taken to his office because, as he kept telling those who rushed to his assistance, he was to make a statement on the Sedition Bill in the Senate that day. After his doctor ordered him taken home and put to bed with a nurse at his side, Stone continued to fret about missing an important vote. He died four days later, still urging that he be permitted to get up and transact business by telephone. In character and achievements Stone ranks among the more noteworthy members of the United States Senate and the greatest Missouri statesmen of the Progressive Era.

RUTH WARNER TOWNE

Link, Arthur Stanley. *Wilson: Campaigns for Progressivism and Peace.* Vol. 5. Princeton: Princeton University Press, 1965.

Stone, William Joel. Papers. Western Historical Manuscripts Collection, Columbia.

Towne, Ruth Warner. *William J. Stone and the Politics of Compromise.* Port Washington, N.Y.: Kennikat Press, 1979.

Wilson, Woodrow. Papers. Library of Congress, Washington, D.C.

STOVER, CLARA (1893–1975); STOVER, RUSSELL (1888–1954)

Russell Stover was born near Alton, Kansas, on May 6, 1888, and Clara Lewis was born near Oxford, Iowa, on September 25, 1893. The couple met while attending high school at the Iowa City Academy in 1906. They did not see each other for several years after graduation, but reestablished their friendship in 1909. They were married on June 17, 1911, in Chicago. They moved to Hume, Saskatchewan, Canada, where Russell unsuccessfully operated a 580-acre farm for a year. Abandoning agriculture, he worked for the next four years in the production and sale of candy in Winnipeg, Manitoba, Canada.

In 1915 the Stovers returned to the United States where Russell sold candy for A. G. Morris and for the Bunte Candy Company in Chicago. He became the superintendent of the Irwin Candy Company of Des Moines, Iowa, in 1918. When Irwin was purchased by Graham Ice Cream Company, Stover retained his position. His first financial success came in 1921 when he designed, named, and patented the Eskimo Pie ice cream bar. Thousands of orders for the confection poured into Des Moines, as did requests for manufacturing rights. Russell and Clara Stover fought for possession of exclusive manufacturing rights but were eventually forced to sell for a mere thirty thousand dollars.

The Stovers began making their own candy on a small scale while they were living in Chicago. Clara Stover made hand-dipped chocolate candy in their apartment, and Russell sold it to neighboring druggists on the weekend. In 1922 the couple used the money and recognition from Eskimo Pies to begin a candy-production business in Denver. They operated from their home for two years, using the name "Mrs. Stover's Bungalow Candies." In 1924 they built their first candy factory in Denver. The following year, they built a second factory in Kansas City, Missouri, and in 1942 they opened a third in Lincoln, Nebraska.

The Stovers' business prospered in the 1920s. Russell Stover received patents for dipping tables and other processes related to making candy and ice cream. Stover candy stores were opened as far away as Chicago and New York City. The couple took five children of a distant relation into their home in Denver for five years, and in 1928 they adopted a daughter, Gloria Virginia.

In late 1929 the Stovers moved into a large apartment in Chicago, along with their daughter and two of the five children in their care. Although they were aware of the stock market crash, they did not realize how it would affect them personally. During the next three years they were forced to close thirteen of their stores, almost half the number they had opened. Their creditor foreclosed on their Denver home, and they also lost the lease on the apartment in Chicago.

In 1931 the Stovers moved their headquarters to Kansas City, Missouri, hoping to save their business. In addition to candy, they began selling ice cream and cakes in their Kansas City and Denver stores. Innovative marketing techniques saved the business, and by 1942 the Stover corporation was debt free. The war years brought increased prosperity to the Stovers, and Russell Stover became chairman of the committee representing the National Confectioners Association in Washington, D.C. In 1946 he became the first individual recipient of the Candy Kettle Award from the National Association of Confectioners.

According to Clara Stover's account, Mrs. Stover's Bungalow Candies was incorporated in 1925, with Clara as president and secretary and Russell as vice president and treasurer. The venture was a true partnership, in which the couple regularly consulted with each other before making business and personal decisions. Russell designed and decorated Stover stores and even candy boxes, while Clara traveled throughout the country as a scout and consultant. In 1943 the business was reorganized into three corporations, and the name was changed to Russell Stover Candies, with Russell Stover as president. Thirty-five older employees were taken into the business, and headquarters for the new corporation were moved to Denver.

In 1943 Russell surprised Clara when he purchased a run-down mansion in the Mission Hills district of Kansas City. It had been built by Frank Jones in the 1920s, but had not been occupied for a number of years. Clara Stover described the grounds as "wildly overgrown." The couple took several years to refurbish and redecorate the home, making it their permanent residence, while maintaining another home in Miami.

Russell Stover died at his Miami home on May 11, 1954. At the time of his death, there were forty Stover candy shops across the country, and the candy was sold in more than two thousand department and drugstores. Clara Stover succeeded her husband as president for seven years following his death. In those seven years the business doubled its output of candy, from 11 to 22 million pounds annually. Clara Stover lived in the Kansas City home until her death on June 9, 1975.

YVONNE JOHNSON

Dains, Mary K., ed. *Show Me Missouri Women: Selected Biographies.* Kirksville, Mo.: Thomas Jefferson University Press, 1989.

Fucini, Joseph J., and Suzy Fucini. *Entrepreneurs: The Men and Women behind Famous Brand Names and How They Made It.* Boston: G. K. Hall, 1985.

Kansas City Times, June 10, 1975.

National Cyclopedia of American Biography. S.v. "Stover, Russell."

Stover, Clara, and Phil A. Koury. *The Life of Russell Stover: An American Success Story.* New York: Random House, 1957.

SUBLETTE, WILLIAM (1799–1845)

William Lewis Sublette was born at Stanford, Kentucky, on September 21, 1799. The family moved to St. Charles, Missouri, in 1817, where his father kept a tavern, speculated in land, and engaged in farming and town politics. As a young man William followed these various pursuits and served as town constable from 1820 to 1823. Life in St. Charles did not satisfy his adventurous and entrepreneurial spirit, however. His younger brother Milton had already ventured to the upper Missouri as a trapper, and William decided to follow him.

Sublette joined **William H. Ashley**'s second expedition to the upper Missouri and the Yellowstone in 1823. He took a prominent part in the fight with the Arikara, which stopped Ashley's ascent of the river, and in the subsequent punitive raid led by Col. Henry Leavenworth.

Sublette then joined a party sent by Ashley to find an overland route to the Rocky Mountains. He spent the next two years in the mountains, trapping with **Jedediah Smith** and other Ashley men. In 1826 Sublette, Smith, and David Jackson bought Ashley's business in the mountains. They soon learned, as Ashley had, that the real profits were to be made in St. Louis, supplying trappers and selling their furs. Frustrated by the declining supply of fur-bearing animals and the intense competition from the British, Indians, and John Jacob Astor's American Fur Company, the partners sold out to the new Rocky Mountain Fur Company in 1830.

After an unsuccessful attempt to break into the Santa Fe trade, Sublette formed a new partnership with an old friend, **Robert Campbell,** while maintaining close ties with William Ashley. Drawing on Ashley's connections with eastern suppliers

and credit, the two continued to supply and market furs for the Rocky Mountain Fur Company and other trappers. They opened posts along the Missouri River, successfully challenging the powerful American Fur Company's monopoly of the river trade. While Campbell managed the river posts, Sublette, a shrewd and calculating businessman, took charge of supply, credit, and marketing. In 1834 he maneuvered the partners of the American Fur Company into an agreement dividing the river and mountain trade between the two companies. He and Campbell withdrew from the Missouri River and established Fort William on the Laramie Fork of the North Platte.

In 1836 Sublette and Campbell sold their interests in the mountains to the Rocky Mountain Fur Company and opened a wholesale and retail business in St. Louis. For a few years the store prospered, and Sublette continued to invest widely in land, insurance companies, and other ventures. His pride was Sulphur Springs, a 779-acre tract outside St. Louis, where he built a fine house in 1834. In addition to experiments with new crop varieties and livestock breeding, he sold coal and lumber from his land, and in 1837 opened a resort hotel at its mineral springs. Sublette served on the board of directors for the Bank of Missouri, and was active in state politics as a hard-money Democrat.

By 1840 the effects of a national depression stifled commerce in St. Louis, and Sublette again decided to withdraw from a declining business. In 1842 he and Campbell dissolved their partnership, and Sublette turned his attention to his farm, real estate, business investments, and state politics. In 1843 he joined his friend Sir William Drumond Stewart on a pleasure trip to the Rocky Mountains to relive their memories of the fur trade a decade before.

Sublette actively campaigned for Democratic candidates in the election of 1844, and served as a presidential elector that year. He was appointed director of the State Bank of Missouri, but was disappointed in his hope for an appointment as an Indian agent.

In 1845 Sublette married Frances Hereford, the daughter of the manager of his Sulphur Springs resort, and later that year took his new bride on a trip to the East. His health had been declining for some years, probably from tuberculosis. He became seriously ill at the outset of the trip, and died at Pittsburgh on July 23, 1845.

Five Sublette brothers sought their fortune in the fur trade. The youngest, Pinckney, was killed by Indians on his first trip west in 1828. Milton (1801–1837) was one of five partners of the Rocky Mountain Fur Company, though financial success always eluded him. Andrew (1808–1853) and Solomon (1810–1857) moved between trapping, the Santa Fe trade, and other ventures, without leaving their mark on any. Only William achieved prominence: he helped pioneer the Overland Trail, and he was the first to prove that wagons and cattle could be taken across the Great Plains. One of the more adventurous and successful of the St. Louis merchants, he helped build St. Louis as the commercial center of the West. His life provides a case study of the early-nineteenth-century western entrepreneur.

MARY ELLEN ROWE

Hafen, LeRoy R., ed. *The Mountain Men and the Fur Trade of the Far West*. 10 vols. Glendale, Calif.: Arthur H. Clark, 1968–1972.
Sunder, John E. *Bill Sublette: Mountain Man*. Norman: University of Oklahoma Press, 1959.

SULLIVAN, LEONOR ALICE KRETZER (1902–1988)

Leonor Alice Kretzer Sullivan was the first woman elected to the United States Congress from a Missouri district, and she served in the House of Representatives for twenty-four years (1953–1977). She was born on August 21, 1902, in St. Louis to Frederick W. and Nora Jostrand Kretzer. After receiving her education in public and private schools in St. Louis, she attended evening classes at Washington University, where she studied vocational psychology. Sullivan's early work experiences included teaching business arithmetic and accounting, and serving as director of a business school in St. Louis.

On December 27, 1941, Leonor Kretzer married John Berchmas Sullivan, a Democratic congressman from Missouri's Eleventh District who served in the Seventy-seventh, Seventy-ninth, Eighty-first, and until his death in the Eighty-second sessions. Leonor Sullivan became his administrative assistant, and she also managed his election campaigns. After her husband died on January 29, 1951, she was an administrative aid to another Missouri representative, Leonard Irving, who served the Fourth Congressional District.

In May 1952 Sullivan returned to Missouri to campaign for the Democratic nomination for St. Louis's Third Congressional District, which had recently been redrawn. The previous year, in the special election to fill her husband's unexpired term, Democratic Party leaders refused to nominate her because they believed a woman could not win. However, she proved them wrong by defeating six men in the Democratic primary and then winning the general election by a two-to-one margin over the Republican incumbent. Although her first victory was mainly seen as a vote for the widow of John B. Sullivan (in fact, she was allowed to be listed on the ballot as Mrs. John B. Sullivan), Leonor Sullivan won the next eleven elections on her own record. She was

a member of the Eighty-third through the Ninety-fourth Congresses; and after 1969 she was recognized as the "dean" of congresswomen. Sullivan served on the Banking and Currency Committee, and on the Merchant Marine and Fisheries Committee. She was also a member of the National Commission on Mortgage and Interest Rates, the National Commission of Consumer Finance, the Joint Committee on Defense Production, and the National Commission on Food Marketing.

Throughout her years in Congress, Sullivan made consumer interests her urgent concern. She sponsored measures to make the Food, Drug, and Cosmetic Act more effective by requiring, among other things, labeling of ingredients on cosmetics, by banning flavored aspirin for children, and by adding more FDA inspectors to check for unfit food products at processing plants. Sullivan led a major fight in Congress for "truth in lending" when she sponsored the Consumer Credit Protection Act, designed to inform consumers of the actual annual interest rates they would pay on loans, especially on "revolving charge accounts" that many department stores offered customers. In signing the bill into law in 1968, President Lyndon B. Johnson gave special recognition to Sullivan's role in its passage.

Sullivan authored the Food Stamp plan as early as 1954, but not until 1959 was it included in an agriculture bill that passed Congress. Other bills she sponsored or cosponsored included tire safety, housing for the elderly, and training for teachers of gifted children as well as handicapped children. She successfully fought to allow the *Delta Queen* and the *Mississippi Queen* to continue to operate as overnight excursion boats after an interpretation of the Safety at Sea Act threatened to eliminate their trips on the Mississippi River.

From her first year in Washington, Sullivan worked with others from Missouri to provide funding for construction of the Jefferson National Expansion Memorial on the St. Louis riverfront. In honor of her efforts in making the Gateway Arch and the Westward Expansion Museum realities, the city of St. Louis in 1983 renamed Wharf Street as Leonor K. Sullivan Boulevard.

Although Sullivan was a cosponsor of the Equal Pay Act of 1963, she was the only woman in the House who did not vote for the Equal Rights Amendment. However, she definitely believed that more women needed to serve in Congress to see that measures affecting the family and general social issues received sufficient attention.

Upon her retirement in 1977 Sullivan headed the Consumer Advisory Council of the Federal Reserve Board, and in 1980 she was elected for a term as president of the Jefferson National Expansion Memorial Association. Among the awards and honors bestowed upon her were the Distinguished Service Award from the Consumer Federation of America, the Americanism Award from the Jewish War Veterans of Missouri, and the Levee Stone Award from Downtown St. Louis Incorporated.

Four years after she retired, Sullivan married Russell G. Archibald, who preceded her in death on March 19, 1987. Leonor K. Sullivan died in St. Louis County on September 1, 1988.

PATRICIA ASHMAN

Chamberlin, Hope. *A Minority of Members: Women in the U.S. Congress.* New York: Praeger Publishers, 1973.

Dains, Mary K., ed. *Show Me Missouri Women: Selected Biographies.* Kirksville, Mo.: Thomas Jefferson University Press, 1989.

Who's Who of American Women. Chicago: A. N. Marquis, 1973.

SWARTHOUT, GLADYS (1904–1969)

Gladys Swarthout, a concert and operatic mezzo-soprano, was born in Deepwater, Missouri, to Frank L. and Ruth W. Swarthout on December 25, 1904. Born with absolute pitch and a full, mature voice for a child, Swarthout gave evidence of great talent and an interest in singing at an early age. By the time she was nine, passersby would inquire who the woman with the beautiful voice was. Many refused to believe she was so young. The unusual maturity "was due to the formation of my throat and vocal chords," Swarthout once explained.

After her family moved from Deepwater to Kansas City, Swarthout began serious vocal instruction with Belle Vickers at age eleven. She made her first public appearance as a singer the next year as a soloist in a church choir. During her first public recital in her early teens, her performance so impressed a wealthy Kansas City family that they decided to finance her career.

After graduation in 1920 from Kansas City's Central High School Swarthout attended the Bush Conservatory of Music in Chicago. She also studied opera with Leopoldo Mugnone. She remained in Chicago for three years to continue her musical education. To help finance her study she performed as a church soloist and on one occasion embarked upon a joint concert tour with her older sister Roma, who was a pianist.

In 1924, without opera experience or a repertoire, Swarthout arranged to audition for Herbert Johnson, manager of the Civic Opera. She was given a contract for the next season. Without a single operatic role to her credit, she managed to learn twenty-three roles within a few months. Her debut took place in Chicago during the 1924–1925 season in the part of the offstage shepherd in Puccini's *Tosca.* During the 1924–1929 seasons she sang in fifty-six performances. Swarthout continued to sing with the Chicago Civic Opera during its regular season and in the summers with the Ravinia Opera Company of Chicago.

Swarthout's work attracted the attention of the Metropolitan Opera in New York and eventually led to an engagement with that company. She first appeared with the company on October 29, 1929, in Philadelphia. Her debut at the Metropolitan Opera House in New York City came on November 15, 1929, in the role of LaCieca in *La Gioconda.* Two months later she sang in the American premiere of Rimsky-Korsakov's *Sadko.* Swarthout stayed with the Metropolitan for thirteen seasons. During that time she sang a total of twenty-four roles in twenty-one different works. The number of performances came to 264.

Although Swarthout performed many different roles, she was best known for her portrayal of Carmen in Bizet's opera of the same name. Her talents as an actress and singer were broad. While playing Carmen in 1942 before forty thousand people in Chicago's Soldier Field, she was "spurned" with such gusto during the love quarrel scene that she was knocked unconscious. In 1948 in the same role, she accidentally stabbed another Metropolitan star in the wrist.

Swarthout gained national and world fame not only in the realm of opera but also on national radio and in motion pictures. She made her first radio appearance on the *General Motors Hour* in 1930. She was also heard on such major programs as *The Ford Symphony.* For three years she was the star on her own show, *The Prudential Family Hour.* American and Canadian critics for five consecutive years voted her the leading female classical singer to perform on radio. Arturo Toscanini selected her to sing Juliet in his NBC radio production of Berlioz's *Romeo and Juliet* on New Year's Day in 1950. In 1936 she went to Hollywood where she was cast in five motion pictures. Like so many other opera stars who appeared in movies these pictures were disappointments. The first, *Rose of the Rancho* (1936), was judged fair. In the last, *Ambush* (1939), she had only a speaking role and did not sing.

Swarthout married Harry Richmond Kern on March 22, 1925, but he died six years later. In 1932 she wed Frank Chapman Jr., a concert baritone who continued his singing career for a time but eventually became her manager and directed her career.

Throughout her career, Swarthout recorded extensively for RCA-Victor Records. In 1943 she published a "career book," *Come Soon, Tomorrow.* Among her many honors, she was the first woman member of the honorary music fraternity Mu Pi

Delta and was awarded an honorary degree, doctor of music, from the Bush Conservatory. Probably the greatest honor conferred on the Missouri-born mezzo-soprano occurred on the 150th anniversary of the federal legislature when she sang before the president, the Supreme Court, the entire Congress, and the diplomatic corps.

A heart attack forced Swarthout to retire completely in 1954. She moved to Florence, Italy, and she died there on July 7, 1969.

ALFRED E. TWOMEY

Ewen, David. *Music and Musicians since 1900.* New York: H. W. Wilson, 1978.

Rasponi, Lanfranco. *The Last Prima Donnas.* New York: Knopf, 1983.

Swarthout, Gladys. *Come Soon, Tomorrow: The Story of a Young Singer.* New York: Dodd, Mead, 1943.

SWEETS, NATHANIEL ALLEN, SR. (1901–1988)

Born on September 23, 1901, in Appleton, Missouri, Nathaniel Sweets was the youngest of seventeen children born to freed slaves Pete and Hannah Sweets. He received his high school and college education in Jefferson City at the Lincoln High School and Lincoln University. After his graduation in 1928, and at the recommendation of Lincoln University's president, **Nathan B. Young,** Sweets took the position of advertising and business manager of the newly founded *St. Louis American,* a weekly newspaper serving the black community. By 1933 he owned the paper, and he and his wife, Melba, fashioned it into a leading voice for civil rights, fair housing and employment, and black participation in politics.

As an advocate for African Americans in Missouri and elsewhere, Sweets joined a small delegation that met with Illinois governor Adlai E. Stevenson in 1952 when Stevenson ran for president on the Democratic ticket. Sweets and the others recommended Stevenson to black voters because he had promised full employment, full educational opportunities, and full black participation in all phases of American life.

Sweets was active in a number of civic projects and fought for improved race relations in St. Louis. In 1948 he served as vice president of a citizens committee for a $16 million slum-clearance bond issue. In 1950 he editorialized against a city-charter proposal because it failed to address civil rights issues. "Any charter, drafted during the current nationwide drive for human rights that ignores the Negro's plea for the right to be treated as a first-class citizen, ought to be defeated," he wrote. The charter was defeated. In 1951 and 1952 Sweets served on the Mayor's Council on Human Relations and the Police Relief

and Retirement Board. He failed in his attempts to be elected to the St. Louis Board of Aldermen in 1947 and in 1959.

As a graduate of Lincoln University, Sweets was one of its biggest boosters, especially during critical times. The *St. Louis American* frequently called attention to political interference in Lincoln University's management. Sweets also criticized the "makeshift," "illegal," and "fraudulent" underfinancing of facilities at Lincoln. He frequently spoke out against these educational inequities, both as an alumnus and as president of the school's national alumni association.

Beginning in 1968 the *St. Louis American* sponsored a summer-long festival of ragtime music produced in St. Louis between 1895 and 1915. Before the Black Expos that began during the 1970s, Sweets hosted annually what he called the *St. Louis American* Home Show and Cooking School. It included an entertainment segment as well as a portion where representatives of area companies demonstrated various products.

In 1981 Sweets retired and sold the *St. Louis American.* After a prolonged illness he died on October 10, 1988. Throughout his adult life, Nathaniel Allen Sweets Sr. exemplified the motto that graced the masthead of the early *St. Louis American:* "Christianity, Opportunity, Liberty."

ANTONIO F. HOLLAND AND DEBRA F. GREENE

Encyclopedia of Black America. S.v. "Sweets, Nathaniel Allen."

Lincoln Collection. *Lincoln University Bulletin, 1949–1950.* Jefferson City, Mo.: Lincoln University Press, 1951.

Quill 1928. Jefferson City, Mo.: Hugh Stephens Press, 1928.

Sweets, Nathaniel A. Papers. Lincoln Collection. Inman E. Page Library, Lincoln University, Jefferson City, Mo.

SWITZLER, WILLIAM FRANKLIN (1819–1906)

William Franklin Switzler, a journalist, politician, and historian, was born on March 16, 1819, in Fayette County, Kentucky. The eldest of two sons of Simeon and Elizabeth Cornelius Switzler, he migrated with his family to central Missouri in 1826, where they eventually settled on a farm in Howard County, near Franklin. After attending Mount Forest Academy, he undertook semiformal legal study in 1839–1840 with prominent attorneys **Abiel Leonard** and Joseph Davis. In 1841 he moved to Columbia to continue his studies with Leonard's old student **James Sidney Rollins,** a rising Whig politician. Although Switzler was admitted to the bar in 1842, he was never truly "called" and gave up all pretense of legal practice by 1845. On August 31, 1843, he married Mary Jane Royall. They subsequently had two sons and a daughter.

Switzler lost interest in the law because he found his true vocation in journalism. Through his mentor Rollins, a co-owner of the *Columbia Whig,* Switzler became interested in reporting. Although Rollins sold his interest in the publication in 1840, Switzler remained involved, and the following year he became its editor and purchased a half-interest in the paper. In late 1842 he became its sole proprietor and in early 1843 changed its name to the *Missouri Statesman.* Switzler would eventually find fame as a newspaperman. Although he was noted for his partisan editorial stance, he was equally noted for his fairness and accuracy in reporting the news, and he acquired an influence that transcended the central-Missouri community he purported to serve. In the years after the Civil War he came to be regarded as the dean of Missouri's journalists.

Switzler was not only a newspaperman but also an educational and civic promoter. He helped found Christian College, a school for women, in 1851 as well as Baptist (later Stephens) College in 1856, and worked tirelessly on behalf of the University of Missouri as a longtime member of its board of curators. If James Rollins was the university's acknowledged father, then Switzler was its uncle. In 1909, three years after his death, the first building constructed for the University of Missouri School of Journalism was christened Switzler Hall. Switzler also helped found Columbia's first public library, headed the local lyceum, strongly encouraged new agricultural advances, and was a passionate temperance advocate, especially as a young man. He was, moreover, an articulate speaker who was frequently called upon to address community gatherings about worthy causes and commemorative holidays.

Switzler's Whig partisanship extended to active politics, and he won three terms as the state representative from Boone County in 1846, 1848, and 1856. He took a particular interest in economic development, internal improvements, and the support of education. He strongly opposed the successful effort to tighten the slave codes to forbid the teaching of slaves to read and write and the requirement that whites be present at all slave worship services. A conservative but ardent Unionist, Switzler attended the National Constitutional Union Convention in Baltimore in 1860 and supported John Bell for president. In 1863 President Abraham Lincoln appointed Switzler as secretary of state for the provisional government of Arkansas. Despite the favoritism shown him, Switzler strongly disapproved of repressive federal measures in Missouri, and supported Democrat George McClellan for president in 1864. Elected as a delegate to Missouri's 1865 Constitutional Convention, Switzler despised the document produced by the Radical Republicans who dominated the convention and actively campaigned against it, as he did the subsequent harsh measures applied against those considered sympathetic to the South.

In 1866 and 1868 Switzler received the majority of votes in U.S. congressional races, but each time a politically corrupt Missouri secretary of state threw out sufficient votes to give his victory to his Republican opponent. Although upon appeal a congressional committee found in his favor on each occasion, the Republican-dominated House eventually seated his opponents. In 1875, with Missouri Republican rule ended, Switzler was elected to the Constitutional Convention of 1875, at which he chaired the education committee.

During the 1870s and 1880s Switzler turned to history writing. Among his works are *Early History of Missouri* (1872), the lengthy historical section in C. R. Barn's *Commonwealth of Missouri* (1877), *Switzler's Illustrated History of Missouri* (1879), and *History of Boone County* (1882). In 1885 President Grover Cleveland appointed him the chief of the Bureau of Statistics, a division of the Treasury Department. In 1888 he produced *History of Statistics and Their Value.* Upon his return to Missouri he briefly edited newspapers in St. Joseph, Chillicothe, and from 1893 to 1898 in Boonville, but finally resettled in Columbia. He was at work on a book-length history of the University of Missouri when he died on May 24, 1906.

KENNETH H. WINN

Hall, Elizabeth Dorsett. "William Franklin Switzler: Editor, Politician, and Humanitarian." Master's thesis, University of Missouri, 1951.

Lyon, William H. *The Pioneer Editor in Missouri, 1808–1860.* Columbia: University of Missouri Press, 1965.

SWOPE, THOMAS HUNTON (1827–1909)

Thomas Hunton Swope, a real estate developer and philanthropist in Kansas City, was born on October 21, 1827, in Lincoln County, Kentucky. After graduating from Centre College in Danville, Kentucky, in 1848, Swope earned a law degree from Yale but never practiced that profession. Instead, he moved west to try his hand at urban land speculation, arriving in Kansas City, Missouri, in 1856, where he purchased some thirty acres south of the original town site in what became the central business district. Within months he received offers of $300 per town lot on land that originally cost him $250 per acre. As the value of Swope's real estate additions soared in coming years, he poured the profits into acquisition of more landholdings in and around the city. Not content merely to wait for rising land prices, Swope strove to encourage the market. He helped organize the city's original chamber of commerce, participated in railroad promotions with the rest of the local business elite, and took the honorific title "colonel" to denote his status.

In 1859 a Kansas City newspaper listed Swope as one of the ten richest men in town, with property worth more than ten thousand dollars. Regarded in his lifetime as a farsighted entrepreneur for having anticipated the city's southward development, Swope often remarked that he had grown rich in spite of himself. He had sold much of his early land acquisitions cheaply and later had to repurchase them at much higher prices when the city's commercial center expanded. Two of the lots that eventually netted him enormous rents he had retained only because they had seemed too rugged for construction sites. His sizable fortune owed largely to luck, Swope claimed.

However he had acquired it, Swope reportedly took little pleasure in his wealth. Bookish and delicate as a youth, the adult Swope initially attended the fashionable parties in Kansas City but refused either to court or to dance with the young ladies present. Instead, he worked unceasingly to extend his real estate holdings and slipped into a reclusive, eccentric solitude, spending his little free time medicating himself for dyspepsia. Even his philanthropies he carried out almost in secret. Yet, notoriety would surround the retiring millionaire in his later years.

Unwelcome public notice began in 1893 when civic reformers proposed an ambitious plan to beautify the city with parks and boulevards. Because the project was to be paid for partly by taxes on vacant real estate parcels, of which Swope owned many, he actively opposed the plan. The *Kansas City Star* excoriated him as a greedy mossback who sat by "evading taxes, fighting progress, and getting rich." After voters approved the plan, Swope donated a parcel of 1,334 acres to the city in 1896 for use as a public park. He probably hoped that his generous gift, still one of the largest urban parks in the nation, would slake the public's desire for recreation grounds and put an end to the costlier proposals. Nonetheless, eighteen thousand Kansas Citians attended the opening day for Swope Park to hear two hours of speeches hailing his benefactions while the colonel wandered anonymously among the crowd. Meanwhile, landscape designer **George Kessler** redesigned the proposed system to incorporate Swope Park as the principal jewel in a necklace of parks and boulevards, thus making the system still more attractive to the electorate. In 1900 the antipark mossbacks admitted defeat, and Kansas City proceeded with construction of one of the finest examples of the City Beautiful movement

in the country. And Thomas Swope became a hero of the parks movement in spite of himself.

Still more notoriety followed Swope's death. The bachelor millionaire's will provided amply for his nieces and nephews, but he reserved the bulk of his estate for dispersal to charity during his lifetime. Any of these funds not yet distributed at the time of his death would revert to his heirs. So matters stood when Swope died on October 3, 1909, apparently a victim of his chronic dyspepsia. Three months later, however, Bennett Clark Hyde, a physician and the husband of a Swope niece, was indicted for murdering Swope. According to the charges, Hyde first dispatched Col. Moss Hunton, Swope's business manager and the executor of Swope's will, by bleeding him to death while treating him for a stroke. Hyde next poisoned Thomas Swope with cyanide, the indictment held, and then tried to do away with the other heirs by introducing typhoid bacilli to the family's water supply. Hyde stood trial for only Thomas Swope's murder. Seven years and three trials resulted in one guilty verdict set aside on appeal, a mistrial, and a hung jury. In 1934 Hyde died in relative obscurity in Lexington, Missouri, where he had maintained an unremarkable medical practice.

Sherry Lamb Schirmer

Garwood, Darrell. *Crossroads of America: The Story of Kansas City.* New York: W. W. Norton, 1948.

Swope, Thomas H. Native Sons Archives. Microfilm Roll 12, Book 1, Missouri Valley Room, Kansas City Public Library, Kansas City.

Whitney, Carrie Westlake. *Kansas City, Missouri: Its History and Its People, 1800–1908.* Vol. 2. Chicago: S. J. Clarke, 1908.

Wilson, William H. *The City Beautiful Movement in Kansas City.* Columbia: University of Missouri Press, 1964.

SYLVESTER, FREDERICK OAKES (1869–1915)

During his relatively brief life, Frederick Oakes Sylvester was known as the poet-painter of the Mississippi. That sobriquet is now rarely used, for Sylvester's reputation rests at this time primarily and almost exclusively on the ageless beauty of his paintings alone. His poetry, overladen with Victorian imagery, has fallen into a gentle oblivion. However, his paintings have not received that same fate, and they have achieved an ever increasing appreciation and desirability by an ever expanding public. His reputation is no longer confined by a naive regionalism that had at one time been assumed to be the raison d'être of his fame. His work is justly known and sought far beyond the confines of the St. Louis and Elsah, Illinois, areas where they were produced.

Sylvester was not a native to St. Louis nor even to Missouri. He was born on October 8, 1869, in what is now Brockton, Massachusetts, into a family that traced its roots to the 1620 immigration of the Soule, Alden, and Standish families. His training in the fine arts was acquired at the Massachusetts Normal School in Boston, and he completed the prescribed six-year course in just three years. Except for a trip to Italy in 1906 for further study, these were the only years of formal training that he received.

Sylvester first moved to New Orleans where he had his initial contact with the Mississippi and then to St. Louis, arriving in that city in 1892, in order to teach art at Central High School and at the Principia, a private school operated by the Christian Scientists. He was to remain in St. Louis and Elsah until his death in 1915, at the age of forty-five.

Whereas every artist of note has a unique and identifiable style, Sylvester's works contain the additional stylistic depiction of a transcendental ideal. He portrayed not just the river, its bluffs, and the sky above. He created a mass of work that conveyed his most idealized interpretation of the actual physical world that intruded upon his utopian longings for a world of simplicity and serenity.

Sylvester's work is easily divisible into two periods. Prior to his discovery of the idyllic village of Elsah in the summer of 1902, he painted the realistic, industrialized, and utilitarian levees and factories of the St. Louis riverfront. There was no hint of idealization of the subject matter, nor was there any attempt to beautify that which was not. He painted in the mildly postimpressionistic fashion that was then favored by a majority of native American artists.

After 1902 Sylvester continued to paint in that same postimpressionistic fashion, but his subject matter became the antithesis of his earlier work. The content of his work changed abruptly from the depiction of industrialization to the depiction of a bucolic calm in an Arcadian setting. There had been no evolution of Sylvester's work. His change of subject matter had occurred with suddenness and finality. Henceforward, he would paint only his interpretation of perfection. In that interpretation there was no place for the appearance of man or his machines.

Sylvester had an almost mystical attachment to the Mississippi. His entire artistic life had been determined by his association with the river. When he became aware of its primal beauty at Elsah, he used it as a metaphor for the eternal quest of man in his pursuit of perfection. In that quest there could be no distractions; those distractions were the accoutrements of mankind. He simply refused to accept their existence and subsequently refused to portray them.

Sylvester's Elsah paintings are a beautiful depiction of an unsullied Eden. They convey a beauty so transcendent and so purified of reality that metaphorically they embrace not only man's quest for perfection but the possibility of his actually achieving that goal as well.

Sylvester died on March 2, 1915, in St. Louis, probably of tuberculosis. He had been ill for the few years prior to his death, and the gradual change in the tonalities of his paintings tell us of his knowledge of his impending demise. His early Elsah works were canvases of color, vibrant and dramatic. He had maintained that palette until 1911, when there appears a slow but progressive change in tone. The last portrayals of his beloved Mississippi were somber and elegiac. Nonetheless, the grandeur of the river, the bluffs, and the sky with its huge billowing clouds were still present, and even in their muted portrayal they convey to us Sylvester's love of perfection.

Frederick O. Sylvester's ashes were strewn on the river that he so loved. He had become one with his transcendent ideal.

THOMAS E. MORRISSEY

Morrissey, Thomas E. "Frederick Oakes Sylvester: Transcendental Regionalist." *Gateway Heritage* 8 (summer 1987): 12–19.

SYMINGTON, WILLIAM STUART (1901–1988)

William Stuart Symington III, the first secretary of the United States Air Force and four-term senator from Missouri (1953–1976), was born on June 26, 1901, in Amherst, Massachusetts, where his father, William Stuart Symington, was a professor of foreign languages at Amherst College. His mother, Emily Harrison Symington, was a direct descendant of the Benjamin Harrison who signed the Declaration of Independence, and of the same family as Presidents **William Henry Harrison** and Benjamin Harrison. Stuart's grandfather, also named William Stuart Symington, served as an officer in the Confederate army during the Civil War. Stuart never used the designation "III" after his name or "William" and ultimately abandoned the use of the initial "W."

Professor Symington, deciding that he could not support his growing family—Stuart was the eldest of six children—on a professor's salary, resigned to study law. After completing his law degree at New York University, he took his family to Baltimore where he had grown up and where most of his brothers were in business. He became prominent in Baltimore's public life, serving as a judge at the time of his death, but his law practice provided few financial rewards. This, combined with some unfortunate business ventures, resulted in a life that varied from modest affluence to genteel poverty.

Stuart attended private and public schools in Baltimore. Upon graduation in the spring of 1918, he entered officers' training and when commissioned was the youngest second lieutenant in the army—he had lied about his age to get in. His commission came after the armistice, so he was mustered out without seeing service beyond training. In the fall of 1919 he enrolled at Yale University, where he received an A.B. degree. In 1924 he married Evelyn Wadsworth, the daughter of Sen. James Wadsworth of New York and granddaughter of John Hay. They had two sons, William Stuart Symington IV and James Wadsworth Symington. The latter represented Missouri's Second District in Congress from 1969 to 1977.

Symington's first job after college was as an iron molder in one of his uncle's factories in Rochester, New York. He soon moved into executive ranks, and held a succession of managerial positions in his uncles' various manufacturing companies in Rochester, Buffalo, and Baltimore. He became president of Colonial Radio Company, moving to New York City, where he sold that business (at a substantial profit) and took over the presidency of the Rustless Iron and Steel Company. He developed a reputation as a manager who could turn failing businesses into profitable enterprises. Stuart and Evelyn Symington were also very much a part of New York's "café society" in the 1930s, and Eve, as she was called, gained fame as a society nightclub singer.

In 1938 Symington became president of the Emerson Electric Company, a manufacturer of electric fans and small electric motors in St. Louis. The company had just gone through a bitter fifty-three-day sit-down strike—the longest to that date in American history—and was close to bankruptcy. In a relatively short time Symington restored Emerson to profitability, and began to develop a reputation as one of the nation's most promising young business executives. Part of his reputation came as the result of his innovative and highly successful labor relations, though many of his associates in St. Louis thought he was too liberal. The War Department asked him to go to England in the spring of 1941 to study the manufacture of movable gun turrets for use on bombardment aircraft, and Emerson became the largest manufacturer of gun turrets in the United States. The company won five "E's" for excellence during the war, a record number.

Symington became well acquainted with Sen. **Harry S. Truman** in connection with the latter's investigation of the defense effort. Although he was not a strong Roosevelt supporter—he had voted for Willkie in 1940—his political affiliations were essentially Democratic, and he helped Truman in his campaign for the vice presidency in 1944, working especially with John W. Snyder, the St. Louis banker who was one of Truman's closest friends. After Truman became president he asked Symington to take over the disposition of the billions of dollars of surplus property the government had accumulated during the war. As chairman of the Surplus Property Board and then as head of the Surplus Property Administration (when the board was replaced with a single administrator), Symington developed policies to govern disposal, while the Reconstruction Finance Corporation (RFC) and other agencies administered actual disposal. He worked effectively to reduce monopolies in various industries and was especially successful in helping create competition in the aluminum industry.

When the War Assets Administration took over surplus-property disposal late in 1946, President Truman appointed Symington as assistant secretary of war for air, in which post he represented the War Department in the complicated and often acrimonious interservice negotiations that accompanied Truman's efforts to bring about the unification of the armed services through the creation of a single Department of Defense. He deserves much of the credit for the establishment of a separate air force as coequal with the army and the navy.

On September 18, 1947, President Truman appointed Symington as the first secretary of the air force. His tenure was controversial from the beginning, as he battled to advance the air force as the nation's first line of defense. In particular, his efforts to build the air force to Seventy-Group strength, an idea pushed by air force planners from the end of World War II, came into conflict with the concern of his longtime friend Secy. of Defense James Forrestal that a balanced strength be achieved among the army, the navy, and the air force. Symington also found himself at odds with the president's desire to reduce defense spending as much as possible. He resigned in 1950, in part as a protest against inadequate support for the air force and in part because of disagreements with Louis Johnson, who had succeeded Forrestal as secretary of defense.

President Truman, not wanting to lose Symington from his administration, appointed him as chairman of the National Security Resources Board (NSRB), giving him the responsibility for mobilizing homefront resources for the Korean War, a position that was characterized as one of the most important in Washington. As the functions of the NSRB were taken over by other agencies, Truman appointed Symington as administrator of the RFC. Symington moved quickly to reform the "scandal-ridden" RFC in preparation for phasing it out of existence. That job finished, he resigned in January 1952 "to get a little rest." During the past seven years he had held five appointive positions that required senatorial confirmation, and in each case he had been confirmed unanimously. He had become known as "Truman's Trouble Shooter." The president recognized his achievements by awarding him the Distinguished Service Medal.

Symington's first thought was to return to business. At the insistence of friends in St. Louis, however, he became a candidate for the Democratic nomination for U.S. senator. He faced an uphill fight, because his good friend Harry Truman, long before Symington announced his candidacy, had endorsed Atty. Gen. J. E. "Buck" Taylor. Nonetheless, with the aid of his attractive family, who campaigned with him all over the state, and with the active support of many young Democrats who wanted to break the domination of the old Pendergast machine in Missouri politics, Symington won the nomination by a two-to-one margin. In the general election, with Truman's enthusiastic endorsement, he easily defeated Sen. **James P. Kem,** running for reelection, even though Eisenhower carried the state in the presidential campaign.

Symington immediately assumed a position of leadership in the Senate. From the beginning he was recognized as probably the Senate's best-informed member on matters of national defense. As a member of the Armed Services Committee, he frequently criticized the Eisenhower administration's tendency to put a balanced budget ahead of the nation's defense needs. After the Soviet Union launched the *Sputnik* satellite in 1957, Symington was appointed chairman of a subcommittee to investigate the preparedness of the air force, and in that role he was largely responsible for creating the idea of the missile gap in the nation's position vis-à-vis the Soviet Union. Senators Lyndon Johnson and John F. Kennedy strongly supported Symington's position, and Kennedy used it in his campaign for the presidency in 1960, though the "missile gap" was later demonstrated to have been an exaggeration.

As a member of the Committee on Government Operations, Symington achieved national recognition for his vigorous opposition to Sen. Joseph McCarthy in the televised Army-McCarthy hearings, though critics complained that he was slow to challenge McCarthy. He served on the Committee on Foreign Relations as well as on the Armed Services Committee—the only person in the Senate to be a member of both committees at the same time. He also served on the Aeronautical and Space Sciences Committee. In his second term he became a member of the Democratic Policy Committee and the Agriculture and Forestry Committee where he was a highly vocal critic of Eisenhower's farm policies.

Although he did not think of himself as a liberal, Symington was regarded as one of the most liberal members of the Senate: Americans for Democratic Action repeatedly listed him as voting the "liberal position" 100 percent of the time. He consistently cast prolabor votes, and was recognized as one of the Senate's most "pro–civil rights" members. His support of labor and civil rights positions conformed to his earlier attitudes as president of Emerson Electric Company, where he had worked cooperatively with organized labor and desegregated the company's operations. He was also largely responsible for the effective way in which the air force carried out President Truman's order to desegregate the armed services.

In 1956 the Democratic Party in Missouri put Stuart Symington forward as a "favorite son" candidate for president. When it appeared that there might be a long, drawn-out battle between Adlai Stevenson and Estes Kefauver for the nomination, Democrats outside Missouri began to express an interest in Symington as an alternative, but he indicated that he had no interest in becoming a candidate for either president or vice president. In 1960, however, he became an active candidate, though he did not enter the presidential primaries. He had strong support from organized labor and civil rights groups, plus the endorsement of former president Truman. He reasoned that Kennedy and Johnson, the two leading candidates, would neutralize each other and the convention would turn to him. Kennedy's relatively easy victory in the convention, of course, prevented this from transpiring. There was strong support in the Kennedy camp for Symington as the vice presidential nominee—and there is some evidence that Kennedy actually offered the post to him—but in the end the position went to Lyndon Johnson as a means of securing support for the ticket in Texas. Symington campaigned actively for Kennedy, and, at the candidate's request, headed a committee to make recommendations for the reorganization of the Department of Defense, which, though highly publicized, were little followed by the new administration.

As the years wore on Symington became increasingly concerned about the costs of maintaining the country's commitments abroad, both foreign aid and military. At the beginning of the Vietnam War, he supported the administration's position, but trips to Vietnam and intense study of the situation convinced him that the war could not be won as it was being pursued, and in 1967 he announced his opposition to continuing, thus creating an irreparable break with President Johnson, a longtime close personal and political friend. Symington spoke out frequently against the war. He played a major role in exposing and ending the secret bombing of Cambodia that the Nixon administration had conducted from 1969 to 1971. He became a strong advocate of arms control and of measures to prevent nuclear proliferation.

Symington remained highly popular in Missouri throughout his senatorial career, even though many Missourians disapproved of his liberal voting record and his positions on such matters as arms control and the Vietnam War, and despite the fact that he was always something of an outsider: when he first announced his candidacy for the Senate, he had been a resident of Missouri for only fourteen years, seven of which had been spent in Washington, and he had never been to Jefferson City. Moreover, his elegant good looks, his custom-tailored clothes, and his urbane manner hardly fit the mold of the conventional Missouri politician. Yet, he became the quintessential Missouri statesman, second only to Harry Truman as *the* man from Missouri. Part of the reason for his popularity is that Missourians were proud of the tall, handsome man who represented them in the Senate with such style; part of it derives from the recognition that Stuart Symington—aided by his legendary administrative assistant, Stanley Fike— could get things done for Missouri. Communities and institutions in all parts of the state can point to federally aided projects that were made possible by influence from Senator Symington's office. Among the most prominent examples of his influence are the Jefferson Expansion National Memorial, with its monumental Gateway Arch, in St. Louis, and the Royals baseball team in Kansas City.

Symington easily won reelection each time he ran, always leading the ticket, but in 1970 his margin of victory over Atty. Gen. John Danforth, while still comfortable, was considerably smaller than that achieved in earlier elections. Although it was generally assumed that he would run for a fifth term in 1976, on April 22, 1975, he announced that he would not seek reelection. He cited the death of his wife, Eve (of a heart attack on December 24, 1972), as a major factor in his decision. Others also suggested that in the face of a resurgent Republican Party in Missouri,

he realized that he might have difficulty defeating Danforth in a second match. After Danforth won the Senate seat, Symington, despite the bitterly personal campaign Danforth had waged in 1970, in a typically gracious act, resigned a few days early so that the new senator could achieve a degree of seniority over others who had been newly elected in 1976.

After his retirement Symington continued to live in Washington. In 1978 he married Ann Watson, the widow of Arthur K. Watson, the chairman of the IBM World Trade Corporation and former ambassador to France, and moved to New Canaan, Connecticut. He died in his sleep at his home in New Canaan on December 14, 1988. He was buried beside his first wife in a crypt in the National Cathedral in Washington.

JAMES C. OLSON

Emerson Electric Company: A Century of Manufacturing, 1890–1990. St. Louis: Emerson Electric, 1989.

Martin, Ralph G., and Ed Plaut. *Front Runner, Dark Horse.* Garden City, N.Y.: Doubleday, 1960.

Symington, Stuart. Papers. Harry S. Truman Library, Independence, Mo.

———. Papers. Western Historical Manuscripts Collection, Columbia.

Watson, George W. *The Office of the Secretary of the Air Force, 1947–1965.* Washington, D.C.: U.S. Government Printing Office, 1993.

Wellman, Paul I. *Stuart Symington: Portrait of a Man with a Mission.* Garden City, N.Y.: Doubleday, 1960.

T

TALLEY, MARION (1907–1983)

Marion Talley was born on December 20, 1907, in Nevada, Missouri, the daughter of a Missouri Pacific Railroad telegraph operator who was later transferred to Kansas City, Missouri. Early on she demonstrated a love for and interest in music. She pestered her parents for music lessons and, as a child, was given instruction in piano and singing. While still quite young she persuaded her mother, Florence, who sang in church choirs in northeast Kansas City, to allow her to join in and sing. She quickly became a church soloist whose singing received a favorable notice from other choir members and from local music critics. She saved the money she received from these performances to pay for further study.

In 1922, at the age of fifteen, Talley caused a sensation when she sang in a Kansas City performance of Ambroise Thomas's opera *Migon.* The concert drew more than two thousand Kansas City residents who had taken an interest in her career and contributed ten thousand dollars to fund further study for her in New York and abroad. The following year, 1923, she went to New York to audition at the Metropolitan Opera. The audition received widespread press coverage. Critics called her voice exceptional. Although the audition did not produce a contract with the Metropolitan, Talley remained in New York to study with the famous voice teacher Frank LaForge, and later she continued her study in Europe.

Talley's great opportunity arrived in the winter of 1925–1926, when Giulio Gatti-Casazza, the general manager of the Metropolitan Opera Company, engaged the nineteen-year-old Kansas Citian to sing with the company in New York. Her professional debut was as Gilda in Verdi's *Rigoletto* on February 17, 1926. Gatti-Casazza had wanted Talley's debut to be unheralded, but loyal Kansas City citizens and civic organizations decided otherwise. They generated an extraordinary amount of interest and publicity. A large delegation, including the mayor and various civic officials, traveled by special train from Kansas City to New York to attend the performance. Four-dollar tickets were scalped for ten times their cost. A telegraph was set up backstage at the Metropolitan Opera so her father could report news of the event to people in Kansas City and nationwide. Although the friendly audience awarded numerous curtain calls, her performance did not live up to the expectations created by all the publicity.

Her career at the Metropolitan lasted for only four seasons (1926–1929). During that time she appeared in only seven productions and gave a total of eighty-four performances. In addition to Gilda in *Rigoletto,* she also created the roles of the Queen of the Night in Mozart's *Die Zauberflöte,* Donizetti's Lucia in *Lucia di Lammermoor,* and the Nightingale in Stravinsky's *Le Rossignol.*

Upon her retirement from the Metropolitan Opera Talley announced she intended to take up farming in Kansas, but that plan never materialized. In 1933 she returned to the concert stage and also sang with the Chicago Opera without much success in either venture. In 1936 she began singing on the radio and was given a series on the NBC network. That same year she made her only film, *Follow Your Heart,* a musical set in the pre–Civil War era that proved disappointing. In 1940 Talley attempted a return to grand opera, but it failed to revive her career.

Talley married twice. Her first marriage in 1932 to a German pianist was annulled after only a few months. In 1935 she married the New York music critic Adolf Eckstrom, and they had a daughter. When their marriage failed, Talley sued Eckstrom for custody of their daughter in 1939. The ensuing custody battle was bitter and generated a great deal of publicity. Following the dispute, which she won, Talley gradually sank into obscurity. On January 3, 1983, she died in a southern California hospital. Her death went unrecorded in the trade newspapers. It was as the youngest prima donna in the Metropolitan Opera history probably would have wanted it.

ALFRED E. TWOMEY

Bakers Biographical Dictionary of Musicians. S.v. "Talley, Marion."
International Encyclopedia of Music and Musicians. S.v. "Talley, Marion."

TANDY, CHARLTON H. (1836–1919)

Charlton H. Tandy, an outspoken leader of the nineteenth-century black civil rights movement, was born in Lexington, Kentucky, on December 16, 1836. Although little is known concerning his childhood, historians are aware that he and his family were involved in the Underground Railroad, assisting slaves fleeing from Covington, Kentucky, to freedom in Cincinnati, Ohio. Upon reaching adulthood, Tandy migrated to St. Louis in 1857 in search of greater opportunities and new experiences. He quickly secured employment as a waiter and later as a porter and a coachman for a local white family. Two years later he married Missouri Bell, the daughter of Proctor and Senia Bell, and settled down to begin a family.

The Civil War disrupted the Tandy household. In response to **Thomas C. Fletcher**'s call for volunteers, in 1864 Tandy enthusiastically enlisted as a private in Company B of the Thirteenth Regiment of the Missouri Volunteers. He and his unit engaged Gen. **Sterling Price** and his forces when they returned to Missouri in 1864. By the conclusion of the war Tandy had risen to the rank of captain.

Following the Civil War Tandy spent much of his time and his resources aggressively advocating equal rights for freedmen in St. Louis. Because of his outspoken nature, education, and charisma, he, along with other African Americans such as **James Milton Turner**, became a leader within the St. Louis black community. For example, in the fall of 1865 Tandy helped organize "Missouri's first black political movement," the Missouri Equal Rights League. This group gave voice to the black demand for political rights and pressured the state government to endorse suffrage and complete political rights for freedmen.

Unlike some Missouri blacks during the immediate postbellum period, Tandy supported the Liberal Republican faction headed by **B. Gratz Brown** rather than the Radical Republicans headed by **Joseph W. McClurg**. In 1870 Tandy helped organize Liberal Republican clubs and urged blacks to vote for gubernatorial candidate Brown. In exchange for Liberal successes at the polls, the Republicans rewarded Tandy with desirable patronage positions that included chief messenger of U.S. Customs, deputy city collector, and deputy marshal.

However, Tandy's relationship with the city's Liberal leaders was not always cordial. By the late 1870s he and other black leaders argued that the St. Louis Republican machine had failed to commit itself completely to black equality. For example, in 1879 Tandy emphasized that the Republicans had not adequately acknowledged the value of blacks' support by either integrating them into the party machinery or dispensing to them a fair share of patronage positions. He argued that though black votes had led to Republican successes, African Americans occupied only two seats on the Republican Central Committee. Tandy warned Republican leaders that if they failed to take black civil rights seriously, African American voters would leave the Republican fold. In response to Tandy and other black critics, a number of outraged white Republicans publicly stated that they "would not be dictated to by any damned nigger." These

struggles continued throughout the remainder of the nineteenth century.

During the post–Civil War years Tandy pursued the quest for black equality in other important ways. For instance, in the late 1870s thousands of black refugees know as "exodusters" fled the oppressiveness of Southern existence in search of new lives in Kansas. In the fall of 1879 large numbers of destitute black men, women, and children suffering from malnutrition and fatigue gathered in St. Louis unable to continue their journey. Tandy and other St. Louis black leaders, having failed to obtain sufficient assistance from local white authorities, quickly organized their own relief effort. Tandy and his associates assisted the exodusters in securing employment and arranging for food, clothing, medical care, and shelter. They also financed the remainder of their journey to Kansas. Afterward, Tandy traveled to Washington, D.C., where he spoke about the racist conditions that had motivated this black migration as well as the urgent need for federal aid to assist future waves of black refugees.

In the late 1860s and early 1870s Tandy helped organize boycotts of St. Louis's segregated street railways. He also participated in acts of civil disobedience such as sitting in the white sections of streetcars. On several occasions he was arrested, only to be bailed out hours later by white Republican friends. Tandy also fought for better education for African Americans in St. Louis and was one of the early promoters of Lincoln Institute in Jefferson City, Missouri. Although he was often overshadowed by other Missouri black leaders such as Turner, Tandy was a major force behind the black struggle for civil rights in St. Louis. He continued this important work until he died on September 1, 1919.

CHRISTOPHER K. HAYS

Black History Collection. 1911–1983. Western Historical Manuscripts Collection, St. Louis.

Tandy, Charlton. Papers. 1868–1967. Western Historical Manuscripts Collection, St. Louis.

TAYLOR, MAXWELL D. (1901–1987)

Maxwell Taylor is one in a trio of outstanding twentieth-century Missouri soldiers. Interestingly, he was born on August 26, 1901, at Keytesville in north-central Missouri, within thirty-five miles of the birthplaces of both **John J. Pershing** and **Omar Nelson Bradley**. An intellectual with a wide-ranging and inquisitive mind, Taylor was the son of John Maxwell Taylor, an attorney, and Pearle Davenport Taylor. His breadth of vision helped create the modern American military with its doctrine of flexible response. His successful career was not, however, without setbacks. Taylor's reasoned, analytical approach to national policy, without reference to political advantage or false economies, cost him the support of powerful figures, including presidents of the United States. Blessed with intelligence, self-assurance, and a liberal dose of Missouri determination, however, Taylor lived to see his convictions substantiated by history.

Taylor, unlike Pershing, never considered any career but the military. Influenced by his grandfather, a Confederate cavalryman, the young boy decided to attend the military academy at West Point and prepared well. At Northeast High School in Kansas City, he excelled in languages and debate. After graduation in 1917 he first attended Kansas City Junior College, then applied and was accepted as a cadet at West Point. Even then, Taylor usually obtained what he wanted.

As a cadet Taylor began a brilliant military career. He made the tennis team, nurtured a remarkable facility for foreign languages, was named captain of the Corps, and finished fourth in the class of 1922. He was also the youngest graduating cadet. Like his fellow Missourians Pershing and Bradley, Taylor left no trail of long-remembered exploits along the Hudson; but, also like them, he laid the foundations for a lifetime of achievement. If not as commanding in form as the imposing Pershing, or as beloved as the affable Bradley, Taylor found his strength in his wide knowledge and shrewd insights.

By the time Lieutenant Taylor entered the United States Army in 1922, the forces were experiencing the sharp post–world war cuts that spelled meager advancement and long tours of duty in isolated posts for all officers. Taylor joined the engineers at posts such as Camp Meade in Maryland, Camp Lewis in Washington, and Schofield Barracks in Hawaii. It was unexciting duty, but it brought him friends and colleagues and valuable experience. The year 1925, on the other hand, provided the young officer with sufficient excitement in the form of a bride. He married Lydia Garner Happer of El Paso, and she eventually gave him two sons, John Maxwell and Thomas Happer Taylor.

A stint in Paris in 1927 led to a five-year appointment as an instructor in French and Spanish at West Point. After an abrupt shift to artillery training at Fort Sill came the essential tour at the Command and General Staff School at Fort Leavenworth, Kansas. Without that experience, an officer could not expect advancement to high rank in the United States Army. Naturally, Taylor performed well and was soon on his way to Tokyo in 1935 to study Japanese and to observe conditions in that increasingly militaristic society. He also paid a short visit to Peking, but was back in Washington in 1939 to attend the War College.

War came to Europe again in September 1939, and Taylor was given command of the Twelfth Field Artillery at Fort Sam Houston in 1940. America was hoping to avoid war, but the army had to be prepared. Experienced officers such as Taylor moved up quickly in rank and were tested for higher command. After Pearl Harbor the Missourian was called to Washington to become the chief aide of Gen. Matthew Ridgeway who was fashioning America's first airborne division, the Eighty-second. Promoted to brigadier general, Taylor began to master the demanding fundamentals of airborne operations and assumed command of the division's artillery.

American forces invaded Axis North Africa in late 1942. Success led to the Anglo-American invasion of first Sicily and then Italy in the summer and autumn of 1943. Taylor, fighting with the Eighty-second, caught the attention of superiors and was selected, after volunteering, for a sensitive mission. Along with Col. William Gardiner he landed on the Italian coast in September 1943, made his way to Rome, and consulted with the Badoglio government, which had overthrown the dictator, Mussolini, and secretly surrendered to the Allies. Taylor wanted to determine if an American airborne descent on Rome at the time of a surrender announcement was feasible. He decided it was not, and transmitted that judgment to Gen. Dwight Eisenhower. His action undoubtedly saved the lives of many American troops. The exploit won him the praise of Eisenhower and a Silver Star.

Taylor was by late 1943 a man with an enviable reputation, and it gained him important assignments. Meanwhile, General Eisenhower had been sent to Britain to begin planning the long-awaited Allied invasion of France to liberate Europe from Nazi control. As supreme commander, "Ike" wanted his best men with him in this epochal campaign. Thus, Taylor was called to London and given command of the newly formed 101st Airborne Division, a force that would have a critical role in the coming invasion.

In the early hours of June 6, 1944, D day, Maxwell Taylor parachuted into German-occupied Normandy with the crack troops of the 101st. He was the first American general on French soil that memorable day, and his men performed with valor and distinction. Following the Allied breakout into France later that summer, Taylor's troops took part in the ill-fated Market Garden, the airborne invasion of the Netherlands. Slightly wounded, the general returned to America, but returned in December when the 101st was surrounded at Bastogne during the Battle of the Bulge. Eluding German troops, Taylor rejoined his men and took part in the heroic battle that ended the last German offensive of the war. The 101st went down in history as the "Battling Bastards of Bastogne."

At war's end, Taylor became superintendent at West Point. His four years there were marked by the introduction of a major liberal arts component in the curriculum and a deemphasis on football. The cold war with the Soviet Union soon developed, however, and he returned to Germany as chief of staff of U.S. forces and commandant of the U.S. military government. There followed a tour as deputy chief of staff in Washington when the cold war turned hot in Korea. By 1953 General Taylor had assumed personal command of the United States Eighth Army fighting the North Koreans and Chinese. Stabilizing the front, he could have taken the offensive, but the Eisenhower administration desired a negotiated settlement. In July a truce was signed, and the fighting ceased. Taylor, as Far Eastern commander, and the Eighth Army stayed on, however, to help rebuild South Korea, an effort with long-term results.

In June 1955 Taylor was named army chief of staff and was immediately embroiled in questions of basic U.S. strategy in the face of Soviet nuclear expansion. Differing with Adm. Arthur Radford, the chair of the joint chiefs, and the Eisenhower administration, he rejected massive nuclear retaliation as America's basic reply to possible Soviet aggression and called for a flexible stance that included a large conventional army. Unable to find common ground, he retired in 1959.

Taylor was recalled by President John Kennedy to be his military representative and to overhaul the U.S. intelligence system after the failure of the CIA at the Bay of Pigs. Taylor's book, *The Uncertain Trumpet,* a critical analysis of U.S. policy, influenced Kennedy and led to a reconsideration of U.S. conventional forces. By 1962 Kennedy had named Taylor chairman of the joint chiefs and leaned heavily on him for guidance. After Kennedy's murder, President Lyndon Johnson continued Taylor as his principal military adviser.

As U.S. operations in Vietnam began to expand in 1965, Johnson sent Taylor to Saigon as U.S. ambassador. Taylor had his doubts about the capacity of South Vietnam to defend itself and soon returned to Washington. He remained an adviser to Johnson until 1969, however, and was inevitably associated with the American failure in Southeast Asia, whatever his personal views.

In later years Taylor published updated policy analyses, including *Responsibility and Response* (1967) and *Precarious Security* (1976). His keen mind comprehended the Vietnam experience, and he shrewdly observed, among other things, that the United States should never again ally itself with a government that was either unable or unwilling to make effective use of American assistance. Taylor died at age eighty-five of Lou Gehrig's disease in Washington, D.C., on April 19, 1987, and was interred at Arlington National Cemetery.

Maxwell Taylor's insistence on the maintenance of a credible U.S. conventional force survived the Vietnam debacle and was vindicated in the decades of the 1980s and 1990s when U.S. conventional forces scored impressive victories, especially in the Persian Gulf War. Once again, and as usual, Maxwell Taylor was absolutely correct.

C. DAVID RICE

Current Biography Yearbook. New York: H. W. Wilson, 1961.

Krebs, Albin. "Maxwell D. Taylor, Soldier and Envoy." *New York Times Biographical Service* 18 (January–June 1987): 1–6.

Taylor, Maxwell D. *Precarious Security.* New York: W. W. Norton, 1976.

———. *Responsibility and Response.* New York: Harper and Row, 1967.

———. *The Uncertain Trumpet.* New York: Harper, 1960.

TEASDALE, SARA (1884–1933)

Although Sara Teasdale never became a modernist as did **T. S. Eliot** and **Marianne Moore,** who were, like Teasdale, born in St. Louis in the decade of the 1880s, her work reflected the tensions of the radical changes that occurred in the early twentieth century. As John Gould Fletcher, a winner of the Pulitzer Prize for poetry, noted, Teasdale's poems combined "the quietism of Christina Rossetti and the emotional intensity of Emily Dickinson." This paradoxical combination also expressed the life that led to the writing of her poems.

Born on August 8, 1884, in St. Louis, Teasdale was a late, unexpected child of relatively wealthy parents. Her brother and sister were twenty and seventeen years older than she. Her childhood was one of indulgence tempered by the rigorous morality of her parents and shaped by her own physical frailty. Throughout her life she experienced various and recurrent physical ailments. She graduated in 1903 from Hosmer Hall in St. Louis, where one of her classmates was **Zoë Byrd Akins,** the winner of the Pulitzer Prize for drama in 1935 for *The Old Maid.*

Although she and Akins were never close, Teasdale had friendships in St. Louis that helped her develop her poetic interests. She joined a group of young women who called themselves the Potters. From November 1904 to October 1907 they published the *Potter's Wheel,* a magazine—limited to one copy—that included their poems, stories, and artwork. In 1907 her parents paid for the publication of her first book of poems, *Sonnets to Duse and Other Poems.* Many of the poems in this collection focused on the subject of women such as Helen of Troy, Sappho, Guinevere, and the famous actress Eleonore Duse.

Women played important roles in Teasdale's poetic career. In 1908 she met Marion Cummings Stanley, a poet and university instructor in Arizona, who helped her gain a stronger sense of herself as a poet. On her first trip to New York City in early 1911, Teasdale met Jessie Rittenhouse, one of the founders of the Poetry Society of America, who became a life-long friend. Teasdale published her first professional book of poems, *Helen of Troy and Other Poems,* in 1911, and in the next summer she and Rittenhouse traveled to Europe. In 1913 she became friends with Harriet Monroe, the editor of *Poetry Magazine.*

Monroe introduced Teasdale to the poet Vachel Lindsay, who came to see her as his poetic muse. However, Teasdale had a romantic interest in another poet, John Hall Wheelock. Although the relationship never developed as Teasdale had wished, Wheelock played a considerable role, as did Lindsay, in her emotional and professional life. In December 1914 Sara Teasdale married a St. Louis businessman, Ernst Filsinger. Her third collection of poems, *Rivers to the Sea,* appeared in 1915, and in 1916 she and Filsinger moved, much to Teasdale's delight, to New York, which would be her home for the rest of her life.

In 1917 Teasdale published two works, a collection of love lyrics by women, *The Answering Voice,* and a collection of her own love poems, *Love Songs,* which won the Columbia-Poetry Society of America Prize, a forerunner of the Pulitzer Prize for poetry. Despite her fragile health, Teasdale continued to travel and to write and publish poems. In 1920 she published *Flame and Shadow.* She edited the volume *Rainbow Gold* (1922), a collection of poems aimed at children between ten and fourteen years of age. In 1926 she met Margaret Conklin, a college student who soon became Teasdale's closest companion. They traveled together to England in 1927. She and Filsinger, despite his devotion to her, divorced in 1929.

In 1930 Teasdale published her last book of poems, *Stars Tonight,* and began research for a biography of the English poet Christina Rossetti, making trips to England in 1931 and 1932. During the second trip she became ill with pneumonia. She returned to New York still fatigued and depressed by her illness. On January 29, 1933, at the age of forty-eight, Sara Teasdale died from an overdose of sleeping pills. Her volume *Strange Victory* appeared posthumously later that year. Margaret Conklin and John Hall Wheelock edited *The Collected Poems of Sara Teasdale* (1937), which was reissued in 1945 and in 1966.

LARRY VONALT

Carpenter, Margaret Haley. *Sara Teasdale: A Biography.* Norfolk, Va.: Pentelic Press, 1977.

Drake, William. *Sara Teasdale: Woman and Poet.* San Francisco: Harper and Row, 1979.
Schoen, Carol. *Sara Teasdale.* Boston: Twayne, 1986.
Teasdale, Sara. *The Collected Poems of Sara Teasdale.* New York: Collier Books, 1966.
———. Correspondence. Missouri Historical Society, St. Louis.
———. Papers. Beinecke Rare Book and Manuscript Library, Yale University, New Haven, Conn.

THOMPSON, GEORGE (1817–1893)

George Thompson, instigator of one of the most radical abolitionist acts in Missouri's history, was born on August 12, 1817, in Madison, New Jersey. He was educated at the same New Jersey school as the infamous John Brown; at Oberlin College in Ohio, newly founded by abolitionist Theodore Weld; and at the Mission Institute in Quincy, Illinois, established by David Nelson, who was forced from Missouri for antislavery speeches. With Nelson and **Elijah P. Lovejoy,** Thompson established the Illinois State Anti-Slavery Society at Alton in 1837.

In July 1841 Thompson, James Burr, and Alanson Work crossed the Mississippi to Marion County where they were caught trying to entice five slaves to flee from their masters. They were tried by a jury that included John M. Clemens (Mark Twain's father), found guilty of slave stealing, and sentenced to twelve years in the state penitentiary in Jefferson City. The case was widely reported by antislavery newspapers in the North and in Britain as one of the first instances of whites putting their lives at risk to rescue slaves and also for a questionable verdict, since Missouri at the time had no law against abolitionist activities. The case also mobilized Missourians to safeguard slavery by organizing vigilante committees in counties near the river and by passing legislation introduced by Sen. John Campbell of Marion County to prohibit the spread of antislavery doctrines and any action to interfere with slavery.

Motivated largely by numerous petitions from the North and Britain and also from Marion County, Gov. **John Cummins Edwards** pardoned the abolitionists in 1846. Thompson subsequently published two books he had written in the penitentiary: *Prison Life and Reflections* (1847), an account of the Underground Railroad, prison conditions, and his views on the effects of slavery on a slaveholding state; and *The Prison Bard* (1848), a collection of religious poems. He then worked as a missionary with freed slaves in West Africa for six years, served from 1861 to 1879 as a home missionary in Michigan, and then returned to Oberlin, where he continued to support equal rights for blacks until his death on February 4, 1893.

OLETA PRINSLOO

Aptheker, Herbert. *Abolitionism: A Revolutionary Movement.* Boston: Twayne, 1989.

Fladeland, Betty. *Men and Brothers: Anglo-American Antislavery Cooperation.* Urbana: University of Illinois Press, 1972.

Harrold, Stanley. *The Abolitionists and the South, 1831–1861.* Lexington: University Press of Kentucky, 1995.

Kilby, Clyde S. "Three Antislavery Prisoners." *Journal of the Illinois State Historical Society* 3 (1959): 1–13.

Merkel, Benjamin. "The Antislavery Movement in Missouri, 1819–1865." Ph.D. diss., Washington University, 1939.

THOMPSON, VIRGIL (1896–1989)

Pulitzer Prize–winning composer and music critic Virgil Thompson was born in Kansas City, Missouri, on November 25, 1896. His roots in America go back to the early period of colonization. The forefathers of his father, Quincy Alfred Thompson, came to America in 1717. Virgil's mother, Clara May Gaines Thompson, could trace her ancestry even further, to the founding of Jamestown in 1607. Virgil's ancestors found their way to Missouri, and for a time his family lived on a farm in Saline County. In 1888 the family moved to Kansas City where Quincy Thompson found work as a cable-car conductor and later a position with the post office.

According to his sister Ruby Thompson, Virgil's musical talent was revealed at an early age. A cousin gave him his first piano lessons, and he then went on to study piano with Geneve Lichtenwalter and music theory with Gustave Schoettle. The organist of Grace Episcopal Church, Clarence Sears, gave him organ lessons, while Robert L. Murray gave him singing lessons. According to Virgil, it was Murray who exercised the greatest influence on his early artistic development.

Young Thompson gained local notice as a musical prodigy in Kansas City. By the age of twelve he was performing professionally, giving recitals and substituting as the organist at Calvary Baptist Church. He also excelled in his academic studies. He attended Central High School from 1908 to 1913 and the Kansas City Polytechnic Institute and Junior College in 1915–1917 and 1919. While in junior college, Thompson first demonstrated his talents as a journalist. Bored with the usual college activities, he published a small magazine called *Pans* in which his and other Pansophists' writings appeared.

In 1917 Thompson left school to enlist in the United States Army. He served in a field artillery unit. He was also trained in radio telephony and at the air service school at Columbia University. Commissioned a second lieutenant, he was ready for shipment to France when the war ended. In 1918 he left the service and returned to Kansas City. At this point in his life he made two important decisions: to attend Harvard and to have a music career.

Thompson entered Harvard in the fall of 1919. He was chosen to be a member of the Harvard Glee Club in 1921 and made a summer tour of Europe with the group. When the tour was over he remained in Paris to study with the famed Nadia Boulanger. In 1923 he graduated from Harvard at which time he received a Juilliard Fellowship for advanced study. After a year he began to write articles on music for *Vanity Fair,* to compose, and to teach.

Thompson left for Paris in September 1925, declaring at the time that if he were going to starve as a composer, he "preferred to starve where the food is good." While in Paris his most important artistic association in his career began. In the fall of 1926 he met the famous writer Gertrude Stein. Their meeting led to a period of collaboration, principally the opera *Four Saints in Three Acts.* The opera had its premiere in Hartford, Connecticut, on February 8, 1934. Twelve days later it opened on Broadway. Thompson and Stein also collaborated on *The Mother of Us All,* an opera about Susan B. Anthony, which was performed in New York in 1947.

In the mid-thirties, Thompson again took up residence in Paris, often returning to the United States to do commissioned work. He composed incidental music for several plays, among them *Antony and Cleopatra, Hamlet,* and *Macbeth.* He remained in Paris until after the German invasion of France in 1940.

Upon his return to New York, Thompson was hired as the chief music critic for the *New York Herald Tribune.* During the next fourteen years, until his retirement in 1954, he established himself as one of the major critics of the era. His newspaper articles furnished material for several anthologies, among them *The Musical Scene* and *The Art of Judging Music.* While working as a critic, Thompson continued to compose. One of these compositions, the score for the documentary film *Louisiana Story,* won the 1948 Pulitzer Prize. This was the only time a motion picture score has received the award.

While working as a critic, Thompson often clashed with other critics. His opinions were plain, concise, often provocative, and sometimes outrageous. He carried on a guerrilla war against the Italian conductor Arturo Toscanini, he labeled Jascha Heifetz's repertory "silk-underwear" music, and observed that the Metropolitan Opera was "not a part of New York's intellectual life." Thompson called his reviews "sassy but classy." His tendency to fall asleep during performances was well known.

As a composer Thompson helped pioneer America's musical nationalism. Deriving inspiration from sources such as Baptist hymns and early American popular music, his works ranged through several different styles, owing much to Erik Satie and French neoclassicism. His works included operas, ballets, orchestral and choral works, film scores, and incidental music for plays by numerous authors.

Although his music reflected a decidedly French influence, Thompson maintained that his musical mission was to let people know, through his music, what it was like "to put your feet in the Missouri River." He never lost his love for his native state. In 1947 he dedicated his tone poem *The Seine at Night* to the Kansas City Symphony. The Lyric Opera of Kansas City produced *The Mother of Us All* in 1983, and the State Ballet of Missouri performed his 1937 ballet *Filling Station* in 1989.

After his stint as a critic for the *New York Herald Tribune,* Thompson traveled widely, conducted, gave lectures, wrote more music, and attended conferences. Affected by deafness for the last years of his life, his appearances and work became more limited. Laden with tributes throughout his life, his many awards included sixteen honorary doctorates—three from Missouri institutions: Park College, the University of Missouri–Kansas City, and William Jewell College. He was a member of the National Institute of Arts and Letters and the American Academy of Arts and Letters. He became a chevalier and officer of the French Légion d'Honneur and a recipient of the Kennedy Center Award for Lifetime Achievement. "Under a cosmopolitan exterior," Kathleen Hoover observed, "he remained a solid Midwesterner—sensible, genial, beaver-busy, tolerant of all things but snobbery and sham."

Thompson, who never married, died in his sleep on September 30, 1989, in New York. He was buried in a family plot at Slater in Saline County, Missouri.

ALFRED E. TWOMEY

Hoover, Kathleen, and John Cage. *Virgil Thompson.* New York: Thomas Yoseloff, 1959.
International Encyclopedia of Music and Musicians. S.v. "Thompson, Virgil."
Thompson, Virgil. *Virgil Thompson: An Autobiography.* New York: E. P. Dutton, 1966.

TIBBE, HENRY (1819–1896)

Mark Twain, Gen. Douglas McArthur, and President Gerald Ford are just a few of the many famous Americans who at times in their lives preferred the simple pleasure of smoking tobacco in a corncob pipe. These men, along with millions of other ordinary Americans and citizens in many foreign lands, owe their smoking pleasure to a Dutch wood turner named Hendrik, or Henry, Tibbe. Through his ingenuity and industry, the state of Missouri has garnered worldwide recognition as the "birthplace of the corncob pipe industry." With a virtual Missouri monopoly on the production of "nearly all the country's corncob pipes," along with the fact that Henry Tibbe's factory was the first, finest, and largest corncob pipe producer in the United States, the city of Washington, Missouri, has earned the title of "Corncob Pipe Capital of the World."

Henry Tibbe was born on May 21, 1819, in Enschede, Holland, where he made wooden articles, handles, and spinning wheels. Tibbe, his wife, Johanna, son Anton, stepdaughter Margaret, and brother Fritz emigrated to America after a citywide fire in 1862 destroyed their Enschede home and Henry's wood-turning factory. The family arrived in New York on January 6, 1866, and traveled westward to South Point, Missouri. In South Point the family lived with Henry's younger brother until 1867 when they moved to Washington. In Washington, a bustling railway center and Missouri River port, Tibbe set up a small wood-turning business and resumed the trade he had learned in Holland. Letters to relatives reveal that while times were hard for the family during those early years the Tibbes felt a "kindred spirit" with the many German settlers in and around Washington.

The year 1869 proved a turning point for the Tibbe family. In his small shop, where he made and sold spinning wheels for nine dollars apiece, Henry Tibbe turned his first corncob on his foot-powered lathe. Tradition has it that he cut the cob in half, bored out the pith, and inserted a reed for a stem. Historical accounts conflict as to whether he performed this task on his own or at the request of a local farmer. Whether it was Tibbe's idea or that of someone else matters little. Many a farmer had whittled a pipe out of a cob, but it was Tibbe's lathe that turned out the smoothed version. And it was Tibbe, after making similar pipes for himself and his friends, who began to sell the pipes commercially.

From inception, durability was a major problem with the pipe. When smoked, the cob burned right along with the tobacco. To solve this dilemma tradition has it that Tibbe, "a great smoker," consulted with his friend Otto L. Muench. The by-product of their conversations led Tibbe to experiment with sealing the cob with plaster of paris. While there is some discrepancy as to whether he did anything more than use someone else's idea, it was Tibbe who applied the mixture that fireproofed, sealed, and hardened the oversized cob, allowing it to be worked on his lathe while not destroying the "sweeter smoke." The firm H. Tibbe and Son applied for and was granted a patent on the process in 1878. This process revolutionized the corncob pipe industry and gave the Tibbes a virtual monopoly on the production of corncob pipes.

By 1879 the company had moved to a larger building. To turn the lathes, a steam engine replaced foot power, and pipe production rose. Henry's son, Anton, was now successfully marketing the unique product, and for a variety of reasons, not the least of which being the need for capital, Henry and his son decided to seek a partner. One-third interest in the company was sold to George Kahmann, son of one of Washington's most influential and prominent citizens. Business flourished, and the family wrote to relatives that they no longer "desire to return to Enschede." The company was now advertising in larger newspapers and small trade journals and had begun labeling their pipes, "A genuine Missouri Meerschaum pipe, made in Missouri, U.S.A." Some accounts credit Henry's brother Fritz with naming the pipe. Whether it was Fritz's idea or merely Henry's way of identifying his pipes with the elaborate meerschaum pipes he had enjoyed in Holland is immaterial. The name became synonymous with the state of Missouri and an excellent corncob pipe.

Over the next five years the company prospered. In 1883, with Anton Tibbe and George Kahmann managing the company, a new and larger building was built on the site of the previous factory. That same year a patent was granted on the trademark "Missouri Meerschaum." From a workforce of ten men in 1879 the company by 1884 employed approximately one hundred workers, infusing prosperity into the local community.

In 1887 a new company was incorporated under the name "Missouri Meerschaum." Henry and Anton Tibbe, George Kahmann, and Upton Weirick were stockholders. With increased demand and sales, more production space was needed. The company responded by building a larger, three-story structure on the same site as the previous factory, and production increased to fifteen thousand pipes a day. In 1888 active management of the company was turned over to Weirick and Kahmann's brother, Guy. In 1895 the Tibbes' patent on their corncob pipe expired. The following year, on October 20, 1896, Henry Tibbe died at his home in Washington at the age of seventy-seven. It was reported that at his funeral "every employee of the factory marched in the funeral procession, thereby showing their respect for their benefactor."

Missouri's production of tobacco and corn facilitated development of the corncob pipe industry, but it was the fortitude of Henry Tibbe and the foresight of his son that "put the business over in a big way" and brought recognition to the state of Missouri. In 1921 Henry Tibbe's son, Anton, disposed of his interest in the pipe factory, thus ending the Tibbe family's direct supervision of the company. Today, with minor changes, the Missouri Meerschaum Company still produces Tibbe's corncob pipes, and Washington, Missouri, is still called the "Corncob Pipe Capital of the World."

Henry Tibbe was an immigrant wood turner from Holland who found opportunity in a simple idea and left a lasting legacy. In his lifetime he accumulated a large fortune and helped bring prosperity to a considerable section of Missouri. He would have been pleased to hear Mark Twain utter the words, "I always said a Missouri Meerschaum was the best smoking in the world."

MARTHA HERVEY

History of Franklin, Jefferson, Washington, Crawford, and Gasconade Counties, Missouri. Chicago: Goodspeed Publishing, 1888.

Jarvis, Charles A. "Clarence Cannon, the Corn Cob Pipe, and the Hawley-Smoot Tariff." *Missouri Historical Review* 84 (January 1990): 154–56.

Keil, Herman Gottlieb, comp. *The Centennial Biographical Directory of Franklin County, Missouri.* Washington, D.C.: n.p., 1925.

McNeill, Paula. "The Missouri Meerschaum Pipe." *Missouri Historical Review* 77 (October 1983): 15–16.

Tibbe-Cuthbertson Family Papers. Western Historical Manuscripts Collection, Columbia.

TOLSON, MELVIN B. (1898–1966)

Through most of his life Melvin B. Tolson claimed he was born with the twentieth century in 1900. He was in fact born on February 6, 1898, in Moberly, Missouri. His father, a novice Methodist minister, was moved to churches in various Missouri and Iowa towns until the family settled in the Kansas City area when Tolson was of high school age. He graduated from Kansas City's Lincoln High School and entered Fisk University in 1919. He transferred to Lincoln University in Pennsylvania the following year because of costs.

During his junior year Tolson married Ruth Southall, and his first son was born the month he graduated, June 1923. The Tolsons moved to Marshall, Texas, and that fall he began teaching in the English department at Wiley College. Two more sons and a daughter soon followed. All three sons became Ph.D.'s, and both daughter and wife earned M.A. degrees. Despite a few notable conflicts Wiley College provided the Tolson family a congenial and stimulating community for twenty-four years.

Tolson became a challenging teacher, a legendary debate coach, and an effective drama director. In 1931 he was given leave to work on an M.A. degree at Columbia University. His master's thesis, a study of the Harlem Renaissance, focused his long-held writing ambitions. Harlem's promise as the cultural capital of his people seized his imagination and never let go. Over the next several years he wrote more than 150 poems for *A Gallery of Harlem*

Portraits, modeled on Edgar Lee Masters's *Spoon River Anthology.* The book was never published during his lifetime, but V. F. Calverton, a friend and supporter, published some of its poems in *Modern Quarterly.*

From 1937 to 1944 Tolson wrote a provocative weekly column, "Caviar and Cabbage," for the *Washington Tribune,* but his big publishing break came when "Dark Symphony" was chosen as the prize poem of the American Negro Exposition in Chicago in 1939 and was later published in *Atlantic Monthly.* When Mary Lou Chamberlain moved from *Atlantic* to Dodd, Mead, she admired the poem sufficiently to invite Tolson to submit a manuscript, which became his first published book, *Rendezvous with America* (1944).

Rendezvous earned Tolson a considerable recognition just as former classmate Horace Mann Bond became president of Lincoln University. Originally named Ashmun Institute after Jehudi Ashmun, a founder of Liberia, Lincoln continued to maintain close ties with Liberia's contemporary leaders. In 1947 Tolson was named Liberia's poet laureate, and his growing recognition brought an offer from Oklahoma's Langston University that Wiley College could not match.

The challenge of responding to his new honor led Tolson to a profound change in his poetry. He embraced the modernist revolution in poetry signaled by the examples of **T. S. Eliot** and Ezra Pound, but he continued to insist on the need for revolutionary social change. In 1949 he asked Alan Tate to write a preface for his *Libretto for the Republic of Liberia.* Karl Shapiro then published Tate's preface and section "Ti" from the *Libretto* in *Poetry* in 1950. Decker Press, *Libretto*'s scheduled publisher, abruptly folded when one of its leaders died in an auto accident, delaying *Libretto*'s appearance as a book until 1953. Meanwhile, *Poetry* awarded Tolson its Bess Hokim Prize for his ironic meditation on the racial dilemma then confronting an African American poet, "E. & O. E."

Langston, Oklahoma, was founded, and continued, as an African American community. The Tolsons bought a modest house there in 1950, and in 1954 Melvin was elected mayor. He was reelected three times, and bowed only reluctantly to his family's insistence he give up his civic role to have more time for his writing. Also in 1954 Liberia conferred upon Tolson the Order of the Star of Africa; Robert Frost's home base, the Breadloaf Writers' Conference, offered him a fellowship in poetry and drama; and Lincoln University conferred upon him an honorary doctorate of letters.

In 1956 Tolson attended President Tubman's third inauguration in Monrovia, and stopped overnight in Paris to visit Richard Wright and Melvin Jr., then studying at the Sorbonne. He had already begun the demanding task of composing his epic *Harlem Gallery,* but did not read galley proofs of *Book 1: The Curator*—there would be four more books—until the spring of 1964, just as he was diagnosed with terminal cancer. His family was told he had six months to live.

Karl Shapiro wrote a much publicized introduction for Tolson's final book, and praised him even more highly than Tate, but took sharp issue with Tate's previous praise. Shapiro's grand liberal claims for Tolson, however, were as culturally questionable as Tate's conservative paternalism and triggered a reaction among African American critics that gave all too easy an excuse for readers to avoid the challenge of Tolson's poems.

However, *Harlem Gallery* brought Tolson attention, if not understanding. Lincoln University conferred a second honorary doctorate of letters, and Tuskegee University invited him to assume the Avalon Chair of Humanities for 1965–1966. In 1966 he was inducted into the American Academy of Arts and Letters along with John Barth, James Dickey, Josephine Herbst, and Gary Snyder. He lived a rewarding two years after his cancer was diagnosed, dying on August 29, 1966.

The life of Tolson's poetry in American culture is still in doubt, but Michael Berube, after detailing the failure of critics, both white and black, to engage Tolson's major achievement, has outlined a reception theory that makes *Harlem Gallery* available to postmodernist readers in *Marginal Forces/Cultural Centers: Tolson, Pynchon, and the Politics of the Canon.*

ROBERT M. FARNSWORTH

Berube, Michael. *Marginal Forces/Cultural Centers: Tolson, Pynchon, and the Politics of Canon.* Ithaca: Cornell University Press, 1992.

Farnsworth, Robert M. *Melvin B. Tolson, 1898–1966: Plain Talk and Poetic Prophecy.* Columbia: University of Missouri Press, 1984.

———, ed. *Caviar and Cabbage: Selected Columns by Melvin B. Tolson from the "Washington Tribune," 1937–1944.* Columbia: University of Missouri Press, 1982.

———. *A Gallery of Harlem Portraits.* Columbia: University of Missouri Press, 1982.

Flasch, Joy. *Melvin B. Tolson.* New York: Twayne, 1972.

Russell, Mariann. *Melvin B. Tolson's "Harlem Gallery": A Literary Analysis.* Columbia: University of Missouri Press, 1980.

TOLTON, AUGUSTUS (1854–1897)

Augustus Tolton, the first recognized black Catholic priest in the United States, was born a slave in

Ralls County, Missouri, on April 1, 1854, the son of Martha Chisley, a slave of the Manning family of Kentucky, and Peter Paul Tolton, a slave on the Hagar plantation in Ralls County. Martha Chisley had come to Ralls County in 1849 as part of the marriage dowry of Susan Manning who married Stephen Elliott, a farmer.

In 1851 Martha Chisley married Peter Paul Tolton in a Catholic ceremony at St. Peter's Catholic Church, in Brush Creek, Missouri. They had three children. Augustus, baptized at St. Peter's Church, was the second child. He had an older brother and a younger sister. Peter Paul Tolton escaped from slavery in 1861 and went to St. Louis to join the Union army, dying shortly thereafter.

Martha Tolton fled with her children across the Mississippi River at Hannibal, Missouri, and found refuge in Quincy, Illinois. Her oldest child died. A determined Catholic, she sought to place her children in a Catholic school. Despite initial racial hostility in one Catholic parish, she was able, with the help of Father McGirr, pastor of the Irish parish, to place her children in the parish school. Still, education was intermittent; poverty forced young Tolton to work in a cigar factory.

Tolton developed an interest in the Catholic priesthood and was encouraged by priests in Quincy and by the bishop of Alton, Peter Baltes, but no seminary in the United States was willing to accept a black student. Tolton began his studies with private tutoring from two of the pastors in Quincy as well as with some private classes at Quincy College, operated by the Franciscans. Finally, through the intervention of Father Bernardino dal Vago, the minister general of the Franciscan friars, Tolton was admitted to the Urban College in Rome. This seminary, attached to the Congregation of the Propaganda Fide (the Roman congregation in charge of all Catholic missionary activity), had many students who were Africans and Asians.

Augustus Tolton entered the college in March 1880. He was one of 142 students. The student register of the Urban College gives his first name as "Augustus," the name that was habitually used after his ordination. In later life he always signed his name "A. Tolton," though at times he seems to have used "Augustine." He was ordained a priest on April 24, 1886, in the basilica of St. John Lateran in Rome. Contrary to the original understanding, the prefect of the Congregation of the Propaganda, Cardinal Simeoni, had determined that Tolton was not to go to Africa as a missionary but was to return as a priest to the United States. Tolton quoted him as saying, "If America has never seen a black priest, it has to see one now."

Arguably, Augustus Tolton was not the first African American priest. James Augustine Healy, Francis Patrick Healy, and Sherwood Alexander Healy were all sons of a slave mother and a white father, Michael Morris Healy, a plantation owner in Georgia. All three brothers studied for the priesthood in Europe and were ordained priests between the years 1854 and 1864. James Augustine Healy became the first African American bishop in 1875. Gifted and fair-skinned, the brothers were not readily identified with the African American community.

Tolton's return to the United States as the first nationally known black priest was a triumph. He celebrated mass before a throng of black Catholics in New York on July 11, 1886, and an even greater crowd in Quincy a week later. His first assignment was as pastor of the black parish in Quincy. In time the racial animosity of the neighboring pastor forced Tolton to seek permission to move to Chicago. Cardinal Simeoni agreed to the move with great reluctance. Nineteen members of his parish accompanied Tolton in 1889. The archbishop of Chicago, Patrick Feehan, gave him the task of establishing a parish for the black Catholics of the city. St. Monica's Church was opened in 1893.

Known throughout the country, Tolton spoke at the black Catholic lay congresses and other events. Black Catholics wrote from all over. His own letters revealed his loneliness and his pressures. Humble and simple, rarely assertive, always compassionate, he was greatly revered. He lived in poverty; his mother was his housekeeper. He died at the age of forty-three on July 9, 1897, from heat exhaustion. Following his wishes, he was buried in Quincy, Illinois.

CYPRIAN DAVIS

Davis, Cyprian, O.S.B. *The History of Black Catholics in the United States.* New York: Crossroad, 1990.

Foley, Albert, S.J. *God's Men of Color: The Colored Catholic Priests of the United States, 1854–1954.* New York: Farrar, Straus, 1955.

Hemesath, Caroline. *From Slave to Priest: A Biography of the Rev. Augustine Tolton (1864–1897), First Afro-American Priest of the United States.* Chicago: Franciscan Herald Press, 1973.

TRAUBEL, HELEN FRANCESCA (1903–1972)

One of the world's great Wagnerian sopranos, Helen Traubel was born in south St. Louis on June 16, 1903. Her father, Otto Ferdinand Traubel, was a druggist. The family lived in a six-room flat above the store until Helen was six years old. During her years of growing up, she constantly focused on becoming a singer. Her parents often attended concerts and the opera with Helen. Her mother, Clara, had been a concert singer before her marriage and encouraged her daughter's interest in music. By the time Helen was twelve she had heard more than thirty operas. Her musical instruction began with piano lessons. In her sophomore year she left high school to concentrate on studying voice. At age thirteen she started singing lessons with her first and only teacher, Louise Meyerson Vetta-Karst.

From the third grade, Traubel sang whenever and wherever the opportunity presented itself. She first sang professionally in a hall at Washington University, and she also sang in a local Catholic church choir. After fourteen months, at the insistence of her voice teacher, she stopped giving public performances and devoted herself to her vocal studies. When Traubel was seventeen, she began earning a living by singing at the Pilgrim Congregational Church and the United Hebrew Temple.

In 1924 Traubel appeared in concert with Rudolph Ganz and the St. Louis Symphony. Later she toured with the orchestra and in the summer of 1926 appeared at Lewishon Stadium in New York where Ganz was the guest conductor. Giulio Gatti-Casazza, general manager of the Metropolitan Opera, heard her performance and invited her to join the Metropolitan. Traubel declined the offer and returned to St. Louis to continue her studies and her work as a soloist for religious services. Her refusal to enter a contract with the Metropolitan became a familiar pattern.

In 1934 Traubel was invited to be the featured soloist at the National Saengerfestr to be held in St. Louis. Walter Damrosch, the well-known guest conductor, was so impressed with her voice that he invited her to appear in his new opera, *The Man without a Country.* After much persuasion and the creation of the role Mary Rutledge just for her, Traubel agreed to appear. In the spring of 1937 she made her operatic debut in this work at the Metropolitan Opera in New York. The opera was not a success, and Traubel sang in only five performances. She stayed in New York, appearing on NBC Radio and studying with Giuseppe Boghetti. In 1938 she married William L. Bass, a real estate and investment broker who later became her manager. This was the second marriage for both. Traubel had married Louis Franklin Carpenter in 1922, but they divorced in 1936.

After many highly acclaimed appearances on the concert stage and involved negotiations with Edward Johnson, the general manager, Traubel signed with the Metropolitan for the 1939–1940 season. She appeared in her first Wagner role, Sieglinde in *Die Walkure,* on December 28, 1939. Her performances at the Metropolitan launched her career as one of the foremost Wagnerian sopranos in modern times. Until 1941 she shared Wagnerian roles with Kirsten Flagstad, the Norwegian soprano and leading Wagnerian singer at the Metropolitan Opera. With the departure of Flagstad in 1941, Traubel became the company's principal Wagnerian soprano. She remained with the Metropolitan for sixteen seasons, leaving at the end of the 1952–1953 season. During that time she appeared in ten different roles, in nine works, for 176 performances.

Traubel's resignation from the Metropolitan Opera came as a result of a highly public clash with the general manager, Rudolf Bing. He believed her appearances in nightclubs, on radio, in films, and on television diminished her dignity and the Met's. She replied that "artistic dignity is not a matter of where one sings. To assert that art can be found at Metropolitan Opera House but not in a night club is rank snobbery that underrates both the taste of the American public and the talents of its composers."

Traubel now focused on appearances in concerts and nightclubs, on radio and television, in a Broadway musical, *Pipe Dream,* and in a motion picture, *Deep in My Heart.* Among the many artists she worked with were Groucho Marx, Jimmy Durante, Red Skelton, Ed Sullivan, Perry Como, Jerry Lewis, and Milton Berle. Traubel was a baseball fan, and in 1950 she became a part owner of the St. Louis Browns. That same year she briefly turned to writing. Her first full-length mystery novel, *The Metropolitan Opera Murders,* was published in October 1951. Critics gave it lukewarm reviews.

Traubel recorded for RCA-Victor and Columbia Records. She was the first singer to ever record with Arturo Toscanini and the NBC Symphony. She spent three years coaching Margaret Truman, who had asked for help in launching a singing career. Her last engagement was with Jimmy Durante in a hotel resort at Lake Tahoe, California, in 1964. Traubel died of a heart attack at her home in Santa Monica, California, on July 28, 1972.

During her lifetime Traubel received many awards and honors, among them honorary doctorates from the Universities of Missouri and Southern California, the King Christian Medal of Liberation, and the Citation of Merit of the National Association for American Composers and Conductors. Throughout her life she was to remain true to her St. Louis roots. As Vincent Sheean wrote, "Helen Traubel was as American as Mark Twain."

ALFRED E. TWOMEY

Encyclopedia of the Opera. S.v. "Traubel, Helen Francesca."

Traubel, Helen. *St. Louis Woman.* 1959. Reprint, Columbia: University of Missouri Press, 1999.

TROOST, BENOIST (1786–1859)

Considered the first physician to reside in Kansas City, Benoist Troost combined medical knowledge, business acumen, personal charm, and a fortunate marriage to become one of the young city's elite. He was born on November 17, 1786, in Bois-le-Duc in a region of Holland that was later annexed by Napoléon's French Empire. Having been extensively educated in medicine, surgery, and all the natural sciences, Benoist and his elder brother Gerard were serving as surgeons to Napoléon's regiments when the pair were selected to join a French scientific expedition to the West Indies. Because France's enemy Britain controlled the seas, the expedition chose for safety's sake to travel on an American merchant ship, only to find themselves stranded in Philadelphia.

Electing to stay in the United States when the expedition returned to France, the brothers remained in Philadelphia a short time before moving to Pittsburgh in 1815 or 1816. There they established one of the earliest factories in the country to produce white lead, a pigment used in paint. In 1831, when the state of Tennessee appointed Gerard as its state geologist, the Troosts disposed of their factory, and Benoist headed for St. Louis with a new bride. Expecting to make a new start among the city's large French-speaking population, the Troosts remained just long enough to meet Samuel Owens, a prosperous Santa Fe trader from Independence. Owens convinced Troost that he could establish a thriving practice among Jackson County's increasingly wealthy and respectable population. An added inducement was the presence of a French-speaking population at nearby Westport Landing. Thus, Troost came to Independence, where his wife, Rachel, died in 1841. He appears not to have located permanently there until 1844, however, when he announced the establishment of his practice in the *Independence Journal.*

Troost's medical practice grew satisfactorily because of his surgical skill, and the energetic and personable widower was a frequent visitor at the homes of Jackson County's wealthy, including one of its richest citizens, the Indian trader and land speculator **William Gilliss.** There Troost met Gilliss's niece, the "sprightly widow" Mary Ann Kennerly. In 1846 she and Troost were married.

It proved an advantageous alliance for Troost. In the year of his marriage, his name appeared as one of the purchasers of town lots in Kansas City, then numbering three hundred residents. In 1849 he built the first brick hotel on the town's busy levee, originally calling it Troost House and later Gilliss House. Whether Troost relied on the financial backing of his wealthy in-law is uncertain, but his fortunes took a decidedly upward turn upon his marriage. Although he lost control of his hotel, he became a member of the city's business and political elite. He served as one of the first trustees governing the Town of Kansas following its incorporation in 1850, and he ran unsuccessfully as the Democratic Party's first mayoral candidate upon the incorporation of the "City of Kansas" in 1853. Like his colleagues among Kansas City's elite, he was an indefatigable booster of the young town's enterprise, purchasing lengthy advertisements and writing newspaper pieces to attract westward emigrants and serving on the health inspection committee assembled to combat a disastrous cholera epidemic that had driven away business in 1852 and 1853.

Benoist Troost died on February 8, 1859, before seeing his ambitions for Kansas City realized. His widow, Mary Ann Troost, would leave a more tangible imprint on the city that burgeoned after the Civil War. When he died in 1868, William Gilliss left his entire estate to Mary Ann Troost. Upon her own death in 1872, she bequeathed the bulk of that estate to establish the Gilliss Orphans' Home and to build the Gilliss Theater in her uncle's honor. Revenues from the elegant theater, which opened in 1883, were used for the support of the orphans' home. Benoist Troost is himself remembered in Troost Avenue, and his portrait hangs in the city's Nelson-Atkins Museum of Art. One of a pair of portraits of the Troosts by **George Caleb Bingham,** the painting of Benoist Troost is considered one of Bingham's finer pieces because it captures the optimism and ebullient personality of its subject.

SHERRY LAMB SCHIRMER

Brown, A. Theodore. *Frontier Community: Kansas City to 1870.* Columbia: University of Missouri Press, 1963.

Troost, Dr. Benoist. Vertical File. Native Sons Archives. Missouri Valley Room, Kansas City Public Library, Kansas City, Mo.

Troost, Mrs. Mary Ann. Vertical File. Native Sons Archives. Missouri Valley Room, Kansas City Public Library, Kansas City, Mo.

TRUDEAU, ZENON (1748–?)

While serving as Upper Louisiana's lieutenant governor between 1792 and 1799, Zenon Trudeau showed himself to be a prudent but pragmatic administrator who adopted a commonsense approach in dealing with the manifold and complex problems that confronted his administration. A Frenchman born in New Orleans on November 28, 1748, Trudeau enlisted in the Spanish army in 1769, served in the conquests of Baton Rouge in 1779 and Pensacola in 1781, and advanced to the rank of captain. He married Eulalie Delassise in 1781, and the couple had several children. Trudeau assumed command in St. Louis in July 1792. The turbulent 1790s presented him with more than his share of problems in Upper Louisiana. He had to prepare for threatened invasions by British, French, and American forces as well as for assaults from hostile Osage bands. Loyal to the Spanish government he served but realistic in the measures he advocated, Trudeau provided a steady hand at the helm in St. Louis.

Following his arrival Trudeau sought to confront the growing British domination of the Indian trade north of St. Louis. Unable to provide enough merchandise for the fur trade, the Spaniards had in effect forced many of Louisiana's Indian tribes to turn to the better-supplied British traders to the north. Upper Louisiana's Spanish-licensed traders also had to look to foreign suppliers for merchandise. Trudeau quickly grasped that any attempts to prevent local merchants from doing business with British firms in Canada would be ruinous to commerce in St. Louis, so he chose to turn a blind eye to their illicit traffic.

However, while willing to allow St. Louis merchants to enter the northern markets, Trudeau was determined not to let British traders engage in direct trade with Indians in Spanish territory. In 1793 he dispatched an expedition to the Des Moines River to arrest foreign traders. Later that year he summoned all of Upper Louisiana's traders to St. Louis to consider proposed new regulations designed to make government-controlled trading operations more equitable and efficient. When **Jacques Clamorgan** spearheaded the formation of a company to promote Spanish trade along the upper Missouri, Trudeau gave the venture his unqualified support. The Missouri Company was organized in 1794 and eventually sent three costly but unsuccessful trading expeditions up the Missouri. Their poor showing caused Trudeau to conclude it was unlikely that Spain could ever gain control of the Indian trade along the upper reaches of the Missouri and Mississippi Rivers.

Closer at hand, Trudeau had to confront the continuing Osage threats to Upper Louisiana's exposed settlements. Not long after he arrived in St. Louis, Trudeau received directives from Louisiana's governor-general, the Baron de Carondelet, suspending all trade with the errant Osages and declaring war on them. Trudeau, who doubted the efficacy of Carondelet's strategy, procrastinated in carrying out his orders to launch a general attack against the main Osage villages. With solid support from St. Louis traders, he continued to urge his superiors to exercise caution in dealing with the powerful Osages.

The outbreak of war between Spain and France compounded Trudeau's problems, especially after rumors of a pending Franco-American invasion led by George Rogers Clark began circulating throughout the region in 1794. Although that threat never materialized, it persuaded Carondelet to heed Trudeau's counsel and call off the Osage war. That decision cleared the way for a new approach to the Osage problem. With Trudeau's backing, St. Louis fur merchant **Auguste Chouteau** renewed his offer to assist the Spaniards in bringing the Osages under control by constructing a fort adjacent to the Osage River villages in return for a monopoly of the Osage trade. Carondelet accepted Chouteau's proposal, and following the establishment of an installation in present-day Vernon County, Missouri, known as Fort Carondelet, tensions with the Osages gradually subsided, to the relief of all parties.

The resumption of warfare between Great Britain and Spain in 1796 along with continuing rumors of French intrigues in Spanish Louisiana prompted Carondelet to dispatch additional military forces to St. Louis in 1797. These imminent dangers also led to renewed Spanish efforts to encourage American settlement in Upper Louisiana. Trudeau favored American immigration and was instrumental in persuading members of the legendary **Daniel Boone** family to leave Kentucky and take up residence in present-day Missouri along the Femme Osage Creek. During his final days in St. Louis, Trudeau allegedly signed numerous blank land-concession forms that were distributed after his departure and filled in illegally by those who secured them.

When Trudeau completed his term as lieutenant governor in 1799, the Spanish government offered him a pension, which he declined. He returned to lower Louisiana and continued in Spanish service until 1803 when Spain relinquished its control of the province. Trudeau remained in Louisiana until his death a few years later in St. Charles Parish.

WILLIAM E. FOLEY

Din, Gilbert C., and Abraham P. Nasatir. *The Imperial Osages: Spanish-Indian Diplomacy in the Mississippi Valley.* Norman: University of Oklahoma Press, 1983.

Nasatir, Abraham P. *Before Lewis and Clark: Documents Illustrating the History of the Missouri, 1785–1804.* 2 vols. 1952. Reprint, Lincoln: University of Nebraska Press, 1990.

———. *Spanish War Vessels on the Mississippi.* New Haven: Yale University Press, 1968.

TRUMAN, ELIZABETH "BESS" VIRGINIA WALLACE (1885–1982)

Born in Independence, Missouri, on February 13, 1885, Elizabeth Virginia Wallace, who as the wife of the thirty-third president of the United States was accustomed to sign her name as Bess W. Truman, graduated from Independence High School in 1901, in the same class as her later husband. Her mother, Margaret Elizabeth "Madge" Gates Wallace, was the daughter of one of the wealthiest men in the town, the owner of the Waggoner-Gates Milling Company, which produced Queen of the Pantry flour, the well-known cake and biscuit flour sold throughout the

Midwest. Her father was David Willock Wallace, holder of various appointive political offices in Jackson County.

In the years after graduation, Bess Wallace assisted her mother with the household, until 1903 when the stark tragedy of her father's suicide persuaded the family to remove to Colorado Springs for a year, after which mother and daughter and three younger brothers lived with the maternal grandparents in a seventeen-room house at 219 North Delaware Street. Bess attended Barstow School, a finishing school, in 1905–1906. She remained in the family house until her marriage to **Harry S. Truman** on July 28, 1919.

The courtship with the future president began in 1910, when Truman was assisting his father on a large farm near the village of Grandview, twenty miles south of Kansas City. Truman had met Bess Wallace in Presbyterian Sunday school in 1890 and, as he put it, fell in love with the then-five year old. Throughout high school they saw each other daily. At that time Truman lived three or four short blocks from Bess. There is no evidence that the couple saw each other between 1901 and 1910. Almost at once Truman expressed his desire to marry Bess, but she gently refused, perhaps because she felt that her mother needed her to help with the large house and the family that now included aging grandparents. Her beau's participation in World War I brought an engagement and then marriage upon his return.

Bess Truman and her new husband chose to live in the Gates house, which after the death of Madge Wallace in 1952 became the Truman house by purchase from Bess's brothers.

During the 1920s, while Bess's husband first conducted a haberdashery in Kansas City (1919–1922) and then was eastern judge of Jackson County (1923–1924) and presiding judge (1927–1934), the Truman family lived at 219 North Delaware. A daughter, Mary Margaret, was born in 1924. Beginning with the Senate years of Harry, Bess and Margaret spent half years in Washington, D.C., until World War II, when Margaret enrolled at George Washington University and they became permanent residents of the capital. They of course resided at the White House during the presidency, 1945–1953.

Bess Truman did not find politics interesting, and sought to remain largely apart from her husband's preoccupation beginning in 1923. During the Senate years and those of the presidency she often returned to Independence where she enjoyed her bridge club and otherwise occupied herself with seeing her many friends. It is perhaps of special interest that after a rather awkward period in Washington at the beginning of the Senate years in her husband's life, Bess Truman became acclimated to life in the capital. However, she did not wish her husband to aspire to

higher office, and when his nomination for the vice presidency loomed in the early weeks of the summer of 1944 she displayed considerable animus over the prospect, which she thoroughly understood, not merely of the vice presidency (for President Franklin D. Roosevelt was obviously going to be reelected in November 1944) but of the presidency. Roosevelt's health, so the leaders of the Democratic Party saw, was deteriorating, and he could not possibly survive a fourth term. Margaret Truman has written that during the trip back from Chicago, where the Democratic National Convention nominated her father for the vice presidency, the temperature in the Truman automobile was close to arctic. The reasons are difficult to be sure of. One might have related to the suicide of Bess's father, which fact had never been communicated to Margaret; at the turn of the century suicides were considered family disgraces. The vice presidential campaign, not to mention the presidency, was bound to bring it out. Another might have been Bess Truman's belief that the White House was an improper environment, almost a goldfish bowl, for a young daughter. Another may have been dislike for the rigmarole of being a president's wife, though when in Washington during her husband's presidency (she often went back to Independence, sometimes remaining for months on end) she performed her duties as first lady with aplomb if not with the wide-ranging zest of her predecessor, Eleanor Roosevelt.

Upon return to Independence after the presidency, Bess Truman took up the life she had known. It was a routine that seldom varied. She rose each morning two or three hours after her early-rising husband and made breakfast for him. Her longtime house helper Vietta Garr provided the other meals. Her husband spent much of his time at the Harry S. Truman Library, a few blocks to the north, or was away for speeches and other Democratic Party events. Bess Truman survived her husband by a decade, dying on October 20, 1982. Burial was in the courtyard of the library, beside the grave of her husband.

ROBERT H. FERRELL

Ferrell, Robert H., ed. *Dear Bess: The Letters from Harry to Bess Truman, 1910–1959.* New York: Norton, 1983.
Truman, Margaret. *Bess W. Truman.* New York: Macmillan, 1986.

TRUMAN, HARRY S. (1884–1972)

Born in Lamar, Missouri, on May 8, 1884, to John Anderson Truman, a farmer and livestock trader, and Martha Ellen Young Truman, Harry Truman was the oldest of three children. He spent most of his childhood and adolescence in Independence, Missouri, ten miles from the rapidly growing metropolis of

Kansas City. The county seat of Jackson County, Independence had been the eastern terminus of the Santa Fe and Oregon Trails. An upper-South town in its ambience and racial mores, it had been the site of Civil War skirmishes in which most of its citizens had sympathized with the Confederacy.

Afflicted with myopic vision from birth and fitted at the age of eight with thick, fragile eyeglasses, Truman appears to have had an awkward childhood in which he worked hard to relate to other boys and, as he put it in his *Memoirs,* was "always afraid of the girls my age and older." Instructed to avoid sports and rough games, ordered to run away from fights if necessary, he was closer to his mother than to his rough, two-fisted father. He learned to play the piano, began to take serious instruction, and for a time aspired to a career as a concert pianist. Yet, possibly out of a desire to establish a more masculine identity, he also venerated great soldiers and sought an appointment to the United States Military Academy, an ambition made impossible by his vision problems.

As a student Truman was bookish but not outstanding. Unlike most teenage boys of that time and place, he completed high school, graduating in 1901. Perhaps because his father was beginning to have financial problems, he seems to have never considered a university education. Instead, he studied briefly at a Kansas City business college, then went to work. (In 1923 and 1924 he successfully completed a series of night classes at the Kansas City School of Law, but he never finished the curriculum.)

For five years Truman plugged away at low-paying jobs as a construction timekeeper, then a Kansas City bank clerk. In 1906 he joined his parents, his younger brother, and his sister in managing the six-hundred-acre farm owned by his elderly grandmother, Harriet Louisa Young, and his uncle, Harrison Young. They left it to the Trumans at their deaths. For the next ten years Truman was a farmer. The hard manual labor probably left him more confident of his masculinity and strengthened his relationship with his father, but he also heartily disliked it.

Not an isolated hayseed, Truman joined the Masonic order and numerous other fraternal organizations, dabbled in local politics, visited Kansas City frequently, and served in a National Guard artillery battery based there (1905–1911). Sometime toward the end of 1910 he began to court **Bess Wallace,** a socially prominent Independence woman to whom he had first been attracted when they were in Sunday school together at the age of five. She appears to have been the only serious romantic interest of his life.

After the death of his father in November 1914, Truman's activities began to move away from the farm. With two partners he made a disastrous investment in an Oklahoma lead and zinc mine; after six months, they each had lost five thousand dollars and exhausted their funds. Truman then converted his remaining share of the farm into equity for an oil exploration venture (1917–1919) that ultimately did little more than return his original investment.

As the United States moved toward war in 1917, Truman rejoined the National Guard and participated in a drive to expand the Kansas City and Independence batteries into an artillery regiment. Elected a lieutenant by the newly formed outfit (which became the 129th Regiment, Sixtieth Field Artillery Brigade, Thirty-fifth Division), he was an outstanding junior officer in regular army training at Fort Sill, Oklahoma. Especially successful as manager of the regimental canteen, he was also one of ten officers selected for advanced artillery training in France. He was recommended for promotion to captain just before his departure; the commission eventually reached him in France.

In July 1918 Truman was given command of the regiment's Battery D. Although its men had a reputation for unruliness, he led them firmly through the war, won the affection of most of them, and emerged with justifiable pride in his leadership. The battery saw combat action in the Vosges, was kept in reserve for the Saint-Mihiel offensive, provided close support to American infantry in the bloody Argonne campaign, and concluded the war in the rear guard to the east of Verdun. In the Argonne Truman received the dangerous assignment of forward spotter for the regiment; he is generally credited with relaying information that led to the destruction of an enemy battery.

Returning home in 1919 Truman married Bess Wallace, who would remain his wife until his death fifty-two years later. They had one child, Mary Margaret, who was born on February 17, 1924. In partnership with army comrade Eddie Jacobson, Truman opened a haberdashery shop in downtown Kansas City at the end of 1919. He wanted to be active in civic affairs and aspired to membership in the metropolitan decision-making elite. During this period he was a leading figure in the Reserve Officers Association, the American Legion, and the Triangle Club, a civic improvement group. A few years later he would serve as president of the National Old Trails Association, a good-roads and historical-commemoration association.

Although Truman achieved a degree of public prominence, his business, caught in the severe economic downturn of 1920–1922, fared badly. Heavily in debt, it closed in September 1922. Truman also lost a Kansas farm he had acquired as a real estate investment. For years he was saddled with debts that he paid off a bit at a time. He was also periodically harassed by court judgments and efforts to garnish his bank accounts.

In 1922 Truman was elected Eastern District judge of the county court, an administrative position akin to that of county commissioner. While he ran as a war veteran and enjoyed considerable independent support, his most important backing came from Boss **Thomas J. Pendergast**'s Kansas City machine, with which he and his father had long been loosely affiliated. His wide connections and good reputation made him a valuable candidate for the organization, which was attempting to extend its influence into rural, small-town Jackson County.

During his two-year term, Truman established himself as an advocate of economy, efficiency, and better rural roads. He was also a machine loyalist who distributed patronage primarily to his own party faction and awarded county contracts to "pet" suppliers. Then and later he cast a blind eye toward the ballot-box stuffing, thuggery, and illegal activities of his own backers, while routinely condemning the lesser sins of civic reformers and other good-government types. Nevertheless, he won wide respect as a personally honest politician striving for as clean an administration as circumstances would allow.

Defeated for reelection in 1924 because of an intraparty conflict, Truman supported himself as the membership director of the local auto club; he also helped establish a savings and loan association. However, he remained interested in politics. In 1926, with the Democratic Party reunited and under firm Pendergast domination, he easily won election as presiding judge of the county court; he was reelected in 1930.

A shrewd practitioner of coalition politics, Truman moved easily from a homogenous rural, small-town political base to a large and heterogeneous urban political setting. He worked easily with diverse groups, including African Americans, who had become increasingly important as a machine constituency. Advocating numerous administrative reforms, he also solidified his standing with the antimachine civic establishment while continuing the patronage and contract politics that the machine required of him. A firm and creative chief county administrator, he won special acclaim for the building of a modern county road system and a downtown Kansas City courthouse without a whiff of the scandal that had usually been associated with such projects.

Truman's second term, impacted by the Great Depression, was difficult. He had to institute sharp salary reductions and lay off hundreds of county employees; by 1934 the county was for all practical purposes operating in a state of bankruptcy. Still, he received little blame for what was widely understood as a catastrophe beyond his control. He briefly assayed a race for governor of Missouri, but, unable to develop the requisite backing, turned his attention to a seat in the United States Congress, which he hoped to claim in 1934.

Instead, the machine slotted Truman for the United States Senate. He waged an exhausting personal campaign in the Democratic primary; ultimately, however, he owed his victory to the Kansas City organization, which turned out an enormous vote for him and influenced the state administration to use its patronage in his behalf. He easily won the general election.

Throughout his senatorial career Truman was a reliable supporter of President Franklin Roosevelt's New Deal, though until World War II he received little recognition from the White House. His association with the Pendergast machine tarnished him in the eyes of some liberals; nonetheless, he was widely popular among his fellow senators, who appreciated his modesty, hard work, and capacity for friendship.

During his first term in the Senate Truman was most prominent for his engagement with transportation issues. Appointed to the Interstate Commerce Committee, he worked closely with its chairman, Burton K. Wheeler, on an investigation of railroad financing and advocated a major overhaul of the Interstate Commerce Act. The inquiry demonstrated a distrust of big business and finance that he shared with older "insurgent" progressives such as Wheeler. It also allowed him to establish close ties to the railway unions. The ultimate outcome, the Transportation Act of 1940, gave some assistance to the railroads by subjecting inland water carriers to federal regulation. Truman also played a role in developing the Civil Aeronautics Act of 1938 and won recognition as a promoter of civil aviation.

Truman developed a strong interest in foreign policy, establishing himself as an advocate of military preparedness to meet the Axis challenge. An old Wilsonian, he believed in the ideal of an international organization, but his World War I combat experience had left him with a realistic appreciation of the role of power. During the war years he would be an important advocate of postwar international involvement and the United Nations.

Truman was reelected to the Senate in 1940, though Boss Pendergast was in prison and his organization in tatters. His opponents in the primary were U.S. District Atty. **Maurice M. Milligan,** who had prosecuted Pendergast, and Gov. **Lloyd Stark,** a one-time friend who had joined the anti-Pendergast movement. Waging a hard campaign, Truman capitalized heavily on his incumbency, his military expertise, and the record of his first term. He drew important support from the railway unions, African Americans (drawn by his public support of civil rights bills), his Senate colleague **Bennett Champ Clark** (who saw Stark as a rival for leadership of the state Democratic Party), and a network of friends and professional politicians (especially in Kansas City, St. Louis, and southeast Missouri). Carrying both Kansas City and St. Louis, he overcame a solid outstate plurality for Stark and won the primary by less than eight thousand votes. In November, with Roosevelt at the head of the ticket, he narrowly defeated his Republican opponent.

In 1941 the newly elected senator received authorization for a select committee to investigate defense production. Starting from modest beginnings, the "Truman Committee" emerged as a major force on Capitol Hill. It probed almost every aspect of the war effort except actual military operations, concentrating on incompetence, waste, and extravagance in military construction. The committee made little or no difference in the course of the war and rarely stopped military waste. It nonetheless attracted praise because it established itself as a guardian of the interests of the ordinary American against the military brass, big business, and big labor.

In 1944 Truman, popular among both liberal and conservative Democrats, was a natural compromise choice for the vice presidential nomination. Elected with Roosevelt that November, he became president upon Roosevelt's death on April 12, 1945.

A mediocre speaker, a man of erratic temperament, with an unprepossessing presence, Truman had the misfortune to replace the most dominant political personality of the century. His popularity moved up and down sharply with events. As measured by the polls, his approval rating was below 50 percent more often than not. His relations with Congress were usually shaky. His last two and a half years, dominated by the Korean War, McCarthyism, and numerous instances of small-bore administration corruption, were politically disastrous. When he left office at the beginning of 1953 he was widely unpopular. Yet, his presidency ranks among the three or four most important of the twentieth century.

At home, Truman consolidated the political revolution that Roosevelt had initiated in the 1930s. His liberal "Fair Deal" program backed labor unions and civil rights for African Americans, and enhanced social welfare (housing, aid to education, and national health insurance). His legislative agenda was mostly stalled in a Congress dominated by a coalition of Republicans and conservative Democrats. In the area of civil rights, however, he was able to take significant administrative action, including the desegregation of the armed forces and support for pathbreaking antisegregation federal court cases. Maintaining neo–New Deal liberalism as the unifying theme of the Democratic "presidential party," he won an upset victory in the 1948 election and preserved the Roosevelt coalition.

Truman's foreign policy established a post–World War II world order that endured for forty-five years,

ending in triumph with the collapse of Communism. He had no diplomatic experience, but he possessed a strong vision based on the Victorian idealism in which he had been educated, the aspirations of Woodrow Wilson, his own World War I experience, and an instinctive understanding that the totalitarianism of the left was as deadly a threat to Western civilization as that of the right.

Although the most partisan of politicians on domestic issues, Truman was largely successful during his first term in working with internationalist Republicans on foreign policy issues. His major achievement was the containment of Soviet expansion in Western Europe and the Middle East through the Truman Doctrine, the Marshall Plan, and the North Atlantic Treaty. These were buttressed by international trade and monetary agreements that fostered Western unity and prosperity.

The unavoidable fall of China to the Communists in 1949 and the perhaps avoidable Korean War, which lasted from June 1950 to July 1953, laid bare weak spots in the administration's conceptualization and policy execution vis-à-vis Asia. Nonetheless, the preservation of a liberal Atlantic community and the maintenance of Japan in the Western camp were far more critical to American interests than the setbacks on the Asian mainland.

As president, Truman had little time for Missouri, but he kept in close touch with political developments there and openly intervened in three Democratic primary elections. In 1946 he succeeded in "purging" Rep. Roger Slaughter, a conservative Democrat from eastern Jackson County. The victory became an embarrassment when investigators found that Slaughter was a victim of massive vote fraud; the subsequent theft of the evidence prevented indictments against the president's machine allies but greatly magnified the scandal. Throughout his presidency Truman's enemies used his Pendergast connections against him.

Truman also did nothing for his reputation by supporting mediocre party regulars for Democratic senatorial nominations against the ultimate victors, **Thomas C. Hennings Jr.** in 1950 and **Stuart Symington** in 1952. No scandals were involved, but the episodes showed Truman was out of touch with the changing politics of his own state. All the same, he remained popular in Missouri. For a time in early 1952 he toyed with the idea of declaring for the Senate himself and running from the White House. Had he done so, he surely would have been nominated and elected.

Upon leaving the White House Truman returned to his home in Independence. For a decade he remained a significant voice in American public life, working first out of an office in Kansas City, then from the Harry S. Truman Library, which became the premier research center for his presidency. He wrote his *Memoirs* (two volumes, published in 1955–1956), *Mr. Citizen* (1960), and occasional newspaper columns, spoke extensively, and participated in a television documentary series about his presidency.

Truman hoped to maintain considerable influence in the Democratic Party, but his efforts to block the nominations of Adlai Stevenson in 1956 and John F. Kennedy in 1960 were futile. Instead, he oscillated between public identities as a fierce partisan campaigner and a respected elder statesman.

After 1963 advancing age and declining health ended Truman's public career. He lived quietly in Independence until his final hospitalization and death in Kansas City on December 26, 1972. In retirement he had increasingly become esteemed as a traditional, genuine American leader with no trace of the artificiality of the generation of media-oriented politicians who succeeded him. The myth grew after his death, until most Americans vaguely thought of him as a quintessential representative of American democracy.

ALONZO L. HAMBY

Ferrell, Robert H. *Harry S. Truman: A Life.* Columbia: University of Missouri Press, 1996.

Hamby, Alonzo L. *Man of the People: The Life of Harry S. Truman.* New York: Oxford University Press, 1995.

McCullough, David. *Truman.* New York: Simon and Schuster, 1992.

Truman, Harry S. *Memoirs.* 2 vols. Garden City, N.Y.: Doubleday, 1955–1956.

TURNBO, SILAS C. (1844–1925)

Silas C. Turnbo collected stories from Ozarkers in the upper–White River country of Arkansas and Missouri from as early as the 1860s continuing into the early twentieth century. His collection, transcribed into around twenty-five hundred typed pages, constitutes the largest single manuscript holding of nineteenth-century Ozarks reminiscences and genealogy. The family, as institution, is Turnbo's common threshold of departure in what could be described as a "regional prosopography." The collection includes history, folklore, and tales of pioneers' heroic adventures on the antebellum frontier and in the Civil War.

The Turnbo family followed other upland southerners through Pennsylvania, South Carolina, Tennessee, and into the Ozarks. Silas, born in Taney County, Missouri, on May 26, 1844, was the eldest of eleven children and grew up along the White River while his father farmed, worked in the timber, and participated in the river trade. The family was Southern in its sympathies, and Silas served three years in active duty with the Twenty-seventh Arkansas Infantry (1862–1865).

While soldiering, Turnbo kept wartime diaries that burned shortly after the war. They were obviously important to him because he soon rewrote them from memory, later expanding them into a history now transcribed as the *History of the Twenty-seventh Arkansas Confederate Infantry,* edited by Desmond Walls Allen (1988). In Turnbo's larger collection of reminiscences he reported that he began collecting stories as early as 1866. He collected intermittently until the 1890s when he envisioned a much larger effort.

As a middle-aged man past fifty, Turnbo sought first- and second-generation settlers who would talk to him about "old times." From 1898 to 1907 he wrote numerous articles for newspapers in Taneyville, Forsyth, Gainesville, and Kansas City, Missouri, and Lead Hill, Harrison, and Yellville, Arkansas. Most of his oral history is set in Taney and Ozark Counties, Missouri, and in Boone and Marion Counties, Arkansas. In 1905 he assembled his nostalgic writings into a modest book, *Fireside Stories of the Early Days in the Ozarks.* He and a few merchants peddled the fifty-cent books, and in 1907 Turnbo published a much shorter volume two of his *Fireside Stories.* He planned a series, but the book sales simply did not return profits to support it.

During his early years of journalism, Turnbo mortgaged his 160-acre farm and lost it in a foreclosure suit in 1902. For the rest of their lives, he and his wife, Matilda, lived with various children in Missouri, Oklahoma, and New Mexico, except for three short terms Silas spent at the Confederate Soldiers' Home in Higginsville, Missouri. Determined in his literary endeavor, Turnbo's most active period of collecting and writing occurred from 1902 to 1908 while he lived with a daughter in Ozark County, Missouri.

Shortly after publication of his first *Fireside Stories* in 1905, the chronicler began an eight-year correspondence with William E. Connelley, a prolific author and publisher of western, Kansas, and Civil War history books. The letters reveal a modest and polite Ozarker, fully aware of his limited writing skills, who hoped that Connelley would edit and publish his collection. Connelley encouraged Turnbo in his efforts by sending him books on frontier and western lore. He offered to find a publisher for Turnbo who, in turn, approved of Connelley as editor of the stories; Turnbo asked for joint copyright and a share of the proceeds, if any.

By 1913, with no prospect of seeing more of his collection published, increasing health problems, and his need for a train ticket from New Mexico to Missouri, Turnbo sold all rights to his collection to Connelley for $27.50. He returned to the Ozarks, continued collecting stories (that apparently were lost or destroyed), and wrote that it was his intention to spend the rest of his life and be buried in the White River Hills, a wish unfulfilled.

Aged Ozarkers in the late twentieth century remembered Turnbo walking the dusty Ozarks back roads during the early 1920s. They saw him aided with a walking stick and carrying his personal belongings in a red handkerchief. He made unannounced appearances throughout the White River neighborhoods, accepting local hospitality. Some relatives thought he was cursed with a strange idiosyncrasy—he never really worked, just mused about old times and the thrill of the chase in the great Ozarks outdoors. At age eighty, in March 1925, he passed away in Broken Arrow, Oklahoma.

Turnbo's writings continued to have a life as they were sold to collectors and deposited in private and public libraries, and selections were reprinted by local historical societies, magazines, and newspapers. Complete manuscript sets are housed at the Springfield–Greene County Public Library in Springfield, Missouri, and in the Heiskell Collection at the University of Arkansas–Little Rock.

LYNN MORROW

Morrow, Lynn. " 'I Am Nothing but a Poor Scribbler' ": Silas Turnbo and His Writings." *White River Valley Historical Quarterly* 10 (spring 1991): 3–9.

———. "The Ozarks Eden of Silas Turnbo." *Ozarks Watch* 6 (summer–fall 1992): 8–14.

Morrow, Lynn, and James Keefe, eds. *The White River Chronicles: The Writings of S. C. Turnbo.* Fayetteville: University of Arkansas Press, 1994.

TURNER, JAMES MILTON (1839?–1915)

Although numerous secondary accounts of James Milton Turner's life list his birth date as May 16, 1840, he recorded in 1871 that he was born on August 22, 1839. Whichever date is accurate, he was born in St. Louis County, the son of John Turner, a free black farrier, and Hannah, the slave of the Reverend Aaron Young and his wife, Theodosia. Hannah and James Milton were freed by Theodosia Young on December 5, 1843.

James Milton Turner was educated in secretly run schools in the St. Louis area during the late 1840s and early 1850s. An 1847 Missouri law prohibited the education of blacks, slave or free, even in the privacy of one's own home. In either 1854 or 1855 Turner's parents sent him to Ohio to attend Oberlin College's preparatory department. At the time Oberlin was a hotbed for Christian abolitionism. Turner seems to have been deeply affected by the antislavery rhetoric

he heard at Oberlin and by the identification of slave owners as evil persons deserving of chastisement and revenge.

Turner returned to St. Louis during the late 1850s and worked as a porter until the Civil War broke out. He reportedly entered the Civil War as a body servant to Col. Madison Miller, a St. Louis railroad entrepreneur. According to Turner, his involvement in the war ended at the Battle of Shiloh when he received a hip wound that caused him to limp the remainder of his life and Colonel Miller was captured by Confederate forces.

Turner became involved with the Missouri Equal Rights League in late 1865. This organization was formed as a consequence of the so-called convention movement of 1864–1865, under the umbrella of a national organization known as the National Equal Rights League. The Missouri Equal Rights League was made up of African Americans and their white supporters who sought legislative allowances for black political and civil rights, including the franchise. As secretary of the league, Turner traveled throughout the state making public speeches in support of its causes.

In 1868 Turner found employment in a black public school in Kansas City. The next year he and his wife taught in a black school in Boonville. That same year Turner worked as an agent of both the Freedmen's Bureau and the Missouri Department of Education to investigate the condition of black education in Missouri and to establish more public schools for African Americans. During much of the next year he logged approximately ten thousand miles, establishing thirty-two new schools in various parts of the state. He also sought and obtained state financial support for Lincoln Institute, an all-black normal school located in Jefferson City.

During the 1870 election Turner campaigned tirelessly for Radical Republican candidates and against the reenfranchisement of Rebel sympathizers. When the Radical candidate for governor, **Joseph W. McClurg,** lost his race, Turner turned to President **Ulysses S. Grant** for a federal appointment. Grant named Turner the U.S. minister resident and consul general to Liberia in early 1871, making him the first African American to hold that position. Turner served as the minister to Liberia until 1878, weathering the storms of a civil war in 1875, recurring bouts with malaria, and the tedium and drudgery of what was largely a clerical post. He also alienated many African Americans by speaking out vigorously and often against American blacks emigrating to Africa in any large numbers. He thought the African climate and way of life were too alien for American blacks.

Upon his return to America in 1878, Turner launched a bid for a congressional seat from Missouri's Third District. Failing in this effort, he next turned his attention and energies to relief efforts on behalf of the so-called exodusters. These were blacks who were fleeing the South in the wake of the restoration of home rule following the removal of federal troops after the Compromise of 1877. Turner's relief efforts, including those of the Colored Emigration Aid Association, which he established, were minimally successful. In 1881 he embarked on an effort to settle southern black immigrants in Oklahoma. This effort failed because a federal court ruled that Indian Territory was not open to settlement by blacks or whites.

Turner's trips to Oklahoma, however, made him aware of conflict between the Cherokee Indians who lived in Indian Territory and their former black slaves who claimed tribal rights. In 1883 the United States Congress ordered that the Cherokee Nation be paid three hundred thousand dollars for the cession of several millions of acres of land west of the Arkansas River. The money was to be distributed among members of the Cherokee Nation as its council saw fit. Blacks protested when the council voted to limit the distribution of money to full-blooded Cherokees, thus excluding black freedmen.

Turner entered the conflict as an advocate for the freedmen. Acting as an attorney for the former slaves, though he had no formal legal training, Turner sought first legislative and then judicial relief on their behalf. His contemporary critics argued, with some justification, that he used chicanery and deceit in the pursuit of his goal. In 1888 Congress passed a law that provided for the distribution of seventy-five thousand dollars among the Cherokee freedmen and other "adopted citizens" of the Cherokee Nation. Turner's fee for legal services was 25 percent of the gross amount paid by the U.S. government, plus expenses.

Although the freedmen's claim appeared settled in 1888, in reality the matter was far from over. Confusion reigned; for example, it was unclear who among the freedmen was entitled to money, and how much. It was a controversy that engaged Turner throughout the remainder of his life.

Meanwhile, Turner, the once ardent advocate of the Republican Party, had grown increasingly disenchanted with the party of Abraham Lincoln. In 1888 he urged blacks to abandon the Republican Party because it had ceased to respond to their needs. He played a key role in a convention of black independents and Democrats held in Indianapolis in July 1888.

Although Turner made repeated efforts to wield power in the way he had in the 1870 election, he never again enjoyed the same prominence. As the years passed, and his frustration grew, he became increasingly embittered. During the 1890s he turned to Prince Hall Freemasonry for companionship and

recognition. Although he achieved some level of notoriety among black Missouri Masons, recognition by an elite group among a black minority was less than satisfying.

Turner died on November 1, 1915, in Ardmore, Oklahoma, of injuries he had suffered in a tank-car explosion on September 27, 1915. He is buried in Father Dickson Cemetery in Crestwood, Missouri. Three elementary schools in the St. Louis area are named for him, as is a playground.

GARY R. KREMER

Christensen, Lawrence O. "J. Milton Turner: An Appraisal." *Missouri Historical Review* 70 (October 1975): 1–19.

———. "Schools for Blacks: J. Milton Turner in Reconstruction Missouri." *Missouri Historical Review* 76 (January 1982): 121–35.

Dilliard, Irving. "James Milton Turner: A Little-Known Benefactor of His People." *Journal of Negro History* 19 (October 1934): 372–411.

Kremer, Gary R. *James Milton Turner and the Promise of America: The Public Life of a Post–Civil War Black Leader.* Columbia: University of Missouri Press, 1991.

TURNER, SARAH LUCILLE (1898–1972)

One of the first two women in the Missouri House of Representatives, Democrat Sarah Lucille Turner won election to the Fifty-second General Assembly from the Sixth District of Jackson County, in Kansas City, in 1922.

Turner was born on March 28, 1898, at Centralia, Illinois. The family moved to Kansas City, Missouri, ten years later, where Sarah attended public school and graduated with honors from Northeast High School in 1915. After graduation she worked during the day for Havens Structural Steel Company and attended evening classes at the Kansas City School of Law. She completed law studies in 1922 and went to work in the law offices of Hagerman and Jost in Kansas City.

Turner did not plan to seek a political office until some of the men in her law class voiced objections to women holding office. She had visited the legislature when she took the bar examination in Jefferson City, and she knew she could do as well as some of the men she saw there. Thus, she decided to run. In her campaign Turner had the support of **Joseph B. Shannon,** a friend and a leader of the Democratic Party's "Rabbit" faction. She received a majority of several hundred votes over her Republican opponent in the November 1922 general election.

The youngest member of the General Assembly, Turner expressed an interest in legislation for women and children, though she was not a member of any women's organizations. Five of her bills were passed. She introduced House Bill 15, making the obsolete mothers' pension law in Jackson County conform with the rest of the state. Other bills she introduced pertained to the employment of children, increased appropriations for the state reformatory farm for women, and the licensing of boarding homes for children. Her most notable legislation, House Bill 135, designated the hawthorn as the official state flower.

Turner chaired the Children's Code Committee, and she served as a member of the Civil and Criminal Procedure, Constitution Amendments and Criminal Jurisprudence, and the University and School of Mines Committees. She favored better education facilities and increasing teachers' salaries. Turner became the first woman to preside as the acting Speaker of the House, on March 16, 1923. Well informed and with sound judgment, she had demonstrated her independence by entering the race for the legislature against her parents' wishes. She believed in equality with men, never asked for favors because she was a woman, and expected to be treated as a fellow member of the legislature.

In 1924 Turner ran for a second term in the House, but was defeated in the general election in November by a Republican landslide. After moving to New York she worked as a secretary for Frank Walsh, a former Kansas Citian and prominent labor attorney. Later she served as a secretary to Malcom Muir, vice president of McGraw-Hill Publishing Company.

In 1933, during the early days of the Franklin Roosevelt administration, Turner went to Washington, D.C., to work with Gen. Hugh S. Johnson, director of the National Recovery Act. When Muir became publisher of *Newsweek,* Turner again served as his secretary. In the 1950s she became the personnel manager for the magazine and worked there until her retirement at the age of sixty-five.

In 1932 Turner married Walter C. Jepson, a New York real estate agent, World War I veteran, and a captain in the United States Air Force during World War II. Following retirement in 1964, the couple moved to Southern Pines, North Carolina, where Sarah Turner died of cancer on April 12, 1972.

MARY K. DAINS

Dains, Mary K. "Women Pioneers in the Missouri Legislature." *Missouri Historical Review* 85 (October 1990): 40–52.
———, ed. *Show Me Missouri Women: Selected Biographies.* Kirksville, Mo.: Thomas Jefferson University Press, 1989.
Kansas City Star, November 8, 1922–January 3, 1923.
Kansas City Times, April 14, 1972.
Official Manual of the State of Missouri, 1923–1924. Jefferson City: Secretary of State, 1924.
Turner, George F. Letter to Mary K. Dains, February 16, 1977.

TWAIN, MARK. *See* Clemens, Samuel Langhorne.

TYLER, RUTH "IDA" HISEY (1894–1976)

Ruth "Ida" Hisey Tyler, a writer and musician, was born on April 22, 1894, near Kansas City, Missouri, the daughter of John Henry and Louisa Jane Kerr Hisey. Although both parents were natives of Illinois, at least one branch of her family came from Kentucky. Her father was a carpenter and farmed near Bonner Springs, Kansas. Ruth "stayed with an old couple from Kaintucky to go to High School [in Kansas City] and Granny learn't me all she knew (which was a-plenty)." In 1913 the family moved to Neosho where her mother ran the Hisey Tea Room. Later the family ran a regionally known restaurant along Shoal Creek between Neosho and Joplin.

On May 15, 1917, Ruth Hisey married Ray Earl Tyler. The couple settled in Neosho about 1920. A sign painter by trade, Tyler, as Ruth always called him, also ran the projection machine at a Neosho motion picture house during the days of silent films, while Ruth played the piano. They also tinted slides and photographs. The couple had no children. Of these years Ruth wrote: "I raised canaries and sold them, red Tabby Persian cats—not both at the same time, though to be sure. . . . I made gardens and grew flowers, raised chickens, geese, and ducks—ran a large kennel of fine hunting dogs—baby sat for their babies—helped rear a passel o' neighbor young'uns."

In 1939 Turner organized a folk festival as part of Neosho's centennial celebration. Encouraged by May Kennedy McCord of Springfield, she began a study of Ozark speech and music. She also worked with **Vance Randolph** and Booth Campbell. Acquiring a forty-seven-string dulcimer, she performed at the first Ozarks Folk Festival at the University of Arkansas in 1949 and subsequently recorded seven tunes for the university. In the early 1950s she performed at the National Folk Festival in St. Louis, at Eureka Springs, and at other regional gatherings. In 1955 she appeared on NBC's *Monitor Radio.* Her last public appearance was at the Ozark Folk Festival in Eureka Springs, Arkansas, in 1970.

Turner was frequently photographed in costume, usually a gray calico-print dress, often with an apron, and a black- or blue-checked gingham slat bonnet. Carrying a handmade white-oak basket, she wore her mother's gold spectacles. "The costume worn is definitely not hillbilly nor meant to be humorous. It is the prim dress of a pioneer Lady at home."

Turner's first published work, the poem "Somewhere in the Ozarks," appeared in McCord's "Hillbilly Heartbeat" column in the *Springfield Leader and Press* in 1936 and was reprinted in the *Neosho Times* and the *Kansas City Star.* Later she became a columnist, writing "Ozark Almanac" in *Ozark Guide Magazine,* and "Ozark Lady in Print" for the *Neosho Daily News.* "Somewhere in the Ozarks" in the *Ozarks Mountaineer* ran from September 1952 to August 1974. "Rhymes, riddles and receets" was her literary formula for what she styled her "hillosophy." Besides publishing "receets," she won a regional baking contest in 1951 with her recipe for Ozark persimmon holler cake. She published more than sixty-three poems and served as guest editor of the *Kansas City Poetry Magazine* in June 1950. Her poems were frequently read on the radio. Other radio work included writing scripts for the "Mirandy" segment of the *National Farm and Home Hour.* She was an honorary member of the National Pen Women.

A "sort of a local character," Turner, Vance Randolph noted, "is downright amusing, sometimes salty, sometimes she has words of deep philosophy and true faith." Although she was not a native of the Ozarks, she studied folkways carefully. In her writings she preserved the flavor of regional dialect, while her dulcimer performances played a major role in returning that instrument to popularity. In her later years the music served to introduce her stories, and it was as an Ozarks storyteller that she was most appreciated. She died on September 10, 1976.

MICHAEL B. DOUGAN

Dougan, Michael B. *Arkansas Odyssey: The Saga of Arkansas from Prehistoric Times to Present.* Little Rock: Rose Publishing, 1994.

Lawless, Ray M. *Folksingers and Folksongs of America.* 1960. Reprint, Westport, Conn.: Greenwood Press, 1981.

Tyler, Ruth. Recordings. Folklore Collection. Special Collections. Mullins Library, University of Arkansas, Little Rock.

———. Scrapbooks and Memorabilia. Neosho Public Library, Newton County Historical Museum, Neosho, Mo.

VALLÉ, FRANÇOIS, I (1716–1783)

François Vallé I was born in Beauport, Canada (near Quebec City) on January 2, 1716, and emigrated to the Mississippi River valley sometime during the early 1740s. Coming from illiterate peasant stock, Vallé settled in the then-metropolis of the Illinois Country, Kaskaskia, determined to improve his lot in life. He engaged in agriculture, lead mining, and the Indian trade and by 1748 had acquired enough wealth and status to marry Marianne Billeron, the literate daughter of the royal notary in Kaskaskia, Leonard Billeron, and Marie-Claire Catoire.

Vallé was not one of the original settlers in Ste. Genevieve, the French village founded on the west bank of the Mississippi around 1750, for he appears as a citizen of Kaskaskia in the 1752 census of the Illinois country conducted by Maj. Jean-Jacques Macarty, commandant at Fort de Chartres. In 1754, however, Vallé and his wife took the plunge, crossed the Mississippi, and tied their futures and their fortunes to the developing town of Ste. Genevieve.

By 1760 Vallé had been appointed captain of the Ste. Genevieve militia by Major Macarty. In French colonial society of the Mississippi River Valley this position meant that one was the preeminent citizen of a community. However, Vallé was honored with an additional title: special lieutenant and civil judge. This title meant that Vallé, as the lieutenant of the commandant at Fort de Chartres, was in fact the local government in the outpost of Ste. Genevieve, the only French community on the west bank of the Mississippi at that time.

The French and Indian War of 1754–1763 did not penetrate to remote Ste. Genevieve, but the geopolitical changes wrought by the war had a significant impact upon the town and the career of François Vallé, its leading citizen. Unbeknownst to Ste. Genevieve's citizens, King Louis XV of France decided in 1762 to convey all of Louisiana west of the Mississippi (in addition to New Orleans on the east side of the river) to his cousin, Carlos III of Spain. The purpose of this extraordinary conveyance was to prevent Great Britain from acquiring sovereignty over both banks of the Mississippi. However, affairs moved slowly in colonial Louisiana, and it was only after several years that Spain took an interest in Upper Louisiana (or Spanish Illinois) and that Ste. Genevieve's citizens became aware they had become subjects of the king of Spain.

However, when a small group of Spanish administrators and soldiers arrived in Upper Louisiana in 1770, Vallé welcomed them heartily and provided them with all the hospitality that could be mustered in that remote region of the Spanish colonial empire. The Spaniards reciprocated by permitting Vallé to keep the titles conveyed to him by the French government, thereby anointing him as the premier citizen of Ste. Genevieve. Even when Spanish military commandants were sent to the town (such as Louis de Villars, Sylvio Cartabona, and Antonio de Oro), Vallé remained the community's most powerful citizen. He was wealthy, he had important commercial connections up and down the Mississippi River, and he could appeal directly to Spanish colonial authorities in St. Louis and New Orleans. Indeed, the first Spanish commandant in Ste. Genevieve, Louis Dubreuil de Villars, deemed it prudent to marry Vallé's eldest daughter, Marie-Louise.

Vallé's deepest commitments were to his family and his community, but he consistently demonstrated his loyalty to the Spanish regime in Upper Louisiana. When in 1780 the British launched an attack (with a few redcoats and many allied Indians) against St. Louis, he dispatched all three of his surviving sons to the beleaguered capital of the upper province. Charles, François II, and Jean-Baptiste all participated in this curious episode in the American Revolution that was fought in Spanish Illinois, and all three survived. Their older brother, Joseph, had been killed by a Chickasaw attack at Mine la Motte in 1776.

By the time François Vallé I was dying in 1783 he could face his future in eternity with some equanimity. His family was wealthy from his enterprises in agriculture, lead mining, and commerce. A reliable measure of this wealth was his relatively large holding of African slaves: twenty men, women, and children. One son had been killed and another, Charles, was destroying his career with strong drink and sexual excesses, but his other children (including an illegitimate daughter, Marguerite) had married well and provided assurance that the Vallés would remain for another generation the preeminent family in the community. François Vallé I died in the Old Town of Ste. Genevieve on September 29, 1783, and was interred in the local cemetery.

CARL J. EKBERG

Ekberg, Carl J. *Colonial Ste. Genevieve: An Adventure on the Mississippi Frontier.* Gerald, Mo.: Patrice Press, 1985.

Houck, Louis. *The Spanish Regime in Missouri: A Collection of Papers and Documents Relating to Upper Louisiana.* 2 vols. Chicago: R. R. Donnelley and Sons, 1909.

Ste. Genevieve Archives. Microfilm. Missouri Historical Society, St. Louis.

Ste. Genevieve Parish Records. Microfilm. State Historical Society of Missouri, Columbia.

Vallé, Capt. Francis. Collection. Missouri Historical Society, St. Louis.

VALLÉ, FRANÇOIS, II (1758–1804)

François Vallé II, the fourth child of **François Vallé I** and **Marianne Billeron Vallé,** was born and baptized in 1758, probably in Kaskaskia (there is no extant baptismal record). While he was still an infant his family moved to the recently founded community of Ste. Genevieve on the west side of the Mississippi.

François II was brought up during the 1760s and 1770s in a family whose economic and political fortunes were steadily rising. The Vallé family was closely connected to the Spanish colonial regime in Louisiana; François II's father maintained his French title of "special lieutenant and civil judge," and his sister, Marie-Louise, married the first Spanish commandant of Ste. Genevieve, Louis Dubreuil de Villars. By the time of the Anglo-Indian attack on St. Louis in 1780, twenty-two-year-old François II was a lieutenant in the Ste. Genevieve militia company, which meant that he could use a Spanish aristocratic title, Don Francisco. His Spanish service record remarks that he displayed "great valor and application, poor capacity, and exemplary conduct."

On January 20, 1777, François II married in Ste. Genevieve Marie Carpentier, the daughter of one of the few local families possessing status equivalent to that of the Vallé family. Between 1778 and 1801 the couple had twelve children baptized in Ste. Genevieve, of whom six lived to adulthood. These high rates of fertility and infant mortality were not unusual in colonial Ste. Genevieve.

By the mid-1780s François II's parents had died; one older brother, Joseph, had been killed by Indians at Mine la Motte; his other older brother, Charles, had destroyed his career with liquor and sexual excess; and his older sister, Marie-Louise de Villars, had moved to Lower Louisiana with her husband. These occurrences left François II as the leader of the most important family in Ste. Genevieve and one of the most important figures in Upper Louisiana. He maintained close social and political ties with the

Spanish lieutenant governors in St. Louis and was a friend and correspondent of **Auguste Chouteau.**

The Spanish censuses of 1787 and 1791 reveal François II to have been one of the wealthiest persons in Ste. Genevieve. He engaged in agriculture, lead mining, salt making, and commerce, and he consistently owned upwards of forty African slaves, more than anyone else in town, a clear measure of his economic and social position.

Between 1787 and 1794 François II fought a bitter political battle with **Henri Peyroux de la Coudrenière,** the appointed Spanish commandant of Ste. Genevieve and an outsider to the community. This fight demonstrated the political strength of the Vallé family in Upper Louisiana. With help from his friends in St. Louis, François II succeeded in undermining Peyroux's position, and in 1794 the latter was removed as commandant on the grounds (later proved to have no substance) that he was politically suspect. François II was appointed to replace Peyroux as commandant in 1794, and for the next decade he exercised as much power in the town as his father had during the 1760s and 1770s.

François II was the first and only commandant of the colonial New Town of Ste. Genevieve. Along with his friends and his younger brother, **Jean-Baptiste Vallé,** he probably moved to the New Town in 1793. This move was portentous for the future of the region, for it meant that other possible loci of settlement—the Old Town of Ste. Genevieve, New Bourbon, and the Saline—would be condemned either to oblivion or to second-class status. François II and his wife built their vertical-log residence (the nucleus of which may still remain) on the north bank of South Gabouri Creek, and during the 1790s this structure was known as the "government house" in Ste. Genevieve. In 1794, as a consequence of wild rumors (totally unfounded) of an imminent American attack on Spanish Illinois, François II oversaw the building of the only fort ever erected in Ste. Genevieve, which was located on the brow of a hill on the south side of South Gabouri Creek, facing François II's residence.

François II died prematurely and was interred on March 6, 1804, under the floor of the Ste. Genevieve parish church, next to the grave of his infant daughter Odile, who had died three years earlier. Burial within the parish church was a signal honor, reserved for only the most distinguished persons, and these grave sites are marked by plaques on the floor of the present church. François II died never having lived under American rule in Upper Louisiana, which in any case probably would not have pleased him anymore than it did the other eminent French Creoles in Ste. Genevieve. His wife, **Marie Carpentier Vallé,** survived him by seven years, and his brother Jean-Baptiste became the preeminent citizen of early American Ste. Genevieve.

CARL J. EKBERG

Ekberg, Carl J. *Colonial Ste. Genevieve: An Adventure on the Mississippi Frontier.* Gerald, Mo.: Patrice Press, 1985.

Houck, Louis. *The Spanish Regime in Missouri: A Collection of Papers and Documents Relating to Upper Louisiana.* 2 vols. Chicago: R. R. Donnelley and Sons, 1909.

Ste. Genevieve Archives. Microfilm. Missouri Historical Society, St. Louis.

Ste. Genevieve Parish Records. Microfilm. State Historical Society of Missouri, Columbia.

Vallé, Capt. Francis. Collection. Missouri Historical Society, St. Louis.

VALLÉ, JEAN-BAPTISTE (1760–1849)

Jean-Baptiste Vallé was born on September 25, 1760, the fifth child of **François Vallé I** and **Marianne Billeron Vallé.** Although he was born in Kaskaskia, Jean-Baptiste's parents were at that time preparing to move across the Mississippi River to the recently founded town of Ste. Genevieve.

Growing up in the premier family of Ste. Genevieve, Jean-Baptiste was probably taught to read and write by his mother, the daughter of a royal notary, and taught business and politics by his father, who held the title of "special lieutenant and civil judge." The fact that Ste. Genevieve, together with the rest of Louisiana, became Spanish territory in 1762 had little effect on Jean-Baptiste's upbringing. He lived and died a French Creole, no matter what sovereign claimed possession of Ste. Genevieve.

As a junior officer Jean-Baptiste accompanied the Ste. Genevieve militia to St. Louis in 1780 to help thwart the British-Indian attack on the capital of Upper Louisiana. In 1783 he married one of the most eligible women in the Illinois country, Marie-Jeanne Barbeau, daughter of Jean-Baptiste Barbeau, captain of the militia in Prairie du Rocher, and Marie-Jeanne Legras. Although the Mississippi River had become an international frontier, the French Creole settlements in the Illinois country remained a tightly knit community. Indeed, within months of her marriage, Marie-Jeanne's family became Americans. The oil-on-canvas portraits done of Jean-Baptiste and Marie-Jeanne reveal a highly respectable French Creole couple.

Jean-Baptiste and Marie-Jeanne Vallé had four children baptized in Ste. Genevieve between 1783 and 1800. All four of these children survived to maturity, a rare occurrence in that time and place.

Jean-Baptiste, like his older brother **François Vallé II,** abandoned the Old Town of Ste. Genevieve and moved to the higher ground of the New Town. In 1793 Jean-Baptiste had a house built on the northwest corner of La Grande Rue (Main Street) and Rue à l'Eglise (Church Street, now Market Street). Constructed in the French Creole style of the time, the walls of this residence were of vertical logs, with galleries on all four sides. The core of this structure (the roof and galleries having been altered) still stands in the same location, and the extensive gardens to the rear of the residence approximate those of the colonial period.

The brothers Jean-Baptiste and François II worked closely together, and like all enterprising men in colonial Ste. Genevieve they invested in whatever was profitable—agriculture, lead mining, salt making, slave trading, and commerce. Either out of deference to François II or by inclination Jean-Baptiste avoided politics and focused his attention on business.

In the Spanish census of 1791 Jean-Baptiste Vallé, descended from French Canadian peasant stock, was enumerated as a Spanish aristocrat, Don Juan Baptista. His position as a captain in the local militia probably accounts for the fancy title. The Spanish service sheet on Jean-Baptiste remarks that he had "great Valor, poor application, great capacity, and good conduct." Presumably, his poor application betrays his general lack of interest in military affairs. The 1791 census also reveals a good deal about Jean-Baptiste's economic activities. He was one of the few entrepreneurs in town who produced the five principal products of the region: wheat, maize, tobacco, salt, and lead. Indeed, his annual production of tobacco, two thousand pounds, was the largest in all of Upper Louisiana. Ownership of slaves was consistently a good index of wealth in colonial Louisiana, and Jean-Baptiste owned thirty-eight African slaves, more than anyone in town except his brother, who owned an identical number.

With the death of his older brother François II in March 1804, Jean-Baptiste became the preeminent citizen of Ste. Genevieve. Therefore, when Capt. **Amos Stoddard** arrived in Ste. Genevieve shortly thereafter, Jean-Baptiste was the obvious choice to be appointed as the town's first American commandant, which position he held for less than a year. The coming of American sovereignty to Ste. Genevieve did not please Jean-Baptiste any more than it did the other French Creole entrepreneurs in town, and he obstinately adhered to his old ways and habits, never, for example, learning to speak English.

Jean-Baptiste's refusal to Americanize himself had little impact on his economic position, however. Tax rolls from the first several decades of the nineteenth century reveal that he remained the wealthiest person in the community. He also lived to witness the burgeoning economic successes of his youngest child, Felix Vallé, a business partner of Pierre Menard, whose residence and commercial establishment were within sight of Jean-Baptiste's own residence.

Jean-Baptiste's wife, Marie-Jeanne Barbeau, died in 1842 at the age of eighty-two, and Jean-Baptiste himself died, as veritable patriarch of Ste. Genevieve, August 3, 1849 at age eighty-eight. They are both buried in the historic cemetery in Ste. Genevieve.

CARL J. EKBERG

Ekberg, Carl J. *Colonial Ste. Genevieve: An Adventure on the Mississippi Frontier.* Gerald, Mo.: Patrice Press, 1985.

Houck, Louis. *The Spanish Regime in Missouri: A Collection of Papers and Documents Relating to Upper Louisiana.* 2 vols. Chicago: R. R. Donnelley and Sons, 1909.

Ste. Genevieve Archives. Microfilm. Missouri Historical Society, St. Louis.

Vallé, Capt. Francis. Collection. Missouri Historical Society, St. Louis.

VALLÉ, MARIANNE BILLERON (1729?–1781)

Marianne Billeron Vallé was born in Kaskaskia around 1729, the daughter of Marie-Claire Catoire and Leonard Billeron dit La Fatigue. Her parents were French Canadian, and her father was a royal notary and therefore a person of some status in Kaskaskia. She grew up in a well-off household during the heyday of French Kaskaskia, the 1730s and 1740s. She received at least a rudimentary education, learning to write in French with an attractive, clear hand. This education was conducted either by her parents or by the French Jesuit fathers who dominated the religious and cultural life of the community. The only dark spot in Marianne's early life was the death of her father in 1740. This left Marianne's mother, known as Widow La Fatigue, to raise five children, Marianne and her four brothers. Marianne's mother was clearly a formidable person, who after the death of her husband took in lodgers and even made business trips to New Orleans.

On January 7, 1748, Marianne married **François Vallé I,** who, despite his illiteracy, was one of the most eligible bachelors in Kaskaskia. Their civil marriage contract, which was drafted according to the Customary Law of Paris, had been signed the day before. This traditional French law ensured that wives had much financial security and were in general the economic equals of their husbands. When important family business was conducted—the sale or purchase of real estate or a slave—husband and wife were considered co-owners, and both signed the contract of exchange.

The 1752 census of Kaskaskia shows Marianne Billeron Vallé's young family as already prosperous; they owned five African slaves, which were precious possessions in the Illinois country. By 1753 they owned real estate in the fledgling community of Ste. Genevieve on the west side of the Mississippi, and a year later they sold their house in Kaskaskia. It seems likely therefore that Missouri acquired in 1754 what would become one of the first families in the early history of the region. Vallé's husband soon became Ste. Genevieve's leading citizen, holding two important offices: captain of the militia and civil judge.

Marianne and François Vallé had six children over a twenty-five-year period: Marie-Louise was born around 1750, married Louis Dubreuil de Villars, the Spanish commandant of Ste. Genevieve, in 1771, and was killed by lightning in Ste. Genevieve in 1801. Charles was born around 1751, married Pelagie Carpentier in 1769, but became an abusive husband, which led his wife to sue for separation of bed and board. Joseph was born around 1754, was killed by Indians at Mine la Motte in 1774, and he had not yet married. François II was born in 1758, married Marie Carpentier in 1777, and went on to become commandant of Ste. Genevieve in the 1790s. Jean-Baptiste was born in 1760, married Marie-Jeanne Barbeau in Prairie du Rocher in 1783, and lived to an advanced age, dying in Ste. Genevieve in 1849. Marianne was born around 1774 and died three years later. Infant and childhood mortality was high in the eighteenth-century Mississippi River Valley.

In addition to these six children there was a seventh child, Marguerite, whom Vallé raised in her household. Marguerite was the illegitimate daughter of François Vallé, but the evidence suggests that Marianne accepted her into the family as one of her own. Marguerite was perhaps the product of a passing liaison between François and an Indian woman, but in any case Marianne's acceptance shows a wonderful generosity of spirit.

Marianne Billeron Vallé died and was interred in Ste. Genevieve in October 1781 at around the age of fifty-two, which was a normal life span for a woman in the eighteenth-century Illinois country. She was much mourned in Upper Louisiana, for she had been popular in both Ste. Genevieve and St. Louis, where she had socialized with the lieutenant governor, **Pedro Joseph Piernas.** During Vallé's lifetime her family became the leading family in Ste. Genevieve and one of the most important in all of Upper Louisiana.

CARL J. EKBERG

Belting, Natalia M. *Kaskaskia under the French Regime.* Urbana: University of Illinois Press, 1948.

Ekberg, Carl J. *Colonial Ste. Genevieve: An Adventure on the Mississippi Frontier.* Gerald, Mo.: Patrice Press, 1985.

Ste. Genevieve Civil Records. Microfilm. Missouri Historical Society, St. Louis.

Ste. Genevieve Parish Records. Microfilm. State Historical Society of Missouri, Columbia.

VALLÉ, MARIE CARPENTIER (1759–1811)

Marie Carpentier was born in 1759 in the village of Nouvelle Chartres, which stood outside of Fort de Chartres, the governmental center of the French Illinois country. Her parents, Henri and Marie Aubuchon Carpentier, were of French Canadian background and were highly respected members of French Creole society in the Illinois country. Many habitants on the east side of the Mississippi bridled at living under British rule after the French and Indian War, and Marie's parents became part of a sizable westward migration during the 1760s. These immigrants preferred living under the Spanish Bourbon regime on the west side of the river, and the Carpentiers selected Ste. Genevieve in which to make their new home. Henri Carpentier quickly became a member of the Ste. Genevieve elite, and was soon an officer in the local militia.

Marie Carpentier was one of the most heavily courted young women in Ste. Genevieve during the 1770s. On January 20, 1777, after signing an elaborate civil marriage contract, she married **François Vallé II** in Ste. Genevieve. For the last twenty-five years of the colonial regime in Ste. Genevieve, Marie and François II were the most prominent couple in the community and one of the most important in all of Upper Louisiana.

Marie and François Vallé were also a fertile couple, and between 1778 and 1801 she bore a dozen children. In colonial Ste. Genevieve the interval between births was often somewhat less than twenty-four months. Menopause ordinarily set in at about age forty-five, halting the childbearing process. Marie had her last child when she was forty-two years old. Life expectancy was short in colonial Ste. Genevieve, and roughly one-third of the children died before reaching their first birthdays (the rate in the United States is now 1.25 percent). Of Marie's twelve children, only seven lived to age five.

François Vallé II was commandant in Ste. Genevieve for the last ten years of the colonial regime in Louisiana. When Perrin du Lac called at the Vallé residence in the 1790s, he was flabbergasted by the appearance of Marie Carpentier Vallé, whom he called "la Commandante," or mistress commandant. He provided an unforgettable description of Vallé, whose appearance struck him as so odd, that is, grotesque, that "it would have been impossible to have clothed her in a fashion so at odds with the adopted customs of the civilized world." Perhaps Marie Carpentier Vallé's attire was aberrant even in Ste. Genevieve, but more likely the women of the frontier town had adopted enough Indian clothing styles, moccasins and buckskin jerkins, for example, so that they appeared bizarre to a metropolitan Frenchman such as du Lac. He was too sophisticated, however, to judge Vallé merely on the basis of her appearance, and he went on to point out that she was a "humane, generous, and compassionate" person.

The townspeople of Ste. Genevieve came to rely upon Vallé for medical advice that was based upon her rich experience as a mother. She, "to whom long experience has given some knowledge of childhood diseases, never refuses her aid when an aggrieved mother comes to her. Day and night she serves the sick, from whom she does not even ask for thanks."

François Vallé II died at age forty-six in 1804, the same year that American government came to Ste. Genevieve. Marie Vallé outlived her husband by seven years, dying in 1811 at age fifty-two. Her estate inventory reveals that she died a wealthy person, owning much real estate and fifteen slaves. In addition to her Roman Catholic faith, Vallé had two things with which to comfort her body and soul when she was on her deathbed: a Franklin stove, which was a newfangled device in Upper Louisiana, and the knowledge that much of the social, economic, and political life of Ste. Genevieve revolved around her extended family.

CARL J. EKBERG

Belting, Natalia M. *Kaskaskia under the French Regime.* Urbana: University of Illinois Press, 1948.

Ekberg, Carl J. *Colonial Ste. Genevieve: An Adventure on the Mississippi Frontier.* Gerald, Mo.: Patrice Press, 1985.

Ste. Genevieve Civil Records. Microfilm. Missouri Historical Society, St. Louis.

Ste. Genevieve Parish Records. Microfilm. State Historical Society of Missouri, Columbia.

VANDIVER, WILLARD DUCAN (1854–1932)

Willard Ducan Vandiver served as an educator, congressman, Missouri insurance commissioner, and director of the United States Subtreasury in St. Louis. He is credited with publicizing the phrase, "I'm from Missouri; you've got to show me," delivered in a Philadelphia speech in 1900. Vandiver drew national attention to the phrase because of a humorous incident prior to the speech and the media attention it attracted, though he did not originate it.

Vandiver was born on March 30, 1854, in Hardy County, Virginia. When he was three, his father, Louis, moved the family to Missouri, finally settling in Fayette in 1871, the location of Central College from which Vandiver graduated in 1877. At Central he received the coveted Adam Hendrix Gold Medal for the best original oration delivered during commencement week.

After graduation Vandiver accepted a professorship of mathematics at Bellevue Collegiate Institute in Caledonia and three years later became president of that institution, a position he held until 1889. In that year he accepted a professorship at Southeast Missouri Normal School in Cape Girardeau. In 1893 he was selected as the school's president.

Because of a decline in enrollment at the normal school, Vandiver was instructed by the board of regents to engage in speaking tours throughout the district. These recruitment trips provided a vehicle for him to become familiar with the Fourteenth Congressional District.

By the end of 1895 Vandiver sought the Democratic nomination for Congress; as he said, "the confinement of the school room was getting a little irksome." **Louis Houck,** president of the board of regents, at first advised Vandiver not to run, but soon became one of his strongest supporters. Vandiver received the nomination in July 1896, and went on to win the election in November. In 1898 he was a Bryan Free Silver Democrat and was greatly influenced by rural Missouri Populism. He favored the primary, income tax, regulation of trusts, and the prohibition of corporate political contributions.

During Vandiver's eight congressional years, he served on the Naval, Manufactures, and Education Committees. He frequently addressed foreign policy issues of the period, including Panama, the Philippines, and Cuba. He supported the declaration of war against Spain in 1898 but strongly opposed the annexation of the Philippines and military occupation of Cuba. After a 1902 Senate investigation revealed acts of atrocity committed against Philippine natives by American soldiers, Vandiver raised the issue on the floor and demanded a congressional investigation. As a member of the Naval Committee, he championed the development of the submarine. Although his support was in part motivated by his desire to save money, he believed that the submarine would revolutionize naval warfare. A submarine cost a half million dollars compared to five million for a battleship. Vandiver was among the first to go down in the *Holland,* the first modern U.S. submarine.

Vandiver represented the Fourteenth District for four consecutive terms, but in 1904 chose not to seek reelection. He seriously considered entering the race for governor, but when he discovered that **Joseph W. Folk** had the support of a significant faction of the Democratic Party he also announced his support for Folk.

Vandiver managed Folk's campaign, which was done with flair and brought to a successful conclusion. Governor Folk then appointed Vandiver as state insurance commissioner, a position he held from 1905 until 1909. As commissioner, Vandiver fought company rebates to favored policyholders. He took the position that everyone was entitled to insurance on equal terms.

Shortly after leaving the commissioner's office, Vandiver accepted the presidency of the Federal Trust Company but soon resigned to accept the position of vice president and treasurer of the Central States Life Insurance Company, a position he held until 1913.

In 1912 Vandiver supported Woodrow Wilson's nomination as the Democratic candidate for president. He attempted to prevent **Champ Clark**'s supporters from securing all the Missouri Democratic delegates to the national convention. As a reward for his support, Vandiver was appointed by President Wilson as assistant secretary of the treasury and director of the subtreasury in St. Louis, a position he held until 1920. Thereafter he retired to Columbia, dying on May 30, 1932.

BOB WHITE

Houck, Louis. Papers. Kent Library Archives. Southeast Missouri State University, Cape Girardeau.

Mattingly, Arthur M. *Normal to University: A Century of Service.* Cape Girardeau: Missourian Litho and Printing, 1979.

Mitchell, Ewing Young. Papers. Western Historical Manuscripts Collection, Columbia.

St. Louis Post-Dispatch, August 8, 1971.

Vandiver, Willard D. Autobiography. Kent Library Archives. Southeast Missouri State University, Cape Girardeau.

VAN HORN, ROBERT THOMPSON (1824–1916)

Robert Thompson Van Horn was born on a farm near East Mahoney, Pennsylvania, on May 19, 1824. When he was fifteen he was apprenticed for four years at the *Indiana Register.* A jack of all trades, he worked as a printer, taught school, practiced law, and worked on an Erie Canal boat. Van Horn married Adela H. Cooley in Pomeroy, Ohio, in 1848; they had five children, three of whom lived to adulthood. In 1854 he and his family settled in Cincinnati where he published the *Union,* a pro-Whig newspaper. When a fire destroyed his printing office the following year,

Van Horn took a job as a clerk on a Mississippi River steamboat.

In October 1854 Van Horn bought a Kansas City newspaper, the *Enterprise,* from William A. Strong for one thousand dollars. He came to Kansas City in July 1855 and successfully managed the *Enterprise,* which in 1857 he renamed the *Kansas City Journal* and made a daily paper.

Van Horn became a staunch business and railroad promoter. In an 1857 speech he spoke of the "west of commerce," a West that would be joined to the East by railroads. The following year at a railroad banquet in Kansas City, he introduced a resolution calling on Congress to provide legislation for the construction of a continental railroad. He believed that his adopted city was the gateway to the West and encouraged eastern investors to assist in its development.

As editor of the *Journal,* Van Horn adopted a moderate, proslavery stance, but he later admitted that in 1855 he had supported an attempt to annex Kansas City to the territory of Kansas. The 1856 attack on Lawrence and John Brown's Pottawatomie massacre threatened commerce and trade in Kansas City and its environs. When proslavery forces disrupted mercantile shipments to Kansas City, Van Horn warned that future marauders "should be careful to bring their coffins with them," as they would meet with violent opposition. While he often excoriated Kansans such as John Brown and James H. Lane, he was first and foremost an editor and businessman. He stressed economic rather than political issues and encouraged friendly relations between Missourians and settlers in the Kansas Territory.

After coming to Missouri, Van Horn styled himself a Union Democrat, and in the presidential election of 1860 he supported John Bell and the Constitutional Union ticket. Before the war his editorials seldom mentioned the prospect of civil war. The firing on Fort Sumter persuaded him to cast his lot with the Union and the Republican Party.

Shortly after the war began, approximately one thousand pro-Southern men gathered at a farm on the road between Independence and Westport with the intention of invading Kansas City on behalf of the Confederacy. Local businessmen backed Van Horn's election as mayor of Kansas City in April 1861. Following his election he quietly left the city and headed for St. Louis where Union authorities commissioned him a major and gave him command of the Enlisted Missouri Militia with the power to enlist a Union battalion in Kansas City. He returned to Kansas City at the end of May 1861, and with the backing of Capt. W. E. Prince of Fort Leavenworth, Kansas, he secured a large part of the city for the Union forces. Although Kansas City was beleaguered and occupied throughout much of the war, it did not fall to Confederate forces.

Van Horn and his troops took part in the Battle of Lexington, where he was wounded and briefly taken prisoner. He returned to Kansas City for the duration of the war. During the war years he was twice elected mayor of Kansas City, and served in the military and as a state senator.

After the Civil War, Van Horn returned to editing the *Journal,* but he devoted more of his time to politics. He promoted Kansas City as a railroad hub, arranging to sell Kansas City land to Boston investors at low prices. He was elected to the United States Congress in 1864, 1866, and 1868 where he concentrated on getting approval for a bridge over the Missouri River at Kansas City. Van Horn joined other Kansas City businessmen in securing completion of the Union Pacific Railroad and the opening of the Hannibal Bridge across the Missouri River in 1869. He was a delegate to Republican National Conventions in the years following the Civil War, and served as collector of U.S. internal revenue from 1875 to 1881. In 1881 he was reelected to Congress where he served intermittently until 1897.

As a prominent member and intellectual leader of an elite group of businessmen who developed and molded Kansas City, Van Horn remained an active participant in city affairs until his death on January 4, 1916. Van Horn High School now stands on the site of "Honeywood," his first home in Kansas City.

YVONNE JOHNSON

Brown, A. Theodore. *Frontier Community: Kansas City to 1870.* Columbia: University of Missouri Press, 1963.

Deatherage, Charles P. *Early History of Greater Kansas City.* Vol. 1. Kansas City: Interstate Publishing, 1927.

Glaab, Charles N., and A. Theodore Brown. *A History of Urban American.* New York: Macmillan, 1967.

Green, George Fuller. *A Condensed History of the Kansas City Area: Its Mayors and Some VIPs.* Kansas City: Lowell Press, 1968.

Haskell, Henry C., Jr., and Richard B. Fowler. *City of the Future: A Narrative History of Kansas City, 1850–1950.* Kansas City: Frank Glenn Publishing, 1950.

VAN RAVENSWAAY, CHARLES (1911–1990)

Charles van Ravenswaay, an author, horticulturist, and museum director, was most of all devoted to preserving the history and physical culture of his native Missouri. In a career that spanned nearly sixty years, he documented the state's architectural heritage, fought to save its historic buildings, and studied the early arts and crafts of the region.

Born on August 10, 1911, in Boonville, Missouri, van Ravenswaay began as a boy to gather items related to local history; some of his family's friends worried that he was becoming a junk collector. After attending Kemper Military School, he went to Washington University in St. Louis, where he earned a B.A. degree in 1933 and an M.A. in 1934. He became the business manager of a clinic in Boonville founded by his father, a doctor.

At the same time, van Ravenswaay teamed up with two St. Louis–based photographers—the brothers Alexander and Paul Piaget—to document distinctive and often endangered early buildings throughout the state. The result was a 1,694-image collection, which was later restored by the Historic American Building Survey and is now owned by the Library of Congress.

In 1938 van Ravenswaay was chosen to direct the Missouri Writers' Project, a state branch of the Federal Writers' Project, which was under the auspices of the Works Progress Administration. Led by van Ravenswaay, a team of talented writers produced essays on such disparate topics as Missouri's contribution to literature and its country sausage. The resulting guidebook was titled *Missouri: A Guide to the "Show Me" State.*

When World War II began, van Ravenswaay interrupted his budding career in cultural conservation to serve for four years in the United States Navy. In 1946 he was appointed as the first paid director of the Missouri Historical Society (MHS) in St. Louis, where he remained for sixteen years.

During van Ravenswaay's tenure the MHS underwent sweeping changes: the membership grew eight times larger, an active educational program for children was established, nearly every gallery was refurbished, and the museum came to national prominence. Talented at acquisition, van Ravenswaay also greatly expanded the society's collection. From descendants of early St. Louis families he coaxed books, portraits, historical documents, old furniture, and other artifacts.

During the same period van Ravenswaay took on community projects, serving as chairman of the St. Louis Bicentennial Planning Commission from 1958 to 1960 and as chairman of the St. Louis County Buildings Commission from 1957 to 1962. He received a citation for civic service from Washington University in 1955 and a Page One Civic Award from the St. Louis Newspaper Guild in 1959.

Van Ravenswaay also fought to save a number of buildings throughout the region. In 1936–1937 he had chaired an effort to preserve historic Thespian Hall in Boonville; later, he worked as instigator, adviser, or consultant on nearly every restoration or preservation project undertaken in Missouri, including the Saxon

Lutheran Memorial in Frohna and Creole homes in Ste. Genevieve.

In 1962 van Ravenswaay left the MHS to become director of Old Sturbridge Village in Massachusetts; four years later he was appointed director of the Henry Francis DuPont Winterthur Museum and Gardens in Winterthur, Delaware, and held that position until his retirement in 1976.

Both during his career and in retirement, van Ravenswaay was an active researcher and writer who produced several well-regarded books: *The Arts and Architecture of German Settlements in Missouri* (1977), *Drawn from Nature: The Botanical Art of Joseph Prestele and His Sons* (1984), and *St. Louis: An Informal History of the City and Its People* (1991). His last major work was a book about apple cultivation.

Among various leadership positions in national organizations, van Ravenswaay served as trustee of the National Trust for Historic Preservation and president of the American Association of Museums. He held honorary doctorate degrees from the University of Missouri–Columbia and Maryville University. In 1987 he was given the Conservation Services Award of the United States Department of the Interior.

Throughout his life van Ravenswaay maintained a strong interest in horticulture and was himself a serious gardener. He had a particular interest in flowers and grapes brought to Missouri by German immigrants.

Charles van Ravenswaay died in Hockessin, Delaware, on March 20, 1990.

CANDACE O'CONNOR

"In Memoriam: Charles Van Ravenswaay." *Missouri Folklore Society Newsletter* 14:3 and 4 (August 1990).

St. Louis Post-Dispatch, July 15, 1990.

Van Ravenswaay, Charles. *The Arts and Architecture of German Settlements in Missouri: A Survey of a Vanishing Culture.* Columbia: University of Missouri Press, 1977.

———. *St. Louis: An Informal History of the City and Its People, 1764–1865.* St. Louis: Missouri Historical Society Press, 1991.

VÁSQUEZ, BENITO (1738–1810)

Benito Vásquez was described by his associates as intensely loyal, honest, and courageous, and of extraordinary energy and enthusiasm, but of questionable good sense and judgment, an appraisal that the facts of his life confirm. He was born in 1738 in Santiago de Compostela, in northern Spain. In 1762 he joined the Spanish infantry as a private. When Spain took over Louisiana from France following the French and

Indian War, Vásquez was sent first to New Orleans and then to St. Louis in 1769.

St. Louis was a village of fewer than five hundred French colonials, a third of them black and Indian slaves and the rest lighthearted, sociable Frenchmen. Spanish governors wisely allowed the inhabitants to retain their language and customs, which Vásquez quickly adopted, learning French and serving as an interpreter. He was one of four Spaniards living in St. Louis.

In 1772 Vásquez resigned from the army to enter the fur trade, the town's principal business. At first he prospered, shipping furs to New Orleans to trade for merchandise. In 1773 he captured two enemy English traders from the east side of the Mississippi, and was rewarded with half the Englishmen's furs. On November 27, 1774, he married Julie Papin *dit* Baronet who made a happy home for Benito and thirteen children. In 1780 he bought a fine house of posts with sixty-two hundred pounds of peltry (furs were the only currency), and he owned fifteen slaves—more than any other man in the village except **Auguste Chouteau** and **Charles Gratiot.**

In 1780 St. Louis was attacked by 950 Englishmen and their Indian allies. Vásquez behaved so well in the successful defense of the village that he was given a special commendation by the governor. Then his fortunes began to decline. In 1782 pirates seized his boat and goods, and left him without capital. He then became a fur trader.

Louisiana governors ignored the Spanish law against monopolies and tried to balance trade by granting licenses for trade with specific tribes. Vásquez's license for 1784 and 1785 was for trade with the profitable Great Osages, which came to an end when the chiefs accused Vásquez of trying to influence them against the governor. The chiefs had lied, as an investigation determined, and the governor punished the Indians by denying them traders, which left Vásquez with no trade, or with unprofitable small tribes such as the Panimaha.

As the number of St. Louis fur traders grew, the system of exclusive trade privileges broke down. Governors favored powerful traders, and small traders like Vásquez were squeezed out. He became poor and desperate; he made an unwise investment in the "Company of Explorers of the Upper Missouri" in 1793, which ended in financial disaster, and he continued to carry on his hapless trade with impoverished tribes until he was denied all privileges. He traveled to New Orleans in 1797 to beg the governor of Louisiana for a trade privilege, but the governor declined. In a fit of anger Vásquez publicly denounced the governor and was put in jail for thirty-five days. The lieutenant governor in St. Louis was moved by Vásquez's misfortune and granted him privileges from 1799 to 1801, but after Vásquez signed a petition against his benefactor in 1801 there is no evidence that he ever traded again.

Vásquez's last years were full of more misfortune. As St. Louis became a rough and lively American city after 1804, poverty forced him and his wife to move out of their house of posts, and his children had to support him. Everything had changed; even his children violated the old customs of society: his daughter Julie married a French revolutionary; his son Baronet hired out to the despised Americans as an interpreter to Lt. Zebulon Pike; and Benito Jr. took service with the unpopular fur trader **Manuel Lisa.** Old St. Louis had passed away, and so, on February 12, 1810, did Benito Vásquez.

JANET S. LECOMPTE

Foley, William E., and C. David Rice. *The First Chouteaus: River Barons of Early St. Louis.* Urbana: University of Illinois Press, 1983.

Houck, Louis. *A History of Missouri, from Earliest Explorations and Settlements until the Admission of the State into the Union.* 3 vols. Chicago: R. R. Donnelley and Sons, 1909.

Kinnaird, Lawrence. "Spain in the Mississippi Valley, 1765–1794." Washington, D.C.: Annual Report of the American Historical Association for the Year 1945, 1946.

Lecompte, Janet. "Don Benito Vásquez in Early St. Louis." *Bulletin of the Missouri Historical Society* 26 (July 1970): 285–305.

Vásquez Papers. Missouri Historical Society, St. Louis.

VAUGHN, GEORGE L. (1880–1949)

George L. Vaughn, a prominent black St. Louis attorney and political activist, was born in Columbus, Kentucky, on March 9, 1880, the son of former slaves Monroe and Josephine Vaughn. Little is known of his early life. He attended Lane College in Jackson, Tennessee, and completed his legal training at Walden University in Nashville. Early in the twentieth century he established a law practice in St. Louis, where he became involved in local politics.

Around 1908 Vaughn, Joseph E. Mitchell, Charles Turpin, and **Homer G. Phillips** formed the Citizens Liberty League to promote and endorse black political candidates. Their activism resulted in the election of Turpin to the position of St. Louis constable in 1910, the first black candidate elected to a public office in Missouri.

After serving as an officer in an artillery unit during World War I, Vaughn resumed his law practice in St. Louis. He also became active in the St. Louis chapter of the NAACP and served for many years as chairman of its executive committee. He was an ardent antilynching crusader and investigated the 1923 lynching of **James T. Scott** in Columbia, Missouri. He later wrote a report of the incident for the national office of the NAACP, which appeared in the *St. Louis Argus* on May 4, 1923.

Vaughn was an especially important figure in Democratic politics in St. Louis during the New Deal. In 1936 he received an appointment as a justice of the peace in the city's Fourth District. In 1941 he ran for alderman on the Democratic ticket but lost. He also served as an assistant attorney general of the state of Missouri until the time of his death in 1949. Vaughn delivered the minority report at the 1948 Democratic National Convention held in Philadelphia. This report recommended the unseating of the Mississippi delegation to the convention because of its declaration of "undying devotion" to the principle of white supremacy. The report failed to carry the convention by a slim margin.

Vaughn is best remembered for his role as the attorney of record in a restrictive covenant case decided by the United States Supreme Court in 1948. Restrictive covenants were written stipulations placed in property deeds that prohibited property from being sold to African Americans. In 1945 J. D. and Ethel Shelley of St. Louis purchased a home. A few days after the Shelleys moved into the house, two of their neighbors, Louis and Fern Kraemer, sued to evict the Shelleys from their new home, citing a restrictive covenant attached to the house's deed. The restriction, dating back to 1911, barred any owners of the property, their heirs, legal representatives, or subsequent owners from selling or renting the property to people who were not of the "Caucasian Race." While a St. Louis circuit court refused to evict the Shelleys, the Missouri Supreme Court overturned its ruling and called for the enforcement of the covenant. Vaughn, the Shelleys' attorney from the beginning of the lawsuit, appealed the case to the United States Supreme Court. The high court accepted Vaughn's argument that the enforcement of restrictive covenants by the courts was a state action in violation of the equal protection clause of the Fourteenth Amendment. The May 3, 1948, ruling of the Court in *Shelley v. Kraemer* struck down the enforcement of restrictive covenants in nineteen states and the District of Columbia. Later, Thurgood Marshall, NAACP attorney and future Supreme Court justice, remarked that the *Shelley* case "Gave thousands of prospective buyers throughout the United States new courage and hope in the American form of government."

Vaughn was a founding member and first president of the Mound City Bar Association. He was also active in the African-Methodist Episcopal Church and in several fraternal lodges, including the Masons and the Elks. George L. Vaughn died at his home in St. Louis on August 17, 1949. Burial was in the Washington Park Cemetery in St. Louis. He was survived by his wife, Eva Vaughn; a son, George L. Vaughn Jr.; and two daughters, Mary and Carolyn.

GARY R. KREMER AND PATRICK J. HUBER

"George L. Vaughn." *Journal of Negro History* 34 (October 1949): 490–91.

Higginbotham, A. Leon, Jr. "Race, Sex, Education, and Missouri Jurisprudence: *Shelley v. Kraemer* in a Historical Perspective." *Washington University Law Quarterly* 67 (fall 1989): 674–708.

Kansas City Call, August 26, 1949.

St. Louis Argus, August 19, 1949.

Vose, Clement E. *Caucasians Only: The Supreme Court, the NAACP, and the Restrictive Covenant Cases.* Berkeley and Los Angeles: University of California Press, 1959.

VEBLEN, THORSTEIN BUNDE (1857–1929)

This iconoclastic social scientist and cultural critic published groundbreaking analyses of capitalism, taking up a wide range of subjects from the concrete movements of consumers to theoretical explorations of the preconceptions of orthodox economists. Veblen saw business infiltrating everything in America and corrupting all that it touched, whether academe, athletics, or patriotic displays. He considered human interactions tarnished by the emphasis on ownership—in particular, the desire to own *more* than one's neighbors—which he believed encouraged people to invidious and competitive acts rather than cooperative and peaceful ones.

Thorstein Bunde Veblen was born on a Wisconsin farm on June 30, 1857, to Norwegian immigrants Thomas Anderson and Kari Bunde Veblen. In 1865 the Veblens moved to a largely Norwegian settlement (later named Nerstrand) in Minnesota, where they acquired 290 acres of prime farmland. The comfortable farmhouse where Veblen spent much of his youth and young manhood has recently been meticulously restored. Along with several siblings, he attended Carleton College where he met his first wife, Ellen Rolfe, and graduated a year early after completing the junior and senior courses in a single year. He interspersed stretches of "loafing" in Nerstrand with a brief teaching appointment at Monona Academy in Madison, Wisconsin (1880–1881), and graduate work at Johns Hopkins (1881) and Yale (1881–1884), which granted him a Ph.D. in philosophy in 1884. In 1888 he married Ellen Rolfe, and they spent an unconventional honeymoon on Iowa farmland owned by her parents. This bucolic interlude ended when Veblen returned to academe, seeking a social science fellowship at Cornell in 1891. In 1892 he went to the newly opened University of Chicago, where he taught until 1906 while serving as managing editor of the *Journal of Political Economy.*

The Chicago years saw the publication of Veblen's first two books, *The Theory of the Leisure Class* (1899) and *The Theory of Business Enterprise* (1904). Although the fame of *Leisure Class* has overshadowed all his other works, it was *Business Enterprise* that Malcolm Cowley and Bernard Smith included as one of twelve entries in *Books That Changed Our Minds* (1940).

Veblen's travels resumed when he secured a short-lived appointment at Stanford University (1906–1909). Driven out by scandal, he landed at the University of Missouri, thanks in part to support from the head of economics, Horace Davenport. Veblen was not fond of Columbia, comparing it to Gopher Prairie (the fictional town immortalized in Sinclair Lewis's *Main Street*), but he remained a lecturer at the university from 1911 to 1918, living for a while in Davenport's basement. For the bulk of the Missouri years Veblen's appointment was in the School of Commerce—ironically enough, given his contempt for business—where he taught such courses as Economic Factors in Civilization and History of Economics. The divorce he had long desired from Ellen Rolfe came through in 1912, and in 1914 he married Ann Fessenden Bradley Bevans, a former student at the University of Chicago.

Perhaps in part because of more satisfying domestic circumstances, including his becoming stepfather to Ann's two daughters, Veblen published three important books while in Columbia: his most anthropological work and reportedly his favorite, *The Instinct of Workmanship and the State of the Industrial Arts* (1914); an analysis of "the penalty of taking the lead" and indictment of Germany in *Imperial Germany and the Industrial Revolution* (1915); and a penetrating analysis of patriotism in times of war, *An Inquiry into the Nature of Peace and the Terms of Its Perpetuation* (1917).

Veblen's colleague Jacob Warshaw's "Recollections of Thorstein Veblen," held by the Western Historical Manuscripts Collection in Columbia, recounts Veblen's Missouri years. Warshaw emphasizes Veblen's erudition, particularly in the humanities, noting, "He absorbed knowledge as if it were a disease to which he was peculiarly susceptible." Warshaw also provides a glimpse of Veblen's legendary status at the University of Missouri, noting the student fable that the professor knew twenty-six languages.

In February 1918 Veblen took a leave of absence from Missouri to serve briefly in the Food Administration in Washington, D.C., shortly thereafter publishing his brilliant exposé of academe, *The Higher Learning in America.* In the fall of 1918 he moved his family to New York City, where he served as an editor of the *Dial* for a year before joining the faculty of the New School for Social Research in 1919.

The later years of Veblen's life featured the publication of the darkly conspiratorial *The Vested Interests and the Common Man* (1919); an accessible collection of previously published essays, *The Place of Science in Modern Civilization* (1919); one of his rhetorical masterpieces and an influential work in the technocracy movement, *The Engineers and the Price System* (1921); a synthesis of many of his ideas, *Absentee Ownership and Business Enterprise in Recent Times* (1923); and his translation of an Icelandic epic, *The Laxdæla Saga* (1925). *Essays, Reviews, and Reports* was published posthumously in 1934.

After retiring, Veblen returned to California, settling near Stanford. He died on August 3, 1929, shortly before the stock market collapsed.

Veblen requested shortly before his death that "no tombstone, slab, epitaph, effigy, tablet, inscription, or monument of any name or nature, be set up in my memory or name in any place or at any time; that no obituary, memorial, portrait, or biography of me, nor any letters written to or by me be printed or published." Veblen's distaste for publicity complements his aversion for the "conspicuous" behaviors anatomized in *Leisure Class* (1899). Thus, when Joseph Dorfman began work on his biography during Veblen's life, the subject did not cooperate with the biographer, even when it became clear to family members that Dorfman's account distorted certain basic facts. In the interest of promulgating a dubious thesis of pathological marginalization to account for Veblen's ideas, for instance, Dorfman characterized the Veblen family as poorer and more socially marginal than they actually were. *Thorstein Veblen and His America* has nevertheless decisively influenced further interpretations of Veblen, and researchers have only recently begun to reconstruct his biography.

Many other factors make Veblen's achievement difficult to assess. Always a wide-ranging intellect, his thought does not fit into neat cubbyholes, in terms of either academic discipline or ideology. A committed Darwinian, he was contemptuous of the teleological presumptions of his contemporary social Darwinists. A leftist, Veblen was skeptical of reform movements, and, while sympathetic to Marx, found Marxism too romantic, optimistic, and impossibly teleological. The amount of satire in his social science, and his penchant for making deadly serious points in a humorous manner, continues to unsettle many readers. Since Veblen spent much of his career assailing economic orthodoxies, it is not surprising that few practitioners today (outside of the institutionalist school) consider him an economist at all. In fact, when offered the nomination for president of the American Economics Association,

Veblen characteristically declined. His prose style is distinctive, difficult, and often tortured, yet he influenced numerous literary figures, such as John Dos Passos and Sinclair Lewis.

The lack of a comfortable niche no doubt would have suited Veblen. His works fuse sociology, satire, and economics into an iconoclastic form of cultural criticism that still illuminates American culture. His admirers have long pointed out that his ideas were in advance of his time.

CLARE VIRGINIA EBY

Diggins, John P. *The Bard of Savagery: Thorstein Veblen and Modern Social Theory.* New York: Seabury Press, 1978.

Dorfman, Joseph. *Thorstein Veblen and His America.* New York: Viking, 1934.

Tilman, Rick. *The Intellectual Legacy of Thorstein Veblen: Unresolved Issues.* Westport, Conn.: Greenwood Press, 1996.

———. *Thorstein Veblen and His Critics: Conservative, Liberal, and Radical Perspectives.* Princeton: Princeton University Press, 1992.

VEST, GEORGE GRAHAM (1830–1904)

George Graham Vest, who served four terms as a U.S. senator from Missouri (1879–1903), was born in Frankfort, Kentucky, on December 6, 1830, to John Jay and Harriet Graham Vest. After graduating from Centre College in Danville, Kentucky, in 1848, Vest may have either taught school or worked as a journalist for a short period. He also began reading law with James Harlan, the Kentucky attorney general. Vest then attended the law department at Transylvania University in Lexington, graduating as valedictorian in 1853.

Shortly after graduation Vest started for Santa Fe to establish a law practice. While visiting acquaintances in Georgetown, Missouri, he was asked to defend a slave accused of murder. Although he gained an acquittal, a mob soon burned the slave and threatened Vest. In response to these threats, the young lawyer decided to open a practice in Georgetown.

In 1856 Vest moved to Boonville. He practiced law first with J. W. Draffen, then with Joseph L. Stephens. Becoming active in Democratic Party politics, Vest served as a presidential elector for Stephen Douglas and was elected to the Missouri House of Representatives in 1860. The following year he became an outspoken advocate for secession and a leader of the secessionist contingent in the convention held to determine Missouri's relation to the federal government.

Vest fought in the Battle of Wilson's Creek in August 1861 and attended the rump legislature meeting in Neosho and Cassville in October and November. He was named as one of the commissioners to the provisional Confederate Congress and then elected to the Confederate House of Representatives, which organized in February 1862. He served as a representative until Gov. **Thomas Caute Reynolds** appointed him to the Confederate Senate in January 1865, a post he held through the end of the war.

Returning to Missouri some months after the war, Vest established a law practice in Sedalia with Russell Hicks and **John Finis Philips.** After Hicks left the firm in 1869, Vest and Philips remained as partners until Vest's election to the United States Senate in 1879. One a former Confederate legislator and one a Union veteran, the partners appealed to all factions in the divisive years following the Civil War.

In an appeal trial before the Johnson County Court of Common Pleas in 1870, Vest and Philips represented Charles Burden, who had brought suit against Leon Hornsby for directing another man to shoot his hunting dog, Old Drum. Philips handled the bulk of the case, and Vest presented only the closing argument. In an eloquent plea subsequently known as "Eulogy to the Dog," Vest praised the faithfulness of dogs to their masters and gained lasting fame as an orator.

During the 1870s Vest again became active in the Democratic Party. A delegate to the national convention in 1872, he was an unsuccessful candidate for the party's gubernatorial nomination in 1876. The state legislature elected him to the United States Senate in January 1879.

As a senator Vest was renowned for his oratorical and debate skills. One of his particular interests was the preservation of Yellowstone National Park. Throughout much of his tenure he fought interest groups who sought to profit from park leases and decimate the area's scenery and wildlife. Vest also developed a deep interest in the welfare of Native Americans and urged reform in their treatment by the federal government. A longtime proponent of the free coinage of silver, the senator actively participated in the filibuster against the repeal of the Sherman Silver Purchase Act in 1893. He also provided leadership on tariff questions, consistently fighting for lower rates. Although usually in the minority on tariff issues, Vest scored a victory during his final days in the Senate when he successfully advocated the suspension of the duty on anthracite coal.

In poor health during his last years in the Senate, Vest retired in 1903. He returned to Missouri and spent his final months dictating a series of articles titled "A Senator of Two Republics" for publication in the *Saturday Evening Post.* The final surviving member of the Confederate Senate, Vest died in his home in Sweet Springs on August 9, 1904. Survivors included his wife, Sallie Elizabeth Sneed

Vest, and two children, Alexander S. and Mollie Vest Jackson. Vest ably represented Missouri in the United States Senate during the final quarter of the nineteenth century but is best remembered for his speech eulogizing the relationship between a dog and its master.

LYNN WOLF GENTZLER

Botts, Virginia Mullinax. "George Graham Vest: United States Senator from Missouri." Master's thesis, University of Kansas, 1926.

Chaney, Walter L. "The True Story of 'Old Drum.'" *Missouri Historical Review* 19 (January 1925): 313–24.

Dawes, Marian Elaine. "The Senatorial Career of George Graham Vest." Master's thesis, University of Missouri, 1932.

Kuhr, Manuel Irvin. "How George Vest Came to Missouri." *Missouri Historical Review* 59 (July 1965): 424–27.

Lamm, Henry. "George Graham Vest." In *Proceedings of the Twenty-Second Annual Meeting of the Missouri Bar Association.* Columbia, Mo.: E. W. Stephens, 1905.

VILES, JONAS (1875–1948)

Jonas Viles, a longtime professor of history at the University of Missouri, was born in Waltham, Massachusetts, on May 3, 1875. His parents, Charles Lowell and Almira Hubbard Viles, operated a prosperous truck and dairy farm where Jonas worked during his youth. After graduating from Waltham High School, Viles entered Harvard University in 1892. There he received a bachelor of arts degree in 1896 and a master of arts degree in history the following year. In 1901 he received a doctor of philosophy degree from the same institution.

Viles taught for two years, 1896–1898, at the Dalzell School for Boys in Worcester, Massachusetts. From 1898 to 1901 he held a graduate-assistant appointment in Harvard's history department. He traveled and engaged in research in Europe and England following the granting of his doctoral degree.

In 1902 Viles accepted a position as an instructor in history at the University of Missouri and moved to Columbia. He rose rapidly in the academic ranks, becoming an assistant professor in 1905 and a full professor in 1907. Although he was trained primarily in English history, Viles taught courses in American and Missouri history at the university. He became most well known for his work on the history of the state. In addition to his teaching duties, he served as chairman of the department of history from 1925 to 1936.

Active scholastically and socially in the university environs, Viles served on committees dealing with enrollment procedures, scholarships, and the 1939 centennial celebration of the university. In the latter capacity, he wrote much of *The University of Missouri: A Centennial History, 1839–1939.* Other faculty members contributed chapters on the modern development of certain departments, but Viles penned the first part of the volume detailing the university's history.

In 1904 the Public Archives Commission of the American Historical Association requested that the young professor survey the condition of state archives in Missouri. During the next three years Viles explored the offices, storage areas, and basement of the capitol to determine the extent and condition of the state's records. His report, which documented the deplorable storage conditions and the lack of intellectual control of the records, appeared in the American Historical Association's 1908 *Annual Report.* This survey benefited the state when the capitol burned in February 1911. Viles arrived at the building while the fire still burned, and under his guidance some of the records were retrieved from the burning structure. Following the disaster he arranged for the records to be transferred to the State Historical Society of Missouri in Columbia for drying, cleaning, and preservation. In the 1911 American Historical Association's *Annual Report,* Viles, now a member of the Public Archives Commission, published an account of the fire, "Lessons to Be Drawn from the Fire in the State Capitol."

Viles's interest in Missouri history stimulated him to publish numerous articles and reviews in professional journals and to write two books for use in the public schools. In 1912 he published *A History of Missouri for the Grades,* which appeared with **Isidor Loeb**'s *Government in Missouri: Local, State, and National;* the volume was revised and reprinted at least two times. *A History of Missouri for High Schools* was published in 1933, then updated and reprinted in 1944. In addition to these volumes and the centennial history of the university, Viles wrote *An Outline of American History for Use in High Schools,* coedited with William B. Parker *The Letters and Addresses of Thomas Jefferson,* and edited *The Letters and Addresses of George Washington.*

Viles held memberships in the American Historical Association, Alpha Pi Zeta, Phi Beta Kappa, and the Mississippi Valley Historical Association. He served as president of the Mississippi Valley group in 1933–1934. An involved member of the State Historical Society, he served as a trustee from 1904 until his death in 1948 and as first vice president from 1907 to 1916.

In 1945 Viles ended his forty-three-year teaching career at the university. He died in Columbia on February 6, 1948. Survivors included his wife, Ruth

Bennett Hayes Viles, whom he had married in Providence, Rhode Island, in 1903; and two sons, Charles and Phillip. Two sons, Jonas and Peter, predeceased their father. Viles's career as an educator and his interest in preserving primary sources contributed significantly to historical scholarship in Missouri.

LYNN WOLF GENTZLER

Columbia Missourian, February 6, 1948.

Viles-Hosmer Papers. Western Historical Manuscripts Collection, Columbia.

Williams, Walter, ed. *A History of Northeast Missouri.* Vol. 3. Chicago: Lewis Publishing, 1913.

Wrench, Jesse E., ed. "News Notes from the Faculty: Jonas Viles, A.B., A.M., Ph.D." *Missouri Alumnus* 25 (March 1937): 9.

VIOLETTE, EUGENE MORROW (1873–1940)

Seldom does a hall on a university campus bear the name of one whose forte was teaching. At Northeast Missouri State University, however, an impressive classroom building, Violette Hall, honors a man who devoted his life almost exclusively to the study and teaching of history with a purpose of improving history teaching in secondary schools.

Eugene Morrow Violette was born on September 4, 1873, on a farm not far north of Holden, Missouri, the second of three sons born to Thomas H. and Julie Horn Violette. Six years later the family moved to Clinton, where Eugene entered the public schools, graduating from Clinton's Franklin High School in 1889. Five years later he started work at the local Lamkin Academy before going to Central College in Fayette to earn in 1898 an A.B degree. While at Central Violette set as his life's goal a full professorship at a major university. Accordingly, he undertook graduate work at the University of Chicago, where he received a master of arts degree in 1899. He did additional graduate work at Harvard University in 1902–1903 and 1906–1907, as well as at the University of London in 1914. He added to his education by traveling extensively on several occasions in Great Britain and on the Continent.

Violette's first teaching position was at the University of Missouri as acting assistant professor of history when **Isidor Loeb** was on a leave of absence in 1899–1900. He then accepted the professorship of history and head of the department of history and government at the First District Normal School in Kirksville, which in 1919 became the Northeast Missouri State Teachers College. He retained this position for twenty-three years, taking leaves of absence only to do graduate work, travel, and teach in summer sessions at the University of Missouri, the University of Minnesota, and a full academic year at Washington University in St. Louis.

During his years on the Kirksville campus Violette's contributions to the school, besides teaching and recruiting students, included amassing materials for what is now the university archives, collecting items for the presently named E. M. Violette Museum, inaugurating the library's Missouriana Collection, helping organize the historical society, and aiding in launching the student paper, the *Index.* At the same time, he did not neglect the community. He founded the Adair County Historical Society and served as its secretary-treasurer as long as he was in Kirksville, participated in minor ways in local politics, strongly supported "drys" that the temptation to drink be removed from young people, and during World War I was one of Adair County's "Four Minute Men" who spoke in support of the war and the sale of liberty bonds. He served further afield as one of the original trustees of the State Historical Society of Missouri and as a member of its board of trustees from 1901 to 1924. Moreover, he was a member of the State Centennial Commission in 1921 and participated in several aspects of that celebration.

Violette was a lifelong member of the Methodist Church and frequently taught Bible classes both at the church and on the campus. He had little use for orthodoxy, believing that it turned more people away from the church than it attracted. He delighted in sermons that challenged him to think, no matter the denomination of the preacher.

Although Violette was interested in party politics, he played almost no role in campaigns. He voted a straight Democratic ticket until 1904, when he disliked the candidates on the state ticket, with the exception of the gubernatorial candidate, **Joseph W. Folk,** whom he admired. The first time he favored a Republican presidential candidate was in 1928, when Herbert C. Hoover, a "dry," ran against Alfred E. Smith, a "wet."

Despite his fair salary and successes in the school and community, Violette was not satisfied—he had not reached his Central College goal. He soon became aware of one obstacle to his advancement, namely, historians in major colleges and universities looked down their noses at professors in normal schools and teachers colleges. To them such professors were mere pedagogues, not academicians. Violette hoped to overcome this obstacle by attending nearly all annual meetings of the American Historical Association and the Mississippi Valley Historical Association (MVHA). At each he met many of the leaders and sought recognition. He met with some success. In 1915 when he urged the MVHA to support the proposition that normal school students be taught history as an academic subject, he was hooted down. The next year, however, he won acceptance of his idea and was appointed to the MVHA executive committee, quite an honor for a normal school professor.

Violette did not have to "publish or perish," but knew publication was a sine qua non for receiving an offer from a major university. Because of this and for other reasons he was almost always readying a manuscript or two for publication. He was the author of *History of the First District Normal School* (1905), which was a financial drag; *History of Adair County* (1911), which ultimately sold for four to five hundred dollars a copy until reprinted in 1977; and *A History of Missouri* (1918), which he hoped would be used in the secondary schools in connection with the study of American history, not as a separate study. Actually, his Missouri history, reprinted in 1953, was used as a text for decades in both high schools and colleges. Violette also wrote numerous historical articles for newspapers, especially the *St. Louis Post-Dispatch,* and had several articles published as brochures, including "Early Settlements in Missouri" (his master's thesis), "The Battle of Kirksville," and "The Missouri and Mississippi Railroad Debt."

In June 1923 Violette received an offer of an associate professorship at Louisiana State University in Baton Rouge. Although the salary would be lower, he accepted, chiefly because it would secure him recognition he could never get while at a teachers college. Moreover, it was a step toward a full professorship at a respected university. Indeed, in June 1925 he was named professor of modern European history, changed later to professor of English history, thus realizing his lifelong ambition. The years at Louisiana State University were the happiest and most satisfying of his career.

Violette married Hallie Hall, a teacher at the First District Normal and a member of a prominent Trenton, Missouri, family, on September 18, 1902. They had two children, Homer Newton and Rachel. Hallie died on October 6, 1935. On December 25, 1937, Violette married Elizabeth Smith Starr of Kirksville, who died a few weeks after their marriage while with her husband aboard a ship they were taking to England. He died in Baton Rouge on March 26, 1940, following a heart attack, and was buried beside Hallie at Trenton. At the time of his death he was completing a text in English history that had been accepted for publication, and a new Missouri history was in the hands of his publisher.

DAVID D. MARCH

Ryle, Walter H. *Centennial History of the Northeast Missouri State Teachers College.* Kirksville: Northeast Missouri State Teachers College, 1972.

Selby, Paul O., comp. *123 Biographies of Deceased Faculty Members.* Kirksville: Northeast Missouri State Teachers College, 1963.

Violette, Eugene M. Diary, MSS. Special Collections. Pickler Library, Northeast Missouri State University, Kirksville.

————. Scrapbook. Special Collections. Pickler Library, Northeast Missouri State University, Kirksville.

VON DER AHE, CHRISTIAN FREDERICK WILHELM (1851–1913)

Christian Frederick Wilhelm Von der Ahe, a pioneering figure in early professional baseball, was born on October 7, 1851, in Hille, Germany, and emigrated to the United States in 1867. Beginning in St. Louis as a grocery clerk, Von der Ahe had saved enough by 1870 to acquire a small combination grocery and saloon. Four years later he opened a spacious establishment at Grand and St. Louis Avenues that served as a grocery, delicatessen, saloon, and beer garden.

Grand Avenue Park was a block away. Its baseball diamond had been built by Augustus Solari in 1866. By 1875 Grand Avenue Park hosted the home games of the Brown Stockings, the city's first professional ball club. The original Brown Stockings, besieged by financial losses and a gambling scandal, resigned from the National League in December 1877. They continued as a semiprofessional ball club, but Solari grew disenchanted over dwindling attendance at their games and announced plans to dismantle Grand Avenue Park.

Von der Ahe stepped in to save St. Louis baseball by taking over the lease of the ballpark in the fall of 1880. Although he did not understand much about the game, he quickly recognized the potential profits available in concession rights. At the time, Grand Avenue Park languished in shambles. Von der Ahe supplied most of the money to construct a new double-deck grandstand and a beer garden in right field.

The attractive ballpark, now renamed Sportsman's Park, boosted ticket sales, especially on Sunday afternoons when most workers enjoyed their only day off. Ball games entertained weary workers with a sporting event, sunshine, fresh air, and beer. Attendance rose dramatically, and Von der Ahe purchased a controlling interest in the Browns near the end of the 1881 season.

This St. Louis baseball revival coincided with renewed enthusiasm in other large cities excluded from the National League. Consequently, Von der Ahe and his St. Louis Browns joined five other clubs to create the first profitable baseball league, the American Association. The association catered to the working class through Sunday games, liquor sales, and twenty-five-cent tickets (half the National League's admission price). The National League, on the other hand, appealed on moral grounds to the middle and upper classes by scrupulously avoiding Sunday games and liquor sales.

During the American Association's 1882 debut, the public indicated a preference for its approach. While National League clubs had rarely enjoyed a profitable season, all six association teams turned profits in 1882. The following year, when the Browns narrowly missed winning the association championship, Von der Ahe claimed to have made seventy thousand dollars.

Von der Ahe's new venture also saw success on the playing field. Under player-manager Charles Comiskey, the Browns claimed four consecutive American Association championships from 1885 through 1888, winning the World Series in 1885 and 1886 (though the outcome of the 1885 series was disputed and many viewed it as a tie).

During his 1880s heyday, Von der Ahe earned approximately five hundred thousand dollars from the Browns. He used this baseball income to advance within business and political circles. He speculated wildly in real estate, building whole blocks in the area around Sportsman's Park and placing neighborhood bars on every corner. He also chaired the Democratic Party's Eighth Congressional District Committee, which helped elect John O'Neill, the Browns' vice president, to five terms in Congress. The *St. Louis Post-Dispatch* described Von der Ahe's main saloon as a place where "baseball history was written, political careers were launched, and beer flowed in an endless stream." These political connections served Von der Ahe well in 1887 after the Missouri legislature passed laws that would have banned Sunday ball games. Von der Ahe defied the law, and later won his case through the favorable decision of a judge with political aspirations.

After 1889 fierce rivalry between leagues (including the ephemeral Players' League) severely weakened the Browns. The American Association dissolved in December 1891, and four of its clubs, including the Browns, were consolidated into an expanded twelve-team National League. The National League dropped its long-standing opposition to Sunday games, beer sales, and twenty-five-cent tickets. Instead, each team received the right to decide these questions for itself.

The 1890s would be as frustrating for Von der Ahe as the 1880s had been glorious. The Browns in the National League, stripped of practically their whole lineup, including Charles Comiskey, never gave Von der Ahe another winning record. Without Comiskey's assistance, Von der Ahe lacked the skill and patience to rebuild the team. Over the next seven years he employed eighteen managers, even trying the job himself. His reckless real estate ventures left him heavily indebted to the Northwestern Savings Bank of St. Louis. To pay his debts Von der Ahe resorted to selling the services of many talented players. In the last two years of his ownership, the Browns finished last in the league.

One of Von der Ahe's major real estate investments was the new Sportsman's Park, built in 1893 at the corner of Vandeventer Avenue and Natural Bridge Road. On April 16, 1898, a disastrous fire virtually destroyed the ballpark. Von der Ahe sank his cash reserve into rebuilding, but the fire hounded him. Some spectators who had been trampled in the rush to flee the burning ballpark filed personal injury lawsuits against Von der Ahe. Confronted by too many creditors, he declared bankruptcy. He could not pay off the bonds used to finance the original construction of the new Sportsman's Park, and in March 1899 the Browns were sold at a public auction.

Von der Ahe faded into the obscurity of the St. Louis saloon business. He died on June 5, 1913, of cirrhosis of the liver. Hundreds attended his funeral. Comiskey, then owner of the Chicago White Sox, eulogized his former boss as "the grandest figure baseball has ever known." Von der Ahe is buried at Bellefontaine Cemetery in St. Louis beneath a life-size marble statue of himself. His major league baseball franchise lives on, now known as the Cardinals.

JON DAVID CASH

Biographical Dictionary of American Sports: Baseball. S.v. "Von der Ahe, Chris."

Cash, Jon David. "The Spirit of St. Louis in the History of Major League Baseball, 1875–1891." Ph.D. diss., University of Oregon, 1995.

Rygelski, Jim. "Baseball's 'Boss President': Chris Von der Ahe and the Nineteenth-Century St. Louis Browns." *Gateway Heritage* 13 (summer 1992): 42–53.

Tiemann, Robert L. *Cardinal Classics: Outstanding Games from Each of the St. Louis Baseball Club's 100 Seasons, 1882–1981.* St. Louis: St. Louis Histories, 1982.

VON PHUL, ANNA MARIA (1786–1823)

In 1817–1818 a young artist named Anna Maria von Phul came to St. Louis to visit relatives in the area. During her stay she sketched the people and places of the town. Her watercolors of Creole life in St. Louis provide the earliest known images of the city and serve as an extremely valuable artistic and historic resource.

Born in Philadelphia in 1786, Anna Maria von Phul moved to Lexington, Kentucky, in 1800 with her widowed mother, brothers, and sister. As did most well-bred young women at the time, von Phul studied French and took lessons in drawing and watercolor. Her teachers were George and Mary Beck, artists who owned a collection of European prints and operated a young-ladies academy in Lexington. Art was a genteel hobby for most girls, but von Phul showed talent, and her family and teachers encouraged her to continue her studies. Among her acquaintances in Lexington was Matthew Harris Jouett, the well-known Kentucky portraitist who had studied with Gilbert Stuart. He painted von Phul's portrait in 1817; the young artist is depicted with portfolio in hand.

Despite her talent, von Phul never seriously pursued a career in art, though she continued to paint and draw, giving many of her works to family and friends. Art became an avocation as von Phul devoted her time to her family. After her mother's death in 1810, Anna Maria lived with her sister, Sarah, who had recently been widowed. Their brother, who had moved to Baltimore, sent Anna Maria art supplies, which she would have found difficult to obtain on the frontier.

In the fall of 1817 von Phul traveled to St. Louis to visit her sister who had married and moved to Edwardsville, Illinois, and her brother **Henry von Phul,** a successful businessman living in St. Louis. While there she filled several sketchbooks with ink and watercolor sketches of St. Louis and the surrounding area. Her drawings depict the people and architecture of the frontier town, as well as nearby landscape scenes, including Indian mounds in St. Louis and St. Charles.

Von Phul made a second visit to the St. Louis area to visit relatives in 1820, and moved to St. Louis to settle in the fall of 1821. Unfortunately, no artwork from her later stays in the city survive. Perhaps as she grew older she had less time to devote to an activity that many considered a frivolous pursuit for a woman. She spent her time at the homes of her siblings and their children. While staying with her sister in Edwardsville, Anna Maria von Phul died on July 28, 1823. Her obituary in the *Edwardsville Spectator* remembered her for "the pleasure of her conversation," "her lively imagination," and "the virtues of her heart." The writer did not mention her artwork, though family members commented on her art frequently in letters.

Von Phul's sketchbooks had been handed down through the family and were largely forgotten, until rediscovered in an attic in 1953. Descendants donated the artwork, along with family letters and papers, to the Missouri Historical Society where they are preserved as an invaluable resource for those studying St. Louis during its early years.

Anna Maria von Phul's watercolors depict with style and accuracy the town's Creole inhabitants—their clothing (both everyday and dress), accessories, hairstyles, and furnishings. Her renderings of the St. Louis riverfront and buildings reveal details of Creole architecture, fences, and horse-drawn carts.

Many of her sketches are in color, which adds to their significance, giving modern viewers a glimpse into the colors of Creole clothing, furniture, and landscape. The sketches are small, delicately drawn details of life in early St. Louis: a mother holding her baby close, a boy slouched in a chair reading a book, a girl holding a basket of flowers, an Indian woman wrapped in a blanket, a man driving a horse-drawn cart, a mother and son hauling water in a bucket, a young woman seated on a decoratively painted chair. The drawings offer an intimate look at everyday life in Creole St. Louis.

Although not a professional artist, Anna Maria von Phul drew and painted with skill and a sensitive eye. Her brush and pen help bring to life St. Louis during its days as the Creole capital of Louisiana Territory.

BETH RUBIN

Van Ravenswaay, Charles. "Anna Maria von Phul." *Missouri Historical Society Bulletin* 10 (April 1954): 367–84.
Von Phul Family Papers. Missouri Historical Society, St. Louis.

VON PHUL, HENRY (1784–1874)

In 1764 Johann Wilhelm (later William) von Phul emigrated from Westhofen, Central Pfalz, to Lancaster, Pennsylvania, where he became a prosperous businessman and married Catharine Graff in 1775. Both were members of the Moravian Brethren, and it is possible that von Phul had left Germany for religious reasons. The family moved to Philadelphia where in 1784 Henry, the fifth of eight children, was born and later attended common school. In 1792 William and probably two children died in a yellow fever epidemic; eight years later Catharine moved her family to Lexington, Kentucky.

In Kentucky Henry von Phul found work with Lexington merchant Thomas Hart Jr., later becoming a merchant's apprentice with Snead and Anderson in Louisville. During these years he made frequent trips north in keelboats loaded with commodities for trade with Indians and planters, gaining experience for his future career. His mother died in 1810; the following year he moved to St. Louis where he established his own mercantile firm, trading primarily in furs.

When von Phul arrived in St. Louis in 1811, the population was around fourteen hundred; Indian attacks were still common along the Missouri River. Indeed, von Phul joined the Missouri Rangers, serving on the frontier as an aide-de-camp to commander **Nathan Boone.** Despite this distraction—and despite a fire in 1814 that damaged his interests—his business flourished. In June 1816 he married Rosalie Saugrain, the daughter of a respected French-born physician; the couple had fifteen children.

In 1817 von Phul was among the crowd who witnessed the arrival of the first steamboat in St. Louis, the *General Zebulon Pike*. Within a few years he became part owner of a number of steamboats, and he and his associates were the first to run boats from St. Louis to New Orleans. Senior partner of the respected mercantile firm Von Phul and McGill (later Von Phul, Waters, and Company, and finally H. von Phul, Sons, and Company), he pursued his business ventures successfully. However, beyond his own interests, he promoted the future of St. Louis as a center of trade and finance. To this end in 1836 he and twenty-four other prominent men founded the St. Louis Chamber of Commerce. Moreover, throughout his life he involved himself in civic as well as business affairs.

As early as 1817 von Phul demonstrated an interest in the well-being of the city. In that year he and **Auguste Chouteau** raised funds to buy a fire engine and build a firehouse. In 1819 von Phul became a town trustee; in 1823, the city's first auditor; in 1826, an alderman; and in 1838–1840, a member of the school board. In addition, he sat on the board of Kemper College, established in 1836. Although in later years he converted to Roman Catholicism, in 1819 he was elected as a member of the vestry of the newly established Christ Episcopal Church.

Von Phul's business activities were no less diverse. In 1821 he became director of the Bank of Missouri, St. Louis; from 1829 to 1830, director of the Branch Bank of the United States, St. Louis; in 1831, director of the Missouri Insurance Company; in 1832, organizer of the Union Insurance Company; in 1836, vice president of the Merchants' Exchange and in 1840, president; in 1837, organizer of the Marine Insurance Company; and in 1855, director of Iron Mountain Railroad. As one contemporary assessed von Phul's contribution: "[He] had done much to build up the mercantile interest of St. Louis, and on the credit of his name alone had brought more commerce to the city and more credit to her firms than any one man of his generation."

Near the end of his life, von Phul suffered a setback in an otherwise remarkably successful career. In 1872 his New Orleans branch—managed by his sons—went under. The eighty-eight year old insisted upon paying his sons' creditors, though doing so forced him to relinquish his personal fortune, "even to his wife's dower." This act of "unfailing integrity" seems to have earned him only greater admiration among his colleagues.

Henry von Phul died in St. Louis on September 8, 1874. Three days later the Merchants' Exchange resolved to pay "appropriate tributes of respect" to their member and drape the hall of exchange in mourning for thirty days. After the burial von Phul's friends presented a full-length portrait of the "old and honored merchant" to be hung—fittingly—in the Union Merchants' Exchange.

CAROL HEMING

Edwards, Richard, and M. Hopewell. *Edwards's Great West and Her Commercial Metropolis, Embracing a General View of the West, and a Complete History of St. Louis, from the Landing of Ligueste, in 1764, to the Present Time; with Portraits and Biographies of Some of the Old Settlers, and Many of the Most Prominent Business Men.* St. Louis: Edwards's Monthly, 1860.

Scharf, J. Thomas. *History of St. Louis City and County: From Earliest Periods to the Present Day.* Vol. 1. Philadelphia: Everts, 1883.

Van Ravenswaay, Charles. "Anna Maria von Phul." *Missouri Historical Society Bulletin* 10 (April 1954): 367–84.

Von Phul Family Papers. Missouri Historical Society, St. Louis.

WADDELL, WILLIAM BRADFORD (1807–1872)

William Bradford Waddell typified the mid-nineteenth-century entrepreneur who shaped the American West through capitalist venture. Although he is sometimes overlooked as a marginal figure in American history, he bears distinction as co-owner of the famed Pony Express. Waddell's involvement in the conveyance of goods and information across the United States facilitated settlement of the western territories and linked those outlying areas to midwestern commercial centers.

Catherine Bradford Waddell, a descendant of Plymouth's Gov. William Bradford, gave birth to the first of two sons on October 14, 1807, in Fauquier County, Virginia. Named for his famous ancestor, William also descended from the strong paternal line of John Waddell of Glasgow, Scotland. Catherine died in 1811 and William's father, John Waddell Jr., married Sarah Crown two years later. In 1815 the family moved to Mason County, Kentucky. Biographers claim that the family's relocation, which reflected a national fervor for westward migration, influenced William to explore opportunities beyond the cane ridge. At age seventeen he briefly worked in lead mines near Galena, Illinois, before moving to St. Louis, where he worked in the Berthold and McCreery general store. This experience particularly influenced Waddell because he glimpsed the profitability of provisioning fur traders and miners for their western journeys. At this point, however, he returned to Kentucky, where he worked briefly in a store in Washington and then as a farm laborer.

The return proved beneficial, for Waddell met, then married, Susan Byram on January 1, 1829. After a few years of farm life, the couple moved to Mayslick, Kentucky, and opened a dry goods store. The business prospered, but by 1835 the Waddells sought new opportunities in Missouri. William built a general store in Lexington, on the Missouri River near Jack's Ferry. He helped build a viable community in Lexington, joining the Baptist Church, participating in the Lexington First Addition Company, organizing the Lexington Mutual Fire and Marine Insurance Company, and constructing a large brick store and hemp warehouse. The California gold rush of 1849 quickened Lexington's development because it became a primary outfitting station for would-be miners. During this period Waddell seized his

opportunity and formed lucrative partnerships to provision those who ventured across the "Great American desert."

Beginning in 1853 Waddell joined William H. Russell in many interesting enterprises. The first, carried out under the auspices of Waddell and Russell, fulfilled a contract to deliver military supplies to Fort Riley, in Kansas Territory. This foray launched a shipping and freight business conducted by Russell, Majors, and Waddell, a partnership incorporated on January 1, 1855. The new firm outfitted emigrants and wagon trains that crossed the Plains, and transported freight and supplies for the federal government to military posts spanning the western region. Russell primarily lobbied federal officials in Washington, D.C., and solicited investors from the New York financial circuit. **Alexander Majors** had directed a successful wagon train business from Westport, now Kansas City, with offices in Denver and Leavenworth before joining the trio and consequently handled daily operations. Waddell managed the firm's bookkeeping and financial affairs from Lexington, with occasional trips to a branch office in Leavenworth. The partnership proved to have such potential that Russell sought to diversify its operations.

Unfortunate circumstances, overextension, and financial mismanagement, however, led Russell, Majors, and Waddell to a swift decline. Wagon trains venturing into the Utah Territory became entrenched in the Mormon War of 1857–1858 and the Pah Ute War of 1860. The firm suffered heavy losses of cargo, capital stock, and reputable standing in the competitive freighting business. Russell further burdened his partners with investment in a failed stagecoach line and an express mail delivery service. The partners managed the Pony Express from St. Joseph, Missouri, for a scant eighteen months, from April 1860 to October 1861, while teetering on the brink of financial ruin. Perceptions of Confederate sympathies wounded the Pony Express, and the telegraph killed it. Russell complicated these business losses with financial scandal that dragged the partnership into insolvency.

By incorporating, the partners avoided personal responsibility for the firm's debts, but creditors hounded them nevertheless. Waddell retired to Lexington and endured Missouri's intrastate skirmishes during the Civil War. He deeded the family home to his son in 1861, and in 1869 ownership passed to the Lexington Baptist Female College. William B. Waddell lived his remaining years on his daughter's nearby farm. He died there on April 1, 1872, and was buried in the Machpelah Cemetery.

Although he is most remembered for the famed Pony Express, Waddell played a greater role in the settlement of the West by providing settlers and soldiers with the means to accomplish their goals. His business acumen awakened small Missouri towns to the excitement and profitability of national expansion, briefly unifying an otherwise fractured nation.

RACHEL FRANKLIN WEEKLEY

Settle, Raymond W., and Mary Lund Settle. "The Early Careers of William Bradford Waddell and William Hepburn Russell: Frontier Capitalists." *Kansas Historical Quarterly* 26 (winter 1960): 355–82.

———. *Empire on Wheels.* Stanford: Stanford University Press, 1949.

———. "Origin of the Pony Express: A Centennial Commemoration." *Bulletin of the Missouri Historical Society* 16 (April 1960): 199–212.

———. *Saddles and Spurs: The Pony Express Saga.* Harrisburg, Pa.: Stackpole, 1955.

———, eds. *The Story of the Pony Express.* San Francisco: Hesperian House, 1960.

WALDO, DAVID (1802–1878)

Born on April 30, 1802, in Harrison County, Virginia (present-day West Virginia), David Waldo migrated to Gasconade County, Missouri, in 1820, where two of his older brothers had already settled. Like his father, Waldo was an agrarian, but he is best known for his activities in the Southwest and his ventures as a mercantile capitalist.

Waldo won appointment as assessor of Gasconade County and clerk of the circuit court in 1822. Two years later he became the county treasurer. In 1826 he attended medical lectures at Transylvania University in Lexington, Kentucky. He then returned to Gasconade County to practice his new profession and resume the duties of his various county offices. By 1827 Waldo was serving as clerk of the circuit court, justice of the peace, coroner, deputy sheriff, postmaster, and a major in the militia. He had also become a land speculator.

In 1828 Waldo vacationed in the Southwest and became acquainted with Santa Fe traders Ceran St. Vrain and Richard Campbell. They convinced Waldo of the profitability of the trade, and on September 2 he received permission from Mexican officials to transport and trade merchandise in Chihuahua and Sonora. He also became the first American-trained physician to practice in Santa Fe and Taos. Waldo continued to profit from Santa Fe trade ventures for many years. In 1844 he reportedly returned from the Southwest with a fortune in gold and silver. A portion of his profits were used to buy land, particularly in Jackson County.

His time in the Southwest made Waldo acutely aware of the growing hostility between the United States and Mexico. When war with Mexico was declared in 1846, Waldo, in Independence, Missouri, promptly offered his services, becoming the captain of Company A of the Missouri Mounted Volunteers. The company, attached to Col. **Alexander W. Doniphan**'s regiment, was part of Gen. **Stephen Watts Kearny**'s Army of the West.

The territory of New Mexico surrendered to Kearny's troops without bloodshed. Waldo, considered the best Spanish scholar in Kearny's army, translated a new constitution for the territory and the Constitution of the United States into Spanish for the American civil government. Taking advantage of Waldo's southwestern experience, Kearny consulted him on all civil appointments. Waldo also played a significant part in the Treaty of Ojo del Oso between the Americans and the Navajos and participated in the Battles of Brazito and Sacramento. After serving, without pay, for ten months, Waldo was discharged at New Orleans and returned to Independence, where he resumed supervision of his landholdings, started farming, and purchased more land.

In 1848 Waldo and other traders formed a company to transport goods for the army to its various outposts in the Southwest. Less than a year later Waldo and Company successfully bid on a freighting contract to transport more than five hundred thousand pounds of goods. This venture proved a disaster. Bad weather caused Waldo and his partners to lose some eight hundred oxen. That same year he married Eliza-Jane Norris, of Independence, the daughter of a business associate. She bore Waldo five children.

Waldo and Company continued to bid on government business, and in 1850 he formed another company that won a four-year contract to deliver mail from Independence to Santa Fe. The company also received a license to trade with the Kansa Indians. After the mail contract ended, Waldo devoted more time to land speculation and farming and became a partner in a coal company. Since he had made numerous personal loans for many years, he decided to engage in banking, becoming a partner in Independence's Southern National Bank.

By 1860 Waldo was worth $225,000. Although he was a slave owner, he was not enthusiastic about involuntary servitude. Throughout the Civil War he maintained a strong allegiance to the Union. During 1863 he ended his association with the Southern National Bank and became a partner and cashier of the First National Bank of Independence.

As a result of the war Waldo suffered serious losses in personal wealth, though he remained a wealthy man and a large landowner. The fact that he had continued to be so successful financially was surprising because he had suffered severe bouts of depression and periods of mental delusion since the mid-1850s. In January 1867 his wife, doctor, and some friends admitted the suicidal Waldo to the Fulton Lunatic Asylum. He remained there until the end of August, then returned to Independence and again supervised his extensive business and banking affairs.

Waldo's health steadily worsened in the mid-1870s. For years he had used morphine, a common procedure to induce sleep. On May 20, 1878, he apparently took an overdose of the sedative and died. His death occurred five months after the First National Bank ceased business.

JAMES W. GOODRICH

Barry, Louis. *The Beginning of the West: Annals of the Kansas Gateway to the American West.* Topeka: Kansas State Historical Society, 1972.
Dictionary of American Biography. S.v. "Waldo, David."
Goodrich, James W. "In the Earnest Pursuit of Wealth: David Waldo in Missouri and the Southwest." *Missouri Historical Review* 66 (January 1972): 155–84.
———. "The Waldo Brothers and the Westward Movement." Ph.D. diss., University of Missouri, 1974.

WALKER, JOHN HARDEMAN (1794–1860)

John Hardeman Walker, the man responsible for putting a boot on Missouri, was born on February 13, 1794, in Fayette County, Tennessee. (There are varying accounts of his birth and death dates.) In 1810 he moved to La Petite Prairie (Little Prairie) in New Madrid County, Missouri, now in Pemiscot County. Members of the Walker family were there during the New Madrid earthquake of 1811. They were one of only two families who remained in the area of the epicenter following the quake.

Walker and his wife, Sarah, with their one daughter, Mary P., operated a plantation and raised cattle in the swampy land along the Mississippi River. Walker took a leading role in area politics and has been called the "Monarch of the Southeast." He served as sheriff of New Madrid County in 1821–1822 and later as a judge of the county court.

In 1857 Walker and his son-in-law, the Reverend George W. Bushey, platted the town of Caruthersville on the Walker plantation. It was named in honor of Samuel Caruthers, a lawyer and judge.

In 1818 when Congress separated the territory of Arkansas from the territory of Missouri, Walker expressed unhappiness with the boundary lines. He lobbied to have land between the St. Francis and the Mississippi Rivers, now known as the Bootheel, included in the soon-to-be state of Missouri. He worked through the Missouri territorial legislature and "wined and dined" the survey team to get lines changed. He reportedly also traveled to Washington, D.C., to lobby Congress for the proposed boundary.

John Hardeman Walker died on April 30, 1860. Sarah Walker died on March 18, 1870. They are buried in Caruthersville.

KAY HIVELY

Caruthersville (Mo.) Democrat-Argus, June 4, 1929.
Douglas, Robert Sidney. *History of Southeast Missouri.* Vol. 1. Chicago: Lewis Publishing, 1912.
Shoemaker, Floyd Calvin. *Missouri and Missourians: Land of Contrasts and People of Achievement.* Chicago: Lewis Publishing, 1943.

WALKER, MADAM C. J. (1865–1919)

Sara Breedlove McWilliams Davis Walker was born in Delta, Louisiana, on December 23, 1865, to former slaves Owen and Minerva Breedlove. Born on a cotton plantation, she was the youngest of three children and the first member of her family born free. When her parents died of yellow fever in 1874, older brother Alex moved the family to Vicksburg, Mississippi.

Working as a laundress, Walker met Moses McWilliams, a day laborer, in Vicksburg. The couple married in 1882, and their daughter, Lelia, was born on June 6, 1885. Following her husband's death in 1887 Walker moved to St. Louis. She married John Davis in 1888, but soon filed for divorce because of his drinking.

Determined to make a better life for herself and her daughter, Walker launched a self-improvement campaign. Membership at St. Paul's African Methodist Episcopal Church, boasting the most influential congregation in St. Louis's African American community, was the logical choice for combining worship with the development of a social network. Moreover, she became an active participant in the local chapter of the National Association of Colored Women (NACW).

While searching for an appropriate business venture, Walker claimed she had a dream about an old man who gave her a formula for moisturizing and promoting hair growth. Many African American women, including Walker, suffered from brittle, thinning hair. Her mixture improved the quantity and quality of her own hair, and had significant restorative effects on her friends' hair. She began selling her product door-to-door.

Walker realized that she would face stiff competition in St. Louis from **Annie Malone**'s Poro hair care products. Malone began marketing the Poro line in 1902 and already had name recognition for her formula. On advice from her good friend C. J. Walker, a local newsman, Walker moved to Denver, Colorado, in 1905. C. J. became her husband on January 4, 1906.

Walker, now using the name Madam C. J. Walker, moved her business headquarters to Pittsburgh, Pennsylvania, in 1908. Her daughter, a college graduate, joined the family business. Walker established a chain of beauty parlors, factories, and laboratories throughout the country, the Caribbean, and South America. By 1910 her company employed five thousand black women, and Walker became the first African American woman millionaire.

Although she was enjoying a luxurious lifestyle, Walker was equally known for her philanthropy. She gave generously to educational and welfare institutions, especially those that benefited black women. She agreed to chair a fund-raising campaign for the NACW at the request of future president Mary McLeod Bethune in 1909. In 1916 the NACW voted to redeem the mortgage on the home of the late Frederick Douglass. To ensure its preservation, the Frederick Douglass Memorial and Historical Association was incorporated. NACW president Mary Talbert awarded the honor of burning the mortgage papers to the woman donating the final five hundred dollars— Madam C. J. Walker. Walker's generosity continued until her death on May 25, 1919. Her will stipulated that her heirs divide two-thirds of her estate among various charities and that her company be controlled by a woman.

Suzanna Maupin Long

Black Women in America: An Historical Encyclopedia. S.v. "Walker, Madame C. J."

Bundles, A'Lelia Perry. *Madam C. J. Walker.* New York: Chelsea House Publishing, 1991.

Giddings, Paula. *When and Where I Enter.* New York: William Morrow, 1984.

WALSER, GEORGE H. (1834–1910)

George H. Walser was born in Dearborn County, Indiana, on May 26, 1834, and died in Liberal, Missouri, on May 1, 1910. In 1856 he was admitted to the Illinois bar. Five years later he responded to the appeal of President Abraham Lincoln and volunteered for service in the Union army. He reenlisted for three additional years. By the end of his Civil War service Walser had reached the rank of lieutenant colonel in the Twentieth Illinois Volunteers. When the war was over he moved to Barton County, Missouri, to begin the practice of law in Lamar.

As a Republican Walser entered Barton County politics and served as the county superintendent of schools and the prosecuting attorney. In 1868 he was elected to the Missouri House of Representatives where he served two terms. In the area he was known as an effective trial lawyer.

Although Walser was born into a Christian home, he became increasingly critical of the faith after the Civil War. He was particularly impressed with the books and speeches of Robert G. Ingersoll who mesmerized crowds with his eloquent defense of agnosticism and converted many Americans—outraged others—with his writings, such as "Some Mistakes of Moses" or "Why I Am an Agnostic." Walser became convinced that he should take up the challenge of establishing a free-thought community. In 1880 he bought land in western Barton County, platted a new town that he called Liberal, and began publicizing his development.

Walser in the 1880s must have been a bundle of energy as he developed and directed his new community, which had eight city blocks, twenty-five business lots, fifty-seven residential lots, and a city park. (From 1887 to 1889 the estimates of the population of Liberal varied from five to eight hundred.) Walser continued to practice law. He established and published a newspaper called the *Liberal.* He operated a coal mine. He built a hotel for the community, the National Hotel, which was advertised as operating on "a liberal basis." He was the founder of Freethought University in Liberal, and the catalog identifies him as the teacher of commercial law. In addition, he found time to write for the magazine the *Orthopaedians* and also published three volumes of esoteric poetry—full of classical allusions.

Among his other activities, Walser developed a cemetery at Liberal and, of course, sold lots. When he died in 1910 his fourth wife, Esther Jaemision Walser, made the unusual decision not to bury him in his own cemetery. Instead she had the body interred in Lake Cemetery at Lamar.

In the history of Missouri, Walser stands alone as the developer of a community that emphasized that religion was not welcome in the new town. He was vocally anti-Christian, and described Liberal in these words: "We have here neither priest, preacher, justice of the peace, or other peace officer, no church, saloon, prison, drunkard, loafer, beggar, or person in want, nor have we a disreputable character. This cannot be truthfully said of any christian town on earth."

Liberal was distinctive because of its free-thought ties. For example, they used a different dating system. Instead of utilizing the supposed date for the birth of Jesus Christ as the base for their system, they used the year 1600 A.D., to honor Giordano Bruno who that year was burned at the stake by the Catholic Church for his freethinking. Thus, the year 1882, using their system, was called E of M 282, or Era of Man 282. Such a dating system had been recommended by the National Liberal League.

Freethought University, which appears to have begun operation in 1886 or 1887 in Liberal, was established to provide a place where freethinkers could confidently send their children. The catalog described it as "the only institution of learning in America that is absolutely free from superstition." Walser was intent on making Liberal a community where freethinkers would feel comfortable. In his own words, "Liberals should come here because it is the only established Liberal town in the world with institutions for promulgating the ideal advancement of liberated minds."

Conflict erupted between freethinkers and Christians in Liberal in the 1880s. William H. Waggoner platted and began building an addition just north of Liberal in 1881. He let it be known that he hoped Christians would flock to his settlement. Walser then constructed a high barbed-wire fence to keep Christians out of Liberal. For two years there were verbal exchanges along the barbed-wire fence. Finally, in 1883, Walser bought out Waggoner, and the conflict ended.

The declining support for freethinking led to a surprising development in 1889. Walser announced the sale of a plot of land and the Universal Mental Liberty Hall to the Methodist Episcopal Church for the sum of $485. The hall was to be used as a Methodist Sunday school. Its sale marked the end of the freethinking movement in Liberal, less than a decade after the settlement's founding.

It is interesting to note that in 1889 when the freethought movement in Liberal ended, a new religious movement, the Spiritual Science Association, was gaining prominence in the town. Spiritualists encamped at Walser's Catalpa Park in July and August each year until 1903 by which time spiritualism in Liberal had also waned.

In a period of little more than two decades, Liberal, Missouri, went through both freethinker and spiritualist phases, and Walser embraced both. There have been few long-term results for the town from its unusual anti-Christian background. Today, Liberal is a typical struggling southwest Missouri town with both Christian churches and saloons and with neither a free-thought nor a spiritualist association.

DUANE G. MEYER

Lamar Democrat, 1880s.

Liberal, Mo., Promotional Booklet. Item H1481.35 W168L. State Historical Society of Missouri, Columbia.

Meyer, Duane. *The Heritage of Missouri.* Springfield, Mo.: Emden Press, 1993.

Missouri: The WPA Guide to the "Show Me" State. St. Louis: Missouri Historical Society Press, 1998.

Moore, James Proctor. *This Strange Town: Liberal, Missouri.* Liberal, Mo.: Liberal News, 1963.

WALTON, LESTER A. (1882–1965)

Born in St. Louis on April 20, 1882, Lester A. Walton became a prominent member of the black community in the mid-twenties and remained a leader until his death on October 16, 1965. The son of a custodian in the public schools, he graduated from Sumner High School, a segregated school in St. Louis.

After passing an exam for a graduate certificate from a business school, Walton went to work for the daily *St. Louis Star-Sayings* in 1902 as a reporter and writer on golf. After an episode in which he won access to a segregated elevator by confronting his editor, Walton moved to New York to try his luck as a playwright.

In 1908 Walton returned to reporting, becoming managing editor of the *New York Age,* a black newspaper. Married on June 29, 1912, he and his wife, Gladys Moore, had two daughters. During the periods 1914–1916 and 1919–1921, he managed the Lafayette Theater in Harlem. In the intervening years, he continued working for the *Age.*

In 1918 Walton traveled to France with a party headed by Robert Russa Moten, the principal of Tuskegee Institute. President Woodrow Wilson and Secy. of War Newton Baker had created the committee to inspect the living conditions of black soldiers. In 1919, as a reporter for the *Age,* Walton went to the Versailles peace conference.

From 1922 to 1931 Walton was a columnist for the *New York World,* eventually becoming one of the most prominent black journalists in America. Briefly moving to the *New York Herald Tribune* in 1931, he returned to the *World* as an associate editor. In 1931 he also conducted public relations for the Tuskegee Institute on its fiftieth anniversary. He was the publicity director for the National Negro Business League from 1926 until 1935.

During the twenties and early thirties, Walton became heavily involved in the Democratic Party, which was something of an anomaly since most blacks remained Republicans until Franklin Delano Roosevelt's emergence on the national scene. In the presidential elections of 1924, 1928, and 1932 Walton directed public relations for the Democratic National Committee's black division. In June 1935 President Franklin Roosevelt rewarded him for his diligent service by appointing him envoy extraordinary and minister plenipotentiary to Liberia.

Walton greatly improved American-Liberian relations by negotiating treaties of consular relations, navigation, conciliation, aviation, extradition, and commerce. Through his effort Liberia granted the United States the rights to construct a military base and to land troops in 1946. Two years later an agreement was reached on port construction. In 1948–1949 Liberia chose Walton as its delegatory adviser to the United Nations.

Walton spent his postwar years serving on the Municipal Commission on Intergroup Relations (the name was later changed to Human Rights). A founding member of the Negro Actors Guild, Walton also held an honorary master of arts degree from Lincoln University and an honorary doctor of laws from Wilberforce University. Always a strong advocate of black civil rights, he strove continually to combat racism, which included leading the campaign to have "Negro" capitalized when it appeared in newspapers or magazines, as well as criticizing slum stereotypes of Harlem.

MICHAEL P. BOYLE

Dictionary of American Biography. Supp. 7, 1961–1965. S.v. "Walton, Lester Aglar."

New York Times, October 19, 1965.

Who Was Who in America. Vol. 4. Chicago: A. N. Marquis, 1961–1968.

WALTON, SAMUEL MOORE (1918–1992)

Samuel Moore Walton, whose Wal-Mart merchandising empire made him the richest man in America, was born in Kingfisher, Oklahoma, on March 29, 1918, the son of Thomas Gibson and Nancy Lee Walton. In 1923 the Walton family moved to Missouri, and young Sam spent his boyhood years in Springfield, Marshall, Shelbina, and eventually Columbia where he attended Hickman High School.

While growing up in rural Missouri during the Great Depression, Walton acquired many of the attributes that made him successful in the business world: a propensity for hard work, a strong desire to succeed, and a well-known sense of frugality. He enrolled at the University of Missouri and earned a degree in economics. His classmates elected him president of the class of 1940, and following his graduation that year he accepted a position with the J. C. Penney Company that launched his career in retailing.

During World War II Walton served in the United States Army and attained the rank of captain. In 1943 he married Helen Robson, an Oklahoman who had attended Christian College in Columbia, Missouri, before graduating from the University of Oklahoma.

The couple had four children: Samuel Robson, John Thomas, James Carr, and Alice.

After the war ended, at the urging of his wife who preferred living in a small town, Walton purchased a Ben Franklin variety store in Newport, Arkansas. In 1950 he acquired a variety store in Bentonville, Arkansas, which he renamed Walton's 5 and 10. During the 1950s and 1960s Walton and his brother James "Bud" expanded their operations with the opening of additional stores in the Ben Franklin chain in Arkansas and Missouri. When executives in the Ben Franklin organization turned down Walton's proposal to create a new discount-store chain to be based in small towns, he ventured out on his own and opened the first Wal-Mart Discount City in Rogers, Arkansas, in 1962.

Walton's concept was simple. He proposed to offer shoppers in America's smaller towns a wide variety of brand-name merchandise in no-frills stores at discount prices by taking advantage of volume purchasing and a low-cost delivery system. Walton recognized the buying potential of this underserved market. The formula proved immensely successful, and following its incorporation in 1969 Wal-Mart Stores grew dramatically.

After the firm opened a general headquarters and distribution center in Bentonville, Arkansas, in 1970, Walton gradually phased out his original variety stores in favor of the new discount stores. By the end of the 1970s the firm operated stores in eleven states, and its annual sales exceeded $1 billion. During the next decade Wal-Mart went nationwide, ventured into larger cities, and expanded its operations to include wholesale outlets known as Sam's Wholesale Club, and Wal-Mart Supercenters and Hypermarts that also offered customers groceries. In 1985 *Forbes* proclaimed Sam Walton the richest man in the United States.

Walton stepped down as the company's chief executive officer in 1988, but he continued as chairman of the board. He died in Little Rock, Arkansas, on April 5, 1992. By then Wal-Mart had gone international with the establishment of joint retailing ventures in Mexico, and the Walton family had amassed a fortune estimated to be in excess of $20 billion. Shortly before Walton's death, President George Bush awarded him the Presidential Medal of Freedom.

WILLIAM E. FOLEY

Vance, Sandra, and Roy V. Scott. *Wal-Mart: A History of Sam Walton's Retail Phenomenon.* New York: Twayne Publishers, 1994.

Walton, Sam, with John Huey. *Sam Walton, Made in America: My Story.* New York: Doubleday, 1992.

WATKINS, BRUCE RILEY, SR.
(1924–1980)

Bruce Riley Watkins made innumerable contributions to the development of Kansas City and toward the advancement of civil rights for African Americans. His accomplishments encompass many areas. He was a politician, a businessman, a civic leader, and an elected official. For a period of more than twenty years in the Kansas City metropolitan area, he was a leading proponent for social and economic progress.

Born in Parkville, Missouri, on March 20, 1924, Watkins was the youngest of three children of Bruce Riley and Olivia Watkins. He attended elementary school in Parkville until his family moved to Kansas City when he was in the third grade. After divorcing Riley, his mother and the children moved to New York where Bruce attended high school, graduating from school in Bordentown, New Jersey. As a young man he entered the military service and was trained in the air force at Tuskegee Airbase where he earned the rank of lieutenant, bombardier-navigator. While he was in the service his mother returned to Kansas City and married T. B. Watkins, a pioneer funeral director. Upon completion of his military service, Watkins graduated from Worsham School of Mortuary Science of Chicago in 1947. He then joined his family in Kansas City where he worked in the family business of Watkins Brothers Memorial Chapel for more than thirty years.

Inspired by his stepfather, Watkins became intrigued with politics. In 1960 he and **Leon Jordan** created the political organization known as Freedom Incorporated. His career as an elected official began in 1963, when he won the Third District council seat, becoming the first African American to serve on the Kansas City Council. It was during his civic service that he quickly gained public attention in his fight for human rights. In 1966 he was elected as the first African American circuit clerk of Jackson County, Missouri, and was reelected again in 1970. In 1975 he was again elected to the city council of Kansas City, representing the Sixth District.

Bruce Watkins's race for Kansas City mayor in 1979 brought him citywide and national recognition. He entered the city's nonpartisan primary for mayor as an underdog in a six-person field. He won first place with a large and solid outpouring of support from the city's six inner-city wards. He was defeated by Republican Richard L. Berkley in the general election by a margin of twenty thousand votes. Nevertheless, he continued to campaign for equality and representation of the people in public accommodations, fair housing, and equal opportunity.

Watkins actively participated in many community organizations, boards, and committees, and he was a driving force in his family mortuary business.

He was a member of Friendship Baptist Church. He considered the black church the most valuable institution of his race.

Watkins was married twice, first to Lola Plummer of Kansas City, Kansas, from which union two sons, Bruce Jr. and Robert, were born. He later married Rhae Tate of Los Angeles. Both marriages ended in divorce. At the age of fifty-six, the longtime community leader and cofounder of Freedom Incorporated died of cancer on September 13, 1980. The Bruce R. Watkins Cultural Center in Kansas City is named in his honor.

JULIE MAURER

Archives. Bruce R. Watkins Cultural Center, Kansas City, Mo.
Kansas City Call, September 19–October 2, 1980.
Kansas City Times, September 16, 1980.
Ploski, Harry A., and James Williams, ed. *The Afro-American.* New York: John Wiley and Sons, 1983.

WATKINS, WALTUS LOCKETT
(1806–1884)

The eldest son of the thirteen children of Benjamin and Jane Minter Watkins, Wathal "Waltus" Watkins was born on October 30, 1806, near Versailles, Kentucky. Although his father was a gentry farmer, the young man was apprenticed to his maternal uncles to learn mechanics and cotton textile manufacturing. Reportedly, he assisted in building a model locomotive for display at Louisville and rose to the position of mill superintendent at Frankfort.

In 1830, the same year that his father died, Watkins migrated to western Missouri. He chose Liberty, at Clay County's center, as his base of operations. He set up cotton-processing machinery, a tannery, and a sawmill near the courthouse square. Good fortune, however, was not with him. He overestimated the available cotton supply, was set back by a fire that destroyed his workshop, and subsequently retreated to the northeast corner of the county—in Washington Township—to reestablish himself in agrarian pursuits.

Between 1839 and 1861 Watkins regained prosperity amid tumult. He seized opportunities and met challenges to become the recognized leader of his rural community. Despite sporadic financial panics he gradually amassed landholdings, improved his acreage, and recruited kin and other settlers to the region along the Plattsburg-Richmond Road. At the height of his farming career, Watkins reportedly controlled thirty-six hundred acres, known as Bethany, some of which he assigned to his sons while others he leased to tenants. As a highly regarded livestock man, he raised mules, shorthorn cattle, and Berkshire hogs. He also farmed commercially, in fodder, fruit, and honey. By 1849 he expanded his operations as he added buhrstones to grind both corn and wheat, sawmills to process nearby timberlands, and brick kilns to exploit clay deposits.

As the local squire Watkins simultaneously developed paternal concerns for the community's institutions. He was in the forefront of cultural uplift that led to construction of a subscription school, the Franklin Academy. First a log cabin and then a distinctive octagonal brick building a half mile from the Watkins homestead, this structure housed a lending library and a debate society. In the 1850s Watkins was a major solicitor, trustee, and examiner for the fledgling William Jewell College in Liberty. A convert to the temperance movement in the late 1830s, he also became a devout Baptist following his conversion at age forty-two. From that time forward he was a pillar in the Mount Vernon Missionary Baptist Church, also located adjacent to Bethany.

Although he never ran for public office—he was a lifelong Democrat—Watkins proudly held the postmastership for Bethany from 1842 to 1849 and was a revered justice of the peace. As turmoil on the Missouri-Kansas border intensified, he supported the migration of slaveholders to Kansas. Yet, when the question of secession arose, Watkins, like his fellow Clay Countian **Alexander Doniphan,** preferred union. Although he was an election official in 1864, during the Reconstruction period he refused to swear a loyalty oath and favored a soft rather than hard approach to resolving postwar turmoil.

Near the age of fifty-five in 1860–1861 Watkins began his most auspicious endeavor: the construction of a three-story woolen mill just down the hill from the twenty-room Greek Revival homestead he had erected the previous decade. In a local newspaper advertisement for May 1861 Watkins asserted that "the machinery is of the very best quality, of superior polish and finish, and is well adapted to making any goods that may be wanted in the State." Between 1861 and 1886 this residentiary manufactory, powered by a one-hundred-horsepower steam engine, operated regularly; for the next ten years it ran intermittently. It operated under four successive names, as Watkins took in son John, who in turn enlisted two other brothers but ultimately ran the business himself. The factory performed custom work such as carding for local farmers as well as commercial production of yarn, cloth, blankets, and shawls for a market within a seventy-five-mile radius. Watkins had opportunely entered the woolen market in the Midwest when it was on the ascent. When he died on January 24, 1884, the peak had already passed. In its prime Watkins Woolen Mill was one of the larger establishments of its kind in Missouri. At its distinctive pastoral setting, thirty to forty operatives labored in tandem with farm laborers at Bethany.

Waltus Watkins sought to epitomize the successful blend of industrialism and agrarianism, an endeavor apparent to visitors who tour the historic site operated by the state since 1964.

LOUIS W. POTTS

Caldwell, Dorothy J. "Missouri's National Historic Landmarks, Part III, Watkins Mill." *Missouri Historical Review* 63 (April 1963): 364–77.

Crockett, Norman L. *The Woolen Industry in the Midwest.* Lexington: University Press of Kentucky, 1970.

Gross, Laurence F. "The Importance of Research outside the Library: Watkins Mill, a Case Study." *IA: The Journal of the Society for Industrial Archaeology* 7 (1981): 15–26.

Potts, Louis W. "From Speculator to Gentleman: Waltus L. Watkins and the Case for Land Speculation on the Missouri Frontier." *Gateway Heritage* 13 (fall 1992): 46–55.

WEBSTER, RICHARD M. (1922–1990)

An active Republican from age sixteen, Richard Melton Webster served in the Missouri House of Representatives for fourteen years and in the state senate for twenty-eight years, longer than any other Republican in Missouri history. Webster's most significant legislative achievement was his sponsorship of a bill leading to the creation of Missouri Southern State College.

Born on April 29, 1922, in Carthage, Missouri, Webster attended public schools in Carthage, graduating from Carthage High School in 1940. He earned his law degree from the University of Missouri in Columbia in 1948 after serving on active duty in the United States Coast Guard from 1941 to 1945. In the Philippine campaign in the South Pacific he directed the first landing barge ashore during the invasion of the islands of Masbate and Lubang. He served in the United States Navy Reserves until 1968. Webster married Janet Poston Whitehead on July 3, 1948, and the couple raised two sons, Richard Melton Jr. and William Lawrence.

Admitted to the Missouri bar in 1948, Webster began practicing law in Carthage. The same year he organized young voters for the Republican State Committee and won election to the Missouri House as the representative from Jasper County. Reelected to the House in 1950, Webster secured the Republican Party's nomination for attorney general in 1952, but lost in the general election. From 1949 to 1951 he served as president of the Missouri Federation of Young Republicans. Reelected to the House in a special election in 1953, and in regular elections in 1954, 1956, 1958, and 1960, he served as Speaker of the House in 1954, the youngest in Missouri history up until that time. In 1962 voters of Missouri's Thirty-second District elected Webster to the state senate. He continued to win reelection to the Senate from 1966 to 1986, posting the Thirty-second Senatorial District's largest-ever vote majority in 1966 and running without opposition in both the primary and the general elections in 1970. From 1983 to 1986 he served as the Senate minority floor leader.

During his career as a state legislator, Webster supported the disadvantaged, education, civil rights, and workers' benefits and helped create strict legislation against child abuse. Deemed his most impressive contribution, he sponsored legislation supporting the establishment of Missouri Southern State College in Joplin. The school began as a two-year institution in 1965 and, with Webster's support, became a four-year college in 1977. The first permanent dormitory at Missouri Southern bears the name Richard M. Webster Hall in his honor.

After practicing law in Carthage and Joplin for more than thirty years, Webster retired in 1981. He continued to serve in the state senate until his death on March 4, 1990, only a few days after undergoing heart surgery.

ERIKA K. NELSON

Obituary. *Missouri Historical Review* 84 (July 1990): 485–86.
Official Manual of the State of Missouri, 1973–1974. Jefferson City: Secretary of State, 1974.
Official Manual of the State of Missouri, 1985–1986. Jefferson City: Secretary of State, 1986.
Who's Who in the Midwest, 1982–1983. 18th ed. Chicago: A. N. Marquis, 1982.

WELCH, CASIMIR JOHN JOSEPH MICHAEL (1873–1936)

Casimir John Joseph Michael "Cas" Welch was a colorful Kansas City Democratic machine politician of the Pendergast era. He earned a place in a triumvirate with **Thomas J. Pendergast** and **Joseph B. Shannon.** Welch, defined by his fists and a tapestry of small incidents, accepting factional differences, seldom digressed or questioned the purposes or policies of the machine. He regarded politics as a ruthless game in which nearly everything was fair. Kansas City "reformers" thought Welch was dishonest and dependent on underworld support.

For three decades Welch controlled thirty-six precincts east of downtown Kansas City. His densely populated, heavily African American district contained many rooming house floaters, manual laborers, petty artisans, and indigents. A large percentage of Welch's electorate believed he had a genuine interest in their welfare, considering him a friend and voting for the ticket of his Jefferson Democratic Club. From 1910 to 1936 Welch was a justice of the peace in his "Little Tammany." He knew little law, settling domestic quarrels and other disputes on the basis of experience and common sense. During Prohibition he set a policy of refusing to hear criminal cases on the grounds they involved too many of his constituents, hurting him as a political satrap. In 1922 he put aside his disdain for Blackstone long enough to pass a probably rigged bar examination.

Welch was born in Jackson, Michigan, on March 3, 1873, the son of two Irish immigrants, Michael and Anne Welch, who named him after Saint Casimir, a Polish Roman Catholic saint. The Welch family of modest means moved to Kansas City in 1882. Cas proved a difficult student and said he stayed in primary school only long enough to reach the phrase "Ned had a sled" in an English primer. Becoming a newsboy, Welch enlarged his territory by bullying and beating up competitors. He moved on to the plumbing trade, joining Plumbers' Union no. 8. He found his chosen profession working as a ruffian at election time for Shannon's Rabbit-faction Democrats. A burly and foulmouthed brute, Welch dressed in sartorial splendor, a Beau Brummell of the boilermakers and ward heelers.

In the early 1900s Welch and Pendergast, a rising member of the Goat-faction Democrats, organized a messenger service. They used their political connections to thwart competition and used their fists to keep in line their delivery boys, young toughs considered "veritable gorillas" by critics. After Pendergast took over the Goats in 1911 and Welch emerged as a Rabbit ward captain, the two men alternately cooperated and opposed one another. In 1924 as Rabbit strength waned, Welch switched his allegiance to the increasingly dominant Pendergast organization.

Welch lived life to the fullest. Somewhat of a daredevil, he owned and piloted his own airplane. He drove carriages and automobiles with abandon, winning a ten-thousand-dollar judgment after a street accident. He promoted prizefights, hunted, and golfed. A number of his henchmen met violent ends during Prohibition. Welch often fought and brawled, once shooting and wounding a political opponent in a street battle. In 1909, after aggravating seasickness by drinking brandy on a voyage to Europe—where he mistakenly called Trafalgar Square "Alfalfa Square," derided artists at the Louvre for copying each other, and asserted Paris was not as wild as expected (nothing compared to what he was used to in Kansas City)—he swore off hard liquor. Arrested in a Prohibition raid holding a large glass of whiskey, he beat an indictment by citing his teetotaling reputation. He was a partner in the Welch-Sandler Concrete Company and owned several oil wells.

Welch thought women were too tricky and vainglorious to participate in politics, but loved them just the same. His marriage to Elizabeth Allbright in 1910 culminated in a separation. A long affair with Mabel Brown, a music and art teacher, ended with her 1921 suicide. His marriage on February 5, 1935, to Pawnee Clark, resulted in tragedy when she and a baby girl died within several weeks of each other from separate illnesses.

Welch, with a history of coronary trouble, died of a heart attack on April 17, 1936. Earlier in the day, looking in splendid physical condition after noticeably losing weight during a hospital stay, he had responded to an inquiry concerning his health, smiling and saying, "I never felt better; everything is fine."

LAWRENCE H. LARSEN

Kansas City Star, April 17, 1936.
Kansas City Times, April 18, 1936.
Reddig, William M. *Tom's Town: Kansas City and the Pendergast Legend.* 1947. Reprint, Columbia: University of Missouri Press, 1986.

WELLS, ROBERT WILLIAM (1795–1864)

Robert William Wells was a pioneer federal jurist in Missouri who played a major role in the *Dred Scott* case. Born on November 29, 1795, in Winchester, Virginia, he received only primary school training, but educated himself in the liberal arts. From 1816 to 1819 he worked as a federal deputy surveyor, probably on crews in Illinois and Missouri. He studied for the bar in law offices in Virginia and Ohio and in 1820 began to practice in St. Charles. In December 1821, while acting as an adviser to the General Assembly, Wells broke a legislative deadlock, performing the unusual but important task of designing the Missouri State Seal. He won elections to the Missouri House of Representatives in 1822 and 1824. He served in the appointed position of state attorney general from 1826 to 1836. Running twice for Congress, he lost close contests in 1831 and 1832. Mentioned as a possible candidate for governor, he never again ran for an important public office.

In 1836, following the death of Judge **James Hawkins Peck,** President Andrew Jackson appointed Wells as the U.S. district judge of the District of Missouri. Judge Wells, in addition to his judicial duties, engaged in many other activities. He became a leader of the Democratic Party, presided as an elected delegate over the 1845 Constitutional Convention, promoted economic projects in Missouri, wrote legal monographs, collected art, and farmed near Jefferson City. Asked about the profitability of his agricultural operation, he once replied, "Very well, but what troubles me is that lawyer Wells has to pay too many of Farmer Wells' bills."

Wells's legal work reflected a combination of his concern about English common-law precedents and his experiences as a frontier lawyer. He usually stood on the side of property, as in *In re Klein,* when he unsuccessfully struck down the Bankruptcy Act of 1841, which he considered too lenient under British practices. In criminal matters he generally favored the accused. He wrote learned and carefully crafted opinions, most noteworthy in several Spanish land-grant cases left over from colonial days. According to a memorial, "His perceptions were keen, his habit of thought and analysis were clear, and he expressed his conclusions with marked precision."

Wells's participation in *Dred Scott* started on June 17, 1854, during the federal phase of the case in the United States Circuit Court in St. Louis. (On occasion, Wells sat as a federal circuit judge.) The jury trial swirled around the question of whether Scott, a slave trying to win his freedom, had enough of the rights of American citizenship to sue in a federal court. Wells, relying on a Missouri Supreme Court interpretation of a United States Supreme Court decision, instructed the jury that Scott was a slave with no legal rights. Accordingly, the jury ruled against Scott. On a writ of error over a technical plea of abatement concerning the jurisdiction of the circuit court, the case went to the Supreme Court. Chief Justice Roger Taney, in his famous and controversial March 1857 opinion, upheld Wells. In a letter to a friend Wells said that he felt sorry for Scott and that he wished the law had favored his freedom.

In 1857 Congress divided Missouri into two federal judicial districts, and Wells became the first judge of the United States District Court for the Western District of Missouri.

Even though he owned slaves, Wells felt that slavery hurt Missouri's economy. He strongly supported the Union and was the Cole County delegate to the June 1862 State Emancipation Convention. In September 1863 he served as president of the Missouri State Radical and Union Convention.

Wells continued to hold court under difficult wartime conditions, but his health failed, and he died on September 22, 1864. A man of an older slaveholding Missouri, he made a strong impact on the life of the state and helped to hold it together through difficult times; he was a true state builder.

LAWRENCE H. LARSEN

Bay, W. V. N. *Reminiscences of the Bench and Bar of Missouri.* St. Louis: F. H. Thomas, 1878.
King, Roy T. "Robert Williams Wells: Jurist, Public Servant, and Designer of the Missouri State Seal." *Missouri Historical Review* 30 (January 1936): 107–31.

Larsen, Lawrence H. *Federal Justice in Western Missouri: The Judges, the Cases, the Times.* Columbia: University of Missouri Press, 1994.

Wells, Robert William. Papers. Western Historical Manuscripts Collection, Columbia.

WELLS, ROLLA (1856–1944)

Rolla Wells, a businessman and mayor of St. Louis, was born in St. Louis on June 1, 1856, to Erastus and Isabella Bowman Henry Wells. The senior Wells had emigrated to St. Louis from New York in 1843, and had made his fortune operating the city's first mass-transit system. Active in city politics for many years, Erastus represented Missouri in Congress from 1869 until 1877.

Rolla's parents sent him to the Vermont Episcopal Institute, a semimilitary school near Burlington, Vermont, in 1868. Favored by prominent St. Louis families, the institute prepared him to attend Washington University in 1871 and to enroll subsequently in Princeton University. He was awarded honorary degrees by Washington University in 1915 and by Princeton in 1916.

Wells became superintendent of the Missouri Railroad Company, the St. Louis streetcar system owned by his family, in 1878. Following its sale in 1882 he invested in unsuccessful cattle-ranching and mining ventures in the New Mexico Territory, but maintained his business interests in St. Louis. Wells was a director of the St. Louis Fair from 1885 until 1890, and its president from 1890 until 1893. An 1891 investment in a steel foundry led to the organization of the highly successful American Steel Foundry Company in 1894, and Wells acted as its president until 1901, when he became mayor of St. Louis.

A Democrat like his father, Wells did not actively participate in politics until 1894, when he accepted the presidency of a local political club, the St. Louis Democracy (later the Jefferson Club). His political independence had made him acceptable to the warring factions of city Democrats, but it also led him to oppose the free-silver policy of presidential-hopeful and fellow Missourian **Richard Parks Bland** in 1896. An active "gold bug" at the Chicago convention, Wells subsequently opposed candidate William Jennings Bryan, and participated as a delegate in the Indianapolis convention that nominated John Palmer and Simon Buckner as the Democratic Sound Money candidates. Those activities led to Wells's resignation as president of the St. Louis Democracy, which supported Bryan.

Wells reentered politics in 1901 at the urging of the "silk stocking independents," who insisted upon his candidacy for mayor as the price of their cooperation with party regulars. Elected and installed as mayor, Wells faced an obstructive legislative body, the House of Delegates, which was greatly influenced by a political machine typical of the era. **Edward Butler** ran the machine, obtaining his revenue and power from operating the city garbage-disposal contract. Wells personally bought an island in the Mississippi River and sent the city's garbage there, breaking the power of the machine. "It seems to be quite appropriate," he later wrote, "that the extinction of boss rule should be achieved in a controversy . . . over the problem of garbage."

Wells proved a progressive during his eight years in office, exemplifying the goals of most urban reformers of the period. He sought honest, efficient government conducted according to sound business practices and responsive to the needs of the people and their city. Plans for the Louisiana Purchase Exposition, or St. Louis World's Fair, in 1904 gave added impetus as well as added burdens to municipal improvements. Wells counted as one of his proudest achievements the clarification of the city's muddy water supply before the opening of the World's Fair, but other accomplishments during his two terms present a roster of progressive goals. City planning, a parks and playground program, public baths, more than three hundred miles of streets paved, public health measures, improved utility services and rates, and an extensive public buildings and works program brought St. Louis—the largest city in the state—into the twentieth century. Wells himself was given much of the credit for those successes, as he both represented and led a coalition of progressive urban reformers.

Wells refused to run for a third term in 1909. A supporter of Woodrow Wilson, he served as treasurer of the Democratic National Committee from 1912 through 1916. He was governor of the Federal Reserve Bank of St. Louis from 1914 until 1919, and then was appointed receiver for the United Railways Company of St. Louis from 1919 to 1927. Wells was again actively involved in politics in 1922 in opposing the renomination of Sen. **James A. Reed.** When Reed won the primary, Wells publicly declared his support for the Republican candidate.

Wells married Jennie Howard Parker on October 2, 1878, and the couple had five children. Jennie Wells died on April 9, 1917. Wells's second marriage, to Carlota Clark Church, took place on November 17, 1923. Rolla Wells died at his home in St. Louis on November 30, 1944.

STEPHANIE L. O'NEAL

St. Louis Post-Dispatch, November 30–December 1, 1944.

Wells, Rolla. *Episodes of My Life.* St. Louis: n.p., 1933.

Who Was Who in America. Vol. 2. Chicago: A. N. Marquis, 1950.

WETMORE, ALPHONSO (1793–1849)

A soldier, pioneer, lawyer, and man of letters, Alphonso Wetmore was born in Winchester, Connecticut, on February 17, 1793, to a family that prized culture. He served as an ensign in the War of 1812, losing his right arm in the abortive invasion of Canada. He married Mary Smith of New York on September 5, 1813, and was appointed paymaster of the Sixth Infantry in the following year. When that regiment was transferred to the Missouri frontier in 1819, he brought his family with him, establishing them in the thriving town of Franklin, a point of supply for travelers along the Santa Fe Trail. There he remained for fourteen years, as paymaster for a large geographical area. In this position he was required to travel constantly, often in considerable danger. His loss of a large sum of government money in a mishap on the flood-swollen Missouri River became the subject of contention between himself and the army, though he was eventually exonerated.

While residing in Franklin, Wetmore was often in St. Louis; there, in 1821, he oversaw the first production of his play *The Pedlar.* Published by J. A. Paxton, who also took a part in it, *The Pedlar* was remarkable in several respects. It was certainly the first play written west of the Mississippi, and may well have been the first English-language play to be staged there. It is among the earliest instances of what came to be called "local-color" writing, and a direct forerunner of the work of frontier humorists such as **Mark Twain.** Finally, it contains the first known reference in print to the legendary riverman Mike Fink.

Wetmore's generous use of local color showed that he had come to know the terrain and settlers of Missouri intimately, and had become familiar with the tall tales of the trappers and rivermen, as well as with the ways of Native Americans, especially the Pawnee and Omaha tribes. As early as 1822 he was turning this material to journalistic account. His sketch "Mike Shuck, the Beaver Hunter," which appeared in two parts in the *Missouri Intelligencer,* was praised by the editor as "the best description of a backwoodsman ever published" and was widely reprinted in the East.

In 1833 Wetmore was listed as among the trustees of the newly established town of New Franklin, but by the end of the year he had resigned his army commission and was practicing law in St. Louis. In 1837 Col. **Charles Keemle** of St. Louis published Wetmore's *Gazetteer of the State of Missouri.* In addition to maps and geography and information about local customs, some of which is distinctly literary in style, the *Gazetteer* includes an appendix of seventy pages containing seven sketches of frontier life. These pieces vary in manner and quality, but the best are remarkable for their vivid diction and for the stoic self-sufficiency of their characters. They constitute an important early collection of literary journalism.

In January 1838 Wetmore undertook, in association with Keemle, the publication of the *Missouri Saturday News,* which was "devoted to literature, political information, commercial intelligence, agriculture, Et. Cetera." In effect, this was the first literary journal in Missouri. From the prospectus in the first issue to the extended fictionalization of his own experience called "Lieutenant Random Ranger's Adventures," Wetmore as editor and writer promoted western themes and values, though his readers also enjoyed reprints of conventional eastern and even European stories and poems.

Political differences caused Wetmore to fall out of favor with both Keemle and Sen. **Thomas Hart Benton.** The forty-third issue of the *Saturday News,* dated October 27, 1838, bears the names of Wetmore and his son Leonidas as editor and publisher, respectively; they continued as joint proprietors of the paper until it ceased publication following its fifty-third issue, in January 1839.

Wetmore lived another decade as a lawyer and man of political affairs in St. Louis. He raised a company of one thousand men in 1847, intending them for service in the Mexican War, only to have them turned down at the behest of Benton. Home from a long-planned trip to California, he was overcome by cholera and died on June 13, 1849, within days of his return to St. Louis. He was survived by his wife and six of their eight children.

Alphonso Wetmore was a man of letters, like Washington Irving, whom he admired. If, for all his literary ambition, he never attained the grace that marks the work of his great model, he nevertheless can be said to have pioneered in a literary landscape as fresh and as little known as the Missouri countryside with which he was so intimate.

ROBERT C. BOYD

Boyd, Robert C. "Literary Activity in Antebellum St. Louis, Missouri." Ph.D. diss., Indiana University, 1989.

Gregg, Kate L. "Major Alphonso Wetmore." *Missouri Historical Review* 45 (April 1941): 385–93.

Spotts, Carleton Brooks. "The Development of Fiction on the Missouri Frontier." Ph.D. diss., Pennsylvania State University, 1934.

WHITE, PEARL (1889–1938)

Pearl Fay White, one of the first great silent-movie stars, was born on March 4, 1889, in Greenridge, Missouri, the daughter of Edward Gilman and Lizzie

G. House White. The family eventually moved to Springfield, Missouri, where Pearl attended public school. She entered high school in 1903 but never graduated. At age sixteen she began her acting career by taking small roles in Springfield's Diemer Theater and, at age eighteen, left home to work in stock theater and traveling companies.

In 1910 White found work in silent movies with the Powers Film Company in New York City. She continued her career in the silent movies at the Lubin Company in Philadelphia and then moved to Pathé Frères in Jersey City, New Jersey. By 1912 she was filming an average of one slapstick comedy a week for Crystal Films of New York. In 1914 she returned to Pathé to star in *The Perils of Pauline,* a series of films (sometimes called "chapterplays") that brought her fame, fortune, and millions of loyal fans. As the perilous Pauline, she became the movies' unchallenged "Serial Queen," a title she never relinquished. Pathé filmed all the *Perils,* mostly in the outdoors, in Ithaca, New York, and Port Lee, New Jersey. In her role as Pauline, White was described by a reviewer as "a pretty, wide-eyed young woman, who covered her natural red hair with a blond wig on the screen. She was an actress who looked good in both formal gown and dirty dungarees."

While at Pathé White also appeared in *The Iron Claw, Pearl of the Army, The Exploits of Elaine, The Fatal Ring,* and *The Black Secret.* All her serial movies placed her character in peril: falling a great distance, trapped in a fire, lying in the path of a freight train, being thrown into the sea, or jumping across something dangerous. The films were cliff-hangers, filled with action and suspense, and featuring last-minute escapes. In each *Perils* film, good always overcame evil. White, who was quite athletic, always wanted to do her own stunts. However, as she became increasingly valuable to the studios, directors insisted that in dangerous scenes she give way to stuntmen in blond wigs.

In 1919, in an effort to prove herself a dramatic actress, White worked at Fox Film Corporation. Over the next two years she made ten films, but never succeeded in gaining recognition or stardom in a dramatic role.

White married fellow actor Victor C. Sutherland on October 12, 1907. They divorced in 1914. In 1919 she married another actor, Wallace McCutcheon, but they divorced in 1921. A year later White moved to France where she lived until her death on August 4, 1938. She died in the American Hospital in Paris and is buried in Passy Cemetery.

In 1947 Paramount Pictures released a fictionalized biography of Pearl White, which starred Betty Hutton.

KAY HIVELY

Dictionary of American Biography. Vol. 1, supp. 1. S.v. "White, Pearl."

Harmon, J. M., and Donald F. Glut. *The Great Movie Serials.* Garden City, N.Y.: Doubleday, 1972.

WHITE HAIR (PAW-HIU-SKAH) (?–1809?)

A succession of Osage leaders from the 1790s to the 1870s were known as "Cheveux Blancs" in French or "White Hair" in English. This is probably a mistranslation of the Osage name by which these men were also known, Paw-Hiu-Skah or Pawhuska, meaning "white-headed eagle." (There seems to be no basis to a story published by Timothy Flint in 1826 that the name referred to an American soldier's wig captured in battle.) Since the name Paw-Hiu-Skah was popular among several Osage clans, it is often difficult to identify the particular individual meant in a given reference. Still, two White Hairs who were prominent in tribal affairs during the last years the Osages occupied their traditional homelands in Missouri may be identified with some certainty.

The first White Hair was born in the early 1700s, and was related, perhaps a half brother, to the first **Clermont,** peace chief (Tsi-zhu Gahige) of the main village of the Big Osage in present Vernon County. While Clermont remained somewhat skeptical and aloof in his dealings with French and Spanish fur traders and government officials, White Hair welcomed the potential wealth and power these newcomers offered. A serious rivalry developed between the two men, probably representing factions within the village and tribe.

This factionalism played into the hands of St. Louis traders **(Jean) Pierre** and **Auguste Chouteau.** In 1795, after the Spanish government granted them a monopoly on the Osage trade, the Chouteaus built a trading post near the Big Osage villages. Pierre spent much time among the Osage, involving himself deeply in tribal politics to further his business interests. Clermont resented the interference and tried to limit Chouteau's influence; Chouteau in turn lent his support to the more cooperative White Hair.

About this time, perhaps in late 1795 or 1796, Clermont died. With the Chouteaus' support, White Hair claimed to be head chief of all the Osages. The Chouteaus convinced Spanish officials to confirm this title, but they had less success with the Osages. A single chief was contrary to Osage tradition: each village governed its own affairs through a complicated balance of peace chiefs, war chiefs, and council of elders. Moreover, **Clermont II** claimed his father's title of Tsi-zhu Gahige, now usurped by White Hair. The younger Clermont and his supporters abandoned their village to join a breakaway Osage band on the Arkansas River. This was the first in a series of defections as White Hair's people moved away rather than submit to his claims of authority over them.

Through the Chouteaus, White Hair attempted to enlist the aid of the Spanish government, and subsequently that of the United States, in pressuring the dissidents to reunite under his authority. In 1804 he traveled to Washington, D.C., with Pierre Chouteau, where President Jefferson and other officials accepted him as head chief of the Osages, though this did little to shore up his sagging prestige at home.

White Hair continued in close alliance with the Chouteaus. About this time his daughter married Pierre Chouteau's interpreter, Noel Mongrain. Government officials in Missouri considered White Hair the tool of the Chouteaus, of whom they were generally suspicious; nevertheless, they were willing to make use of the chief. Relying on the government to support his authority, White Hair was always accommodating to U.S. demands. After an abjectly humble speech he signed a treaty ceding most of the Osage homeland in Missouri and Arkansas to the United States in 1808, and further undermined his credibility among many Osages.

White Hair died not long after the treaty council of November 1808, probably sometime in 1809. His son, Che-sho-hung-ga, assumed the name of White Hair and his father's status as "government chief" and leader of an ever dwindling Osage faction. He proved as pliable as his father to the interests of the Chouteaus and the demands of the U.S. government. In 1822 he signed a treaty absolving the government from commitments it had made in the 1808 treaty. In 1825 he signed treaties ceding yet more Osage land and granting a right-of-way for the Santa Fe Trail through the remainder.

At the Chouteaus' urging White Hair moved his village to the Neosho River, in present southeastern Kansas, near a trading post established by Pierre's sons, Paul Liguest and **Auguste Pierre Chouteau.** He died in the spring of 1832, and was succeeded by another equally cooperative White Hair. Other White Hairs figured prominently in Osage affairs in the 1850s and 1860s, one signing a treaty with the Confederate States of America in 1861. Pawhuska, Oklahoma, is named for the White Hair who settled near there about 1870.

MARY ELLEN ROWE

Din, Gilbert C., and Abraham Nasatir. *The Imperial Osages: Spanish-Indian Diplomacy in the Mississippi Valley.* Norman: University of Oklahoma Press, 1983.

Foley, William E., and C. David Rice. *The First Chouteaus: River Barons of Early St. Louis.* Urbana: University of Illinois Press, 1983.

Mathews, John Joseph. *The Osages: Children of the Middle Waters.* Norman: University of Oklahoma Press, 1961.

Rollings, Willard H. *The Osage: An Ethnohistorical Study of Hegemony on the Prairie-Plains.* Columbia: University of Missouri Press, 1992.

WHITFIELD, OWEN (1892–1965)

Owen Whitfield was born in Jamestown, Mississippi, in 1892. He attended a college in Mississippi that he admitted was no more than an equivalent to high school. In the 1920s several thousand African Americans migrated from the South to the rich soils of southeast Missouri. Most, including Whitfield, became sharecroppers. In addition to farming he started preaching. By the mid-1930s he was the pastor for a number of black churches in the area.

In 1934 the Southern Tenant Farmers Union was established in Arkansas, and three years later Whitfield became a member. At least in part as a result of his preaching renown, he became the organization's most influential member. The union had been started by whites and, partially in an attempt to attract African Americans, named Whitfield its vice president in 1938.

During the 1930s the sharecropping system began to decline, hastened by federal legislation that made it more profitable for landowners to dismiss sharecroppers and replace them with day laborers. Under the legislation sharecroppers received a portion of government payments to cotton farmers; day laborers received none.

In January 1938 Whitfield wrote to President Franklin D. Roosevelt:

> For first time in the life of a lowly sharecropper write you in regards to the plight of more than 10,000 families now hungry . . . and about to be evicted. . . .
> Their reasons for evicting us is as follows
> 1. to git all government benefits without sharing with the share tenants
> 2. to evict us into submission to work for an average of 75 cents per 14 hour day to do all the work that tractors and modern machinery can't do
> We petition your Honor to do all that is your power to get protection for us. . . . These families are the most exploited class they were not allowed to rais hogs or chickens or rais corn for bread or have a milk cow but just rais cotton alone therefore they are homeless and hungry.

Whitfield received a courteous but evasive answer from a Farm Security Administration employee.

Next Whitfield sought a means to illustrate the plight of the cotton laborers. He chose a mass highway demonstration. On the morning of January 9,

1939, approximately eleven hundred demonstrators, most of them black, marched to two federal highways. During the first two days of the camp out, most local officials and landowners believed that the demonstration would quickly fail. They were wrong. Whitfield's chief goal was to gain attention for the workers' plight, and he succeeded. The exodus became front-page news in many American newspapers, causing local and state officials to criticize Whitfield. They asserted that most of the demonstrators had not been evicted, which in a legal sense was correct. Landowners and officials could not believe that a rather sophisticated demonstration could have been the work of an African American. They placed the outrage on others, such as local activist **Thad Snow,** employees of the Farm Security Administration, or the white leaders of the Southern Tenant Farmers Union. Nonetheless, they were wrong again; the leader was Whitfield.

In less than one week, the state government, acting on grounds that the highway camps constituted a health menace, began removing the demonstrators to either their old homes or special camps far removed from the highways. Clearly, officials sought to remove the demonstrators from sight, as the new camps were at least as unsanitary as the original camps. Whitfield spent most of his time elsewhere seeking support for his cause.

Hostility toward Whitfield remained intense throughout 1939. However, late that year state officials met with him and large landowners. At that meeting landowners agreed that tenants would not be evicted. Furthermore, the group recommended that the Farm Security Administration increase its activities in southeast Missouri. This was a major concession, as most landowners disliked the Farm Security Administration, accusing it of promoting the rights of sharecroppers and farm laborers at their expense. In the next two years the agency established various loan-grant programs for sharecroppers and laborers, built group labor camps, and created several cooperatives for some sharecroppers and laborers. This increased involvement was a direct result of Whitfield's work. The gains were not as great as many had hoped, but the overall lot of farm laborers improved.

Ironically, Whitfield's activities destroyed the Southern Tenant Farmers Union. He had not informed the national office of the upcoming demonstration. Financially weak and in constant need of help from wealthy sympathizers, the union saw its financial assistance diverted to assist those in southeast Missouri. The union received increased condemnation from its critics, but little aid from its supporters. Whitfield soon left the union, and by late 1940 it had few members.

At the time of his death in 1965 Whitfield was the pastor at the Pilgrims Rest Baptist Church in Mounds, Illinois. He lived long enough to see the tactics he employed in 1939 used again in the quest for full civil rights.

LEON P. OGILVIE

Cantor, Louis. "A Prologue to the Protest Movement: The Missouri Sharecropper Roadside Demonstration of 1939." *Journal of American History* 55 (March 1969): 804–22.

Ogilvie, Leon Parker. "The Development of the Southeast Missouri Lowlands." Ph.D. diss., University of Missouri–Columbia, 1967.

Snow, Thad. *From Missouri.* Boston: Houghton Mifflin, 1954.

WHITTAKER, CHARLES EVANS (1901–1973)

Charles Evans Whittaker, born on February 22, 1901, near Troy in northeastern Kansas, grew up on a farm. He was the son of Charles and Ida Miller Whittaker. As a youth he performed the usual chores and earned money trapping animals for their fur. He dropped out of school after the ninth grade and spent the next two years farming and trapping. He developed a taste for the law by reading newspaper reports of legal proceedings and attending court in Troy. Despite his limited education, he set a personal goal of becoming a lawyer. He once said, "I have loved the law from my earliest recollection."

Whittaker, like so many Kansas farm boys before and after him, went to Kansas City, Missouri. In 1920 he started work as an office boy at Watson, Gage, and Ess, beginning an association that lasted thirty-four years. Whittaker showed enough merit to secure entrance to the Kansas City School of Law, concurrently using tutors to successfully complete his high school studies. He passed the Missouri bar examination in 1923 and graduated from the Kansas City School of Law the following year. While he and **Harry S. Truman** were in law school together they never attended the same classes.

Whittaker married Winfred Pugh in July 1928, and they had three sons. Over the years he gained high esteem as a trial lawyer. One of his greatest strengths was a mastery of detail, which he attributed to a combination of hard work and understanding that the practice of law was an exact science. A friendly and wiry man of average height, he enjoyed talking about legal affairs and current events with friends at daily luncheons. A nominal Republican, active in legal circles, he built a reputation as a "lawyer's lawyer," and in 1954 he was president of the Missouri Bar Association.

On July 8, 1954, President Dwight D. Eisenhower named Whittaker a federal district judge of the United States District Court of the Western District of

Missouri. There was general agreement that having been an attorney for the strongly Republican *Kansas City Star* played a part in his appointment. Whittaker never had an opportunity to define his working philosophy as a trial judge, because in the summer of 1956 President Eisenhower named him to the Eighth Circuit Court of Appeals. Less than a year later, in March 1957, Eisenhower nominated Whittaker, and he was soon confirmed, to the United States Supreme Court to replace Justice Stanley F. Reed.

Not long after his appointment, Whittaker indicated that he was a pragmatist and not a political partisan. This assertion may shed light on why he felt uncomfortable and unhappy on the Supreme Court. Even many of his friends felt that he had trouble making up his mind on cases that came before the Court and that his great talent as a trial lawyer did not serve him well on what was essentially a policy-making body. During a relatively brief tenure Whittaker usually voted with the majority on the Warren Court. His own opinions were considered undistinguished by some constitutional scholars, reflecting no consistent legal philosophy. Justice Whittaker's duties physically impaired him, and he retired on April 1, 1962.

Whittaker returned to Kansas City, where he maintained chambers and wanted to try cases at the federal district level. Chief Justice Earl Warren would not allow it on the grounds that he had certified Whittaker as disabled. Whittaker ended his retirement from the Supreme Court by officially resigning in 1965. He resumed an active career, writing and speaking widely, especially on what he considered the threat of world communism. He served on the International Court of Arbitration in Stockholm, Sweden, and acted as an arbitrator for General Motors. He died in Kansas City on November 26, 1973. The Charles Evans Whittaker U.S. Courthouse in Kansas City was named in his honor.

LAWRENCE H. LARSEN

"Charles E. Whittaker, 1901–1973." *Journal of the Missouri Bar* 30 (January–February 1974).
"The Honorable Charles E. Whittaker Installed as United States District Judge." *Kansas City Bar Journal* 29 (September 1954): 8–9.
Kansas City Times, November 27, 1973.
Larsen, Lawrence H. *Federal Justice in Western Missouri: The Judges, the Cases, the Times.* Columbia: University of Missouri Press, 1994.
New York Times, November 27, 1973.

WIENER, NORBERT (1894–1964)

A mathematician, scientist, educator, and philosopher, Norbert Wiener is best remembered for having coined the term *cybernetics,* which he defined as the science of control and communication in the animal and the machine.

The son of Leo and Bertha Kahn Wiener, Norbert Wiener was born in Columbia, Missouri, on November 26, 1894. His father, a professor of Slavic languages at the University of Missouri, soon moved the family to Massachusetts where he became the first professor of Slavonic languages at Harvard University.

A child prodigy, young Norbert could read and write at three and had mastered arithmetic, algebra, and geometry at age six. He completed high school by age eleven and earned an A.B. degree from Tufts at fifteen, a master of arts degree from Harvard at eighteen, and a Ph.D. at nineteen. Following postdoctoral work at Cambridge (where he studied with Bertrand Russell) and Göttingen, he earned a science doctorate from Columbia University in 1915. He had completed his formal education, including two doctoral degrees, by age twenty-one.

For the next four years, 1915–1919, Wiener served as a lecturer at Harvard, an instructor at the University of Maine, and a staff writer for the *Encyclopedia Americana,* and he did newspaper work for the *Boston Herald.* In 1919 he became an instructor in mathematics at the Massachusetts Institute of Technology (MIT). He remained on the faculty at MIT until his official retirement from active academic life in 1960.

In 1926 Wiener earned a Guggenheim Fellowship and conducted research at Göttingen and Copenhagen. His reputation as a mathematician earned him invitations to serve as a visiting scholar at Cambridge and at Tsing Hua University in China during the 1930s.

Wiener devoted his technical expertise to goal-seeking mechanisms during World War II, but, disturbed with the destructive potential of the military hardware he and other scientists created, he announced in 1947 that he would no longer contribute to military research. By the 1940s he had become preoccupied with the potential of computers and automatic control devices. He believed computers had the potential to usher in a new industrial revolution that had the awesome potential of devaluing the human brain for customary tasks in the same manner as the historic industrial revolution had diminished the need for human muscle.

In 1948 Wiener published the seminal book of his career, *Cybernetics; or, Control and Communication in the Animal and the Machine.* Cybernetics, he explained, sought to discover the elements common to the function of automatic machines and the human nervous system. This extended Wiener's fame beyond the academic community. For the remainder of his career this eclectic scholar's study of the relationship of the human mind to machines led him to explore a variety of academic disciplines, including biophysics, electrical engineering, philosophy, and religion.

Wiener believed talking differentiated the human being from other animals. The need to communicate served as the guiding motive of human life. Understanding the physiology of human memory, in turn, held the key to the development of memory in machines. Wiener predicted that human genes might ultimately replace magnetic tape as the memory core of computers.

Certain risks would accompany the relative perfection of machines. Wiener warned that intellectual laziness might ultimately give machines the upper hand: "The machine's danger to society is not from the machine itself, but from what man makes of it."

A consummate scholar, Wiener seemed void of humor and never made peace with the world. A prolific writer, he authored books across a broad spectrum, including autobiography, mathematics, cybernetics, logic, and even detective mysteries written under the pseudonym "W. Norbert." In his final years Wiener sought a relationship between the science of cybernetics and religion. The result was *God and Golem, Inc.* (1964), for which he posthumously received the National Book Award.

Honors included election to the National Academy of Sciences, the Bocher Prize of the American Mathematical Society, the Lord and Taylor American Design Award, and the National Medal of Science, awarded by President Lyndon Johnson for his contributions to mathematics, engineering, and logical science.

Wiener died on March 18, 1964. Survivors included his wife, Margaret, and two daughters. He is buried in East Sandwich, New Hampshire.

JACK B. RIDLEY

Heims, Steve J. *John von Neumann and Norbert Wiener: From Mathematics to the Technologies of Life and Death.* Cambridge: MIT Press, 1980.

Hilton, Alice Mary. *Logic, Computing Machines, and Automation.* Washington, D.C.: Spartan Books, 1963.

Wiener, Norbert. *Cybernetics; or, Control and Communication in the Animal and the Machine.* New York: Wiley, 1948.

———. *Ex-Prodigy: My Childhood and Youth.* Cambridge: MIT Press, 1953.

———. *God and Golem, Inc.: A Comment on Certain Points Where Cybernetics Impinges on Religion.* Cambridge: MIT Press, 1964.

———. *I Am a Mathematician: The Later Life of a Prodigy.* Garden City, N.Y.: Doubleday, 1956.

WILD, JOHN CASPER (1804?–1846)

Little is known about the life and career of John Casper Wild, a painter and lithographer who lived and worked in St. Louis from 1839 to 1845. Nevertheless, he remains an important artist in the history of the state, for his lithographs of St. Louis and the Mississippi Valley are some of the earliest views published of the area.

Wild was born in Switzerland around 1804 and educated in Paris, where he worked as an artist, producing views of several European cities. He came to the United States in the early 1830s, first to Philadelphia, and later to Cincinnati. He produced paintings and lithographic views of both cities, issuing a set of twenty views of Philadelphia that sold well at ten dollars each.

In 1839 Wild moved to St. Louis, where he found work as a painter and lithographer. He began to paint landscape scenes of the city, which he then lithographed, publishing a set of eight prints of St. Louis sites in the fall of 1840, which sold for four dollars in black and white and eight dollars in color. Unlike most artists, Wild maintained complete control of the process, painting the original artwork, drawing his painting on stone, and publishing the print himself.

The success of these views encouraged Wild to embark on a more ambitious project: a series of lithographs, accompanied by text, of scenes along the Mississippi and Ohio Rivers. The book, titled *The Valley of the Mississippi Illustrated,* was issued in sets of four views, accompanied by "historical descriptions" written by Lewis Foulk Thomas. The introduction to the volume describes the goals of Wild, the artist and publisher: "It is the design of this work, in presenting views of the principal places and picturesque scenes, on the Ohio and Mississippi, accompanied by brief, but succinct descriptions, to give the reader an opportunity of forming something like a correct idea of that portion of the valley, denominated, 'The Great West.'" The intended audience was not only local citizens interested in images of their home, but also readers back east who knew little about the West and were eager for images of the frontier. City leaders hoped that the publication of views of their towns would promote interest and growth in the area. In addition to views of St. Louis, the series contained images of Alton, Kaskaskia, Cairo, and Illinois Town (now East St. Louis) in Illinois, and St. Charles, Selma, and Carondelet in Missouri— all the earliest printed images of these towns. The final number contained a unique "panorama" of St. Louis: four views of the city, looking east, south, west, and north from the top of the Planters' House Hotel, which could be joined to form a picture of the entire city.

The first set was released in July 1841, and subsequent numbers followed monthly until March 1842, each set selling for one dollar. The project was planned to encompass two hundred pages with fifty lithographs, but only thirty-two were completed. Wild reworked several of his earlier St. Louis views for the volume, but he also painted new views of other sites in the city along the river. He may have planned to use some of his previous Cincinnati works to fill out the Ohio River portion of the volume, but no views of the Ohio River were ever issued.

The set did not sell as well as Wild had hoped, though he received unanimous praise for his accurate and attractive views. Because of its commercial failure, complete volumes are extremely rare today; those that have survived were often cut apart over the years to sell the lithographs individually. The volume was perhaps too ambitious a project for St. Louis in the 1840s when the art of lithography was new and St. Louis was still a frontier town. Wild continued to live in St. Louis for several years after the failed project, supporting himself as a printer of bills, circulars, business cards, letterheads, and steamboat manifests.

Perhaps in search of new towns to paint, Wild moved to Davenport, Iowa, in the summer of 1845. He painted landscape scenes and published lithographs of Davenport, Galena, Dubuque, and Muscatine, apparently with some success. He died in August 1846 in Davenport while at work on a scene of that city.

Although Wild spent only six years in Missouri, as the first important landscape painter to depict the area he played a significant role in the artistic development of the state. His *Valley of the Mississippi Illustrated,* despite its lack of commercial success, is valuable as an early example of the art of printmaking and as a rare and historic resource.

BETH RUBIN

McDermott, John Francis. "J. C. Wild: Western Painter and Lithographer." *Ohio State Archaeological and Historical Quarterly* 60 (April 1951): 111–25.

Reps, John W. "John Casper Wild and St. Louis in the Early 1840s." In *Saint Louis Illustrated: Nineteenth-Century Engravings and Lithographs of a Mississippi River Metropolis.* Columbia: University of Missouri Press, 1989.

WILDER, LAURA INGALLS (1867–1957)

When Laura Ingalls Wilder published her first book, *Little House in the Big Woods,* in 1932, she was already sixty-five years old. By the time she finished her last one, *These Happy Golden Years,* eleven years later, she had become one of America's best-loved children's writers. Sometimes referred to as an untutored genius, Wilder had actually been preparing for the task of novel writing for two decades, publishing articles in farm papers and other outlets on topics relating to her own experiences as a housekeeper, farmer's wife, and community citizen in the Missouri Ozarks.

Although she lived sixty-three of her ninety years in south-central Missouri among neighbors whose families had come primarily from Kentucky, Tennessee, Virginia, and the Carolinas, Wilder's own roots traced back to New York and New England. Her parents were part of the Yankee migration that edged out into Illinois, Wisconsin, and Minnesota during the years before the Civil War. Her father, Charles Philip Ingalls, was born on January 11, 1836, in Allegheny County, New York, the third of eleven children. Her mother, Caroline Lake Quiner, was born on December 12, 1839, in Milwaukee County, Wisconsin, the fifth in a family of seven children that had migrated from Connecticut. (In both families one child died in infancy.) Charles and Caroline—immortalized as "Pa" and "Ma" in their daughter's novels—were living on neighboring farms when they married on February 1, 1860.

After living for a while with Charles's parents in Wisconsin, the young couple moved with them and several of his siblings to northwestern Wisconsin, purchasing a farm seven miles from the Mississippi River town of Pepin. There in the "little house in the big woods" were born two girls, Mary Amelia in January 1865 and Laura Elizabeth on February 7, 1867. Two years later, searching for better opportunities to make a living from the land, Charles Ingalls took his family west to Montgomery County, Kansas.

Caroline Celestia was born in their prairie cabin in August 1870. After learning that they were illegally squatting on land still controlled by the Osage Indians, the family moved back to their Pepin County farm in early 1871, and Laura started attending school with her elder sister, Mary. In 1874 the family left Wisconsin for good, taking up farming along Plum Creek, a mile north of the new railroad town of Walnut Grove, Minnesota. A baby boy, Charles Frederick, arrived in 1875, but he died the following year. Poor crops and other adversities forced them to retreat east for a year to the little town of Burr Oak, Iowa, where the parents kept a hotel and worked at other jobs. The fourth girl and last child, Grace Pearl, was born there in 1877, and by the end of the year they were back in Walnut Grove making another try at farming.

In 1879 the extension westward into Dakota Territory of a branch of the Chicago and Northwestern Railroad provided Charles Ingalls with a job as timekeeper and paymaster for a construction gang and the opportunity to locate a free government homestead on the edge of the agricultural frontier. After moving to De Smet, the family finally settled down for good. Laura spent her adolescence there and on the family's farm a mile and a half southeast of town. High school courses were rudimentary. She dropped out of school altogether at the age of sixteen, and after teaching several terms in nearby rural schools married a homesteader from New York named Almanzo James Wilder on August 25, 1885. She was eighteen, he ten years older.

Trying to wrest a living from the land turned out to be an impossible task for the young couple. Almanzo, weakened by a bout of diphtheria, suffered a stroke that left one leg permanently lame. Hot winds, grasshoppers, fire, poor crops, low farm prices, and other calamities forced them to try making a new start in Florida. They also lived for a time with Laura's parents in De Smet and with Almanzo's parents in Spring Valley, Minnesota. Their one consolation through all their adversities was their daughter, Rose, born on December 5, 1886. A baby boy, born during the drought-ridden summer of 1889, survived only a few days. Finally, in July 1894 the young family packed its belongings in a wagon and headed for "the land of the big red apple"—the Missouri Ozarks—which they had learned about from advertising brochures and friends.

Purchasing a forty-acre farm a mile east of Mansfield, a railroad town that had been established twelve years earlier, the Wilders set out to make something for themselves. The going was hard and setbacks were many, but gradually the farm began producing—lumber, apples, strawberries, chickens, and other products. Eventually, with several additions purchased over the years, it grew to nearly two hundred acres. For a time the family moved into town, where Rose went to school and Almanzo ran a dray business and took odd jobs, but they finally moved back to the farm to stay, building a rambling clapboard house that became something of a showplace in the area.

In 1911 Wilder's life changed significantly when a farm-journal editor happened to hear a talk about chicken raising that she had prepared for a farmers' institute but had been unable to deliver in person. At his invitation she began writing articles for the *Missouri Ruralist*—slowly at first, but by 1916 on a regular basis. It was a trip to visit her daughter, Rose, in San Francisco during the Panama-Pacific International Exposition in 1915 that stimulated Wilder to write more frequently. Between 1916 and 1924 her biweekly column appeared in the *Ruralist* almost without fail.

Wilder's daughter, **Rose Wilder Lane,** who had earned a solid reputation as a journalist and author of popular biographies and short stories by the 1920s, encouraged her to branch out into popular-magazine

writing and helped edit and place several of her articles in national outlets such as *McCall's* and *Country Gentleman.* Writing remained only a part-time avocation for Wilder before 1930, however. Besides housework and helping Almanzo on the farm, she remained active in the Methodist Church, Eastern Star, and a variety of women's clubs. Two study groups that she helped organize and actively participated in were the Athenian Club and the Justamere Club. She also helped initiate and from 1917 to 1928 served as secretary-treasurer of the Mansfield Federal Farm Loan Association, which was affiliated with the Federal Land Bank.

During the time that Lane lived near her parents at Rocky Ridge Farm between 1928 and 1935, Wilder started paying serious attention to her writing career. In 1930 she wrote an autobiographical account called "Pioneer Girl." Lane failed to find a publisher for it in New York, but an expanded version of the first section about her family's life on the Wisconsin frontier was published in 1932 as a novel for children by Harper and Brothers under the title of *Little House in the Big Woods.* Even before it hit bookstore shelves, Wilder was at work on *Farmer Boy,* a story based on her husband's boyhood recollections. Every year or two after that until the last book was published in 1943, another volume chronicling her own childhood and adolescence appeared: *Little House on the Prairie, On the Banks of Plum Creek, By the Shores of Silver Lake, The Long Winter, Little Town on the Prairie,* and *These Happy Golden Years.*

Lane collaborated with her mother in organizing, editing, and polishing the volumes. After leaving Mansfield in 1936, she continued to edit and flesh out the handwritten manuscripts before they were sent to the publisher. A final posthumously published novel, *The First Four Years,* became available after the manuscript was discovered among Lane's papers after her death in 1968.

During the 1940s and 1950s Laura Ingalls Wilder accumulated growing accolades from readers, both young and old, librarians, and children's book critics. Thousands of letters from admiring fans poured in from all over the world. In September 1951 the local Mansfield library was named in her honor. Three years later the American Library Association instituted a Laura Ingalls Wilder Award to honor authors making lasting contributions to children's literature.

After her husband's death in 1949, Wilder became more and more reclusive, though she still enjoyed visiting with friends, doing her weekly shopping in Mansfield, and being driven around the countryside in her Oldsmobile. Health problems, including a heart attack, slowed her down; diabetes was diagnosed not long before her death on February 10, 1957. Her reputation, well established by then, continued to grow in subsequent years, especially with the airing of the television program *Little House on the Prairie* (whose stories bore little actual relation to her life or writings). Today her books are more popular than ever, and tens of thousands of loyal fans and curiosity seekers annually visit the sites that have been established at the places where she and her family lived.

JOHN E. MILLER

Anderson, William T. *Laura Ingalls Wilder.* New York: HarperCollins, 1992.

Holtz, William. *The Ghost in the Little House: A Biography of Rose Wilder Lane.* Columbia: University of Missouri Press, 1993.

Miller, John E. *Becoming Laura Ingalls Wilder: The Woman behind the Legend.* Columbia: University of Missouri Press, 1998.

Spaeth, Janet. *Laura Ingalls Wilder.* Boston: Twayne, 1987.

Zochert, Donald. *Laura: The Life of Laura Ingalls Wilder.* New York: Avon, 1977.

WILFLEY, XENOPHON PIERCE (1871–1931)

A lawyer with a brief career in national politics, Xenophon Pierce Wilfley was born on March 18, 1871, in Audrain County, Missouri. The son of James and Sarah Wilfley, he graduated from Clarksburg College in 1891 and earned a master's degree from Central College in Fayette, Missouri, in 1894. He taught at Central College for one year and at Sedalia High School for three years before deciding to attend law school at Washington University.

After he completed law school and passed his bar exam, Wilfley practiced law in St. Louis in the office of his brother, Judge L. R. Wilfley. He became involved in local Democratic Party politics and served as the chairman of the St. Louis Board of Election Commissioners in 1917 and 1918.

In 1918 Gov. **Frederick D. Gardner** appointed Wilfley to fill the vacancy in the United States Senate caused by the death of Sen. **William Joel Stone.** Wilfley was not the governor's first choice for the appointment, but was chosen after W. W. Graves, chief justice of the Missouri Supreme Court, declined the position. Wilfley was unknown in state political circles, and his selection to fill the Senate vacancy can be attributed to his fondness of golf. Wilfley met Governor Gardner, another avid golfer, at the Bellerive Golf Club in St. Louis.

Wilfley served in the United States Senate during the final months of World War I, from April 30 to November 5, 1918. During his brief tenure in office, he proved an enthusiastic supporter of fellow Democrat Woodrow Wilson as the president prepared

for the armistice and anticipated the peace conference in Paris.

Apparently, Missouri Democrats lacked enthusiasm for Wilfley, for he failed to receive his party's nomination for the Senate post. The unsuccessful politician returned to St. Louis to practice law after spending less than seven months in the United States Senate.

A senior partner in his law firm, Wilfley earned the respect of his peers and became the president of the Missouri Bar Association in 1925. In 1928 the loyal Democrat reentered political life by actively supporting Alfred E. Smith, the Democrats' presidential candidate.

Xenophon Pierce Wilfley died in St. Louis on May 4, 1931, after a brief illness. He was survived by his wife, Rosamund Guthrie Wilfley, and two daughters.

KATHARINE L. RIDLEY

Biographical Directory of the United States Congress, 1774–1989. Bicentennial ed. S.v. "Wilfley, Xenophon Pierce." Washington, D.C.: U.S. Government Printing Office, 1989.

The National Cyclopedia of American Biography. S.v. "Wilfley, Xenophon Pierce."

New York Times, April 30, 1918–May 5, 1931.

WILKINS, ROY O. (1901–1981)

Roy O. Wilkins was born on August 30, 1901, in St. Louis. Five years earlier, the United States Supreme Court issued its decision in *Plessy v. Ferguson,* the case that endorsed racial segregation. Within a few years an elaborate system of state-sanctioned segregation controlled virtually every aspect of race relations in the United States. Under this system African Americans were relegated to a subordinate legal status, and an era of unquestionable white supremacy reigned. These conditions prevailed when William and Mayfield Wilkins migrated to St. Louis from Mississippi in 1900. Roy Wilkins would later dedicate his life to the elimination of this system.

The Wilkins family lived in St. Louis long enough to allow Roy to enter grammar school, but a few years later Mayfield Wilkins died. Roy, his brother Earl, and his sister Armanda were sent to live with an aunt and uncle in St. Paul, Minnesota. Roy attended public elementary and high schools in St. Paul. During his high school years he developed an interest in writing and was eventually elected president of the school's literary club.

Wilkins graduated from high school in 1919. He enrolled as a freshman at the University of Minnesota that fall. While attending the university he became a reporter for the college newspaper, the *Minnesota Daily.* During his undergraduate years Wilkins also worked as the editor of a local black weekly, the *St.*

Paul Appeal. Shortly before his graduation Wilkins was offered an editor's position by the owner of a Missouri newspaper, the *Kansas City Call.* He accepted the offer and moved to Kansas City.

The *Kansas City Call* was a black-owned newspaper that served Kansas City's African American community. Wilkins frequently reported episodes of racial injustice and authorized numerous editorials that advocated the cause of civil rights. He soon established a reputation as a crusader for equal rights. Wilkins met Minnie Badeau, who had moved to Kansas City from St. Louis, and the two were married in 1929.

Wilkins joined the Kansas City branch of the NAACP and later became the secretary of that organization. During a national convention he met Walter White, the executive secretary of the civil rights organization. In 1930 Wilkins received an offer from W. E. B. DuBois to serve as the business manager of the *Crisis,* the NAACP's in-house publication. Although the *Crisis* had enjoyed enormous success as the most influential publication in the African American community, it had fallen on hard times by 1930. When DuBois offered him the position Wilkins declined based on numerous reports he had heard about DuBois's prickly personality.

A few months later White offered Wilkins another position at the national headquarters. After a visit to New York Wilkins accepted the position of assistant secretary. Not long after Wilkins joined the NAACP's staff, the organization underwent a dramatic change in direction. DuBois, a founder and the nationally known voice of the organization, published a series of editorials that ran under the heading of "Segregation." In these 1934 essays DuBois argued that rather than concentrating on what he deemed a futile effort to eliminate segregation, the black community needed to devote its energies to establishing and strengthening black institutions—schools, churches, and black-owned business enterprises. Although they were not intended as such, the editorials were widely construed as advocating the abandonment of the NAACP's long-standing struggle for the civil rights of African Americans. This sent shock waves throughout the black community. Not long afterward the NAACP's board reacted by demanding preapproval of all future editorials. DuBois, who had long enjoyed editorial independence, angrily resigned.

Wilkins succeeded DuBois as the editor of the *Crisis.* At about the same time the NAACP embarked on a long-range, carefully orchestrated litigation campaign in which the separate-but-equal doctrine of *Plessy* was challenged in the Supreme Court. By 1940 the NAACP had established the Legal Defense and Education Fund, headed by Thurgood Marshall, which was responsible for the litigation effort. Lobbying and other activities were directed by White. Wilkins took over the day-to-day operations of the NAACP's New York office.

With the advent of World War II in 1941, the NAACP turned its attention to fighting segregation and discrimination in the military. Wilkins and White were at the center of these efforts. During this period the NAACP continued, without success, to persuade Congress to pass federal antilynching legislation. At the conclusion of the war, however, years of lobbying and litigation began to bear fruit. In 1948 President **Harry S. Truman** issued an executive order that banned discrimination in the federal civil service and in the military. During the same year an impressive Supreme Court victory was won in a housing discrimination case, *Shelley v. Kraemer.*

In 1950 three significant desegregation opinions were issued. In *Sweatt v. Painter, McLaurin v. Oklahoma,* and *Sipuel v. Oklahoma,* the Supreme Court held that states could not operate segregated graduate schools unless equal facilities were provided for black students. Since the southern states had failed to provide any graduate training opportunities for black students, they were forced to admit black students to the all-white graduate schools. While these cases were pending, a series of cases involving primary schools were working their way through the lower courts. In 1954 these cases were decided by the Supreme Court's opinion in *Brown v. Board of Education,* which declared racial segregation in public education a violation of the Fourteenth Amendment. *Brown* represented the culmination of the NAACP's litigation strategy. State-sanctioned segregation was on the way out.

In 1955 White died from a heart attack. Wilkins succeeded him as executive director as the final phase of the civil rights movement was about to unfold. During the same year Rosa Parks's refusal to relinquish her seat on a bus led to the Montgomery, Alabama, boycott. Martin Luther King Jr. quickly emerged as the leader of the grassroots civil rights movement. This "direct action" phase of the civil rights movement—protests and mass marches—was not consistent with the NAACP's philosophy. Wilkins preferred litigation and lobbying, but by then a movement larger than the NAACP was under way.

By the early 1960s college students began to sit in at segregated lunch counters in the South. "Freedom riders" traveled on buses to southern terminals, challenging segregated travel facilities. Several new organizations were spawned. King's Southern Christian Leadership Conference, the Congress of Racial Equality, the Student Nonviolent Coordinating Committee, and others competed with the NAACP for the leadership of the civil rights movement. At times the various groups cooperated. The 1963 march on Washington was the product of such an effort, but there were deep ideological differences.

The NAACP was essentially a conservative organization. It had formally adopted an anticommunist policy during the early 1950s. DuBois, who had gradually drifted toward a more radical ideology, was all but ignored. The leftist and sometimes separatist views of the student radicals of the 1960s created deep divisions within the civil rights movement. With the emergence of charismatic leaders such as King, the NAACP's influence began to wane. In the mid-1960s, however, the NAACP still retained institutional primacy, and Wilkins was heavily involved in lobbying for the far-reaching civil rights legislation that was enacted during those years. These federal laws were the culmination of the organizational effort begun with the founding of the NAACP in 1909. The legal barriers that forced African Americans into a subordinate legal status were finally eliminated. This was largely the result of the efforts of organizations such as the NAACP. Wilkins remained the executive director of the NAACP until his retirement in 1977. He died on September 8, 1981.

LELAND WARE

Myers, Samuel L., Jr. " 'The Rich Get Richer . . .': The Problem of Race Inequalities in the 1990s." *Law and Inequality* 11 (June 1993): 369.

New York Times, March 3, 1978.

Wilkins, Roy. "The Conspiracy to Deny Equality." In *Negro Protest Thought in the Twentieth Century,* ed. Francis L. Broderick and August Meier. Indianapolis: Bobbs-Merrill, 1965.

———. "Smiling Racism." *Nation* 437 (November 3, 1984).

Wilkins, Roy, and Tom Mathews. *The Autobiography of Roy Wilkins: Stand Fast.* New York: Penguin Books, 1984.

WILKINSON, JAMES (1757–1825)

Hidden among the thousands of musty documents in the archives of the Indies, Cuban Papers, in Seville, Spain, are documents confirming that Gen. James Wilkinson was a paid agent of the Spanish government. Most likely his deception began early in the 1790s and spanned at least the next two decades. Historians who tracked his intrigues believe his code name was "Spy No. 13." If so, the number was far more unlucky for the United States than for the wily general. Even two hundred years after his masquerades and trickeries, his political survival skills and uncanny sense of danger can still provoke a heated historical debate.

James Wilkinson, born in Benedict, Maryland, in 1757, came from a respected and substantial merchant family. Any thoughts of a classical education, however, were cut short by the American Revolutionary War. In the early days of the conflict he enlisted in the colonial army, served under George Washington, and rose quickly to the rank of brigadier general. During these trying years he formed, ironically, a close relationship with Benedict Arnold and Aaron Burr. Wilkinson's proclivity toward double-dealing manifested itself when he and others conspired to remove Washington as commander in chief of the Continental army and to replace him with Gen. Horatio Gates. After discovering the plot, referred to as the "Conway Cabal," forty-nine officers of senior grade petitioned Congress to rescind Wilkinson's appointment. Faced with such opposition, the general resigned but retained the rank of colonel.

Following the war the former general moved west where he first worked for Kentucky's separation from Virginia. It was roughly at this time that he was placed on the Spanish payroll. His assignment was to encourage the secession of trans-Appalachia, with the ultimate goal of establishing it as a satellite of the Spanish empire. Using bribery and deceit, he further tried to obtain exclusive trading rights from his foreign benefactors in New Orleans. When these schemes failed he sought and obtained reinstatement in the army around 1791. He served under Gen. "Mad Anthony" Wayne and battled the Indians of the Northwest. During these years he labored as diligently to discredit Wayne as he had earlier tried to undermine Washington. In 1792 his intrigues paid off, and he was again promoted to the rank of brigadier general. Four years later, after Wayne's death, Wilkinson became commanding general of the entire army. Even this honor and responsibility did not quell his appetite for greater fame and glory.

The general's ambitions were given an unexpected boost when President Thomas Jefferson appointed him as the first territorial governor of the newly constructed territory of Louisiana. Wilkinson's acceptance of the appointment was far easier to explain than Jefferson's offer. Perhaps the president did not believe or could not confirm the persistent rumors of his subordinate's duplicity. It was also possible that Jefferson's advisers convinced him that the mere presence of the highest ranking officer in the military on the western frontier might help contain the restlessness and violence in that region. As for Wilkinson, the new assignment proffered a fortuitous turn of events. Even though the new position paid him an additional two thousand dollars per year, he continued to seek further ways to line his pockets. Equally, if not more important, he was now in a position to probe Spanish defenses, gather tactical information, and then, as in the cases of Zebulon Pike, **Meriwether Lewis,** and **William Clark,** inform Spanish authorities of the explorers' whereabouts and encourage their arrests. Thus, Wilkinson could ingratiate himself with his Spanish paymasters while exacerbating international tensions that might later prove advantageous.

No one can be sure how long the general plotted an invasion of the Southwest. Nonetheless, his arrival in St. Louis in the early summer of 1805 afforded him an opportunity to speed up the timetable for his filibustering activities. Shortly before assuming his new duties, Wilkinson found a willing accomplice in Aaron Burr. Discredited within the Republican Party and under indictment for murder in the killing of Alexander Hamilton in a duel, the former vice president's association nevertheless strengthened the plan. Burr was generally well liked in the southern and western regions of the country and enjoyed the confidence of men such as Andrew Jackson and Henry Clay. In addition, the New Yorker brought with him a charisma and sense of derring-do that the cautious Wilkinson lacked.

The final plan hatched by these two men of incredible egos can be only conjectured, since neither would ever be convicted of treason. Nonetheless, it appears that they planned to float a small armada down the Mississippi River and to attack a vulnerable part of the Spanish defenses. Missouri was to play a vital role as a source of men, supplies, and, most important, lead for the rifles and cannons. Toward this end Wilkinson began to establish a network of loyal supporters in the government of Upper Louisiana. Joseph Browne, Burr's brother-in-law, became the territorial secretary and deputy governor. Col. **Samuel Hammond** served as commandant in St. Louis, and Col. **John Smith T** took over **Moses Austin**'s official position in the lead-mining district in Ste. Genevieve. Wilkinson also allied himself with the pro–French Creole families. This group, along with some prominent Americans living in Missouri prior to the 1804 transfer, were dubbed the "junto" by the editor of the *Missouri Gazette,* **Joseph Charless.** At the time the "junto" was the most powerful faction in the St. Louis–Ste. Genevieve area.

Within a relatively short time Wilkinson's support of the junto, the intrigues with Burr, and his efforts to control the lead-mining district divided the territory and produced considerable civil disorder. By the time of his departure for the Spanish frontier in the summer of 1806 he had created a first-class state of disarray. His troubles, however, were far from over. Mistrustful of Burr and increasingly suspicious that the president had discovered the plot, Wilkinson sent Lt. Thomas Smith to Washington with a secret note implicating Burr in treason. Jefferson acted quickly. On November 27, 1806, he authorized the arrest of Burr and his cohorts. Many months would elapse before a Richmond, Virginia, jury acquitted the former vice president. In the interim prosecutors tried to build a case against wily Wilkinson, but the task proved difficult.

Eventually, in 1811, Wilkinson was court-martialed; the verdict was "not guilty." Although he was unnerved by the ordeal of the trial and discredited in the eyes of many of his countrymen, this Talleyrand of the early Republic rebounded once again. In 1813, with the military in shambles, he was promoted to major general in the United States Army. This time it was Britain rather than Spain that was the beneficiary of his ambition. The general's incompetency contributed to the military debacle in the Montreal campaign later that year. Relieved of command in April 1814, he was, in January of the following year, once again court-martialed and once again acquitted.

History often deals her more infamous players a final ironic hand. So it was for the general. Even in death this veteran of so many nefarious schemes was fated to play out his final game in typical style. In 1822 Wilkinson left for Mexico to represent American claimants and to secure land grants for himself and his associates. He was also an agent of the Protestant American Bible Society. He died in Mexico City on December 28, 1825. As a non-Catholic, however, he could not be buried in a reputable cemetery. He therefore had "to be perjured into his grave" by someone of an equally mendacious character who would swear that the general was in fact a Catholic. Upon finding a perjurer, the proper forms were completed, and Wilkinson was placed in a crypt in the city that was "at the center of his dreams of empire." Years later, as the city expanded, the church and the burial grounds were destroyed, and Wilkinson's remains were scattered, like his dreams, across the lands of Mexico.

DICK STEWARD

Burke, Harry S. Papers. "Notes on John Smith T." Missouri Historical Society, St. Louis.

Conard, Howard L., ed. *Encyclopedia of the History of Missouri.* New York: Southern History, 1901.

Cox, Isaac J. "General Wilkinson and His Later Intrigues with the Spaniards." *American Historical Review* 19:4 (July 1914): 794–812.

Jacobs, James R. *Tarnished Warrior: Major-General James Wilkinson.* New York: Macmillan, 1938.

Wilkinson, James. *Memoirs of My Own Times.* 3 vols. Philadelphia: Abraham Small Publishing, 1816.

———. *Wilkinson: Soldier and Pioneer.* New Orleans: Rogers Printing, 1935.

WILLIAMS, ABRAHAM J. (1781–1839)

Missouri's third governor, Abraham J. Williams served in that office for less than six months. He is also the only person to have advanced to the office of governor from the position of president pro tempore of the Senate.

Elected to the Missouri State Senate in 1822, Williams was the first resident of Boone County elected to that office. He won reelection in 1824. During his second term, the Senate chose him as its president pro tempore. Upon the death of Gov. **Frederick Bates** on August 4, 1825, Williams became governor since Lt. Gov. Benjamin H. Reeves had previously resigned. In a constitutionally mandated special election held on December 8, 1825, the voters elected **John Miller** as the new governor. Williams stepped down following Miller's inauguration on January 20, 1826.

Williams's short term as governor was uneventful. The General Assembly was not in session, and he made no major political pronouncements, nor did he offer any recommendations for governmental action. Williams was not a candidate in the special gubernatorial election of 1825.

During his few years in the Senate, Williams appears to have been a relatively important member of that body. He served on the committees of accounts and education—both major committees. He also achieved recognition for his skill in presiding over the Senate. Williams, however, lost in his bid for reelection in 1826. He held no later public office.

Williams centered his lifelong career more around business and farming than politics. Born in Hardy County, Virginia (now Grant County, West Virginia), on February 26, 1781, he entered life with a serious physical impairment: he was born with only one leg. Williams did not allow this handicap to interfere with an active and productive life.

Arriving in Missouri sometime between 1816 and 1820, Williams first located in Franklin. In 1820 he and a partner, James Harris, operated a tobacco warehouse in Nashville, in the southern part of Boone County. In the early 1820s Williams moved to Columbia where he opened a dry goods store, allegedly the first of its kind in the town. He bought land in Boone County and engaged in large-scale farming operations. In recognition for his extensive farm operations, Williams was chosen in 1835 as the president of the first agriculture fair organized in Columbia.

Without any encouragement on his part, Williams's name was placed before the General Assembly as a candidate for election to the United States Senate in 1832. However, 1832 was **Thomas Hart Benton**'s year, and the popular senator won a third term with an overwhelming margin.

Abraham J. Williams died on December 30, 1839, at the age of fifty-eight. He had not married, and appears to have been a private person. Even so, he lived a strenuous and successful life and contributed to the development of frontier Missouri as a businessman,

a public servant, and a farmer. He was buried in the Columbia cemetery.

PERRY MCCANDLESS

Leopard, Buel, and Floyd C. Shoemaker, eds. *The Messages and Proclamations of the Governors of the State of Missouri.* Vol. 1. Columbia: State Historical Society of Missouri, 1922.

Shoemaker, Floyd Calvin. *Missouri and Missourians: Land of Contrasts and People of Achievements.* Vol. 2. Chicago: Lewis Publishing, 1943.

WILLIAMS, ARSANIA M. (1875?–1954)

Born in Baton Rouge, Louisiana, around 1875, Arsania M. Williams was the third of five children of George and Julia Williams. Seeking the perceived greater financial opportunities of the North for African Americans, the family moved to St. Louis before Williams was one year old. She was educated in the segregated St. Louis public school system and earned a teaching certificate from the Sumner Normal School in 1895. Her first teaching position was at Dumas Elementary School. Later, she taught at L'Ouverture, Simmons, and Marshall Schools in St. Louis. At her retirement she was head assistant for John Marshall School.

Williams's keen intelligence and strong personality quickly drew the attention of leaders of both the African American and the white communities in St. Louis. She enjoyed highly public roles and was a recognized black leader in secular and religious education and community affairs. Williams served as the only woman on the committee that organized "Negro Day" at the St. Louis World's Fair in 1904. Part of the black community's effort to stimulate improved race relations, "Negro Day" highlighted activities of African Americans, such as **George Washington Carver** and Booker T. Washington. In 1908 the *St. Louis Post-Dispatch* sent twelve local schoolchildren to the inauguration of President William Taft; the newspaper selected Williams as a chaperon for the black children. She was the first African American selected by the St. Louis Christmas Carol Association to direct activities in black neighborhoods.

A strong proponent of using the system to improve race relations, Williams used examples and effective organizations to soften segregation. Typical of strong female leaders of the period, she worked through women's clubs and behind the scenes of male-dominated organizations, such as the St. Louis Urban League. Active in the St. Louis club-woman movement, Williams founded the Young Ladies Reading Club and the Help-A-Lot Club under the St. Louis Association of Colored Women's Clubs in 1910. She also cofounded the Phillis Wheatley branch of the

St. Louis YWCA in 1911. She believed strongly in the ideals of the YWCA, and helped organize the Wheatley branch because segregation kept young black women from membership in existing chapters. Williams served on the board of directors and later as president of the Phillis Wheatley branch, St. Louis's first black YWCA. Later, she served as president of the St. Louis Association of Colored Women's Clubs and the Missouri Association of Colored Women's Clubs from 1924 to 1926. She served as vice president at large of the National Association of Colored Women's Clubs from 1938 to 1940. The St. Louis association, like the state and national associations, promoted education, cooperation, and economic opportunity for African Americans.

Secular and religious education were Williams's driving passions. She organized the St. Louis Negro Grade School Teachers' Association in 1917, and in 1930 the Missouri Association of Negro Teachers elected her as its president. Equally committed to religious education, Williams organized and served as dean of the St. Louis Standard Leadership Training School at the Union Memorial Methodist Episcopal Church in 1922, the first school of its kind in St. Louis devoted to training church-school and religious leaders.

In 1938 Douglass University in St. Louis awarded Williams an honorary master of arts degree. Arsania M. Williams died in St. Louis at Homer G. Phillips Hospital, a segregated hospital, on March 24, 1954.

SUZANNA MAUPIN LONG

Long, Suzanna Maupin. " 'I Made It Mine Tho' the Queen Waz Always Fair': The St. Louis Black Clubwoman Movement, 1931–1946." Master's thesis, University of Missouri–St. Louis, 1988.

Malcolm, Dolores B. *Herstory in Silhouette: A Curriculum Supplement about Black Women in American History for Middle Schools.* Vol. 2, unit 7. St. Louis: St. Louis Public Schools, 1986.

Metropolitan St. Louis Negro Directory: A Classified Publication of Biographies. St. Louis: Booker T. Washington Trading Stamp Association, 1943.

Mongold, Jeanne. "Vespers and Vacant Lots: The Early Years of the St. Louis Phillis Wheatley Branch YWCA." Western Historical Manuscripts Collection, St. Louis.

WILLIAMS, GEORGE HOWARD (1871–1963)

George Howard Williams, a U.S. senator from Missouri, was born in California, Missouri, on December 1, 1871, the son of John Morrow and Alice Gray Howard Williams. His father was a prominent lawyer who served as a prosecuting attorney, circuit court judge, and state senator. After graduating from California High School in 1889, George completed a preparatory course at Drury College in Springfield prior to enrolling at Princeton University. He graduated from Princeton in 1894 and returned to his hometown.

Williams briefly taught Latin at California High School while reading law at his father's firm. He then studied law at Washington University in St. Louis where he received a bachelor of law degree in 1897. Following his admission to the Missouri bar, he established a legal practice in St. Louis. Williams married Harriet Chase Stewart on June 12, 1900, and the couple had two sons, Stewart and Howard. In 1902 Williams joined his father-in-law as a partner in his law firm.

Active in Republican politics, Williams helped draft the 1904 state platform for the party. He served as a St. Louis circuit court judge from 1906 to 1912, during which time he was instrumental in the creation of a new juvenile code for Missouri. After stepping down from the bench, Williams continued his interest in neglected and delinquent youths and supported closing the St. Louis House of Refuge. As chairman of the Board of Children's Guardians, he helped establish Bellefontaine Farms to care for abandoned and troubled children in St. Louis.

Williams maintained an active legal practice in association with Stewart, Bryan, Williams, and Cave, a firm that specialized in banking and corporate law and counted among its clients the First National Bank of St. Louis, the St. Louis Union Trust Company, Emerson Electric, and Ralston Purina.

As a member of the 1922 Missouri Constitutional Convention, Williams chaired several important committees. In recognition of his service Missouri Valley College in Marshall awarded him an honorary doctor of laws in 1923.

Following the death of Sen. **Seldon Palmer Spencer** in 1925, Gov. **Sam Baker** appointed Williams to fill the vacancy in the United States Senate. During his brief tenure Williams took part in debates concerning the World Court. In the election of 1926 he lost his bid for a full Senate term to Democrat **Harry Hawes.** After failing to retain his Senate seat, Williams returned to his legal practice in St. Louis.

Williams's interest in history led to his involvement in efforts to preserve the **Daniel Boone** farm in St. Charles County and his service as a trustee of the State Historical Society of Missouri. He retired from his legal practice in 1943 and settled in Matson, Missouri, where he lived until he moved to Sarasota, Florida, in 1950. Williams was a major benefactor of several educational institutions, including Drury College, Princeton University, Westminster College, Washington University, and the School of the Ozarks.

He died in Sarasota on November 25, 1963, and was buried in California, Missouri.

ANN NICHOLS

Official Manual of the State of Missouri, 1923–1924. Jefferson City: Secretary of State, 1924.

Official Manual of the State of Missouri, 1925–1926. Jefferson City: Secretary of State, 1926.

Shoemaker, Floyd Calvin. *Missouri and Missourians: Land of Contrasts and People of Achievements.* Chicago: Lewis Publishing, 1943.

St. Louis Globe-Democrat, November 26, 1963.

St. Louis Post-Dispatch, November 25, 1963.

WILLIAMS, SARA LOCKWOOD (1889–1961)

Recognized primarily for her activist role as the wife of **Walter Williams,** who founded the world's first school of journalism, Sara Lockwood Williams was an outstanding personality in her own right— an author, journalist, world traveler, and leader in professional organizations. She was also the first woman ever to hold a professorship in a journalism school in the United States.

Sara Lockwood was born on April 13, 1889, in Rock Port, Missouri, the youngest of nine children of John and Mary Jane Duncan Lockwood. A cattle drover turned shopkeeper, Lockwood later moved his large family to Columbia, home of the state university, to improve the children's opportunities to receive a college education. After graduating from Columbia High School in 1907, Sara Lockwood entered the University of Missouri. As a junior she was admitted to the School of Journalism, which, under the determined leadership of Walter Williams, had become the first formal program of its kind. Energetic as well as talented, she wrote for the school's laboratory newspaper, the *Columbia Missourian,* and became a leader in professional and community organizations.

Upon her graduation in 1913 Lockwood was hired by the *St. Joseph Gazette,* becoming that paper's first woman journalist. Quickly proving herself as a skilled reporter, she also became a popular figure in the community and, in 1915, was one of the organizers of the St. Joseph Press Club, which, at that time, was said to be the only press club in the country where women were admitted to membership.

Later that same year, however, Lockwood left the newspaper to return to Columbia and the bedside of her ailing mother. She was hired by Dean Williams as a graduate assistant, where she graded papers and started the library and clipping file, or morgue, in the School of Journalism. At the end of the academic year she accepted a reporting job at the *Tulsa Times and Democrat,* where she was soon promoted to women's editor. Two years later she was hired by the *Philadelphia Evening Public Ledger.* Her assignments took her throughout the East, and many of her features were syndicated to national audiences. However, after three years with the *Ledger* and a brief stint as a publicist, she was ready for a return to friends and family in Missouri. In 1921 she accepted an assistant professorship in the School of Journalism.

By now the school, begun on a shoestring by the self-educated Williams in 1908, was a going concern, respected across the United States and abroad as the leading professional program of its type. Sara Lockwood, who could now draw upon a wealth of professional experience as well as her academic training, taught writing and editing classes and was active in professional organizations. In 1925 she was elected president of Theta Sigma Phi, the national women's honorary in the mass communications field. She was also involved in a lengthy courtship with her dean, Walter Williams, twenty-five years her senior. His first wife had died in 1918. In 1927 Walter and Sara were married.

Resigning her teaching position, Williams launched a number of writing projects, among them *Twenty Years of Education for Journalism,* a history of the school, and began work on a graduate degree. Her master's thesis, a study of the *Columbia Herald* and, especially, Walter Williams's editorship of it, would become *The Biography of a Country Newspaper,* her second published book. Her master's diploma was presented to her in 1931 by her husband, who had since been elevated to the presidency of the university.

Walter Williams's international interests, which had done so much to promote the School of Journalism, continued apace, even during the dark days of the depression. With Sara at his side, he traveled throughout Europe, Asia, Australia, the Middle East, and Latin America. They met with many chiefs of state, including, in 1933, Adolf Hitler, and were widely acclaimed: Walter Williams for his efforts at raising the status and ethical performance of journalists, and Sara Williams for her concerns with improving professional opportunities for women.

In 1935, however, Walter Williams died of cancer, following a lengthy illness. Grief-stricken, Sara Williams left Missouri to accept a visiting professorship at Yenching University in Beijing, China. When she returned to the United States she settled in St. Louis, teaching at Washington University and hosting her own radio program, *Sara Lockwood Williams's Scrapbook,* over KSD. In 1944 she moved to Rockford College to handle public relations duties and teach. In 1951 she returned to Columbia, rejoining the journalism faculty. She died of cancer in Columbia on July 6, 1961.

In addition to her two books, Williams wrote hundreds of newspaper and magazine articles, bulletins, and pamphlets, and was in demand as a public speaker. Her contributions as a pathbreaking educator and her leadership in women's service and professional organizations secure her reputation not only in Missouri history but in the history of her profession of journalism as well.

RONALD T. FARRAR

Williams, Sara Lockwood. Papers. Western Historical Manuscripts Collection, Columbia.
———. *Twenty Years of Education for Journalism.* Columbia, Mo.: E. W. Stephens, 1929.
Williams, Walter. Papers. Western Historical Manuscripts Collection, Columbia.

WILLIAMS, THOMAS LANIER "TENNESSEE" (1911–1983)

Tennessee Williams, born on March 26, 1911, was one of the greatest of American playwrights. Although many of his themes—alcoholism, homosexuality, cannibalism, torture, rape, impotence, and so on—shocked some playgoers, his sympathetic depictions of passion, employing Chekhovian sensibility to illuminate the irrational unconscious, lifted his work to the highest levels of dramatic art. As he once said, "Let us not deny all the dark things of the human heart, but let us cast a clear light on them in our work."

He was born Thomas Lanier Williams, the second of three children, in Columbia, Mississippi, to Cornelius Coffin and Edwina Dakin Williams. His father was a traveling clothing salesman; Williams grew close to his grandfather, an Episcopal minister, as well as his sister, Rose. He suffered from diphtheria as a child and had barely recovered the use of his legs when the family moved to St. Louis, where Cornelius Williams worked as a sales manager for the International Shoe Company.

Because Williams could not compete in sports, other students called him a sissy. His sister retreated into her collection of glass animals, while his mother dreamed of her former life as a southern belle. Williams began writing and published his first story, "The Vengeance of Nitocris," in the August 1928 issue of *Weird Tales.* In 1931 he entered the University of Missouri at Columbia but was an unsuccessful student, though he actually failed only ROTC. He dropped out in 1933 to take a clerk's job at the International Shoe Company for two years, writing at night. He suffered a nervous breakdown, quit the job, traveled a bit, attended Washington University in 1936–1937, and eventually graduated from the University of Iowa the next year.

Williams received a Rockefeller Fellowship of one thousand dollars, which sustained him while he wrote *Battle of Angels,* produced by the Theater Guild in Boston in 1940. Outraged audience reaction kept it from reaching New York City. After he drifted around the country and ushered at a movie theater in New York in 1942, his agent, Audrey Wood, secured him a job as a Hollywood screenwriter. He outlined a screenplay titled "The Gentleman Caller," but the studio rejected it; he later transformed it into *The Glass Menagerie.*

After a successful production in Chicago, *Menagerie,* starring Laurette Taylor as Amanda, opened on Broadway on March 31, 1945. A smash hit, it won the New York Drama Critics' Circle best-play award, the Donaldson Award, and the Sidney Howard Memorial Award. Critics praised the acting more than the script, but all agreed it was "a masterpiece of make-believe," "completely fascinating theatre," and "an event of the first importance," and most predicted great things to come from Williams.

Williams's next script, which he had dramatized with Donald Windham from D. H. Lawrence's short story "You Touched Me!" garnered only lukewarm reviews on Broadway, but Williams was already at work on *A Streetcar Named Desire,* which he based on his experiences and observations in New Orleans. Opening December 3, 1947, *Streetcar* ran 855 performances on Broadway. The script won the Drama Critics' Circle Award, as well as the Pulitzer Prize for drama in 1948; critics began to compare Williams to Eugene O'Neill. Described as "a feverish, squalid, tumultuous, painful, steadily arresting and oddly touching study of feminine decay along the lower Mississippi," the play won almost universal praise. John Chapman called the production "the answer to a playgoer's prayer"; Brooks Atkinson called it a "superb drama," revealing Williams as "a genuinely poetic playwright whose knowledge of people is honest and thorough and whose sympathy is profoundly human."

On October 6, 1948, Williams's *Summer and Smoke* opened to lackluster reviews, later touring as *Eccentricities of a Nightingale* in 1964. *The Rose Tattoo* opened on February 3, 1951, and revealed Williams's capacity for dealing with more traditional sexual themes than he had previously employed. He followed it with *Camino Real,* a confusing melange of hidden meanings and literary allusions, which survived for only sixty performances.

Williams's next show, *Cat on a Hot Tin Roof,* ran 694 performances, beginning March 24, 1955. Again Williams won the Drama Critics' Circle Award and the Pulitzer Prize for drama. The dean of Broadway critics at the time, Brooks Atkinson, considered it Williams's finest drama; William Hawkins said, "it writhes and yowls and bares the souls of its participants with a shameless tongue." Williams followed *Cat* with *Garden District,* composed of *Something*

Unspoken and *Suddenly Last Summer,* the latter dealing with cannibalism and a lobotomy, produced off Broadway in 1958. The next year *Sweet Bird of Youth* began a run of 383 performances on Broadway. Critics pronounced it a blockbuster, "hypnotic theatre," and "a magnificently theatrical storm of passion, bigotry and tolerance."

An odd comedy, *Period of Adjustment,* appeared in 1960. Late in 1961 Williams's last masterpiece, *The Night of the Iguana,* set in Mexico, dealing with life's losers, appeared, winning the Antoinette Perry Award in 1962. Director Frank Corsaro said of *Iguana,* "Sensibility and a sense of God were intermixed in a way that Tennessee always sought for." Williams's next script, *The Milk Train Doesn't Stop Here Anymore,* premiered at the Spoleto Festival of Two Worlds in 1962 and moved to Broadway the next year, but ran only sixty-nine performances.

In 1966 Williams presented a pair of one-act plays, *The Mutilated* and *Gnadiges Fraulein,* which the playwright collectively called *Slapstick Tragedy.* There followed *In the Bar of a Tokyo Hotel,* which had a brief run off Broadway in 1969. A minor piece, presented in London as *The Two-Character Play* in 1967, premiered in Chicago in 1971 as *Outcry.* In 1972 *Small Craft Warnings* opened off Broadway, with Williams himself taking a small role in the production, his professional debut as an actor. In 1973 *The Red Devil Battery Sign* closed in Boston, but it was later produced in London. *Vieux Carré* ran briefly on Broadway in 1979, the same year Williams produced *A Lovely Sunday at Creve Coeur.* His last Broadway play was *Clothes for a Summer Hotel,* a script about F. Scott and Zelda Fitzgerald, a production that failed totally. Williams nevertheless continued writing for noncommercial theaters such as the Jean Cocteau Theater, which produced his *Something Cloudy, Something Clear* in 1981. The Goodman Theater in Chicago produced his final play, *A House Not Meant to Stand,* in 1982.

Williams also wrote screenplays, such as *Baby Doll,* a tale of southern depravity directed by Elia Kazan, who also directed many of Williams's Broadway successes. Williams had a hand in the screen adaptations of several of his theatrical pieces: *The Glass Menagerie, A Streetcar Named Desire, The Rose Tattoo, Suddenly Last Summer, The Fugitive Kind* (derived from *Orpheus Descending*), and *Boom,* based on *The Milk Train Doesn't Stop Here Anymore.* Warner Brothers filmed Williams's only novel, *The Roman Spring of Mrs. Stone,* in 1961, starring Vivien Leigh.

Williams also published an anthology of poetry, *In the Winter of Cities* (1956) and three anthologies of short stories: *One Arm and Other Stories* (1948), *Hard Candy: A Book of Stories* (1954), and *The Knightly Quest* (1968). He published eleven one-act plays in *"Twenty-seven Wagons Full of Cotton," and Other One-Act Plays* (1946).

Williams claimed never to have written for money, only for his own expression, concluding that writing "nor any form of creative work was never meant by nature to be man's way of making a living . . . when it becomes one, it almost certainly loses a measure of purity." For thirty-five years he almost always worked three hours or more each day, citing the writers who had the most influence upon him as Hart Crane, D. H. Lawrence, Rainer Maria Rilke, and Anton Chekhov. Williams could write almost anywhere, but came to prefer solitude, such as that found in his Key West apartment, a spartan facility near the sea. As he put it, "I write because I love writing. It's what I know how to do, and I work eight hours a day. What else is there?" He usually worked on an empty stomach, except for coffee, suggesting this gave him a chance to do his best work. However, he felt, "Out of a year's writing days, there are only five good ones," days with "wayward flashes."

Williams once said that "high station in life is earned by the gallantry with which appalling experiences are survived with grace." He had experienced adversity of the most appalling type: the childhood bout with diphtheria, a mother who dreamed of a lost southern aristocracy, a father, rarely home, who sneered at his son's writing, calling him "Miss Nancy," and a schizophrenic sister who had a prefrontal lobotomy in 1937. From these biographical dregs Williams fashioned high art, most recognizably in *The Glass Menagerie,* but clearly in many other of his scripts.

Williams's homosexuality magnified his themes of the alienated modern man's existential dilemma, striving to reconcile one's idealism with the dross of reality. Critic Jack Kroll spoke of Williams's life being divided between "puritanism and hedonism, flesh and spirit, pure and impure." Williams himself said he could identify with Blanche (in *Streetcar*), but also with Stanley, adding, "Hell is yourself." The only redemption a human being could find, according to the playwright, was in putting one's self aside to feel deeply for another person. Williams's homosexuality caused him much pain, pain that he encompassed in his work, but when urged to change his sexual orientation he responded, "If I got rid of my demons I'd lose my angels."

Williams's obsession with writing revealed his escape from more mundane matters. "It doesn't make much sense . . . life, you know . . . and so . . . you give it some sort of meaning by creative work . . . frightening process . . . like terror . . . as a white page in the typewriter . . . the fear that they cannot deface it respectably." In a 1962 *Time* interview he voiced a similar theme: "There is a horror in things, a horror at heart of the meaninglessness of existence.

Some people cling to a certain philosophy that is handed down to them and which they accept. Life had a meaning if you're bucking for heaven. But if heaven is a fantasy, we are in this jungle with whatever we can work out for ourselves. It seems to me that the cards are stacked against us. The only victory is how we take it." Tennessee Williams took the stacked deck and made from it a corpus of drama unsurpassed in the twentieth century, and when asked what he wanted audiences to take away from his work, he drawled, "Oh, that other people have been through it, too." Williams died on February 25, 1983.

STEPHEN M. ARCHER

Arnott, Catherine M. *Tennessee Williams on File.* New York: Methuen, 1985.

Devlin, Albert J., ed. *Conversations with Tennessee Williams.* Jackson: University Press of Mississippi, 1986.

Gunn, Drewey Wayne. *Tennessee Williams: A Bibliography.* 2d ed. Metuchen, N.J.: Scarecrow Press, 1991.

Maxwell, Gilbert. *Tennessee Williams and Friends.* Cleveland: World, 1965.

Smith, Bruce. *Costly Performances: Tennessee Williams, the Last Stage.* New York: Paragon, 1990.

Williams, Tennessee. *Memoirs.* Garden City, N.Y.: Doubleday, 1975.

WILLIAMS, WALTER (1864–1935)

Founder and dean of the world's first school of journalism, which he established at the University of Missouri in 1908, author of one of the first ethical codes for journalists, and the driving force behind the successful effort to give journalism schools standards and recognition, Walter Williams was the father of journalism education and one of the eminent journalists of his time. Beyond that, he was an international spokesman for the field and, later, president of the University of Missouri, an academic and professional career all the more remarkable in light of the fact that Williams himself had never attended college.

Williams was born on July 2, 1864, in Boonville, Missouri, the youngest of six brothers in a family of Southern sympathizers whose fortunes had suffered during the Civil War. His parents died before he was fourteen, and his formal education ended the following year when he left Boonville High School for a job as a printer's devil, at seventy cents per week, on the weekly *Boonville Topic.* He was soon allowed to try his hand at writing for the paper and, despite his youth, produced articles that showed exceptional talent and mature news judgment. When the *Topic* was merged with the larger *Boonville Advertiser,* Williams was named editor, though he was not yet twenty-one years of age. Two years later he had become a part owner of the paper and had been elected president of the Missouri Press Association.

In 1890 Williams was hired by E. W. Stephens, a prominent publisher, to edit the weekly *Columbia Herald,* which already enjoyed a reputation as one of the most outstanding community newspapers in the country. Under Williams's editorship the *Herald*'s reputation grew apace; the paper carried articles by **Mark Twain, Eugene Field,** and other notables of the era, and won awards for its enterprise, typography, and editorial leadership. Williams himself attracted national prominence by launching a monthly trade publication, the *Country Editor,* and with his speeches and editorials aimed at raising the standards of journalism. A small, wiry man with a remarkable capacity for sustained hard work, Williams managed to edit two other newspapers in addition to the *Herald* and to contribute to Sunday newspapers in Kansas City and St. Louis. He was editor of the *St. Louis Presbyterian* and, for a time, also edited, via telephone, the *Daily State Tribune* at Jefferson City.

Williams liked to refer to himself as "a country newspaperman," but his ideas were anything but parochial. In 1902 he went to Switzerland and was elected president of the International Press Congress, and in 1904 he organized the World Press Parliament, which he convened in St. Louis—the first time the group had met outside Europe—during the World's Fair. As press commissioner for the fair he had traveled around the world in 1902, publicizing the fair and inviting foreign governments to send exhibits and representatives.

Williams had long believed that the university in his hometown should establish a school of journalism. At his urging the Missouri Press Association began to apply pressure on the university's board of curators in 1898 to establish a chair in journalism. The proposal encountered stiff resistance, however, largely from other university faculty who had not been consulted and who expressed doubt at the academic and intellectual value of offering what were perceived to be vocational courses at the university level. Williams persisted, however, and six years later was appointed to the board of curators himself, and then named chairman of the executive committee. From this strategic position he was able, in 1905, to secure the formation of a broad-based committee to study the establishment of some form of journalism instruction on the campus. Eventually the curators voted to establish a school of journalism if and when a suitable dean could be found to direct the new enterprise. Several prominent newspaper executives were offered the position, but rejected it as being too speculative. Eventually the curators turned to Williams himself, who accepted the challenge eagerly. Ninety-seven students chose to cast their lots with the new school at its first registration in September 1908, and

Williams and his three-man faculty sensed, correctly, that the school would succeed.

At the heart of the school's curriculum was the *Columbia Missourian,* a daily newspaper Williams established as a working laboratory for his students. While highly effective as a teaching tool, the paper was perceived as a threat to private enterprise, a state-supported competitor for readers' time and advertisers' dollars, and Williams came under strong pressure to abandon the *Missourian* altogether. He resisted, and the hands-on approach to journalism education that the *Missourian* reflected would characterize the University of Missouri School of Journalism throughout its history.

While Williams and the Missouri experiment were criticized by some scholars—the sociologist A. M. Lee dismissed Williams as merely "a dyed-in-the-wool printer and newspaperman, blessed with a high-school education and an honorary L.L.D."—Williams never wavered from his vision that journalism schools should be "co-ordinate, equal in rank, with the great schools or colleges of law, medicine, engineering, agriculture, and the teachers' colleges." Within a few years journalism programs had been established on other university campuses from coast to coast.

The rapid growth brought concerns about the professional and academic quality of some of the new programs, and Williams soon realized that his own sternly held notions of what a journalism school should be were not universally shared by colleagues around the country. In 1916 Williams, after having studied journalism programs elsewhere, invited administrators of what he regarded as the stronger programs to join him in forming the Association of American Schools and Departments of Journalism. This organization would later develop an accreditation agency to give academic journalism standards and recognition.

Williams's international interests, whetted when he was a young editor, intensified during his deanship, and he roamed the globe to promote the School of Journalism. He lectured in South America, conferred with chiefs of state (including, in 1933, Adolf Hitler) in Europe, developed extensive exchange programs (especially in China), and addressed professional groups in Australia and the Middle and Far East—becoming known, as the *New York Times* observed, "in virtually every country as editor, author, and good-will ambassador."

Williams also wrote *The Journalist's Creed,* which spelled out his editorial philosophy and high-minded sense of professional responsibility. Written in the early 1920s, this code of ethics was one of the first ever developed in the mass communications field; it has been translated into about fifty languages and reprinted throughout the world and had an important influence on editors, publishers, and reporters, in this country and abroad. *The Creed* was widely credited with helping to curtail the biased, subjective element that characterized much of the news reporting of the period.

Williams married Hulda Harned of Vermont, Missouri, on June 30, 1892. She died in 1918. They had three children, Walter Jr., Helen Harned Williams Rhodes, and Edwin Moss. In October 1927 Williams married Sara Lockwood, a 1913 graduate of the School of Journalism and former newspaper writer, teacher, and author. **Sara Lockwood Williams** died in 1961.

Williams was the author of numerous articles and pamphlets about journalism. He also wrote ten books, largely dealing with his travels. A gifted orator, he was in demand as a speaker to civic and professional groups, not only in Missouri but throughout the country and the world. He was a devout Presbyterian, a leader in state and local Presbyterian organizations, and for years taught a well-attended adult Bible class in Columbia.

During the dark days of the depression, the curators of the University of Missouri turned to Williams, by now in his mid-sixties and the senior dean on the campus, to assume the presidency of the institution. Thus, he became, as was widely noted at the time, "the only college president who never went to college." In one of his first official acts as president, Williams reduced his own salary, from $12,500 per year to $10,000, coupling this action with a request for an increase in salaries for the faculty. Williams's diplomacy, and the esteem he commanded throughout the state, was credited with helping sustain the university through harsh economic times.

On July 29, 1935, after a prolonged illness, Williams died at his home in Columbia. He was seventy-one years old. Personal and editorial tributes poured in from around the world, many of them echoing the theme expressed by the *New York Times:* "He found journalism a trade and helped make it a profession."

RONALD T. FARRAR

Farrar, Ronald T. *A Creed for My Profession: Walter Williams, Journalist to the World.* Columbia: University of Missouri Press, 1998.

Rucker, Frank W. *Walter Williams.* Columbia: Missourian Publishing Association, 1964.

Williams, Sara Lockwood. Papers. Western Historical Manuscripts Collection, Columbia.

———. *Twenty Years of Education for Journalism.* Columbia, Mo.: E. W. Stephens, 1929.

Williams, Walter. Papers. Western Historical Manuscripts Collection, Columbia.

WIMAR, CHARLES "CARL" FERDINAND (1828–1862)

From his studio in St. Louis, Charles "Carl" Ferdinand Wimar painted the Missouri River frontier in the final decade prior to the Civil War. A native German, he participated in the first wave of mass German immigration to Missouri in the 1830s. He joined a generation of artist-explorers, including **Peter Rindisbacher, George C. Catlin, Karl Bodmer,** and **Charles Deas,** who used St. Louis as their base of operations and who together established a tradition of St. Louis as a center for artists of the West during the second quarter of the nineteenth century. Among these artists Wimar's depictions of the life and landscape of the Missouri River frontier stand as important documents of the territory and Native cultures prior to the dramatic transformation that occurred during the mass settlement of the trans-Mississippi West after the Civil War.

Wimar spent his youth in Germany during a difficult political social era, driving his family to emigrate. He was born on February 19, 1828, in Siegbueg, Germany (near Bonn), to a scrivener, Ludwig Gottfried Wimar, and a washerwoman, Elizabeth Schmitz. His father died soon after his birth, and his mother supported the family until she married a merchant named Matthias Becker and moved the family to Cologne in 1835. At this time many Germans experienced economic hardships and political repression, resulting in the first major wave of German emigration to the United States. A significant impetus for German emigration were the popular guides published by **Gottfried Duden.** Evidently Duden inspired Becker, who appeared to follow the author's advice "to travel directly to Saint Louis on the Mississippi" in 1839, where he opened a public house. By 1844, once his business was established, his family joined him.

During this period numerous German artists, scientists, and authors expressed a fascination with the American West. The German appetite for the romantic American West was stoked by the immensely popular literary genre *Wildwestgeschichten* (Wild West stories). Arriving in St. Louis at the age of fifteen, Wimar found himself on the edge of the frontier that had been mythologized by the German literature with which he was probably familiar. The oral history of his youth relates the young Wimar's enchantment with the Indians, who camped next to his stepfather's public house during trade missions to St. Louis. Early biographers of the artist relate the family tradition that an Indian befriended the young German boy and taught him about Native American lifestyle, culture, and customs.

Demonstrating a talent for drawing as a youth, Wimar was apprenticed to a local house and steamboat painter shortly after his arrival from Germany. He expressed dissatisfaction with the painting trade and switched to the studio of the French émigré Leon Pomarede, a local painter and decorator, by 1846. During his apprenticeship Wimar assisted Pomarede in the creation of his monumental Mississippi River panorama, *Portrait of the Father of the Waters* (1849). In preparation for the project, Wimar accompanied his teacher on a series of sketching trips up the Mississippi River to make studies for the panorama. Early biographer William Tod Helmuth wrote that it was on one of these excursions that Wimar realized his lifework, when Pomarede advised him to adopt frontier subject matter in his art and "follow it exclusively, as through it [Wimar] might achieve a reputation that, in years to come when the Indians would be a 'race clean gone,' would increase to a peculiar brightness, not only in this country but on the continent."

Around 1850 Wimar left Pomarede and embarked on his first professional venture as an artist, opening a business with a partner that he advertised in the *St. Louis Directory* as "Wimar and Boneau, painters." Little is known about this partnership, but Wimar's surviving paintings from this period suggest that he painted primarily portraits and a few genre subjects. The most interesting of these surviving genre paintings is the dramatic *Three Children Attacked by a Wolf* (ca. 1851), in which he creatively adapted Thomas Gainsborough's *Two Shepherd Boys with Dogs Fighting* to a frontier subject where children encounter an aggressive wolf.

At this time Wimar's artistic ambitions were motivated by the success of fellow German American Emmanuel Leutze's *Washington Crossing the Delaware* (1851). Unveiled to the American public in November 1851, critics hailed Leutze's picture as the most important American history painting ever created. Wimar proclaimed that it "surpasses everything I have ever seen before," and decided to follow Leutze's career path of painting the history of his adopted country. In December 1851 Wimar departed for Germany to study with Leutze in Düsseldorf.

After a Rhine tour and a reunion with family members, Wimar arrived in spring 1851 in Düsseldorf where he would spend the next four years learning the German academic painting style and applying it to American frontier subjects. Because of his chosen subject and his appearance, Wimar earned the appellation "the Indian painter" from his German colleagues. In his student years his paintings focused on images of conflict and confrontation between Native Americans and the Euramerican colonizers, drawn largely from popular literature of the day. His first major painting, *The Abduction of Daniel Boone's Daughter by the Indians* (1853), exemplifies Wimar's fascination with dramatic frontier subjects, with the terrified Jemima Boone kneeling in her canoe, praying to the menacing Indians for mercy. By contrasting the "civil" white woman posed as a saint kneeling in prayer to the "heathen" Natives, Wimar attempts to establish the moral superiority of the Euramericans and exploits the traditional captivity narrative type of the "savage" Indian.

During his fourth year Wimar created the consummate painting of his Düsseldorf period, *Attack on an Emigrant Train* (1856). Inspired by a French author of Wild West stories, Gabriel Ferry, Wimar appropriated a fictitious tale of Indians attacking a wagon train to compose a tableau portraying the heroic attempts of Native Americans to repel the settlers' inevitable progress across the frontier. Wimar's novel conception of the wagon-train attack provided the prototype for subsequent images copied from the 1860 Leopold Grozelier lithograph of the painting that enjoyed mass distribution.

The academic method that Wimar learned in Düsseldorf emphasized drawing directly from nature. He realized that his epic paintings of the American West were informed by popular literature and not direct observation. Following the completion of *Attack on an Emigrant Train* he traveled to St. Louis, determined to explore the Missouri River frontier "to collect the necessary studies" and then return to Düsseldorf to paint grand history paintings of the American West.

The painter arrived in St. Louis during the winter of 1856–1857, but was initially unsuccessful in securing passage on one of the steamboats traveling up the Missouri into Indian territory. Finally, in the summers of 1858 and 1859, Wimar received permission to accompany government-sponsored expeditions to deliver annuities to the Natives along the river and to explore the upper reaches of the Missouri River. On these expeditions Wimar recorded the exciting experiences that he witnessed in his encounters with the Native cultures and sketched the incredible natural formations that he discovered on the upper Missouri.

Back in his St. Louis studio, Wimar created an extraordinary series of panoramic Missouri River paintings that drew from his storehouse of memorable experiences reinforced by the wealth of sketches that he produced and artifacts that he collected. In these paintings he abandoned his obsession with images of conflict and confrontation and demonstrated his new romantic appreciation for what he perceived was the quickly passing life, land, and culture of the Native inhabitants of the Plains. Within the broad panoramic format of these paintings, Wimar combined his nostalgic vision of the West with realistic depictions of the landscape and the Native Americans.

Wimar's panoramic paintings of the frontier established his artistic reputation and commercial success. *The Buffalo Hunt* (1860) marked the pinnacle of his career. The painting presents a dynamic and ethnographically accurate portrayal of two Sioux Indians on horseback hunting buffalo. Wimar entered this painting in the Western Academy of Art's first, and only, exhibition where it earned popular accolades and the attention of the English Lord Lyons, who, while traveling with the entourage of the Prince of Wales, commissioned a copy. Like *The Attack on an Emigrant Train*, Wimar's *Buffalo Hunt* is a seminal image of this subject that introduced the metaphors of death through the gravelike stone and, in his later versions, skulls to convey the metaphor of the demise of the Indians as well as the buffalo.

The success of his *Buffalo Hunt* motivated a group of St. Louis civic leaders to award Wimar, in partnership with his half brother, August Becker, the commission to decorate the dome of the St. Louis Courthouse with murals. The largest commission of his career, Wimar drew upon his academic training to design a complex mural scheme that presented events in St. Louis's history and its ambitions for the future of the city as the gateway to the West. St. Louis civic leaders envisioned the dome and its decoration to precede and rival the murals for the Capitol in Washington, D.C. They aspired to poise St. Louis as the western counterpart and parallel to the nation's eastern capital.

Above two levels of portraits of historically significant St. Louisans, Wimar composed the epic centerpiece for his mural scheme on four lunettes at the cardinal points, presenting *DeSoto Discovering the Mississippi* (south), *The Landing of Laclède* (east), *The Year of the Blow* (north), and *Westward the Star of Empire* (west). The three early scenes depict moments in history when the Spanish first claimed the Mississippi, the French founded St. Louis, and the settlers defeated British-incited Indians during the American Revolution. The culminating image in the western lunette depicts the Cochetopa Pass in Colorado through which the transcontinental railroad would have passed if Congress had chosen the central route through St. Louis for the railroad. Unfortunately, Congress selected the northern route through Chicago only months before Wimar's mural was completed, dashing St. Louis's ambitions for the national transportation thoroughfare.

During the year that Wimar painted the courthouse murals, he struggled to complete the commission. A frail man, he suffered from tuberculosis. Journalists of the day reported that his advanced condition required his assistants to carry him up to the scaffolds to execute the work. Yet, he managed to complete the ambitious mural project before succumbing to tuberculosis on November 28, 1862.

Wimar's civic legacy, the courthouse murals, preserved the important moments in St. Louis history and the grandiose civic aspiration of the civic leaders at this crucial transition point in American history. In his brief career Wimar created compelling images of the American West, some of which still define our conception of such events as wagon-train attacks and buffalo hunts. Wimar's death at the young age of thirty-four occurred at the close of an era in American art and history precipitated by the Civil War. The subsequent course of history also closed the door on an era of artist-explorers who utilized St. Louis as their home base. Wimar's paintings stand among the final images of the Missouri River frontier prior to mass settlement following the Civil War.

JOSEPH D. KETNER

Rathbone, Perry. *Charles Wimar, 1828–1862: Painter of the Indian Frontier.* St. Louis: City Art Museum, 1946.

Stewart, Rick, Joseph D. Ketner, and Angela Miller. *Carl Wimar: Chronicler of the Missouri River Frontier.* Fort Worth, Tex.: Amon Carter Museum, 1990.

Wimar, Carl. Papers. Missouri Historical Society, St. Louis.

WOERNER, JOHN GABRIEL (1826–1900)

John Gabriel Woerner, a celebrated St. Louis lawyer, legal scholar, journalist, and politician, was admired by St. Louisans for his promotion of local artistic, literary, and philosophical efforts. In addition to his contributions to the study of American law, Woerner composed and published numerous plays and novels (in both German and English), the most significant of which was his semiautobiographical novel, *The Rebel's Daughter: A Story of Love, Politics, and War.* He was one of the founding members of the St. Louis Philosophical Society in 1866, an organization that channeled the energy of the so-called St. Louis Hegelians into the St. Louis movement in philosophy, education, and municipal reform. Woerner married Emilie Plass in 1852, with whom he had three daughters and a son. The son, William F., followed in his father's footsteps in becoming a noted St. Louis lawyer.

Born on April 28, 1826, in the German state of Württemberg, Woerner emigrated with his family to Philadelphia before landing in St. Louis in 1837. Soon thereafter the senior Woerner, a carpenter by trade, died, and John Gabriel received what his nineteenth-century biographers Hyde and Conard described as "but a scant education." Woerner passed his later teen years clerking in country stores in southwestern Missouri before returning to St. Louis to secure a job as a printer's devil for the German-language *Tribune.* In 1848 he became captivated by the revolutionary events in Germany. From motives equally journalistic and political, he spent the years 1848–1850 in Germany as a correspondent for the *St. Louis Tribune* and the *New York Herald.* Hyde and Conard suggest that Woerner's disillusioned return to St. Louis was inspired not so much by the ultimate failure of the 1848 revolution as by his disagreement with the aims and tactics of some of the Forty-eighters.

Upon return to St. Louis Woerner purchased the *Tribune* and as proprietor-editor changed its alignment from Whig to Democrat. Yet, his political migration by no means involved agreement with mainstream Democrats; he became a spokesman for the aging former senator **Thomas Hart Benton** at a time when the latter grew more critical of the Southern wing of his party's position on the extension of slavery.

In 1852 Woerner severed all connections with the *Tribune* to begin the study of law. He passed the bar in 1853 and in the same year gained the clerkship of the St. Louis Recorder's Court. He served successively over the next ten years as clerk of the Board of Aldermen, city attorney, and city councillor.

Of Woerner's career as a practicing lawyer his biographers remark upon "his absolute fidelity to the interests of his clients and his great ability in conducting their litigation to a successful issue." Among his clients between the late 1850s and the late 1860s was the Pacific Railroad. Since he was simultaneously a state senator (as a minority conservative or Union Democrat) for much of that period, Woerner was involved in some ethically suspect actions, though formal charges were never brought against him. In part due to his influence in the Senate, agents of the Pacific Railroad were able to persuade the state in 1868 to sell its $11 million investment in the company for a mere $5 million. This arrangement amounted not only to an enormous state grant to the company (in addition to millions in grants during the 1850s), but it restored to the Pacific Railroad enough control over its finances to forestall a takeover by eastern investors. Woerner's involvement in the affair was compounded by the fact that he chaired the joint investigative committee that on March 24, 1868, hastily cleared both legislators and railroad lobbyists of charges of wrongdoing. Historian James Neal Primm suggests that Woerner and his fellow "conspirators" escaped public censure and indictment because the connivance of public officials and private entrepreneurs in the Pacific Railroad and other cases meant "progress" and prosperity for Missouri, especially for St. Louis financial interests.

Woerner returned to the judiciary in 1870 when he was elected as a judge of the probate court, and he served in this capacity for a total of twenty-four years. Hyde and Conard describe Woerner as a charitable judge who did much to reduce the cost of judicial administration in St. Louis. His long tenure as probate judge made him a national as well as a local expert in his field, and his experience and erudition found expression in two major legal texts, *The American Law of Administration* and *The American Law of Guardianship*. Woerner saw himself in the German tradition of the administrator-scholar-poet whose role it was to serve the public as well as the world of culture. He died on January 20, 1900.

DENYS P. LEIGHTON

Hyde, William, and Howard L. Conard, eds. *Encyclopedia of the History of St. Louis.* New York: Southern History, 1899.

Primm, James Neal. *Lion of the Valley: St. Louis, Missouri, 1764–1980.* 3d ed. St. Louis: Missouri Historical Society Press, 1998.

Rowan, Steven, trans. *Germans for a Free Missouri: Translations from the St. Louis Radical Press, 1857–1862.* Columbia: University of Missouri Press, 1983.

Woerner, John Gabriel. *The Rebel's Daughter: A Story of Love, Politics, and War.* Boston: Little, Brown, 1899.

WOOD, REUBEN T. (1884–1955)

Reuben T. Wood, a union leader and congressman, was born on August 7, 1884, in Greene County, Missouri, the son of Henry N. R. and Martha A. Wood. He was educated by his parents and in the public schools of Springfield. As a young man he became a cigar maker and took an interest in labor union politics. From 1902 until 1939 he was a labor union officer. In 1912 he became president of the Missouri State Federation of Labor and served nearly thirty years in that office. From 1913 until 1933 he attended every session of the Missouri General Assembly, lobbying for unions. On November 8, 1932, he was elected to the United States House of Representatives and served until 1941, representing what was then the Sixth District of Missouri. On December 31, 1936, he married Mary Ellen Eshman.

Wood was one of eighty-three delegates to the Missouri Constitutional Convention that gathered in Jefferson City on September 21, 1943, with a charge to rewrite the constitution of the state of Missouri. Wood, a delegate-at-large, was considered one of the voices for labor at the convention. He served on four convention committees: Initiative and Referendum Revisions and Amendments, Legislative Department, Suffrage and Elections, and Labor.

Reuben T. Wood died on July 15, 1955, in Springfield, Missouri.

KAY HIVELY

Official Manual of the State of Missouri, 1942–1943. Jefferson City: Secretary of State, 1943.

Schmandt, Henry J. "The Personnel of the 1943–1944 Missouri Constitutional Convention." *Missouri Historical Review* 45 (April 1951): 241.

Who Was Who in America. Vol. 3. Chicago: A. N. Marquis, 1966.

WOODS, WILLIAM STONE (1840–1917)

William Stone Woods was born on November 1, 1840, the son of James Harris and Martha Jane Stone Woods. He was one of five children. He graduated from the University of Missouri in 1861 and obtained a medical education at St. Louis Medical College and at Jefferson Medical College in Philadelphia. Subsequently, he practiced medicine in Middle Grove and Paris, Missouri, both in Monroe County. He married Albina McBride of Paris in her hometown on July 10, 1866. In 1867 he began a general merchandising business in Paris. The next year he and his brother established a traveling wholesale grocery business through which they sold groceries and supplies to workers employed to build the Union Pacific Railroad between Omaha, Nebraska, and Ogden, Utah. He used the profits from this venture to establish the Rocheport Savings Bank in Rocheport, Missouri, in 1869. Apparently he did not practice medicine after 1866.

Woods moved from Rocheport to Kansas City in 1881, where he became a partner in a wholesale dry goods business. He also became president of the Kansas City Savings Association, which he reorganized into the Bank of Commerce in 1882. This reorganization allowed the bank to operate more fully as a retail lending institution to businesses and individuals. Upon assuming the presidency of the bank, Woods embarked on an expansion plan into the state of Kansas. One of his first ventures was the acquisition of the Elk City Bank in Montgomery County, Kansas. Later, he bought or established banks in Medicine Lodge, Garnett, and other Kansas communities. In 1900 he joined with nephew C. Q. Chandler II in purchasing Kansas National Bank in Wichita (which changed its name in 1919 to the First National Bank in Wichita). The *Medicine Lodge Cresset* of May 11, 1900, reported, "The new stockholders [which included Woods] have a string of banks from Kansas City to Carlsbad, New Mexico, and their objective in securing a bank at Wichita is to have a central institution convenient for handling the big cattle business of the southwest." Woods had served as a surrogate father to his nephew, whose own father had died in 1875. Years later, Woods's nephew would recall his uncle's influence: "My Uncle W. S. Woods coming into my life at such an early age had much to do in shaping my life, especially from a business standpoint. He was a splendid financier and very shrewd and far-seeing. He was of that positive nature like my Mother, knew his ground and stood by his decisions. He was a bold and fearless man, always true to his friends." By 1903 Woods, Chandler, and other partners controlled eighteen banks, ranging from Humboldt, Kansas, in the East to Clayton, New Mexico, in the Southwest. These included banks in Oklahoma Territory and Texas. Ultimately, Chandler brought other Woods nephews into the Wichita-based banking empire.

Among the people Woods brought into the banking business at the Commerce Bank was **William T. Kemper,** whom Woods hired as a vice president in 1906. The bank crisis of 1907 forced the closure of the Commerce Bank. It was reorganized by Kemper and reopened as the Commerce Trust Company. In 1917, shortly after the death of Woods, James Kemper, son of William Kemper, married Woods's granddaughter, Gladys Woods Grissom.

Woods seems to have taken an interest in the Female Orphans School of the Christian Church of Missouri while it was still located at Camden Point, north of Kansas City, in Platte County. The school had been established in 1870 for the orphaned daughters of Civil War veterans. Woods donated some property in Kansas City to the Reverend Thomas P. Haley of the Linwood Avenue Christian Church for the benefit of the school. In 1890 the struggling school moved to Fulton, Missouri, where it barely survived under a cloud of debt. In 1900 Woods paid off mortgages against the school, after which the institution's trustees changed the name of the school to William Woods College. By 1910 he was paying for the cost of educating approximately forty of the students who attended the school and supplementing the costs of an additional forty students. A number of the students in those years were from towns in which Woods owned or had owned a bank. Over the years he and his wife continued to be important benefactors of the school that bore his name. In 1915 they contributed money to build McBride Gymnasium, which was named in memory of Albina Woods's parents, Mr. and Mrs. Ebenezer McBride.

William Stone Woods died on July 5, 1917, in Excelsior Springs, Missouri. He left an estate worth an estimated $5 million, approximately 10 percent of which went to William Woods College. Albina Woods left a bequest to the college for a new building to be named for her late husband, and construction began on that building in 1919. Woods also left a legacy in the banking world through the banks he helped establish and maintain, and through his efforts in launching two of the most prominent banking families in the Midwest: the Chandlers and the Kempers. In 1996 the William T. Kemper Foundation contributed $1 million to William Woods University for the building of the Gladys Woods Kemper Center for the Arts. She was the granddaughter of William S. Woods and the first woman to serve on the school's board of directors.

GARY R. KREMER

Fulton Daily Sun, July 13, 1917.
Fulton Gazette, July 12, 1917.
Hamlin, Griffith A. *In Faith and History: The Story of William Woods College.* St. Louis: Bethany Press, 1965.
Jones, Billy M. *The Chandlers of Kansas: A Banking Family.* Wichita, Kans.: Wichita State University, 1983.
Kansas City Post, July 13, 1917.
Kansas City Star, July 5–9, 1917.

WOODSON, SILAS (1819–1896)

Born in Kentucky on May 18, 1819, Silas Woodson left the bluegrass country for Missouri in 1854, at age thirty-five, to establish his career in St. Joseph. He brought with him valuable credentials and experience. He had been admitted to the Knox County bar at age twenty-one and two years later was elected to the Kentucky General Assembly. He served as circuit attorney from 1843 to 1848 and then as a delegate to Kentucky's 1849 Constitutional Convention. In 1852 he returned to the Kentucky legislature for a final term.

Why Woodson chose to leave such a promising future remains a matter for conjecture. Some suggest that his call for the gradual emancipation of slaves was too liberal for Kentucky, but Kentucky was as divided as Missouri on this issue. Others think chaos in his Whig Party caused an irreparable rift, but Missouri's political scene between 1850 and 1870 also exhibited division over complex issues, producing splinter parties and cliques. Woodson relatives who had preceded Silas and located in northwestern counties may have encouraged him to come. Finally, St. Joseph, Missouri, itself could have been an enticement. It had a favorable location on the Missouri River, and construction of the Hannibal–St. Joseph Railroad had begun. Impressive development had taken place since it began operation as an outpost for people and goods westward bound. Extensive land openings offered options for speculation. It seemed the most promising of the towns along the western frontier. The combination of enticements may have been irresistible.

The Kentucky transplant quickly adapted to his new surroundings, and as senior partner opened the law firm of Woodson and Hughes, the first of several firms in St. Joseph that would eventually include his name.

Nature blessed Silas Woodson with a handsome physique. His sonorous voice, enhanced with cultivated oratory and sharpened by practiced debate, was greatly admired by his colleagues. Juries were influenced by his commanding figure and exceptional presentations of reason, eloquence, and persuasion; colleagues respected him as a formidable courtroom opponent.

Woodson married in 1842, and his first child, a son, Miller, was born in 1844. A year later Woodson became a widower. His second marriage, to Olivia Adams, took place in 1846. Olivia and Miller accompanied him to St. Joseph.

Woodson became an active Democrat, but by the late 1850s issues of states' rights and slavery created party upheaval and divisiveness. He supported **Robert M. Stewart** (also from St. Joseph) for the governor's seat in 1857. In 1860 he was elected as judge for the Twelfth Judicial Circuit in St. Joseph.

During the Civil War Woodson was a strong Union supporter. Although he was not in the front lines, he received the rank of colonel and the position of inspector general in the Missouri State Militia. In 1863 he was appointed assistant provost marshal for the exclusive purpose of enlisting black volunteers in accordance with General Orders no. 135, a directive designed to increase enlistment of black able-bodied men, both freedmen and slaves, in the military.

Personal tragedy struck again when Miller, now twenty-one and still Woodson's only child, died on June 22, 1865. Four months later, Olivia died, on October 26, at the age of thirty-five. In 1866 Woodson married Virginia Juliet Lard (called Jennie), who was only twenty; Silas, at forty-seven, was the same age as her father, Moses E. Lard, a prominent leader in the Disciples of Christ movement. Silas and Jennie Woodson's first child, Mary Alice, was born in 1870; twins—a boy, Silas Solomon, and a girl, Virginia Lard—arrived in 1875.

In 1868 Woodson ventured into a race for the state legislature but lost, probably because a number of Democratic voters had been disfranchised by the Radical Republican "Iron Clad" rule of 1865.

In an effort to regain their party strength the Democrats formed a coalition with the Liberal Republicans in 1872 and scheduled concurrent nominating conventions in Jefferson City. Delegates elected Woodson as permanent chairman of the convention. The two parties decided upon a single slate represented by candidates from both parties. A Democrat would head the ticket. There were six candidates when the balloting began, and it quickly narrowed to four strong men whose political ties and forceful positions during the contentious past decade made them unacceptable to the whole. When none of the four contenders garnered a sufficient majority Woodson made an impassioned plea for compromise and party unity. The delegate from Jasper County

asked if another nomination might be made from the floor; if permitted, he said, he would like to suggest the name of Silas Woodson. Immediately the convention recognized its savior candidate. Cheers resounded throughout the hall as celebratory hats sailed through the air.

Woodson campaigned well, carrying the state in the November 5, 1872, general election. His Republican opponent, **John B. Henderson,** polled 121,889; Woodson, 156,777.

The governor's two-year term, limited by the 1865 constitution, curtailed Woodson's ability to adequately implement a platform; nonetheless, his messages to the General Assembly resound with those interests and principles he advocated throughout his life: respect for the electorate, efficient management, and economy of operation. The judicial system held particular interest, and Woodson believed his experience as a prosecuting attorney, trial lawyer, and circuit judge qualified him to make recommendations for restructuring and correcting gross financial abuses associated with the criminal justice system.

In spite of his brief term Woodson did see the state's indebtedness reduced and the tax rate lowered. Principal criticisms were directed toward the ineffectiveness of curbing bank and train robberies by marauders terrorizing the state and bringing notorious attention to the Missouri outlaws. Woodson pleaded for additional funds, but received too small an appropriation to combat the lawlessness.

St. Joseph friends and associates regarded Woodson as a man of integrity who dispensed justice with fairness and welcomed his return at the conclusion of his term. His firm's practice thrived.

In 1880 Woodson was elected to a four-year term as judge of the circuit court. Subsequent years saw him elected for repeated terms in the recently established Buchanan County criminal court.

A cerebral hemorrhage ended Woodson's illustrious career in April 1895; death came on October 9, 1896. Much to the surprise of his friends and colleagues Woodson converted to the Roman Catholic faith during the summer of 1895. He is buried in Mount Mora Cemetery in St. Joseph.

When the Democrats selected Woodson as their compromise candidate in 1872 their enthusiasm for his nomination reflected their profound relief; his tenure justified their ringing endorsement. The time had come for healing wounds that had long pained a state so divided and confused about its destiny. In his inaugural speech he begged, "Forget the past, consecrate official lives to the service of the state." Woodson's integrity and moderate philosophy enabled a rebuilding process to begin. Democrats regained the confidence of the people and dominated subsequent elections for more than thirty years.

MARIAN M. OHMAN

Avery, Grace Gilmore, and Floyd C. Shoemaker, eds. *The Messages and Proclamations of the Governors of the State of Missouri.* Vol. 5. Columbia: State Historical Society of Missouri, 1924.

Mitchell, Charles Reed. "Silas Woodson: Governor of Missouri." *Knox Countian* 6 (spring 1994): 1–11.

WORNALL, JOHN BRISTOW (1822–1892)

John Bristow Wornall, a successful farmer and early leader in Jackson County, Missouri, was born in Clark County, Kentucky, on October 12, 1822, the oldest son of Richard and Judith Wornall. Financial losses caused members of the Wornall family to leave Kentucky in 1843 and head farther west in search of new opportunities. They settled in Westport, Missouri, where Richard Wornall purchased approximately five hundred acres of land from **John C. McCoy.** Good crops the first year enabled the elder Wornall to recoup the entire twenty-five-hundred-dollar purchase price. During the mid-1840s Richard and Judith sold the productive land to their sons John and Thomas. When Thomas died of cholera on the western Plains in 1849, John became sole owner of the property.

In 1850 John Wornall married Matilda Polk, but she died the following year. In 1854 he remarried, taking as his second wife Eliza Schalcross Johnson, whose father, the Reverend Thomas Johnson, had founded the Shawnee Methodist Indian Mission in Kansas in 1831. The couple had seven children, only two of whom lived beyond infancy: Francis Clay and Thomas Johnson. Eliza died in 1865, and the following year Wornall married her cousin Roma Johnson. Two of their children, John B. and Charles H., survived to adulthood.

Wiley Britton, now best known as the author of an account of the Civil War on the western border, came to the Wornall farm as a hired hand in the spring of 1858. He later recalled his one-time employer fondly: "He was a good man, a true gentleman and regarded by everybody in that section as one of its best and leading citizens, and a boy from home in my condition could not have fallen in with a better man, and surrounded with better influences than I found while living in his home, treated as one of the family. . . . He owned a beautiful farm . . . and treated me with genuine respect." Wornall was one of Jackson County's more prosperous farmers, and in 1858 he constructed a handsome Greek Revival–style home on his Westport farm. In 1860 the *Kansas City Enquirer and Star* listed him among the "Solid Men of Jackson County," individuals whose taxable property exceeded ten thousand dollars. That same year Wornall's name headed a list of Southern sympathizers who had formed a temporary vigilance committee known as the Westport Minute Men.

Wornall operated his farmstead with the assistance of slaves and hired hands. He was an original member of the Jackson County Agricultural and Mechanical Association founded in 1853 for the purpose of encouraging better farming methods and introducing superior types of crops. He was the organization's president in 1856. A strong Baptist, Wornall served as treasurer and moderator of the Big Blue (later Westport) Baptist Church and as chairman of the board of trustees of William Jewell College.

In 1857 Wornall and his brother-in-law A. S. Johnson acted as incorporators for the Shawnee Town Company of Johnson County, Kansas, and an 1867–1868 business directory listed Wornall's occupation as real estate. He also helped found the Kansas City National Bank and served as its president. A Democrat, he was elected in 1870 to represent Cass, Jackson, and Bates Counties in the Missouri State Senate. He served in that post for four years, but declined to seek reelection.

Wornall died in Kansas City on March 24, 1892. His 1858 home, now surrounded by Kansas City, has been restored to its original period and is operated by the Jackson County Historical Society to interpret the daily life of nineteenth-century farm families.

BETSY JOHNSON

Conard, Howard L., ed. *Encyclopedia of the History of Missouri.* New York: Southern History, 1901.

WRIGHT, CLEO (1916–1942)

Born in Jefferson County, Arkansas, on June 16, 1916, Ricelor Cleodas Watson was the son of farmer Albert Leak and schoolteacher Alonzo Woolfolk Humphrey Watson. He was raised in a religious, close-knit family near Gethsemane, eighteen miles northeast of Pine Bluff, on forty-five acres of property that Alonzo had inherited from her first husband. He received an eighth-grade education and enjoyed a typical childhood, along with older half brother Wiley and younger siblings Alice, James, and Linetta. He entered the Civilian Conservation Corps in 1934 and enlisted in the United States Navy the following year, only to be given an undesirable discharge within seven months for disobeying orders. Back in Arkansas, he drove a truck in Pine Bluff and was reunited with Wiley, who returned after a decade away (including time spent in prison for stealing). Ricelor soon lost his job in the depression economy and, in 1937, teamed with Wiley, a cousin, and a friend to hold up a Chinese grocer in a nearby rural community. With Wiley's capture a few days later, Ricelor left the state and went to Sikeston, Missouri, where he became known as Cleo Wright.

Over the next four and one-half years, Wright lived an uneasy and ambiguous life. He became well liked in the black community of Sunset Addition and among many whites who deemed him quiet and hardworking, despite initially spending time in the county jail for attempting to steal a state trooper's pistol. He married Ardella Gay of Mississippi in February 1940. Losing his job as a chauffeur within months of their wedding, he stole from his former employer and received a two-year prison term for burglary. Released on probation the next summer, he found work at the cotton oil mill and learned that he would be a father in the coming year.

Standing five-feet-ten and weighing 175 pounds, the dark-skinned, dark-haired, and dark-eyed Wright was an athletic and handsome man. Yet, for all his apparent confidence, he seemed deeply troubled by childhood lessons to achieve in a world fraught with racist obstacles preventing success. Demeaned and frustrated, he had challenged his parents, his military officers, and his white bosses. On Sunday, January 25, 1942, his rebellion exploded into violence.

Even though Wright's intentions, whether rape or robbery or both, were never verified and his guilt never proved, he seems to have entered the home of Grace Sturgeon in the early morning hours, slashed her badly, and fled. After being caught by the night marshal and a neighbor, he attacked the officer, who shot him several times. Upon receiving first aid at the local hospital (where his victims survived emergency surgery), he was taken to his wife and then placed in jail. At noon, Wright—dying from his wounds—was dragged from his cell by a mob that pushed aside policemen and state troopers. Representing every class of whites in Sikeston, the mob pulled him outside to the cheers of hundreds of spectators, attached him to a car, dragged him through Sunset Addition, and set him ablaze before the black residents.

Occurring shortly after U.S. entry into World War II, Wright's lynching bore international repercussions as Axis powers broadcast it worldwide as proof of democratic hypocrisy. Local, state, and federal officials quickly investigated the murder. Following the county prosecutor's failure to obtain indictments of citizens involved in the murder, U.S. Justice Department attorneys presented the case to a federal body that refused to recommend prosecution of local officers for not protecting Wright. These legal efforts ended the incident, yet the federal lawyers produced a strategy—based on sections 51 and 52, Title 18, of the United States Code—that would prove significant twenty-two years later when their successors prosecuted killers, including lawmen, who denied due process and equal protection to civil rights workers in Mississippi and Georgia.

Hence, Wright's execution influenced *United States v. Price* (1966) and *United States v. Guest* (1966), setting a precedent for government intervention in lynching cases long denied by the absence of a federal antilynching law. His death also brought an end to an era of eighty-five Missouri lynchings that had begun in 1889, supposedly for crimes so heinous that whites rationalized the need to take the law into their own hands. Ironically, his killing, like the war in which it occurred, symbolized the beginning of the end of the very racial segregation and social control that his killers sought to preserve.

DOMINIC J. CAPECI JR.

Capeci, Dominic J., Jr. "The Lynching of Cleo Wright: Federal Protection of Constitutional Rights during World War II." *Journal of American History* 72 (March 1986): 859–87.
———. *The Lynching of Cleo Wright.* Lexington: University Press of Kentucky, 1998.
Greene, Lorenzo J., Gary R. Kremer, and Antonio F. Holland. *Missouri's Black Heritage, Revised Edition.* Columbia: University of Missouri Press, 1993.
Mitten, Lyman Russell, II. "The Lynching of Cleo Wright: A Study." Senior thesis, Southeast Missouri State University, 1974.
Pfeifer, Michael J. "The Ritual of Lynching: Extralegal Justice in Missouri, 1890–1942." *Gateway Heritage* 13 (winter 1993): 22–33.

WRIGHT, HAROLD BELL (1872–1944)

Harold Bell Wright was one of the five most popular American authors in the first quarter of the twentieth century. His second novel, *The Shepherd of the Hills* (1907), set in the scenic Ozark hills of southwestern Missouri, was a best-seller and his most popular work. Born on May 4, 1872, in a settlement near Rome, New York, he was the second son of William A. and Alma T. Watson Wright. His mother, a gentle woman with some formal education, died of tuberculosis when he was ten years old. Unable to support his two sons, the impoverished father farmed them out to relatives and neighbors. Wright was estranged from his father until a few years before the elder Wright's death.

A drifter by his late teens, Wright wandered through New York and northeastern Ohio, working at odd jobs, painting drays, wagons, and houses. In the early 1890s he settled in Grafton, Ohio, where he joined the Christian Church (Disciples of Christ). His conversion experience caused him to consider the ministry as his lifework. He enrolled in the preparatory department of Hiram College in Ohio in 1893, where he remained for two years. However, he dropped out because of a lack of funds, as well as a respiratory problem that plagued him throughout his life.

In 1895 Wright accepted an invitation from a kinsman in the Missouri Ozarks in the vicinity of Branson to come and visit while he regained his health. Wright arrived early in 1896. One Sunday he was asked to substitute for the pastor of a small country church. His reputation as a speaker spread, and he was soon preaching in other small churches in the area. Then the Christian Church in Pierce City called him to be its weekend minister for forty dollars a month. From there he served Christian Churches in Pittsburg, Kansas (1898–1903); Kansas City, Missouri (1903–1905); Lebanon, Missouri (1905–1907); and Redlands, California (1907–1908).

While in Pittsburg, Wright wrote a series of sermons and stories to be given in serial form at the Sunday-evening service. They were published by solicitation under the title *That Printer of Udell's: A Story of the Middle West* (1902). Its publication planted in his mind the idea that he might write stories, as well as preach sermons to carry out his ministry. Because of poor health he took long summer vacations to recuperate. Wright returned to the Ozarks, where he outlined *The Shepherd of the Hills,* which would change his life and career. In Lebanon he completed the book. Published in 1907 it was a phenomenal success, introduced him to the literary world, and convinced him that he could devote his full attention to being an author. At Redlands in 1908 he quit the ministry to devote his time to writing books. From material he had gathered at Lebanon, he wrote *The Calling of Dan Matthews* (1909), the sequel to *The Shepherd of the Hills.* One other novel, *The Re-Creation of Brian Kent* (1919), also had an Ozarks setting. During his literary career he published nineteen books, averaging a book every two years, until the publication of his autobiography, *To My Sons* (1934).

Before ill health forced him to move from California to the Arizona desert near Tucson, Wright wrote his first western, *The Winning of Barbara Worth* (1911), which in the 1920s was made into a silent motion picture. Other westerns were *When a Man's a Man* (1916) and *The Mine with the Iron Door* (1923).

Many literary critics panned Wright's books as being overly sentimental, untrue to real life, and lacking in originality. However, they were bought and read by millions of people, especially in rural and small-town America. Many Americans in those early decades of the twentieth century grew up in homes where only two books, the Bible and Harold Bell Wright's latest novel, lay on the parlor table.

Wright married Frances E. Long in 1899, and they were the parents of three sons. Following their divorce in 1917, Wright married Winifred Potter Duncan in 1920.

After he returned to California in the mid-1920s Wright's popularity slowly declined. His final novel, *The Man Who Went Away* (1942), sold less than seven thousand copies. He died of pulmonary complications on May 24, 1944.

Harold Bell Wright's greatest legacy to Missouri is *The Shepherd of the Hills.* No book gives a clearer description of early Ozarkers, their ways and lore, as well as their country of deep hollows, rushing streams, and winding trails through the scenic Ozark highlands before the region became a major tourist attraction.

CHARLES T. JONES JR.

Jones, Charles T., Jr. "Brother Hal: The Preaching Career of Harold Bell Wright." *Missouri Historical Review* 78 (July 1984): 387–414.

Nye, Russel. *The Unembarrassed Muse: The Popular Arts in America.* New York: Dial Press, 1970.

Wright, Harold Bell. *The Shepherd of the Hills.* New York: A. L. Burt, 1907.

———. *To My Sons.* New York: Harper and Brothers, 1934.

Y

YATES, JOSEPHINE SILONE (1859–1912)

Josephine Silone was born in Mattituck, New York, in 1859, the youngest daughter of Alexander and Parthenia Reeve Silone. She attended a local school until, at the age of eleven, she was sent by her parents to the Institute for Colored Youth, a famous school in Philadelphia directed by noted African American educator Fannie Jackson Coppin. At age fourteen Silone moved to Newport, Rhode Island, to attend Rogers High School while living with an aunt. She completed the four-year course in three years and graduated valedictorian of her class in 1877. Silone next attended the Rhode Island State Normal School, graduating with honors in 1879. She was the first African American certified to teach in the schools of Rhode Island.

In 1881 Silone moved to Jefferson City, Missouri, to take a teaching job at Lincoln Institute, the state's all-black normal school. She was among the first faculty members hired by **Inman Edward Page,** the school's first black president, whose goal was to replace all the white teachers with black instructors. Silone taught chemistry, elocution, and English literature.

Silone left Lincoln Institute in 1889 when she married William W. Yates, the principal of the black Wendell Phillips School in Kansas City. In 1890 she gave birth to a daughter, whom she named Josephine Silone Yates Jr. In 1895 she bore a son, William Blyden Yates, called "Blyden," presumably in honor of the famed pan-Africanist Edward W. Blyden.

In 1893 Yates became the leading force behind and first president of the Women's League of Kansas City, a self-help and social-betterment organization of African American women. The Women's League was among the black women's clubs that joined the National Association of Colored Women (NACW) in 1896. Yates was elected fourth vice president of the national organization at its first biennial meeting, held in Nashville in September 1897. She was elected president in 1901, succeeding Mary Church Terrell, and held that office until 1906.

During her years as president of the NACW, Yates spoke and wrote widely on issues of racial uplift. Her writing appeared in, among others, the *Southern Workman,* the *Voice of the Negro,* the *Woman's Era,* the *Indianapolis Freeman,* and the *Kansas City Rising Son.* Yates returned to teach at Lincoln Institute in 1902. In addition to serving as an instructor of English and drawing, she served as the women's adviser. She also served as a faculty sponsor of the Olive Branch, "a musical and literary society composed of the young ladies of the senior and junior classes." The Olive Branch held membership in the NACW.

Yates moved back to Kansas City after the death of her husband in 1910. She taught for a time at Lincoln High School. Yates died in Kansas City on September 3, 1912, after a two-day illness, at the age of fifty-three. The *Indianapolis Freeman,* a black newspaper, eulogized Yates as a person "who was especially concerned . . . for the betterment of colored women, and for the betterment of the race generally."

GARY R. KREMER

Black Women in America: An Historical Encyclopedia. Vol. 2. S.v. "Yates, Josephine Silone."
Brown, Hallie Q. *Homespun Heroines and Other Women of Distinction.* Xenia, Ohio: Aldrine Publishing, 1926.
Indianapolis Freeman, September 21, 1912.
Kremer, Gary R., and Cindy M. Mackey. " 'Yours for the Race': The Life and Work of Josephine Silone Yates." *Missouri Historical Review* 90 (January 1996): 199–215.
Notable Black American Women. S.v. "Yates, Josephine Silone."
Scruggs, Lawson. *Women of Distinction.* Raleigh: L. A. Scruggs, 1893.

YEATMAN, JAMES ERWIN (1818–1901)

James Erwin Yeatman, a banker, philanthropist, and civic leader, was born on August 27, 1818, at Beechwood, near Wartrace, Tennessee, to Thomas and Jane Patton Erwin Yeatman. His father was a merchant, iron manufacturer, and banker in Nashville, and Yeatman was reared in surroundings of affluence. He was educated in private schools and at the New Haven Commercial School in preparation for a career in his father's business enterprise. After a European tour he returned to begin an apprenticeship in the family ironworks at Cumberland, Tennessee. In 1842 he moved to St. Louis to establish a branch of the business there. It would be his home for the remainder of his life.

From the outset of his business career in St. Louis, Yeatman established a reputation for scrupulous honesty. He helped organize the Merchant Bank in 1850 while pursuing a highly successful commission business in the decade that followed. He gave up the latter in 1860 to become president of the bank, a position that he occupied for the next thirty-five years, during which time he made it a major force in the city's economic life. He also served as one of the incorporators of the Pacific (later Missouri Pacific) Railroad in the 1850s and worked to secure a subscription of five hundred thousand dollars from the city of St. Louis for the Ohio and Mississippi Railroad, which helped link the metropolis with the East.

Yeatman also found time to engage in a variety of civic enterprises, including the establishment of St. Louis Mercantile Library (of which he was the first president), the incorporation of Bellefontaine Cemetery, the Missouri School for the Blind (which he also served as first president), and the founding of Washington University (which he served for many years as a trustee). In the post–Civil War era he was named as one of the original trustees of the Missouri Botanical Garden in the will of **Henry Shaw** in 1889, and he also served as secretary and trustee of the St. Louis Medical College.

Yeatman is best noted, however, for his work as president of the Western Sanitary Commission during the Civil War. Established in September 1861 by order of Gen. **John C. Frémont** to assist in caring for the wounded following the Battle of Wilson's Creek, the commission, under the leadership of Yeatman and **William Greenleaf Eliot,** expanded its work over the next four years to include the organization of hospitals, the equipping of hospital boats and trains, the recruitment of nurses, the distribution of sanitary supplies to the armed forces, assistance with the massive influx of refugees (both black and white), the maintenance of soldiers' rest homes for veterans on leave, and the establishment of freedmen's schools and orphanages for children of both races. In all these efforts Yeatman proved a dedicated and improvising leader. He spent a great deal of time in the field with the troops, who affectionately called him "Old Sanitary." His report on a trip down the lower Mississippi in December 1863 sought to alleviate the conditions of the freedmen there and led to an investigation of abuses in the hiring system that had been inaugurated. When President Lincoln asked him to head the newly established Freedmen's Bureau in 1865, however, Yeatman declined, wishing to remain in St. Louis. In its final report, the Western Sanitary Commission revealed that it had received $770,998 in cash donations and sanitary stores valued at $3.5 million, all of which it had faithfully used in the Union cause.

Following the war Yeatman returned to his various business and civic enterprises. Much of his wealth was contributed to a variety of charitable endeavors so that at his death he left little by way of an estate except an extensive library. He married twice: in 1838 to Charlotte Thompson, who died in 1849, and in 1851 to Cynthia Ann Pope, who died in 1854. He had five children. He died on July 7, 1901. The novelist **Winston Churchill** used Yeatman as the inspiration for the character Calvin Brinsmade in his 1901 Civil War novel *The Crisis,* calling him "the flower of the American tradition."

WILLIAM E. PARRISH

Forman, J. G. *The Western Sanitary Commission.* St. Louis: R. P. Studley, 1864.

Parrish, William E. "The Western Sanitary Commission." *Civil War History* 36 (March 1990): 17–35.

Scharf, J. Thomas. *History of St. Louis City and County: From Earliest Periods to the Present Day.* 2 vols. Philadelphia: Everts, 1883.

YOCUM BROTHERS

The Yocums, a prolific clan in the interior Ozarks for two centuries, are inextricably bound by history and folklore with significant events in the White River country. Anglicized from *Joachim,* the surname appears in many expressions, including Yocum, Yokum, Yoachum, Yoakum, Yochum, and more. They were among the "first families" in the interior Ozarks, families who sought the hunter's wilderness life and fur trade and followed migrating eastern and southern Indians into the White River valley. The Indians and Yocum history have been interwoven ever since.

No reliable published Yocum family history yet exists. However, four brothers—Solomon, Jacob, Jess, and Mike—came through Ste. Genevieve and into the James fork of the White River valley about 1818; they were descendants of Palatinate Germans who already had much westering experience. They arrived in time to host traveler **Henry Rowe Schoolcraft** during his famous journey in 1818–1819. The Yocums lived and traded on the rivers until Solomon and others moved onto Delaware Indian land on the James River (in Christian County, Missouri) during the 1820s. The Delawares received silver specie annuities and manufactured goods and temporarily "owned" their reservation lands. Their resources attracted others to rent their land, and to trade in pelts, stock, agricultural products, weapons—and illicit alcohol.

In 1825 John Campbell, subagent to Gen. **William Clark,** superintendent of Indian affairs in St. Louis, who was living among the Delawares, named certain "outlaw characters" who refused to pay rent to the

Delawares and, worse, sold them alcohol. Among them were Solomon Yocum and John Denton whom agent Campbell ordered off the reservation. Yocum did not go far. He and others set up a new facility just south of the Indian reservation boundary at the mouth of Finley Creek where it joined the James. There they processed legal whiskey and brandy, intended for the illegal market among the Indians.

The persistent Yocums were after the Delawares' silver specie coins. To mask the accumulation of federal specie from alcohol sales, the Yocums laundered their profits. Perhaps remembering the European *Joachimsthaler* (literally, Yocum dollar), the Yocums devised a clever scheme to produce their own silver coins, "Yocum Dollars," by melting down specie and recasting them in a crude smelting process, probably located in a nearby "silver cave." This silver speculation proved successful, and they probably provided the same service for their fellow distillers for a share of the profits.

The Delawares removed to Kansas reservations during 1829–1831, taking their annuities with them, and the source of Yocum silver dollars disappeared. To cover their imaginative design, the Yocums took advantage of their neighbors' gullibility by promoting the myth of a silver cave. This myth, originating in John Law's famous eighteenth-century Mississippi Bubble land speculation in the Mississippi Valley, was already more than a century old in the Ozarks, and, for fun, Anglicized Indians passed it on to successive settlers in the late-antebellum decades. Scholarly publications during the nineteenth century by Thomas Nuttall, G. W. Featherstonhaugh, Missouri geologists, and others warned of specious legends of precious metals, but the myth continued to thrive in Ozarks folklore.

The Yocum silver dollars continued as good currency for several years. They contained more silver than federal dollars, so silver speculators soon bought them up, melted them down to sell the ore, and the Yocum coins disappeared from circulation.

The Yocums, however, diversified their investments. They acquired land, livestock, and mills. By 1835 Jacob owned one of the largest cattle herds in southwest Missouri. By 1850 Solomon was a major swine producer. At the junction of Finley Creek, Solomon's nephew George owned the largest milling business in the county. At the close of the nineteenth century the now venerable *Reminiscent History of the Ozark Region* proclaimed Solomon Yocum was one of the most praiseworthy of all old Ozark pioneers, and he probably was.

Little did the Yocums realize that their name and the legend they spawned would become synonymous with twentieth-century Ozark stereotypes and tourism. Al Capp's *Li'l Abner* family was called Yocum, and Dogpatch USA is located a few miles south of where the Yocum Dollar was minted. Just east of the Yocum settlements lies sprawling Silver Dollar City, on Indian Point, the real Ozarks silver mine.

LYNN MORROW

Ayres, Artie. *Traces of Silver.* Reeds Spring, Mo.: Ozark Mountain Country Historical Preservation Society, 1982.

Marshall, Howard, and James Goodrich, eds. *The German-American Experience in Missouri: Essays in Commemoration of the Tricentennial German Immigration to America, 1683–1983.* Columbia: Missouri Cultural Heritage Center No. 2, University of Missouri, 1986.

Morrow, Lynn, and Dan Saults. "The Yocum Silver Dollar: Sorting Out the Strands of an Ozarks Frontier Legend." *Gateway Heritage* 5 (winter 1984–1985): 8–15.

YOUNG, HIRAM (1812?–1882)

Free black businessman Hiram Young of Independence, Missouri, who manufactured wagons and ox yokes for the Santa Fe and immigrant trades, was born in Tennessee about 1812, though the exact date of his birth is unknown. He moved to Missouri as a slave and later "purchased his freedom from George Young of Greene County, Missouri, in 1847." It is said that he earned his freedom and that of his wife, Matilda, by whittling and selling ox yokes. He moved to Independence, Missouri, in 1850.

By 1851 Young worked in the "manufactory of yokes and wagons—principally freight wagons for hauling govt [*sic*] freight across the plains." Independence's first mayor, **William McCoy,** served as his business manager. Until 1855 Young had a free black partner, Dan Smith. However, when Smith was forced to leave town, Young continued on his own.

By 1860 Young was turning out thousands of ox yokes and between eight and nine hundred wagons a year. He employed around twenty men. Seven forges operated in the shop. Census officials noted three hundred completed wagons and six thousand yokes in 1860. Young identified his products by branding them with "Hiram Young and Company" and also with the initials of the purchaser. Built for the Mexican trade, they were capable of hauling approximately six thousand pounds and were constructed for oxen drayage. Young's wagon factory was one of the largest industries in Jackson County in 1860 and by far the largest such concern in the county seat of Independence. Young rightly described himself as "a colored man of means."

In 1861 Young fled war-torn Missouri with his family to Fort Leavenworth, Kansas, about fifty miles northwest of Independence, where he continued his business as a private wagon manufacturer. After the war he returned to Independence. In a later suit against the federal government he claimed $22,100 in war damages to his Independence property.

Young's daughter, Amanda, attended Oberlin College in 1871. She later taught school and briefly served as principal in the local black school named for her father. Young and his wife were members of the Independence, Missouri, St. Paul A.M.E. Church.

Young died in 1882, leaving large business debts. His wife died in 1896. Young's case against the federal government continued until 1907, when it was finally dismissed. Amanda Jane Young Brown died in Kansas City in 1913.

WILLIAM PATRICK O'BRIEN

Curtis, William J. *A Rich Legacy: A Black History of Independence, Missouri.* Atlanta: Traco Enterprises, 1985.
Greene, Lorenzo J., Gary R. Kremer, and Antonio F. Holland. *Missouri's Black Heritage, Revised Edition.* Columbia: University of Missouri Press, 1993.
O'Brien, William Patrick. "Hiram Young: Pioneering Black Wagonmaker for the Santa Fe Trade." *Gateway Heritage* 14 (summer 1993): 56–67.

YOUNG, NATHAN B. (1862–1933)

Nathan B. Young was born in slavery during the Civil War on September 15, 1862, in Newbern, Alabama, the son of Susan Smith and a father whose identity is not known. Susan Smith was born in slavery in Chatham, Virginia, in 1842. When she was fourteen years old her master died, and in the settlement of his estate she was sold to a slave trader for $750. In Newbern, near Mobile, the slave trader sold her to a cotton planter for more than a 100 percent profit.

At the end of the Civil War when Nathan was three years old his mother made good their escape. Soon his mother established herself in her own home near Tuscaloosa. She met and married a local black man, Frank Young, who provided adequately for the family.

Young was reared in rural Alabama during the Reconstruction period, and he witnessed some of the most violent activities of the Ku Klux Klan in Alabama. His mother wanted him to receive an education, and enrolled him in a small ungraded school. Young's first formal education was at Talladega College, where he received a classical education in the normal school branch. Upon receiving a diploma from Talladega College, Young took charge of a secondary school in Jackson, Mississippi.

Deciding to make teaching his career, Young sought better preparation at Oberlin College in Ohio. He received a liberal arts education, earned his master's degree, and became the head of a black elementary school in Birmingham, Alabama. Later, Talladega College and Selma University awarded Young honorary degrees of doctor of letters.

On December 1, 1891, Young married Emma Mae Garette of Selma. They had two children, Nathan B. Young Jr. and a daughter, Gareth. Emma Young died of fever in 1904 in Tallahassee, Florida, and in 1908 Young married Margaret Buckley, originally from Charleston, South Carolina. They had three children, two sons, William and Frank DeForrest Young, and one daughter, Julia.

In 1892 Booker T. Washington employed Young to teach at Tuskegee Institute. He stayed at Tuskegee for five years, serving as the head of the academic department. Conflict developed between Young and Washington over the latter's efforts to emphasize vocational education, and in 1897 Young accepted the position of director of teacher training at Georgia State Industrial College. He worked cooperatively under Richard R. Wright, but he became somewhat disillusioned by the efforts of white southerners to proscribe black education to agriculture and the trades.

In 1901 Young was called to serve as president of Florida A&M College. He tried to balance the agricultural and vocational education program with a liberal arts program. After World War I, however, white state officials became intolerant of the teaching of liberal arts to black youths and forced Young out in 1922.

During his battle in Florida, Young accepted the presidency of Lincoln University in Missouri, the former Lincoln Institute. From 1923 to 1927 he made a determined effort to establish Lincoln University as a first-class institution of higher learning. In a remarkably short time he successfully campaigned to raise the academic standards and to get its high school and teacher-training programs accredited by the North Central Association of Colleges and Secondary Schools. Unfortunately, for many years the school had been controlled by politics, and with the state elections of 1924 political forces again dominated the university. By 1927 Missouri political leaders had forced Young out of the presidency, and in 1927–1928 he served as state inspector of black schools. After the heated election of 1928, where the future course of Lincoln University was made a campaign issue by the black press, Young was returned to the presidency in 1929. Politics, however, entered the picture again, and he was forced to retire for a second time in 1931. Nearing seventy years of age, Young decided not to fight, and retired to Tampa, Florida, where he lived with his daughter until his death on July 19, 1933.

Young left a great legacy to black higher education. Two important black institutions of higher education continue to exist and grow as a result of his influence and leadership. His model for Florida A&M and Lincoln Universities was a good one, and continued to guide those institutions for several decades. His courage helped push state politicians out of the schools' affairs.

ANTONIO F. HOLLAND

Holland, Antonio F. "Nathan B. Young: The Development of Black Higher Education." Ph.D. diss., University of Missouri–Columbia, 1984.

Savage, W. Sherman. *The History of Lincoln University.* Jefferson City: New Day Press, 1939.

YOUNGER, THOMAS COLEMAN "COLE" (1844–1916)

Thomas Coleman "Cole" Younger left his family's Missouri farm in 1862, at age seventeen, to join **William Clarke Quantrill**'s guerrillas. In the ensuing months he met **Frank James,** discovered that his father had been killed by a Union soldier, and lost a sister who died in the collapse of an old house in Kansas City that served as a Union prison for housing the female relatives of guerrillas. The impact of these personal events and of the larger Civil War seemed to mark Younger and his three brothers, Jim, John, and Bob. After the war the Youngers joined Frank and **Jesse James** as outlaws and gained notoriety for their criminal acts.

Born on January 15, 1844, Cole Younger began life in a large and affluent family residing in the vicinity of Lee's Summit, Missouri. Cole's father, Henry Washington Younger, who sired fourteen children, owned several thousand acres of land in Jackson and Cass Counties. By 1859 the family had moved to Harrisonville, where the elder Younger operated a store and held a partnership in a livery stable. That year voters elected him as their mayor.

Technically, Cole became an outlaw before he joined Quantrill. Following an altercation with a militiaman named Irvin Walley, Cole's father sent him into hiding. Cole armed himself, violating an order by Gen. **John C. Frémont,** commander of Union forces in Missouri, allowing only those in organized military units to carry weapons. Younger's brother-in-law, John Jarrette, persuaded him to join Quantrill. A short time later, gunmen shot and killed Henry Younger while on his way home from Kansas City, and Cole blamed Walley for his father's death.

When a Union officer assaulted his eighteen-year-old sister, Younger killed him. Cole's mother, Bursheba, moved the family to Jackson County, and militiamen burned their house, leaving the family dependent on relatives. Cole fought with Quantrill, participated in the raid on Lawrence, Kansas, in 1863, served in Colorado with Col. George S. Jackson,

and spent time in Texas and Mexico. In 1864 Cole's brother Jim also joined the Quantrill band, accompanied it to Kentucky in May 1865, and was captured during the engagement in which Quantrill was mortally wounded. Jim was held briefly at the federal prison at Alton, Illinois.

By the winter of 1865 Cole and Jim had returned to Missouri. Jim had taken the loyalty oath prescribed by Missouri's 1865 Constitution. Cole, who was still a wanted man, had come back home after a brief stay with an uncle in California. On February 12, 1866, Cole and Jesse and Frank James led a gang that robbed the Liberty, Missouri, bank of some sixty thousand dollars. In the holdup one of the bandits killed a student from William Jewell College. On March 26, 1868, the James-Younger gang robbed the Nimrod Long Banking Company in Russellville, Kentucky. John Jarrette probably participated in this robbery with Cole, Jesse, Frank, and Oliver and George Shepard. The robbery netted fourteen thousand dollars. That fall the Younger family moved to Dallas County, Texas, where Cole used some of his loot to establish a cattle business.

Moving back and forth between Texas and Missouri, Cole joined the James boys and Clell Miller, another ex-guerrilla fighter, in robbing the bank in Corydon, Iowa, on June 3, 1871. About a year later, on April 29, 1872, the gang hit the Columbia, Kentucky, bank, gaining only six hundred dollars and leaving a cashier dead. On May 27, 1873, the Ste. Genevieve Savings Bank fell victim to a four-thousand-dollar robbery. The gang robbed its first train near Adair, Iowa, on July 21, 1873. All four of the Youngers took part. The first train robbery in Missouri occurred at Gad's Hill, about one hundred miles south of St. Louis, on January 31, 1874. The James-Younger gang took the contents in the express safe and robbed the affluent-looking passengers, proclaiming "that they did not wish to take the hard-earned money of working men or ladies." Subsequent robberies occurred in Muncie, Kansas, on December 8, 1874, and Huntington, West Virginia, where the gang stole thirty thousand and ten thousand dollars, respectively.

To finance the Northfield, Minnesota, expedition, the gang took fifteen thousand dollars off a train near Otterville, Missouri, on July 7, 1876. Jim Younger, never an enthusiastic robber, refused to join his brothers in that escapade. Apparently, Jesse James planned the Northfield holdup and persuaded Bob Younger to go along. Cole expressed reluctance, but since Bob remained adamant Cole telegraphed Jim, who had moved to California, urging him to return home.

The Northfield robbery proved a debacle. The gang entered the town on September 7, 1876. Not long after Bob Younger and the James brothers entered the bank, someone alerted the townsmen of the robbery. Armed citizens began peppering Cole, Jim, and the others with gunfire. The outlaws failed to gain entry into the bank's vault and left with only twenty-six dollars. As they attempted to make their getaway, two of the gang lay dead; Jim Younger had a wound in his shoulder; Bob had received a shot in the elbow that broke his arm; Cole had been hit in the shoulder and the side; Frank James had injured his hand and shoulder when a bank employee tried to close the vault door on him; Jesse received a wound in the side; and the sixth bandit, Charlie Pitts, took a shot on his way out of town and later died. A posse captured the Youngers, but the James brothers managed to escape. The Youngers pleaded guilty to "accessory to the murder of J. L. Heywood, attacking A. E. Bunker with intent to do bodily harm, and the robbery of the First National Bank of Northfield, Minnesota." The court found them guilty and sentenced them to life imprisonment.

Bob Younger died in the Stillwater penitentiary in 1889. Cole and Jim received paroles in 1901, and Jim committed suicide the following year. Their brother John had met a violent death at the hands of Pinkerton detectives in 1874. Following Cole Younger's return to Missouri in 1902, he and Frank James briefly worked in a Wild West show named for them. The next year Younger published a largely fabricated autobiography titled *Cole Younger by Himself.* He worked for the Lew Nichols Carnival Company until 1908, and then toured as a lecturer, delivering a speech titled "What My Life Has Taught Me" until he retired in 1912. When he died in Lee's Summit on March 21, 1916, his body still bore eleven bullets collected during his days as a guerrilla fighter and holdup man.

LAWRENCE O. CHRISTENSEN

Brant, Marley. *The Outlaw Youngers: A Confederate Brotherhood: A Biography.* Lanham, N.Y.: Madison Books, 1992.
Encyclopedia of Western Gunfighters. S.v. "Younger, Thomas Coleman."
Henry County Democrat, November 5, 1903.
Norborne (Mo.) Democrat and Leader, January 3, 1936.
Shoemaker, Floyd C., ed. *Missouri, Day by Day.* Vol. 1. Columbia: State Historical Society of Missouri, 1942.

Z

ZIMMERMAN, THOMAS FLETCHER (1912–1991)

Thomas Fletcher Zimmerman led the Assemblies of God (AG), the second largest Pentecostal body, from 1959 to 1985. During his twenty-six-year tenure as general superintendent, the longest in the denomination's history, the AG experienced both remarkable growth and significant cultural change.

Born in Indianapolis on March 26, 1912, one year before the formation of the AG, Zimmerman converted to Pentecostalism at the age of seven. He entered the Pentecostal pulpit while still in his teens without benefit of formal theological training. In the late twenties and early thirties he pastored a number of AG churches in the Midwest and received ordination papers from the organization in 1935. In 1933 he married Elizabeth Price, the daughter of an AG minister. In each pulpit Zimmerman exhibited an ability to interact with community leaders and other evangelical ministers. These skills, combined with a successful radio ministry conducted in Granite City, Illinois, in cooperation with other local ministers, brought him to the attention of the AG national leadership in Springfield, Missouri.

In 1942 Zimmerman was asked to join the AG delegation to the convention of the newly formed National Association of Evangelicals (NAE), in part to act as the AG representative on NAE committees dealing with radio access. This began a career-long participation in the NAE, which enhanced Zimmerman's public visibility and his reputation. In 1944 he helped found the National Religious Broadcasters, an auxiliary of the NAE, and in 1960 the NAE selected him as its first Pentecostal president. The 1942 convention also marked the beginning of Zimmerman's rise within the AG.

In 1943 Zimmerman moved to Springfield to assume the important pulpit of Central Assembly of God, and in 1945 he was chosen to run the newly established AG Radio Department. He obtained national office in the denomination in 1953 when he was elected as one of four assistant general superintendents. He served under General Superintendent Ralph Riggs, a mentor who used his influence to advance Zimmerman's career. During the next eight years Zimmerman functioned as Riggs's first lieutenant on a number of key issues, including the establishment of Evangel College in Springfield. In 1959

Riggs failed to secure reelection, but by then Zimmerman had created a sufficient reservoir of goodwill to succeed him as general superintendent.

During Zimmerman's twenty-six years at the helm of the AG, the organization grew numerically—more than doubling in size—and in affluence as the constituency moved into the middle class, thus making available resources that allowed Zimmerman to expand the denomination's institutional base. He also worked to improve the denomination's higher educational programs. Under his direction college programs were added and upgraded, and the denomination established its first independent theological graduate school.

The general tone of Zimmerman's administration was moderately progressive. In 1965 he supported a resolution by the denomination's governing body condemning racial discrimination and encouraging more outreach to minorities than had been customary in the past.

However, Zimmerman's tenure did not lack controversy. Many old-line Pentecostals expressed concern that the close communion with other Evangelicals compromised the movement's Pentecostal distinctiveness, and, in fact, Zimmerman's coolness toward the charismatic movement may have been a reflection of the influence from his evangelical contacts. Others within the denomination feared that the general level of holiness and spirituality had been diluted by affluence and seeping secularism, a problem that Zimmerman recognized and sought to address by initiating an internal self-study.

Zimmerman retired in 1985, leaving behind a denomination no longer confined to the social margins but still uncertain about how to respond to modern culture. He died on January 2, 1991.

RICHARD COTNER

Blumhofer, Edith. *The Assemblies of God: A Chapter in the Story of American Pentecostalism.* New York: Oxford Press, 1989.

Dictionary of Pentecostal and Charismatic Movements. S.v. "Zimmerman, Thomas F."

Zimmerman, Thomas F. "The Making of a Minister." Parts 1–4. *Heritage* 10 (winter 1990): 91; 11:1 (spring 1991); 11:3 (fall 1991); 12:2 (summer 1992).

Index